C0-AOE-631

HAYDN'S BOOK OF DIGNITIES
1894

THE BOOK OF DIGNITIES

By JOSEPH HAYDN

Continued to the Present Time (1894)
And with an Index to the Entire Work
By Horace Ockerby

THIRD EDITION

With a New Preface
By Norris and Ross McWhirter

GENEALOGICAL PUBLISHING CO., INC.
BALTIMORE 1970

Originally Published
Third Edition
London, 1894

Reprinted with a new Half-title page, Title-page, and Preface
Firecrest Publishing Limited
Bath, 1969

Reissued with a new Title-page
Genealogical Publishing Company
Baltimore, 1970

Library of Congress Catalog Card Number 70-140398
International Standard Book Number 0-8063-0431-6

Printed and Reproduced by
Redwood Press Limited
Trowbridge & London
England

THE

BOOK OF DIGNITIES

CONTAINING

LISTS OF THE OFFICIAL PERSONAGES OF THE BRITISH EMPIRE, CIVIL, DIPLOMATIC, HERALDIC, JUDICIAL, ECCLESIASTICAL, MUNICIPAL, NAVAL, AND MILITARY, FROM THE EARLIEST PERIODS TO THE PRESENT TIME; TOGETHER WITH THE SOVEREIGNS AND RULERS OF THE WORLD, FROM THE FOUNDATION OF THEIR RESPECTIVE STATES; THE ORDERS OF KNIGHTHOOD OF THE UNITED KINGDOM AND INDIA, ETC., ETC.

RE-MODELLED, AND BROUGHT DOWN TO 1851, BY THE LATE

JOSEPH HAYDN,

CONTINUED TO THE PRESENT TIME, WITH NUMEROUS ADDITIONAL LISTS AND AN INDEX TO THE ENTIRE WORK, BY

HORACE OCKERBY,

THIRD EDITION.

DEDICATED, BY PERMISSION, TO THE

RIGHT HON. W. E. GLADSTONE.

LONDON:

W. H. ALLEN & CO., LIMITED, 13, WATERLOO PLACE, S.W.

Publishers to the India Office.

1894.

TO THE RIGHT HONOURABLE

WILLIAM EWART GLADSTONE, M.P.,

&c. &c. &c.

AT WHOSE SUGGESTION IT WAS UNDERTAKEN, AND WHO HAS THROUGHOUT EVINCED THE GREATEST INTEREST IN ITS PROGRESS,

THIS EDITION OF

THE BOOK OF DIGNITIES

IS MOST RESPECTFULLY INSCRIBED BY

THE AUTHOR.

PREFACE TO 1969 EDITION

JOSEPH HAYDN'S *Book of Dignities*, first published in 1851 was revised for the twelfth, and alas the last, time in 1894. By the middle of this century this book had become so scarce that many reference libraries and historians were without copies of their own.

The *Book of Dignities* is an invaluable source book for any student of world and particularly British Empire affairs whether political, diplomatic, ecclesiastical or military.

Haydn himself built on Dr. Robert Beatson's *Political Index* which was last published in 1806. Haydn's list of office holders – many of the offices themselves have now of course lapsed – holds much fascination whether they are of kings, queens, princes, ministers, ambassadors, governors, admirals, generals, bishops, lord mayors, or indeed Knights of the Royal Guelphic Order of Hanover.

This work is of the greater value because of a generously full index and thanks to the author's practice of giving the detailed sources of his authorities.

Of Joseph Haydn, who died in London on 18 Jan. 1856, we know remarkably little for one whose name adorns this great reference work and his much more famous *Haydn's Dictionary of Dates*, which is happily far less scarce since it was continuously published from 1841 to 1910.

Haydn's work however attracted the attention of Lord Palmerston (1784–1865) Britain's most colourful Foreign Secretary. He thought that the industrious Haydn should be given some Government recognition. All the Treasury would produce was £25 ($60) per annum, which, even allowing for modern inflation, seems a contemptibly small amount. Palmerston it is recorded much increased this derisory stipend out of his private pocket and insisted, on Haydn's death only months later, that his widow should continue to be paid.

In making *Haydn's Book of Dignities* more widely available again we hope not only to have reproduced a very useful reference work but an entertaining and intriguing book.

NORRIS & ROSS McWHIRTER.

London 1969

PREFACE.

Beatson's Political Index, on which the Book of Dignities is founded, was first published in 1786. It went through three editions, the last of which was published in 1806, and has, of course, been long out of print. It contained many lists of little practical utility, and its usefulness was also impaired by a want of systematic arrangement. Still it was, without doubt, a valuable book; and the fact of three large editions having been issued and speedily exhausted, shows that a work of this character is always appreciated.

In the year 1851 the late Joseph Haydn, well known as the compiler of the *Dictionary of Dates* and other similar works of reference, published a new edition of the Political Index, under the title of *The Book of Dignities*. In the preparation of this edition Haydn took Beatson's work as the foundation, eliminated from it such lists as he considered superfluous, re-arranged the remainder somewhat more methodically, and brought the book down to date. The general opinion appears to have been that

Haydn was rather too sweeping in his excisions, and that some of the lists omitted by him might have been retained with advantage.

Like its predecessor, the *Book of Dignities* in its turn was soon out of print, and has almost, if not quite, attained the rank of a "scarce" book. It seldom occurs in auctioneers' or booksellers' catalogues, and, when a stray copy comes into the market, it fetches a price as high as or higher than that at which it was originally published, although nearly forty years out of date, and consequently useless as a modern or correct guide.

Under these circumstances it seemed to me that the time had arrived when a new and revised edition of so useful a book might be published with advantage; and I can only express a hope that my opinion may be justified by the event. I have restored some of the more useful of the lists omitted by Haydn, and have added many others, so as to make the work as complete as possible.

As examples of the additional lists, I may mention the Deans, the Lord-Lieutenants, the Officers of the Heralds' College, the County Court Judges, the Queen's Counsel, the Colonial Governors and Bishops, and many of the minor orders of knighthood. Besides these, a large number of Dignities have been created since 1851, so that altogether whilst Haydn's edition contained only about four hundred lists, the present work contains over thirteen hundred. I have omitted the so-called "PEERAGE," which was very meagre and incomplete, as all information under this head can now be easily supplied from sources well known, and easily accessible; and, in order to economise space, I have greatly curtailed the introductory notes, which were frequently incorrect or obsolete. I have, however, added to each Dignity a reference to the Statutes, Orders in Council, or Letters Patent, creating or affecting it. This will enable the reader to obtain full and accurate information on the subject.

But the great feature of the present edition is the INDEX OF NAMES, which now appears for the first time, and which, I think and hope, cannot fail greatly to increase the utility of the work. It is so arranged as to give to the name of each person a list of every dignity or office held by him. I need not dwell upon the labour such a task has involved, it being nearly a repetition of the book itself, although, by the use of abbreviations, compressed into fewer pages. In compiling this Index, I was met with a formidable difficulty by reason of the different ways in which the same name was spelt, which rendered it almost impossible to adhere to the usual alphabetical or lexicographical arrangement. I was to some extent prepared for this, but I own I was surprised to find how little regard was, even down to comparatively modern times, paid to uniformity of spelling. I have endeavoured to overcome the difficulty by a plentiful use of cross-references, and would ask the reader's careful attention to the observations prefixed to the Index at pages 943–4. The preparation of this Index has greatly delayed the publication of the book. I could not even commence to arrange the names until the whole body of the work was in type; and, being actively engaged in the duties of my profession, I was only able to devote a few hours each day to the task.

It is so obvious that a work of this kind, where every line contains a name and a date, cannot be free from errors, that it seems hardly necessary to make the usual conventional apology for unavoidable mistakes. In compiling the Index, a number of small errors were brought to light, a list of which will be found at pages vii–x. I have not attempted systematically to revise the old lists throughout, as to do so would have been virtually to re-write the entire book; but where, in searching for additional names, I have had an opportunity of collating Haydn's lists with others I have done so. I may mention as instances that the judges, &c., have been collated with Foss's lists, and the orders of knighthood with those of Sir Harris Nicolas.

Had I known what lay before me when I first undertook the task of preparing this edition, I frankly confess that I should have hesitated to attempt it. I anticipated that I should finish the work in a little over six months, but it has occupied almost all my leisure time for more than four years. It has, however, been essentially a labour of love, and I can only hope that I have accomplished my task in such a manner as to merit the approbation of the public, into whose hands the book is now committed.

HORACE OCKERBY.

July 1890.

ERRATA.

Page	Col.	Line	Correction.
15	2	45	For "Alexandra" read "Alexander."
25	2	10	For "*supra*" read "*infra*."
37	2	47	For "2nd time" read "3rd time."
38	1	36	*Dele.* "(2nd time)."
41	1	24	For "Curvus" read "Corvus."
42	1	15	To "P. Decius Mus" add "(5th time)."
43	1	8	To "M. Pomponius Matho" add "(2nd time)."
,,	2	24	To L. Veturius Philo" add "(2nd time)."
44	1	3	For "Gemilius" read "Æmilius."
45	1	57	For "Scarus" read "Scaurus."
,,	2	15	To "Cu. Domitius Ahenobarbus" add "(2nd time)."
46	1	20	To "M. Æmilius Lepidus" add "(2nd time)."
,,	2	59	To "M. Antonius, *abd.*" add "(2nd time)."
68	1	32	For "Rupert II." read "Rupert I."
105	1	last	For "Carrua" read "Carrera."
112	1	30	For "Geo. Granville, E. Gower" read "Geo. Granville, ld. aft. E. Gower."
114	1	6	To "Jno. Savile Lumley" add "aft. Sir J."
146	2	32	For "Vesey Fitzgerald" read "Charles Vesey Fitzgerald."
147	1	7	For "ld. Ellice" read "Edwd. Ellice."
,,	2	9	For "Spring Rice" read "Thos. Spring Rice."
147	2	14	For "Mr. Poulett Thomson" read "Chas. Poulett Thomson."
153	2	22	For "Sudley" read "Sudeley."
168	1	13	For "1736" read "1764."
179	3	54	For "Wm. Visc. Duncannon" read "Wm. 2nd E. of Bessborough."
180	1	17	For "Wm. Visc. Duncannon" read "Wm. 2nd E. of Bessborough."
181	3	3	For "Sir Geo. Hope" read "Sir Geo. J. Hope."
188	2	5	For "Dudley Ryder, E. of Harrowby" read "Dudley, E. of Harrowby."
,,	2	20	For "Jas., ld. Wharncliffe" read "Jas. Archd., ld. Wharncliffe."
,,	2	44	For "Aberdeen" read "Aberdare."
,,	2	49	For "Parkinson" read "Samuel."
193	2	53	(Lowther.) For "baron" read "ld."
195	1	58	For "Thos., E. of Derby" read "Jas., 10th E. of Derby."
,,	2	17	For "Queensbury" read "Queensberry."
207	1	4	(Dartmouth.) For "1810" read "1801."
209	1	29	(Bentinck.) *Dele.* "gov.-gen. of India, May, 1833," and insert "Tr. Hhold."
211	1	13	(Bentinck.) Add "gov.-gen. Ind. 1833."
,,	2	20	For "Jas. Horatio" read "Geo. Jas. Horatio."

Page	Col.	Line	Correction.
212	1	26	For "Wm., visc. Anson" read "Thos. Wm., visc. Anson."
,,	2	5	At end of year 1831 add "Dec. 7, Hon. Thos. Erskine, ch. judge in Bankruptcy."
215	1	7	(Wood.) For "ld. Halifax" read "visc."
217	2	63	For "Lopus" read "Loftus."
218	1	2	(Napier.) Add "and ld. chanc. Ir."
220	1	57	(Gibson.) For "ld. chambn." read "ld. chanc."
,,	2	38	For "Wm. Schomberg Rt." read "Schomberg Hy."
223	1	4	For "1408" read "1480."
229	1	44	For "Harvey" read "Hervey."
230	1	20	After "Edw. Jno. Stanley" add "aft. ld. Eddisbury, &c."
,,	2	24	For "Boyce" read "Bryce."
,,	2	42	For "Corrie" read "Currie."
233	1	8	(Stanley.) For "Hon." read "Col."
234	1	37	(Hillsborough.) For "Wm." read "Wills."
239	2	1	After "Lyon Playfair, C.B.," add "aft. Sir L."
241	2	3	For "Jno., aft. E. of Durham," read "Jno. Geo., aft.," &c.
242	1	45	For "Moore" read "More."
252	1	37	*Dele.* "Grosvenor."
254	2	21	Between "Baring" and "ld." insert "aft."
256	1	25, 26	For "Visc. Dumblane" read "Visc. Osborne of Dumblane."
259	1	10, 11	*Dele.* "aft. D. of Rutland."
,,	2	27, 28	*Dele.* "aft. D. of Rutland."
260	2	32	For "Sir Edwd. G. R. Owen" read "Sir Edwd. C. R. Owen."
262	2	28	(Booth.) For "Gen." read "Geo."
289	1	12	(Arundel.) For "Wm." read "Hy."
294	1	20	(Orford.) After "Edwd." insert "Russell"
294	1	37	(Arundel.) For "Hy." read "Wm."
,,	2	26	Read "Gilbert Elliot, aft. Sir G."
298	1	23, 24	*Dele.* "aft. ld. Hatton."
,,	1	40	(Manchester.) After "Chas." insert "Visc. Mandeville, aft."
300	1	1	(Evelyn.) For "E. of" read "Visc."
,,	1	4	(St. John.) For "Geo. Richd., visc.," read "St. Andrew, ld."
312	1	41	(Somerset.) After "Algernon" insert "ld. Percy, aft. D. of."
318	2	25	(Asheton.) After "Robt." insert "(?) Richd."
319	1	5	For "1847" read "1487."
323	1	15	For "Grenville" read "Granville."
,,	1	17	(Granville.) For "Jas." read "Jno."
347	–	34	For "four" read "three."
355	1	54	(Nevill.) For "Canterbury" read "York."
356	1	43	(Ley.) For "John" read "James."
364	1	30	For "Comhill" read "Cornhill."
399	1	49, 50	(North.) *Dele.* "and E. of."
401	1	33	(Roswell.) For "Richd." read "Wm."
408	1	3 & 24	For "— Brooke" read "Rd. Brooke."
411	1	39	For "Eyres" read "Eyre."
415	1	40	After "Winnington Jeffreys" insert "Wm. Lee."
429	2	11	For "Maddore" read "Maddox."
435	1	13	For "1445" read "1454."
438	1	50	For "Barry" read "Parry."
456	1	2	For "1614" read "1605."
461	1	16	For "Beleanquall" read "Balcanquall."
477	1	21	For "Strafford" read "Stratford."
484	2	12	(Eden.) For "succ. to that title" read "succ. to the title of ld. Auckland."
488 to 492			Until the alteration of the "Style" in 1753 Lord Mayor's Day was Oct. 29th and not Nov. 9th. The list of Lord Mayors should be altered accordingly.

Page	Col.	Line	Correction.
507	1	38	(Balmerino.) For “Jas.” read “Jno.”
509	1	7	(Mansfield.) For “Wm. 3rd E.” &c., read “David Wm.” &c.
511	1	26	(Elibank.) For “Geo., ld.” &c., read “Alex., 7th ld.” &c.
515	2	13	(Huntley.) For “2nd E.” read “4th E.”
,,	2	18	(Huntley.) For “2nd E.” read “5th E.”
517	1	10	(Rothes.) For “Wm.” read “Wm. (?Geo.)”
522	1	39	(Craufurd.) For “Andrew” read “Andrew (? David).”
,,	1	52	(Dalrymple.) For “Hy.” read “Hew.”
524	–	12	For “p. 521” read “p. 523.”
525	1	20	(Dunbar.) For “David” read “Gavin.”
545	2	36	To Gillan's name add “(? bp. of Dunblane).”
546	2	16	(Glasgow.) For “David” read “Jno.”
550	1	15	For “1881” read “1181.”
552	1	25	(Ormond.) For “3rd E.” read “4th E.”
553	2	25	(Brereton.) *Dele.* “ld. chanc.”
559	2	17	(Fitzwilliam.) To “visc.” add “(? ld.)”
562	1	51	(Hervey.) For “Jno. Aug.” read “Aug. Jno.”
570	1	2	(Ormonde.) For “Walter, 18th E.,” read “Jas., 19th E.”
582	1	12	To “1784” add “(?1785).”
583	2	13, 15	(Willes.) *Dele.* “app. solr. gen. in England. and in 1768 a just. K.B.”
597	1	43	(Reeves.) For “John” read “Wm.”
599	2	40	(Townshend.) For “Lismore” read “Waterford.”
613	2	32	For “1543” read “1743.”
627	2	27	For “Dayaly” read “Daly.”
648	–	1	For “1704” read “1764.”
,,	–	32	(Minto.) For “Geo.” read “Gilbert.”
650	1	20, 32	(Cornwallis.) For “Geo.” read “Chas.”
659	1	33, 34	(Fitzgerald.) *Dele.* “aft. ld. F. and V.”
668	–	29	For “Hern” read “Herm.”
672	2	41	(Tennent.) For “Jno.” read “Jas.”
713	1	10	(Mulgrave.) For “Hy.” read “Constantine Hy.”
720	1	20, 22, 24, 33, 35	(Dotin.) read “Jas. or Jno.”
724	2	52	(Goldsworthy.) For “aft. sir G.” read “aft. sir R.”
734	1	55	For “Ostrevart” read “Ostrevant.”
736	1	18	Aft. Lord Bonvill's name insert “Sir Thos. Kyriell; *d.* 1461.” “Sir Jno., aft. ld. Wenlock; *d.* 1471.”
737	2	31	(Ferrers.) For “3rd ld.” read “8th ld.”
740	2	56	(Feversham.) For “1st E.” read “2nd E.”
741	2	10, 11	(Pr. Fk. Lewis.) *Dele.* “D. of Gloucester.”
742	2	5	(Grafton.) For “Sept. 29” read “Sept. 20.”
,,	2	11	(Rochford.) For “5th E.” read “4th E.”
744	1	17	Read “Robt., 2nd Earl Grosvenor and 1st M. of Westminster.”
746	1	20	(King.) For “bp. Salisbury, 1491” read “bp. Exeter, 1492.”
747	1	46	For “Sunderland” read “Sutherland.”
748	1	1	Read “Wm. Hy., 4th M. of Lothian.”
755	1	31	For “Aldeburh” read “Aldeburgh.”
,,	2	45	For “5th ld. Latimer” read “ld Latimer.”
756	1	25	(Westmoreland.) For “Rd.” read “Ralph.”
,,	1	29	For “Cormvale” read “Cornvale.”
758	1	27	(Dudley.) For “6th ld.” read “5th ld.”
759	2	54	For “Skelton” read “Shelton.”
760	1	6	(Dorset.) For “5th M.” read “3rd M.”
762	1	8	(Ratcliffe.) *Dele.* “and aft.”
764	1	35	(Bolton.) For “3rd D.” read “2nd D.”
766	2	4	(Cochrane.) For “Sept.” read “May.”
767	1	3	(Hutchinson.) For “Gen.” read “Jno.”
768	1	5	(Harcourt.) For “2nd E.” read “3rd E.”

Page	Col.	Line	Correction.
771	1	32	(Cooper.) For "Anthy." read "Astley."
772	1	34	(Sydenham.) *Dele.* "Wm."
776	2	61	(Rigny.) For "Re" read "de."
781	2	3	(Tanner.) For "Orel" read "Oriel."
784	2	9	(West.) For "Algernon" read "Algernon Edw." After West's name insert "Col. Donald Matheson."
,,	2	25	*Dele.* "Lt.-Col. Donald Matheson."
,,	–	39	For "Couriers" read "Coursier."
786	1	20	Aft. Gen. Murray's name insert "Gen. Sir Robt. Macfarlane, K.C.B."
,,	2	51	For "Champange" read "Champagne."
788	2	19	(Brooke.) For "John Saml." read "Saml. Jno."
792	1	47	(Munster.) For "Hy." read "Herbert."
794	1	18	For "Cornuto" read "Comuto."
,,	1	25	(Guildford.) For "6th E." read "5th E."
798	2	23	(Vivian.) For "Chas." read "Hussey."
817	2	39	(Nagle.) For "G.C.B." read "G.C.H."
852	–	19	(Wilson.) For "Fabie" read "Fahie."
856	1	52	(Hulse.) *Dele.* "G.C.M.G."
861	2	60	For "Houstoun" read "Houston or Houstoun."
865	1	35	For "Guilford" read "Bedford."
,,	2	31	(Oughton.) Read "Jas. Adolphus, aft. Sir J."
866	1	60	(Craufurd.) *Dele.* "G."
874	2	55	(Hawker.) For "K.C.B." read "K.C.H."
877	–	59	(Fagan.) *Dele.* whole line. See correct entry p. 876, 10 Jan. 1837.
884	–	5	For "Jno. Home" read "Jno. Home Home."
,,	–	61	(Wymer.) *Dele.* whole lines. See correct entries p. 886, 20 Jun.1854
,,	–	62	(Pastle.)
886	–	8	Read "John Mitchel or Mitchell, C.B., aft. sir J."
886	–	27	Read "Geo. Petre Wymer... | 20 Jun. 54 | | 8 Jun. 56 | 9 Sep. 63 |."
887	–	3	For "Dyer" read "Dyce."
,,	–	12	(Wylie.) *Dele.* whole lines. See correct entries p. 888.
,,	–	14	(Garstin.)
,,	–	55	(Conran.) *Dele.* whole line. See correct entries same page, line 13.
888	–	11	Read "Edw. Garstin... | 28 Nov. 54 | 21 Dec. 65 | 1 Mar. 67."
,,	–	14	(Vivian.) Add "and sir R."
,,	–	34	(Dickinson.) *Dele.* whole line. See correct entry same page, line 60
,,	–	51	Read "Wm. Wylie, C.B. | 28 Nov. 54 | 24 Oct. 62 | 24 Feb. 70."
891	–	35	For "Butter" read "Butler."
893	–	23	(Brooke.) *Dele.* whole line. See correct entry p. 887, 28 Nov. 54.
894	–	30	(Abbott.) *Dele.* whole line. See correct entry same page, 13 Apr. 1860.
895	–	3	(Morris.) *Dele.* whole line. See correct entry p. 894, 30 Apr. 1860.
,,	–	19	After Campbell, insert Edwin Hy. Atkinson.
896	–	34	(Hodgson.) *Dele.* whole line. See correct entry p. 894, 11 Apr. 1860.
,,	–	38	(Shirley.) *Dele.* whole line. See correct entry p. 897, 24 Oct. 1862.
,,	–	39	(Lawrence.) *Dele.* whole line. See correct entry p. 897, 1 June 1862.
898	–	54	(Smith.) *Dele.* whole lines. See correct entries p. 897, 21 Dec.1862.
,,	–	55	(Sutton.)
900	–	49	(Tapp.) *Dele.* whole line. See correct entry p. 903, 6 Mar. 1868.
906	–	41	(Briggs.) *Dele.* whole line. See correct entry same page, line 54.
,,	–	61	(Ballard.) *Dele.* whole line. See correct entry p. 907, 16 Aug. 1868.

Page	Col.	Line	Correction.
907	–	40	(Sandham.) *Dele.* whole line. See correct entry p. 904, 6 Mar. 1868.
909	–	48	(Lefroy.) *Dele.* whole line. See correct entry p. 906, 6 Mar. 1868.
915	–	28	(Vine.) *Dele.* whole line. See correct entry p. 914, 26 Nov. 1875.
,,	–	58	(Cockburn.) *Dele.* whole line. See correct entry p. 917, 1 Oct. 1877
917	–	55	(Harrison.) *Dele.* whole line. See correct entry p. 918, 24 Nov. 1877.
918	–	14	(Cockburn.) *Dele.* whole line. See correct entry p. 917, 1 Oct. 1877.
921	–	35	(Thomas.) *Dele.* whole line. See correct entry p. 920, 31 Dec. 1878
924	–	33	(Williams.) *Dele.* whole line. See correct entry same page, line 22
925	–	45	After H. A. Cockburn insert "Peter Hy. Scratchley, m.-gen., 1 Oct. 1882."
,,	–	48	Read "Hy. Augs. Smyth | 1 Nov. 82 | 1 Nov. 86 | . . . . |
,,	–	49	(Dormer.) Read "hon. J. C. Dormer, C.B. | 18 Nov. 82 | 1 Nov. 85 | . . . . |
928	–	41	(Dormer.) *Dele.* whole line. See correct entry p. 925, 18 Nov. 1882.
967	1	2	(Beach.) Add "C. Sec. 235."

LIST OF ABBREVIATIONS USED IN THE BODY OF THE WORK.

abb.	abbot.
abd.	abdicated.
abp.	archbishop.
abt.	about.
actg.	acting.
adm.	admitted.
——	admiral.
admr.	administrator.
admy.	admiralty.
aft.	afterwards.
aldn.	alderman.
amb.	ambassador.
amb. ex.	ambassador extra-ordinary.
app.	appointed.
——	appeal.
appt.	appointment.
archd.	archduke.
archdn.	archdeacon.
arr.	arrival or arrived.
assass.	assassinated.
att. gen.	attorney general.
b.	born.
bar. ex.	baron of the exchequer.
bd.	board.
bp.	bishop.
bt.	baronet.
C.B.	companion of the bath.
c.c.	commonly called.
C.G.	consul general.
C.I.E.	companion of the Indian empire.
C.M.G.	companion of St. Michael and St. George.
C.S.I.	companion of the star of India.
canc.	cancelled.
capt. yeom. gu.	captain of the yeomen of the guard.
capt. gent. pens.	captain of the gentlemen pensioners.
cardl.	cardinal.
ch.	chief.
ch.bar.ex.	chief baron of the exchequer.
ch. commr.	chief commissioner.
ch. d'a.	chargé d'affaires.
ch. ex.	chancellor of the exchequer.
chambn.	chamberlain.
chanc. d. Lanc.	chancellor of the duchy of Lancaster.
chapl.	chaplain.
coadj.	coadjutor.
coffr.	cofferer.
col.	colonial.
comm. admy.	commissioner of the admiralty.
comm.ch.	commander in chief.
comm. serjt.	common serjeant.
comm. treasy.	commissioner of the treasury.
com-mend.	commendator.
commr.	commissioner.
compt. hhold.	comptroller of the household.
conf.	confirmed.
conq.	conquered.
consec.	consecrated.
const.	constable.
——	constituted.
contd.	continued.
contr.	control.
coron.	coronation.
cr.	created.
——	crowned.
Cr. I.	crown of Indi
cr. pr.	crown prince.
Css.	Countess.
D.	duke.
d.	died.
dau.	daughter.
decl.	declared.
——	declined.
degr.	degraded.
dep.	deposed.
——	deputy or depute.
dep. e. marsh.	deputy earl marshal.
depr.	deprived.
desc.	descended.
dethr.	dethroned.
dict.	dictator.
dipl. rel. susp.	diplomatic relations suspended.
dism.	dismissed.
disp.	dispensed.
div.	divorced.
Dss.	duchess.
E.	earl.
earl marsh.	earl marshal.
East. T. or Vac.	Easter Term or Vacation.
elect.	elected.

elect. pal.	elector palatine.
emp.	emperor.
env. ex.	envoy extraordinary.
estab.	established.
exp.	expelled.
ext. ld. of sess.	extraordinary lord of session.
F.M.	field marshal.
fin.	financial.
first ld. adm.	first lord of the admiralty.
first ld. treas.	first lord of the treasury.
for.	foreign.
form.	formerly.
G.	London gazette, *i.e.* the date of the Gazette Notice.
G.C.B.	Knight Grand Cross of the Bath.
G.C.H.	Knight Grand Cross of the order of the Guelphs.
G.C.I.E.	Knight Grand Commander of the Indian Empire.
G.C.M.G.	Knight Grand Cross of St. Michael and St. George.
G.C.S.I.	Knight Grand Commander of the Star of India.
gen.	general.
gent. bedch.	gentleman of the bedchamber.
gov. gen.	governor general
govr.	governor.
gr. d.	grand duke.
gr. seal.	great seal.
gr. stole.	groom of the stole.
hhold.	household.
Hil. T. or Vac.	Hilary Term or Vacation.
introd.	introduced.
inv.	invested.
iss.	issued.
judge prerog.	judge of the prerogative court.
just. C.P.	justice of the common pleas.
just. K.B.	justice of the king's bench.
K.	King.
K.B.	Knight or Knight Companion of the Bath.
K.C.	King's Counsel.
K.C.B.	Knight Commander of the Bath.
K.C.H.	Knight Commander of the order of the Guelphs.
K.C.I.E.	Knight Commander of the Indian Empire.
K.C.M.G.	Knight Commander of St. Michael and St. George.
K.C.S.I.	Knight Commander of the Star of India.
K.G.	Knight of the Garter.
K.H.	Knight of the order of the Guelphs.
K.P.	Knight of St. Patrick.
K.T.	Knight of the Thistle.
knt.	knight.
L.G.	Lieutenant Governor.
L.P.	Letters Patent.
ld.	lord.
ld. admy.	lord of the admiralty.
ld. bed-ch.	lord of the bedchamber.
ld.ch.bar. ex.	lord chief baron of the exchequer.
ld. ch. just. C.P.	lord chief justice of the common pleas.
ld. ch. just. K.B.	lord chief justice of the king's bench.
ld. chambn.	lord chamberlain.
ld. chanc.	ld chancellor.
ld. clk. reg.	lord clerk register of Scotland.
ld. gr. chambn.	lord great chamberlain.
ld. just.	lord justice.
ld. kpr.	lord keeper.
ld. lieut.	lord lieutenant.
ld.marsh.	lord marshal.
ld.pr.seal.	lord privy seal.
ld. pres. council.	lord president of the council.
ld. st.	lord steward.
ld. treasr.	lord treasurer.
ld. treasy.	lord of the treasury.
ld. wden. stann.	lord warden of the stanneries.
loc. gov. bd.	local government board.
lt.-gen.	lieutenant-general.
lt.-gen. ord.	lieutenant - general of the ordnance.
M.	Marquis.
m.	married.
m.g. ordn.	master general of the ordnance.
m.-gen.	major-general.
m. horse.	master of the horse.
m. mint.	master of the mint.
m. ordn.	master of the ordnance.
m. rolls.	master of the rolls.
mahar.	maharajah.
mart.	martyred.
mast.	master.
mast.gen. ord.	master general of the ordnance.
mast. gr. wardr.	master of the great wardrobe.
Michs. T. or Vac.	Michaelmas Term or Vacation.
mil. tri.	military tribune.
min.	minister.
min. plen.	minister plenipotentiary.
min. res.	minister resident.
miss. extr.	mission extraordinary.
Mss.	Marchioness.
natl.	natural.
nom.	nominated.
obt.	obtained.
ordn.	ordnance
p. l. bd.	poor law board
P.P.	Patent of Precedence.
parl.	parliamentary.
parlt.	parliament.
paym. gen.	paymaster general.
pat.	patent.
perm. pres.	permanent president.
plant.	plantations.
pol.	political.
postm. gen.	postmaster general.
pr.	prince.
—	privy.
pr. seal.	privy seal.
pr. serjt.	prime serjeant.
preb.	prebendary.
prec.	precentor.
prem.	premier or prime minister.
pres.	president.
pres. council.	president of the council.
procl.	proclaimed.
prov.	provost.
prov. gov.	provisional government or governor.
prov.pres.	provisional president.
provl.	provisional.
Prss.	Princess.
Q.	queen.
Q.C.	Queen's Counsel.
q.v.	*quid vide.*
raj.	rajah.
rang.	ranger.
rec.	recorder.
rect.	rector.
regr.	registrar.
relinq.	relinquished.
rem.	removed.
remembr.	remembrancer.
rep.	representative.
res.	resident.
—	resigned.
rest.	restored.
ret.	retired.
s. and h.	son and heir.
S.L.	Serjeant at Law.
s.p.	*sine prole.*
sec.	secretary.
sec. st.	secretary of state.
sign.	signet.
sp. ho. comm.	speaker of the house of commons.
sp. miss.	special mission.
succ.	succeeded.
surn.	surnamed.
surr.	surrender.
surrend.	surrendered
susp.	suspended.
sw.	sworn.
T.	Trailbaston (justice of).
tell. ex.	teller of the exchequer.
tr.	trade.
—	translated.
treasr.	treasurer.
treasy.	treasury.
Trin. T. or Vac.	Trinity Term or Vacation.
unm.	unmarried.
v.	vice.
v.	*vice.*
v. chambn.	vice chamberlain.
v. chanc.	vice chancellor.
vic.	vicar.
Visc.	Viscount.
Viscss.	Viscountess.
warrt.	warrant.

TABLE OF CONTENTS.

	PAGE
PREFACE	iii
ERRATA	vii
LIST OF ABBREVIATIONS USED IN THE BODY OF THE WORK	xi
TABLE OF CONTENTS	xiii

LISTS OF DIGNITIES.

THE Lists are divided into XVI. Parts, as under:—

PART I.—ROYAL.

Sovereigns and Rulers of the Principal Countries in the World.

PART II.—DIPLOMATIC.

Ambassadors, Envoys Extraordinary, Ministers Plenipotentiary, &c., from Great Britain and the United Kingdom of Great Britain and Ireland to Foreign States.

PART III.—POLITICAL AND OFFICIAL.

Government Officials, Officers of State, Officers of the Household, &c.

PART IV.

Lord-Lieutenants of Counties, Governors and Constables of Castles, &c.

PART V.—HERALDIC.

Earl-Marshals, Kings of Arms, Heralds, and Pursuivants.

PART VI.—LEGAL.

Judges and other Legal Dignitaries.

PART VII.—ECCLESIASTICAL.

Archbishops, Bishops, and Deans of England and Wales.

PART VIII.—LONDON.

PART IX.—SCOTLAND.

PART X.—IRELAND.

PART XI.—INDIA.

PART XII.—THE COLONIES.

Governors and Bishops of the Colonies and other Dependencies of the British Empire.

PART XIII.—ORDERS OF KNIGHTHOOD.

Orders of Knighthood, &c., connected with the British Empire.

PART XIV.—NAVAL.

PART XV.—MILITARY.

PART XVI.—MISCELLANEOUS.

PART I.—ROYAL.

Sovereigns and Rulers of the Principal Countries in the World.

EUROPE.

Sovereigns, &c. of— PAGE
- Alençon 26
- Anhalt 66
- —— -Bernburg . . 66
- —— -Dessau . . 66
- Anjou 27
- Arragon 86
- Austria 58
- Baden 66
- —— -Baden . . . 67
- —— -Durlach . . 67
- Bavaria 67
- Belgium 84
- Bohemia 58
- Brabant 29
- Brandenburg . . 65
- Brittany 27
- Brunswick . . . 68
- Bulgaria 95
- Burgundy . . . 28
- Castile 85
- Danubian Principalities 94
- Denmark 93
- Eastern Empire . . 49
- England—
  - Sovereigns . . 1
  - Kings Consort . 7
  - Queens Consort . 7
  - Princes of Wales 8
  - Princes and Princesses of . . 9
- Ferrara 52
- Flanders 81
- France 22
- Franconia . . . 71
- Friesland (*see* Holland) 82–3
- Germany 61
- German Confederation, North . . 64
- German Empire . 61, 64
- German States, South 64
- Germanic Confederation 63

Sovereigns, &c. of— PAGE
- Great Britain (*see* under separate Kingdoms) . . 1–17
- Greece 96
- Hainault 81–2
- Hanover 70
- Hesse 71
- —— -Cassel . . . 72
- —— -Darmstadt . 72
- —— -Homburg . . 72
- Hildbourghausen (*see* Saxe-Altenburg) 78
- Holland 82–3
- Hungary 59
- Ionian Islands (Part II.) 129
- Ireland 20
- Italy, Ancient . . 49
- —— Modern . . 51
- Liechtenstein . . 73
- Lippe-Detmold . . 73
- —— -Schaumburg . 73
- Lombardy (*see* Ancient Italy) . . 49
- Lorraine 29
- Lucca 52
- Luxemburg . . . 84
- Mecklenburg . . . 73
- —— -Schwerin . . 74
- —— -Strelitz . . 75
- Modena 52
- Moldavia 94
- Monaco 30
- Montenegro . . . 95
- Naples 55
- Nassau 75
- Navarre . . . 85, 87
- Netherlands . . . 82–3
- Normandy . . . 30
- Norway 91
- Oldenburg . . . 76
- Orange (Pr. of) . . 83
- Parma 53
- Piacenza 53
- Placentia 53

Sovereigns, &c. of— PAGE
- Poland 90
- Portugal 88
- Prussia 65
- Reggio 52
- Reuss-Greiz . . . 76
- —— -Schleiz . . . 77
- Rhine, Confederation of 63
- Rhine, Palatinate of 68
- Rome—
  - Consuls, Dictators, &c. . . 37
  - Emperors . . . 47
  - Kings 36
  - Popes 32
- Roumania . . . 95
- Russia 89
- Sardinia 54
- Savoy 54
- Saxony 77
- Saxe-Altenburg . . 78
- —— -Coburg-Gotha 78
- —— —— -Saalfeld 78
- —— -Gotha Altenburg 78
- —— -Meiningen . 79
- —— -Royale . . 77
- —— -Weimar . . 79
- Schwarzburg-Rudolstadt 79
- —— -Sondershausen 79
- Scotland 17
- Servia 95
- Sicily and Two Sicilies 55
- Spain 84
- Suabia 80
- Sweden 91
- —— and Norway . 92
- Switzerland . . . 31
- Transylvania . . 60
- Turkey (*see* Asia) . 97
- Tuscany 56
- Two Sicilies . . . 55

Sovereigns, &c. of— PAGE
- United Kingdom of G. B. and I. (*see under* separate Kingdoms) . . 1-20
- Waldeck-Pyrmont . 80
- Wales, Sovereigns of 16
- —— Princes of . . 8
- Wallachia. . . . 94
- Western Empire 48
- Wurtemburg 80
- Zell (*see* Brunswick) 70

ASIA.
- Arabia. 98
- China 100
- Egypt 98
- Japan 100
- Jerusalem . . 96
- Ottoman Empire . 97
- Persia 99
- Siam 100
- Trebizond . . 98
- Turkish Empire . 97

AFRICA.

Sovereigns, &c. of— PAGE
- Liberia 100
- Madagascar . . . 101
- Morocco 101
- Orange Free State . 101
- Transvaal . . . 101
- Tunis 101
- Zanzibar 102

AMERICA.
- America, Central . 105
- —— U.S. of . . . 102
- Argentine Confederation 109
- —— Republic . . 109
- Bolivia 109
- Brazil 108
- Buenos Ayres . . 110
- Central America . 105
- Chili 111
- Colombia, Republic of 107
- —— U.S. of . . . 107
- Costa Rica . . . 106

Sovereigns, &c. of— PAGE
- Dominican Republic 105
- Ecuador 108
- Granada, New . . 107
- Guatemala . . . 105
- Hayti 104
- Honduras . . . 106
- Mexico 103
- New Granada . . 107
- Nicaragua . . . 106
- Panama 107
- Paraguay 110
- Peru 108
- St. Domingo . . . 105
- St. Salvador . . . 106
- U.S. of America . 102
- —— of Colombia . 107
- Uruguay 111
- Venezuela . . . 107
- Vera Cruz . . . 103

- Hawaiian or Sandwich Islands . . 111

PART II.—DIPLOMATIC.

AMBASSADORS, ENVOYS EXTRAORDINARY, MINISTERS PLENIPOTENTIARY, &c., FROM GREAT BRITAIN AND THE UNITED KINGDOM OF GREAT BRITAIN AND IRELAND TO FOREIGN STATES.

From the Accession of George III., 1760.

Ambassadors to—
- Abyssinia . . . 131
- America, Central . 133
- America, U.S. of . 132
- Argentine Confederation and Republic 136
- Austria 116-7
- Baden, &c. . . . 119
- Barbary States . . 131
- Bavaria 119
- Belgium 123
- Bolivia 135
- Borneo 131
- Brazil 135
- Bulgaria 128
- Central America . 133
- Chili 137
- China and Corea . 130-1
- Colombia, Republic of 134
- Corea, China and . 130-1
- Costa Rica . . . 133
- Danubian Principalities 128
- Denmark 127

Ambassadors to—
- Dominican Republic 133
- Ecuador (addendum) 942
- Egypt 130
- France 112
- German States . . 121
- Germany 116
- Granada, New . . 134
- Greece 128
- Guatemala . . . 133
- Hanover 120
- Hanse Towns . . 120
- Hawaiian Islands . 137
- Hayti 133
- Hesse-Darmstadt . 119
- Honduras . . . 133
- Ionian Islands (Ld. High Commrs.) 129
- Italy, Modern . . 114
- Japan 131
- Lucca, &c. . . . 115
- Mexico 133
- Modena, &c. . . 115
- Moldavia 128
- Montenegro . . . 128

Ambassadors to—
- Morocco 132
- Muscat 130
- Naples and the Two Sicilies 114
- Netherlands, &c. . 122
- New Granada . . 134
- Nicaragua . . . 133
- Norway and Sweden 127
- Ottoman Empire . 129
- Panama 134
- Paraguay 136
- Parma, &c. . . . 115
- Persia 130
- Peru 135
- Plata, Rio de la . . 136
- Poland 126
- Portugal 124
- Prussia 117
- Rio de la Plata . . 136
- Roumania . . . 128
- Russia 125
- San Salvador. . . 133
- Sandwich Islands . 137
- Sardinia 114
- Saxony 120

Ambassadors to— PAGE
Servia 128
Siam 131
Sicilies, Naples and the Two . . . 114
Spain 123
Sweden 126
—— and Norway . 127
Swiss Confederation 113

Ambassadors to— PAGE
Texas 132
Tunis 132
Turkey 129
Tuscany, &c. . . 115
Two Sicilies, Naples and 114
United States of America . . . 132

Ambassadors to— PAGE
United States of Colombia . . . 134
Uruguay 136
Venezuela . . . 134
Venice 116
Wallachia 128
Wurtemburg, &c. . 118-9
Zanzibar 132

PART III.—POLITICAL AND OFFICIAL.

Government Officials, Officers of State, Officers of the Household, &c.

Administrations—
Treasury—
Lord High Treasurers, &c. . . . } 152
Commissioners . . }
Secretaries, parliamentary and financial 163
Secretaries, assistant 164
Secretaries, permanent 164
Exchequer (*see also* Part VI)
Chancellors . . . 164
Chamberlains . . 166
Auditors 166
Tellers 167
Clerk of the Pells . 168
Comptrollers-General 168
Auditors-General of Public Amounts . 168
Assistant ditto . . 169
Admiralty—
Lord High Admirals, &c. . . . . . } 169
Commissioners . . }
Secretaries, first . 186
Secretaries, second . 187
Secretaries, permanent 187
Privy Council—
Lord Presidents . 187
Privy Councillors . 189
Judicial Committee (*see* Part VI.) . . 360
Ireland—
(*See* Part X.)
Secretaries of State—
Introduction . . . 221
Principal Secretaries to 1782 . . 222
Under Secretaries to ditto 225

Home Department—
Secretaries . . . 226
Under Secretaries, parliamentary . 227
Under Secretaries, permanent . . . 228
Foreign Department—
Secretaries . . . 226
Under Secretaries, parliamentary . 229
Under Secretaries, permanent . . 230
Under Secretaries, permanent, assistant 230
War and Colonial Department
Secretaries . . . 230
Under Secretaries, parliamentary . 231
Under Secretaries, permanent . . 232
War Department—
Secretaries . . . 232
Under Secretaries, parliamentary . 232
Under Secretaries, financial . . . 233
Under Secretaries, permanent . . 233
Secretaries of War 233
Secretaries of War, deputy 234
Colonial Department—
Secretaries . . . 234
Under Secretaries, parliamentary . 235
Under Secretaries, permanent . . 235
Under Secretaries, permanent, assistant 236

India (and *see* Part XI., and Board of Control, *infra*)
Secretaries . . . 236
Under Secretaries, parliamentary . 236
Under Secretaries, permanent . . . 236
Scotland (*see* Part IX.)
Post Office—
Postmasters - General 237
Secretaries . . . 239
Secretaries, second . 239
Secretaries, financial 239
Lord Chancellors, &c. (*see* Part VI.)
Lords Privy Seal . 240
Chancellors of the Duchy of Lancaster 241
Paymasters-General . 243
Paymasters-General of the Forces . . 243
Wardens and Masters of the Mint . . 245
Judge Advocates General (Part XV.) . 937
Speakers of the House of Commons . . 247
Control, Board of (*see also* "Indian Secretaries," *supra*, and Part XI.)—
Introduction . . . 251
Presidents and Commissioners to 1841 252
Presidents from 1841 254
Secretaries . . . 254
Education, Board of—
Vice-Presidents . . 254
Health, Board of—
Presidents . . . 255

	PAGE
Local Government Board—	
Presidents . . .	256
Secretaries, parliamentary . . .	256
Secretaries, permanent	256
Navy Boards—	
Treasurers of the Navy	256
Comptrollers . . .	257-8
Surveyors . . .	257
Ordnance, Board of—	
Masters-General of the Ordnance . .	258
Lieutenants-General of the Ordnance .	259
Surveyors-General of the Ordnance .	259
Clerks of the Ordnance	260
Storekeepers . . .	260
Police—	
Chief Commissioners, &c. . . .	261
Poor Law Board—	
Commissioners . .	262
Presidents . .	262
Secretaries . . .	262
Trade, Board of—	
Original Boards to 1786	263
Subsequent Members	268
Presidents from 1786	268
Vice-Presidents from 1786	269
Secretaries, parliamentary . . .	269
Secretaries, permanent	270
Woods and Forests.	
Land Revenues.	
Works and Public Buildings—	
Introduction . . .	270
Surveyors-General of Woods, Forests, Parks, and Chases	271
Surveyors of Land Revenues . . .	271
Commissioners of Woods, Forests, and Land Revenues . .	271, 273
Commissioners of Woods, Forests, Land Revenues, Works, and Buildings	272
First Commissioners of Works and Public Buildings . .	272
Revenue—	
Commissioners of Customs, England and Wales, to 1722	273
Commissioners of Customs, Great Britain, 1723–42 .	275
Commissioners of Customs, England and Wales, 1742–1823	275
Commissioners of Customs, United Kingdom, from 1823	277
Commissioners of Excise, England and Wales, to 1823	277
Commissioners of Excise, United Kingdom, from 1823–49 . . .	282
Commissioners of Stamps, England and Wales, to 1834	283
Commissioners of Taxes, England and Wales, to 1834	284
Commissioners of Stamps & Taxes, England & Wales, 1834–49 . . .	285
Commissioners of Inland Revenue from 1849 . .	285
Lord High Stewards .	286
Lord Great Chamberlains	287
Deputy Chamberlains	288
Lord High Constables	288
Earls Marshal and their Deputies (*see* Part V.) . . .	325
Lord Steward's Department—	
Lord Stewards of the Household .	289
Treasurers of the Household . .	291
Comptrollers of the Household . . .	292
Cofferers of the Household . . .	293
Treasurers of the Chamber . . .	294
Lord Chamberlain's Department—	
Lord Chamberlains of the Household	294
Vice-Chamberlains of the Household	296
Masters of the Great Wardrobe . . .	295
Governors and Constables of Windsor Castle (Part IV.)	322
Captains of the Yeomen of the Guard	297
Captains of the Gentlemen Pensioners	299
Captains of the Gentlemen-at-Arms .	300
Poets Laureate . .	300
Examiners of Stage Plays	301
Master of the Horse's Department—	
Masters of the Horse	301
Masters of the Buckhounds	302
Grooms of the Stole .	303
Mistresses of the Robes	304

PART IV.—LORD LIEUTENANTS OF COUNTIES, GOVERNORS AND CONSTABLES OF CASTLES, &c.

Lord Lieutenants of Counties.

	PAGE
Introduction	305
England.	
Lord Lieutenants of—	
Bedfordshire	306
Berkshire	306
Buckinghamshire	306
Cambridgeshire	306
Cheshire	306
Cornwall	307
Cumberland	307
Derbyshire	307
Devonshire	307
Dorsetshire	307
Durham	308
Essex	308
Gloucestershire	308
Hampshire	311
Herefordshire	308
Hertfordshire	308
Huntingdonshire	309
Kent	309
Lancashire	309
Lord Lieutenants of—	
Leicestershire	309
Lincolnshire	310
Middlesex	310
Monmouthshire	310
Norfolk	310
Northamptonshire	310
Northumberland	310
Nottinghamshire	311
Oxfordshire	311
Rutlandshire	311
Shropshire	311
Somersetshire	311
Southamptonshire	311
Staffordshire	312
Suffolk	312
Surrey	312
Sussex	312
Tower Hamlets	319
Warwickshire	312
Westmoreland	313
Wiltshire	313
Worcestershire	313
Lord Lieutenants of—	
Yorkshire, E. Riding	313
,, N. ,,	313
,, W. ,,	313
North Wales.	
Lord Lieutenants of—	
Anglesey	314
Carnarvonshire	314
Denbighshire	314
Flintshire	314
Merionethshire	314
Montgomeryshire	315
North Wales	314
South Wales.	
Lord Lieutenants of—	
Brecknockshire	315
Cardiganshire	315
Carmarthenshire	315
Glamorganshire	315
Haverfordwest	316
Pembrokeshire	316
Radnorshire	317
South Wales	315

Scotland, *see* Part IX., and Ireland, *see* Part X.

Governors and Constables of Castles, &c.

Constables of Dover Castle	316
Wardens of the Cinque Ports	316
Constables of the Tower of London	319
Lord Lieutenants of the Tower Hamlets	319
Lieutenants of the Tower of London	321
Governors and Constables of Windsor Castle	322
Lord Wardens of the Stannaries	323

PART V.—HERALDIC.

Earls Marshal, Kings of Arms, Heralds, and Pursuivants.

Introduction	324
Sec. I.—Heraldic Offices still Existent.	
Lords Marshal	325
Earls Marshal	326
Deputy Earls Marshal	327
Kings of Arms—	
Garter	327
Clarencieux	328
Kings of Arms—	
Norroy	329
Bath and Gloucester	330
Heralds—	
Chester	330
Windsor	331
Somerset	332
Lancaster	332
Richmond	333
York	334
Heralds Extraordinary—	
Surrey	334
Maltravers	335
Pursuivants of Arms—	
Rouge Croix	335
Bluemantle	336
Portcullis	337
Rouge Dragon	337

SEC. II.—HERALDIC OFFICES NOW EXTINCT.

Kings of Arms— PAGE
Ireland 338
Lancaster . . . 338
Leicester 339
Marche 339

Heralds and Heralds Extraordinary—
Arundel 339
Blanc Coursier . . 339
Buckingham . . . 339
Carlisle 339
Clarencieux . . . 340
Gloucester . . . 340
Hanover 340
Leicester 340
Marche 340
Mowbray 340

Heralds and Heralds Extraordinary— PAGE
Norfolk 341
Suffolk 341

Pursuivants Extraordinary—
Antelope 341
Athlone 341
Barnes 341
Berwick 341
Blanch Lion . . . 341
Blanch Rose . . . 342
Blanch Sanglier . 342
Calais 342
Comfort 342
Cork 342
Eagle 342
Falcon 342
Fitzalan 343

Pursuivants Extraordinary— PAGE
Guisnes 343
Hampnes 343
Kildare 343
Mont-Orgueil . . 343
Nottingham . . . 343
Portsmouth . . . 344
Risebank 344
Rose 344
Rose Blanche . . 344
Rose Rouge . . . 344

Scotch Officers (Part IX.)—
Lyon Kings of Arms 513
Lyons Depute . . 513

Irish Officers (Part X.)—
Ulster Kings of Arms 572

PART VI.—LEGAL.

JUDGES AND OTHER LEGAL DIGNITARIES.

Introduction . . . 345
Lord High Chancellors 352
Lord Keepers . . . 352
Commissioners of the Great Seal . . . 352
Lords of Appeal . . 358
Judicial Committee of the Privy Council . 358
Chief Justiciaries . . 362
Justiciaries 363
Justices Itinerant . . 365
Justices of Trailbaston 365

King's and Queen's Bench—
Chief Justices, K.B. and Q.B. . . . 369
Presidents, H.C.J., Q.B. DIV. . . . 371
Puisne Justices, K.B. and Q.B. . . . 371
Puisne Justices, H.C.J., Q.B. DIV. 374

Common Pleas—
Chief Justices, C.P. 375
Presidents, H.C.J., C.P. DIV. . . . 376
Puisne Justices, C.P. 376
Puisne Justices, H.C.J., C.P. DIV. 380

Exchequer—
Chancellors (Part III.) 164
Chief Barons Exch. 381
Presidents, H.C.J., EXCH. DIV. . . 382
Puisne Barons Exch. . . . 382
Puisne Justices, H.C.J., EXCH. DIV. 385
Cursitor Barons . 386

County Palatine of Chester or Welsh Judges—
Chief Justices . . 386
Second or Puisne Justices . . . 386

Chancery—
Lord Chancellors, &c. (*vide supra*) . 352
Masters of the Rolls 387
Lord Justices of Appeal 388
Vice Chancellors . 390
Justices, H.C.J., CH. DIV. 390
Masters in Chancery 392
Accountants General (Chancery) . 392

Appeal—
Lords of Appeal (*vide supra*) . . 358
Lords Justices of Appeal before the Judicature Acts . 388
Lords Justices of Appeal after the Judicature Acts . 389

Probate, Divorce, Admiralty—
Judges, Probate and Divorce, 1858–75 391
Judges, H.C.J., Probate, Divorce, and Admiralty Divs. 391
(*For earlier Judges, see Ecclesiastical and Admiralty Courts, inf.*)

Bankruptcy—
Judges of the Court of Review . . 392
Chief Judges in Bankruptcy . . 392
Bankruptcy Judges 392
County Court Judges . 403
Attorneys General . 397
Solicitors General . . 400
Serjeants-at-law . . 406
Kings Counsel, Queen's Counsel, Patents of Precedence 414

Ecclesiastical Courts—
Deans of the Arches 420
Judges of the Prerogative Court of Canterbury . . 421
Vicars General to the Archbishop of Canterbury . . 421
Judges of the Consistory Court (Chancellors of the diocese of London) . 422
King's and Queen's Advocates . . . 422

Admiralty Court (and *vide supra*) . . 391
Judges 422
Admiralty Advocates 423
Recorders and Common Serjeants of London (Part VIII) 493–5

PART VII.—ECCLESIASTICAL.

Archbishops, Bishops, and Deans of England and Wales.

Those marked * are Bishops Suffragan.

Archbishops, Bishops, and Deans of	Abp. or Bp. PAGE	Dean. PAGE
Bangor	425	426
Bath and Wells	427	—
*Bedford	447 & 452	—
*Berwick	479	—
Bristol	439	440
—— Gloucester and	439	—
Canterbury	429	431
Carlisle	475	476
Chester	476	477
Chichester	432	433
Christ Church, Oxford	—	457
—— College, Manchester	—	481
*Colchester	460–1	—
Cornwall	436	—
—— Devon and	436	—
Coventry	443	—
—— Lichfield and	443	—
Devon and Cornwall	436	—
Devonshire	436	—
Dorchester	446	—
—— and Sidnacester	446	—
*Dover	431	—
Dunwich	454	—
—— Elmham and	454	—
Durham	478	479
East Angles	452	—
Elmham	454	—
—— and Dunwich	454	—
Ely	434	435
Exeter	436	437
Gloucester	438	440
—— and Bristol	439	—
*Guildford	471	—
Hereford	441	442
Hexham	480	—
Holy Island	478	—
*Hull	486	—
*Ipswich	455	—
Lichfield	443–4	445
—— and Coventry	443	—
*Leicester	458	—
Lincoln	446	447
Lindisfarne	478	—
Liverpool	480	—
Llandaff	448	449
London	450	452
Manchester	480	481
*Marlborough	452 & 467	—
Newcastle-on-Tyne	481	—
Norwich	454	455
*Nottingham	447	—
Oxford	456	457
Penrith	476 & 482	—
Peterborough	457	458
Ripon	482	482
Rochester	459	461
St. Alban's	461	—
St. Asaph	461	462
St. David's	463	465
St. Paul's	—	452
Salisbury	466	468
Selsey	432	—
*Shaftesbury	467	—
Sherborne	466	—
*Shrewsbury	444	—
Sidnacester	446	—
—— Dorchester and	446	—
Sodor and Man	483	—
Southwell	468	—
*Taunton	428	—
*Thetford	455	—
Truro	468	—
Wakefield	484	—
Wells	427	428
—— Bath and	427	—
Westminster	469	469
Wilton	466	—
Winchester	470	471
Windsor	—	474
Worcester	472	473
York	484	486

PART VIII.—LONDON.

	PAGE
Portreeves, Mayors, and Lord Mayors of London	488
Chamberlains of London	493
Recorders	493
Common Serjeants	494

PART IX.—SCOTLAND.

SOVEREIGNS OF SCOTLAND. *See* Part I., p. 17.

OFFICERS OF STATE, &c., OF SCOTLAND.

Treasury— PAGE
- Lord High Treasurers, &c. . . . 496
- Comptrollers . . 498

Admiralty—
- Lord High Admirals 499
- Vice-Admirals . . 499

Privy Council—
- Lord Presidents . 500
- Vice Presidents for Education . . . 500
- Lords Privy Seal . 500

Secretaries of State—
- Secretaries of State in Scotland from 13— to the Union 501
- Principal Secretaries of State for Scotland in England from the Union to 1746 . 502
- Secretaries for Scotland under 48 & 49 Vict. cap. 61 502

Post Office—
- Postmasters-General 502

Lord Chancellors, *vide infra* 514
Lord Keepers of the Great Seal from Union to present time 503

Revenue—
- Commissioners of Customs . . . 503
- Commissioners of Excise 504

Lord High Stewards . 505
Lord Great Chamberlains 505
Lord High Constables 506
Earls Marischal . . 507
Knights Marischal 507
Lord High Commissioners to the Parliaments of Scotland 507

LORD LIEUTENANTS OF COUNTIES—SCOTLAND.

Lord Lieutenants of— PAGE
- Aberdeenshire . . 508
- Argyleshire . . . 508
- Ayrshire 508
- Banffshire . . . 508
- Berwickshire . . 508
- Buteshire 508
- Caithness-shire . . 509
- Clackmannanshire . 509
- Cromarty 509
- Dumbartonshire . 509
- Dumfries-shire . . 509
- Edinburghshire . . 509
- Edinburgh City . 509
- Elginshire . . . 509
- Fifeshire 510
- Forfarshire . . . 510
- Haddingtonshire . 510
- Inverness-shire . . 510
- Kincardineshire . 510
- Kinross-shire . . 510
- Kirkcudbright, Stewartry . . . 510
- Lanarkshire . . . 511
- Linlithgowshire . 511
- Midlothian . . . 509
- Nairnshire . . . 511
- Orkney and Zetland 511
- Peebleshire . . . 511
- Perthshire . . 511
- Renfrewshire . . 511
- Ross-shire . . . 512
- Roxburghshire . . 512
- Selkirkshire . . . 512
- Shetland 511
- Stirlingshire . . . 512
- Sutherlandshire . . 512
- Wigtonshire . . . 512
- Zetland, Orkney, &c. 511

HERALDIC OFFICERS—SCOTLAND.

Lyon Kings of Arms . 513
Lyons Depute . . . 513

JUDGES AND OTHER LEGAL DIGNITARIES OF SCOTLAND.

Lord Chancellors, &c. 514

Court of Session—
- Introduction . . . 515
- Lord Presidents . . 516
- Lord Justice Clerks 516
- Extraordinary Lords of Session . . . 517
- Ordinary ditto . . 518

Court of Justiciary—
- Introduction . . . 521
- Lords Justices General 522
- Lord Justice Clerks 516
- Judges or Commissioners of Justiciary 522

Exchequer— PAGE
- Introduction . . . 523
- Chief Barons . . 523
- Barons 524

Admiralty Court—
- Judges 524

Lord Clerk Registers . 524
Lord Advocates . . 525
Solicitors General . . 526
Deans of Faculty . . 527

ARCHBISHOPS AND BISHOPS OF SCOTLAND.

Part. 1.—*Ante - Revolution Bishops.*

Archbishops and Bishops of—
- Aberdeen 530
- Argyll 537
- Brechin 530
- Caithness 531
- Dunblane 532
- Dunkeld 532
- Edinburgh . . . 533
- Galloway 538
- Glasgow 535
- Isles, The 539
- Moray 534
- Mortlach 530
- Orkney 534
- Ross 535
- St. Andrew's . . 528
- The Isles 539

Part 2.—*Post - Revolution Bishops.*

Archbishops and Bishops of—
- Aberdeen 540
- —— and Orkney . 541
- Argyll and the Isles 541
- Brechin 541
- Caithness 541
- —— Moray, Ross, &c. 544
- —— Ross and . . . 545
- Dunblane 542
- —— Dunkeld and . 542
- —— Fife, Dunkeld and 543
- —— St. Andrew's, Dunkeld and . . 545
- Dunkeld 542
- —— and Dunblane . 542
- —— (Fife, Dunkeld and Dunblane) . 543
- —— (St. Andrew's, Dunkeld and Dunblane) 545

Archbishops and Bishops of— PAGE
Edinburgh . . . 542
Fife. 543
—— Dunkeld and Dunblane . . . 543
Galloway 543
—— Glasgow and . 544
Glasgow 543
—— and Galloway. 544
Isles, Argyll and the 541
Moray 544
—— and Ross . . 544

Archbishops and Bishops of— PAGE
Moray, Ross and Caithness . . . 544
Orkney 545
—— Aberdeen and. 541
"*Primus*" Bishops. 540
Ross 545
—— and Caithness. 545
—— Moray and. . 544
—— (Moray. Ross and Caithness) . 544
St Andrew's, Dunkeld and Dunblane 545

Archbishops and Bishops of— PAGE
The Isles, Argyll and 541
Scotch Bishops without Sees 545

General Assembly of the Kirk of Scotland—
Lord High Commissioners . . . 546
Moderators . . . 547

Lord Provosts of Edinburgh . . . 547

PART X.—IRELAND.

Sovereigns of Ireland.—*See* Part I., p. 20.

Officers of State, &c., of Ireland.
Lord Lieutenants and Chief Governors of Ireland, including Lord Deputies and Lord Justices 549
Treasury—
Lord Treasurers . 558
Vice-Treasurers . 558
Treasury Commissioners 558
Secretaries . . . 561
Chancellors of the Exchequer. . . 561
Secretaries of State—
Principal Secretaries of State . 562
Chief Secretaries to the Lord Lieutenant 562
Under Secretaries to the Lord Lieutenant, permanent. 563
Under Secretaries to the Lord Lieutenant, parliamentary . . . 564
Post Office—
Postmasters - General 564
Commanders of the Forces 564
Revenue—
Commissioners of Customs . . . 565
Commissioners of Excise 566
Commissioners of Accounts . . . 567
Commissioners of Stamps 568

Lord Lieutenants of Counties—Ireland.
Lord Lieutenants of—
Antrim 568
Armagh 568
Carlow 568
Cavan 569
Clare 569
Cork 569
Donegal 569
Downshire . . . 569
Dublin (County) . 569
Fermanagh . . . 569
Galway 569
Kerry 569
Kildare 569
Kilkenny 570
King's County . . 570
Leitrim 570
Limerick (County) . 570
Londonderry . . . 570
Longford 570
Louth 570
Mayo 570
Meath 570
Monaghan . . . 570
Queen's County . . 571
Roscommon . . . 571
Sligo 571
Tipperary . . . 571
Tyrone 571
Waterford . . . 571
Westmeath . . . 571
Wexford 571
Wicklow 571

Heraldic Officers.—Ireland.
Ulster Kings of Arms 572

Judges and other Legal Dignitaries of Ireland.
Introduction . . . 572
Lord Chancellors . . 574
Deputy Chancellors . 574
Vice-Chancellors . . 574
Lord Keepers . . . 574
Deputy Keepers . . 574
Commissioners of the Great Seal. . . 574
King's and Queen's Bench—
Chief Justices, K.B. and Q.B. . . . 577
Presidents, H.C.J., Q.B. DIV. . . . 578
Puisne Justices, K.B. and Q.B. . . . 578
Puisne Justices, H.C.J., Q.B. DIV. . 579
Common Pleas—
Chief Justices, C.P. 580
Presidents, H.C.J., C.P. DIV. . . . 581
Puisne Justices, C.P. 581
Puisne Justices, H.C.J., C.P. DIV. . 582
Exchequer—
Chancellors (*vide supra*) 561
Chief Barons, EXCH. 582
Presidents, H.C.J., EXCH. DIV. . . 583
Puisne Barons, EXCH. 583
Puisne Barons, H.C.J., EXCH. DIV. 584
Chancery—
Lord Chancellors, &c. (*vide supra*) . 574
Masters of the Rolls 585
Lord Justices of Appeal 585
Vice-Chancellors . 586
Justices, H.C.J., CH. DIV. 586
Land Courts—
Judges of the Landed Estate Court 587

	PAGE
Land Court—(cont.)—	
Land Judges	586
Irish Land Commissioners	588
Appeal—	
Lord Justices of Appeal before the Judicature Acts	585
Lord Justices of Appeal after the Judicature Acts	586
Probate and Matrimonial—	
Judges before the Judicature Acts	587
Judges after the Judicature Acts	587
Admiralty Court—	
Judges	587
Bankruptcy Court—	
Judges	587
Attorneys General	588
Solicitors General	589
Serjeants-at-Law	590

Archbishops, Bishops, and Deans of Ireland.

Archbishops, Bishops, and Deans of	Abp. or Bp. PAGE	Dean. PAGE
Achonry	612	614
—— Killala and	613	—
—— Tuam, Killala, and	613	—
Aghadoe, Ardfert and	639	—
—— Limerick, Ardfert, and	639	—
Ardagh	607	609
——Kilmore and	607	—
—— Kilmore, Elphin, and	608	—
Ardfert	—	640
——and Aghadoe	639	—
—— (Limerick, Ardfert, and Aghadore)	639	—
Armagh	595 & 597	597
——and Clogher	597	
Cashel	624	627
—— and Emly	626	—
—— Emly, Waterford, and Lismore	627	—
Christ Church, Dublin	—	618
Clogher	596 & 597	597
——Armagh and	597	
Clonard	598	
Clonfert	635	637
—— and Kilmacduagh	636	—
—— (Killaloe, Kilfenora, Clonfert, and Kilmacduagh)	636	—
Clonmacnois	599	600
Cloyne	630	632
—— Cork and	631	—
—— (Cork, Cloyne, and Ross)	631–2	—
Connor	603	605
Connor, Down and	604	—
——(Down, Connor, and Dromore)	605	—
Cork	630	632
——and Cloyne	631	—
—— Cloyne, and Ross	631–2	—
—— and Ross	632	—
Derry	600	602
——and Raphoe	602	—
Down	603	605
——and Connor	604	—
—— Connor, and Dromore	605	—
Dromore	604	606
—— Down, Connor, and	605	—
Dublin	615	617, 618
—— and Glendalough	615	—
—— Glendalough, and Kildare	617	—
Elphin	608	609
—— (Kilmore, Elphin, and Ardagh)	608	—
Emly	625	628
——Cashel and	626	—
——(Cashel, Emly, Waterford, and Lismore)	627	—
Enachdune	—	613
Ferns	621	623
——and Leighlin	622	—
—— (Ossory, Ferns, and Leighlin)	622	—
Glendalough	615	619
——Dublin, and	615	—
Glendalough (Dublin, Glendalough, and Kildare)	617	—
Kildare	616	619
—— Dublin, Glendalough, and	617	—
Kilfenora	635	637
—— Killaloe, and	635	—
—— (Killaloe, Kilfenora, Clonfert, and Kilmacduagh)	636	—
Killala	612	614
——and Achonry	613	—
—— (Tuam, Killala, and Achonry)	613	—
Killaloe	634	637
—— and Kilfenora	635	—
—— Kilfenora, Clonfert, and Kilmacduagh	636	—
Kilmacduagh	636	637
—— Clonfert, and	636	—
—— Killaloe, Kilfenora, Clonfert, and	636	—
Kilmore	607	609
——and Ardagh	607	—
—— Elphin, and Ardagh	608	—
Leighlin	621	623
—— Ferns and	622	—
—— Ossory, Ferns and	622	—
Limerick	638	639
—— Ardfert, and Aghadoe	639	—
Lismore	626	628

Archbishops, Bishops, and Deans of	Abp. or Bp.	Dean.	Archbishops, Bishops, and Deans of	Abp. or Bp.	Dean.	Archbishops, Bishops, and Deans of	Abp. or Bp.	Dean.
	PAGE	PAGE		PAGE	PAGE		PAGE	PAGE
Lismore, Cashel, Emly, Waterford, and	627	—	Ossory, Ferns, and Leighlin.	622	—	Tuam . . .	611	613
—— Waterford and . . .	626	—	Raphoe . . .	601	602	—— Killala, and Achonry	613	—
Louth . . .	—	598	—— Derry, and	602	—	Waterford . .	626	628
Mayo . . .	611	—	Ross	631	633	——(Cashel, Emly, Waterford, and Lismore) . . .	627	—
Meath . . .	599	—	—— Cork, and	632	—	—— & Lismore	626	—
Ossory . . .	620	622	—— Cork, Cloyne, and .	631–2	—			
			St. Patrick's	—	617			

Lord Mayors of Dublin 640 | Recorders 642

PART XI.—INDIA.

Introduction . . . 643

SECTION I.—HOME OFFICIALS.

Presidents, Commissioners, and Secretaries of the Board of Control (Part III.) 251-4
Chairmen and Deputy Chairmen of the East India Co. . 644
Secretaries and Under Secretaries of State for India (Part III.) . . 236
Members of the Council of India . . 646

SECTION II.—INDIAN OFFICIALS.

Supreme Government of India—
Administrators prior to 1773 . . 647
Governors-General, 1773 to 1858 . . 648
Viceroys and Governors-General from 1858 649
Commanders - in - Chief 650

Bengal—
Governors, *see* Governors - General of India . . . 647-9

Bengal—
Lieutenant - Governors 652
Commanders - in - Chief 652
and *see* Commanders-in-Chief—India . 650
Chief Justices, Supreme Court . . 652
Chief Justices, High Court of Judicature 653
Bishops of Calcutta 653

North-West Provinces and Oudh—
Lieut.-Governors — North-West Provinces 653
Chief-Commissioners, Oudh 654
Lieut. - Governors, North-West Provinces, and Chief Commissioners, Oudh, united . . 652
Chief Justices, North-West Provinces 654

Punjab—
Presidents of Board of Administration 654
Chief Commissioners 654
Lieut.-Governors . 654
Bishops of Lahore . 655

Central Provinces—
Chief Commissioners 655

Burma—
Chief Commissioners 655
Bishops of Rangoon 655

Assam—
Chief Commissioners 656

Madras—
Governors . . . 656
Commanders - in - Chief 657
Chief Justices, Supreme Court . . 658
Chief Justices, High Court of Judicature 658
Bishops 658

Bombay—
Governors 659
Commanders - in - Chief 659
Chief Justices, Supreme Court . . 660
Chief Justices, High Court of Judicature 660
Bishops 661

Prince of Wales' Island or Penang, Malacca, Singapore (*see* Straits Settlements, Part XII.) 674

PART XII.—THE COLONIES.

Governors and Bishops of the Colonies and other Dependencies of the British Empire.

Introduction, containing a *classified* list of the various Indian and Colonial Dioceses . . PAGE 662

Colonial Governors.

Governors of—
Africa, *see* South Africa and West Africa.
Alderney 668
America, *see* North America.
Anguilla, *see* pp. 726-30
Antigua . . . 727-8
Auckland Islands . 710
Australasia . . 702-12
Australia, *see* Australasia, North Australia, South Australia, and Western Australia.
Bahama Islands . . 716
Barbados . . 719-21
Barbuda, *see* p. 726.
Basutoland . . . 681
Bechuanaland, British 680
Belize 714
Berbice 715
Bermudas . . . 701
Borneo — British North 676
British Bechuanaland 680
—— Columbia . . 698
—— Guiana . . . 714-5
—— Honduras . . 714
—— Kaffraria . . 680
—— New Guinea . 711
—— North Borneo 676
Canada 691-2
——— Dominion of 689-99
—— Govrs.-Gen. . 692
—— Lower (and *see* Quebec) . . 691-3
—— Upper (and *see* Ontario) . . . 691-2
Cape Breton . . . 696
Cape of Good Hope . 678
Ceylon 672
Channel Islands . 667
Christmas Island . 674-5
Cyprus 671

Governors of— PAGE
Demerara . . . 715
Dominica . . . 727-30
Essequibo . . . 715
Falkland Islands . 731
Fiji 711
Gambia 686
Gibraltar 669
Gold Coast . . . 686
Grenada . . . 719-20-4
Grenadines, *see* p. 718
Griqualand West . 681
Guernsey, &c. (Governors) . . . 668
—— (Bailiffs). . 669
Guiana, British . 714-5
Heligoland . . . 670
Herm 668
Honduras, British . 714
Hong Kong . . . 673
Ionian Islands (Part II.) 129
Isle of Man . . . 664
Jamaica 712
Jersey (Bailiffs) . 668
—— (Governors) . 667
Kaffraria, British . 680
Labuan 675
Lagos 687
Leeward Islands 726-31
Malacca 674-5
Malta 671
Man, Isle of . . . 664
Manitoba 696
Martinique . . . 719
Mauritius 683
Montserrat . . . 727-8
Moreton Bay, *see* Queensland.
Natal 680
Nevis 727-9
New Brunswick 691-2-5-6
New Guinea, British 711
New South Wales . 702
New Zealand . . 708
Newfoundland . . 699
Niger Protectorate . 688
North American Provinces . . . 692
North Australia . 705
North Borneo, British 676
North Western Territory and North West Territories 696-7
Nova Scotia . 691-2-4-5

Governors of— PAGE
Ontario (and *see* Canada, Upper) . 692
Pacific, Western— High Commrs. . 711
Penang 674-5
Port Jackson, *see* New South Wales.
Port Philip *see* Victoria.
Prince Edward Island . . . 691-2-9
Prince of Wales' Island . . . 674-5
Quebec (and *see* Canada, Lower) . 693
Queensland . . . 705
Red River Settlement 696
Redonda, *see* p. 726
Rodriguez . . . 684
Rupert's Land . . 696
St. Christopher . 727-9
St. Helena . . . 682
St. Kitts, *see* St. Christopher.
St. Lucia . . 719-20-5
St. Vincent . 719-20-5
Sark 668
Seychelles Islands . 684
Sierra Leone . . 685
Singapore . . . 674-5
Somers Islands . . 701
South Africa— High Commrs. . 679
South African Colonies . . 677-82
South Australia . 706
Straits Settlements 674-5
Swan River Settlement, *see* Western Australia.
Tasmania . . . 708
Tobago . . . 719-20-3
Trinidad . . 719-20-1
Turks and Caicos Islands . . . 713
Vancouver Island . 699
Van Diemen's Land 708
Victoria 704
Virgin Islands . 727-31
West Africa Settlements . . 684-8
Western Australia 707
Western Pacific High Commrs. . 711
Windward Islands 717-26

COLONIAL BISHOPS.

For Classified list of dioceses, *see* p. 662

Bishops of—	PAGE
Adelaide	707
Africa, *see* Central Africa, and Eastern Equatorial Africa.	
Algoma	693
Antigua	728
Armidale, Grafton &	704
Assiniboia	698
Athabasca	697
Auckland	709
Australia	703
Ballarat	705
Barbados	721
Bathurst	704
Bloemfontein	680
Bombay (Part XI.)	661
Brisbane	706
British Columbia	698
Calcutta (Part XI.)	653
Caledonia	698
Cape Town	679
Central Africa	688
China, Mid	676
China, North	676
China, Travancore and	676
Christchurch, N.Z.	709
Colombo	673
Columbia	698
Dunedin	710
Eastern Equatorial Africa	688
Falkland Islands	730
Fredericton	696
Gibraltar	670
Goulburn	704
Grafton and Armidale	704
Grahamstown	680
Guiana	715
Hong Kong	673
Honolulu	712
Huron	693
Jamaica	713
Japan	677
Jerusalem	677
Jersey (Deans)	668
Kaffraria	681
Labuan	675
Lahore (Part XI.)	655
Mackenzie River	697
Madagascar	689
Madras (Part XI.)	658
Maritzburg	680
Mauritius	684
Melanesia	711
Melbourne	705
Mid-China	676
Montreal	694
Moosonee	697
Nassau	717
Natal	680
Nelson	710
Newcastle, N.S.W.	703
Newfoundland	700
New Westminster	698
New Zealand	709
Niagara	693
Niger District	689
North China	676
North Queensland	706
Nova Scotia	695
Ontario	693
Orange Free State	681
Perth, W.A.	707
Pretoria	682
Qu'appelle	698
Quebec	694
Queensland, North	706
Rangoon (Part XI.)	655
Riverina	704
Rupert's Land	697
St. Helena	682
St. John's Kaffraria	681
Saskatchewan	697
Sierra Leone	685
Sydney	703
Tasmania	708
Toronto	693
Travancore and China	676
Trinidad	723
Victoria (Hong Kong)	673
Waiapu	710
Wellington	710
Zambesi	688
Zululand	681

PART XIII.—ORDERS OF KNIGHTHOOD.

ORDERS OF KNIGHTHOOD, &c., CONNECTED WITH THE BRITISH EMPIRE.

	PAGE
Introduction	732
Garter—	
Introduction	732
Knights (K.G.)	733
Prelates	745
Chancellors	745
Registrars	746
Kings of Arms	746
Thistle—	
Introduction	746
Knights (K.T)	747
Deans	749
Secretaries	749
Kings of Arms	749
St. Patrick—	
Introduction	749
Grand Masters	750
Knights (K.P.)	750
Prelates	752
Chancellors	752
Secretaries	752
Genealogists	752
Kings of Arms	752
Bath—	
Introduction	752
Great Masters	753
Acting Masters	754
Knights Companions (K.B.)	754
Knights Grand Cross (G.C.B.)—	
Military	766
Civil	771
Knights Commanders (K.C.B.)—	
Military	773
Civil	782
Deans	784
Genealogists	784
Registrars	784
Secretaries	784
Kings of Arms	785
Guelphs—Hanover—	
Introduction	785
Knights Grand Cross (G.C.H.)	785
Knights Commanders (K.C.H.)	787
Knights (K.H.)	789
Chancellors	792
Vice-Chancellors	792
Secretaries	792
Kings of Arms	793
St. Michael and St. George—	
Introduction	793
Grand Masters, &c.	794

St. Michael and St. George— PAGE
Knights Grand Cross (G.C.M.G.) . . . 794
Knights Commanders (K.C.M.G.) . 796
Prelates 799
Chancellors . . . 799
Secretaries . . . 799
Kings of Arms . . 799
Registrars . . . 799
Star of India—
Introduction . . . 800

Star of India— PAGE
Grand Masters . . 800
Knights Grand Commanders (G.C.S.I.) . . . 800
Knights Commanders (K.C.S.I.) . 802
Registrars . . . 804
Secretaries . . . 804
Indian Empire—
Introduction . . . 804
Grand Masters . . 804

Indian Empire— PAGE
Knights Grand Commanders (G.C.I.E.) 805
Knights Commanders (K.C.I.E.) . 805
Companions (C.I.E.) 805
Registrars . . . 808
Secretaries . . . 808
Crown of India—
Introduction . . . 809
Members (Cr. I.) . 809
Registrars . . . 810

PART XIV.—NAVAL.

Lord High Admirals, Commissioners of Admiralty, &c. (Part III.) . . . 169
Secretaries to the Admiralty (Part III.) 186
Treasurers of the Navy (Part III.) . 256
Comptrollers of the Navy (Part III.) . 257
Surveyors of the Navy (Part III.) . 257
Judges, High Court of Admiralty, England (Part VI.) . 422
Judges, High Court of Admiralty, Scotland (Part IX.) . . 524
Judges, High Court of Admiralty, Ireland (Part X.) 587
Admiralty Advocates (Part VI.) . . . 423

Admirals (List **A**)—
Admirals from the Restoration to 1836, with the dates of their first promotion as Rear-Admirals . 813
Admirals (List **B**)—
Admirals of the Fleet from 1837 . 821
Admirals (List **C**)—
Admirals of the United Kingdom from 1837 . . . 822
Admirals (List **D**)—
Admirals of the Red, White, and Blue, from 1837 to the discontinuance of the division into three squadrons in 1864 . . . 823

Admirals (List **E**)—
Admirals on the Active List from 1864 824
Admirals (List **F**)—
Promotions of Admirals tranferred from the Active to the Retired List 838
Admirals (List **G**)—
Admirals on the Reserve Half-Pay List from 1851 to the closing of the List 840
Admirals (List **H**)—
Captains promoted to the List of Retired Admirals . 844
Governors of Greenwich Hospital . . 854
Lieut.-Governors of Greenwich Hospital 854

PART XV.—MILITARY.

Commanders-in-Chief 855
Captains-General . . 855
Field-Marshals . . 856
Generals (List **A**)—
Officers who attained the rank of GENERAL, down to June 1854 . . 857
Generals (List **B**)—
Officers who attained the rank of LIEUT.-GENERAL down to November 1846 . . . 864
Generals (List **C**)—
Officers who attained the rank of MAJOR-GENERAL down to January 1837 871
Generals (List **D**)—
MAJOR-GENERALS, including the Indian General Officers, from 1837; with their subsequent promotions to LIEUT.-GENERALS and GENERALS 876
Governors of Chelsea Hospital 936
Lieut.-Governors of Chelsea Hospital . 936
Judge Advocates General 936

PART XVI.—MISCELLANEOUS.

	PAGE
Presidents of the Royal College of Physicians	938
Presidents of the Royal College of Surgeons	938
Presidents of the Royal Society	940
Presidents of the Royal Institution	940
Presidents of the Royal Academy of Arts	941
Astronomers-Royal	941

List of Abbreviations used in Index of Names 944
Index of Names 943

THE BOOK OF DIGNITIES.

PART I. ROYAL.

SOVEREIGNS AND RULERS OF THE PRINCIPAL COUNTRIES IN THE WORLD.

SOVEREIGNS AND RULERS OF EUROPE.

ENGLAND.

SOVEREIGNS OF ENGLAND.

KINGS OF THE HEPTARCHY.

KENT.

Co-extensive with the shire of Kent.

455. Hengist.
488. Æsc, Esca, or Escus, son of Hengist, in honour of whom the kings of Kent were for some time called Æscings.
512. Octa, son.
542. Hermenric, or Ermenric, son.
560. St. Ethelbert, 1st Christian king.
616. Eadbald, son.
640. Ercenbert, or Ercombert, son.
664. Ecbert, or Egbert, son.
673. Lother, or Lothair, brother.
685. Edric; slain in 687.

The kingdom was now subject for a time to various leaders.

694. Wihtred, or Wightred.
725. Eadbert } sons of Wihtred, succeeding each other.
748. Ethelbert II. }
760. Alric }
794. Edbert, or Ethelbert Pryn; dep.
796. Cuthred, or Guthred.
805. Balred; who in 823 lost his life and kingdom to Egbert, K. of Wessex.

SOUTH SAXONS.

Sussex and Surrey.

490. Ella.
514. Cissa, son.

The South Saxons here fell into an almost total dependence on the kingdom of Wessex, and the names of the princes who were possessed of this titular sovereignty are scarcely known.

648. Edilwald, Edilwach, or Adelwalch.
688. Anthun and Berthun, brothers; they reigned jointly; both were vanquished by Ina, K. of Wessex, and the kingdom was finally conquered in 725.

West Saxons.

Berks, Southampton, Wilts, Somerset, Dorset, Devon, and part of Cornwall.

519. Cerdicus.
534. Cynric, or Kenric, son.
559. Ceawlin, son; banished by his subjects; *d.* 593.
591. Ceolric, nephew.
597. Ceolwulf.
611. {Cynegils, and in
614. {Cwichelm, his son, reign jointly.
643. Cenwal, Cenwalh, or Cenwald.
672. Sexburga, his queen, sister to Penda, K. of Mercia; dep.
674. Escwine, in conjunction with Centwine. On the death of Escwine
676. Centwine rules alone.
685. Ceadwal, or Cœdwalla.
688. Ina, or Inas.
728. Ethelheard, or Ethelard, related to Ina.
740. Cuthred, brother.
754. Sigebryt, or Sigebert.
755. Cynewulf, or Kenwulf, of the line of Cerdic.
784. Bertric, or Beorhtric.
800. Egbert, aft. sole monarch of England.

East Saxons.

Essex, Middlesex, and parts of Herts.

527. Erchenwin, or Erchwine.
587. Sledda, son.
597. St. Sebert, or Sabert, son; first Christian king.
614. Saxred, or Sexted, or Serred, jointly with Sigebert and Seward; all slain.
623. Sigebert II., surn. the Little, son of Seward.
655. Sigebert III., surn. the Good, brother of Sebert; put to death.
661. Swithelm, son of Sexbald.
663. Sigher, or Sigeric, jointly with Sebbi, or Sebba, who became a monk.
693. Sigenard, or Sigehard, and Suenfrid.
700. Offa.
709. Suebricht, or Selred.
738. Swithred, or Swithed.
792. Sigeric.
799. Sigered.
823. The kingdom seized upon by Egbert, K. of Wessex.

Northumbria.

Lancaster, York, Cumberland, Westmoreland, Durham, and Northumberland.

Northumbria was at first divided into two separate governments, *Bernicia* and *Deira;* the former stretching from the river Tweed to the Tyne, and the latter from the Tyne to the Humber.

547. Ida, Saxon.
560. Adda, son, K. of Bernicia
— Ella, K. of Deira; aft. sole K. of Northumbria.
567. Glappa, Clappa, or Elappea; Bernicia.
572. Heodwulf; Bernicia.
573. Freodwulf; Bernicia.
580. Theodric; Bernicia.
588. Ethelric; Bernicia.
593. Ethelfrith, surn. the Fierce.
617. Edwin, son of Ella, K. of Deira in 590; slain in battle with Penda, K. of Mercia.
634. The kingdom again divided; Eanfrid ruled in Bernicia, and Osric in Deira; both put to death.
635. Oswald; slain in battle.
644. Osweo, or Oswy.
670. Ecfrid, or Egfrid, K. of Northumbria.
685. Alcfrid, or Ealdferth.
705. Osred, son.
716. Cenred; sprung from Ida.
718. Osric, son of Alcfrid.
729. Ceolwulf; *d.* a monk.
738. Eadbert, or Egbert; retired to a monastery.
757. Oswulf, or Osulf; slain in a sedition.
759. Edilwald, or Mollo; slain by Alred.
765. Alred, Ailred, or Alured; dep.
774. Ethelred, son of Mollo; expelled.
778. Elwald, or Celwold; dep. and slain.
789. Osred, son of Alred; fled.
790. Ethelred rest.; aft. slain.
795. Erdulf, or Ardulf; dep.
808. Alfwold; succ. by Erdulf, and perhaps by others.

East Angles.

Norfolk, Suffolk, Cambridge, Isle of Ely.

575. Uffa; a noble German.
582. Titilus, or Titulus, son.
599. Redwald, son.
624. Erpwald, or Eorpwald.
629. Sigebert, half-brother.
632. Egfrid, or Egric, cousin.
635. Anna, or Annas; killed.
654. Ethelric, or Ethelhere; slain in battle.
655. Ethelwald, brother.
664. Aldulf, or Aldwulf.
713. Selred, or Ethelred.
746. Alphwuld.
749. Beorn and Ethelred, jointly.
758. Beorn, alone.
761. Ethelred.
790. Ethelbert, or Ethelbyrht; put to death in Mercia in 792, when Offa, K. of Mercia, overran the country, which was finally subdued by Egbert, K. of Wessex.

Mercia.

Counties of Gloucester, Hereford, Chester, Stafford, Worcester, Oxford, Salop, Warwick, Derby, Leicester, Bucks,

Northampton, Notts, Lincoln, Bedford, Rutland, Huntingdon, and parts of Herts.

586. Crida, or Cridda.
593. Interregnum.
597. Wibba, son.
615 Ceorl, or Cheorl, nephew.
626. Penda; killed in battle.
655. Peada, son; murdered.
656. Wulfhere, brother, to make way for whom Peada was slain.
675. Ethelred; became a monk.
704. Cenred, Cendred, or Kendred; became a monk at Rome.
709. Ceolred, or Celred, or Chelred, son of Ethelred.
716. Ethelbald; slain in a mutiny by one of his own chieftains, his successor, after a defeat in battle.
755. Beornred, or Bernred; himself slain.
755. Offa.
794. Egfrid, or Egferth, son; he had ruled jointly with his father for some years; *d.* suddenly.
794. Cenulf, or Kenulph; slain.
819. Kenelm, or Cenelm, a minor reigned five months; killed by his sister Quendreda.
819. Ceolwulf, uncle; driven from the throne.
821. Beornulf, or Burnwulf; killed by his own subjects.
823. Ludecan; slain.
825. Withlafe, or Wiglaf.
838. Berthulf, or Bertulf.
852. Burhred, or Burdred.

This last kingdom merged, like the other kingdoms of the Heptarchy, into that of England.

The Saxons, although they were divided into seven different kingdoms, yet were for the most part subject to one king alone, who was entitled *Rex gentis Anglorum*, or King of the English nation; those which were stronger than the rest giving the law to them in their several turns, till, in the end, they all became incorporated in the empire of the West Saxons, under Egbert. The term "Octarchy" is sometimes applied, by writers, to the Saxon kingdoms, inasmuch as Northumbria, the seventh kingdom, was at different periods divided into two kingdoms, Bernicia and Deira, ruled by separate kings. Other writers apply the term to the successive kings whose authority was acknowledged by the other princes of the Heptarchy; these they call *Octarchs.*

Kings, or Octarchs, of the English Saxons during the Heptarchy.

457. Hengist, 1st K. of Kent.
490. Ella, 1st K. of the South Saxons.
519. Cerdic, 1st K. of the West Saxons.
534. Kenric, 2nd K. of the West Saxons.
560. Ceawlin, 3rd K. of the West Saxons.
593. Ethelbert, 5th K. of Kent.
616. Redwald, 3rd K. of the East Angles.
630. Edwin, 4th K. of Northumbria.
635. Oswald, 5th K. of Northumbria.
644. Osweo, 8th K. of Bernicia.
670. Wulfhere, 6th K. of Mercia.
675. Ethelred, 7th K. of Mercia.
704. Cenred, 8th K. of Mercia.
709. Celred, 9th K. of Mercia.
716. Ethelbald, 10th K. of Mercia.
758. Offa, 11th K. of Mercia.
796. Egferth, 12th K. of Mercia.
796. Kenulph, 13th K. of Mercia.
820. Egbert, 17th K. of the West Saxons; first and absolute monarch of the whole Heptarchy, who vanquished all or most of the Saxon kings, and added their dominions to his own.

Kings of England before the Conquest.

827. Egbert, first sole Monarch of England.
837. Ethelwolf, son.
857. Ethelbald, son.
860. Ethelbert, 2nd son of Ethelwolf.
866. Ethelred, brother; mortally wounded by the Danes in battle; *d.* April 27, 871.
871. Alfred, surn. the Great, 4th son of Ethelwolf; *d.* Oct. 26, 901.
901. Edward the Elder, son; *d.* 925.
925. Athelstan, natural son of Edward, whose legitimate sons were too young to govern; *d.* Oct. 17, 941.
941. Edmund, son of Edward; *d.* May 26, 947.
947. Edred, brother.
955. Edwy, son of Edmund.
959. Edgar, brother; *d.* July 1, 975.
975. Edward the Martyr, son; stabbed at Corfe Castle, at the instance of his step-mother Elfrida, Mar. 18, 978.
978. Ethelred II., half-brother. This prince retired to Normandy during the Danish usurpation, when Sweyn was procl. king, 1013. Sweyn *d.* a few months afterwards, and was succ. by his son, Canute the Great. While the latter was absent in Denmark, the exiled king returned. Ethelred *d.* April 24, 1016.

1016. Edmund II., surn. Ironside, son of Ethelred. The English and Danish nobility, tired of war, obliged Edmund and Canute to divide the kingdom between them. Canute ruled the northern portion, while the southern was held by Edmund, who, however, did not long survive the treaty; he was murdered at Oxford by two of his chamberlains, accomplices of Duke Edric, Nov. 30, 1016.

The Danish Race.

1016. Canute, styled the Great, and the Dane; established himself as K. of England in 1017; *d.* Nov. 12, 1035.

1035. Harold I., surn. Harefoot, from his agility in running; *d.* April 14, 1039.

1039. Hardicanute, or Canute the Hardy, so named from his bodily powers, brother; *d.* June 8, 1041.

The Saxons Repossessed.

1041. Edward the Confessor, son of Ethelred II. by Emma, his 2nd queen; *d.* Jan. 5, 1066, naming William of Normandy his heir.

1066. Harold II., son of Godwin, E. of Kent; reigned only nine months; killed at the battle of Hastings.

William of Normandy invaded England in Sept. 1066 with a powerful fleet and army, and on Oct. 14 following, gave battle, at Hastings, to Harold, over whom he obtained a complete victory. Harold being slain, William was proclaimed king by his triumphant army on the spot.

Sovereigns of England after the Conquest.

The Norman Line.

1066. William the Conqueror, natural son of Robert, D. of Normandy, by Harlotta, a tanner's dau., at Falaise, *b.* 1025; *m.* Matilda, dau. of Baldwin, Count of Flanders; *d.* at Rouen, Sept. 9, 1087.

1087. William Rufus, or the Red, from the colour of his hair, second son of William I., *b.* 1057; *d.* unm., Aug. 2, 1100.

1100. Henry I., surn. Beauclerk, youngest son of William I., *b.* 1070; *m.* 1st, Matilda, dau. of Malcolm Canmore, K. of Scotland; and, 2nd, Adelicia, dau. of Godfrey, D. of Louvaine; *d.* Dec. 1, 1135.

1135. Stephen, son of the E. of Blois (by Adela, dau. of William I.), and nephew of Henry I., *b.* 1105. The Empress Maud, dau. of Henry, and rightful heir to the throne, contended for it with Stephen, but ultimately concluded a peace with him, by which she secured the succession to her son. *See next Reign.* Stephen *m.* Matilda, dau. of Eustace, count of Boulogne; *d.* Oct. 25, 1154.

The Plantagenet Line.

1154. Henry II., son of the Empress Maud and Geoffrey Plantagenet, Earl of Anjou, her second husband, *b.* 1133; *m.* Eleanor, dau. of the D. of Guienne and divorced queen of Louis VII. of France; *d.* July 6, 1189.

1189. Richard I., *Cœur de Lion*, son of Henry I., *b.* 1157; *m.* Berengaria, dau. of Sancho VI., K. of Navarre; *d.* Apr. 6, 1199.

1199. John, surn. Lackland, brother, *b.* Dec. 24, 1166; *m.* 1st, Avisa, dau. of William, Earl of Gloucester, whom he divorced upon the ground of consanguinity; and, 2nd, Isabella, dau. of Aymer, count of Angoulême, the affianced wife of the Count de la Marche; *d.* Oct. 19, 1216.

1216. Henry III., son, *b.* Oct. 1, 1206; *m.* Eleanor, dau. of Raymond, count de Provence; *d.* Nov. 16, 1272.

1272. Edward I., surn. Longshanks, son, *b.* June 17, 1239; *m.* 1st, Eleanor, dau. of Ferdinand III., K. of Castile; and, 2nd, Margaret, dau. of Philip III., the Hardy, K. of France; *d.* July 7, 1307.

1307. Edward II., son, *b.* Apr. 25, 1284; *m.* Isabella, dau. of Philip IV., the Fair, K. of France; deth. Jan. 25, 1327; and murdered at Berkeley Castle Sept. 21 following.

1327. Edward III., son, *b.* Nov. 13, 1312; *m.* Philippa, dau. of William, count of Holland and Hainhault; *d.* June 21, 1377.

1377. Richard II., son of Edward the Black Prince and grandson of Edward III., *b.* Jan. 6, 1367; *m.* 1st, Anne, dau. of the Emp. Charles IV.; and, 2nd, Isabel, dau. of Charles VI. of France; deth. Sep. 29, 1399, and murdered at Pomfret Castle, Feb. 13 following.

THE LINE OF LANCASTER.

1399. HENRY IV., surn. Bolingbroke, son of John of Gaunt, D. of Lancaster, who was fourth son of Edward III., *b.* 1367; *m.* 1st, Mary de Bohun, dau. and co-heiress of the E. of Hereford; and, 2nd, Joanna of Navarre, widow of John de Montfort, D. of Bretagne; *d.* Mar. 20, 1413.

1413. HENRY V., of Monmouth, son, *b.* 1388; *m.* Katherine, youngest dau. of Charles VI., K. of France; *d.* Aug. 31, 1422.

1422. HENRY VI., son, *b.* Dec. 6, 1421; *m.* Margaret of Anjou, dau. of René or Regnier, D. of Anjou, titular K. of Sicily and Jerusalem; deth. Mar. 4, 1461, and *d.* in the Tower (supposed to have been murdered there by Richard, D. of Gloucester), June 20, 1471.

THE HOUSE OF YORK.

1461. EDWARD IV., eldest surviving son of Richard, D. of York, son of Richard, E. of Cambridge, and Anne, his wife, who was dau. of Roger, E. of March, the son of Edmund Mortimer and Philippa, his wife, who was dau. of Lionel, D. of Clarence, the third son of Edward III., *b.* Apr. 29, 1441; *m.* Elizabeth Widvile, (or Woodville), dau. of Sir Richard Widvile, afterwards E. Rivers, widow of Sir John Grey, of Groby; *d.* Apr. 9, 1483. Edward, pr. of Wales, son of Henry VI., was murdered in this reign.

1483. Edward V., eldest son, *b.* Nov. 4, 1470. Dep. June 22, 1483. He was shortly afterwards murdered, with his brother Richard, in the Tower, by their uncle Gloucester, who had usurped the throne.

1483. RICHARD III., D. of Gloucester, eighth and youngest son of Richard, D. of York, and brother of Edward IV., *b.* 1443; *m.* Anne, dau. of the great E. of Warwick, and widow of Edward, pr. of Wales, above-mentioned. Slain at the battle of Bosworth Field, Aug. 22, 1485.

THE FAMILIES OF YORK AND LANCASTER UNITED IN THE HOUSE OF TUDOR.

1485. HENRY VII., E. of Richmond, grandson of Owen Tudor and Catharine, widow of Henry V., *b.* July 26, 1455; claimed his title to the crown in right of his mother, descended from John of Gaunt, 4th son of Edward III.; *m.* Elizabeth, eldest dau. of Edward IV., by which marriage the houses of Lancaster and York were united. Overcame Richard III. at the battle of Bosworth, and was crowned king upon the spot; *d.* Apr. 22, 1509.

1509. HENRY VIII., son, *b.* June 28, 1491; *m.* (1), Katharine of Arragon (widow of his elder brother, Arthur), whom he repudiated and afterwards formally divorced. (2) Anne Boleyn (dau. of sir Thomas Boleyn, and maid of honour to queen Katharine), whom he beheaded. (3), Jane Seymour (dau. of Sir John Seymour and maid of honour to Anne Boleyn), who died in childbirth of a son, aft. Edward VI. (4), Anne of Cleves (sister of William, D. of Cleves), whom he divorced. (5), Katharine Howard (niece of the D. of Norfolk), whom he beheaded. (6), Katharine Parr (dau. of sir Thomas Parr and widow of Edward Nevill, lord Latimer, her 2nd husband), who survived him; *d.* Jan. 28, 1547.

1547. EDWARD VI., son, by Jane Seymour *b.* Oct. 12, 1537; *d.* unm., July 6, 1553.

1553. MARY, eldest dau. of Henry VIII., by Katharine of Arragon, *b.* Feb. 11, 1516; *m.* Philip II. of Spain, who was joined with her in the government, July 25, 1554; *d.* Nov. 17, 1558.

In the beginning of this reign lady Jane Grey, dau. of the D. of Suffolk, and wife of lord Guildford Dudley, was proclaimed queen; Edward VI., when dying, having been persuaded to alter the succession in her favour. In 10 days afterwards she returned to private life; but was tried Nov. 13, 1553, and beheaded Feb. 12, 1554, being then but seventeen years of age. Her nominal reign extended from July 6 to July 17 1553.

1558. ELIZABETH, second dau. of Henry VIII. by Anne Boleyn, *b.* Sept. 7, 1533; *d.* unm. Mar. 24, 1603; and in her ended the Tudors.

HOUSE OF STUART.

1603. JAMES I. of England, and VI. of Scotland, son of Mary, Q. of Scots, by Henry Stuart, lord Darnley; and grandson of James IV. of Scotland, by Margaret, dau. of Henry VII. of England; *b.* June 19, 1566; *m.* Anne, dau. of Frederick II. of Denmark; *d.* Mar. 27, 1625.

1625. **Charles** I., eldest surviving son, *b.* Nov. 19, 1600; *m.* Henrietta-Maria, dau. of Henry IV. and sister of Louis XIII. of France. This monarch was brought to trial on a charge of making war against the parliament, sentenced to be beheaded, Jan. 27, 1649, and executed on the 30th.

1649. **Commonwealth.** Oliver Cromwell, was decl. protector of England, Dec. 12, 1653; *d.* Sept. 3, 1658. Succ. by his son, Richard Cromwell, who was made protector, Sept. 4; he resigned the office, Apr. 22, 1659.

1649. **Charles** II., son of Charles I., *b.* May 29, 1630. This king's reign commenced, in effect, with his restoration to the throne, May 29, 1660; but it is reckoned by historians from the day of his father's death, Jan. 30, 1649; *m.* the infanta Catharine of Portugal, dau. of John IV. and sister of Alphonso VI.; *d.* Feb. 6, 1685.

1685. **James** II., brother, *b.* Oct. 13, 1633; *m.* 1st, lady Anne Hyde, dau. of Edward, E. of Clarendon, who died before he ascended the throne; and, 2nd, Mary Beatrice Eleanor d'Este, pr. of Modena, dau. of Alphonso d'Este, D. of Modena. James abd. by flight, finally quitting England Dec. 23, 1688; *d.* in exile Sept. 6, 1701.

1689. **William** III., pr. of Orange, and **Mary** II., his queen. The former was the posthumous son of William of Nassau and Orange by the pr. Mary, eldest dau. of Charles I., *b.* Nov. 14, 1650. The latter was the elder dau. of James II., by lady Anne Hyde; *b.* April 30, 1662. Procl. Feb. 13, 1689; this event consummating the Revolution of 1688. Mary *d.* Dec. 28, 1694; and William, Mar. 8, 1702.

1702. **Anne**, second dau. of James II. by lady Anne Hyde, *b.* Feb. 6, 1665; *m.* pr. George of Denmark, July 28, 1683; *d.* Aug. 1, 1714.

House of Hanover.

1714. **George** I. (George Lewis), the nearest Protestant heir to the crown; son of Ernest Augustus, elector of Hanover and D. of Brunswick-Luneburg, by the pr. Sophia, youngest dau. of Frederick V., elector palatine and K. of Bohemia, and the pr. Elizabeth, dau. of James I., *b.* May 28, 1660; *m.* Sophia Dorothea, dau. of George William, D. of Zell; *d.* June 11, 1727.

1727. **George** II. (George Augustus), son, *b.* Oct. 30, 1683; *m.* Wilhelmina Caroline, dau. of John Frederick, margrave of Brandenburg-Anspach; *d.* Oct. 25, 1760.

1760. **George** III. (George William Frederick), son of Frederick Lewis, pr. of Wales, and grandson of George II., *b.* June 4, 1738; *m.* Charlotte Sophia, dau. of Charles Lewis Frederick, D. of Mecklenburg-Strelitz, Sept. 8, 1761. His son, George, pr. of Wales, declared regent of the kingdom, Feb. 5, 1811. and so continued until Jan. 29, 1820, when the king died.

1820. **George** IV. (George Augustus Frederick), eldest son, *b.* Aug. 12, 1762; *m.* his cousin Caroline Amelia Elizabeth, dau. of Charles William Ferdinand, D. of Brunswick-Wolfenbuttel, by Augusta, eldest sister of George III., Apr. 8, 1795. Became prince regent, Feb. 5, 1811; and succ. to the throne, Jan. 29, 1820; *d.* June 26, 1830.

1830. **William** IV. (William Henry), D. of Clarence, third son of George III., *b.* Aug. 21, 1765; *m.* Amelia Adelaide Louisa Theresa Caroline, dau. of George Frederick Charles, D. of Saxe-Meiningen, July 11, 1818; *d.* June 20, 1837.

1837. **Victoria** (Alexandrina Victoria), dau. of Edward, D. of Kent, fourth son of George III., *b.* May 24, 1819; *m.* Feb. 10, 1840, her cousin, Francis Albert Augustus Charles Emmanuel D. of Saxe, pr. of Saxe-Coburg and Gotha.

Wales was finally subdued by England in 1282–3, and the "Statute of Wales," 12 Edw. I., was passed May 19, 1284. Wales was "incorporated, united, and annexed to and with" England in 1535 by 27 Hen. VIII. cap. 26. Scotland was united to both on and after May 1, 1707, by 6 Anne cap. 11, and the three were then styled "Great Britain." Ireland was united to Great Britain on and after Jan. 1, 1801, by 39 and 40

Geo. III. cap. 67, and the four countries were then and are still styled "The United Kingdom of Great Britain and Ireland."

CONSORTS OF THE QUEENS OF ENGLAND.

Philip, Consort of Q. Mary; son of Charles, K. of Spain (Charles I.) and Emp. of Germany (Charles V.); styled King Philip, *b.* May 21, 1527; *m.* (1) to Q. Mary, July 25, 1554, and (2) to Isabella, dau. of Henry II., K. of France, June 24, 1559; succ. to throne of Spain as Philip II. Jan. 16, 1556; *d.* Sept. 13, 1598.

George, Consort of Q. Anne, son of Frederick III., K. of Denmark; styled Pr. George or Pr. George of Denmark, *b.* Apr. 21, 1653; *m.* July 28, 1683; cr. D. of Cumberland, Apr. 9, 1689; *d.* Oct. 28, 1708.

Albert (Francis Albert Augustus Charles Emmanuel), Consort of Q. Victoria, son of Ernest-Anthony, D. of Saxe-Coburg and Gotha; styled Pr. Albert, until June 25, 1857, when he received the style or title of the Pr. Consort; *b.* Aug. 26, 1819; *m.* Feb. 10, 1840; *d.* Dec. 14, 1861.

CONSORTS OF THE KINGS OF ENGLAND.

Including those who died before their husbands accession to the throne. Compiled, chiefly, from Miss Agnes Strickland's *Queens of England*, the dates in which have been followed.

Styled "Queen."

Matilda of Flanders, consort of William I., dau. of Baldwin, Count of Flanders, *b.* abt. 1031; *m.* 1050; *d.* Nov. 2, 1083.

Matilda of Scotland, 1st consort of Henry I., dau. of Malcolm Canmore, K. of Scotland, *b.* 1079; *m.* Nov. 11, 1100; *d.* May 1, 1118.

Adelicia of Louvaine, 2nd consort of Henry I., dau. of Godfrey, D. of Brabant, *b.* 1102; *m.* Jan. 24, 1121; *d.* Apr. 1151.

Matilda of Boulogne, consort of Stephen, dau. of Eustace, Count of Boulogne, *m.* 1128; *d.* May 3, 1151.

Eleanor of Aquitaine, consort of Henry II., dau. of the D. of Guienne and divorced Q. of Louis VII. of France, *b.* 1122; *m.* May 1, 1152; *d*, June 26, 1204.

Berengaria of Navarre, consort of Richard I., dau. of Sancho VI., K. of Navarre; *m.* May 12, 1191; ret. to the Abbey of Espan in 1230, and *d.* there some years aft.

Avisa or Hawise, 1st consort of John, dau. of William, E. of Gloucester; *m.* 1191; divorced, on ground of consanguinity, 1200. This lady was not crowned or acknowledged as Queen.

Isabella of Angoulême, 2nd consort of John, dau. of Aymer, Count of Angoulême, *b.* abt. 1185; *m.* Aug. 24, 1200; *d.* 1246.

Eleanor of Provence, consort of Henry III., dau. of Raymond, Count de Provence, *b.* 1222; *m.* Jan. 4, 1236; *d.* June 24, 1291.

Eleanor of Castile, 1st consort of Edward I., dau. of Ferdinand III., K. of Castile, *b.* abt. 1244; *m.* Aug. 1254; *d.* Nov. 9, 1290.

Margaret of France, 2nd consort of Edward I., dau. of Philip III., K. of France, *b.* abt. 1281; *m.* Sept. 8, 1299; *d.* Feb. 14, 1317.

Isabella of France, consort of Edward II., dau. of Philip IV., K. of France, *b.* 1295; *m.* Jan. 22, 1308; *d.* Aug. 22, 1358.

Philippa of Hainhault, consort of Edward III., dau. of William, Count of Holland and Hainhault, *b.* 1311; *m.* Jan. 24, 1328; *d.* Aug. 15, 1369.

Anne of Bohemia, 1st consort of Richard II., dau. of Charles IV., Emp. of Germany, *b.* May 11, 1366; *m.* Jan. 14, 1382; *d.* June 7, 1394.

Isabella of Valois, 2nd consort of Richard II., dau. of Charles VI., K. of France, *b.* Nov. 9, 1387; *m.* Nov. 1, 1395; *d.* Sept. 13, 1410.

Mary de Bohun, 1st consort of Henry IV., dau. of the E. of Hereford, *m.* 1384; *d.* 1394; before Henry became King.

Joanna of Navarre, 2nd consort of Henry IV., dau. of Charles, K. of Navarre, and widow of John de Montfort, D. of Bretagne, *b.* abt. 1360; *m.* Feb. 7, 1403; *d.* July 9, 1437.

Katherine of Valois, consort of Henry V., dau. of Charles VI., K. of France, *b.* Oct. 27, 1401; *m.* June 3, 1420; *d.* Jan. 3, 1437.

Margaret of Anjou, consort of Henry VI., dau. of René or Regnier, D. of Anjou, *b.* Mar. 23, 1429; *m.* Apr. 22, 1445; *d.* Aug. 26, 1481.

Elizabeth Woodville, consort of Edward IV., dau. of Sir Richard Widvile or Woodville, aft. E. Rivers; widow of Sir John Grey, of Groby, aft. ld. Ferrars, *b.* abt. 1435; *m.* privately May 1, 1464; marriage announced Sept. 29, 1464; *d.* June 8, 1492.

ANNE OF WARWICK, consort of Richard III., dau. of the E. of Warwick, widow of Edward pr. of Wales, *b.* June 11, 1454; *m.* Aug. 1470; *d.* March 16, 1485.

ELIZABETH OF YORK, consort of Henry VII., dau. of Edward IV., *b.* Feb. 11, 1466; *m.* Jan. 18, 1486; *d.* Feb. 11, 1503.

KATHARINE OF ARRAGON, 1st consort of Henry VIII., dau. of Ferdinand, K. of Arragon, and widow of Henry's elder brother Arthur, *b.* Dec. 15, 1485; *m.* June 11 1509; divorced May 25, 1533; *d.* Jan. 7, 1536.

ANNE BOLEYN, 2nd consort of Henry VIII., dau. of Sir Thomas Boleyn, *b.* 1501; *m.* Jan. 25, 1533, and Apr. 12, 1533; beheaded May 19, 1536.

JANE SEYMOUR, 3rd consort of Henry VIII., dau. of Sir John Seymour; *m.* May 20, 1536; *d.* Oct. 24, 1537.

ANNE OF CLEVES, 4th consort of Henry VIII., dau. of John, D. of Cleves, *b.* Sept. 22, 1516; *m.* Jan. 6, 1540; divorced July 9, 1540; *d.* July 16–17, 1557.

KATHARINE HOWARD, 5th consort of Henry VIII., dau. of ld. Edmund Howard, niece of the D. of Norfolk, *b.* 1521 or 1522; *m.* July 1540; beheaded Feb. 12, 1542.

KATHARINE PARR, 6th consort of Henry VIII., dau. of Sir Thomas Parr, widow of Edward, ld. Borough of Gainsborough, and of John Neville, ld. Latimer, her second husband, *b.* (*teste* Miss Strickland), 1513, but according to other authorities in 1509 or 1510; *m.* July 12, 1543; *d.* Sept. 7, 1548.

ANNE OF DENMARK, consort of James I., dau. of Frederick II., K. of Denmark, *b.* Dec. 12, 1574; *m.* Nov. 23, 1589; *d.* Mar. 2, 1619.

HENRIETTA MARIA, consort of Charles I., dau. of K. Henry IV., and sister of K. Louis XIII. of France, *b.* Nov. 25, 1609; *m.* June 13, 1625; *d.* Sept. 10, 1669.

CATHARINE OF BRAGANZA, consort of Charles II., dau. of K. John IV., and sister of K. Alphonso VI. of Portugal, *b.* Nov. 25, 1638; *m.* May 20, 1662; *d.* Dec. 31, 1705.

ANNE HYDE, 1st consort of James II., dau. of Edward, E. of Clarendon, *m.* Sept. 3, 1660; *d.* Mar. 31, 1671, before James became King. Anne was the mother of Q. Mary and Q. Anne.

MARY BEATRICE ELEANOR D'ESTE OF MODENA, 2nd consort of James II., dau. of Alphonso D'Este, D. of Modena, *b.* Oct. 5, 1658; *m.* Nov. 21, 1673; *d.* May 7, 1718

SOPHIA DOROTHEA OF ZELL, consort of George I., dau. of George William, D. of Zell, *b.* Sept. 15, 1666: *m.* 1682; *d.* Nov. 13, 1726.

WILHELMINA CAROLINE, consort of George II., dau. of John Frederick, Margrave of Brandenburg-Anspach, *b.* Mar. 1, 1683; *m.* 1705; *d.* Nov. 20, 1737.

CHARLOTTE SOPHIA, consort of George III., dau. of Charles Lewis Frederick, D. of Mecklenburgh-Strelitz, *b.* May 19, 1744; *m.* Sept. 8, 1761; *d.* Nov. 17, 1818.

CAROLINE AMELIA ELIZABETH, consort of George IV., dau. of Charles William Ferdinand, D. of Brunswick-Wolfenbuttel, *b.* May 17, 1768; *m.* Apr. 8, 1795; *d.* Aug. 7, 1821.

AMELIA ADELAIDE LOUISA THERESA CAROLINE, consort of William IV., dau. of George Frederick Charles, D. of Saxe-Meiningen, *b.* Aug. 13, 1792; *m.* July 11, 1818; *d.* Dec. 2, 1849.

PRINCES OF WALES OF THE BLOOD ROYAL OF ENGLAND.

1284. Edward, of Carnarvon, son of Edward I.; aft. Edw. II.

1343. Edward, the Black Prince, eldest son of Edward III.

1376. Richard, of Bourdeaux, only surviving son of the Black Prince; aft. Richard II.

1399. Henry, of Monmouth, eldest son of Henry IV.; aft. Henry V.

1454. Edward, of Westminster, only son of Henry VI., murdered by the dukes of Gloucester and Clarence, in 1471.

1472. Edward, of Westminster, eldest son of Edward IV.; aft. Edward V.

1483 Edward, E. of Salisbury, only son of Richard III.; cr. Sept. 8, 1483; *d.* April, 1484.

1490. Arthur Tudor, eldest son of Henry VII.; *d.* 1502.

1503. Henry, D. of York, second son of Henry VII., cr. pr. of Wales on his brother's death; aft. Henry VIII.

1537. Edward Tudor, son of Henry VIII.; aft. Edward VI. The patent of creation to the dignity was never actually passed.

1610. Henry Frederick, eldest son of James I.; *d.* 1612.

Charles, D. of York, second son of

James I.; aft. Charles I. Not cr. pr. of Wales.

Charles, eldest son of Charles I.; aft. Charles II. Not cr. pr. of Wales.

1714. George Augustus, only son of George I.; aft. George II.

1729. Frederick Lewis, eldest son of George II.; cr. Jan. 9, 1729; *d.* before his father, Mar. 20, 1751.

1751. George William Frederick, eldest son of the preceding; cr. Apr. 20, 1751; aft. George III.

1762. George Augustus Frederick, eldest son of George III.; cr. Aug. 17, 1762; aft. George IV.

1841. Albert Edward, eldest son of Q. VICTORIA; cr. Dec. 7, 1841.

PRINCES AND PRINCESSES OF ENGLAND.

BORN OF THE NORMAN LINE.

ISSUE OF WILLIAM I.

1. Robert, D. of Normandy.
2. Richard, said to have been killed by a stag in the New Forest.
3. WILLIAM-RUFUS, aft. William II.
4. HENRY, aft. Henry I.
5. Cicely, *d.* abbess of the convent of the Holy Trinity at Caen.
6. Constance, *m.* to Alan, E. of Brittany, and of Richmond, in England.
7. Alice, contracted to Harold (who afterwards refused her), she died unmarried.
8. Adela, *m.* to Stephen, E. of Blois, by whom she had (besides three other sons), William, Theobald, and Henry.

   STEPHEN, aft. King.
9. Gundred, *m.* to William, E. of Warren and Surrey.
10. Agatha (called Margaret by *Ralphe Brooke*), betrothed to Alphonso, K. of Galicia, but died on her journey to join her bridegroom.

ISSUE OF HENRY I.

1. William, drowned on his passage from Normandy; the prince's newly married bride, Matilda, dau. of Fulke, E. of Anjou, shared the same fate.
2. Maud, or Matilda, *m.* 1st, to the emp. Henry V., and 2nd, to Geoffrey Plantagenet, son of Fulke, E. of Anjou, by whom she had:
   - I. HENRY, aft. Henry II.
   - II. Geoffrey (Pembroke) E. of Nantes.
   - III. William, E. of Poitou.
   - IV. Emma, *m.* to David, by usurpation pr. of North Wales.

ISSUE OF STEPHEN.

1. Baldwin, *d.* in infancy.
2. Eustace, E. of Boulogne.
3. William, E. of Mortaigne.
4. Maud, *d.* young.
5. Mary, *m.* to Matthew, son of Theodore, count of Flanders.

BORN OF THE PLANTAGENET LINE.

ISSUE OF HENRY II.

1. William, who died in childhood.
2. Henry, *m.* Margaret, dau. of the French king; *d.* before his father.
3. RICHARD, aft. Richard I.
4. Geoffrey, E. of Brittany and Richmond, *m.* Constance, dau. of Conan, D. of Brittany; accidentally killed at a tournament in Paris, leaving
   - I. Arthur, E. or D. of Brittany, who was rightful heir of his uncle Richard.
   - II. Eleanor, *d.* unm.
5. Philip, *d.* young.
6. JOHN, aft. King.
7. Eleanor, *m.* to Alphonso VIII., K. of Castile.
8. Maud, *m.* to Henry the Lion, D. of Brunswick, ancestor of the present royal family of England.
9. Joan, *m.* 1st, to William II., count of Sicily; and, 2nd, Raymond, count of Toulouse.

[Henry had two sons by Rosamond Clifford; *viz.* William Longespee, or Longsword, so named from the sword he usually wore; and Geoffrey, abp. of York.]

ISSUE OF KING JOHN.

1. HENRY, aft. Henry III.
2. Richard, E. of Poitou and Cornwall; elected K. of the Romans in 1256.
3. Joan, *m.* to Alexander II., K. of Scotland.
4. Eleanor, *m.* 1st, to William Marshall the younger, E. of Pembroke; and, 2nd, to Simon de Montfort, E. of Leicester.
5. Isabel, *m.* to the Emp. Frederick II.

ISSUE OF HENRY III.

1. EDWARD, aft. Edward I.
2. Edmund Plantagenet, surn. Crouchback, E. of Lancaster.
3. Richard; 4. John; 5. William; all *d.* young.
6. Henry, assass. at mass in Italy.
7. Margaret, *m.* to Alexander III., K. of Scotland.

8. Beatrice, *m.* to John, 1st D. of Brittany.
9. Catherine, *d.* in infancy.

Issue of Edward I.

1. John; 2. Henry; 3. Alphonso; *d.* young.
4. **Edward**, pr. of Wales; aft. Edward II.
5. Eleanor, *m.* 1st, to Alphonso of Arragon, who died soon after; and, 2nd, to Henry, comte de Barre.
6. Joan, *m.* 1st, to Gilbert de Clare, E. of Gloucester; and 2nd, to Ralph de Monthermere.
7. Margaret, *m.* to John, D. of Brabant.
8. Berangera or Berenice, *d.* in infancy.
9. Alice, *d.* young.
10. Mary, a nun at Amesbury in Wiltshire, and aft. at Fontevraud, in Normandy.
11. Elizabeth, *m.* 1st, to John, E. of Holland; and, 2nd, to Humphrey, E. of Hereford and Essex.
12. Beatrice, *d.* in infancy.
13. Blanch, *d.* in infancy.
14. Thomas, E. of Norfolk and marshal of England.
15. Edmund, of Woodstock, E. of Kent; beheaded in 1329.
16. Eleanor, second of the name; *d.* young.

Issue of Edward II.

1. **Edward**, aft. Edward III.
2. John, of Eltham, E. of Cornwall.
3. Joan, *m.* to David, pr. of Scotland son of Robert Bruce.
4. Eleanor, *m.* to Reynald or Reginald, E. of Gueldres.

Issue of Edward III.

1. Edward, surn. the Black Prince, pr. of Wales, *b.* June 15, 1330; *m.* his cousin Joan, the "Fair Maid of Kent," dau. of Edmund, E. of Kent, repudiated wife of Thomas Montacute, E. of Salisbury, and widow of sir Thomas Holland; *d.* July 8, 1876, having had issue
   - I. Edward, who died in his seventh year.
   - II. **Richard**, aft. Richard II.
2. William, of Hatfield, died early.
3. Lionel, D. of Clarence. *m.* 1st, Elizabeth de Burgh, dau. of William, E. of Ulster, by whom he had an only daughter, Philippa, *m.* to Edmund Mortimer, E. of March. Lionel espoused, 2nd, Violante, dau. of the D. of Milan, and died in Italy soon after. For the issue of Philippa, *see below.*
4. John, of Ghent, or Gaunt (so called from the place of his birth), D. of Lancaster. From this prince sprang that branch which afterwards possessed the crown. *See below.*
5. Edmund, of Langley, E. of Cambridge, and aft. D. of York, *m.* 1st, Isabel, dau. of Peter, K. of Castile and Leon; and 2nd, Joan, dau. of Thomas, E. of Kent. For his issue (by his first duchess), *see below.*
6. William, of Windsor, *d.* young.
7. Thomas, of Woodstock, D. of Gloucester, *m.* Eleanor, eldest dau. and coheiress of Humphrey de Bohun, E. of Hereford, Essex, and Northampton. The duke was murdered at Calais, Sept. 8, 1397.
8. Isabel, *m.* to Ingelram de Courcy, cr. E. of Bedford.
9. Joan, contracted in marriage to Alphonso, K. of Castile, but died before its celebration.
10. Blanch de la Tour (born in the Tower), *d.* an infant.
11. Mary, *m.* to John de Montfort. surnamed the Valiant, D. of Brittany.
12. Margaret, *m.* to John Hastings, E. of Pembroke, who was poisoned.

The following are given under separate heads, as materially serving to elucidate the claims to, and the descent of, the crown.

Issue of Philippa

Daughter of Lionel, duke of Clarence, 3rd son of Edward III. See above.

1. Roger Mortimer, E. of March, *m.* Eleanor, dau. of Thomas Holland, E. of Kent; killed in Ireland, leaving issue
   - I. Edmund, E. of March, who, on the death of Richard II. became rightful heir to the crown; he was kept in confinement by Henry IV., and *d.* in prison, 1424.
   - II. Anne Mortimer, who became heiress of her house, and conveyed its claims on the crown to the house of York, by her marriage with Richard E. of Cambridge.
   - III. Eleanor, *m.* to Edward Courtenay, E. of Devon.
2. Edmund Mortimer, who settled in North Britain.
3. John Mortimer, put to death in 1424.
4. Elizabeth, *m.* to Henry, lord Percy, surn. Hotspur.
5. Philippa, *m.* 1st, to John, E. of Pembroke; and, 2nd, to Richard Fitz-Alan, E. of Arundel.

Issue of John of Gaunt, D. of Lancaster.

4th son of Edward III.

This prince *m.* 1st, Blanch, youngest daughter and co-heiress of Henry, D. of Lancaster, and had issue

1. Henry, aft. Henry IV.
2. Philippa, *m.* to John I., K. of Portugal.
3. Elizabeth, *m.* 1st to John, D. of Exeter, and 2nd, to sir John Cornewall, cr. baron Fanhope.

He *m.* 2nd, Constance, eldest dau. and co-heiress of Peter, K. of Castile and Leon, by whom he had

4. Catherine, *m.* to Henry, pr. of Asturias, aft. king of Castile and Leon.

He *m.* 3rd, Catherine, dau. of sir Payn Roelt, knt., and widow of sir Hugh Swynford. By this lady he had, before marriage

5. John, marq. of Dorset and Somerset, ancestor of the present D. of Beaufort.
6. Henry, bp. of Winchester.
7. Thomas, D. of Exeter.
8. Joan, *m.* 1st, to Robert, lord Ferrers; and 2nd, to Ralph Nevill, E. of Westmoreland.

These last, by act of parliament, 20 Richard II., were declared legitimate for all purposes but inheriting the crown.

Issue of Edmund, E. of Cambridge.

5th son of Edward III.

1. Constance, *m.* to Thomas le Despencer, E. of Gloucester.
2. Edward, D. of York and Albemarle; slain at the battle of Agincourt.
3. Richard, E. of Cambridge, *m.* Anne Mortimer, great-grand-daughter, and eventually heiress of her uncle Lionel, D. of Clarence. Through her the house of York derived its title to the crown in preference to the house of Lancaster, which, though descended in an unbroken male line from Edward III. was the line of a younger son. The earl was beheaded for a plot against the life of Henry V., leaving issue
   - I. Isabel, *m.* to Henry Bourchier, E. of Essex.
   - II. Richard, D. of York and protector of England, *m.* Cicely, dau. of Ralph Nevill, E. of Westmoreland; he was slain at the battle of Wakefield in 1160. His issue follows:

Issue of Richard, D. of York.

1. Henry, *d.* in infancy.
2. Edward, aft. Edward IV.
3. Edmund, E. of Rutland; slain at Wakefield, aged only 12 years.
4. William, *d.* in infancy.
5. John, *d.* in infancy.
6. George, D. of Clarence; *m.* Isabel, dau. of Richard Nevill, E. of Warwick; attainted, and *d.* 1477; he left issue
   - I. Edward, E. of Warwick; beheaded in 1499.
   - II. Margaret, countess of Salisbury, *m.* to sir Richard Pole; attainted, and beheaded in 1541.
7. Thomas, *d.* in infancy.
8. Richard, aft. Richard III.
9. Anne, *m.* 1st, Henry Holland, D. of Exeter; and 2nd, sir Thomas St. Leger, knt.
10. Elizabeth, *m.* to John Delapole, D. of Suffolk.
11. Margaret, *m.* to Charles, D. of Burgundy.
12. Ursula.

Edward, earl of Warwick, beheaded as above, in 1499, was the last of the male line of the Plantagenets.

Born of the House of Lancaster.

Issue of Henry IV.

1. Henry, surn. Monmouth, pr. of Wales, aft. Henry V.
2. Thomas, of Lancaster, D. of Clarence, who fell at the battle of Beague, in 1421.
3. John, of Lancaster, D. of Bedford, regent of France in the minority of Henry VI.
4. Humphrey, D. of Gloucester, regent of England in the same minority. It is supposed that he died by violence or poison.
5. Blanch, *m.* 1st, to Louis, pr. palatine of Bavaria; 2nd, to the K. of Arragon; and, 3rd, to the D. of Barre.
6. Philippa, *m.* to Eric, K. of Denmark.

Issue of Henry V.

Henry, pr. of Wales, aft. Henry VI.

The widow of Henry V. married sir Owen Tudor of the principality of Wales, said to be of royal lineage, by whom she had

- I. Edmund Tudor, cr. E. of Richmond, who *m.* Margaret, dau. of John, first D. of Somerset, and great-grand-daughter of John of Gaunt. He left an

only son, HENRY, E. of Richmond; aft. Henry VII.
II. Jasper Tudor, cr. E. of Pembroke.
III. Tacina Tudor, *m.* to Reginald, lord Grey, of Wilton.

ISSUE OF HENRY VI.

Edward, pr. of Wales, *b.* Oct. 31, 1452, *m.* in 1470, the lady Anne Nevill, second dau. and co-heiress of Richard, Nevill, E. of Warwick. This prince was, with his mother, taken prisoner at the battle of Tewkesbury, in 1471, and was murdered a few days afterwards by the dukes of Gloucester and Clarence, and lord Hastings. His widow, Anne, subsequently married Gloucester, one of his murderers, who became king as Richard III.

BORN OF THE HOUSE OF YORK.

ISSUE OF EDWARD IV.

1. EDWARD, pr. of Wales, aft. Edward V., and
2. Richard, D. of York. These two princes were murdered in the Tower, at the instance of their uncle Richard, D. of Gloucester, in 1483.
   The latter prince, Richard, was married in his infancy to Anne, heiress of the house of Mowbray, only child of John Mowbray, D. of Norfolk and earl marshal of England, she being also an infant.
3. George, who *d.* young.
4. Elizabeth, *m.* to Henry VII.
5. Cicely, *m.*, 1st, to John, lord Wells; and, 2nd, to Sir J. Kyme.
6. Anne, *m.* to Thomas Howard, D. of Norfolk.
7. Bridget, who became a nun.
8. Mary, who *d.* unm.
9. Margaret, and
10. Katharine, *m.* to William Courtenay, E. of Devonshire.

ISSUE OF RICHARD III.

Edward, E. of Salisbury, cr. pr. of Wales; upon whom the crown was entailed by parliament; but he died *vitâ patris.*

BORN OF THE HOUSE OF TUDOR.

ISSUE OF HENRY VII.

1. Arthur, pr. of Wales, *b.* Sept. 20, 1486; *m.* Nov. 1501, the infanta Catharine, daughter of Ferdinand of Arragon, but died in a few months afterwards. His widow became the first wife of his brother Henry VIII., to whom she was married June 3, 1509.
2. HENRY, aft. Henry VIII.
3. Edmund, who died young.
4. Margaret, *m.* 1st, to James IV. of Scotland, by whom she had an only son, James V. of Scotland, father of Mary, Q. of Scots, whose son, James VI., ascended the English throne as James I. Margaret *m.* 2nd, Arthur Douglas, E. of Angus, from whom she was divorced; and 3rd, Henry Stuart, E. of Methven. By her second husband she had an only daughter, Margaret, who espoused Matthew Stuart, E. of Lenox, and was mother of Henry, E. of Darnley, the husband of Mary, Q. of Scots, and father of James I. of England.
5. Elizabeth, *d.* in infancy.
6. Mary, *m.* 1st, to Louis XII. K. of France; and, 2nd, to Charles Brandon, D. of Suffolk; by whom she left
   I. Henry, E. of Lincoln; *d.* unm.
   II. Frances, *m.* to Henry Grey, marq. of Dorset, aft. D. of Suffolk; and had three daughters, of whom the eldest was lady Jane Grey.
   III. Eleanor, *m.* to Henry Clifford, E. of Cumberland, and left a daughter, Margaret, who *m.* Henry Stanley, E. of Derby.

ISSUE OF HENRY VIII.

1. Henry, *d.* young.
2. MARY (by Katharine of Arragon), aft. Q. Mary.
3. ELIZABETH (by his second queen, Anne Boleyn), aft. Q. Elizabeth.
4. EDWARD (by his third queen, lady Jane Seymour), aft. Edward VI.

The king had by his first queen, besides Henry and Mary, other children not named, who died in infancy.

BORN OF THE HOUSE OF STUART.

ISSUE OF JAMES I.

1. Henry Frederick, cr. after his father's accession, D. of Cornwall, and in May 1610, pr. of Wales; *d.* at the age of eighteen, Nov. 6, 1612.
2. Robert, *d.* young.

3. **Charles**, aft. Charles I.
4. Elizabeth, *m.* to Frederick, count palatine of the Rhine, who, in 1620, was elected K. of Bohemia, but aft. driven from his dominions. She had issue:
   - I. Frederick Henry; drowned in 1529, in his fifteenth year.
   - II. Charles Lewis II., who, by the treaty of Munster, was created the eighth elector of the empire.
   - III. Rupert, so renowned in the civil war of England as "Prince Rupert," cr. D. of Cumberland.
   - IV. Maurice, known in English history as "Prince Maurice," perished by shipwreck in 1654.
   - V. Lewis, *d.* young.
   - VI. Edward, count palatine of the Rhine.
   - VII. Philip, slain at the battle near St. Stephen's in 1640.
   - VIII. Gustavus; *d.* in 1641, in his minority.
   - IX. Elizabeth, who became abbess of Hervorden, in Westphalia, and *d.* in 1680.
   - X. Louisa Hollandia, became abbess of Maubisson, near Paris.
   - XI. Henrietta, *m.* Sigismund, pr. of Transylvania, and *d.* a few months after.
   - XII. Charlotte, *d.* in infancy.
   - XIII. Sophia, on whose descendants the crown of England devolved by the act of Settlement, *b.* Oct. 13, 1630; *m.* 1658, Ernest Augustus, D. of Brunswick-Luneburg, aft. elector of Hanover, by whom she had issue, **George Lewis**, who ascended the English throne as George I.
5. Margaret, *d.* young, 1598.
6. Mary, *d.* in her third year, 1607.
7. Sophia, *d.* two days after her birth, 1606.

Issue of the Princess Sophia.

Grand-daughter of James I.

1. **George** Lewis, aft. George I.
2. Frederick Augustus. slain in battle against the Turks, 1690.
3. Maximilian William, *d.* Dec. 1666.
4. Charles Philip, slain in battle, 1690.
5. Christian, drowned in the Danube, July 1703.
6. Ernest Augustus, bishop of Osnaburg, cr. in 1716, D. of York and Albany, and E. of Ulster; *d.* Aug. 1728.
7. Sophia Charlotte, *m.* to Frederick William, elector of Brandenburg, K. of Prussia.

Issue of Charles I.

1. Charles, who died the day he was born.
2. **Charles**, pr. of Wales, aft. Charles II.
3. **James**, D. of York, aft. James II.
4. Henry, D. of Gloucester; *d.* unmarried in 1660.
5. Mary, *m.* to William II. of Nassau, pr. of Orange, by whom she had an only son, **William**, who ascended the throne of England as William III.
6. Elizabeth, who died of grief, a prisoner in Carisbrook Castle in Sept. 1650, aged 15 years.
7. Anne, *d.* young.
8. Henrietta Maria, *m.* to Philip, D. of Anjou, aft. D. of Orleans, only brother to Louis XIV.

Issue of Charles II.

This prince left no legitimate issue, but had many natural children by various mistresses; among these was James, D. of Monmouth, by Lucy Walters.

Issue of James II.

1. Charles, *d.* young.
2. **Mary**, *m.* to William Henry of Nassau, pr. of Orange; she and her husband aft. ascended the English throne as Mary II. and William III.
3. James, D. of Cambridge, *b.* July 1663; *d.* 1667.
4. **Anne**, aft. Q. Anne.
5. Charles, D. of Kendal; *d.* in infancy.
6. Edgar, D. of Cambridge, *b.* Sept. 14, 1667; *d.* 1671.
7. Henrietta, *d.* in infancy.
8. Catherine, *d.* in infancy.

   These four sons and four daughters were by lady Anne Hyde, and none of them, except Mary and Anne, afterwards queens regnant, survived four years of age. By his second wife, the princess of Modena, James had:
9. Catherine Laura, *d.* in infancy.
10. Charles, D. of Cambridge; *d.* in infancy.
11. Isabella, *d.* in her 4th year.
12. Charlotte Maria, *d.* in infancy.
13. James Francis Edward, known after his father's death as the **Pretender**, and supposed by many at the time to have been of fictitious birth, *b.* June 18, 1668; *m.* in 1719, Mary Clementina, dau. of pr. James Sobieski, and grand-dau. of John,

K. of Poland, by whom he had issue:

I. Charles Edward, known as the Chevalier St. George, or YOUNG PRETENDER, *b.* in 1720; *m.* the princess Stohlberg, known as countess of Albany; *d.* in 1788.

II. Henry Benedict, known as CARDINAL YORK, *d.* in 1807, when the whole issue of James II. became extinct.

14. Louisa Maria Theresa, *b.* in 1692; *d.* 1712.

James had also several natural children, amongst whom was James Fitz-James, D. of Berwick, by lady Arabella Churchill; he followed his father, after his abdication, into France; became general of the French and Spanish armies, and was killed at the siege of Philipsburgh in 1734.

ISSUE OF QUEEN ANNE.

1. A daughter, still-born.
2. Mary, *b.* June 9, 1685; *d.* Feb. 8, 1686.
3. Anne Sophia, *b.* May 12, 1686; *d.* Feb. 2, 1687.
4. William, D. of Gloucester, *b.* July 24, 1689; *d.* July 30, 1700.
5. Mary, *b.* and *d.* in Nov. 1690.
6. George, *b.* and *d.* Apr. 17, 1692.

BORN OF THE HOUSE OF HANOVER.

ISSUE OF GEORGE I.

1. GEORGE Augustus, aft. as George II.
2. Sophia Dorothea, *b.* March 16, 1685; *m.* to Frederick William, of Prussia, Nov. 28, 1706; *d.* July 5, 1757.

Both the above were born long before the king ascended the throne; his queen was kept confined on the continent during his reign, and never came to England.

ISSUE OF GEORGE II.

1. Frederick Lewis, pr. of Wales, *b.* Jan. 20, 1707; *m.* Augusta, dau. of Frederick II., D. of Saxe-Gotha; *d.* in the life-time of his father. For his issue, *see separate notice below.*
2. Anne, princess-royal, *b.* Oct. 22, 1709; *m.* to William Charles Henry, pr. of Orange.
3. Amelia Sophia Eleanora, *b.* May 30, 1711; *d.* unm., Oct. 31, 1786.
4. Elizabeth Caroline, *b.* May, 1713; *d.* unm. Dec. 28, 1757.
5. George William, *d.* in infancy.
6. William Augustus, D. of Cumberland, *b.* April 15, 1721; *d.* Oct. 31, 1765.
7. Mary, *b.* Feb. 22, 1723; *m.* to pr. Frederick of Hesse-Cassel; *d.* Jan. 14, 1771.
8. Louisa, *b.* Dec. 7, 1724; *m.* to Frederick V. of Denmark; *d.* Dec. 8, 1751.

ISSUE OF FREDERICK LEWIS.
Prince of Wales.

1. Augusta, *b.* July 31, 1737; *m.* to Charles William Ferdinand, hereditary pr. of Brunswick-Wolfenbuttel. *See that family.*
2. GEORGE William Frederick, aft. George III.
3. Edward Augustus, D. of York, *b.* March 14, 1739; *d.* Sept. 17, 1767.
4. Elizabeth Caroline, *b.* Dec. 30, 1740, *d.* Sept. 4, 1759.
5. William Henry, D. of Gloucester, *b.* Nov. 25, 1743; *m.* Maria, countess dowager of Waldegrave, dau. of the hon sir Edward Walpole; *d.* Aug. 25, 1805; he had issue:

   I. Sophia Matilda, *b.* May 29, 1773; *d.* Nov. 29, 1844.

   II. Caroline Augusta Maria, *b.* June 24, 1774; *d.* in infancy.

   III. William Frederick, *b.* Jan. 15, 1776; *m.* the princess Mary, dau. of George III.; *d.* Nov. 30, 1834.
6. Henry Frederick, D. of Cumberland, *b.* Nov. 7, 1745; *m.* Anne, dau. of E. Carhampton and widow of Christopher Horton, esq., of Catton Hall, Derbyshire; *d.* Sept. 18, 1790.
7. Louisa Anne, *b.* March 8, 1749; *d.* May 13, 1768.
8. Frederick William, *b.* May 30, 1750; *d.* Dec. 1765.
9. Caroline Matilda, *b.* (after her father's death) July 11, 1751; *m.* Christian VII., K. of Denmark; she *d.* imprisoned in the castle of Zell, May 10, 1775.

ISSUE OF GEORGE III.

1. GEORGE Augustus Frederick, pr. of Wales, and, in 1811, prince regent; aft. George IV.
2. Frederick, D. of York and Albany, *b.* Aug. 16, 1743; *m.* Frederica Charlotte Ulrique, dau. of William II. K. of Prussia; *d.* Jan. 5, 1827.
3. WILLIAM Henry, D. of Clarence; aft. William IV.
4. Charlotte Augusta Matilda, princess royal, *b.* Sept. 29, 1766; *m.* Frederick Charles William, hered. pr. of Wurtemburg; *d.* Oct. 6, 1825.
5. Edward, D. of Kent and Strathern, *b.* Nov. 2, 1767; *m.* May 29, 1818, Victoria Mary Louisa, dau. of Francis Frederick Anthony, D. of Saxe-

Coburg - Saalfeld, and widow of Emich Charles, pr. of Leiningen; the Duke *d.* Jan. 23, 1820, leaving an only daughter,

Alexandrina VICTORIA, the present QUEEN. The Duchess of Kent *d.* Mar. 16, 1861.

6. Augusta Sophia, *b.* Nov. 8, 1768; *d.* Sept. 22, 1840.
7. Elizabeth, *b.* May 22, 1770; *m.* to Frederick Joseph Louis, landgrave of Hesse-Homburg; *d.* Jan. 10, 1840.
8. Ernest Augustus, D. of Cumberland and Teviotdale, *b.* June 5, 1771. *See Hanover.*
9. Augustus Frederick, D. of Sussex, *b.* Jan. 27, 1773; *m.* April 3, 1793, lady Augusta Murray, dau. of John, E. of Dunmore; this marriage was dissolved (being contrary to the statute 12 George III. c. 11.) in Aug. 1794; *d.* April 21, 1843.
10. Adolphus Frederick, D. of Cambridge, *b.* Feb. 24, 1774; *m.*, May 7, 1818, Augusta Wilhelmina Louisa, dau. of Frederick, landgrave of Hesse-Cassel, *d.* July, 1850, leaving issue:
    - I. George Frederick William Charles, *b.* March 26, 1819, the present Duke.
    - II. Augusta Caroline Charlotte Elizabeth, *b.* July 19, 1822; *m.* June 28, 1843, Frederick William Gustavus, hereditary Grand D. of Mecklenburg-Strelitz; and has issue.
    - III. Mary Adelaide Wilhelmina Elizabeth, *b.* Nov. 27, 1833; *m.* June 12, 1866, Francis Louis Paul Alexander, D. of Teck; and has issue.
11. Mary, *b.* April 25, 1776; *m.* July 22, 1816, her cousin, William Frederick, D. of Gloucester. (*See D. of Gloucester.*)
12. Sophia, *b.* Nov. 3, 1777; *d.* May 27, 1848.
13. Octavius, *b.* Feb. 23, 1779; *d.* May 3, 1783.
14. Alfred, *b.* Sept. 22, 1780; *d.* Aug. 26, 1782.
15. Amelia, *b.* Aug 7, 1783; *d.* Nov. 2. 1810.

ISSUE OF GEORGE IV.

Charlotte Caroline Augusta, *b.* Jan. 7, 1796; *m.* to pr. Leopold George Frederick of Saxe-Coburg-Saalfeld, aft. K. of the Belgians, May 2, 1816; *d.* in childbed, Nov. 6, 1817. Issue, a son, still-born, the day before.

ISSUE OF WILLIAM IV.

1. Charlotte Augusta Louisa, *b.* March 27, 1819; *d.* next day.
2. Elizabeth Georgina Adelaide, *b.* Dec. 10, 1820; *d.* Mar. 4, 1821.

ISSUE OF QUEEN VICTORIA.

1. Victoria Adelaide Mary Louisa, Princess Royal, *b.* Nov. 21, 1840; *m.* Jan. 25, 1858, Fredk. Wm., crown pr. of Germany, and has had issue:
    - I. Frederick William Victor Albert, *b.* Jan. 27, 1859; *m.* Feb. 27, 1881, Augusta Victoria princess of Schleswig-Holstein, and has issue.
    - II. Victoria Elizabeth Augusta Charlotte, *b.* July 24, 1860; *m.* Feb. 18, 1878, Bernard, hered. pr. of Saxe Meiningen, and has issue.
    - III. Albert William Henry, *b.* Aug. 14, 1862.
    - IV. Sigismund, *b.* Sep. 15, 1864; *d.* June 18, 1866.
    - V. Frederica Wilhelmina Amelia Victoria, *b.* Apr. 12, 1866.
    - VI. Waldimar, *b.* Feb. 10, 1868, *d.* Mar. 27, 1879.
    - VII. Sophia Dorothea Ulrica Alice, *b.* June 14, 1870.
    - VIII. Margaret Beatrice Feodora, *b.* Apr. 22, 1872.
2. Albert Edward, pr. of Wales, &c., *b.* Nov. 9, 1841; *m.* Mar. 10, 1863, Alexandra Caroline Maria Charlotte Louisa Julia, dau. of Christian IX. K. of Denmark, and has had issue:
    - I. Albert Victor Christian Edward, *b.* Jan. 8. 1864.
    - II. George Frederick Ernest Albert, *b.* June 3, 1865.
    - III. Louisa Victoria Alexandra Dagmar, *b.* Feb. 20, 1867.
    - IV. Victoria Alexandra Olga Mary, *b.* July 6, 1868.
    - V. Maud Charlotte Mary Victoria, *b.* Nov. 26, 1869.
    - VI. Alexandra, *b.* Apr. 6, 1871; *d.* Apr. 7, 1871.
3. Alice Maud Mary, *b.* Apr. 25, 1843; *m.* July 1, 1862, Fredk. Wm. Louis, Gr. D. of Hesse, *d.* Dec. 14, 1878, having had issue:
    - I. Victoria Alberta Elizabeth Matilda Mary, *b.* Apr. 5, 1863; *m.* Apr. 30, 1884, pr. Louis of Battenburg.
    - II. Elizabeth, *b.* Nov. 1, 1864; *m.* June 15, 1884, Gr. D. Sergius of Russia.
    - III. Irene Marie Louise Anna, *b.* July 11, 1866.
    - IV. Ernest Louis Charles Albert William, *b.* Nov. 25, 1868.
    - V. Frederick William, *b.* Oct. 1870; *d.* June 29, 1873.

VI. Victoria Alix Helene Louise Beatrix, *b.* June 7, 1872.
VII. Mary Victoria, *b.* May 24, 1874; *d.* Apr. 20, 1884.

4. Alfred Ernest Albert, D. of Edinburgh, &c., *b.* Aug. 6, 1844; *m.* Jan. 23, 1874, Gr. D. Marie Alexandrovina, only dau. of Alexander II. Emp. of Russia, and has had issue:
I. Alfred Alexander William Ernest Albert, *b.* Oct 15, 1874.
II. Marie Alexandra Victoria, *b.* Oct. 30, 1875.
III. Victoria Melita, *b.* Nov. 25, 1876.
IV. Alexandra Louise Olga Victoria, *b.* Sep. 1, 1878.
V. Beatrice Leopoldine Victoria, *b.* Apr, 20, 1884.

5. Helena Augusta Victoria, *b.* May 25, 1846; *m.* July 5, 1866, pr. Fredk. Christian Chas. Aug. of Schleswig-Holstein-Sonderburg-Augustenburg, and has had issue:
I. Christian Victor Albert Ludwig Ernest Anton, *b.* Apr. 14. 1867.
II. Albert John Charles Frederick Alfred George, *b.* Feb. 26, 1869.
III. Victoria Louise Sophia Augusta Amelia Helena, *b.* May 3, 1870.
IV. Francisca Josepha Louise Augusta Marie Christiana Helena, *b.* Aug. 14, 1872.
V. Harold, *b.* Mar. 12, 1876; *d.* May 20, 1876.

6. Louisa Caroline Alberta, *b.* Mar. 18, 1848; *m.* Mar. 21, 1871, Jno. Douglas Sutherland Campbell, M. of Lorne, eldest son of D. of Argyll.

7. Arthur William Patrick Albert, D. of Connaught, &c., *b.* May 1, 1850; *m.* May 13, 1879, pr, Louise Margaret, 3rd dau. of pr. Fredk. Chas. of Prussia, and has had issue:
I. Margaret Victoria Augusta Charlotte Nora, *b.* Jan. 15, 1882.
II. Arthur Frederick Patrick Albert, *b.* Jan. 13, 1883.
III. Victoria Patricia Helena Elizabeth, *b.* Mar. 17, 1886.

8. Leopold George Duncan Albert, D. of Albany, &c., *b.* Apr. 7, 1853; *m.* Apr. 27, 1882, pr. Helena Frederica Augusta, dau. of pr. of Waldeck-Pyrmont; *d.* Mar. 28, 1884, having had issue:
I. Alice Mary Victoria Augusta Paulina, *b.* Feb. 25, 1883.
II. Leopold Charles Edward George Albert, *b.* July 19, 1884.

9. Beatrice Mary Victoria Feodore, *b.* Apr. 14, 1857; *m.* July 23, 1885, pr. Hy. Maurice of Battenburg, and has had issue:
I. Alexander Albert, *b.* Nov. 23, 1886.
II. Victoria Eugénie Julia Eva, *b.* Oct. 24, 1887.

WALES.

Kings and Princes of Wales.

Kings of Wales.

640. Dyvnwal Moelmud K. of the Cymry.
688. Idwallo.
720. Rhodri, or Roderic.
755. Conan, or Cynan.
818. Mervyn, or Merfyn.
843. Roderic, surn. the Great. This prince divided Wales between his three sons, allotting to each his part. To the eldest he gave North Wales; to the second, South Wales; and to the third, Powys-land.

Princes of North Wales.

Counties of Merioneth, part of Denbigh, Flint, Carnarvon, and the Isle of Anglesea. At Aberfraw, in this last, was the prince's seat.

877. Anarawd.
913. Edwal Voel.
939. Howel Dha, or Hywel Dha, surn. the Good, pr. of all Wales.
948. Jevaf or Jevav, and Iago.
972. Howel ap Jevaf, or Hywel ab Jevav.
984. Cadwallon ab Jevaf.
985. Meredith ap Owen ap Howel Dha, or Meredydd ap Owain ab Hywel Dha.
992. Edwal ab Meyric ab Edwal Voel.
998. Aedan, an usurper.
1015. Llewelyn ab Sitsyllt, and Angharad his wife.
1021. Iago ab Edwal ab Meyric.
1038. Griffith, or Grufydd ab Llewelyn ab Sitsyllt.
1061. Bleddyn and Rygwallon.
1073. Trahaern ab Caradoc.
1079. Griffith ap Conan, or Grufydd ab Cynan.
1137. Owain Gwynedd.
1169. David ab Owain Gwynedd
1194. Leolinus Magnus.

1240. David ab Llewelyn.
1246. Llewelyn ap Griffith, or Grufydd, last pr. of the blood; slain after battle, 1282.

PRINCES OF SOUTH WALES.

Counties of Glamorgan, Pembroke, Carmarthen, Cardigan, and part of Brecknock. Dynevor Castle was the prince's seat.

877. Cadeth, or Cadell
907. Howel Dha, or Hywel Dha, the Good, pr. of all Wales.
948. Owen ap Howel Dha, or Owain ap Hywel Dha, son.
987. Meredith ap Owen, or Meredydd ab Owain, all Wales.
993. Llewelyn ap Sitsyllt, and Angharad his wife.
1021. Rytherch, or Rhydderch ab Jestyn, an usurper.
1031. Hywell and Meredydd.
1042. Rhydderch and Rhys, sons of the usurper.
1061. Meredydd ab Owain ab Edwyn.
1073. Rhys ab Owen, or Owain, and Rhydderch ab Caradoc.
1077. Rhys ab Tewdwr Mawr.
1092. Cadwgan ab Bleddyn.
1115. Griffith, or Grufydd ab Rhys.
1137. Rhys ab Grufydd, or Griffith, called the lord Rhys.
1196. Grufydd ab Rhys.
1202. Rhys ab Grufydd.
1222. Owain ab Grufydd.
1235. Meredith, or Meredydd ab Owain; *d.* 1267.

PRINCES AND LORDS OF POWYS-LAND.

Counties of Montgomery and Radnor, and parts of Denbigh, Brecknock, Merioneth, and Shropshire. The prince's seat was at Matraval, in the first-named county.

877. Merfyn, or Mervyn.
900. Cadeth, or Cadell, also pr. of South Wales.
927. Howel Dha, or Hywel Dha, the Good, pr. of all Wales.

* * * * * *

985. Meredydd ab Owain.

* * * * * *

1061. Bleddyn ab Cynvyn.
1073. Meredydd ab Bleddyn.†
1087. Cadwgan ab Bleddyn.
1132. Madoc ab Meredydd.
1160. Griffith, or Grufydd ab Meredydd.

* * * * * *

1256. Gwenwinwin, or Gwenwynwyn.
1256. Owain ab Grufydd.

† The last Prince who held this dominion entire. He divided it between his two sons, Madoc and Grufydd.

South Wales was conquered by Henry II. about 1157. The rest of the country was finally subdued by Edward I. about 1282–3. The annexation of the country to England is recorded by the *Statute of Wales*, 12 Edward I., passed March 19, 1284. The country was "incorporated, united, and annexed to and with" England in 1535 by 27 Hen. VIII. cap. 26.

PRINCES OF WALES OF THE BLOOD ROYAL OF ENGLAND.

(*See ante, p.* 8.)

SCOTLAND.

KINGS OF SCOTLAND.

BEFORE CHRIST.

The early accounts of these kings are, by many historians, deemed, in a measure, fabulous. The antiquity of the kings is carried as far back as Alexander the Great.

330. Fergus I.; lost in the Irish Sea.
305. Fritharis, brother; poisoned.
290. Mainus, nephew.
261. Dornadilla, son.
233. Northatus, brother; slain.
213. Reutherus, son of Dornadilla.
187. Reutha, brother; res. in favour of his nephew.
170. Thereus, son of Reutherus, dep. and exiled.
158. Josina, brother.
134. Finanus, son.
104. Durstus, son; slain in civil war.
95. Evenus.
76. Gillus, his illegitimate son, who, usurping the royal power, caused the murder of the rightful heirs; dep. by his nobles, and beheaded.

75. Evenus II., nephew of Finanus; chosen in his room.
59. Ederus, grandson of Durstus.
12. Evenus III., son; dep. and strangled in prison.
4. Metellanus, nephew of Ederus.

AFTER CHRIST.

35. Caratacus or Caractacus, nephew.
55. Corbred, brother.
72. Dardanus, son; his subjects slew him.
76. Corbred II., surn. Galdus. Some suppose this king to be the Galgacus whom Tacitus mentions as having fought valiantly against Julius Agricola.
110. Luctacus or Lugthacus, son; murdered by his nobles.
113. Mogaldus, grandson of Corbred II.; murdered.
149. Conarus, son; conspired in his father's murder, dep. and *d.* in prison.
163. Ethodius I.; slain by an Irish harper in revenge for the murder of a kinsman.
195. Satreal or Satrahel, brother; strangled by his courtiers.
199. Donald I., brother.
216. Ethodius II., son of Ethodius I.; slain by his guards in a domestic tumult.
231. Athirco, son; slew himself to avoid a severer death.
242. Nathalocus, who usurped the throne on the king's death; killed by his domestics.
253. Findochus, son of Athirco; murdered in a conspiracy, in which his brother, Carantius, was a principal.
264. Donald II., a third son of Athirco; slain in a battle with Donald of the Isles, who succeeded.
265. Donald III., lord of the Isles, usurped the throne; slain by his successor.
277. Carthilinthus or Crathilinthus, son of Findochus.
301. Fincormachus, son of Donald II.
348. Romachus, nephew; slain by his nobles.
351. Angusianus or Æneanus, cousin; fell in battle with the Pictish king, who was also slain.
354. Fethelmachus, also cousin of Romachus, defeated the Picts and mortally wounded their new king in battle; murdered by a Pictish minstrel who feigned himself a Scot, hired by Hergustus, the succeeding king of the Picts.
357. Eugenius I., son of Fincormachus; slain in battle by Maximus, the Roman general, and the confederate Picts.

With this battle ended the kingdom of the Scots, after having existed from the coronation of Fergus I., a period of 706 years; the royal family fled to Denmark.

Interregnum of 27 years.

404. Fergus II., great-grandson of Eugenius and 40th king; slain in battle with the Romans. "Some call this Fergus the *first* king, and suppose either that the previous kings are fabulous, or that they were only chiefs or generals of armies, having no royal authority. The controversy thus arising, I leave to be decided by the antiquaries, and must follow the received histories of Scotland."—*Anderson.*
420. Eugenius II. or Evenus, son.
451. Dongardus or Domangard, brother; defeated and drowned.
457. Constantine I., brother; assass. by Dugall, a noble, whose daughter he had dishonoured.
479. Congallus I., nephew.
501. Goranus, brother; murdered.
535. Eugenius III., nephew.
558. Congallus II., brother.
569. Kinnatellus, brother; res. in favour of Aidanus.
570. Aidanus or Aldan, son of Goranus.
605. Kenneth or Kennett I., son of Congallus II.
606. Eugenius IV., son of Adianus.
621. Ferchard or Ferquhard, son.
632. Donald IV., brother; drowned in Loch Tay.
646. Ferchard II., son of Ferchard I.; *d.* from the bite of a mad wolf.
664. Malduinus, son of Donald IV.; strangled by his wife for his supposed infidelity, for which crime she was immediately afterwards burnt.
684. Eugenius V., brother.
688. Eugenius VI., son of Ferchard II.
698. Amberkeletus, nephew; fell by an arrow from an unknown hand.
699. Eugenius VII., brother.
715. Mordachus, son of Amberkeletus.
730. Etfinus, son of Eugenius VII.
761. Eugenius VIII., son of Mordachus; killed by his nobles.
764. Fergus III., son of Etfinus; killed by his queen in a fit of jealousy; she immediately afterwards stabbed herself to escape a death of torture.
767. Solvathius, son of Eugenius VIII.
787. Achaius.
819. Congallus III.
824. Dongal or Dougal, son of Solvathius; drowned in the Spey.

831. Alpine, son of Achaius; taken prisoner and beheaded, with many of his nobles, by the Picts.
834. Kenneth II., son, surn. MacAlpine; defeated the Picts, and slew their king and his nobility. United the Picts and Scots under one sceptre, and became the first sole monarch of all Scotland, 843.
854. Donald V., brother; deth., and *d.* in prison by his own hand.
858. Constantine II., son of Kenneth; taken in battle by the Danes, and beheaded.
874. Eth or Ethus, surn. Lightfoot; *d.* of grief in prison.
876. Gregory, called the Great.
893. Donald VI., 2nd son of Constantine.
904. Constantine III., son of Ethus; res. after a long reign, and retired to a monastery.
944. Malcolm I., son of Donald VI.; murdered in Moray.
953. Indulfus or Gondulph; killed by the Danes in an ambuscade.
961. Duff or Duffus, son of Malcolm; murdered by Donald, governor of Forres Castle.
965. Cullen or Culenus, son of Indulfus; avenged the murder of his predecessor; assass. at Methven by a Thane, whose daughter he had dishonoured.
970. Kenneth III., brother of Duffus; murdered by Fenella, the lady of Fettercairn.
994. Constantine IV., son of Culenus, usurped the throne; slain.
995. Grimus or the Grim, son of Duffus; routed and slain in battle by Malcolm, the rightful heir to the crown, who succeeded.
1003. Malcolm II., son of Kenneth III.; assass. on his way to Glamis.
1033. Duncan I., grandson; assass. by his cousin Macbeth, who asc. the throne.
1039. Macbeth, usurper; slain by Macduff, the Thane of Fife, and the rightful heir succeeds.

Historians so differ up to this reign, in the number of the kings, the dates of succession, and the circumstances narrated, that no account can be taken as precisely accurate.

1057. Malcolm III., (Cean-Mohr or Canmore), son of Duncan; killed while besieging Alnwick Castle.
1093. Donald VII., or Donald Bane, brother, usurped the throne; fled to the Hebrides.
1094. Duncan II., natural son of Malcolm, also an usurper; murdered.
1094. Donald Bane, again; dep.
1098. Edgar, son of Malcolm, and rightful heir. Henry I. of England married his sister Maud.
1107. Alexander, brother, surn. the Fierce
1124. David, brother, *m.* Matilda, dau. of Waltheof, E. of Northumberland.
1153. Malcolm IV., grandson.
1165. William, brother, surn. the Lion.
1214. Alexander II., son, *m.* Joan, dau. of John, K. of England.
1249. Alexander III., *m.* Margaret, dau of Henry III., of England; dislocated his neck, when hunting, near Kinghorn.
1285. Margaret, called the "Maiden of Norway," grand-dau., "recognized by the States of Scotland though a female, an infant, and a foreigner"; *d.* on her passage to Scotland.

On the death of Margaret, a competition arose for the vacant throne, which Edward I. of England decided in favour of

1292. John Baliol, who aft. surrendered his crown, and *d.* in exile.

Interregnum.

1306. Robert (Bruce) I., "the Bruce of Bannockburn."
1329. David (Bruce) II., son; Edward Baliol disputed the throne with him.
1332. Edward Baliol, son of John, res.
1342. David II., *again*, 11 years a prisoner in England.
1371. Robert (Stuart) II., nephew, *d.* Apr. 19, 1371.
1390. Robert III., son, *d.* Apr. 4, 1406; his proper name was John, changed on his accession.
1406. James I., 2nd son, imprisoned 18 years in England, set at liberty in 1423; conspired against and murdered in his bed-chamber, Feb. 21, 1437–8.
1438. James II., son, succ. at seven years of age; killed at the siege of Roxburgh Castle by a cannon bursting, Aug. 3, 1460.
1460. James III., son, killed in a revolt of his subjects at Bannockburn, June 11, 1488.
1488. James IV., *m.* Margaret Tudor, dau. of Henry VII. of England; killed at the battle of Flodden, Sept. 9, 1513.
1513. James V., son, succ. when little more than a year old; *d.* Dec. 14, 1542.
1542. Mary, dau., better known as Mary

Q. of Scots, *b.* Dec. 7, 1542; *m.* 1st, Francis, dauphin of France, aft. Francis II., Apr. 24, 1558; 2nd, Henry Stuart, Lord Darnley, July 29, 1565; 3rd, James, E. of Bothwell, May 15, 1567; res. July 22, 1567, in favour of her son, James VI.; beheaded at Fotheringay Castle, Feb. 8, 1587.

1567. James VI., son, *b.* June 19, 1566; *m.* Anne of Denmark, dau. of Frederick II.; *d.* Mar. 27, 1625. In 1603, on the death of Q. Elizabeth, he succ. to the throne of England.

For subsequent Sovereigns of Scotland see *Sovereigns of England*, *ante* p. 5. The two Kingdoms, though governed by the same Monarch, remained separate Kingdoms until the Act of Union 6 Anne cap. 11. They were, on and after May 1, 1707, united and styled "Great Britain."

IRELAND.

Kings of Ireland.

According to Keating.

Before Christ.

So much fable is mixed up with the early history of this country, and the dates and the orthography of the names so vary in every account, it is impossible to do more than compile from accepted authorities.

From the Milesian Conquest.

1300. Heber and Heremon.
1291. Heremon, alone.
1285. Muirmhne, Luighne, and Laighne, sons, succ. their father, Heremon, reigning jointly; the first died, and the other two were slain in battle by the sons of Heber.
1282. Er, Orbha, Fearon, and Feargna, sons of Heber; all slain in battle by their successor.
1281. Irial, or Irial-Faidh; slew and succ. the four sons of Heber.
1271. Eithrial; slain in battle by his successor.
1251. Conmaol, or Conveal, "first absolute monarch of the Hibernian race"; slain in battle.
1221. Tigermas; introduced idolatry into Ireland.
1171. Eochaidh-Eadgothac.
1147. Cearmna and Sobhair, brothers; partitioned Ireland into south and north.
1107. Fiachade-Labhruin; slain by his successor.
1083. Eochaidh-Mumho; slain by his successor.
1061. Aongus - Olmuchac; slain by his successor.
1043. Eadna-Airgtheach, and
1016. Rotheachta; both slain by their successors.
991. Seadhna; slain by his own son.
986. Fiachadh - Fionsgothach; slain by his successor.
966. Muinheamhoin, or Muinimone; *d.* of the plague.
961. Aildergoith, son; slain by his successor.
934. Odlamh-Fodhla.
924. Fionachta, son.
909. Slanoll, brother; *d.* at Tara.
894. Geide - Olgothach, also a son of Odlamh - Fodhla; slain by his nephew and successor.
877. Fiachadh; slain by his successor.
853. Bearngall; slain by his successor.
841. Oilliol; slain by his successor.
825. Siorna - Saoghalach; slain by his successor.
804. Rotheachta; burnt.

Six succeeding kings, among whom was Nuadha-Fionn-Fail, died violent deaths.

735. Fion-Fin, of the line of Er, or Ir.
715. Seadhna; slain by his successor.
695. Simeon Breac; slain by his successor.
689. Duach-Fionn or Fin; slain by his successor.
684. Muireadach, and two succeeding kings, died violently.
659. Siorlamh; slain by his successor.

Eleven princes succeeded, who all died in civil wars or broils, or by assassination.

540. Aodh-Ruadh; drowned.
519. Diothorba; *d.* of a malignant distemper.
498. Coimbaoth; *d.* of the plague.
478. Machadh - Mongruadh, Q., cousin, surn. the Red-haired Princess; slain by her successor.

471. Reachta-Righdhearg; slain by his successor.
451. Ugaine Mor, or the Great, "had 22 sons and 3 daughters, among whom he partitioned his kingdom"; slain by his brother and successor.
421. Laoghaire-Lorck; slain by his brother and successor.
419. Cabhthaick, slew his brother and nephew; himself slain by his grand-nephew.

Ten kings succeeded, of whom three only died natural deaths.

275. Feargus - Forthamhuil; killed in battle.
263. Aongus-Tuirimheach; slain at Tara.

Of 15 succeeding princes, 11 died in battle, or were murdered.

66. Conaire Mor, or the Great; depr. of his crown and life by his successor.
36. Lughaidh-Riebdearg; killed himself by falling on his sword.

Two kings succeeded, of whom the latter died A.D. 4.

AFTER CHRIST.

4. Fearaidhach-Fionfachtna; slain by his successor.
24 Fiachadh-Fion; slain by his successor.
27. Fiachadh-Fionohudh, the Prince with the white cows; "murdered by the Irish plebeians of Connaught."
54. Cairbre-Cinncait; murdered in a conspiracy.
59. Elim; slain in battle.
79. Tuathal-Teachtmar; slain by his successor.
109. Mal or Mail; slain by his successor.
113. Feidhlimhidh; *d.* a natural death.
122. Cathoire Mor, or the Great, "had 30 sons."
125. Conn Ceadchadhach, called the Hero of the hundred battles; slain.
145. Conaire; killed.
152. Art-Aonfhir, the Melancholy; slain in battle.
182. Lughaidh, surn. Mac Conn; thrust through the eye with a spear, in a conspiracy.
212. Feargus, surn. Black-teeth; murdered at the instigation of his successor.
213. Cormac-Ulfhada; choked by the bone of a fish at supper.
253. Eochaidh-Gunait; killed.
254. Cairbre-Liffeachair; slain in battle.
282. Fiachadh, son; slain in battle by his three nephews.
315. Cairioll or Colla-Uais; deth. and retired to Scotland.
319. Muirreadhach-Tireach; slain by his successor.
352. Caolbhach; slain by his successor.
353. Eochaidh - Moidhmeodhain; *d.* a natural death.
360. Criomthan; poisoned by his own sister to obtain the crown for her son.
375. Niall, surn. of the nine hostages; killed in France, on the banks of the Loire.
398. Dathy; killed by a thunderbolt at the foot of the Alps.
421. Laoghaire; killed by a thunderbolt.
453. Oilioll-Molt; slain in battle.
473. Lughaidh; killed also by a thunderbolt.
493. Murtough; *d.* a natural death.
515. Tuateal-Maolgarbh; assass.
528. Diarmuid; fell by the sword of Hugh Dubh.
550. Feargus, in conjunction with his brother Daniel; the manner of their deaths uncertain.
551. Eochaidh, jointly with his uncle Baodan; both slain.
554. Ainmereach; depr. of his crown and life.
557. Baodan; slain by the two Cuimins.
558. Aodh or Hugh; killed in battle.
587. Hugh Slaine; assass.
591. Aodh-Uaireodhnach; killed in battle.
618. Maolcobha; defeated and slain in battle.
622. Suibhne-Meain; killed.
635. Daniel; died a natural death.
648. Conall Claon, jointly with his brother Ceallach; the first was murdered, the other drowned in a bog.
661. Diarmuid and Blathmac; both died of the plague.
668. Seachnasach; assass.
674. Cionfaola, brother; murdered.
678. Fionachta-Fleadha; murdered.
685. Loingseach; killed in battle.
693. Congal Cionmaghair; *d.* suddenly.
702. Feargal; routed and slain in battle.
718. Fogartach; slain in battle.
720. Cionaoth; defeated, and found dead on the battle-field.
724. Flaithbheartagh; became a monk.
731. Aodh or Hugh Alain; killed in battle.
740. Daniel; *d.* on a pilgrimage at Joppa, in Palestine.
782. Niall-Freasach; became a monk.
786. Donagh or Donchad; "*d.* in his bed."
815. Aodh or Hugh; slain in battle.
837. Connor or Conchabhar; "died of grief."
851. Niall-Caillie; drowned in the river Caillie.
866. Turgesius, the Norwegian chief, possessed himself of the sovereign power; "expelled the Irish historians, and burnt their books;"

made prisoner, and thrown into a lough, and drowned.
879. Maol Ceachlin, or Malachy I.
897. Hugh Fionnliath.
913. Flann Sionna.
951. Niall-Glundubh; "died on the field of honour."
954. Donnagh or Donough.
974. Congall; slain by the Danes at Armagh.
984. Daniel; became a monk.
1004. Maol Ceachlin II.; res. on the election of Brian Boiroimhe as king of Ireland.
1027. Brian Boromy, or Boiroimhe, defeated the Danes in the memorable battle of Clontarf, on Good Friday, 1039; assass. in his te the same night.

Brian Boiroimhe was 30 years K. of Munster, and 12 K. of Ireland.

1039. Maol Ceachlin II.; restored.
1048. Donough or Denis O'Brian, 3r son.
1098. Tirloch or Turlough, nephew.
1110. Muriertagh or Murtough; res., an became a monk.
1130. Turlough (O'Connor) II., the Great
1150. Murtough Mac Neil Mac Lachlin slain in battle.
1168. Roderic or Roger O'Connor.
1172. Henry II. K. of England; conq the country, and became lord o Ireland.

The English monarchs were styled "Lords of Ireland," until th reign of Henry VIII., who styled himself *King;* and this title con tinued down to the Union.

For subsequent Sovereigns of Ireland see *Sovereigns of England, ant* p. 4. By the Act of Union 39 & 40 Geo. III. cap. 67, Ireland was on and after Jan. 1, 1801, united to Great Britain (England and Scotland) the three Kingdoms being thenceforth styled "the United Kingdom of Great Britain and Ireland."

FRANCE.

THE following are the principal dates relating to this country:—

Merovingians	418	Elder line of Bourbons	April, 1814
Carlovingians	752	"The Hundred Days,"	Mar. 20 to June 29, 1815
Hugh Capet, cr. at Rheims	July 3, 987	Line of the Orleans Bourbons	Aug. 9, 1830
Line of Valois	April 1, 1328	2nd Republic	Feb. 24, 1848
Elder line of Bourbons	Aug. 2, 1589	2nd Empire	Dec. 2, 1852
1st Republic	Sept. 21, 1792	3rd Republic	Sept. 4, 1870
1st Empire	May 18, 1804		

KINGS OF FRANCE.

MEROVINGIAN RACE.

418. Pharamond.
427. Clodion, or Clodius, the Hairy, supposed son of Pharamond.
448. Merovæus or Merovée, son-in-law of Clodion; this race of kings called from him Merovingians.
458. Childeric, son.
481. Clovis the Great, son, and the real founder of the monarchy. He left four sons, who divided the empire between them:—
511. Childebert, Paris.
— Clodomir, Orleans.
— Thierry, Metz; and
— Clotaire or Clotharius, Soissons.
534 Theodebert, Metz.
548. Theodebald, succ. in Metz.
558. Clotaire, now sole ruler of France. Upon his death the kingdom was again divided between his four sons, viz.:—
561. Charebert, ruled at Paris.
— Gontran, in Orleans and Burgundy.
— Sigebert, at Metz, and } both
— Chilperic at Soissons } assass.

France continued at times afterwards to be ruled in various divisions by separate kings.

575. Childebert II.
584. Clotaire II., Soissons.

596. Thierry II., son of Childebert, in Orleans.
— Theodebert II., Metz.
613. Clotaire II., became sole king.
628. Dagobert the Great, son; he divided the kingdom, of which he had become sole monarch, between his two sons
638. Clovis II., who had Burgundy and Neustra; and
— Sigebert II., who had Austrasia.
656. Clotaire III., son of Clovis II.
670. Childeric II.; he became king of the whole realm of France; assass. with his queen, and his son Dagobert.

At this time Thierry III. rules in Burgundy and Neustra, and Dagobert II., son of Sigebert, in Austrasia. Dagobert is assass., and Thierry reigns alone.

691. Clovis III. Pepin, mayor of the palace, rules the kingdom in the name of this sovereign, who is succ. by his brother.
695. Childebert III., surn. the Just; in this reign Pepin also exercises the royal power.
711. Dagobert III., son.
716. Chilperic II. (Daniel); he is governed, and at length deposed, by Charles Martel, mayor of tbe palace.
719. Clotaire IV., of obscure origin; raised by Charles Martel to the throne; dies soon after, and Chilperic is recalled from Aquitaine, whither he had fled for refuge.
720. Chilperic II., rest.; he shortly afterwards dies at Noyon, and is succ. by
— Thierry IV., son of Dagobert III., surn. *de Chelles; d.* 737. Charles Martel now rules under the new title of "D. of the French."
737. Interregnum, till the death of Charles Martel, in 741; and until
742. Childeric III., son of Chilperic II., surn. the Stupid. Carloman and Pepin, the sons of Charles Martel, share the government of the kingdom in this reign.

THE CARLOVINGIANS.

752. Pepin the Short, son of Charles Martel; he is succ. by his two sons
768. Charlemagne and Carloman; the former, surn. the Great, crowned emp. of the West, by Leo III., in 800. Carloman reigned but three years.
814. Louis I., *le Debonnaire*, son, emp.; dethr., but restored to his dominions.
840. Charles, surn. the Bald, emp. in 875; poisoned by Zedechias, a Jew physician.
877. Louis II., the Stammerer, son.
879. Louis III., son, and Carloman II.; the former *d.* 882; and Carloman reigned alone.
884. Charles *le Gros*, an usurper, in prejudice to Charles the Simple.
887. Eudes or Hugh, count of Paris.
893. Charles III. the Simple; dep. and *d.* in prison 929; *m.* Edgina, dau. of Edward the Elder, of England, by whom he had a son, who was aft. king.
922. Robert, brother of Eudes, crowned at Rheims; but Charles marched an army against him, and killed him in battle.
923. Rodolf, D. of Burgundy, elect. king, but never acknowledged by the southern provinces.
936. Louis IV. *d'Outremer*, or Transmarine (from having been conveyed by his mother into England), son of Charles III. and Edgina; *d.* by a fall from his horse.
954. Lothaire, son; he had reigned jointly with his father from 952, and succeeds him, at 15 years of age, under the protection of Hugh the Great; poisoned.
986. Louis V. the Indolent, son; also poisoned, it is supposed by his queen, Blanche. In this prince ended the race of Charlemagne.

THE CAPETS.

987. Hugh Capet, eldest son of Hugh the Abbot, and the Great, count of Paris, &c.; he seized the crown, in prejudice to Charles of Lorraine, uncle of Louis Transmarine. From him this race of kings is called Capevingians, and Capetians.
996. Robert II., surn. the Sage, son.
1031. Henry I., son.
1060. Philip I. the Fair, and *l'Amoureux*; succ. at eight years of age, and ruled at fourteen.
1108. Louis VI., son, surn. the Lusty, or *le Gros*.
1137. Louis VII., son, surn. the Young, to distinguish him from his father, with whom he was for some years associated on the throne.
1180. Philip II. (Augustus), succ. to the crown at fifteen; crowned at Rheims in his father's lifetime.
1223. Louis VIII., *Cœur de Lion*, son.
1226. Louis IX., son, called St. Louis; ascended the throne at fifteen,

under the guardianship of his mother, who was also regent; *d.* in his camp before Tunis, and was canonized.

1270. Philip III., the Hardy, son; *d.* at Perpignan.

1285. Philip IV., the Fair, ascended the throne in his 17th year.

1314. Louis X., son, surn. *Hutin*, an old French word signifying head-strong or mutinous.

1316. John, a posthumous son, lived a few days only.

— Philip V., the Long (on account of his stature), brother of Louis X.

1322. Charles IV., the Handsome; this king, and Louis X., John, and Philip V., were kings of Navarre. *See Navarre, post.*

House of Valois.

1328. Philip VI., de Valois, grandson of Philip the Hardy.

1350. John II., the Good; *d.* suddenly in the Savoy in London.

1364. Charles V., surn. the Wise, the first prince who had the title of Dauphin.

1380. Charles VI., the Beloved.

1422. Charles VII., the Victorious.

1461. Louis XI., son.

1483. Charles VIII., the Affable.

1498. Louis XII., D. of Orleans.

1515. Francis I., of Angoulême.

1547. Henry II., *d.* at a tournament, when celebrating the nuptials of his sister with the D. of Savoy, from a wound accidently given him by the count de Montmorency.

1559. Francis II., *m.* Mary Stuart, aft. Q. of Scots.

1560. Charles IX.; Catherine of Medicis, his mother, obtained the regency.

1574. Henry III., elect. K. of Poland; murdered Aug. 1, 1589, by Jacques Clement, a Dominican friar. In this prince was extinguished the house of Valois.

House of Bourbon.

1589. Henry IV., the Great, of Bourbon, K. of Navarre; murdered by Francis Ravaillac.

1610. Louis XIII., the Just, son.

1643. Louis XIV., son.

1715. Louis XV., great-grandson, the Well-beloved.

1774. Louis XVI., grandson, *m.* the archd. Maria Antoinette, of Austria, May 1770. Deth. in the great revolution; guillotined Jan. 21, 1793, and his queen, Oct. 16, following.

1793. Louis XVII., son. Though numbered with the kings, this prince never reigned; he died in prison supposed by poison, June 8, 1795, aged ten years and two months.

Republic.

1792. Republic established by the National Convention, Sept. 20–21.

1795. The Directory established Oct., nominated Nov. 1.

1799. The Directory abolished Nov. 8, 9, 10, and a consulate of three established. Napoleon Buonaparte 1st consul; Cambacérès and Le Brun appointed Dec. 24.

1802. Napoleon B. appointed 1st consul for 10 years, May 6, and 1st consul for life, Aug. 2.

French Empire.

1804. Napoleon B., *b.* Aug. 15, 1769; decl. emp. May 18, 1804. Divorced his first wife, the empress Josephine; and *m.* Maria Louisa of Austria, April 7, 1810; abd. and retired to Elba, April 5, 1814.

Again appears in France, March 1, 1815; defeated at Waterloo, and finally abdicates in favour of his infant son, June 22. Banished to St. Helena, where *d.* May 5, 1821.

See Imperial Line, post, p. 25.

Bourbons Restored.

1814. Louis XVIII., next brother of Louis XVI., *b.* Nov. 17, 1755; *m.* Maria Josephine Louise, of Savoy. Entered Paris and took possession of the throne, May 3, 1814; obliged to flee, March 20, 1815; returned, July 8, same year; *d.* Sept. 16, 1824.

1824. Charles X., brother, *b.* Oct. 9, 1757; *m.* Maria Therese, of Savoy; dep. July 30, 1830; *d.* Nov. 6, 1836.

See Legitimate Line, post, p. 25.

House of Orleans.

1830. Louis Philippe, son of the D. of Orleans, called *Egalité*, *b.* Oct. 6, 1773; *m.* Nov. 25, 1809, Maria Amelia, dau. of Ferdinand I. (IV.), K. of the Two Sicilies. Raised to the throne, as "king of the French," Aug. 1830; elect. 7th, sw. 9th; dep. Feb. 24, 1848; *d.* Aug. 26, 1850.

See Orleanist Line, post, p. 25.

Second Republic.

1848. The revolution commenced in a popular insurrection at Paris, Feb. 22. The royal family escaped by flight to England, a prov. govt.

was estab., monarchy abolished, and France decl. a republic.

Louis Napoleon (Charles L. N. Buonaparte), *b.* April 20, 1808, son of Louis Buonaparte some time K. of Holland, and nephew of the late emp. Napoleon I.; elect. pres. of the republic, by 6,048,872 votes, out of 8,040,604; having a majority of 4,600,770 votes over his rival, general Cavaignac, Dec. 11, 1848.

Louis Napoleon declared by the national assembly pres. of the republic of France, Dec. 19, and procl. next day, Dec. 20, 1848.

The Second Empire.

Napoleon II. (Francis Joseph Charles Napoleon), son of the emp. Napoleon I., *b.* March 20, 1811; cr. K. of Rome, and aft. made D. of Reichstadt; *d.* July 22, 1832; he never reigned, but on the establishment of the second empire was recognised as Napoleon II.

1852. Napoleon III. (Louis Napoleon) above-named, the pres. of the Republic, decl. Emperor Dec. 2; *m.* Eugenie de Montijo, countess of Teba, Jan. 29, 1853; dep. Sept. 4, 1870; *d.* Jan. 9, 1873.

See Imperial Line, supra.

Third Republic.

1870. Republic procl., Sept. 4; prov. govt. by Committee of Public Defence, until election of

Presidents.

1871. Louis Adolphe Thiers, Aug. 31.

1873. Marshal Marie Edme Patrice Maurice de Mac Mahon, D. of Magenta, May 24.

1879. François Paul Jules Grévy, Jan. 30.

1887. Marie François Sadi-Carnot, Dec. 3.

THE LEGITIMATE LINE.

Charles X. (*see ante*, p. 24), abdicated, July 1830, and on Aug. 2, following, his eldest son the Dauphin, Louis Antoine, renounced his rights in favour of his nephew

Henry V. (Henry Charles Frederick Marie Dieudonné, of Artois), D. of Bordeaux, better known as the Count of Chambord. He was son of pr. Charles Ferdinand, of Artois, D. of Berri, who was *b.* Jan. 24, 1778, and *d.* Feb. 14, 1820. Henry V. was *b.* Sept. 29, 1820; *d.* Aug. 24, 1883. On his death the elder branch of the Bourbons became extinct and the succession passed to the house of Orleans.

THE ORLEANIST LINE.

Louis Philippe (*see ante*, p. 24), *d*, Aug. 26, 1850. His eldest son was Ferdinand Philippe Louis Charles Henry Joseph, of Orleans, D. of Orleans, pr. royal; *b.* Sept. 3, 1810; *m.* May 30, 1837, Helena Louisa Elizabeth, dau. of Frederick Louis, hered. Gr. D. of Mecklenburg-Schwerin; *d.* July 13, 1842, leaving as his eldest son Louis Philippe Albert d'Orleans, Count of Paris, *b.* Aug. 24, 1838, who became entitled to the throne of France, as rep. of the Orleans line, on death of his grandfather, Louis Philippe, Aug. 26, 1850, and as rep of the Legitimate line, on death of the Count of Chambord (Henry V.), Aug. 24, 1883.

THE IMPERIAL LINE.

Empresses of Napoleon I.

Josephine (Marie Rose Joseph), dau. of — Tascher de la Pagerie, *b.* June 24, 1768; *m.* 1st, Alexr. de Beauharnais; 2nd, the emp. March 8, 1796; div. Dec. 16, 1809; *d.* May 29, 1814.

Maria Louisa, archd. of Austria, *b.* Dec. 12, 1791; *m.* Apr. 2, 1810; *d.* Dec. 18, 1847. *See Parma, post*, p. 53.

Issue of Napoleon I.

See Napoleon II., supra.

Brothers of Napoleon I.

1. Joseph Buonaparte, K. of Naples, aft. K. of Spain; *m.* Maria Julia de Clary; *d.* July 28, 1844.
2. Lucien Buonaparte, pr. of Canino; *m.* 1st, Christine Elenore Boyer, 1794; 2nd, Marie Alexandrine Charlotte Louise Lawrence de Bleschamps; *d.* June 30, 1840.
3. Louis Buonaparte, K. of Holland, *m.* Hortensia Eugenia de Beauharnais, dau. of the Emp. Josephine; *d.* July 25, 1846. The father of Napoleon III.
4. Jerome Buonaparte, K. of Westphalia, *m.* 1st, Elizth. Patterson, Dec. 24,

1803, an American; 2nd, Frederica, dau. of the K. of Wurtemberg, Aug. 1807.

SISTERS OF NAPOLEON I.

1. Elizabeth, gr. duch. of Florence, and pr. of Piombino, *m.* to general Felix Bacciochi, actual pr. of Piombino.
2. Maria Paulette, or Pauline, *m.* 1st., general Leclerc; 2nd., pr. Borghese.
3. Annonceade Caroline, *m.* to Joachim Murat, aft. K. of Naples.

HIS OTHER RELATIVES.

Cardinal Fesch, abp. of Lyons, uncle to Napoleon I.

Eugene de Beauharnais, son of Josephine, viceroy of Italy, Gr. D. of Frankfort, and aft. D. of Leuchtenberg and pr. of Eichstadt; *m.* Amelia Augusta, pr. of Bavaria.

Stephanie de la Pagerie, niece of Josephine, pr. of Baden.

NAPOLEON'S GREAT OFFICERS OF STATE, MARSHALS, &c.

OFFICERS OF STATE.

Cambacérès, D. of Parma.
Caulaincourt, D. of Vicenza.
Champagne, D. of Cadore.
Duroc, D. of Friuli.
Fouché, D. of Otranto.
Le Brun, D. of Piacenza.
Maret, D. of Bassano.
Savary, D. of Rovigo.
Talleyrand de Perigord, pr. of Benevento.

MARSHALS.

Arrighi, D. of Padua.
Augereau, D. of Castiglione.
Bernadotte, pr. of Ponte Corvo, aft. K. of Sweden.
Berthier, pr. of Neufchatel and Wagram.
Bessieres, D. of Istria.
Davoust, pr. of Eckmuhl and D. of Auerstadt.
Jourdan, peer of France.
Junot, D. of Abrantes.
Kellerman, D. of Valmy.
Lannes, D. of Montebello.
Lefebre, D. of Dantzic.
Macdonald, D. of Tarento.
Marmont, D. of Ragusa.
Massena, pr. of Essling and D. of Rivoli.
Moncey, D. of Conegliano.
Mortier, D. of Treviso.
Murat, K. of Naples.
Ney, pr. of Moskwa and D. of Elchingen.
Oudinot, D, of Reggio.
Soult, D. of Dalmatia.
Suchet, D. of Albufera.
Victor, D. of Belluno.

REMARKABLE GENERALS.

Andreossi, Gouvion St. Cyr, Grouchy, Hulin, Rapp, Regnier, Sebastiani, Serrurier, Vandamme, &c.

NAPOLEON III.

Had issue one child only, Napoleon Eugene Louis Jean Joseph, known as the Prince Imperial, who was killed in the Zulu War, June 1, 1879, and *d.* unmarried.

ALENÇON.

COUNTS OF ALENÇON.

1268. Peter.
1293. Charles I. of Valois.
1325. Charles II.
1346. Charles III.
1361. Peter.

DUKES OF ALENÇON.

1404. John I.
1415. John II.
1476. Charles IV, defeated at the battle of Pavia in 1525, and the duchy was merged in the Kingdom of France.

ANJOU.

IN 877, Louis the Stammerer, son and successor of Charles the Bald of France, upon his accession to that crown, bestowed many largesses on his friends. In order to reconcile the malcontents who had not

hared them, Louis found it expedient to dismember great portions of ıis domains; and hence arose many seignories, duchies, and counties, ›ossessed by various individuals and families. This is believed to be he origin of the Counts of Anjou.

COUNTS OF ANJOU.

Fulco (Fulke), surn. the Red. after having united the counties of Eudo and Ingelger, *d.* 938.

938. Fulco II. surn. the Good.

958. Geoffrey I., son; he obtained for himself and his successors the dignity of seneschal of France.

987. Fulco III., the Black, *d.* returning from Jerusalem.

1040. Geoffery II., Martel (the Hammer), son, *d.* without male issue.

1060. { Geoffrey III., the Bearded, and Fulco IV.; the latter imprisoned his brother, and was excommunicated by the pope; his consort, Bertrade of Montfort, was carried off by K. Philip I. of France, who married her.

1106. Geoffrey IV., released his uncle, who died soon after, leaving Anjou to his nephew. Geoffrey fell in a war with his father by a poisoned arrow, discharged at him, it is said, at the instance of Bertrade.

1100. Fulco V., son, became K. of Jerusalem, and *d.* 1142.

1129. Geoffrey V., Plantagenet, 3rd son, obt. Anjou from his father this year; his two elder brothers succeeded the father as kings of Jerusalem.

Geoffrey V., *m.* Mathilde d'Angleterre (Maud, dau. of Henry I.); he conq. Normandy, which he gave, in 1149, to his son Henry, aft. Henry II., K. of England. From this marriage of Maud of England with Geoffrey of Anjou, sprung the line of the Plantagenets of our own country, a race of fourteen kings, commencing with Henry II. in 1154, and terminating with Richard III. in 1485, a period of 331 years.

1150. Geoffrey VI., second son, *d.* without an heir.

1158. William, E. of Poitou, third son of Geoffrey V., *d.* 1164.

Anjou from this time became a possession of the kings of England. It was, however, in the reign of John, taken, together with Normandy, by Philip Augustus of France, and incorporated with that kingdom, and given, as a fief, first to

* * John, son of Louis VIII., who died early, and next to

1264. Charles, his brother, who, later, became Charles I. of Sicily, and whose descendants were called the house of Anjou.

Alfonso V., of Arragon and Naples, achieved a victory over René of Anjou in 1422. The dukedom of Anjou afterwards became nothing more than a mere title, taken by the second sons of the Kings of France. This title has long since ceased.

BRETAGNE OR BRITTANY.

THIS name, in the earliest ages, was common to all that tract of country situated between the mouths of the Seine and the Loire. When, however, the Bretons were obliged to abandon the Isle of Albion (England), and to take refuge in a part of Armorica in the 5th century, they gradually communicated their name as well to the inhabitants as to the province itself.

COUNTS AND DUKES OF BRITTANY.

560. Conober, about this time.

* * * *

590. Waroc, about this time.

* * * *

824. Nomenoe.

851. Erispoe or Herispoe.

857. Salomon, cousin.

874. Pasquito de Vannes, and Gurvan de Rennes.

877. Alain III., de Vannes, and Judicael de Rennes.

907. Gurmallion.
930. Berenger de Rennes.
937. Alain IV. de Vannes.
952. Drogo.
980. Gueroc, de Nantes.
987. Conan I., de Rennes.
992. Geoffrey I.
1008. Alain V.
1040. Conan II.
1066. Hoel V.
1084. Alain Fergent, the Red.
1112. Conan III. the Fat.
1148. Eudes, Hoel VI., and Geoffrey II.
1156. Conan IV.
1171. Geoffrey III.
1196. Arthur, and Constance, dau. of Conan IV., and wife of Geoffrey, son of Henry II. of England.
1203. Guy de Tours, regent.
1213. Peter Mauclerc.
1237. John I., the Red.
1286. John II.
1305. Arthur II.
1312. John III., styled the Good.
1341. Charles, count of Blois, and John IV., de Montfort, brother to John the Good.
1345. Charles de Blois, alone.
1364. John V., styled the Valiant.
1399. John VI.
1442. Francis I.
1450. Peter II.
1457. Arthur III.
1458. Francis II.
1488. Anne, dau.
1513. Claude, dau.
1524. Francis I., of France.
1532. The dukedom of Brittany annexed to the crown of France.

BURGUNDY.

THE Kingdom of the Burgundians began in Alsace in 413, and continued for 119 years, the Franks stripping them of their dominions in 532. In the division of France among the sons of Clotaire in 561, Gontran had Orleans and Burgundy; in 638, Clovis II. had Burgundy and Neustra; and, on the death of Charles le Gros, in 888, Rodolph became king of Transjuran Burgundy. The Kingdom was soon afterwards united to that of Arles, and both passed, on the death of Rodolph III., in 1032, to Conrad the Salique, emperor of Germany. The Burgundians, who settled in Celtic Gaul, gave name to the county and duchy of Burgundy. Burgundy is now a part of France.

KINGS OF BURGUNDY.

413. Gundicar.
436. Gunderic.
466. Chilperic.
491. Gundebaud.
516. Sigismund.
523. Gondemar.
532. Conq. by the Franks under Childebert aud Clotaire, kings of Paris and Soissons.
888. Rodolph I. K. of Transjuran Burgundy.
911. Rodolph II., K. of Arles. Burgundy and Provence united in 933.
937. Conrad the Pacific, second K. of Arles.
993. Rodolph III., *le Faineant*.
1032. Rodolph bequeaths his kingdom to Conrad the Salique, emp.

DUKES OF BURGUNDY.

877. Richard *le Justicier*.
921. Rodolph, K. of France in 923.
923. Giselbert or Gilbert.
938. Hugh, styled the Great.
956. Otho.
965. Henry, brother, styled the Great, bequeathed his dukedom to the K. of France.
1015. Henry II., aft. K. of France.
1031. Robert, brother.
1075. Hugh I.
1078. Eudes I.
1102. Hugh II., surn. the Pacific.
1142. Eudes II.
1162. Hugh III.
1193. Eudes III.
1218. Hugh IV.
1272. Robert II
1305. Hugh V.
1315. Eudus IV.

1350. Philip I. *de Rouvre.*
1363. Philip II. sur. the Hardy, for gallantly fighting near his father K. John of France, at the battle of Poitiers; founded the second royal house of Burgundy.
1384. Flanders united to Burgundy by the marriage of Philip with Margaret, heiress of the counts of Flanders.
1404. John, surn. *Sans Peur* or the Fearless; murdered on the bridge of Montereau.
1419. Philip III., surn. the Good.
1421. Namur sold to Burgundy.
1429. Brabant united to Burgundy.
1433. Holland and Hainault united to Burgundy.
1444. Luxemburg sold to Burguudy.
1467. Charles the Bold, son of Philip the Good, killed in an engagement with the D. of Lorraine. With him ended the second house of Burgundy in 1477.
1477. Burgundy now passed to Austria, by the marriage of Mary, its heiress, with Maximilian I., emp. of Germany.
1479. The Duchy of Burgundy was annexed to France by Louis XI.

LORRAINE. BRABANT.

THIS country took its name from Lothaire, or Lotharius, son of the emperor of the same name, and was given to the prince as an independent dominion in 851. The kingdom eventually was divided in the 10th century into two parts. Lower Lorraine was governed by its dukes, afterwards Dukes of Brabant, until Brabant became united with Burgundy in 1429. The late province subsisted until 1766, when it was finally united to France.

DUKES.

LOWER LORRAINE.

959. Godfrey I.
964. Godfrey II.
976. Charles, of France.
1001. Otho I.
1005. Godfrey III.
1023. Gothelon, styled the Great.
1043. Godfrey IV., surn. the Hardy.
1048. Frederick of Luxemburg.
1065. Godfrey IV., again.
1069. Godfrey V., Bossu.
1076. Conrad.
1089. Godfrey VI., of Bouillon.
1101. Henry I.
1106. Godfrey VII. styled the Great.
1128. Walleran, and Godfrey VII.
1140. Godfrey VIII. *le Jeune.*
1143. Godfrey IX., surn. the Valiant.

BRABANT.

1190. Henry II.
1235. Henry III.
1248. Henry IV.
1261. John I., surn. the Victorious.
1294. John II., surn. the Pacific.
1312. John III., styled the Triumphant.
1355. Jane and Wenceslas of Luxemburg.
1383. Jane gov. alone.
1405. Antony.
1415. John IV.
1427. Philip.
1429. Brabant united to Burgundy.

LORRAINE.

916. Giselbert or Gilbert.
940. Henry I.
944. Conrad, the Red.
953. Bruno, Abp. of Cologne.
959. Frederick I.
984. Thierry I.
1026. Frederick II.
1033. Gothelon or Gothelo I.
1043. Gothelon II.
1046. Albert d'Alsace.
1048. Gerard d'Alsace.
1070. Thierry, surn. the Valiant.
1115. Sigismund I.
1139. Matthew I.
1176. Sigismund II.
1205. Ferri I.
1206. Ferri II.
1213. Theobald I.
1220. Matthew II.
1251. Ferri III., gov. 53 years.
1304. Theobald II.
1312. Ferri IV.
1328. Raoul. French for Rollo.
1346. John I.
1391. Charles I., surn. the Hardy.
1431. René d'Anjou, styled the Good. The succession disputed by Antony de Vaudemont.
1453. John II.
1470. Nicholas.
1473. Jolantha and René II.

1508. Antony, surn. the Good.
1544. Francis I.
1545. Charles II. styled the Great; reigned 63 years.
1608. Henry II., styled the Good.
1624. Francis II., Charles III., and Nicholas Francis, gov. jointly.
1670. Charles, alone
1675. Charles IV., nephew.
1690. Leopold, son.
1729. Francis Stephen, Gr. D, of Tuscany in 1737, *m.* Maria Theresa of Austria. Emp. of Germany in 1745.
1737. Stanislaus, of Poland.
1766. Lorraine united to France. *See note to "Tuscany,"* 1735-7.

In 1871, part of Lorraine was ceded by France to Germany.

NORMANDY.

THE Normans, enticed by plunder, having made many descents upon France, Charles the Simple, at length wearied by their aggressions, came to an accommodation with them, and concluded the famous treaty of St. Clair upon the Epte, whereby he gave them a part of Neustra, which from their incursions had already taken the name of Normandy. Charles also gave his daughter Giselle to their chief, Rollo, in marriage, on the condition of his embracing Christianity, and giving it encouragement among his followers.

DUKES OF NORMANDY.

911. Rollo, the Dane, 1st D., yielded homage for his dukedom to Charles the Simple, K. of France.
927. William *Longespée*, or Longsword, son.
943. Richard I., surn. the Fearless, a minor, son.
996. Richard II., son; this duke's sister, Emma, *m.* to Ethelred II., K. of England.
1026. Richard III.
1028. Robert I., surn. *le Diable.*
1035. William the Bastard, natural son of Richard III. (our William I. or the Conqueror); became K. of England in 1066.
1087. Robert, surn. Courthose,* eldest son of William, became D. of Normandy on his father's death, his brother William succeeding to the crown of England; gov. until 1106; *d.* 1134.

* This Robert had a son, William, to whom (and not to his father) the French historians give the surname Courthose (*Courtecuisse*), short-thigh.

The contention between the last Duke, Robert, and his brother Henry (third son of the Conqueror, and then king of England), terminated with the battle of Tinchebray, in Lower Normandy, Sept, 28, 1106. Robert was defeated, made prisoner, and sent to England, where he died in captivity. Normandy was then annexed to England, but was re-united to the crown of France in the reign of King John.

MONACO.

THE sovereignty of this little State has been held by the family of Grimaldi since 968.

PRINCES OF MONACO.

— Grimaldo I., L. of Monaco, living 920.
— Guido I., 1st Pr.
— Grimaldo II.
— Guido II.
— Grimaldo III., living 1184.
— Hubert.
1223 or 1232. Grimaldo IV.
1257. Francis.
1293. Rainer I.

1314. Rainer II.
1330. Charles I., styled the Great!!!
1346. Rainer III.
1407. John I.
1454. Catalan.
1457. Claudia, *m.* Lambert Grimaldi.
1493. John II.
1505. Lucian.
1525. Honorius I.
1581. Charles II.
1589. Hercules I.
1604. Honorius II.
1662. Hercules II.
1651. ? Louis I.
1701. Anthony.
1731. Louisa Hippolyta.
1731. ? Honorius III.
1780. Honorius IV.
1819. Honorius V.
1841. Florestan I. (Tancred Florestan Roger Louis), Oct. 2.
1856. Charles III. (Charles Honorius), June 20.

SWITZERLAND.

This country became subject to Germany about 1032. The revolt under William Tell occurred in 1306, and Swiss independence was first declared in 1307. A series of wars ensued, but the Swiss maintained their freedom and formed themselves into a federation ultimately consisting of thirteen cantons, and known as the Helvetic Confederation. From 1648 this Confederation enjoyed tranquility except from internal dissensions; but in 1798 it was conquered by France, the Helvetic Confederation dissolved, and the Helvetian Republic, under the control of France, formed in its place. Some minor changes were subsequently made, but ultimately, in 1815, under the provisions of the treaty of Vienna, the federal form of government was definitely restored under the name of the Swiss Confederation, and the number of cantons was increased to 22. A new federal constitution was established in 1848.

Presidents of the Swiss Confederate Council.

From the year 1848.

Term of office, one year from January 1st.

1849. Jonas Furrer.
1850. Heinrich Druck.
1851. J. Munzinger.
1852. Jonas Furrer *again.*
1853. Wilhelm Räff.
1854. Frederich Frey Herosee.
1855. Jonas Furrer *again.*
1856. Jacob Stämpfli.
1857. Constant Fornerod.
1858. Jonas Furrer *again.*
1859. Jacob Stämpfli *again.*
1860. F. Frey Herosee *again.*
1861. Martin Knüsel.
1862. Jacob Stämpfli *again.*
1863. Constant Fornerod *again.*
1864. Jacob Dubs.
1865. Karl Schink.
1866. Martin Knüsel *again.*
1867. Constant Fornerod *again.*
1868. Jacob Dubs *again.*
1869. Emil Welti.
1870. Jacob Dubs *again.*
1871. Karl Schink *again.*
1872. Emil Welti *again.*
1873. Paul Ceresole.
1874. Karl Schink *again.*
1875. J. J. Scherer.
1876. Emil Welti *again.*
1877. Joachim Heer.
1878. Karl Schink *again.*
1879. Bernhard Hammer.
1880. Emil Welti *again.*
1881. Numa Droz.
1882. Simon Bavier.
1883. Louis Ruchonnet.
1884. Emil Welti *again.*
1885. Karl Schink *again.*
1886. Adolf Deucher.
1887. Numa Droz *again.*
1888. J. Zemb.

POPES OF ROME.

The list in the former edition has been collated with that appended to Mosheim's Ecclesiastical History, which follows Bower's History of the Popes. The dates of the earlier popes differ in various writers, and must, probably, be all considered as more or less "approximate."

Bishop Pearson gives the following dates :—

Linus, 55–67.
Anacletus, 67–69.
Clement, 69–83.
Evaristus, 83–91.
Alexander, 91–101.
Sixtus, or Xystus, 101–111.
Telesphorus, 111–122.
Hyginus, 122–126.
Pius, 127–142.
Anicetus, 142–161.
Soter, 161–170.

Dodwell says Anicetus *d.* 153, and Soter in 162.

St. Peter is given in the following list as the first Bishop of Rome. in accordance with the popular tradition; but the better opinion seems to be that the Church of Rome was really settled by St. Peter and St. Paul jointly, and that Linus was appointed the first Bishop by their joint authority. See the notes to Mosheim's List, which contain much useful information on the subject.

The temporal sovereignty of the popes nominally commenced about 720, in the papacy of Gregory III.; but it was not until 754, in the papacy of Stephen II., that it can be said to have had any real foundation. It continued with frequent additions and reductions of territory and with some intervals of conquest by foreign powers till 1859–60, when the greater part of the papal dominions was swept away and soon afterwards incorporated in the new kingdom of Italy. The then Pope, Pius IX, was maintained in Rome under the protection of a French garrison until 1870, when the garrison was withdrawn, the troops of the King of Italy entered the city, and on September 21, 1870, the temporal power of the popes came to an end.

List of the Popes of Rome.

Except when otherwise stated, they died in the same year as that in which their successor was appointed.

42. St. Peter, crucified, his head downwards, in 66.
— St. Clement (*Clemens Romanus*), according to *Tertullian.*
66. St. Linus; mart.
78. St. Anacletus; mart.
91. St. Clement; abd.
100. St. Evaristus; mart.
109. St. Alexander; mart.
119. St. Sixtus; mart.
128. St. Telesphorus; mart.
139. St. Hyginus; the first who was called *pope.*
142. St. Pius; mart.
157. St. Anicetus.
168. St. Soterus; mart.
176. St. Eleutherus.
192. St. Victor; mart.
201. St. Zephirinus; *d.* 218.
219. St. Calixtus, or Callistus; *d.* 222.
222. Throne vacant.
223. St. Urban; beheaded.
230. St. Pontianus; banished
235. St. Anterus; mart.
236. St. Fabian; mart. 250.
250. Throne vacant.
251. St. Cornelius.
252. St. Lucius; mart. the same year. Novatianus, antipope.
253. St. Stephen; mart.
257. Sixtus II., his coadjutor; mart. 258.
258. Throne vacant.
259. Dionysius.
269. Felix I.; mart. 274

275. Eutychianus; mart.
283. Caius.
296. Marcellinus.
304. Throne vacant.
308. Marcellus.
310. St. Eusebius; *d.* the same year.
311. St. Melchiades; coadjutor to Eusebius.
314. Silvester; *d.* 335.
336. Marcus, or Mark; *d.* the same year.
337. Julius.
352. Liberius; banished, and in
356. Felix II., antipope; placed in the chair by Constans, during the exile of Liberius, on whose return he was driven from it with ignominy.
358. Liberius, *again*; abd.
358. Felix became legal pope, but he was made away with by Liberius
359. Liberius, *again*; *d.* 366.
366. Damasus.
384. Siricius.
398. Anastasius.
402. Innocent I.
417. Zosimus; canonized.
418. Boniface I.; canonized.
422. Celestine I.; canonized.
432. Sixtus III.
440. Leo I. the Great; canonized.
461. St. Hilary.
468. St. Simplicius.
483. Felix III., sometimes styled Felix II.; canonized.
492. Gelasius; canonized.
496. Anastasius II.; canonized.
498. Symmachus; canonized.
514. Laurentius, antipope.
514. Hormisdas, July 20; canonized; *d.* Aug. 6.
523. John I., Aug. 13; *d.* May 18.
526. Felix IV., July 12; canonized; *d.* Sept. 15.
530. Boniface II., Sept. 22; *d.* Oct. 17, 532.
532. John II., Dec. 31; *d.* May 27.
535. Agapetus, June 3; *d.* April 22.
536. Silverius, June 8; banished; *d.* June 20, 538.
537. Vigilius, banished, but rest., March 29, 555; *d.* June 7.
555. Pelagius I., June; *d.* March 31.
560. John III., July 14; *d.* July, 573.
573. Throne vacant.
574. Benedict I., surn. Bonosus, June 3; *d.* July 31.
578. Pelagius II., Nov. 27; *d.* Jan. 8.
590. Gregory the Great, Sept. 3; *d.* March 12.
604. Sabinianus, Sept. 13; *d.* Feb. 22, 606.
607. Boniface III., Feb. 19; *d.* Nov. 12.
608. Boniface IV., Sept. 15; *d.* May 25.
615. Deusdedit, Oct. 19; *d.* Nov. 8.
618. Boniface V., Dec. 23; *d.* Oct. 25.
625. Honorius I., Nov. 3; *d.* Oct. 12, 638.
639. Throne vacant.
640. Severinus, May 28; *d.* Aug. 2.
640. John IV., Dec. 24; *d.* Oct. 12.
642. Theodorus, Nov. 24; *d.* May 13.
649. Martin, July 5; *d.* Sept. 16, 655.
654. Eugenius, Aug. 10; canonized; *d.* June 3.
657. Vitalianus, July 30; *d.* Jan. 27.
672. Adeodatus, April 11; *d.* June 16.
676. Donus, Nov. 2; *d.* April 11.
678. Agatho, June 27; *d.* Jan. 10.
682. Leo II., Aug. 7; *d.* July 3, 683.
683. Throne vacant.
684. Benedict II., June 26; *d.* May 7.
685. John V., July 23; *d.* Aug. 2.
686. Conon, Oct. 21; *d.* Sept. 22, 687.
686. Theodore and Pascal, antipopes.
687. Sergius, Dec. 15; *d.* Sept. 7.
701. John VI., Oct. 30; *d.* Jan. 9.
705. John VII., March 1; *d.* Oct. 17, 707.
708. Sisinnius, Jan. 18; *d.* Feb. 6.
708. Constantine, March 25; *d.* April 8.
715. Gregory II., May 19; canonized; *d.* Feb. 11.
731. Gregory III., March 18; *d.* Nov. 29.
741. Zacharias, Dec. 3; *d.* March 14.
752. Stephen II. With this pope commenced the temporal power of the Church of Rome; March 26; *d.* April 26.
757. Paul, May 29; *d.* June 28, 767.
768. Stephen III., Aug. 7; *d.* Feb. 1.
772. Adrian, or Hadrian, I., Feb. 9; *d.* Dec. 25.
795. Leo III., Dec. 27; *d.* June 11.
816. Stephen IV., June 22; *d.* Jan. 24.
817. Pascal, June 25; *d.* May.
824. Eugenius II., May; *d.* Aug.
827. Valentinus; *d.* 827.
828. Gregory IV.; *d.* Jan. 25.
844. Sergius II., Feb. 10; *d.* Jan. 27.
847. Leo IV., April 10; *d.* July 17.

Between Leo IV. and the next pontiff, Benedict III., an absurd story, not worth refutation, places "Pope Joan."

855. Benedict III., Sept. 29; opposed by an antipope called Anastasius; *d.* April 7.
858. Nicholas, styled the Great, April 24; *d.* Nov. 13.
867. Adrian, or Hadrian, II., Dec. 14; *d.* Nov. 26.
872. John VIII., Dec. 14. It is to this John that some authors refer the scandalous fabrication of Pope Joan, but they err even in point of time. *See above.* *d.* Dec. 15.
882. Martin II., or Marinus I., Dec.; *d.* May.
884. Adrian or Hadrian III., May; *d.* Sept.
885. Stephen V., Sept.; *d.* Sept.
891. Formosus, Sept.; *d.* May 23.

896. Boniface VI., May; deposed or *d.* June 896.
896. Stephen VI., June 896; *d.* July 897.
897. Romanus, antipope, July; *d.* Nov 897.
897. Theodorus II., gov. 22 days.
898. John IX., June; *d.* July.
900. Benedict IV., July; *d.* Aug.
903. Leo V., Aug.; driven from his seat a few months after his election, and died in prison, Sept. 903.
903. Christoper, Oct.; *d.* Jan.
904. Sergius III., Jan. 29; *d.* Sept.
911. Anastasius III., Sept.; *d.* Nov.
913. Landonius, or Lando, Nov.; *d.* May.
914. John X., May 15; resigned and *d.* 929.
928. Leo VI., July; considered an intruder by many Roman Catholic historians; *d.* Feb.
929. Stephen VII., Feb.; *d.* Mar.
931. John XI., Mar.; *d.* Jan.
936. Leo VII., Jan.; *d.* July.
939. Stephen VIII., July; *d.* Oct.
942. Martin III., or Marinus II., Oct.; *d.* April.
946. Agapetus II., April; *d.* Nov.
955. John XII. (Octavian).
This pope is said to have been the first who changed his name on his elevation to the papal chair. Nov.; *d.* May 14, 964.
963. Leo VIII., Dec. 6; *d.* Mar. 965.
964. Benedict V., chosen on the death of John XII., but opposed by Leo. VIII., who was supported by the emp. Otho; the Roman people were obliged to abandon his cause. May; *d.* July 4.
965. John XIII., elect. by the authority of the emp. against the popular will, Oct. 1; *d.* Sept. 6, 972.
973. Benedict VI., Jan. 19; *d.* July.
974. Boniface VII.
974. Donus II.
974. Benedict VII., Oct.; *d.* Oct.
983. John XIV. (Peter), Dec.; *d.* Aug. 20.
984. John; *d.* before consecration. (By some omitted and by others called John XV.).
985. John XV. or XVI., Sept.; *d.* April.
996. Gregory V. (Bruno), May 3; *d.* Feb. 18, 999. An antipope, named John XVII., was set up, but exp. by the emp.
999. Silvester II. (Gerbert), April 2; *d.* May 12.
1003. John XVI or XVII., legitimate pope, June 13; *d.* Dec. 7.
1003. John XVII. or XVIII. (Fasanus), Dec. 26; *d.* May.
1009. Sergius IV. (Peter), July; *d.* June.
1012. Benedict VIII., John, June 22, *d.* April 7.
1024. John XVIII. or XIX., June; *d.* Jan.
1033. Benedict IX., Theophylact, Jan; expelled.
1045. Gregory VI., John Gratian, May; abd.
1046. Clement II., Suidger, Dec. 25; *d.* Oct. 9.
1047. Benedict IX. *again*; again deposed.
1048. Damasus II., Popponius, July 17; *d.* Aug. 8, 1048.
1049. Leo IX., Bruno, canonized; Feb. 12; *d.* April 19, 1054.
1054. Throne vacant 1 year.
1055. Victor II., Gebehard, April 13; *d.* July 28.
1057. Stephen IX., Frederick, Aug. 2; *d.* Mar. 29.
1058. Benedict X., John Mincius, Mar. 30; exp.
1058. Nicholas II., Gerard, Dec. 20; *d.* July 22.
1061. Alexander II., Anselm, Oct. 1; *d.* April 21.
1073. Gregory VII., Hildebrand, April 22; *d.* May 25.
1085. Throne vacant 1 year.
1086. Victor III., Desiderius, May 24; *d.* Sept. 16, 1087.
1088. Urban II., Otho, Mar. 12; *d.* July 29.
1099. Pascal II., Rainerius, Aug. 14; *d.* Jan. 21.
1118. Gelasius II., John Cajetan, Jan. 25; retired to a monastery.
1119. Calixtus II., Guido, Feb. 1; *d.* Dec. 14.
1124. Honorius II., Lambert, Dec. 21; *d.* Feb. 14.
1130. Innocent II., Gregory, Feb. 14; *d.* Sept. 24.
1143. Celestine II., Guido del Castello, Sept. 26; *d.* Mar. 8.
1144. Lucius II., Gerard Caccianemici, Mar. 12; *d.* Feb. 15.
1145. Eugenius III., Bernard, canonized; Feb. 18; *d.* July 8.
1153. Anastasius IV., Conrad, July 9; *d.* Dec. 3.
1154. Adrian or Hadrian IV., Nicholas Brakespeare, an Englishman, *b.* at St. Albans; Dec. 4; *d.* Sept. 1.
1159. Alexander III., Roland, Sept. 7; *d.* Aug. 30.
1181. Lucius III., Hubald Allucingolo, Sept. 1; *d.* Nov. 25.
1184. Urban III., Humbert Crivelli, Dec. 1; *d.* Oct. 20.
1187. Gregory VIII., Albert, Oct. 25; *d.* Dec. 17.
1187. Clement III., Paul, Dec. 20; *d.* Mar. 27.
1191. Celestine III., Hyacinth Bobo, April 14; *d.* Jan. 8.

1198. Innocent III., Lothario Conti di Segni, Feb 22; *d.* July 16.
1216. Honorius III., Centius Savelli, July 24; *d* Mar. 18.
1227. Gregory IX., Ugolino dei Conti di Segni, Mar. 19; *d.* Aug. 21.
1241. Celestine IV., Godfrey Castiglione, Oct. 22; *d.* Nov. 9.
1241. Throne vacant 1 year and 7 months.
1243. Innocent IV., Sinibald Fieschi, June 28; *d.* Dec. 7.
1254. Alexander IV., Raynald dei Conti di Segni, Dec. 12; *d.* May 25.
1261. Urban IV., James Pantaleon, Aug. 29; *d.* Oct. 2, 1264.
1265. Clement IV., Guido Foulquois, Feb.; *d.* Nov. 29.
1268. Throne vacant 2 years and 9 months.
1271. Gregory X., Theobald, Sept. 1; *d.* Jan. 10.
1276. Innocent V., Peter de Tarantaise, Feb. 23; *d.* June 22.
1276. Adrian or Hadrian V., Ottobon Fieschi, July 11; *d.* Aug. 18.
1276. Vicedominus; *d.* the next day.
1276. John XX. or XXI., João Pedro, Sept. 15; *d.* May 16.
1277. Nicholas III., John Cajetan Orsini, Nov. 25; *d.* Aug. 22, 1280.
1281. Martin IV., Simon de Brie, Mar. 23; *d.* Mar. 29.
1285. Honorius IV., James Savelli, April 2; *d.* April 3, 1287.
1288. Nicholas IV., Jerome of Ascoli, Feb. 22; *d.* April 4.
1292. Throne vacant 2 years and 3 months.
1294. Celestine V., Peter de Murrho, Aug. 29, resigned; *d.* May 19, 1296.
1295. Boniface VIII., Benedict Cajetan, Jan. 24; *d.* Oct. 11.
1303. Benedict XI., Nicholas Bocasini, Oct. 27; *d.* July 6.
1304. Throne vacant 11 months.
1305. Clement V. Bertrand the Goth; removed the papal seat from Rome to Avignon, Nov. 13; *d.* April 20, 1314.
1314. Throne vacant 2 years and 4 months.
1316. John XXII., James D'Euse, Sept. 5; *d.* Dec. 4, 1334.
1335. Benedict XII., (Nicholas V., antipope, at Rome), James Fournier, Jan. 8; *d.* April 25.
1342. Clement VI., Peter Roger, May 19; *d.* Dec. 6.
1352. Innocent VI., Stephen Aubert, Dec. 30; *d.* Sept. 12.
1362. Urban V., William de Grimsard, Nov. 6; *d.* Dec. 19, 1370.
1371. Gregory XI., Peter Beaufort, Jan. 5; *d.* Mar. 27.
1378. Urban VI., Bartholomew Prignano, April 18; *d.* Oct. 18.
1389. Boniface IX., Peter Tomacelli, Nov. 9; *d.* Oct., 1404.
1394. Benedict (called XIII.), antipope at Avignon.
1404. Innocent VII., Cosmato Megliorati, Oct. 17; *d.* Nov. 6.
1406. Gregory XII., Angelo Corario; elec. during the schism in the East; Benedict XIII. being the other pope; both popes were dep. Dec. 2.
1409. Alexander V., Peter of Candia, June 26; *d.* May 3.
1410. John XXIII., Balthasar Cossa, May 17, deposed.
1417. Martin V., Otho Colonna, Nov. 11; *d.* Feb. 20.
1431. Eugenius IV., Gabriel Condelmerio; dep. by the council of Basil, and Amadeus of Savoy chosen, as Felix V. in 1439; antipope, Mar. 3; *d.* Feb. 23.
1447. Nicholas V., Thomas of Sarzana, Mar. 6; *d.* Mar. 24.
1455. Calixtus III., Alphonso Borgia, April 8; *d.* Aug. 8.
1458. Pius II., Æneas Silvius Piccolomini, Aug. 27; *d.* Aug. 14.
1464. Paul II., Peter Barbo, Aug. 31; *d.* July 25.
1471. Sixtus IV., Francis della Rovere, Aug. 9; *d.* Aug. 13.
1484. Innocent VIII., John Baptist Cibò, Aug. 29; *d.* July 25.
1492. Alexander VI., Roderic Borgia, Aug. 11; *d.* Aug. 18.
1503. Pius III., Francis Todeschini or Piccolomini, Sept. 22; *d.* Oct. 18.
1503. Julius II., Julian de la Rovere, Oct. 31; *d.* Feb. 21.
1513. Leo X., John de Medici, Mar. 11; *d.* Dec. 1, 1521.
1522. Adrian or Hadrian VI., Hadrian Boyens, Jan. 9; *d.* Sept. 14.
1523. Clement VII., Julius de Medici, Nov. 19; *d.* Sept. 25.
1534. Paul III., Alexander Farnese, Oct. 13; *d.* Nov. 10, 1549.
1550. Julius III., John Maria del Monte, Feb. 7; *d.* Mar. 23.
1555. Marcellus II., Marcellus Cervini, April 5; *d.* May 1.
1555. Paul IV., John Peter Caraffa, May 23; *d.* Aug. 18.
1559. Pius IV., John Angelo de Medici, Dec. 28; *d.* Dec. 9, 1565.
1566. Pius V., Michael Ghislieri, Jan. 8; *d.* May 1.
1572. Gregory XIII., Hugh Buoncompagno, May 13; *d.* April 10.
1585. Sixtus V., Felix Peretti, April 24; *d.* Aug. 27.
1590. Urban VII., John Baptist Castagna, Sept. 15; *d.* Sept. 27.
1590. Gregory XIV., Nicolas Sfondrati, Dec. 5; *d.* Oct. 15.

1591. Innocent IX., John Antony Facchinetti, Oct. 29; *d.* Dec. 30, 1591.
1592. Clement VIII., Hippolytus Aldobrandini, Jan. 30; *d.* Mar. 3.
1605. Leo XI., Alexander de Medici, April 1; *d.* April 26.
1605. Paul V., Camillus Borghese, May 16; *d.* Jan. 22.
1621. Gregory XV., Alexander Ludovisi, Feb. 9; *d.* July 8.
1623. Urban VIII., Maffeo Barberini, Aug. 6; July 29.
1644. Innocent X., John Baptist Pamphili, Sept. 15; *d.* Jan. 7.
1655. Alexander VII., Fabius Chigi, April 8; *d.* May 22.
1667. Clement IX., Julius Rospigliosi, June 20; *d.* Dec. 9, 1669.
1670. Clement X., John Baptist Æmilius Altieri, April 29; *d.* July 22.
1676. Innocent XI., Benedict Odeschalchi, Sept. 21; *d.* Aug. 12.
1689. Alexander VIII., Peter Ottoboni, Oct. 6; *d.* Feb. 1.
1691. Innocent XII., Antonio Pignatelli, July 12; *d.* Sept. 17.
1700. Clement XI., John Francis Albani, Nov. 23; *d.* Mar. 19.
1721. Innocent XIII., Michael Angelo Conti, May 8; *d.* Mar. 7.
1724. Benedict XIII., Peter Francis Orsini, May 29; *d.* Feb. 21.
1730. Clement XII., Laurence Corsini, July 12; *d.* Feb. 6.
1740. Benedict XIV., Prosper Laurence Lambertini, Aug. 17; *d.* May 2.
1758. Clement XIII., Charles Rezzonico, July 6; *d.* Feb. 2.
1769. Clement XIV., John Vincent Ganganelli, May 18; *d.* Sept. 22, 1774.
1775. Pius VI., John Angelo Braschi, Feb. 15; *d.* Aug. 29, 1799.
1800. Pius VII., Barnabas Chiaromonti, Mar.; dep. by Buonaparte in 1809, rest. in 1814; *d.* Aug. 20.
1823. Leo XII., Annibal della Genga, Sept. 28; *d.* Feb. 10.
1829. Pius VIII., Francis Xavier Castiglioni, Mar. 31; *d.* Nov. 30.
1831. Gregory XVI., Maurus Cappellari, Feb. 2; *d.* June 1.
1846. Pius IX., John Maria Mastai Ferretti, June 16; *d.* Feb. 7.
1878. Leo XIII., Joachim Pecci, elect. Feb. 20.

ROME. ANCIENT ITALY. WESTERN EMPIRE. EASTERN EMPIRE. LOMBARDS.

Rome was first governed by kings, who ruled for a period of 243 years. It afterwards became a commonwealth, which existed under consnls 479 years. The Roman empire commonly dates from 31 B.C., the year in which was fought the battle of Actium, which gave to Augustus (the title afterwards conferred by the senate upon Octavius Cæsar) the supreme power.

ROME.

Kings of Rome.

Before Christ.

753. Romulus, murdered by the senators. Tatius, K. of the Cures, removed to Rome in 747, and ruled jointly with Romulus six years.
716. Interregnum.
715. Numa Pompilius, son-in-law of Tatius the Sabine, elected; *d.* at the age of 82.
672. Tullus Hostilius; murdered by his successor.
640. Ancus Martius, grandson of Numa.
616. Tarquinius Priscus, son of Demaratus, a Corinthian emigrant, chosen king.
578. Servius Tullius, a manumitted slave, *m.* the king's dau., and succ. by the united suffrages of the army and the people.
534. Tarquinius Superbus, grandson of Tarquinius Priscus; assass. his father-in-law, and usurps the throne.
510. The rape of Lucretia, by Sextus, son of Tarquin, leads to the abolition of royalty, and the establishment of a Republic.

Roman Republic.

First Period.—From the expulsion of Tarquin to the dictatorship of Sulla or Sylla 510 to 82 B.C.

Second Period.—From Sylla to Augustus 82 to 31 B.C. During the Republic the chief magistrates were the Consuls, who were elected annually. Their powers being limited, Dictators were occasionally appointed to meet emergencies which required an absolute ruler. A dictatorship could not be lawfully held longer than six months, and this rule appears to have been adhered to except in the instances of Sylla and Julius Cæsar. During a dictatorship the Consuls remained in office but were subordinated to the Dictator.

Consuls continued to be elected after the establishment of the Empire, but they then became of comparatively minor importance, the supreme power being exercised by the Emperors.

It will be seen that during the Republic, the supreme government was occasionally placed in the hands of Consular Tribunes, Decemvirs, and Triumvirs, but these departures from the regular course of government were only temporary.

Consuls, Dictators, &c., of Rome.

B.C.

509. *Cons.* L. Junius Brutus, *d.*
L. Tarquinius Collatinus, *abd.*
Sp. Lucretius Tricipitinus, *d.*
M. Horatius Pulvillus.
P. Valerius Poplicola.

508. *Cons.* P. Valerius Poplicola (2nd time).
T. Lucretius Tricipitinus.

507. *Cons.* P. Valerius Poplicola (3rd time).
M. Horatius Pulvillus (2nd time).

506. *Cons.* Sp. Lartius Flavus, or Rufus.
T. Herminius Aquilinus.

505. *Cons.* M. Valerius Volusus.
P. Postumius Tubertus.

504. *Cons.* P. Valerius Poplicola (4th time).
T. Lucretius Tricipitinus (2nd time).

503. *Cons.* P. Postumius Tubertus (2nd time).
Agrippa Menenius Lanatus.

502. *Cons.* Opiter Virginius Tricostus.
Sp. Cassius Viscellinus.

501. *Cons.* Postumius Cominius Auruncus.
T. Lartius Flavus, or Rufus, made *Dict.*

500. *Cons.* Ser. Sulpicius Camerinus Cornutus.
M. Tullius Longus, *d.*

499. *Cons.* T. Æbutius Elva.
P. Veturius Geminus Cicurinus.

498. *Cons.* T. Lartius Flavus, or Rufus (2nd time).
Q. Clœlius (Volcula) Siculus.
Dict. A. Postumius Albus Regillensis.

497. *Cons.* A. Sempronius Atratinus.
M. Minucius Augurinus.

496. *Cons.* A. Postumius Albus Regillensis.
T. Virginius Tricostus Cæliomontanus.

495. *Cons.* Ap. Claudius Sabinus Regillensis.
P. Servilius Priscus Structus.

494. *Cons.* A. Virginius Tricostus Cæliomontanus.
T. Verturius Geminus Cicurinus.
Dict. M. Valerius Volusus Maximus.

493. *Cons.* Sp. Cassius Viscellinus (2nd time).
Postumus Cominius Auruncus (2nd time).

492. *Cons.* T. Geganius Macerinus.
P. Minucius Augurinus.

491. *Cons.* M. Minucius Augurinus (2nd time).
A. Sempronius Attratinus (2nd time).

490. *Cons.* Q. Sulpicius Camerinus Cornutus.
Sp. Lartius Flavus or Rufus (2nd time).

489. *Cons.* C. Julius Julus.
P. Pinarius Mamercinus Rufus.

488. *Cons.* Sp. Nautius Rutilus.
Sex. Furius Medallinus Fusus.

487. *Cons.* T. Sicinius Sabinus.
C. Aquilius Tuscus.

486. *Cons.* Proculus Virginius Tricostus Rutilus.
Sp. Cassius Viscellinus (2nd time).

485. *Cons.* Ser. Cornelius Cossus Meluginensis.
Q. Fabius Vibulanus.

484. *Cons.* L. Æmilius Mamercus.
K. Fabius Vibulanus.

483. *Cons.* M. Fabius Vibulanus.
L. Valerius Potitus.

482. *Cons.* C. Julius Julus (2nd time).
Q. Fabius Vibulanus (2nd time)

481 *Cons.* K. Fabius Vibulanus (2nd time)
Sp. Furius Medullinus Fusus.

480. *Cons.* Cn. Manlius Cincinnatus.
M. Fabius Vibulanus (2nd time).
479. *Cons.* K. Fabius Vibulanus (3rd time).
T. Virginius Tricostus Rutilus.
478. *Cons.* L. Æmilius Mamercus (2nd time).
C. Servilius Structus Ahala, *d.*
Opiter Virginius Tricostus Esquilinus.
477. *Cons.* C. Horatius Pulvillus.
T. Menenius Lanatus.
476. *Cons* A. Virginius Tricostus Rutilus.
Sp. Servilius Priscus Structus.
475. *Cons.* P. Valerius Poplicola.
C. Nautius Rutilus.
474. *Cons.* A. Manlius Vulso.
L. Furius Medullinus Fusus.
473. *Cons.* L. Æmilius Mamercus (3rd time).
Vopiscus Julius Julus.
472. *Cons.* L. Pinarius Mamercinus Rufus.
P. Furius Medullinus Fusus.
471. *Cons.* Ap. Claudius Sabinus Regillensis.
T. Quinctius Capitolinus Barbatus.
470. *Cons.* L. Valerius Potitus (2nd time).
Ti. Æmilius Mamercus.
469. *Cons.* A. Virgius Tricostus Cæliomontanus.
T. Numicius Priscus.
468 *Cons.* T. Quinctius Capitolinus Barbatus (2nd time).
Q. Servilius Priscus Structus (2nd time).
467. *Cons.* Ti. Æmilius Mamercus (2nd time).
Q. Fabius Vibulanus.
466. *Cons.* Sp. Postumius Albus Regillensis.
Q. Servilius Priscus Structus (2nd time).
465. *Cons.* Q. Fabius Vibulanus (2nd time).
T. Quinctius Capitolinus Barbatus (3rd time).
464. *Cons.* A. Postumius Albus Regillensis.
Sp. Furius Medullinus Fusus.
463. *Cons.* P. Servilius Priscus Structus.
L. Æbutius Elva.
462. *Cons.* L. Lucretius Tricipitinus.
T. Veturius Geminus Cicurinus.
461. *Cons.* P. Volumnius Amintinus Gallus.
Ser. Sulpicius Camerinus Cornutus.
460. *Cons.* C. Claudius Sabinus Regillensis.
P. Valerius Poplicola, *d.* (2nd time).
L. Quinctius Cincinnatus.
459. *Cons.* Q. Fabius Vibulanus (3rd time).
L. Cornelius Maluginensis.
458. *Cons.* L. Minucius Esquillinus Augurinus.
C. Nautius Rutilus (2nd time).
Dict. L. Quinctius Cincinnatus.
457. *Cons.* C. Horatius Pulvillus (2nd time)
Q. Minucius Esquillinus Augurinus.
456. *Cons.* M. Valerius (Lactuca) Maximus.
Sp. Virginius Tricostus Cæliomontanus.
455. *Cons.* T. Romilius Rocus Vaticanus.
C. Veturius Geminus Cicurinus.
454. *Cons.* Sp. Tarpeius Montanus Capitolinus.
A. Aternius Varus Fontinalis.
453. *Cons.* Sex. Quinctilius Varus.
P. Curiatius Festus Trigeminus
452. *Cons.* P. Sestius Capitolinus Vaticanus.
T. Menenius Lanatus.
451. *Cons.* Ap. Claudius Crassinus Regillensis Sabinus (2nd time), *abd.*
T. Genucius Augurinus, *abd.*
Decemviri—
Ap. Claudius Crassinus Regillensis Sabinus.
T. Genucius Angurinus.
Sp. Veturius Crassus Cicurinus
C. Julius Julus.
A. Manlius Vulso.
Ser. Sulpicius Camerinus Cornutus.
P. Sestius Capitolinus Vaticanus.
P. Curiatius Festus Trigeminus.
T. Romilius Rocus Vaticanus.
Sp. Postumius Albus Regillensis.
450. *Decemviri*—
Ap. Claudius Crassinus Regillensis Sabinus (2nd time).
M. Cornelius Maluginensis.
L. Sergius Esquilinus.
L. Minucius Esquilinus Augurinus.
T. Antonius Merenda.
Q. Fabius Vibulanus.
Q. Poetilius Libo Visolus.
K. Duilius Longus.
Sp. Oppius Cornicen.
M. Rabuleius.
449. *Cons.* L. Valerius Poplicola Potitus.
M. Horatius Barbatus.
448. *Cons.* Lar. Herminius Aquilinus (Continisanus).
T. Virginius Tricostus Cæliomontanus.
447. *Cons.* M. Geganius Macerinus.
C. Julius Julus.
446. *Cons.* T. Quinctius Capitolinus Barbatus (4th time).
Agrippa Furius Medullınus Fusus.
445. *Cons.* M. Genucius Augurinus.
C. Curtius Philo.
444. *Cons.* L. Papirius Mugillanus.
L. Sempronius Atratinus.

443. *Cons.* M. Geganius Macerinus (2nd time).
T. Quinctius Capitolinus Barbatus (5th time).
442. *Cons.* M. Fabius Vibulanus.
Postumus Æbutius Elva Cornicen.
441. *Cons.* C. Furius Pacilus Fusus.
M. Papirius Crassus.
440. *Cons.* Proculus Geganius Macerinus.
L. Menenius Lanatus.
439. *Cons.* T. Quinctius Capitolinus Barbatus (6th time).
Agrippa Menenius Lanatus.
Dict. L. Quinctius Cincinnatus (2nd time).
438. 3 Military Tribunes with consular power.
437. *Cons.* M. Geganius Macerinus (3rd time).
L. Sergius (Fidenas).
Dict. Mam. Æmilius Mamercinus.
436. *Cons.* M. Cornelius Meluginensis.
L. Papirius Crassus.
435. *Cons.* C. Julius Julus (2nd time).
L. Virginius Tricostus.
Dict. Q. Servilius Priscus Structus (Fidenas).
434. 3 Mil. Tri.
433. 3 do.
Dict. Mam. Æmilius Mamercinus (2nd time).
432. 3 Mil. Tri.
431. *Cons.* T. Quinctius Pennus Cincinnatus.
C. Julius Mento.
Dict. A. Postumius Tubertus.
430. *Cons.* C. Papirius Crassus.
L. Julius Julus.
429. *Cons.* L. Sergius Fidenas (2nd time).
Hostus Lucretius Tricipitinus.
428. *Cons.* A. Cornelius Cossus.
T. Quinctius Pennus Cincinnatus (2nd time).
427. *Cons.* C. Servilius Structus Ahala.
L. Papirius Mugillanus (2nd time).
426. 4 Mil. Tri.
Dict. Mam. Æmilius Mamercinus (3rd time).
425. 4 Mil. Tri.
424. 4 do.
423. *Cons.* C. Sempronius Atratinus.
Q. Fabius Vibulanus.
422. 4 Mil. Tri.
421. *Cons.* N. Fabius Vibulanus.
T. Quinctius Capitolinus Barbatus.
420. 4 Mil. Tri.
419. 4 do.
418. 3 do.
Dict. Q. Servilius Priscus Fidenas (2nd time).
417. 4 Mil. Tri.
416. 4 do.
415. 4 Mil. Tri.
414. 4 do.
413. *Cons.* A. Cornelius Cossus.
L. Furius Medullinus.
412. *Cons.* Q. Fabius Vibulanus Ambustus.
C. Furius Pacilus.
411. *Cons.* M. Papirius Mugillanus.
C. Nautius Rutilus.
410. *Cons.* M. Æmilius Mamercinus.
C. Valerius Potitus Volusus.
409. *Cons.* Cn. Cornelius Cossus.
L. Furius Medullinus (2nd time).
408. 3 Mil. Tri.
Dict. P. Cornelius Rutilus Cossus.
407. 4 Mil. Tri.
406. 4 do.
405. 6 do.
404. 6 do.
403. 6 do.
402. 6 do.
401. 6 do.
400. 6 do.
399. 6 do.
398. 6 do.
397. 6 do.
396. 6 do.
Dict. M. Furius Camillus.
395. 6 Mil. Tri.
394. 6 do.
393. *Cons.* L. Valerius Potitus, *abd.*
P. Cornelius Maluginensis Cossus, *abd.*
L. Lucretius Flavus (Tricipitinus).
Ser. Sulpicius Camerinus.
392. *Cons.* L. Valerius Potitus.
M. Manlius Capitolinus.
391. 6 Mil. Tri.
390. 6 do.
Dict. M. Furius Camillus (2nd time).
389. 6 Mil. Tri.
Dict. M. Furius Camillus (3rd time).
388. 6 Mil. Tri.
387. 6 do.
386. 6 do.
385. 6 do.
Dict. A. Cornelius Cossus.
384. 6 Mil. Tri.
383. 6 do.
382. 6 do.
381. 6 do.
380. 6 do.
Dict. T. Quinctius Cincinnatus Capitolinus.
379. 6 Mil. Tri.
378. 6 do.
377. 6 do.
376. 6 do.
375 to 371. C. Licinius and L. Sextius re-elected Tribunes every year and prevented the election of the Consular Tribunes.
370. 6 Mil. Tri.
369. 6 do.

368. 6 Mil. Tri.
Dict. M. Furius Camillus (4th time).
P. Manlius Capitolinus.
367. 6 Mil. Tri.
Dict. M. Furius Camillus (5th time).
366. *Cons.* L. Æmilius Mamercinus.
L. Sextius Sextinus Lateranus.
365. *Cons.* L. Genucius Aventinensis.
Q. Servilius Ahala.
364. *Cons.* C. Sulpicius Peticus.
C. Licinius Calvus Stolo.
363. *Cons.* Cn. Genucius Aventinensis.
L. Æmilius Mamercinus (2nd time).
Dict. L. Manlius Capitolinus Imperiosus.
362. *Cons.* Q. Servilius Ahala (2nd time).
L. Genucius Aventinensis (2nd time).
Dict. Ap. Claudius Crassinus Regillensis.
361. *Cons.* C. Sulpicius Peticus (2nd time).
C. Licinius Calvus Stolo (2nd time).
Dict. T. Quinctius Pennus Capitolinus Crispinus.
360. *Cons.* C. Poetelius Libo Visolus.
M. Fabius Ambustus.
Dict. Q. Servilius Ahala.
359. *Cons.* M. Popilius Lænas.
Cn. Manlius Capitolinus Imperiosus.
358. *Cons.* C. Fabius Ambustus.
C. Plautius Proculus.
Dict. C. Sulpicius Peticus.
357. *Cons.* C. Marcius Rutilus.
Cn. Manlius Capitolinus Imperiosus (2nd time).
356. *Cons.* M. Fabius Ambustus (2nd time).
M. Popilius Lænas (2nd time).
Dict. C. Martius Rutilus.
355. *Cons.* C. Sulpicius Peticus (3rd time).
M. Valerius Poplicola.
354. *Cons.* M. Fabius Ambustus (3rd time).
T. Quinctius Pennus Capitolinus Crispinus.
353. *Cons.* C. Sulpicius Peticus (4th time).
M. Valerius Poplicola (2nd time).
Dict. T. Manlius Imperiosus Torquatus.
352. *Cons.* P. Valerius Poplicola.
C. Marcius Rutilus (2nd time).
Dict. C. Julius Julus.
351. *Cons.* C. Sulpicius Peticus (5th time).
T. Quinctius Pennus Capitolinus Crispinus (2nd time).
Dict. M. Fabius Ambustus.
350. *Cons.* M. Popilius Lænas (3rd time).
L. Cornelius Scipio.
Dict. L. Furius Camillus.
349. *Cons.* L. Furius Camillus.
Ap. Claudius Crassinus Regillensis, *d.*
Dict. T. Manlius Imperiosus Torquatus (2nd time).
348. *Cons.* M. Valerius Corvus.
M. Popilius Lænas (4th time).
Dict. C. Claudius Crassinus Regillensis.
347. *Cons.* T. Manlius Imperiosus Torquatus.
C. Plautius Venno Hypsæus.
346. *Cons.* M. Valerius Corvus (2nd time).
C. Poetelius Libo Visolus.
345. *Cons* M. Fabius Dorso.
Ser. Sulpicius Camerinus Rufus.
Dict. L. Furius Camillus (2nd time).
344. *Cons.* C. Marcius Rutilus (3rd time).
T. Manlius Imperiosus Torquatus (2nd time).
Dict. P. Valerius Poplicola.
343. *Cons.* M. Valerius Corvus (3rd time).
A. Cornelius Cossus Arvina.
342. *Cons.* C. Marcius Rutilus (4th time).
Q. Servilius Ahala.
Dict. M. Valerius Corvus.
341. *Cons.* C. Plautius Venno Hypsæus (2nd time).
L. Æmilius Mamercinus Privernas.
340. *Cons.* T. Manlius Imperiosus Torquatus (3rd time).
P. Decius Mus.
Dict. L. Papirius Crassus.
339. *Cons.* Ti. Æmilius Mamercinus.
Q. Publilius Philo.
Dict. Q. Publilius Philo.
338. *Cons.* L. Furius Camillus.
C. Mænius.
337. *Cons.* C. Sulpicius Longus.
P. Ælius Pætus.
Dict. C. Claudius Crassinus Regillensis.
336. *Cons.* L. Papirius Crassus.
K. Duilius.
335. *Cons.* M. Valerius Corvus (Calenus) (4th time).
M. Atilius Regulus.
Dict. L. Æmilius Mamercinus Privernas.
334. *Cons.* T. Veturius Calvinus.
Sp. Postumius Albinus (Caudinus).
Dict. P. Cornelius Rufinus.
333. *Cons.* L. Papirius Cursor.
C. Poetelius Libo Visolus (2nd time).
332. *Cons.* A. Cornelius Cossus Arvina (2nd time).
Cn. Domitius Calvinus.
Dict. M. Papirius Crassus.
331. *Cons.* M. Claudius Marcellus.
C. Valerius Potitus Flaccus.
Dict. Cn. Quintilius Varus.

330. *Cons.* L. Papirius Crassus (2nd time)
L. Plautius Venno.
329. *Cons.* L. Æmilius Mamercinus Privernas (2nd time).
C. Plautius Decianus.
328. *Cons.* C. Plautius Decianus (Venox) (2nd time).
P. Cornelius Scipio Barbatus.
327. *Cons.* L. Cornelius Lentulus.
Q. Publilius Philo (2nd time).
Dict. M. Claudius Marcellus.
326. *Cons.* C. Poetelius Libo Visolus (3rd time).
L. Papirius Mugillanus (Cursor) (2nd time).
325. *Cons.* L. Furius Camillus (2nd time).
D. Junius Brutus Scæva.
Dict. L. Papirius Cursor.
324. Dict. continued without any Consuls.
323. *Cons.* C. Sulpicius Longus (2nd time).
Q. Aulius Cerretanus.
322. *Cons.* Q. Fabius Maximus Rullianus.
L. Fulvius Curvus.
Dict. A. Cornelius Cossus Arvina.
321. *Cons.* T. Veturius Calvinus (2nd time).
Sp. Postumius Albinus (2nd time).
Dict. Q. Fabius Ambustus.
M. Æmilius Papus.
320. *Cons.* Q. Publilius Philo (3rd time).
L. Papirius Cursor (3rd time).
Dict. C. Mænius.
L. Cornelius Lentulus.
T. Manlius Imperiosus Torquatus.
319. *Cons.* L. Papirius Cursor (Mugillanus) (3rd time).
Q. Aulius Cerretanus (2nd time).
318. *Cons.* M. Foslius Flaccinator.
L. Plautius Venno.
317. *Cons.* C. Junius Bubulcus Brutus.
Q. Æmilius Barbula.
316. *Cons.* Sp. Nautius Rutilus.
M. Popilius Lænas.
Dict. L. Æmilius Mamercinus Privernas (2nd time).
315. *Cons.* Q. Publilius Philo (4th time).
L. Papirius Cursor (4th time).
Dict. Q. Fabius Maximus Rullianus.
314. *Cons.* M. Poetelius Libo.
C. Sulpicius Longus (3rd time).
Dict. C. Mænius (2nd time).
313. *Cons.* L. Papirius Cursor (5th time).
C. Junius Bubulcus Brutus (2nd time).
312. *Cons.* M. Valerius Maximus.
P. Decius Mus.
Dict. C. Sulpicius Longus.
311. *Cons.* C. Junius Bubulcus Brutus (3rd time).
Q. Æmilius Barbula (2nd time).
310. *Cons.* Q. Fabius Maximus Rullianus (2nd time).
C. Marcius Rutilus (Censorinus).
309. No Consuls.
Dict. L. Papirius Cursor (2nd time).
308. *Cons.* Q. Fabius Maximus Rullianus (3rd time).
P. Decius Mus (2nd time).
307. *Cons.* Ap. Claudius Cæcus.
L. Volumnius Flamma Violens.
306. *Cons.* P. Cornelius Arvina.
Q. Marcius Tremulus.
Dict. P. Cornelius Scipio Barbatus.
305. *Cons.* L. Postumius Magellus.
Ti. Minucius Augurinus, *d.*
M. Fulvius Corvus Pætinus.
304. *Cons.* P. Sulpicius Saverrio.
P. Sempronius Sophus.
303. *Cons.* L. Genucius Aventinensis.
Ser. Cornelius Lentulus (Rufinus).
302. *Cons.* M. Livius Denter.
M. Æmilius Paullus.
Dict. C. Junius Bubulcus Brutus.
301. No Consuls.
Dict. Q. Fabius Maximus Rullianus (2nd time).
M. Valerius Corvus (2nd time).
300. *Cons.* Q. Appuleius Pansa.
M. Valerius Corvus (5th time).
299. *Cons.* M. Fulvius Pætinus.
T. Manlius Torquatus, *d.*
M. Valerius Corvus (6th time).
298. *Cons.* L. Cornelius Scipio.
Cn. Fulvius Maximus Centumalus.
297. *Cons.* Q. Fabius Maximus Rullianus (4th time).
P. Decius Mus (4th time).
296. *Cons.* L. Volumnius Flamma Violens (2nd time).
Ap. Claudius Cæcus (2nd time).
295. *Cons.* Q. Fabius Maximus Rullianus (5th time).
P. Decius Mus (4th time).
294. *Cons.* L. Postumius Magellus (2nd time).
M. Atilius Regulus.
293. *Cons.* L. Papirius Cursor.
Sp. Carvilius Maximus.
292. *Cons.* Q. Fabius Maximus Gurges.
D. Junius Brutus Scæva.
291. *Cons.* L. Postumius Magellus (3rd time).
C. Junius Brutus Bubulcus.
290. *Cons.* P. Cornelius Rufinus.
M. Curius Dentatus.
289. *Cons.* M. Valerius Maximus Corvinus.
Q. Cædicius Noctua.
288. *Cons.* Q. Marcius Tremulus (2nd time).
P. Cornelius Arvina (2nd time).
287. *Cons.* M. Claudius Marcellus.
C. Nautius Rutilus.
286. *Cons.* M. Valerius Maximus Potitus.
C. Ælius Pætus.
Dict. Q. Hortensius.
285. *Cons.* C. Claudius Canina.
M. Æmilius Lepidus.

284. *Cons.* C. Servilius Tucca.
L. Cæcilius Metellus Denta.
283. *Cons.* P. Cornelius Dolabella Maximus.
Cn. Domitius Calvinus Maximus.
282. *Cons.* C. Fabricius Luscinus.
Q. Æmilius Papus.
281. *Cons.* L. Æmilius Barbula.
Q. Marcius Philippus.
280. *Cons.* P. Valerius Lævinus.
Ti. Coruncanius.
Dict. Cn. Domitius Calvinus Maximus.
279. *Cons.* P. Sulpicius Saverrio.
P. Decius Mus.
278. *Cons.* C. Fabricius Luscinus (2nd time).
Q. Æmilius Papus (2nd time).
277. *Cons.* P. Cornelius Rufinus (2nd time).
C. Junius Brutus Bubulcus (2nd time).
276. *Cons.* Q. Fabius Maximus Gurges (2nd time).
C. Genucius Clepsina.
Dict. P. Cornelius Rufinus.
275. *Cons.* M. Curius Dentatus (2nd time).
L. Cornelius Lentulus.
274. *Cons.* M. Curius Dentatus (3rd time).
Ser. Cornelius Merenda.
273. *Cons.* C. Claudius Canina (2nd time).
C. Fabius Dorso Licinus, *d.*
C. Fabricius Luscinus (3rd time).
272. *Cons.* L. Papirius Cursor (2nd time).
Sp. Carvillius Maximus (2nd time).
271. *Cons.* C. Quinctius Claudus.
L. Genucius Clepsina.
270. *Cons.* C. Genucius Clepsina (2nd time).
Cn. Cornelius Blasio.
269. *Cons.* Q. Ogulnius Gallus
C. Fabius Pictor.
268. *Cons.* Ap. Claudius Crassus Rufus.
P. Sempronius Sophus.
267. *Cons.* M. Atilius Regulus.
L. Julius Libo.
266. *Cons.* N. Fabius Pictor.
D. Junius Pera.
265. *Cons.* Q. Fabius Maximus Gurges (3rd time).
L. Mamilius Vitulus.
264. *Cons.* Ap. Claudius Caudex.
M. Fulvius Flaccus.
263. *Cons.* M. Valerius Maximus (Messala).
M. Otacilius Crassus.
Dict. Cn. Fulvius Maximus Centumalus.
262. *Cons.* L. Postumius (Magellus).
Q. Mamilius Vitulus.
261. *Cons.* L. Valerius Flaccus.
T. Otacilius Crassus.
260. *Cons.* Cn. Cornelius Scipio Asina.
C. Duilius.
259. *Cons.* L. Cornelius Scipio.
C. Aquilius Florus.
258. *Cons.* A. Atilius Calatinus.
C. Sulpicius Paterculus.
257. *Cons.* C. Atilius Regulus (Serranus).
Cn. Cornelius Blasio (2nd time).
Dict. Q. Ogulnius Gallus.
256. *Cons.* L. Manlius Vulso Longus.
Q. Cædicius, *d.*
M. Atilius Regulus (2nd time).
255. *Cons.* Ser. Fulvius Pætinus Nobilior.
M. Æmilius Paullus.
254. *Cons.* Cn. Cornelius Scipio Asina (2nd time).
A. Atilius Calatinus (2nd time).
253. *Cons.* Cn. Servilius Cæpio.
C. Sempronius Blæsus.
252. *Cons.* C. Aurelius Cotta.
P. Servilius Geminus.
251. *Cons.* L. Cæcilius Metellus.
C. Furius Pacilus.
250. *Cons.* C. Atilius Regulus (Serranus) (2nd time).
L. Manlius Vulso (Longus) (2nd time).
249. *Cons.* P. Claudius Pulcher.
L. Junius Pullus.
Dict. M. Claudius Glicia, *abd.*
A. Atilius Calatinus.
248. *Cons.* C. Aurelius Cotta (2nd time).
P. Servilius Geminus (2nd time).
247. *Cons.* L. Cæcilius Metellus (2nd time).
N. Fabius Buteo.
246. *Cons.* M. Otacilius Crassus (2nd time).
M. Fabius Licinus.
Dict. Ti. Coruncanius.
245. *Cons.* M. Fabius Buteo.
C. Atilius Bulbus.
244. *Cons.* A. Manlius Torquatus Atticus.
C. Sempronius Blæsus (2nd time).
243. *Cons.* C. Fundanius Fundulus.
C. Sulpicius Gallus.
242. *Cons.* C. Lutatius Catulus.
A. Postumius Albinus.
241. *Cons.* A. Manlius Torquatus Atticus (2nd time).
Q. Lutatius Cerco.
240. *Cons.* C. Claudius Centho.
M. Sempronius Tuditanus.
239. *Cons.* C. Mamilius Turrinus.
Q. Valerius Falto.
238. *Cons.* Ti. Sempronius Gracchus.
P. Valerius Falto.
237. *Cons.* L. Cornelius Lentulus Caudinus.
Q. Fulvius Flaccus.
236. *Cons.* P. Cornelius Lentulus Caudinus.
C. Licinius Varus.
235. *Cons.* T. Manlius Torquatus.
C. Atilius Bulbus (2nd time).

234. *Cons.* L. Postumius Albinus.
Sp. Carvilius Maximus.
233. *Cons.* Q. Fabius Maximus Verrucosus.
M. Pomponius Matho.
232. *Cons.* M. Æmilius Lepidus.
M. Publicius Malleolus.
231. *Cons.* M. Pomponius Matho.
C. Papirius Maso.
Dict. C. Duilius.
230. *Cons.* M. Æmilius Barbula.
M. Junius Pera.
229. *Cons.* L. Postumius Albinus (2nd time).
Cn. Fulvius Centumalus.
228. *Cons.* Sp. Carvilius Maximus (2nd time.
Q. Fabius Maximus Verrucosus (2nd time).
227. *Cons.* P. Valerius Flaccus.
M. Atilius Regulus.
226. *Cons.* M. Valerius Messala.
L. Apustius Fullo.
225. *Cons.* L. Æmilius Papus.
C. Atilius Regulus, *d.*
224. *Cons.* T. Manlius Torquatus (2nd time).
Q. Fulvius Flaccus (2nd time).
Dict. L. Cæcilius Metellus.
223. *Cons.* C. Flaminius.
P. Furius Philus.
222. *Cons.* Cn. Cornelius Scipio Calvus.
M. Claudius Marcellus.
221. *Cons.* P. Cornelius Scipio Asina.
M. Minucius Rufus.
Dict. Q. Fabius Maximus Verrucosus.
220. *Cons.* L. Veturius Philo.
C. Lutatius Catulus.
219. *Cons.* M. Livius Salinator.
L. Æmilius Paullus.
218. *Cons.* P. Cornelius Scipio.
Ti. Sempronius Longus.
217. *Cons.* Cn. Servilius Geminus.
C. Flaminius (2nd time), *d.*
Dict. M. Atilius Regulus (2nd time).
Q. Fabius Maximus Verrucosus (2nd time).
L. Veturius Philo.
216. *Cons.* C. Terentius Varro.
L. Æmilius Paullus (2nd time), *d.*
Dict. M. Junius Pera.
M. Fabius Buteo.
215. *Cons.* Ti. Sempronius Gracchus.
L. Postumius Albinus (3rd time), *d.*
M. Claudius Marcellus (2nd time), *abd.*
Q. Fabius Maximus Verrucosus (3rd time).
214. *Cons.* Q. Fabius Maximus Verrucosus (4th time).
M. Claudius Marcellus (3rd time).
213. *Cons.* Q. Fabius Maximus.
Ti. Sempronius Gracchus (2nd time).
Dict. C. Claudius Centho.
212. *Cons.* Q. Fulvius Flaccus (3rd time).
Ap. Claudius Pulcher.
211. *Cons.* Cn. Fulvius Centumalus.
P. Sulpicius Galba Maximus.
210. *Cons.* M. Claudius Marcellus (4th time).
M. Valerius Lævinus.
Dict. Q. Fulvius Flaccus.
209. *Cons.* Q. Fulvius Flaccus (4th time).
Q. Fabius Maximus Verrucosus (5th time).
208. *Cons.* M. Claudius Marcellus (5th time), *d.*
T. Quinctius (Pennus Capitolinus) Crispinus, *d.*
Dict. T. Manlius Torquatus.
207. *Cons.* C. Claudius Nero.
M. Livius Salinator (2nd time).
Dict. M. Livius Salinator.
206. *Cons.* L. Veturius Philo.
Q. Cæcilius Metellus.
205. *Cons.* P. Cornelius Scipio Africanus.
P. Licinius Crassus Dives.
Dict. Q. Cæcilius Metellus.
204. *Cons.* M. Cornelius Cethegus.
P. Sempronius Tuditanus.
203. *Cons.* Cn. Servilius Cæpio.
C. Servilius.
Dict. P. Sulpicius Galba Maximus.
202. *Cons.* M. Servilius Pulex Geminus.
Ti. Clandius Nero.
Dict. C. Servilius.
201. *Cons.* Cn. Cornelius Lentulus.
P. Ælius Pætus.
200. *Cons.* P. Sulpicius Galba Maximus (2nd time).
C. Aurelius Cotta.
199. *Cons.* L. Cornelius Lentulus.
P. Villius Tappulus.
198. *Cons.* Sex. Ælius Pætus Catus.
T. Quinctius Flamininus.
197. *Cons.* C. Cornelius Cethegus.
Q. Mincius Rufus.
196. *Cons.* L. Furius Purpureo.
Q. Claudius Marcellus.
195. *Cons.* L. Valerius Flaccus.
M. Porcius Cato.
194. *Cons.* P. Cornelius Scipio Africanus (2nd time).
Ti. Sempronius Longus.
193. *Cons.* L. Cornelius Merula.
Q. Minucius Thermus.
192. *Cons.* L. Quinctius Flamininus.
Cn. Domitius Ahenobarbus.
191. *Cons.* L. Cornelius Scipio Nasica.
M. Acilius Glabrio.
190. *Cons.* L. Cornelius Scipio Asiaticus.
C. Lælius.
189. *Cons.* M. Fulvius Nobilior.
Cn. Manlius Vulso.

188. *Cons.* M. Valerius Messala.
C. Livius Salinator.
187. *Cons.* M. Gemilius Lepidus.
C. Flaminius.
186. *Cons.* Sp. Postumius Albinus.
Q. Marcius Philippus.
185. *Cons.* Ap. Claudius Pulcher.
M. Sempronius Tuditanus.
184. *Cons.* P. Claudius Pulcher.
L. Porcius Licinus.
183. *Cons.* M. Claudius Marcellus.
Q. Fabius Labeo.
182. *Cons.* Cn. Bæbius Tamphilus.
L. Æmilius Paullus.
181. *Cons.* P. Cornelius Cethegus.
M. Bæbius Tamphilus.
180. *Cons.* A. Postumius Albinus.
C. Calpurnius Piso, *d.*
Q. Fulvius Flaccus.
179. *Cons.* Manlius Acidinus Fulvianus.
Q. Fulvius Flaccus (2nd time).
178. *Cons.* M. Junius Brutus.
A. Manlius Vulso.
177. *Cons.* C. Claudius Pulcher.
Ti. Sempronius Gracchus.
176. *Cons.* Q. Petilius Spurinus, *d.*
Cn. Cornelius Scipio Hispallus, *d.*
C. Valerius Lævinus.
175. *Cons.* P. Mucius Scævola.
M. Æmilius Lepidus (2nd time).
174. *Cons.* Sp. Postumius Albinus Paullulus.
Q. Mucius Scævola.
173. *Cons.* L. Postumius Albinus.
M. Popillius Lænas.
172. *Cons.* C. Popillius Lænas.
P. Ælius Ligus.
171. *Cons.* P. Licinius Crassus.
C. Cassius Longinus.
170. *Cons.* A. Hostilius Mancinus.
A. Atilius Serranus.
169. *Cons.* Q. Marcius Philippus (2nd time).
Cn. Servilius Cæpio.
168. *Cons.* L. Æmilius Paullus (2nd time).
C. Licinius Crassus.
167. *Cons.* Q. Ælius Pætus.
M. Junius Pennus.
166. *Cons.* M. Claudius Marcellus.
C. Sulpicius Gallus.
165. *Cons.* T. Manlius Torquatus.
Cn. Octavius.
164. *Cons.* A. Manlius Torquatus.
Q. Cassino Longinus, *d.*
163. *Cons.* Ti. Sempronius Gracchus (2nd time).
M. Juventius Thalna.
162. *Cons.* P. Cornelius Scipio Nasica, *abd.*
C. Marcius Figulus, *abd.*
P. Cornelius Lentulus.
Cn. Domitius Ahenobarbus.
161. *Cons.* M. Valerius Messala.
C. Fannius Strabo.
160. *Cons.* L. Anicius Gallus.
M. Cornelius Cethegus.
159. *Cons.* Cn. Cornelius Dolabella.
M. Fulvius Nobilior.
158. *Cons.* M. Æmilius Lepidus.
C. Popillius Lænas (2nd time).
157. *Cons.* Sex. Julius Cæsar.
L. Aurelins Orestes.
156. *Cons.* L. Cornelius Lentulus Lupus.
C. Marcius Figulus (2nd time).
155. *Cons.* P. Cornelius Scipio Nasica (2nd time).
M. Claudius Marcellus (2nd time).
154. *Cons.* Q. Opimius.
L. Postumius Albinus, *d.*
M. Acilius Glabrio.
153. *Cons.* Q. Fulvius Nobilior.
T. Annius Luscus.
152. *Cons.* M. Claudius Marcellus (3rd time).
L. Valerius Flaccus, *d.*
151. *Cons.* L. Licinius Lucullus.
A. Postumius Albinus.
150. *Cons.* T. Quinctius Flamininus.
M. Acilius Balbus.
149. *Cons.* L. Marcius Censorinus.
M. Manilius.
148. *Cons.* Sp. Postunius Albinus Magnus.
L. Calpurnus Piso Cæsoninus.
147. *Cons.* P. Cornelius Scipio Africanus Æmilianus.
C. Livius Drusus.
146. *Cons.* Cn. Cornelius Lentulus.
L. Mummius Achaicus.
145. *Cons.* Q. Fabius Maximus Æmilianus.
L. Hostilius Mancinus.
144. *Cons.* Ser. Sulpicius Galba.
L. Aurelius Cotta.
143. *Cons.* Ap. Claudius Pulcher.
Q. Cæcilius Metellus (Macedonicus).
142. *Cons.* L. Cæcilius Metellus Calvus.
Q. Fabius Maximus Servilianus.
141. *Cons.* Cn. Servilius Cæpio.
Q. Pompeius.
140. *Cons.* L. Lælius Sapiens.
Q. Servilius Cæpio.
139. *Cons.* Cn. Calpurnius Piso.
M. Popillius Lænas.
138. *Cons.* P. Cornelius Scipio Nasica Serapio.
D. Junius Brutus (Callaicus).
137. *Cons.* M. Æmilius Lepidus Porcina.
C. Hostilius Mancinus, *abd.*
136. *Cons.* L. Furius Philus.
Sex. Atilius Serranus.
135. *Cons.* Ser. Fulvius Flaccus.
Q. Calpurnius Piso.
134. *Cons.* P. Cornelius Scipio Africanus Æmilianus (2nd time).
C. Fulvius Flaccus.
133. *Cons.* P. Mucius Scævola.
L. Calpurnius Piso Frugi.

132. *Cons.* P. Popillius Lænas.
P. Rupilius.
131. *Cons.* P. Licinius Crassus Mucianus.
L. Valerius Flaccus.
130. *Cons.* C. Claudius Pulcher Lentulus.
M. Paperna.
129. *Cons.* C. Sempronius Tuditanus.
M. Aquillius.
128. *Cons.* Cn. Octavius.
T. Annius Luscus Rufus.
127. *Cons.* L. Cassius Longinus Ravilla.
L. Cornelius Cinna.
126. *Cons.* M. Æmilius Lepidus.
L. Aurelius Orestes.
125. *Cons.* M. Plautius Hypsæus.
M. Fulvius Flaccus.
124. *Cons.* C. Cassius Longinus.
C. Sextius Calvinus.
123. *Cons.* Q. Cæcilius Metellus (Ballaricus).
T. Quinctius Flamininus.
122. *Cons.* Cn. Domitius Ahenobarbus.
C. Fannius Strabo.
121. *Cons.* L. Opimius.
Q. Fabius Maximus (Allobrogicus).
120. *Cons.* P. Manilius.
C. Papirius Carbo.
119. *Cons.* L. Cæcilius Metellus (Dalmaticus).
L. Aurelius Cotta.
118. *Cons.* M. Porcius Cato, *d.*
Q. Marcius Rex.
117. *Cons.* P. Cæcilius Metellus Diadematus.
Q. Mucius Scævola.
116. *Cons.* C. Licinius Geta.
Q. Fabius Maximus Eburnus.
115. *Cons.* M. Æmilius Scaurus.
M. Cæcilius Metellus.
114. *Cons.* M. Acilius Balbus.
C. Porcius Cato.
113. *Cons.* C. Cæcilius Metellus Caprarius.
Cn. Papirius Carbo.
112. *Cons.* M. Livius Drusus.
L. Calpurnius Piso Cæsoninus.
111. *Cons.* P. Cornelius Scipio Nasica, *d.*
L. Calpurnius Bestia.
110. *Cons.* M. Minucius Rufus.
Sp. Postumius Albinus.
109. *Cons.* Q. Cæcilius Metellus (Numidicus).
M. Julius Silanus.
108. *Cons.* Ser. Sulpicius Galba.
L. Hortensius, *d.*
M. Aurelius Scarus.
107. *Cons.* L. Cassius Longinus, *d.*
C. Marius.
106. *Cons.* C. Atilius Serranus.
Q. Servilius Cæpio.
105. *Cons.* P. Rutilius Rufus.
Cn. Mallius Maximus.
104. *Cons.* C. Marius (2nd time).
C. Flavius Fimbria.
103. *Cons.* C. Marius (3rd time).
L. Aurelius Orestes, *d.*
102. *Cons.* C. Marius (4th time).
Q. Lutatius Catulus.
101. *Cons.* C. Marius (5th time).
M. Aquilius.
100. *Cons.* C. Marius (6th time).
L. Valerius Flaccus.
99. *Cons.* M. Antonius.
A. Postumius Albinus.
98. *Cons.* Q. Cæcilius Metellus Nepos.
T. Didius.
97. *Cons.* Cn. Cornelius Lentulus.
P. Licinius Crassus.
96. *Cons.* Cn. Domitius Ahenobarbus.
C. Cassius Longinus.
95. *Cons.* L. Licinius Crassus.
Q. Mucius Scævola.
94. *Cons.* C. Cœlius Caldus.
L. Domitius Ahenobarbus.
93. *Cons.* C. Valerius Flaccus.
M. Herennius.
92. *Cons.* C. Claudius Pulcher.
M. Perperna.
91. *Cons.* L. Marcius Philippus.
Sex. Julius Cæsar.
90. *Cons.* L. Julius Cæsar.
P. Rutilius Lupus, *d.*
89. *Cons.* Cn. Pompeius Strabo.
L. Porcius Cato, *d.*
88. *Cons.* L. Cornelius Sulla (Felix).
Q. Pompeius Rufus, *d.*
87. *Cons.* Cn. Octavius, *d.*
L. Cornelius Cinna, *abd.*
L. Cornelius Merula, *d.*
86. *Cons.* L. Cornelius Cinna (2nd time).
C. Marius (7th time), *d.*
L. Valerius Flaccus (2nd time).
85. *Cons.* L. Cornelius Cinna (3rd time).
Cn. Papirius Carbo.
84. *Cons.* Cn. Papirius Carbo (2nd time).
L. Cornelius Cinna (4th time), *d.*
83. *Cons.* L. Cornelius Scipio Asiaticus.
L. Norbanus Balbus.
82. *Cons.* C. Marius, *d.*
Cn. Papirius Carbo (3rd time), *d.*
Dict. L. Cornelius Sulla Felix.
81. *Cons.* M. Tullius Decula.
Cn. Cornelius Dolabella.
Sulla continues *Dict.*
80. *Cons.* L. Cornelius Sulla Felix (2nd time).
Q. Cæcilius Metellus Pius.
Sulla continues *Dict.* as well as *Cons.*
79. *Cons.* P. Servilius Vatia (Isauricus).
Ap. Claudius Pulcher.
78. *Cons.* M. Æmilius Lepidus.
Q. Lutatius Catulus.
77. *Cons.* D. Junius Brutus.
Mam. Æmilius Lepidus Livianus.
76. *Cons.* Cn. Octavius.
L. Scribonius Curio.

75. *Cons.* L. Octavius.
C. Aurelius Cotta.
74. *Cons.* L. Licinius Lucullus.
M. Aurelius Cotta.
73. *Cons.* M. Terentius Varro Lucullus.
C. Cassius Varus.
72. *Cons.* L. Gellius Poplicola.
Cn. Cornelius Lentulus Clodianus.
71. *Cons.* P. Cornelius Lentulus Sura.
Cn. Aufidius Orestes.
70. *Cons.* Cn. Pompeius Magnus.
Licinius Crassus Dives.
69. *Cons.* Q. Hortensius.
Q. Cæcilius Metellus (Creticus).
68. *Cons.* L. Cæcilius Metellus, *d.*
Q. Marcius Rex
67. *Cons.* C. Calpurnius Piso.
M. Acilius Glabrio.
66. *Cons.* M. Æmilius Lepidus.
L. Volcatius Tullus.
65. *Cons.* P. Cornelius Sulla, did not act.
P. Autronius Pætus, did not act.
L. Aurelius Cotta.
L. Manlius Torquatus.
64. *Cons.* L. Julius Cæsar.
C. Marcius Figulus.
63. *Cons.* M. Tullius Cicero.
C. Antonius.
62. *Cons.* D. Junius Silanus.
L. Licinius Murena.
61. *Cons.* M. Pupius Piso Calpurnianus.
M. Valerius Messala Niger.
60. *Cons.* L. Afranius.
Q. Cæcilius Metellus Celer.
1st *Triumvirate*:—Cæsar, Pompeius, and Crassus.
59. *Cons.* C. Julius Cæsar.
M. Calpurnius Bibulus.
58. *Cons.* L. Calpurnius Piso Cæsoninus.
A. Gabinius.
57. *Cons.* P. Cornelius Lentulus Spinther.
Q. Cæcilius Metellus Nepos.
56. *Cons.* Cn. Cornelius Lentulus Marcellinus.
L. Marcius Philippus.
55. *Cons.* Cn. Pompeius Magnus (2nd time).
M. Licinius Crassus (2nd time).
54. *Cons.* L. Domitius Ahenobarbus.
Ap. Claudius Pulcher.
53. *Cons.* Cn. Domitius Calvinus.
M. Valerius Messala.
52. *Cons.* Cn. Pompeius Magnus (3rd time).
Q. Cæcilius Metellus Pius Scipio.
51. *Cons.* Ser. Sulpicius Rufus.
M. Claudius Marcellus.
50. *Cons.* L. Æmilius Paullus.
C. Claudius Marcellus.
49. *Cons.* C. Claudius Marcellus (2nd time).
L. Cornelius Lentulus Crus.
Dict. C. Julius Cæsar.
48. *Cons.* C. Julius Cæsar (2nd time).
P. Servilius Vatia Isauricus.
47. *Dict.* C. Julius Cæsar (2nd time).
Cons. Q. Fufius Calenus.
P. Vatinius.
46. *Cons.* C. Julius Cæsar (3rd time).
M. Æmilius Lepidus.
45. *Dict.* C. Julius Cæsar (3rd time).
Cons. C. Julius Cæsar (4th time); made *Cons.* for 10 years and *Dict.* for life.
Q. Fabius Maximus, *d.*
C. Caninius Rebilus.
C. Trebonius.
44. *Dict.* C. Julius Cæsar (4th time).
Cons. C. Julius Cæsar (5th time); assass. 15th March.
M. Antonius.
P. Cornelius Dolabella.
43. *Cons.* C. Vibius Pansa, *d.*
A. Hirtius, *d.*
C. Julius Cæsar Octavianus (aft. emp. Augustus), *abd.*
C. Carrinas.
Q. Pedius, *d.*
P. Ventidius.
2nd *Triumvirate*:—Octavianus, Antonius, and Lepidus.
42. *Cons.* L. Munatius Plancus.
M. Æmilius Lepidus (2nd time).
41. *Cons.* L. Antonius Pietas.
P. Servilius Vatia Isauricus (2nd time).
40. *Cons.* Cn. Domitius Calvinus (2nd time), *abd.*
C. Asinius Pollio.
L. Cornelius Balbus.
P. Canidius Crassus.
39. *Cons.* L. Marcius Censorinus.
C. Calvicius Sabinus.
38. *Cons.* Ap. Claudius Pulcher.
C. Norbanus Flaccus.
37. *Cons.* M. Agrippa.
L. Caninius Gallus, *abd.*
T. Statilius Taurus.
Renewal of the Triumvirate for another period of 5 years.
36. *Cons.* L. Gellius Poplicola, *abd.*
M. Cocceius Nerva, *abd.*
L. Munatius Plancus (2nd time).
C. Sulpicius Quirinus.
Lepidus ceases to be one of the Triumvirs.
35. *Cons.* L. Cornificius.
Sex. Pompeius.
34. *Cons.* L. Scribonius Libo.
M. Antonius, *abd.*
L. Sempronius Atratinus.
Paullus Æmilius Lepidus (from July).
C. Memmius (from July).
M. Herennius Picens (from Nov.).

33. *Cons.* C. Julius Cæsar Octavianus (2nd time), *abd.*
L. Volcatius Tullus.
P. Autronius Pætus.
L. Flavius (from May).
C. Fonteius Capito (from July).
M. Acilius (Aviola) (from July).
L. Vinucius (from Sept.).
L. Laronius (from Oct.).

32. *Cons.* Cn. Domitius Ahenobarbus.
C. Sosius.
L. Cornelius (from July).
N. Valerius (from Nov.).

31. *Cons.* C. Julius Cæsar Octavianus (3rd time).
M. Valerius Messala Corvinus.
M. Titius (from May).
Cn. Pompeius (from Oct.).

30. *Cons.* C. Julius Cæsar Octavianus (4th time).
M. Licinius Crassus.
C. Antistius Vetus (from July).
M. Tullius Cicero (from Sept.).
L. Sænius (from Nov.).

29. *Cons.* C. Julius Cæsar Octavianus (5th time).
Sex. Appuleius.
Potitus Valerius Messala (from July).
C. Furnius (from Nov.).
C. Cluvius (from Nov.).

28. *Cons.* C. Julius Cæsar Octavianus (6th time).
M. Agrippa (2nd time).

27. *Cons.* C. Julius Cæsar Octavianus (7th time).
M. Agrippa (3rd time).

EMPERORS OF ROME.

B.C.

31. Octavianus Cæsar; in the year 27 B.C. styled Augustus Imperator.

A.D.

14. Tiberius (Claudius Nero).
37. Caius Caligula; murdered by a tribune.
41. Claudius (Tiber. Drusus); poisoned by his wife Agrippina, to make way for
54. Claudius Nero, dep.; put himself to death.
68. Servius Sulpicius Galba; slain by the prætorian band.
69. M. Salvius Otho; stabbed himself, after a reign of three months.
69. Aulus Vitellius; dep. by Vespasian, and put to death.
69. Titus Flavius Vaspasian.
79. Titus (Vespasian), son.
81. Titus Flavius Domitian, brother of Titus, last of the 12 Cæsars; assass.
96. Cocceius Nerva.
98. Trajan (M. Ulpius Crinitus).
117. Adrian or Hadrian (Publius Ælius).
138. Antoninus Titus, surn. Pius.
161. Marcus Aurelius, and Lucius Verus, his son-in-law; the latter *d.* 169.
180. Commodus (L. Aurelius Antoninus), son; poisoned by his favourite mistress, Martia.
193. Publius Helvius Pertinax; put to death by the prætorian band.

Four emperors now start up; Didius Julianus, at Rome; Pescennius Niger, in Syria; Lucius Septimius Severus, in Pannonia; and Clodius Albinus, in Britain.

193. Lucius Septimius Severus; *d.* at York, in Britain, in 211; succ. by his sons.
211. M. Aurelius Caracalla, and Septimius Geta. Geta murdered the same year by his brother, who reigned alone until 217, when he was slain by his successor.
217. M. Opilius Macrinus, præfect of the guards; beheaded in a mutiny.
218. Heliogabalus (M. Aurelius Antoninus), a youth; put to death by his subjects.
222. Alexander Severus; assass. by some soldiers corrupted by Maximinus.
235. Caius Julius Verus Maximinus; assass. in his tent before the walls of Aquileia.
237. M. Antonius Gordianus, and his son; the latter having been killed in a battle with the partisans of Maximinus, the father strangled in a fit of despair, at Carthage, in his 80th year.
237. Balbinus and Pupienus; put to death.
238. Gordianus junior, grandson of the elder Gordianus, in his 16th year; assass. by the guards, at the instigation of his succ.
244. Phillip, the Arabian; assass. by his own soldiers; his son Philip was murdered, at the same time, in his mother's arms.
249. Metius Decius; he perished, with his two sons, and their army, in an engagement with the Goths.
251. Gallus Hostilius, and his son Volusianus; both slain by the soldiery.
253. Æmilianus; put to death after a reign of only 4 months.

253. Valerianus, and his son, Gallienus; the first was taken prisoner by Sapor, king of Persia, and flayed alive.

260. Gallienus reigned alone.

About this time 30 pretenders to the imperial power started up in different parts of the empire; of these, Cyriades was the first, but he was slain.

268. Claudius II. (Gallienus having been assass. by the officers of the guards) succ; *d.* of the plague.

270. Quintillus, his brother, elect. at Rome by the senate and troops; Aurelian by the army in Illyricum. Quintillus, despairing of success against his rival, who was marching against him, opened his veins, and bled himself to death.

270. Aurelian; assass. by his soldiers in his march against Persia, Jan. 275.

275. Interregnum of about 9 months.

275. Tacitus, elect. Oct. 25; *d.* at Tarsus in Cilicia, April 13, 276.

276. Florian, brother; his title not recognised by the senate.

276. M. Aurelius Probus; assass. by his troops at Sirmium.

282. M. Aurelius Carus; killed at Ctesiphon by lightning.

283. Carinus and Numerianus, sons; both assass. after transient reigns.

284. Diocletian; who associated as his colleague in the government

286. Hercules Maximianus; the two emperors resign in favour of

305. Constantius Chlorus and Galerius Maximianus; the first *d.* at York, in Britain, in 306, and the troops saluted as emperor, his son

306. Consantine, aft. styled the Great; whilst at Rome the prætorian band proclaimed

306. Maxentius, son of Hercules Maximianus. Besides these were

306. Hercules Maximianus, who endeavoured to recover his abdicated power,

306. Flavius Valerius Severus, murdered by the last named pretender, and

307. Flavius Valerianus Licinius, the brother-iu-law of Constantine.

Of these, Hercules Maximianus was strangled in Gaul in 310; Galerius Maximianus *d.* 311: Maxentius was drowned in the Tiber in 312; and Licinius was put to death by order of Constantine in 324.

324. Constantine the Great now reigned alone; *d.* Whitsunday, May 22, 337.

337. Constantine II., Constans, Constantius II. — Sons of Constantine, divided the empire between them; the first was slain in 340, and the second murdered in 350, when the third became sole emperor.

361. Julian, the apostate, so called for abjuring Christianity, having been educated for the priesthood; mortally wounded in a battle with the Persians.

363. Jovian; reigned 8 months; found dead in his bed; supposed to have died from the fumes of charcoal.

The Roman Empire may be said to have terminated here, as a single dominion.

DIVISION OF THE EASTERN AND WESTERN EMPIRE.

Western Empire.

Some writers date the Western Empire from the death of Theodosius the Great, January 17, 303; and as completed by Odoacer, on the defeat of Orestes by that prince, on August 23, 476.

Emperors of the Western Empire.

346. Valentinian, son of Gratian, takes the Western Empire, and his brother, Valens, the Eastern Empire.

367. Gratian, son of Valentinian, made a colleague in the government by his father.

375. Valentinian II., another son, was, on on the death of his father, associated with his brother in the empire. Gratian assass. by his general, Andragathius, in 383; Valentinian murdered by one of his officers, Arbogastes, in 392.

392. Eugenius, an usurper, assumes the imperial dignity; he and Arbogastes are defeated by Theodosius the Great, who becomes sole emperor.

Andragathius throws himself into the sea, and Arbogastes dies by his own hand.

395. Honorius, son of Theodosius, reigns,

on his father's death, in the West, and his brother, Arcadius, in the East. Honorius dies in 423.
Usurpation of John, the Notary, who is defeated and slain, near Ravenna.
425. Valentinian III., son of the Empress Placidia, dau. of Theodosius the Great; murdered at the instance of his successor.
455. Maximus; *m.* Eudoxia, widow of Valentinian, who, to avenge the death of her first husband and the guilt of her second, invites the African Vandals into Italy, and Rome is sacked. Maximus stoned to death.
456. Marcus Macilius Avitus, forced to resign, and dies in his flight towards the Alps.
457. Julius Valerius Majorianus; murdered at the instance of his minister Ricimer; who raises
461. Libius Severus to the throne, but holds the supreme power. Severus is poisoned by Ricimer.
465. Interregnum. Ricimer retains the authority, without assuming the title of emperor.
467. Anthemius, chosen by the joint suffrages of the senate and army; murdered by Ricimer, who dies soon after.
472. Flavius Anicius Olybrius; slain by the Goths soon after his accession.
473. Glycerius; forced to abd. by his successor
474. Julius Nepos; deposed by his general, Orestes, and retires to Salonæ.
475. Romulus Augustulus, son of Orestes. Orestes is slain, and the emperor deposed by
476. Odoacer, king of the Heruli, who takes Rome, assumes the style of king of Italy, and completes the fall of the Western Empire.

Ancient Italy.

Kings of Italy.

476. Odoacer, chief of the Heruli.
493. Theodoric, the Ostrogoth.
526. Athalaric.
534. Theodatus.
536. Vitiges.
540. Theodebald.
541. Araric.
541. Totila, or Baduilla.
552. Teïa, the last of the Goths.
553. Narses, duke or governor of Italy.
Narses was succ. by Longinus, who made the chief towns of Italy exarchates; he governed at Ravenna, which was afterwards ruled by imperial lieutenants called exarchs, until 752, when it was reduced by the Lombards.
568. Alboinus, the Lombard.
573. Cleophis.
575. Interregnum of 10 years, during which the Lombards were governed by elective dukes.

Kings of the Lombards.

584. Autharis.
590. Romanus.
591. Agilulphus.
615. Adawaldus, with his mother, Theodolinda.
625. Ariwaldus.
636. Rotharis, D. of Brescia.
652. Rodoaldus.
653. Aribert I.
661. Pertharitus; dep.
661. Gondibert.
662. Grimoald.
671. Pertharitus, rest.
686. Cunibert, son.
700. Luitpert, or Leutbert.
701. Ragimbertus.
701. Aribert II.
712. Luitprandus.
744. Hildebrand.
744. Ratchis, D. of Friuli.
749. Astolphus.
756. Desiderius, or Didier.
In 774, Desiderius, the last of the Lombards, was taken prisoner by Charlemagne, and the kingdom of Italy was united, first to France, and afterwards to the empire, until 888, when it was separated from the latter, on the death of Charles le Gros.
888. Berenger, D. of Friuli; dep.
900. Louis, the blind.
905. Berenger, rest.
922. Rodolph, K. of Burgundy.
926. Hugh, count of Provence.
945. Lothaire.
950. Berenger II.; dep.
962. The emperor Otho reduced Italy, and re-united it to the German empire.
The title of King of Italy was revived in 1805, and again in 1861. *See Modern Italy.*

Eastern Empire.

Emperors of the Eastern Empire.

364. Valens, son of Gratian, takes the Eastern, and his brother Valentinian the Western, Empire; defeated by the Goths and wounded

in his retreat; his soldiers placed him in a cabin, which the enemy burnt, not knowing he was there.
379. Theodosius the Great, becomes sole emperor in 392; succ. by his sons
395. Arcadius in the East, and Honorius in the West. Arcadius is succ. by
408. Theodosius II., son, under the guardianship of his sister Pulcheria.
450. Marcianus.
457. Leo I., surn. the Thracian.
474. Leo II., the younger, grandson.
474. Zeno, the Isaurian, father, (having married Ariadne, daughter of Leo I.); dep. but rest.
491. Anastatius I., the Silentiary.
518. Justin, the Thracian.
527. Justinian I., nephew; collector of the body of laws called the *Digest*, now the *Pandectæ Florentinæ*, and of the *Novellæ*; and founder of the magnificent church of St. Sophia at Constantinople. The renowned Belisarius was his general.
565. Justin II., nephew.
578. Tiberius II.
582. Maurice, the Cappadocian; murdered, with all his children, by his successor.
602. Phocas, the Usurper, whose crimes and cruelties led to his own assass. in 610.
610. Heraclius, by whom Phocas was dethr.
641. Constantine III. (Heraclius Constantine), reigned a few months; poisoned by his step-mother, Martina.
641. Constans II.; assass. in a bath.
668. Constantine IV., Pogonatus.
685. Justinian II., son; dethr. and mutilated by his succ.
695. Leontius; dethr. and mutilated by Tiberius Aspimar.
698. Tiberius III. Aspimar.
705. Justinian II. rest. Leontius and Tiberius degraded in the Hippodrome, and put to death. Justinian slain in 711.
711. Phillippicus Bardanes; assass.
713 Anastatius II., fled on the election of Theodosius in 716; aft. delivered up to Leo III. and put to death.
716. Theodosius III.
718. Leo III., the Isaurian.

In this reign (726) commences the great Iconoclastic controversy; the alternate prohibition and restoration of images involves the peace of several reigns.

741. Constantine V. Copronymus, son.
775. Leo IV., son.
780. Constantine VI., and his mother Irene.
790. Constantine, alone, by the desire of the people, Irene having become unpopular.
792. Irene, *again*, jointly with her son, and aft. alone; dep. and exiled.
802. Nicephorus I., surn. Logothetes; slain.
811. Staurachius; reigns a few days only.
811. Michael I., defeated in battle; abd. the throne, and retires to a monastery.
813. Leo V., the Armenian; killed in the temple at Constantinople on Christmas-day, 820, by conspirators in the interest of his successor.
820. Michael II., the Stammerer.
829. Theophilus.
842. Michael III., surn. Porphyrogennetes, or the Sot, son, succ. under the regency of his mother, Theodora; put to death by Basilius.
867. Basilius I., the Macedonian.
886. Leo VI., styled the Philosopher.
911. Alexander, and Constantine VII., brother and son of Leo., the latter only six years of age; the former dying in 912, Zoe, mother of Constantine, assumes the regency.
919. Romanus Lecapenus usurps the imperial power.
920. Constantine VIII., son.
928. Stephen and Christopher.

Five emperors now reign; of these, Christopher *d.* 931; Romanus is exiled by his' sons, Constantine and Stephen, who are themselves banished the next year.

945. Constantine VII. now reigns alone; poisoned by his daughter-in-law, Theophania.
959. Romanus II., son.
963. Nicephorus II., Phocas; *m.* Theophania, his predecessor's consort, who has him assassinated.
969. John I., Zemisces, celebrated general, takes Basilius II. and Constantine IX., sons of Romanus II., as colleagues; John *d.* by poison, and
975. Basilius II. and Constantine IX. reign alone; the former *d.* in 1025; the latter in 1028.
1028. Romanus III., Argyropulus; poisoned by his consort Zoe, who raises
1034. Michael IV., the Paphlagonian, to the throne; on his death Zoe places
1041. Michael V., surn. Calaphates, as his succ.; him she dethr., has his eyes put out, and *m.*
1042. Constantine X., Monomachus, who,

and Zoe, reign jointly; Zoe *d.* 1050.
1054. Theodora, widow of Constantine.
1056. Michael VI., Stratiotic; dep.
1057. Isaac I., Comnenus; abd.
1059. Constantine XI., surn. Ducas.
1067. Eudocia, consort of the preceding, and Romanus IV., surn. Diogenes, whom she marries; reign to the prejudice of Michael, Constantine's son.
1071. Michael VII., Parapinaces, recovers his throne, and reigns jointly with Constantine XII.
1078. Nicephorus III.; dethr. by
1081. Alexius I., Comnenus.
1118. John Comnenus, son, surn. Kalos; *d.* of a wound from a poisoned arrow.
1143. Manuel I., Comnenus, son.
1180. Alexius II., Comnenus, son, under the regency of the empress Maria, his mother.
1183. Andronicus I., Comnenus; causes Alexius to be strangled, and seizes the throne; put to death by
1185. Isaac II., Angelus Comnenus, who is dep., imprisoned, and dep. of his eyes by his brother.
1195. Alexius III., Angelus, called the Tyrant; this last dep. in his turn, and his eyes put out; *d.* in a monastery.
1203. Isaac II., again, associated with his son, Alexius IV.; dep.

LATIN EMPERORS.

1204. Baldwin I., E. of Flanders, on the capture of Constantinople by the Latins, elected Emperor; made a prisoner by the K. of Bulgaria, and never heard of afterwards.
1206. Henry I., brother; *d.* in 1217.
1217. Peter de Courtenay, brother-in-law.
1221. Robert de Courtenay, son.
1228. Baldwin II., brother, a minor, and John de Brienne, of Jerusalem, regent and associate emperor.
1261. Constantinople recovered, and the empire of the Franks or Latins terminates.

GREEK EMPIRE AT NICE.

1204. Theodore Lascaris.
1222. John Ducas, Vataces.
1255. Theodore Lascaris II., son.
1259. John Lascaris, and
1260. Michael VIII., Palæologus.

EMPERORS AT CONSTANTINOPLE.

1261. Michael VIII., now at Constantinople; he puts out the eyes of John, and reigns alone.
1282. Andronicus II., Palæologus, the Elder, son; dep. by his grandson, Andronicus the Younger.
1332. Andronicus III., the Younger.
1341. John Palæologus, under the guardianship of John Cantacuzenus; the latter procl emp. at Adrianople.
1347. John Cantacuzenus.
1355. John Palæologus, rest.
1391. Manuel Palæologus, son.
1425. John Palæologus II., son.
1448. Constantine XIII., Palæologus, son.
1453. Constantinople taken on May 29, 1453, by the Ottomans, under their Sultan, Mahomet II.; Constantine is slain, and with him ends the Eastern Empire.

MODERN ITALY.

THE Kings of ancient Italy will be found in succession to the Sovereigns of the Western Empire (*ante* p. 49). The Emperor Napoleon I. of France revived the title of King of Italy in 1805, but it did not long endure, and is not now recognized. The modern Kingdom of Italy dates from 1861, when Victor Emmanuel, King of Sardinia, assumed the title.

KINGS OF MODERN ITALY.

1861. Victor Emmanuel II. (Victor Emmanuel Mary Albert Eugène Ferdinand), K. of Sardinia, took the title of K. of Italy, Mch. 17.
1878. Humbert I. (Humbert Rénière Chas. Emmanuel John Mary Ferd. Eugène), son, June 9.

LUCCA.

Charlemagne having destroyed the empire of the Lombards, a.d. 774, Lucca came into the possession of the Franks, and in two centuries afterwards was annexed to Germany by Otto the Great. After many subsequent revolutions it was sold to Florence, and in a short time it obtained its complete freedom by purchase from the Emperor Charles IV., and retained it until modern times.

Napoleon having conferred Piombino upon his sister Elizabeth and her husband, Prince Bacciocchi, as an hereditary principality, the prince was chosen, in 1805, constitutional chief of the republic of Lucca. In 1806, Massa, Carrara, and Garfagorano, were united to the principality of Lucca. Finally, the congress of Vienna conferred Massa and Carrara upon the archduchess Beatrice d'Este; Piombino upon Prince Ludovisci Buoncampagni; and the Duchy of Lucca, with an annual pension of £20,000 upon—

Maria Louisa, dau. of Charles IV. of Spain, and widow of Louis, K. of Etruria; she *d.* March 13, 1824, and was succ. by her son

1824. Charles Louis, duke, *b.* Dec. 22, 1799; *m.* Aug. 1820, Maria Theresa, dau. of Victor Emmanuel I., K. of Sardinia. Relinquished the dukedom, Oct. 1847.

On the death of Maria Louisa, widow of the Emperor Napoleon I., of France, and duchess of Parma, Piacenza, and Guastalla (see *Parma*), which took place Dec. 18, 1847, Charles Louis, Duke of Lucca, was invested with the Government of the duchy of Parma, as had been agreed upon by the treaty of Paris of June 10, 1817, and congress of Frankfort, July 20, 1819; and, in conformity with the conditions of succession arranged by these acts, and by the subsequent treaty of Florence (Nov. 28, 1844), the duke Louis Charles resigned Lucca to the grand-duke of Tuscany, Oct. 5, 1847.

MODENA. REGGIO. FERRARA.

Albert Azon, or Azzo II. (great-grandson of Albert Azon I., who died a.d. 964), espoused Cunegunda, daughter of Guelph II., count of Altdorf and duke of Lower Bavaria, and, dying in 1097, left two sons. Of these, the elder, Guelph, inherited the states of Altdorf at the decease of his uncle, Guelph, duke of Carinthia; and from him sprang the branch of Guelph-Este. From the second son, Fulke, emanated the branch of Fulke-Este. The illustrious house of Este governed as *Signori* of Ferrara in the 12th century; and Modena, Reggio, and Ferrara became ducal territories, by concession, partly of the emperor and partly of the pope, in favour of Borso and Hercules d'Este, in 1452.

Sovereigns of Modena, &c.

Signori and Marquesses of Ferrara.

1067. Frederic I.
1118. Guy Salinguerra.
1150. Taurello.
1196. Salinguerra II.

Azzo VI., marq. d'Este; to the ascendancy of whose house the Tarrelli afterwards gave way.

1212 Aldovrandino.
1215 Azzo VII. d'Este.
1264. Obizzo II.
1293. Azzo VIII. d'Este.
1308. Folco or Fulke d'Este.
1317. Rinaldo. Obizzo III. Niccolo I. On the death of Rinaldo (1335) and Niccolo (1344) Obizzo ruled alone.
1352. Aldovrandino II.
1361. Niccolo II.
1383. Alberto.
1393. Niccolo III.
1441. Lionello.

DUKES OF MODENA, &c.

1450. Borso; elevated by the emp. Frederick II. and the pope, 1452, to the dukedom of Modena and Reggio.
1471. Ercole (Hercules) I.
1505. Alfonso I.
1534. Ercole (Hercules) II.
1559. Alfonso II.
1597. Cæsar d'Este. This pr. obt. possession of Modena as a fief of the empire. Ferrara was attached to the Church by Clement VIII.
1628. Alfonso III.
1629. Francis I.
1658. Alfonso IV.
1662. Francis II.
1694. Reginald.
1737. Francis III.
1780. Ercole (Hercules) III. This prince acquired, in dowry with his consort, the principalities of Massa and Carrara. He was expelled in 1796, and *d.* 1803, leaving an only child and heiress
1803. Maria Beatrix, duchess of Modena and princess of Massa and Carrara.
She espoused the archd. Ferdinand of Austria, and conferred the dukedom upon her husband; he *d.* Dec. 24, 1086, and was succ. in the dukedom by their son
1806. Francis IV., duke; the duchess, his mother, retaining the principalities.
Modena, which had been incorporated in 1797 with the Cisalpine Republic, and, in 1805, with the kingdom of Italy founded by Napoleon I., was rest. to Francis IV. upon the dissolution of the kingdom of Italy in 1814.
1829. Francis IV., now inherited Massa and Carrara, on the death of his mother, Maria Beatrix, Nov. 14.
1846. Francis V., (Francis Ferdinand Gemenien), son, Jan. 21; *d.* Nov. 20, 1875.

1860. United to the kingdom of Sardinia by Decree, Mar. 18, and now forms part of the kingdom of Italy. *See Modern Italy.*

PARMA. PLACENTIA, OR PIACENZA, &c.

IN 1346, Parma and Piacenza formed part of the territory of the counts of Milan, and were subsequently in the possession of Louis XII. of France; but were ceded by his successor, Francis I., under the league of Cambray, to pope Julius IV., when they were attached to the dominion of the Church. In 1545, pope Paul III. erected Parma and Piacenza into a duchy, and conferred it upon his natural son, Peter Louis Farnese .in whose family it continued for nearly two centuries. The subsequent details are given below.

DUKES.

1545. Peter Louis Farnese, first D.
1547. Octavius Farnese.
1586. Alexander Farnese.
1592. Ranutio I.
1622. Edoard.
1646. Ranutio II.; Edoard, his eldest son, who dying *vitâ patris*, left a dau., Elizabeth, who *m.* Philip V. of Spain.
1694. Francis I.
1727. Antony.
Upon the extinction of the male line of the old dukes, the duchy devolved upon the grandson of Edoard.
1731. Don Carlos, who, upon ascending the throne of the Sicilies, ceded the duchy to the house of Austria, with whom it remained until the treaty of Aix-la-Chapelle, Oct. 18, 1748.
1749. Don Philip, brother of Don Carlos.
1765. Don Ferdinand.

1803. The duchy now passed under the dominion of France, and pr. Louis, son of Ferdinand, became K. of Etruria.
1814. Maria Louisa of Austria, widow of the emp. Napoleon I. She became duchess of Parma, Piacenza, and Guastalla; *d.* Dec. 18, 1847.

Parma, &c., were given by the convention of April 11, 1814, to the arch-duchess Maria Louisa, ex-empress of France. After her death (Dec. 18, 1847) Charles Louis, Duke of Lucca, was given the government of this duchy, as had been arranged by the Treaty of Paris, June 10, 1817, and by the congress of Frankfort, July 20, 1819; and comformably with these acts, and with a subsequent Treaty (that of Frankfort, Nov. 28, 1844), Charles Louis, of Lucca relinquished that duchy to the grand-duke of Tuscany.

1847. Charles II. (Charles Louis de Bourbon, D. of Lucca), succ. by Manifesto, Dec. 26, 1847.
1848. Regency established Mar. 20., Prov. govt. substituted Apr. 9. Charles II. left the country Apr. 19, and *abd.* in favour of his son, Mar. 14, 1849.
1849. Charles III. (Ferd. Charles Joseph Mary Victor Balthasar de Bourbon) Aug. 27.
1854. Robert I. (Robert Charles Louis Mary de Bourbon), son, Mar. 27, a minor, his mother appointed regent.
1860. Parma was annexed to Sardinia by decree, Mar. 18, and now forms part of the Kingdom of Italy.

See Modern Italy.

SAVOY. SARDINIA.

Savoy, after various changes, was erected into a county in the beginning of the 11th century, and at the close of the 14th the governing count obtained the title of duke. The Dukes of Savoy, who acquired Sicily in 1713, exchanged it with Austria, in 1718, for Sardinia, and became kings of Sardinia. This state became involved in the great war between France and Austria, which closed with the treaty of Aix-la-Chapelle in 1748. After enjoying a long term of peace, it took part in the war of the French revolution, and in 1798 the continental territories were parcelled out into departments of the French empire, and were not restored to the legitimate sovereign until the overthrow of Napoleon in 1814. Genoa was added to Sardinia by the congress of Vienna in 1815. Savoy was ceded to France in 1860, and Sardinia became part of the new kingdom of Italy in 1861.

Counts and Dukes of Savoy.

Counts of Maurienne.

1020. Beroald, surn. the Saxon,
1027. Humbert I., "with the White Hands."
1048. Amadeus I., Longtail.
1072. Humbert II. *le Renforce.*

Counts of Savoy.

1108. Amadeus II.
1148. Humbert III., surn. the Saint.
1188. Thomas.
1233. Amadeus III.
1253. Boniface Rolando.
1263. Peter, or Charlemagne *le Petit.*
1268. Philip.
1285. Amadeus IV., styled the Great.
1323. Edward.
1329. Aimon, styled the Peace-maker.
1343. Amadeus V. (or VI.), the Green Count.
1383. Amadeus VII., the Red Count.

Dukes of Savoy.

1391. Amadeus VIII., surn. the Pacific, D. in 1416. Elected pope in 1439, as Felix. V., antipope.
1451, Louis.
1465. Amadeus IX., surn. Benevolent.
1472. Philibert, the Hunter.
1482. Charles I., the Warrior.
1489. Charles II.
1496. Philip II., *Sans Terre*, or Lackland.
1497. Philibert II., surn. the Beau.
1504. Charles III., the Good.
1553. Emmanuel Philibert, surn. the Iron-hand.

580. Charles Emmanuel, styled the Great.
630. Victor Amadeus I.
637. Francis Hyacinth.
638. Charles Emmanuel II.
675. Victor Amadeus II.
1713. He obtained Sicily this year, and in 1718 exchanged it for Sardinia, taking the title of king. Of this dominion, Piedmont and Savoy formed the continental part.

Kings of Sardinia.

720. Victor Amadeus I., K. (II. as duke), res. in 1730, in favour of his son; *d.* 1732.
730. Charles Emmanuel I., son.
773. Victor Amadeus II., son.
792. Savoy conquered by France.
796. Charles Emmanuel II., son; res. in favour of his brother.
1802. Victor Emmanuel I.
1805. Sardinia merged in the kingdom of Italy, of which the emp. Napoleon I. was crowned king, May 26, 1805.
1814. Savoy restored to Sardinia.
1814. Victor Emmanuel, rest. Res. Mar. 1821; and *d.* 1824. On his death the elder branch of the House of Savoy, became extinct in the male line.
1821. Charles Felix.
1831. Charles Albert, nephew. This prince provoked a war with Austria, was defeated in battle, and *abd.* in favour of his son, Mar. 23, 1849; *d.* July 28, 1849.
1849. Victor Emmanuel II. (Victor Emmanuel Mary Albert Eugene Ferdinand), Mar. 23.
1860. Savoy ceded to France under Plebiscite, Apr. 23.
1861. Victor Emmanuel assumed the title of K. of Italy, and his Sardinian dominions were merged in that Kingdom. *See Modern Italy.*

SICILY. NAPLES. THE TWO SICILIES.

The Greek emperors, upon the expulsion of the Ostrogoths by Belisarius in the 6th century, took possession of Lower Italy, and retained it for more than 200 years. The duchy of Benevento (Naples), however, founded by the Lombards in the same century, attained such importance and territorial extent that it possessed, within 120 years, the greater part of the country now comprising the kingdom of Naples. In the 9th century the Arabs conquered the island of Sicily, which was wrested from them in the 11th century by count Roger I., who inherited Naples from his elder brother, Robert Guiscard, by whom it had been acquired by conquest.

Kings of Sicily.

Counts and Dukes of Apulia.

1043. William I., *Bras de Fer*, or Iron Arm.
1046. Drogo.
1051. Humfrey.
1054. Robert Guiscard, D. in 1060.
1085. Roger.

Counts and Kings of Sicily.

1072. Roger I., count of Sicily.
1101. Roger II., son; obt. from pope Honorius II., in 1130, the style of "*king* of Sicily."
1154. William, surn. the Wicked.
1166. William II., surn. the Good.
1189. Tancred, count de Leccé, grandson of Roger II.
1194. William III., son; dethr.
1194. Henry (Husband of Constantia, dau. of William III.); emp., as Henry VI., 1190.
1197. Frederick I., son; emp. in 1212, as Frederick II.
1250. Conrad I., son; emp. as Conrad IV.
1254. Conrad II., or Conradin, son; dep. in his minority by his uncle Manfred; aft. beheaded.
1258. Manfred or Mainfroy, an usurper; slain in battle by his successor.
1266. Charles of Anjou, youngest son of Louis VIII. of France; dep. in 1282 by the bloody revolution known as the "*Silician Vespers.*"
1282. Sicily now separated from Naples; Charles of Anjou retaining the

style of lord paramount of Naples, and governing there.
1282. Peter, the Great, K. of Arragon, consort of Constantia, dau. of Manfred, the Usurper.
1285. James I.; succ. to the kingdom of Arragon as James II. in 1291.
1295. Interregnum.
1296. Frederick II.
1337. Peter II.
1342. Louis I.
1355. Frederick III., surn. the Simple.
1377. Mary, dau. of Frederick; aft. jointly with her consort.
1391. Mary and Martin, pr. of Arragon.
1402. Martin, alone.
1409. Martin, the Elder.

Sicily united to Arragon.
(*See Arragon.*)

1410. Ferdinand, K. of Arragon.
1435. Alfonso, K. of Arragon.
1458. John, K. of Arragon.
1479. Ferdinand the Catholic.
In 1503 this prince took entire pos session of Naples, which he ha previously seized, and divided i with Louis XII. of France. Sicil remained subject to the sove reigns of Spain until 1713.
1713. Victor Amadeus, D. of Savoy, obt the crown of Sicily from Spain.
1718. He exchanged Sicily with Austri for Sardinia, which became kingdom. *See Naples and Sardinia.*

Kings of Naples.

1282. Charles of Anjou, lord paramount.
1285. Charles II., the Lame.
1309. Robert, the Wise.
1343. Joanna I.; dethr. by her cousin
1382. Charles III., Durazzo.
1386. Ladislas, son, and father of
1414. Joanna II., or Janella, or Johannilla, of Bourbon.
1435. Alfonso, the Wise; Alfonso V., as K. of Arragon. Succ. by his natural son
1458. Ferdinand I., the Bastard.
1494. Alfonso II.
1495. Ferdinand II.
1496. Frederick III., son.
1501. Partitioned by France and Spain; but two years afterwards Ferdinand the Catholic became master of the whole, and it remained under the dominion of Spain until 1707.
1707. Charles, of Austria; aft. the emp. Charles VI.
1713. The possession of Naples confirmed to Austria by the treaty o Utrecht.
1734. Sicily and Naples (the Two Sicilies) lost to Austria, and became veste in the royal family of Spain.
1735. Charles, son of Philip V. of Spain he succeeded to his father's dominions, and ceded the Two Sicilie to his third son, Ferdinand.
1759. Ferdinand IV., ascended at eigh years of age; dep. by the French in 1798, and again in 1806. In the latter year, the emperor Napoleon I. placed his brother Joseph on the throne of Naples.
1806. Joseph Buonaparte; advanced in 1808 to the throne of Spain.
1808. Joachim Murat, brother-in-law to Napoleon I., succ. as king.
1815. Ferdinand IV., restored.
It was now decreed that Naples and Sicily should, as formerly, be united in one monarchy, under the designation of the "Kingdom of the Two Sicilies."

Kings of the Two Sicilies.

1815. Ferdinand I. (late IV.), king of the Two Sicilies.
1825. Francis I., son, Jan. 24.
1830. Ferdinand II. (Ferdinand Charles), Nov. 8.
1859. Francis II. (Francis Mary Leopold), May 22.
1860. Annexed to the kingdom of Sardinia by plebiscite, Oct. 21; Victor Emmanuel procl. king, Nov. 7. Now forms part of the kingdom of Italy.
See Modern Italy.

TUSCANY.

Tuscany became subject to Rome in the 5th century before the Christian era, and was possessed by that empire for about 800 years. Tuscany was governed by a succession of marquesses or dukes from the

9th until the 13th century. The continual divisions by which the country was agitated led to a change in the form of government, and eventually to the ascendancy of the great family of the Medici as Grand Dukes. The ancient name, Etruria, was revived for a time in 1801.

Marquesses or Dukes of Tuscany.

828. Boniface I., marq.
847. Adalbert I., D. and marq.
890. Adalbert II., surn. the Rich, D. and marq.
919. Guy, D.
929. Lambert, D.
931. Boson, D.
936. Hubert, D.
961. Hugh, surn. the Great.
1001. Adalbert III.
1014. Rinaldo, D. and marq.
1027. Boniface II., styled the Pious, D. and marq.
1052. Frederick.
1055. Beatrice, and Godfrey the Bearded.
1076. Matilda, styled the Great, countess.
1119. Ratbod, or Radboton.
1119. Conrad, president and marq.
1131. Rampret, president and marq.
1133. Henry of Bavaria, count.
1139. Ulderic, marq.
1153. Guelph.
1195. Philip, elected emp. in 1198; assass at Bamberg in 1208.
1208. Florence became a republic, gov. chiefly by *Signori*, until 1531. In that year Alexander de Medici was appointed its chief, as doge of Florence; assass. in 1537.

Grand Dukes of Tuscany.

House of Medici.

1537. Cosmo de Medici, son of Alexander; cr. gr. d. in 1569 by pope Pius V.
1574. Francis Mary, de Medici, son; to whom the dignity of gr. d. was confirmed by the emp. Maximilian II.
1587. Ferdinand I., de Medici.
1609. Cosmo II., de Medici.
1621. Ferdinand II., de Medici.
1670. Cosmo III., de Medici.
1723. John Gastone de Medici; last representative of the family. By the treaty of peace in 1735 between France and Austria, the D. of Lorraine was named to succeed to the grand-duchy of Tuscany on the death of John Gastone de Medici, which took place in 1737; and upon this arrangement being effected, the duchy of Lorraine lapsed to the French crown, subject to a life interest of Stanislas Lezinski, ex-king of Poland.

House of Lorraine.

1737. Francis II., D. of Lorraine, *m.* Maria Theresa, emp. and Q. of Hungary and Bohemia; elected emp. in 1745.

By a decree of this monarch it was settled that in future the Grand Duchy should be the patrimony of a younger son of the Imperial house; the emp. was accordingly succ. in 1765 by his second son.

1765. Peter Leopold; on the demise of his brother, the emp. Joseph II., he became emp. as Leopold II., and was succ. as gr. d. by his youngest son
1790. Ferdinand III.; dep. by the treaty of Luneville, in 1801.
1801. Louis, pr. of Parma, succ. by the style of "King of Etruria," conformably with the above-mentioned treaty.
1803. Charles Louis, his infant son, under the regency of the Q., Maria Louisa, his mother; afterwards duchess of Parma. *See Parma.*
1807. Tuscany united by the emp. Napoleon I. to the kingdom of Italy.
1814. Ferdinand III., rest.
1824. Leopold II. (Leopold John Joseph Ferdinand Charles), June 18; abd
1859. Ferdinand IV. (Ferdinand Salvator Mary, &c.), son, July 21.
1860. Tuscany united to the kingdom of Sardinia by decree, Mar. 22, and now forms part of kingdom of Italy. *See Modern Italy.*

AUSTRIA.

Austria was part of the German empire. The margraves of Austri were established by Charlemagne between 791 and 796, and were after wards declared princes of the empire. In 1156 the margravate wa made an hereditary duchy, which, in its turn, was, in 1453, raised to a archduchy. The dukes of Germany were frequently elected emperor of Germany, and at length, from 1493 to 1804, the imperial title wa hereditary in the Austrian line. In 1804 the emperor Francis II. o Germany became emperor Francis I. of Austria only.

Margraves of Austria.

928. Leopold I.
1018. Albert I.
1056. Ernest.
1075. Leopold II.
1096. Leopold III.
1136. Albert II.
1136. Leopold IV.
1142. Henry II., made a D. 1156.

Dukes of Austria.

1156. Henry II., above-named.
1177. Leopold V.
1194. Frederick I., the Catholic.
1198. Leopold VI., the Glorious.
1230. Frederick III., the Warlike; killed in battle with the Hungarians, 15 June, 1246.

Interregnum.

1282. Albert I. and his brother Rodolph Albert, elect. emp. of Germany, 1292.
1308. Frederick II.
1330. Albert II. and Otho, his brother.
1358. Rodolph.
1365. Albert III. and Leopold VII.; kille at Sempach.
1395. William and other brothers, an their cousin, Albert IV.
1411. The same. The provinces divide into the duchies of Austria an Corinthia, and the county Tyrol.
1411. Albert V., D. of Austria, obtain Bohemia and Moravia; elect. K of Hungary and emp. of Ger many, 1437; *d.* 1439.
1439. Ladislaus, posthumous son; mad an archduke in 1453.

Archdukes of Austria.

1453. Ladislaus, above-named; *d.* childless, 1457.
1457. The emp. Frederick III. and Albert VI.
1493. Maximilian I., son of the archduke Frederick III., emp. of Germany His descendants took the title o emp. of Germany until 1804.

See "Emperors of Germany."

Emperors of Austria.

1804. Francis I., late Francis II., emp. of Germany, commenced his reign as emp. of Austria only, Aug. 11; *d.* Mar. 2, 1835.
1835. Ferdinand, son; abd. in favour of his nephew, Dec. 2, 1848.
1848. Francis Joseph (Francis Joseph Charles), *b.* Aug. 18, 1830; came to the throne on the abdication of his uncle and the relinquishment of his right to the succession by his father, archd. Francis Charles Joseph, the presumptive heir, Dec. 2, 1848.

BOHEMIA.

Bohemia had formerly an elective government, but Ferdinand I. declared it hereditary in the house of Austria in 1547; and the kingdom may be said to have remained since that time in the undisturbed possession of that house. In the early part of the 17th century, the Bohemians made an attempt to shake of the imperial yoke, and offered the crown to the elector palatine Frederick, then the most powerful Protestant prince in Germany; but he was driven out of Bohemia by the emperor's generals, stripped of his other dominions, and obliged to depend on James I. of England, whose daughter Elizabeth he had married, for a scanty subsistence.

Dukes and Kings of Bohemia.

Dukes.

890. Borzivoi.
902. Spitigneus I.
907. Wratislas I.
916. Wenceslas I.
936. Boleslas I.
967. Boleslas II. *le Débonnaire.*
999. Boleslas III.
1002. Jaromir.
1012. Udalric.
1037. Bretislas I.
1055. Spitigneus II.
1061. Wratislas II.; the title of king conferred upon him by the emp. Henry IV.
1092. Conrad I.
1093. Bretislas II.
1100. Borzivoi II.
1107. Suatopluc.
1109. Ladislas II.
1125. Sobieslas.
1140. Ladislas III.; 2nd king.
1174. Sobielas II.
1178. Frederic.
1190. Conrad II.
1191. Wenceslas II.
1193. Henry Bretislas.
1196. Ladislas IV.

Kings.

1197. Premislas I., styled the Victorius; 3rd king.
1230. Wenceslas III.
1253. Premislas II.
1278. Wenceslas IV.
1305. Wenceslas V.
1306. Henry and Rodolph, of Hapsburg.
1310. John, count of Luxemburg, brother to the emperor.
1346. Charles, son; elect. emp. in 1347.
1378. Wenceslas VI., son; dep. as emp. in 1400.
1419. Sigismund, emp.
1437. Albert, D. of Austria and K. of Hungary, and emp.
1440. Ladislas V.
1458. George Podiebrad, the Protestant chief.
1471. Ladislas VI.
1516. Louis I. (Louis II. of Hungary); killed at the battle of Mohatz.
1526. Ferdinand I., who by his marriage with Anne, sister of Louis, succ. to the crown.

For the succeeding kings, see "Emperors of Germany," and "Emperors of Austria."

The crown of this kingdom having remained in the Austrian family from the days of Ferdinand I. with a form of election on each vacancy, it was, in 1648, by the treaty of Westphalia, secured to that house in hereditary succession.

HUNGARY.

Hungary was annexed to the German Empire under Charlemagne, but it became an independent kingdom in the 10th century.

Kings of Hungary.

997. Stephen, D. of Hungary; he received from the pope the title of Apostolic King, still borne by the emperor of Austria, as K. of Hungary.
1038. Peter, the German; dep.
1041. Aba or Owen.
1044. Peter, *again*; again dep. and his eyes put out.
1047. Andrew I.; dep.
1061. Bela I.; killed by the fall of a ruinous tower.
1064. Salamon, son of Andrew.
1075. Geisa I., son of Bela.
1077. Ladislas I., surn. the Pious.
1095. Coloman, son of Geisa.
1114. Stephen, surn. Thunder.
1131. Bela II.
1141. Geisa II.
1161. Stephen III, son.
1174. Bela III., brother.
1196. Emeric, son.
1204. Ladislas II., son; reigned six months only.

1205. Andrew II., son of Bela III.
1235. Bela IV.
1270. Stephen IV., son.
1272. Ladislas III., killed.
1290. Andrew III., surn. the Venetian, son of Rodolph of Hapsburg, emp. of Germany.
1309. Charobert or Charles Robert.
1342. Louis the Great; elect. K. of Poland in 1370.
1382. Mary, called *King* Mary, dau. of Louis the Great.
1392. Mary and her consort Sigismund, who became K. of Bohemia, and was elected emp. of Germany in 1410.
1437. Albert, D. of Aurtria, *m.* the dau. of Sigismund, and succ. to the thrones of Hungary, Bohemia, and Germany.
1440. Ladislas IV., K. of Poland, of which kingdom he was Ladislas VI.
1444. Interregnum.
1453. Ladislas V., posthumus son of Albert, under the guardianship of the great Huniades; poisoned.
1458. Matthias Corvinus, son of Huniades, the late regent.
1490. Ladislas VI., K. of Bohemia; the emp. Maximilian laid claim to both Kingdoms.
1516. Louis II. of Hungary (I. of Bohemia), killed at the battle of Mohatz.
1526. { John Zapolski, elect. by the Hungarians, and supported by the sultan Solyman, and Ferdinand I., K. of Bohemia, bro. to the emp. Charles V.; rival kings. }
1541. Ferdinand, alone; elect. emp. of Germany in 1558.
1561. Maximilian, son; emp. in 1564.
1573. Rodolphus, son; emp. in 1576.
1609. Matthias II., brother; emp. in 1612.
1619. Ferdinand II., cousin, emp.
1625. Ferdinand III., son; emp. in 1637.
1647. Ferdinand IV.; *d.* 1654, 3 years before his father.
1655. Leopold I., son of Ferdinand III.; emp. in 1658.
1687. Joseph I., son; emp. in 1705.
1711. Charles (Charles VI. of Germany), brother of Joseph, and nominal K. of Spain.
1740. Maria Theresa, dau., empress; surv. her consort, Francis I., emp., from 1765 until 1780. (*See Germany.*)
1780. Joseph II., son, emp. in 1765; succ. to Hungary on the death of his mother.
1790. Leopold II., brother, emp.
1792. Francis I., son, Francis II. as emp. of Germany; in 1804 he became *emp. of Austria* only.
1835. Ferdinand V., son; Ferdinand I. as emp. of Austria.
This Emperor would have been Ferdinand IV. of Germany, but for the change of style in 1804; abd.
1848. Francis Joseph, nephew; Dec. 2.

For the last three centuries the succession of the kings of Hungary varies little from the succession of the emperors of Germany and Austria, the crown having continued in the house of Austria.

TRANSYLVANIA.

Transylvania was a province of Austria. It was an independent principality from 1526 to 1699, when it was again united to Austria, and so remained until 1848, when it was joined to the kingdom of Hungary

Princes of Transylvania.

1526. John Zapoly.
1540. John Sigismund.
1571. Stephen I., (Stephen Zapoly Bathori).
1576. Christopher Bathori.
1581. Sigismund Bathori.
1602. Rodolph, (emp. of Germany).
1605. Stephen II., Bottskai.
1607. Sigismund Ragotski.
1608. Gabriel I., Bathori.
1613. Gabriel II., (Bethlem Gabor).
1631. George I. Ragotski.
1648. George II., Ragotski.
1660. John Kemin.
1662. Michael I., Abaffi.
1690. Michael II., Abaffi.

GERMANY. CONFEDERATION OF THE RHINE. GERMANIC CONFEDERATION. NORTH GERMAN CONFEDERATION. SOUTH GERMAN STATES. GERMAN EMPIRE.

GERMANY.

Germany was anciently divided into several independent states. The Germans withstood the attempts of the Romans to subdue them; and although that people conquered some parts of the country, they were expelled before the close of the 3rd century. In the 5th century the might of the Huns and other nations prevailed over the greater portion of Germany; it was not, however, totally reduced until Charlemagne made himself master of the whole. This great prince took the title of emperor, entailing the dignity of his family; but after his race became extinct in 911, the empire went to the Germans, and the title was afterwards made elective. The house of Austria enjoyed the distinction almost uninterruptedly from 1438 (when one of its princes was raised to the imperial throne) until 1804. In that year Francis II. resigned the honour and office of emperor of Germany, and became emperor of *Austria* only; the latter title being hereditary.

Kings and Emperors of Germany.

Carlovingian Race.

800. Charlemagne.
814. Louis *le Debonnaire*, K. of France.
840. Lothaire, or Lother, son; *d.* in a monastery at Treves.
855. Louis II., son.
875. Charles II., called the Bald, K. of France; poisoned by his physician, Zedechias.
877. Interregnum.
880. Charles III., *le Gros*, crowned K. of Italy; dep.
887. Arnulf, or Arnoul, crowned emp. at Rome in 896.
899. Louis III., called IV., the last of the Carlovingian race in Germany.

Saxon Dynasty.

911. Otho, D. of Saxony, refused the dignity on account of his age.
911. Conrad I., D. of Franconia.
918. Henry I., surn. the Fowler, son of Otho, D. of Saxony, King.
936. Otho I., son, styled the Great. Many writers withhold the imperial title from him until crowned by pope John XII. in 962.
973. Otho II., the Bloody; so stigmatised for his cruelties; wounded by a poisoned arrow.
983. Otho III., son, surn. the Red, yet in his minority; poisoned.
1002. Henry II., D. of Bavaria, surn. the Holy, and the Lame.
1024. Conrad II., surn. the Salique.
1039. Henry III., the Black, son.
1056. Henry IV., son, a minor, under the regency of his mother Agnes; dep. by his son and successor.
1106. Henry V., *m.* Maud or Matilda, dau. of Henry I. of England.
1125. Lothaire II., surn. the Saxon.
1138. Interregnum.
1138. Conrad III., D. of Franconia.
1152. Frederick Barbarossa; drowned by his horse throwing him into the river Salphet, or the Cydnus.
1190. Henry VI., son, surn. Asper, or the Sharp; this emperor detained Richard I. of England a prisoner in his dominions.
1198. Philip, brother; assass. at Bamberg by Otto, of Wittelsbach.
1208. Otho IV., surn. the Superb, recognised as K. of Germany, and crowned as emp. the next year; excommunicated and deposed.
1212. Frederick II., K. of Sicily, son of Henry VI.; dep. by his subjects, who elected Henry, landgrave of Thuringia. Frederick *d.* 1250, naming his son Conrad his succ. but the pope gave the imperial title to William, E. of Holland.
1250. Conrad IV., son.

From the death of Frederick II. until the accession of Rodolph, in 1273, the time that elapsed may be regarded as an interregnum, Conrad IV. being opposed; one party of the electors at Frankfort chose Richard, earl of Cornwall, brother of Henry III. of England, and the other chose Alphonsus, king of Castile. The first lost the dignity, by attending the civil wars of England; and the last it by negligence; so neither is reckoned in the list of emperors.

1250. William, E. of Holland; *d.* Dec. 1255. The electors could not agree in the choice of a successor.

1256. Interregnum.

HOUSES OF HAPSBURG, LUXEMBURG, AND BAVARIA.

1273. Rodolph, count of Hapsburg, the first of the Austrian family.

The Hapsburg family was founded in 1026, by Radboton, grandson of Gontram, count of Brisgau, and derived its name from the castle of Hapsburg on the river Aar, in Switzerland. This was the cradle, as it were, of the house of Austria. The male line of Hapsburg became extinct in 1740, in the person of Charles VI., after giving twenty-two sovereigns to Austria, sixteen emperors to Germany, eleven kings to Hungary and Bohemia, and six to Spain.

1291. Interregnum.

1292. Adolphus, count of Nassau, to the exclusion of Albert, son of Rodolph, dep.; slain at the battle of Spires.

1298. Albert, D. of Austria, Rodolph's son; killed by his nephew at Rheinfels.

1308. Henry VII. of Luxemburg.

1313. Interregnum.

1314. Louis IV. of Bavaria, and Frederick III. of Austria, son of Albert, rival emperors; Frederick *d.* 1330.

1330. Louis reigns alone.

1347. Charles IV. of Luxemberg. In this reign was given at Nuremberg in 1356, the famous *Golden Bull*, which became the fundamental law of the German empire.

1378. Wenceslas, son, K. of Bohemia; twice imprisoned, and at length forced to resign, but continued to reign in Bohemia.

1400. Frederick III., D. of Brunswick; assass. immediately after his election, and seldom placed in the list of emperors.

1400. Rupert, count palatine of the Rhine, crowned at Cologne; *d.* 1410.

1410. Jossus, marq. of Moravia, chosen by a party of the electors; *d.* th next year.

1410. Sigismund, K. of Hungary, electe by another party. On the death o Jossus, he was recognised by a parties; K. of Bohemia in 1419

HOUSE OF AUSTRIA.

1438. Albert II., surn. the Great, D. o Austria, and K. of Hungary an Bohemia; *d.* Oct. 27, 1439.

1439. Interregnum.

1440. Frederick IV., surn. the Pacific elect. emperor Feb. 2; but no crowned until June 1442.

1493. Maximilian I., son, *d.* 1519. Franci I. of France and Charles I. o Spain became competitors for the empire.

1519. Charles V. (I. of Spain), son of Joan of Castile and Philip of Austria, elected; res. both crowns, and retired to a monastery, where he died soon after.

1558 Ferdinand I., brother, K. of Hungary.

1564. Maximilian II., son, K. of Hungary and Bohemia.

1576. Rodolph II., son.

1612. Matthias, brother.

1619. Ferdinand II., cousin, son of the archd. Charles, K. of Hungary.

1637. Ferdinand III., son.

1658. Leopold I., son.

1705. Joseph I., son.

1711. Charles VI., brother.

1740. Maria Theresa, daughter, Q. of Hungary and Bohemia, whose right to the empire was sustained by England.

At the decease of the emp. Charles VI. in 1740, his hereditary dominions devolved of right (by the pragmatic sanction) upon his only daughter and heiress the archduchess Maria Theresa, but were claimed by the husband of his niece, (Maria Amelia, daughter of Joseph I.), Charles, elector of Bavaria, who was declared king of Bohemia in 1741, and crowned emp. of Germany at Frankfort the following year, as Charles VII. This dispute disturbed the tranquillity of Europe, and occasioned a war in which all the great European powers were involved, and which did not terminate until 3 years after the death of Charles VII., when Maria Theresa had her patrimonial dominions guaranteed to her by the treaty of Aix-la-Chapelle in 1748.

1742. Charles VII., elector of Bavaria,

whose claim was supported by France; rival emperor, and contested the succession. Charles *d.* Jan. 1745. *See Maria Theresa, supra.*

1745. Francis I. of Lorraine, Gr. D. of Tuscany, consort of Maria Theresa.

1765. Joseph II., son of the emp. Francis and of Maria Theresa.

1790. Leopold II., brother.

1792. Francis II., son.

This monarch surrendered the dignity of emp. of Germany on August 11, 1804, and assumed the title of emp. of Austria only. In 1806 the German princes seceded from the German empire, and placed themselves under the protection of Napoleon I. of France.

See "*Confederation of the Rhine,*" *infra.*

House of Prussia.

1871. Jan. 18. The title of emp. of Germany was revived, and William I., K. of Prussia, was proclaimed emperor.

THE CONFEDERATION OF THE RHINE

was established July 12, 1806, under the auspices of Napoleon I. emp. of France, and by the Act of Confederation a number of states dissolved their connection with the German empire and allied themselves with France. Other states subsequently joined the Confederation from time to time, most of them under the coercion of Napoleon.

Original Members of the Confederation.

Jly. 12. 1806. France.
Bavaria.
Wurtemberg.
Ratisbon.
Baden.
Berg & Cleves.
Hesse - Darmstadt.
Nassau - Weilburg.
Nassau-Usingen.
Hohenzollern-Hechingen.
Hohenzollern-Sigmaringen.
Salm-Salm.
Salm-Kirburg.
Isemburg-Birchstein.
Aremberg.
Liechtenstein-Darmberg.
Count de la Leyen.

Subsequent Members.

1806. Würtzburg.
1806. Saxony, Dec. 12.
1807. Westphalia.
Anhalt.
Reuss.
Schwartzburg.
Waldeck.

During the reverses of Napoleon in 1813 many of the states seceded from the Confederation, which they had only joined under compulsion, and on June 8, 1815, the German States were formed into

THE GERMANIC CONFEDERATION

which held its first Diet at Frankfort, Nov. 16, 1816.

This Confederation consisted of portions of Austria and Prussia, and of the following minor States:—

Kingdoms.

Bavaria.
Saxony.
Hanover.
Wurtemberg.

Electorate.

Hesse.

Grand Duchies.

Baden.
Hesse.
Mecklenburg-Schwerin.
Mecklenburg-Strelitz.
Oldenburg.
Luxemburg & Limburg.
Saxe-Weimar-Eisenach.

Duchies.	Principalities.	Landgraviate.
Nassau. Brunswick. Holstein-Lauenburg. Saxe-Meiningen. Saxe-Coburg-Gotha. Saxe-Altenburg. Anhalt-Dessau-Köthen. Anhalt-Bernburg.	Schwarzburg-Rudolstadt. Schwarzburg-Sonderhausen. Lippe-Detmold. Schaumburg-Lippe. Reuss-Greiz. Reuss-Schleiz. Waldeck. Liechtenstein.	Hesse. **Free Cities.** Frankfort-on-the-Maine. Hamburg. Bremen. Lubeck.

The Germanic Confederation continued till 1866, when, in consequence of the quarrels between Austria and Prussia, it was dissolved, the Diet holding its last sitting Aug. 24, 1866.

THE NORTH GERMAN CONFEDERATION

was then formed under the leadership of Prussia, whose influence over the other States was paramount.

This Confederation consisted of the following States:—

Under Treaty of Aug. 18, 1866.

1. Prussia.
2. Oldenburg.
3. Brunswick.
4. Saxe-Weimar.
5. Anhalt.
6. Saxe-Coburg-Gotha.
7. Saxe-Altenburg.
8. Waldeck.
9. Lippe-Detmold.
10. Schwartzburg-Rudolstadt.
11. Schwartzburg-Sonderhausen.
12. Reuss Schleiz.
13. Schaumberg Lippe.
14. Hamburg.
15. Lubeck.
16. Bremen.

Joined Subsequently, 1866.

17. Mecklenburg - Schwerin, Aug. 21.
18. Mecklenburg-Strelitz, Aug. 21.
19. Hesse (north of the Maine), Sept. 3.
20. Reuss Greiz, Sept. 26.
21. Saxe-Meiningen, Oct. 8.
22. Saxon, Oct. 21.

The following States in South Germany:—

1. Bavaria.
2. Wurtemburg.
3. Baden.
4. Hesse Darmstadt.

were allowed to remain nominally independent, but were bound by secret treaties to place their armies at the disposal of Prussia in case of war.

The following States were annexed to Prussia:—

1. Hanover.
2. Hesse-Cassel.
3. Nassau.
4. Frankfort.
5. Schleswig-Holstein.

During the Franco-German war of 1870–1, the North and South German States were united under the title of

THE GERMAN EMPIRE.

William I., K. of Prussia, was proclaimed emp. Jan. 1871, and the 1st Parliament of the empire was held at Berlin Mar. 21, 1871.

The German Empire comprises the following States:—

1. Prussia.
2. Bavaria.
3. Saxony.
4. Wurtemburg.
5. Baden.
6. Hesse-Darmstadt.
7. Mecklenburg-Schwerin.
8. Saxe-Weimar.
9. Mecklenburg-Strelitz.
10. Oldenburg.
11. Brunswick.
12. Saxe-Meiningen.
13. Saxe-Altenburg.
14. Saxe-Coburg and Gotha.
15. Anhalt.
16. Schwarzburg-Rudolstadt.
17. Schwarzburg-Sondershausen.
18. Waldeck.
19. Reuss Greiz.
20. Reuss Schleiz.
21. Schaumburg-Lippe.
22. Lippe.
23. Lubeck.
24. Bremen.
25. Hamburg.
26. Alsace-Lorraine.

PRUSSIA. BRANDENBURG.

PRUSSIA continued long under the dominion of Poland, but at length threw off the dependence of its dukes upon that power. Frederick William laid the foundation of the present monarchy, and his son and successor, in Jan. 1701, assumed the title of the king, and was acknowledged as king by the emperor Leopold and all his allies. Prussia is now the ruling German State, and its king is also emperor of Germany.

MARGRAVES, ELECTORS, DUKES, AND KINGS.

MARGRAVES OR ELECTORS OF BRANDENBURG.

1134. Albert I., surn. the Boar, first elector of Brandenburg.
1170. Otho I.
1184 Otho II.
1206. Albert II.
1221. John I. and Otho III.
1266. John II.
1282. Otho IV.
1309. Waldemar.
1319. Henry I., *le Jeune*.
1320. Interregnum.
1323. Louis I., of Bavaria.
1352. Louis II., surn. the Roman.
1365. Otho V., *le Faineant*.
1373. Wenceslas, of Luxemburg.
1378. Sigismund, of Luxemburg.
1388. Jossus, the Bearded.
1411. Sigismuud, *again*.
1415. Frederick I. of Nuremburg.
1440. Frederick II., surn. Ironside.
1470. Albert III., surn. the German Achilles.
1476. John III., son, as margrave.
1486. The same, as elector.
1499. Joachim I., son.
1535. Joachim II.
1571. John George.
1598. Joachim Frederick.
1608. John Sigismund.

AND DUKES OF PRUSSIA.

1616. John Sigismund, above named.
1619. George William.
1640. Frederick William, son.
1688. Frederick, son, crowned K. Jan. 18, 1701.

KINGS OF PRUSSIA.

1701. Frederick I., above named.
1713. Frederick William I., son.
1740. Frederick II. (Frederick the Great), son.
1786 Frederick William II., nephew.
1797. Frederick William III.
1840. Frederick William IV., son, June 7. His brother, aft. William I., app. Regent, Oct. 23, 1857, and the appointment was made permanent, Oct. 7, 1858.
1861. William I. (Fredk. Wm. Louis), brother, Jan. 2. Declared emp. of Germany Jan. 18, 1871. *See Germany.*

ANHALT.

Bernard, son of Albert the Bear, Margrave of Brandenburg, 1st count of Anhalt; *d.* 1212.

1212. Henry I., *d.* 1252.

On his death Anhalt was divided into three parts; Ascania, Bernburg, and Zerbst.

* * * * * *

1570. Anhalt united under Joachim Ernest; *d.* 1586.

* * * * * *

1603. Anhalt divided into four parts: Dessau, Bernburg, Köthen, and Zerbst.

* * * * * *

1793. The Zerbst line became extinct, and this portion of the principality was divided amongst the three remaining branches.

1807. The counts of Anhalt assumed the title of duke.

1847. The Köthen line became extinct by the death of duke Henry, Nov. 23, and this part of the duchy is now incorporated with Dessau.

Dukes of Anhalt-Bernburg.

* * *

* * Alexis.

1834. Alexander Charles, Mar. 24; *d.* Aug. 19, 1863. On his death the male line became extinct, and the whole of the duchy is now under the branch of Anhalt-Dessau.

Dukes of Anhalt-Dessau.

* * *

* * Leopold Frederick Francis.

1817. Leopold Frederick, Aug. 9.

1871. Frederick (Leopold Frederick Francis Nicholas), May 22.

BADEN. BADEN-BADEN. BADEN-DURLACH.

The house of Baden descends from Gerold, who, as well as his son, appears in the ancient records towards the close of the 8th century, as Landgraves of the Barr. From him, after many descents, came Bertholdus, who had two sons. The elder, Herman I., possessed, *vitâ patris,* Hochberg in Brisgau, to which Baden belonged; he took the title of margrave, and died in 1074. His heir was Herman II., who called himself "margrave of Baden," and was the head and founder of the present house of Baden, 1130.

From Christopher I., who united the branches of Hochberg and Baden, and died in 1527, proceeded the branches of Baden-Baden and Baden-Durlach, which were united in 1771. He had two sons, Bernard and Ernest, *of whom below.*

Margraves of Baden.

* * Herman I.

1130. Herman II.

1160. Herman III

1190. Herman IV.

1243. Herman V.

1250. Rodolph I.

1288. Herman VI.

1291. Frederick II.

1333. Herman IX.
1353. Rodolph VIII.
1372. Rodolph X.
1391. Bernhard I.
1431. James I.
1453. Charles I.
1475. Christopher I., *d.* 1527.

Margraves of Baden-Baden.

1527. Bernhard IV.
1537. Philibert.
1569. Philip.
1588. Edward.
1600. William.
1677. Louis William.
1707. Louis George.

* * Augustus William George, *d.* 1771. On his death the line of Baden-Baden became extinct and the territory reverted to Charles Frederick, Margrave of Baden-Durlach.

Margraves of Baden-Durlach.

1527. Ernest.
1553. Charles II., son.
1577. (? 1584.) Ernest Frederick, son.
1604. George Frederick, brother; abd.
1622. Frederick V., son.
1659. Frederick VI., son.
1677. Frederick VII., son.
1709. Charles William, son.
1746. Charles Frederick, grandson. On the death of Augustus William George, Margrave of Baden-Baden, he succ. to that Margravate. He was created an Elector of the empire in 1803 and a Gr. D. in 1806.

Grand Dukes of Baden.

1806. Charles Frederick, above-named.
1811. Charles Louis Frederick, grandson.
1818. Louis William Augustus, uncle.
1830. Charles Leopold Frederick, brother, Mar. 30.
1852. Louis II., son, Apr. 24; *d.* Jan 22. 1858. Being an imbecile, his younger brother, Frederick William Louis, was appointed Regent, and in
1856. Sep. 5, took the title of Gr. D.

BAVARIA.

After undergoing various revolutions, Bavaria became a duchy in the 9th century, and the title of duke was possessed by its rulers until 1623, when Maximilian I. was invested with the electoral dignity by the emperor Ferdinand II. In 1805 Napoleon raised Bavaria to the rank of a kingdom; and on Jan. 1, 1806, Maximilian Joseph was proclaimed king at Munich in the presence of the French Emperor.

Dukes, Electors, and Kings of Bavaria.

Dukes.

895. Leopold.
907. Arnulph, surn. the Bad.
937. Eberhard.
939. Berthold.
942. Henry, surn. the Quarreller.
955. Henry II.
995. Henry III., the Holy and the Lame, elected emp. in 1002.
1004. Herny IV.
1025. Henry V.
1047. Conrad I.
1052. Henry VI.
1054. Conrad II.
1056. Agnes, empress dowager.
1061. Otho.
1071. Guelph I.
1101. Guelph II., son.
1120. Henry VII., surn. the Black, brother.
1126. Henry VIII., surn. the Proud, son.
1138. Leopold II., of Austria.
1142. Henry IX., of Austria.
1154. Henry X., surn. the Lion, son of Henry the Proud.
1180. Otho the Great, cr. D. by the emp. Frederick Barbarossa.
1183. Louis I., son.
1231. Otho II., the Illustrious, son, elector palatine.
1253. Louis II., the Severe, son, elector palatine.
1294. Louis III., son, elected emp. in 1314.

1347. Stephen, son.
1375. John, surn. the Pacific, brother.
1397. Ernest, brother.
1438. Albert I., surn. the Pious, son.
1460. John II., and Sigismund, sons, res.
1465. Albert II., brother.
1508. William I., son.
1550. Albert III., son.
1579. William II., surn. the Religious, son, abd.

ELECTORS.

1596. Maximilian, son, cr. elector by the emp. Ferdinand II., Feb. 25, 1623.
1651. Ferdinand Mary.
1679. Maximilian Emmanuel, son, May 26.
1726. Charles Albert, son, Feb. 26; elected emp. in 1742, opposed by Maria Theresa.
1745. Maximilian Joseph I., son, Jan. 20.
1777. Charles Theodore, elector palatine, succ. to Bavaria, Dec. 30.
1799. Maximilian Joseph II., as elector.

KINGS OF BAVARIA.

1805. Maximilian Joseph I., as King.
1825. Louis Charles, son, Oct. 13; abd. Mar. 21, 1848; *d.* Feb 29, 1868.
1848. Maximilian Joseph II., son.
1864. Louis II. (Louis Otho Frederick William), son, Mar. 10; committed suicide.
1886. Otho William Leopold, brother, June 13; of unsound mind. His brother, Leopold, app. Regent.

PALATINATE OF THE RHINE.

ONE of the ancient electorates of Germany, long united to Bavaria; separated therefrom in 1294, and again united thereto in 1777.

COUNTS PALATINE OF THE RHINE.

1156. Conrad, of Suabia, first elector.
1196. Henry, of Saxe.
1227. Otho, surn. the Illustrious, elector of Bavaria in 1231.
1253. Louis II., surn. the Severe, elector of Bavaria, and elector palatine.
1294. Rodolphus I., *le Begue.*
1319. Adolphus, surn. the Simple.
1327. Rodolphus II., the Blind.
1353. Rupert II., surn. the Red.
1390. Rupert II., *le Petit.*
1398. Rupert III., elected emp. in 1400.
1410. Louis III., surn. Barbatus, or Longbeard.
1436. Louis IV.
1442. Frederick I., surn. the Victorious
1476. Philip, surn. the Ingenuous or Sincere.
1508. Louis V., surn. the Pacific, refused the imperial crown.
1544. Frederick II., surn. the Wise.
1556. Otho Henry.
1559. Frederick III., surn. the Pious.
1576. Louis VI., surn. the Easy.
1583. Frederick IV.
1610. Frederick V., K. of Bohemia, dethroned and stript of his hereditary dominions; *d.* 1632.
1648. Charles Louis, son; by the treaty of Westphalia, in 1648, he had the greater part of the palatinate restored to him.
1680. Charles II.
1685. Philip William, cousin.
1690. John William.
1716. Charles Philip.
1743. Charles Theodore, who, on Dec. 30, 1777, succ. to the dominions of the Bavarian branch of his family.
See Bavaria, suprà.

BRUNSWICK. HANOVER.

THE house of Brunswick owes its origin to Azo IV. of the family of Esté, son of Hugo III., marquess of Ferrara, in Italy. Azo, who died in 1055, left by his consort Cunegonde, daughter and heiress of Guelph, duke of Bavaria, a son, who was great-grandfather of Henry, surnamed the Lion. (See *Bavaria*, p. 67.) This prince married Maud, eldest daughter of Henry II. of England, and is always looked upon as the ancestor of our persent royal family. The dominions possessed by Henry the Lion were very extensive; but he having refused to assist Frederick Barbarossa in a war against pope Alexander III., that emperor's resentment was drawn upon him, and in the diet of Wurtzburg, in 1180, he was proscribed. The duchy of Bavaria was given to Otho, count Wittelsbach, from whom is descended the present royal family of Bavaria; the duchy of Saxony was conferred upon Bernard Ascanius, founder of the house of Anhalt; and his other possessions were disposed of to different princes. Thus despoiled, Henry retired to England; but ultimately, after much intercession, Brunswick and Luneberg were restored to him. He left three sons. The two elder having no male issue, William, the third son, carried on the line of his family, and from him all the succeeding dukes of Brunswick and Luneberg have descended.

The house of Brunswick has from time to time divided into several branches. The principal are:

Brunswick-Luneburg.
Brunswick-Wolfenbuttel, 1st branch.
Brunswick-Zell, or Brunswick-Luneburg-Zell, from which the house of Hanover descended.
Brunswick-Wolfenbuttel, 2nd branch, or Brunswick-Luneburg-Wolfenbuttel.

Rulers of Brunswick and Hanover.

1139. Henry the Lion. *See Introduction, suprà.*
1195. William, son, D. of Luneburg.

Dukes of Brunswick.

1213. Otho I., son, cr. 1st D. of Brunswick in 1235.
1252. Albert I., son, styled the Great.
1279. Albert II. son, styled the Fat.
1318. Magnus I., son.
1368. Magnus II., son. On his death the house of Brunswick was divided into two branches, as under:—

Dukes of Brunswick-Luneburg.

1373. Frederick, son, elect. emp. of Germany 1400.
1400. Bernard, brother.
1434. Frederick the Just, *d.* 1478. }
Otho the Magnanimous, *d.* 1471. }
1478. Henry the Young, son of Otho.
1532. Ernest I., styled the Confessor, *d.* 1546.

On his death the family was again divided into two branches:

I. Brunswick-Zell or Brunswick-Luneburg-Zell (*See below*

Dukes of Brunswick Wolfenbuttel, (1st Branch.)

* * Henry I., son.
1416. William I. and Henry II., sons.
1482. Frederick and William II., sons of William I.
1495. Henry III. and Eric, sons of William I.
1514. Henry IV., son of Henry II.

II. Brunswick - Wolfenbuttel, 2nd Branch, or Brunswick-Luneburg - Wolfenbuttel. *(See opposite column.)*

Dukes of Brunswick-Zell or Brunswick-Luneburg-Zell.

1546. William, the second son of Ernest the Confessor, became D. of Zell.
1592. Ernest II.
1611. Christian, brother, bp. of Minden.
1633. Augustus, brother, administrator of Ratesburg.
1636. Frederick, bro., pres. of the Chapter of Bremen; succ. by his nephew
1648. Christian Lewis, son of his brother George, pr. of Calenberg.
1665. George William. His only dau. Sophia Dorothea, *m.* 1682, George Lewis, his nephew, eldest son to his brother Ernest Augustus, D. of Hanover.

(See below.)

House of Hanover.

Dukes of Hanover.

1665. John, 2nd son of Christian Lewis, D. of Brunswick-Zell *(see above)*, became D. of Hanover.
1679. Ernest Augustus, son, *m.* the pr. Sophia, dau. of Frederick, elector palatine, and of Elizabeth, dau. of James I. of England.

This is the prs. Sophia, to whose descendants (being Protestants) the crown of England was limited by the act of settlement, 1701. She was *b.* Oct. 13, 1630, and had issue by the above marriage six sons and one daughter: namely, George Lewis, afterwards George I.; Frederick Augustus, *b.* 1661, *d.* 1690, unm.; Maximilian William, *b.* 1666, *d.* 1726, unm.; Charles Philip, *b.* 1669, *d.* 1690; Christian, *b.* 1671, *d.* 1703, unm.; Ernest Augustus, bp. of Osnaburg, *b.* 1674, cr. 1716, D. of York and Albany and E. of Ulster, *d.* 1728, unm.; Sophia Charlotte, *b.* 1668, *m.* to Frederick William, elector of Brandenburg. The prs. Sophia *d.* June 8, 1714, in her 84th year.

Electors of Hanover.

1692. Ernest Augustus, above named, cr. Elector.
1698. George Lewis, son, *m.* his cousin, the heiress of the D. of Brunswick-Zell. Became K. of Great Britain Aug. 1, 1714, as George I.

1568. Julius, son.

1589. Henry Julius, son.

1613. Frederick Ulrick, son, *d.* 163[illegible] without issue.

On his death the succession passe[d] under certain family arrange[-]ments to Augustus, a descendan[t] of Henry, the eldest son of Ernes[t] the Confessor, and he became I[D.] of Brunswick-Wolfenbuttel.

Dukes of Brunswick-Wolfenbuttel (2nd Branch), or Brunswick-Luneburg-Wolfenbuttel.

1634. Augustus, above-named. He lef[t] three sons, Rodolphus Augustus[,] Anthony Ulrick, and Ferdinan[d] Albert; the two first succ., th[e] third was the founder of th[e] Bevern line.

1666. Rodolphus Augustus, who associate[d] his next brother, Anthony Ulrick[,] in the government from 1685; *d.* 1704.

1704. Anthony Ulrick, brother, now rule[d] alone; erected Blankenburg int[o] a principality in 1707, became [a] Roman Catholic in 1710; *d.* 1714.

1714. Augustus William, son; *d.* withou[t] issue 1731.

1731. Ludowick Rodolphus, brother (pr. o[f] Blankenburg from his father'[s] death in 1714); *d.* without mal[e] issue in 1735.

This pr. left three daughters, wh[o] were married, Elizabeth Christin[a] to the emp. Charles VI., Christin[a] to the gr.-D. Alexius of Russia and Antonie Amelia to the D. o[f] Bevern.

1735. Ferdinand Albrecht, *d.* same year.

1735. Charles, son, who transf. the ducal residence to Brunswick.

1780. Charles William Ferdinand, son, *m.* the prs. Augusta of England killed at the battle of Jena, commanding the Prussian army, Oct. 14, 1806; succ by his 4th son his eldest sons being blind, and abd. in favour of

1806. Frederick William. His reign may

27. George Augustus, son; GEORGE II. of England.
60. George William Frederick, grandson; GEORGE III. of England.

KINGS OF HANOVER.

814. George William Frederick, abovenamed, 1st K. of Hanover, Oct. 2.
820. George Augustus Frederick, son; GEORGE IV. of England.
830. William Henry, brother; WILLIAM IV. of England.
837. Hanover separated from the crown of Great Britain.
Ernest Augustus, brother to William IV. of England, on whose demise he succ. (as a distinct inheritance) to the throne of Hanover, June 20, 1837.
851. George (George Frederick Augustus, Charles Ernest), Nov. 18, dep. Sept. 20, 1866; *d.* June 12, 1878.
Hanover was annexed to Prussia by Decree Sept. 20, 1866.

be dated from the battle of Leipsic in Oct. 1813; fell at the battle of Quatre-Bras commanding the *avant-garde* under Wellington, June 16, 1815.

1815. Carl, son (Charles Frederick William Augustus), *b.* Oct. 30, 1804. Dep. by his younger brother William in 1830.

1830. William (Augustus Louis William Maximilian Frederick), *b.* April 25, 1806; succ. Sept. 7, 1830; *d.* Oct. 18, 1884.
On his death Ernest Augustus William Adolphus George Fredk., D. of Cumberland and titular K. of Hanover, should have succ. to the dukedom, but this was not permitted by the German Imperial Authorities, and pr. Albrecht of Prussia was appointed Regent, Oct. 21, 1884.

FRANCONIA.

PHARAMOND is the first of the Franconian kings of whom we have any distinct mention; see *France.* They were conquered by Charlemagne, and Franconia was subsequently governed by dukes.

In modern times, Franconia consisted of two principalities, Bayreuth and Anspach; three bishoprics, Bamburg, Wursburg, and Eichstadt; seven counties, and three lordships. These divisions are now altered, one district having been given to Wurtemburg, another to Baden, a third to the house of Hesse, and the tract called Henneberg to the house of Saxe. All the rest has been made over to Bavaria.

DUKES OF FRANCONIA.

891. Conrad I., about this time.
912. Eberhard.
939. Conrad II.
955. Otho I.
1004. Conrad III.
1011. Conrad IV.
1038. The dukedom extinct until 1116.
1116. Conrad V., emp. as Conrad III. in 1138.
1152. Frederick, and D. of Suabia
1167. Conrad VI.
1191. Conrad VII., and D. of Suabia.

HESSE.

HESSE-CASSEL, HESSE-DARMSTADT, HESSE-HOMBURG.

HESSE.

ALL the Hessian branches proceed from Philip the Generous, who at the death of his father, William II., in 1509, inherited the entire principality of Hesse. Dying in 1567, he left four sons, who divided the territory, so that four lines originated:—(1) Hesse-Cassel, (2) Hesse-Marburg, which lapsed in 1583, (3) Hesse-Rheinfels, which lapsed in 1604 and (4) Hesse-Darmstadt. Of the two principal branches, the eldest son, William IV., became the founder of that of Hesse-Cassel; and George, the youngest son, became the founder of the branch of Hesse-Darmstadt.

Landgraves of Hesse.

* * * * * *

1509. Philip, surn. the Generous. On his death in 1567 Hesse was divided as above.

HESSE-CASSEL, OR ELECTORAL HESSE.

Landgraves.

1567. William IV., eldest son of Philip, surn. the Wise.
1592. Maurice, son, abd. in favour of
1627. William V., son, surn. the Constant. His three younger brothers were the founders of the three lines of Rothenberg, Eschwegen, and Rheinfels. William died during the campaign of East Friedland, supposed by poison; his consort,
1637. Amelia Elizabeth, governed until 1650, when she handed over the rule to her son,
1650. William VI., surn. the Good and the Wise.
1663. Charles, brother.
1730. Frederick I., son, who became, in right of his consort, K. of Sweden in 1719; his bro. acted as viceroy, and, at his death, succ. in Hesse.
1751. William VII., brother.
1760. Frederick II., son.
1785. William IX. (VIII.), son, obtained the electorship 1801, and called himself William I., elector 1803.

Electors.

1801–3. William I. (as above).
After the battle of Jena he fled to Denmark, and, by the treaty of Tilsit, Hesse-Cassel became part of the kingdom of Westphalia. Returned in 1813; *d.* 1821.
1821. William II., son, retired to Hanau in 1831. The hereditary pr. made co-regent, Sept. 30, 1831.
1847. Frederick William I., son, late co-regent, Nov. 20; *d.* January 6, 1875.

Hesse-Cassel was annexed to Prussia by Decree, Sept. 20, 1866.

HESSE-DARMSTADT, OR GRAND-DUCAL HESSE.

The founder of this line, as already mentioned, was George I., youngest son of Philip the Generous. The princes of Hesse-Darmstadt were elevated to the rank of grand dukes by the French emperor Napoleon.

Landgraves.

1567. George I.
1596. Louis V., son, surn. the Faithful.
1624. George II., son.
1661. Louis VI.
1678. Louis VII., reigned only a few months.
1678. Ernest Louis, brother.
1733. Louis VIII., son.
1768. Louis IX., son.
1790. Louis X., son, became Gr. D.

Grand-Dukes.

1803. Louis I. (late Louis X.), first Gr. D.
1830. Louis II., son, was thrice married.
1848. Louis III., son, June 16.
1877. Louis IV., nephew (Frederick William Louis Charles), June 13.

HESSE-HOMBURG.

This house owes its origin to a junior branch of Hesse-Darmstadt.

George I. left in 1596 three sons, of whom Frederick became the founder of this line. The later princes were as under:—

Landgraves.

* * *

1751. Frederick Louis V.
1820. Frederick Joseph, son.
1829. Louis William Frederick, brother.
1839. Philip Augustus Frederick, brother.
1846. Gustavus Adolphus Frederick, brother.
1848. Ferdinand Henry Frederick, brother, Sept. 8; *d.* March 24, 1866. On his death the male line became extinct, and Hesse-Homburg reverted to the Grand Duchy of Hesse-Darmstadt, by whom it was ceded to Prussia as from Oct. 8, 1866, by treaty dated Sept. 15, 1866.

LIECHTENSTEIN.

Princes of Liechtenstein.

* * *

1836. Alois Joseph, April 20.
1858. John II. (John Maria Francis Placidus), Nov. 12.

LIPPE-DETMOLD.

Princes of Lippe-Detmold.

* * *

* * Frederick William Leopold.
1802. Paul Alexander Leopold, April 4.
1851. Leopold (Paul Frederick Emile Leopold), Jan. 1.
1875. Woldemar (Gonthier Frederick Woldemar), Dec. 8.

LIPPE-SCHAUMBURG.

Princes of Lippe-Schaumburg.

* * *

* * Philip Ernest.
1787. George William, Feb. 13.
1860. Adolphus George, Nov. 21

MECKLENBURG.
MECKLENBURG-SCHWERIN. MECKLENBURG-STRELITZ.

Charlemagne, during his wars with the Saxons, entered Mecklenburg, a.d. 789, and compelled the inhabitants to embrace Christianity. Louis, his successor, had the country governed by the dukes of Saxony; the people, however, threw off that yoke, and Nicolas and Premislas, prince divided the territory between them. In 1147, Nicolas being slain i battle, Henry the Lion conquered Mecklenburg, and divided it amon his generals and knights. But to the son of Nicolas (Premislas II.) h restored a part of his father's dominions, with the title of "Prince o Mecklenburg," instead of the former title, which was "King of th Wenden." After the death of Premislas II. followed Henry Borwir his son, founder of the house of Mecklenburg. The modern division o the duchy was made at the commencement of the 18th century. Th dignity of grand duke was conferred on the princes of Mecklenburg b the Congress of Vienna in 1815.

MECKLENBURG.

Princes.

* * Henry Borwin I. From this prince and his consort Matilda, dau. of Henry the Lion, sprang the house of Mecklenburg.

* * Henry Borwin II., *d.* 1236, and left four sons, who divided Mecklenburg into four parts, viz.: MECKLENBURG, GUSTROW, ROSTOCK, and PARCHIM, which existed till 1611. The eldest son of Henry Borwin succ.

1236. John, surn. Theologus.

1264. Henry I. (called III.), son. Went to Jerusalem, and was therefore surn. *Hierosolymitanus;* was made prisoner, and was supposed to be dead.

1302. Henry II. (IV.), son. The former prince returned from captivity, and governed with Henry II., who *d.* 1329; and through his sons, Albrecht and John, sprung up the new lines of MECKLENBURG and STARGARD. In the line of Mecklenburg, succ.

1349. Albrecht or Albert I., who was succ. by his three sons

1380. { Albert II., elect. K. of Sweden 1363. Henry, who took but little part in the government, and Magnus I., to whom Albert res. the principality. }

1412. { Albert III., son of Albert II., governed, together with John, son of Magnus I., whose two sons succ. }

1423. { Henry III. (V.), surn. the Fat and John II., who *d.* 1442. }

Henry the Fat again unite Stargard to Mecklenburg, and dying in 1477, left three sons who succ.

1477. { Albert IV. Magnus II. Balthazar } Co-regents. Th three sons o Magnus II. succ

1503. { Henry IV. (VI.) Erich, and Albert the Fair. } Co-regents.

1547. John Albert I., the eldest of five sons of Albert the Fair.

His brother Ulrick made claims to the co-regency, and caused thereby a division in the country.

1553. Ulrick, above-named.

1603. Charles, brother, who governed, instead of his minor cousins, Adolphus Frederick and John Albert until 1610.

The Territory was again divided into two lines, MECKLENBURG and GUSTROW; the latter line became extinct in 1695.

1610. Adolphus Frederick.

1658. Christian Louis, son.

1679 Frederick William, nephew. His disputes with his cousin, Frederick Adolphus (II.) led to the Hambro treaty, by which, in 1701, the two lines of MECKLENBURG-SCHWERIN and MECKLENBURG-STRELITZ were formed.

MECKLENBURG-SCHWERIN.

Princes and Grand Dukes.

Princes.

1701. Frederick William, the above-mentioned prince. He retained three-fourths of the territory.

1713. Charles Leopold, brother. His brother, Christian Louis, who afterwards succ., was appointed administrator by the emp. in 1732.

1747. Christian Louis II., brother.
1756. Frederick, surn. the Kind.
1785. Frederick Francis I., nephew. The dignity of Gr. D. was conferred upon this pr. by the Congr. of Vienna 1815.

GRAND DUKES.

1815. Frederick Francis I., above named.
1837. Paul Frederick, grandson.
1842. Frederick Francis II., son, Mar. 7.
1883. Frederick Francis III., son, Apr. 15.

MECKLENBURG-STRELITZ.

PRINCES AND GRAND DUKES.

PRINCES.

1701. Adolphus Frederick II., founder of this line.
1708. Adolphus Frederick III., son.
1749. Charles Louis Frederick I., brother.
1752. Adolphus Frederick IV., son.
1794. Charles Louis Frederick II., brother. The dignity of Gr. D. was conferred upon this pr. by the Congr. of Vienna 1815.

GRAND DUKES.

1794. Charles Louis Frederick II., above named.
1816. George Frederick Charles Joseph, son, Nov. 6.
1860. Frederick William Charles George Ernest Adolphus Gustavus, son, Sept. 6.

NASSAU.

WALRAM III., who possessed, in 1195, all the territory belonging to Nassau, died in 1198; and his sons, Henry I. and Rupert V., reigned jointly until the latter entered into the union of the German knighthood in 1230. The sons of Henry I. (who was surnamed the Rich) were Walram and Otho. They governed in common until 1255, and became the founders of two distinct principal lines. That of Walram became possessed of the principality of NASSAU, and that of Otho is represented by the NETHERLANDS' dynasty. Walram's successor was his son,

Adolphus, elected emp. in 1292; fell in battle with Albert of Austria, at Gellheim (Spires), in 1298.

1298. Gerlach, son, reigned until 1361. This prince's two sons, Adolphus II. and John I., divided Walram's line again into two branches, Nassau-Idstein-Weisbaden and Nassau-Weilburg; the latter created by John I., the former by Adolphus.

LINE OF NASSAU-IDSTEIN-WEISBADEN.

1361. Adolphus II.
1370. Walram, son.
1393. Adolphus III, son.
1426. John, son.
1480. Adolphus IV., son.
1511. Philip, son.
1568. Balthazar, second son.
1568. John Louis, son. His son died *vitâ patris*, and this line and its possessions fell to the younger branch.

LINE OF NASSAU-WEILBURG.

1361. John I., who enlarged his territories by marriage, and was invested by the emp. Charles IV. with the coronet of a prince; *d.* 1371.
1371. Philip I., son.
1429. Philip II., second son; the elder, John II., founded a separate line.
1492. Louis I., grandson.
1523. Philip III., son, he left two sons, Albert and Philip IV., who divided their territory; the line of the latter became extinct in 1602, and his part fell back to his brother's line.
1559. Albert, son.
1593. Louis II., son, who inherited in 1602 the possessions of Philip IV., and after the death of John Louis (*see above*) he inherited all the possessions of the Walram line.

Louis *d.* 1627; his three sons became founders of three distinct lines, of which the most important

was that of Nassau-Weilburg, ruled by his third son, Ernest Casimir.
1629. Ernest Casimir, third son.
1655. Frederick, son.
1675. John Ernest, son.
1719. Charles Augustus, son, who again assumed the princely title conferred on his ancestors by the emp. Charles IV.
1753. Charles Christian.
1788. Frederick William. This prince lost by the peace of Luneville a part of his possessions on the left border of the Rhine; the Confederation of the Rhine, however, which he joined in 1816, enlarged his territory, and conferred upon him the ducal title.

DUKES.

1806. Frederick William, above named.
1816. William George, son, who inherited in March, 1816, the possessions of Nassau-Usingen, and thus united all the territory of the elder Walram line of the house of Nassau.
1839. Adolphus William Charles Augustus, Frederick, son, Aug. 20.
Nassau was annexed to Prussia by Decree, Sept. 20, 1866.

OLDENBURG.

OLDENBURG comprises (1) the duchy of Oldenburg, (2) the principality of Lubeck, and (3) the principality of Birkenfeld.

1180 (about). The independence of Oldenburg established.

* * * * * *

1448. Count Christian VIII., of Oldenburg, elected K. of Denmark, and Oldenburg transferred to his brother Gerhard.

* * * * * *

1531. Anton I., *d.* 1573.

* * * * * *

16—. Anton Günther, *d.* 1667.
1667. On his death the succession passed to the K. of Denmark, and so continued until 1773, when it was resigned to the Holstein-Gothorp line, who renounced their claims to Schleswig-Holstein. Oldenburg was at this time created a duchy.

DUKES AND GRAND DUKES OF OLDENBURG.

DUKES.

1773. Frederick Augustus, bp. of Lubeck.
1785. Peter Frederick.
* * Peter Frederick Louis.
The Duchy was seized and annexed to the French Empire by Napoleon I. about 1811, but its independence was restored at the Congress of Vienna (1814–5), and it was, at the same time, created a Grand Duchy.

GRAND DUKES.

1815. Peter Frederick Louis above named.
1829. Augustus (Paul Frederick Augustus) succ. May 21, decl. Gr. D., May 28.
1853. Peter I. (Nicholas Frederick Peter), Feb. 27.
1881. Augustus (Frederick Augustus), May 14.

REUSS-GREIZ.

(*The Elder Branch.*)

PRINCES.

* * *

* Henry XX.
1836. Henry XXI., Oct. 31.
1859. Henry XXII., son, Nov. 8

REUSS-SCHLEIZ.

(The Younger Branch.)

PRINCES.

* * *

* * Henry XI.

1818. Henry XII., son, Apr. 17.

1854. Henry XIII., brother, June 19.

1867. Henry XIV., son, July 11.

SAXONY OR SAXE-ROYALE. SAXE-ALTENBURG, LATE HILDBOURGHAUSEN. SAXE-COBURG AND GOTHA, LATE SAXE-COBURG-SAALFELD. SAXE-GOTHA-ALTENBURG. SAXE-MEININGEN. SAXE-WEIMAR.

LITTLE is known of Saxony until Charlemagne directed his arms to the right bank of the Rhine. He experienced much resistance from the Saxons under Wittikind, but they, in the end, submitted to him; and among the consequences of their subjection to this great conqueror, was the conversion of the country to Christianity. He conferred the title of duke upon their chief. The first who became elector was Bernard III. of the House of Ascania, and, on the extinction of that line, Frederick the Warlike, margrave of Misnia or Meissen was made elector. Saxony continued an electorate until 1806, when the title of elector was changed to king, conformably with the treaty of peace between France and Frederick Augustus, signed at Posen, Dec. 11, in that year.

SAXONY OR SAXE-ROYALE.

DUKES, ELECTORS, AND KINGS.

DUKES.

880. Otho I., styled the Great.
912. Henry, surn. the Fowler, elect. emp. 918.
936. Otho II., son, elect. emp.
959. Herman Billing.
973. Bernard I.
1010. Bernard II.
1062. Otho III.
1073. Magnus.
1106. Lothaire, elect. emp. 1125, and surn. the Saxon.
1136. Henry, surn. the Proud, of Bavaria, dep.
1138. Henry, surn. the Lion, dep. by the emp. Frederick Barbarossa; this prince is regarded as the ancestor of the present royal family of England.—(*See Brunswick*).

ELECTORS.

1180. Bernard III., of the house of Ascania, first elector.
1212. Albert I.
1260. Albert II.
1298. Rodolphus I.
1356. Rodolphus II.
1370. Wincelaus.
1389. Rodolphus III.
1419. Albert III.
1423. Frederick I., surn. the Warrior, Landgrave of Thuringia and marq. of Misnia of the ancient House of Saxony.
1428. Frederick II., the Peaceable and the Good. This pr. *d.* 1464, and left two sons, Ernest and Albert. The first gave name to the elder, or *Ernestine* branch of the family; the second, to the younger, or *Albertine* branch.

ERNESTINE BRANCH.

1464. Ernest, eldest son of Frederick II.
1486. Frederick III., the Wise; he refused the imperial crown.
1525. John, brother, surn. the Constant.

1532. John Frederick, styled the Magnanimous, dep. by the emp. Charles V., and the electorate conferred upon the

Albertine Line.

Of this line were previously, in 1464, Albert, already mentioned; in 1500, George the Rich; and in 1539, Henry the Pious.

1548. Maurice, cousin to the deposed elector John Frederick.
1553. Augustus, the Just and the Pious, brother.
1586. Christian I., son.
1591. Christian II., son.
1611. John George I., brother.
1656. John George II., son.
1680. John George III., son.
1691. John George IV., son.
1694. Frederick Augustus I., brother, K of Poland.
1733. Frederick Augustus II., son, K. c Poland.
1763. Frederick Christian, son. Feb.
1763. Frederick Augustus III. Dec Ruled as elector until 1806.

Kings of Saxony.

1806. Frederick Augustus, above named first king, conformably with th treaty of Posen, signed Dec. 11.
1827. Anthony Clement Theodore, brother
1836. Frederick Augustus II., nephew. June 6.
1854. John (John Népomuck Maria Joseph) brother. Aug. 9.
1873. Albert (Albert Frederick Antoine &c.), son. Oct. 29.

SAXE-ALTENBURG, LATE HILDBOURGHAUSEN.

Dukes.

1675. Ernest, the 6th son of Ernest I. of Gotha.
1715. Ernest Frederick I., son.
1724. Ernest Frederick II., son.
1745. Ernest Frederick Charles, son.
1780. Frederick, son. Became, by the convention of Nov. 12, 1826, D. of Saxe-Altenburg.
1834. Joseph George Frederick, son, Sept. 29.
1848. George Charles Frederick, second son of Duke Frederick, succ. on his elder brother's abdication, Nov. 30.
1853. Ernest Frederick Paul George Nicholas, son. Aug. 3.

SAXE-COBURG AND GOTHA, LATE SAXE-COBURG-SAALFELD.

Dukes.

1675. John Ernest, 7th son of Ernest I. of Gotha.
1729. Christian Ernest, son.
1745. Francis Joseph, brother.
1764. Ernest Frederick, son.
1800. Francis Frederick, son.
1806. Ernest Anthony, son. Father-in-law of Q. Victoria. Became, by the convention of Nov. 12, 1826, D. of Saxe-Coburg and Gotha, as Ernest I.; *d.* 1844.
1844. Ernest II., son, (Ernest Augustus Charles John Leopold Alexander Edward), Jan. 29.

SAXE-GOTHA-ALTENBURG.

Dukes.

1605. Ernest I., surn. the Pious, 7th son of John, of Saxe-Weimar, who was duke in 1573.
1675. Frederick I., son.
1691. Frederick II., son.
1732. Frederick III., son.
1772. Ernest Louis, son.
1804. Emilius Augustus, son.
1822. Frederick IV., brother; *d.* Feb. 11, 1825, when the male line of the family became extinct.

On the extinction of the line of Saxe-Gotha-Altenburg, in 1825, a new arrangement or political division took place between the princes of

Saxony. By a convention concluded Nov. 12, 1826, Hildbourghausen and Saalfeld were transferred to the house of Meiningen, and the rights of the late duke of Saxe-Gotha Altenburg were assigned to the two conceding powers. *See Saxe-Meiningen, Saxe-Altenburg, and Saxe-Coburg-Gotha.*

SAXE-MEININGEN.

Dukes.

1675. Bernard, 3rd. son of Ernest I., of Saxe-Gotha.
1706. Ernest Louis, son.
1724. Ernest Louis, II., son.
1729. Charles Frederick, brother.
1743. Anthony Ulric, uncle.
1763. Augustus Frederick, son.
1782. George Frederick, brother.
1803. Bernard Erich, a minor, son, Dec. 24. Assumed the reins of Government, Dec. 17, 1821. Succ. by the convention of Nov. 12, 1826, to Hildbourghausen, Saalfeld, &c.; abd.
1866. George II., son., Sept. 20.

SAXE-WEIMAR.

Dukes and Grand Dukes.

Dukes.

1554. John William.
1573. John, son.
1605. John Ernest I., son.
1626. William, brother.
1662. John Ernest II., son.
1683. William Ernest, son.
1728. Ernest Augustus, nephew.
1748. Ernest Augustus Constantine, son.
1758. Charles Augustus, son, assumed the title of grand-duke in 1815.

Grand Dukes.

1815. Charles Augustus, above named.
1828. Charles Frederick, son, June 14.
1853. Charles Alexander Augustus, son, July 8.

SCHWARZBURG-RUDOLSTADT.

Princes.

* * *

* * Louis Frederick.
1807. Frederick Gunther, son, Apr. 28.
1867. Albert, brother, June 28.
1869. George Albert, son, Nov. 26.

SCHWARZBURG-SONDERSHAUSEN.

Princes.

* * *

* * Gunther, abd. and succ. by his son
1835. Gunther Frederick Charles, Sept. 3 abd. and succ. by his son
1880. Charles Gunther, July 17.

SUABIA.

SUABIA was erected into a duchy in the 5th century, and continued to be governed by its dukes until the 13th, when the reigning family became extinct on the death of Conradin, who was beheaded at Naples in 1268. Suabia was eventually divided among a number of petty princes.

DUKES.

The early dukes are too indistinctly recorded to be named consecutively.

867. Hugh.
916. Burchardt I.
926. Herman I.
949. Ludolph.
954. Burchardt II.
973. Otho I.
982. Conrad I.
997. Herman II.
1004. Herman III.
1012. Ernest I.
1015. Ernest II.
1030. Herman IV., and Conrad II., emp.
1039. Henry I., emp. as Henry III.
1045. Otho II.
1047. Otho III.
1057. Rodolph.
1080. Frederick I., de Buren.
1105. Frederick II., de Borgne.
1138. Conrad, D. of Franconia, and emp. as Conrad III.
1147. Frederick III. Barbarossa, emp. in 1152.
1152. Frederick IV., de Rothemburg, and D. of Franconia.
1167. Interregnum.
1169. Frederick V.
1191. Conrad, and D. of Franconia.
1196. Philip, elect. emp. in 1198.
1208. Frederick VI., elect. emp. in 1212 as Frederick II.
1219. Henry II.
1235. Conrad IV., elect. emp. in 1250; *d.* 1254, supposed to have been poisoned by his illegitimate brother, Manfred.
1254. Conradin, son of Conrad, an infant; this young prince was dep. by his uncle, Manfred, and beheaded at Naples, after a defeat in battle by Charles, D. of Anjou, in 1268.

WALDECK—WALDECK AND PYRMONT.

PRINCES.

* * *

* * George Frederick Henry.

1845. George Victor, May 15.

WURTEMBERG.

THE old duchy of Wurtemburg was erected into a kingdom by the French emperor Napoleon I. in Dec. 1805. This rank was confirmed by the provisions of the peace of Presburg. The elector Frederick II. was proclaimed king, Jan. 1, 1806.

DUKES AND KINGS OF WURTEMBERG.

DUKES.

1457. Eberhard I., the Bearded, first duke.
1496. Eberhard II., *le Jeune.*
1498. Ulric; dispossessed of his dominions by the emp. Charles V. in 1519, but they were restored to him in 1534.
1550. Christopher, styled the Pacific.

1568. Louis.
1593. Frederick I.
1608. John Frederick.
1628. Eberhard III.
1674. William Lewis.
1677. Eberhard Louis.
1733. Charles Alexander.
1737. Charles Eugene.
1793. Louis Eugene.
1795. Frederick Eugene.
1797. Frederick II., son, became elector in 1803, and king, Dec. 12, 1805.

KINGS.

1806. Frederick I. (late elector Frederick II.), procl. king, Jan. 1.
1816. William I. (William Frederick Charles), son, Oct. 30.
1864. Charles I. (Charles Frederick Alexander), son, June 25.

FLANDERS.

THIS country passed early into the hands of France, and was governed by its counts or earls, chiefly subject to that crown, from A.D. 862, until united with Burgundy in 1384. In 862, Baldwin, the great forester or ranger of France, having carried off Judith, the daughter of Charles the Bald, widow of a king of England, after much difficulty obtained the king's consent to marry her, and was made earl of Flanders.

COUNTS OF FLANDERS.

862. Baldwin I., *Bras de Fer*, first count.
879. Baldwin II., surn. the Bald.
918. Arnulph I. and Baldwin III.
965. Arnulph II., *le Jeune.*
989. Baldwin IV., surn. the Bearded.
1036. Baldwin V., *le Débonnaire.*
1067. Baldwin VI., surn. the Good.
1070. Arnulph III.
1071. Robert I., *le Frison.*
1093. Robert II., of Jerusalem.
1111. Baldwin VII., *à la Hache.*
1119. Charles the Good, assass. in the church of Donatianus during divine service.
1127. William de Clito, or Cliton, mortally wounded at the siege of Alost.
1128. Thierry.
1168. Philip d'Alsace.
1191. Margaret I. and Baldwin VIII.
1194. Baldwin IX., of Constantinople, Eastern emp. in 1204.
1206. Jane and Ferdinand.
1233. Jane governs alone.
1244. Margaret II., of Constantinople.
1280. Guy de Dampierre, son; another son, John d'Avennes, became count of Holland.
1305. Robert III., de Bethune.
1322. Louis I., de Crecy, grandson.
1346. Louis II., de Male.
1384. On the death of Louis II., Philip the Hardy, D. of Burgundy, succ. by marriage with his dau. and heiress, and united Flanders to his own dukedom.

HAINAULT.

COUNTS.

875. Regner I
916. Regner II.
932. Regner III.
958. Richer I.

* * * * *

972. Garner and Rainald
973. Godfrey the Old and Arnulph.
998. Regner IV.
1013. Regner V.
1030. Rechila, Herman, and Baldwin I.
1051. Rechila.
1070. Baldwin II., of Jerusalem.
1099. Baldwin III.
1120. Baldwin IV., surn. the Builder.
1171. Baldwin V., surn. the Valiant.
1195. Baldwin VI.

1206. Jane.
1244. Margaret, countess of Flanders.
1280. John d'Avennes, her son; another son, Guy de Dampierre, by another husband, became count of Flanders.
1299. John d'Avennes succ. to Holland. The provinces united.

HOLLAND. THE NETHERLANDS. BELGIUM. PRINCES OF ORANGE.

About the 10th century, Holland and other provinces were governed by their own counts or dukes. The Netherlands subsequently fell to Burgundy, next to Austria; and the emperor Charles V. annexed them to Spain. The tyranny of Philip II. and the barbarities of the duke of Alva exasperated the people, and under the conduct of William, prince of Orange, was formed the famous League of Utrecht, which proved the foundation of the Republic of the Seven United Provinces. The Netherlands were conquered by Napoleon I. and annexed to France, but recovered their independence and became a kingdom in 1815; the southern part, Belgium, separated from it, and became a kingdom in 1830–1.

Counts of Holland, &c.

Counts of Friesland.

Thierry I.

* * * * *

963. Thierry II.
988. Arnulph the Great.
1003. Thierry III., of Jerusalem.
1039. Thierry IV.
1049. Florence I., of Holland; in whom the title became merged.

Counts of Holland.

1049. Florence I.
1061. Thierry V.
The previous counts of this name, Thierry I. II. III. and IV., were counts of Friesland. *See above.*
1091. Florence II., surn. the Fat.
1122. Thierry VI.
1157. Florence III.
1190. Thierry VII.
1203. William I.
1223. Florence IV.
1234. William II. The pope gave the imperial title to this prince on the death of the emp. Frederick II.
1256. Florence V.
1296. John I.; on his death, the ancient house of the counts of Holland became extinct.
1299. John II. (John d'Avennes) count of Hainault, succ., and the provinces became united.

Holland and Hainault.

1304. William III., surn. the Good.
1337. William IV.
1345. Margaret, countess.
1356. William V., surn. the Senseless.
1389. Albert.
1404. William VI.
1417. Jacquelina of Bavaria, countess.
1433. Holland and Hainault came under the dominion of Philip the Good, of Burgundy.

Governors of the Netherlands.

1477. Adolphus of Cleves.
1485. Engilbert, count of Nassau.
1489. Albert of Saxony.
1494. Philip *le Beau*, assumed the government.
1505. William de Croi.
1507. Margaret of Austria.
1531. Mary of Austria, dowager Q. of Hungary, and niece of Margaret.
1555. Emmanuel, D. of Savoy.
1559. Margaret of Austria, duchess of Parma.
1567. Ferdinand, D. of Alva.
1573. Louis de Requisens.
1576. John of Austria.
1578. Alexander of Parma.
1592. Peter Ernest, count of Mansfeldt.
1594. Archd. Ernest.
1595. Pedro de Fuentes.
1596. Albert of Austria.

1599. The infanta of Spain, Isabella, *m.* the archd. Albert, and both were invested with the sovereign power.
1621. Isabella, alone.
1633. Ferdinand.
1641. Francisco Mello.
1644. Marq. de Castel Rodrigo.
1647. Archd. Leopold.
1656. John of Austria.
1659. Marq. de Fromiata.
1664. Marq. de Castel Rodrigo.
1668. D. de Feria.
1670. Comte de Monterei.
1675. D. de Villahermosa.
1678. Pr. of Parma.
1682. Marq. de Castanaga.
1692. The elector of Bavaria.
1701. M. Bedmar.
1702. The elector of Bavaria, *again.*
1706. Council of state.
1710. Conseil la Conference.
1714. Comte de Koenigseck.
1716. Prince Eugene of Savoy.
1725. Mary Elizabeth of Austria.
1741. Count de Harrac Rohrau.
1744. Mary Anne of Austria.
1745. Charles, pr. of Lorraine.
1781. Mary Christina of Austria, and Albert of Saxony, jointly.
1793. The archd. Charles.
1795. United to France.

DUTCH STADTHOLDERS.

1579. William of Nassau, first stadtholder. *See* "Princes of Orange," *infrà.*
1587. Prince Maurice of Nassau.
1625. Frederick Henry of Orange.
1647. William II. of Orange.
1650. The stadtholderate suppressed and the office administered by the states.
1672. William III., pr. of Orange. In 1689 he became K. of England.
1702. The stadtholderate again resumed by the states, on the death of William.
1747. William IV. The stadtholderate revived in William IV., and made hereditary in the house of Orange.

PRINCES OF ORANGE.

The years of the stadtholderate are not always in unison with those of the princes of Orange.
1502. Philibert de Chalons.
1530. René de Nassau.
1544. William of Nassau, styled the Great, cousin to René. To this prince the republic of the Seven United Provinces owed its foundation. Elected stadtholder in 1579; killed by an assassin hired by Philip II. of Spain, June 30, 1584.
1584. Philip William, son, stolen away from the university of Louvaine; the Dutch would never suffer him to reside in their provinces; *d.* 1618.
1618. Maurice, the renowned general, stadtholder in 1587; he was the younger son of William by a second marriage.
1625. Frederick Henry.
1647. William II., *m.* Mary, dau. of Charles I., of England, by whom he had a posthumous son, who succeeded as
1660. William III., stadtholder in 1672. This pr. *m.* Mary, eldest dau. of James II. of England, and both afterwards ascended the English throne.
1702. William IV.
1711. William V.
1751. William VI., retired on the invasion of the French in 1795; *d.* in 1806.
1795. Holland and Belgium united to the French republic.
1806. William Frederick succ. his father, William VI., as pr. of Orange *de jure.*
1806. Louis Buonaparte, made K. of Holland by his brother Napoleon, June 5, 1806; abd. July 1, 1810.
1810. Holland again united to France.
1813. House of Orange rest. William Frederick, pr. of Orange, procl. Dec. 6, 1813; took the oath of fidelity as sov. pr. Mar. 30, 1814, and assumed the style of K. of the Netherlands, Mar. 16, 1815.

KINGS OF THE NETHERLANDS.

1815. William I., late pr. of Orange, abovenamed, first king, abd. in favour of his son, Oct, 7, 1840; *d.* Dec. 12, 1843.
1840. William II., succ. on his father's abdication, Oct. 7.

KINGS OF HOLLAND.

1849. William III. (William Alexander Paul Frederick Louis), Mar. 17. Since the separation of Belgium in 1830, the K. of the Netherlands is often called in popular language, the K. of Holland.

THE Belgian Revolution commenced Aug. 25, 1830. A provisional Government was appointed, who declared Belgium independent, Oct. 4. The sovereignty was offered to Louis Charles, duc de Nemours, second son of Louis Philippe, king of the French, but declined. It was next offered to Leopold, pr. of Coburg, by whom it was accepted.

KINGS OF THE BELGIANS.

1831. Leopold I. (Leopold George Christian Frederick), elected July 12.

1865. Leopold II. (Leopold Louis Philippe Maria Victor), son, Dec. 10.

LUXEMBURG.

SIGEFRID was first count in the 10th century, and the province continued to be governed by independent counts or dukes until it was sold to Burgundy in 1444. The princes of Luxemburg became of considerable note, and several of them have been emperors of Germany. The present dynasty of the Netherlands has the title of grand-duke of Luxemburg.

COUNTS OR DUKES OF LUXEMBURG.

965. Sigefrid.
998. Frederic.
1019. Gilbert or Giselbert.
1057. Conrad I.
1086. Henry I.
1096. William.
1128. Conrad II.
1136. Henry II., surn. the Blind, gov. 60 years.
1196. Ermensind and Theobald.
1214. Ermensind and Waleran.
1226. Henry III., surn. the Great.
1275. Henry IV.
1288. Henry V., elect. emp. in 1308, as Henry VII.; said to have been poisoned.
1309. John, K. of Bohemia; killed at the battle of Creçy, in 1346.
1346. Charles, elect. emp. in 1347, as Charles IV.
1353. Wenceslas I., D.
1383. Wenceslas II., emp.
1388. Jossus, *le Barbu.*
1411. Antony of Burgundy.
1451. Elizabeth de Gorlitz.
1444. Luxemburg united to Burgundy.

SPAIN. ARRAGON. CASTILE.

SPAIN was anciently divided into a number of petty states. The counts of Castile became possessed of Leon, Oviedo, and Toledo, which had been separate territories; and, after many years, the kingdom of Castile was united to that of Arragon by the marriage of Isabella, queen of Castile, with Ferdinand, king of Arragon, in 1474. Ferdinand, by the conquests of Navarre and Granada, entirely put an end to the dominion of the Moors; and we may hence date the foundation of the present monarchy.

KINGS OF SPAIN.

REIGN OF THE GOTHS.

406. Alaric, K. of the Goths.
411. Ataulfo; murdered by his soldiers.
415. Sigerico; reigned a few weeks only.
415. Valia, or Wallia.
420. Theodoric I.; killed in a battle, which he gained, against Attila.
421. Thorismund, or Torrismund; assass. by his favourite.
452. Theodoric II.; assass.

466. Euric, or Evarico.
484. Alaric II.; killed in battle.
507. Gesalric, his bastard son.
511. Almaric, legit. son of Alaric.
531. Theudis, or Theodat; assass.
548. Theudisela, or Theodisele; murdured for female violation.
549. Agila; taken prisoner, and put to death.
554. Atanagildo.
567. Liuva, or Levua I.
568. Leuvigildo; associated on the throne with Liuva, in 568, and sole king in 572.
585. Recaredo I.
601. Liuva II.; assass.
603. Vitericus; assass.
610. Gundemar.
612. Sisibut, or Sisebuth, or Sisebert.
621. Recaredo II.
621. Suintila; dethr.
631. Sisenando.
640. Tulga, or Tulca.
641. Cindasuinto; *d.* 652.
649. Recesuinto; associated on the throne this year, and in 652 became sole king.
672. Vamba, or Wamba; deth. and *d.* in a monastery.
680. Ervigius, or Ervigio.
687. Egica, or Egiza.
698. Vitiza, or Witiza; associated on the throne; in 701 sole king.
711. Rodrigo, or Roderic; slain in battle.

SECOND MONARCHY.

718. Pelagius, or Pelayo; overthrew the Moors, and put a stop to their conquests.
737. Favila; killed in hunting.
739. Alfonso the Catholic.
757. Froila I.; murdered his brother Samaran, in revenge for which he was murdered by his brother and successor,
768. Aurelius, or Aurelio.
774. Silo, the Saracen.
783. Mauregato, the Usurper.
788. Veremundo (Bermuda) I.
791. Alfonso II., the Chaste.
842. Ramiro I.
850. Ordogno, or Ordono I.
866. Alfonso III., surn. the Great, relinquished his crown to his son,
910. Garcias.
914. Ordogno, or Ordono II.
923. Froila II.
925. Alfonso IV., the Monk; abd.
927. Ramiro II.; killed in battle.
950. Ordogno, or Ordono III.
955. Ordogno, or Ordono IV.
956. Sancho I., the Fat; poisoned.
967. Ramiro III.
982. Veremundo II. (Bermuda) the Gouty.
999. Alfonso V.; killed in a siege.
1027. Veremundo III. (Bermuda); killed.

The above were kings of Asturias, of Oviedo, or of Leon.

KINGS OF NAVARRE.

905. Sancho Garcias (Sancho I.)
926. Garcias I.
970. Sancho II.
994. Garcias II., surn. the Trembler.
1000. Sancho III., surn. the Great.
1035. Garcias III.
1054. Sancho IV.
1076. Sancho Ramirez (Sancho V.), K. of Arragon.
1094. Peter of Arragon.
1104. Alfonso I. of Arragon.
1134. Garcias Ramirez.
1150. Sancho VI., surn. the Wise.
1194. Sancho VII., surn. the Infirm.
1234. Theobald I., count of Champagne.
1253. Theobald II.
1270. Henry Crassus.
1274. Juanna; *m.* Philip the Fair of France, 1285.
1305. Louis Hutin of France.
1316. John; lived but a few days.
1316. Philip V. the Long, of France.
1322. Charles I., the IV. of France.
1328. Juanna and Philip, count d'Evereux.
1343. Juanna alone.
1349. Charles II., or the Bad.
1387. Charles III., or the Noble.
1425. John II., aft. K. of Arragon.
1479. Eleanor.
1479. Francis Phœbus.
1483. Catharine and John d'Albret.
1512. Navarre conq. by Ferdinand the Catholic.

KINGS OF CASTILE.

1035. Ferdinand the Great, of Leon and Castile.
1065. Sancho II. the Strong, son. Alfonso in Leon and Asturias, and Garcias in Galicia.
1072. Alfonso VI. the Valiant, K. of Leon.
1109. Urraca and Alfonso VII.
1126. Alfonso VIII., Raymond.
1157. Sancho III., surn. the Beloved.
1158. Alfonso IX., the Noble.
Leon is separated from Castile, and Ferdinand king.
1214. Henry I.
1217. Ferdinand III., the Saint, and the Holy. In him Leon and Castile were perpetually united.
1252. Alfonso X. the Wise.

1284. Sancho IV., the Great, and the Brave.
1294. Ferdinand IV.
1312. Alfonso XI.
1350. Peter the Cruel, dep. Reinstated by Edward the Black Prince of England; aft. slain by his subjects.
1368. Henry II., the Gracious; poisoned.
1379. John I.; he united Biscay to Castile.
1390. Henry III., the Sickly.
1406. John II., son.
1454. Henry IV., the Impotent.
1474. Ferdinand V., the Catholic, in whom, by his marriage with Isabella, queen of Castile, the kingdoms of Castile and Arragon were united.
1504. Joan, or Jane, dau. of Ferdinand and Isabella, and
Philip I. of Austria. On her mother's death Joan succ., jointly with her husband Philip; but Philip dying in 1506, and Joan becoming an imbecile, her father Ferdinand continued the reign; and thus perpetuated the union of Castile with Arragon.

KINGS OF ARRAGON. (*See Sicily.*)

1035. Ramiro I.
1063. Sancho Ramirez. } K. of Navarre. (*See Navarre.*)
1094. Peter of Navarre.
1104. Alfonso the Warrior.
1134. Ramiro II., the Monk.
1137. Petronilla, and Raymond, count of Barcelona.
1162. Alfonso II.
1196. Peter II.
1213. James I.
1276. Peter III., son. This prince contrived the horrible massacre known as the *Sicilian Vespers*, in 1282.
1285. Alfonso III., the Beneficent.
1291. James II., surn. the Just.
1327. Alfonso IV.
1336. Peter IV., the Ceremonious.
1387. John I.
1396. Martin I.
1410. Interregnum.
1412. Ferdinand the Just, K. of Sicily.
1416. Alfonso V., the Wise.
1458. John II., K. of Navarre, brother; *d.* 1479.
1479. Ferdinand V., the Catholic, the next heir; by his marriage with Isabella of Castile, the kingdoms were united.

KINGS OF SPAIN.

1512. Ferdinand V., the Catholic. This prince having conquered Granada and Navarre, became king of al Spain.
1516. Charles I., grandson, son of Joan o Castile and Philip of Austria became emp. of Germany, a Charles V. in 1519; res. both crowns, and retired to a monastery.
1556. Philip II., son, K. of Naples and Sicily; *m.* Mary, queen regnant of England; annexed Portuga 1580.
1598. Philip III., son.
1621. Philip IV., son, who lost Portuga in 1640.
1665. Charles II., son, the last prince o the Austrian line; nominated, by will, as his successor
1700. Philip V., D. of Anjou, grandson o Louis XIV., of France; hence arose the war of the succession, terminated by the treaty of Utrecht in 1713.
1724. Louis I., who reigned only a few months.
1724. Philip V., *again.*
1745. Ferdinand VI., surn. the Wise.
1759. Charles III., K. of the two Sicilies, brother; on ascending the Spanish throne he renounced the Sicilies to his third son Ferdinand.
1788. Charles IV., son; abd. in favour of his son and successor
1808. Ferdinand VII., whom Napoleon I. forced to resign.
1808. Joseph Buonaparte, brother of Napoleon I.; dep.
1814. Ferdinand VII., rest.
1833. Isabella II., dau. (Maria Isabella Louisa), *b.* Oct. 10, 1830; succ. her father Sept. 29, while yet in her third year. The Salic law, existing in Spain, had been formally abolished by Ferdinand, under a decree, March 29, 1830, by virtue of which the order of succession was altered in favour of his daughter, to the exclusion of his brothers, Don Carlos and Don Francis.

REPUBLIC.

1868. Revolution commenced about Sept. 17, and Prov. Govt. apptd. Sept. 19.
The Queen deprived of the crown by the Prov. Govt. Sept. 29, and leaves Spain Sept. 30; aft. abd. in favour of her son, Alfonso, June 25, 1870. A "Junta" appointed to carry on the Government, Pres., — D'Aguirre.
Marshal Francisco Serrano y Dominguez duc de la Torre apptd. Pres. of Prov. Govt., Oct. 4.

1869. Serrano's appointment confirmed by the Cortes, Feb. 22-25; hereditary monarchy resolved on by the Cortes as the future form of Govt., May 21.
New constitution procl., June 6.
Serrano procl. Regent of the monarchy, June 18.

MONARCHY RESTORED.—ITALIAN LINE.

1870. Amadeus Ferdinand Maria, Duke of Aosta, son of Victor Emmanuel II., K. of Italy, chosen king, Nov. 16; procl., Nov. 17; accepts the crown, Dec. 4; takes possession, Dec. 30.
1873. K. Amadeus abdicates, Feb. 11, and leaves Spain.

SECOND REPUBLIC.

1873. New Govt. chosen by the Cortes.
Pres.—1. Figueras.
2. Pi y Margall.
3. Nicholas Salmeron y Alonso, July 18.
4. Emilio Castelar, Sept. 8.
1874. Castelar resigns, Salmeron takes his place, and the Cortes dissolved by force by Gen. Pavia, Jan. 3.
New Ministry under Presidency of Serrano, Jan. 4.

MONARCHY RESTORED.—BOURBON LINE.

1874. Alphonso XII. (A. Francis d'Assise Ferdinand, &c.), son of Isabella II., procl. Dec. 30; *d.* Nov. 25, 1885, leaving two daughters, the elder Maria Mercedes Isabella, and a widow, Maria Christina, who gave birth to a son
1886. Alphonso XIII.; *b.* May 17, and succ. to the throne at his birth. His mother, Q. Maria Christina, was appointed Regent.

NAVARRE.

See France and Spain.

NAVARRE was conquered by Charlemange in 778, but shortly afterwards obtained or asserted its independence. Garcias Ximines (860) is named as the first king. The principal dates and changes of monarchy are given below. The greater part of Navarre, that lying to the south of the Pyrenees, now belongs to Spain. The part lying to the north of the Pyrenees, sometimes called lower Navarre, now belongs to France.

SOVEREIGNS OF NAVARRE.

778. Navarre conquered by Charlemagne.
* * * *
860. Independence of Navarre decl. and Garcias Ximines made king.
* * * *
10—. Sancho III., K., *d.* 1035. He divided his dominions and Navarre fell to his son
1035. Garcia III.
10—. Sancho IV., son, who was in
1076. Conq. and succ. by his cousin Sancho V. (Sancho Ramirez of Arragon), (*see Spain and Arragon*); and the two kingdoms remained united until the death of Alfonso I. in
1134. when Garcia IV. was elected K.
* * * *
* * Sancho VII.
1234. Theobald I., Count of Champagne, adopted heir of Sancho VII.
* * * *
1274. Joanna I., grand-dau. of Theobald I., *m.* 1284, Philip of France, aft. Philip IV., whereby for some years the crown of France and Navarre were united; *d.* 1305.
1305. Louis, son, aft. Louis X. of France.
1316. John I., K. of France, posthumous son, lived a few days only.
1316. Philip V. of France, bro. to Louis X.
1322. Charles I. (Charles IV. of France); *d.* without male issue; whereupon France and Navarre were again separated.
1328. Joanna II., dau. of Louis X., and wife of Philip Count d'Evereux, crowned 1329.
1349. Charles II., son.
1387. Charles III., son.
1425. Blanche, dau., wife of John, son of Ferdinand, K. of Arragon.
1441. John II, husband, who seized the crown to the prejudice of Blanche's sonCharles; became K. of Arragon in 1458.
1479. Eleanor, dau., wife of Gaston de Foix; *d.* same year.

1479. Francis Phœbus, son or grandson.
1483. Catherine, sister, wife of John D'Albret, who being placed under a ban by the pope

1512. Ferdinand V. of Arragon, seized t whole of his dominions south the Pyrenees and annexed the to Spain.

LOWER NAVARRE, NOW PART OF FRANCE.

1516. Henry II., son of Catherine and John D'Albret, succeeded to the remnant of his parents dominions.
1555. Joanna III., wife of Anthony de Bourbon.

1572. Henry III., son or grandson, b came Henry IV. of France 1589.
1607. Lower Navarre united to France.

PORTUGAL.

PORTUGAL submitted to the Roman arms about 250 B.C., and under went the same changes as Spain on the fall of the Roman empire Conquered by the Moors A.D. 713. They kept possession till they wer vanquished by Alfonso VI., the Valiant, of Castile, assisted by man other princes and volunteers. Among those who shone most in thi expedition was Henry of Burgundy, grandson of Robert, king of France Alfonso bestowed upon him Theresa, his natural daughter, and, as he marriage portion, the kingdom of Portugal, which he was to hold o him. Portugal fell under the Spanish yoke in 1580, but shook it off i 1640, since which time the Braganza family has reigned.

KINGS OF PORTUGAL.

1093. Henry, count or Earl of Portugal.
1112. Alfonso I., son, and Theresa.
1128. Alfonso, alone.
1139. Alfonso decl. king, having obtained a signal victory over a prodigious army of Moors on the plains of Ourique.
1185. Sancho I., son.
1212. Alfonso II., surn. Crassus, or the Fat.
1223. Sancho II., or the Idle; dep.
1248. Alfonso III.
1279. Denis, or Dionysius.
1325. Alfonso IV.
1357. Peter the Severe.
1367. Ferdinand I., son.
1384. John I., the Bastard, and the Great, natural brother; *m.* Philippa, dau. of John of Gaunt, D. of Lancaster.
1433. Edward.
1438. Alfonso V., the African.
1481. John II., the Great, and the Perfect.
1495. Emmanuel, the Fortunate, cousin.
1521. John III., son.
1557. Sebastian; slain in the battle of Alcazar, in Africa, Aug. 4, 1578, when the crown reverted to his great uncle

1578. Henry, the Cardinal, son of Em manuel.
1580. Anthony, prior of Crato, son c Emmanuel; dep. by Philip II. o Spain, who united Portugal t his other dominions, till 1640.

1640. John IV., D. of Braganza, dis possessed the Spaniards in bloodless revolution, and wa procl. king, Dec. 1.
1656. Alfonso VI., dep. in 1668, and hi brother and successor Peter mad regent; the latter ascended th throne in
1683. Peter II.
1706. John V., son.
1750. Joseph, son. The daughter an successor of this prince *m.* hi brother, by dispensation from th pope, and they ascended th throne, as
1777. Maria (Frances Isabella) and Peter III., jointly.
1786. Maria, alone; this princess afterwards fell into a state of melancholy and derangement.

792. Regency. John, son of the queen, and aft. king, decl. regent of the kingdom.

816. John VI., previously regent. He had withdrawn in 1807, owing to the French invasion of Portugal, to his Brazilian dominions, but returned in 1821; *d.* in 1826.

826. Peter IV. (Dom Pedro), son, making his election of the empire of Brazil, abd. the throne of Portugal in favour of his daughter

826. Maria II. (da Gloria), who became queen at 7 years of age.

1828. Dom Miguel, brother to Peter IV., usurped the crown, which he retained, amid civil contentions, until 1833.

1833. Maria II., rest., decl. in Sept. 1834 (being then 15) to be of age, and assumed the royal power accordingly.

1853. Pedro V., son, Nov. 15. His father, pr. Ferdinand of Saxe-Coburg-Gotha, acted as regent until Sept. 16, 1855.

1861. Louis I. (Louis Philippe Mary), brother, Nov. 11.

RUSSIA.

Russia was peopled by numerous tribes who were comprehended in the general name of Scythians. Rurick was great duke in the 9th century; and Vladimir or Waldimir, called the Apostle and the Solomon of Russia, was the first Christian sovereign in the 10th. His marriage with Ann, sister of the Eastern emperors Basil and Constantine, led to the adoption of the doctrines of the Greek Church in his dominions. The history of Russia previous to the last three or four centuries is involved in much obscurity, and it does not appear that any of the states existing in this vast tract of country were considerable, or that the events connected with them differed much from those of other barbarous nations.

Dukes, Czars, and Emperors.

Dukes of Kiov.

862. Rurick.
878. Igor.
945. {Olega, regent. / Swiatoslaw or Spendoblos.}
972. Jaropalk I.
980. Vladimir, Wladimir, or Waldimir I., styled the Great.
1015. Jaraslaw or Jaroslaf I.
1054. Isjialaw I.
1078. Wsewolod I.
1093. Swiatopalk.
1114. Vladimir II.
1125. Mtislaw or Michael I.
1132. Jaropalk II.
1138. {Wiatschelaw.
1139. Wsewolod II.}
1146. {Isjialaw II.
1154. Rostislaw.}
1155. Jurie or George I.; the city of Moscow was built by this duke.

Grand-Dukes of Wladimir.

1157. {Andrew I. until 1175, first Gr. D. / Michael II.}
1177. Wsewolod III.
1213. {Jurie or George II. / Constantine, until 1218.}
1238. Jaraslaw II.
1245. Alexander Nevski or Newski, the Saint, son.
1263. Jaraslaw III.
1270. Vasali or Basil I.
1277. *Dmitri or Demetrius I.
1284. *Andrew II.
1294. *Daniel Alexandrowitz.
1302. *Jurie or George III., dep.
1305. *Michael III.
1320. *Vasali or Basil II.
1325. *Jurie or George III., rest.

Grand-Dukes of Moscow.

1328. Ivan or John I.
1340. Simon, surn. the Proud.
1353. Ivan or John II.
1359. Demetrius II., pr. of Susdal.
1362. Demetrius III., Donskoi.
1389. *Vasali or Basil III., Temnoi.
1425. Vasali or Basil IV.
1462. Ivan (Basilovitz) or John III., laid the foundation of the present monarchy.
1505. Vasili or Basil V., obt. the title of emp. from Maximilian I.

* Doubtful, owing to the difficulty that occurs at every step in early Russian annals.

Czars of Muscovy.

1533. Ivan (Basilovitz) IV. first tzar or czar (great king) in 1547.
1584. Feodor or Theodore I.; supposed to have been poisoned, and his son Demetrius murdered by his successor
1598. Boris Godonof, who usurped the throne.
1606. Demetrius, the Impostor, a young Polonese monk, pretended to be the murdered pr. Demetrius; put to death.
1606. Vasili Chouiski, or Zuinski.
1610. Interregnum.
1613. Michael Federowitz, of the house of Romanof, desc. from the czar John Basilovitz.
1645. Alexis, son, styled the Father of his country.
1676. Feodor or Theodore II.
1682. {Ivan V. and Peter I., brothers.

Emperors.

1689. Peter I. the Great, alone; took the title of emp. in 1721, founded St. Petersburg, and elevated the empire.
1725. Catherine I., his consort; at first the wife of a Swedish dragoon who is said to have been killed on the day of marriage.
1727. Peter II., son of Alexis Petrowitz and grandson of Peter the Great; dep.
1730. Anne, duchess of Courland, dau. of the czar Ivan.
1740. Ivan VI., an infant, grand-nephew to Peter the Great, immured in a dungeon for 18 years; murdered in 1762.
1741. Elizabeth, dau. of Peter the Great, reigned during Ivan's captivity.
1762. Peter III., son of Anne and of Charles Frederick, D. of Holstein Gottorp; dep., and died soon after, supposed to have been murdered.
1762. Catharine II., his consort. She extended the Russian territories on all sides; *d.* 1796.
1796. Paul, son, found dead in his chamber; supposed to have been murdered.
1801. Alexander, son.
1825. Nicholas I. (Nicholas Paulowitch), brother, Dec. 1.
1855. Alexander II. (Alexander Nicolaewitch), son, Mar. 2; assass.
1881. Alexander III. (Alexander Alexandrowitch), son, Mar. 13.

POLAND.

The Poles were originally a tribe of Sclavonians, settled on the banks of the Danube, but they removed at an early period to the Vistula, where they became intermingled with the Goths. Their early history is very obscure, and is known chiefly from the accounts of writers of other nations. The country was for a long time governed by elective chiefs bearing the title of duke, no dynasty having been established before the sway of Piastus (842) whose family ruled for several centuries. The Crown became afterwards strictly elective by a Diet, or assembly of the nobles, who chose from among themselves a king, upon every vacancy occasioned on the throne by death. Since the dismemberment of Poland, each portion has been under the sovereignty of the power by which it was seized.

Dukes and Kings of Poland.

Dukes.

842. Piastus.
861. Ziemovitus, son.
892. Lesko or Lescus IV.
913. Ziemomislas, son.
964. Miecislas I.

Kings.

992. Boleslas I., surn. the Lion-hearted; obt. the title of king from the emp. Otho III.
1025. Miecislas II.
1034. Richense or Richsa, his consort, regent; driven from the government.
1037. Interregnum.
1041. Casimir I., her son, surn. the Pacific; he had retired to a monastery, but was invited to the throne.
1058. Boleslas II., surn. the Intrepid.
1081. Ladislas, surn. the Careless.

1102. Boleslas III., surn. Wry-mouth.
1138. Ladislas II., son.
1146. Boleslas IV., surn. the Curled.
1173. Miecislas III., surn. the Old; dep.
1177. Casimir II., surn. the Just.
1194. Lesko V., surn. the White; res.
1200. Miecislas IV.; his tyranny restored Lesko, but the latter was again forced to resign.
1203. Ladislas, res.
1206. Lesko V., a third time; assass.
1227. Boleslas V., an infant son, surn. the Chaste.
1279. Lesko VI., surn. the Black.
1289. Interregnum.
1295. Premislas; assass.
1296. Ladislas IV., surn. the Short; dep.
1300. Wenceslas, K. of Bohemia.
1304. Ladislas, the Short, again.
1333. Casimir III., surn. the Great; killed by a fall from his horse.
1370. Louis, K. of Hungary.
1382. Interregnum.
1385. Hedwige, dau. of Louis, and her consort, Jagello, D. of Lithuania, by the style of Ladislas V.
1399. Ladislas V. alone; he united Lithuania to Poland.
1434. Ladislas VI., son, succ. as K. of Hungary 1440.
1445. Interregnum.
1445. Casimir IV.
1492. John (Albert) I., son.
1501. Alexander, pr. of Livonia, brother.
1506. Sigismund I., brother.
1548. Sigismund II. (Augustus), son, added Livonia to his kingdom.
1573. Interregnum.
1574. Henry, D. of Anjou, brother to the K. of France: aft. succ. to the French throne.
1575. Stephen Batthori, pr. of Transylvania, established the Cossacks as a militia.
1586. Interregnum.
1587. Sigismund III., son of the K. of Sweden, to the exclusion of Maximilian of Austria, elected by the nobles.
1632. Ladislas VII. (Vasa), son.
1648. John II., or Casimir V.; abd. and retired to France, where he *d.* 1672.
1668. Interregnum.
1669, Michael Koributh Wiesnowiski. In this reign the Cossacks joined the Turks, and ravaged Poland.
1674. John III. (Sobieski), whose victories over the Cossacks, Turks, and Tartars procured him the crown.
1697. Interregnum.
1697. Frederick Augustus I., son of John George, elector of Saxony, and elector in 1694; depr.
1704. Stanislas I. (Lezinski), forced to retire from his kingdom.
1709. Frederick Augustus, *again.*
1734. Frederick Augustus II., son.
1763. Interregnum.
1764. Stanislas II. (Augustus Poniatowski).
1772. The Austrians, Russians, and Prussians make their first partition of Poland.
1793. Second division of the kingdom by the same powers.
1795. Final partition of Poland, and deposition of the king, who died at St. Petersburg, a state prisoner, in 1798.

SWEDEN AND NORWAY.

The internal state of Sweden is little known previously to the 11th century. By the union of Calmar, in 1394, Sweden became a mere province of Denmark, and was not rescued from this subjection until 1521, when Gustavus Vasa recovered the kingdom from the Danish yoke. For this he was raised to the throne in 1523, and the crown made hereditary in his descendants, who reigned until 1809. In this year, Gustavus IV., having brought the nation to the verge of ruin by his misgovernment, was deposed, and the duke of Sudermania became king. The next year Bernadotte was elected successor to the throne, which he ascended in 1818.

NORWAY, which had belonged to Denmark from 1397, was ceded to Sweden by the treaty of Kiel, signed January 14, 1814, and confirmed by the Diet, October 14, same year.

Kings of Sweden.

Many antiquaries trace the reigns of the kings of Sweden as early as from the 5th century, and place Swartman as sovereign in 481, A.D. But the authorities so differ in the early successions, that the present list is made to commence with the 11th century.

1001. Olaf Skotkonung, or Olif Schœtkonung.
1026. Amund or Edmund Colbrenner.
1051. Amund or Edmund Slemme.
1056. Stenkill or Stenchil.
1066. Halstan.
1090. Ingeld or Ingo, surn. the Good.
1112. Philip.
1118. Ingo II.
1129. Swerker or Suercher I.
1150. Eric X.
1162. Charles VII.; made prisoner by his succ.
1168. Canute, son of Eric X.
1192. Swerker or Suercher II.; killed in battle.
1210. Eric XI.
1220. John I.
1223. Eric XII., *le Begue*.
1251. Waldemar.
1279. Magnus I.
1290. Birger II.
1320. Magnus II.; dethr.
1363. Albert of Mecklenburg; his tyranny caused a revolt of his subjects, who invited Margaret of Denmark to the throne.
1387. Margaret, Q. of Sweden and Norway, now also of Denmark, and Eric XIII.
1397. Union of Calmar, by which the three kingdoms were united under one sovereign.
1412. Eric XIII. governs alone; deprived.
1441. Christopher III.
1448. Charles VIII., surn. Canuteson.
1470. Interregnum.
1483. John II. (I. of Denmark).
1502. Interregnum.
1520. Christiern or Christian II. of Denmark, styled the "Nero of the North"; dep.
1523. Gustavus Vasa, by whom the Swedes were delivered from the Danish yoke.
1560. Eric XIV., son, deth.; *d.* in prison.
1568. John III., brother.
1592. Sigismund, K. of Poland, son; disputes for the succession continued the whole of this reign.
1604. Charles IX., brother of John III.
1611. Gustavus (Adolphus) II., the Great; fell on the plains of Lutzen.
1633. Interregnum.
1633. Christina, dau. of Gustavus Adolphus; res. the crown to her cousin; *d.* 1689.
1654. Charles X. (Gustavus), son of John Casimir, count palatine of the Rhine.
1660. Charles XI., son.
1697. Charles XII., styled the "Alexander," the "Quixote," and the "Madman of the North"; killed at the siege of Fredrickshall.
1719. Ulrica Eleanora, sister, and her consort Frederick I. Ulrica relinquished the crown, and in
1741. Frederick reigned alone.
1751. Adolphus Frederick, of Holstein Gottorp, descended from the family of Vasa.
1771. Gustavus (Adolphus) III.; assass. by count Ankerstrom at a masked ball.
1792. Gustavus (Adolphus) IV. Deth., and the government assumed by his uncle, D. of Sudermania.
1809. Charles XIII., D. of Sudermania.
1814. Treaty of Kiel, by which Norway fell under the sovereignty of Sweden. Signed Jan. 12, confirmed by the Diet, Oct. 12.

Kings of Sweden and Norway.

1814. Charles XIII., above-named.
1818. Charles XIV. Feb. 5. Jean Baptiste Jules Bernadotte, one of the Marshals of Napoleon I. of France. On being nominated successor to Charles XIII. Aug. 21, 1810, he took the name of Charles John.
1844. Oscar I. (Joseph Francis Oscar), son, Mar. 8.
1859. Charles XV. (Charles Louis Eugène), son, July 8.
1872. Oscar II. (Oscar Frederick), brother, Sept. 18.

DENMARK.

THE name Denmark is supposed to be derived from *Dan*, a founder of the Danish monarchy, and *mark*, a German word signifying country, *i.e.* Dan-mark, the country of Dan. The people, however, were but little known in history until they began to made inroads into Germany and to commit piracies in the northern seas under various designations, as Norwegians or Northmen, Swedes, Frizans, Jutes, or Scuyths, or Danes. Norway was possessed by Denmark from the reign of the celebrated Margaret, "the Semiramis of the North," in the 15th century, until 1814, when it was united, as an integral state, to the sovereignty of Sweden.

KINGS OF DENMARK.

The *Danish Chronicles* mention 25 kings to the reign of Harald; but the accounts differ much from the modern histories of Denmark by the best authors.

813. Harald, or Harold.
850. Eric I.
854. Eric II., or the Child.
883. Gormo, the Old; reigned 53 years.
935. Harald II., surn. Blue-tooth.
985. Suenon, or Sweyn, surn. the Forked-beard.
1014. Canute II., K. of Denmark and England.
1036. Canute III., son, the Hardicanute of England.
1042. Magnus, surn. the Good, of Norway.
1047. Suenon or Sweyn II.
1073. Interregnum.
1077. Harald III., surn. the Simple.
1080. Canute IV.
1086. Olaus IV., surn. the Hungry.
1095. Eric III., surn. the Good.
1103. Interregnum
1105. Nicholas I.; killed at Sleswick.
1135. Eric IV., surn. Harefoot.
1137. Eric V., the Lamb.
1147. { Suenon or Sweyn III.; beheaded. / Canute V., until 1154. }
1157. Waldemar, styled the Great.
1182. Canute VI., surn. the Pious.
1202. Waldemar II., the Victorious.
1241. Eric VI.
1250. Abel, assass. his elder brother Eric; killed in an expedition against the Frisons.
1252. Christopher I.; poisoned.
1259. Eric VII.
1286. Eric VIII.
1320. Christopher II.
1334. Interregnum of 7 years.
1340. Waldemar III.
1375. Interregnum.
1376. Olaus V.
1387. Margaret, styled the "Semiramis of the North," Q. of Sweden, Norway, and Denmark.
1397. Margaret and Eric IX. (Eric XIII. of Sweden) jointly.
1412. Eric IX. reigns alone; res. both crowns.
1438. Interregnum.
1440. Christopher III., K. of Sweden.
1448. Christian I., count of Oldenburg, elect. K. of Scandinavia, which comprehended Denmark, Sweden and Norway.
1481. John, son.
1513. Christian II., son, called the Cruel, and the "Nero of the North," deth. 1523; *d.* 1559.

    In this reign, Sweden succeeded in separating itself from the crown of Denmark.
1523. Frederick I., D. of Holstein, uncle to Christian II.
1534. Christian III., son.
1559. Frederick II., son.
1588. Christian IV., son; head of the Protestant league against the emp.
1648. Frederick III., changed the constitution from an elective to an hereditary monarchy vested in his own family.
1670. Christian V., son.
1699. Frederick IV., son, leagued with the Czar Peter and the K. of Poland against Charles XII. of Sweden.
1730. Christian VI., son.
1746. Frederick V., son, *m.* the prs. Louisa of England, dau. of George II.
1766. Christian VII., son, *m.* Caroline Matilda, sister of George III. In a fit of jealousy he banished his queen to Zell, where she died in

1775, and put to death his ministers Brandt and Struensee.
1784. Regency. The cr. pr. Frederick decl. regent, in consequence of the mental derangement of his father.
1808. Frederick VI., previously regent, now king.
1839. Christian VIII., son, Dec. 3.
1848. Frederick VII. (Frederick Charles Christian), son, Jan. 20.
1863. Christian IX., son of Frederick William, D. of Schleswig-Holstein-Sonderburg - Glucksburg, Nov. 15. Succ. under the convention of London, May 8, 1852, and the Danish Law of Succession of July 31, 1853.

TURKEY.

THE sovereigns of Turkey are given under ASIA, but the subordinate princes of its European Provinces are given under EUROPE.

See Table of Contents.

DANUBIAN PRINCIPALITIES.

WALLACHIA. MOLDAVIA. ROUMANIA.

Under the sovereignty of Turkey and protection of Russia.

WALLACHIA AND MOLDAVIA.

FROM 1832 to 1834 the government of the two principalities of Wallachia and Moldavia was administered by General Kisseleff. It was intended that as soon as he had established a settled form of government separate "Hospodars" for the two principalities should be elected.

HOSPODARS OF WALLACHIA.

1834. Alexander Ghika, Oct. 14; dep. Oct. 1842.
1842. George Bibesco, res., June 25, 1848; Prov. Gov. until appointment of
1849. Dimitri Barbo Stirbey, June 16.
1856. Prince Alexander Dimitri Ghika, July.

HOSPODARS OF MOLDAVIA.

1834. Michel Stourdza, res.
1849. Gregory Alexander Ghika, June 16.
1856. Theodore Ritza Balsch, July 19.
1857. Nicolas Stefanaki Vogorides, Mar. 7.

WALLACHIA AND MOLDAVIA UNITED.

CONSTITUTIONAL government established under Treaty of Paris, March 30, 1856, and Convention, August 19, 1858.

PRINCES.

1859. Alexander I. — Alexander John (Colonel A. J. Couza), elect. for Moldavia, Jan. 17, and for Wallachia, Feb. 5.
1861. The two principalities united under the name of Roumania, Dec. 23, Pr. Alexander becoming Hospodar.

Hospodar, Prince, and Kings of Roumania.

1861 Alexander I., above-named, became Hospodar, Dec. 23; abd. Feb. 22, 1866; and Prov. Gov. procl.

1866. Charles I., second son of pr. Charles Antony, of Hohenzollern-Sigmaringen, elect. hered. pr., Mar. 26; election confirmed Oct. 24; procl. K. of Roumania, Mar. 26, 1881.

BULGARIA.

This principality is under the sovereignty of Turkey. It was created under the Treaty of Berlin, July 13, 1878. Eastern Roumelia was united to it September 1885.

Princes of Bulgaria.

1879. Alexander I. (Alexander Joseph), son of pr. Alexander of Hesse, and of pr. Julia of Battenburg; elect. by the National Assembly, April 29; forcibly abducted, Aug. 21, 1886, returned to Sophia, Sept. 3, 1886; abd. Sept. 7, 1886. Regency appointed, Aug. 26, 1886; continued to act after pr. Alexander's abdication.

1887. Ferdinand, pr. of Saxe-Coburg; elect. July 7.

SERVIA.

This principality formerly belonged to Turkey, and is still nominally subject to that empire.

Princes of Servia.

* * * * *

1829. Milosch I., recog. as hered. pr. by Turkey, Aug. 15; abd. June 1839.

1839. Michael, son; abd. 1842.

1842. Alexander Carageorgevics, recog. by Turkey Sept. 29, and gov. from Oct. 26; abd. 1858.

1858. Milosch II. (Alexander Milosch Obrenovitch), Dec. 23.

1860. Michael III. (Michael Obrenovitch), son, Sept. 26; assass. June 10, 1868.

1868. Milan IV. (Milan Obrenovitch), June 30; procl. K. Mar. 6, 1882.

Kings of Servia.

1882. Milan IV., above-named, Mar. 6.

MONTENEGRO.

A small state under the administration of the family of Pétrovich Njegosch.

Princes of Montenegro.

* * *

* * Daniel I.

1860. Nicholas I., Aug. 13.

GREECE.

This country anciently consisted of the peninsula of the Peloponnesus, Greece outside the Peloponnesus, Thessaly, and the islands; the limits of modern Greece are much more confined. It became subject to the Turkish empire in the 15th century, and has but recently again become a separate state. The treaty of London, on behalf of Greece, between England, France, and Russia, was signed in Oct. 1827; count Capo d'Istria was declared president in Jan. 1828, and assassinated 9th Oct., 1831. The Porte acknowledged the independence of Greece in April, 1830. It was afterwards erected into a kingdom, of which Otho I. of Bavaria was made king.

King of Greece.

1832. Otho, 2nd son of Louis Charles, K. of Bavaria, *b.* June 1, 1815, elect. K. subject to a regency, Mar. 7; assumed power, June 1, 1835; dep. 22nd, and quitted Greece 24th Oct. 1862; *d.* July 26, 1867.

Change of dynasty under the Protocol signed by France, England, and Russia, dated 5th June, 1863. Under this the Ionian Islands were annexed to Greece.

King of the Hellenes.

1863. George I. (Pr. William, of Schleswig - Holstein - Sonderburg - Glucksburg), son of Christian IX., K. of Denmark, accepted the crown, June 6; sworn to constn. Oct. 31.

IONIAN ISLANDS.

The Ionian Islands are now united to Greece. For a list of the English Lord High Commissioners appointed prior to the union *see Part II. "Diplomatic."*

SOVEREIGNS AND RULERS OF ASIA.

JERUSALEM.

This kingdom began with its capture by the first crusaders, who elected as king, in 1099, Godfrey de Bouillon, the chief commander of the expedition, though he chose to be called, from motives of piety, the "advocate or defender of the holy sepulchre." The crown of Jerusalem descended from Godfrey de Bouillon to the house of Anjou, afterwards to Guy de Lusignan, and, in 1210, to John de Brienne. The emperor

Frederick having married the daughter of this last, was invested with all her rights, which, however, he did not care to assert; and the possession of Jerusalem being no longer an object of ambition the city became, what it had been before Godfrey's invasion, a place of pilgrimage.

Kings of Jerusalem.

1099. Godfrey de Bouillon, chosen by the first crusaders. Took Jerusalem from the Turks, 1099, and was procl. king.
1100. Baldwin I.
1118. Baldwin II.
1131. Fulke, count of Anjou.
1142. Baldwin III., son.
1162. Amaurus I.
1173. Baldwin IV.
1185. Baldwin V.
1186. Guy de Lusignan.
1192. Conrad and Isabella.
1192. Henry.
1197. Frederick.
1197. Amaurus de Lusignan, K. of Cyprus.
1205. Interregnum.
1210. John de Brienne; aft. associate emp. of the East.
1229. Jerusalem surrendered by the sultan of Egypt to the emp. Frederick.

OTTOMAN OR TURKISH EMPIRE.

The Turks are of Tartar descent. There is a rapid river called *Turk*, running into the Caspian Sea, from which some suppose this people to take their name. About the year A.D. 800 they obtained possession of a part of Armenia, called from them Turcomania; and they afterwards gradually extended their power. Their dominions, divided for some time into petty states, were united under Othman, from whom his subjects obtained the name of Ottomans. He established his empire Prusa, in Bithynia, in the year 1299, and his successors extended their conquests over the adjacent parts of Asia, Africa, and Europe. In 1453 Constantinople was taken by Mahomed II., which put an end to the Eastern Empire.

Turkish Emperors or Sultans.

1299. Othman, or Ottoman, who assumed the title of Grand Seignior.
1326. Orchan, son.
1360. Amurath I.; stabbed by a soldier.
1389. Bajazet I., son; defeated by Tamerlane, and died imprisoned.
1402. Solyman, son; dep. by his brother and successor.
1410. Musa Chelebi; strangled.
1413. Mahomed I., also son of Bajazet.
1421. Amurath II.
1451. Mahomed II., son; by whom Constantinople was taken, in 1453.
1481 Bajazet II.; dep. by his son
1512. Selim I., who succ.
1520. Solyman the Magnificent, son.
1566. Selim II., son.
1574. Amurath III., son; on his accession he caused his five brothers to be murdered, and their mother, in grief, stabbed herself to death.
1595. Mahomed III., son; commenced his reign by strangling all his brothers, and drowning all his father's wives.
1603. Ahmed, or Achmet I., son.
1617. Mustapha I., brother; dep. by the Janissaries, and imprisoned.
1618. Osman I., nephew; strangled by the Janissaries, and his uncle restored.
1622. Mustapha I., *again*; again dep., sent to the Seven Towers, and strangled.
1623. Amurath IV.
1640. Ibrahim, brother; strangled by the Janissaries
1649. Mahomed IV., son; dep. and died imprisoned.
1687. Solyman III., brother.
1691. Ahmed, or Achmet II.
1695. Mustapha II., nephew, eldest son of Mahomed IV.; dep.
1703. Ahmed, or Achmet III., brother; dep.; *d.* 1736.
1730. Mahmud, or Mahomed V., nephew.

1754. Osman II., brother.
1757. Mustapha III., brother.
1774. Abdul Ahmed I.
1788. Selim III.; dep. by the Janissaries, and his nephew raised to the throne.
1807. Mustapha IV.; dep., and, with the late sultan, Selim, murdered.
1808. Mahmud II.
1839. Abdul Medjid, son, July 1.
1861. Abdul Aziz, brother, June 25; dep. May 29, 1876; committed suicide (?), June 4.
1876. Amurath V. (Mahomed Murad), nephew, procl. May 30, 1876; dep. Aug. 30.
1876. Abdul Hamid II., brother, procl. Aug. 31.

EGYPT.

This country is still nominally under the suzerainty of Turkey, who conquered it in 1517. It was then governed by Beys till about 1799, when the French took possession and remained till expelled by the English in 1801, when the Turkish government was restored. Shortly afterwards Mehemet Ali was appointed pacha, and he from time to time rebelled against the sovereignty of Turkey with a view to establishing Egyptian independence. These struggles terminated in 1841 by the Pachalic or Viceroyalty of Egypt being made hereditary in Mehemet Ali's family.

Viceroys of Egypt.

1841. Mehemet Ali, July 15, abd.
1848. Ibrahim, adopted son, Sept. 1.
— Abbas, son of Tussun Bey, eldest son of Mehemet Ali, Nov. 10.
1854. Säid, 4th son of Mehemet Ali, July 14.
1863. Ismaïl, son of Ibrahim, Jan 18; dep. or abd., June 26, 1879.
1879. Tewfik (Mahomed Tewfik), son, June 26.

TREBIZOND.

Emperors.

1204. Alexis I.
1222. Andronicus I.
1235. John I.
1238. Manuel I.
1263. Andronicus II.
1266. George.
1280. John II.
1285. Theodora.
1285. John II., *again.*
1297. Alexis II.
1330. Andronicus III.
1332. Manuel II.
1332. Basil.
1340. Irene.
1341. Anna.
1343. John III.
1344. Michael.
1349. Alexis III.
1390. Manuel III.
1417. Alexis IV.
1446. John IV.
1458. David.
1461. Conquered by the Turks.

ARABIA.

Caliphs of Arabia, sometimes styled Caliphs of Bagdad

632. Abubeker.
634. Omar.
644. Othman.
655. Ali.
661. Hassan.
The Ommiades ruled 661–750.
The Abbasides ruled 750–1258.
786. Haroun-Al-Raschid, *d.* 809

PERSIA.

At the partition of the dominions of Alexander the Great among his captains, Persia was annexed to the Syrian kingdom of Seleucus Nicator, but did not continue long so, for in the reign of Antiochus Theos, Arsases vindicated the independence of his country, and founded the monarchy of the Parthians. In the 3rd century of the Christian era a great internal convulsion took place, which terminated in the accession of the dynasty of the Sassanides, who restored the name, with the religion and laws of Ancient Persia. This government was overthrown by the Saracens; and the successive invasions by the descendants of Zingis or Zenghis Khan, Timur, and by the Turks, changed entirely the aspect of Western Asia. Persia was the main theatre on which the Saracens contended for mastery with these invaders, and she suffered all the miseries to which a nation can be exposed from the devastation of barbarous and sanguinary hordes. At length, early in the 16th century, a new dynasty arose.

Kings of Persia.

B.C.
559. Cyrus.
529. Cambyses.
522. Smerdis.
521. Darius I.
485. Xerxes I.
465. Artabanus.
465. Artaxerxes I.
425. Xerxes II.

B.C.
425. Sogdianus.
424. Darius II.
405. Artaxerxes II.
359. Ochus.
338. Arses.
336. Darius III.

* * * *

Shahs of Persia.

1502. Ismail, or Ishmael.
1523. Tamasp, or Thamas I.
1576. Ismail Meerza.
1577. Mahomed Meerza.
1582. Abbas I., the Great; *d.* 1627.
1627. Shah Soofe.
1641. Abbas II.
1666. Solyman.
1694. Hessein, dep.
1722. Mahmoud.
1725. Ashraff, the Usurper; slain in battle.
1729. Tamasp, or Thamas II., recovered the throne of his ancestors from the preceding.
1732. Abbas III., infant son, under the regency of Kouli Khan, who aft. caused himself to be procl. as Nadir Shah.
1736. Nadir Shah (the victorious Regent), assass. by his nephew at Korassan.
1747. Adil Shah.
1748. Shah Rokh.
1750. Interregnum.
1753. Kureem Khan.
1779. Abool Fatteh Khan.
1780. Interregnum.
1781. Ali Moorad Khan.
1785. Jaffier Khan.
1788. Interregnum.
1789. Looft Ali Khan; betrayed into the hands of his successor, who put him to death.
1794. Aga Mahomed Khan, assass.
1798. Feth Ali Shah.
1834. Mahomed Shah, grandson.
1848. Nasr-ul-Din, or Nausser-ood-deen, or Nasser-ud-deen Shah, son, Sept. 4 or 10.

CHINA.

Emperors.

* * * *

1627. Chwang-lei.
1644. Shun-che.
1662. Kang-he.
1723. Yung-ching.
1736. Keen-lung.
1795. Kea-King.
1821. Taou-Kwang.
1850. Hienfung, succ. Feb. 25, to dat[e] from Feb. 1, 1851.
1861. Ki-tsiang, or Tsai-sung, changed t[o] T'oungchih, Aug. 22.
1875. Tsai-t'ien, changed to Kuangsu Jan. 12.

JAPAN.

Mikados or Emperors.

* * * *

* * Komei Tonno.

1867. Moutz Hito, Feb. 13.

SIAM.

Kings.

First King.

1868. Phra Bat Somditch Phra Paramindr Maha Chulalon-Korn Phra Cula Chom Klaochow Yu Hua, Oct. 1.

Second King.

His son, Kroma Phraratscha, &c.

Note—The spelling of these sovereigns' names differs in every authority consulted b[y] the Editor.

SOVEREIGNS AND RULERS OF AFRICA.

LIBERIA.

This republic was founded in 1822 by the American Colonizatio[n] Society, and declared independent in July 1847.

Presidents of Liberia.

1848. Joseph Jenkins Roberts. Jan.
1856. Etienne A. Benson. Jan.
1864. Daniel Basil Warner. Jan.
1868. James Spriggs Payne. Jan.
1870. Edward James Roye, Jan. 3; dep. Oct. 1871.
1872. Joseph Jenkins Roberts, *again* Jan. 1.
1876. James Spriggs Payne, *again*. Jan. 3.
1878. Anthony W. Gardner. Jan. 7.
1883. A. J. Russell. Jan.
1884. Hilary R. W. Johnson. Jan. 7.

MADAGASCAR.

Kings and Queens.

1810. Radama I., K.
1828. Ranavolona I., Q.
1861. Radama II., K.
1863. Rasoherina I., Q. May.
1868. Ranavolona II., Q. Apr. 1.
1883. Ranavolona III., Q. July 13.

MOROCCO.

Sultans.

* * * *
1822. Muley Abd-er-Rhaman.
1859. Sidi Muley Mahomed. Sept.
1873. Muley Hassan, son, succ. Sept. 20, procl. Sept. 25.

ORANGE FREE STATE.

Placed under the sovereignty of the British Government Feb. 3, 1848; declared independent Feb. 23, 1854; constitution proclaimed April 10, 1854; revised Feb. 9, 1866.

Presidents.

1854. * * * * *
1859. J. T. Hoffmann.
1864. John Henry Brand, 1st time.
1869. ,, 2nd. May 4.
1874. John Henry Brand, 3rd. May 5.
1879. ,, 4th. Feb. 10.
1883. ,, knighted.
1884. ,, 5th.

TRANSVAAL REPUBLIC.

Declaration of independence, Jan. 17, 1852; constitution proclaimed, Feb. 13, 1858.

Presidents.

* * * *
1869. M. W. Pretorius. May 19.
1872. T. F. Burgers. May 27, to act from July 1.
1877. Annexed to Great Britain, Apr. 12.
1881. Independence restored under suzerainty of Great Britain, Aug.
1880. S. J. P. Krüger, M. W. Pretorius, P. J. Joubert } Elected a triumvirate until the election of a president, Dec.
1883. S. J. P. Krüger, elect. pres., May 9.

TUNIS.

Beys.

* * * *
1835. Mustapha.
1855. Sidi Mahomed. June.
1859. Mahomed Es Sadok, brother. Sept. 23.
1882. Sidi Ali. Oct. 28.

ZANZIBAR.

Sultans.

* * * *

1856. Seyyid Majid.

1870. Seyyid Bargash-Ben-Saïd, brother. Oct. 7.

1888. Seyyid Khalif, Mar. 26.

SOVEREIGNS AND RULERS OF AMERICA.

UNITED STATES OF AMERICA.

The provinces of North America which revolted from the sovereignty of Great Britain were first styled "the United States," by a resolution of congress, Sept. 9, 1776. Their independence was acknowledged by Great Britain, Nov. 30, 1782, and a definitive treaty of peace between Great Britain, France, Spain, and the United States, was signed at Paris, Sept. 3, 1783. The United States now comprise—

Original States.

New Hampshire.
Massachusetts.
Rhode Island.
Connecticut.
New York.
New Jersey.
Pennsylvania.
Delaware.
Maryland.
Virginia.
North Carolina.
South Carolina.
Georgia.

States subsequently added.

Vermont.
Tennessee.
Kentucky.
Ohio.
Louisiana.
Indiana.
Mississippi.
Illinois.
Alabama.
Maine.
Missouri.
Arkansas.
Michigan.
Florida.
Texas.
Iowa.
Wisconsin.
California.
Minnesota.
Oregon.
Kansas.
Nevada.
Colorado.
West Virginia.
Nebraska.

Territories.

New Mexico.
Utah.
Washington.
Dakota.
Arizona.
Idaho.
Montana.

District.

Columbia.

Presidents of the United States.

1789. Gen. George Washington, first president. Apr. 30.
1793. Gen. Washington, *again.* Mar. 4.
1797. John Adams. Mar. 4.
1801. Thomas Jefferson. Mar. 4.
1805. Jefferson, *again.* Mar. 4.
1809. James Madison. Mar. 4.
1813. Madison, *again.* Mar. 4.
1817. James Monroe. Mar. 4.
1821. Monroe, *again.* Mar. 4.
1825. John Quincy Adams. Mar. 4.
1829. Gen. Andrew Jackson. Mar. 4.
1833. Gen. Jackson, *again.* Mar. 4.
1837. Martin Van Buren. Mar. 4.
1841. Gen. Wm. Henry Harrison. Mar. 4.; *d.* Apr. 4.
— John Tyler, vice-pres. Apr. 4.
1845. James Knox Polk. Mar. 4.
1849. Gen. Zachary Taylor. Mar. 4; *d.* July 9, 1850.
1850. Millard Fillmore, vice-pres. July 9.
1853. Gen. Franklin Pierce. Mar. 4.
1857. James Buchanan. Mar. 4.
1861. Abraham Lincoln. Mar. 4.

1865. Lincoln, *again*. Mar. 4; assass. Apr. 14, *d.* Apr. 15, 1865.
— Andrew Johnson, vice-pres., Apr. 15.
1869. Gen. Ulysses Simpson Grant. Mar. 4.
1873. Gen. Grant, *again*. Mar. 4.
1877. Rutherford B. Hayes. Mar. 4.
1881. James Abram Garfield. Mar. 4. Shot July 2, *d.* Sept. 19, 1881.
— Chester A. Arthur, vice-pres., Sept. 19.
1885. Grover Cleveland. Mar. 4.

Note.—The President's term of office commences on the 4th March, but he is elected in the November previous.

MEXICO. VERA CRUZ.

MEXICO.

MEXICO became independent of Spain in 1821. It has since been in a very unsettled condition, as will be seen by the following

SUMMARY OF THE PRINCIPAL CHANGES OF GOVERNMENT.

1821. Independence declared. Aug.
1836. Recognised by Foreign States, and ultimately by Spain, under treaty of Dec. 28.
1821. Regency from Sept. 28.
1822. Empire under Iturbidi (Augustin 1st). May 18.
1823. Prov. Gov. Mar. 19.
1824. Federal Repub. Oct. 10.
1837. Central Republican Gov. Jan. 1.
1841. Dictatorship. Oct. 10.
1844. New Central Gov. June 4.
1846. Re-establishment of the Federal Repub. Aug. 4.
1853. Prov. Gov. Jan. 6.
1853. Repub. under Santa Anna and his successors. April 20.
1858. Separation of Vera Cruz. Feb.
1861. Vera Cruz re-united. June.
1862–1864. Civil war; intervention of France; ultimate establishment of an empire under Archd. Maximilian of Austria, April 10, 1864.
1867. Emp. Maximilian shot, June 19. Repub. re-established.

RULERS OF MEXICO—EMPERORS, PRESIDENTS, AND DICTATORS.

It is believed that the following list contains every ruler who held the Government for any definite period, but in the many revolutions and insurrections which have taken place dictators or presidents were sometimes in power only a few weeks or even a few days.

1821. Augustin Iturbidi, Generalissimo.
1822. Ditto, emp. as Augustin I.
1823. Gens. Guerrero, Bravo, and Negreti, dict.
1824. Gen. G. Victoria, pres.
1827. Gen. Guerrero, pres.
1829. Ditto, dict.
1830. Gen. Anastasio Bustamente, pres.
1832. Gen. Pedraza, pres.
1835. Gen. Antonio Lopez de Santa Anna, pres.
1836. José J. Caro, pres.
1837. Bustamente, *again*, pres. April.
1840. Gen. Farias, pres.
1841. Bustamente, *again*, pres.
1843. Gen. Valentine Canalizo, pres., *ad. int.*
1845. Gen. José Joaquim Herrera, pres Sept. 26.
1847. Gen. Paredes, pres.
1848. Herrera, *again*, pres. May 3.
1851. Gen. Mariano Arista, pres. June 23
1852. M. J. Ceballos, pres.
1853. S. M. Lombardini, pres.
1853. Santa Anna, *again*, dict., Mar. 17, pres. April 25.
1855. Juan Alvarez, pres. Oct. 31.
1856. Gen. Ignatio Comonfort, pres., *ad int.*

1858. Gen. Felix Zuloago, pres. Jan. 22.
1859. Gen. Miguel Miramon, pres. Feb.
1859. Gen. Benito Juarez, pres. Dec.
1861. Juarez, dict.
1864. Maximilian I. (archd. of Austria), emp., April 10; shot June 19, 1867.
1867. Juarez, *again*, pres. Dec.; *d* July 18, 1872.
1872. Sebastian Lerdo de Tejada, pres. Nov
1877 Porfirio Diaz, pres. May 5.
1880. Manuel Gonzales, pres. Dec. 1.
1884. Diaz, *again*, pres. Dec. 1, as from Jan. 1, 1885.

VERA CRUZ.

Vera Cruz was separated from Mexico Feb. 1, 1858, and re-united in June 1861. During its separation it was under the presidency or dictatorship of Gen. Benito Juarez.

HAYTI. ST. DOMINGO. DOMINICAN REPUBLIC.

This island (whose Indian name of Hayti was changed by the Spaniards to Hispaniola and afterwards to St. Domingo) was a Spanish colony from Dec. 1492 to 1630. It was then seized by French freebooters, and ultimately taken possession of by the French Government in 1697. The native negroes revolted against the French in Aug. 1791, and massacred the whites in June 1793. The French Directory recognised the insurgent general, Toussaint L'Ouverture, as general of the army in 1794, and he declared the island independent of France, and granted a separate constitution, May 9, 1801. He was afterwards defeated by the French, by whom he was made prisoner, May 7, 1802, and died in France 1803. Soon after his defeat there was a fresh insurrection by the negroes under Dessalines, and eventually the island was evacuated by the French in Nov. 1803. Dessalines then became emp. as James I., Oct. 8, 1804, but was assassinated, Oct. 17, 1806. The island was then divided, the negroes forming a kingdom in the north under the name of Hayti, and the mulattoes forming a republic in the south under the name of St. Domingo. In Nov. 1820 these two divisions were re-united and formed into a free state under the presidency of Boyer, who was named Regent for life, and the independence of the Republic was recognised by France, April 17, 1825. In 1843 another revolution occurred, which resulted in the deposition and the secession of St. Domingo and the eastern part of Hayti, who formed themselves into a separate state under the title of the Dominican Republic. Hayti has since maintained a separate existence, sometimes as an empire and sometimes a republic.

The Dominican Republic was re-united to Spain by declaration of March 18, 1861, accepted by the Queen of Spain on May 20 following; but it again revolted in 1863, and was finally renounced by Spain, May 5, 1865. Since that time it has continued a republic.

RULERS OF HAYTI AND ST. DOMINGO.

The whole Island.

1794. Toussaint L'Ouverture, gen. in chief; made prisoner May 7, 1802; *d.* 1803.
1802–3. The island under the dominion of France.
1804. John James Dessalines, emp. under title of James I., Oct. 8, 1804; assass Oct. 17, 1806, and the island divided

Hayti.

- 07. Hy. Christopher, pres. Feb.
- 11. Ditto, made emp. under title of Henry I. Mar.; *d.* Oct. 1820.

St. Domingo.

- 1807. Alexander Petion, pres.; *d.* 1818.
- 1818. John Peter Boyer, pres.; under whom the Island was again united.

The whole Island.

- 20. John Peter Boyer, elected regent for life, Nov.; dep. 1843, and the island again divided.

Hayti.

- 43. — Pierrot, pres.
- 46. John Baptist Riche, pres.
- 47. Faustin Soulouque, pres. Mar.
- 49. Ditto, made emp. as Faustin I. Aug. 26. Abd. Jan. 15, 1859; *d.* Sept. 1, 1867.
- 858. Dec. Revolution, under which, in
- 858. A republic procl., and Gen. Nicholas Fabre Geffrard made pres. Feb. 22.
- 862. Victoriano Castellanos, pres.
- 866. Gen. Sylvanus Salnave, pres.
- 870. Gen. Nissage Saget. Mar. 19, to act from May 15.
- 874. Gen. Michel Domingue. June 14, to act from May 15.
- 876. Gen. Boisrond Canal. July 17, to act from May 15.
- 879. Gen. Salomon. Oct. 22, to act from Nov. 17; re-elect. July 6, 1886.

Dominican Republic.

- 1844. Pedro Santana, pres.
- 1849. Bonaventura Baez, pres.
- 1853. Santana, *again*, pres. Mar. 23.
- 1856. Baez, *again*, pres. Oct. 8.
- 1858. José Desiderio Valverde, pres.
- 1859. Santana, *again*, pres. Feb. 5.
- 1861. Reunited to Spain.
- 1865 Baez, *again*, pres. of Prov. Gov., but dep. Nov. 14.
- 1865. José Maria Cabral, pres.
- 1865. Baez, *again*, pres.
- 1866. Cabral, *again*, pres. Oct. 6.
- 1868. Baez, *again*, pres.
- 1873. Gen. Ganier d'Abin. Oct.
- 1876. Igucio Maria Gonzales.
- 1879. Gen. Cæsareo Guillermo, pres. May 10.
- 1880. Fernando Arturo de Merino, pres. July, to act from Sept. 10.
- 1882. Gen. Ulysses Heureaux, pres. July, to act from Sept. 4.
- 1884. Francisco G. Bellini, pres. July, to act from Sept.
- 1886. Heureaux, *again*, pres. July, to act from Sept.

CENTRAL AMERICA.

GUATEMALA. SAN SALVADOR. NICARAGUA. COSTA RICA. HONDURAS.

The large tract of country, now known as "Central America," was formerly part of the Spanish province of Guatemala. It declared its independence Sept. 21, 1821, separated from the Mexican Confederation July 1, 1823, and formed a federal republic until 1839–40, when it was divided into five separate states, viz.:—

Guatemala. San Salvador. Nicaragua. Costa Rica. Honduras.

Presidents of Guatemala.

* * * *

1847. Gen. Raphael Carrua; re-elect. 1851; elect. for life, 1854; *d.* 1865.

1865. Vincent Cerna. May 3.
1871. Miguel Garcia, prov. pres. Oct.
1873. J. Rufino Barrios. May 7.
1882. José Maria Orantes, prov. pres. July 1.
1883. J. Rufino Barrios, pres. Jan. 10.
1885. Manuel L. Barillas, pres. *ad int.* Apr. 10. Perm. pres. Mar. 16, 1886.

Presidents of San Salvador.

* * * *

* * Vasconcelos.
1852. Françisco Dueñas. Mar. 1.
* * José Maria San Martin.
1856. Raphael Campo.
1858. Miguel Santin del Castillo. Jan. 25.
1859. Gerard Barrios, charged with executive power Mar. 15.
1860. Barrios, elect. pres. for 6 years, Feb. 1.
1863. Dueñas, *again*, prov. pres., Nov.; pres. April 1865.
1871. Gen. St. Juan Gonzales, prov. pres. April; pres. Feb. 1, 1872.
1876. Andrew Valle. Feb.
1876. Rafael Zaldivar y Lazo. May, to act from July 22.
1885. Gen. Francisco Menendez. June 19.

Presidents of Nicaragua.

* * * *

* * Laureano Pineda.
1853. Gen. Fruto Chamorro. Feb. 26.
1855. Gen. Nanose, supreme director.
1856. Gen. Patricio, supreme director.
1857. Gen. Thomas Martinez. Nov. 15.
1867. Fernando Guzman. Mar. 1.
1871. Vicente Cuadra. Feb. 1.
1875. Pedro Joaquin Chamorro. Feb. 1.
1879. Joaquin Zavala. Mar. 3.
1883. Adan Cardenas. Mar. 4.
1885. Chamorro *again.* Mar.
1887. Evaristo Cavaza.

Presidents of Costa Rica.

* * * *

1853. Juan Raphaël Mora, May; re-elect. May 4, 1859.
1859-1860. Revolution took place in which the pres. Mora was expelled, Aug. 14, and José Maria Montealegra app. prov. pres.; he was aft. elect. pres. Feb. 7, 1860.
1863. Jésus Ximenes. April.
1866. José Maria Castro. May 8.
1872. Gen. Tomas Guardia. May 8.
1876. Aniceto Esquivel. May 8.
1876. Vicente Herrera. July 31.
1877. Sergio Camargo. May.
1878. Constitution susp. and Guardia app. prov. pres.
1882. Prospero Fernandez. Aug. 10.
1885. Gen. Bernardo Soto. Mar.; re-elect. May 11, 1886.

Presidents of Honduras.

* * * *

1852. Gen. Trinidad Cabañas.
1855. Gen. Santos Guardiola; assass. Jan. 11, 1862.
1862. Vittoriano Castellanos, vice-pres., succ.
1863. Castellanos *d.*, and José Francisco Montez. app. prov. pres.
1863. Gen. José Maria Medina, prov. pres.; elect pres. Feb. 1864.
1872. Celeo Arias, prov. pres., Aug.
* * P. Leiva, prov. pres.
1877. Marco Aurelio Soto. May 29.
1883. Gen. Luiz Bogran. Nov. 27.

COLOMBIA.

REPUBLIC OF COLOMBIA. UNITED STATES OF COLOMBIA. NEW GRANADA. VENEZUELA. ECUADOR. PANAMA.

These countries originally constituted the old Spanish colony of New Granada. They revolted against the mother country in 1811, and the war continued until 1824. In 1819 they formed themselves into the Republic of Colombia, but during the years 1829–31, dissensions arose, and they were ultimately divided into the three separate republics of

NEW GRANADA. VENEZUELA. ECUADOR.

NEW GRANADA. UNITED STATES OF COLOMBIA.

New Granada continued as a separate republic until 1863. In 1855 Panama seceded from it, but was reunited in 1863, the two countries then taking the title of the United States of Colombia.

PRESIDENTS OF NEW GRANADA.

* * * *

1845. Tomas Cipriano de Mosquera. April.
1853 Gen. José Maria y Obando. April.
1855. Manuel Maria Mallarino. April.
1856. Mariano Ospina. Elected Sept. 30, to act from April 1, 1857.
1861. Gen. Tomas Cipriano de Mosquera. July 20.

PRESIDENTS OF UNITED STATES OF COLOMBIA.

1863. Gen. T. C. de Mosquera above-named. Feb.
1864. Manuel Murillo Toro.
1866. Gen. Mosquera *again*; dep. 1867.
1867. Gen. Santos Acosta, prov. pres., May 23.
1868. Gen. Santiago Gutierrez. April 3.
1870. Gen. Eustorjio Salgar. April.
1872. Toro *again*. April.
1874. Santiago Perez. April.
1876. Aquileo Parra. April.
1878. Gen. Julian Trujillo. April.
1880. Gen. Rafael Nuñez. April.
1882. Francisco J. Zaldua. April.
1883. T. E. Otálora. April.
1884. Nuñez *again*. Aug. 11.

PANAMA.

Panama separated from New Granada by Act of Congress, Feb. 27, 1855.

PRESIDENTS OF PANAMA.

1855. Justo Arosemena, prov. chief.
1856. Gen. Bartolomeo Calvo, Oct. 11.
1858. José de Obaldia. Sept.
1862. Santiago de la Guardia; killed in an insurrection, Sept. 1862.
1862. Manuel Maria Diaz.
1863. New Federal Constitution of May 8 procl. June 15, 1863, and Panama became part of the United States of Colombia.

VENEZUELA.

Venezuela separated from the Republic of Colombia about 1829. (See *Republic of Colombia supra.*)

PRESIDENTS OF VENEZUELA.

1831. José Antonio Paëz.
   At the expiration of his term of office, Vargas was nominated his succ., but was opposed by José Tadeo Monagas. Disputes arose, to settle which Paëz was called in to restore order, and he remained in power first as vice-pres., and then as pres., until 1842.
1842. Carlos Soublette.
1846. Civil war broke out between the coloured population, headed by Paëz, and the European population, headed by Monagas, who was again set up as pres. Ultimately, in January 1848, Paëz was forced to fly, and on Aug. 14, 1849, was taken prisoner.

* * Gen. José Tadeo Monagas, pres. Re-elect. Jan 20, 1855.
1858. Gen. Julian Castro ; abd. July 1859, and Pedro Gual adm. the gov. until the arrival of the vice-pres., Manuel Felipe Tovar.
1860. Tovar, pres. April 10.
1861. Paëz *again*, pres., with power of dict. Sept. 8.
1863. Gen. Juan Chrysostôme Falcon; prov. pres. June 17 ; procl. pres. by Congress Mar. 18, and sw. June 8, 1865.
1868. Monagas *again*, prov. pres.
1869. Ruperto Monagas, prov. pres.
1870. Revolution under which Gen. Antonio Guzman Blanco proclaimed chief of Prov. Gov., April 27 ; confirmed by Congress as prov. pres. of the Repub., July 13 ; elected pres. Feb. 20, 1873.
1877. Gen. Francisco Linarez Alcantara. Feb. 27.
1879. Gen. Blanco *again*, prov. pres. May 12 ; pres. Mar. 20, 1880.
1884. Gen. Joaquin Crespo. May.
1886. Gen. Blanco *again*. Sept. 14.

ECUADOR.

Ecuador separated from the Republic of Colombia in 1830. (See *Republic of Colombia, supra.*)

Presidents of Ecuador.

1830. Gen. Juan José Flores.
1835. Vicente Rocafuerte.
1839. Gen. Flores *again*.
1845. Vicente Ramou Roca. Dec.
1851. Diego Noboa. Feb. ; dep.
1852. José Maria Urbina. Sept.
1856. Gen. Francisco Robles. Oct. ; abd.
1859. Aug. Pres. Robles dismissed, and two Prov. Gov. formed:
  1. Guayaquil under Gen. Guillernio Franco.
  2. Quito under Gabriel Garcia Moreno, Manuel Gomez de la Torre and José Maria Aviles.
1861. Apr. These two provinces re-united under presidency of Gabriel Garcia Moreno.
1865. Geronimo Carrion. Aug. 4.
1868. Xavier Espinosa. Jan. 23.
1869. Moreno *again*. Aug. ; assass. Aug. 14, 1875.
1875. Antonio Borrero. Dec. 28.
1877. Ignacio de Veintimilla. Jan. 17 ; confirmed May 1878.
1883. José Maria Placido Cadmaño. Oct. 23 ; to act from Feb. 27, 1884.

BRAZIL.

The French having seized on Portugal in 1807, the royal family of that kingdom embarked for Brazil at the close of the same year. Brazil was erected into an empire in Nov. 1825, when Dom Pedro took the title of emperor soon after his abdication of the throne of Portugal.

Emperors of Brazil.

1825. Pedro I. (of Portugal), Nov. 18; first emperor, abd. throne of Brazil, in favour of his infant son, April 7. 1831 ; *d.* Sept. 24, 1834.
1831. Pedro II., succ. on his father's abd., April 7 ; assumed the government July 23, 1840 ; crowned July 18, 1841.

PERU.

Peru revolted from Spain in 1821, and has since been a republic. Like most of its neighbours, it has experienced numerous revolutions and insurrections, which renders it difficult to give a strictly accurate list of its rulers.

RULERS OF PERU. PRESIDENTS AND DICTATORS.

1821. San Martin, Protector, procl. independence July 28; res. Sept. 20, 1822.
1823. José de la Riva Aguero, pres. Feb. 26.
1824. Bolivar, dict. Feb.
1824. Mariano Prado, pres. Nov. 28.
1827. Gen. Laman, pres. Aug. 24.
1829. Gen. Agustin Gamarra, pres. Aug. 31.
1834. Luis José Orbegoso, pres.
1835. Felipe Santiago Salaverry, pres.
1836. Andres Santa Cruz, pres.
1839. Gamarra, *again*, pres.
1841. Manuel Menendez, pres.
1845. Gen. Ramon Castilla, pres. April 19.
1851. Gen. José Rufino Echénique, pres.
1855. Castilla, *again*, pres. Jan.
1862. Marshal San Ramon, pres. May.
1863. Gen. Juan Antonio Pezet, pres. April 3.
1865. Pedro Diez Canseco, pres., *ad. int.* Nov.
1865. Gen. Mariano Ignacio Prado, dict. Nov. 28; prov. pres., Feb. 15, 1867; pres., Aug. 31, 1867.
1867. Luis La Puerta, pres. *ad. int.* Oct.
1868. Col. José Balta, pres. Aug. 2.
1872. Manuel Prado, pres. Aug. 2.
1876. Prado, *again*, pres. Aug. 2.
1879. Nicholas de Pierola, dict. Dec. 23.
1881. Francisco Garcia Calderon, prov. pres., Mar.; pres., July 10.
Pierola as dict. continued the war against Chili.
1883. Gen. Miguel Iglesias, dict. Oct. 20; prov. pres., April 1884.
1884. Andres Avelino Caceres, dict.; pres. April 1886.

BOLIVIA.

THIS republic was formerly part of Peru. It declared its independence August 6, 1824, and took the name of Bolivia August 11, 1825. The first congress was held May 25, 1826.

PRESIDENTS OF BOLIVIA.

1826. Gen. Suero.
1828. Santa Cruz.
1839. Gen. Velasco. Feb. 3.
1844. José Ballivian. Aug.
1850. Manuel Isidore Belzu. Aug.
1855. Gen. George Cordova. Aug. 15.
1857. José Maria Linares, prov. pres. Nov.
1861. Revolution, and Linares dep. Jan. 15.
1861. José Maria d'Acha, prov. pres., May; perm. pres., Aug. 1862.
1864. Gen. Mariano Melgarejo, prov. pres., Dec.; perm. pres., Feb. 1865.
1871. Col. Augustin Morales, prov. pres., Jan.; perm. pres., June 20.
1872. Thomas Frias. Dec.
1873. Lt. Col. Adolfo Ballivian. May 8.
1874. Frias, *again*. Feb. 14.
1877. Gen. Hilarion Daza. Nov.
1880. Narciso Campero. June 20.
1884. Gregorio Pacheco. Aug. 1.

ARGENTINE CONFEDERATION OR ARGENTINE REPUBLIC. BUENOS AYRES.

THIS confederation consists of the following states or provinces, besides some Indian territories or frontier districts:—

Buenos Ayres.
Entre Rios.
Corrientes.
Santa Fé.
Mendoza.
San Juan.
Catamarca.
La Rioja.
Cordova.
San Luis.
Santiago.
Tucuman.
Jujuy.
Salta.

These states were formerly part of Peru. They were separated in 1778, and with others now forming the republics of Bolivia, Paraguay, and Uruguay, were called the Rio de la Plata. They still remained subject to Spain, but declared their independence in 1816.

Presidents of Argentine Republic.

1816. Payridon. Mar. 25.
Separation from Spain formally declared July 9, but the independence of the states was not recognised by Spain till 1842.

* * *

1825. National constitution for the federal states decreed.

* * *

* * Gen. Juan Manuel de Rosas.
1840. Gen. de Rosas re-elected. Mar. 5.
1852. Prov. Gov. established, Feb. 5, and Vincent Lopez appointed Prov. Gov.; Gen. Justo José Urquiza elect. Prov. Director, May 20; Dr. Alsina elected gov. and capt.-gen., Oct. 30. He retired, and Gen. Pinto elected Prov. Gov. in his place, Dec. 6.
1853. Buenos Ayres secedes and becomes an independent state. Oct 12.
1853. Gen. Justo José d'Urquiza. Nov. 20.
1859. Buenos Ayres re-united to the Argentine Republic. Nov. 10.
1860. Santiago Derqui. Feb. 8.
1861. Victory of Gen. Mitre at Pavon, in consequence of which Derqui resigned, Sept. 17; Prov. Gov. under Gen. Bartholomew Mitre.
1862. Gen. Mitre elected perm. pres. Oct. 12.
1868. Col. Dominique Faustino Sarmiento. Oct. 12.
1874. Nicolas Avellaneda. Oct. 12.
1880. Gen. Julio A. Roca. Oct. 12.
1886. Miguel Juarez Celman. Oct. 12.

BUENOS AYRES.

Buenos Ayres separated from the Argentine Republic, Oct. 12, 1853, and was re-united thereto, Nov. 10, 1859.

Governors or Presidents.

1853. Pastor Obligado. Oct. 12.
1857. Valentine Alsina. May.
1860. Gen. Bartholomew Mitre. May 1.
1859. Re-united to Argentine Republic by peace of S. José de Floris, Nov. 10, 1859, and Act of Union, June 6, 1860.

PARAGUAY.

Paraguay revolted from Spain in 1811, and declared itself an independent state.

Dictators and Presidents of Paraguay.

Dictators.

1814. José Gaspar Rodriguez Francia, elect. Nom. for life, 1817.
1840. Vibal succ. Francia.
1844. Carlos Antonio Lopez elect.
1862. Francisco Solano Lopez, son, Sept.; went to war with Uruguay, Brazil, and the Argentine Republic and was killed in battle, Mar. 1, 1870.
1869. Prov. Gov. composed of C. Loizaga, Cyril Antonio Rivarola, and J. Diaz de Bedoya, Aug. 15.
1870. Treaty of peace between (1) Brazil and the Argentine Republic, and (2) Paraguay, June 20, under which Rivarola was app. prov. pres.
1870. Paraguay becomes a constitutional republic.

Presidents.

1871. Salvador Jovellanos. Dec. 12.
1874. Juan Baptista Gill. Nov. 25.
1877. Higinio Uriarte. April 12.
1878. Candido Bareiro. Nov. 25.
1880. Gen. Bernardino Caballero, Sept. 14; re-elect. Nov. 1882.
1886. Gen. Escobar. Sept. 25.

URUGUAY.

This republic was formerly a part of Buenos Ayres. It declared its independence in 1825, and was recognised as a separate republic by the treaty of Montevideo, signed between Brazil and Buenos Ayres, Aug. 27, and ratified Oct. 4, 1828.

Presidents of Uruguay.

1830. Fructuoso Rivera. Oct. 22.
1835. Manuel Oribe. Mar. 1.
1838. Rivera *again*. Oct. 21.

* * *

* * Joaquim Suarez.
1852. Juan Francisco Giró. Mar. 1.
1854. Col. Venancio Florez. Mar. 12.
1855. Manuel Basilico Bustamente. Oct.
1856. Gabriel Antonio Pereira. Mar. 1.
1860. Bernardo Prudencio Berro. Mar. 1.
1864. Athanase Cruz Aguirre. Mar. 1.
1865. Gen. Venancio Florès, prov. gov. Feb.
1866. Francisco Antonio Vidal.
1868. Col. Lorenzo Battle. Mar. 1.
* * Sarmiento.
1872. Tomas Gomensoro. Mar. 1.
1873. José Ellauri. Mar. 1.
1875. Pedro Varela. Mar. 15.
1876. Col. L. Latorre. Mar. 11.
1880. Vidal *again*. Mar. 17.
1882. Gen. Maximo Santos. Mar. 1
1886. Maximo Tagès. Nov. 19.

CHILI.

This republic declared its independence from Spain, Sept. 18, 1810, but, a long war ensuing, its actual independence dates from Feb. 12, 1817. New constitutions were promulgated in 1828 by General Pinto, and in May 1833, by General Prieto.

Directors and Presidents of Chili.

1817. Gen. Demetrius O'Higgins. Res. 1823.

1823. The government was administered by a prov. triumvirate until Gen. Freire was chosen director. He res. 1826.

1826–1830. During these years the government was administered by six different directors, besides a second provisional triumvirate.

1831. Gen. Prieto, who became pres. under constitution of May 25, 1833.

Presidents.

1833. Gen. Prieto, above named.
1841. Gen. Manuel Bulnès. Sept.
1851. Manuel Montt. Sept. 18.
1861. José Joaquim Perez. Sept. 7.
1871. Frederico Errazuriz. Sept. 18.
1876. Anibal Pinto. Sept. 18.
1881. Domingo Santa Maria. Sept. 18.
1886. José Manuel Balmaceda. Sept. 18.

HAWAIIAN OR SANDWICH ISLANDS.

Kings and Queens.

* * Kamehameha I., *d.* 1819.
1819. Kamehameha II., son, *d.* in England, with his queen, July 1824.
1824. Kamehameha III.
1854. Kamehameha IV.
1863. Kamehameha V., brother, Nov.; Dec. 11.
1873. Lunalilo I. (Q), Jan. 8; *d.* Feb. 3 1874.
1874. Kalakaua. Feb. 12.

PART II. DIPLOMATIC.

AMBASSADORS, ENVOYS EXTRAORDINARY, MINISTERS PLENIPOTENTIARY, &c., FROM GREAT BRITAIN AND THE UNITED KINGDOM OF GREAT BRITAIN AND IRELAND TO FOREIGN STATES.

From the accession of George III., 1760.

TO FRANCE.

1761. Hans Stanley, ch. d'a.
1762. John, D. of Bedford, amb. Sept. 4.
1763. Fras. Seymour, E. of Hertford, amb.
1765. Chas., D. of Richmond, amb.
1766. Wm. Hy. Nassau, E. of Rochford, amb. July 2.
1768. Simon Harcourt, E. Harcourt, amb.
1772. David Murray, visc. Stormont, aft. E. of Mansfield, amb. Sept. 9.
1783. Fras. Godolphin Osborne, M. of Carmarthen, amb. Feb. 10.
— Geo. Montagu, D. of Manchester, amb. Apr. 9.
— John Frederick Sackville, D. of Dorset, amb.
1784. Daniel Hailes, min. plen., *ad int.* Apr. 28.
1785. Wm. Eden, aft. ld. Auckland, env. ext. and plen. for commercial affairs. Dec. 9.
1790. Geo. Granville, E. Gower, amb. June 11. Recalled Sept. 1792.
The war interrupted the diplomatic relations between the two countries.
1796. Jas., ld., aft. E. of Malmesbury, amb. ext. and min. plen. for negotiating a treaty of peace. Oct. 13.
1797. Jas., ld. Malmesbury, *again*, for negotiating a peace with the plens. of the French republic at Lisle. June 30.
1801. Chas., M. Cornwallis, plen. at the congress held at Amiens. Oct. 29.
— Fras. James Jackson, min. plen. Dec. 2.
1802. Anth. Merry, min. plen. Apr. 1.
— Chas., ld., aft. visc. and E. Whitworth, amb. June 18, G. Left Paris, May 19, 1803.
The war with Napoleon I. again interrupted the diplomatic relations between the two countries.
1806. Fras. Seymour, E. of Yarmouth, and James, E. of Lauderdale, commrs. for negotiating a peace with France. Aug. 1.
1814. Sir Chas. Stuart, aft. ld. Stuart de Rothesay, env. ext. and min. plen. *ad int.* June 4.

— Chas. Bagot, aft. Sir C., min. plen. July 11.
— Arthur, D. of Wellington, amb. Aug. 8.
1815. Lord Fitzroy Jas. Hy. Somerset, min. plen. Jan. 18.
— Sir Chas. Stuart, *again*, amb., *ad int.* Mar. 26.
1824. Granville, visc., aft. E. Granville, sp. miss. to congratulate Charles X. on his accession to the throne. Oct. 7.
— Hon. Algernon Percy, min. plen., *ad int.* Oct. 12.
— Granville, visc. Granville, *again*, amb. Nov. 3
1825. Hugh, D. of Northumberland, sp. embassy; coronation of Charles X. Apr. 30.
1828. Lord Stuart de Rothesay, amb. July 1.
1830. Visc. Granville, *again*, amb. Dec. 8.
1832. Hamilton Chas. Jas. Hamilton, min. plen., *ad int.* Mar. 23.
1833. Arthur Aston, aft. Sir A., min. plen., *ad int.* Apr. 19.
1835. Hy., ld. Cowley, amb. Mar. 13.
— Granville, E., late visc. Granville, amb. Mar. 29.
1837. Arthur Aston, *again*; min. plen., *ad int.* Aug. 25. Permanent July 17, 1838.
1839. Hy. Lytton Bulwer, aft. Sir H. and ld. Dalling and Bulwer, min. plen., *ad int.* July 29.
1841. Lord Cowley, *again*, amb. Oct. 16.
1845. Lord Wm. Hervey, min. plen., *ad int.* July 29.
1846. Constantine Hy., M. of Normanby, amb. Aug. 18.
1848. M. of Normanby, *continued*; sp. and temporary miss. to the French National Assembly. Aug. 18.
1849. M. of Normanby, *continued*, amb. Jan. 31.
1852. Hy Rd. Chas., ld., aft. E. Cowley, amb., ext. and plen. to the French Republic. Feb. 3.
1856. Geo. Wm. Frederick, E. of Clarendon, plen. to Congress at termination of war with Russia. Feb.
1860. Hon. Wm. G. Grey, ch. d'a., *ad int.* Jan. 2.*
1866. Hon. Julian Hy. Chas. Fane, min. plen., *ad int.**
1867. Richd. Bickerton Pemell, ld., aft. visc. Lyons, amb., ext. and plen. July 6.
1869. Hon. Lionel Sackville West, min. plen., *ad int.**
1871. Ld. Lyons, *again*, amb., ext. and plen. to French Republic. Feb. 18.
1871. Hon. L. S. West, *again*, min. plen., *ad int.* Sept. 15.*
1873. Edwd. Robt., ld. aft. E. Lytton, min. plen., *ad int.* Apr. 10.*
1875. Fras. Ottiwell Adams, aft. sir F., min. plen., *ad int.* Mar. 23.*
1882. Hon. Fras. Richd. Plunket, min. plen., *ad int.* Mar. 11.*
1884. Sir Jno. Walsham, bart., min. plen., *ad int.* July 31.*
1886. Edwin Hy. Egerton, min. plen., *ad int.* Mar. 30.*
1887. Robt., Earl Lytton, G.C.B., G.C.S.I., amb., ex. and plen. Nov. 1.

* During temporary absence of the ambassador.

TO SWISS CONFEDERATION.

* * Arthur Villettes, min.
1765. Wm. Norton, min. Jan. 1.
* * Col. Braun, ch. d'a.
1792. Lord Rob. Stephen Fitzgerald, min. plen. May 12.
1795. Wm. Wickham, min. plen. July 11.
1798. James Talbot, min., *ad int.* Jan. 22.
1814. Stratford Canning, aft. Sir S., and visc. Stratford de Redcliffe, env. ext. and min. plen. June 14, **G.**
1820. Edw. Cromwell Disbrowe, aft. sir E., ch. d'a., *ad int.* June 12.
1822. Hy. Watkin Williams Wynn, aft. sir H., env. ext. and min. plen. Feb. 12.
1823. Chas. Rd. Vaughan, aft. sir C., min. plen. Feb. 28.
1825. Hon. Algernon Percy, min. plen. Oct. 10.
1832. David Rd. Morier, min. plen. June 21.
1847. Gilbert, E. of Minto; ext. miss. to the Italian States, Sardinia, Sicily, and Switzerland. Sept. 14.
— Sir Stratford Canning, *again*, ext. miss. to Belgium, Germany, Greece, and Switzerland. Nov. 26.
1848. Hy. Rd. Chas., ld., aft. E. Cowley, min. plen. Feb. 29.
1849. Sir Edmund Lyons, min. plen. Feb. 9.
1851. Arthur Chas. Magenis, aft. sir A., min. plen. Jan. 27.
1852. Andrew Buchanan, aft. Sir A., min. plen. Feb. 12.
1853. Hon. Chas. Aug. Murray, aft. sir C., min. plen. Feb. 9.

1854. Geo. Jno. Robt. Gordon, min. plen. Sept. 19.
1858. Capt. Hon. Edwd. Alfred Jno. Harris, R.N., min. plen. Mar. 31.
1867. Jno. Savile Lumley, env. ext. and min. plen. Aug. 22.
1868. Alfred Guthrie Graham Bonar, env. ext. and min. plen. Oct. 19.
1874. Edwin Corbett, min. res. May 23.
1878. Sir Horace Rumbold, bt., min. res. Jan. 17.
1879. Hon. Hussey Crespigny Vivian, C.B., min. res. Oct. 10; env. ext. and min. plen. Mar. 1, 1881.
1881. Fras. Ottiwell Adams, C.B., aft. sir F., K.C.M.G., env. ext. and min. plen. July 8.

TO THE MODERN KINGDOM OF ITALY.

For Ambassadors, &c., to the various states composing the modern kingdom of Italy prior to the formation of that kingdom, see under the names of those states.

1861. Sir Jas. Hudson, env. ext. and min. plen.
1863. Hon. Hy. Geo. Elliot, env. ext. and min. plen. Sept. 12.
1867. Sir Augs. Berkeley Paget, K.C.B., env. ext. and min. plen. July 6; amb., ext. and min. plen. Mar. 24, 1876.
1883. Sir Jno. Savile-Lumley, K.C.B., aft. G.C.B., and subseq. Sir Jno. Savile, only; amb. ext. and plen. Aug. 26.

TO SARDINIA.

* * Hon. Jas. Stuart Mackenzie, env. ext.
1761. Geo. Pitt, aft. ld. Rivers, env. ext.
1768. Sir Wm. Lynch, env. ext. Oct. 1.
1779. John, visc. Mountstuart, env. ext. and plen. Aug. 16.
1783. Hon. John Trevor, env. ext. Feb. 22; min. plen., June 16, 1789.
1799. Thos. Jackson, min. plen. Apr. 13.
1807. Hon. Wm. Hill, env. ext. and min. plen. Dec. 9.
1824. Aug. John Foster, aft. knt., env. ext. and min. plen. Sept. 10, **G.**
1840. Hon. Ralph Abercromby, env. ext. and min. plen. May 30.
1847. Gilbert, E. of Minto, ext. miss. to Italy, Sardinia, Sicily, and Switzerland. Sept. 14.
Hon. Ralph Abercromby, remaining minister to Sardinia.
1852. Jas. Hudson, env. ext. and min. plen. Jan. 19, **G.**

Sardinia now forms part of the kingdom of Italy. *See Italy.*

TO NAPLES AND THE TWO SICILIES.

* * Sir Jas. Gray, bt., env. ext.
1764. Wm. Hamilton, aft. sir W., env. ext.
1800. Hon. sir Arthur Paget, env. ext. and min. plen. Jan. 17.
1801. Wm. Drummond, env. ext. Aug. 4.
1803. Hugh Elliot, env. ext. and min. plen. Jan. 29.
1806. Gen. Hy. Edwd. Fox, env. ext. and min. plen. (military). May 29.
— Wm. Drummond, *again*, env. ext. and min. plen. Oct. 3.
1809. Wm. Pitt, ld., aft. E. Amherst, env. ext. and min. plen. Feb. 1.
1811. Ld. Wm. Cavendish Bentinck, env. ext. and min. plen. Feb. 15, **G.**
1812. Hon. Fredk. Jas. Lamb, aft. sir F. and ld. Beauvale, and succ. as visc. Melbourne, min. plen., *ad int.* May 18.

1814. Wm. A'Court, aft. sir W. and ld. Heytesbury, env. ext. and min. plen. Oct. 1, **G.**

1822. Wm. Rd. Hamilton, env. ext. and min. plen. Feb. 12.

1824. Wm. Noel Hill, env. ext. and min. plen. Sept. 14.

1825. John, ld. Burghersh, succ. as E. of Westmoreland; sp. miss. on the accession of the king (Francis I.), as king of the Two Sicilies. Feb. 23.

1830. John, ld. Burghersh, *again;* env. ext. and min. plen. Nov. 16. *Not sent.*

1832. John, ld., aft. visc. Ponsonby, env. ext. and min. plen. June 8.

— Hon. Wm. Temple, aft. sir W., env. ext. and min. plen. Nov. 27, (?) 1833.

1847. Gilbert, E. of Minto; ext. miss. to Italy, Sardinia, Sicily, and Switzerland. Dec. 17; the hon. Wm. Temple, remaining minister to the Two Sicilies.

1856. Geo. Glyn Petre, ch. d'a. July 28. Diplomatic relations suspended Oct. 1856 to June 1859, in consequence of the king's tyrannical government.

1859. Hon. Hy. Geo. Elliot, aft. Sir H.; sp. miss. to Francis II. on his accession. June 1.

1859. Sir Arthur Chas. Magenis, K.C.B. June 6; env. ext. and min. plen. *Not sent.*

1859. Hon. Hy. Geo. Elliot, *again*, env., ext. and min. plen. July 4 until Nov. 1860.

The Two Sicilies now form part of the kingdom of Italy. *See Italy.*

TO TUSCANY, PARMA, MODENA, AND LUCCA.

UNLESS otherwise stated the mission was to Tuscany only.

* * Sir Horace Mann, bt., env. ext.; *d.* Nov. 1786, having been forty-six years minister at this court.

1787. Wm. Fawkener, env. ext. *pro tem.* April 27.

1787. John Aug., ld. Hervey, env. ext. Aug. 4. Min. plen. July 22, 1791.

1794. Hon. Wm. Fredk. Wyndham, env. ext. Jan. 25. Min. plen., Feb. 8, 1800.

1814. John, ld. Burghersh, aft. E. of Westmoreland, env. ext. and min. plen. Aug. 14.

1818. The same, in the same character, to Parma, and Modena. Feb. 14.

— The same, in the same character, to Lucca, Mar. 5.

1830. Ld. Geo. Hamilton Seymour, aft. sir G., min. res. Nov. 3.

— John, ld. Burghersh, min. plen. to Parma, &c. Nov. 16. *Not sent.*

1831. Sir Geo. Hamilton Seymour, min. res. to Parma, Lucca, and Modena. June 13.

1835. Hon. Ralph Abercromby, min. res. to Tuscany, Parma, and Lucca. Dec. 26.

1839. Hon. Hy. Edw. Fox, aft. ld. Holland, min. plen. to Tuscany, Parma, and Lucca. Jan. 2.

1841. Hy. Edw., ld. Holland, min. plen. to Modena. May 14.

1846. Sir Geo. Baillie Hamilton, min. plen. to Tuscany, Parma, Modena, and Lucca. May 23.

1847. Gilbert, E. of Minto; ext. miss. to the Italian States, Sardinia, Sicily, and Switzerland. Sept. 14.

— Sir Geo. Baillie Hamilton; *d.* at Florence while min. plen. in Sept. 1850.

1850. Hon. Peter Campbell Scarlett, ch. d'a.

— Rd. Lalor Sheil, min. plen., ch. d'a. Oct. 24.

1851. Jas. Hudson, C.B., env. ext. and min. plen. Aug. 29, **G.**

1852. Sir Hy. Lytton Bulwer, G.C.B., aft. ld. Dalling and Bulwer, env. ext. and min. plen. Jan. 19, **G.**

1854. Constantine Hy., M. of Normanby, K.G., env. ext. and min. plen. Dec. 16, **G.**

1858. Hon. Hy. Geo. Howard, env. ext. and min. plen. Mar. 31, **G.**

1858. Hon. Rd. Bickerton Pemell Lyons, aft. ld. and visc. Lyons, env. ext. and min. plen. June 16, **G.**

1858. Hon. Peter Campbell Scarlett, C.B., *again*, env. ext. and min. plen. Dec. 13, **G.**

Tuscany now forms part of the Kingdom of Italy. *See Italy.*

TO VENICE.

* * John Murray, resident.
1761. Chas. Compton, E. of Northampton, amb. ext. and min. plen.
1762. John Murray, resident.
1765. Jas. Wright, aft. sir J., bt., resident.
1773. John Strange, resident. Oct. 19.
1788. Robt. Ritchie, ch. d'a.
1789. Sir Fras. Vincent, bt., resident. Sept. 26; *d.* Aug. 1791.
1791. Wm. Lindsay, resident. Nov. 3.
1793. Fras. Drake, resident. Jan. 19.
— Sir Rd. Worsley, bt., resident July 27.

The republic of the Venetian State was wholly overthrown in 1797 The emperor of Germany took possession of these dominions in that year; it being settled by a private article in the treaty of Campo Formio, that he accepted them in compensation for the Netherlands.

Venice now forms part of the kingdom of Italy. *See Italy.*

TO GERMANY AND AUSTRIA.

THE various states constituting geographical Germany have been from time to time united in various combinations for diplomatic purposes. Hence there is some difficulty in arranging the ambassadors under each separate state. Where an ambassador is accredited to one state where it was the custom to have a separate diplomatic representative, he will be found under that state, but where he is accredited to several states or to one of the confederations of German states, or was sent, as an exception, to one particular state generally associated with others, he should be searched for under the heading "*German States and Confederations.*"

The name of each separate state mentioned in the credentials will be found both in the Table of Contents and in the Index.

TO THE EMPERORS OF GERMANY PRIOR TO 1804.

SEE "AUSTRIA," AND "GERMAN STATES AND CONFEDERATIONS."

TO THE EMPIRE OF GERMANY AND THE KINGDOM OF PRUSSIA SINCE 1871.

1871. Lord Odo Wm. Leopold Russell, amb. ext. and plen. to emp. of Germany and K. of Prussia. Oct. 16.
1878. Benj. E. of Beaconsfield, Robt. Arthur Talbot Gascoigne, M. of Salisbury, and ld. Odo Wm. Loftus Russell, plens. to Congress at close of Russo-Turkish War June 3.
1884. Sir Edw. Baldwin Malet, K.C.B., amb ext. and plen. to emp. of Germany and K. of Prussia. Sept. 20.
1885. Garnet Jos., visc. Wolseley, sp miss. of congratulation. Dec. 30

TO AUSTRIA.

DOWN to 1804 the ambassadors to Austria were accredited to the sovereigns by their title of

EMPERORS OF GERMANY.

1763. David Murray, visc. Stormont, aft. E. of Mansfield, amb. May 7.
1772. Sir Robert Murray Keith, amb Aug. 14.

1790. Thomas, E. of Elgin, amb. ext. to congratulate Leopold II. on his accession to the throne.
1792. Thomas, E. of Elgin, amb. to the emp. Francis II. Aug. 18.
1793. Sir Morton Eden, aft. ld. Henley, env. ext. and min. plen.
1794. George John, E. Spencer, amb. ext. on particular affairs.
1799. Gilbert, ld. Minto, env. ext. and min. plen. July 2.
1801. Hon. Arthur Paget. aft. sir A., env. ext. and min. plen. Aug. 21.

In 1804, the emperor Francis II. became emperor of Austria only, and the ambassadors were thenceforward accredited to him and his successors as

Emperors of Austria.

1805. Charles, E. of Harrington, ext. min. Nov. 28.
1806. Robt. Adair, aft. sir R., env. ext. and min. plen. May 7.
1807. Geo. Aug., E. of Pembroke and Montgomery, amb. May 14.
1809. Benj. Bathurst, ext. miss. Feb. 14.
1813. Geo. Hamilton Gordon, E. of Aberdeen, amb. July 29.
— Hon. Fredk. Jas. Lamb, aft. sir F. and lord Beauvale, succ. as visc. Melbourne, min. plen., *ad. int.* Aug. 6.
1814. Chas. Wm. ld. Stewart, aft. succ. as M. of Londonderry, amb.
— Robt., visc. Castlereagh, aft. M. of Londonderry, Rd. E. of Clancarty, Wm., E. Cathcart, and Chas. Wm., ld. Stewart, plens. to the congress at Vienna. Aug. 11.
1815. Arthur, D. of Wellington, first plen. to the congress at Vienna. Jan. 18.
— Hon. Robt. Gordon, aft. sir R., min. plen. *ad. int.* Mar. 27.
1817. The same, *ad. int.* June 24.
1818. Robt., visc. Castlereagh, and Arthur, D. of Wellington, plens. to the conference at Aix-la-Chapelle. Aug. 18.
1821. Hon. Robt. Gordon, *again*, min. plen. *ad int.* Jan. 19.
— Arthur, D. of Wellington, plen. to the conference at Vienna. Sept. 9.
1822. The same, ext. miss.; congress at Verona. Sept. 14.
1823. Sir Hy. Wellesley, aft. ld. Cowley, amb. Feb. 3.
1831. Hon. Fras. Reginald Forbes, min. plen., *ad. int.* April 22.
— Hon. sir Fredk. Jas. Lamb, *again*, amb. May 13.
1832. John Geo. ld., aft. E. of Durham, ext. miss. to Austria, Prussia, and Russia. Sept. 14.
1834. Hon. Wm. Thos. Horner Fox-Strangways, min. plen. *ad. int.* Oct. 8.
1835. Sir Chas. Bagot, sp. miss. April 7.
— Hon. Hy. Edw. Fox, aft. ld. Holland, min. plen., *ad. int.* July 2.
1838. John Ralph Milbanke, aft. sir J. R. M. Huskisson, bt., min. plen. *ad. int.* Nov. 7.
1841. Sir Robt. Gordon, amb. Oct. 16.
1845. Arthur Chas. Magenis, aft. sir A., min. plen., *ad. int.* June 18.
1846. John, visc. Ponsonby, amb. Aug. 10.
1849. A. C. Magenis, *again*, min. plen., *ad. int.* April 20.
1851. John, E. of Westmoreland, env. ext. and min. plen. Jan. 27.
1855. Sir Geo. Hamilton Seymour, G.C.B., env. ext. and min. plen. Nov. 23.
1855. Ld. John Russell, aft. E. Russell, sp. miss. Feb. 11.
1858. Ld. Aug. Wm. Fredk. Spencer Loftus, env. ext. and min. plen. March 31.
1859. Hy. Rd. Chas., E. Cowley, sp. miss. Feb. 23.
1860. John Arthur Douglas, ld. Bloomfield, G.C.B., amb. ext. and plen. Nov. 22.
1871. Sir Andw. Buchanan, G.C.B., amb. ext. and plen. Oct. 16.
1877. Sir Hy. Geo. Elliot, G.C.B., amb. ext. and min. plen. Dec. 31.
1884. Sir Aug. Berkeley Paget, G.C.B., amb. ext. and plen. Jan. 1.

TO PRUSSIA.

1765. And. Mitchell, aft. sir A., env. ext. Dec. 13.
1771. Robt. Gunning, aft. sir R., bt. env. ext. Feb. 13.

1772. Jas. Harris, aft. Sir J., ld. and E. of Malmesbury, env. ext. Jan. 3.
1776. Hugh Elliot, env. ext. Oct. 13.
1782. Geo. Jas., E. of Cholmondeley, env. ext. June 14.
— Sir John Stepney, bt., env. ext. Sept. 21.
1784. John, visc. Dalrymple, aft. E. of Stair, env. ext.
1788. Jos. Ewart, env. ext. Aug. 5.
1791. Sir Morton Eden, aft. ld. Henley, env. ext. and min. plen. Nov. 3.
1793. James, ld. Malmesbury, *again*, env. ext. and min. plen.
1795. Lord H. John Spencer, env. ext. and min. plen.; *d.* July, 1795.
— Thos., E. of Elgin, env. ext. and min. plen. Aug. 15.
1800. John Joshua, E. of Carysfort, env. ext. and min. plen. July 12.
1802. Fras. Jas. Jackson, env. ext. and min. plen. Oct. 24.
1805. Edwd. Thornton, aft. sir E., min. plen. to Denmark, the Hanse Towns, Lower Saxony, Mecklenburg-Schwerin, and Mecklenburg-Strelitz. May 4.
— Dudley, ld., aft. E. of Harrowby; ext. miss. to Prussia and Russia. Oct. 25.
1806. Ld. Granville Leveson Gower, aft. E. Granville, ext. miss. Jan. 8.
— Chas., E. of Harrington, ext. miss. Jan. 9.
— Geo. Howard, visc. Morpeth, succ. as E. of Carlisle. Sept. 29.
— John Hely, lord Hutchinson, succ. as E. of Donoughmore. Nov. 18.
1807. John Hookham Frere, env. ext. and min. plen. June 17.
— Benj. Garlike, env. ext. and min. plen, *ad int.* July 17.
1813. Hon. sir Chas. Wm. Stewart, aft. ld. Stewart, and M. of Londonderry, env. ext. and min. plen. Apr. 7.
— Robt., visc. Castlereagh, aft. M. of Londonderry, ext. miss., Dec 27.
1815. Geo. Hy. Rose, aft. sir G., env. ext and min. plen. Sept. 10.
1822. Arthur, D. of Wellington, ext. miss to the congress at Verona. Sept 14.
1823. Rd. Meade, E. of Clanwilliam, env ext. and min. plen. Feb. 3.
1827. Sir Brook Taylor, env. ext. and min plen. Dec. 28.
1830. Geo. Wm. Chad, env. ext. and min plen. Sept. 20.
1832. Gilbert, E. of Minto, env. ex. and min. plen. Aug. 22.
— John Geo., ld. Durham, aft. E. of Durham; ext. miss. to Austria Prussia, and Russia. Sept. 14.
1834. Sir Geo. Shee, bt., env. ext. and min. plen. Oct. 31.
1835. Sir Robt. Adair, sp. miss. July 28.
— Lord Geo. Wm. Russell, env. ext and min. plen. Nov. 24.
1841. John, lord Burghersh, aft. E. of Westmoreland, env. ext. and min. plen. Oct. 16.
1846. Hy. Fras. Howard, ch. d'a. *ad int.* May 28.
1851. Jno. Arthur Douglas, ld. Bloomfield, env. ext. and min. plen. Apr. 28.
1860. Ld. Aug. Wm. Fredk. Spencer Loftus, env. ext. and min. plen. Nov. 22.
1861. Jno., M. of Breadalbane, sp. miss. Feb. 7.
1861. Geo. Wm. Fredk., E. of Clarendon, K.G., K.C.B., amb. ext. to K. of Prussia on coronation. Oct. 1.
1862. Sir And. Buchanan, K.C.B., amb. ext. and plen. Oct. 28.
1864. Francis, ld. Napier, K.T., amb. ext. and plen. Sept. 15.
1866. Ld. A. W. F. S. Loftus, K.C.B., *again*, amb. ext. and plen. Jan. 19. Accredited to N. Germ. Confed., Feb. 24, 1868.

See "German States and Confederations."

The North German Confederation was dissolved in 1871, and the modern empire of Germany was then founded, the king of Prussia being chosen emperor. Since that time the ambassadors have been accredited "to the emperor of Germany and king of Prussia." *See Empire of Germany.*

TO WURTEMBURG, BADEN, AND HESSE-DARMSTADT

SEE ALSO "GERMAN STATES AND CONFEDERATIONS."

TO WURTEMBURG.

1803. John Spencer Smith, env. ext. to the elector of Wurtemburg. June 25, **G.**

The electorate of Wurtemburg was, by the provisions of the treaty of Presburg, erected into a kingdom, and the elector, Frederick II., was procl. king, Jan. 1, 1806

14. Brook Taylor, aft. sir B., env. ext. and min. plen. July 11.

20. Alex. Cockburn, env. ext. and min. plen. Mar. 6.

23. Hy. Watkin Williams Wynn, aft. sir H., bt., env. ext. and min. plen. Feb. 8, **G.**

24. David Montagu, lord Erskine, env. ext. and min. plen. Sept. 10, **G.**

1828. Edwd. Cromwell Disbrowe, aft. sir E., env. ext. and min. plen. Jan. 4, **G.**

1833. Lord Wm. Russell, min. plen. Nov. 26.

1835. Sir Geo. Shee, bt., env. ext. and min. plen. Nov. 24.

For subsequent Ambassadors see below.

To Wurtemburg and Baden.

41. Sir Geo. Shee, bt., env. ext. and min. plen. to Wurtemburg, made also min. plen. to Baden. June 29.

44. Sir Alex. Malet, bt., env. ext. and min. plen. Sept. 17.

1852. Arthur Chas. Magenis, aft. sir A., env. ext. and min. plen. Feb. 12.

1854. Hon, Geo. Sulyarde Stafford Jerningham, env. ext. and min. plen. May 20.

1859. Geo. Jno. Robt. Gordon, env. ext. and min. plen. Nov. 11, **G.**

To Wurtemburg only.

871. Robt. Burnett David Morier, C.B., aft. sir R., ch. d'a. July 18, **G.**

872. Geo. Glynn Petre, ch. d'a. Feb. 13, **G.**

1881. Gerard Fras. Gould, C.B., min. res. Apr. 16, **G.**

1883. Sir Hy. Page Turner Barron, bt., C.M.G., min. res. Oct. 1, **G.**

To Baden and Hesse-Darmstadt.

871. Evan Montagu Baillie, ch. d'a. Jly. 18.

873. Fras. Clare Ford, aft. sir F., ch. d'a. Oct. 11.

1878. Hon. Wm. Nassau Jocelyn, ch. d'a. Mar. 27.

TO BAVARIA.

For Ambassadors prior to 1814, see "German States and Confederations."

Diplomatic relations between England and the king of Bavaria were established at the close of the war in 1814.

1814. Geo. Hy. Rose, aft. sir G., env. ext. and min. plen. Jan. 31.

1815. Hon. Fredk. Jas. Lamb, aft. sir F., and lord Beauvale; succ. as visc. Melbourne, env. ext. and min. plen. July 25, **G.**

1820. Brook Taylor, aft. sir B., env. ext. and min. plen. Mar. 6.

1828. David Montagu, lord Erskine, env. ext. and min. plen. Jan. 4.

1843. John Ralph Milbanke, aft. sir J. R. M. Huskisson, bt., env. ext. and min. plen. Nov. 24.

1862. Lord Aug. Wm. Freak Spencer Loftus, K.C.B., env. ext. and min. plen. Oct. 28.

1866. Sir Hy. Fras. Howard, K.C.B., env. ext. and min. plen. Jan. 19.

1872. Robt. Burnett David Morier, C.B., aft. sir R., ch. d'a. Jan. 30.

1876. Maj.-Gen. Edwd. Stanton, C.B., aft. sir E., ch. d'a. May 10.

1882. Hugh Guion Macdonell, ch. d'a. Feb. 23.

1885. Victor Arthur Wellington Drummond, ch. d'a. Nov. 5.

TO HANOVER.

Hanover was separated from the crown of Great Britain by th demise of his Britannic Majesty, William IV., June 20, 1837, an Ernest, duke of Cumberland, ascended the throne.

1838. Hon. John Duncan Bligh, env. ext. and min. plen. May 2.
1857. Sir Jno. Fiennes Twistleton Crampton, bt., K.C.B., env. ext. and min. plen. Mar. 2.
1858. Geo. Jno. Robt. Gordon, env. ext. and min. plen. Mar. 31.
1859. Hy. Fras. Howard, env. ext. ar min. plen. Nov. 11.
1866. Sir Chas. Lennox Wyke, K.C.I env. ext. and min. plen. Ja 19.

Mission ceased on annexation Hanover to Prussia, Sept. 1866.

TO THE HANSE TOWNS.

See also "German States and Confederations."

* * Philip Stanhope, resident.
1762. Robt. Colebrooke, resident.
1763. Ralph Woodford, resident. Mar. 22.
1772. Emmanuel Matthias, resident. Aug. 14.
1790. Chas. Hy. Fraser, resident, and min. plen. to Lower Saxony. Aug. 13.
1798. Sir Jas. Craufurd, bart., resident, and min. plen. to Lower Saxony. July 28.
1803. Sir Geo. Berriman Rumbold, bart., resident. Seized by the French government, and conveyed to Paris, Oct. 25, 1804; rest. to liberty, and arrived in London, Nov. 18, following.
1805. Edwd. Thornton, aft. sir E., res dent, and min. plen. to Denmarl Lower Saxony, Mecklenbur Schwerin, and Mecklenbur Strelitz. Feb. 22, **G.**
1813. Alex. Cockburn, sp. miss. Mar.
1815. The same, env. ext. to the Hans Towns and Lower Saxony. Ma 2, **G.**
1836. Hy. Canning, ch. d'a. to the Hans Towns and to Lower Saxon Nov. 29.
1841. Colonel Lloyd Hodges, ch. d' July 31.
1860. Jno. Ward, ch. d'a. July 1, (Min. res., Oct. 30, 1861.

TO SAXONY.

Electorate.

* * David Murray, visc. Stormont, aft. E. of Mansfield, env. ext.
1764. Philip Stanhope, env. ext. Apr. 3.
1768. Robt. Murray Keith, aft. sir R., env. ext. Nov. 27.
1771. John Osborne, env. ext. Feb. 11.
1775. Sir John Stepney, bart., env. ext. Nov. 30.
1783. Morton Eden, aft. sir M., and lord Henley, env. ext.
1789. The same, min. plen.
1791. Hugh Elliot, env. ext. and min. plen. Nov. 13.
1803. Hy. Watkin Williams Wynn, aft. sir H., bt., env. ext. June 25.

Kingdom.

Saxony was erected into a kingdom conformably with the treaty (Posen (signed Dec. 11, 1806 between France and Frederic Augustus, the then elector, aft king.

1816. John Philip Morier, env. ext. Jan. 5
1824. Geo. Wm. Chad, min. plen. De 11.
1828. Edwd. Michael Ward, min. plen Feb. 12, **G.**
1832. Hon. Fras. Reginald Forbes, min plen. Nov. 26.
1842. Thos., E. of Wilton, env. ext. an min. plen., sp. miss. Sept. 24.

57. Hon. Fras. Reginald Forbes *again*, env. ext. and min. plen. May 2.
58. Augs. Berkeley Paget, aft. sir A., env. ext. and min. plen. Dec. 13.
59. Hon. Chas. Augs. Murray, C.B., aft. sir C., env. ext. and min. plen. June 6.
1866. Jno. Savile Lumley, aft. sir J., env. ext. and min. plen. June 16.
1867. Josh. Hume Burnley, ch. d'a. Dec. 9.
1873. Geo. Strachey, ch. d'a. Oct. 25.

For Ambassadors to Lower Saxony see " German States and Confederations."

O THE SEVERAL GERMAN STATES AND CONFEDERATIONS DETAILED BELOW.

SEE INTRODUCTION TO " GERMANY AND AUSTRIA."

763. Philip Stanhope, env. ext. to the diet of the empire. Mar. 22.
— Jas. Porter, aft. sir J., min. plen. to the emp. of Germany's court at Brussels. May 7.
764. Wm. Gordon, aft. sir Wm., min. plen. to the diet of Ratisbon. April 3; min. plen. to the emp's Court at Brussels. Nov. 23, 1765.
765. Fulke Greville, env. ext. to the elector of Bavaria, and min. plen. to the diet of Ratisbon. Nov. 23.
769. Lewis de Visme, min. plen. to the elector of Bavaria and diet of Ratisbon.
.773. Hugh Elliot, min. plen. to the elector of Bavaria, and min. to the diet of Ratisbon. Dec. 24.
776. Morton Eden, aft. sir M., and lord Henley, to the same. Oct. 31.
.777. Alleyne Fitzherbert, aft. lord St. Helens, min. at Brussels. Mar. 4.
.779. Rd. Oakes, min. to the diet of Ratisbon.
1780. Hon. John Trevor, min. plen. to the elector palatine, and min. to the diet of Ratisbon. April 7.
1781. Ralph Heathcote, min. plen. to the elector of Cologne, &c. Mar. 3.
1783. George Byng, visc. Torrington, env. ext. to the emp's. court at Brussels.
— Robert, visc. Galway, env. ext. to the elect. pal., and min. to the diet of Ratisbon. Feb. 22.
— Hon. Thos. Walpole, env. ext. to the elect. pal. Nov. 19; env. ext. and plen. to same. 1788.
1790 Chas. Hy. Fraser, min. plen. to the circle of Lower Saxony, and res. at the Hanse Towns. Aug. 14.
1792. Thos. E. of Elgin, env. ext. to the emp's. court at Brussels. Aug. 18.
1796. Wm. Elliot, min. plen. to the elect. pal., and min. to the diet of Ratisbon.
1798. Hon. Arthur Paget, aft. sir A., env. ext. to the elect. pal., and min. to the diet of Ratisbon. May 22.
— Sir Jas. Craufurd, bart., min. plen. to the circle of Lower Saxony, and res. at the Hanse Towns. July 28.
1799. Fras. Drake, env. ext. to the same, and min. to the diet of Ratisbon. June 11.
1800. The same, to the elect. pal., *new credentials*, and env. ext. to the diet of Ratisbon. May.
1801. Brook Taylor, aft. sir B., min. plen. to Hesse-Cassel and to the elect. of Cologne. Aug. 4.
1802. Fras. Drake, min. plen. to the elect. pal., in addition to his former character. July 1; min. plen. to the diet of Ratisbon, Feb. 27, 1803.
1805. Hon. Wm. Hill, env. ext. and plen. to the circle of Franconia. Mar. 1.
— Edw. Thornton, aft. sir E., min. plen. to Denmark, the Hanse Towns, and the circle of Lower Saxony, to Mecklenburgh-Schwerin, and to Mecklenburgh Strelitz. May 4.
1815. Alex. Cockburn, env. ext. to the Hanse Towns and to Lower Saxony. June 1.
1817. Hon. Fredk. Jas. Lamb, aft. sir F., and lord Beauvale; succ. as visc. Melbourne, min. plen. to the Germ. Confed. Nov. 28.
1820. The same, env. ext. and min. plen. Apr. 17, **G.**
1823. Geo. Hamilton Seymour, aft. sir G., ch. d'a., *ad. int.*, to the Germ. Confed. Oct. 7.
1824. Hon. Fredk. Cathcart, min. plen. to the Germ. Confed. Jan. 15, **G.**

1826. Hon. F. Cathcart, min. plen. to Hesse-Cassel. Feb. 2.
1827. John Ralph Milbanke, aft. sir J. R. M. Huskisson, bt., ch. d'a., *ad int.*, to the same. Mar. 20.
1828. Hy. Unwin Addington, min. plen. to the Germ. Confed. and to Hesse-Cassel. Feb. 18.
1829. Geo. Wm. Chad, min. plen. to the Germ. Confed. and to Hesse-Cassel. July 30, **G.**
1830. Thos. Cartwright, aft. sir T., min. plen. to the Germ. Confed. Nov. 3, **G.**
1831. The same, min. plen. to Hesse-Cassel. Jan. 14.
1836. Hy. Canning, ch. d'a. to the Hanse Towns and to Lower Saxony.
1838. Hon. Hy. Edwd. Fox, aft. lord Holland, min. plen. to the Germ. Confed. Apr. 17, **G.**
— The same, to Hesse-Cassel. May 2.
1838. Hon. Ralph Abercromby, min. plen. to the Germ. Confed. Dec. 6, **G.**
— The same to Hesse-Cassel. July 25.
1840. Hon. Wm. Thos. Horner Fox Strangways, env. ext. and min. plen. to the Germ. Confed, and min. plen. to Hesse-Cassel, Mar. 17, **G.**
1841. Hon. Fras. Reginald Forbes, min. plen. to Saxe Coburg Gotha. June 29.
1843. Hon. Fras. Geo. Molyneux, ch. d'a. to the Germ. Confed. Jan. 24.
1847. John, E. of Westmoreland, min. plen. to Mecklenburgh-Schwerin, and to Mecklenburgh-Strelitz. Apr. 20.
— Hon. John Duncan Bligh, min. plen. to Oldenburg. Apr. 20.
— The same, min. plen. to Brunswick. Oct. 15.
— John, E. of Westmoreland, min. plen. to Anhalt Dessau. Oct. 15.
— Hon. Fras. Reginald Forbes, min. plen. to Saxe Weimar Eisenach, Saxe Altenburg, and Saxe Meiningen. Oct. 15.
— Hon. Wm. Thos. Horner Fox Strangways, min. plen. to Hesse-Darmstadt, and to Nassau. Oct. 15.
— Sir Stratford Canning, aft Visc. Stratford de Redcliffe, ext. miss. to Belgium, Germany, Greece, and Switzerland. Nov. 26.
1848. Hy. Rd. Chas., ld., aft. E. Cowley, sp. miss. to Germ. Confed. *without credentials.* July 29. Env. ext. and min. plen. to Germ. Confed. May 12, 1851.
1851. Hon. Rd. Edwardes, ch. d'a. to Germ. Confed. Dec. 13.
1852. Sir Alexr. Malet, bart., env. ext. and min. plen. to Germ. Confed. Feb. 12.
1853. Hon. Rd. Edwardes, *again*, ch. d'a. to Germ. Confed. June 11.*
1868. Lord Aug. Wm. Fredk. Spencer Loftus, amb. ext. and plen. to N. Germ. Confed. Feb. 24, **G.**†

* The mission to the Germanic Confederation ceased in 1866 in consequence of the Austro-Prussian war; the Confederation was then dissolved, and Frankfort annexed to Prussia.

† The North German Confederation was established in April 1867. It ceased in 1871 on the formation of the German Empire. *See "Empire of Germany."*

TO THE NETHERLANDS, &c.

* * Hon. Jos. Yorke, aft. Sir J.; env. ext. and plen.
1784. Sir Jas. Harris, aft. lord and E. of Malmesbury, env. ext. and plen. to the states-general of the United Provinces. July 3.
1788. The same, amb. ext. and plen. to the states-general, &c. Feb. 8.
1789. Alleyne Fitzherbert, aft. lord St. Helens, env. ext. and plen. to the states-general, &c. May 16.
— Wm. Eden, lord Auckland, amb. to the states-general, &c. Nov. 28.
1790. Lord Hy. John Spencer, min. plen., *ad int.*, to their high mightinesses. April 7.
1793. Hon. Wm. Eliot, aft. lord Eliot and E. of St. Germans, min. plen., *ad int.*
1794. Alleyne, lord St. Helens, env. ext. and plen.
1802. Robt. Liston, aft. sir R., env. and min. plen. to the Batavian republic. Aug. 14.
1813. Rd., E. of Clancarty, amb. to the pr. of Orange. Nov. 25.
1814. Sir Chas. Stuart, aft. lord Stuart de Rothesay, amb. to the pr. of Orange. Oct. 8, **G.**
1815. Sir Chas. Stuart, aft. lord Stuart de Rothesay, amb. to the Low Countries. Mar. 21.
— John James, min. plen., *ad int.* June 29.

16. Rd., E. of Clancarty, *again*, amb. May 23, G.
19. Geo. Wm. Chad, min. plen., *ad int.* Mar. 23.
24. Granville, visc., aft. E. Granville, amb. Feb. 14.
— Andrew Snape Douglas, min. plen., *ad int.* Oct. 6.
— Sir Chas. Bagot, amb. Nov. 27.
29. Thos. Cartwright, aft. sir Thos., min. plen., *ad int.* July 28.
32. Hon. John Duncan Bligh, min. plen. *ad int.* June 16.
33. Hon. Geo. Sulyarde Stafford Jerningham, ch. d'a.
35. Sir Edw. Cromwell Disbrowe, env. ext. and min. plen. Dec. 30.
51. Hon. sir Ralph Abercromby, aft. lord Dunfermline, env. ext. and min. plen. Nov. 26.
1858. Francis, lord Napier, env. ext. and min. plen. Dec. 15.
1860. Sir Andrew Buchanan, K.C.B., env. ext. and min. plen. Dec. 11.
1862. Sir Jno. Ralph Milbanke, aft. sir J. R. M. Huskisson, bt., env. ext. and min. plen. Oct. 28.
1867. V. adm., aft. adm. hon. Edw. Alf. Jno. Harris, C.B., env. ext. and min. plen. Aug. 22.
1877. Hon. Wm. Stuart, C.B., aft. Sir Wm., K.C.M.G., env. ext. and min. plen. Oct. 31.
1879. The same to K. Netherlands, as Gr. D. of Luxembourg. Nov. 27, G.
1888. Sir Horace Rumbold, bt., K.C.M.G., env. ext. and min. plen. Feb. 1.

TO BELGIUM.

ROM the separation of Belgium from the kingdom of the Netherlands, nd the establishment of a distinct monarchy, 1830–31.

830. John, visc. Ponsonby, sp. miss. to Prov. Gov. Dec. 1.
831. Sir Robt. Adair, sp. miss. Aug. 3.
832. Col. hon. John Hobart Caradoc, aft. succ. as baron Howden, military sp. miss. Nov. 15.
835. Hy. Lytton Bulwer, aft. sir Hy., and ld. Dalling and Bulwer, ch. d'a. Dec. 3.
836. Sir Geo. Hamilton Seymour, env. ext. and min. plen. April 4.
845. Thos. Wathen Waller, ch. d'a. Oct. 18.
846. Chas. Aug., lord Howard de Walden and Seaford, env. ext. and min. plen. Dec. 10.
1847. Sir Stratford Canning, aft. visc. Stratford de Redcliffe, ext. miss. to Belgium, Germany, Greece, and Switzerland. Nov. 26.
1856. Jno. Fane, E. of Westmoreland, sp. miss. July 16.
1866. Jno. Robt., E. Sydney, sp. miss. Feb. 7.
1868. Jno. Savile Lumley, aft. Sir J., env. ext. and min. plen. Oct. 19.
1878. Geo., visc. Torrington, sp. miss. Aug. 12.
1883. Sir Edwd. Baldwin Malet, env. ext. and min. plen. Aug. 29.
1884. Hon. Hussey Crespigny Vivian, C.B. aft. Lord Vivian, K.C.M.G., env. ext. and min. plen. Dec. 15.

TO SPAIN.

* Geo. Wm. Hervey, E. of Bristol, ambassador.
763. John Montagu, E. of Sandwich, amb. Feb. 19.
— Wm. Hy. Nassau, E. of Rochford, amb. June 18.
766. Sir Jas. Gray, bt., amb. Nov. 25.
770. Geo. Pitt, aft. lord Rivers, amb. Feb. 19.
771. Thos., ld. Grantham, amb. Jan. 25.
— Jas. Harris, aft. sir J., and lord and E. of Malmesbury, min. plen. *ad. int.* Feb. 22.
1783. John, visc. Mountstuart, aft. E. and M. of Bute, amb. Mar. 12.
— Philip, E. of Chesterfield, amb. Dec. 31.
1784. Robt. Liston, aft. sir R., min. plen., *ad int.*
1787. William Eden, aft. lord Auckland, amb. Aug. 18.
1789. Chas. Hy. Fraser, min. plen. *ad int.* July 18.

1794. Sir Morten Eden, aft. lord Henley, amb. Mar. 15.
1795. John, E., aft. M. of Bute, *again*, amb. Apr. 23.
1802. John Hookham Frere, env. ext. and min. plen. Sept. 20.
1809. Rd., Marq. Wellesley, amb. June 9.
— Bartholomew Frere, min. plen., *ad int.* Sept. 17.
1810. Hon. Hy. Wellesley, aft. sir H., and ld. Cowley, env. ext. and min. plen. Jan. 3; amb., Oct. 1, 1811.
1813. Chas. Rd. Vaughan, aft. Sir C., min. plen., *ad int.* July 16.
1820. Lionel Hervey, min. plen., *ad int.* Nov. 25.
1822. Sir Wm. A'Court, aft. lord Heytesbury, env. ext. and min. plen. Aug. 8.
1825. Hon. Fredk. Jas. Lamb, aft. sir F., and lord Beauvale, succ. as visc. Melbourne; env. ext. and min. plen. Feb. 18.
1829. Hy. Unwin Addington, env. ext. and min. plen. Dec. 7.
1832. Sir Stratford Canning, aft. visc. Stratford de Redcliffe, sp. miss. Dec. 13.
1833. Hon. Geo. Wm. Fredk. Villiers, aft. sir G., succ. as E. of Clarendon; env. ext. and min. plen. Sept. 5.
1835. Lord Elliot, military miss.
1839. Hon. Geo. Sulyarde Stafford Jerningham, ch. d'a. Oct. 18.
1840. Arthur Aston, aft. sir A., env. ext. and min. plen. Feb. 13.
1843. Hy. Lytton Bulwer, aft. Sir H., and ld. Dalling and Bulwer, env. ext. and min. plen. Nov. 25. In May 1848, Mr. Bulwer was ordered by the Spanish government to quit Madrid within forty-eight hours, on the alleged ground of his improper interference in the internal affairs of the kingdom. The minister of Spain in London (M. Isturiz) was, in consequence, informed by the British government that he could not be allowed to continue at the court of Great Britain as minister from the Q. of Spain. M. Isturiz took his departure, therefore, from London on the 14th June following; and diplomatic relations were not renewed between the two countries until April 1850; when lord Howden was appointed British minister to the court of Madrid, and M. Isturiz returned to the court of London.
1850. John Hobart, lord Howden, env. ext. and min. plen. May 9.
1858. Andrew Buchanan, C.B., aft. sir A., env. ext. and min. plen. Mar. 31.
1860. Sir Jno. Fiennes Twistleton Crampton, bt., K.C.B., env. ext. and min. plen. Dec. 11.
1869. Austen Hy Layard, aft. Sir A., env. ext. and min. plen. Oct. 23.
1878. Hon. Lionel Sackville Sackville West, aft. sir L., env. ext. and min. plen. Jan. 11.
1881. Robt. Burnett David Morier, C.B., aft. sir R., env. ext. and min. plen. June 22.
1884. Fras. Clare Ford, C.B., C.M..G, aft. sir F., env. ext. and min. plen. Dec. 15; amb. ext. and plen. Dec. 8, 1887.

TO PORTUGAL.

* * Hon. Edw. Hay, env. ext. and min. plen.
1766. Wm. Hy. Lyttleton, aft. lord Westcote, env. ext. and min. plen. Oct. 25.
1771. Hon. Robt. Walpole, env. ext. and min. plen. June 12.
1786. Wm. Fawkener, env. ext. and min. plen., for negotiating commercial affairs in conjunction with the hon. Robt. Walpole. Oct. 4.
1800. John Hookham Frere, env. ext. and and min. plen. Oct. 14.
1802. Lord Robt. Stephen Fitzgerald, env. ext. and min. plen. Sept. 25.
1806. James, E. of Rosslyn, John, E. of St. Vincent, and gen. Simcoe; ext. miss. Aug. 9.
— Percy Clinton, visc. Strangford, min. plen., *ad int.* Dec. 1. Env. ext. and min. plen. Apr. 16, 1808.

Visc. Strangford went to the Brazils on the court of Portugal going thither.

— John Chas. Villiers, env. ext. and min. plen. Nov. 27.
1810. Chas. Stuart, aft. sir C. and lord Stuart de Rothesay, env. ext. and min. plen. Jan. 10.
1814. Thos. Sydenham, env. ext. and min. plen. May 26.
— George Canning, amb., to congratulate the king on his return to his European dominions. Oct. 17.

1817. Edw. Thornton, aft. sir Ed., env. ext. and min. plen. July 29.
Mr. Thornton went to the Brazils same year.
1819. The same, amb. *pro tem.* Apr. 12.
1820. Edw. Michael Ward, ch. d'a. Mar. 6.
1823. Sir Edw. Thornton, *again*, env. ext. and min. plen. Aug. 7.
1824. Sir Wm. A'Court, aft. lord Heytesbury, amb. Aug. 16.
1825. Sir Chas. Stuart, aft. lord Stuart de Rothesay, sp. miss. Mar. 14.
1827. Sir Fredk. Jas. Lamb, aft. lord Beauvale; succ. as visc. Melbourne, amb. Dec. 28.
1833. Lord Wm. Russell sp. miss. Aug. 7.
— Chas. Augs., lord Howard de Walden, aft. lord Howard de Walden and Seaford, env. ext. and min. plen. Nov. 26.
1847. Sir Geo. Hamilton Seymour, env. ext. and min. plen. Feb. 2.
1851. Sir Rd. Pakenham, env. ext. and min. plen. Apr. 28. Sp. miss. Aug. 17, 1855.
1855. Hy. Fras. Howard, aft. Sir H., env. ext. and min. plen. Oct. 10.
1858. Jno. Alexr., M. of Bath, env. ext. and min. plen., sp. miss. Apr. 27.
1859. Sir Arthur Chas. Magenis, K.C.B., env. ext. and min. plen. Nov. 11.
1865. Wm. Philip, E. of Sefton, sp. miss. Apr. 17.
1866. Sir Aug. Berkeley Paget, K.C.B., env. ext. and min. plen. June 9.
1867. Edwd. Thornton, C.B., aft. Sir E., env. ext. and min. plen. Sept. 3.
1867. Hon. Sir Chas. Aug. Murray, K.C.B., env. ext. and min. plen. Dec. 13.
1874. Edwd. Robt., ld., aft. E. Lytton, env. ext. and min. plen. Nov. 26.
1876. Robt. Burnett David Morier, C.B., aft. sir R., env. ext. and min. plen. Mar. 1.
1881. Sir Chas. Lennox Wyke, G.C.M.G., K.C.B., env. ext. and min. plen. June 22.
1884. Geo. Glynn Petre, env. ext. and min. plen. Jan. 16.

TO RUSSIA.

* * Robt. Murray Keith, aft. sir R., env. ext.
1762. John, E. of Buckinghamshire, amb. ext. and min. plen. July 17.
1764. Sir Geo., aft. ld., visc., and E., Macartney, env. ext. Aug. 31.
1766. Hans Stanley, amb. ext. and min. plen. Aug. 12.
1767. Sir Geo. Macartney, *again*, amb. ext. and min. plen. Oct. 14.
1768. Chas. Shaw, lord Cathcart, amb. ext. and min. plen. Feb. 23.
1771. Robt. Gunning, aft. sir R., bt., env. ext. and min. plen. Dec. 13.
1776. Sir Jas. Harris, aft. ld., and E. of Malmesbury, env. ext. and min. plen. Nov. 30.
1783. Alleyne Fitzherbert, aft. ld. St. Helens, env. ext. and min. plen. Aug. 19.
1788. Chas. Whitworth, aft. sir C., and ld., visc., and E. Whitworth, env. ext. and min. plen. Oct. 13.
1790. Wm. Fawkener, env. ext. and min. plen, *ad int.*
1801. Alleyne, ld. St. Helens, amb. to the emp. Alexander on his accession. Apr. 24.
— Benj. Garlike, min. plen., *ad int.* July 13.
1802. Sir John Borlase Warren, bt., amb. Sept. 5.
1804. Lord Granville Leveson Gower, aft. E. Granville, amb. Aug. 10.
1806. Wm. Shaw, ld., aft. visc. and E., Cathcart, amb. Nov. 28.
— Dudley, ld., aft. E. of Harrowby; ext. miss. (and to Prussia). Nov. 28.
1806. Lord G. L. Gower, *again*, amb. May 17.
— Alex., M. of Douglas and Clydesdale, succ. as D. of Hamilton, amb. May 28.
1812. Wm. Shaw, visc. Cathcart, amb. July 25.
— Horatio, ld. Walpole, succ. as E. of Orford, min. plen., *ad int.* Aug. 4.
1813. Robt., visc. Castlereagh, succ. as M. of Londonderry, sp. miss. Dec. 27.
1817. Lewis Casamajor, min, plen., *ad int.* July 5.
1820. Sir Chas. Bagot, amb. May 23.
— Lt.-col. hon. Fredk. Cathcart, min. plen., *ad int.*
1822. Arthur, D. of Wellington, ext. miss. to the congress of Verona. Sept. 14.
1824. Edwd. Michael Ward, min. plen., *ad int.* June 30.
— Stratford Canning, aft. sir S. and visc. Stratford de Redcliffe, sp. miss. Dec. 8.

1825. Edwd. Cromwell Disbrowe, aft. sir E., min. plen., *ad int.* Feb. 23.
1825. Percy Clinton, visc. Strangford, amb. Oct. 10.
1826. Arthur, D. of Wellington, *again*, sp. miss. Feb. 6.
— Wm. Spencer, D. of Devonshire, sp. embassy, coronation of the emp. Nicholas. May 5.
— Edwd. Cromwell Disbrowe, *again*, min. plen., *ad int.* May 31.
1828. Hon. Wm. Temple, min. plen., *ad int.* Jan. 4.
— Wm. lord Heytesbury, amb. June 7.
1832. John Geo., lord, aft. E. of Durham, ext. miss. to Austria, Russia, and Prussia. July 3.
1832. Hon. John Duncan Bligh, min. plen., *ad int.* Sept. 3.
1835. John Geo., E. of Durham, amb. July 8.
1836. John Ralph Milbanke, aft. sir J. R. M., min. plen., *ad int.* Sept. 29.
1838. Ulick John M. of Clanricarde, amb. Oct. 6.
1840. Hon. John Arthur Douglas Bloomfield, aft. ld. Bloomfield, min. plen., *ad int.* Mar. 28.
1841. Chas., lord Stuart de Rothesay, amb. Oct. 16.
1844. J. A. D., ld. Bloomfield, *again*, env. ext. and min. plen. Mar. 9.
1851. Sir Geo. Hamilton Seymour, env. ext. and min. plen. Apr. 28.
Dipl. rel. suspended Feb. 1854, till termination of Crimean war.
1856. Jno., ld. Wodehouse, env. ext. and min. plen. May 4.
1856. Geo. Granville, E. Granville, amb. ext. to emp. Alexander II. on coronation.
1858. Sir Jno. Fiennes Twistleton Crampton, bart., K.C.B., env. ext. and min. plen. Mar. 31.
1860. Francis, lord Napier, amb. ext. and plen. Dec. 11.
1864. Hon. Sir Andrew Buchanan, K.C.B., amb. ext. and min. plen. Sept. 15.
1871. Lord Aug. Wm. Fredk. Spencer Loftus, G.C.B., amb. ext. and plen. Oct. 16.
1879. Fredk. Temple Hamilton, E. of Dufferin, K.P., G.C.M.G., K.C.B., amb. ext. and plen. Feb. 8, **G.**
1881. Sir Edwd. Thornton, K.C.B., amb. ext. and plen. May 26.
1884. Sir Robt. Burnett David Morier, K.C.B., amb. ext. and plen. Dec. 1.

TO POLAND.

* * Thos. Wroughton, aft. sir T., min. plen.
1778. Rd. Oakes, min. plen. June 10.
1779. Jas. Hare, min. plen. Oct. 19.
1782. John, visc. Dalrymple, aft. E. of Stair, min. plen. Jan. 5.
1784. Chas. Whitworth, aft. sir C., ld., visc., and E. Whitworth, min. plen. June 25.
1788. Daniel Hailes, min. plen. Sept. 13.
1791. Wm. Gardiner, min. plen. Dec. 14.
Poland was finally partitioned by Russia, Austria, and Prussia, in 1795.

SWEDEN. SWEDEN AND NORWAY.

To Sweden.

* * Sir John Goodricke, bt., env. ext.
1773. Lewis de Visme, env. ext. Nov. 29; *d.* 1776.
1776. Horace St. Paul, env. ext. Oct. 31.
1778. Thos. Wroughton, aft. sir T., env. ext. June 10. Min. plen., Apr. 27, 1787; *d.* Sept. this year.
1787. Chas. Keene, ch. d'a. Sept. 22.
1788. Robt. Liston, aft. sir R., min. plen. Sept. 13.
1793. Lord Hy. John Spencer, env. ext July 13.
1795. Daniel Hailes, min. plen. July 11.
1802. Chas. Arbuthnot, env. ext. Sept. 5.
1804. Hon. Hy. Manvers Pierrepont, env. ext. and min. plen. Apr. 20.
1807. Alexr. Straton, env. ext. and min. plen. Jan. 19.
— Hon. Hy. M. Pierrepoint, *again*, sp. miss. May.
— Edwd. Thornton, aft. sir E., env. ext. and min. plen. Dec. 10.
1808. Anthy. Merry, env. ext. and min. plen. Nov. 1.
1811. Edwd. Thornton, *again*, sp. miss. Oct.
1812. Edwd. Thornton *again*, env. ext. and min. plen. Aug. 5.
1814. Norway united to Sweden.

To Sweden and Norway.

1817. Percy Clinton, visc. Strangford, env. ext. and min. plen. July. 18.

1820. Wm. Fitzgerald Vesey Fitzgerald, aft. ld. Fitzgerald and Vesci, env. ext. and min. plen. Aug. 7.

1823. Sir Benj. Bloomfield, aft. lord Bloomfield, env. ext. and min. plen. Apr. 24.

1832. Chas. Aug., ld. Howard de Walden, aft. ld. Howard de Walden and Seaford, env. ext. and min plen. Sept. 21.

1833. Sir Edwd. Cromwell Disbrowe, env. ext. and min. plen. Nov 26.

1835. Hon. John Duncan Bligh, env. ext and min plen. Nov. 3.

1838. Sir Thos. Cartwright, env. ext. and min. plen. Oct. 6.

1850. Geo. John Robt. Gordon, ch. d'a., May 2, during absence of sir T. Cartwright.

1851. Sir Edmd. Lyons, bt., aft. ld. Lyons, env. ext. and min. plen. Jan. 27.

1853. Hon. Geo. Sulyarde Stafford Jerningham, env. ext. and min. plen. Nov. 23; (appt. cancelled).

1854. Arthur Chas. Magenis, aft. sir A., env. ext. and min. plen. May 20.

1859. Augs. Berkeley Paget, aft. sir A., env. ext. and min. plen. June 6.

Note.—This appointment was cancelled and A. C. Magenis remained until

1859. Hon. Geo. Sulyarde Stafford Jerningham, *again*, env. ext. and min plen. Nov. 11.

1872. Hon. Edwd. Morris Erskine, env. ext. and min. plen. July 24.

1881. Sir Horace Rumbold, bt., env. ext. and min. plen. Apr. 1.

1884. Edwin Corbett, env. ext. and min. plen. Dec. 24.

1888. Hon. Fras. Rd. Plunkett. Apr.

TO DENMARK.

1763. Dudley Alex. Sydney Cosby, aft. ld. Sydney, of Leix, in Ireland, resident. Sept. 10.

1765. Wm. Gordon, aft. sir W., bt., env. ext. June 29.

— Robt. Gunning, aft. sir R., resident. Nov. 23.

1771. Robt. Murray Keith, aft. sir R., env. ext. Feb. 13.

1772. Ralph Woodford, env. ext. Aug. 14.

1774. Daniel de Laval, resident. July 15. Env. ext., June 10, 1778.

1779. Morton Eden, aft. sir M., and ld. Henley, env. ext. Mar. 17.

1782. Hugh Elliot, env. ext. and aft. min. plen.

1791. Daniel Hailes, env. ext. Dec. 14.

1795. Lord Robt. Stephen Fitzgerald, env. ext. and min. plen. July 7.

1800. Chas., ld., aft. visc. and E. Whitworth, ext. miss. Aug. 1.

1803. Sir Jas. Craufurd, env. ext. and min. plen. Feb. 27.

— Robt. Liston, aft, sir R., ext. miss. June 23.

1804. Benj. Garlike, env. ext. and min. plen. Dec. 31.

1805. Edwd. Thornton, aft. sir E., min. plen. to Denmark, the Hanse Towns, Lower Saxony, Mecklenburg-Schwerin, and Mecklenburg-Strelitz. May 4.

1807. Brook Taylor, aft. sir B., env. ext. and min. plen., *ad int.* July 17.

— Fras. Jas. Jackson, env. ext. and min. plen., *ad int.* July 24.

1807. Anthy. Merry, env. ext. and min. plen. Oct. 3.

1812. Edwd. Thornton, *again*, env. ext. and min. plen. July 5.

1813. Gen. hon. Alexr. Hope, env. ext. and min. plen. Jan. 15.

1814. Aug. John Foster, aft. sir A., env. ext. and min. plen. May 19.

1824. Hy. Watkin Williams Wynn, aft. sir H., bt., env. ext. and min. plen. Sept. 14.

1853. Andrew Buchanan, aft. sir A., env. ext. and min. plen. Feb. 9.

1858. Hon. Hy. Geo. Elliot, aft. Sir H., env. ext. and min. plen. Mar. 31.

1859. Augs. Berkeley Paget, aft. sir A., env. ext. and min. plen. July 4.

1863. Jno., ld. Wodehouse, aft. E. of Kimberley, sp. miss. to congrat. K. Christian IX. on his accession. Dec. 9.

1866. Hon. Chas. Aug. Murray, C.B., aft. sir C., env. ext. and min. plen. June 9.

1867. Sir Chas. Lennox Wyke, K.C.B., env. ext. and min. plen. Dec. 16.

1881. Hon. Hussey Crespigny Vivian, C.B., env. ext and min. plen. July 1.

1884. Hon. Edmund Jno Monson, C.B., aft. sir E., env. ext. and min. plen. Dec. 29.

1888. Hugh Guion Macdonell, env. ext. and min. plen. Feb. 1.

TO THE DANUBIAN PRINCIPALITIES OF MOLDAVIA AND WALLACHIA.

United in 1861 under the name of ROUMANIA.

1851. Robt. Gilmour Colquhoun, aft. sir R., agent and C.G. Nov. 18.
1859. Jno. Green, aft. sir J., agent and C.G. July 17.
1874. Hon. Hussey Chas. Vivian, agent and C.G. Feb. 16.
1876. Lt.-col. Chas. Edw. Mansfield, agent and C.G. May 10.
1878. Wm. Arthur White, C.B., aft. sir W., agent and C.G. July 1. Env. ext. and min. plen., Feb. 20, 1880. **G.**
1882. Percy Sanderson, apptd. C.G. and Commr. for Danube arrangements. Jan. 1. **G.**
1887. Sir Frank Cavendish Lascelles, K.C.M.G., env. ext. and min. plen. Jan. 1.

TO BULGARIA.

1879. Wm. Gifford Palgrave, agent and C.G. June 20.
1879. Frank Cavendish Lascelles, aft. sir F., agent and C.G. Nov. 26.
1887. Nichs. Roderick O'Conor, agent and C.G. Jan. 1.

TO SERVIA.

1868. Jno. A. Longworth, agent and C.G. Mar. 17.
1875. Wm. Arthur White, aft. sir A. agent and C.G. Feb. 27.
1878. Gerard Fras. Gould, agent. July 1. Ch. d'a., Jan. 8, 1879. Min. res. Mar. 3, 1879.
1881. Sidney Locock, min. res. Apr. 16.
1885. Geo. Hugh Wyndham, C.B., min. res., Feb. 25; env. ext. and min plen. Sept. 8, 1886.
1888. Fredk. Robt. St. John, env. ext. and min. plen. Feb. 1.

TO MONTENEGRO.

1879. Wm. Kirby Green, ch. d'a. Montenegro, and C.G., Scutari. Jan. 6.
1886. Walter Baring, ch. d'a. July 20.

TO GREECE.

Greece became a kingdom, October 5, 1832; and Otho, of Bavari ascended the throne, as first king, January 25, 1833.

1833. Edw. Jas. Dawkins, min. plen. Jan. 1.
1835. Sir Edmd. Lyons, min. plen. July 2.
1847. Sir Stratford Canning, aft. visct. Stratford de Redcliffe, ext. miss. to Belgium, Germany, Greece, and Switzerland. Nov. 26.
1849. Thos. Wyse, aft. sir T., min. plen. Feb. 9. **G.**
Dipl. rel. susp. from Jan. 22 to Apr. 28, 1850.

1862. Hon. Hy. Geo. Elliot, after sir H., sp. miss. to K. Otho. Apr. 24, **G.** Sp. miss. to Prov. Gov. Dec. 13.
1862. Hon. Peter Campbell Scarlett, C.B., env. ext. and min. plen. June 12.
1864. Hon. Edw. Morris Erskine, env. ext. and min. plen. May 7.
1871. Hon. Wm. Stuart, sp. miss. May 1. Env. ext. and min. plen., July 29, 1872.
1878. Edwin Corbett, env. ext. and min. plen. Jan. 7.
1881. Fras. Clare Ford, C.B., C.M.G., aft. sir F., env. ext. and min. plen. Mar. 5.
1884. Sir Horace Rumbold, bt., env. ext. and min. plen. Dec. 17.

TO THE IONIAN ISLANDS.

CORFU, CEPHALONIA, ZANTE, ST. MAURA, ITHACA, CERIGO, AND PAXO.

THESE islands, called the "REPUBLIC OF THE SEVEN ISLANDS," were placed under the protection of Great Britain, by the congress of Vienna, in 1815, and "LORD HIGH COMMISSIONERS" were from time to time appointed and sent out. A list of these is given here, in the absence of any more appropriate place, although their functions differed considerably from those of ordinary diplomatic representatives.

LORD HIGH COMMISSIONERS.

1816. Lt.-gen. sir Thos. Maitland, G.C.B. May 7.
1824. Lt.-gen. sir Fredk. Adam, K.C.B. Apr. 7.
1832. Sir Jas. Macdonald. June 2, **G.**
— Geo., ld. Nugent. Aug. 13, **G.**
1835. Lt.-gen. sir Howard Douglas, bt. Mar. 13.
1840. Jas. Alex. Stewart Mackenzie. Dec. 2.
1843. Lt.-gen. John, ld. Seaton, G.C.B. Feb. 24.
1849. Hy. Geo. Ward. May 2.
1855. Sir Jno. Young, bt. Mar. 20, **G.**
1858. Wm. Ewart Gladstone, commr. ext., Nov. 6, **G.**; ld. high commr., Jan. 25, 1859, **G.**
1859. Col. sir Hy. Knight Storks, K.C B., Feb. 2, **G.**

The Ionian Islands were united to Greece in 1863. *See "Greece."*

TO TURKEY.

* * James Porter, aft. sir Jas., amb.
1761. Hon. Hy. Grenville, amb.
1765. Robt. Colebrooke, amb. July 31.
— John Murray, amb. Nov. 30; *d.* at Venice, Aug. 9, 1775.
1775. Sir Robt. Ainslie, amb. Sept. 20.
1793. Robt. Liston, aft. sir R., amb. Oct. 1.
1796. Fras. Jas. Jackson, amb. July 23.
— John Spencer Smith, min. plen., *ad. int.*
1799. Thos., E. of Elgin, amb. Apr. 13.
1803. Wm. Drummond, amb. Feb. 9.
1804. Chas. Arbuthnot, amb. June 5.
1807. Hon. sir Arthur Paget, amb. May 15.
1808. Robt. Adair, aft. sir R., sp. miss. July 5; amb. April 14, 1809.
1809. Stratford Canning, aft. sir S. and visc. Stratford de Redcliffe, min. plen. July 17.
1812. Robt. Liston, *again*, amb. Mar. 2.
1820. Bartholomew Frere, min. plen. Mar. 6.
1820. Percy Clinton, visc. Strangford, amb. Aug. 7.
1824. Wm. Turner, min. plen., *ad int.* May 18.
1825. S. Canning, *again*, amb. Oct. 10.
1827. Col. the hon. John Hobart Caradoc, aft. lord Howden, sp. miss. to Egypt and Greece. July 4.
1829. Robt. Gordon, aft. sir R., amb. Apr. 8.
1831. Sir S. Canning, *again*, amb. Oct. 31.
— John Hy. Mandeville, min. plen., *ad int.* Nov. 7.
1832. John, ld., aft. visc. Ponsonby, amb. Nov. 27.
1837. Sir Chas. Rd. Vaughan, amb. Mar. 1.
1841. Chas. Bankhead, min, plen., *ad int.* Mar. 30.
— Sir S. Canning, *again*, amb. Oct. 16.
1845. Hon. Hy. Rd. Chas. Wellesley, aft. ld. and E. Cowley, min. plen., *ad int.* June 14.
1858. Sir Hy. Lytton Bulwer, G.C.B., aft.

ld. Dalling and Bulwer, amb. ext. and plen. May 10.
1865. Rd. Bickerton Pemell, ld. Lyons, G.C.B., amb. ext. and plen. Aug. 10.
1867. Hon. Hy. Geo. Elliot, aft. sir H. amb. ext. and plen. July 6.
1876. Robt. Arth. Talbot, M. of Salisbury, sp. amb. Nov. 8.
1877. Austen Hy. Layard, aft. sir A., sp. amb., *ad int.* Mar. 31.
1871. Edw. Baldwin Malet, aft. sir E., min. plen., *ad int.* Feb. 18.
1880. Geo. Joachim Goschen, sp. amb. ext. and plen. May 6.
1881. Fredk. Temple Hamilton E. of Dufferin, K.P., G.C.M.G., K.C.B., amb. ext. and plen. May 26.
1884. Sir Edw. Thornton, G.C.B., amb. ext. and plen. Dec. 1.
1885. Sir Wm. Arthur White, K.C.M.G., env. ext. and min. plen. *ad int.* Apr. 18.
1885. Sir Hy. Drummond Wolff, G.C.M.G., K.C.B., env. ext. and min. plen., sp. miss. on Egyptian affairs. Aug. 3.
1886. Sir W. A. White, G.C.M.G., *again*, sp. amb. ext. and plen. Oct. 11. Amb. ext. and plen. Jan. 1, 1887.

TO EGYPT.

1858. Robt. Gilmour Colquhoun, aft. sir R., agent and C.G. Dec. 13.
1865. Col. Edw. Stanton, aft. gen. sir. E., agent and C.G. May 15.
1875. Stephen Cave, aft. sir S., sp. miss. Dec. 1.
1876. Hon. Hussey Crespigny Vivian, agent and C.G. May 10.
1879. Edw. Baldwin Malet, C.B., aft. sir E., agent and C.G. Oct. 10.
1882. Fredk. Temple Hamilton, E. of Dufferin, K.P., G.C.M.G., K.C.B., sp. miss. Nov. 2.
1883. Maj. sir Evelyn Baring, K.C.S.I., agent and C.G. Aug. 29.
1884. Thos. Geo., E. of Northbrook, sp. miss. as high commr. Aug. 12.
1885. Sir Hy. Drummond Wolff, G.C.M.G., K.C.B., high commr. Nov. 2. Transf. to Persia, Dec. 1887, leaving Sir E. Baring, agent and C.G.

TO MUSCAT.

1872. Sir Hy. Bartle Edwd. Frere, Sp. Env., Nov. 9.

TO PERSIA.

1807. Sir Harford Jones, aft. sir H. Jones Brydges, env. ext. June 5.
1810. Sir Gore Ouseley, bt., amb. Mar. 6.
1814. Jas. Morier, min. plen., *ad int.* April 18.
— Hy. Ellis, min. plen., *ad int.*, in the event of Mr. Morier's absence. April 18.
1826. Col. Macdonald, env. ext. from the supr. govt. of India. July 29.
1835. Hy. Ellis, *again*, amb. July 8.
1836. John M'Neill, env. ext. and min. plen. May 25.
1844. Lt.-col. Justin Sheil, aft. sir J., env. ext. and min. plen. Sept. 17.
1854. Hon. Chas. Augs. Murray, env. ext. and min. plen. Sept. 3.
Dipl. rel. susp., Dec. 5, 1855.
1859. Lt.-col. sir Hy. Creswicke Rawlinson, K.C.B., env. ext. and min. plen. Apr. 16.
1860. Chas. Alison, env. ext. and min. plen. Apr. 7.
1872. Wm. Taylour Thomson, aft. sir W., env. ext. and min. plen. July 15.
1879. Ronald Ferguson Thomson, aft. sir R., env. ext. and min. plen. June 14.
1887. Sir Hy. Drummond Wolff, G.C.M.G., K.C.B., env. ext. and min. plen. Dec. 3.

TO CHINA AND COREA.

To China.

1792. Geo., ld., aft. visc. and E. Macartney, amb. ext. and min. plen.; sp. miss. May 22.
Commrs. to the embassy, Hy. Browne, Eyles Irwin, and Wm. Jackson.
Sec. of legation, sir Geo. L. Staunton.

1816. Wm. Pitt, ld. Amherst, amb.; sp. miss. Jan. 20.
— Hy. Ellis, aft. sir H., min. plen., *ad int.* Jan. 24.
1841. Sir Hy. Pottinger, supt. of Brit. trade. Aug. 16.
1844. Sir Jno. Fras. Davis, plen. and supt. Feb. 9.
1848. Sir Saml. Geo. Bonham, plen. and supt. Apr. 27.
1853. Sir Jno. Bowring, plen. and supt. Dec. 24.
1857. Jas., E. of Elgin and Kincardine, sp. miss. Apr. 17.
Dipl. rel. susp. during war from May 25, 1857.
1859. Hon. Fredk. Wm. Adolphus Bruce, aft. sir F., env. ext. and min. plen. Jan. 14.
Dipl. rel. again susp. during war from June 25, 1859.
1860. Jas., E. of Elgin and Kincardine *again*, sp. miss. Mar. 20.
1865. Sir Rutherford Alcock, K.C.B., env. ext. and min. plen. Mar. 28, **G.**
1871. Thos. Fras. Wade, C.B., aft. sir T., env. ext. and min. plen. July 22.
1883. Sir Harry Smith Parkes, G.C.M.G., K.C.B., env. ext. and min. plen. July 1.

To China and Corea.

1884. Sir Harry Smith Parkes, G.C.M.G., K.C.B., accredited as env. ext. and min. plen. to K. of Corea. Feb. 27, **G.**
1885. Sir Robt. Hart, K.C.M.G., env. ext. and min. plen. to emp. China and K. Corea. May 2. Did not proceed to China.
1885. Sir Jno. Walsham, bt., env. ext. and min. plen. to China and Corea. Nov. 24.

TO JAPAN.

1858. Jas., E. of Elgin and Kincardine, sp. miss.
1859. Rutherford Alcock, aft. sir R., env. ext. and min. plen. Nov. 30.
1865. Sir Harry Smith Parkes, K.C.B., env. ext. and min. plen. Mar. 28.
1883. Hon. Fras. Rd. Plunkett, aft. sir F., env. ext., min. plen. and C.G. July 1.
1888. Hugh Fraser, env. ext. and min. plen. May.

TO SIAM.

1855. Sir Jno. Bowring, sp. miss. Mar. 12.
1875. Thos. Geo. Knox, agent and C.G. Feb. 8.
1879. Wm. Gifford Palgrave, agent and C.G. Nov. 26.
1884. Ernest Mason Satow, agent and C.G. Jan. 16; Min. res. and C.G. Feb. 17, 1885.

TO BORNEO.

1847. Jas. Brooke, aft. Sir J., commr. and C.G., Mar. 19.

TO ABYSSINIA.

1884. R.-Adm. Sir Wm. Hewett, sp. miss., Jan. 2.

TO THE BARBARY STATES. TUNIS. MOROCCO.

To the Barbary States.

1813. Wm. A'Court, aft. Sir W. and Lord Heytesbury, env. ext. and min. plen. Jan. 5.

To Tunis.

1821. Sir Thos. Reade, agent.
1849. Sir Edwd. Stuart Baynes, agent. Oct. 25.
1855. Rd. Wood, aft. sir R., agent and C.G. Aug. 30.
1879. Thos. Fellowes Reade, agent and C.G. June 23. Retired Feb., 1885. No successor appointed.

To Morocco.

1829. Edwd. Wm. Auriol Drummond Hay, agent. May 11.
1845. Jno. Hay Drummond Hay, aft. sir J., and K.C.B., agent. Aug. 9. Min. res., June 9, 1860. Min. plen., Sept. 1, 1872. Env. ext. and min. plen., Feb. 27, 1880.
1886. Wm. Kirby Greene, C.M.G., env. ext. and min. plen. July 1.

TO ZANZIBAR.

1872. Sir Hy. Bartle E. Frere, sp. env. Nov. 9.
1880. John Kirk, aft. sir J., agent and C.G. Jan. 5.
1887. Col. Chas. Bean Euan-Smith, agent and C.G. Dec. 1.

TO THE UNITED STATES OF AMERICA.

1791. Geo. Hammond, min. plen. July 5. Mr. Hammond was the first minister sent from Great Britain to America.
1796. Robt. Liston, aft. sir R., env. ext. and min. plen. Mar. 10.
1803. Anth. Merry, env. ext. and min. plen. Sept. 16.
1806. Hon. David Montagu Erskine, aft. succ. as ld. Erskine, env. ext. and min. plen. July 21, G.
1807. Geo. Hy. Rose, sp. miss. Oct. 23.
1809. Fras. Jas. Jackson, env. ext. and min. plen. July 6.
1811. Aug. John Foster, aft. sir A., env. ext. and min. plen. Feb.
1815. Hon. Chas. Bagot, aft. sir C., env. ext. and min. plen. July 31.
1820. Sir Stratford Canning, aft. visc. Stratford de Redcliffe, env. ext. and min. plen. July 18.
1825. Chas. Rd. Vaughan, aft. sir C., env. ext. and min. plen. May 21.
1835. Hy. Stephen Fox, env. ext. and min. plen. Oct. 2.
1842. Alex. Baring, lord Ashburton, ext. and sp. miss. Jan. 18.
1843. Rd. Pakenham, aft. sir R., env. ext. and min. plen. Dec. 14.
1849. Sir Hy. Lytton Bulwer, aft. ld. Dalling and Bulwer, env. ext. and min. plen. Apr. 27.
1852. Jno. Fiennes Twistleton Crampton, aft. sir J., bt., env. ext. and min. plen. Jan. 19.
1854. Jas., E. of Elgin and Kincardine, sp. miss. May.
Dipl. rel. susp. from May 28, 1856.
1857. Fras., ld. Napier, aft. ld. Napier and Ettrick, env. ext. and min. plen. Jan. 20.
1858. Rd. Bickerton Pemell, ld. Lyons, env. ext. and min. plen. Dec. 13.
1865. Hon. sir Fredk. Wm. Adolphus Bruce, K.C.B., env. ext. and min. plen. Mar. 1.
1867. Edwd Thornton, C.B., aft. sir E., env. ext. and min. plen. Dec. 6.
1881. Hon. Lionel Sackville Sackville West, aft. sir L., env. ext. and min. plen. June 22.

TO TEXAS.

1842. Capt. Chas. Elliot, ch. d'a., June 28.

Texas was admitted to the United States of America in 1846.

TO MEXICO.

1835. Rd. Pakenham, aft. sir R., min plen. Mar. 12.
1843 Percy Wm. Doyle, ch. d'a. Jan. 4.
— Chas. Bankhead, min. plen. Nov. 24, G.
1847. P. W. Doyle, *again*, ch. d'a.
1850. C. Bankhead, *again*, ch. d'a.
1851. P. W. Doyle, *again*, min. plen. Dec. 24.
1855. Wm. Garrow Lettsom, ch. d'a. May 4.
Dipl. rel. susp. Nov. 1, 1855, to Nov. 1856, when Mr. Lettsom resumed his functions.
1858. Loftus Chas. Otway, C.B., min. plen. Feb. 19.
1860. Chas. Lennox Wyke, C.B., aft. sir C., env. ext. and min. plen. Jan. 23.
Dipl. rel. susp. July 25, 1861.
1864. Hon. Peter Campbell Scarlett, C.B., env. ext. and min. plen. Nov. 9.
Dipl. rel. susp. in consequence of the murder of the emp. Maximilian, from Dec. 21, 1867, to
1883. Sir Spenser St. John, K.C.M.G., sp. miss. May 29. Env. ext. and min. plen. Nov. 28, 1884.

TO HAYTI.

1859. Thos. N. Ussher, ch. d'a. and C.G. May 13.
1861. Spenser St. John, aft. sir S., ch. d'a. and C.G. May 20. Min. res. and C.G., Dec. 12, 1872.
1874. Major Robt. Stuart, min. res. and C.G. Oct. 28. Ret. May, 1883. No successor app.

TO THE DOMINICAN REPUBLIC.

1871. Spenser St. John, after sir S., ch. d'a. June 28.
1874. Major Robt. Stuart, ch. d'a. Oct. 28. Ret. May, 1883. No successor app.

TO CENTRAL AMERICA. GUATEMALA. COSTA RICA.

To Guatemala.

1849. Fredk. Chatfield, ch. d'a., June 16.

To Guatemala and Costa Rica.

1850. Fredk. Chatfield, apptd. ch. d'a. to Costa Rica in addition to his previous appt. to Guatemala, Feb. 20.

To Central America.

Comprising Guatemala, San Salvador, Nicaragua, Costa Rica, Honduras.

1854. Chas. Lennox Wyke, aft. sir C., ch. d'a. Oct. 31.
1857. Sir Wm. Gore Ouseley, sp. miss. Oct. 30.
1859. C. L. Wyke, *again*, env. ext. and min. plen. Aug. 8.
1860. Geo. Fagan, ch. d'a. and C.G. April 7.

1861. Geo. Benvenuto Mathew, aft. sir G., ch. d'a. and C.G., May 25; min. plen., Aug. 21.
1865. Robt. Bunch, ch. d'a. and C.G., Aug. 30, **G**. Appt. canc. and Mr. Bunch appt. to U.S. Colombia from Jan. 15, 1866.
1866. G. B. Mathew, appt. to U.S. Colombia, canc. and re-appt. to Cent. America from Jan. 15, 1866.
1866. Edwin Corbett, ch. d'a. and C.G. April 27; min. res. and C.G. Dec. 12, 1872.
1874. Sidney Locock, min. res. and C.G. May 23.
1881. Fredk. Robt. St. John, min. res. and C.G. Feb. 12.
1884. Jas. Plaister Harriss-Gastrell, min. res. and C.G. Mar. 25.

TO COLOMBIA.

THE REPUBLIC OF COLOMBIA, UNITED STATES OF COLOMBIA, NEW GRANADA, VENEZUELA, ECUADOR, PANAMA.

For the history of these states and their unions with and their separation from each other, see "Colombia," Part I., page 106.

To the Republic of Colombia.

Comprising New Granada, Venezuela, and Ecuador.

1825. Alex. Cockburn, env. ext. and min. plen. Dec. 24, **G**.
1828. Geo. Wm. Chad, env. ext. and min. plen. Feb. 12, **G**.
1829. Wm. Turner, env. ext. Sept 21.

To New Granada.

1837. Wm. Turner, env. ext. and min. plen. June 27.
1841. Robt. Stewart, ch. d'a. Aug. 16, **G**.
1843. Danl. Florence O'Leary, ch. d'a. and C.G. Nov. 28.
1854. Edwd. Thornton, aft. sir E., ch. d'a. May 6.
— Philip Griffith, ch. d'a. Sept 19.

To the United States of Colombia.

Comprising New Granada and Panama.

1865. Geo. Benvenuto Mathew, c.b., aft. sir G., min. plen., Aug. 26; appt. canc. and Mr. Mathew re-appt. to Cent. America from Jan. 15, 1866.
1866. Robt. Bunch, ch. d'a. and C.G., Jan. 15; min. res. and C.G., Dec. 12, 1872.
1878. Col. Chas. Edwd. Mansfield, min. res. and C.G. July 1.
1881. Aug. Hy. Mounsey, min. res. and C.G. Apr. 26.
1882. Jas. Plaister Harriss-Gastrell, min. res. and C.G. May 10.
1884. Fredk. Robt. St. John, min. res. and C.G. Mar. 25.
1885. Wm. Jno. Dickson, min. res. and C.G. Mar. 14.

To Venezuela.

1835. Sir Robert Ker Porter, ch. d'a. July 2.
1842. Belford Hinton Wilson, aft. sir B., ch. d'a. and C.G. Nov. 30.
1852. Hon. R. C. Bingham, ch. d'a. and C.G. Nov. 23.
1858. Philip Edmund Wodehouse, aft. sir P., sp. miss. Feb. 22.
1858. Fredk. Doveton Orme, ch. d'a. and C.G. Apr. 1
1864. Hon. Rd. Edwardes, ch. d'a. and C.G. May 26.

865. Geo. Fagan, ch. d'a. and C.G. Aug. 10.
869. Robt. Thos. Chas. Middleton, ch. d'a. and C.G., July 5; min. res. and C.G., Dec. 12.
1878. Robt. Bunch, min. res. July 1.
1881. Col. Chas. Edwd. Mansfield, min. res. Apr. 26.
1884. Fredk. Robt. St. John, min. res. Dec. 24.

TO BRAZIL.

SINCE the separation of Brazil from Portugal, and its erection into an Empire in November 1825.

1826. Hon. Robt. Gordon, aft. sir R., env. ext. and min. plen. July 31.
1828. John, ld., aft. visc., Ponsonby, env. ext. and min. plen. Feb. 12.
— Percy Clinton, visc. Strangford, sp. miss. Aug. 19.
1832. Hy. Stephen Fox, env. ext. and min. plen. June 1.
1835. Hamilton Chas. Jas. Hamilton, env. ext. and min. plen. Oct. 2.
1838. Wm. Gore Ouseley, ch. d'a. Apr. 20.
1842. Hy. Ellis, aft. sir H., ext. and sp. miss. Aug. 27.
1847. John Hobart, ld. Howden, env. ext. and min. plen. Jan. 25.
1850. James Hudson, aft. sir James, env. ext. and min. plen. May 13.
1851. Hy. Southern, C.B., env. ext. and min. plen. Aug. 29.
1853. Hy. Fras. Howard, aft. sir H., env. ext. and min. plen. May 3.
1855. Hon. Peter Campbell Scarlett, C.B., env. ext. and min. plen. Dec. 31.
1858. Hon. Fras. Regd. Forbes, env. ext. and min. plen. Dec. 13.
1859. Wm. Dougal Christie, env. ext. and min. plen., Sept. 2.
Dipl. rel. susp., July 5, 1863.
1865. Edwd. Thornton, C.B., aft. sir E., sp. miss., July 27; env. ext. and min. plen. Aug. 10.
1867. Geo. Buckley Mathew, C.B., aft. sir G., env. ext. and min. plen. Sept. 19.
1879. Fras. Clare Ford, C.B., C.M.G., aft. sir F., env. ext. and min. plen. June 14.
1881. Edwin Corbett, env. ext. and min. plen. Mar. 5.
1885. Sidney Locock, env. ext. and min. plen. Feb. 11; did not proceed.
1885. Hugh Guion Macdonell, env. ext. and min. plen. Nov. 5.
1888. Geo. Hugh Wyndham, C.B., env. ext. and min. plen. Feb. 1.

TO PERU.

1842. Wm. Pitt Adams, ch. d'a. and C.G. Nov. 30, G.
1852. Capt. Hon. Edwd. Alfd. Jno. Harris, aft. adm. sir E., ch. d'a. and C.G. Dec. 11.
1853. Stephen Hy. Sulivan, ch. d'a. and C.G. Jan. 17.
1857. Hon. Wm. Geo. Stafford Jermingham, ch. d'a. and C.G., Dec. 21; min. res. and C.G., Dec. 12, 1872.
1874. Spenser St. John, aft. sir S., min. res. and C.G. Oct. 14.
1884. Col. Chas. Edwd. Mansfield, aft. sir C., min. res. and C.G. Dec 24.

TO BOLIVIA.

1837. Belford Hinton Wilson, ch. d'a. Nov. 18.
1842. Wm. Pitt Adams, ch. d'a. Nov. 30.
1848. Hon. Fredk. Wm. Aug. Bruce, ch. d'a. Apr. 14.
1851. Geo. Aug. Lloyd, ch. d'a. Dec. 4.
1852. Sir Chas. Hotham, sp. miss., April 17; did not proceed.
Dipl. rel. susp., Oct. 21, 1853 to July 6, 1857.
1858. Fredk. Doveton Orme, ch. d'a. and C.G. Apr. 1; did not proceed.
1858. Wm. Garrow Lettsom, ch. d'a. and C.G. July 24; did not proceed.
1875. Spenser St. John, after sir S., sp. miss. July 18.

TO RIO DE LA PLATA. ARGENTINE CONFEDERATIO ARGENTINE REPUBLIC.

To Rio de la Plata.

1825. Jno., ld., aft. visc. Ponsonby, env. ext. and min. plen. Dec. 24, **G**.

1828. Hy. Stephen Fox, min. plen. April 18, **G**.

1832. Hamilton Chas. Jas. Hamilton, m plen. June 1.

1835. Jno. Hy. Mandeville, min. pl Sept. 23.

To the Argentine Comfederation.

1844. Wm. Gore Ouseley, aft. sir W., min. plen. Dec. 13.

1847. John Hobart, lord Howden, sp. miss. Jan. 25.

1848. Hy. Southern, min. plen. May 31.

1851. Capt. hon. Robt. Gore, R.N., ch. d'a. Aug. 29.

1852. Sir Chas. Hotham, sp. miss. A 17.

1854. Wm. Dougal Christie, ch. d Oct. 10; min. plen., Jan. 1856.

1859. Edwd. Thornton, aft. sir E., m plen. Sept. 9.

To the Argentine Republic.

1865. Hon. Rd. Edwardes, min. plen. Aug. 10; did not proceed.

1866. Geo. Buckley Mathew, C.B., aft. sir G., min. plen. April 13.

1867. Wm. Lowther, aft. hon. W., min. plen. Sept. 26.

1868. Hon. Wm. Stuart, min. plen. Jan. 11.

1872. Hon. Lionel Sackville Sackville-West, aft. sir L., env. ext. and min. plen. Sept. 17.

1878. Fras. Clare Ford, C.B., C.M. aft. sir F., env. ext. and m plen. Feb. 9.

1879. Sir Horace Rumbold, bt., env. e and min. plen. Aug. 15.

1881. Geo. Glynn Petre, env. ext. and m plen. Apr. 1.

1884. Hon. Edmd. Jno. Monson, env. e and min. plen. Jan. 16.

1885. Hon. Fras. Jno. Pakenham, e ext. and min. plen. Feb. 1.

TO PARAGUAY.

1852. Sir Chas. Hotham, sp. miss. April 17.

1854. Chas. Alan Henderson, consul. Apr. 24.

1858. Wm. Dougal Christie, sp. miss.

Dipl. rel. susp. from Aug. 5, 1859.

1863. Edwd. Thornton, aft. sir E., min. plen. Oct. 30.

1866. Geo. Buckley Mathew, aft. sir min. plen. Dec. 6.

1868. Hon. Wm. Stuart, min. plen. J 22; did not proceed.

1882. Geo. Glynn Petre, min. pl Mar. 2.

1884. Hon. Edmd. Jno. Monson, C. min. plen. Jan. 16.

1885. Hon. Fras. Jno. Pakenham, m plen. Feb. 1.

TO URUGUAY.

1843. Adolphus Turner, ch. d'a. and C.G. April 11.

1847. Wm. Gore Ouseley, aft. sir Wm., min. plen. and sp. miss. Jan. 2.

1847. John Hobart, lord Howden, sp. mi Jan. 25.

— Capt. hon. Robt. Gore, R.N., d'a. Oct. 26, **G**.

1851. Hon. Fredk. Wm. Adolphus Bruce, aft. sir F., ch. d'a. and C.G. Aug. 29.

1852. Sir Chas. Hotham, sp. miss. Apr. 17.

1853. Geo. Jno. Robt. Gordon, ch. d'a. and C.G. Sept. 23.

1854. Edwd. Thornton, aft. sir E., ch. d'a. and C.G. Sept. 19.

1859. Wm. Garrow Lettsom, ch. d'a. and C.G. Sept. 9.

1869. Hon. Wm. Stuart, ch. d'a., Sept. 24.

Dipl. rel. susp., Nov. 13, 1871.

1879. Fras. Clare Ford, C.B. and C.M.G., aft. sir C., min. plen. and C.G. Feb. 24.

1879. Hon. Edmd. Jno. Monson, C.B., min. res. and C.G. June 21.

1884. Wm. Gifford Palgrave, min. res. and C.G. Jan. 16.

TO CHILI.

1841. Col. hon. Jno. Walpole, ch. d'a. May 24.

1849. Stephen Hy. Sulivan, ch. d'a. and C.G. May 30.

1853. Capt. hon. Edwd. Alfred Jno. Harris, aft. adm. sir E., ch. d'a. and C.G. Jan. 17.

1858. Wm. Taylour Thomson, aft. sir W., ch. d'a. and C.G. Feb. 24.

1872. Horace Rumbold, aft. sir H., min. res. and C.G. Oct. 24.

1878. Hon. Fras. Jno. Pakenham, min. res. and C.G. Mar. 8.

1885. Hugh Fraser, min. res. and C.G. Feb. 17. Transf. to Japan 1888.

TO THE HAWAIIAN OR SANDWICH ISLANDS.

1866. Maj. Jas. Hay Wodehouse, commr. and C.G., June 21.

PART III. POLITICAL AND OFFICIAL.

GOVERNMENT OFFICIALS, OFFICERS OF STATE, OFFICERS OF THE HOUSEHOLD, &c.

THE ADMINISTRATIONS OF ENGLAND, GREAT BRITAIN, AND THE UNITED KINGDOM.

THE higher officers of the Government, holding their offices during the sovereign's pleasure, and removable on political change, are collectively called "the Administration," and are almost invariably members of one or other house of parliament. A select number of these, filling the most important offices, who assemble to concert on and conduct the measures of the Government, are now called the CABINET, a name not known to the constitution, but which is, in fact, a committee of the privy council, who constitute the responsible advisers of the Crown. The following lists are confined to cabinet ministers, or to those who in former times exercised analogous powers.

ADMINISTRATIONS OF ENGLAND.

From the Accession of King Henry VIII.

KING HENRY VIII.

1509. Wm. Warham, abp. of Canterbury, ld. chanc.; Thos. Howard, E. of Surrey, aft. D. of Norfolk, ld. treas.; Richd. Fox, bp. of Winchester, former sec. to Henry VII., pr. seal; Geo., E. of Shrewsbury, ld. stewd.; Chas., lord Herbert, ld. chambn.; John Fisher, bp. of Rochester and cardinal, &c.

1514. Thos. Wolsey, abp. of York and cardinal, ld. chanc.; Thos. D. of Norfolk, ld. treas.; Chas., E. of Winchester, ld. chamb.; Thos. Routhal, bp. of Durham, sec. st. (made pr. seal), &c. The D. of Norfolk aft. res. in favour of his son.

1523. Thos., E. of Surrey, ld. h. treas.; Cuthbert Tunstall, bp. of London, pr. seal; Richd. Pace, succ. by Dr. Knight, sec. st.

1529. Sir Thos. More, ld. chanc.; Thos. Howard, D. of Norfolk, ld. h. treas.; Cuthbert Tunstall, bp. of London, pr. seal; Stephen Gardiner, aft. bp. of Winchester, sec. st.; Thos. Cranmer, aft. abp. of Canterbury, &c.

1532 Sir Thos. Audley, aft. ld. Audley, ld. kpr.; Thos. Boleyn, E. of Wiltshire, pr. seal; Thos Cromwell, aft. E. of Essex, Thos. Cranmer, aft. abp. of Canterbury, &c.

1540. Thos., ld. Audley, ld. chanc., Thos., D. of Norfolk, ld. h. treas. Chas., D. of Suffolk, ld. pres.; Hy., E. of Surrey, bp. Gardiner, ld. Russell, &c. Sir Thos, aft. ld. Wriothesley, and sir Ralph Sadler, secs. st.

1544. Thos., ld. Wriothesley, ld. chanc. Thos. D. of Norfolk, ld. treas.; Chas., D. of Suffolk, ld. pres.; John, ld. Russell, pr. seal; Wm., ld. St. John, John, ld. Lisle, sir Anthy. Brown, &c. Sir Wm. Petre and sir Wm. Paget, secs. st.

KING EDWARD VI.

1547. Wm., ld. St. John, ld. kpr. and ld. pres., succ. by Rd., ld. Rich. as ld. chanc.; Edwd., E. of Hertford, ld. protector, cr. D. of Somerset, and made ld. treas.; John, ld. Russell, pr. seal; Hy., E. of Arundel, ld. chambn.; Thos., ld. Seymour, sir Anth. Brown, &c. Sir Wm. Paget and sir Wm. Petre, secs. st.

1551. Thos. Goodrich, bp. of Ely, ld. kpr., aft. ld. chanc.; John Dudley, late ld. Lisle, E. of Warwick, cr. D. of Northumberland, ld. h. adm.; Wm., late ld. St. John, now E. of Wiltshire, ld. treas. in 1550, pres. of the council; John, E. of Bedford, pr. seal; Thos., ld. Wentworth, ld. chambn., &c. Sir Wm. Petre and Sir Wm. Cecil, secs. st.

QUEEN MARY.

1554. Stephen Gardiner, bp. of Winchester, ld. chanc.; Wm., M. of Winchester, late ld. Wiltshire, ld. treas.; E. of Arundel, ld. pres.; John, E. of Bedford, succ. by Edwd., E. of Derby, pr. seal; Wm., ld. Howard, ld. h. adm.; sir Edw. Hastings, sir John Baker, Edmd. Bonner, bp. of London, &c. Sir Wm. Petre, sir John Cheke, and sir John Bourne, secs. st.

It appears by the council Register, folio 725, that three secretaries of state were appointed 7 Edward VI., June 2, 1553.

QUEEN ELIZABETH.

1558. Sir Nicholas Bacon, ld. kpr. and pr. seal; Wm., M. of Winchester, ld. treas.; Edw., ld. Clinton, ld. adm.; sir Robt. Dudley, aft. E. of Leicester, ld. Howard of Effingham, ld. Arundel, sir Fras. Knollys, &c. Sir Wm. Cecil, sec. st. This last statesman, aft. ld. Burleigh, continued secretary or chief minister during almost the whole of this reign.

1572. Sir Wm. Cecil, now ld. Burleigh, ld. h. treas.; sir Nichs. Bacon, ld. chanc.; ld. Howard of Effingham, pr. seal; Robt. Dudley, E. of Leicester, m. horse; sir Hy. Cocks, the E. of Sussex, &c. Sir Francis Walsingham, sec. st.

1579. Sir Thos. Bromley, ld. chanc.; Wm. ld. Burleigh, ld. treas.; Edw., E. of Lincoln, ld. h. adm.; Ambrose, E. of Warwick, ordnance; Thos., E. of Sussex, Robt., E. of Leicester, sir Walter Mildmay, Jas. Windebank, &c. Sir Fras. Walsingham and sir Thos. Wilson, secs. st.

1587. Sir Christ. Hatton, ld. chanc.; Wm., ld. Burleigh, ld. treas.; Robt. Devereux, E. of Essex, &c.

1599. Thos. Sackville, ld. Buckhurst, aft. E. of Dorset, ld. h. treas.; sir Thos. Egerton, aft. ld. Ellesmere and subsequently visc. Brackley, ld. kpr.; Chas., ld. Howard of Effingham, &c. Sir Robt. Cecil, son of lord Burleigh, sec. st.

KING JAMES I.

1603. Thos., E. of Dorset, ld. treas.; Thos., ld. Ellesmere, ld. chanc.; Chas., E. of Nottingham, ld. adm.; Thos., E. of Suffolk, Edwd., E. of Worcester, sir Rd. Vernon, Geo., ld. Hume of Berwick, Jas. Hay, ld. Hay, &c. Robt. Cecil, aft. E. of Salisbury, sec. st.

1609. Robt. Cecil, E. of Salisbury, ld. h. treas.; Thos., ld. Ellesmere, ld. chanc.; Hy., E. of Northampton, pr. seal; Chas., E. of Nottingham, Thos., E. of Suffolk, &c.

1612. Hy., E. of Northampton, first commr. of the treas.; Thos., ld. Ellesmere, ld. chanc.; Robt. Carr, visc. Rochester, aft. E. of Somerset, ld. chambn.; Edwd., E. of Worcester, sir Ralph Winwood, Chas., E. of Nottingham, &c.

1615. Thos., E. of Suffolk, ld. treas.; Thos., ld. Ellesmere, ld. chanc.; Edwd., E. of Worcester, pr. seal; Chas., E. of Nottingham, sir Geo. Villiers, aft. visc. Villiers, and successively E., M., and D. of Buckingham, ld. h. adm. in 1619; sir Ralph Winwood, sir Thos. Lake, &c.

1620. Sir Hy. Montagu, aft. visc. Mandeville, and E. of Manchester, ld. treas.

1621. Lionel, ld. Cranfield, aft. E. of Middlesex, Edwd., E. of Worcester, John, E. of Bristol, John Williams, dean of Westminster, Geo. Villiers, now M. of Buckingham, sir Edwd. Conway, aft. ld. Conway, &c.

KING CHARLES I.

1628. Rd., ld. Weston, aft. E. of Portland, ld. treas.; sir Thos. Coventry, aft. ld. Coventry, ld. kpr.; Hy., E. of Manchester (succ. by Jas., E. of Marlborough, who, in turn, gave place to Edwd., ld., aft. visc. Conway), pr. seal; Wm. Laud, bp. of London, sir Albertus Morton, &c.

1635. Wm. Laud, now abp. of Canterbury, first commr. of the treas.; Frs., ld. Cottington, Jas., M. of Hamilton, Edwd., E. of Dorset, sir John Coke, sir Fras. Windebank, &c. The great seal in commission.

1640. Wm. Juxon, bp. of London, ld. treas.; sir John Finch, aft. ld. Finch, ld. kpr.; Fras., ld. Cottington, Wentworth, E. of Strafford, Algernon, E. of Northumberland, Jas., M. of Hamilton, Laud, abp. of Canterbury; and sir Fras. Windebank and sir Hy. Vane, secs. st.

COMMONWEALTH.

1653. Oliver Cromwell, made protector. He named a council whose number at no time was to exceed twenty-one members, nor be less than thirteen.

1658. Rd. Cromwell, son of Oliver, succ. on the death of the latter. A council of officers ruled at Wallingford House.

KING CHARLES II.

From the Restoration of the King.

Until this time there was not, in point of fact, anything that could be properly called a CABINET. The sovereign had latterly governed by a collection of privy councillors, sometimes of larger, sometimes of smaller number, not always holding the same offices, and still less the same men.

1660. Sir Edwd. Hyde, aft. E. of Clarendon, ld. chanc.; Geo. Monk, general of the king's forces in the three kingdoms, and m. horse, cr. D. of Albemarle; Thos., E. of Southampton, soon made ld. treas.; Edwd. Montagu, cr. E. of Sandwich, general and adm.; Jas., D. of York, brother to the king, ld. h. adm.; lord Sey and Sele, pr. seal; sir Robt. Long, ch. ex.; E. of Manchester, lord Seymour, &c. Sir Edwd. Nicholas and sir Wm. Morrice, secs. st.

1667. Geo. Monk, D. of Albemarle, made first commr. of the treas., &c.

1670. "The CABAL" Ministry. Sir Thos. Clifford, aft. ld. Clifford (C); Anthy. Ashley, aft. E. of Shaftesbury (A); Geo. Villiers, D. of Buckingham (B); Hy., ld. Arlington, aft. E. of Arlington (A) and John, D. of Lauderdale (L). This Ministry obtained the name of *Cabal* from the initial letters of their five names, which composed the word. At the time that this appellation had generally obtained, about 1672, ld. Clifford held the office of ld. treas.; ld. Ashley had become ld. chanc.; the D. of Buckingham was ld. pres.; ld. Arlington, sec. st.; and the D. of Lauderdale, ld. pres. of Scotland.

1672. Thos., ld. Clifford, Anthy., E. of Shaftesbury, late ld. Ashley, Hy., E. of Arlington, E. of Anglesey, sir Thos. Osborne, cr. visc. Latimer, Hy. Coventry, sir John Duncombe, sir Geo. Carteret, Edwd. Seymour, &c.

1673. Thos., visc. Latimer, aft. E. of Danby, made ld. h. treas. June 26.

1679. Arthur, E. of Essex, made first commr. of the treas., Mar. 26; succ. by Laurence Hyde, aft. E. of Rochester, Nov. 21, both in this year. Robt., E. of Sunderland, sec. st., *vice* sir Joseph Williamson, &c.

The king nominated a new council this year, on April 21, consisting of thirty members only, of whom the principal were the great officers of state and great officers of the household.

1684. Sidney, ld. Godolphin, Lawrence, E. of Rochester, Danl., E. of Nottingham, Robt., E. of Sunderland, sir Thos. Chicheley, Geo., ld. Dartmouth, Hy., E. of Clarendon, EE. of Bath and Radnor, &c.

KING JAMES II.

1685. Lawrence, E. of Rochester, Geo., M. of Halifax, sir Geo. Jeffreys, aft. lord Jeffreys and ld. chanc., Hy., E. of Clarendon, sir John Ernley, D. of Queensberry, visc. Preston, &c.

1687. The E. of Rochester was displaced, and John, ld. Belasyse, made first commr. of the treas. in his room. Jan. 4; the E. of Sunderland made pres. of the council; visc. Preston, sec. st.; and various other changes took place in this and the following year.

1688. The king left Whitehall in the night of Dec. 17, and, quitting the kingdom, landed at Ambleteuse, in France, Dec. 23.

KING WILLIAM III.

1689. Chas., visc. Mordaunt, first commr. of the treas.; Thos. Osborne, E. of Danby, cr. M. of Carmarthen, aft. D. of Leeds, ld. pres.; Geo., M. of Halifax, pr. seal; Arthur Herbert, aft. lord Torrington, first commr. of the admy.; EE. of Shrewsbury, Nottingham, and Sunderland, E. of Dorset and Middlesex, Wm., E., aft. D. of Devonshire, ld. Godolphin, ld. Montagu, ld. De la Mere, &c. The great seal in commission.

1690. Sidney, ld. Godolphin, first commr. of the treas.; Thos., E. of Danby, ld. pres.; Rd. Hampden, ch. ex.; Thos., E. of Pembroke, adm.; Hy., visc. Sydney, and Daniel, E. of Nottingham, secs. st., &c. The great seal and pr. seal in commission.

1698. Chas. Montagu, aft. ld. Halifax, first commr. of the treas., May 1; succ. by Ford, E. of Tankerville, Nov. 15, 1699.

QUEEN ANNE.

The formation of a ministry under a "Premier" began about this time.

1702. SIDNEY, LORD, aft. E. GODOLPHIN, ld. treas.; Thos., E. of Pembroke and Montgomery, ld. pres.; John Sheffield, M. of Normanby, aft. D. of Normanby and Buckingham, pr. seal; hon. Hy. Boyle, ch. ex; sir Chas. Hedges and the E. of Nottingham (the latter succ. by Robt. Harley, cr. E. of Oxford in 1704), secs. st., &c.

1711. ROBT., E. OF OXFORD, ld. treas.; sir Simon, aft. lord Harcourt, ld. kpr.; John, D. of Normanby and Buckingham, ld. pres.; John, bp. of Bristol, aft. of London, pr. seal; Hy. St. John, aft. visc. Bolingbroke, and Wm., lord Dartmouth, secs. st.; Robt. Benson, aft. ld. Bingley, ch. ex., &c.

1714. Chas., D. of Shrewsbury, ld. treas., July 30, two days before the queen's death. Patent revoked Oct. 13 following.

KING GEORGE I.

1714. CHAS., E. OF HALIFAX, first ld. treas., succ. on his death by the E. OF CARLISLE; Wm., ld. Cowper, aft. E. Cowper, ld. chanc.; Danl., E. of Nottingham, ld. pres.; Thos., M. of Wharton, pr. seal; Edwd., E. of Oxford, first ld. admy.; Jas. Stanhope, aft. E. Stanhope, and Chas., visc. Townshend, secs. st.; sir Rd. Onslow, ch. ex., DD. of Montrose & Marlborough, lord Berkeley, Robt. Walpole, Wm. Pulteney, aft. E. of Bath, &c.

1715. ROBT. WALPOLE, first ld. treas. and ch. ex., &c.

1717. JAS. STANHOPE, aft. E. Stanhope, first ld. treas. and ch. ex.; Wm., ld. Cowper, Chas., E. of Sunderland, D. of Kingston, ld. Berkeley, Joseph Addison, &c.

1718. CHAS., E. OF SUNDERLAND, first ld. treas; Thos., ld. Parker, aft. E. of Macclesfield, ld. chanc.; E. Stanhope, D. of Kent, ld. Berkeley, Jas. Craggs, Jno. Aislabie, &c.

1721. ROBT. WALPOLE, aft. sir Robt., first ld. treas. and ch. ex.; Thos., ld. Parker, cr. E. of Macclesfield, ld. chanc.; Hy., ld. Carleton, succ. by Wm., D. of Devonshire, ld. pres.; Evelyn, D. of Kingston, succ. by ld. Trevor, pr. seal; Jas., E. of Berkeley, first ld. adm.; Chas., visc. Townshend, and John, lord Carteret (the latter succ. by the D. of Newcastle), secs. st.; John, D. of Marlborough, succ. by the E. of Cadogan, ordnance; Geo. Treby, succ. by Hy. Pelham, sec.-at-war; visc. Torrington, &c.

KING GEORGE II.

1727. SIR ROBT. WALPOLE, &c. *contd.*

The following was the state of the Cabinet near the close of sir Robt. Walpole's long administration.

1740. SIR ROBT. WALPOLE, first ld. treas. and ch. ex.; Philip, ld. Hardwicke, ld. chanc.; Spencer, E. of Wilmington, ld. pres.; John, ld. Hervey, pr. seal; John Potter, abp. of Canterbury; D. of Newcastle and E. of Harrington, secs. st.; sir Chas. Wager, first ld. admy.; D. of Dorset, ld. stewd.†; D. of Grafton, ld. chambn.†; D. of Richmond, m. horse†; E. of Pembroke, gr. stole,† &c.

† These great household officers were at this period always in what was called the *Cabinet*, but there was an interior council, of Walpole, the chancellor, and the secretaries of state, who, in the first instance, consulted together on the more confidential points.*

* *Lord Hervey's Memoirs of the Reign of George II. edited by John Wilson Croker.*—Mr. Croker adds, "The duke of Bolton, without a right to it from his office

1742. Sir Robt. Walpole res. Feb. 8, having been first minister twenty-one consecutive years. He was cr. E. of Orford, visc. Walpole, and baron Houghton. The E. of Wilmington was made minister in his room.

1742. Feb. SPENCER, E. OF WILMINGTON, first ld. treas.; ld. Hardwicke, ld. chanc.; Saml. Sandys, ch. ex.; E. of Harrington, pres. of the council; E. Gower, pr. seal; ld. Carteret and the D. of Newcastle, secs. st.; E. of Winchilsea, first ld. admy.; D. of Argyll, com. of the forces and m. g. ordn.; Hy. Pelham, paym. of the forces, &c.

The D. of Argyll res., and was succ. by the E. of Stair, as com. of the forces, and by the D. of Montagu as m. g. ordn.

1743. Aug. 25. HY. PELHAM, first ld. treas. and ch. ex., *vice* Spencer, E. of Wilmington, deceased.

1744. Nov. The "BROAD BOTTOM" Administration: Hy. Pelham, first ld. treas. and ch. ex.; ld. Hardwicke, ld. chanc.; D. of Dorset, pres. of the council; E. Gower, pr. seal; D. of Newcastle, sec. st. for the Southern, and the E. of Harrington for the Northern dept.; D. of Montagu, m. g. ordn.; D. of Bedford, first ld. adm.; D. of Argyll, kpr. of the gr. seal of Scotland; M. of Tweeddale, sec. st. for Scotland; D. of Grafton, ld. chambn.; D. of Richmond, m. horse.

1746. Mr. Pelham and his friends having tendered their resignation to the king, the formation of a new administration, which expired within two days while yet incomplete, was undertaken by the E. of Bath; the members of it actually appointed, and submitted for approval to his majesty were:—

1746. Feb. 10 to Feb. 12. The "SHORT-LIVED" MINISTRY: WM., E. OF BATH, first ld. treas.; ld. Carlisle, pr. seal; ld. Winchilsea, first ld. admy.; and ld. Granville, sec. st. Expired Feb. 12.

1746. Feb. 12. HY. PELHAM returned, with his colleagues, to power.

The D. of Bedford res. the admy. to the E. of Sandwich, and succ. the E. of Chesterfield as sec. st., Feb. 1748; and the E. of Holdernesse succ. the D. of Bedford, June 1751, in the same office. Mr. Pelham *d.* Mar. 6, 1754.

1754. Apr. THOS. HOLLES PELHAM, D. OF NEWCASTLE, first ld. treas.; hon. Hy. Bilson Legge, ch. ex.; E. of Holdernesse and sir Thos. Robinson, aft. ld. Grantham, secs. st.; the latter succ. by Hy. Fox; ld. Anson, first ld. admy.; ld. Granville, ld. pres.; ld. Gower, succ. by the D. of Marlborough, pr. seal; D. of Grafton, E. of Halifax, Geo. Grenville, &c. E. of Hardwicke, ld. chanc.

1756. Nov. WM., D. OF DEVONSHIRE, first ld. treas.; WM. PITT, sec. st. for the Southern dept.; hon. Hy. Bilson Legge, ch. ex.; E. Granville, ld. pres.; E. Gower, pr. seal; E. of Holdernesse, sec. st. for the Northern dept.; Geo. Grenville, E. of Halifax, DD. of Rutland and Grafton, E. of Rochford, &c. The gr. seal in commission.

1757. June. D. OF NEWCASTLE and WM. PITT'S ADMINISTRATION. Thos. Holles Pelham, D. of Newcastle, first ld. treas.; Wm. Pitt, aft. ld. Chatham, sec. st. for the Northern dept., and leader of the house of commons; ld. Henley, ld. kpr.; ld. Granville, ld. pres.; E. Temple, pr. seal; Hy. Bilson Legge, ch. ex.; E. of Holdernesse, sec. st. for the Southern dept.; D. of Devonshire, ld. chambn.; D. of Rutland, ld. stewd.; ld. Anson, first ld. admy.; D. of Marlborough, succ. by lord Ligonier, m. g. ordn.; Hy. Fox, aft. ld. Holland, paym.; Geo. Grenville, lords Halifax and Gower, Jas. Grenville, &c.

KING GEORGE III.

1760. D. OF NEWCASTLE and WM. PITT'S ministry, *contd.*

The following were among the changes subsequent to the acc. of George III.: sir Robt. Henley, cr. lord Henley, ld. chanc., Jan. 1761; the E. of Bute, sec. st., *vice* the E. of Holdernesse, Mar.;

of captain of the Band of Pensioners, in which employment he succeeded the duke of Montagu on his removal to the ordnance, was likewise admitted to the cabinet council, because he had been of the cabinet seven years previously, at the time he was turned out of all his offices." And he further says, "Sir John Norris (vice-admiral of England) was called in, as an auxiliary, when anything was under deliberation in relation to our then maritime war with Spain."

and the E. of Egremont, *vice* Wm. Pitt, Oct. same year; ld. North, a ld. of the treas., &c.

1762. May. JOHN, E. OF BUTE, first ld. treas.; ld. Henley, ld. chanc.; sir Fras. Dashwood, aft. ld. le Despencer, ch. ex.; ld. Granville, ld. pres.; D. of Bedford, pr. seal; E. of Halifax, first ld. admy.; E. of Egremont and Geo. Grenville, secs. st.; ld. Ligonier, ordn.; Hy. Fox, paym.; visc. Barrington, ld. Sandys, D. of Marlborough, lords Huntingdon and North, &c.

1763 May. *et seq.* GEO. GRENVILLE, first ld. treas. and ch. ex.; E. Granville, succ. by JOHN, D. of BEDFORD, ld. pres.; D. of Marlborough, pr. seal; ld. Henley, aft. E. of Northington, ld. chanc.; EE. of Halifax and Sandwich, secs. st.; E. Gower, ld. chambn.; ld. Egmont, first ld. admy.; M. of Granby, ordn.; ld. Holland, late Mr. Fox, paym.; Welbore Ellis, sec.-at-war; ld. Hillsborough, first ld. of trade; D. of Rutland, lord North, &c.

1765. July. *et seq.* CHAS., M. OF ROCKINGHAM, first ld. treas; Wm. Dowdeswell, ch. ex.; E. of Winchilsea and Nottingham, ld. pres.; D. of Newcastle, pr. seal; D. of Portland, ld. chamb.; D. of Rutland, m. horse; ld. Talbot, ld. stewd.; gen. the hon. H. Seymour Conway, and the D. of Grafton, secs. st.; ld. Egmont, first ld. admy.; M. of Granby, ordn.; visc. Barrington, sec.-at-war; visc. Howe, treas. of the navy; hon. Chas. Townshend, paym.; E. of Dartmouth, first ld. of trade; ld. John Cavendish, Thos. Townshend, &c. E. of Northington (late Lord Henley), ld. chanc.

1766. Aug. E. of CHATHAM (late WM. PITT), first min. and pr. seal; D. of Grafton, first ld. treas.; hon. Chas. Townshend, ch. ex.; E. of Northington, ld. pres; Wm. E. of Shelburne and gen. Conway, secs. st.; sir Chas. Saunders, succ. by Sir Edw. Hawke, first ld. admy.; M. of Granby, ordn.; ld. Hillsborough, first ld. of trade; lord Barrington, sec.-at-war; Fredk., lord North, a joint paym.; visc. Howe, &c. Lord Camden, ld. chanc.

1767. Wm., lord Mansfield, ld. c. j. of the king's bench, became, *ex officio*, ch. ex., *pro. tem.*, on the death of Mr. Townshend, Sept. this year; and Fredk., lord North, was app. ch. ex. Dec. following.

1767. Dec. AUG. HY., D. OF GRAFTON, first ld. treas.; Fredk., ld. North, ch. ex.; E. Gower, ld. pres.; E. of Chatham, ld. pr. seal until Oct. 1768, then succ. by the E. of Bristol; E. of Shelburne, sec. st. for the Southern dept.; visc. Weymouth, Northern dept.; and ld. Hillsborough, colonies; sir Edwd. Hawke, first ld. admy.; M. of Granby, ordn.; lords Sandwich and le Despencer, joint postm. gen.; Lord Hertford, Thos. Townshend, &c. Lord Camden, ld. chanc.

1768. Nov. Visc. Weymouth, sec. st. for the Southern dept., *vice* lord Shelburne; E. of Rochford, sec. st. for the Northern dept., *vice* lord Weymouth.

1770. Jan. FREDK., LORD NORTH, first ld. treas. and ch. ex.; E. Gower, ld. pres.; E. of Halifax, pr. seal; ld. Rochford, ld. Weymouth (succ. by ld. Sandwich), and ld. Hillsborough (colonies), secs. st.; Sir Edwd. Hawke, first ld. admy.; ld. Granby, ordn.; sir Gilbert Elliot, treas. of the navy; lord Barrington, sec.-at-war; lord Hertford, lord Carteret, &c. The great seal was delivered to Mr. Attorney-gen. Yorke, who was made ld. chanc.; but before the patent for his peerage, under the title of lord Morden, was completed, he died suddenly, and the seal, after being a year in commission, was given to the hon. Henry Bathurst, one of the commrs., who was cr. lord Apsley.

Lord North continued minister eleven years, during the whole of the American war. The changes within this period were numerous; among them were:

1771. Lord Halifax, sec. st., *vice* ld. Sandwich, who went to the admiralty; succ. as ld. pr. seal by the E. of Suffolk and Berkshire. Jan. The latter gave place to the D. of Grafton, and became sec. st. June.

1772. Lord Dartmouth, sec. st., *vice* ld. Hillsborough. Aug. Visc. Townshend, ordn, *vice* M. of Granby. Oct.

1775. Visc. Weymouth, *again* sec. st., *vice* Rochford; and ld. Geo. Sackville Germaine, *vice* Dartmouth, made pr. seal. Nov.

1778. Lord Thurlow, ld. chanc. June.

1779. Lords Stormont and Hillsborough secs. st. E. Bathurst, ld. pres. Nov.

1782. Mar. CHAS., M. OF ROCKINGHAM, first ld. treas.; ld. John Cavendish, ch. ex.; ld. Camden, pres. of the council; D. of Grafton, pr. seal; Wm., E. of Shelburne, and Chas. Jas. Fox, secs. st.; Augs. Keppel, first ld. admy.; D. of Richmond, ordn.; Thos. Townshend, sec.-at-war; Isaac Barré, treas. of the navy; Edm. Burke, paym., &c. Lord Thurlow, ld. chanc.

The death of the M. of Rockingham (July 2, 1782) led to the administration of lord Shelburne, who accepted the office of first minister, without the privity of his colleagues, and Mr. Fox, lord John Cavendish, and others, resigned.

1782. July. WM., E. OF SHELBURNE, aft. M. of Lansdowne, first ld treas.; Wm. Pitt, ch. ex.; ld., aft. E. Camden, pres. of the council; D. of Grafton, pr. seal; Thos., ld. Grantham, home, and Thos. Townshend, foreign, secs.; Aug., visc. Keppel, first ld. admy.; D. of Richmond, ordn.; Hy. Dundas, treas. of the navy; Isaac Barré, paym.; Sir. Geo. Yonge, sec.-at-war; &c. Lord Thurlow, ld chanc. chanc.

1783. Apr. "*THE* COALITION" MINISTRY, so called from the coalition of LD. NORTH AND MR. FOX, who had, for years previously, opposed and even abused each other. D. of Portland, first ld. treas.; visc. Stormont, pres. of the council; E. of Carlisle, pr. seal; Fredk., ld. North, and Chas. Jas. Fox, home and foreign secs.; ld. John Cavendish, ch. ex.; visc. Keppel, first ld. admy.; visc. Townshend, ordn.; Chas. Townshend, treas. of the navy; Edm. Burke paym.; R. Fitzpatrick, sec.-at war; &c. The great seal in commission; lord Loughborough, c. j. of the common pleas, first commr.

1783. Dec. WM. PITT, first ld. treas. and ch. ex.; E. Gower, pres. of the council; D. of Rutland, pr. seal; M. of Carmarthen, and E. Temple, (the latter immediately succ. by lord Sydney), secs. st.; D. of Richmond, ordn.; visc. Howe, first ld. admy.; ld. Mulgrave and Wm. Wyndham Grenville, aft. ld. Grenville, joint-paym.; Hy. Dundas, &c. Lord Thurlow, ld. chanc.

During Mr. Pitt's long administration numerous changes in the ministry took place; among these were: EE. Camden, Fitzwilliam, Mansfield, and Chatham, successively pres. of the council; M. of Stafford, and EE. of Chatham, Spencer, and Westmoreland, pr. seal; E. of Chatham and E. Spencer, first lds. admy. and Mr. Grenville, aft. lord Grenville, Mr. Dundas, and D. of Portland, secs. st.; &c. Mr. Pitt res. in 1801.

1801. Mar. *et seq.* HY. ADDINGTON, first ld. treas. and ch. ex.; D. of Portland, pres. of the council; E. of Westmoreland, pr. seal; lord Pelham, home, lord Hawkesbury, foreign, and lord Hobart, colonial secs.; E. St. Vincent, first ld. admy.; E. of Chatham, ordn.; Chas. Yorke, sec.-at-war; visc. Lewisham, India Board; lord Auckland, bd. tr.; &c. Lord Eldon ld. chanc.

CHANGES: visc. Castlereagh, India board; Sept. 1802; Chas. Yorke, home sec. July 1803.

1804. May. *et seq.* WM. PITT, first ld. treas.; D. of Portland (succ. by lord Sidmouth, late Mr. Addington, Jan. 1805), pres. of the council; E. of Westmoreland, pr. seal; ld. Hawkesbury, home sec.; ld. Harrowby (succ. by ld. Mulgrave), for. sec.; and E. Camden (succ. by visc. Castlereagh), col. sec.; visc. Melville (succ. by ld. Barham), first ld. admy.; D. of Montrose, bd. tr.; ld. Mulgrave, duchy of Lanc.; Mr. Dundas, Geo. Canning, &c. Lord Eldon, ld. chanc.

The death of Mr. Pitt, on Jan. 23, 1806, led to the formation of another cabinet.

1806. Feb. "ALL THE TALENTS"* administration: WM. WYNDHAM, LORD GRENVILLE, first ld. of the treas.; ld. Hy. Petty, ch. ex.; E. Fitzwilliam, pres. of the council; visc. Sidmouth, pr. seal; Chas. Jas. Fox, for., E.

* The friends of this ministry gave it the appellation of *All the Talents*, which, being echoed in derision by the opposition, became fixed upon it. Besides the members above named, it consisted of Rd. Brinsley Sheridan, treas. of the navy; E. of Derby, ch. of the duchy of Lancaster; gen. Fitzpatrick, sec. at war; earls of Buckinghamshire and Carysfort, postmasters-gen.; E. Temple, vice pres. of the board of trade; lord John Townshend, paym. of the forces; lord Charles Spencer, mast. of the mint; Arthur Piggot, attorney-gen.; Saml. Romilly, solicitor-gen., &c. D. of Bedford, lord lieut. of Ireland.

Spencer, home, and Wm. Windham, war, secs.; E. of Moira, ordn.; sir Chas. Grey, aft. visc. Howick and E. Grey, first ld. admy.; ld. Minto, bd. of control; ld. Auckland, bd. of tr., &c. Lord Erskine, ld. chanc. Lord Ellenborough, ld. c. j. of the K. B., had a seat in this cabinet.

1806. The death of Mr. Fox, on Sept. 13, caused several changes: viz.: visc. Sidmouth, pres. of the council; ld. Holland, pr. seal; ld. Howick, for. sec., *vice* Mr. Fox; Thos. Grenville, first ld. admy.; Geo. Tierney, bd. of control, &c.

1807. Mar. Wm. Hy. Cavendish, D. of Portland, first ld. treas.; E. Camden, ld. pres. of the Council; E. of Westmoreland, pr. seal; hon. Spencer Perceval, ch. ex. and leader of the House of Commons; ld. Hawkesbury, Geo. Canning, and visc. Castlereagh, home, for., and col. secs.; E. Bathurst, bd. of tr.; Hy. Dundas, bd. of control; ld. Mulgrave, first ld. admy.; E. of Chatham, ordn., &c. Lord Eldon, ld. chanc.

1809. A quarrel and duel on Sept. 22, between ld. Castlereagh and Mr. Canning (the latter wounded) led to the retirement of both. This, with the subsequent retirement of the D. of Portland, who died shortly after (Oct. 30, 1809) dissolved the administration, which, after some negotiation with the Whigs, was reconstituted under

1809. Nov. & Dec. Spencer Perceval, first ld. treas., ch. ex., and ch. duch. Lanc.; E. Camden, pres. of the Council; E. of Westmoreland, pr. seal; hon. Rd. Ryder, home, M. Wellesley, for., and E. of Liverpool, col. secs.; lord Mulgrave, first ld. admy.; Hy. Dundas, bd. of control; E. Bathurst, bd. of trade; E. of Chatham, ordn.; visc. Palmerston, sec.-at-war, &c. Lord Eldon, ld. chanc.

1810. May. Lord Mulgrave went to the ordn., and was succ. at the admy. by Chas. Yorke. Some subordinate changes took place.

Regency of George, Prince of Wales.

1811. Feb. Spencer Perceval and his colleagues, *continued.*

The death of Mr. Perceval, who was assassinated by a man named *Bellingham*, in the lobby of the House of Commons on May 11, 1812, led to several changes. After much fruitless negotiation with the Whigs the former govt. was reconstituted under the

1812. May & June. Robt. Banks, E. of Liverpool, first ld. treas.; E. of Harrowby, pres. of the council; E. of Westmoreland, pr. seal; Nichs. Vansittart, ch. ex.; E. of Mulgrave, ordn.; ld. Melville, first ld. admy.; visc. Sidmouth, visc. Castlereagh, and E. Bathurst, home, for., and col. secs.; E. of Buckinghamshire, bd. of control; Marq. Camden, ld. Palmerston, E. of Clancarty, &c. Lord Eldon, ld. chanc.

1814. to 1819. Among the changes that afterwards took place, were the following: Chas. Bragge Bathurst, ch. duch. Lanc., a cabinet minister, and W. Wellesley Pole advanced to the cabinet as m. mint, 1814. Geo. Canning made pres. bd. control, 1816. Fredk. John Robinson, pres. bd. tr., 1818; and the D. of Wellington, m. g. ordn., 1819.

King George IV.

1820. Jan. E. of Liverpool and his colleagues, *continued.* The cabinet at the commencement of this reign was constituted thus: E. of Liverpool, first ld. treas.; E. of Harrowby, pres. of the council; E. of Westmoreland, pr. seal; Mr. Vansittart, ch. ex.; visc. Melville, first ld. admy.; D. of Wellington, ordn.; visc. Sidmouth, visc. Castlereagh, and E. Bathurst, home, for., and col. secs.; Geo. Canning, bd. of control; Fredk. J. Robinson, bd. tr.; Chas. B. Bathurst, ch. duch. Lanc.; W. Wellesley Pole, m. mint; E. of Mulgrave without office. Lord Eldon, ld. chanc.

1822. Robt. Peel became home sec., Jan., and W. W. Wynn, pres. bd. tr., Feb.; and, on the death of visc. Castlereagh, then M. of Londonderry, Geo. Canning became for. sec., Sept. Visc. Sidmouth continued a member of the cabinet, without office. In 1823, Wm. Huskisson united the board of trade with the treasurership of the navy; and a few other changes subsequently occurred.

1827. E. of LIVERPOOL, *continued.* At the close of lord Liverpool's long administration, it consisted of the following members; E. of Liverpool, first ld. treas.; Fredk. J. Robinson, ch. ex.; lords Harrowby and Westmoreland, pres. of the council and pr. seal; Robt. Peel, Geo. Canning, and E Bathurst, secs. st. for the home, for., and col. depts.; lord Melville, first ld. admy.; D. of Wellington, ordn.; lord Bexley, late Mr. Vansittart, duchy of Lanc.; Chas. W. W. Wynn and Wm. Huskisson, bds. of control and trade; ld. Sidmouth, without office, &c. Lord Eldon, ld. chanc. Dissolved, owing to lord Liverpool's illness, April 1827.

1827. Apr. GEO. CANNING, first ld. treas. and ch. ex.; ld. Harrowby, pres. of the council; D. of Portland, pr. seal; ld. Dudley, visc. Goderich, and Sturges Bourne, for., col., and home secs.; C. W. W. Wynn, bd. of control; Wm. Huskisson, bd. of trade; ld. Palmerston, sec.-at-war; ld. Bexley, duch. Lanc.; D. of Clarence, ld. h. adm. Lord Lyndhurst, ld. chanc.

The marquess of Lansdowne had a seat in the cabinet, to which were soon added the seals of the home department.

The death of Mr. Canning on Aug. 8, following, led to several changes.

1827. Aug. VISC. GODERICH, late FREDK. JNO. ROBINSON, aft. E. of Ripon, first ld. treas.; D. of Portland, pres. of the council; E. of Carlisle, pr. seal; visc. Dudley, Wm. Huskisson, and M. of Lansdowne, for., col., and home secs.; ld. Palmerston, sec.-at-war; C. W. W. Wynn, bd. of control; Chas. Grant, bd. of trade; Geo. Tierney, m. mint, &c. Lord Lyndhurst, ld. chanc.

1828. Jan. ARTHUR, D. of WELLINGTON, first ld. treas.; Hy. Goulburn, ch. ex.; E. Bathurst, pres. of the council; ld. Ellenborough, pr. seal; Robt. Peel, E. Dudley, and Wm. Huskisson, home, for., and col. secs.; visc. Melville, bd. of control; Chas. Grant, bd. of trade; ld. Palmerston, sec.-at-war; J. C. Herries, m. mint; E. of Aberdeen, ch. duch. Lanc.; — Arbuthnot, Chas. V. Fitzgerald, &c. Lord Lyndhurst, ld. chanc.

Mr. Huskisson, E. Dudley, visc. Palmerston, and Mr. Grant, quit the ministry, and changes follow.

1828. May & June. D. OF WELLINGTON, first ld. treas.; E. Bathurst, pres. of the council; ld. Ellenborough, pr. seal; Robt. Peel, E. of Aberdeen, and sir Geo. Murray, home, for., and col. secs.; visc. Melville and Chas. V. Fitzgerald, bds. contr. and tr.; sir Hy. Hardinge, sec.-at-war; visc. Lowther, first commr. of land revenues, &c. Lord Lyndhurst, ld. chanc.

The D. of Clarence surrendered the office of ld. h. adm., Aug. 12; and lord Melville became first ld. admy., Sept. 19; lord Ellenborough became pres. bd. contr., and lord Rosslyn pr. seal.

KING WILLIAM IV.

D. OF WELLINGTON and his colleagues, *continued.*

1830. Nov. CHAS., EARL GREY, first ld. treas.; visc. Althorpe, ch. ex.; M. of Lansdowne, pres. of the council; E. of Durham, pr. seal; viscs. Melbourne, Palmerston, and Goderich, home, for., and col. secs.; sir Jas. Graham, first ld. admy.; ld. Auckland and Chas. Grant, pres. of the bds. of trade and control; ld. Holland, ch. duch. Lanc.; ld. John Russell, paym. of the forces (not of the cabinet at first); D. of Richmond, E. of Carlisle, C. W. W. Wynn, &c. Lord Brougham, ld. chanc.

Sir Hy. Parnell aft. became sec.-at-war, *vice* Wynn; and subsequently sir Hy. Parnell was succ. by sir John Hobhouse.

1832. EARL GREY resigned, owing to a majority against him in the lords on a question relating to the Reform Bill, May 10, but resumed office, May 18.

The E. of Ripon, late visc. Goderich succ. the E. of Durham as pr. seal, April 3, 1833, when, also, E. G. S. Stanley, aft. E. of Derby (previously sec. for Ireland), became col. sec., and Ed. Ellice, sec.-at-war.

1834 July. WM., VISC. MELBOURNE, first ld. treas.; M. of Lansdowne, pres. of the council; E. of Mulgrave, pr. seal; visc. Althorpe, ch. ex.; visc. Duncannon, home sec.; visc.

Palmerston, for. sec.; Spring Rice, war and col.; ld. Auckland first ld. admy.; Chas. Grant and C. P. Thomson, bds. of control and trade; ld. John Russell, paym. forces; sir John Hobhouse, Ed. Ellice, M. of Conyngham, Mr. Littleton, &c. Lord Brougham, ld. chanc.

1834. Visc. Melbourne's administration dissolved. The D. of Wellington takes the helm of state provisionally, waiting the return of sir Robert Peel from Italy. Nov. 14.

1834. Nov. & Dec. Sir Robt. Peel, first ld. treas. and ch. ex.; ld. Wharncliffe, pr. seal; E. of Rosslyn, pres. of the council; Hy. Goulburn, D. of Wellington, and E. of Aberdeen, home, for. and col. secs; E. de Grey, first ld. admy.; ld. Ellenborough and Alex. Baring, aft. ld. Ashburton, bds. of control and trade; sir Edw. Knatchbull, paym. forces; J. C. Herries, sec.-at-war; sir Geo. Murray, ordn., &c. Lord Lyndhurst, ld. chanc.

1835. Apr. Visc. Melbourne, again first ld. treas.; M. of Lansdowne, pres. of the council; visc. Duncannon, pr. seal, with the woods and forests; Th. Spring Rice, ch. ex.; ld. John Russell, visc. Palmerston, and ld. Glenelg, late Chas. Grant, home, for., and col. secs.; E. of Minto, first ld. admy.; sir John Hobhouse and Chas. Poulett Thomson, pres. bds. of contr. and tr.; ld. Holland, ch. duch. Lanc.; visc. Howick, sec.-at-war; sir Hy. Parnell, Hy. Labouchere, ld. Morpeth, &c. The gr. seal in commission.

The chancellorship, which had been in commission from the formation of this ministry, was given to sir Chas. C. Pepys, Jan. 1836, with the title of lord Cottenham.

Queen Victoria.

1837. Visc. Melbourne and his colleagues, *contd.* June 20.

F. T. Baring aft. becomes ch. ex., *vice* Spring Rice, cr. lord Monteagle; M. of Normanby, late E. of Mulgrave, home sec., *vice* ld. John Russell, made col. sec.; T. B. Macaulay, sec.-at-war, *vice* visc. Howick; E. Clarendon, ld. pr. seal, *vice* visc. Duncannon; Hy. Labouchere, pres. bd. trade, *vice* C. P. Thomson, &c.

1839. Ministers announced their determination to resign, in consequence of the division in the Commons on the Jamaica Bill, in which they had a majority of only *five*, May 7. Sir Robt. Peel received the queen's commands to form a new administration, May 8; but owing to the refusal of her majesty to dismiss the ladies of her household, on which sir Robt. Peel insisted, this command was withdrawn, and on May 10 lord Melbourne and his friends returned to power.

1841. Aug. & Sept. Sir Robt. Peel, first ld. treas.; D. of Wellington, without civil office, comm.-in-chief; ld. Wharncliffe, pres. of the council; D. of Buckingham, pr. seal; sir Jas. Graham, E. of Aberdeen, and ld. Stanley, home, for., and col. secs.; Hy. Goulburn, ch. ex.; E. of Haddington, first ld. admy.; E. of Ripon, bd. trade; ld. Ellenborough, bd. control; sir Hy. Hardinge, sir Edwd. Knatchbull, sir Geo. Murray, &c. Lord Lyndhurst, ld. chanc.

1841. to 1846. Among the many succeeding changes were: ld. Fitzgerald and Vesey to the bd. of control, *vice* lord Ellenborough app. gov.-gen. of India, Oct. 1841; D. of Buccleuch, pr. seal, Feb. 1842. E. of Ripon, from the bd. of trade to the bd. of control, *vice* lord Fitzgerald, decd., May 1843. Sir Thos. Fremantle, sec.-at-war, *vice* sir Henry Hardinge, app. gov.-gen. of India, May 1844. E. of Dalhousie, to the bd. of trade, and Sidney Herbert, sec.-at-war, Feb. 1845. W. E. Gladstone, col. sec., *vice* ld. Stanley, res.; D. of Buccleuch, pres. of the council, *vice* ld. Wharncliffe, decd.; E. of Haddington, pr. seal; and E. of Ellenborough, first ld. admy., Jan. 1846.

1846. July. Lord John Russell, first ld. treas. and prem.; M. of Lansdowne, ld. pres. council; E. of Minto, ld. pr. seal; sir Geo. Grey, home sec,; visc. Palmerston, for. sec.; E. Grey, war and col. sec.; Chas. Wood, ch. ex.; E. of Auckland, first ld. admy.; sir Jno. Hobhouse, aft. Lord Broughton, pres. bd. control; E. of Clarendon, pres. bd. trade; visc. Morpeth, aft. E. of Carlisle, first commr. woods and forests; M. of Clanricarde, postm.-gen.; T. B. Macaulay, paym.-gen.; lord Cottenham, ld. chanc.; lord Campbell, chanc. d. Lanc.

CHANGES: Hy. Labouchere, app. pres. bd. trade, July 22, 1847, *vice* E. of Clarendon; E. Granville, app. paym.-gen. May 1848, *vice* Macaulay; to be of cabinet, Oct. 1851; sir F. T. Baring, app. first ld. admy., Jan. 18, 1849, *vice* E. of Auckland, decd.; hon. Fox Maule, sec.-at-war, to be of cabinet, Nov. 1849; E. of Carlisle, app. chanc. d. Lanc., Mar. 6, 1850, *vice* lord Campbell, app. ld. ch. just. q. b.; lord Cottenham, ld. chanc., res. June 19, 1850, and commrs. app.; sir Thos. Wilde, ld. ch. just. c. p., app. ld. chanc., July 15, 1850, and cr. lord Truro; ld. Seymour, app. first commr. works, &c., Aug. 1851; to be of cabinet, Oct. 1851; E. Granville, app. for. sec., Dec. 26, 1851, *vice* lord Palmerston, res; hon. F. Maule (aft. ld. Panmure), app. pres. bd. control, *vice* Hobhouse, res. Feb. 1852.

1852. Feb. EDWD. G., E. OF DERBY, first ld. treas. and prem.; E. of Lonsdale, ld. pres. of the council; M. of Salisbury, ld. pr. seal; Spencer Horatio Walpole, home sec.; E. of Malmesbury, for. sec.; sir Jno. S. Pakington, bt., war and col. sec.; Benjn. Disraeli, ch. ex.; D. of Northumberland, first ld. admy.; Jno. Chas. Herries, pres. bd. cont.; Josh. Warner Henley, pres. bd. tr.; E. of Hardwicke, postm.-gen.; sir Edwd. B. Sugden, cr. lord St. Leonards, ld. chanc.; ld. Jno. Manners, first commr. works, &c. Wm. Beresford, app. sec.-at-war with seat in cabinet, Feb. 28, 1852, *vice* R. V. Smith, who was not in cabinet.

1852. Dec. GEO. HAMILTON, E. OF ABERDEEN, first ld. treas. and prem.; E. Granville, ld. pres. of the council; D. of Argyll, ld. pr. seal; visc. Palmerston, home sec.; lord John Russell, for. sec.; D. of Newcastle, war. and col. sec.; hon. Sidney Herbert, sec.-at-war; Wm. Ewart Gladstone, ch. ex.; sir Jas. R. G. Graham, bt., first ld. admy.; sir Chas. Wood, bt., pres. bd. cont.; sir Wm. Molesworth bt., first commr. works, &c.; ld. Cranworth, ld. chanc.; M. of Lansdowne, without office.

CHANGES.—E. of Clarendon, app. for. sec., Feb. 21, 1853, *vice* ld John Russell, who remained in the cabinet without office; secretaryship of st. for war and colonies divided June 12, 1854, D. of Newcastle app. sec. war, sir Geo. Grey app. sec. col.; E. Granville, app. chanc. d. Lanc., June 21, 1854 *vice* E. Strutt, who was not in cabinet; ld. John Russell, app. ld. pres. of the council, June 12, 1854, *vice* E. Granville.

1855. Feb. 10. HY. JNO., VISC. PALMERSTON, first ld. treas. and premier; E. Granville, ld. pres. council; D. of Argyll, ld. pr. seal; Sidney Herbert, home sec., Feb. 8, succ. by Sir Geo. Grey, bt., Feb. 28; E. of Clarendon, for. sec.; Sidney Herbert, col. sec.; ld. Panmure, war sec.; W. E. Gladstone, ch. ex.; Sir Jas. R. G. Graham, bt., first ld. admy.; Sir Chas. Wood, bt., pres. bd. cont.; lord Cranworth, ld. chanc.; E. of Harrowby, chanc. d. Lanc. (app. Mar. 1855); sir Wm. Molesworth, bt., first commr. works, &c.; visc. Canning, postm.-gen.; M. of Lansdowne, without office.

CHANGES.—Sidney Herbert, W. E. Gladstone, and sir J. R. G. Graham, res., Feb. 22, 1855; sir Chas. Wood, bt., app. first ld. admy., Mar. 3, 1855, *vice* Graham, res.; Robt. Vernon Smith, app. pres. bd. cont., Mar. 13, 1855, *vice* Wood; sir Geo. C. Lewis, bt., app. ch. ex., Mar. 5, 1855, *vice* Gladstone, res.; lord Jno. Russell, app. col. sec., May 1, 1855, *vice* Sidney Herbert, res.; sir Wm. Molesworth, app. col. sec., July 21, 1855, *vice* lord John Russell, res.; Hy. Labouchere, app. col. sec., Nov. 21, 1855, *vice* Molesworth, decd.; D. of Argyll, app. postm. gen., July 1855, *vice* visc. Canning, app. gov. gen. India; E. of Harrowby, app. ld. pr. seal, Dec. 7, 1855, *vice* D. of Argyll; Matthew Talbot Baines, app. chanc. d. Lanc., Dec. 7, 1855, *vice* E. of Harrowby; ld. Stanley of Alderley, pres. bd. tr., to be of cabinet, — 1855; M. of Clanricarde, app. ld. pr. seal, Feb. 3, 1858, *vice* E. of Harrowby, res.

1858. Feb. 25. EDWD. G., E. OF DERBY, first ld. treas. and premier; M. of Salisbury, ld. pres. council; E. of Hardwicke, ld. pr. seal; Spencer H. Walpole, home sec.; E. of Malmesbury, for. sec.; lord Stanley, col. sec.; Jonathan Peel, war sec.; Benjn. Disraeli, ch. ex.; sir Jno. S. Pakington, bt., first ld. admy.; E. of Ellenborough, pres. bd. cont.; Jos. Warner Henley, pres. bd. tr.; lord Jno. Manners, first commr. works, &c.; sir Fk. Thesiger, cr. ld. Chelmsford, ld. chanc.

Changes.—E. of Donoughmore, app. pres. bd. tr., Feb. 1859, *vice* Henley; lord Stanley, app. pres. bd. cont., June 5, 1858, *vice* E. of Ellenborough; sir E. Bulwer-Lytton, app. col. sec., June 5, 1858, *vice* lord Stanley; Board of control abolished by 21 & 22 Vic., cap. 106, and Secretaryship of State for India created; lord Stanley, app. first sec. st. for India, Sept. 2, 1858; F. H. S. Sotheron Estcourt, app. home sec., Mar. 3, 1859, *vice* Walpole, res.

859. une 18. Hy. Jno., Visc. Palmerston, first ld. treas. and prem.; E. Granville, ld. pres. council; D. of Argyll, ld. pr. seal; sir Geo. Cornewall Lewis, bt., home sec.; Lord Jno. Russell, cr. E. Russell, 1861, for. sec.; D. of Newcastle, col. sec.; Sidney Herbert, war sec.; sir Chas. Wood, bt., India sec.; Wm. Ewart Gladstone, ch. ex.; D. of Somerset, first ld. admy.; Thos. Milner Gibson, pres. p. l. bd., and then pres. bd. tr.; Edw. Cardwell, Irish sec.; Jas. E. of Elgin, postm. gen.; Chas. P. Villiers, pres. p. l. bd., *vice* Gibson. Ld. Campbell, ld. chanc.; sir Geo. Grey, bt., chanc. d. Lanc.

Changes.—Ld. Stanley of Alderley, app. postm.-gen., Aug. 17, 1860, *vice* E. of Elgin, sent as amb. to China; sir Richd. Bethell, app. ld. chanc. and cr. ld. Westbury, June 26, 1861, *vice* ld. Campbell, decd.; Sidney Herbert, res. and cr. ld. Herbert of Lea, July 1861, *d.* Aug. 2, 1861; sir G. C. Lewis, app. sec. war, July 23, 1861, *vice* Herbert; sir Geo. Grey, app. home sec., July 25, 1861, *vice* Lewis; Edw. Cardwell, app. chanc. d. Lanc., July 25, 1861, *vice* Grey; Sir Robt. Peel, app. Irish sec. (without seat in cabinet) July, 1861, *vice* Cardwell; E. De Grey and Ripon, app. sec. war, Apr. 28, 1863, *vice* Lewis, decd.; Edw. Cardwell, app. col. sec., Apr. 7, 1864, *vice* D. of Newcastle, res.; E. of Clarendon, app. chanc. d. Lanc., Apr. 7, 1864, *vice* Cardwell; ld. Cranworth, app. ld. chanc., July 7, 1865, *vice* ld. Westbury, res.

1865. Nov. 6. Jno., Earl Russell, first ld. treas. and prem.; E. Granville, ld. pres. council; D. of Argyll, ld. pr. seal; sir Geo. Grey, bt., home sec.; E. of Clarendon, for. sec.; Edw. Cardwell, col. sec.; E. De Grey and Ripon, war sec.; sir Chas. Wood, bt., India sec.; Wm. Ewart Gladstone, ch. ex.; D. of Somerset, first ld. admy.; Thos. Milner Gibson, pres. bd. tr.; Chas. Pelham Villiers, pres. p. l. bd.; ld. Stanley of Alderley, postm. gen.; ld. Cranworth, ld. chanc.; Geo. Joachim Goschen, chanc. d. Lanc. (app. Jan. 1866).

Changes.—E. De Grey and Ripon, app. India sec., Feb. 16, 1866, *vice* sir Chas. Wood, res. and cr. visc. Halifax; M. of Hartington, app. sec. war, Feb. 16, 1866, *vice* E. De Grey and Ripon.

1866. July. Edwd. G., E. of Derby, first ld. treas. and prem.; D. of Buckingham and Chandos, ld. pres. council; E. of Malmesbury, ld. pr. seal; Spencer H. Walpole, home sec.; ld. Stanley, for. sec.; E. of Carnarvon, col. sec.; Jonathan Peel, war sec.; visc. Cranborne, India sec.; Benjn. Disraeli, ch. ex.; sir J. S. Pakington, bt., first ld. admy.; sir Stafford Hy. Northcote, bt., pres. bd. tr.; Gathorne Hardy, pres. p. l. bd.; ld. Chelmsford, ld. chanc.; ld. Naas, aft. E. of Mayo, Irish sec.; lord Jno. Manners, first commr. works, &c.

Changes.—E. of Carnarvon, gen. Peel, and lord Cranborne, res., Mar. 1867; D. of Buckingham and Chandos, app. col. sec., Mar. 8, 1867, *vice* E. of Carnarvon; D. of Marlborough, app. ld. pres. council, Mar. 8, 1867, *vice* D. of Buckingham; sir J. S. Pakington, app. sec. war, Mar. 8, 1867, *vice* Peel; Hy. Thos. Lowry Corry, app. first ld. admy., Mar. 8, 1867, *vice* Pakington; sir Stafford Hy. Northcote, app. sec. India, Mar. 8, 1867, *vice* lord Cranborne; D. of Richmond, app. pres. bd. tr., Mar. 8, 1867, *vice* Northcote; Gathorne Hardy, app. home sec., May 17, 1867, *vice* Walpole, res.; E. of Devon, app. pres. p. l. bd. (without seat in cabinet), May 17, 1867, *vice* Hardy.

E. of Derby res. through ill-health, Feb. 1868, and *d.* Oct. 23, 1869.

1868. Feb. BENJN. DISRAELI, first ld. treas. and premier; D. of Marlborough, ld. pres. council; E. of Malmesbury, ld. pr. seal; Gathorne Hardy, home sec.; ld. Stanley, for. sec.; D. of Buckingham and Chandos, col. sec.; sir J. S. Pakington, bt., war sec.; sir Stafford Hy. Northcote, bt., India sec.; Geo. Ward Hunt, ch. ex.; Hy. Thos. Lowry Corry, first ld. admy.; D. of Richmond, pres. bd. tr.; E. of Mayo, Irish sec. (res. Sept. 1868, and succ. by Col. Jno. Wilson Patten, not in cabinet); lord Jno. Manners, first commr. works, &c.; ld. Cairns, ld. chanc.

1868. Dec. WM. EWART GLADSTONE, first ld. treas. and prem.; E. De Grey and Ripon, ld. pres. council; E. of Kimberley, ld. pr. seal; Hy. Austin Bruce, home sec.; E. of Clarendon, for. sec.; E. Granville, col. sec.; Edw. Cardwell, war sec.; D. of Argyll, India sec.; Robt. Lowe, ch. ex.; Hugh C. E. Childers, first ld. admy.; Jno. Bright, pres. bd tr.; Chichester S. Fortescue, Irish sec.; M. of Hartington, postm.-gen.; Geo. Joachim Goschen, pres. p. l. bd.; sir Wm. Page Wood, cr. ld. Hatherley, ld. chanc.

CHANGES.—W. E. Foster, v. pres. educatn., brought into the cabinet, July 1870; E. Granville, app. for. sec., July 6, 1870, *vice* E. of Clarendon, decd.; E. of Kimberley, app. col. sec., July 6, 1870, *vice* E. Granville; visc. Halifax, app. ld. pr. seal, July 6, 1870, *vice* E. of Kimberley; Chichester S. Fortescue, app. pres. bd. tr., Jan. 14, 1871, *vice* Bright, res.; M. of Hartington, app. Irish sec., Jan. 1871, *vice* Fortescue; Wm. Monsell, app. postm. gen., Jan. 9, 1871, *vice* ld. Hartington, but without seat in cabinet; Geo. Joachim Goschen, first ld. admy., Mar. 9, 1871, *vice* Childers, res.; Jas. Stansfeld, app. pres. loc. gov. bd., Aug. 1871; Hugh C. E. Childers, app. chanc. d. Lanc., Aug. 9, 1872, *vice* ld. Dufferin, who was not in cabinet; sir Roundell Palmer, app. ld. chanc. and cr. ld. Selborne, Oct. 15, 1872, *vice* ld. Hatherley, res.; H. A. Bruce, app. ld. pres. council, Aug. 9, 1873, and cr. lord Aberdare, *vice* E. De Grey and Ripon, res.; R. Lowe, app. home sec., Aug. 9, 1873, *vice* Bruce; W. E. Gladstone, app. ch. ex., *vice* Lowe, Aug. 9, 1873, and held the offi jointly with that of first ld. trea and premiership; Jno. Brigh app. chanc. d. Lanc., Sept. 3 1873, *vice* Childers, res.

1874. Feb. BENJN. DISRAELI, first ld. treas. a prem.; D. of Richmond, ld. pre of the council; E. of Malme bury, ld. pr. seal; Richd. Assh ton Cross, home sec.; E. of Derb for. sec.; E. of Carnarvon, co sec.; Gathorne Hardy, war sec M. of Salisbury, India sec.; s Stafford Hy. Northcote, bt., ch ex.; Geo. Ward Hunt, first l admy.; ld. Jno. Manners, postm gen.; ld. Cairns, (cr. E. Cairn Sept. 23, 1878), ld. chanc.

CHANGES.—B. Disraeli, aft. E. Beaconsfield, app. ld. pr. seal, *vi* E. of Malmesbury, Aug. 12, 187 and held the office jointly wi first ld. treas. and premiershi sir Michl. E. Hicks-Beach, bt., Iri sec., to be of cabinet, Feb. 187 Wm. Hy Smith, app. first l admy., Aug. 14, 1877, *vice* Hun decd.; D. of Northumberlan app. ld. pr. seal, Feb. 4, 1878, *vi* E. of Beaconsfield, res.; s Michael E. Hicks-Beach, bt., ap col. sec., Feb. 4, 1878, *vice* E. Carnarvon, res.; Jas. Lowthe app. Irish sec., without seat cabinet, Feb. 1878, *vice* Hick Beach; M. of Salisbury, app. fo sec., Apr. 2, 1878, *vice* E. Derby, res.; Gathorne Hard app. sec. India, Apr. 2, 187 (cr. visc. Cranbrook, May 1878), *vice* Salisbury; col. Fredk Arthur Stanley, app. sec. wa Apr. 2, 1878, *vice* Hardy; vis Sandon, app. pres. bd. trad with seat in cabinet, Apr. 1878, *vice* Adderley.

1880. Apr. 28. WM. EWART GLADSTONE, first l treas., ch. ex. and prem.; E. Spe cer, ld. pr. council; D. of Argyl ld. pr. seal; Wm. G. G. Ve non Harcourt, home sec.; E Granville, for. sec.; E. Kimberley, col. sec.; Hugh E. Childers, war sec.; M. Hartington, India sec.; E. Northbrook, first ld. admy.; Jo Chamberlain, pres. bd. trad John Geo. Dodson, pres. loc. gv bd.; Wm. Edwd. Forster, Iri sec.; ld. Selborne, ld. chanc. (c E. Selborne, Dec. 29, 1881); Jn Bright, chanc. d. Lanc.

CHANGES.—Ld. Carlingford, app. l pr. seal, May 2nd, 1881, *vice* D. Argyll, res.; earl Spencer, ap ld. lieut. Ireland, Apr. 28, 1882, *vice* E. Cowper, who was not in cabinet; lord Fredk. Chas. Cavendish, app. Irish sec., without seat in cabinet, May, 1882, (assass. May 6, 1882) *vice* Forster, res.; Geo. Otto Trevelyan, app. Irish sec., without seat in cabinet, May 9, 1882, *vice* Cavendish; E. of Kimberley, app. chanc. d. Lanc., July 25, 1882, *vice* Bright, res.; H. C. E. Childers, app. chanc. ex., Dec. 16, 1882, *vice* Gladstone, res.; M. of Hartington, app. war sec., Dec. 16, 1882, *vice* Childers; E. of Kimberley, app. India sec., Dec. 16, 1882, *vice* M. of Hartington; E. of Derby, app. col. sec., Dec. 16, 1882, *vice* E. of Kimberley; J. G. Dodson, app. chanc. d. Lanc., Dec. 28, 1882, *vice* E. of Kimberley; sir Chas. Wentworth Dilke, bt., app. pres. loc. gvt. bd., Dec. 28, 1882, *vice* Dodson; ld. Carlingford, app. ld. pres. council, Mar. 19, 1883, *vice* E. Spencer, res.; G. O. Trevelyan, app. chanc. d. Lanc., Oct. 29, 1884, *vice* Dodson, res.; H. Campbell-Bannerman, app. Irish sec., without seat in cabinet, Oct. 29, 1884, *vice* Trevelyan; G. J. Shaw-Lefevre (app. postm.-gen., without seat in cabinet, *vice* Fawcett, decd., also not in cabinet), to be of cabinet, Feb. 1885; E. of Rosebery, app. first commr. works, Feb. 1885, *vice* Shaw-Lefevre; E. of Rosebery, app. ld. pr. seal, Mar. 5, 1885, *vice* ld. Carlingford, res.

1885 June. ROBT. ARTHUR TALBOT, M. OF SALISBURY, for. sec. and prem.; sir Stafford Hy. Northcote, bt. (cr. E. of Iddesleigh), first ld. treas.; visc. Cranbrook, ld. pres. council; E. of Harrowby, ld. pr. seal; sir Rd. Assheton-Cross, home sec.; sir Fredk. A. Stanley, col. sec.; Wm. Hy. Smith, war sec.; ld. Randolph H. S. Churchill, India sec.; sir M. E. Hicks-Beach, bt., chanc. ex.; ld. Geo. F. Hamilton, first ld. admy.; D. of Richmond and Gordon, pres. bd. tr.; E. of Carnarvon, ld. lieut. Ireland; ld. Jno. J. R. Manners, postm.-gen.; hon. E. Stanhope, v. pres. educatn.; sir H. S. Giffard (cr. ld. Halsbury), ld. chanc.; ld. Ashbourne, ld. chanc. Ireland.

CHANGES.—Hon. Edwd. Stanhope, app. pres. bd. tr., Aug. 19, 1885, *vice* D. of Richmond and Gordon, app. sec. Scotland; W. H. Smith, app. Irish sec. Jan. 25, 1886, *vice* sir W. Hart-Dyke, who was not in cabinet.

1886. Feb. WM. EWART GLADSTONE, first ld. treas., ld. pr. seal, and prem.; E. Spencer, ld. pres. council; Hugh C. E. Childers, home sec.; E. of Rosebury, for. sec.; E. Granville, col. sec.; Hy. Campbell-Bannerman, war sec.; E. of Kimberley, India sec.; Geo. Otto Trevelyan, sec. Scotland; sir Wm. G. G. V. Harcourt, chanc. ex.; M. of Ripon, first ld. admy.; Anthy. Jno. Mundella, pres. bd. tr.; Jos. Chamberlain, pres. loc. gvt. bd.; John Morley, Irish sec.; sir Farrer Herschell (cr. lord Herschell), ld. chanc.

CHANGES.—E. of Dalhousie, app. sec. Scotland, without seat in cabinet, Apr. 3, 1886, *vice* Trevelyan, res.; Jas. Stansfeld, app. pres. loc. gvt. bd., Apr. 3, 1886, *vice* Chamberlain, res.

1886. Aug. 3. ROBT. ARTHUR TALBOT, M. OF SALISBURY, first ld. treas. and prem.; visc. Cranbrook, ld. pres. council; Hy. Matthews, home sec.; E. of Iddesleigh, for. sec.; hon. Edwd. Stanhope, col. sec.; Wm. Hy. Smith, war. sec.; sir Rd. Assheton Cross, G.C.B., (cr. visc. Cross, Aug. 8, 1886), India sec.: ld. Randolph H. S. Churchill, chanc. ex.; ld. Geo. F. Hamilton, first ld. admy.; sir Fredk. Arthur Stanley (cr. ld. Stanley of Preston, Aug. 6, 1886), pres. bd. tr.; sir Michl. E. Hicks-Beach, bt., Irish sec.; ld. Halsbury, ld. chanc.; visc. Cranbrook (*pro tem*), and then ld. Jno. Manners, chanc. d. Lanc.; ld. Ashbourne, ld. chanc. Ireland.

CHANGES.—Arthur Jas. Balfour, sec. Scotland, brought into cabinet, Nov. 1886; M. of Salisbury, app. for. sec., Jan. 14, 1887, *vice* E. of Iddesleigh, res.; the marquis retained the premiership; W. H. Smith, app. first ld. treas., Jan. 14, 1887, *vice* M. of Salisbury; hon. Edw. Stanhope, app. war sec., Jan. 14, 1887, *vice* Smith; sir Hy. Thurstan Holland, (cr. ld. Knutsford, Feb. 27, 1888), app. col. sec., Jan. 14, 1887, *vice* Stanhope; Geo. Joachim Goschen, app. chanc. ex., Jan. 14, 1887, *vice* ld. R. Churchill, res.; Arthur Jas. Balfour, app. Irish sec., Mar. 8, 1887, *vice* Hicks-Beach, who res., but remained in the cabinet without office; M. of Lothair, app. sec. Scotland, Mar. 11, 1887, *vice* Balfour; Earl Cadogan, ld. pr. seal, and C. T. Ritchie, pres. loc. gvt. bd.; brought into cabinet May 1887. Sir M. Hicks-Beach retired from the cabinet, Jan. 1888, but rejoined it in the following month as pres. bd. tr., *vice* Stanley of Preston, app. gov.-gen. Canada.

LORD TREASURERS. LORD HIGH TREASURERS. LORDS COMMISSIONERS OF THE TREASURY.

THE lord treasurership, though not highest in nominal rank, has generally been the highest political office in the state. For many years past the office has been executed by commissioners known as lords of the treasury. The first lord is almost invariably the head of the government, and the second lord is, generally, also the chancellor of the exchequer.

LORD TREASURERS, &c., OF ENGLAND.

WILLIAM THE CONQUEROR.

Odo, E. of Kent.

KING HENRY I.

Geoffry de Clinton.
Ranulph Flambard, bp. of Durham.
Roger, bp. of Salisbury.
Nigellus, bp. of Ely.

KING HENRY II.

Geoffrey Ridel, bp. of Ely.
Richd. de Ely.

KING RICHARD I.

The same, *contd.*
Wm. de Ely.

KING JOHN.

The same, *contd.*
Dean of St. Paul's, London.
Walter de Grey, bp. of Worcester.
Geoffrey, archd. of Norwich.

KING HENRY III.

John Ruthal.
1217. Eustace de Fauconbridge, aft. bp. of London.
— John de Fontibus, bp. of Ely.
— Walter Maclerk, or Lacklatine, bp. of Carlisle.
— Hubert de Burgo.
— Peter de Orial.
Under him, Robert Passelewe was ch. ex., or deputy treasurer.
1234. Hugh de Patteshull.
— Galfridus Templarius.
— Wm. Haverhull, canon of St. Paul's, London.
— Richd. de Barking, abbot of Westminster.
— Philip Lovel, dep. by the barons in the year 1258.
1258. John Crackhall, archd. of Bedford.
1260. John, abbot of Peterborough, made treas. by the barons.
1263. Nicholas de Ely, archd. of Ely.
1266. Thos. de Wymundham.
1269. John de Chishull, dean of St. Paul's, London, aft bp. of London.
1271. Philip de Ely.

KING EDWARD I.

1274. Joseph de Clancy.
1275. Walter Giffard, bp. of Bath and Wells, aft. abp. of York.
— Robt. Burnel, bp. of Bath and Wells.
1278. John de Clancy, prior of St. John's of Jerusalem, in England.
1279. Thos. Beck, archd. of Dorchester.
1280. Richd. de Warren, or de Ware, abbot of Westminster.
1284. Walter Wenlock, abbot of Westminster.
1286. Roger de Longespee, *alias* de Molend, bp. of Lichfield.
— John de Kirkeby, archd. of Coventry, aft. bp. of Ely.
1290. Wm. de Marchia, bp. of Bath and Wells.
1293. Peter de Leicester, baron of the exch., who, with the two chamberlains of the exch., executed the office of treasr. until the appointment of
1295. Walter de Langton, bp. of Lichfield.
Under him, Peter Willeby was ch. ex.

KING EDWARD II.

1307. Walter Reynolds, bp. of Worcester, aft. abp. of Canterbury. He had been schoolmaster to the king.
Under him, John de Sandale was ch. ex.
1311. John de Sandale.
1312. Sir Walter de Norwich.
1313. John de Sandale, bp. of Winchester, *again.*
1315. Sir Walter de Norwich, *again.*
— John de Drokenesford, bp. of Bath and Wells.
Hervey de Stanton, ch. ex.
1317. John Hotham, bp. of Ely.

318. Wm. Walwaine.
— John de Stratford, bp. of Winchester.
319. Walter Stapleton, bp. of Exeter.
321. Sir Walter de Norwich, *again.*
322. Roger de Northburgh, bp. of Lichfield and Coventry.
324. Walter Stapleton, bp. of Exeter, *again.* He was beheaded in the year 1326, by order of the queen regent, Isabella.
324. Wm. de Melton, ábp. of York.

King Edward III.

326. John de Stratford, bp. of Winchester, *again.*
— Adam de Orleton, bp. of Hereford.
327. Hy. de Burghersh, bp. of Lincoln.
329. Thos. Charleton, bp. of Hereford.
330. Robt. Woodhouse.
331. Wm. Melton, abp. of York, *again.*
332. Wm. Ayremin, bp. of Norwich.
333. Robt. le Ailstone.
336. Hy. de Burghersh, bp. of Lincoln, *again.*
1337. Richd. de Bury, bp. of Durham.
1338. Wm. de la Zouch, or le Zouch, abp. of York.
1340. Sir Richd. Sodington.
— Roger de Northburgh, bp. of Lichfield and Coventry, *again.*
1342. The same, *again.*
1343. Wm. de Cusans.
1345. Wm. de Edington, bp. of Winchester.
1358. John de Shepey, bp. of Rochester.
1361. Simon Langham, bp. of Ely, aft. abp. of Canterbury, ld. chanc., and a cardinal.
1363. John Barnet, bp. of Worcester. Under him, Wm. Ashby, archd. of Northampton, was ch. ex.
1371. Richd., ld. Scrope, of Bolton, No. 1.
1376. Sir Richd. Ashton, ld. wden. of the Cinque Ports.
1377. Hy. Wakefield, bp. of Worcester.

King Richard II.

1377. The same, *contd.*
1378. Thos. Brentingham, bp. of Exeter.
1379. Richd. Fitzalan, E. of Arundel and Surrey.
1380. Thos. Brentingham, bp. of Exeter, *again.*
1389. John Gilbert, bp. of St. David's.
1390. John Waltham, bp. of Salisbury.
1395. Roger Walden, sec. to the king, and treasr. of Calais. He was elected abp. of Canterbury, but rejected by pope Innocent VII., who aft. confirmed him bp. of London.
1398. Guy de Mona, bp. of St. David's.
— Sir Wm. le Scrope, E. of Wiltshire; beheaded at Bristol in 1399.

King Henry IV.

1399. Sir John Northbury.
1403. Hy. Bowet, bp. of Bath and Wells.
1404. Wm., ld. Roos or Ros.
1405. Thos., ld. Furnival.
1408. Nicholas Bubbewith, bp. of London.
— Richd., ld. Scrope, of Bolton, No. 2.
1409. John de Tiptoft.
1410. Hy., ld. Scrope, of Masham; beheaded at Southampton, 1415.

King Henry V.

1413. Thos., E. of Arundel and Surrey.
1416. Sir Philip Lech.
1417. Hy., ld. Fitz-Hugh.

King Henry VI.

1422. John Stafford, dean of Wells, made bp. of Bath and Wells; aft. abp. of Canterbury.
1425. Walter, ld. Hungerford.
1431. John, ld. Scrope, of Upsal.
1434. Ralph, ld. Cromwell.
1444. Ralph, ld. Sudley.
1447. Marmaduke Lumley, bp. of Carlisle.
1448. Jas., ld. Say and Sele; beheaded by the Kentish rebels under Jack Cade.
1450. John, ld. Beauchamp of Powyk.
1452. John, E. of Worcester.
1455. Jas., E. of Wiltshire and Ormond.
— Thos. Thorpe, ch. ex.
— Hy., visc. Bourchier.
1456. John, E. of Shrewsbury; killed at the battle of Northampton, 1460.
1458. Jas., E. of Wiltshire and Ormond, *again*; beheaded at Newcastle-upon-Tyne, 1461.
1460. Hy., visc. Bourchier, *again.*

King Edward IV.

1460. Thos. Bourchier.
1462. John, E. of Worcester, *again;* beheaded in 1470 or 1471.
1464. Edmd., lord Grey of Ruthyn, cr. E. of Kent.
1465. Sir Walter Blount, aft. lord Montjoy.
1466. Richd., E. Rivers; beheaded at Northampton, 1469.
1469. John Longstrother, prior of St. John's of Jerusalem, in England.
— Wm. Grey, bp. of Ely.
1471. Hy., visc. Bourchier, now E. of Essex, *again.*

King Edward V.

1483. Hy., E. of Essex, *contd.*

King Richard III.

1483. The same, *contd.*
1484. Sir Richd. Wood.

KING HENRY VII.

1485. Sir Reginald Bray.
— Sir Wm. Stanley, ch. ex.
1486. John, lord Dynham.
1501. Thos., E. of Surrey, aft. D. of Norfolk.

KING HENRY VIII.

1509. The same, *contd.*
* * Thos. Cromwell, aft. E. of Essex; and ch. ex.; beheaded 1540.
1522. Thos., E. of Surrey, son to the last ld. treasr.; beheaded 1547.

KING EDWARD VI.

1547. Edwd., E. of Hertford, aft. D. of Somerset; beheaded 1551.
1551. Wm., E. of Wiltshire, aft. M. of Winchester.

QUEEN MARY.

1553. Wm., M. of Winchester, *contd.*

QUEEN ELIZABETH.

1558. The same, *contd.*
— Richd. Sackville, ch. ex.
1566. Sir Wm. Mildmay, ch. ex.
1572. Sir Wm. Cecil, ld. Burleigh, held office 27 years.
1589. Sir John Fortescue, ch. ex.
1599. Thos. Sackville, ld. Buckhurst, aft. E. of Dorset; *d.* Apr. 19, 1609.

KING JAMES I.

1603. Geo., ld. Hume, of Berwick, ch. ex.
— Sir Fulke Greville, ch. ex.
1609. Robt., E. of Salisbury; *d.* May 24, 1612.
1612. Hy., E. of Northampton, and others (first commrs.) by pat., June 16.
1614. Thos. Egerton, ld. Ellesmere, ld. chanc., and others, commrs., Jan. 24.
1614. Thos., ld. Howard de Walden and E. of Suffolk, res.
1618. Geo. Abbott, abp. of Canterbury, and others, commrs., by successive patents, dated July 21, 1618, and Jan. 25, 1619.
1620. Sir Richd. Weston, bt., aft. E. of Portland, ch. ex.
— Sir Hy. Montagu, ld. ch. just. k. b.; cr. baron Kimbolton, and visc. Mandeville; aft. E. of Manchester.
1621. Lionel, ld. Cranfield, aft. E. of Middlesex; sent to the Tower, and deprived, May 14, 1624.
1622. Commission enabling the ld. treas. to act as ch. ex., Apr. 22.
1624. Sir Richd. Weston, aft. ld. Weston, chanc. and under treas. of the ex.; commr. during the vacancy, by pat., May 25.
1624. Sir Jas. Ley, knt. and bt., ld. ch. just. k. b.; cr. lord Ley, aft. E. of Marlborough.

KING CHARLES I.

1625. The same, *contd.*
1628. Rd., ld. Weston, ch. ex.; cr., in 1633, E. of Portland.
— Fras. Cottington, aft. ld. Cottington, ch. ex.
1635. Wm. Laud, abp. of Canterbury,
Hy., E. of Manchester, ld. pr. seal,
Fras., ld. Cottington, late ch. ex.,
Sir John Coke, and
Sir Fras. Windebank, principal secs. of st., commrs.
1636. Wm. Juxon, bp. of London.
— Edwd., ld. Newburgh, in Fifeshire, ch. ex.
1641. Sir Edwd. Littleton, ld. kpr. of the gr. seal,
Hy., E. of Manchester, ld. pr. seal,
Sir John Bankes, ld. ch. just. c. p.,
Edwd., lord Newburgh, ch. ex., and
Sir Hy. Vane, commrs.
1642. Sir John Colepeper, ch. ex.
— Sir Edwd. Hyde, ch. ex.
1643. Fras., ld. Cottington, by pat., dated Oct. 3.

COMMONWEALTH.

1654. Bulstrode Whitelocke,
Sir Thos. Widdrington, and
John Lisle, lds. commrs. of the gr. seal.
Hy. Rolle, and
Oliver St. John, lds. ch. just. of the upper and common bench;
Edwd. Montagu,
Wm. Sydenham, and
Wm. Matham, commrs. of the treasy., by pat., dated Aug. 3.
When Richd. Cromwell became protector, another commission issued.
1658. Bulstrode, ld. Whitelocke, const. of the castle of Windsor,
Edwd., ld. Montagu, one of the generals at sea,
Wm., ld. Sydenham, gov. of the Isle of Wight, and
Sir Thos. Widdrington, ch. bar. exch., commrs. of the treasy., by pat., dated Sept. 18.
After Richd. Cromwell ceased to be protector, another commission issued under the "Keepers of the Liberty of England."
1659. John Disbrowe,
Wm. Sydenham,
Richd. Salwey,
Cornelius Holland,
John Clerke, and
John Blackwell, commrs. of the treasy.

KING CHARLES II.

he dates given below are se of the patents, except se marked **G.**, which are dates of the Gazette ices.

COMMISSIONERS.

June 19, 1660.

EDWARD HYDE, (ld. hanc.), aft. E. of Clarendon.
o. Monk, gen. of the king's orces.
os., E. of Southampton.
n, ld. Robartes.
os., ld. Colepeper.
n. Edwd. Montagu.
Edwd. Nicholas and sir Wm. Morrice, principal secs. of st.

LORD TREASURER.

Sept. 8, 1660.

IOS., E. OF SOUTHAMPTON.
Robt. Long, ch. ex.

COMMISSIONERS.

May. 24, 1667.

EO., D. OF ALBEMARLE.
nthy., ld. Ashley, ch. ex.
r Thos. Clifford, comptr. of the household.
r Wm. Coventry.
r John Duncombe.

Apr. 8, 1669.

EO., D. OF ALBEMARLE.
nthy., ld. Ashley, ch. ex.
r Thos. Clifford, comptr. of the household.
r John Duncombe.

LORD TREASURERS.

Nov. 28, 1672.

HOS., LORD CLIFFORD.
ir John Duncombe, ch. ex.

June 24, 1673.

IR THOS. OSBORNE, BARON OSBORNE, and VISC. LATIMER and DUNBLAIN. Cr. E. of Danby; aft. M. of Carmarthen and D. of Leeds.

COMMISSIONERS.

Mar. 26, 1679.

ARTHUR, E. of ESSEX.
Ion. Laurence Hyde, ch. ex.
ir John Ernley.
ir Edwd. Deering, bt.
idney Godolphin.

Nov. 21, 1679.

ION. LAURENCE, aft. LORD HYDE.
ir John Ernley, ch. ex.
Sir Edwd. Deering, bt.
Sidney Godolphin.
Sir Stephen Fox.

July 9, 1684.

LAURENCE, VISC. HYDE, now E. of ROCHESTER.
Sir John Ernley, ch. ex.
Sir Stephen Fox.

July 26, 1684.

LAURENCE, E. of ROCHESTER.
Sir John Ernley, ch. ex.
Sir Dudley North.
Hy. Fredk. Thynne.

Sept. 9, 1684.

SIDNEY, LORD GODOLPHIN.
Sir John Ernley, ch. ex.
Sir Stephen Fox.
Sir Dudley North.
Hy. Fredk. Thynne.

KING JAMES II.

LORD TREASURER.

Feb. 16, 1685.

LAURENCE, E. OF ROCHESTER.

COMMISSIONERS.

Jan. 4, 1687.

JOHN, LORD BELASYSE.
Sidney, ld Godolphin.
Hy., ld. Dover.
Sir John Ernley, ch. ex.
Sir Stephen Fox.

WILLIAM AND MARY.

Apr. 9, 1689.

CHAS., VISC. MORDAUNT.
Hy., ld. Delamere, ch. ex.
Sidney, ld. Godolphin.
Sir Hy. Capel, K.B.
Richd. Hampden.

Mar. 18, 1690.

SIR JOHN LOWTHER, bt.
Richd. Hampden, ch. ex.
Sir Stephen Fox.
Thos. Pelham.

Nov. 15, 1690.

SIDNEY, LORD GODOLPHIN.
Sir John Lowther, bt.
Richd. Hampden, ch. ex.
Thos. Pelham.
Sir Stephen Fox.

Mar. 21, 1691.

SIDNEY, LORD GODOLPHIN.
Richd. Hampden, ch. ex.
Sir Stephen Fox.
Chas. Montagu, aft. lord Halifax.
Sir Edwd. Seymour, bt.

May 3, 1694.

SIDNEY, LORD GODOLPHIN; and ch. ex.
Sir Stephen Fox.
Chas. Montagu.
Sir Wm. Trumbull.
John Smith.

KING WILLIAM III.

Nov. 1, 1695.

SIDNEY, LORD GODOLPHIN.
Chas. Montagu, ch. ex.
Sir Stephen Fox.
John Smith.

May 2, 1696.

SIDNEY, LORD GODOLPHIN.
Chas. Montagu, ch. ex.
Sir Stephen Fox.
John Smith.
Sir Thos. Littleton, bt.

May 1, 1698.

CHAS. MONTAGU, and ch. ex.
Sir Stephen Fox.
John Smith.
Sir Thos. Littleton, bt.
Thos. Pelham.

June 1, 1699.

CHAS. MONTAGU, and ch. ex.
Ford, E. of Tankerville.
Sir Stephen Fox.
John Smith.
Hon. Hy. Boyle

Nov. 15, 1699.

FORD, E. OF TANKERVILLE.
John Smith, ch. ex.
Sir Stephen Fox.
Hon. Hy. Boyle.
Richd. Hill.

Dec. 9, 1700.

SIDNEY, LORD GODOLPHIN.
John Smith, ch. ex.
Sir Stephen Fox.
Hon. Hy. Boyle.
Richd. Hill.

Mar. 29, 1701.

SIDNEY, LORD GODOLPHIN.
Hon. Hy. Boyle, ch. ex.
Sir Stephen Fox.
Richd. Hill.
Thos. Pelham.

Dec. 30, 1701.

CHAS., E. OF CARLISLE.
Hon. Hy. Boyle, ch. ex.
Sir Stephen Fox.
Richd. Hill.
Thos. Pelham.

QUEEN ANNE.

LORD TREASURER.

May 8, 1702.

SIDNEY, LORD GODOLPHIN, aft. visc. Rialton and E. of Godolphin.

Union with Scotland.

Lord Treasurers, &c., of Great Britain.

Commissioners.
Aug. 10, 1710.
John E. Poulet.
Robt. Harley, ch. ex.
Hon. Hy. Paget.
Sir Thos. Mansell, bt.
Robt. Benson.

Lord Treasurer.
May 30, 1711.
Robt. E. of Oxford and E. Mortimer.

Lord Treasurer.
Chas., D. of Shrewsbu[ry]
He was at the same ti[me] ld. chambn. of the hsho[ld.] and ld. lieut. of Ireland

King George I.

From the accession of George I. to the present time the office of lord treasurer h[as] been executed by commissioners; the duke of Shrewsbury being the last person w[ho] executed the office as an individual.

Commissioners.

Oct. 13, 1714.
Chas., E. of Halifax.
Sir Richd Onslow, bt., ch. ex.
Sir Wm. St. Quintin, bt.
Edwd. Wortley Montagu.
Paul Methuen.

May 23, 1715.
Chas., E. of Carlisle.
Sir Richd. Onslow, bt., ch. ex.
Sir Wm. St. Quintin, bt.
Edwd. Wortley Montagu.
Paul Methuen.

Oct. 11, 1715.
Robt. Walpole, and ch. ex.
Daniel, ld. Finch.
Sir Wm. St. Quintin, bt.
Paul Methuen.
Hon. Thos. Newport.

June 25, 1716.
Robt. Walpole, and ch. ex.
Sir Wm. St. Quintin, bt.
Paul Methuen.
Hon. Thos. Newport, aft. Lord Torrington.
Richd. Edgcumbe.

Apr. 15, 1717.
Jas. Stanhope, aft. E. Stanhope, and ch. ex.
Thos., ld. Torrington.
John Wallop.
Geo. Baillie.
Thos. Micklethwaite, aft. visc. Micklethwaite, in Ireland.

Mar. 20, 1718.
Chas., E. of Sunderland.
John Aislabie, ch. ex.
John Wallop, aft. visc. Lymington and E. of Portsmouth.
Geo. Baillie.
Wm. Clayton.

June 11, 1720.
Chas., E. of Sunderland.
John Aislabie, ch. ex.
Geo. Baillie.
Sir Chas. Turner, bt.
Richd. Edgcumbe.

Apr. 3, 1721.
Robt. Walpole, aft. sir R. and E. of Orford; and ch. ex.
Geo. Baillie.
Sir Chas. Turner, bt.
Richd. Edgcumbe, aft. ld. Edgcumbe.
Hon. Hy. Pelham.

Mar. 23, 1724.
Robt. Walpole, and ch. ex.
Geo. Baillie.
Sir Chas. Turner, bt.
Hon. Hy. Pelham.
Wm. Yonge.

Apr. 2, 1724.
Robt. Walpole, and ch. ex.
Geo. Baillie.
Sir Chas. Turner, bt.
Wm. Yonge.
Geo. Dodington, aft. lord Melcombe.

May 27, 1725.
Sir Robt. Walpole, and ch. ex.
Sir Chas. Turner, bt.
Sir Wm. Yonge, K.B.
Geo. Dodington.
Sir Wm. Strickland, bt.

King George II.
July 28, 1727.
Sir Robt. Walpole, K.G.; and ch. ex.
Sir Chas. Turner, bt.
Geo. Dodington.
Sir Geo. Oxenden, bt.
Wm. Clayton.

May 11, 1730.
Sir Robt. Walpole, K.G. and ch. ex.
Geo. Dodington.
Sir Geo. Oxenden, bt.
Wm. Clayton, aft. lord Su[n]don, of Ireland.
Sir Wm. Yonge, K.B.

May 1735.
Sir Robt. Walpole, K.G. and ch. ex.
Geo. Dodington.
Sir Geo. Oxenden, bt.
Wm., lord Sundon.
Geo., visc. Malpas.

May 1736.
Sir Robt. Walpole, K.G. and ch. ex.
Geo. Dodington.
Sir Geo. Oxenden, bt.
Wm., lord Sundon.
Thos. Winnington.

June 1737.
Sir Robt. Walpole, K.G. and ch. ex.
Geo. Dodington, aft. lo[rd] Melcombe.
Wm., Lord Sundon.
Thos. Winnington.
Giles Earle.

1741.
Sir Robt. Walpole, K.G. and ch. ex.
Thos. Winnington.
Giles Earle.
Geo. Treby.
Thos. Clutterbuck.

Feb. 16, 1742.

SPENCER, E. OF WILMINGTON, K.G.
Saml. Sandys, ch. ex.
Hon. Geo. Compton.
Sir John Rushout, bt.
Philip Gibbons.

Aug. 25, 1743.

HY. PELHAM; and ch. ex.
Hon. Geo. Compton, aft. E. of Northampton.
Philip Gibbons.
Chas. E. of Middlesex, aft. D. of Dorset.
Hy. Fox, aft. lord Holland.

Dec. 25, 1744.

HY. PELHAM; and ch. ex.
Charles, E. of Middlesex.
Hy. Fox.
Hon. Richd. Arundel.
Geo. Lyttelton.

June 1746.

HY. PELHAM; and ch. ex.
Chas., E. of Middlesex.
Geo. Lyttelton, aft. sir G. and ld. Lyttelton.
Hon. Hy. Bilson Legge.
John Campbell.

June 1747.

HY. PELHAM; and ch. ex.
Geo. Lyttelton.
Hon. Hy. Bilson Legge.
John Campbell,
Hon. Geo. Grenville.

May 1749.

HY. PELHAM; and ch. ex.
Geo. Lyttelton.
John Campbell.
Hon. Geo. Grenville.
Hon Hy. Vane, aft. E. of Darlington.

Mar. 18, 1754.

THOS. PELHAM HOLLES, D. OF NEWCASTLE, first commr.

April 6, 1754.

THOS. PELHAM HOLLES, D. OF NEWCASTLE.
Hy., E. of Darlington.
Hon. H. B. Legge, ch. ex.
Thos., visc. Dupplin, aft. E. of Kinnoul.
Robt. Nugent, aft. E. Nugent.

Nov. 22, 1755.

THOS. PELHAM HOLLES, D. OF NEWCASTLE.
Hy., E. of Darlington.
Sir Geo. Lyttelton, bt., ch. ex.
Thos., visc. Dupplin.
Robt. Nugent.

Dec. 20, 1755.

THOS. PELHAM HOLLES, D. OF NEWCASTLE.
Sir Geo. Lyttelton, bt., ch. ex.
Robt. Nugent.
Percy Wyndham O'Bryen.
Hy. Furnese.

Nov. 16, 1756.

WM., D. OF DEVONSHIRE.
Hon. H. B. Legge, ch. ex.
Robt. Nugent.
Wm. visc. Duncannon.
Hon. Jas. Grenville.

July 2, 1757.

THOS. PELHAM HOLLES, D. OF NEWCASTLE.
Hon. H.B. Legge, ch. ex.
Robt. Nugent.
Wm., visc. Duncannon, aft. E. of Besborough.
Hon. Jas. Grenville.

June 2, 1759.

THOS. PELHAM HOLLES, D. OF NEWCASTLE.
Hon. H. B. Legge, ch. ex.
Robt. Nugent.
Hon. Jas. Grenville.
Fredk., lord North.

Dec. 22, 1759.

THOS. PELHAM HOLLES, D. OF NEWCASTLE.
Hon. H. B. Legge, ch. ex.
Hon. Jas. Grenville.
Fredk., lord North.
Jas. Oswald.

KING GEORGE III.

Mar. 12, 1761.

THOS. PELHAM HOLLES, D. OF NEWCASTLE.
Wm., visc. Barrington, ch. ex.
Fredk., lord North.
Jas. Oswald.
Gilbert Elliot.

May 28, 1762.

JOHN, E. OF BUTE.
Sir Fras. Dashwood, bt., aft. lord le Despencer, ch. ex.
Fredk., lord North.
Jas. Oswald.
Sir John Turner, bt.

April 15, 1763.

GEO. GRENVILLE, and ch. ex.
Fredk., lord North.
Sir John Turner, bt.
Thos. Orby Hunter.
Jas. Harris.

July 10, 1765.

CHAS., M. OF ROCKINGHAM.
Wm. Dowdeswell, ch. ex.
Lord John Cavendish.
Thos. Townshend, aft. lord Sydney.
Geo. Onslow, aft. ld. Cranley, and ld. Onslow.

Aug. 2, 1766.

AUG. HY., D. OF GRAFTON.
Hon. Chas. Townshend, ch. ex.
Thos. Townshend.
Geo. Onslow.
Pryse Campbell.

Dec. 1, 1767.

AUG. HY., D. OF GRAFTON.
Fredk., lord North, ch. ex.
Geo. Onslow.
Pryse Campbell.
Chas. Jenkinson.

Dec. 31, 1768.

AUG. HY., D. OF GRAFTON.
Fredk., lord North, ch. ex.
Geo. Onslow.
Chas. Jenkinson.
Jeremiah Dyson

Feb. 6, 1770

FREDK., LORD NORTH; and ch. ex.
Geo. Onslow.
Chas. Jenkinson, aft. lord Hawkesbury.
Jeremiah Dyson.
Chas. Townshend.

Jan. 9, 1773.

FREDK., LORD NORTH; and ch. ex.
Geo. Onslow.
Jeremiah Dyson.
Chas. Townshend.
Hon. Chas. Jas. Fox

Mar. 12, 1774.

FREDK., LORD NORTH; and ch. ex.
Geo. Onslow.
Chas. Townshend.
Fras. Seymour Conway, visc. Beauchamp.
Chas. Wolfran Cornewall.

June 5, 1777.

FREDK., LORD NORTH; and ch. ex.
Geo. Onslow, now ld. Onslow and Cranley.
Fras., visc. Beauchamp.
Chas. Wolfran Cornewall.
Wm. Hy., ld. Westcote.

Dec. 14, 1777.

FREDK., LORD NORTH; and ch. ex.
Fras., visc. Beauchamp.
Chas. Wolfran Cornewall.
Wm. Hy., ld. Westcote.
Henry, visc. Palmerston.

Sept. 6, 1780.

FREDK., LORD NORTH; and ch. ex.
Wm. Hy., ld. Westcote.
Hy., visc. Palmerston.
Sir Richd. Sutton, bt.
John Buller.

Mar. 27, 1782.

CHAS., M. OF ROCKINGHAM.
Lord John Cavendish, ch. ex.
Geo. John, visc. Althorpe.
Jas. Grenville.
Fredk. Montagu.

July 13, 1782.

WM., E. OF SHELBURNE.
Wm. Pitt, ch. ex.
Jas. Grenville.
Richd. Jackson.
Edwd. Jas. Elliot.

April 4, 1783.

WM. HY., D. OF PORTLAND.
Lord John Cavendish, ch. ex.
Chas., E. of Surrey.
Fredk. Montagu.
Sir Grey Cooper, bt.

Dec. 27, 1783.

WM. PITT, and ch. ex.
Jas., M. of Graham.
John Buller.
Edwd. Jas. Elliot
John Aubrey, aft. sir J.

Sept. 19, 1786.

WM. PITT; and ch. ex.
Jas., M. of Graham.
Hon. Edwd. Jas. Elliot.
Sir John Aubrey, bt.
Richd., E. of Mornington.

April 8, 1789.

WM. PITT; and ch. ex.
Hon. Edwd. Jas. Elliot.
Richd., E. of Mornington.
John Jeffreys, visc. Bayham.
Hy., lord Apsley.

June 20, 1791.

WM. PITT; and ch. ex.
Hon. Edwd. Geo. Elliot.
Richd., E of Mornington.
John Jeffreys, visc. Bayham.
Richd. Hopkins.

June 22, 1793.

WM. PITT; and ch. ex.
Richd., E. of Mornington.
John Jeffreys, visc. Bayham.
Richd. Hopkins.
Hon Jno. Thos. Townshend.

May 7, 1794.

WM PITT; and ch. ex.
Richd., E. of Mornington.
Richd. Hopkins.
Hon. John Thos. Townshend
John Smyth.

Feb. 3, 1797.

WM. PITT; and ch. ex.
Richd., E. of Mornington.
Hon. John Thos. Townshend.
John Smyth.
Sylvester Douglas.

Aug. 3, 1797.

WM. PITT; and ch. ex.
Hon. John Thos. Townshend.
John Smyth.
Sylvester Douglas.
Chas. Small Pybus.

July 28, 1800.

WM. PITT; and ch. ex.
John Smyth.
S. Douglas, lord Glenbervie.
Chas. Small Pybus.
Lord Granville Leveson Gower.

Dec. 9, 1800.

WM. PITT; and ch. ex.
John Smyth.
Chas. Small Pybus.
Lord Granville Leveson Gower.
John Hiley Addington.

Mar. 21, 1801.

HY. ADDINGTON; and ch.ex.
John Smyth.
Chas. Small Pybus.
Lord Geo. Thynne.
Nathl. Bond.

July 5, 1802.

HY. ADDINGTON; and ch.ex.
Chas. Small Pybus.
Lord Geo. Thynne.
Nathl. Bond.
John Hiley Addington.

Nov. 13, 1803.

HY. ADDINGTON; and ch.ex.
Chas. Small Pybus.
Lord Geo. Thynne.
Nathl. Bond.
Hon. Wm. Brodrick.

Nov. 19, 1803.

HY. ADDINGTON; and ch.ex.
Lord Geo. Thynne.
Nathl. Bond.
Hon. Wm. Brodrick.
Edwd. Golding.

May 16, 1804.

WM. PITT; and ch. ex.
Geo., ld Lovaine.
Jas. Edwd., visc. Fitzharris.
Hon. Hy. Wellesley.
Chas. Long.

Aug. 6, 1804.

WM. PITT; and ch. ex.
Geo., ld. Lovaine.
Jas. Edwd., visc. Fitzharris.
Chas. Long.
Geo., M. of Blandford.

Feb. 10, 1806.

WM., LORD GRENVILLE.
Lord Hy. Petty, ch. ex.
John Chas., visc. Althorpe.
Wm. Wickham.
John Courtenay.

Mar. 31, 1807.

WM. HY., D. OF PORTLAND.
Spencer Perceval, ch. ex.
Wm. Hy., M. of Titchfield.
Hon. Wm. Eliot.
Wm. Sturges Bourne.

Sept. 16, 1807.

WM. HY., D. OF PORTLAND.
Spencer Perceval, ch. ex.
John Foster.
Hon. Wm. Eliot.
Wm. Sturges Bourne.
Hon. Richd. Ryder.

Dec. 2, 1807.

WM. HY., D. OF PORTLAND.
Spencer Perceval, ch. ex.
John Foster.
Hon. Wm. Brodrick.
Hon. Wm. Eliot.
Wm. Sturges Bourne.

Dec. 6, 1809.

ENCER PERCEVAL; and ch. ex.
hn Foster.
on. Wm. Brodrick.
on. Wm. Eliot.
hn Otway, E. of Desart.
owden Barne.

June 23, 1810.

ENCER PERCEVAL; and ch. ex.
hn Foster.
on. Wm. Brodrick.
on. Wm. Eliot.
owden Barne.
on. Berkeley Paget.

Jan. 6, 1812.

SPENCER PERCEVAL; and ch. ex.
Hon. Wm. Wellesley Pole.
Hon. Wm. Brodrick.
Snowden Barne.
Hon. Berkeley Paget.
Richd. Wellesley.

June 16, 1812.

ROBT., E. OF LIVERPOOL.
Nicholas Vansittart, ch. ex.
Snowden Barne.
Hon. Berkeley Paget.

Oct. 5, 1812.

ROBT., E. OF LIVERPOOL.
Nichs. Vansittart, ch. ex.
Wm. Vesey Fitzgerald.
Hon. Berkeley Paget.
Fdk. Jno. Robinson, aft. visc. Goderich, and E. of Ripon.
Jas. Brogden.

Nov. 25, 1813.

ROBT., E. OF LIVERPOOL.
Nichs. Vansittart, aft. ld. Bexley, ch. ex.
Wm. Vesey Fitzgerald.
Hon. Berkeley Paget.
Jas. Brogden.
Wm., visc. Lowther.

Dec. 20, 1813.

ROBT., E. OF LIVERPOOL.
Nichs. Vansittart, ch. ex.
Wm. Vesey Fitzgerald.
Hon. Berkeley Paget.
Wm., visc. Lowther.
Chas. Grant, jun.

REVENUES OF GREAT BRITAIN AND IRELAND UNITED, UNDER 56 GEO. III., c. 98.

LORD TREASURERS, &c., OF THE UNITED KINGDOM.

COMMISSIONERS.

Jan. 7, 1817.

OBT., E. OF LIVERPOOL.
ichs. Vansittart, ch. ex.
on. Berkeley Paget.
m., visc. Lowther.
has. Grant, jun.
ohn Maxwell Barry.
m. O'Dell. *The two last from the Irish Treasury.*

Mar. 25, 1819.

OBT., E. OF LIVERPOOL.
ichs. Vansittart, ch. ex.
on. Berkeley Paget.
m., visc. Lowther.
ord Granville Chas. Hy. Somerset.
ohn Maxwell Barry.
dmd. Alexr. MacNaughten.

Feb. 10, 1823.

OBT., E. OF LIVERPOOL, K.G.
redk. John Robinson, ch. ex.
Ion. Berkeley Paget.
Vm., visc. Lowther.
ord Granville Chas. Hy. Somerset.
ohn Maxwell Barry.
dmd. Alexr. MacNaughten.

May 3, 1823.

ROBT., E. OF LIVERPOOL, K.G.
Fredk. John Robinson, ch. ex.
Hon. Berkeley Paget.
Wm., visc. Lowther.
Lord Granville Chas. Hy. Somerset.
Edmd. Alexr. MacNaughten.

June 13, 1826.

ROBT., E. OF LIVERPOOL, K.G.
Fredk. John Robinson, ch. ex.
Wm., visc. Lowther.
Lord Granville Chas. Hy. Somerset.
Fras. Nathl. Conyngham, E. of Mount Charles.
Edmd. Alexr. MacNaughten.

Apr. 30, 1827.

GEO. CANNING, and ch. ex.
Fras. Nathl., E. of Mount Charles.
Lord Fras. Leveson Gower.
Edwd. Granville, lord Eliot.
Edmd. Alexr. MacNaughten.

July 31, 1827.

GEO. CANNING, and ch. ex.
Fras. Nathl., E. of Mount Charles.
Lord Fras. Leveson Gower.
Edwd. Granville, lord Eliot.
Maurice Fitzgerald.
Edmd. Alexr. MacNaughten.

Sept. 8, 1827.

FREDK. JOHN ROBINSON, cr. visc. GODERICH.
John Chas. Herries, ch. ex.
Fras. Nathl., E. of Mount Charles.
Edwd. Granville, lord Eliot.
Maurice Fitzgerald.
Edmd. Alexr. MacNaughten.

Jan. 26, 1828.

ARTHUR, D. OF WELLINGTON, K.G.
Hy. Goulburn, ch. ex.
Lord Granville Chas. Hy. Somerset.
Fras. Nathl., E. of Mount Charles.
Edwd. Granville, lord Eliot.
Edmd. Alexr. MacNaughten.

Apr. 24, 1830.

ARTHUR, D. OF WELLINGTON, K.G.
Hy. Goulburn, ch. ex.
Lord Granville Chas. Hy. Somerset.
Edwd. Granville, lord Eliot.
Geo. Bankes.
Edmd. Alexr. MacNaughten.

July 24, 1830.

ARTHUR, D. OF WELLINGTON, K.G.
Hy. Goulburn, ch. ex.

Lord Granville Chas. Hy. Somerset.
Edwd. Granville, lord Eliot.
Geo. Bankes.
Wm. Yates Peel.

Nov. 24, 1830.

CHAS., E. GREY, K.G.
John Chas., visc. Althorpe, ch. ex.
Geo., lord Nugent.
Robt. Vernon Smith.
Fras. Thornhill Baring.
Hon. Geo. Ponsonby.

Nov. 22, 1832.

CHAS., E. GREY, K.G.
John Chas., visc. Althorpe, ch. ex.
Robt. Vernon Smith.
Fras. Thornhill Baring
Hon. Geo. Ponsonby.
Thos. Fras. Kennedy.

Apr. 9, 1834.

CHAS., E. GREY, K.G.
John Chas., visc. Althorpe, ch. ex.
Robt. Vernon Smith.
Fras. Thornhill Baring.
Hon. Geo. Ponsonby.
Robt. Graham.

June 20, 1834.

CHAS., E. GREY, K.G.
John Chas., visc. Althorpe, ch. ex.
Robt. Vernon Smith.
Hon. Geo. Ponsonby.
Robt. Graham.
Capt. Geo. Stevens Byng.

July 18, 1834.

WM. VISC. MELBOURNE.
John Chas., visc. Althorpe, ch. ex.
Robt. Vernon Smith.
Hon. Geo. Ponsonby.
Robt. Graham, and
Capt. Geo. Stevens Byng.

Nov. 21, 1834.

ARTHUR, D. OF WELLINGTON, K.G.
Jas., E. of Rosslyn, G.C.B.
Edwd. ld. Ellenborough.
Wm., ld. Maryborogh.
Sir John Becket, bt.
Joseph Planta.

The duke of Wellington held office provisionally, waiting the return of sir Robt. Peel from Italy.

Dec. 26, 1834.

SIR ROBT. PEEL, bt., and ch. ex.
Wm. Yates Peel.
Hy. Pelham Clinton, E. of Lincoln.
Wm. David, visc. Stormont.
Chas. Ross.
Wm. Ewart Gladstone.

Mar. 14, 1835.

SIR ROBERT PEEL, bt., and ch. ex.
Wm. Yates Peel.
Hy. Pelham Clinton, E. of Lincoln.
Wm. David, visc. Stormont.
Chas. Ross.
John Nicoll.

Apr. 18, 1835.

WM., VISC. MELBOURNE.
Thos. Spring Rice, aft. ld. Monteagle, ch. ex.
Edwd. Adolphus Seymour, lord Seymour.
Wm. Hy. Ord.
Robt. Steuart.

May 16, 1835.

WM., VISC. MELBOURNE.
Thos. Spring Rice, ch. ex.
Edwd. Adolphus, ld. Seymour.
Wm. Hy. Ord.
Robt. Steuart.
Richd. More O'Ferral.

July 18, 1837.

WM., VISC. MELBOURNE.
Thos. Spring Rice, ch. ex.
Edwd. Adolphus, ld. Seymour.
Robt. Steuart.
Richd. More O'Ferral.
John Parker.

Aug. 28, 1839.

WM., VISC. MELBOURNE.
Fras. Thornhill Baring, ch. ex.
Edwd. Adolphus, ld. Seymour.
Robt. Steuart.
John Parker.
Thos. Wyse, jun.

Nov. 2, 1839.

WM., VISC. MELBOURNE.
Fras. Thornhill Baring, ch. ex.
Robt. Steuart.
John Parker.
Thos. Wyse, jun.
Hy. Tuffnell.

May 26, 1840.

WM., VISC. MELBOURNE.
Fras. Thornhill Baring, ch. ex.
John Parker.
Thos. Wyse, jun.
Hy. Tuffnell.
Edwd. Horsman.

June 23, 1841.

WM., VISC. MELBOURNE.
Fras. Thornhill Baring, ch. ex.
Thos. Wyse, jun.
Hy. Tuffnell.
Edwd. Horsman.
Wm. Fras. Cowper.

Sept. 6, 1841.

SIR ROBT. PEEL, bt.
Hy. Goulburn, ch. ex.
Jas. Milne Gaskell.
Hy. Bingham Baring.
Alexr. Perceval.
Alexr. Pringle.

Sept. 16, 1841.

SIR ROBT. PEEL, bt.
Hy. Goulburn, ch. ex.
James Milnes Gaskell.
Hy. Bingham Baring.
Alexr. Pringle.
John Young.

May 21, 1844.

SIR ROBT. PEEL, bt.
Hy. Goulburn, ch. ex.
Jas. Milnes Gaskell.
Hy. Bingham Baring.
Alexr. Pringle.
Lord Arthur Lenox.

Apr. 26, 1845.

SIR ROBT. PEEL, bt.
Hy. Goulburn, ch. ex.
Jas. Milnes Gaskell.
Hy. Bingham Baring.
Lord Arthur Lenox.
Wm. Forbes Mackenzie.

Aug. 8, 1845.

SIR ROBT. PEEL, bt.
Hy. Goulburn, ch. ex.
Jas. Milnes Gaskell.
Hy. Bingham Baring.
Wm. Forbes Mackenzie.
Wm. Cripps.

Mar. 11, 1846.

Robt. Peel, bt.
. Goulburn, ch. ex.
. Bingham Baring.
ı. Cripps.
n. Swynfen Thos. Carnegie.
ph Neville.

July 6, 1846.

rd John Russell, aft. E. Russell.
ıs. Wood, ch. ex.
gh, visc. Ebrington.
e O'Conor Don.
n. Gibson Craig.
. Rich.

Aug. 6, 1847.

rd John Russell.
Chas. Wood, bt., ch. ex.
gh, visc. Ebrington.
n. Gibson Craig.
. Rich.
hd. Montesquieu Bellew.

Dec. 24, 1847.

rd John Russell.
Chas. Wood, bt, ch. ex.
n. Gibson Craig.
. Rich.
hd. Montesquieu Bellew.
., E. of Shelburne, retd., Aug. following.
On the retirement of lord Shelburne, the office of one of the junior lordships of the treasury was abolished.

Feb. 28, 1852, **G.**

wd. Geoffrey, E. of Derby.
njn. Disraeli, ch. ex.
chd. P. C. T. N., M. of Chandos.
rd Hy. Geo. Chas. Gordon Lennox.
os. Bateson.

Jan. 1, 1853, **G.**

o. Hamilton, E. of Aberdeen.
m. Ewart Gladstone, ch. ex.
rd Alfred Hervey.
n. Fras. Wemyss Charteris.
o. Sadleir.

Mar. 6, 1854, **G.**

eo. Hamilton, E. of Aberdeen, k.t.
m. E. Gladstone, ch. ex.
rd Alfred Hervey.
rd Elcho.
hichester Saml. Fortescue.

Feb. 10, 1855, **G.**

Hy. Jno., visc. Palmerston, g.c.b.
Wm. Ewart Gladstone, ch. ex.
Lord Alfred Hervey.
Lord Elcho.
Chichester Saml. Fortescue.

Mar. 7, 1855, **G.**

Hy. Jno., visc. Palmerston, g.c.b.
Sir Geo. Cornewall Lewis, bt., ch. ex.
Chas Stanley, visc. Monck.
Adam Duncan Haldane, c.c. visc. Duncan.
Chichester Saml. Fortescue.

Apr. 16, 1855, **G.**

Hy. Jno., visc. Palmerston, k.c.b.
Sir Geo. Cornewall Lewis, bt., ch. ex.
Chas. Stanley, visc. Monck.
Adam Duncan Haldane, c.c. visc. Duncan.
Hon. Hy. Bouverie Wm. Brand.

Mar. 1, 1858, **G.**

Edwd. Geoffrey, E. of Derby.
Benjn. Disraeli, ch. ex.
Lord Hy. Geo. Chas. Gordon Lennox.
Thos. Edwd. Taylor.
Hy. Whitmore.

Mar. 15, 1859, **G.**

Edwd. Geoffrey, E. of Derby.
Benjn. Disraeli, ch. ex.
Thos. Edwd. Taylor.
Hy. Whitmore.
Peter Blackburn.

June 24, 1859, **G.**

Hy. Jno., visc. Palmerston, k.g.
Wm. Ewart Gladstone, ch. ex.
Edwd. Hugessen Knatchbull-Hugessen.
Sir Wm. Dunbar, bt.
Jno. Bagwell.

Mar. 25, 1862, **G.**

Hy. Jno., visc. Palmerston, k.g.
Wm. Ewart Gladstone, ch. ex.
Edwd. Hugessen Knatchbull-Hugessen.
Sir Wm. Dunbar, bt.
Lt.-Col Luke White.

Apr. 21, 1865, **G.**

Hy. Jno., visc. Palmerston, k.g.
Wm. Ewart Gladstone, ch. ex.
Edwd. Hugessen Knatchbull-Hugessen.
Wm. Patrick Adam.
Lt.-Col. Luke White.

Nov. 6, 1865, **G.**

Jno, E. Russell.
Wm. E. Gladstone, ch. ex.
Edwd. Hugessen Knatchbull-Hugessen.
Lt.-Col. Luke White.
Wm. Patrick Adam.

June 2, 1866, **G.**

Jno., E. Russell, k.g.
Wm. E. Gladstone, ch. ex.
Jno. Bonham-Carter.
Wm. Patrick Adam.
Jno. Esmonde.

July 12, 1866, **G.**

Edwd. Geoffrey, E. of Derby, k.g.
Benjn. Disraeli, ch. ex.
Hon. Gerard Jas. Noel.
Sir Graham Graham Montgomery, bt.
Hy. Whitmore.

Feb. 29, 1868, **G.**

Benjn. Disraeli, aft. E. of Beaconsfield.
Geo. Ward Hunt, ch. ex.
Gerard Jas. Noel.
Sir Graham Graham Montgomery, bt.
Hy. Whitmore.

Nov. 2, 1868, **G.**

Benjn. Disraeli.
Geo. Ward Hunt, ch. ex.
Claud Jno. Hamilton, c.c. lord C. J. Hamilton.
Sir Graham Graham Montgomery, bt.
Hy. Whitmore.

Dec. 16, 1868, **G.**

Wm. Ewart Gladstone.
Robt. Lowe, ch. ex.
Jas. Stansfeld, jun.
Hy. Chas. Keith, M. of Lansdowne.
Wm. Patrick Adam.
Hon. Jno. Cranch Walker Vivian.

Nov. 2, 1869, **G.**

Wm. Ewart Gladstone.
Robt. Lowe, ch. ex.

Hy. Chas. Keith, M. of Lansdowne.
Wm. Patrick Adam.
Hon. Jno. Cranch Walker Vivian.
Wm. Hy. Gladstone.

Aug. 8, 1873, **G.**

Wm. Ewart Gladstone, ch. ex.
Fredk. Chas. Cavendish, c.c. lord F. C. Cavendish.
Wm. Hy. Gladstone.
Hon. Algernon Wm. Fulke Greville

Mar. 4, 1874, **G.**

Benjn. Disraeli.
Sir Stafford Hy. Northcote, bt., ch. ex.
Arthur Philip Hy. Stanhope, c.c. visc. Mahon.
Rowland Winn.
Sir Jas. Dalrymple Howard Elphinstone, bt.

Feb. 16, 1876, **G.**

Benjn. Disraeli, (cr. visc. Hughenden, and E. of Beaconsfield, Aug. 16, 1876.)
Sir Stafford Hy. Northcote, bt., ch. ex.
Jno. Hy. Crichton, c.c. visc. Crichton.
Rowland Winn.
Sir Jas. Dalrymple Howard Elphinstone, bt.

May 5, 1880, **G.**

Wm. Ewart Gladstone, and ch. ex.
Sir Arthur Divett Hayter, bt.
Jno. Holms.
Chas. Cecil Cotes.

Aug. 24, 1881, **G.**

Wm. Ewart Gladstone, and ch. ex.
Sir Arthur Divett Hayter, bt.
Jno. Holms.
Chas. Cecil Cotes.
Herbert Jno. Gladstone.

June 26, 1882, **G.**

Wm. Ewart Gladstone, and ch. ex.
Chas. Cecil Cotes.
Herbert Jno. Gladstone.
Robt. Wm. Duff.

Jan. 1, 1883, **G.**

Wm. Ewart Gladstone.
Hugh Culling Eardley Childers, ch. ex.
Chas. Cecil Cotes.
Herbert Jno. Gladstone.
Robt. Wm. Duff.

June 29, 1885, **G.**

Sir Stafford Hy. Northcote, bt., g.c.b., first ld., but under the premiership of the M. of Salisbury the for. sec. cr. visc. St. Cyres and E. of Iddesleigh, July 2, 1885.
Sir Michael Edwd. Hick Beach, bt., ch. ex.
Chas. Dalrymple.
Hon. Sidney Herbert.
Lt.-Col. Wm. Hood Wa rond.

Feb. 13, 1886, **G.**

Wm. Ewart Gladstone.
Sir Wm. Geo. Granvil Venables Vernon Ha court, ch. ex.
Sir Edwd. Jas. Reed, k.c.
Cyril Flower.
Geo. Granville Leveso Gower.

Aug. 9, 1886, **G.**

Robt. Arthur Talbot, M of Salisbury.
Randolph Hy. Spenc Churchill, c.c. ld. R. I S. Churchill, ch. ex.
Hon. Sidney Herbert.
Col. Wm. Hood Walrond.
Sir Herbert Eustace Ma well, bt.

Jan. 17, 1887, **G.**

Wm. Hy. Smith, first ld., b under the premiership the M. of Salisbury, t for. sec.
Geo. Joachim Goschen, c ex.
Hon. Sidney Herbert.
Col. Wm. Hood Walrond.
Sir Herbert Eustace Ma well, bt.

SECRETARIES AND UNDER SECRETARIES TO THE TREASURY.

The time of the first appointment of a secretary to the Treasury Boar is uncertain; but it is presumed there must always have been a secr tary or some officer acting in that capacity to the lord treasurer, or th board. It is probable that Lord Burleigh was the first treasurer wh used a secretary to notify his directions to the officers of the recei side of the exchequer. Sir George Downing was secretary in May 166 In the reign of James II., when the earl of Rochester was treasurer, h had two secretaries, Henry Guy and Francis Gwyn, as is stated in subsequent Treasury Minute Book (year 1711). In the Treasur Minute Book, 1695, No. 6, page 12, is the following memorandum:

"This evening the king was graciously pleased to bestow on me th place of Secretary to the Treasury." "William Lowndes."

Fron this it would appear that there was only *one* secretary in 169.

as Mr. Lowndes distinctly states *the place of secretary* to have been bestowed upon him. It is quite certain there were two secretaries in 1714.

Both the secretaries to the Treasury are political officers who go out of office with their party. One is termed the "parliamentary" or "patronage" secretary, and generally acts as the principal government "whip" in the House of Commons. The other is termed the "financial" secretary, and attends to what is, really, Treasury business.

Besides the two political secretaries there is a permanent official formerly called the "assistant," but now called the "permanent" secretary.

Secretaries to the Treasury.

From the accession of George III.

In 1760. Jas. West, and
Saml. Martin
1762. Saml. Martin, and
Jeremiah Dyson, May 29.
1763. Jeremiah Dyson, and
Chas. Jenkinson, Apr. 16.
1764. Chas. Jenkinson, and
Thos. Whateley, Apr. 5.
1765. Wm. Mellish, and
Chas. Lowndes, July 12.
1765. Chas. Lowndes, and
Grey Cooper, July 30.
1766. Grey Cooper, and
Thos. Bradshaw, Aug. 2.
1770. Sir Grey Cooper, bt., and
John Robinson, Feb. 6.
1782. Hy. Strachey, and
Edwd. Chamberlain, Mar. 29.
1782. Hy. Strachey, and
Richd. Burke, Apr.
1782. Thos. Orde, and
Geo. Rose, July 15.
1783. Richd. Brinsley Sheridan, and
Richd. Burke, Apr. 5.
1783. Geo. Rose, and
Thos. Steele, Dec. 27.
1791. Geo. Rose, and
Chas. Long.
1801. John Hiley Addington, Mar. 24; and
Nichls. Vansittart, Apr. 9.
1802. Nichls. Vansittart, and
John Sargent.
1804. Wm. Huskisson, and
Wm. Sturges Bourne, May 21.
1806. Nichls. Vansittart, and
John King, Feb. 10.
1806. Nichls. Vansittart, and
Wm. Henry Fremantle.
1808. Wm. Huskisson, and
Hon. Hy. Wellesley.
1809. Richd. Wharton, and
Chas. Arbuthnot.
1814. Chas. Arbuthnot, and
Stephen Rumbold Lushington.
1823. Stephen Rumbold Lushington, and
John Chas. Herries, Feb. 7.
1827. Jos. Planta, *vice* Lushington, Apr. 19, and
Thos. Frankland Lewis, *vice* Herries, Sept. 4.
1828. Geo. Robt. Dawson, *vice* Lewis, Jan. 28.
1830. Thos. Spring Rice, and
Edw. Ellice, Nov. 26.
1832. Chas. Wood, *vice* Ellice, Aug. 10.
1834. Fras. Thornhill Baring, *vice* Spring Rice, June 6
1834. Sir Geo. Clerk, bt., Dec. 19.
Sir Thos. Fras. Fremantle, bt., Dec. 20.
1835. Fras. Thornhill Baring, and
Edwd. J. Stanley, Apr. 21.
1839. Robt. Gordon, *vice* Baring, Sept. 6.
1841. Richd. More O'Ferral, June 9.
Sir Denis Le Marchant, June 19.
1844. Sir Geo. Clerk, bt., and
John Young, May 21.
1845. Edwd. Cardwell, *vice* Clerk, Feb. 4.
1846. Hy. Tufnell, and
John Parker, July 7.
1849. Wm. Goodenough Hayter, *vice* Parker, May 22.
1850. Geo. Cornewall Lewis, aft. sir G., bt., *vice* Tufnell, July 9.
1852. Geo. Alex. Hamilton (Fin.), and
Wm. Forbes Mackenzie (Parl.), Feb.
1853. Wm. Goodenough Hayter (Parl), and
Jas. Wilson (Fin.), Jan.
1858. Geo. Alex. Hamilton (Fin.); app. perm. assist. sec., 1859, and
Sir Wm. Geo. Hilton Jolliffe (Parl.), Mar.
1859. Samuel Laing (Fin.), and
Hon. Hy. Bouverie Wm. Brand, aft. sir H. and visc. Hampden (Parl.), June 9.
1859. Fredk. Peel (Fin.), *vice* Laing.
1865. Hugh Culling Eardley Childers (Fin.), *vice* Peel.
1866. Thos. Edwd. Taylor (Parl.), and
Geo. Ward Hunt (Fin.), July.

1868. Geo. Sclater Booth (Fin.), *vice* Hunt, Feb.
1868. Hon. Geo. Grenfell Glynn, aft. lord Wolverton (Parl.), and
Acton Smee Ayrton (Fin.), Dec.
1869. Jas. Stansfeld (Fin.), *vice* Ayrton, Oct.
1871. Wm. Edwd. Baxter (Fin.) *vice* Stansfeld, Aug.
1873. Arthur Wellesley Peel (Parl.), *vice* Glyn, Aug.
1873. John Geo. Dodson, aft. lord Monk-Bretton (Fin.), *vice* Baxter.
1874. Wm. Hart Dyke, aft. sir W., bt., (Parl.), and
Wm. Hy. Smith (Fin.), Feb.
1877. Col. Fredk. Arthur Stanley, aft. lord Stanley of Preston (Fin.), *vice* Smith, Aug.
1878. Sir Hy. Jno. Selwin-Ibbetson (Fin.), *vice* Stanley, Apr.
1880. Lord Richard Grosvenor (Parl.), and Lord Fredk. Cavendish (Fin.), Apr.
1882. Leonard Hy. Courtney (Fin.), *vice* Cavendish, May.
1885. John Tomlinson Hibbert (Fin.), *vice* Courtney.
1885. Aretas Akers-Douglas (Parl.), and Sir Hy. Thurstan Holland, aft. ld. Knutsford (Fin.), June.
Sir Matthew White Ridley, bt., (Fin.), Sept.
1886. Wm. Lawies Jackson (Fin.), *vice* Ridley, Jan.
Arnold Morley (Parl.), and
Hy. Hartley Fowler (Fin.), Feb.
1886. Aretas Akers Douglas (Parl), and Wm. Lawies Jackson (Fin.), Aug.

ASSISTANT OR PERMANENT SECRETARIES TO THE TREASURY.

From the institution of the Office.

ASSISTANT SECRETARIES.

1805. Geo. Harrison, aft. sir Geo., Aug. 19.
1826. Wm. Hill, Feb. 24.
1828. Hon. Jas. Keith Stewart, July 4.
1836. Alexr. Young Spearman, aft. sir A., bt., Jan. 22.
1840. Chas. Edw. Trevelyan, aft. sir C., bt., Jan. 21.
1859. Geo. Alex. Hamilton.

PERMANENT SECRETARIES.

1867. Geo. Alex. Hamilton, above named.
1870. Ralph Robt. Wheeler Lingen, C.B., aft. sir R., K.C.B.
1885. Sir Reginald Earle Welby, K.C.B.

CHANCELLORS OF THE EXCHEQUER.

THE Chancellor of the Exchequer is one of the lords of the treasury, except on particular emergencies, when the office is held by the lord chief justice of the queen's bench.

CHANCELLORS OF THE EXCHEQUER.

From the restoration of King Charles II. to the present time.

The earlier chancellors will be found in the list of lord treasurers.

KING CHARLES II.

1660. Sir Robt. Long, Sept. 8.
1667. Anthy, ld. Ashley, aft. E. of Shaftesbury, May 24.
1672. Sir John Duncombe, Nov. 13.
1679. Hon. Lawrence Hyde, aft. visc. Hyde and E. of Rochester, Mar. 26.
— Sir John Ernle (Ernley), Nov. 21.

KING JAMES II.

Sir John Ernley, *contd.*

WILLIAM and MARY.

1689. Henry, ld. De la Mere, aft. E. of Warrington, Apr. 8.
1690. Richd. Hampden, Mar. 18.
1694. Sidney, ld. Godolphin, and first commr. treas.; aft. E. of Godolphin, May 3.

King William III., *alone.*

1695. Chas. Montagu, Nov. 1.
1697. Chas. Montagu, and first commr. treas, May 1.
1699. John Smith, aft. sp. of the ho. of commons, Nov. 15.
1701. Hon. Hy. Boyle, aft. baron Carleton, Mar. 29.

Queen Anne.

Hon. Hy. Boyle, *contd.*
1708. John Smith, *again*, Feb. 11.
1710. Robt. Harley, aft. E. of Oxford and Mortimer, Aug. 10.
1711. Robt. Benson, aft. ld. Bingley, June 14.
1713. Sir Wm. Wyndham, bt., Nov. 1.

King George I.

1714. Sir Richd. Onslow, bt., previously sp. of the ho. of commons, Oct. 13; cr. ld. Onslow in 1716.
1715. Robt. Walpole, aft. sir Robt., and first commr., treas., Oct. 11.
1717. Jas. Stanhope, and first ld. treas., aft. E. Stanhope, Apr. 15.
1718. John Aislabie, Mar. 18.
1721. Sir John Pratt, ld. ch. just. of the k. b., *pro tem.*, Jan. 25.
— Robt. Walpole, *again*, and first ld. treas., Apr. 3.

King George II.

Robt. Walpole, *contd.*
1742. Saml. Sandys, aft. Baron Sandys, Feb. 16.
1743. Hon. Hy. Pelham, and first ld. treas., Aug. 25.
1754. Sir Wm. Lee, ld. ch. just. of the k. b., *pro tem.*, Mar. 9.
— Hon. Hy. Bilson Legge, Apr. 6.
1755. Sir Geo. Lyttelton, bt., aft. ld. Lyttelton of Frankley, Nov. 22.
1756. Hon. Hy. Bilson Legge, *again*, Nov. 15.
1757. Wm., ld. Mansfield, ld. ch. just. of the k. b., *pro tem.*, Apr. 9.
— Hon. Hy. Bilson Legge, *again*, July 2.

King George III.

1761. Wm. Wildman, visc. Barrington, Mar. 12.
1762. Sir Fras. Dashwood, bt., aft. lord Le Despencer, May 28.
1763. Geo. Grenville; and first ld. treas., Apr. 15.
1765. Wm. Dowdeswell, July 10.
1766. Hon. Chas. Townshend, Aug. 2; *d.* Sept. 4, 1767.
1767. Wm., ld. Mansfield, ld ch. just, of the k. b., *pro tem.*, Sept. 12.
— Fredk., ld. North, Dec. 10.
1770. Fredk., ld. North, *again*, and first ld. treas., Feb. 10.
1782. Lord John Cavendish, Mar. 27.
— Wm. Pitt, July 13.
1783. Lord John Cavendish, *again*, Apr. 4.
— Wm. Pitt, *again*, and first ld. treas., Dec. 27.
1801. Hy. Addington, and first ld. treas.; previously sp. of the ho. of commons; aft. visc. Sidmouth, Mar. 21.
1804. Wm. Pitt, *again*, and first ld. treas., May 16.
1806. Edwd., ld. Ellenborough, ld. ch. just. of the k. b., on Mr. Pitt's decease, *pro tem.*, Jan.
— Lord Hy. Petty, aft. M. of Lansdowne, Feb. 10.
1807. Spencer Perceval, Mar. 31.
1809. Spencer Perceval, *again*, and first ld. treas., Dec. 6; assass. May 11, 1812.
1812. Nicholas Vansittart, June 9.

King George IV.

Nicholas Vansittart, *contd.*; res. Jan. 1823; and cr. ld. Bexley, Mar. 1, 1823.
1823. Fredk. John Robinson, aft. visc. Goderich and E. of Ripon, Jan. 31.
1827. Geo. Canning, and first ld. treas., Apr. 24; *d.* Aug. 8, same year.
— John Chas. Herries, Aug. 17.
1828. Hy. Goulburn, Jan. 26.

King William IV.

Hy. Goulburn, *contd.*
1830. John Chas., visc. Althorpe, aft. E. Spencer, Nov. 22.
1834. Thos., ld. Denman, ld. ch. just. of the k. b., *pro tem.*, Dec. 2.
— Sir Robt. Peel, bt., and first ld. treas., Dec. 10.
1835. Thos. Spring Rice, aft. ld. Monteagle, Apr. 18.

Queen Victoria.

Thos. Spring Rice, *contd.*; cr. lord Monteagle in Sept. 1839.
1839. Fras. Thornhill Baring, aft. sir Fras., bt., Aug. 26.
1841. Hy. Goulburn, *again*, Sept. 3.
1846. Chas. Wood, aft. sir Chas., bt., July 6.

In some instances the date of the commission to the lords of the treasury instead of that of the separate appointment of the Chancellor of the Exchequer is adopted in the preceding list. In the following list the date when the chancellor was sworn is adopted.

1852. Benjn. Disraeli, aft. E. of Beaconsfield, Feb. 27.
— Wm. Ewart Gladstone, Dec. 30.
1855. Sir Geo. Cornewall Lewis, bt., Mar. 5.
1858. Benjn. Disraeli, *again*, Feb. 28.
1859. Wm. Ewart Gladstone, *again*, June 18.
1866. Benjn. Disraeli, *again*, July 6.
1868. Geo. Ward Hunt, Feb. 29.
— Robt. Lowe, Dec. 9.
1873. Wm. Ewart Gladstone, *again*, and first ld. treas., Aug. 11.
1874. Sir Stafford Hy. Northcote, bt., aft. E. of Iddesleigh, Feb. 21.
1880. Wm. Ewart Gladstone, *again*, and first ld. treas., Apr. 28.
1882. Hugh Culling Eardley Childers Dec. 16.
1885. Sir Michael Edwd. Hicks-Beach, bt., June 24.
1886. Sir Wm. Geo. Granville Vernon Harcourt, Feb. 6.
1886. Lord Randolph Hy. Spencer Churchill, Aug. 6.
1887. Geo. Joachim Goschen, Jan. 14.

THE TWO CHAMBERLAINS OF THE EXCHEQUER.

From the restoration of King Charles II. to the abolition of the office in 1826 under 23 Geo. III., cap. 82.

1.

1660. Hy. Hildeyerd, adm. July 27, "to the office formerly had by sir Edwd. Bash, decd.," under pat. dated July 10.
1675. Philip Hildeyerd, son of the foregoing, adm. under pat. dated Feb. 16; including the reversion to
* * Chas. Cole, son of Hy. Cole. His admission under the preceding pat. is not recorded.
1712. Sir Simeon Stuart, bt. (grandson and heir of sir Nichs. Steward or Stuart, formerly a chamberlain, *see below*), adm. July 8, under pat. dated July 7.
1761. Sir Simeon Stuart, bt., son of the foregoing; by pat. dated Dec. 12.
1779. Hon. Fredk. North, aft. E. of Guildford, by pat. dated Dec. 13; office surr. by him, Oct. 10, 1826.

2.

1660. Sir Nichs. Steward or Stuart, bt., adm. . . . . . 1660, "to the office formerly had by sir Nichs. Carew, alias Throckmorton, decd.," under pat. dated Oct. 1, this year.
1710. Sir Wm. Ashburnham, bt., adm. June 15, under pat. dated May 25, preceding; *d.* Nov. 8, 1755.
1755. Sir John Miller, bt., adm. Nov. . . . ., under pat. in reversion, dated Apr. 7 preceding.
1772. Montagu Burgoyne, by pat. dated July 17; office surr. by him, Oct. 10, 1826.

AUDITORS OF THE RECEIPT OF THE EXCHEQUER.

From the restoration of King Charles II. to the abolition of the office in 1834 under 4 & 5 Will. IV., cap. 15.

1660. Sir Robt. Pye, bt., adm. Jan. 24, 1620; rest. June 25, 1660.
1662. Sir Robt. Long, bt., adm. May 21.
1673. Sir Robt. Howard, adm. July 14.
1698. Chris. Montagu, adm. Sept. 5; surr. 1699.

1699. Chas. Montagu, aft. baron and E. of Halifax, adm. Nov. 17; res. 1714.

1714. Geo. Montagu, adm. Sept. 30; succ. as E. of Halifax.

1739. Robt., lord Walpole, adm. May 9; succ. his father as E. of Orford.

1751. Hy., E. of Lincoln, aft. D. of Newcastle, by const. dated Apr. 1.

1794. Wm. Wyndham, baron Grenville, by const. dated Feb. 27.

1834. Geo., baron Auckland, by const. dated Jan. 14.

Office abolished Oct. 10, 1834.

THE FOUR TELLERS OF THE RECEIPT OF THE EXCHEQUER.

From the restoration of King Charles II. to the abolition of the office in 1834 under 4 & 5 Will. IV., cap. 15.

1.

1660. Geo. Downing, aft. sir G., bt., contd. in the office by Oliver Cromwell, Sept. 8, 1656; *d.* July, 1684.

1684. Simon Clifford, pat. dated June 3, 1671. Forfeited as a "recusant papist," 1689.

1689. Thos. Howard, adm. Jan. 16.

1701. Sir John Stanley, bt., adm. July 11, under pat. dated July 8, during pleasure only; determined by the next grant.

1702. Jas. Vernon, late sec. st.; pat. dated June 29; during pleasure only.

1710. John Smith, late ch. ex., adm. Oct. 13; during pleasure only.

1712. Thos., ld. Mansell, adm. July 23; during pleasure only.

1714. John Smith, re-adm. Nov. 6; during pleasure only; *d.* Oct. 1723.

1724. Geo. Treby, adm. Apr. 25; during pleasure only; "removed."

1727. Thos. Townshend, adm. Aug. 12.

1780. John Jeffreys Pratt, aft. E. and M. Camden, by pat. dated Aug. 18, 1766.

Office abolished Oct. 10, 1834.

1689. Hy. Maynard, adm. Apr. 16.

1694. Guy Palmes, adm. Monday, . . . under pat. dated Oct. 24; "removed," 1702.

1702. Sir Christ. Musgrave, bt., adm. June 30.

1704. Fras. Robartes, adm. Sept.; quitted office, Oct. 27, 1710.

1710. Russell Robarts, adm. Oct. 31.

1714. John, ld. De la Warr, adm. Nov. 6.

1715. Sir Richd. Onslow, bt., aft. ld. Onslow, adm. Nov. 7.

1718. Thos., ld. Torrington, adm. Mar. 21; *d.* May, 1719.

1719. Geo. Parker, aft. visc. Parker, and E. of Macclesfield, adm. July 4, under a pat. in reversion, dated May 3, 1718.

1764. Geo. Grenville, jun., aft. Geo. Nugent, E. Temple, and M. of Buckingham, entered this office, Mar. 21, under a pat. in reversion, dated May 2, 1763; *d.* Feb. 1813.

1813. Spencer Perceval, entered this office Feb. 16, under pat. dated Feb. 15.

Office abolished Oct. 10, 1834.

2.

1660. Leonard Pinckney, adm. July 25, by pat. dated July 16; during the life of his son, "into the place formerly occupied by John Brooke, esq., deceased."

1661. Wm. Pinckney, adm. in his father's place. Jan. 28.

1667. Sir Wm. Doyly, adm. Mar. 19. Susp. Jan. 25, 1673, and on Nov. 17, 1677, two deputies were app. to act in his stead by ld. treas. warrant, Aug. 15, 1678; *d.* April 1680.

1680. Geo. Downing, jun, aft. sir Geo., bt., adm. Apr. 21. Refused to serve king William, and so "abdicated" in 1689.

3.

1660. John Loving, adm. by royal sign manual warrant, dated June 17, on pat. dated Dec. 14, 18th Car. I., (1642), "into the place formerly occupied by Authur Squibb, esq., deceased."

1693. Hy. Carew, adm. July 18.

1699. Fras. Godolphin, adm. June 8; surr. in 1704.

1704. Thos. Coke, adm. May 26; exchanged with his successor, for the office of v. chamb. to the queen.

1706. Hon. Peregrine Bertie, adm. Dec.

1711. Geo. Hay, visc. Dupplin, aft. E. of Kinnoull, adm. Sept. 6; during pleasure only.

1715. Sir Roger Mostyn, bt., adm. Jan. 8; during pleasure only.
1716. Richd. Hampden, adm. June 27; during pleasure only.
1718. Thos., ld. Onslow, adm. Mar. 21; during pleasure only.
1741. Horatio Walpole, aft. ld. Walpole, adm. Apr. 28; *d.* Feb. 1757.
1757. Jas., E. of Waldegrave, entered this office about Feb. 9, under a pat. in reversion, dated Nov. 6, preceding.
1736. Hon. Robt. Henley, aft. succ. as E. of Northington, entered this office Apr. 13, under a pat. in reversion dated July 22, 1758.
1786. Edwd., ld. Thurlow, entered this office July 13, when ld. chanc., under a pat. in reversion, dated June 5, 1784.
1806. Hon. Wm. Fredk. Elliot Eden, entered this office Sept. 15, under a pat. in reversion, dated July 31, 1790; found drowned in the river Thames, Feb. 24, 1810.
1810. Hon. Chas. Philip Yorke, sw. Mar. 2, under a pat. dated Mar. 1; *d.* Mar., 1834.
1834. Chas. Wm. Manningham (formerly deputy to Mr. Yorke, from Mar. 3, 1810), app. by treas. minute, Apr. 25, and by pat. Apr. 29; sw. May 10.

Office abolished, Oct. 10, 1834.

4.

1660. Laurence Squibb, adm. June this year, under pat. in reversion, dated June 9, 11th Car. I. (1635); *d.* Dec. 1674.
1674. Thos. Vernon, adm. Dec. 22.
1685. Fras. Villiers, sw. Feb. 23.
1694. John, visc. Fitzhardinge, adm. Feb. 16; *d.* Dec. 1712.
1713. Basil, E. of Denbigh, adm. Aug 31.
1715. Wm., ld. Paulet, adm. Nov. 7; during pleasure only.
1729. Sir Chas. Turner, bt., adm. May 6; during pleasure only.
1738. Hon. Philip Yorke, aft. visc. Royston and E. of Hardwicke, adm. Dec. 14, under a pat. in reversion, dated Mar 9, 1737.
1786. Hy. Bathurst, ld. Apsley, aft. E. Bathurst, pat. dated Aug. 22.

Office abolished, Oct. 10, 1834.

CLERKS OF THE PELLS.

From the restoration of King Charles II. to the abolition of the office in 1834 under 4 & 5 Will. IV. cap. 15.

1660. Wm. Wardour, adm. or rest. July 7, under constitution dated 17 Apr., 22 Car. I. (1646), and confirmed by patent, Aug. 22, this year.
1698. Hy. Pelham, adm. Feb. 1.
1721. Robt. Walpole, jun. (son of the prime minister), adm. Apr. 12, under const. dated Apr. 5, preceding. Aft. cr. *vitâ patris*, baron Walpole. Surr. May 9, 1739, to take the office of auditor of the Ex.
1739. Edwd. Walpole, aft. sir E., K.B., adm. May 9.
1784. Isaac Barré, by const., dated Jan. 13.
1802. Hy. Addington, junr. aft. hon. Hy. by const., dated July 21.
1823. Edwd. Roberts, by const., dated July 21.
1825. Hy. Ellis, by const., dated Jan. 25.

Office abolished Oct. 10, 1834.

COMPTROLLERS-GENERAL OF THE EXCHEQUER AND AUDITORS-GENERAL OF PUBLIC ACCOUNTS.

On the abolition of the offices of auditor and tellers of the exchequer, and clerk of the pells, as from October 11, 1834, under 4 & 5 Will IV., cap. 15, the office of Comptroller-General of the Exchequer was created, to perform the functions of the suppressed departments. As far back as 1785 commissioners were appointed to audit the public accounts, and numerous acts were passed defining their duties. By 28 & 29 Vict., cap. 23 (July 5, 1855), it was provided that on the next vacancy in the office of comptroller-general of the exchequer the duties were to be performed by the chairman for the time being of the audit commissioners. On July 5, 1865, lord Monteagle, the then comptroller, surrendered his office, and on July 25, 1865, Sir Wm. Dunbar, the then audit chairman, was appointed comptroller in his place. By 29 & 30 Vict., cap. 39, the crown was empowered to appoint the person holding the offices of comptroller-general of the exchequer and chairman of the audit commissioners to be comptroller-general of the exchequer and auditor-general of the public accounts (now usually styled comptroller and auditor-general), and one of the audit commissioners to be assistant-comptroller and auditor; and, on these appointments, the offices of comptroller-general of the exchequer and of audit-commissioners were abolished.

The comptroller and his deputy hold office during good behaviour, and are removable only on the joint address of both houses of parliament. They are thus rendered independent of the executive government and are enabled to exercise freely their functions of considering the strict legality of every payment demanded by the treasury for the public service.

Comptrollers-General of the Exchequer.

Since the creation of the office, in 1834.

1834. Sir John Newport, Oct. 11.
1839. Thos., ld. Monteagle of Brandon, Sept. 9; surr. his office July 5, 1865.
1865. Sir Wm. Dunbar, bt. Chairman of Audit. Commrs. App. under 28 & 29 Vict., cap. 23, July 25.

Comptrollers and Auditors-General.

Under 29 & 30 Vict., cap. 39.

1867. Sir Wm. Dunbar, bt., above named. Mar. 15, **G.** Res. Apr. 1888.
1888. Sir Chas. Lister Ryan, K.C.B., May.

Assistant Comptrollers and Auditors.

Under 29 & 30 Vict., cap. 39.

1867. Wm. Geo. Anderson, Mar. 15, **G.**
1873. Chas. Lister Ryan, aft. sir C., Mar. 20, **G.**

LORD HIGH ADMIRALS AND LORDS COMMISSIONERS OF THE ADMIRALTY.

This, as may be readily supposed, is an office of the highest importance, and in former times was frequently filled by the king himself, or by a member of the royal family. For many years it has, like the office of lord treasurer, been executed by commissioners, who are known as lords of the admiralty. The first lord is always a cabinet minister, and some of the other lords are also appointed on political grounds, and go out with the ministry. There are, however, always one or two permanent officials on the board, whose names are inserted in the successive commissions.

The lord high admiral of England appears always to have had jurisdiction over Ireland, as well before as after the Union; but the lord high admiral of Scotland was a separate office until the appointment of prince George of Denmark as lord high admiral of Great Britain on June 28, 1707.

Lord High Admirals, &c., of England.

The letter N *subjoined to the names denotes the Northern, the letter* W *the Western, and* S *the Southern station.*

871. King Alfred, to his death in 901.
925. King Athelstan, to his death, in 941.
959. King Edgar, to his death, in 975.
1016. The duke Edric.
1066. King Harold.
1106. King Henry I.
1172. King Henry II.
1177. Wm. Mandeville, E. of Essex.
1189. King Richard I.
1189. Gerard, abp. of Aix.
Bernard, bp. of Bayonne.
Robt. de Sabloil.
Richd. de Camville.
Wm. de Fortze, of Oleron.
Leaders and governors of all the king's navy, and governors of the king's ships going to the Holy Land.
1191. Sir Stephen de Turnham, and
Sir Robt. de Turnham.
1199. King John.
1213. Wm. Longespee (claiming to be E. of Salisbury), nat. son of Henry II., by Rosamond Clifford.
* * The E. of Boulogne.

Many of the kings in this list were in sea-battles, or went upon expeditions with their fleets.

King Henry III.

1217.

Sir Hubert de Burgh.
Sir Philip de Albini.

1224.

Sir Geoffrey de Lucy.
Richd. de Aguillon.

1235.

Peter de Rivall, a priest?

1264.

Sir Thos. de Moleton, capt. and keeper of the sea and coasts.

King Edward I.

1293.

Sir Robt. Tiptoft.

1294.

Sir John de Botetourt, for the coasts of Yarmouth. N.
Sir Wm. de Leybourne, for the coasts of Portsmouth. S.
Sir —— Ormond, for Ireland.

1297.

Sir John de Botetourt, keeper of the northern seas.
Sir Wm. de Leybourne, capt. of the mariners.

1300.

Gervase Alard, adm. of the fleet of the Cinque Ports.

1306.

Gervase Alard, capt. and adm. of the king's fleet. W.
Edwd. Chas., capt. and adm. of the king's fleet. N.

King Edward II.

1308.

Wm. de Betour, capt. of the king's ships going to the relief of Aberdeen.

1310.

Sir John de Caunton, capt. and gov. of the king's fleet going to Scotland.
Sir Simon de Montacute, adm. of the king's navy.

1311.

Sir John of Argyle, coast of Argyle.

1314.

Sir John Sturmy, and Peter Bard. } Joint adms. against the Scots.

1315.

Wm. de Creye, W., Scotland and Ireland.
Thos. de Hewys.

March 15, 1315.

John, ld. Botetourt; adm. and capt. of all the mariners from the Thames, to Berwick-on-Tweed.

July 3, 1315.

John de Athey, capt. and leader of the expedition from Bristol against the Scots.

Sept. 18, 1315.

Sir Humphrey Littlebury, adm.-in-chief of one part of the king's navy.
Sir John Sturmy, adm.-in-chief of one part of the king's navy.

Nov. 3, 1316.

Sir Robt. Leybourne, adm. of the fleet going against the Scots.

Dec. 9, 1316.

Sir Nichs. Kyriel, adm. of the fleet of the Cinque Ports, westward.

March 28, 1317.

John de Athey, capt. of the fleet in Ireland.
John de Perburn, or Perbroun, adm. of the king's fleet. N.
Sir Robt. Leybourne, adm. of the king's fleet west of the Thames.

April 24, 1318.

Wm. Gettour, capt. and leader of the king's fleet going to Scotland.

May 23, 1319.

Simon de Dryby.
Robt. Ashman.
Wm. de Thewell. } Adms. of the ships against the Scots.

1321.

Sir Hugh le Despenser, adm.

May 19, 1232.

Robt. Battayle, Cinque Ports.
John de Perburn, or Perbroun. N.
Robt. de Leybourne, W.

July 16, 1324.

Sir John de Cromwell, adm. of the seacoasts, and capt. of the king's mariners going to Gascony.

Aug. 5, 1324.

Sir Robt. Beaudyn. W.
Sir John Sturmey. N.

Sept. 18, 1324.

Stephen Alard, adm. in the absence of sir Robt. Beaudyn.

1325.

Sir Jno. Sturmey.
Sir Nichs. Kyriel.
Sir John Felton. } Adms. of the three English seas.

Jan. 2, 1326.

Sir Nichs. Kyriel.
Sir John Sturmey. } Adms. of the Western fleets.

Sept. 19, 1326.

Sir Robt. de Leybourne. N.

KING EDWARD III.

April 21, 1327.

John de Perburn, or Perbroun. N.

May 24, 1327.

Waresius de Valoignes. W.

April 6, 1333.

Hy. Randolph, capt. and adm. for the Scottish War.

July 16, 1333.

Sir Wm. Clinton, capt. and adm. of the Cinque Ports and places west of the Thames.

Jan. 2, 1335.

Sir John de Norwich. N.
Sir Roger Higham. W.

April 4, 1335.

Sir John Howard, capt. and adm. of the king's fleet of Great Yarmouth and the ports north of the Thames.

April 6, 1335.

Sir Robt. Holand, capt. and adm. of the fleet on the coast of Wales and part of Ireland.

April 24, 1335.

Sir John Athy or Athey, capt. and adm. of the Irish fleet.

July 6, 1335.

Sir John Cobham, capt. and adm. of the Cinque Ports and places west of the Thames.
Peter Bard, capt. and adm. of Cinque Ports and other western ports, to proceed against the Scots.

Feb. 10, 1336.

Sir Thos. Ughtred, capt. and adm. N.

April 10, 1336.

Sir John de Norwich, capt. and adm. N.
Sir Geoffrey Say, or Galfrid de Say, capt. and adm. W.

Nov. 8, 1336.

Sir John Roos, or de Ros. N.

Jan. 14, 1337.

Sir Robt. Ufford, and
Sir John Roos, app. jointly adms. of the king's northern fleet.
Sir Wm. Montacute, capt. and adm. W.

May 30, 1337.

Sir Geoffrey de Say, and
Sir Otho Grandison, commanders of the W. fleet.

Aug. 11, 1337.

Sir Walter Manny, capt. and adm. N.
Sir Wm. Burghersh, capt. and adm. W.

July 28, 1338.

Sir Thos. Drayton or Draiton. N.
Peter Bard. W.

Feb. 18, 1339.

Sir Robt. Morley. N.
Sir Wm. Trussell. W.

Feb. 20, 1340.

Sir Richd. Fitz-Alan, E. of Arundel. W.

Mar. 6, 1340.

Sir Robt. Morley, capt. and adm. N.

April 5, 1341.

Sir Robt. Morley, adm. N.

June 12, 1341.

Sir Wm. Clinton, E. of Huntingdon, capt. and adm. of the W. fleet.

April 10, 1342.

Sir John de Montgomery. W.

Dec. 20, 1342.

Sir Wm. Trussell. N.
Sir Robt. Beaupel. W.

May 8, 1344.

Sir Robt. Ufford, E. of Suffolk. N.
Sir Reginald de Cobham, capt. and adm. W.

Feb. 23, 1345.

Richd., E. of Arundel. W.

Jan. 25, 1347.

King Edward III., styled *King of the Seas.*

Feb. 23, 1347.

Sir John de Montgomery. W.

Mar. 8, 1347.

Sir John Howard. N.

Mar. 14, 1348.

Sir Walter Manny. N.
Sir Reginald Cobham. W.

June 6, 1348.

Sir Robt. Morley. N.

Aug. 17, 1349.

Sir John Beauchamp, adm. of a fleet off Calais.

1350.

Robert de Causton. N.—*Spelman.*

July 22, 1350.

Sir Robt. Morley, *again.—Spelman.*

Mar. 8, 1351.

Sir Wm. de Bohun, E. of Northampton, capt. and adm. W.

1352.

Thos., E. of Warwick. W.—*Spelman.*

Mar. 1354.

John Gybon, adm. of a squadron.

Mar. 5, 1355.

Sir Robt. Morley. N.
Sir John Beauchamp. W.

Jan. 1356.

Robt. Ledrede, adm. of a fleet going to Gascony for wine.

Aug. 8, 1356.

Robt. Drouss, of Cork, adm. of the Irish fleet.

July 18, 1360.

Sir John Beauchamp, adm. of the king's N., S., and W. fleets.

Jan. 26, 1361.

Sir Robt. Herle, adm. of the N., S., and W. fleets.

July 7, 1364.

Sir Ralph Spigurnell, adm. of the N. and W. fleets.

April 28, 1369.

Sir Robt. Ashton. W.

June 12, 1369.

Sir Nichs. Tamworth. N.

Feb. 6, 1370.

Sir Guy Bryan. W.

Sir Guy Bryan was at sea in command of a squadron in Jan. 1370.

May 30, 1370.

John, lord Neville. N.
Sir Guy Bryan. W.

July 8, 1370.

Sir Ralph Ferrers, adm. of the king's fleet going to Britanny.

Oct. 6, 1371.

Sir Robt. Ashton, adm. W.
Sir Ralph Ferrers, adm. N.

Mar. 7, 1372.

Sir Philip Courtenay, adm. W.
Sir Wm. de Neville. N.

Feb. 16, 1373.

E. of Salisbury app. capt. of all ships and barges going to sea.

July 16, 1376.

Wm., E. of Suffolk. N.

Nov 24, 1376.

Sir Michael de la Pole. N.
Sir Robt. Hales, prior of St. John's of Jerusalem, adm. W.

King Richard II.

Aug. 14, 1377.

Sir Michael de la Pole. N.
Sir Robt. Hales. W.

Dec. 5, 1377.

Thos., E. of Warwick. N.
Richd., E. of Arundel. W.

Sept. 10, 1378.

Sir Hugh Calverley. W.

Nov. 5, 1378.

Sir Thos. Percy. N.

Mar. 8, 1380.

Sir Philip Courtenay. W.

April 8, 1830.

Sir Wm. de Elmham. N.

May 22, 1382.

Sir John Roche, or Roches, adm. of a fleet from Southampton, westward.

Oct. 26, 1382.

Sir Walter Fitz-Walter. N.
Sir John Roche. W.

Nov. 13, 1383.

Edwd., E. of Devonshire. W.

Dec. 2, 1383.

Hy., E. of Northumberland. N.

Jan. 29, 1385.

Sir Thos. Percy. N.; aft. E of Worcester, and beheaded in 1402.
Sir John Radington, or Radlington, prior of St. John's of Jerusalem. W.

Feb. 22, 1386.

Sir Philip Darcy. N.

Dec. 10, 1386.

Richd., E. of Arundel, adm. of the N. and W. fleets; held that office until May 18, 1389.

May 20, 1389.

John, ld. Beaumont. N.
John, E. of Huntingdon. W.

May 31, 1389.

Sir John Roche, adm. of the W. and N. fleets.

June 22, 1389.

John, ld. Beaumont. N.
John, E. of Huntingdon. W.

Mar. 22, 1391.

Edwd., E. of Rutland. N.; aft. D. of Albemarle.

Nov. 29, 1391.

Edwd., E. of Rutland, adm. of the N. and W. fleets.

Aug. 30, 1393.

Matthew Swetenham and Nichs. Macclesfield, made adms. of Ireland.

May 9, 1398.

John, M. of Dorset, high adm. of the N. and W. fleets for life. He had been made adm. of the Irish fleet for life, Feb. 2, 1398.

KING HENRY IV.

Nov. 15, 1399.

Thos., E. of Worcester, adm. of the N. and W. fleets, and adm. of the Irish fleet.

April 21, 1401.

Sir Thos. Rampston, or Rempston. W.

April 26, 1401.

Richd., ld. Grey, of Codnor. N.

Nov. 5, 1403.

Thos., ld. Berkeley. W.

Nov. 18, 1403.

Sir Thos. Beaufort. N.; aft. E. of Dorset and D. of Exeter.

July 5, 1404.

James Dartasso, made adm. of Ireland.

Feb. 20, 1405.

Sir Thos. Lancaster (Plantagenet), 2nd son of the king, aft. D. of Clarence, high adm. of England.

April 28, 1406.

Nichs. Blackburne. N.
Richd. Clyderow. W.

Dec. 23, 1406.

John, M. of Dorset (E. of Somerset), adm. of the N. and W. fleets.

May 8, 1407.

Edmd., E. of Kent, high adm. of England.

Sept. 21, 1408.

Sir Thos. Beaufort, adm. of the N. and W. fleets for life.

KING HENRY V.

June 3, 1413.

Thos., E. of Dorset, adm. of England, Ireland, Aquitaine, and Picardy.

Sept. 28, 1414.

Patrick Coterell and Jas. Cornewalsche, app. the king's adms. of Ireland, from Wykynglone Head to Leperisylond, for their lives.

Feb. 18, 1415.

Sir Thos. Carew, and
Sir Gilbert Talbot, app. capts. and leaders of men at arms at sea, in the absence of the E. of Dorset, with the usual powers of adms.

July 6, 1416.

Thos., ld. Morley, adm. of a fleet going from London to Southampton.

July 26, 1416.

Sir Walter Hungerford, adm. of an expedition under the D. of Bedford, the king's lieut. at sea.

July 20, 1417.

Edmd., E. of March, app. the king's lieut. at sea to bring the fleet to England, and then conduct it again with troops to the king.

July 25, 1417.

John, E. of Huntington, app. the king's lieut., with all the powers of adm., during the king's absence.

Mar. 2, 1421.

Sir Wm. Bardolf, app. adm. of a fleet.

John, E. of Richmond and D. of Bedford, ld. adm.

King Henry VI.

1422.

John, D. of Bedford, *contd.*

Oct. 21, 1437.

John, D. of Exeter and E. of Huntingdon, and Hy. his son, for their lives, ld. adms. of England, Ireland, and Aquitaine.

1448—1451.

Wm. de la Pole, ditto; during the minority of Hy. Holland, D. of Exeter.

July 23, 1451.

Hy., D. of Exeter.

King Edward IV.

1461.

Richd., E. of Warwick and Salisbury, styled the "King maker."

July 30, 1462.

Wm., E. of Kent.

Oct. 12, 1462.

Richd., D. of Gloucester, brother to the king.

Jan. 2, 1470.

Richd., E. of Warwick; capt. of the town and citadel of Calais, const. of Dover Castle, and ld. warden of the Cinque ports.

1472.

Richd., D. of Gloucester.

King Richard III.

July 25, 1483.

John, D. of Norfolk.

King Henry VII.

1485—1512.

John de Vere, E. of Oxford.

King Henry VIII.

John de Vere, E. of Oxford, *contd.*

Aug. 15, 1513.

Lord Edwd. Howard.

May 4, 1514.

Thos., D. of Norfolk

1525—1536.

Hy. Fitzroy (natural son to the king), D. of Richmond and Somerset, and E. of Nottingham.

Aug. 16, 1536.

Wm., E. of Southampton.

July 18, 1540.

John, ld. Russel.

June 27, 1542.

John, visc. Lisle, and baron of Malpas, aft. D. of Northumberland, high adm.

King Edward VI.

Feb. 17, 1547.

Thos., ld. Seymour, of Sudley, high adm. of England, Ireland, Wales, Calais, Boulogne, Marches of ditto, Normandy, Gascony, and Aquitaine, capt.-gen. of the navy and seas; beheaded 20th January 1549.

Oct. 28, 1549.

John, visc. Lisle, aft. D. of Northumberland, high adm.

May 4, 1550.

Edwd., ld. Clinton and Say.

Queen Mary.

Mar. 20, 1554.

Wm., ld. Howard, of Effingham, high adm.

Mar. 3, 1556.

Edwd., ld. Clinton and Say, aft. E. of Lincoln.

Queen Elizabeth.

Edwd., E. of Lincoln, *contd*

1585—1619.

Chas., ld. Howard of Effingham, aft. E. of Nottingham.

King James I.

Chas., E. of Nottingham, *contd.*

Jan. 28, 1619.

Geo., M. of Buckingham, aft. E. of Coventry and D. of Buckingham.

King Charles I.

Geo., D. of Buckingham, *contd.*

Mar. 16, 1636.

Commissioners.

Richd., ld. Weston, and Robt., E. of Lindsey, gr. chambn. of England.
Edwd., E. of Dorset, ld. chambn. to the queen.
Fras., ld. Cottington, chanc. and under treas. of the exchequer.
Sir Hy. Vane, compt. of the household.
Sir John Coke and Sir Fras. Windebank, secs. st.

Mar. 23, 1636.

Algernon, E. of Northumberland, ld. adm.

KING CHARLES I.

Robt., E. of Warwick, ld. high adm. of England, for the parliament. *Surrendered his commission by an ordinance that members should have no employments.*

April 15, 1645.

A committee appointed by both Houses.

Arthur, E. of Essex.
Robt., E. of Warwick.
Wm., visc. Say and Sele.
Dudley, ld. North.
Wm. Earle, Philip Stapleton, J. Levelyn, jun., Christr. Wray, J. Rolle, G. Greene, D. Hollis, J. Selden, F. Rouse, T. Eden, J. Lisle, Bulstrode Whitelocke.

April 28, 1645.

Appointed by the Commons.

Robt., E. of Warwick.
Messrs. Bense and H. Pelham.

Feb. 12, 1649.

Messrs. Dean, Fras. Popham, and R. Blake

KING CHARLES II.

June 6, 1660.

JAMES, D. of York, brother to the king, lord high adm. of England. Res. on the passing of the Test Act.

COMMISSIONERS.

July 9, 1673.

PRINCE RUPERT.
Anthy., E. of Shaftesbury, ld. high chanc.
Thos., visc. Latimer, aft. E. of Danby, ld. high treas.
Arthur, E. of Anglesey, ld. pr. seal.
Geo., D. of Buckingham.
Jas., D. of Monmouth.
John, D. of Lauderdale.
Jas., D. of Ormond.
Hy., E. of Arlington, sec. st.
Sir Geo. Carteret, bt., vice chambn.
Hy. Coventry, sec. st.
Edwd. Seymour.

Sept. 29, 1674.

PRINCE RUPERT.
Heneage, ld. Finch, ld. high chanc.
Thos., E. of Danby, ld. high treas.
Arthur, E. of Anglesey, ld. pr. seal.
Jas., D. of Monmouth.
John, D. of Lauderdale.
Jas., D. of Ormond.
Hy., E. of Arlington.
Sir Geo. Carteret, bt., vice chambn.
Hy. Coventry.
Sir Jos. Williamson.
Edwd. Seymour.

July 28, 1675.

PRINCE RUPERT.
Heneage, ld. Finch, ld. high chanc.
Thos., E. of Danby, ld. high treas.
Arthur, E. of Anglesey, ld. pr. seal.
Jas., D. of Monmouth.
Jas., D. of Ormond.
Hy., E. of Arlington, sec. st.
Thos., E. of Ossory.
Wm., E. of Craven.
Sir Geo. Carteret, bt., vice chambn.
Hy. Coventry.
Sir Jos. Williamson, sec. st.
Edwd. Seymour.

Sept. 14, 1677.

PRINCE RUPERT.
Heneage, ld. Finch, ld. high chanc.
Thos., E. of Danby, ld. high treasr.
Arthur, E. of Anglesey, ld. pr. seal.
Jas., D. of Monmouth.
John, D. of Lauderdale.
Jas., D. of Ormond.
Thos., E. of Ossory.
Hy., E. of Arlington, ld. chambn. of the hshold.
Wm., E. of Craven.
Sir Geo. Carteret, bt., vice chambn.
Sir Jos. Williamson, sec. st.
Sir John Ernley, bt.
Sir Thos. Chicheley, mast. of the ordn.
Edwd. Seymour.

Feb. 14, 1679.

SIR HY. CAPEL.
Hon. Danl. Finch.
Sir Thos. Lee, bt.
Sir Humphrey Winch, bt.
Sir Thos. Meeres.
Edwd. Vaughan.
Edwd. Hales.

Feb. 19, 1680.

HON. DANL. FINCH, aft. ld. Finch, & E. OF NOTTINGHAM.
Sir Humphrey Winch, bt.
Sir Thos. Meeres.
Edwd. Hales.
Wm., visc. Brouncker, of Ireland.
Sir Thos. Littleton, bt.

Jan. 20, 1682.

DANL. LORD FINCH, aft. E. OF NOTTINGHAM.
Sir Humphrey Winch, bt.
Sir Thos. Meeres.
Edwd. Hales.
Wm., visc. Brouncker.
Hy. Savile.
Sir John Chicheley.

Aug. 28, 1683.

DANL., E. OF NOTTINGHAM.
Sir Humphrey Winch, bt.
Sir Thos. Meeres.
Sir Edwd. Hales, bt.
Hy. Savile.
Sir John Chicheley.
Arthur Herbert.
John, lord Vaughan.

Apr. 17, 1684.

DANL., E. OF NOTTINGHAM.
Sir Humphrey Winch, bt.
Sir Thos. Meeres.
Sir Edwd. Hales, bt.
Hy. Savile.
Sir John Chicheley.
Arthur Herbert.
John, lord Vaughan.

This commission was revoked May 22, 1684.

1684–5. KING CHARLES II., lord high adm.

KING JAMES II.

King JAMES II. declared himself in council, lord high adm. and lord general of the navy; and he managed the admiralty affairs by Mr. Secretary Pepys all his reign.

KING WILLIAM III.

COMMISSIONERS.

Mar. 8, 1689.

HON. ARTHUR HERBERT.
John, E. of Carberry.
Sir Michael Wharton.
Sir Thos. Lee, bt.
Sir John Lowther, bt., of Whitehaven.
Wm. Sacheverell.

Jan. 20, 1690.

THOS., E. OF PEMBROKE and MONTGOMERY.
John, E. of Carberry.
Sir Thos. Lee, bt.
Sir John Lowther, bt.
Sir John Chicheley.

Jan. 23, 1691.

THOMAS, E. OF PEMBROKE and M.
Sir Thos. Lee, bt.
Sir John Lowther, bt.
Sir Richd. Onslow, bt.
Hy. Priestman.
Anthy., visc. Falkland.
Robt. Austen.

Nov. 16, 1691.

THOMAS, E. OF PEMBROKE and M.
Sir John Lowther, bt.
Sir Richd. Onslow, bt.
Hy. Priestman.
Anthy., visc. Falkland.
Robt. Austen.
Sir Robt. Rich., bt.

Mar. 10, 1692.

CHAS., LORD CORNWALLIS.
Sir John Lowther, bt.
Sir Richd. Onslow, bt.
Hy. Priestman.
Anthy., visc. Falkland.
Robt. Austen.
Sir Robt. Rich., bt.

Apr. 15, 1693.

ANTHY., VISC. FALKLAND.
Sir John Lowther, bt.
Hy. Priestman.
Robt. Austen.
Sir Robt. Rich, bt.
Hy. Killegrew, bt.
Sir Ralph Delaval, bt.

May 2, 1694.

EDWD. RUSSELL, aft. E. OF ORFORD.
Sir John Lowther, bt.
Hy. Priestman.
Robt. Austen.
Sir Robt. Rich, bt.
Sir Geo. Rooke.
Sir John Houblon.

Feb. 24, 1696.

EDWD. RUSSELL, aft. E. OF ORFORD.
Hy. Priestman.
Robt. Austen.
Sir Robt. Rich, bt.
Sir Geo. Rooke.
Sir John Houblon.
Jas. Kendal.

June 5, 1697.

EDWD. RUSSELL, now E. OF ORFORD.
Hy. Priestman.
Robt. Austen.
Sir Robt. Rich, bt.
Sir Geo. Rooke.
Sir John Houblon.
Jas. Kendal.
Goodwin Wharton.

June 2, 1699.

JOHN, E. OF BRIDGEWATER.
John, lord Haversham.
Sir Robt. Rich, bt.
Sir Geo. Rooke.
Sir David Mitchell.

Apr. 4, 1701.

THOS., E. OF PEMBROKE and M.
John, lord Haversham.
Sir Geo. Rooke.
Sir David Mitchell.
Geo. Churchill.

Jan. 18, 1702.

THOS., E. of PEMBROKE and MONTGOMERY, ld. high adm.

QUEEN ANNE.

May 20, 1702.

Pr. GEORGE of DENMARK, ld. high adm. of England; and,

June 28, 1707.

Pr. GEORGE, ld. high adm. of *Great Britain*; on account of the Union between England and Scotland.

Commissioners appointed by Pr. George of Denmark to be his Council.

May 20, 1702.

SIR GEO. ROOKE.
Sir David Mitchell.
Geo. Churchill.
Richd. Hill.

April 30, 1704.

SIR GEO. ROOKE.
Sir David Mitchell.
Geo. Churchill.
Richd. Hill.
Hon. Jas. Bridges, aft. D. of Chandos.
Hon. Hy. Paget, aft. E. of Uxbridge.

Feb. 8, 1706.

SIR DAVID MITCHELL.
Geo. Churchill.
Richd. Hill.
Hon. Hy. Paget.

June 28, 1707.

SIR DAVID MITCHELL.
Geo. Churchill.
Richd. Hill.
Hon. Hy. Paget.
Sir Cloudesley Shovel.
Robt. Walpole, aft. sir R. & E. of Orford.
Sir Stafford Fairborne.

April 19, 1708.

DAVID, E. OF WEMYSS.
Geo. Churchill.
Richd. Hill.
Hon. Hy. Paget.
Sir Stafford Fairborne.
Sir John Leake.

June 20, 1708.

DAVID, E. OF WEMYSS.
Geo. Churchill.
Richd. Hill.
Hon. Hy. Paget.
Sir John Leake.
Sir Jas. Wishart.
Robt. Fairfax.

The Prince died October 28, 1708, *and Queen Anne acted by Secretary Burchett.*

UNION WITH SCOTLAND.

LORD HIGH ADMIRALS, &c., OF GREAT BRITAIN.

1707. June 28. Pr. George, ld. high adm. *Vide supra.*
1708. Nov. 29. Thos., E. of Pembroke & Montgomery, ld. high adm.

COMMISSIONERS.

Nov. 8, 1709.

EDWD., E OF ORFORD.
Sir John Leake.
Sir Geo. Byng, aft. visc. Torrington.
Geo. Dodington.
Paul Methuen.

Oct. 4, 1710.

SIR JOHN LEAKE.
Sir Geo. Byng.
Geo. Dodington.
Paul Methuen.
Sir Wm. Drake, bt.
John Aislabie.

Sept. 30, 1712.

THOS., E. OF STRAFFORD.
Sir John Leake.
Sir Geo. Byng.
Sir Wm. Drake, bt.
John Aislabie.
Sir Jas. Wishart.
Geo. Clarke.

Apr. 9, 1714.

THOS., E. OF STRAFFORD.
Sir John Leake.
Sir Wm. Drake, bt.
Sir Jas. Wishart.
Geo. Clarke.
Sir Geo. Beaumont, bt.

KING GEORGE I.

Oct. 14, 1714.

EDWD., E. OF ORFORD.
Sir Geo. Byng.
Geo. Dodington.
Sir John Jennings.
Sir Chas. Turner.
Abraham Stanyan.
Geo. Baillie.

Apr. 16, 1717.

JAMES, E. OF BERKELEY.
Matt. Aylmer, aft. lord Aylmer.
Sir Geo. Byng.
Sir John Jennings.
John Cockburne.
Wm. Chetwynd.

March 19, 1718.

JAS., E. OF BERKELEY.
Sir Geo. Byng.
Sir John Jennings.
John Cockburne.
Wm. Chetwynd.
Sir John Norris.
Sir Chas. Wager.

Oct. 10, 1721.

JAS., E. OF BERKELEY.
Sir John Jennings.
John Cockburne.
Wm. Chetwynd.
Sir John Norris.
Sir Chas. Wager.
Danl. Pulteney.

June 11, 1725.

JAS., E. OF BERKELEY.
Sir John Jennings.
John Cockburne.
Wm. Chetwynd.
Sir John Norris.
Sir Chas. Wager.
Sir Geo. Oxenden, bt.

KING GEORGE II.

Aug. 2, 1727.

GEO., VISC. TORRINGTON.
John Cockburne.
Sir John Norris.
Sir Chas. Wager.
Sir Thos. Lyttleton, bt.
Geo., visc. Malpas, K.B.
Saml. Molyneux.

June 1, 1728.

GEO., VISC. TORRINGTON.
John Cockburne.
Sir John Norris.
Sir Chas. Wager.
Sir Thos. Lyttleton, bt.
Geo., visc. Malpas, K.B., aft. E. of Cholmondeley.
Sir William Yonge, K.B.

May 19, 1729.

GEO., VISC. TORRINGTON.
John Cockburne.
Sir John Norris.
Sir Chas. Wager.
Sir Thos. Lyttleton, bt.
Sir Wm. Yonge, K.B.
Lord Archd. Hamilton.

May 13, 1730.

GEO., VISC. TORRINGTON.
John Cockburne.
Sir Chas. Wager.
Sir Thos. Lyttleton, bt.
Lord Archd. Hamilton.
Sir Thos. Frankland, bt.
Thos. Winnington.

June 15, 1732.

GEO., VISC. TORRINGTON.
Sir Chas. Wager.
Sir Thos. Lyttleton, bt.
Lord Archd. Hamilton.
Sir Thos. Frankland, bt.
Thos. Winnington.
Thos. Clutterbuck.

Jan. 25, 1733.

Sir CHAS. WAGER.
Sir Thos. Lyttleton, bt.
Lord Archd. Hamilton.
Sir Thos. Frankland, bt.
Thos. Winnington.
Thos. Clutterbuck.
Lord Harry Poulett, aft. D. of Bolton.

May 22, 1736.

Sir CHAS. WAGER.
Sir Thos. Lyttleton, bt.
Lord Archd. Hamilton.
Sir Thos. Frankland, bt.
Thos. Clutterbuck.
Lord Harry Poulett.
John Campbell.

Mar. 13, 1738.

SIR CHAS. WAGER.
Sir Thos. Lyttleton, bt.
Sir Thos. Frankland, bt.
Thos. Clutterbuck.
Lord Harry Poulett.
John Campbell.
Lord Vere Beauclerk, aft. ld. Vere.

May 14, 1741.

Sir CHAS. WAGER.
Sir Thos. Frankland, bt.
Lord Harry Poulett.
John Campbell.
Lord Vere Beauclerk.
John, visc. Glenorchy.
Edwd. Thompson.

Mar. 19, 1742.

DANL., E. of WINCHILSEA and NOTTINGHAM.
John Cockburne.
Lord Archd. Hamilton.
Chas., ld. Baltimore.
Philip Cavendish.
Geo. Lee.
Hon. John Trevor.

Dec. 13, 1743.

DANL., E. of WINCHILSEA and NOTTINGHAM.
John Cockburne.
Lord Archd. Hamilton.
Chas., ld. Baltimore.
Geo. Lee.
Sir Chas. Hardy.
Thos. Philipson.

Dec. 27, 1744.

JOHN, D. of BEDFORD.
John, E. of Sandwich.
Lord Arch. Hamilton.
Lord Vere Beauclerk.
Chas., ld. Baltimore.
Geo. Anson.
Geo. Grenville.

April 20, 1745.

JOHN, D. of BEDFORD.
John, E. of Sandwich.
Lord Archd. Hamilton.
Lord Vere Beauclerk.
Geo. Anson.
Geo. Grenville.
Hon. Hy. Bilson Legge.

Feb. 22, 1746.

JOHN, D. of BEDFORD.
John, E. of Sandwich.
Lord Vere Beauclerk.
Geo. Anson.
Geo. Grenville.
Hon. Hy. Bilson Legge.
Wm. Wildman, visc. Barrington.

Feb. 1747.

JOHN, D. of BEDFORD.
John, E. of Sandwich.
Lord Vere Beauclerk.
Geo. Anson, aft. lord Anson.
Wm. Wildman, visc. Barrington.
Wm., visc. Duncannon.
Welbore Ellis.

Feb. 10, 1748.

JOHN, E. of Sandwich.
Lord Vere Beauclerk.
Geo., ld. Anson.
Wm. Wildman, visc. Barrington.
Wm., visc. Duncannon.
Welbore Ellis.
Hon. John Stanhope.

Nov. 18, 1749.

JOHN, E. of SANDWICH.
Geo., ld. Anson.
Wm. Wildman, visc. Barrington.
Wm., visc. Duncannon.
Welbore Ellis.
Hon. Thos. Villiers.
Granville Leveson, visc. Trentham, aft. E. Gower.

June 22, 1751.

GEO., ld. ANSON.
Wm. Wildman, visc. Barrington.
Wm., visc. Duncannon.
Welbore Ellis.
Hon. Thos. Villiers.
Wm. Rowley.
Hon. Edwd. Boscawen.

April 6, 1754.

GEO., ld. ANSON.
Wm., visc. Duncannon.
Welbore Ellis.
Hon. Thos. Villiers.
Sir Wm. Rowley, K.B.
Hon. Edwd. Boscawen.
Hon. Chas. Townshend.

Dec. 23, 1755.

GEO., ld. ANSON.
Wm., visc. Duncannon, aft E. of Besborough.
Hon. Thos. Villiers.
Sir Wm. Rowley, K.B.
Hon. Edwd. Boscawen.
John, visc. Bateman.
Hon. Richd. Edgcumbe, aft ld. Edgcumbe.

Nov. 19, 1756.

RICHD., E. TEMPLE.
Hon. Edwd. Boscawen.
Temple West.
John Pitt.
George Hay.
Thos. Orby Hunter.
Gilbert Elliot.

Dec. 11, 1756.

RICHD., E. TEMPLE.
Hon. Edwd. Boscawen.
Temple West.
Geo. Hay.
Thos. Orby Hunter.
Gilbert Elliot.
Hon. John Forbes.

April 6, 1757.

DANL., E. of WINCHILSEA and NOTTINGHAM.
Sir Wm. Rowley, K.B.
Hon. Edwd. Boscawen.
Gilbert Elliot.
John, ld. Carysfort.
Savage Mostyn.
Hon. Edwin Sandys, aft lord Sandys.

July 2, 1757.

GEO., ld. ANSON.
Hon. Edwd. Boscawen.
Temple West.
Geo. Hay.
Thos. Orby Hunter.
Gilbert Elliot.
Hon. John Forbes.

KING GEORGE III.

March 21, 1761.

GEO., ld. ANSON.
Hon. Edwd. Boscawen.
Geo. Hay.
Thos. Orby Hunter.

Hon. John Forbes.
Hans Stanley.
Geo. Bussey, visc. Villiers.
Thos. Pelham.

June 19, 1762.

Geo. Montagu Dunk, E. of Halifax.
Geo. Hay.
Thos. Orby Hunter.
Hon. John Forbes.
Hans Stanley.
Geo. Bussey, visc. Villiers.
Thos. Pelham, aft. lord Pelham.

Jan. 1, 1763.

Hon. Geo. Grenville.
Geo. Hay.
Thos. Orby Hunter.
Hon. John Forbes.
Hans Stanley.
John, ld. Carysfort.
Jas. Harris.

April 23, 1763.

John, E. of Sandwich.
Geo. Hay.
Hans Stanley.
John, ld. Carysfort.
Ricd., visc. Howe.
Hy., ld. Digby.
Thos. Pitt.

Sept. 10, 1763.

John, E. of Egmont.
Geo. Hay.
Hans Stanley.
John, ld. Carysfort.
Richd., visc. Howe.
Hy., ld. Digby.
Thos. Pitt.

Aug. 30, 1765.

John, E. of Egmont.
Thos. Pitt, aft. lord Camelford.
Sir Chas. Saunders, K.B.
Hon. Aug. Keppel.
Chas. Townshend.
Sir Wm. Meredyth, bt.
John Buller.

Dec. 21, 1765.

John, E. of Egmont.
Sir Chas. Saunders, K.B.
Hon. Aug. Keppel.
Chas. Townshend.
Sir Wm. Meredyth, bt.
John Buller.
Hon. John Yorke.

Sept. 10, 1766.

Sir Chas. Saunders, K.B.
Hon. Aug. Keppel, aft. visc. Keppel.
Chas. Townshend.
Sir Wm. Meredyth, bt.
John Buller.
Hy., visc. Palmerston.
Sir Geo. Yonge, bt.

Dec. 10, 1766.

Sir Edwd. Hawke, K.B.
Chas. Townshend.
John Buller.
Hy., visc. Palmerston.
Sir Geo. Yonge, bt.
Sir Piercy Brett.
Chas. Jenkinson.

March 19, 1768.

Sir Edwd. Hawke, K.B.
Chas. Townshend.
John Buller.
Hy., visc. Palmerston.
Sir Geo. Yonge, bt.
Sir Piercy Brett.
Lord Chas. Spencer.

Feb. 24, 1770.

Sir Edwd. Hawke, K.B., aft. lord Hawke.
John Buller.
Hy., visc. Palmerston.
Lord Chas. Spencer.
Wilmot, visc. Lisburne.
Fras. Holburne.
Hon. Chas. Jas. Fox.

Jan. 12, 1771.

John, E. of Sandwich.
John Buller.
Hy., visc. Palmerston.
Lord Chas. Spencer.
Wilmot, visc. Lisburne.
Fras. Holburne.
Hon. Chas. Jas. Fox.

Jan. 26, 1771.

John, E. of Sandwich.
John Buller.
Hy., visc. Palmerston.
Lord Chas. Spencer.
Wilmot, visc. Lisburne.
Hon. Chas. Jas. Fox.
Hon. Aug. John Hervey.

May 6, 1772.

John, E. of Sandwich.
John Buller.
Hy., visc. Palmerston.
Lord Chas. Spencer.
Wilmot, visc. Lisburne.
Hon. Aug. John Hervey.
Thos. Bradshaw.

Dec. 4, 1774.

John, E. of Sandwich.
John Buller.
Hy., visc. Palmerston.
Lord Chas. Spencer.
Wilmot, visc. Lisburne.
Hon. Aug. John Hervey, aft. E. of Bristol.
Hy. Penton.

April 6, 1775.

John, E. of Sandwich.
John Buller.
Hy., visc. Palmerston.
Lord Chas. Spencer.
Wilmot, visc. Lisburne.
Hy. Penton.
Sir Hugh Palliser, bt.

Dec. 4, 1777.

John, E. of Sandwich.
John Buller.
Lord Chas. Spencer.
Wilmot, now E. of Lisburne.
Hy. Penton.
Sir Hugh Palliser, bt.
Constantine John, lord Mulgrave.

April 1779.

John, E. of Sandwich.
John Buller.
Lord Chas. Spencer.
Wilmot, E. of Lisburne.
Hy. Penton.
Constantine John, lord Mulgrave.
Robt. Man.

July 6, 1779.

John, E. of Sandwich.
John Buller.
Wilmot, E. of Lisburne.
Hy. Penton.
Constantine John, lord Mulgrave.
Robt. Man.
Bamber Gascoigne.

Sept. 6, 1780.

John, E. of Sandwich.
Wilmot, E. of Lisburne.
Hy. Penton.
Constantine John, lord Mulgrave.
Bamber Gascoigne.
Hon. Chas. Fras. Greville.
Geo. Darby.

March 30, 1782.

Hon. Aug. Keppel, aft. visc. Keppel.
Sir Robt. Harland, bt.
Hugh Pigot.
Wm., visc. Duncannon.
Hon. John Townshend.
Chas. Brett.
Richd. Hopkins.

July 13, 1782.

Aug., visc. Keppel.
Sir Robt. Harland, bt.

Hugh Pigot.
Chas. Brett.
Richd. Hopkins.
Hon. John Jeffreys Pratt.
John Aubrey.

Jan. 28, 1783.

RICHD., visc. HOWE.
Hugh Pigot.
Chas. Brett.
Richd. Hopkins.
Hon. John Jeffreys Pratt.
John Aubrey.
Hon. John Leveson Gower.

April 8, 1783.

AUG., visc. KEPPEL.
Hugh Pigot.
Wm., visc. Duncannon.
Hon. John Townshend.
Sir John Lindsay, K.B.
Wm. Jolliffe.
Whitshed Keene.

Dec. 30, 1783.

RICHD., visc. HOWE.
Chas. Brett.
Hon. John Jeffreys Pratt.
Hon. John Leveson Gower.
Hy., ld. Apsley.
Hon. Chas. Geo. Perceval, aft. ld. Arden.
Jas. Modyford Heywood.

April 2, 1784.

RICHD., visc. HOWE, aft. E. Howe.
Chas. Brett.
Richd. Hopkins.
Hon. John Jeffreys Pratt, aft. visc. Bayham.
Hon. John Leveson Gower.
Hy., ld. Apsley.
Hon. Chas. Geo. Perceval, lord Arden.

July 16, 1788.

JOHN, E. of CHATHAM.
Richd. Hopkins.
John Jeffreys, visc. Bayham.
Hon. John Leveson Gower.
Hy., ld. Apsley.
Chas. Geo., ld. Arden.
Saml., ld. Hood.

Aug. 12, 1789.

JOHN, E. of CHATHAM.
Richd. Hopkins.
Chas. Geo., ld. Arden.
Saml., ld. Hood.
Robt., visc. Belgrave.
Sir Fras. S. Drake, bt., *d.* Nov. 1789.
Hon. John Thos. Townshend.

Jan. 19, 1790.

JOHN, E. of CHATHAM.
Richd. Hopkins.
Chas. Geo., ld. Arden.
Saml., ld. Hood.
Robt., visc. Belgrave.
Hon. John Thos. Townshend.
Alan Gardner.

June 25, 1791.

JOHN, E. of CHATHAM.
Chas. Geo., ld. Arden.
Saml., ld. Hood.
Hon. John Thos. Townshend.
Alan Gardner.
John Smyth.
Chas. Small Pybus.

May 4, 1793.

JOHN, E. of CHATHAM
Chas. Geo., ld. Arden.
Saml., ld. Hood.
Alan Gardner.
John Smyth.
Chas. Small Pybus.
Philip Affleck.

May, 1794.

JOHN, E. of CHATHAM.
Chas. Geo., ld. Arden.
Saml., ld. Hood.
Alan Gardner.
Chas. Small Pybus.
Philip Affleck.
Sir Chas. Middleton, bt.

Dec. 20, 1794.

GEO. JOHN, E. SPENCER.
Chas. Geo., ld. Arden.
Saml., ld. Hood.
Sir Alan Gardner, bt.
Chas. Small Pybus.
Philip Affleck.
Sir Chas. Middleton, bt.

Mar. 2, 1795.

GEO. JOHN, E. SPENCER.
Chas. Geo., ld. Arden.
Chas. Small Pybus.
Sir Chas. Middleton, bt., aft. ld. Barham.
Lord Hugh Seymour.
Sir Philip Stephens, bt.
Jas. Gambier.

Dec. 2, 1795.

GEO. JOHN, E. SPENCER.
Chas. Geo., ld. Arden.
Chas. Small Pybus.
Lord Hugh Seymour.
Sir Philip Stephens, bt.
Jas. Gambier.
Wm. Young.

July 1797.

GEO. JOHN, E. SPENCER.
Chas. Geo., ld. Arden.
Lord Hugh Seymour.
Sir Philip Stephens, bt.
Jas. Gambier.
Wm. Young.
Thos. Wallace.

Sept. 18, 1798.

GEO. JOHN, E. SPENCER.
Chas. Geo., ld. Arden.
Sir Philip Stephens, bt.
Jas. Gambier.
Wm. Young.
Thos. Wallace.
Robt. Man.

July 10, 1800.

GEO. JOHN, E. SPENCER.
Chas. Geo., ld. Arden.
Sir Philip Stephens, bt.
Jas. Gambier.
Wm. Young.
Robt. Man.
Hon. Wm. Eliot.

Feb. 19, 1801.

JOHN, E. ST. VINCENT.
Sir Philip Stephens, bt.
Hon. Wm. Eliot.
Sir Thos. Troubrdge, bt.
Jas. Adams.
John Markham.
Wm. Garthshore.

Jan. 17, 1804.

JOHN, E. ST. VINCENT.
Sir Philip Stephens, bt.
Sir Thos. Troubridge, bt.
Jas. Adams.
John Markham.
John Lemon.
Sir Harry Burrard Neale, bt.

May 15, 1804.

HY., visc. MELVILLE.
Sir Philip Stephens, bt.
Jas. Gambier.
Sir Harry Burrard Neale, bt.
Sir John Colpoys, K.B.
Philip Patton.
Wm. Dickinson, jun.

Sept. 13, 1804.

HY., visc. MELVILLE.
Sir Philip Stephens, bt.
Jas. Gambier.
Sir John Colpoys, K.B.
Philip Patton.
Wm. Dickinson, jun.
Sir Evan Nepean, bt.

May 2, 1805.

Sir CHAS. MIDDLETON, bt., cr. lord BARHAM.

r Philip Stephens, bt.
.s. Gambier.
ilip Patton.
m. Dickinson, jun.
r Evan Nepean, bt.
eo., ld. Garlies.

Feb. 10, 1806.

on. CHAS. GREY.
r Philip Stephens, bt.
hn Markham.
r Chas. Morice Pole, bt.
r Harry Burrard Neale, bt.
ord Wm. Russell.
m., ld. Kensington.

Sept. 29, 1806.

IOS. GRENVILLE.
r Philip Stephens, bt.
hn Markham.
r Chas. Morice Pole, bt.
r Harry Burrard Neale, bt.
rd Wm. Russell.
m., ld. Kensington.

Oct. 23, 1806.

HOS. GRENVILLE.
hn Markham.
r Harry Burrard Neale, bt.
ord Wm. Russell.
m., ld. Kensington.
hos. Fras. Fremantle.
m. Frankland.

April 6, 1807.

Y., ld. MULGRAVE.
as. Gambier.
r Richd. Bickerton, bt.
m. Johnstone Hope.
obt. Ward.
y. John, visc. Palmerston.
as. Buller.

May 9, 1808.

Y., lord MULGRAVE.
r Richd. Bickerton, bt.
m. Johnstone Hope.
obt. Ward.
y. John, visc. Palmerston.
as. Buller.
m. Domett.

Nov. 24, 1809.

Y., lord MULGRAVE.
ir Richd. Bickerton, bt.
obt. Ward.
as. Buller.
m. Domett.
obt. Moorsom.
m., visc. Lowther.

May 1, 1810.

HAS. YORKE.
Sir Richd. Bickerton, bt.
Robt. Ward.
Jas. Buller.
Wm. Domett.
Sir Jos. Sydney Yorke.
Hon. Fredk. John Robinson.

June 17, 1811.

CHAS. YORKE.
Sir Richd. Bickerton, bt.
Jas. Buller.
Wm. Domett.
Sir Jos. Sydney Yorke.
Hon. Fredk. John Robinson.
Horatio, ld. Walpole.

Mar. 25, 1812.

ROBT., visc. MELVILLE.
Wm. Domett.
Sir Jos. Sydney Yorke.
Hon. Fredk. John Robinson, aft. visc. Goderich and E. of Ripon.
Horatio, ld. Walpole.
Wm. Dundas.
Geo. Johnstone Hope.

Oct. 5, 1812.

ROBT., visc. MELVILLE.
Wm. Domett.
Sir Jos. Sydney Yorke.
Wm. Dundas.
Geo. Johnstone Hope.
Sir Geo. Warrender, bt.
John Osborn.

May 18, 1813.

ROBT., visc. MELVILLE.
Wm. Domett.
Sir Jos. Sydney Yorke.
Wm. Dundas.
Sir Geo. Warrender, bt.
John Osborn.
Lord Hy. Paulet.

Oct. 23, 1813.

ROBT., visc. MELVILLE.
Sir Jos. Sydney Yorke.
Wm. Dundas.
Geo. Johnstone Hope.
Sir Geo. Warrender, bt.
John Osborn.
Lord Hy. Paulet.

Aug. 23, 1814.

ROBT., visc. MELVILLE.
Sir Jos. Sydney Yorke.
Geo. Johnstone Hope.
Sir Geo. Warrender, bt.
John Osborn.
Lord Hy. Paulet.
Barrington Pope Blachford.

May 24, 1816.

ROBT., visc. MELVILLE.
Sir Jos. Sydney Yorke, K.C.B.
Sir Geo. Hope, K.C.B.
Sir Geo. Warrender, bt.
John Osborn.
Sir Graham Moore, K.C.B.
Hy., M. of Worcester.

April 2, 1818.

ROBT., visc. MELVILLE.
Sir Geo. Warrender, bt.
John Osborn, aft. bt.
Sir Graham Moore, K.C.B.
Hy., M. of Worcester.
Sir Geo. Cockburn, G.C.B.
Sir Hy. Hotham, K.C.B.

Mar. 15, 1819.

ROBT., visc. MELVILLE.
Sir Geo. Warrender, bt.
Sir John Osborn, bt.
Sir Graham Moore, K.C.B.
Sir Geo. Cockburn, G.C.B.
Sir Hy. Hotham, K.C.B.
Sir Geo. Clerk, bt.

Mar. 13, 1820.

ROBT., visc. MELVILLE.
Sir Wm. Johnstone Hope, K.C.B.
Sir Geo. Warrender, bt.
Sir John Osborn, bt.
Sir Geo. Cockburn, G.C.B.
Sir Hy. Hotham, K.C.B.
Sir Geo. Clerk, bt.

Feb. 8, 1822.

ROBT., visc. MELVILLE.
Sir Wm. Johnstone Hope, K.C.B.
Sir John Osborne, bt.
Sir Geo. Cockburn, G.C.B.
Sir Hy. Hotham, K.C.B.
Sir Geo. Clerk, bt.
Wm. Robt. Keith Douglas.

March 23, 1822.

ROBT., visc. MELVILLE.
Sir Wm. Johnstone Hope, K.C.B.
Sir John Osborn, bt.
Sir Geo. Cockburn, G.C.B.
Sir Geo. Clerk, bt.

Feb. 16, 1824.

ROBT., visc. MELVILLE.
Sir Wm. Johnstone Hope, K.C.B.
Sir Geo. Cockburn, G.C.B.
Sir Geo. Clerk, bt.
Wm. Robt. Keith Douglas.

Lord High Admiral.

May 2, 1827.

Wm. Henry, D. of Clarence, aft. Wm. IV., Ld. High Adm. of the U. K. of Gr. Brit and Ireland, assisted by the following.

Councils.

H.R.H. Council.
V. adm. sir Wm. Johnstone Hope, g.c.b.
V. adm. sir Geo. Cockburn, g.c.b.
Wm. Robert Keith Douglas.
John Evelyn Denison.

Feb. 4, 1828.
V. adm. sir Wm. Johnstone Hope, g.c.b.
V. adm. sir Geo. Cockburn, g.c.b.
Sir Geo. Clerk, bt.
Geo. Chas., E. of Brecknock.

March 12, 1828.
V. adm. sir Geo. Cockbu g.c.b.
Sir Geo. Clerk, bt.
Geo. Chas., E. of Brecknock
R. adm. sir Edwd. Wm. Car bell Rich Owen, k.c.b.

The D. of Clarence res. the office of ld. high adm., Aug. 12, 1828.

Commissioners.

Sept. 19, 1828.
Robt., visc. Melville.
V. adm. sir Geo. Cockburn, g.c.b.
V. adm. sir Hy. Hotham.
Sir Geo. Clerk, bt.
Geo. Chas., E. of Brecknock.

July 15, 1829.
Robt., visc. Melville.
V. adm. sir Geo. Cockburn, g.c.b.
V. Adm. sir Hy. Hotham.
Sir Geo. Clerk, bt.
Fredk., visc. Castlereagh.

July 31, 1830.
Robt., visc. Melville.
V. adm. sir Geo. Cockburn, g.c.b.
V. adm. sir Hy. Hotham.
Fredk., visc. Castlereagh.
Chas. Ross.

Nov. 25, 1830.
Sir Jas. Robt. Geo. Graham, bt.
R. adm. sir Thos. Masterman Hardy.
R. adm. hon. Geo. Heneage Lawrence Dundas.
Sir Saml. John Brooke Pechell, bt.
Hon. Geo. Barrington.

June 8, 1832.
Sir Jas. Robt. Geo. Graham, bt.
R. adm. sir T. M. Hardy.
R. adm. hon. Geo. Heneage L. Dundas.
Sir Saml. John Brooke Pechell, bt.
Hon. Geo. Barrington.
Hy. Labouchere.

Apr. 13, 1833.
Sir Jas. R. G. Graham, bt.
R. adm. sir T. M. Hardy.
R. adm. hon. Geo. Heneage L. Dundas.
Sir Saml. John Brooke Pechell, bt.
Hy. Labouchere.
Hon. Maurice Fredk. Fitzhardinge Berkeley.

June 11, 1834.
Geo., lord Auckland.
R. adm. sir T. M. Hardy.
R. adm. hon. Geo. Heneage L. Dundas.
Sir Saml. John Brooke Pechell, bt.
Hy. Labouchere.
Hon. Maurice Fredk. Fitzhardinge Berkeley.

Aug. 1. 1834
Geo., lord Auckland.
Hon. Geo. Heneage L. Dundas.
Sir Saml. John Brooke Pechell, bt.
Hy. Labouchere, and
Hon. M. F. Fitzhardinge Berkeley.

Nov. 1, 1834.
Geo., ld. Auckland.
R. adm. sir Chas. Adam.
R. adm. sir Wm. Parker.
Sir Saml. John Brooke Pechell, bt.
Hy. Labouchere, aft. ld. Taunton.
Hon. M. F. Fitzhardin Berkeley.

Dec. 23, 1834.
Thos. Philip, E. de Gre
V. adm. sir Geo. Coc burn, g.c.b.
Sir John Poo Beresford, b
Sir Chas. Rowley, k.c.b.
Anthy, ld. Ashley.
Maurice Fitzgerald.

Apr. 25, 1835.
Geo., lord Auckland.
R. adm. sir Chas. Adam.
R. adm. sir Wm. Parker.
Capt. Geo. Elliot.
Sir Edwd. Thos. Tro bridge, bt.
Archd., ld. Dalmeny.

Sept. 19, 1835.
Gilbert, E. of Minto.
R. adm. sir Chas. Adam.
R. adm. sir Wm. Parker.
Capt. Geo. Elliot.
Sir Edwd. Thos. Tro bridge, bt.
Archd., ld. Dalmeny.

July 22, 1837.
Gilbert, E. of Minto.
V. adm. sir Chas. Adam.
R. adm. sir Wm. Parker.
Sir Edwd. Thos. Tro bridge, bt.
Archd., ld. Dalmeny.
Hon. M. F. Fitzhardin Berkeley.

Mar. 5, 1839.
Gilbert, E. of Minto.
Sir Chas. Adam.
Sir Wm. Parker.

ir. Edwd. Thos. Troubridge, bt.
ir Saml. John Brooke, Pechell, bt.
rchd., ld. Dalmeny.

June 25, 1841.

ILBERT, E. of MINTO.
ir Chas. Adam.
ir Edwd. Thos. Troubridge, bt.
ir Saml. John B. Pechell, bt.
rch., ld. Dalmeny.
apt. Jas. Whitley Deans Dundas, C.B.

Sept. 8, 1841.

THOS., E. OF HADDINGTON.
dm. sir G. Cockburn, G.C.B.
. adm. sir Wm. Hall Gage.
ir Geo. Fras. Seymour.
apt. hon. Wm. Gordon, R.N.
Ion. Hy. Thos. Lowry Corry.

May 22, 1844.

THOS., E. OF HADDINGTON.
Adm. sir G. Cockburn, G.C.B.
V. adm. sir Wm. Hall Gage.
R. adm. Wm. Bowles.
Hon. Wm. Gordon.
Hon. Hy. Thos. Lowry Corry.

Feb. 12, 1845.

THOS., E. OF HADDINGTON.
Adm. sir G. Cockburn, G.C.B.
V. adm. sir Wm. Hall Gage.
R. adm. Wm. Bowles.
Hon. Wm. Gordon.
Hon. Hy. Fitzroy.

Jan. 13, 1846.

EDWD., E. OF ELLENBOROUGH.
Adm. sir G. Cockburn, G.C.B.
V. adm. sir Wm. Hall Gage.
R. adm. Wm. Bowles.
Hon. Wm. Gordon.
Hon. Hy. Fitzroy.

Feb. 17, 1846.

EDWD., E. OF ELLENBOROUGH.
Adm. sir G. Cockburn, G.C.B.
V. adm. sir Wm. Hall Gage.
R. adm. Wm. Bowles.
Hon. Hy. Fitzroy.
Hon. Hy. John Rous.

July 13, 1846.

GEO., E. OF AUCKLAND.
V. adm. sir Wm. Parker.
R. adm. Jas. Whitley Deans Dundas, C.B.
Capt. hon. Maurice Fredk. Fitzhardinge Berkeley, C.B.
Capt. lord John Hay, C.B.
Hon. Wm. Fras. Cowper.

July 24, 1846.

GEO., E. OF AUCKLAND.
V. adm. sir Chas. Adam.
R. adm. J. W. D. Dundas, C.B.
Capt. hon. M. F. Fitzhardinge Berkeley, C.B.
Capt. lord John Hay, C.B.
Hon. Wm. Fras. Cowper.

July 20, 1847.

GEO., E. OF AUCKLAND.
R. adm. Jas. W. D. Dundas, C.B.
R. adm. Hy. Prescott.
Capt. hon. M. F. Fitzhardinge Berkeley, C.B.
Capt. lord John Hay, C.B.
Hon. Wm. Fras. Cowper.

Dec. 23, 1847.

GEO., E. OF AUCKLAND.
R. adm. J. W. D. Dundas, C.B.
Capt. hon. M. F. Fitzhardinge Berkeley, C.B.
Capt. lord John Hay, C.B.
Capt. Alex. Milne.
Hon. Wm. Fras. Cowper.

Jan. 18, 1849.

SIR FRAS. THORNHILL BARING, bt.
R. adm. J. W. D. Dundas, C.B.
Hon. M. F. Fitzhardinge Berkeley, now r. adm., C.B.
Capt. lord John Hay, C.B.
Capt. Alex. Milne.
Hon. Wm. Fras. Cowper.

Jan. 30, 1850.

SIR FRAS. THORNHILL BARING, bt.
R. adm. J.W.D. Dundas, C.B.
R. adm. hon. M. F. Fitzhardinge Berkeley, C.B.
Capt. Houston Stewart, C.B.
Capt. Alex. Milne.
Hon. Wm. Fras. Cowper.

Feb. 12, 1852, **G.**

SIR FRAS. THORNHILL BARING, bt.
R. adm. hon. M. F. Fitzhardinge Berkeley, C.B.
R. adm. Houston Stewart, C.B.
Adm. Sir Jas. Stirling.
Capt. Alex. Milne.
Hon. Wm. Fras. Cowper.

Feb. 28, 1852, **G.**

ALGERNON, D. OF NORTHUMBERLAND.
R. adm. Hyde Parker, C.B.
R. adm. Phipps Hornby, C.B.
Capt. sir Thos. Herbert, K.C.B.
Capt. hon. Arthur Duncombe.
Capt. Alex. Milne.

Dec. 30, 1852.

SIR JAS. ROBT. GEO. GRAHAM, bt.
V. adm. Hyde Parker, C.B.
R. adm. hon. M. F. Fitzhardinge Berkeley, C.B.
Capt. hon. Richd. Saunders Dundas, C.B.
Capt. Alex. Milne.
Hon. Wm. Fras. Cowper.

June 1, 1854.

SIR JAS. ROBT. GEO. GRAHAM bt., G.C.B.
R. adm. hon. M. F. Fitzhardinge Berkeley, C.B.
R. adm. hon. Richd. Dundas, C.B.
Capt. Peter Richards, C.B.
Capt. Alex. Milne.
Hon. Wm. Fras. Cowper.

Mar. 13, 1855, **G.**

Sir Chas. Wood, bt.
R. adm. hon. M. F. Fitzhardinge Berkeley, C.B.
R. adm. Hy. Eden.
Capt. Peter Richards, C.B.
Capt. Alex. Milne.
Sir Robt. Peel, bt.

Mar. 28, 1857, **G.**

SIR CHAS. WOOD, bt., G.C.B.
V. adm. hon. sir M. F. Fitzhardinge Berkeley, K.C.B.
R. adm. hon. sir Richd. Saunders Dundas, K.C.B.
R. adm. Hy. Eden.
Capt. Alex. Milne.
Sir Robt. Peel, bt.

May 27, 1857, **G.**

SIR CHAS. WOOD, bt., G.C.B.
V. adm. hon. sir M. F. Fitzhardinge Berkeley, K.C.B.
R. adm. hon. sir Richd. S. Dundas, K.C.B.
R. adm. Hy. Eden.
Capt. Alex. Milne.
Thos. Geo. Baring.

Nov. 21, 1857, **G.**
SIR CHAS. WOOD, bt., G.C.B., aft. visc. Halifax.
R. adm. hon. sir Richd. S. Dundas, K.C.B.
R. adm. Hy. Eden.
Capt. Alex. Milne.
Capt. hon. Fredk. Thos. Pelham, C.B.
Thos. Geo. Baring, aft. E. of Northbrook.

Mar. 8, 1858, **G.**
SIR JNO. SOMERSET PAKINGTON, bt.
V. adm. Wm. Fanshawe Martin.
V. adm. hon. sir Richd. S. Dundas, K.C.B.
R. adm. Alex. Milne.
Capt. hon. Jas. Robt. Drummond, C.B.
Algernon Geo., ld. Lovaine.

Jan. 26, 1859, **G.**
SIR JNO. SOMERSET PAKINGTON, bt.
V. adm. Wm. F Martin.
V. adm. hon. sir Richd. S. Dundas, K.C.B.
R. adm. sir Alex. Milne, K.C.B.
Capt. hon. Swynfen Thos. Carnegie, C.B.
Algn. Geo. ld. Lovaine.

Mar. 9, 1859, **G.**
SIR JNO. SOMERSET PAKINGTON, bt.
V. adm. Wm. F. Martin.
V. adm. hon. sir Richd. S. Dundas, K.C.B.
R. adm. sir Alex. Milne, K.C.B.
Capt. hon. Swynfen Thos. Carnegie, C.B.
Hon. Fredk. Lygon.

Apr. 20, 1859, **G.**
SIR JNO. SOMERSET PAKINGTON, bt.
V. adm. Wm. F. Martin.
V. adm. hon. sir Richd. S. Dundas, K.C.B.
R. adm. sir Hy. Jno. Leeke, K.C.B.
R. adm. sir Alex. Milne, K.C.B.
Hon. Fredk. Lygon.

June 27, 1859, **G.**
EDWD. ADOLPHUS, D. OF SOMERSET.
V. adm. hon. sir Richd. S. Dundas, K.C.B.
R. adm. hon. Fredk. Thos. Pelham, C.B.
Capt. Chas. Eden, C.B.
Capt. Chas. Frederick.
Saml. Whitbread.

June 14, 1861, **G.**
EDWD. ADOLPHUS, D. OF SOMERSET.
R. adm. hon. sir Fredk. Wm. Grey, K.C.B.
Capt. Chas. Eden, C.B.
Capt. Chas. Frederick.
Capt. hon. Jas. Robt. Drummond, C.B.
Saml. Whitbread.

Mar. 23, 1863, **G.**
EDWD. ADOLPHUS, D. OF SOMERSET, K.G.
V. adm. hon. sir Fredk. Wm. Grey, K.C.B.
R. adm. Chas. Eden, C.B.
R. adm. Chas. Frederick.
Capt. hon. Jas. Robt. Drummond, C.B.
Spencer Compton Cavendish, c.c. M. of Hartington.

May 2, 1863, **G.**
EDWD. ADOLPHUS, D. OF SOMERSET, K.G.
V. adm. hon. sir Fredk. Wm. Grey, K.C.B.
R. adm. Chas. Eden, C.B.
R. adm. Chas. Frederick.
Capt. hon. Jas. Robt. Drummond, C.B.
Jas. Stansfeld, jun.

April 21, 1864, **G.**
EDWD. ADOLPHUS, D. OF SOMERSET, K.G.
V. adm. hon. sir Fredk. Wm. Grey, K.C.B.
R. adm. Chas. Eden, C.B.
R. adm. Chas. Frederick.
R. adm. hon. Jas. Robt. Drummond, C.B.
Hugh Culling Eardley Childers.

Mar. 13, 1865, **G.**
EDWD. ADOLPHUS, D. OF SOMERSET.
V. adm. hon. sir Fredk. Wm. Grey, K.C.B.
R. adm. Chas. Eden, C.B.
R. adm. Edwd. Gennys Fanshawe.
R. adm. hon. Jas. Robt. Drummond, C.B.
Hugh C. E. Childers.

Jan. 22, 1866, **G.**
EDWD. ADOLPHUS, D. OF SOMERSET, K.G.
Adm. hon. sir Fredk. Wm. Grey, K.C.B.
R. adm. Chas. Eden, C.B.
R. adm. Edwd. Gennys Fanshawe, C.B.
Hon. Jas. Robt. Drummond, C.B.
Hy. Fenwick.

April 7, 1866, **G.**
EDWD. ADOLPHUS, D. OF SOMERSET, K.G.
Adm. hon. sir Fredk. Wm. Grey, K.C.B.
R. adm. Chas. Eden, C.B.
R. adm. Edwd. Gennys Fanshawe, C.B.
Hon. Jas. Robt. Drummond, C.B.
Capt. John Hay, c.c. Lord John Hay, C.B.

May 8, 1866, **G.**
EDWD. ADOLPHUS, D. OF SOMERSET, K.G.
Adm. hon. sir Fredk. Wm. Grey, G.C.B.
V. adm. Chas. Eden, C.B.
R. adm. Edwd. Gennys Fanshawe, C.B.
Capt. John Hay, c.c. lord John Hay, C.B.
Geo. John Shaw-Lefevre.

July 12, 1866, **G.**
SIR JNO. SOMERSET PAKINGTON, bt., G.C.B.
V. adm. sir Alex. Milne K.C.B.
V. adm. sir Sydney Colpoys Dacres, K.C.B.
R.adm. Geo. Hy. Seymour, C.B.
R. adm. sir John Chas. Dalrymple Hay, bt.
Chas. Du Cane.

March 8, 1867, **G.**
HY. THOS. LOWRY CORRY.
V. adm. sir Alex. Milne K.C.B.
V. adm. sir Sydney Colpoys Dacres, K.C.B.
R. adm. Geo. Hy. Seymour, C.B.
R. adm. sir John Chas. Dalrymple, Hay, bt.
Chas. Du Cane.

Aug. 29, 1868, **G.**
HY. THOS. LOWRY CORRY.
V. adm. sir Alex. Milne, K.C.B.

V. adm. sir Sydney Colpoys Dacres, K.C.B.
R. adm. Geo. Hy. Seymour, C.B.
R. adm. sir Jno. Chas. Dalrymple Hay, bt.
Hon. Fredk. Arthur Stanley, aft. ld. Stanley of Preston.

Dec. 21, 1868, **G.**

HUGH CULLING EARDLEY CHILDERS.
V. adm. sir Sydney Colpoys Dacres, K.C.B.
V. adm. sir Robt. Spencer Robinson, K.C.B.
Capt. John Hay, c.c. lord John Hay, C.B.
Geo. Otto Trevelyan, aft. bt.

July 11, 1870, **G.**

HUGH CULLING EARDLEY CHILDERS.
Adm. sir Sydney Colpoys Dacres, K.C.B.
V. adm. sir Robt. Spencer Robinson, K.C.B.
Capt. John Hay, c.c. lord John Hay, C.B.
Robt. Adam Philips Haldane, E. of Camperdown.

Feb. 9, 1871, **G.**

HUGH CULLING EARDLEY CHILDERS.
Adm. sir Sydney Colpoys Dacres, K.C.B.
Capt. Robt. Hall, C.B.
Capt. John Hay, c.c. lord John Hay, C.B.
Robt. A. P. H., E. of Camperdown.

Mar. 9, 1871, **G.**

GEO. JOACHIM GOSCHEN.
Adm. sir Sydney Colpoys Dacres, K.C.B.
Capt. Robt. Hall, C.B.
Capt. John Hay, c.c. lord John Hay, C.B.
Robt. A. P. H., E. of Camperdown.

June 28, 1871, **G.**

GEO. JOACHIM GOSCHEN.
Adm. sir Sydney Colpoys Dacres, K.C.B.
Capt. Robt. Hall, C.B.
R. adm. John Walter Tarleton, C.B.
Robt. A. P. H., E. of Camperdown.

May 4, 1872, **G.**

GEO. JOACHIM GOSCHEN.
Adm. sir Sydney Colpoys Dacres, G.C.B.
R. adm. Jno. Walter Tarleton, C.B.
R. adm. Fredk. Beauchamp Paget Seymour, C.B.
Robt. A. P. H., E. of Camperdown.

Nov. 27, 1872, **G.**

GEO. JOACHIM GOSCHEN.
Adm. sir Alex. Milne, G.C.B.
R. adm. Jno. Walter Tarleton, C.B.
R. adm. Fredk. Beauchamp Paget Seymour, C.B.
Robt. A. P. H., E. of Camperdown.

Mar. 4, 1874, **G.**

GEO. WARD HUNT.
Adm. sir Alex. Milne. G.C.B.
V. adm. sir Jno. Walter Tarleton, K.C.B.
Capt. Richd. Jas. Meade, c.c. ld. Gilford.
Sir Lopes Massey Lopes, bt.

Dec. 29, 1874, **G.**

GEO. WARD HUNT.
Adm. sir Alex. Milne, G.C.B.
R. adm. Geoffrey Thos. Phipps Hornby.
Capt. Richd. Jas. Meade, c.c. ld. Gilford.
Sir Lopes Massey Lopes, bt.

Sept. 7, 1876, **G.**

GEO. WARD HUNT.
Adm. sir Hastings Reginald Yelverton, G.C.B.
V. adm. Geoffrey Thos. Phipps Hornby.
Capt. Richd. Jas. Meade, c.c. ld. Gilford.
Sir Lopes Massey Lopes, bt.

Jan. 11, 1877, **G.**

GEO. WARD HUNT.
Adm. sir Hastings Reginald Yelverton, G.C.B.
R. adm. Arthur Wm. Acland Hood, C.B.
R adm. Richd. Jas. Meade, c.c. ld. Gilford.
Sir Lopes Massey Lopes, bt.

Aug. 14, 1877, **G.**

WM. HY. SMITH.
Adm. sir Hastings Reginald Yelverton, G.C.B.
R. adm. Arthur Wm. Acland Hood, C.B.
R. adm. Richd. Jas. Meade, c.c. ld. Gilford, C.B.
Sir Lopes Massey Lopes, bt.

Nov. 5, 1877, **G.**

WM. HY. SMITH.
Adm. Geo. Greville Wellesley, C.B.
R. adm. Arthur Wm. Acland Hood, C.B.
R. adm. Richd. Jas. Meade, c.c. ld. Gilford, C.B.
Sir Lopes Massey Lopes, bt.

Aug. 12, 1879, **G.**

WM. HY. SMITH.
Adm. sir Astley Cooper Key, K.C.B.
R. Adm. Arthur Wm. Acland Hood, C.B.
R adm. Richd. Jas. Meade, c.c. ld. Gilford, C.B., aft. E. of Clanwilliam.
Sir Lopes Massey Lopes, bt.

Dec. 4, 1879, **G.**

WM. HY. SMITH.
Adm. sir Astley Cooper Key, K.C.B.
R. adm. Richd. Jas., E. of Clanwilliam, C.B.
R. adm. sir Jno. Edmd. Commerell, K.C.B., V.C.
Sir Lopes Massey Lopes, bt.

May 12, 1880, **G.**

THOS. GEO., E. OF NORTHBROOK, G.C.S.I.
Adm. sir Astley Cooper Key, K.C.B.
V. adm. John Hay, c.c. ld. John Hay, C.B.
R. adm. Anthy. Hiley Hoskins, C.B.
Thos. Brassey.

Apr. 12, 1882.

THOS. GEO., E. OF NORTHBROOK, G.C.S.I.
Adm. sir Astley Cooper Key, K.C.B.
V. adm. sir John Hay, c.c. ld. John Hay, K.C.B.
R. adm. Thos. Brandreth.
R. adm. Anthy. Hiley Hoskins, C.B.

July 22, 1882.

THOS. GEO., E. OF NORTHBROOK, G.C.S.I.
Adm. sir Astley Cooper Key, K.C.B.
V. adm. sir John Hay, c.c. ld. John Hay, K.C.B.
R. adm. Thos. Brandreth.
R. adm. sir Fredk. Wm. Richards, K.C.B.
Sir Thos. Brassey, K.C.B.
Geo. Wightwick Rendel.

Mar. 3. 1883, G.

THOS. GEO., E. OF NORTHBROOK, G.C.S.I.
Adm. sir Astley Cooper Key, G.C.B.
Adm. Fredk. Beauchamp Paget, ld. Alcester, G.C.B.
R. adm. Thos. Brandreth.
R. adm. sir Fredk. Wm. Richards, K.C.B.
Sir Thos. Brassey, K.C.B., aft. ld. Brassey.
Geo. Wightwick Rendel.

Nov. 24, 1884.

THOS. GEO., E. OF NORTHBROOK, G.C.S.I.
Adm. sir Astley Cooper Key, G.C.B.
Adm. Fredk. Beauchamp Paget, lord Alcester, G.C.B.
V. adm. Thos. Brandreth.
R. adm. sir Fredk. Wm. Richards, K.C.B.
Wm. Sproston Caine.
Geo. Wightwick Rendel.

May 25, 1885, G.

THOS. GEO., E. OF NORTHBROOK, G.C.S.I.
Adm. sir Astley Cooper Key, G.C.B.
Adm. Fredk. Beauchamp Paget, lord Alcester, G.C.B.
V. adm. sir Wm. Nathan Wrighte Hewett, K.C.B., K.C.S.I.
V. adm. Thos. Brandreth.
Wm. Sproston Caine.
Geo. Wightwick Rendel.

July 1, 1885, G.

GEO. FRAS. HAMILTON, C.C. LORD GEORGE HAMILTON.
V. adm. Arthur Wm. Acland Hood, C.B.
V. adm. sir Anthy. Hiley Hoskins, K.C.B.
V. adm. Thos. Brandreth.
Capt. Wm. Codrington, C.B.
Ellis Ashmead Bartlett.

Feb. 15, 1886, G.

GEO. FREDK. SAML., M. OF RIPON, K.G., G.C.S.I.
Adm. sir John Hay, c.c. ld. John Hay.
Adm. sir Anthy. Hiley Hoskins, K.C.B.
V. adm. Wm. Graham, C.B.
R. adm. Jas. Elphinstone Erskine.
Robt. Wm. Duff.

Aug. 9, 1886, G.

GEO. FRAS. HAMILTON, C.C. LORD GEO. HAMILTON.
Adm. sir Arthur Wm. Acland Hood, K.C.B.
V. adm. sir Anthy. Hiley Hoskins, K.C.B.
V. adm. Wm. Graham, C.B.
Capt. lord Chas. Wm. De la Poer Beresford, C.B.
Ellis Ashmead Bartlett.

Jan. 30, 1888, G.

GEO. FRAS. HAMILTON, C.C. LORD GEO. HAMILTON.
Adm. sir Arthur Wm. Acland Hood, K.C.B.
V. adm. sir Anthy. Hiley Hoskins, K.C B.
V. adm. sir Wm. Graham, K.C.B.
R. adm. Chas. Fredk. Hotham, C B.
Ellis Ashmead Bartlett.

FIRST SECRETARIES OF THE ADMIRALTY.

THIS is now a political office, the holder of which goes out with the ministry.

FIRST SECRETARIES OF THE ADMIRALTY SINCE THE REVOLUTION.

Saml. Pepys, the then sec., was dismissed at the Revolution.

1689. Phineas Bowles. Mar.
1690. Jas. Southerne. Jan. 17.
1694. Wm. Bridgeman. Aug. 1.
1695. Wm. Bridgeman and Josiah Burchett, jointly. Jan.
1698. Josiah Burchett, *alone*. June 24.
1742. Thos. Corbett. Oct. 14.
1751. John Cleveland. May 1.
1763. Philip Stephens, aft. sir P., bt. June 19.
1795. Evan Nepean, aft. sir E., bt. Mar. 3.
1804. Wm. Marsden. Jan. 21.
1807. Hon. Wm. Wellesley Pole, aft. lord Maryborough. June 24.
1809. John Wilson Croker. Oct. 9. Mr Croker was the first admy. sec who resigned on a change of ministry.
1830. Hon. Geo. Elliot, capt. R.N. Nov 29.
1834. Geo. Robt. Dawson. Dec. 24.
1835. Chas. Wood, aft. sir C., bt., and visc. Halifax. Apr. 27.
1839. Richd. More O'Ferrall. Oct. 4.
1841. John Parker. June 9.
— Hon. Sidney Herbert, aft. lord Herbert of Lea. Sept. 10.
1845. Hy. Thos. Lowry Corry. Feb. 13.
1846. Hy. Geo. Ward. July 13.
1849. John Parker. May 21.

52. Aug. O'Brien Stafford. Mar. 3.
53. Ralph Bernal Osborne. Jan. 6.
58. Hy. Thos. Lowry Corry, *again*. Mar. 9.
59. Lord Clarence Paget. June 30.
66. Hon. Thos. Geo. Baring, aft. E. of Northbrook. Apr. 30.
— Lord Hy. Gordon Lennox. July 16.
'68. Wm. Edwd. Baxter. Dec. 18.
71. Geo. John Shaw-Lefevre. Mar. 17.
1874. Hon. Algn. Fulke Egerton. Feb.
1880. Geo. Otto Trevelyan, aft. sir G., bt. Apr.
1882. Hy. Campbell Bannerman. May.
1884. Sir Thos. Brassey, K.C.B., aft. lord Brassey. Oct.
1885. Chas. Thomson Ritchie. June.
1886. John Tomlinson Hibbert. Feb.
— Arthur Bower Forwood. Aug.

SECOND SECRETARIES TO THE ADMIRALTY.

HE office of "second secretary" existed at first only at intervals, and nder various titles; but the succession has been regular since the year 756, and the name has been the same from Jan. 13, 1783, till 1871, hen it was changed to that of "permanent secretary."

Second Secretaries to the Admiralty since 1702.

02. Geo. Clarke, joint sec., to Oct. 25, 1705. May 20.
'28. Thos. Corbett, dep. and aft. joint sec., to Oct. 13, 1742. June 25.
'44. Robt. Osborne, dep. sec. Nov. 17.
46. John Cleveland, second sec., to May 1, 1750. Aug. 4.
'56. John Milnes, dep. sec. June 15.
'59. Philip Stephens, second sec. Oct. 16.
64. Chas. Fearne, dep. sec. June 28.
'66. Sir Geo. Jackson, dep. sec. Nov. 11.
82. John Ibbotson, dep. and second sec. June 3.

Second Secretaries.

'95. Wm. Marsden. Mar. 3.
04. Benjn. Tucker. Jan. 21.
— John Barrow, aft. Sir J. May 22.
1806. Benjn. Tucker, *again*. Feb. 10.
1807. John Barrow, aft. sir J., bt. Apr. 9.
1845. Capt. Wm. Alexr. Baillie Hamilton, R.N. Jan. 28.
1855. Thos. Phinn.
1857. Wm. Govett Romaine.
1869. Vernon Lushington.

Permanent Secretaries.

1871. Vernon Lushington, above named; ceased 1877.
1873. R. adm. Robt. Hall, R.N., naval sec., jointly with Lushington until 1877, and then alone. Ceased 1882.
1882. Capt. Geo. Tryon, perm. sec.
1884. Evan Macgregor, C.B., perm. sec.

LORD PRESIDENTS OF THE COUNCIL.

HE lord president of the council presides at the privy council in the bsence of the sovereign. He is appointed to his office by a declaration the sovereign in council, and holds it *durante bene placito*. He is *officio* president of all committees of the privy council, with the exception of the board of trade, which has a president of its own. The ffice is now purely a political one, and the holder changes with the inistry.

Lord Presidents of the Council.
Since the Council was remodelled in 1679.

King Charles II.

679. Anthy., E. of Shaftesbury. Apr. 21. *Struck off the council Oct. 15, same year*
— John, E. of Radnor. Oct. 24.
684. Laurence, E. of Rochester. Aug. 24.

King James II.

1685. Geo., M. of Halifax. Feb. 18.
— Robt., E. of Sunderland. Dec. 4.

King William III.

1689. Thos., E. of Danby, aft. M. of

Carmarthen and D. of Leeds. Feb. 14.
1699. Thos., E. of Pembroke and Montgomery. May 18.
1701. Chas., D. of Somerset. June 28.

QUEEN ANNE.

1702. Thos., E. of Pembroke and Montgomery, *again*. July 14.
1708. John, lord Somers. Nov. 25.
1710. Laurence, E. of Rochester. Sept. 21.
1711. John, D. of Normanby and Buckinghamshire. June 14.

KING GEORGE I.

1714. Daniel, E. of Nottingham. Sept. 22.
1715. Lionel Cranfield, E., aft. D. of Dorset. Jan. 3.
1716. Wm., D. of Devonshire. July 5.
1717. Chas., E. of Sunderland. Mar. 16.
1719. Evelyn, D. of Kingston. Feb. 6.
1720. Chas., visc. Townshend. June 11.
1721. Hy., lord Carleton. June 25.
1725. Wm., D. of Devonshire, *again*. Mar. 27.

KING GEORGE II.

1727. D. of Devonshire, *contd*.
1730. Thos., lord Trevor. May 8.
— Spencer, E. of Wilmington. Dec. 31
1742. Wm., E. of Harrington. Feb. 13.
1745. Lionel Cranfield, D. of Dorset *again*. Jan. 3.
1751. John, E. Granville. June 17.

KING GEORGE III.

1760. E. Granville, *contd*.
1763. John, D. of Bedford. Sept. 9.
1765. Daniel, E. of Winchilsea and Nottingham. July 12.
1766. Robt., E. of Northington. July 30.
1767. Granville Leveson, E. Gower. Dec 22.
1779. Hy., E. Bathurst. Nov. 24.
1782. Chas., ld. Camden. Mar. 27.
1783. David, visc. Stormont. Apr. 2.
— Granville Leveson, E. Gower, *again*. Dec. 19; aft. M. of Stafford.
1784. Chas., ld. Camden, *again*, Dec. 1; aft. E. Camden.
1794. Wm. Wentworth, E. Fitzwilliam. July 11.
1794. David, E. of Mansfield. Dec. 17.
1796. John, E. of Chatham. Dec. 21.
1801. Wm. Hy., 4th D. of Portland July 30.
1805. Hy., visc. Sidmouth. Jan. 14.
— John Jeffreys, E. Camden. July 10.
1806. Wm. Wentworth, E. Fitzwilliam, *again*. Feb. 19.
1806. Hy., visc. Sidmouth, *again*. Oct. [illegible]
1807. John, E. Camden, aft. M. Camden *again*. Mar. 26.
1812. Hy., visc. Sidmouth, *again*. April [illegible]
— Dudley Ryder, E. of Harrowby June 11.

KING GEORGE IV.

1820. E. of Harrowby, *contd*.
1827. Wm. Hy., 5th D. of Portland. Aug 17.
1828. Hy., E. Bathurst. Jan. 28.

KING WILLIAM IV.

1830. E. Bathurst, *contd*.
— Hy., M. of Lansdowne. Nov. 22.
1834. Jas., E. of Rosslyn. Dec. 15.
1835. Hy., M. of Lansdowne, *again*. Apr 18.

QUEEN VICTORIA.

1837. M. of Lansdowne, *contd*.
1841. Jas., ld. Wharncliffe. Sept. 3.
1846. Walter Francis, D. of Buccleuch Jan. 21.
— Hy., M. of Lansdowne, *again* July 6.
1852. Wm., E. of Lonsdale. Feb. 27.
— Granville Geo., E. Granville. Dec 28.
1854. Lord John Russell. June 12.
1855. Granville Geo., E. Granville *again*. Feb. 8.
1858. Jas. Brownlow Wm., M. of Salisbury. Feb. 24.
1859. Granville Geo., E. Granville, K.G. *again*. June 18.
1866. Richd. Plantagenet Campbell Temple Nugent Brydges Chandos, D of Buckingham and Chandos July 6.
1867. John Winston, D. of Marlborough Mar. 8.
1868. Geo. Fredk. Saml., E. de Grey and Ripon. Dec. 9.
1873. Hy. Austin Bruce, Aug. 9; cr. ld Aberdare Aug. 20, G.
1874. Chas. Hy., D. of Richmond, K.G Feb. 21.
1880. John Poyntz, E. Spencer, K.G April 28.
1883. Chichester Parkinson, ld. Carlingford. Mar. 19.
1885. Gathorne, visc. Cranbrook. June 24.
1884. John Poyntz, E. Spencer, *again* Feb. 6.
1886. Gathorne, visc. Cranbrook, G.C.S.I. *again*. Aug. 3.

PRIVY COUNCILLORS.

'HE number of the council was anciently about twelve, when it discharged the functions of state, now confined to the members of the abinet; but it had grown to an unwieldy size before 1679, in which ear it was remodelled upon Sir William Temple's plan, and reduced to hirty members. The number is now unlimited, but no members attend nless specially summoned. The members are selected by the sovereign, nd are, or ought to be, distinguished by high office, wisdom, and olitical experience. The council includes the principal ministers of the rown, some of the judges, many diplomatists, and peers and commoners vhose services to the state and whose position in it, whether past or resent, render them eligible to advise upon public affairs. A privy ouncillor, even though a commoner only, is styled " right honourable," nd has precedence of all knights, baronets, and the younger sons of arons and viscounts. He is admitted a member upon taking the oath rescribed by law, and forthwith takes his seat at the board, according o his rank.

Privy Councillors.

The first names on this list are those of the persons who formed he privy council of Charles II. at the period of the Commonwealth. They were sworn at councils held at the Hague, at Breda, and elsewhere, nd were not re-sworn at the Restoration.

1649.

Sir Richd. Lane, ld. kpr., sw. at the Hague, May 13.

Fras., ld. Cottington, ld. treasr., same time and place.

John, ld. Culpeper (Colepeper), m. rolls.

Ralph, ld. Hopton, same time and place.

Sir Edwd. Hyde, ch. ex., same time and place; aft. ld. chanc. and E. of Clarendon.

Robt. Long, sec. to his majesty, May 14.

Patrick, E. of Brentford (county of Middlesex) and Forth (in Scotland), sw. at Peronne, July 12.

Sir Edwd. Nicholas, sec. st. to his late majesty, sw. at Jersey, Oct. 4.

He became sec. st. to Charles II., and was again sw. of the council in 1660.

1650.

Geo., D. of Buckingham, sw. at Breda, Apr. 6.

Wm., M. of Newcastle, same time and place.

Wm., D. of Hamilton, sw. at Breda, Apr. 7.

The following privy councillors are named in the records; but there is no mention of the times when they were sworn.

James, D. of York, aft. K. James II.

Hy., D. of Gloucester.

Jas., M. of Ormond.

Geo., E. of Bristol.

Murrough, E. of Inchiquin.

Thos., ld. Wentworth.

Hy., ld. Jermyn, aft. E. of St. Albans.

The king first sat at a council held at Canterbury, May 27, 1660, *when were sworn:*

Sir Geo. Monk, genl. of all the forces in the three kingdoms, and m. horse, made D. of Albemarle, July 7, 1660.

Thos., E. of Southampton, made ld. treasr., Sept. following.

Sir Wm. Morrice, sec. st.

Sir Anthy. Ashley Cooper, bt., cr. ld. Ashley, Apr. 1661; and baron Cooper and E. of Shaftesbury, Apr. 1772; ld. chanc., Nov., same year. *Struck from the list, May* 19, 1674.

THE RESTORATION.

1660.

May 31. Wm., M. of Hertford, sw. in London.
Algernon, E. of Northumberland.
Robt., E. of Leicester.
Thos., E. of Berkshire.
Fras., ld. Seymour.
Arthur Annesley, aft. baron Annesley, in Ireland, and E. of Anglesey, in Wales, sw. of the council, and obtained these honours in reward of his services for the king's restoration.
Susp. from the office of treasr. of the Navy, Nov. 1668; made ld. pr. seal, Apr. 1673.

June 1. Montagu, E. of Lindsey, ld. gr. chambn. of England.
Edwd., E. of Manchester, ld. chambn.
Geo., E. of Norwich.
Hy., E. of St. Albans, late ld. Jermyn; sat as a pr. councillor before being re-sw., May 31, this year; amb. to France.
Wm., visc. Say and Sele.
John, lord Robartes, of Truro, aft. visc. Bodmin and E. of Radnor; ld. pr. seal, May 1661.
Denzil Holles, cr. baron Holles, Apr. 1661. *Struck from the list, Jan.* 7, 1675.

June 2. Col. Chas. Howard.

June 14. Gen. Edwd., ld. Montagu, K.G., cr. baron Montagu, of St. Neot's, visc. Hinchinbroke, and E. of Sandwich, July following.
Killed in the great sea-fight with the Dutch fleet off Southwold bay, May 28, 1672.

July 6. Sir Fredk. Cornwallis, knt. and bt., treasr. hhold.; cr. lord Cornwallis, Apr. 1661.
Sir Chas. Berkeley, comptr. hhold., cr. visc. Fitzhardinge, 1665.

July 11. Sir Geo. Carteret, knt. and bt., v. chambn.

Aug. 27. Hy., M. of Dorchester.

1661.

Jan. 2. John, E. of Lauderdale, sec. st. for Scotland, aft. D. of Lauderdale.

June 28. Wm., E. of Glencairn, ld. chanc. of Scotland.

Sept. 13. Richd., ld. Vaughan and E. of Carberry, ld. pres. of Wales.

1662.

Jan. 29. Christr., ld. Hatton, made gov. of Jersey.
Sir Hugh Pollard, comptr. hhold.

Apr. 3. Jerome, E. of Portland.
Sir Wm. Compton.

Apr. 28. His highness pr. RUPERT, adm of the council without bein sworn, as a near relative of th king's.
Geo., D. of Buckingham.
John, E. of Middleton, H.M high commr. for Scotland.

Oct. 15. Sir Hy. Bennet, sec. st.; c ld. Arlington, Mar. 1663; an E. of Arlington, Apr. 1672.

1663.

Apr. 3. Gilbert Sheldon, bp. of Lon don; transl. to Canterbury Aug. 1663.

Apr. 6. Wm. Juxon, abp. of Canterbur

June 17. John, ld. Berkeley, of Stratton ld. lieut. of Ireland in 1670.

July 26. John, E. of Bath, gr. stole.

Oct. 2. Sir Richd. Fanshawe, knt. an bt., one of the masters requests.

Nov. 4. John, E. of Rothes, H. M. hig commr. for Scotland.

Dec. 9. Humphrey Henchman, bp. London.

1664.

Aug. 17. Sir Thos. Ingram, chanc. d Lanc.

1665.

May 26. Roger, E. of Orrery, late ld. just in Ireland.

1666.

Apr. 11. Wm., E. of Craven.

June 13. Thos., E. of Ossory.

Dec. 5. Sir Thos. Clifford, kt. comptr hhold; cr. lord Clifford, Apr 1672, and made treas., 28th same month.

Dec. 12. Robt., E. of Lindsey, ld. gr chambn. of England.

1667.

Feb. 13. John, E. of Bridgewater.

May 22. Sir John Duncombe, a comm of the treas. and ch. ex.

Sept. 4. Sir Orlando Bridgeman, sw. a pr councillor and ld. kpr., at th same time.

1668.

July 1. Fras., lord Newport, comptr hhold.; cr. visc. Newport Mar. 1675, and E. of Bradford May 1694.

Sept. 29. Sir John Trevor, sec. st.

1670.

ne 10. Sir Thos. Chicheley, m. g. ordn.
ne 15. Hy., E. of Ogle. Became D. of Newcastle, succeeding his father, in 1676.

1671.

n. 5. Aubrey de Vere, E. of Oxford.
r. 29. JAMES, duke of MONMOUTH, natural son to the king.

1672.

n. 2. Ralph Montagu, mast. gr. wardr.
b. 14. Sir Robert Carr, knt. and bt., chanc. d. Lanc.
pr. 17. Hy., M. of Worcester, ld. pres. of Wales.
Arthur E. of Essex, app. ld. lieut. of Ireland.
Thos., visc. Fauconberg.
Geo. visc. Halifax. *Struck from the list Jan. 7*, 1675.
ay 3. Sir Thos., Osborne, treasr. of the navy; cr. visc. Latimer, Aug. 1673; E. of Danby, June, 1674; made ld. treasr. of England. Cr. M. of Carmarthen, Apr., 1689, and D. of Leeds, May 1694.
ly 3. Hy. Coventry, sec. st.
Sir Robt. Long, bt.
ov. 29. Wm., ld. Maynard, comptr. hhold.

1673.

ar. 7. Jas., E. of Northampton.
pr. 9. Edwd. Seymour, aft. sir E., bt., sp. ho. commons.
Nov. 12. Sir Heneage Finch, bt., ld. kpr.; cr. ld. Finch, of Daventry, Jan. 1674; and E. of Nottingham, May 1681.
Made ld. chanc. of England, Dec. 1675.

1674.

May 27. Robt., E. of Sunderland, sec. st. in 1679.
June 3. Alex., E. of Kincardine. *Struck from the list, Ang.* 1676.
July 10. Hy., E. of Peterborough.
Sept. 11. Sir Jo . Williamson, sec. st.
Dec. 4. Wm., E. of Strafford.

1675.

June 23. Giles Strangways.
July 21. Geo. Morley, bp. of Winchester.
Oct. 15. Christr., D. of Albemarle.

1676.

Jan. 21. Hy. Compton, bp. of London.
Apr. 26. Nathl., ld. Crew, bp. of Durham.
May 10. Sir John Ernle (Ernley), ch. ex.

1678.

Feb. 6. Wm. Sancroft, abp. of Canterbury.
July 17. Geo., ld. Berkeley.
Oct. 10. Robt., E. of Ailesbury.

1679.

Jan. 3. Jas., E. of Salisbury.
Jan. 8. Hy., E. of Clarendon, ld. lieut. of Ireland in 1685.

On the 21st April, 1679, His Majesty King Charles II. was pleased dissolve the whole of the privy council, and in their room to choose *irty* privy councillors, principally selected out of the old list. This umber was not in future to be exceeded, with the exception only f such persons as were to be privy councillors *ex officio*, as the lord resident, the secretary of state for scotland, the princes of the blood, c., who were not reckoned in the thirty. Conformably with this order ne following were sworn at the council board:—

1679.

pr. 21. His Highness Pr. RUPERT.
Anthy., E. of Shaftesbury, as ld. pres. *His name again struck from the list Oct. 15 following.*
Heneage, lord Finch, ld. chanc. of England.
Arthur, E. of Anglesey, ld. pr. seal.
Christr., D. of Albemarle, capt. of the life guards.
JAS., D. of MONMOUTH, m. horse. Beheaded on Tower Hill for rebellion against king James, in 1685.
Chas., M. of Winchester.
Hy., E. of Arlington, ld. chambn. hhold.
Jas., E. of Salisbury. *Struck from the list, Jan.* 18, 1681.
John, E. of Bridgewater.
Robt., E. of Sunderland, sec. st. *Struck out Jan.* 24, 1681 *Readm.*

Sept. 20, 1682; decl. ld. pres,. Dec. 4, 1685.

Apr. 21. Arthur, E. of Essex, first ld. of the treas. *Struck from the list, Jan.* 24, 1681.

John, E. of Bath, gr. stole.

Geo., visc. Halifax, cr. E. of Halifax, July, 1679, and M. of Halifax, Aug. 1682; decl. ld. pres. in the next reign. *Struck from the list Oct.* 21, 1685.

Hy. Compton, bp. of London. *Struck from the list, Dec.* 23, 1685.

John, lord Robartes, cr. visc. Bodmin and E. of Radnor, July following; decl. ld. pres., Oct. 24, 1679.

Wm., lord Russell. Beheaded in Lincoln's-Inn-Fields, July 21, 1683.

Wm., lord Cavendish.

Hy. Coventry, sec. of st.

Sir Fras. North, ld. ch. just. c. p.; made ld. kpr., Dec. 1682.

Sir Hy. Capel., K.B., first commr. of the admy.

Sir John Ernle (Ernley), ch. ex.

Sir Thos. Chicheley, mast. ordn. *Struck from the list, March* 2, 1687.

Sir Wm. Temple, bt. *Struck from the list, Jan.* 24, 1681.

Sir Edwd. Seymour, bt.

Hy. Powle, aft. m. rolls.

1679.

Apr. 22. Wm. Sancroft, abp. of Canterbury.

John, D. of Lauderdale, sec. st. for Scotland.

Hy., M. of Worcester, cr. D. of Beaufort, Nov. 1682.

Thos., visc. Fauconberg, cr. E. of Fauconberg, Apr. 1689.

Apr. 27. Hy., D. of Newcastle.

June 24. Denzil, lord Holles.

Nov. 19. Laurence Hyde, first commr. of the treas.; cr. E. of Rochester, Nov. 1682; decl. ld. pres., Aug. 24, 1684; ld. treasr. in the next reign.

1680.

Feb. 4. Danl. Finch, first commr. of the admy.; succ. as E. of Nottingham, and aft. as E. of Winchilsea. *Struck from the list, Mar.* 12, 1695.

Sidney Godolphin, a commr. of the treas.; cr. lord Godolphin, Sept. 1684, and made first ld. of the treas.

Feb. 11. Sir Leoline Jenkins, judge of t high court of admy., made s st.

Apr. 16. Thos., E. of Ossory, late ld. ju in Ireland; admiral.

May 26 Hy., E. of Clarendon, app. l lieut. of Ireland in 1685.

Oct. 15. Sir Robt. Carr, knt. and l chanc. d. Lanc.

1681.

Jan. 26. Aubrey, E. of Oxford.

Philip, E. of Chesterfield, l warden and ch. just. in eyre this side Trent..

Robt,, E. of Ailesbury, aft. l chambn. to king James II.

Feb. 2. Edwd., E. of Conway, sec. st.

Mar. 9. Wm., E. of Craven.

1682.

Mar. 3. Adm. Geo. Legge, cr. ld. Dar mouth, Nov. 2, following.

May 23. Jas., D. of Ormond, ld. steward ld. lieut. of Ireland.

June 29. Robt., E. of Lindsey, ld. g chambn. of England.

Dec. 22. Sir Fras. Pemberton, knt., ld. c just. of k. b. *Struck from t list, Oct.* 24, 1683

1683.

Feb. 28. Theophilus, E. of Huntingdon.

Hy., E. of Peterborough.

Oct. 4. Sir Geo. Jeffreys, ld. ch. just. b.; cr. ld. Jeffreys, and ma ld. chanc., Oct. 1685.

1684.

July 11. Alexr., E. of Moray, ld. pr. seal Scotland.

Chas., E. of Middleton, made se st.

1685.

Jan. 7. John Drummond.

KING JAMES II.

1685.

Feb. 9. GEORGE., pr. of DENMARK; *intro duced* to the council, not sworn Consort of the princess Ann Cr. ld. Wokingham, E. Kendal, and D. of Cumberland Apr. 9, 1689.

Mar. 27. Wm., D. of Queensberry, l high commr. for Scotland.

Jas., E. of Perth, ld. chanc. Scotland.

May 15. Hy., D. of Newcastle.

July 24. John, E. of Mulgrave, ld. chamb Oct. this year.

July 31. Geo., E. Berkeley.

Oct. 16. Sir Edwd. Herbert, ld. ch. jus k. b.

Oct. 21. Richd., visc. Preston.

Oct. 30. Thos., E. of Plymouth.

1686.

[Ja]n. 8. Nathl., ld. Crewe, bp. of Durham, re-sw.

[J]uly 17. Wm., E. of Powis, cr. M. of Powis next year.

He was cr. M. of Montgomery and D. of Powis by the king after his abdication, but these titles were never allowed in England.

Hy., ld. Arundel, of Wardour, sw. ld. pr. seal, Mar. 1687.

John, ld. Belasyse.

Hy., ld. Dover.

[O]ct. 8. Richd., E. of Tyrconnell, ld. lieut. of Ireland.

Roger, E. of Castlemaine, amb. to the pope.

[O]ct. 14. Wm., D. of Hamilton.

Sir Nichs. Butler.

[N]ov. 11. Edwd. Petre.

Many of the lords and gentlemen sworn of the council in this reign were Roman Catholics.

WILLIAM and MARY.

Upon the accession of their majesties the following persons were sworn of the privy council.

1689.

[F]eb. 14. Hy., D. of Norfolk, earl marsh. and hered. marsh. of England.

Chas., M. of Winchester, cr. D. of Bolton, Apr. this year.

Geo., M. of Halifax, made ld. pr. seal Feb. 19. *Struck from the list, June* 23, 1692.

Robt., E. of Lindsey, ld. gr. chambn. of England.

Wm., E. of Devonshire, ld. stewd., cr. M. of Hartington and D. of Devonshire, May 1694.

Chas., E. of Dorset, ld. chambn.

Aubrey, E. of Oxford.

Chas., E. of Shewsbury, sec. st. *Struck from the list, June* 23, 1692.

Wm., E. of Bedford, cr. M. of Tavistock and D. of Bedford, May 12, 1684.

Chas., E. of Macclesfield.

Thos., visc. Fauconberg.

Chas., visc. Mordaunt, first commr. treasy., Apr. following; cr. E. of Monmouth, same time. *Struck from the list, Jan.* 21, 1696.

Fras., visc. Newport, treasr. hhold., cr. E. of Bradford, May 1694.

Richd., lord Lumley (visc. Lumley, in Ireland), gent. bed-ch., cr. visc. Lumley, of England, Apr. following, and E. of Scarborough, Apr. 1690.

Feb. 14. Hy. Compton, bp. of London, dean of the chapel.

Ralph, ld. Montagu, mast. gr. wardr.; cr. visc. Monthermer and E. of Montagu, Apr. this year; D. of Montagu, Apr. 1705.

Hy., ld. de la Mere, ch. ex.; cr. E. of Warrington, Apr. 1690.

John, ld. Churchill, gen.; cr. E. of Marlborough, Apr. 1689. *Struck from the list, June* 23, 1692. Aft. cr. M. of Blandford and D. of Marlborough. *See year* 1698.

Wm. Bentinck, gr. stole, cr. ld. Cirencester, visc. Woodstock, and E. of Portland, Apr. 1689.

Hy. Sydney, gent. bed-ch., cr. ld. and visc. Sydney, Apr. 1689; ld. lieut. of Ireland in 1692; E. of Romney, May 1694.

Sir Robt. Howard.

Sir Hy. Capel, commr. treasy., cr. ld. Capel, Apr. 1692; aft. ld. dep. in Ireland.

Hy. Powle, sp. ho. commons.

Edwd. Russell, adm., first ld. admy., May, 1614; cr. ld. Shingay, visc. Barfleur, and E. of Orford, May 1697.

Richd. Hampden, commr. treasy.

Hugh Boscawen, cr. lord Boscawen and visc. Falmouth, June, 1720.

Feb. 19. Thos. Wharton, aft. ld. Wharton, compt. hhold.; cr. visc. Winchendon and E. of Wharton Dec. 1706, and visc. Malmesbury and M. of Wharton, Jan. 1715; ld. pr. seal, 1714. In 1709, he was app. ld. lieut. of Ireland, of which kingdom he became baron of Trim, E. of Rathfarnham, and M. of Catherlogh.

Sir John Lowther, of Lowther, bt., v. chamb.; cr. ld. Lowther and visc. Lonsdale, May, 1696; ld. pr. seal, May 1699.

Feb. 26. Arthur Herbert, first commr. admy., cr. ld. Torbay and E. of Torrington, May following. *Struck from the list, June* 23, 1692.

Mar. 8. Wm. Harbord, amb. to Turkey in 1692.

Apr. 25. Fredk., D. of Schomberg, field-marsh.; mast. gen. ordn.

Sep. 26. Sir John Holt, bt., ld. ch. just. k. b.

Oct. 14. Thos., E. of Pembroke and Montgomery, first commr. admy., Jan. 1690; ld. pr. seal, Mar. 1692; ld. pres., May 18, 1699; and *again* ld. pres., July 9, 1702.

1690.

Feb. 13. Sir Hy. Goodricke, bt., lieut. gen. ordn.

June 3. Chas., M. of Winchester, cr. D. of Bolton, Feb. 1698.

Nov. 20. Sidney, ld. Godolphin, first commr. treasy., ld. treasr. in 1702; cr. visc. Rialton and E. of Godolphin, Dec. 1706.

1691.

Jan. 1. Sir John Trevor, sp. ho. commons, prev. and subs. m. rolls.

May 7. John, E. of Bridgewater.

June 4. John Tillotson, abp. of Canterbury.

1692.

Mar. 1. Laurence, E. of Rochester, ld. lieut. of Ireland, in 1701.

Richd., E. of Ranelagh, paym. of the forces.

Chas., ld. Cornwallis, first commr. admy.

Sir Edwd. Seymour, bt., commr. treasy.

Mar. 17. Anthy., visc. Falkland, commr. admy.

Robt., ld. Lexinton.

1693.

Mar. 23. Sir John Somers, ld. kpr.; cr. ld. Somers and made ld. chanc., Dec. 1697.

Sir John Trenchard, sec. st.

Apr. 13. Thos., ld. Coningsby, of Ireland, late ld. just. in that kingdom; aft. ld. Coningsby, of Lincoln, and E. of Coningsby. *Struck from the list, Nov.* 7, 1724.

1694.

Mar. 4. Chas., E. of Shrewsbury, sec. st.; cr. M. of Alton and D. of Shrewsbury, Apr. following.

May 3. John, M. of Normanby. *Struck from the list, Mar.* 12, 1695.

Chas., visc. Dursley, succ. as E. Berkeley.

May 10. Thos., E. of Stamford.

Chas. Montague, ch. ex., first ld. treasy., May 1697; cr. ld. Halifax, Dec. 1700.

King William III., alone.

1695.

Jan. 31. Thos. Tennyson, abp. of Cant[e]bury.

May 3. Sir Wm. Trumbull, sec. st.

May 5. Meinhardt, D. of Schomber[g], comm. in ch.

Ford, E. of Tankerville, aft. fi[rst] commr. treasy. and ld. pr. se[al].

Peregrine Bertie, v. chambn.

May 23. John Smith, commr. treasy., a[ft.] ch. ex. and sp. ho. commons.

1696.

Apr. 9. Jas., D. of Ormond, aft. com[m.] in ch.

Nov. 19. Sir Jos. Williamson, app., wi[th] the E. of Pembroke and vis[c.] Villiers, plen. to treat for pea[ce] with France.

1697.

Nov. 25. Edwd., E of Jersey, app. [l.] just. of Ireland; aft. ld. chamb[n.] to the king; sec. st. 1700.

Dec. 5. Jas. Vernon, sec. st.

1698.

May 18. Robt., ld. Ferrers, cr. visc. Ta[m]worth and E. Ferrers, Ju[ne] 1711.

June 9. Chas., E. of Manchester, cr. D. [of] Manchester, Apr. 1719.

June 19. John, E. of Marlborough, cr. [M.] of Blandford and D. of Ma[rl]borough, Dec. 1702. His nar[me] had been removed from the li[st] of pr. councillors, June 2[?] 1692; but it was now restore[d] and he re-sworn. *See year* 168[?]

1700.

May 21. Sir Nathan Wright, ld. kpr.

Nov. 5. Sir Chas. Hedges, sw. a seco[nd] time; sec. st., May 2, 1702.

1701.

Mar. 27. Hy. Boyle, ch. ex.; sec. st., Fe[b.] 1708.

June 19. Robt., E. of Lindsey, ld. g[reat] chambn. of England; cr. M. [of] Lindsey, Dec. 1706, and D. [of] Ancaster and Kesteven, Ju[ly] 1715.

Chas., E. of Carlisle, earl mars[hal] during minority of Thos., D. [of] Norfolk, the hered. earl mars[hal] of England.

June 28. Chas., D. of Somerset, ld. pres.

1702.

Jan. 1. Chas. Bodville, E. of Radnor.

Jan. 8. Chas., E. of Burlington.

QUEEN ANNE.

1702.

Apr. 21. John, M. of Normanby, ld. pr. seal; cr. D. of Buckinghamsh. and D. of Normanby, Mar. 1703.
Montagu, E. of Abingdon, const. T. Lond.
Sir John Leveson Gower, chanc. d. Lanc.; cr. ld. Gower, of Sittenham, Mar. 1703.
John How, aft. joint paym. gen. of the forces.
May 2. Danl., E. of Nottingham sec. st.
May 21. Geo., E. of Northampton.
June 18. Thos., visc. Weymouth.
Wm., ld. Dartmouth, cr. visc. Lewisham and E. of Dartmouth, Sept. 1711.
Hon. John Granville, ld. wden. stanns.; cr. ld. Granville, Mar. 1703.
Sir Thos. Trevor, ch. just. c. p.; cr. ld. Trevor, of Bromham, Dec. 1711.
Nov. 19. Sir Geo. Rooke, v. adm. of England.
Dec. 10. John, ld. Poulett, cr. visc. Hinton and E. Poulett, Dec. 1706.

1703.

Mar. 20. John Sharp, abp. of York.
Thos., E. of Thanet.
Heneage, ld. Guernsey; cr. E. of Aylesford, Oct. 1714, and made chanc. d. Lanc.

1704.

Apr. 27. Hy., E. of Kent, ld. chambn.; cr. visc. Goderick, E. of Harold, and M. of Kent, Dec. 1706.
Robt. Harley, sp. ho. commons; sec. st., May following; cr. E. of Oxford and E. Mortimer, May 1711.
Thos. Mansell, compt. hhold.; cr. ld. Mansell, Dec. 1711.

1705.

Mar. 29. John, D. of Newcastle, ld. pr. seal.
Chas., E. of Peterborough, gen.
Hugh, visc. Cholmondeley, in Ireland, cr. visc. Malpas and E. of Cholmondeley, Dec. 1706; aft. treasr. hhold.
May 3. Thos. Erle, lt. gen. ordn.
Oct. 11. Wm. Cowper, ld. kpr.; cr. ld. Cowper, of Wingham, and E. Cowper; ld. chanc., May 1711.

1706.

June 10. Thos., E. of Derby, chanc. d. Lanc.
Dec. 3. Chas., E. of Sunderland, sec. st., appd. ld. lieut. of Ireland in 1714, *but never went over*; first ld. treasy., Mar. 1718.
Dec. 5. Thos. Coke, v. chambn.; aft. ld. Lovel, visc. Coke, and E. of Leicester.

1707.

Sept. 8. Wm., D. of Devonshire, ld. st. hhold.

1708.

June 26. Evelyn, M. of Dorchester, cr. D. of Kingston, July 1715.
Hy., E. of Bindon, dep. earl marsh. of England; first ld. tr., 1715.
Aug. 18. John, E. of Mar, sec. st. for Scotland.
Chas., visc. Townshend, aft. sec. st.
Oct. 6. Jas., D. of Queensbury, now sec. st. for Scotland.
Jas., E. of Seafield, late ld. high treasr. for Scotland; succ. as E. of Findlater; last ld. chanc. of Scotland.
Nov. 25. Jas., D. of Montrose, late ld. high adm. of Scotland.
Richd., E. Rivers, gen.
Algernon, E. of Essex.
Hugh, E. of Loudoun, one of the commrs. for the union with Scotland; ld. kpr. in that kingdom.

1709.

Feb. 3. John, D. of Argyle (Argyll), genl. cr. bar. of Chatham and E. of Greenwich, Nov. 1705, and D. of Greenwich, Apr. 1719.
Mar. 3. John, D. of Roxburgh.
June 2. Sir John Holland, compt. hhold.
Nov. 8. Edwd., E. of Orford.

1710.

Feb. 18. Richd., E. of Bradford.
Mar. 30. Sir Thos. Parker, ld. ch. just. q. b.; cr. ld. Parker, Mar. 1716, and made ld. chanc., May 1718; visc. Parker and E. of Macclesfield, Nov. 1721. *Struck from the list, May* 31, 1725, having previously (Jan. 4, 1725) surr. the seal.
June 15. Sir Richd. Onslow, bt., sp. ho. commons; ch. ex., Oct. 1714.
July 10. John, E. of Anglesey, v. treasr. in Ireland; *d.* Sept. following.
Sept. 21. Hy. St. John, late sec. at war, now sw. sec. st.; aft. ld. St. John, of Battersea, and visc. St. John and visc. Bolingbroke.
Oct. 19. Sir Simon Harcourt, ld. kpr.; cr. ld. Harcourt, of Stanton-Harcourt; ld. chanc. in 1713; visc., Sept. 1721.
Hy., ld. Hyde, joint v. treasr. of Ireland; succ. as E. of Clarendon and Rochester, in 1723.

Oct. 19. Arthur, E. of Anglesey, brother of the late John, made joint v. treasr. of Ireland in his room.

1711.

Feb. 9. Chas., E. of Orrery, app. env. ex. to the States General, and to the council of state in the Low Countries.

Mar. 1. Geo., E. of Orkney, gen.

Apr. 19. Wm., M. of Annandale, ld. high commr. to the kirk of Scotland; ld. kpr. pr. seal in that kingdom in 1715.

June 14. Chas., E. of Winchilsea; *d.* the next year.

Robt Benson, ch. ex.; cr. ld. Bingley, July 1713; sent amb. to Spain.

Hy. Paget, capt. yeom. gd.; cr. ld. Burton, *vitâ patris*, Dec. following; succ. his father as ld. Paget, 1713; cr. E. of Uxbridge, 1714.

June 23. Thos., ld. Raby, amb. to the States General; cr. visc. Wentworth and E. of Strafford, Sept. following; first ld. admy., Sept. 1712.

Wm. Bromley, sp. ho. commons; aft. sec. st.

Sept. 3. John Robinson, bp. of Bristol, ld. pr. seal; tr. to London; plen. at Utrecht.

Dec. 13. Edwd., E. of Clarendon.

Archd., E. of Islay, ld. just. gen. of Scotland; succ. his brother as D. of Argyle (Argyll), Oct. 1743.

Wm., ld. North and Grey, made gov. of Portsmouth.

1712.

Apr. 17. John, D. of Atholl, extry. ld. of sess.; comm. in ch. of all the land forces in Scotland.

Aug. 18. Geo., ld. Lansdowne of Bideford, treasr hhold.

Oct. 20. David, E. of Portmore, gen., gov. of Gibraltar.

John Hill, brigadier, lieut. gen. ordn.

Dec. 11. Fras., ld. Guilford.

1713.

Apr. 7. Geo., D. of Northumberland.

Sir John Stonehouse, bt., compt. hhold.

Nov. 1. Sir Wm. Wyndham, bt., ch. ex.

KING GEORGE I.

1714.

Sept. 22. GEO. pr. cf WALES (aft. George II.), introd., not sw.

Sept. 22. Sir Wm. Dawes, bt., abp. o York.

Sept. 27. Jas. Stanhope, sec. st., first ld treasy., &c., Apr. 1717; cr. ld. and visc. Stanhope, July 1717 and E. Stanhope, Apr. 1718.

Oct. 1. Robt. Walpole, aft. sir R., paym. of the forces; cr. ld. Houghton, visc. Walpole, and E. of Orford, Feb. 1742. Filled various offices in the state, and was upwards of twenty-one years prime minister.

Oct. 29. John, E. of Stair, ambass. to France.

Paul Methuen, commr. of the treasy., amb. to Spain; sec. st., July 1716.

Nov. 16. Lionel, E. of Dorset, ld. wden. of Cinque Ports, and gov. of Dover castle; decl. ld. pres., Jan. 1715; D. of Dorset, June 1720.

Hy., E. of Uxbridge, capt. yeom. gd.

Nov. 22. Hy., ld. Carleton, decl. ld. pres. June 25, 1721.

1715.

Mar. 29. Sir Peter King, ld. ch. just. c. p., cr. ld. King, and made ld. chanc., June 1, 1725.

Aug. 31. Chas., D. of Grafton, app. ld. just. Ireland.

Sept. 23. Hy., E. of Galway, app. ld. just. Ireland.

Oct. 26. Jas., E of Derby, capt. yeom. gd.

Hy., E. of Lincoln, paym. forces.

1716.

Jan. 20. Wm. Wake, abp. of Canterbury.

July 6. Chas., E. of Tankerville.

Richd., ld. Cobham, const. of Windsor Castle, and kpr. of the parks, forests, and warrens there; cr. visc. Cobham, May 17 8.

Spencer Compton, sp. ho. commons; cr. ld. Wilmington, Jan. 1728; and visc. Pevensey and E. of Wilmington, May 1730; decl. ld. pres., Dec. 31, same year; first ld. treasy., Feb. 1742.

Wm. Pulteney, sec. at war. *Struck from the list July*, 1, 1731. *See year* 1742.

July 12. John Aislabie, treasr. navy; ch. ex., Mar. 1718. *Struck from the list* some time between Sept. 13, 1720, and May 21, 1722.

1717.

Mar. 2. John Smith, tell. ex.
Mar. 30. Thos., ld. Torrington, commr. treasy.
Wm., ld. Cadogan, gen. of all H. M.'s foot forces; cr. E. of Cadogan, May 1718.
Apr. 16. Thos. Pelham Holles, D. of Newcastle, ld. chambn.; filled various high offices in the state; first ld. treasy., Mar. 18, 1754.
Thos., E. of Westmoreland, ch. just. in eyre of H. M.'s forests south of the Trent; first commr. of tr. and plant., May 1719.
Jas., E. of Berkeley, first ld. admy.
Jos. Addison, sec. st.
July 31. Sir Jos. Jekyll, m. rolls.
Nov. 27. Geo., E. of Halifax.

1718.

Feb. 13. Robt., E. of Holdernesse, first commr. of tr. and plant.
Mar. 16. Jas. Craggs, jun., sec. st.
Mar. 31. Richd. Hampden, treasr. navy.
July 1. Sir Nichs. Lechmere, att.-gen.; made chanc. d. Lanc.; cr. ld. Lechmere, Aug. 1721.
Oct. 9. Sir John Pratt, ld. ch. just. k. b.

1719.

May 9. Chas. Wills, lt. gen. ordn.

1720.

Mar. 22. Wm., E. of Coventry.

1721.

Jan. 3. John, E. of Sutherland.
Sir Geo. Byng, adm.; cr. ld. Byng, of Southill, and visc. Torrington, Sept. following.
Mar. 5. John, ld. Carteret, sec. st.; app. ld. lieut. of Ireland, 1724; succ. as E. Granville, Oct. 1744; ld. pres., June 17, 1751.
Nov. 11. Jas., D. of Chandos.
David, E. of Portmore.
Chas., ld. Cornwallis, late joint postm. gen.; *d.* the next year.

1722.

May 9. Sir Robt. Sutton, amb. successively to Constantinople, to Holland, and to France.

1723.

May 26. Fras., E. of Godolphin, gr. stole.
Edmd. Gibson, bp. of London.
May 29. Jas., E. of Findlater.

1724.

Jan. 23. Peregrine, D. of Ancaster and Kesteven, ld. gr. chambn. of England.
Dec. 10. Lancelot Blackburn, abp. of York.

1725.

Apr. 12. Sir Robt. Raymond, ld. ch. just, k. b.; cr. ld. Raymond, Jan. 1731.
June 1. Chas., D. of Bolton, const. T. Lond.
Danl., ld. Finch, compt. hhold.; succ. as E. of Winchilsea and Nottingham on his father's decease in 1730; ld. pres. July 12, 1765.
Sir Robt. Eyre, ld. ch. just. c. p.
Hy. Pelham, sec. at war.; paym. gen. in 1730; first ld. treasy., Aug. 1743. Mr. Pelham was the head of the celebrated "*Broad-Bottom*" administration.

1726.

Mar. 11. Thos., ld. Trevor, ld. pr. seal.
May 31. Chas., D. of Queensberry and Dover, v. adm. of Scotland.
Alexr., E. of Marchmont.
Nov. 4. Hy., visc. Lonsdale, const. T. Lond.

1727.

May 31. Wm. Stanhope, v. chambn.; cr. ld. Harrington, Dec. 1729; ld. pres., Feb. 13, 1742.

King George II.

1727.

June 15. Richd., E. of Scarborough, m. horse.
July 5. Hy., E. of Grantham, ld. chambn. to the queen.
July 17. John, D. of Rutland, chanc. d. Lanc.
Aug. 5. Talbot, E. of Sussex, dep. earl marsh.

1728.

Feb. 26. Philip, E. of Chesterfield, app. amb. to France; ld. lieut. of Ireland, 1745.
June 25. Arthur Onslow, sp. ho. commons.
Dec. 18. Fredk., prince of Wales, introd., not sw.

1729.

May 15. Richd., E. of Burlington, aft. capt. gent. pens.

1730.

May 8. John, ld. Hervey, v. chambn.; cr., *vitâ patris*, ld. Hervey, of Ickworth, June 1733.

June 11. Robt. ld. Bingley, treasr. hhold.
Sir Conyers D'Arcy, compt. hhold.
Sir Wm. Strickland, bt., sec. at war.

Sept. 12. Horatio Walpole, coffr. hhold.; cr. ld. Walpole, of Woolterton, June 1756.

1731.

June 12. Wm., D. of Devonshire, ld. pr. seal; ld. lieut. of Ireland in 1737.
John, ld. de la Warr, treasr. hhold.

Nov. 29. John, E. of Leicester, const. T. Lond.

1732.

May 4. Hon. Pattee Byng, treasr. navy; succ. his father as visc. Torrington, Jan. 1733.

1733.

Jan. 25. Sir Chas. Wager, adm.; first ld. admy.

Nov. 1. Chas., E. of Selkirk, ld. clk. reg. of Scotland.
Sir Philip Yorke, ld. ch. just. k. b.; cr. ld. Hardwicke, Nov. 23 following, and E. of Hardwicke, Apr. 1754; ld. chanc. Feb. 21, 1737. He continued, it is said, ch. just. until June 7, though he had kissed hands for the great seal.

Nov. 29. Chas. Talbot, ld. chanc.; cr. ld. Talbot, Dec. 5, following.

1734.

Jan. 31. Jas., D. of Atholl, ld. kpr. gr. seal of Scotland.

1735.

Jan. 9. Chas., D. of Richmond, m. horse.
Hy., E. of Pembroke, gr. stole.

Feb. 12. Wm., E. of Essex, aft. capt yeom. gd.
Jas., E. of Waldegrave, v. adm. of Essex.
Stephen Poyntz, recr. gen. of excise. He res. this office to his brother, Wm. Poyntz.
Benjn., E. Fitzwalter, first commr. of tr. and plant.

Nov. 6. Sir Wm. Yonge, bt., sec. at war.

1736.

Jan. 22. John, D. of Montagu, capt. gent. pens.

Feb. 19. Sir Thos. Reeve, ld. ch. just. c. p.; *d.* Jan. the next year.

May 21. Geo., E. of Cholmondeley, chanc d. Lanc.

1737.

Mar. 17. John Potter, abp. of Canterbury.
Sir John Willes, ld. ch. just. c. p.

July 21. John, lord Monson, first commr. of tr. and plant.
Sir Wm. Lee, ld. ch. just. k. b.

1738.

July 20. Jas., E. of Abercorn, ld. bed-ch.

Oct. 12. Hon. John Verney, m. rolls; *d.* Aug. 1741.

1739.

Sept. 6. Sir John Norris, v. adm. of England.

1740.

May 1. Lord Sidney Beauclerk, v. chambn. hhold.

May 12. Chas., ld. Cornwallis, const. T. Lond.; cr. E. Cornwallis, June 1753.

1741.

Apr. 27. Thos. Winnington, commr. treasy.; cr. a bt.; made paym. forces.

Nov. 19. Wm. Fortescue, m. rolls.

1742.

Feb. 16. John, M. of Tweeddale, sec. st. for Scotland.
Saml. Sandys, ch. ex.; cr. ld. Sandys, Dec. 1743; coffr. hhold, 1747; ch. just. in eyre, 1759; first ld. of tr. and plant, Mar. 1761.

Feb. 20. Peregrine, D. of Ancaster and Kesteven (son of Peregrine, pr. councr., Jan. 1724), ld. gr. chambn. of England.
Wm. Pulteney, whose name had been struck from the council, July 1731, now rest. Cr. E. of Bath, July 1742. *See year* 1716. First minister as head of the "*Short-lived*" administration, which endured but two days.

May 17. Wm., D. of Cumberland, introd., not sw.

June 24. Geo. Wade, lt. gen. ordn.; aft. field-marsh. and comm. in ch.
Thos. Clutterbuck, treasr. navy.

July 13. John, ld. Gower, ld. pr. seal; cr. E. Gower, July 1746.
Allen, ld. Bathurst, capt. gent. pens.; cr. E. Bathurst, Aug. 1772.
Hon. Wm. Finch, v. chambn. hhold.

1743.

Apr. 25. Thos. Herring, abp. of York; tr. to Canterbury.

1744.

Jan. 5. Richd., ld. Edgcumbe, chanc. d. Lanc.

Jan. 19. Sir John Rushout, bt., treasr. navy.

Dec. 17. John, D. of Bedford, first ld. admy.; ld. lieut. of Ireland, Sept. 1757; ld. pr. seal, Nov. 1761; ld. pres., Sept. 9, 1763.

1745.

Jan. 3. John, ld. Hobart, capt. gent. pens.; cr. E. of Buckinghamshire, Aug. 1746.

Geo. Dodington, treasr. navy; *again*, Jan. 1756; cr. ld. Melcombe, Apr. 1761.

1746.

Wm. Pitt, paym. gen. of the forces; sec. st., Dec. 1756; *again* sec., June, 1757; cr. E. of Chatham, and made ld. pr. seal, July 1766.

July 23. Hy. Fox, sec. at war; sec. st., Nov. 1755; paym. gen. of the forces, 1757; cr. ld. Holland, Apr. 1763.

1747.

Jan. 15. Wm., E. of Jersey.

1748.

Feb. 10. Matthew Hutton, abp. of York; tr. to Canterbury.

1749.

Jan. 11. Geo. Dunk, E. of Halifax, first commr. of tr. and plant.; ld. lieut. of Ireland, 1761; first ld. admy., June 1762; sec. st., Nov. 1763; ld. pr. seal, Feb. 1770; *again* sec. st., Jan. 1771.

Thos. Sherlock, bp. of London.

Feb. 1. John, E. of Sandwich, late min. plen. to the congress at Aix-la-Chapelle, first ld. admy.; sec. st., 1763; *again* first ld. admy., Jan. 1771.

Sir John Ligonier, lieut. gen. ordn.; cr. visc. Ligonier, in Ireland, Dec. 1757; ld. Ligonier, of Ripley, Apr. 1763; and E. Ligonier, Sept. 1766. Field-marsh. and comm. in ch., 1757.

June 12. Chas., D. of Marlborough, ld. st. hhold.

June 28. Hon. Hy. Bilson Legge, treasr. navy; ch. ex. Apr. 1754; *again*, Nov. 1756.

1750.

Jan. 17. Sir John Strange, m. rolls.

Mar. 29. John, E. of Hyndford, late min. to the empress of Russia.

Geo., ld. Anson, v. adm. of England; first ld. admy., June 1751; *again*, July 1757.

Sir Thos. Robinson, dep. master of the gr. wardr.; sec. st., Apr. 1754; cr. ld. Grantham, Apr. 1761.

1751.

Apr. 30. Simon, E. Harcourt; aft. env. to Mecklenburg, France, &c.; ld. lieut. of Ireland, Nov. 1772.

June 21. Robt., E. of Holdernesse, sec. st.

July 12. Wm., M. of Hartington, m. horse. Called to the house of peers, *vitâ patris*, as ld. Cavendish, same time; ld. lieut. of Ireland, 1755; succ. as D. of Devonshire on his father's decease, Dec. 1755; first ld. treasy. 1756. *Struck from the list, Nov.* 3, 1762.

Wm. Anne, E. of Albemarle, gr. stole.

1752.

Feb. 13. John, ld. Berkeley, of Stratton, late capt. yeom. gd., treasr. hhold., 1755.

Sir Geo. Lee, judge prerog. court.

Dec. 20. Jas., E. of Waldegrave, gov. to the pr. of Wales.

1754.

June 21. Wills, E. of Hillsborough, comptr. hhold., first ld. of trade, Sept. 1763; *again* Aug. 1766; joint postm. gen. Dec. 1766; and *again* ld. of trade, Jan. 1768; cr. E. of Hillsborough, in England, Aug. 1772; and M. of Downshire, in Ireland, Aug. 1789.

Hon. Geo. Grenville, treasr. navy; *again* treasr. navy, Nov. 1756; first ld. admy., Jan. 1763; first ld. treasy. Apr. following.

Sir Dudley Ryder, ld. ch. just. k. b.

Sir Thos. Clarke, m. rolls.

Sir Geo. Lyttelton, bt., coffr. hhold.; ch. ex., Nov. 1755; cr. ld. Lyttelton, Nov. 1756.

1755.

Jan. 9. Harry, D. of Bolton.

John, E. of Egmont, joint postm. gen., Aug. 1762; first ld. admy., Sept. 1763.

Mar. 11. Wm. Hy., E. of Rochford, gr. stole.

Wm., visc. Barrington, mast. gr. wardr.; sec. at war, Nov. same year; ch. ex., Mar. 1761; treasr. navy, June 1762; *again* sec. at war, July 1765.

Dec. 22. Granville, E. Gower, ld. pr. seal; ld. pres., Dec. 22, 1767; *again*, Dec. 19, 1783; cr. M. of Stafford, Feb. 1786.

1756.

Jan. 27. John, ld. Hobart, compt. hhold.; succ. as E. of Buckinghamshire on his father's decease, Sept. following; amb. to Russia, July 1762; ld. lieut. of Ireland, Jan. 1777.

July 7. Robt., ld. Raymond.

Nov. 19. Richd., E. Temple, first ld. admy.; ld. pr. seal, June following.

John, visc. Bateman, treasr. hhold.

Wm., ld. Mansfield, ld. ch. just. k. b.

Hon. Richd. Edgcumbe, compt. hhold.; succ. as ld. Edgcumbe on the death of his father in 1758.

Dec. 15. Hugh, visc. Falmouth, capt. yeom. gd.

1757.

Mar. 26. Thos., D. of Leeds, coffr. hhold.

Apr. 1. Hon. Chas. Townshend, treasr. of the chamber and a ld. of tr. and plant.; paym. gen. of the forces, Mar. 1761, and ch. ex., Aug. 1766.

June 30. John Gilbert, abp. of York.

Sir Robt. Henley, ld. kpr., cr. ld. Henley, Mar. 1760; made ld. chanc., Jan. 1761; and E. of Northington, May following; ld. pres., July 30, 1766.

July 8. Percy Wyndham, E. of Thomond, treasr. hhold.

1758.

Jan. 27. Lord Geo. Sackville (Germaine). *Struck from the list*, *Apr.* 25, 1760. *See Dec.* 1765.

Thos., visc. Dupplin, chanc. d. Lanc.; succ. as E. of Kinnoul on his father's decease, June following.

May 8. Thos. Secker, abp. of Canterbury.

Dec. 22. Chas. Paulett, M. of Winchester, succ. as D. of Bolton on his father's decease, Oct. 1759.

1759.

Feb. 2. Hon. Edwd. Boscawen, adm., ld. admy., and gen. of marines.

Dec. 15. Robt. Nugent, ld. treasy.; cr. ld. Nugent and visc. Clare, of Ireland, Dec. 1766; and E. Nugent, 1776.

1760.

Feb. 9. Basil, E. of Denbigh, aft. ld. bed-ch.

Mar. 20. Welbore Ellis, joint v. treas. in Ireland; sec. at war, Dec. 1762; and aft. filled various offices, that of sec. st., Feb. 1782; cr. ld. Mendip, Aug. 1794.

May 2. John, M. of Granby, lieut. gen. ordn., aft. mast. gen.; comm. in ch., Aug. 1766.

King George III.

1760.

Oct. 27. Edwd., D. of York, introd., not sworn.

John, E. of Bute, gr. stole; sec. st., Mar. 1761; first ld. treasy., May 1762.

Dec. 2. Fras., E. of Huntingdon, m. horse.

Hon. Geo. Townshend, gen.; lieut. gen. ordn., 1763; succ. as visc. Townshend, Mar. 1764; ld. lieut. of Ireland, Oct. 1767; mast. gen. ordn., 1772; M. of Townshend, Oct. 1787.

Dec. 17. Philip, visc. Royston, succ. as E. of Hardwicke, Mar. 1764.

1761.

Jan. 28. Geo., E. of Albemarle, gov. of Jersey.

Mar. 17. Anthy., E. of Shaftesbury.

Mar. 20. Sir Fras. Dashwood, bt., treasr. of the chamber; ch. ex., May 1762; joint postm. gen., Dec. 1766; succ. to title of ld. Le Despencer, 1763.

Mar. 25. Wm., E. Talbot, ld. stewd. hhold.

Apr. 3. Hon. Jas. Grenville, coffr. hhold.; aft. joint v. treasr. of Ireland.

June 25. Hy. Arthur, E. of Powis, compt. hhold.

July 8. Chas., E. of Egremont; sec. st., Oct. following.

Sept. 4. Hon. Jas. Stuart Mackenzie, min. to Sardinia; ld. pr. seal of Scotland, 1763.

Nov. 7. Robt. Drummond, abp. of York.

Thos. Hayter, bp. of London: *d.* 1762.

1762.

Jan. 2. John, D. of Argyll.

Feb. 15. Lord Geo. Cavendish, compt. hhold.

Sir Chas. Pratt, ld. ch. just. c. p.; cr. ld. Camden, July 1765; ld. chanc., July 1766; ld. pres., Mar. 27, 1782; E. Camden, May 1786.

Mar. 13. Richd. Osbaldeston, bp. of London; *d.* 1764.

July 14. Geo. Hy., E. of Lichfield, capt. gent. pens.

Sir John Cust, bt., sp. ho. commons.

Gilbert Elliot, late ld. treasy.; treasr. of the chamber; succ. as bt. on his father's decease; treasr. navy, Mar. 1770.

Nov. 17. Jas., ld. Tyrawley, gen., late gov. of Gibraltar; field marsh., 1763.

Nov. 22. Geo., D. of Marlborough, ld. chamb. hhold.

Hugh, E. of Marchmont, kpr. gr. seal of Scotland, 1764.

Hugh, E. of Northumberland, queen's ld. chamb.; ld. lieut. of Ireland, 1763.

Nov. 26. Hans Stanley, ld. admy.

Dec. 15. Jas., ld. Strange, chanc. d. Lanc.

1763.

Jan. 10. Humphry Morrice, compt. hhold.

Sir John Phillips, bt.

Apr. 20. Wm., E. of Shelburne, first commr. of tr. and plant.; sec. st., Aug. 1766; first ld. treasy., July 1782; cr. M. of Lansdowne, Nov. 1784.

Lord Chas. Spencer, comptr. hhold.

Jas. Oswald, joint v. treasr. in Ireland.

Apr. 22. Stephen, E. of Ilchester, *honoris causâ.*

June 1. Fras., E. of Hertford, cr. E. of Yarmouth and M. of Hertford, July 1793.

July 20. David, visc. Stormont, amb. ext. to Germany; sec. st., Oct. 1779; ld. pres., Apr. 2, 1783; succ. as E. of Mansfield, Mar. 1793; *again* ld. pres., Dec. 1794.

Sept. 9. Thos., lord Hyde, joint postm. gen.; chanc. d. Lanc., June 1771; cr. E. of Clarendon, June 1776.

1764.

July 11. Richd. Terrick, bp. of London.

Dec. 12. Sir Thos. Sewell, m. rolls.

Dec. 19. Wm. Hy., D. of Gloucester, introd., not sworn.

1765.

May 29. Thos., visc. Weymouth, app. ld. lieut. of Ireland, but did not go over; sec. st. in 1768; *again* in 1775; cr. M. of Bath, Aug. 1789.

Lord Fredk. Campbell, kpr. pr. seal of Scotland.

July 10. Wm. Hy., D. of Portland, ld. chamb.; ld. lieut. of Ireland, 1782; first ld. treasy., Apr. 1783; ld. pres., July 30, 1801; *again* first ld. treasy., Mar. 1807.

Aug. Hy., D. of Grafton, sec. st.; first ld. of the treasy., Aug. 1766; first min. of the cr., Dec. 1767; ld. pr. seal, 1771.

Chas., M. of Rockingham, first ld. treasy.; *again*, Mar. 1782.

Hon. Hy. Seymour Conway, sec. st.; comm. in ch., 1782.

Wm. Dowdeswell, ch. ex.

July 12. Richd., E. of Scarborough, coffr. hhold.; app. dep. earl marsh. of England shortly afterwards.

John, E. of Ashburnham, kpr. gr. wardr.

Wm., E. of Besborough, joint postm. gen.

Geo. Bussy, visc. Villiers, v. chambn.; succ. as E. of Jersey on his father's decease, Aug. 1769.

July 26. Wm., E. of Dartmouth, first commr. of tr. and plant.; sec. st., Aug. 1772.

Richd., visc. Howe, treasr. navy; first ld. admy, Jan. 1783.; cr. earl Howe, July 1788.

Geo., ld. Edgcumbe, treasr. hhold.; cr. visc. Mount-Edgcumbe and Valletort, Mar. 1781; and E. of Mount-Edgcumbe, Aug. 1789.

Sept. 6. Thos. Pelham, compt. hhold.; succ. as ld. Pelham on the decease of his cousin, the D. of Newcastle, Nov. 1768; cr. E. of Chichester, June 1801.

Oct. 23. Chas., D. of Richmond, aft. sec. st.

Nov. 22. Ralph, earl Verney, of the kingdom of Ireland.

Dec. 20. Lord Geo. Sackville (his name, struck out in 1760, now rest.), app. a v. treasr. of Ireland; sec. st., Jan. 1776; took the name of Germaine on succeeding to the estates of lady Germaine; cr. visc. Sackville, Feb. 1782. *See* Jan, 1758.

1766.

Feb. 10. Chas., D. of Dorset, ld. lieut. of Kent.

May 12. John, E. of Breadalbane, kpr. of the pr. seal of Scotland.

Sept. 10. Sir John Eardley Wilmot, ld. ch. just. c. p.

Sir Chas. Saunders, first ld. admy.

Isaac Barré, a v. treasr. in Ireland; treasr. navy, Apr. 1782; paymr. of the forces, July same year.

Sept. 26. Geo. William, E. of Bristol, app. ld. lieut. of Ireland, but did not go over; ld. pr. seal, Nov. 1768.

Dec. 3. Hy. Fredk., D. of Cumberland, introd., not sworn.

John Shelley, aft. sir J., treasr. hhold.

Dec. 10. Harry, D. of Bolton, gov. of the Isle of Wight and of Carisbrook Castle.

Fredk., ld. North, joint paymr. of the forces; ch. ex., Dec. 1767; and first ld. treasy., Feb. 1770; succ. his father as E. of Guilford, Aug. 1790.

Sir Edwd. Hawke, first ld. admy.; cr. lord Hawke, May 1776.

1767.

Dec. 23. Thos. Townshend, jun., joint paym. of the forces; sec. at war, Mar. 1782; sec. st., July same year; cr. ld. Sydney, Mar. 1783; and visc., June 1789.

Geo. Onslow, ld. treasy.; cr. ld. Cranley, May 1776; and visc. Cranley and E. of Onslow, June 1801.

1768.

May 27. Hon. Thos. Harley, ld. mayor Lond.

June 29. Chas., ld. Cathcart, amb. to Russia.

Sir Jos. Yorke, amb. to the st. gen. at the Hague; cr. ld. Dover, Sept. 1788.

Oct. 7. Hon. Fredk. Cornwallis, abp. of Canterbury.

Dec. 16. Hy., D. of Newcastle, ld. lieut. of Notts, and kpr. of Sherwood forest.

1769.

Mar. 22. Sir Fletcher Norton, ch. just. in eyre; sp. ho. commons, Jan. 1770; cr. ld. Grantley, Mar. 1782.

Nov. 1. Sir Jas. Gray, bt., amb. ext. to Spain.

1770.

Jan. 17. Hon. Chas. Yorke, app. ld. chanc., and cr. lord Morden, but *d.* before the seals were put to his patent. He died on Jan. 20, having held the great seal but three days.

Jan. 19. Edwd., D. of Somerset.

Feb. 26. Hon. Thos. Robinson, v. chambn. to the queen; succ. as ld. Grantham, Sept. following; amb. to Spain, Feb. 1771; sec. st., July 1782.

May 4. Geo. Rice, treasr. chamb.; late a ld. of tr.

Nov. 21. Chas., earl Cornwallis, const. T. Lond.; cr. M. Cornwallis, Aug. 1792; gov. gen. of Bengal thrice, betw. Feb. 1786 and Oct. 1805; comm. in chief in India at the same time.

Dec. 19. Hon. Hy. Fredk. Thynne, joint postm. gen.; cr. ld. Carteret, Jan. 1784.

1771.

Jan. 22. Hy., E. of Suffolk and Berkshire, ld. pr. seal; sec. st. June following.

Jan. 23. Hy., ld. Apsley, ld. chanc.; succ. his father as earl Bathurst, Sept. 1775; decl. ld. pres., Nov. 1779. Ld. high stewd. of Gr. Britain for the trial of Eliz., duchess of Kingston, on an indictment for bigamy, Feb. 1776.

Feb. 6. John Montagu, visc. Hinchinbrook, v. chambn.; succ. his father as E. of Sandwich, Apr. 1792.

Sir Wm. de Grey, ld. ch. just. c. p.; cr. ld. Walsingham, Sept. 1780.

Mar. 1. Geo., E. of Pomfret, ranger of Windsor Little Park.

Oct. 9. Sir Lawrence Dundas, bt., v. adm. of Shetland and Orkney.

1772.

Nov. 6. Sir Jeffrey Amherst, lt. gen. ordn; cr. ld. Amherst, May 1776; comm. in ch., Mar. 1778.

Nov. 20. Sir Thos. Parker, late ld. ch. bar. ex.

1773.

Feb. 8. Chas. Jenkinson, joint v. treasr. of Ireland; clerk of the pells in Ireland, Aug. 1775; m. mint, Sept. 1776; sec. at war, Dec. 1778; cr. ld. Hawkesbury, July 1786; chanc. d. Lanc., and pres. bd. tr., same year; cr. E. of Liverpool, May 1796. He filled these and various other offices in the state from 1763 until 1804.

Aug. 4. Sir Wm. Lynch, min. to Sardinia.
Sept. 1. Sir John Goodricke, bt., late env. ext. to Sweden.

1774.

Mar. 9. Sir Wm. Meredith, comptr. hhold.
Jeremiah Dyson, coffr. hhold; filled various offices in the state.

1775.

May 12. Jas., D. of Chandos.
Nov. 17. Thos., ld. Lyttelton, warden, and ch. just. in eyre beyond Trent.

1776.

May 31. Thos. Bruce, ld. Bruce; cr. E. of Ailesbury, June 8 following.
June 5. Geo. Montagu, D. of Montagu, gov. to the pr. of Wales; m. horse, Dec. 1780.
Sept. 20. Hy. Flood, joint v. treasr. in Ireland. *Struck from the list by the king's own hand.*

1777.

Jan. 31. Wm. Markham, abp. of York.
June 13. Fredk., E. of Carlisle, treasr. hhold.; pres. bd. tr., Nov. 1779 ld. lieut. of Ireland, 1780.
Robt. Louth, bp. of London.
June 20. Chas. Townshend, joint v. treasr. in Ireland; cr. ld. Bayning, Oct. 1797.
Dec. 3. Sir Sidney Stafford Smythe, late ld. ch. bar. ex.
Dec. 24. Fras., M. of Carmarthen, chambn. of the queen consort's hhold.; succ. as D of Leeds on his father's decease, Mar. 1789.

1778.

June 3. Edwd., ld. Thurlow, ld. chanc.

1779.

Feb. 12. Robt., D. of Ancaster and Kesteven, ld. lieut. of Lincolnsh.; *d.* July 8, following. He was hered. ld. gr. chambn. of England, and on his death the office fell into abeyance, and remained in dispute for more than a year.
Aug 4. John, visc. Mountstuart, env. ext. to Sardinia; succ. his father as E. of Bute, Mar. 1792; cr. visc. Mountjoy, E. of Windsor, and M. of Bute, Feb. 1796.

1780.

Feb. 2. Fras., visc. Beauchamp, ld. treasy.
Feb. 9. Sir Richd. Worsley, bt., gov. of the Isle of Wight.
June 9. Alex. Wedderburn, ld. ch. just. c. p.; cr. ld. Loughborough; ld. chanc. of England, Jan. 1793; cr. E. of Rosslyn, Apr. 1801.
Sept. 27. Jas., E. of Salisbury, treasr. hhold; ld. chambn., Dec. 1783; cr. M. of Salisbury, Aug. 1789.
Nov. 8. Chas. Wolfran Cornewall, sp. ho. commons.

1782.

Jan. 9. Richd., E. of Shannon, joint. v. treasr. in Ireland.
Feb. 11. John, D. of Dorset.
Mar. 27. Lord John Cavendish, ch. ex.
Mar. 30. John Dunning, formerly sol.-gen.; cr. ld. Ashburton; chanc. d. Lanc.
Chas. Jas. Fox, sec. st. *Struck from the list May* 9, 1798. *See year* 1806.
Hon. Aug. Keppel, first ld. admy.; cr. visc. Keppel, Apr. 27, following.
Edmd. Burke, paym. forces.
Apr. 10. Geo., D. of Manchester, ld. chambn.
Thos., E. of Effingham, treasr. hhold; m. mint, Jan. 1784.
Peter, E. Ludlow, compt. hhold.
Sir Geo. Yonge, bt., joint v. treasr. in Ireland; sec. at war, July following.
Apr. 25. Geo., ld. de Ferrars, capt. gent. pens.; became M. of Townshend, 1807.
May 3. Geo., visc. Chewton, v. chambn. hhold; succ. on the death of his father as E. of Waldegrave, Oct. 1784.
June 5. Lord Robt. Spencer, a commr. of tr. and plant.
June 21. Hon. sir Wm. Howe, lt. gen. ordn.; succ. as visc. Howe, Aug. 1799.
July 10. Hon. Wm. Pitt, ch. ex.; first ld. treasy., Dec. 27, 1783; *again*, May 12, 1804, until his death, Jan. 23, 1806.
July 31. Geo., E. Temple, app. ld. lieut. of Ireland; sec. st., Dec. 1783; cr. M. of Buckingham, Nov. 1784; *again* ld. lieut. of Ireland in 1787.
Hy. Dundas, treasr. navy; *again*, Jan. 1784; home sec. June, 1791; col. sec. July, 1794; pres. bd. contr. from July,

1793, to May, 1801; cr. ld. Dunira and visc. Melville, Dec. 1802. *Struck from the list, May* 9, 1805. *See April*, 1807.

Oct. 2 Chas., E. of Tankerville, joint postm. gen.

1783.

Feb. 17. Chas., D. of Rutland, ld. stewd. hhold.

Apr. 7. Wm. Eden, late a ld. of tr., joint v. treasr. in Ireland; amb. to France in 1857; aft. to Spain, and to Holland; cr. ld. Auckland, Sept. 1789; joint postm. gen., Mar. 1798.

Apr. 9. Chas. Greville, treasr. hhold.

Apr. 14. Geo. Jas., E. of Cholmondeley, capt. yeom. gd.

Col., the hon. Richd. Fitzpatrick, sec. at war; lieut. gen. ordn., 1804; *again* sec. at war, Feb. 1806.

Fredk. Montagu, ld. treasy.

Apr. 30. John Moore, abp. of Canterbury.

Robt., E. of Northington, app. ld. lieut. of Ireland.

Aug. 29. Edwd., E. of Derby, chanc. d. Lanc.

GEO. AUGS. FREDK., pr. of WALES, aft. George IV.; introd., not sw.

Dec. 26. Jas. Grenville, a ld. of tr., Aug. 1786; cr. ld. Glastonbury, Oct. 1797.

Dec. 31. Heneage, E. of Aylesford, capt. yeom. gd.

Thos., ld. Walsingham, late a ld. of tr., joint. v. treasr. in Ireland; joint postm. gen., July, 1787. For twenty years chairman of the committees of the house of lords.

Wm. Wyndham Grenville, joint paym. gen., v. pres. bd. tr., Aug. 1786; sp. ho. commons, Jan. 1789; home sec., June same year, and pres. bd. contr. Mar. 1790; cr. ld. Grenville, Nov. 1790; for. sec., June 1791; first ld. treasy., Feb. 1806.

1784.

Jan. 7. Philip, E. of Chesterfield, amb. ext. to Spain; joint postm. gen., Mar. 1790; m. horse, Feb. 1798.

Feb. 9. Lord Geo. Lenox, const. T. Lond.

Apr. 2. Lloyd Kenyon, m. rolls, cr. a bt. this year; ld. ch. just. k. b. June, 1788, and cr. ld. Kenyon.

Apr. 16. Robt., visc. Galway, comptr. hhold.

Apr. 23. Constantine John, ld. Mulgrave, joint paym. gen.; a ld. of tr. and commr. bd. contr.

Aug. 20. Jas., E. of Courtown, treasr. hhold.

Sept. 3. Sir Jas. Harris, env. ext. to the States General; cr. ld. Malmesbury, Sept. 1788, and visc. Fitz-Harris and E. of Malmesbury, Dec. 1800; min. to several courts of Europe.

Nov. 17. Geo., ld. Herbert, v. chambn. hhold; succ. his father as E. of Pembroke, Feb. 1794.

1785.

Nov. 23. Thos. Orde (Powlett), sec. in Ireland; a ld. of tr Aug. 1786. Assumed the name of Powlett on the decease of the last D. of Bolton, 1794; cr. ld. Bolton, Oct. 1797.

1786.

Sept. 6. John Foster, sp. ho. commons of Ireland; cr. ld. Oriel, July 1821.

John Beresford, first commr. of rev. in Ireland.

Oct. 27. Sir John Parnell, bt., ch. ex. in Ireland.

1787.

Jan. 5. John Hely Hutchinson, sec. st. in Ireland. Held a plurality of appointments.

Feb. 19. John Chas. Villiers, compt. hhold.

Mar. 23. Sir John Skynner, ld. ch. bar. ex.

Aug. 8. FREDK., D. of YORK, introd., not sw.

Nov. 30. Alleyne Fitz-Herbert, ch. sec. Ireland, env. ext. to the Hague, May, 1789; cr. ld. St. Helen's of Ireland, 1791; and of England, July, 1801.

Dec. 7. Beilby Porteus, bp. of London.

1788.

June 18. Sir Richd. Pepper Arden, m. rolls, ld. ch. just. c. p., 1801; cr. ld. Alvanley, May, same year.

1789.

April 3. John, E. of Chatham, first ld. admy.; decl. ld. pres., Dec. 21, 1796; mast. gen. ordn., June, 1801; *again*, Apr., 1807.

Apr. 29. Sir Robt. Murray Keith, K.B., late amb. to Germany.

May 15. Sir Wm. Wynne, judge of the prerog. court, &c.; a ld. of tr. in 1790.

June 23. WM. HY., D. of CLARENCE, aft. William IV.; introd., not sw.

Hy. Addington, sp. ho. commons; first ld. treasy., Mar., 1801; cr. visc. Sidmouth, Jan. 1805; ld. pres., Jan. same year; ld. pr. seal, Feb., and *again* ld. pres., Oct. 1806; *a third time* ld. pres., Apr. 1812; home sec. from June 1812, to Jan. 1822.

Aug. 8. Jas., M. of Graham, v. pres. bd. tr., and, in Sept. following, joint paym. gen.; succ. as D. of Montrose, Sept. 1790; m. horse, Dec. same year.

Oct. 14. John, E. of Westmoreland, ld. lieut. of Ireland; ld. pr. seal, Feb. 1798; and *again*, Mar. 1807.

1790.

Mar. 3. Geo. Evelyn, visc. Falmouth, capt. gent. pens.

Hon. Dudley Ryder, compt. hhold., commr. bd. contr.; v. pres. bd. tr., Oct. 1790; treasr. navy, June 1800; succ. as ld. Harrowby, June 1803; chanc. d. Lanc., July 1805; cr. visc. Sandon and E. Harrowby, July 1809; pres. bd. contr., July, same year; decl. ld. pres., June 1812.

May 28. Geo. Granville Leveson, earl Gower, succ. his father as M. of Stafford, Oct. 1803.

Oct. 1. John, ld. Fitzgibbon, ld. chanc. of Ireland; cr. visc. Fitzgibbon, of Limerick, Dec. 1793; E. of Clare, June 1795; and ld. Fitzgibbon, of Sidbury, in the English peerage, Sept. 1799.

1791.

Mar. 9. Thos. Steele, joint paym. gen.; prev. sec. treasy., &c.

Apr. 21. Geo., visc. Parker, compt. hhold., succ. his father as E. of Macclesfield, Feb. 1795.

June 8. Sir Wm. Hamilton, K.B., amb. to Naples.

1792.

May 2. Geo., ld. Macartney, amb. to China; earl Macartney in Ireland, 1794.

June 15. Sir Jas. Eyre, ld. ch. bar. ex.; aft. ld. ch. just. c. p.

1793.

Feb. 15. Sir Archd. Macdonald, ld. ch. bar. ex.

May 1. Hon. Robt. Hobart, sec. in Ireland; col. sec., Mar. 1801; summoned to parlt. in his father's barony, *vitâ patris*, as ld. Hobart, 1798; succ. as E. of Buckinghamshire, Nov. 1804; joint postm. gen., Feb. 1806; pres. bd. contr., Apr. 1812.

June 21. Richd., E. of Mornington; gov. gen. of Bengal, Oct. 1797; cr. marq. Wellesley, Dec. 1799; for. sec., Dec. 1809; ld. lieut. of Ireland, Dec. 1821; ld. stewd., Nov. 1830; *again* ld. lieut. of Ireland, Sept. 1833; ld. chambn., Apr. 1835.

Hy., ld. Apsley, succ. his father as earl Bathurst, Aug. 1794; m. mint, July 1804; pres. bd. tr., Mar. 1807; for. sec., Oct. 1809; and col. sec. from June 1812, to Apr. 1827.

John Jeffreys, visc. Bayham, a commr. of tr.; succ. as earl Camden, Apr. 1794; ld. lieut. of Ireland, Mar. 1795; ld. pres., July 10, 1805; *again*, Mar. 26, 1807; cr. E. of Brecknock and marq. of Camden, Sept. 1812.

Sept. 25. Sir Gilbert Elliott, bt., viceroy of the kingdom of Corsica, June 1795; cr. ld. Minto, of Roxburgh, Oct. 1797; env. ext. to Germany, June 1799; pres. bd. contr., Feb. 1806; gov. gen. of Bengal, July, same year; cr. visc. Melgund and E. of Minto, Feb. 1813.

1794.

May 4. Sylvester Douglas, ch. sec. Ireland; commr. bd. contr., June 1795; ld. treasy., Feb. 1797; cr. ld. Glenbervie, Nov. 1800; joint paym. gen., Mar. 1801; v. pres. bd. tr., Nov., same year; surv. gen. of woods and forests, 1803; first commr. of woods and forests, July 1810.

July 11. Wm. Wentworth Fitzwilliam, E. Fitzwilliam, dec. ld. pres.; *again*, ld. pres., Oct. 19, 1805. He was app. ld. lieut. of Ireland, Dec. 1794; but was recalled

Mar. following, and succ. by ld. Camden.

July 11 Geo. John, earl Spencer, ld. pr. seal; ld. admy., Dec. same year; home sec., Feb. 1806.

July 16. Wm. Windham, sec. at war; sec. st. for war and cols., Feb. 1806.

Nov. 12. Sir Morton Eden, K.B., amb. to Germany, and prev. to several courts of Europe; cr. ld. Henley, Nov. 1799.

Dec. 17. Geo. Damer, visc. Milton, sec. for Ireland; succ. his father as E. of Dorchester, Feb. 1798.

1795.

Mar. 11. Hon. Thos. Pelham, sec. for Ireland; summoned to the house of peers, *vitâ patris*, as ld. Pelham, June 1801; home sec., July, same year; chanc. d. Lanc., Nov. 1803; succ. his father as E. of Chichester, Jan. 1805; postm. gen., May 1807.

July 29. Sir Geo. Howard, K.B., field marsh.; gov. of Jersey.

1796.

Apr. 29. Robt. Auriol Drummond, E. of Kinnoul.

Sir Grey Cooper, bt., some time sec. treasy.

Nov. 30. John, D. of Roxburgh, gr. stole.

1797.

Mar. 29. Sir Jos. Banks, bt., pres. of the Royal Society; app. a commr. bd. tr.

Apr. 26. Lord Chas. Somerset, compt. hhold.; joint paym. gen., July 1804; *again*, Apr. 1807.

June 28. John, D. of Athole.

Sept. 27. Hon. John Trevor, amb. to Sardinia.

Oct. 4. Sir Chas. Grey, K.B., gov. of Jersey; cr. ld. Grey, June 1801, and visc. Howick and E. Grey, Apr. 1806.

1798.

Sept. 28. Wm. Shaw, ld. Cathcart; cr. visc. Cathcart, Nov. 1807; and E. Cathcart, July 1814.

Oct. 24. Chas., E. of Harrington.

Oct. 31. Sir Wm. Scott, a commr. bd. tr.; judge of the high court of admy.; cr. ld. Stowell, July 1821.

Dec. 5. Thos. Grenville., ch. just. in eyre, July 1800; pres. bd. contr., July 1806; first ld. admy., Sept. same year.

Dec. 19. Robt., visc. Castlereagh, sec. in Ireland; pres. bd. contr., Sept. 1802 col. sec., July 1805; *again*, Mar. 1807; for. sec. from Mar. 1812, until his death, Aug. 1822; succ. his father as M. of Londonderry, Apr. 1821.

1799.

Jan. 23. Sir Wm. Fawcett, K.B., gen.

Mar. 13. Robt. Banks Jenkinson, ld. Hawkesbury, m. mint; for. sec., Feb. 1801; home sec., May 1804; summoned to the house of peers, *vitâ patris*, in his father's barony, Aug. 1806; *again* home sec., Mar. 1807; succ. as E. of Liverpool, Dec. 1808; col. sec., Dec. 1809; first ld. treasy. from June 1812 to Apr. 1827.

June 5. EDWD., D of KENT, introd., not sw.

ERNEST AUG., D. of CUMBERLAND, introd., not sw.

July 3. Thos., E. of Elgin, amb. to Turkey.

July 18. Sir John Scott, ld. ch. just. c. p.; cr. ld. Eldon; ld. chanc., Apr. 1801; *again*, Apr. 1807; cr. E. of Eldon, July 1821.

Sept. 25. Isaac Corry, ch. ex. in Ireland.

Oct. 30. Ralph, ld. Lavington, K.B., gov. of the Carribean islands.

1800.

May 28. Geo. Canning, joint paym. gen; for. sec., Mar. 1807; pres. bd contr., June 1816; *again* for sec., Sept. 1822; first ld. treasy April 1827

June 25. Wm. Dundas, commr. bd. contr.; sec. at war, May 1804.

Nov. 5. Chas., ld. Whitworth, late amb. to Russia; negociated a peace with Denmark, 1801; plen. to France, June 1802; cr. visc Whitworth, June 1813; ld. lieut. of Ireland, Aug. same year; cr. earl Whitworth, Nov 1815.

1801.

Jan. 25. Wm. Stuart, abp. of Armagh and primate of Ireland.

Feb. 18. Sir John Mitford, sp. ho. commons; app. ld. chanc. of Ireland, and cr. ld. Redesdale, Feb. 1802.

Feb. 20. John, earl St. Vincent, first ld. admy.

Sir Chas. Yorke, sec. at war; home sec., July 1803; first ld. admy., May 1810.

Mar. 17. Philip, E. of Hardwicke, ld. lieut. Ireland.

Mar. 17. Geo., visc. Lewisham, pres. bd. contr.; cr., *vitâ patris*, ld. Dartmouth; succ. his father as E. of Dartmouth, Nov. 1810.

May 21. Sir Wm. Grant, m. rolls.
Chas. Abbot, ch. sec. Ireland; sp. ho. commons, Feb. 1802; cr. ld. Colchester, June 1807.
Thos. Wallace, commr. bd. contr.; *again*, Apr. 1807; v. pres. bd. tr., Jan. 1818; m. mint, Oct. ld. Wallace, Jan. 1828.

Nov. 18. Chas. Bragge, aft. Bragge Bathurst, treasr. navy; sec. at war, Aug. 1803; pres. bd. contr., Jan. 1821.

1802.

Jan. 13. Wm. Wickham, commr. of tr.; amb. to Switzerland.
Geo. Rose, commr. of tr.; v. pres. bd. tr., Mar. 1804; joint paym. gen., July 1804; *again* v. pres. bd. tr., Mar. 1807; and treasr. navy, Apr., same year.
Chas. Long, ld. treasy., May 1804; ch. sec. Ireland, 1806; paym. gen., Apr. 1807; cr. ld. Farnborough, Aug. 1826.

Feb. 3. ADOLPHUS FRED., D. OF CAMBRIDGE, introd., not sw.

Apr. 21. Edwd., ld. Ellenborough, ld. ch. just. k. b.

Sept. 8. Sir John Borlase Warren, bt., adm.; amb. to Russia.

Sept. 22. Sir Chas. (Gould) Morgan, bt., judge adv. gen.
John Smyth, late ld. treasy.; m. mint.

1803.

Feb. 16. John Hiley Addington, joint paym. gen.; commr. bd. contr., Feb. 1806.
Geo. Tierney, treasr. navy; pres. bd. contr., Oct. 1806; m. mint, May 1827.

Nov. 23. Hon. Thos. Maitland, aft. sir T., G.C.B., commr. bd. contr.
Nathl. Bond, ld. treasy.; v. pres. bd. tr., Feb. 1804; judge adv. gen., Feb. 1806.

1804.

Jan. 4. Hon. Arthur Paget, aft. sir A., K.C.B., amb. to Germany, and aft. to Turkey.

Jan. 20. Sir Evan Nepean, bt., ch. sec. Ireland; prev. sec. admy., and subs. ld. admy.

May 8. Sir Jas. Mansfield, ld. ch. just. c. p.

May 14. Geo., E. of Winchilsea and Nottingham, gr. stole.
Lord Geo. Thynne, compt. hhold.

June 6. Hy. ld. Mulgrave, chanc. d. Lanc.; for. sec., Jan. 1805; first ld. admy., Apr. 1807; mast. gen. ordn., May 1810; cr. visc. Normanby and E. of Mulgrave, Sept. 1812.

June 27. Wm. Drummond, late amb. to Turkey.
Chas. Arbuthnot, amb. ext. to Turkey; sec. treasy., 1810; first commr. woods and forests, Feb. 1823; chanc. d. Lanc., June 1828.

July 11. Lord John Thynne, v. chamb. hhold.; succ. as ld. Carteret, Feb. 1838.

July 19. Granville Leveson, ld. Gower, amb. ext. to Russia and to France; cr. visc. Granville, Aug. 1815, and earl Granville, May 1833.
AUG., D. OF SUSSEX, introd., not sw.

1805.

Jan. 14. John Hookham Frere, amb. to Spain.
Nichs. Vansittart, ch. sec. Ireland; sec. treasy., 1806; ch. ex. from June 1812 to Jan. 1823; cr. ld. Bexley, Mar. 1, 1823.
Reginald Pole Carew, late u. s. home dep., commr. of tr.
John Sullivan, late u. s. cols., commr. of tr.; aft. commr. bd. contr.

Feb. 21. Chas. Manners Sutton, abp. of Canterbury.

May 1. Chas. ld. Barham, first ld. admy.

Nov. 21. Edwd., E. of Powis, app. ld. lieut. of Ireland, but did not go over.

1806.

Feb. 1. WM. FREDK., D. of GLOUCESTER, introd., not sw.

Feb. 5. Fras., E. of Moira, mast. gen. ordn.; Bengal and comm. in ch. in India, Nov. 1812; cr. visc. Loudoun, E. Rawdon, and M. of Hastings, Dec. 1816.
Richd. Chandos, E. Temple, joint paym. gen. and v. pres. bd. tr.; cr. M. of Chandos and D. of Buckingham, Feb. 2.
Lord Hy. Petty, ch. ex.; succ. as M. of Lansdowne, Nov. 1809; home sec., 1827; ld. pres.,

Nov. 22, 1830; *again*, Apr. 18, 1835; and *a third time*, July 6, 1846.

Feb. 5. Hon. Chas. Grey, first ld. admy.; for. sec., Sept. 1806; succ. his father as E. Grey and visc. Howick, Nov. 1807; first ld. treasy., Nov. 1830.

Chas. James Fox, for. sec.; *d.* while holding this office, Sept. 13, 1806.

Feb. 7. Geo., visc. Morpeth, commr. bd. contr.; succ. his father as E. of Carlisle, Sept. 1825; ld. pr. seal in 1827, and 1834.

Lord John Townshend, joint paym. gen.

Thos., ld. Erskine, ld. chanc.

Richd. Brinsley Sheridan, treasr. navy.

Feb. 12. John, D. of Bedford, ld. lieut. of Ireland.

Hy., E. of Carnarvon, m. horse.

John Joshua, E. of Carysfort, joint postm. gen.

Chas. Aug., lord Ossulston, treasr. hhold.

St. Andrew, ld. St. John, of Bletsoe, capt. gent. pens.

Wm. Elliot, ch. sec. Ireland.

Mar. 5. Geo. Ponsonby, ld. chanc. of Ireland.

Mar. 12. Sir John Newport, bt., ch. ex. of Ireland.

May 7. Richd., E. of Donoughmore, commr. bd. tr.; joint postm. gen. in Ireland.

June 18. Alexr., M. of Douglas and Clydesdale; summoned to the house of peers, *vitâ patris*, as ld. Dutton, Nov. 1806; succ. as D. of Hamilton, Feb. 1819.

July 21. Jas., E. of Lauderdale, kpr. gr. seal of Scotland.

Aug. 27. Hy. Richd., ld. Holland, ld. pr. seal.

Nov. 19. Sir Arthur Anstruther, bt., late ch. just. of the supr. court of judic. in Bengal.

1807.

Mar. 26. Hon. Spencer Perceval, ch. ex.; first ld. treasy. from Dec. 6, 1809, to May 4, 1812, when he was assass. by a person named Bellingham, in the lobby of the house of commons.

Hon. Robt. Dundas, pres. bd. contr.; ld. pr. seal of Scotland, 1811; succ. his father as visc. Melville, May, same year; first ld. admy., Mar. 1812.

Mar. 30. Sir Jas. Pulteney, bt., sec. at war.

April 1. Chas., D. of Richmond and Lenox, app. ld. lieut. of Ireland; *d.* gov. gen. of Canada, July 1819.

April 8. Hy., visc. Melville, commr. bd. tr. (*his name which had been struck out of the list May* 9, 1805, *now rest., he being re-sw.*)

John, ld. Teignmouth, commr. bd. contr. App. Sept. 1792, to succ. ld. Cornwallis as gov. gen. of Bengal.

Hon. sir Arthur Wellesley, K.B., ch. sec. to the ld.-lieut. of Ireland; aft. D. of Wellington; com. in ch. of the army, Jan. 1827; first ld. treasy., Jan. 1828, and *again*, Nov. 1834; and *again* com. in ch., Aug. 1842.

April 22. Thos., ld. Manners, ld. chanc. of Ireland.

May 13. Richd., E. of Clancarty, comm bd. tr.; m. mint, Oct. 1812; joint postm. gen., Sept. 1814; employed in several diplomatic missions.

May 20. Hon. Hy. Manvers Pierrepont, late min. to Sweden.

Nov. 25. Hon. Richd. Ryder; sec. st., Nov. 1809.

1808.

Jan. 20. Edwd. Venables Vernon (aft. Harcourt), abp. of York.

Mar. 9. Richd., E. of Mount Edgcumbe.

Mar. 16. Percy Clinton Sidney Smythe, visc. Strangford; env. ext. to Portugal.

1809.

Feb. 6. Sir John Nicholl, late kings's adv. gen.; commr. bd. tr.; aft. dean of the arches court, judge of the high court of admy., &c.

Sept. 27. John Randolph, bp. of London.

Oct. 18. Hon. Wm. Wellesley Pole, ch. sec. Ireland; m. mint, 1814.; cr. ld. Maryborough, July 17, 1821; succ. as E. of Mornington, on the death of his brother, the marq. Wellesley, Sept. 26, 1842.

Nov. 1. Hy. John, visc. Palmerston, sec. at war from this time until May 1828; for. sec., Nov. 1830; *again*, Apr. 1835; and *a third time*, July 1846.

Nov. 8. Chas. Manners Sutton, judge adv. gen.; sp. ho. commons from June 2, 1817, to Aug. 15, 1834;

cr. ld. Botesford and visc. Canterbury, Mar. 10, 1835.

Dec. 20. John, ld. Sheffield, commr. bd. tr.; cr. visc. Pevensey and E. of Sheffield, Jan. 22, 1816.

Hon. Hy. Wellesley, late sec. treasy.; env. ext. to Spain; aft. amb. to France; cr. ld. Cowley, Jan. 21, 1828.

1810.

Aug. 29. Sir John Sinclair, bt., pres. of the agricult. secy., *honoris causâ.*

REGENCY OF GEORGE, PRINCE OF WALES.

1812.

Mar. 20. Chas. Ingoldsby, M. of Winchester, gr. stole.

Fras., E. of Yarmouth, v. chambn.; succ. as M. of Hertford, June 17, 1822.

John McMahon, aft. sir John, bt.; private sec. and keeper of the pr. purse to the pr. regent.

Mar. 26. Robt., visc. Jocelyn, treasr. hhold.; aft. v. chambn.; succ. as E. of Roden, June 29, 1820.

Robt. Liston.

Aug. 13. Lord Wm. Chas. Cavendish Bentinck; gov. gen. of India, May 1833.

Lord Geo. Beresford, compt. hhold.

Wm. Fitzgerald, ch. ex. in Ireland.

Robt. Peel, aft. sir R., bt., sec. for Ireland; home sec., Jan. 1822; *again*, Jan. 1828; first ld. treasy. and ch. ex., Dec. 1834; and *again* first ld. treasy., Sept. 1841.

1813.

May 20. Sir Thos. Plumer, v. chanc. of England.

Oct. 5. Wm. Howley, bp. of London; transl. to Canterbury, Aug. 4, 1828.

Nov. 30. Sir Vicary Gibbs, ld. ch. bar. ex.

1814.

Mar. 19. Hugh Elliot, gov. of Madras.

Apr. 21. Sir Alexr. Thomson, ld. ch. bar. ex.

May 6. Warren Hastings, formerly gov. gen. of Bengal.

July 22. Cropley, E. of Shaftesbury.

Geo. E. of Aberdeen; chanc. d. Lanc., Jan. 1828; for. sec., June, same year; col. sec., Dec. 1834; and *again* for. sec., Sept. 1841.

July 22. Chas. Wm., ld. Stewart; succ. his brother as M. of Londonderry, Aug. 12, 1822.

July 29. Thos., ld. Binning; succ. as E. of Haddington; ld. lieut. of Ireland, Dec. 1834; first ld. admy. Sept. 1841.

Wm. Huskisson, first commr. of woods and forests; pres. bd. tr. and treasr. navy, Feb. 1823; col. and war. sec., Sept. 1827.

Aug 10. Wm. Sturges Bourne; commr. bd. contr. July 1818; home sec., Apr. 1827; first commr. of woods and forests, July, same year.

1815.

Mar. 17. Wm. Adam, chief of the civil jury court of Scotland.

Dec. 4. Hon. Chas. Bagot, aft. sir C., G.C.B., min. plen. to the Netherlands; aft. min. to the United States; gov. gen. of Canada 1841.

Dec. 30. Wm. Pitt, ld. Amherst, on his embassy to China; cr. E. Amherst, Dec. 19, 1828; gov. gen. of Bengal from Oct. 1822 to Mar. 1828.

1816.

June 8. Edwd. Thornton, aft. sir E., G.C.B.; min. plen. to Sweden 1812; to Portugal 1823.

June 27. Sir Hy. Russell, bt., late ch. just. Bengal.

July 1. LEOPOLD, pr. of SAXE-COBURG SAALFELD, consort of CHARLOTTE AUGUSTA, princess of WALES; aft. K. of the Belgians; introd., not sw.

1817.

Apr. 26. Sir Richd. Richards, ld. ch. bar. ex.

May 31. Sir Geo. Fitzgerald Hill, bt., v. treasr. Ireland.

July 11. John Becket, aft. sir J., bt., judge adv. gen.

July 15. Sir Benjn. Bloomfield, private sec. and kpr. of the pr. purse to the prince regent; cr. ld. Bloomfield, May 11, 1825; min. to Sweden.

Sept. 17. Chas. Chetwynd, E. Talbot, app. ld. lieut. of Ireland.

Dec. 30. John Leach, aft. sir J., v. chanc.; m. rolls, Apr. 1827.

Sir Wm. A'Court, bt., min. to the Two Sicilies, &c.; cr. ld. Heytesbury, Jan. 23, 1828; ld. lieut. of Ireland, July 1844.

1818.

April 6. Geo. Hy. Rose, amb. to Prussia.
Nov. 19. Sir Chas. Abbott, ld. ch. just. k. b.; cr. ld. Tenterden, Apr. 30, 1827.
Sir Robt. Dallas, ld. ch. just. c. p.

1819.

May 28. Chas. Grant, ch. sec. Ireland; pres. bd. tr., Sept. 1827; of the bd. contr., Dec. 1830; col. sec., Apr. 1835; cr. ld. Glenelg, May 11, same year.
July 23. Sir Saml. Shepherd, ld. ch. bar. ex. in Scotland.

King George IV.

1820.

April 8. David Boyle, ld. just. clk. in Scotland.
June 7. Peter, ld. Gwydir, dep. gt. chambn. of England.
July 20. Stratford Canning, aft. sir S. and ld. Stratford de Redcliffe; amb. to Turkey, 1841.
Oct. 10. Sir Gore Ouseley, bt.; prev. amb. ext. to Persia and to Russia.
Thos., ld. Manners, ld. chanc. of Ireland; re-sw.

1821.

Feb. 6. Wm. Carr, ld. Beresford; lt.-gen. ordn., 1823; mast. gen., Apr. 1828; cr. visc. Beresford, Mar. 28, 1823.
Feb. 23. Jas., M. of Graham, v. chambn. hhold.; succ. his father as D. of Montrose in 1836.
June 30. Peter Robt., ld. Gwydir, son of the preceding ld. Gwydir, hered. gr. chambn. of England; ld. Willoughby d'Eresby in 1828.
Dec. 10. Chas., D. of Dorset, m. horse.
Hy., M. of Conyngham, ld. st. hhold.
Hy. Goulburn, ch. sec. Ireland; ch. ex., Jan. 1828; home sec., Dec. 1834; *again* ch. ex., Sept. 1841.

1822.

Jan. 17. Chas. Watkin Williams Wynn, pres. bd. contr.; sec. at war, Nov. 1830; chanc. d. Lanc., Dec. 1834.
Wm. Hy. Fremantle, commr. bd. contr.
Feb. 4. Sir Geo. Warrender, bt., commr. bd. contr.
Mar. 28. John, ld. Burghersh, min. to Tuscany; min. to Prussia, 1841; succ. his father as E. of Westmoreland, Dec. 15 1841.
Mar. 28. Aug. John Foster, min. to Denmark and aft. to Sardinia.
Hon. Fredk. Jas. Lamb, amb. to Vienna, Spain, Portugal, &c. cr. ld. Beauvale, Apr. 30 1839; succ. his brother as visc. Melbourne, Nov. 24, 1848
Aug. 17. Chas. Hope, ld. pres. court of session in Scotland.

1824.

Jan. 19. Sir Robt. Gifford, bt., ch. just c. p.; cr. ld. Gifford, Jan. 31 following.
Sir Wm. Alexander, ld. ch. bar. ex.
Apr. 7. Wm. Noel Hill, min. to Naples.
May 25. Sir Wm. Draper Best, ld. ch. just. c. p.; cr. ld. Wynford, June 5, 1829.

1825.

Mar. 23. Hugh, D. of Northumberland, ld. lieut. of Ireland, Mar. 1829.
Chas. Vaughan, aft. sir C., min. to the United States.
Sept. 30. Hy. Watkin Williams Wynn.

1826.

June 1. Jas., M. of Salisbury.
July 27. Hon. sir Robt. Gordon, min. to Brazil; aft. min. to Austria.
Nov. 20. Sir John Singleton Copley, m. rolls; cr. ld. Lyndhurst, April 25, 1827, and made ld. chanc. May 2, following; ld. ch. bar. ex., Jan. 1831; *again* ld. chanc. Dec. 1834, and *again* Sept. 1841

1827.

Apr. 30. Wm. Spencer, D. of Devonshire ld. chambn.
Wm. Hy., D. of Portland, ld. pr seal; decl. ld. pres., Aug. 17 following.
Hy. Wm., M. of Anglesey, mast. gen. ord.; ld. lieut. of Ireland Mar. 1828; *again* ld. lieut. Dec. 1830; and *again* mast gen. ordn., July 1846.
John Wm., visc. Dudley and Ward, for. sec.; aft. earl Dudley.
Sir Anthy. Hart, v. chanc. of England; ld. chanc. of Ireland same year.
Hon. Wm. Lamb, sec. for Ireland succ. as visc. Melbourne, 1828 home sec., Nov. 1830; first ld. treasy., July 1834; *again* April 1835.
Sir Geo. Cockburn, v. admiral first naval councillor to the ld. high adm.

May 10. Wm. Conyngham Plunket, ch. just. c. p. in Ireland; subs. ld. chanc. in that kingdom, and cr. ld. Plunket.

May 23. Jas. Abercromby, judge adv. gen.; m. mint, July 1834; sp. ho. commons from Feb. 1835 to May 1839; cr. ld. Dunfermline, June 7 following.

June 30. Stephen Rumbold Lushington, gov. of Madras.

Aug. 17. Lord Wm. Hy. Cavendish Bentinck.

John Chas. Herries, chanc, ex.; m. mint, Feb. 1828; pres. b. tr., Feb. 1830; and sec. at war, Dec. 1834.

Nov. 16. Sir Lancelot Shadwell, v. chanc. of England.

Sir Jas. Mackintosh, some time recorder of Bombay; commr. bd. contr.

Sir Wm. Keppel, gov. of Guernsey.

1828.

Jan. 28. Edwd., ld. Ellenborough, ld. pr. seal; pres. bd. contr., Sept. this year; *again*, Dec. 1834; *and a third time*, Sept. 1841; gov. gen. of India, Oct. 1841; cr. E. of Ellenborough, Oct. 1844.

Feb. 5. Thos. Frankland Lewis, v. pres. bd. tr.; treasr. navy, Feb. 1830; cr. a bt. 1846.

Feb. 13. Rowland, ld. Hill, gen. on the staff, commanding in ch.

Mar. 5. Sir Christr. Robinson, judge of the admy. court.

May 30. Wm., visc. Lowther, first commr. of woods and forests; v. pres. bd. tr., Dec. 1834; postm. gen., Sept. 1841; and cr., *vitâ patris*, ld. Lowther; succ. as E. of Lonsdale, Mar. 1844.

Sir Geo. Murray, sec. st. war and cols.; mast. gen. ordn., Dec. 1834; *again*, Sept. 1841.

Sir Hy. Hardinge, sec. at war; ch. sec. Ireland, 1834; *again* sec. at war, Sept. 1841; app. gov. gen. of India, May 2, 1844; cr. visc. Hardinge, Apr. 1846.

Thos. Peregrine Courtenay, v. pres. bd. tr.

June 16. John Wilson Croker, sec. admy.

John Calcraft, paym. of the forces.

June 28. Lord Fras. Leveson Gower (aft. ld. Fras. Egerton), ch. sec. Ireland; sec. at war, July 1830; cr. E. of Ellesmere, June 1846.

Hy. Hobhouse, kpr. of the state papers, and *honoris causâ*.

July 23. Robt. Adair, aft. sir R., G.C.B., late min. to Austria, &c.

July 31. Chas. Jas. Blomfield, bp. of Chester; tr. to London Aug. following.

1829.

June 10. Jas., E. of Rosslyn, ld. pr. seal; decl. ld. pres., Dec. 1834.

Sir Nicholas Conyngham Tindal, ld. ch. just. c. p.

Oct. 12. Sir Brook Taylor, G.C.H., late min. to several courts.

1830.

Apr. 7. Geo., D. of Gordon, kpr. gr. seal of Scotland.

KING WILLIAM IV.

1830.

June 28. Bernard Edwd., D. of Norfolk, hered. earl marsh. of England.

July 19. Jas. Horatio, M. of Cholmondeley, dep. gr. chamb. of England.

Geo., E. of Jersey, ld. chambn.; *again*, Dec. 1834; m. horse, Sept. 1841.

Geo., E. of Belfast, v. chambn.; cr. ld. Ennishowen, Aug. 1841; succ. as M. of Donegal, Oct. 1844.

Sir Wm. Rae, bt., ld. adv. of Scotland.

July 28. Hy., visc. Hereford.

Aug. 25. John, E. of Clare, gov. of Bombay.

Nov. 22. Chas., D. of Richmond, postm. gen.; postm. gen. of Gr. Britain and Ireland, by a new patent, Apr. 1831.

Wm. Chas., E. of Albemarle, m. horse; *again*, April 1835.

John, ld. Durham, ld. pr. seal; cr. E. of Durham, Mar. 1833; amb. to Russia, 1835; gov. gen. of Canada, 1838.

Geo., ld. Auckland, pres. bd. tr., to which was joined the mastership of the mint, Dec. 14 following; first ld. admy., June 1834; *again*, April 1835; gov. gen. of India, Aug. same year; E. of Auckland, Dec. 1839; *again* first ld. admy., July 1846.

Hy., ld. Brougham, ld. chanc.

John Chas. Spencer, visc. Althorpe, ch. ex.; succ. his father as earl Spencer, Nov. 1834.

Geo. Jas. Agar Welbore Ellis, first commr. of woods and forests.

Lord John Russell, paym. gen.; home sec., April 1835; sec. st.

war and cols., Aug. 1839; first ld. treasy., July 1846 and Nov. 1865; cr. E. Russell, July 30, 1861.

Nov. 22. Hon. Edwd. Geoffrey Smith Stanley, ch. sec. Ireland; col. sec., April 1833; *again* col. sec., Sept. 1841; summoned to the house of peers, as lord Stanley, of Bickerstaffe, Oct. 1844; succ. his father as E. of Derby, 1851; first ld. treasy., Feb. 1852, Feb. 1858, and July 1866.

Sir Jas. Robt. Geo. Graham, bt., first ld. admy; home sec., Sept. 1841.

Geo. Robt. Dawson, late sec. treasy. and admy.

Chas. Poulett Thompson, v. pres. bd. tr.; treasr. navy, Dec. 13 following; pres. bd. tr., June 1834; aft. gov. of Canada; cr. ld. Sydenham, Aug. 1840.

Nov. 24. Sir Wm. Johnstone Hope, adm.

Wm., visc. Anson, m. buckhounds.

Robt. Grant, judge adv.-gen.; aft. sir R., G.C.H.

Dec. 1. Ulick John, M. of Clanricarde, amb. to Russia; postm. gen., July 1846.

Hon. Robt. Grosvenor, compt. hhold; cr. ld. Ebury, Sept. 10, 1857.

Dec. 8. Thos., ld. Foley, capt. gent. arms.

Sir Jas. Kempt, mast. gen. ordn.; gov. gen. and commr. in ch. in Canada, Aug. 1828.

1831.

Jan. 31. Wm. Geo., E. of Errol, hered. ld. high const. of Scotland; m. horse to the queen consort; ld. st. hhold, Nov. 1839.

Richd. Wm., E. Howe, ld. chambn. to the queen consort.

Feb. 23. Archd., E. of Rosebery.

John, visc. Duncannon, first commr. of woods and forests; home sec., July 1834; ld. pr. seal, and first commr. of woods and forests *again*, May 1835; succ. as E. of Bessborough, Feb. 1844.

Michael Angelo Taylor, *honoris causâ.*

Mar. 23. Edwd., E. of Derby.

Wm. Conyngham, ld. Plunket, ld. chanc. of Ireland; *again* ld. chanc. of Ireland, Apr. 1835.

June 29. Aug. Fredk., D. of Leinster.

Sir Fredk. Adam, ld. high commr. of the Ionian Islands.

Sir Edwd. Hyde East, bt., late ch. just. of Bengal.

1832.

Feb. 6. Sir John Cam Hobhouse, bt., sec. at war; sec. for Ireland, 1834; first commr. of woods and forests, July same year; pres. bd. contr., Apr. 1835 and Apr. 1846.

Chas. Tennyson, who assumed the name of D'Eyncourt, in 1835, *honoris causâ.*

Feb. 22. Sir Wm. Garrow, bt., late bar. ex.

May 30. Hy. Constantine Phipps, E. of Mulgrave; aft. M. of Normanby; ld. pr. seal, July 1834; ld. lieut. of Ireland, April 1835; cr. M. of Normanby, June 1838; col. sec., Feb. 1839; home sec., Aug. same year; amb. to France, Aug. 18, 1846.

July 11. Holt Mackenzie, commr. bd. contr.

Hy. Ellis, min. to Persia.

Aug. 15. Gilbert, E. of Minto, min. to Prussia: first ld. admy., Sept. 1835; ld. pr. seal, July 1846.

Nov. 6. Sir Thos. Denman, ld. ch. just. k. b.; cr. ld. Denman, Mar. 1834.

1833.

Feb. 4. Basil Percy Fielding, E. of Denbigh, ld. chambn. to the queen consort.

Feb. 4. Geo. Fitzclarence, E. of Munster.

Apr. 3. Edwd. Ellice, sec. at war.

June 12. Edwd. John Littleton, apptd. ch. sec. Ireland; cr. ld. Hatherton, May 1835.

Aug. 14. Sir Jas. Parke, bar. ex.

Sept. 4. Sir John Bernard Bosanquet, just. c. p.

Sir Alex. Johnstone, late ch. just. Ceylon; assessor to the jud. comm.

Sept. 11. Geo. Wm., D. of Argyll, ld. st. hhold.

1834.

Jan. 24. Howe Peter, M. of Sligo, gov. of Jamaica.

Mar. 5. Sir John Bayley, late bar. ex.

Apr. 16. Sir Robt. Graham, ld. treasy.

June 5. Thos. Spring Rice, col. sec.; ch. ex., Apr. 1835; cr. ld. Monteagle, Aug. 1839.

Sir John Vaughan, late bar. ex., now just. c. p.

uly 16. Robt. Cutlar Fergusson, judge adv. gen.

pt. 3. Archd., E. of Gosford, gov. of Canada.

ct. 1. Sir Chas. Christr. Pepys, m. rolls; first commr. of the gr. seal, Apr. 1835; made ld. chanc. and cr. ld. Cottenham, Jan. 1836; cr. E. of Cottenham, June, 1850.

Oct. 29. Sir Herbert Jenner (Fust), vicar-gen., dean of the arches' court, &c.

Dec. 16. Stapleton, visc. Combermere, general.

Jas. Arch., ld. Wharncliffe, ld. pr. seal; decl. ld. pres., Sept. 3, 1841.

Sir Edwd. Knatchbull, bt., pay-m. of the forces; *again*. Sept. 1841.

Sir Jas. Scarlett, ld. ch. bar. ex.; cr. ld. Abinger, Jan. 1835.

Sir Edwd. Sugden, app. ld. chanc. of Ireland; *again*, ld. chanc. of Ireland, Oct. 1841; app. ld. chanc. of Eng., Feb. 27, 1852, and cr. ld. St. Leonards.

Alexr. Baring, pres. bd. tr., and immediately aft. m. mint; cr. ld. Ashburton, Apr. 1835.

Dec. 20. Lord Granville Chas. Hy. Somerset, first commr. of woods and forests; chanc. d. Lanc., Sept. 1841.

Wm. Yates Peel, ld. treasy.

Joseph Planta, late sec. and ld. treasy.

Dec. 29. Geo., E. of Chesterfield.

Thos. Philip, E. De Grey, first ld. admy.; ld. lieut. of Ireland, Sept. 1841.

1835.

Feb. 18. Thos., E. of Wilton, ld. st. hhold.

Feb. 23. Fredk. visc. Castlereagh, v. chambn. hhold.

Hon. Hy. Thos. Lowry Corry, compt. hhold.

Apr. 18. Hy., visc. Howick, sec. at war; succ. as E. Grey, July 1845; sec. for war and cols., July 1846.

May 6. Hy. Labouchere, aft. ld. Taunton, v. pres. bd. tr. and m. mint; pres. bd. tr., Aug. 1839; ch. sec. Ireland, 1846; *again* pres. bd. tr., July 1847.

May 20. Fras. Nathl., M. of Conyngham, postm. gen; aft. ld. chambn.

Geo., visc. Morpeth, ch. sec. Ireland; first commr. of woods and forests, July 1846; succ. as E. of Carlisle, Oct. 1848; chanc. d. Lanc., Mar. 1850.

May 27. Sir Richd. Hussey Vivian, bt., general; mast. gen. ordn.; cr. ld. Vivian, Aug. 1841.

Hon. Geo. Stevens Byng, compt. hhold; visc. Enfield on his father's creation as E. of Strafford, Sept. 1847; succ. as E. of Strafford, June 3, 1860.

June 24. Sir Harford Jones Brydges, bt., late sir H. Jones, form. min. to Persia.

July 1. Lord Chas. Fitzroy, v. chambn. hhold.

Sir Chas. Edwd. Grey, bt., a commr. for investigating the grievances affecting Canada.

1836.

Jan. 16. Hy. Bickersteth, m. rolls; cr. ld. Langdale, Jan. following; first commr. gr. seal, June, 1850.

Aug. 3. John, ld. Elphinstone.

1837.

Mar. 1. Lucius, visc. Falkland, gov. of Nova Scotia.

Apr. 5. J. A. Stewart Mackenzie, gov. of Ceylon.

Queen Victoria.

1837.

July 12. Hy. Stephen, E. of Ilchester, capt. yeom. guard.

July 19. Hy. Chas. Howard, E. of Surrey, treasr. hhold.; cr. ld. Maltravers, Aug. 1841; succ. as D. of Norfolk, Mar. 1842; m. horse. July 1846.

1838.

Nov. 5. Stephen Lushington, judge admy. court.

1839.

Mar. 1. Hugh, visc. Ebrington, app. ld. lieut. of Ireland; summoned to the house of peers, *vitâ patris*, as ld. Fortescue; succ. as E. Fortescue, June 1841; ld. std. hhold., July 1846.

Sir Geo. Grey, bt., judge adv. gen.; chanc. d. Lanc., June 1841; home sec., July 1846.

May 22. Hy., E. of Uxbridge, ld. chambn.; aft. M. of Anglesey.

June 3. Chas. Shaw Lefevre, sp. ho. commons; aft. visc. Eversley.

July 31. Sir Chas. Theophilus Metcalfe, gov. of Canada; cr. ld. Metcalfe, June 1845.

Aug. 26. Fras. Thornhill Baring, chanc. ex.; first ld. admy., Jan. 1849; aft. ld. Northbrook.

Aug. 29. Richd. Lalor Sheil, v. pres. bd. tr.; judge adv. gen., June 1841; m. mint, July 1846; min. to Tuscany, Oct. 1850.

Sept. 30. Thos. Babington Macaulay, sec. at war; paym. gen., July 1846; aft. ld. Macaulay.

1840.

Jan. 3. Geo., E. of Clarendon, ld. pr. seal; chanc. d. Lanc., Oct., same year; pres. bd. tr., July 1846; ld. lieut. of Ireland, May 1847.

Jan. 15. Geo., ld. Kinnaird, m. buckhounds.

Sept. 11. Prince ALBERT, consort to the queen, introd., not sw.

1841.

Feb. 25. Sir Jos. Littledale, late just q. b.

June 23. Lord Arthur Marcus Cecil Hill, compt. hhold; *again* compt., July 1847; aft. ld. Sandys.

John, ld. Campbell, ld. chanc. Ireland; chanc. d. Lanc., July 1846; ld. ch. just. q. b., Mar. 1850; ld. chanc. Eng., June 18, 1859.

June 28. Hon. Fox Maule, v. pres. bd. tr.; sec. at war, July 1846; aft. ld. Panmure and E. of Dalhousie.

Aug. 11. Hon. Edwd. John Stanley, paym. gen.; cr. ld. Eddisbury, *vitâ patris*, May 1848; succ. as ld. Stanley of Alderley, Oct. 1850.

Aug. 21. Robt. Vernon Smith, und. sec. cols.; aft. ld. Lyveden.

Sept. 3. Richd. Plantagenet, D. of Buckingham and Chandos, ld. pr. seal.

Chas. Cecil, E. of Liverpool, ld. st. hhold.

Edwd. Granville, ld. Eliot, ch. sec. Ireland; succ. as E. of St. Germans, Jan. 1845; postm. gen., Jan. 1846.

Lord Ernest Bruce, v. chambn.; aft. M. of Ailesbury.

Hy. Pelham, E. of Lincoln, first commr. of woods and forests; ch. sec. Ireland, 1846.

Wm. Ewart Gladstone, v. pres. bd. tr. and m. mint; pres. bd. tr., June 1843; col. sec., Dec. 1845; ch. ex., Dec. 1852, June 1859, Aug. 1873, and Apr. 1880; first ld. treasy., Dec. 1868, Apr. 1880, and Feb. 1886; ld. pr. seal, Feb. 1886.

Sept. 14. Brownlow, M. of Exeter, hered. grand almoner; gr. stole to pr. Albert.

Sept. 14. John Wm. Robt., M. of Lothian capt. yeom. guard.

Geo. John, ld. De la Warr, ld chambn.

Jas. Alex., E. of Rosslyn, m buckhounds.

John Geo., lord Forrester, capt gent. arms.

Hon. Geo. Lionel Dawson Damer compt. hhold.

John Nicholl, judge adv. gen. ld. of tr., Jan. 1846.

Oct. 6. Fredk. Wm., E. Jermyn, treasr hhold.; aft. M. of Bristol.

1842.

Jan. 15. Geo., E. of Beverley.

Sir Jas. Lewis Knight Bruce, v. chanc.

Sir Jas. Wigram, v. chanc.

Feb. 2. Walter Fras., D. of Buccleuch and Queensberry, ld. pr. seal; decld. ld. pres., Jan. 21, 1846.

1843.

June 10. Jas., E. of Dalhousie, v. pres. bd. tr.; *again* Feb. 1845; gov. gen. of India, Aug. 1847; cr. M. of Dalhousie.

Sir Edwd. Ryan, late ch. just., Bengal.

Thos. Pemberton Leigh, chanc. and kpr. of the gr. seal to the D. of Cornwall; cr. ld. Kingsdown, Aug. 28, 1858.

Dec. 13. Richd. Pakenham, env. ex. to the United States; aft. sir R.

1844.

Apr. 17. John Hope, ld. just. clk. Scotland.

Sir Fredk. Pollock, ld. ch. bar. ex.

May 23. Sir Thos. Fras. Fremantle, bt., sec. at war; ch. sec. Ireland; aft. ld. Cottesloe.

Sir Hy. Pottinger, bt., late plen. in China; app. gov. of Madras, Aug. 1847.

1845.

Feb. 3. Hon. Sidney Herbert, sec. at war; aft. ld. Herbert of Lea.

Feb. 5. Sir Geo. Clerk, bt., v. pres. bd. tr. and m. mint.

June 30. Wm. Bingham Baring, paym. gen.; succ. as ld. Ashburton, May 1848.

Hy. Lytton Bulwer, aft. sir H. and then lord Dalling and Bulwer; min. plen. to Spain; subs. to the United States, &c.

1846.

Feb. 25. Jas., M., aft. D. of Abercorn, gr. stole to pr. Albert.

eb. 23. Hon. Jas. Arch. Stuart Wortley, judge adv. gen.

ar. 18. Chas. John, visc. Canning, first commr. of woods and forests.

ly 6. Fras., D. of Bedford.
Chas. Wood, ch. ex.; aft. sir C., bt., and ld. Halifax.

ly 8. Fredk., E. Spencer, ld. chambn. hhold.
Lord Edwd. Geo. Fitz-Alan Howard, v. chambn.; aft. ld. Howard of Glossop.
Thos. Milner Gibson, v. pres. bd. tr.

ug. 1. Granville Geo., E. Granville, m. buck-hounds; v. pres. bd. tr. and paym. gen., May 1848.

ct. 30. Sir Thos. Wilde, ch. just. c. p.; aft. ld. chanc., and cr. lord Truro in 1850.
Edwd. Strutt, first commr. of railways; aft. ld. Belper.

1847.

une 17. Sir Geo. Arthur, bt., late gov. of Bombay.

uly 22. Hon. Wm. Sebright Lascelles, compt. hhold.
Sir Wm. Meredyth Somerville, bt., ch. sec. Ireland; aft. ld. Athlumley.

ct. 30. Jas. Stephen, aft. sir James, K.C.B., late und. sec. war and cols.

Nov. 22. Richd. More O'Ferrall, gov. of Malta.

1848.

Feb. 11. Thos. Musgrave, abp. of York.
Wm. Goodenough Hayter, judge adv. gen.; joint sec. treasy., May 1849; aft. sir W., bt.

Apr. 15. John Bird Summer, abp. of Canterbury.

June 27. John Geo., E. of Besborough, m. buck-hounds.
Saml. March Phillips, late und. sec. home.

Sept. 4. John, M. of Breadalbane, ld. chambn.

1849.

Feb. 13. Thos. Wyse, min. plen. to Greece; aft. sir T.

June 29. Sir David Dundas, judge adv. gen.

July 30. Matt. Talbot Baines, first commr. p. law bd.

1850.

Mar. 22. Richd., M. of Westminster, ld. st. hhold.

July 13. Hy. Tufnell, late sec. treasy.

Aug. 14. Sir John Jervis, ld. ch. just. c. p.

Nov. 13. Sir Robt. Monsey Rolfe, late a bar. ex., v. chanc.; cr. ld. Cranworth, Dec. 1850; ld. chanc., Dec. 28, 1852, and July 6, 1867.

1851.

Apr. 14. Sir John Romilly, m. rolls.
Geo. Jas. Turner, aft. sir G., v. chanc.

May 5. Andw. Rutherford, ld. sess., Scotland.

Aug. 7. Geo. Aug. Constantine Hy Phipps, c.c. E. Mulgrave, compt. hhold.
Lawrence Sulivan, dep. sec. at war.

Oct. 23. Edwd. Adolphus St. Maur, c.c. ld. Seymour, first commr. woods, forests, &c., 1849-51; first commr. works, &c., 1851.

1852.

Feb. 2. Hy. R. C., ld. Cowley, amb. to France.
Sir Jno. Patteson, late just. q. b.

Feb. 27. Algernon, D. of Northumberland, first ld. admy.
John Wm., E. of Sandwich, capt. gent. arms.
Archd. Hamilton, E. of Eglinton, ld. lieut. Ireland.
Chas. Philip, E. of Hardwicke, postm. gen.
Jas., E. of Malmesbury, for. sec.
Jno. Jas. Robt. Manners, c.c. lord John Manners, ch. commr. works, &c.
Lord Claude Hamilton, treasr. hhold.
Wm., ld. de Ros, capt. yeom. guard.
Chas., ld. Colchester, v. pres. bd. tr.
Hon. Geo. Cecil Weld Forester, compt. hhold.
Sir Jno. Somerset Pakington, sec. war and cols.
Spencer Horatio Walpole, home sec.
Benjn. Disraeli, ch. ex.
Jos. Warner Henley, pres. bd. tr.
Robt. Adam Christopher, chanc. d. Lanc.
Wm. Beresford, sec. at war.
Geo. Bankes, judge adv. gen.

Mar. 5. Orlando Geo. Chas., visc. Newport, v. chambn.
Sir Jno. Trollope, pres. p. law bd.

Apr. 5. Sir Jno. Dodson, judge prerog. court, Canterbury.

May 15. Richd. Southwell, ld. Naas, ch. sec. Ireland.

Oct. 16. Fitzroy Jas. Hy., ld. Raglan, m. gen. ordn.

Dec. 28. Sir Wm. Molesworth, bt., first commr. works, &c.
Sir Jno. Young, bt., ch. sec. Ireland.
Edwd. Cardwell, pres. bd. tr.

1853.

Jan. 4. Geo. Douglas, D. of Argyll, ld. pr. seal.
John Robt., visc. Sydney, capt. yeom. guard.
Feb. 7. Arthur Richd., D. of Wellington, m. horse.
Archd. Wm., visc. Drumlanrig, compt. hhold.
Chas. Pelham Villiers, judge adv. gen.
Aug. 8. Duncan McNeill, ld. just. gen., Scotland.
Oct. 24. Jno. Parker, late sec. admy.

1854.

Apr. 15. Hy. Unwin Addington, late und. sec. for.
Aug. 11. Sir Robt. Harry Inglis, bt.
Nov. 14. Sir Benjn. Hall, bt., pres. bd. health.

1855.

Feb. 8. Hon. Hy. Fitzroy, und. sec. home.
Feb. 28. Sir Geo. Cornewall Lewis, bt., ch. ex.
Mar. 10. Edwd. Horsman, ch. sec. Ireland.
Mar. 31. Edwd. Pleydell Bouverie, v. pres. bd. tr.
Dudley, E. of Harrowby, chanc. d. Lanc.
July 21. Sir Wm. Hy. Maule, late just. c. p.
Aug. 13. Hon. Wm. Fras. Cowper, pres. bd. health.
Sir Maurice Fredk. Fitzh. Berkeley, ld. admy.
Robt. Lowe, v. pres. bd. tr.
Wm. Monsell, clk. ordn.
Nov. 21. Sir Geo. Hamilton Seymour, G.C.B.

1856.

Apr. 4. Sir Lawrence Peel, late ch. just., Calcutta.
July 28. GEO. WM. FREDK. CHAS., D. of CAMBRIDGE; introd., not sw.
Nov. 28. Archd. Campbell Tait, bp. of London.

1857.

Feb. 2. Sir Alex. Jas. Edmd. Cockburn, ld. ch. just. c. p.
Feb. 7. Valentine Augs. V. Castlerosse, compt. hhold.
Mar. 21. Jas., E. of Elgin and Kincardine, late gov. gen. Canada; euv. sp. miss. to China.
May 6. Jno. Evelyn Denison, sp. commons.
Sir Jno. McNeill, G.C.B., pres l. bd. Scotland.
Fredk. Peel, late und. war.
June 25. Hy. Arthur Herbert, ch. Ireland.
Aug. 27. Sir Edmd. Walker Head, bt., g gen. Canada.

1858.

Feb. 3. Sir Creswell Creswell, judge ct. of prob. and div.
Feb. 26. Hy. Chas. FitzRoy, D. of Be fort, m. horse.
Hy. Jno., Earl Talbot, ca gent. arms.
Edwd. Hy., lord Stanley, sec.
Sir Fredk. Thesiger, ld. Chel ford, ld. chanc.
Jon. Peel, war sec.
Thos. Hy. Sutton Sotheron-E court, pres. p. l. bd.
Chas. Bowyer Adderley, v. comm. education.
Apr. 6. Richd. John, E. of Donoughmc pres. bd. tr.
Jno. Robt. Mowbray, judge a gen.
June 5. Sir Edwd. Geo. Earle Lyt Bulwer-Lytton, bt., col. sec.
Sir Jno. Taylor Coleridge, l just. q. b.

1859.

Feb. 2. Jno. Inglis, ld. just. clk. Sc land.
Mar. 3. Chas. Hy. Gordon Lennox, c.c. of March, pres. p. l. bd.
Algernon Geo. Percy, lc Lovaine, v. pres. bd. tr.
May 13. Sir Jno. Laird Mair Lawren bt., G.C.B., M.C.I.
June 11. Hugh, visc. Gough, comm. c India.
June 18. Geo. Wm. Fredk., M. of Ail bury, m. horse.
Sir Wm. Geo. Hylton Jolliffe, b late sec. treasy.
Jas. Wilson, v. pres. bd. tr.
Thos. Emerson Headlam, jud adv. gen.
July 6. Jno. Poyntz, Earl Spencer, g stole to pr. Albert.
Hy. Jno., E. of Ducie, cap yeom. guard.
Wm. Coutts Keppel, c.c. vis Bury, treasr. hhold.
Granville Leveson Proby, c.c. l Proby, compt. hhold.
Sir Wm. Erle, ld. ch. just. c. p
Sir Jas. Wm. Colvile, late c just. Calcutta.

1860.

b. 22. Wm. Hutt, v. pres. bd. tr.
ne 9. Chas Thos. Longley, abp. design. York.
c. 17. John Arthur Douglas, ld. Bloomfield, amb. to Prussia.

1861.

b. 4. Fras., lord Napier, amb. to Russia.
ne 26. Sir Rd. Bethell (ld. Westbury), ld. chanc.
ly 25. Sir Robt. Peel, bt., ch. sec. Ireland.

1863.

b. 3. Wm. Thomson, abp. York.
Sir Andrew Buchanan, K.C.B., amb. to Prussia.
pr. 28. Geo. Fred. Saml., E. De Grey and Ripon, sec. war.
c. 8. ALBERT EDWD. Pr. of WALES, introd., not sw.
Sir Wm. Gibson Craig, bt.

1864.

pr. 7. Chichester Saml. Fortescue, und. sec. cols.
pr. 26. Sir Jas. Plaisted Wilde, judge of ct. of prob. and. div.
Hy. Austin Bruce, v. pres. comm. education.
ov. 1. Jno., ld. Wodehouse.

1865.

eb. 4. Wm. Nathaniel Massey, M.C.I.
ar. 9. Richd. Bickerton Pemell, ld. Lyons, amb. U. S. America, Turkey, France, &c.
Sir Edwd. Vaughan Williams, late just. c. p.
ov. 29. Geo. Joachim Göschen, v. pres. bd. tr.

1866.

eb. 16. Spencer Compton Cavendish, c.c. M. of Hartington, sec. war.
ay 9. Richd. Edmd., E. of Cork and Orrery, m. buckhounds.
Clarence Edwd. Paget, c.c. ld. Clarence Paget.
PR. ALF. ERN. ALB., aft. D. of EDINBURGH, introd., not sw.
une 11. Otho FitzGerald, c.c. ld. Otho Fitzgerald, treasr. hhold.
Edmund Hammond, und. sec. for.
Russell Gurney, Recorder of London.
une 27. Horatio Waddington, und. sec. home.
uly 6. Rd. Plantagenet Campbell Temple Nugent Brydges Chandos, D. of Buckingham and Chandos, ld. pres. council.
Hy. Howard Molyneux, E. of Carnarvon, sec. st. cols.
July 6. Robt. Arthur Talbot Cecil, c.c. visc. Cranborne, sec. st. India.
Sir Staffd. Hy. Northcote, bt., pres. bd. tr.
Hy. Bouverie Wm. Brand, sec. treasy.
Gathorne Hardy, pres. p. l. bd.
July 10. Jno. Winston Spencer, D. of Marlborough, ld. st. hhold.
Wm. Reginald, E. of Devon, chanc. d. Lanc.
Chas. Aug., E. of Tankerville, capt. gent. arms.
Hy. Chas., E. of Cadogan, capt. yeom. guard.
Wm. Alleyne Cecil, c.c. ld. Burghley, treasr. hhold.
Chas. Philip Yorke, c.c. visc. Royston, compt. hhold.
Chas. Jno., ld. Colville of Culross, m. buckhounds.
Stephen Cave, v. pres. bd. tr.
Aug. 9. Hy. Jas. Baillie, M.P. Inverness.
Nov. 10. Sir FitzRoy Edwd. Kelly, ld. ch. bar. ex.
Sir Hugh MacCalmont Cairns, l. j. app.
Sir Rd. Torin Kindersley, late v. chanc.
M.-gen. sir Hy. Knight Storks, G.C.B., gov. Malta.
Dec. 28. Sir Wm. Bovill, ld. ch. just. c. p.
Wm. Robt. Seymour Vesey Fitz-Gerald, gov. Bombay.

1867.

Mar. 19. Robt. Montagu, c.c. lord Robt. Montagu, v. p. comm. education.
Hon. Percy Egerton Herbert, C.B., treasr. hhold.
June 26. Col. Jno. Wilson Patten, chanc. d. Lanc.
Aug. 3. Sir Jno. Rolt, l. j. app.
Sir Robt. Josh. Phillimore, judge admy. court.
Aug 20. Hon. Hy. Geo. Elliot, amb. Turkey.
Nov. 4. Geo. Patton, ld. just. clk. Scotland.
Dec. 20. Sir Fras. Bond Head, bt., late lt. gov. Upp. Canada.

1868.

Feb. 29. Geo. Ward Hunt, ch. ex.
Mar. 28. Sir Wm. Page Wood, l. j. app.
Sir Chas. Jasper Selwyn, l. j. app.
Nov. 7. Col. Thos. Edwd. Taylor, late sec. treasy.; chanc. d. Lanc., *pro. tem.*
Nov. 11. Aug. Wm. Fredk. Spencer Loftus, G.C.B., c.c. lord W. F. S. Lopus, amb. Prussia.

Nov. 11. Sir Jos. Napier, bt., v. chanc. univ. Dublin, and late ld. chanc. Ireland.
Sir Jas. Fergusson, bt., gov. S. Australia.
Dec. 9. Jno. Bright, pres. bd. tr.
Hugh Culling Eardley Childers, first ld. admy.
Austen Hy. Layard, first commr. works, &c.
Wm. Edwd. Forster, v. p. comm. education.
Dec. 12. Fredk. Temple, ld. Dufferin, K.P., K.C.B., chanc. d. Lanc.
Sir Colman Michael O'Loghlen, bt., judge adv. gen.

1869.

Feb. 4. Geo., ld. de Tabley, treasr. hhold.
Sir Geo. Markham Giffard, l. j. app.
Jas. Stansfeld, ld. treasy.
Feb. 15. Wm. Amelius Aubrey De Vere, D. of St. Albans, capt. yeom. guard.
Geo. Wm., ld. Lyttelton, formerly und. sec. cols.
May 13. Jno. Jackson, bp. of London.
Aug. 7. Chas. Stanley, visc. Monck, gov. gen. Canada.
Thos. Geo., ld. Northbrook, und. sec. war.
Geo. Alexr. Hamilton.
Oct. 7. Jas. Moncrieff.
Nov. 11. Sir Alex. Young Spearman, bt., commr. works and nat. debt.
Acton Smee Ayrton, ch. commr. works, &c.

1870.

May 18. Jas. Anthy. Lawson, just. c. p. Ireland.
July 6. Sir Wm. Milbourne James, l. j. app.
Sir Barnes Peacock, late ch. just. Bengal.
Aug. 9. Sir Wm. Heathcote, bt., late M.P. univ. Oxford.
Sir Geo. Mellish, l. j. app.

1871.

Feb. 8. Jno. Robt. Davison, judge adv. gen.
Mar. 24. Sir Jno. Macpherson Macleod, late Madras civ. service.
Sir Jno. Stuart, late v. chanc.
May 16. PR. ARTH. WM. PATR. ALBT., aft. D. of CONNAUGHT, introd., not sw.
Fras. Thos. de Grey, E. Cowper, K.G., capt. gent. arms.
June 29. Sir Fredk. Rogers, K.C.M.G., und. sec. cols.
Mountague Bernard, D.C.L., prof. at Oxford, member jud. comm.
Aug. 19. Sir Edwd. Thornton, K.C.B., en ext. U. S. America.
Nov. 3. Sir Jas. Shaw Willes, late ju c. p.
Sir Montague Edwd. Smith, mem ber jud. comm.
Sir Edwd. Lugard, G.C.B., un sec. war.
Sir Robt. Porrett Collier, memb jud. comm.

1872.

Feb. 5. Sir Jas. Weir Hogg, bt., la M.C.I.
Odo Wm. Leopold Russell, am Germany.
Mar. 19. Richd. d'Aguilar Grosvenor, c. ld. Richd. Grosvenor, chambn. hhold.
Aug. Fredk. Geo. Warwick, l Poltimore, treasr. hhold.
Sir Wm. Thos. Knollys, K.C. comptr. pr. Wales.
May 10. John Geo. Dodson, chairman committees, and dep. sp. h commons.
Aug. 9. Geo. Young, ld. adv. Scotland.
Oct. 15. Sir Roundell Palmer (ld. Se borne), ld. chanc.
Nov. 27. Peter Erle, late charity commr.
Sir Jas. Hannen, judge of ct. prob. and div.

1873.

Mar. 3. Sir John Barnard Byles, late jus c. p.
Mar. 24. Wm. Edwd. Baxter, late se treasy.
Edwd. Hugessen Knatchbul Hugessen, und. sec. cols.
Aug. 4. Geo. Grenfell, ld. Wolverton, se treasy.
Sir Hy. Bartle Edwd. Frere, K.C.B M.C.I.
Aug. 9. Wm. Patrick Adam, paym.-gen &c.
Aug. 30. Sir Geo. Jessel, m. rolls.
Dec. 12. Sir John Duke Coleridge, ld. c just. c. p.
Lyon Playfair, postm. gen.

1874.

Feb. 2. Wm. John, ld. Monson, treas hhold.
Sir Saml. Martin, late bar. ex.
Feb. 21. Hy. Edwd, E. of Ilchester, ca gent. arms.
Richd. Assheton Cross, home sec
Mar. 2. Fras. Hugh Geo., M. of Hertford ld. chambn. hhold.
Hy. Geo. Percy, c.c. E. Percy treasr. hhold.
Fredk., E. Beauchamp, ld. st hhold.

[M]ar. 2. Hy. Richd. Chas. Somerset, c.c. ld. Somerset, compt. hhold.
Geo. Wm., visc. Barrington, v. chambn. hhold.
Dudley Fras. Stuart Ryder, c.c. visc. Sandon, v. p. comm. educatn.
Edwd., ld. Skelmersdale, capt. yeom. guard.
Sir Michael Edwd. Hicks-Beach, bt., ch. sec. Ireland.
Sir John Chas. Dalrymple Hay, bt., commr. pub. works loan bd.
Geo. Sclater Booth, pres. l. g. bd.
[M]ar. 17. Edwd. Strathearn Gordon, ld. adv. Scotland.
[M]ay 12. Hon. Gerard Jas. Noel, form. sec. treasy., aft. first commr. wks., &c.
[J]uly 7. Hy. Chas. Geo. Gordon Lennox, c.c. ld. Hy. Gordon Lennox, first commr. wks., &c.
[A]ug. 6. John Gellibrand Hubbard, first commr. pub. wks. loan bd.
[O]ct. 20. Pr. Leop. Geo. Duncan Albt., aft. D. of Albany, introd., not sw.

1875.

[F]eb. 4. Chas. John, E. of Shrewsbury and Talbot, capt. gent. arms.
Sir Hy. Singer Keating, late just. c. p.
[M]ar. 17. John Douglas Sutherland Campbell, c.c. M. of Lorne, M.P. Argyleshire.
[M]ay 13. Hon. sir Chas. Augs. Murray, K.C.B., groom in waiting.
[N]ov. 27. Sir Richd. Baggallay, l. j. app.
Sir Richd. Couch, late ch. just. Bengal.
Geo. Augs. Fredk. Cavendish Bentinck, judge adv. gen.

1876.

[F]eb. 12. Hon. Hy. Fk. Thynne, c.c. ld. Hy. Fk. Thynne. treasr. hhold.
[M]ar. 24. Sir John Burgess Karslake, late att. gen.
[J]uly 21. Sir Augs. Berkeley Paget, K.C.B., amb. to Italy.
Nov. 28. Colin, ld. Blackburn, ld. of app.
Sir Hy. Conyngham Montgomery, bt., late M.C.I.
Sir Geo. Wm. Wilshere Bramwell, l. j. app.
Sir Wm. Baliol Brett, l. j. app.
Sir Richd. Paul Amphlett, l. j. app.

1877.

[J]uly 11. Hy. Cotton, l. j. app.
[A]ug 13. Geo. Wm., E. of Coventry, capt. gent. arms.
Wm. Hy. Smith, first ld. admy.
Dec. 12. Hon. Alf. Hy. Thesiger, l. j. app.
Dec. 22. Lt.-gen. sir Thos. Myddelton Biddulph, K.C.B., kpr. pr. purse, &c.

1878.

Feb. 22. Jas. Lowther, ch. sec. Ireland.
Mar. 26. Wm., D. of Devonshire, K.G.
Wm. Watson, ld. adv. Scotland.
April 2. Col. hon. Fredk. Arthur Stanley, sec. war.
April 4. Geo. Fras. Hamilton, c.c. ld. Geo. Fras. Hamilton, v. p. comm. educatn.
Aug. 14. John Arthur Roebuck.

1879.

Feb. 22. Hugh de Grey Seymour, c.c. E. of Yarmouth, compt. hhold.
May 17. Wm. Hy., E. of Mount Edgcumbe, ld. chambn. hhold.
Sir Robt. Lush, l. j. app.
June 26. Sir John Mellor, late just. q. b.
Aug. 14. Sir John Alexr. Macdonald, K.C.B., prem. of Canada.

1880.

Mar. 18. Gilbert Hy., ld. Aveland, dep. ld. gr. chambn.
Hy. Cecil Raikes, chairm. comm. ways and means and dep. sp. ho. of commons.
Mar. 24. David Robt. Plunket, paym. gen.
Geo. Cubitt, M.P. West Surrey.
Apr. 20. Hon. Robt. Bourke, late und. sec for.
Sir Wm. Hart-Dyke, late sec. treasy.
Lt.-gen. sir Hy. Fredk. Ponsonby, K.C.B., kpr. pr. purse.
Alexr. Jas. Beresford Beresford-Hope, M.P. Camb. Univ.
Apr. 28. Hugh Lupus, D. of Westminster, K.G., m. horse.
Sir Wm. Geo. Granville Venables Vernon Harcourt, home sec.
May 3. Gavin, E. of Breadalbane, treasr. hhold.
Alexr. Wm. Geo., E. of Fife, capt. gent. arms.
Chas. Wm. Brudenell Bruce, c.c. ld. C. W. B. Bruce, v. chambn. hhold.
Wm., ld. Kensington, compt. hhold.
Jos. Chamberlain, pres. bd. tr.
Anthony John Mundella, v. p. comm. educatn.
Hy. Fawcett, postm. gen.
Geo. Osborne Morgan, judge adv. gen.
Mountstuart Elphinstone Grant Duff, und. sec. cols.
Dec. 16. Geo. John Shaw Lefevre, first commr. wks., &c.

1881.

Mar. 2. Chas., M. of Huntley, capt. gent. arms.

Mar. 2. Sir Arth. Hobhouse, K.C.S.I., memb. jud. comm.
May 18. Sir Richd. Malins, late v. chanc.
July 15. Chas. Robt., ld. Carrington, capt. gent. arms.
Aug. 26. Archd. Philip, E. of Rosebery, und. sec. home.
Dec. 19. Sir Nathl. Lindley, l. j. app.

1882.

Feb. 6. Sir John Holker, l. j. app.
June 29. John David FitzGerald, ld. of app.
Sir Chas. Synge Christopher Bowen, l. j. app.
Geo. Otto Trevelyan, ch. sec. Ireland.
Dec. 28. Sir Chas. Wentworth Dilke, bt., pres. l. g. bd.

1883.

Mar. 19. Edwd. White Benson, abp. of Canterbury.
Apr. 20. Sir Edwd. Fry, l. j. app.
May 22. Sir Hercules Geo. Robt. Robinson, G.C.M.G., gov. C. G. Hope.
Aug. 23. Sir Louis Mallet, C.B., late und. sec. India.
Sir Thos. Dyke Acland, M.P. North Devon.
John Baird Balfour, ld. adv. Scotland.
Dec. 12. Sir John Savile Lumley, K.C.B., amb. Italy.

1884.

May 19. Arthur Wellesley Peel, sp. ho. commons.
Aug. 11. Sir Thos. Erskine May, K.C.B., clk. ho. commons.
Adm. Sir Astley Cooper Key, G.C.B., ld. admy.
Nov. 29. Hy. Campbell Bannerman, ch. sec. Ireland.

1885.

Jan. 27. Sir Robt. Burnett David Morier, K.C.B., amb. Russia.
Mar. 26. Sir Edmd. Baldwin Malet, K.C.B., amb. Germany.
May 19. Fredk. Temple, bp. of London.
Sir John Lambert, K.C.B., form. sec. l. g. bd.
June 24. Sir Hy. James, late atty.-gen.
Randolph Hy. Spencer Churchill, c.c. ld. R. H. S. Churchill, sec. India.
Hon. Edwd. Stanhope, v. pres. comm. educatn.
Edwd. Gibson (ld. Ashbourne), ld. chambn. Ireland.
Sir Hy. Selwin-Ibbetson, bt., form. und. sec. home, sec. treasy., &c.
June 24. Sir Hy. Drummond Wolff, G.C.M.G., K.C.B., high commr., &c., to Egypt.
Sir Hardinge Stanley Giffard (ld. Halsbury), ld. chanc.
Hy. Chaplin, chanc. d. Lanc.
Arthur Jas. Balfour, pres. l. g. bd.
June 27. John Hy., M. of Waterford, K.P., m. buckhounds.
Geo. Hy., earl Cadogan, ld. pr. seal.
Arth. Wm. Hill, c.c. lord A. W. Hill, compt. hhold.
Wm. Pleydell, Bouverie, c.c. visc. Folkestone, treasr. hhold.
Wm. Heneage Legge, c.c. visc. Lewisham, chambn. hhold.
July 9. Sir Arth. John Otway, bt., chairman committees and dep. sp. ho. commons.
Wm. Thackeray Marriott, judge adv. gen.
Sir Massey Lopes, bt., form. ld. admy.
Sir Harry Verney, bt., M.P. Buckm.
Sir Fras. Richd. Sandford, K.C.B., und. sec. Scotland.
Aug. 12. John Hay Athol Macdonald, ld. adv. Scotland.
Sept. 17. Sir Hy. Thurstan Holland, bt., K.C.M.G., v. p. comm. educatn.
Dec. 12. Sir Hy. Chas. Lopes, l. j. app.
Stephen Woulfe Flanagan, late land judge chanc. div. Ireland.

1886.

Feb. 6. Wm. Schomberg Robt., M. of Lothian, kpr. pr. seal, Scotland.
Sir Chas. Lennox Wyke, G.C.M.G., K.C.B., late dipl. service.
Chas. Newdigate Newdigate, late M.P., N. Warwicksh.
John Campbell, E. of Aberdeen, ld. lieut. Ireland.
Sir Farrer Herschell (lord Herschell), ld. chanc.
John Morley, ch. sec. Ireland.
Edwd. Heneage, chanc. d. Lanc.
Feb. 10. Chas. Douglas Richd., ld. Sudeley, capt. gent. arms.
Hon. Edwd. Marjoribanks, compt. hhold.
Feb. 17. Victor Alexr., E. of Elgin, treasr. hhold.
Albert Edmd., E. of Morley, first commr. wks., &c.
Fredk. Edwd. Gould, visc. Kilcoursie, v. chambn. hhold.
Chas., ld. Suffield, m. buckhounds.
John Tomlinson Hibbert, sec. admy.

Mar. 8. John Wm. Mellor, judge adv. gen.
Apr. 3. John Wm., E. of Dalhousie, kpr. gr. seal, Scotland.
Thos. John, ld. Thurlow, paym. gen.
Col. John Sidney North, late M.P. Oxfordsh.
Apr. 16. Sir Ughtred Jas. Kay-Shuttleworth, bt., chanc. d. Lanc.
June 26. Hy. Hartley Fowler, sec treasy
Aug. 3. Sir John Rose, bt., G.C.M.G.
Sir John Hay Drummond-Hay, G.C.M.G., K.C.B.
Chas. Stewart, M. of Londonderry, ld. lieut. Ireland.
Aug. 3. Hy. Matthews, home sec.
Chas. Thomson Ritchie, pres. l. g. bd.
Aug. 16. Wm. John Arth. Chas. Jas., D. of Portland, m. horse.
Algn. Hawkins Thomond, E. of Kintore, capt. yeom. gd.
Nov. 26. Fras. Robt., E. of Rosslyn, capt. gent. arms.
Sir Jas. Bacon, late v. chanc.
Sir Geo. Ferguson Bowen, G.C.M.G., gov. Hong Kong.

1887.

Jan. 25. Edwd. Macnaghten, aft. ld. Macnaghten, ld. of app.
July 12. Adelbert Wellington Brownlow, E. Brownlow, paym. gen.
Sir Jno. Clayton Cowell, K.C.B., mast. hhold.
Nov. 28. Sir Wm. Robt. Grove, late just. q.b.

1888.

Feb. 21. Sir Rd. Garth, late ch. just. Bengal.
June 29. Edw. Robt. Earl Lytton, G.C.B., G.C.S.I., amb. to France.
Sir Wm. Arth. White, G.C.B., G.C.M.G., amb. to Turkey.

LORDS LIEUTENANT OF IRELAND.
CHIEF SECRETARIES TO THE LORDS LIEUTENANT.
PARLIAMENTARY SECRETARIES AND UNDER SECRETARIES TO THE LORDS LIEUTENANT.

See Part X. "Ireland," *post.*

THE PRINCIPAL SECRETARIES OF STATE.

The earliest mention of a king's secretary (*secretarius noster*) occurs in 1253 (37 Hen. III.). There was only one secretary of state until 1539, when Henry VIII. increased the number to two, of equal rank and authority. These secretaries were either at the time of their first appointment, or soon afterwards, styled secretaries for the "northern" and "southern" departments. Both attended to home affairs, but foreign affairs were divided between them—the "northern" secretary taking the Low Countries, Germany, Sweden, Poland, Russia; and the "southern" secretary taking France, Switzerland, Italy, Spain, Portugal, Turkey, &c. Irish affairs were under the charge of the senior secretary.

In 1708, soon after the union between England and Scotland, a third secretary of state was appointed, styled the secretary of state for Scotland. This office was abolished in 1746; but in 1885, by 48 & 49 Vict., cap. 61, a "secretary for Scotland" was again appointed. He, however, does not rank as a secretary of state, and is not always a cabinet minister.

In 1768 a third secretary of state was again appointed, to attend to American affairs. He was styled the secretary of state for the colonies. This office was abolished in 1782 by 22 Geo. III., cap. 82. In the same year the terms "northern" and "southern" departments were discontinued, and the secretaryships were divided into "home" an "foreign," Ireland and the colonies being allotted to the former.

The "secretary at war" was not a principal secretary of state, but a official of inferior rank. On July 11, 1794, a secretary of state fo war was appointed, and on March 17, 1801, the duties connected wit the colonies were transferred to his department, he being thencefort styled secretary of state for war and the colonies. The secretary a war was continued as a separate office, but from 1855 it was always hel jointly with the secretaryship of state for war, and it was ultimatel abolished in 1863 by 26 & 27 Vict., cap. 12.

On June 12, 1854, a fourth secretary of state was appointed, and th duties of the "war" and "colonial" departments were separated.

In 1858 the board of control was abolished by 21 & 22 Vict., cap. 106 and a fifth secretary of state was appointed for Indian affairs. He i styled the secretary of state for India.

The Irish secretary is not a secretary of state, but is chief secretary t the lord lieutenant of Ireland. He is not always a cabinet minister.

There are now five principal secretaries of state viz. :—

I. Home.
II. Foreign.
III. War.
IV. Colonies.
V. India.

These are always members of the Cabinet, and retire from office on change of ministers.

The division of the duties of the principal secretaries of state int departments is purely a matter of arrangement for greater convenienc in the despatch of business. Each secretary has full power to transac the business of any or every department.

PRINCIPAL SECRETARIES OF STATE DOWN TO 1782.

See Introduction, *ante* p. 221.

The earlier dates represent the time when they were *found* to be secre taries, not their appointments, unless expressly so mentioned.

King Henry III.

1253. John Maunsell, described as "*secretarius noster.*"

King Edward I.

1278. Francis Accursii.
1299. John de Benstede.

King Edward II.

1308. Wm. de Melton.

* * * *

King Richard II.

1379. Robt. Braybrooke.

King Henry IV.

1402. John Profit, held the office until 1412, when he was app. ld. pr. seal.

King Henry V.

1415. John Stone, who, before 1421, wa succ. by Wm. Alnwick.

King Henry VI.

1432. Wm. Hayton, dismissed and no pe son at that time appointed to su ceed him.
1439. Thos. Beckington, who held th office until 1443, when he wa app. ld. pr. seal.
1460. Thos. Manning.

King Edward IV.

1464. Wm. Hatcliffe, called "one of th king's secretaries," called secr tary and councillor, in 1467; he the office until 1480, when a c adjutor, Oliver King, was giv him on account of his age: Oliver King was to succeed him; Hatcliffe died same year.

1408. Oliver King.

KING RICHARD III.

1483. John Kendal; Oliver King having been removed. Kendal was sec. on Aug. 1, 1485.

KING HENRY VII.

1485. Richd. Fox, made bp. of Exeter in 1487, probably succ. by

1487. Oliver King, who was certainly sec. in 1489 and in 1492, when he was made bp. of Exeter; probably succ. by

1500. Thos. Ruthal, or Routhall, who was certainly sec. in 1500 and to 1509, when he became bp. of Durham.

KING HENRY VIII.

1509. Routhall, *contd.* Sec. until May 1516, when he became ld. pr. seal.

1516. Richd. Pace.

1526. Wm. Knight.

1528. Stephen Gardiner, bp. of Winchester in 1531.

1533. Thos. Cromwell, aft. ld. Cromwell and E. of Essex; ld. pr. seal, July 2, 1536.

1536. Thos. Wriothesley.

FIRST APPOINTMENT OF TWO SECRETARIES.

1539. Thos. Wriothesley, and
Sir Ralph Sadler.

1543. Sir Wm. Petre, *vice* Wriothesley.
Sir Wm. Paget, *vice* Sadler, April 23.

KING EDWARD VI.

1547. Sir Wm. Petre, and
Sir Wm. Paget, *contd.*

1548. Sir Wm. Petre, and
Sir Thos. Smith.

1549. Nichs. Wotton, and
Sir Wm. Petre.
Sir Wm. Cecil, *vice* Wotton.

1551. Sir Wm. Petre and sir Wm. Cecil, "our secretaries."

1553. Sir John Cheke, in addition to sir Wm. Petre and sir Wm. Cecil.

QUEEN MARY.

1553. Sir Wm. Petre, and sir John Bourne.

1557. John Boxall, the first sec. app. by letters pat.

QUEEN ELIZABETH.

1558. Sir Wm. Cecil, aft. ld. Burleigh; ld. treasr. in 1572.

1572. Sir Thos. Smith.

1574. Sir Fras. Walsingham.

1578. Thos. Wilson, app. by pat., Jan. 5, in addition to sir Fras. Walsingham.

1586. Wm. Davison, app. "one of the chief secretaries" by pat.

1596. Sir Robt. Cecil, also app. "one of the chief secretaries" by pat. July 13.
He continued sec. during the remainder of this reign.

KING JAMES I.

1603. Sir Robt. Cecil. *contd.*; aft. E of Salisbury.

1609. Sir Alexr. Hay.

1612. Thos. Hamilton.

1616. Sir Ralph Winwood.
Sir Thos. Lake.

1618. Sir John Herbert, *vice* Winwood.
Sir Robt. Naunton, *vice* Herbert.

1619. Sir Geo. Calvert, aft. ld. Baltimore. *vice* Lake.

1622. Sir Edwd. Conway, aft ld. Conway, *vice* Naunton.

KING CHARLES I.

1625. Sir Albertus Morton. Apr. 9.
Sir Edwd., ld. Conway, *contd.* Apr. 23.
Sir John Coke, *vice* Morton. Nov. 9.

1630. Sir Dudley Carleton, ld. Carleton, aft visc. Dorchester, *vice* Conway.

1632. Fras., ld. Cottington, *vice* Dorchester.
Sir Harry Vane, *vice* Coke.
Sir Fras. Windebanke, *vice* Cottington.

1641. Sir Edwd. Nicholas, *vice* Windebanke.

1642. Lucius, visc. Falkland, *vice* Vane.
Geo., ld. Digby, *vice* Falkland.
On the commencement of the civil war all went into confusion. The name of Secretary of State was abolished during the Commonwealth.

FROM THE RESTORATION OF KING CHARLES II.

1660. Sir Edwd. Nicholas. June 1.
Sir Wm. Morrice. June 30.

1662. Sir Hy. Bennet, aft. E. of Arlington, *vice* Nicholas.

1668. Sir John Trevor, *vice* Morrice. Sept. 29.

1672. Hy. Coventry, *vice* Trevor. July 18.

1674. Sir Jos. Williamson, *vice* Arlington. Sept. 11.

1678. Robt., E. of Sunderland, *vice* Williamson. Feb. 20.

1680. Sir Leoline Jenkins, *vice* Coventry. Feb. 11.

1681. Edwd., E. of Conway, *vice* Sunderland. Mar. 9.

1683. Robt., E. of Sunderland, *again*, *vice* Conway. Mar. 6.
1684. Sidney Godolphin, aft. E. of Godolphin, *vice* Jenkins. May 1.
Chas., E. of Middleton, *vice* Godolphin. Sept. 25.

KING JAMES II.

1685. Robt., E. of Sunderland, *again*. Mar. 13.
1688. Richd., visc. Preston, *vice* Middleton.

KING WILLIAM III.

1689. Chas., E. of Shrewsbury. Feb. 19.
Danl., E. of Nottingham.
1690. Hy., visc. Sydney, aft. E. Romney, *vice* Shrewsbury. Dec. 26.
1692. Sir John Trenchard, *vice* Sydney.
1694. Chas., E. of Shrewsbury, *again*, *vice* Nottingham. Mar. 4.
1695. Sir Wm. Trumbull, *vice* Trenchard. May 3.
1697. Jas. Vernon, *vice* Trumbull. Dec 5.
1700. Edwd., E. of Jersey, *vice* Shrewsbury. May 26.
Sir Chas. Hedges, *vice* Vernon. Nov. 5.
1701. Chas., E. of Manchester, *vice* Jersey. Jan. 4.

QUEEN ANNE.

1702. Danl., E. of Nottingham, *again* May 15.
Sir Chas. Hedges, *again*, May 2.
1704. Robt. Harley, aft. E. of Oxford and E. Mortimer, *vice* Nottingham. May 18.
1706. Chas., E. of Sunderland, *vice* Hedges. Dec. 3.
1708. Hy. Boyle, aft. ld. Carleton, *vice* Harley. Feb. 15.
1710. Wm., ld. Dartmouth, aft. E. of Dartmouth, *vice* Sunderland. June 15.
Hy. St. John, aft. visc. Bolingbroke, *vice* Boyle. Sept. 21.
1713. Wm. Bromley, *vice* Dartmouth.

KING GEORGE I.

1714. Chas., visc. Townshend, *vice* Bolingbroke. Sept. 27.
Jas. Stanhope, aft. E. Stanhope, *vice* Bromley. Sept. 27.
1716. Paul Methuen, in the absence of Mr. Stanhope. June 23.
1717. Chas., E. of Sunderland, *vice* Stanhope. Apr. 16.
Jos. Addison, *vice* Townshend. Apr 16.
1718. Jas. Craggs, *vice* Addison. Mar. 16.
Jas., E. Stanhope, *again*, *vice* Sunderland. Mar. 18.
1721. Chas., visc. Townshend, *vice* Stanhope. Feb. 10.
John, ld. Carteret, aft. E. Granville, *vice* Craggs. Mar. 5.
1724. Thos. Pelham Holles, D. of Newcastle, *vice* Carteret. Apr. 14.

KING GEORGE II.

1727. D. of Newcastle, and
Visc. Townshend, *contd.*; patents dated July 27.
1730. Wm., ld. Harrington, aft. E. of Harrington, *vice* Townshend. June 27.
1742. John, ld. Carteret. *again* *vice* Harrington. Feb. 15.
1744. Wm., E. of Harrington, *again*, *vice* Carteret. Nov. 27.
1746. John, E. Granville, *vice* Harrington. Feb. 10.
1746. Wm., E. of Harrington, *again*, *vice* Granville. Feb. 14.
Philip Dormer, E. of Chesterfield, *vice* Harrington, Nov. 4.
1748. John, D. of Bedford, *vice* Chesterfield, Feb. 13.
1751. Robt., E. of Holdernesse, *vice* Bedford, June 21.
1754. Sir Thos. Robinson, aft. ld. Grantham, *vice* Newcastle, Apr. 15.
1755. Hy. Fox, aft. ld. Holland, *vice* Robinson, Nov. 25.
1756. Wm. Pitt, aft. E. of Chatham, *vice* Fox, Dec. 14; res. Apr. 1757.
1757. Wm. Pitt, *again*, June 30.

KING GEORGE III.

1760. Wm. Pitt, and
Robt., E. of Holdernesse, *contd.*
From this time the two departments are distinguished, "N. Dep." signifying Northern Department, and "S. Dep." Southern Department.
1761. John, E. of Bute, *vice* Holdernesse (S. Dep.), Mar. 25; pat. dated Apr. 13.
Chas., E. of Egremont, *vice* Pitt (N. Dep.), Oct. 9; pat. dated Oct. 23.
1762. Hon. Geo. Grenville, *vice* Bute (S. Dep.), May 29; pat. dated June 19.
1763. John, E. of Sandwich, *vice* Egremont (N. Dep.), Sept. 2; pat. dated Sept. 23.
Geo., E. of Halifax, *vice* Grenville (S. Dep.), Oct. 14; pat. dated Nov. 15.
1765. Aug. Hy., D. of Grafton, *vice* Halifax (S. Dep.), July 10.
Hon. Hy. Seymour Conway, *vice* Sandwich (N. Dep.), July 10; pat. dated July 19; transf. to S. Dep., May 26, 1766.
1766. Chas., D. of Richmond, *vice* Grafton (N. Dep.), May 6; pat. dated June 3.
Wm., E. of Shelburne, aft. M. of Lansdowne, *vice* Richmond (N. Dep.), July 30; pat. dated Aug. 18.
1768. Thos., visc. Weymouth, aft. M. of

Bath, *vice* Conway (S. Dep.), Jan. 20; pat. dated Feb. 5; transf. to N. Dep., Oct. 21.

1768. Wm. Hy., E. of Rochford, *vice* Shelburne (S. Dep.), Oct. 21; transf. to N. Dep., Dec. 19, 1770.

1770. John, E. of Sandwich, *again*, *vice* Weymouth (S. Dep.), Dec. 19.

1771. Geo., E. of Halifax, *vice* Sandwich (S. Dep.), Jan. 22.

1771. Hy., E. of Suffolk and Berkshire, *vice* Halifax (S. Dep.), June 12.

1775. Thos., visc. Weymouth, aft. M. of Bath, *again*, *vice* Rochford (N. Dep.), Nov. 10.

1779. David, visc. Stormont, aft. E. of Mansfield, *vice* Suffolk (S. Dep.), Oct. 27; pat. dated Nov. 30.

Wills, E. of Hillsborough, aft. M. of Downshire (N. Dep.), Nov. 24; pat. dated Jan. 19.

UNDER SECRETARIES OF STATE DOWN TO 1782.

See Introduction, *ante* p. 221.

1680. John Cooke. Apr. 14.
Fras. Gwynn. Apr. 26.
1682. Wm. Bridgeman, *vice* Gwynn.

William and Mary and King William III.

Southern Department.

1689. Richd. Warr.
John Isham.
1699. Robt. Yard.
Matt. Prior.

Northern Department.

1692. Wm. Bridgeman.
Jas. Vernon.
Thos. Hopkins, *vice* Vernon.
1697. Thos. Hopkins.
John Ellis, *vice* Bridgeman.
1700. John Ellis.
John Tucker, *vice* Hopkins.

Queen Anne.

Southern Department.

1702. Richd. Warr.
Wm. Aglionby.
1704. John Isham, *vice* Aglionby.
1707. John Tucker.
Jos. Addison.
1710. Thos. Hopkins.
Robt. Pringle.

Northern Department.

1702. John Ellis, John Tucker, } *contd.*
1704. Richd. Warr.
Erasmus Lewis.
1710. Geo. Tilson.
Horatio Walpole.

King George I.

Southern Department.

1714. Robt. Pringle, *contd.*
Chas. Stanhope.
1717. Temple Stanian.
Thos. Tickell.
1718. — Corbiere.
Chas. de la Faye.
1724. Chas. de la Faye.
Temple Stanian.

Northern Department.

1714. Geo. Tilson, Horatio Walpole, } *contd.*
1717. Geo. Tilson.
Chas. de la Faye.
1724. Geo. Tilson.
Thos. Townshend.

King George II.

Southern Department.

1735. John Couraud, *vice* Stanian.
1736. And. Stone, *vice* de la Faye.
1743. Thos. Ramsden, *vice* Couraud.

Northern Department.

1730. Geo. Tilson.
Edwd. Weston.
1740. Thos. Stanhope, *vice* Tilson.

SOUTHERN DEPARTMENT (*continued*).

1748. Richd. Nevill Aldworth.
John Potter.
Hon. Richd. Leveson Gower, *vice* Potter.

1751. Claudius Amyand.
Richd. Pottinger.

1754. Claudius Amyand.
Jas. Rivers.

1755. Claudius Amyand.
Jas. Rivers.
Hy. Rivers.

1756. Robt. Wood.
Jas. Rivers.

NORTHERN DEPARTMENT (*continued*).

1742. Edwd. Weston.
— Balaguier.

1745. Edwd. Weston.
— Chetwynd.

1746. — Chetwynd.
John Potter.

1748. Andw. Stone.
Thos. Ramsden.

1750. Claudius Amyand.
Hugh Valence Jones, *vice* Ramsden.

1751. Jas. Wallis, *vice* Amyand.
Andw. Stone.

1754. Jas. Wallis.
Richd. Pottinger, *vice* Stone.

1760. Michael Peter Morin, *vice* Pottinger.
Wm. Fraser, *vice* Wallis.

KING GEORGE III.

SOUTHERN DEPARTMENT.

1761. Robt. Wood, Jas. Rivers, } *contd.*

1762. Edwd. Sedgwick.
Lovel Stanhope.

1765. Wm. Burke.
Michael Peter Morin.
John Chas. Roberts.

1768. Robt. Wood.
Wm. Fraser.

1773. Fras. Willis.
Sir Stanier Porten.

1775. Sir Stanier Porten.
Sir Anthy. Chamier, *vice* Willis.

1779. Robt. Bell, *vice* Chamier.

NORTHERN DEPARTMENT.

1761. Edwd. Weston.
Chas. Jenkinson.

1762. Edwd. Weston.
Edwd. Sedgwick.
Lovell Stanhope, *vice* Weston.

1763. Richd. Phelps.
Jas. Rivers.

1765. Rd. Stonehewer.
Wm. Fraser.

1766. Wm. Fraser.
Wm. Burke.

1768. Wm. Fraser.
David Hume, *vice* Burke.
Robt. Wood.

1769. R. Sutton.
Stanier Porten.

1770. Richd. Phelps.
Wm. Fraser.

1771. Edwd. Sedgwick.
Lovel Stanhope.
Wm. Eden.
Wm. Fraser.

1772. Wm. Fraser.
Thos. Whately.

1773. Wm. Eden, *vice* Whately.

1779. Wm. Fraser.
Benj. L'Anglois.

SECRETARIES OF STATE FOR THE HOME DEPARTMENT.

See Introduction, *ante* p. 221, and "Secretaries of State," *ante* p. 222.

1782. Wm., E. of Shelburne, *vice* ld. Stormont, Mar. 27.
Thos., ld. Grantham, July 17; res. Apr. 1783.

1783. Fredk., ld. North, aft. E. of Guildford, Apr. 2.
Fras., M. of Carmarthen, aft. succ. as D. of Leeds, Dec. 23.

1789. Wm. Wyndham Grenville, aft. ld. Grenville, June 5.

1791. Hy. Dundas, aft. ld. Melville, June 8.

1794. Wm. Hy., D. of Portland, July 11.

1801. Thos., ld. Pelham, aft. E. of Chichester, July 30.

1803. Chas. Philip Yorke, Aug. 7; res. May 1804.

1804. Robt., ld. Hawkesbury, aft. E. of Liverpool, May 12.
1806. Geo. John, E. Spencer, Feb. 5.
1807. Robt., ld. Hawkesbury, *again*, Mar. 25.
1809. Richd. Ryder, Nov. 1.
1812. Hy., visc. Sidmouth, June 11.
1822. Robt. Peel, aft. sir R., bt., Jan. 17.
1827. Wm. Sturges Bourne, Apr. 30.
Hy., M. of Lansdowne, July 16.
1828. Robt. Peel, *again*, Jan. 26.
1830. Wm., visc. Melbourne, Nov. 22.
1834. John, visc. Duncannon, aft. E. of Besborough, July 19.
Hy. Goulburn, Dec. 15.
1835. Ld. John Russell, aft. E. Russell, Apr. 18.
1839. Constantine Hy., M. of Normanby, Aug. 30.
1841. Sir Jas. Robt. Geo. Graham, bt., Sept. 6.
1846. Sir Geo. Grey, bt., July 6.
1852. Spencer Horatio Walpole, Feb. 27.
Hy. Jno., visc. Palmerston, Dec. 28.
1855. Hon. Sidney Herbert, aft. ld. Herbert of Lea, Feb. 8.
1855. Sir Geo. Grey, bt., *again*, Feb. 28.
1858. Spencer Horatio Walpole, *again*, Feb. 26.
1859. Thos. Hy. Sutton Sotheron-Estcourt, Mar. 3.
Sir Geo. Cornewall Lewis, bt., June 18.
1861. Sir Geo. Grey, bt., G.C.B., *again*, July 25.
1866. Spencer Horatio Walpole, *again*, July 6.
1867. Gathorne Hardy, aft. visc. Cranbrook, May 17.
1868. Hy. Austin Bruce, aft. ld. Aberdare, Dec. 9.
1873. Robt. Lowe, aft. visc. Sherbrooke, Aug. 9.
1874. Rd. Assheton Cross, aft. visc. Cross, Feb. 21.
1880. Sir Wm. Geo. Granville Venables Vernon Harcourt, Apr. 28.
1885. Sir Rd. Assheton Cross, G.C.B., *again*, June 24.
1886. Hugh Culling Eardley Childers, Feb. 6.
Henry Matthews, Aug. 3.

UNDER SECRETARIES OF STATE FOR THE HOME DEPARTMENT.

There are two under secretaries for this department, one parliamentary, the other permanent.

Parliamentary Under Secretaries of State for the Home Department.

From the year 1782, when the "Southern" was changed into the "Home" Department.

1782. Thos. Orde, and
Hy. Strachey.
1783. Hon. G. North.
1784. Hon. John Thos. Townshend, Feb. 10.
1796. Chas. Greville.
1798. Wm. Wickham.
1800. Edwd. Finch Hatton.
Sir Geo. Shee, bt.
1803. Reginald Pole Carew.
1804. John Hy. Smyth.
1806. Chas. Watkin Williams Wynn, Feb. 19.
1807. Hon. Chas. Cecil Cope Jenkinson, aft. E. of Liverpool, Oct. 10.
1810. Hy. Goulburn, Feb. 27.
1812. John Hiley Addington, Aug. 21.
1818. Hy. Clive, Apr. 21.
1822. Geo. Robt. Dawson, Jan. 17.
1827. Spencer Perceval, Apr. 30.
Thos. Spring Rice, aft. ld. Monteagle, July 16.
1828. Wm. Yates Peel, Apr. 5.
1830. Sir Geo. Clerk, bt., Aug. 5.
Hon. Geo. Lamb, Nov. 22.
1834. Hy., visc. Howick, aft. E. Grey, Jan. 13.
Edwd. John Stanley, aft. ld. Eddisbury, and ld. Stanley of Alderly, July 23.
Wm. Gregson, Jan. 3.
1835. Hon. Fox Maule, aft. ld. Panmure and E. of Dalhousie, Apr. 18.
1841. Edwd. Adolphus, ld. Seymour, June 15.

1841. Hon. John Hy. Thos. Manners Sutton, Sept. 3.
1842. Sir Wm. Marcus Somerville, bt., July 5.
1847. Sir Denis Le Marchant, July 22.
1848. Geo. Cornewall Lewis, aft. sir G., bt., May 15.
1850. Hon. Edwd. Pleydell Bouverie, July 9.
1852. Sir Wm. Geo. Hilton Jolliffe, bt., Feb.
1853. Hon. Hy. Fitzroy, Dec.
1855. Wm. Nathl. Massey, Feb.
1858. Gathorne Hardy, aft. visc. Cranbrook, Feb.
1859. Geo. Clive, June.
1863. Hy. Austin Bruce, aft. Lord Aberdare.
1864. Hon. Thos. Geo. Baring, aft. ld. and E. of Northbrook.
1866. Saml. Richd. Lowry, E. of Belmore, July.
1867. Sir Jas. Fergusson, bt.
1868. Sir Michael Hicks-Beach, bt., Feb.
Edwd. Hugessen Knatchbull-Hugessen, aft. ld. Brabourne, Dec.
1871. Hy. Selfe Page Winterbotham.
1874. Sir Hy. Jno. Selwin-Ibbetson, bt., Feb.
1878. Sir Matthew White Ridley, bt.
1880. Leonard Hy. Courtney, May.
1881. Arch. Philip, E. of Rosebery.
1883. John Tomlinson Hibbert.
1884. Hy. Hartley Fowler.
1885. Chas. Beilby Stuart-Wortley, June.
1886. Hy. Broadhurst, Feb.
Chas. B. Stuart-Wortley, *again*, Aug

Permanent Under Secretaries of State for the Home Department.

1782. Evan Nepean, aft. sir E., bt.
1789. Scrope Bernard.
1792. John King.
1806. John Beckett, jun., aft. sir J., bt., Feb. 19.
1817. Hy. Hobhouse, June 28.
1827. Saml. March Phillips, July 16.
1848. Horatio Waddington, May 15.
1867. Hon. Adolphus Freak Octavius Liddell, aft. sir A., K.C.B.; d June 27, 1885.
1885. On Liddell's death, Sir Hy. J. S Maine, K.C.S.I., was appointed but, being unable through ill health to perform the duties, he retired in favour of Godfrey Lushington, July.

SECRETARIES OF STATE FOR FOREIGN AFFAIRS.

See Introduction, *ante* p. 221, and "Secretaries of State," *ante* p. 222.

1782. Chas. Jas. Fox, Mar. 27; res. July 5.
Thos. Townshend, aft. ld. and visc. Sydney, July 13.
1783. Chas. Jas. Fox, *again*, Apr. 2.
Geo., E. Temple, aft. M. of Buckingham, Dec. 19.
Thos., ld., aft. visc. Sydney, *again*, Dec. 23; res. May 1791.
1791. Wm. Wyndham, lord Grenville, June 8.
1801. Robt., ld. Hawkesbury, aft. E. of Liverpool, Feb. 20.
1804. Dudley, ld., aft. E. of Harrowby, May 14.
1805. Hy., ld., aft. E. of Mulgrave, Jan. 11.
1806. Chas. Jas. Fox, *again*, Feb. 7; *d.* Sept. 13, 1806.
Chas., ld. Howick, aft. E. Grey, Sept. 24.
1807. Geo. Canning, Mar. 25; res. Sept. 1809.
1809. Hy., E. Bathurst, Oct. 11.
Richd., M. Wellesley, Dec. 6.
1812. Robt. Hy., visc. Castlereagh, aft M. of Londonderry, Mar. 4; *d* Aug. 12, 1822.
1822. Geo. Canning, Sept. 16.
1827. John Wm., visc. Dudley and Ward Apr. 30.
1828. Geo., E. of Aberdeen, June 2.
1830. Hy. John, visc. Palmerston, Nov 22.
1834. Arthur, D. of Wellington; entrusted with the three seals of secs. of st. Nov. 15; he retained the seal o for. sec., Dec. 9, 1834.
1835. Hy. John, visc. Palmerston, *again* Apr. 18.
1841. Geo., E. of Aberdeen, *again*, Sept. 2
1846. Hy. John, visc. Palmerston, *again* July 6.
1851. Granville Geo., E. Granville, Dec 26.
1852. Jas. Howard, E. of Malmesbury Feb. 27.
Lord John Russell, aft. E. Russell Dec. 28.

1853. Geo. Wm. Fredk., E. of Clarendon, K.G., Feb. 21.
1858. Jas. Howard, E. of Malmesbury, *again*, Feb. 26.
1859. Lord John Russell, aft. E. Russell, *again*, June 18.
1865. Geo. Wm. Fredk., E. of Clarendon, *again*, Nov. 3.
1866. Hon. Edwd. Hy. Stanley, c.c. lord Stanley; aft. E. of Derby, July 6.
1868. Geo. Wm. Fredk., E. of Clarendon, K.G., *again*, Dec. 9.
1870. Granville Geo., E. Granville, *again*, July 6.
1874. Edwd. Hy., E. of Derby, *again*, Feb. 21.
1878. Robt. Arthur Talbot, M. of Salisbury Apr. 2.
1880. Granville, Geo., E. Granville, K.G., *again*, Apr. 28.
1885. Robt. Arthur Talbot, M. of Salisbury, K.G., *again*, June 24; held with the premiership.
1886. Archd. Philip, E. of Rosebery, Feb. 6.
Stafford Hy., E. of Iddesleigh, G.C.B., Aug. 3; *d.* Jan. 12, 1887.
1887. Robt. Arthur Talbot, M. of Salisbury, *again*, Jan. 14; held with the premiership.

UNDER SECRETARIES OF STATE FOR FOREIGN AFFAIRS.

See "Under Secretaries of State," *ante* p. 225.

THERE were at first two under secretaries for foreign affairs, both parliamentary; but in 1790 one of the under secretaryships was made a permanent appointment. In 1824 a third under secretary (parliamentary) was appointed, but this was discontinued in 1827. An assistant under secretary was appointed on Oct. 1, 1858, a legal assistant under secretary on July 14, 1876, and on the promotion of this officer to the permanent under secretaryship on Sept. 23, 1882, a second assistant under secretary was appointed; all these appointments being permanent.

PARLIAMENTARY UNDER SECRETARIES OF STATE FOR FOREIGN AFFAIRS.

From the year 1782, when the "Northern" was changed into the "Foreign" department.

1782. Richd. Brinsley Sheridan.
Wm. Fraser.
Geo. Maddison, *vice* Sheridan.
1783. St Andrew St. John, *vice* Maddison.
Wm. Fraser, sole sec.
1789. Jas. Bland Burgess, *vice* Fraser, Aug. 22.
Hon. Dudley Ryder, aft. ld. and E. of Harrowby, Aug. 24.

In 1790 George Aust was appointed Permanent Under Secretary, *vice* Ryder. See "Permanent Under Secretaries," below.

PARLIAMENTARY UNDER SECRETARIES—*continued.*

1789. Jas. Bland Burgess, above named, Aug. 22.
1796. Geo. Canning, Jan. 5.
1799. John Hookham Frere, Apr. 1.
1800. Edwd. Fisher, Sept. 25.
1801. Fredk., ld. Harvey, aft. E. and M. of Bristol, Feb. 20.
1803. Chas. Arbuthnot, Nov. 8.
1804. Hon. Wm. Eliot, aft. E. of St. Germans, June 5.
1805. Robt. Ward, Feb. 25.
1806. Hon. Geo. Walpole, Feb. 20.
Sir Fras. Vincent, bt., Feb. 20.
1807. Jas. Edwd., visc. Fitz Harris, aft. E. of Malmesbury, Mar. 30.
Hon. Chas. Bagot, Aug. 19.
1809. Culling Chas. Smith, Dec. 13.
1812. Edwd. Cooke, Feb. 28.
1822. Richd. Chas. Fras., E. of Clanwilliam, Jan. 22.
1823. Lord Fras. Nathaniel Conyngham, aft. E. of Mount Charles and M. Conyngham, Jan. 6.
1824. Chas. Aug., ld. Howard de Walden, aft. ld. Seaford, app. third under sec. July 5.

1826. Ulick John, M. of Clanricarde, Jan. 2, *vice* Conyngham; retired Aug. 17, 1827, and the third under secretaryship was not filled up.
1828. Cospatrick Alexr., lord Dunglas, June 9.
1830. Sir Geo. Shee, bt., Nov. 26.
1834. Geo., visc. Fordwich, Nov. 13.
Philip Hy., visc. Mahon, Dec. 17.
1835. Hon. Wm. Thos. Horner Fox Strangways, aft. E. of Ilchester, Aug. 15.
1840. Granville Geo. Leveson, visc. Leveson, aft. E. Granville, Mar. 7.
1841. Chas. John, visc. Canning, aft. E. Canning, Sept. 4.
1846. Hon. Geo. Aug. Fredk. Percy Sydney Smythe, aft. visc. Strangford, Jan. 27.
Edwd. John Stanley, aft. ld. Eddisbury and ld. Stanley of Alderley, July 6.
1852. Austen Hy. Layard, aft. sir A., Feb. 12.
Hon. Edwd. Hy. Stanley, c.c. ld. Stanley; aft. E. of Derby, May 18.
1852. John, ld. Wodehouse, aft. E. of Kimberley, Dec. 28.
1856. Hy. Petty, E. of Shelburne, aft. M. of Lansdowne, July 5.
1858. Wm. R. Seymour Vesey Fitzgerald, aft. Sir W., Feb. 26.
1859. John, ld. Wodehouse, aft. E. of Kimberley, *again*, June 19.
1861. Austen Hy. Layard, aft. sir A., *again*, Aug. 15.
1866. Edwd. Christr. Egerton, July 6.
1868. Arthur John Otway, aft. sir A., Dec. 12.
1871. Geo. Hy. Chas., visc. Enfield, Jan. 9.
1874. Hon. Robt. Bourke, aft. ld. Connemara, Feb. 23.
1880. Sir Chas. Wentworth Dilke, bt., Apr. 28.
1883. Lord Edmond Geo. Petty Fitzmaurice, Jan. 1.
1885. Hon. Robt. Bourke, aft. ld. Connemara, *again*, June 24.
1886. James Boyce, Feb.
Sir Jas. Fergusson, bt., G.C.S.I., Aug.

Permanent Under Secretaries of State for Foreign Affairs.

1790. Geo. Aust, Feb. 20.
1795. Geo. Hammond, Oct. 16; res. 1806.
1807. Geo. Hammond, re-app. Mar. 30.
1809. Wm. Richd. Hamilton, Oct. 16.
1817. Josh. Planta, July 25.
1827. John Backhouse, Apr. 23.
1842. Hy. Unwin Addington, Mar. 4.
1854. Edmd. Hammond, aft. ld. Hammond, Apr. 10.
1873. Chas. Stuart Aubrey, lord Tenterden, K.C.B., Oct. 10.
1882. Sir Julian Pauncefote, C.M.G., C.B., Sept. 23.

Assistant Permanent Under Secretaries of State for Foreign Affairs.

From their first appointment in 1858.

1858. Jas. Murray, Oct. 1.
1869. Hon. Thos. Chas. Wm. Spring Rice.
1870. Odo W. L. Russell, c.c. ld. O. Russell, and aft. ld. Ampthill, Aug. 10.
1871. Chas. Stuart Aubrey, ld. Tenterden, Jan. 9; app. perm. under sec., Oct. 10, 1873.
1873. Thos. Villiers Lister, aft. sir T., K.C.M.G., Oct. 10.
1876. Sir Julian Pauncefote, July 14, legal assist. under sec.; app. perm. under sec., Sept. 23, 1882.
1882. Philip Hy. Wodehouse Corrie, C.B., aft. sir P., K.C.B., second assist. under sec., Oct. 24.

SECRETARIES OF STATE FOR WAR AND COLONIES.

From the establishment of the War Department in 1794.

See Introduction, *ante* p. 221, "Secretaries of State," *ante* p. 222, and "Secretaries of State for the Colonies from 1768 to 1782," *post* p. 234.

1794. Hy. Dundas, aft. visc. Melville, sec. for war, July 11.
The business of the Colonies, which was carried on at the Home Office, was transferred in 1801 to the War Department.
1804. Robt., ld. Hobart, Mar. 17.
John, E., aft. M. Camden, May 12.

1805. Robt., visc. Castlereagh, July 10.
1806. Wm. Windham, Feb. 14.
1807. Robt., visc. Castlereagh, *again*, Mar. 25.
1809. Robt., E. of Liverpool, late ld. Hawkesbury, Oct. 11.
1812. Hy., E. Bathurst, June 11.
1827. Fredk. John, visc. Goderich, aft. E. of Ripon, Apr. 30.
1827. Wm. Huskisson, Aug. 17.
1828. Sir Geo. Murray, May 30.
1830. Fredk. John, visc. Goderich, aft. E. of Ripon, *again*, Nov. 22.
1833. Hon. Edwd. Geoffrey Smith Stanley, c.c. ld. Stanley; aft. ld. Stanley of Bickerstaffe and E. of Derby; Apr. 3.
1834. Thos. Spring Rice, aft. ld. Monteagle, and
Geo., E. of Aberdeen, June 5.
1835. Chas. Grant, aft. ld. Glenelg, Apr. 18.
1839. Constantine Hy., M. of Normanby, Feb. 20.
Lord John Russell, aft. E. Russell, Aug. 30.
1841. Hon. E. G. Stanley, c.c. ld. Stanley; aft. ld. Stanley of Bickerstaffe and E. of Derby, *again*, Sept. 3.
1845. Wm. Ewart Gladstone, Dec. 23.
1846. Hy., E. Grey, July 3.
1852. Sir John Somerset Pakington, bt., Feb. 27.
Hy., D. of Newcastle, Dec. 28.

The secretaryship was divided 10th June, 1854. See "Secretaries of State for the War Department," *post* p. 232, and "Secretaries of State for the Colonies," *post* p. 234.

UNDER SECRETARIES OF STATE FOR WAR AND COLONIES.

From the establishment of the War Department in 1794.

See Introduction, *ante* p. 221, "Under Secretaries of State," *ante* p. 225, and "Under Secretaries of State for the Colonies from 1768 to 1782," *post* p. 235.

War.

1794. Evan Nepean, aft. sir E., bt.
1795. Wm. Huskisson.

War and Colonies.

1801. John Sullivan.
1804. Edwd. Cooke.
1806. Sir Geo. Shee, bt.
Sir Jas. Cockburn, *additional appt.*
1807. Edwd. Cooke, *vice* Shee.
Hon. Chas. Wm. Stewart, *vice* Cockburn.
1809. Hon. Fredk. John Robinson, *vice* Stewart.
Hon. Cecil Jenkinson, *vice* Cooke.
Lt.-col. Hy. E. Bunbury, *vice* Robinson.
1810. Robt. Peel, aft. sir R., bt., *vice* Jenkinson.
1812. Hy. Goulburn, *vice* Peel.
1816. Lt.-col. Bunbury's appointment was this year set aside.
1821. Robt. Wilmot Horton, *vice* Goulburn.
1828. Hon. Edwd. Geoffrey Smith Stanley, c.c. ld. Stanley; aft. ld. Stanley of Bickerstaffe and E. of Derby; *vice* Horton.
Lord Fras. Leveson Gower, aft. ld. Fras. Egerton, and E. of Ellesmere, *vice* Stanley.
Horace Twiss, *vice* Gower.
1830. Hy., visc. Howick, aft. Earl Grey, *vice* Twiss.
1833. John G. Shaw-Lefevre, aft. sir J., *vice* Howick.
1834. Sir Geo. Grey, bt., *vice* Shaw-Lefevre.
1835. Wm. Ewart Gladstone, *vice* Grey.
Sir Geo. Grey, bt., *again*; *vice* Gladstone.
1839. Hy. Labouchere, aft. ld. Taunton, *vice* Grey.
Robt. Vernon Smith, aft. ld. Lyveden, *vice* Labouchere.
1841. Geo. Wm. Hope, *vice* Vernon Smith, Sept. 8.
1846. Geo. Wm., ld. Lyttelton, *vice* Hope, Jan. 8.
Benj. Hawes, *vice* Lyttelton, July 6.
1851. Fredk. Peel, aft. sir F.

Permanent Under Secretaries of State for War and Colonies

1825. Robt. Wm. Hay.
1835. Jas. Stephen, aft. sir J.
1847. Herman Merivale.

The under secretaryship was divided 10th June, 1854. See "Under Secretaries of State for the War Department," *infra*, and "Under Secretaries of State for the Colonies," *post* p. 235.

SECRETARIES OF STATE FOR THE WAR DEPARTMENT

See Introduction, *ante* p. 221, and "Secretaries of State for War and Colonies," *ante* p. 230.

1854. Hy., D. of Newcastle, June 12.
1855. Fox, ld. Panmure, aft. E. of Dalhousie, Feb. 8.
1858. Jonathan Peel, Feb. 26.
1859. Sidney Herbert, aft. ld. Herbert of Lea, June 18.
1861. SirGeo. Cornewall Lewis, bt., July 23.
1863. Geo. Fredk. Saml., E. de Grey and Ripon, Apr. 28.
1866. Hon. Spencer Compton Cavendish, c.c. M. of Hartington, Feb. 16.
1866. Jonathan Peel, *again*, July 6.
1867. Sir John Somerset Pakington, bt., Mar. 8.
1868. Edwd. Cardwell, aft. visc. Cardwell, Dec. 9.
1874. Gathorne Hardy, aft. visc. Cranbrook, Feb. 21.
1878. Col. Fredk. Arthur Stanley, aft. ld. Stanley of Preston, Apr. 2.
1880. Hugh Culling Eardley Childers, Apr. 28.
1882. Hon. Spencer Compton Cavendish, c.c. M. of Hartington, *again*, Dec. 16.
1885. Wm. Hy. Smith, June 24.
1886. Hy. Campbell-Bannerman, Feb. 6.
Wm. Hy. Smith, *again*, Aug. 3.
1887. Hon. Edwd. Stanhope, Jan. 14.

UNDER SECRETARIES OF STATE FOR THE WAR DEPARTMENT.

There were originally two under secretaries for this department, one parliamentary, the other permanent. In 1870, under the provisions of 33 & 34 Vict., cap. 17, a third under secretary was appointed, with the title of "financial secretary of the war office." His office is parliamentary.

Parliamentary Under Secretaries of State for the War Department.

1855. Fredk. Peel, aft. sir F.
1857. Sir John Wm. Ramsden, bt.
1858. Lord Hardinge.
1859. Geo. Fredk. Saml., Earl de Grey and Ripon.
1863. Hon. Spencer Compton Cavendish, c.c. M. of Hartington.
1866. Wm. Lygon, E. of Longford.
1868. Thos. Geo., ld., aft. E. of Northbrook, Dec.
1872. Hy. Chas. Keith, M. of Lansdowne. Mar. or Apr.
1874. Geo. Robt. Chas., E. of Pembroke, Feb.
1875. Geo. Hy., E. of Cadogan.
1878. Wm. Coutts, visc. Bury.
1880. Albert Edmd., E. of Morley, Apr.
1885. Wm. Coutts, visc. Bury, *again*, June 24.
1886. Wm., ld. Sandhurst, Feb.
Geo. Robt. Canning, ld. Harris, Aug.

FINANCIAL SECRETARIES OF THE WAR OFFICE.

Appointed under 33 & 34 Vict., cap. 17.

1870. Hon. John Cranch Walker Vivian; app. perm. und. sec. Aug 29, 1871.
1871. Hy. Campbell, aft. Hy. Campbell-Bannerman.
1874. Col. Fredk. Arthur Stanley, aft. ld. Stanley of Preston, Feb.
1877. Lt.-col. Robt. Jas. Loyd Lindsay.
1880. Hy. Campbell-Bannerman, *again*, Apr.
1882. Sir Arthur Divett Hayter, bt.
1885. Hon. Hy. Stafford Northcote, aft. sir H., bt., June.
1886. Herbert John Gladstone, Feb.
Wm. St. John Fremantle Brodrick, Aug.

PERMANENT UNDER SECRETARIES OF STATE FOR THE WAR DEPARTMENT.

1855. Col. G. C. Mundy.
1857. Sir Benj. Hawes, K.C.B., late dep. sec. at war.
1861. Sir Edwd. Lugard, K.C.B.
1871. Hon. John Cranch Walker Vivian.
1878. Ralph Wood Thompson, aft. sir R.

SECRETARIES AT WAR.

See Introduction, *ante* p. 221.

KING CHARLES I.

1644. Edwd. Walker was sec. at war this year.—*Harleian Catalogue, No.* 6802.

COMMONWEALTH.

Wm. Clarke, aft. sir W. He was sometimes called "Clerk to the General" (Monk), sometimes "Secretary to the Forces"; but the title of the office was, probably, "Secretary to the Council of War."—*Council Book during the Interregnum. State Paper Office.*

KING CHARLES II.

1661. Sir Wm. Clarke, *contd.*, Jan. 28.
1666. Matthew Locke, June 5.
1683. Wm. Blathwayte, Aug. 18.

KING JAMES II.

1685. Wm. Blathwayte, *contd.*

KING WILLIAM III.

1692. Geo. Clarke, Mar. 3.

QUEEN ANNE.

1704. Hy. St. John, aft. ld. and visc. St. John, and visc. Bolingbroke, Apr. 20.
1708. Robt. Walpole, aft. sir R. and E. of Orford, Feb. 25.
1710. Geo. Granville, aft. ld. Lansdowne, of Bideford, Sept. 28.
1712. Sir Wm. Wyndham, bt., June 28.
1713. Fras. Gwyn, Aug. 21.

KING GEORGE I.

1714. Wm. Pulteney, aft. E. of Bath, Sept. 25.
1717. Jas. Craggs, jun., Apr. 13.
1718. Christr. Wandesford, visc. Castlecomer, Mar. 14.
Robt. Pringle, May 18.
Geo. Treby, Dec. 24.
1720 & 1721. It is stated in TINDAL, ii., 631, that Mr. Trevor was sec. at war in these years.
1724. Hon. Hy. Pelham, Apr. 1.

KING GEORGE II.

1730. Sir Wm. Strickland, bt., June 11.
1735. Sir Wm. Yonge, bt., May 9.
1741. Thos. Winnington, Apr. 27.—*Kearsley's Annals.*
This name does not appear in the authorised lists; nor can it be traced at the Rolls' office.
1746. Hy. Fox, aft. ld. Holland, July 23.
1755. Wm. Wildman, visc. Barrington, Nov. 14.

KING GEORGE III.

1761. Chas. Townshend, Mar. 18.
1762. Welbore Ellis, aft. ld. Mendip, Dec. 17.
1765. Wm. Wildman, visc. Barrington, *again*, July 19.

1778. Chas. Jenkinson, aft. ld. Hawkesbury and E. of Liverpool, Dec. 16.
1782. Thos. Townshend, aft. visc. Sydney, Mar. 27.
1782. Sir Geo. Yonge, bt., July 11.
1783. Col. hon. Richd. Fitzpatrick, Apr. 11.
Sir Geo. Yonge, bt., *again*, Dec. 24.
1794. Wm. Windham, July 11.
1801. Chas. Yorke, Feb. 20.
1803. Chas. Bragge (Bathurst), Aug. 17.
1804. Wm. Dundas, May 15.
1806. Gen. hon. Richd. Fitzpatrick, *again*, Feb. 7.
1807. Lt.-gen. sir Jas. Murray Pulteney, bt., Mar. 30.
1809. Lord Granville Leveson Gower, aft. E. Granville, June 27.
1809. Hy. John, visc. Palmerston, Oct. 27.

King George IV.

1820. Visc. Palmerston, *contd.*
1828. Sir Hy. Hardinge, aft. visc. Hardinge, May 31.

King William IV.

1830. Lord Fras. Leveson Gower, aft. ld. Fras. Egerton and E. of Ellesmere, July 30.
1830. Chas. Watkin Williams Wynn, Nov 30.
1831. Sir Hy. Brooke Parnell, bt., aft ld. Congleton, Apr. 4.
1832. Sir John Cam Hobhouse, bt., Feb. 1.
1833. Edwd. Ellice, Apr. 4.
1834. John Chas. Herries, Dec. 16.
1835. Hy., visc. Howick, aft. E. Grey, Apr. 20.

Queen Victoria.

1837. Visc. Howick, *contd.*
1839. Thos. Babington Macaulay, aft. lord Macaulay, Sept. 26.
1841. Sir H. Hardinge, aft. visc. Hardinge *again*, Sept. 4.
1844. Sir Thos. Fras. Fremantle, bt. May 17.
1845. Hon. Sidney Herbert, aft. ld. Herbert of Lea, Feb. 4.
1846. Hon. Fox Maule, aft. ld. Panmure and E. of Dalhousie, July 6.
1852. Robt. Vernon Smith, aft. ld. Lyveden, Feb. 6.
Wm. Beresford, Feb. 28.
Sidney Herbert, aft. ld. Herbert of Lea, *again*, Dec. 30.

Office held by Secretary of State for War from 1854 until 1863, when it was abolished by 26 & 27 Vict., cap. 12.

Deputy Secretaries at War.

* * * *

1797. Matt. Lewis (dep. sec. in this year).
1803. Fras. Nison, aft. sir F.
1810. Wm. Merry.
1826. Lawrence Sulivan.
1851. Benjn. Hawes, aft. sir B.; made permanent und. sec. war, 1857. *Vide* that title, *supra*.

SECRETARIES OF STATE FOR THE COLONIES.

See Introduction, *ante* p. 221.

I. From 1768 to 1782.

1768. Wm. E. of Hillsborough, aft. M. of Downshire, Feb. 27.
1772. Wm., E. of Dartmouth, Aug. 27.
1776. Lord Geo. Sackville Germaine, aft. visc. Sackville, Jan. 25.
1782. Welbore Ellis, aft. ld. Mendip, Mar. 8.

The office was abolished in 1782, and the duties transferred to the Home Secretary until 1794, when the Secretary of State for War was appointed, and the duties transferred to him. See " Secretaries of State for War and Colonies," *ante* p. 230.

II. From 1854 to the present time.

1854. Sir Geo. Grey, bt , June 2.
1855, Hon. Sidney Herbert, aft. ld. Herbert of Lea, Feb.
1855. Lord John Russell, aft. E. Russell, May 1.
Sir Wm. Molesworth, bt., July 21.

1855. Hy. Labouchere, aft. ld. Taunton, Nov. 21.
1858. Hon. Edwd. Hy. Stanley, c.c. ld. Stanley, aft. E. of Derby, Feb. 26.
Sir Edwd. Geo. Earle Lytton Bulwer Lytton, bt., aft. ld. Lytton, May 31.
1859. Hy. Pelham, D. of Newcastle, June 18.
1864. Edwd. Cardwell, aft. visc. Cardwell, Apr. 4.
1866. Hy. Howard Molyneux, E. of Carnarvon, July 6.
1867. Richd. Plant. Campbell Temple Nugent Brydges Chandos, D. of Buckingham and Chandos, May 8.
1868. Granville Geo., E. Granville, Dec. 9.
1870. John, E. of Kimberley, July 6.
1874. Hy. Howard Molyneux, E. of Carnarvon, *again*, Feb. 21.
1878. Sir Michael Edwd. Hicks-Beach, bt., sw. Feb. 4.
1880. John, E. of Kimberley, *again*, Apr. 28.
1882. Edwd. Hy., E. of Derby, *again*, Dec. 16.
1885. Fredk. Arth. Stanley, aft. ld. Stanley of Preston, June 24.
1886. Granville Geo., E. Granville, K.G., *again*, Feb. 6.
Hon. Edwd. Stanhope, Aug. 3.
1887. Sir Hy. Thurstan Holland, bt., G.C.M.G., Jan. 14, sw.; cr. ld. Knutsford, Feb. 27, 1888, **G.**

UNDER SECRETARIES OF STATE FOR THE COLONIES.

See Introduction, *ante* p. 221, and see note to "Secretaries of State for the Colonies," *ante* p. 234.

I. From 1768 to 1782.

1768. Richd. Philips.
John Pownall.
1772. Wm. Knox, *vice* Philips.
1776. Christian D'Oyly, *vice* Pownall.
1778. Thos. De Grey, junr., *vice* D'Oyly.
1780. Benjn. Thompson, *vice* De Grey.

II. From 1854 to the present time.

There are now two under secretaries of state for the colonies, one parliamentary, the other permanent. There are also two permanent assistant under secretaries.

Parliamentary Under Secretaries of State for the Colonies.

1854. Fredk. Peel, aft. sir F.
1855. John Ball, Feb.
1857. Chichester Saml. Fortescue, aft. ld. Carlingford.
1858. Hy. Howard Molyneux, E. of Carnarvon, Feb.
1859. C. S. Fortescue, aft. lord Carlingford, *again*, June.
1865. Wm. Edwd. Foster, Nov.
1866. Chas. Bowyer Adderley, aft. sir C., bt., and ld. Norton, July.
1868. Wm. Monsell, aft. ld. Emly, Feb.
1871. Edwd. Hugessen Knatchbull-Hugessen, aft. ld. Brabourne, Jan.
1874. Jas. Lowther, Feb.
1878. Geo. Hy., E. Cadogan, Feb.
1880. Mountstewart Elphinstone Grant-Duff, aft. sir M., Apr.
1881. Leonard Hy. Courtney.
1882. Hon. Anthy. Evelyn M. Ashley.
1885. Wyndham Thos., E. of Dunraven, June.
1886. Geo. Osborne Morgan, Feb.
W. T., E. of Dunraven. *again*, Aug.
1887. Wm. Hillier, E. of Onslow, Feb. 17.
1888. Baron Hy. de Worms.

Permanent Under Secretaries of State for the Colonies.

1825. Robt. Wm. Hay, war and colonies.
1835. Jas. Stephen, aft. sir J., war and colonies, 1836.
1847. Herman Merivale, war and colonies till June 1854, and then colonies, May 1848.
1859. Sir Fred. Rogers, aft. ld. Blachford.
1871. Robt. Geo. Wyndham Herbert, aft. sir R.

Permanent Assistant Under Secretaries of State for the Colonies.

1849. T. Fredk. Elliot, aft. sir T.; war and colonies till June 1854, and then colonies.
1868. Sir Fras. R. Sandford.
1870. Robt. Geo. Wyndham Herbert, aft. sir R.; app. perm. und. sec. 1871.
Hy. Thurstan Holland, aft. sir H., bt., and ld. Knutsford, *addtnl. appt.*
1871. Hon. Robt. Hy. Meade, *vice* Herbert.
1874. W. R. Malcolm, *vice* Holland.
Sir Julian Pauncefote, *additional appt., making three assist und. secs.*
1876. John Bramston, *vice* Pauncefote.
1878. Edwd. Wingfield, *vice* Malcolm.

SECRETARIES OF STATE FOR INDIA.

Appointed after the passing of 21 & 22 Vict. cap. 106.

See Introduction, *ante*, p. 221.

1858. Hon. Edwd. Hy. Stanley, c.c. lord Stanley, aft. E. of Derby, Sept. 2.
1859. Sir Chas. Wood, bt., aft. visc. Halifax, June 18.
1866. Geo. Fredk. Saml., E. de Grey and Ripon, Feb. 16.
Robt. Arth. Talbot Cecil, c.c. visc. Cranborne, aft. M. of Salisbury, July 6.
1867. Sir Stafford Hy. Northcote, bt., aft. E. of Iddesleigh, Mar. 8.
1868. Geo. Douglas, D. of Argyll, Dec. 9.
1874. Robt. Arth. Talbot, M. of Salisbury, *again*, Feb. 21.
1878. Gathorne Hardy, aft. visc. Cranbrook, Apr. 2.
1880. Hon. Spencer Compton Cavendish, c.c. M. of Hartington, Apr. 28.
1882. John, E. of Kimberley, Dec. 16.
1885. Randolph Hy. Spencer Churchill, c.c. ld. Randolph Churchill, June 24.
1886. John, E. of Kimberley, *again*, Feb. 6.
Sir Richd. Assheton Cross, G.C.B., aft. visc. Cross, Aug. 3.

UNDER SECRETARIES OF STATE FOR INDIA.

There are two under secretaries for this department, one parliamentary, the other permanent.

Parliamentary Under Secretaries of State for India.

1858. Hy. Jas. Baillie.
1859. Hon. Thos. Geo. Baring, aft. ld. and E. of Northbrook.
1864. Fredk. Temple, ld., aft. E. Dufferin.
1866. Sir Jas. Fergusson, bt.
1867. Chas. Hy. Rolle, ld. Clinton.
1869. Mountstuart Elphinstone Grant-Duff, aft. sir M.
1874. Hon. Geo. Fras. Hamilton, c.c. ld. Geo. Hamilton, Feb.
1878. Hon. Edwd. Stanhope.
1880. Geo. Hy. Chas., visc. Enfield, aft. E. Strafford, May.
1883. John Kynaston Cross.
1885. Geo. Robt. Canning, ld. Harris, June.
1886. Sir Ughtred James Kay-Shuttleworth, Feb.
Edwd. Stafford Howard, Apr.
Sir John Eldon Gorst, Aug.

Permanent Under Secretaries of State for India.

1858. Sir Geo. R. Clerk, K.C.B.
1860. Herman Merivale.
1874. Sir Louis Mallet, C.B.
1883. John Arth. Godley, C.B.

SECRETARIES OF STATE FOR SCOTLAND

from 1708 to 1746, and

SECRETARIES FOR SCOTLAND.

appointed under 48 & 49 Vict. cap. 61. *See* Part IX. "Scotland," *post.*

POSTMASTERS-GENERAL.

"It does not appear at what precise period the crown undertook to be the regular carrier of letters for its subjects. The crown, doubtless, at a very early period, found it necessary to the exercise of the functions of sovereignty, to be able to convey with speed and security its own despatches from one part of the realm to another, and for that purpose it appointed certain messengers or runners called the 'Posts.' These posts were also employed for the personal convenience of the sovereign and the individuals composing the royal court. In course of time a 'Master of the Posts' was appointed, and the first of these on record was Brian Tuke, esq., afterwards sir Brian Tuke, knt., who held that office in 1516. The joint successors of sir Brian Tuke were sir William Paget, one of Henry VIII.'s chief secretaries of state, and John Mason, esq., secretary for the French tongue. The letters patent, dated Nov. 12, 1545, conveying to them this office, grant to them during their lives and the live of the survivor, the office of 'Master of the Messengers, Runners, or Posts,' as well within the kingdom of England as parts beyond the seas, with the wages or fee of £66 13s. 4d. a year, to be held by themselves or their sufficient deputy or deputies. But, besides his fee, the 'Master of the Posts' received from the crown the amount of his expenses for conveying the letters, of which he rendered an account. There is a succession of patents granting the same office, at the same fee, to other parties for life, in the reigns of Elizabeth, James I., and Charles I."—*House of Commons' Report*, July 2, 1844.

Down to 1823 this office was generally held by two joint postmasters of equal rank and authority, but from that time only one postmaster has been appointed. The office is now a political one, the holder resigning with the ministry of which he is a member.

Postmasters-General.

From the earliest official accounts to the present time. The earlier names are taken from a return made to the House of Commons, dated March 25, 1844.

King Charles II.

1687 to 1688. Philip Frowde, acting for the D. of York.

King William III.

1690 to 1708. Sir Robt. Cotton, and Thos. Frankland.

QUEEN ANNE.

1708 to 1715. Sir Thos. Frankland, and Sir John Evelyn, bt.

KING GEORGE I.

1715 to 1720. Chas., ld. Cornwallis, and Jas. Craggs.
1720 to 1725. Edwd. Carteret, and Galfridus Walpole.
1725 to 1732. Edwd. Carteret, and Edwd. Harrison.

KING GEORGE II.

1732. Edwd. Carteret, *alone*, from Christmas 1732 to midsummer 1733.
1733 to 1739. Edwd. Carteret, and Thos., ld. Lovel, aft. visc. Coke and E. of Leicester.
1739 to 1744. Sir John Eyles, bt., and Thos., ld. Lovel, aft. visc. Coke and E. of Leicester.
1744 to 1745. Thos., now E. of Leicester, *alone*.
1745 to 1758. Thos., E. of Leicester, and Sir Everard Fawkener.
1758 to 1759. Thos., E. of Leicester, from Nov. 1758 to Apr. 1759.
1759. Wm., E. of Besborough, and Hon. Robt. Hampden, June 2.

KING GEORGE III.

1762. John, E. of Egmont, and Hon. Robt. Hampden, Nov. 27.
1763. Thos., ld. Hyde, and Hon. Robt. Hampden, Sept. 23.
1765. Wm., E. of Besborough, and Thos., ld. Grantham, July 19.
1766. Wills, E. of Hillsborough, and Fras., ld. Le Despencer, Dec. 29.
1768. John, E. of Sandwich, and Fras., ld. Le Despencer, Apr. 26.
1771. Fras., ld. Le Despencer, and Hy. Fredk. Carteret, Jan. 16.
1781. Hy. Fredk. Carteret, *alone*, Dec. 11.
1782. Wm., visc. Barrington, and Hy. Fredk. Carteret, Jan. 24.
Chas., E. of Tankerville, and Hy. Fredk. Carteret, Apr. 25.
1783. Thos., ld. Foley, and Hy. Fredk. Carteret, May 1.
1784. Chas., E. of Tankerville, and Hy. Fredk. Carteret, Jan. 7; cr. ld. Carteret, Jan. 29, 1784.
1786. Thos., E. of Clarendon, and Hy. Fredk., ld. Carteret, Sept. 19.
Hy. Fredk., ld. Carteret, *alone*, Dec. 10 to July 6, 1787.
1787. Hy. Fredk., ld. Carteret, and Thos., ld. Walsingham, July 6.
1789. Thos., ld. Walsingham, and John, E. of Westmoreland, Sept. 19.
1790. Thos., ld. Walsingham, and Philip, E. of Chesterfield, Mar. 13.
1794. Philip, E. of Chesterfield, and Geo., E. of Leicester, July 28.
1798. Geo., E. of Leicester, and Wm., ld. Auckland, Mar. 1.
1799. Wm., ld. Auckland, and Geo., ld. Gower, Feb. 27.
1801. Wm., ld. Auckland, and Lord Chas. Spencer, Mar. 31.
1804. Lord Chas. Spencer, and Jas., D. of Montrose, July 19.
1806. Robt., E. of Buckinghamshire, and John Joshua, E. of Carysfort, Feb. 20.
1807. John, E. of Sandwich, and Thos., E. of Chichester, May 5.
1814. Thos., E. of Chichester, *alone*, June 6.
Thos., E. of Chichester, and Richd., E. of Clancarty, Sept. 30.
1816. Thos., E. of Chichester, and Jas., M. of Salisbury, Apr. 6. M. of Salisbury *d.* June 13, 1823.

KING GEORGE IV.

Appointed by Letters Patent dated as under.

1823. Thos., E. of Chichester, *alone*, Nov. 27; *d.* July 4, 1826.
1826. Lord Fredk. Montague, Aug. 18; res. Sept. 17, 1827.
1827. Wm., D. of Manchester, Sept. 27.

KING WILLIAM IV.

1830. Chas., D. of Richmond, Dec. 14.
1831. Chas., D. of Richmond, Apr. 14, as postm.-gen. of Great Britain and Ireland, conformably with the provisions of 1 Will. IV., cap. 8 (March 11, 1831), whereby the two separate offices of postm.-gen. of Great Britain and postm.-gen. of Ireland were united into one, to possess the same powers, and to be subject to the same penalties, as the former two; and the appointments of secs. and other officers of the Post-Office at Dublin were thereafter vested in the postm.-gen.
1834. Fras. Nathaniel, M. Conyngham, July 5.
Wm., ld. Maryborough, Dec. 31; sw. Jan. 1, 1835.
1835. Fras. Nathaniel, M. Conyngham, *again*, May 8; sw. May 9.
Thos. Wm., E. of Lichfield, May 30; sw. June 1.

QUEEN VICTORIA.

1837. Thos. Wm., E. of Lichfield, *contd.*
1841. Wm., visc. Lowther, Sept. 15; sw. same day.
1846. Edwd. Granville, E. of St. Germans, Jan. 2; sw. Jan. 3.
Ulick John, M. of Clanricarde, July 14.

1852. Chas. Philip, E. of Hardwicke, Mar. 1, G.
1853. Chas. John, visc. Canning, Jan. 5, G.
1855. Geo. Douglas, D. of Argyle, Dec.
1858. Chas., ld. Colchester, Feb.
1859. Jas., E. of Elgin, June.
1860. Edwd. Jno., ld. Stanley of Alderley, Aug. 17, G.
1866. Jas., D. of Montrose, July.
1868. Hon. Spencer Compton Cavendish, c.c. M. of Hartington, Dec. 9, sw.
1871. Wm. Monsell, Jan. 9, G.
1873. Hon. Lyon Playfair, C.B., Nov. 18, G.
1874. John Jas. Robt. Manners, c.c. ld. John Manners, aft. D. of Rutland, Feb. 21, sw.
1880. Hy. Fawcett, May 3, sw.
1884. Geo. John Shaw-Lefevre, Nov. 18.
1885. Sir John Jas. Robt. Manners, G.C.B., c.c. ld. John Manners, aft. D. of Rutland, *again*, June 24, sw.
1886. Geo. Grenfell, ld. Wolverton, Feb. 17, sw.
Hy. Cecil Raikes, Aug. 9, sw.

SECRETARIES TO THE GENERAL POST OFFICE.

There is no *complete* record in the department of the General Post office of the persons by whom the office of secretary was held previously to the year 1762, when Anthony Tod., esq., was appointed.

1720. The name of Jas. Craggs appears on the records of the Post-office as sec. in this year.
1723. In this year, Jos. Godman is found to be filling the office of sec.
1738. John David Barbutt, app. sec., *vice* T. Robinson, decd. Sept. 17.
1742. Geo. Shelvocke, *vice* Barbutt, removed July 22.
1762. Anthy. Tod, app. (in whose room is not stated), Dec. 1.
1797. Fras. Freeling (who had acted for a short time previously as joint sec.), *vice* Tod, decd.; cr. a bt. Mar. 11, 1828.
1836. Lt.-Col. Wm. Leader Maberly, Sept. 29.
1854. Rowland Hill, aft. sir R., K.C.B.
1864. John Tilley, Mar.
1880. Stevenson Arthur Blackwood, aft. sir S., K.C.B.

SECOND SECRETARY TO THE GENERAL POST OFFICE.

1869 to 1875. Frank Ives Scudamore.

FINANCIAL SECRETARIES TO THE GENERAL POST OFFICE.

1875. Stevenson Arthur Blackwood, aft. sir S., K.C.B.
1880. Algernon Turner.

LORD HIGH CHANCELLORS,

LORD KEEPERS,

AND

COMMISSIONERS OF THE GREAT SEAL.

Vide Part VI., "Legal," *post*.

LORDS PRIVY SEAL

AND

COMMISSIONERS FOR EXECUTING THAT OFFICE.

THIS office is now a political one, the holder retiring with the ministry.

KING HENRY VIII.

* * Richd. Fox, bp. of Winchester.
1516. Thos. Routhall, bp. of Durham.
Hy., ld. Marney.
1523. Cuthbert Tunstal, bp. of London.
1533. Wm., E. of Southampton.
Thos., E. of Wiltshire and Ormond.
1536. Thos., ld. Cromwell, aft. E. of Essex; beheaded in 1540.
1543. John, ld. Russell, aft. E. of Bedford.

KING EDWARD VI.

1547. Lord Russell, *contd.*

QUEEN MARY.

1553. Lord Russell, *contd.*
1554. Edwd., E. of Derby.
1556. Wm., ld. Paget.

QUEEN ELIZABETH.

1558. Sir Nicholas Bacon.
1572. Wm., ld. Howard of Effingham.
Jas. Windebank.

KING JAMES I.

1608. Hy., E. of Northampton.
1614. Edwd., E. of Worcester.

KING CHARLES I.

1625. E. of Worcester, *contd.*
1627. Hy., E. of Manchester.

KING CHARLES II.

1660. Wm., visc. Saye and Sele.
1661. John, ld. Robartes, aft. E. of Radnor.
1669. Sir Edwd. Deering, bt., sir Thos. Strickland, and Robt. Milward, commrs. during lord Robartes' absence in Ireland as ld. lieut., Sept. 22.
1673. Arthur, E. of Anglesey, Apr. 24.
1682. Geo., M. of Halifax, Feb. 24.

KING JAMES II.

1685. Hy., E. of Clarendon, Feb. 18.
Robt., visc. Tiviot, Robt. Phillips, and John Evelyn, commrs. during the earl's absence in Ireland as ld. lieut.
1686. Hy., ld. Arundel of Wardour, Mar. 11.

KING WILLIAM III.

1689. Geo., M. of Halifax, Feb. 19.
1690. Wm. Cheney, sir John Knatchbull, bt., and sir Wm. Pulteney, commrs.
1691. Thos., E. of Pembroke.
1697. Sir Thos. Montpesson, sir Chas. Cotterel, jun., and Jas. Tyrrell, commrs. during the earl's absence in Ireland as ld. lieut., Apr. 13.
1699. John, visc. Lonsdale, May 16.
1700. Ford, E. of Tankerville.
1701. Edwd. Southwell, Christr. Musgrave, and Jas. Vernon, commrs. June 11.

QUEEN ANNE.

1702. John, M. of Normanby, aft. D. of Normanby and Buckinghamshire, Apr. 27.
1705. John, D. of Newcastle, Mar. 31.
1711. John Robinson, bp. of Bristol, aft. bp. of London, Apr. 23.
Sir Geo. Beaumont, bt., Robt. Byerly, and Edwd. Nicholas, commrs. during the bishop's absence at the treaty of Utrecht, Dec. 22.
1713. Wm., E. of Dartmouth.

KING GEORGE I.

1714. Thos., M. of Wharton, Sept. 24; *d.* Apr. 12, 1715.
1715. Edwd. Southwell, sir Christr. Musgrave, bt., and Andrew Charleton, commrs., Apr. 30.
Chas., E. of Sunderland, Aug. 20.
1716. Edwd. Southwell, Jas. Vernon, and Andrew Charleton, commrs. during the earl's absence at Aix-la-Chapelle, Aug. 28.
Evelyn, D. of Kingston, Dec. 19.
1718. Hy., D. of Kent, Feb. 6.
1720. Evelyn, D. of Kingston, *again*, June 11.
1726. Thos., ld. Trevor, Mar 11.

KING GEORGE II.

1727. Lord Trevor, *contd.*
1730. Spencer, E. of Wilmington, May 8.
1731. Wm., D. of Devonshire, June 12.
1733. Hy., visc. Lonsdale, May 5.
1735. Francis, E. of Godolphin, May.
1740. John, ld. Hervey, eldest son of the E. of Bristol, Apr. 7.

1742. John, ld. Gower, July 13.
1743. Geo., E. of Cholmondeley, Dec.
1744. John, ld. Gower, *again*, Dec. 27.
1755. Chas., D. of Marlborough. Jan. 8.
Granville, E. Gower, Dec. 22.
1757. Richd., E. Temple, June 30.

KING GEORGE III.

1760. Earl Temple, *contd.*
1761. John, D. of Bedford, Nov. 25.
1763. Geo., D. of Marlborough, Apr. 22.
1765. Thos. Pelham Holles, D. of Newcastle, Aug. 25.
1766. Wm., E. of Chatham, July 30.
1768. Richd. Sutton, Wm. Blair, and Wm. Fraser, commrs. for six weeks, or other sooner determination, Feb.
The seal re-delivered to the E. of Chatham, Mar. 21.
Geo. Wm., E. of Bristol, Nov. 2.
1770. Geo., E. of Halifax, Feb. 26.
1771. Hy., E. of Suffolk and Berkshire, Jan. 22.
Aug. Hy., D. of Grafton, June 12.
1775. Wm., E. of Dartmouth, Nov. 4.
1782. Aug. Hy., D. of Grafton, *again*, Mar. 27.
1783. Fredk., E. of Carlisle, Apr. 2.
Chas., D. of Rutland, Dec. 23.
1784. Wm. Fraser, Stephen Cotterell, and Evan Nepean, commrs., Mar. 8.
Granville Leveson, E. Gower, aft. M. of Stafford, Nov. 27.
1794. Geo. John, E. Spencer, July 16.
Evan Nepean, Stephen Cotterell, and Jas. Bland Burgess, commrs. during the absence of E. Spencer, July 26.
John, E. of Chatham, Dec. 17.
1798. John, E. of Westmoreland, Feb. 14.
1806. Hy., visc. Sidmouth, Feb. 5.
Hy. Richd., ld. Holland, Oct. 15.
1807. John, E. of Westmoreland, *again*, Mar. 25.

KING GEORGE IV.

1820. E. of Westmoreland, *contd.*
1827. Wm. Hy., D. of Portland, Apr. 30.
Geo., E. of Carlisle, July 16.
1828. Edwd.. ld. Ellenborough, Jan. 26.
1829. Jas., E. of Rosslyn, June 10.

KING WILLIAM IV.

1830. E. of Rosslyn, *contd.*
John, ld., aft. E. of Durham, Nov. 22.
1833. Fredk. John, E. of Ripon, Apr. 3.
1834. Geo., E. of Carlisle, *again*, June 5.
Constantine Hy., E. of Mulgrave, aft. M. of Normanby, July 30,
Jas. Archibald, ld. Wharncliffe, Dec. 15.
1835. John Wm., visc. Duncannon, aft. E. of Bessborough, Apr. 23

QUEEN VICTORIA.

1840. Geo. Wm. Fredk., E. of Clarendon, Jan. 15.
1841. Richd., D. of Buckingham, Sept. 3.
1842. Walter, D. of Buccleuch, Feb. 2.
1846. Thos., E. of Haddington, Jan. 21.
Gilbert, E. of Minto, July 6.
1852. Jas. Brownlow Wm., M. of Salisbury, Feb. 27.
1853. Geo. Douglas, D. of Argyll, Jan. 4.
1855. Dudley, E. of Harrowby, Dec. 7.
1858. Ulick Jno., M. of Clanricarde, Feb. 3.
Chas. Philip, E. of Hardwicke, Feb. 26.
1859. Geo. Douglas, D. of Argyll, *again*, Juue 18.
1866. Jas. Howard, E. of Malmesbury, July 6.
1868. Jno., E. of Kimberley, Dec. 9.
1870. Chas., visc. Halifax, July 6.
1874. Jas. Howard, E. of Malmesbury, G.C.B., *again*, Feb. 21.
1876. Benj. Disraeli, Aug. 12. Also first ld. treasy. and premier.
1878. Algernon Geo., D. of Northumberland, Feb. 4.
1880. Geo. Douglas, D. of Argyll, K.T., *again*, Apr. 28.
1881. Chichester Saml., ld. Carlingford, May 2.
1885. Arch. Philip, E. of Rosebery, Mar. 5.
Dudley Fras. Stuart, E. of Harrowby, June 24.
1886. Wm. Ewart Gladstone, Feb. 17. Also first ld. treasy. and premier.
Geo. Hy., E. Cadogan, Aug. 3.

CHANCELLORS OF THE DUCHY OF LANCASTER.

THE Chancellor of the Duchy of Lancaster formerly sat as judge of the Duchy court of Lancaster, held at Westminster, in which causes relating to the revenue of the Duchy of Lancaster were tried. Another branch of the same court was established at Preston, in Lancashire, called the court of the county palatine of Lancaster.

The office of Chancellor of the Duchy of Lancaster is now, practically, a sinecure. It is held by a member of the ministry, who resigns with his party.

Chancellors of the Duchy of Lancaster.

From the creation of the Dukedom.

King Edward III.

1360–1. Sir Hy. de Haydok, chanc. of Henry, 1st D. of Lancaster.
1372–3. Ralph de Ergham, bp. of Salisbury.
1377. Thos. de Thelwall, Apr. 16.

King Richard II.

1377–8. Sir Jno. De Yerborough.
1382. Sir Thos. Stanley, Nov. 10, *pro tem.*
Sir Thos. Scarle, Nov. 29.
1383. Sir Wm. Okey, Oct.

King Henry IV.

1399–1400. Jno. de Wakering.
Wm. Burgoyne.
1404. Sir Thos. Stanley, May 15.
1410. Jno. Springthorpe, Mar. 30.

King Henry V.

1413. Jno. Woodhouse, Apr. 4.

King Henry VI.

1423. Jno. Woodhouse, *contd.*, Jan. 20.
1424. Wm. Troutbecke, June 10.
1431. Walter Sherington, Feb. 16.
1439. The same, May 7, for life.
1442. Wm. Tresham, July 3, in reversion.
1447. The same, Nov. 1.
1449. Jno. Say, aft. sir J., June 10.

King Edward IV.

1461. Jno. Say, *contd.*, June 16.
1462. Sir Richd. Fowler, June 10; and ch. ex.
1477. Sir Jno. Say, *again*, Nov. 3.
1478. Thos. Thwaites, April 2; and ch. ex.

King Richard III.

1483. Thos. Metcalfe, July 7.

King Henry VII.

1486. Sir Reginald Bray, Sept. 13.
1504. Sir Jno. Mordant, June 24.
1505. Sir Richd. Empson, Oct. 3.

King Henry VIII.

1509. Sir Henry Marny, May 14.
1524. Sir Richd. Wingfield, Apr. 14.
1525. Sir Thos. Moore, Dec. 31, aft. ld. chanc.
1529. Sir Wm. Fitzwilliams, aft. E. of Southampton, Nov. 3.
1533. Sir Jno. Gage, May 10.

King Edward VI.

1547. Sir Wm. Pagett, July 1.
1552. Sir Jno. Gate, July 7.

Queen Mary and Philip and Mary.

1553–4. Sir Robt. Rochester.
1558. Sir Edwd. Walgrave, June 22.

Queen Elizabeth.

1558–9. Sir Ambrose Cave.
1568. Sir Ralph Sadler, May 16.
1577. Sir Fras. Walsingham, June 15.
1589–90. Sir Thos. Heneage.
1595. Sir Robt. Cecil, Oct. 7.
1601. Sir John Fortescue, Sept. 16.

King James I.

1615. Sir Thos. Parry and Jno. Daccombe, aft. sir J., May 27.
1616. Sir Jno. Daccombe, alone, June 5.
1618. Sir Humphrey May, Mar. 23.

King Charles I.

1629. Edwd., ld. Newburgh, Apr. 16.
1644. Wm., ld. Grey of Wake, and Wm. Lenthall, Feb. 10.

Commonwealth.

1649. Jno. Bradshawe, Aug. 1.
1655. Thos. Fell.
1659. Sir Gilbert Gerrard, May 14.

King Charles II.

1660. Fras. (? Chas.), ld. Seymour, July 9.
1664. Sir Thos. Ingram, July 21.
1672. Sir Robt. Carr, bt., Feb. 22.
1682. Sir Thos. Chichely, Nov. 21.

William and Mary.

1689. Robt., ld. Willoughby d'Eresby, Mar. 21.

King William III.

1697. Thos., E. of Stamford, May 4.

Queen Anne.

1702. Sir John Leveson Gower, bt., aft. ld. Gower, May 12.
1706. Jas. E. of Derby, June 10.
1710. Wm., ld. Berkeley of Stratton, Sept. 21.

King George I.

1714. Heneage, E. of Aylesford, Nov. 6.
1716. Richd., E. of Scarborough, Mar. 12.
1717. Nicholas Lechmere, aft. ld. Lechmere, for life, June 19.

King George II.

1727. John, D. of Rutland, July 17.
1735. Geo., E. of Cholmondeley, May 21.

1742. Richd., ld. Edgcumbe, Dec. 22.
1760. Thos. Hay, visc. Dupplin, aft. E. of Kinnoul, Feb. 27.

KING GEORGE III.

1762. Jas., ld. Strange, Dec. 13.
1771. Thos., ld. Hyde, aft. E. of Clarendon, June 14.
1782. John, ld. Ashburton, Apr. 17.
1783. Edwd., E. of Derby, Aug. 29.
Thos., E. of Clarendon, Dec. 31.
1787. Chas., ld. Hawkesbury, aft. E. of Liverpool, Sept. 6.
1803. Thos., ld. Pelham, aft. E. of Chichester, Nov. 11.
1804. Hy., ld. Mulgrave, June 6.
1805. Robt., E. of Buckinghamshire, Jan. 14.
Dudley, ld., aft. E. of Harrowby, July 10.
1806. Edwd., E. of Derby, *again*, Feb. 12.
1807. Spencer Perceval, Mar. 30.
1812. Robt., E. of Buckinghamshire, *again*, May 23.
Chas. Bathurst June 23

KING GEORGE IV.

1823. Nichs. Vansittart, aft. ld. Bexley, Feb. 13.
1828. Geo., E. of Aberdeen, Jan. 26.
Chas. Arbuthnot, June 2.

KING WILLIAM IV.

1830. Hy. Richd., ld. Holland, Nov. 25.
Thos. E. of Haddington, Dec. 20.
1834. Chas. Watkin Williams Wynn, Dec. 26.
1835. Hy. Richd., ld. Holland, *again*, Apr. 23.

QUEEN VICTORIA.

1840. Geo. Wm. Fredk., E. of Clarendon, Oct. 31.
1841. Sir Geo. Grey, bt., June 23.
Lord Granville Chas. Hy. Somerset, Sept. 3.
1846. John, ld. Campbell, July 6.
1850. Geo. Fredk. Wm., E. of Carlisle, Mar. 6.
1852. Robt. Adam Christopher, Mar. 1.
1853. Edwd. Strutt, Jan. 1.
1854. Granville Geo., E. Granville, June 21.
1855. Dudley, E. of Harrowby, Mar. 31.
Matthew Talbot Baines, Dec. 7.
1858. Jas., D. of Montrose, Feb. 26.
1859. Sir Geo. Grey, bt., *again*, June 22.
1861. Edwd. Cardwell, aft. ld. Cardwell, July 25.
1864. Geo. Wm. Fredk., E. of Clarendon, K.G., G.C.B., *again*, Apr. 7.
1866. Geo. Joachim Göschen, Jan. 26.
Wm. Regd., E. of Devon, July 10.
1867. Col. Jno. Wilson Patten, June 26.
1868. Thos. Edwd. Taylor, Nov. 7.
Fredk. Temple, ld. Dufferin, K.P., K.C.B., aft. E. Dufferin, Dec. 12.
1872. Hugh Culling Eardley Childers, Aug. 9.
1873. Jno. Bright, Sept. 30.
1874. Thos. Edwd. Taylor, *again*, Mar. 2.
1880. Jno. Bright, *again*, Apr. 28.
1882. John, E. Kimberley, July 25.
1882. Jno. Geo. Dodson. Dec. 28.
1884. George Otto Trevelyan, aft. sir G., bt., Oct. 29.
1885. Hy. Chaplin, June 24.
1886. Edwd. Heneage, Feb. 6.
Sir Ughtred Jas. Kay-Shuttleworth, Apr. 16.
Gathorne, visc. Cranbrook, *pro tem.*, Aug. 3.
Hon. sir Jno. Jas. Robt. Manners, c.c. ld. John Manners, aft. D. of Rutland, Aug. 16.

PAYMASTERS-GENERAL OF THE FORCES

AND

PAYMASTERS-GENERAL.

THE office of Paymaster-General of the Forces was formerly one of the most lucrative in the gift of the crown, not so much on account of the salary annexed to it, as on account of the vast sums of public money that lay in the Paymaster's hands for long spaces of time; the whole of the money voted by parliament for the land forces passing through his department. In 1782 the office underwent a reform, and the Paymaster-General and his deputy were allowed fixed salaries in lieu of perquisites.

On the 1st December, 1836, by Treasury warrant, under 5 & 6 Will.

IV. cap. 35, the offices of Paymaster-General of the Forces, Treasurer of Chelsea Hospital, Treasurer of the Navy, and Treasurer of the Ordnance were abolished and the duties transferred to a new officer, styled the Paymaster-General. By 11 & 12 Vict. cap. 55 (Aug. 14, 1848), the offices of Paymaster of Exchequer Bills and Paymaster of Civil Services were also abolished, and the duties transferred to the Paymaster-General. By 35 & 36 Vict. cap. 44 (Aug. 6, 1872), and subsequent rules of court, the office of Accountant-General of the Court of Chancery was abolished and the duties transferred to the Paymaster-General.

This office was generally held jointly with that of Vice-President of the Board of Trade from 1848 until the abolition of the latter office in December 1868, under 30 & 31 Vict. cap. 72.

Paymasters-General of the Forces.

1660. Sir Stephen Fox.
1679. Nichs. Johnson, and
Chas. Fox.
1682. Chas. Fox.
1689. Richd., E. of Ranelagh.
This nobleman was charged with the misapplication of large sums of the public money ; he resigned to avoid prosecution, and was expelled the house of commons, 1702.
1703. John Howe, for guards and garrisons at home, Jan. 4.
Chas. Fox, for the other troops and Chelsea Hospital.
1707. Hon. Jas. Brydges, aft. D. of Chandos.
1713. Thos. Moore, for her majesty's forces abroad.
Edwd. Nicholas, treasr. and paym. of her majesty's pensioners.
1714. Robt. Walpole, aft. sir R., and E. of Orford.
1715. Hy., E. of Lincoln, Oct. 26.
1720. Robt. Walpole, *again.*
1721. Chas., ld. Cornwallis; *d.* 1722.
1722. Hon. Spencer Compton, aft. E. of Wilmington.
1730. Hon. Hy. Pelham.
1743. Sir Thos. Winnington, bt.
1746. Wm. Pitt, aft. E. of Chatham.
1755. Hy., E. of Darlington.
Thos. Hay, visc. Dupplin, aft. E. of Kinnoul.
1757. Hy. Fox, aft. ld. Holland.
1765. Hon. Chas. Townshend.
1766. Fredk., ld. North, and
Geo. Cooke, Dec. 10.
1767. Geo. Cooke, and
Thos. Townshend, Dec. 23.
1768. Richd. Rigby.
1782. Edmund Burke, Mar. 27.
Isaac Barré, July 17.
1783. Edmd. Burke, *again*, Apr. 8.
1784. Wm. Wyndham Grenville, aft. ld. Grenville, Jan. 8.
Wm. Wyndham Grenville, and
Constantine John, ld. Mulgrave, Apr. 7.
1789. Lord Mulgrave, and
Jas., M. of Graham, Sept. 4.
1791. Dudley Ryder, and
Thos. Steele, Mar. 7.
1800. Thos. Steele, and
Geo. Canning, July 5.
1801. Thos. Steele, and
Sylvester, ld. Glenbervie, Mar. 26.
1803. Thos. Steele, and
John Hiley Addington, Jan. 3.
1804. Geo. Rose, and
Lord Chas. Hy. Somerset, July 7.
1806. Richd, Earl Temple, and
Lord John Townshend, Feb. 17
1807. Chas. Long, aft. sir C. and ld. Farnborough, and
Lord Chas. Hy. Somerset, *again*, Apr. 4.
1813. Chas. Long, *again*, and
Fredk. John Robinson, aft. visc. Goderich and E. Ripon, Nov. 13.
1817. Sir Chas. Long, *alone*, Aug. 14.
1826. Wm. Vesey Fitzgerald, aft. ld. Fitzgerald and Vesci, July 15.
1828. John Calcraft, July 15.
1830. Lord John Russell, aft. E. Russell, Dec. 16.
1834. Sir Edwd Knatchbull, bt., Dec. 23.
1835. Sir Hy. Parnell, bt., aft. ld. Congleton, May 14.

Paymasters-General.

1836. Sir Hy. Parnell, bt., above named.
1841. Edwd. John Stanley, aft. ld. Eddisbury and ld. Stanley of Alderley, July 1.
Sir Edwd. Knatchbull, bt., *again*, Sept. 12.
1845. Wm. Bingham Baring, aft. ld. Ashburton, Mar. 1.
1846. Thos. Babington Macaulay, aft. ld. Macaulay, July 12.
1848. Granville Geo., E. Granville, May 11.

1852. Edwd. John, ld. Stanley of Alderley, *again*, Feb. 12, **G.**
Chas., ld. Colchester, Feb. 28, **G.**
1853. Edwd. John, ld. Stanley of Alderley, *again*, Jan. 5, **G.**
1855. Edwd. Pleydell Bouverie, Mar.
Robt. Lowe, aft. visc. Sherbrooke, Aug. 28, **G.**
1858. Richd. John, E. of Donoughmore, Apr.
1859. Algernon Geo. Percy, ld. Lovaine, Mar.
Jas. Wilson, June.
Wm. Fras. Cowper, Aug.
1860. Wm. Hutt, Feb.
1865. Geo. Joachim Göschen.
1866. Wm. Monsell, aft. ld. Emly, Mar.
Stephen Cave, July.
1868. Fredk. Temple, ld. Dufferin and Clandeboye, K.P., K.C.B., aft. Earl Dufferin, Dec.
1872. Hugh Culling Eardley Childers.
1873. Wm. Patrick Adam.
1874. Stephen Cave, Apr. 20, sw.
1880. Geo. Grenfell, ld. Wolverton, May 24, sw.
1885. Fredk., E. Beauchamp, June.
1886. Thos. John, ld. Thurlow, Apr. 3, sw.
Fredk., E. Beauchamp, *again*, Aug. 19, sw.
1887. Aldebert Wellington Brownlow, E. Brownlow, July.

WARDENS AND MASTERS OF THE MINT.

The Warden was anciently the chief officer of the Mint, but his office was abolished by 57 George III. cap. 67 (July 7, 1817), and the duties were directed to be performed by the Master, who was by that act constituted Master, Warden, and Worker.

For many years the office of Master was a political one, the holder being, sometimes, a member of the cabinet. From 1835 to 1850 the office was generally held jointly with the vice-presidency of the Board of Trade. In 1850 sir John Herschel was appointed Master, and he was succeeded by Professor Graham, both these appointments being non-political. Professor Graham died in Sept. 1869, and by 33 & 34 Vict. cap. 10 (Apr. 4, 1870), it was enacted that the office and title of Master of the Mint should be held by the Chancellor of the Exchequer for the time being, and the duties of the office were transferred to the deputy Master.

Wardens of the Mint.

* * * * *

* * John Jeffries.
1766. Gen. Wm. Whitmore, Feb.
1771. Robt. Pigot, Oct. 1.
1798. Sir Walter J. James, bt.

Masters of the Mint.

King Henry I.

* * Godwin Socche, Winchester.

King Edward I.

1275. Gregory Rokesley.
1280. Wm. de Turnemire, of Marseilles.
Richd. de Lothebury.
1281. Alexr. Norman de Luic, Dublin.
1282. Gregory Rokesley, *again*.
1285. Wm. de Turnemire, *again*, in Gascony.
1286. John de Caturco and Gerald Mauhan, London and Canterbury.
1287. John de Caturco.
1297. John Porcher.
Roger de Rede, St. Edmundsbury.
1300. Hubert Elion, Wm. de Turnemire, *again*, and his brother.

King Edward II.

1308. John de Puntoyse.
1313. John de Puntoyse, *again*, and Lapine Roger; Lond. and Cant.
1317. Giles de Hertesburg and Terric de Lose; Lond. and Cant.

King Edward III.

1327. Roger Rykeman, Lond. and Cant.
1344. Geo. Kyrkin, and Lotto Nicholyn of Florence.
Hy. de Brusele.
1345. Percival de Porche, de Lucca.
Walter de Dunflower.
1347. Geo. Kyrkin and Lotto Nicholyn, *again*.
1348. Bertrand de Polirac, meistre du coigne et de monoies de la duchée de Guien.—*Rolls of Parlt.*

1351. Anthy. Bache, of Geneva, and Nichs. Choue.
1352. Hy. de Brusele, *again*, and John de Chichester.
1354. Hy. de Brusele, *again*, Lond. and Cant.
1357. John Donative, of the castle of Florence, and Philip John Denier.
1361. Peter de Bataile, Rochelle.
1362. Gauter de Barde.
1363. Robt. de Porche.
1366. Thos. Kyng, Calais.
1367. John de Chichester, *again*.
1372. Bardet de Malepilys.

KING RICHARD II.

1377. Gauter de Barde.
1395. Nichs. Malakine, a Florentine.
John Wildeman.
1396. Nichs. Malakine, *again*.

KING HENRY IV.

1402. Walter Merwe, magister moneta, Lond.
1413. Richd. Garner.
John Lowys, or Lodowic John.

KING HENRY V.

1418. Conrad Melwer, Normandy.
1421. John Marceur, St. Looe.

KING HENRY VI.

1422. Bartholomew Goldbeter, London, York, Bristol, and Calais.
1426. Robt. Manfeld.
1432. Wm. Russe, London, Calais, Bristol, and York.
1433. John Paddesley, the same places.
1446. Robt. Manfeld, *again*, London and Calais.
1459. Sir Richd. Tonstall.
1461. Robt., bp. of Ross.
Germayne Lynch, Ireland.

KING EDWARD IV.

1461. Wm., ld. Hastings, "keeper of all manner of the king's exchaunges and outchaunges in the Tower of London, realm of England, territory of Ireland, and town of Calais."—*Patent*.
1480. Hugh Brice, Calais.
1483. Bartholomew Rede.
Thos. Galinole, "master and worker of the money of silver in Develyn (Dublin) and Waterford."

KING RICHARD III.

1483. Robt. Brackenbury.

KING HENRY VII.

1485. Giles, ld. Daubeney, and Bartholomew Rede, *again*.
Robt. Bowley, "maister of the cunage and mynt, within the cities of Dyvelyn and Waterford."—*Rolls of Parlt.*
1491. John Shaa and Barth. Rede, *again*.
1492. Robt. Fenrother and B. Rede, *again*

KING HENRY VIII.

1509. Wm., ld. Montjoy.
1524. Wm. Wright, York.
1527. Ralph Rowlet and Martin Bowes.
1531. Wm., ld. Montjoy, *again*.
1534. Wm. Tilesworth, archbishop's mint, Canterbury.
1543. Sir Martin Bowes and Ralph Rowlet.
1544. Sir Martin Bowes, *alone*.
1545. Sir Martin Bowes, *again*, Stephen Vaughan, and Thos. Knight.
Nichls. Tyery.

KING EDWARD VI.

1547. John York and others, Southwark.
Wm. Tillesworth, Canterbury.
Sir Martin Bowes, *again*, Tower.
1548. Geo. Gale, York.
1549. Sir Edmd. Peckham, and others.
Sir Wm. Sharrington.
1550. Martin Pirri, Dublin.—*Cotton. MSS.*
Geo. Gale, *again*, and others, York.

PHILIP AND MARY.

1554. Thos. Egerton.

QUEEN ELIZABETH.

1559. Sir Thos. Stanley and others.
1572. John Lonison.—*Harleian MSS.*
1573. Thos. Stanley.—*Lansdowne MSS.*
1581. Sir Richd. Martin.
1582. Richd. Martin.—*Harleian MSS.*
1584. Sir Richd. Martin, *again*, and Richd Martin, his son.—*Lowndes*.

KING JAMES I.

1603. Sir Richd. Martin and Richd. Martin, his son, *contd.*
1615. Thos., ld. Knyvet, and Edwd. Doubleday.
1619. Randal Cranfield.
1623. Sir Edwd. Villiers.
1624. Sir Hy. Villiers and Hy. Twedy.
1625. Sir Hy. Villiers, *alone*.

KING CHARLES I.

1625. Sir Robt. Harley.
1635. Sir Ralph Freeman.
1637. Thos. Bushell, Aberystwith.
1641. Sir Wm. Parkhurst and Thos. Bushel, *again*, Oxford.
1643. Sir Robt. Harley, *again*.
1647. Hy. Slingsby.
John Faulkener, or Falconer, Edinburgh.

THE COMMONWEALTH.

1649. Aaron Guerdain.

KING CHARLES II.

1660. Sir Wm. Parkhurst.
Sir Ralph Freeman, *again*.

1660. Sir Thos. Vyner, Robt. Vyner, and Danl. Bellingham, Dublin.
1670. Hy. Slingsby, *again*.
1679. Thos. Neale.
John Falconer, *again*, Edinburgh.

KING JAMES II.

1685. Thos. Neale, *again*.
1688. John Trinder, Thos. Goddard, Wm. Talbot, Wm. Bromfield, Fras. Rice, and Edwd. Fox, Dublin; Walter Plunket, Limerick. — Commissioners for brass money.

KING WILLIAM III.

1689. Thos. Neale, *again*.
1699. Isaac Newton, previously warden, aft. sir I.
Major Wyvil, York.

QUEEN ANNE.

1702. Isaac Newton, *contd.*, knt. in 1705.

KING GEORGE I.

1714. Sir Isaac Newton, *contd.*
1727. John Conduit,

KING GEORGE II.

1727. John Conduit, *contd.*
1737. Hon. Richd. Arundel.
1744. Hon. Wm. Chetwynd, aft. visc. Chetwynd.

KING GEORGE III.

1760. Visc. Chetwynd, *contd.*
1769. Hon. Chas. Sloane Cadogan, aft. E. Cadogan.
1784. Thos., E. of Effingham, Jan.
1789. Philip, E. of Chesterfield, Feb. 12.
1790. Geo., E. of Leicester, Jan. 20.
1794. Sir Geo. Yonge, bt., July.
1799. Robt. Banks, ld. Hawkesbury, Feb. 14.
1801. Chas. Geo., ld. Arden, Apr. 18.
1802. John Smyth, July 2.
1804. Hy., E. Bathurst, July 7.
1806. Lord Chas. Spencer, Feb. 20.
Chas. Bathurst, Oct. 27.
1807. Earl Bathurst. *again*, Apr. 25.
1812. Richd., E. of Clancarty, Oct. 30.
1814. Wm. Wellesley Pole, aft. ld. Maryborough, Sept. 28.

KING GEORGE IV.

1820. Wm. Wellesley Pole, aft. ld. Maryborough, *contd.*
1823. Thos. Wallace, aft. ld. Wallace, Oct 9.
1827. Geo. Tierney, May 29.
1828. John Chas. Herries, Feb. 12.

KING WILLIAM IV.

1830. John Chas. Herries, *contd.*
Geo., ld. Auckland, Dec. 14.
1834. Jas. Abercromby, July 1.
1835. Alexr. Baring, Jan. 1.
Hy. Labouchere, aft. ld. Taunton, May 9.

QUEEN VICTORIA.

1837. Hy. Labouchere, *contd.*
1841. Wm. Ewart Gladstone, Sept. 21.
1845. Sir Geo. Clerk, bt., Feb. 12.
1846. Richd. Lalor Shiel, July 14.
1850. Sir John Fredk. Wm. Herschel, bt., Dec. 13; res. 1855.
1855. Thos. Graham, Mar.; *d.* Sept. 1869.

The dates in this roll, which differ, in some instances materially, from those found in other works, are taken from Ruding's "*Coinage of Great Britain*," or from the Records of the Mint.

By 33 & 34 Vict. cap. 10 (Apr. 4, 1870) the office of master of the mint was to be held by the chancellor of the exchequer for the time being. See Introduction, *ante*, p. 245.

JUDGE ADVOCATES GENERAL.

See Part XV. "Military," *post*.

SPEAKERS OF THE HOUSE OF COMMONS.

The Speaker is chosen by the House of Commons from its own members, subject to the approval of the sovereign, and holds his office until the dissolution of the parliament by which he was elected. As Chairman of the House, his duties are the same as those of any other preside of a deliberative assembly. Generally speaking, the business of tl House could not be transacted in the absence of the Speaker, although this rule there was an exception in the year 1606, when, during the il ness of a Speaker, a prisoner was released from custody by order of tl House. By 18 & 19 Vict. cap. 34 (Aug. 14, 1855), and certain standin orders of the House, power is now given to appoint a deputy Speak when necessary. The Speaker has a casting vote upon divisions which the votes prove equal.

Speakers of the House of Commons.

From the earliest authentic Records of Parliament.

The county, town, or borough following each name is the place for which the Speaker w returned as a member of the House.

England & Wales.

King Henry III.

1260. Peter de Montfort. *Killed at the battle of Evesham.*

King Edward II.

1326. Wm. Trussell.*

King Edward III.

1327. Wm. Trussell,* *contd.*
1332. Sir Hy Beaumont.*
*These must have been Speakers to both lords and commons.
1376. Sir Peter de la Mare, Herefordshire. He is supposed to have been the first regular Speaker.
1377. Sir Thos. Hungerford, Wilts.

King Richard II.

1377. Sir Peter de la Mare, Herefordshire.
1378. Sir Jas. Pickering, Westmoreland.
1380. 1381. } Sir John Goldsborough, Essex.
1382. Sir Richd. Waldegrave, Suffolk.
1386. Sir Jas. Pickering, Westmoreland.
The next speaker on record is
1394. 1397. 1398. } Sir John Bushey, Lincolnshire.

King Henry IV.

1399. Sir John Cheney, Gloucestershire; he, growing infirm and unable to serve,
John Doreword, Essex, was delegated to serve in his place.
1400. Sir Arnold Savage, Kent.
1403. Sir Hy. Redeford, Lincolnshire.
1404. Sir Arnold Savage, *again*, Kent.
1405. Sir Wm. Esturmy, Devonshire.
Sir Wm. Esturmy, *again*, same year.
Sir John Cheney, Cornwall, also appears to have been Speaker in this parliament.
1406. Sir John Tiptoft, Hunts.
1408. 1409. 1412. } Thos. Chaucer, Oxfordshire.

King Henry V.

1413. Wm. Stourton, Dorsetshire; but l being unwell, John Dorewor Essex, was chosen in his room.
1414. Walter Hungerford, Wilts.
1415. Thos. Chaucer, *again*, Oxfordshire
Richd. Redman, Yorkshire.
Sir Walter Beauchamp, Wilts.
1416. 1417. 1419. } Roger Flower, Rutlandshire.
1421. Richd. Baynard, Essex.

Henry VI.

1422. Roger Flower, *again*, Rutlandshire
1423. John Russell, Herefordshire.
1425. Sir Thos. Waughton or Wauto Beds.
1426. Richd. Vernon, Derbyshire.
1428. John Tyrrell, Essex.
1430. Wm. Allington, Cambs.
1431. John Tyrrell, *again*, Essex.
1432. John Russell, *again*, Herefordshir
1433. Roger Hunt, Hunts.
1436. John Bowes. Here the records a imperfect, but it is presumed l sat for Northumberland.
1439. Sir John Tyrrell, *again*, for a thi and fourth time, Essex.
Wm. Boerley, Shropshire.
1440. Wm. Tresham, Northamptonshire.
1445. Wm. Boerley, *again*, Shropshire.
1447. Wm. Tresham, *again*, Northampto shire.
1449. John Saye, Cambs.
1450. John Popham, Hants.; but he e cusing himself,
Wm. Tresham, Northamptonshir was chosen *again*.
1451. Sir Wm. Oldhall, Herefordshire.
1453. Thos. Thorpe, Essex.
Thos. Thorpe, *again*, same year.
Sir Thos. Charlton, Middlesex.
1455. Sir John Wenlock, Beds.
1459. Sir Wm. Tresham, Northampto shire, *again*, fourth time.
1460. John Green, Essex.

KING EDWARD IV.

60. Sir Jas. Strangeways, Yorks.
63. } John Saye, Herts.
67. }
72. Wm. Allington, Cambs.
77. Wm. Allington, *again*, Lincolnshire.
82. John Wode, Surrey or Sussex.

KING RICHARD III.

83. Wm. Catesby, Northamptonshire.

KING HENRY VII.

85. Thos. Lovel, Northamptonshire or Oxfordshire.
88. John Mordaunt, Beds.
89. Sir Thos. Fitzwilliam, Yorks.
92. Richd. Empson, Northamptonshire.
96. Sir Reginald Bray, Beds. or Northhamptonshire.
Robt. Drury, Sussex.
97. Thos. Englefield, aft. Sir T., Berks.
04. Edmd. Dudley, Staffs.

KING HENRY VIII.

509. Sir Thos. Englefield, *again*, Berks.
512. Sir Thos. Sheffeild, Lincolnshire.
514. Sir Thos. Nevill, perhaps Kent.
523. } Sir Thos. More, Middlesex.
524. }
530. Sir Thos. Audley, perhaps Essex.
537. Richd. Rich, Essex.
540. Sir Nichs. Hare, Norfolk.
542. Thos. Moyle, Kent; he continued Speaker all the rest of this reign.

KING EDWARD VI.

547. Sir John Baker, Hunts.
553. Jas. Dyer, Cambs.

QUEEN MARY.

553. John Pollard, Oxfordshire.
554. Robt. Brooke, London city.

PHILIP AND MARY.

555. Clement Higham, West Looe.
556. John Pollard, *again*, Chippenham.
558. Wm. Cordell, Essex.

QUEEN ELIZABETH.

559. Sir Thos. Gargrave, Yorks.
563. Thos. Williams, Exeter city; *d.* 1566; when Richd. Onslow, Steyning, was chosen in his room.
571. Christr. Wray, Ludgershall.
572. Robt. Bell, Lynn Regis; made ch. bar. of the ex. in 1577, when
577. John Popham, Bristol city, solicitor-gen., was chosen in his place.
585 & 586. John Puckering, { Bedford town. / Gatton, Surrey.
589. Thos. Snagg, Bedford town.
592. Edwd. Coke, Norfolk.
597. Christr. Yelverton, Northamptonshire.
601. John Croke, London; recorder of the city.

KING JAMES I.

1603. Edwd. Philipps, Somersetshire.
1614. Randolph Crew.
No records of this parliament are to be found; but it is presumed he sat for Brackley, Northhamptonshire.
1620. Thos. Richardson, St. Alban's.
1623. Thos. Crewe, aft. Sir T., Ailesbury.

KING CHARLES I.

1625. Sir Thos. Crewe, *again*, Gatton.
1626. Sir Heneage Finch, London; recorder of the city.
1628. Sir John Finch, Canterbury.
1640. John Glanville, Bristol.
1641. Wm. Lenthal, Woodstock; he continued till 1653.

KING CHARLES II.

Commonwealth.

1653. Fras. Rous, nom. for Devonshire.
1654. Wm. Lenthal, rest., Oxfordshire.
1656. Sir Thos. Widdrington, nom. for York city.
1659. Chaloner Chute, sen., Middlesex; but, being unable to attend, the commons chose
Sir Lisleborne Long, Wells, to supply his place. Sir Lisleborne, on Mar. 9, gave up the office after seven days' possession, and on Mar. 16th the commons delegated to the office
Thos. Bampfield, Exeter. Chute dying on Apr. 15 following, Bampfield was then chosen speaker.

THE RESTORATION.

1660. Sir Harbottle Grimstone, bt., Colchester.
1661. Sir Edwd. Turnor, bt., Hertford town. On his being app. ch. bar. of the ex., May 23, 1671, the commons chose at their meeting in
1673. Sir Job Charlton, bt., Ludlow, but he desiring leave to resign on account of his health,
Edwd. Seymour, aft. bt., Hindon, was elected in his place. On Seymour's indisposition, the commons chose
Sir Robt. Sawyer, Wycombe; but he, excusing his attendance, they *again* chose
1678. Sir Edwd. Seymour, bt., Hindon. To this choice the king refused his approval, whereupon the commons returned to their house, and elected
Serjt. Wm. Gregory, Weobly.
1680. Wm. Williams, Chester city.

KING JAMES II.

1685. Sir John Trevor, Denbigh town.

WILLIAM AND MARY AND KING WILLIAM III.

1689. Hy. Powle, Windsor.
1690. Sir John Trevor, *again*, Yarmouth, Hants.
Sir John Trevor was expelled the chair and the house for taking a bribe of 1000 guineas from the city of London, on the passing of the Orphans' Bill, Mar. 12, 1695.
1695. Paul Foley, Hereford city.
1698. Sir Thos. Lyttelton, bt., Woodstock.
1700 & 1701. Robt. Harley, New Radnor.

QUEEN ANNE.

1702. Robt. Harley, *again*, New Radnor.
1705. John Smith, Andover.

UNION OF ENGLAND AND SCOTLAND UNDER THE STYLE OF GREAT BRITAIN.

1707. John Smith, *again*, Andover, Hants.
1708. Sir Richd. Onslow, bt., Surrey.
1710. Wm. Bromley, Oxford univ.
1713. Sir Thos. Hanmer, bt., Suffolk.

KING GEORGE I.

1714 & 1722. Hon. Spencer Compton, Sussex, filled the chair all this reign.

KING GEORGE II.

1727. 1734. 1741. 1747. 1754. Arthur Onslow, Surrey, chosen by these five parliaments successively; and so filled the chair during the whole reign of this king, embracing a period of 33 years.

KING GEORGE III.

1761. Sir John Cust, bt., Grantham.
1768. Sir John Cust, bt., *again*, Grantham. Res. on account of ill-health, Jan. 17, 1770, and on the 23rd of same month the commons elected
1770 Sir Fletcher Norton, Guildford.
1774. Sir Fletcher Norton, *again*.
1780. Chas. Wolfran Cornewall, Winchelsea.
1784. Chas. Wolfran Cornewall, *again*, Rye; *d.* Jan. 2, 1789.
1789. Wm. Wyndham Grenville, aft. ld. Grenville, Bucks, Jan. 5; res. June 5 following.
Hy. Addington, Devizes, June 8.
1790. Hy. Addington, *again*, Nov. 25.
1796. Hy. Addington, *again*, Sept. 27.

UNION OF ENGLAND, SCOTLAND, AND IRELAND, UNDER THE STYLE OF THE UNITED KINGDOM OF GREAT BRITAIN AND IRELAND.

1801. Hy. Addington, *again*, fourth time, Jan. 22; res. Feb. 10, and became first ld. treasy. and ch. ex., Mar. following; cr. visc. Sidmout Jan. 1805.
1801. Sir John Mitford, Beeralston, Fe 11; res. Feb. 9, 1802, on bei cr. ld. Redesdale, and made chanc. of Ireland.
1802. Chas. Abbot, Helston, Feb. 10.
Chas. Abbot, *again*, Nov. 16.
1806. Chas. Abbot, *again*, Dec. 15.
1807. Chas. Abbot, *again*, June 22.
1812. Chas. Abbot, *again*, fifth time, No 24. Ret., and cr. ld. Colcheste June 1817.
1817. Chas. Manners Sutton, Scarboroug June 2.
1819. Chas. Manners Sutton, *again*, Ja 15.

KING GEORGE IV.

1820. Chas. Manners Sutton, *again*, Ap 22.
1826. Chas. Manners Sutton, *again*, No 15.

KING WILLIAM IV.

1830. Chas. Manners Sutton, *again*, Oc 26.
1831. Chas. Manners Sutton, aft. sir C *again*, June 14.
1833. Sir Chas. Manners Sutton, nc member for Cambridge uni *again*, seventh time, Jan. 29.
1835. Jas. Abercromby, Edinburgh cit Feb. 19. In the memorable co test for the speakership, in 183 Mr. Abercromby had 316 vote and Sir C. Manners Sutton, 30 the majority in favour of M Abercromby being *ten*. Sir Manners Sutton retired fro political life immediately aft this contest, and was cr. vis Canterbury. He *d.* 1845.

QUEEN VICTORIA.

1837. Jas. Abercromby, *again*, Nov. 1 ret. and cr. bar. Dunfermlin June 7, 1839.
1839. Chas. Shaw Lefevre, Hampshire, div., May 27.
1841. Chas. Shaw Lefevre, *again*, Au 19.
1847. Chas. Shaw Lefevre, *again*, No 18.
1852. Chas. Shaw Lefevre, *again*, four time, Nov. 4; ret. and cr. vis Eversley, Apr. 11, 1857.
1857. John Evelyn Denison, Notts., Div., Apr. 30.
1859. J. E. Denison, *again*, May 31.
1866. J. E. Denison, *again*, Feb. 1.
1868. J. E. Denison, *again*, fourth tim Dec. 10; ret. and cr. visc. O sington, Feb. 13, 1872, **G.**

372. Hy. Bouverie Wm. Brand, Cambridgeshire, Feb. 9.
374. H. B. W. Brand, *again*, Mar. 5.
380. H. B. W. Brand, *again*, third time, Apr. 29; made G.C.B. Sept. 20, 1881; ret. and cr. visc. Hampden, Mar. 3, 1884, **G.**

1884. Arthur Wellesley Peel, Warwick, Feb. 26.
1886. A. W. Peel, *again*, Warwick and Leamington, Jan. 12.
A. W. Peel, *again*, third time, Aug. 5.

THE BOARD OF CONTROL.

COMMONLY CALLED

THE INDIA BOARD.

'HIS Board was originally established by Mr. Pitt's celebrated East ndia Bill, 24 Geo. III. cap. 25 (May 18, 1784). This act empowered he crown to appoint six privy councillors to be commissioners for the ffairs of India, with very extensive powers; they having the "control nd superintendence of all the British territorial possessions in the East ndies, and over the affairs of the United Company of Merchants rading thereto." One of the principal secretaries of state was contituted president; in his absence the chancellor of the exchequer, nd in the absence of both, then the senior commissioner was to be resident. Subsequently, however, to the passing of this act, it was ound necessary to alter the constitution of the Board, and by 33 Geo. II. cap. 52 (June 11, 1793), it was enacted that any three or more ommissioners might form a board, that the first-named commisioner in the letters patent or commission for the time being should be he president of such board; and that when any board should be formed n the absence of the president, the senior commissioner present should or that turn preside at the board.

The president was always specially appointed, and was one of the nost important members of the cabinet, entering upon office and retiring n every change in the administration.

The lord president of the council, the lord privy seal, the first lord of he treasury, the principal secretaries of state, and the chancellor of the xchequer, for the time being, were *ex officio* members of the board, nd the sovereign might appoint any other persons to be members lso.

By the 3 & 4 Will. IV. cap. 85 (Aug. 28, 1833), the provisions of the revious act as to *ex officio* and additional members were repealed; but t will be seen that from the passing of this act fewer commissioners, ther than *ex officio* commissioners, were named, and that, latterly, ut *one* commissioner was named. The letters patent, since Sept. 1841, vere addressed to one commissioner only, exclusive of the *ex officio* ommissioners, and the whole powers of the former boards were pracically vested in that one commissioner.

By the 21 & 22 Vict. cap. 106 (Aug. 2, 1858) the board of control was bolished, the government of India transferred from the East India Company to the sovereign, and the secretaryship of state for India created.

Presidents and Commissioners of the Board of Control.

The following dates are those of the patents, in all cases, excep those marked "G.", the dates of which are those of the notice in th *London Gazette.*

King George III.

Sept. 3, 1784.

Thos., ld. Sydney, pres.
Wm. Pitt, ch. ex.
Hy. Dundas.
Thos., ld. Walsingham.
Wm. Wyndham Grenville.
Constantine John, ld. Mulgrave.

Mar. 12, 1790.

Wm. Wyndham Grenville, pres.
Hy. Dundas.
Constantine John, ld. Mulgrave.
Thos., ld. Sydney.
Thos., ld. Walsingham.
Lord Fredk. Campbell.
Dudley Ryder.

May 16, 1791.

Wm. Wyndham Grenville, aft. ld. Grenville, pres.
Wm. Pitt.
Hy. Dundas.
Lord Fredk. Campbell.
Jas., D. of Montrose.
Thos. Steele.

June 28, 1793.

Hy. Dundas, the first paid pres.
Jas., D. of Montrose.
Richd., E. of Mornington.
Robt. Grosvenor, visc. Belgrave.
Hy., ld. Apsley.
Hon. Edwd. Jas. Eliot.
Hon. Robt. Banks Jenkinson.

June 29, 1795.

Hy. Dundas, pres.
Jas., D. of Montrose.
Richd., E. of Mornington, aft. M. Wellesley.
Robt., visc. Belgrave.
Hy., E. Bathurst (late ld. Apsley).
Hon. Edwd. Jas. Eliot.
Hon. Robt. Banks Jenkinson.
Sylvester Douglas.

Nov. 16, 1797.

Hy. Dundas, pres.
Jas., D. of Montrose.
Robt., visc. Belgrave.
Hy., E. Bathurst.
Robt. Banks, ld. Hawkesbury.
Sylvester Douglas.
Wm. Dundas.

Mar. 28, 1799.

Hy. Dundas, pres.
Jas., D. of Montrose.
Robt., visc. Belgrave.
Hy., E. Bathurst.
Sylvester Douglas.
Wm. Dundas.
Geo. Canning.

July 2, 1800.

Hy. Dundas, aft. visc. Melville, pres.
Jas., D. of Montrose.
Robt., visc. Belgrave.
Hy., E. Bathurst.
Sylvester Douglas.
Geo. Canning.
Thos. Wallace.
Richd. Temple Nugent, E. Temple.

May 19, 1801.

Geo., visc. Lewisham, pres. succ. as E. of Dartmouth.
Jas., D. of Montrose.
Hy., E. Bathurst.
Sylvester Douglas, now ld. Glenbervie.
Wm. Dundas.
Thos. Wallace.
Chas. Geo., ld. Arden.
Thos. Pelham.
Edwd. Golding.

July 12, 1802.

Robt., visc. Castlereagh, pres.
Jas., D of Montrose.
Sylvester, ld. Glenbervie.
Wm. Dundas.
Thos. Wallace.
Chas. Geo., ld. Arden.
Edwd. Golding.

Oct. 22, 1803.

Robt., visc. Castlereagh, pres.
Sylvester, ld. Glenbervie.
Thos. Wallace.
Edwd. Golding.
Hon. Thos. Maitland.

May 31, 1804.

Robt., visc. Castlereagh, pres.
Sylvester, now visc. Glenbervie.
Thos. Wallace.
Richd. Trench, visc. Dunl aft. E. of Clancarty.

Feb. 12, 1806.

Gilbert, ld. Minto, aft. E of Minto, pres.
Geo., visc. Morpeth.
John Hiley Addington.
John Sullivan.

July 16, 1806.

Thos. Grenville, pres.
Geo., visc. Morpeth.
John Hiley Addington.
John Sullivan.
John Joshua, E. of Carysfort.

Oct. 1, 1806.

Geo. Tierney, pres.
Geo., visc. Morpeth, aft. E of Carlisle.
John Hiley Addington.
John Sullivan.
John Joshua, E. of Carysfort.

April 6, 1807.

Robt. Dundas, pres.
Geo., ld. Lovaine.
John, ld. Teignmouth.
Thos. Wallace.
Geo. Johnstone.

July 17, 1809.

Dudley, E. of Harrowby, pres.
Robt. Dundas.
Geo., ld. Lovaine.
John, ld. Teignmouth.
Thos. Wallace.
Thos., ld. Binning.

Nov. 13, 1809.

Robt. Dundas, pres.
Geo., ld. Lovaine.
John, ld. Teignmouth.
Thos. Wallace.
Lord Fras. Almaric Spencer

July 7, 1810.

ROBT. DUNDAS, pres.
Geo., ld. Lovaine.
John, ld. Teignmouth.
Thos. Wallace.
Wm., visc. Lowther

April 7, 1812.

ROBT., E. of BUCKINGHAMSHIRE, pres.
Geo., ld. Lovaine.
John, ld. Teignmouth.
Thos. Wallace.
Wm., visc. Lowther.
John Sullivan.

Sept. 8, 1812.

ROBT., E. of BUCKINGHAMSHIRE, pres.
John, ld. Teignmouth.
Thos. Wallace.
Wm., visc. Lowther.
John Sullivan.
Hy., ld. Apsley.

Sept. 7, 1814.

ROBT., E. of BUCKINGHAMSHIRE, pres.
John, ld. Teignmouth.
Thos. Wallace.
Wm., visc. Lowther.
John Sullivan.
Hy., ld. Apsley.
Thos., ld. Binning.
Wm. Sturges Bourne.

June 20, 1816.

GEO. CANNING, pres.
John, ld. Teignmouth.
Wm., visc. Lowther.
John Sullivan.
Hy., ld. Apsley.
Thos., ld. Binning.

June 17, 1818.

GEO. CANNING, pres.
John, ld. Teignmouth.
John Sullivan.
Thos., ld. Binning.
Wm. Sturges Bourne.
Jas. Brownlow Wm., visc. Cranborne.
Horatio, ld. Walpole.

KING GEORGE IV.

Jan. 16, 1821.

CHAS. BATHURST, pres.
John, ld. Teignmouth.
John Sullivan.
Thos., ld. Binning, aft. E. of Haddington.
Wm. Sturges Bourne.
Jas. Brownlow Wm., visc. Cranborne.
Horatio, ld. Walpole, aft. E. of Orford.

Feb. 8, 1822, G.

CHAS. WATKIN WILLIAMS WYNN, pres.
John, ld. Teignmouth.
John Sullivan.
Jas. Brownlow Wm., visc. Cranborne, aft. M. of Salisbury.
Wm. Hy. Fremantle.
Sir Geo. Warrender, bt.
Jos. Phillimore.

June 2, 1826, G.

CHAS. WATKIN WILLIAMS WYNN, pres.
Jas. Brownlow Wm., M. of Salisbury.
John, ld. Teignmouth.
John Sullivan.
Sir Geo. Warrender, bt.
Jos. Phillimore.
Wm. Yates Peel.

June 4, 1827.

CHAS. WATKIN WILLIAMS WYNN, pres.
John, ld. Teignmouth.
John Sullivan.
Sir Geo. Warrender, bt.
Jos. Phillimore.
Sir Jas. Macdonald, bt.

Feb. 7, 1828.

ROBT. DUNDAS, visc. MELVILLE, pres.
Thos., ld. Wallace.
John Sullivan.
Anthy., ld. Ashley.
Jas., M. of Graham.
Laurence Peel.

July 31, 1828.

ROBT., visc. MELVILLE, pres.
Thos., ld. Wallace.
John Sullivan.
Anthy., ld. Ashley.
Jas., M. of Graham.
Laurence Peel.
Thos. Peregrine Courtenay.

Sept. 24, 1828.

EDWD., ld. ELLENBOROUGH, pres.
Thos., ld. Wallace.
John Sullivan.
Anthy., ld. Ashley.
Jas., M. of Graham.
Laurence Peel.
Thos. Peregrine Courtenay.

Feb. 24, 1830.

EDWD., ld. ELLENBOROUGH, pres.
John Sullivan.
Anthy., ld. Ashley.
Jas., M. of Graham.
Thos. Peregrine Courtenay.
Geo. Banks.

KING WILLIAM IV.

Dec. 6, 1830.

CHAS. GRANT, pres.
Chas. Watkin Williams Wynn.
John Sullivan.
Sir Jas. Macdonald, bt.
Sir Jas. Mackintosh.
Robt. Grant.
Hy. Ellis.

July 28, 1832.

CHAS. GRANT, pres.
Chas. Watkin Williams Wynn.
John Sullivan.
Robt. Grant.
Hy. Ellis.
Holt Mackenzie.
Robt. Gordon.
Thos. Babington Macaulay.

Dec. 21, 1832.

CHAS. GRANT, aft. ld. GLENELG, pres.
John Sullivan.
Robt. Grant.
Hy. Ellis.
Holt Mackenzie.
Robt. Gordon.
Jas. Alex. Stewart Mackenzie.

Dec. 20, 1834.

EDWD., ld. ELLENBOROUGH, pres.
John Sullivan.
Jos. Planta.
Sir Alexr. Cray Grant.

April 29, 1835.

Sir JOHN HOBHOUSE, bt., pres.
John Sullivan.
Sir Chas. Cockerell, bt.

QUEEN VICTORIA.

July 21, 1837.

Sir JOHN HOBHOUSE, bt., pres.
John Sullivan.

Presidents of the Board of Control.

1841. Edwd. ld., aft. E. of Ellenborough, *again*, Sept. 9, **G.**
Wm. Vesey Fitzgerald, lord Fitzgerald and Vesci, Oct. 28.
1843. Fredk. John, E. of Ripon, May 23.
1846. Sir John Hobhouse, bt., *again*, July 10.
1852. Fox Maule, aft. ld. Panmure and E. of Dalhousie, Feb. 5, **G.**
1852. John Chas. Herries, Feb. 28, **G.**
Sir Chas. Wood, bt., aft. visc. Halifax, Dec. 30, **G.**
1855. Robt. Vernon Smith, aft. ld. Lyveden, Mar. 3, **G.**
1858. Edwd., E. of Ellenborough, *again*, Mar. 6, **G.**
1858. Edwd. Hy., ld. Stanley, aft. E. of Derby, June 5, **G.**

Office abolished by 21 & 22 Vict. cap. 106. *Vide supra*; Secretary of State for India substituted. See that title, *ante*, p. 236.

Secretaries to the Board of Control.

1784. C. W. Broughton Rouse, Sept. 8.
1791. Hy. Beaufoy, May 10.
1793. Wm. Broderick, July 3.
1803. Benjn. Hobhouse, aft. sir B., Nov. 19.
1804. Geo. Peter Holford, May 22.
1806. Thos. Creevy, Feb. 14.
1807. Geo. Peter Holford, *again*, Apr. 8.
1810. Sir Patrick Murray, Jan. 6.
1812. John Bruce, Mar. 14.
Thos. Peregrine Courtenay, Aug. 20.
1829. Geo. Bankes, May 2.
1830. Hon. John Stuart Wortley, aft. ld. Wharncliffe, Feb. 16.
Dudley, ld. Sandon, aft. E. of Harrowby, Dec. 18.
1831. Thos. Hyde Villiers, May 18.
1832. Thos. Babington Macaulay, aft. ld. Macaulay, Dec. 19.
1833. } Robt. Gordon, Dec. 26, and
1834. } Jas. Alexr. Stewart Mackenzie, Apr. 22; joint secs.
1834. } Winthrop M. Praed, Dec. 20 and
1835. } Hon. Sidney Herbert, aft. ld. Herbert of Lea, Jan. 8; joint secs.
1835. { Robt. Gordon, *again*, and Robt. Vernon Smith, aft. ld. Lyveden, Apr. 21.
1839. { Edwd. Adolphs., ld. Seymour, and Wm. Clay, aft. sir W., bt., Sept. 30.
1841. Chas. Buller, *vice* ld. Seymour, June 21.
1841. { Jas. Emerson Tennent, aft. sir J., and Hon. Wm. Bingham Baring, ld. Ashburton, Sept. 8.
1845. { Robt., visc. Jocelyn, Feb. 17. Philip Hy., visc. Mahon, Aug. 5.
1846. { Geo. Stevens Byng, aft. visc. Enfield and E. of Strafford, and Thos. Wyse, July 6.
1847. Geo. Cornewall Lewis, aft. sir G., bt., Nov. 30, *vice* Byng.
1848. Jas. Wilson, May 16, *vice* Lewis.
1849. Hon. John Edmund Elliot, Jan. 26, *vice* Wyse.
1852. { Hy. Jas. Baillie, and Chas. Lennox Cumming Bruce, Mar.
1852. { Robt. Lowe, aft. visc. Sherbrooke, and Sir Thos. N. Redington, Dec.
1855. Hy. Danby Seymour, *vice* Lowe.
1857. Sir Geo. Russell Clerk, K.C.B., *vice* Redington.

Office abolished by 21 & 22 Vict. cap. 106. *Vide supra.*

VICE-PRESIDENTS OF THE COMMITTEE OF THE PRIVY COUNCIL FOR EDUCATION IN ENGLAND AND WALES.

Annual grants in aid of education were first made in 1834, and a committee of the privy council to superintend the distribution of these grants was first appointed Jan. 20, 1846. The lord president of the council is president of this committee, and from Feb. 1857, a vice-president has been from time to time appointed. The management of the Education Department is practically in his hands, he is the representative of the department in parliament, his office is a political one, and he retires with his party.

Vice-Presidents of the Committee of the Privy Council for Education in England and Wales.

1857. Hon. Wm. Fras. Cowper, Feb. 5, **G.**
1858. Chas. Bowyer Adderley, aft. sir C., bt., and ld. Norton, Mar. 12, **G.**
1859. Robt. Lowe, aft. visc. Sherbrooke, June 24, **G.**
1864. Hy. Austin Bruce, aft. ld. Aberdare, Apr.
1866. Hy. Thos. Lowry Corry, July 12, **G.**
1867. Robt. Montagu, c.c. ld. Robt. Montagu, Mar. 19.
1868. Wm. Edwd. Forster, Dec. 9.
1874. Dudley Fras. Stuart Ryder, c.c. visc. Sandon, Mar. 2.
1878. Geo. Fras. Hamilton, c.c. ld. Geo. Hamilton, Apr. 4.
1880. Anthony John Mundella, May 3.
1885. Hon. Edwd. Stanhope, June 29, **G.**
Sir Hy. Thurstan Holland, bt., K.C.M.G., aft. ld. Knutsford, Sept. 17.
1886. Sir Lyon Playfair, K.C.B., Feb. 6.
Sir H. T. Holland, *again*, Aug. 6.
1887. Sir Wm. Hart Dyke, bt.. Jan. 24.

PRESIDENTS OF THE BOARD OF HEALTH.

Boards of Health appear to have been first established by orders in council, dated June 21, Nov. 14, and Nov. 21, 1831, made under 6 Geo. IV. cap. 78. In 1848, under 11 & 12 Vict. cap. 63, a "General Board of Health" was created, consisting of the first commissioner of woods, forests, &c., as president, and two other members appointed by the crown. In 1854, under 17 & 18 Vict. cap. 95, the "General Board of Health" was reconstituted, and thenceforth consisted of a president appointed by the crown and a board composed of the secretaries of state and the president and vice-president of the Board of Trade. In 1858 the powers of the Board were transferred to the privy council under 21 & 22 Vict. cap. 97, and in 1871 these powers were (*inter alia*) again transferred to the Local Government Board under 34 & 35 Vict. cap. 70

Presidents of the General Board of Health from its Reconstruction in 1854.

1854. Sir Benjn. Hall, bt., aft. ld. Llanover, Oct. 14, **G.**
1855. Hon. Wm. Fras. Cowper, Aug. 13, **G.**
1857. Wm. Monsell, aft. lord Emly, Feb. 9, **G.**
1857. Hon. Wm. Fras. Cowper, *again*, Sept. 24, **G.**
1858. Chas. Bowyer Adderley, aft. sir C., bt., and ld. Norton, Mar. 8, **G.**

Powers transferred to the Privy Council and subsequently to Local Government Board. *Vide supra.*

THE LOCAL GOVERNMENT BOARD.

This Board was established in 1871 under 34 & 35 Vict. cap. 70, and in it were vested all the powers of the Poor Law Board, which thenceforth ceased to exist, and also all the powers of the home secretary and the privy council in matters of public health, local government, &c.

Presidents of the Local Government Board.

1871. Jas. Stansfeld, Aug. 19.
1874. Geo. Sclater Booth, Mar. 2.
1880. John Geo. Dodson, May 3.
1882. Sir Chas. Wentworth Dilke, bt., Dec. 28.
1885. Arthur Jas. Balfour, June 24.
1886. Jos. Chamberlain, Feb. 6.
Jas. Stansfeld, *again*, Apr. 3.
Chas. Thomson Ritchie, Aug. 3.

Parliamentary Secretaries to the Local Government Board.

1871. John Tomlinson Hibbert, Aug.
1874. Clare Sewell Read, Feb.
1876. Thos. Salt.
1880. John Tomlinson Hibbert, *again*, May.
1883. Geo. Wm. Erskine Russell.
1885. Adelbert Wellington Brownlow, E. Brownlow, June.
1886. Jesse Collings, Feb.
Wm. Copeland Borlase, Apr.
Walter Hume Long, Aug.

Permanent Secretaries to the Local Government Board.

1871. John Lambert, aft. sir J., K.C.B., and
Hy. Fleming; jointly till 1876; then Lambert alone.
1882. Hugh Owen, aft. Sir H., K.C.B.

TREASURERS OF THE NAVY.

This office was abolished Dec. 1, 1836, by 5 & 6 Will. IV. cap 35. See "Paymasters-General," *ante*, p. 243.

Treasurers of the Navy, from the Restoration.

1660. Sir Geo. Carteret, bt.
1667. Arthur, visc. Valentia, in Ireland, and E. of Anglesey.
1672. Sir Thos. Osborne, bt., aft. visc. Dumblane, E. of Danby, M. of Carmarthen and D. of Leeds.
1673. Sir Edwd. Seymour, bt.
1681. Anthy., visc. Falkland, June 24.
1689. Edwd. Russel, aft. E. of Orford, Apr. 8.
1699. Sir Thos. Littleton, bt., May 29.
1710. Robt. Walpole, aft. sir R. and E. of Orford, Jan. 21.
1711. Chas. Cæsar, June 8.
1714. John Aislabie, Oct. 15.
1718. Richd. Hampden, Mar. 27.
1720. Sir Geo. Byng, bt., aft. visc. Torrington, Oct. 24.
1724. Hon. Pattee Byng, his son, aft. visc. Torrington, Apr. 18.
1727. The same, by a new patent, Aug. 12.
1734. Arthur Onslow, Apr. 20.
1742. Hon. Thos. Clutterbuck, May 17.
Sir Chas. Wager, Dec. 20.
1743. Sir John Rushout, bt., Dec. 24.
1744. Geo. Dodington, Dec. 29.
1749. Hon. Hy. Bilson Legge, May 3.
1754. Geo. Grenville, Apr. 4.
1756. Geo. Dodington, *again*, Jan. 13; aft. ld. Melcombe.
Geo. Grenville, *again*, Nov. 25.
1761. The same by a new patent, Mar. 18.
1762. Wm. Wildman, visc. Barrington, June 2.
1765. Richd., visc. Howe, Aug. 9.
1770. Sir Gilbert Elliot, bt., Mar. 19.
1777. Welbore Ellis, aft. ld. Mendip, June 12.
1782. Isaac Barré, Apr. 10.
Hy. Dundas, Aug. 19.
1783. Chas. Townshend, Apr. 11.
1784. Hy. Dundas, *again*, Jan. 5, aft. visc. Melville, held the office upwards of sixteen years.
1800. Hon. Dudley Ryder, June 2.
1801. Chas. Bragge, Nov. 21.
1803. Geo. Tierney, June 3.
1804. Geo. Canning, May 29.
1806. Richd. Brinsley Sheridan, Feb. 22.
1807. Geo. Rose, Apr. 15.
1818. Fredk. John Robinson, aft. visc. Goderich, and E. of Ripon, Feb. 12.
1823. Wm. Huskisson, Feb. 8.

1827. Chas. Grant, aft. ld. Glenelg, Sept. 10.
1828. Wm. Fitzgerald Vesey Fitzgerald, aft. ld. Fitzgerald and Vesci; Feb. 25.
1830. Thos. Frankland Lewis, Feb. 25.
Chas. Poulet Thompson, aft. ld. Sydenham, Dec. 13.
1834. Wm., visc. Lowther, aft. E. of Lonsdale, Dec. 27.
1835. Sir Hy. Parnell, bt., aft. ld. Congleton, Apr. 22.
Sir Hy. Parnell became paym.-gen. when this office ceased.

COMPTROLLERS AND SURVEYORS OF THE NAVY.

Comptrollers.

1688. Sir Richd. Haddock, aft. adm., Sept. 30.
1714. Sir Chas. Wager, aft. adm., Feb. 17.
1718. Thos. Swanton, Mar. 26.
1722. Jas. Mighells, Jan. 18.
1733. Richd. Haddock, jun., Mar. 27.
1749. Savage Mostyn, aft. adm., Mar. 22.
1755. Edwd. Falkingham, Feb. 6.
Chas. Saunders, aft. adm., Nov. 14.
1756. Digby Dent, June 4.
Geo. Cockburne, Dec. 29.
1770. Hugh Palliser, aft. adm. sir H., Aug. 1.
1775. Maurice Suckling, aft. adm., Apr. 5.
1778. Chas. Middleton, aft. adm. sir C., bt., July 18; cr. ld. Barham in 1805.
1790. Sir Hy. Martin, bt., Mar. 13.
1794. Sir Andrew Snape Hamond, bt., Aug. 30.
1806. Hy. Nicholls, Feb. 19.
Sir Thos. Boulden Thompson, bt., aft. adm., June 7.
1816. Sir Thos. Byam Martin, K.C.B., adm., Feb. 9.
1831. Adm. Hon. Geo. Heneage Lawrence Dundas, Nov. 2. Patent revoked June 9, 1832.

By 2 Will. IV. cap. 40 (June 1, 1832) the Navy and Victualling Boards and the offices of Commissioners of Navy and Victualling and Comptroller of the Navy were abolished, and in lieu thereof were appointed five "Principal Officers," viz.:

The Surveyor of the Navy.
Accountant-General of the Navy.
Storekeeper-General.
Comptroller of Victualling, and
Medical Director-General.

To these other departments were afterwards added.

Surveyors.

1668. Sir John Tippetts, Sept. 30.
1692. Edmd. Dummer, June 25.
1699. Danl. Furzer, Sept. 22.
1706. Wm. Lee, Sept. 9.
1715. Jacob Ackworth, aft. sir J., Mar. 30.
1746. Joseph Allin, aft. sir J., June 16.
1755. Thos. Slade, and Wm. Bateley. Aug. 6.
1765. Thos. Slade, aft. sir T., and John Williams. June 22.
1771. John Williams, aft. sir J., with two assistants.
1778. Sir John Williams, and Edwd. Hunt. Mar. 19.
1784. Edwd. Hunt, and John Henslow. Nov. 24.
1793. Sir Wm. Rule, Jan. 26.
1806. Sir Hy. Peake, June 7.
1813. Jos. Tucker, and Sir Robt. Seppings. May 26.
Jos. Tucker superanuated Mar. 1831; and sir Robt. Seppings, June 1832.
1832. Sir Wm. Symonds, June 9.
1848. Sir Baldwin W. Walker, K.C.B., Feb. 5.

17

In 1860 the office of Comptroller of the Navy was revived.

COMPTROLLERS—*continued.*

1860. R.-adm. sir Baldwin W. Walker, bt., K.C.B.
1861. R.-adm. Robt. Spencer Robinson, aft. sir R. and v.-adm.
1871. Capt. Robt. Hall, C.B.
1872. R.-adm. Wm. Houston Stewart, C.B., aft. sir W. and v.-adm.
1881. R.-adm. Thos. E. Brandreth.
1885. V.-adm. Wm. Graham, C.B., aft. sir W., K.C.B.

THE BOARD OF ORDNANCE.

THE Ordnance Department is of very great antiquity. A master of the Ordnance is mentioned *temp.* Richard III., and a clerk of the Ordnance as early as 1418. Henry VIII. constituted a Board of Ordnance by adding to the master and clerk a lieutenant, a surveyor, a storekeeper, and a clerk of the cheque. In 1604 James I. dignified the master and lieutenant with the style of master-general and lieutenant-general. The clerk of the cheque was abolished many years ago, and the lieutenant-general in 1831, but this latter office was revived for a short time in 1854.

By letters patent of May 25, 1855 (**G.**) the appointments of master-general, lieutenant-general, and principal storekeeper of the Ordnance were revoked, and the civil administration of the army and Ordnance vested in lord Panmure, the then secretary of state for war. The Act 18 & 19 Vict. cap. 117 (Aug. 14, 1855) recites these letters patent and vests all statutory powers, lands, &c., of the principal officers of Ordnance in the secretary of state for war.

The office of surveyor-general of the Ordnance was abolished about the same time, but was revived with somewhat different duties, by 33 & 34 Vict. cap. 17 (June 28, 1870).

MASTERS-GENERAL OF THE ORDNANCE.

QUEEN ELIZABETH.

1596. Robt. E. of Essex; beheaded.

KING JAMES I.

1603. Chas., E. of Devonshire.
1609. Geo., E. of Totnes.
1623. Sir Richd. Morrison.

KING CHARLES I.

1628. Sir Thos. Stafford.
1629. Horatio, ld. Vere, of Tilbury.
1634. Montjoy Blount, E. of Newport.

KING CHARLES II.

1660. Sir. Wm. Compton.
1665. John, ld. Berkeley. / Sir John Duncombe. / Sir Thos. Chicheley. } Commissioners.
1670. Sir Thos. Chicheley.
1674. Sir John Chicheley.
1679. Sir John Chicheley. / Sir Wm. Hickman. / Sir Christr. Musgrave. } Commissioners.
1681. Geo. Legge, aft. ld. Dartmouth.

WILLIAM AND MARY.

1689. Fredk., D. of Schomberg.
1693. Hy. visc. Sydney, aft. E. of Romney.

QUEEN ANNE.

1702. John, E., aft. D. of Marlborough, July 1.
1712. Richd., E. Rivers, Jan. 1.
1712. Jas., D. of Hamilton and Brandon, July 1; killed in a duel, Nov. 15, same year.

KING GEORGE I.

1714. John, D. of Marlborough, *again*, Oct. 1.
1722. Wm., E. Cadogan, July 1.

1725. John, D. of Argyll and Greenwich, July 1.

KING GEORGE II.

1740. John, D. of Montagu, July 1.
1742. John, D. of Argyll, *again*.
1743. John, D. of Montagu, *again*.
1756. Chas., D. of Marlborough, Jan. 1.
1759. John, visc., aft. E. Ligonier, July 1.

KING GEORGE III.

1763. John, M. of Granby, aft. D. of Rutland.
1772. Geo., visc. Townsend, Oct. 1.
1782. Chas., D. of Richmond, Lenox, and Aubigny, Mar. 30.
1783. Geo., visc. Townshend, *again*; aft. Marq. Townsend.
Chas., D. of Richmond, *again*, Dec. 23.
1795. Chas., M. Cornwallis, Feb. 13.
1801. John, E. of Chatham, June 16.
1806. Fras., E. of Moira, aft. M. of Hastings, Feb. 14.
1807. John, E. of Chatham, *again*, Apr. 4.
1810. Hy., ld., aft. E. of Mulgrave, May 5.
1819. Arthur, D. of Wellington, Jan. 1.

KING GEORGE IV.

1827. Hy. Wm., M. of Anglesey, Apr. 30.
1828. Wm. Carr, visc. Beresford, Apr. 28.

KING WILLIAM IV.

1830. Sir Jas. Kempt, Nov. 30.
1834. Sir Geo. Murray, Dec. 18.
1835. Sir Richd. Hussey Vivian, bt., aft. ld. Vivian, May 4.

QUEEN VICTORIA.

1841. Sir Geo. Murray, *again*, Sept. 9.
1846. Hy. Wm., M. of Anglesey, *again*, July 6.
1852. Hy., visc. Hardinge, G.C.B., Mar. 5, **G.**
1853. Lt.-gen. ld. Fitzroy Jas. Hy. Somerset, G.C.B., aft. ld. Raglan, Sept. 30, **G.**

Office abolished in 1855.

LIEUTENANTS-GENERAL OF THE ORDNANCE.

From the Union of England and Scotland.

1603. Sir Geo. Carew, aft. E. of Totnes.
1635. Sir Wm. Haydon.
1636. Colin Legge.
1670. David Walter, Nov. 25.
*George Legge, aft. lord Dartmouth, Dec. 7.
1681. Sir Chas. Musgrave, bt.
1687. Sir Hy. Tichborne, bt.
1688. Hy. Goodricke, bt.
1702. John Granville, aft. ld. Granville.
1705. Thos. Erle.
1712. John Hill.
1714. Thos. Erle, *again*.
1717. Thos. Micklethwaite.
1718. Sir Chas. Wills, K.B.
1742. Geo. Wade, field marshal, 1743; comm. in ch., 1745.
1748. *Sir John Ligonier, K.B., aft. visc. and E. Ligonier; field marshal and comm. in ch., 1757.
1757. Lord Geo. Sackville (Germaine); dism. the service in 1759; aft. visc. Sackville.
1759. *John, M. of Granby, aft. D. of Rutland.
1763. *Hon. Geo. Townshend, aft. visc. and M. Townshend.
1767. Hon. Hy. Seymour Conway, aft. comm. in ch., &c.
1772. Sir Jeffrey Amherst, K.B., aft. ld. Amherst, comm. in ch. 1778, *et seq*.
1782. Hon. Sir Wm. Howe, aft. visc. Howe, K.B.
1804. Sir Thos. Trigge.
Richd. Fitzpatrick.
1807. Sir Thos. Trigge, *again*.
1810. Sir Hildebrand Oakes, bt.
1823. *Wm. Carr, visc. Beresford.
1824. *Sir Geo. Murray.
1825. Sir W. H. Clinton.
1829. Lord Robt. Edwd. Hy. Somerset.

The office was abolished in 1831, but temporarily revived in 1854.

1854. Lt.-gen. sir Hew Dalrymple Ross, K.C.B., May 2, **G.** Ceased in 1855.

* Subsequently Masters-General.

SURVEYORS-GENERAL OF THE ORDNANCE.

From the Union of England and Scotland.

* * Wm. Brydges.
1714. Maj.-Gen. Michael Richards.
1722. John Armstrong, aft. maj.-gen.
1742. Thos. Lascelles.

1750. Chas. Frederick, aft. sir C., K.B.
1782. Hon. Thos. Pelham.
1783. John Courtenay.
1784. Hon. Jas. Luttrell.
1789. Hon. G. C. Berkeley.
1795. Maj.-Gen. A. Ross.
1804. Lt.-Col. Jas. M. Hadden, Nov. 22.
1810. Sir Robt. Moorsoom, R.N., July 20.
1820. Lt.-Col. sir Ulysses Burgh, aft. ld. Downes, Mar. 18.
1827. Adm. sir Edwd. Wm. C. R. Owen, May 14.
1828. Lt.-gen. sir Herbert Taylor, Mar. 24.
1829. Lt.-gen. sir Hy. Fane, Apr. 3.
1831. Lt.-Col. Wm. Leader Maberley, Jan. 12.
1832. Lt.-Col. Chas. R. Fox, Dec. 5.
1835. Lord Robt Edwd. Hy. Somerset, Jan. 12.
Lt.-Gen. sir Rufane Shawe Donkin, May 6.
1841. Col. Chas. R. Fox, *again*, May 12.
Col. Jonathan Peel, Sept. 10.
1846. Maj.-Gen. Chas. R. Fox, *again*.
1852. Lt.-Gen. sir Geo. Hy. Fredk. Berkeley, K.C.B., June 28, **G.**
1853. Lt.-Col. hon. Lauderdale Maule, Jan. 15, **G.**

Office abolished, 1855.

OFFICE REVIVED UNDER 33 & 34 VICT. CAP. 17.

1870. Maj.-Gen. sir Hy. Knight Storks, G.C.B.
1874. Lord Eustace B. H. Gascoyne Cecil, Feb.
1880. Lt.-Gen. sir Jno. Miller Adye, K.C.B., Apr.
1883. Hon. Hy. Robt. Brand.
1885. Hon. Guy Cuthbert Dawnay, June.
1886. Wm. Woodall, Feb.
1886. Hon. Hy. Stafford Northcote, aft. Sir H., bt., Aug.

CLERKS OF THE ORDNANCE.

From the Union of England and Scotland.

* * Chas. Musgrave.
1712. Edwd. Ashe.
1714. Lt.-Gen. Wm. Cadogan, aft. ld. and E. Cadogan.
1718. Thos. White.
1733. Leonard Smelt.
1740. Wm. Rowlinson Earle.
1772. Sir Chas. Cocks, bt., aft. ld. Somers.
1781. John Aldridge.
1782. Gibbs Crawford.
1783. Humphrey Minchin, Apr.
Gibbs Crawford, *again*, Dec.
1793. John Sargent.
1802. Hon. Wm. Wellesley Pole, July 5.
1806. John Calcraft, Feb. 15.
1807. Hon. W. W. Pole, *again*, Mar. 31.
Hon. Cropley Ashley Cooper, July 21.
1811. Robt. Ward, June 4.
1823. Sir Hy. Hardinge, aft. visc. Hardinge.
1827. Sir Geo. Clerk, bt., May 4.
1828. Spencer Percival, aft. Sir S., Aug. 4
1830. Chas. Tennyson, aft. Tennyson D'Eyncourt, Dec. 30.
1832. Thos. Fras. Kennedy, Feb. 8.
1833. Lt.-Col. Wm. Leader Maberly.
1834. Col. Andw. Leith Hay, aft. sir A., June 16.
R.-Adm. sir Edwd. G. R. Owen, Dec. 22.
1835. Sir Andw. Leith Hay, *again*, Apr. 18.
1838. Capt., aft. adm., J. W. Deans Dundas, Mar. 21.
1841. Capt. Hy. Geo. Boldero.
1845. Lord Arthur Lennox.
1846. Col. Hon. Geo. Anson.
1852. Lt.-Col. Fras. Plunkett Dunne, Mar. 5, **G.**
1853. Wm. Monsell, aft. ld. Emly, Jan. 13, **G.**

Office abolished, 1857.

PRINCIPAL STOREKEEPERS OF THE ORDNANCE.

From the Union of England and Scotland.

* * Jas. Lowther.
1712. Hon. Dixie Windsor.
1715. Geo. Gregory.
1717. Sir Thos. Wheate, bt.
1721. Geo. Gregory, *again*.
1746. Andw. Wilkinson.
1762. Sir Edwd. Winnington, bt., Dec.
1765. Andw. Wilkinson, *again*, Sept. 7.
1778. Benjn. L'Anglois, July.
1780. Hy. Strachey, aft. sir H., Oct.
1782. John Aldridge, Apr. 30.
1783. Sir Hy. Strachey, *again*, Apr. 12.
John Aldridge, *again*, Dec. 26.
1795. Mark Singleton.

1806. John M'Mahon, Feb.
1807. Mark Singleton, *again*.
1829. Col. Fredk. Wm. French, June 4.
1830. Capt hon. Hy. Duncan, Dec. 30.
1834. Fras. Robt. Bonham, Dec. 22.
1835. Hon. Geo. Anson.
1841. Fras. Robt. Bonham, *again*, Sept. 9.
1845. Capt. sir Thos. Hastings.

Office abolished 1855.

CHIEF COMMISSIONERS OF POLICE OF THE METROPOLIS.

THE Metropolitan Police District was formed by 10 Geo. IV. cap. 44 (June 19, 1829), and by this act two "Justices" were appointed, whose title was afterwards changed by 2 & 3 Vict. cap. 47 (Aug. 17, 1839) to that of "Commissioners of Police of the Metropolis." On the death of one of the commissioners in 1855 an Act, 19 & 20 Vict. cap. 2 (Feb. 28, 1856), was passed enacting that thenceforth there should only be one commissioner (to be styled "the Commissioner of Police of the Metropolis") and two assistant commissioners.

"JUSTICES" UNDER 10 GEO. IV. CAP. 44.

1829. Col. Chas. Rowan, aft. sir C.
Richd. Mayne, aft. sir R., K.C.B.

"COMMISSIONERS" UNDER 2 & 3 VICT. CAP. 47.

1839 Col. Chas. Rowan, aft. sir C.; *d.* 1850.
Richd. Mayne, aft. sir R., K.C.B.
1850. Capt. Wm. Hay, aft. C.B., Apr., *vice* Rowan; *d.* Aug. 29, 1855.

CHIEF "COMMISSIONERS" UNDER 19 & 20 VICT. CAP. 2.

1856. Sir Richd. Mayne, K.C.B.
1869. Col. Edmund Yeamans Walcott Henderson, aft. sir E., K.C.B., Feb. 12, **G.**
1886. Col. sir Chas. Warren, R.E., G.C.M.G., Mar. 29, **G.**

THE POOR LAW BOARD.

THE Poor Law Board was first established by 4 & 5 Will. IV. cap. 76 (Aug. 14, 1834), under which the Crown was authorised to appoint three commissioners, besides assistant commissioners, secretaries, &c. The appointment was limited to five years, but was continued by various Acts down to 1847, when a new Act, 10 & 11 Vict. cap. 109 (July 23, 1847), was passed, under which the power of the Crown to appoint commissioners was continued; but the lord president of the council, the lord privy seal, the home secretary, and the chancellor of the exchequer were made *ex officio* commissioners, and the first-named commissioner in each commission was to be styled the president. Under this Act the appointment was again limited to five years, but was continued by various Acts, and ultimately made permanent by 30 & 31 Vict. cap. 106 (Aug. 20, 1867).

By 34 & 35 Vict. cap. 70 (Aug. 14, 1871) the Poor Law Board was abolished, and its duties and powers transferred to the Local Government Board. *Vide ante*, p. 255.

Poor Law Commissioners for England and Wales.

Under 4 & 5 Will. IV. cap. 76 (Aug. 14, 1834).

Aug. 18. 1833. { Thos. Frankland Lewis, res. Jan. 30, 1839.
John Geo. Shaw Lefevre, res. Nov. 25, 1841.
Geo. Nicholls, res. Dec. 17, 1847.* }
1839. Geo. Cornewall Lewis, aft. sir G., bt., Jan. 30 *vice* Lewis; res. Aug. 2, 1847.*
1841. Sir Edmd. Walker Head, bt., Nov. 25, *vice* Shaw Lefevre; res. Dec. 17, 1847.*
1845. Edwd. Turner Boyd Twistleton, Nov. 5, *additional commr.*; res. July 23, 1847.*

* Resigned on formation of Poor Law Board under 10 & 11 Vict. cap. 109. *Vide infra.*

Presidents of the Poor Law Board.

Under 10 & 11 Vict. cap. 109 (July 23, 1847).

1847. Chas. Buller, jun., *d.* Nov. 29, 1848.
1849. Matt. Talbot Baines, Jan. 1.
1852. Sir John Trollope, bt., Feb.
1852–3. Matt. Talbot Baines, *again.*
1855. Edwd. Pleydell Bouverie, Aug. 13, **G.**
1858. Thos. H. S. Sotheron-Estcourt, Feb.
1859. Chas. Pelham Villiers, June.
1866. Gathorne Hardy, aft. visc. Cranbrook, July 12, **G.**
1867. Wm. Regd., E. of Devon, May 21, **G.**
1868. Geo. Joachim Göschen, Dec. 9, sw.
1871. Jas. Stansfeld, Mar. 9.

Powers transferred to Local Government Board under 34 & 35 Vict. cap. 70. *Vide ante*, p. 255.

Secretaries to the Poor Law Board.

Parliamentary.

1847. Hon. Hugh Fortescue, c.c. visc. Ebrington; aft. E. Fortescue.
1851. Ralph Wm. Grey.
1853. Chas. Lennox Grenville Berkeley.
1856. Ralph Wm. Grey, *again.*
1858. Fredk. Winn Knight, Feb.
1859. Chas. Gilpin, June.
1865. Hon. Geo. Hy. Chas. Byng, c.c. visc. Enfield, aft. ld. and E. of Strafford.
1866. Ralph A. Earle, July.
1867. Gen. Sclater Booth.
1868. Arthur Wellesley Peel, Dec.

Permanent.

1847. Geo. Nicholls.
1850. Hon. Wm. Regd. Courtenay, c.c. visc. Courtenay, aft. E. of Devon.
1859. Hy. Fleming; continued as sec. to loc. gov. bd.

THE BOARD OF TRADE.

Oliver Cromwell seems to have given the first notion of a Board of Trade, as in 1655 he appointed his son Richard, with many lords of his council, judges, and gentlemen, and about twenty merchants of London, York, Newcastle, Yarmouth, Dover, and other places, to meet and consider by what means the traffic and navigation of the republic might be best promoted and regulated, and to report upon the subject. Charles II., on his restoration, established a Council of Trade, "for keeping a control and superintendence upon the whole commerce of the nation," Nov. 7, 1660; and by patent, dated Dec. 1, same year, he also created a Council of Foreign Plantations. In 1672, these Boards were united, and various revisions followed from time to time. In 1782, by statute 22 Geo. III. cap. 82, the Board was abolished, and the business was managed by a committee of the privy council, whose duty was "to examine the custom-house accounts of all goods and merchandise exported and imported to and from the several ports in the kingdom, as well as from foreign ports, in order to inform the government of the advantages and disadvantages of the trade of this nation with other kingdoms and states, in regard to the balance of trade. And also to encourage our plantations abroad by endeavouring to promote their trade, and by discovering and encouraging such branches as were most conducive to their respective interests, as well as to those of the kingdom at large." In 1786, by an order in council, dated Aug. 23, the Board of Trade, as at present constituted, was formed. *Vide infra.* The president is now always a cabinet minister.

The Original Boards.

1660.

Edwd., ld. Hyde, aft. E. of Clarendon, ld. chanc., *ex officio*.
Thos., E. of Southampton, ld. treasr.
Geo., D. of Albemarle.
Montagu, ld. Willoughby d'Eresby.
Wm., E. of Pembroke.
Jas., E. of Marlborough.
Chas., E. of Portland.
Chas., E. of Norwich.
Edwd., E. of Sandwich.
John, ld. Robartes, and others.

Oct. 20, 1668.

All the great officers of state.
The secs. of state.
John, E. of Bridgewater.
Wm., E. of Craven.
Sir Hy. Coventry.
Sir John Ernley.
Sir Geo. Carteret.
Robt. Southwell.

Sept. 16, 1672.

A standing council, of which Anthy., E. of Shaftesbury, and
Thos., ld. Colepeper were pres. and vice-pres.

April 16, 1679.

A new commission, which included many of the preceding commrs., and
Wm., E. of Devonshire.
Geo., visc. Halifax, and
Geo., ld. Berkeley.

Dec. 16, 1695.

The ld. chanc. or keeper of the gr. seal.
Ld. pres. of the council.
Ld. keeper of the pr. seal; all for the time being, together with
John, E. of Bridgewater, and others.

May 15, 1696.

The great officers of state for the time being, and
John, E. of Bridgewater.
Ford, E. of Tankerville.
Sir Philip Meadows.
Wm. Blathwayte.
John Pollexfen.
John Locke.
Abraham Hill.
John Methuen.

June 9, 1699.

By a commission under this date, the following great officers of state were specially mentioned:—
Ld. chanc. or keeper of the gr. seal.
Ld. pres. of the council.
Ld. keeper of the pr. seal.
Ld. treas. or first commr. of the treasy.
Ld. high adm. or first commr. of the admy.
The two principal secs. of state, and
Ch. ex.; all for the time being, with
Thos., E. of Stamford.
Robt., lord Lexinton.
Sir Philip Meadows.
Wm. Blathwayte.
John Pollexfen.
John Locke.
Abraham Hill.
Geo. Stepney.
From this time all the great state officers continued to be members of the board.

June 11, 1700.

The same board, with the addition of Matt. Prior.

Jan. 8, 1702.

The same board, with the addition of Robt. Cecil.

1705.

Thos., E. of Stamford.
Thos., visc. Weymouth.
Wm., ld. Dartmouth.
Sir Philip Meadows.
Wm. Blathwayte.
John Pollexfen.
Geo. Stepney.
Matt. Prior.
Robt. Cecil.

1706.

Thos., E. of Stamford.
Wm., ld. Dartmouth.
Hy., ld. Herbert.
Sir Philip Meadows.
Geo. Stepney.
John Pulteney.
Robt. Monckton.

1707.

Thos., E. of Stamford.
Wm., ld. Dartmouth.

Hy., ld. Herbert of Cherbury.
Robt. Monckton.
John Pulteney.
Sir Chas. Turner.
John Locke.

1710.

Thos., E. of Stamford.
Wm., ld. Dartmouth.
Sir Philip Meadows.
John Pulteney.
Robt. Monckton.
Sir Chas. Turner.
Geo. Baillie.

Oct. 4, 1710.

The same board, with the addition of Arthur Moore.

June 12, 1711.

Chas., E. of Winchilsea, and the same board with the addition of Fras. Gwyn.

Sept. 15, 1713.

Fras., ld. Guildford.
Sir Philip Meadows.
Robt. Monckton.
Arthur Moore.
Sir John Hynde Cotton, bt.
John Sharpe.
Saml. Pitts.
Thos. Vernon.

Sept. 1714.

Wm., ld. Berkeley of Stratton.
Sir Jacob Astley, bt.
Robt. Molesworth, aft. visc. Molesworth.
John Cockburn.
Archibald Hutchinson.
John Chetwynd.
Chas. Cooke.
Paul Docminique.

1715.

Hy., E. of Suffolk and Bindon, and the same board, except Archibald Hutchinson, in whose room came Jos. Addison.
Danl. Pulteney, *vice* Cockburn.
Martin Bladen, *vice* Addison.

July 13, 1717.

Hy., E. of Suffolk and Bindon.
John Chetwynd.
Chas. Cooke.
Paul Docminique.
John Molesworth.
Thos. Pelham, *vice* Astley.

Jan. 31, 1718.

Robt., E. of Holdernesse, *vice* Suffolk, and the same board.

May 11, 1719.

Thos., E. of Westmoreland, *vice* Holdernesse, and the same board.

June 24, 1720.

Thos., E. of Westmoreland.
John Chetwynd.
Sir Chas. Cooke, bt.
Paul Docminique.
Thos. Pelham.
Martin Bladen.
Edwd. Ashe, *vice* Pulteney.

Sept. 4, 1721.

Thos., E. of Westmoreland, and the same board, with the addition of
Richd. Plumer.

Oct. 4, 1721.

Thos., E. of Westmoreland, and the same board, except
Sir John Hobart, bt., aft. E. of Buckinghamshire, *vice* Cooke.

Aug. 8, 1727.

Thos., E. of Westmoreland, and the same board, except
Sir Orlando Bridgeman, bt., *vice* Plumer, and
Walter Carey, *vice* Hobart.

June 1, 1728.

Thos., E. of Westmoreland, and the same board, except
Sir Thos. Frankland, bt., *vice* Chetwynd.

1730.

Thos., E. of Westmoreland, and the same board, except
Hon. Jas. Brudenell, *vice* Frankland.

May 13, 1730.

Thos., E. of Westmoreland, and the same board, except
Sir Archer Croft, bt., *vice* Carey.

May 1735.

Benjn. Mildmay, E. Fitzwalter, *vice* Westmoreland.
Thos. Pelham.
Martin Bladen.
Edwd. Ashe.
Sir Orlando Bridgeman, bt.
Hon. Jas. Brudenell.
Sir Archer Croft, bt.
Richd. Plumer.

June 1737.

John, ld. Monson, *vice* Fitzwalter, and the same board.

Feb. 1742.

John, ld. Monson.
Martin Bladen.
Edwd. Ashe.
Hon. Jas. Brudenell.
Richd. Plumer.
Hon. Robt. Herbert, *vice* Pelham.
Sir Chas. Gilmour, bt., *vice* Bridgeman.
Benjn. Keene, *vice* Croft.

Dec. 25, 1744.

John, ld. Monson.
Martin Bladen.
Edwd. Ashe.
Hon. Jas. Brudenell.
Richd. Plumer.
Hon. Robt. Herbert.
Sir John Phillips, bt., *vice* Gilmour.
John Pitt, *vice* Keene.

May 7, 1745.

John, ld. Monson, and the same board, except
Hon. Baptist Leveson Gower, *vice* Phillips.

Feb. 1746.

John, ld. Monson, and the same board, except
Hon. Jas. Grenville, *vice* Bladen.

Nov. 1746.

John, ld. Monson.
Edwd. Ashe.
Richd. Plumer.
Hon. Robt. Herbert.
John Pitt.
Hon. Jas. Grenville.
Thos., visc. Dupplin, *vice* Brudenell.
Fras. Fane, *vice* Gower.

Nov. 1, 1748.

GEO., E. of HALIFAX, *vice* Monson.
Richd. Plumer.
Hon. Robt. Herbert.
John Pitt.
Hon. Jas. Grenville.
Thos., visc. Dupplin.
Fras. Fane.
Sir Thos. Robinson, K.B., aft. ld. Grantham, *vice* Ashe.

June 1749.

GEO., E. of HALIFAX.
Hon. Robt. Herbert.
John Pitt.
Hon. Jas. Grenville.
Thos., visc. Dupplin.
Fras. Fane.
Sir Thos. Robinson, K.B.
Hon. Chas. Townshend, *vice* Plumer.

Nov. 1749.

GEO., E. of HALIFAX.
Hon. Robt. Herbert.
John Pitt.
Hon. Jas. Grenville.
Thos., visc. Dupplin.
Fras. Fane.
Hon. Chas. Townshend.
Andrew Stone, *vice* Robinson.

Dec. 1751.

GEO., E. of HALIFAX.
John Pitt.
Hon. Jas. Grenville.
Thos., visc. Dupplin.
Fras. Fane.
Hon. Chas. Townshend.
Andrew Stone.
Jas. Oswald, *vice* Herbert.

Apr. 6, 1754.

GEO., E. of HALIFAX.
John Pitt.
Hon. Jas. Grenville.
Fras. Fane.
Andrew Stone.
Jas. Oswald.
Hon. Richd. Edgcumbe, aft. ld. Edgcumbe, *vice* Dupplin.
Thos. Pelham, aft. ld. Pelham, *vice* Townshend.

Dec. 23, 1755.

GEO., E. of HALIFAX.
Fras. Fane.
Andrew Stone.
Jas. Oswald.
Thos. Pelham.
Hon. John Talbot, *vice* Pitt.
Soame Jenyns, *vice* Grenville.
Richd. Rigby, *vice* Edgcumbe.

Apr. 24, 1756.

GEO., E. of HALIFAX, and the same board, with the exception of
Wm. Gerard Hamilton, *vice* Fane.

Dec. 11, 1756.

GEO., E. of HALIFAX, and the same board, with the exception of
Wm. Sloper, *vice* Talbot.

Dec. 24, 1759.

GEO., E. of HALIFAX.
Andrew Stone.
Thos. Pelham.
Soame Jenyns.
Richd. Rigby.
Wm. Gerard Hamilton.
Wm. Sloper.
Edwd. Bacon, *vice* Oswald.

Jan. 1760.

GEO., E. of HALIFAX.
Andrew Stone.
Thos. Pelham, now ld. Pelham.
Soame Jenyns.
Wm. Gerard Hamilton.
Wm. Sloper.
Edwd. Bacon.
Edwd. Eliot, *vice* Rigby.

Mar. 21, 1761.

SAML., ld. SANDYS, *vice* Halifax.
Andrew Stone.
Soame Jenyns.
Edwd. Eliot.
Edwd. Bacon.
Hon. John Yorke, *vice* Pelham.
Sir Edmd. Thomas, bt., *vice* Hamilton.
Geo. Rice, *vice* Sloper.

Oct. 23, 1761.

SAML., ld. SANDYS.
Soame Jenyns.
Edwd. Eliot.
Edwd. Bacon.
Hon. John Yorke.
Sir Edmd. Thomas, bt.
Geo. Rice.
John Roberts, *vice* Stone.

Dec. 28, 1762.

SAML., ld. SANDYS, and the same board, with the exception of
Fras., ld. Orwell, aft. E. of Shipbrooke, *vice* Roberts.

Mar. 1, 1763.

Hon. CHAS. TOWNSHEND, *vice* Sandys, and the same board.

Apr. 20, 1763.

WM., E. of SHELBURNE, aft. M. of Lansdowne, *vice* Townshend.
Soame Jenyns.
Edwd. Eliot.
Edwd. Bacon.
Geo. Rice.
Fras., ld. Orwell.
Jeremiah Dyson, *vice* Yorke.
Bamber Gascoyne, *vice* Thomas.

Sept. 9, 1763.

WILLS, E. of HILLSBOROUGH, *vice* ld. Shelburne, and the same board.

July 20, 1765.

WM., E. of DARTMOUTH, *vice* Hillsborough.
Soame Jenyns.
Edwd. Eliot.
Geo. Rice.
Jeremiah Dyson.
Hon. John Yorke, *vice* Orwell.
John Roberts, *vice* Gascoyne.
Wm. Fitzherbert, *vice* Bacon.

Dec. 1765.

WM., E. of DARTMOUTH.
Soame Jenyns.
Edwd. Eliot.
Geo. Rice.
Jeremiah Dyson.
John Roberts.
Wm. Fitzherbert.
Hy., visc. Palmerston, *vice* Yorke.

Aug. 16, 1766.

WILLS, E. of HILLSBOROUGH, *vice* ld. Dartmouth, and the same board.

Oct. 11, 1766.

WILLS, E. of HILLSBOROUGH.
Soame Jenyns.
Edwd. Eliot.
Geo. Rice.
Jeremiah Dyson.
John Roberts.
Wm. Fitzherbert.
Hon. Thos. Robinson, aft. 2nd ld. Grantham, *vice* Palmerston.

Dec. 1766

ROBT. NUGENT, aft. E. Nugent, *vice* Hillsborough, and the same board.

Jan. 20, 1768.

WILLS, E. of HILLSBOROUGH, and the same board, except
Wilmot, visc. Lisburne, *vice* Dyson.

Apr. 12, 1770.

WILLS, E. of HILLSBOROUGH.
Soame Jenyns.
Edwd. Eliot.
Geo. Rice.
John Roberts.
Wm. Fitzherbert.
Wilmot, visc. Lisburne.
Geo. Greville, ld. Greville, *vice* Robinson.

Apr. 16, 1770.

WILLS, E. of HILLSBOROUGH, and the same board, except
Wm. Northey, *vice* Lisburne.

May 16, 1770.

WILLS, E. of HILLSBOROUGH.
Soame Jenyns.
Edwd. Eliot.
John Roberts.
Wm. Fitzherbert.
Geo., ld. Greville.
Wm. Northey.
Bamber Gascoyne, *vice* Rice.

Jan. 16, 1771.

WILLS, E. of HILLSBOROUGH.
Soame Jenyns.
Edwd. Eliot.
John Roberts.
Wm. Fitzherbert.
Geo., ld. Greville.
Bamber Gascoyne.
Thos. Whateley, *vice* Northey.

Feb. 11, 1772.

WILLS, E. of HILLSBOROUGH, and the same board, except
Wm. Jolliffe, *vice* Fitzherbert.

Aug. 15, 1772.

WILLS, E. OF HILLSBOROUGH.
Soame Jenyns.
Edwd. Eliot.
John Roberts.
Geo., ld. Greville.
Bamber Gascoyne.
Wm. Jolliffe.
John, ld. Garlies, *vice* Whateley.

Aug. 31, 1772.

WM., E. of DARTMOUTH, *vice* Hillsborough.
Soame Jenyns.
Edwd. Eliot.
Geo., ld. Greville, aft. E. of Warwick.
Bamber Gascoyne.
Wm. Jolliffe.
John, ld. Garlies, aft. E. of Galloway.
Lord Robt. Spencer, *vice* Roberts.

Jan. 25, 1774.

WM., E. of DARTMOUTH.
Soame Jenyns.
Edwd. Eliot, aft. ld. Eliot.
Bamber Gascoyne.
Wm. Jolliffe.
Lord Robt. Spencer.
Hon. Chas. Greville, *vice* Warwick.
Whitshed Keene, *vice* Galloway.

Nov. 10, 1775.

Lord GEO. (SACKVILLE) GERMAINE, *vice* Dartmouth, and the same board.

Mar. 9, 1776.

Lord GEO. GERMAINE.
Soame Jenyns.
Bamber Gascoyne.
Wm. Jolliffe.
Lord Robt. Spencer.
Hon. Chas. Greville.
Whitshed Keene.
Wm. Eden, *vice* Eliot.

June 5, 1777.

Lord GEO. GERMAINE.
Soame Jenyns.
Bamber Gascoyne.
Wm. Jolliffe.
Lord Robt. Spencer.
Hon. Chas. Greville.
Wm. Eden.
Thos. de Grey, *vice* Keene.

July 6, 1779.

Lord GEO. GERMAINE, aft visc. Sackville.
Soame Jenyns.
Lord Robt. Spencer.
Hon. Chas. Greville.
Wm. Eden.
Thos. de Grey.
Andrew Stuart, *vice* Gascoyne.
Edward Gibbon, *vice* Jolliffe

Nov. 6, 1779.

FREDK., E. of CARLISLE *vice* Germaine, and the same board.

Sept. 6, 1780.

FREDK., E. of CARLISLE.
Lord Robt. Spencer.
Wm. Eden.
Hon. Thos. de Grey, aft. ld. Walsingham.
Andrew Stuart.
Edwd. Gibbon.
Hans Sloane, *vice* Jenyns.
Benjn. L'Anglois, *vice* Greville.

Dec. 9, 1780.

THOS., 2nd ld. GRANTHAM *vice* Carlisle, and the same board.

1781.

THOS., ld. GRANTHAM.
Lord Robt. Spencer.
Wm. Eden.
Andrew Stuart.
Edwd. Gibbon.
Hans Sloane.
Sir Adam Fergusson, bt. *vice* Walsingham.
Anthy. Storer, *vice* L'Anglois.

Dec. 22, 1781.

THOS., ld. GRANTHAM.
Wm. Eden.
Andrew Stuart.
Edwd. Gibbon.
Hans Sloane.
Sir Adam Fergusson, bt.

Anthy. Storer.
John Chetwynd Talbot, aft. Earl Talbot; *vice* Spencer.
The Board of Trade and Plantations was abolished in June 1782, under 22 Geo. III., cap. 82, and the business was transferred to the secretaries of state.

Mar. 5, 1784.

The abolition of the Board of Trade, being greatly felt by the trading part of the nation, His Majesty was pleased, in order to protect the interests of the mercantile community, to appoint the following Committee of the most honourable Privy Council, for the consideration of all matters relating to Trade and Foreign Plantations.

THOS., ld. SYDNEY, one of the principal secs. of st., pres.
Heneage, E. of Aylesford.
Thos., E. of Effingham.
Thos., E. of Clarendon.
Geo., E. of Leicester.
Lord Fredk. Campbell.
Richd., visc. Howe.
Robt., bp. of London.
Thos., ld. Grantham.
Thos., ld. Walsingham.
Fletcher, ld. Grantley.
Constantine John, ld. Mulgrave.
Hon. Thos. Harley.
Hon. sir Jos. Yorke, K.B.
Chas. Jenkinson.
Sir John Goodricke, bt.
Hy. Dundas.
Jas. Grenville.
Wm. Wyndham Grenville.

ESTABLISHMENT OF THE PRESENT BOARD OF TRADE.

LORDS *of the* COMMITTEE *of* PRIVY COUNCIL *appointed by* KING GEORGE III. *for the consideration of all matters relating to* TRADE *and* FOREIGN PLANTATIONS.

Order in Council, August 23, 1786.

"His Majesty, having thought fit to revoke his Order in Council, bearing date the 5th day of March, 1784, appointing a Committee of Privy Council for the consideration of all matters relating to Trade and Foreign Plantations, and to declare the said Committee dissolved, was pleased to appoint a New Committee of Privy Council for the business above-mentioned, to consist of the following members:—

The Lord Archbishop of Canterbury.
The First Commissioner of the Treasury.
The First Lord Commissioner of the Admiralty.
His Majesty's Principal Secretaries of State.
The Chancellor and Under-Treasurer of the Exchequer.
The Speaker of the House of Commons.

"And also such of the persons of His Majesty's most honourable Privy Council as shall hold any of the following offices:—

The Chancellor of the Duchy of Lancaster.
The Paymaster or Paymaster-general of His Majesty's forces.
The Treasurer of the Navy, and
The Master of His Majesty's Mint.

"And His Majesty was at the same time pleased to order that the Speaker of the House of Commons of Ireland, and such persons as shall hold offices in His Majesty's kingdom of Ireland, and shall be members of His Majesty's Most Honourable Privy Council in this kingdom, shall be members of this Committee; and also that—

Lord Fredk. Campbell,
Robt., ld. bp. of London,
Fletcher, ld. Grantley,
Sir Lloyd Kenyon, bt.,
The Hon. Sir Jos. Yorke,
Sir John Goodricke, bt.,
The Hon. Wm. Eden,
Jas. Grenville, and
Thos. Orde,

"be members of this Committee. And that Charles Lord Hawkesbury, chancellor of the duchy of Lancaster, and, in his absence, William

Wyndham Grenville, joint paymaster-general of the forces (vice-president of the Board, &c.), be President of the Committee."

Subsequent Members of the Board.

1788. Beilby Porteus, bp. of London, Jan. 25.
1790. John Chas. Villiers, Feb. 24.
Sir Richd. Pepper Arden, m. rolls, Mar. 13.
Dudley Ryder, same date.
Sir Wm. Wynne, same date.
1793. John, visc. Bayham, June 21.
Sylvester Douglas, aft. ld. Glenbervie, Mar. 17.
1797. Sir Jos. Banks, bt., Mar. 20.
1798. Sir Wm. Scott, aft. ld. Stowell, Oct. 31.
1799. Robt. Banks, ld. Hawkesbury, aft. E. of Liverpool, Mar. 14.
Sir John Scott, aft. ld. and E. of Eldon, July 17.
1802. John Beresford, Feb. 17.
John Foster, same date.
Wm. Wickham, same date.
Geo. Rose, same date.
Chas. Long, same date.
1803. Chas. Bragge, June 22.
1805. Lord Geo. Thynne, May 1.
Lord John Thynne, same date.
1805. John Smyth, same date.
Nathl. Bond, same date.
Regd. Pole Carew, same date.
John Sullivan, same date.
1806. Fredk. Morton, ld. Henley, Feb. 14.
Richd., ld. Donoughmore, May 23.
John Joshua, E. of Carysfort, June 18.
1807. Isaac Corry, Jan. 28.
Chas., ld. Whitworth, Apr. 15.
Richd., E. of Clancarty, May 20.
1808. John, ld. Redesdale, Mar. 30.
1809. Sir John Nicholl, Feb. 6.
John Randolph, bp. of London Oct. 11.
John, ld. Sheffield, Dec. 20.
1812. Fredk. John Robinson, aft. visc. Goderich and E. of Ripon, Aug. 13.
1813. Wm. Howley, bp. of London, Dec. 2.
1815. Wm. Huskisson, Jan. 7.
1823. Chas. Arbuthnot, Apr. 3.
1846. John Nicholl, aft. sir J., Jan. 21.
1848. Sir Jas. Stephen, Apr. 15.
Sir Edwd. Ryan, Apr. 18.

The Board of Trade, from the time of its reconstruction in 1786, consisted, as before, of six or more members, besides the *ex officio* commissioners; but the business of late years has been wholly conducted by the president, the vice-president, and the secretaries; no other members having been appointed since the year 1823, with the exception of Dr. Nicholl in 1846, and of sir James Stephen and sir Edward Ryan in 1848, all of whom were appointed for special purposes and in reference to certain duties. The vice-presidency was abolished by 30 & 31 Vict. cap. 72 (Aug. 12, 1867) "as from the next vacancy," and a parliamentary secretaryship was substituted. *Vide* "Vice-Presidents of the Board of Trade," *infra.*

Presidents of the Board of Trade from 1786.

1786. Chas., ld. Hawkesbury, aft. E. of Liverpool, first pres., Aug. 23.
1804. Jas., D. of Montrose, June 7.
1806. Wm., ld. Auckland, Feb. 5.
1807. Hy., E. Bathurst, Mar. 31.
1812. Richd., E. of Clancarty, Sept. 29.
1818. Fredk. John Robinson, aft. visc. Goderich and E. of Ripon, Jan. 24.
1823. Wm. Huskisson, Feb. 21.
1827. Chas. Grant, aft. ld. Glenelg, Sept. 4.
1828. Wm. Vesey Fitzgerald, aft. ld. Fitzgerald and Vesci, June 11.
1834. John Chas. Herries, Feb. 2.
1830. Geo., ld., aft. E. of Auckland, Nov. 22.
1834. Chas. Poulett Thomson, aft. ld. Sydenham, vice-pres., acting as pres., June 5.
Alexr. Baring, aft. ld. Ashburton, Dec. 15.
1835. Chas. Poulett Thomson, *again*, Apr. 18.
1839. Hy. Labouchere, aft. ld. Taunton, Aug. 29.
1841. Fredk. John, E. of Ripon, *again*, Sept. 3.

1843. Wm. Ewart Gladstone, June 10.
1845. Jas. Andrew, E., aft. M., of Dalhousie, Feb. 5.
1846. Geo. Wm. Fredk., E. of Clarendon, July 6.
1847. Hy. Labouchere, *again*, July 22.
1852. Jos. Warner Henley, Feb. 27.
Edwd. Cardwell, aft. visc. Cardwell, Dec. 28.
1855. Edwd. Jno., ld. Stanley of Alderley, Mar. 31.
1858. Jos. Warner Henley, *again*, Feb. 26.
Richd. Jno., E. of Donoughmore, Apr. 6.
1859. Thos. Milner Gibson, July 6.
1866. Sir Stafford Hy. Northcote, bt., aft. E. of Iddesleigh, July 6.
1867. Chas. Hy., D. of Richmond, Mar. 8.
1868. Jno. Bright, Dec. 9.
1871. Chichester Saml. Fortescue, aft. ld. Carlingford, Jan. 14.
1874. Sir Chas. Bowyer Adderley, K.C.M.G., aft. ld. Norton, Mar. 2.
1878. Dudley Fras. Smart Ryder, c.c. visc. Sandon, Apr. 4.
1880. Jos. Chamberlain, May 3.
1885. Chas. Hy., D. of Richmond and Gordon, June 24.
Hon. Edwd. Stanhope, Aug. 19.
1886. Anthy. Jno. Mundella, Feb. 6.
Sir Fred. Arthur Stanley, G.C.B., Aug. 3; cr. ld. Stanley of Preston, Aug. 6, **G.**
1888. Sir Michl. Hicks-Beach, bt., Feb. 21.

Vice-Presidents of the Board of Trade from 1786.

1786. Wm. Wyndham Grenville, aft. ld. Grenviile, Aug. 23.
1789. Jas., M. of Graham, aft. D. of Montrose, Aug. 8; aft. pres.
1790. Dudley Ryder, aft. ld. and E. of Harrowby, Oct. 20.
1801. Sylvester Douglas, ld. Glenbervie, Nov. 18.
1804. Nathl. Bond, Feb. 8.
Geo. Rose, June 7.
1806. Richd. Chandos, E. Temple, aft. D. of Buckingham, Feb. 5.
1807. Geo. Rose, *again*, Mar. 30.
1812. Fredk. John Robinson, aft. visc. Goderich and E. of Ripon, Sept. 29; aft. pres.
1818. Thos. Wallace, aft. ld. Wallace, Jan. 28.
1823. Chas. Grant, Apr. 3, aft. pres.
1828. Thos. Frankland Lewis, Feb. 5.
Thos. Peregrine Courtenay, May 30.
1830. Chas. Poulett Thomson, aft. ld. Sydenham, Nov. 22; aft. pres.
1834. Wm., visc. Lowther, Dec. 20.
1835. Hy. Labouchere, aft. ld. Taunton, May 6; aft. pres.
1839. Richd. Lalor Sheil, Aug. 29.
1841. Fox Maule, aft. ld. Panmure and E. of Dalhousie, June 28.
1841. Wm. Ewart Gladstone, Sept. 3; aft. pres.
1843. Jas. Andrew, E., aft. M. of Dalhousie, June 13; aft. pres.
1845. Sir Geo. Clerk, bt., Feb. 5.
1846. Thos. Milner Gibson, July 6; aft. pres.
1848. Granville Geo., E. Granville, May 8.
1852. Edwd. Jno., ld. Stanley of Alderley, Feb. 11; aft. pres.
Chas., ld. Colchester, Feb. 27.
1853. Edwd. Jno., ld. Stanley of Alderley, *again*, Jan. 4; aft. pres.
1855. Edwd. Pleydell Bouverie, Mar. 31.
Robt. Lowe, aft. visc. Sherbrooke, Aug. 13.
1858. Rd. Jno., E. of Donoughmore, Apr. 6.
1859. Algernon Geo. Percy, ld. Lovaine, Mar. 3.
Jas. Wilson, June 18.
Wm. Fras. Cowper, Aug. 12.
1860. Wm. Hutt, Feb. 22.
1865. Geo. Joachim Göschen, Nov. 29.
1866. Wm. Monsell, aft. ld. Emly, Mar. 12.
Stephen Cave, July 10.

By 30 & 31 Vict. cap. 72, (Aug. 12, 1867,) the office of Vice-President of the Board of Trade was abolished, and a Parliamentary Secretary to the Board substituted "as from the next vacancy." Mr. Cave resigned, Dec. 1868.

Parliamentary Secretaries to the Board of Trade.

Appointed under 30 & 31 Vict. cap. 72, in lieu of the Vice-President.

1868. Geo. Jno. Shaw Lefevre, Dec.
1871. Arthur Wellesley Peel.
1874. Geo. Aug. Fredk. Cavendish Bentinck, May.
1875. Hon. Edwd, Stanhope.
1878. John Gilbert Talbot.
1880. Hon. A. Evelyn Ashley, May.
1882. John Holms.
1885. Bar. Hy. de Worms, Aug.
1886. Chas. Thos. Dyke Acland, Feb.
Bar. Hy. de Worms, *again*, Aug.
1888. Wm. Hillier, E. of Onslow, Feb.

Permanent Secretaries to the Board of Trade.

* * Sir Stephen Cottrell, Wm. Fawkener, } In virtue of their office of clerks of the council.

Lord Chetwynd, *vice* Mr. Fawkener.

1810. Thos. Lack, app. assist. sec., Aug. 25.

1829. Jos. Deacon Hume, second assist. sec.; *new app.*, July 15.

1836. Denis le Marchant, aft. sir Denis, bt., *vice* Lack, Feb. 8.

1840. John MacGregor, *vice* Hume, Jan. 24.

1841. John Geo. Shaw Lefevre, *vice* Le Marchant, transferred to the treasury, June 19.

1847. Geo. Richardson Porter, *vice* Mac Gregor, Aug. 6.

1848. Sir Denis Le Marchant, bt., *vice* Lefevre, transferred to the house of lords, May 14.

1850. Jas. Booth, *vice* Le Marchant, transferred to the house of commons, Oct. 10.

1843. Sir Jas. Emerson Tennent, second sec.

1865. The same, first sec.

Thos. Hy. Farrer, second sec.

1867. The same, sole sec.; cr. bt., 1883.

1886. Hy. Geo. Calcraft, sole sec.

WOODS AND FORESTS. LAND REVENUES. WORKS AND PUBLIC BUILDINGS.

The Crown Lands and Palaces were for many years managed by Commissioners or Surveyors, from time to time appointed by the Crown, and various statutes were passed extending, defining, or restricting their powers and duties.

In 1810, by 50 Geo. III. cap. 65, the then offices of Surveyor-General of Woods, Forests, Parks, and Chases, and Surveyor-General of the Land Revenues of the Crown were united under a Board of Commissioners, styled the Commissioners of Woods, Forests, and Land Revenues. The status, powers, and duties of these commissioners were more clearly defined by a subsequent consolidating statute, 10 Geo. IV. cap. 50, which came into operation June 10, 1829.

In 1814, by Geo. III. cap. 157, His Majesty's Works and Public Buildings were placed under the superintendence and control of a Surveyor-General of Works and Public Buildings.

In 1832, by 2 Will. IV. cap. 1, the duties of the Commissioners of Woods, Forests, and Land Revenues, and of the Surveyor-General of Works and Public Buildings were united under a board of commissioners, styled the Commissioners of Woods, Forests, Land Revenues, Works, and Buildings.

In 1851, by 14 & 15 Vict. cap. 42, the two departments were again divided into two separate boards: (1) styled Commissioners of Works and Public Buildings; (2) styled Commissioners of Woods, Forests, and Land Revenues. The first commissioner of the old Board of Woods, Forests, Land Revenues, Works, and Buildings was to be first commissioner of the new Board of Works and Public Building, the remaining commissioners being the principal secretaries of state, and the president and vice-president of the Board of Trade for the time being. The other commissioners of the old Board of Woods, Forests, Land Revenues, Works, and Buildings were to be commissioners of the new Board of Woods, Forests, and Land Revenues. The Crown was empowered to appoint other commissioners as vacancies occurred, and also to appoint a SURVEYOR-GENERAL OF WOODS, FORESTS, AND LAND REVENUES, on whom the duties, rights, powers, &c., of the commissioners of Woods, Forests, and Land Revenues was to devolve, when the appointment of such commissioners was to cease. This last power has not yet been exercised.

The office of first commissioner of Works and Public Buildings is a political one. The other offices are permanent.

SURVEYORS-GENERAL OF WOODS, FORESTS, PARKS, AND CHASES.

See Introduction, *supra*.

1607 (or 1608). John Taverner.
1608. Thos. Morgan.
1608 to 1667: Thos. Morgan and Robt. Treswell, Jointly. Robt. Treswell, Andw. Treswell, and ——— Treswell, Successively.
1667. Thos. Agar, and John Madden. Jointly.
1680. Thos. Agar, and Chas. Strode. Jointly.
1688. Philip Riley.
1701. Thos. Hewett.
1702. Edwd. Wilcox.
1714. Thos. Hewett, *again*.
1716. Edwd. Younge.
1720. Chas. Whithers.
1736. Fras. Whitworth.
1742. Hy. Legge.
1745. John Phillipson.
1756. John Pitt.
1763. Sir Edmond Thomas, bt.
1767. Jehn Pitt, *again*.
1786. John Robinson.
1803. Sylvester, ld. Glenbervie.
1806. Lord Robt. Spencer.
1807. Sylvester, ld. Glenbervie, *again*.

SURVEYOR-GENERAL OF THE LAND REVENUES OF THE CROWN.

See Introduction, *supra*.

1666. Sir C. Harbord.
1682. Wm. Harbord.
1692. Wm. Tailer.
1693. Saml. Travers.
1710. J. Manley.
1714. Alexr. Pendarves.
1715. H. Chomeley.
1722. J. Poulteney.
1726. Phillips Gybbon.
1730. Exton Sayer.
1732. Thos. Walker.
1750. John, visc. Galway.
1751. Robt. Herbert.
1769. Peter Burrell.
1775. John St. John.
1784. G. Aug. Selwyn.
1794. John Fordyce.
1809. Jas. Pillar (*acting*).

COMMISSIONERS OF WOODS, FORESTS, AND LAND REVENUES.

Appointed under 50 Geo. III. cap. 65, and 10 Geo. IV. cap. 50.

See Introduction, *supra*.

DATES OF PATENTS.

July 31, 1810.

SYLVESTER, LD. GLENBERVIE.
Wm. Dacres Adams.
Hy. Dawkins.

Aug. 21, 1814.

WM. HUSKISSON.
Wm. Dacres Adams.
Hy. Dawkins.

Feb. 8, 1823.

CHAS. ARBUTHNOT.
Wm. Dacres Adams.
Hy. Dawkins.

May 30, 1827.

GEO., E. OF CARLISLE.
Wm. Dacres Adams.
Hy. Dawkins.

July 23, 1827.

WM. STURGES BOURNE.
Wm. Dacres Adams.
Hy. Dawkins.

Feb. 11, 1828.

CHAS. ARBUTHNOT.
Wm. Dacres Adams.
Hy. Dawkins.

June 14, 1828.

WM., VISC. LOWTHER.
Wm. Dacres Adams.
Hy. Dawkins.

Dec. 13, 1830.
GEO. JAS. WELBORE AGAR ELLIS.
Wm. Dacres Adams.
Hy. Dawkins.

Feb. 11, 1831.
JOHN WM., VISC. DUNCANNON.
Wm. Dacres Adams.
Hy. Dawkins.

COMMISSIONERS OF WOODS, FORESTS, LAND REVENUES, WORKS, AND BUILDINGS.

Appointed under 2 Will. IV. cap. 1. See Introduction, *ante*, p. 270.

DATES OF PATENTS.

Feb. 22, 1832.
JOHN WM., VISC. DUNCANNON.
Wm. Dacres Adams.
Sir Benjn. C. Stephenson.

July 30, 1834.
SIR JOHN CAM HOBHOUSE, BT.
Wm. Dacres Adams.
Sir Benjn. C. Stephenson.

Aug. 23, 1834.
SIR JOHN CAM HOBHOUSE, BT.
Sir Benjn. C. Stephenson.
Alexr. Milne, C.B.

Dec. 31, 1834.
LORD GRANVILLE CHAS. HY. SOMERSET.
Sir Benjn. C. Stephenson.
Alexr. Milne, C.B.

May 7, 1835.
JOHN WM., VISC. DUNCANNON.
Sir Benjn. C. Stephenson.
Alexr Milne, C.B.

June 18, 1839.
JOHN WM., VISC. DUNCANNON.
Alexr. Milne, C.B.
Hon. Chas. Alexr. Gore.

Sept. 25, 1841.
HY. PELHAM, E. OF LINCOLN.
Alexr. Milne, C.B.
Hon. Chas. Alexr. Gore.

Mar. 10, 1846.
CHAS. JOHN, VISC. CANNING.
Alexr. Milne, C.B.
Hon. Chas. Alexr. Gore.

July 13, 1846.
GEO. FREDK. WM., VISC. MORPETH, aft. E. of CARLISLE.
Alexr. Milne, C.B.
Hon. Chas. Alexr. Gore.

Apr. 15, 1850.
EDWD. ADOLPHUS SEYMOUR, C.C. LORD SEYMOUR.
Alexr. Milne, C.B.
Hon. Chas. Alexr. Gore.

Aug. 28, 1850, **G.**
EDWD. ADOLPHUS SEYMOUR, C.C. LORD SEYMOUR.
Hon. Chas. Alexr. Gore.
Thos. Fras. Kennedy.

FIRST COMMISSIONERS OF WORKS AND PUBLIC BUILDINGS.

Appointed under 14 & 15 Vict. cap. 42. See Introduction, *ante*, p. 270.

The other commissioners are the principal secretaries of state and the president and vice-president of the Board of Trade for the time being.

1851. Edwd. Adolphus Seymour, c.c. ld. Seymour, form. first commr. of w., f., l. r., w., & p. b.
1852. John Jas. Robt. Manners, c.c. ld. John Manners, aft. D. of Rutland, Mar. 4, **G.**
1853. Sir Wm. Molesworth, Jan. 5, **G.**
1855. Sir Benjn. Hall, bt., aft. ld. Llanover, July 21.
1858. Lord John Manners, *again*, Feb. 26.
1859. Hy. Fitzroy, June 18.
1860. Fras. Wm. Cowper, Feb. 9.
1866. Lord John Manners, *again*, July 6.
1868. Austen Hy. Layard, aft. sir A., G.C.B., Dec. 9, sw.
1869. Acton Smee Ayrton, Oct. 26, **G.**, Nov. 11, sw.
1873, Wm. Patrick Adam, Aug. 11, sw.
1874. Hy. Chas. Geo. Gordon Lennox, c.c. lord Gordon Lennox, Mar. 21, sw.
1876. Gerard Jas. Noel, Aug. 14, sw.
1880. Wm. Patrick Adam, *again*, May 3, sw.
Geo. John Shaw Lefevre, Nov. 29, sw.

1885. Archd. Philip, E. of Rosebery, Feb. 13, sw.
Hon. David Robt. Plunket, June 24, sw.
1886. Albert Edmd., E. of Morley, Feb. 6.
1886. Victor Alexr., E. of Elgin and Kincardine, Apr. 16, sw.
Hon. David Robt. Plunket, *again*, Aug. 5, sw.

Commissioners of Woods, Forests, and Land Revenues.

Appointed under 14 & 15 Vict. cap. 42. See Introduction, *ante*, p. 270.

1851. Hon. Chas. Alexr. Gore, and Thos. Fras. Kennedy, form. commrs. of W., F., L. R., W., & P. B.
1855. Hon. Chas. Kenneth Howard, *vice* Kennedy.
1882. Sir Hy. Brougham Loch, *vice* Howard.
1884. Geo. Culley, *vice* Loch.
1885. Col. Robt. Nigel Fitzhardinge Kingscote, C.B., *vice* Gore.

COMMISSIONERS OF CUSTOMS.

From the Restoration of King Charles II.

Commissioners of Customs for England and Wales.

1660. Sir Job Harby, sir John Wolstenholme, sir John Jacob, sir Nichs Crispe, sir John Harrison, and sir John Shawe, Sept. 20.
1671. Sir Geo. Downing, sir Wm. Thompson, sir Wm. Lowther, Wm Garway, Fras. Millington, and John Upton, Sept. 27.
1672. Sir Richd. Temple, sir Geo. Downing, sir Wm. Thompson, sir Wm. Lowther, Wm. Garway, Fras. Millington, and John Upton, Mar. 30.
1675. Sir Richd. Temple, sir Edwd. Deering, sir Geo. Downing, sir Wm. Lowther, Chas. Cheyne, Fras. Millington, and John Upton, Jan. 8.
1677. Sir Richd. Temple, sir Edwd. Deering, sir Fras. Lawley, sir Geo. Downing, sir Wm. Lowther, Chas. Cheyne, and Fras. Millington, Nov. 9.
1679. Sir Richd. Temple, sir Edwd. Deering, sir Fras. Lawley, sir Geo. Downing, Chas. Osborne, Chas. Cheyne, and Fras. Millington, Feb. 14.
Sir Richd. Temple, sir Geo. Downing, Chas. Cheyne, Fras. Millington, and John Upton, Apr. 10.
1680. Chas., visc. Newhaven, sir Richd. Temple, sir Geo. Downing, John Upton, and Nichs. Butler, July 1.
1681. Chas., visc. Newhaven, Andw Newport, sir Richd. Temple, sir Geo. Downing, and Nichs. Butler, Nov. 11.
1684. Chas., visc. Newhaven, sir Dudley North, Andw. Newport, sir Richd. Temple, sir Geo. Downing, and sir Nichs. Butler, Mar. 7.
Chas., visc. Newhaven, Andw. Newport, sir Richd. Temple, sir Nichs. Butler, sir John Buckworth, and Wm. Dickinson, Aug. 1.
Chas., visc. Newhaven, Andw. Newport, sir Richd. Temple, sir Nichs. Butler, sir John Buckworth, Wm. Dickinson, and Thos. Chudleigh, Dec. 31.
1685. Chas., visc. Newhaven, sir John Werden, sir Nichs. Butler, Wm. Dickinson, and Thos. Chudleigh, Feb. 28.
Chas., visc. Newhaven, sir Dudley North, sir John Werden, sir Nichs. Butler, sir John Buckworth, Wm. Dickinson, and Thos. Chudleigh, Apr. 2.
1686. Chas., visc. Newhaven, sir Dudley North, sir John Werden, sir John Buckworth, sir Nichs. Butler, Wm. Dickinson, Thos. Chudleigh, and Saml. Clarke, June 25.
Chas., visc. Newhaven, sir Dudley North, sir John Werden, sir Nichs.

Butler, sir John Buckworth, Wm. Dickinson, Thos. Chudleigh, and Saml. Clarke, July 9.

1687. Sir Dudley North, sir John Werden, sir Nichs. Butler, sir John Buckworth, and Thos. Chudleigh, Feb. 25.

1688. Sir Nichs. Butler, sir Dudley North, sir John Werden, Thos. Chudleigh, and Wm. Culliford, Jan. 14.

Sir Nichs. Butler, Hy. Browne, sir Dudley North, sir John Werden, and Wm. Culliford, Feb. 28.

1689. Geo. Booth, sir Richd. Temple, sir John Werden, sir Robt. Southwell, sir Robt. Clayton, sir Patience Ward, and Thos. Pelham, Apr. 20.

1691. Geo. Booth, sir Richd. Temple, sir John Werden, sir Robt. Southwell, sir Robt. Clayton, sir Patience Ward, and Hy. Guy, Mar. 24.

Geo. Booth, sir Richd. Temple, sir John Werden, sir Robt. Southwell, sir Patience Ward, sir Robt. Clayton, and Chas. Godolphin, July 3.

1694. Sir Robt. Clayton, sir Patience Ward, sir Robt. Southwell, Chas. Godolphin, sir Walter Young, Jas. Chadwick, and Saml. Clarke, Aug. 14.

1696. Sir Robt. Clayton, sir Patience Ward, sir Robt. Southwell, Chas. Godolphin, sir Walter Young, Jas. Chadwick, Saml. Clarke, and Benjn. Overton, Apr. 14.

1697. Chas. Godolphin, sir Walter Young Saml. Clarke, Benjn. Overton, sir Hy. Hobart, sir John Austin, and Robt. Henley, June 21.

1698. Chas. Godolphin, sir Walter Young, Saml. Clarke, Benjn. Overton, sir Hy. Hobart, sir John Austin, Robt. Henley, and sir Wm. St. Quintin, Nov. 22.

1699. Chas. Godolphin, sir Walter Young, Saml. Clarke, Benjn. Overton, Robt. Henley, sir Wm. St. Quintin, and hon. Thos. Newport, Nov. 22.

1701. Chas. Godolphin, Saml. Clarke, Benjn. Overton, Robt. Henley, Thos. Newport, Arthur Maynwaring, and Wm. Culliford, Dec. 18.

1702. The same commrs. to the close of K. William III.'s reign; contd. at the commencement of that of Q. Anne.

1703. Chas. Godolphin, Saml. Clarke, Thos. Newport, Arthur Maynwaring, Wm. Culliford, sir John Werden, and Richd. Bretton, July 14.

1705. Chas. Godolphin, Saml. Clarke, Thos. Newport, Wm. Culliford, sir John Werden, Richd. Bretton, and Thos. Hall, May 15.

1706. Chas. Godolphin, Saml. Clarke, Thos. Newport, Wm. Culliford, sir John Werden, Thos. Hall, and sir Matt. Dudley, June 6.

1708. Chas. Godolphin, Saml. Clarke, Thos. Newport, Wm. Culliford, sir John Werden, sir Matt. Dudley, and sir John Stanley, May 4.

Chas. Godolphin, Thos. Newport, Wm. Culliford, sir John Werden, sir Matt. Dudley, sir John Stanley, and John Shute, Dec. 23.

1711. Chas. Godolphin, sir John Werden, sir John Stanley, Matt. Prior, John Bridges, Robt. Williamson, and Edwd. Gibbons, Jan. 25.

1714. Sir John Werden, sir John Stanley, Matt. Prior, John Bridges, Robt. Williamson, Edwd. Gibbons, Chas. Godolphin, and sir David Nairne, May 17.

Sir John Stanley, John Bridges, Robt. Williamson, sir John Werden, Matt. Prior, Edwd. Gibbons, and sir David Nairne, Nov. 9; their patent revoked, and sir Walter Young, sir Matt. Dudley, sir John Stanley, John Bridges, Robt. Williamson, John Pulteney, and Thos. Walker, app.

Sir Walter Young, sir Matt. Dudley, sir John Stanley, Robt. Williamson, John Pulteney, Thos. Walker, and sir Chas. Peers, Dec. 4.

1715. Sir Walter Young, sir Matt. Dudley, sir John Stanley, John Pulteney, Thos. Walker, sir Chas. Peers, and sir Thos. Frankland, Mar. 17.

1718. Sir Walter Young, sir Matt. Dudley, sir John Stanley, John Pulteney, Thos. Walker, sir Chas. Peers, and Robt. Baylis, Jan. 2.

1720. Sir Walter Young, sir Matt. Dudley, sir John Stanley, John Pulteney, Thos. Walker, sir Chas. Peers, and Robt. Baylis, Oct. 1.

1721. Sir Walter Young, sir John Stanley, John Pulteney, Thos. Walker, sir Chas. Peers, Robt. Baylis, and sir John Evelyn, Sept. 4.

1722. Sir Walter Young, sir John Stanley, Thos. Walker, sir Chas. Peers, Robt. Baylis, sir John Evelyn, and Thos, Maynard, Mar. 27.

Commissioners of Customs for Great Britain.

Fourteen commissioners were appointed, seven to reside in London, five in Edinburgh, and two to attend the outports.

1723. Sir Walter Young, sir John Stanley, Thos. Walker, sir Chas. Peers, Robt. Baylis, sir John Evelyn, Thos. Maynard, sir Jas. Campbell, Humphry Brent, John Campbell, Brian Fairfax, Hy. Hale, Geo. Drummond, and John Hill.

1727. Sir Walter Young, sir John Stanley, Thos. Walker, sir Chas. Peers, sir John Evelyn, Thos. Maynard, sir Jas. Campbell, Humphry Brent, John Campbell, Brian Fairfax, Hy. Hale, Geo. Drummond, John Hill, and Allan Broderick, Oct. 18.

1728. Sir Walter Young, sir John Stanley, Thos. Walker, sir Chas. Peers, sir John Evelyn, sir Jas. Campbell, Humphry Brent, John Campbell, Brian Fairfax, Hy. Hale, Geo. Drummond, John Hill, Allan Broderick, Gwynn Vaughan, and Thos. Maynard, July 19.

1730. Sir Walter Young, sir John Stanley, Thos. Walker, sir Chas. Peers, sir John Evelyn, sir Jas. Campbell, John Campbell, Brian Fairfax, Hy. Hale, Geo. Drummond, John Hill, Gwynn Vaughan, and Geo. Ross, aft. ld. Ross, Sept. 21.

1731. Sir Walter Young, sir John Stanley, Thos. Walker, sir Chas. Peers, sir John Evelyn, sir Jas. Campbell, John Campbell, Brian Fairfax, Hy. Hale, Geo. Drummond, John Hill, Gwynn Vaughan, Geo. Ross, and Wardel Geo. Westby, May 14.

Sir John Stanley, Thos. Walker, sir Chas. Peers, sir John Evelyn, sir Jas. Campbell, John Campbell, Brian Fairfax, Hy. Hale, Geo. Drummond, John Hill, Gwynn Vaughan, Geo. Ross, Wardel Geo. Westby, and sir Robt. Baylis, Aug. 28.

1732. Sir John Stanley, sir Chas. Peers, sir John Evelyn, sir Jas. Campbell John Campbell, Brian Fairfax, Hy. Hale, Geo. Drummond, John Hill, Gwynn Vaughan, Geo. Ross, Wardel Geo. Westby, sir Robt. Baylis, and Edwd. Trelawney. Jan. 2.

1735. Sir John Stanley, sir Chas. Peers, sir John Evelyn, sir Jas. Campbell, John Campbell, Brian Fairfax, Geo. Drummond, John Hill, Gwynn Vaughan, Geo. Ross, Wardel Geo. Westby, sir Robt. Baylis, Edwd. Trelawney, and sir Robt. Corbett, May 24.

1737. Sir John Stanley, sir John Evelyn, John Campbell, Brian Fairfax, John Hill, Gwynn Vaughan, Geo. Ross, Wardel Geo. Westby, sir Robt. Baylis, sir Robt. Corbett, Richd. Chandler, Beaumont Hotham, Richd. Somers, and Colin Campbell, Oct. 15.

1741. Sir John Stanley, sir John Evelyn, JohnCampbell, BrianFairfax, John Hill, Geo. Ross, now ld. Ross, Wardel Geo. Westby, sir Robt. Baylis, Richd. Chandler, Beaumont Hotham, Richd. Somers, Colin Campbell, Edwd. Riggs, and Isaac Leheup, June 29.

1742. Sir John Stanley, sir John Evelyn, John Campbell, Brian Fairfax, John Hill, Wardel Geo. Westby, sir Robt. Baylis, Richd. Chandler, Beaumont Hotham, Richd. Somers, Colin Campbell, and Gwynn Vaughan.

At this time the commission for Great Britain was divided, and nine commissioners were appointed for England and Wales, and five for Scotland.

Commissioners of Customs for England and Wales.

1742. Sir John Stanley, sir John Evelyn, Brian Fairfax, John Hill, sir Robt. Baylis, Richd. Chandler, Wardel Geo. Westby, Beaumont Hotham, and Saml. Mead, Sept.

1744. Sir John Evelyn, Brian Fairfax, John Hill, sir Robt. Baylis, Richd. Chandler, Wardel Geo. Westby, Beaumont Hotham, Saml. Mead, and Gwynn Vaughan.

1747. Sir John Evelyn, Brian Fairfax, sir Robt. Baylis, Richd. Chandler, Wardel Geo. Westby, Beaumont Hotham, Saml. Mead, Gwynn Vaughan, and Wm. Levinz.

1748. Sir John Evelyn, Brian Fairfax, Richd. Cavendish, Wardel Geo. Westby, Beaumont Hotham, Saml. Mead, Gwynn Vaughan, Wm. Levinz, and Edwd. Hooper.

1750. Sir John Evelyn, Richd. Cavendish, Wardel Geo. Westby, Beaumont Hotham, Saml. Mead, Gwynn Vaughan, Wm. Levinz, Edwd.

Hooper, and sir Miles Stapleton.

1752. Sir John Evelyn, Richd. Cavendish, Wardel Geo. Westby, Beaumont Hotham, Saml. Mead, Gwynn Vaughan, Wm. Levinz, Edwd. Hooper, and Thos. Tash.

1756. Sir John Evelyn, Richd. Cavendish, Beaumont Hotham, Saml. Mead, Gwynn Vaughan, Wm. Levinz, Edwd. Hooper, Thos. Tash, and Claudius Amyand.

1758. Sir John Evelyn, Richd. Cavendish, Beaumont Hotham, Saml. Mead, Wm. Levinz, Edwd. Hooper, Thos. Tash, Claudius Amyand, and Hy. Pelham.

1761. Sir John Evelyn, Beaumont Hotham, Saml. Mead, Wm. Levinz, Edwd. Hooper, Thos. Tash, Claudius Amyand, Hy. Pelham, and John Frederick.

1762. Sir John Evelyn, sir Beaumont Hotham, Saml. Mead, Wm. Levinz, Edwd. Hooper, Claudius Amyand, Hy. Pelham, John Frederick, and Hy. Banks, Dec. 11.

1763. Saml. Mead, Edwd. Hooper, Claudius Amyand, Hy. Pelham, sir John Frederick, Hy. Banks, sir Wm. Musgrave, sir Jos. Pennington, and Corbyn Morris, Mar. 15.

1765. Saml. Mead, Edwd. Hooper, Hy. Pelham, sir John Frederick, Hy. Banks, sir Wm. Musgrave, sir Jos. Pennington, Corbyn Morris, and hon. Hy. Grenville, June 8.

1766. Saml. Mead, Edwd. Hooper, Hy. Pelham, sir John Frederick, Hy. Banks, sir Wm. Musgrave, sir Jos. Pennington, Corbyn Morris, and Jas. Jeffreys, Aug. 16.

1769. Saml. Mead, Edwd. Hooper, Hy. Pelham, sir John Frederick, Hy. Banks, sir Wm. Musgrave, Corbyn Morris, Jas. Jeffreys, and Thos. Boone, Dec. 5.

1776. Edwd. Hooper, Hy. Pelham, sir John Frederick, sir Wm. Musgrave, Corbyn Morris, Jas. Jeffreys, Thos. Boone, Welbore Ellis Agar, and Wm. Hay, Oct. 31.

1778. Edwd. Hooper, Hy. Pelham, sir John Frederick, sir Wm. Musgrave, Jas. Jeffreys, Thos. Boone, Welbore Ellis Agar, Wm. Hay, and Thos. Allan.

1782. Edwd. Hooper, Hy. Pelham, sir Wm. Musgrave, Jas. Jeffreys, Thos. Boone, Welbore Ellis Agar, Wm Hay, Thos. Allan, and sir Stanier Porten, Mar. 27

1785. Edwd. Hooper, Hy. Pelham, sir Wm. Musgrave, Jas. Jeffreys, Thos. Boone, Welbore Ellis Agar, Wm. Hay, sir Stanier Porten, and John Pownall, Feb. 8.

Edwd. Hooper, Hy. Pelham, Jas. Jeffreys, Thos. Boone, Welbore Ellis Agar, Wm. Hay, sir Stanier Porten, John Pownall, and Joah Bates, Aug. 10.

1786. Edwd. Hooper, Hy. Pelham, Thos. Boone, Welbore Ellis Agar, Wm. Hay, John Pownall, Joah Bates, sir Alexr. Munro, and Richd. Frewin, Nov. 15.

1788. Edwd. Hooper, Thos. Boone, Welbore Ellis Agar, Wm. Hay, Joah Bates, sir Alexr. Munro, Richd. Frewin, Wm. Stiles, and Wm. Roe, Mar. 18.

1793. Thos. Boone, Welbore Ellis Agar, Wm. Hay, Joah Bates, sir Alexr. Munro, Richd. Frewin, Wm. Stiles, Wm. Roe, and Fras. Fownes Luttrell, Dec. 2.

1797. Thos. Boone, Welbore Ellis Agar, Joah Bates, sir Alexr. Munro, Richd. Frewin, Wm. Stiles, Wm. Roe, Fras. Fownes Luttrell, and John Buller.

1799. Thos. Boone, Welbore Ellis Agar, sir Alexr. Munro, Richd. Frewin, Wm. Stiles, Wm. Roe, Fras. Fownes Luttrell, John Buller, and Gloucester Wilson.

1805. Welbore Ellis Agar, sir Alexr. Munro, Richd. Frewin, Wm. Roe, Fras. Fownes Luttrell, John Buller, Gloucester Wilson, Jas. Hume, and John Williams, Sept. 17.

Sir Alexr. Munro, Richd. Frewin, Wm. Roe, Fras. Fownes Luttrell, John Buller, Gloucester Wilson, Jas. Hume, John Williams, and Jas. Willis, Nov. 26.

1810. Richd. Betenson Dean, *vice* Munro, Sept. 17.

1812. Snowden Barne, previously a commr. of the treasy., Oct. 22.

1813. Hy. Richmond, *vice* Frewin, May 6.

Wm. Boothby, aft. sir Wm., bt., Sept. 15.

1819. Hon. Edwd. Stewart and Wm. Thos. Roe, Feb. 17.

1821. Hon. Jas. Hy. Keith Stewart, Apr. 21.

On September 13, 1823, the consolidation of the Boards of Customs for England and Wales, Scotland, and Ireland, took place, and the commissioners from that time have been commissioners for the United Kingdom.

Commissioners of Customs for the United Kingdom.

323. Richd. Betenson Dean, Wm. Boothby, aft. sir W., bt., Gloucester Wilson, John Williams, Hy. Richmond, hon. Jas. Hy. Keith Stewart, Wm. Thos. Roe, Edwd. Earl, hon. Abraham Hely Hutchinson, Hulton Smith King, Fras. Seymour Larpent, Fredk. Beilby Watson, aft. sir F., bt., and Hy. Jas. Bouverie, Sept. 13.

Of these, Edwd. Earl had been previously commr. in Scotland, and the hon. Abraham Hely Hutchinson and Hulton Smith King commrs. in Ireland.

324. Geo. Wm. Fredk. Villiers, aft. E. of Clarendon, Nov. 27.

1825. Stephen Geo. Lushington, Jan. 3.
Hon. Wm. Cust, Apr. 21.

1826. Hon. Heneage Legge, Apr. 13.
David Munro Binning, July 15.

1827. Culling Chas. Smith, Mar. 13.
Aug. G. Stapleton, Aug. 31.

1834. Lt.-Col. Wm. Leader Maberly, June 28.

1836. Sir Geo. Hy. Freeling, bt., Oct. 21.

1838. Hon. Stephen Edmd. Spring-Rice, Sept. 10.

1841. Geo. Robt. Dawson, Dec. 29.

1845. Fredk. Goulburn, Jan 28.
Thos. Pargiter Dickenson, Apr. 4.

1846. Sir Thos. Fras. Fremantle, bt., Feb. 24.
Capt. Edwd. Saurin, R.N., aft. adm., July 4.

Commissioners in 1851.

'here marked "ceased" the vacancy was not filled up.

r Thos. Fras. Fremantle, bt., aft. ld. Cottesloe, *chairman*; ceased 1875.
eo. Robt. Dawson, *dep. ch.*
y. Richmond, ceased 1851.
;eph. Geo. Lushington, ceased 1854.
ulling Chas. Smith, ceased 1854.
on. Steph. Edmd. Spring-Rice, *dep. ch.*, 1856, *vice* Dawson.
redk. Goulburn, *dep. ch.*, 1859, *vice* Spring-Rice; *chairman* 1875, *vice* Fremantle.
hos. Pargiter Dickenson.
dm. Edwd. Saurin, ceased 1860.

Subsequent Appointments.

1856. Granville C. L. Berkeley, *vice* Dawson; ceased 1886.
Wm. Rathbone Greg, *vice* Dickenson.

1859. Ralph W. Grey, *vice* Spring-Rice.

1865. Col. Fredk. Romilly, *vice* Greg; *dep. ch.* 1875, *vice* Goulburn.

1870. Sir Fras. Hastings Doyle, *vice* Grey.

1878. Sir Chas. Du Cane, K.C.M.G., *chairman*, *vice* Goulburn.

1883. Arthur Sanders Wm. Chas. Fox, visc. Sudley, aft. E. of Arran; *vice* Doyle.

1885. Horace Alfred Damer Seymour, Jan. 1, *vice* Arran.

1887. Herbert Harley Murray, *dep. ch.*, *vice* Romilly.

COMMISSIONERS OF EXCISE, STAMPS, TAXES, AND INLAND REVENUE.

HERE were three distinct boards of Excise, Stamps, and Taxes. In 333 the same persons were by two separate letters patent appointed ommissioners of Stamps and Commissioners of Taxes, and by 4 & 5 Vill. cap. 60 (Aug. 13, 1834) the two boards were consolidated under e style of Commissioners of Stamps and Taxes. In 1849 a similar ourse was adopted. On January 6 the same persons were appointed ommissioners of Excise and Commissioners of Stamps and Taxes, and y 12 & 13 Vict. cap. 1 (Feb. 27, 1849) the boards were consolidated nder the style of Commissioners of Inland Revenue.

COMMISSIONERS OF EXCISE.

Commissioners of Excise for England and Wales.

From the Restoration of King Charles II.

360. Sir Matth. Hale, ld. ch. baron; sir Edwd. Atkyns and sir Christr. Turner, barons of the exch.; sir Rich. Browne, ld. mayor of London; sir Wm. Doyley, sir Hy. Vernon, sir Geo. Bimon, Wm.

Prynne, John Birch, Robt. Scawen, Fras. Finch, Nathl. Martin, and Edwd. Wingate, commrs. for discharging, settling, and recovering the arrears of excise due to the king, Feb. 8.

1660. Sir Geo. Bimon and others, or any three of them, to receive all arrears of excise due to November 8, last past, within London, Westminster, Southwark, Surrey, and Middlesex, South Mimms in Middlesex excepted, Nov. 29.

1664. Sir Denny Ashburnham, sir Geo. Bimon, Fras. Finch, and Edwd. Wingate, Mar. 20.

1665. Sir John James, John James, Richd. Kingdom, and Wm. Hiccocks, commrs. within London, Westminster, Southwark, and counties of Middlesex and Surrey, except South Mimms in Middlesex, on behalf of his majesty's farmers of the excise, June 24.

1666. Robt. Huntingdon, Richd. Kingdom, John James, jun., and Wm. Forthe, commrs. for the abovesaid places for the farmers of the excise, Oct. 11.

Wm. Forthe, Robt. Huntingdon, Richd. Kingdom, and John James.

1670. Sir Saml. Morland, Robt. Huntingdon, Wm. Forthe, and Richd. Kingdom, Aug. 15.

Sir Saml. Morland, sir John James, Robt. Huntingdon, Wm. Forthe, and Richd. Kingdom, Sept. 24

1671. Sir Saml. Morland, sir Robt. Southwell, one of the clerks of his majesty's privy council, sir John James, Robt. Huntingdon, Wm. Forthe, and Richd. Kingdom, May 15.

1672. Sir Saml. Morland, sir John Davys, sir Robt. Southwell, sir John James, Robt. Huntingdon, and Richd. Kingdom, Jan. 31.

1673. Sir Saml. Morland, sir Robt. Wiseman, sir Robt. Southwell, sir John James, sir Robt. Huntingdon, Wm. Forthe, and Richd. Kingdom, Sept. 12.

Sir Saml. Morland, sir Robt. Wiseman, sir Robt. Southwell, sir John James, sir Robt. Huntingdon, Wm. Forthe, Richd. Kingdom, and Richd. Brett, Dec. 1.

1674. Sir Saml. Morland, sir Robt. Wiseman, sir Robt. Southwell, sir John James, Robt. Huntingdon, Richd. Kingdom, Fras. Finch, and Hy. Fred. Thynne, Oct. 23.

1677. Sir Saml. Morland, sir Robt. Wiseman, sir Robt. Southwell, sir John James, Robt. Huntingdon, Fredk. Thynne, Edwd. Wing Fredk. Christian Howard, and John Elves, Nov. 9.

1678. Sir Denny Ashburnham, sir Sa Morland, sir Robt. Wiseman, John Elves, sir Robt. Sou well, sir John James, Robt. H tingdon, Chas. Davenant, Ed Wingate, and Fredk. Christ Howard, Aug. 3.

1679. Sir Denny Ashburnham, sir Ro Wiseman, sir John Elves, Robt. Southwell, sir John Jam Robt. Huntingdon, Chas. Da nant, Edwd. Wingate, Fre Christian Howard, and J Bende, Mar. 11.

Hon. Chas. Bertie, sir Denny A burnham, sir Robt. Southw sir John James, Robt. Hunti don, Chas. Davenant, Edwd. W gate, Fredk. Christian Howa and John Bende, Mar. 21.

Sir Denny Ashburnham, sir Ro Southwell, Robt. Huntingd Chas. Davenant, and Edwd. W gate, May 14.

1681. Sir Denny Ashburnham, Fras. Par Robt. Huntingdon, Chas. Da nant, and Edwd. Wingate, F 14.

1683. Sir Denny Ashburnham, Fras. Par Robt. Huntingdon, Chas. Da nant, John Freind, Felix Calve and Nathl. Hornby, May 19.

1684. Sir Denny Ashburnham, Fras. Par Robt. Huntingdon, Chas. Da nant, John Freind, Felix Calve Nathl. Hornby, Patrick Trau and Wm. Bridges, commrs. excise and hearth-money, A 10.

Sir Denny Ashburnham, Fras. Par Robt. Huntingdon, Chas. Da nant, John Freind, Felix Calve Nathl. Hornby, Patrick Trau Wm. Bridges, and Richd. Graha Sept. 17.

1685. Sir Denny Ashburnham, Fras. Par Robt. Huntingdon, Chas. Da nant, John Freind, Felix Calve Nathl. Hornby, and Richd. G ham, Mar. 11.

Sir Denny Ashburnham, Fras. Par Chas. Davenant, John Frei Felix Calvert, Nathl. Ho by, and Richd. Graham, Au 26.

1688. Sir Denny Ashburnham, Fras. Par sir John Freind, Chas. Dav nant, Nathl. Hornby, Rich Graham, and John Wilcox, ju Feb. 22.

1689. Sir Hy. Fane, sir Hy. Ashurst,

Humphry Edwin, Thos. Frankland, Fras. Parry, John Danvers, and John Wilcox, Apr. 20.

689. Sir Hy. Ashurst, sir John Morden, sir Saml. Dashwood, sir Humphry Edwin, Wm. Strong, John Foche, and Stephen Evance, Oct. 14.

.691. Sir Saml. Dashwood, sir Stephen Evance, Fras. Parry, Wm. Strong, John Foche, Nathl. Hornby, John Wilcox, jun., Thos. Hall, and Thos. Aram, Apr. 13.

.694. Sir Saml. Dashwood, sir Stephen Evance, sir John Foche, Fras. Parry, Wm. Strong, Thos. Hall, Edwd. Clarke, John Danvers, and Foot Onslow, Aug. 14.

1695. Sir Saml. Dashwood, sir Stephen Evance, sir John Foche, Fras. Parry, Wm. Strong, Thos. Hall, Edwd. Clarke, John Danvers, Foot Onslow, and sir Philip Meadows, Mar. 9.

1696. Sir Stephen Evance, sir John Foche, Fras. Parry, Wm. Strong, Edwd. Clarke, John Danvers, Foot Onslow, sir Philip Meadows, and Thos. Everard, June 30.

1698. Edwd. Clarke, Foot Onslow, Philip Meadows, Thos. Everard, sir Wm. Ashurst, Christr. Montagu, John Smith, Wm. Carr, and Wm. Fleming, Aug. 15.

1699. Foot Onslow, sir Philip Meadows, John Smith of Beaufort Buildings, Wm. Fleming, Fras. Parry, Wm. Strong, Geo. Townshend, Philip Ryley, and Richd. Cocks, June 22.

1702. Foot Onslow, sir Philip Meadows, Fras. Parry, Wm. Strong, Geo. Townshend, Philip Ryley, and Richd. Cocks, June 19.

Foot Onslow, sir Philip Meadows, Fras. Parry, Wm. Strong, Geo. Townshend, Philip Ryley, and sir Marmaduke Wyvill, Oct. 8.

1703. Foot Onslow, Wm. Strong, Geo. Townshend, Philip Ryley, sir Marm. Wyvill, Edwd. Noell, and John Boys, Dec. 17.

1706. Foot Onslow, Wm. Strong, Geo. Townshend, Philip Ryley, sir Marm. Wyvill, Edwd. Noell, and Christr. Montagu, June 6.

1710. Wm. Strong, Geo. Townshend, Philip Ryley, sir Marm. Wyvill, Edwd. Noell, Christr. Montagu, sir Wm. Gifford, Nichs. Pollexfen, and Whitelock Bulstrode, May 20.

Wm. Strong, Geo. Townshend, Philip Ryley, sir Marm. Wyvill, Edwd. Noell, Christr. Montagu, Nichs. Pollexfen, Whitelock Bulstrode, and Jas. Vernon, jun., Oct. 20.

1712. Wm. Strong, Geo. Townshend, Philip Ryley, sir Marm. Wyvill, Edwd. Noell, Christr. Montagu, Whitelock Bulstrode, Jas. Vernon, jun., and John Price, July 7.

1714. Geo. Townshend, sen., Philip Ryley, sir Marm. Wyvill, Edwd. Noell, Christr. Montagu, Whitelock Bulstrode, Jas. Vernon, John Price, and John Whetham, Feb. 2.

Geo. Townshend, sen., Philip Ryley, sir Marm. Wyvill, Edwd. Noell, Christr. Montagu, Whitelock Bulstrode, Jas. Vernon, John Whetham, sir Wm. Ashurst, and Wm. Carr, Nov. 12.

1715. Geo. Townshend, sen., sir Marm. Wyvill, Christr. Montagu, Jas. Vernon, John Whetham, sir Wm. Ashurst, Wm. Carr, Roger Gale, and John Brougham, Nov. 24.

1719. Geo. Townshend, sen., sir Marm. Wyvill, Christr. Montagu, Jas. Vernon, John Whetham, Wm. Carr, Roger Gale, John Brougham, and Benjn. Mildmay, Mar. 3.

1720. Geo. Townshend, sen., sir Marm. Wyvill, Christr. Montagu, Jas. Vernon, John Whetham, Roger Gale, John Brougham, Benjn. Mildmay, and Richd. Elliott, June 18.

1721. Geo. Townshend, sen., sir Marm. Wyvill, Christr. Montagu, Jas. Vernon, John Whetham, Roger Gale, John Brougham, Benjn. Mildmay, and Richd. Elliott, Mar. 15.

1722. Geo. Townshend, sen., Christr. Montagu, Jas. Vernon, John Whetham, Roger Gale, John Brougham, Benjn. Mildmay, Richd. Elliott, and Geo. Duckett, Mar. 20.

1724. Geo. Townshend, sen., Christr. Montagu, Jas. Vernon, John Whetham, Roger Gale, Benjn. Mildmay, Richd. Elliott, Geo. Duckett, and Patrick Haldane, May 20.

1726. Geo. Townshend, sen., Christr. Montagu, Jas. Vernon, John Whetham, Roger Gale, Benjn. Mildmay, Richd. Elliott, Geo. Duckett, Patrick Haldane, and Chas. Polhill, June 22.

Christr. Montagu, John Whetham, Roger Gale, Benjn. Mildmay, Richd. Elliott, Geo. Duckett, Patrick Haldane, Chas. Polhill, and John Fowle, jun., Oct. 11.

1727. Christr. Montagu, John Whetham, Roger Gale, Benjn. Mildmay, Richd. Elliott, Geo. Duckett, Chas. Polhill, John Fowle, and Thos. Wylde, Nov. 3.

1728. Christr. Montagu, John Whetham, Roger Gale, Richd. Elliott, Geo. Duckett, Chas. Polhill, John Fowle, Thos. Wylde, and Jas. Vernon, June 26.

1729. Christr. Montagu, John Whetham, Roger Gale, Geo. Duckett, Chas. Polhill, John Fowle, Thos. Wylde, Jas. Vernon, and Robt. Eyre, May 21.

1732. Christr. Montagu, John Whetham, Roger Gale, Chas. Polhill, John Fowle, Thos. Wylde, Jas. Vernon, Robt. Eyre, and Humphry Thayer, Oct. 20.

1735. John Whetham, Chas. Polhill, John Fowle, Thos. Wylde, Jas. Vernon, Robt. Eyre, Humphry Thayer, hon. Horatio Townshend, and sir Thos. Robinson, Nov.

1737. Chas. Polhill, John Fowle, Thos. Wylde, Jas. Vernon, Robt. Eyre, Humphry Thayer, hon. Horatio Townshend, sir Thos. Robinson, and Wm. Burton, Oct.

1738. Chas. Polhill, John Fowle, Thos. Wylde, Jas. Vernon, Robt. Eyre, hon. Horatio Townshend, sir Thos. Robinson, Wm. Burton, and John Orlebar, Jan.

1740. Chas. Polhill, John Fowle, Jas. Vernon, Robt. Eyre. hon. Horatio Townshend, sir Thos. Robinson, Wm. Burton, John Orlebar, and Aug. Earle, Nov.

1742. Chas. Polhill, John Fowle, Jas. Vernon, Robt. Eyre, hon. Horatio Townshend, Wm. Burton, John Orlebar, Aug. Earle, and David Papillon, Feb.

1750. Chas. Polhill, Jas. Vernon, Robt. Eyre, hon. Horatio Townshend, Wm. Burton, John Orlebar, Aug. Earle, David Papillon, and John Wyndham Bowyer, July.

1751. Chas. Polhill, Jas. Vernon, Robt. Eyre, Wm. Burton, John Orlebar, Aug. Earle, David Papillon, John Wyndham Bowyer, and Wm. Mellish, Dec.

1753. Chas. Polhill, Jas. Vernon, Wm. Burton, John Orlebar, Aug. Earle, David Papillon, John Wyndham Bowyer, Wm. Mellish, and Fredk. Frankland, Feb.

1754. Chas. Polhill, Jas. Vernon, Wm. Burton, John Orlebar, Aug. Earle, John Wyndham Bowyer, Wm. Mellish, Fredk. Frankland, and David Papillon, jun., Apr.

1755. Jas. Vernon, Wm. Burton, John Orlebar, Aug. Earle, John Wyndham Bowyer, Wm. Mellish, Fredk. Frankland, David Papillon, jun., and Wm. Cayley, Apr.

1756. Wm. Burton, John Orlebar, Au Earle, John Wyndham Bowy Wm. Mellish, Fredk. Fran land, David Papillon, jun., W Cayley, and Thos. Farringto Apr.

1758. Wm. Burton, John Orlebar, Au Earle, John Wyndham Bowye Wm. Mellish, Fredk. Franklan David Papillon, jun., Wm. Ca ley, and Geo. Lewis Scott, Feb.

1760. Wm. Burton, John Orlebar, Au Earle, John Wyndham Bowye Fredk. Frankland, David Papillo jun., Wm. Cayley, Geo. Lew Scott, and Hy. Poole.

1762. Wm. Burton, John Orlebar, Jo Wyndham Bowyer, Fredk. Fran land, David Papillon, Wm. Ca ley, Geo. Lewis Scott, Hy. Pool and Thos. Bowlby, June 19.

1763. Wm. Burton, John Orlebar, Jo Wyndham Bowyer, David Papillo Wm. Cayley, Geo. Lewis Scot Thos. Bowlby, Hy. Vernon, ar John Bindley, Feb. 15.

1765. Wm. Burton, John Orlebar, Jo Wyndham Bowyer, David Papillo Wm. Cayley, Geo. Lewis Scot Thos. Bowlby, Hy. Vernon, ar Richd. Bagot, Jan. 5.

Wm. Burton, John Orlebar, Joh WyndhamBowyer, David Papillo Wm. Cayley, Geo. Lewis Scot Thos. Bowlby, Richd. Bagot, ar sir Hy. Poole, bt., Aug. 24.

1766. Wm. Burton, John Wyndha Bowyer, David Papillon, Wn Cayley, Geo. Lewis Scott, Th Bowlby, Richd. Bagot, sir H Poole, bt., and Geo. Quarme.

1767. Wm. Burton, John Wyndha Bowyer, David Papillon, Ge Lewis Scott, Thos. Bowlby, Rich Bagot, sir Hy. Poole, bt., Ge Quarme, and Richd. Stonehewe Jan. 17.

Wm. Burton, John Wyndha Bowyer, David Papillon, Ge Lewis Scott, Thos. Bowlby, Rich Bagot, Geo. Quarme, Rich Stonehewer, and Anthy. Luca Aug. 29.

1772. Wm. Burton, John Wyndha Bowyer, David Papillon, Ge Lewis Scott, Thos. Bowlby, Rich Bagot, Geo. Quarme, Anth Lucas, and Wm. Lowndes, Oc 31.

1774. Wm. Burton, John Wyndha Bowyer, David Papillon, Ge Lewis Scott, Thos. Bowlby, Ge Quarme, Anthy. Lucas, Wn Lowndes, and Wm. Burrell, Ma 14.

776. John Wyndham Bowyer, David Papillon, Geo. Lewis Scott, Anthy. Lucas, Wm. Lowndes, Wm. Burrell, Stamp Brooksbank, John Pownall, and Heneage Legge, Oct. 31.

780. David Papillon, Geo. Lewis Scott, Anthy. Lucas, Wm. Lowndes, Wm. Burrell, Stamp Brooksbank, John Pownall, Heneage Legge, and Chas. Garth, Dec. 2.

781. David Papillon, Anthy. Lucas, Wm. Lowndes, Wm. Burrell, Stamp Brooksbank, John Pownall, Heneage Legge, Chas. Garth, and Martin Whish, Aug. 25.

782. David Papillon, Anthy. Lucas, Wm. Lowndes, Wm. Burrell, Stamp Brooksbank, John Pownall, Chas. Garth, Martin Whish, and Geo. Jas. Cholmondeley, June 1.

784. David Papillon, Anthy. Lucas, Wm. Lowndes, Wm. Burrell, Stamp Brooksbank, John Pownall, Martin Whish, Geo. Jas. Cholmondeley, and Hy. Reveley, May 18.

785. David Papillon, Anthy. Lucas, Wm. Lowndes, Wm. Burrell, Stamp Brooksbank, Martin Whish, Geo. Jas. Cholmondeley, Hy. Reveley, and hon. John Luttrell-Olmius, aft. E. of Carhampton, Feb. 5.

789. David Papillon, Wm. Lowndes, Wm. Burrell, Stamp Brooksbank, Martin Whish, Geo. Jas. Cholmondeley, Hy. Reveley, hon. John L.-Olmius, and Timothy Caswell, Sept. 12.

790. Wm. Lowndes, Stamp Brooksbank, Martin Whish, Geo. Jas. Cholmondeley, Hy. Reveley, hon. John L.-Olmius, Timothy Caswell, Robt. Nicholas, and John Buller, Mar. 31.

792. Martin Whish, Wm. Lowndes, Geo. Jas. Cholmondeley, Hy. Reveley, hon. John L.-Olmius, Timothy Caswell, Robt. Nicholas, John Buller, and hon. Aug. Phipps, July 7.

794. Martin Whish, Wm. Lowndes, Geo. Jas. Cholmondeley, Hy. Reveley, hon. John L.-Olmius, Timothy Caswell, Robt. Nicholas, hon. Aug. Phipps, and Wm. Jackson, Jan. 17.

797. Martin Whish, Wm. Lowndes, Geo. Jas. Cholmondeley, hon. John L.-Olmius, Timothy Caswell, Robt. Nicholas, hon. Aug. Phipps, Wm. Jackson, and Richd. Spiller, Aug. 16.

801. Martin Whish, Wm. Lowndes, hon. John L.-Olmius, Timothy Caswell, Robt. Nicholas, hon. Aug. Phipps, Wm. Jackson, Richd. Spiller, and ld. Geo. Seymour, July 24.

1802. Martin Whish, Wm. Lowndes, hon. John L.-Olmius, Robt. Nicholas, hon. Aug. Phipps, Wm. Jackson, Richd. Spiller, ld. Geo. Seymour, and Edwd. Fisher, Sept. 27.

1805. Martin Whish, Wm. Lowndes, hon. John L.-Olmius, Robt. Nicholas, hon. Aug. Phipps, Wm. Jackson, Richd. Spiller, ld. Geo. Seymour, and Geo. Watson, Sept. 14.

1807. Martin Whish, Wm. Lowndes, hon. John L.-Olmius, Robt. Nicholas, hon. Aug. Phipps, Wm. Jackson, ld. Geo. Seymour, Geo. Watson, and Alexr. Campbell, July 7.

1808. Martin Whish, hon. John L.-Olmius, Robt. Nicholas, hon. Aug. Phipps, Wm. Jackson, ld. Geo. Seymour, Geo. Watson, Alexr. Campbell, and Christr. Thompson Maling, July 22.

1809. Martin Whish, hon. John L.-Olmius, Robt. Nicholas, hon. Aug. Phipps, ld. Geo. Seymour, Geo. Watson, Alexr. Campbell, Christr. Thompson Maling, and Benjn. Sydenham, July 15.

1810. Martin Whish, hon. John L.-Olmius, Robt. Nicholas, hon. Aug. Phipps, ld. Geo. Seymour, Geo. Watson, Alexr. Campbell, Benjn. Sydenham, and Wm. Manley, July 14.

1815. Martin Whish, hon. John L.-Olmius, Robt. Nicholas, hon. Aug. Phipps, ld. Geo. Seymour, Alexr. Campbell, Benjn. Sydenham, Wm. Manley, and sir Fras. Hastings Doyle, Oct. 7.

1819. Martin Whish, hon. John L.-Olmius, Robt. Nicholas, hon. Aug. Phipps, ld. Geo. Seymour, Alexr. Campbell, Wm. Manley, sir Fras. Hastings Doyle, and sir John Cheetham Mortlock, Apr. 5.

Hon. John L.-Olmius, Robt. Nicholas, hon. Aug. Phipps, ld. Geo. Seymour, Alexr. Campbell, Wm. Manley, sir Fras. Hastings Doyle, sir John Cheetham Mortlock, and hon. Chas. Rodolph Trefusis, Oct. 15.

1822. Lord Geo. Seymour, *chairman*, sir Fras. Hastings Doyle, *dep. ch.*, hon. John L.-Olmius, now E. of Carhampton, hon. Aug. Phipps, Alexr. Campbell, Wm. Manley, sir John Cheetham Mortlock, hon. Chas. Rodolph Trefusis, and Richd. Dawkins, Mar. 19.

On September 13, 1823, the consolidation of the Boards of Excise for England and Wales, Scotland, and Ireland took place, and the commissioners from that time have been commissioners for the United Kingdom

Commissioners of Excise for the United Kingdom.

1823. Ld.Geo. Seymour, *chairman*, sir Fras. Hastings Doyle, *dep. ch.*, John, E. of Carhampton, hon. Aug. Phipps, Alexr. Campbell, Wm. Manley, sir John Cheetham Mortlock, hon. Chas. Rodolph Trefusis, Richd. Dawkins, hon. Jas. Hewitt, Woodbine Parish, Wm. Plunket, and John Backhouse, Sept.

Abraham Cutto, Patrick P. Fitzpatrick, Saml. Rose, and Jas. Cornwall, asst. commrs., of whom the latter two retired in Sept. 1829, and the former two in May 1830.

1824. Lord Geo. Seymour, *chairman*, sir Fras. Hastings Doyle, *dep. ch.*, John, E. of Carhampton, hon. Aug. Phipps, Alexr. Campbell, sir John Cheetham Mortlock, hon. Chas. Rodolph Trefusis, Richd. Dawkins, hon. Jas. Hewitt, Woodbine Parish, Wm. Plunket, John Backhouse, and Hart Davis, Aug. 11.

1826. Lord Geo. Seymour, *chairman*, sir Fras. Hastings Doyle, *dep. ch.*, hon. Aug. Phipps, Alexr. Campbell, sir John Cheetham Mortlock, hon. Chas. Rodolph Trefusis, hon. Jas. Hewitt, Woodbine Parish, Wm. Plunket, John Backhouse, Hart Davis, Thos. Harrison, and hon. Berkeley Paget, July 28.

1827. Lord Geo. Seymour, *chairman*, sir Fras. Hastings Doyle, *dep. ch.*, hon. Aug. Phipps, Alexr. Campbell, sir John Cheetham Mortlock, hon. Chas. Rodolph Trefusis, hon. Jas. Hewitt, Woodbine Parish, Wm. Plunket, Hart Davis, Thos. Harrison, hon. Berkeley Paget, and Thos., ld. Graves, July 24.

1828. Lord Geo. Seymour, *chairman*, sir Fras. Hastings Doyle, *dep. ch.*, Alexr. Campbell, sir John Cheetham Mortlock, hon. Chas. Rodolph Trefusis, hon. Jas. Hewitt, Woodbine Parish, Wm. Plunket, Hart Davis, Thos. Harrison, hon. Berkeley Paget, Thos., ld. Graves, and hon. Wm. Hy. Percy, July 28.

1830. Lord Geo. Seymour, *chairman*, sir Fras. Hastings Doyle, *dep. ch.*, Alexr. Campbell, sir John Cheetham Mortlock, hon. Chas. Rodolph Trefusis, hon. Jas. Hewitt, Woodbine Parish, Wm. Plunket, Hart Davis, Thos. Harrison, hon. Berkeley Paget, and hon. Wm. Hy. Percy, Feb.

1832. The same board, with the exception of Alexr. Campbell, hon. Jas. Hewitt, and Woodbine Parish, who ceased to be commrs. in Oct. this year.

1833. Lord Geo. Seymour, *chairman*, (until July this year), sir Fras. Hastings Doyle, *dep. ch.*, sir John Cheetham Mortlock, hon. Chas. Rodolph Trefusis, aft. ld. Clinton, Wm. Plunket, Hart Davis, Thos. Harrison, hon. Berkeley Paget, and hon. Wm. Hy. Percy.

1834. Sir Fras. Hastings Doyle, *chairman*, Wm. Plunket, *dep. ch.* (until Sept. 1837), sir John Cheetham Mortlock, Hart Davis, Thos. Harrison, hon. Berkeley Paget, and hon. Wm. Hy. Percy.

1838. Sir Fras. Hastings Doyle, *chairman* (until Dec. 1), Hart Davis, *dep. ch.*, sir John Cheetham Mortlock, hon. Berkeley Paget, hon. Wm. Hy. Percy, Thos. Harrison, and Hy. Fredk. Stephenson.

1839. John Wood, *chairman*, Hart Davis, *dep. ch.*, sir John Cheetham Mortlock, hon. Berkeley Paget (until Nov. 22, 1842), hon. Wm. Hy. Percy, Thos. Harrison, Hy. Fredk. Stephenson, and Chas. John Herries. The last app. Nov. 22, 1842.

1845. John Wood, *chairman*, Hart Davis, *dep. ch.*, sir John Cheetham Mortlock (until Dec. this year), hon. Wm. Hy. Percy, Thos. Harrison, Hy. Fredk. Stephenson, Chas. John Herries, and Chas. Ross. The last app. Dec. 13.

1849. John Wood, *chairman*, John Thornton, *dep. ch.*, Thos. Harrison, Hy. Fredk. Stephenson, Chas. John Herries, Chas. Powlett Rushworth, Alfred Montgomery, and Chas. Pressly, Jan. 6.

Consolidated with the Board of Stamps and Taxes. See Introduction, *ante* p. 277, and "Commissioners of Inland Revenue," *post*, p. 285.

COMMISSIONERS OF STAMP DUTIES FOR ENGLAND AND WALES.

From the reign of William III. to the consolidation of of the Board with the Board of Taxes in 1834.

94. Christr. Montagu, John Stanley, Edwd. Lloyd, Hy. Cornish, Hy. Harris, Jacob Vanderesch, and Jas. Isaacson, commrs. for the several duties upon stamped vellum, parchment, and paper, to commence from June 28; May 21.

98. John Stanley, Edwd. Lloyd, Hy. Cornish, Hy. Harris, Jacob Vanderesch, Jas. Isaacson, and Thos. Farrington, Sept. 13.

00. Edwd. Lloyd, Hy. Cornish, Hy. Harris, Jas. Isaacson, Thos. Farrington, Richd. Uthwayte, and Robt. Pooley, Dec. 7.

2. Edwd. Lloyd, Hy. Cornish, Richd. Uthwayte, Robt. Pooley, and John Weneyve, June 13.

Edwd. Lloyd, Hy. Cornish, Richd. Uthwayte, Robt. Pooley, and Richd. Dyott, Oct. 8.

)6. Edwd. Lloyd, Hy. Cornish, Robt. Poole, Richd. Dyott, and John Molesworth, June 26.

)8. Edwd. Lloyd, Robt. Pooley, Richd. Dyott, John Molesworth, and Richd. Martyn, May 1.

10. Edwd. Lloyd, Robt. Pooley, Richd. Dyott, Richd. Martyn, and Richd. Steele, June 1.

13. Robt. Pooley, Richd. Martyn, Richd. Steele, sir Brocas Gardiner, and Thos. Palmer, June 12.

.4. Robt. Pooley, Richd. Martyn, sir Brocas Gardiner, Thos. Palmer, and Chas. Vivian, Jan. 15.

Sir Brocas Gardiner, Thos. Palmer, Chas. Vivian, Richd. Shelton, and Geo. Cowper, May 5.

Richd. Martyn, Richd. Pye, Thos. Warner, Nichs. Carew, sen., and Roger Gale, Dec. 20.

.5. Sir Brocas Gardiner, Richd. Pye, Thos. Warner, Nichs. Carew, sen., and Roger Gale, May 4.

Sir Brocas Gardiner, Richd. Pye, Thos. Warner, Nichs. Carew, sen., and Richd. Houlditch, Nov. 28.

17. Sir Brocas Gardiner, Richd. Pye, Thos. Warner, Nichs. Carew, sen., and John Shutz, Feb. 21.

!1. Sir Brocas Gardiner, sir Richd. Pye, Thos. Warner, John Shutz, and Geo. Townshend, Jan. 29.

Sir Brocas Gardiner, sir Richd. Pye, John Shutz, Geo. Townshend, jun., and John Turner, May 12.

1722. Sir Brocas Gardiner, John Shutz Geo. Townshend, jun., John Turner, and John Shorter, Oct. 12.

1727. Sir Brocas Gardiner, John Shutz, John Turner, John Shorter, and Wm. Hewett, Mar. 17.

1729. Sir Brocas Gardiner, John Turner, John Shorter, Wm. Hewett, and Richd. Shelly, June 3.

1734. Sir Brocas Gardiner, John Shorter, Richd. Shelley, Wm. Fisher, and Burrington Goldsworthy, June 1.

1736. Sir Brocas Gardiner, John Shorter, Richd. Shelley, Wm. Fisher, and Brinley Skinner, May 6.

1737. Sir Brocas Gardiner, John Shorter, Richd. Shelly, Wm. Fisher, and Wm. Blair, Feb. 2.

Sir Brocas Gardiner, Richd. Shelley, Wm. Blair, Matt. Kenrick, and John Bird, Apr. 2.

1739. Richd. Shelley, Wm. Blair, Matt. Kenrick, John Bird, and John Plumptree, jun., Feb. 7.

1742. Richd. Shelley, Wm. Blair, Matt. Kenrick, John Plumptree, jun., and John Bernard, Aug. 30.

1754. Richd. Shelley, Wm. Blair, Matt. Kenrick, John Bernard, and Robt. Thompson, Apr. 15.

1755. Wm. Blair, Matt. Kenrick, John Bernard, Robt. Thompson, and Geo. Whitmore, Dec. 5.

1762. Wm. Blair, John Bernard, Robt. Thompson, Geo. Whitmore, and John Kenrick, Mar. 17.

1763. John Bernard, Robt. Thompson, sir Jas. Calder, Edwd. Tucker, and Marm. Gwynne, Feb. 8.

1764. John Bernard, sir Jas. Calder, Edwd. Tucker, Marm. Gwynne, and Jas. Bindley, Jan. 4.

1765. Wm. Blair, John Bernard, Geo. Whitmore, John Kenrick, and Jas. Bindley, Aug. 24.

1775. Wm. Blair, Geo. Whitmore, John Kenrick, Jas. Bindley, and Wm. Bailey, Aug. 3.

1776. Wm. Blair, John Kenrick, Jas. Bindley, Wm. Bailey, and Wm. Waller.

1778. John Kenrick, Jas. Bindley, Wm. Bailey, Wm. Waller, and Martin Whish, July 7.

1781. Jas. Bindley, Wm. Bailey, Wm. Waller, Richd. Tickel, and Goo. Jas. Cholmondeley, Aug. 24.

1782. Jas. Bindley, Wm. Bailey, Wm.

Waller, Richd. Tickel, and hon. John Byng, June 1.

1783. Jas. Bindley, Wm. Bailey, Richd. Tickel, hon. John Byng, and Everard Fawkener.

1793. Jas. Bindley, Wm. Bailey, hon. John Byng, Everard Fawkener, and Chas. Mellish.

1795. Jas. Bindley, hon. John Byng, Everard Fawkener, Chas. Mellish, and Lewis Jenkins.

1797. Jas. Bindley, hon. John Byng, Everard Fawkener, Lewis Jenkins, and Wm. Robt. Spencer.

1799. Jas. Bindley, Lewis Jenkins, Wm. Robt. Spencer, Warwick Lake, and Edwd. Finch Hatton.

1800. Jas. Bindley, Everard Fawkener, Lewis Jenkins, Wm. Robt. Spencer, and Warwick Lake.

1804. Jas. Bindley, Wm. Robt. Spencer, Warwick Lake, Edwd. Finch Hatton, and Lewis Jenkins.

1806. Gilbert Neville Neyle, *chairman*, Jas. Bindley, Wm. Robt. Spencer, Warwick Lake, Edwd. Finch Hatton, Hy. Hallam, and Lewis Jenkins.

1807. The same board, with the addition of Hy. Bouverie, *vice* Jenkins.

1817. Jas. Sedgwick, *chairman*, *vice* Neyle, res.; Jas. Bindley, Wm. Robt. Spencer, Warwick Lake, Edwd. Finch Hatton, Hy. Hallam, a[nd] Hy. Bouverie.

1819. Jas. Sedgwick, *chairman*, Wm. Rob[t.] Spencer, Hy. Hallam, Hy. Bo[u]verie, John Kingston, Meyri[ck] Shaw, and Haviland John A[d]dington.

1823. The same board, with the addition [of] Edwd. John Johnston, *vice* Me[y]rick Shaw, and capt. Wm. [A.] Montagu, *vice* Bouverie, both re[s.]

1826. The same board, with the addition [of] Hy. Seymour Montagu, *vice* Spe[n]cer, res.

1827. Hon. Jas. H. K. Stewart, *chairma[n]*, John Thornton, capt. Wm. [A.] Montagu, Hy. Seymour Montag[u], John Wm. Bowden, capt. Edw[d.] Saurin, R.N., and Richd. We[l]lesley.

1828. The same board, with the excepti[on] of hon. Jas. H. K. Stewart, in li[eu] of whom John Thornton becam[e] chairman.

1833. John Thornton, *chairman*, capt. Wm. A. Montagu, Hy. Seymour Montag[u], John Wm. Bowden, capt. Edw[d.] Saurin, R.N., and Richd. Wellesle[y].

John Wood, *chairman*, John Thor[n]ton, *dep. ch.* Chas. Powlett Rus[h]worth, Hy. Seymour Montag[u], John Wm. Bowden, and cap[t.] Edwd. Saurin, R.N.

Consolidated with the Board of Taxes. See Introduction, *ante*, p. 277, and "Commissioners of Stamps and Taxes," *post*, p. 285.

COMMISSIONERS FOR THE AFFAIRS OF TAXES.

From the accession of George III. in 1760 to the consolidation of the Board with the Board of Stamps in 1834.

* * Edwd. Younge, Hy. Kelsall, Christr. Rigby, Richd. Frankland, John Trenchard, and John Fane.

1762. Edwd. Younge, Christr. Rigby, John Trenchard, John Fane, Geo. Quarme, and Thos. Wyndham, Feb. 15.

Hy. Reade, Edwd. Yonge, Christr. Rigby, John Trenchard, John Fane, Geo. Quarme, and Thos. Wyndham, Apr. 27.

1763. Edwd. Younge, John Trenchard, Thos. Wyndham, Wm. Blair, Danl. Bull, Geo. Blount, and Thos. Bradshaw, Feb. 1.

1765. Edwd. Younge, John Trenchard, Thos. Wyndham, Danl. Bull, Geo. Blount, Thos. Bradshaw, and Christr. Rigby, July 24.

1767. Edwd. Younge, Christr. Rigby, John Trenchard, Thos. Wyndham, Danl. Bull, Geo. Blount, and Edwd. Tucker, Oct. 24.

1773. Christr. Rigby, John Trenchar[d], Thos. Wyndham, Danl. Bull, Ge[o.] Blount, Chas. Deering, and Joh[n] Eames, May 29.

1777. Christr. Rigby, John Trenchar[d], Danl. Bull, Geo. Blount, Cha[s.] Deering, John Eames, and Geo[.] Heathcote.

1783. John Trenchard, Danl. Bull, Geo[.] Blount, Chas. Deering, Joh[n] Eames, Geo. Heathcote, an[d] Alexr. Popham.

1784. John Trenchard, Danl. Bull, Geo[.] Blount, Chas. Deering, Joh[n] Eames, Geo. Heathcote, an[d] Fras. Fownes Luttrell, July 6.

1789. John Trenchard, Danl. Bull, Geo[.] Blount, Chas. Deering, Joh[n] Eames, Fras. Fownes Luttrell[,] Alexr. Popham, and Wm. Lowndes[.]

1791. John Trenchard, Geo. Blount, Chas[.] Deering, John Eames, Fras[.] Fownes Luttrell, Alexr. Popham

Wm. Lowndes, and Barne Barne, Apr. 9.
1793. John Trenchard, Geo. Blount, Chas. Deering, John Eames, Alexr. Popham, Wm. Lowndes, Barne Barne, and Edwd. Meadows.
1795. John Trenchard, Geo. Blount, Chas. Deering, Alexr. Popham, Wm. Lowndes, Barne Barne, Edwd. Meadows, and Horace Hayes.
1798. Wm. Lowndes, Barne Barne, Edwd. Meadows, Horace Hayes, Geo. Trenchard Goodenough, and Hy. Hodgson.
1804. Wm. Lowndes, Barne Barne, Edwd. Meadows, Hy. Hodgson, and Thos. Davis Lamb.
1806. Wm. Lowndes, Barne Barne, Edwd. Meadows, Hy. Hodgson, and Thos. Davis Lamb.
1810. Wm. Lowndes, Barne Barne, Hy. Hodgson, Thos. Davis Lamb, and Gabriel Tucker Steward.
1818. Wm. Lowndes, Barne Barne, Thos. Davis Lamb, Gabriel Tucker Steward, and Chas. Powlett Rushworth.
1819. Wm. Lowndes, Barne Barne, Gabriel Tucker Steward, Chas. Powlett Rushworth, and Wm. Rigby Bradshaw.
1820. Wm. Lowndes, Gabriel Tucker Steward, Chas. Powlett Rushworth, Wm. Rigby Bradshaw, and Sir Hy. Campbell.
1823. Robt. Mitford, Gabriel Tucker Steward, Chas. Powlett Rushworth, Wm. Rigby Bradshaw, and Sir Hy. Campbell.
1828. Robt. Mitford, Chas. Powlett Rushworth, Wm. Rigby Bradshaw, and sir Hy. Campbell.
1833. John Wood, *chairman*, John Thornton, *dep. ch.*, Chas. Powlett Rushworth, Hy. Seymour Montagu, John Wm. Bowden, and Capt. Edwd. Saurin, R.N.

Consolidated with the Board of Stamps. See Introduction, *ante*, p. 277, and "Commissioners of Stamps and Taxes," *infra*.

COMMISSIONERS OF STAMPS AND TAXES.

Under 4 & 5 Will. IV. cap. 60.

1834. John Wood, *chairman*, John Thornton, *dep. ch.*, Chas. Powlett Rushworth, Hy. Seymour Montagu, John Wm. Bowden, and Capt. Edwd. Saurin, R.N.
1838. Lewis Wickham, *chairman*, John Thornton, *dep.-ch.*, Chas. Powlett Rushworth, Hy. Seymour Montagu, John Wm. Bowden, and Capt. Edwd. Saurin, R.N.
Mr. Wood, previously chairman of this board, was appointed chairman of the board of Excise.
1840. The same board, with the exception of John Wm. Bowden, deceased.
1846. Hy. Lewis Wickham, *chairman*, John Thornton, *dep. ch.*, Chas. Powlett Rushworth, Hy. Seymour Montagu, and Alfred Montgomery, *vice* Saurin, transf. to the Board of Customs.
1849. John Wood, *chairman*, John Thornton, *dep. ch.*, Thos. Harrison, Hy. Fredk. Stephenson, Chas. John Herries, Chas. Powlett Rushworth, Alfred Montgomery, and Chas. Pressly. Jan. 6.

Consolidated with the Board of Excise. See Introduction, *ante*, p. 277, and "Commissioners of Inland Revenue," *infra*.

COMMISSIONERS OF INLAND REVENUE.

Under 12 & 13 Vict. cap. 1.

Original Board.

Where marked "ceased" the vacancy was not filled up.

1849. John Wood, *chairman*.
John Thornton, *dep. ch.*, ceased 1855.
Thos. Harrison, *d.* May 6, 1851.
Hy. Fredk. Stephenson.
Chas. John Herries, *dep. ch.* 1857, *vice* Pressly; *chairman* Aug. 15, 1877, *vice* W. H. Stephenson.
1849. Chas. Powlett Rushworth, ceased 1855.
Alfred Montgomery, ceased 1881–2.
Chas. Pressly, *dep. ch.* 1855, *vice* Thornton; *chairman* 1857, *vice* Wood.

Subsequent Appointments.

1855. Hy. Roberts, *vice* Thornton or Rushworth.
1858. Sir. Alexr. Duff Gordon, *vice* Wood.

1858. Jas. Disraeli, *vice* H. F. Stephenson; *d.* 1869.
1863. Wm. Hy. Stephenson, aft. sir W., K.C.B.; *commr. and chairman, vice* Pressly.
1872. Algernon Edwd. West, aft. sir A., *vice* Gordon; *dep. ch.* Aug. 15, 1877, *vice* Herries; *chairman* 1881, *vice* Herries.
1874. Major Hon. Chas. Jas. Keith-Falconer, *vice* Roberts.
1877. Walter Stafford Northcote, aft. visc. St. Cyres and E. of Iddesleigh Aug. 15, *vice* Stephenson; *dep. ch.* 1886, *vice* Young.
1881. Adam Young, commr., *vice* Herries, and *dep. ch.*, *vice* West.
1882. John Arthur Godley, C.B., *vice* Montgomery.
1883. Fredk. Lacey Robinson, *vice* Godley.
1888. Sidney Fras. Godolphin Osborne, *vice* Young.

LORD HIGH STEWARDS OF ENGLAND.

THIS office is of great antiquity, having been established prior to the reign of Edward the Confessor. The Lord High Steward was the prime officer under the king, the office was annexed to the lordship of Hinckley, in Leicestershire, and this lordship belonging to the family of Montfort, earls of Leicester, they were in right of it, Lord High Stewards of England. But Simon de Montfort, the last earl of this family, having made a bad use of the power which this office gave him, raised a rebellion against his sovereign Henry III., and was attainted and his estate forfeited. Henry and his successors in some measure abolished the office, and it is now only revived *pro hâc vice*, to officiate at a coronation or on the trial of a peer.

LORD HIGH STEWARDS OF ENGLAND FROM THE RESTORATION OF KING CHARLES II.

1661 Jas., D. of Ormond; for the coron of Charles II., crowned Apr. 23.
1666. Edwd., E. of Clarendon, ld. chanc.; for the trial of Thos., ld. Morley and Monteagle, Apr. 12.
1676. Heneage, ld. Finch, ld. chanc.; for the trial of Chas., ld. Cornwallis, June 15.
1677. The same; for the trial of Philip, E. of Pembroke and Montgomery, Mar. 18.
1679. The same; for the trial of Thos., E. of Danby, May 10.
The same; for the trial of Wm., E. of Powis; Wm., visc. Stafford; Hy., ld. Arundel of Wardour; Wm., ld. Petre; and John, ld. Belasyse, May 27.
1680. The same; for the trial of Wm., visc. Stafford, Nov. 30.
1685. Jas., D. of Ormond; for the coron. of Jas. II., crowned Apr. 23.
Geo., ld. Jeffreys, ld. chanc.; for the trial of Hy., ld. Delamere, Jan. 9.
1689. Wm., E. of Devonshire; for the coron. of William III. and Mary II., crowned Apr. 11.
1692. Thos., M. of Carmarthen; for the trial of Chas., ld. Mohun, Mar. 25.
1699. John, ld. Somers, ld. chanc.; for the trial of Edwd. Hy., E. of Warwick and Holland, and of Chas., ld. Mohun, Jan. 31.
1702. Wm., D. of Devonshire; for the coron. of Queen Anne, crowned Apr. 13.
1714. Chas., D. of Grafton, for the coron. of George I., crowned Oct. 20.
1716. Wm., ld. Cowper, ld. chanc.; for the trial of Jas., E. of Derwentwater; Wm., ld. Widdrington; Wm., E. of Nithsdale; Robt., E. of Carnwath; Wm., visc. Kenmure; and Wm., ld. Nairne, Jan. 10.
The same; for the trial of Geo., E. of Wintoun, Mar. 15.
1717. The same; for the trial of Robt., E. of Oxford and E. Mortimer, June 24.
1725. Peter, ld. King, ld. chanc.; for the

trial of Thos., E. of Macclesfield, May 14.

727. Lionel Cranfield, D. of Dorset; for the coron. of George II., crowned Oct. 11.

746. Philip, ld. Hardwicke, ld. chanc.; for the trial of Wm., E. of Kilmarnock; Geo., E. of Cromarty; and Arthur, ld. Balmerino, July 5.

747. The same; for the trial of Simon, ld. Lovat, Mar. 9.

760. Robt., ld. Henley, ld. keeper; for the trial of Lawrence, Earl Ferrers, Apr.

761. Wm., Earl Talbot; for the coron. of George III., crowned Sept. 22.

765. Robt., E. of Northington, ld. chanc.; for the trial of Wm. Byron, ld. Byron, May.

776. Hy., E. Bathurst, ld. chanc.; for the trial of Elizth. Chudleigh, duchess of Kingston, Feb. 10.

1788. Edwd., ld. Thurlow, ld. chanc.; for the trial of Warren Hastings, Feb. 12.

1793. Alexr., ld. Loughborough, ld. chanc.; for the trial of the same, Jan. 28.

This trial continued seven years, and ended in the acquittal of Mr. Hastings, Apr. 23, 1795.

1806. Thos., ld. Erskine, ld. chanc.; for the trial of Hy., visc. Melville, Apr. 29.

1821. Hy. Wm., M. of Anglesey; for the coron. of George IV., crowned July 19.

1831. Alexr., D. of Hamilton; for the coron. of William IV., crowned Sept. 8.

1838. The same; for the coron. of Queen Victoria, crowned June 28.

1841. Thos., ld. Denman, l. c. j. of the queen's bench; for the trial of Jas. Thos. Brudenell, E. of Cardigan, Feb. 16.

LORD GREAT CHAMBERLAINS OF ENGLAND AND THEIR DEPUTIES.

This office is hereditary, is of great antiquity, and was anciently of much importance. It was granted by Henry I. to the family of De Vere, earls of Oxford, by whom it was enjoyed for nearly six centuries. On the death of the 18th earl of Oxford, of this family, without issue, in 1625, both the office and earldom were claimed, together with other titles, by Robert Bertie, baron Willoughby De Eresby, in right of his mother, who was sister and heiress of Edward, 17th earl of Oxford. The earldom was awarded by the house of lords to the heir male collateral, in whose son it became extinct; while the office of Hereditary Great Chamberlain was adjudged to be descendible through heirs female, and was consequently confirmed to lord Willoughby De Eresby, who took his seat in the house of lords in that capacity in 1626. This nobleman was created duke of Ancaster and Kesteven in July 1715, and the office descended uninterruptedly in his family until the death of the 4th duke in 1779, when the barony of Willoughby De Eresby fell into abeyance, and the chamberlainship was claimed by five distinct branches of the family. The house of lords decided that it became vested in the two sisters of the deceased 4th duke jointly, and that they were competent to appoint a deputy. In favour of the elder of these sisters the abeyance of the barony of Willoughby De Eresby was terminated, and she became a baroness in her own right. The second sister married into the family of Cholmondeley.

Lord Great Chamberlains of England from 1626.

King Charles I.

1626. Robt., ld. Willoughby De Eresby, by descent from the De Veres, earls of Oxford; cr. E. of Lindsey; *killed at the battle of Edgehill, Oct.* 23, 1642.

1642. Montagu, E. of Lindsey.

King Charles II.

1666. Robt., 3rd E. of Lindsey.

King William III.

1701. Robt., 4th E. of Lindsey; cr. M. of Lindsey in 1706, and D. of Ancaster and Kesteven in 1715.

King George I.

1723. Peregrine, 2nd D. of Ancaster and Kesteven.

King George II.

1742. Peregrine, 3rd D. of Ancaster and Kesteven.

King George III.

1778. Robt., 4th D. of Ancaster and Kesteven; *d.* July 8, 1779.

1779. The office vacant, and the claim to it in dispute for upwards of a year.

1780. Priscilla Barbara Elizth., lady Willoughby De Eresby, and Georgiana, countess, aft. marchs. of Cholmondely, jointly; the baroness *d.* Dec. 29, 1828.

King George IV.

1828. Peter Robt., ld. Willoughby De Eresby, and Georgiana, dowager marchs. of Cholmondeley, jointly; the marchs. *d.* June 23 1838.

Queen Victoria.

1838. Peter Robt., ld. Willoughby De Eresby, *d.* Feb. 22, 1865; and Geo. Horatio, 2nd M. of Cholmondeley, jointly.

1865. Geo. Horatio, 2nd M. of Cholmondeley (*d.* May 8, 1870, *s. p.*); and Albyric, ld. Willoughby De Eresby (*d.* Aug. 26, 1870, *s. p.*), jointly.

1870. Wm. Hy. Hugh, 3rd M. of Cholmondeley, and Clementina Elizth., dowager lady Aveland, aft. lady Willoughby De Eresby, and Charlotte Augusta Annabella, dowager lady Carrington, daurs. of Peter Robt., and sisters and coheiresses of Alberic, ld. Willougby De Eresby, jointly. Lady Carrington *d.* July 26, 1879.

1879. Wm. Hy. Hugh, 3rd M. of Cholmondeley, and Clementina Elizth., lady Willoughby De Eresby, and Chas. Robt., ld. Carrington, jointly. The M. of Cholmondeley *d.* Dec. 16, 1884.

1884. Geo. Hy. Hugh, 4th M. of Cholmondeley, Clementina Elizth., lady Willoughby De Eresby, and Chas. Robt., ld. Carrington, jointly.

Deputy Great Chamberlains of England.

1780. Sir Peter Burrell, bt., husband of Priscilla Barbara Elizth., lady Willoughby d'Eresby, aft. ld. Gwydyr; as deputy to his wife, and for Georgiana, countess and aft. marchs. of Cholmondeley.

1821. Peter Robt., ld. Gwydyr, aft. ld. Willoughby De Eresby, as deputy to lady Willoughby De Eresby and the marchs. of Cholmondeley, above named; succ. to the office in his own right on the death of his mother in 1828; *vide supra.*

1871. Gilbert Hy., ld. Aveland, as deputy to Clementina Elizth., dowager lady Aveland, aft. lady Willoughby De Eresby, and Charlotte Augusta Annabella, dowager lady Carrington, *vide supra.*

1879. Gilbert Hy., ld. Aveland, as deputy to lady Willoughby De Eresby, above named.

LORD HIGH CONSTABLES OF ENGLAND.

The office of Constable existed before the conquest, and seems to have been instituted by the Saxons. It was granted in the reign of Stephen to Milo de Gloucester, earl of Hereford, and went with inheritance, and by the tenure of certain manors in Gloucestershire,* by grand sergeantry, into the family of the Bohuns, earls of Hereford and Essex, and afterwards into the family of Stafford, as heirs-general to them. In

* The castle of Caldecot or Caldecote, near Chepstow, in Monmouthshire, was the residence of the Lord High Constables of England, and was held by them in virtue of their office.

1521 this office became forfeited to the king in the person of Edward Stafford, duke of Buckingham, who was in that year attainted of high treason, and it then ceased to be hereditary. The Lord High Constable is now only appointed *pro hâc vice*, to officiate at coronations or at trials by combat.

Lord High Constables at Coronations from that of Edward VI.

KING EDWARD VI.

1547. Hy., M. of Dorset, aft. D. of Suffolk. The king crowned, Sunday, Feb. 20.

QUEEN MARY.

1553. Wm., E. of Arundel. The queen crowned, Oct. 1.

QUEEN ELIZABETH.

1559. Hy., E. of Arundel. The queen crowned, Jan. 15.

KING JAMES I.

1603. Edwd., E. of Worcester. The king crowned, with his queen, Anne, July 25.

KING CHARLES I.

1626. Geo., D. of Buckingham. The king crowned, with his queen, Henrietta Maria, Feb. 2.

KING CHARLES II.

1661. Algernon, E. of Northumberland. The king crowned, Apr. 23.

KING JAMES II.

1685. Hy., D. of Grafton. The king crowned, Apr. 23.

WILLIAM and MARY.

1689 Jas., D. of Ormond. The king and queen crowned, Apr. 11.

QUEEN ANNE.

1702. Wriothesley, D. of Bedford. The queen crowned, Apr. 13.

KING GEORGE I

1714. John, D. of Montagu. The king crowned, Oct. 20.

KING GEORGE II.

1727. Chas., D. of Richmond, Lenox, and Aubigny. The king crowned, with his queen, Wilhelmina Caroline, Oct. 11.

KING GEORGE III.

1761. John, D. of Bedford. The king crowned, with his queen, Charlotte Sophia, Sept. 22.

KING GEORGE IV.

1821. Arthur, D. of Wellington. The king crowned, July 19.

KING WILLIAM IV.

1831. The same. The king crowned, with his queen, Adelaide, Sept. 8.

QUEEN VICTORIA.

1838. The same. The queen crowned, June 28.

EARL MARSHALS AND THEIR DEPUTIES.

See Part V., "Heraldic," *post*.

THE LORD STEWARD'S DEPARTMENT.

LORD STEWARDS OF THE HOUSEHOLD.

KING HENRY VII.

* * Robert, ld. Brooke.
1502. Sir Gilbert Talbot.

KING HENRY VIII.

1509. Geo., E. of Shrewsbury.
1541. Chas., D. of Suffolk.

1544. Wm., ld. St. John of Basing, aft. E. of Wiltshire, and M. of Winchester.

KING EDWARD VI.

1547. Wm., ld. St. John, *contd.*
1551. John, D. of Northumberland, beheaded in 1553.

QUEEN MARY.

1553. Hy., E. of Arundel.

QUEEN ELIZABETH.

1558. Hy., E. of Arundel, *contd.*
1568. Wm., E. of Pembroke.
1570. Robt., E. of Leicester.
1588. Wm., ld. St. Jonn of Basing, eldest son to the M. of Winchester.

KING JAMES I.

1603. Chas., E. of Nottingham.
1618. Ludovick, D. of Richmond and Lenox.
1623. Jas., M. of Hamilton and E. of Cambridge.

KING CHARLES I.

1625. Wm., E. of Pembroke, *d.* in 1630. The office *vacant* for some years.
1640. Thos., E. of Arundel and Surrey.
1644. Jas., D. of Richmond and Lenox.

KING CHARLES II.

1660. Jas., D. of Ormond.

KING JAMES II.

1685. Jas., D. of Ormond, *contd.*

KING WILLIAM III.

1689. Wm., E., aft. 1st D. of Devonshire.

QUEEN ANNE.

1702. Wm., 1st D. of Devonshire, *contd.; d.* Aug. 18, 1707.
1707. Wm., 2nd D. of Devonshire, Sept. 8.
1710. John, D. of Buckinghamshire and Normandy.
1711. John, E. Paulet.

KING GEORGE I.

1714. Wm., 2nd D. of Devonshire, *again.*
1716. Hy., D. of Kent.
1718. John, D. of Argyle and Greenwich.
1725. Lionel Cranfield, D. of Dorset.

KING GEORGE II.

1727. Lionel Cranfield, D. of Dorset, *contd.*
1730. Philip Dormer, E. of Chesterfield.
1733. Wm., 3rd D. of Devonshire.
1737 Lionel Cranfield, D. of Dorset, *again.*
1744 Wm , 3rd D. of Devonshire, *again.*
1749. Chas., D. of Marlborough, June 12.
1755. John, D. of Rutland.

KING GEORGE III.

1760. John, D. of Rutland, *contd.*
1761. Wm., E. of Talbot.
1782. Fredk., E. of Carlisle, May 4.
1783. Chas., D. of Rutland, Feb. 14.
William, E. of Dartmouth, Apr. 9.
Jas., D. of Chandos, Dec. 26; *d.* Oct. 1789.
1789. John Fredk., D. of Dorset, Oct. 7.
1799. Geo., E. of Leicester, Feb. 20.
1802. Geo., E. of Dartmouth, Aug. 15.
1804. Heneage, E. of Aylesford, May 30.
1812. Geo. Jas., E., aft. M. of Cholmondeley, Feb. 19.

KING GEORGE IV.

1821. Hy., M. of Conyngham, Dec. 11.

KING WILLIAM IV.

1830. Richd., D. of Buckingham and Chandos, July 16.
Richd., marq. Wellesley, Nov. 23.
1833. Geo. Wm., D. of Argyll, Sept. 12.
1835. Thos., E. of Wilton, Jan. 5.
Geo. Wm., D. of Argyll, *again*, Apr. 23.

QUEEN VICTORIA.

1839. Wm. Geo., E. of Erroll, Nov. 15.
1841. Chas. Cecil, E. of Liverpool, Sept. 3.
1846. Hugh, E. Fortescue, July 9.
1850. Richd., M. of Westminster, Mar. 22.
1852. Jas., D. of Montrose, K.T., Feb. 27, **G.**
1853. Hy. Chas., D. of Norfolk, K.G., Jan. 4, **G.**
1854. Fredk., E. Spencer, K.G., Jan. 10, **G.**
1857. Edwd. Granville, E. of St. Germans, G.C.B., Nov. 23, **G.**
1858. Brownlow, M. of Exeter, K.G., Feb. 26, **G.**
1859. Edwd. Granville, E. of St. Germans, G.C.B., *again*, June 18, **G.**
1866. John Geo. Brabazon, E. of Bessborough, Jan. 20, **G.**
John Winston, D. of Marlborough, July 10, **G.**
1867. Chas., E. of Tankerville, Mar. 19, **G.**
1868. John Geo. Brabazon, E. of Bessborough, *again*, Dec, 12, sw.
1874. Fredk., E. Beauchamp, Mar. 2, **G.**
1880. John Robt., Earl Sydney, G.C.B., May 3, **G.**
1885. Wm. Hy., E. of Mount-Edgcumbe, June 27, sw.
1886. John Robt., Earl Sydney, G.C.B., *again*, Feb. 10, **G.**
Wm. Hy., E. of Mount-Edgcumbe, *again*, Aug. 16, **G.**

TREASURERS OF THE HOUSEHOLD.

KING HENRY VII.

* * Sir Richd. Croft.
1500. Sir Thos. Lovell.

KING HENRY VIII.

1521. Sir Thos. Boleyn (father of Q. Anna Boleyn), aft. visc. Rochford and E. of Wiltshire, Dec.
1537. Sir Wm. Fitzwilliam, aft. E. of Southampton.
1538. Sir Wm. Paulet, aft. ld. St. John of Basing, E. of Wiltshire and M. of Winchester.
1541. Sir Thos. Cheney.

KING EDWARD VI.

1547. Sir Thos. Cheney, *contd.*

QUEEN MARY.

The office *vacant.*

QUEEN ELIZABETH.

1560. Sir Thos. Parry.
* * Sir Edwd. Montagu.
1586. Sir Fras. Knollys, K.G.
1597. Roger, ld. North.
1601. Sir Wm. Knollys.

KING JAMES I.

1603. Sir Wm. Knollys, *contd.*; aft. ld. Knollys, visc. Wallingford, and E. of Banbury.
1616. Edwd., ld. Wotton.
1618. Sir Thos. Edmonds.

KING CHARLES I.

1625. Sir Thos. Edmonds, *contd.*
1639. Sir Hy. Vane, sen.
1641. Thos., visc. Savile, in Ireland, and ld. Savile of Pomfret, in England.

KING CHARLES II.

1660. Sir Fredk. Cornwallis, bt., aft. ld. Cornwallis.
1663. Chas., visc. Fitz-Harding, of Ireland.
1668. Sir Thos. Clifford, ld. Clifford of Chudleigh.
1672. Fras., ld. Newport, aft. visc. Newport and E. of Bradford.

KING JAMES II.

1686. Wm., E. of Yarmouth.

KING WILLIAM III.

1689. Fras., ld. Newport, *again.*

QUEEN ANNE.

1702. Fras., now E. of Bradford, *contd.*
1708. Hugh, E. of Cholmondeley.
1712. Geo., E. Lansdowne of Bideford, Aug. 18.

KING GEORGE I.

1714. Hugh, E. of Cholmondeley, *again.*
1725. Paul Methuen, aft. sir P., K.B.

KING GEORGE II.

1727. Sir Paul Methuen, *contd.*
1730. Robt., ld. Bingley.
1731. John, ld., aft. E. De la Warr, K.B., June 12.
1737. Benjn., E. Fitzwalter.
1755. John, ld. Berkeley of Stratton.
1756. John, visc. Bateman, Nov. 19.
1757. Percy, E. of Thomond, July 8.

KING GEORGE III.

1760. Percy, E. of Thomond, *contd.*
1761. Hy. Arthur, E. of Powis.
1765. Geo., ld. Edgcumbe, aft. visc. Mount Edgcumbe.
1766. John Shelly, aft. sir J.
1777. Fredk., E. of Carlisle, June 13.
1779. Geo., ld. Onslow and Cranley.
1780. Jas., visc. Cranbourn, aft. E. of Salisbury, Sept.
1782. Thos., E. of Effingham, Apr. 10.
1783. Hon. Chas. Greville, Apr.
1784. Jas., E. of Courtown, Aug.
1793. Jas. Geo., visc. Stopford, June 20.
1806. Chas. Aug., ld. Ossulston, Feb. 12.
1807. Jas. Geo., visc. Stopford, *again*, Mar. 31; aft. E. of Courtown.
1812. Robt., visc. Jocelyn, May 8.
Lord Wm. Chas. Cavendish Bentinck, July 29.

KING GEORGE IV.

1826. Sir Wm. Hy. Fremantle, Apr. 29.

KING WILLIAM IV.

1830. Sir Wm. Hy. Fremantle, *contd.*

QUEEN VICTORIA.

1837. Hy. Chas., E. of Surrey, July 19.
1841. Geo. Stevens Byng, aft. ld. Strafford, visc. Enfield, and E. of Strafford, June 23.
Fredk. Wm., Earl Jermyn, Sept. 9.
1846. Lord Robt. Grosvenor, Aug. 4.
1847. Lord Arthur Marcus Cecil Hill, July 22.
1852. Lord Claude Hamilton, Feb. 27, **G.**
1853. Geo. Aug. Constantine, E. of Mulgrave, aft. M. of Normanby, Jan. 4, **G.**
1858. Lord Claude Hamilton, *again*, Feb. 26, **G.**
1859. Hon. Wm. Coutts Keppel, c.c. visc. Bury, June 23, **G.**

1866. Hon. Otho Aug. Fitzgerald, c.c. ld. Otho Fitzgerald, May 8, **G.**
Wm. Alleyne Cecil, c.c. ld. Burghley, July 10, **G.**
1867. Hon. Percy Egerton Herbert, C.B., Feb. 27, **G.**
1868. Geo., ld. de Tabley, Dec. 12, **G.**
1872. Aug. Fredk. Geo. Warwick, ld. Poltimore, Mar. 1, **G.**
1874. Wm. John, ld. Monson, Jan. 1, **G.**
1874. Hon. Hy. Geo. Percy, c.c. E. Percy, Mar. 2, **G.**
1875. Hon. Hy. Fredk. Thynne, c.c. ld. Hy. Thynne, Dec. 14, **G.**
1880. Gavin, E. of Breadalbane, May 3, **G.**
1885. Wm. Pleydell-Bouverie, c.c. visc. Folkestone, June 27, **G.**
1886. Victor Alexr., E. of Elgin and Kincardine, Feb. 17, **G.**
Wm. Pleydell-Bouverie, c.c. visc. Folkestone, *again*, Aug. 5, **G.**

COMPTROLLERS OF THE HOUSEHOLD.

KING HENRY VII.

* * Sir Richd. Edgcumbe.

KING HENRY VIII.

* * Sir Edwd. Poynings.
1537. Sir John Russell, aft. ld. Russell and E. of Bedford.
1542. Sir John Gage.

KING EDWARD VI.

1547. Sir John Gage, *contd.*
Sir Wm. Paget, aft. ld. Paget.
1550. Sir Anthy. Wingfield.

QUEEN MARY.

1553. Sir Robt. Rochester, K.G.
1557. Sir Thos. Cornwallis.

QUEEN ELIZABETH.

1558. Sir Thos. Parry.
1560. Sir Edwd. Rogers.
1565. Sir Jas. Crofts.
1588. Sir Fras. Knollys.
1590. Sir Wm. Knollys, (his son), aft. ld. Knollys and visc. Wallingford.
1601. Sir Edwd. Wotton, aft. ld. Wotton.

KING JAMES I.

1603. Sir Edwd., now ld. Wotton, *contd.*
Sir Hy. Carey.
1616. Sir Thos. Edmondes, K.B.
1618. Sir Hy. Carey, aft. visc. Falkland.
1621. Sir John Suckling.

KING CHARLES I.

1625. Sir John Savile, aft. ld. Savile, and E. of Sussex.
1628. Sir Hy. Vane, sen.
1640. Sir Thos. Jermyn.
1641. Sir Peter Wyche.
1642. Sir Christr. Hatton, aft. ld. Hatton.

KING CHARLES II.

1660. Sir Chas. Berkeley, aft. visc. Fitzharding.
1660. Sir Hugh Pollard, K.B.
1666. Sir Thos. Clifford, aft. ld. Clifford of Chudleigh.
1668. Fras., ld. Newport, aft. visc. Newport and E. of Bradford.
1672. Wm., ld. Maynard.

KING JAMES II.

1685. Hy., ld. Waldegrave.

KING WILLIAM III.

1689. Hon. Thos. Wharton, aft. ld., E., and M. of Wharton.

QUEEN ANNE.

1702. Sir Edwd. Seymour, bt.
1704. Sir Thos. Mansell, bt., aft. ld. Mansell, Apr. 27.
1708. Hugh, E. of Cholmondeley, May.
Sir Thos. Felton, bt., Oct.
1709. Sir John Holland, bt., June 2.
1711. Sir Thos. Mansell, bt., aft. ld. Mansell, *again.*
1712. Geo., ld. Lansdowne of Bideford.
1713. Sir John Stonehouse, bt.

KING GEORGE I.

1714. Hugh Boscawen, aft. visc. Falmouth.
1720. Paul Methuen, aft. sir P., K.B.
1725. Daniel, ld. Finch, aft. E. of Winchelsea and Nottingham.

KING GEORGE II.

1727. Danl., ld. Finch, *contd.*
1730. Hon. sir Conyers D'Arcy, June 11.
1754. Wills, E. of Hillsborough.
1755. John, ld. Hobart, aft. E. of Buckinghamshire.
1756. Hon. Richd. Edgcumbe, aft. ld. Edgcumbe, Nov. 19.

KING GEORGE III.

1760. Richd., ld. Edgcumbe, *contd.*
1761. Hy. Arthur, E. of Powis, May 31.
Lord Geo. Cavendish, Nov.
1762. Lord Chas. Spencer.
1763. Humphrey Morrice, Jan. 10.
1765. Thos. Pelham, aft. ld. Pelham, Sept. 6.
1774. Sir Wm. Meredith, bt., Mar. 9.
1777. Geo., ld. Onslow and Cranley.
1779. Sir Richd. Worsley, bt.

1782. Peter, earl Ludlow.
1784. Robt., visc. Galway.
1787. Hon. John Chas. Villiers, Feb. 19.
1790. Hon. Dudley Ryder, aft. ld. Harrowby, Feb. 27.
1791. Geo., visc. Parker, aft. E. of Macclesfield, Apr. 21.
1797. Lord Chas. Hy. Somerset, Apr. 27.
1804. Lord Geo. Thynne, May 31.
1812. Lord Geo. Thos. Beresford, July 29.

KING GEORGE IV.

1820. Lord Geo. Thos. Beresford, *contd.*

KING WILLIAM IV.

1830. Lord Robt. Grosvenor, Nov. 23.
1834. Hon. Hy. Thos. Lowry Corry, Dec. 29.
1835. Geo. Stevens Byng, aft. ld. Strafford, visc. Enfield, and E. of Strafford, May 7.

QUEEN VICTORIA.

1837. Geo. Stevens Byng, *contd.*
1841. Lord Arthur Marcus Cecil Hill, June 23.
1841. Hon. Geo. Lionel Dawson Damer, Sept. 9.
1846. Lord A. M. C. Hill, *again*, July 7.
1847. Hon. Wm. Sebright Lascelles, July 22.
1851. Geo. Aug. Constantine, E. of Mulgrave, aft. M. of Normanby, July 23.
1852. Geo. Cecil Weld Forester, Feb. 27, **G.**
1853. Archibald, visc. Drumlanrig, aft. M. of Queensberry, Jan. 4, **G.**
1856. Hon. Val. Aug. Browne, c.c. visc. Castlerosse, aft. E. of Kenmare, July 25, **G.**
1858. Geo. Cecil Weld Forester, *again*, Feb. 26, **G.**
1859. Hon. Granville Leveson, c.c. ld. Proby, June 23, **G.**
1866. Hon. Chas. Philip Yorke, c.c. visc. Royston, July 10, **G.**
1868. Hon. Otho Aug. Fitzgerald, c.c. ld. Otho Fitzgerald, Dec. 12, **G.**
1874. Hon. Hy. Richd. Chas. Somerset, c.c. ld. Hy. Somerset, Mar. 2, **G.**
1879. Hon. Hugh De Grey Seymour, c.c. E. of Yarmouth, Feb. 4, **G.**
1880. Wm., ld. Kensington, May 3, **G.**
1885. Arthur Wm. Hill, c.c. ld. Arthur Hill, June 27, **G.**
1886. Hon. Edwd. Majoribanks, Feb. 10, **G.**
1886. Arthur Wm. Hill, c.c. ld. Arthur Hill, *again*, Aug. 5, **G.**

COFFERERS OF THE HOUSEHOLD.

THIS office was abolished in 1782 by 22 Geo. III. cap. 82, and the duties transferred to the lord steward and the paymaster of the household.

COFFERERS OF THE HOUSEHOLD.

From the reign of Queen Elizabeth to the abolition of the office in 1782.

QUEEN ELIZABETH.

* * Sir Hy. Cocks.

KING JAMES I.

1603. Sir Richd. Vernou.
1615. Sir Arthur Ingram.
1620. Sir Marmaduke Darrell.

KING CHARLES I.

1625. Sir Hy. Vane.
1628. Sir John Suckling.
1642. Wm. Ashburnham.

KING CHARLES II.

* * Wm. Ashburnham, *contd.*

KING JAMES II.

* * Sir Peter Apsley.

KING WILLIAM III.

* * Hy. Herbert, aft. ld. Herbert of Chirbury.

QUEEN ANNE.

1702. Sir Benjn. Bathurst.
1704. Hon. Fras. Godolphin, aft. visc. Rialton, and E. of Godolphin.
1711. Saml. Masham, aft. ld. Masham.

KING GEORGE I.

1714. Francis, E. of Godolphin, *again*.
1723. Wm. Pulteney, aft. E. of Bath.
1725. Hy., 7th E. of Lincoln.

KING GEORGE II.

1727. Hy., E. of Lincoln, *contd.*
1730. Horace Walpole, aft. ld. Walpole.
1741. Sir Wm. Yonge, bt. and K.B.
1743. Saml., ld. Sandys.
1744. Edmd. Waller.
1746. Hy., 9th E. of Lincoln, aft. D. of Newcastle.
1754. Sir Geo. Lyttelton, bt., aft. ld. Lyttelton.
1755. Thos., D. of Leeds.

KING GEORGE III.

1760. Thos., D. of Leeds, *contd.*
1761. Hon. Jas. Grenville, Apr. 17.
Percy, E. of Thomond, Nov. 18.
1765. Richd., E. of Scarborough, July 12.
1766. Hans Stanley.
1774. Jeremiah Dyson.
1776. Hans Stanley, *again.*
1780. Fras., visc. Beauchamp, aft. 2n E. of Yarmouth and M. of Her ford.

Office abolished in 1782 by 22 Geo. III. cap. 82.

TREASURERS OF THE CHAMBER.

THIS office was abolished in 1782 by 22 Geo. III. cap. 82, and th duties transferred to the lord steward and the paymaster of the house hold.

TREASURERS OF THE CHAMBER.

From the Restoration to the abolition of the office in 1782.

KING CHARLES II.

* * Sir Edwd. Griffin, bt.

KING JAMES II.

1685. Sir Edwd. Griffin, *contd.*

KING WILLIAM III.

1689. Sir Rowland Gwin.
1692. Edwd., aft. E. of Orford.

QUEEN ANNE.

1702. Chas., visc. Fitzharding.
1713. John, ld. De la Warr.

KING GEORGE I.

1714. Chas. Bodville, E. of Radnor.
1720. Hon. Hy. Pelham.
1722. Hon. Chas. Stanhope.

KING GEORGE II.

1727. Sir John Hobart, bt., aft. l Hobart and E. of Buckinghar shire.
1744. Sir John Hinde Cotton, bt.
1746. Hon. Richd. Arundel.
1747. Saml., ld. Sandys.
1755. Wills, E. of Hillsborough.
1756. Hon. Chas. Townshend.

KING GEORGE III.

1760. Hon. Chas. Townshend, *contd.*
1761. Sir Fras. Dashwood, bt., aft. ld. I Despencer.
1762. Sir Gilbert Elliot, bt.
1770. Geo. Rice.
1779. Lord Chas. Spencer.

Office abolished in 1782 by 22 Geo. III. cap. 82.

THE LORD CHAMBERLAIN'S DEPARTMENT.

LORD CHAMBERLAINS OF THE HOUSEHOLD.

KING HENRY VII.

1485. Sir Wm. Stanley, *beheaded.*
1508. Sir Chas Somerset, aft. ld. Herbert and E of Worcester.

KING HENRY VIII.

1509. Chas., E of Worcester, *contd.*
1526. Hy., E. of Arundel.
1530. Wm., ld. Sandys of the Vine.
1535. Wm., ld. St. John of Basing.

KING EDWARD VI.

1547. Wm., ld. St. John of Basing, *contd.*
1550. Thos., ld. Wentworth.
1551. Thos., ld. D'Arcy of Chiche.

QUEEN MARY.

1553. John, ld. Williams.
1557. Wm., ld. Howard of Effingham.

QUEEN ELIZABETH.

1558. Wm., ld. Howard of Effingham, *con*
1572. Thos., E. of Sussex.
1585. Hy., ld. Hunsdon.
1596. Geo., ld. Hunsdon.

KING JAMES I.

1603. Geo., ld. Hunsdon, *contd.*
Thos., E. of Suffolk.
1613. Robt., E. of Somerset.
1615. Wm., E. of Pembroke

KING CHARLES I.

1625. Wm., E. of Pembroke, *contd.*
Philip, E. of Montgomery, and aft. of Pembroke.
1641. Robt., E. of Essex.
1642. Edwd., E. of Dorset.

KING CHARLES II.

1660. Edwd., E. of Manchester.
1671. Hy., E. of St. Albans.
1674. Hy., E. of Arlington.
1681. John, E. of Mulgrave, aft. D. of Buckingham.

KING JAMES II.

1685. Robt., E. of Ailesbury and Elgin, July.
Thos., E. of Ailesbury and Elgin, Oct.
1686. John, E. of Mulgrave, aft. D. of Buckingham, *again*.

KING WILLIAM III.

1689. Chas., E. of Dorset and Middlesex.
1695. Robt., E. of Sunderland.
1699. Chas., D. of Shrewsbury.
1700. Edwd., E. of Jersey.

QUEEN ANNE.

1702. Edwd., E. of Jersey, *contd.*
1704. Hy., E. of Kent, aft. M. and D. of Kent.
1714. Chas., D. of Shrewsbury.

KING GEORGE I.

1714. Chas., D. of Shrewsbury, *contd.*
1715. Chas., D. of Bolton, June 19; res. July 4, following.
The office vacant.
1717. Thos., D. of Newcastle, Apr. 14.
1724. Chas., D. of Grafton.

KING GEORGE II.

1727. Chas., D. of Grafton, *contd.*
1757. Wm., D. of Devonshire.

KING GEORGE III.

1760. Wm., D. of Devonshire, *contd.*
1762. Geo., D. of Marlborough, Nov. 22.
1763. Granville, earl Gower, Apr. 22.
1765. Wm. Hy., D. of Portland, July 10.
1766. Fras., E. of Hertford, aft. 1st E. of Yarmouth and M. of Hertford, Dec. 4.
1782. Geo., D. of Manchester, Apr. 10.
1783. Fras., E. of Hertford, aft 1st E. of Yarmouth and M. of Hertford, *again*, Apr. 9.
Jas., E., aft. M. of Salisbury, Dec. 26.
1804. Geo., E. of Dartmouth, May 14.
1812. Fras., 2nd M. of Hertford, Mar. 5.

KING GEORGE IV.

1821. Jas., D. of Montrose, Dec. 11.
1827. Wm. Spencer, D. of Devonshire, May 5.
1828. Jas., D. of Montrose, *again*, Feb. 18.

KING WILLIAM IV.

1830. Geo. Child, E. of Jersey, July 24.
William Spencer, D. of Devonshire, *again*, Nov. 22.
1834. Geo. Child, E. of Jersey, *again*, Dec. 15.
1835. Richd., M. Wellesley, Apr.
Fras. Nathl., Marq. Conyngham, May.

QUEEN VICTORIA.

1839. Hy., E. of Uxbridge, May 6.
1841. Geo. John, E. De la Warr, Sept. 14.
1846. Fredk., earl Spencer, July 8.
1848. John, M. of Breadalbane, Sept. 4.
1852. Brownlow, M. of Exeter, K.G., Feb. 27, **G.**
1853. John, M. of Breadalbane, K.T., *again*, Jan. 15, **G.**
1858. Geo. John, E. De la Warr, Feb. 26, **G.**
1859. John Robt., visc. Sydney, June 23, **G.**
1866. Orlando Geo. Chas., E. of Bradford, July 10, **G.**
1868. John Robt., visc. Sydney, G.C.B., *again*, Dec. 9, **G.**
1874. Fras. Hugh Geo., M. of Hertford, Mar. 2, **G.**
1879. Wm. Hy., E. of Mount-Edgcumbe, May 7, **G.**
1880. Valentine Augustus, E. of Kenmare, K.P., May 3, **G.**
1885. Edwd., E. of Lathom, June 27, **G.**
1886. Valentine Augustus, E. of Kenmare, K.P., *again*, Feb. 10, **G.**
Edwd., E. of Lathom, *again*, Aug. 5, **G.**

MASTERS OF THE GREAT WARDROBE.

THE Master or Keeper of the Great Wardrobe was an officer of great antiquity and dignity. High privileges and immunities were conferred upon him by King Henry VI., and were confirmed to him by his successors. King James I. not only enlarged these, but ordained that the office should be a corporation or body politic for ever. The salary of this officer was £2,000 per annum. He was usually a personage o high political consideration, and subordinate to him were a comptroller a patent clerk, and many other officers and servants.

The wardrobe establishment was abolished in 1782 by 22 Geo. III cap. 82, and the duties transferred to the department of the lord cham berlain.

Masters of the Great Wardrobe.

From the reign of King James I. to the abolition of the office in 1782.

King James I.

* * Geo., ld. Hume of Berwick, aft. E. of Dunbar, in Scotland.
1616. Jas., ld. Hay, aft. E. of Carlisle.
1636. Wm., visc. Fielding, aft. E. of Denbigh.

King Charles I.

* * Spencer, E. of Northampton.
1642. Wm. Legge.

King Charles II.

1660. Edwd., E. of Sandwich.
1672. Ralph Montagu, aft. ld., E., and D. of Montagu.

King James II.

1685. Jas., E. of Arran, aft. D. of Hamilton.

King William III.

1689. Ralph, lord Montagu, aft. E. and D. of Montagu, *again.*

Queen Anne.

1702. Ralph, E., aft. D. of Montagu, *contd*
1709. John, D. of Montagu.

King George I.

1714. John, D. of Montagu, *contd.*

King George II.

1727. John, D. of Montagu, *contd.*
1750. Sir Thos. Robinson, K.B., aft. ld. Grantham, deputy mast.
1754. Wm. Wildman, visc. Barrington.
1755. Sir Thos. Robinson, K.B., aft. ld. Grantham; *again.*

King George III.

1760. Granville, E. Gower.
1763. Fras., ld. Le Despencer.
1765. John, E. of Ashburnham.
1775. Thos., ld. Pelham.

Office abolished in 1782 by 22 Geo. III. cap. 82.

VICE-CHAMBERLAINS OF THE HOUSEHOLD.

King Henry VIII.

* * Sir John Gage.

King Edward VI.

* * Sir Anthy. Wingfield.
* * Sir John Gates.
1550. Sir Thos. D'Arcy.

Queen Mary.

1553. The office *vacant.*

Queen Elizabeth.

* * Sir Edwd. Rogers.
* * Sir Thos. Heneage.
1577. Sir Christr. Hatton, Nov. 11.
1602. Sir John Stanhope, aft. ld. Stanhope of Harrington.

King James I.

1603. John, ld. Stanhope, *contd.*
1616. Sir John Digby, aft. ld. Digby and E. of Bristol.

King Charles I.

1625. Sir Dudley Carleton, aft. ld. Carleton and visc. Dorchester.
1626. Sir Hy. May.
Sir Thos. Jermyn.
1640. Geo., ld. Goring, aft. E. of Norwich.

King Charles II.

1660. Sir Geo. Carteret.
1670. Hy. Savile or Saville.

King Jame

1685. Hy. Savile, *contd.*
1686. Jas. Porter.

King William III

1689. Sir John Lowther, bt., aft. visc. Lonsdale.
1690. Hon. Peregrine Bertie.

QUEEN ANNE.

1702. Hon. Peregrine Bertie, *contd.*
1706. Thos. Coke, aft. ld. Lovel and E. of Leicester, Dec. 5.

KING GEORGE I.

1714. Thos. Coke, *contd.*
1727. Wm. Stanhope, aft. E. of Harrington.

KING GEORGE II.

1727. Wm. Stanhope, *contd.*
1730. Lord John Hervey, May 8.
1740. Lord Sydney Beauclerk, May 1.
1742. Hon. Wm. Finch, July 13.

KING GEORGE III.

1760. Hon. Wm. Finch, *contd.*
1765. Geo. Bussy, visc. Villiers, aft. E. of Jersey, July 12.
1770. Hon. Thos. Robinson, aft. ld. Grantham, Feb. 13.
1771. John, visc. Hinchinbroke, Feb. 6.
1782. Geo., visc. Chewton, aft. E. Waldegrave, May 2.
1784. Geo., ld. Herbert, aft. E. of Pembroke, Nov. 20.
1794. Chas. Fulke Greville, Aug.
1804. Lord John Thynne, July 11.
1812. Fras. Chas., E. of Yarmouth, aft. 3rd M. of Hertford, Mar. 10.
Robt., visc. Jocelyn, Aug. 15.

KING GEORGE IV

1821. Jas., M. of Graham, Feb. 7.
1827. Sir Saml. Hulse, May 5.

KING WILLIAM IV.

1830. Geo., E. of Belfast, aft. M. of Donegal, July 24.
1834. Fredk, visc. Castlereagh, Dec. 27.
1835. Lord Chas. Fitzroy, June 29.

QUEEN VICTORIA.

1838. Geo., E. of Belfast, aft. M. of Donegal, *again*; May 2.
1841. Lord Ernest Aug. Brudenell Bruce, Sept. 8.
1846. Lord Edwd. Geo. Fitz-Alan Howard, July 8.
1852. Orlando Geo. Chas., visc. Newport, aft. E. of Bradford, Mar. 5, **G.**
Lord Ernest Aug. Brudenell Bruce, *again*, Dec. 30, **G.**
1858. Orlando Geo. Chas., visc. Newport, aft. E. of Bradford, *again*, Feb. 26, **G.**
1859. Val. Aug. Browne, c.c. visc. Castlerosse, aft. E. of Kenmare, June 23, **G.**
1866 Claude Hamilton, c.c. ld. Claude Hamilton, July 10, **G.**
1868. Val. Aug. Browne, c.c. visc. Castlerosse, aft. E. of Kenmare, *again*, Dec. 12, **G.**
1872. Richd. De Aquila Grosvenor, c.c. ld. Richd. Grosvenor, Feb. 25, **G.**
1874. Geo. Wm., visc. Barrington, Mar. 2, **G.**
1880. Chas. Wm. Brudenell Bruce, c.c. ld. Chas. Bruce, May 3, **G.**
1885. Wm. Heneage Legge, c.c., visc. Lewisham, June 27, **G.**
1886. Fredk. Edwd. Gould, visc. Kilcoursie, Feb. 17.
Wm. Heneage Legge, c.c. visc. Lewisham, *again*, Aug. 5, **G.**

GOVERNORS AND CONSTABLES OF WINDSOR CASTLE.

See Part IV., *post.*

CAPTAINS OF HER MAJESTY'S BODY-GUARD, OR THE YEOMEN OF THE GUARD.

THE Body-Guard of the Queen is the oldest corps in Her Majesty's service. The corps was instituted by Henry VII. in 1485, neary two hundred years before any regiment that is now in existence was raised; it was, in fact, the only standing force in the kingdom, with the exception of the Honourable Corps of Gentlemen-at-Arms.

The officers of the corps consist of a captain, who is now always a peer, and a member of the privy council, and who carries a gold stick of office; a lieutenant, an ensign, four exons, and an adjutant or clerk of the cheque. All the officers, under the captain, carry, when on duty, a silver stick of office, which they have the privilege of receiving, at a private audience, immediately from the hands of the sovereign.

The office of captain is now a political one, and the holder resigns on a change of ministry.

Captains of the Yeomen of the Guard.

From the institution of the corps by King Henry VII. in 1485.

King Henry VII.

1486. John, E. of Oxford.
1488. Sir Chas. Somerset, aft. ld. Herbert, and E. of Worcester.

King Henry VIII.

1509. Sir Chas. Somerset, *contd.*
1514. Sir Hy. Guilford, K.G.
1521. Sir Hy. Marney, aft. ld. Marney, K.G.
1523. Sir Wm. Kingston, K.G.
1536. Sir Anthy. Wingfield, K.G.

King Edward VI.

1547. Sir Anthy. Wingfield, K.G., *contd.*
1550. Sir Thos. D'Arcy, aft. ld. D'Arcy, K.G.

Queen Mary.

1553. Sir Hy. Jernyngham.

Queen Elizabeth.

1558. Sir Wm. St. Loe.
1569. Sir Fras. Knowlys.
1578. Sir Christr. Hatton, K.G., aft. ld. Hatton.
1587. Sir — Goodier.
1592. John Best, champion of England.
1597. Sir Walter Raleigh.

King James I.

1603. Sir Thos. Erskine, aft. visc. Fenton, and E. of Kellie, K.G.
1617. Hy., E. of Holland.

King Charles I.

1625. Hy., E. of Holland, *contd.*
1630. Sir Christr. Musgrave.
1632. Geo., E. of Kinnoul.
1635. Wm., E. of Morton, K.G.

King Charles II.

1660. Geo., visc. Grandison.
1662. Chas., E. of Norwich.
1670. Chas., E. of Manchester.

Queen Anne.

1702. Wm., M. of Hartington, aft. D. of Devonshire.
1707. Chas., visc. Townshend, K.G.

King George I.

1714. Hy., ld. Paget, aft. E. of Uxbridge.
1715. Jas., E. of Derby.
1723. Philip Dormer, ld. Stanhope, aft. E. of Chesterfield, K.G.
1725. John, E. of Leicester, K.B.

King George II.

1727. John, E. of Leicester, K.B., *contd.*
1731. John, ld. Ashburnham, aft. E. of Ashburnham.
1733. Chas., E. of Tankerville, K.B.
1737. Wm., D. of Manchester, K.B.
1739. Wm., E. of Essex, K.G.
1743. John, ld. Berkeley of Stratton.
1746. Pattee, visc. Torrington.
1747. Hugh, visc. Falmouth.

King George III.

1760. Hugh, visc. Falmouth, *contd.*
1782. John Fredk., D. of Dorset, Feb.
1783. Geo. Jas., E. of Cholmondeley, Apr.
Heneage, E. of Aylesford, Dec. 16.
1804. Thos., ld. Pelham.
Geo., E. of Macclesfield.

King George IV.

1820. Geo., E. of Macclesfield, *contd.*

King William IV.

1830. Ulick John, M. of Clanricarde. Dec. 1.
1834. Archd., E. of Gosford, Sept. 3.
1835. Jas. Geo., E. of Courtown, Jan. 5.
Archd., E. of Gosford, Apr.

Queen Victoria.

1837. Hy. Stephen, E. of Ilchester, July 22.
1841. Hy. Chas., E. of Surrey, July 5.
John Wm., M. of Lothian, Sept. 8.
1842. Geo., E. of Beverley, Jan. 18.
1846. Lucius, visc. Falkland, July 24.
1848. Geo., M. of Donegal, Feb. 16.
1852. Wm. Lennox Lascelles, ld. de Ros, Feb. 27, **G.**
John Robt., visc., aft. E. Sydney, Dec. 30.
1858. Wm. Lennox Lascelles, ld. de Ros, Mar. 17, **G.**
1859. Hy. John, E. of Ducie, June 28, **G.**
1866. Hy. Chas., E. Cadogan, July 10, **G.**
1868. Wm. Amelius Aubrey de Vere, D. of St. Albans, Dec. 22, **G.**
1874. Edwd., ld. Skelmersdale, aft. E. of Lathom, Mar. 2, **G.**
1880. Wm. John, ld. Monson, May 3, **G.**
1885. Geo. Wm., visc. Barrington, June 27, **G.**
1886. Wm. John, ld. Monson, *again*, Feb. 10, **G.**
Algernon Hawkins Thomond, E. of Kintore, Aug. 5, **G.**

CAPTAINS OF THE CORPS OF GENTLEMEN-AT-ARMS, FORMERLY THE BAND OF GENTLEMEN PENSIONERS.

:HE Honourable Corps of Gentlemen-at-Arms (formerly styled the Band of Gentlemen Pensioners) is the oldest corps in England, with he exception of the Yeomen of the Guard and the Sergeants-at-Arms. 'his corps was instituted in 1509, soon after Henry VIII. ascended the hrone, and was composed entirely of gentlemen of noble blood. The fficers of the corps consist of a captain, who is always a peer and a nember of the privy council, a lieutenant, a standard bearer, and an djutant or clerk of the cheque. The office of captain is now a political ne, and the holder resigns on a change of ministry. On March 17, 1834, is late Majesty, William IV., "was graciously pleased to command that the Honourable Band of Gentleman Pensioners should be in future called His Majesty's Honourable Corps of Gentlemen-at-Arms."

Captains of the Corps of Gentlemen Pensioners.

From the institution of the corps by King Henry VIII. in 1509.

King Henry VIII.

509. Hy., E. of Essex, K.G.
539. Sir Anthy. Browne, K.G.

King Edward VI.

549. John, ld. Bray.
550. Wm. (late E. of Essex), M. of Northampton, K.G.

Queen Mary.

553. Wm., M. of Northampton, K.G., *contd.*
Thos., E. of Sussex, K.G.

Queen Elizabeth.

558. Hy., ld. Hunsdon, K.G.
596. Geo., ld. Hunsdon, K.G.

King James I.

.603. Geo., ld. Hunsdon, *contd.*
Hy., E. of Northumberland, K.G., May.
.615. Thos., E. of Suffolk, K.G.
.616. Theophilus, ld. Howard de Walden, aft. E. of Suffolk, K.G.

King Charles I.

.625. Theophilus, ld. Howard de Walden, aft. E. of Suffolk, *contd.*
.635. Wm., E. of Salisbury, K.G., May.
.643. Fras., ld. Dunsmore, aft. E. of Chichester.

King Charles II.

* * Wm., E. of Salisbury, *again.*
1660. Thos., E. of Cleveland.
1661. Geo., E. of Norwich.
1662. Thos., E. of Cleveland, *again.*
1667. John, ld. Belasyse of Worlaby.
.672. Thos., visc. Fauconberg.
1674. Wentworth, E. of Roscommon.
.684. Robt., E. of Scarsdale.

King James II.

1687. Theophilus, E. of Huntingdon.

King William III.

* * John, 3rd ld. Lovelace.
1693. Ralph, E., aft. D. of Montagu.
1695. Chas., D. of St. Albans, K.G.

Queen Anne.

1712. Hy., D. of Beaufort, K.G., Jan. 13.

King George I.

1714. Chas., D. of St. Albans, *again.*
1726. Wm., M. of Hartington, aft. D. of Devonshire, K.G.

King George II.

1727. Wm., M. of Hartington, aft. D. of Devonshire, *contd.*
1731. Richd, E. of Burlington and Cork, K.G.
1734. John, D. of Montagu, K.G. and K.B.
1740. Chas., D. of Bolton, K.G.
1742. Allen, ld., aft. E. Bathurst.
1745. John, ld. Hobart; aft. E. of Buckinghamshire, K.B.
1756. John, ld. Berkeley, of Stratton.

King George III.

1760. John, ld. Berkeley, of Stratton, *contd.*
1762. Geo. Hy., E. of Lichfield, July 17
1772. Geo., ld. Edgcumbe, Dec. 31; aft. visc. Mount-Edgcumbe and Valletort.
1782. Geo., ld. Ferrers, or de Ferrers, aft. E. of Leicester and M. Townshend, Mar. 29.
1783. Geo. Bussy, E. of Jersey, May 14.
Geo., ld. Ferrers, *again*, Dec. 31.

1797. Geo. Evelyn, E. of Falmouth.
1799. Heneage, E. of Aylesford.
1804. Geo., E. of Macclesfield.
1806. Geo. Richd., visct. St. John, Feb. 19.
1808. Richd., E. of Mount-Edgcumbe, Mar. 19.
1812. Jas. Geo., E. of Courtown, Apr. 11.

KING GEORGE IV.

1820. Jas. Geo., E. of Courtown, *contd.*
1827. Hy., visc. Hereford.

KING WILLIAM IV.

1830. Hy., visc. Hereford, *contd.*
Thos., ld. Foley, Dec. 8.
1833. Thos. Hy., ld. Foley, May.

CAPTAINS OF THE CORPS OF GENTLEMEN-AT-ARMS.

From the alteration in the name, March 17, 1834.

1834. Thos. Hy., ld. Foley, above named, Mar 17.
Hy., visc. Hereford, Dec. 30.
1835. Thos. Hy., ld. Foley, *again*, May 6.

QUEEN VICTORIA.

1841. John. Geo., ld. Forester, Sept. 8.
1846. Thos. Hy., ld. Foley, *again*, July 24.
1852. John Wm., E. of Sandwich, Feb. 27, **G.**
Thos. Hy., ld. Foley, *again*, Dec. 30, **G.**
1858. Hy. Jno., E. Talbot, aft. E. of Shrewsbury and Talbot, Feb. 24, **G.**
1859. Thos. Hy., ld. Foley, *again*, June 28, **G.**
1866. Chas., E. of Tankerville, July 10, **G.**
1867. Wm. Alleyne, M. of Exeter, Mar. 20.
1868. Thos. Hy., ld. Foley, *again*, Dec. 12, **G.**
1869. Geo. Aug. Constantine, M. of Normanby, Dec. 17.
1871. Fras. Thos. De Grey, E. Cowper, Apr. 20.
1874. Hy. Edwd., E. of Ilchester, Jan. 1, **G.**
Wm. Alleyne, M. of Exeter, *again*, Mar. 2, **G.**
1875. Chas. Jno., E. of Shrewsbury and Talbot, Feb 4, **G.**
1877. Geo. Wm., E. of Coventry, May 28, **G.**
1880. Alexr. Wm. Geo., E. of Fife, May 3, **G.**
1881. Chas., M. of Huntley Jan. 21, **G.**
Chas. Robt., ld. Carrington, June 27, **G.**
1885 Geo. Wm., E. of Coventry, *again*, July 6, **G.**
1886. Chas. Douglas Richd., ld. Sudeley, Feb. 10, **G.**
Geo. Wm., visc. Barrington, Aug. 5 **G.**
Fras. Robt., E. of Rosslyn, Nov. 24, **G.**

POETS LAUREATE.

THE origin of this office cannot be precisely traced, nor can a complete list be furnished. Warton, in his *History of English Poetry*, states that in the reign of Henry III. there was a *Versificator Regis*, and there is reason to suppose that Chaucer held this or some analogous office. The first mention of a POET LAUREATE was in the reign of Edward IV., when the name of John Kay, or Key, occurs as holding that appointment. The name of Andrew Bernard occurs in the reign of Henry VII., and the name of John Skelton in the reign of Henry VIII. Edmund Spenser was the first Poet Laureate in the reign of Elizabeth, and from this time the succession appears to be tolerably regular. Wherever in the following list the date of the appointment is not given, it was probably shortly after the death of the predecessor.

POETS LAUREATE.

* * * * *

1369. Geoffrey Chaucer.

* * * * *

Edw. IV. John Kay or Key.
Hen. VII. & Hen. VIII. } Andrew Bernard. John Skelton.

* * * * *

Eliz. Edmund Spenser, *d.* Jan. 15, 1599.
* * Saml. Daniel, *d.* Oct. 14. 1619.
1619. Ben Jonson, *d.* Aug. 16, 1637.
* * Sir Wm. Davenant, *d.* Apr. 7, 1668.
1670. John Dryden, removed 1688; *d.* May 1, 1700 or 1701.
1688. Thos Shadwell, *d.* Dec. 6, 1692.
1692 or 1693. Nahum Tate, *d.* Aug 12, 1715.
* * Nicholas Rowe, *d.* Dec. 6, 1718.
1718 or 1719. Laurence Eusden, *d.* Sept. 27, 1730.
1730. ColleyCibber, Dec.; *d.* Dec. 12, 1757.
1757. Wm. Whitehead, Dec. 28; *d.* Apr. 14, 1785.
1785. Thos. Warton, Apr. 30, sw.; *d.* May 21, 1790.
1790. Hy. Jas. Pye, July 17; *d.* Aug. 11, 1813.
1813. Robt. Southey, Nov, 11. **G.**; *d.* Mar. 21, 1843.
1843. Wm. Wordsworth, Apr. 6, **G.**; *d.* Apr. 23, 1850.
1850. Alfred Tennyson, aft. ld. Tennyson, Nov. 21, **G.**

EXAMINERS OF STAGE PLAYS.

THE act 10 Geo. II. cap. 28 provides that after June 24, 1737, every stage play, &c., shall, previous to performance, be submitted to the Lord Chamberlain for approval. This act is now repealed, but these provisions are repeated in 6 & 7 Vict. cap. 68 (Aug. 22, 1843), the act now regulating stage plays.

EXAMINERS OF STAGE PLAYS.

* * * * *
1741. — Lee, "Master of the Revels."
1743. Wm. Chetwynd, "Principal Master of the Revels."
Thos Odell, deputy.
1747. Wm. Chetwynd, inspector of plays.
Thos. Odell, deputy.
1749. Edwd. Capell, deputy, *vice* Odell.
1778. John Larpent, inspector, *vice* Chetwynd, Nov. 20.
1781. Jas. Trail, deputy, *vice* Capell.
1783. John Larpent, *alone.*
1824. Geo. Colman, Feb. 24, **G.**
1836. Chas. Kemble, Oct. 27, **G.**
1840. Jno. Mitchell Kemble, Feb. 22, **G.**
1857. Wm. Bodham Donne, Mar. 31, **G.**
1874. Edwd. Fredk. Smyth Pigott, Aug. 25, **G.**

DEPARTMENT OF THE MASTER OF THE HORSE.

MASTERS OF THE HORSE.

THIS office is always filled by noblemen of great rank. The Master of the Horse has the management and direction of all matters relating to the royal stables and of the revenue appropriated to this branch of the royal household. He has the privilege of using horses belonging to the crown, and of being attended by pages and servants attached to his department. In royal processions and on occasions of state he usually rides in the same carriage with the sovereign or is in immediate attendance. The office is now a political one, and the holder resigns on a change of ministry.

MASTERS OF THE HORSE.

KING HENRY VIII.

* * Sir Thos. Knivet.
* * Sir Nichs. Carew.
1539. Sir Anthy. Brown.

KING EDWARD VI.

1547. Sir Anthy. Brown, *contd.*
1548. Sir Wm. Herbert, aft. ld. Herbert and E. of Pembroke, May.
1552. Ambrose, E. of Warwick.

QUEEN MARY.

1556. Sir Hy. Jernyngham.

QUEEN ELIZABETH.

1559. Sir Robt. Dudley, aft. E. of Leicester; Jan. 11.
1588. Robt., E. of Essex.
1602. Edwd., E. of Worcester.

KING JAMES I.

1603. Edwd., E. of Worcester, *contd.*
1616. Geo., visc. Villiers, aft. D. of Buckingham.

KING CHARLES I.

1625. Geo., D. of Buckingham, *contd.*
1629. Jas., M., and aft. D. of Hamilton.

KING CHARLES II.

1660. Geo., D. of Albemarle.
1665. Jas., D. of Monmouth and Buccleuch.
1672. Geo., D. of Buckingham.
1673. Hy. Guy.
* * { Theophilus Oglethorpe, and Chas. Adderley, Commrs. during the minority of Chas., D. of Richmond and Lenox.
1679. Chas., D. of Richmond and Lenox.

KING WILLIAM III.

1689. Hy. de Nassau d'Auverquerque.

QUEEN ANNE.

1702. Chas., D. of Somerset.

KING GEORGE I.

1714. Chas., D. of Somerset, *contd.*
1715. { Hon. Conyers D'Arcy. Fras. Negus. } Commrs.
1717. Hy. Berkeley, commr., *vice* D'Arcy, June 14.
Fras. Negus, June 27, apptd. and contd. sole commr. till the accession of George II.

KING GEORGE II.

1727. Richd., E. of Scarborough, June 15.
1734. { Hon. Jas. Lumley. Hon. Hy. Berkeley. } Commrs., May.
1735. Chas., D. of Richmond, Lenox, and Aubigny, Jan. 9.
1751. Wm., M. of Hartington, aft. D. of Devonshire.
1755. Lionel Cranfield, D. of Dorset.
1757. Granville, E. Gower.

KING GEORGE III.

1760. Fras., E. of Huntingdon.
1761. John, D. of Rutland.
1766. Fras., E. of Hertford, aft. 1st E. of Yarmouth and M. of Hertford Aug.
Peregrine, D. of Ancaster and Kesteven, Dec.
1778. Hugh, D. of Northumberland, Dec. 10.
1780. Geo., D. of Montagu, Dec. 11.
1790. Jas., D. of Montrose, Dec. 7.
1795. John, E. of Westmorland, Mar.
1798. Philip, E. of Chesterfield, Feb. 14.
1804. Fras., 2nd M. of Hertford, July 21.
1806. Hy., E. of Carnarvon, Feb. 11.
1807. Jas., D. of Montrose, Apr. 4.

KING GEORGE IV.

1821. Chas., D. of Dorset, Dec. 11.
1827. Geo. Wm. Fredk., D. of Leeds, May 4.

KING WILLIAM IV.

1830. Wm. Chas., E. of Albemarle, Nov. 22.
1835. Chas., D. of Dorset, *again*, Jan. 1.
Wm. Chas., E. of Albemarle, *again*, Apr. 25.

QUEEN VICTORIA.

1837. Wm. Chas., E. of Albemarle, *contd.*, June 20.
1841. Geo. Child, E. of Jersey, Sept. 4.
1846. Hy. Chas., D. of Norfolk, July 11.
1852. Geo. Child, E. of Jersey, *again*, Mar. 1, **G.**
1853. Arthur Richd., D. of Wellington, Jan. 21, **G.**
1858. Hy. Chas. FitzRoy. D. of Beaufort, Feb. 26, **G.**
1859. Geo. Wm. Fredk., M. of Ailesbury, June 24, **G.**
1866. Hy. Chas. FitzRoy, D. of Beaufort, *again*, July 18, **G.**
1868. Geo. Wm. Fredk., M. of Ailesbury, K.G., *again*, Dec. 12, SW.
1874. Orlando Geo. Chas., E. of Bradford, Mar. 5, SW.
1880. Hugh Lupus, D. of Westminster, May 3, SW.
1885. Orlando Geo. Chas., E. of Bradford, *again*, June 27, SW.
1886. Richd. Edmd. St. Lawrence, E. of Cork and Orrery, K.P., Feb. 10.
Wm. Jno. Arthur Chas. Jas., D. of Portland, Aug. 9, **G.**

MASTERS OF THE BUCKHOUNDS.

This office is in the department of the Master of the Horse. It is always filled by a nobleman, and, being a political office, the holder resigns on a change of ministry.

MASTERS OF THE BUCKHOUNDS FROM THE ACCESSION OF GEORGE III.

KING GEORGE III.

* * Jno., visc. Bateman.
1782. Geo. Bussy, E. of Jersey.
1783. Jno., visc. Hinchinbroke, aft. E. of Sandwich.
1806. Wm. Chas., E. of Albemarle, Feb. 19, **G.**
Chas., M. Cornwallis.

KING GEORGE IV.

1820. Chas., M. Cornwallis, *contd.*
1823. Wm., ld. Maryborough, Sept. 12, **G.**

KING WILLIAM IV.

1830. Thos. Wm., visc. Anson, aft. E. of Lichfield, Nov. 24.
1834. Geo., E. of Chesterfield, Dec. 30, **G.**
1835. Wm. Geo., E. of Errol, Apr. 30, **G.**

QUEEN VICTORIA.

1839. Geo. Wm. Fox, ld. Kinnaird, Dec. 21, **G.**
1841. Jas. Alex., E. of Rosslyn, Sept. 10, **G.**
1846. Granville Geo., E. Granville, July 9, **G.**
1848. Jno. Geo. Brabazon, E. of Bessborough, May 16, **G.**
1852. Jas. Alexr., E. of Rosslyn, *again*, Feb. 28, **G.**
1853. Jno. Geo. Brabazon, E. of Bessborough, *again*, Dec. 30, **G.**
1858. Jno. Wm., E. of Sandwich, Feb. 26, **G.**
1859. Jno. Geo. Brabazon, E. of Bessborough, *again*, June 18, **G.**
1866. Richd. Edmd. St. Lawrence, E. of Cork and Orrery, Jan. 23, **G.**
Chas. Jno., ld. Colville of Culross, July 10, **G.**
1868. Richd. Edmd. St. Lawrence, E. of Cork and Orrery, *again*, Dec. 12, **G.**
1874. Chas. Philip, E. of Hardwicke, Mar. 2, **G.**
1880. Richd. Edmd. St. Lawrence, E. of Cork and Orrery, K.P., *again* May 3, **G.**
1885. Jno. Hy. De la Poer, M. of Waterford, K.P., June 27, **G.**
1886. Chas., ld. Suffield, K.C.B., Feb. 17, **G.**
Geo. Wm., E. of Coventry, Aug. 16, **G.**

GROOMS OF THE STOLE.

THE Groom of the Stole, a high officer of the royal household, whose office existed until the commencement of the present reign, was first Lord of the Bedchamber, and derived his official distinction from having the custody of the long robe or vestment worn by the king on solemn occasions of state, called the Stole.

GROOMS OF THE STOLE.

From the Restoration to the discontinuance of the office in 1837.

KING CHARLES II.

1660. John, E. of Bath.

KING JAMES II.

1685. Hy., E. of Peterborough.

KING WILLIAM III.

1689. Wm., E. of Portland.
1699. Hy., E. of Romney.

QUEEN ANNE.*

1704. Sarah, duch. of Marlborough.
1710. Elizth., duch. of Somerset.

KING GEORGE I.

1714. Lionel Cranfield, E. of Dorset and Middlesex, aft. D. of Dorset.
1719. Chas., E. of Sunderland.
1723. Fras., E. of Godolphin.

* Though somewhat incongruous in name, the office of groom of the stole was continued when Queen Anne was on the throne, and combined the duties of mistress of the robes.

KING GEORGE II.

1727. Fras., E. of Godolphin, *contd.*
1735. Hy., E. of Pembroke, Jan. 9.
1750. Wm. Anne, E. of Albemarle.
1755. Wm. Hy., E. of Rochford.

KING GEORGE III.

1760. John, E. of Bute.
1761. Fras., E. of Huntingdon.
1770. Geo. Wm., E. of Bristol.
1775. Thos., visc. Weymouth, aft. M. of Bath, Mar.
John, E. of Ashburnham, Nov.
1782. Thos., visc. Weymouth, aft. M. of Bath, *again.*
1796. John, D. of Roxburgh, Nov. 30.
1804. Geo., E. of Winchilsea and Nottingham, May 14.
1812. Chas. Ingoldsby, M. of Winchester.

KING GEORGE IV.

1820. Chas. Ingoldsby, M. of Winchester, *contd.*

KING WILLIAM IV.

1830. Chas. Ingoldsby, M. of Winchester, *contd.*

Office discontinued on the accession of Q. Victoria, in 1837.

MISTRESSES OF THE ROBES.

THIS lady performs for the Queen, whether regnant or consort, duties analogous to those performed by the groom of the stole for the king; but mistress of the robes to a queen regnant is an office of more political importance than that of mistress of the robes to a queen consort. Mary, duchess of Ancaster and Kesteven, held this appointment in the household of Queen Charlotte, consort of George III.; and the duchess dowager of Leeds in that of Queen Adelaide, consort of William IV.

MISTRESSES OF THE ROBES TO QUEEN VICTORIA.

1837. Harriett Elizth. Georgiana, duch. of Sutherland, Aug. 29.
1841. Charlotte, duch. of Buccleugh, Sept. 6.
1846. Harriett Elizth. Georgiana, duch. of Sutherland, *again*, July 6.
1852. Anne, duch. of Athole, Mar. 16, **G.**
1853. Harriett Elizth. Georgiana, duch. of Sutherland, *again*, Jan. 15, **G.**
1858. Louise Fredericke Augusta, duch. of Manchester, Feb. 26, **G.**
1859. Harriett Elizth. Georgiana, duch. of Sutherland, *again*, June 22, **G.**
1861. Elizth., duch. of Wellington, Apr. 25, **G.**
1868. Elizth. Georgiana, duch. of Argyll, Dec. 17, **G.**
1870. Anna, duch. of Sutherland, Jan. 22, **G.**
1874. Elizth., duch. of Wellington, *again*, Mar. 2, **G.**
1880. Elizth., duch. of Bedford, May 3, **G.**
1883. Anne, duch. of Roxburghe, Jan. 11, **G.**
1885. Louisa Jane, duch. of Buccleuch, June 27, **G.**; res. Feb. 1886.
1886. The duch. of Bedford declined to accept the office under Mr. Gladstone's govt., but performed the duties as acting-mistress, Feb.
1886. Louisa Jane, duch. of Buccleuch, *again*, Aug. 5, **G.**

PART IV.

LORD LIEUTENANTS OF COUNTIES, GOVERNORS AND CONSTABLES OF CASTLES, &c.

LORD LIEUTENANTS OF COUNTIES—ENGLAND AND WALES.

The militia, or ancient land force for the protection of the kingdom against invasion, was originally under the command of commissioners of array, who, about the reign of Edward VI., were superseded by commissioners of lieutenancy for each county, at the head of whom was an officer styled a lieutenant, or lord lieutenant. Strype, in his Memorials, gives 1549 as the date of their first appointment, and statutes of 2 & 3 Edwd. VI. and 4 & 5 Ph. and M. speak of the office as then in existence. The right of the crown to appoint these officers, and through them to command the militia, was one of the matters in dispute between Charles I. and his parliament, but on the Restoration, by statutes 13 Chas. II. cap. 6, and 14 Chas. II. cap. 3, the right of the crown was expressly declared, and the militia of each county was placed under the lord lieutenant, in whom the appointment of deputy lieutenants and officers was vested either directly or by recommendation. These rights remained undisturbed until 1871, when, by the "Army Regulation Act" (34 & 35 Vict. cap. 86) the control of the militia was removed from the lord lieutenant and vested wholly in the crown.

Besides his duties as head of the militia, the lord lieutenant is considered the chief magistrate of his county, and justices of the peace are made by the lord chancellor on his recommendation.

Great difficulty has been experienced in procuring complete lists of the lord lieutenants, and in many instances it has been found impossible to commence earlier than the reign of George III. The county histories, which almost invariably give the sheriffs and members of parliament from the earliest times, seldom give a list of the lord lieutenants although undoubtedly the highest office in the county.

ENGLAND.

LORD LIEUTENANTS OF BEDFORDSHIRE.

* * *

1745. John, D. of Bedford, Apr. 23.
1771. John, E. of Upper Ossory, Jan. 24.
1818. Thos. Philip, ld. Grantham, aft. E. de Grey, Feb. 13.
1859. Francis, D. of Bedford, K.G., Nov. 29, sw.
1861. Fras. Thos. De Grey, E. Cowper, Nov. 20, sw.

LORD LIEUTENANTS OF BERKSHIRE.

* * *

1751. Geo., D. of St. Albans, Dec. 15.
1761. Vere, ld. Vere.
1771. Geo., D. of St. Albans, July 19.
1786. Wm., ld. Craven, Mar.
1791. Jacob, E. of Radnor, Dec.
1819. Wm., E. of Craven, Nov. 12.
1826. Montagu, 5th E. of Abingdon, May 3.
1855. Montagu, 6th E. of Abingdon, Feb. 28, sw.
1881. Geo. Grimston, E. of Craven, Aug. 11.
1884. Ernest Aug. Chas., M. of Ailesbury, Jan. 11.
1886. Robt. Jas., ld. Wantage, Nov. 10.

LORD LIEUTENANTS OF BUCKINGHAMSHIRE.

* * *

1758. Richd., E. Temple, Dec. 22.
1763. Fras., ld. le Despencer.
1781. Philip, E. of Chesterfield, Nov.
1782. Geo. Nugent, aft. E. Temple and M. of Buckingham, Mar. 27.
1813. Richd. Chandos, M. of Buckingham, aft. D. of Buckingham, Feb. 23, G.
1839. Robt. John, ld. Carrington, Feb. 20, sw.
1868. Richd. Plantagenet Campbell Temple Nugent Brydges Chandos, D. of Buckingham and Chandos, Apr. 3

LORD LIEUTENANTS OF CAMBRIDGESHIRE.

* * *

1757. Philip, visc. Royston, aft. 2nd E. of Hardwicke, Aug. 23.
1790. Philip, 3rd E. of Hardwicke, June.
1834. Thos. Clifton.
1840. Chas. Philip, 4th E. of Hardwicke.
1874. Chas. Watson Townley, Jan. 17.

LORD LIEUTENANTS OF CHESHIRE.

See "Anglesey," *post*, p. 314.

1569. Edwd., 3rd E. of Derby, Nov. 18.
1574. Hy., 4th E. of Derby, Apr. 24.
1607. Wm., 6th E. of Derby, Dec. 22.
1626. Jas., 7th E. of Derby, Sept. 27.
1660. Chas., 8th E. of Derby, July 30.
1672. John, E. of Bridgewater, during minority of Wm. Richd. Geo., 9th E. of Derby.
1676. Wm. Richd. Geo., 9th E. of Derby; removed by Jas. II.
1688. Same, *again* app.
1689. Hy., ld. Delamere, Apr. 12.
1693. Richd., visc. Colchester.
1708. Hugh, 1st E. of Cholmondeley removed 1713, rest. 1714.
1725. Geo., 2nd E. of Cholmondeley, Mar. 20.
1727. Geo., visc. Malpas, aft. 3rd E. of Cholmondeley, Nov. 2.
1771. Geo. Jas., 4th E. and aft. 1st. M. of Cholmondeley.
1783. Geo. Harry, 5th E. of Stamford and Warrington, May 14.
1819. Geo. Harry, 6th E. of Stamford and

Warrington, June 14, **G.**; Oct. 11, sw.
1845. Richd., M. of Westminster, June 30, sw.
1868. Wm. Tatton, ld. Egerton of Tatton, Jan. 23, sw.
1883. Hugh Lupus, D. of Westminster, Mar. 24.

LORD LIEUTENANTS OF CORNWALL.

1660. John, E. of Bath.
1692. Chas. visc. Lansdowne, son of E. of Bath, joined with him.
1696. Chas. Bodville, E. of Radnor.
1702. John Granville, aft. ld. Granville.
1705. Sidney, ld. Godolphin, aft. visc. Rialton and E. of Godolphin.
1710. Lawrence, E. of Rochester.
1711. Hy., E. of Rochester.
1713. Chas. Bodville, E. of Radnor, *again*; *d.* 1723.
17—. Hy., E. of Radnor.
1740. Hon. Richd. Edgcumbe, aft. ld. Edgcumbe.
1761. Geo., ld. Edgcumbe, aft. visc. and E. of Mount-Edgcumbe.
1795. Richd., E. of Mount-Edgcumbe.
1840. Sir Wm. Trelawny, bt., Jan. 15, sw.
1856. Chas. Crespigny, ld. Vivian, Dec. 29, sw.
1877. Wm. Hy., E. of Mount-Edgcumbe, Nov. 2, **G.**

LORD LIEUTENANTS OF CUMBERLAND.

* * *
1759. Sir Jas. Lowther, aft. visc. Lowther and E. of Lonsdale, Dec. 13.
1802. Wm., visc. Lowther, aft. 1st E. of Lonsdale (second creation), June 16, sw.
1844. Wm., 2nd E. of Lonsdale, Apr. 17, sw.
1868. Hy. Lowther, aft. 3rd E. of Lonsdale, Dec. 2, **G.**
1876. Joselyn Fras., ld. Muncaster, Sept. 27, **G.**

LORD LIEUTENANTS OF DERBYSHIRE.

* * *
1756. Wm., 4th D. of Devonshire, Jan. 17.
1764. John, M. of Granby, Feb. 21.
1766. Lord Geo. Cavendish, June 17.
1782. Wm., 5th D. of Devonshire, June 18.
1811. Wm. Spencer, 6th D. of Devonshire, Aug. 19, sw.
1858. Wm., 7th D. of Devonshire, May 7, sw.

LORD LIEUTENANTS OF DEVONSHIRE.

* * *
1751. John, D. of Bedford, June 21.
1771. Vere, E. Poulett, Jan. 23.
1788. Hugh, ld., aft. 1st E. Fortescue, May.
1839. Hugh, visc. Ebrington, aft. 2nd E. Fortescue, Nov., sw.
1861. Edwd. Adolphus, D. of Somerset, Nov. 20, sw.
1886. Stafford Hy., E. of Iddesleigh, Jan. 21.
1887. Chas. Hy. Rolle, ld. Clinton, Feb. 16, **G.**

LORD LIEUTENANTS OF DORSETSHIRE.

1585. Fras., E. of Bedford.
1588. Wm., M. of Winchester.
1598. Thos., visc. Bindon, *d.* 1619.
1635. Theophilus, E. of Suffolk.
1640. Fras., ld. Cottington.
1641. Jas., E. of Salisbury.
* * Sir John Bankes.
* * Denzil, ld. Holles.
1667. Anthy., ld. Ashley, aft. E. of Shaftesbury, May 27.
1674. John, ld. Paulet of Hinton, July 6.
1680. John, E. of Bristol.
1702. Chas., 2nd D. of Bolton, July 1.
1707. Algernon, E. of Essex.
1708 Chas., 2nd D. of Bolton, *again*.
1727. Chas., 3rd D. of Bolton, Sept. 2.
1733. Anthy., 4th E. of Shaftesbury, Mar. 20.
1771. Hy., ld., aft. E. Digby, June 7.
1793. Geo., ld. Rivers, Oct.
1803. Geo., E. of Dorchester, June 17, sw.
1808. Edwd., E. Digby, Mar. 16, sw.
1856. Anthy., 7th E. of Shaftesbury, June 24, sw.
1885. Hy. Edwd., E. of Ilchester, Nov. 5, **G.**

LORD LIEUTENANTS OF DURHAM.

* * Cuthbert Tunstall, bp. of Durham, ld. pres. of the North and ld. lieut.
1552. Hy., E. of Westmorland, May 7; *d.* 1563.
* * Sir Geo. Bowes, lieut. for the Crown.
* * Algernon Percy, E. of Northumberland, ld. lieut. for the Parlt.
1660. Thos., visc. Fauconberg.
1687. Nathl. Crewe, bp. of Durham, aft ld. Crewe.
1689. Richd., visc. Lumley, aft. E. of Scarborough.
1712. Nathl., ld. Crewe, bp. of Durham, *again.*
1715. Richd., E. of Scarborough, *again.*
1721. Wm. Talbot, bp. of Durham.
1754. Hy., 1st E. of Darlington.
1758. Hy., 2nd E. of Darlington.
1792. Wm. Hy., 3rd E. of Darlington, aft D. of Cleveland.
1842. Chas. Wm., M. of Londonderry Apr. 27, **G.**
1854. Geo. Fredk. D'Arcy, E. of Durham Aug. 11, sw.
1880. Geo. Hy. Robt. Chas. Wm., M. o Londonderry, June 8, **G.**
1884. Jno. Geo., E. of Durham, Dec. 1, **G**

LORD LIEUTENANTS OF ESSEX.

* * John, ld. Petre.
* * Thos., visc. Colchester, aft. E. Rivers.
1641. Robt. Richd., E. of Warwick.
* * Geo., D. of Albemarle.
1675. Christr., D. of Albemarle, Nov.
1714. Hy., E. of Suffolk and Bindon, Oct. 14.
1719. Chas. Wm., E. of Suffolk, Oct. 29.
* * Hy., E. of Thomond.
1741. Benjn., E. Fitzwalter, May.
1756. Wm. Hy., E. of Rochford, Apr. 6.
1781. John, E. Waldegrave, Oct. 12.
1784. John, ld. Howard of Walden, Nov 13.
1798. Richd., ld. Braybrooke, Jan. 19.
1825. Hy., visc. Maynard, Apr. 20.
1865. Thos. Crosbie Wm., ld. Dacre, Nov 14, sw.
1869. Thos. Burch Western, May 8, **G.**
1873. Chichester Saml. Parkinson Fortescue, aft. ld. Carlingford, Aug 27, **G.**

LORD LIEUTENANTS OF GLOUCESTERSHIRE.

See "Anglesey," *post*, p. 314.

* * *

1754. Matthew, 2nd ld. Ducie, Feb. 14.
1761. Jno., ld. Chudworth.
1762. Norbonne Berkeley, aft. ld. Bottetourt.
1766. Fredk., E. of Berkeley, July 5.
1810. Hy. Chas., D. of Beaufort, Aug. 22, **G**
1836. Wm. Fitzhardinge, ld. Seagrave, aft E. Fitzhardinge, Feb. 3, sw.
1857. Hy. John, E. of Ducie, Nov. 4, sw.

LORD LIEUTENANTS OF HAMPSHIRE.

See "Southamptonshire," *post*, p. 311.

LORD LIEUTENANTS OF HEREFORDSHIRE.

See "Anglesey," *post*, p. 314.

* * *

1690. Chas., E., aft. D. of Shrewsbury.
1704. Hy., E., aft. D. of Kent.
1715. Thos., ld. Coningsby.
1727. Jas., D. of Chandos.
1741. Chas. Hanbury Williams.
1747. Jno., visc. Bateman.
1802. Geo., E. of Essex, Mar. 24, sw.
1817. John, ld. Somers, Aug. 26, **G.**
1841. Wm., ld. Bateman.
1845. Jno. Somers, E. Somers, Aug. 8, sw
1852. Wm. Bateman, ld. Bateman, Nov 10, **G.**

LIEUTENANTS AND LORD LIEUTENANTS OF HERTFORDSHIRE.

Lieutenants.

1588. Sir Rowland Lytton.
1605. Robt., E. of Salisbury, Aug. 5.
1612. Wm., E. of Salisbury, July 10.

Lord Lieutenants.

660. Arthur, E. of Essex.
681. Jno., E. of Bridgwater, Feb. 10.
686. Lawrence, E. of Rochester.
689. Chas., E. of Shrewsbury, during minority of E. of Essex.
691. Algernon, E. of Essex.
711. Jas., E. of Salisbury.
714. Wm., E. Cowper.
1764. Wm. Anne Holles, E. of Essex, Oct. 10.
1771. Jas., visc. Cranborne, aft. M. of Salisbury, Mar. 1.
1823. Jas. Walter, 1st E. of Verulam, July 16, sw.
1846. Jas. Walter, 2nd E. of Verulam, Jan. 21, sw.

LORD LIEUTENANTS OF HUNTINGDONSHIRE.

* * *

739. Robt., D. of Manchester, Nov. 3.
762. Geo., D. of Manchester.
789. Geo., D. of Montagu, May 15.
790. Jas., M. of Graham, aft. D. of Montrose, June.
1793. Wm., D. of Manchester, Mar. 1.
1841. Jno. Wm., E. of Sandwich, Sept. 14, sw
1884. Fras. Chas. Hastings, D. of Bedford, K.G., Apr. 7, **G.**

LORD LIEUTENANTS OF KENT.

559. Wm., ld. Cobham.
598. Hy., ld. Cobham, attainted 1 Jas. I.
624. Philip, E. of Montgomery, Mar. 17.
660. Heneage, E. of Winchilsea.
672. Chas., D. of Richmond and Lennox; *d.* 1672.
687. Christr., ld. Tenham, Jan. 16.
692. Vere, E. of Westmoreland, and Hy., visc. Sidney; jointly. The E. of Westmorland *d.* 1693.
702. Danl., E. of Nottingham, May.
704. Chas., E. of Winchilsea.
705. Lewis, ld., aft. 1st E. of Rockingham, Apr. 16.
724. John, E. of Leicester, May 5.
1737. Lewis, 2nd E. of Rockingham, Jan. 12.
1746. Thos., E. of Rockingham.
Lionel Cranfield, D. of Dorset, July.
1766. Chas., D. of Dorset, Feb. 10.
1769. Jno. Fredk., D. of Dorset.
1797. Chas., ld., aft. E. of Romney.
1808. John Jeffreys, E., aft. M. Camden, May 25.
1841. Hy., E. of Thanet.
1846. Geo. Augs., E. Cowper, Nov. 14, sw.
1856. Jno. Robt., visc., aft. E. Sydney, June 24, sw.

LORD LIEUTENANTS OF LANCASHIRE.

Baines, in his history of Lancashire (1831–5), states that the first lord lieutenant or this county was the duke of Norfolk, followed by the earl of Shrewsbury, who was ucceeded by Edward, earl of Derby, and that almost ever since the office has been held y the successive holders of that title.

* * *

* John Smith, c.c. ld. Strange.
771. Edwd., ld. Stanley, aft. 12th E. of Derby, July 19.
834. Edw., 13th E. of Derby, Nov. 20, sw.
1851. Chas. Wm., E. of Sefton, July 17, sw.
1856. Fras., E. of Ellesmere, Apr. 9, sw.
1857. Wm., E. of Burlington, Mar. 20, sw.
1858. Wm. Philip, E. of Sefton, Apr. 6, sw.

LORD LIEUTENANTS OF LEICESTERSHIRE.

* * *

721. John, 3rd D. of Rutland, Apr. 26.
779. Chas., 4th D. of Rutland, July 6.
787. Hy., D. of Beaufort, Dec. 5.
799. John Hy., 5th D. of Rutland, July 10, sw.
1857. Chas. Cecil John, 6th D. of Rutland Mar. 20, sw.
1888. Richd. Wm. Penn, E. Howe, C.B., June 18, **G.**

LORD LIEUTENANTS OF LINCOLNSHIRE.

* * *

1742. Peregrine, 3rd D. of Ancaster and Kesteven, Jan. 1.
1778. Robt., D. of Ancaster and Kesteven, Dec. 15.
1779. Brownlow, D. of Ancaster and Kesteven, Aug. 9.
1809. John, ld., aft. E. Brownlow, Mar. 1, sw.
1852. Chas. Cecil Jno., M. of Granby, a D. of Rutland, Aug. 18, sw.
1857. Chas. Anderson Worsley, E. of Y borough, Feb. 7, **G.**
1862. Gilbert John, ld. Aveland, M 12, sw.
1867. Adelbert Wellington Brownlow, Brownlow, Nov. 22, sw.

LORD LIEUTENANTS OF MIDDLESEX.

* * *

1714. Thos., D. of Newcastle, Oct. 9.
1762. Hugh, E., aft. 3rd D. of Northumberland, *d.* 1786, when the office was placed in commission until
1794. Wm. Hy. Cavendish, M. of Titchfield, aft. D. of Portland, Aug.
1842. Jas. Brownlow Wm., M. of Salisbu Feb. 2, sw.
1868. Arthur Richd., D. of Wellingto May 4, **G.**
1884. Geo. Hy. Chas., visc. Enfield, a E. of Strafford, Sept. 20.

LORD LIEUTENANTS OF MONMOUTHSHIRE.

See "Anglesey," *post*, p. 314, and "Brecknockshire," *post*, p. 315.

* * *

1715. John Morgan, Oct. 27.
1720. Wm. Morgan, June 21.
1728. Sir Wm. Morgan, June 26.
1732. Thos. Morgan, June 18.
1771. Hy., 5th D. of Beaufort, Dec. 24.
1803. Hy. Chas., 6th D. of Beaufort, O 26, sw.
1836. Capel Hanbury Leigh, Feb. 3, sw
1861. Benjn., ld. Llanover, Nov. 20, sw.
1867. Hy. Chas. Fitzroy, 8th D. of Bea fort, May 17, sw.

LORD LIEUTENANTS OF NORFOLK.

* * *

1757. Geo., E. of Orford, June 21.
1792. Geo., Marq. Townshend, Feb. 15.
1808. Wm. Assheton Harbord, aft. ld. Suffield, Mar. 2.
1822. Hon. John Wodehouse, aft. l Wodehouse, Mar. 28, sw.
1846. Thos. Wm., E. of Leicester, Aug. sw.

LORD LIEUTENANTS OF NORTHAMPTONSHIRE.

* * *

1749. Geo. Montagu, E. of Halifax, Nov. 23, sw.
1771. Spencer, E. of Northampton, July 19.
1796. Chas., E., aft. M. of Northampton.
1828. John, E. of Westmorland, June 2 sw.
1842. Brownlow, M. of Exeter, Feb. 2, G
1867. Chas., ld. Southampton, Mar. 1, sw
1872. John Poyntz, E. Spencer, Aug. 10, G

LORD LIEUTENANTS OF NORTHUMBERLAND.

* * *

1753. Hugh, E., aft. 3rd D. of Northumberland, Mar. 20.
1786. Hugh, 4th D. of Northumberland, Sept. 2; res. 1798. The office was then put into commission until June 15, 1798, when the duke wa again app.
1817. Hugh, 5th D. of Northumberland July 24, sw.
1847. Hy., E. Grey, Feb. 27, sw.
1877. Algernon Geo., D. of Northumber land, Dec. 27, **G.**

LORD LIEUTENANTS OF NOTTINGHAMSHIRE.

* * *

63. Evelyn, D. of Kingston, Jan. 10.
65. Thos. Holles, D. of Newcastle, Sept. 7.
68. Hy. Fiennes, D. of Newcastle, Dec. 16.
94. Thos., D. of Newcastle, Apr. 30.
95. Wm. Hy. Cavendish, 3rd D. of Portland, June 20.
1809. Hy. Pelham, 4th D. of Newcastle, Dec. 20, sw.
1840. John, E. of Scarborough.
1857. Hy. Pelham, 5th D. of Newcastle, Feb. 2, sw.
1864. Edwd., ld. Belper, Nov. 25, sw.
1880. Wm. Amelius Aubrey de Vere, D. of St. Albans, Aug. 18, sw.

LORD LIEUTENANTS OF OXFORDSHIRE.

* * *

60. Geo., 4th D. of Marlborough, Mar. 21.
17. Geo., 7th E. of Macclesfield.
42. Geo., 6th D. of Marlborough, Apr. 27, sw.
1857. John Winston, 7th D. of Marlborough, Aug. 27, sw.
1883. Sir Hy. Wm. Dashwood, bt., Aug. 13, **G.**
1887. Victor Albert Geo., E. of Jersey, **G.**

LORD LIEUTENANTS OF RUTLANDSHIRE.

* * *

51. Brownlow, ld. Burghley, aft. 9th E. of Exeter, June 21.
779. Geo., E. of Winchilsea and Nottingham, Mar. 19.
1826. Brownlow, 4th M. of Exeter, Nov. 20.
1867. Chas. Geo., E. of Gainsborough, Mar. 6, sw.
1881. Wm. John Manners, E. of Dysart, Oct. 29, **G.**

LORD LIEUTENANTS OF SHROPSHIRE.

* * *

61. Wm., E. of Bath.
64. Hy. Arthur, E. of Powis, Aug. 17.
72. Robt., ld. Clive, Oct. 9.
775. Edwd., ld. Clive, aft. E. of Powis, Apr. 7.
1839. Geo. Granville, D. of Sutherland, Aug. 26, sw.
1845. Rowland, visc. Hill, Nov. 20, sw.
1875. Orlando Geo. Chas., E. of Bradford, Jan. 23, **G.**

LORD LIEUTENANTS OF SOMERSETSHIRE.

* * *

711. John, 1st E. Poulett, Jan. 30; to Sept., 1714.

* * *

744. John, 2nd E. Poulett, Jan.
764. Percy, E. of Thomond, Nov. 30.
773. John Jas., E. of Egmont, Feb. 12.
774. Fredk., ld. North, aft. E. of Guildford, Mar. 15.
1792. John, 4th E. Poulett, Oct. 26.
1819. Thos., 2nd M. of Bath, Feb. 8, **G.**
1837. Hy., E. of Ilchester, Apr. 19, sw.
1839. Edwd., ld. Portman, May 22, sw.
1864. Richd. Edmund St. Lawrence, E. of Cork and Orrery, K.P., June 24, sw.

LORD LIEUTENANTS OF SOUTHAMPTONSHIRE.

* * *

759. Chas., D. of Bolton, Oct. 25.
763. Jas., M. of Carnarvon, aft. D. of Chandos, June 1.
764. Robt., E. of Northington, Aug. 21.
771. Jas. Brydges, c.c. M. of Carnarvon, aft. D. of Chandos, Jan. 23.
780. Geo., ld. Rivers, May.
782. Harry, D. of Bolton, Apr. 6.
793. Geo. Powlett
Sir Wm. Heathcote, bt., and
Wm. Chute, commrs.
1798. Chas., E. of Wiltshire.
1800. Thos., ld. Bolton, Feb. 21, sw.
1807. Jas., E. of Malmesbury, K.B., Aug. 11, **G.**
1820. Arthur, D. of Wellington, K.G., Dec. 19, sw.
1852. John, M. of Winchester, Nov. 10, sw.
1887. Hy. Howard Molyneux, E. of Carnarvon, Aug. 6, **G.**

LORD LIEUTENANTS OF STAFFORDSHIRE.

* * *

1755. Granville, E. Gower, aft. M. of Stafford, Jan. 7.
1800. Geo. Granville, E. Gower, aft. M. of Stafford and D. of Sutherland, Oct. 21.
1801. Hy., E. of Uxbridge, June 2, **G.**
1812. Chas., E. Talbot, Apr. 8, sw.
1849. Hy. Wm., M. of Anglesey, Jan. 3 sw.
1854. Edw. Jno., ld. Hatherton, June sw.
1863. Thos., E. of Lichfield, June sw.
1871. Arthur, ld. Wrottesley, July 8, **G.**
1887. Wm. Walter, E. of Dartmouth, M 21, **G.**

LORD LIEUTENANTS OF SUFFOLK.

* * *

1763. Chas., ld., aft. visc. Maynard, Feb. 8.
1769. Aug. Hy., D. of Grafton, June 3.
1790. Geo. Hy., E. of Euston, aft. D. of Grafton, June.
1844. John Edwd. Cornwallis, E. Stradbroke, Jan. 31, sw.
1886. Fredk. Wm. John, M. of Brist Feb. 15, **G.**

LORD LIEUTENANTS OF SURREY.

* * *

Jas. I. Edwd., visc. Wimbledon.
1621. Chas., ld. Howard of Effingham, aft. E. of Nottingham, July 27.
1635. Thos., E. of Arundel and Surrey, July 23.
1660. John, visc. Avalon, June 30; *d.* 1675.
* * Prince Rupert, *d.* 1682.
1682. Hy., E. of Arundel, Dec.
1701. Geo., 2nd D. of Northumberland.
1702. Chas., E. of Berkeley, June 7.
1712. Geo., 2nd D. of Northumberlan *again*, Oct. 9.
1714. Chas., E. of Halifax, Nov. 3.
1716. Richd., 1st ld. Onslow, July 6.
1717. Thos., 2nd ld. Onslow, Dec. 9.
1741. Richd., 3rd ld. Onslow, Jan. 29.
1776. Geo., 4th ld. Onslow, aft. Onslow, Oct. 31.
1814. Geo., visc. Middleton, May 30, sw
1830. Chas. Geo., ld. Arden, Nov. 1, sw.
1840. Wm., E. of Lovelace, Aug. 10, sw

LORD LIEUTENANTS OF SUSSEX.

1550. Sir Richd. Sackville.
1553. Hy., E. of Arundel.
1598. Richd., ld. Buckhurst, and Chas., E. of Nottingham.
1608. Chas., E. of Nottingham, and Thos., E. of Arundel.
1626. Thos., E. of Arundel, and Edwd., E. of Dorset.
1670. Richd., E. of Dorset, and Chas., ld. Buckhurst.
1677. Chas., E. of Dorset.
1705. Algernon, D. of Somerset.
1754. John, E. of Ashburnham.
1757. Geo., E. of Abergavenny.
1759. In Commission.
1762. Chas., E. of Egremont.
1763. Chas., 3rd D. of Richmond, Oct. 1
1807. Chas., D. of Norfolk, Jan. sw.
1816. Chas., 4th D. of Richmond, Ja 30, sw.
1819. Geo. O'Brien, 3rd E. of Egremor Nov. 5, **G.**
1835. Chas., 5th D. of Richmond.
1860. Hy. Thos., E. of Chichester, No 23, sw.
1886. Hy. Bouverie Wm., visc. Hampde G.C.B., Apr. 5, **G.**

LORD LIEUTENANTS OF THE TOWER HAMLETS.

See "Constables of the Tower of London," *post*, p. 319.

LORD LIEUTENANTS OF WARWICKSHIRE.

* * *

1750. Fras., E., aft. 1st M. of Hertford, June 30, sw.
1795. Geo., E. of Warwick and Brooke, Jan 4.
1816. Fras., 2nd M. of Hertford, June 2
1822. Hy. Richd., E. of Warwick a E. Brooke, July 5, sw.
1854. Wm., 3rd E. of Craven, Mar. 29, s
1856. Wm. Hy., ld. Leigh, Apr. 4, sw.

LORD LIEUTENANTS OF WESTMORELAND.

* * *

58. Sir Jas. Lowther, bt., aft. E. of Lonsdale, Aug. 14.

92. Wm., visc. Lowther, aft. 1st E. of Lonsdale(second creation),June16.

44. Wm., 2nd E. of Lonsdale, Apr. 17, sw.

1868. Hy. Lowther, aft. 3rd E. of Lonsdale Dec. 2, **G.**

1876. Sir Richd. Courtenay Musgrave, bt., Sept. 27, **G.**

1881. Sir Hy. Jas. Tufton, bt., aft. ld. Hothfield, Mar. 14, **G.**

LORD LIEUTENANTS OF WILTSHIRE.

* * *

61. Hy., 10th E. of Pembroke, Mar. 18.

80. Thos., E. of Ailesbury, Feb. 19.

82. Hy., E. of Pembroke, *again*, Mar. 27.

1794. Geo. Aug., E. of Pembroke, Jan. 26.

1827. Hy., M. of Lansdowne, Nov. 16, sw.

1863. Geo. Wm. Fredk., M. of Ailesbury, Mar. 25, sw.

1878. Jacob, E. of Radnor, Mar. 7, **G.**

LORD LIEUTENANTS OF WORCESTERSHIRE.

See "Brecknockshire," *post*, p. 315.

* * *

51. Geo. Wm., 6th E. of Coventry, June 12.

08. Geo. Wm., visc. Deerhurst, aft. 7th E. of Coventry, Nov. 23, sw.

1831. Thos., ld. Foley, Apr. 27, sw.

1833. Wm. Hy., ld. Lyttleton, May 29, sw.

1837. Thos. Hy., ld. Foley, July 12, sw.

1839. Geo. Wm., ld. Lyttleton, Oct. 21, sw.

1876. Fredk., E. Beauchamp, May 13.

LORD LIEUTENANTS OF YORKSHIRE—EAST RIDING.

* * *

78. Fras. Godolphin, M. of Carmarthen, aft. D. of Leeds, July 11.

80. Fredk., E. of Carlisle, Feb. 9.

82. Fras. Godolphin, M. of Carmarthen, aft. D. of Leeds, *again*, Mar. 27.

99. Fredk., E. of Carlisle, Feb. 26.

07. Hy., ld. Mulgrave, Aug. 19, sw.

1824. Geo., visc. Morpeth, aft. E. of Carlisle, Nov. 20, sw.

1840. Paul Beilby, ld. Wenlock, Jan. 29, **G.**

1847. Geo. Wm. Fredk., visc. Morpeth, aft. E. of Carlisle, Jan. 29.

1864. Beilby Richd., ld. Wenlock, Nov. 22, sw.

1880. Marmaduke, ld. Herries, Dec. 16, **G.**

LORD LIEUTENANTS OF YORKSHIRE—NORTH RIDING.

* * *

40. Robt., E. of Holdernesse, Apr. 15.

77. Hy., E. Fauconberg, Dec.

02. Geo. Wm. Fredk., D. of Leeds, Apr. 7.

1839. Hon. Thos. Jno. Dundas, c.c. ld. Dundas, aft. E. of Zetland, Feb. 3, sw.

1873. Geo. Fredk. Saml., M. of Ripon, K.G., Mar. 19, **G.**

LORD LIEUTENANTS OF YORKSHIRE—WEST RIDING.

* * *

32. Fras., E. of Huntingdon.

65. Chas., M. of Rockingham, *again*, Aug. 7.

82. Chas., E. of Surrey, aft. D. of Norfolk, Sept. 28.

98. Wm., E. Fitzwilliam, Feb. 14.

1819. Hy., visc. Lascelles, aft. 2nd E. of Harewood, Nov. 5, **G.**

1842. Jas. Archibald, ld. Wharncliffe.

1846. Hy., 3rd E. of Harewood, Jan. 21, sw.

1857. Wm. Thos. Spencer, visc. Milton, aft. E. Fitzwilliam, Mar. 20, sw.

NORTH WALES.

LORD LIEUTENANTS OF ANGLESEY.

1660. Richd. Vaughan, E. of Carbery, app. for all counties of S. Wales, and for Haverfordwest, Sept. 18.
The same, re-app. for all counties of N. and S. Wales, and for Haverfordwest, Dec. 22.
1662. The same, re-app., July 19.
1673. Hy. Somerset, 3rd M. and 7th E. of Worcester, aft. D. of Beaufort; app. for all counties of N. and S. Wales, July 20.
1685. The same, re-app. for ditto, and for Haverfordwest, and the counties of Gloucester, Hereford, and Monmouth, Mar. 28.
1689. Chas. Gerard, E. of Macclesfield, app. for ditto, Mar. 22.
1695. The same, re-app. for all counties of N. Wales, Mar. 10.
1702. Wm., E. of Derby, app. for ditto Jan. 18.
Hugh, ld. Cholmondeley, aft. 1st E of Cholmondeley, app. for ditto Dec. 2.
1714. The same, re-app. for ditto, Aug. 21
1725. Geo., 2nd E. of Cholmondeley, app for ditto, and for Cheshire, Apr. 7
1733. Geo., 3rd E. of Cholmondeley, app for ditto, June 14.

ANGLESEY ONLY.

1771. Sir Nicholas Bayley, bt.
1782. Hy., E. of Uxbridge, July 20.
1813. Hy. Wm., E. of Uxbridge, aft. 1s M. of Anglesey.
1854. Hy., 2nd M. of Anglesey, June 8, sw
1869. Hon. Wm. Owen Stanley, Mar. 2, G
1884. Richd. Davies, Mar. 27, **G.**

LORD LIEUTENANTS OF CARNARVONSHIRE.

See "Anglesey," supra.

* * *

1761. Thos. Wynne, aft. ld. Newborough.
1781. Thos. Jas., visc. Bulkeley, Nov. 20.
1822. Thos. Assheton Smith, Sept. 16, sw.
1829. PeterRobt.,ld.WilloughbyDeEresby, Feb. 11, sw.
1851. Sir Richd. Bulkeley Williams Bulkeley, Feb. 11, sw.
1866. Edwd. Gordon, ld. Penrhyn, Sept 18, sw.
1886. Jno. Ernest Greaves.

LORD LIEUTENANTS OF DENBIGHSHIRE.

See "Anglesey," supra.

* * *

* * Watkin Williams, in 1792.
1793. Richd. Myddelton.
1795. Sir Watkin Williams Wynn, bt.
1840. Middleton Biddulph.
1852. Robt. Myddelton Biddulph.
1872. Maj., aft. col., Wm. Cornwalli West, May 9, **G.**

LORD LIEUTENANTS OF FLINTSHIRE.

See "Anglesey," supra.

* * *

1761. Sir Roger Mostyn, bt.
1797. Lloyd, ld. Kenyon.
1798. Robt., visc. Belgrave, aft. E. Grosvenor and M. of Westminster.
1845. Sir Stephen Rd. Glynne, bt., Jun 30, sw.
1874. Hugh Robt. Hughes, Aug. 1 **G.**

LORD LIEUTENANTS OF MERIONETHSHIRE.

See "Anglesey," supra.

* * *

1762. Wm. Vaughan—the grant to the E. of Cholmondeley for all counties in N. Wales revoked, *pro tanto*, Apr. 26.
1775. Sir Watkin Williams Wynn, 4th bt.
1789. Watkin Williams, Aug. 31.
1793. Sir Watkin Williams Wynn, 5th bt June 10.
1830. Sir Watkin Williams Wynn, 6th bt. Dec. 21.
1840. Hon. Edw. Mostyn Lloyd, aft. l Mostyn, June 25.
1884. Robt. Davies Pryce, May 12, **G.**

LORD LIEUTENANTS OF MONTGOMERYSHIRE.

See "Anglesey," *ante*, p. 314.

* * *

72. Robt., ld. Clive, Oct. 9.
75. Fras., E., aft. 1st M. of Hertford, Apr. 7.
76. Geo. Edwd. Hy. Arthur, E. of Powis, Nov. 8.
4. Edwd., E. of Powis, June 6, sw.

1839. Edwd. Herbert, E. of Powis.
1848. Chas., ld. Sudeley, Feb. 11, sw.
1858. Hon. Thos. Chas. Sudeley, aft. ld. Sudeley, Apr. 6, sw.
1863. Sudeley Chas. Geo., ld. Sudeley, Apr. 22.
1877. Edwd. Jas., E. of Powis, May 22.

SOUTH WALES.

LORD LIEUTENANTS OF BRECKNOCKSHIRE.

See "Anglesey," *ante*, p. 314.

* * *

94. Thos. Herbert, E. of Pembroke and Montgomery, app. for all counties of S. Wales and for Haverfordwest and Monmouthshire, May 11.
94. The same, re-app. Jan. 27.
15. John Morgan, app. for Brecknockshire and Monmouthshire, Oct. 7.
20. Wm. Morgan, app. for ditto, June 21.
28. Sir Wm. Morgan, app. for ditto, June 26.
31. Thos. Morgan, app. for ditto, June 18.
71. Chas. Morgan, app. for Brecknockshire only, Dec. 23.

1787. Hy., D. of Beaufort, app. for ditto, June 1.
1803. Hy. Chas., D. of Beaufort, app. for Brecknockshire and Monmouthshire, Oct. 26. sw.

BRECKNOCKSHIRE ONLY.

1836. Penry Williams, Feb. 3, sw.
1847. Lloyd Vaughan Watkins, Feb. 4, sw.
1865. Geo. Chas., M. Camden, Oct. 31, **G.**
1866. Chas. Morgan Robinson Tredegar, Sept. 25, **G.**
1875. Sir Jos. Russell Bailey, bt., June 14, **G.**

LORD LIEUTENANTS OF CARDIGANSHIRE.

See "Anglesey," *ante*, p. 314, and "Brecknockshire," *supra*.

* * *

3. Hon. Wilmot Vaughan, aft. visc. and E. of Lisburne, Jan. 10.
0. Thos. Johnes, July 2, sw.

1816. Wm. Edwd. Powell, Oct. 26, **G.**
1854. Thos. Lloyd, Oct. 18, sw.
1857. Edwd. Lewis Pryse, Aug. 27, sw.
1888. Herbert Davies Evans, July 16, **G.**

LORD LIEUTENANTS OF CARMARTHENSHIRE.

See "Anglesey," *ante*, p. 314, and "Brecknockshire," *supra*.

* * *

* Geo. Rier.
9. Thos. Johnes.
0. Jno. Vaughan, Mar. 25.
4. Geo., ld. Dynevor, June 6, sw.

1852. Jno. Fredk., 1st E. Cawdor, May 15, sw.
1861. Jno. Fredk. Vaughan, 2nd E. Cawdor, Apr. 30.

LORD LIEUTENANTS OF GLAMORGANSHIRE.

See "Anglesey," *ante*, p. 314, and "Brecknockshire," *supra*.

* * *

8. Chas. Paulet, 3rd D. of Bolton, Mar. 22.
2. Other Lewis, E. of Plymouth, Nov. 6.
2. John, ld. Mountstewart, aft. 4th E. and 1st M. of Bute, Mar. 22.

1794. Geo. Aubrey, John Price, and John Richards, } Dep. lieuts. to act during vacancy, Mar.
John, 4th E., aft. 1st M., of Bute, Dec.
1815. John, 2nd M. of Bute, June 2.
1848. Christopher Rice Mansel Talbot Apr. 15, sw.

LORD LIEUTENANTS OF HAVERFORDWEST.

See "Anglesey," *ante*, p. 314, and "Brecknockshire," *ante*, p. 315.

* * *

* * Sir Wm. Owen, bt.
1770. Sir Rd. Philipps, bt., aft. ld. Milford, Jan. 23.
1824. Rd. Bulkeley Philipps Philipps, aft. ld. Milford, Apr. 7, sw.
1857. Jno. Hy. Philipps, aft. sir J. I Philipps-Scourfield, bt., July 1 sw.
1876 Chas. Edwd. Gregg Philipps, Aug 7.

LORD LIEUTENANTS OF PEMBROKESHIRE.

See "Anglesey," *ante*, p. 314, and "Brecknockshire," *ante*, p. 315.

* * *

* * Sir Wm. Owen, bt.
1778. Hugh Owen, Feb. 10.
1780. Richd., ld. Milford.
1824. Sir Jno. Owen, bt.
1861. Wm., 3rd ld. Kensington, Apr. 3 sw.
1872. Wm., 4th ld. Kensington, Feb. 6, G

LORD LIEUTENANTS OF RADNORSHIRE.

See "Anglesey," *ante*, p. 314, and "Brecknockshire," *ante*, p. 315.

* * *

1766. Edwd., E. of Oxford.
1792. Hon. Thos. Harley.
1805. Geo., ld. Rodney, Mar. 21.
1842. Sir Jno. Benn Walsh, bt., aft. l Ormathwaite, Aug. 11, sw.
1875. Hon. Arthur Walsh, aft. ld. Orma thwaite, Apr. 19, G.

SCOTLAND AND IRELAND.

For lord lieutenants of counties in these countries, *see* Part IX., "Scot land," *post*, and Part X., "Ireland," *post*.

GOVERNORS AND CONSTABLES OF CASTLES, &c

CONSTABLES OF DOVER CASTLE AND WARDENS OF THE CINQUE PORTS.

These are very ancient offices, and in former days had importan duties attached to them in protecting the country from invasion. The are now merely honorary posts, generally conferred upon some distin guished statesman, and the only emolument now derived from them i the enjoyment of Walmer Castle as a residence.

The two offices were formerly sometimes separated, but for man years past they have been held by the same person.

In compiling the present list, the lists given in Harris's History o Kent, Hasted's History of Kent, and Lyons' History of Dover have been collated and, as far as possible, reconciled. There are, how ever, some slight differences in some of the earlier names and dates and therefore, although the list now given will probably be found suffi ient for all practical purposes, the works above quoted should, in any ase of difficulty, be consulted, and the ancient records on which they ely examined.

ONSTABLES OF DOVER CASTLE AND WARDENS OF THE CINQUE PORTS.

C. signifies constable *only;* W., warden *only;* C. and W., both constable and warden.

* * Godwin, E. of Kent, gov. in the reign of Edward the Confessor.
1053. Harold, his son, gov., aft. king.
1066. Bertram de Ashburnham, gov.; put to death by William the Conqueror.
Wm. Peverel, gov., *pro. tem.*
Vill. I. Odo, bp. of Baieux, E. of Kent, gov.
Baron John de Fienes, C. and W.
1084. Jas. de Fienes, C. and W.
1111. Baron John de Fienes, *again*; C. and W.
138–9. Wm. Mareschall, E. of Pembroke, C. (4 Stephen).
Steph. Wakelyn de Magminot, C.
Richd., E. of Ewe, C.
Eustace, E. of Boulogne, C. and W.
Hen. II. Hy. de Essex, bar. of Raleigh and E. of Essex, C. and W.; dism. 1163.
Simon de Sandwich, C. and W
Hy. de Sandwich, C. and W.
Alan de Fienes, C. and W.
Rich. I. Jas. de Fienes, C. and W.
Ingelram de Fienes, C. (?).
Richd., otherwise Matth. de Clare, C. and W.
Wm. Longspee, E. of Salisbury, natl. son of Henry II., sometimes called Wm. Devereux, C.
Wm. Longchamp (?).
John. Wm. de Wrotham, C. and W.
1201–2. Thos. Bassett, C. (3 John).
Hubert de Burgh, aft. E. of Kent, C. and W. (3 John).
1203–4. Wm. de Huntingfield, C. and W. (5 John).
1204. Wm. Longspee, E. of Salisbury, *again*; C. and W., Sept. 9.
1206–7. Geoffry Fitz-Pier, aft. E. of Essex, C. May 25.
1215. Hubert de Burgh, aft. E. of Kent, *again*; C. and W., June 30.
1219–20. Hy. de Braibroc, or Braybrooke C. (4 Hen. III.).
1220–1. Sir Robt. de Neresford, C. (5 Hen. III.)
1223. Hugh de Windlesore, or Wynsore, C., Oct. 31.
1225. Sir Geoffry de Shurland, C., Apr. 13.
1226. Wm. de Averenches, or Albrincis and Tergusius, mayor of Dover, joint W., Mar. 14.
Hen. III. John Mansel, C. (?).
1827–8. Hubert de Burgh, *again*; C. (12 Hen. III.)
1231–2. Stephen de Segrave, C. and W. (16 Hen. III.)
Symon, or Harry Hoese, C. (15 Hen. III.)
Bertram de Criol, C. (16 Hen. III.)
1233–4. Hubert de Husato, C. (18 Hen. III.)
1234–5. Hams de Crevequer, or Crêvecœur, C. and joint W. with Walerand de Teyes (19 Hen. III.)
1237–8. Bertram de Criol, *again*; C. (22 Hen. III.); and *again* C. 1240–1 (25 Hen. III.)
1241–2. Peter de Savoy, E. of Richmond, C. (26 Hen. III.)
Humphry de Bohun, E. of Hereford and Essex, C. (26 Hen. III.)
1246–7. Sir Robt. de Neresford, *again*; C. (31 Hen. III.).
1247–8. Peter de Rivallis, C. (32 Hen. III.)
1254–5. Reginald de Cobham, C. and W. (39 Hen. III.)
1258–9. Peter de Savoy, E. of Richmond, *again*; C. and W. (42 Hen. III.)
1258. Roger Northwood, C. and W., June 9.
Nicholas de Moels, C. and W., June 10.
Richd. de Grey, C. and W., July 28.
1259. Hugh, or Roger Bigod, C. and W. (43 & 44 Hen. III.)
1259–60. Wm. de Say, C. (44 Hen. III.)
1261. Robt. Waleran, C., May 3.
1262–3. Hy. Braybrooke, C. (47 Hen. III.)
Edmd. and Robt. de Gascoyne, joint C. (47 Hen. III.)
1263. Hy. de Sandwich, bp. of London, C., July 10.
Walter de Bersted, C. and W. July 20.
Richd. de Grey, C., and aft. W.
Nichs. de Criol, W.; res. in favour of De Grey.
1264. Hy. Montfort, C. and W., May 8.
Roger de Leyborne, W., Nov. 26.
Hy., or Edmd. and Robt. Gascoigne, joint C., July 8.
Hen. III. Walter Berested, C.
Matth. Belers, or Beslīz, W.

1265–6. Simon de Sandwich, aft. sir S., C. (50 Hen. III.)
1266–7. Edwd., pr. of Wales, aft. Edw. I., C. and W. (51 Hen. III.)
1272–3. Sir Steph. de Penchester, C. (1 Edw. I.), and W., July 4, 1273.
1275. Simon de Grey, C. and W., (3 and 4 Edw. I.)
1277–8. Ralph de Sandwich, C. and W. (6 Edw. I.)
1290. Sir Steph. de Penchester, *again*; C. and W., Sept. 24; and *again*, 1293–4 (22 Edw. I.)
Edw. I. Sir Robt. de Shurland, W.
1290–1. Robt. Burgess, or de Burghersh, C. and W. (19 Edw. I); *again*, July 20, 1299.
1305–6. Hy. Cobham, C. and W. (34 Edw. I.)
1307. Robt. de Kendall, C. and W., Nov. 14.
1314–5. Hy. de Cobham, jun., C. and W. (8 Edw. II.)
1315–6. Robt. de Kendall, *again*; C. and W. (9 Edw. II.)
Bartholomew de Badlesmere, grandson of Robt. de Burghersh, C. and W.
1320–1. Sir Hugh de Spencer, or Le Spencer, junr., aft. E. of Gloucester, W. (14 Edw. II.)
1321–2. Edmd., E. of Kent, C. and W. (15 Edw. II.)
Edw. II. Sir Thos. Peache, C.
1325–6. Robt. de Kendall, *again;* C. and W., and Ralph de Camoys, W. (18 Edw. II.)
1326. Ralph Basset, Mar. 18.
Ralph de Camoys and Robt. de Kindale, *again*; C. and W., Sept. 30.
1326–7. Sir Hugh de Spencer or Le Spencer, junr., *again*; W. (20 Edw. II.)
1327. Bartholomew de Badlesmere, or de Burghersh, or ld. Burghersh, *again*; C. and W., Aug. 1.
1327–8. Edmd. of Woodstock, E. of Kent, C. (1 Edw. III.)
1330. Robt. de Burghersh, C. and W., Feb. 28.
1331. Wm. de Clinton, aft. E. of Huntingdon, C. and W., Sept. 4.
1337–8. John de Lancaster (11 Edw. III.)
1339–10. Wm., E. of Huntingdon, *again*; C. and W. (13 Edw. III.)
1343–4. Bartholomew, ld. Burghersh, *again*; C. and W. (17 Edw. III.)
Sir John Peche, C. and W. (17 Edw. III.)
1345–6. Ralph, ld. Bassett, C. and W. (19 Edw. III.)
1346–7. Bartholomew, ld. Burghersh, *again*; C. and W. (20 Edw. III.)
1350–1. Reginald de Cobham, K.G., or ld. Cobham, W. (24 Edw. III.)
1355. Otho de Grandison, C., Aug. 4.
1355–6. Roger de Mortimer, E. of March, C. and W. (29 Edw. III.)
Edw. III. Guy St. Clere, C. and W.
1360–1. Sir John Beauchamp, K.G., C. and W. (34 Edw. III.)
Reginald de Cobham, K.G., C. and W. (34 Edw. III.)
1361–2. Sir Robt. Herle, C. and W. (35 Edw. III.)
1365–6. Sir Ralph Spirgunell, C. and W. (39 Edw. III.)
1369. Sir Richd. de Pembrigg, or Pembridge, C. and W., Mar. 20.
1372. Wm. de Latimer, or ld. Latimer, C. and W., Feb. 7.
1376–7. Edmd. Plantagenet de Langley, E. of Cambridge, C. and W. (50 Edw. III.)
1380–1. Sir Robt. Asheton, C. and W. (4 Rich. II.)
1384. Sir Simon de Burley, K.G., C. and W., Feb. 6.
1388. Sir John Devereux, K.G., C. and W., Jan. 4.
1391–2. Hy. de Cobham, son of Reginald, C. and W. (15 Rich. II.)
1392–3. John, ld. Beaumont, C. and W. (16 Rich. II.)
1396–7. Edwd., D. of York and Albemarle, C. and W. (20 Rich. II.)
1398. John, M. of Dorset, C. and W. Feb. 5.
1401–2. Sir Thos. Erpingham, K.G., C. and W. (3 Hen. IV.)
1409. Hy., pr. of Wales, aft. Hen. V., C. and W., Dec. 12.
1413–4. Sir Thos. Fitz-alan, E. of Arundel, C. and W. (1 Hen. V.)
1420. Humphry, D. of Gloucester, son of Hen. IV., C. and W., Jan. 20.
1425–6. John Reynsford, C. (4 Hen. VI.)
1447. Sir Jas. Fienes, cr. ld. Saye and Sele, C. and W., Feb. 24.
1449–50. Humphry, D. of Buckingham, C. and W. (28 Hen. VI.)
1459–60. Edmd., D. of Somerset, C. and W. (38 Hen. VI.)
1461–2. Simon Montfort, C. and W. (1 Edw. IV.)
Richd., E. of Warwick, C. and W. (1 Edw. IV.)
1470–1. Sir John Scott, C. and W. (10 Edw. IV.)
Wm., E. of Arundel, C. and W. (10 Edw. IV.)
Edw. V. Richd., D. of Gloucester, aft. Richd. III., C. and W.

1483–4. Hy., D. of Buckingham, C. and W. (1 Rich. III.)
1483. Wm., E. of Arundel, *again*; C. and W., Oct. 23.
1847–8. Sir Wm. Scott, C. and W. (3 Hen. VII.)
1493. Hy., D. of York, aft. Hen. VIII., C. and W., Apr. 5.
1504–5. Sir Edwd. Poynings, K.G., C. and W. (20 Hen. VII.)
1510–1. Geo., ld. Abergavenny, C. and W. (2 Hen. VIII.)
1513. Sir Edwd. Poynings, K.G., *again*; C. and W., May 17.
1521–2. Sir Edwd. Guildeford, K.G., C. and W. (13 Hen. VIII.)
1532–3. Geo., visc. Rochford, C. and W. (24 Hen. VIII.)
1536–7. Hy., D. of Richmond, C. and W. (28 Hen. VIII.)
Arth. Plantagenet, visc. Lisle, C. and W. (28 Hen. VIII.)
1539–40. Sir Thos. Cheney, K.G. C. and W. (31 Hen. VIII.)
1558. Wm., ld. Cobham.
1596–7. Hy., ld. Cobham, his son, C. and W. (39 Eliz.)
1603–4. Hy., E. of Northampton, C. and W. (1 Jas. I.)
1615–6. Edwd., ld. Zouch of Haringworth, C. and W. (13 Jas. I.) ? 1614.
1623–4. Geo., D. of Buckingham, C. and W. (21 Jas I.)
1628. Theophilus, E. of Suffolk, C. and W., July 24.
1640. Jas., D. of Richmond, C. and W., June 9.
1648. Robt., E. of Warwick, C.
During the commonwealth the offices were at first executed by the Council of State; afterwards they were put into commission.
John Lambert, John Desborough, Robt. Blake, Chas. Fleetwood. } Held the office of Constable during the commonwealth.
1660. Jas., D. of York, aft. Jas. II., C. and W.
Chs. II. Hy., visc. Sidney, aft. E. of Romney, C. and W.
Anne. Pr. Geo. of Denmark, consort of Q. Anne, C. and W.
1708. Lionel Cranfield, E., aft. D. of Dorset, C. and W., Dec.
1713–4. Jas., D. of Ormond, C. & W., (12 Anne).
Lionel Cranfield, E., aft. D. of Dorset, *again*; C. and W. (1 Geo. I.)
1717. John Sidney, E. of Leicester, C. and W.
Lionel Cranfield, now D. of Dorset, *again*; C. and W. (1 Geo. II.)
1765. Robt., E. of Holderness, C. and W., Oct.
1778. Fredk. North, c.c. Lord North, K.G, aft. E. of Guildford, C. and W.
1792. Wm. Pitt, C. and W., Aug. 18.
1806. Robt. Bankes Jenkinson, c.c. ld. Hawkesbury, aft. E. of Liverpool, C. and W., Jan. 28, **G.**
1829. Arthur, D. of Wellington, C. and W., Jan. 20, **G.**
1853. Jas. Andrew, M. of Dalhousie, K.T., C. and W., Jan. 13, **G.**
1861. Hy. Jno., visc. Palmerston, K.G., C. and W., Mar. 27, **G.**
1865. Granville Geo., E. Granville, K.G., C. and W., Dec. 23, **G.**

CONSTABLES AND LIEUTENANTS OF THE TOWER OF LONDON. LORD LIEUTENANTS OF THE TOWER HAMLETS.

CONSTABLES OF THE TOWER OF LONDON AND LORD LIEUTENANTS OF THE TOWER HAMLETS.

THESE two offices have been united for many years, probably from the first institution of the office of lord lieutenant. The act 14 Chas. II. cap. 3, sec. 31, recites, " Whereas the Militia of the Tower division of Middlesex known as the Tower Hamlets *are, and always have been*, under the command of his majesty's constable or lieutenant of the Tower.

Constables of the Tower of London.

William I.

1066. Geoffrey de Mandeville (No. 1).
* * Wm. de Mandeville, his son.
1140. Geoffrey de Mandeville (No. 2), his grandson.

Stephen.

1153. Richd. de Lucy.

Henry II.

* * Garnerius de Isenei.

Richard I.

1189. Wm. Longchamp, bp. of Ely, with Wm. Piuntellus under him.
1192. Archbp. of Rouen
1194. Roger FitzRenfred.

John.

1205. Roger de la Dune.
1213. Geoffrey de Mandeville (No. 3).

Henry III.

1214. Eustace de Greinville.
1215. Steph. Langton, abp. of Canterbury.
1217. Walter de Verdun.
1220. Stephen de Segrave.
1223. Hugh de Wyndlesore.
1224. Pandulph Masca, bp. of Norwich.
John de Boville.
1225. Thos. de Blunvill.
1226. Hy. Fitz Aucher.
1229. Ralph de Gatel.
1232. Hubert de Burgh, E. of Kent.
1233. W. de St. Edmund.
1234. Geoffrey de Crancumb.
1235. Hugh Giffard.
1241. Walter de Grey, abp. of York, and Bertram de Crioyle, jointly.
1243. Peter de Vallibus.
1244. John de Plessetis.
1245. Peter de Blund.
1255. Aymon Thorimbergh.
1256. Imbert Pugeys.
1260. Richd. de Culwurth.
Richd. de Tilbury.
1261. Hugh de Bigod.
John Mansel.
1262. Hugh le Despenser.
1264. Roger de Leyburn.
Hugh Fitz Otho.
1265. John Walerand and John de la Lind, jointly.
1266. Alan la Zouch.
1267. Thos. dé Ippegrave.
Stephen de Eddeville.
1268. Hugh Fitz Otho, *again*.
1272. Walter Giffard, abp. of York.
1273. John de Burgh.
Philip Basset.
1274. Anthy. Bek.

Edward I.

1283. Ranulph de Dacre.
1286. Ralph de Sandwich.
1289. Ralph de Berners.
Ralph de Sandwich, *again*.

Edward II.

1307. John de Crumbwell.
1320. Guy Frere.
1321. Roger de Swynnerton.
1322. Stephen de Segrave.
1323. Walter Stapleton, bp. of Exeter.
John de Weston.
1326. Thos. Wake.
John de Gisors and Rd. de Betoigne jointly.
1327. Maurice de Berkeley.
Wm. la Zouche.

Edward III.

1329. John de Crumbwell, *again*.
1335. Wm. de Montacute.
Nicholas de la Beche.
1341. Robert de Dalton.
1346. John Darcy (No. 1).
1347. John Darcy (No. 2), son.
1355. Bartholomew de Burghersh.
Robert de Morley.
1360. Jno. de Beauchamp.
1361. Richd. de la Vache.
1365. Alen Buxhill, or Alan de Burchull.

Richard II.

1381. Sir Thos. Murrieux.
1391. Edwd., E. of Rutland.
1397. Ralph de Nevill.
Edwd., D. of Albemarle.
Sir Thos. de Rempston.
1407. Edwd., D. of York.

Henry V.

1413. Robt. de Morley.
John Dabrichcourt.
1415. Sir Wm. Bourchier.
1420. Sir Roger Aston.

Henry VI.

1446. John, D. of Exeter.
Jas., ld. Saye and Sele.

Edward IV.

1461. John, ld. Tiptoft, E. of Worcester.
1473. John, ld. Dudley.
Richd., ld. Dacre.
1478. John, ld. Howard.
* * Thos., M. of Dorset.

Richard III.

1483. Sir Thos. Brackenbury.

Henry VII.

1485. Jno., E. of Oxford.

Henry VIII.

1509. Sir Thos. Lovel.
1524. Sir Wm. Kingston.
1540. Sir John Gage.
1553. Edwd., ld. Clinton.

MARY.

1554. Sir John Gage, *again*.
1556. Sir Edmund Bray.

TEMP. ELIZABETH AND JAMES I.

Thos., ld. Howard of Walden.

CHARLES I.

1640. Fras., ld. Cottington.
1647. Gen. Sir Thos. Fairfax.

CHARLES II.

1660. Sir John Robinson.
1678. Jas., E. of Northampton.
1680. Wm., ld. Allington.
1684. Geo., ld. Dartmouth.

WILLIAM III. TO VICTORIA.

1688. Thos., ld. Lucas.
1702. Montagu, E. of Abingdon.
Algernon, E. of Essex.
1712. Geo., E. of Northampton.
1717. Chas., E. of Carlisle.
1722. Hy., E. of Lincoln.
1725. Chas., D. of Bolton.
1726. Hy., visc. Lonsdale.
* * Richd., E. Rivers.
* * John, E. of Leicester.
1740. Chas., ld., aft. E. Cornwallis.
1762. John, ld. Berkeley of Stratton.
1770. Chas., E., aft. M. Cornwallis.
1783. Ld. Geo. Hy. Lennox.
1785. Chas., E., aft. M. Cornwallis, K.G.
1806. Fras., E. of Moira, aft. M. of Hastings, Feb. 12, sw.
1826. Arthur, D. of Wellington, K.G., Dec. 29, **G.**
1852. Stapleton, visc. Combermere, G.C.B., Oct. 11, **G.**; Feb. 21, 1853, sw.
1865. Gen. Sir John Fox Burgoyne, bt., G.C.B., Apr. 8, **G.**; Apr. 22, sw.
1871. F.-marsh. Sir Geo. Pollock, G.C.B., G.C.S.I., Nov. 14, **G.**
1872. F.-marsh. Sir Wm. Maynard Gomm, G.C.B., Oct. 31, **G.**
1875. Gen. Sir Chas. Yorke, G.C.B., Apr. 5, **G.**
1881. Gen. Sir Wm. Fenwick Williams, of Kars, bt., G.C.B., May 9, **G.**
Gen. Sir Richd. Jas. Dacres, G.C.B., July 2, **G.**
1887. Robt. Cornelis, ld. Napier of Magdala, G.C.B., G.C.S.I., Jan. 6, **G.**

LIEUTENANTS OF THE TOWER OF LONDON.

FROM THE REIGN OF EDWARD I.

EDWARD I.

Giles de Oudenard.

EDWARD II.

Ralph Bavant.

HENRY V.

Sir Roger Aston.

HENRY VII.

Sir John Digby.

HENRY VIII.

Sir Richd. Cholmondeley.
Sir Edwd. Walsingham.
Sir Wm. Sidney.
Sir Anthony Knevit.
— Stoner.

EDWARD VI.

Sir John Markham.
Sir Arthur Darcy.

QUEEN MARY.

Sir John Bridges, aft. ld. Chandos.
Sir Thos. Bridges.
Sir Hy. Bedingfield.
Sir Robt. Oxenbridge.

QUEEN ELIZABETH.

Sir Thos. Carden and Sir Edwd. Warner were app. to take charge of the tower jointly with Sir Robt. Oxenbridge.
Sir Edwd. Warner, alone.
Sir Richd. Blount.
Sir Fras. Jobson.
Sir Owen Hopton.
Sir Michael Blount.
Sir Drue Drury.
Sir Richd. Barkley.
Sir John Peyton.

JAMES I.

Sir Geo. Harvey.
Sir Wm. Waad.
Sir Gervase Helwias.
Sir Geo. More.
Sir Allan Apsley, who continued in office on the accession of

CHARLES I.

Sir Wm. Balfour.
Col. Lunsford.
Sir John Byron.
Sir John Conyers.
Sir Robt. Harlowe.
Alderman Pennington.

COMMONWEALTH.

Col. John Berkstead.
Col. Titchbourn.
Col. Fitch.
Col. Herbert Morley.

CHARLES II.

Sir John Robinson.

JAMES II.

Thos. Cheek.
Sir Edwd. Hales.
Sir Bevill Skelton.
1688. Col. King, as dep. gov.

WILLIAM AND MARY.

Col. John Farewell.

ANNE TO VICTORIA.

Chas. Churchill.
Brig.-gen. Wm. Cadogan.
Lt.-gen. Sir Hatton Compton.
Lt.-gen. Chas. Vernon.
1810. Lt.-gen. Wm. Loftus, Aug. 18, **G.**
1831. Geo., E. of Munster, July 21, **G.**
1833. Ld. Fredk. Fitzclarence, Jan. 19, **G.**
Lt.-gen. John Sulivan Wood, Feb. 26, **G.**
1851. Maj.-gen. Geo. Bowles, July 16, **G.**
1876. Maj.-gen. Chas. Lennox Brownlow Maitland, C.B., July 22, **G.**
1884. Lt.-gen. Fredk. Aug., ld. Chelmsford, G.C.B., July 8, **G.**

GOVERNORS AND CONSTABLES OF WINDSOR CASTLE.

1087. Walter FitzOther.
1100. Wm. FitzWalter.
1153. Richd. de Lucy.
1190. Hugh Pudsey.
Wm. Longchamp.
1191. Wm. de Albini.
E. of Arundel, until 1193.
* * Walter, abp. of Rouen.
* * John FitzHugh.
1216. Engelard de Cygony.
1225. Ralph Tyrell.
1233. Wm. de Millars.
1242. Bernard de Savoy.
1259. Aymon Thurumburd.
1264. Hugh de Barantin.
1267. Nichs. de Yatington.
1273. Geoffrey de Picheford.
1299. John de Loudon.
1305. Roger le Sauvage.
1319. Oliver de Bordeaux.
1326. Thos. de Huntercombe.
1327. John de l'Isle.
1330. Thos. de Foxle.
1360. Richd. la Vache.
1365. Thos. Cheyn.
1377. Sir Simon de Burley.
1390. Peter de Courtney.
1409. Sir John Stanley.
Hen. VI. Walter Hungeford.
1443. Edmd., E., aft M., of Dorset and D. of Somerset (? in 1439).
1461. John, ld. Berners.
1474. Sir Thos. Bourchier.
Richd. III. Thos. Windesor.
1483. Sir John Frilington.
1485. Sir Thos. Bourchier, *again.*
Hen. VII. and Hen. VIII. Hy., ld. Daubeny, aft. E. of Bridgewater.
1562. Ld. Robt. Dudley, aft. E. of Leicester.
1590. Chas., E. of Nottingham, K.G.
Jas. I. Geo., D. of Buckingham.
1637. Hy., E. of Holland.
1648. Philip, E. of Pembroke, 1st E. of Montgomery, &c.
1659. Bulstrode Whitelock.
1660. John, visc. Mordaunt.
1668. Pr. Rupert.
1682. Hy., E. of Arundel, aft. D. of Norfolk.
1701. Geo., D. of Northumberland.
1702. Geo., pr. of Denmark, consort of Q. Anne.
1714. Hy., D. of Kent.
1717. Richd., ld. Cobham.
1723. Chas., E. of Carlisle.
1728. Chas., D. of St. Albans.
1752. Geo., E. of Cardigan, aft. D. of Montagu.
1790. Jas., E. of Cardigan.
1812. Chas., E. of Harrington, Mar. 14, **G.**
1829. Hy., M. of Conyngham, K.B., Sept. 24, **G.**
1833. Geo., E. of Munster, Jan. 19, **G.**
1842. Aug. Fredk., D. of Sussex, Apr. 28, **G.**
1843. Pr. Albert, consort of Q. Victoria, May 18, **G.**
The Prince Consort *d.* Dec. 14, 1861, but the office was not filled up until
1867. Pr. Victor Ferdinand, &c., of Hohenlohe, count Gleichen, capt. R.N., aft. v. adm., July 22, **G.**

LORD WARDENS OF THE STANNARIES.

The term "stannaries" is applied to the tin mines of Devon and Cornwall, over which certain rights and powers are, or were, vested in the dukes of Cornwall. The lord warden of the Stannaries is the principal officer of that duchy.

Lord Wardens of the Stannaries.

Temp. Edwd. VI. Edwd., D. of Somerset.
1553. John, E. of Bedford.
1554. Edwd., ld. Hastings.
Fras., E. of Bedford, abt. 1560.
1584. Sir Walter Raleigh.
1603. Wm., E. of Pembroke.
1630. Philip, E. of Pembroke and Montgomery.
1660. Sir John Grenville, aft. E. of Bath.
1701. Chas., E. of Radnor.
1702. Jos. Granville, aft. ld. Granville.
1705. Fras., ld. Rialton.
1708. Hugh Boscawen, aft. visc. Falmouth.
1734. John Schutz.
1742. Thos. Pitt.
1751. Jas., E. of Waldegrave.
1763. Humphrey Morice.
1783. Geo., visc. Lewisham.
1798. Sir John Morshead, bt.
1800. John Willett Payne.
1803. Thos. Tyrwhitt, aft. Sir T., Dec. 6, **G.**
1812. Fras. Chas. Seymour, c.c., E. of Yarmouth, aft. 3rd M. of Hertford, July 28, **G.**
1842. Pr. Albert, consort of Q. Victoria, Apr. 16, **G.**
1862. Hy. Pelham, D. of Newcastle, Feb. 6, **G.**
1865. Edwd. Berkeley, ld., aft. visc. Portman, Jan. 20, **G.**

PART V. HERALDIC.

EARLS MARSHAL, KINGS OF ARMS, HERALDS, AND PURSUIVANTS.

INTRODUCTION.

THE earlier portions of these lists have been compiled from "Noble's College of Arms," which was published in 1805, and contains an account of the herald's college, and of the various members thereof. As might be expected, there is often, in very early times, some little uncertainty both as to names and dates, and in these cases it will be well to compare the present lists with "Edmondson's Heraldry," from which Noble sometimes differs. From the reign of Henry VII. the succession in each case appears tolerably regular.

The head of the herald's college is the EARL MARSHAL, and under him are a number of officers, divided into three classes :—

KINGS OF ARMS. HERALDS. PURSUIVANTS.

Each officer bears a distinctive title, the origin of which it is, in some cases, not quite easy to trace. The creation and extinction of any particular office were entirely in the discretion of the sovereign, and in many instances the office became extinct on the death or removal of the first holder. In other cases, however, there has been an unbroken succession from the earliest to the present time, and these offices may now be considered permanent.

The following lists are divided into two sections—(1) containing the offices still existing; and (2) containing the offices which have now become extinct.

SECTION I. HERALDIC OFFICES STILL EXISTENT.

LORDS AND EARLS MARSHAL OF ENGLAND.

This office, until it was made hereditary, always passed by grant from he king, and was never held by tenure or sergeantry by any subject, as he offices of lord high steward and lord high constable sometimes were. The marshal was anciently styled lord marshal only; but Richard II., June 20, 1397, granted letters-patent to Thomas Mowbray, earl of Notingham, and to his heirs, the style of earl marshal. James I. by letters-patent, dated August 29, 1622, constituted Thomas Howard, earl of Arundel and Surrey, earl marshal for life; and the next year granted other letters-patent, wherein it was declared that during the vacancy of the office of lord high constable, the earl marshal should have the ike jurisdiction in the court of chivalry as both constable and marshal had jointly exercised. Charles II., on Oct. 19, 1672, granted this office and dignity to Henry, lord Howard, and to his heirs, with power o execute the same by deputy or deputies, in as full and ample a manner as the same had theretofore been executed by any former marshal of England. Under this grant the office is now held by the dukes of Norfolk.

Lords and Earls Marshal of England.

Lords Marshal.

135. Gilbert de Clare, cr. E. of Pembroke by Stephen, 1139.
149. Richd. de Clare, surn. Strongbow, E. of Pembroke, *d.* 1176.
176. John., surn. Marshal, from this office, which was conferred on him by Hen. II., on the death of Richd., E. of Pembroke.
199. Wm. Marshal, grandson of John, who, having married Isabel, dau. and heiress of Richd. Strongbow, was by king John cr. E. of Pembroke in 1201.
219. Wm. Marshal, E. of Pembroke.
231. Richd. Marshal, E. of Pembroke.
234. Gilbert Marshal, E. of Pembroke.
242. Walter Marshal, E. of Pembroke.
245. Anselm Marshal, E. of Pembroke.
245. Roger Bigot or Bigod, E. of Norfolk, in right of Maud, his mother, one of the sisters and co-heiresses of the last five marshals.
269. Roger Bigot or Bigod, E. of Norfolk, whose estate, being confiscated to the crown, came, after his decease, into the king's hands.
307. Robert de Clifford, made ld. marsh. by Edward II., *durante bene placito*.
1308. Nicholas, ld. Segrave.
1315. Thos. Plantagenet de Brotherton, E. of Norfolk; in right of his wife, dau. and heiress of Lord Segrave.

Margaret, dau. and heiress of Thos. Plantagenet, E. of Norfolk; she was often honoured with the title of lady marshal, and was aft. cr. duch. of Norfolk.

Wm. de Montacute, E. of Salisbury.

Thos., E. of Warwick.

Edmd., ld. Mortimer.

These all successively discharged the office of ld. marsh, but whether as deputies to the lady Margaret, *nondum plané constat.*

1377. Hy., ld. Percy, ld. marsh. at the coron. of Richd. II.

John Fitz-Alan, ld. Maltravers.—*Camden*.

1383. Thos., E. of Nottingham, grandson to the lady Margaret by her dau Elizabeth; made the first E. marsh. by Richd. II., and aft cr. D. of Norfolk.

EARLS MARSHAL AND COMMISSIONERS FOR EXECUTING THAT OFFICE.

1397. Thos., E. of Nottingham, aft. D. of Norfolk, above named, June 20.
1398. Thos., E. of Kent and D. of Surrey; made E. marsh. on the banishment of the D. of Norfolk.
Thos., ld. Mowbray, E. of Nottingham; he assumed, on his father's death, the title of E. marsh., but the office was exercised by John, E. of Salisbury.
1400. Ralph, E. of Westmoreland, made ld. marsh. of England for life by Henry IV. in the beginning of his reign.
1412. John, ld. Mowbray, brother of Thos., E. marsh.; rest. to the title of E. of Nottingham and E. marsh. by Henry V., and to that of D. of Norfolk by Henry VI.
1435. John, D. of Norfolk.
1476. Richd. Plantagenet, D. of York, second son to Edward IV.; cr. by his father, D. of Norfolk and E. marsh., in right of his wife Anne, dau. and heiress to John, D. of Norfolk.
Sir Thos. Grey.—*Camden.*
1483. John, ld. Howard, in right of his wife Anne (widow of Richd., D. of York), dau. and heiress of John, D. of Norfolk.
1486. Wm., ld. Berkeley, E. of Nottingham, in right of Isabel, his mother, dau. of Thos., D. of Norfolk; by Henry VII.
1497. Hy. Tudor, D. of York, second son to Henry VII.; aft. Henry VIII.
1509. Thos., E. of Surrey (son to John, ld. Howard, D. of Norfolk, attainted), cr. E. marsh. and rest. as D. of Norfolk.
Chas., D. of Suffolk.—*Camden.*
1546. Thos., D. of Norfolk, attainted in 1546.
1547. Edwd., D. of Somerset, beheaded.
John, D. of Northumberland, beheaded.—*Camden.*
1553. Thos., D. of Norfolk, rest. to his blood and honours by Q. Mary.
1554. Thos., D. of Norfolk, his grandson and heir; beheaded in 1572.
1572. Geo., E. of Shrewsbury, *d.* 1590.
1590. Commissioners:—
Wm., ld. Burleigh, ld. treasr.
Chas., ld. Howard of Effingham, ld. h. adm.
Hy., ld. Hunsdon, ld. chambn.
1597. Robt., E. of Essex, beheaded 1601.
1602. Commissioners:—
Thos., ld. Buckhurst, ld. treasr.
Chas., E. of Nottingham, ld. adm.
Edwd., E. of Worcester, m. horse
1603. Edwd., E. of Worcester, perform the duties of E. marsh. at t coron. of king James; after whi the office was for a long ti executed by commission.
1604. Commissioners:—
Thos., E. of Dorset, ld. treasr.
Lodowick, D. of Lenox.
Chas., E. of Nottingham, ld. adm.
Thos., E. of Suffolk, ld. chambn.
Edwd., E. of Worcester, m. horse
Chas., E. of Devon, m. ordn.
Hy., E. of Northampton, ld. wa Cinque Ports.
1616. Commissioners:—
Edwd., E. of Worcester, ld. seal.
Lodowick, D. of Richmond, steward.
Geo., M. of Buckingham, m. hors
Chas., E. of Nottingham, ld. adm.
Wm., E. of Pembroke, ld. chamb
1622. Thos., E. of Arundel and Sur (grandson of Thos., D. of N folk, by his son Philip, E. Arundel), cr. E. marsh.
1646. Hy., E. of Arundel, &c., *d.* 1652
1661. Jas., E. of Suffolk, Apr. 18.
1662. May 26, Commissioners:—
Thos., E. of Southampton.
John, ld. Roberts.
Hy., M. of Dorchester.
Montagu, E. of Lindsey.
Edwd., E. of Manchester.
Algn., E. of Northumberland.
1672. Hy., his second son, cr. by Cha II. ld. Howard, of Castle Risi in Norfolk, and aft. hereditary marsh. and E. of Norwich; he su his brother as D. of Norfolk.
1684. Hy., ld. Mowbray, and D. of Norfo
1701. Thos., D. of Norfolk.
1732. Edwd., D. of Norfolk, Dec. 23.
1777. Chas., D. of Norfolk, Sept. 20.
1786. Chas., D. of Norfolk, Aug. 31.
1815. Bernard Edwd., D. of Norfolk, D 16.
1842. Hy. Chas., D. of Norfolk, Mar.
1856. Hy. Granville, D. of Norfolk, F 18.
1860. Hy., D. of Norfolk, Nov. 25; Jan. 14, 1869, on attaining majority.

Deputy Earls Marshal of England.

During the legal incapacity of the dukes of Norfolk.

1701. Chas., E. of Carlisle.
1706. Hy., E. of Bindon.
1718. Hy. Bowes, E. of Berkshire.
1725. Talbot, E. of Sussex.
1731. Fras., E. of Effingham.
1743. Thos., E. of Effingham.
1763. Hy., E. of Suffolk and Berkshire.
1765. Richd., E. of Scarborough.
1777. Thos., E. of Effingham.
1782. Chas., E. of Surrey, only son to the D. of Norfolk.
His lordship succ. his father as D. of Norfolk in 1786, and being a Protestant was able to exercise the office in person.
1816. Hy. Thos. Molyneux Howard, brother to Bernard Edward, D. of Norfolk, Jan. 15.
Hy. Thos. Molyneux Howard was the last deputy E. marsh. The dukes of Norfolk were, by 5 Geo. IV. cap. 109 (June 24, 1824), empowered to execute the office of E. marsh. in person notwithstanding their being Roman Catholics.
1861. Lord Edwd. Geo. Fitzalan Howard, during minority of Hy., D. of Norfolk, Feb. 4, **G.**

GARTER KINGS OF ARMS.

This officer was created by Henry V. in the year 1417. He takes his name from the order of the garter, of which he is principal officer of arms. He is also the principal king at arms.

Garter Kings of Arms.

Hen. V. Sir Wm. Brugge or Brugges (1st Garter); cr. by Hen. V. and conf. 24 Hen. VI. (1425–6); *d.* before Mar. 20, 1449.
* * John Smert or Swertz.
* * John Wrexworth.
1478. John Wrythe, July 16; *d.* Mar. or Apr. 1504.
1506. Sir Thos. Writhe or Wriothesley, Jan. 26.
1509. Ditto, by new L. P., dated Oct. 9; *d.* Nov. 24, 1534.
1534. Thos. Wall, aft. sir T., Dec. 9; cr. Dec. 25; *d.* 1535–6.
1536. Christr. Barker, cr. July 9; L. P. July 15; cr. K.B. by Edw. VI.
1549. Sir Gilbert Derrick, cr. Apr. 4; L. P. Apr. 29; *d.* Oct. 3, 1584.
Eighteen months vacancy, during which the duties were discharged by Cook (Clarencieux).
1586. Wm. Dethick, Apr. 21; knt. May 20, 1603; depr. Jan. 1, 1604; *d.* 1612.
1603. Wm. Segar; knt. Nov. 1616; *d.* Dec. 3, 1633.
1633. Sir John Burroughs, Dec. 27; *d.* Apr. 1644.
1644. Sir Hy. St. George (No. 1), Apr.; *d.* Oct. or Nov. 1644.
1645. Sir Edwd. Walker, Feb. 24; depr. by the parlt. Re-instated at the Restoration; *d.* Feb. 19, 1677.
1646. Edwd. Byshe, app. by the parlt.; depr. at Restoration and reduced to his legal office of Clarencieux.
1677. Wm. Dugdale, Apr. 26; *d.* Feb. 10, 1686.
1686. Sir Thos. St. George; signet, Feb.; L. P. Mar. 9; *d.* Mar. 6, 1703.
1703. Sir Hy. St. George (No. 2), cr. Apr. 26; L. P. June 2; *d.* Aug. 1715.
1715. John Anstis (No. 1), received L. P. granting him the reversion of this office, Apr. 2, 1714. On the death of sir Hy. St. George he claimed the office, but his demand was disregarded, and sir John Vanbrugh (Clarencieux) was app. by L. P., Oct. 26, 1715. Ultimately the claims of Anstis were allowed, and he was *created* Garter, Apr. 20, 1718. He afterwards obtained L. P. dated June 8, 1727, granting the office to him and to his son, John Anstis (No. 2), in reversion; *d.* Mar. 4, 1745.
1745. John Anstis (No. 2), Mar. 4; succ. under the L. P. of June 8, 1727 *d.* Dec. 5, 1754.

1754. Stephen Martin Leake, Dec.; *d.* Mar. 24, 1773.
1773. Sir Chas. Townley, Apr. 27; *d.* June 7, 1774
1774. Thos. Browne; *d.* Feb. 22, 1780.
1780. Ralph Bigland (No. 1), app. Feb. 26; cr. Mar. 2; *d.* Mar. 27, 1784.
1784. Isaac Heard, aft. sir I., Apr. 27.; *d.* 1822.
1822. Sir Geo. Nayler, May 10, **G.**; July 2 sw.; *d.* 1831.
1831. Ralph Bigland (No. 2), Nov. 15, **G** knt. Dec. 7; *d.* 1839.
1839. Sir Wm. Woods, July 23, **G.**; *d.* 184
1842. Chas. Geo. Young, aft. sir C., Au 4, **G.**; inv. Aug. 27; sw. Oct. 1844; *d.* 1869.
1869. Albert Wm. Woods, Oct. 25, **G** knt. Nov. 11.

CLARENCIEUX KINGS OF ARMS.

The date and origin of the title of Clarencieux is a little obscure. was apparently created by or in the reign of Edward III., and was take from the dukedom of his son, the Duke of Clarence. The office was first that of Clarencieux *Herald* only, but when Edward IV. su ceeded to the dukedom, on the death of his brother, he raised it Clarencieux *King at Arms*.

The province or jurisdiction of Clarencieux extends south of t Trent.

Clarencieux Kings of Arms.

* * *

* * Clarencieux *Heralds* only:—
Wm. Horseley, cr. by Hen. V.
Roger Lygh, cr. by Hen. VI.
John Ashwell, cr. by Hen. VI.
Thos. Collyer, cr. by Hen. VI.
John Mallet, cr. by Hen. VI.
Wm. Hawkeslow, cr. by Edw. IV.
Clarencieux *K. arms.*

1476. Sir Thos. Holme; *d.* 1493.
1493. Roger Machado. See note to "Norroy," *post*, p. 329; *d.* 1516.
1516. Thos. Benolte; *d.* May 8, 1534.
1534. Thos. Tonge, Aug. 2.
1536. Thos. Hawley, May 19; *d.* Aug. 22, 1557.
1557. Wm. Harvey, cr. Nov. 21; *d.* Feb. 27, 1567.
1567. Robt. Cooke. *d.* 1592.
1594. Richd. Lee; L. P. May 11; cr. May 18; *d.* Sept. 23, 1597.
1597. Wm. Camden, cr. Oct.; L. P. June 6, 1599; *d.* Nov. 19, 1623.
1623. Sir Richd. St. George; L. P. Sept. 17; cr. Dec. 23; *d.* May 17, 1635.
1635. Sir Wm. Le Neve, June 22; depr. by the parlt., 1646. At the Restoration he was found to be insane, so he was not re-appointed; but the place was given to Byshe, the deposed "Garter."
1646. Arth. Squibb, app. by the parlt. about Mar.; *d.* May 22, 1646.
1646. Edwd. Byshe, aft. sir E., who r signed in favour of
* * Wm. Ryley, who was at the Rest ration reduced to his legal ra of Lancaster Herald, and the po of Clarencieux given to Edw Byshe, *ut supra*.
1679. Sir Hy. St. George (No. 2), Jan aft. "Garter."
1704. Sir John Vanbrugh, Mar. 29; re Feb. 9, 1726; *d.* Mar. 26, 1726
1726. Knox Ward, June 9; *d.* Sept. 30, 174
1741. Stephen Martin Leake, Sept. 30; c Dec. 22; aft. "Garter."
1755. Chas. Townley, aft. sir C., Jan. 1 aft. "Garter."
1773. Thos. Browne; aft. "Garter."
1774. Ralph Bigland (No. 1); a "Garter."
1780. Isaac Heard, Mar. 11; aft. "Garter
1784. Thos. Locke, May 18; *d.* Feb. 2 1803.
1803. Geo. Harrison, Mar. 4, **G.**
1820. Sir Geo. Nayler, May 17, **G.**; a "Garter."
1822. Ralph Bigland (No. 2), May 10, **G** aft. "Garter."
1831. Wm. Woods, Nov. 15, **G.**; knt. Ap 12, 1832; aft. "Garter."
1838. Edmd. Lodge, July 23, **G.**; *d.* 183
1839. Jos. Hawker, Jan. 29, **G.**; *d.* 184
1846. Fras. Martin, Apr. 18, **G.**; *d.* 1848
1848. Jas. Pulman, June 14, **G.**
1859. Robt. Laurie, Nov. 19, **G.**
1882. Walter Aston Blount, Mar. 13, **G.**

NORROY KING OF ARMS.

THIS officer takes his name from those over which he has jurisdiction, i.e. the people residing *north* of the Trent, the inhabitants of the north being anciently called NORREYS.

The duties of this office were exercised as early as the reign of Edward I., but it is believed that the title of NORROY was not used until the reign of Edward II. or Edward III. It certainly occurs in the records of the latter reign. From that time until the reign of Edward IV. it is doubtful whether any officer bearing the title was ever created, but there are several records of the duties of the office being discharged by other kings of arms or heralds. Edward IV. revived the dormant title, and it has since continued without interruption.

NORROY KING OF ARMS.

* * *

1478. John Moore, July 9; *d.* 1491.
1485. Roger Machado.
It would seem that upon the accession of Henry VII., in 1485, Moore, who was a partisan of Richd. III., was deprived. Henry VII. created a king at arms with his own former title of RICHMOND, and appointed Roger Machado to the office. He wrote himself "RICHMOND-NORROY": aft. "Clarencieux."
1493. Christr. Carhill, *d.* 1510.
1510. Thos. Benolte, aft. "Clarencieux."
1516. Thos. Wall, May 27. The father or grandfather of "Garter" Wall.
* * John Joyner, *d.* 1522.
1522. Thos. Tonge, Nov. 1 (Allhallow's Day), aft. "Clarencieux."
1526. Christr. Barker, aft. "Garter."
1536. Wm. Fellows, July 9.
1545–6. Gilbert Dethick, cr.; L. P. Aug. 16, 1547.
1550. Wm. Harvey; L. P. Feb. 2; cr. Feb. 4.
1557. Laurence Dalton; L. P. Sept. 6; cr. Dec. 1558; *d.* Dec. 13, 1561.
1562. Wm. Flower, Feb. 8.
1592. Edmd. Knight, Mar. 26; *d.* Oct. 30, 1593.
1593. Wm. Segar, cr.; L. P. June 6, 1602; aft. "Garter."
1603. Sir Richd. St. George; aft. "Clarencieux."
1623. Jno. Burroughs, Dec. 18; cr. Dec. 23; knt, July 17, 1624; aft. "Garter."
1634. Sir Wm. le Neve, Jan. 3; aft. "Clarencieux."
1635. Sir Hy. St. George (No. 1), June 24; aft. "Garter."
1643. Sir Edwd. Walker, cr. end of 1643; L. P., signet, Apr.; gr. seal, June 24, 1644; aft. "Garter." On his promotion to Garter there was a vacancy not legally supplied until the Restoration. In the meantime
1646. Wm. Ryley, Aug. 13; cr. Oct. 20; was app. by the parlt., who afterwards promoted him to "Clarencieux." At the Restoration he was reduced to his previous office of Lancaster Herald.
1658. Geo. Owen, who was reduced at the Restoration to his previous office of York Herald.
1660. Sir Wm. Dugdale, June 12; aft. "Garter."
1677. Sir Hy. St. George (No. 2), Apr. 27; aft. "Clarencieux."
1680. Sir Thos. St. George, Jan.; aft. "Garter."
1685–6. Sir Jno. Dugdale, knt.; *d.* between Mar. and Nov. 1700.
1700. Robt. Devenish, cr. Oct.; L. P. Nov. 22; *d.* Apr. 7, 1704.
1704. Peter le Neve, May 25; *d.* Sept. 24, 1729.
1729. Steph. Martin Leake, Dec. 8; aft. "Clarencieux."
1741. John Cheale, Sept. 30; *d.* May 8, 1751.
1751. Chas. Townley, app. Nov. 2; cr. Nov. 19; aft. "Clarencieux."
1756. Wm. Oldys; *d.* Apr. 15, 1761.
1761. Thos. Browne; aft. "Clarencieux."
1773. Ralph Bigland (No. 1), May; aft. "Clarencieux."
1774. Isaac Heard, Oct.; aft. "Clarencieux."
1780. Peter Dore, Mar. 21; *d.* Sept. 27, 1781.

1781. Thos. Locke, Nov. 8; aft. "Clarencieux."

1784. Geo. Harrison, May 20; aft. "Clarencieux."

1803. Ralph Bigland (No. 2), Apr. 4; aft. "Clarencieux."

1822. Edmd. Lodge, May 30, **G.**; aft. "Clarencieux."

1838. Jos. Hawker, July 23, **G.**; aft. "Clarencieux."

1839. Fras. Martin, Jan. 29, **G.**; af "Clarencieux."

1846. Jas. Pulman, Apr. 18, **G.**; af "Clarencieux."

1848. Edwd. Howard Howard Gibbo June 14, **G.**; *d.* 1849.

1849. Robt. Laurie, July 5, **G.**; af "Clarencieux."

1859. Walter Aston Blount, Nov. 28, **G** aft. "Clarencieux."

1882. Geo. Edwd. Cokayne, June 23, **G**

BATH AND GLOUCESTER KINGS OF ARMS.

THE office of BATH KING OF ARMS was founded by George I. o June 1, 1725.

GLOUCESTER KING OF ARMS was founded by Richard III. in honou of his dukedom. There are prior traces of a Gloucester herald, but h seems to have been merely an officer of the dukes of Gloucester and no of the king. Richard Champney was appointed Gloucester king o arms on Jan. 4, 1484. He was either deprived after the battle o Bosworth, or, more probably, killed in that battle. The office remaine in abeyance until January 14, 1726, when it was revived, and "in separably annexed, united, and perpetually consolidated with" th office of Bath king of arms.

The duties of "Bath" are, as his name implies, principally connecte with the order of knighthood bearing that name. "Gloucester," o his revival, was made principal herald of "the parts of Wales," and ha special jurisdiction over that portion of the United Kingdom.

BATH AND GLOUCESTER KINGS OF ARMS.

Grey Longueville, app. "Bath," June 1, 1725; app. "Gloucester," Jan. 14, 1726; *d.* Sept. 29, 1745.

1745. Hon. Edwd. Young, Oct.

* * Wm. Woodley.

1757 or 1761. Saml. Horsey; *d.* July 28, 1771.

1771. Thos. Gery Cullum, aft. bt., De 14; res.

1801. Jno. Palmer Cullum, app. "Bath, Apr. 3, **G.**; and "Gloucester, Apr. 21, **G.**

1830. Algernon Greville.

1865. V.-Adm. Hon. Geo. Grey.

CHESTER HERALDS.

THIS office is said to have been founded in the reign of Edward III., an there are traces of the title under Richard II., Henry IV., an Henry V.

CHESTER HERALDS.

* * *

Edw. IV. Roger Stamford.*

Rich. III. Roger Bromley.*

* There is some doubt whether these two names do not refer to the same individual.

Rich. III. Thos. Whiting, who was living u to 10 Hy. VII. (1494–5). Th date of his death is uncertain Office vacant for some years.

1534. Randolph Jackson, cr. June 21 at coronation of Q. Ann Boleyn.

1545–6. Wm. Flower; aft. "Norroy."
1562. Robt. Cooke, cr. Jan. 29; L. P. Feb. 8; aft. "Clarencieux."
1566. John Hart.
1574. Edwd. Knight, cr. Oct. 31 (All-hallow's Eve); aft. "Norroy."
1592. Jas. Thomas, Mar. 26.
* * Wm. Penson, under L. P. from Jas. I., which were afterwards declared invalid, and Penson was superseded by
1617. Thos. Knight; L. P. Apr. 5 res., and *d.* Oct. 1618.
1618. Hy. Chitting, July 18; *d.* Jan. 7, 1638.
1638. Edwd. Walker, Jan. 31; cr. Feb. 8; aft. "Norroy."
1644. Wm. Dugdale, Apr. 16; depr. by the Parlt; app. "Norroy" at the Restoration.
1644. — Ryley, "Intruder" during the Commonwealth; the brother of Wm. Ryley, the "intruding" Clarencieux.
* * Thos. Lee; *d.* Apr. 23, 1677.
1677. Thos. May, nom. Apr. 24; L. P. May 6; cr. June 24; *d.* Dec. 1689.
1689. Chas. Mawson; res. Aug. 5, 1720.
1721. Edwd. Stibbs, Dec. 13; *d.* Jan. 10, 1739.
1739. Fras. Hutchenson, Feb. 22; *d.* June 22, 1752.
1752. Jno. Martin Leake, Aug.; res.
1791. Geo. Martin Leake, Dec.; *d.* 1834.
1834. Walter Aston Blount, Nov. 15, **G.**; aft. "Norroy."
1859. Edwd. Steph. Dendy, Dec. 5, **G.**
1864. Hy. Murray Lane, July 18, **G.**

WINDSOR HERALDS.

This office is said to have been founded by Edward III. in the 38th year of his reign (1364–65), but until the reign of Edward IV. the records are uncertain, and the name of Windsor is applied to a king of Arms and to a Herald apparently without much distinction either of person or office.

Windsor Heralds.

* * * *

* * Thos. Holme.
About 8 Edw. IV.
1468–9. Jno. Moore, aft. "Norroy."
Vacancy until
1 Hy. VII.
1485–6. Richd. Slacke; *d.* May 1502.
Vacancy not filled up until
Hy. VII. Thos. Benolte; aft. "Norroy."
Hy. VIII. Fras. Dyes; *d.* Oct. or Nov. 1524.
1524. Thos. Wall; aft. "Garter."
1534. Chas. Wrythe or Wriothesley, cr. Dec. 25; L. P. Jan. 1, 1535; *d.* Jan. 25, 1561.
Vacancy until
1564. Richd. Turpin, app.; cr. Apr. 19, 1565; *d.* Oct. 17, 1581.
1583. Nichs. Dethick, Apr. 24; *d.* Jan. 19, 1596.
1597. Thos. Lant, cr. Oct. 22; L. P. Nov. 19, 1600; *d.* 1600 or 1601.
1603. Richd. St. George, aft. "Norroy."
1617. Saml. Thompson, Apr. 5; *d.* May 15, 1624.
1624. Augustine Vincent, June 1; cr. June 29; *d.* Jan. 11, 1626.
1626. John Bradshaw, Jan.; *d.* 1655.
1633. Edwd. Norgate, Oct. 28; *d.* Dec. 23, 1650.
It is believed that during the Commonwealth, Byshe, the brother of Edwd. Byshe (see Garter K. Arms), "intruded" into this office, and was deprived at the Restoration.
1660. Elias Ashmole, Apr. 22; res. July 21, 1676.
1676. John Dugdale, Oct. 22; aft. "Norroy."
1686. Hy. Ball, cr. Mar. 29; *d.* Feb. 13, 1687.
1687. Thos. Holford (No. 1).
1690. Peers Mauduit; res.
1726. Jas. Whorwood, Dec. 2.
1736. Jno. Kettle, Aug.; cr. Dec. 22, 1741; *d.* May 1745.
1745. Richd. Mawson; *d.* Sept. 2, 1745, the day on which the warrant appointing him was made out.
1746. Thos. Thornborough; *d.* about 1757.
1757. Hy. Hill, Nov. 26; cr. July 4, 1758; *d.* June 1774.
1774. Geo. Harrison, Nov.; aft. "Norroy."
1784. Fras. Townshend, June 5; *d.* 1819.

1819. Fras. Martin, Apr. 12, **G.**; aft. "Norroy."
1839. Robt. Laurie, Feb. 1, **G.**; aft. "Norroy."
1849. Geo. Harrison Rogers-Harrison July 6, **G.**; *d.* 1880.
1880. Wm. Hy. Weldon, Apr. 17, **G.**

SOMERSET HERALDS.

THIS office was created by Henry VII., in the 9th year of his reign (1493–4), in honour of the house of Somerset, from which he was descended.

SOMERSET HERALDS.

9 Hen. VII.
1493–4. John Young; *d.* 1510.
* * John or Thos. Ponde; *d.* about 1542.
* * Wm. Hastings; *d.* May 15.
* * Thos. Traheyron or Trahern.
35 Hen. VIII.
1543–4. Richd. Radcliffe.
37 Hen. VIII.
1545–6. Wm. Harvey, aft. "Norroy."
1551. Edmond Atkynson, Feb. 21; *d.* Dec. 1, 1570.
1570. Robt. Flower, *d.* 1571.
1571. Robt. Glover, *d.* Apr. 1588.
1589. Wm. Segar, Jan. 4; aft. "Norroy."
1597. Robt. Treswell or Creswell, cr. Oct. 22; L. P. Mar. 20, 1603. Sold his office June 14, 1624, to—
1624. Jno. Philipot, July 8; *d.* Nov. 25, 1645.
Vacancy, except for a doubtful "intrusion" by Wm. Dethick, under the Commonwealth until
1660. Sir Thos. St. George, by Signet July; aft. "Norroy."
1679-80. Fras. Burghill; surr. the office.
1700. Saml. Stebbing, May 31; *d.* Aug. 21, 1719.
1720. John Warburton, app. June 6 L. P. June 18; cr. June 24; *d.* May 11, 1759.
1759. Ralph Bigland (No. 1), aft. "Norroy."
1773. Hy. Hastings, June; *d.* Dec. 21 1777.
* * John Chas. Brooke, *d.* Feb. 3 1794.
1794. John Atkinson, Mar. 1; *d.* 1813.
1813. Jas. Cathrow, aft. J. Cathrow Disney, Aug. 25, **G.**
1854. Wm. Courthorpe, Jan. 31, **G.**
1866. Jas. Robinson Planché, June 7, **G.**
1880. Stephen Isaacson Tucker, Aug. 10, **G.**; *d.* Jan. 6, 1887.
1887. Hy. Farnham Burke, Jan. 29, **G.**

LANCASTER HERALDS.

THIS officer takes his name from the Lancaster branch of the Plantagenets. The title is believed to have been first used by Henry IV. who was formerly duke of Lancaster. He created a Lancaster *king of arms*, and appointed to the office Richard del Brugg, who held it till his death. Edward IV. first reduced the office to Lancaster *herald*, and afterwards abolished it. It was revived as Lancaster herald by Henry VII.

LANCASTER HERALDS.

1 Edw. IV.
1461–2. Wm. Jennings.
Edw. IV. Wm. Tyndall.
* * * *
1509. Thos. Wall, Apr. 30, aft. "Norroy."
* * * *
1526. Wm. Jennings, May 2.
1527. Wm. Fellows, cr. Nov. 1 (All hallows Day); aft. "Norroy."
1536. Thos. Mylner, cr. July 9; executed 1538–9 (30 Hy. VIII.).

1539. Fulk ap Howell, Apr. 28; cr. July 9. Expelled, degraded, and executed.
1553. Nichs. Tubman, cr. Nov. 15; L. P. Nov. 22; *d.* Jan. 8, 1559.
1559. John Cocke, Jan. 13; *d.* Mar. 17, 1585.
1588. Nichs. Paddy, June 30.
1602. Fras. Thynne, cr. Apr. 22; *d.* 1608.
1609. Nichs. Charles or Carles, cr. Apr. 21; *d.* Nov. 1613.
1613. Wm. Penson, Dec. 16 (see "Chester Herald"); *d.* Apr. 20, 1637.
1637. Thos. Thompson.
1641. Wm. Ryley, Nov. 11; app. by the Parlt. to "Norroy," but reduced at Restoration to "Lancaster"; *d.* July 1667.
1646. Edwd. Byshe, "intruder," aft. "Clarencieux."
Geo. Barkham, "intruder"; depr. at Restoration.
1665. Robt. Chaloner, *d.* Nov. 1, 1676.
1676. Fras. Sandford, Nov. 16; res.
1689. Gregory King, July; *d.* Aug. 29, 1712.
1712. Rowland Fryth, Nov. 14; *d.* Dec. 7, 1712.
1713. John Hesketh, June 4. Sold his office in
1727. To Stephen Martin Leake; aft. "Norroy."
1729. Chas. Greene, Dec. 8.
1743. Thos. Browne, Apr.; aft. "Norroy."
* * Isaac Heard; aft. "Clarencieux."
1774. Thos. Locke, Nov. 10; aft. "Norroy."
1781. Chas. Townley, Dec. 24; surr. his office July 11, 1793; *d.* Nov. 25, 1800.
1793. Edmd. Lodge, Dec.; aft. "Norroy."
1822. Geo. Fredk. Beltz, May 30, **G.**; *d.* 1841.
1841. Albert Wm. Woods, Nov. 6, **G.**; aft. "Garter."
1870. Geo. Edwd. Adams, Jan. 1.
1873. Geo. Edwd. Cokayne, aft. "Norroy."
1882. Edwd. Bellasis, July 7, **G.**

RICHMOND HERALDS.

According to some writers this title existed as far back as the reign of Edward IV., both as a herald and a king of arms. If it did, it was probably only attached to the household of a prince and not of a reigning monarch. The better opinion seems to be that Henry VII., who prior to his accession had been duke of Richmond, first made "Richmond" an officer of the crown, and the title has ever since continued.

Richmond Heralds.

Hen. VII. Robt. Browne (?).
1485. Roger Machado, Richmond *K. arms.* See his name under "Norroy," *ante*, p. 329.
* * John Joyner, aft. "Norroy."
1522. Christr. Barker, cr. Nov. 1 (All-hallows Day); aft. "Clarencieux."
1536. John Narboone, *d.* 1540.
1540. Gilbert Dethick, Dec. 25; aft. "Norroy."
1547. Laurence Dalton, Apr. 12; aft. "Norroy."
1557. Nicholas Narboone; aft. "Ulster."
1566. Hugh Cotgrave, cr.; L. P. July 27, 1569; *d.* abt. 1584.
1584. Richd. Lee, nom.; cr. June 10, 1585, aft. "Clarencieux."
1597. Wm. Camden, cr. Oct. 22; aft. "Clarencieux." He was only in office one day.
1597. John Raven, cr. Oct. 23; L. P. Aug. 13, 1603; *d.* Feb. 13, 1615.
1615. Hy. St. George (No. 1.), cr. Mar. 22; L. P. Apr. 5, 1617; knt. abt. 1627; aft. "Norroy."
1635. Geo. Mainwaring, June 25.
Everard Exton, "intruded" under the Commonwealth, and was depr. at the Restoration.
1660 or 1666. Hy. St. George (No. 2), June 18; aft. "Norroy."
1677. Hy. Dethick, Apr. 30; *d.* June 1707.
1707. Peter Le Neve; aft. "Norroy."

* * John Hare, *d.* May 14, 1720.
1721. Robt. Dale, May 3; *d.* Apr. 4, 1722.
Geo. I. Chas. Whinyates, res.
1755. Fras. Grose, June; res. 1763; *d.* May 12, 1791.
1763. Hy. Pugolas, Feb. 19; *d.* May 23, 1764.
1764. Peter Dore, July 16, aft. "Norroy."
1780. Ralph Bigland (No. 2), Apr. 8; aft. "Norroy."
1803. Jos. Hawker, May 5, **G.**; aft. "Norroy."
1838. Jas. Pulman, July 23, **G.**; aft. "Norroy."
1846. Matth. Chas. Howard Gibbon, Apr. 24, **G.**
1873. Hy. Harrington Molyneux Seel, Nov. 11, **G.**
1882. Arth. Staunton Larken, Oct. 4, **G.**

YORK HERALDS.

THIS officer was named after the white rose branch of the Plantagenets. The office was probably created either by Edward IV. or Richard III., though some writers date it back to Edward III., whose son was created duke of York. There is some doubt about the order of the earlier names.

YORK HERALDS.

* * Hy. Ffranch, or Franke.
Edw. IV. Thos. Hollingsworth.
1483. John Waters; *d.* 1500.
* * Thos. Tonge, aft. "Norroy."
* * Ralph Lagysse; *d.* 1528.
* * Thos. Bysley; *d.* midsummer, 1530.
* * Allan Dagnall.
24 Hen. VIII.
1532–3. Rowland Playnford.
* * Wm. Writhe, or Wriothesley.
* * John Mynne.
* * Bartholomew Butler; aft. "Ulster."
Vacancy until
1553. Martin Maroffe, cr. Nov. 15; L. P. Nov. 25; *d.* Apr. 1563.
1565. Wm. Colborne, Jan. 25; cr. Apr. 19; *d.* Sept. 13, 1567.
1567. Ralph Langman.
1569. Wm. Dethick, aft. "Garter."
1587. Humphry Hales, cr. June 4; *d.* June 16, 1591.
1593. Ralph Brooke, Mar. 2; *d.* Oct. 15, 1625.
1625. Wm. Le Neve, aft. sir W., Nov. 25; aft. "Norroy."
1633. Geo. Owen; warr. to E. marsh., Dec. 9; advanced to "Norroy" by the Commonwealth, but reduced to York at Restoration; surr. his office 1663; *d.* May 13, 1665 or 1666.
1658. — Owen, bro. of the preceding; depr. at Restoration.
1663. John Wingfield; surr. his office, Dec. 22, 1674; *d.* Dec. 30, 1678.
1675. Robt. Devenish, cr. Feb. 23; aft. "Norroy."
1700. Lawrence Cromp; L. P. Nov. 23; cr. Dec. 11; *d.* June 11, 1715.
1717. Thos. Whitwick, cr. Oct. 4; *d.* June 20, 1722.
1722. Philip Jones, Nov. 9; sold his office to his successor.
1735. Chas. Townley, app. July; cr. Dec.; L. P. Aug. 26, 1736; aft. "Norroy."
1753. Geo. Fletcher, Nov. 23; *d.* Nov. 9, 1785.
1786. Benjn. Pingo, Feb. 4; *d.* Feb. 3, 1794.
1794. Geo. Nayler, Mar. 15; aft. "Clarencieux."
1820. Chas. Geo. Young, May 18, **G.**; aft. "Garter."
1842. Edwd. Howard Gibbon, Aug. 5, **G.**; aft. "Norroy."
1848. Thos. Wm. King, June 17, **G.**
1872. John Von Sonnentag de Haviland, Mar. 20, **G.**; *d.* 1886.
1886. Alf. Scott Gatty, Oct. 9, **G.**

SURREY HERALDS EXTRAORDINARY.

1856. Edwd. Stph. Dendy, Aug. 23; aft. "Chester."
1880. Chas. Alban Buckler, July 16, **G.**

MALTRAVERS HERALD EXTRAORDINARY.

1887. Jos. Jackson Howard, Nov. 26, **G.**

ROUGE CROIX PURSUIVANTS.

THIS name was taken from the colour of the St. George's Cross. The office was created by Henry V.

ROUGE CROIX PURSUIVANTS.

* * *

* * John Wrythe.

* * *

Edwd. IV. or Rich. III. John Waters, aft. "York."

Rich. III. Geo. Berry.

Hy. VII. Rich. Grinwode.

Robt. Browne, aft. "Richmond."

John Joyner, aft. "Richmond."

Thos. Waters, aft. "Carlisle."

Wm. Jennings, aft. "Lancaster."

Thos. Benolte, aft. "Windsor."

1509. Thos. Hawley, Aug. 29; aft. "Carlisle."

Hy. VIII. Laurence de la Gatta.

John or Thos. Ponde, aft. "Somerset."

1521. Thos. Wall, cr. May 4; L. P. May 10; aft. "Windsor."

* * Chas. Wrythe or Wriothesley, aft. "Windsor."

1535. Barthw. Butler, Jan. 12; aft. "York."

* * Justinian Barker.

1540. Gilbert Dethick, Dec.; aft. "Richmond."

* * Wm. Flower, aft. "Chester."

1546. Laurence Dalton, Nov. 15; aft. "Richmond."

* * Simon Nymbolthe or Newbald; *d.* 1550 or 1551.

1551. Nicholas Tubman, Jan. 19; aft. "Lancaster."

1553. Hugh Cotgrave, cr. Nov. 15; L. P. Nov. 20; aft. "Richmond."

1566. Wm. Dethick; aft. "York."

1559. Thos. Dawes; L. P. Mar. 24; cr. Mar. 25, 1570.

1580. Ralph Brooke, aft. "York."

1592. Thos. Knight, Mar. 26; aft. "Chester."

1604. Wm. Wyrley, May 5; *d.* Feb. 1619.

1619. John Gwillim, Feb. 26; *d.* May 7, 1621.

1621. Augustine Vincent; L. P. May 29; cr. June 6; aft. "Windsor."

1624. John Bradshaw; L. P. June 8; cr. June 23; aft. "Windsor."

1626. Geo. Owen; pr. seal, Mar. 2; warrt. July 26; aft. "York."

1637. Edwd. Walker; sign. May; gr. seal, May 19; cr. June 5; aft. "Chester."

1638. Hy. Lilley; sign. Jan.; *d.* Aug. 19, 1638.

1639. Wm. Dugdale, Mar. 18; aft. "Chester," in 1644.

Vacancy until

1646. Everard Exton "intruded" during the Commonwealth, and promoted to "Richmond."

* * Robt. Brown "intruded" during the Commonwealth; res. or depr. at the Restoration.

1660. Hy. Dethick; sign. July; aft "Richmond."

1677. Hy. Ball; sign. Apr.; aft. "Windsor."

1686. Chas. Mawson, cr. Mar. 29; aft "Chester."

1688. Saml. Stebbing, May 17; aft. "Somerset."

1701. Peter Le Neve, Jan. 17; aft "Richmond."

* * John Bound, *d.* Mar. 30, 1721.

1722. Richd. Graham, Aug. 4.

1725. John Pomfret, July 26; *d.* Mar. 24, 1751.

1751. Alexr. Cozens.

1752. Hy. Hastings, Aug.; aft. "Somerset."

1773. John Chas. Brooke, aft. "Somerset."

1777. Fras. Townshend, aft. "Windsor."

1784. John Atkinson, June 5; aft. "Somerset."

1794. Jos. Hawker, Apr. 19; aft. "Richmond."

1803. Wm. Radcliffe, May 17; res.

1823. Robt. Laurie, Aug 11, **G.**; aft. "Windsor."

1839. Wm. Courthope, Feb. 1, **G.**; aft. "Somerset."
1854. Jas. Robt. Planché, Feb. 13, **G.**; aft. "Somerset."
1866. John Von Sonnentag de Havilland, Aug. 16, **G.**; aft. "York."
1872. Stephen Isaacson Tucker, Sept. 9, **G.**; aft. "Somerset."
1880. Hy. Farnham Burke, Aug. 27, **G.**; aft. "Somerset."
1887. Geo. Wm. Marshall, Jan.

BLUE MANTLE PURSUIVANTS.

According to some this name was adopted by Edward III., in honour of the colour of the "field" of the French coat of arms, which he assumed. According to others, and more probably, it was taken from the colour of the garter.

The office was founded either by Edward III. or by Henry V., probably by the former.

Blue Mantle Pursuivants.

* * *

Edw. IV. Roger Bromley, aft. "Chester."
Rich. III. John Brice.
Hy. VII. — Coller.
* * Thos. Franche.
* * Laurence Alford.
* * John Younge.
* * Fras. Dyes; aft. "Windsor."
Hy. VIII. Thos Wall; aft. "Lancaster."
6 Hy. VIII.
1514–5. Ralph Lago.
10 Hy. VIII.
1518–9. John Hutton.
1522. Thos. Bysley, Nov. 5; aft. "York."
1528. John Narboone, cr. Nov. 1 (All-hallows day); aft. "Richmond."
* * Rowland Playnford; aft. "York."
1536. Richd. Ratcliffe, May 16; aft. "Somerset."
* * Leonard Warcup; aft. "Carlisle."
* * Wm. Harvey; L. P. June 18; aft. "Somerset."
1544. Edmd. Atkynson, Sept. 28; aft. "Somerset."
1550–1. Nicholas Narboone; aft. "Richmond."
1557. John Hollingworth, nom.; cr. Dec. 9, 1558; L. P. Sept., 1559; *d.* Oct. 10, 1559.
1559. Richd. Turpin, app.; cr. Jan. 22, 1561; aft. "Windsor."
1564. Nichs. Dethick, app.; cr. Apr. 19, 1565; aft. "Windsor."
1583. Humphry Hales, app.; cr. Nov. 3, 1584; aft. "York."
1587. Jas. Thomas; sign. Apr. 24; L. P. Apr. 25; cr. June 4; aft. "Chester."
1588, Robt. Treswell or Creswell; sign. Feb. 21; L. P. May 18; cr. Mar. 26, 1592; aft. "Somerset."
1597. Mercury Patten, cr. Oct. 22; L. P. May 8, 1604; sold his office to his successor.
1611. Hy. St. George (No. 1), Dec. 23; aft. "Richmond."
1616. Sampson Lennard, cr. Mar. 22; L. P. Mar. 23 and Apr. 29, 1617; *d.* Aug. 1633.
* * Edwd. Norgate, aft. "Windsor."
1633. Wm. Ryley, Sept. 4; aft. "Lancaster."
1641. Robt. Browne, *d.* Oct. 14, 1646.
1646. John Watson, "intruder" during the Commonwealth; depr. at Restoration.
1660. Robt. Chaloner, July; aft. "Lancaster."
1665. R. Hornebrock, *d.* July, 1667.
* * Thos. Segar, *d.* 1670.
1668. John Gibbon; L. P. Feb. 10; cr. May 25, 1671.
1719. Jas. Green, June 3; inv. June 24; *d.* Sept. 4, 1737.
1737. Thos. Browne, Oct.; aft. "Lancaster."
1743. John Pine, Dec.; *d.* May 4, 1756.
1757. Ralph Bigland (No. 1), Mar.; aft. "Somerset."
1759. John Ward, Dec.
1761. Isaac Heard, aft. "Lancaster."
1762. Hy. Pugolas, aft. "Richmond."
1763. Peter Dore, Apr. 21; aft. "Richmond."
1764. Geo. Browne, Nov. 2; *d.* 1767.
1767. Geo. Harrison; aft. "Windsor."
1774. Chas. Townley, Dec. 31; aft. "Lancaster."

1781. Edmd. Lodge, aft. "Lancaster."
1793. Geo. Nayler, Dec.; aft. "York."
1794. John Havers, May 13.
1796. Fras. Martin, jun., aft. "Windsor."
1819. Wm. Woods, Apr. 13, **G.**; aft. "Norfolk."
1831. Geo. Harrison Rogers Harrison, Nov. 15, **G.**; aft. "Windsor."
1849. Hy. Murray Lane, Aug. 11, **G.**; aft. "Chester."
1864. Hy. Harington Molyneux-Seel, Nov. 14, **G.**; aft. "Richmond."
1873. Edwd. Bellasis, Dec. 13, **G.**; aft. "Lancaster."
1882. Chas. Harold Athill, July 24, **G.**

PORTCULLIS PURSUIVANTS.

THE name of this officer was taken from one of the cognizances of the house of Somerset, which was a favourite badge with Henry VII., by whom the office was founded.

PORTCULLIS PURSUIVANTS.

Hy. VII. Ralph Lagysse, aft. "York."
Wm. Fellows, aft. "Lancaster."
1526. Wm. Hastings, Apr. 29.
Hy. VIII. Allan Dagnall, aft. "York."
* * Thos. Traheyron or Trahern, aft. "Somerset."
* * Robt. Fayery, *d.* 1549–50, (3 Edwd. VI.)
Edw. VI. Richd. Withers.
1553. Jno. Cocke, cr. Dec. 25; L. P. Jan. 3, 1555; aft. "Lancaster."
1559. Edwd. Merlin, *d.* same year.
Ralph Langman, app.; cr. Dec 4, 1561; aft. "York."
1567. Robt. Glover, aft. "Somerset."
1571. Richd. Lee, cr. Mar. 30; aft. "Richmond."
1585. Wm. Segar, cr. June 10; L. P. June 14; aft. "Somerset."
1588. Thos. Lant, aft. "Windsor."
1597. Saml. Thompson, cr. Oct. 22; L. P. May 15, 1602; aft. "Windsor."
1619. Philip (? John) Holland, Feb. 23.
1625. Thos. Preston, Dec. 22; aft. "Ulster."
1633. John Beauchamp.
1660. John Wingfield, sign. and pr. seal, July 27; aft. "York."
1663. Thos. Holford (No. 1.); aft. "Windsor."
Chas. II. Thos. Holford (No. 2.); res.
1689. Lawrence Cromp, aft. "York."
W. & M. John Hesketh, aft. "Lancaster."
1713. Thos. Wightwick, aft. "York."
1718. Rd. Mawson, Dec. 11.
1746. Peter Toms, Jan.; *d.* Jan. 1, 1777.
1780. Jno. Doddington Forth, Mar. 3.
1817. Geo. Fredk. Beltz, May 3, **G.**; aft. "Lancaster."
1822. Jas. Pulman, May 30, **G.**; aft. "Richmond."
1838. Albt. Wm. Woods, July 23, **G.**; aft. "Lancaster."
1841. Geo. Wm. Collen, Nov. 6, **G.**
1878. Arthur Staunton Larken, Feb. 20, **G.**; aft. "Richmond."
1882. Wm. Alexr. Lindsay, Dec. 27, **G.**

ROUGE DRAGON PURSUIVANTS.

THIS office was created by Henry VII. prior to his coronation, to commemorate the banner which he bore at the battle of Bosworth.

ROUGE DRAGON PURSUIVANTS.

* * Wm. Tyndall.
1506. Thos. Miller, pr. seal, Nov. 2.
* * Christr. Barker.
Vacancy.
1525. Richd. de la Towre, July 5.
1531. Thos. Mylner, cr. Nov. 8; aft. "Lancaster."
Fulk app. Howell, cr. July 6, 1536; L. P. July 6, 1538; aft. "Lancaster."

* * Richd. Croke.
1546. Martin Maroffe, Mar. 4; aft. "York."
1553. Wm. Colborne, cr. Dec. 25; L. P. Jan. 11, 1555; aft. "York."
1565. Edmd. Knight, cr. Apr. 19; aft. "Chester."
1574. Nicholas Paddy, L. P. Sept. 30; cr. Oct. 31 (Allhallows Eve); aft. "Lancaster."
1588. JohnRaven,June 8; aft."Richmond."
1597. Wm. Smith, cr. Oct. 22; L. P. Mar. 20, 1603; *d.* Oct. 1618.
1618. John Philipot, cr. Nov. 19; aft. "Somerset."
1624. Thos. Thompson, L. P. June 29; cr. July 8; aft. "Lancaster."
1638. Wm. Crowne, L. P. Sept. 14; cr. Sept. 24; res.
1661. Fras. Sandford, June 6; aft. "Lancaster."
1676. Thos. May, aft. "Chester."
1677. Gregory King, Mar. 7; cr. June 24; aft. "Lancaster."
1689. Peers Mauduit, aft. "Windsor."
* * Hugh Clopton.
* * John Hare, aft. "Richmond."
1704. Dudley Downs, May 27; *d.* Oct. 27, 1720.
* * Arth. Shepherd, *d.* Mar. 2, 1756.
1756. Hy. Hill, aft. "Windsor."
1758. Thos. Sheriff, May 23; sold hi[s] office to his successor.
1763. Thos. Locke, Nov.; aft. "Lancaster."
1774. Ralph Bigland (No. 2.), Nov.; aft "Richmond."
1780. Benj. Pingo, May 15; aft. "York."
1786. Jas. Monson Philips, Apr. 13.
1797. Jas. Cathrow, aft. "Somerset."
1813. Chas. Geo. Young, Aug. 28, **G.**; aft "York."
1820. Fras. Townsend, May 27, **G.**; *d* 1833.
1833. Jas. Rock, Apr. 23, **G.**; *d.* 1833.
Thos. Wm. King, May 20, **G.**; aft "York."
1848. Edwd. Steph. Dendy, June 19, **G.** aft. "Surrey."
1859. Geo. Edwd. Adams, Dec. 10, **G.** aft. "Lancaster."
1870. Wm. Hy. Weldon, Jan. 27, **G.**; af "Windsor."
1880. Alf. Scott Gatty, Apr. 27, **G.**; af "York."
1886. Albt. Wm. Woods (No. 2), Oct. 2[0] **G.**

SECTION II. HERALDIC OFFICES NOW EXTINCT.

IRELAND KINGS OF ARMS.

Kings of Arms of this name appear to have existed as early a[s] Richard II. Their jurisdiction was no doubt over Ireland.

* * *
Hy. V. John Kirby.
Hy. VI. Thos. Collyer.
* * *

This office seems to have continued down to the reign of Edward IV., but it is unce[r]tain whether from the death of that king it existed or not. On the accession [of] Edward VI. the office was superseded by that of Ulster King of Arms, *q.v.* und[er] "Ireland." Part X., *post.*

LANCASTER KINGS OF ARMS.

See Lancaster Heralds, *ante*, p. 332.

LEICESTER KINGS OF ARMS.

See LEICESTER HERALDS, *post*, p. 340.

MARCHE KINGS OF ARMS.

FOUNDED by Edward IV., formerly earl of March. There are prior traces of a Marche *Herald*.

Edw. IV. John Ferrant.

Edw. IV. Wm. Ballard.

ARUNDEL HERALDS EXTRAORDINARY.

THIS title was no doubt taken from the second title of the dukes of Norfolk, who were hereditary earls marshal.

1735. Fras. Hutchenson, L. P. July; cr. Sept.; aft. "Chester."

* * Jno. Cheale.

* * Thos. Bewes.

BLANC COURSIER HERALDS.

THIS title was taken from the White Horse in the Brunswick arms. The office was afterwards consolidated with that of genealogist of the Bath.

Geo. I. John Anstis (No. 2); aft. "Garter."

Geo. II. Sackville Fox, res.; *d.* Dec. 18, 1760.

1757. John Suffield Brown, res.

1792. Geo. Nayler, Sept.; aft. "York," &c., but continued "Blanc Coursier" and "Bath" genealogist until his death in 1831.

1831. Walter Aston Blount, Dec. 20, **G.**; aft. "Chester," &c., continued "Blanc Coursier" and "Bath" genealogist until app. to "Norroy" in 1859; no succ. app.

BUCKINGHAM HERALDS.

THIS officer is mentioned as attending the funeral of Edward IV., but nothing further appears to be known of him.

CARLISLE HERALDS.

THIS office was founded by Richard III., who was formerly earl of Carlisle.

Rich. III. Christopher Carhill; aft. "Norroy."

1493. Thos. Waters.

1514. Thos. Hawley cr. Nov. 1 (Allhallows Day); L. P. Jan. 2 and 30, 1515; aft. "Clarencieux."

1544. Leonard Warcup.

CLARENCIEUX HERALDS.

See Clarencieux Kings of Arms, *ante*, p. 328.

GLOUCESTER HERALDS.

See Bath and Gloucester Kings of Arms, *ante*, p. 330.

HANOVER HERALDS.

This office was founded by George I. in honour of his Hanoveria[n] dominions. It was annexed to Bath and Gloucester king of arms, *q.v.* *ante*, p. 330.

1726. Grey Longueville, Feb. 1; *d.* Sept. 29, 1745.
1745. Hon. Edwd. Young, Oct.
* * Wm. Woodley.
1757 or 1761. Saml. Horsey, Jan. 4.; [d.] July 28, 1771.

LEICESTER HERALDS.

This office was founded by Henry IV., formerly Earl of Leicester.

Hy. IV. Hy. Grene, Leicester Herald; aft. cr. Leicester K. Arms.
A Leicester Herald appears in the records of the reigns of Hy. IV., Hy. V., Edw. IV[.], Rich. III., and Hy. VII., but th[e] names are unknown.

MARCHE HERALDS.

See Marche Kings of Arms, *ante*, p. 339.

MOWBRAY HERALDS EXTRAORDINARY.

Mowbray was the ancient family name of the dukes of Norfolk, the hereditary earls marshal.

1623. Jas. Borough or Burroughs, June; aft. "Norroy."
1624. Wm. Le Neve, L. P., June 24; cr. June 29; aft. "York."
1677. Fras. Burghill, cr. June 24; aft. "Somerset."
1694–5. Robt. Plot, Feb. 2.
Anne. Rowland or Richd. Fryth; a[ft.] "Lancaster."
Geo. I. Jno. Dugdale; *d.* Aug. 4, 174[9]
1764. Jos. Edmondson, Mar.; *d.* Fe[b.] 17, 1786.
1842. Edwd. Howard Gibbon, Apr. [..] G.; aft. "Norroy,"

NORFOLK HERALDS EXTRAORDINARY.

Geo. I. Jno. Anstis (No. 1), aft. "Garter."
1761. Stephen Martin Leake (No. 2); *d.* Feb. 19, 1797.
1825. Wm. Woods, May 9, **G**; aft. "Clarencieux."

SUFFOLK HERALDS EXTRAORDINARY.

This office was founded by George III. The title was taken from the earldom, which belongs to a branch of the Howard family.

1774. John Ives, junr., Oct.; *d.* Jan. 9, 1776.

ANTELOPE PURSUIVANTS EXTRAORDINARY.

Henry V. John Wrythe, aft. "Rouge Croix."

ATHLONE PURSUIVANTS EXTRAORDINARY.

1552. Philip Butler, June 22.

BARNES PURSUIVANTS EXTRAORDINARY.

Henry VII. Richard Ratcliffe, or Radcliffe.

BERWICK PURSUIVANTS EXTRAORDINARY.

Edw. IV. Wm. Jennings, aft. "Rouge Croix."
Hy. VII. Thos. Wall, aft. "Rouge Croix."
1523. Leonard Warcup, cr. Nov. 1 (Allhallows Day); aft. "Bluemantle."
Hy. VIII. Chas. Wrythe or Wriothesley, aft. "Rouge Croix."
Hy. Ray; *d.* about 1565.
1602. Richd. St. George, Apr. 22; aft. "Windsor."

BLANC LION PURSUIVANTS EXTRAORDINARY.

Jas. 1. Nicholas Charles, or Carles; aft. "Lancaster."
1618. John Philipot, sign. Oct.; L. P. Nov. 13; aft. "Rouge Dragon."
1623. Thos. Hamelin, Feb. 14.
Chas. I. Edwd. Walker, aft. "Rouge Croix."
1686. Thos. Holford, junr., May 3; aft. "Portcullis."
1690. Hugh, or Hy. Clopton, May 29; aft. "Rouge Dragon."
Anne. Robt. Dale.
1720. Arth. Shepherd, sw. June 24; aft. "Rouge Dragon."
1782 Alexr. Ocherlony.

BLANCHE ROSE PURSUIVANTS EXTRAORDINARY.

See Rose Blanche, *post*, p. 344.

BLANC SANGLIER PURSUIVANTS EXTRAORDINARY.

The White Boar was Richard the third's cognizance and one of hi supporters.

A pursuivant extraordinary with this title appears to have been ap pointed by Richard III., and it is believed his name was St. Leger, bu there is no certainty on the point.

CALAIS PURSUIVANTS EXTRAORDINARY.

Edw. IV.	Thos. Wall, aft. "Blue Mantle."
Hen. VIII.	Ralph Lagysse, aft. "Portcullis."
	Christr. Barker, aft. "Rouge Dragon."
Hen. VIII.	Thos. Mylner, aft. "Rouge Dragon."
28 or 30 Hen. VIII.	Martin Maroffe, L. P. Mar. 4 aft. "Rouge Dragon."
Hen. VIII.	Laurence Dalton, aft. "Roug Croix."
	Nichs. Fairlewe, or Fellow killed in the attack o Calais, 1558, and with hin the office expired.

COMFORT PURSUIVANTS EXTRAORDINARY.

Hen. VII. John Joyner, aft. "Rouge Croix"; on his promotion the office wa not filled up.

CORK PURSUIVANTS EXTRAORDINARY.

This office was created by Henry VII., but the name of the officer is unknown.

EAGLE PURSUIVANTS EXTRAORDINARY.

This office was created by Henry VII., but the name of the officer unknown.

FALCON PURSUIVANTS EXTRAORDINARY.

The title of Falcon was given to a herald or a pursuivant by Henry V., by Edward IV., possibly by Richard III., and by Henry VII. The names of the officers are not known.

FITZALAN PURSUIVANTS EXTRAORDINARY.

Named from the duke of Norfolk's family.

1837. Albert Wm. Woods, June 27, G.; aft. "Portcullis."

GUISNES PURSUIVANTS EXTRAORDINARY.

Guisnes was the name of a town in Picardy, France.

w. IV. Robt. Browne, aft. "Rouge Croix."

h. III. Thos. Ffranch, or Franke, aft. "Blue Mantle."

n. VII. Wm. Fellows, aft. "Portcullis."

Wm. Tyndall, aft. "Rouge Dragon."

* * *

1521. Wm. Jennings, aft. "Lancaster."

Hen. VIII. John Hutton, aft. "Blue Mantle."

Allan Dagnall, cr. Nov. 1 (Allhallows Day), 1528; aft. "Portcullis."

1523. Fulk ap Howell, L. P. July 6; cr. Nov. 1 (Allhallows Day); aft. "Rouge Dragon."

1536. Wm. Flower, cr. July 10.

Hen. VIII. Richd. Withers, aft. "Portcullis."

Edw. VI. Hy. Fellow.

HAMPNES PURSUIVANTS EXTRAORDINARY.

Hampnes was the name of a castle near Calais.

Hen. VIII. 1530–1. Bartholomew Butler, aft. "Rouge Croix."

1536. Gilbert Dethick, cr. June 16; L. P. June 18; aft. "Rouge Croix."

n. VIII. Wm. Harvey, aft. "Blue Mantle."

Hen. VIII. Edmond Atkynson, aft. "Blue Mantle."

Nichs. Tubman, aft. "Rouge Croix."

Edw. VI. Richd. Turpin, aft. "Blue Mantle."

KILDARE PURSUIVANTS EXTRAORDINARY.

pursuivant bearing this title, but name unknown, attended the funeral of Henry VII.

MONT-ORGUEIL PURSUIVANTS EXTRAORDINARY.

Hen. VII. Randolph Jackson.

NOTTINGHAM PURSUIVANTS EXTRAORDINARY.

Created by Henry VIII. and named after his illegitimate son, Henry Fitzroy, Earl of Nottingham.

len. VIII. Wm. Hastings, aft. "Portcullis."

1528. Richd. Croke, May 17; aft. "Rouge Dragon."

22 Hen. VIII. 1530–1. Thos. Traheyron, or Trahern, aft. "Portcullis."

PORTSMOUTH PURSUIVANTS EXTRAORDINARY.

Named after the Town.

Jas. I. John Gwillim, aft. "Rouge Croix."

RISEBANK PURSUIVANTS EXTRAORDINARY.

Risebank, or Rysbrook, was the name of a fortress in the English dominions in France.

Hen. VII. Thos. Bysley, aft. "Blue Mantle,"
Hen. VIII. John Narboone, aft. "Blue Mantle."
1528. Richd. Storke, cr. Nov. 1 (All-hallows Day); *d.* same year.
Hen. VIII. Justinian Barker, aft. "Rouge Croix."
Wm. Lambarde.
1554. John Hollingworth, Apr. 2[illegible] aft. "Blue Mantle."

ROSE PURSUIVANTS EXTRAORDINARY.

Edwd. VI. }
Mary. } "Richard."

ROSE BLANCHE PURSUIVANTS EXTRAORDINARY.

Created by Edward IV., the white rose being the badge of his family.

Edw. IV. John Waters.
Rich. III. Laurence Alford.
Hen. VII. Thos. Hawley.
1561. Robt. Cook, cr. Jan. 25; aft. "Chester."
Chas. II. Name unknown.

ROSE ROUGE PURSUIVANTS EXTRAORDINARY.

1602. Philip Holland, Apr. 22; aft. "Portcullis."
1610. Hy. St. George, cr. May; L. P. Dec. 18; aft. "Blue Mantle."
1615. Sampson Lennard, sign. Feb.; L. P. Mar. 11; aft. "Blue Mantle."
1616. Augustine Vincent, L. P. Feb. 22; inv. Mar. 22; aft. "Rouge Croix."
1623. John Bradshaw, inv. Feb. 14; aft. "Rouge Croix."
1630. Wm. Ryley, July 31; aft. "Blue Mantle."
* * Hy. Lilley, aft. "Rouge Croix."
Anne. Thos. Coote.

LYON KINGS OF ARMS. LYONS DEPUTE.

See Part IX, "Scotland," *post.*

ULSTER KINGS OF ARMS.

See Part X, "Ireland," *post.*

PART VI. LEGAL.

JUDGES AND OTHER LEGAL DIGNITARIES.

INTRODUCTION.

[ost of the lists in the previous editions of this work were compiled :om Dugdale, or from some later writers who simply adopted his ıaterials and added to them. These lists have now been collated with, ›rrected by, and compiled from those given by the late Mr. Foss in his *udges of England*, a work of great authority and research, to which ›ference should be made in all cases of difficulty, as the learned author ot only gives the authorities on which he relies, but is careful, where e differs from other writers, to give his reasons for so doing.

It would be beyond the scope of the present work to enter into ıything like a detailed history of the origin of the various Courts ı which sat the Judges whose names figure in the following list. [any volumes have been written on the subject, but the information ›ntained in Mr. Foss's book will probably be found sufficient for l practical purposes. Here the barest outline must suffice.

Prior to the Norman Conquest each hundred or other subdivision f a county had its separate Court, which exercised both civil and 'iminal jurisdiction. Besides these, each county had its "County ourt," which then possessed extensive powers and was altogether a ır different tribunal to the County Court of the present day, the ırisdiction of which is very limited, and which is, as a rule, only ›sorted to in trivial matters. Finally, there was the "Witenagemote,") which cases of great importance were sometimes brought by way f appeal.

William the Conqueror introduced an entirely new system of juris-rudence, adopted from that established in Normandy, and the leading rinciple of which was to make the Sovereign the supreme head or ›untain of justice, and to have the laws administered, if not by him ı person, by judges appointed directly by and dependent upon him.

Under this system the ancient local Courts were practically sup seded. They gradually became extinct or obsolete, or, if they s vived, their jurisdiction was limited to petty local disputes.

The tribunal founded by William the Conqueror was styled CURIA REGIS, and was composed of the King himself, some of principal officers, and of the Bishops and Lords; or, as they were th styled, the Barons of the Kingdom. The King sometimes presided person; in his absence the head of the Court was an official styled CHIEF JUSTICIARY, or the JUSTICIARY OF ENGLAND.

It was soon found that judicial aptitude can only be attained judicial training, and that a judge, to do his duty properly, must a skilled lawyer. Hence there were gradually added to the bishops a barons who composed the Curia Regis a body of men who w called JUSTICIARIES, who probably acted as deputies for the Ch Justiciary, and, afterwards, as the business of the Court increas divided the duties with him. They also went on *itinera*, or as it now called, on *circuit*, to administer justice throughout the Kingdo and on these occasions some men of rank or learning in each cou were joined with them in their Commissions, *all* the Commissioners bei designated JUSTICES ITINERANT. Towards the end of the reign Edward I., commissions of Trailbaston were issued for the trial of cert offences, the Commissioners being termed JUSTICES OF TRAILBAST The appointment both of these justices, and also of the Justi Itinerant, ceased early in the reign of Edward III., when the regu Judges went circuit, as at the present day.

For some time after the Curia Regis was established, great inc venience was experienced from the fact that it followed the person the King, so that suitors were frequently compelled to travel gr distances to prosecute or defend their suits. This was one of grievances redressed by Magna Charta, which provides that "comm pleas," *i.e.* the Court for the decision of suits between subjects, sho "not follow the Court, but be held in some certain place," which v then or soon afterwards fixed at Westminster Hall. This was t origin of the Court of COMMON PLEAS. Other changes gradually f lowed, into the details of which it is impossible here to enter; but the reign of Edward I., the Chief Justiciary had been superseded a the Curia Regis, divided into three distinct Courts, known by the nan of the KING'S BENCH, the COMMON PLEAS, and the EXCHEQUER, EXCHEQUER OF PLEAS; and these Courts continued until they w absorbed into the SUPREME COURT OF JUDICATURE in 1875.

THE COURT OF KING'S BENCH originally had jurisdiction only criminal matters, or in cases where the Crown was otherwise interest or was called on to interfere, in order to compel some inferior tribu or some official or corporation to fulfil its duties, or to prohibit it fr exceeding its powers. But, as the emolument of the Judges depend to a great extent upon fees, and, consequently, upon the amount business done, and as suits between individuals were found to be pro able, the Judges of the King's Bench, by means of certain le fictions, whereby a defendant was presumed to be in the custody the Marshal of the Court, under a *latitat* or a *bill of Middlesex*, a therefore liable to be sued in that Court on any cause of acti gradually acquired or assumed cognizance of private suits.

THE COURT OF COMMON PLEAS confined itself to its original jurisd ion over private suits, but its exclusive jurisdiction in this respect was gradually encroached upon by the other Courts. It, however, for many years, retained exclusive jurisdiction over "real actions," *i.e.* actions brought for the specific recovery of land.

The Court of Exchequer was founded upon a department of the Curia Regis called the Scaccarium, and originally had jurisdiction only in cases concerning the Revenues of the Crown. Afterwards, jurisdiction over private suits was acquired by means of a writ of *quo minus* issued by a plaintiff who pretended to be a debtor to the Crown and "*less able* to discharge his indebtedness for want of the debt owing to him by the defendant," which debt he was thereby able to sue for in the Exchequer Court. So long as the business of this Court was confined to Revenue Cases the Judges were frequently *laymen, i.e.* men not bred to the profession of the law, and it was not until the reign of Elizabeth or James I. that they were, invariably, selected from the serjeants-at-law like the Judges of the other Courts. It then became necessary to appoint another Judge to attend exclusively to the purely revenue or exchequer business. This functionary was styled a Cursitor Baron. His duties were gradually transferred to various Government departments not connected with the administration of justice, and the office was ultimately abolished in 1856.

The Court of Exchequer, besides its revenue and common law jurisdiction, had also jurisdiction in equity cases; but this branch was abolished in 1841 by the 5 Vict., cap. 5, and the equity suits then pending were transferred to the Court of Chancery. The Judges of the Court of Exchequer retained their original title of Barons down to the establishment of the Supreme Court of Judicature, whilst the Judges of the other Courts were styled Justices.

At the head of each Court was a Chief Justice or Chief Baron, the other Judges being styled "Puisnes."

At first the number of Judges in each Court varied from time to time, being increased or diminished at the pleasure of the Sovereign; but in the Reign of Henry VIII. the number had become fixed at four in each Court (the Chief and four puisnes), and so remained, with very rare exceptions, until 1830, when by 1 Wm. IV., cap. 70, the number was increased to five in each Court. In 1868, by 31 & 32 Vict., cap. 125, the number was again increased to six in each Court.

In 1831, by the "Uniformity of Process Act" 2 & 3 Wm. IV., cap. 39, the legal fictions above mentioned were abolished and statutory jurisdiction in all private suits given to each Court. The King's Bench retained its exclusive jurisdiction in all Crown suits and criminal cases, and all revenue cases were still confined to the Exchequer.

The Court of Chancery rose from a department of the Curia Regis called the Cancellaria, where all writs, charters, and other documents were prepared for the Great Seal. The chief of this department was the Cancellarius, or Chancellor, who held the Great Seal. He was at first inferior in rank to the Chief Justiciary, but ultimately he became the head of the law, and in former times was generally also the King's chief minister. His title was, at first, The Chancellor of the King, then Chancellor of England, then Lord Chancellor, and finally Lord High Chancellor. The Great Seal was sometimes delivered to a Lord Keeper instead of to a Lord Chancellor; but even Mr. Foss admits himself unable to distinguish between the two, either in point of dignity or duties, and in 1563 by 5 Eliz. cap. 18, their ider tity in rank, power, and privileges was explicitly declared. Ther has been no appointment of a Lord Keeper since 1760, but both befor and since that date the Great Seal has been occasionally "put into com mission," *i.e.*, delivered into the custody of several persons style "COMMISSIONERS OF THE GREAT SEAL," who jointly performed th Chancellor's duties.

Occasionally, a deputy or VICE CHANCELLOR was, in early time appointed to assist the Lord Chancellor or act in his absence; but th office was not permanently established until 1813, when by 53 Geo. III cap. 24, a VICE CHANCELLOR OF ENGLAND was appointed. Afte wards, in 1841, by 5 Vict., cap. 15, extended by 14 & 15 Vict cap. 4, and 15 and 16 Vict., cap. 80, two additional Vice Chancello were appointed. On the death of Sir Lancelot Shadwell in 1850, th title of Vice Chancellor of England was discontinued and the thre Vice Chancellors thenceforward ranked according to seniority of appin ment.

By the statutes above referred to, the Lord Chancellor's jurisdictic as a judge of first instance was practically abolished and his dutie as an equity judge were confined to hearing appeals. By 14 & 1 Vict., cap. 83, the "Court of Appeal in Chancery" was establishe being composed of the Lord Chancellor and two new Judges style LORDS JUSTICES.

The Lord Chancellor had a number of Clerks or MASTERS to assis him in the minor details of his many duties. The principal of thes was styled THE MASTER OF THE ROLLS, the others MASTERS IN CHAN CERY. The Master of the Rolls soon became a very important pe sonage, and ranked next after the Chief Justice of the King's Bench and before the chiefs of the Common Pleas and Exchequer. In additio to having the custody of the Records or ROLLS, he assisted the Chan cellor in his judicial duties, his powers being gradually increased b 3 Geo. II., cap. 30, and 3 & 4 Wm. IV., cap. 94.

The Masters in Chancery also assisted in working out the details o the Chancellor's decrees and in other minor matters. They wer abolished in 1852, by 15 & 16 Vict., cap. 80, their duties being trans ferred to the Vice Chancellors, to be performed either by them i person or by a staff of "Chief Clerks," of whom at first two and after wards three were attached to each Judge's Court.

The proceedings in the various Courts were, for many years, conducte in Latin or Norman-French, languages with which the ordinary suito was unacquainted. He was, probably, equally ignorant of the law an practice of the Courts, and hence there was, from the very earlies times, a distinct class of men bred to the law who represented th suitors and pleaded their causes before the Judges, and from whos ranks the Judges soon came to be selected. These were ancientl divided into SERJEANTS-AT-LAW and APPRENTICES. The Serjeant were appointed by the Crown, and it would seem that in very early time they were appointed without regard to their preliminary legal training but it soon became the settled practice to promote them from the ap prentices or ordinary barristers, according to their seniority, merit, o interest at Court. Down to the establishment of the Supreme Court o Judicature, every Common Law Judge must have been a Serjeant, and i as frequently happened in more recent times, the person selected did no possess the necessary qualification, he was made a Serjeant, *pro formâ*, and appointed a Judge immediately afterwards.

As much of the business brought before the Courts affected the interests of the Crown, either in its revenues or its prerogatives, it was necessary that those interests should be properly protected. Hence the appointment of the Attornatus Regis or Attorney General about 1277, (5 Edw. I.), and of the Sollicitor Regis or Solictor General in 1461, (1 Edw. IV.). These officers had a right of pre-audience over all the other members of the bar except the two most ancient of the King's Serjeants, which exception was abolished in 1813. Rights of pre-audience were also enjoyed by King's Serjeants and by those members of the bar who received the appointment of King's Counsel, a dignity which, with one or two doubtful exceptions, was not conferred until the reign of Charles I. At first, the office was what its name implied, and certain small fees and perquisites were annexed to it; but it gradually became a mere step of professional rank, and all the emoluments were abolished in 1830.

From the time of George I., to the present day, the Crown has also on special occasions, granted Patents of Precedence to eminent members of the bar, whether Serjeants, King's Counsel, or ordinary Barristers, giving them certain rights of pre-audience over their fellows as fixed by their patents. Holders of Patents of Precedence have the same privileges as King's Counsel, but are able to hold briefs against the Crown, which a King's Counsel cannot do without a "licence to plead."

In addition to the Courts above mentioned which were generally known as the Superior Courts, it is necessary to refer to the Ecclesiastical Courts and the High Court of Admiralty because, although formerly inferior Courts, their jurisdiction has now been transferred to the Supreme Court of Judicature.

The Ecclesiastical Courts were of very great antiquity. Every Bishop had his own Court, and, besides dealing with questions of theology and church discipline, had jurisdiction within his diocese over testamentary and matrimonial causes; but as the Archbishop of Canterbury's jurisdiction extended over the whole of his province, most of the important litigation came before his tribunals, the Prerogative Court of Canterbury, and the Court of Arches. The Bishop's Courts were presided over by their Chancellors, the Prerogative Court of Canterbury by a "Master Keeper, or Commissary," and the Court of Arches by a Dean. In 1857, by 20 & 21 Vict., cap. 77, the jurisdiction of all the Ecclesiastical Courts in testamentary matters was transferred to the newly established Court of Probate, and in the same year, by 20 & 21 Vict., cap. 85, their jurisdiction in matters matrimonial was transferred to another new tribunal called The Court for Divorce and Matrimonial Cases. These two Courts were distinct tribunals but were presided over by the same Judge.

The advocates who practised before the Ecclesiastical Courts were Doctors of Civil Law, and the Crown was represented by a King's Advocate.

The High Court of Admiralty was a very ancient tribunal with jurisdiction over all maritime matters including, in time of war, all questions of prize. It was presided over by the Lord High Admiral and in modern times by his deputy, who was styled The Judge of the

ADMIRALTY. The Court was thoroughly re-organized, and its practic of procedure much improved in 1840 by the 3 & 4 Vict., caps. 65 an 66. The Crown was represented in this Court by an ADMIRALTY ADVO CATE.

The present SUPREME COURT OF JUDICATURE was formed by con solidating the old Courts of Chancery, Queen's Bench, Common Plea Exchequer, Probate, Divorce, and Admiralty. It was established b the following Acts:—

(1) The Supreme Court of Judicature Act, 1873 (36 & 37 Vict., cap. 66
(2) " " 1875 (38 & 39 Vict., cap. 77
(3) The Appellate Jurisdiction Act, 1876 (39 & 40 Vict., cap. 59
(4) The Supreme Court of Judicature Act, 1877 (40 & 41 Vict., cap. 9).
(5) The Judicature (Officers) Act, 1879 (42 & 43 Vict., cap. 78
(6) The Supreme Court of Judicature Act, 1881 (44 & 45 Vict., cap. 68

the combined effect of which was that the Supreme Court of Judica ture was divided into two permanent divisions:—

I. Her Majesty's High Court of Justice.
II. Her Majesty's Court of Appeal.

I. HER MAJESTY'S HIGH COURT OF JUSTICE.

THIS COURT originally consisted of five divisions:—

1. THE CHANCERY DIVISION, consisting of the Lord Chancello (President), the Master of the Rolls, and the Vice Chancellor of the old Court of Chancery.
2. THE QUEEN'S BENCH DIVISION, consisting of the L. C. J. o England (President), and the other Judges of the old Cour of Queen's Bench.
3. The COMMON PLEAS DIVISION, consisting of the L. C. J. of th Common Pleas (President), and the other Judges of the ol Court of Common Pleas.
4. THE EXCHEQUER DIVISION, consisting of the L. C. B. of th Exchequer (President), and the other Judges of the old Cour of Exchequer of Pleas.
5. THE PROBATE, DIVORCE, AND ADMIRALTY DIVISION, consisting o the then existing Judge of the Court of Probate and Divorc (President), and the then existing Judge of the Court o Admiralty.

Power was given to reduce or increase the number of divisions an to abolish (on vacancy) any of the following offices: the L. C. J. o England, the Master of the Rolls, the L. C. J. of the Common Pleas and the L. C. B. of the Exchequer. Under these powers the Com mon Pleas and Exchequer Divisions, and the offices of L. C. J. of th Common Pleas and L. C. B. of the Exchequer, were abolished by Orde in Council dated December 16, 1880. Power was also given to appoin other judges from time to time, as vacancies arose, under the title o JUDGES OF THE HIGH COURT, altered by the Supreme Court of Judi cature Act, 1881, to JUSTICES OF THE HIGH COURT, the old titles o Vice Chancellor and Baron of the Exchequer being for the futur abolished.

Under the Supreme Court of Judicature Act, 1881, the Master of the Rolls was removed from the High Court of Justice and is now a Judge of the Court of Appeal only.

II. HER MAJESTY'S COURT OF APPEAL.

This Court, as ultimately settled, consists of:—

1. Three *ex-officio* Judges, viz., the Ld. Chanc., the L. C. J. of England, and the President of the Probate, Divorce, and Admiralty Division. The Master of the Rolls, the L. C. J. of the Common Pleas, and the L. C. B. of the Exchequer were originally made *ex-officio* judges, but the Master of the Rolls is now exclusively a Judge of the Court of Appeal, and the offices of L. C. J. of the Common Pleas and L. C. B. of the Exchequer have been abolished.
2. The Master of the Rolls.
3. Five (reduced from six) Ordinary Judges to be appointed from time to time under the style of Justices of Appeal, altered by the Supreme Court of Judicature Act, 1881, to Lords Justices of Appeal.

The two Lord Justices of Appeal in Chancery were appointed two of these Ordinary Judges.

There has been for centuries a final appeal from the Superior Courts of Common Law, and from the Court of Chancery, to the "High Court of Parliament." This appellate jurisdiction has always been exercised by the House of Lords, and was expressly disclaimed by the House of Commons in the reign of Henry IV.

There is nothing to prevent the *lay* Lords from hearing and voting on appeals to their House; but for many years the judicial powers have been exercised by the "*law* Lords" alone, *i.e.* by such of the Lords as either hold or have held judicial offices. By the Appellate Jurisdiction Act, 1876, it was enacted that no appeal should be heard and determined by the House of Lords unless there were present not less than three of the following persons, who were designated Lords of Appeal:—

1. The Lord Chancellor of Great Britain for the time being.
2. The Lords of Appeal in Ordinary, to be appointed under the Act.
3. Such peers as were holding or had held any "high judicial office," which term was by the interpretation clause defined to mean (1) Lord Chancellor of Great Britain or Ireland; (2) paid Judge of Judicial Committee of Privy Council; and (3) Judge of one of the Superior Courts of Great Britain or Ireland.

By this Act the Crown was empowered at once to appoint two Lords of Appeal in Ordinary, with life peerages, to appoint one additional Lord of Appeal in ordinary, on the death or resignation of any two paid Judges of the Judicial Committee of the Privy Council, and another additional Lord of Appeal in ordinary on the death or resignation of the remaining two paid Judges of that Committee.

By this Act, also, the Lords of Appeal in Ordinary if Privy Councillors were made Members of the Judicial Committee of that body, and were required to sit and act as such.

Either by virtue of the royal prerogative or under the provisions of various statutes too numerous to quote, a final appeal from the Ecclesiastical and Admiralty Courts, and from the Courts of India and the British Colonies a final appeal lay to the King or to the King in Council. This appellate jurisdiction was in practice exercised by a JUDICIAL COMMITTEE composed of privy councillors who held or had held judicial office. For many years such a committee was appointed *pro hâc vice* as occasion required; but in 1833, by 3 & 4 Wm. IV., cap. 41, a permanent committee was formed, the constitution of which has been modified from time to time by subsequent statutes. The principal change effected by the establishment of a permanent committee was the addition of paid members; but under the Appellate Jurisdiction Act, 1876, the places of these are gradually being supplied by the Lords of Appeal in Ordinary (see *ante* p. 351.) Appeals in probate and admiralty cases, which are now heard by a division of the High Court of Justice, now lie to the House of Lords, and not to the Judicial Committee.

In many of the following lists there is some little uncertainty about the earliest names. It must be borne in mind that in ancient times the various changes in judicial procedure were introduced very gradually, indeed almost imperceptibly, and by authority of the King or of the judges only, and not, as now, by an elaborate Act of Parliament, in which every detail is carefully set forth. Hence, it is frequently impossible to say *exactly* when a particular change took place or what was the exact status of particular officials during a transition period.

LORD HIGH CHANCELLORS. LORD KEEPERS. COMMISSIONERS OF THE GREAT SEAL.

SEE INTRODUCTION, *ante*, p. 347.

The Lord Chancellor, in addition to his judicial duties, presides over the House of Lords, his office being analogous to that of Speaker of the House of Commons, though there are some points of difference between the two; the most important being that the Lord Chancellor is at liberty both to speak and vote upon every question before the House. He is always an important member of the Government and of the Cabinet, and goes out of office with his party.

LORD HIGH CHANCELLORS, &c., OF ENGLAND.

Where no other title is given, that of Chancellor is to be presumed.

Those marked thus † are omitted from Foss's list, for reasons which he explains; but, as they are given in Hardy's list, they are included here with this distinguishing mark.

WILLIAM I.

1067. Arfastus, or Herefast, aft. bp. of Elmham.
1070. Osbert, aft. bp. of Exeter.
1073. Osmund de Seez, aft. bp. of Salisbury.
1078. Maurice, aft. bp. of London.
1083. Wm. Velson, or Welson (de Bellofago), aft. bp. of Thetford.
1086. Wm. Giffard, aft. bp. of Winchester.

William II.

1087. Wm. Giffard, *contd.*
1090. Robt. Bloet, or Bluet, July; aft. bp. of Lincoln.
1093. Baldric, or Galdric, and (?) Drogo, kpr. under him.
1094. Wm. Giffard, *again.*

Henry I.

1100. Wm. Giffard, now bp. of Winchester, *contd.*
1101. Roger, Sept.; aft. bp. of Salisbury.
1103. Wm. Giffard, bp. of Winchester, *again*, Mar.
1104. Waldric, Jan.
1107. Ranulph, or Arnulph; *d.* 1123.
1124. Geoffrey Rufus, aft. bp. of Durham.

Stephen.

1135. Roger Pauper, son of Roger, bp. of Salisbury.
1139. Philip.
1142. Theobald, abp. of Canterbury, const. by the emp. Maud.
* * Wm. Fitzgilbert, const. by the emp. Maud.
* * Wm. de Vere, also const. by the empress, in reversion.
* * Robt. de Gant; *d.* 1153.

Henry II.

1154. Thos. à Becket, Dec., aft. abp. of Canterbury; res. 1162.
From 1162-1173 no chancellor can with certainty be placed.—*Foss.*
1173. Ralph de Warneville, treasr. of York.
1177. †Walter de Constantiis, bp. of Lincoln and abp. of Rouen; v. chanc. or deputy.
1181. Geoffrey Plantagenet, bp. of Lincoln; aft. abp. of York.

Richard I.

1189. Wm. de Longchamp, Sept. 3; aft. bp. of Ely; *d.* 1197.
1190. John de Alençon, archd. of Lisieux, v. chanc., Jan.
1191. Roger Malus Catulus, v. chanc., Mar.
Benet, v. chanc., Oct.
1194. Eustace, dean of Salisbury, May; aft. bp. of Ely; v. chanc.
1198. Warine, or Guarinus, prior of Loches in Touraine, v. chanc., Feb. 28.
Eustace, bp. of Ely, chanc., Feb. (?)
Roceline, v. chanc. Nov.

John.

1199. Hubert Walter, abp. of Canterbury, May.
1205. Walter de Grey, Oct. 2; aft. bp. of Worcester and abp. of York.
1213. Peter de Rupibus, bp. of Winchester, Oct.
1214. Walter de Grey, *again*, Jan. 2.
Richd. de Marisco, aft. bp. of Durham, Oct. 29.

Henry III.

1216. Richd. de Marisco, *contd.*
1218. Ralph. de Nevill, aft. bp. of Chichester, kpr. or v. chanc.
1226. Ralph de Nevill, chanc.
The king took the gr. seal from him in 1238, and delivered it to Geoffrey, a Templar, and to John de Lexinton; but Ralph had still the emoluments of the chancellorship.
1238. Simon Normannus, or de Cantilupe, kpr., Aug.
1240. Richd. Crassus, abbot of Evesham, kpr.
1244. Silvester de Everdon, or Eversden, kpr., Nov. 14.
1246. John Mansel, provost of Beverly, kpr., Nov. 8.
1247. John de Lexinton, kpr., in the absence of John Mansel on an embassy, Aug. 28.
1248. John Mansel, on his return, *again*, kpr., Aug. 10.
1249. John de Lexinton, *again*, kpr., Sept. 8.
1250. Wm. de Kilkenny, aft. bp. of Ely, kpr.
1255. Hy. de Wingham, bp. of London, kpr.
1260. Nichs. de Ely, aft. bp. of Worcester and Winchester, kpr.
1261. Walter de Merton, bp. of Rochester, July 5.
1263. Nichs. de Ely, July 12.
1265. Thos. de Cantilupe, bp. of Hereford, Feb. 21.
Walter Giffard, bp. of Bath and Wells, Aug.
1267. Godfrey Giffard, bp. of Worcester.
1268. John de Chishull, aft. bp. of London, kpr., Oct. 30.
1269. Richd. de Middleton, kpr.; aft. chanc. July.
1272. John de Kirkeby, aft. bp. of Ely, Aug. 7.

Edward I.

1272. Walter de Merton, bp. of Rochester, *again*, Nov.
1273. Robt. Burnell, archd. of York, Sept. 21; aft. bp. of Bath and Wells.
1292. Wm. de Hamilton, kpr., Oct. 25.
John de Langton, Dec. 17; aft. bp. of Chichester.
1302. Adam de Osgodby, kpr., Aug. 26.
Wm. de Grenefield, dean of Chichester; aft. abp. of York.
1304. Wm. de Hamilton, dean of York, Dec. 29.
John de Benstede, kpr., until the new chancellor's arrival to receive the seal.
1307. Ralph de Baldoc, Baldok, or Beaudake, bp. of London, Apr. 21.

Edward II.

1307. Ralph. de Baldoc, *contd.*
John de Langton, bp. of Chichester, *again.*
1310. Adam de Osgodby, Wm. de Melton, Robt. de Bardelby, Ingelard de Warlegh, and John Fraunceis, kprs.
Walter Reginald, bp. of Worcester, July 6.
1311. Adam de Osgodby, m. rolls, Robt. de Bardelby, and Wm. de Ayremynne, kprs.
1312. Walter Reginald, bp. of Worcester, *again,* kpr., Oct. 6; aft. abp. of Canterbury.
1314. John de Sandale, Sept. 26; aft. bp. of Winchester.
1318. John de Hotham, bp. of Ely, June 11.
1320. John Salmon, bp. of Norwich, Jan. 26.
1323. Robt. de Baldock, archd. of Middlesex, Aug. 20; aft. bp. of Norwich.
1326. Wm. de Ayremynne, bp. of Norwich, *again,* kpr., Nov. 30.
Hy. de Cliff, kpr., Dec. 17.

Edward III.

1327. John de Hotham, bp. of Ely, *again,* Jan.
1328. Hy. de Cliff, m. rolls, *again,* and Wm. de Herlaston, kprs., Mar. 1.
Hy. de Burghersh, bp. of Lincoln, May 12.
1330. John de Stratford, bp. of Winchester, Nov. 28.
1334. Richd. de Angarville, or Bury, bp. of Durham, Sept. 28.
1335. John de Stratford, *again,* now abp. of Canterbury, June 6.
1337. Robt. de Stratford, archd. of Canterbury, Mar. 24.
1338. Richd. de Bynteworth, or Wentworth, bp. of London, July 6.
John de St. Paul, m. rolls, and Thos. de Baumburgh, kprs., *pro tem.*, July.
1339. John de St. Paul, Michl. de Wath, and Thos. de Baumburgh, kprs., Dec. 8.
1340. John de St. Paul, kpr., Feb. 6.
John de Stratford, abp. of Canterbury, *again,* chanc., Apr. 28.
Robt. de Stratford, *again,* now bp. of Chichester, June 28.
Wm. de Kildesby, kpr., Dec. 1.
Sir Robt. Burgchier, or Bourchier, Dec. 14.
1341. Sir Robt. Parnyng, Oct. 29; *d.* Aug. 26, 1343.
1343. John de Thoresby, m. rolls, John de St. Paul, Thos. de Brayton, and Thos. de Beauchamp, E. of Warwick, kprs., Aug. 27.
1343. Robt. de Sadyngton, Sept. 29.
1345. John de Offord, or Ufford, dean of Lincoln, Oct. 26; app. abp. of Canterbury, but *d.* May 20, 1349, before consecration.
1349. David de Wollore, m. rolls, John de St. Paul, Thos. de Brayton, and Thos. Cotyngham, kprs., May 20.
John de Thoresby, bp. of St. David's, June 16.
1356. Wm. de Edington, bp. of Winchester, Nov. 27.
1363. Simon Langham, bp. of Ely, Feb. 19; aft. abp. of Canterbury.
1367. Wm. de Wyckham, or Wykeham, bp. of Winchester, Sept.
1371. Sir Robt. de Thorpe, Mar. 26; *d.* June 29, 1372.
1372. Richd. le Scrope, ld. Scrope of Bolton; kpr., June 29.
Sir John Knyvet, July 5.
1377. Adam de Houghton, or Hoghton, bp. of St. David's, Jan. 11.

Richard II.

1377. Adam de Houghton, *contd.*
1378. Richd., ld. Scrope, *again,* Oct. 29.
1379. Simon de Sudbury, abp. of Canterbury, July 4; beheaded by the rebels under Wat Tyler, June 14, 1381.
1381. Richd., E. of Arundel, kpr., June 14.
Hugh de Segrave, stewd. of the king's household, kpr., June 16.
Wm. Courtenay, bp. of London, Aug. 10.
Richd., ld. Scrope, *again,* Nov. 18.
1382. Hugh de Segrave, treasr., Wm. de Dighton, pr. seal, John de Waltham, m. rolls, and Walter de Skirlawe; kprs., July 11.
Robt. de Braybroke, bp. of London, Sept. 20.
1383. John de Waltham, m. rolls, kpr., Mar. 10.
Sir Michael de la Pole, Mar. 13.
1386. Thos. de Arundel, or FitzAlan, bp. of Ely, Oct. 24; aft. abp. of York and of Canterbury.
1389. Wm. de Wykeham, bp. of Winchester, *again,* May 4.
1391. Thos. de Arundel, now abp. of York, *again,* Sept. 17.
1396. Edmund Stafford, bp. of Exeter, Nov. 23.
1399. Thos. de Arundel, now abp. of Canterbury, *again,* Aug.
John de Scarle, m. rolls, Sept.

HENRY IV.

1399. John de Scarle, *contd.*
1401. Edmund Stafford, bp. of Exeter, *again*, Mar. 9.
1403. Hy. de Beaufort, bp. of Lincoln, Feb.
1405. Thos. Longley, or Langley, kpr. of the pr. seal, Feb. 28; bp. of Durham in 1406.
1407. Thos. de Arundel, abp. of Canterbury, *again*, Jan. 30.
1410. John Wakering, kpr., Jan. 19.
Sir Thos. de Beaufort, aft. E. of Dorset and D. of Exeter, Jan. 31.
1412. Thos. de Arundel, abp. of Canterbury, *again*, Jan. 5.

HENRY V.

1413. Hy. de Beaufort, bp. of Winchester, (transl. from Lincoln), Mar. 21.
1417. Thos. Longley, or Langley, bp. of Durham, *again*, July 23.

HENRY VI.

1422. Simon Gaunstede, m. rolls, kpr., Sept. 28.
Thos. Longley, or Langley, bp. of Durham, *again*, Nov. 16.
1424. Hy. de Beaufort, bp. of Winchester, *again*, July 6.
1426. John Kempe, bp. of London, Mar. 16; aft. abp. of York.
1432. Humphrey, D. of Gloucester, kpr., Feb. 25.
John Stafford, bp. of Bath and Wells, Mar. 4; aft. abp. of Canterbury.
1450. John Kempe, now a cardinal, and abp. of York, Jan. 31; *d.* Mar. 2, 1454.
1454. Richd., E. of Salisbury, Apr. 2.
1455. Thos. Bourchier, abp. of Canterbury, Mar. 7.
1456. Wm. de Waynflete, bp. of Winchester, Oct. 11.
1460. Thos. Bourchier, abp. of Canterbury, *again*, kpr., July 7.
Geo. Nevill, bp. of Exeter, July 25; aft. abp. of York.

EDWARD IV.

1461. Geo. Nevill, *contd.*
1463. Robt. Kirkham, m. rolls, kpr. during the chancellor's absence, Aug. 23, and subsequently.
1467. Robt. Kirkham, kpr., June 9.
Robt. Stillington, bp. of Bath and Wells, June 20.
1470. Geo. Nevill, now abp. of York, Oct. 9 to Apr. 1471, during restn. of Hen. VI.
1471. Apr., Edw. IV. resumed the throne, and bp. Stillington remained chanc.
1473. John Morton, m. rolls, June 18; aft. bp. of Ely and abp. of Canterbury, kpr.
Hy., E. of Essex, kpr., June 23.
1473. John Morton, *again*, kpr., July 17.
Lawrence Booth, bp. of Durham, July 27; aft. abp. of York.
1474. Thos. Rotheram, bp. of Lincoln, May 25; aft. abp. of York.
1475. John Alcock, bp. of Rochester and m. rolls, Apr. 27; aft. bp. of Worcester and of Ely.
Thos. Rotheram, bp. of Lincoln, *again*, Sept. 28.

EDWARD V.

1483. John Russell, bp. of Lincoln

RICHARD III.

1483. John Russell, *contd.*
1485. Thos. Barowe, m. rolls, kpr., Aug. 1.

HENRY VII

1485. John Alcock, now bp. of Worcester, Aug. 22; aft. bp. of Ely.
1486. John Morton, now abp. of Canterbury, Mar. 6. He had been made bp. of Ely in 1478; *d.* Sept. 1500.
1500. Richd. Nikke, dean of the chapel royal, kpr., Sept. 16.
Hy. Deane, bp. of Salisbury, Oct. 13; aft. abp. of Canterbury, kpr.
1502. Wm. Barnes, or Barons, m. rolls, kpr., July 27.
Wm. Warham, bp. elect of London, kpr., Aug. 11.
1504. Wm. Warham, now bp. of London, and abp. elect of Canterbury, ld. chanc., Jan. 21.

HENRY VIII.

1509. Wm. Warham, *contd.*
1515. Thos. Wolsey, cardl., and abp. of York, Dec. 22.
1529. Thos., D. of Norfolk, treasr., and Chas., D. of Suffolk, earl marsh., kprs., Oct. 17.
Sir Thos. More, Oct. 25.
1532. Sir Thos. Audley, kpr., May 20; chanc., Jan. 26, 1533; cr. ld. Audley of Walden, Nov. 29, 1538.
1544. Thos., ld. Wriothesley, kpr., Apr. 22; chanc., May 3.

EDWARD VI.

1547. Lord Wriothesley, *contd.*; cr. E. of Southampton.
Wm., ld. St. John, kpr., Mar. 25.
Richd., ld. Rich., Oct. 23.
1551. Thos. Goodrich, bp. of Ely, kpr., Dec. 22; chanc., Jan. 19, 1552.

MARY.

1553. Stephen Gardiner, bp. of Winchester, Aug. 23.
1556. Nichs. Heath, abp. of York, Jan. 1.

ELIZABETH.

1558. The QUEEN, kpr., Nov. 18.
Sir Nichs. Bacon, kpr., Dec. 22; the first kpr. that ranked as ld. chanc. under 5 Eliz., cap. 18; *d.* Feb. 20, 1579.

1579. The QUEEN, Feb. 20.
Wm. Cecil, ld. Burleigh, and Robt., E. of Leicester, kprs., Feb. 24.
Sir Thos. Bromley, Apr. 26; *d.* Apr. 12, 1587.

1587. Hy., ld. Hunsdon, Wm., ld. Cobham, and sir Fras. Walsingham; kprs., Apr. 15.
Wm., ld. Burleigh, Robt., E. of Leicester, and sir Fras. Walsingham; kprs., Apr. 26.
Sir Christr. Hatton, Apr. 29; *d.* Nov. 20, 1591.

1591. Wm., ld. Burleigh, Hy., ld. Hunsdon, Wm., ld. Cobham, and Thos., ld. Buckhurst; commrs. gr. seal, Nov. 22.
Sir Gilbert Gerrard, m. rolls, and others; commrs. to hear causes, Nov. 22.

1592. Sir John Puckering, kpr., May 28; *d.* Apr. 30, 1596.

1596. Sir Thos. Egerton, m. rolls, kpr., May 6.

JAMES I.

1603. Sir Thos. Egerton, *contd.*; cr. ld. Ellesmere, July 19; chanc., July 24; aft. cr. visc. Brackley; *d.* Mar. 15, 1617.

1617. Sir Fras. Bacon, ld. kpr., Mar. 7; chanc., Jan. 4, 1618; cr. ld. Verulam, and aft. visc. St. Albans; removed May 1, 1621.

1621. Sir Julius Cæsar, m. rolls, and others, commrs. to hear causes in chancery, May 1.
Sir John Ley, knt. and bt., ch. just. and others; commrs., to hear causes in the lords, May 1.
Hy., visc. Mandeville, ld. treasr., Ludowic, D. of Richmond, and the E. of Arundel; to use the seal, May 1.
John Williams, dean of Westminster, aft. bp. of Lincoln, kpr., July 10.

CHARLES I.

1625. John Williams, *contd.*; res. Oct. 30.
Sir Thos. Coventry, kpr., Nov. 1; aft. ld. Coventry; *d.* Jan. 13, 1640.

1640. Sir John Finch, ch. just, C. P., kpr., Jan. 17; aft. ld. Finch.

1641. Sir Edwd. Lyttleton, ch. just. C.P., kpr., Jan. 19; aft. ld. Lyttleton.

1642. The KING, May 21.

1643. Hy., E. of Kent, Oliver, E. of Bolingbroke, Oliver St. John, John Wilde, Saml. Browne, and Edmd. Prideaux; parly. commrs. o kprs., Nov. 10.

1645. Sir Richd. Lane, royal kpr., Oct. 25

1646. Wm., E. of Salisbury, parly. commr *vice.* E. of Bolingbroke, July 3.
Edwd., E. of Manchester, sp. ho lords, and Wm. Lenthall, sp. ho commons and m rolls; parly commrs. or kprs., Oct. 30.

1648. Hy., E. of Kent, and Wm., ld Grey of Werke; parly. commrs or kprs., Mar. 15.
Sir Thos. Widdrington, and Bulstrode Whitelocke, joined to th preceding, Apr. 12.

THE COMMONWEALTH.

Parliamentary Commissioners or Keepers.

1649. Bulstrode Whitelocke, John Lisle, and Richd. Keeble, Feb. 8.

1654. Bulstrode Whitelocke, sir Thos Widdrington, and John Lisle Apr. 5.
Sir Thos. Widdrington, alone Whitelocke being abroad, an Lisle unwell, May 30.
Bulstrode Whitelocke, sir Thos Widdrington, and John Lisle *again*, July 14.

1656. Nathl. Fiennes and John Lisle, Jan.15

1659. Nathl. Fiennes, now styled ld Fiennes; John Lisle, now style ld. Lisle; and Bulstrode Whitelocke, now styled ld. Whitelocke Jan. 22.
Wm. Lenthall, May 14.
John Bradshaw, Thos. Terryll, and John Fountain, June 3.
Bulstrode, ld. Whitelocke, Nov. 1.

1660. Wm. Lenthall, *again*, Jan. 13.
Sir Thos. Widdrington, Thos Terryll, and John Fountain, Jan 17.
Edwd., E. of Manchester, joined to the above, May 5.

CHARLES II.

Keepers of the Great Seal for the King during the Commonwealth.

1649. Sir Richd. Lane, *contd.*; *d.* 1650.

1653. Sir Edwd. Herbert, kpr., Apr. 5 res. June 1654.

1658. Sir Edwd. Hyde, knt. and bt. made kpr. at Bruges, Jan. 13 and chanc., Jan. 29.

THE RESTORATION.

1660. Sir Edwd. Hyde, *contd.*, June 1 aft. ld. Hyde, visc. Cornbury and E. of Clarendon; removed Aug. 1667.

1667. Sir Orlando Bridgeman, knt. and bt., kpr., Aug. 30.
1672. Anthy. Ashley, E. of Shaftesbury, Nov. 17.
1673. Sir Heneage Finch, bt., kpr., Nov. 9; cr. ld. Finch, Jan. 10, 1674; chanc., Dec. 19, 1675; aft. E. of Nottingham; *d.* Dec. 18, 1682.
1682. Sir Fras. North, aft. ld. Guildford, kpr., Dec. 20.

JAMES II.

1685. Lord Guildford, *contd.*; *d.* Sept. 5, 1685
Geo., ld. Jeffreys, ch. just., K. B., Sept. 28.

WILLIAM AND MARY.

1689. Sir John Maynard, sir Anthy. Keck, and sir Wm. Rawlinson; commrs., Mar. 4.
1690. Sir John Trevor, sir Wm. Rawlinson, and sir Geo. Hutchins; commrs., May 14.
1693. Sir John Somers, kpr., Mar. 23; chanc., Apr. 22, 1697; aft. ld. Somers; depr., Apr. 27, 1700.
1700. Sir Jno. Holt, ch. just. K. B., sir Geo. Treby, ch. just. C. P., sir Edw. Ward, ch. bar. ex., and sir John Trevor, m. rolls, commrs., May 5.
Sir Nathan Wright., kpr., May 21.

ANNE.

1702. Sir Nathan Wright, *contd.*; removed in 1705.
1705. Wm. Cowper, kpr., Oct. 11; aft. ld. Cowper; chanc., May 4, 1707; res. Sept. 25, 1710.
1710. Sir Thos. Trevor, ch. just. C. P., Robt. Tracy, just. C. P., and bar. Jno. Scrope, of Scotland; commrs., Sept. 26.
Sir Simon Harcourt, atty. genl., kpr., Oct. 19; aft. ld. Harcourt; chanc., Apr. 7, 1713.

GEORGE I.

1714. Lord Harcourt, *contd.*; depr., Sept. 21.
Wm., ld. Cowper, Sept. 21; aft. E. Cowper.
1718. Sir Robt. Tracy, just. C. P., sir John Pratt, just. K. B., and sir Jas. Montague, bar. ex.; commrs., Apr. 18.
Thos., ld. Parker, May 12, aft. E. of Macclesfield; surr. the seal, Jan. 4, 1725.
1725. Sir Jos. Jekyll, m. rolls, sir Jeffrey Gilbert, bar. ex., and sir Robt. Raymond, just. K. B.; commrs., Jan. 7.
1725. Sir Peter King, cr. ld. King, June 1.

GEORGE II.

1727. Lord King, *contd.*
1733. Hon. Chas. Talbot, Nov. 29, aft. ld. Talbot; *d.* Feb. 1737.
1737. Philip, ld. Hardwicke,* ch. just. K. B., Feb. 21.
1756. Sir John Willes, ch. just. C. P., sir Sidney Stafford Smythe, bar. ex., and sir John Eardley Wilmot, just. K. B.; commrs., Nov. 9.
1757. Sir Robt. Henley, atty. gen., kpr., June 20; aft. ld. Henley.

GEORGE III.

1760. Lord Henley, *contd.*; chanc., Jan. 16, 1761; aft. visc. Henley, and E. Northington.
1766. Chas., ld. Camden, ch. just. C. P., July 30.
1770. Hon. Chas. Yorke, atty. gen., cr. ld. Morden, Jan. 17; *d.* Jan. 20, before the seals were put to his patent of peerage. He held the gr. seal only three days.
Sir Sidney Stafford Smythe, bar. ex., hon. Hy. Bathurst, just. C. P., and sir Richd. Aston, just. K. B.; commrs., Jan. 21.
1771. Hon. Hy. Bathurst, cr. ld. Apsley, Jan. 23; succ. his father as E. Bathurst, 1775.
1778. Edwd. Thurlow, atty. gen., cr. ld. Thurlow, June 3.
1783. Alexr., ld. Loughborough, ch. just. C. P., sir Wm. Hy. Ashhurst, just. K. B., and sir Beaumont Hotham, bar. ex.; commrs., Apr. 9.
Edwd., lord Thurlow, *again*, Dec. 23.
1792. Sir Jas. Eyre, ch. bar. ex., sir Wm. Hy. Ashurst, just. K. B., and sir John Wilson, just. C. P.; commrs., June 15.
1793. Alexr., ld. Loughborough, ch. just. C. P., Jan. 28; cr. E. of Rosslyn on his resignation.
1801. John, ld. Eldon, ch. just. C. P., Apr. 14.
1806. Hon. Thos. Erskine, cr. ld. Erskine, Feb. 7.
1807. John, ld. Eldon, *again*, Apr. 1.

GEORGE IV.

1820. Lord Eldon, *contd.*, aft. E. of Eldon.
1827. John Singleton Copley, m. rolls, cr. ld. Lyndhurst, May 2.

* Lord Hardwicke continued, it is said, chief justice of the king's bench until June 7, 1737, though he had kissed hands for the great seal.

WILLIAM IV.

1830. Lord Lyndhurst, *contd.*
Hy. Brougham, cr. ld. Brougham and Vaux, Nov. 22.
1834. Lord Lyndhurst, *again*, Nov. 21.
1835. Sir Chas. Christr. Pepys, m. rolls, sir Launcelot Shadwell, v. chanc., and sir J. B.Bosanquet, just. C. P.; commrs., Apr. 23.
1836. Sir Chas. Christr. Pepys, cr. ld. Cottenham, chanc., Jan. 16.

VICTORIA.

1837. Lord Cottenham, *contd.*
1841. Lord Lyndhurst, *again*, Sept. 3.
1846. Lord Cottenham, *again*, July 4; cr. E. of Cottenham on his resignation.
1850. Hy., ld. Langdale, m. rolls, sir Launcelot Shadwell, v. chanc., and sir Robt. Monsey Rolfe, bar. ex.; commrs., June 19.
Sir Thos. Wilde, ch. just. C. P., cr. ld. Truro, July 15.
1852. Sir Edwd. Burtenshaw Sugden (formerly ld. chanc. for Ireland), cr. ld. St. Leonards, Feb. 27.
1852. Robt. Monsey, ld. Cranworth, ld. just. app.
1858. Sir Fredk. Thesiger, cr. ld. Chelmsford, Feb. 26.
1859. John, ld. Campbell, ch. just. Q. B., June 18; *d.* June 23, 1861.
1861. Sir Richd. Bethell, atty.-gen., cr. ld. Westbury, June 26.
1865. Ld. Cranworth, *again*, July 7; *d.* July 26, 1868.
1866. Ld. Chelmsford, *again*, July 6; *d.* Oct. 5, 1878.
1868. Hugh McCalmont, ld. Cairns, ld. just. app., Feb. 29.
Sir Wm. Page Wood, ld. just. app., cr. ld. Hatherley, Dec. 9.
1872. Sir Roundell Palmer, cr. ld. Selborne, Oct. 15.
1874.* Ld. Cairns, *again*, Feb. 21; cr. E. Cairns, Sept. 23, 1878; *d.* Apr. 2, 1885.
1880. Ld. Selborne, *again*, Apr. 28; cr. E. Selborne, Dec. 29, 1881.
1885. Sir Hardinge Stanley Giffard, cr. ld. Halsbury, June 24.
1886. Sir Farrer Herschell, cr. ld. Herschell, Feb. 6.
Ld. Halsbury, *again*, Aug. 3.

* Under the S. C. J. Acts 1873 & 1875 (See *ante*, p. 350), the ld. chanc., on the 1st Nov. 1875, became President of the Chancery Division of the High Court of Justice and one of the *ex-officio* judges of the Court of Appeal.

LORDS OF APPEAL.

APPOINTED UNDER THE "APPELLATE JURISDICTION ACT, 1876" (39 & 40 Vict. cap. 59), WITH PEERAGES FOR LIFE.

See Introduction, *ante*, pp. 351–2.

1876. Sir Colin Blackburn, just. Q. B. div.; cr. ld. Blackburn, Oct. 5, **G.**; res., Jan. 1887.
Edwd. Strathearn Gordon, ld. adv. Scotland; cr. ld. Gordon, Oct. 6, **G.**; *d.* Aug. 21, 1879.
1880. Wm. Watson, *vice* Gordon; cr. ld. Watson, Apr. 26, **G.**
1882. Jno. David Fitzgerald, just. Q. B. div., Ireland; addl. ld. app.; cr. ld. Fitzgerald, June 19, **G.**
1887. Edwd. Macnaghten, *vice* Blackburn; cr. ld. Macnaghten, Jan. 25, **G.**

JUDICIAL COMMITTEE OF THE PRIVY COUNCIL.

See Introduction, *ante*, p. 352.

This committee was first established by 3 & 4 Wm. IV., cap. 41 (Aug. 14, 1833), and its constitution has been enlarged by various subsequent Acts. It is composed partly of *ex-officio* members, and partly of persons specially appointed. See the following table.

Qualification.	Qualifying Statute.	Remarks.
ll persons *being Privy Councillors* who hold, or have held, any of the following offices:—		
Ld. Pres. of the Council - -	3 & 4 Wm. IV., c. 41, s. 1	
Ld. Chancellor - - -	,,	
Ld. Keeper - - - -	,,	
First Commr. of the Great Seal-	,,	
L. C. J. of the Queen's Bench.	,,	Now styled L. C. J. of England.
Justice of the Queen's Bench -	,,	Now Justice of the Q.B. Division of the H. C. J.
L. C. J. of the Common Pleas -	,,	Office now abolished
Justice of the Common Pleas -	,,	,,
L. C. B. of the Exchequer -	,,	,,
Baron of the Exchequer - -	,,	,,
Judge of the Prerog. Court of Canterbury - - -	,,	,,
Judge of the Court of Probate -	20 & 21 Vict., c. 77, s. 15	Now Pres. of the Probate Division of the H. C. J.
Judge of the High Court of Admiralty - - - -	3 & 4 Wm. IV., c. 41, s. 1	Office now abolished.
Chief Judge in Bankruptcy -	,,	,,
Master of the Rolls - -	,,	
Vice Chancellor of England -	,,	,,
Vice Chancellor - - -	5 & 6 Vict., c. 5, s. 24	,,
Judge of the Court of Appeal in Chancery - - -	14 & 15 Vict., c. 83, s. 15	,,
Judge of the Court of Appeal under S. C. J. Acts - -	44 & 45 Vict., c. 3, s. 1	
Lords of Appeal - - -	39 & 40 Vict., c. 59, ss. 6 & 14.	
Archbishop or Bishop - -	3 & 4 Vict., c. 86, s. 16, & 39 & 40 Vict., c. 59, s. 14	To sit on appeals under Church Discipline Act, and in Ecclesiastical cases.
Any two retired East Indian or Colonial Judges appointed by the Crown - - -	3 & 4 Wm. IV., c. 41, s. 30	
Any two other persons being Privy Councillors, and appointed by the Crown -	3 & 4 Wm. IV., c. 41, s. 1	
Four persons who have been Judges of the Superior Courts, or C. J. of the High Court of Judicature of Bengal, Madras, or Bombay; or of the late Supreme Court of Bengal - -	34 & 35 Vict., c. 91	These persons are, under 39 & 40 Vict., c. 59, s. 14, now being gradually superseded by the Lords of Appeal.

The Judicial Committee first sat on November 27, 1833.

MEMBERS OF THE JUDICIAL COMMITTEE OF THE PRIVY COUNCIL.

* Appointed under 3 & 4 Wm. IV., cap. 41, ss. 1 & 30.
† Do. 34 & 35 Vict., cap. 91.
‡ Do. 3 & 4 Vict, cap. 86, s. 16.

The rest are *ex-officio* members. The date of appointment is, except where otherwise stated, also the date of being sworn a member of the Privy Council.

ORIGINAL MEMBERS, Aug. 14, 1833.

Hy., ld. Brougham, ld. chanc.
Hy., M. of Lansdowne, ld. pres.
Wm. Hy., D. of Portland, ex ld. pres.
Jno. Jeffreys, M. Camden, do.
Jno., E. of Chatham, do.
Hy., E. Bathurst, do.
Dudley, E. of Harrowby, do.
Jno., E. of Eldon, ex ld. chanc.
Hy., visc. Sidmouth, ex ld. pres.
Wm., ld. Stowell, ex judge admy. ct.
Jno. Singleton, ld. Lyndhurst, ch. bar. ex.
Wm. Draper, ld. Wynford, ex ch. just. C. P.
Thos., ld. Denman, ch. just. K. B.
Sir Jno. Nicholl, judge prerog. ct. Canterbury, &c.
Sir Jno. Leach, m. rolls.
Sir Wm. Alexander, ex ch. bar. ex.
Sir Lancelot Shadwell, v. chanc. England.
Sir Nichs. Conygham Tindal, ch. just. C. P.
Hon. Thos. Erskine, ch. judge bkptcy.
Sir Wm. Garrow, ex bar. ex.
Sir Jas. Parke, aft. ld. Wensleydale, just. K. B.
*Sir Edwd. Hyde East, ex. ch. just., Calcutta.

SUBSEQUENT APPOINTMENTS.

1833. Sir Jno. Bernard Bosanquet, just. C. P., Sept. 4.
Sir Alexr. Johnston, ex. ch. just., Ceylon, Sept. 4.
1834. Sir Jno. Bayley, ex. bar. ex., Mar. 5.
Sir Robt. Graham, ex. bar. ex., Apr. 16.
Sir Jno. Vaughan, just. C. P., June 5.
Sir Chas. Christr. Pepys, aft. ld. Cottenham, m. rolls, Oct. 1.
Sir Herbt. Jenner, (Fust) judge prerog. ct., Canterbury, &c., Oct. 29.
Jas., E. of Rosslyn, Dec. 15; sw. June 10, 1829.
1834. Sir Jas. Scarlett, aft. ld. Abinger ch. bar. ex., Dec. 16.
1836. Hy. Bickersteth, aft. ld. Langdale m. rolls, Jan. 16.
1838. Stephen Lushington, judge admy. ct
1840. ‡Wm. Howley, abp. of Canterbury sw. Oct. 5, 1813.
‡Edwd. Venables Vernon Harcourt abp. of York; sw. Jan. 20, 1808.
‡Chas. Jas. Blomfield, bp. of London sw. July 31, 1828.
1841. Sir Jos. Littledale, ex. just. Q. B. Feb. 25.
Jno., ld. Campbell, ex. ld. chanc Ireland, June 23.
Jas. Archd., ld. Wharncliffe, ld. pres., Sept. 3; sw. Dec. 16, 1834.
1842. Sir Jas. Lewis Knight Bruce, v. chanc., Jan. 15.
Sir Jas. Wigram, v. chanc., Jan. 15.
1843. *Thos. Pemberton Leigh, aft. ld Kingsdown, chanc. d. Cornwall, June 10; *d.* 1867.
*Sir Edwd. Ryan, ex. ch. just. Bengal, June 10; res. 1859.
1844. Sir Fredk. Pollock, knt., aft. bt., ch. bar. ex., Apr. 17.
1846. Walter Fras., D. of Buccleuch, ld. pres., Jan. 21; sw. Feb. 2, 1842.
Sir Thos. Wilde, aft. ld. Truro, ch. just. C. P., Oct. 30.
1848. ‡Thos. Musgrave, abp. of York, Feb. 11.
‡Jno. Bird Sumner, abp. of Canterbury, Apr. 15.
1850. Sir Jno. Jervis, ch. just. C. P., Aug. 14.
Sir Robt. Monsey Rolfe, aft. ld. Cranworth, v. chanc., Nov. 13.
1851. Sir John Romilly, aft. ld. Romilly, m. rolls, Apr. 14.
Geo. Jas. Turner, aft. Sir G., v. chanc. Apr. 14.
1852. Sir Jno. Patteson, ex. just. Q. B., Feb. 2.
Wm., E. of Lonsdale, ld. pres., Feb. 27; sw. May 30, 1828.
Edwd. Burtenshaw, ld. St. Leonards, ld. chanc., Feb. 27; sw. Dec. 16, 1834.
Sir Jno. Dodson, judge prerog. ct., Canterbury, Apr. 5.

852. Granville Geo., E. Granville, ld. pres., Dec. 28; sw. Aug. 1, 1846.
054. Ld. Jno. Russell, aft. E. Russell, ld. pres., June 12; sw. Nov. 22, 1830.
855. Sir Wm. Hy. Maule, ex. just. c. p., July 21.
856. *Sir Lawrence Peel, ex. ch. just. Calcutta, Apr. 4.
‡Archd. Campbell Tait, bp. of London, Nov. 28.
857. Sir Alexr. Jas. Edmd. Cockburn, knt., aft. bt., ch. just. c. p., Feb. 2.
858. Sir Cresswell Cresswell, judge prob. and div. cts., Feb. 3.
Jas. Brownlow Wm., M. of Salisbury, ld. pres., Feb. 24; sw. June 1, 1826.
Fredk., ld. Chelmsford, ld. chanc., Feb. 26.
Sir Jno. Taylor Coleridge, ex. just. q. b., June 5.
859. Sir Wm. Erle, ch. just. c. p., July 6.
*†Sir Jas. Wm. Colvile, ex. ch. just. Calcutta; sw. July 6, and app. under 3 and 4 Wm. IV., cap. 41, s. 1; app. under s. 30, Nov. 20, 1865, **G.**, *vice* Ryan, res.; app. under 34 and 35 Vict., cap. 91, Nov. 1871.
860. ‡Chas. Thos. Longley, abp. of York, June 1, **G.**
861. Richd., ld. Westbury, ld. chanc., June 26.
863. ‡Wm. Thomson, abp. of York, Feb. 3.
864. Sir Jas. Plaisted Wilde, aft. ld. Penzance, judge prob. and div. cts., Apr. 26.
865. Sir Edwd. Vaughan Williams, ex. just. c. p., Mar. 9.
866. Richd. C. T. N. B. C., D. of Buckingham, ld. pres., July 6.
Sir FitzRoy Edwd. Kelly, ch. bar. ex., Nov. 10.
Sir Hugh McCalmont Cairns, aft. ld. and E. Cairns, ld. just. app., Nov. 10.
Sir Richd. Torin Kindersley, ex. v. chanc., Nov. 10.
Sir Wm. Bovill, ch. just. c. p., Dec. 28.
867. Jno. Winston, D. of Marlborough, ld. pres. Mar. 8; sw, July 10, 1866.
Sir Jno. Rolt, ld. just. app., Aug. 3.
Sir Robt. Jos. Phillimore, judge admy. ct., &c., Aug. 3.
868. Sir Wm. Page Wood, aft. ld. Hatherley, ld. just. app., Mar. 28.
Sir Chas. Jasper Selwyn, ld. just. app., Mar. 28.
*Sir Jos. Napier, bt., ex. ld. chanc. Ireland, Nov. 11.
Geo. Fredk. Saml., E. de Grey and Ripon, ld. pres., Dec. 9; sw. Apr. 28, 1863.

1869. Sir Geo. Markham Giffard, ld. just. app., Feb. 4.
‡Jno. Jackson, bp. of London, May 13.
1870. Sir Wm. Milbourne James, ld. just. app., July 6.
*†Sir Barnes Peacock, ex. ch. just. Bengal; sw. July 6, and app. under 3 and 4 Wm. IV., cap. 41; app. under 34 and 35 Vict., cap. 91, June 10, 1872, **G.**
Sir Geo. Mellish, ld. just. app., Aug. 9.
1871. Sir Jno. Stuart, ex. v. chanc., Mar. 24.
Sir Jas. Shaw Willes, ex. just. c. p., Nov. 3.
†Sir Montague Edwd. Smith, ex. just. c. p., Nov. 3.
†Sir Robt. Porrett Collier, ex. just. c. p., Nov. 3.
*Mountague Bernard, *vice* Colvile, Nov. 24, **G**; sw. June 29.
1872. Roundell, ld., aft. E. Selborne, ld. chanc., Oct. 15.
Sir Jas. Hannen, judge prob, and div. cts., Nov. 27.
1873. Sir Jno. Barnard Byles, ex. just. c. p., Mar. 3.
Hy. Austin Bruce, aft. ld. Aberdare, ld. pres., Aug. 9; sw. Apr. 26, 1864.
Sir Geo. Jessel, m. rolls, Aug. 30.
Sir Jno. Duke Coleridge, aft. ld. Coleridge, ld. ch. just. c. p., Dec. 12.
1874. Sir Saml. Martin, ex. bar. ex., Feb. 2.
Chas. Hy., D. of Richmond, ld. pres., Feb. 21; sw. Mar. 3, 1859.
1875. Sir Hy. Singer Keating, ex. just. c. p., Feb. 4.
Sir Richd. Baggallay, ld. just. app., Nov. 27.
1876. Edwd. Strathearn, ld. Gordon, ld. of app., Oct. 5, **G.**; sw. Mar. 17, 1874.
Colin, ld. Blackburn, ld. of app., Nov. 28.
Sir Geo. Wm. Wilshere Bramwell, aft. ld. Bramwell, ld. just. app., Nov. 28.
Sir Wm. Baliol Brett, aft. ld. Esher, ld. just. app., Nov. 28.
Sir Richd. Paul Amphlett, ld. just. app., Nov. 28.
1877. Hy. Cotton, aft. Sir H., ld. just. app., July 11.
Hon. Alf. Hy. Thesiger, ld. just. app., Dec. 12.
1879. Sir Robt. Lush, ld. just. app., May 17.
Sir Jno. Mellor, ex just. q. b., June 26.
1880. Jno. Poyntz, E. Spencer, ld. pres., Apr. 28; sw. July 6, 1859.

1880. Wm., ld. Watson, ld. of app., Apr. 26, G.; sw. Mar. 26, 1878.
1881. *Sir Richd. Couch, ex. ch. just. Bengal, *vice* Bernard, Jan. 24, G.; sw. Nov. 27, 1875.
*Sir Arthur Hobhouse, K.C.S.I., aft. ld. Hobhouse, *vice* Napier, July 2, G.; sw. Mar. 2.
Sir Richd. Malins, ex. v. chanc., May 18.
Sir Nathl. Lindley, ld. just. app., Dec. 19.
1882. Sir Jno. Holker, ld. just. app., Feb. 6.
Jno. David Fitzgerald, aft. ld. Fitzgerald, ld. of app., June 29.
Sir Chas. Synge Christr. Bowen, ld. just. app., June 29.
1883. Chichester Saml., ld. Carlingford, ld. pres., Mar. 19; sw. Apr. 7, 1864.
1883. ‡Edwd. White Benson, abp. of Ca terbury, Mar. 19.
Sir Edwd. Fry, ld. just. app., Ap 20.
1885. Sir Hardinge Stanley Giffard, a ld. Halsbury, ld. chanc., June 2
Gathorne, visc. Cranbrook. ld. pre. June 24; sw. July 6, 1866.
Sir Hy. Chas Lopes, ld. just. app Dec. 12.
‡Fredk. Temple, bp. of Londo May 19.
1886. Sir Farrer Herschell, aft. ld. He schell, ld. chanc., Feb. 6.
Sir Jas. Bacon, ex v. chanc., No 26.
1887. Edwd. Macnaghten, aft. ld. Ma naghten, ld. of app., Jan. 25.
Sir Wm. Robt. Grove, ex just. Q. B Nov. 28.

CHIEF JUSTICIARIES. JUSTICIARIES. JUSTICES ITINERANT. JUSTICES OF TRAILBASTON.

See Introduction, *ante*, p. 346.

Chief Justiciaries.

Those marked † are omitted from Foss's lists, and must be considered doubtfu It is also doubtful whether those marked ? were Chief Justiciaries or Justiciarie Those marked ‡ were possibly Chief Justices of the King's Bench and not Chi Justiciaries of the *Aula Regis*.

1067. Odo., bp. of Bayeux and E. of Kent, ch. justr. of the southern div., and
Wm. Fitz-Osborne, E. of Hereford, ch. justr. of the northern div. of the kingdom.
1073. Wm. de Warenne, and Richd. Fitz-Gilbert or de Benefacta.
1078. Lanfranc, abp. of Canterbury.
Geoffrey, bp. of Coutance, in Normandy, and
Robt., E. of Moreton, or Mortagne.
1087. Bp. Odo, *again*.
1088. Wm. de Carilefo, bp. of Durham.
Ranulph Flambard, aft. bp. of Durham.
1100. Robt. Bloet, bp. of Lincoln.
1107–8. Roger, aft. bp. of Salisbury.
* * †Hugh de Bocland, canon of St. Paul's.
* * ? Geoffrey Ridel.
* * ? Ralph Basset, baron of Weld.
* * ? Richd. Basset, son of Ralph.
* * ? Geoffrey de Clinton, treasr.
* * ? Alberic de Vere.
1153. Hy., D. of Normandy, Nov.
? Richd. de Luci, or Lucy.
1154. Robt. de Beaumont, E. of Leice ter, and
Richd. de Luci, or Lucy, jointl Dec.
1167. Richd. de Lucy, only.
1179. Richd. Tocliffe, bp. of Winchester
Geoffrey Ridel, bp. of Ely, and
John of Oxford, bp. of Norwich.
1180. Ranulph de Glanville.
1189. Hugh Pusar, or Pudsey, bp. Durham. and
Wm. de Mandeville, E. of Alb marle, Sept. 15.
Hugh Pusar, or Pudsey, *again*, an
Wm. de Longchamp, bp. of El Dec. 11.
1191. Walter de Constantiis, bp. of Li coln and abp. of Rouen. Oct.
1193. Hubert Walter, abp. of Canterbur Sept.
1198. Geoffrey Fitz-Peter, aft. E. Essex, July.
1214. Peter de Rupibus, bp. of Winche ter, Feb. 1.
1215. Hubert de Burgh, E. of Kent, Jun He was regent of England in 121 during the minority of Henry II

1225. ‡ Martin de Pateshull.
1232. Stephen de Segrave, July.
1234. ‡ Robt. de Lexinton, July.
1236. ‡ Thos. de Muleton.
1240. ‡ Wm. of York, aft. bp. of Salisbury.
1250. ‡ Hy. de Bathonia.
1258. Hugh Bigot, June 22.
1259. ‡ Roger de Thurkilby, Dec. 29.
1260. Hugh le Despencer, Oct. 18.
1261. Philip Basset, July 5.
‡ Wm. de Wilton.
1263. Hugh le Despencer, *again*, Oct.
1265. ‡ Hy. de Bracton, Aug.
1267. Nichs. de Turri.

JUSTICIARIES.

It is doubtful whether those marked ? were Justiciaries or Chief Justiciaries, and whether those marked † were regular Justiciaries at all. In the reign of Hen. III. (1216–1272) those Justiciaries marked B have been called JUSTICIARII DE BANCO, and those marked F have had fines levied before them, and for these reasons have been considered as belonging to the Court of Common Pleas, though it is doubtful whether at the dates of their service the Court of Common Pleas had been actually established as a separate court.

* * ? Hugh de Bocland, canon of St. Paul's.
* * ? Geoffrey Ridel.
* * ? Ralph Basset, baron of Weld.
* * ? Rd. Basset, son of Ralph.
* * ? Geoffrey de Clinton, treasr.
* * ? Alberic de Vere.
1153. ? Rd. de Luci, or Lucy.
1164–5. Nigel, bp. of Ely.
Geoffrey Ridel, archdn. of Canterbury.
Rd. Tocliffe, archdn. of Poictiers.
Rd. Fitz-Nigel, treasr.
Guy, dean of Waltham.
Hy. Fitz-Gerold.
Wm. Malduit.
Simon Fitz-Peter.
Alan de Nevil.
Geoffrey Monachus.
Wm. Fitz-Andelm.
Philip de Davencester.
1169–70. Wm. Fitz-Martin.
John Malduit.
1174–5. Thos. Basset.
Wm. Basset.
Wm. Fitz-Ralph.
Bertram de Verdun.
1176–7. Hugh de Cressi.
Walter Fitz-Robert.
Turstin Fitz-Simon.
Wm. Fitz-Stephen.
Robt. Mantel.
1178–9. Roger Fitz-Reinfrey.
Godfrey de Luci.
John Cumin.
Hugh de Gaerst.
Ranulph de Glanville, aft. ch. justiciary.
Wm. de Bendings.
Alan de Furnellis.
1181–2. Wm. de Auberville.
Michael Belet.
Gilbert de Coleville.
Gervase de Cornhill.
Thos. Fitz-Bernard.
Osbert Fitz-Hervey.
1181–2. Ralph de Gedding.
Osbert de Glanville.
Wm. Rufus.
Wm. Torell.
1183–4. Hugh Bardolf.
Ralph Fitz-Stephen.
Robt. Marmium.
Hugh de Morewic.
Robt. de Whitefeld.
1184–5. Nigel Fitz-Alexander.
Hubert Walter, dean of York.
1186–7. Thos. de Husseburn.
Robt. de Inglesham, archdn. of Gloucester.
Josceline, archdn. of Chichester.
Ralph, archdn. of Hereford.
1188–9. Ralph, archdn. of Colchester.
Wm., archdn. of Totnes.
1189–90. Michael Belet.
Ralph Murdac.
1193–4. Roger Bigot, E. of Norfolk.
Ranulph Blundevil, E. of Chester.
Walter de Constantiis, abp. of Rouen.
Rd. Fitz-Neale, bp. of London.
Hugh Pusar, bp. of Durham.
Stephen de S. Jacobo.
Wm. de S. Mariæ Ecclesia, dean of St. Martin's; aft. bp. of London.
Geoffrey Fitz-Peter.
Otho Fitz-William.
Gilbert de Glanville, bp. of Rochester.
Wm. de Longchamp, bp. of Ely, chanc.
Wm. Mareschall.
Simon de Pateshull.
1194–5. Richd. de Herierd.
Herbert Pauper, bp. of Salisbury.
Hugh Peverel.
1195–6. Richd. Barre, archdn. of Ely.
Geoffrey de Bocland.
Wm. Briwer.

1195–6. Wm. Chanvill, archdn. of Richmond.
Hy. de Chastillon, archdn. of Canterbury.
Oger Fitz-Oger.
Osbert Fitz-Simon.
Wm. de Glanville.
Wm. de Kunill.
Wm. de Vere, bp. of Hereford.
Wm. de Warenne.
1197–8. John de Gestling, F.
James de Poterna.
Stephen de Turnham.
Hy. de Wichinton.
1198–9. Eustace, bp. of Ely, chanc.
Robert Fitz-Roger.
Osbert Fitz-William.
Richd. Flandrensis.
Godfrey de Insula.
Philip of Poictiers, bp. of Durham.
Ralph de Welford.
Wm. de Wrotham, archdn. of Taunton.
1199-1200. Hugh le Bobi.
Geoffrey de Bocland, archdn. of Norfolk and dean of St. Martin's, F.
Walter de Crepping.
Reginald de Comhill.
Wm. de Faleise.
Eustace de Fauconberg, F; aft. bp. of London.
Hy. de Furnellis.
Hy. of London, archdn. of Stafford; aft. abp. of Dublin.
1200–1. Ralph de Stoke.
1201–2. Reg. de Argentine.
John de Grey, bp. of Norwich.
1202–3. Jordan de Turri.
1203–4. Wm. de Cantilupe.
Thos. de Samford.
Josceline de Wells, aft. bp. of Bath and Wells.
1204–5. Richd. de Mucegros.
Hugh de Wells, archdn. of Wells, aft. bp. of Lincoln.
1206-7. Hy. Fitz-Ailwyn, mayor of London.
1207–8. Walter de Grey, chanc.
Hy. de Ponte Audomare.
1208–9. Robt. de Aumari.
Wm. de Ely, treasr.
Wm. de Furnellis.
John Fitz-Hugh.
Ralph Hareng, F.
Robt. Malduit.
Peter de Rupibus, bp. of Winchester, aft. ch. just.
1209–10. John de Briwes.
Robt. (? Roger) Huscarl.
1211–12. Saherus de Quincy, E. of Winchester.
1212–13. Richd. de Marisco, archdn. of Richmond; aft. chanc.
1213–14. Josceline de Stivicle.
1216–7. Richd. de Seinges, F.
1217–8. †Wm. de Albini, E. of Arundel, F.
†Alan Basset, F.
Simon de Insula, F.
Martin de Pateshull, archdn. of Norfolk and dean of St. Paul's, F.
Stephen de Segrave, aft. ch. just., F.
1218–9. Maurice de Audeley, F.
†Hugh Foliot, F.
†Geoffrey Gibbewin, F.
Thos. de Heydon, B.
†Robt. de Neville, F.
†Benedict de Sansetun, bp. of Rochester, F.
1219–20. Robt. de Lexinton, B.
1222–3. Geoffrey le Sauvage, F.
1223–4. Thos. de Muleton, B.
1225–6. Warin Fitz-Joel, F.
1226–7. Hy. de Braybroc, B.
1227–8. Wm. de Insula, F.
Roger de Northwold, F.
1228–9. †Thos. de Camviel, F.
Wm. de London, F.
Wm. de Raleigh, aft. bp. of Norwich and Winchester, F.
Robt. de Shardelow, F.
1229–30. Ralph de Norwich, B.
†Richd. Reinger, F.
1230–1. Wm. of York, aft. bp. of Salisbury, F.
1231–2. Adam Fitz-William, B.
1232–3. Wm. de St. Edmund, F.
1233–4. Robt. de Beauchamp, B.
Regd. de Moyun, B.
Robt. de Rockele, B.
Robt. de Ros, B.
1235–6. Wm. de Culeworth, F.
John de Kirkeby, F.
1237–8. Hy. de Bathonia, F.
Hugh Giffard, F.
1241–2. Jollan de Neville, F.
Gilbert de Preston, B.
Roger de Thurkelby, B.
1242–3. Robt. de Esseby, F.
1243–4. Jeremiah de Caxton.
John de Cobbeham, F.
1244–5. Robt. de Nottingham, F.
1245–6. Alan de Watsand, F.
1246–7. Simon de Wauton, F.
Wm. de Wilton, F.
1247–8. John de Lexinton.
1248–9. Wm. le Breton or Brito.
Hy. de Mara.
1249–50 Hy. de Bracton or Bretton
Robt. de Brus, B.
John de Gatesden, F.
†Alan de Zouche.
1250–1. Giles de Erdington, F
Gilbert de Segrave.
Nichs. de Turri.
Robt. Walerand.

1251–2. Roger de Whitchester, F.
Wm. Trussel, B.
1253–4. † John le Fraunceys.
1254–5. John de Caleto, F.
John de Cave, F.
Nichs. de Hadlow, or Handlo, F.
Robt. de Shottinden, F.
1255–6. John de Cokefield, F.
John de Wyvile, B.
1256–7. Peter de Percy.
1259–60. Wm. de Englefield.
1260–1. Martin de Littlebiri.
1261–2. † Thos. Basset.
Wm. Bonquer, or Boncour, B.
Richd. de Middeton, B.
1264–5. Hervey de Boreham, F.
† Fulco Fitz-Warine.
Richd. de Hemington.
Geoffrey de Leuknore.
1265–6. Walter de Berstede, F.
Adam de Greinvill, B.
John de la Lynde, B.
John le Moyne.
1265–6. Wm. de Poywick.
1266–7. John le Bretun, aft. bp. of Hereford.
Robt. Fulcon, B.
Roger de Messenden, B.
Hy. de Monteforti, B.
1267–8. Lawrence del Brok.
Adam de Castreton.
Roger de Seyton, B.
1268–9. Walter de Helynn.
John de Oketon.
John de Reygate.
Wm. de St. Omera.
Richd. de Stanes.
Thos. Trevet.
Hy. de Wollaveston.
1269–70. John de Cobbeham, B.
Nich. de Yattenden.
1270–1. Stephen Heym, F.
Ralph de Hengham.
Jas. de Paunton.
1271–2. † Walter de Merton.
Wm. de Weyland.

Justices Itinerant.

Prior to 1155 these lists are very imperfect, but from that date they are tolerably complete. Those marked † are doubtful, and those marked T were Justices of Trailbaston (See Introduction, *ante*, p. 346). Many of the Justices Itinerant were also Justiciaries or Judges, and will we found repeated in the other lists.

Those marked * are included in Dugdale's list, but Foss considers them to be only Commissioners appointed to deal with certain complaints which had been made against the Sheriffs of particular counties.

1155–6. Robt. de Beaumont, E. of Leicester.
Thos. Becket, chanc.
Henry de Essex.
1162–3. Wm. Fitz-John.
1165–6. Geoffrey de Mandevil, E. of Essex.
Richd. de Luci, or Lucy, ch. justr.
1167–8. Wm. Basset.
Guy Rufus, dean of Waltham.
Richd., archdn. of Poictiers.
Regd. de Warenne.
1168–9. Gervase de Cornhill.
John Cumin.
1169–70. Hy. Fitz-Gerold.
Hugh de Morevill.
Alan de Nevil, jun.
Oger.
Robt. de Stuteville.
1170–1. *The Abbot of St. Augustin, Canterbury.
*The Abbot of Chertsey.
*Roger, E. of Clare.
*Wm. de Abrincis.
*Manaserins de Dammartin.
*Gerold Fitz-Ralph.
*Gilbert de Pinkeni.
*Wm. Fitz-Helton.
*Wm. Fitz-Nigel.
*Wm. Fitz-Martin.
*Ralph de Hospitali.
1170–1. *Ralph de Dene.
1172–3. Hugh de Bocland.
Turstin Fitz-Simon.
Adam de Gernemue.
Regd. de Luci.
Robt. Mantel.
Walter Map.
Richd. Fitz-Nigel, treasr.
Wm. Rufus.
Sefred, archdn. of Chichester.
Nichs. de Sigillo.
Richd. de Wilton.
— Wimer.
1173–4. Alard Banastre.
Wm. Bastard.
Alexr. le Boteler.
Wm. de Braiosa.
John le Clerk.
John le Dover.
Mathew de Escuris.
Philip Fitz-Ernise.
Wm. Fitz-Ralph.
Wm. Fitz-Richard.
Ralph Fitz-Stephen.
Hugh de Gundevil.
Walter de Hadfield.
John Jukel.
Leonard.
Alured de Lincoln.
Robt. de Luci.

1173–4. John Malduit.
Hamon Morgan.
Milo de Mucegros.
Const. de Oxenford.
Walter de St. Quintin.
Guy le Strange.
1174–5. Thos. Basset.
Hugh de Cressi.
Ranulph de Glanville.
Wm. de Lamvallei.
Roger Fitz-Reinfred.
Walter Fitz-Robert.
Wm. Fitz-Stephen.
Bertram de Verdun.
Robt. Fitz-Bernard.
Richd. Giffard.
Robt. Pikenot.
Gilbert Pipard.
Robt. de Vaux.
1176–7. Michael Belet.
Ralph Briton.
Gilbert de Columbiers.
1177–8. Thos. Fitz-Bernard.
Richd. Tocliff, bp. of Winchester.
Geoffrey Ridel, bp. of Ely.
Jno., of Oxford, bp. of Norwich.
Wm. de Bending.
Nich. Fitz-Torold.
Alan de Furnellis.
Hugh de Gaerst.
Geoffrey Hose.
Godfrey de Luci.
Hugh Murdac.
Richd. de Pec.
Regd. de Wisebec.
Robt. de Witefeld.
1179–80. Richd. Rufus, or Giffard.
1181–2. Samson de Totington, abbot of St. Edmunds.
1184–5. Thos. de Husseburn.
Hugh de Morewic.
Ralph Murdac.
Wm. Vavasour, No. 1.
1186–7. Hugh Bardolf.
Wm. Briwer.
Richd., archd. of Wilts.
1189–90. Ralph de Arden.
Roger Arundel.
Maurice de Berkeley.
Richd. Brito, archdn. of Coventry.
Wm. Fitz-Alan.
Geoffrey Fitz-Peter.
Gilbert de Glanville, bp. of Rochester.
Robt. de Hardres.
Hy. de Northampton.
Hugh Pantulf.
Hugh Pusar, bp. of Durham.
Peter de Ros.
Wm. de Stuteville.
Wm. de Vere, bp. of Hereford.
1191–2. Simon de Kyme.
Adam de Tornoura.
1193–4. Regd. de Argentine.
Walter Fitz-Robert.
Wm. de Warenne.
1195–6. Wm. de Braiosa.
Simon de Pateshull.
Jno. Suthill, abbot of Hyde.
1196–7. Hugh de Bobi.
Walter de Crepping.
Hy. Fitz-Hervey.
Jno. de Garland.
Eustace de Ledenham.
Roger de Stikesward.
1197–8. Wm. Achard.
Simon Basset.
Baldwin de Cuserugge.
Osbert Fitz-Hervey.
Robt. Fitz-Roger.
Geoffrey, archdn. of Berks.
Hy. de Kingeston.
Wm. de Rideware.
Roger de St. Edmund.
Theobald Walter.
Wm. de Albini.
Philip Fitz-Robert.
Geoffrey Hachet.
Ranulph.
Ralph de St. Martin.
1199–1200. Alan, abbot of Tewkesbury.
Robt. de Braybroc.
Ralph de Welleford.
1200–1. Stephen de Clay.
Ralph Morin.
1201–2. Rd. Malebysse.
1202–3. Roger Arundel.
Wm. Fitz-Richard.
Hy. de Northampton.
Alexr. de Poynton.
1203–4. Hugh de Chaucomb.
1204–5. Robt. Marmion.
1206–7. Humphrey de Bassingborn, archdn. of Sarum.
Walter de Bovington.
Roger de Huntingfield.
Simon de Kyme.
Wm. de Percy.
Rd. de Seinges.
Robt. de Veteriponte.
1207–8. Ralph de Arden.
1208–9. Robt. de Berkeley.
Gerard de Camvill.
Wm. de Cornhill, archdn. of Huntingdon, aft. bp. of Lichfield and Coventry.
Hy. Fitz-Hervey.
Wm. de Huntingfield.
Roger de Lacy.
Robt. de Percy.
Rd. de Ponte.
Adam de Port.
Wm., archdn. of Hereford.
1210–11. Simon de Waldhull.
1218–9. Gilbert de Abbingworth.
Jno. de Bayeux.

1218–9. Faukes de Breaute.
Wm. de Cantilupe.
Hy. de Cobbeham.
Wm. de Cressy.
Ralph de la Ferte.
Matth. Fitz-Herbert.
Wm. Fitz-Roger.
Walter Foliot.
Ralph Gernum.
John Marescallus.
Walter Mauclerk, aft. bp. of Carlisle.
Thos. de Muleton.
Adam de Newmarket.
Walter de Pateshull.
Rd. Poore, bp. of Chichester, Salisbury, and Durham.
Walter de Ripariis.
Jordan de Sackville.
James le Sauvage.
Ralph Tablir.
Wm. de Trumpington.
Maurice de Turvil.
Walter de Verdun.
Wm. de Vernon.
Robt. de Veteriponte.
Philip de Ulecot.
Hugh de Wells, bp. of Lincoln.
Josceline de Wells, bp. of Bath and Wells.
John Wigenholt.
Laurence de Wilton.
John de Winchestede.
1219–20. Stephen de Ebroicis.
Waren de Granden.
John de Monmouth.
Robt. de Vere, E. of Oxford.
1220–1. Ralph Musard.
Randolph, abbot of Evesham.
Simon, abbot of Reading.
1223–4. Hy. de Braybrok.
Warin Fitz-Joel.
Wm. de Houbrug.
Ralph de Neville, bp. of Chichester.
1224–5. Herbert de Alençun.
Wm. de Ambly.
Roger de Auntreseye.
John de Baalun.
Roger de Baalun.
Roger Bertram.
Rd. de Beynvill.
Nich. le Boteler, or Pincerna.
Hugh de Glahaul.
Robt. de Cokefield.
Hugh de Droes.
Rd. Duket.
Walter Duredent.
Alan de Englefield.
Jordan de Esseby.
Hy. le Evesk.
Brian Fitz-Alan.
Walter Fitz-Robert.
Wm. Fitz-Rosceline.
Richd. Fitz-Simon.
1224–5. Wm. Fitz-Warine.
Adam Fitz-William.
Robt. Fitz-William.
Wm. de Frenchvill.
Barth. de Glanville.
Simon de Hale.
Wm. de Haunsarde.
Jordan Heyrun.
Jno. de Houton, archdn. of Bedford.
Wm. de Insula.
Regd. de Kaune.
Richd. de Kellesay.
Richd. de Levinton.
Alured de Lincoln.
Ralph de Lydiard.
Roger de Merelay.
Richd. de Montfichet.
Jordan Oliver.
Peter, abbot of Tewkesbury.
Adam de Porteseye.
Jno. de Reiny.
Walter de Romsey.
Jno. de St. Helena.
Jno. de St. John.
Richd. de Stoke.
Theobald de Valoines.
Richd. de Veym.
Wm. de Waleis.
Jno. de Wauton.
Wm. de Welles.
Wm. de Wichinton.
1225–4. Wm. Basset.
Walter de Beauchamp.
Peter de Brus.
Jno. de Daivill.
Jno. Fitz-Robert.
Randolph Fitz-Robert.
Alexr. Holdernesse.
Brian de Insula.
Jno. de Lacy, const. of Chester, aft. E. of Lincoln.
Wm. de Lancaster.
Walter le Poer.
Roger de Scarborough.
Wm. de Tametone.
Thos., abbot of Winchecumbe.
1226–7. Fulco Baynard.
Maurice de Gant.
Wm. de Hengham.
Jno. de Kirkeby.
Wm. de London.
Wm. de Sorewell.
Wm. of York.
1227–8. Hugh de Bolebec.
Stephen de Luci.
1229–30. Ralph Fitz-Reginald.
Jno. de Ulecot.
1230–1. Wm. Loudham.
1231–2. Walter de Cantilupe, aft. bp. of Worcester.
1232–3. Hy. de Tracy.
1233–4. Norman de Aresey.
Adam de Ascwardby.
Roger Bigot, E. of Norfolk.
Ranulph Fitz-Henry.

1233-4. Thos. Fitz-John.
Simon de Furnellis.
Robt. Grimbald.
Jollam de Neville.
Robt. de Salceto.
Oliver de Vaux.
1239-40. Warner Engaine.
Robt. de Haya.
Gilbert de Preston.
Ralph de Sudley.
Roger de Thurkelby.
1244-5. Hy. de Bracton, or Bretton.
1245-6. Hugh Fitz-William.
Simon de Wauton.
1247-8. Wm. le Breton, or Brito.
Regd. de Cobbeham.
1250-1. Silvester de Everdon, bp. of Carlisle.
Adam de Hilton.
Jno. Plessitis, E. of Warwick.
1251-2. Hy. de Coleville.
Robt. de Ripariis.
Simon de Trop.
1252-3. Giles de Argentine.
1253-4. Wm. de Spaldewick.
1254-5. Wm. de Cobbeham.
Wm. de Englefield.
Geoffrey de Leuknore.
Nichs. de Romesei.
1255-6 Peter de Percy.
1259-60. James de Audley.
Humphrey de Bohun, E. of Hereford.
Hugh le Depenser.
Jno. de Grey.
Jno de Montealto.
Jno. de Verdun.
Jno. de Warenne, E. Warren.
1260-1. Adam de Greinvill.
Martin de Littlebiri.
Roger de Sumeri.
Gilbert Talebot.
1261-2. Jno. de Aure.
Walter de Berstede.
Ralph Fitz-Ranulph.
Richd. de Hemington.
Robt. de Neville.
Wm. de Nottingham.
Wm. de Poywick.
Wm. de Staunton.
1267-8. Regd. de Acle.
Peter de Brus.
Roger de Clifford.
Matth. de Columbariis.
Walter de Helynn.
Jno. de Oketon.
Richd. de Stanes.
Jno. de la Strode.
Thos. Trevet.
Hy. de Wollaveston.
1269-70. Wm. de Boscehall.
Peter de Chester.
Geoffrey de Neville.
Geoffrey de Upsale.
1271-2. Ralph de Marsh.
1271-2 Jno. de Spalding.
Thos. de Weyland.
Wm. de Weyland.
1272. Walter de Hopton.
1273-4. Elias de Beckingham.
Solomon de Rochester.
1274-5. Wm. de Northbury.
Wm. de St. Omera.
† Jno. de Saunford.
1275-6. Roger Loveday.
Geoffrey de Newbald.
Thos. de Sadington.
1277-8. Godfrey Giffard, bp. of Worcester.
Geoffrey de Picheford.
Jno. de Vaux.
Richd. de Ware.
1278-9. Richd. de Boyland.
1279-80. Wm. de Brabœuf.
† Roger de Clifford, senr.
† Matth. de Columbiers.
† Adam Gurdon.
† Wm. de Hamilton.
Alan de Walkingham.
1280-1. Thos. de St. Vigore.
1284-5. Nichs. le Gras.
Hamon Hauteyn.
1285-6. † Richd. de Crepping.
† Thos. de Normanville.
Wm. de Vesey.
1286-7. Roger de Brabazon.
Walter de Stircheleye
Wm. Wyther.
1291-2. † Wm. de Bereford.
Jno. de Berewyk.
Hugo de Cressingham.
† Jno. de Crokesley.
† Simon de Ellesworth.
Peter Heym.
Jno. Lovel.
Wm. de Mortimer.
Wm. de Ormesby.
Roger le Strange.
Jno. Wogan.
1292-3. Jno. de Batesford.
Jno. de Bosco.
Walter de Cambhou.
Hugh de Cave.
Adam de Crokedayk.
Hy. de Eynefeld.
Thos. Fisheburn.
Wm. Howard.
Wm. Inge.
Jno. de Insula.
Gilbert de Kirkeby.
Jno. de Lythegrenes.
1294-5. Robt. de Retford.
1298-9. Jno. de Bankwell.
Lambert de Trikingham.
1301-2. Wm. de Burnton.
Jno. Randolf.
Hervey de Staunton.
1303-4. Hy. de Guldeford.
1304-5. Jno. de Barton, T.

1304–5. Roger de Bellaforgo.
Jno. de Botetourt, T.
Jno. le Breton, T.
Thos. de Burnham, T.
Wm. de Cressy, T.
Edmd. D'Eyncourt, T.
Nichs. Fermbaud.
Ralph FitzWilliam, T.
Robt. de Harwedon, T.
Thos. de la Hyde, T.
Wm. de Kardeston, T.
Gilbert de Knovill, T.
Peter de Malo Lacu, or Mauley, T.
Wm. Martyn, T.
Adam de Middleton, T.
Gerard Salveyn, T.
Milo de Stapleton, T.
Wm. le Vavasour, T.
Richd. de Walsingham, T.
1306–7. Geoffrey de Hertelpole.
Hugh de Louthere, T.
Jno. de Mutford, T.
Thos. de Snyterton, T.
Jno. de Thorp, T.
1310–1. Richd. de Bereford.
Nichs. de Bolinbroke.
Robt. de Clyderhou, or Clider-hou.
Wm. de Colneye.
1310–1. Wm. de Goldington.
Walter de Gloucester.
Milo de Rodborough.
Jno. de Westcote.
1313–4. Richd. de Berningham.
1314–5. Robt. de Maddingley.
1317–8. Gilbert de Toutheby.
1329. Ralph de Bereford.
Adam de Brome.
Jno de Ifeld.
Jno. de Radenhale.
Jno. Randolph.
Lambert de Trikingham.
1330. Hugh de Courtney.
Nichs. Fastolf.
Peter de Middleton.
Thos. de Radclyve.
Robt. de Thorpe.
Wm. de Zouche.
1333. Jno. Claver.
1349. Wm. de Herlaston.
Wm. de Scothou.
1370. Robt. Bealknap.
Jno. de Cavendish.
Edmd. Chelreye.
Wm. de Wakebrug.
Jno. de Fencotes.
Roger de Fulthorpe.
Roger de Meres.

CHIEF JUSTICES OF THE KING'S OR QUEEN'S BENCH AND LORD CHIEF JUSTICES OF ENGLAND. PUISNE JUSTICES OF THE KING'S OR QUEEN'S BENCH. PRESIDENTS AND JUSTICES OF THE HIGH COURT OF JUSTICE, QUEEN'S BENCH DIVISION.

See Introduction, *ante*, p. 346.

CHIEF JUSTICES OF THE KING'S OR QUEEN'S BENCH, SOMETIMES STYLED CHIEF JUSTICES OF ENGLAND.

1268. Robert de Brus, or Brius, in modern times spelt Bruce; the first judge who was distinctly constituted ch. just. of the K. B.—*Foss*.
Ralph de Hengham, just. K. B. *Foss* gives the date of his appt. as 1273–4.
1290. Gilbert de Thornton.
1296. Roger le Brabazon, just. K. B.
1316. Wm. Inge, Mar.
1317. Hy. le Scrope, June 15.
1323. Hervey or Hy. de Staunton, Sept.
1324. Geoffrey le Scrope, just. C. P., Mar. 21.
1329. Robt. de Malberthorp, just. K. B., May 1.
Hy. le Scrope, *again*, Oct. 28.
1330. *Geoffrey le Scrope, *again*, Dec. 19.
1332. *Richd. de Wyllughby, just. K. B., Mar. 28.
*Geoffrey le Scrope, *again*, Sept. 20.
1333. *Richd. de Wyllughby, *again*, Sept. 10.
1337. *Geoffrey le Scrope, *again*.
1338. *Richd. de Wyllughby, *again*, Oct.
1340. Sir Robt. Parning, just. C. P., July 21.
1341. Sir Wm. Scot, Jan. 8.
1346. Sir Wm. de Thorpe, just. K. B., Nov. 26; hanged for malpractices in 1351.
1350. Sir Wm. de Shareshull, just. K. B., Oct. 26.
1357. Sir Thos. de Seton, just. K. B., July 5.
1361. Sir Hy. Greene, May 24.

* These changes were occasioned by Geoffrey Le Scrope's absences abroad with the king, during which Wyllughby was appointed chief justice in his place.

1365. Sir Jno. Knivet, or Knyvet, Oct. 29.
1372. Jno. de Cavendish, July 15; beheaded by the Kentish rebels.
1381. Sir Robt. Tresylian, just. K. B., June 22; executed in 1388.
1388. Sir Walter de Cloptone, Jan. 31.
1400. Sir Wm. Gascoigne, Nov. 15.
1413. Sir Wm. Hankford, Mar. 29.
1424. Sir Wm. Cheyne, just. K. B., Jan. 21.
1439. Sir John Ivyn, or Juyn, ch. just. C. P., Jan. 20.
1440. Sir John Hody, Apr. 13.
1442. Sir John Fortescue, Jan. 25.
1461. Sir John Markham, just. K. B., May 13.
1469. Sir Thos. Billing, just. K. B., Jan. 23.
1481. Sir Wm. Huse, or Hussey, May 7.
1495. Sir John Fineux, just. C. P., Nov. 24.
1526. Sir John Fitz-James, just. K. B., Jan. 23.
1539. Sir Edwd. Montague, Jan. 21; aft. ch. just. C. P.
1545. Sir Richd. Lyster, Nov. 9.
1552. Sir Roger Chomeley, Mar. 21.
1553. Sir Thos. Bromley (No. 1), just. K. B., Oct. 4.
1555. Sir Wm. Portman, just. K. B., June 11.
1557. Sir Edwd. Saunders, just. C. P., May 8; aft. ch. bar. ex.
1559. Sir Robt. Catlyn, just. C. P., Jan. 22.
1574. Sir Christr. Wray, just. K. B., Nov. 8.
1592. Sir John Popham, June 2.
1607. Sir Thos. Fleming, or Flemynge, bar. ex., June 25.
1613. Sir Edwd. Coke, ch. just. C. P., Oct. 25; disch. Nov. 1616.
1616. Sir Hy. Montagu, Nov. 16; made ld. treasr. 1620.
1621. Sir Jas. Ley, knt. and bt., Jan. 29, aft. ld. Ley; made ld. treasr. and cr. E. of Marlborough 1626.
1625. Sir Ranulph Crewe, Jan. 26.
1627. Sir Nichs. Hyde, Feb. 5.
1631. Sir Thos. Richardson, ch. just. C. P., Oct. 24.
1635. Sir John Brampston, or Bramstone, Apr. 14; removed Oct. 1643.
1642. Sir Robt. Heath, just. K. B., Oct. 31; removed by a vote of parlt., Oct. 1645.
1645. "There now sat only two judges in each court of law, until the close of this troubled reign." *Whitelocke.*
1648. Hy. Rolle, just. K. B., apptd. by the parlt. under the Commonwealth, Oct. 12.
1655. John Glyn, ch. just. of the "upper bench" under the Commonwealth, June 15; confirmed to him Oct. 11, 1656. *Whitelocke.*
1660. Sir Richd. Newdigate, ch. just. of the "upper bench," Jan. 17.
Sir Robt. Foster, just. C. P., Oct. 1.
1663. Sir Robt. Hyde, just. C. P., Oct. 19.
1665. Sir John Kelynge, just. K. B., Nov. 21.
1671. Sir Matth. Hale, just. C. P., May 18; res. 1676, and *d.* on Christmas Day following.
1676. Sir Richd. Raynsford, or Rainsford, just. K. B., Apr. 12; removed May 1678.
1678. Sir Wm. Scroggs, just. C. P., May 31; removed 1681.
1681. Sir Fras. Pemberton, just. K. B., Apr. 11; aft. ch. just. C. P.
1683. Sir Edmd. Saunders, Jan. 3.
Sir Geo. Jeffreys, bt., Sept. 28; aft. ld. chanc., and cr. ld. Jeffreys.
1685. Sir Edwd. Herbert, Oct. 23; aft. ch. just. C. P.
1687. Sir Robt. Wright, ch. just. C. P., Apr. 22.
1689. Sir John Holt, Apr. 17.
1710. Sir Thos. Parker, Mar. 11; aft. ld Parker, ld. chanc., and E. of Macclesfield.
1718. Sir John Pratt, just. K. B., May 15.
1725. Sir Robt. Raymond, just. K. B., Mar. 2; aft. ld. Raymond.
1733. Sir Philip Yorke, Oct. 31; aft. ld. Hardwicke, ld. chanc., and E. of Hardwicke.
1737. Sir Wm. Lee, just. K. B., June 8; became a bt. on the death of his brother, in 1749.
1754. Sir Dudley Ryder, atty.-gen., May 2.
1756. Wm. Murray, atty.-gen., cr. ld. Mansfield, Nov. 8; cr. E. of Mansfield in 1776; res. June 1788.
1788. Lloyd, ld. Kenyon, m. rolls, June 4; *d.* Apr. 1802.

1802. Sir Edwd. Law, atty.-gen., Apr. 11, cr. ld. Ellenborough; res. Nov. 1818; *d.* Dec. following.
1818. Sir Chas. Abbott, just. K. B., Nov. 2; aft. ld. Tenterden.
1832. Sir Thos. Denman, atty.-gen., Nov. 4; cr. ld. Denman, Mar. 22, 1834; res. Feb. 28, 1850.
1850. John, ld. Campbell, Mar. 5; app. ld. chanc. June 18, 1859.
1859. *Sir Alexr. Jas. Edmd. Cockburn, bt., ch. just. C. P., June 24.

* Transferred Nov. 1, 1875, to the H. C. J., Q. B. Division, and also made an *ex-officio* judge of the Court of Appeal, under Supreme Court of Judicature Acts, 1873 and 1875. (See *ante*, pp. 350–1.)

Presidents of the High Court of Justice, Queen's Bench Division.

(Lord Chief Justices of England.)

875. Sir Alexr. Jas. Edmd. Cockburn, bt., transf. from court of Q. B. Nov. 1; *d.* Nov. 20, 1880.

1880. John Duke, ld. Coleridge, pres. of C. P. div., Nov. 29.

Puisne Judges of the King's or Queen's Bench.

Those marked † are omitted from *Foss's* lists and must be considered doubtful.

Dugdale commences his list with—

250. †Alanus de Zouch, ld. mayor of London in 1267 and 1268.
253. †Hy. de Bathonia.
258. †Roger de Thorkelby, or Thurkilby.
†Gilbert de Preston.
†Nichs. Handlo, or Hadlow.
262. †Thos. Basset.
265. †John le Breton, or Bracton.
269. †Wm. de St. Omero.
†Richd. de Stanes.
270. †Jas. Panton.
†Ralph de Hengham, aft. ch. just.
271. †John de Cokefeud, or Cokefield.

Some of the above were probably only "Justiciaries." According to *Foss* the following were the puisne judges of the king's bench at the death of Henry III. in Nov. 1272.

John de Cobbeham.
Walter de Helynn, or Helyun.
Martin de Littlebire or Littlebiri.
John de Reygate (?).
Rd. de Stanes (?).

The following are the subsequent appointments.

274–5. Nichs. de Stapelton.
Wm. de Saham.
Walter de Hopton.
275. Martin de Letilbir.
John de Cobham, or Cobbeham.
275–6. John de Metingham.
Walter de Wymburne.
1282–3. †John de Cave, *Dugdale*; doubted by *Foss*.
1284–5. Elias de Suttone.
1288–9. Ralph de Sandwic.
289–90. Roger de Brabazon, aft. ch. just.
Robt. Malet, or Mallet.
1293–4. John Lovel.
1294–5. Gilbert de Roubury.
1295–6. Wm. de Ormesby.
1300–1. Hy. Spigurnell.
1316. Geoffrey le Scrope, aft. ch. just.
Lambert de Trikingham, Aug. 6.
1320, Robt. de Malberthorpe, Aug.; aft. ch. just.
1327. Walter de Friskeney, Mar. 6.
1327. Robt. Baynard, Mar. 9.
1328. Hy. de Hanbury.
1330. Richd. de Wyllughby, Dec. 15; aft. ch. just.
Thos. de Louthere, or Louthe, Dec. 15.
1331. Geoffrey Edenham, Jan. 18.
1332. Thos. Bacon, Jan. 28.
1333. Wm. de Shareshull, Mar. 20; aft. ch. just.
1334. Robt. de Scardeburgh, Sept. 14; transf. to C. P., 1339.
1338. Robt. Brundish, Apr. 4.
Wm. Faunt, Apr. 4.
1339. Wm. Scot, May 2.
John de Shardelow, or Cherdelawe, just. C. P., Sept. 6.
1341. Robt. de Scardeburgh, *again*; from the C. P., Jan. 8.
Roger de Bankewell.
Wm. Bassett, Oct. 28.
1342. Adam de Staingrave, Jan. 10.
1345. Wm. de Thorpe, aft. ch. just.
1354. Thos. de Seton, aft. ch. just.
1355. Wm. de Notton, Oct. 12.
1361. Thos. de Ingelby, Sept. 30.
1378. Robt. Tresylian, May 6; aft. ch. just.
1383. David Hanemere, Feb. 26.
1387. John de Lokton, or Lockton, Oct. 25.
1389. John Hull, or Hill, May 20.
Hugh Hulse, May 20.
1409. Robt. Thirwit, or Tirwhit, May.
1415. Roger Horton, June, 16.
Wm. Cheyne, June 16; aft. ch. just.
1424. John Halls, Jan. 21.
1426. Wm. Westbury, Feb. 6.
1434. Wm. Goderede, July 3.
1443. Wm. Yelverton.
1444. John Markham, Feb. 6; aft. ch. just.
1445. Richd. Bingham, aft. sir R.
1452, Ralph Pole, July 3.
1464. Thos. Billing, Aug. 9; aft. ch. just.
1465. Wm. Lakene, June 4.
1470. Richd. Neele, Oct. 9.
1471. John Needham, June 17.
1475. Thos. Young, Apr. 29.

1477. Guido Fairfax.
1481. Wm. Jenney.
1484. John Sulyard, or Sulliard, Oct. 26.
1488. Thos. Tremayle, July 16.
1495. Robt. Read, Nov. 24.
1507. Robt. Brudnell, or Brudenell, Apr. 28; transf. to C. P.
1509. Humfrey Coningsby, May 21.
1520. Jno. Moore, Apr.
1522. John Fitz-James, Feb. 6; aft. ch. just.
1529. John Port, Nov.
1532. John Spelman.
Wm. or Walter Luke, Aug. 23.
1540. Wm. Coningsby, July 5.
Edwd. or Edmd. Mervin, Nov. 22.
1544. Robt. Brooke, or Broke.
Thos. Bromley (No. 1), Nov. 4; aft. ch. just.
1546. Wm. Portman, May 14; aft. ch. just.
1553. John Whyddon, Oct. 4.
1556. Wm. Dallison, Jan.
1558. Fras. Morgan, Jan. 23.
Sir Jas. Dyer, just. C. P., Apr. 23. Held both offices *pro tem.*; aft. ch. just. C. P.
Wm. Rastal, Oct. 27; res.
1559. Regd. Corbet, Oct. 16.
1563. John Southcote, Feb. 10.
1566. Thos. Carus.
1572. Christr. Wray, May 14; aft. ch. just.
1574. Thos. Gawdy, aft. sir T., Nov. 16.
1576. John Jefferay, May 15; aft. ch. bar. ex.
1577. Wm. Ayloffe,
1584. John Clench, bar. ex., May 24.
1586. Robt. Schute, bar. ex., Feb. 8.
1588. Fras. Gawdy, aft. sir F., Nov. 25.; aft. ch. just. C. P.
1590. Edwd. Fenner, aft. sir E., May 26.
1602. Christr. Yelverton, aft. sir C., Feb. 8.
1604. David Williams, aft. Sir D., Feb. 4.
1606. Laurence Tanfield, aft. sir L., Jan. 13.
1607. Sir John Croke, late sp. ho. comm., June 25.
1612. Sir John Doderidge, Nov. 25.
1613. Sir Robt. Houghton, Apr. 21.
1620. Sir Thos. Chamberlain, Oct. 8.
1624. Sir Wm. Jones, just. C. P., Oct. 17.
Sir Jas. Whitelock, Oct. 18.
1625. Sir Hy. Yelverton.
1628. Sir George Croke, just. C. P., Oct. 28.
1632. Sir Robt. Berkeley, Oct. 11; removed. "Taken off the bench." —*Whitelocke.*
1641. Sir Robt. Heath, Jan. 23; aft. ch. just.
Sir Thos. Mallet, July 1; removed by the parlt. 1645.
1642. Sir Fras. Bacon, Oct. 14.
1644. Sir Robt. Brerewood, Jan. 31.
1645. Hy. Rolle, Sept. 30; under the parlt aft. ch. just.
1648. Philip Jermin, Oct. 12.
Saml. Browne, Oct. 12.
1649. Justice Bacon and Justice Brow (with judges of other court refused to act under the ne commission, Feb. 8.
Robt. Nicholas, June.
Richd. Ask, June 1.
1654. Richd. Newdigate, aft. sir R., June aft. removed.
It appears that there now sat thre judges in this court.
1655. Peter Warburton, June; removed 1659.
Richd. Newdigate, now sir Richd *again*, Jan. 17; aft. ch. just.
1660. Robt. Nicholas, and
Roger Hill, *vice* Newdigate (no ch. just.) and Warburton, Ja 17.
Sir Thos. Mallet, rest. by Charles II May 31; disp. with in June 1663.
Sir Thos. Twisden, July 2; dis with in 1678, "but continu judge until his death in Ja 1682."—*Raymond.*
Sir Wadham Wyndham; Nov. 24.
1663. Sir John Kelyng, June 18.
1665. Sir Wm. Morton, Nov. 23.
1669. Sir Richd. Raynsford, or Rainsfor bar. ex., Feb. 6; aft. ch. just.
1673. Sir Wm. Wylde, knt. and bt., jus C. P., Jan. 21; removed Apr. 2 1679.
1676. Sir Thos. Jones, Apr. 13, aft. c just. C. P.
1678. Sir Wm. Dolben, Oct. 23.
1679. Sir Fras. Pemberton, *vice* Wyld May 1; removed Feb. 17, 168 aft. ch. just. K. B. and C. P.
1680. Sir Thos. Raymond, just. C. Apr. 29; *d.* July 14, 1683.
1683. Sir Fras. Wythens, Apr. 25.
Sir Richd. Holloway, or Hallowa Sept. 25; removed June, 1688.
Sir Thos. Walcot, Oct. 22.
1685. Sir Robt. Wright, bar. ex., Oct. 2 aft. ch. just. C. P. and K. B.
1687. Sir John Powell, sen., just. C. Apr. 16; removed June, 1688.
Sir Richd. Allibone, Apr. 22.
1688. Sir Thos. Powell, bar. ex., July 7.
Sir Robt. Baldock, July 7.
Sir Thos. Stringer, Aug.
Sir Richd. Holloway and Sir Jo Powell were removed for givi their opinions against the cou in favour of the seven bishop and Sir Thos. Powell and S Robt. Baldock, the king's serjea were made justices in their roo
1689. Sir Wm. Dolben, Mar. 11.

689. Sir Wm. Gregory, bar. ex., May 4.
Sir Giles Eyre, May 4.
1694. Sir Sam. Eyre, Feb. 22.
695. Sir Thos. Rokeby, just. C.P., Oct. 29.
696. Sir John Turton, bar. ex., July 1; rem. June 9, 1702.
1699. Sir Hy. Gould, Jan. 26.
701. Sir Lyttelton Powys, bar. ex., Jan. 26; res. Oct. 1725.
1702. Sir John Powell, jun. just. C. P. June 24.
1710. Sir Robt. Eyre, *vice* Powell, May 5; aft. ch. bar. ex. and ch. just. C. P.
1713. Sir Thos. Powis, June 8; removed Oct. 14, 1714.
.714. Sir John Pratt, *vice* Powis, Nov. 22; aft. ch. just.
718. Sir John Fortescue Aland, *vice* Pratt, May 15; transf. to C. P. 1729, and cr. ld. Fortescue, of Credan, in Ireland, 1746.
1724. Sir Robt. Raymond, *vice* Eyre, Feb. 1; aft. ch. just., and cr. ld. Raymond.
1725. Sir Jas. Reynolds, sen., *vice* Raymond, Mar. 16; aft. ch. bar. ex.
1726. Sir Edmd. Probyn, Nov. 3, aft ch. bar. ex.
1727. Sir Fras. Page, just. C. P., Sept.
1730. Sir Wm. Lee, June 1, aft. ch. just.
1737. Sir Wm. Chapple, *vice* Lee, June 16.
1740. Sir Martin Wright, bar. ex., *vice* Probyn, Nov. 28; res. 1755.
1741. Sir Thos. Denison, Dec.
1745. Sir Michl. Foster, Apr. 22.
1755. Sir John Eardley Wilmot, Feb. 3; aft. ch. just. C. P.
1764. Sir Jos. Yates, Jan. 23; transf. to C. P. in 1770.
1765. Sir Richd. Aston, Apr. 19; res., *d.* 1778.
1766. Jas. Hewitt, Nov. 6; made ld. chanc. of Ireland in 1767, and cr. ld. Lifford.
1768. Edwd. Willes, *vice* Hewitt, Jan. 27.
1770. Sir Wm. Blackstone, Feb. 12; transf. to C. P. same year.
Sir Wm. Hy. Ashhurst, *vice* Blackstone, June 22; res. 1799.
1778. Sir Fras. Buller, knt., aft. bt., *vice* Aston, May 6; transf. to C. P. 1794.
1787. Sir Nash Grose, *vice* Willes, Feb. 9
1794. Sir Soulden Lawrence, just C. P. Apr. 9; transf. to C. P., *again*, 1808.
1799. Sir Simon Le Blanc, June 6.

---

808. John Bayley, *vice* Lawrence, May 9; knt., May 11; transf. to ex., Nov. 1830.
1813. Hy. Dampier, *vice* Grose, June 23; knt., July 14; *d.* Feb. 1816.
1816. Geo. Sowley Holroyd, *vice* Dampier, Feb. 20; knt., May 14; res., Nov. 1828.
Chas. Abbott, just. C. P., *vice* Le Blanc, Apr.; knt., May 13; aft. ch. just. and ld. Tenterden.
.818. Wm. Draper Best, ch. just. Chester, *vice* Abbott, Nov. 30; knt. June 1819; aft. ch. just. C. P. and ld. Wynford.
1824. Jos. Littledale, aft. sir J., *vice* Best, Apr. 30; res., Feb. 1841.
1828. Jas. Parke, *vice* Holroyd, Nov. 8; knt. Dec. 1; transf. to ex., Apr. 1834, by exchange with Williams; aft. ld. Wensleydale.
1830. Wm. Elias Taunton, *vice* Bayley, Nov. 12; knt. Nov. 17; *d.* Jan. 11, 1835.
Jno. Patteson, Nov. 12; knt. Nov. 17; additl. or fifth judge under 1 Wm. IV., cap. 70 (July 23, 1830); res. Feb. 1852; *d.* June 28, 1861.
1834. Sir John Williams, bar. ex., *vice* Parke, Apr. 29; *d.* Sept., 14, 1846.
1835. John Taylor Coleridge, aft. Sir J., *vice* Taunton, Jan. 27; res. May 1858; *d.* Feb. 11, 1876.
1841. Wm. Wightman, aft. Sir W., *vice* Littledale, Feb. 17; *d.* Dec. 10, 1863.
1846. Sir Wm. Erle, just. C. P., *vice* Williams, Oct. 27; aft. ch. just. C. P., June, 1859.
1852. Chas. Crompton, *vice* Patteson, Feb.; knt., Feb. 26; res. Oct. 6, and *d.* Oct. 10, 1865.
1858. Hugh Hill, *vice* Coleridge, May 29; knt. Apr. 18; res. Dec. 1861.
1859. *Colin Blackburn, *vice* Erle, June; knt. Apr. 14, 1860.
1861. *Jno. Mellor, *vice* Hill, Dec. 3; knt. June 11, 1862.
1863. Wm. Shee, *vice* Wightman, Dec. 18; knt. June 10, 1864; *d.* Feb. 19, 1868.
1865. *Robt. Lush, *vice* Crompton, Nov. 2; knt. Nov. 20.
1868. Jas. Hannen, *vice* Shee, Feb. 25; knt. May 14; apptd. judge of prob. and div. ct., Nov. 1872.
1868. Geo. Hayes, Aug. 25; additl. or

sixth judge under 31 & 32 Vict. cap. 125 (July 31, 1868); knt. Dec. 9, 1868; *d.* Nov. 25, 1869.

1872. *Jno. Richd. Quain, *vice* Hayes, Jan. 5; knt. Apr. 22.

1872. Thos. Dickson Archibald, *vice* Hannen, Nov. 20; knt. Feb. 5, 1873 transf. to C. P., Feb. 6, 1875.

1875. *Wm. Ventris Field, *vice* Archibald, Feb. 6; knt. May 13.

* On Nov. 1, 1875, these Judges were transf. to the H. C. J., Q. B. Div., under Supreme Court of Judicature Acts, 1873 and 1875. (See *ante*, pp. 350–1.).

Puisne Judges of the Queen's Bench Division of the High Court of Justice.

Transferred from the old Court of Queen's Bench, Nov. 1, 1875.

Sir Colin Blackburn, made ld. app., Oct. 1876.

Sir Jno. Mellor, res. 1879.

Sir Robt. Lush, made ld. just. app. Nov. 5, 1880.

Sir Jno. Rd. Quain; *d.* Sept. 12 1876.

Sir Wm. Ventries Field.

Subsequent Appointments.

1876. Hy. Manisty, *vice* Quain, Oct. 31; knt. Nov. 28.

Hy. Hawkins, *vice* Blackburn, Nov. 2, G.; transf. to ex. div., Nov. 14, 1876.

1879. Chas. Synge Christr. Bowen, *vice* Mellor, June 16; knt. June 26 made ld. just. app. June 2, 1882.

1880. Chas. Jas. Watkin Williams, *vice* Lush, Nov. 5; knt. Dec. 1; *d.* July, 1884.

Upon the abolition of the Com. Pleas and Exch. Divisions under the Supreme Court of Judicature Act, 1873, secs. 22 and 75, and Order in Council, Dec. 16, 1880 (see *ante*, p. 350), the following Judges became, on Feb. 26, 1881, judges of this division, but with relative rank according to their original appointments:—

From the Common Pleas Division.

Sir Wm. Robt. Grove, res. Sept. 1887.

Hon. Geo. Denman.

Sir Nathl. Lindley, made ld. just. app., Nov. 1, 1881.

Sir Hy. Chas. Lopes, made ld. just. app., Dec. 1, 1885.

From the Exchequer Division.

Sir Chas. Edwd. Pollock.

Sir Jno. Walter Huddleston.

Sir Hy. Hawkins.

Sir Jas. Fitzjames Stephen, K.C.S.I

Subsequent Appointments.

1881. Sir Hy. Mather Jackson, bt., *vice* ld. Coleridge, Mar. 2; *d.* before taking his seat.

Jas. Chas. Mathew, *vice* Kelly, Mar. 3; knt. Apr. 1.

Lewis Wm. Cave, *vice* Jackson, Mar. 14; knt. Apr. 1.

Ford North, *vice* Lindley, Nov. 1; knt. Dec. 7; transf. to ch. div. Apr. 1883.

1882. Jno. Chas. Day, *vice* Bowen, June 3; knt. June 29.

1883. Archd. Levin Smith, *vice* North, Apr. 12; knt. Apr. 20.

1884. Alfred Wills, *vice* Watkin Williams, July 21; knt. Aug. 11.

1886. Wm. Grantham, *vice* Lopes, Jan. 4; knt. Jan. 19.

1887. Arthur Charles, *vice* Grove, Sept. 8; knt., Nov. 28.

IIEF AND PUISNE JUSTICES OF THE COMMON PLEAS, RESIDENTS AND JUSTICES OF THE HIGH COURT OF JUSTICE, COMMON PLEAS DIVISION.

See Introduction, *ante*, pp. 346–7.

Chief Justices of the Common Pleas.

'hose marked † are omitted from *Foss's* lists, and must be considered doubtful.

Dugdale commences his list with—
'7. †Robt. de Lexinton.
5. †Thos. de Muleton.
8. †Hy. de la Mare or Mara.
1. †Wm. de Wyltone or Wilton.
But *Foss* considers it doubtful whether the division of the *aula regis* had yet actually taken place and whether the office of chief justice of the common pleas had yet been clearly established. He therefore begins with—
2. Gilbert de Preston, just. C. P., Nov.
3–4. Roger de Seytone or Seyton.
7–8. Thos. de Weyland, just. C. P.; removed 1288.
9–90. John de Metingham.
1. Ralph deHengham,just.C.P.,Sept.19.
9. Wm. de Bereford, just. C. P., Mar.15.
6. Hervey deStaunton,just.C.P.,July18.
7. Wm. de Herle, just. C. P., Jan. 25.
9. John de Stonore, just. C. P., Sept. 2.
1. William de Herle, *again* chief, and John de Stonore,second just., Mar. 2.
5. John de Stonore, *again*, July 7.
1. Roger Hillary, just. C. P., Jan. 8.
2. John de Stonore, *again*, May 9.
4. Roger Hillary, *again*, Feb. 20.
6. Robt. de Thorpe, June 27.
1. Wm. de Fyncheden,just.C.P.,Apr.14.
4. Robt. de Bealknap,aft. sirR.,Oct.10.
0. †Sir Robt. de Preston, Oct. 5.
8. Robt. de Carleton, Jan. 30.
6. Wm. Thirning or Thyrnynge, just. C. P., Jan. 15.
13. Richd. Norton, June 26.
23. Wm. Babington, ch. bar.ex. and just. C. P., May 5.
36. John Ivyn, or Juyn, bar. ex., Feb. 9.
39. John Cottesmore, just. C. P., Jan.20.
Richd. Newton, just. C. P., Oct. 14.
49. John Prysot, Jan. 16.
70. Robt. Danby, aft. sir R., just. C. P., Oct. 9.
†Richd. Choke, Sept. 5.
71. †Sir Robt. Danby, *again*.
Thos. Bryan, May 29.
00. Thos. Wood, just. C. P., Oct. 28.
02. Thos. Frowyk, Sept. 30.
06. Sir Robt. Read, Apr. 26.
19. John Ernley, Jan. 27.
1521. Robt. Brudnel, just. C. P., Apr. 13.
1531. Robt. de Norwich, just. C. P., Feb.
1535. Sir John Baldwin, Apr.
1545. Sir Edwd. Montague, ch. just. K. B., Nov. 6.
1553. Sir Richd. Morgan, Sept. 5.
1554. Sir Robt. Brooke, or Broke, Oct. 8.
1558. Sir Anthy. Browne, Oct. 5; aft. just. only.
1559. Sir Jas. Dyer, just. C. P. and K. B., Jan. 22.
1582. Sir Edmd. Anderson, May 2.
1605. Sir Fras. Gawdy, just. K. B.,Aug. 26.
1606. Sir Edwd. Coke, June 30; aft. ch. just. K. B.
1613. Sir Hy. Hobart, bt., Nov. 26..
1626. Sir Thos. Richardson, Nov. 28; aft. ch. just. K. B.
1631. Sir Robt. Heath, Oct. 26; removed Sept. 1634; aft. ch. just. K. B., whence he was removed by a vote of parlt.
1634. Sir John Finch, just. C. P. (?), Oct. 14; aft. ld. Finch and ld. kpr.
1640. Sir Edwd. Lyttelton, Jan. 27; aft. ld. Lyttelton and ld. kpr.
1641. Sir John Banks, Jan. 29; *d.* Dec. 1644.
The chief justiceship was not filled up until
1648. Oliver St. John, Oct. 12.
1660. Sir Orlando Bridgman, ch. bar. ex., Oct. 22; aft. ld. kpr.
1668. Sir John Vaughan, May 23.
1675. Sir Fras. North, Jan. 23; aft. ld. kpr. and ld. Guilford.
1683. Sir Fras. Pemberton, ch. just. K. B., Jan. 22; removed Sept. same year.
Sir Thos. Jones, just. K. B., Sept. 29; removed Apr. 1686.
1686. Sir Hy. Bedingfield, just. C. P., Apr. 21; *d.* next year.
1687. Sir Robt. Wright, just. K. B., Apr. 16; immediately aft. made ch. just. K. B.
Sir Edwd. Herbert, ch. just. K. B., Apr. 22.
1689. Sir Hy. Pollexfen, May 4.
1692. Sir Geo. Treby, May 3.

1701. Sir Thos. Trevor June 28; aft. ld. Trevor; removed, Oct. 1714.
1714. Sir Peter King, Oct. 14; aft. ld. chanc., and ld. King.
1725. Sir Robt. Eyre, ch. bar. ex., June 3.
1736. Sir Thos. Reeve. just. C. P., Jan. 26; *d.* Jan. 13, 1737.
1737. Sir John Willes, Jan. 28; aft. commr. gr. seal.
1762. Sir Chas. Pratt, Jan. 23; cr. ld. Camden; aft. ld. chanc.
1766. Sir John Eardley Wilmot, just. K. B., Aug. 21; res. 1771.
1771. Sir Wm. de Grey, Jan. 25; res. June 1780, and cr. ld. Walsingham, Oct. following.
1780. Alexr. Wedderburn, June 9; cr. ld. Loughborough; aft. ld. chanc. and E. of Rosslyn.
1793. Sir Jas. Eyre, ch. bar. ex., Jan. 28; *d.* July 1799.
1799. Sir John Scott, atty.-gen., July 18; cr. ld. Eldon; aft. ld. chanc. and E. of Eldon.

1801. Sir Richd. Pepper Arden, m. rolls, May 30; cr. ld. Alvanley; *d.* Mar. 1804.
1804. Sir Jas. Mansfield, May 8; res. Fe 1814.
1814. Sir Vicary Gibbs, ch. bar. ex., Fe 24; res. Oct. 1818.
1818. Sir Robt. Dallas, just. C. P., Nov. res. Nov. 1823.
1824. Sir Robt. Gifford, Jan. 9; cr. Gifford, Jan. 30; aft. m. rolls.
Sir Wm. Draper Best, just. K. Apr. 15; res. June, 1829, and ld. Wynford.
1829. Sir Nicolas Conyngham Tind solr.-gen., June 9; *d.* July 184
1846. Sir Thos. Wilde, atty.-gen., July aft. ld. chanc., and ld. Truro.
1850. Sir John Jervis, atty.-gen., July 1 *d.* Nov. 1, 1856.
1856. Sir Alexr. Jas. Edmd. Cockbu knt., aft. bt.; atty.-gen., Nov. 2 aft. ch. just. Q. B.
1859. Sir Wm. Erle, just. Q. B., June 2 res. Nov. 26, 1866.
1866. Sir Wm. Bovill, solr.-gen., Nov. 2 **G.**; *d.* Nov. 1873.
1873. *Sir John Duke Coleridge, att gen., Nov. 19, **G.**; cr. ld. Co ridge, Jan 1, 1874, **G.**

* Transferred Nov. 1, 1875, to the H. C. J., C. P. Div., and also made an *ex offi* judge of the Court of Appeal under the Supreme Court of Judicature Acts, 18 and 1875. (See *ante*, pp. 350–1.)

Presidents of the High Court of Justice, Common Ple Division.

(Chief Justices of the Common Pleas.)

1875. John Duke, ld. Coleridge, transf. from court of C. P., Nov. 1; made ld. ch. ju of England and pres. of the Q. B. div., Nov. 29, 1880.

The C. P. Div. and the office of ch. just. thereof were abolished under Supreme Co of Judicature Act, 1873, secs. 22 & 75, and Order in Council Dec. 16, 1880. (See *an* p. 350.)

Puisne Justices of the Common Pleas.

Those marked † are omitted from *Foss's* lists, and must be considered doubtful.

Dugdale commences his list with—
1234. †Robt. de Bello Campo, or Beauchamp.
†Regd. dé Moyun, or Mohun.
†Robt. de Rockele.
1235. †Adam, son of William.
†John de Kirkeby.
1236. †Wm. de Culeworth.
1238. †Hugh Giffard, const. Tower of London.
1241. †Jollanus de Neville.
1242. †Gilbert de Preston, aft. ch. just.
1243. †Roger de Thurkilby.
†Robt. de Esseburne, or Esseby.
1244. †John de Cobbeham.
1245. †Robt. de Nottingham.
1247. †Alanus de Watsand, or Wassand.
†Wm. de Wyltone.
†Hy. de la Mare.
1250. †Hy. de Bathonia.
†John de Gatesden, canon of S Paul's.
1251. †Simon de Wauton, aft. bp. of No wich.

1. †Giles de Erdington.
2. †Wm. Trussell.
4. †Roger de Wircestre,orWhitchester.
†Nichls. Handlo, or Hadlow.
6. †John de Wyville.
†John de Cokefield.
7. †Robt. de Briwes.
2. †Nichls. de Turri.
†Richd. de Middelton.
†Wm. de Bonquer, or Boncour.
3. †John de Wyville, *again*.
5. †Wm. de Wylton, *again*.
†Fulco, son of Warren.
†Hervey de Boreham.
66. †John de la Lynde.
†Walter de Berestede.
†Adam de Greynville.
67. †John le Breton, aft. bp. of Hereford.
†Hy. de Monteforti, or Montfort.
†Roger de Messenden.
68. †Martin de Litelbiri.
†Roger de Seyton, or Seytone.
71. †Robt. Fulke, or Fulc.
†Stephen Hayme, or Heym.
†Ralph de Hengham, chanc. of Exeter; aft. ch. just.
72. †Wm. de Weyland.

Foss considers it uncertain whether the judges above named were justices of the common pleas or justiciaries of the *aula regis*, and begins his list of undoubted justices of the common pleas with the following as being those in office at the end of the reign of Henry III., Nov. 1272:—

Robt. Fulcon.
Ralph de Hengham.
Stephen Heym.
Hy. de Monteforti.
Roger de Seyton.
Wm. de Weyland.

The following are the subsequent appointments:

73–4. Richd. de Stanes.
Thos. de Weyland, aft. ch. just.
74–5. Ralph de Frenyngham.
John de Lovetot.
75–6. Roger de Leicester.
†Roger Loveday.
†Geoffrey de Leuknore.
†Geoffrey de Newbold.
Walter de Helynn, or Helyun.
77–8. Wm. de Brompton.
83–4. †Stephen de Pencestre.
84–5. Elias de Bekingham.
89–90. Robt. de Hertford.
Robt. de Thorpe.
Wm. de Giselham.
90–1. Wm. de Bereford, aft. ch. just.
91. †Wm. de Ormesby.
91–2. Peter Malore.
96–7. Wm. Howard.
99–1300. Lambert de Trikingham.

1304–5. †Hy. de Guldeford.
1305–6. Hervey de Staunton; aft. ch. just.
1308. Hy. le Scrope, Nov. 27; aft. ch. just.
1309. John de Benstede, Sept. 29.
Wm. de Burne, Sept. 29.
1313. John Bacon, or Bacoun, Feb. 19.
1314. Wm. Inge, Sept. 28.
1316. Gilbert de Roubury, Mar. 10.
John de Mutford, Apr. 20.
1319. John de Doncaster, June 5.
1320. Wm. de Herle, Oct. 16; aft. ch. just.
John de Stonore, Oct. 16; aft. ch. just.
1321. John de Bousser, May 21.
1323. Walter de Friskeney, July 9.
Geoffrey le Scrope, Sept. 27; aft. ch. just. K. B.
1338. Richd. de Wyllughby, Mar. 6.
1329. John Travers, Mar. 2.
Thos. Bacon, or Bacoun, Sept. 30.
1331. Robt. de Malberthorpe, Jan. 18.
John de Cantebrig, Jan. 18.
John Inge, Jan. 18.
John de Stonore, late ch., now a puisne just., Apr. 1.
1332. John de Shardelow, or Cherdelawe, Jan. 28.
Richd. de Aldeburgh, Feb. 3.
1333. Wm. de Shareshull, May 30.
1334. †Geoffrey le Scrope, *again*(?), July16.
John de Trevaignon, Sept. 24.
1337. Wm. Basset, Jan.
Roger Hillary, Mar. 18; aft. ch. just.
Wm. Scot, Mar. 18; aft. ch. just.
1339. Robt. de Scardeburgh, Sept. 6.
1340. Jas. de Wodestoke, Feb. 4.
Robt. Parning, May 23; aft. ch. just. K. B.
Richd. de Wyllughby, *again*, Oct. 9.
Stonore, Shareshull, Shardelowe, and Wyllughby were removed about Nov., 1340.
1341. Thos. de Heppescotes, Jan. 8.
Richd. de Kelleshull, May 30.
Adam de Staingrave, Oct. 28.
1342. Wm. de Thorpe, Apr. 23.
John de Stonford, Apr. 23.
Wm. de Shareshull, rest. May 10.
John de Shardelowe, rest. May 10.
Richd. de Wyllughby, rest. May 10.
Roger Hillary, res. ch. justiceship to Stonore, and became a puisne just.
1348. Thos. de Fencotes, Jan. 14.
1354. Hy. Greene, Feb. 6.
1355. Thos. de Seton.
1357. Hy. de Motelow, July 4.
1359. John de Moubray, July 11.
Wm. de Skipwith, Oct. 25.
1361. John Knivet, Sept. 30.
1364. John Delves, Feb. 3.

1365. Wm. de Fyncheden, Oct. 29; aft. ch. just.
Wm. de Winchingham, Oct. 29.
1371. Roger de Meres, Nov. 2.
John de Cavendish, Nov. 27.
1372. Roger de Kyrketon.
1374. Robt., or Roger de Fulthorp, Nov. 28.
1376. Wm. de Skipwith, Oct. 8.
1377. Hy. de Perchehay, or Percehay, Nov. 26.
†Thos. de Ingleby.
1380. Hy. Asty, Dec. 6.
1383. John Holt.
Wm. Burgh.
1388. John Wadham.
Richd. Sydenham.
Wm. Thirning, or Thyrnynge, Apr. 11; aft. ch. just.
1389. Wm. Rickhill, May 20.
1391. John Penros, or Penrose, Jan. 15.
1391. †John Hull.
1396. John Markham, July 7.
1398. Wm. Hankford, May 6.
1399. Wm. Brenchesley.
1400. †John Hulse. ? Hugh.
1405. John Cokayne, May 14.
1406. John Colepeper, June 17.
1408. Robt. Hill, May 14.
1409. †Robt. Thirwit.
1415. Wm. Lodington, June 16.
John Preston, June 16.
†Wm. Cheyne.
†Roger Horton.
1420. Wm. Babington, ch. bar. ex., June 30; held both offices until app. ch. just. in 1423.
John Martin, June 30.
†Robt. Hull.
1423. John Ivyn, or Juyn, May 5; app. ch. bar. ex. same time; aft. ch. just. C. P. and K. B.
John Halls, May 5.
1426. Jas. Strangways, Feb. 6.
†Wm. Westbury.
1429. John Cottesmore, Oct. 15; aft. ch. just.
Wm. Pastone.
1438. Richd. Newton, Nov. 8; aft. ch. just.
1439. Thos. Fulthorpe, Jan.
1440. Wm. Ayscoghe, Apr. 17.
1443. John Portington.
1444. Richd. or Nichs. Ayshton, June.
1448. Peter Arderne, Nov.
1450. Robt. Danvers, Aug. 14.
1452. Robt. Danby, June 28; aft. sir R., and ch. just.
1454. Robt. or Walter Moyle, July 9.
1457. John Needham, May 9.
1461. Richd. Choke, Sept. 5.
1466. Thos. Littelton, Apr. 17.
1467. Thos. Young, Nov. 4.
1471. Sir Richd. Neele, May 29.
1481. Sir John Catesby, Nov. 20.
* * Humphrey Starkey, ch. bar. ex.; held both offices.
1484. Roger Townsend, Jan.
1487. Wm. Calowe, or Collow, Jan. 31.
John Haugh, Jan. 31.
1488. Wm. Danvers, Feb. 5.
1490. John Vavasour, Aug. 14.
1494. John Fineux, Feb. 11; aft. ch. ju K. B.
1495. Thos. Wood, Nov. 24; aft. ch. ju
1501. John Fisher, Nov. 3.
1503. John Kingsmill, July 2.
1508. John Boteler, or Butler, Apr. 26.
1509. Robt. Brudnel, just. K. B., A aft. ch. just.
Wm. Fairfax, Apr.
Wm. Grevyle, or Greville, May 2
1513 Richd. Elliot, Apr. 26.
1514. Lewis Pollard, May 29.
1518. John More, father of Sir Thos. M Jan.
1520. Richd. Brooke, or Broke, Apr.
1523. Anthy. Fitzherbert, Apr.
1526. Thos. Englefield, or Englefeld.
Wm. Shelley.
1530. Robt. de Norwich, Nov. 22; aft. just.
1537. Sir Thos. Willoughby, Oct. 9.
1538. Sir Christr. Jenny, June 30.
1542. Sir Humfrey Brown, Nov. 20.
1545. John Hinde, Nov. 5.
1549. Sir Jas. Hales, May 20.
1550. Sir Edwd. Molyneux, Oct. 22.
1552. Wm. Cooke, or Coke, Nov. 16.
1553. Edwd. Saunders, Oct. 4.
1554. Wm. Staunford, Oct.
1557. Sir Jas. Dyer, May 8; aft. just. K. held both offices *pro tem.*; aft. just. C. P.
1558. Robt. Catlyn, Oct. 28; aft. ch. j K. B.
1559. Ch. just. sir Anthy. Browne, justice, Jan. 22.
Richd. Weston, Oct. 16.
1563. John Welsh, or Walsh, Feb. 10.
1567. Richd. Harper.
1571. Christr. Wray, aft. ch. just. K.
1572. Roger Manwood, Oct. 14; aft. bar. ex.
Robt. Monson, Oct. 31; res. 157
1577. Thos. Meade, Nov. 20.
1579. Fras. Windham.
1581. Wm. Periam, Feb. 13; aft. ch. ex.
1585. Fras. Rodes. June 29.
1589. Sir Thos. Walmesley, May 10.
1593. Fras. Beaumond, or Beaumont, Ja
1594. Thos. Owen, Jan. 21; *d.* 1598.
1598. John Glanvile, or Glanville, Jun
1599. Sir Geo. Kingsmill, Feb.; res. 1
1600. Peter Warburton, Nov. 24.
1604. Sir Wm. Daniel, Feb. 3.
1606. Sir Thos. Coventry, Jan.
1607. Sir Thos. Foster, Nov. 24.
1611. Sir Humphrey Winch, Nov. 7.
1612. Sir Augustine Nichols, Nov. 26.
1617. Sir Richd. Hutton, May 3.
1621. Sir Wm. Jones, aft. just. K. B.

624. Sir Geo. Crooke, or Croke, Feb. 11; aft. just. K. B.
Sir Fras. Harvie, or Harvey, Oct. 18.
625. Thos. Chamberlayne, *pro tem.*, Mar.
Sir Henry Yelverton, bt., May.
630. Sir Humphrey Davenport, Feb. 2; aft. ch. bar. ex.
631. Sir Geo. Vernon, bar. ex., May 8.
632. Sir Fras. Crawley, Oct. 11.
634. †Sir John Finch, aft. ch. just.
639. Sir Edmund Reve, or Reeve, Mar. 24; *d.* 1647.
640. Sir Robt. Foster, Jan. 27.
645. Just. Crawley and just. Foster (with several judges of other courts) removed by the parlt.
Peter Phesant, Sept. 30.
647. John Godbolt, Apr. 30; *d.* 1648.
648. †John Creswell (*Dugdale*).
Rd. Cresheld (*Foss*), Oct. 12.
Thos. Bedenfield, Oct. 12.
649. Just. Creswell and just. Bedenfield refused to act, under the new commission.
{John Puleston, and
Peter Warburton, just. of the "common bench," June 1.
Edwd. Atkins, Oct. 19, *vice* Phesant, decsd.
654. Matthew Hale, Jan. 25, *vice* Warburton, transf. to the "upper bench."
Hugh Wyndham, June 2; removed 1660; made bar. ex. 1670.
658. Just. Hale threw up his commission about Sept.
659. John Archer, May 15.
660. Sir Robt. Foster, *again*, May 31; aft. ch. just. K. B.
Sir Robt. Hyde, May 31; aft. ch. just. K. B.
Sir Thos. Tyrrell, July 27.
Sir Saml. Browne, Nov. 3.
663. Sir John Archer, Nov. 4.
668. Sir Wm. Wylde, knt. and bt., Apr. 16; transf. to K. B.
672. Sir Robt. Atkyns, knt., Apr. 15; aft. ch. bar. ex.
Sir Wm. Ellis, or Ellys, Dec. 18; removed Oct., 1676.
673. Sir Hugh Wyndham, *again*, Jan. 22. He had been made bar. ex. in 1670, and now returned to this court.
676. Sir Wm. Scroggs, Oct. 23; aft. ch. just. K. B.
678. Vere Bertie, bar. ex., June 15; removed Apr. 1679.
679. Sir Wm. Ellis, or Ellys, *again*, Apr. 30.
680. Sir Thos. Raymond, bar. ex., Feb. 7.
Sir Job Charlton, Apr. 26; removed Apr. 1686.
681. Sir Creswell Levinz, or Levinge, Feb. 12; removed Feb. 1686.
684. Sir Thos. Street, bar. ex., Oct. 29.

1686. Sir Hy. Bedingfield, Feb. 13; aft. ch. just.
Sir Edwd. Lutwyche, Apr. 21.
Sir John Powell, sen., Apr. 26; transf. to K. B.
1687. Sir Christr. Milton, bar. ex., Apr. 16; res. next year.
1688. Sir Thos. Jenner, bar. ex., July 6.
1689. Sir John Powell, sen., *again*, Mar. 11.
†Sir Wm. Gregory, bar. ex., Apr. 18; immediately aft. to K. B.
Sir Thos. Rokeby, May 4; transf. to K. B.
Sir Peyton Ventris, May 4.
1691. Sir Edwd. Neville, bar. ex., Oct. 30.
1695. Sir John Powell, jun., bar. ex., Oct. 29; transf. to K. B.
1697. Sir John Blencowe, bar. ex., Nov. 23; res. 1722.
1702. Sir Robt. Tracy, bar. ex., June 24; aft. a commr. gr. seal; res.
1706. Sir Robt. Dormer, Jan. 8.
1722. Alexr. Denton, June 25.
1726. Sir Robt. Price, bar. ex., Oct. 16.
Sir Fras. Page, bar. ex., Nov. 4.
1727. Spencer Cowper, Oct. 24; *d.* Dec. 1728.
1729. Sir John Fortescue Aland, just. K. B., Jan. 27; aft. ld. Fortescue; res. 1746.
1733. Thos. Reeve, Apr. 16; aft. ch. just.
1736. Sir John Comyn, bar. ex., Jan. 5; aft. ch. bar. ex.
1738. Wm. Fortescue, aft. sir W., bar. ex., July 7; made m. rolls 1741.
1740. Sir Thos. Parker, jun., bar. ex., Apr. 21; aft. ch. bar. ex.
1741. Sir Thos. Burnet, Nov. 8.
1743. Sir Thos. Abney, bar. ex., Feb. 10.
1746. Sir Thos. Birch, June 24.
1750. Sir Nathl. Gundry, June 23.
1753. Sir Edwd. Clive, bar. ex., Jan. 30; res. 1770.
1754. Hon. Hy. Bathurst, May 2; aft. ld. chanc. and ld. Apsley; succ. as E. Bathurst, 1775.
1757. Hon. Wm. Noel, Mar. 3.
1763. Sir Hy. Gould, bar. ex., Jan. 24.
1770. Sir Jos. Yates, just. K. B., Feb. 16; *d.* June 16 following.
Sir Wm. Blackstone, just. K. B., June 22; *d.* 1780.
1771. Sir Geo. Nares, Jan. 26.
1780. Sir John Heath, *vice* Blackstone, July 19.
1786. Sir John Wilson, Nov. 7.
1793. Sir Giles Rooke, Nov. 13; res. 1808.
1794. Sir Soulden Lawrence, Mar. 8; transf. to K. B. by exchange with—
Sir Fras. Buller, knt. and bt., just. K. B., Apr.

1800. Alan Chambre, aft. Sir A., bar. ex., *vice* Buller, June 13; res. Dec. 1815.

1808. Sir Soulden Lawrence, *again*, *vice* Rooke, Mar. 31; res. at Easter, 1812.

1812. Sir Vicary Gibbs, atty.-gen., *vice* Lawrence, May 29; aft. ch. bar. ex. and ch. just. C. P.

1813. Sir Robt. Dallas, solr.-gen., *vice* Gibbs, Nov. 18; aft. ch. just.

1816. James Alan Park, *vice* Chambre, Jan. 24; knt. May 14; *d.* Dec. 8, 1838.

Chas. Abbott, *vice* Heath, Feb. 1; knt. May 14; aft. just. and ch. just. K. B. and ld. Tenterden.

Jas. Burrough, *vice* Abbott, May 4; knt. May 14; res. 1829.

1818. John Richardson, *vice* Dallas, Nov. 30; knt. June 1819; res. May 1824.

1824. Stephen Gaselee, aft. sir S., *vice* Richardson, July 5; res. 1837.

1830. John Bernard Bosanquet, *vice* Burrough, Feb. 1; knt. Feb. 2; res. 1842.

Edwd. Hall Alderson, Nov. 12; knt. Nov. 17; addl. or *fifth* judge under 1 Wm. IV., cap. 70 (July 23, 1830); transf. to ex. by exchange with—

1834. Sir John Vaughan, bar. ex., Apr. 27; *d.* Sept. 1, 1839.

1837. Thos. Coltman, *vice* Gaselee, Feb. 24; knt. Mar. 1; *d.* July 1849.

1839. Hon. Thos. Erskine, *vice* Park, Jan. 9; res. Nov. 1844.

Sir Wm. Hy. Maule, bar. ex., *vice* Vaughan, Nov. 11; res. June 1855.

1842. Cresswell Cresswell, *vice* Bosanquet, Jan. 22; knt. May 4; app. to court of prob. and div., Ja 1858.

1844. Wm. Erle, *vice* Erskine, Nov. knt. Apr. 23, 1845; transf. Q. B., 1846.

1846. Edwd. Vaughan Williams, *vice* Erl Oct. 27; knt. Feb. 4, 1847; re Jan. 1865.

1849. Thos. Noon Talfourd, *vice* Coltma July 28; knt. Jan. 30, 1850; Mar. 13, 1854.

1854. Richd. Budden Crowder, *vice* Ta fourd, Mar.; knt. May 3; Dec. 5, 1859.

1855. Jas. Shaw Willes, *vice* Maule, Ju 3; knt. Aug. 14; *d.* 1872.

1858. Jno. Barnard Byles, *vice* Cresswel Jan.; knt. Apr. 14; res. Jan. 187

1859. Sir Hy. Singer Keating, solr.-gen *vice* Crowder, Dec. 14, **G.**; res. 187

1865. Montague Edwd. Smith, *vi* Vaughan Williams, Feb. 2; kn May 18; app. to jud. comm. C., 1871.

1868. *Sir Wm. Baliol Brett, solr.-gen Aug. 24, **G.**; addl. or *six* judge under 31 & 32 Vict. ca 125 (July 31, 1868).

1871. Sir Robt. Porrett Collier, atty.-ge *vice* Smith, Nov. 7, **G.**; app. jud. comm. P. C., 1871.

*Wm. Robt. Grove, *vice* Collie Nov. 30, **G.**; knt. Feb. 21, 187

1872. *Hon. Geo. Denman, *vice* Wille Oct. 17, **G.**

1873. Sir Geo. Essex Honyman, bt., *vi* Byles, Jan. 23, **G.**; res. 1875.

1875. *Sir Thos. Dickson Archibald, ju Q. B., *vice* Keating, Feb. 6.

Jno. Walter Huddleston, *vice* Hon man, Feb. 22, **G.**; transf. to e May 12, 1875.

*Nathl. Lindley, *vice* Huddlesto May 12, **G.**; knt. May 13.

* On Nov. 1, 1875, these judges were transferred to the H. C. J., C. P. Div., unde Supreme Court of Judicature Acts, 1873 and 1875. (See *ante*, pp. 350-1.)

Puisne Judges of the Common Pleas Division of the High Cou of Justice.

Transferred from the Old Court of Common Pleas, Nov. 1, 1875.

Sir Wm. Baliol Brett, made ld. just. app., Oct. 27, 1876.

*Sir Wm. Robt. Grove.

*The Hon. Geo. Denman.

Sir Thos. Dickson Archibald; 1876.

*Sir Nathl. Lindley.

Subsequent Appointments.

1876. *Hy. Chas. Lopes, *vice* Archibald, Nov. 7, **G.**; knt. Nov. 28.

* Under Supreme Court of Judicature Act 1873, secs. 22 and 75 (see *ante*, p. 350), a Order in Council, Dec. 16, 1880, the Common Pleas Division was abolished, and the judges became, on Feb. 26, 1881, judges of the Q. B. Div., but with relative ra according to their original appointments.

CHIEF, PUISNE, AND CURSITOR BARONS OF THE EXCHEQUER. PRESIDENTS AND JUSTICES OF THE HIGH COURT OF JUSTICE, EXCHEQUER DIVISION.

See Introduction, *ante*, p. 347.

Chief Barons of the Exchequer.

Those marked † are omitted from *Foss's* lists, and must be considered doubtful.

The title of chief baron of the exchequer was, according to *Foss*, first used in the reign of Edwd. II. The following were *senior* barons :—

1303. Wm. de Carleton, July 26.
1308. Thos. de Cantebrig, Oct. 24.
1310. Roger le Scotre, July 17 ; but *Foss* considers it doubtful whether they actually enjoyed the title of *chief*. Then comes—
1312. Walter de Norwich, Mar. 3, who was a few days afterwards designated " Capitalis Baro " in certain letters patent, appointing John Abel a puisne baron. Walter retired from his office whilst holding the treasurership, and on his re-appointment, May 30, 1317, he was distinctly appointed " Capitalem Baronem."
1327. †Hervey de Staunton, July 17.
1329. John de Stonore, Feb. 22.
1330. Hy. le Scrope, Dec. 20.
1337. Robt. de Sadington, Mar. 24.
1344. Wm. de Shareshull, July 2.
1345. John de Stouford, Nov. 10.
Robt. de Sadington, *again*, Dec. 8.
1350. Gervase de Wilford, Apr. 7.
1362. Wm. Skypwith, or Skipwith.
1365. Thos. de Lodelow, Oct. 29.
1374. Wm. Tanks, or Tant, Feb. 3.
1375. Hy. Asty, Nov. 12.
1380. Robt. de Plesyngton, Dec. 6.
1384. †Wm. de Karleol, June 27.
1386. Jno. Cary, Nov. 5.
1387. †Robt. de Plesyngton, *again*, Aug 8.
1388. Thos. Pynchebek, Apr. 24.
1389. John Cassy, or Cassey, May 12.
1400. John Cokayne, Nov. 15.
1413. Wm. Lasingby, Apr. 28.
1419. Wm. Babington, Nov. 4.
1423. John Ivyn, or Juyn, May 5 ; app. just. C. P. same time ; aft. ch. just. C. P. and K. B.
1436. John Fray, Feb. 9.
1448. Peter Arderne, May 2.
1462. Sir Richd. Illingworth, Sept. 10.
1471. Sir Thos. Urswyk, May 22.
1479. Wm. de Nottingham, Apr. 3.
1483. Sir Humfrey Starkey, June 15; just. C. P. same time.
1486. Wm. Hody, Oct. 29.
1513. John Scot, Jan. 8.
1522. John Fitz-James, Feb. 8.
1526. Richd. Brooke, or Broke, Jan. 4.
1529. Richd. Lyster, or Leicester, May 12.
1545. Sir Roger Cholmeley, Nov. 11.
1552. Hy. Bradshaw, May 21.
1553. Sir David Brooke, Sept. 1.
1558. Sir Clement Higham, Mar. 2.
1559. Sir Edwd. Saunders, ch. just. K. B., Jan. 22.
1577. Sir Robt. Bell, Jan. 24 ; *d.* the summer assizes following.
Sir John Jefferay, or Jeffrey, just. K. B., Oct. 12.
1578. Roger Manwood, Nov. 17.
1593. Sir Wm. Periam, just. C. P., Feb.
1604. Sir Thos. Fleming, or Flemynge, Oct. 27 ; aft. ch. just. K. B.
1607. Sir Laurence Tanfield, just. K. B., June 25.
1625. Sir John Walter, May 10.
1631. Sir Humphrey Davenport, just. C.P., Jan. 10.
1644. Sir Richd. Lane, Jan. 25 ; aft. (Oct. 23, 1645) ld. kpr. ; his place was not filled up until
1648. John Wild, app. under the Commonwealth, Oct. 12.
1655. Wm. Steele, under the Commonwealth, *vice* Wild, May 1 ; aft. ld. chanc. of Ireland.
1658. Sir Thos. Widdrington, under the Commonwealth, *vice* Steele, June 26.
1660. John Wild, *again*, *vice* Widdrington, Jan. 17.
Sir Orlando Bridgman, knt. and bt., June 1 ; aft. ch. just. C. P. and ld. kpr.
Sir Matthew Hale, just. C. P., Nov. 7 ; aft. ch. just. K. B.
1671. Sir Edwd. Turner, May 23.
1676. Sir Wm. Montagu, Apr. 12 ; removed Apr. 1686.
1686. Sir Edwd. Atkyns, bar. ex., Apr. 21.
1689. Sir Robt. Atkins, Apr. 18.

1695. Sir Edwd. Ward, June 8; *d.* July 1714.
1714. Sir Saml. Dodd, Nov. 22.
1716. Sir Thos. Bury, bar. ex., June 10.
1722. Sir Jas. Montague, bar. ex., May 4.
1723. Sir Robt. Eyre, just. K. B., Nov. 16; aft. ch. just. C. P.
1725. Sir Jeffrey Gilbert, bar. ex., June 3.
1726. Sir Thos. Pengelly, Oct. 16.
1730. Sir Jas. Reynolds, just. K. B., Apr. 30; res. July, 1738.
1738. Sir John Comyns, just. C. P., July 7; *d.* Nov. 13, 1740.
1740. Sir Edmd. Probyn, just. K. B., Nov. 24.
1742. Sir Thos. Parker, jun., just. C. P., Nov. 29; res. Oct. 1772.
1772. Sir Sydney Stafford Smythe, bar. ex., Oct. 28; res. Dec. 1777.
1777. Sir John Skynner, Nov. 27; res, Dec. 1786.
1787. Sir Jas. Eyre, bar. ex., Jan. 26; aft. ch. just. C. P.
1793. Sir Arch. Macdonald, atty. gen. Feb. 13; res. Mich. term, 1813.

1813. Sir Vicary Gibbs, just. C. P., Nov. 8 aft. ch. just. C. P.
1814. Sir Alexr. Thomson, bar. ex., Feb 14; *d.* Apr. 1817.
1817. Sir Richd. Richards, bar. ex., Apr 22; *d.* Nov. 1823.
1824. Wm. Alexander, mast. chanc., Jan. 9 knt. Jan. 19; res. Jan. 1831.
1831. John Singleton, ld. Lyndhurst, ld chanc., Jan. 18; *again* ld. chanc 1834.
1834. Sir Jas. Scarlett, Dec. 24; cr. ld Abinger, Jan. 1835; *d.* Apr 1844.
1844. Sir Fredk. Pollock, atty. gen., Apr 15; res. July 1866, and cr. a bt. *d.* Aug. 22, 1870.
1866. *Sir Fitzroy Edwd. Kelly, July 16 G.

* Transferred Nov. 1, 1875, to the H. C. J., Ex. Div., and also made an *ex-offici* Judge of the Court of Appeal under Supreme Court of Judicature Acts 1873 and 187. (See *ante*, pp. 350–1.)

Presidents of the High Court of Justice, Exchequer Divisio (Chief Barons of the Exchequer).

1875. Sir Fitzroy Edwd. Kelly, transf. from Court of Ex., Nov. 1; *d.* Sept. 17, 1880.

The Ex. Division and the office of ch. bar. thereof were abolished under Suprem Court of Judicature Act 1873, secs. 22 & 75, and Order in Council Dec. 16, 1880. (Se *ante*, p. 350.)

Puisne Barons of the Exchequer.

Those marked † are omitted from *Foss's* lists, and must be considered doubtful.

1212. † G*** *fil. Petri Justiciarius Regis.*
1215. † Saherus, *comes* Winton.
1221. † Wm. Briwer.
* * † Richd. de Marisco.
1233. Wm. de Beauchamp (Bello-Campo).
Alexr. de Swereford, archdn. of Salop, compiler of the *Red Book* of the exchequer.
Richd. de Montfichet.
1237–8. Michael Belet.
John Fitz-Robert (?).
1240–1. Ralph de Ely.
Peter de Grimbald.
1242–3. Richd. de Barking, abbot of Westminster.
John le Fraunceys.
1247–8. Edwd. de Westminster.
1250–1. Richd. de Crokesley, abbot of Westminster.
1252–3. Peter de Ryevalis, or Orivallis.
John de Wyville.
1256–7. Simon Passelewe.
1257–8. Elerius, abbot of Pershore.
John Reinger.
1257–8. Thos. de Wymundham.
John de Launfare.
1260–1. Hy. de Tracey.
1263–4. Arnald de Berkeley.
Roger de la Laye, or Leye, archdn of Essex and dean of London.
1264–5. Nichs. de Criol.
Alexr. le Seculer.
Wm. de Mareschal.
1267–8. Wm. de Grancurt.
1270–1. Wm. de Cliff, or Clifford.
1272–3. Hervey de Boreham.
1273–4. Walter de Hopton.
Roger de Northwood.
John de St. Valerico.
1274–5. Philip de Wilighby, or Wiliby.
1275–6. John de Cobham, or Cobbeham
1283–4. Peter de Cestria or de Chester
1285–6. Wm. de Middleton.
1290–1. Wm. de Karleton, or Carleton.
Peter de Leycestre.
1291. Adam de Straton, or Stratton (?)
1293. Roger de Leycestre (?).
1295. † Richd. de Saham.

1295. John de Insula, Oct. 21.
1297–8. Roger de Hegham.
1299. Richd. de Abendon, or Abyndon, Oct. 17.
1306. Humfrey de Waledene, Oct. 19.
1307. Thos. de Cantebrig, Sept. 16.
John de Banquel, or Bankwell, Nov. 10.
John de Everdon, Nov. 28.
1308. Richd. de Abyndon, rest. Jan. 20.
1309. John de Foxle, Feb. 28.
1310. Roger de Scotre, July 17.
1311. Walter de Gloucester, July 5.
Walter de Norwico, or Norwich, Aug. 29; aft. ch. bar.
1312. John Abel, Mar. 8.
1313. John de Insula, *again*, Jan. 30.
1314. Hervey de Staunton, Sept. 28; aft. ch. bar.
1315. John Abel, *again*, May 4.
1316. Ingelardus de Warlee, or Warle, Dec. 29.
1317. John de Okeham, June 18.
1318. Robt. de Wodehouse, July 24.
1320. Lambert de Trikingham, Aug. 6.
Walter de Friskeney, Aug. 6.
1322. Roger Beler, July 20.
1323. Wm. de Fulburn, June 1.
Edmd. de Passele, Sept. 20.
1324. Robt. de Ayleston, May 21.
Wm. de Everdon, June 18.
Humfrey de Waldene, *again*, June 18.
1326. John de Redeswell, Sept. 1.
1327. Wm. de Boudon, Feb. 4.
Robt. de Nottingham, Oct. 15.
1330. Wm. de Coshale, Dec. 20.
1331. Thos. de Garton, Oct. 10.
1332. Adam de Steyngrave, July 24.
Wm. de Denum, Sept. 24.
Thos. de Blaston, Nov. 2.
Robt. de Scorburgh, or Scarburgh, Nov. 2.
John de Hildersley, Dec. 18.
1334. Adam de Lymbergh, Nov. 9.
1336. Nichs. Hawman, or Haghman, Oct. 3.
John de Shoredich, Nov. 10.
1339. Wm. de la Pole, Sept. 26.
1340. Wm. de Northwell, June 21.
1341. Wm. de Broclesby, Jan. 20.
Gervase de Wilford, Jan. 20; aft. ch. bar.
Wm. de Stow, Jan. 20.
1344. Alanus de Ashe, July 2.
1347. John de Houton, Mar. 8.
1350. Jas. Husse, Apr. 16.
1352. Wm. de Thorpe, May 24.
1354. Wm. de Retford, Nov. 27.
1356. Hy. de Greystoke, Oct. 6.
1357. John de Bukyngham.
1362. Robt. de Pleste.
1365. Almeric de Shirland, Oct. 29.
John de Stokes, Nov. 3.
1373. Wm. Gunthorpe.
John de Blockley.
1375. Hy. de Percehay, Oct. 5.
Lawrence Allerthorpe, Nov. 27.
1376. Nichs. de Drayton, Nov. 14.
1377. Richd. Stokes, Oct. 9.
1384. Wm. Ford, July 20.
1387. †John Carey.
1388. Wm. Doubridge.
1389. †Lawrence Allerthorpe, *again*.
†Wm. Ford, *again*.
1393. Ralph de Selby, Oct. 24.
1399. Thos. Ferriby.
John Staverton.
1401. Thos. Tuttlebury, June 27.
Wm. Ermyn, June 27.
1402. Thos. Overton, Jan.
1403. Roger Westwode, Mar. 1.
1407. Hy. Merston.
Hy. Somer, Nov. 8.
1410. Richd. Banke, June 19.
1413. Robt. Malton, Nov. 14.
1418. Roger Waltham.
1421. Wm. Hesill, July 13.
1423. Nichs. Dixon, Jan. 26.
Thos. Banaustre, or Bannister, Nov. 4.
1424. Thos. Banke, May 18.
1426. Wm. Warde, May 26.
1425–6. John Fray, aft. ch. bar.
1435. Wm. Derby, Feb. 8.
1436. Wm. Fallan, June 16.
1438. Roger Hunt, Nov. 3.
Robt. Frampton.
1444. John Arderne.
Wm. Levesham, Feb. 5.
1446. John Holme, Feb. 3.
1447. Gilbert Haltoft.
1449. John Durem, May 27.
1453. Thos. Thorpe.
1458. Bryan Roucliffe, Nov. 2.
1460. John Clerke, Oct. 10.
1462. John Ingoldesby, Nov. 4.
1467. Ralph Wolseley, Sept. 29.
Nichs. Stathum, Oct. 30.
1471. Thos. Urswyke, May 22.
1481. Thos. Whittington, Feb. 3.
1483. Edwd. Goldesburg, or Goldsborough, June 26.
1485. John Holgrave, Aug.
1487. Nichs. Lathelle, Nov.
1488. Thos. Roche, Dec. 5.
1489. †Thos. Goldesburg or Goldsborough.
1494. Thos. Barnewall, Oct. 1.
1496. Andrew Dymocke, May 2.
1501. Barthw. Westby, May 12.
Wm. Bolling, Oct. 11.
1504. John Alleyn, Feb. 18.
1511. †John Stag.
Robt. Blagge, June 26.
1513. Edmd. Denny, May 6.
1521. Wm. Wotton, July 10.
1522. John Hales or Halys, Oct. 2.
1523. Wm. Ellis.
1527. John Petit, Nov.
1528. John Scot, May 15; aft. ch. bar.
1536. Thos. Walshe, king's remembr., Apr. 27.

1538. John Danaster, Nov.
1539. John Smith, Nov.
1540. Nichs. Luke, Apr. 14.
1542. Lewis Fortescue, Aug. 6.
1545. John Pilborough, Nov. 28.
1547. Robt. Curzon, Feb. 15.
1548. John Darnall, or Darnell, May 5.
1549. Edwd. Saxelby or Saxby, Nov. 28.
1550. Robt. Browne, May 6.
1559. Geo. Frevyle, Jan. 31.
1562. Thos. Pyne or Pymme, Sept. 30.
1564. John Birch, May 9.
1566. Jas. Lord, Nov. 12.
1576. Thos. Greeke, Jan. 20.
1577. Christr. Muschampe, Nov. 28.
1579. Robt. Schute, June 1.
John Sotherton, June 16.
1581. John Clench, Nov. 27; aft. just. K. B.
1584. Edwd. Flowerdew, Oct. 23.
1586. Thos. Gent, Jan.
1587. Sir Robt. Clerke, or Clarke, June 22.
1594. Mattw. Ewens, Feb. 1.
1598. Sir John Savil or Savile, July 1.
1604. Sir Geo. Snigge, Oct. 14.
1607. Sir Jas. Altham, Feb. 9.
Sir Edwd. Heron, Nov. 5.
1610. Sir Edwd. Bromley, Feb. 6.
1617. Sir John Denham, May 2.
1625. Sir Thos. Trevor, May 10.
1627. Sir Geo. Vernon, July 4.
1631. Sir Jas. Weston, May 16; *d.* 1633.
1634. Sir Richd. Weston, sen., Apr. 30.
1637. Sir Edwd. Henden, Jan. 22; left about 1642.
1645. Baron Weston was removed by the parlt., Oct.
Edwd. Atkins, *vice* Weston, Sept. 30.
1648. Thos. Gates, app. by the parlt., Oct. 12.
1649. Barons Trevor and Atkins refused to act under the new commission.
Fras. Thorpe, June 1.
Alexr. Rigby, June 1.
1650. Barons Gates and Rigby, *d.* of an infection, on their circuits.
1654. Robt. Nicholas, from the "upper bench," *vice* Thorpe, removed; Nicholas aft. returned to the "upper bench."
1654. Rd. Pepys, June 2.
1655. John Parker.
1657. Roger Hill, aft. just. of the "upper bench."
1660. Fras. Thorpe, rest. Jan. 17.
Sir Edwd. Atkyns, June 23.
Sir Christr. Turner, July 7.
1663. Sir Richd. Raynsford, or Rainsford, Nov. 16; aft. just. and ch. just. K. B.
1670. Sir Timothy Littleton, Feb. 1.
Sir Hugh Wyndham, just. C. P., June 20; aft. just. C. P.
1673. Sir Edwd. Thurland, Jan. 24; res.
1675. Vere Bertie, June 4; aft. just. C. P.
1678. Sir Fras. Bramstone, June 17.
1679. Sir Wm. Gregory, sp. ho. commons, May 1.
Wm. Leak, May 8.
Sir Thos. Raymond, *vice* Thurland, May 8; aft. just. C. P.
Sir Edwd. Atkyns, jun., June; aft. ch. bar.
1680. Sir Richd. Weston, Feb. 7; *d.* next year.
1681. Sir Thos. Street, Apr. 23; aft. just. and ch. just. C. P.
1684. Sir Robt. Wright, Oct. 30; aft. just. K. B., ch. just. C. P., and ch. just. K. B.
†Sir Richd. May, Feb. 7.
1685. Sir Edwd. Neville, Oct. 11; pat. revoked Apr. 21, 1686.
1686. Sir Thos. Jenner, Feb. 13; aft. just. C. P.
Sir Richd. Heath, Apr. 21.
Sir Christr. Milton, Apr. 26; aft. just. C. P.
1687. Sir Thos. Powell, Apr. 22; aft. just. K. B.
1688. Sir Chas. Ingleby, July 7.
Sir John Rotherham, July 7.
1689. Sir Edwd. Neville, *again*, Mar. 11; aft. just. C. P.
Nichs. Lechmere, or Letchmere, May 4; res. aft. Trin. term, 1700.
Sir John Turton, May 4; aft. just. K. B.
1691. Sir John Powell, Oct. 27; aft. just. C. P.
1695. Sir Lyttleton Powys, Oct. 29; aft. just. K. B.
1696. Sir John Blencowe, Sept. 18; aft. just. C. P.
1697. Sir Hy. Hatsell, Nov. 23; removed June 8, 1702.
1700. Sir Robt. Tracy, Nov. 14; aft. just. C. P.
1701. Sir Thos. Bury, Jan. 26; aft. ch. bar.
1702. John Smith, just. C. P., Ireland, June 24; aft. ch. bar. ex., Scotland.
Sir Robt. Price, June 24; aft. just. C. P.
1708. Sir Salathiel Lovel, *vice* Smith, June 17; *d.* May, 1713.
1713. Sir Wm. Banister, June 8; removed Oct., 1714.
1714. Sir Jas. Montague, Nov. 22; aft. commr. gr. seal and ch. bar.
1717. Sir John Fortescue Aland, Jan. 24; aft. just. K. B.
1718. Sir Fras. Page, May 15; aft. just. C. P.
1722. Sir Jeffray Gilbert, May 24; aft. ch. bar.
1725. Sir Bernard Hale, June 1.
1726. Sir Laurence Carter, Nov. 7.
Sir John Comyn, Nov. 7; aft. just C. P. and ch. bar.
1729. Sir Wm. Thomson, Nov. 27.

1736. Sir Wm. Fortescue, Feb. 9; aft. just. C. P. and m. rolls.
1738. Sir Thos. Parker, jun., July 7; aft. just. C. P. and ch. bar. ex.
1739. Sir Martin Wright, Nov. 5; aft. just. K. B.
1740. Sir Jas. Reynolds, jun., May.
Sir Thos. Abney, Nov. 27; aft. just. C. P.
1743. Chas. Clarke, Feb. 11.
1745. Sir Edwd. Clive, Apr.; aft. just. C. P.
1747. Hon. Heneage Legge, June 23.
1750. Sir Sidney Stafford Smythe, May; aft. a commr. gr. seal and ch. bar.
1753. Sir Richd. Adams, Feb. 3.
1759. Sir Richd. Lloyd, Sept.; *d.* Sept., 1761.
1761. Sir Hy. Gould, Nov. 7; aft. just. C. P.
1763. Sir Geo. Perrott, Jan. 24; res. May 1775.
1772. Sir Jas. Eyre, Nov. 6; aft. ch. bar. and ch. just. C. P.
1774. Sir John Burland, Apr. 8.
1775. Sir Beaumont Hotham, May 10; aft. ld. Hotham.
1776. Sir Richd. Perryn, Apr. 15.
1787. Sir Alexr. Thomson, Feb. 7; aft. ch. bar.
1799. Sir Alan Chambre, July 2; aft. just. C. P.

1800. Robt. Graham, *vice* Chambre, June 16; knt June 19; res. Feb. 1827.
1805. Sir Thos. Manners Sutton, solr. gen., *vice* Hotham, Feb. 4; aft. ld. Manners; ld. chanc. Ireland, Apr. 1807.
1807. Geo. Wood, aft. sir G., *vice* Manners Sutton, Apr.; res. Feb. 1823.
1814. Richd. Richards, *vice* Thompson, Feb. 26; knt. May 11; ch. bar., Apr. 1817.
1817. Sir Wm. Garrow, atty. gen., *vice* Richards, May 4; res. 1832.
1823. John Hullock, *vice* Wood, Mar. 1; knt. Apr. 21; *d.* Sept., 1829.
1827. John Vaughan, *vice* Graham, Feb. 24; knt. Nov. 24; transf. to C. P. Apr., 1834, by exchange with Alderson.
1829. Wm. Bolland, *vice* Hullock, Nov. 16; knt. Feb. 2, 1830; res. Jan., 1839.
1830. Sir John Bayley, just. K. B., Nov. 11; additl. or *fifth* judge under 1 Wm. IV. cap. 70 (July 23, 1830); res. Feb. 1834.
1832. John Gurney, *vice* Garrow, Feb. 13; knt. Feb. 22; res. Jan. 1845.
1834. John Williams, *vice* Bayley, Feb. 28; knt. Apr. 16; transf. to K. B. Apr. 1834, by exchange with Parke.
Sir Jas. Parke, just. K. B., *vice* Williams, Apr. 29; res. 1855, and cr. ld. Wensleydale.
Sir Edwd. Hall Alderson, just. C. P. *vice* Vaughan, Apr. 29; *d.* Jan. 27, 1857.
1839. Wm. Hy. Maule, aft. sir W., *vice* Bolland, Feb. 14; transf. to C. P. Nov. same year.
Sir Robt. Monsey Rolfe, solr. gen., *vice* Maule, Nov. 11; aft. commr. gr. seal; v. chanc.; ld. Cranworth, and ld. chanc.
1845. Thos. Joshua Platt, *vice* Gurney, Jan. 28; knt. Apr. 23; res. 1856.
1850. Saml. Martin, *vice* Rolfe, Nov. 6; knt. Nov. 13; res. Jan., 1874.
1856. * Geo. Wm. Wilshere Bramwell, *vice* Parke, Jan.; knt. Jan. 30.
Wm. Hy. Watson, *vice* Platt, Nov. 3; knt. Nov. 28; *d.* Mar. 12, 1860.
1857. Wm. Fry Channell, *vice* Alderson, Feb. 12; knt. June 18; res. 1873; *d.* Feb. 26, 1873.
1860. Jas Plaisted Wilde, *vice* Watson, Apr. 13, **G.**; knt. Apr. 24; made judge of prob. and div. ct., Aug. 1863.
1863. Gillery Pigott, *vice* Wilde, Oct. 2, **G.**; knt. Nov. 1; *d.* Apr. 28, 1875.
1868. * Anthy. Cleasby, Aug. 25, **G.**; additl. or *sixth* judge under 31 & 32 Vict. cap. 125 (July 31, 1868); knt. Dec. 9.
1873. * Chas. Edwd. Pollock, *vice* Channell, Jan. 10, **G.**; knt. Feb. 5.
1874. * Richd. Paul Amphlett, *vice* Martin, Jan. 23; knt. Jan. 27.
1875. * John Walter Huddleston, just. C. P., *vice* Pigott; May 12, **G.**; knt. May 13.

* On Nov. 1, 1875, these Judges were transferred to the H. C. J., Exch. Div., under Supreme Court of Judicature Acts, 1873 and 1875 (see *ante*, p. 350). By these Acts the title of Baron of the Exchequer was abolished, except as to the judges then holding that office.

Puisne Judges of the Exchequer Division of the High Court of Justice.

Transferred from the old Court of Exchequer, Nov. 1, 1875.

1875. Sir Geo. Wm. Wilshere Bramwell; made ld. just. app. 1876.
Sir Anthy. Cleasby, res. 1878.
* Sir Chas. Edwd. Pollock.
1875. Sir Richd. Paul Amphlett; made ld. just. app. Oct. 27, 1876.
* Sir John Walter Huddleston.

Subsequent Appointments.

1876. * Hy. Hawkins, *vice* Amphlett, transf. from Q. B. div., Nov. 14, **G.**; knt. Nov. 28.

1879. * Sir Jas. Fitzjames Stephen, K.C.S.I., *vice* Cleasby, Jan 15.

* Under the Supreme Court of Judicature Act, 1873, secs. 22 and 75 (see *ante*, p. 320), and Order in Council Dec. 16, 1880, the Exch. Div. was abolished, and these judges became, on Feb. 26, 1881, judges of the Q. B. Div., but with relative rank according to their original appointments.

Cursitor Barons of the Exchequer.

1606. Nowell Southerton, July 8.
1610. Thos. Cæsar, May 26.
John Southerton, Oct. 24.
1631. Jas. Paget, Oct. 24.
1638. John or Wm. Page, Oct. 29.
1642. Thos. Leeke, Nov. 25.
1645. Richd. Tomlins, app. by the parlt., Sept. 2.
1660. Thos. Leeke, re-app. on the restoration.
1663. Clement Spelman, Mar. 9.
1679. Fras. Crawley, May 8.
1683. Richd. May, aft. Sir R., Mar. 17.
Jas. II. Wm. Carr.
1689. Geo. Bradbury, July 9.
1696. Richd. Wallop, Feb. 12.
1697. Wm. Simpson, Aug. 22.
1726. Wm. Thomson, May 23.
1729. John Birch, Dec. 11.
1735. Geo. Clive, Nov. 6.
1740. Wm. Kynaston (?), Feb.
1744. Edwd. Barker, May.
1755. John Tracy Atkyns, Apr. 22.
1773. Fras. Maseres, Aug.
1824. Geo Bankes, July 6; *d.* July, 1856.

Office abolished by 19 & 20 Vict. cap. 86.

JUDGES OF THE COURT OF SESSION OF THE COUNTY PALATINE OF CHESTER, &c.

From the Accession of King James I. to the abolition of the Courts in 1830, under 1 Wm. IV. cap. 70.

Chief Justices.

1 Jas. I. Sir Rd. Lewknor or Leuknor.
1616. Thos. Chamberlayne.
1620. Jas. Whitlock, Oct. 29.
1626. Sir Jno. Bridgman.
1647. John Bradshaw.
1660. Timothy Turner, Aug. 21.
1661. Sir Geoffrey Palmer, July 8.
1662. Sir Job Chorleton, Mar. 14.
1680. Sir Geo. Jeffreys.
1684. Sir Edw. Herbert, Oct. 25.
1686. Edw. Lutwyche, Mar.
Sir Job Chorleton, *again*, Oct.
1689. John Trenchard, May 10.
1695. John Coombe.
1707. Joseph Jekyll.
1717. Spencer Cowper.
1729. John Willes.
1734. Hon. Jno. Verney.
1738. Matth. Skynner, Nov. 26.
1749. Wm. Noel.
1763. John Morton.
1780. Lloyd Kenyon.
1784. Rd. Pepper Arden.
1788. Edw. Bearcroft.
1797. James Adair.
1798. Wm. Grant, Aug. 1.
1799. Jas. Mansfield, July 11.
1804. Vicary Gibbs, July 17.
1805. Robt. Dallas, Jan.
1813. Rd. Richards, May.
1814. Sir Wm. Garrew, Mar. 1.
1817. Jno. Leach.
1818. Wm. Draper Best.
John Singleton Copley, Michs. Vac.
1819. Chas. Warren, Trin. Term.

Second or Puisne Justices.

1603–4. H. Townsend, 1 Jas. I.
1622. Marm. Lloyd, Mar. 24.
1636. Rd. Prytherg, Feb. 20.
1638. Sir Thos. Milward, Mar. 23.
1647. Peter Warburton.
1649. Homfrey Macworth, dep. to Bradshaw.
Thos. Fell, Aug. 10.

1661. Robt. Milward, Aug. 12.
1674. Geo. Johnson.
1681. John Warren, July 23.
1689. Lyttleton Powis, Aug. 12.
Jno. Coombe, dep. to ch. just.; aft ch. just.
1696. Salathiel Lovel, Nov. 7.
1707. John Pocklington, Apr. 28.
1711. John Ward.
1714. Edw. Jeffreys.
1726. John Willes, aft. ch. just.
1729. Wm. Jessop, Feb. 24.
1735. Rd. Pottinger, May 12.
1739. John Skynner, Apr. 3.
1740. Hon. John Talbot.
1757. Taylor White.
1777. Fras. Buller, Nov.
1778. Hon. Daines Barrington, May.
1788. Fras. Burton.
1811. Wm. Draper Best, Mar. 1; *again*, Jan. 31, 1817; aft. ch. just.
1818. Saml. Marshall.
1823. Michl. Nolan.
Robt. Mathew Casberd.
1824. Thos. Jervis, Feb. 24.
1825. Sir Giffin Wilson, July 16.

MASTERS OF THE ROLLS.

See Introduction, *ante*, p. 348.

In addition to his judicial duties, which are fully explained in the introduction, the Master of the Rolls is, under 1 & 2 Vict. cap. 94 (August 10, 1838), constituted keeper of all the records in the Public Record Office, founded by that act.

The earlier part of the following list is founded on that compiled by the late Sir Thos. Duffus Hardy.

Masters of the Rolls.

From the earliest appointment to the office in the reign of Edward 1.

1286. John de Langton, Sept. 2 (?), aft. ld. chanc.
1295. Adam de Osgodeby, Oct. 1.
1316. Wm. de Ayremynne, Aug. 19.
1324. Richd. de Ayremynne, May 26.
1325. Hy. de Clyff, July 4.
1334. Michl. de Wath, Jan. 20.
1337. John de St. Paul, Apr. 28; aft. ld. kpr.
1341. Thos. de Evesham, Jan. 10.
John de Thoresby, Feb. 21; aft. ld. chanc.
1346. David de Wollore, or Wallore, July 2; aft. ld. kpr.
1371. Wm. Burstall, Mar. 28.
1381. John de Waltham, Sept. 8; aft. ld. kpr.
1386. John de Burton, Oct. 24.
1394. John de Scarle, July 22; aft. ld. chanc.
1397. Thos. Stanley, Sept. 11.
1402. Nichs. de Bubbewyth, Sept. 24; aft. bp. of London.
1405. John de Wakering, Mar. 2.
1415. Simon de Gauntstede, June 3; aft. ld. kpr.
1423. John Fraunke, or Frank, Oct. 28.
1438. John Stopynden, Nov. 13.
1447. Thos. de Kirkeby, Mar. 29 (? May).
1461. Robt. Kirkeham, Dec. 23; aft. ld. kpr.
1471. Wm Morland, Feb. 12.
John Alcock, bp. of Rochester; aft. bp. of Worcester, and ld. chanc.; Apr. 29.
1472. John Morton, Mar. 16; aft. bp. of Ely, &c., and ld. chanc.
1479. Robt. Morton, Jan. 9, under L. P. dated May 30, 1477, granting him the mastership in reversion; aft. bp. of Worcester.
1483. Thos. Barrow, or Barowe, Sept. 22.
1485. Robt. Morton, *again*, Aug. 22.
1485. Robt. Morton and Wm. Eliot, jointly.
1487. David William, Feb. 26 (? Nov. 26).
1492. John Blyth, May 5; aft. bp. of Salisbury.
1494. Wm. Warham, Feb. 13; aft. bp. of London, &c., and ld. chanc.
1502. Wm. Barnes, or Barons, Feb. 1; aft. ld. kpr.
1504. Christr. Bainbrigge, or Benebrigge, Nov. 13; aft. abp. of York.
1508. John Yonge, dean of York, Jan. 22.
1516. Cuthbert Tunstall, May 12; aft. bp. of London.
1522. John Clarke, archdn. of Colchester, Oct. 20.
1523. Thos. Hannibal, Oct. 9.
1527. John Taylor, June 26.

1534. Thos. Cromwell, Oct. 8; aft. ld. Cromwell and E. of Essex; beheaded in 1540.
1536. Christr. Hales, or Halys, July 10.
1541. Sir Robt. Southwell, July 1.
1550. John de Beaumont, Dec. 13.
1552. Sir Robt. Bowes, June 18.
1553. Sir Nichs. Hare, Sept. 18.
1557. Sir Wm. Cordell, Nov. 5.
1581. Sir Gilbert Gerrard, atty. gen., May 30. *See Chancellors*, 1591.
1594. Sir Thos. Egerton, Apr. 10; aft. ld. kpr. and ld. chanc.; cr. ld. Ellesmere; aft. visc. Brackley.
1603. Edwd. Bruce, May 18; cr. ld. Kinloss; aft. E. of Elgin.
1611. Sir Edwd. Phelips, or Phillips, Jan. 14.
1614. Sir Julius Cæsar, Sept. 1; *d.* Apr. 18, 1636. *See Chancellors*, 1621.
Sir Humphrey May had the mastership granted to him in reversion, Apr. 10, 1629; but he *d.* soon after, before it fell into possession.
1636. Sir Dudley Digges, Apr. 18; he had had the mastership granted to him in reversion in 1630, on the death of May.
1639. Sir Chas. Cæsar, Mar. 30.
1643. Sir John Colepeper, Jan. 28; aft. ld. Colepeper.
Wm. Lenthall, parly. m. rolls, Nov. 10. *See Chancellors*, 1659.
1660. John, ld. Colepeper, *again*, June 1.
Sir Harbottle Grimstone, bt., Nov. 3.
Geo. Johnson had the mastership granted to him in reversion, Aug. 15, 1667, but *d.* before it fell into possession.
1685. John Churchill, aft. Sir J., Jan. 12.
Sir John Trevor, Oct. 20; aft. commr. gr. seal.
1689. Sir Hy. Powle, Mar. 13.
1693. Sir John Trevor, *again*, Jan. 13.
1717. Sir Jos. Jekyll, July 13; aft. ld. kpr.
1738. Hon. John Verney, Oct. 9.
1741. Wm. Fortescue, just. C. P., Nov. 5.
1750. Sir John Strange, Jan. 11.
1754. Sir Thos. Clarke, May 29.
1764. Sir Thos. Sewell, Dec. 4.
1784. Sir Lloyd Kenyon, knt., and aft. bt. atty. gen., Mar. 30; aft. ch. just K. B., and ld. Kenyon.
1788. Sir Richd. Pepper Arden, atty. gen. June 4; aft. ch. just. C. P., and ld. Alvanley.
1801. Sir Wm. Grant, solr. gen., May 27 res. 1818.
1818. Sir Thos. Plumer, v. chanc. of England, Jan. 6; *d.* 1824.
1824. Robt., ld. Gifford, ch. just. C. P. Apr. 5.
1826. Sir John Singleton Copley, atty gen., Sept. 14; aft. ld. chanc. and ld. Lyndhurst.
1827. Sir John Leach, v. chanc. of England, May 3.
1834. Sir Chas. Christr. Pepys, solr. genl. Sept. 29; aft. ld. chanc., and ld Cottenham.
1836. Hy. Bickersteth, Jan. 16, cr. ld Langdale; res. 1851.
1851. Sir John Romilly, atty. gen., Mar 28, cr. ld. Romilly, 1866; res Aug. 1873; *d.* Dec. 23, 1874.
1873. Sir Geo. Jessel, solr. gen., Aug 30

On Nov. 1, 1875, the M. Rolls was made a judge of the H. C. J., Chancery Div., and also an *ex officio* judge of the Court of Appeal, under the Supreme Court of Judicatur Acts, 1873 and 1875 (see *ante*, pp. 350–1).

On Aug. 27, 1881, the M. Rolls was made exclusively a judge of the Court of Appeal under the Supreme Court of Judicature Act, 1881. (See *ante*, p. 351.)

Sir Geo. Jessel, *d.* Mar. 21, 1883.
1883. Sir Wm. Baliol Brett, ld. just. app., Apr. 3; cr. ld. Esher, July 23, 1885.

LORDS JUSTICES (JUDGES OF THE COURT OF APPEAL IN CHANCERY). JUSTICES OF APPEAL. LORDS JUSTICES OF APPEAL.

See Introduction, *ante*, p. 348.

Judges of the Court of Appeal in Chancery.

The lord chancellor was an *ex officio* judge of the Court of Appeal, and with him were associated the following

Lords Justices.

Appointed under 14 & 15 Vict. cap. 83.

1851. Sir Jas. Lewis Knight-Bruce, v. chanc., Oct. 8; res. Oct. 14, 1866; *d.* Nov. 7, 1866.
1851. Robt. Monsey, ld. Cranworth, v. chanc., Oct. 8; app. ld. chanc Dec. 28, 1852.

853. Sir Geo. Jas. Turner, v. chanc., *vice* Cranworth, Jan. 10, **G.**; *d.* July 9, 1867.
866. Sir Hugh McCalmont Cairns, atty. gen., *vice* Knight-Bruce, Oct. 29, **G.**; cr. ld. Cairns, Feb. 22, 1867; app. ld. chanc., Feb. 29, 1868.
867. Sir John Rolt, atty. gen., *vice* Turner, July 18, **G.**; res. 1868; *d.* June 6, 1871.
868. Sir Chas. Jasper Selwyn, solr. gen., *vice* Rolt, Feb. 8, **G.**; *d.* Aug. 11, 1869.

1868. Sir Wm. Page Wood, v. chanc., *vice* Cairns, Mar. 5, **G.**; app. ld. chanc., Dec. 11, 1868 and cr. ld. Hatherley.
1869. Sir Geo. Markham Giffard, v. chanc. *vice* Page Wood, Jan. 1, **G.**; *d* July 13, 1870.
1870. *Sir Wm. Milbourne James, v. chanc., *vice* Selwyn, July 2, **G.**
*Geo. Mellish, *vice* Giffard, Aug. 4, **G.**; knt., Aug. 9.

* On Nov. 1, 1875, these judges were trans. to the Court of Appeal under the Supreme ourt of Judicature Acts 1873 and 1875. (See *ante*, pp. 350–1.)

Judges of the Court of Appeal.

Ex-Officio Judges under the Supreme Court of Judicature Acts, 1873 and 1875.

The Lord Chancellor.
The Ld. Ch. Just. of England.
The Master of the Rolls.
The Ch. Just. of the Common Pleas; (office abolished by Supreme Court of Judicature Act 1873, secs. 22 and 75, and order in Council, Dec. 16, 1880).
The Ch. Bar. of the Exchequer; (office abolished *ut supra*).

Additional Ex-Officio Judge under the Supreme Court of Judicature Act, 1881.

The president of the Prob., Div., and Adm. Div. of the H. C. J.

)rdinary Judges, at first styled Justices of Appeal, and afterwards, under the Supreme Court of Judicature Act, 1877, styled Lords Justices of Appeal.

Transferred from the old Court of Chancery, Nov. 1, 1875.

878. Sir Wm. Milbourne James, Nov. 1; *d.* 1881.
Sir Geo. Mellish, Nov. 1; *d.* 1877.

Additional appointment under Supreme Court of Judicature Act, 1875.

875. Sir Richd. Baggallay, Oct. 29, **G.**; res. 1885; *d.* Nov. 13, 1888.

Additional appointments under Appellate Jurisdiction Act, 1876.

876 Sir Geo. Wm. Wilshere Bramwell, judge ex. div. H. C. J., Oct. 27, **G.**; res. 1881; cr. ld. Bramwell, 1882.
Sir Wm. Baliol Brett, judge C. P. div. H. C. J., Oct. 27, **G.**; m. rolls, Apr. 3, 1883; cr. ld. Esher, 1885.
Sir Richd. Paul Amphlett, judge ex. div. H. C. J., Oct. 27, **G.**; res. 1877; *d.* Dec. 7, 1883.

Subsequent Appointments.

877. Hy. Cotton, *vice* Mellish, June 28; knt. July 11.
Hon. Alfred Hy. Thesiger, *vice* Amphlett, Nov. 2, **G.**; *d.* Oct. 20, 1880.
1880. Sir Robt. Lush, judge Q. B. div. H. C. J., *vice* Thesiger, Nov. 5, **G.**; *d.* Dec. 27, 1881.
1881. Sir Nathl. Lindley, judge Q. B. div. H. C. J., *vice* Bramwell, Nov. 1, **G.**
1882. Sir John Holker, *vice* Lush, Jan. 14, **G.**; res. 1882; *d.* May 24, 1882.
Sir Chas. Synge Christr. Bowen, judge Q. B. div. H. C. J., *vice* Holker, June 2.
1883. Sir Edwd. Fry, judge ch. div. H. C. J., *vice* Brett, Apr. 9.
1885. Sir Hy. Chas. Lopes, judge Q. B. div H. C. J., *vice* Baggallay, Dec. 1, **G.**

VICE CHANCELLORS OF ENGLAND. VICE CHANCELLORS. JUSTICES OF THE HIGH COURT OF JUSTICE, CHANCERY DIVISION.

See Introduction, *ante*, p. 348.

Vice Chancellors of England.

Appointed under 53 Geo. III., cap. 24.

1813. Sir Thos. Plumer, atty. gen., Apr. 10; aft. m. rolls.

1818. Jno. Leach, aft. sir J., Jan. 6; aft. m. rolls.

1827. Sir Anthy. Hart, May 2; aft. ld chanc. Ireland.

Lancelot Shadwell, Nov. 1; knt. Nov 16; *d.* Aug. 10, 1850, and with him the title ceased.

Vice Chancellors.

Appointed under 5 Vict. cap. 5.

1841. Jas. Lewis Knight-Bruce, aft. sir J., Oct. 28; knt. 1842; app. ld. just. app., Oct. 8, 1851.

Jas. Wigram, aft. sir J., Oct. 28; res. 1850.

1850. Sir Robt. Monsey Rolfe, bar. ex. *vice* Shadwell, Nov. 2; cr. ld Cranworth, Nov. 7; app. ld. just app., Oct. 8, 1851.

Appointed under 14 & 15 Vict. cap. 4, and 15 & 16 Vict. cap. 80.

1851. Geo. Jas. Turner, *vice* Wigram, Apr. 2; knt. Apr. 14; app. ld. just. app., Jan. 10, 1853.

Richd. Torin Kindersley, mast. in chanc., *vice* Knight-Bruce, Oct. 20, **G.**; knt. Oct. 23; res. Nov. 1866; *d.* Oct. 22, 1879.

Jas. Parker, *vice* Cranworth, Oct. 20, **G.**; knt. Oct. 23; *d.* Aug. 13, 1852.

1852. John Stuart, *vice* Parker, Sept. 20, **G.**; knt. June 13, 1853; res. 1871; *d.* Oct. 29, 1876.

1853. Sir Wm. Page Wood, *vice* Turner, Jan. 10, **G.**; app. ld. just. app., Mar. 5, 1868.

1866. *Richd. Malins, *vice* Kindersley, Dec 1, **G.**; knt. Feb. 2, 1867.

1868. Geo. Markham Giffard, *vice* Page Wood, Mar. 11, **G.**; knt. May 14; made ld. just. app., Jan. 1 1869.

1869. Wm. Milbourne James, *vice* Giffard Jan. 2, **G.**; knt. Feb. 4; made ld. just. app., July 2, 1870.

1870. *Jas. Bacon, *vice* James, July 4, **G.** knt. Jan. 14, 1871.

1871. John Wickens, *vice* Stuart, Apr. 18 **G.**; knt. June 29; *d.* Oct. 23 1873.

1873. *Chas. Hall, *vice* Wickens, Nov. 11 **G.**; knt. Dec. 12.

* On Nov. 1, 1875, these judges were transf. to the H. C. J., Chancery Div., unde Supreme Court of Judicature Acts, 1873 and 1875. (See *ante*, pp. 350–1.) By thes acts the title of vice-chancellor was abolished, except as to the judges then holding tha office.

Judges of the Chancery Division of the High Court of Justice.

Transferred from the old Court of Chancery, Nov. 1, 1875.

The Lord Chancellor, President. See "Lord Chancellors."

The Master of the Rolls. See "Masters of Rolls."

By the S. C. J. Act, 1871, the m. rolls was made exclusively a judge of the court of appeal.

Sir Richd. Malins, v. chanc.; res 1881; *d.* Jan. 15, 1882.

Sir Jas. Bacon, v. chanc.; res. Nov 1886.

Sir Chas. Hall, v. chanc.; res. 1882 *d.* Dec. 12, 1883.

Subsequent Appointments.

These new judges were styled justices, and not vice chancellors.

7. Edwd. Fry, Apr. 27; knt. Apr. 30; additl. judge under S. C. J. Act, 1877; app. ld. just. app., Apr. 9, 1883.

1. Edwd. Ebenezer Kay, *vice* Malins, Mar. 30, **G.**; knt. May 2.

Jos. Wm. Chitty, *vice* Jessel, m. rolls, who was made exclusively a judge of the court of app. *ut supra*, Sept. 6, **G.**; knt. Dec. 7.

1882. John Pearson, *vice* Hall, Oct. 24, **G.**; knt. Nov. 30; *d.* May 13, 1886.

1883. Sir Ford North, *vice* Fry; transfd. from Q. B. div. with relative rank from date of orignl. appt. (Nov. 1, 1881.)

1886. Jas. Stirling, *vice* Pearson, May 20, **G.**; knt. Nov. 26.

Arthur Kekewich, *vice* Bacon, Nov. 12; knt. Nov. 26.

DGES OF THE PROBATE AND DIVORCE COURTS, AND OF THE PROBATE, DIVORCE, AND ADMIRALTY DIVISIONS OF THE HIGH COURT OF JUSTICE.

See Introduction, *ante*, p. 349.

JUDGES OF HER MAJESTY'S COURT OF PROBATE.

Appointed under 20 & 21 Vict. cap. 77,

AND

UDGES ORDINARY OF HER MAJESTY'S COURT FOR DIVORCE AND MATRIMONIAL CAUSES.

Appointed under 20 & 21 Vict. cap. 85.

his jurisdiction was previously exercised by the judges of the Ecclesiastical Court. Introduction, *ante*, p. 349, and the lists of those judges, *post*.

8. Sir Cresswell Cresswell, just. C. P., Jan. 6, **G.**; *d.* July 29, 1863.

3. Sir Jas. Plaisted Wilde, bar. ex., Aug. 26, **G.**; cr. ld. Penzance, Apr. 6, 1869; res. 1872.

1872. *Sir Jas. Hannen, just. Q. B., Nov. 14, **G.**

Transferred on Nov. 1, 1875, to the H. C. J., Prob., Div., and Adm. Div., under Supreme Court of Judicature Acts, 1873 and 1875 (see *ante*, p. 350).

UDGES OF THE PROBATE, DIVORCE, AND ADMIRALTY DIVISION OF THE HIGH COURT OF JUSTICE.

Transferred from the old Courts of Probate and Divorce.

5. Sir Jas. Hannen, president, Nov. 1; made an *ex-officio* judge of the ct. of app. on Aug. 27, 1881, under S. C. J. Act, 1881 (see *ante*, p. 389).

Transferred from the old Court of Admiralty, Nov. 1, 1875.

5. Sir Robt. Jos. Phillimore, Nov. 1; cr. bt. Dec. 15, 1881; res. 1883; *d.* Feb. 4, 1885.

Subsequent Appointments.

3. Chas. Parker Butt, *vice* Phillimore, Apr. 3, **G.**; knt. Apr. 30.

JUDGES OF THE COURT OF REVIEW IN BANKRUPTCY

APPOINTED UNDER 1 & 2 WILL. IV. CAP. 56 (OCT. 20, 1831).

Dec. 2, 1831, **G.**

1. Hon. Thos. Erskine, ch. judge; res. Nov. 1842; app. just. C. P., Jan. 9, 1839, and held both offices for nearly four years.
2. Albert Pell; knt. Dec. 7; *d.* 1832.
3. John Cross; knt. Dec. 7; *d.* 1842.
4. Geo. Rose; knt. Dec. 7; res. Dec 1840, on appt. as mast. in chanc

Vice chancellor Sir Jas. Lewis Knight-Bruce was app. ch. judge in Nov. 1842, o the resignation of Erskine. He held both offices until the Court of Review was abolishe in 1847 by 10 & 11 Vict. cap. 102, by which Act the jurisdiction of the court was tran ferred to such of the vice chancellors as the lord chancellor might name for th purpose.

By the Bankrupt Law Consolidation Act, 1849 (12 & 13 Vict. cap. 106), as amende by the 14 & 15 Vict. cap. 83, extended by 30 & 31 Vict. cap. 64, the Bankruptcy Appella Jurisdiction was transferred to the Court of Appeal in Chancery. (See list of th judges of that court, *ante*, p. 388-9.) This jurisdiction was continued by the 32 & 3 Vict. cap. 71, and on the passing of the Supreme Court of Judicature Acts (*ante*, p 350–1), was transferred to the Court of Appeal thereby established.

By the 46 & 47 Vict. cap. 52, and 47 & 48 Vict. cap. 9, the London Bankrupto Court was transferred to the High Court of Justice, and appellate jurisdiction in bank ruptcy was given to the Divisional Courts of the High Court of Justice, with an appe therefrom to the Court of Appeal.

CHIEF JUDGE IN BANKRUPTCY.

APPOINTED UNDER 32 & 33 VICT. CAP. 71.

1869. Jas. Bacon, Dec. 31; app. v. chanc. July 4, 1870; knt. Jan. 14, 1871. Held both offices until Dec. 31, 1883, when the office of ch. judg in bankruptcy was abolished b 46 & 47 Vict., cap. 52.

BANKRUPTCY JUDGE.

APPOINTED UNDER 46 & 47 VICT. CAP. 52.

1884. Sir Lewis Wm. Cave, just. Q. B. div. H. C. J., Jan. 1.

MASTERS IN CHANCERY. ACCOUNTANTS GENERAL O THE COURT OF CHANCERY.

See Introduction, *ante*, p. 248.

THE list of masters prior to 1597 is compiled from *Foss.* The list sub sequent to that date is founded on that compiled by the late Sir Tho Duffus Hardy.

The office of master in chancery was abolished in 1852 by 15 & 1 ict. cap. 80, and the duties transferred to the vice chancellors and eir chief clerks. The then existing masters were gradually released om their duties, the last retiring Aug. 8, 1860.

The office of accountant general of the Court of Chancery was created 1726 by 12 Geo. I. cap. 32. Although there is nothing in that statute hich requires such a qualification, yet no person has been appointed to e office without having first become a Master in Chancery. This fice was abolished in 1872 by 35 & 36 Vict. cap. 44, and the duties ansferred to the paymaster-general (see *ante*, p. 244).

Masters in Chancery prior to 1597.

A. R. EDWARD I.

-12. Jno. de Kirkeby.
– . Thos. Bek.
-19. Hugh de Kendal.
-12. Walter de Odyham.
-33. Wm. de Hamilton.
– . Wm. de Chyrinton.
-35. Jno. de Cadomo.
-35. Robt. de Radeswell.
-29. Jno. de Derby.
-33. Jno. de Craucombe.
-30. Wm. de Grenefield, aft. chanc.
-33. Wm. de Kilkenny.
-35. Peter de Dene.
-33. Regd. de Braundon.
-29. Jno. de Lacy.
-35. Thos. de Logore.
-33. Wm. de Birlaco.
-33. Peter de Insula.
-35. Robt. de Pykering.
-35. Wm. de Pykering.
-30. Wm. de Sardenne.
-33. Philip Martel.
-35. Rd. de Plumstok.
-35. Robt. de Bardelby.
-35. Jno. Busshe.
– . Jno. Fraunceis.
– . Geoffrey de Welleford.

EDWARD II.

-2. Robt. de Radeswell, *contd.*
-15. Peter de Dene, *contd.*
-7. Thos. de Logore, *contd.*
-3. Jno. de Cadomo, *contd.*
-19. Robt. de Pykering, *contd.*
– . Wm. de Pykering, *contd.*
– . Rd. Plumstok, *contd.*
-18. Robt. de Bardelby, *contd.*
-16. Jno. Busshe, *contd.*
-7. Jno. Franceis, *contd.*

A. R.

1–14. Geoffrey de Welleford, *contd.*
1–12. Robt. de Askeby.
6–20. Adam de Brome.
8– . Jno. Bray.
8–20. Wm. de Herlaston.
9–16. Edmund de London.
10– . Hugh de Burgh.
10– . Jno. Terlyng.
10–15. Jno. de Merton.
10–18. Jno. de Crosseby.
12–14. Roger de Sutton.
12-18. Wm. de Leycester.
13–16. Wm. de Cliff.
18– . Hy. de Edenstowe.

EDWARD III.

1–3. Adam de Brome, *contd.*
1–27. Wm. de Herlaston, *contd.*
1–2. Jno. de Crosseby, *contd.*
1–8. Wm. de Leycester, *contd.*
1–20 Hy. de Edenstowe, *contd.*
1–14. Thos. de Baumburgh.
2– . Adam de Herwynton.
6–12. Jno. de Blebury.
6–33. Thos. de Brayton, or Drayton.
7–14. Jno. de Longtoft.
9–27. Edmd. de Grymesby.
11– . Thos. de Elingham.
11–20. Robt. de Kettleseye.
12– . Wm. de Kyldesbury.
12– . Thos. Durant.
12–15. Jno. de Wodehouse, aft. ch. ex.
12–20. Hy. de Iddesworth.
14– . Hy. de Stratford.
14–25. Thos. de Sibthorp.
14–44. Thos. de Cotyngham
15– Thos de Pardishowe.

A. R.

15–17. Jno. de Marton.
15–36. Elyas de Grymesby.
18– . Gilbert de Chishull.
18–21. Thos. de Capenhurst.
18–28. Wm. de Emelden.
19–29. Andr. de Offord.
22– . Jno. de Chestrefeld.
25–29. Jno. Gogh.
25–29. Wm. de Newnham.
25–47. Walter Power.
33– . Jno. de Rokyngham.
33–43. Jno. de Codington.
36–48. Jno. de Branketre.
36–49. Wm. de Mirfield.
36–51. Rd. de Ravenser.
45–48. Nichs. de Spaigne.
45–50. Robt. de Wykford, aft. abp. Dublin and chanc. Ireland.
45–51. Thos. de Newnham.
46–49. Simon de Multon.
49–51. Hy. de Codington.
50– . Rd. de Tissyngton.
50–51. Thos. de Thelwall.
50–51. Jno. de Fretton, or Frethorne.
50–51. Michl. de Ravendale.
50-51. Peter de Barton.
50–51. Jno. de Bouland.
51– . Walter Skirlawe, dean of St. Martins, aft. bp. of Lichfield, Bath and Wells, and Durham.

RICHARD II.

1–10. Rd. de Ravenser, *contd.*
1–15. Thos. de Newnham, *contd.*
1–4. Hy. de Codington, *contd.*
1–5. Thos. de Thelwall, *contd.*

A. R.
1-7. Jno. de Fretton, *contd.*
1-6. Michl. de Ravendale, *contd.*
1-18. Peter de Barton, *contd.*
1-10. Jno. de Bouland, *contd.*
1-4. Walter Skirlawe, *contd.*
4-23. Robt. de Faryngton.
6-8. Robt. de Muskham.
10- . Robt Manfield.
11-23. Rd. Ronhale, or Rouhale.
13-18. Thos. de Midelton.
16- . Jno. de Folkynham.
16-23. Jno de Chitterne.
19- . Wm. Rouden.
19-23. Jno de Roderham.
19-23. Jno. Wakering, aft. bp. of Norwich.
19-23. Nichl. Bubbewyth, aft. bp. of London.
19-23. Simon Gaunstede.
20- . Robt. Claydon.
20-21. Hugh de Gaudeby.
20-23. Jno. Springthorpe.
22-23. Jno. Rome.

HENRY IV.

1-5. Robt. de Faryngton, *contd.*
1- . Rd. Ronhale, or Rouhale, *contd.*
1-3. Jno. de Chitterne, *contd.*
1-13. Jno. de Roderham, *contd.*
1-13. Simon Gaunstede, *contd.*
1-13. Jno. Springthorpe, *contd.*
1-13. Jno. Rome, *contd.*
2-11. Jno. Kyngton.
7-13. Jno. Hertelpole.
12- . Ralph Grenehurst.
13- . Hy. Malpas.
13- . Wm. Waltham.

HENRY. V.

1- . Jno. de Chitterne, *contd.*
1-2. Jno. de Roderham, *contd.*
1-9. Jno. Springthorpe, *contd.*
1-2. Jno. Rome, *contd.*
1-9. Jno. Hertelpole, *contd.*
1-2. Hy. Malpas, *contd.*

A. R.
2-9. Jno. Frank.
2-3. Jno. Roland.
3- . Thos. Haxey.
3- . Wm. Aghton.
3-9. Jno. Thoralby.
3-9. Jno Mapilton.
3-9. Hy. Shelford.
4-9. Hy. Keys.

HENRY VI.

1- . Jno. Springthorpe, *contd.*
1-10. Jno. Hertelpole, *contd.*
1-9. Jno. Thoralby, *contd.*
1-10. Jno. Mapilton, *contd.*
1-18. Hy. Shelford, *contd.*
1-2. Hy. Keys, *contd.*
1-2. Jno. Roland, *contd.*
2-27. Jno. Stokes.
2-29. Nichl. Wymbysh.
3-14. Wm. Prestwyk.
4-32. Wm. Hill.
10-39. Jno. Faukes.
15-39. Jno. Bate.
18-29. Robt. Monter.
20-29. Jno. Cammell.
20-27. Jno. Stokes.
20- . — Shecfield.
28-39. Rd. Wetton.
31- . Thos. Kent.
31- . Dean of St. Severino de Bourdeaux.
31- . Rd. Langport.
31-39. Rd. Fryston.
32-39. Robt. Kirkham.
32- . Wm. Normanton.
33- . John Derby.
38- . Gilbert Haydock.
38- . Thos. Manning.
39- . Jno. Chamberlayn.
39- . Jno. Pemberton.

EDWARD IV.

1-7. Jno. Faukes, *contd.*
1-3. Rd. Wetton, *contd.*
1-3. Jno. Bate, *contd.*
1-12. Rd. Fryston, *contd.*
1-7. Jno. Chamberlayn, *contd.*
1-7. Jno. Pemberton, *contd.*
1- . Wm. Swerendon.
1-17. Hy. Sharpe.
3-23. Wm. Bolton.
3- . Thos. Westhorp.
12-23. Jno. Gunthorp, dean of Wells.
12- . Jno. Davyson.
12-17. Rd. Martyn.
12- . Rd. Woodward.
22-23. Jno. Brown.
22-23. Wm. Kelet.

RICHARD III.

A. R.
1-3. Wm. Morland, *con*
1-3. Wm. Bolton, *cont*
1-3. Jno. Gunthorp, *con*
1-3. Jno. Brown, *contd*
1-3. Wm. Kelet, *contd.*
1- . Thos. Hutton.
1-3. Rd. Skipton.
1-3. Robt. Blackwall.

HENRY VII.

1-11. Wm. Morland, *contd.*
1- . Wm. Bolton, *cont*
1-12. Jno. Gunthorp, *con*
1-11. Jno. Brown, *contd*
1-7. Wm. Kelet, *contd.*
1-12. Rd. Skipton, *cont*
1-19. Robt. Blackw *contd.*
1-12. Thos. Barowe, (rolls under Ri ard III.)
1-11. Jno. Morgan.
7- . Edwd. Chaderton
7-12. Jno. Jamys.
11- . Edmd. Martyn.
12-19. Rd. Hatton.
19- . Geoffrey Simeon.
19- . Rd. Maihewe.
19- . Jas. Hubert.

HENRY VIII.

There appears to no record of re-appointment the Masters liv at the death Hen. VII.
7-21. Wm. Throgmorto
21-28. Rd. Wolman, dea Wells.
21- . Roger Lupton.
21- . Edwd. Hygons.
21-25. Rowland Lee, bp. Lichfield and Coventry.
21-24. Thos. Newman.
30-35. Wm. Peter, aft. W.
30- . Thos. Wetherall.
30- . Rd. Layton, dea York.
30- . Edwd. Carne, a sir E.
30- . Jno. London, d of Oxford.
30-36. Thos. Legh, aft. T.
30-38. John Tregonwell, sir J.

A. R.
36–38. Jno. Oliver, dean of Christchurch.
36–38. Anthony Bellasis.
37–38. — Mitchell.
38– Wm. Leeson.

EDWARD VI.

1–4. Sir Jno. Tregonwell, *contd.*
1–4. Jno. Oliver, *contd.*
1–7. Anthy. Bellasis, *contd.*
1–2. Wm. Leeson, *contd.*
2– . — Grimstead.
2–4. — Standish.
3–4. — Hussey.
3–6. Jno. Croke.
4– . Wm. Cooke.
4– . — Breten.
4–7. Sir Rd. Read.
5– . Rd. Goodrich.

A. R.
5– . Jno. Gosnold.
6–7. Rd. Lyell.
6–7. David Lewes.

MARY.

1– . Anthony Bellasis, *contd.*
1–2. Jno. Croke, *contd.*
1–6. Sir Rd. Read, *contd.*
1– . Rd. Lyell, *contd.*
1– . David Lewes, *contd.*
? Wm. Awbrey.
? Wm. Mowse.

ELIZABETH.

1–17. Sir Rd. Read, *contd.*
1–26. David Lewes, *contd.*
3–4. — Vaughan.
3–17. Thos. Huyck, chanc. of London.

A. R.
4–9. Robt. Weston, dean of Wells, aft. chanc. of Ireland.
? Jno. Belley.
11–26. Hy. Hervey.
17– . David (? Thos.) Yale.
–25. Robt. Lougher.
21– . — Forth.
25– . — Harris.
25–45. Sir Matth. Carew.
25–45. Sir Rd. Swale.
30–33. Julius Cæsar.
36–45. Sir Edwd. Stanhope.
–42. Thos. Bynge.
38–45. Thos. Legge.
38–45. Jno. Hone.
–40. Rd. Cosin.
38–44. Lawrence Hussey.
38–40. Wm. Lewen.
38–45. Wm. or Jno. Hunt.
38–45. Sir Jno. Amye.

MASTERS IN CHANCERY SUBSEQUENT TO 1597.

The Accountants General are marked *

1597. Dec. 2. Wm. Lambard, *vice* Cossyne.
1598. Apr. 17. John Tyndall, *vice* Lewen.
1599. Dec. 21. Geo. Carewe, *vice* Bynge.
1601. Aug. 27. Edwd. Grymstone, *vice* Lambard.
1602. Feb. 23. Hy. Hickman, *vice* Hussey.
1607. July 17. Hy. Thoresbye, *vice* Legge.
1608. Mar. 18. Sir John Bennett, *vice* Stanhope.
June 2. Sir Thos. Crompton, *vice* Swale.
1609. Feb. 8. Thos. Ridley, aft. Sir T., *vice* Crompton.
1612. Nov. 24. Gregory Bonhault, *vice* Geo. Carewe.
1614. Apr. 12. Fras. James, *vice* Bonhault.
1615. May 17. Jas., or Jno. Wolveridge, *vice* Thoresbye.
May 19. Sir Chas. Cæsar, *vice* Hunt.
1616. Feb. 17. Richd. More, *vice* Hickman.
Nov. 13. John Hayward, aft. sir J., *vice* Tyndall.
1617. Jan. 11. Ewball Thelwall, *vice* Hone.
1618. Aug. 7. Robt. Rich, *vice* sir M. Carew.
1619. Oct. 30. John Michell, *vice* Ridley.
1621. July 11. Edwd. Salter, *vice* Amye.
July 16. Edwd. Leech, *vice* Bennett.
* * Sir Wm. Birde, *vice* Grymstone (19–22 Jas. I.)
1624. Oct. 14. Sir Peter Mutton, *vice* Birde.
1624. Dec. 18. Edwd. Clarke, *vice* Wolveridge.
1625. July 22. Thos. Eden, *vice* James.
1627. July 3. John Page, *vice* Hayward.
1631. Jan. 22. Sir Dudley Digges, *vice* Thelwall.
1635. June 8. Thos. Bennett, aft. sir T., *vice* More.
1637. Mar. 20. Wm. Griffith, *vice* Digges.
1638. Jan. 29. Robt. Aylett, *vice* Mutton.
1639. Jan. 28. Wm. Child, *vice* Clarke.
May 20. Jas. Littleton, *vice* Cæsar.
1640. Nov. 10. Thos. Heath, *vice* Eden.
1641. July 22. Justinian Lewen, aft. sir J., *vice* Griffith.
1643. Apr. 12. Sir Thos. Mainwaring, *vice* Salter.
1644. June 1. John Sadler, *vice* Michell.
1645. Aug. 2. Arthur Duck, *vice* Littleton.
1646. Feb. 6. Edwin, or Edwd. Rich. *vice* Heath.
Nov. 21. Wm. Hakewell, *vice* Rich.
1647. June 2. Edwd. Eltonhed, *vice* Mainwaring.
1650. May 22. John Bonde, *vice* Duck.
1651. Aug. 6. Robt. Keylway, *vice* Lewen.
1652. July 12. Thos. Estcourt, *vice* Hakewell.
July 14. Nathl. Hobart, *vice* Leech.
1655. May 3. Arthur Barnardiston, *vice* Bonde.
June 21. Wm. Harrington, *vice* Barnardiston.
Nov. 15. Wm. Glascocke, *vice* Page.
Nov. 22. Edmd. Gyles, *vice* Aylett.

1656. Feb. 4. Thos. Bulstrode, *vice* Sadler.
1659. May 30. Robt. Warsup, *vice* Glascocke.
June 7. Wm. Eden, *vice* Child.
1660. May 31. Wm. Child, *again*, *vice* Eden.
Justinian Lewen, *again*, *vice* Keylway.
June 1. Thos. Estcourt, re-app.
June 2. Thos. Bird, *vice* Gyles.
June 4. Thos. Bennett, re-app.
Mounteford Brampston, *vice* Rich.
June 5. Nathl. Hobart, re-app.
Wm. Glascocke, *vice* Warsup.
June 6. Walter Littleton, *vice* Harrington.
Sir Edmund, or Edwd. Pearce, *vice* Bulstrode.
June 18. Toby Woolrich, *vice* Eltonhed.
1664. Oct. 1. John Coell, *vice* Woolrich.
1665. June 26. Wm. Lisle, *vice* Bird.
Nov. 15. Richd. Proctor, *vice* Lisle.
1667. Oct. 3. Thos. Croft, *vice* Pearce.
1669. Nov. 19. John Halsey, *vice* Proctor.
1670. June 29. Robt. Steward, *vice* Bennett.
Timothy Baldwin, *vice* Halsey.
Dec. 10. Andrew Hacket, *vice* Littleton.
Dec. 26. Wm. Beversham, *vice* Croft.
1672. July 5. Wm. Howell, *vice* Lewen.
1673. Jan. 2. Edwd. Lowe, aft. sir E., *vice* Howell.
Jan 9. Wm. Pargeter, *vice* Steward.
Feb. 11. Saml. Clarke, *vice* Pargeter.
June 7. Sir Lacon Wm. Child, *vice* Wm. Child.
Dec. 24. Miles Cooke, *vice* Hobart.
1675. July 7. John Franklyn, *vice* Glascocke.
1676. Jan. 29. John Hoskins, *vice* Brampston.
1680. June 28. Adam Oatley, *vice* Hacket.
1682. Apr. 12. Robt. Legard, *vice* Baldwin.
1683. Apr. 27. Jas. Astry, *vice* Estcourt.
1684. May 13. John, or Jas. Edisbury, *vice* Lowe.
1685. June 20. John Methwen, *vice* Coell.
1688. Mar. 26. Roger Meredith, *vice* Clarke.
1689. Mar. 8. Saml. Keck, *vice* Beversham.
1694. Oct. 20. Thos. Pitt, *vice* Oatley.
June 28. Richd. Holford, *vice* Astry.
1699. Feb. 23. Hy. Newton, aft. sir H., *vice* Cooke.
1700. July 1. Thos. Gery, *vice* Meredith
1701. Aug. 20. Wm. Rogers, *vice* Newton.
1703. July 20. Jno. Hiccocks, *vice* Hoskins.
1706. Aug. 7. Jas. Medlycott, *vice* Methwen.
1708. Aug. 22. Wm. Fellows, *vice* Franklyn.
1709. Mar. 17. John Meller, *vice* Edisbury.
1710. July 24. John Orlebar, *vice* sir L. W. Child.
Dec. 2. Fleetwood Dormer, *vice* Holford.
1711. June 6. Saml. Browning, *vice* Keck.
1712. Oct. 17. Robt. Holford, *vice* Legard
Nov. 3. Hy. Lovibond, *vice* Pitt.
1717. Mar. 10. John Bennett, *vice* Medlycott.
1719. Oct. 14. Richd. Godfrey, *vice* Gery.
1720. Jan. 7. Jas. Lightbourn, *vice* Browning.
July 29. John Borrett, *vice* Meller.
1721. Jan. 10. Edwd. Conway, *vice* Orlebar.
May 18. Hy. Edwards, *vice* Dormer.
Aug. 9. Wm. Kynaston, *vice* Rogers.
1723. June 1. Thos. Bennett, *vice* Hiccocks.
1724. Feb. 1. Fras. Elde, *vice* Fellows.
Aug. 5. Mark Thurston, *vice* Borrett.
1726. June 29. *Hy. Edwards, app. acct. gen.
Dec. 12. *Fras. Cudworth Masham, app. acct. gen., *vice* Edwards.
1727. Feb. 17. Saml. Burroughs, *vice* Godfrey.
Robt. Yard, *vice* Conway.
1728. May 29. Anthy. Allen, *vice* Yard.
John Tothill, *vice* Lovibond.
1731. May 19. *Mark Thurston, app. acct. gen., *vice* Masham.
June 2. Wm. Spicer, app. master, *vice* Thurston.
1732. Mar. 31. Richd. Edwards, *vice* Tothill.
1738. May 12. Edmd. Sawyer, *vice* Lightbourn.
1739. Feb. 10. Hy. Montague, *vice* John Bennett.
1749. Mar. 2. Thos. Lane, *vice* Kynaston.
Aug. 9. *John Waple, app. acct. gen., *vice* Thurston.
1750. Aug. 14. Peter Holford, *vice* Robt. Holford.
1754. Apr. 24. Thos. Harris, *vice* Allen.
1759. Oct. 27. *Peter Davall, app. acct. gen., *vice* Waple.
Peter Bonner, *vice* Sawyer
1760. Mar. 8. John Browning, *vice* Elde
1761. Sept. 21. Thos. Anguish, *vice* Spicer

1761. Nov. 7. Wm. Graves, *vice* Burroughs.
1763. Jan. 10. *Thos. Anguish, app. acct. gen., *vice* Davall.
Jan. 15. Saml. Pechell, app. master, *vice* Anguish.
1764. June 20. John Eames, *vice* Thos. Bennett.
1765. June 24. Edwd. Montague, *vice* Bonner.
Dec. 3. Thos. Cuddon, *vice* Hy. Montague.
1767. Aug. 6. Robt. Pratt, *vice* Richd. Edwards.
1773. Jan. 21. Edwd. Leeds, *vice* Lane.
1775. July 26. Wm. Weller Pepys, *vice* Pratt.
Dec. 19. John Hett, *vice* Cuddon.
1778. Mar. 6. Fras. Ord, *vice* Harris.
1780. Apr. 11. Robt. Bicknell, *vice* Browning.
1781. Aug. 6. John Wilmot, *vice* Bicknell.
1782. May 11. Alexr. Thomson, *vice* Pechell.
1786. Jan. 4. *Alexr. Thomson, app. acct. gen., *vice* Anguish.
Apr. 1. Alexr. Popham, app. master, *vice* Thomson.
1787. Feb. 13. *Thos. Walker, app. acct. gen., *vice* Thomson.
1790. Nov. 11. John Spranger, *vice* Hett.
1795. May 16. Nichs. Smith, *vice* Eames.
Nov. 20. John Simeon, *vice* Edwd. Montague.
1801. June 2. John Campbell, *vice* Graves.
1802. Feb. 1. *Nichs. Smith, app. acct. gen., *vice* Walker.
Nichs. Ridley, app. master, *vice* Smith.
1803. Mar. 28. Fras. Paul Stratford, *vice* Leeds.
1804. Jan. 13. John Springett Harvey, *vice* Wilmot.
July 18. Saml. Compton Cox, *vice* Holford.
July 23. Jas. Stanley, *vice* Spranger.
1805. Jan. 16. Robt. Steele, *vice* Ridley.
1807. Apr. 1. Edwd. Morris, *vice* Weller.
1809. Feb. 10. Chas Thomson, *vice* Popham.
Nov. 9. Wm. Alexander, *vice* Ord.
1811. Feb. 20. Jas. Stephen, *vice* Stanley.
1815. June 22. Jos. Jekyll, *vice* Morris.
1817. July 30. Wm. Courtenay, *vice* Steele.
1819. Nov. 29. *John Campbell, app. acct. gen., *vice* Smith.
1820. Feb. 8. John E. Dowdeswell, app. master, *vice* Campbell.
1821. July 12. Fras. Cross, *vice* Thomson.
1823. Mar. 3. Jas. Trower, *vice* Jekyll.
1824. Feb. 16. Wm. Wingfield, *vice* Alexander.
Mar. 9. Jas. Wm. Farrer, *vice* Simeon.
1826. Feb. 2. *John Springett Harvey, app. acct. gen., *vice* Campbell.
Mar. 23. Robt. Henley Eden, aft ld. Henley, *vice* Courtenay.
Sir Giffin Wilson, app. master, *vice* Harvey.
1831. Mar. 4. Geo. B. Roupell, *vice* Cox.
Hy. Martin, *vice* Stratford.
Mar. 29. Wm. Brougham, *vice* Stephen.
June 9. *Wm. Geo. Adam, app. acct. gen., *vice* Harvey.
1836. June 7. Nassau Wm. Senior, *vice* Trower.
1838. Feb. 17. Andw. Hy. Lynch, *vice* Roupell.
1839. Mar. 15. Saml. Duckworth, *vice* Cross.
Apr. 30. *Wm. Russell, app. acct. gen., *vice* Adam.
July — Sir Wm. Horne, *vice* Martin.
1840. Dec. 7. Sir Geo. Rose, *vice* ld. Henley.
1841. Oct. — Richd. Richards, acct. gen. and mast. of the ct. of exch., app. under 5 Vict. cap. 5.
1847. Dec. 20. Wm. Hy. Tinney, *vice* Duckworth.
1848. Mar. 10. Richd. Torin Kindersley, *vice* Wilson.
1849. Dec. 6. John Elijah Blunt, *vice* Wingfield.
1850. Dec. 7. Jos. Humphry, *vice* Dowdeswell.

Offices abolished by 15 & 16 Vict. cap. 80, and 35 & 36 Vict. cap. 44. (See *ante*, pp, 392–3.)

ATTORNEYS GENERAL.

See Introduction, *ante*, p. 349.

THE ATTORNEY GENERAL for the time being is the head of the bar, and his office is esteemed the highest below the bench. It has subsisted for six hundred years, though not under its present designation, the original title being ATTORNATUS REGIS. The appointment, which is by letters patent, was formerly "*quamdiu se bene gesserit*," but is now "*durante bene placito*," and the holder retires with his political friends on every change of administration.

ATTORNEYS GENERAL.

From the reign of Edward I.

EDWARD I.

1277–8. Wm. de Boneville.
1278–9. Wm. de Giselham.
1279–80. Gilbert de Thornton.
1280–1. Alanus de Walkingham.
1281–2. Jno. le Fawconer.
1284–5. Wm. de Seleby.
1286. Gilbert de Thornton, *again* (?).
1286–7. Wm. Inge.
1289–90. Jno. de Bosco.
Nichs. de Warwick
Jno. de Haydell.
1291–2. Richd. de Breteville.
Hugh de Louther.
1292–3. Roger de Hegham.
1293–4. Jno. de Mutford.
1300–1. Jno. de Cestria, or Chester.
1302. Jno. de Mutford, *again*.
1304–5. Jno. de Drokenesford (?).

EDWARD II.

1307–8. Jno. de Chester, *again*.
1309–10. Matt. de Scaccario.
1312–3. Jno. de Norton.
1315–6. Wm. de Langeley.
1318–9. Adam de Fyncham.
1320–1. Geoffrey le Scrope.
1322–3. Geoffrey de Fyngale.
1325. Adam de Fyncham, *again*.

EDWARD III.

1327. Alexr. de Hadenham.
Wm. de Merston, or Mershton, Feb. 26.
1329. Richd. de Aldeburgh.
1334. Simon de Trewythosa.
Wm. de Hepton, or Hopton.
1338. Jno. de Lincoln, May 28.
Jno. de Clone, or Clove, Aug. 4.
Wm. de Merington.
1339. Jno. de Clone, *again*.
1342. Wm. de Thorpe.
1343. Jno. de Lincoln, *again*.
Jno. de Clone, *again*.
1349. Simon de Kegworth.
1353. Hy. de Greystok.
1356. Jno. Gaunt, or de Gaunt.
1360. Richd. de Fryseby, May 4.
1362. Wm. de Pleste (? Robt.).
1363. Wm. de Nessefield.
1366. Thos. de Shardelow, Nov. 9.
1367. Jno. de Ashwell, May 20.
Michl. Skilling.

RICHARD II.

1378. Thos. de Shardelow, *again*.
1381. Wm. Ellis.
Laurence Dru.
1384. Wm. de Horneby.
1386. Edmd. Brudnell, or Brudenell.
1398. Thos. Coveley.

HENRY IV.

1399. Wm. de Lodington, Sept. 30.
1401. Thos. Coveley, *again*.
1407. Thos. Dereham, July 13.
Roger Hunt, Aug. 17.
1410. Thos. Tickhill.

HENRY V.

1414. Wm. Babington, Jan. 16.
1420. Wm. Babthorpe.

HENRY VI.

1429. Jno. Vampage, Oct. 28.
1452. Wm. de Nottingham, June 30.

EDWARD IV.

1461. Jno. Herbert, ? Aug. 12.
Hy. Sothill, or Sotill.
1471. Wm. Husee, or Hussee, June 16.
1481. Wm. Huddersfield, May 7.

EDWARD V. AND RICHARD III.

1483. Morgan Kydwelly, May 28.

HENRY VII.

1485. Wm. Hody, Sept. 20.
1486. Jacob Hubbard, Nov. 3.

HENRY VIII.

1509. Jno. Ernley, Apr.
1518. Jno. Fitz-James, Jan. 26.
1522. Jno. Roper, Feb.
1524. Ralph Swillington, Apr. 1.
1525. Richd. Lyster, ? Aug.
1529. Christr. Hales, June 3.
1535. Sir Jno. Baker, July 10.
1540. Wm. Whorwode, Nov. 8.
1545. Hy. Bradshaw, June 18.

EDWARD VI. AND MARY.

1552. Edwd. Griffin, May 21.

ELIZABETH.

1559. Sir Gilbert Gerrard, Jan. 22; aft. m. rolls.

1581. Sir Jno. Popham, June 1; aft. ch. just. Q. B.
1592. Sir Thos. Egerton, June 2; aft. ld. kpr., ld. chanc., and ld. Ellesmere.
1594. Sir Edwd. Coke, Apr. 10; aft. ch. just. C. P. and K. B.

JAMES I.

1606. Sir Hy. Hobart, bt., July 4; aft. ch. just. C. P.
1613. Sir Fras. Bacon, Oct. 27; aft. ld. kpr., ld. chanc., and ld. Verulam.
1617. Sir Hy. Yelverton, bt., Mar. 12; aft. just. C. P.
1621. Sir Thos. Coventry, Jan. 11; aft. ld. kpr., and ld. Coventry.

CHARLES I.

1625. Sir Robt. Heath, Oct. 31; aft. ch. just. C. P. and K. B.
1631. Wm, Noy, Oct. 27.
1634. Sir Jno. Banks, Sept. 27.
1641. Sir Edwd. Herbert, Jan. 29; aft. ch. just. C. P.
1645. Thos. Gardner, Nov. 3.

COMMONWEALTH.

1644. Oliver St. John, (?) May.
St. John is named as atty. gen. by *Whitelocke*, but *Foss* says he was merely continued in his old office of king's solr. gen., and that the ordinance of the Commons, on which *Whitelocke* relies, merely enabled him to perform the duties of atty. gen.
1649. Wm. Steele, Jan. 10; aft. recorder of London, and ch. bar. ex.
Edmd. Prideaux, Apr. 9.
1659. Robt. Reynolds.

CHARLES II.

1649. Edwd. Herbert held the nominal title during the king's exile until 1653.
1660. Sir Geoffrey Palmer, bt., May 31.
1670. Sir Heneage Finch, knt, and bt., May 10; aft. ld. chanc., ld. Finch of Daventry, and E. of Nottingham.
1673. Sir Fras. North, Nov. 12; aft. ch. just. C. P., ld. kpr., and ld. and E. of Guilford.
1675. Sir Wm. Jones, Jan. 25.
1679. Sir Creswell Levinz, or Levinge, Oct. 27; aft. just. C. P.
1681. Sir Robt. Sawyer, Feb. 24.

JAMES II.

1687. Sir Thos. Powis, Dec. 13.

WILLIAM III.

1689. Sir Hy. Pollexfen, Feb.; aft. ch. just. C. P.
1689. Sir Geo. Treby, May 4; aft. ch. just. C. P.
1692. Sir Jno. Somers, May 3; aft. ld. kpr., ld. chanc., and ld. Somers.
1693. Sir Edwd. Ward, Mar. 30; aft. ch. bar. ex.
1695. Sir Thos. Trevor, June 8; aft. ch just. C. P., and ld. Trevor.
1701. Sir Edwd. Northey, June 28.

ANNE.

1707. Sir Simon Harcourt, Apr. 26.
1708. Sir Jas. Montague, Oct. 22.
1710. Sir Simon Harcourt, *again*, Sept. 19; aft. ld. kpr., ld. Harcourt, and ld. chanc.
Sir Edwd. Northey, *again*, Oct. 19.

GEORGE I.

1718. Sir Nichs. Lechmere, Mar. 18; aft. ld. Lechmere.
1720. Sir Robt. Raymond, May 7; aft. just. and ch. just. K. B., and ld. Raymond.
1724. Sir Philip Yorke, Feb. 1; aft. ch. just. K. B., ld. Hardwicke, ld. chanc., visc. Royston, and E. Hardwicke.

GEORGE II.

1734. Sir Jno. Willes, Jan.; aft. ch. just. C. P.
1737. Sir Dudley Ryder, Jan. 28; aft. ch. just. K. B.
1754. Hon. Wm. Murray, May; aft. ch. just. K. B., and ld. and E. of Mansfield.
1756. Sir Robt. Henley, Nov. 3; aft. ld. kpr., ld. and visc. Henley, E. of Northington, and ld. chanc.
1757. Sir Chas. Pratt, July 1; aft. ch. just. C. P., ld. chanc., and ld. and E. Camden.

GEORGE III.

1762. Hon. Chas. Yorke, Jan. 25.
1763. Sir Fletcher Norton, Dec. 16; aft. sp. ho. comns., and ld. Grantley.
1765. Hon. Chas. Yorke, *again*, Sept. 17; aft. ld. chanc.
1766. Wm. de Grey, Aug. 6; aft. ch. just., C. P., and ld. Walsingham.
1771. Edwd. Thurlow, Jan. 26; aft. ld. chanc. and ld. Thurlow.
1778. Alexr. Wedderburn, June 11; aft. ch. just. C. P., ld. Loughborough, ld. chanc., and E. of Rosslyn.
1780. Jas. Wallace, July 21.
1782. Lloyd Kenyon, Apr. 18.
1783. Jas. Wallace, *again*, May 2; *d.* Nov. following.
John Lee, Nov. 22.
Lloyd Kenyon, *again*, Dec. 26; aft. m. rolls, a bt., ch. just. K. B., and ld. Kenyon.

1784. Richd. Pepper Arden, Mar. 31; aft. m. rolls, ch. just. C. P., and ld. Alvanley.

1788. Sir Archd. Macdonald, June 28; aft. ch. bar. ex.

1793. Sir John Scott, Feb. 14; aft. ch. just. C. P., ld. Eldon, ld. chanc. and E. of Eldon.

1799. Sir John Mitford, July 18; aft. sp. ho. commons; ld. chanc. Ireland, and ld. Redesdale.

1801. Sir Edwd. Law, Feb. 14; aft. ch. just. K.B., and ld. Ellenborough.

1802. Hon. Spencer Perceval, Apr. 15; assass. by Bellingham, while prime minister, May 11, 1812.

1806. Sir Arthur Pigott, Feb. 12.

1807. Sir Vicary Gibbs, Apr. 1; aft. just. C. P. ch. bar. ex., and ch. just. C. P.

1812. Sir Thos. Plumer, June 26; aft. v. chanc. of England, and m. rolls.

1813. Sir Wm. Garrow, May 4; aft. bar. ex.

1817. Sir Saml. Shepherd, May 7; aft. a judge in Scotland.

1819. Sir Robt. Gifford, July 24; aft. ch. just. C. P., ld. Gifford, and m. rolls.

George IV.

1824 Sir John Singleton Copley, Jan. 9; aft. m. rolls, ld. Lyndhurst, ld. chanc. (three times), and ch. bar. ex.

1826. Sir Chas. Wetherell, Sept. 20.

1827. Jas. Scarlett, aft. sir J., Apr. 27.

1828. Sir Chas. Wetherell, *again*, Feb. 19.

1829. Sir Jas. Scarlett, *again*, June 29; aft. ch. bar. ex., and ld. Abinger.

William IV.

1830. Thos. Denman, Nov. 19 (? 26); knt. Nov. 24; aft. ch. just. K. B. and ld. Denman.

1832. Sir Wm. Horne, Nov. 26; aft. mast. in chanc.

1834. Sir John Campbell, Mar. 1.
Fredk. Pollock, Dec. 17; knt. Dec. 29.

1835. Sir John Campbell, *again*, Apr. 30; aft. ld. chanc. Ireland, ld. Campbell, ch. duch. lanc., ch. just. Q. B., and ld. chanc.

Victoria.

1841. Sir Thos. Wilde, July 3.
Sir Fredk. Pollock, *again*, Sept. 6; aft. ch. bar. ex., and a bt.

1844. Sir Wm. Webb Follett, Apr. 15; *d.* June 28, 1845.

1845. Sir Fredk. Thesiger, June 29.

1846. Sir Thos. Wilde, *again*, July 7; aft. ch. just. C. P., ld. chanc., and ld. Truro.
John Jervis, July 17; knt., Aug. 1; ch. just. C. P.

1850. Sir John Romilly, July 11; aft. m. rolls, and ld. Romilly.

1851. Sir Alexr. Jas. Edmd. Cockburn, Mar. 28.

1852. Sir Fredk. Thesiger, *again*, Feb. 27, aft. ld. chanc., and ld. Chelmsford.
Sir Alexr. Jas. Edmd. Cockburn, *again*, Dec. 28; aft. ch. just. C. P. and Q. B.

1856. Sir Richd. Bethell, Nov., knt. Nov. 15.

1858. Sir Fitzroy Kelly, Feb. 26; aft. ch. bar. ex.

1859. Sir Richd. Bethell, *again*, June 18; aft. ld. chanc. and ld. Westbury.

1861. Sir Wm. Atherton, June 27.

1863. Sir Roundell Palmer, Oct. 2, **G.**; aft. ld. chanc. and ld. and E. Selborne.

1866. Sir Hugh McCalmont Cairns, July 10, **G.**; aft. ld. just. app., ld. Cairns, ld. chanc., and E. Cairns.

1866. John Rolt, Oct. 29, **G.**; knt. Nov. 10; aft. ld. just. app.

1867. Sir John Burgess Karslake, July 18.

1868. Sir Robt. Porrett Collier, Dec. 12, **G.**; aft. just. C. P., and jud. com. P. C.

1871. Sir John Duke Coleridge, Nov. 10, **G.**; aft. ch. just. C. P., ld. Coleridge, and ch. just. Q. B.

1873. Hy. James, Nov. 20, **G.**; knt. Dec. 12.

1874. Sir John Burgess Karslake, *again*, Feb. 27, **G.**

1874. Sir Richd. Baggallay, Apr 20; aft. ld. just. app.

1875. Sir John Holker, Nov. 25, **G.**; aft. ld. just. app.

1880. Sir Hy. James, *again*, May 3, **G.**

1885. Richd. Everard Webster, June 26; knt. July 9.

1886. Chas. Arthur Russell, Feb. 9, **G.**; knt. Mar. 8.

1886. Sir Richd. Everard Webster, *again*, Aug. 5.

SOLICITORS GENERAL.

The Solicitor General is next in rank to the Attorney General. The office, which was originally styled Sollicitor Regis, was first instituted in the reign of Edward IV. It is created by letters patent, and is held on the same tenure as that of the attorney-general. The honour of knighthood is now always conferred both upon the attorney and the solicitor-general, and, together, they are usually styled the "Law Officers of the Crown."

Solicitors General.

From the reign of Edward IV.

Those marked * afterwards became attorneys general. *See* "Attorneys General," *ante* p. 398, where their subsequent promotions are noted.

Edward IV.

1461. Richd. Fowler, Mar. 12.
1470. Richd. Page, Jan. 31.

Richard III.

1483. Thos. Lynom, Aug. 26.

Henry VII.

1485. Andrew Dimmock or Dymock, Nov. 15.
1503. Thos. Lucas.
1507. *John Ernley, July 9.

Henry VIII.

1514. John Port.
1521. Richd. Lyster, July 8.
1525. *Christr. Hales, Aug. 14.
1531. Baldwin Mallet.
1533. Richd. Rich, Oct. 4.
1536. *Wm. Whorwode, Apr. 13.
1540. Hy. Bradshaw, Nov.
1545. *Edwd. Griffin, June 18.

Edward VI.

1552. John Gosnel or Gosnold, May 21.

Mary.

1553. Wm. Cordell, Sept. 30.
1557. Richd. Weston, sen., Nov. 20.

Elizabeth.

1559. Richd. Roswell, Feb. 1.
1566. Richd. Onslow, June 27.
1569. Thos. Bromley, jun., Mar. 13; aft. sir T. and ld. chanc.
1579. *Sir John Popham, June 26.
1581. *Sir Thos. Egerton, June 28.
1592. *Sir Edwd. Coke, June 16.
1595. Thos. Fleming, or Flemynge, Nov. 6.

James I.

1604. Sir John Doderidge, Oct.
1607. *Sir Fras. Bacon, June 25.
1613. *Hy. Yelverton, Oct. 29.
1617. *Sir Thos. Coventry, Mar. 14.
1621. *Robt. Heath, Jan. 22.

Charles I.

1625. Sir Richd. Sheldon, or Shilton, Nov. 1.
1634. Sir Edwd. Littleton, Oct. 17; aft. ld. Littleton and ld. kpr.
1640. *Sir Edwd. Herbert, Jan. 25.
1641. Oliver St. John, Jan. 29.
1643. Sir Thos. Gardner, knt. and bt., Oct. 30.
1645. Geoffrey Palmer, Nov. 3.

Commonwealth.

1643. Oliver St. John, continued in office by the parliament.
1548. *Edmd. Prideaux, Oct. 12.
1649. John Cook, Jan. 10.
1650. *Robt. Reynolds.
1654. Wm. Ellis, May 24.

Charles II.

1660. *Sir Heneage Finch, June 6.
1670. Sir Edwd. Turner, May 11; aft. ch. bar. ex.
1671. *Sir Fras. North, May 20.
1673. *Sir Wm. Jones, Nov. 11.
1674. Sir Fras. Winnington, Dec.
1679. Hon. Heneage Finch, Jan. 13.

James II.

1686. *Sir Thos. Powys, or Powis, Apr. 26.
1687. Sir Wm. Williams, Dec. 13.

William III.

1689. *Sir Geo. Treby, Feb.
*John Somers, May 4.
1692. *Sir Thos. Trevor, May 3.
1695. Sir John Hawles, June 8.

Anne.

1702. *Sir Simon Harcourt, June 1.
1707. *Sir Jas. Montagu, Apr. 26.
1708. Robt. Eyre, Oct. 22; aft. just. Q. B., ch. bar. ex., and ch. just. C. P.
1710. *Sir Robt. Raymond, May 13.

George I.

1714. *Nichs. Lechmere, Oct. 14.
1715. John Fortescue Aland, Dec. 6; aft. bar. ex., just. K. B., just. C. P., and. ld. Fortescue, in Ireland.
1717. Sir Wm. Thomson Jan. 24; aft. bar. ex.
1720. *Sir Philip Yorke, Mar. 23.
1724. Sir Clement Wearg, Feb. 1; *d.* next year.
1726. Chas. Talbot, Apr. 23; aft. ld. chanc. and ld. Talbot.

George II.

1734. *Sir Dudley Ryder, Jan.
1737. John Strange, Jan. 28; aft. m. rolls.
1742. *Hon. Wm. Murray, Nov. 27.

1754. Sir Richd. Lloyd, May; aft. bar. ex.
1756. *Hon. Chas. Yorke, Nov. 3.

GEORGE III.

1762. *Fletcher Norton, Jan. 25.
1763. *Wm. de Grey, Dec. 16.
1766. Edwd. Willes, Aug. 6; aft. just. K. B.
1768. John Dunning, Jan. 28; aft. ld. Ashburton.
1770. *Edwd. Thurlow, Mar. 30.
1771. *Alexr. Wedderburn, Jan. 26.
1778. *Jas. Wallace, June 11.
1780. Jas. Mansfield, Sept. 1.
1782. *John Lee, Apr. 18.
*Richd. Pepper Arden, Nov. 7.
1783. *John Lee, *again*, Apr. 18.
Jas. Mansfield, *again*, Nov. 22; aft. ch. just. C. P.
*Richd. Pepper Arden, *again*, Dec. 26.
1784. *Archd. Macdonald, Apr. 8.
1788. *John Scott, aft. sir J., June 28.
1793. *John Mitford, aft. sir J., Feb. 14.
1799. Wm. Grant, aft. sir W., July 18; aft. m. rolls.
1801. *Hon. Spencer Perceval, Feb. 14.
1802. Thos. Manners Sutton, May 11; knt. May 19; aft. bar. ex., ld. chanc. Ireland, and ld. Manners.
1805. *Vicary Gibbs, Feb. 12; knt. Feb. 20.
1806. Saml. Romilly, aft. sir S., Feb. 12.
1807. *Thos. Plumer, aft. sir T., Apr. 1.
1812. *Wm. Garrow, June 26; knt. July 17.
1813. Robt. Dallas, May 4; knt. May 9; aft. just. and ch. just. C. P.
*Saml. Shepherd, Dec. 22; knt. May 11, 1814.
1817. *Robt. Gifford, May 9; knt. May 29.
1819. *John Singleton Copley, aft. sir J., July 24.

GEORGE IV.

1824. *Chas. Wetherell, Jan. 12; knt. Mar. 10.
1826. Nicolas Conyngham Tindal, Sept. 20; knt. Nov. 27; aft. ch. just. C. P.
1829. Sir Edwd. Burtenshaw Sugden, June 29; knt. June 10; aft. ld. chanc. Ireland, ld. St. Leonards, and ld. chanc.

WILLIAM IV.

1830. *Wm. Horne, Nov. 26; knt. Nov. 24.
1832. *John Campbell, Nov. 26; knt. Dec. 3.
1834. Chas. Christr. Pepys, Feb. 25; knt. Feb. 26; aft. m. rolls, ld. Cottenham, ld. chanc., and E. of Cottenham.
1834. Robt. Monsey Rolfe, Nov. 6.
*Wm. Webb Follett, Dec. 20; knt. Dec. 22.
1835. Robt. Monsey Rolfe, *again*, May 4; knt. May 6; aft. bar. ex., v. chanc., ld. Cranworth, ld. just. app., and ld. chanc.

VICTORIA.

1839. *Thos. Wilde, Dec. 2; knt. Feb. 19, 1840.
1841. *Sir Wm. Webb Follett, *again*, Sept. 6.
1844. *Fredk. Thesiger, Apr. 15; knt May 23.
1845. Fitzroy Kelly, July 17; knt. Aug. 8.
1846. *John Jervis, July 4.
David Dundas, July 18; knt. Feb. 24, 1847.
1848. *John Romilly, Mar.; knt. May 17.
1850. *Alexr. Jas. Edmd. Cockburn, July 11; knt. Aug. 14.
1851. Wm. Page Wood, Mar. 28; knt. Apr. 14; aft. v. chanc.; ld. just. app., ld. chanc., and ld. Hatherley.
1852. *Sir Fitzroy Kelley, *again*, Feb. 27.
*Richd. Bethell, Dec. 28; knt. June 13, 1853.
1856. Hon Jas. Stuart Wortley, Nov. 22.
1857. Hy. Singer Keating, May 28; knt. June 18.
1858 *Hugh MacCalmont Cairns, aft. sir H., Feb. 26.
1859. Sir Hy. Singer Keating, *again*, June 18; aft. just. C. P.
*Wm. Atherton, Dec. 16, **G.**; knt. Feb. 23, 1860.
1861. *Roundell Palmer, June 28; knt. Aug. 5.
1863. *Robt. Porrett Collier, Oct. 2, **G.**; knt. Nov. 23.
1866. *Wm. Bovill, July 10, **G.**; knt. July 26; aft. ch. just. C. P.
*John Burgess Karslake, Nov. 29, **G.**; knt. Dec. 28.
1867. Chas. Jasper Selwyn, July 18; knt. Aug. 31; aft. ld. just. app.
1868. Wm. Baliol Brett, Feb. 10; knt Feb. 29; aft. just. C. P., ld. just app., m. rolls, and ld. Esher.
*Richd. Baggallay, Sept. 14; knt. Dec. 9.
*John Duke Coleridge, Dec. 12, **G.**; knt. Dec. 12.
1871. Geo. Jessel, Nov. 10, **G.**; knt. Feb. 21, 1872; aft. m. rolls.
1873. *Hy. James, Sept. 26, **G.**; knt. Dec. 12.
Wm. Geo. Granville Venables Vernon Harcourt, Nov. 20, **G.**; knt. Dec. 12; aft. ch. ex., &c.

874. *Sir Richd. Baggallay, *again*, Feb. 27, G.
*John Holker, Apr. 20; knt. Dec. 12.
875. Hardinge Stanley Giffard, Nov. 25, G.; knt. Nov. 27; aft. ld. chanc. and ld. Halsbury.
880. Farrer Herschell, May 3, G.; knt. May 13.; aft. ld. chanc. and ld. Herschell.
1885. John Eldon Gorst, July 2, G.; knt. Aug. 1.
1886. Horace Davey, Feb. 15, G.; knt. Mar. 8.
Edwd. Geo. Clarke, Aug. 6; knt. Aug. 16.

JUDGES OF THE COUNTY COURTS.

[T]HESE courts were established under 9 & 10 Vict. cap. 95 (Aug. 28, [1]846), and Orders in Council dated Dec. 19, 1846, and Feb. 4, and Mar. [.], 1847.

The judges' style and precedence are fixed by Order in Council dated [A]ug. 7, 1884. They are to be "called, known, and addressed as 'his [h]onour' prefixed to the word 'judge' before their respectives names," [a]nd to have "rank and precedence next after knight bachelors."

This list has been compiled and very kindly furnished by Mr. F. [B]oase, the librarian to the Incorporated Law Society.

JUDGES OF THE COUNTY COURTS.

ORIGINAL APPOINTMENTS.

March, 1847.

[J]as. Manning, S.L., res. Feb. 1863.
[H]y. Storks, S.L., res. Sept. 1859.
[T]hos. Starkie, Q.C., *d.* Apr. 15, 1849.
[J]ohn Herbert Koe, Q.C., *d.* Sept. 3, 1860.
[N]athl. Richd. Clarke, S.L., *d.* July 31, 1859.
[J]ohn Billingsley Parry, Q.C., res. Sept. 1874.
[F]ras. King Eagle, *d.* June 8, 1856.
[J]ohn Wilson, *d.* Dec. 6, 1851.
[J]ohn Tyrrell, res. Dec. 1864.
[G]eo. Hutton Wilkinson, res. May 1853.
[J]oseph Grace Smith, *d.* Mar. 26, 1859.
[U]vedale Corbett, res. Sept. 1865.
[J]ohn Farquhar Fraser, *d.* Feb. 1865.
[J]ohn Addison, *d.* July 14, 1859.
[W]m. Lowndes, *d.* Mar. 31, 1850.
[A]ndrew Amos, res. Sept. 1852.
[C]has. Heneage Elsley, res. 1854.
[A]rthur Palmer, res. 1854.
[R]obt. Brandt, *d.* Apr. 15, 1862.
[J]ohn Hildyard, *d.* Feb. 13, 1855.
[T]hos. Horncastle Marshall, *d.* Feb. 18, 1875.
[W]m. Mackworth Praed, *d.* Oct. 2, 1857.
[E]dwd. Everett, res. Dec. 1867.
[R]obt. Griffiths Temple, *d.* Jan. 11, 1859.
[R]ichd. Leigh Trafford, res. Oct. 1862.
[H]y. Downer Stapylton, res. Jan. 1873.
[B]enj. Parham, res. 1859.
[W]m. Adam Hulton, res. 1886.
[J]as. Espinasse, *d.* Mar. 16, 1867.
Geo. Granville Kekewich, *d.* Jan. 7, 1857.
John Collyer, *d.* Sept. 1, 1870.
Chas. Harwood, *d.* Sept. 25, 1866.
John Dick Burnaby, *d.* Dec. 29, 1855.
Wm. Gurdon, res. Mar. 1871.
Denis Creagh Moylan, *d.* 1849.
Richd. Wildman, res. Apr. 1881.
John Stock Turner Green, res. Mar. 1872; no successor app.
Geo. Clive, res. Feb. 1857.
John Geo. Stapylton Smith, *d.* Oct. 23, 1862.
Jos. Thos. Cantrell, *d.* Apr. 6, 1862.
John Johnes, res. Oct. 1861.
Thos. Jacob Birch, *d.* Apr. 26, 1868.
David Leahy, *d.* June 21, 1847.
Chas. Jas. Gale, res. Oct. 1874.
Robt. Wharton, *d.* Oct. 27, 1848.
Jas. Francillon, *d.* Sept. 3, 1866.
Wm. Raines, *d.* Jan. 28, 1874.
Wm. Walker, res. Nov. 10, 1863.
John Monson Carrow, *d.* May 8, 1853.
Fredk. Trotter Dimsdale, *d.* July 8, 1872; no successor app.
Theoph. Hastings Ingham.
Arthur Jas. Johnes, res. Dec. 1870.
Douglas Devon Heath, res. Sept. 1865.
John Maurice Herbert, *d.* Nov. 3, 1882.
Jos. St. John Yates, res. July 1882.
John Wm. Harden, *d.* Apr. 16, 1875.
Edwd. Lewis Richards, *d.* June 25, 1863.
John W. Wing, *d.* June 18, 1855.
Jas. Stansfeld, res. Sept. 1871.
Wm. Furner, res. Sept. 1877.

SUBSEQUENT APPOINTMENTS.

1847. Geo. Chilton, Q.C., June, *vice* Leahy, dec.; *d.* Nov. 1, 1852.

1848. Alf. Sept. Dowling, S.L., Nov. 9, *vice* Wharton, dec.; *d.* Mar. 3, 1868.

1849. Herbt. Geo. Jones, S.L., Apr. 16, *vice* Starkie, dec.; *d.* Feb. 17, 1866.

Fras. Bayley, Nov. 28, *vice* Moylan, dec.

1850. Wm. Ramshay, Apr., *vice* Lowndes, dec.; rem. Nov. 1851.

1851. Jos. Pollock, Nov., *vice* Ramshay, rem.; res. Oct. 1857.

Thos. Falconer, Dec. 22, *vice* Wilson, dec.; res. Dec. 1881.

1852. Jno. Leycester Adolphus, Oct., *vice* Amos, res.; *d.* Dec. 24, 1862.

Jno. Pitt Taylor, Nov. 2, *vice* Chilton, dec.; res. Oct. 1885.

1853. Graham Willmore. Q.C., May, *vice* Carrow, dec.; *d.* June 19, 1856.

James Losh, May, *vice* Wilkinson, res.; *d.* Oct. 1, 1858.

1854. Sir Jno. Eardley Eardley-Wilmot, bt., Jan. 26, *vice* Palmer, res.; res. Nov. 1871.

Edwd. Cooke, Jan., *vice* Elsley, res.; res. 1861.

1855. Jas. Jno. Lonsdale, Feb. 14, *vice* Hildyard, dec.; res. Mar. 1884.

Christr. Temple, Q.C., June, *vice* Wing, dec.; *d.* Jan. 21, 1871.

1856. Robt. Miller, S.L., Jan. 1, *vice* Burnaby, dec.; *d.* Aug. 5, 1876.

Jno. Worlledge, June 9, *vice* Eagle, dec.; res. June 1880.

Chas. Saunders, June 23, *vice* Willmore, dec.; *d.* Apr. 8, 1872. No successor appointed.

1857. Chas. Shapland Whitmore, Feb. 10, *vice* Clive, res.; *d.* May 17, 1877.

Chas. Dacres Bevan, Jan. 22, *vice* Kekewich, dec.; *d.* June 24, 1872.

Matt. Fortescue, Oct. 8, *vice* Praed, dec.; *d.* Mar. 27, 1883.

Jas. Kennedy Blair, Oct. 22, *vice* Pollock, res.; res. Feb. 28, 1872.

1858. Jno. Bury Dasent, Oct. 2, *vice* Losh, dec.; res. Jan. 1884.

1859. Sir Walter Buchanan-Riddell, bt., Jan. 12, *vice* R. G. Temple, dec.; res. July 1879.

Camille Felix Desiré Caillard, Mar. 27, *vice* J. G. Smith, dec.

Robt. Segar, July, *vice* Addison, dec.; *d.* May 1862.

1859. Allan Maclean Skinner, Q.C., Aug 1, *vice* Clarke, dec.; res. Sept. 1872.

Rupert Alf. Kettle, aft. Sir R., Oct 15, *vice* Parham, res.

Wm. Hy. Willes, Sept., *vice* Storks, res.; *d.* Feb. 2, 1863.

1860. Jas. Whigham, Sept. 5, *vice* Koe, dec.

1861. Fras. Ellis, aft. Ellis-McTaggart May 4, *vice* E. Cooke, res.; *d.* Mar. 15, 1872.

Hy. Ridgard Bagshawe, Q.C., Oct. 30, *vice* J. Johnes, res.; *d.* May 16, 1870.

1862. Wm Elmsley, Q.C., Apr. 16, *vice* Cantrell, dec.; *d.* Dec. 20, 1866.

Edwd. Ovens, May 8, *vice* Brandt, dec.; *d.* Feb. 19, 1869.

Thos. Wheeler, S.L., May 26, *vice* Segar, dec.; *d.* June 17, 1883.

Wm. Nichols, Oct. 22, *vice* Trafford, res.; *d.* Dec. 29, 1864.

Jno. Godfrey Teed, Q.C., Oct. 31, *vice* J. G. T. Smith, dec.; *d.* Oct. 20, 1871.

1863. Wm. Blanshard, Jan. 10, *vice* Adolphus, dec.; res. 1871.

Edwd. Jno. Lloyd, Q.C., Feb. 18 *vice* Willes, dec.; res. Sept 1874.

Wm. Spooner, Feb. 13, *vice* Manning, res.; *d.* May 19, 1880.

Robt. Vaughan Williams, July 7, *vice* Richards, dec.; res. Sept 1874.

Thos. Ellison, Nov. 10, *vice* Walker, res.

1865. Chas. Erdman Petersdorff, S.L., Jan 1, *vice* Tyrrell, res.; res. Dec. 1885.

Rd. Griffiths Welford, Jan. 11, *vice* Nichols, dec.; *d.* Sept. 2, 1872.

Hy. Jas. Stonor, Feb. 17, *vice* Fraser dec.

Geo. Lake Russell, Sept. 21, *vice* Heath, res.; *d.* Nov. 16, 1878.

Josiah Wm. Smith, Q.C., Sept. 26 *vice* Corbett, res.; res. Jan. 1879

1866. Thos. Hull Terrell, Feb. 23, *vice* H. G. Jones, dec.; res. Dec. 1877

Wm. Carmalt Scott, Sept. 7, *vice* Francillon, dec.; *d.* Mar. 3 1874.

Chas. Sumner, Sept. 28, *vice* Harwood, dec.; *d.* Dec. 23, 1885.

Geo. Russell, aft. Sir G., Dec., *vice* Elmsley, dec.; res. Feb. 1884.

1867. Wm. Thos. Shave Daniel, Q.C. Mar. 20, *vice* Espinasse, dec.; res Apr. 1884.

68. Thos. E. P. Lefroy, Jan. 1, *vice* Everett, res.; res. Oct. 1880.
Edmd. Robt. Turner, Mar. 11, *vice* Dowling. dec.
Wm. Hy. Cooke, Q.C., Apr. 29, *vice* Birch, dec.
69. Jno. Archd. Russell, Q.C., Mar. 2, *vice* Ovens, dec.
70. Gordon Whitbread, May 21, *vice* Bagshawe, Q.C., dec.; *d.* Jan. 29, 1883.
Edmd. Beales, Sept. 17, *vice* Collyer, dec.; *d.* June 26, 1881.
Hy. Tindal Atkinson, S.L., Dec. 16, *vice* A. J. Johnes, res.; res. Nov. 1888.
71. Jno. Osborne, Q.C., Jan. 26, *vice* C. Temple, dec.; *d.* Nov. 23, 1872.
Jno. Thos. Abdy, Apr. 1, *vice* Gurdon, res.
Delamere Robt. Blaine, Apr., *vice* Blanshard, res.; *d.* Dec. 13, 1871.
Homersham Cox, Oct. 1, *vice* Stansfeld, res.
Thos. Jos. Cavendish Bradshaw, Nov. 10, *vice* Eardley-Wilmot, res.; *d.* Dec. 17, 1884.
Jas. Stephen, Nov. 16, *vice* Teed, dec.
72. Rd. Harington, aft. Sir R., bt., Jan. 6, *vice* Blaine, dec.
Hy. Tyrwhitt Jones Macnamara, Apr. 1, *vice* Ellis-McTaggart, dec.; res. Aug. 1873.
Thos. Perronet Edwd. Thompson, Apr. 1, *vice* Blair, res.
Montagu Bere, Q.C., June 28, *vice* Bevan, dec.; *d.* Oct. 19, 1887.
Hy. Warwick Cole, Q.C., Sept. 11, *vice* Welford, dec.; *d.* June 19, 1876.
Alfred Martineau, Oct. 4, *vice* Skinner, res.
Crompton Hutton, Dec. 27, *vice* Osborne, dec.
73. Edgar Jno. Meynell, Feb. 1, *vice* Stapylton, res.
Jno. Fras. Collier, Aug. 9, *vice* Macnamara, res.
74. C. Chapman Barber, Feb., *vice* Raines, dec.; res. Mar. 1874.
Fras. Alford Bedwell, Mar. 16, *vice* Barber, res.
Woodforde Ffooks Woodforde, Mar. 24, *vice* Scott, dec.
Robt. Alexr. Fisher, Oct. 1, *vice* E. J. Lloyd, res.; *d.* Sept. 30, 1879.
Patr. Marcellinus Leonard, Oct. 1, *vice* Gale, res.
Edwin Plumer Price, Oct. 5, *vice* Parry, res.
Horatio Lloyd, Oct. 5, *vice* Vaughan Williams, res.

1875. Jno. Walter de Longueville Giffard, Mar. 15, *vice* Marshall, dec.; *d.* Oct. 23, 1888.
Wm Wynne Ffoulkes, May 6, *vice* Harden, dec.
1876. Jas. Motteram, Q.C., June 20, *vice* Cole, dec.; *d.* Sept. 19, 1884.
Fras. Barrow, Aug. 23, *vice* Miller, S.L., dec.; res. Nov. 1883.
1877. Wm. Downes Griffith, June 9, *vice* Whitmore, dec.
Vernon Lushington, Q.C., Oct. 1, *vice* Furner, res.
1878. Wm. Beresford, Jan. 1, *vice* Terrell.
Fras. Hy. Bacon, Nov. 23, *vice* G. L. Russell, dec.
1879. Arundel Rogers, Feb. 6, *vice* J. W. Smith, res.
Wm. Jas. Metcalfe, Q.C., Oct. 20, *vice* Fisher, dec.
1880. Hy. Holroyd, May 27, *vice* Spooner, dec.
Saml. Boteler Bristowe, Q.C., July 1, *vice* Worlledge, res.
Wm. Thos. Greenhow, Oct. 9, *vice* Lefroy, res.
1881. Fras. Roxburgh, Q.C., aft. sir F., May 1, *vice* Wildman, res.
Wm. Hy. Gunning Bagshawe, Q.C., July 1, *vice* Beales, dec.
Benjn. Thos. Williams, Q.C., Dec. 13, *vice* Falconer, res.; res. June 1885.
1882. Thos. Hughes, Q.C., July 21, *vice* Yates, res.
Wm. Lyon Selfe, Nov. 8, *vice* Herbert, dec.
1883. Arthur Shelly Eddis, Q.C., Feb. 1, *vice* Whitbread, dec.
Thos. Wm. Snagge, Mar. 31, *vice* Fortescue, dec.
Thos. Hudson Jordan, June 18, *vice* Wheeler, dec.
Jas. J. Hooper, Dec. 1, *vice* Barrow, res.
1884. Saml. Prentice, Q.C., Jan. 14, *vice* Dasent, res.
Wm. Stevenson Owen, Feb. 9, *vice* Sir G. Russell, res.
Gwilym Williams, Apr. 1, *vice* Lonsdale, res.
Jno. Jos. Powell, Q.C., Apr. 12, *vice* Daniel, res.
Mackenzie Dalzell Chalmers, Sept. 27, *vice* Motteram, dec.
Wm. Haworth Holl, Q.C., Dec. 19, *vice* Bradshaw, dec.
1885. David Brynmor Jones, July 1, *vice* B. T. Williams, res.
Philip Chasemore Ga tes, Q.C., Nov 2, *vice* Pitt-Taylo r, res.
1886. Jno. Bishop, Jan. 1, *vice* Sumner dec.
Wm. Paterson, Jan. 19, *vice* Petersdorff, res. 1885; *d.* 29 July, 1886.

1886. Millis Coventry, Mar., *vice* Hulton, res.
1887. Jno. Morgan Howard, Q.C., Nov., *vice* Bere, dec.
1888. Jas. Broughton Edge, Nov., Giffard, dec.
Jas. Mackonochie, Nov., *vice* Atl son, res.

SERJEANTS-AT-LAW.

See Introduction, *ante*, p. 348.

The serjeants formerly enjoyed the exclusive right of pleading in Court of Common Pleas during term time, but this privilege was a lished by 9 & 10 Vict. cap. 54 (Aug. 18, 1846).

The rule which required every judge of the common law courts take, or to have taken, the degree of a serjeant before his appointm was abolished by the Supreme Court of Judicature Act, 1873. Si that Act came into operation in 1875 no serjeants have been appoint and the order is gradually dying out. A few years ago, their inn sold and the proceeds divided amongst the then surviving members.

Full information concerning this ancient order will be found in S jeant Pulling's "Order of the Coif."

Serjeants-at-Law.

Those marked * were afterwards raised to the bench. *See* Lists of Judges, *a* where their subsequent promotions are noted.

K. signifies King's Serjeant; Q. Queen's Serjeant; C. Serjeant for the Comm wealth; P.P. Patent of Precedence.

1274–5.
*Thos. de Weyland, K.
*John de Metingham, K.
*John de Cobbeham, K.
*Elias de Beckingham, K.

1280–1.
*Gilbert de Thornton, K.
*Wm. de Giselham, K.

1291–2.
*Wm. Inge, K.

1292–3.
*Nichs. de Warwick, K.

1296–7.
Thos. le Mareschall, K.

1309–10.
*Roger le Scotre, ? K.
*Edmd. Passele, ? K.

1315–6.
*Wm. de Herle, ? K.
*Gilbert de Toutheby, K.
*Geoffrey le Scrope, K.
*John de Stonore, ? K.

1320–1.
John de Denum.

1329.
*Richd. de Aldeburgh, K.
*John de Cantebrig, K.

1330.
*John de Trevaignon, K.

1331.
*Wm. de Denum, K.
John de Munden.
*Wm. de Shareshull, K.
Richd. de Bellishall.
Thos. de Lincoln.

1334.
*Wm. Scot, K.
*Robt. Parning, K.
Simon de Trewythosa, K.
Lucas de Burgh, K.

1335.
Wm. de Hopton, K.

1338.
Arnold de Doresme, ? K.
— Spigurnel, K.

1340.
*John de Stovard, or St ford, K.

1341.
*Wm. de Thorpe, K.

1343.
*Thos. de Fencotes, ? K.

1344.
— Rokel, ? K.

1345.
*Robt. de Thorpe, K.
*Hy. Green, K.
*Thos. de Setone, K.

1346.
*Wm. de Notton, K.

1350.
— Burton, ? K.

1354.
*Wm. de Shipwith, K.
*John de Moubray, K.

1356.

Vm. de Fishide.

1357.

ohn Knyvet.

1362.

dmd. Chillery, K.
Vm. de Wychingham, K.
Vm. de Fyncheden, K.

1363.

— "Richm," ? K.

1366.

obt Bealknap, K.
oger de Meres, K.
ohn de Cavendish.
ohn de Fencotes.
— Hillam.
oger de Kirketon.
— Moris.
illardus de Ufflete.

1370.

oger de Fulthorpe, K.
Iy. de Percehay, K.

1371.

— Wakbruge, ? K.

1375.

Valter Persey, ? K.
avid Hannemere, K.

1377.

ohn Holt.
obt. Tresilian, K.
Valter de Clopton, K.
ohn de Middleton, K.

1383.

ohn Cary.
dmd. de Clay.
ohn Hill.
Vm. Rickhill, K.

1385.

ohn de Lokton, K.

1390.

ohn Markham, K.
ohn Wadham, K.
Vm. Hankford, K.
Vm. Brenchesley, K.

1397.

Vm. Gascoigne, K.

1399.

obt. Tirwhit, K.
Vm. Hornby, K.
obt. Hill, K.

1401.

ohn Read.
m. Frisby.

1402.

Thos. Tildeslegh, K.
*John Colepeper, K.

1407.

*Richd. Norton, K.

1408.

Wm. Skrene, K. 1413.

1410.

*John de Preston.
*Wm. Lodington, K. 1413.
*Jas. Strangeways, K. 1415.
*Wm. Cheyne.
John Barton, jun.
Walter Askham.
*John Martin.
Wm. Wynard.

1413.

*John Halls, K. 1413.

1415.

John Barton, sen.
Thos. Lopham.
Wm. Poulet.

1418.

*Wm. Babington.
*John Martin.
Wm. Pole.
*John Cotismore.
*Wm. Westbury.
*John Ivyn, or Juyn.
Thos. Rolfe.

1421.

*Wm. Paston.

1424.

John Ellarker.
*Wm. Goderede, K. 1430.
Wm. Hall.
*Richd. Newton.
*Thos. Fulthorpe.
Wm. Chantrell.
Robt. Caundish.
John Weston.

1429.

*John Fortescue, K. 1441.

1440.

*Wm. Yelverton.
*John Markham, K. 1443.
John Portington, K.

1443.

*Nichs. de Ayshtone.
*Richd. Bingham.
*Ralph Pole.
*Robt. Danby.
*John Prisot.
*Walter Moyle, K. 1454.
*Peter Arderne.
*Robt. Danvers, K.

1453.

Wm. Hyndestone.
*Wm. Laken.
Wm. Wangford.
Wm. Boeff.
*Thos. Lyttelton, K.
*Richd. Choke.
*John Needham, K. 1454.
Thos. Billing, K. 1456.

1463.

*Thos. Young, K.
*Richd. Neele, K. 1464.
*Wm. Jenney.
*Guy Fairfax, K. 1467.
*Thos. Brian.
John Grenefield.
*John Catesby, K. 1469.
Richd. Pigot, K. 1467.

1472.

Richd. Higham.

1478.

*Wm. Huse, or Hussey.
*Humphrey Starkey.
*Thos. Tremayle, K. 1481.
*John Sulyard.
*Wm. Calowe, or Collow.
*John Vavasour, K. 1483.
*Roger Townsend, K. 1483.
Thos. Brigges.
Thos. Rogers.

1481.

Walter Keeble.

1485.

*Thos. Wood, K. 1487.
*Robt. Read, K. 1493.
*John Haws.
*John Fineux.
*Wm. Danvers.
Thos. Keeble, K. 1498.
Richd. Jay.
*Wm. Hody.
John Huddersfield, K.
*John Fisher, K.

1494.

*Humphrey Coningsby, K. 1500.
*John Boteler.
Thos. Keeble.
Thos. Oxonbridge.
*Thos. Frowy.
Richd. Highkam, K. 1498.
John Kingsmill, K. 1496.
John Yaxley.
John Mordaunt, K. 1495.
Robt. Constable.

1502.

Wm Cutler.

1503.

— Brooke.
*Robt. Brudenell, K. 1504
Wm. Grevill.
Thos. Marrow.
Geo. Edgore.
*John More.
John Cutler.
*Richd. Eliot, K. 1506.
*Lewis Pollard, K. 1506.
Guy Palmer, K. 1513.
*Wm. Fairfax.
Thos. Piggot, K. 1513.

1504.

— Griffin.

1505.

John Newport.

1510.

John Newdigate, K. 1520.
Brian Palmys, jun.
John Carrell, K. 1514.
— Brooke.
John Roe.
*Anthy. Fitzherbert, K. 1516.

1520.

Baldwin Malet, called but exonerated.

1521.

Wm. Rudhale.
John FitzJames.
*John Port.
Thos. Fairfax.
*John Spelman, K. 1528.
John Brown.
*Wm. Shelley.
*Thos. Willoughby, K. 1530.
*Robt. Norwich, K. 1522.
*Thos. Englefield.

1531.

*Humphrey Brown, K. 1535.
*Thos. Audley, K.
*Walter Lake.
*John Baldwin, K.
*John Hinde, K. 1535.
*Christr. Jenney, K. 1535.
John Densell.
*Edmd. Mervin, K. 1539.
Edmd. Knightley.
*Roger Cholmley, K. 1544.
*Edwd. Montagu, K. 1537.
Roger York.
John Pakington, K.

1540.

Thos. Rushedon.
Robt. Townsend, K. 1543.
John Harris, K. 1546.
*Thos. Bromley, K.
John Carrell.
Robt. Chidley.
*Wm. Coningsby.
*Wm. Portman, K.
*Edwd. Saunders, K. 1547.
*Jas. Hales, K. 1544.
Jas. Missenden.

1542.

*Edwd. Molineux, K.

1547.

*David Brook, K. 1551.
*John Whiddon, K. 1551.
John Pollard.
Robt. Meynell.
*Richd. Morgan.
*Wm. Coke, K. 1550.
Wm. Croke.

1552.

*Jas. Dyer, K. 1552; Q. 1553.
John Carrell.
Thos. Gawdy, sen.
Richd. Catlin, Q. 1555 and 1566.
Ralph Rokeby.
*Wm. Staunford, Q. 1553.
*Wm. Dalison, Q. 1555.
Robt. Keilwey.
Robt. Brooke.

1555.

John Caryl.
John Prideaux, Q, 1558.
Geo. Wood.
*Fras. Morgan.
*Robt. Catlin, Q. 1556.
*Anthy. Browne, Q.
Geo. Seintpoll.
Wm. Bendlowes.
Geo. Brown.
John Walpole.
*Wm. Rastall.

1558.

*Thos. Carus, Q. 1562.
*Regd. Corbet.
*John Walsh.
*John Southcote.
Wm. Simmonds.
Geo. Wall.
*Richd. Harpur.
Ranulph Cholmley.
Nichs. Powtrell, Q. 1562.
John Birch.

1559.

*Richd. Weston, Q.

1566.

— Baker, Q.

1567.

*Thos. Gawdy.
*Roger Manwood.
*Christr. Wray, Q.
*Thos. Meade.
Nichs. Barham, Q. 1573
*John Jeffrey, Q. 1572.
Wm. Lovelace.

1572.

*Robt. Monson.

1577.

*Robt. Bell, Q.
*Wm. Ayloff.
Edwd. Baber.
*Fras. Wyndham.
*Fras. Gawdy, Q. 1582.
*Edmd. Anderson, Q. 15
*Robt. Shute.
*Edwd. Fenner.

1578.

*Fras. Rodes, Q. 1582.
*John Popham.

1580.

*John Clench.
*John Puckering, Q. 15 or 1588.
Thos. Walmsley.
Wm. Fleetwood, Q. 1592
*Edwd. Flowerdew.
Thos. Snagge, Q. 1590.
*Wm. Periam.
Robt. Halton.

1584.

*Thos. Gent.
*Richd. Shuttleworth.

1587.

Robt. Gardener.
*Robt. Clarke.

1589.

*Christr. Yelverton, Q. 15
Thos. Hamond.
Thos. Harris.
Edwd. Drew, Q. 1596.
John Cooper.
*John Glanville.
*Thos. Owen, Q. 1593.
*Fras. Beaumont.

1593–4.

Richd. Lewkenor.
*Peter Warburton.
Richd. Branthwaite.
*John Savile.
John Heale, Q. 1602.
*Thos. Fleming.
*David Williams.
*Matth. Ewens.
John Spurling.
*Geo. Kingsmill, Q.
*Edwd. Heron.
*Wm. Daniell, Q.

1601.

dmd. Pelham.

1603.

ohn Croke, K.
hos. Coventry, K. 1606
awrence Tanfield.
hos. Foster.
obt. Barker.
dwd. Phelips, K.
ugustine Nichols.
obt. Houghton.
hos. Harris.
enry Hobart.
as. Altham.
ohn Shirley.
eo. Snigg.
ichd. Hutton.
ohn Doderidge, K. 1607.
as. Ley.

1606.

dwd. Coke.
ohn Davies, K. 1612.
umphrey Winch.

1609.

ohn Denham.
dwd. Bromley.

1610.

y. Montagu, K. 1611.

1611.

m. Methwould.

1614.

obt. Hicham, K. 1616.
anulph Crewe, K.
eo. Wilde.
m. Towse.
ras. Moore.
ras. Hervey.
y. Finch, K. 1616.
hos. Chamberlayne.
hos. Athowe.
eonard Bawtry.
ohn More.
ohn Chibon.
hos. Richardson, K. 1624.

1616.

dwd. Henden.
m. Jones.

1617.

ras. Ashley, K. 1625.

1620.

ohn Shirley.
as. Whitelock.

1623.

eo. Croke, K.
ice Gwyn.
ohn Bridgman.
eneage Finch.
Richd. Amherst.
Thos. Crew, K. 1624.
*Humphrey Davenport, K. 1625.
Thos. Headley.
Fras. Crawley.
Richd. Diggs.
John Dany.
John Hoskins.
Egremont Thyn.
*John Bramston, K. 1634.

1625–6.

John Lloyd.
*John Walter, K.
*Thos. Trevor, K.
Hy. Yelverton, K.

1626–7.

*Nichs. Hyde, K.

1627–8.

Rowley Ward.
*Robt. Berkeley, K.
Wm. Ayloff.
*Robt. Callice.
*Geo. Vernon.

1631–2.

*Jas. Weston.
*Robt. Heath, K. 1637.

1633–4.

*Richd. Weston.

1634–5.

*John Finch.
Ralph Whitfield, K.

1635–6.

*Thos. Malet.

1636–7.

Timothy Leving.
*John Wilde.
*Robt. Foster.
Hy. Clarke.
Thos. Milwarde.
*Richd. Cresheld.
*Edmd. Reeve.
*John Godbolt.
*Arth. Turner.
Nath. Finch, K. 1640–1.
Gilbert Boone.
*Philip Jermyn.

1637–8.

John Glanville, K. 1640–1 and 1660.

1639–40.

*Edwd. Lyttleton.

1640–1.

John Stone.
John Whitwich.
*Hy. Rolle.
Wm. Lyttleton.
*Robt. Brerewood, K.
Robt. Hyde.
Richd. Taylor.
Edwd. Atkyns.
John Greene, C. 1650.
*Peter Pheasant.
*Fras. Bacon.
Sampson Evre (? Eyre), K. 1640–1.
*John Banks.

1643–4.

*Richd. Lane.

The following being called by the authority of Parliament only, the call was subsequently declared to be invalid. The survivors were subsequently recalled at the Restoration.

1648.

*Thos. Widdrington, K.; C. 1650.
*Thos. Bedingfield.
*Richd. Keble.
*Fras. Thorpe.
*John Bradshaw.
*Oliver St. John.
*Saml. Browne.
*John Glynne, C. 1654.
Erasmus Erle, or Earle, C. 1654.
*Bulstrode Whitelock, K.
Wm. Coniers.
*John Puleston.
Thos. Chapman.
*Thos. Gates.
Wm. Lyttleton.
Wm. Powel.
John Clerke.
John Eltonhead.
*Robt. Nicholas.
*John Parker.
Robt. Bernard.
Robt. Hutton, or Hatton.

1649.

*Peter Warburton.
*Alexr. Rigby.
Evan Seys.
*Richd. Aske.

1654.

*Richd. Pepys.
Thos. Fletcher.
*Matt. Hale.
*Wm. Steele.
*Richd. Newdigate.
Thos. Twisden.
*Hugh Wyndham.
*John Maynard, C. 1658
Unton Croke.

1655.

*Roger Hill.

1656.

Wm. Shephard.

1658.

*John Fountaine.
*John Archer.

1659.

*Thos. Tyrrell.
— Steel.
Thos. Waller.
— Wroth.
— Finch.
— Lynne.
John Corbet.
— Hyde.

June 1, 1660.

*Sir Orlando Bridgeman.

June 22, 1660.

At the Restoration the following fifteen old serjeants were recalled:—
*Sir Thos. Widdrington.
*Thos. Bedingfield.
*Saml. Brown.
*John Glynne, K.
Erasmus Earle.
Sir Robt. Bernard.
*Matthew Hale.
*John Maynard, K.
*Richd. Newdigate.
*Thos. Twisden.
*Hugh Wyndham.
John Fountain.
Evan Seys.
*John Archer.
Thos. Waller.

July 6, 1660.

*Thos. Tyrrell.
*Christr. Turner.
Geo. Beare.
Edmd. or Edwd. Hoskins.
*Wadham Wyndham.
*Job Charlton, K. 1668.
*Sir Wm. Morton, K. 1663.
John Parker.
John Merefield.
*John Kelyng, sen. K. 1661.
Chas. Holloway.
Chas. Dalison.
Thos. Broome, or Brome.

Oct. 5, 1660.

*Sir Wm. Wylde, K. 1661.
*Richd. Raynsford, or Rainsford.
Fredk. Hyde.

May 22, 1668.

*Sir John Vaughan.

Oct. 30, 1669.

Timothy Tourner, K. 1670.
*Wm. Ellis, or Ellys, K. 1671.
Nichs. Willmot.
Thos. Hardy, or Hardres, K. 1676.
Guibon Goddard.
Sir Richd. Hopkins.
Thos. Flint.
John Turner.
John Barton.
Sir John Howell.
*Fras. Bramstone.
Sir Hy. Peckham.
Christr. Goodfellow.
Saml. Baldwin, K. 1672.
Thos. Powys.
*Thos. Jones, K. 1671.
*Sir Wm. Scroggs, K. 1669.

1670.

*Timothy Littleton.

May 23, 1671.

*Sir Edwd. Turner.

April 24, 1672.

*Sir Robt. Atkyns.
*Sir Edwd. Thurland.

Jan. 23, 1673.

*Sir Fras. North.

April 21, 1675.

Edwd. Pecke, K.
Tristram Conyers.
Sir Thos. Skipwith, K. 1685.
Richd. Croke.
Sir Richd. Stote, K. 1676.
Sir Nichs. Pedley.
L'Estrange Calthorp, K.
Sir Robt. Shaftoe.
Fras. Barrell, or Barwell.
*Edwd. Rigby.
*Geo. Strode, K. 1676.
*Sir Fras. Pemberton, K.
Robt. Stevens.

June 4, 1675.

*Vere Bertie.

April 12, 1676.

*Wm. Montague.

Oct. 23, 1677.

Thos. Holt.
Thos. Rawlins.
*Wm. Gregory.
*Richd. Weston, K. 1678
Fras. Wingfield.
Geo. Johnson.
*Robt. Baldock, K. 1685
*Richd. Holloway, K 1683.
Thos. Strode.
Sir John Shaw, K. 1685
*Thos. Raymond.
*Sir Thos. Stringer, 1679.
*Thos. Street, K. 1678.
John Simpson, K.
*Sir Wm. Dolben, K.

May 7, 1679.

Edwd. Atkins.
Wm. Leake.

May 12, 1680.

*Sir Geo. Jeffreys, K.
Sir John Kelyng, jun.,
Robt. Hampson.
Edmd. West.
*Thos. Wallcott.
Sir John Boynton, 1685.
Edwd. Bigland.
Wm. Richardson.
Wm. Buckby, Bugby, Buckleby.
*Sir Robt. Wright, K.
Sir Fras. Manley.

Feb. 12, 1681.

*Sir Creswell Levinz, Levinge.

Jan. 23, 1682.

Edmd. Saunders.

April 23.

*Sir Fras. Wythens.

Jan. 23, 1683.

*Sir Thos. Jenner, K.
John Windham.
Edwin Wyatt.
Edwd. Birch.
*Hy. Bedingfield, K. 168
*Sir Edwd. Nevil, K. 168
Sir Paul Barret.
Anthy. Farrington.
John Jeffreson.
*Edwd. Lutwyche, K 1684.
*Richd. Heath.
Hy. Selby.
John Millington.
*Thos. Powell
Owen Wynne.
Sir Geo. Pudsey.

Oct. 23, 1685.
ir Edwd. Herbert.

Apr. 21, 1686.
ohn Holt, K.
hristr. Milton.
ohn Powell.
ohn Tate, K, 1688.
Vm. Rawlinson.
mbrose Phillips, K. and in 1693.
Vm. Killingworth.
ugh Hodges.
hos. Geeres.
eo. Hutchins, K. 1689 and 1693.

1687.
d. Allibone.
has. Ingleby.

June 18, 1688.
alathiel Lovell, K. 1695, Q. 1702.
y. Chauncey.
m. Moses.
ras. Fuller.
y. Trinder.
m. Thomson, K. 1689.
m. le Hunt.
ohn Rotherham.
incent Denn.

May 1, 1689.
y. Pollexfen.
ichs. Lechmere.
hos. Rookby, or Rokeby.
ohn Thurbone.
m. Woogen, or Wogham, K.
hos. or Wm. Powlett.
athl. Bond, K.
yles Eyres.
y. Hatsel.
ohn Blencow.
eyton Ventris.
oger Belwood.
ohn Tremayne, K.
ohn Trenchard, K. 1693.
ohn Turton.

Apr. 27, 1692.
r Geo. Treby.
aml. Eyre.
ras. Purley.
m. Coward.
m. Edwards (?).
eo. Prickett.
hos. Goodinge.
y. Gould, K. 1693.
oger Moore.
egd. Britland.
ohn Darnell, K. 1698, Q. 1702.
os. Girdler.

*Littleton Powys.
*Nathan Wright, K. 1697.
Chas. Bonython.

June 10, 1695.
*Sir Edwd. Ward.

Oct. 30, 1700.
John Green.
Chas. Whiteacre, K.
Thos. Gibbons.
*Thos. Bury.
John Keen.
Philip Neve.
Nichs. or Richd. Hooper, Q. 1702.
Hy. Turner.
*John Smith.
*Robt. Tracy
*Sir Jos. Jekyll, K.; Q. 1702; K. 1714.
Jas. Mundy.
John Hook.
Lawrence Agar.
*John Pratt.
Wm. Hall.
Jas. Selby.
Thos. Carthew.

July 5, 1701.
*Sir Thos. Trevor.

June 23, 1702.
*Sir Thos. Powys, Q.; K. 1714.
*Robt. Price.

June 8, 1705 (? 1706).
*Thos. Parker, Q.
Hy. Chetham.
Jas. or Jno. Grove.
*Wm. Banister.
John or St. John Brodrick.
Jos. Weld.
John Bennett.
Hy. Lloyd.
Richd. Wynne.
Richd. Richardson.
John Hoo.
John Birch, Q. 1712.
John Cheshire, Q. 1711; K. 1715.
*John Comyns.
Thos. Webb.

Feb. 11, 1706.
*Robt. Dormer.

May 12, 1710.
*Robt. Eyre.
*Thos. Pengelly, K. 1719.

Oct. 26, 1714.
*Sir Peter King.
*Sir Saml. Dodd.
*Sir Jas. Montague.

Jan. 24, 1715.
*Fras. Page, K.
Wm. Earle.
Hy. Stevens.
John Cuthbert.
Wm. Brydges.
Thos. Hanbury.
Edwd. Whiteacre.
Wm. Branthwayt.
John Belfield, or Benfield.
Wm. Salkeld.
Edwd. Miller.
Nathl. Meade.
*Jas. Reynolds

Dec. 3, 1716.
*John Fortescue Aland.

May 31, 1722.
*Jeffrey Gilbert.
*Alexr. Denton.

Jan. 27, 1724.
*Edmd. Probyn.
*Sir Robt. Raymond.

Feb. 1, 1724.
*Lawrence Carter, K.
Thos. Morley.
Fettiplace Nott.
Jos. Girdler, jun.
John Baynes.
John Raby.
Richd. Comyns.
Wm. Hawkins.
*Wm. Chapple, K. 1729.
Jas. Shepherd.
Eyles, or Giles, Eyre, K. 1736.
Matth. Skinner, K. 1745.

1725.
*Bernard Hale.

Oct. 24, 1727.
*Spencer Cowper.
Edwd. Corbet.

Nov. 17, 1729.
*Sir Wm. Thompson.
Simon Urlin (?)

June 13, 1730.
*Wm. Lee.
*Thos. Birch, K. 1745.

Apr. 14, 1733.
*Thos. Reeve.
*Martin Wright.

Union of the Serjeants of the Inn in Fleet Street with the Serjeants Chancery Lane.

April 23, 1733.

1733. Oct. 31. * Sir Philip Yorke.
1736. June 4. * Thos. Parker, K.
Thos. Hussey.
Abraham Gapper.
Robt. Price, jun.
* Michl. Foster.
* Thos. Burnet, K. 1740.
Wm. Wynne.
John Agar.
Richd. Draper.
Robert Johnson Kettleby.
Wm. Hayward.
Saml. Prime, K. 1745.
Thos. Barnardiston.
Edwd. Bootle.
* Wm. Fortescue.
1737. Jan. 27. * John Willes.
1740. June 11. * Jas. Reynolds.
Edwd. Willes (?), K. 1745.
Nov. 27. * Sir Thos. Abney.
Wm. Eyre (? 1745).
1742. Feb. 11. * Thos. Denison.
Edwd. Leeds, K. 1747.
* Chas. Clarke.
1745. May 1. * Edwd. Clive.
1747. June 23. Hon. Heneage Legge.
David Poole, K. 1757.
1750. June 23. * Nathl. Gundry.
* Sidney Stafford Smythe.
1753. Feb. 3. * Sir Richd. Adams.
Geo. Wilson.
1754. May 2. * Sir Dudley Ryder.
* Hon. Hy. Bathurst.
1755. Feb. 11. * Sir John Eardley Wilmot.
* Jas. Hewitt, K. 1759.
Lomax Martin.
Wm. Davy, K. 1763.
1756. Nov. 8. * Hon. Wm. Murray.
1757. May 3. * Hon. Wm. Noel.
Thos. Stanyford, or Stanyforth.
Jas. Forster, K. 1772.
1759. Feb. 6. Wm. Whitaker, K.
* Geo. Nares, K.
Anthony Keck.
Nov. 14. * Sir Richd. Lloyd.
1761. Nov. 7. * Hy. Gould.
Jos. Sayer.
1762. Jan. 23. * Sir Chas. Pratt.
* John Burland, K. 1764.
1763. Jan. 24. * Geo. Perrott.
John Glynn.
John Aspinall.
1764. Jan. 23. * Jos. Yates.
1765. Apr. 24. * Richd. Aston.
Wm. Jephson.
Richd. Leigh, K. 1771.
1768. Jan. 29. * Edwd. Willes.
1770. Feb. 12. * Wm. Blackstone.
1770. June 25. * Wm. Hy. Ashhurst.
1771. Jan. 24. * Wm. de Grey.
1772. May 13. Wm. Kempe.
Thos. Walker.
Harley Vaughan.
Nov. 6. * Sir Jas. Eyre.
Geo. Hill, K.
1774. Apr. 28. * Nash Grose.
Jas. Adair, K. 1782.
1775. May 17. * Sir Beaumont Hotham.
* John Heath.
1776. Apr. 26. * Sir Richd. Perryn.
1777. Nov. 27. * Sir John Skynner.
1778. May 6. * Fras. Buller.
1779. Nov. 29. Jas. Clayton Bolton.
1780. June 14. * Alexr Wedderburn.
1781. Feb. 8. Cranley Thos. Kirby.
* Giles Rooke, K. 1793.
1783. June 25. Thos. Davenport (?).
1786. May 27. Geo. Bond, K. 1795.
Nov. 6. * John Wilson.
1787. Feb. 9. * Sir Alexr. Thompson.
* Simon Le Blanc, K. 17
* Soulden Lawrence.
May. 7. Wm. Cockell, K. 1796.
Nov. 27. Chas. Runnington.
Saml. Marshall.
Jas. Watson.
1788. June 9. * Sir Lloyd Kenyon, bt.
Ralph Clayton.
1789. Nov. 13. Sir John Wm. Rose.
1793. Feb. 12. * Sir Archd. Macdonald.
1794. June 21. John Williams, K. 1804
Saml. Heywood.
1796. Feb. 9. Arthur Palmer.
Apr. 18. Saml. Shepherd, K.
1798. May 14. Baker John Sellon.
1799. Feb. 12. * John Vaughan, K. 181
June 12. John Lens, K. 1806.
* John Bayley.
July 2. * Alan Chambre.
16. * Sir John Scott.
1800. Jan. 24. * Wm. Draper Best, 1806.
June 16. * Robt. Graham.
Arthur Onslow, K. 1816
1801. Feb. 9. Wm. Mackworth Praed
May 22. * Sir Richd. Pepper Ard
1802. Apr. 12. * Sir Edwd. Law.
1804. Apr. 24. * Jas. Mansfield.
1805. Feb. 4. * Sir Thos. Manners Sutt
1807. May 28. * Geo. Wood.
1808. May 30. Wm. Manley.
Albert Pell, K. 1819.
Wm. Rough.
1809. May 15. Robt. Hy. Peckwell.
Wm. Frere.
1812. May 29. * Sir Vicary Gibbs.
1813. June 23. * Hy. Dampier.

813. July 6. * John Singleton Copley, K. 1819.
Nov. 18. * Sir Robt. Dallas.
814. Feb. 26. * Richd. Richards.
Nov. 22. * John Bernard Bosanquet, K. 1827.
816. Jan. 20. * James Alan Park.
Feb. 12. * Chas. Abbott.
20. * Geo. Sowley Holroyd.
May 4. * Jas. Burrough.
June 18. * John Hullock.
817. Feb. 11. Wm. Firth.
May 6. * Sir Wm. Garrow.
818. June 10. Wm. Taddy, K. 1827.
Nov. 30. * John Richardson.
819. Feb. 9. Vitruvius Lawes, P. P. 1834.
John Cross, K. 1827.
Thos. D'Oyley, P. P. 1834.
820. Feb. 9. Thos. Peake, P. P. 1834.
824. Jan. 6. * Sir Robt. Gifford.
* Wm. Alexander.
May 4. * Jos. Littledale.
13. Wm. St. Julien Arabin. P. P. 1834.
* Thos. Wilde, K. 1827.
July 5. * Stephen Gaselee.
Robt. Spankie, P. P. 1830; K. 1832.
John Adams, P. P. 1834.
827. June 25. Thos. Andrews.
Henry Storks, P. P. 1834.
Ebenezer Ludlow, P. P. 1834.
Hy. Alworth Merewether, K. 1832.
Wm. Oldnall Russell.
Edwd. Hobson Vitruvius Lawes.
David Fras. Jones, aft. Atcherley-Jones; P. P. 1830; K. 1832.
27. John Scriven, P. P. 1834.
Hy. John Stephen, P. P. 1834.
Chas. Carpenter Bompas, P. P. 1834.
828. Nov. 18. * Jas. Parke.
829. Feb. 4. Edwd. Goulburn, P. P. 1834.
June 5. * Sir Nicolas Conyngham Tindal.
Nov. 16. * Wm. Bolland.
830. Nov. 11. * Wm. Elias Taunton.
* John Patteson.
* Edwd. Hall Alderson.
22. Geo. Thos. Heath, P. P. 1834.
32. Feb. 14. * John Gurney.
* John Taylor Coleridge, P. P. 1834.
Nov. 7. * Sir Thos. Denman.
33. Jan. 29. * Thos. Noon Talfourd, P. P. 1834; Q. 1846.
34. Feb. 28. * John Williams.

1834. Dec. 24. Sir Jas. Scarlett.
1837. Feb. 24 * Thos. Coltman.
1839. Jan. 9. * Hon. Thos. Erskine.
Feb. 14. * Wm. Hy. Maule.
Nov. 11. * Sir Robt. Monsey Rolfe.
1840. Feb. 19. * Wm. Shee, P. P. 1844; Q. 1857.
Digby Cayley Wrangham, Q. 1857.
* Wm. Fry Channell, P. P. 1845.
Jas. Manning, P. P. 1845; Q. 1846.
John Halcombe.
June 19. Wm. Glover.
Stephen Gaselee, jun.
1841. Feb. 17. * Wm. Wightman.
July 6. John Vincent Thompson.
1842. Jan. 27. * Creswell Creswell.
Feb. 25. Francis Stack Murphy, P. P. 1847.
June 16. Herbert Geo. Jones.
Nov. 12. Alfred Septimus Dowling.
1843. Feb. 6. Nathl. Richd. Clarke.
14. * John Barnard Byles, P. P. 1847; Q. 1857.
1844. Apr. 15. * Sir Fredk. Pollock.
July 10. Chas. Chadwicke Jones.
John Alexr. Kinglake, P. P. 1849.
Edwd. Bellasis.
Nov. 7. * Wm. Erle.
1845. Jan. 28. * Thos. Joshua Platt.
July 3. Robt. Allen, P. P. 1850.
Nov. 12. Edwin Sandys Bain.
Chas. Wilkins, P. P. 1850.
1846. Oct. 27. * Edwd. Vaughan Williams.
1848. July 14. Arnold Wallinger.
1850. Mar. 5. * John, ld. Campbell.
July 16. * Sir John Jervis.
Nov. 7. * Saml. Martin.
19. Robt. Miller.
1852. Feb. * Chas. Crompton.
Trin. Vac. Robt. Matthews.
Ralph Thomas.
1853. Mich. Vac. Geo. Atkinson.
1854. Mar. * Richd. Budden Crowder.
1855. Hil. Vac. Humphry Wm. Woolrych.
July. * Jas. Shaw Willes.
1856. Jan. * Geo. Wm. Wilshere Bramwell.
Hil. Vac. * Geo. Hayes, P. P. 1861.
* Gillery Pigott, P. P. 1857.
Mordaunt Lawson Wells.
Wm. Ballantine, P. P. 1864.
John Humffreys Parry, P. P. 1864.
Nov. * Wm. Hy. Watson.
* Sir Alexr. Jas. Edmd. Cockburn.
1858. East. Vac. Wm. Payne.
John Cross.
John Tozer.
Chas. Erdman Petersdorff.
May. * Hugh Hill.

1859. June. * Colin Blackburn.
Mich. Term. Peter Burke.
Dec. * Sir Hy. Singer Keating
1860. April. * Jas. Plaisted Wilde.
1861. Feb. 23. Thos. Wheeler, **G.**
Dec. * John Mellor.‡
1862. May 13. Michael Wm. O'Brien, **G.**
Fredk. Lowten Spinks, **G.**
1864. Feb. 9. John Simon, **G.**, P. P. 1868.
Alexr. Pulling, **G.**
Hy. Tindal Atkinson, **G.**
1865. Feb. * Montague Edwd. Smith.
17. Benjn. Coulson Robinson, **G.**, P. P. 1874.
Nov. 2. * Robt. Lush, **G.**
1866. July 16. * Sir Fitzroy Edwd. Kelly, **G.**
Nov. 29. * Sir Wm. Bovill, **G.**
1868. Feb. 25. * Jas. Hannen, **G.**
May 29. Edwd. Wm. Cox, **G.**
July 24. Wm. Campbell Sleigh, **G.**
1868. July 24. Augustine Sargood, **G.**, P. P. 1872.
Aug. 24. * Sir Wm. Baliol Brett, **G.**
25. * Anthy. Cleasby, **G.**
1871. Nov. * Sir Robt. Porrett Collier.†
30. * Wm. Robt. Grove, **G.**
1872. Jan. 9. * John Richd. Quain, **G.**
Oct. 17. * Hon. Geo. Denman, **G.**
Nov. 20. * Thos. Dickson Archibald **G.**
1873. Jan. 10. * Chas. Edwd. Pollock, **G.**
23. * Sir Geo. Essex Honyman, bt., **G.**
Nov. 19. * Sir John Duke Coleridge, **G.**
1874. Jan. 24. * Richd. Paul Amphlett, **G.**
1875. Feb. * Wm. Ventris Field.
22. * John Walter Huddleston, **G.**
May 12. * Nathl. Lindley, **G.**

† There is some doubt whether this gentleman was created a serjeant on his elevation to the bench. Serjeant Pulling omits him from his list, giving his reasons for doing so.

KING'S COUNSEL. QUEEN'S COUNSEL. HOLDERS OF PATENTS OF PRECEDENCE.

See Introduction, *ante*, p. 349.

Those marked * were afterwards raised to the bench. *See* "Lists of Judges," *ante* where their subsequent promotions are noted.

Holders of Patents of Precedence are marked P.P.

QUEEN ELIZABETH.

*Fras. Bacon?

KING JAMES I. TO KING JAMES II.

Aug. 25, 1604.

*Sir Fras. Bacon, *again* (?).
*Sir Hy. Montagu?

According to *Pulling* there were no other appointments until 1668; but *Foss* gives the following:—

Mar. 17, 1626.

*John Finch.

Nov. 15, 1632.

Geo. Ratcliffe.

Oct. 7, 1634.

Richd. Shilton.

July 31, 1641.

Thos. Levingston.

Oct. 1, 1646.

Precedence granted by Parliament:

*John Wilde.
*Saml. Browne.
*Edmd. Prideaux.

1660.

Thos. Levingston, *again.*

1668.

*Fras. North.
— Miller.

1670.

*Wm. Jones.

1671.

Fras. Goodricke.

1672.

Fras. Winnington.

1673.

*John Churchill.

1674.

John King.

1678.

*Geo. Jeffreys?
*Creswell Levinz, or Levinge.
*John Kelyng, jun.

1679.

Jas. Butler.

1681.

*Wm. Scroggs, jun.

1683.

*Thos. Jones.
Roger North.
*Fras. Wythens.
*John Trevor.

Feb. 1685.

The following were appointed or re-appointed by Jas. II. on his accession:—

J. Ottway.
Jas. Butler, *re-app.*
*Thos. Hammer.

Wm. Scroggs, *re-app.*
Edwd. Herbert.
Roger North, *re-app.*
Thos. Jones., *re-app.*
Oliver Montague.

Nov. 1686.

Richd. Allibone.

William III.

Wm. Aglionby.
Edwd. Clerk.
Jno. Conyers.
Wm. Cowper.
Wm. Farrar.
John Hawles.
Roger North, *re-app.*
— Osborne.
Nathl. Powell.
Wm. Whitlock.
Wm. Williams.

Anne.

1702.

Wm. Whitlock, *re-app.*
John Conyers, *re-app.*
Wm. Cowper, *re-app.*
Wm. Jennings.

1706.

Wm. Aglionby, *re-app.*
Jas. Montagu.

1707.

Robt. Eyre.

17—.

Edwd. Jeffreys.
Thos. Lutwyche.
John Ward.

George I.

There are no regular lists xtant, but the following ames occur :—
Winnington Jeffreys.
John Willes.

George II.

Kings Counsel and Holders of Patents of Precedence arranged alphabetically :—
*Thos. Abney.
*Richd. Aston.
Hy. Banks.
*Hy. Bathurst.
Thos. Bootle.
A. Hume Campbell.
*Thos. Clarke.
*Wm. De Grey.
*Wm. Fortescue.
*Hy. Gould.
*Nathl. Gundry.
Eliab Harvey.
*Robt. Henley.
Paul Joddrell.
Matth. Lamb.
*Heneage Legge.
*Richd. Lloyd.
John Morton.
*Wm. Noel.
Fletcher Norton
*Geo. Perrott.
*Chas. Pratt.
*Thos. Reeve.
*Thos. Sewell.
*Sidney Stafford Smythe.
*John Strange.
John Trevor.
*John Verney.
*Edwd. Willes.
*Chas. Yorke.

George III.

To the end of 1799.

King's Counsel and Patents of Precedence arranged alphabetically :—
Anthy. Thos. Abdy.
Wm. Adam.
*Wm. Alexander.
Chas. Ambler.
John Anstruther.
*Richd. Pepper Arden.
Daines Barrington.
Edwd Bearcroft.
*Wm. Blackstone.
Nathl. Bond.
Foster Bower.
*Fras. Buller.
*Jas. Burrough.
Fras. Burton.
Richd. Clayton.
Thos. Cooper.
Fras. Cottayne Cust.
Geo. Dallas.
Thos. Davenport.
Sylvester Douglas.
*Hon. Thos. Erskine, No. 1.
*Wm. Garrow.
*Vicary Gibbs.
*Robt. Graham.
*Wm. Grant.
Geo. Harding.
Hy. Howarth.
Rd. Hussey.
Rd. Jackson.
Jos. Jekyll.
*Lloyd Kenyon.
*Edwd. Law.
John Lee.
Hugh Leycester.
John Lloyd.
*Archd. Macdonald.
John Maddocks.
*Jas. Mansfield.
Jno. Mitford.
Jno. Morton.
Geo. Lewis Newnham.
*Jas. Alan Park.
Hy. Partridge.
Spencer Perceval.
*Rd. Perryn.
*Thos. Plumer.
*Chas. Pratt.
Griffith Price.
*Rd. Richards.
Saml. Romilly
*John Scott.
Wm. Selwyn.
*Jas. Skynner.
*Thos. Manners Sutton.
*Edwd. Thurlow.
Jas. Wallace.
John Richmond Webb.
*Alexr. Wedderburn.
John Frost Widmore.

King's and Queen's Counsel and Patents of Precedence, in Order of Date, from 1800 to the present time.

George III.

1804. East. Term.

Richd. Hollist.
Thos. Milles.
Geo. Wilson.
Jas. Topping, P. P.
Jas. Fonblanque, P. P.

1806. Hil. Term.

Thos. Jervis, P. P.

1806. East. Term.

Fras. Hargrave.
Philip Dauncey, P. P.

1807. Hil. Term.

Chas. Thomson.
*Anthy. Hart.
Hy. Martin.
*John Leach.

1808. Trin. Vac.

Nathl. Goodwin Clarke.

1816. East. Term.

*Jas. Burrough.
Chas. Warren.
John Raine.
*Jas. Scarlett.
Jas. Trower.
Wm. Cooke.
Saml. Yate Benyon.
Wm. Agar.
John Bell.
Chas. Wetherell, P. P.
Wm. Harrison.

1816. Mich. Term.

Saml. Marryat.
*John Gurney.

1818. Mich. Term.

Archd. Cullen.
Wm. Owen.
Wm. Wingfield.
Wm. Horne.
Geo. Heald.

1818. Mich. Vac.

Giffin Wilson.
Nichl. Nolan.
*Stephen Gaselee.
Robt. Matth. Casberd, P.P.

George IV.

1820. East. Term.

P. P. renewed with former rank:—

John Fonblanque.
Thos. Jervis.
Chas. Wetherell.

Made K. C.

R. M. Casberd.

1822. Hil. Term.

*Wm. Elias Taunton.
Christr. Puller.
Wm. Geo. Adam.
*Lancelot Shadwell.
*Edwd. Burtenshaw Sugden.

1826. Michs. Term.

*Chas. Christr. Pepys.

1827. East. Vac.

*Hy. Brougham, P.P.
Thos. Crosby Treslove.
*Hy. Bickersteth.
*Geo. Rose.
*John Williams.
*John Campbell.
*Fredk. Pollock.
Horace Twiss.

1827. Trin. Vac.

Chas. Fredk. Williams.
Wm. Selwyn.
*Hon. Thos. Erskine, No. 2.

1828. Michs. Term.

*Thos. Denman, P. P.

1829. Trin. Vac.

Thos. Pemberton.
*Jas. Lewis Knight, aft. Knight-Bruce.
Hon. Chas. Ewan Law.
Wm. Hy. Tinney.

William IV.

1830. Trin. Vac.

Made K. C. with former rank:—

Thos. Jervis.
Sir Chas. Wetherell.
*Hy. Brougham.

P. P. renewed with former rank:—

*Jno. Fonblanque.
*Thos. Denman.

1830. Michs. Vac.

Robt. Spankie, serjt.; P. P. next after F. Pollock.
David Fras. Jones, aft. Atcherley-Jones, serjt.; P. P. next after C. E. Law.
*Thos. Coltman.

1831. East. Term.

Wm. Walton.

1831. Trin. Term.

Wm. Fuller Boteler.
John Aug. Fras. Simpkinson.

1831. Trin. Vac.

Chas. Butler.
Hy. Wm. Tancred.
Philip Williams.
Fras. Ludlow Holt.

1832. Trin. Vac.

John Beames.
Hy. Hall Joy.
Clement Tudway Swanston, No. 1.
*Robt. Monsey Rolfe.

1833. Hil. Vac.

David Pollock.
Philip Courtenay.
John Blackburne.
*Wm. Hy. Maule.

1833. Trin. Vac.

John Balguy.

1834. April 25.

By warrant under the sign-manual it was declared that all barristers should after the first day of Trinity Term have an equal right with the serjeants to practice in the Common Pleas. By the same warrant, precedence was given to the following serjeants, to rank immediately after John Balguy:—

Vitruvius Lawes.
Thos. D'Oyly.
Thos. Peake.
Wm. St. Julien Arabin.
John Adams.
Thos. Andrews.
Hy. Storks.
Ebenezer Ludlow.
John Scriven.
Hy. Jno. Stephen.
Chas. Carpenter Bompas.
Edwd. Goulburn.
Geo. Thos. Heath.
John Taylor Coleridge.
Thos. Noon Talfourd.

The warrant was declare[d] a nullity by the Court [of] Common Pleas in Hilar[y] Term, 1840; but the exclu[]sive privileges of the ser[]jeants was ultimately abo[l]ished by 9 & 10 Vict., cap[.] 54 (Aug. 18, 1846).

1834. Trin. Vac.

*Fredk Thesiger, July 7.
Matth. Davenport Hil[l], P. P., July 7.
*Wm. Erle, July 7.
*Cresswell Cresswell, Aug. 2[]

1834. Mich. Term.

Richd. Preston.

1834. Mich. Vac.

Wm. Webb Follett.
Danl. Wakefield.
Walker Skirrow.
Christr. Temple.
Chas. Hy. Barber.
John Miller.
Geo. Spence.
*Richd. Torin Kindersley.
Wm. Burge.
Edwd. Jacob.
*Jas. Wigram.
Hy. John Shepherd
*Thos. Josh. Platt.
*Fitzroy Kelly.

1835. Hil. Vac.

Robt. Alexander.
Thos. Starkie.

1835. Trin. Term.

Basil Montagu.

1837. Hil. Vac.

Fras. J. Newman Rogers, Feb. 24
Biggs Andrews, Feb. 24.
Geo. Chilton, Feb. 24.
Jno. Evans, Feb. 24.
Richd. Budden Crowde[r], Feb. 24.
*John Jervis, P. P.
*Jas. Fras. Whitmarsh.
Chas. Purton Cooper.

1839. Hil. Vac.

Wm. Goodenough Hayter, P. P.
Saml. Girdlestone.
Robt. Vaughan Richards.
*John Stuart.
Griffith Richards.

1840. Hil. Vac.

Robt. Baynes Armstrong, Feb. 21; to rank before
*Geo. Jas. Turner } Feb. 17.
David Dundas. } Feb. 17.
*Richd. Bethell. } Feb. 17.

1841. Trin. Vac.

Wm. Whately } July 6.
Richd. Godson } July 6.
Sutton Sharpe } July 6.
Chas. Jas. Knowley } July 6.
Matth. Talbot Baines } July 6.
Chas. Austin, P. P. } July 6.
Hon. Jas. Stuart Wortley } July 6.
*Alexr. Jas. Edmd. Cockburn.

1841. Mich. Term.

Edwd. Wilbraham.
Wilkinson Matthews.
John Herbert Koe.
John Godfrey Teed.
Wm. Loftus Lowndes.
Thos. Purvis.
John Walker.
Kenyon Stevens Parker.
Jas. Russell.
Robt. Prioleau Roupell.
Thos. Oliver Anderdon.
Loftus Tottenham Wigram.

1843. Hil. Vac.

Digby Cayley Wrangham, serjt. P. P.

1843. East. Term.

Sir Geo. A. Lewin.
Hon. John C. Talbot.
*Saml. Martin.
John Arthur Roebuck.
*Wm. Hy. Watson.

1843. Mich. Vac.

*John Romilly.

1844. Trin. Vac.

John Hodgson.
Wm. John Alexander.
Chas. H. Whitehurst.
Robt. Chas. Hildyard.
*Jas. Parker.

1845. Hil. Vac.

Jas. Manning, serjt. P. P.
*Wm. Fry Channell, serjt. P. P.
Wm. Lee.
Lebbens Chas. Humfrey.
John Billingsley Parry.
*Wm. Page Wood.
Russell Gurney.
Geo. Medd Butt.
Abrm. Hayward.

1845. Trin. Vac.

*Wm. Shee, serjt.; P. P. after W. P. Wood, *supra*.
Montagu Chambers.

1846. Trin. Vac.

Jos. Humphry.
*Jas. Bacon.
Spencer Horatio Walpole.
*John Rolt.

1847. Trin. Vac.

Fras. Stack Murphy, serjt.; P. P. after A. Hayward, *supra*.
*John Barnard Byles, serjt.; P.P. after F. S. Murphy.

1847. Mich. Term.

Chas. Buller.

1849. Hil. Vac.

Jno. Alex. Kinglake, serjt.; P.P. after J. Rolt, *supra*.
Edwd. John Lloyd.
John Greenwood.
*Richd. Malins.
Fred. Calvert.
*Hy. Singer Keating.
*Roundell Palmer.
Jas. Robt. Hope, P. P.

1850. Hil. Vac.

Michl. Prendergast.
Hy. Bliss.
Chas. Sprengel Greaves.
Wm. Chas. Townsend.
Christr. Argyle Hoggins.
Wm. Carpenter Rowe.
Thos. Colpitts Granger.
Peter Fredc. O'Malley.
Barnes Peacock.
Edwin John James; disbarred, Trin. Vac. 1861.
Kenneth Macaulay.

1850. Mich. Term.

Robt. Allen, serjt. P. P.
Chas. Wilkins, serjt. P. P.

1851. Trin. Vac.

Robt. Ingham.
Jas. Campbell.
Thos. Chandless.
Wm. Elmsley.
John Wm. Willcock.
Walter Coulson.
Graham Willmore.
Wm. Thos. Shave Daniel.
Fredk. Wm. Slade.
John Baily.
John Geo. Phillimore.
Brent Spencer Follett.
*John Mellor.
Wm. Bulkeley Glasse.
Richd. Davis Craig.
Saml. Warren.
Robt. Pashley.
*Geo. Wm. Wilshere Bramwell.
Jas. Anderson.
Thos. Emerson Headlam.
Wm. Atherton.
*Hugh Hill.
Chas. Jas. Hargreave.

1853. Hil. Vac.

*Wm. Milbourne James.
Hy. Alworth Merewether.

1853. Trin. Vac.

Stephen Temple.
Edwd. James.
*Montagu Edwd. Smith.
*Wm. Robt. Grove.

1854. Trin. Vac.

Peter Erle.
Thos. Phinn, P. P.
Edmd. Beckett Denison.
*Robt. Porrett Collier, P. P.

1854. Mich. Vac.

Hy. Ridgard Bagshawe.

1855. Trin. Vac.

Chas. Shapland Whitmore.
Wm. Overend.
Percival Andw. Pickering.
*Jas. Plaisted Wilde.
*Wm. Bovill.

1856. Hil. Vac.

*Chas. Jasper Selwyn.
*Hugh McCalmont Cairns.

1857. Trin. Vac.

Hon. Edwd. Phipps.
Chas. F. F. Wordsworth.
John Locke.
*Gillery Pigott, serjt. P. P.
Allan Maclean Skinner.
*John Walter Huddlestone.
*Robt. Lush.
John Monk.
Wm. Forsyth.
*Hy. Manisty.

1857. Mich. Vac.
Evelyn Bazalgette.
John Shapter.
Saml. Bush Toller.
Thos. Webb Greene.
Fras. Hy. Goldsmid.
*Richd. Paul Amphlett.
Jas. Fleming.

1858. Hil. Term.
Sir John Dorney Harding.
Jesse Adams.
*Robt. Jos. Phillimore.
Jas. Parker Deane.
Travers Twiss.

1858. East. Term.
David Power.

1858. Mich. Vac.
Benj. Bridges Hunter Rodwell.
*Geo. Markham Giffard.
*Hy. Hawkins.

1859. Trin. Term.
Jno. Hinde Palmer.
Archd. Jno. Stephen.
Wm. David Lewis.

Feb. 22, 1861, **G.**
*Geo. Hayes, serjt. P. P.
Wm. Dugmore.
Wm. Anthy. Collins.
*Anthy. Cleasby.
Hy. Warwick Cole.
John Fraser Macqueen.
Thos. Chambers.
Edwin Plumer Price.
Josiah Wm. Smith.
*Richd. Baggallay.
Hy. Mills.
Hon. Adolphus Fred. Octavius Liddell.
*Wm. Baliol Brett.
John Burgess Karslake.
Wm. Digby Seymour.
*John Duke Coleridge.
*Hon. Geo. Denman.
*Geo. Mellish.

Feb. 5, 1862, **G.**
Wm. Matthewson Hindmarch.
Geo. Boden.
Thos. Weatherley Phipson.

Nov. 1, 1862, **G.**
John Robt. Kenyon.
Thos. Southgate.
Arthur Hobhouse.

Nov. 29, 1862, **G.**
John Osborne.
Jas. St. Geo. Burke.

Feb. 3, 1863, **G.**
Geo. Stovin Venables.

June 20, 1863, **G.**
Geo. Loch.

Nov. 4, 1863, **G.**
Wm. Hy. Cooke.
John Gray.
John Jos. Powell.

Jan. 12, 1864, **G.**
Wm. Ballantine, serjt. P. P.

Feb. 9, 1864, **G.**
John Humffreys Parry, serjt. P. P.

Feb. 13, 1864, **G.**
David Deedy Keane.
John James Johnson.
*Wm. Ventris Field.

July 7, 1864, **G.**
John Lee.
John Bridge Aspinall.

Feb. 17, 1865, **G.**
Thos. Webster.
Sir Thos. Phillips.
Jos. Brown.
Clement Milward.
Jas. Redford Bulwer.
*Hardinge Stanley Giffard.

Mar. 30, 1865, **G.**
John Peter De Gex.
Joshua Williams.
Edwd. Fras. Smith.
*Geo. Jessel.
John Shapland Edmonds Stock.

Jan. 9, 1866, **G.**
Hy. Hopley White.
Hon. Anthy. John Ashley.
Hy. Wm. Cripps.
John Robt. Davison.
Wm. Geo. Granville Venables Vernon Harcourt.

June 26, 1866, **G.**
John Blossett Maule.

July 23, 1866, **G.**
Jas. Dickinson.
Robt. Scarr Sowler.
Saml. Prentice.
Thos. Jones.
*Chas. Edwd. Pollock.
Wm. Adam Mundell.
Richd. Garth.
*Sir Geo. Essex Honyman, bt.
*John Richd. Quain.

Dec. 13, 1866. **G.**
Thos. Spinks.
Jos. Trigge Schomberg.
Harris Prendergast.
Geo. Morley Dowdeswell
Chas. Greville Prideaux.
Benj. Hardy.
Geo. Little.
Hy. Thos. Cole.
*John Pearson.
Fras. Roxburgh.
Thos. Jas. Clark.
*Hy. Cotton.
Edwd. Kent Karslake.
Geo. Druce.
*Edwd. Ebenezer Kay.
Thos. Kingdon Kingdon.

Feb. 21, 1868, **G.**
John Simon, serjt. P. P.
Wm. Wyllys Mackeson.
Martin Archer Shee.
John Clerk.
John Archd. Russell.
Edwd. Vaughan Richard
Edwd. Vaughan Keneale patent cancelled Dec. 1874.
Wm. Housman Higgin.
Hy. Wyndham West.
Hy. Matthews.
Alexr. Staveley Hill.
Horace Lloyd.
*Jas. Fitzjames Stephen.
John Holker.
Clement Tudway Swanton, No. 2.
Robt. Stuart.

Dec. 8, 1868, **G.**
Wm. Golden Lumley.
Edmd. FitzMoore.
Sir Patrick MacChombai de Colquhoun, LL.D.
Granville Robt. Hy. Somerset.
*Chas. Parker Butt.
Vernon Lushington.

June 22, 1869, **G.**
Arthur Robarts Adams.
Wm. Cracroft Fooks.
Arthur Shelley Eddis.
Douglas Brown.
Hy. Fox Bristowe.
Peter Hy. Edlin.
Thos. Hughes.
Montagu Bere.
Jos. Kay.
Henry James.
*Hy. Chas. Lopes.
Geo. Osborne Morgan.
*Edwd. Fry.
Saml. Pope.

Feb. 5, 1872, **G.**

Augustine Sargood, serjt. P. P.
Thos. Chas. Renshaw.
Leofric Temple.
Chas. Wm. Wood.
Æneas John McIntyre.
Wm. John Bovill.
Saml. Boteler Bristowe.
*John Chas. Day.
John Berry Torr.
*Nathl. Lindley.
Jos. Napier Higgins.
Thos. Halhed Fischer.
Jas. Kemplay.
Theodore Aston.
Alexr. Edwd. Miller.
Chas. Arthur Russell.
*Farrer Herschell.

1872. Trin. Term.

Judah Philip Benjamin, P. P.

Nov. 1, 1872.

John Farley Leith.
*Alfred Wills.

Feb. 3, 1873, **G.**

Wm. Jas. Metcalfe.
Thos. Hardwicke Cowie.
Morgan Lloyd.
Jas. Wm. Bowen.
*Watkin Williams.
*Hy. Mather Jackson.
Ralph Daniel Makinson Littler.

July 3, 1873, **G.**

*Hon. Alfred Hy. Thesiger.

Feb. 5, 1874, **G.**

Chas. Clark.
Thos. Ewing Winslow.
Saml. Joyce.
Fredk. Waller.
Wm. Hy. Gunning Bagshawe.
Wm. Pearson.
Chas. Hy. Hopwood.
John Westlake.
*Jos. Wm. Chitty.
John Patrick Murphy.
Alfd. Geo. Marten.
Robt. Griffith Williams.
Arthur Cohen.
Saml. Danks Waddy.

Mar. 19, 1874, **G.**

Philip Chasemore Gates.
Fredc. Andw. Inderwick.
Edwd. Hy. Pember.
Fredk. Adolphus Philbrick.
Geo. Parker Bidder.

1874. Trin. Term.

Benj. Coulson Robinson, serjt. P. P.
Alborough Henniker.
Wm. Talfourd Salter.
Hy. Rowcliffe.
John Morgan Howard.
Wm. Ambrose.
John Edwards.

June 28, 1875, **G.**

Thos. Campbell Foster.
Jas. Olliff Griffits.
Chas. Locock Webb.
Geo. Wirgman Hemming.
Jas. Motteram.
Graham Hastings.
Hy. Bret Ince.
Thos. Hy. Baylis.
Wm. Fothergill Robinson.
Benj. Thos. Williams.
*Lewis Wm. Cave.
Montague Hughes Cookson; aft. Cookson-Crackanthorp.
John Wm. Mellor.
Horace Davey.
John Eldon Gorst.

July 7, 1876, **G.**

Andw. Richd. Scoble.

Feb. 14, 1877, **G.**

Wm. St. Jas. Wheelhouse.
Chas. Geo. Merewether.
Wm. Haworth Holl.
Wm. Geo. Harrison.
Fredk. Meadows White.
Wm. Patchett.
Chas. Marshall Griffith.
Thos. Richardson Kemp.
John Compton Lawrance.
Wm. Court Gully.
Arthur John Hammond Collins.
Wm. Willis.
*Arthur Charles.
Marston Clarke Buszard.
*Wm. Grantham.
Hy. Mason Bompas.
Wm. Thackeray Marriott.

May 7, 1877, **G.**

Edwd. Jas. Bevir.
*Ford North.
*Arthur Kekewich.
Richd. Horton Smith.

April, 1878.

Wm. Hy. Michael.
Richd. Everard Webster.

Mar. 24, 1880, **G.**

Hy. Geo. Allen.
Wm. Shaw.
Fredk. Bailey.
Edgar Rodwell.
Jas. Jones Aston.
Fredk. Waymouth Gibbs.
Edmd. Swetenham.
Geo. Browne.
Wm. Cole Beasley.
Fredk. Chas. Jas. Millar.
Lumley Smith.
Wm. Potter.
Jos. Underhill.
John Edmd. Wentworth Addison.
Arthur Richd. Jelf.
John Thos. Crossley.
Edwd. Geo. Clarke.
Sir Wm. Thos. Charley.
Wm. Comer Petheram.

Apr. 23, 1880, **G.**

*Edwd. Macnaghten.

May 31, 1880, **G.**

Jos. Graham.

Mar. 21, 1881, **G.**

Thos. Hutchinson Tristram.
Eugene Comerford Clarkson.
Hon. Edwd. Chandos Leigh.
Herbert Clifford Saunders.
John Forbes.

Apr. 25, 1881, **G.**

Jas. Chas. Whitehorne.
Wm. Wollaston Karslake.
Hugh Shield.
John Rigby.
Robt. Romer.

June 2, 1881, **G.**

Chas. Hall.

Jan. 18, 1882, **G.**

Fras. Wm. Everitt Everitt.
Wm. Barber.
Herbert Hardy Cozens-Hardy.
Pembroke Scott Stephens.
Philip Albert Myburgh.
Jos. Addison McLeod.
Chas. Crompton.
Hy. Alexr. Giffard.
John Freeman Norris.
Robt. Bannatyne Finlay.
Wm. Bowen Rowlands.

Mar. 14, 1882, **G.**

Edwd. Cooper Willis.

Mar. 31, 1882, **G.**

Fras. Savage Reilly.

Dec. 16, 1882, **G.**

Robt. John Biron.
Jas. Anstie.
Hugh Cowie.

John Stratford Dugdale.
Fredk. Albert Bosanquet.
Cornelius Marshall Warmington.
Robt. Threshie Reid.
Frank Lockwood.

Oct. 27, 1883, **G.**

Richd. Henn Collins.
John Chas. Bigham.
Gainsford Bruce.
Fredk. Thos. Durell Ledgard.
John Shiress Will.
Walter Geo. Frank Phillimore, P. P.

July 2, 1885, **G.**

Saml. Taylor.
Sir Arthur Townley Watson, bt.
Arthur Moseley Channell.
Robt. Augs. Bayford.
Chas. Isaac Elton.
Thos. Townsend Bucknill.
John Lawrence Gane.
Wm. Rann Kennedy.
Danl. O'Connell French.
John Fletcher Moulton.

July 13, 1885, **G.**

Fras. Whittaker Bush.
Jas. Marshall Moorsom.
Chas. Hy. Anderson.
Fredc. Octavius Crump.
Hy. David Greene.
John Hutton Balfour Browne.

Nov., 1885.

Wm. Speed.
Benj. Fras. Williams.
Geo. Pitt Lewis.
Chas. John Darling.

May, 1886.

Wm. Lloyd Birkbeck.
John Horne Payne.
John Edge.
Fras. Wm. Maclean.
Clement Higgins.
Alfd. Cock.

Nov., 1886.

Edwd. Cutler.
Wm. Latham.
Emanuel Maguire Underdown.

Walter Chas. Renshaw.
Thos. Whittenbury Wheel[e]
Lindsey Middleton As[h]land.
Hy. Burton Buckley.
Geo. Candy.
Edwd. Tindal Atkinson.
Seward Wm. Brice.
Kenneth Augs. Muir Ma[c]kenzie.

Feb. 13, 1888, **G.**

Geo. Deedes Warry.
Montagu Stephen Wil[l]iams.
Richd. Harris.
David Nasmith.
Arthur Ruscombe Poole.
Edmd. Widdrington Byr[ne].
Wm. Phipson Beale.
Fras. Hy. Jeune.
Edwd. Jas. Castle.
Thos. Milvain.
Saml. Hall.
Ralph Neville.
Hy. Winch.
John Gorell Barnes.

JUDGES OF THE ECCLESIASTICAL COURTS.

DEANS OF THE ARCHES.

From the reign of Henry VIII.

See Introduction, *ante*, p. 349.

1541. Richd. Gwent.
1543. John Cockys.
1545. Wm. Cooke.
1549. Griffin, or Griffith Leyson.
1556. David Pole; bp. of Peterborough in 1557, but lost his preferments in 1559, refusing to take the oath of supremacy.
1557. Hy. Cole; app. dean of St. Paul's by queen Mary, and dean of the arches by cardl. Pole.
1558. Nichs. Harpisfeld.
1559. Wm. Mowse; being unwilling to take the oath of supremacy, he was superseded by
Sir Hy. Hervie, founder of the college of *Doctors' Commons.*
Robt. Weston, aft. sir R.; dean until 1567, when he was made ld. chanc. Ireland, and also became a ld. just. in that kingdom.
1567. Thos. Yale, one of the high comm[r] under queen Elizabeth.
1573. Barthw. Clerk.
1590. Richd. Cosin, chanc. of the dioce[se] of Worcester; *d.* 1598.
* * Thos. Byng, dean in 1598.
1598. Sir Danl. Dun.
1618. Sir Wm. Bird.
1624. Sir Hy. Marten.
1634. Sir John Lamb, chanc. to Quee[n] Henrietta Maria; dean until 164[7].
1647. * * * * *
1660. Sir Geiles Sweit, principal of Alb[an] Hall.
1672. Sir Robt. Wyseman.
1684. Sir Richd. Lloyd.
1686. Sir Thos. Exton.
1694. Geo. Oxenden, master of Trinity Ha[ll].
1703. Sir John Cooke.
1710. John Bettesworth, dean until 1751.
1751. Sir Geo. Lee.

1758. Edwd. Simpson, aft sir E.
1764. Sir Geo. Hay.
1778. Peter Calvert, Oct. 17; *d.* 1788.
1788. Sir Wm. Wynne, knt., Aug. 22.
1809. Sir John Nicholl, res. 1834; *d.* 1838.
1834. Sir Herbert Jenner (Fust).
1852. Sir John Dodson.
1858. Stephen Lushington, July 2; res. 1867; *d.* Jan. 19, 1873.
1867. Sir Robt. Jos. Phillimore; knt., aft. bt., Aug. 23; res. 1875; *d.* Feb. 4, 1885.
1875. Jas. Plaisted, ld. Penzance, Oct. 20.

Under the Pub. Worship Regn. Act, 1874 (37 & 38 Vict. cap. 85), ld. Penzance was app. judge of the Provincial Courts of Canterbury and York, and, as such, he, on the resignation of Sir R. J. Phillimore, became Dean of Arches and Master of Faculties.

JUDGES OF THE PREROGATIVE COURT OF CANTERBURY.

From the reign of King Henry VIII.

See Introduction, *ante*, p. 349.

1545. John Barbar.
1548. Wm. Cooke.
* * Hy. Cole; died in confinement.
1558. Walter Haddon.
1559. Wm. Mowse; removed.
1560. Wm. Parker, aft. Sir W.
Wm. Drurye.
1576. Wm. Lewen; m. in chanc.
1598. Sir John Gibson.
1611. Sir John Benet, or Bennet; judge in this year; but there is no record of his appointment.
1622. Sir Wm. Byrde, or Bird, June 29.
1624. Hy. Marten, Aug. 28.
1641. Sir Wm. Mericke, Sept. 28. Lost his preferments during the Commonwealth; but recovered them at the Restoration.
* * John Godolphin, Wm. Clarke, and Chas. Geo. Cocke; joint commrs. under the Commonwealth.
1658. Wm. Purefoy, June 7.
1659. Walter Walker; app. by the Commonwealth, Mar. 12.
* * Wm. Turner, aft. Sir W.; app. a short time before the Restoration
1668. Sir Leoline Jenkins, Feb. 6; sec. st., 1680; *d.* 1685.
1685. Richd. Raines; judge this year, but no record of his appointment; knt. 1686.
1710. Sir Chas. Hedges, late sec. st., Jan. 10.
1714. John Bettesworth, June 11; *d.* Dec. 1751.
1751. Sir Geo. Lee, M.P., Dec. 20.
1758. Edwd. Simpson, Dec. 2.
1764. Sir Geo. Hay, June 4.
1778. Peter Calvert, Oct. 13.
1788. Sir Wm. Wynne, Aug. 25.
1809. Sir John Nicholl, Jan. 20.
1834. Sir Herbert Jenner (Fust), Oct. 21.
1852. Sir Jno. Dodson.

This office was abolished and the jurisdiction of the Court transferred to the courts of Probate and Divorce by 20 and 21 Vict. cap. 77.

(*See list of judges of those courts, ante, p.* 391.)

VICARS GENERAL TO THE ARCHBISHOP OF CANTERBURY.

From the reign of King Henry VIII.

1543. John Cockys.
1556. David Pole.
1557. Henry Cole.
1559. Wm. Mowse.
1561. Thos. Yale; *d.* 1577.

* * * * *

1583. Richd. Cosin, M.P.
* * Wm. Aubrey; *d.* 1595.
* * Sir Edwd. Stanhope; *d.* 1609.
* * John Cowell, mast. of Trinity Hall; *d.* 1611.
* * Sir Thos. Crompton.
* * Sir Thos. Ridley; *d.* 1629.
1621. Sir Nathl. Brent.
* * Sir Robt. Wyseman; *d.* 1684.
1688. Geo. Oxenden, master of Trinity Hall; *d.* 1703.
1703. John Cooke.
1710. John Bettesworth.

1714. Geo. Paul; *d.* Mar. 1755.
1755. Sir Geo. Hay.
1764. Peter Calvert; res.
1778. Sir Wm. Wynne; res.
1788. Wm. Scott; aft. Sir W. and ld. Stowell; res.
1821. Jas. Hy. Arnold, res.
1832. Herbert Jenner, aft. sir H. Jenner (Fust); res.
1834. Sir John Nicholl; *d.* Aug., 1838.
1838. John Nicholl, aft. sir J.; res.
1844. Sherrard Beaumont Burnaby; *d.* 1849.
1849. Sir John Dodson; res. 1852.
1852. Travers Twiss; knt. 1867; res. 1872.
1872. Jas. Parker Deane; knt. Aug. 1, 1885.

JUDGES OF THE CONSISTORY COURT.

Chancellors of the Diocese of London.

From the reign of King Henry VIII.

1520. Richd. Foxfoord, under bp. Stokesley, chanc. until 1539.

* * * *

1540. John Croke.
1561. Thos. Huick, or Huycke.
1574. John Hamond, or Hammonde.
1583. Sir Edwd. Stanhope.
1607. Sir Thos. Crompton.
1611. Thos. Edwards.
1616. Hy. Marten, aft. sir H.
1627. Arthur Ducke.
1637. Sir Richd. Chaworth.
1663. Sir Thos. Exton.
1685. Sir Hy. Newton.
1715. Humphrey Henchman.
1739. John Andrew.
1747. Sir Edwd. Simpson.
1759. John Bettesworth.
1764. Sir Geo. Hay.
1779. Sir Wm. Wynne.
1788. Wm. Scott; aft. sir W. and ld. Stowell.
1821. Sir Christr. Robinson.
1828. Stephen Lushington; res. 1858.
1858. Travers Twiss; knt. 1867; res. 1872.
1872. Thos. Hutchinson Tristram.

KING'S OR QUEEN'S ADVOCATES.

From the commencement of the Eighteenth Century.

See Introduction, *ante*, pp. 349.

1701. Sir John Cooke, July 25.
1715. Sir Nathl. Lloyd, Jan. 13.
1727. Geo. Paul, Jan. 26.
1755. Geo. Hay, aft. sir G., Apr. 23.
1764. Jas. Marriott, aft. sir J., Sept. 11.
1778. Wm. Wynne, aft. Sir W., Nov. 2.
1798. John Nicholl, aft. Sir J., Nov. 6.
1809. Sir Christr. Robinson, Mar. 1.
1828. Herbert Jenner, aft. Sir H. Jenner (Fust), Feb. 28.
1834. John Dodson, Oct. 18; knt. Oct. 29.
1852. Jno. Dorney Harding, Mar. 5; knt. Mar. 24; res. 1862.
1862. Robt. Jos. Phillimore, Sept. 12; knt. Sept. 17.
1867. Travers Twiss, Aug. 27; knt. Nov. 4; res. 1872.

The office has not since been filled up.

JUDGES OF HIGH COURT OF ADMIRALTY.

From the reign of Henry VIII.

See Introduction, *ante*, pp. 349-50.

1514. Christr. Myddleton, or Middylton.
1524. John Tregonwell, aft. sir J.
1542. Anthy. Huse.
1549. Richd. Lyell.
Griffith Leyson.
1554. Wm. Cooke.
1558. David Lewes, or Lewis.
1575. David Lewes and sir John Harbert, joint commrs.
1584. Julius Cæsar; aft. sir J., m. rolls and commr. gr. seal.
* * Valentine Dale; *d.* Nov. 1589.
* * Sir Thos. Crompton, after the death of Dale.

1608. Sir Danl. Dun, and sir Richd. Trevor, joint. commrs., Feb. 7.
1617. Sir Hy. Marten, or Martin.
1641. Richd. Zouch, app. by the E. of Northumberland, ld. h. adm.
1643. Wm. Sams; *d.* Oct. 1646.
1647. Wm. Clark and John Exton, joint commrs.
1648. Isaac Dorislaus, added to Clark and Exton, Apr.; app. by the Commonwealth.
1649. Wm. Clark and John Exton, continued by patent from the parlt. Feb. 15.
Wm. Stephen and Nathl. Bacon, added, Aug. 30.
1653. John Godolphin and Chas. Geo. Cocke, added to Clark, by Cromwell.
1654. The same, by patent dated Oct. 28.
1658. Godolphin and Cocke; patent renewed by Richd. Cromwell.
1659. Walter Walker, app. 1st judge.
Sir Wm. Turner, app. 2nd judge.
1660. Richd. Zouch, re-app.
Thos. Hyde, app. by the D. of York ld. h. adm., Mar. 12.
1661. John Exton, re-app by the D. of York, Oct. 26.
1668. Sir Leoline Jenkins, knt., originally app. by the D. of York; aft. sec. st.
1673. Sir Robt. Wyseman, Aug. 12.
1685. Sir Richd. Lloyd, Oct. 1.
1686. Sir Thos. Exton, July 6.
Sir Richd. Raines, Dec. 17.
1689. Chas. Hedges, aft. Sir C., June 1.

* * * *

1714. Humphrey Henchman, June 22.
Sir Hy. Newton. on the death of Henchman, Dec. 1.
1715. Hy. Penrice, Aug. 23.
1751. Sir Thos. Salusbury, Dec. 19; *d.* Nov. 1773.
1773. Sir Geo. Hay, Nov. 4.
1778. Sir Jas. Marriott, Oct. 12.
1798. Sir Wm. Scott, aft. ld. Stowell, Oct. 26.
1828. Sir Christr. Robinson, Feb. 22.
1833. Sir John Nicholl, May 30; *d.* Aug., 1838.
1838. Stephen Lushington, Oct. 17; res. 1867.

Court removed from Doctors Commons to Westminster Hall by Order in Council, dated Jan. 23, 1860.

1867. * Sir Robt. Jos. Phillimore, Aug. 23; cr. a bt. Dec. 15, 1881.

* Transferred on Nov. 1, 1875, to the High Court of Justice Prob., Div., and Adm. Division under Supreme Court of Judicature Acts, 1873 and 1875 (see *ante*, pp. 350-1.)

(See judges of that division, ante, p. 391.)

ADMIRALTY ADVOCATES.

From the Restoration of King Charles II. to the present time.
See Introduction, *ante*, p. 350.

1661. Wm. Turner, Oct. 29.
1674. Richd. Lloyd, May 19; *vice* sir Walter Walker, whose appointment does not seem to be recorded.
1685. Thos. Pinfold, Sept. 13.
1686. Wm. Oldyss, or Oldiss, July 17.
1693. Fisher Littleton, Sept. 17.
1694. Hy. Newton, *pro tem.*; Littleton being absent from indisposition, Jan. 26; permanently app. Mar. 16, 1697.
1704. Nathl. Lloyd, deputy, during the absence of Newton, Nov. 15.
1714. Hy. Penrice, Oct. 28.
1715. Richd. Fuller, Aug. 15.
1727. Exton Sayer, Mar. 30.
1731. Edmd. Ishan, Oct. 1.
1741. Wm. Strahan, Mar. 20.
1748. Thos. Salusbury, Aug. 9.
1751. Chas. Pinfold, jun., Nov. 14.
1756. John Bettesworth, Feb. 15.
1764. Geo. Harris, June 14.
1782. Wm. Scott, aft. sir W. and ld. Stowell, May 1.
1788. Thos. Bever, Sept. 4.
1791. Wm. Batline, Nov. 12.
1809. Sir Christr. Robinson, Mar. 1.
1811. Jas. Hy. Arnold, Nov. 25.
1829. John Dodson, aft. sir J., Mar. 11.
1834. Jos. Phillimore, Oct. 25.
1855. Robt. Jos. Phillimore, aft. sir R.
1862. Travers Twiss, aft. sir T.
1867. Jas. Parker Deane; knt. Aug. 1, 1885.

RECORDERS AND COMMON SERGEANTS OF THE CITY OF LONDON.

See Part VIII. "London," *post*.

PART VII. ECCLESIASTICAL.

ARCHBISHOPS, BISHOPS, AND DEANS OF ENGLAND AND WALES.

THE ecclesiastical government of England and Wales is divided into two provinces, Canterbury and York. Canterbury comprises the dioceses of—

Bangor.	Lichfield.	St. Albans.
Bath and Wells.	Lincoln.	St. Asaph.
Canterbury.	Llandaff.	St. David's.
Chichester.	London.	Salisbury.
Ely.	Norwich.	Southwell.
Exeter	Oxford.	Truro.
Gloucester and Bristol.	Peterborough.	Winchester.
Hereford.	Rochester.	Worcester.

and York the dioceses of—

Carlisle.	Manchester.	Sodor and Man.
Chester.	Newcastle-on-Tyne.	Wakefield.
Durham.	Ripon.	York.
Liverpool.		

By 26 Hen. VIII., cap. 14 (1534), power was given to the crown to appoint bishops suffragan to assist the other bishops in their duties. Under this act sundry appointments were made, but after 1567 the act remained in abeyance until 1870, when the practice of appointing bishops suffragan was revived. The following are the titles of the suffragan bishoprics.

Bedford.	Hull.	Penrith.
Berwick.	Ipswich.	Shaftesbury.
Bristol.	Leicester.	Shrewsbury.
Colchester.	Marlborough.	Taunton.
Dover.	Nottingham.	Thetford.
Guildford.		

The bishop of Sodor and Man has a seat in the House of Lords by courtesy, but cannot vote. The two archbishops and the bishops of London, Durham, and Winchester, always have seats; but since the

10 and 11 Vict. cap. 108 (July 23, 1847), the first of the Acts under which the number of bishoprics was increased, only 21 of the other bishops, according to seniority of consecration, are allowed to sit. In the following lists the bishops of each province are, for convenience, arranged in alphabetical order, but the archbishops of Canterbury and York, and the bishops of London, Durham, and Winchester rank in the order named, and then the other bishops in the order of their consecration.

Each diocese with the exception of—

Liverpool.	Sodor and Man.	Truro.
Newcastle.	Southwell.	Wakefield.
St. Albans.		

has a dean and chapter as well as a bishop.

There are also the following deans and chapters which are not attached to any diocese:

Westminster. Windsor (Chapel Royal).

PROVINCE OF CANTERBURY.

DIOCESE OF BANGOR.

This see is of very great antiquity: the founder is unknown. St. Daniel was bishop here about the year 516, but, for nearly five hundred years afterwards, there is no certain record of the names of his successors.

By the first general report of the Ecclesiastical Commissioners for England, under 6 and 7 Vict. cap. 77 (Aug. 22, 1843), the union of the sees of Bangor and St. Asaph was recommended to take place on the avoidance of the sees, or on the avoidance of either, with the consent of the other bishop; and to this end, an order in council was gazetted Jan. 25, 1839; but public opinion subsequently set in so strongly (particularly in Wales) against this union, that the order was, in effect, annulled by 10 and 11 Vict. cap. 108 (July 23, 1847), and the two sees still subsist separately.

BISHOPS OF BANGOR.

516. St. Daniel.

* * * * *

1107. Hervey, or Hervæus, tr. to Ely.
1109. Urban, also bp. of Llandaff.
1120. David, a Scot.
1139. Mauritius, or Meuricus.
1162. William, prior of St. Austin's, in Bristol.
1177. Guy, Guido, or Guianus.
See vacant 4 years.
1195. Albanus, prior of St. John of Jerusalem.
1197. Robt. de Shrewsbury.
1215. Caducan I.
1236. Howel I.
1240. Richard.
1267. Anianus, archdn. of Anglesey.
1303. Caducan II.
1306. Griffith, or Griffin ap Yerward.
1320. Lewis I. succ. according to *Heylyn*; but
Anian Seys, according to *Le Neve*, in 1309.
1327. Matth. de Englefeld.

1357. Thos. de Ringstede.
1366. Gervase de Castro.
1370. Howel II.
1371. John Gilbert, tr. to Hereford.
1375. John Swaffham, bp. of Cloyne, in Ireland; styled Jo. Clovensis by *Heylyn*.
1400. Richd. Young, tr. to Rochester.
1405. Lewis II.; great uncertainty as to this appointment.—*Le Neve*.
1408. Benedict Nichols, tr. to St. David's.
1418. Wm. Barrow, canon of Lincoln; tr. to Carlisle.
1424. Nicholaus, or John Clederow, canon of Chichester.
1436. Thos. Cheryton.
1448. John Stanbery, or Stanbury, confessor to Henry VI., first provost of Eton; tr. to Hereford.
1454. Jas. Blakedon, bp. of Achad-Fobhair, an ancient bishopric in Ireland.
1464. Thos. Ednam, *alias* Richd. Evynden.
1496. Hy. Dean, prior of Lanthony and ld. chanc. of Ireland; tr. to Salisbury.
1500. Thos. Pigot.
1504. John Penny, tr. to Carlisle.
1509. Thos. Skeffington, abbot of Waverly.
1534. John Salcott, *alias* Capon, abbot of Hyde; tr. to Salisbury.
1539. John Bird, the last provincial of the Carmelites; tr. to Chester.
1541. Arth. Bulkeley; *d.* Mar. 1552.
See vacant 3 years.
1555. Wm. Glynn, master of Queen's College, Cambridge.
1559. Rowland Merrick, chanc. and residentiary of St. David's.
1566. Nichs. Robinson.
1585. Hugh Bellot, tr. to Chester.
1595. Richd. Vaughan, archn. of Middlesex; tr. to Chester.
1598. Hy. Rowlands.
1616. Lewis Bayley.
1631. David Dolben, vicar of Hackney.
1633. Edmd. Griffith, dean of Bangor.
1637. Wm. Roberts, sub-dean of Wells.
1666. Robt. Morgan, archdn. of Merioneth.
1673. Humphrey Lloyd, dean of St. Asaph.
1689. Humphrey Humphreys, dean of Bangor; tr. to Hereford.
1701. John Evans, tr. to Meath, in Ireland.
1715. Benjn. Hoadley, rector of St. Peter's-le-Poor, London; tr. to Hereford.
1721. Richd. Reynolds, dean of Peterborough; tr. to Lincoln.
1723. Wm. Baker, warden of Wadham College, Oxford; tr. to Norwich.
1728. Thos. Sherlock, dean of Chichester; tr. to Salisbury.
1734. Chas. Cecil, tr. from Bristol.
1737. Thos. Herring, dean of Rochester; tr. to York.
1743. Matth. Hutton, tr. to York.
1748. Zacariah Pearce, dean of Winchester; tr. to Rochester.
1756. John Egerton, dean of Hereford; tr. to Lichfield and Coventry.
1769. John Ewer, tr. from Llandaff.
1774. John Moore, dean of Canterbury; tr. to Canterbury.
1783. John Warren, tr. from St. David's.
1800. Wm. Cleaver, Apr. 5; tr. from Chester; tr. to St. Asaph.
1806. John Randolph, Dec. 13; tr. from Oxford; tr. to London.
1809. Hy. Wm. Majendie, Aug. 12; tr. from Chester; *d.* July 9, 1830.
1830. Christr. Bethell, Oct. 10; tr. from Exeter; *d.* Apr. 19, 1859.
1859. Jas. Colquhoun Campbell, archdn. of Llandaff; May 12, **G.**

DEANS OF BANGOR.

603. Jago Ab Beli.
* * Arthur De Bardsey.
* * Adam Decan.
* * Kyndelw.
* * William.
* * Anian Sais.
* * Adam Elias Kenrick.
1359. Hywel Ab Gronow.
* * John David Daron.
* * Wm. Pollard.
1410. Hy. Honore.
1413. Roger Wodhele.
1416. J. Vantort.
* * Nigellus Bonde z.
* * J. Martyn.
* * Hugh Alcock.
* * Hugh Morgan.
* * Nichs. Rewys.
144–. Richd. Kyffin y Deon Du.
1504. Richd. Cowland.
1534. John Glynn.
* * Robt. Evans.
1554. Rhese Powel.
1570. Rowland Thomas.
* * Hy. Rowlands.
1599. Richd. Parry; bp. St. Asaph, 1603.
1605. J. Williams.
1613. Edmd. Griffith; bp. Bangor, 1633.
1634. Gr. Williams.
1673. W. Lloyd; bp. Bangor 1680.
1680. Humphrey Humphreys; bp. Bangor, 1689.
1689. J. Jones.

1727. Peter Maurice.
1750. Hugh Hughes.
1753. Thos. Lloyd.
1793. John Warren.
1838. John Hy. Cotton.
1862. Jas. Vincent Vincent.
1876. Hy. Thos. Edwards.
1884. Evan Lewis.

DIOCESE OF BATH AND WELLS.

THE diocese, although it has a double name, is but one bishopric. The church was built at Wells in 704, and was erected into a bishopric in 905. John de Villula, the sixteenth bishop, having purchased the city of Bath of Hen. I. for 500 merks, transferred his seat to that city in 1088. From this, disputes arose between the monks of Bath, and the canons of Wells, about the election of a bishop; but they were at length compromised by Robert the eighteenth bishop, who decreed that thenceforward the bishop should be styled from both places, that the precedency should be given to Bath; that, in the vacancy of the see, the bishop should be elected by a certain number of delegates from both churches; that he should be installed in them both; that both should constitute the bishop's chapter; and that all his grants and patents should be confirmed in both. So matters stood until the Reformation, when by 35 Hen. VIII., cap. 15, it was enacted that the dean and chapter of Wells should make one sole chapter for the bishop.

In 1538 a bishop suffragan of Taunton was appointed to this see under 26 Hen. VIII., cap. 14, but no subsequent appointments have been made.

BISHOPS OF WELLS.

905. Athelm, or Adelmus, abbot of Glastonbury; tr. to Canterbury.
915. Wolphelmus, or Wulfhelme, or Wulfelm I.; tr. to Canterbury.
924. Elphegus, or Alphegus.
942. Wolphelmus, or Wulfelmus II.
958. Brithelmus, monk of Glastonbury.
973. Kinewardus, or Kinewaldus, abbot of Middleton.
985. Sigarus, abbot of Glastonbury.
997. Alwinus, or Ealfwyn.
1005. Burwaldus, or Burwold.
1008. Leovingus, Livingus, or Elstan; tr. to Canterbury.
1013. Ethelwyn; exp.; rest. 1023.
1021. Brithwyn; exp.; rest. 1024.
1025. Merewith, abbot of Glastonbury.
1031. Dudoco, or Bodeca, of Saxony or Lorraine.
1059. Giso, a Frenchman.

BISHOPS OF BATH AND WELLS.

1088. John de Villula, a Frenchman.
1123. Godfrey, or Godefridus, chanc. to the queen.
1135. Robert, monk of Lewes, Sussex; *d*, 1165.
See vacant 9 years.
1174. Reginald FitzJoceline; tr. to Canterbury.
1192. Savaricus, archdn. of Northampton, and abbot of Glastonbury; whither he removed the bishopric.
1205. Joceline, canon of Wells; *d*. 1242.
The see vacant 2 years.
1244. Roger, chanter of Salisbury.
1247. Wm. Bitton, or Button I., archdn. of Wells.
1264. Walter Giffard, canon of Wells, ld. chanc.; tr. to York.
1267. Wm. Bitton, or Button II., archdn. of Wells.
1274. Robt. Burnel, archdn. of York, ld. chanc. and ld. treasr.
1292. Wm. de Marchia, dean of St. Martin's, ld. treasr.
1302. Walter Haselshaw, dean of Wells.
1310. John Drokenesford, kpr. of the king's wardrobe, and dep. to the ld. treasr.

1329. Ralph de Shrewsbury.
1363. John Barnet, tr. from Worcester; ld. treasr.; tr. to Ely.
1366. John Harewell, chanc. of Gascoigne; chaplain to the Black Prince.
1386. Walter Skirlow, or Skirlaw; tr. from Lichfield and Coventry; tr. to Durham.
1388. Ralph Ergham, or Erghum; tr. from Salisbury.
1401. Richd. Clifford; app. to this see, but before consecration tr. to Worcester.
1402. Hy. Bowet, canon of Wells; tr. to York.
1408. Nichs. Bubwith, or Bubbewith; tr. from Salisbury.
1425. John Stafford, dean of Wells, ld. treasr.; tr. to Canterbury; ld. chanc.
1443. Thos. Beckyngton, warden of New College, Oxford; kpr. pr. seal.
1465. Robt. Stillington, archdn. of Taunton; ld. chanc.
1492. Richd. Fox; tr. from Exeter; tr. to Durham, 1494.
1495. Oliver King; tr. from Exeter.
1504. Adrian de Castello, cardl.; tr. from Hereford; dep. by Pope Leo X.
1518. Thos. Wolsey, cardl.; abp. of York, and ld. chanc.; he held this see *in commendam*, and res. it 1522.
1523. John Clark, m. rolls, dean of Windsor.
1541. Wm. Knight, sec. st., preb. of St. Paul's.
1549. Wm. Barlow, tr. from St. David's; depr. by Queen Mary. See *Chichester*.
1554. Gilbert Bourde, or Bourn, preb. of St. Paul's; ld. pres. of Wales.
1559. Gilbert Berkeley; *d.* 1581.
See vacant 3 years.
1584. Thos. Godwin, dean of Canterbury; *d.* 1590.
See vacant 2 years.
1592. John Still, master of Trinity College, Cambridge, and preb. of Westminster.
1608. Jas. Montague, dean of Worcester.
1616. Arthur Lake, dean of Worcester, and master of St. Cross.
1626. Wm. Laud; tr. from St. David's; tr. to London.
1628. Leonard Mawe, master of Trinity College, Cambridge.
1629. Walter Curle; tr. from Rochester; tr. to Winchester.
1632. Wm. Piers, or Pierce; tr. from Peterborough.
1670. Robt. Creighton, dean of Wells.
1672. Peter Mew, or Mews, dean of Rochester; tr. to Winchester.
1684. Thos. Ken, preb. of Winchester; depr. for not taking the oaths to William and Mary.
1691. Richd. Kidder, dean of Peterborough; *d.* 1703.
1703. Geo. Hooper, tr. from St. Asaph.
1727. John Wynne, tr. from St. Asaph.
1744. Edwd. Willes.
1774. Chas. Moss, tr. from St. David's; *d.* 1802, aged 91 years.
1802. Richd. Beadon, Apr. 17; tr. from Gloucester; *d.* Apr. 21, 1824.
1824. Geo. Hy. Law, May 8; tr. from Chester; *d.* Sept. 22, 1845.
1845. Hon. Richd. Bagot, Oct. 14; tr. from Oxford; *d.* May 15, 1854.
1854. Robt. John, ld. Auckland, June 2, **G**.; tr. from Sodor and Man; res. Sept. 6, 1869.
1869. Arthur Chas. Hervey, c.c. ld. Arthur Chas. Hervey, archdn. of Sudbury, Nov. 11, **G.**

BISHOPS SUFFRAGAN OF TAUNTON.

1538. Wm. Finch.

DEANS OF WELLS.

1150. Ivo.
1160. Richd. de Spakeston.
1180. Alexander.
1205. Leonius.
1218. Ralph de Lechlade.
1220. Peter de Ciceter.
1236. Wm. de Merton.
1241. Joanes Saracenus.
1253. Giles de Bridport; bp. Salisbury, 1256.
1256. Edwd. de la Knoll.
1284. Thos. de Button; bp. Exeter, 1292.
1292. Wm. Burnell.
1295. Walter de Haselshaw; bp. Bath and Wells, 1302.
1302. Hy. Husee.
1305. John de Godelegh.
1332. Richd. de Bury, or de Angarville; bp. Durham, 1333.
1334. Wibert de Littleton.
1335. Walter de London.
1350. John de Carlton.
1361. Wm. de Camell, elect. and refused.
Stephen de Pympell.
1378. John Fordham; bp. Durham, 1381.
1381. Thos. de Sudbury.

1396. Nichs. Slake.
1397. Hy. Beaufort; bp. Lincoln, 1398.
1401. Thos. Tuttebury.
1402. Thos. Stanley.
1410. Richd. Courtney.
1413. Thos. Karnicke
Walter Mitford.
1423. John Stafford; bp. Bath and Wells, 1425.
1425. John Forest.
1446. Nichs. Carent.
1467. Wm. Witham.
1472. John Gunthorp.
1498. Wm. Cosyn.
1526. Thos. Winter.
1529. Richd. Woolman.
1537. Thos. Cromwell.
1540. Wm. Fitzwilliams.
1548. John Goodman.
1550. Wm. Turner.
1570. Robt. Weston.
1574. Valentine Dale.
1589. John Herbert.
1602. Benjn. Heydon.
1607. Richd. Meredith.
1621. Ralph Barlow.
1631. Geo. Warburton.
1641. Walter Raleigh.
Deanery Vacant 14 Years.
1660. Robt. Creighton; bp. Bath and Wells, 1670.
1670. Ralph Bathurst.
1704. Wm. Graham.
1713. Matth. Brailsford.
1733. Isaac Maddore; bp. St. Asaph, 1736.
1736. John Harris, bp. Llandaff.
1739. Saml. Creswicke.
1766. Ld. Fras. Seymour; *d.* Sept. 19, 1785.
Deanery vacant until
1799. Geo. Wm. Lukin. Mar. 26.
1813. Hon. Hy. Ryder, bp. Gloster, Dec. 12, **G.**; aft. bp. Lichfield.
1831. Edmd. Goodenough, Sept. 6, **G.**
1845. Richd. Jenkyns, June 4, **G.**
1854. Geo. Hy. Sacheverell Johnson, Mar. 27, **G.**
1881. Edwd. Hayes Plumptre, Dec. 6, **G.**

DIOCESE OF CANTERBURY.

THIS see was settled by Austin, or Augustin, a monk, who first preached the gospel in England. The diocese included, until recently, a number of parishes in other dioceses; these were called *Peculiars*, it having been an ancient privilege of this see, that, wheresoever the archbishops had either manors or advowsons, that place was exempted from the jurisdiction of the ordinary of the diocese wherein it was situated, and was deemed in the diocese of Canterbury. This privilege was abolished from 1st January 1846.

The archbishop of Canterbury ranks first amongst the English bishops, and is styled Primate and Metropolitan of all England. He is also the first peer in the realm; having the precedence of all dukes not of the blood royal, and all the great officers of state. He is styled His Grace, and he writes himself *Divinâ Providentiâ*; whereas other bishops style themselves *Divinâ Permissione.* At coronations, he places the crown on the king's head; and, wherever the court may be, the king and queen are the proper domestic parishioners of the archbishop. The bishop of London is accounted his provincial dean; the bishop of Winchester, his sub-dean; the bishop of Lincoln, his chancellor; and the bishop of Rochester, his chaplain.

In 1537 a bishop suffragan of Dover was appointed to this see under 26 Hen. VIII. cap. 14, and this appointment was revived in 1870.

ARCHBISHOPS OF CANTERBURY.

597. Augustine, or St. Augustine.
604. Laurentius, or St. Lawrence.
619. Mellitus, or St. Miletus; tr. from London.
624. Justus, or St. Justus; tr. from Rochester.
627. Honorius, or St. Honorius.
655. Deus-dedit, or St. Adeodatus; the first Englishman who ruled this see.
See vacant 4 years.
664. Wigard; *d.* of the plague before consecration.

Adrian; app. by the pope, but refused the see.
668. Theodore, a Grecian.
693. Brihtwald, abbot of Reculver.
731. Tatwine; made primate of all England.
735. Nothelmus.
741. Cuthbert; tr. from Hereford.
759. Bregwin, a noble Saxon.
766. Lambert, or Jaenbert; abbot of St. Augustin's.
793. Ethelhard; tr. from Winchester.
805. Wulfred, a monk of Canterbury.
832. Syred; *d.* before he had obtained full possession.
Theologild, abbot of Canterbury.
833. Ceolnoth, dean of Canterbury.
870. Ethelred; tr. from Winchester.
890. Plegmund, preceptor to king Alfred.
914. Athelm, or Adelmus; tr. from Wells.
923. Wulfelm, or Wolfhelmus; tr. from Wells.
942. Odo Severus; tr. from Wilton.
960. Dunstan, or St. Dunstan; tr. from London.
988. Ethelgarus; tr. from Selsey.
990. Siricius; tr. from Wilton.
995. Elfric, or Aluricius; tr. from Wilton.
1006. Elphege, or St. Elphege; tr. from Winchester.
1013. Leovingus, Livingus, or Elstan; tr. from Wells.
1020. Ethelnoth, or Æthelnotus, dean of Canterbury.
1038. Eadsige, or Eadsimus.
1051 Robt. Gemeticensis.
1052. Stigand, bp. of Winchester; depr. of both sees for simony.
1070. Lanfranc, or St. Lanfranc, abbot of Caen, an Italian; *d.* June 4, 1089.
See vacant 4 years.
1093. Anselm, or St. Anselm, abbot of Becco.
See vacant 5 years.
1114. Ralph, or Rodolphus; tr. from Rochester.
1123. Wm. Corbois, or Corbyl, prior of St. Osyth, in Essex.
See vacant 2 years.
1139. Theobald, abbot of Becco.
See vacant 2 years.
1162. Thomas á Becket, archdn. of Canterbury, provost of Beverley, and ld. chanc.; murdered Dec. 28, 1170.
1174. Richd., prior of Dover.
1185. Baldwin, tr. from Worcester. He followed Richard I. to the Holy Land, and *d.* at the siege of Ptolemais.
1191. Regd. Fitz Jocelin, tr. from Wells; *d.* same year.
See vacant 2 years.
1193. Hubert Walter, tr. from Salisbury; ld. chanc.; *d.* 1205.
1205–6. Reginald, the sub-prior, was chosen by the monks, but was afterwards, at their own request, set aside by the king; they then chose
John Grey, bp. of Norwich, but the pope set him aside in favour of
1207. Stephen Langton, cardl. who *d.* July 1228.
1228. Walter de Hempsham chosen, but the king and the pope set him aside.
1229. Richd. Grant, or Rd. Wethershed, chanc. of Lincoln; *d.* 1231.
1231. Ralph Nevil, bp. of Chichester; John, the sub-prior, and Richard Blundy, severally chosen, but the pope set them aside.
1234. Edmd. Rich, preb. of Salisbury.
1245. Boniface of Savoy, uncle to the queen; *d.* July 1270.
1270. Wm. Chillenden chosen, but set aside by the pope.
1273. Robt. Kilwardby, made a cardl. and res., 1278.
1278. Robt. Burnel, bp. of Bath and Wells chosen, but set aside by the pope.
1279. John Peckham, canon of Lyons, provincial of Friars Minors.
1294. Robt. Winchelsey, archdn. of Essex, chanc. of Oxford.
1313. Thos. Cobham, precentor of York; elected, but not confirmed by the pope.
1313. Walter Reynolds; tr. from Worcester; ld. chanc. and ld. treasr.
1328. Simon Mepeham, preb. of Chichester.
1333. John de Stratford; tr. from Winchester; ld. chanc.
1348. John de Ufford, dean of Lincoln, ld. chanc.; *d.* before consecration.
1349. Thos. Bradwardine, chanc. of London; *d.* two months after.
Simon Islip, preb. of St. Paul's; sec. to the king and kpr. pr. seal.
1366. Wm. Edington, or Edendon, bp. of Winchester, elected; but refused the dignity.
1366. Simon Langham; tr. from Ely; made a cardl. and res. the see.
1368. Wm. Whittlesey, or Wittlesey; tr. from Worcester.
1375. Simon de Sudbury, *alias* Tibold; tr. from London; ld. chanc.; beheaded by the rebels under Wat Tyler, June 14, 1381.
1381. Wm. Courtenay; tr. from London.
1397. Thos. Fitz-Alan, or Arundel (son of the E. of Arundel); tr. from York; ld. chanc.

This prelate was charged with high treason in 1398, and fled the kingdom. Roger Walden, dean of York, was then consecrated; but Fitz-Alan was aft. rest. by Henry IV.

1414. Hy. Chicheley; tr. from St. David's.
1443. John Stafford; tr. from Bath and Wells; cardl., ld. chanc., and ld. treasr.
1452. John Kemp; tr. from York; cardl. and ld. chanc.
1454. Thos. Bouchier; tr. from Ely; cardl. and ld. chanc.
1486. John Morton; tr. from Ely; cardl. and ld. chanc.
1501. Thos. Langton, bp. of Winchester, chosen; but *d.* Jan. 27, 1501, five days after.
Hy. Dene, or Dean; tr. from Salisbury.
1503. Wm. Warham; tr. from London; ld. chanc.
1533. Thos. Cranmer, archdn. of Taunton; first Protestant abp. of Canterbury; burnt at Oxford, Mar. 21, 1556.
1556. Regd. Pole, dean of Exeter; cardl.
1559. Matth. Parker, dean of Lincoln.
1575. Edmd. Grindal; tr. from York.
1583. John Whitgift; tr. from Worcester.
1604. Richd. Bancroft, Oct. 9; tr. from London.
1611. Geo. Abbot, March 4; tr. from London.
1633. Wm. Laud, Aug. 6; tr. from London; beheaded on Tower Hill, Jan. 10, 1644.
See vacant 16 years.
1660. Wm. Juxon, Sept. 3; tr. from London.
1663. Gilbert Sheldon, July 14; tr. from London.
1678. Wm. Sancroft, Jan. 27, dean of St. Paul's; depr. Feb. 1, 1691, for not taking the oaths to William and Mary; *d.* Nov. 1693.
1691. John Tillotson, April 23; dean of St. Paul's.
1694. Thos. Tenison, Dec. 6; tr. from Lincoln.
1715. Wm. Wake; tr. from Lincoln.
1737. John Potter; tr. from Oxford.
1747. Thos. Herring; tr. from York.
1757. Matth. Hutton; tr. from York; *d.* the next year.
1758. Thos. Secker; tr. from Oxford.
1768. Hon. Fredk. Cornwallis; tr. from Lichfield and Coventry.
1783. John Moore; tr. from Bangor; *d.* Jan. 18, 1805.
1805. Chas. Manners Sutton, Feb. 2; tr. from Norwich; *d.* July 21, 1828.
1828. Wm. Howley, Aug. 4; tr. from London; *d.* Feb. 11, 1848.
1848. John Bird Sumner, Feb. 22; tr. from Chester; *d.* Sept. 6, 1862.
1862. Chas. Thos. Longley, Oct. 20, **G.**; tr. from York; *d.* Oct. 27, 1868.
1868. Archd. Campbell Tait, Nov. 26, **G.**; tr. from London; *d.* Dec. 3, 1882.
1883. Edwd. White Benson, Jan. 18, **G.**; tr. from Truro.

BISHOPS SUFFRAGAN OF DOVER.

1537. Richd. Yugworth.
1539. Richd. Taunton.
1567. Richd. Rogers.
1870. Edwd. Parry, archdn. and canon of Canterbury, Jan. 26, **G.**

DEANS OF CANTERBURY.

1542. Nichs. Wotton, Apr. 8; *d.* Jan. 26, 1567.
1567. Thos. Godwin; bp. Bath and Wells, 1584.
1584. Richd. Rogers, Sept. 16; *d.* May 19, 1597.
1597. Thos. Nevil; *d.* May 2, 1615.
1615. Chas. Fotherby; *d.* Mar. 29, 1619.
1619. John Boys; *d.* Sept. 26. 1625.
1625. Isaac Bargrave, Oct. 11; *d.* Jan. 1642.
1642. Geo. Aglionby, Feb. 8; *d.* Nov. 1643.
1643. Thos. Turner; *d.* Oct. 31, 1672.
1672. John Tillotson, Nov. 14; dean of St. Paul's, 1689.
1689. John Sharp, Nov. 25; abp. 1691.
1691. Geo. Hooper, July; bp. St. Asaph, 1703.
1704. Geo. Stanhope, Mar. 23; *d.* Mar. 18, 1728.
1728. Elias Sydall, Apr. 26; bp. St Davids, 1730.
1734. John Lynch, Jan. 18; *d.* May 25 1760.
1760. Wm. Friend, Jan. 14; *d.* Nov. 26, 1766.
1766. John Potter, Dec. 23; *d.* Sept. 20, 1770.
1770. Hon. Brownlow North, Oct. 9; bp. Lichfield and Coventry, 1771.
1771. John Moore, Sept. 20; bp. Bangor, 1775.
1775. Hon. Jas. Cornwallis, Apr. 29; bp. Lichfield and Coventry, 1781.
1781. Geo. Horne, Sept. 22; bp. Norwich, 1790.
1790. Wm. Buller, June 22; bp. Exeter, 1792.
1793. Folliott Herbert Walker Cornewall, Jan. 26; bp. Bristol, 1797.
1797. Thos. Powis, May 13.
1809. Gerard Andrews, Oct. 17, **G.**

1825. Hugh Percy, June 10, **G.**; bp. Rochester, 1827.
1827. Richd. Bagot, Aug. 6, **G.**; also bp. Oxford, 1829; tr. to Bath and Wells, 1845.
1845. Wm. Rowe Lyall, Nov. 26, **G.**; *d.* 1857.
1857. Hy. Alford, Mar. 18, **G.**; *d.* Jan. 12, 1871.
1871. Robt. Payne Smith, Feb. 4, **G.**

DIOCESE OF CHICHESTER.

WILFRIDE, the third archbishop of York, having been obliged to flee his country by Egfrid, king of Northumbria, came and preached the gospel in these parts; and Edilwach, king of the South Saxons, gave him the isle of Selsey, not far from Chichester, for his seat, where he built a church. Cenwal, king of the West Saxons, having won Edilwach's kingdom, built a monastery in the Island of Selsey, which was afterwards erected into a bishopric. Here the seat of this see continued, till Stigand, the twenty-third bishop of Selsey, removed it to Chichester about 1082. Anciently the bishops of Chichester were confessors to the queens of England.

BISHOPS OF SELSEY.

680. Wilfride, exp. from York.
686. Hedda.
705. Daniel.
711. Eadbertus, abbot of Selsey.
719. Eolla; *d.* 782.
See vacant.
733. Sigelmus, or Sigfridus.
761. Alubrithus, or Alubertus.
790. Osa, or Bosa.
817. Giselherus.
844. Tota.
873. Wighthun.
891. Ethelulphus.
905. Beornegus.
923. Coenredus.
942. Guthard.
960. Alfredus.
970. Eadhelmus.
980. Ethelgarus, abbot of the new abbey at Winchester; tr. to Canterbury.
988. Ordbrightus.
1003. Elmarus.
1019. Ethelricus, or Agelred.
1038. Grinketellus; tr. to Norwich.
1047. Heca, confessor to king Edward: he was depr., and imprisoned at Marlborough.
1057. Algericus, monk of Canterbury.
1070. Stigand, chaplain to Wm. I.

BISHOPS OF CHICHESTER.

1082. Stigand, bp. of Selsey from 1070 until 1082, when he became bp. of Chichester; *d.* 1087.
1087. Godfrey; by some authors called William.
1091. Ralph, or Radulphus; *d.* 1123.
1125. Seffridus I., abbot of Glastonbury.
* * Hilary. The date of his consecration is uncertain; some authorities give the year 1133; others 1147.
See vacant 4 years.
1173. John de Greenford, dean of Chichester.
1180. Seffridus II.
1199. Simon de Welles.
1209. Nicholas de Aquila.
1214. Richd. Poor, dean of Salisbury; tr. to Salisbury.
1217. Ralph de Warham, prior of Norwich.
1223. *Ralph de Nevill, ld. chanc.; elected to Canterbury; rejected by the pope; *d.* 1244.
1244. Robt. Papelew chosen, but the election was made void.
1245. St. Richard, surn. de la Wich.
1253. John Clipping, dean of Chichester.
1261. Stephen de Berkestede.
1288. St. Gilbert de Sancto Leofardo, treasr. of Chichester.
1306. John Langton, ld. chanc.
1338. Robt. Stratford, archdn. of Canterbury, ld. chanc., and chanc. of Oxford.
1362. Wm. de Lenne, or Lullimore; tr. to Worcester.
1369. Wm. Reade, fellow of Merton Colledge, Oxford.

1385. Thos. Rushooke; tr. from Llandaff.
1389. Richd. Mitford, ld. treasr. of Ireland; tr. to Salisbury.
1395. Robt. Waldby, abp. Dublin; tr. to York.
1396. Robt. Reade, tr. from Carlisle.
1417. Stephen Patrington, tr. from St. David's; *d.* immediately after.
1418. Hy. Ware, official to the abp. Canterbury, and preb. of St. Paul's.
1422. John Kempe, tr. from Rochester; tr. to London.
Thos. Pulton, or Polton, tr. from Hereford; tr. to Worcester.
1425. John Rickinghale, chanc. of York.
1431. Simon Sidenham, dean of Salisbury.
1437. Richd. Pratty, chanc. of Oxford.
1445. Adam Molins, dean of Salisbury; ld. pr. seal.
1450. Regd. Peacock, tr. from St. Asaph; depr. for opposing the Romish tenets, 1457.
1459. John Arundel, preb. of St. Paul's.
1478. Edwd. Story, tr. from Carlisle.
1504. Richd. Fitz-James, tr. from Rochester; tr. to London, 1506.
1508. Robt. Sherburn, or Sherborne, tr. from St. David's; res. a little before his death; *d.* Aug. 1536, aged 96.
1536. Richd. Sampson, dean of Lichfield; made dean of St. Paul's in 1536; tr. to Lichfield and Coventry.
1543. Geo. Day, provost of King's College, Cambridge; depr. 1551, by Edward VI., and imprisoned; restd. by Mary, 1553.
1551. John Scory, tr. from Rochester; depr. by Queen Mary, 1553, and, in 1559, made bp. Hereford by Elizabeth.
1557. John Christopherson, dean of Norwich; depr. 1559.
1559. Wm. Barlow, the depr. bp. Bath and Wells.
1570. Richd. Curteys, fellow of St. John's College, Cambridge.
See vacant 3 years.
1585. Thos. Bickley, warden of Merton College, Oxford.
1596. Anthy. Watson, dean of Bristol.
1605. Lancelot Andrews, dean of Westminster; tr. to Ely.
1609. Saml. Harsnet, archdn. of Essex; tr. to Norwich.
1619. Geo. Carleton, tr. from Llandaff.
1628. Richd. Montagu, canon of Windsor; tr. to Norwich.
1638. Brian Duppa, dean of Christchurch, Oxford; tr. to Salisbury.
1641. Hy. King, dean of Rochester.
1669. Peter Gunning, master of St. John's College, Cambridge; tr. to Ely.
1675. Ralph Brideoake, dean of Salisbury.
1678. Guy Carleton, tr. from Bristol.
1685. John Lake, tr. from Bristol; depr. for not taking the oaths.
1689. Simon Patrick, dean of Peterborough; tr. to Ely.
1691. Robt. Grove, archdn. of Middlesex.
1696. John Williams, preb. of Canterbury.
1709. Thos. Manningham, dean of Windsor.
1722. Thos. Bowers, archdn. of Canterbury.
1724. Edwd. Waddington, fellow of Eton.
1731. Fras. Hare, tr. from St. Asaph.
1740. Matthias Mawson, tr. from Llandaff; tr. to Ely.
1754. Sir Wm. Ashburnham, bt., dean of Chichester.
1797. John Buckner, rector of St. Giles, London; *d.* May 2, 1824.
1824. Robt. Jas. Carr, dean of Hereford, May 8; tr. to Worcester.
1831. Edwd. Maltby, preb. of Lincoln, Sept. 23; tr. to Durham.
1836. Wm. Otter, principal of King's College, London, Sept. 9; *d.* Aug. 20, 1840.
1840. Philip Nichs. Shuttleworth, warden of New College, Oxford, Sept. 7; *d.* Jan. 7, 1842.
1842. Ashurst Turner Gilbert, principal of Brasenose College, Oxford, Jan. 24; *d.* Feb. 21, 1870.
1870. Rd. Durnford, archdn. of Manchester, May 19, **G.**

DEANS OF CHICHESTER.

1115. Richard (1).
1125. Matthew (1)
1144. Richard (2).
1158. William.
1172. John de Greneforde, bp. Chichester, 1173.
1176. Jordan de Meleborne.
1180. Seffride (1).
Matthew (2).
1180. Nichs. de Aguila.
1196. Ralph.
1197. Seffride (2).
1220. Simon.
1230. Walter.
1232. Thos. de Lichfield.
1250. Geoffrey.
* * John Clipping; bp. of Chichester, 1253.

1262. Walter de Gloucester.
1280. Wm. de Bracklesham.
1296. Thos. de Berghsted.
1299. Wm.de Grenefeld; abp. York, 1303.
1316. John de Sancto Leofardo.
1332. Hy. de Garland.
1342. Walter de Seagrave.
1356. Wm. de Lynne.
1396. Roger de Freton.
1383. Richd. de Scrope.
1391. Wm. Lithington.
1400. John de Maydenhithe.
1402. Hy. de Lovel.
* * Richd. Talbot.
* * Wm. Milton.
1425. John Patten, *alias* Waynflete.
1434. John Hasely.
1481 John Cloos.
1501. John Pychard.
1503. Geoffrey Symeon.
* * Thos. Larke.
1508. John Yonge.
1526. Wm. Fleshmonger.
1543. Richd. Caurden.
1549. Giles Eyre.
1553. Bartholomew Traheron.
Wm. Pye.
1558. Hugh Turnbull.
1566. Richd. Curteys, or Coorteyse.
1570. Anthy. Ruse, or Rushe.
1570. John Bexhall.
1577. Martin Colepepper.
1602. Wm. Thorne.
1630. Fras. Dee; bp. Peterborough, 1634
1634. Richd. Stuart.
1639. Bruno Ryves.
1660. Jos. Henshawe; bp. Peterborough 1663.
1663. Jos. Goulston.
1669. Nathaniel Crewe; bp. Oxford, 1671.
1671. Lambroch Thomas.
1672. Geo. Stradling.
1688. Fras. Hawkins.
1699. Wm. Hayley.
1715. Thos. Sherlock; bp. Bangor, 1728.
1728. John Newry.
1735. Thos. Hayley.
1739. Jas. Hargraves.
1742. Wm. Ashburnham; bp. Chichester, 1754.
1754. Thos. Ball.
1770. Chas. Harward.
1790. Coombe Miller.
1814. Christopher Bethell, Mar. 15, **G.**; bp. Gloucester, 1824.
1824. Saml. Slade, Mar. 12, **G.**
1830. Geo. Chandler, Feb. 20, **G.**
1859. Walter Farquhar Hook, Feb. 24, **G.**; *d.* Oct 20, 1875.
1875. Jno. Wm. Burgon, Nov. 22, **G.**; *d.* Aug. 4, 1888.
1888. Fras. Pigou. Oct. 29, **G.**

DIOCESE OF ELY.

THE church or abbey of Ely was erected into a bishopric by Henry I. in 1109, the diocese being carved out of that of Lincoln. The great privileges the see possessed were much restricted by the act 27 Hen. VIII., cap. 24, which restored to the crown its ancient royalties.

BISHOPS OF ELY.

1109. Hervey, or Hervæus; tr. from Bangor.
See vacant 2 years.
1133. Nigellus, preb. of St. Paul's, and ld. treasr.; *d.* 1169.
See vacant 5 years.
1174. Geoffrey Ridel; bar. ex.
1189. Wm. de Longchamp; ld. chanc. and legate of Rome; *d.* 1197.
1198. Eustace, dean of Salisbury; ld. chanc.; *d.* 1215.
See vacant 5 years.
1220. John de Fontibus, abbot of Fountains, in Yorkshire.
1225. Geoffrey de Burgh, archdn. of Norwich.
1229. Hugh Northwold, abbot of St. Edmundsbury.
1254. Wm. de Kilkenny, archdn. of Coventry; ld. kpr.
1257. Hugh de Balsham, sub-prior of Ely.
1286. John de Kirkeby, canon of Wells and York; ld. treasr.
1290. Wm. de Luda, archdn. of Durham.
1299. Ralph de Walpole, tr. from Norwich.
1302. Robt. de Orford, prior of Ely,
1310. John de Ketene, almoner of Ely.
1316. John Hotham, preb. of York; ld. chanc., and ld. treasr.
1337. Simon de Montacute, tr. from Worcester.
1345. Thos. Lisle, prior of Winchester.
1362. Simon Langham, abbot of Westminster; ld. treasr.; aft. ld. chanc.; tr. to Canterbury.

1366. John Barnet, tr. from Bath, and Wells; ld. treasr.
1374. Thos de Arundel, or Fitz-Alan, archdn. of Taunton; ld. chanc.; tr. to York.
1388. John Frodsham, or Fordham; tr. from Durham.
1425. Philip Morgan, tr. from Worcester.
1438. Louis de Luxemburgh (or Lushborough, according to *Le Neve*), abp. of Rouen; cardl.
1443. Thos. Bourchier; tr. from Worcester; tr. to Canterbury.
1445. Wm. Grey, archdn. of Northampton; ld. treasr.
1478. John Morton, preb. of Salisbury, Lincoln, St. Paul's, and York; m. rolls; ld. chanc., and a cardl.; tr. to Canterbury.
1486. John Alcock, tr. from Worcester; ld. chanc.
1501. Richd. Redman, tr. from Exeter.
1506. Jas. Stanley, warden of Manchester, and dean of St. Martin's.
1515. Nich. West, dean of Windsor.
1534. Thos. Goodrick, or Goodrich, canon of St. Stephen's, Westminster; aft. ld. chanc.
1554. Thos. Thirlby; tr. from Norwich; depr.
1559. Richd. Coxe, dean of Christchurch, Oxford; *d.* 1581.
See vacant 18 years.
1600. Martin Heton, dean of Winchester.
1609. Lancelot Andrews, tr. from Chichester; tr. to Winchester.
1619. Nichs. Felton, tr. from Bristol.
1628. John Buckeridge, tr. from Rochester.
1631. Fras. White, tr. from Norwich.
1638. Matth. Wren, tr. from Norwich.
1667. Benjn. Lancy, or Laney, tr. from Lincoln.
1675. Peter Gunning, tr. from Chichester.
1684. Fras. Turner, tr. from Rochester; depr. for not taking the oaths.
1691. Simon Patrick, tr. from Chichester.
1707. John Moore, tr. from Norwich.
1714. Wm. Fleetwood, tr. from St. Asaph.
1723. Thos. Greene, tr. from Norwich.
1738. Robt. Butts, tr. from Norwich.
1748. Sir. Thos. Gooch, bt., tr. from Norwich.
1754. Matthias Mawson, tr. from Chichester.
1770. Edmd. Keene, tr. from Chester.
1781. Hon. Jas. Yorke, tr. from Gloucester; *d.* Aug. 26.
1808. Thos. Dampier, Sept. 13; tr. from Rochester; *d.* May 13, 1812.
1812. Bowyer Edwd. Sparke, May 23, tr. from Chester; *d.* Apr. 4, 1836.
1836. Jos. Allen, June 15; tr. from Bristol; *d.* Mar. 20, 1845.
1845. Thos. Turton, reg. prof. Divinity, and fellow of Catharine Hall, Cambridge, Mar. 29; *d.* Jan. 7, 1864.
1864. Edwd. Harold Browne, canon of Exeter, Feb. 4, **G.**; tr. to Winchester.
1873. Jas. Russell Woodford, vicar of Leeds, Oct. 27, **G.**; *d.* Oct. 24, 1883.
1885. Alwyne Compton, c.c. ld. Alwyne Compton, Dean of Worcester, Dec. 31, **G.**

DEANS OF ELY.

1541. Robt. Steward, *alias* Wells, Sept. 10; last prior and first dean; *d.* Sept. 22, 1557.
1557. Andrew Perne; *d.* Apr. 26, 1589.
1589. John Bell; *d.* Oct. 31, 1591.
1591. Humphrey Tyndall; *d.* Oct. 12, 1614.
1614. Hy. Cæsar, *alias* Adelmare; *d.* June 27, 1636.
1636. Wm. Beale, nominated but never admitted; *d.* Oct. 1, 1651.
Wm. Fuller, July 14; dean of Durham, 1646; *d.* May 12, 1659.
1660. Richd. Love, Sept. 6; *d.* Jan. 1661.
1661. Hy. Ferne, Feb.; bp. Chester, 1662; *d.* Mar. 16, 1662.
1662. Edwd. Martin, Feb. 22; *d.* Apr. 28, 1662.
Fras. Wilford, May 20; *d.* July, 1667.
1667. Robt. Mapletoft, Aug. 7; *d.* Aug. 20, 1677.
1677. John Spencer, Sept.; *d.* May 27, 1693.
1693. John Lamb, June 20; *d.* Aug. 10, 1708.
1708. Chas. Roderick, Oct. 8; *d.* Mar. 25, 1712.
1713. Robt. Moss, Apr. 30; *d.* Mar. 26, 1729.
1729. John Frankland, Apr. 28; *d.* Sept. 3, 1730.
1730. Peter Allix, Nov. 21; *d.* Jan. 11, 1758.
1758. Hugh Thomas, July 15; *d.* July 11, 1780.
1780. Wm. Cooke, Aug. 9; *d.* Nov. 21, 1797.
1797. Wm. Pearce, Dec. 10.
1820. Jas. Wood, Nov. 21, **G.**
1839. Geo. Peacock, May 7, **G.**
1858. Harvey Goodwin, Dec. 10, **G.**; bp. Carlisle, 1869.
1869. Chas. Merivale, Dec. 11, **G.**

DIOCESE OF EXETER.

THIS diocese comprises the two former bishoprics of Devonshire and Cornwall. The church of the former was at Crediton, and of the latter at Bodmin. About the year 1032, the bishopric of Cornwall was united to that of Devonshire; and, soon after, the then bishop removed the see to Exeter, where it still continues.

BISHOPS OF DEVONSHIRE.

905. Ædulphus, or Werstanus I.
906. Putta.
925. Ædulphus II.
932. Ethelgarus.
942. Algarus.
953. Alfwoldus I.
972. Alfwolfus.
981. Sydemanus.
990. Alfredus, abbot of Malmesbury.
999. Alfwoldus II.
1014. Eadnothus.
1032. Livyngus, who, after the death of Burwoldus, bp. of Cornwall, procured that bishopric to be annexed to his own. He also held the see of Worcester from 1838.

BISHOPS OF CORNWALL.

* * St. Patroe; he lived about the year 850.
909. Athelstan I.
* * Conanus.
* * Ruydocus.
* * Aldredus I.
* * Britwynus.
966. Athelstan II.
966. Wolfi.
* * Woronus.
* * Wolocus.
* * Stidio.
* * Aldredus II.
* * Burwoldus, or Brithwaldus; the last bp. of Cornwall.

BISHOP OF DEVON AND CORNWALL.

1046. Leofric, who removed the see to Exeter in 1049 or 1050.

BISHOPS OF EXETER.

1049–50. Leofric.
1074. Osbert, brother to the E. of Hereford; *d.* 1103.
See vacant 3 years.
1107. Wm. Warelwast, Warlewast, or Warewast, res. 1127; *d.* 1137.
1128. Robt. Chichester, dean of Salisbury.
1150. Robt. Warlewast, dean of Salisbury.
1161. Barth. Iscanus.
1185. John; *d.* 1191.
See vacant 2 years.
1193. Hy. Marshall, dean of York; *d.* 1206.
See vacant above 7 years.
1214. Simon de Apulia, dean of York.
1224. Wm. Brewer, pr. councillor to Hen. III.
1245. Richd. Blondy.
1258. WalterBronscombe,archdn.ofSurrey.
1280. Peter Quivil, canon of Exeter.
1292. Thos. de Button, dean of Wells.
1307. Walter Stapleton, ld. treasr.; beheaded by a mob in London, Oct. 15, 1326.
1326. Jas. de Berkeley; *d.* 1327.
John Godeleigh chosen, but set aside by the pope.
1327. John Grandison.
1370. Thos. Brentingham, ld. treasr.
1395. Edmd. Stafford, ld. chanc.
1419. John Ketterick, tr. from Lichfield and Coventry; *d.* 1420.
1420. Jas. Cary, bp. Lichfield and Coventry; *d.* before he took possession of the see.
Edmd. Lacy, tr. from Hereford.
1456. Geo. Nevill, ld. chanc. and chanc. of Oxford; tr. to York.
1465. John Booth, preb. of St. Paul's.
1478. Peter Courtenay, archdn. of Exeter; tr. to Winchester.
1486. Richd. Fox, preb. of Salisbury; ld. pr. seal; tr. to Bath and Wells.
1492. Oliver King, preb. of St. Paul's; tr. to Bath and Wells.
1495. Richd. Redman, tr. from St. Asaph; tr. to Ely.
1502. John Arundel, tr. from Lichfield and Coventry.
1504. Hugh Oldham, or Oldman, preb. of York and Lichfield.
1519. John Voysey, *alias* Harman, dean of Windsor; res. 1551.
1551. Miles Coverdale, depr. and banished by Mary, 1553. After her death he refused to return to his

bishopric, and lived in retirement until his 81st year.
553. John Voysey, *again*; rest. by Mary on her accession.
555. Jas. Turberville, preb. of Winton; depr. Jan. 1560.
560. Wm. Alley, preb. of St. Paul's.
571. Wm. Bradbridge, dean of Salisbury.
579. John Woolton, can.-res. of Exeter.
594. Gervase Babington, tr. from Llandaff; tr. to Worcester.
598. Wm. Cotton, can.-res. of St. Paul's.
621. Valentine Cary, dean of St. Paul's.
627. Jos. Hall, dean of Worcester; tr. to Norwich 1641.
641. Ralph Brownrigg, preb. of Durham.
660. John Gauden, master of the Temple; tr. to Worcester.
662. Seth Ward, dean of Exeter; tr. to Salisbury.
667. Anthy. Sparrow, archdn. of Sudbury; tr. to Norwich.
676. Thos. Lamplugh, dean of Rochester; tr. to York.
688. Sir Jonn. Trelawney, bt.; tr. from Bristol; tr. to Winchester.
707. Offspring Blackhall, rector of St. Mary Aldermary, London.
1717. Lancelot Blackburn, dean of Exeter; tr. to York.
1724. Stephen Weston.
1743. Nichs. Claggett, tr. from St. David's.
1746. Geo. Lavington, can.-res. of St. Paul's.
1762. Fredk. Keppel, canon of Windsor, and in 1766 dean of Windsor.
1778. John Ross, one of his majesty's chaplains and preb. of Durham.
1792. Wm. Buller, dean of Canterbury.
1797. Hy. Regd. Courtenay, tr. from Bristol; *d.* 1803.
1803. John Fisher, archdn. of Exeter, June 25; tr. to Salisbury.
1807. Hon. Geo. Pelham, July 11; tr. from Bristol; tr. to Lincoln.
1820. Wm. Carey, Oct. 16; tr. to St. Asaph.
1830. Christr. Bethell, Apr. 7; tr. from Gloucester; tr. to Bangor, Oct. 10, same year.
Hy. Phillpotts, preb. of Durham, Nov. 11; *d.* Sept. 18, 1869.
1869. Fredk. Temple, head master of Rugby, Oct. 25, **G.**; tr. to London, 1885.
1885. Edwd. Hy. Bickersteth, dean of Gloucester, Mar. 26, **G.**

DEANS OF EXETER.

225. Serlo, Dec.; *d.* July 25, 1231.
* Roger de Wynklegh; *d.* Aug. 13, 1252.
* Wm. de Stanwey; *d.* Dec. 30, 1268.
* Roger de Thoriz; *d.* Apr. 30, 1274.
274. John Noble, Sept. 20.
* John Pycot.
284. Andrew de Kilkenny, Mar. 13; *d.* Nov. 4, 1302.
* Hy. de Somerset.
* Thos. de Lechlade; *d.* 1309.
311. Barthw. de Sancto Laurentio, June 3.
* Roger de Coleton, was dean in 1328; *d.* 1335.
335. Richd. de Braylegh, Oct. 2.
* Regd. de Bugwell.
* Robt. Sumpter, was dean in 1373 and 1377.
* Thos. Walkyngton, was dean on Feb. 23, 1384.
385. Ralph Tregrision, June.
415. Stephen Payn, Nov. 4; *d* May, 1419.
419. Roger Bolter, elected but declined.
John Cobethorn, Sept. 2.
* John Hals, bp. Lichfield and Coventry, 1459.
459. Hy. Webber, Dec. 26; *d.* Feb. 13, 1477.
477. Peter Courtenay, Apr. 27; bp. Exeter, 1478.
478. Lionel Woodvile, bp. Salisbury, 1482.
1482. John Arundell, bp. Lichfield and Coventry, 1496.
1496. Edwd. Willoughby; *d.* Nov. 23, 1508.
1509. Thos. Hobbys, Feb. 7; *d.* Sept. 1509.
John Veysy, Nov. 19; bp. Exeter, 1519.
1519. Richd. Pace, res. July 8, 1527.
1527. Regd. Pole, Sept. 23; depr.; abp. Canterbury, 1556.
1537. Simon Heynes, July 16; *d.* Oct. 1552.
1553. Jas. Haddon, July 10.
John Moreman; *d.* 1554.
1554. Thos. Reynolds, Feb. 9; depr. by Elizabeth; *d.* Nov. 24, 1559.
1560. Gregory Dodds, Feb. 25; *d.* 1570.
1570. Geo. Carewe; *d.* 1583.
1583. Stephen Townesende, Oct. 5; *d.* 1588.
1588. Matt. Sutcliffe, Oct. 27; *d.* 1629.
1629. Wm. Peterson, July 18; *d.* 1661.
1661. Seth Ward, Dec. 26; bp. Exeter, 1662.
1662. Edwd. Younge, Aug. 21; *d.* 1663.
1663. Geo. Cary, Sept. 5; *d.* Feb. 2, 1681.
1681. Hon. Richd. Annesley, aft. ld. Altham, Apr. 6; *d.* Nov. 16, 1701.
1703. Wm. Wake, Feb. 14; bp. Lincoln, 1705.
1705. Lancelot Blackburne, Nov. 3; bp. Exeter, 1717.

1717. Edwd. Trelawny, Mar. 18; *d.* Oct. 24, 1726.
1726. John Gilbert, Dec. 27; bp. Llandaff, 1740.
1741. Alured Clarke, Jan. 12; *d.* May 31, 1742.
1742. Wm. Holmes, Aug. 14; *d.* Apr. 4, 1748.
1748. Chas. Lyttelton, June 1; bp. Carlisle, 1762.
1762. Jeremiah Milles, Apr. 28; *d.* Feb. 16, 1784.
1784. Wm. Buller, Mar. 25; dean of Canterbury, 1790.
1790. Chas. Harward, July 16; *d.* July 17, 1802.
1802. Chas. Talbot, Dec. 31; dean Salisbury, 1809.
1809. Geo. Gordon, Mar. 25, **G.**; dean Lincoln, 1810.
1810. John Garnett, Feb. 10, **G.**; *d.* Ma 12, 1813.
1813. Whittington Landon, Mar. 30, **G.**
1839. Ld. Wriothesley Russell, Jan. 19, res. same year.
Thos. Hill Lowe.
1861. Chas. John Ellicott, July 1, **G.**
1863. Hon. Wm. John Brodrick, aft. vi Midleton, Apr. 2, **G.**
1867. Archd. Boyd, Nov. 11, **G.**
1883. Benjn. Morgan Cowie, dean of M chester, Nov. 20, **G.**

DIOCESES OF GLOUCESTER AND BRISTOL.

The Diocese of Gloucester was formerly part of that of Worcest and was erected into a separate see by Henry VIII. in 1541.

The Diocese of Bristol was erected into a separate see by Hen VIII. in 1542, and was formed chiefly out of the diocese of Salisbu with small portions of Wells and Worcester. During a great part Queen Elizabeth's reign, this see was held *in commendam* by the bisho of Gloucester.

By 6 and 7 Wm. IV. cap. 77 (Aug. 13, 1836) and an order in coun dated Oct. 7, 1836, the dioceses of Gloucester and Bristol were co solidated.

By 47 and 48 Vict. cap. 66 (Aug. 14, 1884) provision is made for t separation of the two dioceses on the next vacancy of the see, but t act has not yet come into operation.

BISHOPS OF GLOUCESTER.

1541. John Wakeman, the last abbot of Tewkesbury.
1550. John Hooper, held the see of Worcester *in commendam* in 1552; depr. by Mary, 1553; burnt at Gloucester, Feb. 9, 1555.
1554. Jas. Brookes, master of Baliol College, Oxford; *d.* 1558.
See vacant 3 years.
1562. Richd. Cheyney, also bp. Bristol; *d.* 1579.
See vacant 2 years.
1581. John Bullingham, also bp. Bristol; *d.* 1598.
1598. Godfrey Goldsborough, preb. of Worcester.
1604. Thos. Ravis, dean of Christ Church, Oxford; tr. to London.
1607. Hy. Barry, dean of Chester; tr. to Worcester.
1610. Giles Thomson, dean of Windsor.
1612. Miles Smith, can.-res. of Hereford.
1624. Godfrey Goodman, dean of Rochester; his see was sequestrated in 1640, and he *d.* a papist in 1655.
See vacant 5 years.
1660. Wm. Nicholson, archdn. of Brec nock.
1672. John Pritchet, or Pritchard, vi of St. Giles's, Cripplegate.
1681. Robt. Frampton, dean of Glouc ter; depr. for not taking oaths.
1691. Edwd. Fowler, preb. of Gloucest
1715. Richd. Willis, dean of Lincoln; to Salisbury.
1722. Jos. Wilcocks, preb. of Westmins tr. to Rochester.
1731. Elias Sydall, tr. from St. David's
1734. Martin Benson, preb. of Durham
1752. Jas. Johnson, can.-res. of St. Paul tr. to Worcester.
1759. Wm. Warburton, dean of Bris and preacher at Lincoln's Inn.
1779. Hon. Jas. Yorke, tr. from St. Davi tr. to Ely.
1781. Saml. Halifax, tr. to St. Asaph.
1789. Richd. Beadon, archdn. of Lond tr. to Bath and Wells.

802. Geo. Isaac Huntingford, warden of Winchester College, Apr. 21; tr. to Hereford.

815. Hon. Hy. Ryder, July 8; tr. to Lichfield and Coventry.

1824. Christr. Bethell, Mar. 11; tr. to Exeter.

1830. Jas. Hy. Monk, July 11. United to Bristol, 1836.

See "Bishops of Gloucester and Bristol," *infra*.

BISHOPS OF BRISTOL.

538. Hy. Holbeach, bp. suffragan; tr. to Rochester.

542. Paul Bushe, provincial of the *Bonhommes*; res. the see on the accession of Mary in 1553, he being married.

554. John Holyman, monk of Reading; *d.* Dec. 1558.

See vacant 3 years.

562. Richd. Cheney, or Cheyney, archdn. of Hereford; he held the see of Gloucester, by dispensation, along with this see.

See vacant 2 years.

581. John Bullingham, preb. of Worcester and St. Paul's; he held Gloucester by dispensation; res. the see of Bristol, 1589.

589. Richd. Fletcher, dean of Peterborough; tr. to Worcester, 1593.

See vacant 10 years.

603. John Thornborough, tr. from Limerick; tr. to Worcester.

617. Nichs. Felton, preb. of St.. Paul's; tr. to Ely.

619. Rowland Serchfield, vicar of Charlbury, Oxfordshire.

622. Robt. Wright, canon of Wells; tr. to Lichfield and Coventry.

632. Geo.Cook,or Coke,rector of Bygrave, Herts.; tr. to Hereford.

636. Robt. Skinner, rector of Launton, Oxfordshire; tr. to Oxford.

640. Thos.Westfield,archdn.ofSt.Alban's.

644. Thos. Howell, can. of Windsor; *d.* 1646.

See vacant 16 years.

660. Gilbert Ironside, preb. of York.

671. Guy Carleton, dean of Carlisle; tr. to Chichester.

678. Wm.Gulston, rector of Symondsbury, Dorsetshire.

684. John Lake, tr. from Sodor and Man; tr. to Chichester.

685. Sir Jonathan Trelawny, bt.; tr. to Exeter.

1689. Gilbert Ironside, warden of Wadham College, Oxford; tr. to Hereford.

1691. John Hall, master of Pembroke College, Oxford.

1710. John Robinson, dean of Windsor; ld. pr. seal; tr. to London.

1714. Geo. Smallridge, dean of Christchurch, Oxford.

1719. Hugh Boulter,archdn. of Surrey; tr. to Armagh, Ireland.

1724. Wm.Bradshaw,dean ofChristchurch, Oxford.

1732. Chas. Cecil, tr. to Bangor.

1734. Thos. Secker, preb. of Durham; tr. to Oxford.

1737. Thos. Gooch, preb. of Canterbury; tr. to Norwich.

1738. Jos. Butler, preb. of Rochester; tr. to Durham.

1750. John Conybeare, dean of Christchurch, Oxford.

1758. John Hume, can.-res. of St. Paul's; tr. to Oxford.

Philip Younge,can.-res.of St. Paul's; tr. to Norwich.

1761. Thos. Newton, preb. of Westminster, and dean of St. Paul's.

1782. Lewis Bagot, dean of Christchurch, Oxford; tr, to Norwich.

1785. Christr.Wilson,preb.of Westminster.

1792. Spencer Madan, can.-res. of Lichfield; tr. to Peterborough.

1794. Hy. Regd. Courtenay, preb. of Rochester; tr. to Exeter.

1797. Folliot Herbert Walker Cornewall, dean ofCanterbury; tr.toHereford.

1802. Hon. Geo. Pelham, tr. to Exeter.

1807. John Luxmore, dean of Gloucester; tr. to Hereford.

1808. Wm. Lort Mansel; *d.* 1820.

1820. John Kaye, master of Christ's College, Cambridge; tr. to Lincoln.

1827. Robt. Gray; *d.* in 1834.

1834. Jos. Allen; tr. to Ely, 1836. United to Gloucester.

See "Bishops of Gloucester and Bristol," *infra*.

BISHOPS OF GLOUCESTER AND BRISTOL.

836. Jas. Hy. Monk, bp. of Gloucester, Oct. 7; *d.* June 6, 1856.

1856. Chas. Baring, rector of Limpsfield, Surrey, and chaplain in ordy.to the Queen, July 9, **G.**; tr. to Durham.

1861. Wm. Thompson, prior of Queen's College, Oxford; tr. to York.

1863. Chas. Jno. Ellicott, dean of Exeter, Jan. 30, **G.**

DEANS OF GLOUCESTER.

1541. Wm. Jennings, last prior of St. Oswalds and first dean of Gloucester; *d.* Nov. 4, 1565.
1565. John Man; *d.* 1568.
1569. Thos. Cowper; bp. Lincoln, 1570.
1570. Laurence Humphrey; dean of Winchester, 1580; *d.* 1590.
1584. Anthy. Rudd; bp. St. David's, 1594; *d.* 1614.
1594. Lewis Griffith; *d.* 1607.
1607. Thos. Morton, June 22; dean of Winchester, 1609; *d.* Sept. 22, 1659.
1609. Richd. Field; *d.* Nov. 21, 1616.
1616. Wm. Laud; bp. St. David's, 1621.
1621. Richd. Senhouse; bp. Carlisle, 1624.
1624. Thos Winniffe, dean of St. Paul's, 1631; bp. Lincoln, 1641.
1631. Geo. Warburton, June; dean of Wells, Aug. 1631.
Accepted Frewen; bp. Lichfield and Coventry, 1643.
1644. Wm. Brough, nom. by Chas. I., but never enjoyed the dignity.
1671. Thos. Vyner; *d.* 1673.
1673. Robt. Frampton; bp. Gloucest[e] 1681.
1681. Thos. Marshall, Apr. 30; *d.* 1685.
1685. Wm. Jane; *d.* 1707.
1707. Knightly Chetwood, Apr.; *d.* A[p] 11, 1720.
1720. John Waugh, Aug. 4; bp. Carlisl[e] 1723.
1723. John Frankland, dean of Ely, 172
1729. Peter Allix; dean of Ely, 1730.
1730. Danl. Newcombe; *d.* 1758.
1758. Josiah Tucker; *d.* Nov. 4, 1799.
1800. John Luxmore, Jan. 7, **G.**; and b Bristol, 1807; tr. to Hereford, 180
1808. John Plumtree, Aug. 27, **G.**
1825. Hon. Edwd. Rice, Dec. 18, **G.**
1862. Hy. Law, Dec. 1, **G.**
1885. Edwd. Hy. Bickersteth, Jan. 19, bp. Exeter, 1885.
Hy. Montague Butler, May 14, **G.**
1886. Hy. Donald Maurice Spence, De 13, **G.**

DEANS OF BRISTOL.

The dates down to 1781 are those of the installations. The actual appointment were, of course, a short time previous.

1542. Wm. Snow, last prior of Bradenstock and first dean, June 4.
1551. John Whiteheare, or Whytere, July 26.
1552. Geo. Carewe, Nov. 5; depr. by Mary.
1554. Hy. Jolliffe, Sept. 9; depr. by Elizabeth, 1559; *d.* 1573.
1559. Geo. Carewe, rest. Nov. 10; aft. dean of Exeter.
1570. John Sprint, Feb. 16; *d.* 1589.
1590. Anthy. Watson, July 21; bp. Chichester, 1596; held deanery till 1598.
1598. Simon Robson, Apr. 21; *d.* 1617.
1617. Edwd. Chetwynd, July 26; *d.* 1639.
1639. Matth. Nicholas, June 22; dean of St. Paul's, 1660.
1660. Hy. Glenham, Sept. 14; bp. S Asaph, 1667.
1667. Richd. Towgood, May 1; *d.* 1683.
1683. Saml. Crossman, Feb. 4; *d.* 1684.
1684. Richd. Thompson, May 25; *d.* 168
1685. Wm. Levett, Jan. 10; *d.* 1693.
1693. Geo. Royse, Mar. 10; *d.* 1708.
1708. Hon. Robt. Booth, June 20.
1730. Saml. Creswick, Sept. 8.
1739. Thos. Chamberlayne, Dec. 24.
1757. Wm. Warburton, Oct. 25; bp. Glo cester, 1759.
1760. Saml. Squire, June 21; bp. S David's, 1761.
1761. Fras. Ayscough, June 5.
1768. Cutts Barton.
1781. John Hallam, Feb. 22.

The following dates are those of the Gazette notices.

1800. Chas. Peter Layard. Jan. 7, **G.**
1803. Bowyer Edwd. Sparke, May 24, **G.**; bp. Chester, 1809.
1810. John Parsons, Jan. 27, **G.**
1813. Hy. Becke, Dec. 14, **G.**
1837. Thos. Musgrave, Mar 27, **G.**; b Hereford, Aug., 1837.
John Lamb, Oct. 2, **G.**
1850. Gilbert Elliot, May 1, **G.**

DIOCESE OF HEREFORD.

THIS was a bishopric in the time of the Britons, and one of the suffragan to the metropolitan see of St. David's. When the country was co ıered by the Saxons, it became a member of the province of ınterbury.

BISHOPS OF HEREFORD.

0. Putta, tr. from Rochester.
1. Tirhtullus.
3. Tortherus.
8. Walstodus, or Wastoldus.
6. Cuthbert, tr. to Canterbury.
1. Podda.
6. Ecca, or Acca.
2. Cedde.

758. Albertus, or Alberus.
769. Esna.
775. Celmund.
783. Utellus.
788. Wulfehard.
809. Beonna.
829. Edulph.
849. Cuthwolf.
868. Mucellus.
888. Deorlaf.

908. Cunemund, or Ceynemundus.
928. Edgar.
949. Tidhelm.
966. Wulfehelm.
990. Alfric.
997. Athulf.
1012. Athelstan.
1055. St. Leovegard, or Leofgar.
See vacant 4 years.

30. Walter, chaplain to the queen.
79. Robt. Losing, preb. of St. Paul's.
95 Gerard, chanc. to William the conqueror; tr. to York.
01. Rainelm, chanc. to the queen; he rebuilt the cathedral.
15. Geoffrey de Clyve, chaplain to the king.
20. Richd. de Cappella, clerk of the seal.
31. Robt. de Betun, prior of Lanthony.
48. Gilbert Foliot, abbot of Gloucester; tr. to London.
53. Robt. de Melun, prior of Lanthony; *d.* 1166.
See vacant 7 years.
74. Robt. Foliot, archdn. of Oxford.
36. Wm. de Vere, preb. of St. Paul's.
00. Giles de Bruse, or Braose.
16. Hugh de Mapenore, dean of Hereford.
19. Hugh Foliot, archdn. of Salop
34. Ralph de Maydenstune, or Maidstone, dean of Hereford; res. Dec. 1239.
40. Peter de Egueblank, or Egeblaunch, a Savoyard.
38. Johd de Breton.
75. St. Thos. de Cantilupe, archdn. of Stafford; ld. chanc. of England, and chanc. of Oxford.
2. Richd. Swinefield.
7. Adam de Orleton, ld. treasr.; tr. to Worcester.
27. Thos. Charlton, canon of York; ld. chanc. of Ireland.
4. John Trilleck.
31. Lewis de Charleton, canon of Hereford; chanc. of Oxford.
9. Wm. Courteney, canon of York; tr. to London.
75. John Gilbert, tr. from Bangor; ld. treasr.; tr. to St. David's.
39. John Trevenant, or Treffnant, canon of St. Asaph and Lincoln.
4. Robt Maschal, confessor to the king.
7. Edmd. Lacy, canon of Windsor; tr. to Exeter.
20. Thos. Polton, dean of York; tr. to Chichester.

1422. Thos. Spofford, abbot of St. Mary's, York; bp. elect of Rochester, but removed to this see before consecration; res. 1448.
1448. Richd. Beauchamp, archd. of Suffolk; tr. to Salisbury.
1450. Regd. Butler, or Botteler, abbot of Gloucester; tr. to Lichfield and Coventry.
1453. John Stanbery, or Stanbury, tr. from Bangor.
1474. Thos. Milling, abbot of Westminster.
1492. Edmd. Audley, tr. from Rochester; tr. to Salisbury.
1502. Adrian de Castello, preb. of St. Paul's; tr. to Bath and Wells.
1504. Richd. Mayhew, or Mayo, pres. of Magdalen College, Oxford.
1516. Chas. Booth, preb. of Lincoln.
1535. Edwd. Fox, provost of King's College, Cambridge.
1538. Edmd. Bonner, archdn. of Leicester; before consecration, tr. to London.
1539. John Skypp, archdn. of Dorset.
1553. John Harley, preb. of Worcester; depr. for being married.
1554. Robt. Warton, or Parfew, tr. from. St. Asaph.
Thos. Reynolds; nom. by Mary, but on her death, set aside by Elizabeth.
1559. John Scory, the depr. bp. of Chichester; made bp. Hereford by Elizabeth.
1585. Herbert Westphaling, canon of Windsor.
1602. Robt. Bennet, dean of Windsor.
1617. Fras. Godwin, tr. from Llandaff.
Wm. Juxton, dean of Worcester, elected; but before consecration, tr. to London.
Godfrey Goodman. bp. Gloucester, elected; but declined the app.
1634. Augustin Lindsell, tr. from Peterborough; *d.* same year.
Matth. Wren, dean of Windsor; tr. to Norwich.
1635. Theoph. Field, tr. from St. David's Dec. 1635; *d.* June, 1636.

1636. Geo. Cook, or Coke, tr. from Bristol; *d.* 1646.
See vacant 14 years.
1660. Nichs. Monk, provost of Eton.
1661. Herbert Croft, dean of Hereford.
1691. Gilbert Ironside, tr. from Bristol.
1701. Humphrey Humphreys, tr. from Bangor.
1712. Philip Bisse, tr. from St. David's.
1721. Benjn. Hoadley, tr. from Bangor; tr. to Salisbury.
1723. Hon. Hy. Egerton, canon of Christchurch, Oxford.
1746. Lord Jas. Beauclerk, canon of Windsor; *d.* 1787.
1787. Hon. John Harley, dean of Windsor; *d.* 1788.
1788. John Butler, tr. from Oxford; *d.* 1802.
1802. Folliot Herbert Walker Cornewa[ll], tr. from Bristol; tr. to W[or]cester.
1808. John Luxmore, July 16; tr. fr[om] Bristol; tr. to St. Asaph.
1815. Geo. Isaac Huntingford, July 2[?], tr. from Gloucester; *d.* Apr. 18[?]
1832. Hon. Edwd. Grey, dean of He[re]ford, May 7; *d.* June 24, 1837.
1837. Thos. Musgrave, Aug. 7; tr. [to] York.
1847. Renn Dickson Hampden, princi[pal] of St. Mary's Hall, reg. pr[of.] Divinity, and canon of Chri[st]church, Oxford, Dec. 11; [d.] Apr. 23, 1868.
1868. Jas. Atlay, vicar of Leeds, May 1[?] **G.**

DEANS OF HEREFORD.

1140. Ralph (1).
1150. Geffry (1).
1157. Ralph (2).
1172. Geffry (2).
1187. Richard.
1202. Hugh de Breuse.
1203. Hugh de Mapenore; bp. Hereford, 1216.
1216. Henry.
1218. Thos. de Bosbury.
1231. Ralph de Maideston.
1234. Steph. de Thorne.
1247. Ancelinus, or Ancelin.
1271. Giles de Avenbury.
1278. John de Aquablanca.
1320. Steph. de Ledbury.
1352. Thos. de Trilleck.
1363. Wm. de Birmingham.
* * John de Middleton.
1380. John Harold.
1393. John Prophet.
1407. Thos. Felde.
1419. John Stanwey.
1434. Hy. Shelford.
1445. John Berew.
1462. John ap Richard.
* * Richd. Pede.
1481. Thos. Chandeler.
1490. Oliver King.
1491. John Harvey.
1501. Regd. West.
1512. Thos. Wolsey.
Edmd. Frowcester.
1529. Gamaliel Clifton.
1549. Hugh Curwyn; bp. Oxford, 1567.
1558. Edmd. Daniel.
1559. John Ellis.
1576. John Watkins.
1593. Chas. Langford.
1607. Edwd. Doughtie.
1616. Richd. Mountague.
1617. Sylvanus Gryffith.
1623. Danl. Price.
1631. John Richardson.
1635. Jonathan Browne.
1644. Herbert Croft; bp. Hereford, 16[61].
1661. Thos. Hodges.
1672. Geo. Benson.
1692. John Tyler; bp. Llandaff, 1707.
1724. Robt. Clavering.
* * Edwd. Cresset; bp. Llandaff, 17[?]
1748. Edmd. Castle.
1750. John Egerton; bp. Bangor, 1756.
1756. Fras. Webber.
1771. Nathan Wetherell.
1808. Wm. Leigh, Jan. 16, **G.**
1809. Geo. Gretton, Mar. 21, **G.**
1820. Robt. Jas. Carr, Aug. 14, **G.**; a[ft.] bp. Chichester, 1824.
1827. Edwd. Mellish, June 28, **G.**
1830. Hon. Edwd. Grey, Dec. 22, **G.**; b[p.] Hereford, 1832.
1832. John Merewether, May 15, **G.**
1850. Richd. Daws, May 15, **G.**
1867. Hon. Geo. Herbert, Apr. 10, **G.**

DIOCESE OF LICHFIELD, FORMERLY LICHFIELD AND COVENTRY.

This bishopric is said to have been founded by Oswy, king of Nort[h]umbria, about the year 656, and although it had, until very recently, uble name (Lichfield and Coventry), yet, like Bath and Wells, it has ways been a single diocese. Offa, king of Mercia, by the favour of pe Adrian, constituted it an archiepiscopal see; but this title was laid ide on the death of that king. In 1075, Peter, the thirty-fourth shop, removed the see to Chester; in 1102, his immediate successor, obert de Limesey, removed it to Coventry; and bishop Roger de inton, according to some authorities (bishop Hugo Novant being entioned by others), removed it back to Lichfield, but with great position from the monks of Coventry. The dispute was finally settled a manner nearly similar to that adopted between Bath and Wells: it s agreed that the bishop should be styled from both places; that ey should choose the bishop alternately; and that they should both ake one chapter, of which the prior of Coventry should be the chief. atters continued thus until the Reformation, when the priory of ventry was dissolved by Henry VIII., but the style of the bishop ntinued as before.

By an order in council dated Jan. 24, 1837, the archdeaconry of ventry was separated from this see and added to the see of Worcester; d the double name was then discontinued.

In 1537 a bishop suffragan of Shrewsbury was appointed (probably this see) under 26 Hen. VIII., cap. 14, and this title was revived in 88.

BISHOPS OF LICHFIELD.

6. Dwyna, Diuma, or Duma.
8. Cellach, a Scot; he resigned and returned to his own country.
0. Trumhere, abbot of Ingethling.
4. Jaruman.
7. St. Chad, or Ceadda, tr. to York.
2. Winfride, depr. by abp. Theodore.
6. St. Sexulf, or Saxulf, abbot of Medeshamstede, now Peterborough.
1. Headda, or Eatheadus, of Sidnacester.
1. Aldwyn.
7. Witta, or Huitta.
2. Hemel.
5. Cuthfrid; *d.* 768.
8. Berthun; *d.* 785.
5. Higbert, or Sigbert I.
6. Adulphus, the *Archbishop*. This title was laid aside in 799.
* Humbert I.
2. Herewin.
4. Higbert, or Sigbert II.
7. Ethelwald, or Ethelwold.
845. Humbert II.
864. Kinebert, or Kenferth.
872. St. Cumbert, or Cineferth.
898. Tunbright, Tunfrith, or Tumfriht.
928. Ella.
944. Ælfgar.
953. Kinsey, or Kinsius.
964. Winsey, or Winsius.
977. Elphege.
990. Godwin.
1007. Leofgar, or Leosgar.
1027. Brithmar.
1038. Wolfius.
1054. Leofwin, abbot of Coventry.
1067. Peter; he removed the see to Chester in 1075.
1085. Robt. de Limesey, preb. of St. Paul's; he removed the see to Coventry in 1102.
See vacant 4 years.
1117. Robt. Pecham, or Peche, chaplain to Hen. I.; *d.* 1127.
See vacant 2 years.

BISHOPS OF LICHFIELD AND COVENTRY.

29. Roger de Clinton, archdn. of Buckingham; he removed the see to Lichfield.
149. Walter Durdent, prior of Canterbury.
162. Richd. Peche, archdn. of Coventry.
183. Geraldus Puella, or la Pucelle; *d.* Jan. 1185.
185. Hugh Novant, Nunant, or Minant, prior of the Carthusians; he removed the see permanently to Lichfield.
1198. Geoffrey de Muschamp, archdn. of Cleveland.
1208. Walter Grey, ld. chanc.; tr. to Worcester.
1215. Wm. de Cornhull, archdn. of Huntingdon.
1224. Alexr. de Savensby, or Stavenby; *d.* Dec. 26, 1238.

1239. Wm. de Rule, or Raleigh, elected by both chapters; but being chosen bishop of Norwich also, he accepted the latter; the chapter of Lichfield then chose Wm. de Manchestre, their dean, and that of Coventry elected Nichs. de Farnham; and after much controversy, both chapters, at the king's request, agreed in the choice of

Hugh de Pateshull, ld. treasr., conf. Dec. 25; *d.* Dec. 1241.

1242. Richd., surn. Crassus, elected; but *d.* Dec. 8, 1242, before consecration.

1243. Robt. de Monte Pessulano next chosen; but he, finding his election disagreeable to the king, refused the see, and the pope appointed

1245. Roger de Weseham, dean of Lincoln.

1257. Roger de Longespée, or de Molend.

1296. Walter de Langton, ld. treasr. and ld. chanc.

1322. Roger de Northbrugh, or Northburgh, archdn. of Richmond; ld. kpr. and ld. treasr.

1360. Robt. Stretton, canon of Lichfield.

1386. Walter Skirlawe, dean of St. Martin's; tr. to Bath and Wells same year.

Richd. Scrope, tr. to York.

1398. John Burghill, tr. from Llandaff.

1415. John Keterich, tr. from St. David's; tr. to Exeter, 1419.

1419. Jas. Cary, tr. to Exeter; *d.* before taking possession of that see.

Wm. Heyworth, Nov. 20; *d.* Mar. 13, 1447.

1447. Wm. Booth, preb. of St. Paul's; tr. to York.

1452. Nichls. Close, tr. from Carlisle; chanc. of Cambridge.

1453. Regd. Butler, tr. from Hereford.

1459. John Halse, or Hales, preb. of St. Paul's.

1492. Wm. Smith, archdn. of Surrey; tr. to Lincoln.

1496. John Arundel, dean of Exeter; t to Exeter.

1503. Geoffry Blythe, dean of York.

1534. Rowland Lee, chanc. and preb. Lichfield, and ld. pres. of Wal

1543. Richd. Sampson; tr. from Chich ter; ld. pres. of Wales.

1554. Ralph Baines, or Bayne, depr. 15 and *d.* soon after.

1560. Thos. Bentham, fellow of Magdal College, Oxford.

1580. Wm. Overton, preb. of Winchest and Salisbury.

1609. Geo. Abbot, dean of Winchester; to London.

1610. Richd. Neile, or Neale, tr. from R chester; tr. to Lincoln.

1614. John Overal, dean of St. Paul's; to Norwich.

1619. Thos. Morton, tr. from Chester; to Durham.

1632. Robt. Wright, tr. from Bristol.

1643. Accepted Frewen, dean of Glouc ter; tr. to York.

1661. John Hacket, can.-res. of St. Paul

1671. Thos. Wood, dean of Lichfield.

1692. Wm. Lloyd, bp. of St. Asaph; tr. Worcester.

1699. John Hough, tr. from Oxford; t to Worcester.

1717. Edwd. Chandler, preb. of Worce ter; tr. to Durham.

1730. Richd. Smalbroke, tr. from S David's.

1749. Hon. Fredk. Cornwallis, canon Windsor, and, in 1766, dean St. Paul's; tr. to Canterbury.

1768. Hon. John Egerton, tr. from Ba gor; tr. to Durham.

1771. Brownlow North, dean of Cante bury; tr. to Worcester.

1774. Richd. Hurd, master of the Templ tr. to Worcester.

1781. Hon. Jas. Cornwallis, dean of Ca terbury; succ. to the earldom Cornwallis, 1823; *d.* 1824.

1824. Hon. Hy. Ryder, Feb. 4; tr. fro Gloucester; *d.* Mar. 31, 1836.

1836. Saml. Butler, June 15; became b of Lichfield only, Jan. 24, 183

BISHOPS OF LICHFIELD.

1837. Saml. Butler, above named, Jan. 24; *d.* Dec. 4, 1839.

1839. Jas. Bowstead, Dec. 30; tr. from Sodor and Man; *d.* Oct. 11, 1843.

1843. John Lonsdale, archdn. of Middlesex and principal of King's College, London, Nov. 6; *d.* Oct. 19, 1867.

1867. Geo. Augs. Selwyn, Dec. 13, **G** tr. from New Zealand; *d.* Ap 11, 1878.

1878. Wm. Dalrymple Maclagan, vicar St. Mary Abbot, Kensingto May 13, **G.**

BISHOPS SUFFRAGAN OF SHREWSBURY.

1537. Lewis Thomas.

1888. Sir Lovelace Tomlinson Stamer, bt., archdn. of Stoke-on-Trent, Feb. **G.**

DEANS OF LICHFIELD.

140. William (1).
170. Richd. de Balam, or Dalam.
173. William (2).
190. Richard.
193. Bertram.
214. Ralph, or Richd. de Nevill, bp. Chichester, 1222.
222. Wm. de Manchester; *d.* Feb. 7, 1253.
254. Ralph de Sempringham; *d.* Mar. 25, 1280.
280. John de Derby; *d.* Oct. 12, 1319.
320. Stephen de Segrave, Dec. 5; bp. Armagh, 1324.
325. Roger de Covinis, Nov.; *d.* 1328.
328. John Casey, or Gasey.
337. Richd. FitzRalph, Apr. 20; bp. Armagh, 1347.
347. Simon de Borisleyer Briesley, or Griesley, Apr. 20; dean of Lincoln, 1349.
349. John de Bokingham; bp. Lincoln, 1363.
363. Anthy. Rous.
368. Laurence de Ibbestoke, or Ibbestock, Feb. 3.
371. Fras. St. Sabine.
381. Wm. de Packington, Jan. 5; *d.* 1390.
390. Thos. de Stretton, May 15; *d.* July 16, 1426.
426. Robt. Wolveden, Sept. 23; *d.* Nov. 1432.
432. John Verney, Dec. 2; *d.* 1457.
457. Thos. Heywood, Aug.; *d.* Oct. 25, 1492.
493. John Yotton, Feb. 23; *d.* Aug. 2, 1512.
512. Ralph Collingwood, Sept. 26; *d.* Nov. 22, 1521.
522. Jas. Denton, Jan. 7; *d.* Feb. 23, 1533.
533. Richd. Sampson, June 20; bp. Chichester, 1536.
1536. Richd., or Hy. Williams, Nov. 23; depr. 1553.
1554. John Rambridge, Apr. 2; impris. or depr. by Elizabeth.
1559. Lawrence Nowell. Apr. 29; *d.* 1576.
1576. Geo. Boleyn, or Bollen, Nov. 22; *d.* Jan. 1603.
1603. Jas. Montagu, July 16; dean of Worcester, 1604.
1604. Wm. Tooker, or Tucker, Feb. 21; *d.* Mar. 19, 1620.
1620. Walter Curll, or Curle, Mar. 24; bp. Rochester, 1628.
1628. Augustine Lindsell, Oct. 15; bp. Peterboro', 1632.
1633. John Warner, Mar.; bp. Rochester, 1637.
1637. Saml. Fell, dean of Christ Church, 1638.
1638. Griffith Higgs; *d.* Dec. 15, 1659.
1661. Wm. Paul, Apr. 8; bp. Oxford 1663.
1663. Thos. Wood, Feb.; bp. Lichfield, 1671.
1671. Matthew Smallwood, July 7; *d.* Apr. 26, 1683.
1683. Lancelot Addison, July 3; *d.* Apr. 20, 1703.
1703. Wm. Binckes, June 19; *d.* June 19, 1712.
1713. Jonathan Kimberley, July 7; *d.* Mar. 7, 1719.
1720. Wm. Walmisley, May. 7.
1730. Nichs. Penny; *d.* Jan. 15, 1745.
1745. John Addenbrook, Feb. 15; *d.* Feb. 25, 1776.
1776. Baptist Roby, Mar. 25; *d.* 1807.
1807. John Chappel Woodhouse, Jan. 27, **G.**; *d.* Nov. 17, 1833.
1833. Hon. Hy. Edwd. John Howard, Nov. 27, **G.**; *d.* Oct. 8, 1868.
1868. Wm. Weldon Champneys, Nov. 12, **G.**; *d.* Feb. 4, 1875.
1875. Edw. Bickersteth, Feb. 22, **G.**

DIOCESE OF LINCOLN.

HIS diocese was formerly two sees, Sidnacester (not far from Gainsorough, in Lincolnshire), and Dorchester, in Oxfordshire. The former as united to Dorchester, after remaining a long time vacant, subsequent the death of Eadulphus II. its ninth bishop.

The diocese was very large; so large, in fact, that although the ioceses of Ely, Oxford, and Peterborough, when originally formed, were aken from it, it still continued to be the largest in England. Portions f it have since been transferred to other dioceses. The bishops of

Lincoln were heretofore accounted chancellors to the archbishop of Canterbury.

In 1537 a bishop suffragan of Bedford was appointed under 26 Hen VIII. cap. 14. He was probably suffragan to this see, but when, i 1879, the title was revived, the bishop was made suffragan to London.

In 1567, a bishop suffragan of Nottingham was appointed (probabl to this see) under 26 Hen. VIII. cap. 14, and this title was revived i 1870.

BISHOPS OF DORCHESTER.

625. Birinus.
650. Agilbertus.
737. Totta, the first bp. of Leicester.
764. Edbertus.
786. Unwona.
801. Werinbertus.
814. Rethunus.
861. Aldredus.
873. Ceolredus.
Harlardus.
* * * *
905. Ceolulfus, or Kenulphus.

BISHOPS OF SIDNACESTER.

678. Eadhedus.
679. Ethelwinus.
701. Edgarus.
720. Kinebertus, or Embercus.
733. Alwigh.
751. Eadulphus I.
767. Ceolulfus.
783. Unwona.
789. Eadulphus II.; after whose deat the see remained long vacant until it was joined to that of Dor chester.

BISHOPS OF DORCHESTER AND SIDNACESTER.

949. Leofwynus, who first united the sees of Dorchester and Sidnacester
960. Ailnothus.
967. Ascwinus, or Œswy.
994. Alfhelmus.
1004 Eadnothus I.
1016. Eadhericus.
1034. Eadnothus II.
1052. Ulfus Normanus.
1053. Wulfinus.
1070. St. Remigius de Feschamp, who re moved the see to Lincoln in 107

BISHOPS OF LINCOLN.

1075. St. Remigius de Feschamp, above-named.
1092. Robt. Bloet, or Bluet; ld. chanc.
1123. Alexr., archdn. of Salisbury; ld. chanc.
1147. Robt. de Chesney, or Cheney, *alias* Querceto; *d.* 1166.
See vacant 7 years.
1173. Geoffrey Plantagenet; res. 1181.
1183. Walter de Constantiis, archdn. of Oxford; tr. to Rouen, 1184.
See vacant 2 years.
1186. Hugh, prior of the Carthusians at Witham, Somersetshire; canonised.
See vacant 3 years.
1203. Wm. de Blois, preb. of Lincoln.
See vacant 3 years.
1209. Hugo Wallis, or de Wells, archdn. of Wells; ld. chanc.
1235. Robt. Grosthead, or Grouthed, archdn. of Leicester.
1254. Hy. de Lexington, dean of Lincoln.
1258. Benedict, or Richd. de Gravesend dean of Lincoln.
1281. Oliver Sutton, dean of Lincoln.
1300. John Aldberry, or d'Aldreby, chanc of Lincoln.
1319. Thos. Beke, chanc. of Lincoln.
1320. Hy. de Burghersh, ld. treas., and ld chanc.
1343. Thos. le Bec, or Bek.
1351. John Gyndell, Gyndwelle, or Sin well, archdn. of Northampton.
1363. John Bokingham, kpr. pr. seal.
1398. Hy. Beaufort, dean of Wells, an chanc. of Oxford; ld. chanc.; tr to Winchester. This prelate wa third son of John of Gaunt, by Katherine Swinford.
1405. Philip de Repingdon, abbot o Leicester; chanc. of Oxford; res on being made a cardl.
1420. Richd. Fleyming, canon of Lincoln
1431. Wm. Grey, tr. from London.
1436. Wm. Alnewick, tr. from Norwich.

50. Marmaduke Lumley, chanc. of Cambridge; tr. from Carlisle.
52. John Chadworth, archdn. of Wells.
71. Thos. Rotherham, *alias* Scot; tr. from Rochester; kpr. pr. seal, ld. chanc., and chanc. of Cambridge; tr. to York.
80. John Russel, archdn. of Berks; ld. chanc. and chanc. of Oxford.
95. Wm. Smith; tr. from Lichfield and Coventry; chanc. of Oxford, and pres. of Wales.
13. Thos. Wolsey, bp. of Tournay, almoner; dean of York; tr. to York, Aug. 1514; aft. cardl.
14. Wm. Atwater, dean of Salisbury.
20. John Longland, or Langland, principal of Magdalen Hall, Oxford.
47. Hy. Holbeach; tr. from Rochester.
52. John Taylour, dean of Lincoln; depr. 1553.
53. John Whyte, warden of Winchester; tr. to Winchester in 1556.
57. Thos. Watson, dean of Durham; depr. in 1559.
60. Nichs. Bullingham, archdn. of Lincoln; tr. to Worcester, Jan. 1571.
70. Thos. Cowper, dean of Gloucester; tr. to Winchester.
84. Wm. Wickham, dean of Lincoln; tr. to Winchester.
95. Wm. Chaderton; tr. from Chester.
08. Wm. Barlow; tr. from Rochester.
13. Richd. Neile, or Neale; tr. from Lichfield and Coventry; tr. to Durham.
17. Geo. Monteigne, dean of Westminster; tr. to London.
21. John Williams, dean of Westminster, ld. kpr.; tr. to York, Dec. 1641.
1641. Thos. Wineffe, or Winniffe, dean of St. Paul's; *d.* 1654.
See vacant 6 years.
1660. Robt. Sanderson, preb. of Lincoln.
1663. Benjn. Laney, tr. from Peterborough; tr. to Ely.
1667. Wm. Fuller, tr. from Limerick.
1675. Thos. Barlow, provost of Queen's College, Oxford.
1691. Thos. Tenison, vicar of St. Martin's-in-the-Fields; tr. to Canterbury.
1694. Jas. Gardner, sub-dean of Lincoln.
1705. Wm. Wake, dean of Exeter; tr. to Canterbury, Jan. 1716.
1716. Edmd. Gibson, archdn. of Surrey; tr. to London.
1723. Richd. Reynolds, tr. from Bangor.
1743. John Thomas, bp. elect of St. Asaph; tr. to Salisbury.
1761. John Green, dean of Lincoln, and in 1771, can.-res. of St. Paul's; *d.* 1779.
1779. Thos. Thurlow, dean of Rochester, and, in 1781, dean of St. Paul's; tr. to Durham.
1787. Geo. Pretyman Tomline, dean of St Paul's; tr. to Winchester.
1820. Hon. Geo. Pelham, Aug. 19; tr. from Exeter; *d.* Feb 1, 1827.
1827. John Kaye, Feb. 15; tr. from Bristol; *d.* Feb. 19, 1852.
1853. John Jackson, canon of Bristol, &c., Mar. 11, **G.**; tr. to London.
1869. Christr. Wordsworth, archdn. of Westminster; Jan. 30, **G.**; res. 1885.
1885. Edwd. King, reg. prof. pastoral theology, and canon of Christ Church, Oxford; Mar. 5, **G.**

BISHOPS SUFFRAGAN OF BEDFORD.

See Diocese of London, *post*, p. 452.

BISHOPS SUFFRAGAN OF NOTTINGHAM.

67. Richd. Barnes.

---

70. Hy. Mackenzie, archdn. of Notts, and canon of Lincoln, Jan. 22, **G.**; res. 1877; *d.* 1878.
1877. Edwd. Trollope, archdn. of Stow, Dec. 17, **G.**

DEANS OF LINCOLN.

92. Ralph.
10. Simon Bloet.
* Nigellus, between 1123 and 1138.
41. Philip de Harcourt; aft. bp. Bayonne.
45. Adelmus, or Ascelimus.
bt. 1164 Hamelinus.
69. Geoffrey Kirtling.
1184. Richd. Fitz-Neal, or Fitz-Nigel; bp. London, 1189.
1189. Hamo; *d.* 1195.
1195. Roger de Rolveston; *d.* 1223.
1223. Wm. de Tournay; susp. 1232.
1232. Roger de Weseham; bp. Lichfield, 1245.

1245. Hy. de Lexington; bp. Lincoln, 1254.
1254. Richd. de Gravesend; bp. Lincoln, 1258.
1258. Robt. de Mariscis.
* * Wm. de Lexington, in 1263; *d.* 1272.
1273. Richd. Mepham; *d.* 1274.
* * John de Maidston, dean in 1275; *d* same year.
1275. Oliver Sutton, July; bp. Lincoln, 1281.
1281. Nichs. Heigham; *d.* 1288.
1288. Philip Willoughby, June; *d.* 1305.
1305. Josceline de Kirmington, Sept. 9.
1307. Cardl. Raymond de la Goth; dean of Salisbury, 1310.
1310. Roger de Martival; bp. Salisbury, 1315.
1315. Hy. de Mansfield, Jan.; *d.* 1328.
1329. Anthy. Beck; bp. Norwich, 1336.
Deanery vacant till
1338. John de Nottingham, Oct.
1340. Wm. Bateman, *alias* Wm. de Norwich; bp. Norwich, 1344.
1344. John de Ufford, or Offord, nom. abp. Canterbury, 1348, but *d.* before consecration.
1349. Simon de Briesly; *d.* 1360.
* * John de Stretely in 1361 and 1368.
* * Simon, or Simon Sixti, cardl. in 1372.
* * John de Shepey, in 1376; *d.* 1412.
1412. John Mackworth; *d.* 1451.
1451. Robt. Fleming, Jan. 21; *d.* 1483.
1483. Geo. Fitzhugh, Oct. 30; *d.* 1505.
1506. Geoffrey Simeon; *d.* 1508.
1508. Thos. Wolsey, Feb. 2; dean of York, 1512; bp. Lincoln, 1514; abp. York, 1514.
1514. John Constable; *d.* 1528.
1528. Geo. Heneage; res. 1544; *d.* 1548.
1544. John Taylour; bp. Lincoln, 1552.
1552. Matt. Parker, June 8; depr. b Mary, May 21, 1554; abp. Can terbury, 1559.
1554. Fras. Mallet; *d.* 1570.
1571. John Whitgift, Aug. 2; bp. Worces ter, 1577.
1577. Wm. Wickham, May 30; bp. Lin coln, 1584.
1584. Ralph Griffin, Dec. 17.
1593. John Reynolds, Dec. 10; *d.* 1607.
1599. Wm. Cole, June 2; *d.* 1600.
1601. Laurence Staunton, May 8; *d.* 161
1613. Roger Parker, Nov. 29; *d.* 1629.
1629. Anthy. Topham, Sept. 7; *d.* 1655.
Deanery vacant 5 years.
1660. Michl. Honeywood, Oct. 12; *d.* 168
1682. Danl. Brevint, Jan. 3; *d.* 1695.
1695. Saml. Fuller, Dec. 21; *d.* 1699.
1700. Abrm. Campion, Apr. 17; *d.* 1701.
1701. Richd. Willis, Dec. 26; bp Gloucester, 1715.
1721. Robt. Cannon, Sept. 23; *d.* 1722.
1722. Edwd. Gee, Mar. 30.
1730. Edwd. Willes, May; bp. St. David's 1743.
1744. Thos. Cheney, Mar. 28.
1748. Wm. George, Apr. 16.
1756. John Green, Oct. 16; bp. Lincoln, 176
1762. Hon. Jas. Yorke. Jan. 23; bp. St David's, 1774; tr. to Glouceste 1781.
1781. Richd. Cust, Dec. 22; *d.* 1783.
1783. Sir Richd. Kaye, bt., Nov. 11.
1810. Geo. Gordon, Jan. 9, **G.**; *d.* 1845.
1845. John Giffard Ward, Oct. 9, **G.**
1860. Thos. Garmier, Mar. 30, **G.**
1864. Fras. Jeune, Jan. 18, **G.**; bp. Peter borough, May, 1864.
Jas. Amiraux Jeremie, July 4, **G.**
1872. Jos. Williams Blakesley, July 4,
1885. Wm. John Butler, June 22, **G.**

DIOCESE OF LLANDAFF.

THIS is a very ancient see: by whom founded is uncertain. The firs bishop, that is known for certainty, is St. Dubritius.

BISHOPS OF LLANDAFF.

* * *
522. St. Dubritius.
* * Thelian, Teilaus, or Eliud.
* * Oudoceus.
* * Ubylwinus, or Unelbicus.
* * Aydanus.
* * Elgistil.
* * Lunapeius.
* * Comergius, or Comegern.
* * Argwistil.
* * Gurvan.
* * Guodloiu.
* * Edilbinus.
* * Grecielus.
* * Berthgwyn.
* * Tyrcheanus, Tyrchan, or Tridianus.
* * Elvogus.
* * Catguaert, or Cat guaret.
* * Cerenhire.
* * Nobis.
* * Gulfridus.
* * Nudd.
* * Cimeliau, or Cem liauc.
* * Libiau.
* * Marcluith.
* * Pater.

982. Gogwan, Gucanor, or Gucaunus.
993. Bledri.
1022. Joseph.
1059. Herewald.
1107. Urban, archdn. of Llandaff.
See vacant 6 years.
1139. Uhtred.
1148. Galfrid.
1153. Nichs. ap Gwrgant.
1183. Wm. de Salso Marisco, or Saltmarsh.
1191. Hy., prior of Abergavenny.
1219. Wm., prior of Godcliffe.
1230. Elias de Radnor; *d.* 1140.
See vacant 4 years.
1244. Wm. de Burgh, chaplain to the king.
1253. John de la Ware.
1256. Wm. of Radnor.
1266. Wm. de Braose, preb. of Llandaff.
1287. Philip de Staunton.—*Prynne.* But the see is generally considered to have been vacant from 1287 to 1296.
1296. John de Monmouth.
1323. John Eglescliffe, tr. from Connor, Ireland.
1347. John Paschal.
1362. Rodger Cradock, tr. from Waterford, Ireland.
1383. Thos. Rushooke, confessor to the king; tr. to Chichester.
1385. Wm. of Bottlesham, titular bp. of Bethlehem; tr. to Rochester.
1389. Edmd. Bromfeld.
1391. Tideman de Winchecombe, abbot of Beauly; tr. to Worcester.
1395. Andrew Barret.
1397. John Burghill, or Bruchilla, confessor to the king; tr. to Lichfield and Coventry.
1399. Thos. Peverel, tr. from Ossory, Ireland; tr. to Worcester.
1408. John de la Zouche.
Quære, de Johanne Fulford.—*Le Neve.*
1425. John Wells.
1441. Nichs. Ashby, prior of Westminster.
1458. John Hunden, prior of King's Langley; res.
1476. John Smith.
1478. John Marshal.
1496. John Ingleby, prior of Shene.
1500. Miles Salley, or Sawley, abbot of Eynesham.
1516. Geo. Athequa, or Attien, a Spaniard; chaplain to queen Catharine, who brought him out of Spain with her.
1537. Robt. Holgate, prior of Wotton; tr. to York.
1545. Anthy. Kitchin, or Dunstan, abbot of Eynesham,
See vacant three years.
1560. Hugh Jones.
1575. Wm. Blethyn, preb. of York.
1591. Gervase Babington, preb. of Hereford; tr. to Exeter.
1594. Wm. Morgan (he translated the Bible into Welsh); tr. to St. Asaph.
1601. Fras. Godwin, canon of Wells; tr. to Hereford.
1618. Geo. Carleton; tr. to Chichester.
1619. Theoph. Field, rector of Cotton, Suffolk; tr. to St. David's in 1627.
1627. Wm. Murray, tr. from Kilfenora, Ireland.
1639. Morgan Owen.
See vacant 16 years.
1660. Hugh Lloyd, archdn. of St. David's.
1667. Fras. Davis, archdn. of Llandaff.
1675. Wm. Lloyd, preb. of St. Paul's; tr. to Peterborough.
1679. Wm. Beaw, vicar of Adderbury, Oxfordshire.
1707. John Tyler, dean of Hereford.
1724. Robt. Clavering, canon of Christchurch, Oxford; tr. to Peterborough.
1728. John Harris, preb. of Canterbury.
1738. Matthias Mawson, rector of Hadstock, Essex; tr. to Chichester.
1740. John Gilbert, dean of Exeter; tr. to Salisbury.
1748. Edwd. Cresset, dean of Hereford.
1754. Richd. Newcome, canon of Windsor; tr. to St. Asaph.
1761. John Ewer, canon of Windsor; tr. to Bangor.
1769. Jonn. Shipley, dean of Winchester; tr. to St. Asaph.
Hon. Shute Barrington, canon of St. Paul's; tr. to Salisbury.
1782. Richd. Watson, reg. prof. Divinity, Cambridge, and archdn. of Ely; *d.* July 1816.
1816. Herbert Marsh, July 18; tr. to Peterborough.
1819. Wm. Van Mildert, May 15; tr. to Durham.
1826. Chas. Richd. Sumner, Apr. 25; tr. to Winchester.
1827. Edward Copleston, Dec. 12; *d.* Oct. 14, 1849.
1849. Alfred Ollivant, canon of St. David's, reg. prof. Divinity, Cambridge, &c., Nov. 1; *d.* Dec. 16, 1882.
1883. Richd. Lewis, archdn. of St. David's, Feb. 16, **G.**

DEANS OF LLANDAFF

Down to the passing of the act 3 and 4 Vict. cap. 113 (Aug. 11, 1840), the bishops of Llandaff were also the deans and the archdeacons of Llandaff were also the sub-deans.

By that Act. (sec. 1), it was enacted that the archdeacons of Llandaff should be als the deans, but by 6 and 7 Vict. c. 77 (Aug. 22, 1843) and order in council, Novembe 10, 1843, the two offices were afterwards separated.

1840. John Probyn, archdn., now dean also; Aug. 11.
1843. Wm. Bruce Knight.
1845. W. D. Conybeare.
1857. Thos. Williams.
1877. Hy. Lynch Blosse.
1879. Chas. John Vaughan.

DIOCESE OF LONDON.

THIS see was archiepiscopal in the time of the Britons and was intende by pope Gregory to continue so; but St. Augustine, whom his holines had sent to convert the Saxons, was so pleased with his reception fron Ethelbert, king of Kent, that he set up his staff at Canterbury, th capital of Ethelbert's dominions, which has continued the metropolitan see of England ever since. London still remained a bishopric. Th bishop has precedency before all bishops of the realm, next to the tw archbishops, and is dean to the archbishop of Canterbury.

In 1537 a bishop suffragan of Bedford was appointed under 26 Hen VIII. cap. 14. He was probably suffragan to Lincoln, but when, in 1879, the title was revived, the bishop was made suffragan to London.

In 1537 a bishop suffragan of Marlborough was appointed unde 26 Hen. VIII., cap. 14. He was probably suffragan to Salisbury, but when, in 1888, the title was revived, the bishop was made suffragan to London.

The deans of this diocese are styled "Deans of St. Paul's."

ARCHBISHOPS OF LONDON.

"The archbishops' names are set down by Jocelyne of Furnes, in his book of *British Bishops*, and nowhere else that I can find."—*Stowe*.

1. Thean; the first abp. of London, in the time of Lucius, who built the church of St. Peter, in a place called Cornehill, in London, by the aid of Cyran, chief butler to king Lucius.
2. Elvanus.
3 Cadar.
4. Obinus.
5. Conan.
6. Paludius
7. Stephen.
8. Iltute.
9. Dedwin, or Theodwin.
10. Thedred.
11. Hillary.
12. Restitutus I.
13. Guidelium, or Guiteline.
14. Fastidius.
15. Vodimus; slain by the Saxons.
16. Theanus; the sixteenth and last abp.; he fled with the Britons into Wales.

BISHOPS OF LONDON.

514. Restitutus II.
553. Theonus.
604. St. Miletus; tr. to Canterbury. See vacant 39 years.
658. St. Ceadda; *d.* 664. See vacant 2 years.
666. Wina, tr. from Winchester.
675. St. Erkenwald.
697. Waldherus
715. Ingualdus.
746. Egwolfus.
754. Wighedus.

761. Eadbrightus.
768. Edgarus.
773. Kenwalchus.
784. Eadbaldus.
795. Hecbertus, or Heathobertus.
802. Osmundus, or Oswynus.
816. Ethelnothus.
830. Ceolbertus.
841. Renulphus, or Ceolnulfus.
851. Suithulfus.
863. Eadstanus.
898. Wulfius, or Walsius.
Ethelwardus.
926. Elstanus.
938. Theodredus.
Wolstanus.
941. Brithelmus.
958. St. Dunstan, tr. from Worcester ; tr. to Canterbury.
960. Oelfstan, or Ælfstan.
996. Wuffstan,
1004. Aldwin, or Alduinus, tr. from Durham.
1016. Alfwy.
1032. Elfward, or Alword, abbot of Evesham.
1044. Robt. the Norman, Gemiticensis; tr. to Canterbury.
1051. Wm. the Norman.
1075. Hugh d'Orevalle, or de Orwell, a Norman.
1085. Maurice, archdn. of Maine ; ld. chanc.
1108. Richd. de Beaumis Belmis, or Rufus I.
1128. Gilbert, surn. Universalis, canon of Lyons.
See vacant 5 years.
1141. Robt. de Sigello, monk of Reading.
1152. Richd. de Beaumis, or Belmis II., archdn. of Middlesex.
1163. Robt. or Gilbert Foliot; tr. from Hereford.
See vacant 2 years.
1189. Richd. Fitz-Neale, or Fitz-Nigel, dean of Lincoln.
1199. Wm. de St. Mariæ Ecclesiâ, preb. of St. Paul's ; res.
1221. Eustace de Fauconberg, ld. treasr.
1229. Roger Niger, archdn. of Colchester ; canonised.
1241. Fulke Basset, dean of York.
1260. Hy. de Wengham, or Wingham, preb. of St. Paul's ; ld. chanc. ; *d.* July 1262.
1262. Richd. Talbot, dean of St. Paul's ; *d.* Oct. 1262.
Hy. de Sandwich, preb. of St. Paul's.
1273. John de Chishull, dean of St. Paul's ; ld. chanc. and ld. treasr.; *d.* 1280.
1280. Fulke Lovell elected, but declined the dignity.
Richd. de Gravesend, preb. of St. Paul's.
1304. Ralph de Baldoc, or Baudake, dean of St. Paul's.
1313. Gilbert de Segrave, precentor of St. Paul's.
1317. Richd. de Newport, dean of St. Paul's.
1318. Stephen de Gravesend, preb. of St. Paul's.
1338 Richd. de Wentworth, or Bynteworth, preb. of St. Paul's, and ld. chanc.
1340. Ralph de Stratford, preb. of St. Paul's and Salisbury.
1354. Michl. de Northburg, preb. of St. Paul's.
1361. Simon de Sudbury, *alais* Tybold, chanc. of Salisbury; tr. to Canterbury.
1375. Wm. Courtenay, tr. from Hereford; ld. chanc., chanc. of Oxford ; tr. to Canterbury.
1381. Robt. de Braybroke, dean of Salisbury; ld. chanc.
1404. Roger Walden, formerly dean of York; and consec. abp. Canterbury, (*q. v.*) ; ld. treasr.
1406. Nichs. de Bubwith, or Bubbewyth, preb. of Salisbury ; m. rolls, kpr. pr. seal, and ld. treasr. ; tr. to Salisbury.
1407. Richd. de Clifford, tr. from Worcester.
1421. John Kempe, tr. from Chichester ; tr. to York.
1426. Wm. Grey, dean of York ; tr. to Lincoln.
1431. Robt. Fitz-Hugh, archdn. of Northampton, and chanc. of Cambridge.
1436. Robt. Gilbert, dean of York.
1448. Thos. Kempe, archdn. of Middlesex, and chanc. of York.
1489. Richd. Hill, dean of the king'schapel, and preb. of Salisbury.
1496. Thos. Savage, tr. from Rochester ; tr. to York.
1502. Wm. Warham, preb. of St. Paul's ; ld. chanc. ; tr. to Canterbury.
1504. Wm. Barnes, m. rolls.
1506. Richd. Fitz-James, tr. from Chichester.
1522. Cuthbert Tunstall, dean of Salisbury; m. rolls ; tr. to Durham.
1530. John Stockesley, archdn. of Dorset.
1539. EdmundBonner, archdn. of Leicester ; bp. elect of Hereford ; depr. Sept. 1549.
1550. Nichs. Ridley, tr. from Rochester ; burnt at Oxford., Oct. 16, 1555.
1553, Edmd. Bonner, *again* ; rest. by Mary ; again depr. by Elizabeth, May 1559 ; *d.* Sept. 1569.
1559. Edmd. Grindal, master of Pembroke Hall, Cambridge ; tr. to York.
1570. Edwyn Sandys, tr. from Worcester.
1577. John Aylmer, archdn. of Lincoln.
1594. Richd. Fletcher, tr. from Worcester ; *d.* June 15, 1596.

1597. Richd. Bancroft, preb. of Westminster; tr. to Canterbury.
1604. Richd. Vaugham, tr. from Chester.
1607. Thos. Ravis, tr. from Gloucester.
1610. Geo. Abbot, tr. from Lichfield and Coventry; tr. to Canterbury.
1611. John King, dean of Christchurch, Oxford.
1621. Geo. Monteigne, tr. from Lincoln.
1628. Wm. Laud, tr. from Bath and Wells; chanc. of Oxford; tr. to Canterbury.
1633. Wm. Juxon, tr. from Hereford before consecration; ld. treasr.; he attended Charles I. on the scaffold, and at the Restoration was tr. to Canterbury.
1660. Gilbert Sheldon, preb. of Gloucester; tr. to Canterbury.
1663. Humphrey Henchman, tr. from Salisbury; bp. almoner.
1675. Hy. Compton, tr. from Oxford, Dec.
1713. John Robinson, tr. from Bristol.
1723. Edmd. Gibson, tr. from Lincoln.
1748. Thos. Sherlock, tr. from Salisbury.
1761. Thos. Hayter, tr. from Norwich; d. the next year.
1762. Richd. Osbaldeston, tr. from Carlisle; *d.* 1764.
1764. Richd. Terrick, tr. from Peterborough.
1777. Robt. Lowth, tr. from Oxford.
1787. Beilby Porteus, tr. from Chester; d. May 14, 1809.
1809. John Randolph, June 12; tr. from Bangor.
1813. Wm. Howley, Aug. 14; tr. to Canterbury.
1828. Chas. Jas. Blomfield, tr. from Chester, Aug. 15; res. Sept. 1856; d. Aug. 5, 1857.
1856. Archd. Campbell Tait, dean of Carlisle, Oct. 11, **G.**; tr. to Canterbury.
1869. Jno. Jackson, Jan. 4, **G.**; tr. from Lincoln, *d.* Jan. 6, 1885.
1885. Fredk. Temple, Feb. 25, **G.**; tr from Exeter.

BISHOPS SUFFRAGAN OF BEDFORD.

1537. John Hodgkins, probably suffragan to Lincoln.

1879. Wm. Walsham How, hon. canon of St. Asaph and rural dean, July 15 **G.**; tr. to Wakefield, 1888.
1888. Robt. Claudius Billing, preb. of St. Paul's, June 21, **G.**

BISHOPS SUFFRAGAN OF MARLBOROUGH.

1537. Thomas Morley; probably suffragan to Salisbury.
1888. Alfred Earle, archdn. of Totnes, Jan. 27, **G.**

DEANS OF ST. PAUL'S.

* * Leovegarus.
* * Godwinus.
* * Syredus.
* * Guilermus.
* * Elfwinus.
* * Luiredus.
* * Ulstan or Ulstanus, *alias* Ulmannus 1st. dean after Norman conquest.
* * William, dean in 1111; *d.* 1138.
1138. Ralph de Langford.
* * Taurinus de Stamford, dean between 1154 and 1162.
* * Hugh de Marinis, or de Marny, from about 1160 to 1181.
1181. Ralph de Diceto.
* * Alardus de Burnham; *d.* Aug. 14, 1216.
* * Gervase de Hobrugg.
1218. Robt. de Watford, or Dowtford, Nov. 22.
1228. Martin de Pateshull; *d.* Nov. 14, 1229.
* * Walter de Langford.
Geoffrey de Lucy, dean in 1231; *d.* 1240 or 1241.
1241. Wm. de Maris; *d.* Mar. 4, 1243.
1244. Hy. de Cornhill, *d.* Apr 9, 1254.
1254. Walter de Salerne, or de London; Easter abp. of Tuam, Oct. 16, 1256; *d.* Aug. 1258.
1256. Robt. de Barthon, or Barton.
* * Peter de Newport.
* * Richd. Talbot; made bp. London, Aug. 18, 1262; *d.* Sept. 1262.
Geoffrey de Feringes, dean in 1263.
1268. John de Chishull; bp. London, 1273.
1274. Herveius de Borham; *d.* 1276.
1276. Thos. de Inglethorp, or Ingaldesthorp, Mar.; bp. Rochester, 1283; *d.* May 11, 1291.
1283. Roger de la Leye, or Lee, Nov. 8.
1285. Wm. de Mundfort or Montford, *d.* 1294.
1294. Ralph de Baldock, or Baudake, Oct. 18; bp. London, 1304.
1306. Raymond de la Goth; dean of Lincoln, 1307.

1307. Arnaldus Frangeruis de Cantilupe.
John de Sandale, king's treasr., 1313; chanc. 1315; bp. Winchester, 1316; *d.* 1319.
1314. Richd. de Newport; bp. London, 1317.
Vitalis de Testa, dean in 1316.
* * John de Everdon; *d.* Jan. 15, 1336.
1336. Gilbert de Bruera.
1353–4. Richd. de Kilmyngton; *d.* 1361.
1362. Walter de Alderbury.
1363. Thos. Trilleck, Apr. 11; bp. Rochester, 1364; *d.* 1372.
1364. John de Appleby.
1389. Thos. de Eure or Everey; *d.* Oct. 9, 1400.
1400. Thos. Stow, Oct. 25; *d.* before Nov. 19, 1405.
1406. Thos. Moor, Jan.; *d.* 1421.
1421. Regd. Kentwode, Jan. 20; *d.* Oct. 8, 1441.
1441. Thos. Lisieux, Dec. 11, king's pr. seal, 1456.
1456. Laurence Bathe, or Both, or Booth, Nov. 22; bp. Durham, 1457.
1457. Wm. Say, Nov. 21; *d.* Nov. 23, 1468.
1468. Roger Radclyff, Dec. 15; *d.* 1471.
1471. Thos. Wynterburne, Sept. 25; *d.* Sept. 6, 1478.
1479. Wm. Worsely, Jan. 22; *d.* Aug. 14, 1499.
1499. Robt. Sherbon, or Sherburne, bp. St. David's 1505; *d.* Aug. 21, 1536.
1505. John Colet, May; *d.* Sept. 16, 1519.
1519. Richd. Pace, Oct. 25; *d.* 1532.
1536. Richd. Sampson, bp. Chichester, July; tr. to Lichfield and Coventry, 1543; *d.* Sept. 25, 1554.
1540. John Incent, June 4; *d.* 1545.
1545. Wm. May, Feb. 8; depr. by Mary; chosen abp. York, but not consec.; *d.* Aug. 8, 1560.
1553. John Feckenham, Mar. 10; res. 1556; *d.* 1585.
1556. Hy. Cole, Dec. 11; depr. by Elizabeth; *d.* Dec. 1579.
1559. Wm. May, *again*; June 23.
1560. Alexr. Nowell, Nov. 17; *d.* Feb. 13, 1602.
1602. John Overall, May 29; bp. Lichfield and Coventry, 1614; *d.* May 12, 1619.
1614. Valentine Carey, Apr. 8; bp. Exeter, 1621; *d.* 1626.
1621. John Donne, Nov. 27; *d.* Mar. 31, 1631.
1631. Thos. Whinniff, Apr. 18; bp. Lincoln, 1641.
1660. Matthew Nicholas, July 10; *d.* Aug. 14, 1661.
1661. John Barwick, Oct. 15; *d.* Oct. 22, 1664.
1664. Wm. Sancroft, Nov. 11; abp. Canterbury, 1678; *d.* Nov. 24, 1693.
1677. Edwd. Stillingfleet, Jan. 19; bp. Worcester, 1689; *d.* 1699.
1689. John Tillotson, Nov. 19; abp. Canterbury, 1691; *d.* Nov. 22, 1694.
1691. Wm. Sherlock, June 12; *d.* 1707.
1707. Hy. Godolphin, July 14; res. 1726; *d.* July 29, 1733.
1726. Fras. Hare, Oct. 26; bp. St. Asaph, 1727; bp. Chichester, 1731.
1740. Jos. Butler, May 19; bp. Durham, 1750; *d.* June 16, 1752.
1750. Thos. Secker, bp. Oxford, Dec. 4; abp. Canterbury, 1758.
1758. John Hume, May 24; bp. Bristol, 1758.
1766. Fredk. Cornwallis, bp. Lichfield, Nov. 17; abp. Canterbury, 1768.
1768. Thos. Newton, bp. Bristol, Oct. 5.
1782. Thos. Thurlow, bp. Lincoln, Mar. 23; bp. Durham, 1787.
1787. Geo. Pretyman, aft. Tomline, Feb. 28; bp. Lincoln, 1787; bp. Winchester, 1820.
1820. Wm. Van Mildert, bp. Llandaff, Aug. 21; bp. Durham, 1826.
1826. Chas. Richd. Sumner, bp. Llandaff; Apr. 25, **G.**; bp. Winchester, 1827.
1827. Edwd. Copleston, bp. Llandaff; Dec. 12, **G.**
1849. Hy. Hart Milman, Nov. 1, **G.**; *d.* 1868.
1868. Hy. Longueville Mansel, Oct. 1, **G.**; *d.* 1871.
1871. Richd. Wm. Church, Sept. 6, **G.**

DIOCESE OF NORWICH.

This was once two distinct bishoprics, Elmham, in Norfolk, and Dunwich, in Suffolk. Felix, a Burgundian, who first converted the East Angles, founded the first see, and called it by that name. Bifus, the third bishop in succession from him, finding himself, from his great age, unable to bear so great a burden, got his diocese divided into two. Both sees suffered extremely from the Danish invasions, insomuch that, after the death of St. Humbert, they lay vacant for upwards of a hundred years. At length the see of Elmham was revived, and the see of Dunwich was united to it; but Herefast, the twenty-second bishop, removed the seat to Thetford, in Norfolk, where it remained until Herbert Losinga, the twenty-fourth bishop, removed it to Norwich, where it has continued ever since.

In 1536 bishops suffragan of Thetford and Ipswich were appointed (probably to this see) under 26 Hen. VIII., cap. 14, but the appointments were not continued.

BISHOPS OF THE EAST ANGLES.

630. St. Felix, a Burgundian.
647. Thomas, a deacon.
652. Brigilsus, or Bonifacius.
669. Bifus or Bisus, by whom this diocese was divided into those of—

ELMHAM. AND DUNWICH.

ELMHAM.

673. Bedwinus.
696. Northbertus.
720. Headulacus.
736. Eadilfridus.
767. Lanferthus.
771. Athelwolfus.
779. Hunferthus.
786. Sybba.
788. Alherdus.
818. St. Humbertus, or Humbryct, after whose death both sees lay vacant for the space of 100 years.

DUNWICH.

* * Acca.
* * Astwolfus.
* * Eadfarthus.
* * Cuthwynus.
* * Alberthus, or Aldberthus.
* * Eglasius.
* * Hardulfus, or Heardredus.
* * Ælphunus.
* * Thefridus, Tedfrid, or Tydferth.
* * Weremundus.
* * Wilfredus, or Wyredus; the last bp of Dunwich.

BISHOPS OF ELMHAM AND DUNWICH UNITED.

955. Athulf.
962. Alfrid.
967. Theodred.
973. Athelstan.
993. Algar.
1021. Alwyn.
1028. Alfric.
1032. Alifregus.
1034. Stigand; tr. to Winchester.
1043. Grinkettel; tr. from Selsey.
1047. Ethelmar, or Egelmar.
1070. Arfastus, or Herefast, who remove the see to Thetford; ld. chanc in 1067.
1085. Wm. Galfragus, or Galsagus.
1091. Herbert Losinga, abbot of Ramsay ld. chanc.; who in 1094 remove the see to Norwich.

BISHOPS OF NORWICH.

1094. Herbert Losinga, above named.
1121. Everard, archdn. of Salisbury.
1146. Wm. Turbus, a Norman; prior of Norwich.
1175. John of Oxford, dean of Salisbury.
1200. John de Grey; elected to Canterbury, but set aside by the pope. See vacant 7 years.
1218. Pandulph Masca, the pope's legate, and a cardl.
1226. Thos. de Blundeville, clerk of the exch.
1236. Radulph, or Ralph. See vacant 3 years.
1239. Wm. de Raleigh; tr. to Winchester.
1244. Walter de Suthfield, or Calthorp.
1253. Simon de Wauton, or Walton, or of the king's justices.
1265. Roger de Skerwing, prior of Norwich.
1278. Wm. de Middleton, archdn. of Canterbury.
1288. Ralph Walpole, archdn. of Ely; tr. Ely.
1299. John Salmon, or Saleman, prior Ely; ld. chanc.
Robt. de Baldock, archdn. of Middlesex, elected; but the pope having reserved the presentation, he declined; ld. chanc. in 1323.
1325. Wm. Ayremyn; ld. treas.
Thos. de Hemenhale elected; bu

before consecration removed to Worcester.
1336. Anthy. de Beck; poisoned by his own servants.
1344. Wm. Bateman, archdn. of Norwich.
1355. Thos. Percy.
1370. Hy. le Spencer.
1406. Alexr. Totington, prior of Norwich.
1413. Richd. Courtney, chanc. of Oxford; *d.* at the siege of Harfleur.
1416. John Wakering, archdn. of Canterbury.
1426. Wm. Alnewick, archdn.of Salisbury; kpr. pr. seal; tr. to Lincoln.
1436. Thos. Brown; tr. from Rochester.
John Stanbery, provost of Eton; nom. by the king, but set aside by the pope.
1446. Walter Hart, or Lyhert, provost of Oriel College, Oxford.
1472. Jas. Goldwell, dean of Salisbury.
1490. Thos. Jane, archdn. of Essex.
1501. Richd. Nix, canon of Windsor, and dean of the king's chapel.
1536. Wm. Rugg, or Repps, abbot of St. Benedict, in Hulme.
1550. Thos. Thirleby, tr. from Westminster; tr. to Ely.
1554. John Hopton, chaplain to Mary.
1559. Richd. Cox, elected; but before consecration removed to Ely.
1560. John Parkhurst.
1575. Edmd. Freke, tr. from Rochester; tr. to Worcester.
1585. Edmd. Scambler, tr. from Peterborough, Jan. 5; *d.* May 7, 1594, aged 85.
1594. Wm. Redman, archdn. of Canterbury.
1602. John Jeggon, dean of Norwich.
1618. John Overal, tr. from Lichfield and Coventry.
1619. Saml. Harsnet, tr. from Chichester; tr. to York.
1628. Fras. White, tr. from Carlisle; tr. to Ely.
1632. Richd. Corbet, tr. from Oxford.
1634. Matth. Wren, tr. from Hereford; tr. to Ely.
1638. Richd. Montague, tr. from Chichester.
1641. Jos. Hall, tr. from Exeter.
1660. Edwd. Reynolds, dean of Christchurch, Oxford.
1676. Anthy. Sparrow, tr. from Exeter.
1685. Wm. Lloyd, tr. from Peterborough; depr. for not taking the oaths.
1691. John Moore, preb. of Norwich; tr. to Ely.
1707. Chas. Trimnell, preb. of Norwich; tr. to Winchester.
1721. Thos. Green, archdn. of Canterbury; tr. to Ely.
1723. John Leng; *d.* 1727.
1728. Wm. Baker; tr. from Bangor.
1732. Robt. Butts, dean of Norwich; tr. to Ely.
1738. Thos. Gooch, tr. from Bristol; tr. to Ely.
1748. Saml. Lisle, tr. from St. Asaph.
1749. Thos. Hayter, preb. of Westminster; tr. to London.
1761. Philip Yonge, tr. from Bristol; *d.* April, 1783.
1783. Lewis Bagot, tr. from Bristol; tr. to St. Asaph.
1790. Geo. Horne, dean of Canterbury; *d.* Jan. 17, 1792
1792. Chas. Manners Sutton, dean of Peterborough; tr. to Canterbury.
1805. Hy. Bathurst, preb. of Durham; *d.* Apr. 5, 1837.
1837. Edwd. Stanley, Apr. 18; *d.* Sept. 6, 1849.
1849. Saml. Hinds, dean of Carlisle, Sept. 29; res. 1857.
1857. Hon. John Thos. Pelham, rector of Marylebone, and hon. canon of Norwich, Apr. 30, **G.**

BISHOP SUFFRAGAN OF THETFORD.

1536. John Salisbury.

BISHOP SUFFRAGAN OF IPSWICH.

1536. Thos. Manning.

DEANS OF NORWICH.

1538. Wm Castleton, last prior and first dean; res. 1539; *d.* 1548.
1539. John Salisbury; depr. 1554; rest. 1560; bp. Sodor and Man, 1571; *d.* Sept. 1573.
1554. John Christopherson, Apr. 18; bp. Chichester, 1557.
1557. John Boxhall, or Boxall, Dec. 20; *d.* 1570
1558. John Harpsfield, May 16; depr. by Elizabeth; *d.* 1558.
John Salisbury, rest.; *see above.*
1573. Geo. Gardiner, Nov. 28; *d.* 1589.
1589. Thos. Dove, June 16; bp. Peterborough, 1600; *d.* Aug. 30, 1630.
1601. John Jeggon, July 22; bp. Norwich, 1602; *d.* Mar. 13, 1617.

1603. Geo. Montgomery, June 6; bp. Meath, 1614.
1614. Edmd. Suckling, Sept. 30; *d.* 1628.
1628. John Hassal, July 15; depr. by the Commonwealth.
1660. John Crofts, Aug. 7; *d.* July 27, 1670.
1670. Herbert Astley, Sept. 2; *d.* June, 1681.
1681. John Sharp, June 8; dean of Canterbury, 1689; abp. York, 1691.
1689. Hy. Fairfax, Nov. 30; *d.* 1702.
1702. Humphrey Prideaux, June 8; *d* Nov. 1, 1724.
1724. Thos. Cole, May; *d.* Feb. 1730.
1731. Robt. Butts, Apr. 10; bp. Norwich 1732.
1733. John Baron; *d.* July 11, 1739.
1739. Thos. Bullock.
1761. Edwd. Townshend.
1765. Philip Lloyd.
1790. Jos. Turner.
1828. Geo. Pellew, Nov. 29, **G.**
1866. Edwd. Meyrick Goulburn, Nov. 26 **G.**; res. 1888.

DIOCESE OF OXFORD.

THIS diocese constituted a part of the diocese of Lincoln until 1541, whe[n] Henry VIII. erected it into a separate bishopric, endowed it out of th[e] lands of the dissolved monasteries of Abingdon and Osney, and assigne[d] to it the church of the abbey of Osney, for a cathedral. Five year[s] afterwards he removed the seat of the see to Oxford. The presen[t] cathedral of Oxford was anciently dedicated to St. Frideswide; bu[t] when the see was removed to that city, it was styled Christ Church, an[d] part of the lands appropriated by cardinal Wolsey to the maintenanc[e] of his colleges, was allotted to the dean and chapter.

The deans of this diocese are styled "Deans of Christ Church."

BISHOPS OF OXFORD.

1541 Robt. King, the last abbot of Osney; *d.* 1557.
1557. Thos. Goldwell, bp. of St. Asaph, was intended by Mary for this see; but she died before the translation could be perfected.
See vacant 10 years.
1567. Hugh Curwyn, dean of Hereford, abp. of Dublin, and ld. chanc. of Ireland; *d.* the next year.
See vacant 21 years.
1589. John Underhill, rector of Lincoln College, Oxford, and chaplain to the queen; *d.* May 1592.
See vacant 11 years.
1603. John Bridges, dean of Salisbury.
1618. John Howson; tr. to Durham.
1628. Richd. Corbet, dean of Christchurch; tr. to Norwich.
1632. John Bancroft, preb. of St. Paul's.
1640. Robt. Skinner, tr. from Bristol; tr. to Worcester.
1663. Wm. Paul, dean of Lichfield.
1665. Walter Blandford, preb. of Gloucester; tr. to Worcester.
1671. Nathl. Crewe, aft. third ld. Crewe, dean of Chichester; tr. to Dur ham.
1674. Hy. Compton, canon of Christ church; tr. to London, Dec. 167[5]
1676. John Fell, dean of Christchurch.
1686. Saml. Parker, archdn. of Canterbur[y]
1688. Timothy Hall, rector of Horsingto[n] Bucks.
1690. John Hough, preb. of Worcester tr. to Lichfield and Coventry.
1699. Wm. Talbot, dean of Worcester; t[r.] to Salisbury.
1715. John Potter, canon of Christchurch tr. to Canterbury.
1737. Thos. Secker; tr. from Bristol; t[r.] to Canterbury.
1758. John Hume; tr. from Bristol; tr. t[o] Salisbury.
1766. Robt. Lowth; tr. from St. David's tr. to London.
1777. John Butler, preb. of Wincheste[r] and archdn. of Surrey.
1788. Edwd. Smallwell, canon of Chris[t] church, Oxford; tr. from S[t.] David's; *d.* 1799.
1799. John Randolph, canon of Chris[t]

church, and reg. prof. Divinity, Oxford; tr. to Bangor.
1807. Chas. Moss, Jan. 14; *d.* Dec. 16, 1811.
1811. Wm. Jackson, Dec. 31; *d.* Dec. 2, 1815.
1815. Hon. Edwd. Legge, Dec. 30; *d.* Jan. 27, 1827.
1827. Chas. Lloyd, Feb. 14; *d.* May 31, 1829.
1829. Hon. Richd. Bagot, July 13; tr. to Bath and Wells.
1845. Saml. Wilberforce, Nov. 13; tr. to Winchester.
1869. John Fielder Mackarness, rector of Honiton, Devon, Dec. 15, **G.**; res. Nov. 17, 1888, **G.**
1888. Wm. Stubbs, Dec. 11, **G.**; tr. from Chester.

DEANS OF CHRIST CHURCH.

Foundation of Cardinal Wolsey.

1524. John Hygden.

Foundation of Henry VIII.

1532. John Hygden, *contd.*, July 18.
1533. John Oliver, Feb.; *d.* May, 1552.

Deanery Transferred from Osney to Christ Church.

1546. Richd. Coxe, Nov. 4; depr. 1553; bp. Ely, 1559; *d.* July 22, 1581.
1553. Richd. Marhall; depr. by Elizabeth.
1559. Geo. Carew, May 16; res. 1561; *d.* 1583.
1561. Thos. Sampson; depr. for nonconformity; *d.* Apr. 9, 1589.
1565. Thos. Godwyn, June; *d.* 1590.
1567. Thos. Cowper, Hil. term.; dean of Gloucester, 1569; *d.* 1594.
1570. John Piers, East. term.; bp. Rochester, 1576; *d.* 1594.
1576. Toby Mathew, res. 1584; *d.* Mar. 29, 1628.
1584. Wm. James, res. 1594; dean of Durham, 1596.
1594. Thos. Ravys, bp. Gloucester, 1604; res. 1605; *d.* Dec. 14, 1609.
1605. John Kyng, Aug. 4; bp. London, 1611; *d.* 1621.
1611. Wm. Goodwyn, Sept. 13; *d.* 1620.
1620. Richd. Corbet, June 24; bp. Oxford, 1628; *d.* 1635.
1629. Brian Duppa, Nov. 28; bp. Chichester, 1638; *d.* 1662.
1638. Saml. Fell, June 24; ejected 1647; *d.* Feb. 1, 1649.
1648. Edwd. Reynolds; depr. 1650.
1651. John Owen, depr. 1659; *d.* Aug. 24, 1683.
1659. Edwd. Reynolds, rest. Mar. 13; bp. Norwich, 1660; *d.* July 28, 1676.
1660. Geo. Morley, July 27; bp. Worcester, 1660; *d.* Oct. 29, 1684.
John Fell, Nov. 30; bp. Oxford, 1676; *d,* July 10, 1686.
1686. John Massey, Dec. 29; *d.* Aug. 11, 1715.
1689. Hy. Aldrich, June 17; *d.* Dec. 14, 1710.
1711. Fras. Atterbury, Sept. 27; bp. Rochester, 1713; *d.* Feb. 17, 1732.
1713. Geo. Smalridge, July 18; bp. Bristol, 1714; *d.* Sept. 27, 1719.
1719. Hugo Boulter, Nov. 6; bp. Bristol, same date; abp. Armagh, 1724; *d.* Sept. 28, 1742.
1724. Wm. Bradshaw, Sept. 17; bp. Bristol, same date; *d.* Dec. 16, 1732.
1732. John Conybeare, Jan. 27; bp. Bristol, 1750; *d.* July 13, 1755.
1756. David Gregory, May 18; *d.* 1767.
1767. Wm. Markham, Oct. 23; bp. Chester, 1771; abp. York, 1776.
1777. Lewis Bagot, Jan. 25; bp. Bristol, 1782; bp. Norwich, 1783.
1783. Cyril Jackson, June 27.
1809. Chas. Hy. Hall, Oct. 21, **G.**; dean of Durham, 1824.
1824. Saml. Smith, Feb. 11, **G.**; res.
1831. Thos. Gaisford, Oct. 10, **G.**; *d.* June 2, 1855.
1855. Hy. Geo. Liddell, June 16.

DIOCESE OF PETERBOROUGH.

This see was erected by Henry VIII. in 1541, and endowed out of the lands of the dissolved monasteries. It was wholly taken from the diocese of Lincoln. The place was anciently called Medeshamstede;

but Wolpher, king of the Mercians, founding an abbey here, and dedicating it to St. Peter, it came to be called Peterborough.

In 1888 a bishop suffragan of Leicester was appointed to this see.

BISHOPS OF PETERBOROUGH.

1541. John Chambers, the last abbot of Peterborough, and first bp.
1557. David Poole, or Pole, archdn. of Derby; depr. 1559 by Elizabeth.
1560. Edmd. Scrambler, preb. of Westminster and York; tr. to Norwich, Jan. 5, 1585.
1585. Richd. Howland, master of St. John's College, Cambridge.
1600. Thos. Dove, dean of Norwich.
1630. Wm. Peirs, or Pierce, dean of Peterborough; tr. to Bath and Wells.
1632. Augustin Lindsell, dean of Lichfield; tr. to Hereford.
1634. Fras. Dee, dean of Chichester.
1638. John Towers, dean of Peterborough; *d.* Jan. 1648.
See vacant 12 years.
1660. Benjn. Laney, dean of Rochester; tr. to Lincoln.
1663. Jos. Henshaw, dean of Chichester.
1679. Wm. Lloyd, tr. from Llandaff; tr. to Norwich.
1685. Thos. White, archdn. of Northampton; depr. for not taking the oaths.
1691. Richd. Cumberland, rector of All Saints, Stamford.
1718. White Kennet, dean of Peterborough.
1728. Robt. Clavering; tr. from Llandaff.
1748. John Thomas, can.-res. of St. Paul's; tr. to Salisbury.
1757. Richd. Terrick, can.-res. of St. Paul's, preacher at the rolls; tr. to London.
1764. Robt. Lamb, dean of Peterborough.
1769. John Hinchcliffe, mast. of Trinity College, Cambridge.
1794. Spencer Madan, tr. from Bristol; *d.* Oct. 8, 1813.
1813. John Parsons, Nov. 16; *d.* Mar. 12, 1819.
1819. Herbert Marsh, Apr. 25; tr. from Llandaff; *d.* Apr. 8, 1839.
1839. Geo. Davys, dean of Chester, fellow of Christ's College, Cambridge, May 7; *d.* Apr. 8, 1864.
1864. Fras. Jeune, mast. of Pembroke Coll., Oxford, May 21, **G.**; *d.* Aug. 20, 1868.
1868. Wm. Connor Magee, dean of Cork, and of Chap. Royal, Dublin.

BISHOP SUFFRAGAN OF LEICESTER.

1888. Fras. Hy. Thicknesse, archdn. of Northampton, June 18, **G.**

DEANS OF PETERBOROUGH.

1541. Fras. Abree, *alias* Leycester, last prior of St. Andrews, and first dean.
1543. Gerard Carlton; *d.* 1549.
1549. Jas. Curthopp; *d.* 1557.
1557. John Boxall; depr. by Elizabeth.
1560. Wm. Latymer; *d.* 1583.
1583. Richd. Fletcher; bp. Bristol, 1589.
1589. Thos. Nevell, dean of Canterbury, 1597.
1597. John Palmer.
1607. Richd. Cleyton.
1612. Geo. Meriton; dean of York, 1616.
1616. Hy. Beaumont, dean of Windsor; 1622; *d.* 1627.
1622. Wm. Pierse; bp. Peterborough, 1630.
1630. John Towers; bp. Peterborough, 1638.
1638. Thos. Jackson; *d.* 1640.
1640. John Cosin; bp. Durham, 1660.
1660. Edwd. Rainbow; bp. Carlisle, 1664.
1664. Jas. Duport; *d.* 1679.
1679. Simon Patrick; bp. Chichester, 1689.
1689. Richd. Kidder; bp. Bath and Wells, 1691.
1691. Saml. Freeman; *d.* 1707.
1707. White Kennet; bp. Peterborough, 1718.
1718. Richd. Reynolds; bp. Bangor, 1721.
1721. Wm. Gee.
1722. John Mandevil.
1725. Fras. Lockyer.
1740. John Thomas; elect. bp. of St. Asaph, but not consecrated, 1743.
1744. Robt. Lamb; bp. Peterborough, 1764.
1764. Chas. Tarrant.
1791. Chas. Manners Sutton; bp. Norwich, 1792.
1792. Peter Peckard, Apr. 10.
1798. Thos. Kipling.
1822. Jas. Hy. Monk, Feb. 20, **G.**; bp. Gloucester, 1830.

1830. Thos. Turton, Nov. 20, **G.**; dean of Westminster, 1842.
1842. Geo. Butler, Nov. 3, **G.**
1853. Augs. Page Saunders, May 28, **G.**
1878. John Jas. Stewart Perowne, Aug. 26, **G.**

DIOCESE OF ROCHESTER.

THIS see was founded by St. Augustine about ten years after he came to England. The bishop has been styled chaplain to the archbishop of Canterbury; and that archbishop claimed, and, for several centuries, disposed of the see. His patronage was, however, often disputed by the prior and monks here, who at length obtained a papal decree in their favour. In all solemn pomps and processions, the bishop of Rochester was cross-bearer to the archbishop. The revenue of the see was at one time so small, that, for many years, the deanery of Westminster was held *in commendam* with it, for its better support.

In 1536 a bishop suffragan of Colchester was appointed (probably to this see) under 26 Hen. VIII., cap. 14, but only two bishops were appointed. The title was revived in 1882, but the bishop was made suffragan to the newly constituted diocese of St. Albans.

BISHOPS OF ROCHESTER.

604. St. Justus; tr. to Canterbury.
622. Romanus; drowned on his way to Rome.
634. St. Paulinus, abp. of York.
644. St. Ithamar.
656. Damianus; *d.* 664.
See vacant 5 years.
669. Putta; res.
677. Quichelmus, or Gulielmus; res.
681. Godmundus, or Godwin I.
693. Tobias, the first Englishman who was bp. of this see.
727. Adulfus, or Aldulfus.
740. Duina, or Dunnus.
764. Earduff.
775. Diora, or Deora.
790. Weremund.
802. Beornmod, or Beornredus.
804. Tadnoth.
* * Bedenoth.
* * Godwin I., dean of London.
* * Cutherwolf.
* * Swithulf; *d.* 897.
* * Buiric.
* * Cheolmund.
* * Chineferth.
945. Burric, or Burrhieus.
980. Alfstanus.
1001. Godwin II.
1009. Godwin III.; *d.* 1038.
See vacant 20 years.
1058. Siward, abbot of Abingdon.
1076. Ernostus, or Arnolf, monk of Bec, in Normandy; *d.* July 15, same year.
1077. Gundulph, monk of Bec.
1108. Ralph, or Rodolph; tr. to Canterbury, 1114.
1115. St. Earnulph, abbot of Peterborough.
1125. John I., archdn. of Canterbury.
1137. John II.
1142. Ascelyn, a monk.
1147. Walter, archdn. of Canterbury.
1183. Walleran, archdn. of Bayonne.
1185. Gilbert de Glanville, ch. just.
1214. Benet de Sansetun, precentor of St. Paul's.
1226. Hy. de Sanford, archdn. of Canterbury.
1235. Richd. de Wendover, rector of Bromley, Kent.
1250. Lawrence de St. Martin, chaplain and councillor to the king.
1274. Walter de Merton, ld. chanc.
1278. John de Bradfield, monk of Rochester.
John de Kirkeby, archdn. of Coventry; elected, but declined the dignity.
1283. Thos. de Inglethorpe, dean of St. Paul's.
1291. Thos. de Wuldham, or Suthflete, prior of Rochester; chosen, but refused the see; again chosen, and accepted it.

1316. Haymo de Hythe, confessor to the king.
1352. John de Sheppey, prior of Rochester; ld. treasr.
1360. Wm. de Whittlesey, archdn. of Huntingdon; tr. to Worcester.
1364. Thos. Trelleck, dean of St. Paul's; *d.* 1372.
1372. John de Hertley, elected; but set aside by the pope.
1373. Thos. de Brinton, confessor to the king; *d.* 1389.
1389. John Barnet, elected; but set aside by the pope.
Wm. de Bottlesham; tr. from Llandaff.
1400. John de Bottlesham, preb. of York.
1404. Richd. Young; tr. from Bangor.
1419. John Kempe, archdn. of Durham; tr. to Chichester, 1421.
1421. Thos. Spofforth, or Spofford, elected; but set aside by the pope.
1422. John Langdon, monk of Canterbury.
1434. Thos. Browne, dean of Salisbury; tr. to Norwich.
1436. Wm. de Wells, abbot of York, aft. provost of Beverley; kpr. pr. seal.
1444. John Lowe, tr. from Asaph.
1467. Thos. Scott, surn. Rotherham, provost of Beverley; tr. to Lincoln.
1472. John Alcock, dean of Westminster; m. rolls; tr. to Worcester.
1476. John Russell, archdn. of Bucks; tr. to Lincoln.
1480. Edmd. Audley, preb. of York; tr. to Hereford.
1492. Thos. Savage, canon of York, and dean of the king's chapel; tr. to London.
1496. Richd. Fitz-James, preb. of St. Paul's; tr. to Chichester.
1504. John Fisher, chanc. of Cambridge and master of Queen's College; cardl.; beheaded for denying the king's supremacy.
1535. John Hilsey, prior of Dominican friars, in London.
1540. Nichs. Heath, archdn. of Stafford, almoner; tr. to Worcester.
1544. Hy. Holbeach, dean of Worcester, suffragan bp. of Bristol; tr. to Lincoln.
1547. Nichs. Ridley, master of Pembroke Hall, Cambridge; tr. to London.
1550. John Poynet, preb. of Canterbury; tr. to Winchester.
1551. John Scory, one of the six preachers in Canterbury Cathedral; tr. to Chichester, 1552.
See vacant 2 years.
1554. Maurice Griffin, archdn. of Rochester.
1559. Edmd. Gheast, archdn. of Canterbury; tr. to Salisbury.
1571. Edmd. Freake, dean of Salisbury; tr. to Norwich, 1575.
1576. John Piers, dean of Salisbury, and Christchurch, Oxford, almoner; tr. to Salisbury, Oct. 1577.
1578. John Young, preb. of Westminster.
1605. Wm. Barlow, dean of Chester; tr. to Lincoln.
1608. Richd. Neile, dean of Westminster; tr. to Lichfield and Coventry.
1610. John Buckeridge, pres. of St. John's College, Oxford; tr. to Ely.
1628. Walter Curle, dean of Lichfield; tr. to Bath and Wells.
1629. John Bowle, dean of Salisbury.
1637. John Warner, dean of Lichfield.
1666. John Dolben, dean of Westminster; tr. to York.
1683. Fras. Turner, dean of Windsor; tr. to Ely.
1684. Thos. Sprat, dean of Westminster.
1713. Fras. Atterbury, dean of Christchurch, and preacher at the Rolls; dean of Westminster, 1713; depr. and banished; *d.* 1732.
1723. Saml. Bradford, tr. from Carlisle.
1731. Jos. Wilcocks, tr. from Gloucester.
1756. Zach. Pearce; tr. from Bangor; res. the deanery of Westminster, 1758.
1774. John Thomas, dean of Westminster; *d.* 1793.
1793. Saml. Horsley; tr. from St. David's; tr. to St. Asaph.
1802. Thos. Dampier, preb. of Durham, Aug. 3; tr. to Ely.
1808. Walter King, Dec. 3; *d.* Feb. 22, 1827.
1827. Hon. Hugh Percy, June 28; tr. to Carlisle, same year.
Geo. Murray; tr. from Sodor and Man, Nov. 14; *d.* Feb. 16, 1860.
1860. Jos. Cotton Wigram, archdn. of Winchester, Apr. 7, **G.**; *d.* Apr. 6, 1867.
1867. Thos. Legh Claughton, hon. can. of Worcester, Apr. 26, **G.**; tr. to St. Albans.
1877. Anthy. Wilson Thorold, vicar of St. Pancras and rural dean, June 19, **G.**

BISHOPS SUFFRAGAN OF COLCHESTER.

See Diocese of St. Albans, *post*, p. 461.

DEANS OF ROCHESTER.

1533. Walter Philips, June 18; last prior and first dean; *d.* 1570.
1570. Edmd. Freake, Apr. 10; bp. Rochester, May 9, 1571.
1574. Thos. Willoughby, June 23; *d.* Aug. 19, 1585.
1585. John Coldwell, Jan. 7; bp. Salisbury, Dec. 26, 1591.
1592. Thos. Blague, Feb. 1; *d.* Oct. 1611.
1611. Richd. Milbourne, Dec. 11; bp. St. David's, July 9, 1615.
1615. Robt. Scott, July 13; *d.* Dec. 1620.
1620. Godfrey Goodman, Jan. 6; bp. Gloucester, Mar. 6, 1624.
1624. Walter Beleanquall, Mar. 12; dean of Durham, 1638.
1638. Hy. King, Feb. 6; bp. Chichester, Feb. 16, 1641.
1641. Thos. Turner, Feb. 26; dean of Canterbury, 1643.
1660. Benj. Laney, July 24; bp. Peterborough, same year.
1660. Nathl. Hardy, Dec. 10; *d.* June 1, 1670.
1670. Peter Mew; bp. Bath and Wells, 1672.
1673. Thos. Lamplugh, Mar. 6; bp. Exeter, Nov. 12, 1676.
1676. John Castilion, Nov. 15; *d.* Oct. 21, 1688.
1689. Hy. Ullock; *d.* June 20, 1706.
1706. Saml. Pratt; *d.* Nov. 14, 1723.
1724. Nichs. Claggett, Jan. 4; bp. St. David's, Jan. 1731.
1731. Thos. Herring; bp. Bangor, 1737.
1743. Wm. Bernard; bp. Raphoe, 1744.
1744. John Newcombe; *d.* Mar. 10, 1765.
1765. Wm. Markham, dean of Christ Church, 1767.
1767. Benj. Newcombe, Oct.; *d.* Aug. 1775.
1775. Thos. Thurlow, Nov. 8; bp. Lincoln, 1779.
1779. Richd. Cust; dean of Lincoln, 1782.
1782. Thos. Dampier; bp. Rochester, 1802.
1802. Saml. Goodenough; bp. Carlisle 1808.
1808. Wm. Beaumont Busby, Mar. 15, **G.**
1820. Robt. Stevens, Oct. 17, **G.**
1870. Thos. Dale, Feb. 23, **G.**; *d.* May 14, 1870.
Robt. Scott, June 16, **G.**
1887. Saml. Reynolds Hole, Dec. 31.

DIOCESE OF ST. ALBANS.

THIS see was constituted under 38 and 39 Vict. cap. 34, and order in council April 30, 1877, under which its establishment was to date from May 4, 1877. It was formed out of the diocese of Rochester.

The title of bishop suffragan of Colchester was revived in 1882, but the bishop was made suffragan to this see instead of to Rochester as before.

There are at present no dean and chapter attached to this see.

BISHOPS OF ST. ALBANS.

1877. Thos. Legh Claughton, May 11, **G.**; tr. from Rochester; first bishop.

BISHOPS SUFFRAGAN OF COLCHESTER.

1536. Wm. More } Probably suffragan
1567. John Sterne } to Rochester.

1882. Alfred Bloomfield, archdn. of Essex and hon. canon of St. Albans June 6, **G.**

DIOCESE OF ST. ASAPH.

THIS bishopric is of great antiquity, having been founded in the sixth century, by Kentigern, a Scotsman, bishop of Glasgow, who, returning into Scotland, left as his successor a holy man, named St. Asaph, from whom the see takes its name. Who succeeded St. Asaph is uncertain, as no authentic records supply the information, and the list of bishops is not renewed until 1143.

BISHOPS OF ST. ASAPH.

583. Kentigern, bp. of Glasgow.
* * St. Asaph.
* * * *
1143. Gilbertus, or Galfridus.
1152. Geoffrey of Monmouth.
1154. Richard; *d.* the next year.
1155. Godefridus, or Godfrey.
1175. Adam, a Welshman; canon of Paris.
1183. John I., or Johannes.
1186. Reinerus, or Reyner.
1225. Abraham.
1235. Hugo, or Hugh.
1240. Howel ap Ednevet.
See vacant 2 years.
1249. Enion, or Anian I.
1267. John II.
1268. Enion, or Anian II.
1293. Leoline de Bromfeld, canon of St. Asaph.
1314. David I.
1352. John Trevaur I.
1357. Leoline ap Madoc, dean of St. Asaph.
1376. Wm. de Sprinlington, dean of St. Asaph.
1382. Lawrence Child, penitentiary to the pope.
1390. Alexr. Bache.
1395. John Trevaur II., preb. of Hereford; depr, 1402.
1402. David II.
1411. Robt. de Lancaster.
1433. John Lowe, tr. to Rochester.
1444. Regd. Peacock, tr. to Chichester.
1450. Thomas I.
1461. Thomas II.
1472. Richd. Redman, tr. to Exeter.
1495. Michl. Dyacon.
1499. David III.
1503. David IV., abbot of Conway.
1513. Edmd. Birkhead.
1518. Hy. Standish, guardian of the Franciscans.
1535. Wm. Barlow, prior of Bisham; tr. to St. David's.
1536. Robt. Warton, or Parfew, or Purfoy, abbot of Bermondsey; tr. to Hereford.
1554. Thos. Goldwell; he went into voluntary exile.
1559. Richd. Davies, tr. to St. David's.
1561. Thos. Davies.
1573. Wm. Hughes.
1601. Wm. Morgan, tr. from Llandaff.
1603. Richd Parry, dean of Bangor.
1622. John Hanmer, preb. of Worcester.
1629. John Owen, archdn. of St. Asaph; *d.* 1651.
See vacant 9 years.
1660. Geo. Griffith, archdn. of St. Asaph.
1667. Hy. Glenham, dean of Bristol.
1669. Isaac Barrow, tr. from Sodor and Man.
1680. Wm. Lloyd, dean of Bangor; tr. to Lichfield and Coventry.
1692. Edwd. Jones, tr. from Cloyne, Ireland.
1703. Geo. Hooper, dean of Canterbury; tr. to Bath and Wells.
1704. Wm. Beveridge, archdn. of Colchester.
1708. Wm. Fleetwood, canon of Windsor; tr. to Ely.
1714. John Wynne, principal of Jesus College, Oxford; tr. to Bath and Wells.
1727. Fras. Hare, dean of Worcester, and dean of St. Paul's; tr. to Chichester.
1731. Thos. Tanner, canon of Christ Church, Oxford.
1736. Isaac Maddox, dean of Wells; tr. to Worcester.
1743. John Thomas, dean of Peterborough; elected, but not consecrated; tr. to Lincoln.
Saml. Lisle, archdn. of Canterbury; tr. to Norwich.
1748. Hon. Robt. Drummond, preb. of Westminster; tr. to Salisbury.
1761. Richd. Newcombe, tr. from Llandaff.
1769. Jonn. Shipley, tr. from Llandaff.
1789. Saml. Halifax, tr. from Gloucester.
1790. Lewis Bagot, tr. from Norwich.
1802. Saml. Horsley, July 29; tr. from Rochester; *d.* Oct. 4, 1806.
1806. Wm. Cleaver, Oct. 15; tr. from Bangor; *d.* May 15, 1815.
1815. John Luxmore, May 23; tr. from Hereford; *d.* Jan. 21.
1830. Wm. Carey, Feb. 23; tr. from Exeter; *d.* Sept. 13, 1846.
1846. Thos. Vowler Short, Oct. 10; tr. from Sodor and Man; res. Jan. 1870; *d.* Apr. 13. 1872.
1870. Joshua Hughes, Vicar of Llandovery, Mar. 25, **G**.

DEANS OF ST. ASAPH.

* * R——
1244 and 1272. David.
1279. Anian (1).
1294. R——
1299. Anian (2).
1339. Leoline ab Madoc, bp. St. Asaph, 1357.

* * Robt. de Walshum.
1357. Wm. de Spridelington; bp. St. Asaph, 1376.
1376. Alan de Stokes.
1381. David de Calwylegh.
1389. and 1391. Howel ab Madoc Kyffen.
1397. Hugh Collingham; preb. of St. Paul's, 1402; *d.* 1409.
1402. Richd. Courtenay.
1404. Hugh Holbeche; *d.* 1417.
1418. John Blodwell; res. 1441.
1441. David Blodwell; *d.* 1461.
1462. John Tapton; Jan. 27.
1493. Fulke or Fouke, Salisbury.
1544. Richd. Puskin; res. 1556; *d*, 1566.
1556. John Gryffyth, Sept. 27; *d.* 1557.
1557. Maurice Blayne, *alias* Griffith, Aug. 5; contd. until Feb. 27, 1559.
1559. John Lloyd, Apr. 4; depr. 1559.
1560. Hugh Evans, Apr. 26; *d.* Dec. 17, 1587.
1587. Thos. Banks, Dec. 18; *d.* July 31, 1634.
1634. Andrew Maurice, Aug. '28; *d.* 1653–4.
1660. David Lloyd, Sept. 24; *d.* Sept. 7, 1663.
1663. Humphrey Lloyd, Dec. 14; bp. Bangor, 1673; *d.* 1688.
1673–4. Nichs. Stratford, bp. Chester, 1689.
1689. Geo. Bright, Sept. 28; *d.* 1696.
1696. Daniel Price, July 26; *d.* Nov. 7, 1706.
1706. Wm. Stanley, Dec. 7; *d.* Oct. 9, 1731.
1731. Wm. Powell, Oct. 21; *d.* Apr. 14, 1751.
1751. Wm. Herring; *d.* May 13, 1774.
1774. Wm. Davies Shipley, May 27.
1826. C. Scott Luxmoore.
1854. Chas. Butler Clough.
1859. Richd. Bonner Maurice Bonnor.
1886. Herbert Armitage James.
1888. David Evans.

DIOCESE OF ST. DAVID'S.

THIS see was once the metropolitan see of Wales and archiepiscopal; and for many years the seat of the supreme ordinary of the Welsh. When Christianity was first planted in Great Britain there were three archbishops' seats appointed, viz., London, (afterwards removed to Canterbury), York, and Caerleon upon Usk, in Monmouthshire. That at Caerleon being found to be too near to the dominions of the Saxons, was removed, in the time of Arthur, king of the Britons, to a place called Menew, in the furthermost part of Pembrokeshire; and since, in honour of the archbishop who translated it there, the see is called St. David's. It is from the first name that the bishops style themselves *Menevensis.* Bishop Sampson was the last of the archbishops of St. David's; for he, withdrawing himself, on account of a pestilence which raged in his diocese, to Dole, in Brittany, carried the pall with him. His successors, though they lost the name, still preserved the archiepiscopal power; and the Welsh bishops continued to receive consecration at his hands, until the reign of Henry I., when Bernard, the forty-seventh bishop, was forced to submit himself to Canterbury.

ARCHBISHOPS OF ST. DAVID'S.

577. St. David.
* * Cenauc.
* * Eluid.
* * Ceneu.
* * Morvael.
* * Haernunen.
* * Elwaed.
* * Gurnven.
* * Lendivord, or Luedwith.
* * Gorwysc, or Gorwyst.
* * Gorgan, or Gogan.
* * Cledauc, or Cledauke.
* * Anian.
* * Elvoed, or Eludgeth.
* * Ethelmen, or Eldunen.
* * Elanc, Elnaeth, or Elvaoth.
* * Mascoed, Malscoed, or Maelschwythe.
* * Sadermen, Sadurnven, or Madenew.
* * Catellus, or Catulus.
* * Sulnay, or Sulhaithnay.
* * Novis, Nonis, or Namis.
* * Etwal, or Doythwal.
* * Asser.
* * Arthvael, or Alhuael.
* * St. Sampson, the last abp.

BISHOPS OF ST. DAVID'S.

* * Kuclinus, or Ruclinus.
* * Rodheric.
* * Elguni, or Elguen.
* * Lunverd, or Lywarch.
* * Nergu, or Vergu.
* * Sulhidyr, Sulhidwr, or Hubert.
* * Everus, or Eneuris.
* * Morgeneu.
* * Nathan.
* * Jevan.
* * Argusteil.
* * Morgenveth, or Urgeneu.
* * Ervin, or Hernun.
* * Tramarin, or Caermerin.
* * Joseph.
* * Bleithud.
* * Sulgheim, or Sulgeheyn.
* * Abraham.
* * Sulgheim, *again*.
* * Rythmarch.
* * Wilfride, or Griffri.
* * Bernardus, chanc. to queen Adelise. The first bp. who submitted to the see of Canterbury.

1147. David Fitzgerald, archdn. of Cardigan.
1176. Peter de Leia, prior of Wenlock.
1198. Giraldus Cambrensis, the historian; his election was disputed, and he resigned.
1203. Geoffrey.
1214. Gervase; *d.* 1229.
1230. Anselm le Gros.
1248. Thos. Wallensis.
1256. Richd. de Carew.
1280. Thos. Beck, archdn. of Dorset.
1293. David Martyn.
1328. Hy. Gower.
1347. John Thoresby, ld. chanc.; tr. to Worcester.
1350. Regd. Brian; tr. to Worcester.
1353. Thos. Falstoffe, parson of Fakenham, Norfolk.
1361. Adam Houghton, ld. chanc.
Richd. Metford; elected, but set aside by the pope.
1389. John Gilbert, tr. from Hereford; ld. treasr.; *d.* in 1397.
See vacant 4 years.
1401. Guy de Mona, ld. treasr.
1408. Hy. Chicheley, archdn. of Salisbury; tr. to Canterbury.
1414. John Ketterich, or Catryk, archdn. of Surrey; tr. to Lichfield and Coventry.
1415. Stephen Patrington, archdn. of Surrey; tr. to Chichester.
1417. Benedict Nichols, tr. from Bangor.
1433. Thos. Rodeburn, archdn. of Sudbury.
1442. Wm. Lynwood, ld. pr. seal.
1447. John Langton, chanc. of Cambridge; chosen Jan., 1447; *d.* May, 1447.
John Delabere, dean of Wells, Sept. 15.
1460. Robt. Tully, monk of Gloucester.
1482. Richd. Martin, pr. councillor to Edwd. IV.
1483. Thos. Langton, preb. of Wells.
1484. Andrew ——*; his surname does not appear.
1485. Hugh Pavy, or Parry, archdn. of Wilts.
1496. John Morgan, or Young, dean of Windsor; *d.* May 1504.
1505. Robt. Sherborne, dean of St. Paul's; tr. to Chichester.
1509. Edwd. Vaughan, preb. of St. Paul's.
1523. Richd. Rawlins, preb. of St. Paul's.
1536. Wm. Barlow, tr. from St. Asaph; tr. to Bath and Wells.
1549. Robt. Ferrar; depr. by Mary; burnt Mar. 30, 1555.
1553. Hy. Morgan, principal of St. Edward Hall, Oxford; depr. by Elizabeth.
1559. Thos. Young, chanc. of St. David's; tr. to York.
1561. Richd. Davies; tr. from St. Asaph.
1582. Marmaduke Middleton; tr. from Waterford, Ireland; depr. 1592, for publishing a forged will.
See vacant 2 years.
1594. Anthy. Rudd, dean of Gloucester.
1615. Richd. Milbourne, dean of Rochester; tr. to Carlisle.
1621. Wm. Laud, dean of Gloucester; tr. to Bath and Wells.
1627. Theoph. Field, tr. from Llandaff; tr. to Hereford.
1635. Roger Mainwaring, dean of Worcester; *d.*. 1653.
See vacant till the Restoration.
1660. Wm. Lucy, rector of High Clere, Hunts.
1677. Wm. Thomas, dean of Worcester; tr. to Worcester.
1683. Lawrence Womach, archdn. of Suffolk.
1686. John Lloyd, principal of Jesus College, Oxford.
1687. Thos. Watson, fellow of St. John's

* The accounts of the early prelates of this see are very conflicting; *Godwin, Isaacson, Heylyn*, and *Le Neve* frequently differing in names and dates. *Sir Harris Nicholas* appears to follow *Le Neve*, who is also here adopted as an authority in many instances.

College, Cambridge; depr. for simony and other crimes in 1699. See vacant 5 years.
1705. Geo. Bull, archdn. of Llandaff.
1710. Philip Bisse; tr. to Hereford.
1712. Adam Ottley, archdn. of Salop, and preb. of Hereford.
1723. Richd. Smalbroke, treasr. of Llandaff; tr. to Lichfield and Coventry.
1730. Elias Sydall, dean of Canterbury; tr. to Gloucester.
1731. Nichs. Clagget, dean of Rochester; tr. to Exeter.
1743. Edwd. Willes, dean of Lincoln; tr. to Bath and Wells.
1744. Hon. Richd. Trevor, canon of Windsor; tr. to Durham.
1752. Anthy. Ellis, preb. of Gloucester.
1761. Saml. Squire, dean of Bristol.
1766. Robt. Lowth, preb. of Durham; tr. to Oxford.
1766. Chas. Moss, archdn. of Colchester; tr. to Bath and Wells.
1774. Hon. Jas. York, dean of Lincoln; tr. to Gloucester.
1779. John Warren, archdn. of Worcester; tr. to Bangor.
1783. Edwd. Smallwell; tr. to Oxford.
1788. Saml. Horsley, preb. of Gloucester; tr. to Rochester.
1793. Hon. Wm. Stuart, canon of Christ Church, Oxford r. to Armagh.
1800. Lord Geo. Murray, Dec. 20; *d.* June 3, 1803.
1803. Thos. Burgess, preb. of Durham, June 25; tr. to Salisbury.
1825. John Banks Jenkinson, June 18; *d.* July 7, 1840.
1840. Connop Thirlwall, fellow of Trinity College, Cambridge, July 23; *d.* July 27, 1875.
1874. Wm. Basil Jones, archdn., chanc., and can.-res. of York, July 13, **G**.

DEANS OF ST. DAVID'S.

Until the year 1840 the bishops of this see were also the deans. In that year the precentor assumed the title of dean under 3 and 4 Vict., cap. 113, sec. 1 (Aug. 11, 1840).

1840. Ll. Llewellyn, precentor, now dean; Aug. 11.
1878. Jas. Allen.

DIOCESE OF SALISBURY.

This see has undergone many alterations, from the time of its establishment to its final settlement at Salisbury. Its first seat was at Sherborne, in Dorsetshire; and the diocese then had episcopal jurisdiction over all those counties that now constitute the sees of Salisbury, Bristol, Wells, and Exeter. Wells and Exeter were dismembered from it, and erected into two distinct bishoprics. Another see was afterwards formed out of the remaining jurisdiction of Sherborne, and seated at Wilton, in Wiltshire; but this last, after having had eleven bishops of its own, was once more united to Sherborne. Subsequently the seat of the see was removed to Salisbury, the principal city in those parts; but the then bishop removed it to the hill called Old Sarum, and began to build a cathedral church there, which was finished by St. Osmund. This situation was chosen, perhaps, from the strong fortifications with which the hill was surrounded, and as being more out of the reach of the Danes. Bishop Richard Poore, in 1220, once more brought the seat of the see from Old Sarum to Salisbury, or New Sarum, where it has continued ever since. In ancient times the bishops of Salisbury were precentors to the archbishops of Canterbury. Edward IV. annexed the chancellorship of the Garter to the bishops of this see; but in the new statutes made by Henry VIII. this office was left solely at the king's disposal, and might be conferred on a clergyman or a layman. After bishop Ward's time, however, it was conferred without interruption, until recently, on the bishops of Salisbury.

Two bishops suffragan were appointed (probably to this see) under 26 Henry VIII., cap. 14, one with the title of Marlborough in 1537, and the other with the title of Shaftesbury in 1539. Neither appointment was continued; but a bishop suffragan of Marlborough was again appointed in 1888, and made suffragan to London.

BISHOPS OF SHERBORNE.

705. St. Adhelm, or Aldhelm.
710. Fordhere.
738. Herewald.
756. Ethelwald I.
778. Denefrith.
798. Wilbert.
717. Ealstan, or Alfstan.
868. Eadmund, or St. Hamund; martyr.
872. Etheleage.
875. Alfric.
879. Asser, surn. *Menevensis.*
883. Swithelmus, or Sigelmus I.
889. Ethelwald II. After his death the diocese was divided into several sees, Wells, Devonshire, &c., by Plegmund, abp. of Canterbury; and another see was erected at Wilton, whose seat was sometimes there, and sometimes at Ramsbury and Sunning.

SHERBORNE.

906. Werstane.
918. Elthebald.
Sigelmus II.
934. Alfred.
941. Wulfine.
958. Alfwold, or Elfwold.
978. Athelric.
986. Ethelsius.
998. Brithwyn I.
1009. Elmer.
1020. Brithwyn II.
1041. Elfwold; *d.* 1058.
1058. After Elfwold's death in this year Herman, who had before been bp. of Wilton, and resigned that see, was made bp. of Sherborne; and having united both sees, he shortly removed the seat to Salisbury from which place the bishops have since had their name.

WILTON.

906. Ethelstan.
920. Odo Severus.
934. Osulph.
971. Alfstan.
981. Wulfgar, or Alfgar.
986. Siricius; tr. to Canterbury.
990. Alfric, or Aluricius; tr. to Canterbury.
996. Brithwold.
1013. Ethelwin.
1046. Herman, vide *infra.*

BISHOPS OF SALISBURY.

1046. Herman; succ. in 1046 as bp. of Wilton, and in 1058 as bp. of Sherborne; he removed the see, first to Salisbury, and then to Old Sarum.
1078. St. Osmund de Sees, Earl of Dorset, ld. chanc.; *d.* 1099.
See vacant 2 years.
1102. Roger, ld. ch. just. and ld. treasr. *d.* 1139.
See vacant 3 years.
1142. Josceline de Bailol, a Lombard, archdn. of Winchester, and preb. of York; *d.* 1184.
See vacant 4 years.
1188. Hubert Walter, dean of York; tr. to Canterbury, 1193.
1194. Herbert Poore, or Robt. Poore.
1217. Richd. Poore; tr. from Chichester; he removed the see back to Salisbury; tr. to Durham.
1228. Robt. de Bingham, preb. of Salisbury.
1246. Wm. de York, provost of Beverley.
1256. Giles de Bridport, dean of Wells.
1263. Walter de la Wyle, sub-chanter of Salisbury.
1274. Robt. Wykehampton, dean of Salisbury.
1284. Walter Scammel, dean of Salisbury.

1287. Hy. de Brandeston, dean of Salisbury; *d.* Feb. 1288.

Lawrence de Awkeburne, elected; but *d.* before consecration.

1288. Wm. de Corner; he was also elected abp. of Dublin; but was set aside by the pope.

1291. Nichs. Longespee, preb. of Salisbury.

1315. Roger de Martival, dean of Lincoln.

1330. Robt. Wivill.

1375. Ralph Ergham; tr. to Bath and Wells.

1388. John Waltham, m. rolls. and ld. treasr.

1395. Richd. Mitford; tr. from Chichester,

1407. Nichs. Bubbewith; tr. from London.

1408. Robt. Hallam, archdn. of Canterbury, cardl. and chanc. of Oxford.

1417. John Chandeler, dean of Salisbury.

1427. Robt. Nevill, provost of Beverley.

1438. Wm. Aiscough, clerk of the council.

1450. Richd. Beauchamp; tr. from Hereford; the first chanc. of the Garter.

1482. Lionel Woodville, dean of Exeter, chanc. of Oxford.

1485. Thos. Langton; tr. from St. David's; tr. to Winchester; chanc. of the Garter.

1493. John Blyth, m. rolls, chanc. of Cambridge, chanc. of the Garter.

1500. Hy. Deane; tr. from Bangor; tr. to Canterbury.

1501. Edmd. Audley; tr. from Hereford; chanc. of the Garter.

524. Lawrence Campejus, cardl.; depr. for non-residence by act of parliament, 1534. The chancellorship of the Garter in lay hands.

535. Nichs. Shaxton, treasr. of Sarum; res. in consequence of not subscribing to the Six Articles.

539. John Salcott, *alias* Capon; tr. from Bangor; *d.* Oct. 1557.

557–8. Peter Petow, cardl.; app. to this see by the pope; but the queen would not allow him to enter the realm.

558. Fras. Mallet, nominated by the queen, Oct. 14, 1558; but set aside on her death, Nov. 17. following.

559. John Jewell; *d.* 1571.

571. Edmd. Gheast; tr. from Rochester; almoner.

577. John Piers; tr. from Rochester; almoner; tr. to York, Feb. 1, 1589.

See vacant 2 years.

1591. John Coldwell, dean of Rochester.

1598. Hy. Cotton, preb. of Winchester.

1614. Robt. Abbot, master of Baliol College, Oxford.

1618. Martin Fotherby, preb. of Canterbury.

1620. Robt. Tounson, or Thompson, dean of Westminster.

1621. John Davenant, master of Queen's College, Cambridge.

1641. Brian Duppa; tr. from Chichester; tr. to Winchester, 1660; *d.* 1662.

1660. Humphrey Henchman, precentor of Salisbury; tr. to London.

1663. John Earle; tr. from Worcester.

1665. Alexr. Hyde, dean of Winchester.

1667. Seth Ward; tr. from Exeter; chanc. of the Garter.

1689. Gilbert Burnet, preacher at the rolls.

1715. Wm. Talbot; tr. from Oxford; tr. to Durham.

1722. Richd. Willis; tr. from Gloucester; tr. to Winchester.

1723. Benj. Hoadley; tr. from Hereford; tr. to Winchester.

1734. Thos. Sherlock; tr. from Bangor; tr. to London.

1748. John Gilbert; tr. from Llandaff; tr. to York.

1757. John Thomas I.; tr. from Peterborough; tr. to Winchester.

1761. Robt. Drummond; tr. from St. Asaph; tr. to York.

John Thomas II.; tr. from Lincoln.

1766. John Hume; tr. from Oxford.

1782. Hon. Shute Barrington; tr. from Llandaff; tr. to Durham.

1791. John Douglas; tr. from Carlisle; *d.* 1807.

1807. John Fisher, May 30; tr. from Exeter; *d.* July 2, 1825.

1825. Thos. Burgess, May 21; tr. from St David's; *d.* Feb. 19, 1837.

1837. Edwd. Denison, fellow of Merton College, Oxford, Mar. 13; *d.* Mar. 6, 1854.

1854. Walter Kerr Hamilton, can.-res. and precentor, Salisbury, Mar. 27, **G.**; *d.* Aug. 1, 1869.

1869. Geo. Moberly, canon of Chester, Aug. 14, **G.**; *d.* July 6, 1885.

1885. John Wordsworth, Oriel prof. of divinity, Oxford, Sep. 3, **G.**

BISHOPS SUFFRAGAN OF MARLBOROUGH.

See Diocese of London, *ante*, p. 452.

BISHOP SUFFRAGAN OF SHAFTESBURY.

1539. John Bradley.

DEANS OF SALISBURY.

* * Roger.
* * Osbert.
* * Serlo.
* * Robert; *d.* 1111.
* * Robt. Chichester; bp. Exeter about 1128.
1140. Robt. Warlewest.
* * Henry.
1165. John of Oxford; bp. Norwich, 1175.
* * Robert.
* * Jordan, dean in 1192.
* * Eustachius, dean in 1195; bp. Ely, 1198.
1197. Richd. Poor; bp. Chichester, 1214.
1215. Adam de Ilchester; *d.* 1220.
1220. Wm. de Waude.
1238. Robt. de Hertford; *d.* 1257.
1257. Robert. de Wykehampton; bp. Salisbury, 1274.
1274. Walter Scammel; bp. Salisbury, 1284.
1284. Hy. de Blaundeston; bp. Salisbury 1287.
1287. Simon de Mitcham.
1298. Peter of Savoy.
1309. Cardl. Wm. Ruffatus de Cassineto.
1310. Cardl. Raymond de la Goth; *d.* 1346.
1346. Bertrand de Farges.
1347. Reynold Orsini.
1380. Robt. Braybrooke.
1385. Thos. de Montacute; *d.* 1404.
1404. John Chandler; bp. Salisbury, 1417.
1418. Simon Sidenham; bp. Chichester, 1430.
1430. Thos. Browne; bp. Rochester, 1434.
1434. Nichs. Billesdon; *d.* 1441.
1441. Adam Moleyns.
1446. Richd. Leyat; *d.* 1449.
1449. Gilbert Kymer; *d.* 1463.
1463. Jas. Goldwell; bp. Norwich, 1472.
1473. John Davyson; *d.* 1485.
* * Edwd. Cheyne, dean in 1499; *d.* 1502.
1505. Thos. Rowthall; bp. Durham, 1508.
1509. Wm. Atwater; bp. Lincoln, 1514.
1514. John. Longland, or Langland; bp. Lincoln, 1521.
1521. Cuthbert Tunstall; bp. London, 1522.
1522. Raymund Pade.
1539. Peter Vannes; res. 1563.
1563. Wm. Bradbridge; bp. Exeter, 1571.
1570. Edmund Freke; bp. Rochester, 1571.
1571. John Piers; bp. Salisbury, 1577.
1577. John Bridges; bp. Oxford, 1603.
1604. John Gordon; *d.* 1619.
1619. John Williams; dean of Westminster, 1620.
1620. John Bowle; bp. Rochester, 1629.
1629. Edmund Mason; *d.* 1634.
1635. Richd. Baylie; *d.* 1667.
1667. Ralph Brideoake; bp. Chichester, 1675.
1675. Thos. Peirce; *d.* 1691.
1691. Robt. Woodward; *d.* 1701.
1702. Edwd. Young; *d.* 1705.
1705. John Young.
1727. John Clark; *d.* 1757.
1757. Thos. Green; *d.* 1780.
1780. Rowney Noel; *d.* 1786.
1786. John Ekins; *d.* 1808.
1809. Chas. Talbot, Feb 18, **G.**
1823. Nichs. Pearson, Mar. 6, **G.**
1846. Fras. Lear, June 4, **G.**
1850. Hy. Parr Hamilton, Apl. 17, **G.**
1880. John Chas. Ryle, Mar. 22, **G.**; made bp. Liverpool before he was confirmed in his deanery.
1880. Geo. David Boyle, May 5, **G.**

DIOCESE OF SOUTHWELL.

THIS see was constituted under the "Bishoprics Act, 1878," (41 and 24 Vict., cap. 68,) and an order in Council, dated Feb. 2, 1884, under which its establishment was to date from Feb. 5, 1884. It was formed out of portions of the dioceses of Lichfield and Lincoln, and has at present no dean and chapter attached to it.

BISHOP OF SOUTHWELL.

1884. Geo. Ridding, head master of St. Mary's College, Winchester; first bishop; May 4, **G.**

DIOCESE OF TRURO.

THIS see was constituted under the "Bishopric of Truro Act, 1876," (39 and 40 Vict., cap. 52,) and an order in Council, dated Dec. 9, 1876, under which its establishment was to date from Dec. 15, 1876. It was formed out of the diocese of Exeter.

BISHOPS OF TRURO.

1877. Edwd. White Benson, canon of Lincoln; first bishop; Jan. 16, **G.**; tr. to Canterbury.

1883. Geo. Howard Wilkinson, vicar of St. Peter, Eaton Square, and hon. canon of Truro; Mar. 24, **G.**

BISHOPRIC AND DEANERY OF WESTMINSTER.

At the dissolution of the monasteries, Westminster Abbey was by Henry VIII., in 1539, erected into a deanery; and in 1541, he erected it into a bishopric, and appointed John Thirleby bishop. But he, having wasted the patrimony allotted by the king for the support of the see, was translated to Norwich, and with him ended the bishopric of Westminster. The dignity existed only nine years; and Middlesex, which was the diocese, was restored to London. The dean continued to preside until the accession of queen Mary, who restored the abbot; but queen Elizabeth displaced the abbot, and erected the abbey into a collegiate church, of a dean and twelve prebendaries, as it still continues. On the revival of the order of the Bath in 1725, the dean of Westminster was appointed dean of that order, and this honour has been continued to his successors.

BISHOP AND DEANS OF WESTMINSTER.

1539. Wm. Benson, the last abbot and first dean.
1541. Thos. Thirleby, first and only bp.; tr. to Norwich.
1550. Richd. Coxe, dean; aft. bp. Ely.
1553. Hugh Weston, dean; rector of Lincoln College, Oxford.
1556. John Frecknam, abbot; depr.

All the Following were Deans:—

1560. Wm. Bill, mast. Trin. Coll., Cambridge.
1561. Gabriel Goodman, preb. of St. Paul's.
1601. Lancelot Andrews; bp. Chichester, 1605.
1605. Richd. Neyle, or Neale; bp. Rochester, 1608.
1610. Geo. Monteigne; bp. Lincoln, 1617.
1617. Robt. Tounson, or Thompson; bp. Salisbury, 1620.
1620. John Williams, bp. Lincoln, 1621; tr. to York.
1660. John Earle, clerk of the closet; bp. Salisbury, 1662.
1663. John Dolben, bp. Rochester 1666; tr. to York.
1683. Thos. Spratt; bp. Rochester, 1684.
1713. Fras. Atterbury, bp. Rochester, &c.
1723. Saml. Bradford, bp. Rochester, &c.
1731. Jos. Wilcocks, bp. Rochester, &c.
1756. Zach. Pearse, bp. Rochester.
1769. John Thomas, preb. of Westminster; promoted to the deanery on the resignation of bp. Pearse, and on his death, in 1774, succ. him in the bishopric of Rochester.
1793. Saml. Horsley, bp. Rochester.
1802. Wm. Vincent, sub-almoner; Aug. 3, **G.**; *d.* Dec. 21, 1815.
1815. John Ireland, a canon of Westminster; Dec. 30, **G.**; *d.* Sep. 21, 1842.
1842. Thos. Turton, Oct. 10, **G.**; bp. Ely, 1845.
1845. Saml. Wilberforce, May 5, **G.**; bp. Oxford, 1846.
1845. Wm. Buckland, previously canon of Christ Church, Oxford, Nov. 27, **G.**; *d.* Aug. 14, 1856.
1856. Richd. Chevenix Trench, Oct. 14, **G.**; abp. Dublin, 1864.
1863. Arthur Penrhyn Stanley, Dec. 21, **G.**; *d.* July 18, 1881.
1881. Geo. Granville Bradley, Sep. 13, **G.**

DIOCESE OF WINCHESTER.

This see is of great antiquity, and has always continued at Winchester which was anciently the capital of the West Saxon kingdom. The bishop is accounted sub-dean to the archbishop of Canterbury; and by Edward III. the office of prelate of the order of the Garter was conferred upon him, and has been continued to his successors ever since. The bishops were anciently reputed to be earls of Southampton and are so styled in the new statutes of the Garter made by Henry VIII.; but that title does not now belong to them.

In 1874 a bishop suffragan of Guildford was appointed to this see

BISHOPS OF WINCHESTER.

636. St. Birine, or Birinus.
650. Agilbertus.
660. Wina; exp.; aft. bp. London.
670. St. Eleutherius.
677. St. Headda.
705. Daniel, res.
745. Humphrey, or Humfridus.
755. Kinehard, or Kineward.
780. Athelard, tr. to Canterbury.
793. Egbald.
795. Dudda.
799. Kineberth.
808. Alhmund.
814. Withenius, or Wighteinus, or Wigthen.
827. Herefrid, murd. by the Danes.
832. Edmund.
833. Helmstan.
838. St. Swithin.
862. Athelred, tr. to Canterbury.
875. Dunbert, or Dumbert.
879. Denewulf, a hogherd under king Alfred, whom he sheltered when he fled from the Danes.
888. St. Anthelm, or Bertulf.
906. St. Frithstan.
942. St. Brinstan.
935. Elphege, the Bald.
951. Elffine, or Alfsius.
958. Brithelm.
963. St. Ethelwald.
983. St. Elphegus, abbot of Bath.
1006. Kenulph.
1007. St. Brithwold.
1015. St. Elfsinus, or Eadsinus.
1032. Alfwine.
1047. Stigand, tr. to Canterbury.
1070. Walkeline, or Walkin.
See vacant 2 years.
1100. Wm. Giffard, preb. of St. Paul's; ld. chancr.; not consec. until 1107.
1129. Hy. de Blois, abbot of Glastonbury, and cardl.; brother to king Stephen.
See vacant 3 years.
1174. Richd. Tocliffe, or More, abp. of Poitiers.
1189. Godfrey de Lucy, or Luci.
1205. Sir Peter de Rupibus; *d.* 1238.
See vacant 5 years.
1243. Wm. de Raleigh, or Radley, tr. from Norwich.
1250. Gethelmar, Aymer, or Ludomar de Valentia, the king's half brother.
1261. John Exon, or Oxon.
Richd. Moore, elected; but set aside by the abp. of Canterbury.
1267. Nichs. de Ely, tr. from Worcester *d.* Feb. 1280.
1280. John de Pontois, or Sawbridge; *d.* Dec. 1304.
1305. Hy. Woodloke, or de Merewell.
1316. John de Sandale, dean of St. Paul's, ld. chanc., ld. treasr., and chanc. ex.
Adam * * * elected; but set aside by the pope.
1320. Regd. de Asserius, the pope's legate.
1323. John de Stratford, ld. chanc. and ld. treasr.; tr to Canterbury.
1333. Adam de Orleton, tr. from Worcester.
John Devenesche, chosen; but set aside by the pope.
1345. Wm. de Edendon, ld. treasr., and ld. chanc.
1367. Wm. de Wykeham, ld. chanc.
1405. Hy. de Beaufort, third son of John of Gaunt by Catherine Swinford, cardl. and ld. chanc.; tr. from Lincoln.
1447. Wm. de Waynflete, or Pattyn, provost of Eton; ld. chanc.
1487. Peter Courtenay, tr. from Exeter.
1493. Thos. Langton, tr. from Salisbury; elected to Canterbury, but *d.* before his translation was perfected.

01. Richd. Fox, tr. from Durham; ld. pr. seal; *d.* Sept. 1528.

29. Thos. Wolsey, abp. of York, cardl., and ld. chanc.; he held this see, *in commendam*, from Apr. 6, 1529, until his death, Nov. 29, 1530.

31. Stephen Gardiner, mast. Trin. Coll., Cambridge; depr. by Edwd. VI., in 1550, for opposing the Reformation; committed to the Tower, where he was imprisoned during the remainder of Edward's reign.

51. John Poynet, tr. from Rochester; res. in 1553.

53. Bishop Gardiner, *again*; rest. by Mary, and made ld. chanc.; *d.* Nov. 12, 1555.

56. John Whyte, tr. from Lincoln; depr. 1560.

61. Robt. Horne, dean of Durham; *d.* 1580.

80. John Watson, dean of Winchester.

84. Thos. Cowper, tr. from Lincoln.

95. Wm. Wickham, tr. from Lincoln, Jan. 7, 1595; *d.* June 12 following.

95. Wm. Day, dean of Windsor; elected Nov. 3, 1595; *d.* Sept. 20, 1596.

1597. Thos. Bilson, tr. from Worcester.

1616. Jas. Mountague, tr. from Bath and Wells.

1619. Lancelot Andrews, tr. from Ely.

1627. Richd. Neile, or Neale, tr. from Durham; tr. to York.

1632. Walter Curle, tr. from Bath and Wells; bp. almoner; *d.* 1650.

See vacant 10 years.

1600. Brian Duppa, tr. from Salisbury.

1662. Geo. Morley, tr. from Worcester.

1684. Peter Mews, or Mew, tr. from Bath and Wells.

1707. Sir Jonn. Trelawney, bt., tr. from Exeter.

1721. Chas. Trimnell, tr. from Norwich.

1723. Richd. Willis, tr. from Salisbury

1734. Benjn. Hoadley, tr. from Salisbury,

1761. John Thomas, tr. from Salisbury.

1781. Hon. Brownlow North, tr. from Worcester; *d.* July 12, 1820.

1820. Geo. Pretyman Tomline, July 18; tr. from Lincoln; *d.* 1827.

1827. Chas. Richd. Sumner, May 25; tr. from Landaff; res. Nov. 1869; *d.* Aug. 15, 1874.

1869. Saml. Wilberforce, Nov. 11, **G.**; tr. from Oxford; *d.* July 19, 1873.

1873. Edwd. Harold Browne; Aug. 13, **G.**; tr. from Ely.

BISHOPS SUFFRAGAN OF GUILDFORD.

74. John Sutton Utterton, archdn. of Surrey and canon of Winchester, Mar. 9, **G.**; *d.* 1879.

1888. Geo. Hy. Sumner, archdn. and canon of Winchester, Nov. 19, **G.**

DEANS OF WINCHESTER.

40. Wm. Kingsmill, *alias* de Basyng, Mar. 28; last prior of St. Swithin and first dean of Winchester.

49. Sir Jno. Mason, Oct. 9; res. 1553.

54. Edmd. Steward, Mar. 22.

59. Jno. Warner, Oct. 15; *d.* Mar. 21, 1564.

65. Fras. Newton, Mar. 21.

72. Jno. Watson, Feb. 14; bp. Winchester, 1580.

80. Lawrence Humphrey, Oct. 24; *d.* Feb. 1, 1589.

89. Martin Heton, Mar. 20; bp. Ely, 1600.

00. Geo. Abbot, bp. Lichfield and Coventry, 1609.

10. Thos. Morton, Jan. 3; bp. Chester, 1616.

16. Jno. Young, July 8.

1660. Alexr. Hyde, Aug. 8; bp. Salisbury, 1665.

1666. Wm. Clark, Feb. 1.

1679. Richd. Meggott, Oct. 9.

1693. Jno. Wickart, Jan. 14.

1722. Wm. Trimmell, Feb. 16.

1729. Chas. Naylor, May 7; *d.* June 23, 1739.

1739. Zachariah Pearce, Aug. 4; bp. Bangor, 1748.

1749. Thos. Cheyney, Mar. 25; *d.* Dec. 27, 1760.

1760. Jonn. Shipley, Oct. 21; bp. Llandaff, 1769.

1769. Newton Ogle, Oct. 21.

1804. Robt. Holmes, Jan. 31, **G.**

1805. Thos. Rennell, Dec. 7, **G.**

1840. Thos. Garnier, Apr. 9, **G.**

1872. Jno. Bramston, Nov. 15.

1883. Geo. Wm. Kitchin, May 23.

DIOCESE OF WORCESTER.

THIS see was founded by Ethelred, king of the Mercians, in the ye 679; the diocese was taken from Lichfield.

BISHOPS OF WORCESTER.

679. Boselus, Boisel, or Bosel.
691. Ostforus.
693. St. Edwin, or Egwyn.
717. Wilfride.
744. Milred.
775. Weremund.
779. Tilhere.
782. Eathored, or Adored.
799. Denebert.
822. Eadbert, or Hubert.
848. Alwinus.
872. Werefrid.
892. Wilfreth I.
915. Ethelan, or Ethelhune, abbot of Brackley.
922. Wilfreth II.
929. Kenewold.
957. St. Dunstan, abbot of Glastonbury; tr. to London, which he held with this see, till he was tr. to Canterbury.
960. St. Oswald; in 971 made abp. of York, which he held with this see.
993. Adulfe, abbot of Peterborough; succ. to this see, and to York.
1002. Wolstan I.; he likewise succ. to this see, and to York.
1023. Leoffius, abbot of Thorney.
Britteagus, abbot of Pershore.
1038. Livingus, bp. also of Devonshire and Cornwall.
1046. Aldred, tr. to York.
1062. St. Wolstan II., prior of Worcester; the last Saxon bp. of this see.
1097. Sampson, canon of Baion.
1113. Theulph, or Theobald, or Teoldus, canon of Baion; *d.* 1124.
1125. Simon, chanc. to the queen.
* * Alured (?).
1151. John Pagham, or Payham.
1163. Roger, son of Robt., E. of Gloucester.
1180. Baldwin, abbot of Ford; tr. to Canterbury, 1184.
1186. Robt. de Northall, abbot of Gloucester.
1191. Robt. FitzRalph, canon of Lincoln; *d.* the next year.
1192. Hy. de Soilly, abbot of Gloucester.
1196. John de Constance, dean of Rouen, archdn. of Oxford.
1199. Maugere.
1215. Walter de Grey, tr. from Lichfield, ld. chanc.; tr. to York.
1217. Sivester de Evesham, prior of Worcester.
1218. Wm. de Blois, archdn. of Bucks.
1236. Walter de Cantilupe, son to Cantilupe.
1266. Nichs. de Ely, archdn. of Ely, chanc. and pr. treasr; tr. Winchester.
1268. Godfrey Gifford, archdn. of Wel ld. chanc.
John de St. German, elected, but is doubtful if he was ever con crated.
1302. Wm. de Gainsborough, or Gayn burgh, friar minor at Oxford.
Peter of Savoy, nominated by t Pope, but set aside by the king
1308. Walter Reynolds, preb. of St. Pau ld. chanc. and ld. treasr.; tr. Canterbury, 1313.
1314. Walter Maydenstun, or Maidsto preb. of St. Paul's.
1318. Thos. Cobham, sub-dean of Saru *d.* 1327.
Wolstan, prior of Worcester; elect 1327, but was not consecrated.
1327. Adam de Orleton, tr. from He ford; tr. to Winchester.
1333. Simon de Montacute, archdn. of Ca terbury; tr. to Ely.
1337. Thos. Hennibal, monk of Norwich
1338. Wolstan de Brandesford, prior Worcester; probably the W stan not consecrated in 1327.
John de Evesham, prior of Wo cester; elected 1349, but not co secrated.
1349. Jno. Thoresby, tr. from St. David' ld. chanc., cardl.; tr. to York.
1352. Regd. Bryan, tr. from St. David's
1362. John Barnet, archdn. of London, l treasr.; tr. to Bath and Wells.
1363. Wm. de Wittlesey, tr. from Roche ter; tr. to Canterbury.
1369. Wm. de Lynne, or Lenne, tr. fro Chichester.
1375. Hy. Wakefield, archdn. of Cante bury, ld. treasr.
John Green, elected, but set asi by the pope.
1395. Tideman de Winchcombe, tr. fro Llandaff.
1401. Richd. Clifford, dean of York; t to London.
1408. Thos. Peverel, tr. from Llandaff.
1419. Philip Morgan, chanc. of Normand tr. to Ely.

25. Thos. Polton, or Poldon, or Pulton, tr. from Chichester.
34. Thos. Bourchier, dean of St. Mabin's, London; tr. to Ely.
43. John Carpenter, provost of Oriel College, Oxford, chanc. of Oxford.
76. John Alcock, tr. from Rochester; tr. to Ely; ld. chanc.
86. Robt. Morton, preb. of York and Lincoln.
97. John Gigles, preb. of St. Paul's, York, and Lincoln.
99. Silvester Gigles, nephew to the last bishop.
Julius de Medicis, cardl., aft. pope Clement VII.; made administrator of this see in 1521; res. 1522.
23. Jerome de Ghinucci, an Italian; depr. in 1534.
35. Hugh Latimer, consec. Sept. 1535; res. July 1, 1539; burnt at Oxford, Oct. 16, 1555.
39. John Bell, archdn. of Gloucester.
43. Nichs. Heath, tr. from Rochester; displaced by Edwd. VI., and the see granted *in commendam* to
52. John Hooper, bp. of Gloucester; depr. 1553; suffered martyrdom 1555.
53. Nichs. Heath, rest. by Mary; tr. to York.
55. Richd. Pate, archdn. of Lincoln and Winchester; depr.
59. Edwyn Sandys, preb. of Peterborough; tr. to London.
70. John Calfhill chosen; but *d.* before consecration.
71. Nichs. Bullingham, tr. from Lincoln, Jan. 1571.
77. John Whitgift, dean of Lincoln; tr. to Canterbury, Sept. 1583.
84. Edmd. Freke, tr. from Norwich.
1593. Richd. Fletcher, tr. from Bristol; tr. to London, Dec. 1594.
1596. Thos. Bilson, preb. of Winchester; tr. to Winchester.
1597. Gervase Babington, tr. from Exeter.
1610. Hy. Parry, tr. from Gloucester; *d.* Dec. 1616.
1617. John Thornborough, tr. from Bristol.
1641. John Prideaux, canon of Christ-Church, Oxford; *d.* 1650.
See vacant 10 years.
1660. Geo. Morley, dean of Christ-Church, Oxford; tr. to Winchester.
1662. John Gauden, tr. from Exeter.
John Earle, dean of Westminster; tr. to Salisbury.
1663. Robt. Skinner, tr. from Oxford.
1671. Waltr. Blandford, tr. from Oxford.
1675. Jas. Fleetwood, preb. of Lichfield.
1683. Wm. Thomas, tr. from St. David's.
1689. Edwd. Stillingfleet, dean of St. Paul's.
1699. Wm. Lloyd, tr. from Lichfield and Coventry.
1714. John Hough, tr. from Lichfield and Coventry.
1743. Isaac Maddox, tr. from St. Asaph.
1759. Jas. Johnson, tr. from Gloucester.
1774. Hon. Brownlow North, tr. from Lichfield and Coventry; tr. to Winchester.
1781. Richd. Hurd, tr. from Lichfield and Coventry; *d.* May 28, 1808.
1808. Foliot Herbert Walker Cornewall, June 14; tr. from Hereford; *d.* Sept. 5, 1831.
1831. Robt. Jas. Carr, Sept. 10; tr. from Chichester; *d.* Apr. 24, 1841.
1841. Hy. Pepys, Apr. 29; tr. from Sodor and Man; *d.* Nov. 13, 1860.
1861. Hy. Philpott, canon of Norwich, Jan. 7, **G.**

DEANS OF WORCESTER.

40. Hy. Holbeck, Jan. 18; last prior and first dean; bp. Rochester, 1544.
44. Jno. Barlow; depr. by Mary.
* Philip Hawford, *alias* Ballard; *d.* 1557.
57. Seth Holland; depr. by Elizabeth.
59. Jno. Pedor; *d.* Apr. 5, 1571.
71. Thos. Wilson, May 4; *d.* July 20, 1586.
86. Fras. Willis.
96. Richd. Eedes.
02. Jas. Montague; bp. Bath and Wells, 1608.
08. Arthur Lake; bp. Bath and Wells, 1616.
16. Jos. Hall; bp. Exeter, 1627.
27. Wm. Juxon; bp. Hereford, 1633.
1633. Roger Manwaring; bp. St. David's, 1635.
1636. Christr. Potter; dean of Durham, 1646.
1646. Richd. Holdsworth; *d.* Aug. 22, 1649.
1660. Jno. Oliver; *d.* Oct. 27, 1661.
1661. Thos. Warmistry; *d.* 1665.
1665. Wm. Thomas; bp. St. David's, 1677.
1683. Geo. Hickes, Oct. 13; depr. Feb. 1, 1691; *d.* Dec. 15, 1715.
1691. Wm. Talbot, Apr. 23; bp. Oxford, 1699; tr. to Salisbury, 1715.
1715. Fras. Hare, Apr. 27; dean of St. Paul's, 1726.
1726. Jas. Stillingfleet, Dec. 16; *d.* Sept. 1746.
1747. Edmd. Martin, Apr. 24; *d.* 1751.
1751. Jno. Waugh, Nov. 14; *d.* 1765.

1765. Sir Richd. Wrottesley, bt., May 30; d. 1769.
1769. Wm. Digby, Sept. 8; dean of Durham, 1777.
1778. Robt. Foley, Jan. 31; *d.* 1783.
1783. Hon. and rev. St. Andrew St. John, Mar. 29; *d.* Mar. 23, 1795.
1795. Arthur Onslow, May 16.
1817. Jno. Banks Jenkinson, Nov. 20, **G.**; bp. St. David's, 1825.
1825. Jas. Hook, July 26, **G.**
1828. Geo. Murray, bp. Rochester; Ma 19, **G.**
1845. Jno. Peel, Dec. 3, **G.**
1874. Hon. Grantham Munton Yorke, Ju 18, **G.**
1878. Ld. Alwyne Compton, Nov. 11, G bp. Ely, 1886.
1886. Jno. Gott, Feb. 6, **G.**

DEANS OF THE CHAPEL ROYAL, WINDSOR.

Custodes.

* * Jno. de la Chambre.
1348. Wm. Mugge, Aug. 6.
1380. Walter Almaly or Almary.
1403. Thos. Butiler.

Deans.

1412. Thos. Kingestone (first dean).
1417. Jno. Arundel.
1452. Thos. Manning.
1462. Jno. Faux; *d.* 1470.
1470. Wm. Morland or Merland, Feb. 26.
1471. Jno. Davison, Oct. 30.
1473. Wm. Dudley, Dec. 4; bp. Durham, 1476.
1476. Peter Courtney, Oct. 11.
1478. Richd. Beauchamp, bp. Salisbury, Mar. 4; first chanc. of the order of the Garter.
1481. Thos. Danett.
1483. Wm. Benley.
1484. Jno. Morgan; bp. St. David's, 1496.
1495. Christr. Urswicke, Nov. 20.
1505. Christr. Bainbridge or Bainbrigge, dean of York; bp. Durham, 1507.
1507. Thos. Hobbes.
1510. Nichs. West; bp. Ely, 1515.
1515. Jno. Voysey *alias* Harman; bp. Exeter, 1519.
1519. Jno. Clerk.
1523. Richd. Sampson, Nov. 14.
1536. Wm. Franklin, Dec. 19.
1553. Owen Oglethorp; first regr. of the Garter; bp. Carlisle, 1556.
1556. Hugh Weston, dean of Westminster.
1557. Jno. Boxall.
1559. Geo. Carew; res. 1572.
1572. Wm. Day, Aug. 22; bp. Winchester, 1595.
1595. Robt. Bennett, Mar. 24; bp. Hereford, 1602.
1602. Giles Thompson, Mar. 2; bp. Exeter, 1610.
1612. Anthy. Maxey, June 25.
1618. Marcus Antonius de Dominis, ab of Spalato, May 11.
1622. Hy. Beaumont, dean of Pete borough, May 18.
1628. Mathew Wren, July 24; bp. Her ford, 1634.
1635. Christr. Wren, Apr. 4.
1658. Edwd. Hyde, July; *d.* befo installation.
1660. Bruno Ryves, dean of Chicheste Sept. 3.
1677. Jno. Durell, July 27.
1683. Fras. Turner, July 20; bp. Roche ter, same date.
1684. Gregory Hascard, Sept. 29.
1709. Thos. Manningham, Feb. 26; b Chichester, Nov. 1709.
Jno. Robinson, Dec. 3; bp. Brist 1710.
1714. Geo. Verney, ld. Willoughby Broke, Mar. 24.
1729. Penyston Booth, Apr. 26.
1765. Hon. Fredk. Keppel, bp. Exeter.
1778. Hon. Jno. Harley; bp. Herefor 1787.
1788. Jno. Douglas, bp. Carlisle, Ma 22, **G.**; tr. to Salisbury, 1791.
1791. Hon. Jas. Cornwallis, Aug. 20, **G.**
1794. Chas. Manners Sutton, bp. Norwic Feb. 6, **G.**; tr. to Canterbury, 18C
1805. Hon. Edwd. Legge, Feb. 23, G bp. Oxford, 1815.
1816. Hon. Hy. Lewis Hobart, Apr. 6,
1846. Hon. Geo. Neville Grenville, M 23, **G.**
1854. Hon. Gerald Wellesley, June 23,
1882. Geo. Hy. Connor, Oct. 30, **G.**
1883. Randall Thos. Davidson, May 21,

PROVINCE OF YORK.

DIOCESE OF CARLISLE.

This see was erected in 1133 by Henry I., and made suffragan to York.

In 1537 a bishop suffragan of Penrith was appointed under 26 Hen. VIII., cap. 14. He was probably suffragan to this see, but when, in 1888, the title was revived the bishop was made suffragan to Ripon.

BISHOPS OF CARLISLE.

1133. Athelwolf, or Athelward, the last prior of St. Oswald's and first bishop.
1157. Bernard; *d.* 1186.
See vacant 32 years.
During this vacancy, however, king John, in 1200, gave the see to the abp. of Sclavonia; and in 1203 he granted it to Alexr. de Lucy; but the next regular bishop was
1218. Hugh de Bello Loco, abbot of Battle, Sussex.
1223. Walter Maclerk, or Malclerk, ld. treasr.; res.
1246. Silvester de Everdon, archdn. of Chester; ld. chanc.
1255. Thos. Vipont.
1258. Robt. de Cheverel, or Chause, called, by Leland, chaplain to the queen.
1278. Wm. de Rotherfeld, elected but refused the see.
Rodolph or Ralph de Ireton, prior of Gisborne.
1293. John de Halghton, or Halton, canon of Carlisle.
1325. Wm. Ayremyn, canon of York, elected; but the Pope appointed
John de Rosse, canon of Hereford.
1332. John de Kirkeby, canon of Carlisle.
John de Horncastle elected, but set aside by the pope.
1353. Gilbert de Wilton.
1363. Thos. de Appleby, canon of Carlisle.
Wm. Strickland chosen, but set aside by the pope.
1396. Robt. Reade, tr. from Waterford, Ireland; tr. to Chichester same year.
1397. Thos. Merkes; depr. 1399, and aft. vicar of Sturminster, Dorsetshire; in 1404 became rector of Todenham, Gloucestershire; *d.* about 1409.
1399. Wm. Strickland.
1420. Roger Whelpdale, prov. of Queen's Coll., Oxford.
1423. Wm. Barrowe; tr. from Bangor.
1430. Marmaduke Lumley, archdn. of Northumberland, ld. treasr., ld. chanc., and chanc. of Cambridge; tr. to Lincoln.
1450. Nichs. Close, archdn. of Colchester; tr. to Lichfield and Coventry.
1452. Wm. Percy, preb. of York, Lincoln, and Salisbury; chanc. of Cambridge.
1462. Jno. Kingscotes, archdn. of Gloucester.
1464. Richd. Scrope, rector of Fen-Ditton, Cambridgeshire.
1468. Edwd. Story, chanc. of Cambridge; tr. to Chichester.
1478. Richd. Bell, prior of Durham; res.
1495. Wm. Sever, or Seveyer, abbot of St. Mary's, York; tr. to Durham.
1502. Roger Leybourn, archdn. of Durham.
1509. Jno. Penny; tr. from Bangor.
1521. Jno. Kite, abp. of Armagh.
1537. Robt. Aldrich, prov. of Eton and canon of Windsor.
1556. Owen Oglethorpe, dean of Windsor; depr. 1559.
1561. Jno. Best, preb. of Wells.
1570. Richd. Barnes, chanc. and preb. of of York, styled bp. of Nottingham; tr. to Durham.
1577. Jno. Mey, preb. of Ely.
1598. Hy. Robinson, prov. of Queen's Coll., Oxford.
1616. Robt. Snowdon, preb. of Southwell.
1621. Richd. Milbourne; tr. from St. David's.
1624. Richd. Senhouse, dean of Gloucester.
1626. Fras. White, dean of Carlisle; tr. to Norwich.
1629. Barnabas Potter, prov. of Queen's Coll., Oxford.
1641. Jas. Usher, abp. of Armagh; *d.* 1655.
See vacant 5 years.
1660. Richd. Sterne, mast. of Jesus Coll., Cambridge; tr. to York.
1664. Edwd. Rainbow, dean of Peterborough.

1684. Thos. Smith, dean of Carlisle.
1702. Wm. Nicholson, archdn. and preb. of Carlisle; tr. to Derry.
1718. Saml. Bradford, preb. of Westminster; tr. to Rochester.
1723. Jno. Waugh, dean of Gloucester.
1734. Sir Geo. Fleming, bt., dean of Carlisle.
1747. Richd. Osbaldeston, dean of York; tr. to London.
1762. Chas. Lyttelton, dean of Exeter.
1768. Edmd. Law, archdn. of Carlisle.
1787. Jno. Douglas, can.-res. of St. Paul's; tr. to Salisbury.
1791. Hon. Edwd. Venables Vernon, aft. Harcourt; tr. to York.
1808. Saml. Goodenough, Jan. 26; *d.* Aug. 12, 1827.
1827. Hon. Hugh Percy; tr. from Rochester, Sept. 17; *d.* Feb. 1856.
1856. Hon. Hy. Montagu Villiers, canon of St. Paul's, Feb. 25, **G.**; tr. to Durham.
1860. Hon. Saml. Waldegrave, canon of Salisbury, Aug. 29, **G.**; *d.* Oct. 1, 1869.
1869. Harvey Goodwin, dean of Ely, Oct. 28, **G.**

BISHOPS SUFFRAGAN OF PENRITH.

See Diocese of Ripon, *post*, p. 482.

DEANS OF CARLISLE.

1542. Lancelot Salkeld, May 8, last prior and first dean.
1547. Sir Thos. Smith; *d.* Aug. 12, 1571.
1577. Sir Jno. Wooley, Oct. 11; *d.* 1595.
1596. Christr. Perkins; *d.* 1622.
1622. Fras. White; bp. Carlisle, 1626.
1626. Wm. Paterson; dean of Exeter, 1629.
1630. Thos. Coomber; *d.* 1653.
1660. Guy Carleton; bp. Bristol, 1671.
1671. Thos. Smith; bp. Carlisle, 1684.
1684. Thos. Musgrave; *d.* 1686.
1686. Wm. Graham; dean of Wells, 1704.
1704. Fras. Atterbury; dean of Christchurch, 1711.
1711. Geo. Smalridge; dean of Christchurch, 1713.
1713. Thos. Gibbon; *d.* 1716.
1716. Thos. Tullie; *d.* 1726.
1727. Geo. Fleming, aft. sir G., bt.; bp. Carlisle, 1734.
1734. Robt. Bolton; *d.* 1764.
1764. Chas. Tarrent; dean of Peterborough, 1764.
Thos. Wilson; *d.* 1778.
1778. Thos. Percy; bp. Dromore, 1782.
1782. Jeffery Ekins; *d.* 1792.
1792. Isaac Milner.
1820. Robt. Hodgson, Apr. 11, **G.**
1844. Jno. Antony Cramer, Dec. 4, **G.**
1848. Saml. Hinds, Sept. 27, **G.**; bp. Norwich, 1849.
1849. Archd. Campbell Tait, Dec. 3, **G.**; bp. London, 1856.
1856. Fras. Close, Nov. 24, **G.**
1881. Jno. Oakley, Nov. 23, **G.**; made dean of Manchester, 1883.
1884. Wm. Geo. Henderson.

DIOCESE OF CHESTER.

The bishopric of Chester was anciently part of Lichfield. One of the bishops of that diocese removing the seat of his see hither in the year 1075, occasioned his successors to be frequently styled bishops of Chester; but it was not erected into a distinct bishopric until the general dissolution of the monasteries, when Henry VIII., in 1541, raised it to this dignity. He added the bishopric to the province of Canterbury; but, soon after, he disjoined it from Canterbury, and added it to the province of York.

BISHOPS OF CHESTER.

1541. John Bird, tr. from Bangor; depr. by Mary.
1554. Geo. Cotes, master of Baliol College, Oxford.
1556. Cuthbert Scot, preb. of St. Paul's; depr. by Elizabeth.
1561. Wm. Downman, preb. of Westminster; *d.* 1577.
See vacant 2 years.
1579. Wm. Chaderton, preb. of York and Westminster; tr. to Lincoln.
1595. Hugh Bellot, tr. from Bangor.

1597. Richd. Vaughan, tr. from Bangor; tr. to London.
1604. Geo. Lloyd, tr. from Sodor and Man.
1616. Thos. Moreton, dean of Winchester; tr. to Lichfield and Coventry.
1619. John Bridgeman, preb. of Lichfield; *d.* 1657.
See vacant 3 years.
1660. Brian Walton, preb. of St. Paul's; author of the Polyglot Bible.
1662. Hy. Ferne, dean of Ely; consec. in Feb., and *d.* March following.
Geo. Hall, archdn. of Canterbury.
1668. John Wilkins, preb. of York; *d.* Nov. 1672.
673. John Pearson, preb. of Salisbury and Ely.
686. Thos. Cartwright, preb. of Durham; nom. to Salisbury; but he fled.
689. Nichs. Strafford, dean of St. Asaph.
707. Sir Wm. Dawes, bt., preb. of Worcester; tr. to York.
714. Fras. Gastrell, canon of Christ Church, Oxford.
725. Saml. Peploe, warden of Manchester.
752. Edmd. Keene, rector of Stanhope, Durham; tr. to Ely.
1771. Wm. Markham, dean of Christ Church, Oxford; tr. to York.
1777. Beilby Porteus, rector of Hunton, Kent; tr. to London.
1787. Wm. Cleaver, preb. of Westminster; tr. to Bangor.
1800. Hy. Wm. Majendie, can.-res. of St. Paul's, May 24; tr. to Bangor.
1809. Bowyer, Edwd. Sparke, Oct. 7; tr. to Ely.
1812. Geo. Hy. Law, June 20; tr. to Bath and Wells.
1824. Chas. Jas. Blomfield, June 8; tr. to London.
1828. John Bird Sumner, canon of Durham, Aug. 26; tr. to Canterbury.
1848. John Graham, mast. Christ's Coll., Cambridge, Mar. 11; *d.* June 15, 1865.
1865. Wm. Jacobson, reg. prof. divinity and canon of Christ Church, Oxford, July 8; res. 1884; *d.* July 13, 1884.
1884. Wm. Stubbs, reg. prof. mod. hist. Oxford, and canon of St. Paul's, Feb. 29, **G.**; tr. to Oxford, 1888.
1888. Fras. Jno. Jayne, vicar of Leeds; bp. desig.

DEANS OF CHESTER.

541. Thos. Clerke, last abbot of St. Werburghe, and first dean.
* Hy. Mann; bp. Sodor and Man, 1546.
* Wm. Clyve.
* Roger Walker.
* John Piers, bp. Rochester, 1576.
* Richd. Longworth.
* Robt. Dorsell.
* Thos. Modesley.
589. John Nuttall; *d.* 1603.
603. Wm. Barlow; bp. Rochester, 1605.
605. Hy. Parry, Aug. 1; bp. Gloucester, 1607.
607. Thos. Mallory; *d.* Apr. 3, 1644.
544. Wm. Nicols; *d.* 1658.
660. Hy. Bridgeman; bp. Sodor and Man, 1671.
682. Jas. Arderne, July 12; *d.* Aug. 18, 1691.
691. Laurence Fogg, Nov. 14; *d.* Feb. 28, 1718.
718. Wm. Offley, Mar. 6; *d.* 1721.
1721. Thos. Allen, Nov. 12; *d.* May 31, 1732.
1732. Thos. Brooke, July 18; *d.* Dec. 1757.
1758. Wm. Smith, July 28; *d.* Jan. 12, 1787.
1787. Geo. Cotton, Feb. 10; *d.* 1805.
1806. Hugh Cholmondeley, Jan. 28, **G.**; *d.* Nov. 25, 1815.
1815. Robt. Hodgson, Dec. 12, **G.**; dean of Carlisle, 1820.
1820. Peter Vaughan, Apr. 14, **G.**; *d.* 1826.
1826. Edwd. Copleston, Aug. 7, **G.**; dean of St. Paul's and bp. Llandaff, 1828.
1828. Hy. Phillpotts, Mar. 19, **G.**; bp. Exeter, 1830.
1831. Geo. Davys, Jan. 10, **G.**; bp. Peterborough, 1839.
1839. Fredk. Anson, May 9, **G.**; *d.* 1867.
1867. John Saul Howson, June 12, **G.**
1886. John Lionel Darby, Feb. 1, **G.**

DIOCESE OF DURHAM.

THIS see was first fixed at Lindisfarne, or Holy Island, a small island on the coast of Northumberland; but from this spot the monks were driven by the invasions of the Danes. They next fixed themselves at Chester-on-the-Street, where they remained nearly two hundred years, and then settled finally at Durham. The bishops of Durham take precedence next after the bishops of London.

In 1537 a bishop suffragan of Berwick was appointed (probably to this see) under 26 Hen. VIII., cap. 14; but the appointment was not continued.

BISHOPS OF LINDISFARNE, OR HOLY ISLAND.

635. St. Aidan.
652. St. Finan.
661. Colman; res.
664. Tuda.
See vacant 14 years.
678. Eata, St. Eata, or Estata.
685. St. Cuthbert.
688. St. Eadbert.
698. St. Eadfrid, or Egbert I.; *d.* 721.
See vacant 3 years.
724. St. Ethelwold.
740. Kenulf, or Cynewolf.
781. Higbald.
803. Egbert II.
821. Heathured, or Heathored.
828. Egfrid.
846. Eanbert.
854. Eardulph. In 884 he removed the see to Chester-on-the-Street.
900. Cuthard, or Cutheard.
915. Tilred, or Milred.
929. Withred.
944. Uchtred.
947. Sexhelm; held the see only six months.
948. Aldred.
968. Alsius, Alfine, or Elfsig.
990. Aldwin, or Aldune, who removed the see to Durham.

BISHOPS OF DURHAM.

990. Aldwin, or Aldune, above-named.
1020. Eadmund.
1041. Eadred; *d.* in less than 11 months.
1042. Egelric; res. 1056.
1056. Egelwine, his brother; exp. by William the Conqueror, 1070, and *d.* in prison, 1071.
1072. Walcherus de Loraine, E. of Northumberland; slain.
1080. Wm. de Carilepho, ld. ch. just.
See vacant 4 years.
1099. Ralph Flambard, ld. treasr., and ld. ch. just.
1133. Geoffrey Rufus, ld. chanc.
1143. Wm. de St. Barbara, dean of York.
1153. Hugh Pudsey, or Pusar, E. of Northumberland, treasr. of York, and archdn. of Winchester.
1197. Philip de Poitiers; *d.* 1208.
See vacant 9 years.
1217. Richd. de Marisco, archdn. of Northumberland; ld. chanc.
1228. Richd. Poore; tr. from Salisbury.
1240. Nichs. de Farnham, elected Jan. 2; he refused the see of Lichfield, and unwillingly accepted this; res. 1249; *d.* 1256.
1249. Walter de Kirkham.
1260. Robt. Stitchell, prior of Finchdale.
1274. Robt. de Insula.
1283. Anthy. de Beck, archdn. of Durham, patriarch of Jerusalem; he had also, from the king, the principality of Man.
1311. Richd. de Kellawe.
1317. Lewis de Beaumont, treasr. of Salisbury.
Robt. de Greystanes, elected; but set aside by the pope, and *d.* soon after.
1333. Richd. de Angarville, Aungervyle, or de Bury, dean of Wells, ld. pr. seal, ld. chanc., and ld. treasr.
1345. Thos. de Hatfield, preb. of York and Lincoln; sec. st.
1381. John Fordham, dean of Wells, ld. treasr.; tr. to Ely.
1388. Waltr. Skirlaw, tr. from Bath and Wells.
1406. Thos. Langley, or Longley, dean of York, ld. chanc. and cardl.
1438. Robt. Nevill, tr. from Salisbury.
1457. Laurence Booth, dean of St. Paul's, chanc. of Cambridge, ld. chanc.; tr. to York.
1476. Wm. Dudley, dean of Windsor; *d.* 1483.
See vacant 2 years.
1485. John Sherwood, chanc. of Exeter *d.* 1492.
See vacant 2 years.
1494. Richd. Fox, tr. from Bath and Wells; tr. to Winchester, 1501.
1502. Wm. Sever, or Siveyer, tr. from Carlisle; *d.* 1505.
See vacant 2 years.
1507. Christr. Bainbridge, dean of York and Windsor, m. rolls; tr. to York, 1508.
1509. Thos. Ruthal, or Rowthall, dean of Salisbury; ld. pr. seal.
1523. Thos. Wolsey, abp. of York, held this see *in commendam*; tr. to Winchester in 1529.

1530. Cuthbert Tunstall, tr. from London; depr. 1552, and the bishopric dissolved; rest. 1553; depr. *again*, 1559.
1560. Jas. Pilkington.
1577. Richd. Barnes, tr. from Carlisle.
See vacant 2 years.
1589. Matth. Hutton, dean of York; tr. to York.
1595. Tobias Matthew, dean of Durham; tr. to York.
1606. Wm. James, dean of Durham.
1617. Richd. Neile, or Neale, tr. from Lincoln; tr. to Winchester, Dec. 1627.
1627. Geo. Monteigne, tr. from London; tr. to York.
1628. John Howson, tr. from Oxford.
1632. Thos. Moreton, tr. from Lichfield and Coventry; *d.* 1659.
See vacant about a year.
1660. John Cosin, dean of Peterborough.
1674. Nathl. Crewe, ld. Crewe, tr. from Oxford; *d.* 1722.
1722. Wm. Talbot, tr. from Salisbury.
1730. Edwd. Chandler, tr. from Lichfield and Coventry.
1750. Jos. Butler, tr. from Bristol.
1752. Hon. Richd. Trevor, tr. from St. David's.
1771. Hon. John Egerton, tr. from Lichfield and Coventry.
1787. Hon. Thos. Thurlow, tr. from Lincoln.
1791. Hon. Shute Barrington, tr. from Salisbury; *d.* 1826.
1826. Wm. Van Mildert, tr. from Llandaff; *d.* Feb. 21, 1836.
1836. Edwd. Maltby, Mar. 3; tr. from Chichester; res. Sept. 1856; *d.* July 3, 1859.
1856. Chas. Thos. Longley, Oct. 13, **G.** tr. from Ripon; tr. to York, 1860.
1860. Hon. Hy. Montagu Villiers, July 14, **G.**; tr. from Carlisle; *d.* Aug. 10, 1861.
1861. Chas. Baring, Sept. 5, **G.**; tr. from Gloucester; res. Jan. 1879; *d.* Sept. 14, 1879.
1879. Jos. Barber Lightfoot, prof. div. at Cambridge; Feb. 28, **G.**

BISHOP SUFFRAGAN OF BERWICK.

1537. Thos. Sparke.

DEANS OF DURHAM.

1541. Hugh Whitehead, first dean, May 12; *d.* 1548 (?).
1551. Robt. Horn, Nov. 18; depr. by Mary; *d.* June 1, 1579.
1553. Thos. Watson, Nov. 18; bp. Lincoln, 1557; but, it is believed, held the deanery also for some time after.
1557.}
1558.} Thos. Robertson, July 23; depr. by Elizabeth.
1559. Robt. Horn, rest.; bp. Winchester, 1561.
1561. Ralph Skynner, Mar. 5; *d.* Jan. 1563.
1563. Wm. Whittingham, July 19; *d.* June 10, 1579.
1580. Thos. Wilson, Feb. 28; *d.* June 16, 1581.
1583. Tobias Matthew, Aug. 31; bp. Durham, 1595.
1596. Wm. James, June 5; bp. Durham, 1606.
1606. Adam Newton, Sept. 27; res. 1620; cr. knt. and bt.; *d.* Sept. 13, 1626.
1620. Richd. Hunt, May 29; *d.* Nov. 1, 1638.
1639. Waltr. Balcanquall, May 14; *d.* Christmas Day, 1645.
1646. Christr. Potter, Jan.; *d.* Mar. follg., before installation.
Wm. Fuller, Mar. 6; app., but probably never inst.; *d.* May 12, 1659.
1660. Jno. Barwick, Nov. 1; dean of St. Paul's, 1661.
1662. Jno. Sudbury, Feb. 25; *d.* 1684.
1684. Denis Granville, Dec. 14; depr. as a non-juror.
1691. Thos. Comber, June 15; *d.* Nov. 25, 1698.
1699. Hon. Jno. Montague, June 19; *d.* Feb. 23, 1728.
1728. Hy. Bland, May 6; *d.* May 24, 1746.
1746. Hon. Spencer Cowper, July 21; *d.* Mar. 25, 1774.
1774. Thos. Dampier, June 17; *d.* July 31, 1777.
1777. Hon. Wm. Digby, Sept. 20.
1788. Jno. Hinchliff.
1794. Hon. Jas. Cornwallis, aft. E. Cornwallis, bp. Lichfield; *d.* 1824.
1824. Chas. Hy. Hall, dean of Christchurch, Feb. 11, **G.**
1827. Jno. Banks Jenkinson, bp. St David's, May 31, **G.**; *d.* 1840.
1840. Geo. Waddington, Aug. 24, **G.**
1869. Wm. Chas. Lake, Aug. 9, **G.**

DIOCESE OF HEXHAM.

Now Extinct.

This bishopric was founded in the infancy of the Saxon Church. Ten bishops enjoyed it in regular succession, and then, by reason of the spoil and rapine of the Danes, it was discontinued, Tydferth, or Tilford, the last bishop, driven away by these invaders, dying on a journey to Rome. The district in which the see was situated was anciently a county palatine; but is now annexed to the county of Northumberland, and forms part of the diocese of Durham.

BISHOPS OF HEXHAM.

678. Estata, bp. of Lindisfarne.
680. Tumbert.
685. St. John of Beverley, tr. to York.
709. St. Acca.
739. Frithebert.
766. Alhmund.
780. Tilhere.
789. Ethelbert.
797. Heardred.
800. Eanbert.
810. Tydferth, or Tilford, last bp. of Hexham

DIOCESE OF LIVERPOOL.

This see was constituted under the "Bishoprics Act, 1878," (41 & 42 Vict., cap. 68,) and an order in Council, dated March 24, 1880, under which its establishment was to date from April 9, 1880.

It was formed out of the diocese of Chester, and has at present no dean and chapter attached to it.

BISHOP OF LIVERPOOL.

1880. John Chas. Ryle, vicar of Stradbroke, Suffolk, dean desig. of Salisbury, Apr. 19, **G.**; first bishop.

DIOCESE OF MANCHESTER.

This see was constituted by 6 & 7 Wm. IV., cap. 77 (Aug. 13, 1836), and 10 & 11 Vict., cap. 108, and an order in Council, dated Aug. 10, 1847, under which its establishment was to date from Aug. 31, 1847. It was formed out of the diocese of Chester.

BISHOPS OF MANCHESTER.

1847. Jas. Prince Lee, head master of king Edward VI.'s School, Birmingham, Oct. 18; first bp.; *d.* Dec. 24, 1869.
1870. Jas. Fraser, rector of Upton Nervet, Berks, Jan. 18, **G.**; *d.* 1885.
1886. Jas. Moorhouse, Feb. 3; tr. from Melbourne.

DEANS OF MANCHESTER.

For many years prior to the constitution of the see, Manchester possessed a collegiate church originally dedicated to the Virgin Mary; but on its re-constitution by Queen Elizabeth it was called Christ's College. The establishment consisted of a warden and fellows. By an order in Council, December 12, 1838, and gazetted January 25,

1839, it was provided that on the constitution of the see of Manchester (then contemplated at an early date) the "Warden and Fellows" of the Collegiate Church should thenceforward be styled "Deans and Canons," and should be the dean and chapter of the new see. The see of Manchester was not constituted until 1847; but by 3 & 4 Vict., cap. 113, sec. 1 (Aug. 11, 1840), it was provided that the wardens should be styled deans, and they have since borne that title.

Wardens of Christ's College, Manchester.

On Thos. de la Warre's Foundation, 1422.

1422. Jno. Huntingdon.
1459. Jno. Booth.
1465. Ralph Langley.
1481. Jas. Stanley.
1509. Robt. Cliffe.
1514. — Alday (?).
1518. Geo. West.

Philip and Mary's Foundation.

1535. Geo. Collier.
1557. Lawrence Vaux.

Elizabeth's Foundation, 1578.

1560. Wm. Birch.
Thos. Herle.
1578. Jno. Wolton.
1580. Wm. Chaderton.
1595. Jno. Dee.
1608. Richd. Murray

Chas. I.'s Foundation, 1635.

1636 Richd. Heyrick.
1667. Nichs. Stratford.
1684. Richd. Wroe.
1717. Saml. Peploe.
1738. Saml. Peploe (son).
1781. Richd. Assheton
1798. Thos. Blackburn.
1823. Thos. Jackson Calvert.
1840. Hon. Wm. Herbert.

Deans of Christ's College, Manchester.

1840. Hon. Wm. Herbert, above-named, warden, now dean, Aug. 11.
1847. Geo. Hull Bowers, June 19, **G**.

Deans of Manchester Cathedral.

1847. Geo. Hull Bowers. above-named, Aug. 31.
1872. Benjn. Morgan Cowie, Nov. 7, **G.**; dean of Exeter, 1883.
1884. Jno. Oakley, from Carlisle, Feb. 7, **G.**

DIOCESE OF NEWCASTLE-ON-TYNE.

This see was constituted under the "Bishoprics Act 1878" (41 & 42 Vict., cap. 68), and an order in council, dated May 17, 1882, under which its establishment was to date from May 23, 1882. It was formed out of the diocese of Durham.

BISHOP OF NEWCASTLE-ON-TYNE.

1882. Ernest Roland Wilberforce, canon of Winchester, June 26, **G.**; first bishop.

DIOCESE OF RIPON.

THIS see was constituted under 6 & 7 Will. IV., cap. 77 (Aug. 13, 1836), and an order in council, dated Oct. 5, 1836, under which its establishment was to date from October 7, 1836. It was formed out of the dioceses of York and Chester.

In 1557, a bishop suffragan of Penrith was appointed under 26 Hen. VIII., cap. 14. He was probably suffragan to Carlisle, but when in 1888 the title was revived, the bishop was made suffragan to Ripon.

BISHOPS OF RIPON.

1836. Chas. Thos. Longley, head master of Harrow, Oct. 15; first bp.; tr. to Durham, 1856.

1856. Robt. Bickersteth, canon of Salisbury, Dec. 9, **G.**; *d.* Apr. 15, 1884.

1884. Wm. Boyd Carpenter, canon of Windsor, June 12, **G.**

BISHOPS SUFFRAGAN OF PENRITH.

1537. Jno. Bird, probably suffragan to Carlisle.

1888. Jno. Jas. Pulleine, can. of Ripon, Apr. 30, **G.**

DEANS OF RIPON.

Before the constitution of the see, Ripon possessed a collegiate church. It was originally a monastery dissolved by Henry VIII. and refounded by James I., in 1604. By the Act 6 & 7 Will. IV., cap. 77 (Aug. 13, 1836) and order in council, dated Oct. 5, 1836, establishing the see of Ripon, it was provided that the deans and prebendaries of the Collegiate Church should be the dean and canons of the new see.

DEANS OF THE COLLEGIATE CHURCH OF RIPON.

From the restoration by James I.

The dates are those of the installations, except when otherwise stated.

1604. Moses Fowler, Aug. 2 (first dean); *d.* Mar. 1608.

1608. Anthy. Higgins.

1624. John Wilson, *d.* Feb. 1635.

1635. Thos. Dod, Apr. 23; dispossessed; *d.* Feb. 1648.

1660. John Wilkins, Aug. 31; bp. Chester 1668; *d.* Nov. 19, 1672.

1673. John Neile, instituted May 25; installed May 30; *d.* Apr. 14, 1675.

1675. Thos. Tullie, instituted May 5; installed Aug. 21; *d.* Jan. 14, 1676.

1676. Thos. Cartwright, instituted Jan. 31; installed Feb. 1; bp. Chester, Oct. 17, 1686.

1686. Christr. Wyvill, Nov. 6; *d.* Jan. 7, 1711.

1711. Heneage Dering, Mar. 10; *d.* Apr. 8, 1750.

1750. Fras. Wanley, instituted Aug. 13; installed Aug. 16; *d.* July 1791.

1791. Robert Darby Waddilove, app. Oct.; instituted Jan. 14, installed Jan. 21, 1792; *d.* Aug. 18, 1828.

1828. Jas. Webber, app. Nov. 14; installed Nov. 24.

DEANS OF RIPON CATHEDRAL.

1836. Jas. Webber (above-named), Oct. 5; *d.* Sept. 3, 1847.

1847. Hon. Hy. David Erskine, app. Sept. 23, **G.**; installed Nov. 14; *d.* July 27, 1859.

1859. Thos. Garnier, app. Aug. 29, **G.**; installed Oct. 6; made dean of Lincoln Mar. 30, 1860.

1860. Wm. Goode, app. May 10, **G.**; installed July 17; *d.* Aug. 13, 1868.

1868. Hugh McNeile, app. Sept. 9, **G.**; installed Oct. 29; res. 1875; *d.* Jan. 28, 1879.

1875. Sydney Turner, app. Dec. 20, **G.**; installed Jan. 27, 1876; res. same year.

1876. Wm. Robt. Fremantle, app. Apr. 18, **G.**; installed May 9.

DIOCESE OF SODOR AND MAN.

THE bishopric of Man was established or affirmed by pope Gregory IV. It had united to its diocese the Western Isles of Scotland, which, when Man became dependant upon England, withdrew their obedience and had a bishop of their own. The patronage of the diocese was given, together with the island, to the Stanleys, afterwards earls of Derby, from whom it passed to the dukes of Athole. The patrons nominated the bishop to the king, who sent him to the archbishop of York for consecration. The prelates thus appointed were not lords of Parliament, not holding from the king himself, and though allowed to sit in the House of Lords by courtesy, did not enjoy a vote. This disability continues, although, since 1829, when the last remaining rights of the dukes of Athole over the Isle of Man were bought up, the bishops have been directly nominated by the Crown. The bishopric is nominally united to that of Sodor, or Sudreys, *i.e.*, South Hebrides, a diocese which comprehended all the islands, together with the Isle of Man. The bishop is still called "Bishop of Sodor and Man"; but the diocese consists of the Isle of Man only.

There are no dean and chapter attached to this see.

BISHOPS OF SODOR AND MAN.

447. Germanus,
* * Conindrius,
* * Romulus,
498. Machutus, Machilla, or Maughold,
* * Conanus,

} bishops of Man.

* * St. Contentus,
* * St. Bladus,
* * St. Malchus,
889. Torkinus,
* * Roolwer,
* * William,
* * Brendinus,

} bishops of Man; styled also bishops of Sodor.

BISHOPS OF SODOR AND MAN.

1113. Wymundus, or Reymundus; depr.
1151. John, a monk of Sais, in Normandy.
1154. Gamaliel.
* * Reginald, a Norwegian.
* * Christian Orcadensis, or of Orkney.
* * Michael, a Manxman.
1203. Nicholas de Meaux, abbot of Furnes.
1217. Reginald, nephew to king Olave.
1226. John.
1230. Simon Orcadensis, or of Orkney.
1249. Lawrence, archdn. of Man.
See vacant almost 2 years.
1252. Richard.
1275. Mark of Galloway.
1305. Allen, or Onachus, of Galloway.
1321. Gilbert of Galloway.
1324. Bernard, a Scot, abbot of Kilwinning, Scotland.
1334. Thomas, a Scot.
1348. Wm. Russell, a Manxman, abbot of Rushen.
1374. John Donkan, a Manxman.
1381. Robt. Waldby; tr. to Dublin, 1391.
He is said to have been bp. of this see in 1396; but *Le Neve* doubts it.
See vacant many years.
1429. Richd. Pully.
1448. John Green, or Sprotton, vicar of Dunchurch, Warwickshire.
1455. Thos. Burton.
1458. Thos., abbot of Vale Royal, Cheshire.
1480. Richd. Oldham, abbot of Chester.
1487. Huan Hisketh, or Blackleach.
1510. Thos. Stanley, rector of Wigan; depr.
1545. Robt. Farrer, or Ferrar; tr. to St. David's.
1546. Hy. Mann, dean of Chester.
1558. Thos. Stanley, rest.; *d.* 1570.
1571. John Salisbury, dean of Norwich.
1573. Jas. Stanley.
Le Neve says the see was vacant about 3 years; but *Heylyn* states that this prelate held it from 1573 to 1576.
1576. John Merick, vicar of Hornchurch, Essex.
1600. Geo. Lloyd; tr. to Chester.
1604. John Philips, archdn. of Cleveland and Man.
1634. Wm. Forster, preb. of Chester.
1635. Richd. Parr, rector of Eccleston, Lancashire; *d.* 1643.

See vacant 17 years.
1661. Saml. Rutter, archdn. of Man.
1663. Isaac Barrow, fellow of Eton College; tr. in 1669 to St. Asaph; but held this see two years *in commendam.*
1671. Hy. Bridgman, dean of Chester.
1682. John Lake, archdn. of Cleveland; tr. to Bristol.
1684. Baptist Levinge, preb. of Winchester.
See vacant 5 years.
1697. Thos. Wilson, of Trin. Coll., Dublin; *d.* 1755.
1755. Mark Hiddesley, vicar of Hitchen, Herts.
1773. Richd. Richmond, vicar of Walton-on-the-Hill, Lancashire.
1780. Geo Mason; *d.* 1783.
1784. Claudius Crigan; *d.* 1813.
1813. Geo. Murray; tr. to Rochester.
1827. Wm. Ward; *d.* 1838.
1838. Jas. Bowstead; tr. to Lichfield and Coventry.
1839. Hy. Pepys; tr. to Worcester.
1841. Thos. Vowler Short, rector of St. George's, Bloomsbury; tr. to St. Asaph.
1846. Walter Aug. Shirley; app. Nov. 28; *d.* 1847.
1847. Hon. Robt. John Eden, who, on the decease of his brother, the E. of Auckland, in 1849, succ. to that title; tr. to Bath and Wells 1854.
1854. Hon. Horatio Powys, rector of Warrington and rural dean, July 5 **G.**; *d.* May 31, 1877.
1877. Rowley Hill, canon of York, July 17 **G.**; *d.* May 27, 1887.
1887. John Wareing Bardsley, archdn. of Warrington.

DIOCESE OF WAKEFIELD.

THIS see was constituted under the "Bishoprics Act 1878" (41 & 42 Vict., cap. 68), and an order in council dated May 17, 1888, under which its establishment was to date from May 18, 1888. It was formed out of the dioceses of York and Ripon.

There are at present no dean and chapter attached to this see.

BISHOP OF WAKEFIELD.

1888. Wm. Walsham How, tr. from Bedford, May 28, **G.**; first bishop.

DIOCESE OF YORK.

YORK is the most ancient metropolitan see in England, dating, it is said from about A.D. 180, when Christianity was first, although partially planted in England. But this establishment was overturned by the Saxons driving out the Britons. When the former were converted pope Gregory determined that York should be restored to its former dignity, and Paulinus was made archbishop of this see, about A.D. 622 York and Durham were the only two sees in the north of England for many years, until Henry I. erected a bishopric at Carlisle, and Henry VIII. another at Chester. York was the metropolitan see of the Scottish bishops; but during the time of archbishop Nevill they withdrew their obedience, and had archbishops of their own. Many disputes arose between the two English metropolitans about precedency as, by pope Gregory's institutions, it was thought he meant that whichever of them was first confirmed should be the superior. Appeal was made to the Court of Rome by both parties, and it was determined in favour of Canterbury; but York was allowed to style himself primate of England, while Canterbury styles himself primate of *all* England. The archbishop of York ranks next to the archbishop of Canterbury amongst the English bishops; he also has precedence before all dukes not of the blood-royal, as also before all the great officers of state, the lord high chancellor excepted.

In 1538 a bishop suffragan of Hull was appointed (probably to this see) under 26 Hen. VIII., cap. 14, but this appointment was not continued.

ARCHBISHOPS OF YORK.

622. St. Paulinus; *d.* 644, being then bp. Rochester.
See vacant above 30 years.
St. Chad, previously bp. Lichfield; *d.* 672.
669. Wilfride I.
678. St. Bosa.
705. St. John of Beverley; res.
718. St. Wilfride II.
735. St. Egbert, brother to king Eadbert of Northumbria.
767. Adelbert, Albert, Caena, or Coena.
780. Eanbald I.
797. Eanbald II.
812. Wolsius, or Wulfius.
830. Wilmund, or Wymond.
854. Wulfhere, or Wilferus.
895. Ethelbald.
921. Redeward, or Redward.
941. Wolstan, or Wolfstan I.
955. Oskitell.
971. Athelwald.
St. Oswald, } held the see of Worcester *in commendam.*
993. Adulphus, or Adulse, }
1002. Wolfstan, or Wolstan II., }
1023. Alfric, or Putta.
1050. Kinsius.
1061. Aldred; tr. from Worcester.
1070. Thomas I., canon of Baion.
1100. Gerard; tr. from Hereford.
1109. Thomas II., bp. elect of London; but removed, before consecration, to this see.
1114. Thurstan, preb. of St. Paul's; res. Jan. 1139.
1144. William, a kinsman of king Stephen's; depr. by the pope, 1147.
1147. Hilary, bp. of Chichester, chosen by part of the chapter; but the other part chose
Hy. Murdac, abbot of Fountains.
1153. William, who was depr. in 1147; rest.
1154. Roger, archdn. of Canterbury.
See vacant 10 years.
1191. Godfrey Plantagenet, natl. son of Henry II., archdn. of Lincoln, ld. chanc.
See vacant 4 years.
Simon de Langton, brother to Stephen, abp. of Canterbury; elected, but set aside by the pope
1217. Walter de Grey, tr. from Worcester; ld. chanc.
1256. St. Sewall de Bovill, dean of York.
1258. Godfrey de Kinton, or Ludeham, dean of York.
1264. Wm. de Langton, or Ruderfield; elected, but put aside by the pope, who conferred the see on St. Bonaventure, cardl., who soon afterwards resigned it.
1265. Walter Giffard, tr. from Bath and Wells; ld. chanc.
1279. Wm. Wickwane, chanc. of York.
1285. John Romayne, precentor of Lincoln.
1296. Hy. de Newark, or Newerke, dean of York.
1299. Thos. Corbridge, or Corbrigge, preb. of York.
1303. Wm. Greenfield, or Grenfeld, dean of Chichester, ld. chanc.
1316. Wm. de Melton, provost of Beverley, ld. chanc. and ld. treasr.
1340. Wm. le Zouch, or de la Zouch, dean of York, ld. treasr.
1352. John Thoresby, tr. from Worcester; cardl.; ld. chanc.
1373. Alexr. Nevill, archdn. of Durham; banished in 1387.
1388. Thos. Fitz-Alan, or Arundel, ld. chanc.; tr. from Ely; tr. to Canterbury.
1396. Robt. Waldby, tr. from Chichester.
1398. Richd. Scrope, tr. from Lichfield and Coventry; beheaded June 8 1405.
1405. Thos. Langley, or Longley, dean of York; elected, but put aside by the pope.
Robt. Hallum, nom. by the pope; but, the king not consenting, he was removed to Salisbury.
1407. Hy. Bowett, tr. from Bath and Wells.
1424. Richd. Flemyng, bp. of Lincoln; promoted to this see, but the appt. not confirmed.

1426. John Kempe, tr. from London; cardl., and ld. chanc.; tr. to Canterbury.
1452. Wm. Booth, tr. from Lichfield and Coventry.
1465. Geo. Nevill, tr. from Exeter; ld. chanc.
1476. Laurence Booth, tr. from Durham.
1480. Thos. Scott, *alias* Rotheram; tr. from Lincoln; ld. chanc.
1501. Thos. Savage, tr. from London.
1508. Christr. Bainbridge, tr. from Durham; cardl.
1514. Thos. Wolsey, tr. from Lincoln; ld. chanc. and cardl.
1531. Edwd. Lee, chanc. of Salisbury and preb. of York.
1545. Robt. Holgate, tr. from Llandaff; ld. pres. of the north; depr.
1555. Nichs. Heath, late bp. of Worcester; ld. chanc.; depr. 1558.
Wm. May, dean of St. Paul's; chosen, but *d.* before consecration, Aug. 1560.
1560. Thos. Young, tr. from St. David's; ld. pres. of the north.
1570. Edmd. Grindal, tr. from London; tr. to Canterbury, 1575.
1576. Edwyn Sandys, tr. from London.
1588. John Piers, tr. from Salisbury.
1595. Matth. Hutton I.; tr. from Durham.
1606. Tobias Matthew, tr. from Durham
1628. Geo. Monteigne, tr. from Durham; *d.* the same year.
1628. Saml. Harsnet, tr. from Norwich; *d.* May 1631.
1632. Richd. Neile or Neyle, tr. from Winchester.
1641. John Williams, tr. from Lincoln; ld. kpr.; *d.* 1650.
See vacant 10 years.
1660. Accepted Frewen, tr. from Lichfield and Coventry.
1664. Richd. Sterne, tr. from Carlisle.
1683. John Dolben, tr. from Rochester.
1688. Thos. Lamplugh, tr. from Exeter.
1691. John Sharp, dean of Canterbury.
1714. Sir Wm. Dawes, bt., tr. from Chester.
1724. Lancelot Blackburn, tr. from Exeter.
1743. Thos. Herring, tr. from Bangor; tr. to Canterbury.
1747. Matth. Hutton II., tr. from Bangor; tr. to Canterbury.
1757. John Gilbert, tr. from Salisbury.
1761. Hon. Robt. Drummond; tr. from Salisbury; almoner.
1776. Wm. Markham, tr. from Chester; almoner; *d.* Nov. 3, 1807.
1807. Hon. Edwd. Venables Vernon, aft. Harcourt, Dec. 1; tr. from Carlisle; *d.* Nov. 1847.
1847. Thos. Musgrave, Nov. 17; tr. from Hereford; *d.* Nov. 5, 1847.
1860. Chas. Thos. Longley, June 1, **G.**; tr. from Durham; tr. to Canterbury.
1862. Wm. Thomson, Dec. 4, **G.**; tr. from Gloucester and Bristol.

BISHOP SUFFRAGAN OF HULL.

1538. Robt. Sylvester, *alias* Pursglove.

DEANS OF YORK.

Will. II. Hugo.
Steph. Wm. de St. Barbara; bp. Durham, 1142.
1144. Robt. de Gant.
* * Robt. Botevillin; *d.* 1186.
1186. Hubert Walter; bp. Salisbury, 1188.
1189. Hy. Marshall; bp. Exeter, 1193.
1191. Simon de Apulia; bp. Exeter, 1214.
1214. Hamo.
12—. Roger de Insula.
1235. Geoffry de Norwych.
1240. Fulk Bassett; bp. London, 1241.
1244. William.
124–. Walter de Kyrkham.
125–. Sewal de Bovil; abp. York, 1256.
1256. Godfrey de Ludham, *alias* Kinton; abp. York, 1258.
1258. Roger de Holderness.
126–. Wm. de Langueton; *d.* 1279.
1279. Robt. de Scardeburgh; *d.* 1290.
1290. Hy. de Newark, or Newerke; abp. York, 1296.
1298. Wm. de Hameltone.
1309. Reginald de Gote, cardl.; *d.* 1310.
1310. Wm. de Pykering; *d.* 1312.
1312. Robt. de Pykering.
1332. Wm. de Colby.
1333. Wm. le Zouch, or de la Zouch; abp. York, 1340.
1347. Philip de Weston.
135–. Tailerand, B. of Albanen.
1366. Jno. Anglicus, cardl.; depr.
1381. Adam Easton, cardl.; depr.
1385. Edmd. de Strafford.
139–. Roger Walden; consec. abp. Canterbury (*q. v.*), 1398; bp. London, 1404.
1398. Richd. Clifford; bp. Worcester, 1401.
1401. Thos. Langley; bp. Durham, 1406.
1407. Jno. Prophete.
1416. Thos. Polton; bp. Hereford, 1420.

1421. Wm. Grey; bp. London 1426.
1426. Robt. Gilbert; bp. London, 1436.
1437. Wm. Felter.
1454. Richd. Andrews; res. 1477.
1477. Robt. Bothe.
1488. Christr. Urswyk; res. 1494.
1494. Wm. Sheffield.
1496. Geoffry Blythe; bp. Lichfield, 1503.
1503. Christr. Baynbrigge; bp. Durham, 1507.
1507. Jas. Harrington; *d.* 1512.
1512. Thos. Wolsey, dean of Lincoln; bp. Lincoln, Feb. 1514; abp. York, Sept. 1514.
1514. Jno. Young; *d.* 1516.
1516. Brian Higden.; *d.* 1539.
1539. Richd. Layton; *d.* 1544.
1544. Nichs. Wotton; *d.* 1567.
1567. Matth. Hutton; bp. Durham, 1589.
1589. Jno. Thornburgh; held bpks. of Limerick and Bristol *in commendam*; tr. to Worcester, 1617.
1617. Geo. Meriton; *d.* 1624.
1624. Jno. Scott; *d.* 1644.
1660. Richd. Marsh; *d.* 1663.
1663. Wm. Sancroft; dean of St. Paul's, 1664.
1664. Robt. Hitch; *d.* 1676.
1676. Tobias Wickham; *d.* 1679.
1679. Thos. Gale; *d.* 1702.
1702. Hy. Finch; *d.* 1728.
1728. Richd. Osbaldeston; bp. Carlisle, 1747.
1747. Jno. Fountayne; *d.* 1802.
1802. Geo. Markham, Apr. 6, **G.**; *d.* 1822.
1822. Wm. Cockburn, Oct. 17, **G.**
1858. Hon. Aug. Duncombe, May 28.
1880. Arthur Perceval Purey-Cust, Feb. 27.

PART VIII. LONDON.

PORTREEVES, MAYORS, AND LORD MAYORS OF LONDON.

The Lord Mayor is the chief magistrate of London and the head o the Corporation. At first he was chosen for life, and afterwards fo periods of irregular duration; now he is chosen annually, but is capabl of re-election. He must be an alderman, and must have previousl filled the office of sheriff. Those freemen who have been admitted int the livery of their respective companies are the electors of the Lor Mayor; they choose two persons from amongst the aldermen, and th court of aldermen confer the dignity on whichever of the two the please. The practice is for the livery to return the aldermen in rota tion, and of these the court chooses the senior; but instances are no wanting in which this course has been varied, for the purpose of ex cluding some individual on whom the rotation of seniority would other wise have conferred the office. The 29th of September is the day o election, and between that date and the 9th of November, when h enters on his duties, he is styled the Lord Mayor Elect.

Portreeves, Mayors, and Lord Mayors of London.

The year mentioned in the following list is that in which each Mayor *served.* Hi year of office *commenced* on the 9th of November in the year preceding.

Those marked thus * died in their year of office.

Portreeves.

Richd. de Par.
Leofstanus Goldsmith.
Robt. Barquerel.
Andrew Buchevet.

Mayors.

Year ending Nov. 9.	
1189 to 1212.	Hy. Fitz-Alwyn, or Ailwyn, mayor of London 24 years.
1213.	Roger Fitz-Alwyn, or Ailwyn.
1214.	Robt. Serle, mercer.
1215.	Wyllyam Hardell.
1216.	Jacob Alderman. Saml. Basing.
1217 to 1222.	Robt. Serle, *again*, 6 years.
1223 to 1226.	Richd. Renger, 4 years.
1227 to 1231.	Roger le Duc, or Duke, 5 years.
1232 to 1237.	Andw. Bokerell, 6 years.
1238.	Richd. Renger, *again*.
1239.	Wm. Joynour.
1240.	Gerard Bat, or Bate.
1241. 1242.	Reymond or Regd Bongay.
1243.	Rauf Aswy, or Ash way.
1244.	Michl. Tony.
1245. 1246.	Johan de Gysors.
1247.	Pyers Aleyne.
1248.	Michl. Tony, *again*.
1249.	Roger Fitz-Roger.
1250.	John Norman.
1251.	Adam Basing.

Year ending Nov. 9.

252. Johan Tolason, or Tholozane.
253. Nycholas Batte.
254 to 258. Richd. Hardell, 5 years.
259. Johan de Gysors, *again.*
260. 261. Wm Fitz-Richard.
262 to 265. Thos. Fitz-Thomas, 4 years.
266. Wm. Fitz-Richard, *again.*
267. 268. Alan de la Zouch, one of the justices of the kingdom; slain by the earl Warenne.
269. Wm. Fitz-Thomas Fitz-Richard.
270. 271. Johan Adryan.
272. 273. Sir Walter Harvey.
274. Hy. Waleis, or Waleys.
275 to 281. Gregory Rokeslie, 7 years.
282. to 284. Hy. Waleis, *again*, 3 years.
285. Gregory Rokeslie, *again.*
286. Rauf de Sandwitch.
287. Johan Breton, aft. sir J.
288 to 293. Rauf de Sandwitch, *again*, 6 years.
294 to 297. Sir Johan Breton, *again*, 4 years.
298. Hy. Waleis, *again.*
299. 300. Elyas Russell.
301 to 307. Johan Blount, 7 years.
308. Nycholas Faryngdone.
309. Thos. Romayne.
310. Richd. Roffham, or Refham.
311. Johan Gysors.
312. Johan Pounteney, or Pultney.
313. Nycholas Faryngdone, *again.*
314. Johan Gysors, *again.*
315. Stephen de Abyngdone.
316 to 318. Johan Wentgrave, 3 years.

Year ending Nov. 9.

1319. Hamond Chyckwell.
1320. Nycholas Faryngdone, *again.*
1321. 1322. Hamond Chyckwell, *again.*
1323. Nycholas Faryngdone, *again.*
1324. 1325. Hamond Chyckwell, *again.*
1326. Richd. Bretayne.
1327. Hamond Chyckwell, *again.*
1328. Johan Grauntham, or Grantham.
1329. Symon Swanland.
1330. 1331. Johan Pounteney, or Pultney, *again* (?).
1332. Johan Preston.
1333. Johan Pounteney, *again.*
1334. 1335. Reynold at Conduyte.
1336. Johan Pounteney, *again.*
1337. 1338. Hy. Darcey.
1339. 1340. Andw. Awbrey.
1341. Johan de Oxynforde.
1342. Symond Fraunceys.
1343. 1344. Johan Hamond.
1345. Richd. Lacere.
1346. Geoffrey Wychyngham.
1347. Thos. Legge.
1348. Johan Lewkyn, or Loufkin.
1349. Wm. Turke.
1350. Richd. Killingbury.
1351. Andrew Awbrey, *again.*
1352. 1353. Adam Fraunceys.

LORD MAYORS.

1354. Thos. Legge, *again.*
1355. Symond Fraunceys, *again.*
1356. Hy. Pycard, or Pickard.
1357. Johan Stody.
1358. Johan Lewkyn, *again*,
1359. Symond Doffelde.
1360. Johan Wroth, or Worth.
1361. Johan Peche.
1362. Stephen Caundish.
1363. Johan Notte.
1364. Adam de Bury.
1365. 1366. Johan Lewkyn, *again.*
1367. Jas. Andrew.

Year ending Nov. 9.

1368. Symond Mordon.
1369. Johan Chychester.
1370. 1371. Johan Bernes, or Barnes.
1372. Johan Pyell, or Piel.
1373. Adam de Bury, *again.*
1374. Wyllyam de Walworthe.
1375. Johan Warde.
1376. Adam Staple.
1377. Nichs. Brembyr.
1378. Johan Phylpot.
1379. Johan Hadley.
1380. Wyllyam de Walworthe, *again*, aft. sir W.
1381. 1382. Johan de Northampton.
1383 to 1385. Nichs. Brembyr, *again*, 3 years.
1386. 1387. Nycholas Exton.
1388. Nichs. Swynford.
1389. Wyllyam Venour.
1390. Adam Bamme.
1391. Johan Heende, or Hyende, or Hind.
1392. Wyllyam Stondon.
1393. Johan Hadley.
1394. Johan Frenche.
1395. Wyllyam More.
1396. Adam Bamme, *again.*
1397. Richd. Whittington.
1398. Drew Barentyne.
1399. Thos. Knolles.
1400. Johan Fraunceys.
1401. Johan Shadworth.
1402. Johan Walcot.
1403. Wm. Askam.
1404. Johan Heende, *again.*
1405. Johan Woodcock.
1406. Richd. Whittington, *again.*
1407. Wyllyam Stondon, *again.*
1408. Drew Barentyne, *again.*
1409. Richd. Marlowe.
1410. Thos. Knolles, *again.*
1411. Robt. Chycheley.
1412. Wm. Waldern, or Waldren.
1413. Wm. Crowmer.
1414. Thos. Fawconer.
1415. Nichs. Wotton.
1416. Hy. Barton.
1417. Richd. Marlowe, *again.*
1418. Wm. Sevenoak.
1419. Richd. Whittington, *again.*
1420. Wm. Cambrege.
1421. Richd. Chichelee.

Year ending Nov. 9.

1422. Wm. Waldern.
1423. Wm. Crowmer, *again*.
1424. Johan Michell.
1425. Johan Coventre.
1426. Wm. Rynwell.
1427. Johan Gedney.
1428. Hy. Barton, *again*.
1429. Wm. Estfeld, or Eastfield.
1430. Nichs. Wotton, *again*.
1431. Johan Wellis, or Welles.
1432. Johan Parneys, or Parveis.
1433. Johan Brokley, or Brocle.
1434. Robt. Otley, or Roger Otely.
1435. Hy. Frowyk, or Frow.
1436. Johan Michell, or Michael (? *again*).
1437. Wm. Estfeld, *again*.
1438. Stephen Browne.
1439. Robt. Large.
1440. Johan Paddesley.
1441. Robt. Clopton.
1442. Johan Atherley, or Hatherley.
1443. Thos. Chatworth.
1444. Hy. Frowyk, *again*.
1445. Symken or Symon Eyer.
1446. Johan Olney.
1447. Johan Gidney.
1448. Stephen Browne, *again*.
1449. Thos. Chalton.
1450. Niclas Wyfforde.
1451. Wm. Gregory.
1452. Geffrey Feldyng.
1453. Johan Norman.
1454. Stephen Forster.
1455. Wm. Marowe.
1456. Thos. Caning, or Canings.
1457. Geffrey Boleyn, or Boleine.
1458. Thos. Scot.
1459. Wm. Henlyn.
1460. Richd. Lee.
1461. Hugh Wyche.
1462. Thos. Cooke.
1463. Mathew Philip.
1464. Rauf Josselyne.
1465. Rauf Verney.
1466. Johan Yonge.
1467. Thos. Owlgrave.
1468. Wm. Taylour.
1469. Richd. Lee, *again*.
1470. Johan Stockton.
1471. Wm. Edward.
1472. Wm. Hampton.
1473. Johan Tate.

Year ending Nov. 9.

1474. Robt. Drope.
1475. Robt. Basset.
1476. Rauf Josselyne, *again*,
1477. Humphry Heyforde.
1478. Richd. Gardiner.
1479. Bartilmew James.
1480. Johan Browne,
1481. Wm. Haryot.
1482. Edmond Shaa.
1483. Robt. Billesdon.
1484. Thos. Hylle.
1485. Hugh Bryce.
1486. Hy. Colet.
1487. Wm. Horne.
1488. Robt. Tate.
1489. Wm. White.
1490. Johan Mathew.
1491. Hugh Clopton.
1492. Wm. Martyn.
1493. Rauf Astry, or Ostrich.
1494. Richd. Chawry.
1495. Hy. Colet, *again*.
1496. Johan Tate, *again*.
1497. Wm. Purchase.
1498. Johan Percival.
1499. Nichs. Alwyn.
1500. Johan Reymington.
1501. Sir Johan Shaa.
1502. Barthw. Reed.
1503. Sir Wm. Capell.
1504. John Wyngar, or Winger.
1505. Thos. Knesworth.
1506. Sir Richd. Haddon.
1507. Wm. Browne, aft. sir W.
1508. Stephen Jenyns.
1509. Thos. Bradbury.
1510. Hy. Keble.
1511. Roger Aichiley.
1512. Sir Wm. Copinger, *again*
1513. *Sir Wm. Browne, *again*; John Tate.
1514. Geo. Monoux.
1515. Sir Wm. Butler.
1516. John Rest.
1517. Sir Thos. Exmewe.
1518. Thos. Mirfine.
1519. Sir Jas. Yarford.
1520. Sir John Bruge.
1521. Sir John Milborne.
1522. Sir John Munday.
1523. Sir Thos. Baldry, or Baldrie.
1524. Sir Wm. Bailey.
1525. Sir John Allen.
1526. Sir Thos. Seamer.
1527. Sir Jas. Spencer.
1528. Sir John Rudstone.
1529. Ralph Dodmer.
1530. Sir Thos. Pargitor.

Year ending Nov. 9.

1531. Sir Nichs. Lambard.
1532. Sir Stephen Pecocke
1533. Sir Christr. Askew.
1534. Sir John Champneis.
1535. Sir John Allen, *again*
1536. Sir Ralph Waren.
1537. Sir Richd. Gresham.
1538. Wm. Forman.
1539. Sir Wm. Holles.
1540. Sir Wm. Roch.
1541. Sir Michl. Dormer.
1542. John Cootes, or Cotes
1543. { *Sir Wm. Bowyer. / Sir Ralph. Waren *again*. }
1544 Sir Wm. Laxton.
1545. Sir Martin Bowes.
1546. Sir Hy. Hubarthorne
1547. Sir John Gresham.
1548. Sir Hy. Amcotes.
1549. Sir Rowland Hill *first Protestant lord mayor*.
1550. Sir Andw. Jude.
1551. Sir Richd. Dobbes.
1552. Sir Geo. Barnes.
1553. Sir Thos. White.
1554. Sir John Lion.
1555. Sir Wm. Gerard.
1556. Sir Thos. Offley.
1557. Sir Thos. Curteis.
1558. Sir Thos. Leigh, or Lee.
1559. Sir Wm. Huet.
1560. Sir. Wm. Chester.
1561. Sir Wm. Harper.
1562. Sir Thos. Lodge.
1563. Sir John White.
1564. Sir Richd. Malorie.
1565. Sir Richd. Champion
1566. Sir Christr. Draper.
1567. Sir Roger Martin.
1568. Sir Thos. Rowe.
1569. Alexr. Avenon.
1570. Sir Rowland Heyward.
1571. Sir Wm. Allen.
1572. Sir Lionel Ducket.
1573. Sir John Rivers.
1574. Jas. Hawes.
1575. Ambrose Nicholas.
1576. Sir John Langley.
1577. Sir Thos. Ramsey.
1578. Richd. Pipe.
1579. Sir Nichs. Woodrofe
1580. Sir John Branche.
1581. Sir Jas. Harvie.
1582. Sir Thos. Blancke.
1583. Edwd. Osborne.
1584. Sir Edwd. Pullison.
1585. Sir Wolstan Dixie.
1586. Sir Geo. Barne.
1587. Sir Geo. Bond.

Year ending Nov. 9.

1588. Martin Calthorp, or Colthrop.
1589. Sir John Hart.
1590. John Allot.
1591. Sir Wm. Web.
1592. Sir Wm. Rowe.
1593. { * Sir Cuthbert Buckle.
Sir Richd. Martin. }
1594. Sir John Spencer.
1595. Sir Stephen Slany.
1596. { * Thos. Skinner.
Sir Hy. Billingsly. }
1597. Sir Richd. Saltenstall.
1598. Sir Stephen Some, or Soame.
1599. Sir Nichs. Mosley.
1600. Sir Wm. Ryder.
1601. Sir John Gerrard.
1602. Robt. Lee.
1603. Sir Thos. Bennet.
1604. Sir Thos. Low.
1605. Sir Hy. Hollyday.
1606. Sir John Wats.
1607. Sir Hy. Rowe.
1608. Sir Humphrey Weld.
1609. Sir Thos. Cambell.
1610. Sir Wm. Craven.
1611. Sir Jas. Pemberton.
1612. Sir John Swinnerton.
1613. Sir Thos. Middleton.
1614. Sir John Hayes.
1615. Sir John Jolles.
1616. Sir John Leman.
1617. Geo. Bolles.
1618. Sir Sebastian Harvey.
1619. Sir Wm. Cockain.
1620. Sir Fras. Jones.
1621. Sir Edwd. Barkham.
1622. Sir Peter Proby.
1623. Sir Martin Lumley.
1624. Sir John Goare.
1625. Sir Allen Cotton.
1626. Sir Cuthbert Aket.
1627. Sir Hugh Hammersley.
1628. Sir Richd. Deane.
1629. Sir Jas. Cambell.
1630. Sir Robt. Ducy.
1631. Sir Geo. Whitmore.
1632. Sir Nichs. Raynton.
1633. Ralph Freeman.
1634. Sir Thos. Moulson.
1635. Sir Robt. Packhurst.
1636. Sir Christr. Cletheroe.
1637. Sir Edwd. Bromfield.
1638. Sir Richd. Fenn.
1639. Sir Maurice Abbott.
1640. Sir Hy. Garway.
1641. Sir Wm. Acton.
1642. Sir Richd. Gurney.
1643. Sir Isaac Pennington.
1644. Sir John Wollaston.

Year ending Nov. 9.

1645. Sir Thos. Atkins.
1646. Sir Thos. Adams.
1647. Sir John Gayre.
1648. Sir John Warner.
1649. Sir Abrm. Reynardson.
1650. Thos. Foote.
1651. Thos. Andrews.
1652. John Kendrek.
1653. John Fowkes.
1654. Thos. Vyner.
1655. Christr. Pack.
1656. John Dethick.
1657. Robt. Tichborne.
1658. Richd. Chiverton.
1659. Sir John Ireton.
1660. Sir Thos. Alleyne.
1661. Sir Richd. Browne.
1662. Sir John Frederick.
1663. Sir John Robinson.
1664. Sir Anthy. Bateman.
1665. John Lawrence.
1666. Sir Thos. Bludworth.
1667. Sir Wm. Bolton.
1668. Sir Wm. Peake.
1669. Sir Wm. Turner.
1670. Sir Saml. Sterling.
1671. Sir Richd. Ford.
1672. Sir Geo. Waterman.
1673. Sir Robt. Hanson.
1674. Sir Wm. Hooker.
1675. Sir Robt. Vyner.
1676. Sir Jos. Sheldon.
1677. Sir Thos. Davies.
1678. Sir Fras. Chaplin.
1679. Sir Jas. Edwards.
1680. Sir Robt. Clayton.
1681. Sir Patience Ward.
1682. Sir John Moore.
1683. Sir Wm. Pritchard.
1684. Sir Hy. Tulse; app. by the king's commission, during pleasure.
1685. Sir Jas. Smith.
1686. Sir Robt. Jeffery.
1687. Sir John Peake.
1688. * Sir John Shorter.
"Sir John Shorter died Sept. 4, and sir John Eyles was the next day appointed to succeed him by the king."—*Chron. Brit.*
1689. { Sir John Chapman.
Sir Thos. Pilkington. }
1690. } Sir Thos. Pilkington, *again*.
1691. }
1692. Sir Thos. Stamp.
1693. Sir John Fleet.
1694. Sir Wm. Ashurst.

Year ending Nov. 9.

1695. Sir Thos. Lane.
1696. Sir John Houblon.
1697. Sir Edwd. Clarke.
1698. Sir Humphrey Edwin.
1699. Sir Fras. Child.
1700. Sir Richd. Levett.
1701. Sir Thos. Abney.
1702. Sir Wm. Gore.
1703. Sir Wm. Dashwood.
1704. Sir John Parsons.
1705. Sir Owen Buckingham.
1706. Sir Thos. Rawlinson.
1707. Sir Robt. Bedingfield.
1708. Sir Wm. Withers.
1709. Sir Chas. Duncombe.
1710. Sir Saml. Garrard, bt.
1711. Sir Gilbert Heathcote.
1712. Sir Robt. Beachcroft.
1713. Sir Richd. Hoare.
1714. Sir Saml. Stanier, or Stainer.
1715. Sir Wm. Humphreys.
1716. Sir Chas. Peers.
1717. Sir Jas. Bateman.
1718. Sir Wm. Lewen.
1719. Sir John Ward.
1720. Sir Geo. Thorold.
1721. Sir John Fryer.
1722. Sir Wm. Stewart.
1723. Sir Gerard Conyers.
1724. Sir Peter Delme.
1725. Sir Geo. Mertins, or Martyns.
1726. Sir Fras. Forbes.
1727. Sir John Eyles.
1728. Sir Edwd. Beecher.
1729. Sir Robt. Baylis.
1730. Sir Richd. Brocas.
1731. Sir Humphrey Parsons.
1732. Sir Fras. Child.
1733. John Barber.
1734. Sir Wm. Billers.
1735. Sir Edwd. Bellamy.
1736. Sir John Williams.
1737. Sir John Thompson.
1738. Sir John Barnard.
1739. Micajah Perry.
1740. Sir John Salter.
1741. { * Sir Humphrey Parsons.
Danl. Lambert. }
1742. { * Sir Robt. Godschal.
Geo. Heathcote. }
1743. Robt. Willimot, or Willmot.
1744. Sir Robt. Westley.
1745. Sir Hy. Marshall.
1746. Sir Richd. Hoare.
1747. Wm. Benn.
1748. Sir Robt. Ladbroke.

Year ending Nov. 9.

1749. Sir Wm. Calvert.
1750. { * Sir Saml. Pennant. John Blachford.
1751. Fras. Cockayne.
1752. { * Thos. Winterbottom. Robt. Alsop.
1753. Sir Crispe Gascoyne.
1754. { * Edwd. Ironside. Thos. Rawlinson.
1755. Steph. Theod. Janssen.
1756. Slingsby Bethell.
1757. Marshe Dickinson.
1758. Sir Chas. Asgill.
1759. Sir Richd. Glyn, bt.
1760. Sir Thos. Chitty.
1761. Sir Matt. Blakiston.
1762. Sir Saml. Fludyer, bt.
1763. Wm. Beckford.
1764. Wm. Bridgen.
1765. Sir Wm. Stephenson.
1766. Geo. Nelson.
1767. Sir Robt. Kite.
1768. Hon. Thos. Harley.
1769. Saml. Turner.
1770. { * Wm. Beckford. Barlow Trecothick.
1771. Brass Crosby.
1772. Wm. Nash.
1773. Jas. Townshend.
1774. Fredk. Bull.
1775. John Wilkes.
1776. John Sawbridge.
1777. Sir Thos. Halifax.
1778. Sir Jas. Esdaile.
1779. Saml. Plumbe.
1780. Brackley Kennet.
1781. Sir Watkin Lewes.
1782. Sir Wm. Plomer.
1783. Nathl. Newnham.
1784. Robt. Peckham.
1785. Richd. Clark.
1786. Thos. Wright.
1787. Thos. Sainsbury.
1788. John Burnell.
1789. Wm. Gill.
1790. Wm. Pickett.
1791. John Boydell.
1792. John Hopkins.
1793. Sir Jas. Sanderson.
1794. Paul le Mesurier.
1795. Thos. Skinner.
1796. Wm. Curtis, aft. sir W., bt.
1797. Sir Brook Watson, bt.
1798. Sir John Wm. Anderson, bt.
1799. Sir Richd. Carr Glyn, bt.
1800. Harvey Christr. Coombe.

Year ending Nov. 9.

1801. Sir Wm. Staines.
1802. Sir John Eamer.
1803. Chas. Price (bt. 1804).
1804. John Perring.
1805. Peter Perchard.
1806. Sir Jas. Shaw, bt.
1807. Sir Wm. Leighton.
1808. John Ainsley.
1809. Chas. Flower, aft. sir C., bt.
1810. Thos. Smith.
1811. Joshua Jonathan Smith.
1812. Claudius Stephen Hunter, aft. sir C., bt.
1813. Geo. Scholey.
1814. Wm. Domville, aft. sir W., bt.
1815. Saml. Birch.
1816. } Matth. Wood.
1817. }
1818. Christr. Smith.
1819. John Atkins.
1820. Geo. Brydges.
1821. John Thos. Thorpe.
1822. Christr. Magnay.
1823. Wm. Heygate, aft. sir W., bt.
1824. Robt. Waithman.
1825. John Garratt.
1826. Wm. Venables.
1827. Anthy. Browne.
1828. Matthias Prime Lucas.
1829. Wm. Thompson.
1830. John Crowder.
1831. } Sir John Key, bt.
1832. }
1833. Sir Peter Laurie.
1834. Chas. Farebrother.
1835. Hy. Winchester.
1836. Wm. Taylor Copeland.
1837. Thos. Kelly.
1838. Sir John Cowan, bt.
1839. Saml. Wilson.
1840. Sir Chapman Marshall.
1841. Thos. Johnson.
1842. John Pirie, aft. sir J., bt.
1843. John Humphrey.
1844. Wm. Magnay, aft. sir W., bt.
1845. Michael Gibbs.
1846. John Johnson.
1847. Sir Geo. Carroll.
1848. John Kinnersley Hooper, aft. sir J.
1849. Sir Jas. Duke, knt., aft. bt.
1850. Thos. Farncomb.
1851. John Musgrove, aft. sir J., bt.

Year ending Nov. 9.

1852. Wm. Hunter.
1853. Thos. Challis.
1854. Thos. Sidney.
1855. Fras. Graham Moon, aft. sir F., bt.
1856. David Salomons (bt. 1869).
1857. Thos. Quested Finnis.
1858. Sir Robt. Walter Carden, (bt. 1887).
1859. David Williams Wire.
1860. John Carter.
1861. } Wm. Cubitt.
1862. }
1863. Wm. Anderson Rose (knt. 1867).
1864. Wm. Lawrence (knt. 1887).
1865. Warren Stormes Hale.
1866. Benjn. Saml. Phillips, aft. sir B.
1867. Thos. Gabriel, aft. sir T., bt.
1868. Wm. Ferneley Allen.
1869. Jas. Clarke Lawrence aft. sir J., bt.
1870. Robt. Besley.
1871. Thos. Dakin (knt. 1872).
1872. Sills John Gibbons aft. sir S., bt.
1873. Sir Sydney Hedley Waterlow, knt., aft. bt.
1874. Andrew Lusk, aft. sir A., bt.
1875. David Hy. Stone.
1876. Wm. Jas. Richmond Cotton.
1877. Sir Thos. White.
1878. Thos. Scambler Owden, aft. sir T.
1879. Sir Chas. Whetham.
1880. Sir Fras. Wyatt Truscott.
1881. Wm. McArthur, (K.C.M.G. 1882).
1882. John Whitaker Ellis, aft. sir J., bt.
1883. Hy. Edmd. Knight, aft. sir H.
1884. Robt. Nichs. Fowler.
1885. { * Geo. Swan Nottage. Robt. Nichs. Fowler, *again*; aft. sir R., bt.
1886. John Staples, aft. sir J., K.C.M.G.
1887. Sir Reginald Hanson, knt., aft. bt.
1888. Polydore de Keyser, aft. sir P.
1889. Jas. Whitehead.

CHAMBERLAINS OF LONDON.

THIS officer is chosen, annually, on Michaelmas-day; but, as a rule, he continues in office during life. As treasurer of the corporation, he has the receipt of all rents and other revenues, and the payment of all salaries, charges, and other outgoings. He has also the custody of all the Corporation accounts, and keeps all the records concerning freemen.

CHAMBERLAINS FROM THE REVOLUTION.

1688. Sir Peter Rich.
1689. Sir Leonard Robinson.
1696. Sir Thos. Cuddon.
1702. Sir Wm. Fazakerley.
1718. Sir Geo. Ludlam.
1727. Saml. Robinson.
1734. Sir Wm. Bosworth.
1751. Sir Thos. Harrison.
1765. Sir Steph. Theoph. Janssen, bt.
1776. Benjn. Hopkins.
1779. John Wilkes.
1798. Richd. Clarke.
1831. Sir Jas. Shaw, bt.
1843. Sir Wm. Heygate, bt.
1844. Anthy. Brown.
1853. Sir Jno. Key, bt.
1858. Benjn. Scott.

RECORDERS OF LONDON.

THE Recorder of London is the principal legal officer of the corporation, and is appointed for life by the Court of Aldermen. He sits as judge in the Mayor's Court, and also at the Central Criminal Court.

RECORDERS OF LONDON.

1298. Jeffery de Norton, aldn.
1304. John de Wangrave, aldn.
1320. Geoffrey de Hertpoll, aldn.
1321. Robt. de Swalchyne, aldn.
1329. Gregory de Norton, aldn.
1339. Roger de Depham, aldn.
1363. Thos. Lodelow
1365. Wm. de Halden, aldn.
1377. Wm. Cheyne.
1389. John Tremayne, comm. serjt.
1392. Wm. Makenade.
1394. John Cokam, or Cokeyn.
1398. Matth. de Suthworth.
1403. Thos. Thornburgh.
1405. John Preston.
1415. John Barton, sen.; serjt. at law, 1416.
1422. John Fray; bar. ex., 1428, and ch. bar., 1436.
1426. John Simonds, or Symond.
1435. Alexr. Anne.
1440. Thos. Cockayne.
Wm. (? John) Bowes.
1442. Robt. Danvers, comm. serjt.
1451. Thos. Billyng, just. K. B., 1465; and ch. just., 1469.
1455. Thos. Urswyke, comm. serjt.; ch. bar. ex., 1472.
1471. Humphry Starkey, ch. bar. ex., 1483.
1483. Thos. Fitzwilliam, sp. ho. comm., 1489.

The records, up to this time, are imperfect. The subsequent records have been better preserved; and the names and dates that follow are, therefore, regular and consecutive.

1508. Sir Robt Sheffield, or Sheffelde.
John Chalyner.
1511. Richd. Brooke, or Broke, just. C. P. 1521; and ch. bar. ex., 1526
1520. Wm. Shelley, one of the judges of the sheriffs' court; just. C. P., 1527.
1527. John Baker, one of the judges of the sheriffs' court.
1536. Sir Roger Cholmeley, serjt. at law; ch. bar. ex., 1546; ch. just. K. B., 1552.
1546. Robt. Brooke, or Broke, comm. serjt.; serjt. at law, 1552; ch. just. C. P., 1554.
1552. Ranulph Cholmeley, one of the judges of the sheriffs' court.
1563. Richd. Onslow, solr.-gen., 1566.
1566. Thos. Bromley, solr.-gen., 1569.

1569. Thos. Wilbraham; went to the court of wards and liveries, 1571.
1571. Wm. Fleetwood, serjt. at law, 1580.
1591. Edwd. Coke, solr. gen. 1592; atty. gen., 1594; ch. just. C. P., 1606; and ch. just. K. B., 1613.
1592. Edwd. Drew, serjt. at law.
1594. Thos. Flemynge, serjt. at law same year; solr-gen., 1595; ch. bar. ex., 1604; and ch. just. K. B., 1607.
1595. John Croke, sp. ho. commons, 1601; just. K. B., 1607.
1603. Hy. Montagu, ch. just. K. B., 1616; ld. treasr., 1620; cr. ld. Kimbolton and visc. Mandeville, 1620, and E. of Manchester, 1625.
1615. Thos. Coventry, one of the judges of the sheriffs' court; solr.-gen., 1616; atty.-gen., 1620; ld. kpr. 1625; cr. ld. Coventry, 1628.
1616. Anthy. Benn, aft. sir A.
1618. Richd. Martin.
Robt. Heath, aft. sir R., solr.-gen., 1620; atty.-gen. 1625; ch. just. C. P., 1631; dischd., 1634; just. K. B., 1640; ch. just. of that court, 1643.
1620. Robt. Shute.
Heneage Finch, serjt. at law, 1623; sp. ho. commons, 1625.
1631. Edwd. Lyttelton, aft. sir E. and ld. L.; solr.-gen., 1634; ch. just. C. P., 1639; ld. kpr., 1641.
1634. Robt. Mason.
1635. Hy. Calthrop.
1635. Thos. Gardiner.
1643. Peter Pheasant, one of the common pleaders of the city; just. C. P. same year.
1643. John Glynn, recorder of Westminster; serjt. at law, 1649.
1649. Wm. Steele, of Gray's Inn, atty.-gen. to the Commonwealth; made ch. bar. ex., 1656.
1656. Lisleborne Long.
1658. John Green, a judge of the sheriffs' court.
1659. Wm. Wylde, serjt. at law, 1660; just. C. P., 1668; aft. just. K. B.
1660. John Glynn, *again*.
1668. John Howell, aft. sir J., deputy recorder, *vice* Wylde.
1676. Wm. Dolben, *vice* Howell, who surr.; serjt. at law, 1677; just. K. B. in 1678.
1678. Geo. Jeffreys, aft. sir G., and ld. J., comm. serjt; serjt. at law same year; ch. just. K. B., 1683; ld. chanc., 1685.
1680. Geo. Treby, aft. sir G.; depr., 1685; rest. at the revolution; solr.-gen., 1689; atty.-gen., same year; ch. just. C. P., 1692.
1685. Sir Thos. Jenner, bar. ex., 1686; just. C. P., 1688.
1686. Sir John Holt, ch. just. K. B., 1689; commr. gr. seal, 1700.
1687. John Tate, serjt. at law.
1688. Sir Barthw. Shower.
John Somers, elected, but declined, Oct. 23. This personage, aft. sir John and ld. Somers, became ld. kpr. 1693, and ld. chanc. 1697.
Jas. Selby, elected, but also declined, Oct. 25.
1692. Sir Salathiel Lovel, serjt. at law; bar. ex., 1708.
1708. Sir Peter King, aft. ld. King; ch. just. C. P., 1714; ld. chanc., 1725.
1714. Sir Wm. Thompson, solr.-gen., 1717; bar. ex., 1729; *d.* 1739.
1739. Sir John Strange, solr.-gen., aft. m. rolls.
1742. Sir Simon Urlin, serjt. at law; *d.* 1746.
1746. John Stracey, judge of the sheriffs' court; *d.* 1749.
1749. Sir Richd. Adams, senior common pleader, Jan. 17; bar. ex. 1753.
1753. Sir Wm. Moreton, senior judge of the sheriffs' court, Feb. 15; *d.* 1763.
1763. Sir Jas. Eyre; Apr. 7, successively bar. ex., ch. bar. ex., and ch. just. C. P.
1772. John Glynn, serjt. at law, Nov. 17; *d.* 1779.
1779. Jas. Adair, serjt. at law; Oct. 12.
1789. Sir John Wm. Rose, senior common pleader, June. 30; serjt. at law, Nov. 13, following; *d.* 1803.
1803. John Silvester, common serjt., Oct. 20; cr. a bt., 1815; *d.* 1822.
1822. Newman Knowlys, comm. serjt., Apr. 10; res. 1833.
1833. Hon. Chas. Ewan Law, Q.C., comm. serjt; *d.* 1850.
1850. Hon. Jas. Archd. Stuart Wortley, Sept. 25; res. 1856.
1856. Russell Gurney, Q.C.; res. 1878.
1878. Sir Thos. Chambers, Q.C.

COMMON SERJEANTS OF LONDON.

THE Common Serjeant is the second legal officer of the corporation, and sits as a judge in the Mayor's Court, and also at the Central Criminal Court.

Common Serjeants.

Common Serjeants, previous to the Revolution, who became Recorders.

1383. John Tremayne; rec. 1389.
1422. Robt. Danvers; rec. 1442.
1453. Thos. Urswyke; rec. 1455.
1536. Robt. Brooke, or Broke; rec. 1546.
1675. Sir Geo. Jeffreys; rec. 1678.

Common Serjeants from the reign of Charles II.

1678. Hy. Crispe.
1700. Duncan Dee.
1720. John Lingard.
1729. Thos. Garrard.
1758. Thos. Nugent.
1790. John Silvester; rec. 1803.
1803. Newnan Knowlys; rec. 1822.
1822. Thos Denman, aft. ch. just. K. B. and ld. Denman.
1830. Hon. Chas. Ewan Law; rec. 1833.
1833. John Mirehouse.
1850. Edwd. Bullock.
1857. Thos. Chambers; Q. C. 1861; knt. Mar. 14, 1872; rec. 1878.
1878. Wm. Thos. Charley; knt. Mar. 18, 1880.

PART IX. SCOTLAND.

SOVEREIGNS OF SCOTLAND.

See Part I.—"Royal" *ante*.

OFFICERS OF STATE, &c., OF SCOTLAND.

LORD HIGH TREASURERS OF SCOTLAND AND COMMISSIONERS FOR EXERCISING THAT OFFICE. COMPTROLLERS.

THE OFFICE OF TREASURER was established on the return of James I. to Scotland from his long captivity in England.

In 1617 the Treasurer was ranked by an ordinance of James VI. as the first officer of state; and, in 1623, when that king determined the precedency of his counsellors, he was ranked next to the chancellor; in 1663, he was declared president of the exchequer. The office of comptroller, which was sometimes joined with that of Treasurer, and designated *computorum rotulator*, and that of collector of the new augmentations, both distinct offices from that of the Treasurer, were conjoined into one by James VI., and exercised by the Treasurer until the treasury was put in commission.

At the Union the Treasuries of England and Scotland were united, see *ante*, p. 156.

LORD HIGH TREASURERS, &c., OF SCOTLAND.

1420. Sir Walter Ogilvie, of Lintrethan.
* * Thos. de Myrton, dean of Glasgow.
1430. Patrick de Ogilvie.
1439. Sir Walter de Halliburton, ld. of Dirleton.
Robt. Livingston, son to the govr. of the kingdom.
1440. Sir Walter de Halliburton, *again*.
1449. Andrew, abbot of Melrose.
1455. Jas. Stuart, dean of Moray.
1466. Sir David Guthrie, of Guthrie.
1470. Sir Wm. Knowlys, preceptor of Torphichen.
1473. John Laing, parson of Kenland.
1480. Archd. Crawford, abb. of Holyrood House.
* * Sir John Ramsay, of Balmaine.
1490. Hy. Arnot, abb. of Cambus-Kenneth.
1494. Geo. Schaw, abb. of Paisley.
1499. Sir Robt. Lundin, of Balgony.
1507. Sir David Beaton, of Creich.

1509. Geo. Hepburn, abb. of Aberbrothock; aft. bp. of the Isles.
Andrew Stewart, bp. of Caithness.
1512. Cuthbert Baillie, commend. of Glenluce.
1515. Jas. Hepburn, bp. of Moray.
1516. Sir Walter Ogilvie, of Stratheren.
1517. John Campbell, of Lundy.
1520. Archd.Douglas(? sir A.)of Kilspindie.
1528. Robt. Cairncross, abb. of Holyrood House; aft. bp. of Ross.
1529. Sir Robt. Barton, of Over Barnton.
1530. Wm. Stewart, bp. of Aberdeen.
1537. Robt., abb. of Holyrood House.
1546. John Hamilton (brother to the regent), abb. of Paisley; aft. bp. of St. Andrew's.
1548. Sir Jas. Kirkaldie, of Grange.
1555. Gilbert, E. of Cassilis.
1561. Robt. Richardson, commend. of St. Mary Isle.
1564. Wm. Stewart. prov. of Lincluden.
1572. Wm., E. of Gowrie.
1584. John, E. of Montrose.
1585. Sir Thos. Lyon, of Auld Bar, mast. of Glamis.
1595. Walter, ld. Blantyre.
1599. Alexr., ld. Elphinstone.
1601. Sir Geo. Hume, E. of Dunbar.
1611. Sir Robt. Ker, K.B., E. of Somerset.
1616. John, E. of Marr.
1630. Wm., E. of Morton.
1636. John, E. of Traquair.

Commissioners appointed by the Parliament in 1641.

1641. John, E. of Loudoun, ld. chanc.
Archd., M. of Argyll.
Wm., E. of Glencairn.
John, E. of Lindsey.
Sir Jas. Carmichael.

1644. John, E. of Lindsey; ld. treasr. app. by the States.

Commissioners appointed by the States in 1649.

1649. John, E. of Loudoun, ld. chanc.
Archd., M. of Argyll.
Alexr., E. of Eglintoun.
John, E. of Cassilis.
Robt., ld. Burleigh.
Sir Danl. Carmichael.
1660. John, E. of Craufurd and Lindsey.
John, 7th E. of Rothes.
1667. John, 7th E. of Rothes, ld chanc.
John, E., aft. D. of Lauderdale.
John, E. of Tweeddale.
Alexr., E. of Kincardine.
John, ld. Cochrane, eldest son of the E. of Dundonald.
Sir Robt. Murray, ld. just. clk.
1674. John, 7th E., aft. 1st D. of Rothes ld. chanc.
John, D. of Lauderdale.
John, E. of Dundonald.
1674. Colin, E. of Balcarras.
Hon. Chas. Maitland, dep. treasr. and mast. mint.
1682. Wm., M., aft. D. of Queensberry.
1686. Wm., D. of Queensberry.
Jas., E. of Perth, ld. chanc.
Wm., D. of Hamilton.
John, E. of Kintore, treasr. dep.
Geo., visc. Tarbat, clk. regr.
Hon. Wm. Drummond, aft. visc. Strathallan.
1687. Jas., E. of Perth, ld. chanc.
John, M. of Athole, ld. pr. seal.
Wm., D. of Hamilton.
Geo., D. of Gordon.
John, E. of Tweeddale.
Colin, E. of Balcarras.
Geo., visc. Tarbat.
Wm., visc. Strathallan.
Richd., visc. Maitland, eldest son of E. of Lauderdale, treasr. dep.
1689. Wm., E. of Crauford.
John, E. of Cassilis.
John, E. of Tweeddale.
David, ld. Ruthven.
*Hon. Alexr. Melville, eldest son of ld. Melville.
1692. John, E. of Tweeddale, ld. chanc.
*Jas., E. of Drumlanrig, eldest son of the D. of Queensberry.
John, E. of Cassilis.
Geo., E. of Linlithgow.
John, E. of Breadalbane.
Alexr., ld. Rai h, eldest son of the E. of Melville, treasr. dep.
1695. John, M. of Tweeddale, ld. chanc.
Jas., E. of Drumlanrig.
John, E. of Cassilis.
Geo., E. of Linlithgow.
John, E. of Breadalbane.
*John, ld. Yester, eldest son of the M. of Tweeddale.
1696. John, M. of Tweeddale, ld. chanc.
Jan. Jas., D. of Queensberry.
30. Archd., E., aft. D. of Argyll.
Wm., E., aft. M. of Annandale.
Alexr., ld. Raith, treasr. dep.
*Sir John Maxwell, of Pollock, bt.
1696. Patrick, ld. Polwarth, aft. E. of
May Marchmont; ld. chanc.
24. Jas., D. of Queensberry.
Archd., E. of Argyll.
Wm., E. of Annandale.
Hon. Alexr. Hume, eldest son of ld. l olwarth, treasr. dep.
*Sir John Maxwell, of Pollock, bt.
1698. Patrick, E. of Marchmont, ld. chanc.
Jas., D. of Queensberry.
Archd., E. of Argyll.

* See Note, next page.

1698. Wm., E. of Annandale.
Adam Cockburn, of Ormiston, treasr. dep.
*Sir John Maxwell, of Pollock, bt.

1702. Jas., E. of Seafield, ld. chanc.
Jas., D. of Queensberry.
Archd., E. of Argyll.
Wm., E. of Annandale.
Alexr., E. of Eglintoun.
Hugh, E. of Loudoun.
David, ld. Boyle, treasr. dep.
*David, ld. Elcho, eldest son of the countess of Wemyss.

1703. Jas., E. of Seafield, ld. chanc.
Jas., D. of Queensberry.
Archd., D. of Argyll.
Wm., M. of Annandale.
Alexr., E. of Eglintoun.
Hugh, E. of Loudoun.
David, ld. Boyle, eldest son of the E. of Glasgow, treasr. dep.
*Hon. Fras. Montgomery.

1704. John, M. of Tweeddale, ld. chanc.
Wm., M. of Annandale.
Hugh, E. of Loudoun.
Chas., E. of Selkirk.
John, ld. Belhaven.
Geo. Baillie, treasr. dep.

1704. *Hon. Fras. Montgomery.
Sir John Hume, bt.

1705. Jas., E. of Seafield, ld. chanc.

1705. Jas., D. of Queensberry.
Jas., D. of Montrose.
Jas., E. of Galloway.
David, E. of Northesk.
Archd., E. of Forfar.
David, E. of Glasgow, treasr. dep.
*Ld. Archd. Campbell.
Wm., ld. Ross.
Hon. Fras. Montgomery.

1706. Jas., E. of Seafield, ld. chanc.
Jas., D. of Montrose.
Jas., D. of Queensberry.
David, E. of Northesk.
Archd., E. of Forfar.
David, E. of Glasgow, treasr. dep.
Wm., ld. Ross.
*Fras. Montgomery.

1707. Jas., E. of Seafield, ld. chanc.
Jas., D. of Montrose, pres. pr. council.
Jas., D. of Queensberry, kpr. pr. seal.
David, E. of Glasgow, treasr. dep.
Wm., ld. Ross.
*Hon. Fras. Montgomery.

For Lord Treasurers, &c., of Scotland after the Union see "Treasurers, Commissioners, &c., of Great Britain," *ante*, p. 156.

* Note.—The Lord Treasurer of Scotland had, by the law of that country, a seat in its parliament, in virtue of his office, independently of election; and when the treasury was in commission, the king had a right to name any one commissioner to sit and vote as Lord Treasurer in parliament. The member of each treasury board marked thus * was so nominated.

Comptrollers of Scotland.

1426. David Brune.
1429. John Spence.
1446. Alexr. Nairne, of Sanford.
1448. Robt. de Livingston.
1458. Ninian Spot, canon of Dunkeld.
1464. John Colquhoun, of Colquhoun.
1467. David Guthrie, of Guthrie.
1468. Adam Wallace, of Craigie.
1471. Jas. Schaw, of Salquhy.
1472. Alexr. Leslie, of Warderis.
* * Thos. Simson.
1488. Alexr. Inglis, archdn. of St. Andrew's.
1499. Patrick Hume, of Polwarth.
1506. James, abb. of Dunfermline.
1507. Jas. Riddoch, of Aberladenoche.
1513. Robt. Arnot, of Woodmill; killed at Flodden.
1514. Duncan Forrester, of Carden.
1515. Patrick Hamilton.
1616. Alexr. Garden.
1520. Robt. Barton, of Over Barnton.
1525. Sir Jas. Colvill, of Ochiltree.
1538. David Wood, of Craig.
1543. Thos. Menzies.
1546 William, commend. of Culross.
1548. William, abb. of Ross.
1557. Mons. de Ruby; to Q. Mary the Regent.
1560. Barthw. Villemore.
1561. Sir John Wishart, of Pittarrow.
1563. Sir. Wm. Murray, of Tullibardine.
1567. Jas. Cockburn, of Skirling.
1584. Sir Jas. Campbell, of Ardkinglass.
1585. Andrew Wood, of Largo.
1589. David Seton, of Parbroath.
1597. Walter, prior of Blantyre.
1599. Sir Geo. Hume, of Wedderburn
1600. Sir David Murray, of Gospetrie, aft. ld. Scoon.
1603. Peter Rollock, bp. of Dunkeld.
1610. Sir Jas. Hay, of Fingask.
1615. Sir Gideon Murray, of Elibank.
He was the last Comptroller to James VI., in whose reign the office was suppressed, and incorporated with that of lord high treasurer.

See "Lord High Treasurers," *ante*, p. 496.

LORD HIGH ADMIRALS OF SCOTLAND.

This officer in Scotland had very extensive powers. He commanded the king's ships and sailors, and had the inspection of all the sea-ports, harbours, and sea-coasts in the kingdom. He had, also, a particular tribunal, where the judges, appointed by him, decided all causes relating to sea affairs, according to a particular code of naval law. His powers likewise extended to the cognizance of all crimes committed at sea, and to all controversies, actions, and quarrels, concerning crimes, faults, and trespasses committed upon the sea, or in the ports and creeks thereof, or in fresh waters and navigable rivers, so far as the sea flows and ebbs. This duty he executed by a deputy, commissioned by him, called the Deputy Judge-Admiral, who likewise judged in matters purely commercial, arising on the sea. After the Treaty of Union, a vice-admiral only was appointed by the sovereign.

Lord High Admirals of Scotland.

* * Hy., E. of Orkney; to Robert III.
* * Geo., E. of Caithness; to James II.
* * Wm., E. of Caithness and Orkney; to James II.
1476. David, 5th E. of Crauford, aft. D. of Montrose.
1482. Alexr., D. of Albany.
* * Andrew Wood, of Largo; he was never admiral; but, in 1477, was master of the *Yellow Carval.* In the reign of James IV., his son defended the castle of Dumbarton against the English.
1502. Patrick, E. of Bothwell.
* * Jas., E. of Arran.
* * Archd., E. of Angus.
* * Robt., ld. Maxwell.
1511. Adam, E. of Bothwell; heritably.
1544. Patrick, E. of Bothwell.
1567. Jas., E. of Bothwell, and D. of Orkney; attainted.
1578. Jas., E. of Morton; beheaded.
1583. Fras., E. of Bothwell; attainted.
1626. Jas., D. of Lenox and Richmond; heritably.
* * John, E. of Linlithgow; made adm. during the D. of Lenox's minority.
1633. Jas., D. of Lenox and Gordon; *d.* 1672.*
1668. Alexr., E. of Kincardine; vice.-adm.
1673. JAS. D. of YORK and ALBANY; aft. James VII. of Scotland and II. of England.
Wm., D. of Hamilton.
Chas., D. of Richmond and Lenox.
1705. Jas., D. of Montrose.
1706. David, E. of Wemyss.

Office abolished at the Union.

Vice-Admirals of Scotland.

From the Union to the discontinuance of the office.

1708. David, E. of Wemyss.
1714. John, 8th E. of Rothes.
1722. Chas., D. of Queensberry and Dover.
1729. John, E. of Stair.
1733. Geo., E. of Morton.
1738. Jas., E. of Findlater and Seafield.
1764. John, E. of Hyndford, Dec. 22.
1766. Wm., E. of March, aft. D. of Queensberry, Aug. 30.
1776. John, E. of Breadalbane, Sept.
1782. Lord Wm. Gordon, bro. to D. of Gordon, Mar. 20.
1795. Chas. Shaw, ld., aft. visc. and E. Carthcart, K.T.; *d.* June 16, 1843.
Office not filled up.

* On his death, in 1672, the office of Admiral of Scotland reverted to the crown. The king then bestowed it upon his infant natural son, Charles Lenox, afterwards duke of Richmond and Lenox, with a reservation of a term for life to his brother James, duke of York. In 1673, William, duke of Hamilton, was appointed Admiral of Scotland, and after his death the office was managed by commissioners till the duke of Richmond became of age. He resigned the office to the crown in 1703.

LORD PRESIDENTS OF THE PRIVY COUNCIL OF SCOTLAND.

1625. John, E. of Montrose.
1649. John, E. of Loudoun.
1660. John, 7th E., aft. 1st D. of Rothes.
1663. John, E., aft. M. of Tweeddale.
1672. John, D. of Lauderdale.
1681. Sir Geo. Gordon, of Haddo, aft. E. of Aberdeen.
1682. Jas., M. of Montrose.
1686. Wm , D. of Queensberry.
1689. Wm., E. of Craufurd and Lindsey.
1693. Wm., E., aft. M. of Annandale.
1695. Geo., E. of Melville.
1702. Wm., M. of Annandale.
1704. Jas., M., aft. D. of Montrose.
1705. Wm., M. of Annandale.
1706. Jas., D. of Montrose.

The Scotch Privy Council was abolished by 6 Anne, cap. 40 (cap. 6, G. B. Ruffhead's Statutes) [1707].

VICE-PRESIDENTS OF THE COMMITTEE OF THE PRIVY COUNCIL FOR EDUCATION IN SCOTLAND.

By 48 & 49 Vict., cap. 61 (Aug. 14, 1885), the Act creating the office of Secretary for Scotland (see *ante*, p. 221), power was given to the Crown to appoint such secretary vice-president of the Scotch Education Department, and under this power the following appointments have been made:—

Vice-Presidents of the Committee of the Privy Council for Education in Scotland.

1885. Chas. Hy., D. of Richmond and Gordon, Aug. 19, **G.**
1886. Geo. Otto Trevelyan, aft. Sir G., bt., Feb. 13, **G.**
1886. Jno. Wm., E. of Dalhousie, K.T. Apr. 3, **G.**
Arthur Jas. Balfour, Aug. 16, **G.**
1887. Schomberg Hy., M. of Lothian Mar. 25., **G.**

LORDS PRIVY SEAL OF SCOTLAND.

This office was established by James I. on his return to Scotland from his captivity in England. The duties are analogous to those of the corresponding office in England.

Lords Privy Seal of Scotland.

1424. Walter Foote, prov. of Bothwell.
1426. John Cameron, prov. of Lincluden, and bp. of Glasgow.
1432. Wm. Fowlis, prov. of Bothwell.
1442. Wm. Turnbull, canon of Glasgow.
1458. Thos. Spence, bp. of Galloway.
1459. John Arouse.
1463. Jas. Lindsay, prov. of Lincluden.
1467. Thos. Spence, bp. of Aberdeen.
1470. Wm. Tulloch, bp. of Orkney, aft. bp. of Moray.
1472. Andrew Stuart (half brother to James III.), bp. elect of Moray.
1482. David Livingston, prov. of Lincluden.
1489. John, prior of St. Andrew's.
1500. Wm. Elphinstone, bp. of Aberdeen
1507. Alexr. Gordon, bp. of Aberdeen.

1514. David, abb. of Aberbrothock.
1519. Geo., abb. of Holyrood House.
1526. Geo., Crichton, bp. of Dunkeld.
1527. Archd. Douglas (? sir A.), of Kilspindie.
* * Robt. Colvill, of Craufurd; a ld. of sess.
1542. David Beaton, abb. of Aberbrothock; cardl. and abp. of St. Andrew's.
John Hamilton, abb. of Paisley, aft. abp. of St. Andrew's.
1547. Wm., ld. Ruthven.
1533. Geo., ld. Fyvie, aft. E. of Dunfermline.
1563. Sir Richd. Maitland, of Lethington.
1567. John Maitland, prior of Coldingham.
1571. Geo. Buchanan; a ld. of sess., pr. councr., and preceptor to the king.
1583. Walter Stewart, commend. of Blantyre.
1595. Sir Richard Cockburn, of Clerkington.
1626. Thos., E. of Haddington.
1641. Robt., E. of Roxburgh.
1649. John, E. of Sutherland; by the parlt.
1660. Wm., E. marischal.
1661. Chas., E. of Dunfermline.
1672. John, E., aft. M. of Athole.
1689. Archd., E. of Forfar.
1689. John, E. of Kintore.
John, ld. Carmichael, aft. E. of Hyndford.
1690. Geo., E. of Melville.
1695. Jas., D. of Queensberry.
1702. John, M., aft. D. of Athole.
1705. Jas., D. of Queensberry.
1709 Jas., D. Montrose.
1713 John, D. of Athole.
1714. John, D. of Roxburgh.
1715. Wm., M. of Annandale.
1721. Archd., E. of Islay, aft. D. of Argyll.
1733. Jas., D. of Athole.
1763. Hon. Jas. Stuart-Mackenzie, brother to the E. of Bute.
1765. Lord Fredk. Campbell, son of the D. of Argyll.
1765. John, E. of Breadalbane.
1766. Hon. Jas. Stuart-Mackenzie, *again* (for life); *d.* 1800.
1800. Hy. Dundas, aft. visc. Melville; *d.* May, 1811.
1811. Robt., second visc. Melville; *d.* June, 1851.
The office of Lord Privy Seal was not filled up until
1853. Fox, ld. Panmure, aft. E. and M. of Dalhousie, May 25, **G.**
1874. Schomberg Hy., M. of Lothian, Aug. 5.

SECRETARIES OF STATE IN AND FOR SCOTLAND. SECRETARIES FOR SCOTLAND.

THE Scotch Secretaries may be divided into three classes:—

I. The Scotch Secretaries of State who existed from early times and continued down to the Union.

II. The Principal Secretaries of State for Scotland, in England, who were first appointed at the Union, and continued down to 1746.

III. The Secretaries for Scotland who were appointed under 48 & 49 Vict., cap. 61 (Aug. 14, 1885), and whose powers were enlarged by 50 & 51 Vict., cap. 52 (Sept. 16, 1887).

See introduction to English Secretaries of State, *ante*, p. 221.

SECRETARIES OF STATE IN SCOTLAND.

From the reign of King Malcolm IV. to the Union.

* * Nicolaus; to Malcom IV.
1380. Duncan Pecoce; to Robert II.
1410. Andrew de Hawick, rector of Liston.
1418. John, E. of Buchan.
1424. John Cameron, aft. bp. of Glasgow.
1429. Wm. Fowlis.
1432. John Methven.
1448. John Raulston, bp. of Dunkeld.
1452. Wm. Otterburne.
1453. Geo. de Shoreswood.
1454. John Arouse, archdn. of Glasgow.
* * Thos. de Vaus, dean of Glasgow.

1463. Jas. Law, archdn. of Glasgow.
* * Archd. Whitlaw, archdn. of Lothian.
1488. Alexr. Inglis, aft. bp. of Dunkeld.
1490. Patrick Paniter, (*vulgo* Panter), archdn. of Moray; aft. abb. of Cambuskenneth.
1495. Richd. Muirhead, dean of Glasgow.
1496. Michl. Balfour, abb. of Melrose.
1516. Thos. Hay.
1524. Patrick Hepburn, rector of Whiteston.
* * Thos. Erskine, of Halton; aft. sir T. E., of Brechin.
1528. Patrick, abb. of Cambuskenneth, *again*.
1535. Richd. Muirhead, dean of Glasgow, *again*.
1543. David Paniter, bp. of Ross.
* * Jas. Strachan, canon of Aberdeen.
1561. Sir Wm. Maitland, jun., of Lethington.
1464. Sir Jas. Balfour, of Pittendriech; to Q. Mary.
* * Jas. Maxwell, of Cramond, son of sir Wm. Maxwell; to Q. Mary.
* * David Rizzio, frgn. sec. to Q. Mary; murd. by Darnley, 1566.
* * John Lesley, bp. of Ross; sec. until May, 1571.
1572. Robt. Pitcairn, archdn. of St. Andrew's.
1584. Sir John Maitland, of Thirlestane.
1591. Sir Richd. Cockburn, of Clerkington.
1596. Sir John Lindsay, of Balcarras.
1597. Jas. Elphinstone, aft. ld. Balmerino.
1608. Sir Alexr. Hay, of Newton.
1608. Sir John Preston, ld. pres. ct. sess.
1612. Thos., E. of Haddington.
1626. Sir Wm. Alexander, aft. E. of Stirling.
Sir Archd. Acheson, bt., of Glencairn.
1641. Wm., E. of Lanark, aft. D. of Hamilton.
1644. Sir Robt. Spottiswood, of New Abbey, ld. pres. ct. sess.
* * Wm., E. of Lothian; app. by the parlt., when the E. of Lanark fled.
1650. Geo., E. of Seaforth; to Charles II. during his exile.
1659. Alexr., E. of Balcarras.
1661. John, E., aft. D. of Lauderdale.
1682. Alexr., E. of Moray.
Chas., E. of Middleton.
1685. John, visc., aft. E. of Melfort.
1689. Geo., ld., aft. E. of Melville.
1690. Hon. John Dalrymple, eldest son of visc. Stair.
* * Jas. Johnston.
1696. John, ld. Murray, eldest son of M. of Tullibardine.
1696. Jas., ld. Deskford, eldest son of E. of Finlater; visc., aft. E. of Seafield.
Jas., E. of Seafield.
* * John, E. of Hyndford.
1702. Jas., D. of Queensberry, aft. D. of Dover, also.
Geo., visc. Tarbat, aft. E. of Cromarty.
1704. Wm., M. of Annandale.
1705. John, E. of Marr.
* * Hugh, E. of Loudoun.

Principal Secretaries of State for Scotland in England.

From the Union to the year 1746.

1708. Jas., D. of Queensberry and Dover.
1710. John, E. of Marr.
1714. Jas., D. of Montrose; res. 1715.
1716. John, D. of Roxburgh; res. 1725.
1731. Chas., E. of Selkirk.
1742. John, M. of Tweeddale, Feb. 16; res. Jan. 1746.
Office not filled up.

Secretaries for Scotland.

Appointed under 48 & 49 Vict., cap. 61.

1885. Chas. Hy., D. of Richmond and Gordon, Aug. 17, **G.**
1886. Geo. Otto Trevelyan, aft. Sir G., bt., Feb. 8, sw.
1886. Jno. Wm., E. of Dalhousie, K.T., Apr. 3, sw.
Arthur Jas. Balfour, Aug. 4, sw.
1887. Schomberg Hy., M. of Lothian, Mar. 11, sw.

POSTMASTERS-GENERAL OF SCOTLAND.

From a return made to the House of Commons, dated July 2, 1844.

1737. Archd. Douglas, in office this year.
1767 Robt. Oliphant, of Rossie, in office this year.
1799. Thos. Elder, of Forneth
Wm. Robertson.
1802. Robt. Trotter, of Castlelaw.

807. Hon. Fras. Gray, aft. ld. Gray.
811. Jas., E. of Caithness.
823. Sir David Wedderburn, bt. The LAST deputy post.-m. gen. of Scotland.

LORD CHANCELLORS OF SCOTLAND.

See "Judges, &c., of Scotland," *post*.

LORD KEEPERS OF THE GREAT SEAL OF SCOTLAND.

AT the Union the original Great Seal of Scotland was discontinued, or, rather, merged in the Great Seal of Great Britain. Another seal was substituted for various exclusively Scotch purposes, which was declared to have the same effect as, and is still commonly considered and called, the Great Seal of Scotland. The Secretaries for Scotland appointed by 48 & 49 Vict., cap. 61 (Aug. 14, 1885), were by that statute made *ex-officio* keepers of this seal.

LORD KEEPERS OF THE GREAT SEAL OF SCOTLAND.

From the Union to the present time.

708. Hugh, E. of Loudoun.
713. Jas., E. of Finlater and Seafield.
714. Wm., M. of Annandale.
716. Jas., D. of Montrose; *d.* 1731.
733. Archd., E. of Isla, aft. D. of Argyll.
761. Chas., D. of Queensbury and Dover.
763. Jas., D. of Athole; *d.* Jan. 1764.
764. Hugh, E. of Marchmont.
794. Alexr., D. of Gordon.
806. Jas., E. of Lauderdale.
807. Alexr., D. of Gordon, *again*; *d.* Jan. 1827.
827. Geo. Wm., D. of Argyll.
828. Geo., D. of Gordon, G.C.B., Feb. 4, **G.**
830. Geo. Wm., D. of Argyll, *again*; *d.* Oct. 22, 1839.
840. Jno. Hamilton, E. of Stair, Dec. 14, **G.**
841. Jno. Douglas Edwd. Hy., D. of Argyll, Sept. 27, **G.**
1846. Jno. Hamilton, E. of Stair, *again*, Aug. 22.
1852. Dunbar Jas., E. of Selkirk, Aug. 7, **G.**; res. Dec. 1852.
1853. Cospatrick Alexr., E. of Home, May 23, **G.**; res. 1855.
1858. Dunbar, Jas., E. of Selkirk, *again*, Apr. 10, **G.**; *d.* Apr. 11, 1885.

Ex officio Keepers as Secretaries for Scotland, under 48 and 49 Vict., cap. 61.

1885. Chas. Hy., D. of Richmond and Gordon, Aug. 17, **G.**
1886. Geo. Otto Trevelyan, aft. sir G., bt., Feb. 8, sw.
Jno. Wm., E. of Dalhousie, K.T., Apr. 3, sw.
Arthur Jas. Balfour, Aug. 4, sw.
1887. Schomberg Hy., M. of Lothian, Mar. 11, sw.

COMMISSIONERS OF CUSTOMS FOR SCOTLAND.

From the Union until 1823.

COMMISSIONERS FOR SCOTLAND.

1707. Sir Alexr. Rigby, Jas. Isaacson, Lionel Norman, Sir Robt. Dickson, and Wm. Boyle, June 5.
1710. Thos. Fullerton and Jno. Kent, July 18.
1713. Sir Jas. Campbell and Wm. Cleland, Oct. 5.
1714. Wm. Culliford, Jno. Cayley, and Humphrey Brent, Dec. 20.
1715. Jno. Haldane, July 18.
1720. Launcelot Whitehall and Jno. Campbell, July 20.

Commissioners for Great Britain.

For Commissioners for Great Britain from 1723 to 1742, see *ante*, p. 27

In September, 1742, the Commission for Great Britain was divide and five separate Commissioners were appointed for Scotland.

Commissioners for Scotland.

1742. Geo., ld. Ross, Richd. Somers, Colin Campbell, Jas. Cardonnell, and Alexr. Arbuthnot, Sept. 9.
1744. Geo., ld. Ross, Richd. Somers, C. Campbell, A. Arbuthnot, and Mansfeldt Cardonnell, Feb. 18.
1747. Geo., ld. Ross, R. Somers, C. Campbell, M. Cardonnell, and Alexr. Legrand, Oct. 28.
1751. Geo., ld. Ross, C. Campbell, M. Cardonnell, A. Legrand, and Jos. Tudor, July 29.
1754. C. Campbell, M. Cardonnell, A. Legrand, J. Tudor, and Jas., ld. Deskford, July 29.
1758. M. Cardonnell, A. Legrand, J. Tudor, Jas., ld. Deskford, and Robt. Montgomery, Dec. 2.
1763. M. Cardonnell, A. Legrand, J. Tudor. R. Montgomery, and Geo. Clerk Maxwell.
1764. M. Cardonnell, A. Legrand, J. Tudor, G. C. Maxwell, and Basil Cochrane.
1766. M. Cardonnell, J. Tudor, G. C. Maxwell, B. Cochrane, and Jno. West.
1773. M. Cardonnell, J. Tudor, G. C. Maxwell, B. Cochrane, and Archd. Menzies.
1774. M. Cardonnell, G. C. Maxwell, B. Cochrane, A. Menzies, and Wm. Nelthorpe.
1777. M. Cardonnell, G. C. Maxwell, B. Cochrane, W. Nelthorpe, and Adam Smith.
1780. G. C. Maxwell, B. Cochrane, W. Nelthorpe, A. Smith, and Ja Buchanan.
1782. G. C. Maxwell, B. Cochrane, A Smith, J. Buchanan, and Ja Edgar.
1784. B. Cochrane, A. Smith, J. Buchana J. Edgar, and David Reid, Fe 28.
1786. B. Cochrane, A. Smith, J. Edgar, I Reid, and Rt. Hepburn, Aug. 3.
A. Smith, J. Edgar, D. Reid, I Hepburn, and Jno. Hy. Cochran Nov. 6.
1791. J. Edgar, D. Reid, R. Hepburn, H. Cochrane, and Alexr. Mac nochie.
1796. J. Edgar, D. Reid, R. Hepburn, H. Cochrane, and Richd. Ellisto Phillips.
1798. J. Edgar, D. Reid, J. H. Cochran R. E. Phillips, and sir Cha Preston.
1799. D. Reid, J. H. Cochrane, R. I Phillips, sir C. Preston, an Shadrach Moyse.
1800. D. Reid, J. H. Cochrane, R. I Phillips, S. Moyse, and Hy Veitch.
1807. Edwd. Earl, J. H. Cochrane, R. I Phillips, and S. Moyse.
1810. E. Earl, J. H. Cochrane, R. I Phillips, H. Veitch. Alex Osborn, and L. H. Ferrier.
1812. E. Earl, R. E. Phillips, H. Veitcl A. Osborn, and L. H. Ferrier.
1813. E. Earl, H. Veitch, A. Osborn, I H. Ferrier, and Thos. Bruce.

On September 13, 1823, the consolidation of the Boards of Custom for England and Wales, Scotland, and Ireland took place, and th commissioners from that time have been commissioners for the Unite Kingdom. See *ante*, p. 277.

COMMISSIONERS OF EXCISE FOR SCOTLAND.

From the Union until 1823.

1708. Sir Wm. Douglas, Alexr. Wedderburn, John Montgomery, John Whetham, and David Ross.
1710. Alexr. Forbes, Jas. Boyle, and Jas. Moodie.
1714. Gilbert Burnet and sir Wm. Bennet
1715. Geo. Drummond.
1717. Chas. Cockburn, Hy. Robinson, Thos Broughton, Geo. Ross. (aft. ld Ross), and Richd. Somers.

728. Richd. Dodswell.
730. Thos. Cochrane (aft. E. of Dundonald), Christr. Wyvill, and Christr. Rhodes.
749. Alexr. Udny.
758. Richd. Dauber.
761. Geo. Drummond, Alexr. Udny, Richd. Dauber, Basil Cochrane, and Geo. Burgess.
764. G. Drummond, A. Udny, R. Dauber, G. Burgess, and Thos. Lockhart.
766. A. Udny, R. Dauber, G. Burgess, T. Lockhart, and Geo. Brown.
768. A. Udny, R. Dauber, T. Lockhart, Geo. Brown, and David Cuthbert.
— A. Udny, R. Dauber, T. Lockhart, G. Brown, and Gilbert Laurie.
771. A. Udny, T. Lockhart, Geo. Brown, G. Laurie, and Thos. Wharton.
781. A. Udny, G. Brown, T. Wharton, and Jas. Stoddart.
1785. A. Udny, G. Brown, T. Wharton, J. Stoddart, and Jas. Balmain.
1787. T. Wharton, G. Brown, J. Stoddart, J. Balmain, and Robt. Graham.
1790. T. Wharton, G. Brown, J. Stoddart, R. Grieve, and R. Graham.
1803. T. Wharton, G. Brown, J. Stoddart, R. Graham, and Sir John Stuart.
1804. T. Wharton, J. Stoddart, R. Graham, sir J. Stuart, and Fredk. Fotheringham.
1807. T. Wharton, J. Stoddart, R. Graham, F. Fotheringham, and sir Geo. Abercrombie.
1809. T. Wharton, F. Fotheringham, J. Sedgwick, J. Jackson, and S. Rose.
1811. J. Sedgwick, F. Fotheringham, J. Jackson, S. Rose, and David Clephane.
1815. Woodbine Parish, F. Fotheringham, J. Jackson, S. Rose, and J. Douglas.

On September 13, 1823, the consolidation of the Boards of Excise or England and Wales, Scotland, and Ireland took place, and the comnissioners from that time have been commissioners for the United Kingdom. See *ante*, p. 282.

LORD HIGH STEWARDS OF SCOTLAND.

'HE Lord High Steward was judge of the king's household, and he whole family of the royal palace was under his care. This office vas held heritably for many years by one family, who, when surnames came into use, assumed for theirs the name of their office, Steward, or Stuart. This was done by Walter, the son of Alan, who vas at the same time justiciar to king Alexander II., 1230. This amily was frequently nearly allied to the crown, and at last succeeded o it in the person of Robert, eldest son to Walter Steward, or Stuart, n the year 1371. The Robert, just named, was the ninth heritable Lord High Steward of Scotland, and his son, John, afterwards Robert II., was created by his father prince and Steward of Scotland, since which time the eldest son of the king is *natus Senescallus Scotiæ*.

GREAT CHAMBERLAINS OF SCOTLAND.

'HE Great Chamberlain of Scotland was ranked by king Malcolm as he third great officer of the crown, and was called *Camerarius Domini Regis*. Before the appointment of a treasurer, it was his duty to collect he revenue of the crown, and to disburse the money necessary for the king's expenses and the maintenance of the royal household. From he time a treasurer was appointed, his province was limited to the boroughs throughout the kingdom, where he was a sort of justice-general, as he had power to judge all crimes committed within th borough. He was to hold Chamberlain-ayres every year, of whic court he was the supreme judge.

This office was granted heritably to the family of Stuart, dukes o Lenox, afterwards Lenox and Richmond; and when their male lin failed, Charles II. conferred it in like manner, heritably, upon hi natural son James, whom he created duke of Monmouth. On hi forfeiture it went to the new line of dukes of Richmond and Lenox but that family surrendered the office to the Crown in 1703.

LORD GREAT CHAMBERLAINS OF SCOTLAND.

1128. Herbert.
* * Philip.
1147. Herbert, bp. of Glasgow.
1153. Edward.
1165. Walter de Berclay, ld. of Reidcastle.
* * Gilbert Moray, bp. of Caithness.
* * Philip de Valoniis, ld. of Panmure.
* * Wm. de Valoniis, ld. of Panmure.
1224. Hy. de Baliol, ld. of Reidcastle.
1231. Sir John Maxwell, ld. Carlaverock.
1237. David Benham, bp. of St. Andrew's.
1249. Robt. de Meyners.
1256. David Lindsay, ld. Craufurd.
1258. Sir Eumer Maxwell, ld. Carlaverock.
1260. Gilbert de Lempedlar.
1266. Wm., E. of Marr.
1267. Sir Reynold Chyne, of Innerugie.
1269. Sir Thos. Randolph.
1279. John Lindsay, bp. of Glasgow.
1290. Sir Alexr. Baliol, of Cavers.
1317. Sir Wm. Lindsay, rector of Ayr.
1321. Robt. Peebles, canon of Glasgow.
1325. Sir Alexr. Fraser, ld. of Cowie.
1329. Sir Regd. More.
1330. Jas. Bennet, bp. of St. Andrew's.
1335. Sir Wm. Bullock.
1350. Robt. Erskine, ld. of Erskine.
1358. Thos., E. of Marr.
1364. Michl. Monymusk, bp. of Dunkeld.
1368 Walter Biggar, parson of Errol.
1378. John, ld. Glamis.
1383. Robt., D. of Albany.
1406. John, E. of Buchan.
1425. Sir John Forrester, of Corstorphine.
1440. Sir Jas. Crichton, of Frendraught.
1453. Jas., ld. Livingston.
1467. Robt., ld. Boyd; beheaded.
1471. Jas., E. of Buchan; res.
1474. Sir John Colquhoun, of Colquhour killed at siege of Dunbar.
1478. Jas., E. of Buchan.
1484. David, D. of Montrose.
1488. Alexr., ld. Hume; beheaded.
1517. John, ld. Fleming; murd. by Drumelzer.
1524. Malcolm, ld. Fleming; killed a battle of Pinkey, 1547.
1553. Jas., ld. Fleming.
1565. John, ld. Fleming; killed at sieg of Edinburgh castle, 1572.
1580. Esmy, D. of Lenox; heritably.
* * Ludovick, D. of Lenox and Richmond; *d.* 1624.
1624. Jas., D. of Lenox and R.
1655. Esmy, D. of Lenox and R.
1660. Chas., D. of Lenox and R.; *d.* 167: when the male line of the famil failed.
1680. Jas., D. of Monmouth and Bucleugh; beheaded.
1685. Chas., D. of Richmond and Lenox who surrendered the office to th crown in 1703; *ut supra.*

LORD HIGH CONSTABLES OF SCOTLAND,

THE Lord High Constable is an officer of great antiquity. He ha two grand prerogatives:—(1.) The keeping of the king's sword, which th king, at his promotion, when he swears fealty, delivers to him naked Hence the badge of the Constable is a naked sword. (2.) The absolut and unlimited command of the king's armies while in the field, in th absence of the king; but this command did not extend to castles an garrisons. He was likewise judge of all crimes committed within tw leagues of the king's house, a precinct which was called the Chalmer o Peace.

The jurisdiction of this officer came at last to be exercised only as to crimes during the time of parliament, which some extended likewise to all general conventions. The office was conferred heritably upon the noble family of Erroll by king Robert Bruce, and with them it still remains, having been expressly reserved by the Treaty of Union.

Lord High Constables of Scotland.

* * Hugo de Morville; to David I.
* * Edward; to David I.
1163. Richd. de Morville.
* * Wm. de Morville, his son.
* * Allan de Galloway, son to Rowland de Galloway, and Helena de Morville (sister of the last const.); to Alexander II.
* * Sir Leonard Leslie; to Alexander III.
* * Roger de Quincy, E. of Winton; in right of his wife, dau. of the lord of Galloway.
* * Scierus de Quincy, E. of Winton, son to Roger; forfeited to Robert I.
1321. Sir Gilbert Hay, made heritable const., and cr. E. of Erroll.

EARLS MARISCHAL OF SCOTLAND.

The office of Earl Marischal has never been out of the noble family of Keith. It was reserved at the Union; and when the heritable jurisdictions were bought, it was in the crown, having been forfeited by the rebellion of George Keith, Earl Marischal, in 1715.

KNIGHTS MARISCHAL OF SCOTLAND.

* * * *

* * Hon. Jas. Erskine.
1785. Sir Robt. Laurie, bt.
1805. Wm. Hay, E. of Erroll, Feb. 5, **G.**
1819. Alexr. Keith, aft. sir A., July 19, **G.**
1832. Wm. Geo., E. of Erroll, Nov. 12, **G.**
1846. Wm. Alexr. Anthy. Archd. Hamilton Douglas, c.c. M. of Douglas and Clydesdale, June 27, **G.**; aft. 11th D. of Hamilton; *d.* July 15, 1863.
Office not filled up.

LORD HIGH COMMISSIONERS TO THE PARLIAMENTS OF SCOTLAND.

From the accession of king James VI. to the throne of England, to the Union of the two Kingdoms, when the office ceased, there being but one parliament for Great Britain.

1605. John, E. of Montrose.
1607. Ludovick, D. of Lenox and Richmond.
1609. Geo. Keith, E. marischal.
1621. Jas., M. of Hamilton.
1639. John, E. of Traquair.
1641. Jas., ld. Balmerino.
1646. Jas. D. of Hamilton.
1660. John E. of Middleton.
1663. John, 7th E., aft. 1st D. of Rothes.
1669. John, E., aft. D. of Lauderdale.
1670. The same.
1672. The same.
1680. James, D. of York and Albany, aft. king James VII. of Scotland and II. of England.
1685. Wm., D. of Queesberry.
1686. Alexr., E. of Moray.
1689. Wm., D. of Hamilton, elect. pres. of the convention; and when it was

turned into a parliament the same year, he was app. ld. high commr.
1690. Geo., ld., aft. E. of Melville.
Robt., E., aft. M. of Lothian.
1694. John, M. of Tweeddale.
1696. John, E. of Tullibardine, aft. D. of Athole.
1700. Jas., D. of Queensberry.
1702. The same.
1703. The same.
1704. John, M. of Tweeddale, *again*.
1705. John, D. of Argyll.
1707. Jas., D. of Queensberry, *again*. The LAST Lord High Commissioner.

LORD LIEUTENANTS OF COUNTIES—SCOTLAND.

Lord Lieutenants of counties were first appointed in Scotland, May 6, 1794.

LORD LIEUTENANTS OF ABERDEENSHIRE.

1794. Alexr., D. of Gordon, May 6, sw.
1830. Geo., D. of Gordon, July 28.
1836. Wm. Geo. Erroll, K.T., June 6.
1846. Geo., E. of Aberdeen, K.T., Apr. 23.
1861. Chas., M. of Huntly, Feb. 14.
1863. Fras. Alexr., E. of Kintore, Dec. 28, **G.**
1880. John Campbell, E. of Aberdeen, Sept. 18.

LORD LIEUTENANTS OF ARGYLESHIRE.

1794. John, D. of Argyle, May 6, sw.
1806. Geo. Wm., D. of Argyle.
1839. John, M. of Breadalbane, Dec. 7.
1862. Geo. Douglas, D. of Argyle, Nov. 19.

LORD LIEUTENANTS OF AYRSHIRE.

1794. Archibald, E. of Eglintoun, May 6, sw.
1796. Hugh, E. of Eglintoun.
1820. Geo., E. of Glasgow, Jan. 17.
1842. Archd. Wm., E. of Eglinton, Aug. 17.
1861. Archd., M. of Ailsa, Dec. 7.
1870. John Hamilton, 10th E. of Stair, June 18.

LORD LIEUTENANTS OF BANFFSHIRE.

1794. Jas., E. of Fife, May 6, sw.
1813. Jas., E. of Fife, aft. K.T., June 12.
1856. Jas. Duff, aft. E. of Fife and K.T., Mar. 25.
1879. Chas. Hy., D. of Richmond and Gordon, K.G., Aug. 25.

LORD LIEUTENANTS OF BERWICKSHIRE.

1806. Alexr., 10th E. of Home.
1841. Jas., E. of Lauderdale, Nov. 3, **G.**
1860. David Robertson, Dec. 10.
1873. Jas. Hy. Robt., D. of Roxburghe, K.T., July 9.
1879. Chas. Alexr. Home, c.c. ld. Dunglass; aft. E. of Home, June 23.

LORD LIEUTENANTS OF BUTESHIRE.

1806. Jno., 4th E., aft. 1st M. of Bute; *d.* Nov. 16, 1814.
1814 or 1815. John, 2nd M. of Bute.
1848. Ld. Patrick Jas. Herbert Crichton Stuart, Apr. 18, **G.**
1859. Lt.-Col. Jas. Fredk. Dudley Crichton Stuart, Nov. 19.

LORD LIEUTENANTS OF CAITHNESS-SHIRE.

* * Jas., 12th E. of Caithness.
1823. Alexr., 13th E. of Caithness, Aug. 22, **G.**
1856. Jas., 14th E. of Caithness, Mar. 5.
1881. Geo. Philips Alexr., 15th E. of Caithness, May 9, **G.**

LORD LIEUTENANTS OF CLACKMANNANSHIRE.

* * Wm. L. Cathcart.
1803. Wm., 3rd E. of Mansfield, May 4.
1840. Lt.-Col. Hon. Geo. Ralph Abercromby, Apr. 25.
1852. Wm. David, E. of Mansfield, K.T. Aug. 2, **G.**

LORD LIEUTENANTS OF CROMARTY.

* * Robt. Bruce Æneas McLeod.
1833. Roderick McLeod, May 8, **G.**
1853. Geo. Granville Wm. Sutherland-Leveson-Gower, c. c. M. of Stafford; aft. D. of Sutherland, Apr. 6.

LORD LIEUTENANTS OF DUMBARTONSHIRE.

* * John, 11th ld. Elphinstone.
1794. Hon. Wm. Elphinstone.
1799. John, 12th ld. Elphinstone; *d.* 1813.
1813. Jas., 3rd D. of Montrose, K.G.
1837. Sir Jas. Colquhoun, Jan. 16.
1874. Humphrey Ewing Crum-Ewing, Feb. 26.
1887. Sir Jas. Colquhoun, bt., Sept. 1, **G.**

LORD LIEUTENANTS OF DUMFRIESSHIRE.

1794. Wm., D. of Queensberry, May 26; *d.* 1810.
1810. Chas. Wm. Hy., E. of Dalkeith; aft. D. of Buccleugh.
1819. Chas., M. of Queensberry, K.T., June 14.
1837. John, M. of Queensberry, Dec. 13.
1856. Archd. Wm. Douglas, c.c. visc. Drumlanrig; aft. M. of Queensberry, Aug. 28.
1858. Wm. Hy. Walter Montagu Douglas Scott, c.c. E. of Dalkeith; aft. D. of Buccleuch and Queensberry, Mar. 22.

LORD LIEUTENANTS OF EDINBURGHSHIRE, OR MID-LOTHIAN.

1794. Hy., D. of Buccleuch; aft. D. of Buccleuch and Queensberry, May 6, sw.; *d.* Jan. 11, 1813.
1813. Chas. Wm. Hy., D. of Buccleuch and Queensberry; *d.* Apr. 20, 1819.
1819. Wm., 6th M. of Lothian, June 14, **G.**
1824. Geo., E. of Morton, K.T., June 2.
1828. Walter Fras., D. of Buccleuch and Queensberry; aft. K.G., Jan. 3.
1884. Archd. Philip, 5th E. of Rosebery, May 19, **G.**

LIEUTENANTS OF THE CITY OF EDINBURGH.

1837. Jas. Spittal, ld. provost of Edinburgh, and his successors in that office, Nov. 8, **G.**

LORD LIEUTENANTS OF ELGINSHIRE.

1794. Fras., 9th E. of Moray, May 6; *d.* Aug. 28, 1810.
1813 (about). Fras., 10th E. of Moray; aft. K.T.
1848. Gen. Hon. Sir Alexr. Duff, Feb. 17, **G.**
1856. Geo. Skene Duff, Apr. 9, **G.**
1872. Alexr. Wm. Geo. Duff, c.c. visc. Macduff; aft. E. of Fife, Jan. 8.

LORD LIEUTENANTS OF FIFESHIRE.

1798. Geo., 20th E. of Crawford.
1807. Thos., E. of Elgin and Kincardine, Mar. 14.
Geo., 20th E. of Crawford, *again*, May 23; *d.* 1808.
1808. Geo., 18th E. of Morton.
1824. Thos., E. of Kellie, June 11, **G.**
1828. Jas. St. Clair, E. of Rosslyn, Feb. 23, **G.**
1837. Robt. Ferguson, Feb. 15, **G.**
1840. Capt. Jas. Erskine Wemyss, R.N., Dec. 23.
1854. Jas., E. of Elgin and Kincardine, K.T., Apr. 22.
1864. Jas. Hay Erskine Wemyss, Feb. 4, **G.**
Sir Robt. Anstruther, bt, June 11.
1886. Victor Alexr., E. of Elgin and Kincardine, Aug. 6, **G.**

LORD LIEUTENANTS OF FORFARSHIRE.

1794. Archd., ld. Douglas, May 6, sw.
1828. David, E. of Airlie, Feb. 14.
1849. Fox Maule, aft. Ld. Panmure and E. of Dalhousie, June 11, **G.**
1874. Claude, E. of Strathmore and Kinghorn, Aug. 5.

LORD LIEUTENANTS OF HADDINGTONSHIRE.

* * Geo., 7th M. of Tweeddale; *d.* Aug. 9, 1804.
* * Chas., 8th E. of Haddington *d.* Mar. 17, 1828.
1823. Geo., 8th M. of Tweeddale; aft. K.T., Feb. 20, **G.**
1876. Geo., E. of Haddington, Nov. 16.

LORD LIEUTENANTS OF INVERNESS-SHIRE.

* * Sir Jas. Jno. Grant, bt.
1809. Hon. Fras. Wm. Grant, aft. E. of Seafield, Sept. 16, **G.**
1853. Thos. Alexr., ld. Lovat, Aug. 30, **G.**
1873. Hon. Simon Fraser, c.c. Master of Lovat; aft. ld. Lovat, Apr. 18.
1887. Donald Cameron.

LORD LIEUTENANTS OF KINCARDINESHIRE.

* * Anthy., E. of Kintore.
1805. John, 8th Visc. Arbuthnott.
1847. Sir Thos. Burnett, bt., Apr. 24, **G.**
1849. Sir Jas. Carnegie, bt., aft. E. of Southesk, Apr. 2, **G.**
1856. Fras. Alexr., E. of Kintore, May 28, **G.**
1863. Sir Jas. Horn Burnett, bt., Dec. 28, **G.**
1876. Sir Thos. Gladstone, bt., Oct 10, **G.**

LORD LIEUTENANTS OF KINROSS-SHIRE.

1794. Geo. Graham, May 6, sw.
1802. Wm. Adam, June 29, **G.**
1839. V. adm. Sir Chas. Adam, K.C.B., Apr. 1.
1854. Sir Graham Graham Montgomery, bt., Aug. 9, **G.**

LORD LIEUTENANTS OF KIRKCUDBRIGHT STEWARTRY.

1794. Hon. Geo. Stewart, c.c. ld. Garlies, Dec. 26.
1807. Thos., E. of Selkirk, Mar. 28, **G.**
1820. Geo., E. of Galloway, June 15, **G.**
1828. Randolph Stewart, c.c. visc. Garlies; aft. E. of Galloway, July 28.
1845. Dunbar Jas., E. of Selkirk, June 2, **G.**
1885. Marmaduke, ld. Herries, May 28.

LORD LIEUTENANTS OF LANARKSHIRE.

1794. Douglas, D. of Hamilton and Brandon, May 6.
1799. Archd., D. of Hamilton.
1802. Alexr., M. of Douglas; aft. D. of Hamilton and Brandon, K.G., Nov. 13, **G.**
1852. Wm. Alexr. Anthy. Archd., D. of Hamilton and Brandon, Oct. 6, **G.**
1863. Robt. Montgomery, ld. Belhaven, K. T., Aug. 10, **G.**
1869. Sir Thos. Edwd. Colebrooke, bt., Jan. 29, **G.**

LORD LIEUTENANTS OF LINLITHGOWSHIRE.

* * Jas., 3rd E. of Hopetoun.
1816. John, 4th E. of Hopetoun, July 4, **G.**
1825. John, 5th E. of Hopetoun, Jan. 30, **G.**
1843. Archd. John, 4th E. of Rosebery, Apr. 20, **G.**
1863. John Alexr. 6th E. of Hopetoun, Sept. 30, **G.**
1873. Archd. Philip, 5th E. of Rosebery, June 5, **G.**

LORD LIEUTENANTS OF MID-LOTHIAN.

See "Edinburghshire," *ante*, p. 509.

LORD LIEUTENANTS OF NAIRNSHIRE.

* * Jas. Brodie.
1824. Wm. Brodie, Feb. 12, **G.**
1873. Jas. Campbell Jno. Brodie, June 26, **G.**
1880, Hugh Fife Ashley Brodie, Mar. 24, **G.**

LORD LIEUTENANTS OF ORKNEY AND ZETLAND.

1794. Sir Thos. Dundas, bt., aft. ld. Dundas; sw. May 6; *d.* June 14, 1820. Vacancy until
1831. Lawrence, ld. Dundas, May 12, **G.**
1839. Hon. John Chas. Dundas, Apr. 1, **G.**
1866. Fredk. Dundas, Mar. 9, **G.**
1872. John Chas. Dundas, Dec. 21, **G.**

LORD LIEUTENANTS OF PEEBLESHIRE.

1794. Geo. ld. Elibank, June 20, sw.
1821. Fras., 7th E. of Wemyss; aft. E. of Wemyss and March, Mar. 12.
1853. Fras., 8th E. of Wemyss and March, Aug. 10, **G.**
1880. Colin Jas. Mackenzie, Apr. 21, **G.**

LORD LIEUTENANTS OF PERTHSHIRE.

* * John, 4th D. of Athole, K. T.; *d.* Sept. 29, 1830.
1830. Thos. Robt., 10th E. of Kinnoull, Oct. 18, **G.**
1866. Geo. Wm. Fox, ld. Kinnaird, Feb. 28, **G.**
1878. John Jas. Hugh Hy., D. of Athole, K. T., Feb. 12, **G.**

LORD LIEUTENANTS OF RENFREWSHIRE.

1794. Wm. M'Dowall, May 6, sw.
1810. Geo., E. of Glasgow, Apr. 28, **G.**
1820. Robt. Walter, ld. Blantyre, Feb. 25, **G.**
1822. Sir Michl. Shaw Stewart, bt., Dec. 16, **G.**
1826. Archd. Campbell.
1838 or 1839. Alexr. Spiers, Aug. 9.
1844. Jas., E. of Glasgow, Oct. 21, **G.**
1869. Sir Michl. Robt. Shaw Stewart, bt., Apr. 23.

LORD LIEUTENANTS OF ROSS-SHIRE.

* * Fras. Humberstone Mackenzie, aft. ld. Seaforth; *d.* 1814.
1814-5. Sir Hector Mackenzie, bt.
1826. Sir Jas. Wemyss Mackenzie, bt., May 11, **G.**
1843. Col. Hugh Duncan Baillie. Mar. 22, **G.**
1866. Sir Jas. Matheson, July 2, **G.**
1879. Duncan Davidson, Feb. 18, **G.**
1881. Sir Kenneth Smith Mackenzie, bt., Dec. 3, **G.**

LORD LIEUTENANTS OF ROXBURGHSHIRE.

1794. John, D. of Roxburgh, May 6, sw.
1804. Hy., D. of Buccleuch, aft. D. of Buccleuch and Queensberry; *d.* Jan. 11, 1812.
1812. Wm., E. of Ancrum, aft. 6th M. of Lothian; aft. K. T.
1824. John. Wm. Robt.. 7th M. of Lothian, June 2, **G.**
1841. Walter Francis, D. of Buccleuch and Queensberry, K. G.. Dec. 2, **G.**
1884. Jas. Hy. Robt., D. of Roxburgh, May 19, **G.**

LORD LIEUTENANTS OF SELKIRKSHIRE.

1794. Chas. Wm. Hy., E. of Dalkeith; aft. D. of Buccleuch and Queensberry, May 6, sw.; *d.* Apr. 20, 1819.
1819. Fras., ld. Napier; sw.
1823. Hy. Jas., ld. Montagu, Sept. 2, **G.**
1845. Hy. Fras. ld. Polwarth, Dec. 8, **G.**
1867. Alan Eliot Lockhart, Nov. 19, **G.**
1878. Walter Hugh, ld. Polwarth, May 6, **G.**

LORD LIEUTENANTS OF SHETLAND.

See "Orkney and Zetland," *ante*, p. 511.

LORD LIEUTENANTS OF STIRLINGSHIRE.

1794. Jas., 3rd D. of Montrose; aft. K. G., May 6, sw.
1837. Geo., ld. Abercromby, Jan. 23, **G.**
1843. Jas., 4th D. of Montrose, Feb. 28, **G.**
1875. Chas. Adolphs., E. of Dunmore, Feb. 16, **G.**
1885. Douglas Beresford Malise Ronald, 5th D. of Montrose, July 23, **G.**

LORD LIEUTENANTS OF SUTHERLANDSHIRE.

1794. Granville, 2nd E. Gower; aft. 1st M. of Stafford; res. 179-; *d.* 1803.
179-. Geo. Granville Leveson-Gower, c.c. E. Gower; aft. 2nd M. of Stafford and 1st D. of Sutherland; res. 1831; *d.* 1833.
1831. Geo. Granville Leveson-Gower, c.c. E. Gower; aft. c.c. M. of Stafford; aft. second D. of Sutherland; *d.* Feb. 28, 1861.
1861. Geo. Granville Wm., 3rd D. of Sutherland, May 6, **G.**

LORD LIEUTENANTS OF WIGTONSHIRE.

1794. John, 7th E. of Galloway, May 29.
1807. Geo., E. of Galloway, Mar. 28, **G.**
1828. Randolph Stewart, c.c. visc. Garlies; aft. E. of Galloway, July 28, **G.**
1851. John Hamilton Dalrymple, aft. c.c. visc. Dalrymple, and aft. 10th E. of Stair.

LORD LIEUTENANTS OF ZETLAND.

See "Orkney and Zetland," *ante*, p. 511.

HERALDIC OFFICERS OF SCOTLAND.

In Scotland all heraldic matters are transacted in what is called the Lyon Court, at the head of which is Lyon King of Arms. Under him was a deputy called Lyon Depute; but in 1866 the then holder of that office was appointed Lyon King of Arms, and the two offices may now be considered as united. There are also a Lyon Clerk and a Lyon Clerk Depute besides several Heralds and Pursuivants. For further information the reader is referred to Seton's *Scotch Heraldry*, from which the following lists have been compiled.

LYON KINGS OF ARMS.

1437. Alexr. Nairne.
1450–90. Duncan Dundas.
1504. Hy. Thomson.
1512. Sir Wm. Cumyng.
1530. Sir David Lindsay (No. 1), of the Mount, co. Fife.
1555. Sir Robt. Forman.
1567. Sir Wm. Stewart, form. Ross Herald, Feb. 20.
1568. Sir David Lindsay (No. 2), of Rathillet, co. Fife; Aug. 22.
1591. Sir David Lindsay (No. 3), of the Mount, co. Fife.
1621. Sir Jerome Lindsay, June 27.
1630. Sir Jas. Balfour, June 15.
1658. Sir Jas. Campbell, May 13.
1660. Gilbert Stewart, Aug. 21.
1660. Sir Alexr. Durham, Aug. 28.
1663. Sir Chas. Erskine, bt.
1677. Sir Alexr. Erskine.
1726. †— Cocherne, or Cochrane.
†Alexr. Drummond.
1727. Alexr. Brodie, July 6.
1754. John Hooke-Campbell, Apr. 3.
1796. Robt. Auriol, 9th E. of Kinnoull, May 26.
1804. Thos. Robt., 10th E. of Kinnoull, Apr. 12; *d.* Feb. 18, 1866.
1886. Geo. Burnett, lyon dep., app. L. K. A. Aug. 3, **G.**; and the office of lyon dep. not filled up. Burnett acted as *interim* L. K. A. from the death of the E. of Kinnoull.

† These names occur in *Noble's "College of Arms,"* but are considered doubtful by *Seton.*

LYONS DEPUTE.

* * Robt. Innes; in 1681.
1728. John Dundas, Feb. 1.
1744. Thos. Dundas, jr., June 18.
1754. Thos. Brodie, Sept. 7.
1770. Robt. Boswell, Nov. 2.
1796. Jas. Home, Aug. 8.
1819. David Clyne, Feb. 21.
1819. Geo. Tait, Apr. 24.
1823. Geo. Clerk Craigie, Apr. 1.
1827. Jas. Tytler (jointly with Craigie), June 2; sole lyon dep. from 1845.
1863. Geo. Burnett, Feb. 9; made L. K. A. Aug. 3, 1866; and the office of lyon dep. was not filled up.

SCOTCH HERALDS AND PURSUIVANTS.

The following are the names of the various Scotch Heralds and Pursuivants. Those marked * are still existing. The other titles are either extinct or in abeyance.

Heralds.

Islay.
*Rothesay.
*Marchmont.
*Albany.
Ross.
Snowdon.

Pursuivants.

Kintyre.
Dingwall.
*Carrick.
*Bute.
Ormond.
*Unicorn.

JUDGES AND OTHER LEGAL DIGNITARIES OF SCOTLAND.

LORD CHANCELLORS OF SCOTLAND.

The Lord Chancellor was the chief in matters of justice. In the laws of Malcolm II. he is placed before all other officers, and from these laws it appears that he had the principal direction of the Chancery or Chancellary. He had the custody of the great seal of Scotland, and it was his duty to examine the king's grants and other deeds which were to pass under it, and to cancel them if they appeared against law, or were obtained surreptitiously, or by false suggestions.

James VI. ordained that the Lord Chancellor should have the first place and rank in the nation, *ratione officii*, by virtue whereof he presided in the parliament, and in all courts of judicature. After the Restoration of Charles II. the Lord Chancellor was declared by act of parliament, *virtute officii*, president in all the meetings of parliament, or other public judicatures of the kingdom.

The office of Lord Chancellor was abolished at the Union, there being no further use for the judicial part of the office, and a lord keeper of the seal then substituted for the great seal of Scotland was appointed.

Lord Chancellors of Scotland.

From the year 1057 to the abolition of the office.

1057. Evan, surn. Canmore; to Malcolm III.
1093. Oswald; to Donald VII.
1094. Earl Constantine; to Duncan II. the Usurper.
Sphothad, abb. of the religious Culdees; to Duncan.
1097. Earl Rorey; to Donald VII., after the expulsion of Duncan.
1098. Humphrey, bp. of Dunkeld; to Edgar.
1107. Constantine, E. of Fife; to Alexr. I.
1124. Herbert, aft. bp. of Glasgow.
1125. Walter.
1129. John, bp. of Glasgow.
* * Herbert, gr. chambn.
1147. Edward.
* * Wm. Cuming.
* * Hy., E. of Northumberland.
1151. Ingelramus, aft. bp. of Glasgow.
1153. Walter Seneschallus.
1157. Gregory, bp. of Dunkeld.
1161. Nicolaus, chambn.
1163. Willielmus de Ripariis, prior of St. Andrew's.
1165. Hugo de Morville, ld. of Lauderdale.
1171. Walter de Bidun, bp. elect of Dunkeld.
1178. Roger (son to the E. of Leicester), bp. of St. Andrew's.
1183. Walterus de Beide.
1187. Walterus de Vidone.
1189. Hugo de Roxburgh, bp. of Glasgow.
1192. Willielmus de Lundyne.
1199. Wm. Malvoisine, bp. of St. Andrew's.
1202. Florence, bp. elect of Glasgow.
* * Richard, aft. bp. of Dunkeld.
1211. Willielmus de Bosco, or Wood, bp. of Dumblane.
1214. Willielmus Riddel.
Robt. Kildelicht, abb. of Dunfermline.
1216. Walterus de Oliford.
1226. Thos. de Stryvelin, archdn. of Glasgow.
1227. Matth. Scot, bp. of Aberdeen.
1230. Wm. de Lindesay.
1231. Wm. de Bondington, bp. of Glasgow.
* * Richd. de Innerkeithing, aft. bp. of Dunkeld.
* * Wm. de Huntington.
1247. Wm. de Bond.
1251. Gameline, bp. of St. Andrew's.
1253. Richd. de Innerkeithing, bp. of Dunkeld.
1256. Wm. Wisehart, bp. of Glasgow; aft. bp. of St. Andrew's.
1273. Wm. Fraser, dean of Glasgow; aft. bp. of St. Andrew's.
1295. Alexr. de Baliol.

1295. Allan, bp. of Caithness; confirmed in the office by Edward I. of England, as superior.
1298. Maurice, or Marcus, bp. of the Isles.
Adam, aft. bp. of Brechin.
1301. Bernard, abb. of Aberbrothock.
* * Nicolas de Balmyle, bp. of Dumblane.
1327. Walter Twynham, canon of Glasgow.
1345. Patrick de Leuchars, bp. of Brechin.
1347. Thos. de Carnsto, or Charteris de Kinfawns.
1349. Wm. Caldwall, preb. of Glasgow.
1367. Patrick de Leuchars, bp. of Brechin, *again.*
* * Sir John Carrick, preb. of Glasgow.
1377. John Peebles, bp. elect of Dunkeld.
1380. John Lyon, ld. Glamis.
* * Sir John Carrick, *again.*
1395. Sir Alexr. Cockburn, of Langton.
* * Duncan Petit, archdn. of Glasgow.
* * Gilbert Greenlaw, bp. of Aberdeen; to Robert III., and during the administrations of Robert and Murdoch, dukes of Albany.
1422. Sir John Forrester, of Corstorphine.
1424. Wm. Lauder, bp. of Glasgow.
1427. John Cameron, bp. of Glasgow.
* * Sir Wm., aft. ld. Crichton; turned out.
1444. Jas. Kennedy, bp. of St. Andrew's; held office only a few weeks.
Jas. Bruce, bp. of Dunkeld; aft. bp. of Glasgow.
1447. Wm., ld. Crichton, *again.*
1455. Wm., E. of Orkney and Caithness.
1458. Geo. Shoreswood, bp. of Brechin.
1460. Robt., ld. Boyd.
* * Andrew, ld. Evandale.
1482. John Laing, bp. of Glasgow
1483. Jas. Livingston, bp. of Dunkeld.
1484. Colin, 1st E. of Argyll.
1489. Wm. Elphinstone, bp. of Aberdeen.
1493. Archd., E. of Angus.
1498. Geo., E. of Huntly,
1500. Jas. Stuart (second son to James III.), D. of Ross, and abp. of St. Andrew's.
1506. Andr. Foreman, abp. of St. Andrew's.
1510. Alexr. Stuart (natural son to James IV.), abp. of St. Andrew's.
1512. Jas. Bethune, abp. of St. Andrew's.
1525. Archd., E. of Angus; consort to the queen-mother.
1528. Gavin Dunbar, abp. of Glasgow; tutor to James V.
* * David Bethune, cardl., and abp. of St. Andrew's.
1546. John Hamilton, abp. of St. Andrew's.
1561. Geo., 2nd E. of Huntly.
Monsr. de Ruby, a French lawyer; made chancellor for a short time by the queen-regent.
1562. Jas., E. of Morton.
1567. Geo., 2nd E. of Huntly, *again.*
Jas., E. of Morton, *again.*
1572. Archd., E. of Argyll.
1573. John, ld. Glamis.
1578. John Stuart, E. of Athole.
1579. Colin, 6th E. of Argyll.
1584. Jas. Stewart, E. of Arran.
1587. Sir John Maitland, of Thirlestane.
1597. John, E. of Montrose.
1605. Alexr., E. of Dunfermline.
1622. Sir Geo. Hay, aft. visc. Dupplin, and E. of Kinnoull.
1634. John Spottiswood, abp. of St. Andrew's.
1641. John, E. of Loudoun.
1660. Wm., E. of Glencairn.
1664. John, E., aft. D. of Rothes.
1682. Geo., E. of Aberdeen.
1684. Jas., E. of Perth.
1690. Wm., D. of Hamilton, Archd., E. of Argyll, Geo., E. of Sutherland. } commissioners.
1692. John, M. of Tweeddale.
1696. Patrick, ld. Polwarth; aft. E. of Marchmont.
1702. Jas. (son to the 3rd E. of Findlater), 1st visc., and E. of Seafield.
1704. John, M. of Tweeddale.
1705. Jas., 1st E. of Seafield, *again*; aft. 4th E. of Findlater.

Office abolished at the Union.

LORD PRESIDENTS AND JUDGES OF THE COURT OF SESSION.

The Court of Session is the supreme civil court of justice in Scotland. It received its name and derives its constitution under a statute passed in the 20th year of James V., 1532. Previously to this year the functions now discharged by this court were performed by parliamentary committees; and until the period of the Revolution the condition of the court was very defective. The judges, upon their appointment, assume a title from their surnames or their estates, which is conceded to them by ancient usage, and though purely official, is recognised by courtesy in social intercourse.

The Court, the constitution of which has been modified from time to time by a series of statutes too numerous to quote, is now composed of thirteen judges, who sit in an inner house or court of appeal, and an outer house or court of first instance. The inner house sits in two divisions of four judges each, the Lord Justice General (Lord President) presiding in the first division, and the Lord Justice Clerk in the second; the outer house is composed of five judges, who sit in separate courts as judges of first instance.

Lord Presidents of the Court of Session.

1532. Alexr. Milne, abb. of Cambuskenneth.
1543. Robt. Reid, bp. of Orkney.
1558. Hy. Sinclair, bp. of Ross.
1565. John Sinclair, bp. of Brechin.
1566. Wm. Baillie, of Provand.
1567. Sir Jas. Balfour, of Pittendrich.
1593. Sir Alexr. Seton, ld. Urquhart, aft. E. of Dunfermline.
1605. Jas. Elphinstone, ld. Balmerino.
1609. John Preston, of Fenton Barns.
1616. Thos. Hamilton, ld. Binning.
1626. Sir Jas. Skene, of Curriehill.
1633. Sir Robt. Spottiswood, of New Abbey.
1661. Sir John Gilmour, of Craigmiller.
1671. Sir Jas. Dalrymple, aft. visc. Stair.
1681. Sir Geo. Gordon, aft. E. of Aberdeen.
1682. Sir David Falconer, of Newton.
1685. Sir Geo. Lockhart, of Carnwath.
1689. Sir Jas. Dalrymple, *again*; aft. 1st visc. Stair.
1698. Sir Robt. Berwick.
1707. Sir Hew Dalrymple, of North Berwick.
1737. Duncan Forbes, of Culloden.
1748. Robt. Dundas, of Arniston.
1754. Robt. Craigie, of Glendoick.
1760. Robt. Dundas, of Arniston, son of the ld. pres. app. in 1748.
1787. Thos. Miller, of Glenlee, aft. bt.
1789. Ilay Campbell, of Succoth; aft. bt.; res. 1808; *d.* 1823.
1808. Robt. Blair, of Avonton; *d.* 1811.
1811. Chas. Hope, of Granton, res. 1841.

On the death of the D. of Montrose, ld. just. gen. of Scotland in 1836, that office was, under 11 Geo. IV. and 1 Wm. IV., cap. 65, united with that of the ld. pres. of the ct of sess.

1841. David Boyle.
1852. Duncan McNeill, of Colonsay, May 15, **G.**; aft. ld. Colonsay.
1867. Jno. Inglis, of Glencorse, Feb. 25, **G.**

Lord Justice Clerks.

* * Wm. de Camera; to David II.
* * Adam Forrester; to David II.
1478. Wm. Halket, of Belfico.
1491. Richd. Lawson, of Heirigs.
1507. Jas. Henderson, of Fordil.
1513. Jas. Wishart, of Pittarrow.
1524. Nicolas Crawford, of Oxengang.
1537. Adam Otterburn, of Redhall.
Thos. Scott, of Pitgorn.
1539. Thos. Ballenden, of Auchinoul.
1540. Hy. Balneaves.
1547. Sir John Ballenden, of Auchinoul.
1578. Sir Lewis Ballenden, of Auchinoul.
1591. Sir John Cockburn, of Ormistoun.
1625. Sir Geo. Elphinston, of Blythswood.
1634. Sir Jas. Carmichael, of Carmichael.
1637. Sir John Hamilton, of Orbiston.
1661. Sir Robt. Murray.
1663. Sir Jas. Foulis, of Collingtoun.
1688. Sir John Dalrymple, aft. 2nd visc. and 1st E. of Stair.
1689. Sir Robt. Sinclair, of Stevenson.
1693. Sir Wm. Hamilton, of Whitelaw.
1702. Roderick Mackenzie, of Prestonhall
1705. Adam Cokburne, of Ormiston.
1710. Jas. Erskine, of Grange.
1714. Adam Cokburne, of Ormiston *again*.
1735. Andrew Fletcher, of Milton.
1748. Chas. Erskine, of Tinwald.
1763. Sir Gilbert Elliot, of Minto, bt.
1766. Thos. Miller, of Glenlee, aft. sir T., bt.
1788. Robt. Mac Queen, of Braxfield.
1799. David Rae, of Eskgrove, aft. sir D., bt.
1804. Chas. Hope, of Granton.
1811. David Boyle.
1841. John Hope.
1858. Jno. Inglis, of Glencorse, July 9, **G.**
1867. Geo. Patton, Feb. 27, **G.**
1869. Jas. Moncrieff, of Tulliebole, Aug 14, **G.**; aft. ld. Moncrieff; res Oct. 1888.
1888. Jno. Hay Athole Macdonald, of Kingsburgh, Oct. 20, **G.**

Extraordinary Lords of Session.

The designation "Extraordinary Lords of Session," expresses a distinction between those functionaries and the Ordinary Lords of Session. The Extraordinary Lords of Session were lords of parliament appointed by the crown to sit and vote in court along with the permanent judges. This "manifest impropriety," as a writer justly termed it, was abolished by 10 Geo. I., cap. 19 (1723).

1539. Wm., ld. Ruthven.
John, ld. Erskine.
1541. Wm., E. marischal.
Wm., E. of Rothes.
Robt., ld. Maxwell.
John, ld. Lindsay.
1542. Geo., ld, Seton.
Alexr., ld. Livingston.
Jas., ld. Ogilvie.
Jas., ld. Innermeath.
1554. Sir Richd. Maitland, of Lethington.
Adam Livingstone, of Dunipace.
1561. Wm., E. marischal.
Wm. Maitland, of Lethington.
Jas. Balfour, parson of Flisk.
1562. John Wood, of Tulliedairie.
1563. Adam, bp. of Orkney.
1565. Alexr. bp. of Galloway.
1566. Edwd. Henryson.
John Wood, of Tulliedairie, *again.*
Gavin Hamilton, commend. of Kilwinning.
1567. Sir John Wisehart, of Pittarrow.
1569. Mark Ker, commend. of Newbattle.
1570. John, ld. Glamis.
1573. Robt., ld. Boyd.
1574. Sir John Wisehart, of Pittarrow.
1575. Hy. ——, commend. of Balmerino.
1578. Patrick, mast. of Gray.
Robt., ld. Boyd.
Wm., ld. Ruthven.
1583. Jas. Stuart, E. of Arran.
1584. Jas., ld. Doune.
John, E. of Montrose.
Patrick, ld. Gray.
Mark Ker, aft. E. of Lothian.
1585. Alexr. Seton, prior of Pluscardin.
Thos. Lyon, of Balduckie.
1586. Robt., ld. Boyd, *again.*
1587. Sir John Seton, of Barnes.
1588. John Cokburne, of Ormiston.
1591. John, E. of Montrose.
1592. Sir Thos. Lyon, of Auldbar.
1593. Walter Stewart, commend. of Blantyre; aft. ld. Blantyre.
1594. Sir Robt. Melville, of Burntisland.
1596. Peter, bp. of Dunkeld.
1599. Alexr., mast. of Elphinstone.
1601. Sir Robt. Melville, of Burntisland, *again.*
1608. Sir Alexr. Drummond, of Medhope.
1610. Walter, ld. Blantyre.
Alexr., mast. of Livingston, *again.*
SirRbt.Melville,ofBurntisland,*again.*
John, abp. of Glasgow.
Peter Pollock, of Piltoun.
1620. John, ld. Erskine.
1622. Sir Robt.Spottiswood,of New Abbey.
1626. Sir Archd. Napier, of Merchiston.
David, ld. Carnegie.
John, E. of Lauderdale.
Patrick, bp. of Ross.
1628. John, ld. Erskine, *again.*
Sir Archd. Acheson, of Glencairnie.
Wm., E. of Menteith.
Sir Andrew Ker, mast. of Jedburgh.
1629. Sir John Scot, of Scotstarvet.
1630. Sir John Hamilton, of Magdalens.
John, E. of Traquair.
1631. Wm., visc., aft. E. of Stirling.
1633. Sir John Hay, of Barro.
John, bp. of Ross.
1634. Archd., ld. Lorne.
1635. Wm., ld. Alexander.
1639. Archd., ld. Angus.
1641. Archd., E. of Argyll.
Archd., ld. Angus, *again.*
John, ld. Lindsay.
John, ld. Balmerino.
1649. John, ld. Coupar.
John, E. of Cassilis.
1661. John, E. of Crauford.
John, E. of Rothes.
John, E. of Lauderdale.
John, E. of Cassilis, *again.*
1662. John, E. of Middleton.
1664. John, E. of Tweeddale.
Alexr., abp. of Glasgow.
1667. Alexr., E. of Kincardine.
1668. Jas., M. of Montrose.
1669. John, E. of Dumfermline.
1673. John, E. of Athole.
1674. Archd., E. of Argyll.
1680. Alexr., E. of Moray.
1681. Wm., E. of Queensberry.
1682. Jas., E. of Perth.
1684. Chas., E. of Middleton.
1686. Wm., D. of Hamilton.
Patrick, E. of Strathmore.
1693. Wm., D. of Queensberry.
Wm., M. of Annandale.
Patrick, ld. Polwarth, aft. E. of Marchmont.
Wm., D. of Hamilton, *again.*
1694. Archd., E., aft. D. of Argyll.
1696. Jas., D. of Queensberry.
1699. Hugh, E. of Loudoun.
1704. John, D. of Argyll.
1708. Archd., E. of Isla, aft. D. of Argyll.
1712. John, D. of Athole.
1721. John, M. of Tweeddale. The last Extraordinary Lord of Session.

Ordinary Lords of Session.

The title assumed by each lord is affixed to his name; thus "William Scott—Balwerie" (1532), means that this judge was styled Lord Balwerie.

1532. Richd. Bothwell, rect. of Eskirk.
John Dingwall, prov. of Trinity, Edinburgh.
Hy. Whyte, rect. of Finevin.
Wm. Gibson, dean of Restalrig.
Thos. Hay, dean of Dunbar.
*Robt. Reid, abb. of Kinloss.
*Geo. Ker, prov. of Dunglass.
Wm. Scott—Balwerie.
Sir John Campbell—Lundie.
Sir Jas. Colville—Easter Wemyss.
Adam Otterburn—Auldhame.
Nicol Crawford—Oxengang.
Fras. Bothwell.
Jas. Lawson.
Jas. (? John) Foulis—Collington.
1537. Walter Lindesay, ld. St. John.
Sir Thos. Erskine—Brechin.
Thos. Bannatyne.
Robt. Galbraith, parson of Spot.
Hy. Sinclair, dean of Glasgow.
1538. Hy. Balnavis,—Hall Hill (No. 1).
Thos. Scot—Abbotshall.
John Letham, rect. of Kilchrist.
1239. D. Brithman.
Hy. Lauder—St. Germain's.
1540. John Sinclair, dean of Restalrig.
Wm. Lamb, rect. of Conveth.
1541. Geo. Durie, abb. of Dunfermline.
Donald Campbell, abb. of Cupar.
Andrew Durie, abb. of Melrose.
Gavin Hamilton, abb. of Kilwinning.
John Foulis—Collington.
1542. John Waddell, parson of Flisk.
John Gladstaines.
1543. David Strachan.
John Hamilton, abb. of Paisley.
Abb. of Lindores.
Abb. of Culross.
Abb. of Pittenweem.
1544. Thos. Wemyss.
1547. Sir Robt. Carnegie—Kinnaird.
1548. Geo. Hay, parson of Renfrew.
1553. John Hamilton, abp. of St. Andrew's.
Geo. Durie, commend. of Dumfermline.
1554. Jas. Macgill—Rankeilor Nether.
Abrm. Creighton, prov. of Dunglass.
John Stevenson, precentor of Glasgow.
Wm. Baillie—Provand.
Jas. Scott, prov. of Corstorphine.
Sir John Ballenden—Auchinoul.
Thos. Marjoribanks—Ratho.
Wm. Chisolme, bp. of Dunblane.
Sir Wm. Hamilton—Sanquhar.
1560. Archd. Dunbar, sub-chanter of Moray.
1561. Sir Richd. Maitland—Lethington.
John Spence—Condie.
1562. Hy. Balnavis—Hall Hill (No. 2).
1563. Jas. Balfour, parson of Flisk.
1564. John Leslie, parson of Oyne.
Robt. Maitland, dean of Aberdeen.
1565. David Chalmers—Ormond.
Adam Bothwell, bp. of Orkney.
1566. Sir Wm. Maitland—Lethington.
Archd. Craufurd, parson of Eglishame.
1568. Robt. Pitcairne, commend. of Dunfermline.
John Maitland, commend. of Coldingham.
Archd. Douglass, parson of Douglass.
1570. Thos. Macallyean—Clifton Hall.
1573. David Borthwick—Lochill.
1575. Jas. Meldrum—Segie.
Robt. Pont, prov. of Trinity College.
Wm. Douglass—Whittinghame.
Alexr. Colvill, abbot of Culross.
1576. Patrick Vanse—Barnbarrow.
1577. Thos. Bellenden—Newtyle.
1578. Archd. Douglass, parson of Glasgow.
1579. Alexr. Hay—Easter Kennet.
1580. Robt. Creighton, or Crichton —Elliock.
1581. John Maitland—Thirlestane.
John Lindsay, parson of Menmure.
1582. David Macgill—Nisbet.
1584. John Graham—Hallyards.
Sir Lewis Ballenden—Auchinoul.
John Bartane, dean of Dunkeld.
1586. David Chalmers—Ormond.
1587. Jas. Elphinstone—Innernochtie.
John Colvill, chanter of Glasgow.
Alexr. Colvill, commend. of Culross.
Wm. Melville, commend. of Tongland.
1588. Alexr. Seton, ld. Urquhart.
1590. Archd. Douglas—Whittinghame.
1591. Thos. Bellenden—Newtyle.
Richd. Cockburne—Clerkintoun.
Andr. Wemyss—Myrecairnie.
1592. Thos. Hamilton—Drumcairne.
1593. Sir John Cockburn—Ormistoun.
Sir Thos. Lyon—Auldbar.
John Bothwell, commend. of Holyrood House.
1594. John Skene—Currie Hill.
1595. John Preston—Fenton Bars.

* In the original nomination, Robert Chanwell and Arthur Boyes were inserted; but in their absence the abbot of Kinloss and the provost of Dunglass were chosen, and admitted by the king. It does not appear that Robert Chanwell or Arthur Boyes ever officiated.

1597. David Macgill—Cranston Riddel.
Edwd. Bruce—Kinloss.
1598. Sir David Lindsay—Edzell.
1604. Alexr. Hay—Fosterseat.
Sir Jas. Wemyss—Bogie.
Sir Lewis Craig—Wright's Land.
Sir John Wemyss—Craigtoun.
1607. Thos. Hamilton—Prestonfield.
1608. Sir Andr. Hamilton—Redhouse
1609. Sir Wm. Livingston—Kilsyth.
1610. Sir Alexr. Hay—Newton.
1611. Wm. Oliphant—Newton.
1612. Sir Jas. Skene—Currie Hill.
1613. Sir Gideon Murray—Elibank.
1616. David Carnegie—Carnegie.
1617. Sir Geo. Erskine—Innerteil.
1618. John Maitland, visc. Lauderdale.
1621. Sir Alex. Gibson—Durie.
1622. Thos. Henderson—Chesters.
Sir John Hamilton—Magdalens.
1623. Sir Archd. Napier—Merchistoun.
Sir Andr. Fletcher—Innerpeffer.
1627. Sir Robt. Spottiswood—New Abbey.
Alexr. Seton—Kilcreuch.
Sir Geo. Auchinleck—Balmanno.
Sir Alexr. Napier—Laurieston.
Sir Archd. Acheson—Glencairnie.
Jas. Bannatyne—Newhall.
Alexr. Morison—Preston Grange.
Sir Jas. Learmonth—Balcomie.
Geo. Haliburton—Fodderance.
1629. Sir Jas. (? Wm.) Oliphant—Newton.
Sir Jas. Macgill—Cranston Riddel.
1632. Sir John Hope—Craighall.
Sir John Scot—Scotstarvet.
1634. Sir John Hay—Barro.
1636. Patrick Nisbet—Eastbank.
1637. Sir John Hamilton—Orbieston.
Sir Wm. Elphinstone.
Adam Cunninghame—Woodhall.
1639. Sir Jas. Carmichael—Carmichael.
Sir Alexr. Falconer—Halkertoun.

New Commission by Act of Parliament, 13th November, 1641.

1641. Sir Geo. Erskine—Innerteil.
Sir Alexr. Gibson—Durie.
Sir Andr. Fletcher—Innerpeffer.
Sir John Hamilton—Orbiestoun.
Sir Jas. Carmichael—Carmichael.
Sir Jas. Learmonth—Balcomie.
Sir Jas. Macgill—Cranston Riddel.
Sir Geo. Haliburton—Fodderance.
Sir John Hope—Craighall.
Sir John Scot—Scotstarvet.
Sir Alexr. Falconer—Halkertoun.
Sir John Leslie—Newton.
Sir Thos. Hope—Kerse.
Sir Archd. Johnston—Warriston.
Sir Adam Hepburn—Humbie.

1646. Sir Alexr. Gibson—Durie.
Sir Jas. Lockhart—Lee.
Sir Alexr. Belsches—Tofts.
1649. Sir Jas. Hope—Hopetoun.
1649. Robt. Bruce—Broomhall.
Alexr. Pearson—South Hall.
Robt. Macgill—Ford.
Sir Wm. Scott—Clerkintoun.
Geo. Winram—Libbertoun.
Alexr. Brodie—Brodie.
John Dickson—Hartree.
Sir Hew Campbell—Cesnock.

Commissioners for Administration of Justice to the People of Scotland; appointed by Oliver Cromwell.

1654. Geo. Smyth.
Wm. Laurence.
Edwd. Mosely.
1655. John Swinton—Swinton.
Alexr. Pearson—South Hall.
Sir Jas. Learmonth—Balcomie.
Andr. Ker.
1656. Sir Wm. Lockhart.
1657. Jas. Dalrymple—Stair.
Sir Archd. Johnston—Warriston.
Alexr. Brodie—Brodie.

Lords of Session appointed at the Restoration.

1661. Alexr. Falconer—Halkertoun.
Sir Archd. Primrose—Carrington.
Sir Robt. Murray, ld. just.-clk.
Sir Jas. Macgill—Cranston Riddel.
Sir Jas. Lockhart—Lee.
Sir Geo. Mackenzie—Tarbet.
Sir Archd. Stirling—Carden.
Sir Jas. Foulis—Collington.
Sir Jas. Dalrymple—Stair.
Sir Robt. Nairne—Strathurd.
Robt. Burnet—Crimond.
Jas. Roberton—Bedley.
John Scougal—Whitekirk.
Andr. Ayton—Kinglassie.

Sir David Nevoy—Nevoy.
1662. Sir Jas. Dundas—Arniston.
1663. John Hume—Renton.
1664. Sir John Nisbet—Dirleton.
Sir John Baird—Newbyth.
1665. Sir John Lockhart—Castlehill.
1668. Sir Peter Wedderburn—Gosford.
1669. Chas. Maitland—Halton.
1671. Sir Thos. Wallace—Craigie.
Sir Andr. Ramsay—Abbotshall.
Sir Richd. Maitland—Pittrichie.
1672. Sir Robt. Preston—Preston.
1674. Sir David Balfour—Forret.
Sir Thos. Murray—Glendoick.
Sir Jas. Foulis—Reidfurd.
1676. Sir David Falconer—Newton.
1677. Sir Alexr. Seton—Pitmedden.
Sir Roger Hogg—Harcarse.
1679. Sir Andr. Birnie—Saline.
1680. Sir Geo. Gordon—Haddo.
1681. Sir Geo. Mackenzie—Tarbet.
Sir Patrick Ogilvie—Boyne.
Jno. Murray—Drumcairne.
1682. Sir Geo. Nicolson—Kemnay.
Jno. Wauchope—Edmonstone.

1683. Sir Thos. Stewart—Blair.
Sir Patrick Lyon—Carse.
1685. Sir G. Lockhart—Carnwath.
1687. Alexr. Malcolm—Lochore.
1688. Sir Jno. Dalrymple—Stair.
1688. Alexr. Swinton—Mersington.
Lewis Gordon—Auchintoul.

THE REVOLUTION.

1689. Sir Jno. Baird—Newbyth.
Alexr. Swinton—Mersington.
Sir Colin Campbell—Aberuchill.
Jas. Murray—Philiphaugh.
Jas. Dundas—Arniston.
Jno. Hamilton—Halcraig.
David Home—Crocerig.
Sir Jno. Maitland—Ravelrig; aft. 5th E. of Lauderdale.
Sir Robt. Sinclair—Stevenson.
Sir Jno. Lauder—Fountain Hall.
Wm. Anstruther—Anstruther.
Archd. Hope—Rankeilor.
Jas. Falconer—Phesdo.
Robt. Hamilton—Presmennan.

1693. Sir Wm. Hamilton—Whitelaw.
1696. Jas. Scougal—Whitehill.
1699. Sir Jno. Maxwell—Pollock.
1701. Robt. Stewart—Tulliecutrie.
1704. R. Mackenzie—Preston Hall.
Sir A. Campbell—Cesnock.
1705. Adam Cockburn—Ormistoun.
Sir Gilbert Elliot—Minto.
Sir Alexr. Ogilvie—Forglen.
1707. Hon. Jas. Erskine—Grange.
Jno. Murray—Bowhill.
1709. Dougal Stewart—Blairhall.
Sir Fras. Grant—Cullen.
1710. Sir Jas. Mackenzie—Royston.
David Erskine—Dun.
1711. Sir W. Calderwood—Polton.
1712. Jas. Hamilton—Pencaitland.
1714. Hon. Jas. Elphinstone—Coupar; aft. ld. Balmerino.
Sir Andr. Hume—Kimerghame.
1718. Sir Walter Pringle—Newhall.
1724. Andr. Fletcher—Milton.
1726. Sir Gilbert Elliot—Minto.
Hew Dalrymple—Drummore.
1727. Patrick Campbell—Monzie.
1729. Jno. Pringle—Haining.
1730. Alexr Fraser—Strichen.
1732. Patrick Grant—Elchies.
1733. Hon. Jno. Sinclair—Murkle.
1734. Alexr., E. of Leven.
1735. Sir Jas. Fergusson—Kilkerran.
1737. Robt. Dundas—Arniston.
1744. Chas. Areskine or Erskine—Tinwald.
1746. Hon. Patrick Boyle—Shewalton.
1749. Jas. Graham—Easdale.
1751. Geo. Sinclair—Newhall.
1752. Hy. Home—Kames.
1754. Alexr. Boswell—Auchinleck.
Wm. Grant—Preston Grange.
Robt. Pringle—Edgefield.
1754. Thos. Hay—Huntington.
1755. Andr. Macdowal—Bankton.
Patrick Wedderburn—Chesterhall
Geo. Carre—Nisbet.
1756. Geo. Brown—Coalston.
1759. Andr. Pringle—Alemoore.
1761. Jas. Veitch—Elliock.
Jas. Erskine.
1762. Jno. Campbell—Stonefield.
1764. Jas. Ferguson—Pitfour.
Fras. Garden—Gardenston.
Robt. Bruce—Kennet.
1766. Sir David Dalrymple—Hailes.
Thos. Miller—Barskimming, aft. Glenlee.
1767. Jas. Burnett—Monboddo.
1775. Alexr. Lockhart—Covington.
1776. David Ross—Ankerville.
Robt. MacQueen—Braxfield.
1777. David Dalrymple—Westhall.
1782. David Rae—Eskgrove.
Jno. Swinton—Swinton.
1783. Alexr. Murray—Henderland.
Hon. Alexr. Gordon—Rockville.
1786. Wm. Nairne—Dunsinnan; aft. bt.
1787. Jno. Maclaurin—Dreghorn.
1792. Alexr. Abercromby—Abercromby.
Wm. Craig—Craig.
1793. Wm. Baillie—Polkemmet.
David Smythe—Methven.
1795. Sir Wm. Miller—Glenlee.
1796. Allan Maconochie—Meadowbank.
Robt. Cullen—Cullen.
1797. Sir Wm. Honyman, bt.—Armadale.
1799. Wm. MacLeod Bannatyne—Bannatyne.
Claud Irvine Boswell—Balmuto.
Geo. Ferguson—Hermand.
1802. Alexr. Fraser Tytler—Woodhouselee.
1805. Wm. Robertson—Robertson.
1806. Chas. Hay—Newton.
1809. Archd. Campbell—Succoth.
1811. David Boyle—Boyle.
Robt. Craigie—Craigie.
David Williamson—Balgray.
Adam Gillies—Gillies.
1813. David Monypenny—Pitmilly.
David Cathart—Alloway.
David Douglas—Reston.
1816. Jas. Wolfe Murray—Cringletie.
1819. Alexr. Maconochie—Meadowbank.
1822. Wm. Erskine—Kinneder.
Joshua Hy. Mackenzie—Mackenzie.
1823. Jno. Clerk—Eldin.
1825. Jno. Hay Forbes—Medwyn.
1826. Geo. Cranstoun—Corehouse.
Alexr. Irving—Newton.
1829. Jno. Fullerton—Fullerton.
Sir Jas. W. Moncreiff, bt.—Moncreiff.
1834, Fras. Jeffrey—Jeffrey.
Hy. Cockburn—Cockburn.
1837. Jno. Cunninghame—Cunninghame.
1839. Sir Jno. Archd. Murray—Murray.
1840. Jas. Ivory—Ivory.
1842. Alexr. Wood—Wood.

1843. Patrick Robertson—Robertson.
1850. Thos. Maitland—Dundrennan, Feb. 6, **G.**
1851. Andr. Rutherfurd — Rutherfurd, Apr. 7, **G.**
Duncan M'Neill—Colonsay, May 15, **G.**; aft. ld. Colonsay.
Jno. Cowan—Cowan, June 23, **G.**
1852. Adam Anderson—Anderson, May 18, **G.**
John Marshall — Curriehill, *vice* Forbes, Nov. 3, **G.**
1853. Geo. Deas—Deas, *vice* Cunninghame, May 25, **G.**
Robt. Handyside—Handyside, *vice* Anderson, Nov. 15, **G.**
Hercules Jas. Robertson—Benholme, *vice* Fullerton, Dec. 7, **G.**
1854. Chas. Neaves—Neaves, *vice* Cockburn, May 13, **G.**
1855. Jas. Craufurd — Ardmillan, *vice* Rutherfurd, Jan. 10, **G.**
Thos. Mackenzie—Mackenzie, *vice* Robertson, Jan. 29, **G.**
1858. Wm. Penney—Kinloch, *vice* Handyside, May 7, **G.**
1859. Chas. Baillie—Jervis Woode, *vice* Murray, Apr. 15, **G.**
1862. Robt. Macfarlane — Ormidale, *vice* Wood, Jan. 13, **G.**
Edwd Fras. Maitland—Barcaple, *vice* Ivory, Nov. 10, **G.**
1865. David Mure—Mure, *vice* Mackenzie, Jan. 11, **G.**
1868. Geo. Dundas—Manor, *vice* Marshall Oct. 14. **G.**
1870. Adam Gifford—Gifford, *vice* Dundas. Jan. 26, **G.**
Donald Mackenzie—Mackenzie, *vice* Maitland, Mar. 16, **G.**
1872. Alexr. Burns Shand—Shand, *vice* Penney, Dec. 9, **G.**
1874. Geo. Young—Young, *vice* Cowan, Feb. 19, **G.**
John Millar—Craighill, *vice* Baillie, July 15, **G.**
John Marshall — Curriehill, *vice* Robertson, Oct. 29, **G.**
1875. Andrew Rutherfurd-Clark—Rutherfurd-Clark, *vice* Mackenzie.
1876. Jas. Adam—Adam, *vice* Craufurd.
1880. Robt. Lee — Lee, *vice* Neaves, May 5, **G.**
1881. Patrick Fraser—Fraser, *vice* Macfarlane, Feb. 8, **G.**
John McLaren — McLaren, *vice* Gifford, Aug. 15, **G.**
1882. Alexr. Smith Kinnear—Kinnear, *vice* Marshall, Jan. 2, **G.**
1885. John Trayner—Trayner, *vice* Deas, Feb. 26, **G.**
1888. Hy. Jas. Moncrieff—Wellwood, *vice* Millar, Nov. 1, **G.**

LORDS JUSTICES GENERAL AND JUDGES OF THE HIGH COURT OF JUSTICIARY.

THE Lord Chief Justice, or, as he was called in Scotland, the Lord Justice General, was placed next in rank to the lord chancellor. He was anciently, before the court of session was erected, the grand justiciar of Scotland, and his court was originally the only sovereign court of the kingdom, and had a great part of that jurisdiction which now belongs to the court of session. Even after the erection of that court several civil causes came before it; but at length its powers were confined to criminal matters alone, and the Lord Justice General was empowered to name his own deputies. In 1671 the court of justiciary was constituted, nearly as it now stands, by a commission under the great seal, afterwards ratified by regulations made in 1672. The kingdom was divided into three circuits, to which the judges went once a year; but after the suppression of the heritable jurisdictions, the assizes were held twice a year. Anciently the kingdom was divided into two justiciaries, viz. the north and the south of the Frith of Forth. The office of Lord Justice General was hereditary in several families; but the family of Argyll surrendered it to the crown, for a valuable consideration, in 1628, and this arrangement was ratified by parliament in 1633. From that time it was disposed of either for life, or during pleasure, by a commission under the great seal, until the year 1836, when, under

11 Geo. IV. and 1 Wm. IV., cap. 69, the office was united with that of Lord President of the Court of Session.

The High Court of Justiciary was originally composed of the Lord Justice General, or first Jndge of Justiciary, the Lord Justice Clerk, or second Judge of Justiciary, and five other judges or commissioners selected from the Lords of Session; but by 50 & 51 Vict., cap. 35 (Sept. 16, 1887), the constitution and procedure of the court were remodelled, and all the Lords of Session are now commissioners of the High Court of Justiciary.

The Lords Justices General or First Judges of Justiciary.

* * Argadus, capt. of Argyll; in the reign of Ethodius.
* * Comes Dunetus; in the reign of William.
* * The E. of Fife.
* * Wm. Cummin.
* * David, E. of Huntingdon.
* * Walter Cliffer.
1216. Allan; to Alexander II.
1224. Wm. Cummin, E. of Buchan.
1227. Walter Oliphant.
* * Walter, son to Allan; seneschal or steward of Scotland.
1239. Walter, E. of Ross; N. of Forth.
1243. David de Lindsay; S. of Forth.
* * Alexr., seneschal to Alexander II.
* * Hugh de Berkeley; S. of Forth.
1253. Alexr. Cummin, E. of Buchan.
1366. Robt. de Erskine; N. of Forth.
1426. Robt. de Lauder; N. of Forth.
1446. Patrick de Ogilvy; N. of Forth.
1457. John, ld. Lindsay de Byres; N. of Forth.
* * Wm. E. of Orkney; S. of Forth.
1477. John Haldane, of Gleneagles; N. of Forth.
* * Patrick, ld. Hales, and Robt., ld. Lyle.
* * Andrew, E. of Craufurd, and Geo., E. of Huntly.
1488. Robt., ld. Lyle.
1489. John, ld. Glamis, and John, ld. Drummond.
1492. Robt., ld. Lyle, *again*, and John, ld. Glamis, *again*.
1494. John, ld. Drummond, *again*.
1504. Andrew, ld. Gray, and John, ld. Kennedy.
1514. Colin, 3rd E. of Argyll.
1526. Archd. Douglas, of Kilspindie.
1537. Archd., 4th E. of Argyll.
1567. Gilespick, E. of Argyll; heritably.
1578. Colin, 6th E. of Argyll.
1589. Archd., 7th E. of Argyll; he exch. the office for the heritable lieutenancy of Argyllshire, and most of the Isles.
1628. Wm., E. of Menteith.
* * Sir Wm. Elphinstone.
1642. Sir Thos. Hope, jun., of Carse.
1646. Wm., E. of Glencairn.
1649. John, E. of Cassilis.
1663. John, E., aft. M. of Athole.
1678. Sir Geo. Mackenzie, bt., aft. visc Tarbat and E. of Cromartie.
Sir Archd. Primrose, of Carrington.
1680. Wm., E., aft. M. and D. of Queensberry.
1682. Jas., E. of Perth.
1692. Robt., E. of Lothian.
1703. Geo., E. of Cromartie.
1710. Archd., E. of Isla, aft. D. of Argyll; for life.
1761. John, M. of Tweeddale.
1763. Chas., D. of Queensberry and Dover.
1778. David, visc. Stormont, aft. E. of Mansfield.
1795. Jas., D. of Montrose; after whose death, in 1836, this office was united with that of the ld. pres. ct. sess.

For subsequent Lord Justices General, see "Lord Presidents of the Court of Session," *ante*, p. 516.

Lord Justice Clerks or Second Judges of Justiciary.

See List, *ante*, p. 516.

Other Judges or Commissioners of Justiciary.

* * Sir Gilbert Elliott—Minto.
* * Hy. Dalrymple—Drummore.
* * Alexr. Fraser—Strichen.
* * Patrick Grant—Elchies.
* * Sir Jas. Ferguson—Kilkerran.
* * Chas. Arskine, or Erskine—Tinewald
* * Hy. Home—Kames.
* * Alexr. Boswell—Auchinleck.

* * Wm. Grant—Preston Grange.
* * Geo. Brown—Coalston.
* * Andrew Pringle—Alemoore.
* * John Campbell—Stonefield.
* * Fras. Garden—Gardenston.
* * Robt. Bruce—Kennet.
* * Sir David Dalrymple—Hailes.
* * Robt. Mc.Queen—Braxfield.
* * David Rae—Eskgrove.
* * Sir Wm. Nairn, bt.—Dunsinnan.
* * Wm. Craig—Craig.
* * Allan Maconnochie—Meadowbank.
* * Robt. Cullen—Cullen.
* * Sir Wm. Honyman, bt.—Armadale.

* * *

1811. David Boyle—Boyle, Feb. 23, **G.**
1819. Alexr. Maconochie—Meadowbank.
1824. Joshua Hy. Mackenzie—Mackenzie.
1829. Sir Jas. W. Moncreiff—Moncreiff.
1830. John Hay Forbes—Medwyn.
1837. Hy. Cockburn—Cockburn.
1843. Alexr. Wood—Wood, Nov. 15, **G.**
1849. Jas. Ivory—Ivory.
1851. Duncan McNeill—Colonsay, aft. ld. Colonsay, May 30, **G.**
John Cowan—Cowan, June 23, **G.**
1852—Adam Anderson—Anderson, May 18, **G.**
1853. Robt. Handyside—Handyside, Nov. 15, **G.**
1854. John Deas—Deas, May 13, **G.**
1855. Jas. Craufurd—Ardmillan, June 16, **G.**
1858. Chas. Neaves—Neaves, May 7, **G.**
1862. Chas. Baillie—Jervis Woode, June 14, **G.**
1874. Geo. Young—Young, Feb. 19, **G.**
David Mure—Mure, Apr. 1, **G.**
1876. John Millar—Craighill, Mar. 4, **G.**
Jas. Adam—Adam, Dec. 2, **G.**
1885. John McLaren — McLaren, Feb. 26, **G.**

All the Lords of Session are now, under 50 & 51 Vict., cap. 35, Commissioners of the High Court of Justiciary. See Introduction, *ante*, pp. 521–2.

JUDGES OF THE COURT OF EXCHEQUER OF SCOTLAND.

The old Scotch Court of Exchequer was reserved by the Act of Union, but was superseded on May 1, 1708, by a new court established by 6 Anne, cap. 53 (cap. 26, Ruffhead's statutes). This Court was at first composed of a chief and four puisne barons; but by 1 Wm. IV., cap. 69 (1830), it was provided that no vacancies should be filled up until the court was reduced to a chief and one puisne baron; and by 2 Wm. IV., cap. 54 (1832), it was provided that no new judges should be appointed, and that on the death of the last Exchequer Judge the duties should be performed by one of the lords of session to be appointed by the crown. This arrangement was modified by 2 & 3 Vict., cap. 36 (1839), which provided that the duties of Exchequer Judges should be performed by two of the lords of session to be fixed by themselves in rotation; and by 19 & 20 Vict., cap. 56 (1856), a further alteration took place, and it was provided that the duties should be performed by one of the lords of session, to be appointed by the crown, and styled the Lord Ordinary in Exchequer. The administrative duties of the Court of Exchequer were transferred to the Treasury by 3 & 4 Wm. IV., cap. 13 (1833). The old Exchequer Court came to an end on the death of Baron Murray in 1838. Adam Gillies (Lord Gillies), a lord of session, was then appointed under 2 Wm. IV., cap. 54, and on his death in 1839 the other lords of session were appointed in rotation under 2 & 3 Vict., cap. 36.

Chief Barons of the Exchequer of Scotland.

From the accession of George III. to the extinction of the office.

* * — Idle.
* * Robt. Ord.
1775. Jas. Montgomery.
1801. Robt. Sanders Dundas, May 12.
1819. Sir Saml. Shepherd, June 15, **G.**
1830. Jas. Abercrombie, Feb. 20, **G.**; *d.* 1832.

No further appointments. See Introduction, *supra*.

Barons of the Exchequer of Scotland.

From the accession of George III. to the extinction of the office.

In 1760. Edwd. Edline.
Jno. Maule.
Jno. Grant.
Jas. Erskine.
1761. Wm. Mure, *vice* Edline.
Sir Geo. Wynne Allanson, bt., *vice* Erskine.
1776. Hon. Fletcher Norton, *vice* Allanson.
Sir Jno. Dalrymple, bt., *vice* Maule.
1777. Cosmo Gordon, *vice* Grant.
1781. David Stewart-Moncreiffe, *vice* Maule.
1790. Archd. Cockburn, *vice* Moncreiffe.
1801. Geo. Buchan Hepburn, *vice* Gordon.
1809. Jas. Clerk, May 27, **G.**; *vice* Cockburn; res.
1814. Wm. Adam, Nov. 8, **G.**
1820. Sir Patrick Murray, bt.; *d.* 1838.

No further appointments. See Introduction, *ante*, p. 523.

JUDGES OF THE ADMIRALTY COURT OF SCOTLAND.

By the Act of Union the Scottish Admiralty Court was to be continued until regulated by parliament. It was afterwards gradually shorn of its jurisdiction, and ultimately abolished by 6 Geo. IV., cap. 120 (1825). Its prize jurisdiction was transferred to the English Admiralty Court, and by 11 Geo. IV. and 1 Wm. IV., cap 69 (1830) its civil jurisdiction was transferred to the Court of Session and the Sheriff Court; and its criminal jurisdiction to the Court of Justiciary and the Sheriff Court.

Judges of the Admiralty Court of Scotland.

* * Alexr. Cockburn.
1790. Geo. Buchan Hepburn.
1801. R. H. Cay.
1810. Jno. Burnett.
1811. Jas. Wolfe Murray, Feb. 23, **G.**
1816. Jno. Connell, aft. sir J., July 20, **G.**

Office abolished Oct. 5, 1830, *ut supra*.

LORD CLERK REGISTERS OF SCOTLAND.

The Clerk Register was anciently the principal clerk in the kingdom; from him all other clerks, who were his deputies, derived their immediate authority, and he himself acted as clerk to the parliament and council. He was called *Clericus Rotulorum*, because the proceedings of parliament, and the minutes and judgments of other courts, were written upon rolls of parchment (hence the term *Rotuli Parliamenti*), which were preserved by him in the public archives. By the Treaty of Union, the preservation of the registers was particularly provided for; and the return of the election of the sixteen Scottish peers to the British parliament was ordered to be made by the Clerk Register, or by two of the clerks of session deputed by him for that purpose.

Lord Clerk Registers of Scotland.

* * Wm., abp. of St. Andrew's.
* * Simon de Quincy.
* * Nicolaus, *clericus* to Malcolm IV.
* * Wm. de Bosch, and Hugo.
* * Galfrid and Gregory; to Alexander II.
1253. Willielmus Capellanus, and Alexr. de Carrerg.
All the preceding were called *cler. dom. regis.*
1323. Robt. de Dunbar, *cler. rotul.*
* * Jno. Gray; to Robert II.

1426. Jno. Schives.
1440. Richd. Craig, vicar of Dundee.
1442. Geo. Shoreswood, rect. of Culter.
1449. Sir Jno. Methven.
1450. Jno. Arouse, archdn. of Glasgow.
1455. Nicol Otterburn.
1466. Fergus Macdowall.
1471. David Guthrie, of Guthrie.
1473. Jno. Laing, rect. of Newlands.
1477. Alexr. Inglis, chanc. of see of Aberdeen.
1482. Patrick Leith, canon of Glasgow.
* * Alexr. Scot, rect. of Wigtoun.
1488. Wm. Hepburn, vicar of Linlithgow.
1489. Richd. Muirhead, dean of Glasgow.
1492. Jno. Fraser, rect. of Restalrig.
1497. Walter Drummond, dean of Dumblane.
1500. David Dunbar, archdn. of St. Andrew's; aft. bp. of Aberdeen.
* * Sir Stephen Lockhart; to James IV.
1531. Sir Jas. Foulis, of Collington.
1548. Sir Thos. Marjoribanks, of Ratho.
1554. Jas. Macgill, parson of Flisk; depr. for his share in David Rizzio's murder in 1566.
1566. Sir Jas. Balfour.
1567. Jas. Macgill, *again*.
1577. Sir Alexr. Hay, of Easter Kennet.
1594. Sir Jno. Skene, of Curriehill.
1598. Sir Jno. Skene, and his son, Jas. Skene.
1612. Sir Thos. Hamilton, aft. E. of Haddington
* * Sir Alexr. Hay, of Whitburgh.
1616. Sir Geo. Hay, aft. E. of Kinnoull.
1622. Sir Jno. Hamilton, of Magdalens.
1632. Sir Alexr. Hay, of Lands.
1641. Sir Alexr. Gibson, jun., of Durie.
1649. Sir Archd. Johnston, of Warriston.
1660. Sir Archd. Primrose, of Chester.
1681. Sir Geo. Mackenzie, bt., aft. visc. Tarbat, and E. of Cromartie.
1689. John, ld. Belhaven, and four others.
1692. Sir Geo. Mackenzie, *again*.
1696. Chas., E. of Selkirk.
1702. John, M. of Tweeddale.
1704. Jas. Johnston.
1706. Sir Jas. Murray, of Philiphaugh.
1708. David, E. of Glasgow.
1714. Archd., E. of Isla, aft. D. of Argyll.
1716. Jas., D. of Montrose, July.
Alexr., ld. Polwarth, aft. E. of Marchmont, Dec.
1733. Chas., E. of Selkirk.
1739. Wm., M. of Lothian.
1756. Hon. Alexr. Hume Campbell.
1761. Jas., E. of Morton.
1767. Lord Fredk. Campbell, son of the D. of Argyll.
1777. Lord Fredk. Campbell, app. for life; *d.* June 1816.
1821. Wm. Dundas.
1845. Jas. Andrew, E., aft. M. of Dalhousie, Dec. 12, **G.**
1862. Sir Wm. Gibson Craig, bt., July 3, **G.**
1879. Geo. Fredk., E. of Glasgow, Feb. 21, **G.**

LORD ADVOCATES OF SCOTLAND.

The Lord Advocate holds much the same position in Scotland as the Attorney General in England. His business is to pursue and defend in all causes wherein the sovereign has an interest. His office is very honourable, and he is, by virtue of it, styled Lord. And, as it was decided, in 1685, in the parliament of Paris (on which the Court of Session is modelled), that the king's advocate might at the same time be a judge, so in like manner was it allowed in Scotland; and both Sir William Oliphant and Sir John Nesbit were Lords Advocate and Lords of Session at the same time. This practice has, however, now been long discontinued.

Lords Advocate of Scotland.

Those marked * afterwards became Judges. See lists of Judges, *ante*.

1483. Jno. Ross, of Mongrenan.
1494. Jas. Henderson, of Fordel.
1503. Richd. Lawson, of Heirigs.
1521. Jas. Wishart, of Pittarrow.
1525. *Adam Otterburn, of Redhall.
1527. *Jno. (? Jas.) Foulis, and Adam Otterburn, *again*.
1533. *Adam Otterburn, *again*. and Hy. Lauder, of St. Germains.
* * *Hy. Balnavis, to Q. Mary.

* * Thos. Cummin.
1561. *Jno. Spence, of Condie.
* * *Robt. Crichton (or Creighton), of Elliock.
1573. David Brothwick, of Loch-hill.
1582. *David MacGill, of Cranston Riddel, son to sir Jas., ld. clk. regr.
1589. Jno. Skene.
1594. Wm. Hart, of Levelands.
Andr. Logie.
1595. *Sir Thos. Hamilton, aft. E. of Haddington.
*David Macgill, *again*.
* * *Sir Thos. Hamilton, *again*.
1612. *Sir Wm. (? Jas.) Oliphant, of Newton.
1626. *Thos. (? Jno.) Hope, of Craighall, aft. sir T.
1641. *Sir Archd. Johnston, of Warriston.
* * Sir Thos. Nicholson.
1659. *Sir Archd. Primrose.
1661. Sir Jno. Fletcher.
16—. *Sir Jno. Nisbet.
* * *Sir Geo. Mackenzie.
1687. *Jno. Dalrymple, aft. E. of Stair.
*Sir Geo. Mackenzie, *again*.
1689. Sir Wm. Jas. Stewart.
1709. Sir David Dalrymple
1720. *Robt. Dundas, of Arniston (No. 1).
1725. *Duncan Forbes, of Culloden.
1737. *Chas. Areskine, or Erskine, of Tinwald.
1742. *Robt. Craigie, of Glendoick.
1746. *Wm. Grant, of Preston Grange.
1754. *Robt. Dundas, of Arniston (No. 2).
1760. Thos. Miller, of Glenlee.
1766. Jas. Montgomery, aft. sir J. (No. 1).
1775. Hy. Dundas, aft. visc. Melville.
1783. Hon. Hy. Erskine.
1784. *Ilay Campbell of Succoth, aft. sir I., bt.
1789. Robt. Dundas of Arniston (No. 3); son of the 2nd, grandson of the 1st Robt.
1801. Chas. Hope of Granton.
1804. Sir Jas. Montgomery, bt. (No. 2).
1806. Hon. Hy. Erskine, *again*.
1807. Archd. Colquhoun.
1816. *Alexr. (? Allan) Maconochie.
1819. Sir Wm. Rae, bt.
1830. *Fras. Jeffrey.
1834. *Jno. Archd. Murray, aft. sir J.
Sir Wm. Rae, bt., *again*, Dec. 19, **G.**
1835. *Jno. Archd, Murray, *again*, Apr. 20, **G.**
1839. *Andr. Rutherfurd.
1841. Sir Wm. Rae, bt., *again*, Sept. 4, **G.**
1842. *Duncan M'Neill.
1846. *Andr. Rutherfurd, *again*.
1851. *Jas. Moncrieff, Apr. 8, **G.**
1852. *Adam Anderson, Feb. 28, **G.**
*Jno. Inglis, May 19, **G.**
*Jas. Moncrieff, *again*, Dec. 30, **G.**
1858. *Jno. Inglis, *again*, Mar. 1, **G.**
*Chas. Baillie, July 10, **G.**
1859. *David Mure, Apr. 15, **G.**
*Jas. Moncrieff, *again*, June 24, **G.**
1866. *Geo. Patton, July 12, **G.**
1867. *Edwd. Strathearn Gordon, Feb. 28, **G.**
1868. *Jas. Moncrieff, *again*, Dec 10, **G.**
1869. *Geo. Young, Oct. 14, **G.**
1874. *Edwd. Strathearn Gordon, *again*, aft. ld. Gordon, and ld. app., Feb. 26, **G.**
1876. *Wm. Watson, aft. ld. Watson and ld. app, Oct. 13, **G.**
1880. *Jno. McLaren, May 5, **G.**
1881. Jno. Blair Balfour, Aug. 19, **G.**
1885. *Jno. Hay Athole Macdonald, July 2, **G.**
1886. J. B. Balfour, *again*, Feb. 13, **G.**
*J. H. A. Macdonald, *again*, Aug. 6, **G.**
1888. Jas. Patrick Bannerman Robertson. Oct. 24, **G.**

SOLICITORS GENERAL OF SCOTLAND.

THE Solicitor General of Scotland is the crown counsel next in dignity to the Lord Advocate. His office cannot be traced further back than the Union, and the list for the present work has only been procured from 1775.

SOLICITORS GENERAL OF SCOTLAND.

From the year 1775 to the present time.

Those marked † were afterwards Lords Advocates, see list, *ante*, p. 525, where their subsequent promotion is noted. Those marked * afterwards became Judges. See lists of Judges, *ante*.

1775. *Alexr. Murray, of Henderland.
1783. †*Ilay Campbell; of Succoth, aft. sir I., bt.
1789. Robt. Blair of Avonton.
1806. *John Clerk, of Elden.
1807. *David Boyle, of Shewalton.

1811. *David Monypenny, of Pitmilly.
1813. †*Alexr. Maconochie, of Meadowbank.
1810. Jas. Wedderburn, July 20, **G.**
1825. *John Hope.
1830. *Hy. Cockburn.
1834. Andr. Skene.
†*Duncan M'Neill.
1835. *John Cunninghame.
1837. †*Andr. Rutherfurd.
1839. *Jas. Ivory.
1840. *Thos. Maitland of Dundrennan.
1841. †*Duncan M'Neill.
1842. †*Adam Anderson
1846. *Ths.Maitland,ofDundrennan,*again.*
1850. †*Jas. Moncreiff, Feb. 7, **G.**
1851. *John Cowan, Apr. 18, **G.**
*Geo. Deas, June 28, **G.**
1852. †*John Inglis, Feb. 28, **G.**
*Chas. Neaves, May 24, **G.**
1853. *Robt. Handyside, Jan. 17, **G.**
*Jas. Craufurd, Nov. 16, **G.**
1855. *Thos. Mackenzie, Jan. 11, **G.**
*Edwd. Fras. Maitland, Feb. 14, **G.**
1858. †*Chas. Baillie, Mch. 17, **G.**
†*David Mure, July 12, **G.**
1859. †*Geo. Patton, May 3, **G.**
*Edwd. Fras. Maitland, *again* June 27, **G.**
1862. †*Geo. Young, Nov. 11, **G.**
1866. †*Edwd. Strathearn Gordon, aft. ld. Gordon, and ld. app., July 12, **G.**
1867 *John Millar, Mar. 6, **G.**
1868. †*Geo. Young, *again*, Dec. 14, **G.**
1869. *Andr. Rutherfurd-Clark, Oct. 14, **G.**
1874. *John Millar, *again*, Mar. 4, **G.**
†*Wm. Watson, July 21, **G.**
1876. †*Jno. Hay Athole Macdonald, Dec 5, **G.**
1880. †John Blair Balfour, May 6, **G.**
1881. Alexr. Asher, Aug. 19, **G.**
1885. †Jas. Patrick Bannerman Robertson, July 2, **G.**
1886. Alexr. Asher, *again*, Feb. 13, **G.**
†Jas. Patrick Bannerman Robertson, *again*, Aug. 6, **G.**
1888. Moir Tod Stormont Darling, Oct. 27, **G.**

DEANS OF THE FACULTY OF ADVOCATES.

THE Faculty or Society of Advocates in Scotland dates from the year 1532, but the profession of advocate had existed for many years previously. The Faculty is presided over by a Dean, who is elected annually, but who is frequently chosen for several years in succession.

DEANS OF FACULTY OF SCOTLAND.

From the year 1801.

1801. Robt. Blair, of Avonton.
1808. Matth. Ross.
1823. Geo. Cranstoun.
1826. Sir Jas. W. Moncreiff, bt.
1829. Fras. Jeffrey.
1830. John Hope.
1841. Alexr. Wood.
1842. Patrick Robertson.
1843. Duncan M'Neill.
1851. Adam Anderson.
1852. John Inglis.
1858. Jas. Moncreiff.
1869. Edwd. Strathearn Gordon.
1874. Andr. Rutherfurd-Clark.
1875. Wm. Watson.
1876. Robt. Horn.
1878. Patrick Fraser.
1881. Alexr. Smith Kinnear.
1882. John Hay Athole Macdonald.
1885. John Blair Balfour.
1886. Wm. Mackintosh.

ARCHBISHOPS AND BISHOPS OF SCOTLAND.

THE EPISCOPAL CHURCH OF SCOTLAND was the established Church of that country down to the period of the Reformation. From that time it had a chequered existence, being alternately abolished and restored until it was finally disestablished at the Revolution. The history of its vicissitudes is too long to be even epitomised here, but a full account will be found in Burton's *History of Scotland* and in the somewhat numerous histories of the Scottish Church.

PART I.—ARCHBISHOPS AND BISHOPS OF SCOTLAND BEFORE THE REVOLUTION.

Scotland had two Archbishoprics—

I.—St. Andrew's.

to which were suffragan the sees of—

Aberdeen.	Dunblane.	Moray.
Brechin.	Dunkeld.	Orkney.
Caithness.	Edinburgh.	Ross.

II.—Glasgow.

to which were suffragan the sees of—

Argyll.	Galloway.	The Isles.

DIOCESE OF ST. ANDREW'S.

Abernethy, in Perthshire, was the metropolis of the kingdom of the Picts. The collegiate church there was dedicated to St. Bridget, or St. Bryde, who died about 523. Kenneth III., having conquered the Picts, translated the see from Abernethy, and called it St. Andrew's, and the bishop was styled *Maximus Scotorum Episcopus*. It was erected into an Archbishopric in 1470, by Pope Paul II.

Bishops of St. Andrew's.
According to Sir R. Sibbald.

* * Adrian; killed by the Danes, and buried in the island of May, in 872.
872. Kellach I.; sat four years, Constantine II. being King.
877. Malisius I.; sat eight years, Gregory the Great being king.
904. Kellach II.
* * Malmore.
* * Malisius II.
* * Alwinus.
* * Malduinus.
* * Tuthaldus.
* * Fothadus; consec. in 954.
* * Gregorius; sat two years.
* * Turgot, prior of Durham; sat 25 or 26 years.
* * Godericus, who anointed king Edgar; *d.* 1107.
1120. Eadmerus, a monk of Canterbury.
1122. Robert, prior of Scone; founded the priory of St. Andrew's, and obtained land and many privileges for it from David I.
1159. Walter, abb. of Melrose, elected; but did not accept.
* * Ernald, abb. of Kelso; legate in Scotland for the pope; founded the cathedr. ch. of St. Andrew's, but *d.* soon after it was begun.
1163. Richard, chapl. to Malcolm IV.
1178. { John Scot, archdn. of St. Andrew's. / Hugh, chapl. to king William. } A double election.*
1188. Roger (son of the E. of Leicester); ld. chanc.

* John was elected bishop, but the king opposed him, and caused his chaplain, Hugh, to be consecrated. John went to Rome to plead his cause, and the Pope (Alexander III.) was so convinced of the justness of it, that he sent him home with a nuncio, who made Matthew, bishop of Aberdeen, consecrate him in the abbey of Holyrood House. Still the king continued inflexible, and John went a second time to Rome, and continued seven years in voluntary exile. The pope was about to interdict the kingdom; but John prevailed with him to desist, and the bishopric of Dunkeld falling vacant, the king agreed that John should have it, and he accepted it.

1202. Wm. Malvoisine ; tr. from Glasgow ; ld. chanc.
1233. David Benham, grt. chambn. to the king.
1253. Abel, archdn. of St. Andrew's.
1255. Gameline, archdn. of St. Andrew's ; ld. chanc.
1272. Wm. Wiseheart, archdn. of St. Andrew's ; ld. chanc.
1279. Wm. Fraser, dean of Glasgow ; ld. chanc.
1298. Wm. Lamberton, chanc. of diocese of Glasgow.
1328. Jas. Bennet, archdn. of St. Andrew's.
1332. Wm. Bell, D. of Dunkeld, elect. ; but the pope refused to confirm the choice.
See vacant 9 years.
1341. Wm. Landell, rect. of Kinkell.
1383. Stephen de Paye, prior of St. Andrew's ; taken prisoner at sea by the English, on his way to Rome ; *d.* at Alnwick, soon after his election.
* * Walter Trail, canon of St. Andrew's ; app. by the pope without an election ; built the castle of St. Andrew's.
1401. Thos. Stuart (son to Robert II.) ; archdn. of St. Andrew's.
1404. Gilbert Greenlaw, bp. of Aberdeen, ld. chanc. ; elect., but
* * Hy. Wardlaw, prec. of the see of Glasgow ; being at Avignon, he was preferred to this see. instead of Gilbert, bp. of Aberdeen, and was consec. there the same year.
1440. Jas. Kennedy ; tr. from Dunkeld ; ld. chanc. ; a younger son of Jas. Kennedy of Dunure, by the lady Mary, countess of Angus, dau. of Robert III.

Archbishops of St. Andrew's.

1466. Patrick Graham, tr. from Brechin ; he took a journey to Rome, and procured this see to be made an archbishopric, in 1470, by pope Paul II., who made him his legate for Scotland.
1478. Wm. Schives, archdn. of St. Andrew's.
1497. Jas. Stuart, D. of Ross (second son of James III.), ld. chanc ; *d.* 1503.
See vacant 6 years.
1509. Alexr. Stuart (natural son of James IV.) ; killed at the battle of Flodden in 1513.
1514. Andr. Foreman, tr. from Moray.
1522. Jas. Bethune, or Beaton, tr. from Glasgow ; ld. chanc.
1539. David Bethune, or Beaton, abb. of Aberbrothock, nephew to the last abp. ; at different times ld. pr. seal, ld. chanc., and a cardl. ; murd. Feb. 1, 1545.
1543. Jno. Hamilton, transl. from Dunkeld ; at different times ld. pr. seal, ld. treasr., and one of Q. Mary's pr. council ; hanged Apr. 1, 1570.
1572. Jno. Douglas, rector of the univ. of St. Andrew's ; the first protestant abp. here.
1576. Patrick Adamson, parson of Paisley ; *d.* 1591.
The see vacant, and its revenues bestowed on the D. of Lenox.
1606. Geo. Gladstanes, or Gladstone ; tr. from Caithness.
1615. Jno. Spottiswood, tr. from Glasgow ; ld. chanc. ; *d.* 1639.
See vacant 22 years.
1661. Jas. Sharp, prof. of Divinity at St. Andrew's ; murd. May 3, 1679, on Magus-muir, near St. Andrew's.
1679. Alexr. Burnet, tr. from Glasgow ; *d.* 1684.
1684. Arthur Ross, tr. from Glasgow ; the last abp. of this see ; ejected soon after the Revolution in 1688.

There were no post-Revolution bishops of this see.

DIOCESE OF ABERDEEN.

King Malcolm II., having gained a great victory over the Danes in 1010, resolved to found a new bishopric in token of his gratitude for his success, and pitched upon Mortlach, in Banffshire. The see was only inferior, in point of precedence, to St. Andrews, but its revenue was inconsiderable. Nectanus, the fourth and last prelate who sat at

34

Mortlach, was removed by David I., in 1139, to Old Aberdeen, whither the see was entirely transferred in 1154, and where it continued until the Revolution.

Bishops of Mortlach.

1015. St. Beanus.
* * Donortius; *d.* 1098.
* * Cormacus.
1106. Nectanus; he transf. the see to Aberdeen, *ut supra*.

Bishops of Aberdeen.

* * Edward.
* * Galfrid.
1164. Matth. de Kinninmund, archdn. of Lothian.
1200. John, prior of Kelso.
* * Adam Crail.
* * Matth. Scot, archdn. of St. Andrew's; ld. chanc.
1228. Gilbert de Stryvelin.
1238. Randolf de Lambley, abb. of Aberbrothock.
1247. Petre de Ramsay.
1256. Richd. de Potton.
1267. Hugh de Benham.
1281. Hy. le Clen.
1329. Alexr. Kinninmund (No. 1).
1345. Wm. de Deyn.
1351. Jno. Rait.
1357. Alexr. de Kinninmund (No. 2).
1382. Adam de Tinningham, dean of Aberdeen.
1390. Gilbert Greenlaw, ld. chanc.; elect. abp. of St. Andrew's; but the pope preferred Hy. Wardlaw to that see.
1424. Hy. de Leighton, tr. from Moray.
1442. Ingeram Lindsay.
1459. Thos. Spence, tr. from Galloway; ld. pr. seal.
1480. Robt. Blackadder, preb. of Glasgow; tr. to Glasgow.
1484. Wm. Elphinstone, tr. from Ross; at different times ld. chanc. and ld. pr. seal; he founded the university of Old Aberdeen, for which purpose he got a bull from Alexander VI. in 1494; *d.* 1514.
1515. Alexr. Gordon, prec. of Moray.
1518. Gavin Dunbar, archdn. of St. Andrew's.
1532. Wm. Stewart, dean of Glasgow; ld. treasr.; *d.* 1545.
* * Wm. Gordon, rect. of Clatt.
1577. David Cunningham, sub-dean of Glasgow; the first protestant bp. of this see; *d.* 1603.
1603. Peter Blackburn, rect. of St. Nicholas's church, Aberdeen.
1615. Alexr. Forbes, tr. from Caithness.
1635. Adam Ballenden, tr. from Dunblane; depr. by the assembly of Glasgow in 1638, when he retired into England, and *d.* soon after.
1661. David Mitchell, preb. of Westminster.
1662. Alexr. Burnet, chapl. to the garrison of Dunkirk; tr. to Glasgow.
* * Patrick Scougal, parson of Saltoun.
1682. Geo. Haliburton, tr. from Brechin; eject. soon after the Revolution, and *d.* 1715.

For post-Revolution bishops see *post*, p. 540.

DIOCESE OF BRECHIN.

This see was founded by David I. in 1150. There anciently existed here an abbey or convent of Culdees.

Bishops of Brechin.

1155. T. * * *
* * Sampson.
1178. Turpin.
1202. Radulfus; *d.* 1218.
1219. Robt. Mar.
* * Gregory, archdn. of Brechin.
* * Gilbert; *d.* 1249.
* * Albin, or Alwyn.
* * Wm. de Kilconcath, dean of Brechin; *d.* 1275.

* Edwd., a monk of Cupar, Angus.
284. Robt., archdn. of Brechin.
290. William.
304. Jno. de Kynninmonde, or Kinninmund.
328. Adam.
351. Philip.
354. Patrick de Leuchars, a rect. in East Lothian; ld. chanc.
384. Stephen.
401. Walter Forrester, canon of Aberdeen.
424. Dominus G * * *.
435. John de Carnoth.
456. Robert.
* Geo. Shoreswood, chanc. of the see of Dunkeld, and confessor to the king; ld. chanc.
463. Patrick Graham, tr. to St. Andrew's.
470. John Balfour.
* Walter Meldrum.
517. John Hepburn.
558. Donald Campbell, abb. of Cupar, Angus.
* John Sinclair, dean of Restalrig.
566. Alexr. Campbell; the first Protestant bp. of this see; he was made bp. when but a boy, by the interest of the E. of Argyll, to whom he alienated most of the revenues; *d.* 1606.
See vacant 4 years.
1610. Andr. Lamb, parson of Burntisland; tr. to Galloway.
1619. David Lindsay, parson of Dundee; tr. to Edinburgh.
1624 (?). Thos. Sydeserf, tr. to Galloway.
1634. Walter Whitford, or Whitworth, sub-dean of Glasgow, and rect. of Moffat; depr. by the assembly of Glasgow in 1638, and *d.* 1643.
1662. David Strachan, parson of Fettercairn.
1672. Robt. Laurie, dean of Edinburgh.
1678. Geo. Haliburton, parson of Cupar, Angus; tr. to Aberdeen.
1682. Robt. Douglas, dean of Glasgow; tr. to Dunblane.
1684. Alexr. Cairncross, tr. to Glasgow.
* * Jas. Drummond, parson at Muthil; eject. soon after the Revolution in 1688; *d.* 1695.

For post-Revolution bishops see *post*, p. 541.

DIOCESE OF CAITHNESS.

T is uncertain whether this see owes its foundation to Malcolm III. or ɔ Malcolm IV. Its seat was at Dornoch.

Bishops of Caithness.

150. Andrew.
185. John.
213. Adam, abb. of Melrose; murd. by the E. of Caithness.
222. St. Gilbert Moray, chambn. of Scotland; *d.* 1245.
* A * *; *d.* 1260.
261. William.
* Walter de Baltroddi.
273. Nicholas; but the pope would not confirm him.
275. Archibald, archdn. of Moray; *d.* 1288.
290. Alan St. Edmunds; ld. chanc.
* Andrew.
301. Ferquhard de Belleganach.
* David; *d.* 1348.
348. Thos. de Fingask.
389. Alexr. Man.
410. Malcolm.
444. Robt. Strathbrock.
1447. Jno. Innes, dean of Ross; *d.* 1448.
1448. Wm. Moodie; *d.* 1460.
* * Prosper, elected bp., but res. in favour of
* * Jno. Sinclair, son of the E. of Caithness.*
1490. Andr. Stewart, abb. of Fearn, Ross, shire; ld. treasr.
1518. Andr. Stewart, son of the E. of Athol; tr. from Dunkeld.
1542. Robt. Stewart, brother of the E. of Lenox, and aft. E. of Lenox; prov. of Dumbarton; became a protestant, and retained the revenues of the see; he lived a long time privately at St. Andrew's. and *d.* there 1586.
See vacant 14 years.
1600. Geo. Gladstanes, or Gladstone, minister of St. Andrew's; tr. to St. Andrew's.

* Archbishop Spottiswood says that neither Prosper nor Sinclair was ever concrated; that the see continued vacant twenty-four years, and that the affairs of it ere governed by Adam Gordon, the dean, third son of the earl of Huntly.

1606. Alexr. Forbes, rect. of Fettercairn; tr. to Aberdeen, 1615.
The see vacant.
1624. Jno. Abernethy, parson of Jedburgh; depr. by the assembly of Glasgow, 1638.
1662. Patrick Forbes.
1680. Andr. Wood; tr. from the Isles eject. soon after the Revolutic in 1688, and *d.* at Dunba 1695.

For post-Revolution bishops see *post*, p. 541.

DIOCESE OF DUNBLANE.

In Dunblane, a small town in Strathallan, there existed anciently convent of Culdees, which David I. erected into an episcopal see abou the year 1142. The church was dedicated to St. Blaan, who had bee superior of the convent in the time of Kenneth III.; and from th saint the place took its name.

The list of the Bishops is very incorrect; but the fault is now beyon remedy.

Bishops of Dunblane.

* * M * *.
1160. Laurentius.
* * Simon.
* * Jonathan.
1210. William.
1220. Abraham.
* * Radulphus.
1230. Osbert.
1233. Clement.
1258. Robt. de Præbenda, dean of Dunblane.
* * Alpin.
1290. William.
1307. Nichs. de Balmyle; ld. chanc.
1319. Mauritius, abb. of Inchaffray.
1353. William.
1362. Walter Cambuslang.
* * Andreas.
* * Dougal.
1406. Finlay.
1420. Wm. Stephen, divinity reader at St. Andrew's.
1430. Michl. Ochiltree, dean of Dunblane.
1448. Robt. Lauder.
1459. Thomas.
1467. Jno. Hepburn.
1486. Jas. Chisholm, chapl. to Jas. III. res. in favour of his brother
1527. Wm. Chisholm (No. 1); he alienate great part of the revenues of th see, which he bestowed upon h kinsman, sir Jas. Chisholm, an on his illegitimate children.
1564. Wm. Chisholm (No. 2), nephew t the last bp; coadj. in 1561; fo feited his see, and withdrew t France, where he became a bp.
1575. Andr. Graham.
1606. Geo. Graham, parson of Scone tr. to Orkney.
1615. Adam Bellenden, rect. of Falkirk tr. to Aberdeen.
1636. *Jas. Wedderburn, prof. of divinit at St. Andrew's; depr. by th Assembly of Glasgow in 1638 *d.* 1639.
1661. Robt. Leighton, prof. of divinit at Edinburgh; tr. to Glasgow.
1673. Jas. Ramsay, dean of Glasgow tr. to Ross.
1684. Robt. Douglas; tr. from Brechin eject. soon after the Revolutic in 1688; *d.* 1716.

For post-Revolution bishops see *post*, p. 542.

DIOCESE OF DUNKELD.

Constantine III., king of the Picts, founded a monastery of Culdee here, which was dedicated to St. Columba, the patron saint of th nation. King David, or, as he is generally called, St. David, expelle

* In this bishop's time the prelates of Dunblane were made deans of the Chap Royal, which formerly appertained to the bishops of Galloway.

e Culdees, changed their church into a cathedral, and founded the see out the year 1127.

Bishops of Dunkeld.

* Gregory (No. 1); *d.* about 1169.
59. Richd. de Præbenda (No. 1).
77. Cormacus.
* Gregory (No. 2).
78. Walter de Bidun, ld. chanc.
00. Jno. Scot, archdn. of St. Andrew's. See note to that bishopric, *ante*, p. 528.
* Richd. de Præbenda (No. 2).
11. John of Leicester, archd. of Lothian; got part of his diocese disjoined to form the see of Argyll.
14. Hugh de Sigillo.
* Matth. Scot, ld. chanc.; tr. from Aberdeen.
* Gilbert.
36. Galfrid Liverance.
19. Richard.
50. David.
* Richd. de Inverkeithing, a preb. of this see.
2. Robt. de Stuteville, dean of Dunkeld.
38. Matth. de Crambeth.
9. Wm. Sinclair; bp. before this year. —*Keith.*
24. Walter.
51. Duncan.
56. John.
* Michl. Monymusk, gr. chambn. of Scotland.
7. Jno. Peebles, archdn. of St. Andrew's, and ld. chanc.
6. Robt. de Cairny.
36. Donald MacNaughton; *d.* on his way to Rome for confirmation.
38. Jas. Kennedy, abb. of Scone; tr. to St. Andrew's.
0. Alexr. Lawder.
1. Jas. Bruce, ld. chanc.; tr. to Glasgow.
1447. Wm. Turnbull, archdn. of Lothian, and ld. pr. seal; tr. to Glasgow.
1448. Jno. Raulston, dean of Dunkeld; kpr. of the pr. seal, sec. st., and ld. treasr.
1452. Thos. Lawder, prec. of Soutray.
1476. Jas. Livingtoun, dean of Dunkeld; ld. chanc.
1483. Alexr. Inglis, dean of Dunkeld, and kpr. of the rolls.
1484. Robert.
* * Geo. Brown, chanc. of the see of Aberdeen.
1515. Andr. Stuart (son of the E. of Athole); tr. to Caithness.
1516. Gavin Douglas, prov. of St. Giles's, Edinburgh; brother of the E. of Angus.
1527. Geo. Crichton, ld. kpr. pr. seal.
1545. Jno. Hamilton (natl. son of the E. of Arran), abb. of Paisley; tr. to St. Andrew's.
1550. Robt. Crichton (nephew to bp. Geo. Crichton); forfeited.
1571. Jas. Paton, the first Protestant bp. of this see; res.
1603. Peter Rollock, a ld. of sess.
1606. Jas. Nicholson, parson of Meigle.
1638. Alexr. Lindsay, parson of St. Mado's.
1662. Geo. Haliburton, parson of Perth.
1664. Hy. Guthrie, form. parson of Stirling, but depr. in 1648.
1677. Jas. Lindsay, min. of Perth.
1679. Andr. Bruce, archdn. of St. Andrew's; depr. in 1686; but aft. made bp. of Orkney, May, 1688.
1686. Jno. Hamilton; *d.* one of the ministers of Edinburgh, after the Revolution.

For post-Revolution bishops see *post*, p. 542.

DIOCESE OF EDINBURGH.

is see was founded by Charles I., when in Scotland, in 1633. The urch of St. Giles, in the city of Edinburgh, was made the cathedral.

Bishops of Edinburgh.

4. Wm. Forbes, one of the ministers of Edinburgh; *d.* same year.
David Lindsay; tr. from Brechin; depr. by the assembly of Glasgow, 1638.
2. Geo. Wiseheart, rect. of Newcastle-upon-Tyne.
1671. Alexr. Young, archdn. of St. Andrew's; tr. to Ross.
1679. John Patterson; tr. from Galloway; tr. to Glasgow.
1687. Alexr. Rose; tr. from Moray; eject. soon after the Revolution in 1688.

For post-Revolution bishops see *post*, p. 542.

DIOCESE OF MORAY.

THE bishopric of Moray was founded by king Malcolm III., surnam Canmore. The seat of the see was at Elgin, situated on the river Lossi about three miles from its mouth. The cathedral was dedicated to t Holy Trinity.

BISHOPS OF MORAY.

1115. Gregory.
* * William; made apostolic legate in 1159.
* * Felix; *d.* 1170.
1171. Simeon de Tonei, a monk of Melrose.
1187. Richard, chapln. to K. William.
1203. Brice, or Bricius, prior of Lesmahagow.
* * Andr. de Moravia.
1242. Simon, dean of Moray.
1253. Archd., dean of Moray.
1299. David Moray; founded the Scots' College at Paris.
1325. John Pilmore, bp.-elect of Ross.
1362. Alexr. Bar; whilst this prelate was bp., Alexr., E. of Buchan, youngest son of Robert II., burnt the cathedral church, and the whole town of Elgin, with the churches and hospitals.
1397. Wm. Spynie, chanter of Elgin.
1407. John Innes, archdn. of Caithness.
1414. Hy. Leighton, chanter of Moray; tr. to Aberdeen.
1425. David.
1429. Columba Dunbar.
1437. John Winchester (an Englishman), prov. of Lincluden, and ld. clk. regr.; often employed as ambass. to the English court.
1459. Jas. Stewart, ld. treasr.
1462. David Stewart (bro. to the last bp.); parson of Spynie.
1477. Wm. Tulloch; tr. from Orkney; pr. seal.
1482. Andr. Stewart, sub-dean of Glasgo ld. pr. seal; called "the Bla Knight of Lorn."
1501. Andr. Forman; tr. to St. Andrew
1516. Jas. Hepburn, abb. of Dunfermlin and ld. treasr.
1524. Robt. Schaw, abb. of Paisley.
1527. Alexr. Stuart, son of Alexr., D. Albany, son of James II. Katharine Sinclair, then his wi daur. of Wm., E. of Orkney a Caithness. He was abb. of Sco when advanced to this see.
1535. Patrick Hepburn, son of Patric first E. of Bothwell; prior of Andrew's, and sec. st.
1573. Geo. Douglas, natl. son of Arch E. of Angus; first protestant b of this see.
1606. Alexr. Douglas, parson of Elgin.
1623. John Guthrie, parson of Edinburg depr. with other bps. in 1638.
1662. Murdoch Mackenzie; tr. to Or ney.
1677. Jas. Aitkin; tr. to Galloway.
1680. Colin Falconer; tr. from Argyll.
1687. Alexr. Rose, principal of St. Mary College, St. Andrew's.
1688. Wm. Hay, parson of Perth; he w eject. soon after the Revolution 1688; *d.* 1707.

For post-Revolution bishops see *post*, p. 544.

DIOCESE OF ORKNEY.

THE accounts of the founding of this see are various and uncertai and considering that the Orkney and Shetland islands were subje sometimes to the Norwegians, and sometimes to the Scots, litt authenticated matter can be expected. The seat of the see was Kirkwall. The church was dedicated to St. Servanus, and was one the only two cathedral churches in Scotland (that of Glasgow being t other) that escaped the fury of the mob. The foundation of this see by some ascribed to St. Servanus, who was ordained a bishop by S Palladius, and sent to the Scots by pope Celestine I. in the beginning the fifth century; others say that St. Columb was the founder. T diocese contained the islands of Orkney and Shetland.

Bishops of Orkney.

* Radulphus, who lived in the time of David I.
* William (No. 1), reckoned by Torpheus to be the first bp. resident in Orkney.
* William (No. 2); *d.* 1188.
* Biarn; *d.* Sept. 1223.
223. Jofreir; *d.* 1246.
248. Hervey, or Hausir.
* Henry (No. 1).
270. Petrus.
286. Dolgfinnus.
310. William (No. 3).
* William (No. 4); murd.
390. William (No. 5).
394. Henry (No. 2).
422. Thos. de Tulloch.
448. William (No. 6).
468. Wm. Tulloch; tr. to Moray.
478. Andrew.
511. Edwd. Stewart.
* Thomas.
* Robt. Maxwell, prov. of the collegiate ch., Dumbarton.
540. Robt. Reid, prior of Beaulieu; pres. ct. sess.
1562. Adam Bothwell; *m.* Q. Mary to the E. of Bothwell, and aft. became a protestant.
See vacant 13 years.
1606. Jas. Law, parson of Kirkliston; tr. to Glasgow.
1615. Geo. Graham; tr. from Dunblane; deposed.
1638. Robt. Baron, prof. of divinity in Marischal College, Aberdeen, chosen; but the ruling powers depr. him of the benefit of his election.
1662. Thos. Sydeserf, prev. bp. of Galloway; he was the only surviving bp. at the Restoration.
1664. Andr. Honyman, archdn. of St. Andrew's.
1677. Murdoch Mackenzie; tr. from Moray.
1688. Andr. Bruce; he had been formerly bp. of Dunkeld, but had been depr.; lost this see at the Revolution.

For post-Revolution bishops see *post*, p. 545.

DIOCESE OF ROSS

[T]HE see of Ross was founded in the twelfth century by king David I.

Bishops of Ross.

* Macbeth.
* Simon.
161. Gregory.
195 Reinaldus; *d.* 1213.
* Andr. Murray; elect., but refused to be consec.
214. Robert (No. 1), chapl. to K. William.
* St. Duthac.
269. Robert (No. 2).
270. Robert (No. 3), archdn. of Ross.
273. Matthæus, or Machabæus; *d.* at Lyons, having gone to attend the council there.
274. Thos. de Fifyne.
284. Robert (No. 4).
309. Thos. de Dundemore, or Dundumore.
325. John Pilmore; elect., but before consec. chosen bp. of Moray.
328. Rogerus (No. 1).
334. John (No. 1).
340. Roger (No. 2).
357. Alexander (No. 1).
* * Alexander (No. 2).
1420. John (No. 2).
1449. Thos. Urquhart.
1463. Henry.
1481. Thomas.
1482. Wm. Elphinstone, archdn. of Argyll; tr. to Aberdeen.
1485. John Fraser, abb. of Melrose.
1508. Robt. Cockburn.
1525. Jas. Hay, abb. of Dundrennan, in the stewartry of Kirkcudbright.
1539. Robt. Cairncross abb. of Holyrood House; ld. treasr.
1546. David Paniter (*vulgo* Panter), sec. st.
1560. Hy. Sinclair, dean of Glasgow; ld. pres. ct. sess.
1565. John Lesley, sec. to Q. Mary; *d.* at Brussels, 1596.
1600. David Lindesay; the first protestant bp. of this see.
1613. Patrick Lindesay, parson of St. Vigians, Angus; tr. to Glasgow.

1633. John Maxwell, one of the ministers of Edinburgh; depr. in 1638. In 1640 he was made bp. of Killala, Ireland; and in 1645, abp. of Tuam; *d.* suddenly in 1646.

1662. John Paterson, parson of Aberdee
1679. Alexr. Young; tr. from Edinburg
1684. Jas. Ramsay; tr. from Dunblan eject. soon after the Revolution 1688.

For post-Revolution bishops see *post*, p. 545.

DIOCESE OF GLASGOW.

Historians disagree with respect to the foundation of this see: that is, next to St. Andrews, of higher antiquity than any other in Scotlan is, however, beyond all doubt. The founder is nowhere mentione with any certainty. Kennet says, the see was instituted by St. Kent gern, *alias* Mungo, in the year 560. Yet some doubt whether Kentige was ever bishop of Glasgow, and speak of him as being only a ho man, who had a cell there, and whose sanctity was held in such hig veneration, that when the cathedral church was dedicated, it was to hir Dr. Heylyn, speaking of the see of St. Asaph, in Wales, says, "th the see was founded in 583 by St. Kentigern, a Scot, then bishop Glasgow. In *that* see he was the first bishop; and on his return Scotland, he was succeeded as bishop by St. Asaph, to whom tl cathedral there is dedicated." From this it may be inferred that S Kentigern, *alias* Mungo, founded the see of Glasgow, and was the fir bishop. The see was made an archbishopric in 1491.

The diocese was of great extent, till the see of Edinburgh was part taken out of it. The want of records leaves a vast blank in the catalog of its bishops.

Bishops of Glasgow.

* * *

1115. John, ld. chanc.
1147. Herbert, abb. of Kelso; ld. chanc.
1164. Ingelram, archdn. of Glasgow.
1174. Joceline, abb. of Melrose.
1199. Hugo de Roxburgh, archdn. of St. Andrew's, and ld. chanc.
1200. Wm. Malvoisine, ld. chanc.; tr. to St. Andrew's.
1202. Florentius (son of the E. of Holland), ld. chanc.; res.
1208. Walter, chapl. to the king.
1233. Wm. de Bondington, archdn. of St. Andrew's, and ld. chanc.
1260. John de Cheyam, archdn. of Bath, England; chapl. to pope Alexander IV., and by him forced into the see; he was so disagreeable both to king and people, that he retired to France, where he died.
1268. Nichs. de Moffat, archdn. of Tiviotdale; never consec.
1270. Wm. Wiseheart, archdn. of St. Andrew's, and ld. chanc.; tr. to St. Andrew's.
1272. Robt. Wiseheart, archdn. of St. A drew's.
1317. Stephen de Dundemore, chanc. the see of Glasgow; never conse *d.* on his way to Rome.
1319. John Wiseheart, archdn. of Gla gow.
1325. John Lindsay; *d.* 1335.
1335. Wm. Rae.
1368. Walter Wardlaw, archdn. of Lothia and sec. to the king.
1389. Matth. Glendoning, preb. of Gla gow.
1408. Wm. Lauder, archdn. of Lothian.
1426. John Cameron, prov. of Linclude and ld. pr. seal.
1446. Jas. Bruce; tr. from Dunkel ld. chanc.; *d.* before he was i stalled.
1448. Wm. Turnbull, archdn. of St. A drew's, and ld. pr. seal.
1455. Andr. Muirhead, rect. of Cadzo (now Hamilton).
1474. John Laing, ld. treasr.
1483. Geo. Carmichael, treasr. of the s of Glasgow; *d.* before consec.

Archbishops of Glasgow.

1484. Robt. Blackadder ; tr. from Aberdeen; he had so much interest at Rome, that he got this see erected into an archbishopric in 1491, and had the bps. of Argyll, Galloway, and the Isles assigned him as suffragans.

1508. Jas. Beaton, or Bethune (No. 1); tr. from Galloway; ld. chanc.; tr. to St. Andrew's.

1524. Gavin Dunbar; tr. from Aberdeen; ld. chanc.

1551. Jas. Beaton, or Bethune (No. 2); abb. of Aberbrothock; he sent the records of this see to the Scots' college at Paris; quitted the see in 1560; rest. 1588.

The see vacant.

1571. John Porterfield; the first Protestant abp. of Glasgow; he seems to have been appointed merely to get the lands belonging to the see alienated in a legal manner; remained here till the year 1572.

1572. Jas. Boyd, one of the ministers of Glasgow.

581. Robt. Montgomery, parson of Stirling; res.

585. Wm. Erskine, titular abp., not being in orders; turned out by the king in 1587; the diocese given to Walter Stewart, commend. of Blantyre, with power to feu what remained of the see lands.

1588. Jas. Beaton, or Bethune (No. 2); rest. by act of parlt.

1603. John Spottiswood, parson of Calder, Mid Lothian; tr. to St. Andrew's.

1615. Jas. Law; tr. from Orkney.

1633. Patrick Lindsay ; tr. from Ross; depr. and excomm. 1638; *d.* at Newcastle 1641.

1661. Andr. Fairfowl, parson at Dunse.

1664. Alexr. Burnet; tr. from Aberdeen; forced to resign by the D. of Lauderdale, in 1669.

1671. Robt. Leighton; tr. from Dunblane; res. 1674.

1674. Alexr. Burnet; rest. by the D. of Lauderdale; tr. to St. Andrew's.

1679. Arthur Ross; tr. from Argyll; tr. to St. Andrew's.

1684. Alexr. Cairncross; tr. from Brechin; removed in 1686.

1687. John Paterson; tr. from Edinburgh; son of the bp. of Ross; ejected soon after the Revolution in 1688.

For post-Revolution bishops see *post*, p. 543.

DIOCESE OF ARGYLL.

John Scot, bishop of Dunkeld, finding his see so large that he could not pay that attention to it which his conscience dictated, made a representation to that effect to the court of Rome; whereupon pope Innocent III. disjoined from his diocese all that now constitutes the shire of Argyll, on the main land, together with some of the Western Islands, particularly the island of Lismore, which was made the bishop's seat of the new see: hence the bishops of Argyll are frequently styled bishops of Lismore. The church was dedicated to St. Molocus, who lived about 1160, and whose bones were translated to the island. The diocese contained Argyllshire, Lochaber, and some of the isles.

Bishops of Argyll.

200. Evaldus.
228. Harald.
240. William.
250. Alan.
261. Laurence.
304. Andrew.
330. David.
342. Martin.

Here some of the names are wanting.

* * *

1425. Finlay, a Dominican friar; chapl. to Murdoch, D. of Albany; retired to Ireland with the duke's son James.

1437. Geo. Lauder, prec. of St. Laurence Peebles.

1473. Robt. Colquhoun, rect. of Luss.

1499. John.

1505. David Hamilton; this prelate held *in commendam* the two abbeys of Dryburgh and Glenluce; and procured the abbey of Sandal, in Kintyre, to be annexed to his see.
1539. Wm. Cunningham, bro. to the E. of Glencairn.
* * Robt. Montgomery, rect. of Kirkmichael.
1558. Jas. Hamilton. natl. bro. to the D. of Chatelherault; sub-dean of Glasgow; the first Protestant bp. of this see.
1580. Neil Campbell, parson of Kilmartin; res.
1608. John Campbell, son of the last bp.
1613. Andr. Boyd, natl. son of ld. Boyd; preb. of Glasgow.
1637. Jas. Fairley, min. in Edinburgh; he was, with other bps., depr. 1638; but became the presbyteri parson of Leswade.
1661. John Young, prof. of divinity Glasgow; *d.* before consecratio
1662. David Fletcher, parson at Melrose
1666. Wm. Scrogie, parson of Ratha Aberdeenshire.
1675. Arthur Ross, parson of Glasgo tr. to Glasgow.
1679. Colin Falconer, parson of Forre tr. to Moray.
1680. Hector Maclean, parson at Eastwo
1688. Alexr. Monro, principal of the c lege of Edinburgh; he had a *con d'elire* to the dean and chapter this see; but it is uncertain wh ther he was elected before t Revolution.

For post-Revolution bishops see *post*, p. 541.

DIOCESE OF GALLOWAY.

This was a very ancient see, said to have been founded by St. Ninia who was the first bishop, and who had previously converted many of t inhabitants to the Christian religion. This saint, about the close of t fifth or beginning of the sixth century, built a church of white ston in honour of St. Martin, and from it the place took its name Whiter or Whitehorn.

Bishops of Galloway.

* * St. Ninian (No. 1).
* * Octa.
730. Pecthelmus.
764. Frethewaldus.
776. Pictuinus.
777. Ethelbertus.
790. Radvulf.
* * *
1154. Christianus.
1189. John.
1209. Walter.
1225. Gilbert, abb. of Kinloss.
1255. Henry, abb. of Holyrood House.
1296. Thomas (No. 1).
1321. Simon.
1334. Henry.
1357. Michael.
1359. Adam.
1362. Thomas (No. 2).
1368. Andrew.
1415. Elisæus.
1415. Thomas (No. 3).
1426. Alexander.
1451. Thos. Spence; res.
1459. Ninian (No. 2).
1489. Geo. Vaus.
1508. Jas. Beaton, or Bethune (No. abb. of Dunfermline; ld. treas tr. to Glasgow.
1509. David Arnot, abb. of Cambus Ke neth.
1526. Hy. Weems.
1541. Andr. Durie, abb. of Melrose.
1558. Alexr. Gordon, tr. from the Isle titular abp. of Athens; the fi protestant bp. of this see; su pended from his function by t kirk, he assigned his bishopric his son, which assignment w afterwards confirmed by a chart under the great seal; *d.* 1576.
1576. John Gordon, not consec.
1606. Gavin Hamilton, parson of Hamilt
* * Wm. Coupar, parson of Perth.
1619. Andr. Lamb, tr. from Brechin.
1634. Thos. Sydeserf, tr. from Brechi depr. in 1638 by the assembly Glasgow; he was the only Sco bp. that survived the usurpati and in 1662 was made bp. Orkney.
1661. Jas. Hamilton, bro. to the first

Belhaven; parson of Cambusnethan.
674. John Paterson, dean of Edinburgh.
679. Arthur Ross, tr. from Argyll; tr. to Glasgow.
680. Jas. Aitkin, tr. from Moray.
1688. John Gordon, chapl. to the king; he followed James II., after his abdication, into France, and aft. into Ireland, but still continued a protestant.

For post-Revolution bishops see *post*, p. 543.

DIOCESE OF THE ISLES.

'HIS see contained, formerly, not only the Æbudæ, or Western Isles, ut the Isle of Man, which for more than four hundred years has been separate bishopric. The prelates had three places of residence, viz., he isles of Icolumkill, Man, and Bute; and, in ancient writs are ariously styled *Episcopi Manniæ et Insularum, Episcopi Æbudarum*, and *'piscopi Sodorenses*, which last title is still retained by the bishops of he Isles, and the bishops of the Isle of Man.

During the great contest between the houses of Bruce and Baliol for he throne of Scotland, Edward III. of England made himself master f the Isle of Man, and it has ever since remained an appendage of the rown of England. The lords of the isle of Man set up bishops of heir own, and the Scottish monarchs continued their bishops of the sles, of which the records are but imperfect.

Bishops of the Isles.

360. Amphibalus.
447. Germanus.
* * Conindicus.
* * Romulus.
498. St. Machatus.
648. St. Conan.
* * St. Contentus.
* * St. Bladus.
* * St. Malchus.
889. Tarkinus.
* * Roolwer.
* * William.
* * St. Brandan, to whom the cathedral in the Isle of Man is dedicated.
113. Wymundus, a monk of Sais.
151. John (No. 1), a monk of Sais.
154. Gamaliel, an Englishman.
* Reginald (No. 1), a Norwegian.
* Christian.
* Michael.
203. Nicholas.
217. Reginald (No. 2), nephew to Ottaus, K. of Norway.
226. John (No. 2).
* Simon.
249. Laurence, archdn. of Man.
252. Richard (No. 1).
253. Stephen.
* Richard (No. 2); in his time, the Scots regained the island of Man.
275. Marcus, ld. chanc. of Scotland.
304. Onacus.
1305. Allan.
1321. Gilbert.
1328. Bernard de Linton, abb. of Aberbrothock, and ld. chanc.
1334. Thomas.
1348. Wm. Russell, abb. of Rushen.
1374. John Dunkan, a Manxman, consec. at Avignon; made prisoner on his return at Balonia, and redeemed for five hundred merks.
1388. John (No. 3); the Isle of Man was now separated from this see.
1409. Michael.
1427. Angusius (No. 1).
1476 Angusius (No. 2).
1492. Robert.
* * John (No. 4), the king, with the consent of the pope, got the abbey of Icolumkill annexed to the see.
1510. Geo. Hepburn, abb. of Aberbrothock; ld. treasr.; killed at the battle of Flodden, Sept. 9, 1513.
See supposed to be vacant.
1524. John (No. 5), elected.
1530. Ferquhard. res. in favour of
1544. Roderick Maclean, archdn. of the Isles.
1553. Alexr. Gordon, titular abp. of Athens; held the abbey of Inchaffray *in commendam*; tr. to Galloway.
1558. John Campbell, prior of Ardchattan.
* * John Carswell; titular.

1606. Andr. Knox, parson of Paisley, the first protestant bp. of this see; tr. to Raphoe, Ireland.

1622. Thos. Knox, son of the last bishop.

1628. John Lesley, tr. to Raphoe, Ireland, 1633, but depr.; made bp. of Clogher, 1661; and *d.* in 1671.

1634. Neil Campbell, parson of Glastrey; depr. by the Glasgow assem 1638.

1661. Robt. Wallace, parson of Barnwe in Ayrshire.

1675. Andr. Wood, parson of Dunbar, to Caithness.

1680. Archd. Graham, parson of Rothsa ejected soon after the Revolut in 1688.

For post-Revolution bishops see *post*, p. 541.

PART II.—BISHOPS OF SCOTLAND AFTER TH REVOLUTION.

At the Revolution of 1688 the episcopal Church of Scotland w disestablished, and thenceforward became a mere voluntary associati The apostolical succession of bishops was, however, continued, and t names of most of the former dioceses have been retained or revive From time to time two or more sees have been united under o bishop and again separated, a system which, though no doubt adopt for good practical reasons, renders the succession of the post-Revoluti bishops somewhat intricate and difficult to follow.

BISHOPS OF SCOTLAND WHO HAVE HELD THE OFFICE OF *PRIMUS*.

Anciently, no bishop in Scotland had the title of archbishop, but o bishop had a precedency under the title of *Primus Scotiæ Episcop* In consequence of the Revolution, and after the death of bishop Ro of Edinburgh, the Scottish bishops resumed the old form, one of th being elected *Primus*, with the power of convocating and presidi according to their canons.

1704. *Alexr. Rose, bp. of Edinburgh.
1720. *Jno. Fullarton, bp. of Edinburgh.
1727. *Arthur Millar, bp. of Edinburgh.
*Andrew Lumsden, bp. of Edinburgh.
1731. *David Freebairn, minister of Dunning; aft. bp. of Edinburgh.
1739. Thomas Rattray, bp. of Dunkeld.
1743. Robert Keith, bp. of Fife.
1757. Robert White, bp. of Fife.
1761-2. William Falconar, bp. of Moray; aft. bp. of Edinburgh.
1784. Robert Kilgour, bp. of Aberdeer
1788–9. John Skinner, bp. of Aberdeer
1816. George Gleig, bp. of Brechin.
1837. James Walker, bp. of Edinburgh
1841. William Skinner, bp. of Aberdee
1857. Chas. Hugh Terrot, bp. of Ed burgh.
1862. Robert Eden, bp. of Moray Ross.
1886. Hugh Willoughby Jermyn, bp. Brechin.

* Some authorities style these bishops "Administrators," and not "*Primi.*"

POST-REVOLUTION BISHOPS OF ABERDEEN.

1721. Hon. Archd. Campbell; consec. Aug. 24. 1711; res. 1724.

1724. Jas. Gadderar, min. at Kilmaurs; consec. Feb. 24, 1712.

1733. Wm. Dunbar, tr. from Moray; 1746.

1747. Andr. Gerard, presbyter in Ab deen; consec. July 17; *d.* Oct. 17

1768. Robt. Kilgour, presbyter in Peterhead; consec. Sept. 21; *primus* on the death of bp. Falconar in 1784; res. 1786; *d.* Mar. 1790.

1786. John Skinner, presbyter in Aberdeen; consec. and app. coadj. to bp. Kilgour, Sept. 25, 1782; succ. that bp. on his resign. in 1786; *primus* in 1788–9; *d.* July 1816.

1816. Wm. Skinner, presbyter in Aberdeen, son of the preceding bp.; consec. Oct. 27; *primus* in 1841.

1857. Thos. G. Suther.

In 1864 Orkney was united to this see, and bp. Suther was thenceforth styled bp. of Aberdeen and Orkney.

See "Aberdeen and Orkney," *infra*.

POST-REVOLUTION BISHOPS OF ABERDEEN AND ORKNEY.

See "Aberdeen," *supra*, and "Orkney," *post*, p. 545.

1864. Thos. G. Suther, bp. of Aberdeen; now bp. of Aberdeen and Orkney.

1883. Hon. Arthur Gascoigne Douglas.

POST-REVOLUTION BISHOPS OF ARGYLL AND THE ISLES.

Since the Revolution the sees of Argyll and the Isles have never existed independently, being joined to Moray and Ross, or to Ross alone. In 1847, however, Argyll and the Isles were made to form an independent diocese, and a bishop was appointed thereto.

1847. Alex. Ewing, consec. at Aberdeen, Oct. this year.

1874. Geo. Richd. Mackarness.

1883. Jas. Robt. Alex. Chinnery-Haldane.

POST-REVOLUTION BISHOPS OF BRECHIN.

1731. John Ouchterlonie; consec. Nov. 29, 1726; *d.* 1742.

1742. Jas. Rait, presbyter in Dundee; consec. Oct. 4; *d.* 1777.

1778. Geo. Innes; consec. Aug. 13; *d.* May 1781.

See vacant some years.

1787. Wm. Abernethy Drummond, presbyter in Edinburgh; consec. Sept. 26; tr. soon afterwards to Edinburgh.

1787–8. John Strachan, presbyter in Dundee; consec. with bp. Drummond, to whom he was coadj. On Drummond being elected to Edinburgh, he had the undivided charge of Brechin; *d.* Jan. 1810.

1810. Geo. Gleig, presbyter in Stirling; consec. as coadj. to bp. Strachan, Oct. 12, 1808; succ. him in 1810; *primus* in 1816.

1837. David Moir, consec. Oct. 8, as coadj. to bp. Gleig, whom he succ. in 1841.

1847. Alex. Penrose Forbes.

1876. Hugh Willoughby Jermyn, *primus* in 1886.

POST-REVOLUTION BISHOPS OF CAITHNESS.

1662. Patrick Forbes, June 1.

1727. Robt. Keith; June 18; tr. to Fife, 1733.

1741. Wm. Falconar, Sept. 10; tr. to Moray, 1742.

See "Ross and Caithness," *post*, p. 545.

POST-REVOLUTION BISHOPS OF DUNBLANE.

1731. John Gillan; consec. June 11, 1727; assumed the charge of this diocese, but his authority was not fully recognised until 1731.

1735. Robt. White, presbyter at Cupar; consec. June 24; tr. to Fife, 1743.

See some years vacant.

1774. Chas. Rose, presbyter at Doune; consec. Aug. 24; succ. bp. Alexander in Dunkeld in 1776, when the bishoprics of Dunkeld and Dunblane were united.

See "Dunkeld and Dunblane," *infra*.

POST-REVOLUTION BISHOPS OF DUNKELD.

1727. Thos. Rattray, of Craighall; consec. June 4; *primus* in 1739; *d.* May 1743.

1743. John Alexander, presbyter at Alloa consec. Aug. 9; *d.* 1776.

On his death the bishoprics of Dunkeld and Dunblane were united. See "Dunkeld and Dunblane," *infra*.

POST-REVOLUTION BISHOPS OF DUNKELD AND DUNBLANE.

See "Dunkeld," and "Dunblane," *supra*.

1776. Chas. Rose, bp. of Dunblane, became also bp. of Dunkeld; *d.* Apr. 1791.

1792. Jonathan Watson, presbyter at Laurence Kirk; consec. Sept. 20; *d.* 1808.

1808. Patrick Torry, presbyter at Peterhead; consec. Oct. 12; made bp. of Fife 1837, and thenceforward styled bp. of Fife, Dunkeld, and Dunblane.

See "Fife, Dunkeld, and Dunblane," *post*, p. 543.

POST-REVOLUTION BISHOPS OF EDINBURGH.

PASSING over bishop Alexander Rose, whose name is found in the preceding lists of ante-Revolution bishops, and who connects the established Episcopal Church of Scotland with that form of it which is now only voluntary, the first of the post-Revolution bishops, properly so described, chosen to superintend the clergy of Edinburgh, was

1720. John Fullarton, form. min. of Paisley; consec. Jan. 25, 1705; app. to Edinburgh in 1720, on the death bp. of Alexr. Rose.

1727. Arthur Millar, min. of Inveresk; consec. Oct. 22, 1718; app. to Edinburgh; *primus* in 1727; *d.* same year.

Andrew Lumsden, min. of Duddington; consec. Nov. 22, and at once made *primus*.

1733. David Freebairn, min. of Dunning; consec. Oct. 17, 1722; *primus* in 1731; app. to Edinburgh 1733; *d.* 1739.

From 1739 to 1776 there was no appointment of a bishop of Edinburgh.

1776. Wm. Falconar; tr. from Moray; *primus* 1761–2; *d.* 1784.

Arth. Petrie was his coadj. in 1777.

1787. Wm. Abernethy Drummond; tr. from Brechin; res. 1805.

1806. Daniel, or David, Sandford, elect. in Jan. and consec. Feb. 9 this year; *d.* 1830.

1830. Jas. Walker, consec. Mar. 7; *primus* in 1837; *d.* Mar. 1841.
1841. Chas. Hughes Terrot.
1863. Thos. Baker Morrell, coadj.
1872. Hy. Cotterill.
1886. John Dowden.

POST-REVOLUTION BISHOPS OF FIFE.

1733. Robt. Keith; tr. from Caithness; *primus* in 1743; *d.* Jan. 1757.
1743. Robt. White; tr. from Dunblane; *primus* in 1757; *d.* 1761.
1761. Hy. Edgar, consec. in 1759; coadj. to bp. White, whom he succeeded: there is no record of his death.

Fife was united to Edinburgh from bp. Edgar's death, until 1837, when it was transferred to Dunkeld and Dunblane. This bishopric has been styled St. Andrew's. since Sept. 1844.

See "Edinburgh," *ante*, p. 542, "Fife, Dunkeld, and Dunblane," *infra*, and "St. Andrew's, Dunkeld, and Dunblane," *post*, p. 545.

POST-REVOLUTION BISHOPS OF FIFE, DUNKELD, AND DUNBLANE.

See "Fife," *supra*, and "Dunkeld and Dunblane," *ante*, p. 542.

1837. Patrick Torry, bp. of Dunkeld and Dunblane, was this year made bp. of Fife also. In Sept. 1844 the title of Fife was changed to St. Andrew's, and bp. Torry was thenceforward styled bp. of St. Andrew's, Dunkeld, and Dunblane.

See "St. Andrew's, Dunkeld, and Dunblane," *post*, p. 545.

POST-REVOLUTION BISHOPS OF GALLOWAY.

It is doubtful whether there was a bishop of this see until it was united with Glasgow in 1848; but David Freebairn, who was consec. Oct. 17, 1722, is, by some, given as bp. of Galloway in 1731.

See "Glasgow and Galloway," *post*, p. 544.

POST-REVOLUTION BISHOPS OF GLASGOW.

It is doubtful whether any named before 1837 were more than *titular* bishops, but the following are given by some authorities:—

172-. Alexr. Duncan, consec. 1724; (? bp. in 1721, and *d.* 1733),
1724. Robt. Norrie, consec. this year.
1726. Jas. Rose, consec. this year.
1727. David Rankine, consec. this year.
1732 (? 1722). Andrew, or David, Cant, consec. Oct. 17.
1837. In this year a mandate was issued to the dean and clergy to elect a bishop, and accordingly, on Oct. 8, Michl. Russell was consec. and app. He *d.* 1848, and his successor was consec. as bp. of Glasgow and Galloway.

See "Glasgow and Galloway," *post*, p. 544.

POST-REVOLUTION BISHOPS OF GLASGOW AND GALLOWAY.

See "Glasgow" and "Galloway," *ante*, p. 543.

1848. Walter Jno. Trower; consec. Sept. as bp. of Glasgow and Galloway.

1859. Wm. Scot Wilson.

1888. Wm. Thos. Harrison.

POST-REVOLUTION BISHOPS OF THE ISLES.

See "Argyll and the Isles," *ante*, p. 541.

POST-REVOLUTION BISHOPS OF MORAY.

1727. Wm. Dunbar, min. at Cruden; consec. June 18; tr. to Aberdeen 1733.

1742. Wm. Falconar; tr. from Caithness; tr. to Edinburgh.

1776. Arthur Petrie, presbyter at Micklefolla, in Fyvie; consec. June 27; *d.* 1787.

1787. Andr. Macfarlane, presbyter in Inverness; consec. Mar. 7.

Hitherto the diocese of Ross had since the Revolution been under the charge of the bps. of Moray, but in

1796. Alexr. Jolly, presbyter at Frazerburgh, was consec. June 24, and app. coadj. to bp. Macfarlane, who immediately afterwards res. the charge of Moray to him, retaining that of Ross, with the title of bp. of that diocese. See "Ross," *post*, p. 545.

1838. On the death of bp. Jolly in this year, Moray was again united to Ross under bp. Low, conformably with a decree of an episcopal synod held in Edinburgh in 1837.

See "Ross," *post*, p. 545, and "Moray and Ross," *infra*.

POST-REVOLUTION BISHOPS OF MORAY AND ROSS.

See "Moray," *supra*, and "Ross," *post*, p. 545.

1838. Conformably to a decree of an episcopal synod held in Edinburgh in 1837, the bishoprics of Moray and Ross were united under David Low, then bp. of Moray, who was thenceforward styled bp. of Moray and Ross, and who res. 1851.

1851. Robt. Eden, who, in 1864, was styled bp. of Moray, Ross, and Caithness.

See "Moray, Ross, and Caithness," *infra*.

POST-REVOLUTION BISHOPS OF MORAY, ROSS, AND CAITHNESS.

See "Moray and Ross," *supra*, and "Ross and Caithness," *post*, p. 545.

1864. Robt. Eden, above named.

1886. Jas. Butler Kelly, consec. 1867.

POST-REVOLUTION BISHOPS OF ORKNEY.

It is doubtful whether there were any post-Revolution bishops of this see until it was united to Aberdeen in 1864. The following names are given by some, but, as will be seen, they had other preferment from which they took their titles.

1703. Robt. Keith, consec. June 18, 1727; also bp. of Caithness.

1741. Wm. Falconar, consec. Sept. 10; also bp. of Caithness.

1762. Robt. Forbes, consec. June 21; also bp. of Ross and Caithness.

1787–8. Andr. Macfarlane, consec. Mar. 7, 1787; also bp. of Moray.

See "Aberdeen and Orkney," *ante*, p. 541.

POST-REVOLUTION BISHOPS OF ROSS.

It is not clear by whom the duties of some of the remoter districts of Scotland were performed about the middle of the last century. Ross appears to have been usually united with Moray, until bp. Macfarlane, in 1796, res. Moray to bp. Jolly, and retained, together with Ross, the superintendence of Argyll.

1796. Andr. Macfarlane, previously consec. bp. of Moray; *d.* 1819. See "Moray," *ante* p. 544.

1819. David Low, presbyter of Pittenween; consec. Nov. 14.

See "Moray and Ross," *ante*, p. 544.

POST-REVOLUTION BISHOPS OF ROSS AND CAITHNESS.

1762. Robt. Forbes, consec. June 24.

See "Moray, Ross, and Caithness," *ante*, p. 544.

POST-REVOLUTION BISHOPS OF ST. ANDREW'S, DUNKELD, AND DUNBLANE.

See "Fife Dunkeld, and Dunblane," *ante*, p. 543.

1844. St. Andrews was anciently the principal archiepiscopal see of Scotland, but the title was dropped at the Revolution, and was not revived until Sept. 5 of this year, when it was substituted for that of Fife by Patrick Torry, until then styled bp. of Fife, Dunkeld, and Dunblane, but thenceforward styled bp. of St. Andrews, Dunkeld and Dunblane; *d.* 1853.

1853. Chas. Wordsworth.

SCOTCH POST-REVOLUTION BISHOPS WITHOUT SEES.

1705. John Sage, consec. Jan. 25.
John Fullarton, consec. Jan. 25.

1709. John Falconer, consec. Jan. 25.
Hy. Christie, consec. Apr. 28.

1711. Hon. Archd. Campbell, consec. Aug. 24.

1718. Wm. Irvine, consec. Oct. 22.

1722. Andr. Cant, consec. Oct. 17; (? David Cant, bp. Glasgow, 1732.

1726. Jas. Rose, consec. Nov. 29 (? bp. of Glasgow).

1727. John Gillan, consec. June 11.
David Rankin, consec. June 11. (? bp. of Glasgow)

THE GENERAL ASSEMBLY OF THE KIRK OF SCOTLAND.

THE government of the established Presbyterian Kirk of Scotland is superintended by a supreme court, called the General Assembly, consisting of commissioners from each presbytery, royal burgh, and university in the kingdom, with a proportion of Kirk elders, nearly as three to four. Meetings of this court take place annually, under the presidency of a Lord High Commissioner, as the representative of the crown, and of a moderator chosen by the members present.

LORD HIGH COMMISSIONERS APPOINTED TO REPRESENT THE SOVEREIGN IN THE GENERAL ASSEMBLIES OF THE KIRK OF SCOTLAND.

1638. Jas., M., aft. D., of Hamilton.
1639. John, E. of Traquair.
1640. No commr.
1641. John, E. of Wemyss.
1642. Chas., E. of Dunfermline.
1643. Sir Thos. Hope, of Craighall, king's advocate.
1644–49. No commissioners; but the king wrote a letter to the Assembly in 1646 showing that he could not conveniently send a commr.

* * * *

1690. John, ld. Carmichael.
1692. Robt., E., aft. M., of Lothian.
1694–99. John, ld. Carmichael, aft. E. of Hyndford.
1700. Jas., 1st visc. Seafield, aft. 1st E. of Seafield, and 4th E. of Findlater.
1701. Wm., E., aft. M. of Annandale.
1702. Patrick, E. of Marchmont.
1703. Jas., E. of Seafield, *again.*
1704. Wm., ld. Ross.
1705. Wm., M. of Annandale, *again.*
1706–10. David, E. of Glasgow.
1711. Wm., M. of Annandale, *again.*
1712–14. John, D. of Athole.
1715–21. John, E. of Rothes.
1722. Hugh, E. of Loudoun.
1723. Chas., E. of Hopetoun.
1724. Jas., E. of Findlater and Seafield, *again.*
1725–26. Hugh, E. of Loudoun.
1727. Jas., E. of Findlater and Seafield, *again.*
1728. Hugh, E. of Loudoun, *again.*
1729. David, E. of Buchan.
1730–31. Hugh, E. of Loudoun, *again.*
1732–38. Wm., M. of Lothian.
1739–40. John, E. of Hyndford.
1741–53. Alexr., E. of Leven and Melville.
1754. John, E. of Hopetoun.
1755–63. Chas. Schaw, ld. Cathcart.
1764–72. David, E. of Glasgow.
1773–76. Chas. Schaw, ld. Cathcart, *again.*
1777–82. Geo., E. of Dalhousie.
1783–1801. David, E. of Leven and Melville.
1802–16. Fras., ld. Napier.
1817–19. Wm., E. of Erroll.
1820–24. Geo., E. of Morton.
1825–30. Jas., ld. Forbes.
1831–41. Robt. Montgomery, ld. Belhaven.
1842–46. John, M. of Bute.
1847–51. Robt. Montgomery, ld. Belhaven, *again.*
1852. Wm. David, E. of Mansfield, K. T.
1853–57. Robt. Montgomery, ld. Belhaven, *again.*
1858–59. Wm. David, E. of Mansfield, K. T., *again.*
1860–66. Robt. Montgomery, ld. Belhaven, K. T. 1861.
1867–68. Geo., E. of Haddington.
1869–71. John, E. of Stair, K. T.
1872–73. David Graham Drummond, E. of Airlie, K. T.
1874–75. Fras. Robt., E. of Rosslyn.
1876–77. Alan Plantagenet, E. of Galloway.
1878–80. Fras. Robt., E. of Rosslyn, *again.*
1881–85. John Campbell, E. of Aberdeen.
1886. Thos. John, ld. Thurlow.
1887–89. John Adrian Louis, E of Hopetoun.

MODERATORS OF THE GENERAL ASSEMBLY OF THE KIRK OF SCOTLAND.

From the beginning of the Century.

THIS list has been compiled from those given in Oliver & Boyd's "Edinburgh Almanac," a work which contains a large amount of useful information on all Scotch subjects.

1801. Wm. Ritchie.
1802. Jas. Finlayson.
1803. Gilbert Gerard.
1804. John Inglis.
1805. Geo. Hamilton.
1806. Wm. Taylor.
1807. Jas. Sheriffs.
1808. Andr. Grant.
1809. Fras. Nicol.
1810. Hugh Meiklejohn.
1811. Alexr. Rankine.
1812. W. McMorine.
1813. Andr. Brown.
1814. David Ritchie.
1815. Lewis Gordon.
1816. John Cook.
1817. Gavin Gibb.
1818. John Campbell.
1819. Duncan Macfarlane (No. 1.)
1820. Thos. Macknight.
1821. D. Mearns.
1822. David Lamont.
1823. Alexr. Brunton.
1824. Andr. Duncan.
1825. Geo. Cook.
1826. Thos. Taylor.
1827. Robt. Haldane.
1828. Stevenson Macgill.
1829. Patrick Forbes.
1830. Wm. Singer.
1831. Jas. Wallace.
1832. Thos. Chalmers.
1833. John Stirling.
1834. Patrick Macfarlan.
1835. W. A. Thomson.
1836. Norman McLeod (No. 1).
1837. Matt. Gardiner.
1838. Wm. Muir.
1839. Hy. Duncan.
1840. Angus Makellar.
1841. Robt. Gordon.
1842. David Walsh.
1843. Duncan Macfarlan (No. 2).
1844. John Lee.
1845. Alexr. Hill.
1846. Jas. Paull.
1847. John Paul.
1848. Geo. Buist.
1849. Alexr. L. Simpson.
1850. John Graham.
1851. John McLeod,
1852. Lewis W. Forbes.
1853. Jas. Barr.
1854. Jas. Grant.
1855. Andr. Bell.
1856. John Crombie.
1857. Jas. Robertson.
1858. Matt. Leishman.
1859. John Cook.
1860. Jas. Maitland.
1861. Colin Smith.
1862. Jas. Besset.
1863. Jas. Craik.
1864. Wm. Robinson Pirie.
1865. Jas. Macfarlane.
1866. John Cook.
1867. Thos. T. Crawford.
1868. Jas. S. Barty.
1869. Norman Macleod (No. 2).
1870. Geo. Ritchie.
1871. Robt. Horne Stevenson.
1872. Robt. Jamieson.
1873. Robt. Gillan.
1874. Saml. Trail.
1875. Jas. Sellar.
1876. Geo. Cook.
1877. Kenneth M. Phin.
1878. John Tulloch.
1879. Jas. Chrystal.
1880. Archd. Watson.
1881. Jas. Smith.
1882. Wm. Milligan.
1883. John Rankin.
1884. Peter McKenzie.
1885. Alexr. F. Mitchell.
1886. John Cunningham.
1887. Geo. Hutchison.
1888. Wm. H. Gray.

THE LORD PROVOSTS OF EDINBURGH.

THE municipal affairs of the city of Edinburgh are administered by a corporation called the Town Council, the constitution of which has been altered from time to time, and as now settled consists of forty-one persons. These are the Lord Provost, six bailies, a dean of guild, a treasurer, a convener of trades, and thirty-one counsellors.

Lord Provosts of Edinburgh from 1760.

1760–1. Geo. Lind.
1762–3. Geo. Drummond.
1764–5. Jas. Stewart.
1766–7. Gilbert Laurie.
1768–9. Jas. Stewart.
1770–1. John Dalrymple.
1772–3. Gilbert Laurie, *again*.
1774–5. Jas. Stoddart.
1776. Alexr. Kincaid; *d.* in office, Jan. 1777.
1777. John Dalrymple.
1778–9. Walter Hamilton.
1780–1. David Steuart.
1782–3. John Grieve.
1784–5. Jas. Hunter Blair.
1786–7. John Grieve, *again*.
1788–9. Thos. Elder.
1790–1. Jas. Stirling, aft. bt.
1792–3. Thos. Elder, *again*.
1794–5. Sir Jas. Stirling, bt., *again*.
1796–7. Thos Elder, *again*.
1798–9. Sir Jas. Stirling, bt., *again*.
1800–1. Wm. Fettes, aft. bt.
1802–3. Neil Macvicar.
1804–5. Wm. Fettes, aft. bt., *again*.
1806–7. Donald Smith.
1808–9. Wm. Coulter; *d.* Apr. 1809.
1809–10. Wm. Calder
1811–12. Wm. Creech.
1813–14. Jno. Marjoribanks, aft. bt.
1815–16. Wm. Arbuthnot, aft. bt.
1817–18. Kincaid Mackenzie.
1819–20. John Manderston.
1821–22. Wm. Arbuthnot, aft. bt., *again*.
1823–24. Alexr. Henderson.
1825–26. Wm. Trotter.
1827–28. Walter Brown.
1829–30. Wm. Allan.
1831–32. John Learmouth.
1833–36. Jas. Spittal, aft. Sir J.
1837–42. James Forrest, aft. bt.
1843–47. Adam Black.
1848–50. Wm. Johnston, aft. Sir W.
1851–53. Duncan McLaren.
1854–58. John Melville, aft. Sir J.
1859–61. Fras. Brown Douglas.
1862–64. Chas. Lawson.
1865–68. Wm. Chambers.
1869–71. Wm. Law.
1872–73. Jas. Cowan.
1874–76. James Falshaw, aft. bt.
1877–81. Thos. Jamieson Boyd, aft. Sir T.
1882–84. Geo. Harrison, aft. Sir G.
1885–88. Thos. Clark, aft. bt.

PART X. IRELAND.

SOVEREIGNS OF IRELAND.

For the sovereigns of Ireland prior to 1172 see Part I. "Royal," *ante*,). 20. The subsequent sovereigns will be found under those of England, *ante*, p. 4.

OFFICERS OF STATE, &c., OF IRELAND.

LORD-LIEUTENANTS AND CHIEF GOVERNORS OF IRELAND.

VHEN the English established themselves in Ireland, in the reign of Ienry II., the Government of the country was constituted much upon he model of that of England. The executive government was vested n officers who in the early ages of the English power in Ireland were ariously denominated; as Custos or Keeper, Warden, Justiciary, Procuator, Seneschal, Constable, Lord-Lieutenant, and Lord Deputy, the last eriving his power sometimes from the superior Governor and sometimes rom the crown; for many years the title has been Lord-Lieutenant.)uring his absence his powers are delegated to two, three, or someimes four Officers of State, styled "Lords Justices." Formerly iese officers frequently administered the government for considerable eriods, and their names are therefore included in these lists. Since ie union of Great Britain and Ireland, in 1801, the absence of the ord-Lieutenant has been but temporary, generally for a few days only, nd it has therefore not been necessary to notice the appointment of ords Justices since that time. They were generally three—(1) the ord Chancellor, (2) the commander of the Forces, and (3) until the isestablishment of the Irish Church on Jan. 1, 1871, the Archbishop of rmagh.

LORD-LIEUTENANTS AND CHIEF GOVERNORS OF IRELAND.

L. L. Lord Lieutenant; L. J. Lord Justice; L. D. Lord Deputy; L. W. Lor Warden; Cust. Custos, Proc. Procurator; Sen. Seneschal; L. Const. Lor Constable; all governors under those names.

HENRY II.

1173. Hugh de Lacy, ld. of Meath, L. J.
Rd. de Clare, E. of Pembroke, L. J.
1177. Raymond Le Gros, by the council elected *Proc.*
JOHN, E. of Morton, son to the king. Lord of Ireland.
Wm. Fitzaldelm, the king's purser. *Sen.*
1179. Hugh de Lacy, ld. of Meath. *Proc.*
1881. John de Lacy, const. of Chester; and Rd. de Peche, bp. of Coventry, LL. J.; sent by the king to deprive Hugh de Lacy, who by his marriage with a daughter of Roderick, king of Connaught, had displeased Henry.
Wm. Fitzaldelm, *again*, L. D.
1184. Philip de Braos, *alias* Philip of Worcester, *Proc.*
1185. JOHN, E. of Morton, *again.* Lord of Ireland.
John de Courcy, E. of Ulster, L. D.

RICHARD I.

1189. Hugh de Lacy the younger, ld. of Meath, aft. E. of Ulster, L. J.
1191. Wm. le Petit, L. J.
Wm., E. of Pembroke and E. marshl. of England, *Sen.* of Leinster.
Peter Pipard, L. J.
1194. Hamo de Valois, a gentleman of Suffolk, L. J.

JOHN.

1199. Meiler Fitzhenry, nat. son of Henry II., L. J.
1203. Hugh de Lacy the younger, *again*, L. D.
1205. Meiler Fitzhenry, *returns.*
1208. Hugh de Lacy, now E. of Ulster, L. D.
1209. King JOHN, in person. Lord of Ireland.
Wm., E. of Pembroke, left by the king as L. D.
1210. John de Grey, bp. elect of Norwich, L. J.
1213. Hy. de Londres, abp. of Dublin, L. J.
1215. Geoff. de Marisco. *Cust.*

HENRY VIII.

1216. The same, *contd.*
1219. Hy. de Londres, *again*, L. J.
1224. Wm., E. of Pembroke, L. J.
1226. Geoff. de Marisco, *again*, L. J.
1227. Hubert de Burgh, E. of Kent, an justiciar of England, L. J.
Rd. de Burgh, L. D.
1229. Maurice Fitzgerald, L. J.
1230. Geoff. de Marisco, *again*, L. D.
1232. Maurice Fitzgerald, *returned*, L. J.
1245 Sir John Fitz-Geoffrey de Marisco L. J.
1247. Theobd. Butler, ld. of Carrick; an John Cogan, LL. J.
1248. Sir John Fitz-Geoffrey de Marisco *again*, L. J.
1252. Prince EDWARD, eldest son to th king, L J.
1255. Alan de la Zouche, L. J.
1259. Steph. de Longespee, L. J.
1260. Wm. Den, or Dene, L. J.
1261. Sir Rd. de Rupella, or Capella, L.
1266. Sir John Fitz-Geoffrey de Marisco *again*, L. J.
1267. Sir David de Barry, L. J.
1268. Sir Robt. de Ufford, L. J.
1269. Rd. de Exonia, or d'Exeter, L. J.
1270. Sir Jas. Audley, or d'Aldithley, L.
1272. Maurice Fitzmaurice Fitzgeral elected L. J.

EDWARD I.

1272. The same, *contd. by commission.*
1273. Sir Geoff. de Geneville, L. J.
1276. Sir Rt. de Ufford, *again*, L. J.
1277. Steph. de Fulburn, bp. of Wate ford, L. D.
Sir Robt. de Ufford, *returned*, L. J.
1279. Steph. de Fulburn, *again*, L. J.
1280. Sir Robt. de Ufford, *returned*, L. J
1282. Steph. de Fulburn, *again*, aft. ab of Waterford, L. J.
1287. John de Saunford, abp. of Dubli elected L. J.
1290. Wm. de Vesci, L. J.
1293. Wm. de la Haye, L. D.
1294. Wm. de Odinsele, or Dodinsele, L.
1295. Thos. Maurice Fitzgerald, Nappag elected L. J.
Sir John Wogan, L. J.
1302. Sir Maurice Rochfort, L. D.
Sir John Wogan, *returned*, L. J.

EDWARD II.

1307. The same, *contd.*
1308. Sir Wm. Burke, or Burgh, *D. Cu*
Piers Gaveston, E. of Cornwall, L.
1309. Sir John Wogan, L. J.
1312. Sir Edmd. Boteler, or Butler, *Cust.*

1314. Sir Theobald de Verdun, or Verdan, *D. Const.*
1315. Sir Edmd. Butler, *again*, *D. Cust.*
1317. Sir Roger Mortimer, aft. E. of March, L. J.
1318. Wm. Fitz-John, abp. of Cashel, *D. Cust.*
Alexr. de Bicknor, abp. of Dublin, L. D.
1319. Sir Roger Mortimer, *returned*, L. J.
1320. Thos., second E. of Kildare, L. D.
1321. Sir John Bermingham, E. of Louth, L. J.
1322. Ralph de Gorges, L. D.
Sir John Darcy, L. D.
1323. Sir Thos. Bourke, L. D.
1324. Sir John Darcy, *returned* as L. J.
1326. Thos., second E. of Kildare, *again*, L. J.

EDWARD III.

1328. Roger Oatlawe, or Outlawe, ld. chanc., elected L. J.
Sir John Darcy, *again*, L. J.
1329. Jas. Boteler, or Butler, E. of Ormonde, L. L.
1330. Roger Outlawe, *again*, L. D.
1331. Sir Anthy. Lucy, L. L.
1332. Sir John Darcy, L. J.
1333. Sir Thos. de Burgh, ld. treasr., L. D.
1334. Sir John Darcy, *returned*, L. J.
1337. Sir John Charlton, L. J.
1338. Thos. Charlton, bp. of Hereford, bro. to sir John, and ld. chanc., L. D.
1340. Roger Outlawe, *again*, L. J.
Sir John Darcy, *again*, for life, L. J.
1341. Sir John Morice, L. D.
1344. Sir Ralph Ufford (consort to the countess of Ulster), L. J.
1346. Sir Roger Darcy (second son of sir John Darcy), elected L. J.
Sir Walter Bermingham, L. J.
1347. John Archer, prior of Kilmainham, L. D.
1348. Sir Walter Bermingham, *returned*.
1349. Sir John de Carew, baron de Carew, L. J.
Sir Thos. Rokeby, L. J.
1351. Maurice de Rochfort, bp. of Limerick, L. D.
1353. Sir Thos. Rokeby, *returned*, L. J.
Maurice, 4th E. of Kildare, for life, L. J.; *d.* Jan. 25, following.
1356. Sir Thos. Rokeby, L. J.; *d.* same year.
1357. Sir Almeric de St. Amand, L. J.
1359. Jas., 2nd E. of Ormond, L. J.
1360. Maurice, 4th E. of Kildare, *again*, L. D.
Jas., 2nd E. of Ormond, *returned*, L. J.
1361. LIONEL, D. of Clarence, E. of Ulster, ld. of Connaught; son to the king, L. L.
1364. Jas., 2nd E. of Ormond, *again*, L. D.
LIONEL, D. of Clarence, &c., *returned*, L. L.
1365. Sir Thos. Date, L. D.
1367. LIONEL, D. of Clarence, &c., *returned*, L. L.
Maurice, 4th E. of Kildare, *again*, L. J.
1369. Sir Wm. de Windsor, L. L.
1371. Maurice, 4th E. of Kildare, *again*, L. D.
1372. Sir Robt. de Assheton, L. J.
Ralph Chene, or Cheney, L. D.
Wm. Tany, prior of Kilmainham, elect. upon Cheney resigning, L. D.
1374. Sir Wm. de Windsor, *again*.
1375. Maurice, 4th E. of Kildare, *again*, L. D.
1376. Jas., E. of Ormond, L. J.

RICHARD II.

1378. Alexr. Balscot, bp. of Ossory, L. J.
1379. John de Bromwich, L. J.
1380. Edmd. Mortimer, E. of March and Ulster, L. L.; for three years; *d.* 1831.
1381. John Colton, dean of St. Patrick's, ld. chanc., elect. L. J., Jan. 10.
The same, by patent, Jan. 20.
Roger Mortimer, E. of March and Ulster, son of Edmund, L. L.
1383. Philip de Courtenay, the king's cousin, L. L.
1384. Jas., 3rd E. of Ormond, L. D.
Philip de Courtenay, *returned*.
The KING in person.
Robt. de Vere, E. of Oxford, aft. M. of Dublin, and D. of Ireland,* L. L. He never came over; banished and attainted in 1388.
1385. Sir John Stanley, L. L.
1386. Philip de Courtenay, L. L.
1387. Alexr. de Balscot, now bp. of Meath, *again*, L. J.
1389. Sir John Stanley, L. L.
Richd. White, prior of Kilmainham, ld. treasr., and sir Robt. Preston, ld keeper, LL. D.
1391. Alexr. de Balscot, bp. of Meath, *again*, L. J.
1392. Jas., 3rd E. of Ormond, *again*, L. J.
1393. Thos. of Woodstock, D. of Gloucester, L. L., July.
The KING in person; landed at Waterford, Oct. 2.
1394. Sir Thos. le Scrope, L. D.

* This nobleman was summoned to Parliament, 11 Richard II. 1387, as "*Charissimo consanguieneo Regis Roberti duci Hiberniæ*"; but no notice of his creation to the dukedom of Ireland occurs in the rolls of Parliament; he was Marquess of Dublin, with the lordship and dominion of Ireland.—*Sir Harris Nicolas.*

1395. Roger Mortimer, E. of March and Ulster, L. L.; *d.* 1398.

1398. Roger Gray, elect. on the death of Mortimer, L. J.

Thos. de Holland, E. of Kent and D. of Surrey, half-brother to the king, L. L.; aft. attainted and his honours forfeited.

1399. The KING in person; landed at Waterford, June 1.

HENRY IV.

1399. Alexr. de Balscot, bp. of Meath, *again*, L. J., Oct.

1399. Sir John Stanley, L. L., Dec. 1.

1400. Sir Wm. Stanley, bro. to sir John, L. D.

1401. THOS. de Lancaster,* the king's son, seneschal of England, L. L. Patent at Westminster, June 27.

1401. Sir Steph. le Scrope, L. D., Dec. 19.

1402. THOS, de Lancaster, *again*, L. L.

1403. Sir Steph. le Scrope, *again*, L. D.; *d.* 1408.

1404. THOS. de Lancaster, *again*, L. L.

1405. Jas., 3rd E. of Ormond, in the absence of sir Steph. le Scrope.

Gerald, 5th E. of Kildare, elected on Ormond's death.

1407. Jas., 4th E. of Ormond, L. D.

1408. THOS. de Lancaster, *again*, L. L., June 4.

Wm. Fitz-Thos. le Botiller, prior of St. John's of Jerusalem, L. D.

HENRY V.

1413. Sir John Stanley, L. L., Sept.; *d.* Jan. following.

1414. Thos., abp. of Dublin, elected on Stanley's death, L. J.

Sir John Talbot, of Hallamshire, ld. of Furnyvall; aft. E. of Shrewsbury, L. L.

1419. Rd. Talbot, abp. of Dublin, bro. to sir John, L. D.

Jas., 4th E. of Ormond, *again*, L. L.

HENRY VI.

1423. Edmd. Mortimer, E. of March and Ulster, L. L., May 9.

Edwd. Dantsey, bp. of Meath, L. D., Aug. 4. His patent was deemed insufficient by the council, having been signed by Mortimer only; but his authority was afterwards recognised.

1424. Jas., 4th E. of Ormond, *again*, L. L.

1426. The same; now L. J. only.

1427. Sir John de Grey, L. L. on Ormond' patent being revoked.

1428 Sir John Sutton, ld. Dudley, L. L.

1429. Sir Thos. Straunge, L. D.

1430. Rd. Talbot, abp. of Dublin, L. D.

1431. Sir Thos. Stanley, L. L.

1432. Sir Christr. Plunket, L. D.

1435. Sir Thos. Stanley, *returned*, L. L.

1436. Rd. Talbot. abp. of Dublin, *again* L. D.

1438. Lionel de Welles, ld. Welles, L. L.

It is said he did not come over but he certainly did, and per formed public acts at Dubli castle, held a council at Trim, ar other at Drogheda, &c.

1440. Jas., 4th E. of Ormond, *again*, L. D

1442. Wm. Welles, L. D. to his brother, ld Welles, aft. Dec. 5, in this year.

1443. Jas., 4th E. of Ormond, *again*, L. I

1445. Rd. Talbot, abp. of Dublin, *agai* L. D.

1446. John Talbot, E. of Shrewsbur L. L.

1447. Rd. Talbot, abp. of Dublin, *agai* L. D.

1449. RD. Plantagenet, D. of York, E. c Ulster, March, Cork, &c., L. L July.

Rd. Nugent, baron of Delvin, L. D.

1450. Jas., E. of Wilts, aft. 5th E. Ormond, L. L.

1452. Sir Edwd. Fitz Eustace, L. D.

1453. Jas., 5th E. of Ormond, *again*, L. L May.

John Mey, abp. of Armagh, L. D June.

1454. Sir Edwd. Fitz Eustace, *again*, L. D *d.* this year.

1459. RD. Plantagenet, D. of York, &c *again*, L. L. for ten years; 1460.

1460. Thos., 7th E. of Kildare, L. D.

EDWARD IV.

1461. The same, *contd.*

GEO., D. of Clarence, bro. to tl king, L. L. for seven years.

1462. Roland Fitz Eustace, ld. of Por lester, L. D.

Wm. Sherwood, bp. of Meath, L.

1463. Thos., 7th E. of Kildare, *again*, L.

1467. John, ld. Tiptoft, E. of Worceste *d.* 1470.

1468. Thos., 7th E. of Kildare, *again*, L.

1475. Wm. Sherwood, bp. of Meath, *aga* L. D.

1478. RD., of Shrewsbury, D. of York, s

* Thomas de Lancaster is by some authors styled *Duke* of Lancaster, but err neously, for Henry IV. had no son who bore that title. Thomas of Lancaster, he mentioned, was Henry's second son by Queen Mary de Bohun, and was afterwar (July 9, 1411) created earl of Albemarle and duke of Clarence; slain 1421. The la Mr. Lascelles, in his *Liber Hiberniæ*, correctly states that his patent as "lord Ireland" is of record at Westminster.

cond son to the king, L. L.; he never went over. Murdered (with his brother Edwd. V.) in the Tower of London, 1483, by ord. of his uncle, Rd., D. of Gloucester.
Robt., visc. Gormanstown, L. D.
Gerald, 8th E. of Kildare, L. D.
1483. EDWD., pr. of Wales, son to the king, L. L.; he never went over. He, too, was murdered this year, when king, by order of his uncle, Rd., D. of Gloucester.

RICHARD III.

1483. Gerald, 8th E. of Kildare, *again*, L. D.
1484. John de la Pole, E. of Lincoln, L. L.
Gerald, 8th E. of Kildare, *again*, L. D.

HENRY VII.

1485. Jasper, E. of Pembroke and D. of Bedford, uncle to the king, L. L.
Gerald, 8th E. of Kildare, *again*, L. D.
1490. Jasper, D. of Bedford, *again*, by a "new constitution," L. L.
1492. Walter Fitzsimons, abp. of Dublin, L. D.
1493. Robt., visc. Gormanstown, *again*, L. D.
Wm. Preston, his son, L. D.
1494. HY., D. of York, second son to the King, aft. Hy. VIII., L. L.; he never went over.
Sir Edwd. Poynings, L. D. to Henry, the king's son.
1495. Hy. Deane, bp. of Bangor, and ld. chanc., L. J.
1496. Gerald, 8th E. of Kildare, *again*, L. D.
1498. HY., aft. Hy. VIII., *again*, L. L.
Gerald, 8th E. of Kildare, *again*, L. D.
1503. Walter Fitzsimons, abp. of Dublin, L. D. to Kildare.
Gerald, 8th E. of Kildare, *returned*, L. D.

HENRY VIII.

1509. The same, *contd.*
1510. The same, by a new patent.
1513. Gerald, 9th E. of Kildare, elect. on the death of his father, L. J.
The same, by patent, L. D.
1515. Wm., visc. Gormanstown, L. J.
Gerald, 9th E. of Kildare, *again*, L. D. to the king.
1519. Sir Maurice Fitzgerald, of Lackagh, L. D. to Kildare.
1521. Thos. Howard, E. of Surrey, L. L.
Pierce, 8th E. of Ormond and E. of Ossory, L. D.
1524. Gerald, 9th E. of Kildare, *again*, L. D.
1526. Sir Jas. Fitzgerald, of Leixlip, bro. to E. of Kildare, his dep.
Richd. Nugent, ld. Delvin, L. D.
1528. Pierce, E. of Ossory, *again*, L. J. The title of Ormond was taken from him, and conferred on sir Thos. Boleyn, father of Anna Boleyn, aft. queen; elect. by council on Nugent's being made prisoner by O'Connor; L. J.
1529. Hy. Fitzroy, D. of Richmond and Somerset, nat. son to the king, L. L.
1530. Sir Wm. Skeffington, L. D.
1532. Gerald, 9th E. of Kildare, *again*, L. D.
1534. Thos., ld. Offaley, son and dep. to E. of Kildare.
1535. Leonard, ld. Grey, visc. Graney, in Ireland, son to the M. of Dorset; elect. on Skeffington's death in 1541; L. D.
1540. Sir Wm. Brereton, ld. chanc., L. J.
Sir Anthy. St. Leger, L. D.
1543. Sir Wm. Brabazon, L. J.
1544. Sir Anthy. St. Leger, *again*, L. D.
1546. Sir Wm. Brabazon, *again*, L. J.
Sir Anthy. St. Leger, *again*, L.D.

EDWARD VI.

1547. Sir Wm. Brabazon, *again*, L. J.
1548. Sir Edwd. Bellingham, L. J.
1549. Sir Fras. Bryan; elect. on Bellingham's going to England, L. J.
Sir Wm. Brabazon, *again*, elect. on Bryan's death; L. J.
1550. Sir Anthy St. Leger, *again*, L. D.
1551. Sir Jas. Croft, a gentleman of the privy chamber, L. D.
1552. Sir Thos. Cusack, ld. chanc.; elect. on Croft's going to England; and Sir Gerald Aylmer, ld. ch. just. K. B.; LL. J.

MARY.

1553. The same, *contd.*
Sir Anthy. St. Leger, *again*, L. D.
1556. Thos., visc. Fitz-Walter, aft. E. of Sussex, L. D.
1557. Hugh Curwen, ld. chanc., and Sir Hy. Sidney, LL. J.
1558. Sir Hy. Sidney, *again*, L. J.
Thos., E. of Sussex, *again*, L. D.
Sir Hy. Sidney, *again*, during Sussex's expedition to Scotland, L. D.
Thos., E. of Sussex, *again*, by a new commission, L. D.

ELIZABETH.

1558. The same *contd.* for a time, without a new commission, L. D.
Sir Hy. Sidney, *again*, elect. by the council, L. J.

1559. Thos., E. of Sussex, *again*, L. D.
1560. Sir Wm. Fitzwilliam, in Sussex's absence, L. D.
Thos., E. of Sussex, *again*, L. L.
1561. Sir Wm. Fitzwilliam, *again*, in the absence of Sussex, by a commission from the queen, L. D.
Thos., E. of Sussex, *again*, by a new patent, L. L.
1562. Sir Wm. Fitzwilliam, *again*, L. J.
Thos., E. of Sussex, *again*, by a new patent, L. L.
1564. Sir Nichs. Arnold, L. J.
1565. Sir Hy. Sidney, *again*, L. D.
1567. Robt. Weston, ld. chanc., and Sir Wm. Fitzwilliam, LL. J.
1568. Sir Hy. Sidney, *again*, L. D.
1571. Sir Wm. Fitzwilliam, *again*, elect. in the absence of Sidney, L. J.
1572. The same, elect. by the council, L. D.
1575. Sir Hy. Sidney. *again*, L. D.
1578. Sir Wm. Drury, elect. L. J.
1579. Sir Wm. Pelham, elect. on Drury's death, L. J.
1580. The same, by patent, L. J.
Arthur, ld. Grey, of Wilton, L.D.
1582. Adam Loftus (No. 1), abp. of Dublin and ld. chanc.; and
Sir Hy. Wallop, LL. J.
1584. Sir John Perrot, L. D.
1588. Sir Wm. Fitzwilliam, *again*, L. D.
1594. Sir Wm. Russell, youngest son of the E. of Bedford, L. D.
1597. Thos., ld. Burgh, of Gainsborough, K. G. and L. D.
Sir Thos. Norris, elect. on ld. Burgh's death, L. J.
Sir Thos. Norris, by patent, L. J.
Adam Loftus (No. 1), *again*; and
Sir Robt. Gardiner, ch. just., LL. J. for civil affairs; and
Thos., 10th E. of Ormond, L. J. for military affairs; elect. by the queen's commission on Norris's death.
1599. Robt. Devereux, E. of Essex, L. L.; *d.* 1601.
Adam Loftus (No. 1), *again*; and
Sir Geo. Cary; elect. on Essex's going to England, LL. J.
1600. Sir Chas. Blount, ld. Mountjoy, K.G., L. D.

JAMES I.

1603. The same *contd.*
The same, by a new patent, L. D.
The same, as L. L.
Sir Geo. Cary, L. D.
1604. Sir Arthur Chichester, aft. ld. Chichester. L. D.
1606. The same, by a new commission.
1613. Sir Richd. Wingfield, aft. visc. Powerscourt; and
Thos. Jones, abp. of Dublin; LL. J.
1614. Arth., ld. Chichester, L. D.
1615. Abp. Jones, *again*; and
Sir John Denham, ch. just. K. B. LL. J.
1616. Sir Oliver St. John, aft. visc. Grandison, L. D.
1622. Hy., visc. Falkland, L. D.
1623. Adam Loftus (No. 2), now visc Loftus of Ely, ld. chanc.; and
Richd., visc. Powerscourt, *again* LL. J.

CHARLES I., COMMONWEALTH, AND CHARLES II,

1625. Hy., visc. Falkland, *again*, L. D.
1629. Adam, visc. Loftus of Ely, ld chanc., *again*; and Richd., E. of Cork, LL. J.
1633. Thos., visc. Wentworth, aft. E. of Strafford, L. D.
1636. Adam, visc. Loftus of Ely, ld chanc., *again*; and
Christr. Wandesford, m. rolls, LL. J.
Thos., visc. Wentworth, *returned* L. D.
1639. Robt., ld. Dillon; and
Christr. Wandesford, *again*, LL. J.
1640. Thos., now E. of Strafford, *again* L. L.; *d.* 1641.
Sir Christ. Wandesford, *again*, L. D.
Robt., ld. Dillon, *again*; and
Sir Wm. Parsons, LL. J.
1641. Robt., E. of Leicester, L. L.; he never came over.
1643. Sir John Borlase; and
Sir Hy. Tichborne, gov. of Drogheda, LL. J.
1644. Jas., 1st M. and aft. 1st D. Ormond, L. L.
1647. Philip, ld. Lisle, son to the E. of Leicester, under the parliament L. L.
Arthur Annesley, sir Robt. King, sir Robt. Meredith, col. John Moore, col. Michael Jones, parl. commrs.
1648. Jas., 1st M. of Ormond., *returned* L. L.
1649. Oliver Cromwell, under the parl L. L.
1650. Hy. Ireton, son-in-law to Cromwell L. D.
Ulick, M. of Clanricade, deputy M. of Ormond, L. D.
1651. Maj.-gen. Lambert, under the parl L. D.
1653, Chas. Fleetwood, lt.-gen.; Edmund Ludlow, lt.-gen. of the horse Miles Corbet, John Jones, Jo. Weever, commrs.
1654. Chas. Fleetwood, lt.-gen. under the parlt., L. D.
1655. Hy. Cromwell, comm. in chief of the army, Matt. Thomlinson, Miles Corbet, Robt. Goodwin, to whom

afterwards was added Wm. Steel, commrs.
1657. Hy. Cromwell, son to the protector Oliver, L. L.
1658. The same, brother to the protector Richd., for three years, L. L.
1659. Edmd. Ludlow, John Jones, Matth. Tomlinson, Miles Corbet, maj. Wm. Bury, commrs.
1660. Roger, ld. Broghill; sir Chas. Coote, maj. Wm. Bury, commrs.
1660. Geo., D. of Ablbemarle; declared L. L.; but did not go over.
John, ld. Robartes, ditto, ditto, L. D.
Sir Maurice Eustace, ld. chanc.; sir Chas. Coote, E. of Mountrath; and Roger, E. of Orrery, LL. J.
1661. Sir Maurice Eustace, ld. chanc.; and Roger, E. of Orrery, *again*, upon the death of Mountrath, LL. J.
1662. Jas., 1st D. of Ormond, *again*, L. L.
1664. Thos., E. of Ossory, son to the D. of Ormond, L. D.
1665. Jas., 1st D. of Ormond, *returned*, L. L.
1668. Thos., E. of Ossory, *again*, L. D.
1669. John, ld. Robartes, *again*, L. L.
1670. John, ld. Berkeley of Stratton, L. L.
1671. Michl. Boyle, abp. of Dublin & ld. chanc.; and
Sir Arth. Forbes, marshl.-genl., LL. J.
John, ld. Berkeley, *returned*, L. L.
1672. Arth. E. of Essex, L. L.
1675. Michl. Boyle, abp. of Dublin and ld. chanc; and
Arth., visc., aft. E. Granard, LL. J.
1676. Arth., E. of Essex, *returned*, L. L.
1677. Jas., 1st D. of Ormond, L. L.
1682. Richd., E. of Arran, son to the D. of Ormond, L D.
1684. Jas., 1st D. of Ormond, *returned*, L.L.

James II.

1684. The same, *contd.*, L. L.
Michl. Boyle, now abp. of Armagh and ld. chanc.; and
Arth., now E. of Granard, *again*, LL. J.
1685. Hy., E. of Clarendon, L. L.
1686. Richd., E. of Tyrconnel, L. L.
1687. Sir Alexr. Fitton, ld. chanc.; and Wm., E. of Clanricade, in absence of Tyrconnel, LL. J.
1687. Richd., E. of Tyrconnel, *returned*, L. L.
1689. The King in person, arrived at Dublin, Mar. 20.

William III.

1690. King Wm. in person, landed at Carrickfergus.
Hy., visc. Sydney; sir Chas. Porter, and Thos. Coningsby, LL. J.
1692. Hy., visc. Sydney, L. L.
1693. Hy., ld. Capel; sir Cyril Wyche; and Wm. Duncombe, esq.; in absence of ld. Sydney, LL. J.
1693. Sir Chas. Porter, ld. chanc.; and sir Cyril Wyche, *again*, LL. J.
1695. Hy., ld. Capel, L. D.
1696. Murrough, visc. Blesinton; and brigadier Wm. Wolesley, LL. J. Elected upon ld. Capel's illness, but their commissions were not sealed, nor were they sworn.
Sir Chas. Porter, ld. chanc., *again*; elected on ld. Capel's death.
Sir Chas. Porter, ld. chanc., *again*; Chas., E. of Mountrath; and Hy., E. of Drogheda, LL. J.
1697. Hy., E. of Galway, on sir Chas. Porter's death, L. J.
Chas., M. of Winchester; Hy., E. of Galway; and Edw., visc. Villiers, aft. E. of Jersey, LL. J.
1699. Chas., D. of Bolton; Hy., E. of Galway, *again*; Edw., E. of Jersey, *again*; and Narcissus Marsh, abp. of Dublin; or any two of them, LL. J.
Chas., D. of Bolton, *again*; Chas., E. of Berkeley; and Hy., E. of Galway, *again*, LL. J.
1701. Laurence, E. of Rochester, L. L.
1702. Narcissus Marsh, abp. of Dublin, *again*; Hy., E. of Drogheda, *again*; and Hugh, E. of Mount Alexander, LL. J.
The same, by a new commission, LL. J.

Anne.

Hugh, E. of Mount Alexander, *again*; Thos. Earl, lt.-gen.; and Thos. Keightley, LL. J.
1703. Jas., 2nd D. of Ormond, L. L.
Sir Richd. Cox, bt., ld. chanc.; Hugh, E. of Mount Alexander, *again*; and Thos. Earl, lt.-gen., *again*, LL. J.
1704. Jas., 2nd D. of Ormond, *returned*, L. L.
1705. Sir Richd. Cox, bt., ld. chanc., *again*; and John, ld. Cutts, of Gowran, lt.-gen., LL. J.
1707. Narcissus Marsh, now abp. of Armagh; and sir Richd. Cox, ld. chanc., *again*, on the death of ld. Cutts, LL. J.
Thos., E. of Pembroke, L. L.
Narcissus Marsh, abp. of Armagh, *again*; and Richd. Freeman, ld. chanc., LL. J.
1709. Thos., E. of Wharton, L. L.
Richd. Freeman, ld. chanc., *again*; and Richd. Ingoldsby, lt.-gen., LL. J.
1710. Thos., E. of Wharton, *returned*, L. L.
Richd. Freeman, ld. chanc.; and Richd. Ingoldsby, *again*, LL. J.

1710. Jas., 2nd D. of Ormond, *again*, L. L. Narcissus Marsh, abp. of Armagh, *again*; and Richd. Ingoldsby, *again*, LL. J.

1711. Sir Const. Phipps, ld. chanc.; and Rd. Ingoldsby, *again*, LL. J.

Jas., 2nd D. of Ormond, *returned*, L. L.

Sir Const. Phipps, ld. chanc., *again*; and Richd. Ingoldsby, *again*, LL. J.

1712. Sir Const. Phipps, ld. chanc., *again*; and John Vesey, abp. of Tuam; on Ingoldsby's death, LL. J.

1713. Chas., D. of Shrewsbury, L. L.

1714. Thos. Lindsay, abp. of Armagh; John Vesey, abp. of Tuam, *again*; and sir Const. Phipps, *again*, LL. J.

GEORGE I.

1714. Wm. King, abp. of Dublin; John Vesey, abp. of Tuam, *again*; and Robt., 19th E. of Kildare, LL. J.

Chas., E. of Sunderland, L. L.; *he never came over.*

1715. Chas., D. of Grafton; and Hy., E. of Galway, LL. J.

1716. Chas., visc. Townshend, L. L.; *he never came over.*

1717. Alan, ld. Brodrick, aft. visc. Midleton, ld. chanc.; Wm. King, abp. of Dublin, *again*; and Wm. Conolly, sp. ho. comm., LL. J.

Chas., D. of Bolton, L. L.

1718. Alan, visc. Midleton, ld. chanc.; Wm. King, abp. of Dublin; and Wm. Conolly, sp. ho. comm., *again*, LL. J., May 22.

1719. Chas., D. of Bolton, *returned*, L. L., Mar. 31.

Alan, visc. Midleton, ld. chanc.; and Wm. Conolly, sp. ho. comm., *again*, LL. J., Nov. 20.

1721. Chas., D. of Grafton, L. L., Aug. 28.

1722. Wm. King, abp. of Dublin, *again*; Richd., visc. Shannon; and Wm. Conolly, sp. ho. comm., *again*, LL. J., Feb. 24.

1723. Alan, visc. Midleton, ld. chanc.; Wm. King, abp. of Dublin; Richd., visc. Shannon; and Wm. Conolly, sp. ho. comm., *again*, LL. J., June 13.

Chas., D. of Grafton, *returned*, L. L., Aug. 13.

1724. Alan, visc. Midleton, ld. chanc.; Richd., visc. Shannon; and Wm. Conolly, sp. ho. comm., *again*, LL. J., May 9.

John, ld. Carteret, aft. E. Granville, L. L., Oct. 22.

1726. Hugh Boulter, abp. of Armagh; Richd. West, ld. chanc.; and Wm. Conolly, sp. ho. comm., *again*, LL. J., Apr. 2.

1726. Hugh Boulter, abp. of Armagh, *again*; Thos. Wyndham, aft. ld. Wyndham, ld. chanc.; and Wm. Conolly, sp. ho. comm., *again*, LL. J., Dec. 23.

GEORGE II.

1727. John, ld. Carteret, by a new commission, L. L., Nov. 19.

1728. The same lords justices, May 15.

1729. John, ld. Carteret, *returned*, L. L., Sept. 13.

1730. The same lords justices, Apr. 22.

1731. Lionel Cranfield, D. of Dorset, L. L., Sept. 11.

1732. Hugh Boulter, abp. of Armagh, *again*; Thos., ld. Wyndham, ld. chanc. *again*; and sir Ralph Gore, sp. ho. comm., LL. J., Apr. 24.

1733. Sir Ralph Gore, *d.* in the govt.; and Hy. Boyle, the new speaker, became L. J. in his room.

Lionel Cranfield, D. of Dorset, *returned*, L. L., Sept. 24.

1734. The same lords justices, May 3.

1735. Lionel Cranfield, D. of Dorset, *returned*, L. L., Sept. 26.

1736. The same lords justices, May 19.

1737. Wm., 3rd D. of Devonshire, L. L., Sept. 7.

1738. The same lords justices, Mar. 28.

1739. Wm., 3rd D. of Devonshire, *returned*, L. L., Sept. 27.

1740. Hugh Boulter, abp. of Armagh, *again*; Robt. Jocelyn, aft. ld. Newport and visc. Jocelyn, ld. chanc.; and Hy. Boyle, sp. ho. comm., *again*, LL. J., Apr. 18.

1741. Wm., 3rd D. of Devonshire, *returned*, L. L., Sept. 23.

1742. John Hoadly, abp. of Armagh; Robt. Jocelyn, aft. ld. Newport, &c., ld. chanc. *again*; and Henry Boyle, sp. ho. comm., *again*, LL. J., Dec. 3.

1743. Wm., 3rd D. of Devonshire, *returned*, L. L., Sept. 29.

1744. The same lords justices, Apr. 12.

1745. Philip Dormer, E. of Chesterfield, L. L., Aug. 31.

1746. The same lords justices, Apr. 25. The abp. of Armagh *d.* in the govt.

1747. Geo. Stone, abp. of Armagh; Robt., ld. Newport, ld. chanc., *again*; and Hy. Boyle, sp. ho. comm., *again*, LL. J., Apr. 10.

Wm., E. of Harrington, L. L., Sept. 13.

1748. The same lords justices, Apr. 20.

1749. Wm., E. of Harrington, *returned*, L. L., Sept. 20.

1750. The same lords justices, Apr. 19.

1751. Lionel Cranfield, D. of Dorset, *again*, L. L., Sept. 19.

1752. The same lords justices, May 27.

1753. Lionel Cranfield, D. of Dorset, *returned*, L. L., Sept. 21.
1754. Geo. Stone, abp. of Armagh, *again*; Robt., ld. Newport, ld. chanc., *again*; and Brabazon, E. of Besborough, LL. J., May 11.
1755. Wm., M. of Hartington; aft. 4th D. of Devonshire, L. L., May 5.
1756. Robt., now visc. Jocelyn, ld. chanc., *again*; Jas., 20th E. of Kildare, aft. 1st M. of Kildare and D. of Leinster; and Brabazon, E. of Besborough, *again*, LL. J.; the three, or any two or one of them, to act separately, Sept. 20.
1757. John, 7th D. of Bedford, L. L., Sept. 25.
1758. Geo. Stone, abp. of Armagh, *again*; Hy., E. of Shannon; and John Ponsonby, sp. ho. comm., LL. J., May 10.
1759. John, 7th D. of Bedford, *returned*, L. L.
1760. The same lords justices, May 20.

GEORGE III.

1760. The same lords justices, *contd.*
1761. Geo., E. of Halifax, L. L., Oct. 6.
1762. The same lords justices, May 3.
1763. Hugh, E. of Northumberland, L. L., Sept. 22.
1764. The same lords justices, May 15.
The abp. of Armagh *d.* Dec. 19, and the E. of Shannon Dec. 28, 1764.
1765 Thos., visc. Weymouth, L. L.: *did not come over.*
John, ld. Bowes, ld. chanc.; and John Ponsonby, sp. ho. comm., *again*, LL. J.
Fras., 17th E., aft. 1st M. of Hertford, L. L., Oct. 18.
1766. John, ld. Bowes, ld. chanc., *again*; Chas., E. of Drogheda; and John Ponsonby, sp. ho. comm., *again*, LL. J., June 11.
Wm. Geo., E. of Bristol, L. L.; *he did not come over.*
The same lords justices.
1767. Geo., visc. Townshend, L. L., Oct. 14.
1772. Simon, E. Harcourt, L. L., Nov. 30.
1777. John, E. of Buckinghamshire, L. L., Jan. 25.
1780. Fred., E. of Carlisle, L. L., Dec. 23.
1782. Wm. Hy., D. of Portland, L. L., Apr. 14.
Geo., E. Temple, aft. M. of Buckingham, L. L., Sept. 15.
1783. Robt., E. of Northington, L. L., June 3.
1784. Chas., 4th D. of Rutland, L. L., Feb. 24; *d.* in the govt., Oct. 22, 1787.
1787. Richd., ld. Rokeby, abp. of Armagh; Jas., visc. Lifford, ld. chanc.; and John Foster, sp. ho. comm., LL. J., Oct. 27.
Geo., now M. of Buckingham, *again* L. L., Nov. 2.
1789. John, ld. Fitzgibbon, ld. chanc.; and John Foster, sp. ho. comm., *again*, LL. J., June 30.
1790. John, E. of Westmoreland, L. L. Jan. 5.
1794. Wm., E. Fitzwilliam, L. L., Dec. 10; recalled Mar. 1795.
1795. John Jeffreys, E. Camden, L. L., Mar. 11.
1798. Chas. M. Cornwallis, L. L., June 13.

LORD LIEUTENANTS SINCE THE UNION.

The lords justices are no longer given, for the reasons stated *ante*, p. 549.
1801. Philip, E. of Hardwicke, Mar. 17.
1805. Edw., E. Powis; app. Nov. 16; *did not come over.*
1806. John, 9th D. of Bedford, Mar. 18.
1807. Chas., D. of Richmond, Apr. 19.
1813. Chas., visc., aft. E. Whitworth, Aug. 26.
1817. Chas., E. Talbot, Oct. 9.

GEORGE IV.

1820. The same, *contd.*
1821. The KING, in person; landed in Dublin Aug. 12; left Ireland Sept. 5.
Chas., E. Talbot, *resumed.*
1821. Richd., M. Wellesley, Dec. 29.
1828. Hy. Wm., M. of Anglesey, Mar. 1.
1829. Hugh, D. of Northumberland, Mar. 6.

WILLIAM IV.

1830. Hy. Wm., M. of Anglesey, *again*; Dec. 23.
1833. Richd., M. Wellesley, *again*; Sept. 26.
1834. Thos., E. of Haddington, Dec. 29; sw. Jan. 6, 1835.
1835. Hy. Constantine, E. of Mulgrave; aft. M. of Normanby Apr. 23; sw. May 11.

VICTORIA.

1837. The same *contd.*
1839. Hugh, visc. Ebrington, aft. E. Fortescue, Apr. 3.
1841. Thos. Philip, E. De Grey, Sept. 15.
1844. Wm., ld. Heytesbury, July 26.
1846. John Wm., E. of Bessborough, July 11; *d.* in the govt., May 16, 1847.
1847. Geo. Wm. Fredk., E. of Clarendon, K. G., May 26.
1852. Archd. Wm., E. of Eglinton, Feb. 27.
1853. Edwd. Granville, E. of St. Germans, Jan. 4.
1855. Geo. Wm. Fredk., E. of Carlisle, K. G., Feb. 28.

1858. Archd. Wm., E. of Eglinton, *again*, Feb. 26.
1859. Geo. Wm. Fredk., E. of Carlisle, K. G., *again*, June 18.
1864. John, ld. Wodehouse, aft. E. of Kimberley, Nov. 1.
1866. Jas., M., aft. D. of Abercorn, K. G., July 6.
1868. John Poyntz, E. Spencer, K. G., Dec. 11.
1874. Jas. D. of Abercorn, K. G., *again*, Mar. 2.
1876. John Winston, D. of Marlborough, K. G., Nov. 28.
1880. Fras. Thos. De Grey, E. Cowper, K. G., May 3.
1882. John Poyntz, E. Spencer, K. G., *again*, May 3.
1885. Hy. Howard Molyneux, E. of Carnarvon, July.
1886. John Campbell, E. of Aberdeen, K. G., Feb. 6.
Chas. Stewart, M. of Londonderry, Aug. 3.

LORD TREASURERS, VICE TREASURERS, AND TREASURY COMMISSIONERS FOR IRELAND.

Lord Treasurers and Vice Treasurers of Ireland.

V. T. Vice Treasurer; *when no initials Lord Treasurer is understood.*

Henry III.

1217. John de St. John.
1232. Peter de Rivallis.
1233. Eustace, canon of Chichester.
1234. Geoffrey de Turville, archdn of Dublin.
1251. Hugh de Mapilton, bp. of Ossory.
1258. Hugh de Tachmon, bp. of Meath.

Edward I.

1274. Steph. de Fulburn, bp. of Waterford.
1277. Robt. le Poer.
1278. Steph. de Fulburn, *again*.
1281. Hugh de Tachmon, *again*.
1289. Nichs. le Clerc, or Clerk.
1294. John ap Rees, or Rice.
Sir Wm. de Essendon.
1300. Richd. de Bereford.
1304. Sir Wm. de Essendon, *again*.
1305. Richd. de Bereford, *again*.
Richd. de Sahan.

Edward II.

1307. Alexr. de Bicknor, or Bython.
1309. John de Hotham.
1312. John Leck, or Lich, abp. of Dublin.
1315. Walter de Istlep, or Isteley.
John de Hotham, *again*.
1317. Walter de Istlep, *again*.
1325. Adam de Hermington.

Edward III.

1327. Walter de Istlep, *again*.
Robt. Fitz-Eustace.
1330. Sir Thos. de Burgh.
1335. Sir John de Ellerker.
1344. John de Burnham, canon of St. Patrick's.
1349. John de Boukton.
1354. Wm. de Bromley.
1357. Nichs. Allen, bp. of Meath.
1367. Alexr. Balscot, bp. of Ossory.
1371. Peter Curragh, bp. of Limerick.
Steph. de Valle, bp. of Meath.
1374. John de Colton, dean of St. Patrick's.

Richard II.

1377. Alexr. Balscot, *again*.
1381. John de Colton, *again*.
1385. Wm. Chambers, archdn. of Dublin.
1392. Richd. Mitford, bp. of Chichester.
1395. Stephn., abbot of St. Mary's, Dublin.

Henry IV.

1399. Robt. de Faryngton.
1400. Thos. Bathe, or Batche.
1401. Sir Laurence Merbury.
1409. Wm. Allington.

Henry V.

1413. Hugh Burgh.
1414. John Coryngham.
1421. Wm. Tynebegh, or Thynbegh.

Henry VI.

1424. Hugh Banent.
1426. Edwd. Dantsey, bp. of Meath.
1427. Sir Nichs. Plunket.
1429. Sir Thos. Strange.
1432. Christr. Barnewall.
1437. Ægidius Thorndon, or Thornton.
1441. Thos. Barry, bp. of Ossory.
1443. Wm. Cheevers, just. K. B.
1446. Ægidius Thorndon, *again*.
1450. John Blackston.
1453. Sir Hy. Bruyn.
1454. Sir Rowland Fitz-Edwd. Fitz-Eustace, aft. ld Portlester.

EDWARD IV.

1461. John, ld. Wenlock, and Rowland, ld. Portlester, for their lives, and survivor.
1471. Portlester, who survived Wenlock, had his pat. confirmed by act of parlt.

HENRY VII.

1492. Sir Jas. Ormond, natl. son of the E. of Ormond.
1494. Sir Hugh Conway.
1504. Gerald Fitzgerald, eldest son of the E. of Kildare.

HENRY VIII.

1514. Christr., ld. Slane.
1516. Barth. Dillon, ch. bar. ex., V. T.
1517. John Rawson, prior of Kilmainham.
1520. Sir John Stile, V. T.
1524. John, ld. Trimleston.
1530. John Rawson, prior of Kilmainham, *again*.
1532. Jas. Butler, aft. visc. Thurles, and 9th E. of Ormond.
1533. Wm. Bath of Dollardstown, V. T.
1534. Wm. Brabazon. He continued V. T. until his death in 1552.
1540. Jas., 9th E. of Ormond.
1542. Jas., 15th E. of Desmond.

EDWARD VI.

* * The same, *contd.*
1552. Andr. Wise, on Brabazon's death, V. T.

MARY.

1553. Sir Edmd Rouse, L. T. and V. T.
* * Jas., 15th E. of Desmond.

ELIZABETH.

1559. Sir Hy. Sydney, V. T.
* * Sir Thos. Fitz-William, V. T.
1559. Thos., 10th E. of Ormond.
1573. Sir Edwd. Fitton, V. T.
1582. Sir Hy. Wallop, V. T.
1586. Thos., 10th E. of Ormond.

JAMES I.

1603. The same, *contd.*
1616. Arth., ld. Chichester of Belfast.
1625. Sir Archd. Blundell, V. T.

CHARLES I.

1625. Sir Fras. Annesley, bt., V. T.
* * Oliver, visc. Grandison.
1629. Sir Fras. Annesley, *again*, V. T.
1631. Richd., E. of Cork.
1636. Sir Adam Loftus, V. T.

THE COMMONWEALTH.

1654. Jas. Standish, under the parlt., V. T.

CHARLES II.

1660. Arth., visc. Valentia, aft. E. of Anglesey, V. T., Aug. 21.
Richd., ld. Clifford, E. of Cork and aft. of Burlington, Nov. 15.
1662. The same, by a new patent. Mar. 20.
1667. Sir Geo. Carteret, bt., V. T., July 18.
1673. Sir John Temple, V. T., Nov. 26.

JAMES II

1685. John Price, V. T., June 17.
1686. Thos. Knightley, V. T., Apr. 3.
1689. Richd., D. of Tyrconnel (so cr. after the abdn.); Hy., ld. Dover; Thos., ld. Riverston; Jenico visc. Gormanstown; visc. Fitzwilliam, Bruno Talbot, and sir Steph. Rice, commrs.

WILLIAM III.

1690. Wm. Harbord, V. T., Dec. 11.
1693. Thos., ld. Coningsby, V. T., Jan. 9.
1695. Chas., ld. Clifford of Lanesborough, visc. Dungarvan, May 4.
1698. Thos., ld. Conyngsby, *again*, V. T., Oct. 7.

ANNE.

1702. Chas., E. of Cork and Burlington, son of Chas., ld. Clifford, Sept. 12.
1704. Hy. Boyle, cr. ld. Carleton (bro. of the E. of Cork) during the minority of Richd., E. of Cork and Burlington, May 5.
1710. John, E. of Anglesey, V. T., Aug. 3; *d.* Sept. following.
Arth., E. of Anglesey; and Hy., ld. Hyde, aft. E. of Clarendon and Rochester, V. T., Oct. 19.

GEORGE I.

1715. Richd., E. of Cork and Burlington, Aug. 25.
1716. Chas., E. of Sunderland, and Hy., E. of Rochester, V. TT., Mar. 1.
Chas., E. of Sanderland, now sole V. T.
1717. Matt. Ducie Morton, aft. ld. Ducie, V. T., May 2.
Richd., E. of Scarborough, and Matt. Ducie Morton, V. T., May 31.
Hugh Boscawen, aft. visc. Falmouth; and Matt. Ducie Morton, V. T., Oct. 10.
1720. Hugh Boscawen, and sir Wm. St. Quintin, bt., V. TT., June 16.
1724. Hugh Boscawen, now visc. Falmouth, and Richd. Edgcumbe, aft. ld. Edgcumbe, V. TT., Apr. 7.

GEORGE II.

1727. Richd., E, of Cork, *contd.* by a new pat., Oct. 24.
1734. Richd. Edgcumbe, and Pattee, visc. Torrington, v. TT., Apr. 24.
1742. Pattee, visc. Torrington, and Hy. Vane, v. TT., Aug. 2.
1744. Pattee, visc. Torrington, and Geo., E. of Cholmondeley, v. TT., Jan. 11.
Geo., E. of Cholmondeley, and Wm. Pitt, v. TT., Mar. 6.
1746. Geo., E. of Cholmondeley, and sir Wm. Yonge, bt., v. TT., May 22.
1754. Wm., ld. Cavendish of Hardwyck, M. of Hartingon, aft. 4th D. of Devonshire, Mar. 2.
1756. John, E. of Sandwich, Geo., E. of Cholmondeley, and Welbore Ellis, v. TT., Jan. 20.
1757. John, E. of Sandwich, Welbore Ellis, and Thos. Potter, v. TT., Aug. 2.
1760. John, E. of Sandwich, Welbore Ellis, and Robt. Nugent, aft. visc. Clare and E. Nugent, v. TT., Jan. 7.

GEORGE III.

1761. Wm., fourth D. of Devonshire, *contd.*, Mar. 3.
1763. John, E. of Sandwich, Robt. Nugent, and Richd. Rigby, v. TT., Jan. 5.
Robt. Nugent, Richd. Rigby, and Jas. Oswald, v. TT., May 4.
1765. Richd. Rigby, Jas. Oswald, and Welbore Ellis, v. TT., July 12.
1766. Jas. Oswald, ld. Geo. Sackville, aft. visc. Sackville, and Welbore Ellis, v. TT., Jan. 21.
Wm., 5th D. of Devonshire, *vice* his father, decd., Mar. 13. Continued ld. treasr. until the abolition of the office in 1793, *ut infra*.
1766. Jas. Oswald, Welbore Ellis, and hon. Jas. Grenville, v. TT., Aug. 3.
Jas. Oswald, hon. Jas. Grenville, and Isaac Barré, v. TT., Sept. 17.
1768. Hon. Jas. Grenville, Isaac Barré and Richd. Rigby, v. TT., Feb. 22
Hon. Jas. Grenville, Isaac Barré, and Robt., visc. Clare, v. TT., July 4.
1769. Hon. Jas. Grenville; Robt., visc. Clare, and Chas., E. Cornwallis, v. TT., Feb. 27.
1770. Robt., now visc. Clare; Chas. E. Cornwallis, and Welbore Ellis, v. TT., Apr. 21.
1771. Robt., visc. Clare; Welbore Ellis, and Geo., ld. Edgcumbe, aft. visc. Mount Edgcumbe and Valletort, v. TT., May 5.
1773. Robt., visc. Clare; Welbore Ellis, and Chas. Jenkinson, aft. bt., ld. Hawkesbury, and E. of Liverpool, v. TT. Jan. 18.
1775. Robt., visc. Clare; Welbore Ellis, and Henry Flood, v. TT., Oct. 27.
1777. Robt., now E. Nugent; Welbore Ellis, and Hy. Flood, v. TT., Mar. 7.
Robt., E. Nugent; Hy. Flood, and Chas. Townshend, v. TT., Sept. 17.
1781. Robt., E. Nugent; Chas. Townshend, and Richd., E. of Shannon, v. TT., Nov. 21.
1782. Richd., E. of Shannon; Richd., E. of Scarborough, and sir Geo. Yonge, bt., v. TT., Apr. 20.
Richd., E. of Shannon; sir Geo. Yonge, bt., and ld. Robt. Spencer, v. TT., May 24.
Richd., E. of Shannon; ld. Robt. Spencer, and ld. Chas. Spencer, v. TT., Sept. 9.
1783. Richd., E. of Shannon; ld. Chas. Spencer, and Wm. Eden, v. TT., Apr. 18.
1784. Richd., E. of Shannon; Geo., visc. Mount Edgcumbe, and Thos., ld Walsingham, v. TT., Mar. 8.
1787. Richd., E. of Shannon; Geo., visc. Mount Edgcumbe, and ld. Fredk. Campbell, v. TT., July 20.
1789. Geo., visc. Mount Edgcumbe; and ld. Fredk, Campbell, v. TT., June 18.

In 1793, the patents to the lord treasurer and vice-treasurers were revoked, and commissioners were from time to time appointed for executing those offices.

COMMISSIONERS OF THE TREASURY FOR IRELAND.

1793.

Richd., E. of Shannon.
Sir John Parnell, bt.
John Beresford.
Sir Hy. Cavendish, bt.
Wm. Burton Conyngham.
Robt., ld. Hobart.

1795.

Richd., E. of Shannon.
Sir John Parnell, bt.
Wm. Burton Conyngham.
Hon. Thos. Pelham.
John Monk Mason.

1796.

Richd., E. of Shannon.
Sir John Parnell, bt.
Thos., ld. Pelham.
John Monk Mason.
Lodge Morris.

1797.

Richd., E. of Shannon.
Isaac Corry.
Hon. Thos. Pelham.
John Monk Mason.
Lodge Morris.
Robt., visc. Castlereagh.

1800.

Richd., E. of Shannon.
Isaac Corry.

Robt., visc. Castlereagh.
Lodge, ld. Frankfort.
John, ld. Loftus.
Wm. Wickham.
Maurice Fitzgerald.

1801.

Richd., E. of Shannon.
Isaac Corry.
Chas. Abbot.
Lodge, ld. Frankfort.
John, visc. Loftus.
Maurice Fitzgerald.

1802.

Same Board.

1803.

Richd., E. of Shannon,
Isaac Corry.
Lodge, ld. Frankfort.
John, visc. Loftus.
Maurice Fitzgerald.
Wm. Wickham.

1804.

John Foster.
Sir Evan Nepean, bt.
Lodge, ld. Frankfort.
John, visc. Loftus.
Maurice Fitzgerald.

1804.

John Foster.
Lodge, ld. Frankfort.
John, visc. Loftus.
Maurice Fitzgerald.
Hon. George Knox.
Nichs. Vansittart.

1805.

John Foster.
Lodge, ld. Frankfort.
John, visc. Loftus.
Maurice Fitzgerald.
Hon. Geo. Knox.
Sir Lawrence Parsons, bt.
Chas. Long.

1806.

Wm. Wyndham, ld. Grenville.
Sir John Newport.
Maurice Fitzgerald.
Sir Lawrence Parsons, bt.
Chas. O'Hara.
Hy. Parnell.
Wm. Burton.
Wm. Elliot.

1807.

Geo., E. of Ross.
John Foster.
Arth. Wellesley, aft. Sir A., &c.
Hon. Thos. Hy. Foster
Sir Geo. FitzGerald Hill, bt.
John Maxwell Barry.
Chas. Vereker.

1810.

Hon. Spencer Perceval.
John Foster.
Wm. Wellesley Pole.
Geo., E. of Ross.
Sir G. Fitz-G. Hill, bt.
John M. Barry.
Thos. H. Foster.
Chas. Vereker.
W. W. H. Guarden.

1811.

Hon. Spencer Perceval.
John Foster.
Wm. W. Pole.
Geo., E. of Ross.
Sir G. Fitz-G. Hill, bt.
John M. Barry.
Thos. H. Foster.
Chas. Vereker.
Wm. Odell.

1812.

John Foster.
Wm. W. Pole.
Sir G. Fitz-G. Hill, bt.
John M Barry.
Thos. H. Foster.
Chas. Vereker.
Wm. Odell.

1813.

The same Board, with the addition of—
Hy. John Clements.
Edmd. Alexr. Macnaghten.

1814.

Robt. Banks, E. of Liverpool.
Wm. Vesey Fitzgerald.
Robt. Peel, aft. bt.
Sir G. Fitz-G. Hill, bt.
John M. Barry.
Wm. Odell.
Hy. John Clements.
Edmd. Alexr. Macnaghten.

In 1817, the revenues of Great Britain and Ireland were united, under 56 Geo. III. cap. 98.

See "Lord High Treasurers, &c., of the United Kingdom," *ante*, p. 159.

SECRETARIES TO THE TREASURY—IRELAND.

1793. Thos. Burgh, L. P., Dec. 25.
1799. Sir Geo. Shee, bt., L. P., July 18.
1801. Hon. Geo. Cavendish, L.P., Aug. 29.

CHANCELLORS OF THE EXCHEQUER OF IRELAND.

* * Wm. de Bromleye, *temp*. Edwd. III.
1346. Robt. de Emeldon.
1385. Wm. Fitzwilliam, kpr. of the seal.
* * Robt. de Herford, *temp*. Richd. II.
1399. Hugh Banent.
1423. Sampson Dartas; he app. Jas. Blakeney his deputy.
1431. Jas. Blakeney, now chanc.
1461. Robt. Norreys.
* * Robt. de St. Lawrence.
1495. Edwd. Barnewall.
1532. Richd. Delahyde.
1535. John Alen, clerk or kpr. of the rolls.
1536. Thos. Cusake, just. C. P.
1561. Hy. Dracote, serjt.-at-arms.
1572. Robt. Dillon.
1577. John Bathe.
1586. Sir Edwd. Waterhouse; surrend.
1589. Sir Geo. Clive.
1590. Thos. Molynex, or Molyneux.

1596. Sir Richd. Cooke.
1612. Sir Dudley Norton; in reversion aft. Cooke.
1616. Hy. Holcrofte; surrend.
1617. Thos. Hibbotts, Oct. 27.
Hy. Holcrofte, *again*; in reversion after Hibbotts; L. P. same date.
1634. Sir Hy. Meredith.
1668. Richd. Jones; aft. visc. and E. of Ranelagh.
1674. Sir Chas. Meredith.
1687. Bruno Talbot.
1695. Philip Savage.
1702. Philip Savage, *again*, by new pat.
1717. Sir Ralph Gore, bt.
1733. Hy. Boyle; res.
1735. Marmaduke Coghill.
1739. Hy. Boyle, *again*; pat. revoked.
1754. Arth. Hill; pat. revoked.
1755. Hy. Boyle, *again*; aft. ld. Castlemartyr, and visc. and E. of Shannon.
1757. Anthy. Malone.
1761. Sir Wm. Yorke, bt., ch. just. C. P., Mar. 28; res.
1763. Wm. Gerard Hamilton, May 31.
1784. John Foster, Apr. 23.
1785. Sir John Parnell, bt., Sept. 22.
1799. Isaac Corry, Jan. 28.
1804. John Foster, July 19.
1806. Sir John Newport, bt., Feb. 25.
1807. John Foster, *again*, May 2.
1811. Wm Wellesley Pole, aft. ld. Maryborough, July 1.
1812. Wm. Vesey Fitzgerald, aft. ld. Fitzgerald and Vesey, Aug 17.
1817. Nichs. Vansittart, aft. ld. Bexley; ch. ex. England, July 12.

In 1817, the exchequers of Great Britain and Ireland were consolidated under 56 Geo. III. cap. 98.

See "Chancellors of the Exchequer," *ante*, p. 165.

PRINCIPAL SECRETARIES OF STATE, OR PRINCIPAL SECRETARIES OF THE COUNCIL.

1576. John Chalenor; L. P. before this date.
1581. Sir Geoff. Fenton. Another secretary was joined with him.
1603. Sir Richd. Cooke.
1612. Sir Dudley Norton.
1616. Sir Fras. Annesley, aft. ld. Mountnorris.
1634. Philip Mainwaring.
1661. Sir Paul Davys; in reversion after Mainwaring.
1665. Sir Geo. Lane, knt., aft. visc. Lanesborough; in reversion after Davys.
1678. Sir John Davys; in reversion after Lane.
1690. Sir Robt. Southwell.
1702. Edwd. Southwell, son of sir Robt.
1720. Edwd. Southwell, and
Edwd. Southwell, his son.
1755. Thos. Carter, on the demise of the Southwells.
1763. Thos. Carter, and
Philip Tisdall, solr.-gen.
1766. John Hely-Hutchinson; in reversion after Tisdall; succ. 1777.
1795. Edmd. Hy., ld. Glentworth.
1796. Hon. Thos. Pelham.
1797. Robt. Stewart, visc. Castlereagh, aft. M. of Londonderry.
1801. Chas. Abbot, aft. sp. ho. comm. of England, and ld. Colchester.

Office abolished at the union of Great Britain and Ireland in 1801.

CHIEF SECRETARIES TO THE LORD LIEUTENANT, OR CHIEF SECRETARIES FOR IRELAND.

1760. Richd. Rigby; before this date.
1761. Wm. Gerard Hamilton.
1764 Chas., E. of Drogheda.
1765. Edwd. Thurlow, app. ch. sec. to visc. Weymouth; *but his lordship did not come over.*
1765. Fras., visc. Beauchamp.
1766. Hon. John Aug. Hervey, app. ch. sec. to the E. of Bristol; *but the earl did not come over.*
1767. Lord Fredk. Campbell.
1768. Sir Geo, Macartney, K. B.
1772. Sir John Blaquiere, aft. ld. de Blaquiere.
1777. Sir Richd. Heron, bt.
1780. Wm. Eden, aft. ld. Auckland.
1782. Hon. R. Fitzpatrick.
Wm. Wyndham Grenville, aft. ld. Grenville.
1783. Wm. Windham.

1783. Hon. Thos. Pelham.
1784. Thos. Orde.
1787. Alleyne Fitzherbert, aft. ld. St. Helens.
1789. Robt. Hobart, Apr.; aft. E. of Buckinghamshire.
1794. Sylvester Douglas, Jan.; aft. ld Glenbervie.
1795. Hon. Geo. Damer, c.c. visc. Milton, Jan.; aft. E. of Dorchester.
Hon. Thos. Pelham, Mar. 31; aft. E. of Chichester.
1798. Robt. visc. Castlereagh, Mar. 29; aft. M. of Londonderry.
1801. Chas. Abbot, aft. sp. ho. comm. of England, and ld. Colchester; May 25.
1802. Wm. Wickham, Feb. 13.
1804. Sir Evan Nepean, bt., Feb. 6.
1805. Nichs. Vansittart, aft. ld. Bexley, Mar. 23.
Chas. Long, aft. ld. Farnborough, Sept. 21.
1806. Wm. Elliot, Mar. 28.
1807. Sir Arth. Wellesley, K. B., aft. D. of Wellington. Apr. 19.
1809. Hon. Robt. Dundas, aft. visc. Melville, Apr. 13.
Wm. Wellesley Pole, aft. ld Maryborough, and E. of Mornington, Oct. 18.
1812. Robt. Peel, aft. bt., Aug. 4.
1818. Chas. Grant, aft. ld. Glenelg, Aug. 3.
1821. Hy. Goulburn, Dec. 29.
1827. Hon. Wm. Lamb, aft. visc. Melbourne, Apr. 29.
1828. Ld. Fras. Leveson Gower, aft. ld. Fras. Egerton, and E. of Ellesmere, June 21.
1830. Sir Hy. Hardinge, aft. visc. Hardinge, July 30.
Hon. Edwd. Geoff. Smith-Stanley, aft. ld. Stanley of Bickerstaffe and 14th E. of Derby, Nov. 26.
1833. Sir John Cam Hobhouse, aft. ld. Broughton, Mar. 29.
1833. Edwd. John Littleton, aft. ld. Hatherton, May 17.
1834. Sir Hy. Hardinge *again*, Dec. 17.
1835. Geo. Wm. Fredk. Howard, visc. Morpeth, aft. E. of Carlisle, Apr. 22.
1841. Edwd., ld. Eliot, aft. E. of St. Germans, Sept. 6.
1845. Sir Thos. Fras. Fremantle, bt., aft. ld. Cottesloe, Feb. 1.
1846. Hy., E. of Lincoln, Feb. 14.
Hy. Labouchere, aft. ld. Taunton, July 6.
1847. Sir Wm. Meredyth Somerville, bt., aft. ld. Athlumney and ld. Meredyth.
1852. Rd. Southwell Bourke, c.c. ld. Naas, aft. E. of Mayo, Feb.
1852. Sir Jno. Young, bt., Dec.
1855. Edwd. Horsman, Feb.
1857. Hy. Arth. Herbert.
1858. Ld. Naas *again*, Feb.
1859. Edwd. Cardwell, aft. visc. Cardwell, June.
1861. Sir Robt. Peel, bt., July.
1865. Chichester Samuel Fortescue, aft. ld. Carlingford, Nov.
1866. Ld. Naas *again*, July.
1868. Col. Jno. Wilson Patten, Sept.
Chichester S. Fortescue, *again*, Dec.
1871. Spencer Compton Cavendish, c.c. M. of Hartington, Jan.
1874. Sir Michl. Edwd. Hicks-Beach, bt., Mar. 3.
1878. Jas. Lowther, Mar. 11, **G.**
1880. Wm. Edwd. Forster, May 10, **G.**
1882. Lord Fredk. Chas. Cavendish, May.
Geo. Otto Trevelyan, May 9.
1884. Hy. Campbell Bannerman, Oct.
1885. Sir Wm. Hart Dyke, July 2, sw.
1886. Wm. Hy. Smith, Jan.
Jno. Morley, Feb.
Sir Michl. Edwd. Hicks-Beach, bt., *again*, Aug.
1887. Arth. Jas. Balfour, Mar. 8.

UNDER SECRETARIES TO THE LORD LIEUTENANT OF IRELAND.

1780. Sackville Hamiton, Feb. 17.
1795. Lodge Morris, Feb. 7.
Sackville Hamilton, *again*; May 15.
1796. Edwd. Cooke, Jan. 6.
1801. Alexr. Marsden, Oct. 21.
1806. Jas. Trail, Sept. 8.
1808. Sir Chas. Saxton, bt., Sept. 6.
1812. Wm. Gregory, Oct. 5.
1831. Lt.-col. sir Wm. Gossett, Jan. 1.
1835. Thos. Drummond, July 25.
1840. Norman H. Macdonald, May 28.
1841. Edwd. Lucas, Sept. 15.
1845. Rd. Pennefather, Aug. 21.
1846. Thos. N. Redington, aft. sir T., July 11.
1852. Jno. Wynne, Feb.
1853. Maj.-gen. sir Thos. Aiskew Larcom, K.C.B.
1848. Col. sir G. R. Wetherall, K.C.S.I., C.B.
1869. Thos. Hy. Burke, May 20; **G.**
1882. Robt. Geo. Crookshank Hamilton, C.B., May.
1886. Maj.-gen. sir Redvers Hy. Buller, K.C.M.G., V.C.
1887. Col. sir Jos. West Ridgeway, K.C.B., K.C.S.I., V.C.

Parliamentary Under Secretaries to the Lord-Lieutenant of Ireland.

In April 1887 Col. Edward Robert King-Harman was appointed to this office, without salary. In the following year a bill was introduced into Parliament to place the office on a permanent footing and to provide a salary for it. Col. King-Harman died on June 10, 1888, and on his death the office was not filled up, and the bill was not proceeded with.

POSTMASTERS-GENERAL OF IRELAND.

From a Return made to the House of Commons in 1844.

* * Sir T. Prendergast.
* * Wm Hy., E. of Clermont.
1784. Jas., visc. Clifden, and Wm. Brabazon Ponsonby. July 16.
1789. Wm. Brabazon Ponsonby, and Chas., ld. Loftus, aft. E. and M. of Ely. Jan. 14.
Chas., ld. Loftus, and Chas., E. of Bellamont. July 18.
1797. Chas., now E. of Ely, and Chas., M. of Drogheda. July 14.
1806. Richd. Hely, E. of Donoughmore, and Hy. Fitzgerald, c.c. ld. H. Fitzgerald. Apr. 19.
1807. Chas. Hy. St. John, Earl O'Neill, and Richd., E. of Clancarty. May 2.
1809. Chas. Hy. St. John, Earl O'Neill, and Laurence, E. of Rosse. Dec. 1.

By 1 Wm. IV. cap. 8 (1831), the two separate offices of Postmaster-General of Great Britain and Postmaster-General of Ireland were consolidated and united into one.

See "Postmasters-General," *ante*, p. 237.

COMMANDERS OF THE FORCES IN IRELAND.

* * Gen. John Leslie, E. of Rothes.
1774. Gen. sir Geo. Aug. Elliot.
1775. Lt.-gen. sir John Irvine, K.B.
1782. Lt.-gen. John Burgoyne.
1784. Gen. Wm. Aug. Pitt.
1791. Gen. Geo. Warde.
1793. Gen. Robt. Cunninghame, aft. ld. Rossmore.
1796. Gen. Hy., E. of Carhampton.
1797. Lt.-gen. sir Ralph Abercrombie, K.B.
1798. Gen. Chas., M. Cornwallis.
1801. Gen. sir Wm. Medows, K.B.
1803. Lt.-gen. hon. Hy. Edwd. Fox.
Gen. Wm., ld. Cathcart.
1806. Gen. Chas., E. of Harrington.
1812. Gen. sir J. Hope, K.B.
1813. Gen. sir Geo. Hewett, bt.
1816. Gen. sir Geo. Beckwith, G.C.B.
1820. Gen. sir David Baird, bt., G.C.B.
1822. Lt.-gen. sir Saml. Auchmuty, G.C.B.
Lt.-gen. Stapleton, ld. aft. visc. Combermere, G.C.B., &c.; Nov.
1825. Lt.-gen. sir Geo. Murray, G.C.B.
1828. Lt.-gen. sir John Byng, K.C.B.
1831. Lt.-gen. sir Rd. Hussey Vivian, bt., K.C.B., &c.; aft. ld. Vivian, &c.
1836. Lt.-gen. sir Edwd. Blakeney, K.C.B., Aug. 26.
1855. Gen. John, ld. Seaton, G.C.B.
1860. Gen. sir Geo. Brown, G.C.B.
1865. Gen. sir Hugh Hy. Rose, aft. ld. Strathnairn, G.C.B., G.C.S.I.
1870. Gen. sir Wm. Rose Mansfield, aft. ld. Sandhurst, G.C.B., G.C.S.I.
1875. Gen. sir John Michel, G.C.B.
1880. Gen. sir Thos. Montagu Steele, K.C.B.
1885. Gen. Pr. W. A. Edwd. of Saxe-Weimar, G.C.B.

COMMISSIONERS OF CUSTOMS AND EXCISE FOR IRELAND,

SOMETIMES CALLED COMMISSIONERS OF REVENUE.

Sometimes the Commissioners for Customs and Excise were appointed by the same and sometimes by separate Letters Patent; but, as a rule, some of the Commissioners, if not all, filled both offices. In order to avoid confusion the lists are here divided and the various appointments given separately as in the *Lib. Mun. Publ. Hib.*

Commissioners of Customs.

1761. Hon. John Ponsonby; John Bourke, aft. ld. Naas and E. of Mayo; Hon. Arthur Trevor, aft. visc. Dungannon; Benj. Burton, sir Richd. Coxe, Hugh Valence Jones, and Brinsley Butler, c.c. ld. Newtown, aft. E. of Lanesborough; L. P., Apr. 21.

1765. Hon. J. Ponsonby, J. Bourke, Arthur, now visc. Dungannon, B. Burton, H. V. Jones, Brinsley, ld. Newton, and John Millbanke; L. P., Apr. 8.

1767. Hon. J. Ponsonby, J. Bourke, Arth., visc. Dungannon, H. V. Jones, Brinsley, ld. Newtown, J. Millbanke, and Bellingham Boyle; L. P., Dec. 3.

1770. J. Bourke, Arth., visc. Dungannon, H. V. Jones, Brinsley, ld. Newtown, J. Millbanke, B. Boyle, hon. John Beresford, and sir Wm. Osborne; L. P., May 1.

1772. J. Bourke, hon. J. Beresford, Jno. Staples, Jas. Agar, Thos. Allan, Chas. Tottenham, aft. ld. Loftus, and Richd. Gore; L. P., Feb. 3.

J. Bourke, hon. J. Beresford, J. Staples, J. Agar, T. Allan, C. Tottenham, and Robt. Clements, aft. ld. Leitrim; L. P., Nov. 19.

1773. J. Bourke, hon. J. Beresford, John Monck Mason, J. Staples, Richd. Townshend, sir Fras. Bernard, and J. Agar; L. P., Dec. 25.

1774. J. Bourke, hon. J. Beresford, J. M. Mason, J. Staples, R. Townshend, J. Agar, and Hercules Langrishe, aft. sir H.; L. P., Dec. 24.

1776. J. Bourke, hon. J. Beresford, J. M. Mason, R. Townshend, J. Agar, H. Langrishe, and Robt. Waller; L. P., July 13.

1780. Hon. J. Beresford, J. M. Mason, R. Townshend, Jas., ld. Clifden, sir H. Langrishe, Robt. Ross, and John Parnell, aft. sir J.; L. P., Dec. 16.

1784. Hon. J. Beresford, J. M. Mason, Jas., ld. Clifden, sir H. Langrishe. Robt. Ross, sir John Parnell, and Gervas Parker Bushe; L. P., Jan. 28.

1785. Hon. J. Beresford, J. M. Mason, sir H. Langrishe, R. Ross, sir J. Parnell, G. P. Bushe, and hon. Richd. Hely-Hutchinson, aft. ld. visc. and E. of Donoughmore; L. P., Mar.

1786. Hon. J. Beresford, J. M. Mason, sir H. Langrishe, R. Ross, G. P. Bushe, Richd., now ld. Donoughmore, and hon. Richd. Annesley, aft. E. of Annesley; L. P., Jan. 9.

1789. Hon. J. Beresford, J. M. Mason, sir H. Langrishe, Rd., ld. Donoughmore, hon. Rd. Annesley, Isaac Corry, and ld. Chas. Fitzgerald; L. P., Sept. 28.

1792. Hon. J. Beresford, J. M. Mason, sir H. Langrishe, Richd., ld. Donoughmore, hon. R. Annesley, I. Corry, and John Wolfe; L. P., Mar. 1.

1793. Hon. J. Beresford, J. M. Mason, sir H. Langrishe, Richd., ld. Donoughmore, hon. R. Annesley, Isaac Corry, J. Wolfe, and hon. Geo. Knox; L. P., Dec. 31.

1795. Hon. J. Beresford, sir H. Langrishe, R. Ross, I. Corry, J. Wolfe, hon Geo. Knox, and Chas. Hy. Coote, aft. ld. Castlecoote; L. P., Oct. 27.

1798. Hon. J. Beresford, sir H. Langrishe, R. Ross, hon. R. Annesley, J. Wolfe, hon. G. Knox, C. H. Coote, and hon. Thos. Hy. Foster; L. P., Feb. 27.

1799. Hon. J. Beresford, sir H. Langrishe, Richd., now visc. Donoughmore, Maurice Fitzgerald, John Ormsby Vandeleur, John Townshend, and Mountefort Longfield; L. P., Aug. 5.

1801. Hon. J. Beresford, sir H. Langrishe, Rd., now E. of Donoughmore, J. O. Vandeleur, J. Townshend, M. Longfield, and Wm. Rowley; L. P., Feb. 13.

1802. Rd., E. of Donoughmore, hon. Rd. Annesley, Chas. Hy., now ld. Castlecoote, Mountefort Longfield, Wm. Rowley, Robt. Wynne, and Thos. Burgh; L. P., Mar. 26.

1803. Rd., E. of Donoughmore, Rd., now Earl Annesley, Wm. Rowley, Robt. Wynne, T. Burgh, Rd. Longfield, and hon. John Jocelyn; L. P., June 2.

1806. Chas. Hy., ld. Castlecoote, J. O. Vandeleur, W. Rowley, R. Wynne, T. Burgh, hon. John Jocelyn, and hon. Abrm. Hely Hutchinson; L. P., Sept. 3.

1807. Chas. Hy., ld. Castlecoote, J. O. Vandeleur, W. Rowley, R. Wynne, T. Burgh, hon. A. Hely Hutchinson, and Geo. Knox; L.P., July 15

1809. Chas. Hy., ld. Castlecoote, J. O. Vandeleur, W. Rowley, R. Wynne, T. Burgh, hon. A. Hely-Hutchinson, and hon. J. Jocelyn; L. P., Sept. 9.
1810. Chas. Hy., ld. Castlecoote, J. O. Vandeleur, W. Rowley, A. Hely-Hutchinson, hon. J. Jocelyn, and Robt. Molesworth; L. P., Nov. 5.
1811. Chas. Hy., ld. Castlecoote, J. O. Vandeleur, R. Wynne, hon. A. Hely-Hutchinson, hon. J. Jocelyn, hon. Robt. Molesworth, and Hy. Hamilton; L. P., May 4.
1814. Chas. Hy., ld. Castlecoote, J. O. Vandeleur, R. Wynne, A. Hely-Hutchinson, hon. J. Jocelyn, H. Hamilton, and Hulton Smith King; L. P., May 20.
1820. Chas. Hy., ld. Castlecoote, J. O. Vandeleur (ceased 1822), hon. A. Hely-Hutchinson, Hy. Hamilton, and H. S. King; L. P. July 25.
1823. Wm. Boothby, Hy. Jas. Keith Stewart, A. Hely-Hutchinson, H. S. King, and Chas. Boyd, Feb. 6.

On September 13, 1823, the consolidation of the Boards of Customs for England and Wales, Scotland and Ireland, took place, and the commissioners, from that time, have been commissioners for the United Kingdom. See *ante*, p. 277.

Commissioners of Excise.

1761. Hon. Jno. Ponsonby, Jno. Bourke, aft. ld. Naas and E. of Mayo, hon. Arth. Trevor, aft. visc. Dungannon, Benj. Burton, and sir Rd. Coxe; L. P., Apr. 21.
1765. Hon. J. Ponsonby, J. Bourke, Arth., now visc. Dungannon, Benj. Burton, and Brinsley Butler, c.c. ld. Newtown, aft. E. of Lanesborough; L. P., Apr. 8.
1767. Hon. J. Ponsonby, J. Bourke, Arth., visc. Dungannon, B. Butler, c.c. ld. Newtown, and Bellingham Boyle; L. P., Dec. 3.
1770. J. Bourke, Arth., visc. Dungannon, B. Boyle, hon. J. Beresford, and sir Wm. Osborne; L. P., May 1.
1772. Sir Wm. Osborne, sir Fras. Bernard, Jno. Monck Mason, Robt. Waller, and Wm. Montgomery; L. P., Feb. 3, and Nov. 19.
1773. Sir Fras. Bernard, J. M. Mason, R. Waller, W. Montgomery, and Richd. Townshend; L. P., Jan. 22, and Apr. 13.
J. Bourke, hon. J. Beresford, J. M. Mason, Jno. Staples, and R. Townshend; L. P., Dec. 25, and Dec. 24, 1774.
1776. J. Bourke, hon. J. Beresford, J. M. Mason, R. Townshend, and Jas. Agar; L. P., July 13.
1780. Hon. J. Beresford, J. M. Mason, R. Townshend, Jas., ld. Clifden, and sir Hercules Langrishe; L. P., Dec. 16.
1784. Hon. J. Beresford, J. M. Mason, Jas., ld. Clifden, sir H. Langrishe, and Robt. Ross; L. P., Jan. 28.
1785. Hon. J. Beresford, sir H. Langrishe, R. Ross, and sir J. Parnell; L. P., Mar. 1.
Hon. J. Beresford, J. M. Mason, sir H. Langrishe, R. Ross, Gervas Parker Bushe; L. P., Dec. 30, Sept. 28, 1789, and Mar. 1, 1792.
1793. Hon. J. Beresford, J. M. Mason, sir H. Langrishe, R. Ross, and Rd. ld. aft. visc. and E. of Donoughmore; L. P., Dec. 31.
1795. Hon. J. Beresford, sir H. Langrishe, Robt. Ross, Rd. ld. Donoughmore, and Rd. Annesley, aft. E. of Annesley; L. P., Oct. 27, and Feb. 27, 1798.
1799. Hon. J. Beresford, sir H. Langrishe, Rd., ld. Donoughmore, Rd. Annesley, and Chas. Hy. Coote, aft. ld. Castlecoote; L. P., Aug. 5, and Feb. 13, 1801.
1802. Rd., now E. of Donoughmore, Rd. Annesley, Chas. Hy., now ld. Castlecoote, John Ormsby Vandeleur, and Jno. Townshend; L. P., Mar. 26, July 26, 1802, and June 2, 1803.
1806. Richd., now E. of Annesley, John Townshend, Alexr. Marsden, Geo. Macquay, Ralph Peter Dundas, Edw. Taylor, and John Therry; L. P., Sept. 3.
1807. Richd. E. of Annesley, J. Townshend, A. Marsden, R. P. Dundas, J. Therry, Rd. Longfield, and Thos. Odell; L. P., July 15.
1810. A. Marsden, J. Townshend, R. P. Dundas, J. Therry, R. Longfield, T. Odell, and Wm. Gregory; L. P., June 18.
A. Marsden, J. Therry, R. P. Dundas, R. Longfield, T. Odell, W. Gregory, and Robt. Langrishe, aft. bt.; L. P., Sept. 17.
1812. A. Marsden, J. Therry, R. P. Dundas, R. Longfield, T. Odell, sir R. Langrishe, bt., and hon. Jas. Hewitt; L. P., Dec. 31.

815. Chas. Stewart Hawthorne, J. Therry, R. P. Dundas, R. Longfield, T. Odell, sir R. Langrishe, and hon. J. Hewitt; L. P., Feb. 2.

C. S. Hawthorn, J. Therry, R. Longfield, T. Odell, sir R. Langrishe, hon. J. Hewitt, and Wm. Plunkett; L. P., Mar. 2.

1823. Sir Cheetham Mortlock, Chas. Rudolph Trefusis, hon. J. Hewitt, Wm. Plunkett, and Abraham Culto; L. P., Feb. 6.

On Sept. 13, 1823, the consolidation of the Boards of Excise for England and Wales, cotland, and Ireland took place, and the commissioners from that time have been ommissioners for the United Kingdom. See *ante*, p. 282.

COMMISSIONERS OF ACCOUNTS FOR IRELAND.

From 1761.

761. Jno. ld. Bowes, ld. chanc., sir Wm. Yorke, ch. ex., Edw. Willes, ch. bar. ex., Rd. Mounteney, bar. ex., and Arthur Dawson, bar. ex.; L. P., Aug. 26.

771. Jas. ld. Lifford, ld. chanc., Wm. Gerard Hamilton, ch. ex., Anthy. Foster, ch. bar. ex., Wm. Scott, bar. ex., and Geo. Smyth, bar. ex.; L. P., Dec. 13.

Chas. O'Hara, Gervas Parker Bushe, Hy. Loftus, Edwd. Tighe, and St. John Jefferies; L. P., Dec. 13.

775. G. P. Bushe. H. Loftus, E. Tighe, St. John Jefferies, and John Damer; L. P., July 17.

776. H. Loftus, E. Tighe, St. J. Jefferies, Richd. Hely-Hutchinson, aft. ld., visc., and E. of Donoughmore, and Edwd. Bellingham Swan; L. P., July 11.

781. H. Loftus, Edwd. Tighe, R. Hely-Hutchinson, E. B. Swan, and sir Fredk. Flood, bt.; L. P., May 26.

85. Hy. Loftus, E. Tighe, E. B. Swan, sir F. Flood, and Peter Holmes; L. P., Mar. 1.

89. E. Tighe, sir F. Flood, C. H. Coote, aft. ld. Castlecoote, John Reilly, and auditor of imprests for time being; L. P., July 18.

90. E. Tighe, C. H. Coote, J. Reilly, Richd. Neville, and auditor &c.; L. P., Sept. 3.

95. E. Tighe, C. H. Coote, J. Reilly, R. Neville, hon. Geo. Jocelyn, and auditor &c.; L. P., Oct. 28.

97. J. Reilly, R. Neville, hon. Geo. Jocelyn, Cromwell Price, and auditor &c.; L. P., June 26.

98. J. Reilly, R. Neville, Richd. Townshend Herbert, Wm. Rowley, and auditor &c.; L. P., May 25.

1799. J. Reilly, W. Rowley, R. T. Herbert, T. Burgh, and auditor &c.; L. P., July 20.

1800. R. T. Herbert, W. Rowley, Thos. Burgh, Rd. Martin, and auditor &c.; L. P., Aug. 16.

R. T. Herbert, Rd. Magenis, W. Rowley, T. Burgh, R. Martin, and auditor &c.; L. P., Sept. 18.

1801. R. T. Herbert, T. Burgh, R. Martin, R. Magenis, Arth. Browne, and auditor &c.; L. P., Apr. 25.

1802. R. T. Herbert, T. Burgh, R. Martin, R. Magenis, Edm. Stanley, and auditor &c.; L. P., Feb. 6.

R. T. Herbert, R. Martin, R. Magenis, E. Stanley, Chas. McDonald, and auditor &c.; L. P., May 29.

R. T. Herbert, R. Martin, E. Stanley, C. McDonald. Maurice Cane, and auditor &c.; L. P., Nov. 15.

R T. Herbert, R. Martin, C. McDonald, M. Cane, Redmond Barry, and auditor &c.; L. P., Dec. 4.

1803. R. T. Herbert, R. Martin. M. Cane, R. Barry, and Hulton Smith King; L. P., Jan. 8.

1812. R. T. Herbert, R. Magenis, M. Cane, H. S. King, and hon. Jas. Hewitt; L. P., Mar. 28, and July 6.

1813. R. T. Herbert, M. Cane, H. S. King, Richd. Magenis, junr., and hon. Hans Blackwood; L. P., Jan. 1.

1814. R. T. Herbert, M. Cane, Richd. Magenis, junr., hon. H. Blackwood, and John Mahon; L. P., May 20.

1830. R. Magenis, junr., hon. H. Blackwood, and John Mahon.

Abolished about 1832.

COMMISSIONERS OF STAMPS FOR IRELAND.

First appointed in 1774.

The same Commissioners as for the Account Office until 1789.

See "Commissioners of Accounts," *ante*, p. 567.

Commissioners of Stamps from 1789.

1789. Peter Holmes, Richd. Townshend Herbert, Edwd. Fitzgerald, Saml. Hayes, and Geo. Rawson; L. P., July 18.
1796. P. Holmes, R. T. Herbert, E. Fitzgerald, Geo. Hatton, and hon. Hugh Howard; L. P., Feb. 15.
1798. P. Holmes, E. Fitzgerald, G. Hatton, hon. H. Howard, and Wm. Arthur Crosbie; L. P., May 25.
1802. P. Holmes, E. Fitzgerald, hon. H. — Hugh Howard, W. A. Crosbie, and Wm. Gore; L. P., Jan. 19.
Hon. H. Howard, E. Fitzgerald, W. A. Crosbie, W. Gore, and Jno. French; L. P., Mar. 18.
1802. Hon. H. Howard, E. Fitzgeral W. Gore, J. French, and Rich Pennefather; L. P., July 20.
1807. Hon. H. Howard, E. Fitzgerald, Gore, John French, and Matt Pennefather Jacob; L. P., A 8.
1808. Hon. H. Howard, W. Gore, J. Frenc M. P. Jacob, and Thos. Burt Fitzgerald; L. P., July 20.
1812. Hon. H. Howard, W. Gore, Jo French, T. B. Fitzgerald, Edw Glasscock; L. P., May 2.
1824. Wm. Campbell, John S. Cooper, a D'Arcy Mahon.

About 1827 the Commissioners were superseded by a Comptroller.

LORD LIEUTENANTS OF COUNTIES—IRELAND.

Lord Lieutenants of the Irish Counties were first appointed und 1 & 2 Wm. IV. cap 17 (August 23, 1831). Prior to this Act "Governo of Counties" were appointed, there being frequently several Governors a county. Under the new Act the chief authority was vested in o Lord Lieutenant, who had power to appoint deputies, in like manner in England and Scotland.

LORD LIEUTENANTS OF ANTRIM.

1831. Chas. Hy., E. O'Neill.
1842. Geo. Hamilton, E. of Belfast, aft. M. of Donegal.
1884. Robt. Alexr. Shafto, ld. Wavene
1886. Sir Edwd. Porter Cowan.

LORD LIEUTENANTS OF ARMAGH.

1832. Archd., 2nd E. of Gosford; *d.* Mar. 27, 1849.
1849. Jas. M. Caulfield.
1864. Chas., 2nd ld. Lurgan; *d.* Jan. 1882.
1883. Archd. Brabazon Sparrow, 4th of Gosford, K.P.

LORD LIEUTENANTS OF CARLOW.

1831. Hon. John Wm. Ponsonby, c.c. visc. Duncannon, aft. 4th E. of Bessborough; *d.* May 16, 1847.
1847. John Geo. Brabazon, 5th E. of Be borough; *d.* Jan. 28, 1880.
1880. Arthur MacMorrough Kavanagh.

LORD LIEUTENANTS OF CAVAN.

831. Thos., 2nd M. of Headfort; *d.* Dec. 6, 1870.
871. John, ld. Lisgar; *d.* Oct. 6, 1876.
1877. John Vansittart Danvers, 6th E. of Lanesborough.

LORD LIEUTENANTS OF CLARE.

831. Wm. Vesey Fitzgerald, aft. ld. Fitzgerald and Vesey.
843. Sir Lucius O'Brien, bt., aft. ld. Inchiquin.
1872. Hon. Chas. W. White
1879. Edwd. Donough, ld. Inchiquin

LORD LIEUTENANTS OF CORK.

831. Hy., 3rd E. of Shannon; *d.* Apr. 22, 1842.
842. Jas., 2nd E. of Bandon; *d.* Oct. 31, 1856.
1857. Edmd. Burke, ld. Fermoy; *d.* Sept 17, 1874.
1874. Fras., 3rd E. of Bandon; *d.* Feb. 17, 1877.
1877. Jas. Fras., 4th E. of Bandon.

LORD LIEUTENANTS OF DONEGAL.

831. Geo. Aug., 2nd M. of Donegal; *d.* Oct. 5, 1844.
1845. Jas., M. of Abercorn, aft. 1st D. of Abercorn.
1886. Jas., 2nd D. of Abercorn.

LORD LIEUTENANTS OF DOWNSHIRE.

831. Arth. Blundell Sandys Trumbull, 3rd M. of Downshire; *d.* Apr. 12, 1845.
845. Fredk. Wm. Robt., visc. Castlereagh, aft. 4th M. of Londonderry; *d.* Nov. 1872.
1864. Fredk. Temple, ld. Dufferin and Clandeboye, aft. E. of Dufferin and M. of Dufferin and Ava.

LORD LIEUTENANTS OF THE COUNTY OF DUBLIN.

831. John Chambre, 10th E. of Meath; *d.* Mar. 15, 1851.
1851. Thos., 3rd E. of Howth; *d.* Feb. 4, 1874.
1874. Chas. Stanley, visc. Monck.

LORD LIEUTENANTS OF FERMANAGH.

831. John Willoughby, 2nd E. of Enniskillen; *d.* Mar. 31, 1840.
1840. Col. John Crighton, aft. E. Erne.

LORD LIEUTENANTS OF GALWAY.

831. Ulick John, M. of Clanricarde; *d.* Apr. 10, 1874.
1874. Robt., ld. Clonbrock.

LORD LIEUTENANTS OF KERRY.

831. Valentine, 2nd E. of Kenmare; *d.* Oct. 31, 1853.
854. Hy. Arthur Herbert.
1866. Val. Aug., visc. Castlerosse, aft. E. of Kenmare.

LORD LIEUTENANTS OF KILDARE.

831. Aug. Fredk., 3rd D. of Leinster, Oct. 10, 1874.
1875. Hy. Fras. Seymour, 3rd M. of Drogheda.

LORD LIEUTENANTS OF KILKENNY.

1831. Walter, 18th E. and 1st M. of Ormonde; *d.* May 18, 1838.
1838. Jno. Wm., visc. Duncannon, aft. 4th E. of Bessborough.
1847. W. Fredk. Tighe.
1878. Jas. Edwd. Wm. Theobald, 3rd M. of Ormonde.

LORD LIEUTENANTS OF KINGS COUNTY.

1831. Wm., ld. Oxmantown, aft. E. of Rosse; *d.* Oct. 31, 1867.
1867. Col. Thos. Bernard.
1883. Fras. Travers Dames Longworth, Q

LORD LIEUTENANTS OF LEITRIM.

1831. Nath., 2nd E. of Leitrim; *d.* Dec. 31, 1854.
1855. Edwd. King Tenison, Jan. 31, **G.**
1857. Geo. Arth. Hastings, E. of Granard.
1872. Thos. Arth. Jos., visc. Southwell; *d.* Apr. 26, 1878.
1878. Wm. Richd., 2nd ld. Harlech.

LORD LIEUTENANTS OF THE COUNTY LIMERICK.

1831. Hon. Richd. Hobart Fitzgibbon, aft. 3rd E. of Clare; *d.* Jan. 10, 1864.
1864. Edwin Richd. Windham, 3rd E. of Dunraven; *d.* Oct. 6, 1871.
1871. Col. Wm. Monsell, aft. ld. Emly.

LORD LIEUTENANTS OF LONDONDERRY.

1831. Geo., ld. Garvagh; *d.* Aug. 20, 1840.
1840. Sir Robt. A. Ferguson, bt.
1860. Acheson Lyle.
1870. Col. R. Peel Dawson.
1878. Sir Hy. Hervey Bruce, bt.

LORD LIEUTENANTS OF LONGFORD.

1831. Geo. Jno., visc. Forbes; *d.* Nov. 13, 1836.
1836. Luke White.
1850–1. Hy. White, aft. ld. Annaly; *d.* Sept. 3, 1873.
1874. Wm. Lygon, E. of Longford.

LORD LIEUTENANTS OF LOUTH.

1831. Sir Patrick Bellew.
1867. Col. Jno. McClintock, aft. ld. Rathdonnell.
1879. Clotworthy Jno. Eyre, visc. Massereene and Ferrard.

LORD LIEUTENANTS OF MAYO.

1834. Dominick Browne, aft. ld. Oranmore and Browne.
1842. Howe Peter, 2nd M. of Sligo; *d.* Jan. 26, 1845.
1845. Geo. Chas., 3rd E. of Lucan; *d.* Nov. 10, 1888.
1888. Arth. Saunders Wm. Chas., 5th E. of Arran.

LORD LIEUTENANTS OF MEATH.

1831. Edwd., 5th E. of Darnley; *d.* Feb. 12, 1835.
1835. Edwd. Wadding, 14th ld. Dunsany; *d.* Dec. 11, 1848.
1849. Arth. Jas., 9th E. of Fingall, Apr. 22, 1869.
1869. Fras. Nathl., 2nd M. of Conyngham; *d.* July 17, 1876.
1876–7. Thos., 3rd M. of Headfort.

LORD LIEUTENANTS OF MONAGHAN.

1831. Hy. Robt., 3rd ld. Rossmore.
1858. Chas. Powell Leslie.
1871. Richd., E. of Dartrey.

LORD LIEUTENANTS OF QUEENS COUNTY.

1831. Jno., 2nd visc. De Vesci; *d.* Oct. 19, 1855.

1855. Jno. Wilson Fitzpatrick, aft. ld. Castletown; *d.* Jan. 22, 1883.

1883. Jno. Robt. Wm., 4th visc. de Vesci.

LORD LIEUTENANTS OF ROSCOMMON.

1831. Robt. Edwd., 1st visc. Lorton; *d.* Nov. 20, 1854.

1855. Arth., ld. de Freyne; *d.* Sept. 29, 1856.

1857. Edwd. King Tenison.

1878. Edwd. Robt. King-Harman; *d.* June 10, 1888.

1888. Hy. Ernest Newcomen, E. of Kingston.

LORD LIEUTENANTS OF SLIGO.

1831. Arth. Knox Gore.

1871. Sir Robt. Bootle, bt.

1877. Lt.-col. E. H. Cooper.

LORD LIEUTENANTS OF TIPPERARY.

1831. Jno., 3rd E. of Donoughmore; *d.* Sept. 14, 1851.

1851. Geo. Ponsonby, visc. Lismore.

1885. Cornwallis, visc. Hawarden, aft. E. de Montalt.

LORD LIEUTENANTS OF TYRONE.

1831. Du Pre, 2nd E. of Caledon; *d.* 1839.

1839. Fras. Wm., 2nd E. of Charlemont; *d.* Dec. 26, 1863.

1864. Jas. Molyneux, 3rd E. of Charlemont.

LORD LIEUTENANTS OF WATERFORD.

1831. Hy. Villiers Stuart, aft. ld. Stuart de Decies.

1874. Jno. Hy. de la Poer, M. of Waterford.

LORD LIEUTENANTS OF WESTMEATH.

1831. Anthy. Fras., M. of Westmeath.

1871. Fulke Southwell, 1st ld. Greville of Clonyn; *d.* Jan. 5, 1883.

1883. Sir Benjn. Jas. Chapman, bt.; *d.* Nov. 3, 1888.

1888. Richd., 4th ld. Castlemaine.

LORD LIEUTENANTS OF WEXFORD.

1831. Robt. Shapland Carew, aft. 2nd ld. Carew; *d.* Sept. 9, 1881.

1881. Ld. Maurice Fitzgerald.

LORD LIEUTENANTS OF WICKLOW.

1831. Wm. Forward, 4th E. of Wicklow; *d.* Mar. 22, 1869.

1869. Wm., 11th E. of Meath.

HERALDIC OFFICERS—IRELAND.

ULSTER KINGS OF ARMS.

This office was created by Edward VI.

The dates are those of the Letters Patent.

1552. Barth. W. Butler, *alias* York, June 1.
1566. Nichs. Narbon, or Narboone, July 7.
1588. Christr. Ussher, June 30.
1597. Danl. Molineux, June 28.
1629. Danl. Molineux and Adam Ussher, Apr. 25.
1633. Thos. Preston, Sept. 21.
1643. Wm. Roberts, Apr. 15.
1655. Sir Richd. Kerney, or Carney, Feb. 19.
1660. Sir Richd. St. George, Aug. 20.
1683. Sir Rd. Carney, *again*, and Geo. Wallis, May 25.
1698. Wm. Hawkins (No. 1), Apr. 13.
1722. Wm. Hawkins (No. 1), and Jnc Hawkins, his son, July 19.
1759. Jas. McCulloch, Mar. 22.
1765. Wm. Hawkins (No. 2), aft. sir W May 17.
1787. Gerald Fortescue, Apr. 26.
1788. Chichester Fortescue, aft. sir C Apr. 26.
1820. Wm. Betham, aft. sir W.
1854. Jno. Bernard Burke, aft. sir J.

JUDGES AND OTHER LEGAL DIGNITARIES OF IRELAND.

The earlier portions of these lists have been compiled from the *Libe Munerum Publicorum Hiberniæ*, a work in two immense volumes, imperia folio, which was completed by the late Mr. Rowley Lascelles, from th compilations of Mr. Lodge, formerly Deputy Keeper of the Rolls an Keeper of the State Papers in Ireland, and printed by order of th House of Commons. It has never been published. A few copies onl were issued to high personages in the state, and to certain public offices as records. A copy is in the British Museum, and may be seen there There is no index to the book, but a separate index has been prepare and embodied in the 9th Report of the Record Office, Ireland (1877) Smyth's *Chronicle of Irish Law Officers*, a very useful little work published in 1839, has also been consulted.

The Irish Law Courts were modelled on those of England, the origi of which is shortly given at pp. 345-352, *ante*.

The embarrassed condition of many of the Irish landowners led t the establishment first of an Incumbered Estates Court and afterward of a Landed Estates Court.

The Irish Supreme Court of Judicature is formed by a con solidation of the old Irish Courts of Chancery, Queen's Benct Common Pleas, Exchequer, Probate, and Matrimonial Causes, and th Landed Estates Court, with a provision for the inclusion of the Cou of Admiralty on the next vacancy in the judgeship thereof. It wa established by the Supreme Court of Judicature (Ireland) Act, 187 (40 & 41 Vict. c. 57), whereby a "Supreme Court of Judicature i Ireland" was established, to consist of two permanent divisions.

1. Her Majesty's High Court of Justice in Ireland.
2. Her Majesty's Court of Appeal in Ireland.

. HER MAJESTYS HIGH COURT OF JUSTICE IN IRELAND.

President, the Lord Chancellor of Ireland for the time being; in his bsence the L.C.J. of Ireland for the time being.

This Court originally consisted of five divisions :—

1. THE CHANCERY DIVISION, consisting of the Lord Chancellor (President), the Master of the Rolls, the Vice Chancellor, and the Judges of the Landed Estates Court, who were to be called the Land Judges of the Chancery Division.
2. THE QUEEN'S BENCH DIVISION, consisting of the L.C.J. of Ireland (President), and the other Judges of the old Court of Queen's Bench, in all four Judges.
3. THE COMMON PLEAS DIVISION, consisting of the L.C.J. of the Common Pleas (President) and the other Judges of the old Court of Common Pleas, in all three judges.
4. THE EXCHEQUER DIVISION, consisting of the L.C.B. of the Exchequer (President) and the other Judges of the old Court of Exchequer, in all (after the next vacancy) three Judges.
5. THE PROBATE AND MATRIMONIAL DIVISION, consisting of the Judge of the Courts of Probate and for Matrimonial Causes. Upon the Admiralty jurisdiction falling into the Supreme Court it was to be exercised by the Judge of this division, which was thenceforward to be called the PROBATE, MATRIMONIAL, and ADMIRALTY DIVISION.

The titles of Lord Chancellor, Lord Chief Justice of Ireland, Master f the Rolls, L.C J. of the Common Pleas, and L.C.B. of the Exchequer vere to be retained, but all other future judges were to be styled "Judges f Her Majesty's High Court of Justice in Ireland."

By the Supreme Court of Judicature (Ireland) Act, 1887, (50 & 51 'ict. cap. 6), power was given on the next vacancies to abolish the offices f L.C.J. of the Common Pleas and L.C.B. of the Exchequer, to fill up he vacancies with ordinary puisne judges, and to "direct the amalgaation and fusion" of the Common Pleas and Exchequer Divisions vith the Queen's Bench Division of the High Court. This power has een acted on as regards the Common Pleas Division, which by Order n Council (Ireland) dated July 6, 1887, was abolished as from Oct. 20, 887.

II. HER MAJESTY'S COURT OF APPEAL IN IRELAND.

HIS COURT originally consisted of :—

1. Five *ex officio* Judges, viz., the Lord Chancellor of Ireland, the L.C.J. of Ireland, the Master of the Rolls, the L.C.J. of the Common Pleas, and the L.C.B. of the Exchequer, but under the Supreme Court of Judicature (Ireland) Act, 1887 (50 & 51 Vict., cap. 6), power was given to abolish the last two offices; *vide supra*.
2. Two ordinary Judges to be from time to time appointed. The first ordinary Judges were to be the existing Lord Justice of Appeal, and one other to be appointed either before or after the commencement of the Act.

3. Power was given to appoint as additional Judges any retire[d] Lord Chancellor, Lord Chief Justice, Master of the Rolls, o[r] Lord Chief Baron willing to serve.

The ordinary and additional Judges are styled "Lords Justices o[f] Appeal."

The new system came into operation on Jan. 1, 1878.

LORD CHANCELLORS, &c., OF IRELAND.

The abbreviations signify, V. C. Vice Chancellor; D. C. Deputy Chancellor; L. K. Lord Keeper; D. L. K. Deputy Lord Keeper; where no abbreviations appear the person named is Lord Chancellor.

RICHARD I.

1189. Steph. Ridel.

HENRY III.

1219. John de Worcheley.
1230. Fromond le Brun.
1232. Ralph Nevill, bp. of Chichester, Sept. 28.
Geoffrey Turville, archdn. of Dublin, V. C.
1235. Alan de Sancta Fide.
1236. Robt. Luttrell, friar of St. Patrick's, Dublin, V. C.
The same, as ld. chanc.
1237. Geoffrey Turville, *again*, as ld. chanc.
Ralph, bp. of Norwich.
1245. Wm. Welward, Nov. 4.
1249. Ralph, bp. of Norwich *again*, July 9.
1259. Fromond le Brun.

EDWARD I.

1272. Fromond le Brun, *contd.*
1283. Walter de Fulburn.
1288. Wm. de Buerlaco.
1292. Thos. Cantoc, aft. bp. of Emly.
1293. Walter de Thornburg.
1294. Adam Wodington.
1295. Thos. Cantoc, *again*.

EDWARD II.

1307. Thos. Cantoc, *contd.*
1314. Richd. de Bereford.
1317. Wm. Fitzjohn, abp. of Cashel, Aug. 10.
1321. Roger Outlawe, or Utlagh, prior of St. John of Jerusalem.
1325. Alexr. de Bicknor, abp. of Dublin.
1326. Roger Outlawe, or Utlagh, *again*.

EDWARD III.

1330. Adam de Limberg.
1331. Wm., prior of St. John's, near Dublin.
1332. Adam de Limberg, *again*.
Roger Outlawe, or Utlagh, *again*.
1334. Adam de Limburg, *again*.
1335. Roger Outlawe, *again*.
1337. Thos. Charlton, bp. of Hereford.
1338. Robt. de Henningberg.
John de Battail, L. K.
1339. Roger Outlawe, *again*.
Thos. Charlton, *again*.
1341. Robt. de Askeby.
John le Archer, prior of St. John o[f] Jerusalem.
1342. Roger Darcy, L. K.
1343. John de Battail, *again*; app. b[y] parlt., L. K.
John le Archer, *again*.
1346. John Morice, or Morys, May 20.
Roger Darcy, *again*, L. K.
1349. John le Archer, *again*.
1350. Wm. Bromley, L. K.
John de St. Paul, abp. of Dublin.
1354. Richd. de Assheton.
1355. John de St. Paul, *again*.
1356. John de Frowyk (? 1357).
1357. Thos. Burley, prior of Kilmainham.
Friar John de Mora, and Wm. Draiton, clerk, D. C.
1359. Thos. Burley, prior of Kilmainham *again*.
1363. Richd. de Assheton, *again*.
1366. Thos. Scurlock, abb. of St. Thomas's, Dublin, D. C.
1367. Thos. le Reve, first bp. of the *united* see of Waterford and Lismore.
1368. Thos. Burley, prior of Kilmainham *again*.
1370. John de Botheby (? 1371).
1372. Wm. Tany, prior of Kilmainham.
1374. John de Botheby, *again*.
Wm. Tany, prior of Kilmainham, *again*, Mar. 2.
1375. John Keppock, just. K. B., D. C., Apr. 13.

RICHARD II.

1377. Robt. de Wikeford, or Wickford, abp. of Dublin.
Alexr. Balscot, bp. of Ossory.
1379. John Colton, dean of St. Patrick's, Dublin.
1381. Wm. Tany, prior of Kilmainham, *again*, Feb.

1381. Ralph Chene, or Cheney, L. K.
1385. Robt. de Wickford, abp. of Dublin, *again.*
Robt. Sutton, V. C.
1386. Alexr. Balscot, bp. of Ossory, *again.*
Thos. de Everdon, V. C.
The same, L. K., with power to hear causes.
1387. Richd. White, prior of Kilmainham.
1388. Sir Robt. Preston, L. K.
1389. Alexr. Balscot, bp. of Ossory, *again*, Aug. 27.
1391. Sir Robt. Preston, *again*, as ld. chanc.
1392. Robt. Waldby, abp. (? archdn.) of Dublin.
1393. Richd. Northalis, bp. of Ossory, May 29.
1394. Alexr. Balscot, now bp. of Meath, *again.*
1395. Robt. de Wickford, abp. of Dublin, *again.*
1397. Alexr. Balscot, bp. of Meath, *again.*
Robt. de Braybrooke, bp. of London.
Robt. Sutton, D. L. K.
Thos. Cranley, abp. of Dublin.

HENRY IV.

1399. Thos. Cranley, *contd.*
1400. Alexr. Balscot, bp. of Meath, *again*, Jan. 4.
1401. Thos. Cranley, abp. of Dublin, *again*, Aug. 23.
1402. Thos. de Everdon, *again*, D. C.
1405. Richd. Rede, ch. just. K. B., and John Bermingham, 2nd just. C. P., jointly, D. C. C., Feb. 13.
Robt. Sutton, *again*, D. C.
1407. Laurence Merbury, or Marbury, aft. sir L., D. C., July 14.
1410. Patrick Barret, bp. of Ferns, June 13.
1412. Robt. Sutton, *again*, D. C., May 4.
Thos. Cranley, abp. of Dublin, *again.*

HENRY V.

1414. Sir Laurence Merbury, *again*, ld. chanc., Mar. 2.
1415. Thos. Cranley, abp. of Dublin, *again.*
Patrick Barret, bp. of Ferns, *again.*
1416. Wm. Fitzthomas, prior of Kilmainham.
1419. Sir Laurence Merbury, *again.*
1421. Wm. Fitzthomas, *again*, May 24.

HENRY VI.

1422. Sir Laurence Merbury, *again*, Oct. 4.
1423. Richd. Sedgrave, or Segrave.
Richd. Talbot, abp. of Dublin, May 19.
1426. Wm. Fitzthomas, *again*, Apr. 25.
Sir Richd. Fitz-Eustace (No. 1), Sept. 10.
Richd. Talbot., abp. of Dublin, *again*, Oct. 23.
Robt. Sutton, *again*, L. K.
1434. Thos. Chase, clerk, L. K.
1435. Thos. Strange, aft. sir T., D. C.
1436. Sir Richd. Fitz-Eustace (No. 1), *again*, D. C.
Robt. Dyke, Dyce, or Dyche, archdn. of Dublin, L. K.
1441. Sir Thos. Strange, *again*, as ld. chanc.
1444. Richd. Wogan.
1445. Wm. Cheevers, D. C.
1446. Sir John Talbot, son and heir to the E. of Shrewsbury.
Robt. Dyke, *again*, D. C.
1448. Thos. Fitzgerald, prior of St. Thomas's, D. C.
Thos. Talbot, prior of Kilmainham, D. C.
1451. Sir John Talbot, *again.*
1453. Sir Edwd. Fitz-Eustace.
1454. Sir Wm. Wells, D. C.
1460. Edmd. (? E. of Rutland), younger son of the D. of York.
John Dynham, Nov. 5, for life.

EDWARD IV.

1461. Sir Robt. Preston, D. C.
Sir Wm. Wells, July 8, for life; conf. by parlt. 2 Edw. IV.
1462. John, E. of Worcester, for life.
1464. Thos., 7th E. of Kildare, for life; conf. by parlt.
1468. Robt. Allaunston.
1469. Sir Wm. Dudley.
1472. Robt., ld. Portlester.
The same, and John Taxton, jointly, and to the survivor of them, Apr. 10; conf. by parlt.
1474. Gilbert de Venham.
Sir Richd. Fitz-Eustace (No. 2).
1480. Wm. Sherwood, bp. of Meath.
1481. Lawrence de St. Lawrence.
Wm. Sherwood, bp. of Meath, *again*, Aug. 5.
1482. Walter Champflower, abb. of St. Mary's, L. K.
1483. Sir Robt. de St. Lawrence, bar. of Howth, July 10.
Thos. Fitzgerald, of Lackagh; const. by parlt.

HENRY VII.

1486. Roland, ld. Portlester.
1492. Alexr. Plunket, June 11
1494. Hy. Deane, prior of Lanthony, bp. of Bangor, Sept. 13.
1496. Walter Fitzsimons, abp. of Dublin, Aug. 6.
1498. Wm. Rokeby, aft. bp. of Meath, and abp. of Dublin.
1501. Walter Fitzsimons, abp of Dublin, *again.*

HENRY VIII.

1509. Nichs., ld. Howth, June 11.
Walter Fitzsimons, abp. of Dublin, *again.*
1513. Sir Wm. Compton, Nov. 6, for life.

1515. Wm. Rokeby, now abp. of Dublin, *again*; Mar. 24.
1527. Hugh Inge, abp. of Dublin.
1528. John Allen, abp. of Dublin, Sept. 19.
1532. Geo. Cromer, abp. of Armagh, July 5.
1534. John, ld. of Trimleston, Aug. 16.
1538. John Allen, aft. sir J., L. K., July 25.
The same, ld. chanc., Oct. 18.
1546. Sir Thos. Cusake, or Cusack, L. K., May 1.
Sir Richd. Read, L. C., Nov. 6.

EDWARD VI.

1547. Sir Richd. Read, L. K., Feb. 26.
1548. Sir John Allen, Apr. 22.
1550. Sir Thos. Cusack, in Sir John Allen's absence, D. C., app. ld. chanc., Aug. 5, 1551.

MARY.

1553. Sir Thos. Cusack, *contd.*
1555. Sir Wm. Fitzwilliam, L. K., July 3.
Hugh Curwen, abp. of Dublin, Sept. 13; by a separate pat. he had power to hear causes.

ELIZABETH.

1559. Hugh Curwen, abp. of Dublin, *contd.*, during pleasure, June 8.
1567. Robt. Weston, dean of Arches, London, June 10.
1573. Adam Loftus, abp. of Dublin, L. K., May 29.
1576. Wm. Gerrard, dean of St. Patrick's, Apr. 23.
1577. Adam Loftus (No. 1), in Wm. Gerard's absence, L. K., Sept. 15.
1578. Adam Loftus (No. 1), as ld. chanc.

JAMES I.

1605. Thos. Jones, bp. of Meath, aft. abp. of Dublin;
Sir Jas. Ley, ch. just. K.B.;
Sir Edmd. Pelham, ch. bar. ex.;
Sir Anthy. St. Leger, m. rolls.; L.K.K., Apr. 5.
1605. Thos. Jones, now abp. of Dublin, Oct. 14.
1619. Sir Wm. Jones, ch. just. K. B.;
Sir Wm. Methwold, ch. bar. ex.;
Sir Fras. Aungier; L.K.K., Apr. 10.
1619. Adam Loftus (No. 2), aft. visc. Loftus of Ely, Apr. 26.

CHARLES I.

1625. Adam, visc. Loftus of Ely, *contd.*, Mar. 30.
1638. Robt., ld. Dillon;
Sir Adam Loftus (No. 3);
Christr. Wandesford;
Sir Ph. Mainwaring, L. K. K., May 25
1639. Sir Richd Bolton, Dec. 6.

CHARLES II.

1655. Rd. Pepys, ch. just. K. B.;
Sir Gerard Lowther, ch. just. C. P.;
Miles Corbet, ch. bar. ex. Commrs.
1656. Wm. Steele, under the parlt., Aug. 20.

THE RESTORATION.

1660. Sir Maurice Eustace, Oct 9.
1665. Michl. Boyle, abp. of Dublin, aft. abp. of Armagh, June 22.

JAMES II.

1685. Michl. Boyle, now abp. of Armagh, *again*, Feb. 19.
1686. Sir Chas. Porter, Mar. 22.
1687. Sir Alex. Fitton, Jan. 13.

WILLIAM III.

1690. Richd. Pyne;
Sir Richard Ryves;
Robt. Rochfort; L. K. K., Aug. 1.
Sir Chas. Porter, Dec. 3.
1696. Sir John Jeffreyson;
Thos. Coote;
Nehemiah Donellan; Commrs., Dec. 31.
1697. John Methuen, Jan. 24.

ANNE.

1702. John Methuen, *contd.*, July 26.
1703. Sir Richd. Cox, July 29; res. 1707.
1707. Richd. Freeman, June 12.
1710. Robt., E. of Kildare;
Wm., abp. of Dublin;
Thos. Keightley; Commrs., Nov. 22.
1710. Sir Constantine Phipps, Dec. 22 res. Sept., 1714.

GEORGE I.

1714. Alan Brodrick, aft. ld. and visc Midleton, Sept. 30; res. 1725.
1725. Richd. West, May 29.
1726. Thos. Wyndham, aft. ld. Wyndham Dec. 3.

GEORGE II.

1727. Thos. Wyndham, *contd.*
1739. Robt. Jocelyn, aft. ld. Newport and visc. Jocelyn, Aug. 30; *d.* Dec. 3 1756.
1757. John Bowes, aft. ld. Bowes, of Clonlyon, Mar. 11.

GEORGE III.

1761. John. ld. Bowes, *contd.*, Jan. 19; *d.* 1767.
1767. Jas. Hewitt, just. K. B. in England Nov. 24; cr. ld. and aft. visc Lifford; *d.* 1789.
1789. Robt. Fowler, abp. of Dublin;
Sir Hugh Carleton, ch. just. C. P.; an
Sir Samuel Bradstreet, just. K. B. Commrs., May 5.

1789. John Fitzgibbon, cr. ld. and aft. visc. Fitzgibbon and E. of Clare, June 13; *d.* Jan. 28, 1802.
1802. Sir John Mitford, cr. ld. Redesdale, Feb. 15.
1806. Geo. Ponsonby, Feb. 14; res. next year.
1807. Thos. Manners Sutton, bar. ex. in England, Apr. 23; cr. ld. Manners.

George IV.

1820. Thos., ld. Manners, *contd.*
1827. Sir Anthy. Hart, v. chanc. England, Nov. 5; res. Nov. 1830; *d.* 1831.

William IV.

1830. Wm. Conyngham, ld. Plunket, ch. just. C. P., Dec. 23; surr. Nov. 1834.
1835. Sir Edwd. Burtenshaw Sugden, Jan. 13; aft. ld. St. Leonards; surr. Apr. 1835.
Wm. Conyngham, ld. Plunket, *again*, Apr. 30.

Victoria.

1837. Wm. Conyngham, ld. Plunket, *contd.*
1841. Sir John Campbell, atty.-gen. in England; cr. ld. Campbell, June 22; res. Sept.
Sir Edwd. Burtenshaw Sugden, aft. ld. St. Leonards, *again*, Oct. 3, Oct. 8 (?); res. 1846.
1846. Maziere Brady, ch. bar. ex., July 16; res. 1852.
1852. Fras. Blackburne, ch. just. Q. B., Mar. 10; res. Dec. 1852.
1853. Maziere Brady, *again*, Jan. 13; res. Feb. 1858.
1858. Sir Joseph Napier, bt., 1867, Mar. 10; res. June 1859.
1859. Maziere Brady, *again*, June 27; res. July 1866.
1866. Fras. Blackburne, *again*, July 24; res. Mar. 1867.
1867. Abraham Brewster, Mar. 29; res. Dec. 1868.
1868. Thos. O'Hagan, just. C. P., Dec. 18; cr. ld. O'Hagan 1870; res. Feb. 1874.
1874. Commissioners.
Sir Jos. Napier, bt.
Mr. Justice Lawson.
Wm. Brooke. Mar. 11.
1875. *John Thos. Ball, Jan. 1; res. Apr. 1880.
1880. Ld. O'Hagan, *again*, May; res. Nov. 1881.
1881. Hugh Law, Nov. 11; *d.* Sept. 10, 1883.
1883. Sir Edwd. Sullivan, bt., Dec. 11; *d.* Sept. 13, 1885.
1885. John Naish, May 21.
Edwd. Gibson, July 1; cr. ld. Ashbourne.
1886. John Naish, *again*, Feb. 11.
Ld. Ashbourne, *again*, Aug. 5.

* Under the S.C.J.I. Act, 1877 (see *ante*, p. 573), the Ld. Chanc., on Jan. 1, 1878, became President of the Chancery Division of the High Court of Justice and one of the *ex-officio* judges of the Court of Appeal.

CHIEF AND PUISNE JUSTICES OF THE KING'S OR QUEEN'S BENCH, IRELAND. PRESIDENTS AND JUSTICES OF THE HIGH COURT OF JUSTICE (IRELAND), QUEEN'S BENCH DIVISION.

Chief Justices of the King's Bench.

1300. Walter L'Enfant.
1342. Elias de Asshebournham.
1346. John Hunt.
1354. John de Redenesse, Nov. 4.
1371. Wm. de Skipwith, Apr. 25.
1373. John Keppok, or Keppock, Apr. 22.
1382. Sir Thos. de Mortimer, Mar. 3.
1384. John Penros, or Penrose, Feb. 27.
1385. John Shriggely; from the ex., June 26.
1388. Richd. Plunket, July 10.
Peter Rowe, Sept. 23.
1403. Steph. Bray; from the C. P.
1426. Hy. Fortescue, June 25.
1429. Steph. Bray, *again*, Feb. 18.
1434. Christr. Bernevall, or Barnewall, 2nd just., Feb. 14.
1461. Thos. Plunket, May 11.
* * Wm. Bermingham; *d.* 1489.
1496. John Topcliffe; from the ex., Oct. 3.
1521. Patr. Bermingham, Feb. 28.
1532. Sir Barth. Dillon, 2nd just.; from the ex.; Jan. 15.
1534. Patr. Fynglass; from the ex., May 8.
1535. Sir Gerald Aylmer; from the ex., Aug. 12.

1559. John Plunket, Oct. 12.
1562. The same, by new pat., Oct. 5.
1583. Jas. Dowdall, 2nd just., May 13.
1585. Robt. Gardener, or Gardiner, serjt. in England, Feb. 19.
1604. Sir Jas. Ley, aft. E. of Marlborough; res.
1608. Sir Humfrey Winche, ch. bar. ex.; aft. just. C. P. in England, Dec. 26.
1612. Sir John Denham, ch. bar. ex., Feb. 28.
1617. Sir Wm. Jones, serjt. in England, Jan. 6.
1620. Sir Geo. (? Jno.) Shirley, serjt. in England, Mar. 4.
1655. Richd. Pepys; under the Commonwealth.
1658. John Santhey, Jan. 19; *pro tem.* on Pepys' death.
Wm. Basil, atty.-gen., Jan. 24.
1660. Sir Jas. Barry, aft. ld. Santry, Nov. 17.
1673. Sir John Povey; from the ex., Mar. 21.
1679. Sir Robt. Booth, Mar. 28; *d.* next year.
1680. Sir Wm. Davys, or Davies, pr. serj., Feb. 21.
1687. Thos. Nugent, Oct. 7; rem.
1690. Sir Richd. Reynell, knt. and bt., Nov. 3; res.
1695. Sir Richd. Pyne, ch. just. C. P., May 16.
1709. Alan Brodrick, Dec. 24; rem.
1711. Sir Richd. Cox, kt. and bt., June 4; rem.
1714. Wm. Whitshed, Sept. 30; rem. to the C. P.
1727. John Rogerson, atty.-gen., Apr. 3.
1741. Thos. Marlay; from the ex., Dec. 29; res.
1751. St. Geo. Caulfield, atty.-gen., Aug. 27; res.
1760. Warden Flood, atty.-gen., July 31.
1764. John Gore, aft. ld. Annaly, solr.-gen., Aug. 24.
1784. John Scott, cr. ld. Earlsfort; aft. visc. and E. of Clonmel, Apr. 29.
1798. Arth. Wolfe, aft. visc. Kilwarden, June 13; murd. in the streets of Dublin by rebels in Emmett's insurrection, July 23, 1803.
1803. Wm. Downes, aft. ld. Downes, Sept. 12.
1822. Chas. Kendal Bushe, solr.-gen., 1805, Feb. 14.
1841. Edwd. Pennefather, solr.-gen., Nov. 10.
1846. Fras. Blackburne, m. rolls, Jan. 23.
1852. Thos. Lefroy, Feb.; res. 1866.
1866. Jas. Whiteside, July 24; *d.* Nov. 1876.
1877. *Geo. Augs. Chichester May, Feb. 2, **G.**

* Transferred Jan. 1, 1878, to the H.C.J., Q.B. Division, and also made an *ex-officio* Judge of the Court of Appeal, under the S.C.J.I. Act, 1877. See *ante*, p. 572.

Presidents of the High Court of Justice, Queen's Bench Division. (Lord Chief Justices of Ireland.)

1878. Geo. Augs. Chichester May, transf. from court of Q. B., Jan. 1.
1887. Michl. Morris, aft. bt.; ch. just., C. P. div.; transf. to Q. B. div. on abolition of C. P. div., *ut ante*, p. 573.

Puisne Justices of the King's Bench.

1322. Robt. Bagod, Bigod, or Bigot.
1326. Nichs. Fastolf.
* * Roger de Preston.
* * John Hunter del Nash.
1344. Jeffrey Foljambe.
1352. John de Redenesse.
1357. Peter Malorre.
* * Nichs. Meones.
1371. John Keppok, or Keppock.
1381. The same, by pat. dated Trym, Mar. 3.
1382 Jas. Penkeston.
1385. John Sothern.
1388. Robt. Coterell, July 10.
Walter Penkeston; pat. same date.
1402. John de Bermingham.
1404. John Lumbard.
1415. Roger Hakenshawe.
1434. Christr. Bernevall, or Barnewall; aft. ch. just.
1434. Wm. Cheevers, or Chevyrs.
1461. John Beg, or Begg, of Drogheda.
* * * *
1513. Sir John Barnewall, ld. Trimleston.
* * Sir Barth. Dillon.
1527. Christr. Delahyde.
1535. Patr. White, *vice* Delahyde, Jan. 26.
* * Thos. St. Lawrence, or Howth, Aug. 12.
1553. Sir Robt. Dillon, aft. ch. just. C. P.
1559. Luke Netterville, *vice* Dillon.
1560. Richd. Dillon, *vice* Netterville.
1566. Barth. Russell, clerk; 3rd just.
1575. Jas. Dowdall, 2nd just.
1577. The same; new appt.
1583. Barth. Russell; new appt., May 26; 3rd just.
Edmond Butler, atty.-gen.; 2nd just.

1584. Sir Nichs. Walshe, 2nd just.; aft. ch. just C. P.
1590. Hy. Burnell, 3rd just., Oct. 15.
Gerald Dillon, 3rd just., Nov. 26.
1599. Wm. Saxey, 2nd just.
1602. John Everard, 2nd just.
1604. Lewis Prowde, 3rd just.
1605. Geoffrey Osbaldeston, 2nd just.
1606. Sir Dominick Sarsfield, 3rd just.
1607. Sir Christr. Sibthorpe, 2nd just.; rem.
1609. Sir Dominick Sarsfield, made 2nd just.
1610. Sir Wm. Sparke; "made a 4th or additional judge by the king's letters patent, in order to ride the circuits, and avoid the protraction of suits; and to be 2nd justice when sir Dominick Sarsfield should be made chief judge of the common pleas."—*Lib. Mun. Publ. Hib.*
Sir Dominck Sarsfield was directly aft. app. to the C. P.
1623. Sir Edwd. Harris, 3rd just.
1625. Sir Christr. Sibthorpe, 2nd just.
1632. Hugh Cressy, 2nd just.
1636. Sir Wm. Ryves, atty.-gen.; 3rd just.
1644. Thos. Dongan, 2nd just.; aft. bar. ex.
1659. John Cooke; under the Commonwealth, 3rd just.
1660. Sir Wm. Aston, 2nd just., Nov. 3.
Thos. Stockton, 3rd just., Nov. 23.
1671. Oliver Jones, from the C. P., 2nd just.
1682. John Lyndon, 3rd serj., 2nd just.
1684. Sir Richd. Reynolds (called in some records Reynell), kt. and bt., 3rd just.; aft. ch. just.
1685. Thos. Nugent, 3rd just,; aft. ch. just.
1687. Sir Bryan O'Neile, bt., 3rd just.; rem.
1690. Sir Richd. Stephens, 3rd just., *vice* O'Neile.
1691. Sir Hy. Echlin, 3rd just.; from the ex.
1693. Thos. Coote, 3rd just., *vice* Echlin, who returned to the ex.
1699. Robt. Tracy, 2nd just.; aft. bar. ex. England.
1701. Jas. Macartney, 2nd just.; rem.
1711. Richd. Nutley, 2nd just.; rem.
1714. Jas. Macartney, *again*; transf. to the C. P.
1715. Jeffrey Gilbert, 2nd just.; aft. ch. bar. ex.
Wm. Caulfield, 3rd just.
1716. Godfrey Boate, pr. serjt., 2nd just.
1722. John Parnell, 2nd just.
1729. Michl. Ward, *vice* Parnell, 2nd just.
1734. Hy. Rose, *vice* Caulfield, 3rd just.
1743. Arth. Blennerhassett, pr. serjt., *vice* Rose.
1758. Chas. Robinson.
1759. Wm. Scott, pr. serj.; aft. bar. ex.
1768. Wm. Henn, *vice* Scott, July 12.
1784. Sir Saml. Bradstreet, recorder of Dublin; addl. or 4th just., Jan. 13.
1787. John Bennett, *vice* Robinson, May 10.
1791. Robt. Boyd, *vice* Bradstreet, June 27.
Jos. Hewett, 2nd serjt., July 27.
1792. Wm. Downes, *vice* Bennett, Mar. 12; aft. ch. just.
1794. Tankerville Chamberlain, *vice* Hewett, June 20.
1798. Robt. Day, *vice* Boyd, Feb. 28.
1802. Chas. Osborne, *vice* Chamberlain, July 20.
1803. St. George Daly, *vice* Downes, Nov. 3.
1817. Edwd. Mayne, *vice* Osborne, Oct. 24.
1818. Richd. Jebb, *vice* Day, Dec. 1.
1820. Chas. Burton, *vice* Mayne, Dec. 2.
1822. Thos. B. Vandeleur, *vice* St. George Daly res.; Mar. 4.
1834. Philip Cecil Crampton, solr.-gen., *vice* Jebb, Oct. 21.
1835. Louis Perrin, atty.-gen., *vice* Vandeleur, Aug. 31.
1847. Richd. Moore, Dec. 13.
1856. *Jas. O'Brien.
1859. Edmd. Hayes; res. 1866.
1860. *Jno. David Fitzgerald, Feb.
1866. John George; Oct. 18, **G.**; *d.* 1871.
1872. *Chas. Robt. Barry, aft. ld. just. app., Jan. 13, **G.**

* On Jan. 1, 1878, these judges were transferred to the H.C.J. Q.B. Div., under the S.C.J.I. Act, 1877. See *ante*, p. 573.

Puisne Judges of the Queen's Bench Division of the High Court of Justice.

Transferred from the old Court of Queen's Bench, Jan. 1, 1878

Jas. O'Brien, *d.* 1882.
John David Fitzgerald, made ld., app. 1882. See *ante* pp. 351–2 and 358.
Chas. Robt. Barry, made ld. just., app. 1883.

Subsequent Appointments.

1882. Jas. Anthy. Lawson (transf. from C.P. div.); *d.* 1887.
1883. Wm. Moore Johnson.
1883. Wm. O'Brien (transf. from C.P. div.).

Upon the abolition of the C.P.D. under the S.C.J.I. Act, 1887 (see *ante*, p. 573), the following judges became, on Oct. 20, 1887, judges of this Division, but with relative rank according to their original appointments.

Michl. Harrison, app. 1878.
Jas. Murphy, app. 1883.
Hugh Holmes, app. 1887.

Subsequent Appointments.

1888. John Geo. Gibson, Jan.

CHIEF AND PUISNE JUSTICES OF THE COMMON PLEAS, IRELAND. PRESIDENTS AND JUSTICES OF THE HIGH COURT OF JUSTICE, IRELAND, COMMON PLEAS DIVISION.

Chief Justices of the Common Pleas.

* * Richd. de Exon.
1326. Hy. de Hambury.
1334. Robt. le Poer, May 10.
Simon Fitz-Richard (2nd just.), *vice* le Poer, Oct. 13.
1343. John Gernoun, Apr. 13.
1353. Thos. de Dent.
1358 Sir Robt. de Preston, Oct. 14.
1378. Hy. Michell, Apr. 3.
1381. Steph. Bray, Mar. 8.
1384. Edmd. del Clay, Feb. 27.
1414. John Fitz-Adam.
1419. Wm. de Tynbegh, July 20.
1425. John Blakeney, June 16.
1428. Sir Jas. Alleyne, Nov. 23.
1430. John Blakeney, *again*, May 13.
1446. Robt. Dowdall.
1461. Nichs. Barnewall, Aug. 1.
1464 Philip Bermingham, June 25.
1496. Thos. Bowryng, Oct. 3.
* * * *
1532. Richd. Delahyde, Aug. 22.
1534. Thos. Luttrell, of Luttrellstown, Oct. 17; aft. sir T.
1554. Sir John Bathe, K. serj., July 7.
1559. Robt. Dillon, of Newtoun, near "Trym," Sept. 3.
1562. The same; new appt.
* * Nichs. Nugent, *vice* Dillon, Oct. 5; res.
1581. Sir Robt. Dillon, of Riverstown, Westmeath (one of the justices), June 28; res.
1593. Sir Wm. Weston, Oct. 10.
1595. Sir Robt. Dillon; rest. on death of Weston.
1597. Sir Nichs. Walsh; from the K. B., Oct. 22.
1610. Sir Dominick Sarsfield, aft. ld. Kilmallock; from the K. B.; June 21; in reversion after Walsh.
1615. Sir Dominick Sarsfield, succ. on Walsh's death, Nov. 28; depr. by sentence of the court of Star-chamber in England.
1634. Sir Gerard Lowther, bar. ex. on Sarsfield being depr., Mar. 13.
1658. The same, by new pat. from Richd. Cromwell, protector, Oct. 7.
1660. Sir Jas. Donellan, Nov. 30.
1665. Sir Edwd. Smith; res. June 13.
1669. Sir Robt. Booth, one of the justices, Jan. 28; made ch. just. K. B.
1679. John Keating, Apr. 25.
1691. Sir Richd. Pyne, Jan. 5; made ch. just. K. B.
1695. Sir John Hely; from the exch., May 10.
1701. Sir Richd. Cox, 2nd just., May 4; made ld. chanc.
1703. Robt. Doyne, ch. bar., Dec. 27; pat. revoked.
1714. John Forster, recorder of Dublin, Sept. 20.
1720. Sir Richd. Levinge, knt. and bt., July 2.
1724. Thos. Wyndham, Oct 22; aft. ld. chanc.

1726. Wm. Whitshed; from the K. B., Jan. 23.
1727. Jas. Reynolds, Nov. 3; res. and made a judge in England.
1740. Hy. Singleton, pr. serj., May 11; res., and made m. rolls.
1753. Sir Wm. Yorke, 2nd just., Sept. 4; aft. chanc. ex.
1761. Sir Richd. Aston, May 5, made just. K. B. in England.
1765. Richd. Clayton, K. C. in England, Feb. 21; res.
1770. Marcus Paterson, atty. gen., June 18.
1787. Hugh Carleton, Apr. 30; aft. ld. and visc. Carleton.
1800. John Toler, atty. gen.; aft. ld. and E. Norbury, Oct. 22.
1827. Wm. Conyngham, ld. Plunket, June 18; aft. ld. chanc.
1830. John Doherty, solr. gen., Dec. 23.
1850. Jas. Hy. Monahan, atty. gen., Sept. 23; res. 1876; *d.* 1879.
1876. *Michl. Morris, aft. bt., Feb. 9, **G.**

* Tranferred Jan. 1, 1878, to the H.C.J., C.P. Division, and also made an *ex-officio* judge of the Court of Appeal under the S.C.J.I. Act, 1877 (see *ante*, p. 573).

Presidents of the High Court of Justice, Common Pleas Division.

(Chief Justices of the Common Pleas.)

1878. Michl. Morris, aft. bt., transf. from court of C. P. Jan. 1: made ld. ch. just. of Ireland and pres. of the Q. B. div.

The C.P. Div., and the office of ch. just. thereof, were abolished Oct. 20, 1887, under S.C.J.I. Act, 1887. See *ante*, p. 573.

Puisne Justices of the Common Pleas.

* * Robt. Bagot.
* * Simon Fitz-Richard.
1334. Richd. Broun, or Brown.
1342. Roger de Preston.
1346. Nichs. de Synterby.
1358. Barth. Dardys.

* * * *

1439. Wm. Baldewyne.
1461. Barnaby Barnewall.

* * * *

1528. Gerald Aylmer, aft. ch. bar. ex. and ch. just. K. B.
1535. Thos. Cusake, or Cusack, May 24; pat. rev.
* * Walter Kerdyffe, Aug. 12.
* * Richd. Talbot.
* * Jas. Dowdall, 3rd just.; rem. to K. B.
* * Robt. Dillon, of Riverstown; rem. to K. B.
1581. Wm. Bathe, 2nd just.
1592. Thos. Dillon, 3rd just.
1600. Patr. Fitzgerald, 2nd just.
Peter Palmer, 3rd just.
1602. Geo. Robinson; "appointed to supply the office of a justice in the absence of the other judges."—*Lodge.*
1604. John Ady, 3rd just.
1606. Chas. Calthorpe, atty. gen., 2nd just.
1610. Gerald Lowther, addl. judge.
1621. John Phillpott, 3rd just.
1624. Saml. Mayart, *vice* Lowther.
1637. Jas. Donellan, 3rd just.
1644. Wm. Hilton, at same time bar. ex.
1655. Jas. Donellan, *again*; his commission signed by Oliver Cromwell, "*quam diu se bene gesserit*"; aft. ch. just.
1660. Sir Jerome Alexander, 2nd just., *vice* Mayart.
Sir Robt. Booth, *vice* Donellan, 3rd just.; aft. ch. just. K. B.
1669. Robt. Johnson, 3rd just.; pat. rev.
1670. Oliver Jones, 3rd just.; rem. to the K. B.
1672. Adam Cusake, or Cusack, 3rd just.
1674. Sir Richd. Reynell, 2nd serjt. 2nd just.; rem. to the K. B.
1682. Arthur Turner, 3rd just.
1684. Saml. Gorges, 3rd just.
1685. Robt. Johnson, *vice* Reynell, 2nd just.
1686. Denis Daly, *vice* Johnson, 2nd just.
1687. Peter Martin, *vice* Gorges.
1690. Sir Richd. Cox, *vice* Daly; aft. ld. chanc., Sept. 2.
* * †John Jefferson, serjt., Dec. 6.
1701. John Smyth, *vice* Jefferson, Feb. 20.
Sir Gilbert Dolben, bt., June 24.
1702. Anthy. Upton, *vice* Smith.
1714. Jas. Macartney, from the K. B., *vice* Upton.
1720. Geo. Gore, atty. gen., *vice* Dolben.
1726. Fras. Bernard, pr. serjt., *vice* Macartney.
1731. Robt. Dixon, 2nd serjt., *vice* Bernard.
1732. Robt. Lindsay, *vice* Dixon.

† This name seems doubtful.

1742. Wm. Yorke, *vice* Lindsay, aft. ch. just.
1745. Robt. French, *vice* Gore.
1753. Robt, Marshall, *vice* Yorke; app. ch. just.
1761. Thos. Tennison, pr. serjt., *vice* French.
1767. Edmd. Malone, *vice* Marshall, Dec. 11.
1774. Godfrey Lill, *vice* Malone, Dec. 15.
1779. Robt. Hellen, *vice* Tennison, May 4.
1784. Thos. Kelly, *vice* Lill, Jan. 9.
Alexr. Crookshank, addl. or 4th just., Jan. 14.
1793. Tankerville Chamberlain, *vice* Hellen, Dec. 6.
1794. Matthias Finucane, *vice* Chamberlain, res., June 20.
1800. Luke Fox, *vice* Crookshank, Feb. 27.
1801. Robt. Johnson, *vice* Kelly, June 23.
1806. Edwd. Mayne, *vice* Finucane, Fe 21; aft. just. K. B.
Wm. Fletcher, *vice* Johnson.
1816. Arthur Moore, 1st serjt., *vice* F res. July 23.
1817. Wm. Johnson, 1st serjt., *vice* Mayn Oct. 25.
1823. Robt. Torrens, chairman of Ki mainham, *vice* Fletcher, July 1 *d.* 1856.
1839. Nichs. Ball, atty. gen., *vice* Moor Feb. 23; *d.* 1865.
1842. Jos. Devonshire Jackson, Sept. *d.* 1858.
1856. *Wm. Keogh, Mar.
1858. Jonn. Christian, Feb.; aft. ld. jus app.
1865. Thos. O'Hagan; aft. ld. chan Ireland.
1867. Michl. Morris; aft. ld. ch. just. C.
1868. *Jas. Anthy. Lawson.

* On Jan. 1, 1878, these judges were transferred to the H.C.J., C.P. Div., und the S.C.J.I. Act, 1877. See *ante*, p. 573.

Puisne Judges of the Common Pleas Division of the High Cour of Justice.

Transferred from the Old Court of Common Pleas, Jan. 1, 1878.

Wm. Keogh, res. 1878.
Jas. Anthy. Lawson; transf. to Q. div. 1882.

Subsequent Appointments.

1878. *Michl. Harrison, Dec. 12, **G.**
1882. Wm. O'Brien, June 27, **G.**; transf. to Q. B. div. 1883.
1883. *Jas. Murphy, June 18, **G.**
1887. *Hugh Holmes, June.

* Under the S.C.J.I. Act, 1887, (see *ante*, p. 573), the C.P. Div. was abolished, an these judges became, on Oct. 20, 1887, judges of the Q.B. Div., but with relative ran according to their original appointments.

CHIEF AND PUISNE BARONS OF THE EXCHEQUER IRELAND. PRESIDENTS AND JUSTICES OF TH HIGH COURT OF JUSTICE, IRELAND, EXCHEQUE DIVISION.

Chief Barons of the Exchequer.

1346. Hugh de Burgh.
1374. Robt. de Holywode, dism.
1376. Hy. Michell, Nov. 23; aft. ch. just. C. P.
1378. Steph. Bray, Apr.; aft. ch. just. C. P.
1381. Thos. Bathe, Mar. 8.
1399. Richd. Rede.
1403. Thos. Bathe, archdn. of Meath, Oct. 14.
1414. Wm. de Tynbegh, atty.-gen., Mar. 2
1419. Jas. Uriell, Dec. 8.
1420. Jas. Cornewalsh, Apr. 24.
1423. Rd. Sydgrave, or Segrave, Aug. 12.
1446. Michl. Griffin.

* * * *

* * John Topcliffe; (in 1496); aft. ch just. K. B.
1513. Sir Barth. Dillon, Feb. 1.

1525. Patr. Fynglass; aft. ch. just. K. B.
1534. Sir Gerald Aylmer, June 25; aft. ch. just. K. B.
1546. Jas. Bathe, Aug.
1570. Lucas Dillon, atty.-gen., May 17.
1593. Sir Robt. Napper, Apr. 10.
1602. Sir Edmd. Pelham, July 6.
1606. Sir Humfrey Winche, Nov. 8; aft. ch. just. K. B.
1609. Sir Jno. Denham, serjt. in England, June 5; aft. ch. just. K. B.
1611. Sir Wm. Methwould, serjt. in England, Feb. 28.
1620. Sir John Blennerhassett, bar. ex., Mar. 12.
1625. Sir Rd. Bolton; aft. ld. chanc.
1639. Sir Edwd. Bolton, solr.-gen., son of Sir Rd., Oct. 7.
1655. Miles Corbet; app. under the Commonwealth.
1660. John Bysse, July 9.
1679. Hy. Hene, one of the barons, Feb. 20.
1687. Sir Stephen Rice, one of the barons, Mar. 9; rem.
1690. Sir John Hely, Nov. 3; aft. ch. just. C. P.
1695. Robt. Doyne, May 10; aft. ch. just. C. P.; pat. rev.
1703. Nehemiah Donellan, one of the barons, Dec. 27.
1706. Rd. Freeman, June 25; aft. ld. chanc.
1707. Robt. Rochfort, atty.-gen., June 12; rem.
1714. Jos. Deane, Sept. 30.
1715. Geffrey Gilbert; from the K. B., June 16; aft. bar. ex. in England.
1722. Bernard Hale, May 25; aft. bar. ex in England.
1725. Thos. Dalton, Sept. 2.
1730. Thos. Marlay, atty.-gen., June 25, aft. ch. just. K. B.
1741. John Bowes, atty -gen., Dec. 21; aft ld. chanc.
1757. Edwd. Willes, serjt., Mar 11; app solr.-gen. in England, and in 1768 a just. K. B., *vice* Hewitt, made ld. chanc. of Ireland.
1766. Anthy. Foster, *vice* Willes, Sept. 5.
1777. Jas. Dennis, July 3; aft. ld. Tracton.
1782. Walter Hussey Burgh, July 2.
1783. Barry Yelverton; aft. ld. and visc. Avonmore, Nov. 29.
1805. Standish O'Grady, Oct. 5; res. 1831; cr. visc. Guillamore.
1831. Hy. Joy, atty.-gen., Jan. 6.
1838. Steph. Woulfe, atty.-gen., July 20; aft. ld. chanc.
1840. Maziere Brady, atty.-gen., Feb. 11.; aft. ld. chanc.
1846. David Richd. Pigot, Sept. 1; *d.* 1873.
1874. *Christr. Palles, atty.-gen., Feb. 25; **G.**

* Transferred, Jan. 1, 1878, to the H.C.J. Ex. Division, and also made an *ex-officio* judge of the Court of Appeal, under the S.C.J.I. Act, 1877. See *ante*, p. 573.

Presidents of the High Court of Justice, Exchequer Division (Chief Barons of the Exchequer.)

1878. Christr. Palles, transf. from Court of Ex., Jan. 1.

Puisne Barons of the Exchequer.

335. Hugh de Burgh.
Robt. Poer.
336. John de Carleton.
343. Nichs. de Synterby.
356 Thos. de Doughes.
369. John Brettan, ch. remembr.
371. Wm. de Karlett.
* * Robt. de Holywode; aft. ch. bar.
377. John Pembroke.
378. Wm. Archebold.
380. Thos. Bathe, aft. ch. baron.
381. Walter de Brugge.
382. Thos. Taillor, clerk.
* * John Shriggely; pat. rev.; aft. ch. just. K. B.
385. John Brekdene.
399. Hugh de Faryngton.
401. Richd. Sydgrave, or Segrave; aft. ch. bar.
1402. Robt. Burnell.
1415. John Gland.
1419. John Wyche.
1422. John de Lydington.
1425. Fras. Toppesfeld.
1426. Regd. Sneterby.
* * Thos. Shorthalls.
1435. Peter Clinton, or Clynton.
1461. Wm. Sutton.
* * * * *
1529. Patr. White; aft. sir P.
1534. Walter Hussey.
1535. Walter Golding.
1561. Robt. Cusake, or Cusack.
1562. Hy. Draycott; res.
1566. Richd. Edwarde, 3rd bar.
1570. Nichs. Nugent, 2nd bar.
1575. John Durninge, 3rd bar.
1577. Roger Mainweringe, 3rd bar.

1578. Robt. illon, 2nd bar., Apr. 17.
Richd. Sedgrave, or Segrave, 2nd bar., June 16.
1580. Michl. Cusake, or Cusack, 3rd bar.
1589. Sir John Elliott, 3rd bar.
1598. Patr. Sedgrave, 2nd bar.: "removed for divers causes by the judgment of the lord deputy and council at Dublin castle."—*Lodge.*
1603. Gerald Comerford, 2nd bar.
1604. Thos. Cary, of Gray's Inn, London, *vice* Comerford.
1605. Sir Robt. Oglethorpe, of Gray's inn, London, *vice* Cary.
1609. Sir John Blennerhassett, aft. ch. bar.
1617. Sir Lancelot Lowther, 3rd bar.
1624. Sir Laurence Parsons, *vice* Oglethorpe.
1628. Gerald Lowther. aft. ch. just. C. P.
1634. Jas. Barry, pr. serjt.; aft. ch. just. K. B., and ld. Santry.
1637. Wm. Hilton, 3rd bar. He was continued a bar. ex. after he was app. a just. C. P. in 1644. and held both offices together by a clause in his patent.—*Lib. Mun. Publ. Hib.*
1659. John Santhey 2nd bar., in the interregnum. See *C. J. K. B.*, *ante*, p. 578.
1660. Sir Richd. Kennedy, 2nd bar.
Thos. Dongan, late just. K. B.
1663. Sir John Povey, 3rd bar.
1673. Hy. Hene, 2nd serjt., 2nd bar.; aft. ch. bar.
1679. Sir Standish Hartstonge, bt., *vice* Hene; rem.
Wm. Worth, 2nd bar.
1686. Sir Chas. Ingleby, *vice* Worth, 2nd bar.
Sir Steph. Rice, *vice* Hartstonge; aft. ch. bar.
1687. Sir Hy. Lynch, bt., *vice* Rice.
1688. Sir John Barnewall, 3rd serjt., and recorder of Dublin.
1690. Sir Hy. Echlin, knt. and bt.; aft. just. K. B.
Sir Standish Hartstonge, *again*, *vice* Lynch.
1692. Sir Richd. Ryves, 2nd serjt.; aft. ch. bar.
1693. Sir Hy. Echlin, *again*; from th K. B.; a second time a baron this court.
1695. Nehemiah Donellan.
1703. Robt. Johnson, *vice* Donellan.
1714. John Pocklington, *vice* Echlin.
* * St. John St. Leger, *vice* Johnson res.
1732. John Wainwright, *vice* Pocklington.
1741. Richd. Mountney, of the Inner Temple, London, *vice* Wainwright.
1742. Arth. Dawson, *vice* St. Leger.
1768. Wm. Scott, just. K. B., *vice* Mountney, Aug. 1.
* * Geo. Smith, or Smyth, *vice* Dawson Nov. 25.
1772. Richd. Power, *vice* Smyth.
1776. Geo. Hamilton, 3rd serjt., *vice* Scott
1784. Peter Metge, addl. or 4th bar.
1793. Michl. Smith, aft. bt., *vice* Hamilton; aft. m. rolls.
1794. Denis George, recorder of Dublin *vice* Power.
1801. St. Geo. Daly, pr. serjt., *vice* Smith; aft. just. K. B.
Wm. Cusack Smith, sol.-gen., *vice* Metge.; aft. bt.
1803. Jas. M'Clelland, solr.-gen., *vice* St. Geo. Daly.
1821. Richd. Pennefather, *vice* George res. Feb. 1; *d.* 1859.
1830. John Leslie Foster, *vice* M'Clelland July 13; *d.* 1841.
1836. Michl. O'Loghlen, atty.-gen., *vice* Sir Wm. C. Smith, Nov. 5; aft. m. rolls.
1837. John Richards, atty.-gen., *vice* O'Loghlen, Nov. 5; res. 1859.
1841. Thos. Lefroy, Nov. 17; aft. ch. just. Q. B.
1852. Richd. Wilson Greene; res. 1861.
1859. *Fras. Alexr. Fitzgerald.
Hy. Geo. Hughes; *d.* 1872.
1861. Rickard Deasy, atty.-gen.; aft. l. just. app.
1872. *Richd. Dowse, atty-gen., Nov. G.

* On Jan. 1, 1878, these judges were transf. to the H.C.J., Exch. Div., under the S.C.J.I. Act, 1877. See *ante*, p. 573.

Puisne Judges of the Exchequer Division of the High Court of Justice.

Transferred from the old Court of Exchequer, Jan. 1, 1878.

Fras. Alexr. Fitzgerald, res. 1882. | Richd. Dowse.

Subsequent Appointments.

1882. Wm. Drennan Andrews.

MASTERS OF THE ROLLS—IRELAND.

1334. Wm. de Bardelby.
1372. Thos. de Thelwall.
1373. Robt. de Sutton, Nov. 4.
1374. Thos. de Everdon, and Robt. de Sutton. jointly, Feb. 4.
1377. Robt. de Sutton, alone, June 20.
1382. The same, new appt., Jan. 21.
1385. Thos. de Everdon, *again*, Jan. 15.
1399. John Kirkeby.
1401. Thos. de Everdon, *again*, Jan. 10.
1423. Robt. de Sutton, *again*, Apr. 27.
1430. Wm. Sutton, Dec. 10.
1446. Robt. Dyke, Dyce, or Dyche, archdn. of Dublin.
1461. Patr. Cogley, May 2.
Peter Travers, Aug. 4.
1478. Thos. Dovedall, or Dowdall.
1496. John Payne, or Pain, Oct. 3; bp. of Meath in 1483.
1522. Thos. Darcy, rect. of Howth, July 7.
1528. Robt. Cowley, Jan. 10.
1533. John Allen, July; aft. ld. chanc.
1542. Sir John Cusake, or Cusack, June 10.
1550. Patr. Barnewall, K. serjt., Aug. 5.
1552. John Parker, Dec.
1566. Hy. Draycott, ch. remembr. Oct. 5.
1572. Nichs. Whyte, of Whyte's Hall, July 18; "sequestrated."—*Lodge*.
1578. Edwd. Fitz-Symon, Apr. 28.
1593. Anthy. St. Leger, aft. sir A., Apr. 10.
1609. Sir Fras. Aungier, aft. ld. Aungier, June 5.
1632. Christr. Wandesford, Jan. 4.
1640. Sir John Temple, Jan. 31.
1644. Sir Maurice Eustace, June 22; in reversion after sir Jno. Temple.
1664. Wm. Temple (son of sir J.) aft. bt., Apr. 7; in reversion after his father and Eustace.
1677. Sir Wm. Temple, bt.; new appt., Nov. 23, on death of his father, who survived Eustace; rem.
1689. Sir Wm. Talbot, bt., Apr. 22.
1696. Wm. Berkeley, aft. ld. Berkeley; pr. seal Apr. 28; L. P. June 20.
1717. John Shute, *alias* Barrington, aft. visc. Barrington, Feb. 28; in reversion after ld. Berkeley.
1731. Thos. Carter, Oct. 26; he was formerly dep. to ld. Berkeley, and was now app. on surrend. of lds. Berkeley and Barrington.
1754. Hy. Singleton, Apr. 11.
The office of Master of the Rolls ceased to be a judicial office, 1759.
1759. Richd. Rigby, Nov. 21.
1761. The same, new appt., Feb. 11.
1788. Wm. Robt., D. of Leinster, June 7.
1789. John, E. of Glandore, and John Joshua, E. of Carysfort, jointly, July 15.
By 41 Geo. III. cap. 25, (Apr. 18, 1801), the office of master or keeper of the rolls was re-made a judicial office, with an augmented salary, and the future masters were constituted assistants to the lord chancellor.
1801. Sir Michl. Smith, bt., bar. ex.; app. the first judicial master under the Act, June 24.
1806. John Philpot Curran, June 28.
1814. Sir Wm. MacMahon, aft. bt., Mar. 1.
1837. Sir Michl. O'Loghlen, aft. bt., Jan. 28.
1842. Fras. Blackburne, atty. gen., Nov. 1; aft. ch. just. K. B.
1846. Thos. Berry Cusack Smith, grandson of sir Michl. Smith, atty. gen.; *d.* 1866.
1866. John Edwd. Walsh, Oct. 27, **G.**; *d.* 1869.
1870. *Edwd. Sullivan, aft. bt., Jan. 12, **G.**; aft. ld. chanc.
1883. Andrew Marshall Porter, Dec. 14, **G.**

* On Jan. 1, 1878, the Master of the Rolls was made a judge of the H.C.J., Chanc. Div., and also an *ex-officio* judge of the Court of Appeal, under the S.C.J.I. Act, 1877. See *ante*, p. 573.

LORDS JUSTICES AND JUDGES OF APPEAL.

Lords Justices of the Court of Appeal in Chancery in Ireland.

Appointed under 19 & 20 Vict. c. 92.

1856. Fras. Blackburne, ld. chanc. in 1852 and 1866.
1866. Abraham Brewster, aft. ld. chanc., Aug. 15, **G.**
1867. *Jonathan Christian, just. C. P.

* On Jan. 1, 1878, this judge was transferred to the Court of Appeal under the S.C.J.I. Act, 1877. See *ante*, p. 573.

Judges of the Court of Appeal.

Ex-officio Judges under the S.C.J.I. Act, 1877.

The ld. chancellor.
The ld. ch. just. of Ireland.
The master of the rolls.
The ch. just. of the common pleas (office abolished by S.C.J.I. A[ct] 1887).
The ch. baron of the exch. (offi[ce] to be abolished *ut supra*).

Ordinary Judges, styled Lord Justices of Appeal.

Transferred from the old Court of Chancery, Jan. 1, 1878.

1878. Jonn. Christian, Jan. 1.

Subsequent Appointments.

1878. Rickard Deasy, bar. ex., Jan. 1, **G.**; *d.* 1883.
Gerald FitzGibbon, solr. gen., Dec. 12, **G.**
1883. Chas. Robt. Barry, just. Q. B. di[v.], June 18, **G.**
1885. John Naish, ex. ld. chanc.

VICE CHANCELLORS OF IRELAND. JUSTICES OF TH[E] HIGH COURT OF JUSTICE, IRELAND, CHANCER[Y] DIVISION.

Vice Chancellors of Ireland.

Appointed under 33 & 31 Vict. c. 44.

For previous Deputy or Vice Chancellors see "Lord Chancellors of Ireland," *ante*, p. 5[..]

1867. Hedges Eyre Chatterton.

On Jan. 1, 1878, this judge was transferred to the H.C.J., Chancery Div., under t[he] S.C.J.I. Act, 1877. See *ante*, p. 573.

Judges of the Chancery Division of the High Court of Justice.

Transferred from the old Courts of Chancery, Jan. 1, 1878.

The ld. chancellor, president (see *ante*, p. 573).
The master of the rolls (see *an[te]*, p. 573).
Hedges Eyre Chatterton.

LAND JUDGES.

Transferred from the Landed Estates Court, Jan. 1, 1878.

See *ante*, p. 573.

Steph. Woulfe Flanagan, res. 1885.
Hy. Ormsby, res. 1885.

Subsequent Appointment.

1885. Jno. Monroe.

JUDGES OF THE PROBATE COURT AND THE COURT FOR MATRIMONIAL CAUSES—IRELAND.

Appointed under
20 & 21 Vict. c. 79 (Probate).
33 & 34 Vict. c. 110 (Matrimonial Causes).

1858. Richd. Keatinge, formerly judge of H.M. court of prerogative in Ireland, Jan. 1; judge of prob. court only; res. 1868.

1868. Robt. Richd. Warren, judge of prob. court only; became judge of matrimonial causes court Jan. 1, 1871.

On Jan. 1, 1878, this judge was transferred to the H.C.J., Prob. and Matrim. Div., under the S.C.J.I. Act, 1877. See *ante*, p. 573.

JUDGES OF THE LANDED ESTATES COURT.

Appointed under 21 & 22 Vict. c. 72.

1858. Nov. 1. } Hy. Martley; *d.* 1859.
Mountifort Longfield; res. 1867.
Chas. Jas. Hargreave; *d.* 1866.

1859. Wm. Cary Dobbs, *vice* Martley; *d.* 1869.

1867. David Lynch, *vice* Longfield; *d.* 1872.

1869. *Steph. Woulfe Flanagan, *vice* Dobbs, May 27.

1875. *Hy. Ormsby, *vice* Lynch, Nov. 12.

* On Jan. 1, 1878, these judges were transferred to the H.C.J., Chanc. Div., under the S.C.J.I. Act, 1877. See *ante*, p. 573.

JUDGES OF HIGH COURT OF ADMIRALTY—IRELAND.

First appointed by the Crown in 1785 under 23 & 24 Geo. III. (Ireland) cap. 14 (1783-4). Continued by Act of Union 39 & 40 Geo. III. cap. 67 (1800). Practice and procedure of the court altered by 30 & 31 Vict. cap. 114 (1867).

1785. Warden Flood; *d.* 1797.

1797. Sir Jonah Barrington; L. P. rev. 1830.

1830. John Hy. North; *d.* 1831.

1831. Sir Hy. Merdyth, bt.; res. 1838; *d.* 1859.

1838. Jos. Stock; *d.* 1855.

1855. Thos. F. Kelly, res. 1867.

1867. John Fitzhenry Townshend.

By the S.C.J.I. Act, 1877, the jurisdiction of this Court will, upon the next vacancy in the office of judge thereof, fall into the S.C.J., and be exercised by the judge of the Prob. and Matrim. Div. thereof. See *ante*, p. 573.

JUDGES OF THE COURT OF BANKRUPTCY—IRELAND.

Appointed under 20 & 21 Vict. c. 60.

1857. Nov. 1. { John Macan; *d.* 1859. Hon. Patrick Plunket; *d.* 1859. } Commrs. of bankruptcy; succ. as judges under 20 & 21 Vict. cap. 60.

1859. Walter Berwick, *vice* Macan; *d.* 1868.

1859. David Lynch, *vice* Plunket; app. judge land. est. court, 1867.

1867. Stearne Ball Miller, *vice* Lynch.

1868. Michl. Harrison, *vice* Berwick.

1879. Fredk. Wm. Walsh, *vice* Harrison, Jan. 16, **G.**; *d.* 1885.

1885. Walter Boyd, *vice* Walsh.

THE IRISH LAND COMMISSION.

Commissioners appointed under the Land Law (Ireland) Act, 1881, 44 & 45 Vict. Cap. 49.

Judicial Commissioner.

John O'Hagan, with the title of Justice O'Hagan, and the same rank, &c., as a puisne com. law judge.

Edwd. Falconer Litton, Q. C. (2nd Commr.) | Fredk. S. Wrench (3rd Commr.)

Commissioners appointed under the Purchase of Land (Ireland) Act, 1885, 48 & 49 Vict. Cap. 73.

Stanislaus J. Lynch. | John Geo. MacCarthy.

ATTORNEYS GENERAL FOR IRELAND.

Those marked * were afterwards raised to the bench.

1357. John de Leycestre.
1372. Hy. Michell, May 4.
1379. Robt. Hore.
1381. Thos. Malalo, Jan. 15.
1385. Robt. Hemynborgh, July 28.
1400. *Wm. de Tynbegh, Jan. 20.
1401. John Barry, Feb. 6.
1422. John Whyte, or White, Oct. 19.

* * *

1532. Thos. St. Lawrence, Aug. 19.
1535. *Robt. Dillon, Aug.
1554. Barnaby Scurloke, or Scurlog.
1559. James Barnewall, Sept. 3.
1566. *Lucas Dillon, Nov. 8.
1570. Edwd. Fitz-Symons, June 4.
1574. John Bathe, Feb. 21.
1577. Thos. Snagg, Sept. 13.
1580. Christr. Flemyng, Sept. 9.
1582. *Edmd. Butler, Aug. 8.
1584. *Chas. Calthorpe, aft. sir C., June 22.
1606. Sir John Davys, or Davies, Apr. 19.
1619. *Sir Wm. Ryves, Oct. 30.
1636. Richd. Osbaldeston, of Gray's Inn, London, Aug. 2.
1640. Thos. Tempest, of Lincoln's Inn, July 20.
1649. *Wm. Basil, under the Commonwealth, July 18.
1660. Sir Wm. Domville, June 23.
1686. Sir Richd. Nagle, Dec. 31.
1690. Sir John Temple, Oct. 30.
1695. *Robt. Rochfort, May 10.
1707. Alan Brodrick, June 12.
1709. John Forster, Dec. 24.
1711. Sir Richd. Levinge, bt., June 4.
1714. *Geo. Gore, Nov. 8.
1720. *John Rogerson, May 14.
1727. *Thos. Marlay, May 5.
1730. Robt. Jocelyn, Sept. 29.
1739. *John Bowes, Sept. 3.
1741. *St. Geo. Caulfield, Dec. 23.
1751. *Warden Flood, Aug. 27.
1760. Philip Tisdall, July 31.
1777. *John Scott, Oct. 17.
1782. *Barry Yelverton, July 2.
1783. *John Fitzgibbon, Nov. 29.
1789. *Arthur Wolfe, July 16.
1798. *John Toler, June 26.
1799. John Stewart, Dec. 9; aft. bt.
1803. *Standish O'Grady, May 28.
1805. *Wm. Conyngham Plunket, Oct. 15.
1807. Wm. Saurin, May 15.
1822. *Wm. Conyngham Plunket, *again*, Jan. 15.
1827. *Hy. Joy, June 18.
1831. *Fras. Blackburne, Jan. 11.
1835. *Louis Perrin, Apr. 29.
*Michl. O'Loghlen, Aug. 31.
1836. *John Richards, Nov. 10.
1837. *Steph. Woulfe, Feb. 3.
1838. *Nichs. Ball, July 11.
1839. *Maziere Brady, Feb. 23.
1840. *David Richd. Pigot, Aug. 14.
1841. *Fras. Blackburne, *again*, Sept. 23.
1842. *Thos. Berry Cusack Smith, Nov. 1.
1846. *Richd. Wilson Greene, Feb. 2.
*Richd. Moore, July 16.
1847. *Jas. Hy. Monahan, Dec. 24.
1850. John Hatchell, Sept. 23.
1852. *Jos. Napier, Feb.
1853. *Abraham Brewster, Apr.
1855. *Wm. Keogh, Mar.
1856. *John David Fitzgerald, Mar.
1858. *Jas. Whiteside, Feb.
1859. *John David Fitzgerald, *again*, June.
1860. *Rickard Deasy, Feb.
1861. *Thos. O'Hagan.
1865. *Jas. Anthy. Lawson.
1866. *John Edwd. Walsh, July 25, **G.**
*Michl. Morris, Nov. 1, **G.**
1867. *Hedges Eyre Chatterton.
*Robt. Richd. Warren.
1868. *John Thos. Ball.
*Edwd. Sullivan.

1870. *Chas. Robt. Barry, Jan. 26, **G.**
1872. *Richd. Dowse, Jan. 13, **G.**
*Christr. Palles, Nov. 5, **G.**
1874. *John Thos. Ball, *again*, Mar. 12, **G.**
1875. *Hy. Ormsby, Jan. 21, **G.**
*Geo. Augs. Chichester May, Nov. 27, **G.**
1877. *Edwd. Gibson, Feb. 15, **G.**
1880. *Hugh Law, May 10, **G.**
1881. *Wm. Moore Johnson, Nov. 17, **G.**
1883. *Andrew Marshall Porter, Jan. 3, **G.**
*John Naish, Dec. 19, **G.**
1885. Saml. Walker.
*Hugh Holmes, July 3, **G.**
1886. Saml. Walker, *again*.
*Hugh Holmes, *again*.
1887. *John Geo. Gibson.
1888. Peter O'Brien.

SOLICITORS GENERAL FOR IRELAND.

From the appointment of solicitor-general Cowley, in 1537, to the death of Richard Finglas, in 1574, there appears to have been *two* solicitors for Ireland, subsisting at the same time; the one by the name of Principal or Chief Solicitor (*Solicitoris Principalis sive capitalis aut Solicitatoris regni Hiberniæ*), and the other by the name of General Solicitor (*Solicitoris Generalis, alias Solicitatoris regni Hiberniæ*).—*Lib. Mun. Publ. Hib.*

Solicitors General for Ireland.

Those marked † afterwards became Attorneys General. See "Attorneys General" *ante*, p. 588, where their subsequent promotions are noted. Those marked * were afterwards raised to the Bench without having been Attorneys General.

Principal Solicitors and Solicitors General.

1532. Thos. Luttrell, solr.-gen., Sept. 9.
1534. Patr. Barnewall, solr.-gen., Oct. 17.
1537. Walter Cowley, pr. solr., Sept. 7.
1546. †John Bathe, pr. solr., Feb. 7.
1550. †The same, solr.-gen.; new pat., Oct. 16.
Richd. Finglas, pr. solr., Oct. 17.
1551. †John Bathe, *again*, solr.-gen.; new pat., July 24.
Richd. Finglas, *again* pr. solr.; new pat., July 24.
1554. Jas. Dowdall, pr. solr. and solr.-gen., July 20.
1565. Nichs. Nugent, solr.-gen., Apr. 17.
1570. †John Bathe, *again*, pr. solr., Oct. 20.
1574. Richd. Bellyng, pr. solr., Feb.

Solicitors General only.

1584. Jesse Smythes, July 7.
1586. Roger Wilbraham, Feb. 11.
1603. †Sir John Davys, or Davies, of the Middle Temple, London, Sept. 18.
1606. Sir Robt. Jacobe, Apr. 19.
1618. Sir Richd. Bolton, Dec. 31.
1622. Sir Edwd. Bolton, son of sir Richd., Dec. 5.
1640. Sir Wm. Sambach, June 8.
1657. Wm. Ellys, or Ellice; under the Commonwealth.
1658. Robt. Shapcott; under the Commonwealth; Hil. T.
1660. †Sir John Temple, July 10.
1689. Sir Theobald Butler; after the abdication of Jas. II.; rem., July 25.
1690. †Sir Richd. Levinge, *vice* Butler, Nov. 3.
1695. †Alan Brodrick, May 10.
1704. †Sir Richd. Levinge, *again*; now bt Apr. 4.
1709. †John Forster, recorder of Dublin, Sept. 8.
Wm. Whitshed, Dec. 24.
1711. Fras. Bernard, June 4.
1714. †John Rogerson, Nov. 8.
1720. †Thos. Marlay, Oct. 13.
1727. †Robt. Jocelyn, Apr. 5.
1730. †John Bowes, Sept. 29.
1739. †St. Geo. Caulfield, Sept. 24.
1741. †Warden Flood, Dec. 24.
1751. †Philip Tisdall, Aug. 27.
1760. *John Gore, July 31.
1764. *Marcus Paterson, Aug. 29.
1770. *Godfrey Lill, June 18.
1774. †John Scott, July 13.
1777. *Robt. Hellen, Oct. 31.
1779. *Hugh Carleton, Apr. 7.
1787. †Arth. Wolfe, May 1.
1789. †John Toler, July 16.
1798. †John Stewart, June 26.
1800. †Wm. Cusack Smith, aft. bt., Dec 6.
1801. †Jas. McClelland, Dec. 17.
1803. †Wm. Conyngham Plunket, Oct. 22
1805. *Chas. Kendal Bushe, Oct. 15.
1822. †Hy. Joy, Feb. 20.
1827. *John Doherty, June 18.

1830. *Philip Cecil Crampton, Dec. 23.
1834. †Michl. O'Loghlen, Oct. 21.
1835. *Edwd. Pennefather, Jan. 27.
†Michl. O'Loghlen, *again*, Apr. 29.
†John Richards, Sept. 21.
1836. †Stephen Woulfe, Nov. 10.
1837. †Maziere Brady, Feb. 3.
1839. †David Richd. Pigot, Feb. 11.
1840. †Richd. Moore, Aug. 14.
1841. *Ed. Pennefather, *again*, Sept. 23.
*Jos. Devonshire Jackson, Nov. 10.
1842. †Thos. Berry Cusack Smith, Sept. 21.
†Richd. Wilson Greene, Nov. 1.
1846. †Abraham Brewster, Feb. 2.
†Jas. Hy. Monahan, July 16.
1847. †John Hatchell, Dec. 24.
1850. *Hy. Geo. Hughes, Sept. 26.
1852. †Jas. Whiteside, Feb.
1853. †Wm. Keogh, Apr.
1855. †John David Fitzgerald, Mar.
1856. *Jonathan Christian, Mar.
1858. *Hy. Geo. Hughes, *again*, Feb.
*Edmd. Hayes.
1859. *John George, June.
†Rickard Deasy.
1860. †Thos. O'Hagan, Feb.
1861. †Jas. Anthy. Lawson.
1865. †Edwd. Sullivan.
1866. †Michl. Morris, Aug. 3, **G.**
†Hedges Eyre Chatterton, Nov. 8, **G**
1867. †Robt. Richd. Warren.
*Michl. Harrison.
1868. †John Thos. Ball.
†Hy. Ormsby.
†Chas. Robt. Barry.
1870. †Richd. Dowse, Feb. 14, **G.**
1872. †Christr. Palles, Feb. 6, **G.**
†Hugh Law, Nov. 18, **G.**
1874. †Hy. Ormsby, *again*, Mar. 12, **G.**
1875. Hon. David Robt. Plunket, Jan. 29 **G.**
1877. †Gerald FitzGibbon, jun., Mar. 3, **G**
1878. †Hugh Holmes, Dec. 14, **G.**
1880. †Wm. Moore Johnson, May 24, **G.**
1881. †Andrew Marshall Porter, Nov. 18, **G**
1883. †John Naish, Jan. 9, **G.**
†Saml. Walker, Dec. 19, **G.**
1885. The MacDermot.
*John Monroe, July 3, **G.**
†John Geo. Gibson.
1886. The MacDermot, *again*.
†John Geo. Gibson, *again*.
1887. †Peter O'Brien.
1888. Dodgson Hamilton Madden.

SERJEANTS-AT-LAW—IRELAND.

In Ireland, as in England, the office of serjeant-at-law is one of very great antiquity, but in Ireland the title was conferred upon a much more limited number. Down to 1627 only one person held the dignity of serjeant, and from the patents quoted in "Smyth's Chronicle" (*ante*, p. 572) he seems to have beenstyled the king's serjeant. In 1627 a second serjeant was appointed, and the senior serjeant was then styled the prime serjeant. In 1682 a third serjeant was appointed. In 1805 on the death of Arthur Browne, the then prime serjeant, the title was altered to first serjeant.

The serjeants, or at all events the prime and second serjeants formerly ranked before the attorney and solicitor general, but from 1805 this precedence has been abolished.

Name.	Third Serjeant.	Second Serjeant.	Serjeant or King's Serjeant to 1627, Prime Serjeant to 1805, and then First Serjeant.
			Serjeant or King's Serjeant.
Simon Fitz-Richard	—	—	1326, Feb. 12.
Hugh Brown	—	—	1341, Dec. 3.
Wm. le Petit	—	—	1343, June 1.
Robt. de Preston	—	—	134–.
Edmd. de Berford or Bereford	—	—	1357, Nov. 19
John Tyrell	—	—	1373–4.

NAME.	THIRD SERJEANT.	SECOND SERJEANT.	SERJEANT OR KING'S SERJEANT TO 1627, PRIME SERJEANT TO 1805, AND THEN FIRST SERJEANT.
			SERJEANT OR KING'S SERJEANT.
Richd. Plunket	——	——	1375, Apr. 18.
Walter Cotterell	——	——	1375.
John Bermyngham	——	——	1388, Sept. 24.
Chas. Barnewall	——	——	1422, Oct. 20.
Sir Thos. Fitz-Christr. Plunket	——	——	1434, Nov. 8.
Robt. Dowdall	——	——	1435, June 20.
Edwd. Somerton	——	——	1437, Feb. 4.
Sir Thos. Luttrell	——	——	1532.
Patr. Barnewall	——	——	1534.
Sir John Bathe	——	——	1550.
Richd. Finglas	——	——	1554, Sept. 11.
Edwd. Fitz-Symon	——	——	1574, Feb. 21.
Arthur Corye	——	——	1594, May 9.
Edwd. Loftus	——	——	1597, Nov. 1.
Edwd. Kerdiffe	——	——	1601, June 8.
Sir John Beere	——	——	1609, Feb. 9.
Sir John Brereton	——	——	1617, May 13.
Sir Nathl. Catelyn	——	1627, May 23.	——
		——	PRIME SERJEANTS.
Jas. Barry, aft. ld. Santry	——	——	1629, Oct. 6.
Sir Maurice Eustace	——	1637, Apr. 14.	1634, Aug.
Sir Wm. Sandbach	——		——
Sir Audley Mervyn	——	1661, Mar. 4.	1660, Sept. 20.
Robt. Griffith	——	1670, Apr. 6.	——
Hy. Hene	——	1673, May 10.	——
Sir Richd. Reynell	——	1674, May 26.	——
John Osborne	——		1676, Aug. 29, in reversion; in possession 1680; depr. 1686; rest. 1690, Sept. 29.
Sir Wm. Davys or Davies	——	——	1675, Oct. 26.
Sir Richd. Stephens	——	1680, Apr. 7; dism. 1682; rest. 1690, Nov. 14.	
John Lyndon	1682, July 24.	——	——
Wm. Beckett	——	1682, Oct. 24.	——
Sir Richd. Ryves	1683, Feb. 19.	1683, Aug. 7; rem.; rest. 1691, Jan. 5.	——
Sir Hy. Echlin	1683, Aug. 3.	1687, May.	——
Gerald Dillon	——	——	1687, Feb. 15.
Sir John Barnewall	1687, May 6.	——	——
Sir Theob. Butler	1688, Mar.	——	——
Alan Brodrick	1691, Jan. 5.	——	——
Nehemiah Donellan	——	——	1692, Dec. 29.
Sir Thos. Packenham	——	1692, Feb. 8.	1695, Nov. 5.
Wm. Neave	——	1696, Jan. 13.	1708, Dec. 1.
Robt. Saunders	——		1703, Feb. 28.
Wm. Caulfield	——	1708, Dec. 1; res.	1714, Dec. 8.
Robt. Blennerhassett	——	——	1711, Aug. 11.
Morley Saunders	——	1711, Aug. 14.	1712, Feb. 9.

Name.	Third Serjeant.	Second Serjeant.	Serjeant or King's Serjeant to 1627, Prime Serjeant to 1805, and then First Serjeant.
			Prime Serjeants.
John Cliffe	1711, Nov. 29.	1712, Feb. 12.	——
John Staunton	1712, Feb. 25.	——	——
Robt. Fitzgerald	——	1714, Dec. 18.	1716, June 23.
Godfrey Boate	——	——	1715, June 13.
John Witherington	1714, Dec. 14.	1716, Aug. 23.	——
Wm. Brodrick	——	1718, Dec. 23.	——
Fras. Bernard	——	——	1724, Jan. 26.
Hy. Singleton	——	——	1726, June 22.
Robt. Jocelyn	1726, Mar. 28.	——	——
John Bowes	1727, May 4.	——	——
Robt. Dixon	——	1728, Jan. 5.	——
Hy. Purdon	1730, Oct.	——	——
Richd. Bettesworth	——	1731, Apr. 29.	——
Robt. Marshall	1737, Apr. 18.	1741, Mar. 31.	——
Arthur Blennerhassett ...	——	——	1742, Jan. 14.
Philip Tisdall	1742, Jan. 21.	——	——
Anthy. Malone	——	——	1743, May 9.
Richd. Malone	1751, Oct. 28.	1757, Nov. 25.	——
Eaton Stannard	——	——	1754, Jan. 24.
Wm. Scott	——	——	1757, Oct. 6.
Marcus Paterson	1757, Nov. 24.	——	——
Thos. Tennison	——	——	1759, July 27.
Edmd. Malone	——	1759, Sept. 10.	——
John Hely-Hutchinson ...	——	——	1761, Dec. 11.
Jas. Dennis	1764, Oct. 10.	1767, Jan. 14.	1774, July 18.
Godfrey Lill	1767, Jan. 15.	——	——
Maurice Coppinger	1770, July 12.	1774, July 19.	——
Geo. Hamilton	1774, July 20.	——	——
Hugh Carleton	1776, May 15.	1777, Nov. 5.	——
Walter Hussey Burgh ...	——	——	1777, July 24, to June 14, 1780; *again* June 1, 1782.
Attiwell Wood	1777, Nov. 6.	1779, May 8.	——
Jas. Fitzgerald	1779, May 8.	1784, Apr. 8.	1787, June 21.
Jas. Browne	——	——	1780, June 14, to June 1, 1782; *again* May 21, 1784.
Peter Metge	1782, July 25.	——	——
Thos. Kelly	——	——	1782, July 13.
John Scott	——	——	1783, Dec. 31.
John Toler	1784, Jan. 15.	1787, June 27.	——
Jos. Hewett	1787, June 27.	1789, Aug. 17.	——
Hy. Duquerry	1789, Aug. 17.	1791, July 30.	——
Jas. Chatterton	1791, July 30.	1793, Dec. 10.	——
Edmd. Stanley	1793, Dec. 10.	——	1801, July 1.
St. George Daly	——	——	1799, Jan. 28.
Arthur Browne	——	——	1802, Dec. 29; *d.* 1805; and his successor was styled first serjt.
			First Serjeants.
Arthur Moore	1801, Oct. 30.	——	1805, July 25.
Chas. Kendal Bushe	1805, July 25.	——	——
John Ball	1805, Oct. 25.	1806, Apr. 23.	——

Name.	Third Serjeant.	Second Serjeant.	Serjeant or King's Serjeant to 1627, Prime Serjeant to 1805, and then First Serjeant.
			First Serjeants.
Wm. McMahon	1806, Apr. 23.	1813, Dec. 3.	——
Wm. Johnson	1813, Dec. 4.	1814, Mar. 4.	1816, July 25.
Hy. Joy	1814, Mar. 19.	1816, July 26.	1817, Oct. 28.
Richd. Jebb	1816, July 27.	1817, Oct. 29.	——
Chas. Burton	1817, Oct. 30.	1818, Dec. 1.	——
Thos. Lefroy	1818, Dec. 1.	1820, Dec. 3.	1822, May 13.
Thos. B. Vandeleur	1821, Feb. 13.	——	——
John Lloyd	——	1822, May 13.	——
Robt. Torrens	1822, May 13.	——	——
Thos. Goold	1823, July 13.	——	1830, Apr.
Fras. Blackburne	——	1830, Apr. 19.	——
Edwd. Pennefather	1830, Apr.	1831, Jan. 18.	1832, Feb.
Michl. O'Loghlen	1831, Jan. 18.	1832, Feb. 13.	——
Louis Perrin	1832, Feb. 7.	——	——
Richd. Wilson Greene ...	——	——	1835, May 23.
Jos. Devonshire Jackson ...	——	1835, Jan. 27.	——
Stephen Woulfe	1835, May 23.	——	——
Nichs. Ball	1836, Nov. 10.	——	——
Wm. Curry	1838, July 20.	——	——
Richd. Moore	1840, May.	——	——
Jos. Stock	1840, Aug.	1841, Nov.	1842, Nov.
Richd. B. Warren	1841, Nov.	1842, Nov.	——
Richd. Keating	1842, Nov.	——	——
John Howley	1843, Sept.	1848, July.	1851, June.
Jas. O'Brien	1848, July.	1851, June.	——
Jonathan Christian	1851, June.	——	——
Walter Berwick	1855.	1858, Feb. 5.	——
Rickard Deasy	1858, Feb. 5.	——	——
Gerald Fitzgibbon	1859.	1859.	——
Thos. O'Hagan	1859.	——	——
Jas. Anthy. Lawson	——	1860, Feb. 25.	——
Edwd. Sullivan	1860, Oct. 24.	1861, Feb. 21.	——
Richd. Armstrong	1861, Feb. 21.	1865, Feb. 18.	1866, Feb. 27.
Sir Colman O'Loghlen, bt. ...	1865, Feb. 18.	1866, Feb. 24.	——
Chas. Robt. Barry	1866, Feb. 24.	——	——
Richd. Dowse	1867, Jan. 12.	——	——
David Sherlock	1870, Mar. 11.	1877, Nov. 29.	1880, Oct. 25.
Jas. Robinson	1877, Nov. 29.	1880, Oct. 25.	1884, May 20.
Denis Caulfield Heron ...	1880, Oct. 25.	——	——
John O'Hagan	1881, May 30.	——	——
Chas. Hare Hemphill ...	1881, Sept. 13.	1884, May 20.	1885, July 19.
Peter O'Brien	1884, May 26.	1885, July 19.	——
John Geo. Gibson	1885, July 18.	——	——
Wm. Bennett Campion ...	1885, Dec. 5.	1887, July 14.	——
Dodgson Hamilton Madden ...	1887, July 14.	——	——
Hewitt Poole Jellett	1888, Feb. 14.	——	——

ARCHBISHOPS, BISHOPS, AND DEANS OF IRELAND.

THE number of Irish archbishops and bishops has been gradually reduced by the union of dioceses, chiefly under the provisions of 3 & 4 Wm. IV. cap. 37 (Aug. 14, 1833). The various changes will be found noted in the lists. In the result, Ireland is now, for ecclesiastical purposes, divided into two provinces, Armagh and Dublin. Armagh comprises the dioceses of—

Armagh and Clogher.
Meath.
Derry and Raphoe.
Down, Connor, and Dromore.
Kilmore, Elphin, and Ardagh.
Tuam, Killala, and Achonry.

and Dublin the dioceses of—

Dublin, Glendalough, and Kildare.
Ossory, Ferns, and Leighlin.
Cashel, Emly, Waterford, and Lismore.
Cork, Cloyne, and Ross.
Killaloe, Kilfenora, Clonfert, and Kilmacduagh.
Limerick, Ardfert, and Aghadoe.

The churches of England and Ireland were united on Jan. 1, 1801, on the union of Great Britain and Ireland under 39 & 40 Geo. III. cap. 67, but on Jan. 1, 1871, under 32 & 33 Vict. cap. 42, the Irish Church was disestablished and became a voluntary institution. Since that date the affairs of the Irish Church have been managed by a "Representative Church Body" incorporated under the disestablishing statute.

A great deal of valuable information on the subject of the Irish Protestant Church, and the bishops and deans thereof, will be found in Cotton's *Fasti*, of which use has been made in completing the following lists.

PROVINCE OF ARMAGH.

DIOCESES OF ARMAGH AND CLOGHER.

ST. PATRICK, the Apostle of Ireland, built a church, and fixed a bishop's see, at Armagh, in the year 444 or 445. The bishops were not invested with the *pallium* until March 9, 1152, when it was conferred at the hands of the cardinal-priest, John Paparo, legate from pope Eugene III., on the sees of Dublin, Cashel, and Tuam. About the same time, the dignity of "Primate of all Ireland" was recognised as belonging to the Archbishops of Armagh, of whom Gelasius was the first.

CLOGHER was founded by St. Macartin, who was one of the earliest disciples of St. Patrick. He fixed the see at Clogher, where he also built a monastery.

On the death of Bishop Tottenham, in 1850, ARMAGH AND CLOGHER were united under 3 & 4 Wm. IV. cap. 37.

BISHOPS OF ARMAGH.

444. St. Patrick founded this see about this year.
455. St. Benen; res.
465. St. Jarlath, the son of Trien.
482. Cormac.
497. Dubtach I.
513. Ailill I.
526. Ailill II.
536. Dubtach II.
548. David (MacGuaire Hua Farannan).
551. Fiedlimid.
578. Cairlan.
588. Eschaid (MacDermod).
598. Senach.
610. MacLaisir (supposed to be St. Ternan).
623. Thomian (MacRonan).
661. Segene.
688. Flan Febla.
715. Suibhney.
730. Congusa.
750. Cele-Peter.
758. Ferdachry.
768. Foendelach; res.
778. Dubdalethy I.
793. Assiat.
794. Cudiniscus.
798. Conmach.
807. Torbach (Mac Gorman).
808. Nuad (MacSegine).
812. MacLoingle (Flangus).
822. Artrigius.
833. Eugene I. (Monaster).
834. Faranan; res.
848. St. Dermod (O'Tigernach).
852. Factna.
872. Ainmire.
875. Catasach I. (MacRabarlach).
883. Mœlcob (MacCrumvail).
885. Mœl-Brigid (Mac Dornan).
927. Joseph.
936. Mœl-Patrick (MacMaoltule).
937. Catasach II. (MacDulgen).
957. Muirdach (MacFergus).
966. Dubdalethy II. (MacKellach).
* * Murechan; res. 998.
1001. Mælmury, or Marian.
1021. Amalgaid.
1050. Dubdalethy III.
1065. Cumasach (O'Herudan).
1065. Mœlisa I. (MacAmalgaid).
1092. Donald (MacAmalgaid).
1106. Celsus (MacAid MacMælisa).
1129. Maurice (MacDonald).
1134. Malachy O'Morgair, tr. from Connor; tr. to Down.
1137. Gelasius (MacRoderick); made abp. 1152.

See "Archbishops of Armagh," *infra*.

ARCHBISHOPS OF ARMAGH

1152. Gelasius (MacRoderick), above named; the 1st abp.
1174. Cornelius (MacConcalede) abb. of St. Peter and St. Paul, Armagh.
1175 Gilbert (O'Caran), tr. from Raphoe.
1184. Mœlisa II. (O'Carrol), tr. from Clogher.
1184. Amlave (O'Murid).
1185. Thos. O'Connor.
1206. Eugene II. (MacGillivider).
1220. Luke Nettervill.
1227. Donato Fidatra, tr. from Clogher. See vacant 3 years.
1240. Albert of Cologne; res.
1247. Reiner.
1257. Abraham O'Conellan.
1261. Patr. O'Scanlan.
1272. Nichs. Mac Molissa.
1305. John Taaf.
1306. Walter de Jorse; res.
1311. Roland de Jorse; res.
1322. Steph. Segrave, rector of Stepney, London.
1334. David O'Hiraghty.
1347. Richd. Fitz Ralph.
1361. Milo Sweetman.
1382. John Colton, dean of St. Patrick; res.
1404. Nichs. Fleming.
1417. John Swayn, rector of Gall Irim, Meath; res.
1439. John Prene.
1444. John Mey.
1457. John Bole, abb. of St. Mary, Navan. See vacant nearly 5 years.
1475. John Foxall.
1477. Edmd. Connesburgh; res.
1480. Octavian de Palatio.
1513. John Kite; res.
1522. Geo. Cromer.
1543. Geo. Dowdall; app. by the king, but the pope would not confirm him in the see, and app. Robt. Wauchope, a Scotsman, who was never allowed possession.
1552. Hugh Goodacre.

The see was vacant for some years, except at the time that abp. Dowdall filled it during the reign of Mary.

1562. Adam Loftus (No. 1) tr to Dublin.
1568. Thos. Lancaster.
1584. John Long.
1589. John Garvey, tr. from Kilmore.
1595. Hy. Ussher, archdn. of Dublin.

1613. Christr. Hampton, bp. elect of Derry.
1624. Jas. Usher, tr. from Meath; *d.* 1655.
1661. John Bramhall, tr. from Derry.
1663. Jas. Margetson, tr. from Dublin.
1678. Michl. Boyle, tr. from Dublin.
1713. Narcissus Marsh, tr. from Dublin.
1714. Thos. Lindsay, tr. from Raphoe.
1724. Hugh Boulter, tr. from Bristol.
1742. John Hoadley, tr. from Dublin.
1747. Geo. Stone, tr. from Derry.
1765. Richd. Robinson, tr. from Kildare; cr. ld. Rokeby, of Armagh, in 1777.
1795. Wm. Newcombe, tr. from Waterford.
1800. Hon. Wm. Stuart; tr. from St. David's.
1822. Lord John Geo. de la Poer Beresford, tr. from Dublin.
See united to Clogher, 1850.

See "Archbishops of Armagh and Bishops of Clogher," *post*, p. 597.

BISHOPS OF CLOGHER.

The lists of the earlier bishops are very imperfect, and differ considerably from each other. Those given below include all whose title is generally admitted, but Sir James Ware names forty-five bishops between 506 and 1126; of whom eleven are named between the death of St. Macartin, in 506, and the death of Laserian, in 571.

* * St. Macartin; *d.* 506.
* * St. Tigernach; *d.* 550.
* * St. Sinell.
* * Feidlimid.
* * St. Laserian; *d.* 571.
* * St. Aidan, made bp. of Lindisfarn; *d.* 651.
* * Airmeadach.
* * Fœldobar; *d.* 731.
* * Ailill; *d.* 898.
* * St. Cenfail; *d.* 929.
1126. Christian O'Morgair.
1139. Edan O'Kelly.
1182. Mœlisa (O'Carol), tr. to Armagh.
1184. Christian O'Macturan, abb. of Clonmacnois.
1191. Mœlisa (Mac-Mail-Ciaran), abb. of Millefont.*
1195. Tigernach, MacGilla Ronan.
1218. Donato Fidatra, tr. to Armagh.
1227. Nehemiah O'Brogan.
1240. David O'Brogan.
1268. Michl. (MacAntsair), archdn.
1287. Matt. MacCatasaid I., chanc. of Armagh.
1316. Gelasius O'Banan.
1320. Nicholas MacCatasaid, archdn.
1356. Bernard MacCamaill, archdn.
1361. Matt. MacCatasaid II., archdn.
* * Odo O'Neal, chanc. of Armagh; *d.* 1370.
1370. O'Corcroin.
1389. Arth. MacCamaill, archdn.
1432. Peter Macguire, archdn.; res.
1449. Roger Macguire.
1485. Edmd. Courcy, tr. to Ross.
See vacant 8 years.
* * Nehemiah Clonin, res. 1502.
1504. Patr. O'Conolly, abb. of St. Peter and St. Paul, Clonmacnois.
1505. Eugene Mac Camœil, dean.
See vacant 4 years.
1519. Patr. Cullin.
See vacant 8 years.
1542. Hugh O'Cervallan.
1570. Miler Magragh, tr. to Cashel, 1571 first Protestant bp.
See vacant many years.
1605. Geo. Montgomery, dean of Norwich. He held the sees of Derry and Raphoe with this; resigning these, he got Meath, which he held with this see until his death.
1621. Jas. Spottiswood.
1645. Hy. Jones, dean of Ardagh; tr. to Meath.
1661. John Lesley, tr. from Raphoe.
1671. Robt. Lesley, tr. from Raphoe.
1672. Roger Boyle, tr. from Down and Connor.
1691. Richd. Tennison, tr. from Killala and Achonry; tr. to Meath.
1697. St. George Ash, tr. from Cloyne; tr. to Derry.
1717. John Sterne, tr. from Dromore.
1745. Robt. Clayton, tr. from Cork and Ross.
1758. John Garnet, tr. from Leighlin and Ferns.
1782. John Hotham, tr. from Ossory.
1796. Wm. Foster, tr. from Kilmore.
1798. John Porter, tr. from Killala.
1819. Lord John Geo. de la Poer Beresford, tr. from Raphoe; tr. to Dublin.
1820. Hon. Percy Jocelyn, tr. from Leighlin and Ferns; depr.
1822. Lord Robt. Ponsonby Tottenham, tr. from Ferns and Leighlin.
See united to Armagh, 1850.

See "Archbishops of Armagh and bishops of Clogher," *post*, p. 597.

* The family name of this bishop is lost; for those he is here called by are assumed names, according to a custom often practised among ecclesiastics, to express their devotion to Christ, or some saint. Mœlisa means "the servant of Christ"; and Mac-Mail-Ciaran, "the son of the servant of St. Kiaran."

ARCHBISHOPS OF ARMAGH AND BISHOPS OF CLOGHER.

850. Lord Geo. John de la Poer Beresford, abp. of Armagh, above-named.

1862. Marcus Gervaise Beresford.

On his death, in 1886, Armagh and Clogher were again separated. *Vide infra.*

ARCHBISHOP OF ARMAGH.

1886. Robert Bent Knox, tr. from Down, &c., May 11.

BISHOP OF CLOGHER.

1886. Chas. Maurice Slack, consec. June 29.

DEANS OF ARMAGH.

238. Mauritius, or Maurus.
256–7. Abraham O'Conellan, made abp. same year.
256–7. Joseph.
272. Brice.
301 to 1330. Dionysius, or Denis.
362. Patr. O'Kerry.
372. Maurice Dovey, or O'Dove.
397. Maurice O'Corry.
406. Thos. O'Luchan, or O'Lucheran.
425 to 1441. Denis O'Culean.
443 to 1474. Chas. O'Niellan.
483. Edmd. McCamaill.
518. Edmd. McKamyll, or McCamaill.
551. Terence Daniel, or Thirlagh O'Donnel.
590. Eugene Woods; *d.* 1610.
610. Robt. Maxwell.
622. Geo. Mackeston, or Makeson.
635. Jas. Frey, L. P. Nov. 15.
636–7. Peter Wentworth.
643. Wm. Sley.
661. Fras. Marsh; bp. of Limerick, 1667.
667. Jas. Downham, L. P. June 19; *d.* 1681.
1681. Barth. Vigors, L. P. June 29; bp. of Ferns, 1690.
1691. Peter Drelincourt, L. P. Feb. 28; *d.* 1722.
1722. Richd. Daniel, L. P. June 28; res. 1731.
1731. John Brandreth, L. P. Mar. 21; res. 1736.
1736. Jas Auchmuty, L. P. July 1; *d.* 1753.
1753. Anthy. Cope, L. P. Feb. 1; *d.* 1764.
1764. Benj. Barrington, L. P. July 7; res. 1768.
1768. Hugh Hamilton, L. P. Apr. 23; bp. of Clonfert, 1796.
1796. Hon. Jas. Hewitt, L. P. Feb. 20; *d.* 1830.
1830. Jas. Edwd. Jackson, L. P. Sept. 4; *d.* 1841.
1841. Edwd. Gust. Hudson, L. P. Sept. 1; *d.* 1851.
1851. Brabazon Wm. Disney, L. P. Dec. 23; *d.* 1874.
1875. John Reeves.
1886. Geo. Alexr. Chadwick.

DEANS OF CLOGHER.

390. Peter O'Heoghain.
414. Donal O'Heoghain.
427 to 1435. Philip.
458. John M'Kathmoyll, or MacCamaill.
498. Chas. Maguire; *d.* 1498.
505. Eugene MacCamaill.
508. Wm. MacCaghwell, or MacCamaill.
530. Odo.
606. Robt. Openshaw, July 7.
617. Robt. Barclay, Barkley, or Berkeley, L. P. Apr. 20.
621. Donald Clogh (? Robert).
634. Robt. Barkley (? *again*), Dec. 13.
661. John Hudson, Feb. 13; bp. of Elphin, 1667.
1662. One Thos. Gowen appears as claiming the deanery, but never was in possession.
1667. John Roane, L. P. Aug. 19; bp. of Killaloe, 1675.
1675. Richd. Tennison, L. P. Apr. 29; bp. of Killala, 1681.
1682. Jos. Williams, L. P. Apr. 20; *d.* 1716.
1716. Wm. Gore, L. P. June 7; res. 1724.
1724. Jonn. Smedley, L. P. Apr. 13; *res.* 1727.
1728. Paschal Ducasse, L. P. Feb. 29; *d.* 1730.
1730. Edwd. Cressett, L. P. July 4.
1738. John Copping, inst. May 25.

1743. Wm. Langton, L. P. Sept. 24; *d.* 1761.
1761, Edwd. Young. L. P. Sept. 29; bp. of Dromore, 1763.
1763. Richd. Woodward, Aug. 27; bp. of Cloyne, 1781.
1781. Cadogan Keatinge, Mar. 2; *d.* 1799.
1799. Lord John Geo. de la Poer Beresford, Dec. 23; bp. of Cork and Ross, 1806.
1806. Richd. Bagwell, Feb. 21; *d.* 1825.
1826. Hon. Robt. Wm. Hy. Maude, inst. May 27; *d.* 1861.
1862. Ogle Wm. Moore, L. P. Jan. 21.
1874. Thos. Le Ban Kennedy.

DEANS OF LOUTH.

* * Donell, dean of Louth; *d.* 1065.
* * O'Robhartaigh, dean of Louth; *d.* 1081.

At a period now unknown, but supposed to be in the eleventh century, the bishopric of Louth was united to that of Clogher.

DIOCESE OF MEATH, INCLUDING CLONARD AND CLONMACNOIS.

THERE were formerly many episcopal sees in Meath, as Clonard, Duleek, Kells, Trim, Ardbraccan, Dunshaughlin, and Slane, besides others of less note. All of these, with the exception of Duleek and Kells, were consolidated, and their common see fixed at Clonard, before the year 1152; at which time the divisions of the bishoprics in Ireland was made by Cardinal Paparo. Subsequently Duleek and Kells were merged into the general see.

The see of CLONARD was founded by St. Finian about 520. Bishop Eugene, who succeeded in 1174, changed the name of the see to Meath, but the see remained at Clonard until about 1206, when bishop Rochfort, of Meath, changed it to Newtown, near Trim, and made the abbey church of St. Peter and St. Paul, which he had just founded for Augustine canons, the cathedral. At the Reformation, King Henry VIII. converted the church of St. Mary's abbey at Ballymore, near Loch Seudy, in Westmeath, into a cathedral for this see; but how long it continued so is uncertain.

CLONMACNOIS was founded by St. Keiran or Kiaran about 549. In 1568, on the death of bishop Wall, the see was united to Meath, and that title was alone preserved by the succeeding bishops. The deans of the united sees still take their title from Clonmacnois.

BISHOPS OF CLONARD.

520. St. Finian.
563. Senach.
* * Fiachre.
* * Colman.
652. Ossenius.
* * Ultan O'Cunga.
665. Becan.
687. Colman O'Heir.
700. Dubdan O'Foelan.
716. Ailchu.
726. Fienmale MacGirthid.
731. Tola MacDunchad.
733. Beglatneu.
755. Fulertach.
774. Algnied.
778. Cormac I. (MacSuibay).
828. Cormac II.
882. Rumold MacCathasach.
919. Colman MacAilill.
924. Ferdomnach MacFlanagan.
930. Moctean.
940. Malfechin.
942. Bechan MacLactnan.
971. Faithman.

1010. Tuethal O'Dunluing.
1028. Cellach O'Clerchen.
1043. Tuathal O'Follanmuin.
1055. Tigernach Boircech.
1061. Murchertach Mac Longsee.
1092. Idunan.
1110. Concovar.
1117. Fiachry.
1135. Christian O'Hagan.
1136. Eochaid O'Kelly.
1140. O'Follomar.
1150. Eleutherius.
1174. Eugene, who changed the name of the see to Meath.

See "Bishops of Meath," *infra*.

BISHOPS OF MEATH.

1174. Eugene, above-named.
1194. Simon Rochfort.
1224. Deodatus.
1227. Ralph le Petit, archdn. of Meath.
1230. Richd. de la Corner, canon of St. Patrick's, Dublin.
1250. Hugh de Tachmon.
1287. Thos. St. Leger.
1321. John O'Carrol, tr. to Cork.
1327. Wm. de St. Paul.
1350. Wm. St. Leger, archdn. of Meath.
1353. Nichs. Allen, abb. of St. Thomas, near Dublin.
1369. Steph. de Valle, dean of Limerick.
1380. Wm. Andrew, tr. from Achonry.
1386. Alexr. de Balscot, tr. from Ossory.
1402. Robt. Montmain.
1413. Edwd. Dantsey, archdn. of Cornwall.
1430. Wm. Hudsor.
1434. Wm. Silk.
1450. Edmd. Ouldhal of Norwich.
1460. Wm. Sherwood.
1483. John Pain, or Payne.
1507. Wm. Rokeby, tr. to Dublin.
1512. Hugh Inge, tr. to Dublin.
1523. Richd. Wilson.
1530. Edwd. Staples, depr. 1554.
1554. Wm. Walsh, depr. 1560.
1563. Hugh Brady.

In 1568 the see of Clonmacnois was united to or merged in that of Meath, the latter title being alone preserved.

1584. Thos. Jones, tr. to Dublin.
1605. Roger Dod, dean of Salop.
1610. Geo. Montgomery, dean of Norwich; bp. of Derry, Raphoe, and Clogher.
1621. Jas. Ussher, tr. to Armagh.
1625. Anth. Martin, dean of Waterford.
1660. Hy. Leslie, tr. from Down and Connor.
1661. Hy. Jones, tr. from Clogher.
1682. Anthy. Dopping, tr. from Kildare.
1697. Richd. Tennison, tr. from Clogher.
1705. Wm. Moreton, tr. from Kildare.
1716. John Evans, tr. from Bangor.
1724. Hy. Downs, tr. from Elphin; tr. to Derry.
1727. Ralph Lambert, tr. from Dromore.
1732. Welbore Ellis, tr. from Kildare.
1734. Arth. Price, tr. from Leighlin, &c.; tr. to Cashel.
1744. Hy. Maule, tr. from Dromore.
1758. Hon. Hy. Carmichael, tr. from Ferns, &c.; tr. to Dublin.
1765. Richd. Pocock, tr. from Ossory.
Arth. Smythe, tr. from Down, &c.; tr. to Dublin.
1766. Hon. Hy. Maxwell, tr. from Dromore.
1798. Thos. Lewis O'Beirne, tr. from Ossory.
1823. Nathl. Alexander, tr. from Down and Connor.
1840. Chas. Dickenson, Dec.
1842. Edwd. Stopford, consec. Nov. 6.
1850. Thos. Stewart Townshend, dean of Lismore, Oct. 3.
1852. Joseph Henderson Singer.
1866. Saml. Butcher.
1876. Wm. Conyngham, ld. Plunket; tr. to Dublin.
1885. Chas. Parsons Reichel, dean of Clonmacnois, consec. Sept. 30.

BISHOPS OF CLONMACNOIS.

549. St. Kiaran, the founder.
* * St. Tigernach.
* * Baitan (O'Cormac), *d.* 663.

* * *

* * Joseph, of Rosmore, *d.* 839.
* * Mœldarius, *d.* 886.
* * Cropery, or Corprey Crom, *d.* 899.
* * Colman, *d.* 924.
* * Cormac O'Killeen, *d.* 964.
* * Tuathal, *d.* 969.
969. Durichad O'Braoin, res.
* * Ectigern O'Ergain, *d.* 1052.
* * Colocair, *d.* 1067.
* * Ailill O'Harretaigh, *d.* 1070.
* * Christian O'Hectigern, *d.* 1103.
* * Donald O'Dubhai, *d.* 1136.
* * Moriertach O'Melider, seated here in 1152.
* * Tigernach O'Mœleoin, *d.* 1172.
* * Mureach O'Murrechan, *d.* 1213.
* * Edan O'Maily, *d.* 1220.
1220. Mælrony O'Modein.

1230 Hugh O'Malone.
1236. Elias.
Thomas.
1252. Thos. O'Quin.
See vacant nearly 2 years.
* * Gilbert, res. 1281.
See vacant 2 years.
1290. Wm. O'Duffy.
1298. Wm. O'Findan, abb. of Kilbeggan.
See vacant some years.
1303. Donald O'Brian.
* * Lewis O'Daly, *d.* 1337.
* * Henry, *d.* 1367.
* * Richard.
* * Philip, *d.* 1388.
1390. Milo Cory.
* * O'Galachor, *d.* 1397.
1398. Peter, abb. of Granard
1411. Philip O'Mœil.
1423. David Brendoc.
See vacant some years
1427. Cormac MacCoughlan.
1444. John Oldais.
* * John, *d.* 1486.
1487. Walter Blake, canon of Enaghdune.
1508. Thomas.
1516. Quintin.
1538. Richard Hogar.
1539. Florence Gerawan.
1556. Peter Wall.
See merged in Meath, 1568.
See *ante*, pp. 598–9.

DEANS OF CLONMACNOIS.

1236. Thomas.
1280. Gilbert.
1426. Cormac MacCoghlan.
1459. Odo O'Molan, or Malone.
1561. Wm. Flynn, Jan. 27.
1579. Miler M'Clery.
1601. Wm. Leicester, Lester, or Lyster.
1628. Marcus Lynch, or Lynche, May 18.
1629. Richd. Price, Mar. 31.
1633. Saml. Clarke, inst. Aug. 29.
1634. Wm. Burley, June 25.
1640. Wm. Meyler, or Meales.
1661. John Kerdiffe.
1668. Hy. Cottingham, Oct. 15.
1681. Theoph. Harrison, inst. Oct. 21.
16—. Steph. Handcock.
1697. Theoph. Harrison (? *again*).
1720. Anthy. Dopping, inst. July 2; bp. of Ossory, 1741.
1742. John Owen, Feb. 18; *d.* 1760.
1761. Arth. Champagnè, Mar. 13; d. 1800.
1800. Chas. Mongan Warburton, Nov. or Dec. 20; bp. of Limerick 1806.
1806. Thos. Vesey Dawson, Aug. 11; *d.* 1811.
1811. Hy. Roper, Dec. 6; *d.* 1847.
1847. Richd. Butler, Dec.; *d.* 1862.
1862. John Brownlow.
1882. Chas Parsons Reichel; bp. Meath, 1885.
1885. Fras. Hy. Swift.

DIOCESE OF DERRY AND RAPHOE.

THE see of DERRY, when first founded, was placed at Ardsrath, whence it was translated, about 597, to Maghera, and in 1158 to Derry, when Flathbert O'Brolcan, abbot of Derry, was made bishop of it. Flathbert built the cathedral in 1164; and the edifice becoming ruinous, it was rebuilt by the colony of Londoners who settled here in the reign of James I.

It is difficult to determine the time when the see of RAPHOE was founded. St. Columb-Cile founded a monastery here, which was afterwards enlarged and repaired by other holy men; but it is the general opinion, that St. Eunan erected the church into a cathedral, and was the first bishop of the see. History is very defective in the account of his successors, until the arrival of the English.

On the death of bishop Bissett, in 1834, DERRY and RAPHOE were united under 3 & 4 Wm. IV. cap. 37.

BISHOPS OF DERRY.

1158. Flathbert O'Brolcan.
* * Maurice O'Coffy, or O'Dubthaic; *d.* 1173.
1173. Amlave O'Coffy.
1185. Florence O'Cherballen, or Carellan I.

1230. German, or Gervase O'Cherballen, or Carellan.
1279. Florence O'Cherballen, or Carellan II.
1295. Huny of Ardagh.
1297. Jeffry Maglathin.
1316. Odo O'Neal.
1319. Michl. MacLaghlin.
* * Simon; seated here in 1367.
* * John Dongan, tr. to Down, 1395.
See 6 years vacant.
1401. John, abb. of Moycoscain.
* * Wm. Quaplode.
* * Donald, seated here in 1423; res.
1429. John.
1458. Barth. O'Flanagan.
See vacant 3 years.
1466. Nichs. Weston, canon of Armagh.
1485. Donald O'Fallon.
See vacant 7 years.
1507. Thos. MacMasson, prior of Knock.
1529. Roderick O'Donnell, dean of Raphoe.
1551. Eugene Magenis.
1603. Denis Campbell, a native of Scotland, and dean of Limerick, was nominated to the sees of Derry, Raphoe, and Clogher, but *d.* in London, July 1603, before consecration.
1605. Geo. Montgomery, dean of Norwich; made bp. of Derry, Raphoe and Clogher; tr. to Meath.
1610. Brutus Babington.
See vacant nearly 2 years.
1612. John Tanner. See *Dromore.*
1616. Geo. Downham.
1634. John Bramhall, archdn. of Meath; tr. to Armagh.
1660. Geo. Wild.
1666. Robt. Mossom, dean of Christ Church, Dublin.
1679. Michl. Ward, tr. from Ossory.
1681. Ezekiel Hopkins.
1691. Wm. King, tr. to Dublin.
1703. Chas. Hickman.
1714. John Hartstonge, tr. from Ossory.
1717. St. Geo. Ash, tr. from Clogher.
1718. Wm. Nicholson, tr. from Carlisle; tr. to Cashel.
1727. Hy. Downs, tr. from Meath.
1735. Thos. Rundle, preb. of Durham.
1743. Carew Reynell, tr. from Down and Connor.
1745. Geo. Stone, tr. from Kildare; tr. to Armagh.
1747. Wm. Barnard, tr. from Raphoe.
1768. Hon. Fred. Hervey, aft. E. of Bristol; tr. from Cloyne.
1803. Hon. Wm. Knox, tr. from Killaloe.
1831. Hon. Richd. Ponsonby, tr. from Killaloe.
See united to Raphoe, 1834.

See "Bishops of Derry and Raphoe," *post*, p. 602.

BISHOPS OF RAPHOE.

* * St. Eunan, founder, and first bp. of Raphoe.
* * Mœlbrigid, or Brigidian Mac Dornan, tr. to Armagh.
* * Malduin Mac Kinfalaid, *d.* about 930.
* * Ængus, or Æneas O'Lapain, *d.* 957.
* * Muredach O'Dubthaigh.
1160. Gilbert O'Caran, tr. to Armagh.
His immediate successors uncertain.
* * * *
1203. Mœlisa O'Dorigh.
* * Patr. O'Scanlain, tr. to Armagh 1261.
1261. John de Alento, res. on account of bad health.
1266. Carbrac O'Scoba.
1275. Florence O'Ferral.
1299. Thos. O'Nathain, archdn.
1306. Hy. Mac-an-Crossain.
1319. Thos. Mac Cormac O'Donnel, abbot of Ashroe.
* * Patr. Magonail, seated here in 1360.
1366. Richd. MacCrossain.
1397. John.
Cornelius MacCarmic.
1399. Anthony.
1414. Robt. Mubire.
1415. John MacCarmic.
1419. Laurence O'Galachor I.
See vacant 4 years.
1442. John MacGilbride.
* * Laurence O'Galachor II., seated here in 1469.
1484. Menelaus MacCarmacan.
Cornelius O'Cahan, seated here in 1550.
Donat Magonail, seated here in 1563; he assisted at the council of Trent, and *d.* 1589.
The see remained vacant until
1605. Geo. Montgomery; he held this see in conjunction with Clogher and Derry; tr. to Meath.
1611. Andr. Knox, tr. from Orkney.
1633. John Leslie, tr. from Orkney; tr. to Clogher.
1661. Robt. Lesley, tr. from Dromore; tr. to Clogher.
1671. Ezekiel Hopkins, tr. to Derry.
1682. Wm. Smith, tr. from Killala and Achonry; tr. to Kilmore.
1693. Alexr. Cairncross, formerly abp. of Glasgow.
1701. Robt. Huntington.
1702. John Pooley, tr. from Cloyne.

1713. Thos. Lindsay, tr. from Killaloe; tr. to Armagh.
1714. Edwd. Singe, tr. to Tuam.
1716. Nichs. Forster, tr. from Killaloe.
1744. Wm. Barnard, dean of Rochester; tr. to Derry.
1747. Philip Twisden.
1753. Robt. Downes, tr. from Down and Connor.
1763. John Oswald, tr. from Dromore.
1780. Jas. Hawkins, tr. from Dromore.
1807. Ld. John Geo. de la Poer Beresford tr. from Cork and Ross; tr. t Clogher.
1819. Wm. Magee, dean of Cork; tr. t Dublin.
1822. Wm. Bissett, chapl. to ld. Wellesley then ld. lieut.

See united to Derry in 1834,

See "Bishops of Derry and Raphoe," nfra.

BISHOPS OF DERRY AND RAPHOE.

1834. Hon. Richd. Ponsonby, bp. of Derry, above-named.
1853. Wm. Higgin, tr. from Limerick.
1867. Wm. Alexander.

DEANS OF DERRY.

1294. Peter.
1319. Thomas.
1365. Arth. McBruyn (McBrien).
1388. Wm. White.
1397. Wm. McCamaill.
1428. Donat, or Donald, O'Cherballen, or Carellan.
1440. Dernot.
1540. Name not given.
15—. Wm. McTagart.
1612. Wm. Webbe, Mar. 2.
1621 or 1622. Hy. Sutton, May 3.
1635. Michl. Wandesford, L. P. Nov. 9; *d.* 1637.
1637. Jas. Margetson, Dec. 22; res. 1639.
1640. Godfrey Rhodes, L. P. Feb. 26.
16—. Peter Wentworth.
1661. Geo. Beaumont, Nov. 8.
1663. Geo. Holland, L. P. Nov. 16.
1670–1. Wm. Lightburne, June 4; *d.* 1671.
1672. John Lesley, inst. Jan. 11.
1672. Peter Manby, Sept. 17.
1690?. Peter Morris; *d.* 1690.
1691. Thos. Wallis, Feb. 10; *d.* 1695.
1695. Coote Ormsby, Sept. 9; *d.* 1699–1700.
1700. John Bolton, Feb. 20; *d.* 1724.
1724. Geo. Berkeley, May 2; bp. c Cloyne, 1733.
1734. Geo. Stone, dean of Ferns, L. P Mar. 11; bp. of Ferns, 1740.
1740. Robt. Downes, Aug. 4; bp. of Ferns 1744.
1744. Arth. Smyth, Aug. 28; bp. of Clon fert, 1752.
1752. Hon. Philip Sydney Smyth, Apr. 7
1769. Thos. Barnard, May 26; bp. of Ki laloe, 1780.
1780. Wm. Cecil Pery, Feb. 17; bp. c Killala, 1781.
1781. Edwd. Emly, L. P. May 25; res 1783.
1783. John Hume, L. P. Mar. 14.
1818. Jas. Saurin, Apr. 7; bp. of Dro more, 1819.
1820. Thos. Bunbury Gough, L. P. Jan 28; *d.* 1860.
1860. Hugh Usher Tighe, L. P. July 13 *d.* 1874.
1874. Chas. Seymour.
1882. John Gwyn, dean of Raphoe.
1883. Andr. Ferguson Smyly.

DEANS OF RAPHOE.

1397. Florence.
1419–20. Laurence (or Loughlin), O'Galchor; *d.* 1438.
1438. Cornelius McGillewride.
1442. Donald.
1484. Menelaus McCarmacan.
15—. Roderick O'Donnell; bp. of Derry, 1529.
1535. Edmd. O'Gallagher.
1603. John Albright, L. P. Dec. 3.
1609. Phelim O'Doghertie, L. P. July 22.
1622. Archd. Adair, L. P. Nov. 4; bp. of Killala 1630.
1630. Alexr. Cunningham, L. P. Apr. 27; *d.* 1660.
1661. John Lesley, L. P. Feb. 9; res same year.
1661. John Wellwood, L. P. June 25 *d.* 1670.
1671. Thos. Buttolph, L. P. Oct. 30.
1676. Capel Wiseman, Aug. 19; bp. c Dromore, 1683.
1683. Nathl. Wilson, L. P. Sept. 15 bp. of Limerick, 1691.
1692. John French, L. P. Jan. 21; *d* 1725.
1725. Wm. Cotterill, June 26; bp. o Ferns and Leighlin, 1743.
1743. Arthr. Smyth, L. P. Mar. 30; res 1744.

744. Anthy. Thompson, L. P. Sept. 14.
757. Wm. Barker, June 17; *d.* 1776.
776. Thos. Bray.
776. Jas. King, Oct. 25; *d.* 1795.
1795. Richd. Allot, L. P. July 10; *d.* 1832.
1832. Ld. Edwd. Chichester, L.P. Apr. 28.
1873. John Gwyn; dean of Derry, 1882.
1882. Edwd. Bowen.

DIOCESES OF DOWN, CONNOR, AND DROMORE.

The see of Down is said to have been founded by St. Carlan, about 499, but lists of its bishops generally commence with Malachy O'Morgair, who succeeded in 1137. The prior bishops are sometimes styled bishops of Dundalethglass, but this see is generally included in that of Connor.

The first Bishop of Connor was Ængus Macnisius, or St. Macnise, who died about 507. The ancient name of this see was Dailnaraigh.

The see of Dromore was founded by St. Colman about 556.

Down and Connor appear to have been always intimately connected. It is probable that prior to the appointment of bishop Malachy O'Morgair in 1137 they were united, or, rather, that Down was included in Connor. In 1442 the two sees were permanently united.

On the death of bishop Saurin, in 1842, Down, Connor, and Dromore were united under 3 & 4 Wm. IV. cap. 37.

BISHOPS OF DOWN.

* * St. Cailan, seated here in 499.
* * St. Fergus; *d.* 583.
No mention is made of any bishop of this see with any certainty for some centuries; Fingen, Flaghertack, and Samuel are named, but without good authority.
* * * *
1137. Malachy I. (O'Morgair), tr. from Armagh; *d.*
1148. Malachy II. (MacInclericuir).
1175. Gelasius (MacCormac).
1176. Malachy III.
1202. Ralph, abb. of Melrose.
1213. Thomas.
1237. Ranulph.
1258. Regd., tr. to Cloyne.
1266. Thos. Lidell.
1276. Nicholas.
1305. Thomas Kettel.
1314. Thos. Bright, prior of Down.
See vacant 2 years.
1329. Ralph, or Thomas, of Kilmessan.
1353. Richd. Calfe I,, prior of Down.
1365. William.
1368. John Logan, archdn.
1369. Richd. Calfe II.
1387. John Ross.
1395. John Dongan, tr. from Derry.
1413. John Cely, depr. 1441.
See united to Connor 1442.

See "Bishops of Down and Connor," *post*, p. 604.

BISHOPS OF CONNOR.

* * St. Ængus Macnisius; *d.* 507.
Lugade, Dima, Duchonna, Ægedearus, and Malbrigid, are mentioned by some as bishops of this see, but without certainty.
1124. Malachy O'Morgair, tr. to Armagh.
1152 Patr. O'Bainan, res.
1172. Nehemiah.
1183. Reginald.
* * Christian O'Kerney, abb. of St. Columb, Derry; *d.* 1210.
No account of his successor.
1225. Eustachius, archdn.
1242. Adam, abb. of Warden, Bedfordshire.
1245. Isaac, of Newcastle-upon-Tyne.

1257. William, of Port Royal.
1261. Wm. de Hay.
1264. Robert, of Flanders.
1274. Peter, of Dunath.
1293. John.
* * Richard, seated here before 1320.
1321. Jas. Couplith.
1322. John, of Eglescliffe, tr. to Llandaff.
1324. Jas. Kerney.
1353. Wm. Mercier archdn. of Kildare.
1376. Paul.
* * John, seated here in 1411.
* * Eugene, seated here in 1427.
* * Cornelius.
* * John, seated here before 1440.
See united to Down, 1442.

See ' Bishops of Down and Connor," *infra*.

BISHOPS OF DOWN AND CONNOR.

1442. John, bp. of Connor, above-named.
1451. Robt. Rochfort.
1456. Thomas.
1469. Thady.
* * Richd. Wolsey; *d.* about 1502.
* * Tiberius; *d.* about 1526.
* * Robt. Blyth, abb. of Thorney, Cambridgeshire; res.
1541. Eugene Magenis.
1568. John Merriman.
1573. Hugh Allen, tr. to Ferns.
1593. Edwd. Edgeworth.
1596. John Charden.
1602. Robt. Humston.
1606. John Todd, dean of Cashel; he held the see of Dromore in *commendam* with this; depr.
1612. Jas. Dundas, chanter of Moray in Scotland.
1613. Robt. Echlin.
1635. Hy. Leslie, dean of Down; tr. to Meath.
1660. Jeremy Taylor, also bp. of Dromore in 1661.
1667. Roger Boyle, tr. to Clogher.
1672. Thos. Hacket, depr.
1694. Saml. Foley.
1695. Edwd. Walkington, archdn. o Ossory, and chapl. to the ho. c comm.
1699. Edwd. Smith, dean of St. Patrick's
1721. Fras. Hutchinson.
1739. Carew Reynell, tr. to Derry.
1743. John Ryder, tr. from Killaloe; tr to Tuam.
1752. John Whitcombe, tr. from Clonfert tr. to Cashel.
1752. Robt. Downes, tr. from Ferns an Leighlin; tr. to Raphoe.
1753. Arth. Smyth, tr. from Clonfert; tr to Meath.
1765. Jas. Trail, chapl. to the ld. lieut.
1783. Wm. Dickson, chapl. to the ld lieut.
1804. Nathl. Alexander, tr. from Killaloe tr. to Meath.
1823. Richd. Mant, tr. from Killaloe.
See united to Dromore, 1842.

See "Bishops of Down, Connor, and Dromore," *post*, p. 605.

BISHOPS OF DROMORE.

* * St. Colman, a Florentine, about 556. There are no certain accounts of the successors of St. Colman, till after the arrival of the English. It is probable that this see was united to Armagh, as its revenues were then very inconsiderable.

* * * *

1227. Gerard, abbot of Mellifort.
1245. Andrew, archdn.
* * Tigernach I., seated here before 1287.
* * Gervase, about 1290.
* * Tigernach II., *d.* 1309.
1309. Florence MacDonegan, canon.
1369. Christopher.
* * Cornelius.
1382. John O'Lannube.
* * John Volcan, tr. to Ossory, 1404.
See vacant 4 years.
1408. Richd. Messing.
1410. John, res.
1419. Nichs. Wartre.
1427. David of Chirbury.
1434. Thos. Scrope, *alias* Bradley; res.
1440. Thos. Radcliffe.
1489. Geo. Brann, tr. to Elphin.
1500. William.
* * Galeatius, *d.* 1504.
1504. John Baptist.
1511. Thady.
1536. Quintin Cogley.
1550. Arth. Magenis.
1606. John Todd, also bp. of Down and Connor, *q. v.*; depr. 1611.
John Tanner was, in 1611, app. by James I. to succeed bp. Tod; but the bishopric of Derry just then falling void by the death of bp Babington, he was advanced to that see.
See vacant 2 years.
1613. Theoph. Buckworth; *d.* 1652.
See vacant 8 years.
1660. Robt. Lesley, tr. to Raphoe.

1661. Jeremy Taylor, also bp. of Down and Connor.
1667. Geo. Rust.
1670. Essex Digby, dean of Cashel.
1683. Capel Wiseman, dean of Raphoe.
1695. Tobias Pullen, tr. from Cloyne.
1713. John Sterne, dean of St. Patrick's; tr. to Clogher.
1717. Ralph Lambert, dean of Down; tr. to Meath.
1727. Chas. Cobbe, tr. from Killala and Achonry; tr. to Kildare.
1732. Hy. Maule, tr. from Cloyne; tr. to Meath.
1744. Thos. Fletcher, Dean of Down; tr. to Kildare.
1745. Jemmet Brown, tr. from Killaloe; tr. to Cork and Ross.
1745. Geo. Marlay (?).
1763. John Oswald, tr. from Clonfert; tr. to Raphoe.
Edwd. Young, tr. to Ferns and Leighlin.
1765. Hon. Hy. Maxwell, tr. to Meath.
1766. Wm. Newcombe, tr. to Ossory.
1775. Jas. Hawkins, tr. to Raphoe.
1780. Hon. Wm. Beresford, tr. to Ossory.
1782. Thos. Percy, dean of Carlisle.
1811. Geo. Hall, prov. of Trinity College, Dublin.
1812. John Leslie, dean of Cork; tr. to Elphin.
1819. Jas. Saurin, archdn. of Dublin, and dean of Derry.

See united to Down and Connor 1842.

See "Bishops of Down, Connor, and Dromore," *infra*.

BISHOPS OF DOWN, CONNOR, AND DROMORE.

1842. Richd. Mant, bp. of Down and Connor, above-named.
1849. Robt. Knox, Apr. 14.
1886. Wm. Reeves, consec. June 29.

DEANS OF DOWN.

1541. Connor Magennis, McGenis, McGinnis, or McGanysa.
1609. John Gibson, July 20.
1622. John Yorke, Oct. 18.
1623. Robt. Dawson, Nov. 25; bp. of Clonfert, 1627.
1627. Hy. Leslie, L. P. May 30; made bp. 1635.
1635. Wm. Coote, Oct. 14.
1662. Thos. Bayley, Feb. 13.
1664. Danl. Wytter, L. P. Mar. 19; bp. of Killaloe, 1669.
1669. Wm. Sheridan, Aug. 25; bp. of Kilmore, 1681.
1682. Benjn. Phipps, L. P. Apr. 24.
1683. John McNeale, L. P. Jan. 9; *d.* 1709.
1709. Ralph Lambert, May 10; bp. of Dromore, 1717.
1717. Benjn. Pratt, June 17.
1722. Chas. Fairfax, Feb. 21.
1724. Wm. Gore, L. P. Jan. 20; *d.* 1731.
1731. Richd. Daniel, Feb. 18; *d.* 1739.
1739. Thos. Fletcher, Oct. 4; bp. of Dromore, 1744.
1744. Patr. Delany, July 16; *d.* 1768.
1768. Jas. Dickson, July 2; *d.* 1787.
1787. Hon. Wm. Annesley, June 16; *d.* 1817.
1817. Hon. Edmd. Knox, Aug. 2; bp. of Killaloe, 1831.
1831. Hon. Thos. Plunket, Oct. 8; bp. of Tuam, 1839.
1839. Theoph. Blakeley, L. P. May 11; *d.* 1855.
1856. Thos. Woodward, L. P. Jan. 20; *d.* 1874.
1876. Edwd. B. Moeran.
1887. Edwd. Maguire.

DEANS OF CONNOR.

1609. Milo Whale, res. 1615.
1615. Robt. Openshaw, Dec. 23.
1628. Richd. Shuckburgh, June 23.
1640. Robt. Price, Apr. 1; bp. of Ferns and Leighlin, 1660.
1661. Fras. Marsh, Feb. 8; res.
Geo. Rust, L. P. Aug. 3; bp. of Dromore, 1667.
1667. Patr. Sheridan, L. P. Nov. 9; bp. of Cloyne, 1679.
1679. Thos. Ward, Apr. 28.
1694. Geo. Walter Story, Dec. 19.
1704. Martin Baxter, Dec. 21.
1710. Eugene (or Owen) Lloyd, Feb. 28.
1739. (?) Geo. Cuppage, *d.* 1743.
1743. John Walsh, June 20, *d.* 1775.
1775. Richd. Dobbs, June 19; *d.* 1802.
1802. Thos. Graves, L. P. Apr. 29; res. 1811.
1811. Theoph. Blakeley, May 4; res. 1824.
1825. Hy. Leslie, L. P. Jan 10; res. 1838.
1839. John Chaine, L. P. Feb. 26; res. 1855.
1855. Geo. Bull, L. P. Sept. 13.
1886. Jno. Walton Murray.

DEANS OF DROMORE.

1309. Patrick.
1369. Augustus.
1604. Isaac Plume, Feb. 1.
1609. Wm. Todd.
1621. Thos. Wilson, Nov. 27.
1622. Jno. Wall, June 15.
1623. Robt. Dawson, July 9.
1629. Wm. Moore, Feb. 10.
1635. Geo. Synge, Feb. 21; bp. of Cloyne, 1638.
1638. Robt. Forward, L. P., Nov. 26.
1642. Nichs. Graves, Mar. 21.
1673. Wm. Smyth, Aug. 23; bp. of Killala, 1681.
1681. John Leslie, May 5; *d.* 1721.
1722. Hy. Leslie, Feb. 5.
Geo. Berkeley, L. P., Feb. 16; dean of Derry, 1724.
1724. John Hamilton, May 2; *d.* 1729.
1729. Saml. Hutchinson, Nov. 6; bp. o Killala, 1759.
1759. Walter Cope, Aug. 17; bp. of Clon fert, 1772.
1772. Hon. Jos. Deane Bourke, L. P. Mar. 4; abp. of Tuam, 1772.
1772. Ralph or Raphael Walsh, Oct. 6; *d* 1808.
1809. Jas. Mahon, Jan. 6.
1841. Wm. Hy. Wynne; elected by th chapter.
1842. Holt Waring, L. P., Nov. 10; *d* 1850.
1850. Dan. Bagot, L. P., Nov. 26.
1876. Jeffrey Lefroy.
1885. Hy. Stewart.
1887. Theophs. Campbell.

DIOCESES OF KILMORE, ELPHIN, AND ARDAGH.

Kilmore signifies a great church. The bishops of Kilmore borrowed their title from a territory called *Brefiny* or *Brefne:* they were sometimes called Brefinienses, and sometimes Triburnenses (bishops of Triburna); because they are said to have had their residence near a village of that name; but in 1454, Andrew Mac Brady, bishop of Triburna erected the parish church of St. Fedlemid or Felimy, which he found to be in a more commodious situation, into a cathedral.

St. Patrick founded a cathedral at Elphin about the middle of the fifth century, and placed over it St. Asicus, a monk, whom he consecrated bishop. After some centuries, and a little before the arrival of the English, Elphin was enriched with many large estates, on its union with the see of Roscommon; and the sees of Ardcarn, Drumclive, and others of less note, were also annexed to it. By these unions, the see of Elphin became one of the richest in Ireland.

Ardagh is among the most ancient sees in Ireland, having been founded by St. Patrick, who made his nephew the first bishop. In 1742 Ardagh was joined to or held *in commendam* with Tuam until that archdiocese was reduced to a bishopric, on the death of Archbishop Trench, in 1839.

Ardagh was held *in commendam* by the bishops of Kilmore during the first half of the seventeenth century, and the two sees were united in 1661. On the deprivation of bishop Sheridan, in 1691, they were separated for a short time, but were again re-united under bishop Smith in 1693. They were again separated in 1742, and Ardagh was then united to or held *in commendam* with Tuam.

On the death of bishop Trench, of Tuam, in 1839, Kilmore and Ardagh were united under 3 & 4 Wm. IV. cap. 37, and on the death of ishop Beresford, in 1841, KILMORE, ELPHIN, and ARDAGH were united nder the same Statute.

BISHOPS OF KILMORE AND OF KILMORE AND ARDAGH.

See Introduction, *ante*, p. 606.

KILMORE ONLY.

* Florence O'Conacty; *d.* 1231.
231. Congolach MacEneol.
251. Simon O'Ruirk.
286. Maurice; abbot of the convent B.V. at Kells.
307. Matt. MacDuibne
314. Patrick.
* Cornelius MacConoma; *d.* 1355.
* Rd. O'Reley; *d.* 1370.
389. Thomas, of Rushop.
* John O'Reley; *d.* 1393.
See vacant 3 years.
396. Roderick Brady.
* Nichs. Brady; *d.* 1421.
421. Donat.
* Andr. MacBrady, archdn.; *d.* 1456.
456. Thady.
* Fursey Mac Duibne; *d.* 1464.
464. John.
489. Thos. Brady.
511. Dermod.
541. Edmd. Nugent.
John or Richd. Brady; promoted to this see by the pope's authority; depr. by sir John Perrot, ld. dep. by whose recommendation
585. John Garvey, dean of Christ-Church, Dublin, was app.; tr. to Armagh.
See vacant till 1603.

KILMORE AND ARDAGH.

603. Robt. Draper.
612. Thos. Moygne, dean of St. Patrick's, Dublin.
29. Wm. Bedell.
1643. Robt. Maxwell, dean of Armagh; bp. of Kilmore only until 1661, and then bp. of Kilmore and Ardagh.
1672. Fras. Marsh, tr. from Limerick; tr. to Dublin.
1681. Wm. Sheridan, dean of Down; depr. for not taking the oaths, 1691.
1693. Wm. Smith, tr. from Raphoe.
1699. Edw. Wetenhall, tr. from Cork and Ross.
1714. Timothy Godwin, archdn. of Oxford; tr. to Cashel.
1727. Josiah Hort, tr. from Leighlin and Ferns: tr. to Tuam, to which see Ardagh then became attached. *See* "Archbishops of Tuam," *post*, p. 611.

KILMORE ONLY.

1742. Jos. Story, tr. from Killaloe, &c.
1757. John Craddock, tr. to Dublin.
1772. Dennis or Denison Cumberland, tr. from Clonfert.
1774. Geo. Lewis Jones, chapl. to Earl Harcourt, ld.-lieut.; tr. to Kildare.
1790. Wm. Foster, tr. from Cork and Ross; tr. to Clogher.
1796. Hon. Chas. Brodrick, tr. from Clonfert, &c.; tr. to Cashel.
1802. Geo. de la Poer Beresford, tr. from Clonfert.

KILMORE AND ARDAGH.

1839. Geo. de la Poer Beresford, abovenamed. On his death in 1841 Kilmore and Ardagh were united to Elphin under bp. Leslie of that see.

See "Bishops of Kilmore, Elgin, and Ardagh, *post*, p. 608.

BISHOPS OF ARDAGH.

* St. Mell, before 454; *d* 488.
488. St. Melchuo.
* * * *
754. St. Erard.
* Ceili; *d.* 1048.
* * * *
* Macrait O'Moran; *d.* 1168.
* Christian O'Heothy; *d.* 1179.
* O'Tirlenan; *d.* 1187.
* O'Hislenan; *d.* 1189.
* Adam O'Murredai; *d.* 1217.
217. Robt., abb. of St. Mary's, Dublin.
224. Simon MacGraith.
230. Jos. Magodaig, archdn.
233. Jocelin O'Tormaig.
238. Brendan Magodaig.
256. Milo, of Dunstable.
1290. Matt. O'Heothy.
1331. John Mageoir, or Magee.
See vacant 3 years.
1347. Owen O'Ferral, archdn.
1367. Wm. MacCasac.
1373. Chas. O'Ferral.
1378. John O'Fraic.
1396. Gilbert MacBrady.
* * Adam Lyns; *d.* 1416.
1418. Cornelius O'Ferral.
1425–7. Richd. O'Ferral.
1445. MacSamrhadhan.
1460. Cormac.
* * Wm. O'Ferral (uncertain).
* * Thos. O'Congalan; *d.* 1508.
1508. Owen.
1541. Richd. Ferral, abb. of Granard.

1553. Pat. MacMahon.
Vacant from 1577, to the appointment of
1583. Lisach Ferral.
Robt. Draper, Thos. Moygne, and Wm. Bedell.
See these prelates under *Kilmore*, *ante*. p. 607 ; Bedell res. Ardagh, in 1630, but retained Kilmore.
1633. John Richardson, archdn. of Derry.
Robt. Maxwell, Fras. Marsh, and Wm. Sheridan.
See these prelates under *Kilmore*, *ante*, p. 607.
1692. Ulysses Burgh.
On the deprivation of bp. Sheridan, Ardagh, which had gone wit Kilmore from the restn. of Charl II., was now separated from i and Ulysses Burgh, dean of Emly promoted to it by William an Mary in 1692. Bp. Burgh *d.* th same year, and the union of th two sees was restored under bp Smith. In 1742 Ardagh was onc more disjoined from Kilmore, an was held *in commendam* with th of Tuam, until the death of abp Trench in 1839. See "Arch bishops of Tuam," *post*, pp 611–3. In 1839, Ardagh wa again united to Kilmore.

See "Bishops of Kilmore and Ardagh," *ante*, p. 607.

BISHOPS OF ELPHIN.

* * St. Asicus; seated here in the fifth century.
* * * *
* * Donnald O'Dubhai, or O'Duffy, bp. of Clonmacnois; *d.* 1136.
1168. Flanachan O'Dubhai, or O'Duffy.
1174. Mœlisa O'Conactain.
* * Florence MacRiagan O'Mulrony; *d.* 1195.
1215. Ardgall O'Connor.
1224. Denis O'Mulkyran, bp. of Ardcarn.
* * Denis O'Morda; res. 1229; *d.* 1231.
1244. Donat O'Connor.
1245. John, archdn.
1246. Cornelius Rufus.
Thos., or Tumultach O'Connor, dean of Achonry; tr. to Tuam.
1260. Milo O'Connor, archdn. of Clonmacnois.
1262. Thos. MacFerall MacDermot.
1266. Maurice O'Connor.
1285. Gelasius MacInlianaig, abb. of Lochkee.
1296. Malachy MacBrien, abb. of Boyle.
1303. Donat O'Flanagan, abb. of Boyle.
1308. Chas. MacInlianaig, abb. of Lochkee; his election annulled by the pope, 1310.
1310. Malachy MacÆda.
1313. Laurence O'Laghnan.
1326. John O'Findsa, canon.
1356. Gregory, prov. of Killala.
1372. Thos. Barret, archdn. of Enaghdune.
1405. John O'Grada, or O'Grady.
1418. Robt. Foster, or Fostin.
* * Wm. O'Etegan; seated here in 1444.
* * Cornelius; seated here in 1450.
* * Nichs.; res. 1494.
See vacant nearly 5 years.
1499. Geo. Brann.
* * Christr. Fisher; *d.* 1511.
* * John; *d.* 1536.
1544. Conat O'Siagal, abb.
* * Bernard O'Higgin; seated here 1552.
1552. Roland de Burgo, also bp. of Clo fert; he held the two sees durin his life; *d.* 1580.
1580. Thos. Chester; *d.* 1584.
1584. John Linch; res. 1611.
1611. Edwd. King.
1639. Hy. Tilson, dean of Christ Church *d.* 1655.
See vacant until the Restorati in 1660.
1661. John Parker, dean of Killala; tr. Tuam.
1667 John Hudson, dean of Clogher; *d.* 168
See vacant from 1685 to 1691
1691. Simon Digby, tr. from Limerick.
1720. Hy. Downs, tr. from Killala a Achonry; tr. to Meath.
1724. Theoph. Bolton, tr. from Clonfer tr. to Cashel.
1730. Robt. Howard, tr. from Killala a Achonry.
1740. Edwd. Synge, tr. from Ferns a Leighlin.
1762. Wm. Gore, tr. from Clonfert; tr. Limerick.
1772. Jemmet Brown, tr. from Cork; t to Tuam.
1775. Chas. Dodgson, tr. from Ossory.
1795. John Law, tr. from Killala a Achonry.
1810. Hon. Power Trench, tr. from Wate ford and Lismore; tr. to Tuam
1819. John Leslie, tr. from Dromore.
See united to Kilmore a Ardagh, 1841.

See "Bishops of Kilmore, Elphin, and Ardagh," *infra*.

BISHOPS OF KILMORE, ELPHIN, AND ARDAGH.

1841. John Leslie, bp. of Elphin, abovenamed.
1854. Marcus Gervais Beresford, tr. Armagh.

862. Hamilton Verschoyle.
870. Thos. Carson, dean of Kilmore.
874. John R. Darley.
1884. Saml. Shone, archdn. of Kilmore; Mar. 26.

DEANS OF KILMORE.

325. Thos. O'Coinderi (O'Connery).
369. O'Bardain.
426. Andrew.

* * * *

6—. Thos. Robinson, res. 1619.
619. John Hill, L. P. Apr. 30.
627. Nichs. Bernard, L. P. Jan. 21; res. 1637.
638?. Hy. Jones, July 10.
662. Lewis Downes, May 13.
673. Edwd. Orme. It does not appear that he was ever in possession.
691–2. Enoch Reader, May 18.
700. Richd. Reader, July 10.
700. Jeremiah Marsh, Dec. 3; *d.* 1734.
1734. John Madden, L. P. Jan. 16; *d.* 1751.
1751. Hon. Hy. Maxwell, Dec. 19; bp. of Dromore, 1765.
1765. Chas. Agar, May 3; bp. of Cloyne, 1768.
1768. Thos. Webb, May 19; *d.* 1797.
1797. Geo. de la Poer Beresford, Mar. 25; bp. of Clonfert, 1801.
1801. Wm. Magenis, Jan. 29; *d.* 1825.
1825. Hy. Vesey Fitzgerald, L. P. Mar. 16; *d.* 1860.
1860. Thos. Carson, L. P. Apr. 16; made bp. of Kilmore, &c., Sept.16,1870.
1872. John M. Massey-Beresford.
1886. Wm. Hy. Stone.

DEANS OF ELPHIN.

240. Gilla na Naomh O'Dreain, *d.*
258. Gilchreest O'Carmacain, *d.*
271. Simon Magrath, *d.*
444. O'Flannagan.
487. Malachi O'Flannagan, *d.*
* Thos. O'Heidigein, or Edigein, or Edigen.
591. Thos. Burke, or Bourke; *d.* 1603.
603. Edwd. King, L. P. May 28.
606. Eriell O'Higgin, L. P. Apr. 30.
614. John Evatt, Jan. 18.
634. Richd. Jones, May 31; *d.* 1642.
642. Jos. Ware, Mar. 10; *d.* 1648.
6—. Edwd. Synge.
662. Clement Payman, Paman, or Paynem, Feb. 12.
1664. Danl. Neylan, or Neyland, June 12.
1665. Thos. Crofton, Aprl. 12; *d.* 1683.
1683. Anthy. Cope, Aug. 28; res. 1700.
1700. Edwd. Goldsmith, May 30; *d.* 1722–3.
1723. Peter Mahon, Feb. 12; *d.* 1739.
1739. Christr. Lloyd, Oct. 6; *d.* 1757.
1757. Jas. Dickson, L. P. Nov. 12; res. 1768.
1668. Robt. Bligh, July 9; *d.* 1778.
1778. John Barry, May 12; *d.* 1794.
1794. Fras. Browne, Mar. 5; *d.* 1797.
1797. John French; *d.* 1848.
1848. Wm. Warburton.

DEANS OF ARDAGH.

373. Richd. Ferral, or O'Ferrall.
407. Charles.
451. Gerald.
460. John.
512. Pierce M'Graidin.
552. John Bowerman.
563. Wm. Brady, L. P. Sept. 10.
595. Robt. Richardson, L. P. May 27.
606. Lewis Jones, June 26; res. 1625.
625. Hy. Jones, May 24.
637. Nichs. Bernard, L. P. June 22; *d.* 1661.
661. John Kerr, or Carr, L. P. Sept. 15.
703. John Barton, L. P. Mar. 21.
719. Chas. Cobbe, L. P. Jan. 22; bp. of Killala, 1720.
720. Josiah Hort, L. P. June 17; bp. of Ferns and Leighlin, 1721.
1721–2. Robt. Howard, L. P. Apr. 27; bp. of Killala, 1726.
1727. Lewis Saurin, Mar. 22.
1749. Geo. Sandford, Nov. 3.
1757. Thos. White, Nov. 30; *d.* 1769.
1769. Wm. French, Oct. 20; *d.* 1785.
1785. Lilly Butler, Mar. 19; res. 1790.
1790. Chas. Mongan (Warburton), Apr. 15.
1800. Hon. Richd. Bourke, Dec. 15; bp. of Waterford and Lismore, 1813.
1814. Richd. Graves, Mar. 1.
1829. Richd. Murray, inst. Nov. 10; *d.* 1854.
1854. Hugh Usher Tighe, L. P. Sept. 15; res. 1860.
1860. Aug. Wm. West, L. P., Aug. 23.
1880. Alexr. Orme.

DIOCESES OF TUAM (INCLUDING ENACHDUNE AND MAYO), KILLALA, AND ACHONRY.

St. Jarlath, the son of Loga, is looked upon as the founder of the cathedral of Tuam, about the beginning of the sixth century. Tuam was anciently called Tuiam-da-Gualand, and the cathedral, dedicated to St. Jarlath, was known as *Tempull Jarleith* or St. Jarlath's Church, having been dedicated to its founder. By means of assistance from Turlough O'Connor, the then king of Ireland, it was rebuilt, in 1152, by Edan O'Hoisin, first archbishop of Tuam, or at least the first who had the *pallium*, but several of his predecessors are sometimes called archbishops by the Irish historians.

The see of Enachdune has long been united to Tuam, and the title has ceased. The sees of Ardagh and Kilfenora have also at various times been held *in commendam* with Tuam. Particulars will be found under those dioceses. On the death of archbishop Trench, in 1839, Tuam was reduced to a bishopric.

St. Gerald, a native of England, and a disciple of St. Colman, bishop of Lindisfarne, followed that saint upon his expulsion out of England, in company with many persons of the same nation. St. Colman founded a monastery about the year 665 or 670, at Mayo, and placed in it the Englishmen who had followed him; whence it took the name of Mayo-na-Sasson, or Mayo of the Saxons, by which name the natives called the natives of England. St. Gerald enlarged this monastery, and erected it into an episcopal see, of which he was the first bishop. He died on the 13th of March, about the year 697.

St. Muredach, the first bishop of Killala, was consecrated by St. Patrick; whence it is manifest that he flourished in the fifth century; but the time of his death is uncertain. The date of the foundation of the see is pretty nearly to be guessed at; for St. Patrick made his journey into Connaught about 440–1. Few traces remain of the successors of Muredach, before the arrival of the English. The names of two only occur in history.

St. Finian, bishop of Clonard, founded the church of Achad, latterly commonly called Achonry and Achad-Conair, and anciently Achad-Chavin, about the year 530. St. Finian, having built this church, immediately gave it to his disciple Nathy, called in Irish Dathi, *i.e.* David, who went by two names; for he was commonly called Comrah or Cruimthir, and was a man of great sanctity. The latter of these names signifies, in old Irish, a priest; the other has a religious meaning. His festival is celebrated on the 9th of August, and the church was dedicated to him. In the ancient annals of Ireland, the prelates of this see are, for the most part, called bishops of Luigny or Liny, from the barony or subdivision of the county in which it is situated. No account is to be had of the successors of St. Nathy, until the arrival of the English in Ireland.

Mayo was united to or merged in Tuam about 1559, and the name was no longer preserved.

Achonry was held *in commendam* with Killala from 1607, and on the death of bishop Verschoyle, in 1834, Tuam, Killala, and Achonry were united under 3 & 4 Wm. IV. cap. 37.

BISHOPS OF TUAM.

* St. Jarlath, seated here in 501, *d.* 540.
* * * *
* Ferdomnach, *d.* 781.
* * * *
* Eugene Macclerig, *d.* 969.
* * * *
* Murchad O'Nioc, *d.* 1033.
* * * *
* Aid O'Hoisin, *d.* 1085.
* * Ercad O'Mœlomair, *d.* 1086.
1092. Cormac O'Cairil.
* * Catasch O'Cnail, or O'Conuil, *d.* 1118.
* * Murgesius O'Nioc, *d.* 1128.
* * Donald O'Dubhai, *d.* 1136.
* * Maurice, or Muredach O'Dubhai, *d.* 1150.
1150. Edan O'Hoisin, abp. 1152.

ARCHBISHOPS OF TUAM.

152. Edan O'Hoisin, above named; invested with the *pallium* at the hands of cardinal Paparo, 1152; *d.* 1161.
.161. Catholicus O'Dubhai, or O'Duffy.
* Felix O'Ruadan, res. 1201.
.235. Marian O'Laghnan, dean.
1250. Florence MacFlin, chancellor.
.257. Walter de Salern, dean of St. Paul's London.
.259. Thos. O'Connor, tr. from Elphin.
286. Steph. of Fulburn, tr. from Waterford.
289. Wm. de Birmingham.
.313. Malachy Mac Æda.
349. Thos. O'Carrol, archdn. of Cashel; tr. to Cashel.
.365. John O'Grady, archdn. of Cashel.
372. Gregory, tr. from Elphin.
.385. Gregory O'Moghan, depr. 1386.
.386. Wm. O'Cormacain, tr. to Clonfert.
394. Maurice O'Kelly, tr. from Clonfert.
See vacant from 1407 to 1410.
410. John Babynghe.
411. Cornelius.
427. John Baterley.
438. Thos. O'Kelly, tr. from Clonfert.
441. John de Burgo.
458. Donat O'Murry.
485. Wm. Shioy, or Joy.
503. Philip Pinson.
506. Maurice de Portu, *alias* O'Fehely.
531. Thos. O'Mullaly, or Laly.
536. Christr. Bodekin, tr. from Kilmacduach.
1559. The see of Mayo was annexed to Tuam about this time.
1573. Wm. Mullaly, or Laly, dean of Tuam.
1595. Nehemiah Donellan, res. 1609.
1609. Wm. Daniel.
1629. Randolph Barlow, dean of Christ Church.
1638. Rd. Boyle, tr. from Cork.
1645. John Maxwell, tr. from Killala and Achonry; *d.* 1646.
See vacant until the Restoration.
1661. Saml. Pullen, dean of Clonfert; he also held the bishopric of Kilfenora *in commendam.*
1667. John Parker, tr. from Elphin; tr. to Dublin.
1678. John Vesey, tr. from Limerick.
1716. Edwd. Singe, tr. from Raphoe.
1742. Josiah Hort, tr. from Kilmore and Ardagh; he held Ardagh *in commendam* with this see, and it continued with Tuam up to 1839.
1752. John Ryder, tr. from Down and Connor.
1775. Jemmet Brown, tr. from Elphin.
1782. Hon. Jos. Deane Bourke, tr. from Ferns and Leighlin; succ. as E. of Mayo, 1792.
1795. Hon. Wm. Beresford, tr. from Ossory.
1819. Hon. Power Trench, tr. from Elphin; *d.* 1839.
See united to Killala and Achonry, 1834.

See "Archbishops of Tuam and Bishops of Killala and Achonry," *post*, p. 613.

BISHOPS OF MAYO.

* St. Gerald, *d.* about 697.
* Muredach, *d.* 726.
* Aidan, *d.* 768.
* * * *
* * Cele O'Dubhai, *d.* 1209.
* * Stephn. O'Braoin, *d.* 1231.

* * * *

1428. Wm. Pendergast, depr. for not expediting his letters of provision, by pope Martin V.

1430. Nichs. Wagomai.

* * O'Higin, *d.* 1478.

* * Odo, *d.* 1493.

1493. John Bell.

* * * *

Eugene MacBreohan, or Brethemain, was the last bp. of Mayo in 1559. In his time the see was annexed to Tuam.

See "Archbishops of Tuam," *ante*, p. 611.

BISHOPS OF KILLALA.

* * St. Muredach, seated here about 440.

* * * *

* * Kellach, *d.* 544.

* * * *

* * O'Mœl Fogamair, *d.* 1151.

1177. Imar O'Ruadan.

1207. Donat O'Beoda.

1226. Cormac O'Tarpaid, or O'Torpy.

1234. John O'Malfagamair.

1275. O'Laidig, or O'Loyn.

1281. John O'Laidig, or O'Loyn.

1281. Donat O'Flaherty.

1306. John Tankard, archdn.

* * John O'Laitin, *d.* 1343.

See vacant 3 years.

1347. Wm. O'Dowda.

1350. Robert.

1381. Thos. Lodowis.

1389. Thos. Orwell.

1400. Thomas, archdn.

* * Muredach Clerach, *d.* 1403.

1416. O'Haneki, dean.

* * Connor O'Connell I., *d.* 1426.

* * Martin, *d.* 1431.

* * Manus Fitz Fultagh O'Dowda, archdn.; *d.* 1436.

* * Connor O'Connell II., slain in 1461 by Manus O'Dowda's son.

1461. Donat O'Concubhair, or O'Connor.

* * John O'Cashin, res. about 1490.

* * Thomas, *d.* 1497.

* * Thos. Clerk, or Cleragh, res.

1505. Malachy O'Clowan, or Cluan.

* * Rd. Barrett, seated here in 1523.

* * Redmund Gallakan, seated here in 1549.

1591. Owen O'Connor, dean.

He sat about 16 years; and on his death, Miler Magrath, abp. of Cashel, held this see, together with Achonry, *in commendam*, for almost 15 years. On *his* death, archdn. Hamilton was advanced to the see of Killala, and held that of Achonry *in commendam*, and this union has continued ever since.

See "Bishops of Killala and Achonry," *post*, p. 613.

BISHOPS OF ACHONRY.

St. Nathy, or Cruimthir Nathy; promoted about 530.

* * * *

* * Melruan O'Ruadan; *d.* 1170.

1214. Gillasius O'Ruadan.

1219. Clemens O'Sinadaig.

1226. Carus O'Tarpa, abb. of Mellifont.

1230. Gelisa O'Clery.

1237. Thos. O'Ruadan.

1238. Oengus O'Clumain.

1251. Thos. O'Miachan.

1266. Dennis O'Miachan, archdn.

1286. Benedict.

* * Hy. MacO'Reghty, *d.* 1297.

* * Benedict O'Brogan, *d.* 1311.

1312. David.

* * Murchard O'Hara, *d.* 1344.

* * David, *d.* 1348.

1373. Nichs. O'Hedram.

1374 Wm. Andrew, tr. to Meath.

1445. Laurence Peter Jacopin.

* * Thady, *d.* 1448.

1449. Gasper, abb. of Boyle.

Jas. Blakedon, tr. to Bangor, 1452.

* * Cornelius, *d.* 1472.

1473. Robt. Wellys.

* * Bernard, *d.* 1488.

1489. John de Bustamento, a Spaniard never visited the see.

* * Richard, *d.* 1492.

1492. Thos. Fort, Augustine canon.

Cormac, seated here in 1523.

* * * *

1585. Eugene.

1607. Miler Magragh, abp. of Cashel, obtained this see in 1607, and also that of Killala, and held them both till his death, from which time the two sees have always gone together.

See "Bishops of Killala and Achonry," *post.* p. 613.

BISHOPS OF KILLALA AND ACHONRY.

1607. Miler Magrath, abp. of Cashel. See *Killala, ante*, p. 612.
1623. Archd. Hamilton, of Glasgow; tr. to Cashel.
1630. Archd. Adair, dean of Raphoe; depr.
1640. John Maxwell, tr. from Ross, in Scotland; tr. to Tuam.
The see continued vacant from his translation in 1645 to the Restoration.
1660. Hy. Hall, chapl. to the ld.-lieut.
1663. Thos. Bayly, dean of Down.
1670. Thos. Otway, tr. to Ossory.
1679. John Smith, dean of Limerick.
1681. Wm. Smith, dean of Dromore; tr. to Raphoe.
1681–2. Richd. Tennison, dean of Clogher; tr. to Clogher.
1690. Wm. Lloyd, dean of Achonry.
1717. Hy. Downs, minister of Darlington, Northamptonshire; tr. to Derry.
1720. Chas. Cobbe, dean of Ardagh; tr. to Dromore.
1726. Robt. Howard, dean of Ardagh; tr. to Elphin.
1730. Robt. Clayton, tr. to Cork and Ross.
1735. Mordecai Cary, tr. from Clonfert.
1752. Richd. Robinson, tr. to Ferns and Leighlin.
1759. Saml. Hutchinson.
1781. Wm. Cecil Pery, dean of Derry; tr. to Limerick.
1784. Wm. Preston, tr. to Ferns and Leighlin.
1787. John Law, tr. from Clonfert; tr. to Elphin.
1795. John Porter, chapl. to the abp. of Canterbury; tr. to Clogher.
1798. Jos. Stock, chapl. to the ld.-lieut.
1810. Jas. Verschoyle, dean of St. Patrick's; *d.* 1834.

See united to Tuam, 1834.

See "Archbishops of Tuam, and Bishops of Killala and Achonry," *infra*.

ARCHBISHOP OF TUAM, AND BISHOP OF KILLALA AND ACHONRY.

1834. Hon. Power Trench, abp. of Tuam. See *Tuam, ante*, p. 611; *d.* 1839.

On his death Tuam was reduced to a bishopric.

See "Bishops of Tuam, Killala, and Achonry," *infra*.

BISHOPS OF TUAM, KILLALA, AND ACHONRY.

1839. Hon. Thos. Plunket.
1867. Hon. Chas. Brodrick Bernard.

DEANS OF TUAM.

1230. Marian, or Mael-Murry O'Laghnan.
1282. Constantine O'Dowd.
133–. Philip Hanlain; *d.* 1339.
1339. Denis.
1394. James.
1399. Jas. Caer, Carr, or Cahir.
1523. Thomas.
1558. Wm. Mullaly, or Laly, Nov. 7; made abp. 1573.
1573. Edwd. Browne, Apr. 21.
1610. Abel Walsh, Feb. 6.
1625. Thos. Peyton.
1638 (?). John King.
1661. Wm. Buchanan, L. P. June 21.
1669. Jas. Wilson, L. P., May 18.
1686. Robt. Echlin, June 30; *d.* 1712.
1712. John Hinton, Aug. 31.
Thos. Butler (?).
1716. Wm. White; res. 1724.
1724. Jonn. Bruce.
1543. Isaac Gervais, May 29; *d.* 1756.
1756. Robt. Johnson, June 1; bp. of Cloyne, 1759.
1759. Danl. le Tablere, Aug. 12; *d.* 1775.
1775. Robt. Clarke; *d.* 1782.
1782. Joshua Berkeley, Apr. 13; *d.* 1807.
1807. Jas. Mahon, Aug. 11.
1809. John Wm. Keatinge, Jan. 7; res. 1810.
1810. Richd. Bourne, June 1.
1813. Thos. Carter, July 27; *d.* 1849.
1850. Hon. Robt. Plunket, L. P., May 11; *d.* 1867.
1867. Chas. Hy. Seymour, L. P., June 14.
1879. Wm. Chambers Townsend.

DEANS OF ENACHDUNE.

1523. Donald O'Flaherty.
1558. Patr. Blach, or Black.
1638. The deanery of Enachdune is returned as vacant, and the office ceased to exist.

DEANS OF KILLALA.

* * O'Haneki, made bp. 1416.
1442. Mac Wm. Barrett, *d.* same year.
* * * *
1613. Wm. Flanagan, June 11.
1629. Wm. Buchanan, Feb. 21.
1636. Robt. Forgie, Feb. 26.
1664. Hy. Dodwell, L.P. July 7.
1674. Alexr. Murray, May 20.
1701. Fras. Knapp, Dec. 24; *d.* 1718.
1718. Jonn. Smedley, Sept. 6.
1724. Peter Maturin, May 4.
1741. Theoph. Brocas, Dec. 24.
1770. John Brocas, June 30; *d.* 1795.
1795. Thos. Vesey Dawson, June 11.
1796. Thos. Thompson, Mar. 16; *d.* 1799.
1800. Walter Blake Kirwan, Jan. 25.
1806. Edmund Burton, Feb. 5; *d.* 1817.
1817. Hon. Geo. Gore, Aug. 21; *d.* 1844.
1844. Jas. Collins, Oct. 21.
1872. Wm. Jackson.
1885. Wm. Skipton.

DEANS OF ACHONRY.

1246. Thos. or Tomultach O'Connor.
1442. MacMulroona M'Donagh.
1582. Owen O'Connor, Aug. 24.
1615. Wm. Flanagan.
1629. Wm. Buchanan, Feb. 21.
1661. Randal (or Rodolph) Hollingworth, Mar. 22.
1662. Jas. Vaughan, Apr. 9.
1683. Wm. Lloyd, Aug. 11; bp. of Killala 1690.
1691. Saml. Foley, Apl. 4; bp. of Down and Connor 1694.
1695. John Yeard, Feb. 12; *d.* 1733.
1733. Sutton Symes, Nov. 30.
1752. Richd. Handcock, Sept. 15; *d.* 1791.
1792. Jas. Langrishe, Jan. 14; res. 1806.
1806. Jas. Hastings, Aug. 13.
1812. Arth. Hy. Kenney, June 10; res. 1821.
1821. Wm. Greene, June 11; res. 1824.
1824. Theoph. Blakeley, Dec. 6; res. 1839.
1839. Edwd. Newenham Hoare, June 14.
1850. Hon. Harvey de Montmorency, L. P. Dec. 17; *d.* 1872.
1875. Arthur Moore.
1883. Hamilton Townsend.

PROVINCE OF DUBLIN.

See p. 594.

DIOCESES OF DUBLIN, GLENDALOUGH, AND KILDARE.

THE SEE OF DUBLIN is supposed to have been founded by St. Patrick, about the year 448. It became archiepiscopal in 1152. See *Armagh, ante*, p. 594. There are two cathedrals, both situated in the city of Dublin; one is dedicated to the Holy Trinity, and is called Christ Church; the other is dedicated to St. Patrick. The Archbishop is primate of Ireland.

GLENDALOUGH or GLANDALAGH has been united to Dublin since the year 1214. The catalogue of its bishops is extremely incorrect; and it has been so long united to the archiepiscopal see of Dublin that their names are seldom to be met with in history. St. Kevin seems to have been the founder of the see. There existed both a cathedral and an abbey; the first was dedicated to the apostles St. Peter and St. Paul, and both were situated in a small valley surrounded by lofty mountains. The place is now commonly known by the name of the "Seven Churches," from the remains of so many buildings which are contiguous to the cathedral.

KILDARE is one of the earliest episcopal foundations in Ireland. It was founded, probably, at the close of the fifth century, as the first bishop on record died in the year 519. St. Bridget, the illegitimate daughter of an Irish chieftain, born in the year 453, receive i the veil while in her fourteenth year, from the hands of St. Patrick, and prior to 484 she founded a nunnery here. To this saint, who died in 523, the cathedral was dedicated.

GLENDALOUGH was united to DUBLIN in 1214. On the death of Bishop Lindsay, in 1846, DUBLIN, GLENDALOUGH, and KILDARE were united under 3 & 4 Wm. IV. cap. 37.

BISHOPS OF DUBLIN.

* * * *

* * Livinius; suffered martyrdom in the Low Countries in 633.
* * St. Wiro or Wirus, *d.* 650.
* * Disibode, res. 675.
* * Gualafer.
* * St. Rumold, murd. near Mechlin, 775.
* * St. Sedulius, *d.* 785.
* * Cormac.

* * * *

* * Donat, *d.* 1074.
1074. Patrick.
1084. Donat O'Haingly.
1095. Samuel O'Haingly.
1121. Gregory, abp. 1152.

ARCHBISHOPS OF DUBLIN.

1152. Gregory, above named, the first abp.
1162. St. Laurence O'Toole.
1182. John Comyn.
1213. Hy. de Londres.

See united to Glendalough, 1214.

See "Archbishops of Dublin and Bishops of Glendalough," *infra.*

BISHOPS OF GLENDALOUGH OR GLANDALAGH.

* * St. Coemgene, or Kevin; res. about 612.
612. Molibba, or Libba.
* * Aidan.
* * Ampadan.
* * Dungal Mac Baithen, *d.* 899.
925. Cormac MacFitzbran.
1085. Gilda na Naomh I.
1101. Cormac O'Mail.
1152. Gilda na Naomh II.
Kinad O'Ronan, seated here about 1166.
1179. Malchus, or Macrobius.
Wm. Piro, seated here in 1192.

See united to Dublin 1214.

See "Archbishops of Dublin and Bishops of Glendalough," *infra.*

ARCHBISHOPS OF DUBLIN AND BISHOPS OF GLENDALOUGH.

1214. Hy. de Londres, abp. of Dublin, above named.
1228. Luke, dean of St. Martin's, London.
1256. Fulk de Saunford.
1279. John de Derlington.
1284. John de Saunford, dean of St. Patrick's.
Thos. de Chadsworth, dean of St. Patrick's, was elected in 1294, but the king would not confirm him.
1297. Wm. de Hotham, dean of St. Patrick's.
He died the same year, and Adam de Balsham, prior of Christ-Church, was elected by that convent; but the dean and chapter of St. Patrick's made choice of *their* dean, the before-mentioned Thos. de Chadsworth. This occasioned much trouble; for the pope, claiming a right to name to the see, it not having been filled within three months after the death of the last bishop, named
1299. Rd. de Ferings, archdn. of Canterbury, who got possession after some difficulty; *d.* 1306.
1310. John Leck, bp. elect of Dunkeld.
The same scene ensued on bp. Fering's death, in 1306, as had occurred on bp. Hotham's, and ended in both elections being declared void. Bp. Leck *d.* 1313.
1317. Alexr. de Bicknor.
On bp. Leck's death, the contest of election was renewed: one party made choice of Walter Thornbury; the other of Bicknor; but the former was wrecked going to France, and the latter easily obtained possession.
1349. John de St. Paul, canon of Dublin.

1363. Thos. Minot.
1373-5. Robt. de Wikeford, archdn. of Winchester.
1391. Robt. Waldby, bp. of Aire, in Gascony.
1396. Rd. Northalis, tr. from Ossory.
1397. Thos. Cranley.
1417. Rd. Talbot.
1449. Michl. Tregury.
1472. John Walton, abb. of Osney, near Oxford; res.
1484. Walter Fitzsimons, chanter of St. Patrick's, Dublin.
1511. Wm. Rokeby, tr. from Meath.
1521. Hugh Inge, tr. from Meath.
1528. John Allen, or Allan; murd. by the Fitzgeralds.
1535. Geo. Brown, of London; the first Protestant abp. of this see; depr. by Q. Mary, 1554.
1555. Hugh Curwen, or Curwyn; tr. to Oxford.
1567. Adam Loftus (No. 1), tr. from Armagh.
1605. Thos. Jones, tr. from Meath.
1619. Lancelot Bulkeley, archdn. of Dublin.
1660. Jas. Margetson, dean of Christ Church, Dublin; tr. to Armagh.
1660. Michl. Boyle, tr. from Cork, &c.; tr to Armagh.
1678. John Parker, tr. from Tuam.
1681. Fras. Marsh, tr. from Kilmore, &c.
1694. Narcissus Marsh, tr. from Cashel; tr. to Armagh.
1703. Wm. King, tr. from Derry.
1729. John Hoadley, tr. from Ferns and Leighlin; tr. to Armagh.
1742-3. Chas. Cobbe, tr. from Kildare.
1765. Hon. Wm. Carmichael, tr. from Meath.
1766. Arth. Smythe, tr. from Meath.
1772. John Craddock, tr. from Kilmore.
1778. Robt. Fowler, tr. from Killaloe and Kilfenora.
1801. Chas. Agar, visc. Somerton, aft. E. of Normanton; tr. from Cashel.
1809. Euseby Cleaver, tr. from Ferns and Leighlin.
1820. Lord John Geo. de la Poer Beresford, tr. from Clogher; tr. to Armagh.
1822. Wm. Magee, tr. from Raphoe.
1831. Rd. Whately, principal of St. Alban's Hall, Oxford.
See united to Kildare, 1846.

See " Archbishops of Dublin and Bishops of Glendalough and Kildare," *post* p. 617.

BISHOPS OF KILDARE.

Those with an (A.) after their names, were probably only *abbots* of Kildare.

* * St. Conlæth, *d.* 519.
638. St. Aid.
694. Lochin.
697. St. Forannan (A.).
708. Mœldoborean.
732. Tola.
743. Diman.
747. Cathald O'Forannan (A.).
782. Lomtuil.
785. Snedbran.
Muredach O'Cathald (A.).
793. Eudocius O'Diocholla (A.).
799. Fœlan O'Kellach (A.).
813. Lœtan O'Muctigern.
820. Murtogh O'Kellach (A.).
828. Siedhul, or Sedulius (A.).
833. Tuadcar.
840. Orthanach.
862. Ædgene.
868. St. Cobthack O'Muredach (A.).
870. Mœngal.
874. Robertæ MacNaserda.
Lanfran MacMogtigern.
880. Suibney O'Fianacta.
884. Scandalus, or Scannail.
885. Largisius.
920. Flanagan O'Riagan (A.).
929. Crunmoel.
949. Mælfinan.
953. Culean MacKellach (A.).
965. Mured MacFœlan (A.).
981. Amucaid.
985. Murechad MacFlan.
1028. Moel Martin.
1042. Moel Brigid, or Brigidian.
1085. Fin MacGuffan (MacGorman).
1097. Moel Brigid (or Brigidian O'Brolcan).
1100. Aid O'Heremon.
1102. Ferdomnac.
1108. MacDongail.
1144. Cormac O'Cathsuigh.
1148. O'Dubhin.
1160. Finan (MacTiarcain) O'Gorman.
1176. Malachy O'Beirn.
1177. Nehemiah.
1206. Cornelius MacGelany.
1223. Ralph of Bristol.
1233. John of Taunton, canon of St. Patrick's.
1258. Simon of Kilkenny.
1279. Nichs. Cusack.
1299. Walter de Veele, chanter of Kildare.
1334. Richd. Hulot, archdn.
1353. Thos. Gifford, chanter of Kildare.
1366. Robt. of Askeaton.
1368. George.
1401. Hy. of Wessenberch.
1405. Thomas, *d.* 1405.
John Madock, archdn.; *d.* 1431.
1432. William, archdn.

See vacant nearly 3 years.
1449. Geoff. Hereford.
1464. Richd. Lang; elected to Armagh, but disappointed of it.
1474. David.
* * Jas. Wale; res. 1475.
* * Wm. Barret; res. before 1482.
1482. Edmd. Lane.
1523. Thos. Dillon.
1531. Walter Wellesley.
1540. Wm. Miagh.
On the death of bp. Wellesley, the pope named Donald O'Beachan to be bishop; he died a few days after; the pope then named Thady Reynolds, but the king set him aside.
1550. Thos. Lancaster, the first Protestant bp.; depr. 1554.
1554. Thos. Liverous, or Leverous, dean of St. Patrick's; depr. for refusing the oath of supremacy.
1560. Alexr. Craik, dean of St. Patrick's.
1564. Robt. Daly.
1583. Daniel Neylan.
1604. Wm. Pilsworth.
1635. Robt. Usher, archdn. of Meath.
1644. Wm. Golbourn, archdn.; *d.* 1650.
See vacant about 10 years.
1661. Thos. Price, dean of Kilmore; tr. to Cashel.
1667. Ambrose Jones, archdn. of Meath.
1678. Anthy. Dopping, tr. to Meath.
1681. Wm. Moreton, dean of Christ Church; tr. to Meath.
1705. Welbore Ellis, tr. to Meath.
1732. Chas. Cobbe, tr. from Dromore; tr. to Dublin.
1743. Geo. Stone, tr. from Ferns and Leighlin; tr. to Derry.
1745. Thos Fletcher, tr. from Dromore.
1761. Richd. Robinson, tr. from Ferns and Leighlin; tr. to Armagh.
1765. Chas. Jackson, tr. from Ferns and Leighlin.
1790. Geo. Lewis Jones, tr. from Kilmore.
1804. Hon. Chas. Dalrymple Lindsay, tr. from Killaloe; *d.* 1846.
See united to Dublin and Glendalough, 1846.

See "Archbishops of Dublin, and Bishops of Glendalough and Kildare," *infra.*

ARCHBISHOPS OF DUBLIN AND BISHOPS OF GLENDALOUGH AND KILDARE.

1846. Richd. Whately, abp. of Dublin, &c. See *Dublin and Glendalough, ante* p. 616.
1864. Richd. Chenevix Trench; res. Nov., 1884.
1884. Wm. Conyngham, ld. Plunket; tr. from Meath.

DEANS OF ST. PATRICK'S.

The earlier names differ in the various lists. Those marked (?) in the list below were probably sub-deans only.

1219. Wm. Fitz-Guy, or Fitz-Guido, the first dean recorded.
1223. Ralph de Bristol (?).
1234. John de Taunton (?).
1235. Richd. Gardiner, or de Gardino (? 1240).
1250. Richd. de St. Martin.
1251. Hugh de Mapilton, or de Glandelagh; ld. treasr. same year (?).
1260. John de Saunford, just. K. B.; abp. of Dublin, 1284.
1275. Wm. de Salinis (?).
1277. Adam de Wadenhall (?).
1284. Thos. de Chaddesworth; *d.* about 1311.
* * James de Ispania (?).
1289. Stephn. de Brogan (?).
1294. Adam de Furneis (?).
1310. Alexr. de Byknore, or Bicknor, preb. of Maynooth; ld. treasr. 1307 (?).
1312. Wm. Rudyard, treasr. of St. Patrick's; elect. dean.
1348. Adam de Kingston.
1349. Wm. de Bromley; ld. treasr. of Ireland, 1354; *d.* 1374.
1363. Thos. Minot, preb. of Malihidert, or Mullahithart (?).
1374. Wm. Lawless and Nichs. Bromley; "the dean being very old and infirm, the king authorised them to prosecute his affairs at Rome and elsewhere."
John Colton, ld. treasr.; ld. chanc. of Ireland, 1379.
1382. The deanery sequestered; dean Colton made abp. of Armagh this year.
1390. Hy. Bowett.
1392. Wm. Chambre.
1396. Thos. de Everdon. Cardl. Randulph, who had intruded himself into the deanery, was evicted, after a trial of *quare impedit.*
1399. John Prene; abp. of Armagh, 1439.
1439. Nichs. Hill (?).

1449. Michl. Tregury.
1457. Peter Norreis, or Norreys.
1465. John Alleyne, precentor of the cathedral; *d.* 1505.
1505. Thos. Rochfort, son of Roger, ld. of Killadown.
1522. John Rycarde, rector of Trim; res. 1523 (? 1527).
1523 (? 1527). Robt. Sutton, archdn. of Dublin.
1528. Thos. Darcy, preb. of Howth, and m. rolls.
1529. Geo. Fyche, archdn. of Glendalough; *d.* Mar. 1537.
1537. Edwd. Bassenet de Devonshire.
1555. Thos. Liverous, or Leverous, bp. of Kildare, *q. v.*; L. P. Mar. 26.
1560. Alexr. Craik, preb. of Clonmethan, Aug. 21; bp. of Kildare same year; *d.* 1564.
1564. Adam Loftus (No. 1), abp. of Armagh.
1567. Robt. Weston, dean of Arches in London; aft. ld. chanc. of Ireland, and dean of Wells, 1570.
1576 (? 1573). Wm. Gerrard, aft. ld. chanc. of Ireland.
1581. Thos. Jones; bp. of Meath, 1584; aft. tr. to Dublin.
1584. Richd. Meredyth, L. P. June 13; bp. of Leighlin Apr. 1589; *d.* 1597.
1597. Sir John Ryder.
1608. Thos. Moigne, archdn. of Meath; res. 1625; *d.* 1628.
1625. Benjn. Culme, rector of Rathmore, diocese of Meath; L. P. Oct. 23.
1660. Wm. Fuller, L. P. July 3; res. 1666.
1666. Thos. Seele, precentor of Christ Church; L. P. Mar. 30; *d.* Feb. 1675.
1675. Benj. Parry, chaplain to the ld.-lieut.; L. P. Feb. 17; *d.* 1678.
1678. John Worth, L. P. Jan. 17; having conformed to the Roman Catholic persuasion, he was depr.
1688. Wm. King, chaplain to Parker, abp. of Tuam, Jan. 26; bp. Derry, 1690.
1691. Michl. Jephson, L. P. Jan. 15; *d.* 1693.
1693. Thos. Lindsay, chanc. of Christ Church; L. P. Feb. 6; bp. of Killaloe, 1625.
1695. Edwd. Smith, L. P. Mar. 3; *d.* 1698.
1699. Jerome Ryves, L. P. Feb. 22; *d.* June, 1704.
1704. John Sterne, Mar. 30; bp. of Dromore, 1713; aft. tr. to Clogher.
1713. Jonathan Swift, L. P. May 6; *d.* 1745.
1745. Gabriel Jas. Maturin, dean of Kildare, Nov. 20; *d.* 1746.
1746. Fras. Corbet, preb. of Malahide, Nov. 13; *d.* 1775.
1775. Wm. Cradock, Sept. 11; *d.* Sept. 1793.
1793. Robt. Fowler, Oct. 15; res., and *d.* soon after.
1794. Jas. Verschoyle, Apr. 23; bp. of Killala, &c., 1810.
1810. John Wm. Keatinge, L. P. May 31; *d.* 1817.
1817. Hon. Richd. Ponsonby, inst. July 1818; bp. of Killaloe, 1828; tr. to Derry, 1831.
1828. Hy. Richd. Dawson, Mar. 3.
Dean Dawson died in Oct. 1840. Two candidates were thereupon proposed, viz. Dr. Daly and Dr. Wilson; the latter disputed certain votes given to the other, and on Dec 9, 1842, the Court of Delegates decided in favour of Dr. Daly.
1842. Robt. Daly; inst. dean Dec. 13; bp. of Cashel, same year.
1843. Hon. Hy. Pakenham, Feb. 7; *d.* Dec. 25, 1863.
He was made dean of Christ Church also in 1846. and the two deaneries were united until 1885.
1864. John West, Feb. 5.

DEANS OF CHRIST CHURCH, DUBLIN.

1539-41. Robt. Payswick, L. P. May 11, 1541; *d.* 1543.
1543. Thos. Lockwood, Dec. 1; *d.* Apr. 1565.
1565. John Garvey, May; *d.* Mar. 2, 1594.
1595. Jas. Wheeler, L. P. Mar. 9; bp. of Ossory, 1613.
1618. Randolph (or Ranulph) Barlow, L. P. Feb. 25.
1634. Hy. Tilson, L. P. Dec. 23; bp. of Elphin, 1639.
1639. Jas. Margetson, L. P. Dec. 2; abp. of Dublin, 1660.
1661. Robt. Mossom, Feb. 1; bp. of Derry, 1666.
1666. John Parry, L. P. Apr. 2; bp. of Ossory, 1672.
1677. Wm. Moreton, L. P. Dec. 22.
1705. Welbore Ellis, L. P. Sept. 23.
1731. Chas. Cobbe, Mar. 16; abp. of Dublin, 1742–3.
1743. Geo. Stone, bp. of Ferns and Leighlin, June 15.
1745. Thos. Fletcher, L. P. May 14; *d.* 1761.
1761. Richd. Robinson, bp. of Kildare; L. P. Apr. 13; made abp. of Tuam, 1765.
1765. Chas. Jackson, L. P. Feb. 25.

1790. Geo. Lewis Jones, L. P. June 5.
1804. Hon. Chas. Lindsay, L. P. May 14; d. 1846.
1846. Hon. Hy. Pakenham, dean of St. Patrick's. Held the two deaneries; *d.* Dec. 25, 1863.
1864. John West, Feb. 5; also dean of St. Patrick; res. Christ Church, but retained St. Patrick's.
1885. Wm. Conyngham, ld. Plunket, abp. Dublin, &c.
1887. Wm. Conyngham Greene.

DEANS OF GLENDALOUGH.

1218. Robt. de Bedford, bp. of Lismore same year. "It is likely that on the annexation of the bishopric to Dublin, the chapter, of whatever members it may have consisted, became gradually extinguished." —*Cotton.*

DEANS OF KILDARE.

1212. Daniel.
1215 (about). Alan.
1260. Wm. Punchard.
1279. Stephen.
1291. Petrus Capellanus.
1307. John.
1319 (about). John de Conall.
1333. Roger.
1352. Gregorius de Salter (? Leixlip).
1357. Gregory Holgin (? same man).
1366. Wm. Whyte.
1432. Nichs. Sherlock.
1472–78. Malachy Malvane, or O'Malone.
1500. Nichs. Conyll.
1521. Edwd. Dillon.
1540. Wm. Miagh, or Meagh.
15—. David Stubin.
1553. Denis Ellan.
15—. Thos. Ellis.
1610–15. Walter Walsh, *d.* 1621.
1626. Wm. Cleborne, inst. Mar. 8.
1661. Christr. Golborne, Mar. 21.
1675. John Worth, L. P. Sept. 7; dean of St. Patrick, 1677.
1678. Simon Digby, Feb. 12; bp. of Limerick, 1678–9.
1679. Saml. Synge, L. P. Apr. 17.
1708. John Clayton, Dec. 7; *d.* 1725.
1725. Sankey Winter, Oct. 5; *d.* 1736.
1737. Gabriel Jas. Maturin, Feb. 15; aft. dean of St. Patrick's; *d.* 1746.
1746. Philip Fletcher, Dec. 9; *d.* 1765.
1765. Wm. Fletcher, June 5; *d.* 1771.
1772. Edwd. Ledwich, May 6; *d.* 1782.
1787. Dixie Blundell, Oct. 27; *d.* 1808.
1808. Arth. John Preston, Dec. 15; dean of Limerick, 1809.
1809. Thos. Trench, Aug. 7; *d.* 1834.
1834. Jas. Gregory, Mar. 16; *d.* 1859.
1859. John Wolseley, Apr. 2.

DIOCESES OF OSSORY, FERNS, AND LEIGHLIN.

The see of Ossory was first planted at Saiger, in the territory of Ely O'Carrol, about the year 402, thirty years, it is said, before the arrival of St. Patrick. It was removed to Aghavoe, it is supposed, in 1052. Felix O'Dullany, bishop of Ossory, translated the see to Kilkenny about the close of Henry II.'s reign.

Ferns took its name from the "hero Ferna, son of Caril, king of the Decies, who was slain in battle at this place by Gallus, the son of Morna." The see was anciently archiepiscopal for a time; for in the early ages of Christianity, the title of Archbishop in Ireland, except in the case of Armagh, was not fixed to any particular see, but sometimes belonged to one, and sometimes to another city, according to the sanctity and merits of the presiding bishop; and he was not denominated from his see, but from the province in which his bishopric was situated.

Leighlin, commonly called Old Leighlin, is situated about a mile and a half to the westward of the river Barrow. Here St. Laserian constituted an episcopal see about the year 628.

FERNS and LEIGHLIN were united in 1600, and on the death of bishop Elrington, in 1835, OSSORY, FERNS, and LEIGHLIN were united under 3 & 4 Wm. IV., cap. 37.

BISHOPS OF OSSORY.

In the ancient writings the name *abbot* is frequently used instead of bishop; so that the abbots of Saiger may have been bishops likewise.

BISHOPS OR ABBOTS OF SAIGER.

* * St. Kiaran, *d.* 549.
* * St. Carthagh, the Elder.
* * St. Sedna, flourished in 570.
* * St. Killene MacLubney, archdn.; *d.* 695.
* * Laigdene MacDonennach, abbot; *d.* 739.
* * Tuntgall, abbot; *d.* 771.
* * Mocoach, abbot; *d.* 783.
* * Cucathach, abbot; *d.* 788.
* * Cobthach, abbot; *d.* 801.
* * Feredach, abbot; *d.* 809.
* * Conchovar, abbot; *d.* 810.
* * Conmach, abbot; *d.* 826.
* * Irgalach, abbot; *d.* 832.
* * Anluain, abbot; *d.* 846.
* * Cormac MacCladach, *d.* 867.
* * Geran, abbot; *d.* 868.
* * Slogad O'Raithnin, abbot; *d.* 885.
* * Cormac, *d.* 907.
* * Fergall MacMoelmorra, abbot; *d.* 919.
* * Fogartach I., abbot; *d.* 941.
* * Kenfœlad MacSwiny, abbot; *d.* on a pilgrimage at Glendalough.
* * Flathlem, *d.* 984.
* * Fogartach II., abbot (and of Glendalough); *d.* 1004.
* * Dunchad O'Kellechuir, *d.* 1048.
* * Kellach Ramhar, *d.* 1079.

Here is a blank of 73 years.

* * * *

BISHOPS OF OSSORY.

* * Donald O'Fogarty, seated here in 1152.

1178. St. Felix O'Dullany.
1202. Hugh I. (Rufus).
1218. Peter Mannesin, canon of Ossory.
1229. Wm, of Kilkenny, chanc. of Ossory; res.
1232. Walter Brackell, or Bracknell.
1244. Geoff. of Turvill, archdn. of Dublin.
1251. Hugh II. (de Mapilton), archdn. of Dublin.
1257. Hugh III.
1260. Jeffr. St. Leger.
1287. Roger of Wexford, dean of Kilkenny.
1289. Michl. of Exeter, canon of Kilkenny.
1302. Wm. FitzJohn, tr. to Cashel.
1318. Richd. Ledred.
1360. John of Tatenale.
1371. Alexr. Balscot, canon; tr. to Meath.
1386. Richd. Northalas, tr. to Dublin.
1397. Thos. Peverel, tr. to Llandaff.
1398. John Griffin, tr. from Leighlin.
1399. John Waltham.
1400. Roger of Appleby, prior of Newton dean of Lichfield.
1404. John Volcan, tr. from Dromore.
1405. Thos. Snell, tr. from Lismore.
1417. Patr. Ragged, tr. from Cork.
1421. Dennis O'Dea.
1428. Thos. Barry.
1460. David Hacket.
1479. John O'Hedian, archdn. of Cashel.
1488. Oliver Cantwell.
1527. Milo Baron, *d.* 1550.
  See vacant nearly 2 years.
1552. John Bale, the first Protestant bp.; depr.
1553. John Thonory, a Roman Catholic; *d.* 1565.
  See vacant 2 years.
1567. Christr. Gafney, preb. of St. Patrick's.
1577. Nichs. Walsh, chanc. of St. Patrick's.
1586. John Horsfall.
1609. Richd. Dean, dean of Ossory.
1613. Jonas Wheeler, dean of Christ Church, Dublin.
1641. Griffith Williams.
1672. John Parry, dean of Christ Church, Dublin.
1677. Benjn. Parry, brother to the above; dean of St. Patrick's.
1678. Michl. Ward, dean of Lismore; tr. to Derry.
1679. Thos. Otway, tr. from Killala and Achonry.
1693. John Hartstonge, archdn. of Limerick; tr. to Derry.
1714. Sir Thos. Vesey, bt.; tr. from Killaloe.
1731. Edwd. Tennison, archdn. of Caermarthen.
1735. Chas. Este, archdn. of Armagh; tr. to Waterford.
1740. Anthy. Dopping, dean of Clonmacnois.
1743. Michl. Cox, tr. to Cashel.
1754. Edwd. Maurice.
1756. Richd. Pocock, tr. to Meath.
1765. Chas. Dodgson, tr. to Elphin.
1775. Wm. Newcombe, tr. from Dromore; tr. to Waterford.
1779. John Hotham, archdn. of Middlesex; tr. to Clogher.
1782. Hon. Wm. Beresford, tr. from Dromore; tr. to Tuam.

1795. Thos. Lewis O'Beirne, private sec. to the ld.-lieut., rector of Longford, &c.; tr. to Meath.

1798. Hugh Hamilton, tr. from Clonfert.

1806. John Kearney, provost of Trinity College, Dublin.

1813. Robt. Fowler, archdn. of Dublin.

See united to Ferns and Leighlin, 1835.

See "Bishops of Ossory, Ferns, and Leighlin," *post*, p. 622.

BISHOPS OF FERNS.

* * St. Edan, seated here in 598; *d.* 632.
632. St. Molin.
* * Dachuan, or Mochuan Luachra, abbot; *d.* 652.
* * Tuenoch MacFintan, abbot; *d.* 662.
* * Coman, *d.* 675.
* * Mœdogair, *d.* 676.
* * Diratus, *d.* 692.
* * Cillenius, *d.* 714.
* * Arectacius MacCuanach, abbot; *d.* 737.
* * MacColgan, abbot; *d.* 744.
* * Reodaigh, abbot; *d.* 758.
* * Dubenracht MacFergus, abbot; *d.* 776.
* * Finnachta, *d.* 794.
* * Killene, *d.* 814.

There is a chasm of a hundred years, in which no mention is to be found either of bishop or abbot of Ferns. This is probably owing to the ravages of the Danes, who spread destruction on every side. In 834 Ferns was burnt by them.

* * Laidgnen, *d.* 937.
* * Flathguss, abbot; *d.* 944.
* * Finnacht MacLactan, *d.* 956.
* * Carbre O'Laigdnen, abbot; *d.* 965.
* * Conan MacCathan, abbot; *d.* 975.
* * Constans O'Laigdnen, abbot; *d.* 996.
* * Cornelius O'Laigdnen, *d.* 1042.
* * Dermod O'Rudican, *d.* 1048.
* * Marchad O'Laigdnen, *d.* 1062.
* * Flan O'Corboy.
* * Fogdath O'Haurecan.
* * Nelan MacDonegan.
* * Ugair O'Laigdnen, *d.* 1085.
* * Carbrick O'Kerny, *d.* 1095.
* * Gelasy, or Kellach O'Colman, *d.* 1117.
* * Carthag O'Malgebry.
* * Mœlisa O'Cathlan.
* * Roderick, or Rory O'Traffy.
* * Brigdin O'Cathlan.
1155. Jos. O'Hethe.
1186. Albin O'Mulloy, abbot of Baltinglass.
1223. John St. John.
1243. Jeffrey St. John.
1258. Hugh Lamport.
1282. Richd. de Northampton, canon of Killaloe.
1304. Simon de Evesham.
1305. Robt. Walrand.
1312. Adam de Northampton.
1347. Hugh de Saltu, depr. by the pope.
Geoff. Grosseld.
1349. John Esmond, depr. by the pope.
1350. Wm. Charnels.
1363. Thos. Den, archdn. of Ferns.
1400. Patr. Barret.
1416. Robt. Whittey, or Whitby.
1459. John Purcell I.
1480. Laurence Nevill.

See vacant nearly 2 years.

1505. Edmd. Comerford, dean of Kilkenny.
1509. Nichs. Comyn, tr. to Waterford.
1519. John Purcell II.
1539. Alexr. Devereux.
1566. John Devereux, dean of Ferns.
1582. Hugh Allen, preb. of Sarum; the first Protestant bishop.

See united to Leighlin, 1600.

See "Bishops of Ferns and Leighlin," *post*, p. 622.

BISHOPS OF LEIGHLIN.

628. St. Laserian.

* * * *

865. Manchin.

* * * *

943. Condla MacDunecan.
969. Daniel.

* * * *

1048. Cleirec O'Muinic.

* * * *

1113. Condla O'Flain.
1144. Sluagad O'Catan.
1152. Dungall O'Cellaic.
1158. Donat, *d.* 1185.

See vacant some years.

1199. John, abbot of Rosea Valle.
1201. Harlewin, or Herlewin.
1217. Richd. Fleming.
1227. William, archdn. of Leighlin.
1252. Thomas.
1277. Nichs. Chevers, archdn.
1309. Maurice of Blanchvill, canon.
1320. Miler le Poer.
1341. Wm. St. Leger.
1349. Thos. of Brakenberg.
1363 (? 1360). John Young, Leighlin.
1385. John Griffin, chanc. of Limerick; tr. to Ossory.

1399. Richd. Rocomb.
See vacant 2 years.
1422. John Mulgan, rector of Lin, in Meath.
1432. Thos. Fleming, canon of Kilkenny.
1458. Milo Roche.
1490. Nichs. Maguire.
1513. Thos. Halsay, the pope's prothonotary for Ireland; assisted at the Lateran Council in 1515 and 1516: never saw his bishopric.
See vacant 4 years.
1523. Maurice Doran, murd. by his archdn, Maurice Cavenagh.
1527. Matt. Sanders.
1550. Robt. Travers, depr. 1555.
1555. Thos. Field.
1567. Dan. Cavenagh.
See vacant 2 years.
1589. Richd. Meredyth, dean of St. Patrick's.
See vacant 3 years.
1600. Robt. Grave, dean of Cork.
On whose advancement to the see, it was united to Ferns.

See "Bishops of Ferns and Leighlin," *infra*.

BISHOPS OF FERNS AND LEIGHLIN.

1600. Robt. Grave, above-named.
Nichs. Stafford, chanc. of Ferns.
1605. Thos. Ram, dean of Ferns.
1635. Geo. Andrew, dean of Limerick; *d.* 1648.
See vacant 12 years.
1660. Robt. Price, dean of Connor.
1666. Richd. Boyle, dean of Limerick.
1683. Narcissus Marsh, provost of Dublin College; tr. to Cashel.
1691. Barth. Vigors, dean of Armagh.
1722. Josiah Hort, dean of Ardagh; tr. to Kilmore and Ardagh.
1727. John Hoadly, archdn. of Salisbury; tr. to Dublin.
1729. Arth. Price, tr. from Clonfert; tr. to Meath.
1734. Edwd. Synge, tr. from Cloyne; tr. to Elphin.
1740. Geo. Stone, dean of Derry; tr. to Kildare.
1743. Wm. Cotterell, dean of Raphoe.
1744. Robt. Downes, dean of Derry; tr. to Down and Connor.
1752. John Garnet, tr. to Clogher.
1758. Hon. Wm. Carmichael, tr. from Clonfert; tr. to Meath.
Thos. Salmon.
1759. Richd. Robinson, tr. to Kildare.
1761. Chas. Jackson, tr. to Kildare.
1765. Edwd. Young, tr. from Dromore.
1772. Hon. Jos. Deane Bourke, dean of Dromore; tr. to Tuam.
1782. Walter Cope, tr. from Clonfert and Kilmacduach.
1787. Wm. Preston, tr. from Killala and Achonry.
1789. Euseby Cleaver, tr. from Cork and Ross.
1809. Hon. Percy Jocelyn, tr. to Clogher.
1820. Lord Robt. Ponsonby Tottenham, tr. from Killaloe; tr. to Clogher.
1822. Thos. Elrington, tr. from Limerick; *d.* 1835.
See united to Ossory, 1835.

See "Bishops of Ossory, Ferns, and Leighlin," *infra*.

BISHOPS OF OSSORY, FERNS, AND LEIGHLIN.

1835. Robt. Fowler, bp. of Ossory, see *ante*, p. 621.
1842. Jas. Thos. O'Brien.
1875. Robt. Saml. Gregg, tr. to Cork.
1878. Wm. Pakenham Walsh, dean of Cashel, elect. Aug. 30.

DEANS OF OSSORY.

1210. S****.
1218–28. Odo, or Hugh.
1245–50. Hy. Pembroke.
12—. Robt. de Dunkit.
12—. John de Ballyganran.
1268–71. Wm. de Balreput.
1269. Roger de Wexford, bp. of Ossory, 1287.
1292 to 1312. John Lupus, or de Low.
1309 (?). Jacobus.
1319-24. Nichs. Fitzjohn.
1332. Adam de Trilleck, or Trillock (No. 1).
1333. John le Baron.
1347. Adam de Trilleck, or Trillock (No. 2).
1355. John.
1372. Thos. Waferton, or de Waverton.
1388. Michl. Delafield.
1413. John Stafford, Apr. 14.
1419. John Curk (Cusack?).
Between 1417 and 1426. Nichs. Hacket.
1436. Thos. Gellian.
1469. Thos. Archer.
1471. John Strang, or Strange.
1493. Edmd. Comerford, bp. of Ferns about 1505.
1505. Jas. Cleere.
15—. Wm. Comerford.
15—. Louis Dedder.

1547. Jas. Briton; *d.* 1552.
1552. Thos. Lancaster.
1559. Wm. Johnson.
1582. David Cleere.
1603. Richd. Deane, bp. of Ossory, 1610.
1610. John Todd.
1612. Barnabus Boulger, L. P., Oct. 24.
1617. Absalom Gethin, July 17.
1621. Jenkin Mayes, Dec. 8.
1626. Edwd. Warren, Dec. 19.
1661. Chas. Cullen, L. P., Apr. 15; res. same year.
Thos. Ledisham.
1666. Danl. Neyland, L. P., July 28.
1668. Jos. Teate, L. P., Feb. 20.
1671. Thos. Hill, L. P., Mar. 11; *d.* 1673.
1674. Benj. Parry, L. P., Feb. 19; bp. of Ossory, 1677.
1675. John Pooley, L. P., Mar. 6; bp. Raphoe, 1702.
1703. Robt. Mossom, L. P., Feb. 25; *d.* 1747.
1747. Robt. Watts, L. P., May 14.
1755. John Lewis, L. P., Mar. 20.
1784. Hon. Jos. Bourke, Aug. 29; *d.* 1843.
1843. Chas. Vignoles, L. P., June 10.
1877. Thos. Hare.

DEANS OF FERNS.

1262. Name not mentioned.
1311. Nichs. de Sandford.
1325. Dionysius, or Denis.
1331. Nichs. Moncell.
1345. Geoffry Whitley.
1347. Robert.
1366–76. Wm. St. John.
1401. Thos. Nevylle.
1453. Thos. Petyt.
14—. Wm. Dirle, or Dule.
14—. Hy. Roche.
1531. Thos. Pursell.
1537. Thos. Hay, L. P., Feb. 15; *d.* 1558.
1558. John Garvie, or Garvey.
1559. John Devereux.
1569. Walter Turner, L. P., Jan. 11.
1590. Wm. Campyon, or Champion, L. P., Oct. 9.
1592. Walter Turner, Jan. 18; see 1569.
1601. Thos. Ram.
1610. John Thoms.
1626. Thos. Ram, jun., L. P., Feb. 11.
1629. Robt. Wilson, L. P., Feb. 19.
1643. Anthy. Procter, L. P., Mar. 11.
1662. John Watson, L. P., Mar. 27.
1666. John Creighton, Oct. 26; *d.* 1670.
1670. Benj. Phipps, L. P., May 23.
1671. Robt. Osborne, L. P., Apr. 11 (?).
1682. Tobias Pullen, L. P., Apr. 25; bp of Cloyne, 1694.
1694. Thos. Cox, L. P., Dec. 21.
1719. Wm. Cresse, L. P., Apr. 2.
1720. Arth. Price, L. P., Mar. 31.
1724. Pascal, or Paul Ducasse, L. P. May 5.
1728. Thos. Sawbridge, L. P., Jan. 28.
1733. Geo. Stone, L. P., Aug. 22; aft dean of Derry, &c.
1734. Jos. Story, L. P., Mar. 14.
1740. Robt. Watts, L. P., Mar. 6.
1747. John Alcock, L. P., June 15; *d* 1769.
1769. Richd. Marlay, inst. Dec. 26; bp. of Clonfert, 1787.
1787. Hon. Thos. Stopford, Nov. 21; bp. of Cork and Ross, 1794.
1794. Peter Browne, L. P., Dec. 6; *d.* 1842.
1842. Hy. Newland, inst. Jan. 19, 1843.
1862. Hamilton Verschoyle, L. P., Apr. 4; res. same year.
Wm. Atkins, L. P., Nov. 21.
1879. John Robt. Dowse.

DEANS OF LEIGHLIN.

11—. M.
1199 to 1201. Robert.
1298 to 1312. John Chevars.
1346. Wm. Cryspyn.
1401. John Heygarth (? Heygate).
1432. Nichs. Cloal.
1494. David Corrin, Curwen, Curran, or Curwin,
1506. Cornelius O'Curran.
1521. Cornelius.
1541–63. Dermit Cavanagh, or Kevenagh.
1580. Roger Hooker.
1591. Walter Harpoll (? Hartpoole).
1597. Walter Hatfield, L. P., Nov. 16.
1—. Moses Powell; *d.* 1603.
1604. Thos. Tedder, Feb. 22; *d.* 1614.
1614. Ralph Barlow.
1618. John Parker, L. P., July 6.
1637. Hugh Cressy, inst. Aug. 11.
1666. John Nearne, Mar. 15; res. 1668.
1668. Geo. Burdett, L. P., Feb. 3; *d.* 1671.
1672. Saml. Burgess, L. P., Jan. 1.
1692. Noah Webb, L. P., Aug. 12.
1696. John Francis, L. P., Aug. 12.
1723. Wm. Crosse, L. P., July 19.
1749. Barth. Vigors, L. P., Dec. 26.
1755. John Fetherston, May 26; *d.* 1764.
1765. Chas. Doyne, L. P., Jan. 21; *d.* 1777.
1777. Richd. Stewart, July 25; *d.* 1778.

1778. Stewart Blacker, Apr. 25; res. 1804.
1804. Geo. Maunsell, Oct. 6; res. 1822.
1822. Hon. Richd. Boyle Bernard, L. P., Aug. 22.
1850. Hugh Usher Tighe, L. P., Apr. 22; res. 1854.
1854. Jas. Lyster, L. P., Nov. 14.
1864. Wm. Bernard Lauder, L. P., July 11; *d.* 1868.
1868. Fras. Metcalf Watson, L. P., Apr. 15; *d.* 1876.
1877. Wm. Smyth King.

DIOCESES OF CASHEL, EMLY, WATERFORD, AND LISMORE.

CORMAC, king and bishop of CASHEL, is reputed to have been the founder or the restorer of the cathedral of Cashel, and we have few traces of the bishops before his time. Cashel became archiepiscopal in 1152, but under 3 & 4 Wm. IV., cap. 37, was reduced to a bishopric on the death of Archbishop Laurence in 1839.

EMLY is a very ancient see, and is supposed to have been founded by St. Patrick. The place is mentioned by some of the old historians as a large and flourishing city, but it is now a poor and inconsiderable village. The cathedral is dedicated to St. Ailbe, who is named as the first bishop, and who died September 12, 527.

THE cathedral of WATERFORD, dedicated to the Blessed Trinity was first built by the Ostmen, and by Malchus, the first bishop, after his return from England from his consecration, about 1096.

LISMORE was founded by St. Carthage about 636, and Cormac, the son of Muretus, king of Munster, repaired it before 1130.

There was a see at Ardmore, founded by St. Declan, in the infancy of the Irish Church, but it was united to Lismore, soon after the arrival of the English.

EMLY was united to CASHEL in 1568, and LISMORE was united to WATERFORD in 1358 or 1363. On the death of Bishop Bourke in 1832 CASHEL, EMLY, WATERFORD, and LISMORE were united under 3 & 4 Wm. IV., cap. 37.

BISHOPS OF CASHEL.

901. Cormac MacCulinan, *d.* 908.
* * Donald O'Hene, *d.* 1098.
1118. Miler, or Melmurray O'Dunan.
1131. Mœlisa O'Foglada.
1137. Donat O'Conaing.

ARCHBISHOPS OF CASHEL.

* * Donat O'Lonergan I., seated here before 1152; as in that year he was invested with the *pallium* by cardl. Paparo, the pope's legate.
1158. Donald O'Hullucan.
1182. Maurice.
1192. Matthew O'Heney.
1206. Donat O'Lonergan II.
1216. Donat O'Lonergan III.; res.
1224. Marian O'Brien, tr. from Cork.
1238. David MacKelly, tr. from Cloyne.
1253. David MacCarwill, dean of Cashel.
1291. Steph. O'Brogan, archdn. of Glendalough.
1303. Maurice MacCarwill, archdn.
1317. Wm. Fitz-John, tr. from Ossory.

The pope, at the king's request, made void two elections made by two parties in the chapter and chose this prelate.
327. John O'Carrol, dean of Cork.
330. Walter le Rede, tr. from Cork.
332. John O'Grada, friar of Cashel.
345. Ralph Kelly.
* Geo. Roche, *d.* 1362.
See vacant some years.
365. Thos. O'Carrol, tr. from Tuam.
374. Philip de Torrington, Franciscan friar.
See vacant 4 years.
1384. Peter Hacket, archdn.
1406. Richd. O'Hedian, archdn.
See vacant 10 years.
1450. John Cantwell.
1483. David Creagh.
1504. Maurice Fitzgerald.
1527. Edmd. Butler, *d.* 1550.
See vacant 3 years.
1553. Roland Baron.
See vacant 6 years.
1567. Jas. MacCoghwell, the first protestant abp.
See united to Emly 1568.

See "Archbishops of Cashel and Bishops of Emly," *post*, p. 626.

BISHOPS OF EMLY.

448. St. Ailbe, *d.* 527.
* Conaing O'Daithil, *d.* 660.
* Conamail MacCartiag, *d.* 707.
* Cellach, *d.* 718.
* Senchai, *d.* 778.
* Cuan, *d.* 784.
* Sectabrat, *d.* 819.
* Flan MacFlamchellaic, *d.* 825.
* Olchobar MacKinede, king of Cashel, *d.* 850.
* Maneus Hac Huargusa, *d.* 857.
* Cænfelad, king of Cashel, *d.* 872.
* Rudgall MacFingail, *d.* 882.
* Concen Mathair, *d.* 887.
* Owen MacCenfeolad, *d.* 889.
* Mœlbrigid. *d.* 895.
* Miscelus, *d.* 898.
* Flan MacConail, *d.* 903.
* Tibraid MacMælfin, *d.* 912.
* Edchada MacScanlain, *d.* 941.
* Huarach, *d.* 953.
* Mel Killach, *d.* 957.
* Feolan MacCellaid, *d.* 981.
* Cenfada, *d.* 990.
* Columb MacLagenan, *d.* 1003.
* Cormac O'Fin, *d.* 1020.
* Serbrethæ, *d.* 1027.
* Mælfinan, *d.* 1040.
* O'Flanchua, *d.* 1047.
* Clothna Muimnech, *d.* 1049.
* Mœlmorda, *d.* 1075.
* Mœlisa O'Harachtain, *d.* 1093.
* O'Ligbai, *d.* 1122.
* Mœlmorda MacInclodnai.
* Deicola.
163. Mœlisa O'Lagenan.
172. O'Meiciti, or O'Meleic.
177. Chas. O'Buacalla, abb. of Mellifont.
197. Regd. O'Flanua.
No certainty of his successor.
212. Henry.
228. John Collingham.
1236. Christian.
1251. Gilbert O'Doverty, dean.
1266. Florence of Emly, canon.
1272. Matt. MacGorman, archdn.
1275. David O'Cuffy, or O'Cassy, abbot of Holy Cross, Tipperary.
1282. Wm. de Clifford.
1306. Thos. Cantock, canon.
1309. Wm. Roghened, dean.
1335. Richd. de Walleys.
1356. John Esmond, archdn. of Ferns.
1363. William, archdn.
1422. Nicholas.
John Rishberry, delayed to expedite his letters of provision.
Robt. Windell, app. by the pope; never consec.
Thos. Burgh, delayed to expedite his letters of provision.
Robt. Portland, never consec.
These four were named by the pope, and the disputes which arose were the cause of the episcopal revenues being for a long time returned into the king's exchequer.
1431. Thomas.
Robert, of England, app. by the pope on Thomas's death; but he was either rejected, or app. bp. of Tiberias in Galilee.
1444. Cornelius O'Cunlis, tr. to Clonfert.
1448. Cornelius O'Mulledy, tr. from Clonfert.
See vacant 10 years.
1459. Wm. O'Hedian.
* * Philip, *d.* 1494.
1498. Chas. MacBrien, canon.
* * Thos. Hurley, *d.* 1542.
1543. Æneas O'Heffernan.
1554. Raymund de Burgh, *d.* 1562.
See united to Cashel 1568.

See "Archbishops of Cashel, and Bishops of Emly," *post*, p. 626.

ARCHBISHOPS OF CASHEL AND BISHOPS OF EMLY.

1568. Jas. MacCaghwell, abp. of Cashel; see Cashel, *ante*, p. 624.
1571. Miler Magragh; who, becoming a Protestant, was, by Q. Elizabeth, promoted to this see; *d.* 1622, aged 100 years.
1623. Malcolm Hamilton, chanc. of Down.
1640. Archd. Hamilton, tr. from Killala and Achonry; *d.* 1569.
1661. Thos. Fulwar, tr. from Ardfert.
1667. Thos. Price, tr. from Kildare 1684.
The see vacant until
1691. Narcissus Marsh, tr. from Ferns and Leighlin; tr. to Dublin.
1694. Wm. Palliser, tr. from Cloyne.
1726. Wm. Nicholson, tr. from Derry.
1727. Timothy Godwin, tr. from Kilmore and Ardagh.
1730. Theoph. Bolton, tr. from Elphin.
1744. Arth. Price, tr. from Meath.
1752. John Whitcombe, tr. from Down and Connor.
1754. Michl. Cox, tr. from Ossory.
1779. Chas. Agar, tr. from Cloyne; aft. visc. Somerton and E. of Normanton.
1801. Hon. Chas. Brodrick, tr. from Kilmore.
1822. Richd. Lawrence, reg. prof. of Hebrew, Oxford.

See united to Waterford and Lismore, 1833.

See "Archbishops of Cashel, and Bishops of Emly, Waterford, and Lismore," *post*, p. 627.

BISHOPS OF WATERFORD.

1096. Malchus.
* * Melisa O'Hamire, *d.* 1136.
* * Tuistius, or Tostius, seated here in 1152.
1175. Augustine.
* * Robt. I., seated here in 1200.
1204. David.
1210. Robt. II.
1223. Wm. Wace, dean.
1227. Walter I.
* * Steph. I., seated here in 1238.
1249. Henry, archdn.
1252. Philip, dean.
1255. Walter II.
1273. Steph. de Fulburn II.
1286. Walter de Fulburn III., dean.
1307. Matthew.
1323. Nichs. Welifed, dean.
1338. Richd. Francis.
1349. Robt. Elyot, dep. 1350.
1350. Roger Cradock, tr. to Llandaff.

See united to Lismore 1363.

See "Bishops of Waterford and Lismore," *infra.*

BISHOPS OF LISMORE.

* * St. Carthage, promoted about 631–6; *d.* 637.
* * Hierologus, *d.* 698.
* * Colman, or Mocholmoc, son of Finbar, *d.* 702.
* * St. Cronan, *d.* 717.
* * Colman O'Liathan, *d.* 725.
* * Macoge, *d.* 746.
* * Ronan, *d.* 763.
* * CormacMac Culenan, bp. of Lismore, and prince of Decies, in Munster; *d.* 903.
* * O'Mail Sluaig, *d.* 1025.
* * Moriertach O'Selbaic, *d.* 1034.
* * MacAirthir, *d.* 1064.
* * Mal-Duin O'Rebacain, *d.* 1191.
* * Mac-Mic-Oeducan, *d.* 1113.
* * Gilla-Mocuda O'Rebacain, *d.* 1129.
* * Malchus, seated here in 1134.
1150. Christian O'Conarchy, res. 1175.
* * Felix, *d.* before 1200.
* * O'Heda, *d.* 1206.
An uncertain blank here, impossible to fill up.
1218. Robt. of Bedford.
1223. Griffin Christopher, chanc. of Lismore.
1248. Alan O'Sullivan, tr. from Cloyne.
1253. Thos., treasr. of Lismore.
1270. John Roche, chanter of Lismore.
1279. Richd. Corr, chanc. of Lismore.
1309. Wm. le Fleming, archdn. of Lismore
1324. John Leynagh.
1358. Thos. le Reve.

See united to Waterford 1363.

See "Bishops of Waterford and Lismore," *infra.*

BISHOPS OF WATERFORD AND LISMORE.

1363. Thos. le Reve, bp. of Lismore, abovenamed.
1394. Robt. de Reade, tr. to Chichester.
1396. Thos. Sparkford.
1397. John Deping.
1399. Thos. Snell, archdn. of Glendalough tr. to Ossory.
1405. Roger.

1409. John Gese.
1426. Richd., archdn. of Lismore.
1446. Robt. Poer, dean of Limerick.
1472. Richd. Martin.
1475. John Bolcomp.
1480. Nichs. O'Henisy.
1482. John.
1486. Thos. Pursell.
* * Nichs. Comin, tr. from Ferns; res. 1519.
1551. Patr. Walsh, dean of Waterford.
1579. Marm. Middleton, tr. to St. David's.
1582. Miler Magragh, res. 1589; again succ. 1592; and again res. 1607.
1589. Thos. Wetherhead.
1592. Miler Magragh, *again*.
1607. John Lancaster.
1619. Michl. Boyle, dean of Lismore.
1636. John Atherton, chanc. of Christ-Church.
1641. Archd. Adair, tr. from Killala and Achonry; *d.* 1647.
The see remained vacant till the Restoration.
1661. Geo. Baker.
1666. Hugh Gore, dean of Lismore.
1691. Nath. Foy, minister of St. Bridget's, Dublin.
1708. Thos. Milles.
1740. Chas. Este, tr. from Ossory.
1745. Richd. Chenevix, tr. from Killaloe.
1779. Wm. Newcombe, tr. from Ossory.
1795. Richd. Marlay, tr. from Clonfert.
1802. Hon. Power Trench, tr. to Elphin.
1810. Jos. Stock, tr. from Killala.
1813. Hon. Richd. Bourke, dean of Ardagh; *d.* Nov. 15, 1832.

Sees united to Cashel and Emly 1833.

See "Archbishops of Cashel, and Bishops of Emly, Waterford, and Lismore," *infra*.

ARCHBISHOPS OF CASHEL AND BISHOPS OF EMLY, WATERORD, AND LISMORE.

1833. Richd. Lawrence, abp. of Cashel, and bp. of Emly, above-named; *d.* 1839.

On his death Cashel was reduced to a bishopric.

See "Bishops of Cashel, Emly, Waterford, and Lismore," *infra*.

BISHOPS OF CASHEL, EMLY, WATERFORD, AND LISMORE.

1839. Stephen C. Sandes, tr. from Killaloe, &c.
1843. Robt. Dayaly.
1872. Maurice Fitzgerald Day, Mar. 19.

DEANS OF CASHEL.

Between 1224 and 1238. Thomas.
Before 1238. David MacKelly was dean; bp. Cloyne, 12—; abp. of Cashel, 1238; *d.* Mar. 2, 1253.
Before 1253. David MacCarwill, abp. of Cashel, 1253; *d.* 1269.
1254. Thaddæus O'Brien.
1260. Keran, or Kyran.
1267. Roland.
1269. David.
1282 and 1289. Antonius.
1302–6. Philip Broder.
1346. Richd. Fitzjohn.
1402–12. Richd. Barry.
1429–37. David O'Dwyer.
1452. Cornelius.
1467–85. John Hodian, or Hedian.

* * * *

1616. John Todd, bp. of Down, &c., 1606.
1608. Lewis Jones, June 16; bp. of Killaloe, 1633; *d.* aged 104.
1633. Wm. Chappell, inst. Aug. 20; bp. of Cork, 1638.
1639. Richd. Howlett, inst. Mar. 9.
1661. Essex Digby, inst. Feb. 27; bp. of Dromore, 1670.
1671. Cæsar Williamson, inst. Aug. 9; *d.* May 1676.
1676. John Glandie, inst. July 4; *d.* Jan. 22, 1694.
1694. Hy. Price, inst. Mar. 17; *d.* 1706.
1706. Wm. Mullart, or Maillart, inst. Apr. 4, 1707; *d.* May 8, 1713.
1714. John Wetherby, inst. May 7; *d.* 1736.
1736. Wm. Gore, inst. Nov. 2; bp. of Clonfert, 1758.
1758. Thos. Paul, inst. June 5; res. 1769.
1769. John Jebb, L. P., June 22; *d.* 1787.
1787. Jos. Palmer, inst. June 22; *d.* May 1, 1829.
1829. Saml. Adams, inst. Aug. 29.
1856. Ogle Wm. Moore, L. P., Feb. 25; res. 1861.
1862. John Cotter MacDonnell, L. P., Feb. 24.
1873. Wm. Pakenham Walsh.
1878. Arth. Hy. Leech.

DEANS OF EMLY.

1219. D*****.
1221 and 1227. P*****.
1240. W****.
1245. Gilbert O'Doherty; elect. bp. 1251.
1295. Philip.
1305. Wm. Roghened, or Roughhead, bp. of Emly, 1309.
1542. Donogh Ryan, Aug. 24.
1602. Donat Hogan; *d.* same year.
Hugh Hogan.
Before 1615. Kennedy O'Brian.
1615. John Darling.
1621. Edwd. Warren, Nov. 12.
Andr. O'Donellan.
1627. John Crayford, inst. May 21.
1640. Wm. Burleigh, Apr. 24.
1666. Tempest Illingworth, L.P. Sept. 19.
1669. Geo. Mundy, L. P. Feb. 27.
1675. Robt. Ewing, L. P. Sept. 4; *d.* 1685.
1685. Ulysses Burgh, L. P. May 9; bp. of Ardagh, 1692.
1693. Thos. Smythe, L. P., inst. Apr. 12; bp. of Limerick, &c., 1695.
1697. Richd. Reader, inst. July 2.
1701. Enoch Reader, L. P. July 10; *d.* 1709.
1710. John Wetherby, inst. June 29; res. 1713.
1714. Wm. Perceval, inst. Aug. 28; *d.* 1735.
1735. Jas. Auchmuty, L. P. July 10; res. 1736.
1736. John Brandreth, inst. Oct. 15.
1765. John Averell, inst. Apr. 19; bp. of Limerick, &c., 1771.
1766. Jas. Hawkins, July 17; bp. of Dromore, 1775.
1775. Wm. Evelyn, inst. Sept. 7; *d.* 1776.
1776. Richd. Moore, L. P. June 9; *d.* June 1818.
1818. Hy. Vesey Fitzgerald, inst. July 11; res. 1826.
1826. Thos. Philip Lefanu, inst. Apr. 21; *d.* June 24, 1845.
1845. Brabazon Wm. Disney, inst. Oct. 11.
1852. Denis Browne, L. P. Apr. 28.
1864. Wm. Alexander, L. P. Aug. 24; bp. of Derry and Raphoe, 1867.

Chapter united to Cashel by Statute of the General Synod for 1872.

DEANS OF WATERFORD.

1223. Wm. Wace, dean; bp. this year.
1252. Philip, ditto.
1284. Walter de Fulburn; bp. 1286.
1308. David le Waleys.
1312. David (? the same).
1323. Nichs. Welifed, dean; bp. this year.
1365. Walter le Reve.
1372. Lucas de Londres.
1379. John Reder.
1395. Walter de Ludlow.
1396. Wm. Whyte.
1481. Robt. Bron, or Brown.
1484. John Collyne.
1522. Robt. Lombard; *d.* 1547.
1547. Patr. Walsh; bp. 1551.
1566. Peter White.
1570. David Cleeve, Aug. 9.
1615. Richd. Boyle, bp. of Cork, Cloyne, and Ross, 1620; abp. of Tuam, 1638.
1621. Hy. Sutton, L. P. Nov. 17.
1623. Anthy. Martin, May 18; bp. of Meath, 1625.
1625. Richd. Jones, Mar. 26.
1634. Thos. Gray, May 31.
1635. Jas. Margetson, May 25; abp. of Dublin, 1661; abp. of Armagh, 1663.
1638. Edwd. Parry, inst. Mar. 20.
1640. Gervase Thorpe, L. P. Apr. 28; inst. July 29.
1662. Thos. Potter, L. P. Feb. 6.
1666. Thos. Ledisham, L. P. June 29.
1671. Danl. Burston, L. P. June 9.
1678. Arth. Stanhope. L. P. Jan. 20.
1685. Thos. Wallis, L. P. Nov. 27.
1692. John Dalton, L. P. Feb. 14.
1697. John Eeles, L. P. Apr. 6.
1723. Hugh Bolton, L. P. Jan. 17; *d.* Dec. 1758.
1759. Cutts Harman; presented Mar. 7.
1784. Christr. Butson, Apr. 2; bp. of Clonfert, &c., 1804.
1804. Hon. Wm. Montgomery Cole, inst. Aug. 11; *d.* same year.
Ussher Lee, dean of Kilmacduagh; inst. Dec. 22.
1850. Thos. Stewart Townshend, L. P. Aug. 21; bp. of Meath same year.
Edwd. Newenham Hoare, L. P. Nov. 26; *d.* 1877.
1877. John Morgan.

DEANS OF LISMORE.

1260. Thos. de Wodeford.
1281. Philip.
* * Roger Russell.
1320. Walter le Fleming.
1346. Michl. le Fleming.
1403. Wm. Walshe, Mar. 3.

1421. Philip Wyott.
1548. Edwd. Power.
1551-2. Denis Morris.
15—. Peter Lewis, res. 1564.
1564. Gerald FitzJames Fitzgerald, June 17.
1583. John Prendergast, L. P. Sept. 12.
1610. Thos. Wilson, L. P. Feb. 15; res. 1614.
1614. Michl. Boyle, L. P. Dec. 6; also bp. of Waterford, &c., 1619.
1622. Edwd. Brouncker, L. P. Apr. 30.
Robt. Daborne, L. P. June 14; *d.* Mar. 1628.
1628. John Grey, Apr. 3.
1630. Robt. Naylor, inst. Mar. 24; res. Mar. 1640.
1640. Edwd. Parry, inst. May 11; bp. of Killaloe, 1647.
1647. Robt. Parry, L. P. May 7.
1661, Richd. Underwood, L. P. Feb. 5; *d.* 1664.
1664. Hugh Gore, inst. Apr. 7; bp. 1666.
1666. Richd. Lingard, L. P. Mar. 2; *d.* 1670.
1670. Michl. Ward, L. P. Nov. 29; bp. of Ossory, 1678.
1678. Edwd. Jones, L. P. Nov. 16; bp. of Cloyne, 1682.
1683. Barzillai Jones, adm. Nov. 5.
1692. Wm. Jephson, L. P. Jan. 6; *d.* Apr. 11, 1720.
1719. Arthur Price (?).
1720. Wm. Crosse, L. P. May 28.
1723. John Francis, L. P. Aug. 2; *d.* 1724.
1724. Wm. Burscough (?)
1725. Alexr. Alcock, L. P. July 22.
1747. Washington Cotes, L. P. Dec. 26; *d.* 1762.
1762. John Ryder, L. P. May 22; *d.* Apr. 18, 1791.
1791. John Whetham, inst. Sept. 14; *d.* May 1, 1796.
1796. John Scott, L. P. June 11; *d.* 1828.
1828. John Bayley, inst. July 12; *d.* June 1831.
1831. Sir Geo. Bisshopp, inst. July 30; *d.* 1834.
1834. Hy. Cotton, Dec. 16.
1850. Hy. Montagu Browne.
1884. Hy. Brougham.

DIOCESES OF CORK, CLOYNE, AND ROSS.

THERE is little to be found in ancient writers concerning the foundation of the cathedral of CORK, but it is generally ascribed to St. Barr or Finbarr, in the seventh century. Through length of time the church became quite ruinous, but some years ago it was completely rebuilt, and is now a handsome structure.

ROSS was, most likely, founded by St. Fachnan, who flourished in the beginning of the sixth century, and "who lived in a monastery of his own erection." He was called Fachnan Mongach, or the "Hairy," having been born with hair; and was abbot of a monastery in th island of Molanfid, near the town of Youghal, formerly called Dar-Inis. There a city grew up, in which was a large seminary for scholars, called Ross-Ailithri. When the cathedral was founded, or who was the first bishop of it, it is impossible to ascertain. It seems probable, however, that Fachnan was the first bishop. There are no records of this see until after the arrival of the English.

CLOYNE was founded in the sixth century by St. Colman, the son of Linin, who was himself the first bishop of it. Who his immediate successors in the see were, it is difficult, if not impossible, to ascertain; nor can anything be said, with certainty, of the bishops, until after the arrival of the English.

CORK and CLOYNE were united by Pope Martin V. about 1430. ROSS was added in 1583, and the bishops were styled "CORK, CLOYNE, and ROSS" as at present. In 1638 a separate bishop was appointed to Cloyne; but after the Restoration the three sees were again united, and so continued until 1678, when CLOYNE once more had a separate bishop, CORK and ROSS still remaining united.

On the death of bishop Brinkley in 1835, CORK, CLOYNE, and ROSS were united under 3 & 4 Wm. IV., cap. 37.

BISHOPS OF CORK.

* * St. Barr, or Finbarr; seated here in 630.
Of his immediate successors there are very imperfect accounts until the arrival of the English.
* * St. Nessan.
* * Russin, *d.* 685.
773. Selbaic.
961. Cathmogan.
990. Colum MacCiarucain.
* * Cellach O'Selbaic, *d.* 1026.
* * Neil O'Maildaib, *d.* 1027.
1028. Airtri Sairt.
* * Cathal, *d.* 1034.
1057. Mugron O'Mutan.
1086. Clerech O'Selbaic.
1107. Macloth d O'Hailgenen.
1111. Patr. O'Selbaic.
The see of Cork was vacant about 1140, and then "a certain poor man" was nom., but his name is not mentioned.
* * Gilla Æda O'Mugin, *d.* 1172.
* * Gregory, *d.* 1186.
* * Reginald.
* * — O'Selbaic, *d.* 1205.
* * Geoff. White.
* * Marian O'Brien, tr. to Cashel, 1224.
1225. Gilbert, archdn. of Cork.
* * Laurence, *d.* 1264.
1266. William of Jerepont.
1267. Reginald, treasr. of Cashel.
1277. Robt. Macdonogh.
1302. John MacCarvill, or O'Carrol, dean; tr. to Meath.
1321. Philip of Slane.
1326. John le Blonde, dean of Cloyne (never consec.)
1327. Walter le Rede, canon; tr. to Cashel.
1329. John de Baliconingham. He was made bp. of Down by the king, but his election was not confirmed by the pope.
1347. John Roche, dean.
1359. Gerald de Barry, dean.
1396. Roger Ellesmere.
1406. Gerald.
* * Patr. Raggad, tr. to Ossory, 1417.
1418. Milo FitzJohn, dean.
See united to Cloyne, 1430.

See "Bishops of Cork and Cloyne," *post*, p. 631.

BISHOPS OF CLOYNE.

* * St. Colman, *d.* 604.
* * * *
* * O'Malvain, *d.* 1094.
* * Nehemiah Moriertach, *d.* 1149.
* * O'Dubery, *d.* 1159.
* * O'Flanagan, *d.* 1167.
* * Matthew, *d.* 1192.
* * Laurence O'Sullivan, *d.* 1204.
* * Daniel, *d.* 1222.
1224. Florence.
1226. Patrick.
* * David MacKelly, tr. to Cashel, 1238.
1240. Alan O'Sullivan, tr. to Lismore.
1249. Daniel.
1265. Reginald, tr. from Down.
1274. Alan O'Lonergan.
1284. Nichs. de Effingham.
1320. Maurice O'Solehan, archdn.
1335. John de Cumba.
* * John Bird, or Brid, abbot of Louth, Lincolnshire.
1351. John Whittock, dean.
1363. John de Swaffham.
1376. Richd. Wye; depr.
1394. Gerald Canton.
* * Adam Pay, or Pye, seated here in 1421.
1431. Jordan, chanc. of Limerick.
Cloyne was now united to Cork (see *Cork and Cloyne*, and *Cork, Cloyne, and Ross*, *post*, p. 631), and continued so for nearly 200 years, until the appointment of
1638. Geo. Synge, *d.* 1653.
From the death of bp. Geo. Synge, the see continued vacant until the restoration of Chas. II., when it was again united to Cork and Ross under bps. Boyle and Edwd. Synge. See *Cork, Cloyne, and Ross*, *post*, p. 631. On the death of bp. Edwd. Synge, in 1678, Cloyne again had a separate bishop.
1679. Patrk. Sheridan, dean of Connor.
1682. Edwd. Jones, dean of Lismore; tr. to St. Asaph.
1692. Wm. Palliser, tr. to Cashel.
1694. Tobias Pullen, dean of Ferns; tr. to Dromore.

95. St. Geo. Ash, tr. to Clogher.
97. John Pooley, dean of Ossory, tr. to Raphoe.
02. Chas. Crow, provost of Tuam.
26. Hy. Maule, dean; tr. to Dromore.
32. Edwd. Synge, tr. from Clonfert; tr. to Ferns and Leighlin.
34. Geo. Berkeley, dean of Derry.
53. Jas. Stopford.
59. Robt. Johnson.
67. Hon. Fredk. Hervey, tr. to Derry.
68. Chas. Agar, dean of Kilmore; aft. visc. Somerton and E. of Normanton; tr. to Cashel.
1780. Geo. Chinnery, tr. from Killaloe.
1781. Richd. Woodward, dean of Clogher.
1794. Wm. Bennett, tr. from Cork and Ross.
1820. Chas. Mongan Warburton, tr. from Limerick.
1826. John Brinkley, archdn. of Clogher and royal astronomer of Ireland.

See again united to Cork and Ross 1835.

See "Bishops of Cork, Cloyne, and Ross," *post*, p. 632.

BISHOPS OF CORK AND CLOYNE.

Upon the death of Milo FitzJohn in 1430, the see of Cork was for a time committed Nicholas, bp. of Ardfert, and Richd. Scurlog, archdn. of Cork; but before the close of 30, Jordan, chanc. of Limerick, was advanced by Pope Martin V. to the bishoprics Cork and Cloyne, both vacant at one time, and then canonically united.

31. Jordan, chanc. of Limerick.
* Gerald FitzRichard, *d.* 1479.
79 Wm. Roche, res.
90. Thady MacCarthy.
* Gerald, res. 1499
99 John FitzEdmund.
* John Bennet, *d.* 1536.
1536. Dominick Tirrey.
1557. Roger Skiddy, dean of Limerick.

See vacant 4 years.

1570. Richd. Dixon; depr.
1572. Matth. Sheyn.

Sees united to Ross, 1583.

See "Bishops of Cork, Cloyne, and Ross," *infra*.

BISHOPS OF ROSS.

* St. Fachnan.

* * * *

* St. Finchad.
* Benedict, seated here in 1172.
* Maurice, *d.* 1196.
97. Daniel.
* Florence, *d.* 1222.
* Robert, seated here in 1225.
* Florence, or Finin O'Cloghena; res. 1252.
53. Maurice, chanter of Cloyne.
69. Walter O'Micthian.
75. Peter O'Hullucan.
90. Laurence, canon.
10. Matth. O'Fin.
31. Laurence O'Hullucan.
36. Dennis.
1378. Bernard O'Connor.
1402. Steph. Brown.
Matthew. *d.* 1418.
1418. Walter Formay.
1426. Cornelius MacElchade.
* * Thady, seated here in 1488.
1489. Odo.
1494. Edmd. Courcey.
1519. John Imurily, or Smurily, abbot of Maur.
* * Bonaventure, a Spaniard; was alive in 1523.
1544. Dermod MacDomnuil.
1563. Thos. O'Herlihy, res. 1570.
1582. Wm. Lyon.

See united to Cork and Cloyne, 1583.

See "Bishops of Cork, Cloyne, and Ross," *infra*.

BISHOPS OF CORK, CLOYNE, AND ROSS.

83. Wm. Lyon, bp. of Ross, above-named.
18. John Boyle.
20. Richd. Boyle, dean of Waterford; tr. to Tuam.
38. Wm. Chappel, provost of Dublin College; bp. of Cork and Ross only; *d.* 1649.

The see remained vacant until 1660.

1661. Michl. Boyle, dean of Cloyne; tr. to Dublin.
1663. Edwd. Synge, tr. from Limerick.

Cloyne *separated* 1678.

e "Bishops of Cloyne," *ante*, p. 630; and "Bishops of Cork and Ross," *post*, p. 632.

BISHOPS OF CORK AND ROSS.

1678. Edwd. Wetenhall, chanter of Christ Church; tr. to Kilmore and Ardagh.
1699. Dive Downs, archdn. of Dublin.
1710. Peter Brown, provost of Dublin College.
1735. Robt. Clayton, tr. from Killala; tr. to Clogher.
1745. Jemmet Brown, tr. from Killala; tr. to Elphin.
1772. Isaac Mann, archdn. of Dublin.
1789. Euseby Cleaver, rect. of Petworth, England; tr. to Ferns and Leighlin.
1789. Wm. Foster, chapl. to the house of commons; tr. to Kilmore.
1790. Wm. Bennett, chapl. to the E. of Westmoreland, ld.-lieut.; tr. to Cloyne.
1794. Hon. Thos. Stopford, dean of Ferns.
1806. Ld. John Geo. de la Poer Beresford, dean of Clogher; tr. to Raphoe.
1807. Hon. Thos. St. Lawrence, dean of Cork.
1831. Saml. Kyle, prov. of Trin. Coll., Dublin.

Sees again united to Cloyne, 1835.

See "Bishops of Cork, Cloyne, and Ross," *infra*.

BISHOPS OF CORK, CLOYNE, AND ROSS.

1835. Saml. Kyle, bp. of Cork and Ross, above-named.
1848. Jas. Wilson.
1857. Wm. FitzGerald.
1862. John Gregg.
1878. Robt. Saml. Gregg, tr. from Ossory, &c

DEANS OF CORK.

1288. Philip.
1302. Jno. MacCarvill, or O'Carrol, bp. same year.
1323–26. Dionysius.
1328–36. Philip Albus, or White.
1337. G——.
1347. Jno. de Rupe, or Roche, bp. 1347.
1348. Geraldinus, or Gerald de Barry, bp. 1359.
1370. Wm. Bull, bp. of Ardfert, &c., 1379.
13—. John Walsh.
1404. Milo Fitzjohn, bp. 1418.
15—. Thos. O'Heirnan, or O'Hiffernan.
1582. Thos. Long.
1590. Robt. Grave.
1600. Thos. Ram; also dean of Ferns; bp. of Ferns and Leighlin, 1605.
1605. Geo. Lay, or Lee, L. P. Dec. 9.
1628. John Fitzgerald, L. P. Jan. 31.
1642. Hy. Hall.
1645. Edwd. Worth, L. P. May 1.
1661. Thos. Hackrell, L. P. May 1.
1662. Roger Boyle, L. P. Oct. 9.
1667. John Vesey, inst. Nov. 4; bp. of Limerick, 1672.
1673. Arth. Pomeroy, L. P. Feb. 11.
1710. Rowland Davies, L. P. Feb. 17 *d.* 1721-2.
1722. Robt. Carleton, inst. Mar. 21; *d* 1736.
1736. Wm. Meade, L. P. May 3.
1763. Geo. Chinnery, inst. June 18; bp. o Killaloe, 1779.
1779. John Erskine, inst. Mar. 3; *d* 1795.
1796. Hon. Thos. St. Lawrence, Jan. 25 bp. 1807.
1807. John Leslie, inst. Oct. 24; bp. o Dromore, 1812.
1812. Jas. Saurin, inst. May 2.
1813. Wm. Magee, inst. July 24; bp. o Raphoe, 1819.
1819. Robt. Burrowes, Nov. 20; *d.* Sept 13, 1841.
1841. Jas. Thos. O'Brien, Nov. 9; bp. o Ossory, &c., same year.
1842. Horatio Townshend Newman, inst Mar. 24.
1864. Wm. Connor Magee, L. P. Feb. 5 bp. of Peterborough, 1869.
1869. Arth. Wm. Edwards, inst. Feb. 5.
1875. Achilles Daunt.
1878. Saml. Owen Madden.

DEANS OF CLOYNE.

1251. Gilbert.
1291. Philip Segda.
1317. Chas. O'Donchada, *d.* Oct. 13.
1320. John.
1324–30. John le Blonde.
1351 John Whittock, or Whitcock, bp. same year.
1359. John Went (? West).
1367. John Cantok, *d.* 1376.
1376. Thos. Striker.
1402. Eugenius.
1512. Thaddeus O'Keefe.
1529. David Fitzjames Fitzgerald.
1591. John Edmundi, or Fitzedmund

1612-3. Thos. Winter, *d.* 1615.
1615. Edwd. Clerke, Aug. 27.
1640. Michl. Boyle, Mar. 30, bp. of Cork, Cloyne, and Ross, 1661.
1661. Hy. Rugg, L. P. Feb. 21; *d.* 1671.
1671. Wm. Fitzgerald, L. P. July 13; bp. of Clonfert and Kilmacduagh, 1691.
1691. Hy. Scardeville, L. P. Sept. 4; *d.* 1704.
1704. Thos. Deane, L. P. Mar. 6.
1714. Robt. Sesse, L. P. Aug. 12; held but a few days.
Thos. Simcocks, Sept. 9.
1718. Josiah Hort, L. P. Apr. 3.
1720. Hy. Maule, L. P. June 22; bp. 1726.
1726. Jas. Ward, L. P. Sept. 24.
1736. Isaac Goldsmith, L. P. Sept. 7.
1769. Wm. Pratt, May 26; *d.* 1770.
1770. Eyton Butts, Apr. 21.
1779. Hon. John Hewitt, May 4.
1804. Jas. Archd. Hamilton, Sept. 17.
1816. Alexr. Arbuthnot, Feb. 22; bp. of Killaloe, &c., 1823.
1823. Thos. John Burgh, Oct. 7; *d.* 1845
1845. Hervey de Montmorenci, 4th visc. Mountmorres.
1851. Jas. Howie, L. P. Jan. 9.
1885. Horace Townsend Fleming.

DEANS OF ROSS.

1381-3. Jno. O'Houlachan.
1591. Robt. Sturton, or Shirton.
1615. Hugh Persevall, *d.* 1630.
1631. Wm. Bolton, adm. Jan. 8.
1637. Geo. Horley, or Horsey, L. P. Nov. 19.
1639. John Chappell.
1664. John Everleigh, L. P. Jan. 19.
1679. Rowland Davies, Feb. 10; res. 1710.
1710. Richd. Griffith, L. P. Mar. 24.
1717. Valentine French, L. P. Apr. 20.
1733. Jemmet Brown, L. P. Sept. 14 bp. of Killaloe, 1743.
1743. Arth. St. George, May 16; *d.* 1772.
1772. Wensley Bond, Nov. 5; res. 1813.
1813. Jas. Forward Bond, July 23.
1829. Jas. Stannus, Sept. 9; *d.* Jan. 28, 1876.
1876. Isaac Morgan Reeves.

DIOCESES OF KILLALOE, KILFENORA, CLONFERT, AND KILMACDUAGH.

THE SEE of KILLALOE is supposed to have been founded by St. Molua, abbot, whose disciple, St. Flannan (son of king Theodoric) was consecrated at Rome by pope John IV. about 640, and was first bishop. About the end of the twelfth century, the ancient see of ROSCREA was united to Killaloe. Of Roscrea, St. Cronan, who flourished about 620, was bishop, or, as some say, abbot, and the founder of the church.

There is no certainty concerning the foundation of the see of KILFENORA. Some writers think that St. Fachnan, to whom the church was dedicated, was the founder and first bishop. In the ancient distribution of the bishoprics of Ireland, made by cardinal Paparo, it was suffragan to the archbishopric of Cashel; but when at the Restoration of Charles II. it was annexed to or held with Tuam, it became suffragan to that see.

ST. BRENDAN, the son of Finloga, contemporary with St. Brendan of Birr, and his fellow student, founded an abbey at CLONFERT in 558, and was himself abbot. He died in May 577, at Enaghdune, whence his body was conveyed to Clonfert, and there interred. In his time the cathedral of Clonfert was founded. Colgan makes St. Brendan the founder and first bishop of Clonfert, and says that he abdicated, and placed St. Moena in his room. Others again make St. Moena the first bishop. In the Ulster Annals, under the year 571 or 572, the death of the first bishop of this see is thus mentioned: "Moena, Bishop of Clonfert-Brenain, went to rest." Brendan's true name was Nennius or Nennio; but it is common with the Irish to add the monosyllable *mo*, signifying *mine*, to the proper names of their saints, out of respect and tenderness.

The church of KILMACDUAGH was founded by Colman, the son of Duagh, who was descended from a noble family at Connaught, and very nearly related to Guair, king of that country. To distinguish him from other Colmans, his contemporaries, he was usually called after his father, Macduagh, or the son of Duagh. He was very fond of an ascetic life, and is said to have lived in a wilderness in the southern parts of Connaught seven years with only one companion. From this life of retirement he was, in the end, made bishop, and fixed his see in a place which, from his surname, was called Kilmacduagh, or the "Church of the son of Duagh."

KILFENORA was held with Limerick from 1642 to 1649, with Tuam from 1660 to 1741, and with Clonfert and Kilmacduagh from 1741 to 1752. KILLALOE and KILFENORA were united in 1752. CLONFERT and KILMACDUAGH were united in 1602. On the translation of bishop Knox to Limerick in 1834, KILLALOE, KILFENORA, CLONFERT, and KILMACDUAGH were united under 3 & 4 Wm. IV., cap. 37.

BISHOPS OF KILLALOE.

* * St. Flannan, about 640.
* * * *
* * Carmacan O'Muil Cashel, *d.* 1019.
1055. O'Gernidider.
1083. Teig O'Teig.
* * * *
1161. Thady O'Lonergan.
1165. Donat O'Brien.
* * Constantine O'Brien, seated here in 1179.
* * Dermod O'Coning, depr. 1195.
1195. Chas. O'Heney.
Cornelius O'Heney, seated here in 1215.
1216. Robt. Travers, depr. by the pope's legate.
See vacant 10 years.
1231. Donald O'Kennedy, archdn.
* * Isaac O'Cormacain, dean.
1267. Matt. O'Hogain, dean.
1281. Maurice O'Hogain, chanter.
1299. David MacMahon, dean.
1316. Thos. O'Cormacain, archdn.
1322. Benedict O'Coscry, dean.
1326. David, of Emly.
1343. Thos. O'Hogain.
1355. Thos. O'Cormacain, archdn.
1391. Matt. MacCragh, dean.
1409. Robt. Mulfield.
DonatMacCragh, seated here in 1428.
1429. Eugene O'Felan.
1430. Thady MacCragh.
* * Ired O'Lonergan
* * Jas. O'Ghonelan, seated here in 1441.
* * Terence O'Brien I., murd. 1460.
1460. Thady.
Matt., or Mahoun O'Griffa, *d.* 1482.
1482. Terence O'Brien II.
1525. Richd. Hogan, tr. to Clonmacnois.
1539. Jas. O'Corrin, res.
1546. Cornelius O'Dea.
1555. Terence O'Brien III.; put in by Q. Mary; governed this see until 1566.
* * Maurice O'Brien; he received the profits of this see six years before he was consecrated, which was in 1570; res. 1612.
1612. John Rider, dean of St. Patrick's.
1633. Lewis Jones, dean of Cashel.
1647. Edwd. Parry, dean of Lismore.
See vacant until the Restoration.
1661. Edwd. Worth, dean of Cork.
1669. Daniel Witter, dean of Down.
1675. John Roan, dean of Clogher.
1693. Hy. Rider, archdn. of Ossory.
1696. Thos. Lindsay, tr. to Raphoe.
1713. Sir Thos. Vesey, bt.; tr. to Ossory.
1714. Nichs. Forster, tr. to Raphoe.
1716. Chas. Carr, chapl. to the ho. of comm.
1740. Jos. Story, tr. to Kilmore.
1742. John Ryder, tr. to Down and Connor.
1743. Jemmet Brown, dean of Ross; tr. to Cork and Ross.
1745. Richd. Chenevix, tr. to Waterford, &c.
1746. Nichs. Synge.
See united to Kilfenora 1752.

See "Bishops of Killaloe and Kilfenora," *post*, p. 635.

BISHOPS OF KILFENORA.

* * Christian, *d.* 1254.
1265. Henry, or Maurice.
1273. Florence O'Tigernach.
1281. Chas., dean of Kilfenora.
* * Congal O'Loghlan, *d.* 1300.
* * Simon O'Currin, *d.* 1303.
1303. Maurice O'Brien, dean.
1323. Richd. O'Loghlin.
Patrick, seated here in 1394.
* * Dennis O'Cane, or O'Cahan; res. 1491.
1491. Maurice O'Brien, canon.
* * John O'Hinalan, seated here in 1552.
* * Daniel, seated here in 1585.
See vacant in 1602.
1606. Bernard Adams, bp. of Limerick; held this see from 1606 to 1617 when he resigned it.
1617. John Steere, tr. to Ardfert.
1622. Wm. Murray, tr. to Llandaff.
1628. Richd. Betts, who, on learning the poverty of the see, would not accept it.
1630. Jas. Higate, archdn. of Clogher.
1638. Robt. Sibthorp, tr. to Limerick in 1642.

Held with Limerick from 1642 to 1649. See *Limerick, post*, p. 638.
Held with Tuam from 1660 to 1741. See *Tuam, ante*, p. 611.
Held with Clonfert and Kilmacduagh from 1741 to 1752. See *Clonfert and Kilmacduagh, post*, p. 636.
United to Killaloe, 1752.
See "Bishops of Killaloe and Kilfenora," *infra*.

BISHOPS OF KILLALOE AND KILFENORA.

1752. Nichs. Synge, bp. of Killaloe, abovenamed.
1771. Robt Fowler, canon of Windsor; tr. to Dublin.
1779. Geo. Chinnery, dean of Cork; tr. to Cloyne.
1780. Thos. Bernard, dean of Derry; tr. to Limerick.
1794. Hon. Wm. Knox, chapl. to the ho. of comm.; tr. to Derry.
1803. Hon. Chas. D. Lindsay, vicar of Sutterton, and chapl. to the ld.-lieut.; tr. to Kildare.
1804. Nathl. Alexander, tr. from Clonfert; tr. to Down and Connor.
Lord Robt. Ponsonby Tottenham, tr. to Ferns and Leighlin.
1820. Rd. Mant, rector of Bishopsgate, London; tr. to Down and Connor.
1823. Alexr Arbuthnot, dean of Cloyne.
1828. Hon. Richd. Ponsonby, dean of St. Patrick's, tr. to Derry.
1831. Hon. Edmd. Knox, dean of Down tr. to Limerick 1834.
See united to Clonfert and Kilmacduagh 1834.

See "Bishops of Killaloe, Kilfenora, Clonfert, and Kilmacduagh," *post*, p. 636.

BISHOPS OF CLONFERT.

* * St. Moena, *d.* 571.
Fintan Corach; seated here about the close of the sixth century.
* * St. Senach Garbh, *d.* 620.
* * St. Colman, the son of Comgal; *d.* 620.
662. Cumin Foda, *i.e.* the Long.
825. Rutmel, called "Prince and Bishop of Clonfert."
861. Cathald MacCormac.
921. Cormac MacÆdain.
1116. Gilla MacAiblen.
* * Petro O'Mordai, drowned 1171.
* * Mœlisa MacAward, *d.* 1173.
1186. Malcallan.
1248. Thomas.
1259. Cormac, or Chas. O'Lumlin.
1263. Thos, O'Kelly.
See vacant 3 years.
1266. John, an Italian, the pope's nuncio; tr. to the abpric. of Benevento.
1296. Robert, a monk of Christ-Church, Canterbury.
1308. Gregory O'Brogy, dean.
1319. Robt. le Petit, depr. 1321.
1322. John O'Lean, archdn. of Tuam.
See vacant almost 10 years.
1347. Thos. O'Kelly.
1378. Maurice O'Kelly, tr. to Tuam 1394.
1398. David Corre.
At this time the pope tr. Wm. O'Cormacain, abp. of Tuam, to this see; but the abp. "took the exchange so much to heart," that he neglected to expedite his bull of translation in due time, and was depr.
* * Thos. O'Kelly, tr. to Tuam; seated here in 1415.
1438. John Heyn.
* * Thos. de Burgo, seated here in 1444.

1447. Cornelius O'Mulledy, tr. to Emly.
1448. Cornelius O'Cunlis, tr. from Emly.
* * Matt. MacRaik, *d.* 1507.
1508. David de Burgo.
1509. Denis.
1536. Richd. Nangle.
1541. Roland de Burgo, dean of Clonfert.
1582. Steph. Kerovan, tr. from Kilmac duagh.
1602. Roland Linch, archdn. of Clonfer and bp. of Kilmacduagh; hel both sees.
See united to Kilmacduag 1602.

See "Bishops of Clonfert and Kilmacduagh," *infra.*

BISHOPS OF KILMACDUAGH.

The following is an imperfect catalogue of the Bishops of Kilmacduagh.

* * St. Colman, about 620.
* * * *
* * Indrect, *d.* 814.
* * * *
1178. Rugnad O'Ruadan.
* * Odo, chanter; seated here in 1227.
* * Gelasius MacScelagai, *d.* 1249.
1283. Maurice Ileyan.
1290. David O'Sedaghan.
1306. Laurence O'Laghnan.
1325. Luke.
* * John, dean; seated here in 1347.
* * Nicholas, seated here in 1371.
* * Gregory Ileyan, *d.* 1395.
1399. Nichs. Ileyan.
1401. John Icomaid.
* * John, abbot of Corcumroe; seate here in 1418.
* * * *
* * Cornelius, res. 1502.
1503 Matthew, archdn. of Killaloe.
1533. Christr. Bodekine, tr. to Tuam, an held this see *in commendam.*
1573. Steph. Kerovan, tr. to Clonfert.
1583. Roland Linch.
See united to or held wit Clonfert, 1602.

See "Bishops of Clonfert and Kilmacduagh," *infra.*

BISHOPS OF CLONFERT AND KILMACDUAGH.

1602. Roland Linch above named.
See vacant nearly 2 years.
1627. Robt. Dawson, dean of Down.
1644. Wm. Baily; he did not get possession till the Restoration.
1664. Edwd. Wolley, chapln. to the king.
See vacant from 1684 to 1691. The episcopal revenues were seized into the hands of James II., and paid over to the Roman Catholic bishops.
1691. Wm. Fitzgerald, dean of Cloyne.
1722. Theoph. Bolton, chanc. of St. Patrick's, and vicar-general of the diocese of Dublin; tr. to Elphin.
1724. Arthr. Price, dean of Ferns; tr. to Ferns and Leighlin.
1730. Edwd. Synge, chanc. of St. Patrick's; tr. to Cloyne.
1732. Mordecai Cary, tr. to Killala and Achonry.
1735. John Whitcomb, rector of Louth; tr. to Down, &c.
1752. Arth. Smyth, dean of Derry; tr. Down.
1753. Hon. Wm. Carmichael, tr. to Fer and Leighlin.
1758. Wm. Gore, dean of Cashel; tr. to Elphi
1762. John Oswald, tr. to Dromore.
1763. Denis Cumberland, tr. to Kilmore.
1772. Walter Cope, tr. to Ferns and Leighli
1782. John Law, archdn. of Carlisle.
1787. Richd. Marlay, dean of Ferns; tr. t Waterford.
1795. Hon. Chas. Brodrick, tr. to Kilmor
1796. Hugh Hamilton, dean of Armagh; t to Ossory.
1798. Matt. Young, senior fellow of Tri Coll., Dublin.
1801. Geo. de la Poer Beresford, dean Kilmore; tr. to Kilmore.
1802. Nathl. Alexander, tr. to Down ar Connor.
1804. Christr. Butson, dean of Waterfor
See united to Killaloe and Ki fenora 1834.

See "Bishops of Killaloe, Kilfenora, Clonfert, and Kilmacduagh," *infra.*

BISHOPS OF KILLALOE, KILFENORA, CLONFERT, AND KILMACDUAGH

1834. Christr. Butson, above-named.
1836. Steph. C. Sandes, senior fellow of Trin. Coll., Dublin, May 2; tr. to Cashel.
1839 Hon. Ludlow Tonson, rector Ahern, county Cork Jan. 25.
1862. Wm. Fitz-Gerald.
1884. Wm Bennett Chester, archdn. Killaloe, Jan. 16.

DEANS OF KILLALOE.

53. Isaac O'Cormacain, Apr. 5; aft. bp.
67. Matt. O'Hogain; bp. same year.
80. Luke.
97. Nehemiah.
99. David MacMahon; bp. same year.
317. Luke.
22. Benedict O'Coscry; bp. same year.
29–31. Charles.
81. Matt. McCragh; bp. 1391.
389. David O'Cormagan, July 15.
—. Boetius Clancy; *d.* 1559.
59. Cornelius Ryan.
85. Donogh O'Horan.
02. Hugh O'Hogan; res. Nov. 25, 1624.
24. Richd. Hacket, L. P. Dec. 16.
28. Alexr. Spicer, L. P. Mar. 26.
62. Jasper Pheasant, L. P. Feb. 12.
92. Jerome Ryves, L. P. May 18; res. 1699.
99. Jas. Abbadie, inst. May 13; *d.* 1727.
1728. Julius, or Giles Eyre, Mar. 15; *d.* 1749.
17—.? Chas. Talbot Blayney.
1761. Wm. Henry, Nov. 9.
1768. Hon. Jos. Deane Bourke, Aug. 8; res. 1772.
1772. Wm. Cecil Pery, aft. ld. Glentworth; L.P. Apr. 4; dean of Derry, 1780; bp. of Killala, &c., 1781.
1780. Saml. Rastall, Feb. 18; *d.* 1781.
1781. Hon. Thos. Stopford, Aug. 1; bp. of Cork, 1794.
1787. John Murray, Dec. 1; *d.* June 25, 1790.
1790. Peter Carleton, Oct. 30; res. 1808.
1808. John Bayly, Feb. 11; res. 1828.
1828. Allen Morgan, July 5; *d.* 1830.
1830. John Head, L. P. Oct. 9; *d.* June 2, 1871.
1871. John Hastings Allen.
1880. Jos. F. Robbins.
1886. Robt. Humphreys.

DEANS OF KILFENORA.

281. Charles; bp. this year.
303. Maurice O'Brien; bp. this year.
585. Danl. Shennagh.
591 ? Donald O'Heawo (O'Heney? or Shennagh?).
615. Donat O'Shanny.
617. Hygatus Love, L. P. June 2.
639. Philip Flower, L. P. Sept. 16.
664. Neptune Blood, L. P. Jan. 27.
692. Neptune Blood, jun. L. P. Dec. 8.
716. Wm. White, L. P. June 8.
724 to 1750. Jonathan Bruce, L. P. Oct. 15.
1761. Chas. Coote; *d.* 1796.
1796. Latham Coddington, L. P. May 16 res. 1802.
1802. Geo. Stephenson, L. P. June 14; *d.* 1825.
1825. Wm Hy. Stacpoole, May 24; *d.* 1847.
1847. John Armstrong; *d.* June 16, 1856.
1856. Michl. John Keating, L. P. June 30.
1884. Robt. Humphreys; dean of Killaloe, 1886.
1886. John Robt. Copley.

DEANS OF CLONFERT.

308. Gregory O'Brogy, bp. same year.
319. James.
392. Michl. (or Nichs.) O'Kelly.
407. Thos. O'Longain, or Lonergan.
460. Simon M'Keogh.
534. Roland de Burgo, bp. 1541.
591. Donat O'Lorchan.
598. Arilan Loughlin, Jan. 26.
622. Revatius (or Ryvas) Tully; *d.* 1627.
638. Saml. Pullein, L. P. Nov. 14.
662. Richd. Heaton, Feb. 12.
666. Nichs. Proude, Oct. 31.
1670. Joshua Brooksbank, Feb. 5.
1692. John Burdett; *d.* 1726.
1726. Robt. Taylour, Sept. 8; *d.* 1745.
1745. Wm. Crow, Aug. 9; res. 1766.
1766. Wm. Digby, Oct. 28; *d.* 1812.
1812. Thos. Hawkins, L. P. May 7; *d.* 1850.
1850. Edwd. Mitchell Kennedy, Feb.; *d.* 1864.
1865. Chas. Graves, L. P. Oct. 25; bp. of Limerick, 1866.
1866. Jas. Byrne, L. P. June 25.

DEANS OF KILMACDUAGH.

326. John, aft. bp.
3—. David.

* * * *

558. John Tierney, or O'Tiernay.
1591. Matt. Warde.
1621. John Wingfield, July 5.
1624. John Yorke, Dec. 18.
1662. Dudley Pierse, Feb. 5.

1699–1700. Steph. Handcock, June 7; *d.* 1719.
1719. Chas. Northcott, Aug. 28; *d.* 1730.
1731. John Richardson, Feb. 20.
1748. Jas. Stopford, Feb. 10; bp. of Cloyne, 1753.
1753. Wm. Nethercoat, July 25.
1771. Robt. Gorges, Sept. 26; *d.* 1802.
1803. Ussher Lee, Jan. 22; dean of Waterford, 1804.
1804. Richd. Bagwell, Oct. 30.
1806. Wm. Forster, Feb. 22; *d.* 1823.
1823. Richd. Hood, Oct. 24; *d.* 1836.
1837. John Thos. O'Neil, Oct. 10; re 1838.
1839. Anthy. La Touche Kirwan, ins May 20; dean of Limerick, 184
1849. Jos. Aldrich Bermingham, June 2 *d.* 1874.
1874. Christr. Hy. Gould Butson.

DIOCESES OF LIMERICK, ARDFERT, AND AGHADOE.

Donald O'Brien, king of Limerick, founded and endowed the cathedr of Limerick about the period of the arrival of the English in Irelan The more ancient see of Inis-Scattery was united to Limerick about t beginning of the thirteenth century; but, according to Usher, its po sessions were divided among the sees of Limerick, Killaloe, an Ardfert. Inis-Scattery is said to have been founded by St. Patrick, an to have been governed by him for some time.

The see of Ardfert was formerly called the bishopric of Kerr its cathedral was dedicated to St. Brandon. The cathedral of Aghado dedicated to St. Finian, is situated within two miles of the town Killarney.

Ardfert and Aghadoe have been united from the earliest time and they were both united to Limerick in 1667.

BISHOPS OF LIMERICK.

* * St. Munchin.
* * Gille, or Gillebert, *d.* about 1140.
1140. Patrick.
* * Harold, an Ostman; called by the Irish Erolb; *d.* 1151.
* * Torgesius, an Ostman; seated here about 1152.
* * Brictius, an Ostman; seated here about 1179.
* * Donat O'Brien, *d.* 1207.
* * Geoffry, seated here in 1217.
* * Edmund, *d.* 1222.
1222. Herbert de Burgh, prior of Athassel.
251. Robt. of Emly.
1272. Gerald le Marescall, archdn.
1302. Robt. of Dundovenald, canon.
1311. Eustace de l'Eau, or Waters, dean.
1337. Maurice Rochfort.
1354. Steph. Lawless, chanc. of Limerick.
1360. Steph. de Valle, dean; tr. to Meath.
1369. Peter Currah, res.
1400. Cornelius O'Dea, archdn. of Killaloe; res.
1426. John Mothel, Augustine canon of Kells, abbot of Kilkenny; res.
1459. Wm Creagh.
1472. Thos. Arthur
1486. Richard.
John Dunow, canon of Exeter.
1489. John Folan, canon of Ferns.
1522. John Coyn, or Quin; res. 1551.
1551. Wm. Casey, depr. 1556; rest. 157
1557. Hugh Lacy, or Lees, canon; ap by pope Paul IV. at Q. Mar instance; res. 1571.
1571. Bp. Casey rest. to his see.
1593. John Thornborough, chapl. to Elizabeth; tr. to Bristol.
1604. Bernard Adams; with this see held also Kilfenora from 1606 1617, when he resigned it.
1626. Fras. Gough, chanc. of Limerick.
1634. Geo. Webb, chapl. to Chas. I.
1642. Robt. Sibthorpe, tr. from Kilfenor held both sees; *d.* 1649.
The see was vacant until the Rest ration.
1660. Edwd. Synge, dean of Elphin; tr. Cork, &c.
See united to Ardfert a Aghadoe, 1667.

See "Bishops of Limerick, Ardfert, and Aghadoe," *post*, p. 639.

BISHOPS OF ARDFERT AND AGHADOE.

* Ert.
* Cerpain, *d.* 500.
A blank here, which it is impossible to fill up.
* Dermod Mac-Mel-Brenan, *d.* 1075.
099. Magrath O'Erodain, or O'Ronan.
* MacRonan, seated here before 1152.
* MelBrandan O'Ronan, *d.* 1161.
166. Gilla MacAiblen O'Hanmada.
193. Donald O'Conarchy.
207. David O'Duibditrib.
215. John, depr. 1221.
225. Gilbert, dean; res.
237. Brendan, provost of Ardfert; res. 1242.
His successor uncertain.
252. Christian.
256. Philip.
264. John, archdn. of Ardfert.
285. Nichs. I.
288. Nichs. II., abbot of Odorney.
336. Alan O'Hathern.
1348. John de Valle.
1372. Cornelius O'Tigernach.
1379. Wm. Bull, dean of Cork.
* * Nichs. III., seated here in 1420.
* * Maurice, *d.* 1462.
* * John Stack, after much opposition, was settled here in 1480.
1488. Philip.
1495. John Fitzgerald, canon.
* * * *
* * Jas. Fitzmaurice, seated here about 1551.
1588. Nichs. Keenan.
1600. John Crosby, preb. of Disert.
1622. John Steere, archdn. of Emly.
1628. Wm. Steere, dean.
1641. Thos. Fulwar, tr. to Cashel.
1660. Edwd. Synge, dean of Elphin; tr. to Cork.
1663. Wm. Fuller.
See united to Limerick, 1667.

See "Bishops of Limerick, Ardfert, and Aghadoe," *infra.*

BISHOPS OF LIMERICK, ARDFERT, AND AGHADOE.

667. Wm. Fuller, dean of St. Patrick's; tr. to Lincoln.
672. John Vesey, dean of Cork; tr. to Tuam.
678. Simon Digby, dean of Kildare; tr. to Elphin.
692. Nathl. Wilson, dean of Raphoe.
695. Thos. Smythe, dean of Emly.
725. Wm. Burscough.
755. Jas. Leslie.
771. John Averell, dean of Emly.
772. Wm. Gore, tr. from Elphin.
784. Wm. Cecil Pery, aft. ld. Glentworth; tr. from Killala and Achonry.
1794. Thos. Bernard, tr. from Killaloe.
1806. Chas. Mongan Warburton, dean of Ardagh; tr. to Cloyne.
1820. Thos. Elrington, provost of Trinity College, Dublin; tr. to Ferns and Leighlin.
1822. John Jebb, archdn. of Emly.
1834. Hon. Edmd. Knox, tr. from Killaloe, &c.
1849. Wm. Higgin, dean of Limerick, June; tr. to Derry, &c.
1853. Hy. Griffin.
1866. Chas. Graves.

DEANS OF LIMERICK.

204 to 1207. P * * *
212. J* * *
* W* * *
* Reymundus.
249 to 1278. Thos. of Woodford.
295–8. John de Cotes.
302. Luke.
311. Eustace de l'Eau, or Waters, bp. same year.
360. Steph. de Valle, bp. same year.
366. Adam Owen.
398 to 1409. Rd. Warren, Waryn, or Waryng.
405. Eustathius de Agna.
446. Robt. Poer, bp. of Waterford, &c., same year.
451. Thos. O'Semican.
488. Milo de Burgo.
1493. Philip Water.
1516. Andr. Creagh, res. 1543.
1543. Andr. Stritche, Sep. 30; *d.* 1551.
1552. Roger Skiddy, L.P. May 10; bp. Cork, &c., 1557.
15—. David Arthur, res. 1588.
1588. Denis Campbell.
1603. Geo. Andrews, L.P. Aug. 31; bp. of Ferns and Leighlin, 1635.
1635. Michl. Wandesford, L.P. May 11.
1640. Hy. Sutton, L.P. Nov. 9.
1641. Robt. Naylor, L.P, Apr. 16.
1662. Richd. Boyle, L.P. Feb.; bp. of Ferns and Leighlin 1666.
1666. John Smith, Sep. 13; bp. of Killala and Achonry, 1669.
1680. Ezekiel Webbe, L.P. Jan. 9; *d.* 1704.
1704. Geo. Walter Story, L.P. Dec. 21.

1722. Thos. Bindon, L.P. Feb. 16; *d.* 1740.
1740. Chas. Massy, L.P. July 28; *d.* 1766.
1766. John Averill, L. P. July 14; bp. 1771.
1771. Hon. Maurice Crosbie, L.P. Oct. 3; *d.* 1809.
1809. Arth. John Preston, July 20.
1844. Wm. Higgins, Dec.
1849. Anthy. La Touche Kirwan, dean Kilmacduagh; *d.* July 1868.
1868. Maurice Fitzgerald Day, L.P. No 13; bp. of Cashel 1872.
1872. Thos. Bunbury.

DEANS OF ARDFERT.

1225. Gilbert, bp. this year.
1237. Brendan.
1313. Thomas.
1323. Michl. O'Colweny.
1365. John FitzThomas.
1603. Richd. Southwell, res. same year. Robt. Chaffe, L.P. Aug. 15.
1620. Wm. Steere, L.P. Feb. 13; bp. 1628.
1630. Giles Baden.
1635. Thos. Gray, L.P. Apr. 29.
1661. Danl. Witter, L.P. Mar. 27; dean of Down, 1664.
1665. Thos. Bladen, L.P. Apr. 6.
1686. John Richards, L.P. Aug. 4.
1728. Jas. Bland, L.P. Feb. 3.
1728. Wm. Smythe, L.P. Apr. 15.
1732. Chas. Meredyth, L.P. June 1; 1747.
1747. Sir Philip Hoby, L.P. Sept. 8; *d.* 17(
1766. Edwd. Bayly, L.P. Nov. 28 or Au 16; *d.* 17 June, 1785.
1785. Thos. Greaves, Oct. 19.
1802. Gilbert Holmes, L.P. Aug. 21; Dec. 23, 1846.
1808. Edwd. Archd. Douglas, July 20.
1847. Alexr. Irwin, *d.* Feb. 7, 1861.
1861. John Godfrey Day, L.P. Apr. 10.
1879. Thos. Moriarty.

LORD MAYORS AND RECORDERS OF DUBLIN.

The Corporation of Dublin originally consisted of the Lord Mayor, sheriffs, 24 aldermen, 124 common councilmen, 28 sheriff-men or sherif peers, and 96 representatives of the 25 civic guilds. It was re-constitut under 3 & 4 Vict., cap. 108 (1840), and now consists of the Lo Mayor, who is chosen from among the aldermen or town councillor 15 aldermen and 45 town councillors.

The chief magistrate of Dublin had conferred upon him the distincti of "Lord" Mayor by Charles I. in 1641; but the first mayor th enjoyed the title was Sir Daniel Bellingham, in 1665.

Lord Mayors of Dublin.

The lord mayors thus marked * died during their mayoralty.

1665–6. Sir Danl. Bellingham.
1666–7. John Desmyniers.
1667–8. Mark Quin.
1668–9. John Forrest.
1669–70. Lewis Desmyniers.
1670–1. Enoch Reader.
1671–2. Sir John Totty.
1672–3. Robt. Deey.
1673–4. Sir Joshua Allen.
1674–5. Sir Fras. Brewster.
1675–6. Wm. Smith.
1676–7. Christr. Lovet.
1677–8. John Smith.
1678–9. John Ward.
1679–80. John Eastwood.
1680–1. Luke Lowther.
1681–3. Sir Humphrey Jervis.
1683–4. Sir Elias Best.
1684–5. Sir Abel Ram.
1685–6. Sir John Knox.
1686–7. Sir John Castleton.
1687–8. Sir Thos. Hacket.
1688–9. Sir Michl. Creagh.
1689–90. Terence M'Dermott.
1690–1. John Otrington.
1691–3. Sir. Michl. Mitchell.
1693–4. Sir John Rogerson.
1694–5. Geo. Blackhall.
1695–6. Wm. Watts.
1696–7. Sir Wm. Billington.
1697–8. Barth. Van Homrigh.
1698–9. Thos. Quin.
1699–1700. * * *
1700–1. Sir Mark Rainsford.

1701–2. Saml. Walton.
1702–3. Thos. Bell.
1703–4. John Page.
1704–5. Sir Fras. Stoyte.
1705–6. Wm. Gibbons.
1706–7. Benj. Burton.
1707–8. John Pearson.
1708–9. Sir Wm. Fownes.
1709–10. Chas. Forrest.
1710–11. Sir John Eccles
1711–12 Ralph Gore.
1712–13. Sir Saml. Cooke.
1713–14. * * *
1714–15. Sir Jas. Barlow.
1715–16. John Stoyte.
1716–17. Thos. Bolton.
1717–18. Anthy. Barkey.
1718–19. Wm. Quail.
1719–20. Thos. Wilkinson.
1720–1. Geo. Forbes.
1721–2. Thos. Curtis.
1722–3. Wm. Dickson.
1723–4. John Porter.
1724–5. John Reyson.
1725–6. Jos. Kane.
1726–7. Wm. Empson.
1727–8. Sir Nathl. Whitwell.
1728–9. *Hy. Burrowes, and John Page, *again*.
1729–30. Sir Peter Verdoen.
1730–1. Nathl. Pearson.
1731–2. Jos. Nuttall.
1732–3. Humphrey French.
1733–4. Thos. How.
1734–5. Nathl. Kane.
1735–6. *Sir Richd. Grattan, and Geo. Forbes, *again*.
1736–7. Jas. Somerville.
1737–8. Wm. Walker.
1738–9. John Macarroll.
1739–40. Danl. Falkiner.
1740–1. Sir Saml. Cooke.
1741–2. Wm. Aldrich.
1742–3. Gilbert King.
1743–4. *David Tew, and Wm. Aldrich, *again*.
1744–5. John Walker.
1745–6. Danl. Cooke.
1746–7. *Richd. White, and Wm. Walker, *again*.
1747–8. Sir Geo. Ribton.
1748–9. Robt. Ross.
1749–50. John Adamson.
1750–1. Thos. Taylor.
1751–2. John Cooke.
1752–3. Sir Chas. Burton.
1753–4. Andr. Murray.
1754–5. Hans Bailie.
1755–6. Percival Hunt.
1756–7. John Forbes.
1757–8. Thos. Mead.
1758–9. Philip Crampton.
1759–60. John Tew.
1760–1. Sir Patr. Hamilton.
1761–2. Sir Timothy Allen.
1762–3. Chas. Rossell.
1763–4. Wm. Forbes.
1764–5. Benj. Geale.
1765–6. Sir Jas. Taylor.
1766–7. Edwd. Sankey.
1767–8. Fras. Fetherston.
1768–9. Benj. Barton.
1769–70. Sir Thos. Blackhall.
1770–1. Geo. Reynolds.
1771–2. *Fras. Booker, and Wm. Forbes, *again*.
1772–3. Richd. French.
1773–4. Wm. Lightburne.
1774–5. Hy. Hart.
1775–6. Thos. Emerson.
1776–7. Hy. Bevan.
1777–8. Wm. Dunn.
1778–9. Sir Anthy. King.
1779–80. James Hamilton.
1780–1. Killner Swettenham.
1781–2. John Darragh.
1782–3. Nathl. Warren.
1183–4. Thos. Green.
1884–5. Jas. Horan.
1785–6. Jas. Shiel.
1786–7. Geo. Alcock.
1787–8. Wm. Alexander.
1788–9. John Rose.
1789–90. John Exshaw.
1790–1. Hy. Howison.
1791–2. Hy. Gore Sankey.
1792–3. John Carleton.
1793–4. Wm. James.
1794–5. Richd. Moncrieffe.
1795–6. Sir Wm. Worthington.
1796–7. Saml. Read.
1797–8. Thos. Fleming.
1798–9. Thos. Andrews.
1799–1800. *John Sutton and John Exshaw, *again*.
1800–1. Chas. Thorp,
1801–2. Richd. Manders.
1802–3. Jacob Poole.
1803–4. Hy. Hutton.
1804–5. Meredith Jenkin.
1805–6. Jas. Vance.
1806–7. Jos. Pemberton.
1807–8. Hugh Trevor.
1808–9. Fred. Darley.
1809–10. Sir Wm. Stamer, bt.
1810–11. Nathl. Hone.
1811–12. Wm. Hy. Archer.
1812–13. Abraham Bradley King.
1813–14. John Cash.
1814–15. John Claudius Beresford.
1815–16. Robt. Shaw, aft. bt.
1816–17. Mark Bloxham.
1817–18. John Alley.
1818–19. Thos. M'Kenny.
1819–20. Sir Wm. Stamer, bt., *again*.
1820–1. Sir Abraham Bradley King, bt.
1821–2. Sir John Kingston James, bt.
1822–3. John Smyth Fleming.
1823–4. Richd. Smyth.
1824–5. Drury Jones.

1825–6. Thos. Abbot.
1826–7. Saml. Wm. Tyndall.
1827–8. Sir Edmd. Nugent.
1828–9. Alexr. Montgomery.
1829–30. Jacob West.
1830–1. Robt. Way Harty, cr. bt. 1831.
1831–2. Sir Thos. Whelan.
1832–3. Chas. Palmer Archer.
1833–4. Sir Geo. Whiteford.
1834–5. Arth. Perrin.
1835–6. Arth. Morrison.
1836–7. Wm. Hodges.
1837–8. Saml. Warren.
1838–9. Geo. Hoyte.
1839–40. Sir Nichs. Wm. Brady.
1840–1. Sir John Kingston James, bt.
1841–2. Danl. O'Connell.
1842–3. Geo. Roe.
1843–4. Timothy O'Brien.
1844–5. John L. Arabin.
1845–6. John Keshan.
1846–7. Michl. Staunton.
1847–8. Jeremiah Dunne.
1848–9. Timothy O'Brien, *again*; cr. bt. 1849.
1849–50. John Reynolds.
1850–1. Benj. Lee Guinness, cr. bt. 1867.
1851–2. John D'Arcy.
1852–3. Robt. H. Kinahan.
1853–4. Sir Edwd. McDonnell.
1854–5. Jos. Boyce.
1855–6. Fergus Farrell.
1856–7. Richd. Atkinson.
1857–8. John Campbell.
1858–9. Jas. Lambert.
1859–60. Redmond Carroll.
1860–1. Richd. Atkinson.
1861–2. Denis Moylan.
1862–3. Hon. John Prendergast Vereker.
1863–4. Peter Paul McSwiney.
1864–5. John Barrington; knt. 1868.
1865–6. Jas. W. Mackey.
1866–7. Wm. Lane Joynt.
1867–8. Wm. Carroll; knt. 1868.
1868–9. The same.
1869–70. Edwd. Purdon.
1870–1. P. Bulfin and J. Campbell.
1871–2. Robt. G. Durdin.
1872–3. Sir Jas. W. Mackey.
1873–4. Maurice Brooks.
1874–5. Peter Paul McSwiney, *again*.
1875–6. Geo. Bolster Owens; knt. 1876.
1876–7. Hugh Tarpey.
1877–8. The same.
1878–9. Sir John Barrington, *again*.
1879–80. Edmd. Dwyer Gray.
1880–1. Geo. Moyers.
1881–2. Chas. Dawson.
1882–3. The same.
1883–4. Wm. Meagher.
1884–5. John O'Connor.
1885–6. Timothy Danl. Sullivan.
1886–7. The same.
1887–8. Thos. Sexton.
1888–9. The same.

RECORDERS OF DUBLIN.

1564. Jas. Stanihurst.
1573. Hy. Burnell.
1575. Geo. Taylor.
1595. Edwd. Loftus.
1597. John Caddell.
1598. Patr. Fitzgerald.
1602. Wm. Talbot.
1605. Sir Richd. Bolton, aft. ch. bar. ex. and ld. chanc.
1608. John Veldon (deputy).
1614. Wm. Dongan.
1627. Nathl. Catelyn.
1634. John Bysse, aft. ch. bar. ex.
1660. Sir Wm. Davys, aft. ch. just. K. B.
1682. Sir Richd. Ryves, aft. bar. ex.
1687. Sir John Barnewell, aft. bar. ex.
1688. Gerald Dillon.
1690. Thos. Coote, aft. just. K. B.
1693. Nehemiah Donnellan, aft. bar. and ch. bar. ex.
1695. Sir Wm. Handcock.
1701. John Forster, aft. ch. just. C. P.
1714. John Rogerson, aft. ch. just. K. B.
1727. Fras. Stoyte.
1733. Eton Stannard.
1750. Fras. Morgan.
1757. Jas. Grattan.
1767. Sir Saml. Bradstreet, bt., aft. just. K. B.
1785. Dudley Hussey.
1786. Denis George, aft. bar. ex.
1795. Wm. Walker.
1822. Sir Jonas Greene.
1828. Sir Fredk. Shaw, bt.
1876. Fredk. Richd. Falkiner, July 10, G.

PART XI. INDIA.

It is impossible within the limits of the present work to give any account of the origin and history of the present British Indian Empire, or even to refer to the numerous acts of parliament, charters, and orders in council relating thereto. The first English East India Company was incorporated by Elizabeth in 1600. Charles I. granted another charter to a new company; but after numerous disputes between the two companies they were united by Oliver Cromwell. In 1698 a rival company was again established, again the two were united in 1702, and finally in 1708 a new East India Company was established under a charter granted by Anne. This charter was modified from time to time, but the company continued until, under 21 & 22 Vict., cap. 106, the Government of India was transferred to the Crown. This act came into operation September 1, 1858, but was not proclaimed in India until November 1, following.

In the year 1784, under 24 Geo. III., cap. 25, the East India Company was placed under a Board of Control (see part III., *ante*, p. 251). This was abolished by 21 & 22 Vict., cap. 106, above mentioned, and a Secretary of State for India appointed (see part III., *ante*, p. 236). A council, composed principally of retired Indian officials, was at the same time appointed to advise and assist the Secretary of State; but he has power to act independently if he thinks fit. Under 39 & 40 Vict., cap. 10, and a proclamation dated and gazetted April 28, 1876, the Queen assumed the title of Empress of India. This title was proclaimed in India January 1, 1877.

British India was originally divided into three provinces or presidencies—

Bengal, or Fort William;
Madras, or Fort St. George;
Bombay;

but after various sub-divisions and acquisition of territory it now consists of eight provinces—

Bengal,	Punjab,	Assam,
North-West Provinces and Oudh,	Central Provinces,	Madras,
	Burma,	Bombay,

which are placed under a governor, a lieutenant governor, or a chief commissioner, according to their relative importance.

Prince of Wales Island or Penang, Malacca, and Singapore, which were formerly under the government of India, now form a separate colony under the title of the Straits Settlements. See "Straits Settlements," *post*, p. 674.

The supreme government of India is vested in a Governor General or Viceroy, whose seat of government is at Calcutta, the chief city of Bengal.

The whole of India is in the ecclesiastical province of CALCUTTA.

SECTION 1.—HOME OFFICIALS.

PRESIDENTS, COMMISSIONERS, AND SECRETARIES OF THE BOARD OF CONTROL.

See Part III., "Official," *ante*, pp. 251-254.

CHAIRMEN AND DEPUTY CHAIRMEN OF THE EAST INDIA COMPANY.

Since the Regulation Act, 1773 (13 Geo. III., cap. 63).

1773. *Chair*. Hy. Crabbe Boulton.
Dep. Edwd. Wheeler.
On the death of Mr. Boulton, the court, on Oct. 12, 1773, app. Edwd. Wheeler, *chair*., and John Harrison, *dep*.
1774. *Chair*. Edwd. Wheeler.
Dep. John Harrison.
1775. *Chair* John Harrison.
Dep. John Roberts.
1776. *Chair*. John Roberts.
Dep. Wm. James.
1777. *Chair*. Geo. Wombwell, aft. bt.
Dep. Wm. Devaynes.
1778. *Chair*. Sir Geo. Wombwell, bt., *again*.
Dep. Wm. James, aft. bt.
1779. *Chair*. Sir Wm. James, bt.
Dep. Wm. Devaynes.
1780. *Chair*. Wm. Devaynes.
Dep. Laurence Sullivan.
1781. *Chair*. Laurence Sullivan.
Dep. Sir Wm. James, bt., *again*.
1782. *Chair*. Robt. Gregory.
Dep. Hy. Fletcher, aft. bt.
Mr. Gregory being disqualified, the court, on July 31, 1782, app. sir Hy. Fletcher, *chair*.; and, the next day, Nathl. Smith, *dep*.
1783. *Chair*. Sir Hy. Fletcher, bt., *again*.
Dep. Nathl. Smith.
Sir Hy. Fletcher being disqualified, the court, on Nov. 26, 1783, app. Nathl. Smith, *chair*.; and, on the day, Wm. Devaynes, *dep*.
1784. *Chair*. Nathl. Smith.
Dep. Wm. Devaynes, *again*.
1785. *Chair*. Wm. Devaynes.
Dep. Nathl. Smith, *again*.
1786. *Chair*. John Michie.
Dep. John Motteux.
1787. *Chair*. John Motteux.
Dep. Nathl. Smith, *again*.
1788. *Chair*. Nathl Smith, *again*.
Dep. John Michie.
Wm. Devaynes, app. Dec. 2, 1788 *vice* Michie, dec.
1789. *Chair*. Wm. Devaynes, *again*.
Dep. Stephen Lushington, aft. bt
1790. *Chair*. Stephen Lushington.
Dep. Wm. Devaynes, *again*.
1791. *Chair*. John Smith Burges.
Dep. Fras. Baring.
1792. *Chair*. Fras. Baring.
Dep. John Smith Burges.
1793. *Chair* Wm. Devaynes, *again*.
Dep. Thos. Cheap.
1794. *Chair*. Wm. Devaynes, *again*.
Dep. John Hunter.
1795. *Chair*. Sir Stephen Lushington, bt. *again*.
Dep. David Scott.
1796. *Chair*. David Scott.
Dep. Hugh Inglis, aft. bt.
1797. *Chair*. Hugh Inglis.
Dep. Jacob Bosanquet.
1798. *Chair*. Jacob Bosanquet.
Dep. Sir Stephen Lushington, bt. *again*.

1799. *Chair*. Sir Stephen Lushington, bt., *again*.
Dep. Hugh Inglis, *again*.
1800. *Chair*. Hugh Inglis, *again*.
Dep. David Scott, *again*.
1801. *Chair*. David Scott, *again*.
Dep. Chas. Mills.
Mr. Scott res. the chair; and, on Sept. 2, 1801, the court app. Chas. Mills, *chair*., and John Roberts, *dep*.
1802. *Chair*. John Roberts.
Dep. Jacob Bosanquet, *again*.
1803. *Chair*. Jacob Bosanquet, *again*.
Dep. John Roberts, *again*.
1804. *Chair*. Hon. Wm. Fullerton-Elphinstone.
Dep. Chas. Grant.
1805. *Chair*. Chas. Grant.
Dep. Geo. Smith.
1806. *Chair*. Hon. W. Fullerton-Elphinstone, *again*.
Dep. Edwd. Parry.
1807. *Chair*. Edwd. Parry.
Dep. Chas. Grant, *again*.
1808. *Chair*. Edwd. Parry, *again*.
Dep. Chas. Grant, *again*.
1809. *Chair*. Chas. Grant, *again*.
Dep. Wm. Astell.
1810. *Chair*. Wm. Astell.
Dep. Jacob Bosanquet, *again*.
1811. *Chair*. Jacob Bosanquet, *again*.
Dep. Sir Hugh Inglis, bt., *again*.
1812. *Chair*. Sir Hugh Inglis, bt., *again*.
Dep. Robt. Thornton.
1813. *Chair*. Robt. Thornton.
Dep. Hon. W. Fullerton-Elphinstone.
1814. *Chair*. Hon. W. Fullerton-Elphinstone, *again*.
Dep. John Inglis.
1815. *Chair*. Chas. Grant, *again*.
Dep. Thos. Reid.
1816. *Chair*. Thos. Reid.
Dep. John Bebb.
1817. *Chair*. John Bebb.
Dep. Jas. Pattison.
1818. *Chair*. Jas. Pattison.
Dep. Campbell Marjoribanks.
1819. *Chair*. Campbell Marjoribanks.
Dep. Geo. Abercrombie Robinson, aft. bt.
1820. *Chair*. G. A. Robinson.
Dep. Thos. Reid.
1821. *Chair*. Thos. Reid.
Dep. Jas. Pattison, *again*.
1822. *Chair*. Jas. Pattison, *again*.
Dep. Wm. Wigram.
1823. *Chair*. Wm. Wigram.
Dep. Wm. Astell, *again*.
1824. *Chair*. Wm. Astell, *again*.
Dep. Campbell Marjoribanks, *again*.
1825. *Chair*. Campbell Marjoribanks, *again*.
1825. *Dep*. Sir G. A. Robinson, bt., *again*.
1826. *Chair*. Sir G. A. Robinson, bt., *again*.
Dep. Hon. Hugh Lindsay.
1827. *Chair*. Hon. Hugh Lindsay.
Dep. Jas. Pattison, *again*.
1828. *Chair*. Wm. Astell, *again*.
Dep. John Loch.
1829. *Chair*. John Loch.
Dep. Wm. Astell, *again*.
1830. *Chair*. Wm. Astell, *again*.
Dep. Robt. Campbell, aft. bt.
1831. *Chair*. Sir Robt. Campbell, bt.
Dep. John Goldsborough Ravenshaw.
1832. *Chair*. J. G. Ravenshaw.
Dep. Campbell Marjoribanks, *again*.
1833. *Chair*. Campbell Marjoribanks, *again*.
Dep. Wm. Wigram, *again*.
Chair. John Loch, *again*.
Dep. Hy. St. Geo. Tucker.
1834. *Chair*. Hy. St. Geo. Tucker.
Dep. Wm. Stanley Clarke.
1835. *Chair*. W. S. Clarke.
Dep. Jas. Rivett-Carnac, aft. bt.
1836. *Chair*. Sir Jas. Rivett-Carnac, bt.
Dep. John Loch, *again*.
1837. *Chair*. Sir Jas. Rivett-Carnac, *again*.
Dep Sir Jas. Law Lushington.
1838. *Chair*. Sir Jas. L. Lushington.
Dep. Richd. Jenkins, aft. sir R.
1839. *Chair*. Sir Richd. Jenkins.
Dep. Wm. Butterworth Bayley.
1840. *Chair*. Wm. B. Bayley.
Dep. Geo. Lyall.
1841. *Chair*. Geo. Lyall.
Dep. Sir Jas. L. Lushington, *again*.
1842. *Chair*. Sir Jas. L. Lushington, *again*.
Dep. John Cotton.
1843. *Chair*. John Cotton.
Dep. John Shepherd.
1844. *Chair*. John Shepherd.
Dep. Sir Hy. Willock.
1845. *Chair* Sir Hy. Willock.
Dep. Jas. Weir Hogg, aft. sir Jas., bt.
1846. *Chair*. as. Weir Hogg.
Dep. Hy. St. Geo. Tucker, *again*.
1847. *Chair*. Hy. St. Geo. Tucker, *again*.
Dep. Sir Jas. L. Lushington, *again*.
1848. *Chair*. Sir Jas. L. Lushington.
Dep. Archd. Galloway, aft. sir A.
1849. *Chair*. Sir A. Galloway.
Dep. John Shepherd.
1850. *Chair*. John Shepherd.
Dep. Sir Jas. Weir Hogg, bt., *again*.

1851. *Chair.* John Shepherd, *again.*
Dep. Sir Jas. Weir Hogg, bt., *again.*
1852. *Chair.* Sir Jas. Weir Hogg, bt., *again.*
Dep. Russell Ellice.
1853. *Chair.* Russell Ellice.
Dep. Jas. Oliphant.
1854. *Chair.* Jas. Oliphant.
Dep. Elliot Macnaghten.
1855. *Chair.* Elliot Macnaghten.
Dep. Wm. Hy. Sykes.
1856. *Chair.* m. Hy. Sykes.
Dep. Ross Donnelly Mangles.
1857. *Chair.* Ross Donnelly Mangles.
Dep. Sir Fredk. Currie, bt.

SECRETARIES AND UNDER-SECRETARIES OF STATE FOR INDIA.

See Part III., "Official," *ante*, p. 236.

THE COUNCIL OF INDIA.

Appointed under 21 & 22 Vict., cap. 106. Secs. 7–13.

By this act a Council of fifteen members was established and styled the Council of India. Of the original members seven were chosen by the East India Company and eight by the Crown. Vacancies occurring amongst the latter were to be filled up by the Crown and all other vacancies by election by the Council. With certain exceptions (see section 10) all members of the Council were to have served or resided in India for ten years at the least.

Council of India.

Original Members, Sept. 21, 1858 (**G.**).

Chosen by the East India Co.

1. Chas. Mills.
2. John Shepherd.
3. Sir Jas. Weir Hogg, bt.
4. Elliot Macnaghten.
5. Ross Donnelly Mangles.
6. Wm. Jos. Eastwick.
7. Hy. Thoby Prinsep.

Chosen by the Crown.

8. Sir Hy. Conyngham Montgomery, bt.
9. Sir Fredk. Currie, bt.
10. Sir John Laird Mair Lawrence, bt., G.C.B.; aft. ld. Lawrence.
11. Maj-gen. Sir Robt. John Hussey Vivian, K.C.B.
12. Col. Sir Proby Thos. Cautley, K.C.B.
13. Lt.-col. Sir Hy. Creswicke Rawlinson, K.C.B.
14. John Pollard Willoughby.
15. Wm. Urquhart Arbuthnot.

Subsequent Appointments.

1859. Col. Hy. Marion Durand, C.B.; aft. sir H., June 18, **G.**
Sir Thos. Erskine Perry, Aug. 8, **G.**
1861. Col. Wm. Erskine Baker, July 18.
1863. Sir Geo. Russell Clerk, K.C.B., K.C.S.I., Dec. 14, **G.**
1866. Sir Hy. Bartle Edwd. Frere, G.C.S.I., K.C.B., Nov. 12, **G.**
1868. Sir Robt. Montgomery, K.C.B., G.C.S.I., Sept. 21.
Sir Fredk. Jas. Halliday, K.C.B., Sept. 29.
Sir Hy. Creswicke Rawlinson, K.C.B., Oct, 9, **G.**
1871. Sir Hy. Jas. Sumner Maine, K.C.S.I., Nov. 2.

1872. Sir Louis Mallet, C.B., Feb. 8.
1874. Sir Geo. Campbell, K.C.S.I., Feb. 16.
Andrew Cassels, Apr. 30.
Maj.-Gen. Edwin Beaumont Johnson, Sept. 1.
1875. Lt.-Gen. Richd. Strachey, Jan. 1.
Hon. Edmd. Drummond, Feb. 9.
Sir Barrow Helbert Ellis, K.C.S.I., July 14.
Col. Hy. Yule, C.B., Oct. 23.
1876. Maj.-gen. sir Alfred Thos. Wilde, K.C.B., C.S.I., Jan. 1.
Maj.-gen. sir Garnet Wolseley, K.C.B., G.C.M.G.; aft. visc. Wolseley, Nov. 13.
Sir Wm. Muir, K.C.S.I., Nov. 28.
1877. Col. sir Wm. Lockyer Merewether, C.B., K.C.S.I., Nov. 1.
Robt. Anstruther Dalyell, Nov. 1.
1878. Sir Hy. Wylie Norman, K.C.B., Feb. 25.
Maj.-gen. Chas. John Foster, C.B., July 22.
1879. Lt.-gen. Richd. Strachey, *again*, Mar. 11.
1880. Bertram Wodehouse Currie, Dec. 11.
1882. Hon. sir Ashley Eden, K.C.S.I., Apr. 24.
1883. Sir Peter Stark Lumsden, K.C.B., C.S.I., Dec. 1.
1884. Jas. Richd. Bullen-Smith, C.S.I., June 6.
1885. Sir Robt. Hy. Davies, K.C.S.I., C.I.E., Mar. 3.
Sir John Strachey, G.C.S.I., C.I.E., July 14.
Gen. sir Donald Martin Stewart, bt., G.C.B., G.C.S.I., C.I.E., Dec. 16.
1887. Col. sir Owen Tudor Burne, K.C.S.I., Jan. 1.
Robt. Hardie, Mar. 17.
Jas. Braithwaite Peile, C.S.I.; aft. Sir J., Nov. 12.
Sir Alexr. John Arbuthnot, K.C.S.I., Nov. 1.
1888. Sir Alfred Comyns Lyall, K.C.B., K.C.I.E., Jan. 17.
Sir Chas. Arthr. Turner, K.C.I.E., Feb. 21.
1889. Lt.-gen. sir Archbd. Alison, bt., G.C.B., Jan. 1.

SECTION II.—INDIAN OFFICIALS.

THE SUPREME GOVERNMENT, CALCUTTA.

ADMINISTRATORS AND GOVERNORS-GENERAL OF INDIA.

ADMINISTRATORS.

Appointed prior to the Regulation Act, 1773, 13 Geo. III., cap. 63.

	App. by the Court.	Assumption of govt.	Time of quitting.
Alexr. Dawson	Jan. 27, 1748	July 18, 1749	Jan. 5, 1752; dism. by the court.
Wm. Fytche	Jan. 8, 1752	July 6, 1752	*d.* Aug. 8, 1752.
Roger Drake, admr., chosen on the spot.	Aug. 8, 1752; succ. on death of Fytche.	Aug. 10, 1752	Res. June 21, 1758.
Messrs. Watts, Manningham, Becker, and Holwell.	App. by the court, *vice* Drake, to govern, each alternately four months, Nov. 11, 1757.	June 21, 1758	Agreed to call col. Clive to the govt.
Col. Robt. Clive, aft. ld. Clive.	Called to the govt. by Messrs. Watts, &c., and aft. app. by the court, Mar. 25, 1758.	June 27, 1758	Res. Jan. 14. 1760.
John Zephaniah Holwell.	Succ. on resign. of Clive, Jan. 24, 1760.	Jan. 28, 1760	Res. on arrival of Vansittart, July 27, 1760.

	App. by the Court.	Assumption of govt.	Time of quitting.
Hy. Vansittart - -	Nov. 23, 1759 - -	July 27, 1760	Res. Nov. 26, 1704.
John Spencer - -	Succ. on resign. of Vansittart, Nov. 26, 1764.	Dec. 3, 1764 -	May 3, 1765; res. on arrival of ld. Clive.
Robt. ld. Clive, *second time.*	June 1, 1764 - -	May 3, 1765 -	Res. Jan. 20, 1767.
Henry Verelst - -	Succ. on resign. of ld. Clive, Jan. 20, 1767.	Jan. 29, 1767	Res. Dec. 16, 1769.
John Cartier - -	Succ. on resign. of Verelst, Dec. 16, 1769.	Dec. 20, 1769	Ordered to quit the govt. in the last ship of the season after Mr. Hastings' arrival.
Warren Hastings - -	Apr. 25, 1771 - -	Apr. 13, 1772. First Council held Oct. 20, 1774.	App. gov.-gen., *vide infra.*

Governors-General.

Under the Regulation Act 1773, 13 Geo. III., cap. 63.

Warren Hastings, *vide supra.*	Named in the act -	*Vide supra* -	Feb. 1, 1785; res. to Macpherson.
John Macpherson, aft. sir John.	Succ. Hastings - -	Feb. 1, 1785 -	Feb. 12, 1786; res. to ld. Cornwallis.
Geo., Earl Macartney -	App. by the court to succ. Hastings, Feb. 17, 1785.	Declined the office.	
Chas., E., aft. M. Cornwallis.	Feb. 24, 1786 - -	Sept. 12, 1786	Res. to Shore, Oct. 28, 1793.
M.-gen. Wm. Medows, aft. sir W.	Apr. 28, 1790 - -	Appt. appr. by Mr. Pitt.	But relinq. by gen. Medows.
Sir John Shore, aft. ld. Teignmouth.	App, Apr. 11, 1786, to succ. to the next vacancy.		
The same - - -	App. Sept. 19, 1792, to succ. E. Cornwallis.	Oct. 28, 1793	Res. to Clarke, Mar. 12, 1798.
Geo., M. Cornwallis, *again.*	Feb. 1, 1797 - -	But did not proceed.	Relinq. the appt., Aug. 2, 1797.
Sir Alured Clarke -	Sept 20, 1797 - -	Apr. 6, 1798 -	May 17, 1798; res. to ld. Mornington.
Rd. Colley, E. of Mornington, aft. ld. and M. Wellesley.	Oct. 4, 1797 - -	May 17, 1798	July 30, 1805; res. to ld. Cornwallis.
Geo., M. Cornwallis, *again.*	Jan. 9, 1805 - -	July 30, 1805	Oct, 5, 1805; *d.* on his way to the upper provinces.
Sir Geo. Hilaro Barlow, bt.	Oct 10, 1805; succ., provisionally, on ld. Cornwallis' death.	Conf. in the govt. by the court, Feb. 19, 1806.	Succ. by ld. Minto, July 31, 1807.
Geo., ld., aft. E. of Minto.	July 9, 1806 - -	July 31, 1807	Oct. 4, 1813; res. to ld. Moira.
Fras., E. of Moira, aft. M. of Hastings.	Nov. 18, 1812 - -	Oct. 4, 1813 -	Jan. 9, 1823.
Hon. John Adam, as senior councillor.	Jan. 13, 1823, under 33 Geo. III., cap. 52.	Jan. 13, 1823	Aug. 1, 1823; res. to ld. Amherst.
Geo. Canning - -	Mar. 27, 1822 - -	Did not go out	Relinq. appt. Sept. 16, 1822.

	App. by the Court.	Assumption of govt.	Time of quitting.
Wm., ld., aft E. Amherst.	Oct. 23, 1822 - -	Aug 1, 1823 -	Mar. 10, 1828.
Wm. Butterworth Bayley.	Succ., provisionally, as senr. councillor.	Mar. 13, 1828	July 4, 1828.
Ld. Wm. Cavendish-Bentinck, G. C. B., G.C.H.	July 18, 1827 - -	July 4, 1828 -	*Vide infra.*

By 3 and 4 Wm. IV., cap. 85 (Aug. 28, 1833), it was declared that the supreme direction and control of the whole of the civil and military government of all the territories and revenues in India should be vested in a governor-general and council, to be styled the governor-general of India in council. And it was further declared that the person who should be governor-general of the presidency of Fort William in Bengal on Apr. 22, 1834, should be the first governor-general of India, under the act. The governor-general of Bengal, as head of the chief presidency, had been usually denominated "Governor-General"; Madras, Bombay, &c., being subject to his supreme control; but it was not until the passing of this act that the "Governor-General of India," actually so constituted, existed as well in name as in authority.

Ld. Wm. Cavendish Bentinck, *vide supra.*	Contd. in the govt., Apr. 22, 1834.	First *Gov.-Gen. of India* under the above act.	Mar. 20, 1835.
Sir Chas. Theoph. Metcalfe, bt., aft. ld. Metcalfe.	Succ. provisionally -	Mar. 20, 1835	Mar. 4, 1836.
Wm., ld. Heytesbury, G.C.B.	Jan. 28, 1835.	Did not proceed.	Appt. vacated by the crown, May 5, 1835.
Geo., ld., aft. E. of Auckland.	Aug. 12, 1835 - -	Mar. 4. 1836 -	Feb. 28, 1842.
Edwd., ld., aft. E., of Ellenborough.	Oct. 20, 1841 - -	Feb. 28, 1842	Removed June 15, 1844.
Wm. Wilberforce Bird, memb. of council.	Succ. provisionally as next in rank in the council.	June 15, 1844	Res. to Hardinge, July 23, 1844.
Sir Hy. Hardinge, aft. visc. Hardinge, G.C.B.	May 2, 1844 - -	July 23, 1844	Jan. 12, 1848.
Jas. Andrew, E., aft. M., of Dalhousie.	Aug. 4, 1847.	Jan. 12, 1848.	
Chas. John, visc. Canning.	- - - - - -	Feb. 29, 1856	Made viceroy, *vide infra.*

Since Nov. 1, 1858, on the passing of 21 and 22 Vict., cap. 106 (see Introduction, *ante*, p. 643), the Governors-General have been appointed by the Crown, and are distinguished by the additional title of Viceroy.

Viceroys and Governors-General of India.

From Nov. 1, 1858.

	App. by the Crown.	Assumption of govt.
Chas. John, visc. Canning, *vide supra.*	Appt. contd. - -	Appt. contd.
Jas., E. of Elgin and Kincardine, K.T., G.C.B.	Jan. 21, 1862 - -	Mar. 12, 1862.
Sir John Laird Mair Lawrence, bt., G.C.B., K.C.S.I.; aft. ld. Lawrence.	Dec. 5, 1863 - -	Jan. 12, 1864.
Richd Southwell, E. of Mayo.	Oct. 27, 1868 - -	Jan. 12, 1869.
Thos. Geo., ld., aft. E., of Northbrook.	Mar. 14, 1872 - -	May 3, 1872.
Edwd. Robt. Lytton, ld., aft. E., of Lytton.	Feb. 12. 1876 - -	Apr. 12, 1876.

	App. by the Crown.	Assumption of govt.
Geo. Fredk. Saml., M. of Ripon, K.G.	May 6, 1880 - -	June 8, 1880.
Fredk. Temple, E. of Dufferin, K.P., G.C.B., G.C.M.G.; aft. M. of Dufferin and Ava.	Oct. 21, 1884 - -	Dec. 13, 1884.
Hy. Chas. Keith, M. of Lansdowne, G.M.S.I., G.C.M.G., G.M.I.E.	1888 - - -	Dec. 10,1888.

COMMANDERS IN CHIEF IN INDIA.

	Appointed.	Assumed command.	Quitted command.
Lt.-gen. John Clavering.	Feb. 7, 1774 - -	Oct. 27, 1774	Aug, 30, 1777, when he *d.*

On the death of gen. Clavering the duties were carried on by the military board; but on Oct. 16 following brigr.-gen. Giles Stibbert, provincial comm.-ch., assumed command of the army, which he held until the arrival of Sir Eyre Coote.

Lt.-gen. sir Eyre Coote.	Apr. 17, 1777 - -	Mar. 25, 1779	Apr. 27, 1783; *d.* Apr. 30, 1783.

Brigr.-gen. Stibbert again assumed the chief command, and held it until lt.-gen. Sloper arrived.

Lt.-gen. Robt. Sloper -	Oct. 27, 1784 - -	July 21, 1785	Sept. 12, 1786.
Geo., E., aft M., Cornwallis, gov.-gen.	Apr. 11, 1786 - -	Sept. 12, 1786	Oct. 28, 1793.

Col. Mackenzie and col. Auchmuty were apptd. to the command-in chief in the absence of ld. Cornwallis in 1790 and 1793.

Maj.-gen. sir Robt. Abercromby.	Sept. 19, 1792 - -	Oct. 28, 1793	Apr. 30, 1797.

Maj.-gen. Morgan held the chief command in the absence of gen. Abercromby.

Lt.-gen. sir Alured Clarke.	Oct. 4, 1797 - -	May 17, 1798	July 31, 1801.

He had held the provl. command from Apr. 30, 1797.

Lt.-gen. Gerard Lake, aft. ld. Lake.	Aug. 13, 1800 - -	July 31, 1801	July 30, 1805.
Geo., M. Cornwallis, *again*; gov.-gen.	Mar. 20, 1805 - -	July 30, 1805	Oct. 5, 1805; *d.* Oct. 5, 1805.

Lord Lake held the provl. command in the absence of ld. Cornwallis.

Lt.-gen. Gerard, ld., aft. visc., Lake	Feb. 19, 1806 - -	Oct. 10, 1805	Oct. 17, 1807.

Ld. Lake held the command from the death of the marq. Cornwallis, in his capacity of provl. comm.-ch.

Lt.-gen. sir Geo. Hewett-	Dec. 23, 1806 - -	Oct. 17, 1807	Dec. 18, 1811.
Lt.-gen. sir Geo. Nugent-	Mar. 13, 1811 - -	Jan. 14, 1812	Oct. 4, 1813.

On the arrival of ld. Moira, sir Geo. Nugent assumed the provl. command, agreeably with the court's resolution of the 18th Nov. 1812.

Gen. Fras., E. of Moira, aft. M. of Hastings, gov.-gen.	Nov. 18, 1812 - -	Oct. 4, 1813 -	Jan. 13, 1823.
Lt.-gen. hon. sir Edwd. Paget, G.C.B.	June 2, 1822 - -	Jan. 13, 1823	Oct. 7, 1825.
Gen. Stapleton, ld., aft. visc., Combermere, G.C.B., G.C.H.	Feb. 9, 1825 - -	Oct. 7, 1825 -	Jan. 1, 1830.

	Appointed.	Assumed command.	Quitted command.
Lt -gen. Geo., E. of Dalhousie, G.C.B	Feb. 17, 1829 - -	Jan. 1, 1830 -	Jan. 10, 1832.
Lt.-gen. sir Edwd. Barnes, G.C.B.	Oct. 17, 1830 - -	Jan. 10, 1832	Oct. 16, 1833.
Ld. Wm. Cavendish Bentinck, G.C.B., G.C.H., gov.-gen.	May 18, 1833 - -	Oct. 16, 1833	*Vide infra.*
Ld. Wm. Cavendish Bentinck, gov.-gen. and commr.-chief.	Re-app. by a new commission under 3 & 4 Wm. IV. cap. 85.	Apr. 22, 1834	Sept. 5, 1835.
Gen. sir Hy. Fane, G.C.B.	Feb. 4, 1835 - -	Sept. 5, 1835	Dec. 7, 1839.
Gen. sir Jasper Nicolls, K.C.B.	Aug. 14, 1839 - -	Dec. 7, 1839 -	Aug. 11, 1843.
Gen. sir Hugh Gough, G.C.B.; aft. visc. Gough.	- - - - - -	Aug. 11, 1843	May 7, 1849.
Gen. sir Chas, Napier, G.C.B.	Mar. 7, 1849 - -	May 7, 1849 -	Dec. 6, 1850
Gen. sir Wm. Maynard Gomm, K.C.B.	Sept. 18, 1850 - -	Dec. 6, 1850.	
Gen. hon. Geo. Anson.	Nov. 20, 1855 - -	Jan. 23, 1856.	
Lt.-gen. sir Colin Campbell, G.C.B.; aft. ld Clyde.	July 11, 1857 - -	Aug. 13,1857.	
Gen. sir Hugh Hy. Rose, G.C.B., K.C.S.I.; aft. ld. Strathnairn.	May 18, 1860 - -	June 4, 1860.	
Gen. sir Wm. Rose Mansfield, K.C.B., G.C.S.I.; aft. ld. Sandhurst.	- - - - - -	Mar. 23,1865.	
Gen. Robt. Cornelis, ld Napier of Magdala, G.C.B, G.C.S.I.	- - - - - -	Apr. 9, 1870.	
Gen. sir Fredk. Paul Haines, K.C.B.	- - - - - -	Apr. 10,1876.	
Gen. sir Donald Martin Stewart, bt., G.C.B., C.I.E.	- . - - - -	Apr. 8, 1881.	
Gen. sir Fredk. Sleigh Roberts, bt., V.C., G.C.B., C.I.E.	- - - - - -	Nov. 28,1885.	

BENGAL.

THE PRESIDENCY OR PROVINCE OF BENGAL, sometimes styled the presidency of Fort William, from the small settlement out of which it has risen, is the youngest of the three presidencies, but has for many years been considered as the principal one, its governor having been, by the Regulation Act 1773 (13 Geo. III., cap. 63), made *ex-officio* governor-general of the whole of the dominions of the East India Company. By the 3 & 4 Wm. IV., cap. 85 (Aug. 28, 1833), the title of "Governor-General of India" was first officially created, and provision was made for the division of Bengal into two provinces, to be called Fort William, in Bengal, and Agra, with a deputy or lieut. governor for each. By the 5 & 6 Wm. IV., cap. 52 (Aug. 31, 1835), the East India Company was empowered to suspend this division, and it was never made. By 16 & 17 Vict., cap. 95 (Aug. 20, 1853), and

17 & 18 Vict., cap. 77 (Aug. 7, 1854), further provision was made for the division of Bengal; and under these various Acts, to which the reader is referred for details, the North-West Provinces were separated, and a lieutenant governor was appointed for the rest of Bengal.

LIEUTENANT GOVERNORS OF BENGAL.

1854. Fredk. Jas. Halliday, aft. sir F., May 1.
1859. John Peter Grant, May 1.
1862. Cecil Beadon, aft. sir C., Apr. 23.
1867. Wm. Grey, aft. sir W.
1870. Geo. Campbell, aft. sir G.
1874. Sir Richd. Temple, bt., K.C.S.I., Apr. 9.
1877. Hon. Ashley Eden, C.S.I., aft. sir A., May 1.
1882. Aug. Rivers Thompson, C.S.I., C.I.E., aft. sir A., Apr. 24.
1887. Sir Stewart Colvin Bayley, K.C.S.I., C.I.E., Apr. 2.

COMMANDERS IN CHIEF IN BENGAL.

	Appointed.	Assumed command.
Lt.-gen. Giles Stibbert	Sept. 26, 1776	Oct. 16, 1777.

Lt.-gen. Stibbert held the provl. command during the absence of sir Eyre Coote. at Madras, and continued to hold it after sir Eyre Coote's death until the arrival of lt.-gen. Sloper.

Col. McKenzie	Dec. 6, 1790	Dec. 6, 1790.

During the absence of ld. Cornwallis.

Col. Saml. Auchmuty, aft. sir S.	Aug. 15, 1793	Aug. 15, 1793.

During the absence of ld. Cornwallis.

Maj.-gen. sir Robt. Abercromby	Sep. 19, 1792	Oct. 5, 1793.

On Oct. 28, 1793, he assumed the chief command in India.

Maj.-gen. Morgan	Jan. 17, 1797	Jan. 17, 1797.

During the absence of gen. Abercromby.

Lt.-gen. sir Alured Clarke, K.B.	Apr. 6, 1796	Apr. 30, 1797.

On May 17, 1798, sir A. Clarke assumed the chief command in India.

Lt.-gen. Gerard, ld., aft. visc. Lake	Apr. 11, 1805	July 30, 1805.

On Oct. 5, 1805, on the death of the M. Cornwallis, ld. Lake assumed the chief command in India.

Lt.-gen. sir Geo. Nugent	Nov. 18, 1812	Oct. 9, 1813.

Pursuant to a resolution of the court, of Nov. 18, 1812, sir Geo. Nugent, on the arrival of the earl of Moira, assumed the provl. command, and held it until Dec. 28, 1814; from which time the separate appointment of commr.-chief in Bengal merged into the general appointment of comm.-chief in India.

(See "Commanders in Chief in India," *ante*, p. 650.)

CHIEF JUSTICES OF BENGAL.

Chief Justices of the Supreme Court of Bengal.

Appointed under 13 Geo. III., cap. 63 (June 16, 1773).

1774. Sir Elijah Impey, first judge, Mar. 26.
1791. Sir Robt. Chambers.
1798. Sir John Anstruther, bt.; res. 1806.
1807. Sir Hy. Russell, knt.; bt. 1812.
1813. Sir Edwd. Hyde East, knt.; bt. 1823.
1821. Sir Robt. H. Blossett, *d.* Feb. 1, 1823.
1823. Sir Christr. Puller, *d.* May 26, 1824.
1825. Sir Chas. Grey, Feb. 2.
1832. Sir Wm. Oldnall Russell.
1838. Sir Edwd. Ryan.
1842. Sir Lawrence Peel.
1855. Sir Jas. Wm. Colvile.
1859. Sir Barnes Peacock.

Supreme Court abolished on establishment of High Court of Judicature under 24 & 25 Vict., cap. 104 (Aug. 6, 1861).

Chief Justices of the High Court of Judicature for the Bengal Division of the Presidency of Fort William.

Appointed under 24 & 25 Vict. cap. 104, and Order in Council dated May 13, 1862.

1862. Sir Barnes Peacock, May 13, **G.**
1870. Sir Richd. Couch, Apr. 1, **G.**
1875. Richd. Garth, Mar. 2; knt. May 13, **G.**
1886. Sir Wm. Comer Petheram, Feb. 26, **G.**

DIOCESE OF CALCUTTA.

The bishopric of Calcutta was constituted under 53 Geo. III., cap. 155 (July 21, 1813). By 3 & 4 Wm. IV., cap. 85 (Aug. 28, 1833), the bishop of Calcutta was declared to be the metropolitan of India.

The ecclesiastical province of Calcutta comprises the sees of—

Bombay.
Calcutta.
Colombo.
Lahore.
Madras.
Rangoon.
Travancore and Cochin

Bishops of Calcutta.

1814. Thos. Fanshawe Middleton, 1st bp., Feb. 18; *d.* July 8, 1822.
1823. Reginald Heber, May 13, **G.**; *d.* Apr. 2, 1826.
1827. John Thos. James, Apr. 25, **G.**; *d.* 1829.
1829. John M. Turner, *d.* 1832.
1832. Danl. Wilson, Apr. 3, **G.**
1858. Geo. Edwd. Lynch Cotton, Mar. 29, **G.**
1867. Robt. Milman.
1876. Edwd. Ralph Johnson, Nov. 21, **G.**

NORTH-WEST PROVINCES AND OUDH.

The North-West Provinces were separated from Bengal in 1853, and were placed under a lieutenant governor. See "Bengal," *ante*, p. 651.

Oudh was annexed in 1856, and placed under a chief commissioner.

Since 1877 the offices of lieutenant governor of the North-West Provinces and chief commissioner of Oudh have been held by the same person.

GOVERNORS, &c., OF THE NORTH-WEST PROVINCES AND OUDH.

Lieutenant Governors of the North-West Provinces.

1853. John Russell Colvin, Oct. 14.
1859. Geo. Fredk. Edmonstone, Jan. 20.
1863. Hon. Edmond Drummond, Mar. 7.
1868. Sir Wm. Muir, K.C.S.I., Mar. 7.
1874. Sir John Strachey, K.C.S.I.
1877. Sir Geo. Ebenezer Wilson Couper, bt., C.B., K.C.S.I., C.I.E., Jan. 17.

Office united to that of Chief Commissioner of Oudh, 1877.

Chief Commissioners of Oudh.

1856. Maj.-gen. sir Jas. Outram, K.C.B.
1858. Robt. Montgomery, aft. sir R.
1859. Chas. John Wingfield.
1866. John Strachey, aft. sir J.
1870. Robt. Hy. Davies.
1871. Maj.-gen. Lousada Barrow.
1874. Sir Geo. Ebenezer Wilson Couper bt.
1876. John Forbes David Inglis.

Office united to that of Lieut. Governor of North-West Provinces, 1877.

Lieutenant Governors of the North-West Provinces and Chief Commissioners of Oudh.

1877. Sir Geo. Ebenezer Wilson Couper, bt., C.B., K.C.S.I., C.I.E.
1882. Sir Alfred Comyns Lyall, K.C.B., Apr. 17.
1887. Sir Auckland Colvin, K.C.M.G., C.I.E., Nov. 21.

CHIEF JUSTICES OF THE NORTH-WEST PROVINCES.

The High Court of Judicature for the North-West Provinces was established in 1866 under 24 & 25 Vict., c. 104, sec. 16.

1866. Walter Morgan, Mar 3, **G.**; knt. June 13.
1871. Robt. Stuart, Sept. 22, **G.**; knt. Oct. 3.
1884. Wm. Comer Petheram, Aug. 26, **G.**; knt. Sept. 26.
1886. John Edge, aft. sir J., May 27, **G.**; aft. knt

THE PUNJAB.

The Punjab was annexed in 1849, and was until 1853 governed by a board of administration. In 1853 it was placed under a chief commissioner, who in 1859 was raised to the rank of lieutenant governor.

GOVERNORS, &c., OF THE PUNJAB.

President of the Board of Administration of the Punjab.

1849. Col. Sir Hy. Montgomery Lawrence, K.C.B.

Chief Commissioner of the Punjab.

1853. Jno. Laird Mair Lawrence, aft. sir J., bt., and ld. Lawrence.

Lieutenant Governors of the Punjab.

1859 Robt. Montgomery, aft. sir R.
1865. Donald Friell McLeod, C.B.
1870. Maj.-gen. sir Hy. Marion Durand, K.C.S.I., C.B.
1871. Robt. Hy. Davies, C.S.I., aft. sir R., Jan. 20.
1877. Robt. Eyles Egerton, C.S.I., aft. sir R., Apr. 2.
1882. Sir Chas. Umpherston Aitchison, K.C.S.I., C.I.E., Apr. 12.
1887. Jas. Broadwood Lyall, aft. sir J. Apr. 2.

DIOCESE OF LAHORE.

The bishopric of Lahore was constituted in 1877, and is in the province of Calcutta.

Bishops of Lahore.

1877. Thos. Valpy French, Dec. 17, **G.**; res.
1887. Hy. Jas. Matthew, Dec. 22, **G.**

THE CENTRAL PROVINCES.

The Central Provinces were constituted in 1861. They were taken from the North-West Provinces and from Madras. They are governed by a chief commissioner.

CHIEF COMMISSIONERS OF THE CENTRAL PROVINCES.

1862. Lt.-col. Edwd. King Elliott.
1865. Richd. Temple, aft. sir R., bt.
1867. Geo. Campbell, aft. sir G.
1870. John Hy. Morris.
1883. Wm. Brittain Jones, C.S.I.
1885. Chas. Haukes Tod Crosthwaite, aft. sir C.
1887. Alexr. Mackenzie, C.S.I.

BURMA.

Burma is now divided into Upper and Lower Burma. Lower Burma, formerly known as British Burma, was annexed to India partly in 1826, after the first Burmese War, and partly in 1852, after the second Burmese War. Upper Burma was annexed in February 1886, after the third Burmese War. The government is vested in a chief commissioner.

CHIEF COMMISSIONERS OF BURMA.

1862. Arthur Purvese Phayre.
1867. Col. Albert Fytche.
1871. Hon. Ashley Eden, aft. sir A., actg. C. C.; app. C. C. 1873.
1877. Augustus Rivers Thompson, aft. sir A.
1878. Chas. Umpherston Aitchison, C.S.I., aft. sir C.
1882. Chas. Edwd. Bernard, aft. sir C.
1887. Chas. Haukes Tod Crosthwaite, C.S.I., aft. sir C.

DIOCESE OF RANGOON.

The bishopric of Rangoon was constituted in 1877, and is in the province of Calcutta.

Bishops of Rangoon.

1877. Jonn. Holt Titcomb, Dec. 17, **G.**; res. 1882.
1882. John Miller Strachan, consec. May 1.

ASSAM.

ASSAM was ceded by Burma in 1824, and was included in the government of Bengal until 1874, when it was made a separate province and placed under a chief commissioner.

CHIEF COMMISSIONERS OF ASSAM.

1874. Col. Richd. Harte Keatinge, V.C., C.S.I.
1880. Sir Stuart Colvin Bayley, K.C.S.I.
1881. Chas. Alfred Elliott, C.S.I., aft. sir C.
1887. Dennis Fitzpatrick, C.S.I.

MADRAS.

THE PRESIDENCY OR PROVINCE OF MADRAS is sometimes called the Presidency of FORT ST. GEORGE, from the settlement in which it had its origin. This settlement was the first acquisition of territory by the original East India Company, who obtained possession of it about 1639.

GOVERNORS OF MADRAS.

First appointed under 24 Geo. III., cap. 25 (Aug. 13, 1784).

	Appointed.	Took his Seat.
Geo., Earl Macartney	Sept. 2, 1784	Feb. 12, 1785
Alexr. Davidson, councillor	Succ. provisionally	June 4, 1785.
Sir Archd. Campbell	Mar. 9, 1785	Apr. 6, 1786.
John Hollond, councillor	Succ. provisionally	Feb. 7, 1789.
E. J. Hollond, councillor	Succ. provisionally	Feb. 13, 1790
M.-gen. Wm. Medows, aft. sir W.	July 7, 1789	Feb. 20, 1790
Sir Chas. Oakeley, bt.	Apr. 28, 1790	Aug. 1, 1792.

He had previously held the office of governor, in the absence of gen. Medows, from Oct. 15, 1790, to Dec. 21, 1791.

	Appointed.	Took his Seat.
Robt. Hobart, c.c. and aft. ld. Hobart; aft. E. of Buckinghamshire	Oct. 23, 1793	Sept. 7, 1794.
M.-gen. Geo. Harris, aft. gen. ld. Harris	Oct, 4, 1797	Feb. 21, 1798
Edwd., ld. Clive, aft. E. of Powis	Dec. 13, 1797	Sept. 5, 1799.

Lord Powis quitted the government, Aug. 30, 1803. The govr.-gen., ld. Mornington, held the office from Jan. 2, preceding.

	Appointed.	Took his Seat.
Ld. Wm. Cavendish Bentinck	Nov. 17, 1802	Aug. 30, 1803

Recalled by the court, Apr. 7, 1807; quitted Sept. 11, following.

	Appointed.	Took his Seat.
Wm. Petrie, councillor	Succ. provisionally	Sept. 11, 1807
Sir Geo. Hilaro Barlow, bt.	May 13, 1807	Dec. 24, 1807
Lt.-gen. hon. John Abercromby	Nov. 20, 1812	May 21, 1813
Hugh Elliot	Dec. 3, 1813	Sept. 16, 1814
Maj.gen. sir Thos. Munro, bt., K.C.B.		June 10, 1820
Hy. Sullivan Græme	Succ. provisionally	July 10, 1827

Took charge of the govt. on the death of Sir Thos. Munro, which took place at Ghooty, July 6, preceding.

	Appointed.	Took his seat.
Stephen Rumbold Lushington - - - -	Jan. 17, 1827	- Oct. 18, 1827.
Lt.-gen. sir Frederick Adam, K.C.B. - - - -	- - - -	- Oct. 25, 1832
John, ld. Elphinstone - - - - - -	- - - -	- Mar. 4, 1837.
Lt.-gen. Geo., M. of Tweeddale, K.T., comm. ch. -	Apr. 13, 1842	- Sept. 24, 1842.
Maj.-gen. sir Hy. Pottinger, bt., G.C.B. - -	Aug. 4, 1847	- Apr. 7, 1848.
Geo. Fras. Robt., ld. Harris - - - - -	- - - -	- Apr. 28, 1854.
Sir Chas. Edwd. Trevelyan, K.C.B. - - -	Jan. 31, 1859	- Mar. 28, 1859.
Sir Hy. Geo. Ward, G.C.M.G. - - - - -	May 19, 1860	-
Sir Wm. Thos. Denison, K.C.B. - - - -	Oct. 30, 1860	- Feb. 18, 1861.
Fras., ld. Napier, K.T. - - - - - -	Jan. 31, 1866	- Mar. 27, 1866.
Vere Hy., ld. Hobart - - - - - -	Mar. 14, 1872	- May 15, 1872.
Richd. Plant, &c., D. of Buckingham and Chandos	July 28, 1875	- Nov. 23, 1875.
Wm. Patrick Adam - - - - - -	Oct. 11, 1880	- Dec. 20, 1880.
Mountstuart Elphinstone Grant-Duff - - -	July 8, 1881	- Nov. 5, 1881.
Robt. Bourke, aft. ld. Connemara, G.C.I.E. -	Sept. 4, 1886, **G.**	- Dec. 8, 1886.

COMMANDERS IN CHIEF IN MADRAS.

	Appointed.	Assumed command.
Lt.-gen. Robt. Sloper - - - - - - -	Oct. 7, 1784	- June 17, 1785.

Assumed chief command in India, July 21, 1785.

Lt.-gen. sir John Dalling, bt. - - - - -	Dec. 7, 1784	- July 21, 1785.
Lt.-gen. sir Archd. Campbell; govr. - - - -	Apr. 11, 1786	- Apr. 6, 1786.
M.-gen. sir Wm. Medows; govr. - - - -	July 7, 1789	- Feb. 20, 1790.

The command was held by the senior officer until Gen. Medows' arrival.

M.-gen. sir Alured Clarke - - - - - -	Apr. 28, 1795	- Jan. 15, 1796.

Proceeded to assume the command in Bengal, Mar. 6, 1797; the command being held by the senior officer until his return.

Lt.-gen. Jas. Stuart - - - - - - -	Dec. 10, 1800	- Aug. 1, 1801.
M.-gen. sir John Fras. Cradock, aft. ld. Howden	Dec. 21, 1803	- Oct. 17, 1804.
Lt.-gen. H. McDowall - - - - - -	May 29, 1807	- Sept. 17, 1807.
Lt.-gen. Geo. Hewett, aft. bt. - - - -	- - - -	- Apr. 10, 1810.
M.-gen. sir Saml. Auchmuty - - - - -	Feb. 14, 1810	- Sept. 27, 1810.
Lt.-gen. hon. John Abercromby - - - -	Feb. 12, 1812	- May 21, 1813.
Lt.-gen. sir Thos. Hislop, bt. - - - - -	Dec. 3, 1813	- May 25, 1814.
Lt.-gen. sir Alexr. Campbell, bt., K.C.B. - -	Dec. 6, 1820	- June 15, 1821; *d.* Dec. 11, 1824.

Gen. Bowser, senr. officer, then held command.

Lt.-gen. sir Geo. Townshend Walker, G.C.B. -	May 11, 1825	- Mar. 3, 1826.
Lt.-gen. Hon. sir Robt. Wm. O'Callaghan, K.C.B.	Oct. 17, 1830	- May 11, 1831
Lt.-gen. sir Peregrine Maitland, K.C.B. - -	Apr. 17, 1836	- Oct. 11, 1836.
Lt.-gen. sir Jasper Nicolls, K.C.B. - - -	- - - -	- Dec. 21, 1838.

Took the office as comm. ch. of the forces in India, Dec. 7, 1839.

Lt.-gen. sir Saml. Ford Whittingham, K.C.B., K.C.H.	Sept. 18, 1839	- Aug. 1, 1840.
Lt.-gen. sir Hugh Gough, bt., G.C.B., aft. visc. Gough.	June 16, 1841.	

Assumed office, commanding the expedition in China. Comm. chief of the forces in India, Aug. 11, 1843.

Lt.-gen. Geo., M. of Tweeddale, K.T.; govr., and comm. chief.	Apr. 20, 1842	- Sept. 24, 1842.
Lt.-gen. sir Geo. Hy. Fredk. Berkeley, K.C.B. -	Sept. 29, 1847	- Mar. 13, 1848.
Lt.-gen. sir Rd. Armstrong, K.C.B. - - - -	- - - -	- Sept. 29, 1851.
Lt.-gen. Wm. Staveley, C.B. - - - - -	- - - -	- Oct., 1853.
Lt.-gen. hon. Geo. Anson, C.B. - - - -	- - - -	- Sept. 23, 1854.

	Appointed.	Assumed command.
Lt.-gen. sir Patrick Grant, K.C.B.	-	June 10, 1856.
Lt.-gen. sir Jas. Hope Grant, G.C.B.	-	Dec. 26, 1861.
Lt.-gen. sir Jno. Gaspart Le Marchant, K.C.B., G.C.M.G.	-	May 25, 1865.
Lt.-gen. W. A. McCleverty	-	Nov. 8, 1867.
Lt.-gen. sir Fredk. Paul Haines, K.C.B.	-	May 22, 1871.
Gen. sir Neville Bowles Chamberlain, G.C.B., G.C.S.I.	-	Feb. 2, 1876.
Lt.-gen. sir Fredk. Sleigh Roberts, bt., V.C., G.C.B., C.I.E.	-	Nov. 28, 1881.
Lt.-gen. sir Herbert Taylor Macpherson, V.C., K.C.B., K.C.S.I.	-	Mar. 7, 1886
Sir Chas. Geo. Arbuthnot, K.C.B.	-	Dec. 9, 1886

CHIEF JUSTICES OF MADRAS.

Chief Justices of the Supreme Court of Madras.

Appointed under 39 & 40 Geo. III., cap. 79 (1799).

1800. Sir Thos. A. Strange, Dec. 26.
1815. Sir John H. Newbolt, Sept. 6.
1820. Sir Edmd. Stanley, May 17.
1825. Sir Ralph Palmer, Jan. 28.
1835. Sir Robt. Buckley Comyns, July 1.
1842. Sir Edwd. J. Gambier, Mar. 11.
1849. Christr. Rawlinson, aft. sir C.
1859. Sir Hy. Davison.
1861. Colley Harman Scotland, aft. sir C., Feb. 8, **G.**

Supreme Court abolished on establishment of High Court of Judicature under 24 & 25 Vict. cap. 104 (Aug. 6, 1861).

Chief Justices of the High Court of Judicature for Madras.

Appointed under 24 & 25 Vict. cap. 104, and Order in Council dated June 23, 1862.

1862. Sir Colley Harman Scotland, June 23, **G.**
1871. Sir Walter Morgan, Sept. 22, **G.**
1879. Hon. Chas. Arthur Turner, C.I.E., Mar. 3, **G.**; knt. Apr. 23.
1885. Arthur John Hammond Collins, Aug. 18, **G.**; knt. same date.

DIOCESE OF MADRAS.

The bishopric of Madras was constituted under 3 & 4 Wm. IV., cap. 85 (Aug. 28, 1833), and is in the province of Calcutta.

Bishops of Madras.

1835. Danl. Corrie, Feb. 14.
1837. Geo. Trevor Spencer.
1849. Thos. Dealtry.
1861. Fredk Gell, May 16, **G.**

BOMBAY.

The island of Bombay, the foundation of the presidency or province of that name, came into possession of the English in 1661, being part of the dowry of the Infanta of Portugal, the queen of Charles II., by whom it was ceded to the East India Company in 1668.

GOVERNORS OF BOMBAY.

First appointed under 24 Geo. III., cap. 25 (Aug. 13, 1784).

	Appointed.	Took his seat.
awson H. Boddam	Sept. 3, 1784	Jan. 6, 1785.
ndr. Ramsay	Sept. 10, 1784	Jan. 9, 1788.
[.-gen. Wm. Medows, aft. sir W.	Sept. 5, 1787	Sept. 6, 1788.
ol. Robt. Abercromby, aft. sir R.	Aug. 5, 1789	Jan. 21, 1790.

Quitted the presidency, Nov. 26, 1792, having been app. comm. ch. in India.

eo. Dick, councillor	Succ. provisionally	Nov. 26, 1792.
ohn Griffith, councillor	Succ. provisionally	Nov. 9, 1795.
onn. Duncan	Nov. 12, 1794	Dec.27,1795; *d.* in the govt., Aug.11,1811.
eo. Browne, councillor	Succ. provisionally	Aug. 11, 1811.
ir Evan Nepean, bt.	Jan. 7, 1812	Aug. 12, 1812.
on. Mountstuart Elphinstone	Oct. 7, 1818	Nov. 1, 1819.
.-gen. sir John Malcolm, G.C.B.	Jan. 17, 1827	Nov. 1, 1827.
ohn, E. of Clare	-	Mar. 21, 1831.
r Robt. Grant, G.C.H.	-	Mar. 17,1835; *d.* in the govt., July 9,1838.
ames Farish, councillor	Succ. provisionally	July 11, 1838.
r Jas. Rivett-Carnac, bt.	-	May 31, 1839.

Res. on account of ill health, Apr. 27, 1841.

eo. Wm. Anderson, aft. sir G.	-	Apr. 27, 1841.
r Wm. Hay Macnaghten, bt.	July 28, 1841.	

At the time of his app. sir Wm. Macnaghten was resident at Cabul, where, on Dec. 23, 1841, he was assassinated during a deliberation respecting the evacuation of the place.

l. sir Geo. Arthur, bt.	-	June 9, 1842.

Res., on account of ill health, Aug. 6, 1846.

stock Robt. Reid, councillor	Succ. provisionally	Aug. 6, 1846.
o. Russell Clerk, aft. sir G.	Nov. 11, 1846	Jan. 23, 1847.
cius, visc. Falkland	Feb. 1, 1848	May 1, 1848.
hn, 13th ld. Elphinstone, G.C.B.	-	Dec. 26, 1853.
Geo. Russell Clerk, K.C.B., *again*	April 23, 1860	May 11, 1860.
Hy. Bartle Edwd. Frere, K.C.B.	-	Apr. 24, 1862.
n. Robt. Seymour Vesey FitzGerald, aft. ld. F. and V.	Nov. 19, 1866	Mar. 6, 1867.
Philip Edmond Wodehouse, K.C.B.	Mar. 2, 1872	May 6, 1872.
Richd. Temple, bt., K.C.S.I.	Feb. 26, 1877	Apr. 30, 1877.
Jas. Fergusson, bt., K.C.M.G.	Mar. 10, 1880	Apr. 28, 1880.
nald Jas., ld. Reay, G.C.I.E.	Feb. 27, 1885	Mar. 30, 1885.

COMMANDERS IN CHIEF IN BOMBAY.

	Appointed.	Assumed command
g.-gen. Lawrence Nilson	Mar. 31, 1784	Jan. 6, 1785.
gen. Wm. Medows, aft. sir W., govr.	Sept. 5, 1787	Sept. 6, 1788.

Previously to the arrival of gen. Medows, Rawson H. Boddam, the govr., was invested with the command of the army.

Robt. Abercromby, aft. sir R., govr.	Aug. 5, 1789	Jan. 21, 1790.
gen. Jas. Stuart	Apr. 6, 1796	Jan. 17, 1797

On Jan. 22, 1801, he proceeded to take the command at Madras. Previously to the arrival of gen. Stuart, the command had been held by the senior officer.

	Appointed.	Assumed command
M.-gen. Oliver Nicolls		Jan. 22, 1801.
M.-gen. Hon. John Abercromby	May 2, 1809	Nov. 28, 1809.

On Oct. 10, 1812, he proceeded to take the command of the forces at Madras. Previously to the arrival of gen. Abercromby, the command was held by the senior officer.

M.-gen. Sir Thos. Hislop, bt.	Feb. 28, 1812.	

This officer was captured on the voyage outwards; and upon being exchanged, he was app. to the command at Madras.

Lt.-gen. sir Miles Nightingall	Jan. 10, 1815	Feb. 24, 1816.
Lt.-gen. hon. sir Chas. Colville	Nov. 4, 1818	Oct. 9, 1819.
Lt.-gen. sir Thos. Bradford, K.C.B.	July 20, 1825	May 3, 1826.
Lt.-gen. sir Thos. Sidney Beckwith, K.C.B.	May 17, 1829	Dec. 3,1829; d in the govt., Jan.15,1831.

The command was assumed by the senior officer.

Lt.-gen. sir Colin Halkett, K.C.B.	July 17, 1831	Jan. 21, 1832
Lt.-gen. sir John Keane, K.C.B., G.C.H., aft. ld. Keane.	Oct. 18, 1833	July 2, 1834.
Lt.-gen. sir Thos. McMahon, bt., K.C.B.	Oct. 16, 1839	Feb. 14, 1840
Lt.-gen. sir Willoughby Cotton, G.C.B.	Jan. 13, 1847	Apr. 8, 1847.
Lt.-gen. sir John Grey, K.C.B.		Dec. 30, 1850
Lt.-gen. ld. Fredk. FitzClarence, G.C.H.		Nov. 22, 1852
Lt.-gen. sir Hy. Somerset, K.C.B.		Mar. 26, 1855
Lt.-gen. sir Wm. Rose Mansfield, K.C.B., aft. ld. Sandhurst		May 16, 1860.
Lt.-gen. sir Robt. Cornelis Napier, G.C.B., G.C.S.I., aft. ld. Napier of Magdala.		Nov. 30, 1865
Lt.-gen. hon. sir Augs. Almeric Spencer, K.C.B.		Aug. 27, 1869
Gen. sir Chas. Wm. Dunbar Staveley, K.C.B.		Oct. 9, 1874.
Lt.-gen. Henry Jas. Warre, C.B.		Oct. 9, 1878.
Lt.-gen. hon. Arthur Edwd. Hardinge, C.B.		Mar. 30, 1881
Sir Chas. Geo. Arbuthnot, K.C.B.		Feb. 16, 1886
Arth. Wm. Patrick Albert, D. of Connaught, &c.		Dec. 14, 1886

CHIEF JUSTICES OF BOMBAY.

Chief Justices of the Supreme Court of Bombay.

Appointed under 4 Geo. IV., cap. 71 (July 11, 1823).

1823. Sir Edwd. West, Dec. 8.
1829. Sir J. Dewar, Apr. 4.
1831. Sir R. H. A. D. Compton, Apr. 11.
1839. Sir J. W. Awdry, Jan. 26.
1840. Sir Hy. Roper, Dec. 26.
1846. Sir David Pollock, Sept. 12.
1847. Sir Thos. Erskine Perry, Sept. 18.
1852. Sir Wm. Yardley.
1858. Sir Hy. Davison.
1859. Sir Matt. Richd. Sausse.

Supreme Court abolished on establishment of High Court of Judicature, under 24 & 25 Vict., cap. 104 (Aug. 6, 1861).

Chief Justices of the High Court of Judicature for Bombay.

Appointed under 24 & 25 Vict., cap. 104, and Order in Council dated June 23, 1862.

1862. Sir Matt. Richd. Sausse, June 23, **G.**
1866. Richd. Couch, Mar. 3, **G.**; knt. June 13.
1870. Sir Michl. Roberts Westropp, Ap[r]. 1, **G.**
1882. Sir Chas. Sargent, May 23, **G.**

DIOCESE OF BOMBAY.

ʼHE bishopric of Bombay was constituted under 3 & 4 Wm. IV., cap. 5 (Aug. 28, 1833), and is in the province of Calcutta.

BISHOPS OF BOMBAY.

837. Thos. Carr.
851. John Harding.
1868. Hy. Alexr. Douglas.
1876. Louis Geo. Mylne, Apr. 29, **G.**

ʼRINCE OF WALES' ISLAND OR PENANG, MALACCA, AND SINGAPORE.

See "STRAITS SETTLEMENTS," *post*, p. 674.

PART XII. THE COLONIES.

GOVERNORS AND BISHOPS OF THE COLONIE AND OTHER DEPENDENCIES OF THE BRITISH EMPIRE.

INTRODUCTION.

THIS section will be found much more complete than in the form editions. As far as possible a complete list of the governors of eve colony is furnished, and lists of the colonial bishops have been added.

There are monographs on most of the more important colonies; b for general information on the colonies as a whole the best authority the official "Colonial List," published annually. This useful work h been of great assistance in the compilation of this section, the lists governors having been in every case collated therewith, and, whe necessary, completed therefrom. The Isle of Man, Heligoland, and th Channel Islands are not strictly colonies, but are included in th section as being that most applicable to them.

The colonies are divided into ecclesiastical provinces and diocese much in the same manner as in England, but the bishops hardl possess the same powers. Sir Travers Twiss, the eminent civilian, i his article "Bishop," in the *Encyclopædia Britannica,* ninth editio says on the subject of colonial bishops:—

> The first colonial bishopric of the Church of England was that of Nov Scotia, founded in 1787, since which time various colonial bishoprics have bee established, some of which were constituted by Letters Patent of the Crow only, whilst others have been confirmed by Acts of the imperial or coloni legislatures. With regard to those bishoprics which have been constituted b Letters Patent of the Crown only, where the bishopric has been established i a Crown colony, the bishop is legally entitled to exercise the jurisdictic conferred upon him by the Letters Patent; but where the bishopric has bee established in a colony possessing at the time an independent legislature, th bishop is not entitled to exercise such jurisdiction unless it has been confirme to him by an imperial or colonial statute. The report of the judicial committe of the Privy Council in the case of the bishop of Natal (Moore's "Privy Counc Reports," N.S., iii., p. 115) is an exposition of the law on this subject. On th other hand, where bishoprics have been constituted by Letters Patent of th

Crown in pursuance of imperial statutes, as was the case of the East Indian bishoprics, or where bishoprics constituted by Letters Patent have subsequently been confirmed or recognised by colonial statutes, the bishop's jurisdiction is complete; otherwise his authority is only pastoral or spiritual. The practice adopted by the Crown, since the decision of the judicial committee in the case of the bishop of Natal revealed the invalidity of the Letters Patent granted to many colonial bishops, has been to grant licences to the archbishop of Canterbury to consecrate bishops for the colonies without any definite diocese, and without any authority to exercise coercive jurisdiction. The Crown has also revoked the Letters Patent erecting Gibraltar into a bishop's see, and the last appointed bishop has been consecrated under a licence from the Crown, and is a titular bishop, having only consensual authority in that colony.

The following are the principal Acts of Parliament bearing on the ppointment of colonial bishops:—

6 Geo. III. cap. 84 (1786).
& 4 Vict. cap. 33 (1840).
& 6 Vict. cap. 6 (1842).
15 & 16 Vict. cap. 52 (1852).
16 & 17 Vict. cap. 49 (1853).
37 & 38 Vict. cap. 77 (1874).

The Orders in Council, or Letters Patent, under which the various olonial bishoprics were constituted will be found noted under each.

The following list of colonial provinces and dioceses is taken from ;rockford's Clerical Directory, where each bishop's antecedents will e found noted.

Province of Canada.

lgoma.
redericton.
:uron.
Montreal.
Niagara.
Nova Scotia.
Ontario.
Quebec.
Toronto.

Province of Rupert's Land.

thabasca, now Mackenzie River and S. Athabasca.
oosonee.
Rupert's Land.
Qu'Appelle, formerly Assiniboia.
Saskatchewan.

Province of Calcutta.

ɔmbay.
alcutta.
olombo.
Lahore.
Madras.
Rangoon.
Travancore and China.

These bishops will be found in Part XI., "India," *ante*, pp. 643–661.

Province of New Zealand.

uckland, formerly New Zealand.
ɪrist Church, N. Z
Dunedin.
Melanesia.
Nelson.
Waiapu.
Wellington.

Province of Sydney.

delaide.
allarat.
athurst.
risbane.
ɔulburn.
Grafton and Armidale.
Melbourne.
Newcastle, N.S.W.
N. Queensland.
Perth.
Riverina.
Sydney.
Tasmania.

Province of Capetown.

Bloemfontein, formerly Orange River Free State.
Capetown.
Grahamstown.
Maritzburg, formerly Natal.
Pretoria.
St. Helena.
St. John's, Kaffraria.
Zululand.

Province of the West Indies.

Antigua.
Barbadoes.
Guiana.
Jamaica.
Nassau.
Trinidad.

Dioceses holding Missions from the Metropolitan See of Canterbury.

British Columbia.
Caledonia.
Falkland Islands.
Mauritius.
Newfoundland.
New Westminster.
Sierra Leone.
Victoria (Hong Kong)
Singapore, Labuan, and Sa[r]wak, formerly Labuan.

Missionary Bishoprics holding Missions from the Metropolita[n] See of Canterbury.

Central Africa.
Eastern Equatorial Africa.
Honolulu.
Japan.
Madagascar.
Mid China.
Niger District.
North China.

European Bishopric.

Gibraltar (see Introduction, *ante*, p. 663).

Asiatic Bishopric.

Jerusalem.

I. COLONIES, &c.—EUROPE.

ISLE OF MAN.

This island is situated in the Irish Sea. Its early history is uncertai[n] but it appears to have belonged first to Scotland, then to Denmar[k] then to Norway, and then again to Scotland. Early in the fifteen[th] century it was seized by Henry IV., who granted it to Sir Joh[n] Stanley, the ancestor of the earls of Derby, in whom it continued unt[il] the death, in 1735, of James, the tenth earl, without issue. It the[n] passed to the duke of Athole, as heir general of James, the sevent[h] earl, and continued in the Athole family until their rights were boug[ht] up by the Crown at various times from 1765 to 1825.

The Isle of Man now constitutes the whole of the diocese of Sodo[r] and Man.

KINGS OF MAN.

Danish Line.

Orry, 1st King (10th century).
Guttred, his son.
Reginald, assass.
Olave I., executed by K. of Denmark.
Olain, his brother.
Allen, poisoned.
Macon.
Fingal.

Norwegian Line.

77. Godred Crovan, the Norwegian Conqueror; *d.* 1093.
93. On his death, the Island was conquered by Magnus, K. of Norway, who appointed Octtan as governor. Some of the inhabitants chose Macmanus as governor in place of Octtan, but he was defeated in battle, and K. Magnus continued to reign until his death in
02. When the line of Godred Crovan was restored in the person of
Lagman, his son, who abdicated, and after a regency of about 3 years was succeeded in
14. By his younger brother Olave II., who was killed by his nephew Reginald about
54. And was succ. by his son Godred, who was conq. in
58. By Summerled, his brother-in-law, who usurped theCrown until conq. by Reginald above-named, who in his turn was conq. by Godred, who *d.* King, 1187.
87. Olave III., son of Godred; *d.* 1237.
37. Harold, his son; *d.* 1248.
48. Reginald, his brother; killed 1249.
49. Magnus, his brother, last of Norwegian line; *d.* 1265.

Scottish Line.

Alexr. III. conq. the island, and governed it by his thanes; then Maurice, Okerfair, and others.

English Line.

1305. Sir Simon Montacute, who claimed through his wife, a descendant of Godred Crovan (*vide supra*).
1344. Sir Wm. Montacute, aft. E. of Salisbury, crowned by order of Edwd. III. He claimed as a descendant of Godred Crovan (*vide supra*).
Antony Beck, bp. of Durham.
Sir Wm. Montacute (now E. of Salisbury), *again*.
1395. Sir Wm. Scroope, aft. E. of Wiltshire, who was beheaded.
1399. Percy, E. of Northumberland: island granted to him by Hen. IV., who aft. depr. him.
6 H. IV. 1404–5. Island granted to Sir John Stanley for life.
1406–7. Island granted to him and his heirs.
1414. Sir John Stanley, his son.
1441. Thos., his son (cr. baron Stanley by Hen. VI.)
1460. Thos., his son (cr. E. of Derby by Hen. VII).
1504. Thos., 2nd E. of Derby, who renounced the title of King.

LORDS OF MAN AND THE ISLES.

House of Derby.

21. Edwd., 3rd E. of Derby.
2. Hy., 4th E. of Derby.
Ferdinand, 5th E. of Derby; *d.* 1594, and succ. by his brother,
4. Wm., 6th E. of Derby, who, being abroad, Sir Thos. Gerrard was app. governor by Q. Eliz. Jas I. gave Wm. a new grant of the Island.
2. Jas., 7th E. of Derby; beheaded at Bolton by the parlt. for supporting Chas. I.
Island besieged by parly. forces and surrendered.
2. Island granted by parlt. to ld. Fairfax.
1660. On the restoration, the Derby family were reinstated in the person of Chas., 8th E. of Derby; *d.* 1672.
1672. Wm., 9th E. of Derby; *d.* 1702.
1702. Jas., 10th E. of Derby; *d.* 1735, *s.p.*

House of Athole.

1735. On the death of Jas., 10th E. of Derby, without issue, the Island devolved on James, 2nd D. of Athole, who was descended from Lady Mary Sophia, youngest daughter of the 7th E. of Derby and wife of John, M. of Athole. The D. *d.* 1764.
1764. John, 3rd D. of Athole, who res. the Island to the British Government in 1765; *d.* 1774.

GOVERNORS OF THE ISLE OF MAN.

From the grant of the Island to Sir John Stanley, *ut supra.*

7. John Letherland, L.G.
8. John Fazakerley, L.G.
2. John Walton, L.G.
8. Hy. Byron, L.G.
* * *
No record until
6. Peter Dutton, L.G.
1497. Hy. Radcliffe, abb. of Rushen, Dep.
1505. Randolph Rushton, Capt.
1508. Sir John Ireland, L.G.
1517. Randolph Rushton, *again*, Capt.
1519. Thos. Danisport, Capt.
1526. Richd. Holt, L.G.

1529. John Fleming, Capt.
1530. Thos. Sherburn, L.G.
1532. Hy. Bradley, dep. L.G.
1533. Hy. Stanley (No. 1), Capt.
1535. Geo. Stanley, Capt.
1537. Sir Thos. Stanley (No. 1), L.G.
1539. Geo. Stanley, *again*, Capt.
1540. Thos. Tydsley, Dep.
1544. Wm. Stanley, Dep.
1552. Hy. Stanley (No 1), *again*, Capt.
1561. Sir Richd. Sherburne.
15 2. Sir Thos. Stanley (No. 2), L.G.
1566. Richd. Ashton, Capt.
1567. Sir Thos. Stanley (No. 2), *again*, L.G.
1569. Edwd. Tarbock, Capt.
1575. John Hanmer, Capt.
1580. Richd. Sherburn, Capt.
1591. Richd. Aderton, L.G.
1592. Cuthbert Gerrard, Capt.
Thos. Martinier, Dep.
1593. Hon. Wm. Stanley. aft. 6th E. of Derby, Capt.
1594. Randolph Stanley, Capt.
1596. Sir Thos. Gerrard, Capt.
Cuthbert Gerrard, *again*, Dep.
1597. Sir Thos. Gerrard, *again*, Capt.
Robt. Molyneux, Dep.
1599. Cuthbert Gerrard, *again*, Capt.
Robt. Molyneux, *again*, Dep.
1600. The same, Capt.
1609. John Ireland and John Birchall, Joint Govrs.
Thos. Gerrard.
1610. John Ireland, *again*, L.G. and Capt.
1612. Robt. Molyneux, *again*, Capt.
1621. Edwd. Fletcher, Dep.
1622. The same, Govr.
1623. Sir Ferd. Leige, Capt.
1625. Edwd. Fletcher, *again*, Dep.
1626. Edwd. Homewood, Capt.
1627. Edwd. Fletcher, *again*, Dep.
1628. Edwd. Christian, L.G. and Capt.
1629. John Ireland, *again*.
1634. Evan Christian, Dep.
1635. Sir Chas. Gerrard, Capt.
1636. John Sharpeless, Dep.
1639. Radcliffe Gerrard, Capt.
1640. John Greenhalgh, Govr.
1651. Sir Phil. Musgrave, kt. and bt., Govr.
1652. Saml. Smith, Dep.
1652. Ld. Fairfax app. Jas. Chaloner Robt. Dinely, and Jonathan Witton, commrs. for governing this year.
1653. Matth. Caldwell, Govr.
1656. Wm. Christian, Govr.
1658. Jas. Challoner, Govr.
1660. Roger Nowell, Govr.
Richd. Stevenson, Dep.
1663. Hy. Nowell for one part of the year and Thos. Stanley for the other part, Deps.
1664. Bishop Barrow, Gov.; H. Nowell Dep.
1669. Hy. Nowell, *again*, Govr.
1677. Hy. Stanley (No. 2), Govr.
1678. Robt. Hegwood, Govr.
1691. Roger Kenyon, Govr.
Wm. Sacheverell, Dep.
1696. Col. Sankey, Govr.
Hon. Capt. Cranston, Dep.
1703. Robt. Maudesley, Govr.
John Rowe, Dep.
1713 John Parr, Govr.
C. Stanley, Dep.
1714. Alexander Horne, Govr.
Major Floyde, Dep.
1726. Thos. Horton, Govr.
1734. James Horton, Govr.
1739. Hon. Jas. Murray, 1st Govr. under D. of Athole.
1747 (? 1741). Patrick Lindesay.
1756. Basil Cochrane, Govr.
John Taubman, Dep.
1763. John Wood, Govr.
1765. Island sold to Gt. Britain.
J. Hope, Dep. Govr.
1776. Richd. Dawson, L.G.
1777. Edwd. Smith, Govr.
1791. Alexander Shaw, L.G.
1798. John, 4th D. of Athole, Govr.
1805. Col. Cornelius Smelt, L.G., June 15 **G.**
1832. Col. Jno. Ready, L.G., Jan. 29, **G.**
1845. Hon. Chas. Hope, L.G., Aug. 9, **G.**
1860. Fras. Pigott, aft. Pigott-Conant L.G., Oct. 22, **G.**
1863. Hy. Brougham Loch, C.B., aft. sir H., L.G., Feb. 14, **G.**
1882. Spencer Walpole, L.G., Apr. 24, **G.**

For bishops, see "Bishops of Sodor and Man," *ante*, p. 483.

THE CHANNEL ISLANDS,

COMPRISING

JERSEY, GUERNSEY, ALDERNEY, SARK, AND HERM.

THESE WELL-KNOWN ISLANDS are the only portions of the old dukedom of Normandy still belonging to the British Crown. The islands were placed under the same governor until the reign of Henry VII., when

;wo separate governors were appointed, one for Jersey and one for Guernsey and its dependencies, the smaller islands of Alderney, Sark, ınd Herm.

Besides the GOVERNOR the Crown appoints for each of the two ›rincipal islands a BAILIFF, who is the chief *civil* officer.

THE CHANNEL ISLANDS are under the ecclesiastical charge of the ›ishops of WINCHESTER.

GOVERNORS OF THE CHANNEL ISLANDS.

Down to the separation of the government, *ut supra*.

111. Prince Jullien du Pracle, Govr. and Ld. of the Isles.
154. Sire Walter Dunker, Govr. of the Holy Isle of Guernsey.
167. Sire Peter Cornet, Govr., kpr., and capt. of the forts, places, and castles of Guernsey, called the Holy Island.
198. John, E. of Mortain, aft. King John held the Islands as an appanage.
199. Sire Wm. Orseth, Govr. Genl. of the Islands.
203. Gregory Balizon, gent.-of-arms, Govr. Genl., capt. and kpr. of the Holy Isle of Guernsey.
226. Richd. Grey, kpr. of the Isles.
227. Wm. de St. John, kpr. of the Isles.
232. Arnauldus de St. Amand and Philip de Carteret, kprs. of the Isles.
* Philip de Albemar and Wm. St. John, kprs. of the Isles.
271. Pr. Edwd., son of Hen. III., and aft. Edwd. I. held the Islands in appanage.
284. Sire Stephen Waller, Govr., capt., and kpr. of all the forts, places, and castles of the king in the Islands.
299. Hy. de Cobham, kpr. of the Isles.
312. Sire Peter Cornet.
323. Otto de Grandison.
* Walter de Weston, L.G. of Guernsey.

1330. John de Roches, warden of the Isles.
1335. Wm. de Montagou, Comte de Salbiere and Hy. de Ferrure, wardens of the Isles.
1339. Thos. de Ferrariis, kpr. of the Isles.
1342. Thos. Hampton, kpr. of the Isles.
1350. John Mantaners, warden of the Isles.
1356. Thos. Holland, warden of the Isles.
1360. Sir Edmond de Chene, kpr. of the Isles.
1374. Edmond Rosse, kpr. of the Isles.
1376. Hugh Calvilegh, kpr. of the Isles.
1388. John Golafre, kpr. of the Isles.
1397. Edmund, E. of Rutland, kpr. of the Isles.
1415. Edwd., D. of York, son of Edmund, D. of York, the 5th son of Edward III., held the Islands in appanage.
1430. John, D. of Bedford, Regent of France, bro. of Hen. V., held the Islands in appanage.
1435. Humphrey, D. of Gloucester, another bro. of Hen. V.
1446. Hy. de Beauchamp, E. of Warwick, king of the Isles of Wight, Guernsey, and Jersey
1447. Wm. Bertram, and Nichs. Hault, } Wardens and Govrs. of the Isles.
1453. John Nanfan, kpr. of the Isles.

GOVERNORS OF JERSEY.

From the separation of the Governments, *ut supra*.

487–8. Matth. Baker.
499–1500. Thos. Overay.
501–2. Sir Hugh Vaughan, David Philips, } jointly; aft. Vaughan alone.
525–6. Sir Anthy. Ughtred.
533–4. Sir Arth. Darcy.
535–6. T. Vaux.
536–7. Edwd. visc. Beauchamp.
550–1. Sir Hugh Paulet.
* Sir Amias Paulet.
* Sir Anthy. Paulet.
500–1. Sir Walter Raleigh.

1603–4. Sir Jno. Peyton.
* * Sir Thos. Jermyn.
* * Hy. Jermyn, aft. E. of St. Albans
* * Sir Geo. de Carteret.
* * Sir Thos. Morgan.
* * Sir Jno. Lanier.
* * Thos. ld. Jermyn.
* * Hy. Lumley.
* * Sir Rd. Temple, aft. visc. Cobham.

* * * *

1807. Jno. E. of Chatham, K.G., Oct. 14, sw.

* * * *

1838. M.-gen. sir Edwd. Gibbs.
1847. M.-gen. sir Jas. Hy. Rugnett, Jan. 1, **G.**
1852. M.-gen. Jas. Fredk. Love, C.B., L.G., Apr. 9.
1857. Col. Godfrey Chas. Mundy, Jan. 31, **G.**
1860. M.-gen. Robt. Percy Douglas, Aug. 22, **G.**
1863. M.-gen. Burke Cuppage, Oct. 23, **G.**
1868. M.-gen. Philip Melmoth Nelson Guy, C.B., Oct. 1, **G.**
1873. M.-gen. Wm. Sherbrooke Ramsay Norcott, C.B., Oct. 1, **G.**
1878. M.-gen. Lothian Nicholson, C.B., R.E., Oct. 1, **G.**
1883. M.-gen. Hy. Wray, C.M.G., R.E., Oct. 1, **G.**; res. Nov. 1, 1887.
1887. Lt.-gen. Chas. Brisbane Ewart, C.B., R.E., Oct. 18, **G.**, to date from Nov. 1, 1887.

BAILIFFS OF JERSEY

* * * *

* * Hy. Fredk., ld. Carteret.
1826. Sir Thos. Le Breton, Aug. 1 and 19, **G.**
1831. Jno. De Veulle, Feb. 26, **G.**; knt. Mar. 2.
1848. Sir Thos. Le Breton, June 22, **G.**
1858. Jno. Hammond, Feb. 16, **G.**
1880. Robt. Pipon Marett, Mar. 10, **G.**; knt., May 3, **G.**
1884. Geo. Clement Bertram Bailiff, Dec. 15, **G.**; knt., Aug. 1, **G.**

For bishops, see "Bishops of Winchester," *ante*, p. 470.

DEANS OF JERSEY.

* * * *

1620. David Bandinel.
1661. Philip Le Couteur.
1672. Clement Le Couteur.
1714. Thos. Le Breton.
1729. Fras. Payn.
1775. Fras. Le Breton.
1802. Edwd. Dupré, Aug. 3, **G.**
1823. Corbet Hue, Ap. 14, **G.**
1838. Fras. Jeune, Feb. 20, **G.**
1844. Jas. Hemery, Oct. 24, **G.**
1849. Wm. Corbet Le Breton, Dec. 26, **G.**
1888. Geo. Orange Balleine, June 23, **G.**

GOVERNORS OF GUERNSEY AND ITS DEPENDENCIES, ALDERNEY, SARK, AND HERN.

From the separation of the Governments, *ut supra*.

1470. Geffrey Wallifly, Capt. of Castle Cornet and Govr. of the I. of Guernsey.
1482. Sir — Difthefield, Capt. of Guernsey.
1483. Edwd. Brampton, Capt. of Guernsey.
1488. John April, Lt. and Capt. of Guernsey.
* * Sir Wm. Weston.
1536. Sir Richd. Weston.
1541. Sir Richd. Lone.
1551. Sir Peter Meautis.
1553. Sir Leonard Chamberlain } Joint Govrs. of Guernsey.
1555. Francis Chamberlain } Joint Govrs. of Guernsey.
1570. Sir Thos. Leighton, Govr.
* * Lord Zouche, Govr.
1580. Thos. Wigmore, L.G. and Bailiff 1581.
1610. Lord Geo. Carew Baron de Clapton, Govr.
1621. Lord Hy. Danvers, Baron of Danby, Govr.
* * Sir Peter Osborne, L.G.
1632. Peter Beauvoir, Dep. L.G.
1643. Robt. Russell, L.G.
1644. Lord Warwick, Govr.
1649. Col. Cox, L.G.
1651. Col. John Bingham, L.G.
1653. John Clarke, L.G.
1654. Chas. Waterhouse, L.G.
1660. Sir Hugh Pollard, Govr.
1661. Capt. Nathl. Darell, L.G.
1662. Christr. ld. Hatton, Govr.
1664–5. Sir Jonn. Atkins, L.G.
1670. Christr. ld. Hatton, *again*, Govr.
1697. Col. Mordaunt, L.G.
1684. Capt. Hon. Chas. Hatton, L.G.
1689. Bernard Ellis, L.G.
1704. Sir Edmond Andros, L.G.
1706. Chas. Churchill, Govr.
1711. Giles Spencer, L.G.
1715. Lt.-gen. Dan. Harvey, Govr.
1726. Lewis Dollon, L.G.
1732. Geo., E. of Cholmondeley, Govr.
1733. M.-gen. Richd. Sutton, Govr.
1735. Hon. John Graham, L.G.
1737. Fras., M. de Montandre, Govr.
1742. Algernon Seymour, c.c. ld. Percy aft. E. of Hertford and E. of Northumberland, Govr.
1745. Hon. Chas. Strahan, L.G.
1750. Sir John Ligonier, K.B., Govr.
1752. John, ld. de la Warr, Govr.
1756. Sir John Milne, bt., L.G.
1766. Sir Richd. Littleton, K.B., Govr.

1770. Sir Jeffery Amherst, aft. ld. Amherst, Govr.
* * Lt.-col. Irving, L.G.
1784. Lt.-col. Wm. Brown, L.G.
1793. Col. Dundas, L.G.
* * Col. Jas. Hy. Craig, L.G.
1794. Col. Hon. John Small, L.G.
1796. Sir Hugh Dalrymple, L.G.
1797. Chas., ld. Grey of Howick, Govr.
1803. Sir John Doyle, bt., K.B., &c., L.G.
1807. Geo. Augs., E. of Pembroke and Montgomery, K.G., Govr., Nov. 25, sw.; re-sw. May 3, 1826.
1829. Sir Wm. Keppel, Govr., Nov. 16, sw.
* * M.-gen. John Ross.
1837. M.-gen. Sir Jas. Douglas, K.C.B., L.G., Apr. 1, **G.**
1842. M.-gen. Wm. Fras. Patr. Napier, L.G., Apr. 1, **G.**
1848. M.-gen. John Bell, C.B., L.G., Jan. 24, **G.**
1854. M.-gen. Wm. Thos. Knollys, L.G., July 1, **G.**
1855. M.-gen. Geo. Judd Harding, C.B., L.G., Nov. 22, **G.**
1859. M.-gen. Marcus John Slade, L.G., Apr. 1, **G.**
1864. M.-gen. Chas. Rochfort Scott, L.G., Apr. 1, **G.**
1869. M.-gen. Edwd. Frome, L.G., May 1, **G.**
1874. M.-gen. Hon. St. Geo. Gerald Foley, C.B., L.G., May 1, **G.**
1879. M.-gen. Alexr. Abercromby Nelson, C.B., L.G., May 1, **G.**
1883. M.-gen. Hy. Andrew Sarel, C.B., L.G., Oct. 10, **G.**
1885. M.-gen. John Hy. Ford Elkington, C.B., L.G., Nov. 2, **G.**

BAILIFFS OF GUERNSEY.

* * * *

* * Robt. Porret le Marchant.
1810. Peter de Havilland, aft. sir P., Apr. 7.
1821. Danl. de Lisle Brock, Apr. 27, **G.**
1842. John Guille, Nov. 28, **G.**
1845. Peter Stafford Carey, aft. sir P., June 28, **G.**
1883. John de Havilland Utermark, July 23, **G.**
1884. Edgar MacCulloch, Sept. 26, **G.**; knt., May 8, 1886.

For bishops, see "Bishops of Winchester," *ante*, p. 470.

GIBRALTAR.

Gibraltar is a mere rock, of little value except as a fortress. It is situated at the entrance to the Mediterranean Sea. It formerly belonged to Spain, of which it is geographically a part. It was captured by the English in 1704, and ceded to Great Britain by the Treaty of Utrecht in 1713.

Gibraltar forms part of the diocese of that name, which comprises Gibraltar and Malta.

GOVERNORS OF GIBRALTAR.

1704. Pr. Geo. of Hesse Darmstadt.
M.-gen. Shrimpton, L.G.
1706. Lt.-gen. David, E. of Portmore, Govr.
1706. M.-gen. Ramos, } Occasional commandants in absence of the Govr.
1710. Col. Roger Elliot, }
1713. Col. Ralph Congreve, }
1716. Col. Stanhope Cotton, }
1720. Brigr.-gen. Richd. Kane, L.G.
1727. Brigr.-gen. Jasper Clayton, L.G.
1730. Lt.-gen. Jos. Sabine, Govr.
1738. Lt.-gen. Fras. Columbine, Govr.
1739. Lt.-gen. Wm. Hargrave, Govr.
1749. Lt.-gen. Humphrey Bland, Govr.
Col. ld. Geo. Beauclerk, } Occasional commandants in absence of the Govr.
Col. hon. Wm. Herbert, }
1752. Lt.-gen. Thos. Fowke, Govr.
1756. Lt.-gen. Jas., ld. Tyrawley, Govr.
1756. M.-gen. Wm., E. of Panmure, second in command.
1758. M.-gen. Wm., E. of Home, Govr.; *d.* 1761.

1758. Col. Wm. Tovey, commandant till the arrival of
1761. M.-gen. Parslow, commandant.
1762. Lt.-gen. hon. Edwd. Cornwallis, Govr.
M.-gen. John Irwin, commandant in the absence of the Govr.
1770. M.-gen. Robt. Boyd, aft. sir R., L.G
1776. Lt.-gen. Geo. Augs. Elliot, aft. ld. Heathfield, Govr., Jan. 16.
1787. M.-gen. Chas. O'Hara, L.G.
1790. Lt.-gen. sir Robt. Lloyd, K.B., Govr., Oct. 16.
M.-gen. sir Hy. Calder, bt., L.G., Oct. 16.
1792. M.-gen. Chas. O'Hara, *again*, L.G., Apr. 10.
1794. Gen. sir Hy. Clinton, K.B., Govr., July 19.
1795. Lt.-gen. Chas. O'Hara, now Govr.
1798. M.-gen. sir Thos. Trigge, L.G.; aft. Govr.
1802. Edward, D. of Kent, Govr., Mar. 24.
1804. Lt.-gen. hon. Hy. Edwd. Fox, L.G.
1810. M.-gen. Colin Campbell, L.G., Aug. 16.
1814. Lt.-gen. Geo. Don, aft. sir G., L.G., Aug. 25.
1820. Gen. John Pitt, E. of Chatham, K.G., Mar. 5.
1825. Gen. sir Geo. Don, G.C.B., *again*, L.G., June 8.
1831. Lt.-gen. sir Wm. Houston, G.C.B., L.G., Apr. 8.
1835. M.-gen. sir Alex. Woodford, K.C.B., L.G., Feb. 28; Govr., Sept. 1, 1836, **G.**
1843. Gen. sir Robt. Thos. Wilson, Govr., Oct. 4, **G.**
1848. M.-gen. sir Robt. Wm. Gardiner, K.C.B., Govr. G., Nov. 21, **G.**
1855. Lt.-gen. sir Jas. Fergusson, K.C.B. Govr., July 26, **G.**
1859. Lt.-gen. sir Wm. Jno. Codrington K.C.B., Govr., May 6, **G.**
1865. Lt.-gen. sir Richd. Airey, K.C.B. Govr., Sept. 20, **G.**
1870. Sir Wm. Fenwick Williams, of Kars bt., K.C.B., Govr., Sept. 12, **G.**
1876. Gen. Robt. Cornelis, ld. Napier of Magdala, R.E., G.C.B., G.C.S.I., Govr., July 30, **G.**
1882. Lt.-gen. sir Jno. Miller Adye, R.A., G.C.B., Govr., Dec. 26, **G.**
1886. Gen. Hon. sir Arth. Edwd. Hardinge, K.C.B., C.I.E., Govr., Oct. 26.

DIOCESE OF GIBRALTAR.

THIS bishopric was originally constituted by Letters Patent, Sept, 29, 1842, **G.**, and included Gibraltar and Malta. These Letters Patent have since been revoked, and the present bishop is titular only. See Introduction, *ante*, p. 663.

BISHOPS OF GIBRALTAR.

1842. Geo. Tomlinson, Sept. 29, **G.**
1863. Walter Jno. Trower, form. bp. Glasgow, Sept. 26, **G.**
1868. Hon. Chas. Amyand Harris, May 1, **G.**
1874. Chas. Waldegrave Sandford.

HELIGOLAND.

THIS is a small island in the North Sea. It originally belonged to Denmark, from whom it was captured in 1807.

GOVERNERS OF HELIGOLAND.

1807. Lt.-Col. J. D'Auvergne, L.G.
1814. Lt.-Col. Hamilton, L.G.
1817. Lt.-Col. Hy. King, aft. sir H., L.G., Nov. 11, **G.**
1840. Capt. Jno. Hindmarsh, R.N., aft. adm. sir J., Sept. 28, **G.**
1857. Maj. Richd. Pattinson, L.G., Mar. 7, **G.**
1863. Maj. Hy. Fitzhardinge Berkeley Maxse, aft. sir H., L.G., May 14, **G.**; app. Govr. Apr. 25, 1864, **G.**
1882. Lt.-Col. Jno. Terence Nicolls O'Brien, C.M.G., aft sir T., Govr., Jan. 9, **G.**
1888. Arth. Cecil Stuart Barkly, Nov. 24.

MALTA.

THE ISLAND OF MALTA is situated in the Mediterranean Sea. In 1530 it was given by Charles V. of Spain to the Knights Hospitallers, who retained it till 1798, when it was taken by France. The British captured it in 1800, but by the Treaty of Amiens (1801–2) agreed to restore it to the knights. In consequence, however, of the threatening attitude of France, possession was retained, and it was ultimately guaranteed to Great Britain by the Treaty of Paris (1814).

MALTA forms part of the diocese of Gibraltar.

GOVERNORS OF MALTA.

CIVIL COMMISSIONERS.

1799. Capt. Alexr. Jno. Ball, R.N., aft. sir A.
1801. C. Cameron.
1802. Adm. sir Alexr. Jno. Ball, bt.
1810. Lt.-gen. sir Hildebrand Oakes, G.C.B.

GOVERNORS.

1813. Lt.-gen. Hon. Thos. Maitland, July 15, sw.
1824. Gen. Fras., M. of Hastings, K.G., G.C.B., G.C.H., Mar. 22, **G.**
1826. M.-gen. sir Fredk. Cavendish Ponsonby, L.G., L.P., Dec. 22.
1836. M.-gen. sir Hy. Fredk. Bouverie, K.C.B., Oct. 18, **G.**
1843. Lt.-gen. Hon. Patr. Stuart, aft. sir P., May 19, **G.**
1847. Richd. More O'Ferrall, Oct. 1, **G.**
1851. Lt.-Col. Wm. Reid, C.B., Sept. 12, **G.**
1858. M.-gen. sir Jno. Gaspard Le Marchant, Apr. 9, **G.**
1864. M.-gen. sir Hy. Knight Storks, G.C.B., G.C.M.G., Nov. 15, **G.**
1867. Lt.-gen. sir Patr. Grant, G.C.B., June 17, **G.**
1872. Lt.-gen. sir Chas. Thos. Van Straubenzee, K.C.B., May 25, **G.**
1878. Gen. sir Arthur Borton, K.C.B., May 13, **G.**
1884. Gen. sir Jno. Lintorn Arabin Simmons, G.C.B., Apr. 19, **G.**
1888. Lt.-gen. sir Hy. D'Oyley Torrens, K.C.B., Aug. 3, **G.**

For bishops, see "Bishops of Gibraltar," *ante*, p. 670.

CYPRUS.

CYPRUS is a large island in the Mediterranean Sea. It has for some centuries belonged to Turkey, and still nominally forms part of the Ottoman Empire. By a treaty between England and Turkey, dated June 4, 1878, Cyprus was granted to England to be occupied and administered by that country so long as Batoum and Kars were retained by Russia.

The government of Cyprus is by high commissioners appointed under the Foreign Jurisdiction Acts (see list in Index to Statutes), and Order in Council dated Sept. 14, and gazetted Oct. 1, 1878.

HIGH COMMISSIONERS OF CYPRUS.

1878. Lt.-gen. sir Garnet Jos. Wolseley, G.C.M.G., K.C.B., aft. visc. Wolseley, July 12, **G.**
1879. Col. Robt. Biddulph, C.B., aft. sir R., May 31, **G.**
1885. M.-gen. sir Hy. Ernest Gascoyne Bulwer, G.C.M.G., Sept. 12.

II. COLONIES, &c.—ASIA.

CEYLON.

Ceylon is an island in the Indian Ocean. The Portuguese visited this island in 1505, and formed settlements there in 1517, but they were ousted by the Dutch about 1658. In 1795-6 the island was conquered by the British, who annexed it to the presidency of Madras. It was formally ceded to Great Britain at the Peace of Amiens (1801-2), and was then made a separate colony.

Ceylon constitutes the diocese of Colombo.

GOVERNORS OF CEYLON.

Dutch Governors.

Taken from the Colonial List.

1640. William Jacobezen Coster.
Jan Thuysz.
Joan Matsoyker.
1650. Jacob Van Kittenstein.
1653, 1656, and 1661, Adrian Van Der Meyden.
1660. Ryckloff Van Goens.
1663. The same *again*, Apr. 6.
Jacob Hustaart, Dec. 27.
1664. Ryckloff Van Goens, *again*, Nov. 19.
1674. Ryckloff Van Goens, the younger, Feb. 24.
1679. Laurens Pye, Dec. 19.
1692. Thos. Van Rhee, Feb. 3.
1697. Gerrit De Heer, Feb. 22.
1702. Members of Council, Nov. 26.
1703. Cornelis Joan Simons, May 12.
1707. Henrick Becker, Dec. 1.
1716. Isaac Augustin Rumpf, Dec. 5.
1723. Members of Council, June 11.
1724. Joannes Hertenberg, Jan. 12.
1725. Members of Council, Oct 19.
1726. Petrus Vuyst, Sept. 16.
1729. Stephanus Versluys, Aug. 29.
1732. Members of Council, Aug. 26.
Jacob Christiaan Pielat, Dec. 2.
1734. Dideric Van Domburgh, Feb. 19.
1736. Members of Council, June 7.
1736. Gustaaf Willem Van Imhoff, July 24.
1740. Willem Maurits Bruynink, Mar. 12.
1742. Daniel Overbeck, *ad. int.*, Feb. 8.
1743. Julius Valentyer Stein Van Gollenesse, May 12.
1751. Gerrard Joan Vreelandt, Mar. 5.
1752. Jacob de Jong, Feb. 26.
Joan Gideon Loten, Sept. 30.
1757. Jan Schrender, Mar. 17.
1762. Lubbert Jan Baron Van Eck,
1765. Members of Council, Apr. 1.
Iman Willem Falk, Aug. 10.
1785. Willem Jacob Van de Graaff, Feb. 7.
1794. Johan Gerard Van Angelbeck, July 5.

British Governors.

Completed from the Colonial List.

1790. The Govr. of Madras in Council.
1798. Hon. Fredk. North, aft. E. of Guildford, Mar. 26.
1805. M.-gen. Thos. Maitland, aft. sir T., Jan. 5, **G.**
1811. M.-gen. Jno. Wilson, L.G.
Lt.-gen. Robt. Brownrigg, Aug. 1, **G.**
1820. M.-gen. sir Edwd. Barnes, L.G.
Lt.-gen. hon. sir Edw. Paget, G.C.B., Sept. 11, **G.**; sw. May 5, 1821.
1822. M.-gen. sir Jas. Campbell, K.C.B., L.G.
1824. M.-gen. sir Edw. Barnes, K.C.B., as Govr., Mar. 12, **G.**
1831. M.-gen. sir Jno. Wilson, K.C.B., L.G.
Robt. Jno. Wilmot Horton, Jan. 26, **G.**; knt., June 22.
1837. Jas. Alexr. Stewart Mackenzie, Mar. 29, **G.**
1840. Lt.-gen. Sir Colin Campbell, K.C.B. (not ld. Clyde), Nov. 17, **G.**
1847. Sir Jno. Emerson Tennent, L.G.
1847. Geo., visct. Torrington, Mar. 12, **G.**
1850. Chas. Justin MacCarthy, aft. sir C., L.G., until arrival of Anderson.
1850. Sir Geo. Wm. Anderson, K.C.B., Oct. 1. **G.**

1855. Chas. Justin MacCarthy, aft. sir C., L.G., until arrival of Ward.
1855. Sir Hy. Geo. Ward, K.C.M.G., Feb. 26, **G.**
1860. Sir Chas. Justin MacCarthy, now Govr., Aug. 23, **G.**
1863. M.-gen. Jno. Terence Nicolls O'Brien, aft. sir T., Actg. Govr. during absence of MacCarthy.
1865. Sir Hercules Geo. Robt. Robinson, Mar. 6, **G.**
1872. Wm. Hy. Gregory, Jan. 8, **G.**
1876. Arthur Nonus Birch, C.M.G., aft. sir A., L.G., May 6, **G.**
1877. Sir Jas. Robt. Longden, K.C.M.G., June 30, **G.**
1878. Jno. Douglas, C.M.G., L.G., Aug. 13, **G.**; Actg. Govr. in 1883 until arr. of Gordon.
1883. Hon. Sir Arthur Hamilton Gordon, G.C.M.G., July 23, **G.**
1885. Cecil Clementi Smith, C.M.G., L.G., Aug. 6, **G.**

DIOCESE OF COLOMBO.

This bishopric was constituted by Letters Patent April 24, 1845, **G.** It is in the province of Calcutta.

Bishops of Colombo.

1845. Jas. Chapman, Apr. 24, **G.**
1862. Piers Calveley Claughton, May 8, **G.**; tr. from St. Helena.
1871. Hugh Willoughby Jermyn, Oct. 26, **G.**
1876. Regd. Stephen Copleston, Jan. 12, **G.**

HONG KONG.

Hong Kong is an island on the south-east coast of China. It was ceded to Great Britain in 1842.

Hong Kong constitutes the diocese of Victoria (Hong Kong).

GOVERNORS OF HONG KONG.

1843. M.-gen. sir Hy. Pottinger, bt., G.C.B., Apr. 5, **G.**
1844. Jno. Fras. Davis, aft. bt., Feb. 9, **G.**
1847. Saml. Geo. Bonham, aft. bt., Nov. 27, **G.**
1852. M.-gen. Wm. Jervoise, acting Govr. until return of Bonham in 1853.
1854. John Bowring, Jan. 10, **G.**; knt. Feb. 16.
Lt.-col. Caine, L. G.
1859. Hercules Geo. Robt. Robinson, June 17, **G.**; knt. June 25; aft. bt.
1862. Wm. T. Mercer, Actg. Govr. until return of Robinson in 1864; *again* in 1865, until arrival of MacDonnell.
1865. Sir Richd. Graves MacDonnell, C.B., Oct. 19, **G.**
1869. M.-gen. Whitfield, L.G., actg. until return of Macdonnell in 1871.
1872. Sir Arthur Edwd. Kennedy, C.B., K.C.M.G., Feb. 20, **G.**
1875. John Gardiner Austin, admr. until return of Kennedy in 1876.
1877. John Pope Hennessy, C.M.G., aft. sir J.; Apr. 13, **G.**
1882. Wm. Hy. Marsh, C.M.G., aft. sir H.; Actg. Govr. until arrival of Bowen.
Sir Geo. Ferguson Bowen, G.C.M.G., Dec. 26, **G.**
1885. Wm. Hy. Marsh, C.M.G., *again* Actg.-Govr. until return of Bowen.
1887. Sir Geo. Wm. Des Vœux, K.C.M.G., July 11, **G.**

DIOCESE OF VICTORIA (HONG KONG).

This bishopric was constituted by Letters Patent, May 11, 1849, **G.** It is classed as one of the dioceses holding mission from the see of Canterbury.

Bishops of Victoria (Hong Kong).

1849. Geo. Smith, May 11, **G.**
1867. Chas. Richd. Alford, Feb. 4, **G.**; res. 1872.
1873. John Shaw Burdon, consec. 1874.

THE STRAITS SETTLEMENTS.

PRINCE OF WALES' ISLAND OR PENANG. MALACCA. SINGAPORE. CHRISTMAS ISLAND.

The Straits Settlements are on the west coast of the Malay Peninsula, and take their name from their situation in the Straits of Malacca. They comprise Prince of Wales' Island or Penang, Malacca, Singapore, Christmas Island, and some minor dependencies.

Prince of Wales' Island is the official name of the island popularly known as Penang, or Pulo-Penang. The East India Company established a settlement here in 1786, which was in 1806 made a presidency of equal rank with Madras and Bombay.

Malacca originally belonged to the Portuguese, who settled there in 1511. They were succeeded by the Dutch in 1641. The Dutch in their turn were dispossessed in 1795 by the British, who restored it in 1818. It was finally ceded by Holland to Great Britain by treaty in 1824.

The settlement of Singapore consists of the island of that name and of a number of small adjacent islands. The English built a factory here in 1819, and acquired the islands by purchase in 1824.

In 1826 Malacca and Singapore were incorporated with the presidency of Penang. The government remained at Penang until 1832, when it was removed to Singapore.

Under 21 & 22 Vict. c. 106 (1858), and 29 & 30 Vict. c. 115 (1866), and Letters Patent Feb. 2, 1867, **G.**, Prince of Wales' Island, Malacca, and Singapore, with their dependencies, were separated from India and formed into an independent colony by the name of the Straits Settlements.

The Cocos or Keeling Islands were transferred from Ceylon to the Straits Settlements by Letters Patent dated Feb. 1, 1886 (Feb. 3, **G.**), revoking Letters Patent of 10th Sept. 1878.

Christmas Island was annexed to the Straits Settlements by Letters Patent, Jan. 9, 1889, **G.**

The territories forming the Straits Settlements were formerly part of the diocese of Calcutta, but were in 1869 annexed to the diocese of Labuan, and are now part of the diocese of Singapore, Labuan, and Sarawak.

GOVERNORS OF STRAITS SETTLEMENTS.

SEAT OF GOVERNMENT, SINGAPORE.

1867. Col. Harry St. Geo. Ord, R.E., C.B.; aft. sir H., Feb. 5. **G.**

1871. Lt.-col. Archd. Edwd. Harbord Anson, R.A., aft. sir A., admr. Mar., until arrival of Clarke.

1873. Sir Andr. Clarke, R.E., K.C.M.G., C.B., Aug. 25, **G.**

1875. Col. sir Wm. Fras. Drummond Jervois, R.E., K.C.M.G., C.B., Apr. 7. **G.**

1877. Col. A. E. H. Anson, R.A., C.M.G., *again* admnr. Apr., until arrival of Robinson in Oct.

1877. Sir Wm. Cleaver Fras. Robinson, K.C.M.G., Dec. 4.

1879. M.-gen. A. E. H. Anson, admr. *again*, Feb., until arrival of Weld in May 1880.

1880. Fredk. Aloysius Weld, C.M.G., aft. sir F., Mar. 18, **G.**

1884. Cecil Clementi Smith, C.M.G., aft. sir C., admr., Mar., until return of Weld in Nov. 1885; app. Govr. Aug. 2, 1887.

DIOCESE OF SINGAPORE.

See under "Labuan," *infra.*

LABUAN.

LABUAN is an island in the Malay Archipelago, on the coast of Borneo. In 1846 it was acquired from the sultan of Borneo by the English, who settled there in the following year.

LABUAN forms part of the diocese of SINGAPORE, LABUAN and SARAWAK.

GOVERNORS OF LABUAN.

1847. Jas. Brooke, aft. sir J., Nov. 27, **G.**

1848. Wm. Napier, L.G.

1850. John Scott, aft. sir J., L.G.

1856. Hon. Geo. Warren Edwardes, Feb. 13, **G.**

1862. Jeremiah Thos. FitzGerald Callaghan, Apr. 10, **G.**

1866. Hugh Low, aft. sir H., Actg. Govr. until arrival of Hennessy.

1867. John Pope Hennessy, aft. sir J., Sept. 16, **G.**

1871. Hy. Ernest Bulwer, C.M.G.; aft. sir H., June 22, **G.**

1875. Herbert Taylor Ussher, C.M.G., Oct. 31, **G.**

1879. Chas. Cameron Lees, C.M.G.; aft. sir C., Sept. 29, **G.**

1881. Peter Leys, Sept. 3; Actg. Govr. during vacancy.

DIOCESE OF SINGAPORE, LABUAN, AND SARAWAK.

THE bishopric of Labuan was constituted under Letters Patent, Aug. 7, 1855, **G.**

Under 32 & 33 Vict. c. 88 (1869), and Letters Patent, dated Nov. 15, and gaz. Nov. 16, 1869, the Straits Settlements were separated from the diocese of Calcutta and added to that of Labuan, whose bishops were thenceforward styled bishops of Singapore, Labuan and Sarawak. It is now classed as a diocese holding mission from the see of Canterbury.

BISHOPS OF LABUAN.

1855. Fras. Thos. McDougall, May 15, **G.**; res. 1868.

1869. Walter Chambers, June 28, **G.**

Bishops of Singapore, Labuan and Sarawak.

1869. Walter Chambers, above-named, Nov. 15, **G.**; res. 1881.
1881. Geo. Fredk. Hose, consec. May 26.

BRITISH NORTH BORNEO.

This territory now belongs to the British North Borneo Company, who hold it under grants from the Sultans of Brunei and Lulu, dated Dec. 29, 1877, and Jan. 28, 1878, and a Royal Charter granted Nov. 1 and gazetted Nov. 8, 1881. The British protectorate was formally assumed May 12, 1888.

There had previously been settlements under the East India Company at Balambagan and Brunei, but these were abandoned early in the present century.

Governors of British North Borneo.

1881. Wm. Hood Treacher, June 1.
1888. Chas. Vandeleur Creagh.

ASIATIC DIOCESES

whose jurisdiction lies outside the British dominions.

DIOCESE OF TRAVANCORE AND CHINA.

This bishopric was constituted in 1879, and is in the province of Calcutta. Its jurisdiction extends over the native States of Travancore and China.

Bishop of Travancore and Cochin.

1879. John Martindale Speechley.

DIOCESES OF NORTH CHINA AND MID-CHINA.

The bishopric of North China was constituted in 1872, and that of Mid-China in 1880. The original bishopric of North China is now called Mid-China, the present bishopric of North China having a different jurisdiction.

Both dioceses are classed as missionary bishoprics holding missions from the metropolitan see of Canterbury.

Bishops of Mid-China, formerly North China.

1872. W. A. Russell.
1880. Geo. Evans Moule, consec. Oct. 28.

Bishop of North China as now Constituted.

1880. Chas. Perry Scott, consec. Oct. 28.

DIOCESE OF JAPAN.

This bishopric was constituted in 1883, and is classed as a missionary bishopric holding missions from the metropolitan see of Canterbury.

Bishops of Japan.

1883. Arth. Wm. Poole.
1885. Edwd. Wm. Bickersteth, consec. 1886.

DIOCESE OF JERUSALEM.

This bishopric was constituted in 1841.

Bishops of Jerusalem.

1841. M. S. Alexander.
1846. Saml. Gobat.
1879. Joseph Barclay, ceased 1881.
1887. Geo. Fras. Popham Blyth, consec. Mar. 25.

III.—COLONIES, &c.—AFRICA.

SOUTH AFRICAN COLONIES.

CAPE OF GOOD HOPE. NATAL. BRITISH BECHUANALAND. BRITISH KAFFRARIA. BASUTOLAND. GRIQUALAND, EAST AND WEST.

The division and government of the British possessions in South Africa have been subject to many changes, a detailed and very accurate account of which will be found in the official Colonial List.

The Cape of Good Hope or Cape Colony originally belonged to the Dutch, who settled there about 1652 and retained it till 1795, when the British took possession of it in order to prevent its capture by the French. It was restored to the Dutch at the Peace of Amiens (1801–2), but on the renewal of hostilities between Great Britain and France it was again captured by the former in 1806, and finally ceded to this country in 1814. The district of Rode Valley was annexed to the Cape by Letters Patent, Aug. 2, 1887, **G.**

Natal was originally colonized by a secession of Dutch Boers from Cape Colony. In Aug. 1843 it was proclaimed a British colony by the authorities at the Cape. In Aug. 1845 it was annexed as a district to Cape Colony, and in Nov. 1845 it was constituted a separate government under a lieutenant governor subordinate to the Cape. By Letters Patent, July 15, 1856, **G.**, Natal was altogether separated from the Cape and constituted a separate colony.

Bechuanaland was taken under British protection by convention of London dated Feb. 27, 1884, and on Sept. 30, 1885, part of that country was declared to be British territory under the name of **British Bechuanaland**, and the governor of the Cape was appointed its governor with a local administrator under him.

The acquisition of **British Kaffraria** was the result of the second and third Kaffir wars (1846–7 and 1850–3). It was at first treated as part of Cape Colony, but in 1861 it was declared a separate colony under a lieutenant governor, subordinate to the Cape. In 1865, under 28 & 29 Vict. cap. 5, British Kaffraria was reunited to the Cape, of which it now forms the two divisions of King Williamstown and East London.

Basutoland became British territory in March 1868, and was annexed to the Cape in Aug. 1871 under an Act of the Colonial Legislature. As from March 13, 1884, it was separated from the Cape and formed into a separate colony under a commissioner subordinate to the High Commissioner for South Africa.

Griqualand West was made British territory on Oct. 27, 1871, and a lieutenant governor appointed, April 2, 1873. It was annexed to the Cape under Colonial Act No. 39, of 1877, and proclamation dated Oct. 15, 1880. (See *London Gazette* of Jan. 25, 1881.)

The South African colonies are in the ecclesiastical province of Cape Town which province comprises the dioceses of

Bloemfontein, formerly Orange River Free State.
Grahamstown.
Maritsburg, formerly Natal.
Pretoria.
St. Helena.
St. John's, Kaffraria.
Zululand.

GOVERNORS OF THE CAPE OF GOOD HOPE.

See Introduction, *ante*, p. 677.

Dutch Governors.

1652. Johan Antony van Riebeck.
1662. Zacharias Wagenaar.
1666. Cornelis van Qualberg.
1668. Jacob Borghorst.
1670. Pieter Hackins.
1671. Coenraad van Breitenbach.
1672. Albert van Breugel.
Ysbrand Goske.
1676. Johan Bax.
1678. Hendrik Crudare.
Simon van der Still.
1699. Wm. Adriaan van der Still.
1707. Johan Cornelis d'Abling.
1708. Louis van Assenburg.
1711. Willem Helot.
1714. Mauritz Pasquess de Chavo.
1724. Jan de la Fontaine; also Actg. Govr. in 1728; Govr. in 1730.
1727. Piet Gysbert Nood.
1736. Adriaan von Kervel.
1737. Daniel van den Henghell.
1739. Hendrik Swellengrebel.
1751. Ryk Tulbagh.
1771. Joachim van Plettenberg.
1773. Pieter Baron van Reed Van Oudtschoorn; *d.* on voyage out.
1785. Cornelius Jacobus van de Graaff.
1791. Johannes Isaac Rhenius.
1793. Abraham Jos. Sluysken, L.G.

British Governors.

1795. J. H. Craig.
1796. Geo., Earl Macartney, L P., Dec. 30.
1798. Sir Fras. Dundas, L.G.
1799. Sir Geo. Yonge, bt., L.P., Mar. 23.
1801. Sylvester, ld. Glenbervie, Jan. 28 G. Did not go over.
Sir Fras. Dundas, *again*, L.G.

Restored to Holland 1803.

1803. Jan Willem Jansens, Dutch Govr.

Re-taken by the British, Jan. 18, 1806.

1806. Sir David Baird.
M.-gen. hon. Hy. Geo. Grey, L.G.; July 21, **G.**
Dupré, E. of Caledon, July 2, **G.**
1811. Lt.-gen. sir John Fras. Cradock, K.B. (aft. ld. Howden); Mar. 8, **G.**
1812. M.-gen. hon. Robt. Meade, L.G.; Feb. 21, **G.**
1813. Lt.-gen. ld. Chas. Hy. Somerset, Nov. 13, **G.**
1820. Sir Rufane Shaw Donkin, actg. until return of Somerset in 1821.
1825. M.-gen. Richd. Bourke, aft. sir R., L.G., July 4, **G.**
1828. Gen. hon, sir Galbraith Lowry Cole, Jan. 9, **G.**
1833. Lt.-col. T. F. Wade, Actg. Govr. until arrival of D'Urban.
M.-gen. sir Benjn. D'Urban, July 4, **G**
1836. Andries Stockenstrom, aft. bt., L.G. eastern division, Feb. 2, **G.**
1837. M.-gen. Geo. Thos. Napier, C.B.; aft. sir G., Oct. 4, **G.**
1839. Col. John Hare, C.B., L.G. eastern division, Oct. 26, **G.**
1843. Lt.-gen. sir Peregrine Maitland, K.C.B., Dec. 12, **G.**
1846. M-gen. sir Henry Pottinger, bt., G.C.B., Sept. 25, **G.**
1847. Hy. Edwd. Fox Young, L.G. eastern division, Feb. 2, **G.**
M.-gen. sir Hy. Geo. Wakelyn Smith, bt., G.C.B., Sept. 10, **G.**
1852. M.-Gen. hon. Geo. Cathcart, Jan. 20, **G.**
Chas, Hy. Darling, aft. sir C., L.G., Jan. 20, **G.**
1854. Sir Geo. Grey, K.C.B., July 24.
Lt.-gen. John Jackson, L.G., Oct. 27, **G.**; until arrival of Grey.
1859. M.-gen. Robt. Hy. Wynyard, L.G., Mar. 14, **G.**; until return of Grey in 1860.
1861. Philip Edmond Wodehouse, C.B., aft. sir P., Oct. 28, **G.**
1864. Sir Robt. Percy Douglas, bt., L.G., July 9.
1870. Sir Hy. Barkly, K.C.B., Aug. 19, **G.**
1877. Lt.-gen. sir Arthur Augs. Thurlow Cunyngham, K.C.B., Mar. 5, **G.**

Governors of the Cape and High Commissioners for South Africa.

1877. Sir Hy. Bartle Edwd. Frere,
1878. M.-gen. hon. Fredk. Augs. Thesiger, C.B.; aft. ld. Chelmsford, L.G., Jan. 30, **G.**
1880. M.-gen. sir Hy. Hugh Clifford, V.C., K.C.M.G. and C.B., admr.
M.-gen. sir Geo. Cumine Strahan, K.C.M.G.; temp. admr. and commr. until arrival of Robinson, Aug. 23, **G.**
1880. Sir Hercules Geo. Robt. Robinson, G.C.M.G., Aug. 23, **G.**
1882. Lt.-gen. hon. sir Leicester Smyth, K.C.M.G. and C.B., admr. until return of Robinson in 1883.
1886. Lt.-gen. D'Oyley Torrens, C.B., admr. until return of Robinson in 1887.

DIOCESES OF CAPE TOWN AND GRAHAMSTOWN.

The bishopric of Cape Town, as originally constituted under Letters Patent, June 28, 1847, **G.**, included the whole of Cape Colony and its dependencies and also St. Helena. By Letters Patent Nov. 23, 1853, **G.**, the Cape portion of the diocese was divided into the separate bishoprics of Cape Town, Grahamstown, and Natal, and by other Letters Patent, Dec. 6, 1853, **G.**, the bishop of Cape Town was made metropolitan to the other two sees. In 1873 the bishopric of St. John's, Kaffraria, was formed from part of that of Grahamstown. By Letters Patent, June 3, 1859, **G.**, St. Helena was constituted a separate bishopric.

Bishops of Cape Town.

1847. Robt. Gray, 1st bp, June 28, **G.**;
1853. The same, Dec. 6, **G.** (on division of diocese *ut supra*). App. bp. of Capetown, and metrop. of the Cape of Good Hope and its dependencies.
1874. Wm. West Jones.

Bishops of Grahamstown.

1853. John Armstrong, 1st bp., Nov. 23, **G.**
1856. Hy. Cotterill, Nov. 4, **G.**
1871. N. J. Merriman.
1883. Allan Becher Webb, tr. fro[m] Bloemfontein.

GOVERNORS OF NATAL.

See Introduction, *ante* p. 677.

Lieutenant Governors prior to Separation from Cape Colony.

1845. Martin West, Dec. 30, **G.**
1849. Benjn. Chilley Campbell Pine, aft. sir B., Nov. 27, **G.**
1856. John Scott, Mar. 15, **G.**

Lieutenant Governors after Separation from Cape Colony.

1856. John Scott, above-named, July 15, **G.**
1864. John Maclean, C.B., Oct. 6, **G.**
1867. Robt. Wm. Keate, Feb. 20, **G.**
1872. Anthy. Musgrave, C.M.G., aft. sir A., May 25, **G.**
1873. Sir Benjn. Chilley Campbell Pine, K.C.M.G., May 31, **G.**
1875. M.-gen. sir Garnet Jos. Wolsele[y], G.C.M.G., K.C.B., aft. visc. Wo[l]seley; Feb. 24, **G.**; to administe[r] the govt. temporarily.
1875. Sir Hy. Ernest Bulwer, K.C.M.G., July 6, **G.**

Governors.

1880. Col. sir Geo. Pomeroy Colley, K.C.S.I., C.B., C.M.G., Apr. 21, **G.**; also high commr. for S.E. Africa.
1881. M.-gen. sir Fredk. Sleigh Roberts, bt., G.C.B., C.I.E., Mar. 7, **G.**; also Govr. Transvaal and high commr. for S.E. Africa.
1882. Sir Hy. Ernest Bulwer, K.C.M.G. Feb. 2, **G.**; also sp. commr. f[or] Zulu affairs.
1885. Sir Arth. Elibank Havelock, K.C.M.G., Sept. 12, **G.**

DIOCESE OF NATAL, NOW STYLED MARITZBURG.

The bishopric was separated from Cape Town by Letters Patent, Nov. 23, 1853, **G.**, and was made suffragan to that province by Letter[s] Patent, Dec. 6, 1853, **G.**

Bishop of Natal.

1853. John Wm. Colenso, 1st bp., Nov. 23, **G.**; deposed (?) 1863; *d.* 1883.

Bishop of Maritzburg.

1869. Wm. Kenneth Macrorie, consec. Jan. 5.

GOVERNORS OF BRITISH BECHUANALAND.

The Governor of the Cape of Good Hope for the time being.

See Introduction, *ante*, p. 677.

Under him is a local administrator.

Administrators of British Bechuanaland.

1884. Sir Chas. Warren, R.E., app. sp. commr. for Bechuanaland, abt. Oct.
1885. Sidney Godolphin Alexr. Shippar[d], aft. sir S., Oct.

For bishops see "Bishops of Bloemfontein," *post* p. 681.

LIEUTENANT-GOVERNORS OF BRITISH KAFFRARIA.

See Introduction, *ante* p. 678.

1860. Jno. Maclean, C.B., Dec. 6, **G.**

Re-united to the Cape in 1865. See *ante*, p. 678.

DIOCESE OF ST. JOHN'S, KAFFRARIA.

This bishopric was formerly part of that of Grahamstown, from which it was separated in 1873. See *ante*, p. 679.

Bishops of St. John's, Kaffraria.

873. Hy. Callaway.

1883. Bransby Lancelot Key (coadj.); made bp. 1886.

RESIDENT COMMISSIONERS GOVERNING BASUTOLAND UNDER THE HIGH COMMISSIONERS FOR SOUTH AFRICA.

See Introduction, *ante*, p. 678.

1884. Lt.-col. sir Marshall Jas. Clarke, Jan.

For bishops see " Bishops of Bloemfontein," *infra*.

LIEUTENANT GOVERNORS OF GRIQUALAND WEST.

See Introduction, *ante* p. 678.

873. Richd. Southey, C.M.G., Apr. 2, **G.**

875. Maj. Wm. Owen Lanyon, aft. sir W., C.M.G., Sept. 1, **G.**

On Oct. 15, 1880, Griqualand West was incorporated with Cape Colony. See *ante*, p. 678.

For bishops see " Bishops of Bloemfontein," *infra*.

SOUTH AFRICAN DIOCESES
OF
BLOEMFONTEIN (FORMERLY ORANGE FREE STATE). ZULULAND. PRETORIA.

The Bishopric of the Orange Free State was established in 1873. In 1886 its jurisdiction was extended and its name changed to Bloemfontein. It now includes the Orange Free State, Griqualand West, Basutoland, and Bechuanaland, and is in the province of Cape Town.

The Bishopric of Zululand was established in 1870. Its jurisdiction extends over Zululand and the territories to the north and north-east thereof. It is in the province of Cape Town.

The Bishopric of Pretoria was established in 1878. Its jurisdiction extends over the Transvaal. It is in the province of Cape Town.

BISHOPS OF BLOEMFONTEIN, FORMERLY ORANGE FREE STATE.

863. Edwd. Twells; consec. Feb. 2.

870. Allan Becher Webb; tr. to Grahamstown, 1883.

1886. Geo. Wyndham Hamilton Knight-Bruce.

BISHOPS OF ZULULAND.

870. Thos. Edwd. Wilkinson; ceased 1876.

1880. Douglas McKenzie; consec. Nov 30.

BISHOP OF PRETORIA.

1878. Hy. Brougham Bousfield, consec. Feb. 2.

ST. HELENA.

St. Helena is an island in the South Atlantic Ocean, and whilst the route for India and Australia was round the Cape of Good Hope, more especially before the introduction of steam, most ships, both homeward and outward bound, called there for provisions and water. Since the opening of the Suez Canal its importance has somewhat declined.

The Island was discovered by the Portuguese, but was first colonized by the Dutch. It came into the possession of England in 1673, and was soon afterwards granted by Charles II. to the East India Company, by whom it was transferred to the Crown in 1833 under 3 & 4 Wm. IV. cap. 85, sec. 112. Prior to that date the governors of the island were appointed by the company, except during the detention of Napoleon Buonaparte from 1816 to 1821, when Sir Hudson Lowe was appointed governor by the Crown.

GOVERNOR OF ST. HELENA
during the detention of Napoleon Buonaparte.

1816. Sir Hudson Lowe, arr. Apr. 14.

GOVERNORS SINCE THE TRANSFER OF THE ISLAND FROM THE EAST INDIA COMPANY TO THE BRITISH GOVERNMENT.

1835. M.-gen. Geo. Middlemore, Oct. 12, **G.**
1841. Lt.-col. Hamelin Trelawny, Aug. 24, **G.**
1846. M.-gen. sir Patrk. Ross, G.C.M.G., June 27, **G.**
1850. Sir Jas. Emerson Tennent, Dec. 31, **G.**; did not proceed.
1851. Lt.-col. Thos. Gore Browne, C.B., aft. sir T., May 20, **G.**
1854. Edwd. Hay Drummond Hay, C.B. aft. sir E., Nov. 6, **G.**
1863. V.-adm. sir Chas. Elliot, K.C.B., May 20, **G.**
1870. Hudson Ralph Janisch, Actg. Govr. until arrival of Patey.
1869. R.-adm. Chas. Geo. Edwd. Patey, Dec. 6, **G.**
1873. Hudson Ralph Janisch, now Govr., Oct. 1, **G.**
1884. Lt.-col. Grant Blunt, R.E., Actg. Govr., Mar. 19.
1887. Wm. Grey-Wilson, Dec. 8, **G.**

DIOCESE OF ST. HELENA.

St. Helena was originally included in the diocese of Capetown, which was constituted under Letters Patent, June 28, 1847, **G.** (See *ante*, p. 679.) By Letters Patent, June 3, 1859, **G.**, St. Helena was formed into a separate diocese comprising that island and the island of Ascension.

Bishops of St. Helena.

1859. Piers Calveley Claughton, June 3, **G.**; tr. to Colombo, 1862.
1862. Thos. Earle Welby, May 8, **G.**

MAURITIUS.

SEYCHELLES ISLANDS. RODRIGUES.

THE ISLAND OF MAURITIUS is in the Indian Ocean. It was discovered by the Portuguese in 1507, colonised by the Dutch in 1598, abandoned by them in 1710, taken possession of by the French in 1710, and captured by Great Britain in 1810.

MAURITIUS has a number of small dependencies, the principal of which are the SEYCHELLES ISLANDS and RODRIGUES. These are governed by commissioners, who are subordinate to the governor of Mauritius. By Letters Patent, Jan. 2, 1889, **G.**, fresh provision was made for the government of the Seychelles by an administrator.

Mauritius and its dependencies constitute the diocese of MAURITIUS.

GOVERNORS OF MAURITIUS.

FRENCH GOVERNORS.

Taken from the Colonial List.

1722. M. de Nyon, Jan.
1726. M. Dumas, Aug. 28.
1728. M. de Maupin, Oct. 26.
1734. M. Mahé de Labourdonnais, Nov. 10.
1746. M. David, Apr.
1750. M. de Lozier-Bouvet.
1755. M. Magon.
1759. M. Desforges Boucher.
1767. Col. M. Dumas, July 17.
1768. Brig.-gen. M. Steinaüer, Nov. 29.
1769. Le Chevalier Des Roches, June 7.
1770. M. Steinaüer, *again*, *ad int.*, July to Nov.
1772. Le Chevalier d'Arzac de Ternay, Aug. 24.
1776. Le Chevalier de Guiran de la Brillanne, Dec. 2.
1779. Le Vicomte de Souillac, *ad int.*, May 3; Govr. July 4, 1781.
1785. Col. Le Chevalier de Fresne, Apr. 5.
Col. Le Chevalier de Fleur, *ad int.*, June 28.
Le Vicomte de Souillac, *again*, Nov.
1787. Le Chevalier de Bruni d'Entrecasteaux, Nov. 5.
1789. Maréchal-de-Camp Le Comte de Conway, Nov. 14.
1790. Maréchal-de-Camp M. David Charpentier de Cossigny, Aug. 26.
1792. Lt.-gen. Le Comte de Malartic, June 21.
1800. Gen. le Comte Magallon de la Morlière, *ad int.*, July 29.
1803. Gen. Charles Decaen, Sept. 26.

BRITISH GOVERNORS.

Completed from the Colonial List.

1810. Robt. Townshend Farquhar, Dec. 3.
1811. M.-gen. H. Warde, Actg. Govr. from Apr. 9, until return of Farquhar, July 12, 1811.
1817. M.-gen. J. Gage Hall, Nov. 19.
1818. Col. Dalrymple, Actg. Govr. from Dec. 10 until app. of Darling.
1819. M.-gen. R. Darling, Actg. Govr. from Feb. 6 until return of Farquhar, July 6, 1820; *again*, from May 20, 1823, till arrival of Cole in June 1823.
1822. Sir Galbraith Lowry Cole, G.C.B., Aug. 31, **G.**; Feb. 21, 1823, sw.
1828. Lt.-gen. hon. sir Chas. Colville, G.C.B., Jan. 9, **G.**
1830. M.-gen. Wm. Nicolay, Jan. 31; May 1, 1832, **G.**
1840. Col. J. Power, Actg. Govr. from Feb. 20 until arrival of Smith, July 16.
1840. Sir Lionel Smith, bt., K.C.B., Jan. 7, **G.**
1842. Col. W. Staveley, Actg. Govr. from Jan. 3 until arrival of Gomm, Nov. 21, 1843.
1842. M.-gen. sir Wm. Maynard Gomm, K.C.B., June 13, **G.**
1846. Lt.-col. T. Blanchard, Actg. Govr. from May 5 until app. of Sweeting.
1848. Lt.-col. H. L. Sweeting, Actg. Govr. from May 21 until arrival of Anderson, June 8, 1849.

1849. Geo. Wm. Anderson, Feb. 9, **G.**; knt. Feb. 22.
1850. M.-gen. W. Sutherland, Actg Govr. from Oct. 19 until arrival of Higginson, Jan. 8, 1851.
1850. Jas. Macaulay Higginson, Oct. 1, **G.**
1854. M.-gen. W. Sutherland, *again*, Actg. Govr. during absence of Higginson from Apr. 14 until app. of Hay.
1855. M.-gen. C. M. Hay, Actg. Govr. from Jan. 18 until return of Higginson, June 12; *again*, from Sept. 11, 1857, until arrival of Stevenson, Sept. 21.
1857. Wm. Stevenson, May 9, **G.**
1863. M.-gen. M. C. Johnstone, Actg. Govr. from Jan. 9 until arrival of Barkly, Aug. 22.
1863. Sir Hy. Barkly, K.C.B., Sept. 17, **G.**
1870. Brig.-gen. E. Selby Smyth, Actg. Govr. from June 4 until arrival of Gordon, Feb. 21, 1871.
1870. Hon. Arthur Hamilton Gordon, C.M.G., Oct. 4, **G.**
1871. E. S. Smyth, Actg. Govr. *again* during absence of Gordon, Aug. 19 to Sept. 29.
1871. Edwd. Newton, Actg. Govr. during absence of Gordon, Oct. 21, 1871, to Oct. 28, 1872; *again*, from Jan. 20 to Oct. 30, 1873; *again*, from Aug. 26, 1874, until arrival of Phayre, Nov. 21, 1874.
1874. M.-gen. Sir Arthur Purves Phayre, K.C.S.I., C.B., Nov. 14, **G.**
1878. Fredk. Napier Broome, Actg. Govr. from Dec. 31 until arrival of Bowen, Apr. 4, 1879.
1879. Sir Geo. Ferguson Bowen, G.C.M.G., Mar. 31, **G.**
1880. Fredk. Napier Broome, C.M.G., L.G., Sep. 2, **G.**
1883. Chas. Bruce, C.M.G., Actg. Govr. from May 5 until arrival of Hennessy, June 1. 1883.
1882. Sir John Pope Hennessy, K.C.M.G., Dec. 26, **G.**
1884. H. N. Duverger Beyts, C.M.G., Actg. Govr. during absence of Hennessy from Sept. 24 to Oct. 15; *again*, from Sept. 30 to Oct. 28, 1886.
1885. Clifford Lloyd, L.G., Nov. 23, **G.**
1886. Sir Hercules Geo. Robinson, G.C.M.G., on sp. missn. in consequence of disputes between P. Hennessy and Lloyd; held govt. from 15 to 18 Dec.
M.-gen. W. H. Hawley, Actg. Govr. Dec. 18, until appt. of Fleming.
1887. Fras. Fleming, Actg. Govr. until return of Hennessy, Dec. 1888.

DIOCESE OF MAURITIUS.

The bishopric of Mauritius was orginally constituted under Letters Patent Nov. 27, 1854, **G.**, but it is now classed as a colonial diocese holding missions from the see of Canterbury. Its jurisdiction extends over the island of Mauritius and its dependencies.

BISHOPS OF MAURITIUS.

1854. Vincent Wm. Ryan, Nov. 27, **G.**, 1st bp.: res. 1868; *d.* Jan. 11, 1888.
1869. Thos. Goodwin Hatchard, Mar. 4, **G.**
1870. Hy. Constantine Huxtable, Nov. 19.
1872. Peter Sorenson Royston, Dec. 15.

CHIEF COMMISSIONERS OF THE SEYCHELLES ISLANDS.

1880. Capt. Fras. Theophilus Blunt, Sept. 11, **G.**; ch. civil commr. Seychelles Islands.
1881. Arth. Cecil Stuart Barkly, Dec. 7, **G.**
1885. G. H. Griffiths.
A. C. S. Barkly, *again*.
1889. Thos. Riseley Griffith, Admr., Jan. 2, **G.**

WEST AFRICA SETTLEMENTS.

SIERRA LEONE. GAMBIA. GOLD COAST. LAGOS.

SIERRA LEONE was first taken possession of by the British Government in 1787, and was in 1791 granted by charter to the Sierra Leone Company. In 1807 it was transferred back to Great Britain.

GAMBIA or the GAMBIA SETTLEMENTS were discovered by the Portuguese. From 1588 to 1807 it was only a trading settlement, but in the latter year it was placed under the governor of Sierra Leone. In 1843 it was formed into an independent colony under 6 & 7 Vict. cap. 13.

The GOLD COAST COLONY, formerly the GOLD COAST SETTLEMENTS, were originally under the government of trading companies, but were in 1843 taken over by the Crown under 6 & 7 Vict. cap. 13, followed by Order in Council dated Sept. 3, 1844 (Sept 6, **G.**).

LAGOS was ceded to Great Britain by king Docemo by treaty dated Aug. 16 and gazetted Sept. 20, 1861, and together with its dependencies was created a distinct settlement by Letters Patent, Mar. 5, 1862, **G.**

By Letters Patent, Feb. 19, 1866, **G.**, SIERRA LEONE, GAMBIA, the GOLD COAST SETTLEMENTS, and LAGOS were united under the title of the WEST AFRICA SETTLEMENTS.

By Letters Patent, July 24, 1874, **G.**, the GOLD COAST SETTLEMENTS and LAGOS were severed from the West Africa Settlements and formed into the GOLD COAST COLONY.

By Letters Patent, Dec. 17, 1874, **G.**, and June 17, 1885, **G.**, the WEST AFRICA SETTLEMENTS were reconstituted by the union of SIERRA LEONE and GAMBIA.

By Letters Patent, Jan. 13, 1886, **G.**, LAGOS was separated from the Gold Coast territory and made a separate colony.

By Letters Patent, Nov. 28, 1888, SIERRA LEONE and GAMBIA were separated and became once more separate colonies. The title of WEST AFRICAN SETTLEMENTS then ceased.

All the West African colonies are in the diocese of SIERRA LEONE.

GOVERNORS OF SIERRA LEONE

prior to its incorporation in the West Africa Settlements in 1866.

See Introduction *ante*, p. 684.

1811. Chas. Maxwell, Apr. 11, **G.**
1815. Chas. McCarthy, Sept. 6, **G.**
1824. M.-gen. Chas. Turner, C.B., June 24, **G.**
1826. M.-gen. sir Neil Campbell, C.B., May 12, **G.**
1833. Octavius Temple, June 15, **G.**
1834. Maj. Hy. Dundas Campbell, Nov. 4, **G.**
1837. Lt.-Col. Richd. Doherty, Mar. 27, **G.**
1840. John Jeremie, Oct. 15, **G.**; knt. Nov. 4.
1845. Wm. Fergusson, May 3, **G.**
1846. Norman Wm. Macdonald, Apr. 7, **G.**
1852. Arth. Edwd. Kennedy, Sept. 13, **G.**
1854. Lt.-col. Stephen John Hill, Nov. 6, **G.**

For subsequent Governors to Nov. 1888, see *post*, p. 688.

1888. Capt. Jas. Shaw Hay, C.M.G., Nov. 29.

DIOCESE OF SIERRA LEONE.

This bishopric was originally constituted by Letters Patent, May 21, 1852, **G.**, but it is now classed as a diocese holding mission from the metropolitan see of Canterbury. Its jurisdiction extends over all the West African Colonies.

Bishops of Sierra Leone.

1852. Owen Emeric Vidal, May 19, **G.**
1855. John Wills Weeks, May 10, **G.**
1857. John Bowen, Aug. 10, **G.**
1860. Edwd. Hyndman Beckles, Jan. 5, **G.**; res. 1870.
1870. Hy. Cheetham, Nov. 10, **G.**; res. 1882.
1883. Ernest Graham Ingham, Feb. 6, **G.**

GOVERNORS OF GAMBIA OR THE GAMBIA SETTLEMENTS.

See Introduction *ante*, p. 685.

Governors.

1843. Commander Hy. Frowd Seagram, R.N., June 23, **G.**
Commander Edmund Norcott, R.N., Nov. 20, **G.**
1844. Commander Chas. FitzGerald, R.N., May 3, **G.**
1847. Richd. Graves MacDonnell, Oct. 1, **G.**
1852 Arth. Edwd. Kennedy, May 25, **G**.
1852. Maj. Luke Smyth O'Connor, Sep. 13, **G.**
1859. Col. Geo. Abbas Kooli D'Arcy, June 17, **G.**

For subsequent Governors, see *post*, p. 688.

Commissioners or Administrators.

1866. R.-adm. Chas. Geo. Edwd. Patey, Oct. 22, **G.**
1871. T. F. Callaghan, C.M.G.
1873. Cornelius Hendericksen Kortright, Aug. 25, **G.**
1875. Surg.-maj. Saml. Rowe, C.M.G., aft. sir S., June 16, **G.**
1877. Surg,-maj. Valesius Skipton Gouldsbury, M.D., C.M.G., Mar. 15, **G.**
1884. Capt. Cornelius Alfd. Moloney, C.M.G., Feb. 2, **G.**
1886. Jas. Shaw Hay, Jan. 14, **G.**
Gilbert T. Carter (actg.); app. admr. Nov. 29, 1888.

For bishops, see "Bishops of Sierra Leone," *supra*.

GOVERNORS, &c. OF THE GOLD COAST.

See Introduction *ante*, p. 685.

Governors and Administrators of the Gold Coast Fort or Settlements.

1843. Commr. Hy. Worsley Hill, R.N., L.G., Mar. 6, **G.**
1845. Commr. Wm Winniett, R.N., aft. sir W., L.G., Oct. 24, **G.**; made Govr., Jan. 24, 1850, **G.**
1851. Maj. Stephen John Hill, Apr. 1, **G.**
1856. Benj. Chilley Campbell Pine, Nov. 4, **G.**; knt. Nov. 28.
1860. Edwd. Bullock Andrews, Mar. 7, **G.**
1863. Richd. Pine, Feb. 9, **G.**

For subsequent Governors to 1874, see *post*, p. 688.

Administrators.

1867. Herbert Taylor Ussher, Admr., July 22, **G.**
1872. Col. Robt. Wm. Harley, C.B., Admr., Sept. 12, **G.**

Gold Coast Colony constituted out of Gold Coast Settlements and Lagos, July 31, 1874, **G.**

Governors of Gold Coast Colony.

1874. Capt. Geo. Cumine Strahan, R.A., aft. sir G., July 31, **G.**
1874. Chas. Cameron Lees, aft. sir C., L.G., Nov. 7, **G.**
1876. Sanford Freeling, C.M.G., aft. sir S., Dec. 4, **G.**
1878. Chas. Cameron Lees, *again*, L.G.

1879. Herbert Taylor Ussher, C.M.G., May 26, **G.**
1879. Wm. Brandford Griffith, C.M.G., aft. sir C., L.G., Nov. 29, **G.**
1881. Surg.-Maj. sir Saml. Rowe, K.C.M.G., Jan. 25, **G.**
1882. Capt. Cornelius Alfred Moloney. C.M.G., Admr. during absence of Rowe.
1882. Wm. Brandford Griffith, C.M.G., *again*, L.G.
1884. Wm. Alex. Geo. Young, C.M.G., Feb. 28, **G.**; Actg. Govr. during absence of Rowe; aft. app. Govr.
1885. W. B. Griffith, C.M.G., *again*, L.G

Lagos separated from Gold Coast Colony, Jan. 13, 1886, **G.**

1886. Wm. Brandford Griffith, C.M.G., aft. sir W.; app. Govr. Jan. 13, **G.**

For bishops, see "Bishops of Sierra Leone," *ante*, p. 686.

GOVERNORS AND ADMINISTRATORS OF LAGOS.

See Introduction *ante*, p. 685.

Governors.

1861. Hy. Stanhope Freeman, Mar. 5, **G.**
1863. J. Hawley Glover, R.N., L.G.
1863. H. S. Freeman, *again*.
1864. J. Hawley Glover, R.N., L.G

For Governors from 1866 to 1874, see *post*, p. 688.

For Governors from 1874 to 1886, see "Gold Coast Colony," *ante*, p. 686.

For Governors from 1886, *vide infra*.

Lieutenant-Governors or Administrators under Governors of the West Africa Settlements.

1866. R.-adm. Chas. Geo. Edwd. Patey. R.N., Admr., Mar. 24, **G.**
Commr. John Hawley Glover, R.N., Admr., Oct. 22, **G.**
1870. W. H. Simpson.
1871. John Hawley Glover, R.N., *again*.
1872. Henry Fowler (actg.).
Geo. Berkeley.
1873. Capt. Chas. Cameron Lees, aft. sir C. (actg.).

Lieutenant-Governors or Administrators under Governors of the Gold Coast Colony.

1874. Capt. C. Cameron Lees, aft. sir C., L.G., July 31.
1875. John D.A.Dumaresq, Actg. Admr.
1878. Malcolm J. Brown, Actg. Admr.
1878. Capt. Cornelius Alf. Moloney, Actg. Admr.
1879. Wm. Brandford Griffith, C.M.G., aft. sir C., L.G., Nov. 29, **G.**
1880. Capt. C. A. Moloney, *again*, Actg. Admr.
1880. Wm. Brandford Griffith, C.M.G., *again*, L.G. from Dec. 1880 to Mar. 1881, Oct. to Dec. 1882, and May to Oct. 1885; Govr. Oct. 6, 1885.
1882. Surg.-maj. Frank Simpson, Actg. Admr.
Capt. C. Alf. Moloney, C.M.G., *again*, Actg. Admr.
1883. Fredk. Evans, C.M.G., Dep. Govr.
1884. Commr. R. Murray Ramsey, R.N., Dep. Govr.
Capt. Robt. Knapp Barrow, C.M.G., Dep. Govr.
1885. Fredk. Evans, C.M.G., Dep. Govr.
1886. Capt. C. Alf. Moloney, C.M.G., *again*, Admr.
Fredk. Evans, C.M.G., Actg. Admr.

Governors after Separation from Gold Coast Colony.

Office of Governor reconstituted Jan. 13, 1886, **G.**

1886. Capt. Cornelius Alfred Moloney, C.M.G., Jan. 13, **G.**

For bishops, see "Bishops of Sierra Leone," *ante*, p. 686.

GOVERNORS OF THE WEST AFRICA SETTLEMENTS,

See Introduction *ante*, p. 685.

Comprising Sierra Leone, Gambier, Gold Coast, and Lagos.

1866. Maj. Saml. Wensley Blackall, Feb. 23, **G.**
1868. Sir Arthur Edwd. Kennedy, C.B., Jan. 15, **G.**
1872. John Pope Hennessy, aft. sir J., Actg. Govr. until arrival of Keate in 1873.
1872. Robt. Wm. Keate, Nov. 30, **G.**
1873. Geo. Berkeley, July 26, **G.**

Comprising Sierra Leone and Gambia only.

1875. Cornelius Hendericksen Kortright, aft. sir C., Jan. 27, **G.**
1877. Surg.-maj. Saml. Rowe, C.M.G., aft. sir S., June 9, **G.**
1881. Arthur Elibank Havelock, C.M.G., aft. sir A., Jan. 26, **G.**
1884. Surg.-maj. sir Saml. Rowe, K.C.M.G., *again*, Dec. 29, **G.**
1886. Capt. Jas. Shaw Hay, C.M.G., July 5. **G.**

Sierra Leone and Gambia separated Nov. 28, 1888. See Introduction, *ante*, p. 685.

For bishops, see "Bishops of Sierra Leone," *ante* p. 686.

THE NIGER PROTECTORATE.

The Territory over which this Protectorate extends was brought under British protection in July 1824, under treaties with the native chiefs. Many of the treaty rights were granted to the Royal Niger Company by charter dated July 10, 1886.

No British governor is appointed, the principal official being the consul, who has a certain jurisdiction over British subjects.

For further particulars see the official Colonial List.

AFRICAN DIOCESES

whose jurisdiction lies outside the British dominions.

DIOCESE OF CENTRAL AFRICA, FORMERLY ZAMBESI.

This bishopric was constituted in 1861. It is classed as a missionary bishopric holding mission from the see of Canterbury.

Bishops of Central Africa.

1861. C. F. Mackenzie.
1863. Wm. Geo. Tozer, aft. bp. Jamaica.
1874. Edwd. Steele.
1883. Chas. Alan Smythies, consec. Nov. 30.

DIOCESE OF EASTERN EQUATORIAL AFRICA.

This bishopric was constituted in 1884. It is classed as a missionary bishopric holding mission from the see of Canterbury.

Bishops of Eastern Equatorial Africa.

1884. Jas. Hannington.
1886. Hy. Perrott Parker, consec. Oct. 18.

DIOCESE OF MADAGASCAR.

This bishopric was constituted in 1874. It is classed as a missionary bishopric holding mission from the see of Canterbury.

Bishop of Madagascar.

1874. Robt. Kestell Kestell-Cornish.

DIOCESE OF THE NIGER DISTRICT.

This bishopric was constituted in 1864. It is classed as a missionary bishopric holding mission from the see of Canterbury.

Bishop of the Niger District.

1884. Saml. Adjai Crowther, consec. June 29.

IV. –COLONIES, &c.—NORTH AMERICA.

DOMINION OF CANADA.

UPPER AND LOWER CANADA. ONTARIO. QUEBEC. NOVA SCOTIA. NEW BRUNSWICK. CAPE BRETON. MANITOBA. RED RIVER SETTLEMENT. RUPERT'S LAND. N W. TERRITORIES. BRITISH COLUMBIA. VANCOUVER ISLAND. PRINCE EDWARD ISLAND.

Canada was discovered by Sebastian Cabot about 1497. It was taken possession of by the French in 1525; but it was not until 1608–9 that Quebec, the first settlement, was founded. In 1759 Quebec was captured by the British under General Wolfe, in 1763 the rest of the country was ceded to Great Britain by the Treaty of Paris, and in that year, and again in 1774, provision was made for the government of the colony. In 1783, on the recognition of the independence of the United States, a considerable part of the Canadian territory was given up to that Republic.

In 1791, under 31 Geo. III. cap. 31, Canada was divided into (1) Upper Canada, now Ontario, and (2) Lower Canada, now Quebec. These provinces were again united, in 1840, under 3 & 4 Vict. cap. 35, by proclamation made under Order in Council dated Aug. 10, and gazetted Aug. 14, 1840.

Nova Scotia was discovered by John Cabot about 1497, colonised by the French in 1598, and, with the exception of its occupation by the English from 1627 to 1632, it was retained by the French until its cession to Great Britain at the Peace of Utrecht in 1714.

New Brunswick orginally belonged to the French, being called by them New France. It was ceded to Great Britain in 1763, and constituted a separated colony in 1785, having up to that time been annexed to Nova Scotia.

Cape Breton originally belonged to France. It was captured by the British forces in 1745, restored to France at the Peace of Aix-la-Chapelle in 1748, again captured by Great Britain in 1758, and ceded to that country by the Treaty of Paris in 1763. It was then united to Nova Scotia, separated from it in 1784, and again united thereto in 1820.

Manitoba, or, rather, the nucleus of that province, was formerly known as the Red River Settlement. It originally belonged to the Hudson's Bay Company as part of Rupert's Land, and was granted by them in 1811 to Thos., 5th Earl of Selkirk, who founded a settlement on the banks of the Red River in 1813. It was repurchased by the Hudson's Bay Company in 1835. By 31 & 32 Vict. cap. 105 (1867) the company surrendered their rights over Rupert's Land to the Crown, and, under this Act and the Canadian Acts 33 Vict. cap. 3 (1870), and 44 Vict. cap. 14 (1881), the province of Manitoba, as now constituted, was formed.

The North-West Territories were created by proclamation of Oct. 7, 1876, under Canadian Act 38 Vict. cap. 49 (1875). This Act was amended by Canadian Act 43 Vict. cap. 25 (1880). The North-West Territories consist of such portions of Rupert's Land and the old North-Western Territory as were not included in Manitoba.

British Columbia was constituted a colony in 1858 under 21 & 22 Vict. cap. 99 (1858).

Vancouver Island was discovered in 1592, but the first regula settlement was by the Hudson's Bay Company in 1843. The island was secured to Great Britain by treaty in 1846, and was constituted a colony in 1849.

Vancouver Island was united to British Columbia in 1866 unde 29 & 30 Vict. cap. 67 (1866).

Prince Edward Island was discovered in 1497, and colonised by the French shortly afterwards. It was taken from them by Grea Britain in 1758, annexed to Nova Scotia in 1763, and made a separat colony in 1770.

The federation of the Canadian colonies, under the title of th Dominion of Canada, is authorised by Acts of the Imperial Parlia ment, 30 Vict. cap 3 (1867), 31 & 32 Vict. cap. 105 (1868), and b Orders in Council or proclamations thereunder; and by Colonial Act 33 Vict. cap. 3 (1870), 30 Vict. cap. 49 (1875), and 43 Vict. cap. 2 (1880).

The dominion was first formed by proclamation dated May 22 an gazetted May 24, 1867, and then consisted of the provinces of Uppe Canada (then re-named Ontario), Lower Canada (then re-name Quebec), Nova Scotia, and New Brunswick. Rupert's Land an the N. W. Territory, afterwards re-divided into the N. W. Territories and Manitoba, were added on July 15, 1870, under Order in Council dated June 23, and gazetted June 24, 1870. British Columbia was added on July 20, 1871, under Order in Council dated May 16, and gazetted May 19, 1871. Prince Edward Island was added on July 1, 1873, by Order in Council dated June 26, and gazetted July 4, 1873. By Order in Council dated July 31, 1880 (not gazetted in England), such parts of the British possessions in North America (except Newfoundland) as had not previously joined the dominion were annexed to it.

The Dominion of Canada forms the ecclesiastical provinces of Canada, which comprises the dioceses of

Algoma, Fredericton, Huron, Montreal, Niagara, Nova Scotia, Ontario, Quebec, Toronto;

and of Rupert's Land, which comprises the dioceses of

Athabasca (now Mackenzie River and S. Athabasca), Moosonee, Rupert's Land, Saskatchewan.

GOVERNORS OF CANADA.

Prior to the division into Upper and Lower Canada in 1791.

See Introduction, *ante*, p. 689.

1765. Lt.-gen. hon. Jas. Murray, Nov. 21.
1766. Paulus Æmilius Irving (president), June 30.
M.-gen. Guy Carleton, L.G., Sept. 24.
1770. Hector C. Cramahé (president), Aug. 9.
1774. Lt.-gen. sir Guy Carleton, aft. ld. Dorchester, Oct. 11.
M.-gen. Jas. Johnstone, L.G., Nov. 26.
1777. Lt.-gen. Fredk. Haldimand, Apr. 21.
1786. Sir Guy Carleton, *again;* aft. ld. Dorchester; Apr. 11.

Governors of Canada.

After the division in 1791.

See Introduction, *ante*, p. 689.

Governors of Upper and Lower Canada, Nova Scotia, New Brunswick, Prince Edward Island, and Cape Breton.

1796. Lt.-gen. R. Prescott.
1807. Lt.-gen. sir Jas. Hy. Craig, K.B., Aug. 31, **G.**
1811. Lt.-gen. sir Geo. Prevost, bt., Sept. 10, **G.**
1814. Lt.-gen. sir Gordon Drummond, L.P., Dec. 28.
1817. Lt.-gen. sir John Coape Sherbrooke, G.C.B., Jan. 29, **G.**
1818. Chas., D. of Richmond, K.G., Apr. 6, **G.**
1819. Lt.-gen. Geo., 9th E. of Dalhousie, G.C.B., Apr. 20, **G.**

In 1820 Cape Breton was re-united to Nova Scotia. See Introduction, *ante*, p. 690.

Governors of Upper and Lower Canada, Nova Scotia, New Brunswick, and Prince Edward Island.

1828. Lt.-gen. sir Jas. Kempt, G.C.B., Aug. 14, **G.**
1830. Lt.-gen. Matth., ld. Aylmer, K.C.B., July 19, **G.**
1835. Archd., E. of Gosford, June 9, **G.**

Governors-General of North American Provinces.

1838. John Geo., E. of Durham, G.C.B., Jan. 16, **G.**
Lt.-gen. sir John Colborne, G.C.B., Dec. 14, **G.**
1839. Chas. Poulett Thomson, aft. ld. Sydenham, Aug. 29, **G.**

In 1840 the provinces of Upper and Lower Canada were united. See Introduction, *ante*, p. 689.

Governors of Canada, New Brunswick, Nova Scotia, and Prince Edward Island, and Governors-General of North American Provinces.

1840. Chas., ld. Sydenham, above-named, Aug. 28, **G.**; *d.* in office, 1841.
1841. Sir Chas. Bagot, G.C.B., Sept. 27. **G.**
1843. Sir Chas. Theoph. Metcalfe, G.C.B., aft. ld. Metcalfe, Jan. 25, **G.**
1846. Lt.-gen. Chas. Murray, E. of Cathcart, K.C.B., Mar. 10, **G.**
1846. Jas., E. of Elgin and Kincardine, Sept. 16, **G.**
1854. Sir Edmd. Walker Head, bt., Sept. 19, **G.**
1861. Chas. Stanley, visc. Monck, Oct. 28, **G.**

In 1867 the Dominion of Canada was formed. See Introduction, *ante*, p. 690.

Governors-General of the Dominion of Canada.

1867. Chas. Stanley, visc. Monck, June 4, **G.**; as from July 1, 1867.
1869. Sir John Young, bt., G.C.B., G.C.M.G., aft. ld. Lisgar, Jan. 2, **G.**
1872. Fredk. Temple, E. of Dufferin, K.P., K.C.B., aft. M. of Dufferin and Ava, June 3, **G.**

The above were also governors of Prince Edward Island, which was not annexed to the Dominion until 1873.

1878. Sir John Douglas Sutherland Campbell, K.T., G.C.M.G., c.c. M. of Lorne, Oct. 14, **G.**
1883. Hy. Chas. Keith, M. of Lansdowne, Aug. 24, **G.**
1888. Fredk. Arthur, ld. Stanley of Preston, G.C.B., May 1.

LIEUTENANT-GOVERNORS OF UPPER CANADA, NOW ONTARIO.

From the division into Upper and Lower Canada in 1791. See Introduction, *ante*, p. 689.

For Governors prior to 1791, see "Governors of Canada," *ante*, p. 691.

Lieutenant-Governors of Upper Canada.

1806. Fras. Gore, Mar, 1, **G.**
1817. M.-gen sir Peregrine Maitland, K.C.B., Jan. 8, **G.**
1828. M.-gen. sir John Colborne, K.C.B., Aug. 14, **G.**
1835. Sir Fras. Bond Head, K.C.H., Nov. 27, **G.**
1837. Col. sir Geo. Arthur, K.C.H., Dec. 22.

In 1840 the provinces of Upper and Lower Canada were united, see Introduction *ante*, p. 689. For governors from 1840 to 1867, see "Governors of Canada, &c.," *supra*. In 1867 the Dominion of Canada was formed, and the name of Upper Canada was changed to Ontario, see Introduction, *ante*, p. 690. For governors since 1867, see "Governors-General of the Dominion of Canada," *supra*, and the following list of

Lieutenant-Governors of Ontario.

Taken from the Colonial List.

1867. Lt.-gen. sir H. W. Stisted, K.C.B.
1868. Wm. Pearce Howland, C.B., aft. sir W.
1873. John W. Crawford.
1875. D. A. Macdonald.
1880. John Beverley Robinson, June 30.
1887. Sir Alexr. Campbell, K.C.M.G., Feb. 8.

DIOCESE OF QUEBEC.

From 1793 to 1850 the bishops of Quebec had jurisdiction over part of Upper Canada.

See "Bishops of Quebec," *post*, p. 694.

DIOCESE OF TORONTO.

This diocese was constituted in 1839. By Letters Patent, Feb. 6, 1862, **G.**, the see was divided and part of it formed into the bishopric of Ontario. Toronto is in the ecclesiastical province of Canada.

Bishops of Toronto.

1839. John Strachan, Aug. 5, **G.**
1868. A. N. Bethune.
1879. Arthur Sweatmam, consec. May 1.

DIOCESE OF ONTARIO.

This bishopric was constituted out of that of Toronto by Letters Patent, Feb. 6, 1862, **G.** It is in the ecclesiastical province of Canada.

Bishop of Ontario.

1862. John Travers Lewis, Feb. 6, **G.**

DIOCESE OF HURON.

This bishopric was constituted in 1857, and is in the ecclesiastical province of Canada.

Bishops of Huron.

1857. Benjn. Cronyn, Oct. 14, **G.**
1871. Isaac Hellmuth, res. 1883.
1883. Maurice S. Baldwin, consec. Nov. 30.

DIOCESE OF ALGOMA.

This bishopric was constituted in 1873. It is in the ecclesiastical province of Canada.

Bishops of Algoma.

1873. F. D. Fauquier.
1882. Edwd. Sullivan, consec. June 29.

DIOCESE OF NIAGARA.

This diocese was constituted in 1875. It is in the ecclesiastical province of Canada.

Bishops of Niagara.

1875. Thos. B. Fuller.
1885. Chas. Hamilton, consec. May 1.

LIEUTENANT GOVERNORS OF LOWER CANADA, NOW QUEBEC.

See Introduction, *ante*, p. 689.

For governors prior to the formation of the Dominion of Canada in 1867, see "Governors of Canada," *ante*, p. 691. On the division of Canada into Upper and

Lower in 1791, Lower Canada was placed under the *governors* thereafter appointed *lieutenant-governors* being appointed for Upper Canada only.

In 1840 the provinces of Upper and Lower Canada were united. For governor from 1840 to 1867, see "Governors of Canada, &c.," *ante*, p. 692. In 1867 the Dominion of Canada was formed, and the name of Lower Canada was changed to Quebec. See Introduction, *ante*, p. 690. For governors since 1867, see "Governors-General of the Dominion of Canada," *ante*, p. 692, and the following list of

Lieutenant-Governors of Quebec.

Taken from the Colonial List.

1867. Sir N. F. Belleau, K.C.M.G.
1873. R. E. Caron.
1876. Luc Letellier de St. Just.
1879. Theodore Robitaille.
1884. Louis François Roderique Masson, Nov. 7.
1887. Auguste Réal Angers, Oct. 24.

DIOCESE OF QUEBEC.

This bishopric was constituted in 1793, and originally extended over both Upper and Lower Canada. By Letters Patent, July 19, 1850, **G.** the district of Montreal was separated from it and erected into a separate diocese. It is in the ecclesiastical province of Canada.

Bishops of Quebec.

Undivided Diocese.

1793. I. Mountain.
1826. C. J. Stewart.
1836. Geo. Jehosophat Mountain, Feb. 13, **G.**

Bishops of Quebec.

After the Separation of Montreal.

1850. Geo. Jehosophat Mountain, above named, July 19, **G.**
1863. Jas. Wm. Williams.

DIOCESE OF MONTREAL.

This bishopric was constituted by Letters Patent July 19, 1850, **G.**, and consists of so much of the original diocese of Quebec as comprised the district of Montreal. It is in the ecclesiastical province of Canada.

Bishops of Montreal.

1850. Fras. Fulford, July 19, **G.**
1869. A. Oxenden.
1879. Wm. Bennett Bond.

GOVERNORS OF NOVA SCOTIA.

See Introduction, *ante*, p. 689.

For Governors, see "Governors of Canada" and "Governors-General of the Dominion of Canada," *ante*, pp. 691–2.

Lieutenant-Governors of Nova Scotia.

The earlier names are taken from the Colonial List.

1714. Saml. Vetch.
1717. Col. Rd. Phillips.
1749. Hon. Edwd. Cornwallis.
1752. Peregrine Thos. Hopson.
1754. Chas. Lawrence.
1756. A. Moulton.

1760. J. Belcher.
1761. Hy. Ellis (?)
1764. Robt. Wilmot.
1766. M. Franklin.
1773. Fras. Legge.
1776. M. Arbuthnot.
1778. R. Hughes.
1781. Sir A. S. Hammond.
1782. Jno. Parr.
1783. P. Fanning.
1786. Sir Guy Carleton, aft. ld. Dorchester.
1791. R. Bulkeley.
1792. Jno. Wentworth, aft. bt.
1808. Sir Geo. Prevost, bt., Jan. 16, **G.**
1811. Gen. Duncan Darroch (acting).
1811. Lt.-gen. sir John Cope Sherbrooke, K.B., Aug. 19, **G.**
1816. Gen. Smyth (acting).
1816. Lt.-gen. Geo., E. of Dalhousie, G.C.B., July 29.
1819. M.-gen. sir Jas. Kempt, G.C.B., Oct. 20, **G.**
1826. M. Wallace (acting).
1828. M.-gen. sir Peregrine Maitland, K.C.B., Aug. 14, **G.**
1834. M.-gen. sir Colin Campbell (not ld. Clyde), Jan. 24, **G.**
1840. Lucius Bentinck, visc. Falkland, **G.**
1846. M.-gen. sir Jno. Harvey, K.C.B., June 26, **G.**
1852. Col. sir Jno. Gaspard Le Marchant, June 18, **G.**
1858. Geo. Augs. Constantine, E. of Mulgrave, aft. M. of Normanby, Jan. 28, **G.**
1864. Sir Richd. Graves Mac Donnell, C.B., May 28, **G.**
1865. Sir Wm. Fenwick Williams, bt., K.C.B., Oct. 20, **G.**

In 1867 the Dominion of Canada was formed, and Nova Scotia became one of its provinces.

Lieutenant-Governors of Nova Scotia.

Since the formation of the Dominion of Canada.

Taken from the Colonial List.

1867. M.-gen. sir Chas. Hastings Doyle, K.C.M.G.
1870. Sir Edwd. Kenny (acting).
1873. Jos. Howe (acting).
1873. Adams G. Archibald, aft. sir A.
1883. Matth. Hy. T. Richey, July 4.
1888. A. W. McLelan, July 9.

DIOCESE OF NOVA SCOTIA.

This is the oldest of all the colonial dioceses, having been constituted as far back as 1787. Its jurisdiction extends over Nova Scotia, Cape Breton, and Prince Edward Island. It is in the ecclesiastical province of Canada.

Bishops of Nova Scotia.

1787. Chas. Inglis.
1816. R. Stanser, May 20, **G.**
1825. J. Inglis.
1851. Hibbert Binney, Mar. 12, **G.**
1888. F. Courtney.

GOVERNORS OF NEW BRUNSWICK.

See Introduction, *ante*, p. 689.

From 1763 to 1785 New Brunswick formed part of Nova Scotia. See lieutenant-governors of that colony, *ante*, p. 694.

Lieutenant-Governors of New Brunswick.

From its formation into a separate colony in 1786.

1786. Sir Guy Carleton, aft. ld. Dorchester.
1787. E. Winslow.
1788. Lt.-col. Johnston.
1809. Gen. Martin Hunter, aft. sir M.
1811. M.-gen. Wm. Balfour.
1817. M.-gen. Geo. Stracey Smith, Feb. 28, **G.**
1823. Ward Chipman, acting until arrival of Douglas.
1824. J. M. Bliss, acting until arrival of Douglas.
1823. M.-gen. sir Howard Douglas, bt., Sept. 5, **G.**
1831. M.-gen. sir Archd. Campbell, G.C.B., Mar. 21, **G.**
1837. M.-gen. sir Jno. Harvey, K.C.B., Mar. 19, **G.**

1841. Lt.-col. sir Wm. Macbean George Colebrook, Mar. 25, **G.**
1847. Sir Edmd. Walker Head, bt., Oct. 26, **G.**
1854. Hon. Jno. Hy. Thos. Manners-Sutton, July 1, **G.**
1861. Hon. Arth. Hamilton Gordon, C.M.G aft. sir A., Sept. 16, **G.**
1866. M.-gen. sir Chas. Hastings Doyl K.C.M.G.

In 1867 the Dominion of Canada was formed, and New Brunswick became one of i provinces.

Lieutenant-Governors of New Brunswick.

Since the formation of the Dominion of Canada.

Taken from the Colonial List.

1867. Col. F. P. Harding, C.B.
1868. Lemuel Allen Wilmot.
1873. Saml. Leonard Tilley, C.B., aft. sir S.
1878. E. B. Chandler.
1880. Robt. Duncan Wilmot.
1885. Sir S. L. Tilley, K.C.M.G., C.I *again*, Oct 31.

DIOCESE OF FREDERICTON.

This bishopric was constituted by Letters Patent, April 24, 1845, (Its jurisdiction extends over the province of New Brunswick. It is i the ecclesiastical province of Canada.

Bishops of Fredericton.

1845. Jno. Medley, Apr. 24, **G.**; made Metrop. of Canada, 1879.
1881. Hollingworth Tully Kingdon, Coad

GOVERNORS OF CAPE BRETON.

See Introduction, *ante*, p. 690, and Nova Scotia, *ante*, p. 694. Tl island is within the ecclesiastical jurisdiction of the bishops of Nov Scotia.

GOVERNORS OF MANITOBA, FORMERLY RED RIVER SETTLEMENT.

See Introduction, *ante*, p. 690.

For Governors, see "Governors-General of the Dominion of Canada," *ante*, p. 692.

Lieutenant-Governors of Manitoba.

Taken from the Colonial List.

1870. Adams, G. Archibald, aft. Sir A.
1873. Alex. Morris.
1877. J. E. Cauchon.
1882. Jas. Cox Aikins, Oct. 8.
1888. Jonn. Christian Schultz, July 1.

For bishops, see "Bishops of Rupert's Land," *post*, p. 697.

GOVERNORS OF RUPERT'S LAND AND THE NORTH-WESTERN TERRITORY.

See Introduction, *ante*, p. 690, Manitoba, *supra*, and North-We Territories, *post*, p. 697. The Governors-General of the Dominion (Canada were appointed Governors by Letters Patent dated April 1870 (June 24, 1870, **G.**).

DIOCESE OF RUPERT'S LAND.

This bishopric was constituted by Letters Patent, May 19, 1849, **G.** Its jurisdiction extends over Manitoba, and also over part of the N. W. Territory. It is in the ecclesiastical province of Rupert's Land.

BISHOPS OF RUPERT'S LAND.

1849. David Anderson, May 19, **G.**
1865. Robt. Machray, consec. June 24.

GOVERNORS OF NORTH-WEST TERRITORIES.

See Introduction, *ante*, p. 690.

LIEUTENANT-GOVERNORS OF THE NORTH-WEST TERRITORIES.

Taken from the Colonial List.

1876. David Laird.
1881. Edgar Dewdney, Dec. 3.
1888. Jos. Royal, July 1.

DIOCESE OF MOOSONEE.

This bishopric was constituted in 1872. It is in the ecclesiastical province of Rupert's Land.

BISHOPS OF MOOSONEE.

1872. John Horden, consec. Dec. 15.

DIOCESES OF ATHABASCA AND MACKENZIE RIVER.

These dioceses are in the ecclesiastical province of Rupert's Land. The original diocese of Athabasca was constituted in 1874, and was divided in 1884, the northern portion being thenceforth styled Mackenzie River and the southern portion retaining the old name of Athabasca.

BISHOP OF ATHABASCA—UNDIVIDED DIOCESE.

1874. Wm. Carpenter Bombas, consec. May 4; became bp. of Mackenzie River on division of the diocese] *ut supra*.

BISHOP OF ATHABASCA—PRESENT DIOCESE.

1884. Richd. Young, consec. Oct 18.

BISHOP OF MACKENZIE RIVER.

1884. Wm. Carpenter Bompas, form. bp. of Athabasca; *vide supra*.

DIOCESE OF SASKATCHEWAN.

This bishopric was constituted in 1874, and is in the ecclesiastical province of Rupert's Land.

BISHOPS OF SASKATCHEWAN.

1874. Jno. McClean.
1887. Wm. Cyprian Pinkham, consec. Aug. 7.

DIOCESE OF QU'APPELLE, FORMERLY CALLED ASSINIBOIA.

This bishopric was constituted in 1884. It is in the ecclesiastical province of Rupert's Land.

Bishop of Qu'Appelle.

1884. Hon. Adelbert Jno. Robt. Anson, June 24.

Part of the N. W. Territories is under the ecclesiastical jurisdiction of the bishops of Rupert's Land.

See "Bishops of Rupert's Land," *ante*, p. 697.

GOVERNORS OF BRITISH COLUMBIA

See Introduction, *ante*, p. 690.

1858. Jas. Douglas, Sept. 3, **G.**
1864. Fredk. Seymour, Feb. 8, **G.**
1869. Anthy. Musgrave, aft. sir A., Nov. 8, **G.**

British Columbia was made part of the Dominion of Canada as from July 20, 1871, under Order in Council dated May 16, and gazetted May 19, 1871.

Lieutenant-Governors of British Columbia.

Since its annexation to the Dominion of Canada.

Taken from the Colonial List.

1871. Joseph Wm. Trutch, C.M.G., aft. sir J.
1876. Albert Norton Richards.
1881. Clement Fras. Cornwall, June 25.
1887. Hugh Nelson, Feb. 8.

DIOCESE OF BRITISH COLUMBIA, NOW COLUMBIA.

British Columbia and Vancouver Island were constituted into the see of British Columbia by Letters Patent, Jan. 12, 1859, **G.** The see has since been divided by the present jurisdiction of the bishop of Columbia, and extends over Vancouver and the adjacent islands. The see is now classed as a colonial diocese holding mission from the see of Canterbury.

Bishop of British Columbia, now Columbia.

1859. Geo. Hills, Jan. 12, **G.**; consec. Feb. 24.

DIOCESE OF CALEDONIA.

This bishopric was constituted in 1879 as a colonial diocese holding mission from the see of Canterbury.

Bishop of Caledonia.

1879. Wm. Ridley.

DIOCESE OF NEW WESTMINSTER.

This bishopric was constituted in 1879 as a colonial diocese holding mission from the see of Canterbury.

Bishop of Caledonia.

1879. Acton Windeyer Sillitoe, consec. Nov. 1.

GOVERNORS OF PRINCE EDWARD ISLAND.

See Introduction, *ante*, p. 690.

For Governors, see "Governors of Canada," *ante*, p. 691, and "Governors-General of the Dominion of Canada," *ante*, p. 692.

From 1763 to 1770, Prince Edward Island formed part of Nova Scotia.

Lieutenant-Governors of Prince Edward Island.

From its formation into a separate colony in 1770.

1770. Walter Paterson.
1786. Lt.-gen. Edmd. Fanning.
1804. Col. Jos. Fredk. Wallett Des Banes, May 19, **G.**
1813. Chas. Douglas Smith.
1824. (? 1822). Lt.-col. Jno. Ready, May 22, **G.**
1831. Capt. sir Murray Maxwell, C.B., Mar. 14, **G.**
Aretas Wm. Young, July 25, **G.**
1836. Col. sir Jno. Harvey, Feb. 2, **G.**
1837. Chas. Augs. FitzRoy, Mar. 19, **G**; knt., June.
1841. Commander Hy. Vere Huntley, R.N., aft. sir H., Aug. 20, **G.**
1847. Sir Donald Campbell, bt., Oct. 26, **G.**
1850. Alexr. Bannerman, aft. sir A., Dec. 3, **G.**
1854. Dominick Daly, aft. sir D., May 8, **G.**
1859. Geo. Dundas, Jan. 5, **G.**
1867. Lt.-col. Archd. Edwd. Harbord Anson, Feb. 27, **G.**
1868. Sir Robt. Hodgson (acting).
1870. Wm. Cleaver Fras. Robinson, aft. sir W., Aug. 19, **G.**

Prince Edward Island was made part of the Dominion of Canada as from July 1, 1873, by Order in Council dated June 26, and gazetted July 4, 1873.

Lieutenant-Governors of Prince Edward Island.

Since its annexation to the Dominion of Canada.

Taken from the Colonial List.

1873. Sir W. C. F. Robinson, K.C.M.G., above named.
Sir Robt. Hodgson, acting L. G. in 1874.
1879. T. H. Haviland.
1884. A. A. Macdonald, Aug. 1.

For bishops, see "Bishops of Nova Scotia," *ante*, p. 695.

GOVERNORS OF VANCOUVER ISLAND.

See Introduction, *ante*, p. 690; and British Columbia, *ante*, p. 698.

Governors of Vancouver Island.

1849. Richd. Blanshard, July 13, **G.**
1851. James Douglas, May 9.
1863. Arth. Edwd. Kennedy, C.B., Dec. 4, **G.**

United to British Columbia, August, 1866.

See "British Columbia," *ante*, p. 698.

For bishops, see "Bishops of Columbia," *ante*, p. 698.

NEWFOUNDLAND.

Newfoundland was discovered in 1497, and was formally taken possession of by the English in 1578. Their right was, however, not admitted by the fishing fleets of the other nations frequenting the coast, and it was not until the Treaty of Utrecht in 1713 that Newfoundland was formally ceded to the British.

NEWFOUNDLAND is the only part of British North America not included in the Dominion of Canada.

GOVERNORS OF NEWFOUNDLAND.

The names of the Governors down to 1757 are taken from the Colonial List.

From 1713 to 1729 the captain of the first ship on the coast was admiral for the fishing season.

1729. Capt. Osborn.
1737. Capt. Vanbrugh.
1740. Capt. ld. Geo. Graham.
1741. Capt. aft. adm. Hon. Jno. Byng (executed at Portsmouth Mar. 14, 1757).
1744. Capt. Sir C. Hardy.
1749. Capt. Geo. Brydges Rodney, aft. adm. ld. Rodney.
1750. Capt. Drake.
1753. Capt. Bonfoy.
1755, Capt. Dorrill.
1757. Captain Edwards.
1760. Capt. aft. adm. Jas. Webb.
1761. Capt. Groves.
1764. Capt. aft. adm. sir Hugh Palliser, bt., Mar. 31.
1769. Capt. hon. John Byron, June 3.
1772. Commodore Molyneux, ld. Shuldham, Mar. 10.
1775. Commodore aft. adm. Robt. Duff, Apr. 24.
1776. Adm. John Montagu, Mar. 31.
1779. Adm. Richd. Edwards, Feb. 19.
1782. Adm. John Campbell, Mar. 24.
1786. Adm. John Elliot, Mar. 25.
1789. Adm. Mark Milbanke, Sept. 21.
1792. Adm. sir Richd. King, bt., July 7.
1794. Adm. sir James Wallace.
1797. Adm. hon. Wm. Waldegrave, aft. ld. Radstock.
1800. Adm. Chas. Morice Pole.
1802. Adm. Jas. Gambier, aft. ld. Gambier.
1804. Adm. sir Erasmus Gower, May 31.
1807. Adm. John Holloway, Apr. 10, **G.**
1810. Adm. sir John Thos. Duckworth, K.B., May 4, **G.**
1813. Adm. sir Richd. Godwin Keats, K.B., Mar. 9, **G.**
1816. Adm. Fras. Pickmore, May 20, **G.**
1818. V.-Adm. sir Chas. Hamilton, bt., May 13, **G.**
1825. Capt. sir Thos. John Cochrane, Apr. 16, **G.**
1834. Capt. Hy. Prescott, Sept. 24, **G.**
1841. Maj.-gen. sir John Harvey, K.C.B., Apr. 29, **G.**
1846. Hon. Fredk. Adolphus Bruce, L.G., June 27, **G.**
Lt.-Col. sir John Gaspard Le Marchant, Dec. 28, **G.**
1852. Ker Baillie Hamilton, Oct. 8, **G.**
1855. Chas. Hy. Darling, aft. sir C. (admr.), May 26, **G.**; Govr. May 3, **G.**
1864. Anthy. Musgrave, aft. sir A., July 29, **G.**
1867. Sir Alexr. Bannerman, Feb. 9, **G.**
1869. Col. Stephen John Hill, C.B., aft. sir S , Sept. 29, **G.**
1876. Commander Sir John Hawley Glover, G.C.M G., Mar. 31, **G.**
1881. Sir Fredk. Bowker Terrington Carter, K.C.M.G., admr. until arrival of Maxse.
Lt.-Col. Sir Hy. Fitzhardinge Berkeley Maxse, K.C.M.G., July 6, **G.**
1882. Carter, *again*, admr. until arrival of Glover.
1883. Sir John Hawley Glover, G.C.M.G., *again*, Dec. 17, **G.**
1885. Carter, *again*, admr. until arrival of Des Voeux.
1886. Sir Geo. Wm. Des Vœux, K.C.M.G.
1887. Hy. Arthur Blake, C.M.G., aft. sir H., July 11, **G.**
1888. Sir John Terence O'Nicolls O'Brien, K.C.M.G., Nov. 24.

DIOCESE OF NEWFOUNDLAND.

This bishopric was founded in 1839. It is now classed as a colonial diocese holding mission from the see of Canterbury.

BISHOPS OF NEWFOUNDLAND.

1839. Aubrey Geo. Spencer, Aug. 5, **G.**
1844. Edwd. Feild, Mar. 22, **G.**
1876. Jas. Butler Kelly, (coadj. 1867), aft. Bishop of Moray.
1878. Llewellyn Jones, consec. May 1; now styled Bishop of Newfoundland and the Bermudas.

THE BERMUDAS OR SOMERS ISLANDS.

THESE ISLANDS are situated in the North Atlantic Ocean, about 600 miles from Cape Hatteras, North Carolina. They were discovered by Bermudez, a Spaniard, in 1527, but remained uninhabited until 1611, when, attention having been drawn to them by the shipwreck of sir Geo. Somers there in 1609, they were included in the grant to the Virginia Company, and have from that time remained a British Colony.

THE BERMUDAS from 1844 to 1877, and from 1879 to the present time, have been attached to the diocese of Newfoundland, the present bishop (Llewellyn Jones) being styled Bishop of Newfoundland and the Bermudas.

GOVERNORS OF BERMUDA.

The earlier names are taken from the Colonial List.

1612. Richd. Moore.
1616. Danl. Tucker.
1619. Capt. N. Butler.
1622. Capt. J. Bernard.
1623. Capt. Woodhouse.
1626. Capt. P. Bell.
1629. Capt. Roger Wood.
1637. Capt. T. Craddock.
1641. Capt. W. Sayle.
1642. Capt. J. Forster.
1643. Capt. W. Sayle, *again*.
1644. W. Sayle, — Paynter, and — Wilkinson (jointly).
1645. Capt. J. Forster.
Sayle, Paynter and Wilkinson, *again*.
1647. Capt. J. Turnor.
1650. John Trimingham.
Capt. J. Forster, *again*.
1659. Capt. W. Sayle, *again*.
1663. Capt. F. Seymour.
1668. Capt. S. Whalley.
1669. Sir John Haydon.
1681. Capt. F. Seymour, *again*.
1684. Richd. Coney.
1686. Sir R. Robinson.
1689. Isaac Richier.
1692. Capt. Goddard.
1698. Saml. Day.
1700. Capt. Bennett.
1713. Hy. Pullein.
1721. John Bruce Hope, aft. sir J.
1727. Capt. John Pitt.
1737. Alured Popple.
1745. Wm. Popple.
1764. Geo. Jas. Bruere.
1781–2. Wm. Browne.
1788. Hy. Hamilton.
1794. Jas. Crawford.
1796. Wm. Campbell, June 1.
1797. Geo. Beckwith, aft. sir G., L.P., Apr. 7.
1805. Fras. Gore. Jan. 23, **G.**
1806. Brig.-gen. John Hodgson, Mar. 1, **G.**
1811. Sir Jas. Cockburn, Mar. 14, **G.**
1819. Lt.-gen. Sir Wm. Lumley, K.B., June 1, **G.**
1825. Lt.-Gen. sir Hilgrove Turner, K.B. and K.C.H., May 28, **G.**
1831. Col. Stephen Remnant Chapman, C.B., April 23, **G.**
1838. Sir Andrew Leith Hay, Feb. 6, **G.**
1839. Lt.-Col. Wm. Reid, C.B.. Nov. 1, **G.**
1846. Capt. Chas. Elliott, R.N., Sept. 25, **G.**
1854. Lt.-Col. Freeman Murray, July 24, **G.**
1861. Lt.-Col. Harry St. George Ord, R.E., Feb. 14, **G.**
1867. Col. sir Fredk. Edwd. Chapman, R.E., K.C.B., Apr. 8, **G.**
1870. Col. sir Thos. Gore Browne, K.C.M.G., C.B., admr., July 11. **G.**
1871. M.-Gen. John Hy. Lefroy, R.A., C.B., Apr. 8, **G.**
1877. Col. Robt. Michl. Laffan, R.E., aft. sir R., Apr. 23, **G.**
1882. Lt.-Gen. Thos. Lionel John Gallwey, R.E., June 2, **G.**
1888. Lt.-Gen. Edwd. Newdigate Newdigate, C.B., Aug. 7, **G.**

For bishops, see Introduction, *supra*, and Diocese of Newfoundland, *ante*, p. 700.

V.—COLONIES, &c.—AUSTRALASIA.

New South Wales, formerly known as Port Jackson, was the foundation of the Australian colonies, and it is from the subsequent division of this territory and from the colonization of other parts of the Australian continent and the adjacent islands that the present Australasian colonies have arisen. These colonies now comprise:—

New South Wales and Norfolk Island,	South Australia,	New Zealand,
Victoria,	Western Australia,	Fiji Islands,
Queensland,	Tasmania (formerly Van Diemen's land),	British New Guinea.

The first discovery of the Australian Continent is involved in some doubt, and still more dispute. It is said to have been known to the Portuguese early in the sixteenth century. During the seventeenth century both Spanish and Dutch navigators made voyages of discovery, some records of which still linger in "Torres" Straits, "Van Diemen's" Land, and other places; but it was not until the voyages of captain Cook (1769–77) that any practical result was obtained. In 1788 the first attempt at colonization was made, Port Jackson (now Sydney, N.S.W.) being founded as a convict settlement by the British, who have been allowed to take undisputed possession of the entire continent, as well as of the neighbouring islands of Tasmania and New Zealand.

The Australasian colonies form the ecclesiastical provinces of Sydney, which comprises the dioceses of—

Adelaide,	Grafton and Armidale,	Perth, W. A.,
Ballarat,	Melbourne,	Riverina,
Bathurst,	Newcastle,	Sydney,
Brisbane,	North Queensland,	Tasmania;
Goulburn,		

and of New Zealand, which comprises the dioceses of

Auckland, formerly New Zealand,	Dunedin.	Waiapu,
Christ Church, N.Z.,	Melanesia,	Wellington,
	Nelson,	

NEW SOUTH WALES.

This is the oldest of the Australian colonies, a convict settlement having been established at Port Jackson in 1788. In earlier times the governors of New South Wales were also appointed governors over the other colonies, which were placed under the direct control of lieutenant-governors only.

GOVERNORS OF NEW SOUTH WALES.

A few of the earlier names are taken from the Colonial List.

1788. Capt. A. Phillip, R.N., Jan. 26.
1792. Capt. F. Grose, R.N., L.G., Dec. 11.
1794. Capt. Wm. Paterson, L.G., Dec. 13.
1795. Capt. Hunter, R.N., Sept. 27.
1800. Capt. P. G. King, R.N., Sept. 28.
1805. Capt. Wm. Bligh, R.N., Apr. 27, **G.**
1808. Lt.-col. G. Johnstone, Lt.-col. Foveaux and col. Wm. Paterson, Jan. 26.

1809. Lt.-col. Lachlan Macquarrie, Apr. 22, **G.**

1821. Gen. sir Thos. Brisbane, K.C.B., Feb. 8, **G.**

1824. Col. Geo. Arthur, Govr. N. S. Wales and V. D. Land.

1825. Col. Stewart. Actg. Govr. until arrival of Darling, Dec. 6 to Dec. 18.

M.-Gen. Ralph Darling, Govr. N. S. Wales and V. D. Land, Apr. 20, **G.**

1831. Col. Lindsay, C.B., Actg. Govr. until arrival of Bourke, Oct. 22 to Dec. 2.

M.-gen. Richd. Bourke, Apr. 27, **G.**

1837. Lt.-col. K. Snodgrass, L.G., Actg. Govr. until arrival of Gipps, Dec. 6 to Feb. 23, 1838.

Sir Geo. Gipps, July 24, **G.**

1846. Sir Maurice O'Connell, Actg. Govr. until arrival of Fitzroy, July 12 to Aug. 2.

Sir Chas. Augs. Fitzroy, Feb. 13, **G.** App. Govr. N. S. Wales, V. D. Land, Victoria, S. Australia, and Gov.-gen. of all the colonies of Australia, including W. Australia, Jan. 27, 1851, **G.**

1854. Capt. Sir Wm. Thos. Denison, Govr. N. S. Wales and Govr.-gen. N. S. Wales, V. D. Land, Victoria, S. Australia, and W. Australia, Sept. 19, **G.**

1857. Col. Hy. Keane Bloomfield, John Hubert Plunkett, and Chas. Cowper, admrs. during absence of Denison, Sept. 17 to Oct. 27.

1859. Col. John Maxwell Perceval, sir Wm. W. Burton, and C. Cowper, admrs. during absence of Denison, June 16 to July 8.

1861. Lt.-col. John Kempt, admr. until arrival of Young, Jan. 23 to Mar. 21.

Sir John Young, bt., K.C.B., G.C.M.G., aft. ld. Lisgar, Mar. 6, **G.**

1867. Sir Trevor Chute, K.C.B., admr. until arrival of Belmore, Dec. 25 to Jan. 7, 1868.

Somerset Richd. Lowry, E. of Belmore, Aug. 22, **G.**

1872. Sir Alfred Stephen, C.B., ch. just.; Actg. Govr. until arrival of Robinson, Feb. 23 to June 2.

Sir Hercules Geo. Robt. Robinson, K.C.M.G., Mar. 4, **G.**

1875. Sir Alfred Stephen, K.C.M.G., C.B., L.G., Nov. 29, **G.**

1879. Sir Augs. Wm. Fredk. Spencer Loftus, G.C.B., c.c. ld. Augs. Loftus, May 3, **G.**

1885. Sir Alfred Stephen, L. G., actg. as Govr. until arrival of Carrington on Dec. 11.

Chas. Robt., ld. Carrington, Apr. 11, **G.**

DIOCESE OF AUSTRALIA.

The bishopric of Australia was first constituted in 1836, and comprised all such parts of the Australian continent as were then colonised. By Letters Patent, June 28, 1847, **G.**, the bishopric was divided into the four dioceses of Sydney, Newcastle, Adelaide, and Melbourne, all in the ecclesiastical province of Sydney.

Bishop of Australia.

1836. Wm. Grant Broughton, June 15, **G.** Became bp. of Sydney, N.S.W., June 28, 1847; *vide supra et infra.*

DIOCESE OF SYDNEY, N.S.W.

This diocese was formed out of that of Australia by Letters Patent, June 28, 1847, **G.** See "Diocese of Australia," *supra.* It is in the ecclesiastical province of Sydney.

Bishops of Sydney, N.S.W.

1847. Wm. Grant Broughton, form. bp. of Australia, June 28, **G.**

1854. Fredk. Barker, Oct. 17, G.

1884. Alfred Barry, consec. Jan. 1.

DIOCESE OF NEWCASTLE, N.S.W.

This diocese was formed out of that of Australia by Letters Patent, June 28, 1847, **G.** See "Diocese of Australia," *supra.* It is in the ecclesiastical province of Sydney.

Bishops of Newcastle, N.S.W.

1847. Wm. Tyrrell, June 28, **G.**

1880. Josiah Brown Pearson.

DIOCESE OF GOULBURN, N.S.W.

This bishopric was formed out of that of Sydney by Letters Patent, March 25, 1863, **G.** It is in the ecclesiastical province of Sydney.

Bishops of Goulburn, N.S.W.

1863. Mesac Thomas, Mar. 25, **G.**

DIOCESE OF BATHURST, N.S.W

This bishopric was constituted in 1869. It is in the ecclesiastical province of Sydney.

Bishops of Bathurst, N.S.W.

1869. Saml. Edwd. Marsden, res. 1885.

1887. Chas. Edwd. Camidge, consec. Oct. 18.

DIOCESE OF GRAFTON AND ARMIDALE.

This bishopric was constituted in 1867. It is in the ecclesiastical province of Sydney.

Bishops of Grafton and Armidale.

1867. W. C. Sawyer.

1869. Jas. Fras. Turner, consec. Feb. 24.

DIOCESE OF RIVERINA.

This bishopric was constituted in 1884. It is in the ecclesiastical province of Sydney.

Bishop of Riverina.

1884. Sydney Linton, consec. May 1.

VICTORIA.

Victoria was, under the name of Port Philip, originally a part of New South Wales. It was separated and constituted a separate colony in 1851, under 13 & 14 Vict. cap. 59.

GOVERNORS OF VICTORIA.

See also "Governors of New South Wales," *ante*, pp. 702–3.

1839. Chas. Jos. La Trobe, supt. of Port Philip, Sept. 30; L.G. Victoria, Jan. 27, 1851, **G.**

1854. John Vesey Fitzgerald Foster, Actg. Govr., May, till arrival of Hotham on June 22.

1853. Capt. Sir Chas. Hotham, K.C.B., L. G., Dec. 6, **G.**; Govr. Feb. 1, 1855, **G.**

1856. M.-gen. Edwd. Macarthur, Actg. Govr., Jan. 1, until arrival of Barkly, Dec. 26.

Sir Hy. Barkly, K.C.B., Nov. 24, **G.**

1863. Sir Chas. Hy. Darling, K.C.B., June 26, **G.**

1866. Brig.-gen. Geo. Jackson Carey, C.B., Actg. Govr., May 7, until arrival of Manners-Sutton, Aug. 15.

1866. Hon. John Hy. Thos. Manners-Sutton, aft. visc. Canterbury, May 19, **G.**
1873. Sir Wm. Foster Stawell, Actg. Govr., Mar. 3, until arrival of Bowen.
1873. Sir Geo. Ferguson Bowen, G.C.M.G., May 31, **G.**
1875. Sir Redmond Barry, Actg. Govr. during absence of Bowen, Jan. 3 to Jan. 10.
1875. Sir W. F. Stawell, *again*, Actg. Govr. during absence of Barry, Jan. 11 to Jan. 14, 1876.
1879. Geo. Augs. Constantine, M. of Normanby, G.C.M.G., Feb. 24, **G.**
1884. Sir F. Stawell, *again*, Actg. Govr., Apr. 18, until arrival of Loch, July 15.
Sir Hy. Brougham Loch, K.C.B., Apr. 18, **G.**

DIOCESE OF MELBOURNE.

This bishopric was formed out of that of Australia, and was constituted by Letters Patent, June 28, 1847, **G.** See "Diocese of Australia," *ante*, p. 703. It is in the ecclesiastical province of Sydney.

Bishops of Melbourne.

1847. Chas. Perry, June 28, **G.**; res. 1876.
1876. Jas. Moorhouse, tr. to Manchester.
1887. Field Flowers Goe, consec. Feb. 24.

DIOCESE OF BALLARAT.

This bishopric was constituted in 1875. It is in the ecclesiastical province of Sydney.

Bishop of Ballarat.

1875. Saml. Thornton, consec. May 1.

NORTH AUSTRALIA.

In 1846 a governor and lieutenant-governor of "North Australia" were appointed, but these titles were not continued; the territory over which their jurisdiction extended would seem to be the northern portion of what are now South Australia and Queensland.

Governors of North Australia.

1846. Sir Chas. Augs. Fitzroy, Govr. Feb. 24, **G.**
1846. Lt.-col. Geo. Barney, L.G Feb. 24, **G.**

QUEENSLAND.

Queensland was, under the name of Moreton Bay, originally a part of New South Wales. It was separated and constituted a separate colony under Letters Patent, June 3, 1859, **G.**

Governors of Queensland.

See also "Governors of New South Wales," *ante*, pp. 702–3.

1859. Sir Geo. Ferguson Bowen, K.C.M.G., June 3, **G.**
1868. Col. Maurice Chas. O'Connell, aft. sir M., admr., Jan. 4, until arrival of Blackall.
1868. Saml. Wensley Blackall, May 4, **G.**
1871. Col. sir M. C. O'Connell, *again*, admr., Jan 2, until arrival of Normanby.

1871. Geo. Augs. Constantine, M. of Normanby, Apr. 8, **G.**

1874. Col. sir M. C. O'Connell, *again*, admr., Nov. 12, until arrival of Cairns.

Wm. Wellington Cairns, C.M.G., aft. sir W., Nov. 14, **G.**

1877. Col. sir M. C. O'Connell, *again*, admr., Mar. 14, until arrival of Kennedy.

Sir Arthur Edwd. Kennedy, K.C.M.G., C.B., Jan. 6, **G.**

1880. Joshua Peter Bell, admr., Mar 19, during absence of Kennedy.

1883. Sir Arthur Hunter Palmer, K.C.M.G., admr., May 2, until arrival of Musgrave.

Sir Anthy. Musgrave, K.C.M.G., July 21, **G.**; *d.* 1888.

1886. Sir A. H. Palmer, *again*, admr. during absence of Musgrave.

1888. Sir Hy. Arth. Blake, K.C.M.G., nom. but declined the appt.

1889. Sir Hy. Wylie Norman, G.C.B., G.C.M.G., C.I.E., Jan. 2, **G.**

DIOCESE OF BRISBANE.

This bishopric was constituted by Letters Patent, June 3, 1859, **G.** It is in the ecclesiastical province of Sydney.

Bishops of Brisbane.

1859. Edwd. Wyndham Tufnell, June 3, **G.**; res. 1875.

1875. Matthew Blagden Hale, tr. from Perth, W. A.; res. 1885.

1885. Wm. Thos. Thornhill Webber, consec June 5.

DIOCESE OF NORTH QUEENSLAND.

This bishopric was constituted in 1878. It is in the ecclesiastical province of Sydney.

Bishop of North Queensland.

1878. Geo. Hy. Stanton, consec. June 24

SOUTH AUSTRALIA.

This colony was constituted under 4 & 5 Wm. IV. cap. 95 (1834-5), and Letters Patent, May 4, 1835, **G.**, and Feb. 2, 1836, **G.** Additions to or alterations in the constitution of this colony have been made by 13 & 14 Vict. cap. 59 (1850), 24 & 25 Vict. cap. 44 (1861), 25 & 26 Vict. cap. 11 (1862), and 28 & 29 Vict. cap. 63 (1865).

Governors of South Australia.

See also "Governors of New South Wales," *ante*, pp. 702–3.

1836. Capt. John Hindmarsh, R.N., Feb. 2, **G.**

Geo. Milner Stephen, Actg. Govr. *ad int.*

1838. Lt.-col. Geo. Gawler, Apr. 28, **G.**

1840. Geo. Grey, aft. sir G., Dec. 15, **G.**

1845. Maj. Fredk. Holt Robe, L.G., July 15, **G.**

1847. Sir Hy. Edwd. Fox Young, L.G., June 11, **G.**

Boyle Travers Finniss, Actg. Govr. *ad int.*

1851. Sir Hy. Edwd. Fox Young, now Govr., Jan. 27, **G.**

1854. Richd. Graves MacDonnell, C.B., aft. sir R., Nov. 6, **G.**

1861. Sir Dominick Daly, Oct. 28, **G.**; *d.* Feb. 1868. On his death lt.-col. Hamley administered the govt. until arrival of Fergusson, Feb. 16, 1869.

1869. Sir Jas. Fergusson, bt., Jan. 1, **G.**

1872. Sir R. D. Hanson, ch. just., admr., Dec. 7, until arrival of Musgrave.

1873. Anthy. Musgrave, C.M.G., aft. sir A., Mar. 6, G.

1877. S. J. Way, ch. just., admr., Jan. 29, until arrival of Cairns, Mar. 24.

Wm. Wellington Cairns, C.M.G., aft. sir W., Jan. 8, **G.**

1877. S. J. Way, *again*, admr., May 18, until arrival of Jervois, Oct. 2.
Col. sir Wm. Drummond Fras. Jervois, R.E., K.C.M.G., C.B., July 5, **G.**
1878. S. J. Way, *again*, admr. during absence of Jervois, Feb. 14 to Aug. 14; and *again* during absence of Robinson in 1883.
1882. Wm. Cleaver Fras. Robinson, K.C.M.G., Dec. 2, **G.**
1889. Algernon Hawkins Thomond, E. of Kintore, Jan. 3, **G.**

DIOCESE OF ADELAIDE.

This bishopric was formed out of that of Australia, and was constituted by Letters Patent, June 28, 1847, **G.** See "Diocese of Australia," *ante*, p. 703. It is in the ecclesiastical province of Sydney.

Bishops of Adelaide.

1847. Augs. Short, June 28, **G.**
1882. Geo. Wyndham Kennion, consec. Nov. 30.

WESTERN AUSTRALIA.

This Colony was originally known as the Swan River Settlement, which was first founded in 1826. The colony was founded June 1, 1829, and its constitution was modified in 1850 by 13 & 14 Vict. cap. 59.

Governors of Western Australia.

See also "Governors of New South Wales," *ante*, pp. 702–3.

1829. Capt. Jas. Stirling, R.N., aft. sir J., L.G. June 1.
1832. Capt. Irving, Actg. L. G., Sept.
1833. Capt. Daniel, Actg. L.G., Sept.
1834. Capt. Beete, Actg. L.G., May 11 to May 24.
Capt. Jas. Stirling, R.N., aft. sir J., Govr. Feb. 15, **G.**
1838. John Hutt, Apr. 28, **G.**
1845. Lt.-col. Andr. Clarke, Aug. 12, **G.** (acted from Feb. 1840).
1847. Lt.-col. Irwin, Actg. Govr., Feb., till arrival of Fitzgerald, Aug. 1848.
Chas. Fitzgerald, commander, R.N., Oct. 1, **G.**
1854. Arthur Edwd. Kennedy, Nov. 6, **G.**
1862. Lt.-col. John Bruce, Actg. Govr., Feb. 17, until arrival of Hampton, Feb. 27.
1861. John Stephen Hampton, Oct. 28, **G.**
1868. Sir Benj. Chilley Campbell Pine, Sept. 10, **G.**; did not act, being transferred to Leeward Islands.
1868. Lt.-col. John Bruce, *again*, Actg. Govr., Nov., until arrival of Weld, Sept. 30, 1869.
1869. Fredk. Aloysius Weld, aft. sir F., Apr. 7, **G.**
1874. Wm. Cleaver Fras. Robinson, C.M.G., aft. sir W., Nov. 14, **G.**
1877. Lt.-col. E. D. Harvest, admr., Aug. 28, till arrival of Ord in Nov.
M.-gen sir Harry St. Geo. Ord, K.C.M.G., C B., Dec. 4, **G.**
1880. Sir Wm. Cleaver Fras. Robinson, K.C.M.G., *again*, Feb. 3, **G.**
1883. Hy. Thos. Wrenfordsley, admr., Feb. 14, until arrival of Broome, June 2.
1882. Fredk. Napier Broome, C.M.G., aft. sir F., Dec. 29, **G.**
1884. Alexr. Campbell Onslow, admr. during absence of Broome, from Nov. 11 to June 15, 1885.

DIOCESE OF PERTH, W.A.

This bishopric was constituted by Letters Patent, January 11, 1856, **G.** It is in the ecclesiastical province of Sydney.

Bishops of Perth, W.A.

1856. Matthew Blagden Hale, Jan 11, **G.**; tr. to Brisbane.
1876. Hy. Hutton Parry, form. coadj. bp. of Barbadoes.

TASMANIA, FORMERLY VAN DIEMEN'S LAND.

VAN DIEMEN'S LAND was discovered by Tasman in 1642. It was taken possession of by the British in 1803, separated from New South Wales and constituted a penal settlement by 4 Geo. IV. cap. 84 (1824) and Order in Council dated June 23, and gazetted August 17, 1824. The name was changed from Van Diemen's Land to TASMANIA in 1853.

GOVERNORS OF VAN DIEMEN'S LAND.

See also "Governors of New South Wales," *ante*, pp. 702–3.

1804. Col. David Collins, Feb. 19.
1810. Lieut. Edwd. Lord, Capt. Murray, } Mar. 24.
1812. Lt.-col. Geils, Feb.
Lt.-col. Thos. Davey, Feb. 21, **G.**; arr. Feb. 4, 1813.
1817. Col. Wm. Sorell, Apr. 9.
1824. Col. Geo. Arthur, May 14.
1825. M.-gen. Ralph Darling, Govr. N. S. Wales, Dec. 3; actg. during absence of Arthur, who returned Dec. 6.
1836. Lt.-col. K. Snodgrass, actg. from Oct. 31, till arrival of Franklin, Jan. 5, 1837.
1836. Capt. sir John Franklin, Apr. 19, **G.**
1843. Sir John Eardley Eardley-Wilmot, bt., Mar. 27, **G.**
1846. Chas. Jos. Latrobe, Oct. 13; actg. until arrival of Denison, Jan. 26, 1847.
1846. Capt. Wm. Thos. Denison, R.E., aft. sir W., June 27, **G.**

GOVERNORS OF TASMANIA.

1854. Sir Hy. Edwd. Fox Young, Sept. 19, **G.**
1862. Col. Thos. Gore Browne, C.B., Mar. 5, **G.**
1868. Lt.-col. W. C. Trevor, C.B., Dec. 30; admnr. until arrival of Du Cane, Jan. 15, 1869.
1869. Chas. Du Cane, aft sir C., Jan. 1, **G.**
1874. Sir Valentine Fleming, admr., Mar. 26 to Nov. 30.
Sir Fras. Smith, admr., Nov. 30 till arrival of Weld, Jan. 13, 1875.
1874. Fredk. Aloysius Weld, aft. sir F., Sept. 7, **G.**
1880. Sir Fras. Smith, admr., Apr. 6 till Oct. 21.
1880. Lt.-gen. sir John Hy. Lefroy, K.C.M.G., C.B., Aug. 23, **G.**; admr. from Oct. 21 till arrival of Strahan, Dec. 7, 1881.
1880. Maj. sir Geo. Cumine Strahan, K.C.M.G., June 30, **G.**
1886. Sir Robt. Geo. Crookshank Hamilton, K.C.B., Dec. 14.

DIOCESE OF TASMANIA.

This diocese was constituted by Letters Patent, Sept. 29, 1842, **G.** It is in the ecclesiastical province of Sydney.

BISHOPS OF TASMANIA.

1842. Fras. Russell Nixon, Sept. 29, **G.**
1864. Chas. Hy. Bromby, June 27, **G.**; res. 1882.
1883. Daniel Fox Sandford, consec. Apr. 25; res. 1889.
1889. H. H. Montgomery; bp. design., Mar.

NEW ZEALAND.

THE SOVEREIGNTY of the islands which form New Zealand was vested in the Crown by treaty of Waitangi, Feb. 5, 1840, and proclamation thereunder dated May 21, and gazetted Oct. 2, 1840. It was constituted a separate colony by Letters Patent, Nov. 20, 1840, **G.** See also 9 & 10 Vict. cap. 103 (1846), and charter thereunder dated Dec. 23, and gazetted Dec. 29, 1846; 11 & 12 Vict. cap. 5 (1848); 15 & 16 Vict. cap. 72 (1852); 20 & 21 Vict. cap. 53 (1857); 25 & 26 Vict. cap. 48 (1862); and 31 & 32 Vict. cap. 92 (1868).

Governors of New Zealand.

1840. Capt. John (? Wm.) Hobson, R.N., Nov. 20, **G.**
1842. W. Shortland, Actg. Govr.
1843. Capt. Robt. Fitzroy, R.N., Apr. 3, **G.**
1845. Geo. Grey, aft. sir G., July 15, **G.**

New Zealand was divided into—
New Ulster, | New Munster,
under 9 & 10 Vict. c. 103 (1846), and L. P. Dec. 23, gaz. Dec. 29, 1846.

1846. Geo. Grey, aft. sir G., Govr. New Zealand, Dec. 28, **G.**
Edwd. John Eyre, L.G. New Ulster and New Munster, Dec. 28, **G.**
1851. Lt.-col. Robt. Hy. Wynyard, L.G New Ulster, Nov. 25, **G.**; Actg. Govr. New Zealand, 1854, until arrival of Browne.

By 15 & 16 Vict. cap. 72 (1852) the division into New Ulster and New Munster was discontinued, and the colony was divided into six provinces, each under a superintendent. This system was again abolished in 1875 under a Colonial Act.

1854. Col. Thos. Gore Browne, C.B., Nov. 6, **G.**
1861. Sir Geo. Grey, K.C.B., admr. June 3, **G.**; Govr. Aug. 7, **G.**
1867. Sir Geo. Ferguson Bowen, G.C.M.G., Nov. 16, **G.**
1873. Sir Jas. Fergusson, bt., Mar. 3, **G.**
1874. Geo. Augs. Constantine, M. of Normanby, K.C.M.G., Nov. 14, **G.**
1879. Sir Hercules Geo. Robt. Robinson, G.C.M.G., Feb. 24, **G.**
1880. Hon. sir Arthur Hamilton Gordon, G.C.M.G., Aug. 11, **G.**
1882. Lt.-gen. sir Wm. Fras. Drummond Jervois, R.E., G.C.M.G., C.B., Dec. 2, **G.**
1888. Wm. Hillier, E. of Onslow, K.C.M.G., Nov. 27, **G.**

DIOCESE OF NEW ZEALAND, NOW AUCKLAND.

This bishopric was first constituted in 1841, and its jurisdiction then extended over the entire colony. The diocese of Christchurch, N.Z., was formed out of it by Letters Patent Aug. 1, 1856, **G.**, and the rest of the district was reconstituted by Letters Patent, Oct. 5, 1858, **G.**, and formed into the four dioceses of New Zealand, Wellington, Waiapu, and Nelson. The name of the diocese of New Zealand was afterwards changed to Auckland. It is in the ecclesiastical province of New Zealand.

Bishops of New Zealand, now Auckland.

1848. Geo. Augs. Selwyn; diocese divided Sept. 27, 1858, *vide supra*; tr. to Lichfield, 1868.
1869. Wm. Garden Cowie.

DIOCESE OF CHRISTCHURCH, N.Z.

This diocese was formed out of that of New Zealand, and was constituted by Letters Patent dated Aug. 1, 1856, **G.** See "Diocese of New Zealand," *supra*. On the reconstitution of the diocese of New Zealand in Sept. 1858, Christchurch was removed from the province of Australia (now Sydney) to that of New Zealand.

Bishop of Christchurch, N.Z.

1856. Hy. Jno. Chitty Harper, Aug. 1, **G.**

DIOCESE OF WELLINGTON.

This bishopric was formed out of that of New Zealand, and wa constituted by Letters Patent Sept. 27, 1858, **G.** See "Diocese o New Zealand," *ante*, p. 709. It is in the ecclesiastical province of New Zealand.

BISHOPS OF WELLINGTON.

1858. Chas. John Abraham, Sept. 27, **G.**; res. 1870.
1870. Octavius Hadfield.

DIOCESE OF WAIAPU.

This bishopric was formed out of that of New Zealand, and wa constituted by Letters Patent, Sept. 27, 1858, **G.** See "Diocese of New Zealand," *ante*, p. 709. It is in the ecclesiastical province of New Zealand.

BISHOPS OF WAIAPU.

1858. Wm. Williams, Sept. 27, **G.**
1877. Edwd. Craig Stuart, consec. Dec.

DIOCESE OF NELSON.

This bishopric was formed out of that of New Zealand, and wa constituted by Letters Patent, Sept. 27, 1858, **G.** See "Diocese o New Zealand," *ante*, p. 709.

BISHOPS OF NELSON.

1858. Edwd. Hobhouse, Sept. 27, **G.**; res. 1865.
1866. Andrew Burn Suter, consec. Au 24.

DIOCESE OF DUNEDIN.

This bishopric was constituted in 1866.

BISHOPS OF DUNEDIN.

1866. Hy. Lascelles Jenner, res. 1871.
1871. Saml. Tarratt Nevill, consec. June

AUCKLAND ISLANDS.

THESE ISLANDS are a dependency of New Zealand. The only separa governor was

1849. Charles Enderby, L.G., June 16, **G.**

The islands were granted by the British Government to Messr Enderby as a whaling station, but were abandoned by them in 1852.

For bishops, see "Bishops of Christchurch, N.Z.," *ante*, p. 709.

FIJI.

THE FIJI ISLANDS were ceded to Great Britain by deed dated Oct. 10, 1874, and created into a colony by Letters Patent dated Feb. 4, and gazetted Feb. 5, 1875. The island of Rotumah and its dependencies were annexed by Letters Patent dated Dec. 17, and gazetted Dec. 31, 1880.

GOVERNORS OF FIJI.

1875. Hon. sir Arth. Hamilton Gordon, Feb. 4, **G.**
1880. Geo. Wm. Des Voeux, C.M.G., aft. sir G., Oct. 5, **G.**
John Bates Thurston, C.M.G., aft. sir J., admr. during absence of Govr., Oct. 17, 1882; *again*, Nov. 10, 1883, to July 23, 1884; *again*, 1885-6, L.G., 1886.
1886. Lt.-col. sir Chas. Bullen Hugh Mitchell, K.C.M.G., Aug. 3
1887. Sir John Bates Thurston, K.C.M.G., now Govr.; Dec. 9.

DIOCESE OF MELANESIA.

This bishopric was constituted in 1861. Its jurisdiction extends over the Islands of the Melanesian Archipelago. It is in the ecclesiastical province of New Zealand.

BISHOPS OF MELANESIA.

1861. J. C. Patteson.
1877. John Richardson Selwyn, consec. Feb. 18.

WESTERN PACIFIC HIGH COMMISSION.

CREATED under 35 & 36 Vict. cap. 19 (1872), and 38 & 39 Vict. cap. 51 (1875), and Orders in Council of 1877, 1879, and 1880 (not gazetted).

HIGH COMMISSIONERS.

1877. Hon. Sir Arthur Hamilton Gordon, K.C.M.G., Sept. 27, **G.**
188–. Geo. Wm. Des Vœux, C.M.G., aft. sir G., assist. commr., 1880; actg. high commr., 1882.
1886. Sir Chas. Bullen Hugh Mitchell, K.C.M.G., Aug. 3.
1887. Sir John Bates Thurston, K C.M.G., Dec. 9.

BRITISH NEW GUINEA.

THIS TERRITORY was constituted by Letters Patent. Oct. 27, 1888, **G.**, as "a separate possession and government," by the name of BRITISH NEW GUINEA.

ADMINISTRATOR OF BRITISH NEW GUINEA.

1888. Wm. Macgregor, C.M.G., June 9, (Oct. 27, **G.**).

DIOCESE OF HONOLULU.

This bishopric was constituted in 1861. It is classed as a missionar bishopric holding mission from the see of Canterbury. Its jurisdic tion is over the Sandwich Islands.

Bishops of Honolulu.

1861. Thos. Nettleship Staley.
1872. Alfred Willis, consec. Feb. 2.

VI.—COLONIES, &c. WEST INDIES.

JAMAICA.

Jamaica is the largest and most important of the British West India possessions. It was discovered by Columbus in 1494, and take possession of by Spain; captured by the English in 1655, and formall ceded to England by Spain in 1670 by the Treaty of Madrid.

The Turks and Caicos Islands were annexed to Jamaica by 36 37 Vict. cap. 6 (1873), and Order in Council dated Aug. 4, 1873. The had previously been made subordinate thereto by Letters Patent, No 21, 1848, **G.** Morant Cays and Pedro Cays were annexed by Lette Patent dated Mar. 13, and gazetted Mar. 14, 1882.

The island now forms the entire diocese of Jamaica.

GOVERNORS OF JAMAICA.

1656. G. D'Oyley.
1661. Thos., ld. Windsor.
1662. Sir Chas. Lyttleton.
1664. Col. sir Thos. Lynch, pres.
1666. Sir Thos. Modyford.
1671. Sir Thos. Lynch, *again*, L.G.
1675. Sir Hy. Morgan, L.G.
John, ld. Vaughan.
1678. Sir Hy. Morgan, *again*, L.G.
Chas., E. of Carlisle.
1680. Sir Hy. Morgan, *again*, L.G.
1682. Sir Thos. Lynch, *again*.
1684. Col. Hender Molesworth, L.G.
Sir P. Howard.
1687. Christr., D. of Albemarle.
1688. Sir Fras. Watson, pres.
1690. Wm., E. of Inchiquin.
1692. John White, pres.
John Bourdon, pres.
1693. Sir Wm. Beeston, L.G.
1701. M.-gen. Wm. Selwyn.
Peter Beckford, L.G.
1702. Chas., E. of Peterborough; did not come over, and in his absence,
M.-gen. Thos. Handasyde acted as govr.
1711. Ld. Archd. Hamilton.
1714. Peter Heywood.
1716. Thos. Pitt.
1718. Sir Nichs. Lawes.
1722. Hy., D. of Portland; *d.* 1726, office.
1726. John Ayscough, pres.
1727. M.-gen. Robt. Hunter.
1734. John Ayscough, *again*, pres.
1735 John Gregory, pres.
Hy. Cunningham.
1736. Edwd. Trelawney.
1752. V.-adm. Chas. Knowles, aft. bt.
1756. Hy. Moore, L.G.
1758. Brig.-gen. Geo. Haldane.
1759. Hy. Moore, *again*, L.G.
1762. Wm. Hy. Lyttelton, aft. ld. Westcot
1766. Roger Hope Elletson, L.G.
1767. Sir Wm. Trelawney, bt., capt. R.N. *d.* Dec. 1772.
1773. Sir Basil Keith, capt. R.N., Mar. 2 *d.* Aug. 1777.
1777. Lt.-gen. John Dalling, Sept. 1.
1782. M.-gen. Archd. Campbell.
1790. Thos., E. of Effingham.
1794. Alexr., E. of Balcarres, Oct. 20.

1801. M.-gen. Geo. Nugent, L.G., May 16, **G.**
1806. Lt.-gen. sir Eyre Coote.
1807. Wm., D. of Manchester, sw. Jan. 6, 1808.
1808. Wm. Anne Villettes, L.G., Jan. 8, **G.**
1809. Lt.-gen. Edwd. Morrison, L.G., June 10, **G.**
1828. Somerset, E. of Belmore, Aug. 9, **G.**
1832. Hy., E. of Mulgrave, Mar. 16, **G.**
1833. Howe Peter, M. of Sligo, Dec. 8, **G.**
1836. M.-gen. sir Lionel Smith, Oct. 15, **G.**
1839. Sir Chas. Theoph. Metcalf, bt., G.C.B., July 11, **G.**
1842. Jas., E. of Elgin and Kincardine, Mar. 16, **G.**
1846. Sir Chas. Edw. Grey, Sept. 25, **G.**
1853. Sir Hy. Barkly, K.C.B., Aug. 9, **G.**
1855. M.-gen. Edwd. Wells Bell, L.G., Mar. 30, **G.**
1857. Chas. Hy. Darling, aft. sir C., Feb. 9, **G.**
1860. M.-gen. Pringle Taylor, K.H., L.G., Mar. 29, **G.**
1864. Edwd. John Eyre, July 15, **G.**
1865. M.-gen. sir Hy. Knight Storks, G.C.B., G.C.M.G., temp. govr. during inquiries, Dec. 12, **G.**; govr. Dec. 21, **G.**
1866. Sir John Peter Grant, K.C.B., July 16, **G.**
1870. Edwd. Everard Rushworth, admr. until return of Grant in 1870, and L.G. in 1872, until return of Grant in 1873.
1873. Wm. Alexr. Geo. Young, admr. until arrival of Grey.
1874. Sir Wm. Grey, K.C.S.I., Mar. 14, **G.**
Edwd. Everard Rushworth, L.G., Apr. 17, **G.**
1877. Sir Anthy. Musgrave, K.C.M.G., June 8, **G.**
1878. Edwd. Newton, C.M.G., L.G., Feb. 23, **G.**; Actg. Govr. from Aug. 7, 1879, until return of Musgrave, June 3, 1880.
1883. M.-gen. Gamble, C.B.; admr. from May 4, until arrival of Norman.
Gen. sir Hy. Wylie Norman, K.C.B., C.I.E., Oct. 27, **G.**
1889. Sir Hy. Arth. Blake, K.C.M.G., Jan. 3, **G.**

DIOCESE OF JAMAICA.

This bishopric was formed in 1824, and is in the ecclesiastical province of the West Indies. The Bahamas and the Turks and Caicos Islands were added to it by Letters Patent, Nov. 21, 1843, **G.**, but were separated from it by Letters Patent, Nov. 6, 1861, **G.**, and formed into the diocese of Nassau, *q.v. post*, p. 716.

Bishops of Jamaica.

1824. Christr. Lipscomb, July 9, **G.**
1843. Aubrey Geo. Spencer, Nov. 20, **G.**
1856. Regd. Courtenay, coadj. bp. of Kingston, Feb. 13, **G.**
1872. Regd. Courtenay, bp. of Jamaica; res. 1879.
1879. Wm. Geo. Tozer, bp. of Jamaica; form. bp. of Centr. Afr.; res. 1880.
1880. Enos Nuttall, consec. Oct. 28.
1888. — Douet, assist. bp.; consec. Nov. 30.

TURKS AND CAICOS ISLANDS.

These islands are situated to the north of Jamaica. They were originally a part of the Bermudas, but were transferred to the Bahamas in 1799. They were separated from the Bahamas and placed under the supervision of the governor of Jamaica by Letters Patent Nov. 21, 1848, **G.** Finally they were annexed to Jamaica by 36 & 37 Vict. cap. 6 (1873), and Order in Council, Aug. 4, 1873. They are locally under the government of a commissioner.

COMMISSIONERS FOR THE TURKS AND CAICOS ISLANDS.

1874. D. T. Smith.
1879. Robt. Baxter Llewelyn, Jan. 10, **G.**
1885. Capt. Hy. Moore Jackson, Oct. 24.

For bishops prior to 1861, see "Bishops of Jamaica," *supra*.
For bishops after 1861, see "Bishops of Nassau," *post*, p. 716.

BRITISH HONDURAS OR BELIZE.

THIS COLONY is situate on the east coast of Central America, in the Caribbean Sea. It was discovered by Columbus in 1502, and the Spaniards claimed sovereignty over it, but did not colonise it. The early government was of a very primitive kind, the settlers practically managing their own affairs. In 1786, superintendents were appointed by the British government, and, with an interval from 1790 to 1797, were continued until 1862, when a lieutenant-governor was appointed subordinate to Jamaica. By Letters Patent proclaimed Oct. 31, 1884, a governor was appointed, and the colony was thenceforward independent of Jamaica.

British Honduras is at present temporarily attached to the bishopric of Jamaica, but is to be shortly formed into a separate diocese, with its own bishop.

GOVERNORS, &c. OF BRITISH HONDURAS.

SUPERINTENDENTS.

Taken from the Colonial List.

1786. Col. Edwd. Marcus Despard
1790. Col. Peter Hunter.
1790–97. Magistrates elected annually.
1797. Col. Thos. Barrow.
1800. Gen. sir Richd. Basset.
1805. Lt.-col. Gabriel Gordon.
1806. Lt.-col. Alexr. Mark Kerr Hamilton.
1809. Lt.-col. John Nugent Smyth.
1814. Maj. Geo. Arthur.
1822. M.-gen. Allan Hampden Pye.
1823. M.-gen. Edwd. Codd.
1829. Maj. Alexr. McDonald (actg.).
1830. Lt.-col. Fras. Cockburn.
1837. Lt.-col. Alexr. McDonald.
1843. Col. Chas. St. John Fancourt, K.H.
1851. Philip Edmd. Wodehouse.
1854. Wm. Stevenson.
1857. Fredk. Seymour.

LIEUTENANT GOVERNORS.

1862. Fredk. Seymour, above named, July 19, **G.**
1864. John Gardiner Austin, Feb. 1, **G.**
1867. Jas. Robt. Longden, Dec. 5, **G.**
1870. Wm. Wellington Cairns, aft. sir W., July 6, **G.**
1871. Lt.-col. Harley, C.B., admr. until return of Cairns in 1872.
1874. Capt. Mitchell, R.N., admr. until arrival of Mundy.
Maj. Robt. Miller Mundy, Mar. 4, **G.**
1876. Capt. Mitchell, R.N., admr. until arrival of Barlee.
1877. Fredk. Palgrave Barlee, May 10, **G.**
1883. Col. Robt. Wm. Harley, C.B., C.M.G., aft. sir R., Apr. 18, G.
Hy. Fowler, admr. until arrival of Goldsworthy.
1884. Roger Tuckfield Goldsworthy, C.M.G., aft. sir R., May 31, **G.**; app. govr., *ut infra*.

GOVERNORS.

1884. Roger Tuckfield Goldsworthy, C.M.G., aft. sir G., above-named, Oct. 7, **G.**

For bishops, see Introduction, *supra*, and "Diocese of Jamaica," *ante*, p. 713.

BRITISH GUIANA.
BERBICE, DEMERARA, ESSEQUIBO.

THESE SETTLEMENTS were first established by the Dutch West India Company in 1580. Afterwards, as the result of various wars, they were from time to time taken by Great Britain, France, and Holland.

Ultimately they were taken by Great Britain in 1803, and finally ceded to that country in 1814.

PRIOR to 1831, DEMERARA and ESSEQUIBO formed one colony, and BERBICE another. In that year they were all united under the title of BRITISH GUIANA.

THIS COLONY constitutes the diocese of Guiana.

LIEUTENANT-GOVERNORS OF DEMERARA AND ESSEQUIBO.

1806. Hy. Bentinck, Feb. 1, **G.**; app. Govr. Dec. 13, 1808, **G.**; sw. Jan. 4, 1809.

1824. M.-Gen. sir Benjn. D'Urban, K.C.B., Jan. 5, **G.**

For subsequent Governors, see "Governors of British Guiana," *infra.*

LIEUTENANT-GOVERNORS OF BERBICE.

1808. Wm. Woodley, Oct. 8, **G.**

1810. Robt. Gordon, May 2, **G.**

1821. Hy. Beard, Jan. 22, **G.**; sw. Jan. 30, 1826.

For subsequent Governors, see "Governors of British Guiana," *infra.*

GOVERNORS OF BRITISH GUIANA.

1831. M.-gen. sir Benjn. D'Urban, K.C.B., Feb. 15, **G.**

1833. M.-gen. sir Jas. Carmichael Smyth, bt., L.G., June 8, **G.**; *again* app. L.G. Feb. 26, 1835, **G.**

1835. M.-gen. sir Lionel Smith, Govr. B. Guiana, Trinidad, and St. Lucia, Feb. 26, **G.**

M.-gen sir Jas. Carmichael Smyth, L.G., June; app. Govr., Oct. 18, 1836, **G.**

1838. Hy. Light, May 1, **G.**

1848. W. Walker, May 20; Actg. Govr. until arrival of Barkly.

Col. sir Wm. Macbean Geo. Colebrooke; app. Apr. 28, **G.**, but did not proceed.

Hy. Barkly, aft. sir H., Dec. 12, **G.**

1854. Philip Edmd. Wodehouse, aft. sir P., Feb. 10, **G.**

1857. W. Walker, July 25, Actg. Govr. until return of Wodehouse, May 10, 1858; *again*, May 9, 1861, until arrival of Hincks.

1861. Fras. Hincks, aft. sir F., Dec. 5, **G.**

1866. Maj. Robt. Miller Mundy, L.G., May 29; until app. of Watson.

1866. Hy. Watson, Oct. 11; admr. until return of Hincks, Aug. 12, 1867.

1868. John Scott, aft. sir J., Dec. 31, **G.** to Dec. 26, 1873.

1873. Edwd. Everard Rushworth, D.C.L., C.M.G., June 27; admr. until arrival of Longden.

1874. Jas. Robt. Longden, C.M.G., aft. sir J., Mar. 14, **G.**

1877. Wm. Alexr. Geo. Young, C.M.G., Mar. 8; admr. until arrival of Kortright.

Cornelius Hendericksen Kortright, C.M.G., aft. sir C., July 14, **G.**

1879. Wm. Alexr. Geo. Young, C.M.G., L.G.; actg. from Apr. 6, 1879, until return of Kortright, Dec. 4, 1879; *again*, from Dec. 13, 1881, until arrival of Irving.

1882. Sir Hy. Turner Irving, K.C.M.G., Mar. 7, **G.**

1884. Wm. Fredk. Haynes Smith, LL.D., actg. from Apr. 26, until return of Irving, Sept. 2, 1884.

1885. Chas. Bruce, C.M.G., L.G, Nov. 2, **G.**; actg. during absence of Irving.

1887. Jenico Wm. Jos., visc. Gormanston, K.C.M.G., Dec. 14, **G.**

BISHOPRIC OF GUIANA.

This diocese was constituted by Letters Patent, Sept. 29, 1842, **G.** It is in the ecclesiastical province of the West Indies.

BISHOP OF GUIANA.

1842. Wm. Piercy Austin, Sept. 29, **G.**

BAHAMA ISLANDS.

THESE ISLANDS lie between Cuba and the coast of Florida on the North American continent. St. Salvador, one of the group, was discovered by Columbus in 1492. Being abandoned by the Spaniards the islands were occupied by the English in 1629, and in 1670 New Providence was granted by Chas. II. to a trading company. From 1703 to 1718 the islands were in the hands of the French and the Spaniards. In 1718 the British resumed possession of them, but surrendered them to the Spaniards in 1781. They were finally restored to Great Britain in 1783 by the Treaty of Versailles.

THE TURKS AND CAICOS ISLANDS, which belong to the group, were separated from it by Letters Patent, Nov. 21, 1848, **G.**, and placed under Jamaica. See "Jamaica," *ante*, p. 712.

The Bahama Islands were formerly a part of the diocese of Jamaica, but with the Turks and Caicos Islands were separated from it in 1861, and formed into the diocese of Nassau.

GOVERNORS OF THE BAHAMA ISLANDS.

The earlier names are taken from the Colonial List.

1671. Wentworth Johnson.
1673. — Chillingworth.
1677. — Clark.
1684. — Lilburne.
1687. — Bridges.
1690. Cadwallader Jones.
1694. — Trott.
Nichs. Webb.
1700. Elias Haskett.
Ellis Lightfoot.
1704. — Birch.
1717. Woodes Rogers.
1721. Geo. Phinny, or Finny.
1728. Woodes Rogers, *again*.
1733. Richd. Fitzwilliam.
1738. John. Tinker.
1759. Wm. Shirley.
1767. Thos. Shirley, aft. sir T.
1774. Mountford Browne.
1779. John Maxwell.
1787. John, 4th E. of Dunmore.
1796. John Forbes, L.G.
1797. Wm. Dowdeswell.
1801. John Halkett, Dec. 2, **G.**
1803. Chas. Cameron, Dec. 22, **G.**; sw. May 3, 1804.
1820. M.-gen Lewis Grant, Jan. 1, **G.**
1829. Sir Jas. Carmichael Smyth, bt., May 8, **G.**
1833. Blayney Townley Balfour, L.G., Mar. 6, **G.**
1834. Lt.-col. Wm. Macbean Geo. Colebrook, L.G., Sept. 9, **G.**
1837. Col. Fras. Cockburn, L.G., Mar. 28, **G.**
1838. Sir Lionel Smith.
1840. Col. Fras. Cockburn, as Govr., Apr. 18, **G.**
1844. Geo. Benvenuto Mathew, Mar. 26, **G.**
1848. John Gregory, Dec. 16, **G.**
1854. Sir Alex. Bannerman, May 8, **G.**
1857. Chas. John Bayley, Feb. 23, **G.**
1864. Rawson Wm. Rawson, C.B., aft. sir R., Nov. 15, **G.**
1869. Sir Jas. Walker, K.C.M.G., C.B., Apr. 15, **G.**
1873 John Pope Hennessy, C.M.G., aft. sir J., Mar. 13, **G.**
1874. Wm. Robinson, C.M.G., aft. sir W., L.G., Oct.; Govr. 1875.
1880. Geo. Wm. Des Vœux, C.M.G., aft. sir G., Aug. 3, **G.**
1880. Thos. Fitzgerald Callaghan, C.M.G., Sept. 11, **G.**
1881. Chas. Cameron Lees, C.M.G., aft. sir C., Oct. 5, **G.**
1884. Hy. Arthur Blake, aft. sir H., Jan. 15, **G.**
1887. Sir Ambrose Shea, K.C.M.G., July 11, **G.**

BISHOPRIC OF NASSAU.

The Bahama Islands were by Letters Patent, Nov. 21, 1843, **G.**, made part of the diocese of Jamaica. By Letters Patent, Nov. 6,

1861, **G.**, the Bahama Islands and its dependencies and the Turks and Caicos Islands were separated from Jamaica, and constituted into the see of Nassau. The diocese is in the ecclesiastical province of the West Indies.

Bishops of Nassau.

1861. Chas. Caulfeild, Nov. 6, **G.**
1863. Addington Robt Peel Venables, Nov. 28 **G.**
1878. Fras. Alexr. Cramer Roberts.
1886. Edwd. Townson Churton.

THE WINDWARD ISLANDS.
MARTINIQUE (now restored to France); BARBADOS, TRINIDAD, AND TOBAGO, (now separate Colonies); AND GRENADA, ST. VINCENT, and ST. LUCIA.

The Windward Islands are the most southern of the West Indian group, and are situated in the Caribbean Sea. Geographically they comprise all the islands above-named, besides some smaller dependencies; but the colonies now grouped together for the purpose of government under the name of the Windward Islands comprise Grenada, St. Vincent, and St. Lucia only.

Martinique was discovered by Columbus in 1493, and colonised by the French in 1635. It was taken by Great Britain in 1762, but restored to France by the Treaty of Paris in 1763. It was again taken by Great Britain in 1794, again restored to France at the Peace of Amiens in 1802–3; again taken by Great Britain in February 1809, and finally restored to France in 1815.

Barbados is believed to have been discovered by the Portuguese. It was colonised by the English in 1625, and has ever since continued one of the British possessions.

Trinidad is the most southerly of the West Indian Islands. It was discovered by Columbus in 1498, colonised by Spain in 1532, captured by Great Britain in 1797, and ceded to that country by the Treaty of Amiens in 1802–3.

Tobago was discovered by Columbus in 1498, but, as with many other of the Spanish discoveries, no attempt was made to colonise the island. It was claimed by the English in 1580, and some attempts made to colonise it, but these failed; and after various disputes concerning it between the English, French, and Dutch, the island was declared neutral by the treaty of Aix-la-Chapelle (1748). In 1763 it was ceded to England by the treaty of Paris, but on the renewal of hostilities it was captured by France in 1781, surrendered to France in 1783, captured by Great Britain in 1793, restored to France in 1802, recaptured by Great Britain in 1803, and ultimately ceded to that country in 1814.

GRENADA was discovered by Columbus in 1498, colonised by French settlers about 1650, annexed to France in 1674, captured by the British in 1762, and ceded to them by the treaty of Paris in 1763. It was re-taken by the French in 1779, but finally restored to Great Britain at the treaty of Versailles in 1783.

THE GRENADINES are a number of small islands lying between Grenada and St. Vincent. They are included in the government of one or other of those colonies.

ST. VINCENT was discovered by Columbus in 1498. It was granted by the kings of England, (by what authority it is rather hard to say), to James, Earl of Carlisle, in 1627; to William, Lord Willoughby of Parham, in 1672; and to John, Duke of Montagu, in 1722; the intervals being filled up by declarations of "neutrality" between England and France. In 1762 the island was taken possession of by the British, and was ceded to them by the treaty of Paris in 1763. It was surrendered to France in 1779 (Sept. 28, **G.**), and ultimately restored to Great Britain in 1783 by the treaty of Versailles.

ST. LUCIA was discovered by Columbus in 1502. Its possession was disputed between England and France with varying success from 1635 to 1763, when it was secured to France by the treaty of Paris. It was conquered by Great Britain in 1782, restored to France by the treaty of Versailles in 1783, surrendered to Great Britain in 1794, restored to France by the treaty of Amiens in 1802–3, again captured, and ever since retained, by Great Britain in 1803 (July 30, **G.**).

THE WINDWARD ISLANDS have from time to time been grouped together in various combinations for the purposes of government, and, for some years, Dominica, which is classed as one of the Leeward Islands, was joined with them. Some care is, therefore, necessary in searching the following lists of governors. In 1763 a governor was appointed for the "SOUTHERN CARIBBEE ISLANDS" of GRENADA, DOMINICA, ST. VINCENT, and TOBAGO. In 1833 (Feb. 13, **G.**), BARBADOS, ST. VINCENT, GRENADA, and TOBAGO were united under one governor resident at Barbados, with lieutenant-governors for the other islands, and ST. LUCIA was added to this federation in 1838. By Letters Patent (May 4, 1885, **G.**) the office of "Governor and Commander in Chief of the WINDWARD ISLANDS," *eo nomine*, was created, with jurisdiction over GRENADA, ST. VINCENT, TOBAGO, and ST. LUCIA. The governor was made resident at Grenada, and the other islands were placed under lieutenant-governors or administrators. BARBADOS thenceforth became a separate and independent colony. The government of Trinidad was generally distinct from that of the other islands, but, as will be seen below, was occasionally joined with them under one governor.

By 50 & 51 Vict. c. 44 (1877), and Order in Council dated Nov. 17, and gazetted Nov. 30, 1888, TOBAGO was separated from the WINDWARD ISLANDS, and as from Jan. 1, 1889, joined with TRINIDAD as one colony, to be called TRINIDAD AND TOBAGO.

The Windward Islands constitute the dioceses of BARBADOS and Trinidad.

GOVERNORS OF THE WINDWARD ISLANDS, or of two or more of them, arranged chronologically, with their appointments specified.

See Introduction, *ante*, pp. 717–8.

Governors of Barbados, Grenada, St. Vincent, and Tobago.

M.-gen. sir Lionel Smith, K.C.B.
1833. App. Govr. Barbados, St. Vincent, Grenada and Tobago, Feb. 13, **G.**
1835. App. Govr. B. Guiana, Trinidad and St. Lucia, Feb. 26, **G.**
1836. Sir Evan John Murray Macgregor, Oct. 17, **G.**

Governor of Barbados, St. Vincent, Tobago, Trinidad, and St. Lucia.

1841. Sir Chas. Edwd. Grey, Aug. 24, **G.**

Governors of Barbados, Grenada, St. Vincent, Tobago, and St. Lucia.

1846. Lt.-col. Wm. Reid, R.E., Sept 25, **G.**
1848. Col. sir Wm. Macbean Geo. Colebrooke, Aug. 11, **G.**
1856. Fras. Hincks, aft. sir F.
1861. Jas. Walker, aft. sir J., Dec, 5, **G.**
1869. Rawson Wm. Rawson, C.B., aft. sir R., Apr. 15, **G.**
1876. John Pope Hennessy, aft. sir J., Jan. 15, **G.**
1876. Capt. Geo. Cumine Strahan, R.A., C.M.G., aft. sir G., Dec. 2.
1882. Sir Wm. Robinson, K.C.M.G.

By Letters Patent dated March 17, 1885, (May 4, 1885, **G.**), Barbados became a separate government, and the colony of the Windward Islands was constituted, consisting only of Grenada, St. Vincent, Tobago, and St. Lucia.

Governors of the Windward Islands.

1885. Walter Jos. Sendall, May 4, **G.**

For bishops, see "Bishops of Barbados," *post*, p. 721.

BRITISH GOVERNORS OF MARTINIQUE.

See Introduction, *ante*, p. 717.

1809. M.-gen. Hon. John Brodrick, June 10, **G.**
1812. M.-gen. Chas. Wale, Feb. 21, **G.**

GOVERNORS OF BARBADOS.

See Introduction *ante*, p. 717.

The earlier names are taken from the Colonial List.

1625. Wm. Dean.
1628. Chas. Wolferston.
1629. Jno. Powell, Robt. Wheatley, Sir Wm. Tufton, } Joint Govrs.
1630. Hy. Hawley.
1633. Richd. Peers, Dep. Govr. until return of Hawley in 1634.
1634. Richd. Peers, *again*, Dep. Govr. until return of Hawley in 1636.
1638. Wm. Hawley, Dep. Govr. until return of H. Hawley in 1639.
1640. Sir Hy. Hunks.
1641. Philip Bell.
1650. Fras., ld. Willoughby of Parham.
1651. Sir Geo. Ayscue.
1652. Daniel Searle, Dep. Govr.
1660. Thos. Modifod.
1663. Fras., ld. Willoughby, *again*.
1666. Hy. Willoughby, Hy. Hawley, Saml. Berwick, } Joint Govrs.
1667. Wm., ld. Willoughby of Parham.
1668. Christr. Codrington, Dep. Govr. in absence of ld. Willoughby,
1669. Wm., ld. Willoughby, *returned*.
1670. Christr. Codrington, *again*, Dep. Govr. in absence of ld. Willoughby.
1672. Wm., ld. Willoughby, *returned*.
1673. Sir Peter Colleton, bt., Dep. Govr.
1674. Sir Jonathan Atkins.
1680. Sir. Richd. Dutton.
1683. Sir John. Witham, Dep. Govr.
1684. Sir Richd. Dutton.
1685. Edwin Stede, Dep. Govr.
1690. Jas. Kendal,
1694. Hon. Fras. Russell.
1696. Fras. Bond, pres.

1698. Hon. Ralph Grey. aft ld. Grey.
1701. John Farmer (? Turner), pres.
1703. Sir Bevil Granville.
1706. Wm. Sharpe, pres.
1707. Metford Crowe.
1710. Geo. Lillington, pres.
1711. Robt. Lowther.
1714. Wm. Sharpe, pres. in absence of Lowther.
1715. Robt. Lowther, *returned.*
1720. John Frere, pres.
1720–1. Saml. Cox, pres.
Richd. Visc. Irwin, app. but *d.* before setting out.
1721. John, ld. Belhaven; drowned on his passage out.
1722. Hy. Worsley.
1728. Edwd. Ashe.
1731. Saml. Barwick, pres.
1733. Jas. Dotin, pres.
Emanuel Scrope, Visc. Howe, *d.* 1735.
1735. Jas. Dotin, pres.
1739. Hon. Robt. Byng.
1740. Jas. Dotin, *again*, pres.
1742. Sir Thos. Robinson, bt.
1747. Hon. Hy. Grenville.
1753. Ralph Weeks, pres.
Chas. Pinfold.
1766. Saml. Rous, pres.
1767-8. Wm. (? Chas.) Spry.
1771. Saml. Rous, *again*, pres.
1772. Hon. Edwd. Hay.
1773. John Dotin, *again*, pres.
1780. Jas. Cunninghame.
1783. John Dotin, *again*, pres.
1784. David Parry.
1790. Hy. Frere, pres. during absence of Parry.
David Parry, *returned; d.* in office.
1793. Wm. Bishop, pres.
1794. Geo. Poyntz Ricketts.
1800. Wm. Bishop, *again*, pres.
1800. Fras. Humberstone, ld. Seaforth Nov. 26, sw.
1803. John Ince, pres. during absence of Seaforth.
1804. Ld. Seaforth, *returned.*
1806. John Spooner, pres.
1807. Hugh Elliot, Apr. 10, **G.**
1808. Lt.-Gen. Geo. Beckwith, aft, Sir G Oct. 8, **G.**
1814. John Spooner, pres.
1815. Lt.-Gen. Sir Jas. Leith, G.C.B., May 10, **G.**
1816. John Spooner, *again*, pres. during absence of Leith.
Sir Jas. Leith, *returned.*
1817. John Foster Alleyne, pres. until arr. of Combermere.
1816. Gen. Stapleton, ld., aft. visc. Combermere, G.C.B., Dec. 24, **G.**
1820. John Braithwaite Skeete, pres.
1821. Saml. Hinds, pres.
Lt.Gen.Sir Hy.Warde, K.C.B., Feb.8, **G.**
1825. J. B. Skeete, *again*, pres. during absence of Warde.
1826. Sir Hy. Warde, K.C.B., *returned.*
1827. J. B. Skeete, *again* pres.
1828. Lt.-Gen. Sir Jas. Lyon, K.C.B., Mar. 17, **G.**
1829. J. B. Skeete, *again*, pres. during absence of Lyon.
Sir Jas. Lyon, *returned.*
1830. J. B. Skeete, *again*, pres. during absence of Lyon.
Sir Jas. Lyon, *returned.*
1832. J. B. Skeete, *again*, pres. until arr. of Smith.

From 1833 to 1885, the Governors of Barbados were appointed Governors of other islands also. See Introduction, *ante*, p. 718. In the following list the Governors marked thus—

* were Governors of Barbados, St. Vincent, Grenada, and Tobago.
† ,, Barbados, St. Vincent, Tobago, Trinidad, and St. Lucia.
‡ ,, Barbados, Grenada, St. Vincent, Tobago, and St. Lucia.

The lieutenant-governors, administrators, and presidents were for Barbados only.

1833. *M. Gen. Sir Lionel Smith, K.C.B. Feb. 13, **G.**
1834. John Alleyne Beccles, pres. during absence of Smith.
*Sir L. Smith, *returned.*
1835. J. A. Beccles, *again*, pres. during absence of Smith.
*Sir L. Smith, *returned.*
1836. J. A. Beccles, *again*, pres. during absence of Smith.
*Sir L. Smith, *returned.*
*Sir Evan John Murray M'Gregor bt., K.C.B., Oct. 17, **G.**
1841. John Brathwaite Skeete, pres. until app. of Darling.
H. C. Darling, L.G.
1841. †Sir Chas Edwd. Grey, Aug, 24, **G.**
1846. ‡Lt.-Col. Wm. Reid, R.E., Sept. 25, **G.**
J. R. Best, pres. during absence of Reid.
1847. ‡Wm. Reid, C.B., *returned.*
1848. J. S. Gaskin, pres. during absence of Reid.
‡Wm. Reid, C.B., *returned.*
Col. Sir Wm. Macbean Geo. Colebrooke, C.B., Aug. 11, **G.**
1849. J. S. Gaskin, *again*, pres. during absence of Colebrooke.
‡Sir W. M. G. Colebrooke, *returned.*
1850. J. R. Best, pres. during absence of Colebrooke.
‡Sir W. M. G. Colebrooke, *returned.*

1851. K. B. Hamilton, admr. until appt. of Gaskin.
1852. J. S. Gaskin, *again*, pres. during absence of Colebrooke.
‡Sir W. M. G. Colebrooke, *returned.*
1856. ‡Fras. Hincks, aft. sir F.
Grant E. Thomas, pres. during absence of Hincks.
1858. Fras. Hincks, *returned.*
1859. Jas. Walker, aft. sir J., admr. during absence of Hincks.
1860. Sir Fras. Hincks, K.C.M.G., C.B., *returned.*
1861. ‡Jas. Walker, C.B., aft. sir J., now Govr., Dec. 5, **G.**
1865. Maj. Robt. Miller Mundy, aft. sir R., admr. during absence of Walker.
‡Sir Jas. Walker, K.C.M.G., C.B., *returned.*
1869. ‡Rawson Wm. Rawson, C.B., aft. sir R., Apr. 15, **G.**
1875. Sanford Freeling, C.M.G., aft. sir S., admr. until arr. of Hennessy.
1876. ‡John Pope Hennessy, C.M.G., aft. sir J., Jan. 15, **G.**
‡Capt. Geo. Cumine Strahan, R.A., C.M.G., aft. sir G., Dec. 2, **G.**
Geo. Dundas, C.M.G., L.G. during absence of Strahan.
‡Maj. G. C. Strahan, *returned.*
1878. Geo. Dundas, C.M.G., *again*, L.G. during absence of Strahan.
1879. ‡Maj. sir G. C. Strahan, K.C.M.G., *returned.*
1880. M.-gen. D. J. Gamble, C.B., admr. until appt. of Robinson.
Wm. Robinson, aft. sir W., L.G.
1881. Col. sir Robt. Wm. Harley, C.B., K.C.M.G., admr. until appt. of Robinson.
1882. ‡Wm. Robinson, aft. sir W., now Govr.
1884. M.-gen. Browne, admr. during absence of Robinson.

SEPARATE GOVERNMENT OF BARBADOS.

See Introduction, *ante*, p. 718.

1884. Sir Wm. Robinson, K.C.M.G., May 4, **G.**
1885. Sir Chas. Cameron Lees, K.C.M.G., Sept. 4.

DIOCESE OF BARBADOS.

This bishopric was originally created by Letters Patent dated July 24, 1824, and enlarged or altered by subsequent patents dated April 2, 1825, May 11, 1826, and Sept. 24, 1838. By Letters Patent (Sept. 29, 1842, **G.**), all previous patents were revoked, and a diocese constituted, comprising Barbados, St. Vincent, St. Lucia, Trinidad, Geneva, and Tobago. A separate diocese of Trinidad was constituted in 1872. Barbados is in the ecclesiastical province of the West Indies.

BISHOPS OF BARBADOS.

1824. W. H. Coleridge.
1842. Thos. Parry, Sept. 29, **G.**
1873. J. Mitchinson.
1882. Herbert Bree, consec. May **1.**

GOVERNORS OF TRINIDAD.

See Introduction, *ante*, pp. 717–8.

The earlier names are taken from, and the whole list corrected by, the Colonial List.

SPANISH GOVERNORS.

1735. Lt.-col. E. S. de Linany Vera, Oct. 11.
1745. F. de la Monteras, Dec. 4.
1746. Juan José Salcedo, June 19.
1752. F. Manclares.
1757. Pedro de la Moneda.
1760. Juan San Juan.
1762. J. A. Gil-Knight.
1765. J. de Bruno, June 19.
1766. Juan de Flores.
1773. J. de Dios Valdez.
1776. Manuel Falquez, Nov. 30.
1779. Maria de Salavaria, Aug.
1783. José Maria de Chaçon, Sept. 1.

British Governors.

1797. Sir Ralph Abercrombie, Feb. 18.
Brig.-gen. Thos. Picton, Apr. (May 26, 1801, **G.**)

1803. Col. Wm. Fullerton, Brig.-gen. Thos. Picton, Commodore Saml. Hood } commrs., Jan.
Brig.-gen. Thos. Hislop, July 20. (Jan. 21, 1806, **G.**)

1810. Lt.-col. Tolly (acting), Jan. 9.

1811. Col. Munro, Apr. 25.

1813. Sir Ralph J. Woodford, bt., June 14. (Sept. 21, 1812, **G.**)

1821. Lt.-col. A. W. Young, Apr. 12; acting until return of Woodford, Feb. 18, 1823.

1828. Maj. Capadose, Apr. 1; acting until arrival of Grant.
Sir Chas. F. Smith, R.E., Apr. 18; acting until arrival of Grant.
Col. Farquharson, July 26; acting until arrival of Grant.

1829. M.-gen. Lewis Grant, Mar. 10. (Aug. 9, 1828, **G.**)
Lt.-col. Doherty, acting during absence of Grant; Nov. 20 to Feb. 15, 1830, and May 15 to June 3, 1830.

1830. Lt.-col. Sir Chas. F. Smith, acting during absence of Grant; June 3 to Dec. 5, 1831.

1833. Sir Geo. Fitzgerald Hill, L.G., June 9.

1835. M.-gen. Sir Lionel Smith, app. Govr. B. Guiana, Trinidad and St. Lucia, and sir G. F. Hill, L. G. Trinidad, Feb. 26, **G.**

1839. Lt.-col. Mein, Mar. 8; acting until arrival of McGregor.
Col. sir E. M. McGregor, Govr., Mar. 24.
Lt.-col. Mein (Feb. 2, 1839, **G.**), acting until arrival of Macleod, Mar. 28.

1840. Col. sir Hy. Geo. Macleod, L.G., Apr. 13; app. Govr. May 31, 1842, **G.**
Note.—Sir Chas. Edwd. Grey was *Governor* from Aug. 24, 1841, **G.**, to Mar. 31, 1842, **G.** See "Barbados," *ante*. p. 720.
Maj. Barlow, acting during absence of Macleod, Nov. 11.
Maj. Tyler, acting during absence of Macleod, Dec. 14.

1841. Lt.-col. sir Chas. Chichester, acting during absence of Macleod, Sept. 25 to May 9, 1842.

1842. Maj. F. Fuller, acting during absence of Macleod, June 29 to Aug. 8.
Lt.-col. sir Chas. Chichester, acting during absence of Macleod, Aug. 8 to May 3, 1843.

1845. Lt.-col. E. C. Archer, acting during absence of Macleod, Feb. 8 to July 2.

1846. Lt.-col. Brown, Apr. 21; acting until arrival of Harris.
Geo. Fras. Robt., ld. Harris, L.G., Apr. 22. (May 5, 1846, **G.**) App. Govr. Nov. 3, 1846, **G.**

1851. Lt.-col. Ward, R.E., acting during absence of Harris, June 12 to Feb. 11, 1853.

1853. Maj. Halliday, acting during absence of Harris, Feb. 11 to Feb. 25.

1854. Maj. L. Bouchier, acting until arrival of Elliott, Jan. 26.
Capt. Chas. Elliott, aft. K.C.B., Mar. 10. (Jan. 11, **G.**)

1856. Lt.-col. B. Brooks, acting until arrival of Keate, Oct. 27.

1857. Robt. Wm. Keate, Jan. 26. (Nov. 6, 1856, **G.**)

1860. Jas. Walker, C.B., L.G., Apr. 7 (Mar. 13, **G.**)

1861. Maj. Holworthy, acting during absence of Keate, Mar. 25 to May.

1864. Maj. Thompson, admr. until arrival of Manners-Sutton, July 5.
Hon. John Hy. Thos. Manners-Sutton, aft. visc. Canterbury, Sept. 6 (June 24, **G.**)

1866. E. E. Rushworth, admr. until arrival of Gordon, Apr. 24.
Hon. Arthur Hamilton Gordon, C.M.G., Nov. 7. (June 30, **G.**)

1868. Maj. Bostock, admr. during absence of Gordon, Apr. 8 to Apr. 2[illegible]
Cornelius Hendericksen Kortright, aft. sir C., admr. during absence of Gordon, June 25 to Dec. 21.

1870. Jas. Robt. Longden, C.M.G., aft. si[illegible] J., June 25. (July 18, **G.**)

1872. W. H. Rennie, admr. during absence of Longden, July 11 to May 2[illegible] 1873.

1874. J. Scott Bushe, admr. until arriv[illegible] of Cairns, Apr. 27.
Wm. Wellington Cairns, C.M.G., af[illegible] sir W., May 2. (Mar. 14, **G.**)
J. Scott Bushe, admr. until arriv[illegible] of Irving, May 27.
Hy. Turner Irving, C.M.G., aft. s[illegible] H., Nov. 20. (Sept. 7, **G.**)

1876. J. Scott Bushe, C.M.G., adm[illegible] during absence of Irving, Dec. to Feb. 3, 1877.

1877. Geo. Wm. Des Vœux, C.M.G., aft. s[illegible] G., L.G., acting during absen[illegible] of Irving, Feb. 3 to Jan. 2, 187[illegible]

1880. W. R. Pyne, admr., acting unt[illegible] arrival of Freeling, July 27 [illegible] Aug. 27.

1880. Wm. Alexr. Geo. Young, C.M.G., admr. until arrival of Freeling, Aug. 27.
Sir Sanford Freeling, K.C.M.G., Nov. 2. (Oct. 4, **G.**)
1882. J. Scott Bushe, C.M.G., admr. during absence of Freeling, June 28 to Sept 1.
1884. J. Scott Bushe, C.M.G., admr., Mar. 28; until arrival of Havelock.
1884. Sir Fredk. Palgrave Barlee, K.C.M.G., L.G., June 19; until arrival of Havelock.
J. Scott Bushe, C.M.G., admr., Aug. 8; until arrival of Havelock.
1885. Sir Arthur Elibank Havelock. K.C.M.G., Jan. 24.
Sir Wm. Robinson, K.C.M.G., Oct. 9.
1886. J. Scott Bushe, admr. during absence of Robinson. May 29 to July 16.

Trinidad and Tobago were united into one colony as from Jan. 1, 1889.
See Introduction, *ante*, p. 718.

For bishops prior to 1872, see "Bishops of Barbados," *ante*, p. 721.

DIOCESE OF TRINIDAD.

This bishopric was constituted in 1872. It is in the ecclesiastical province of the West Indies.

Bishops of Trinidad.

1872. Richd. Rawle, consec. June 29.
1888. Jas. Thos. Hayes.

GOVERNORS OF TOBAGO.

See Introduction *ante*, p. 717.

The earlier names are taken from the Colonial List.

1764. — Browne, L.G.
1768. Brig.-gen. Robt. Melville, Govr. of Grenada, Dominica, St. Vincent, and Tobago.
1770. — Stewart.
1771. Brig.-gen. Wm. Leybourne Leybourne, Govr. of Grenada, Dominica, St. Vincent and Tobago.
Maj. Young, L.G.
— Ferguson, L.G.
From 1781 to 1783 the Island was in the possession of the French.
1784. — Dillon.
1794. — Ricketts.
1795. — Lindsay.
1796. — Delaney.
1800. — Masters.
1802. Sahuhie } French Governors.
1803. Buthtir } French Governors.
1803. — Picton, L.G.
— McDonald, L.G.
— Johnstone, L.G.
John Halkett, Oct. 27.
1806. — Balfourn.
1807. Sir Wm. Young.
1810. — Campbell, pres.
1816. Gen. sir Fredk. Phillip Robinson, K.C.B., Feb. 13, **G.**
1819. — Cumine, pres.
1820. — Robley, pres.
1823. — Nichol, pres.
1826. — Brasnell, pres.
1827. — Piggott, pres.
1828. Gen. sir Colin Campbell, K.C.B., Feb. 27, **G.**
M.-gen. Nathl. Blackwell, Apr. 17, **G.**

For Governors from 1833 to 1885, see "Governors of Barbados," *ante*, pp. 720–1.
For Governors since 1885, see "Governors of Windward Islands," *ante*, p. 719.

Lieutenant-Governors and Administrators of Tobago.

1833. M.-gen. Hy. Chas. Darling, L.G., Mar. 13, **G.**
1845. Maj. Laurence Græme, Aug. 18, **G.**
1851. David Robt. Ross, L.G., Feb. 14, **G.**
1851. Fredk. Daly, L.G., Sept. 16, **G.**
1854. Willoughby Shortland, L.G., Jan. 10, **G.**
1857. Jas. Vickery Drysdale, L.G., Apr. 1, **G.**

1864. Cornelius Hendericksen Kortright, aft. sir C., L.G., Oct. 14, **G.**

1872. Herbert Taylor Ussher, C.M.G., L.G., Sept. 12, **G.**

1875. Col. Robt. Wm. Harley, C.B., C.M.G., aft. sir R., L.G., Aug. 9, **G.**

1877. Augs. Fredk. Gore, L.G., Sept. 29, G

1881. Edwd. Laborde, admr., Oct. 6, **G.**

1883. John Worrell Carrington, admr.

1885. Loraine Geddes Hay, admr.
Robt. Baxter Llewelyn, admr.

1886. Loraine Geddes Hay, *again*, admr.

Trinidad and Tobago were united into one colony as from Jan. 1, 1889. See Intro duction, *ante*, p. 718.

For bishops, see "Bishops of Barbados," *ante*, p. 721.

GOVERNORS OF GRENADA.

See Introduction, *ante*, p. 717.

The earlier names are taken from the Colonial List.

1764. Brig.-gen. Robt. Melville, Govr. of Grenada, Dominica, St. Vincent, and Tobago.

1768. Ulysses Fitzmaurice, L.G.

1771. Brig.gen. Wm. Leybourne Leybourne, Govr. of Grenada, Dominica, St. Vincent, and Tobago.

1775. Wm. Young, L.G.

1776. Sir Geo. Macartney, K.B., aft. ld. M.

1784. Lt.-gen. Edwd. Matthew.

1789. Saml. Williams, Pres.

1793. Ninian Home, L.G.

1796. Alexr. Houstoun, L.G.

1797. Col. Chas. Green, aft. sir C.

1802. Hon. Geo. Vere Hobart, L.G.

1803. Thos. Hislop, L.G., Feb. 5, **G.**
M.-gen. Wm. Douglas McLean Clephane, L.G.

1804. M.-gen. John Stuart, L.G., Jan. 25, **G.**; knt., Aug. 18.

1805. Brig.-Gen. Fredk. Maitland, Ma 29, **G.**

1808. A. C. Adye, pres. during absence c Maitland.

1810. M.-gen. F. Maitland, *returned.*
A. C. Adye, *again* pres. until app of Ainslie.

1812. Col. R. Ainslie. Vice-Govr.

1813. M.-gen. sir Chas. Shipley, Feb. 27 **G.**

1815. M.-gen. sir Geo. Townshend Walker K.C.B., *vice* Stuart decd., Apr. 7 **G.**

1816. M.-gen. Phineas Riall, Feb. 17, **G.**

1817. Andr. Houstoun, pres. during ab sence of Riall.

1821. M.-gen. P. Riall, *returned.*
Geo. Paterson, Pres.

1825. M.-gen. sir Jas. Campbell, K.C.B May 23, **G.**

1831. Felix Palmer, pres.

For Governors from 1833 to 1885, see "Governors of Barbados," *ante*, pp. 720-1.
For Governors since 1885, see "Governors of Windward Islands," *ante*, p. 719.

LIEUTENANT-GOVERNORS AND ADMINISTRATORS OF GRENADA.

1833. M.-gen. Geo. Middlemore, L.G., Feb. 13, **G.**

1835. Lt.-col. John Hastings Mair, L.G., Mar. 26, **G.**

1836. Lt.-col. Chas. Jos. Doyle, L.G., June 26, **G.**

1846. Ker Baillie Hamilton, L.G., Jan. 13, **G.**

1853. Robt. Wm. Keate, L.G., Oct. 11, **G.**

1856. Cornelius Hendericksen Kortright, aft. sir C., L.G., Nov. 15, **G.**

1863. Maj. Robt. Miller Mundy, aft. sir R., L.G., Sept. 18. **G.**

1871. Edwd. Laborde, admr. until arr. of Freeling,

1871. Sanford Freeling, aft. sir S., L.G., Apr. 11, **G.**
Edwd. Laborde, *again* admr. until arr. of Graham.

1876. Cyril Clerke Graham, L.G., Jan. 1 **G.**

1877. Col. Robt. Wm. Harley, C.B., C.M.G aft. sir R., L.G., Sept. 28, **G.**

1878. Thos. Kerr, admr. during absenc of Harley.

1879. Col. R. W. Harley, *returned.*

1881. Capt. Irwin Chas. Maling, adm during absence of Harley.
Col. R. W. Harley, *returned*; trans to Br. Honduras, 1883.

1882. Capt. I. C. Maling, *again*, admr.,
Roger Tuckfield Goldsworthy, C.M.G., aft. sir G., admr.,

1883. Edwd. Laborde, admr.

} during ab sence an after re- tirement of Harle

Since the constitution of the colony of the Windward Islands the seat of governme has been at Grenada, the other islands being under local administrators.

For bishops, see "Bishops of Barbados," *ante*, p. 721.

GOVERNORS OF ST. VINCENT.

See Introduction, *ante*, p. 718.

The earlier names are taken from the Colonial List.

1765. Brig.-gen. Robt. Melville, Govr. of Grenada, Dominica, St. Vincent, and Tobago.
1775. Brig.-gen. Wm. Leybourne Leybourne, Govr. of Grenada, Dominica, St. Vincent, and Tobago.
1776. Valentine Morris.
1783. Jas. Seton.
1798. Wm. Bentinck.
1802. Hy. Wm. Bentinck, Feb. 24, **G.**
1805. M.-gen. Geo. Beckwith, aft. sir G., Jan. 2, sw.
1808. Capt. sir Chas. Brisbane, Oct. 8, **G.**; Nov. 16, sw.
1830. Sir Geo. Fitzgerald Hill, bt.

For Governors from 1833 to 1885, see "Governors of Barbados," *ante*, pp. 720–1.
For Governors since 1885, see "Governors of Windward Islands," *ante*, p. 719.

LIEUTENANT-GOVERNORS AND ADMINISTRATORS OF ST. VINCENT.

1833. Capt. Geo. Tyler, R.N., aft. sir G., L.G., Feb 13, **G.**
1840. Lt.-col. Richd. Doherty, aft. sir R., L.G., Nov. 20, **G.**
1845. Sir John Campbell, bt., L.G., June 9, **G.**
1852. Richd. Graves MacDonnell, C.B., L.G., Feb. 23, **G.**
1854. Edwd. John Eyre, Nov. 6, **G.**
1859. Wm. Chas. Sargeaunt, aft. sir W., admr., Mar. 31, **G.**
1861. Anthy. Musgrave, aft. sir A., admr., May 20; L.G., May 13, 1862, **G.**
1864. Geo. Berkeley, L.G., July 29, **G.**
1871. Wm. Hepburn Rennie, L.G., Apr. 11, **G.**
1872. Edwd. Laborde, admr., July 2.
1874. Augs. Fredk. Gore, admr., May 2.
Geo. Dundas, C.M.G., L.G., Oct. 31, **G.**
1878. Edwd. Laborde, *again*, admr. during absence of Dundas, May 28.
1879. Augs. Fredk. Gore, *ditto*.
Geo. Dundas, *returned* Mar. 27.
1880. Augs. Fredk. Gore, *again*, admr.. May 4, **G.**; L.G., Aug. 5, **G.**
1888. Robt. Baxter Llewelyn, admr.

For bishops, see "Bishops of Barbados," *ante*, p. 721.

GOVERNORS OF ST. LUCIA.

See Introduction, *ante*, p. 718.

* * * *

1801. Brig.-gen. Geo. Prevost, L.G., May 16, **G.**

* * * *

1816. M.-gen. Richd. Augs. Seymour, June 28, **G.**
1818. M.-gen. sir John Keane, K.C.B., Jan. 19, **G.**
1825. M.-gen. John Montagu Mainwaring, Oct. 7, **G.**
1830. M.-gen. Geo. Mackie, July 19, **G.**
1831. M.-gen. Jas Alexr. Farquharson, Nov. 23, **G.**
1834. Col. sir Dudley St. Leger Hill, L.G., Apr. 15, **G.**; and Feb. 26, 1835, **G.**
1835. M.-gen. sir Lionel Smith, Govr. Br. Guiana, Trinidad, and St. Lucia, Feb. 26, **G.**

For Governors from 1838 to 1885, see "Governors of Barbados," *ante*, pp. 720–1.
For Governors since 1885, see "Governors of Windward Islands," *ante*, p. 719.

LIEUTENANT-GOVERNORS AND ADMINISTRATORS OF ST. LUCIA.

1838. Col. sir Dudley St. Ledger Hill, above named, *contd.* as L.G.
1847. Chas. Hy. Darling, L.G., Dec. 21, **G.**
1852. Maurice Power, L.G., Feb. 23, **G.**
1858. H. Hegart Breen, L.G.
1865. J. M. Grant, admr.
1869. Geo. Wm. Des Vœux, aft. sir G., admr.
1877. Capt. Macnamara Dix.
1881. Roger Tuckfield Goldsworthy, C.M.G., aft. sir R., admr., Jan. 10, **G.**
1884. Clement Courtenay Knollys, admr., May.
1885. Edwd. Laborde, C.M.G., admr., Sept. 19, **G.**

For bishops, see "Bishops of Barbados," *ante*, p. 721.

THE LEEWARD ISLANDS.

ANTIGUA, MONTSERRAT, ST. CHRISTOPHER OR ST. KITTS, NEVIS, DOMINICA, VIRGIN ISLANDS, AND THEIR DEPENDENCIES.

The Leeward Islands lie to the north of the Windward Islands. They were discovered by Columbus during the last ten years of the fifteenth century. Besides those mentioned above, which belong to Great Britain, there are others belonging to France, Holland, and Denmark.

The British Leeward Islands were formed into one colony in 1871 as stated below.

Antigua was discovered by Columbus in 1493; colonised by the English in 1632; granted by Chas. II. to Fras., Lord Willoughby of Parham, in 1663; conquered by France in 1666, but reconquered by the English, and confirmed to them by the Treaty of Breda in 1667.

Barbuda and Redonda are dependencies of Antigua.

Montserrat was discovered by Columbus in 1493; colonised by the English in 1632· taken by the French in 1664;· restored to England in 1668, again captured by the French in 1782, and finally restored to Great Britain in 1784.

St. Christopher or St. Kitts and Nevis were discovered by Columbus in 1498, and colonised by the English in 1628.

Anguilla is a dependency of these islands.

Dominica was discovered by Columbus in 1493. It was included in the grant made by Jas. II. to Jas., Earl of Carlisle in 1627; but as the island lay between the French possessions of Guadaloupe and Martinique, the earl's right to it was disputed by France. By the Treaty of Aix-la-Chapelle (1748) the island was declared "neutral," but on the renewal of hostilities it was captured by the British in 1756, and ceded to them by the Treaty of Paris in 1763. It was retaken by the French in 1778, restored to Great Britain in 1783. once more captured by France in 1802, and finally restored to Great Britain in 1814. It was at one time joined, for administrative purposes, with some of the Windward Islands. See "Windward Islands," *ante*, pp. 717–8.

The Virgin Islands are a numerous group. St. Thomas, St. John, and St. Croix belong to Denmark, the rest being British. The principal British islands are Virgin Gorda, Anegada, Jost Van Dyke, Tortola, Bieques, and Peters Island.

These islands were discovered by Columbus in 1494, and the English settled in Tortola in 1666. St. Thomas and St. John were taken from Denmark in 1801, and again in 1807, but restored in 1802 and 1815.

The Leeward Islands were from time to time grouped together in various combinations under one governor, with lieutenant-governors for each separate island.

In 1871, under 34 & 35 Vict. cap. 107, and proclamation thereunder, ntigua, Montserrat, St. Christopher, Nevis, Dominica, and the, 'irgin Islands were formed into six presidencies of one colony called he Leeward Islands, with power to include other West Indian slands in the colony. St. Christopher and Nevis were afterwards nited into one presidency by Colonial Act No. 2 of 1882.

The Leeward Islands constitute the greater part of the diocese f Antigua.

GOVERNORS OF THE LEEWARD ISLANDS,

r of two or more of them, arranged chronologically, and with their appointments specified.

See Introduction, *ante*, p. 726.

Governors of the Leeward Islands.

Taken from the Colonial List.

668. Wm., ld. Willoughby of Parham.
672. Philip Warner.
675. Rowland Williams.
682. Sir Wm. Stapleton.
Nathl. Johnson.
689. Christr. Codrington.
704. Sir Wm. Matthew.
706. Col. Parke.
710. Gen. Hamilton.
711. Walter Douglas.
715. Gen. Hamilton, *again*.
721. John Hart.
728. Ld. Londonderry (Thos. Pitt).
1730. Wm. Matthew.
1752. Sir Geo. Thomas.
1766. James Verchild.
1771. Sir Ralph Payne, aft. ld. Lavington.
1776. Wm. H. Burt.
1781. Sir Thos. Shirley.
1790. The same, *again*.
1795. M.-gen. Leigh.
1801. Ralph, ld. Lavington, *again*.
1808. Hugh Elliot, Oct. 8, **G.**, and Apr. 12, 1809, **G.**
1814. Lt.-gen. sir Jas. Leith, K.C.B., Feb. 15, **G.**

Governors of Antigua and Montserrat.

816. M.-gen. Geo. Wm. Ramsay, Feb. 13, **G.**
1820. M.-gen. sir Benjn. D'Urban, K.C.B., Jan. 22, **G.**; Apr. 8, sw.

Governors of St. Christopher, Nevis, and Virgin Islands.

816. Thos. Probyn, Feb. 13, **G.**
319. Chas. Maxwell, May 21, **G.**
1831. M.-gen. Wm. Nicolay, Jan. 13, **G.**

Governors of Antigua, Montserrat, Barbuda, St. Christopher, Nevis, Anguilla, Virgin Islands and Dominica.

832. Sir Evan John Murray-Macgregor, Dec. 19, **G.**
837. Lt.-col. Wm. Macbean Geo. Colebrook, Jan. 11, **G.**; knt., Mar. 31.
341. Sir Chas. Augs. FitzRoy, Aug. 3, **G.**
346. Jas. Macaulay Higginson, June 26, **G.**
1850. Robt. Jas. Mackintosh, Oct. 1, **G.**
1855. Ker Baillie Hamilton, Mar. 26, **G.**
1860. The same, *again*.
1863. Col. Stephen John Hill, aft. sir S., Feb. 9, **G.**
1867. The same, *again*.
1869. Sir Benjn. Chilley Campbell Pine Apr. 15, **G.**

Governors of the Leeward Islands

n the "Leeward Islands Act, 1871," 34 & 35 Vict. cap. 107, coming into operation; *vide supra*.

371. Sir Benj, Chilley Campbell Pine, now K.C.M.G., Dec. 8.
1873. Hy. Turner Irving, C.M.G., aft. sir H., June 11, **G.**

1874. Geo. Berkeley, C.M.G., aft. sir G. Nov. 14, **G**.
1881. Sir John Hawley Glover, R.N., G.C.M.G., Dec 7, **G**.
1882. Neale Porter, admr.
1884. Sir Chas. Cameron Lees, K.C.M.G., Jan. 2, **G**.
1885. Chas. Monroe Eldridge, admr.
1885. Jenico Wm. Jos., visc. Gormanston Sept. 4.
1887. Sir Chas. Bullen Hugh Mitchell, K.C.M.G., Dec. 14.
1887. Wm. Fredk. Haynes Smith, C.M.G., temporary admr. until arrival of Mitchell, Dec. 14; app. Govr., Nov. 8, 1888.

For bishops, see "Bishops of Antigua," *infra*.

GOVERNORS OF ANTIGUA.

See Introduction, *ante*, p. 726.

For Governors from 1668 to 1824, and from 1832 to present time see "Governors of Leeward Islands," *ante*, p. 727.

Governors of Antigua only, from 1824 to 1832.

1824. Lt.-gen sir Hudson Lowe, K.C.B., Jan. 6, **G**.; did not proceed.
1825. M.-gen. sir Patr. Ross, May 23, **G**.

Lieutenant-Governors, &c., of Antigua.

The earlier names are taken from the Colonial List.

1668. Saml. Winthrope, Dep. G.
1698. Col. John Yeamans, L.G.
1710. The same, *again*, L.G.
1768. Wm. Woodley, L.G.
1788. John Nugent, L.G.
1791. The same, *again*, L.G.
1792. Wm. Woodley, *again*, L.G.
1793. John Stanley, L.G.
1799. Wm. Woodley, *again*, L.G.
1836. Lt.-col. Hy. Senior, L.G., Jan. 14, **G**.
Hy. Light, L.G., Apr. 13, **G**.
1840. Maj. John Macphail, L.G.
1845. C. J. Cunningham, L.G.
1859. Sir Hercules Geo. Robt. Robinson, L.G.
B. E. Jarvis, pres.
Edwd. John Eyre, L.G., Mar. 31.
1860. Sir Wm. Byam, pres.
1863. The same, *again*, pres.

After the passing of the "Leeward Islands Act, 1871," see Introduction, *ante*, p. 727, Antigua was under the direct control of the Governor of the Leeward Islands, the other islands being placed under commissioners or presidents subordinate to him.

Commissioners or Presidents of Antigua during absence of Governor.

1883. Neale Porter, June, to Jan. 1884, and July to Sept. 1884.
1887. Chas. Monroe Eldridge.

DIOCESE OF ANTIGUA.

This bishopric was constituted by Letters Patent (Sept. 29, 1842, **G**.). It comprises the British Islands of Antigua, Barbuda, Montserrat, Dominica, St. Christopher, Nevis, Anguilla, and the Virgin Islands, and also the foreign islands of St. Croix, St. Thomas, Porto Rico, and St. Bartholomew. It is in the ecclesiastical province of the West Indies.

Bishops of Antigua.

1842. Daniel Gateward Davis, Sept. 29, **G**.
1858. Stephen Jordan Rigaud, Jan. 14, **G**.
1860. Wm. Walrond Jackson, May 14, **G**.
1882. Chas. Jas. Branch, coadj.

GOVERNORS OF MONTSERRAT.

See Introduction, *ante*, p. 728.

For Governors, *vide* "Governors of Leeward Islands," &c., *ante*, p. 727.

Commissioners or Presidents of Montserrat.

1854. Hercules Geo. Robt. Robinson, aft. sir H., Feb. 14, **G.**
1868. W. Rowland Pym, actg.
1872. S. S. Odlum.
1872. Neale Porter, June.
1882. Jas. Meade, actg.
1887. John Spencer Churchill.

For bishops, see "Bishops of Antigua," *ante*, p. 728.

GOVERNORS OF ST. CHRISTOPHER.

See Introduction, *ante*, p. 726.

For Governors, see "Governors of Leeward Islands," *ante*, p. 727.

Lieutenant-Governors, &c. of St. Christopher.

1833. Lt.-col. J. Lyons Nixon, L.G., St. Christopher, Nevis, Anguilla and Virgin Islands, Feb. 7, **G.**
1835. W. G. Cooke, pres.
1836. Lt.-col. Hy. Geo. Macleod, L.G., Oct. 8, **G.**
1839. Chas. Cunningham, L.G., Apr. 6, **G.**
1847. Robt. Jas. Mackintosh, L.G., Mar. 12, **G.**
1850. Edwd. Hay Drummond Hay, L.G., Oct. 1, **G.**
1854. Hercules Geo. Robt. Robinson, aft. Sir H.; L.G., Nov. 6, **G.**
1856. Thos. Price, admr.
1859. Sir Benjn. Chilley Campbell Pine, May.
1862. J. E. Tudor, pres. } During absence of Pine.
J. H. King, pres. }
1864. J. H. Holligan, pres. }
1866. J. R. Holligan, pres. until app. of Rumbold.
1867. Sir Arth. Carlos Hy. Rumbold, bt., admr. until arr. of Mackenzie.
1866. Capt. Jas. Geo. Mackenzie, R.N., Sept. 22, **G.**
1869. Wm. Wellington Cairns, aft. Sir W., Jan. 14, **G.**
1870. Fras. Spencer Wigley, C.M.G., admr.

After the passing of the "Leeward Islands Act, 1871," see *ante*, p. 727, commissioners or presidents of St. Christopher were substituted for lieutenant-governors, and, in 1882, the Islands of St. Christopher, Nevis, and Anguilla were united into one presidency. See *ante*, p. 727.

Commissioners or Presidents of St. Christopher.

1872. J. S. Berridge.
1873. Alexr. Wilson Moir.

Commissioners or Presidents of St. Christopher and Nevis.

1883. Chas. Monroe Eldridge, actg.
1885. Fras. Spencer Wigley, C.M.G., actg., May.
1885. Chas. Monroe Eldridge, *again.*
1886. Fras. Spencer Wigley, C.M.G., *again*, actg.

For bishops, see "Bishops of Antigua," *ante*, p. 728.

GOVERNORS OF NEVIS.

See Introduction, *ante*, p. 726.

For Governors, see "Governors of Leeward Islands," &c., *ante*, p. 727.

Lieutenant-Governors, &c., of Nevis.

1833. Lt.-Col. J. Lyons Nixon, L.G. St. Christopher, Nevis, Anguilla, and Virgin Islands, Feb, 7, **G.**
1841. R. B. Cleghorn, pres.
1842. Maj. Graeme, pres.
1845. Willoughby Shortland, pres
1854. Fredk. Seymour, Jan. 10, **G.**, pres.
1857. Sir Arth. Rumbold, bt., pres.

1860. Anthy. Musgrave, aft. sir A., actg. pres. during absence of Rumbold.
1863. J. P. L. Dyett, pres.
1864. Jas. W. Sheriff, pres.
1865. W. Maynard, pres.
1866. Capt. Jas. Geo. Mackenzie, R.N., L.G., Sept. 22, G.
1869. Wm. Wellington Cairns, aft. Sir W., L.G., Jan. 14, G.
1870. Fras. Spencer Wigley, admr.

After the passing of the "Leeward Islands Act, 1871," see *ante*, p. 727, commissioners or presidents of Nevis were again substituted for lieutenant-governors. In 1882 the islands of St. Christopher, Nevis, and Anguilla were united into one presidency. See *ante*, p. 727.

Commissioners or Presidents of Nevis.

1871. Fras. Spencer Wigley, above named.
1873. Capt. Melfort Campbell.
1876. Roger Tuckfield Goldsworthy, aft. sir R., May.
1877. Capt. Arth.. Elibank Havelock, aft Sir A.
1879. John Spencer Churchill, actg.; Apr. C. S. Salmon.
1882. Wm. Hy. Whyham, actg.; July to Dec.

Commissioners or Presidents of United Presidencies of St. Christopher and Nevis.

See *ante*, p. 729.

For bishops, see "Bishops of Antigua," *ante*, p. 728.

ANGUILLA.

Anguilla was formerly a dependency of St. Christopher, *q.v. ante*, p. 729. It is now included in the united presidency of St. Christopher and Nevis, *q.v. ante*, pp. 729–30.

GOVERNORS OF DOMINICA.

See Introduction, *ante*, p. 726.

* * Sir Wm. Young, bt.
1770. Thos. Shirley.
1783. Capt. John Orde, aft. bt.
1794. Hy. Hamilton.
1797. Lt.-col. hon. Andr. Cochrane Johnston.
1802. Col. Geo. Prevost, aft. bt., Sept. 23, G.
1807. Wm. Lukin, Apr. 10, G.
1808. Brig.-gen. Jas. Montgomerie, May 27, G.
1816. Lt.-col. Chas. W. Maxwell, Jan 29, G.
1819. Sir Saml. Ford Whittingham, May 21, G.
1821. Hans Fras., E. of Huntingdon, Dec 12, G.; Mar. 28, 1822, sw.
1824. M.-gen. Wm. Nicolay, Apr. 27 G.
1831. Col. sir Evan John Murray-Mac Gregor, July 25, G.

For subsequent Governors, see "Governors of Leeward Islands," *ante*, p. 727.

Lieutenant-Governors of Dominica.

1813. Lt.-gen. Fredk. Maitland, Jan. 30, G.

* * * *

1833. Capt. sir Chas. M. Schomberg, R.N., Feb. 7, G.
1835. Lt.-col. John Hastings Mair, Feb. 19, G.
1838. Maj. John Longley, May 10, G.
Maj. John Macphail, Nov. 3, G.
1845. Lt.-col. Geo. Macdonald, Jan. 14, G.
1851. Saml. Wensley Blackall, Apr. 1, G.
1857. Maj. Harry St. Geo. Ord, R.E. Sept. 2, G.
1861. Thos. Price, Dec. 30, G.
1865. Jas. Robt. Longden, aft. sir J., Sept 5, G.
1867. Hon. Hy. Ernest Gascoyne Bulwer aft. sir H., C.M.G., actg. L.G., Mar
1868. Sanford Freeling, aft. sir S., Dec 31, G.

After the passing of the "Leeward Islands Act, 1871," see *ante*, p. 727, commissioners or presidents of Dominica were substituted for lieutenant-governors.

COMMISSIONERS OR PRESIDENTS OF DOMINICA.

1872. Chas. Monroe Eldridge.
1882. John Spencer Churchill, Dec.
1887. Geo. Ruthven Le Hunte.

For bishops, see "Bishops of Antigua," *ante*, p. 728.

GOVERNORS OF THE VIRGIN ISLANDS.

See Introduction, *ante*, p. 726.

For Governors, *vide* "Governors of Leeward Islands," *ante*, p. 727.

LIEUTENANT-GOVERNORS OF THE VIRGIN ISLANDS.

* * * * * *

1812. Lt.-col. Chas. Napier, Feb. 21, **G.**
1816. Col. Jas. Bathurst. Jan. 18, **G.**
1833. J. Lyons Nixon, L.G. St. Christopher, Nevis, Anguilla, and Virgin Islands, Feb. 7, **G.**

COMMISSIONERS OR PRESIDENTS OF THE VIRGIN ISLANDS.

1854. Cornelius Hendericksen Kortright, aft. sir C., Mar. 16, **G.** and Apr. 25, 1855, **G.**
1865. Sir Arth. Carlos Hy. Rumbold, bt., Nov. 17; *d.* June 12, 1869.
1869. Alexr. Wilson Moir.
1873. Capt. R. M. Hickson
1879. R. H. Dyett, actg.
John Spencer Churchill, Apr., to Jan. 1881.
1881. R. H. Dyett, *again*, actg.
1885. J. A. Pickering, actg.
1886. R. H. Dyett, *again*, actg.
1887. Edwd. Jas Cameron.

For bishops, see "Bishops of Antigua," *ante*, p. 728.

FALKLAND ISLANDS.

THESE ISLANDS lie in the South Atlantic Ocean, and occupy a position quite isolated from all other British colonies. They were discovered by John Davis in 1592, and after having nominally belonged to France and Spain they were finally taken possession of by Great Britain and colonised.

The islands form the missionary diocese of the Falkland Islands.

GOVERNORS OF THE FALKLAND ISLANDS.

From 1833 to 1842 the Settlement was in charge of a naval officer.
1841. Lieut. Richd. Clement Moody, R.E., L.G., Aug. 20, **G.**; Govr., June 23, 1843, **G.**
1847. Geo. Rennie, Nov 27, **G.**
1855. Capt. Thos. Edwd. Laws Moore, R.N., July 2. **G.**
1862. Capt. Jas. Geo. Mackenzie, R.N., Sept. 10, **G.**
1866. Wm. Cleaver Fras. Robinson, aft. sir W., May 19, **G.**
1870. Col. Geo. A. K. D'Arcy, Feb. 24, **G**
1876. Thos. Fitzgerald Cal aghan, May 18, **G.**
1880. Thos. Kerr, Sept. 13, **G.**
1886. Arthr. Cecil Stuart Barkly, L.G., Jan. 16, **G.**; acted during absence of Kerr.

DIOCESE OF THE FALKLAND ISLANDS.

This bishopric was constituted in 1869. It is classed as a colonial diocese, holding mission from the see of Canterbury.

BISHOP OF THE FALKLAND ISLANDS.

1869. Waite Hockin Stirling.

PART XIII. ORDERS OF KNIGHTHOOD.

ORDERS OF KNIGHTHOOD, &c., CONNECTED WITH THE BRITISH EMPIRE.

THE Orders here dealt with comprise:

THE GARTER.
THE THISTLE.
ST. PATRICK.
THE BATH.
ST. MICHAEL AND ST. GEORGE.
GUELPHIC ORDER.
STAR OF INDIA.
CROWN OF INDIA.
INDIAN EMPIRE.

Many works have been written upon Orders of Knighthood in general, and individual Orders in particular, but the best work on the British Orders is beyond doubt that of Sir Harris Nicolas, published in 1842–7 in four large volumes. The following lists have been carefully collated with, and corrected by, those given by Nicolas, and the Guelphic knights which were not given in the former editions of this work have been compiled entirely from his list.

The Indian Orders are of comparatively recent date, and can hardly yet be said to have a history. Reference is, therefore, simply given to the Letters Patent or Statutes creating or enlarging them.

THE ORDER OF THE GARTER.

THE GARTER is considered both the oldest and the most illustrious Order of Knighthood now existing, not only in this country but in the world. It was undoubtedly instituted by Edward III., but the time is uncertain, various dates from 1344 to 1351 being given by different writers. Sir Harris Nicolas, who is the latest and probably the most trustworthy authority, says, "Edward III. founded the Order in 1344 but did not completely establish it until between Oct. 12, 1347, and Aug. 1348."

The Order originally consisted of the Sovereign and twenty-five knights, and so continued until 1786, when the sons of Geo. III. were made eligible, notwithstanding the chapter being complete. In 1805 this privilege was extended to the lineal descendants of Geo. II. except the Prince of Wales for the time being, who was declared to be "a constituent part of the original institution;" and in 1831 it was further extended to the lineal descendants of Geo. I. The principal foreign sovereigns are frequently admitted by special statutes, which are also occasionally passed for the admission of extra knights. The latter are generally absorbed into the ordinary twenty-five as vacancies arise.

The officers of the Order are:

PRELATE.	REGISTRAR.	USHER.
CHANCELLOR.	KING AT ARMS.	

The Order is styled—

THE MOST NOBLE ORDER OF THE GARTER.

KNIGHTS OF THE GARTER.

(K.G.)

THE reigning sovereign becomes, on his accession to the throne, the head of the Order. As a rule, he has previously been admitted a member of it.

EDWARD III.

THE ORIGINAL KNIGHTS.

K. Edw. III., *d.* 1377.
Edwd., pr. of Wales (the Blk. prince); *d.* 1376.
Hy., D. of Lancaster; *d.* 1362.
Thos., E. of Warwick; *d.* 1369.
Piers or John de Greilly, capt. de Buche; *d.* 1376.
Ralph, E. of Stafford; *d.* 1372.
Wm., E. of Salisbury; *d.* 1397.
Roger, E. of March; *d.* 1360.
Sir John Lisle, or baron Lisle; *d.* 1356.
Sir Barth. Burghersh, or ld. B.; *d.* 1369.
Sir Jno. Beauchamp, *d.* 1360.
Sir John Mohun, or ld. M.; *d.* 1373.
Sir Hugh Courtenay, *d.* 1374.
Sir Thos. Holland, aft. E. of Kent; *d.* 1360.
Sir John Grey, baron of Codnor; *d.* 1392.
Sir Richd. FitzSimon.
Sir Miles Stapleton, *d.* 1373.
Sir Thos. Wale, *d.* 1352.
Sir Hugh Wrottesley, *d.* 1380.
Sir Nele Lorin, or Loring; *d.* 1385.
Sir John Chandos, *d.* —.
Sir Jas. Audley, *d.* 1386.
Sir Otho Holland, *d.* 1359.
Sir Hy. Earn, *d.* —.
Sir Sanchet Daubrichcourt, *d.* —.
Sir Walter Pavely, *d.* 1375.

SUBSEQUENT CREATIONS.

1349 (about). Wm., 1st E. of Northampton; *d.* 1360.
Wm. Fitzwarine, *d.* 1361.
1353 (about). Regd., 1st ld. Cobham, *d.* 1361.
Robt., 1st E. of Suffolk; *d.* 1369.
1356 (about). Richd. de la Vache, *d.* 1366.
Thos., 1st ld. Ughtrede; *d.* 1365.
1360 (about). Walter, 1st ld. Manny; *d.* 1372.
Frank Van Hale, *d.* 1375–6.
Sir Thos. Ufford, *d* 1368.
1361. Lionel, E. of Ulster, and D. of Clarence; *d.* 1368.
John, E. of Richmond, aft. D. of Lancaster and K. of Castile and Leon; *d.* 1399.
Edmd., E. of Cambridge, aft. D. of York; *d.* 1402.
1361 (about). Edwd., 5th ld. le Despencer; *d.* 1375.
1362 (about). Wm., 4th ld. Latimer; *d.* 1381.
John Sully, or Sulby; *d.* 1388.
1365 (about). Humphrey, 7th E. of Hereford; *d.* 1373.
1366 (about). Ingelram, 1st E. of Bedford; *d.* 1397.
Hy. Percy, aft. 4th ld. Percy, and E. of Northumberland; *d.* 1407.
1369 (about). Ralph, 4th ld. Basset of Drayton; *d.* 1390.
Richd. Pembrugge, *d.* 1375.
John, 3rd ld. Neville of Raby; *d.* 1388.
1370 (about). Robt. de Namur, *d.* 1392,
John, 2nd E. of Pembroke; *d.* 1375.
Thos. Granston, or Gramston; *d.* 1375–6.
Guy, 1st ld. Bryan; *d.* 1390.
1372 (about). Guichard D'Angle, aft. E. of Huntingdon; *d.* 1380.

1373. Alan Buxhull, or Boxhall; *d.* 1381.
1373 (about). Thos., 4th E. of Warwick; *d.* 1401.
1376 (about). John de Montfort, D. of Brittany and E. of Richmond; *d.* 1399, (? 1401).
Hugh, 2nd E. of Stafford; *d.* 1386.
Wm., 2nd E. of Suffolk; *d.* 1382.
Thos. Banestre, *d.* 1379.
1376. Thos., E. of Kent; *d.* 1397.
Thos. Percy, aft. E. of Worcester; *d.* 1403.
1378. Wm. Beauchamp, sometimes called ld. Bergavenny or Abergavenny; *d.* 1410.
1377. Apr. 23. Richd., pr. of Wales, aft. K. Richd. II.; dep. 1399; *d.* 1400.
Hy., E. of Derby, aft. D. of Lancaster and K. Hen. IV.; *d.* 1413.

RICHARD II.

1378. Sir John Burley, *d.* —.
Sir Lewis Clifford, *d.* 1404.
1380. Bermond Arnand de Preissac Soudan de la Trau, *d.* —.
1380 (about). Thos., E. of Buckinghamshire, aft. D. of Gloucester; *d.* 1397.
1381. Thos. Felton, *d.* 1381.
1382 (about). John Holand, aft. E. of Huntingdon and 1st D. of Exeter; *d.* 1400.
Sir Simon Burley, *d.* 1388.
Sir Brian Stapleton, *d.* —.
Sir Richd. Burley, *d* —.
1384. Thos., E. of Nottingham, aft. D. of Norfolk; *d.* 1413.
1385. Robt., E. of Oxford, and M. of Dublin; aft. D. of Ireland; *d.* 1392.
1386. Richd., E. of Arundel, aft. E. of Surrey; *d.* 1397.
1387 (about). Sir Nichs. Sarnsfield, *d.* —.
1388 (about). Edwd., E. of Rutland, aft. D. of Albemarle and D. of York; *d.* 1415.
Hy. Percy (Hotspur), *d.* 1403.
* * Sir Matthew de Gournay (?). Said to be a companion in Apr. 1386.
1388–9. Sir John D'Evereux, or ld. Devereux; *d.* 1394.
Sir Peter Courtenay, *d.* 1409.
1389 (about). Thos., 6th ld. le Despencer and 1st E. of Gloucester; *d.* 1400.
1391 (about). Wm., D. of Guelderland; *d.* 1402.
Wm. of Bavaria, E. of Ostrevart, aft. D. of Holland, Hainault, and Zealand; *d.* 1417.
1393 (about). John, 2nd ld. Bourchier; *d.* 1400.
1394 (about). John, ld. Beaumont; *d* 1396.
1395 (about). Wm., ld. Scrope, aft. E. o[f] Wiltshire; *d.* 1399.
1396 (about). Sir Wm Fitzalan, *alia[s]* Arundel, *d.* 1400.
1397 (about). Sir John Beaufort, aft. E of Somerset and M. of Dorset; *d* 1410.
Thos., E. of Kent, aft. D. of Surrey *d.* 1400.
1398 (about). John, 3rd E. of Salisbury *d.* 1400.
Albert, count Palatine, D. o[f] Bavaria and D. of Holland; *d* 1404.
Sir Simon Felbrigge, *d.* —.
1399 (about). Sir Philip de la Vache, *d.* —

---

*Michl., E. of Suffolk; *d.* 1389.
*Sir Robt. Knollys.
*Sir Robt. Dunstavil.
*Sir Standich de Franc, *alias* San[n]chet de la Tour.

HENRY IV.

1399. Henry, pr. of Wales, aft. K. Hen[ry] V., about Sept.; *d.* 1422.
1400 (about). Hy. III., K. of Spain; [*d.*] 1406.
Thos. of Lancaster, E. of Albe[-]marle and D. of Clarence; [*d.*] 1421.
John, E. of Kendal and D. of Bed[-]ford; *d.* 1435.
Humphrey, E. of Pembroke, aft. [D.] of Gloucester; *d.* 1446.
Thos., 7th E. of Arundel; *d.* 1415.
1402 (about). Ralph, 1st E. of Westmo[re]land; *d.* 1425.
Richd. Beauchamp, aft. 5th E. [of] Warwick; *d.* 1439.
Thos. Beaufort, aft. E. of Dors[et] and D. of Exeter; *d.* 1417.
Sir Thos. Rampston, *d.* —.
1401 (about). Sir Thos. Erpingham, *d.* —
1402 (about). Edmd., 5th E. of Stafford *d.* 1403.
Wm., 5th ld. Willoughby de Eresby *d.* 1410.
1403 (about). Edmd., 4th E. of Ken[t] *d.* 1407.
Wm., 7th ld. Roos; *d.* 1414.
Richd., 4th ld. Grey of Codnor; [*d.*] —.
1405 (about). Sir John Stanley, *d.* 1413.
Eric X., K. of Denmark; *d.* 1459.
John, ld. Lovel; *d.* 1408.
Hugh, ld. Burnell; *d.* 1420.

* These names are not included in Sir Harris Nicolas's list, and are doubtfu[l] or more than doubtful.

1407 (about). John I., K. of Portugal; *d.* 1433.
Edwd., ld. Cherleton of Powis; *d.* 1422.
1408. Thos., 4th E. of Salisbury; *d.* 1428.
1409 (about). Sir John Cornwall, aft. ld. Fanhope; *d.* 1443.
Sir John Arundell (?), *d.* —.
1409–13. Sir Robt. de Umfreville, *d.* 1437.
1410 (about). Hy., 3rd ld. Scrope of Masham; *d.* 1415.
1411 (about). Hy., ld. Fitzhugh; *d.* 1424.
Thos., ld. Morley; *d.* 1417.
1413 (about). Gilbert, 5th ld. Talbot; *d.* 1418.

---

*Robt. or Rupert, count Palat., D. of Bavaria, aft. Emp. of Germany; *d.* 1410.

HENRY V.

1413. Sir John Daubrichcourt, about Apr. *d.* —.
1415. Thos. de Camois, or ld. Camois; *d.* 1421.
1415–16. Wm., 4th ld. de la Zouche of Haryngworth; *d.* —.
Sir. Wm. Harrington, *d.* 1457.
John, E. of Huntingdon, aft. D. of Exeter; *d.* 1446.
Richd., 11th E. of Oxford; *d.* 1417.
1416. Sigismund, Emp. of Germany, May; *d.* 1437.
Robt., 6th ld. Willoughby de Eresby; *d.* 1452.
1417. Sir John Blount, *d.* —.
1418 (between Aug. and Nov.). Hugh, ld. Bourchier; *d.* 1421.
1418–19. Sir John Robsart, *d.* 1450.
Sir Wm. Philip, aft. ld. Bardolf; *d.* 1439.
1419–20. John, E. of Tankerville; *d.* 1421.
1421. Sir Walter Hungerford, aft. ld. H., before May 3; *d.* 1449.
1421, May 3. Sir Lewis Robsart, aft. ld. Bourchier; *d.* 1431.
John Mowbray, E. Marshal, aft. 2nd D. of Norfolk; *d.* 1432.
Wm., E. of Suffolk, aft. M. and D. of Suffolk; *d.* 1450.
John, ld. Clifford; *d.* 1422.
Sir Hy. Van Clux, *d. temp.* Hen. V.
1422. Philip le Bon, D. of Burgundy; decl. in Apr. 1424; *d.* 1467

HENRY VI.

1424. John, ld. Talbot, aft. E. of Shrewsbury, Apr. 22; *d.* 1453.
1425. Thos., ld. Scales, Apr. 22; *d.* 1460.
1426. Sir John Falstaff, or Fastolf, Apr. 22; *d.* 1463.
1427. Peter, D. of Coimbra, Apr. 22; *d.* 1449.
1429, Apr. 22. Humphrey, 6th E. of Stafford, aft. D. of Buckingham; *d.* 1459.
Sir John Ratcliffe, *d.* 1437.
1432. John, E. of Arundel and ld. Maltravers, Apr. 12; *d.* 1434.
1433. Richd. Plantagenet, D. of York, Apr. 22; *d.* 1460.
1435. Edwd., K. of Portugal, May 8; *d.* 1438.
1435–6. Edwd. Beaufort, E. of Morton, aft. E. of Dorset and D. of Somerset; *d.* 1455.
Sir John Grey, *d.* —.
1438. Apr. 22. Richd., E. of Salisbury; *d.* 1460.
Albert, D. of Austria, aft. Albert II., Emp. of Germany; *d.* 1439.
1438–9. Gaston de Foix, E. of Longueville, capt. de Beauch; *d.*
1440 (about). John, 3rd E. of Somerset, aft. D. of Somerset and E. of Kendal; *d.* 1444.
Wm., ld. Falconburgh or Fauconberg, aft. E. of Kent; *d.* 1462.
Ralph Boteler, aft. ld. Sudely; *d.* 1473.
1440–3. John, 1st visc. Beaumont; *d.* 1459.
1443 (about). Alphonso V., K. of Portugal; *d.* 1481.
Alphonso V., K. of Arragon; re-elect. 1450; *d.* 1458.
Hy., D. of Visen in Portugal; *d.* 1460.
1445. John, ld. Beauchamp of Powyck, before May; *d.* 1475.
John de Foix, aft. E. of Kendal, May 12; *d.* abt. 1485.
1445, July 11. Alvaro Vasquez d'Alamada, count D'Avranches; *d.* 1449.
Thos. Hoo, aft. ld. Hoo and Hastings; *d.* 1453–5.
Sir Francis Surienne, Nov. 27; *d.* —.
1450, Aug. 4. Casimir IV., K. of Poland; *d.* 1492.
Wm., D. of Brunswick; *d.* 1482.
Richd., ld. Rivers, aft. E. Rivers; *d.* 1469.
1451. John, 3rd D. of Norfolk, May 28; *d.* 1461.
1452 (about). Hy., 1st visc. Bourchier, aft. E. of Essex; *d.* 1483.
Sir Philip Wentworth, *d.* —.

* This name is not included in Sir Harris Nicolas's list, and is doubtful, or more than doubtful.

1453. Sir Edwd. Hull, May 7; *d.* 1453.
1457 (before May 13). John, 2nd E. of Shrewsbury; *d.* 1460.
Lionel, 6th ld. Welles; *d.* 1461.
Thos., 1st ld. Stanley; *d.* 1458.
1457. Fredk. IV., Emp. of Germany, May 14; *d.* 1493.
1458. Jasper, E. of Pembroke, aft. D. of Bedford; *d.* 1495.
1459 (before Apr. 23). Jas., 5th E. of Ormond and 1st E. of Wiltshire; *d.* 1461.
John, 4th ld. Dudley; *d.* 1482.
John, 1st ld. Berners; *d.* 1474.
1460 (about July). Richd. Neville, aft. E. of Warwick and Salisbury; *d.* 1471.
Wm., 1st ld. Bonvill; *d.* 1460.

EDWARD IV.

1461. Geo., D. of Clarence; *d.* 1477.
1461 (about). Ferd. II., K. of Naples; *d.* 1496.
Fras. Sforza, D. of Milan; *d.* 1466.
Jas., E. of Douglas; *d.* 1488.
John, 5th ld. Scrope of Bolton; *d.* 1494.
Gaillard de Durefort, ld. of Duras; *d.* —.
Sir Wm. Chamberlayne, *d.* —.
Sir Robt. Harcourt, *d.* 1470.
1462 (before Mar. 1). John, 1st E. of Worcester; *d.* 1470.
Wm., ld. Hastings; *d.* 1483.
John, ld. Montague, aft. E. of Northumberland and M. of Montague; *d.* 1471.
Wm., 1st ld. Herbert, aft. E. of Pembroke; *d.* 1469.
Sir John Astley, *d.* —.
1466. Richd., D. of Gloucester, aft. K. Richd. III., before Feb. 4; *d.* 1485.
Anthy., ld. Scales and Nucells, aft. E. Rivers; about Apr.; *d.* 1483.
1467. Inigo D'Avalos, count de Monte Odorisio, about Apr.; *d.* —.
1469 (about). Chas., D. of Burgundy; *d.* 1477.
1472 (before). Wm., 11th E. of Arundel; *d.* 1487.
1472, Apr. 23. John, ld. Howard, aft. D. of Norfolk; *d.* 1485.
John, 1st E. of Wiltshire; *d.* 1473.
Walter, 6th ld. Ferrers of Chartley; *d.* 1485.
Walter, ld. Montjoy; *d.* 1474.
John, 4th D. of Norfolk; *d.* 1475.
1472 (about). John, 3rd D. of Suffolk; *d.* 1491.
1474, Feb. 26. Hy., 2nd D. of Buckingham; *d.* 1485.
Thos., ld. Maltravers, aft. E. of Arundel; *d.* 1524.
Sir Wm. Parr, of Kendal; *d.* —
1474, Aug. 18. Fredk., D. of Urbino; *d.* 1482
Hy., 4th E. of Northumberland *d.* 1489.
1475, May 15. Edwd., Pr. of Wales, aft. Edwd. V.; *d.* 1483.
Richd., D. of York; *d.* 1483.
1476. Thos., 1st M. of Dorset; degr. 1483; rest. 1485; *d.* 1501.
1477. Sir Thos. Montgomery, Apr. *d.* —.
1480, Feb. 10. Ferdinand V., K. of Castile and Leon, aft. K. of Spain; *d.* 1516.
Hercules d'Esté, D. of Ferrara *d.* 1505.
1482. John II., K. of Portugal, Sept 15; re-elect. 1488; *d.* 1495.

---

*Richd., ld. Mountgryson, i Apulia.

EDWARD V.

No creations.

RICHARD III.

1483 (before June). Thos., E. of Surrey aft. D. of Norfolk; *d.* 1524.
Fras., 9th ld. and 1st visc Lovell; *d.* 1487.
Sir Richd. Ratcliffe, *d.* 1485.
Between June 1483 and Aug. 1485—
Sir Thos. Burgh, aft. ld. Burgh *d.* 1496.
Thos. ld. Stanley, aft. E. of Derby; *d.* 1504.
Sir Richd. Tunstall, *d.* —.
Sir John Conyers, *d.* 1490.

HENRY VII.

Between Aug. 1485 and May 1486—
John, 13th E. of Oxford; *d.* 1513.
John, 1st visc. Welles; *d.* 1498
John, 1st ld. Dynham, or Denham; *d.* 1509.
Sir Giles D'Aubeney, aft. ld. D.; *d.* 1507.
Between Aug. 1485 and 1487—
Sir Wm. Stanley, *d.* 1494.
Sir John Cheney, *d.* 1495.
1847 (before Apr.). Geo., 3rd ld. Strange; *d.* 1497.

* This name is not included in Sir Harris Nicolas's list, and is doubtful, or more than doubtful.

1487 (before Apr.). Sir Edwd. Wydeville, c.c.ld. Wydeville; *d.* 1488.
1488. Geo., 4th E. of Shrewsbury, Apr. 27; *d.* 1541.
Sir John Savage, Nov. 10; *d.* 1492.
1489. Maximilian, K. of the Romans, aft. Emp. of Germany, Oct.; re-elect. 1502; *d.* 1519.
1491. Arthur, Pr. of Wales, Apr. 8; *d.* 1502.
1493. Alphonso II., D. of Calabria and Naples, K. of Sicily and Jerusalem, Mar.; *d.* 1495.
1494 (before). Edwd., 7th E. of Devonshire; *d.* 1509.
Robt., ld. Brook, or Willoughby de Broke; *d.* 1503.
Sir Edwd. Poynings, *d.* 1521.
John, K. of Denmark; *d.* 1513.
Hy., D. of York, aft. Pr. of Wales and Hen. VIII.; *d.* 1547.
Between Apr. 1494 and Apr. 1499—
Edmd., 3rd D. of Buckingham; *d.* 1521.
Hy., 5th E. of Northumberland; *d.* 1427.
Edmd., 6th E. of Suffolk; *d.* 1513.
Hy., 2nd E. of Essex; *d.* 1539.
Sir Chas. Somerset, aft. ld. Herbert and E. of Worcester; *d.* 1526.
Sir Gilbert Talbot, of Grafton; *d.* 1516.
1499. Sir Richd. Pole, Apr. 23; *d.* —.
1503 (before May). Philip I., Archd. of Austria, &c., aft. K. of Castile; *d.* 1506.
Thos., 2nd M. of Dorset; *d.* 1530.
Sir Regd. Bray, *d.* 1503.
Sir Thos. Lovell, *d.* 1524.
Sir Richd. Guildford, *d.* —.
1504 (before Feb. 20). Guido Ubaldo, D. of Urbino; *d.* 1508.
1504 (before May). Gerald, 8th E. of Kildare; *d.* 1513.
1505 (before May). Hy., ld. Stafford, aft. E. of Wiltshire; *d.* 1523.
1505. Richd., 3rd E. of Kent, Apr. 22; *d.* 1523.
1506 (before May 23). Sir Rys Ap Thomas; *d.* —.
1507. Sir Thos. Brandon, May 10; *d.* —.
1508. Chas., Archd. of Austria, Pr. of Spain, aft. Emp. Chas. V. of Germany, Dec. 20; *d.* 1558.

HENRY VIII.

1509, May 18. Thos., ld. Darcy; *d.* 1538.
Edwd., 5th ld. Dudley; *d.* 1530.
1510, Apr. 23. Emanuel, K. of Portugal; *d.* 1521.
1510, Apr. 23. Thos., ld. Howard and E. of Surrey, aft. 8th D. of Norfolk; *d.* 1552.
Thos., ld. De la Warr; *d.* 1525.
Sir Hy. Marney, aft. ld. Marney; *d.* 1524.
1513, Apr. 23. Geo., 3rd ld. Abergavenny; *d.* 1535.
Sir Edw. Howard, *d.* 1513.
Sir Chas. Brandon, aft. D. of Suffolk; *d* 1545.
1514, Apr. 23. Julian de Medicis, D. of Nemours; *d.* 1516.
Edwd., 1st ld. Monteagle; *d.* 1523.
1518, Apr. 24. Thos., 2nd ld. Dacre of Gillesland; *d.* 1525.
Sir Wm. Sandys, aft. ld. Sandys; *d.* 1542.
1521. Hy., 8th E. of Devonshire, aft. M. of Exeter, Apr. 24; *d.* 1539.
1522. Ferdinand, Pr. and Infant of Spain, Archd. of Austria, aft. Emp. Ferdinand I. of Germany, Apr. 23; *d.* 1564.
Sir Richd. Wingfield; *d.* abt. 1525.
1523. Sir Thos. Bullen, or Boleyn, aft. visc. Rochford and E. of Wiltshire and Ormond, May 10; *d.* 1538.
Walter, 3rd ld. Ferrers, aft. visc. Hereford, July 13; *d.* 1558.
1524, Apr. 23. Arth. Plantagenet, visc. Lisle, nat. son of Edwd. IV.; *d.* 1541.
Robt., visc. Fitzwalter, aft. E. of Sussex; *d.* 1542.
1525, Apr. 23. Wm., E. of Arundel; *d.* 1543.
Thos., ld. Roos, aft. E. of Rutland; *d.* 1543.
1525, June 7. Hy. Fitzroy, nat. son of Hen. VIII.; aft. E. of Nottingham and D. of Richmond and Somerset; *d.* 1536.
Ralph, 4th E. of Westmoreland; *d.* 1549.
1526, Apr. 24. Wm., 4th ld. Montjoy; *d.* 1535.
Sir Wm. Fitzwilliam, aft. E. of Southampton; *d.* 1543.
Sir Hy. Guildford; *d.* —.
1527, Oct. 21. Fras. I., K. of France; *d.* 1547.
John, 15th E. of Oxford; *d.* 1539.
1531. Hy., E. of Northumberland, Apr. 23; *d.* 1537.
1532, Oct. 27. Anne, count de Beaumont and D. de Montmorency; *d.* 1567.
Philip Chabot, E. of Newblanc.
1535. Jas. V., K. of Scotland, Jan. 20; *d.* 1542.
1536. Sir Nichs. Carew, Apr. 23; *d.* 1539.
1537. Hy., E. of Cumberland, Apr. 23; *d.* 1542.

1537. Thos., ld. Cromwell, aft. E. of Essex, Aug. 5; *d.* 1540.
1539, Apr. 24. John, 1st ld. Russell, aft. E. of Bedford, *d.* 1554.
Sir Thos. Cheney, *d.* 1558.
Sir Wm. Kingston, *d.* 1541.
1540, Apr. 23. Thos., ld. Audley of Walden; *d.* 1544.
Sir Anthy. Browne, *d.* 1548.
1541. Edwd., 1st E. of Hertford, aft. D. of Somerset, Jan. 9; *d.* 1552.
1541, Apr. 23. Hy. Howard, c. c. E. of Surrey; *d.* 1546.
Sir John Gage, *d.* 1556.
Sir Anthy. Wingfield.
1543, Apr. 23. John, visc. Lisle, aft. E. of Warwick and D. of Northumberland; *d.* 1553.
Wm., ld. St. John of Basing, aft. E. of Wiltshire and M. of Winchester; *d.* 1572.
Wm., ld. Parr of Kendal, aft E. of Essex and M. of Northampton; *d.* 1571.
1543. Sir John Wallop, Dec. 24; *d.* 1551.
1544, Apr. 24. Hy., E. of Arundel; *d.* 1579.
Sir Anthy. St. Leger, *d* —.
1545, Apr. 23. Fras., E. of Shrewsbury; *d.* 1560.
Thos., ld Wriothesley, aft. E. of Southampton; *d.* 1550.

EDWARD VI.

1547, Feb. 17. Hy., 3rd M. of Dorset, aft. D. of Suffolk; *d.* 1554.
Edwd., 3rd E. of Derby; *d.* 1574.
Thos., ld. Seymour of Sudley; *d.* 1549.
Sir Wm. Paget, aft. ld. Paget; *d.* 1563.
1549, Apr. 24. Fras., 2nd E. of Huntingdon; *d.* 1560.
Geo., 4th ld. Cobham; *d.* 1558.
1549, Dec. 1. Thos., ld. De la Warr; *d.* 1554.
Sir Wm. Herbert, aft. ld. Herbert of Cardiff and E. of Pembroke; *d.* 1559.
1551, Apr. 24. Hy. II., K. of France; d. 1559.
Edwd., 8th ld. Clinton, aft. E. of Lincoln; *d.* 1585.
1551. Thos., ld. Darcy of Chiche, Sept. 28; *d.* 1558.
1552, Apr. 24. Hy., 5th E. of Westmoreland; *d.* 1563.
Sir Andr. Dudley, *d.* —.

MARY.

1554, Apr. 24. Pr. Philip, aft. Philip II., K. of Spain, consort of Q. Mary; *d.* 1598.
Hy., 2nd E. of Sussex; *d.* 1556.
1554. Emanuel Philibert, D. of Savoy, Aug. 6; *d.* 1580.
Wm., ld. Howard of Effingham, Oct. 9; *d.* 1573.
1555, Apr. 23. Anthy., 1st visc. Montagu: *d.* 1592.
Sir Edwd. Hastings, aft. ld. Hastings of Loughborough; *d.* 1558.
1557, Apr. 23. Thos., 3rd E. of Sussex; *d.* 1583.
Wm., 13th ld. Grey of Wilton; *d.* 1562.
Sir Robt. Rochester, *d.* Nov. 28, 1557.

ELIZABETH.

1559, Apr. 24. Thos., D. of Norfolk; *d.* 1572.
Hy., 2nd E. of Rutland; *d.* 1563.
Sir Robt. Dudley, aft. E. of Leicester; *d.* 1588.
1560. Adolphus, D. of Holstein, June 10; *d.* 1586.
1561, Apr. 22. Geo., E. of Shrewsbury; *d.* 1590.
Hy., 1st ld. Hunsdon; *d.* 1596.
1563, Apr. 22. Thos., E. of Northumberland; *d.* 1572.
Ambrose, E. of Warwick; *d.* 1589.
1564, Apr. 23. Chas. IX., K. of France; *d.* 1574.
Fras., 2nd E. of Bedford; *d.* 1585.
Sir Hy. Sydney, *d.* 1586.
1567. Maximilian II., Emp. of Germany, April 23; *d.* 1576.
1570, Apr. 23. Hy., 3rd E. of Huntingdon; *d.* 1595.
Wm., 3rd E. of Worcester; *d.* 1589.
1572, Apr. 23. Fras., D. de Montmorency; *d.* 1579.
Walter., 2nd visc. Hereford, aft. E. of Essex; *d.* 1576.
Wm., 1st ld. Burleigh; *d.* 1598.
Arthr., ld. Grey of Wilton; *d.* 1593.
Edmd., 2nd ld. Chandos; *d.* 1573.
1574, Apr. 24. Hy., 4th E. of Derby; *d.* 1592.
Hy., 2nd E. of Pembroke; *d.* 1601.
1575, Apr. 23. Hy. III., K. of France; *d.* 1589.
Chas., 2nd ld. Howard of Effingham, aft. E. of Nottingham *d.* 1624.
1578, Apr. 24. Rodolph II., Emp. of Germany *d.* 1612.
Fredk. II., K. of Denmark; *d.* 1588.
1579. John Casimir, Ct. Palatine of the Rhine, &c., Feb. 8; *d.* 1592.
1584, Apr. 23. Edwd., E. of Rutland; *d.* 1587.
Wm., 5th ld. Cobham; *d.* 1596.

1584, Apr. 23. Hy., 9th ld. Scrope of Bolton; *d.* 1592.
1588, Apr. 24. Robt., 2nd E. of Essex; *d.* 1600.
Thos., E. of Ormond; *d.* 1614.
Sir Christr. Hatton, *d.* 1591.
1589, Apr. 24. Hy., 4th E. of Sussex; *d.* 1593.
Thos., 1st ld. Buckhurst, aft. E. of Dorset; *d.* 1608.
1590, Apr. 24. Hy. IV., K. of France; *d.* 1610.
Jas. VI., K. of Scotland, aft. K. Jas. I. of England; *d.* 1625.
1592, Apr. 23. Gilbert, E. of Shrewsbury; *d.* 1616.
Geo., E. of Cumberland; *d.* 1605.
1593, Apr. 23. Hy., E. of Northumberland; *d.* 1632.
Edwd., 4th E. of Worcester; *d.* 1628.
Thos., ld. Borough, or Burgh; *d.* 1597.
Edmd., 3rd ld. Sheffield, aft. E. of Mulgrave; *d.* 1646.
1593. Sir Fras. Knollys, June 25; *d.* 1596.
1597, Apr. 23. Fredk., D. of Wurtemberg; *d.* 1608.
Thos., ld. Howard of Walden, aft. E. of Suffolk; *d.* 1626.
Geo., 2nd ld. Hunsdon; *d.* 1603.
Chas., 8th ld. Mountjoy, aft. E of Devonshire; *d.* 1606.
Sir Hy. Lee, *d.* 1611.
1599, Apr. 23. Robt., 5th E. of Sussex; *d.* 1629.
Hy., 8th ld. Cobham; *d.* 1619.
Thos., 10th ld. Scrope of Bolton; *d.* 1612.
1601, Apr. 23. Wm., 6th E. of Derby; *d.* 1642.
Thos., 2nd ld. Burleigh, aft. E. of Exeter; *d.* 1622.

JAMES I.

1603, June 14. Hy. Fredk., aft. Pr. of Wales; *d.* 1612.
Christian IV., K. of Denmark; *d.* 1648.
1603, June 25. Ludwick, D. of Lenox, aft. E. and D. of Richmond; *d.* 1624.
Hy., 3rd E. of Southampton; *d.* 1624.
John, E. of Mar; *d.* 1634.
Wm., 3rd E. of Pembroke; *d.* 1630.
1605, Apr. 24. Ulrick, D. of Holstein; *d.* 1624.
Hy., 1st E. of Northampton; *d.* 1614.
1606, Apr. 24. Robt., 1st E. of Salisbury; *d.* 1612.
Thos., 3rd visc. Bindon; *d.* 1582.
1608, Apr. 23. Geo., 1st E. of Dunbar; *d.* 1611.
Philip, 1st E. of Montgomery, aft. E. of Pembroke; *d.* 1650.
1611, Apr. 23. Thos., E. of Arundel, aft. E. of Norfolk; *d.* 1646.
1611, Apr. 23. Robt., 1st visc. Rochester, aft. E. of Somerset; *d.* 1645.
1611. Chas., D. of York, aft. Chas. I., Apr. 24; *d.* 1649.
1612, Dec. 19. Fredk., Ct. Palatine of the Rhine, aft. K. of Bohemia, son-in-law of Jas. I.; *d.* 1632.
Maurice de Nassau, Pr. of Orange; *d.* 1625.
1615, Apr. 24. Thos., visc. Fenton, aft, E. of Kellie; *d.* 1639.
Wm., 1st ld. Knollys, aft. E. of Banbury; *d.* 1632.
1616, Apr. 24. Fras., 6th E. of Rutland; *d.* 1632.
Sir Geo. Villiers, aft. E., M., and D. of Buckingham; *d.* 1629.
1616. Robt., visc. Lisle, aft. E. of Leicester, May 26; *d.* 1677.
1623. Jas., 2nd M. of Hamilton and 1st E. of Cambridge, Feb. 2; *d.* 1624.
1624. Esmé, D. of Lenox and E. of March, Apr. 22; *d.* 1624.
1624, Dec. 31. Christian, D. of Brunswick-Wolfenbuttel; *d.* 1626.
Wm., 2nd E. of Salisbury; *d.* 1668.
Jas., 1st E. of Carlisle; *d.* 1636.

CHARLES I.

1625, May 15. Edwd., 4th E. of Dorset; *d.* 1652.
Hy., 1st E. of Holland; *d.* 1649.
Thos.. 1st visc. Andover, aft. E. of Berkshire; *d.* 1699.
1625. Claude de Loraine, D. of Chevreuse, July 4, *d.* 1657.
1627, Apr. 24. Gustavus Adolphus, K. of Sweden; *d.* 1632.
Fredk. Hy. of Nassau, Pr. of Orange; *d.* 1647.
Theoph., E. of Suffolk; *d.* 1640.
1628. Wm., 1st E. of Northampton, Sept. 25; *d.* 1630.
1630, Apr. 18. Richd., ld. Weston, aft. E. of Portland; *d.* 1634.
Robt., 1st E. of Lindsey; *d.* 1642.
Wm., 2nd E. of Exeter; *d.* 1640.
1630. Jas., 3rd M. of Hamilton and 2nd E. of Cambridge, aft. D. of Hamilton, Oct. 5; *d.* 1648.
1633, Apr. 18. Chas. Louis, Ct. Palatine of the Rhine and D. of Bavaria; *d.* 1680.
Jas., D. of Lenox, aft. E. of March and D. of Richmond; *d.* 1655.
1633, Nov. 7. Hy., E. of Danby; *d.* 1643.
Wm., E. of Morton; *d.* 1648.
1635. Algernon, E. of Northumberland, Apr. 23; *d.* 1668.

1638. Chas., Pr. of Wales, aft. Chas. II., May 20; *d.* 1688.
1640. Thos., 1st E. of Strafford, Sept. 12; *d.* 1641.
1642, Apr. 20. Jas., D. of York, aft. James II.; *d.* 1710.
Pr. Rupert, Ct. Palatine of the Rhine, &c., aft. D. of Cumberland; *d.* 1682.
1645, Mar. 2. William II. of Nassau, Pr. of Orange; *d.* 1660.
Bernard de Nogaret de Foix, D. d'Espernon, &c.; *d.* 1661.

CHARLES II.

1649, Sept. 18. Pr. Maurice, Ct. Palatine of the Rhine; *d.* 1654.
Jas., 1st M. of Ormond, aft. D. of Ormond; *d.* 1688.
Pr. Edwd., Ct. Palatine of the Rhine; *d.* 1663.
Geo., 2nd D. of Buckingham; *d.* 1687.
1650, Jan. Wm., M. of Hertford, aft D. of Somerset; *d.* 1660.
Wm., 2nd D. of Hamilton and 3rd E. of Cambridge; *d.* 1651.
Thos., 4th E. of Southampton; *d.* 1667.
Wm., 1st M., aft. 1st D. of Newcastle; *d.* 1676.
Jas., M. of Montrose; *d.* 1650.
Jas., 7th E. of Derby; *d.* 1651.
1653. Geo., 2nd E. of Bristol, Jan.; *d.* 1697.
1653, Apr. 4. Hy., D. of Gloucester; *d.* 1669.
Hy. Chas. de la Tremouille, Pr. of Tarente; *d.* 1672.
1653. William III. of Nassau, Pr. of Orange, aft. K. William III. of England, Apr. 25; *d.* 1702.
1654. Fredk. Wm., Margrave and Elector of Brandenburg, D. of Prussia, Jan. 23; *d.* 1688.
1658. Jno. Gaspar Ferd. de Marchin, Count de Graville, &c., Feb 26; *d.* —.
1660. Geo., 1st D. of Albemarle, May 26; *d.* 1670.
Edwd. Montagu, aft. 1st E. of Sandwich, May 27; *d.* 1672.
Aubrey, E. of Oxford, May 31; *d.* 1702.
1661, Apr. 1. Chas., 4th D. of Richmond and Lenox; *d.* 1672.
Montague, 2nd E. of Lindsey; *d.* 1666.
Edwd., E. of Manchester; *d.* 1671.
Wm., 2nd E. of Strafford; *d.* 1695.
1662. Christian, Pr. of Denmark, aft. K. Christian V., Nov. 6; *d.* 1699.
1663. Jas., D. of Monmouth and Buccleuch, Mar. 28; *d.* 1685.
1666. Jas., D. of Cambridge, Dec. 3; *d.* 1667.
1668, June 19. Charles XI., K. of Sweden; *d.* 1697.
Jno. George II., Elector of Saxony; *d.* 1680.
1670. Christr., 2nd D. of Albemarle, Feb. 4; *d.* 1688.
1672. Jno., 2nd E., aft. D. of Lauderdale, Apr. 18; *d.* 1682.
1672, May 29. Hy., 3rd M. of Worcester, aft. D. of Beaufort; *d.* 1699.
Hy., 1st E. of St. Albans; *d.* 1683.
Wm., 5th E., aft. 1st D. of Bedford; *d.* 1700.
1672. Hy., 1st E. of Arlington, June 15; *d.* 1685.
Thos. Butler, c.c. E. of Ossory, Sept. 30; *d.* 1680.
1673. Chas. Fitzroy, c.c. E. of Southampton, aft. D. of Southampton and Cleveland, Apr. 1; *d.* 1730.
1674. Jno., 3rd E. of Mulgrave, aft. D. of Buckingham, Apr. 23; *d.* 1720.
1677. Hy., D. of Newcastle, Feb. 17; *d.* 1691.
Thos., E. of Danby, aft. M. of Carmarthen and D. of Leeds, Apr. 19; *d.* 1712.
1680, Aug. 31. Hy., 1st D. of Grafton; *d.* 1690.
Jas., 3rd E. of Salisbury; *d.* 1683.
1680. Charles II., Ct. Palatine of the Rhine and D. of Bavaria, Sept. 15; *d.* 1685.
1681. Chas., 1st D. of Richmond and Lenox, Apr. 7; *d.* 1723.
1684. Geo., Pr. of Denmark, aft. D. of Cumberland, Consort of Q. Anne, Jan. 1; *d.* 1708.
1684, Jan. 10. Chas., D. of Somerset; *d.* 1748.
Geo., D. of Northumberland; *d.* 1716.

JAMES II.

1685. Hy., D. of Norfolk, May 6; *d.* 1701.
Hy., 2nd E. of Peterborough, June 18; *d.* 1697.
Lawrence, 1st E. of Rochester, June 29; *d.* 1711.
Louis, 1st E. of Feversham, June 30; *d.* 1709.
1687. Robt., E. of Sunderland, Apr. 26; *d.* 1702.
1688, Sept. 28. Jas., D. of Berwick, nat. son of James II. His election declared void, Jan. 1, 1690.
Jas., 2nd D. of Ormond; *d.* 1715.

WILLIAM III.

1689. Fredk., 1st D. of Schomberg, Apr. 3; *d.* 1690.
Wm., 4th E., aft. 1st D. of Devonshire, May 14; *d.* 1707.
1690. Frederick III., Elect. of Brandenburg, aft. K. Frederick I. of Prussia; *d.* 1712.
Geo. Wm., D. of Brunswick and Lunenburg Zell, c.c. D. of Zell, Dec. 30; *d.* —.
1692, Feb. 2. Jno. George IV., D. of Saxony; *d.* —.
Chas., E. of Dorset and 1st E. of Middlesex; *d.* 1706.
1694. Chas., 1st D. of Shrewsbury, Apr. 25; *d.* 1718.
1696. Pr. Wm., c.c. D. of Gloucester, son of Q. Anne, Jan. 6; *d.* 1700.
1697. Wm., 1st E. of Portland, Feb. 19; *d.* 1709.
1698. Jno., D. of Newcastle, May 30; *d.* 1711.
1700, May 14. Thos., 8th E. of Pembroke and 5th E. of Montgomery; *d.* 1733.
Arnold Joost, 1st E. of Albemarle; *d.* 1718.
1701, June 18. Geo. Lewis, Elect. of Hanover, &c., aft. K. Geo. I. of England; *d.* 1727.
Jas., 2nd D. of Queensberry and D. of Dover; *d.* 1711.

ANNE.

1702, Mar. 14. Wriothesley, 2nd D. of Bedford; *d.* 1711.
Jno., E., aft. 1st D. of Marlborough; *d.* 1722.
1703. Meinhardt, 3rd D. of Schomberg and 1st D. of Leinster, Aug. 12; *d.* 1719.
1704. Sidney, 1st ld., aft. 1st E. of Godolphin, July 6; *d.* 1712.
1706. Geo. Augs., Electoral Pr. of Hanover, &c., aft. K. Geo. II. of England, Apr. 4; *d.* 1760.
1710, Mar. 22. Wm., 2nd D. of Devonshire; *d.* 1729.
Jno., D. of Argyle, and E., aft. D., of Greenwich; *d.* 1743.
1712, Oct. 25. Jas., 4th D. of Hamilton and 1st D. of Brandon; *d.* Nov. 15, 1712.
Hy., D. of Kent; *d.* 1740.
Jno., 1st E. Poulett; *d.* 1743.
Robt., 1st E. of Oxford and E. Mortimer; *d.* 1724.
Thos., 3rd E. of Strafford; *d.* 1739.
1712. Hy., 2nd D. of Beaufort, Oct. 26; *d.* 1714.
1713. Chas., 3rd E. of Peterborough and 1st E. of Monmouth, Aug. 3; *d.* 1735.

GEORGE I.

1714, Oct. 16. Chas., 2nd D. of Bolton; *d.* 1722.
Jno., 2nd D. of Rutland; *d.* 1721.
Lionel Cranfield, E., aft. 1st D. of Dorset and Middlesex; *d.* 1763.
Chas., 1st E. of Halifax; *d.* 1715.
1716, July 3. Pr. Fredk. Lewis, aft. D. of Gloucester, D. of Edinburgh, and Pr. of Wales; *d.* 1751.
Ernest Augs., bp. of Osnaburg and D. of York; *d.* 1728.
1718, Mar. 31. Chas., 1st D. of St. Albans; *d.* 1726.
Jno., 2nd D. of Montagu; *d.* 1749.
Thos. Holles, D. of Newcastle; *d.* 1768.
Jas., 3rd E. of Berkeley; *d.* 1736.
1719. Evelyn, 1st D. of Kingston, Apr. 29; *d.* 1726.
Chas., E. of Sunderland, Nov. 21; *d.* 1722.
1721, Mar. 27. Chas., 2nd D. of Grafton; *d.* 1723.
Hy., E. of Lincoln; *d.* 1728.
1722, Oct. 10. Chas., 3rd D. of Bolton; *d.* 1754.
Jno., 3rd D. of Rutland; *d.* 1779.
Jno., 1st D. of Roxburghe; *d.* 1741.
1724, July 9. Richd., E. of Scarborough; *d.* 1740.
Chas., 2nd visc. Townshend; *d.* 1738.
1726, May 26. Chas., D. of Richmond and Lenox; *d.* 1750.
Sir Robt. Walpole, aft. E. of Orford; *d.* 1745.

GEORGE II.

1730, May 18. Wm. Augs., D. of Cumberland; *d.* 1765.
Philip Dormer, E. of Chesterfield; *d.* 1751.
Richd., E. of Burlington and Cork; *d.* 1735.
1733, June 12. Wm. Chas. Hy. Friso, Pr. of Orange; *d.* 1751.
Wm., 3rd D. of Devonshire; *d.* 1755.
Spencer, E. of Wilmington; *d.* 1743.
1738, Feb. 20. Wm., 3rd E. of Essex; *d.* 1743.
Jas., 1st E. Waldegrave; *d.* 1741.
1741, Mar. 20. Frederick III., Pr., aft. Landgrave, of Hesse Cassel; *d.* 1785.
Chas., 2nd D. of St. Albans; *d.* 1751.
Chas., D. of Marlborough; *d.* 1758.

1741, Mar. 20. Evelyn, 2nd D. of Kingston; *d.* 1773.
Wm., 2nd D. of Portland; *d.* 1762.
Frederick III., D. of Saxe Gotha, May 2; *d.* 1772.
1745. John Adolph, D. of Saxe Weissenfels, Apr. 24; *d.* 1746.
1749, June 22. Pr. Geo. Wm. Fredk., aft. Pr. of Wales and Geo. III.; *d.* 1820.
Chas. Wm. Fredk., Margrave of Brandenburg-Anspach; *d.* 1757.
1749, June 22. Thos., 4th D. of Leeds; *d.* 1789.
Jno., 4th D. of Bedford; *d.* 1771.
Wm. Anne, E. of Albemarle; *d.* 1754.
Jno., 1st E. Granville; *d.* 1763.
1752, Mar. 13. Pr. Edwd. Augs., aft. D. of York, bro. to Geo. III.; *d.* 1767.
Wm. V., Pr. of Orange; *d.* 1806.
Daniel, E. of Winchelsea and Nottingham; *d.* 1769.
Geo., 4th E. of Cardigan, aft. D. of Montague; *d.* 1790.
1752. Hy., 9th E. of Lincoln, aft. D. of Newcastle, June 4; *d.* 1794.
1756, Nov. 18. Wm., 4th D. of Devonshire; *d.* 1764.
Hy., E. of Carlisle; *d.* 1758.
Hugh, E., aft. D., of Northumberland; *d.* 1786.
Fras. Seymour, E., aft. M., of Hertford; *d.* 1794.
1757. Jas., E. Waldegrave, June 30; *d.* 1763.
1759. Pr. Ferdinand of Brunswick, Aug. 16; *d.* 1792.
1760. Chas. Watson, 2nd M. of Rockingham, Feb. 4; *d.* 1782.
Richd., 1st E. Temple, May 6; *d.* 1779.

George III.

1762, May 27. Pr. Wm. Hy., bro. to Geo. III., D. of Gloucester and Edinburgh; *d.* 1805.
Jno., E. of Bute; *d.* 1792.
1764, Apr. 23. Adolphus Frederick IV., D. of Mecklenburg-Strelitz; *d.* 1794.
Geo., 5th E. of Halifax; *d.* 1772.
1765, Dec. 26. Geo. Augs., Pr. of Wales, aft. George IV.; *d.* 1830.
Chas. Wm. Ferd., hered. Pr. of Brunswick-Wolffenbuttel; *d.* 1806.
Geo., 3rd E. of Albemarle; *d.* 1772.
1767. Pr. Hy. Fredk., D. of Cumberland and Strathern, Dec. 21; *d.* 1790.
1768. Geo., D. of Marlborough, Dec. 12; *d.* 1817.
1771. Pr. Fredk., bp. of Osnaburgh, aft. D. of York and Albany, July 25; *d.* 1827.
1771. Granville Leveson, E. Gower, aft. 1st M. of Stafford, Feb. 11; *d.* 1803.
1769. Augs. Hy., 3rd D. of Grafton, Sept. 29; *d.* 1811.
1772. Sir Fredk. North, c.c. ld. North, aft. E. of Guilford, June 18; *d.* 1792.
1778, June 3. Hy., E. of Suffolk and Berkshire; *d.* 1779.
Wm. Hy., 5th E. of Rochford; *d.* 1781.
Thos., visc. Weymouth, aft. 1st M. of Bath; *d.* 1796.
1782, Apr. 19. Pr. Wm. Hy., aft. D. of Clarence and William IV.; *d.* 1830.
Chas., 7th D. of Richmond and Lenox; *d.* 1806.
Wm., 5th D. of Devonshire; *d.* 1811.
Wm., 2nd E. of Shelburne, aft. 1st M. of Lansdowne; *d.* 1805.
1782. Chas., 4th D. of Rutland, Oct. 3; *d.* 1787.
1786, June 2. Pr. Edwd., aft. D. of Kent; *d.* 1820.
Pr. Ernest Augs., aft. D. of Cumberland and K. of Hanover; *d.* 1851.
Pr. Augs. Fredk., aft. D. of Sussex; *d.* 1843.
Pr. Adolphus Fredk., aft. D. of Cambridge; *d.* 1850.
Wm. Geo., Landgrave of Hesse-Cassel; *d.* 1821.
Hy., 5th D. of Beaufort; *d.* 1803.
Geo. Nugent Temple, M. of Buckingham; *d.* 1813.
Chas., E., aft. 1st M. Cornwallis; *d.* 1805.
1788, Apr. 9. Jno. Fredk., D. of Dorset; *d.* 1799.
Hugh, D. of Northumberland; *d.* 1817.
1790, Dec. 15. Ernest Lewis Fredk., D. of Saxe-Gotha; *d.* 1800.
Fras. Godolphin, 5th D. of Leeds; *d.* 1799.
Jno., 2nd E. of Chatham; *d.* 1835.
1793, June 14. Jas., 1st M. of Salisbury; *d.* 1823.
Jno., 10th E. of Westmorland; *d.* 1841.
Fredk., E. of Carlisle; *d.* 1825.
1794. Hy., 3rd D. of Buccleuch and 5th D. of Queensberry, May 28; *d.* 1812.
Pr. Wm. Fredk., aft. D. of Gloucester, July 16; *d.* 1834.
Wm. Hy., 3rd D. of Portland, July; *d.* 1809.

1797, June. Richd., E. Howe; *d.* 1799.
Jno. Jeffries, 2nd E., aft. 1st M. Camden; *d.* 1840.
Geo. Jno., 2nd E. Spencer; *d.* 1834.
1801. Jno., 3rd D. of Roxburghe, May 29; *d.* 1804.
1803, Nov. 25. Jno. Hy., 5th D. of Rutland; *d.* 1857.
Philip, E. of Hardwicke; *d.* 1834.
1805, Jan. 17. Hy. Chas., 6th D. of Beaufort; *d.* 1835.
Jno. Jas., 9th M. of Abercorn; *d.* 1818.
Geo. Augs., E. of Pembroke and Montgomery; *d.* 1827.
Geo., 8th E. of Winchelsea and 4th E. of Nottingham; *d.* 1826.
Philip, E. of Chesterfield; *d.* 1813.
1805. Geo., E. of Dartmouth, May 27; *d.* 1810.
1806. Jno., D. of Bedford; *d.* 1839.
Geo. Granville, 2nd M. of Stafford, aft. 1st D. of Sutherland, Mar. 22; *d.* 1833.
1807, July 18. Fras., M. of Hertford; *d.* 1822.
Wm., E. of Lonsdale; *d.* 1844.
1810. Richd. Colley, Marq. Wellesley, Mar. 3; *d.* 1842.
1812, Mar. 26. Chas., D. of Richmond and Lennox; *d.* 1819.
Jas., 3rd D. of Montrose; *d.* 1836.
1812. Fras., E. of Moira, aft. M. of Hastings, June 12; *d.* 1824.
Hy. Pelham, 4th D. of Newcastle, June 19; *d.* 1851.
1813. Arthur, M., aft. D. of Wellington, Mar. 4; *d.* 1852.
Alexander I., Emp. of Russia, July 13; *d.* 1825.
1814. Louis XVIII., K. of France, Apr. 21; *d.* 1824.
1814, June 9. Francis I., Emp. of Austria (form. Francis II., Emp. of Germany); *d.* 1835.
Fredk. William III., K. of Prussia; *d.* 1840.
Robt. Banks, 2nd E. of Liverpool; *d.* 1828.
1814. Sir Robt. Stewart, c.c. visc. Castlereagh, aft. 2nd M. of Londonderry, June 9; *d.* 1822.
Ferdinand VII., K. of Spain, Aug. 10; *d.* 1833.
Wm. Fredk., Pr. of Orange, aft. K. William I. of the Netherlands, Aug. 22; *d.* 1843.
1816. Pr. Leopold, &c., of Coburg, aft. K. of the Belgians, May 23; *d.* 1865.
1817. Hy., E. Bathurst, July 24; *d.* 1834.
1818. Hy. Wm., 1st M. of Anglesey, Feb. 19; *d.* 1854.
1819. Hugh, D. of Northumberland, Nov. 25; *d.* 1847.

GEORGE IV.

1820. Richd., 2nd M., aft. 1st D. of Buckingham, June 7; *d.* 1839.
1822, Feb. 13. Frederick VI., K. of Denmark; *d.* 1839.
John VI., K. of Portugal; *d.* 1826.
1822. Geo. Jas., M. of Cholmondeley, July 22; *d.* 1827.
Fras. Chas., M. of Hertford, Nov. 22; *d.* 1842.
1823. Thos., 2nd M. of Bath, July 16; *d.* 1837.
1825. Charles X., K. of France, June 7; *d.* 1836.
1826. Chas., 5th D. of Dorset, Jan. 30; *d.* 1843.
1827. Nichs. I., Emp. of Russia, Mar. 16; *d.* 1855.
1827, May 10. Geo. Wm. Fredk., 6th D. of Leeds; *d.* 1838.
Wm. Spencer, 6th D. of Devonshire; *d.* 1858.
Brownlow, 2nd M. of Exeter; *d.* 1867.
1829. Chas., D. of Richmond and Lennox, May 13; *d.* 1860.
Geo., E. of Ashburnham, June 22; *d.* 1830.

WILLIAM IV.

1830, July 26. Bernard, D. of Saxe-Meiningen; *d.* —.
Wm. I., K. of Wurtemberg; *d.* 1864.
1831. Chas., 2nd E. Grey, May 27; *d.* 1845.
Augs. Louis Wm. Max. Fredk., D. of Brunswick, June 20; *d.* 1884.
1834. Bernard Edwd., D. of Norfolk, Aug. 13; *d.* 1842.
Geo. Hy., 4th D. of Grafton, Dec. 20; *d.* 1844.
1835. Walter Fras., 5th D. of Buccleugh, and 7th D. of Queensberry, Feb. 23; *d.* 1884.
Pr. Geo. Fredk., &c., of Cumberland, Crown Pr. of Hanover, aft. D. of Cumberland and K. of Hanover, Aug. 15; *d.* 1878.
Pr. Geo. of Cambridge, aft. D. of Cambridge, Aug. 15.
1836, Feb. 5. Alexr., 10th D. of Hamilton and 7th D. of Brandon; *d.* 1852.
Hy., 3rd M. of Lansdowne; *d.* 1863.
1837. Geo., 6th E. of Carlisle, Mar. 17; *d.* 1848.
Edwd. Adolphus. 11th D. of Somerset, Apr. 19; *d.* 1855.

VICTORIA.

1837. Chas. Wm. Fredk. Emicon, Pr. of Leiningen, July 14; *d.* —.

1838. Ernest Anthy. Chas. Lewis, reigning D. of Saxe-Coburg and Gotha, July 16; *d.* 1844.

1839, Apr. 17. Wm. Hy., 1st D. of Cleveland; *d.* 1842.

Edwd. Smith, 13th E. of Derby; *d.* 1851.

1839. Fras. Albert Augs. Chas. Emmanuel, Pr. of Saxe-Coburg and Gotha, aft. consort of Q. Victoria, Dec. 16; *d.* 1861.

1841, Mar. 11. Geo. Granville, 2nd D. of Sutherland; *d.* 1861.

Robt., 2nd E. and 1st M. of Westminster; *d.* 1845.

1842. Fredk. William IV., K. of Prussia, Jan. 25; *d.* 1861.

1842, Apr. 11. Fredk. Augustus II., K. of Saxony; *d.* 1854.

Hy., 7th D. of Beaufort; *d.* 1853.

Richd. Plantgt. &c., 2nd D. of Buckingham and Chandos; *d.* 1861.

Jas. Brownlow Wm., 2nd M. of Salisbury; *d.* 1868.

Hy., 2nd D. of Cleveland; *d.* 1864.

1844. Louis Philippe, K. of the French, Oct. 11; *d.* 1850.

1844, Dec. 12. Ernest II., D. of Saxe-Cobourg and Gotha.

Thos. Philip, E. de Grey; *d.* 1859.

Jas., 2nd M. and 1st D. of Abercorn; *d.* 1885.

Chas., 2nd E. Talbot; *d.* 1849.

Edwd., 2nd E. of Powis; *d.* 1848.

1846, Jan. 19. Geo. Chas., 2nd M. of Camden; *d.* 1866.

Richd., M. of Hertford; *d.* 1870.

1847. Fras., 7th D. of Bedford, Mar. 26; *d.* 1861.

1848. Hy. Chas., D. of Norfolk, May 11; *d.* 1856.

1849, Mar. 23. Geo. Wm. Fredk., 4th E. of Clarendon; *d.* 1870.

Fredk., 4th E. Spencer; *d.* 1857.

1851. Constantine Hy., 1st M. of Normanby, Feb. 19; *d.* 1863.

Chas. Wm., 5th E. Fitzwilliam, Nov. 4; *d.* 1857.

1853, Jan. 19. Algernon, D. of Northumberland; *d.* 1865.

Chas. Wm., 3rd M. of Londonderry; *d.* 1854.

1855, Feb. 7. Geo. Wm. Fredk., 7th E. of Carlisle; *d.* 1864.

Fras., 1st E. of Ellesmere; *d.* 1857.

Geo., 4th E. of Aberdeen; *d.* 1860.

1855. Napoleon III., Emp. of the French, Apr. 18; *d.* 1873.

Victor Emanuel, K. of Sardinia, aft. K. of Italy, Dec. 5; *d.* 1878.

1856, July 12. Hugh, 2nd E. Fortescue; *d.* 1861.

Hy. John, visc. Palmerston; *d.* 1865.

1856. Abdul Medjid, Sultan of Turkey, Nov. 5; *d.* 1861.

1857, July 6. Granville Geo., 2nd E. Granville.

Richd., 2nd M. of Westminster; *d.* 1869.

1858. Fredk. Wm. Nichs. Chas., Cr. Pr. of Prussia, aft. Frederick III. Emp. of Germany and K. of Prussia, Jan. 28; *d.* 1888.

1858, Mar. 25. Arthur Richd., 2nd D. of Wellington; *d.* 1884.

Wm., 7th D. of Devonshire.

1858. Pedro V., K. of Portugal, May 27; *d.* 1861.

Albert Edwd., Pr. of Wales, Nov. 9.

1859, June 28. Dudley, 2nd E. of Harrowby; *d.* 1882.

Edwd. Geoffrey, 14th E. of Derby; *d.* 1869.

1860. Hy. Pelham, 5th D. of Newcastle, Dec. 17; *d.* 1864.

1861. William I., K. of Prussia, aft. emp. of Germany, Mar. 6; *d.* 1888.

1862, May 21. Chas. John, Earl Canning; *d.* 1862.

John, 1st E. Russell; *d.* 1878.

Edwd. Adolphus, D. of Somerset, *d.* 1885.

Anthy., E. of Shaftesbury; *d.* 1886.

Wm. Thos. Spencer, 6th E. Fitzwilliam.

1862, July 5. Pr. Fredk. Wm. Louis Chas. of Hesse, aft. Gr. D. Louis IV.

Fredk Wm., &c., Gr. D. of Mecklenburg-Strelitz.

1863, June 10. Hy. Geo., Earl Grey.

Pr. Alfd. Ernest Albert, aft. D. of Edinburgh.

1864, May 24. Geo. Granville Wm., 3rd D. of Sutherland.

Geo. Wm. Fredk., 2nd M. of Ailesbury; *d.* 1878.

1864. Hy., 4th M. of Lansdowne, Oct. 10; *d.* 1866.

1865. John Poyntz, 5th E. Spencer, Jan. 14.

Harry Geo., 4th D. of Cleveland, Apr. 10.

Christian IX., K. of Denmark, Apr. 25.

Louis, K. of Portugal, May 4.

Louis III., D. of Hesse, June 6; *d.* 1877.

Fras. Thos. De Grey, 7th E. Cowper, Aug. 5.

1866. Hy. Richd. Chas., 1st E. Cowley, Feb. 3; *d.* 1884.
Leopold II., K. of Belgians, Feb. 12.
Pr. Christian of Schleswig-Holstein, July 9.
1867, Feb. 6. Chas. Hy., 6th D. of Richmond and 1st D. of Gordon.
Chas. Cecil John, 6th D. of Rutland; *d.* 1888.
1867. Hy. Chas. Fitzroy, 8th D. of Beaufort, Mar. 19.
Pr. Arthur Wm. Patr. Albert, aft. D. of Connaught, May 31.
Fras. Jos., Emp. of Austria, July 25.
Alexander II., Emp. of Russia, July 28; *d.* 1881.
Abdul Aziz, Sultan of Turkey, Aug. 14; *d.* 1876.
1868. John Winston, D. of Marlborough, May 23; *d.* 1883.
1869. Pr. Leopold Geo. Duncan Albert, aft. D. of Albany, May 29; *d.* 1884.
1869, Dec. 11. Stratford, visc. Stratford de Redcliffe; *d.* 1880.
Geo. Fredk. Saml., E. de Grey and Ripon, aft. M. of Ripon.
1870. Hugh Lupus, 3rd M., aft. 1st D. of Westminster, Dec. 6.
1871. Pedro II., Emp. of Brazil, July 11.
1872. Thos., 2nd E. of Zetland, Dec. 26; *d.* 1873.
1873. Nasr-ul-Din, Shah of Persia, June 26.
Thos. Wm., E. of Leicester June 30.
1876. Geo., 1st K. of the Hellenes (Greece), July 12.
Pr. Fredk. Victor Albert of Prussia, aft. Empr. Wm. II. of Germany, Jan. 27.
1878. Humbert, K. of Italy, Mar. 2.
Pr. Ernest Augs. Wm. Adolphus Geo. Fredk. of Hanover, D. of Cumberland and Teviotdale, July 20.
Benjn., E. of Beaconsfield, July 22; *d.* 1881.
Robt. Arthur Talbot, M. of Salisbury, July 30.
1880. Fras. Chas. Hastings, 9th D. of Bedford, Dec. 1.
1881. Alexander III., Emp. of Russia, Apr. 2.
Oscar II., K. of Sweden and Norway, May 17.
Alfonso XII., K. of Spain, Oct. 24; *d.* 1885.
1882. Albert, K. of Saxony, Feb. 20.
William III., K. of the Netherlands, Apr. 26.
Augs. Chas. Lennox, 7th D. of Grafton, Feb. 3.
Pr. Albert Victor of Wales, Sept. 3.
1884, July 15. Geo. Douglas, D. of Argyle.
Edwd. Hy., 15th E. of Derby.
1884. Pr. Geo. Fredk. Ernest Albert of Wales, Aug. 4.
1885, July 9. John, E. of Kimberley.
Wm., M. of Northampton.
Wm. Philip, 4th E. of Sefton.
1855. Pr. Hy. Maurice of Battenberg, July 22.
1886, Feb. 22. Algernon Geo., D. of Northumberland.
Wm., M. of Abergavenny.
Hy., D. of Norfolk.
1887. Rudolph, Cr. Pr. of Austria, *d.* 1889.
1888. Chas. Stewart, 6th M. of Londonderry, inv. May 7.

OFFICERS OF THE GARTER.

Prelates.

The Bishops of Winchester in regular succession from Wm. de Edington, Edendon, or Edindon, who *d.* 1366.

See "Bishops of Winchester," *ante*, p. 470.

Chancellors.

1475. Richd. Beaucham, bp. of Salisbury, Oct. 10; *d.* 1842.
* * Lionel Wydville, or Woodville, bp. of Salisbury; *d.* 1484.
* * (?) Thos. Langton, bp. of Salisbury, tr. to Winchester, 1493.
1491. John Morgan, or Young, dean of Windsor; bp. of St. Davids, 1496; *d.* 1504.
* * (?) John Blyth, bp. of Salisbury; *d.* 1499.
* * Chas, E. of Worcester. ld. chambn.; chanc. in. Aug. 1523; *d.* 1526.
1553. Sir Wm. Cecil, sec. st., Mar.
Sir Wm. Petre, sec. st., Sept. 27; *d.* 1572.
1572. Sir Thos. Smith, sec. st., Apr. 25; *d.* 1577.
1578. Sir Fras. Walsingham, sec. st., Apr. 22; res. 1588.
1588. Sir Amyas Paulet, Apr. 22; *d.* Sept. 1588.

1589. Sir John Woolley, Apr. 23; *d.* 1596.
1596. Sir Edwd. Dyer, Apr. 23; *d.* 1608.
1608. Sir John Herbert, sec. st.; *d.* 1617.
1623. Sir Geo. More (? 1610); res. 1628.
1628. Sir Fras. Crane, Apr. 23; *d.* 1636.
1636. Sir Thos. Roe, Dec. 5; *d.* abt. 1644.
1638. Sir Jas. Palmer, dep. chanc., May 4; chanc. Mar. 2, 1645: *d.* 1657.
1660. Sir Hy. de Vie, bt., Sept.; *d.* 1671.
1661. Sir Richd. Fanshaw, dep. chanc., Jan. 14.
1671. Seth Ward, bp. Salisbury, Nov. 25, and his successors down to bp. Burgess, who *d.* Feb. 19, 1837.

See "Bishops of Salisbury," *ante*, p. 466.

1837. Hon. Richd. Bagot, bp. of Oxford, Feb. 25, and his successors.

See "Bishops of Oxford," *ante*, p. 456.

Registrars.

* * John Covingham, can. Windsor in 1414; *d.* 1445.
1446. John Depeden, can. Windsor, May.
1460. Jas. or Thos. Goldwell, can. Windsor; bp. Norwich, 1472.
1481. Thos. Danett, can. Windsor.
* * Oliver King, can. Windsor in 1488; bp. Salisbury, 1491.
* * Richd. Nix, or Nikks, can. Windsor in 1496; bp. Norwich, 1501.
* * Christr. Urswick, can. Windsor in 1490, and dean in 1495; *d.* 1505.
* * Thos. Rowthall, dean of Salisbury; bp. Durham, 1508.
1510. Thos. Wolsey, dean of Lincoln, &c.
* * Wm. Atwater, can. Windsor in 1499; bp. Lincoln, 1514.
* * Nichs. West, dean of Windsor in 1510; bp. Ely, 1515.
* * John Vosey, dean of Windsor in 1515; bp. Exeter, 1519.
* * Richd. Sydnor, can. Windsor in 1518; *d.* 1534.
* * Richd. Sampson, dean of Windsor in 1523; bp. Chichester, 1536.
1534. Robt. Aldridge, can. Windsor, May 27; bp. Carlisle, 1537.
1555. Owen Oglethorpe, dean of Windsor, May 1, and his successors.

See "Deans of Windsor," *ante*, p. 474.

Kings of Arms.

See "Garter Kings of Arms," *ante*, p. 327.

THE ORDER OF THE THISTLE.

The Thistle is a Scotch Order. Like the Garter, the date of its institution is somewhat obscure. It is said by some to have been originally formed as far back as 787, and by others to have been founded in 1500, and revived in 1540. King James VII. of Scotland and II. of England, by warrant dated May 29, 1687, ordered Letters Patent to be made out for "reviving and restoring the Order of the Thistle to its full glory, lustre, and magnificency." At the same time a set of statutes and orders was passed for regulating the Order, and it is considered by Sir Harris Nicolas and some other writers that until this date the Order as an organized fraternity did not exist.

The Order remained in abeyance during the reign of William and Mary, but Queen Anne again revived it, by statutes and orders dated Dec. 31, 1703. These were subsequently modified by statutes of Geo. III. dated Feb. 17, 1715, and of Geo. IV. dated May 8, 1827, by the last of which the number of knights of the Order was extended from twelve to sixteen. Extra knights are occasionally admitted by special statute.

The officers of the Order are:

DEAN.
SECRETARY.
KING AT ARMS.
USHER.

The Order is styled—

THE MOST ANCIENT AND MOST NOBLE ORDER OF THE THISTLE.

KNIGHTS OF THE THISTLE.
(K.T.)

From the foundation or restoration of the Order by James II. in 1687.

JAMES II.

1687, June 6. Geo., D. of Gordon; *d.* Dec. 1716.
John, M. of Athole; *d.* May 1703.
Jas., E. of Arran, aft. D. of Hamilton; *d.* 1712.
Alexr., E. of Moray; *d.* Nov. 1700.
Jas., E. of Perth; attainted.
Kenneth, E. of Seaforth; attainted.
Geo., E. of Dumbarton.
John, E. of Melfort; attainted.

ANNE.

1704. John, D. of Argyll, Feb. 4; quitted for the Garter, 1710.
1704, Feb. 7. John, D. of Athole; *d.* Nov. 1724.
Wm., M. of Annandale; *d.* Jan. 1721.
Jas., E. of Dalkeith; *d.* Mar. 1705.
Chas., E. of Moray; *d.* Oct. 1735.
Geo., E. of Orkney; *d.* Jan. 1737.
Jas., E. of Findlater and Seafield; *d.* Aug. 1730.
1705. Oct. 30. Wm., M. of Lothian; *d.* Feb. 1722.
Chas., E. of Orrery; *d.* Aug. 1731.
1706, Aug. 10. John, E. of Marr; attainted 1715.
Hugh, E. of Loudoun; *d.* Nov. 1731.
1710. John, E. of Stair, Mar. 25; *d.* May 1747.
1713. David, E. of Portmore, Jan. 17; *d.* Jan. 1730.

GEORGE I.

1716, June 22. Wm., E. of Cadogan; *d.* July 1726.
John, E. of Sunderland; *d.* June 1733.
1717. Thos., E. of Haddington, Mar. 1; *d.* Nov. 1735.
1721. Chas., E. of Tankerville, Mar. 28; *d.* May 1722.
1725, Mar. 2. Wm., E. of Essex; quitted for the Garter, 1738.
Francis, E. of Dalkeith, aft. D. of Buccleuch; *d.* Apr. 1751.
1725, Mar. 2. Alex., E. of Marchmont; *d.* Feb. 1740.
1726. Jas., D. of Hamilton, Sept. 23; *d.* Mar. 1743.

GEORGE II.

1730. Chas., E. of Tankerville, May 16; *d.* Mar. 1753.
1732. Chas., E. of Portmore, Jan. 2; *d.* July 1785.
1734. Jas., D. of Athole, Feb. 11; *d.* Jan. 1764.
Wm., M. of Lothian; *d.* July 1767.
1738, July 10. Jas., E. of Morton; *d.* Oct. 1768.
Chas., E. of Hopetoun; *d.* Feb. 1742.
John, E. of Bute; quitted for the Garter, 1762.
1739. Augs., E. of Berkeley, June 7; *d.* Jan. 1755.
1741. Jas., E. of Moray, Feb. 23; *d.* July 1767.
1742. John, E. of Hyndford, June 22; *d.* July 1767.
1743. Lionel, E. of Dysart, Mar. 29; *d.* Mar. 1770.
1747. Cosmo Geo., D. of Gordon, Feb. 10; *d.* Feb. 1747.
1752. John, E. of Dumfries and Stair, Mar. 11; *d.* July 1768.
1753, Mar. 29. John, E. of Rothes; *d.* Dec. 1767.
Fras., E. Brooke and E. of Warwick; *d.* July 1773.
1755. Jas., D. of Hamilton and Brandon, Mar. 18; *d.* Jan. 1758.

GEORGE III.

1763, Apr. 13. Wm., E. of March, aft. D. of Queensberry; *d.* Dec. 1810.
Chas., ld. Cathcart; *d.* Aug. 1766.
1765. John, D. of Argyll, Aug. 7; *d.* Nov. 1770.
1767, Dec. 23. Hy., D. of Buccleuch and Queensberry; quitted for the Garter, 1794.
John, D. of Athole; *d.* Nov. 1774.
Fredk., E. of Carlisle; quitted for the Garter, 1793.

1768. Wm., M. of Lothian, Oct. 26; *d.* Apr. 1775.

1768, Nov. 23. David, visc. Stormont, aft. E. of Mansfield; *d.* Sept. 1796.

John, D. of Roxburghe; *d.* Mar. 1804.

1770. Pr. Wm. Hy., aft. D. of Clarence and Wm. IV., Apr. 5; *d.* 1837.

1771. Neil, E. of Rosebery, Mar. 4; *d.* Mar. 1814.

1773. Robt., E. of Northington, Aug. 18; *d.* July 1786.

1775. Alexr., D. of Gordon, Jan. 11; *d.* June 1827.

John, E. of Galloway, Nov. 1; *d.* Nov. 1806.

1776, Oct. 11. Wm. John, M. of Lothian; *d.* Jan. 1815.

Douglas, D. of Hamilton and Brandon; *d.* Aug. 1799.

Thos., E. of Aylesbury; *d.* Apr. 1814.

Jas., D. of Montrose; quitted for the Garter, 1812.

John, Earl Poulett; *d.* Jan. 1819.

Geo., E. of Morton; *d.* July 1827.

John, D. of Athole; *d.* Sept. 1830.

1805. Wm. Schaw, Earl Cathcart, Nov. 23; *d.* June 1843.

1808. Geo., E. of Aberdeen, Mar.; *d.* Dec. 1860.

1812, May 22. Chas. Wm. Hy., D. of Buccleuch and Queensberry; *d.* Apr. 1819.

Hugh, E. of Eglinton; *d.* Dec. 1819.

1814, May 23. Hy., E. of Abergavenny; *d.* Mar. 1843.

Geo., E. of Galloway; *d.* Mar. 1834.

1815. Thos., ld. Erskine, Feb. 23; *d.* Nov. 1823.

1819. Chas. Bruce, 2nd E., aft. 1st M. of Ailesbury, May 20; *d.* Jan. 1856.

George IV.

1820. Wm., M. of Lothian, Apr. 26; *d.* Apr. 1824.

Geo., 8th M. of Tweeddale, May 22; *d.* Oct. 1876.

1821, July 17. Chas., M. of Queensberry; *d.* Dec. 1837.

Archd., E. of Cassilis, aft. M. of Ailsa; *d.* Sept., 1846.

Jas., E. of Lauderdale; *d.* Sept. 1839.

Robt., visc. Melville; *d.* June 1851.

1827, May 10. Geo., E. of Aboyne, M. of Huntley, aft. D. of Gordon; *d.* May 1836.

Hy. Richd., E. Brooke and E. of Warwick; *d.* Aug. 1853.

1827, Sept. 3. Jas., E. of Fife; *d.* Mar. 1857.

Fras., E. of Moray; *d.* Jan. 1848.

William IV.

1830. Augs. Fredk., D. of Sussex, July 19; *d.* Apr. 1843.

Walter Fras., D. of Buccleuch and Queensberry, Nov. 5; quitted for the Garter, 1835.

1834. Wm. Geo., E. of Erroll, Apr. 16; *d.* Apr. 1846.

1835. David Wm., E. of Mansfield, Mar. 4; *d.* Feb. 1840.

Victoria.

1838. John, 2nd M. of Breadalbane, Mar. 21; *d.* Nov. 1862.

1840, Mar. 18. Jas. Hy. Robert, 6th D. of Roxburghe; *d.* Apr. 1879.

Archd. John, E. of Rosebery; *d.* Mar. 1868.

1842. Pr. Albert, consort of Her Majesty; decl. a knt. by spec. stat. Jan. 17; *d.* Dec. 1861.

1843, June 13. John, M. of Bute; *d.* Mar. 1848.

Wm. David, 4th E. of Mansfield.

1845. Jas., 4th D. of Montrose, Mar. 12; *d.* Dec. 1874.

1847, July 12. John Hamilton, 8th E. of Stair; *d.* Jan. 1853.

Jas., 8th E. of Elgin and 12th E. of Elgin and Kincardine; *d.* Nov. 1863.

1848, May 12. Jas. Andr., 10th E., aft. 1st M., of Dalhousie; *d.* Dec. 1860.

Robt. Dundas, 1st E. of Camperdown; *d.* Dec. 1859.

1852. Alexr. Geo., 16th ld. Saltoun, Mar. 25; *d.* Aug. 1853.

1853. Archd. Wm., 13th E. of Eglinton, June 18; *d.* Oct. 1861.

Thos., 9th E. of Haddington, Oct. 25; *d.* Dec. 1858.

1853, Oct. 28. Geo. Aug. Fredk. John, 6th D. of Athole; *d.* Jan. 1864.

Fox, ld. Panmure, aft. E. of Dalhousie; *d.* July 1874.

1856. Geo. Douglas, D. of Argyll, May 2.

1857. Geo. Wm. Fox, 9th ld. Kinnaird, July 6; *d.* Jan. 1878.

1859. Archd., 2nd M. of Ailsa, Mar. 7; *d.* Mar. 1870.

1860. Jas., 5th E. of Fife, Mar. 2; *d.* Aug. 1879.

1861, July 1. Thos., 2nd E. of Zetland; *d.* May 1873.
Robt. Montgomerie, 8th ld. Belhaven and Stenton; *d.* Dec. 1868.
1862. David Graham Drummond, 9th E. of Airlie, Feb.; *d.* Sept. 1881.
1864. Fras., 9th ld. Napier and 1st ld. Ettrick, June.
Thos. Alexr., ld. Lovat; *d.* June 1875.
1865. John Hamilton, 10th E. of Stair.
Pr. Alfred Ernest Albert, aft. D. of Edinburgh.
1867. Albert Edwd., Pr. of Wales.
1868. John Jas. Hugh Hy., 7th D. of Athole.
1869. Pr. Arth. Wm. Patr. Albert, aft. D. of Connaught.
Jas., E. of Southesk.
1870. Wm. Hugh, 3rd E. of Minto.
1871. Pr. Leopold Geo. Duncan Albert, aft. D. of Albany; *d.* Mar. 1884.
John Douglas Sutherland Campbell, c.c. M. of Lorne.
1874. Chas. John, 8th ld. Colville of Culross.
1875. John Patr., 3rd M. of Bute.
Wm. Hy. Walter Scott, c.c. E. of Dalkeith, aft. 6th D. of Buccleuch and 8th D. of Queensberry.
1876. Sir Wm. Stirling-Maxwell, bt.; *d.* Jan. 1878.
1878. Wm. Alex. Louis Stephen, 12th D. of Hamilton and 9th D. of Brandon.
Schomberg Hy., 9th M. of Lothian.
1879. John Chas., 7th E. of Seafield; *d.* Feb. 1881.
Douglas Beresford Malise Ronald, 5th D. of Montrose.
1881. Alex. Wm. Geo., 6th E. of Fife.
John Wm., 13th E. of Dalhousie; *d.* Nov. 1887.
1882. Geo. Wm. Fredk. Chas., D. of Cambridge.
1887. Alan Plantagenet, 10th E. of Galloway, Dec. 16, **G.**

OFFICERS OF THE THISTLE.

Deans.

(*Deans of Chapel Royal, Scotland.*)

1763. John Jardine.
1767. Robt. Hamilton.
1787. Geo. Hill, Apr. 9.
1791. Archd. Davison.
1803. Wm. Laurence Brown, Oct. 4, **G.**
1830. Geo. Cook, June 19, **G.**
1845. Wm. Muir, June 10.
1869. Norman Macleod, July 26, **G.**
1872. John Macleod, Aug. 10, **G.**
1882. John Tulloch, June 19, **G.**
1886. Jas. Cameron Lees.

Secretaries.

1617. Sir Andr. Forrester, May 31; res.
1704. Sir David Nairn, Jan. 29; *d.* Aug. 2, 1734.
1737. Geo. Drummond, Jan. 28.
1765. Lt.-gen. sir Hy. Erskine, bt., Apr. 10; *d.* Aug. 9, 1765.
Geo. Dempster, Aug. 21; *d.* Feb. 13, 1818.
1818. Wm. Bertram, *d.* 1819.
1819. Lt.-col. ld. Robt. Kerr, Aug. 24, **G.**
1843. Sir John Stewart Richardson, bt., Aug. 2, **G.**
1875. Jas. Thos. Stewart Richardson, aft. bt., Nov. 11, **G.**

Kings of Arms.

See "Lyon Kings of Arms," *ante*, p. 513.

THE ORDER OF ST. PATRICK.

This Order is of comparatively recent date, having been instituted by King Geo. III. by warrant dated Feb. 5, 1783, the statutes being signed on Feb. 28, and the first investiture being held on Mar. 11, 1783.

As originally constituted the Order consisted of the Sovereign, the grand master (the lord-lieutenant for the time being), and fifteen knights. The number of knights was temporarily increased by Geo. IV. and Wm. IV. at their coronations, and, in Jan. 1833, was permanently fixed at twenty-two.

The officers of the Order are or were:

PRELATE.
CHANCELLOR.
REGISTRAR.
SECRETARY.
GENEALOGIST (now discontinued).
KING OF ARMS.
USHER.

The Order is styled—

THE MOST ILLUSTRIOUS ORDER OF ST. PATRICK.

GRAND MASTERS OF THE ORDER OF ST. PATRICK.

1783, Feb. 5. Geo. Grenville, 3rd E. Temple, aft. M. of Rockingham; ld. lieut. of Ireland, and his successors.

See "Lord Lieutenants of Ireland," *ante*, p. 557.

KNIGHTS OF ST. PATRICK.

(K.P.)

GEORGE III.

THE ORIGINAL KNIGHTS, NOM. FEB. 5, 1783.

Pr. Edwd., aft. D. of Kent; *d.* Jan. 1820.
Wm. Robt., D. of Leinster; *d.* Oct. 1804.
Hy. Smyth, E., aft. M. of Clanricarde; *d.* Dec. 1797.
Randall Wm., E. of Antrim; *d.* July 1791.
Thos., E. of Westmeath; *d.* Sept. 1792.
Murrough, E. of Inchiquin, aft. M. of Thomond; *d.* Feb. 1808.
Chas., E., aft. M. of Drogheda; *d.* Dec. 1822.
Geo. de la Poer, E. of Tyrone, aft. 1st M. of Waterford; *d.* Dec. 1800.
Richd., E. of Shannon; *d.* May 1807.
Jas., E. of Clanbrassil; *d.* Feb. 1798.
Richd. Colley, E. of Mornington, aft. M. Wellesley; quitted for the Garter, 1810; *d.* Sept. 1842.
Arthr. Saunders, E. of Arran; *d.* Oct. 1809.
Jas., E. of Courtoun; *d.* Mar. 1810.
Jas., E. of Charlemont; *d.* Aug. 1799.
Thos., E. of Bective; *d.* Feb. 1795.
Hy., E. of Ely, nom.; but *d.* May 1783, without having been invested.

SUBSEQUENT CREATIONS.

1784. John Joshua, E. of Carysfort, Feb. 5; *d.* Apr. 1828.
1794. Chas., visc. Loftus, E., aft. M. of Ely, Dec. 12; *d.* Mar. 1806.
1795. Wm. Hy., E. of Clermont, Mar. 30; *d.* Sept. 1806.
1798, Mar. 19. Walter, E. of Ormond and Ossory; *d.* Aug. 1820.
Chas., visc. Dillon; *d.* Nov. 1813.
1800. John Denis, E. of Altamont, aft. M. of Sligo, Aug. 11; *d.* Jan. 1809.
1801. Hy., Marq. Conyngham, Jan. 22; *d.* Dec. 1832.
1806. Hy. de la Poer, 2nd M. of Waterford, Mar. 14; *d.* July 1826.
Thos., M. of Headfort, May 15; *d.* Oct. 1829.
Robt., E. of Roden, Nov. 13; *d.* June 1820.
1807. John, M. of Ely, Nov. 3; *d.* 1845.
1808. Hy., E. of Shannon, Apr. 5; *d.* Apr. 1842.
1809. Chas. Hy., Earl O'Neill, Feb. 13; *d.* Mar. 1841.
Wm., M. of Thomond, Nov. 11; *d.* Aug. 1846.
1810. Howe Peter, M. of Sligo, Mar. 24; *d.* Jan. 1845.

1810. John Willoughby, E. of Enniskillen, Apr. 27; *d.* Mar. 1840.
1813. Thos., E. of Longford, Dec. 17; *d.* May 1835.
1821, Aug. 20. Ernest Augs., D. of Cumberland, aft. K. of Hanover; *d.* Nov. 1851.
Geo. Augs., M. of Donegal; *d.* Oct. 1844.
1821. Dupré, E. of Caledon, Aug. 28; *d.* Apr. 1839.
Chas. Chetwynd, Earl Talbot, July; quitted for the Garter, 1844.
Jas., M. of Ormond, July; *d.* May 1838.
1821, July. John Chambre, E. of Meath; *d.* Mar. 1851.
Arth. Jas., E. of Fingal; *d.* July 1836.
Jas. Geo., E. of Courtown; *d.* June 1835.
Robt., 3rd E. of Roden; *d.* Mar. 1870.
1831, Oct. 7. Arth., 3rd M. of Downshire; *d.* Apr. 1845.
Ulick John, 1st M. of Clanricarde; *d.* Apr. 1874.
Fras. Wm., E. of Charlemont; *d.* Dec. 1863.
Fras. Jas., E. of Landaff; *d.* Mar. 1833.
1833. Fras. Nathl., 2nd Marq. Conyngham, Mar. 27; *d.* July 1876.
1834, Apr. 8. Nathl., 2nd E. of Leitrim; *d.* Dec. 1854.
John, 3rd E. of Donoughmore; *d.* Sept. 1851.
1835, July 22. Edmd., 8th E. of Cork and Orrery; *d.* June 1856.
Thos., 3rd E. of Howth; *d.* Feb. 1874.
1837. Thos. Anthy., 3rd visc. Southwell, Sept. 12; *d.* Feb. 1860.
1839. Thos., 2nd M. of Headfort, Apr. 15; *d.* Dec. 1870.
Wm., 2nd E. of Listowel, Apr. 29; *d.* Feb. 1856.
1841. Jos., 4th E. of Milltown, Mar. 13; *d.* Jan. 1866.
Philip Yorke, 4th E. of Arran, May 6; *d.* 1844.
1842. Wm., 4th E. of Wicklow, Nov. 9; *d.* Mar. 1869.
Pr. Albert, consort of Q. Victoria, by spec. stat. dated Jan. 25; *d.* Dec. 1861.
1845, Jan. 4. Wm., 3rd E. of Rosse; *d.* Oct. 1867.
Hy., de la Poer, 3rd M. of Waterford; *d.* Nov. 1866.
1845, Sept. 17. John, E. of Clare; *d.* —.
John, 2nd M. of Ormond; *d.* Sept. 1854.
1845. Hy., 7th ld. Farnham, Nov. 12; *d.* Aug. 1868.
1846. Arth. Jas., 9th E. of Fingal, Oct. 12; *d.* Apr. 1869.
1851. John Skeffington, visc. Massereene and Ferrard, July; *d.* Apr. 1863.
Geo. Wm. Fredk. Chas., D. of Cambridge.
1855. Richd., ld., aft. E. Dartrey.
Fredk. Wm. Robt., 4th M. of Londonderry; *d.* Nov. 1872.
1857. Geo. Arth. Hastings, 7th E. of Granard.
Geo. Hamilton, 3rd M. of Donegall; *d.* Oct. 1883.
1860. Richd. Edmd. St. Lawrence, 9th E. of Cork and Orrery.
1863. Fredk. Temple, ld., aft. E. Dufferin and M. of Dufferin and Ava.
Chas., 2nd ld. Lurgan; *d.* Jan. 1882.
1865. Jas. Molyneux, 3rd E. of Charlemont.
Edwin Richd., 3rd E. of Dunraven; *d.* Oct. 1871.
1868. Hy. Fras. Seymour, 3rd M. of Drogheda, Feb. 7.
Albert Edw., Pr. of Wales, Apr. 18.
1868, Nov. 17. Jno. Hy. De la Poer, 5th M. of Waterford.
John, 3rd E. of Erne, Nov. 17; *d.* 1885.
1869. Richd. Southwell, 6th E. of Mayo; *d.* Feb. 1872.
Pr. Arth. Wm. Patr. Albert, aft. D. of Connaught, Apr. 2, **G.**
1869, June 2. Archd. Brabazon Sparrow, 4th E. of Gosford.
Granville Leveson, 4th E. of Carysfort; *d.* May 1872.
1871, Aug. 2. Mervyn, 7th visc. Powerscourt.
Thos. Arth. Jos., 4th visc. Southwell; *d.* Apr. 1878.
1872, Feb. 20. Robt. Shapland, 2nd ld. Carew; *d.* Sept. 1881.
Wm., 3rd E. of Listowel.
1872. Val. Aug., 4th E. of Kenmare, June 3.
1874, Aug. 31. Wm., 5th E. of Carysfort.
Geo. Hy. Robt. Chas. Wm., 5th M. of Londonderry; *d.* 1884.
1876. Windham Thos., 4th E. of Dunraven, May 13.
1877. Wm. Drogo, 7th D. of Manchester.
1879. Hy. Jno. Reuben, 3rd E. of Portarlington, Feb. 10.
1880. Alfred Ernest Albert, D. of Edinburgh, May 14, **G.**

1881. Thos., 1st ld. O'Hagan, Jan. 17; *d.* Feb. 1885.
1882. Chichester, Saml., ld. Carlingford, aft. ld. Clermont; Apr. 11.
1884. Wm. Ulick Tristram, 4th E. of Howth, May 8.
1885. Luke, 2nd ld. Annaly, Feb. 9; *d.* 1888.
1885. Thos. Spring, 2nd ld. Monteagle, Feb. 9.
1885, Garnet Joseph, visc. Wolseley.
Nov. 28. Thos. 3rd M. of Headfort.
1887. Pr. Albert Victor of Wales, June 28
1888. Jas. Edw. Wm. Theobald, 3rd M of Ormonde, Apr. 26.
1889. Jno. Hy., 4th E. of Erne, Apr.

OFFICERS OF ST. PATRICK.

Prelates.

1783, Mar. 11. Richd., ld. Rokeby, abp. of Armagh, and his successors.

See "Archbishops of Armagh," *ante*, p. 595.

Chancellors.

1783, Mar. 11. Robt. Fowler, abp. of Dublin, and his successors down to abp. Trench. After his resignation in 1884 the office was transferred to the Chief Secretary for Ireland.

See "Archbishops of Dublin," *ante*, pp. 616–7, and "Chief Secretaries for Ireland," *ante*, p. 563.

Registrars.

1783, Mar. 11. Wm. Cradock, dean of St. Patrick's, and his successors.

See "Deans of St. Patrick," *ante*, p. 618.

Secretaries.

1783. Geo. Fredk. Nugent, c.c. visc. Delvin, aft. 7th E. of Westmeath, Mar. 11; res. Sept. 1791.
1793. Sir Richd. St. George, bt., inst. Feb. 15; res.
* * Sir Fredk. Jno. Falkiner, bt.; *d.* 1815.
1828. M.-gen. Geo. Jno. Forbes, c.c. visc. Forbes; inv. Mar. 17; *d.* Nov. 13, 1836.
1837. Hon. Robt. Edwd. Boyle; inv. Sept. 15; *d.* 1856.
1853. Lowry Vesey Townley Balfour.
1878. Gustavus Wm. Lambart.
1887. Gustavus Fras. Wm. Lambart, Jan. 24.

Genealogists.

1783. Chas. Hy. Coote, aft. ld. Castlecoote, inv. Mar. 11; res.
1804. Sir Stewart Bruce, bt.; inv. Dec. 18; *d.* Mar. 1841.
1841. Sir Wm. Edwd. Leeson; inv. May 6; *d.* 1885; when the office was discontinued.

Kings of Arms.

1783. Feb. 28. Wm. Hawkins (No. 2), aft. sir W., Ulster K. of Arms, and his successors.

See "Ulster Kings of Arms," ante, p. 572.

THE ORDER OF THE BATH.

This Order is of very ancient origin. On the coronation of Hen. IV. "Knights of the Bath" were undoubtedly created *eo nomine*, and this year is frequently treated as being that of the foundation of the Order. It is, however, certain that the ceremonies of watching and *bathing* as a preparation for knighthood are of much more ancient origin, and were practised both in this country and in Germany from very early times. Sir Harris Nicolas begins his list in the reign of King John, but adds that it cannot be treated as accurate or complete until about the reign of Hen. VII.

From the reign of Hen. IV. to that of Chas. I. it was customary on the coronation of the sovereign or his queen, the creation of a prince of Wales, and other occasions of exceptional rejoicing, to create a number of Knights of the Bath. After the coronation of Chas. I., this practice was discontinued, and the Order remained in abeyance until it was revived and remodelled by Geo. I., who, by Statute dated May 18, 1725, decreed that the Order should consist of the Sovereign, a great master, and thirty-six companions.

In 1815 the Order was again remodelled and mnch enlarged, principally with the view of rewarding the services of the numerous military and naval officers engaged in the long war then terminating.

By Statute dated Jan. 2, 1815, the Order was made to consist of three Classes:—

I.—Knights Grand Cross—Not exceeding in number 72, exclusive of the Sovereign and princes of the blood Royal. Of these 72 a number not exceeding 12 might be appointed for civil services. All the then existing Knights of the Bath were to become Knights Grand Cross.

II.—Knights Commanders—Not at first to exceed in number 180, exclusive of foreign officers to the number of 10, but with power to increase the number in the event of future wars, &c.

III.—Companions—Number not limited.

As remodelled, the Bath remained a reward exclusively for military or naval services, except the 10 Civil Knights Grand Cross; but by Statute dated April 1, 1847, the Knights Commanders and the Companions were divided into two divisions, military and civil, and the numbers fixed as under:—

I.—Knights Grand Cross ...	Military	50	...	Civil	25
II.—Knights Commanders ...	„	123	...	„	80
III.—Companions	„	690	...	„	250

These numbers are exclusive of the Royal family, distinguished foreigners, and foreign officers. Power was also reserved to increase the number on special occasions.

The officers of the Order are or were:—

Great Master.
(Now filled by the Sovereign.)
Dean.
King of Arms.

Genealogist.
(Discontinued.)
Usher.

Registrar.
Secretary.
(Now united.)

The Order is styled

The Most Honorable Order of the Bath.

MEMBERS OF THE ORDER OF THE BATH.

GREAT MASTER.

1725. John, 2nd D. of Montagu, May 18; *d.* July 5, 1749.

ACTING GREAT MASTERS.

* * Pr. Fredk., aft. D. of York and Albany, 2nd son of Geo. III.; *d.* Jan 5, 1827.
1827. Wm. Hy., D. of Clarence, aft. Wm. IV.
1837. Aug. Fredk., D. of Sussex, uncle of Q. Victoria, Dec. 16; *d.* Apr. 21, 1843.

The Sovereign is now considered the Great Master of the Order.

KNIGHTS COMPANIONS OF THE BATH.

(K.B.)

From 1204 to 1815.

JOHN.

1204. Thos. Esturmy, July 17.
Theod. le Tyes, Nov. 5.

HENRY III.

1249. Stephen de Salinis, July,
John de Simnevil, Dec. 25.
1252. Alexr. III., K. of Scotland, and 20 others, Dec. 25.
1254-5. Matth. Hanybal.

EDWARD I.

1302-3. Peter de la Foix.
John de Horne.
Robt. de Ufford.
John de Felton.
Richd. de ———.
John de Dagworth.
Richd. de Stratton.
Jno. de Cormailles.
Wm. de Botetourt.
John de Berkeley.
John Giffard.
Philip de Neville.
1304-5. Pain de Tibelot.
Geo. de Thorpe.
Jno. Douvedale.
Jno. de Neville.
1304-5. Thos. de Latimer.
Richd. Grey.
Peter Skerk.
John de Waterville.
John le Strange.
Hugh de Crofte.
Barth. Dynevil.
1306, May 22. Edw. Pr. of Wales, aft. Edw. II
John de Warren.
John de Arundell.
Thos. de Greyley.
1306, May 22. Thos. de Vere, aft. E. of Oxford.
Thos. Bardolf.
and numerous others.

EDWARD II.

1316. Richd. de Rodney, July 3.
1322 Hy. Percy, Sept. 10.
1323. John de la Haye, June 1.
Wm. de Dounton.
Wm. Waykam.
Hy. Tilly.
Hy. Longchamp.
Raymond Durant.
1324. Hugh de Poyntz, Aug. 10.
1324, Aug. 13. Peter de Bexstede.
Richd. Pyke.
Thos. de Marlebergh.
1324. Peter de la Horse, Oct. 24.
Hugh de Plessis, Oct. 31.
1325. Hugh de Neville, Apr. 2.
1326. Jas. Botiller, Mar. 31.
1326, Apr. 19. Wm. de Montacute.
Eubulo le Strange.
Roger de Bourne.
1326, Apr. 19. Roger Only.
Matth. Fitzherbert.
Jno. de Gras.
Thos. West.
Ryce ap Griffith.
Thos. de Weston.
Nichs. de Cantelon.
Thos. de Gonshull.
Hy. de Harnhall.
Adam de Moleston.
Walter de Fauconberge.
Wm. de Albemarle.
John de Kirketon.
Hy. le Vavasour.
Roger Deyncourt.
Wm. Peverell.
1327, Jan. 20. John de Bohun.
Edmund de Mortimer.
Roger de Mortimer.

1327. Geoffry de Mortimer.
Jan. 20. Gerard de la Bret.
Hugh de Courtenay.
Ralph de Wylinton.
Ralph Daubeney.
John de Willoughby.
Edwd. Stradling.
Ralph de Stafford, aft. ld. and E. of Stafford.
John de Moeles.
Wm. de Percy.
Gerard de Lisle.
Peter Breton.
Roger le Strange.
Ernomville de Poitiers.
John de Neville.
Wm. de Willoughby.

1327. John de Ralee.
Jan. 20. Ralph de Bloyon.
Odo Botetourt.
Wm. Daubeney.
Robt. Brente.
John de Chernstone.
John de Sutton.
Alexr. de Cobledyl.
Sayer de Rocheford.
Wm. Cheyney.
Regd. de la Mare.
Robt. de Brens.
Simon FitzRalph.
Hugh Abetot.
John de Rous.
Wm. de Evereux.
John de Hotham.

EDWARD III

1327. The King, Jan. 31.
1329, Jno. de Cambridge (just. itin.).
Oct. 22. Edwd. le Blount.
Peter de Thorntone.
Richd. de Bajocis.
Banco de Lere.
1330. Thos. de Bradeston.
Edmd. de Cornwall.
Wm. de Pomeroy.
1331. Walter de Manny.
1332. Robt. de Scoresburgh (just.itin.).
Wm. de Denum (bar. ex.).
Rd. de Aldeburgh (just. C.P.).
Jno. de Shardelowe (just. C.P.).

1332. Thos. Bacon (just. C.P.).
1333. Jno de Shordich (bar. ex.).
Wm. de Shareshull (just. C.P.).
Nathl. de Bath.
Simon FitzRichard.
Robt. de Scardeburgh (just. C.P and K.B.)
Jno. Petit.
Nichs. Giffard.
1347, Maurice FitzThomas.
Dec. 25. Philip de Staunton.
Thos. de Fencotes (just. C.P.).
Jno. Mowbray (just. C.P.).
Wm. de Skipwith (just. C.P.).

RICHARD II.

1385, Jno. Holt (just. C.P.).
Dec. 25. Wm. Burgh (just. C.P.).
1389. Geoff. de la Vale, Feb. 28.
1389. Walter de Clopton (ch.just.K.B.).
Apr. 23. Robt. de Charleton (ch.just.C.P.).
1390, Roger, 4th E. of March.
Apr. 23. Thos. E. of Stafford.
Alphonso, son of the Count of Denia in Arragor

1394, O'Neale, K. of Meath.
Mar. 25. Brian de Thomond, K. of Thomond.
Arth. MacMorough, K. of Leinster.
Connor, K. of Chenow and de Erpe.
Thos. Ourgham.
Jno. or Jonn. de Pado.

HENRY IV.

On the eve of his coronation. Mar. 17, 1400.

Thomas, aft. D. of Clarence. } Sons of
John, aft. D. of Bedford. } the
Humphrey, aft. D. of Gloucester. } King.
Thos. Fitzalan, E. of Arundel.
Rd. Beauchamp, aft. E. of Warwick.
Edmd., 5th E. of Stafford.
Hugh Courtenay, son of and aft. E. of Devon.
Hy., 5th ld. Beaumont.
—— Willoughby, bro. to Wm., 5th ld. Willoughby.
Hugh Stafford, bro. to the E. of Stafford.
Richd. Camois, son of Thos., ld. Camois.
The Lord of Paule.
Peter, 7th ld. Mawley.

Jno., 5th ld. Latimer.
Ralph, 3rd ld. Deyncourt.
Almaric, 3rd ld. Scyntismond or St. Amand.
Thomas Beauchampe.
Thomas Pelham.
John Luttrell.
John Lisle.
Wm. Hankford (just. C.P.).
Wm. Brenchesley (just. C.P.).
Barth. Rochford.
Giles Daubeney.
Wm. Butler.
John Ashton.
Rd. Snape or Sanope.
Jno. Tiptoft.

Rd. Francis.
Hy. Percy (Hotspur).
Jno. Arundel.
Wm. Strall or Stralley.
Jno. Turpington.
Ailmer Saint.
Edw. Hastings.
John Greisley.
Gerald Sotill.
John Arden.
Robt. Chalons.
Thos. Dymock.
Walter Hungerford.
Wm. Gebethorpe.
Wm. Newport.

HENRY V.

On the eve of his coronation. Apr. 1413.

Edw. E. of March.
Roger Mortimer, his brother.
Jno., E. of Huntingdon.
Richd. Holland, his brother.
Richd., ld. le Despencer.
Jno. Phelip.
Jno. Rothenhale.
Thos. West.

1418, Apr. 23. Lewis Robsart.
Roger Salveine.
Jno. Stewart.
Jno. Shotesbrooke.
Jno. Montgomery, and 10 more.

1421, Apr. 23. Jas. I., K. of Scotland.
Humphrey, E. of Stafford.

HENRY VI.

1426, May 19. The King.
Rd., D. of York.
Thos. Jno. Mowbray, son of Jno., 2nd D. of Norfolk.
Jno., E. of Oxford.
Rd., E. of Westmorland.
Hy. Percy, son of Hy., E. of Northumberland.
Thos., 14th ld. Roos.
Jno. Cornvale.
Lord Maltravers.
Jno., ld. Tankerville.
Wm. Neville, aft. ld. Fauconberg.
Jno., 5th ld. Latimer.
Leo., 6th ld. Welles.
Jas., ld. Berkeley.
Jno., son of Jno., 12th ld. Talbot.
Ralph Gray.
Rd. Gray.
Robt. de Vere. } Bros. to Jno., 12th E. of Oxford.
—— de Vere. }

1426, May 19. Robt. Hungerford, son of Walter 1st ld. Hungerford.
Robt. Wyngfelde.
Jno. Boteler.
Regd. Cobham.
Jno. Paslen.
Thos. Constable.
Thos. Chediok.
Ralph Longford.
Thos. Drusy.
Wm. Ap Thomas.
Richd. Carbonel.
Richd. Wodewyk.
Ralph Shirley.
Nichs. Bloncat.
Ralph Radclyf.
Edmund Trayford.
Wm. Cheyne (just. K.B.).
Wm. Babington (ch. just. C.P.).
Jno. Ivyn or Juyn (just. C.P. an ch. bar. ex.).
Gilbert Bewcham.

Coronation of Henry VI. Nov. 6, 1429.

30 knights made; names not recorded.

1449, Xmas. Edmund Tudor, aft. E. of Richmond. } Half-brothers to the King.
Jasper Tudor, aft. E. of Pembroke. }

1449, Xmas. Thos. Neville. } Sons of Richd., E. of Salisbury.
Jno. Neville. }
Wm. Herbert.
Roger Lewknor.
Wm. Catesby.

EDWARD IV.

At his coronation. Jan. 27, 1461.

Geo., D. of Clarence. } Bros. to the King.
Rd., D. of Gloucester, aft. Rd. III. }
Jno. Mowbray, s. and h. to the D. of Norfolk.
Jno. Stafford, aft. E. of Wiltshire.
Thos. Fitzalan, c c. ld. F., son and aft E. of Arundel.
Jno., ld. Strange of Knokyn.
Jno. Markham.

Robt. Danby.
Wm. Yelverton.
Jno. Wingefield.
Walter Blount.
Robt. Markham.
Robt. Clifden or Clifton.
Wm. Stanley.
Nichs. Byron.
Wm. Cantelewe.

On the coronation of Elizabeth, Q. of Edward IV

May 26, 1464.

Hy., 2nd D. of Buckingham.
—— Stafford, his brother.
Jno., 13th E. of Oxford.
Thos., 2nd Visc. Lisle.
Jno., ld. Maltravers, son of Jno., 2nd E. of Arundel.
Geo. Grey, son of Edwd., 1st E. of Kent.
Richd. Wydvile.
Jno. Wydvile.
Ralph Josselyne.
Richd. Bingham (just. C.P.).
Robt. Danvers (just. K.B.).
Jno. Needham (just. C.P.).
Richd. Choke (just. C.P.).
Walter Moyle (just. K.B.).
Richd. Illingworth (ch. bar. ex.).
—— Hyngham.
Jno. Arundelle.
Wm. Calthorp.
Thos. Brewce or Bruce.
Geo. Darelle.
Richd. Harecourt.
Walter Mauntelle.
Edmd. Rede.
Wm. Hawte.
Jno. Clifford.
Jno. Say.
Jno. Cheney of Canterbury.
Robt. Darcy.
Thos. Ovedale.
Jno. Durward.
Jno. Henyngham.
Jno. Savage.
Roger Corbet of Murtone.
Nichs. (?) Culpeper.
Hugh Whyche.
Thos. Cooke.
Jno. Plomer.
Hy Wafyr.
Matth. Philip.
—— ld. Duras.
Bartelot de Robaire.

At the creation of prince Edward, the King's eldest son, as prince of Wales.

April 18, 1475.

Edw., Pr. of Wales, aft. Edw. V. } The King's sons.
Rd. D. of York. }
Thos., E. of Huntingdon, cr. M. of Dorset.
Rd. Grey, his brother.
Jno., E. of Lincoln, son of Jno., D. of Suffolk.
Geo., E. of Shrewsbury.
Edw., E. of Wiltshire.
Edw. Wydeville.
Ralph (? ld. Neville).
Wm. Berkeley, son of Jas., ld. Berkeley.
Jas. Touchet, son of Jno., ld. Audley.
Rd., ld. St. Amand.
Geo. Stanley, son of Thos., 2nd ld. Stanley.
Jno. Stourton, son of Wm., 2nd ld. Stourton.
Edwd. Hastings, son of Wm., 1st ld. Hastings.
Jno. Devereux, son of Walter, 6th ld. Ferrers.
Herbert (? Richd.), bro. to Wm., E. of Pembroke.
Thos. Vaughan.
Thos. Bryan (ch. just. C.P.).
Thos. Lyttelton (just. C.P.).
Hy. Bodryngam.
Bryan Stapilton.
Wm. Knyvett.
Jno. Pilkynton.
Rd. Ludlow.
Rd. Charleton.

On the marriage of Richd., D. of York, the King's 2nd son, to Ann, daughter of John, D. of Norfolk.

Jan. 17, 1478.

Hy., son of Wm., ld. Bourchier, and grandson of and aft. E. of Essex.
Richd., ld. Latimer.
Jno., ld. Berners or Barnes.
Jno. (?), ld. Powis.
Hy., ld. Morley.
Thos., ld. De la Warr.
Jno., 3rd ld. Mountjoy.
John Beauchamp, son of ld. Beauchamp.
Thos. Howard, son of Jno., 1st ld. Howard.
Thos. (? Jno.) Bourchier.
Thos. St. Leger.
Jno. Elrington (treasr. hhold).
Giles Daubeney.
Wm. Stoner.
Guy Fairfax.

Wm. Gascoigne.
Robt. Broughton.
Thos. Froweck.
Hy. Talboys or Tailboys.
Wm. Redman.
Hy. Wentworth.
Rd. Delabere.
Rd. Lakyn.

Richard III.

On his coronation. July 6, 1483.

Edmd. de la Pole, son of and aft. D. of Suffolk.
Jno. Grey, son of Edmd., E. of Kent.
Wm. Zouche, bro. of Jno., ld. Zouche.
Wm. (? Geo.) Nevill, son of Geo., ld. Abergavenny.
Christr. Willoughby.
Wm. Berkeley.
Hy. Banington.
Thos. Arundel.
Thos. Bolayne, or Boleyn.
Edmd. Bedingfield.
Gervase Clifton.
Wm. Say.
Wm. Enderby.
Thos. Lewkenor.
Thos. Ormond.
Jno. Browne.
Wm. Barkeley.
Edm. Cornwall, bar. of Burford

Henry VII.

On his coronation. Oct. 28, 1485.

Edwd. Stafford, aft. D. of Buckingham.
Jno., 12th ld. Fitzwater.
Thos. Cokesay.
Roger Lewkenor.
Hy. Heydon.
Regd. Bray.
John Verney.

On the coronation of Elizabeth, Q. of Henry VII.

Nov. 1487.

Wm., ld. Courtenay, son of Edwd., E. of Devon.
Edwd., 6th ld. Dudley.
Jno. or Wm. Gascoyne.
Thos. Butler.
Edwd. Berkeley.
Wm. Lucy.
Thos. Hungerford.
Guy de Wolston.
Thos. or Richd. Pemery.
Jno. or Ralph Sheldon.
Hugh Luttrell.
Thos. Pulteney.
Hugh Conway.
Nichs. Lisley.

On the creation of prince Arthur as prince of Wales.

Nov. 29, 1489.

Arthur, Pr. of Wales (the King's son).
Hy., E. of Northumberland.
Thos., ld. Maltravers, aft. E. of Arundel.
Richd. Grey, c.c. ld. Grey of Ruthyn, son of Geo., E. of Kent.
Wm., 4th ld. Stourton.
Thos. West, son of ld. De la Warr.
Jno. St. John.
Hy. Vernon.
Jno. Hastings.
Wm. Griffith.
Wm. Tyndall.
Nichs. Montgomery.
Wm. Uvedall.
Matth. Browne.
Thos. Darcy.
Thos. Cheney.
Edmd. Gorges.
Walter Denis.
Wm. Scott.
Jno. Guyse.

On the creation of prince Henry as D. of York.

Nov. 1, 1491.

Pr. Henry, D. of York, aft. Hen. VIII.
Thos. Grey, ld. Harynton, son of M. of of Dorset.
Hy., 14th ld. Clyfford.
Jno., 11th ld. FitzWarin.
Thos. Fienes.
Thos., 7th ld. Dacre of the South.
Thos. Stanley, son of ld. Strange, and grandson of and aft. E. of Derby.
Jno. Arundell.
Walter Gryffith.
Gervase Clifton.

Edwd. Traford.
Robt. Harcourt, or Hardecourt.
Hy. Marney.
Roger Newburgh.
Ralph Rider.
Thos. Bawde.
Jno. Speke.
Humphry Fulford.
Robt. Lytton, or Litten.
Piers Edgecombe.
Robt. Clere.
Thos. Fairfax.
Richd. Knightby.
Jno. Chooke, or Cheoke.

On the marriage of Arthur, prince of Wales.

Nov. 17, 1501.

Richd., ld. Willoughby de Eresby.
Jno., 10th ld. Clinton.
Geo., son of Edwd., 2nd ld. Hastings.
Wm. Fenys, or Finnis.
Gryffithe ap Rys Thomas.
Robt. Corbet.
Jno. Wogan.
Thos. Laurence.
Hy. Rogers.
Wm. Walgrave.
Wm. Seymour.
Robt. Throgmorton.
Jno. Bassett.
Thos. Grenefield, or Grenville.
Jno. Arundel of Trerico.
Roger Strange.
Jno. Scrope of Castlecomb.
Jno. Paulet.
Walter Baskervyle.
Robt. Waterton.
Jno. Gyfford.
Jno. Aston.
Wm. Fyllioll.
Thos. Ingilfield.
Wm. Martyn.
Wm. Callwey.
Geo. Putnam.
Nich. Biron.
Thos. Hawte.
Richd. Warr.
Alnathe Malyverer.
Wm. Rede.
Jno. Trevelyan.
Jno. Foster.
Walter Strykeland.
Thos. Long
Jno. Philpot.
Jno. Lee of Wiltshire.
Wm. Hartwell.
Nichs. Griffin.
Lancelot Thyrkyll.
Jno. Norton.
Roger Ormiston.
Geo., or Gerard, Fyldynge.
Thos. Curwyn.
Hugh Loder.
Thos. Sampson.
Richd. Fowler.
Thos. Woodhouse.
Philip Bothe.
Geo. Inwardby.
Hy. Frowick.
Jno. Leghe of Stokewell.
Wm. Ascue.
Thos. Kemp.
Morgan Kydwell.
Jno. Gyllot.

On the creation of Henry, D. of York (aft. Henry VIII.), as prince of Wales.

Feb. 18, 1503.

Jno., 4th visc. Lisle.
Thos., ld. Dacre of the North.
Myles Bussy.
Edwd. Pomery.
Jno. Mordaunt.
Brian Stapilton.
Ranff Gray.
Jas. Hubert.

Henry VIII.

On his coronation. June 23, 1509.

Robt., ld. FitzWalter.
Hy., 7th ld. Scroope of Bolton.
Geo., 7th ld. FitzHugh.
Wm., 4th ld. Mountjoy.
Hy., ld. Daubeney.
Robt., 2nd ld. Willoughby de Broke.
Morris Barkeley.
Hy. Clyfford.
Thos. Knevet.
Andr. Windsor.
Thos. Parr.
Thos. Boleyn.
Richd. Wentworth.
Hy. Owtred.
Fras. Cheney.
Hy. Wyotte, or Wyatt.
Geo. Hastings.
Thos. Metham.
Thos. Bedingfield.
Jno. Skelton.
Giles Allington.
Jno. Trevanyon.

Wm. Crowmer.
Jno. Heydon.
Edwd., or Godard Oxenbridge.
Hy. Sackveyle, or Sacheverell.
Steph. Jenyns, ld. may. London, 1508.

On the coronation of Anne Boleyn, Q. of Henry VIII.

May 30, 1533.

Hy., 5th M. of Dorset.
Edwd, 3rd E. of Derby.
Hy. Clifford, c.c. ld. Clifford, son of Hy., 1st E. of Cumberland.
Hy. Ratcliffe, c.c. ld. FitzWalter, son of Robt., E. of Sussex.
Fras. Hastings, c.c. ld. Hastings, son of Geo., E. of Huntingdon.
Wm. Stanley, son of and aft. ld. Monteagle.
Thos., 2nd ld. Vaux of Harroden.
Hy. Parker, son of Hy., 8th ld. Morley.
Wm. Windsor, son of Andr., 1st ld. Windsor.
Jno. Mordaunt, son of Jno., 1st ld. Mordaunt.
Fras. Weston.
Thos. Arundell.
Jno. Hudleston.
Thos. Poynings.
Hy. Savell.
Geo. FitzWilliams of Lincolnshire.
Hy. Jermey.

EDWARD VI.

On his coronation. Feb. 20, 1547.

Hy., D. of Suffolk.
Edwd., E. of Hertford, aft. D. of Somerset.
Jno., 16th E. of Oxford.
Thos., 10th E. of Ormond.
Hy., ld. Maltravers.
Geo. Talbot, c.c. ld. Talbot, son of Fras., E. of Shrewsbury.
Edwd. Stanley, c.c. ld. Strange, son of E. of Derby.
Wm. Somerset, c.c. ld. Herbert, son of and aft. E. of Worcester.
Jno., 4th ld. Lisle.
Gregory, ld. Cromwell.
Hy. Hastings, c.c. ld. Hastings, son of Fras., E. of Huntingdon.
Chas. Brandon, bro. of Hy., D. of Suffolk.
Hy. Scrope, son of Jno., ld. Scrope of Bolton.
Thos. Windsor, son of Wm., 2nd ld. Windsor.
Fras. Russell.
Anthy. Browne (son of m. horse).
Richd. Devereux.
Hy. Seymour.
Jno. Yates.
Anthy. Cook of Essex.
Alexr. Umpton of Oxford.
Geo. Norton.
Val. Knightby.
Robt. Lytton.
Geo. Vernon of the Peak.
Jno. Porte.
Thos. Josselyn.
Edmd. Molyneux, serjt. law, aft. just. C.P.
Christr. Barker, Garter K. A.
Jas. Hailes, or Halles.
Wm. Bapthorpe.
Thos. Brykenell.
Thos. Neville.
Angel Mareyn, or Marnia.
Jno. Holcrofte.
Jno. Cuff, or Cuyt.
Hy. Tyrrell.
Wm. Sherington.
Wimond Carewe.
Wm. Sneath.

MARY.

At her coronation. Sept. 28, 1553.

Edwd., E. of Devon.
Thos. Howard, son of Hy., E. of Surrey.
Hy. Herbert, c.c. ld. Cardiff, son of and aft. E. of Pembroke.
Hy., ld. Abergavenny, or Bergavenny.
Hy., 12th ld. Berkeley.
Jno., 6th ld. Lumley.
Jas., 6th ld. Mountjoy.
Hy. Clinton, son of Edwd., 8th ld. Clinton.
Wm. Paulet, son of Jno., ld. St. John, grandson of and aft. M. of Winchester.
Hugh Rich, son of Richd., 1st ld. Rich.
Hy. Paget, son. of Wm., 1st ld. Paget.
Hy. Parker.
Robt. Rochester (comptr. hhold.).
Hy. Jerningham.
Wm. Dormer.

ELIZABETH.

At her coronation. Jan. 15, 1559.

Jno., 3rd ld. Darcy of the North.
Jno., 2nd ld. Sheffield.
Jno., 2nd ld. Darcy of Chiche.
Robt. Riche.
Roger North.
Jno. Souwche, or Zouche.
Nichs. Poynes.
Jno. Berkeley.
Edwd. Umpton.
Hy. Weston.
Geo. Speke.

JAMES I.

At his coronation. July 25, 1603.

Philip Herbert, aft. E. of Montgomery.
Thos., ld. Berkeley.
Wm., 2nd ld. Evres.
Geo. Wharton.
Robt. Rich, aft. E. of Warwick.
Robt. Carr, aft. E. of Somerset (? Robt. Kerr, aft. E. of Ancram).
Jno. Egerton, aft. E. of Bridgewater.
Hy. Compton, bro. of Wm., ld. Compton, who was aft. E. of Northampton.
Thos. Erskine (son of E. of Mar), aft. E. of Buchan.
Wm. Anstruther.
Patr. Murray, aft. E. of Tullibardine.
Jas. Hay, ld. Yester.
Jno. Lindesay (? ld. Wolmerstown).
Richd. Preston, aft. E. of Desmond.
Oliver Cromwell of Huntingdonshire.
Edwd. Stanley.
Wm. Herbert, aft. ld. Powys.
Fulke Greville, aft. ld. Brooke.
Fras. Fane, aft. E. of Westmorland.
Robt. Chichester.
Robt. Knowles.
Wm., or Gervase, Clifton of Notts.
Fras. Fortescue.
Edwd. Corbet.
Edwd. Herbert, aft. ld. Herbert in England and Ireland.
Thos. Langton.
Wm. Pope.
Arth. Hopton.
Chas. Morison, or Moryson.
Fras. Leigh.
Edwd. Montague, aft ld. Montague of Boughton.
Edwd. Stanhope.
Peter Manwood.
Robt. Harley.
Thos. Strickland.
Christr. Hatton.
Edwd. Griffin.
Robt. Bevill.
Wm. Welby.
Edwd. Harwell.
Jno. Mallet.
Walter Aston.
Hy. Gawdy.
Richd. Musgrave.
Jno. Stowell.
Richd. Amertes.
Thos. Leeds.
Thos. Jermyn.
Ralph Hare.
Wm. Forster.
Geo. Speke, or Speeke.
Goo. Hyde.
Anthy. Felton.
Anthy. Browne.
Thos. Wise.
Robt. Chamberlaine.
Anthy. Palmer.
Edwd. Heron.
Hy. Burton.
Robt. Barker.
Wm. Norris.
Roger Bodenham.

On the creation of prince Charles (aft. Charles I.) as D. of York.
Jan. 5–6, 1605.

Chas., D. of York and Albany, second son of the K., aft. Chas. I.
Robt. Bertie, ld. Willoughby de Eresby, aft. E. of Lindesey.
Wm. Compton, c.c. ld. Compton, aft. E. of Northampton.
Grey, ld. Chandos.
Fras., ld. Norris, aft. E. of Berkshire.
Wm. Cecil, son of Robt., visc. Cranborne, aft. E. of Salisbury
Allan Percy, bro. of Hy., E. of Northumberland.
Fras. Manners, aft. E. of Rutland.
Fras. Clifford, bro. of and aft. E. of Cumberland.
Thos. Somerset, son of Edwd., E. of Worcester; aft. visc. Cashel in Ireland.
Thos. Howard, son of E. of Suffolk; aft. E. of Berkshire.
John Harrington, son of John, ld. Harrington of Exton.

On the creation of prince Henry as prince of Wales.
June 2, 1610.

Henry, 18th E. of Oxford.
Geo. Gordon, c.c. ld. Gordon, son of E. of Huntley, aft. M. of Huntley.
Hy., ld. Clifford, aft. E. of Cumberland.
Hy. Ratcliffe, c.c. ld. Fitzwalter, cousin of and aft. E. of Sussex.
Edwd., ld. Fitzwarine, aft. E. of Bath.
Fras. Hay, c.c. ld. Hay.
Jas. Erskine, c.c. ld. Erskine, son of E. of Mar, and aft. E. of Buchan.
Thomas, ld. Windsor.
Thos., ld. Wentworth, aft. E. of Cleveland.
Chas. Somerset, 3rd son of Edwd., E. of Worcester.
Edwd. Somerset, 4th son of Edwd., E. of Worcester.
Thos. Ratcliffe, 2nd son of E. of Sussex.
Fras. Stuart, son of E. of Moray.
Ferd. Sutton, son of Edwd., ld. Dudley.
Hy. Carey, son of John, ld. Hunsdon, aft. visc. Rochford and E. of Dover.
Oliver St. John, c.c. ld. St. John, son of Oliver, ld. St. John; aft. 1st E. of Bolingbroke.
Gilbert Gerard, son of Thos., ld. Gerard.
Chas. Stanhope, son of and aft. ld. Stanhope of Harrington.
Edwd. Bruce, s. and h. of ld. Kinlosse.
Wm. Stewart, son of Walter, ld. Blantyre.
Robt. Sydney, c.c. ld. Sydney, son of visc. Lisle, aft. 2nd E. of Leicester.
Ferd. or Mervyn, Touchet, son of Geo., ld. Audley, and E. of Castlehaven.
Peregrine Bertie, bro. of Robt., 11th ld. Willoughby de Eresby, who was aft. 1st E. of Lindsey.
Hy. Rich, bro. to E. of Warwick; aft. E. of Holland.
Edwd. Sheffield (son of ld. Sheffield), aft. E. of Mulgrave.
Wm. Cavendish, bro. of ld. Ogle; aft. visc. Mansfield and E. of Newcastle.

On the creation of Charles, D. of York (aft. Chas. I.), as prince of Wales.
Nov. 3, 1616.

Jas. Howard, c.c. ld. Maltravers, son of Thos., E. of Arundel.
Algernon Percy, c.c. ld. Percy, son of E. of Northumberland.
Jas. Wriothesley, c.c. ld. Wriothesley, son of E. of Southampton.
Theoph. Clinton, c.c. ld. Clinton, son of Thos., E. of Lincoln.
Edwd. Seymour, ld. Beauchamp, gr. son of Edwd., E. of Hertford.
John Erskine; Mast. of Fenton, c.c. ld. Erskine, son of E. of Mar.
Hy. Howard, 2nd son of E. of Arundel; aft. ld. Maltravers.
Robt. Howard, 3rd or 5th son of Thos., E. of Suffolk.
Edwd. Sackville, aft. E. of Dorset.
Wm. Howard, 4th or 6th son of Thos., E. of Suffolk.
Edwd. Howard, 5th or 7th son of Thos., E. of Suffolk.
Wm. Seymour, 2nd son of ld. Beauchamp, aft. E. of Hertford.
Montague Bertie, son of Robt., ld. Willoughby, aft. E. of Lindesey.
Wm. Stourton, son of and aft. ld. Stourton.
Hy. Parker, son of and aft. ld. Monteagle.
Dudley North, son of and aft. ld. North.
Wm. Spencer, son of and aft. ld. Spencer.
Spencer Compton, son of Wm., ld. Compton.
Rowland St. John, bro. to Oliver, ld. St. John.
John Cavendish, 2nd son of Wm., E. of Devonshire.
Thos. Neville, son of Edwd., ld. Abergavenny.
John, 1st ld. Teynham.
John North, bro. of Dudley, ld. North.
Hy. Carey, aft. visc. Falkland.

CHARLES I.

At his coronation. Feb. 1, 1625.

Geo. Fielding, c.c. visc. Callan, son of Wm., E. of Denbigh.
Jas. Stanley, c.c. ld. Strange, aft. 7th E. of Derby.
Chas. Cecil, c.c. visc. Cranborne, son of Wm., E. of Salisbury.
Chas. Herbert, c.c. ld. Herbert, son of Philip, E. of Montgomery.
Robt. Rich, c.c. ld. Rich, son of and aft. E. of Warwick.
Jas. Hay, c.c. ld. Hay, son of Jas., E. of Carlisle.
Basil Fielding, c.c. ld. Fielding, son of Wm., E. of Denbigh.
Oliver St. John, c.c. ld. St. John, son of Oliver, E. of Bolingbroke.
Mildmay Fane, c.c. ld. Burghersh, son of E. of Westmorland.
Hy. Paulet, c.c. ld. Hy. Paulet, son of Wm., M. of Winchester.
Edwd. Montagu, son of Hy., visc. Mandeville.

John Cary, son of and aft. visc. Rochford and E. of Dover.
Chas. Howard, son of and aft. visct. Andover of Berkshire.
Wm. Howard, son of Thos., E. of Arundel.
Robt. Stanley, 2nd son of Wm., 6th E. of Derby.
Pawlet St. John, 2nd son of Oliver, E. of Bolingbroke.
Fras. Fane, 2nd son of Fras., E. of Westmoreland.
Jas. Howard, son of Theoph., ld. Howard de Walden.
Wm. Cavendish, eldest son of ld. Cavendish (? E. of Devonshire).
Thos. Wentworth, son of Thos., ld. Wentworth, who was aft. E. of Cleveland.
Wm. Paget, son of Wm., ld. Paget.
Wm. Russell, son of Fras., ld. Russell; aft. E. of Bedford.
Hy. Stanhope, son of Philip, ld. Stanhope of Shelford.
Richd. Vaughan, son of John, ld. Vaughan of Mullingar.
Christr. Neville, 2nd son of Edwd., ld. Abergavenny.
Roger Bertie, 2nd son of Robt., ld. Willoughby de Eresby.
Thos. Wharton, 2nd son of Thos., ld. Wharton.
St. John Blunt, or Blount, bro. of Mountjoy, ld. Mountjoy.
Ralph Clare.
John Maynard, bro. to ld. Maynard.
Fras. Carew.
John Byron.
Roger Palmer (mast. hhold.).
Hy. Edmonds (treasr. hhold.).
Ralph Hopton.
Wm. Brooke.
Alexr. Ratcliffe.
Edwd. Scot.
Christr. Hatton.
Thos. Sackville.
John Manson, or Monson.
Peter Wentworth.
John Butler.
Edwd. Hungerford.
Richd. Lewson.
Nathl. Bacon.
Robt. Poyntz.
Robt. Bevill.
Geo. Sandes.
Thos. Smith, or Smythe, aft. visct. Strangford.
Thos. Fanshawe.
Miles Hobart.
Hy. Hart.
Fras. Carew.
John Baccus, or Backhouse.
Matth. Monins.
John Stowell, or Stawell.
John Jennings.
Stephen Harvey.

CHARLES II.

At his coronation. Apr. 23, 1661.

Edwd. Clinton, c.c. ld. Clinton, grandson of and aft. E. of Lincoln.
John Egerton, c.c. ld. Brackley, son of and aft. E. of Bridgewater.
Philip Herbert, 2nd son of Philip, E. of Pembroke and Montgomery.
Wm. Egerton, 2nd son of John, E. of Bridgewater.
Vere Vane, 2nd son of Mildmay, E. of Westmorland.
Chas. Berkeley, aft. 2nd E. of Berkeley.
Hy. Belasyse, aft. 2nd ld. Belasyse.
Hy. Hyde, son of Edwd., ld. Hyde, ld. chanc.
Rowland Bellasyse, bro. to Thos., visct., aft. E. Fauconberg.
Hy. Capell, 2nd son of Arth., ld. Capell, and E. of Essex.
John Vaughan, 2nd son of E. of Carberry.
Chas. Stanley, gr. son of Chas., 8th E. of Derby.
Fras. Vane and Hy. Vane, "gr. sons of the late E. of Westmorland" (? sons of Mildmay, E. of Westmorland).
Sir Wm. Portman, bt.
Sir Richd. Temple, bt.
Sir Wm. Ducie, bt., aft. visct. Downe.
Sir Thos. Trevor, bt.
Sir John Scudamore, bt.
Sir Wm. Gardiner, bt.
Chas. Cornwallis, son of sir Fredk., aft. ld. Cornwallis.
John Nicholas, son of E. Nicholas, sec. st.
John Monson.
Bourchier Wray.
John Coventry.
Edwd. Hungerford.
John Knyvet.
Philip Butler.
Adrian Scroope.
Richd. Knightley.
Hy. Heron.
John Lewkinor.
Geo. Browne.
Wm. Terringham, or Tiringham.
Fras. Godolphin.
Edwd. Baynton.
Grevill Verney.
Edwd. Harley.
Edwd. Walpole.
Fras. Popham.
Edwd. Wise.
Christr. Calthorpe.
Richd. Edgcumbe.

Wm. Bromley.
Thos. Bridges.
Thos. Fanshawe.
John Denham.
Nichs. Bacon.
Jas. Altham.
Thos. Windy, or Wendy.
John Brampston.
Geo. Freeman.
Nichs. Slaning.
Richd. Ingoldsby.
John Rolles.
Edwd. Heath.
Wm. Morley.
John Bennet.
Hugh Smith.
Simon Leech.
Hy. Chester.
Robt. Atkins.
Robt. Gayer, or Gayre.
Richd. Powle.
Hugh Darcy, or Ducie.
Stephen Hales.
Ralph Bash.
Thos. Whitmore.

Order revived by Geo. I.

May 18, 1725.

See Introduction, *ante*, p. 753.

KNIGHTS COMPANIONS.

(K.B.)

Invested May 27, and Installed June 17, 1725.

Pr. Wm. Aug., 2nd son of Geo., Pr. of Wales, and grandson of Geo. I.; aft. D. of Cumberland.
John, 2nd D. of Montagu (Great Master).
Chas., 6th D. of Richmond (not inv.).
Wm., 2nd D. of Manchester.
Chas. Beauclerk, c.c. E. of Burford, son of and aft. D. of St. Albans.
John, 6th E. of Leicester.
Wm. Anne, 2nd E. of Albemarle.
Hy., 1st E. of Delorain.
Geo., 2nd E. of Halifax.
Talbot, E. of Sussex.
Thos., 1st E. of Pomfret.
Nassau Paulet, c.c. ld. N. Paulet, son of Chas., 3rd D. of Bolton.
Adm. Geo., 1st visct. Torrington.
Geo. Cholmondeley, c.c. visct. Malpas, son of and aft. E. of Cholmondeley.
John Campbell, c.c. visct. Glenorchy, son of and aft. E. of Breadalbane.
John, ld. De la Warr, aft. 1st E. De la Warr.
Hugh, 13th ld. Clinton, aft. E. of Clinton.
Robt., ld. Walpole, aft. 2nd E. of Orford.
Hon. Spencer Compton (son of Jas., 3rd E. of Northampton), aft. E. of Wilmington; quitted for the Garter, Aug. 1733.
Wm. Stanhope, son of Philip, E. of Chesterfield.
Conyers D'Arcy.
Hon. Thos. Lumley Saunderson, aft. 3rd E. of Scarborough.
Paul Methuen.
Sir Robt. Walpole, aft. 1st E. of Orford; quitted for the Garter, 1726.
Robt. Sutton.
Lt.-Gen. Chas. Willis.
Sir John Hobart, bt., aft. ld. Hobart and E. of Buckinghamshire.
Sir Wm. Gage, bt.
Robt. Clifton, son of sir Gervase Clifton, bt. (? aft. sir R.).
Michl. Newton (? aft. bt.).
Wm. Yonge, aft. bt.
Thos. Watson Wentworth, aft. E. of Malton and M. of Rockingham.
John Monson, aft. ld. Monson.
Wm. Morgan.
Thos. Coke, aft. ld. Lovell, visct. Coke, and E. of Leicester.
Wm., 4th E. of Inchiquin, inv. May 28, 1725
John, visct. Tyrconnell, inv. May 28, 1725.

George II.

1732, Jan. 12. Hy. Brydges, c.c. M. of Carnarvon, aft. 2nd D. of Chandos.
Wm., 1st visc. Bateman.
Sir Geo. Downing, bt.
1732. Chas. Gunter Nicol, Jan. 17.
1742. Sir Thos. Robinson, bt., aft. ld. Grantham, June 26.
1743. Lt.-gen. Philip Honywood, July 12.
1743, July 12. Lt.-gen. Hon. Jas. Campbell.
Lt.-gen. John Cope.
F. M. sir John Ligonier, aft. ld visc. and E. Ligonier.
1744, May 28. Rd., 6th visc. Fitzwilliam.
Sir Chas. Hanbury Williams.
Hy. Calthorpe.
Thos. Whitmore.
Sir Wm. Morden Harbord, bt.

1747. R.-adm. Peter Warren, May 29.
V.-adm. Edwd. Hawke, aft. ld. Hawke, Nov. 14.
1749, May 2. Lt.-gen. Hon. Chas. Howard.
Gen. sir John Mordaunt.
M.-gen. Chas. Armand Powlett.
John Savile, aft. ld. Pollington and E. of Mexborough.
1752. Rd., 3rd ld. Onslow, Mar. 12.
1753, Aug. 27. Edwd. Walpole, 2nd son of Robt., 1st E. of Orford.
1753, Aug. 27. Lt.-gen. Chas. Paulet, aft. 5th D. of Bolton.
Edwd. Hussey Montagu, aft. ld. and E. Beaulieu.
Lt.-gen. Hon. Rd. Lyttelton, bro. of Geo. ld. Lyttelton.
1753. Sir Wm. Rowley, adm. of the fl., Dec. 12.
1754. Benj. Keene, Sept 23.
1756. Lt.-gen. Wm. Blakeney, aft. ld. Blakeney, Nov. 27.

George III.

1761, Mar. 23. John, 1st ld. Carysfort.
Lt.-gen. Hon. Jos. Yorke, aft. ld. Dover.
Sir Jas. Gray, bt.
Sir Wm. Beauchamp, bt.
Sir John Gibbons, bt.
Adm. Geo. Pocock.
M.-gen. sir Jeffrey Amherst, aft. ld. Amherst.
M.-gen. John Griffin Griffin, aft. 4th ld. Howard de Walden.
Fras. Blake Delaval.
Chas. Frederick.
1761. Geo. Warren, Mar. 26.
V.-adm. Chas. Saunders, May 16.
1764. Chas. Cook, aft. E. of Belmont or Bellamont, Jan. 16.
M.-gen. Robt., 1st ld. Clive, Apr. 24.
1765. Andr. Mitchell, Dec. 13.
Lt.-gen. Wm. Draper, Dec. 27.
1767. Pr. Fredk., Bp. of Osnaburgh, aft. D. of York; nom. 1st and ppal. compn., Dec. 30.
1768. Sir Horace Mann, bt., Oct. 25.
1770, May 18. Robt., 1st E. of Catherlough.
V.-adm. sir John Moore, bt.
1770, June 28. R.-adm. sir John Lindsay, bt.
M.-gen. Eyre Coote.
1771, Feb. 18. Lt.-gen. sir Chas. Montagu.
Ralph Payne, aft. ld. Lavington; *d.* 1807.
Wm. Lynch.
1772, Jan. 15. M.-gen. sir Chas. Hotham (aft. Hotham-Thompson), bt.
Wm. Hamilton.
1772. Lt.-col. Robt. Murray Keith, Feb. 29.
Geo. Macartney, aft. ld., visc. and E. Macartney, May 29.
1773. Lt.-gen. Jas. Adolphus Oughton, Feb. 22.
Robt. Gunning, aft. bt., June 2.
1774, Aug. 3. Lt.-gen. sir Geo. Howard, bt.
Lt.-col. John Blaquiere, aft. ld. Blaquiere.
1775. Wm. Gordon, Feb. 3.
Lt.-gen. John Irwin, Dec. 15.
1776. Gen. Guy Carleton, aft. ld. Dorchester, July 6.
1776. M.-gen. Hon. Wm. Howe, aft. visc. Howe, Oct. 13.
Lt.-gen. John Clavering, Nov. 9.
1777. M.-gen. sir Hy. Clinton, Apr. 11.
1778. R.-adm. Edwd. Hughes, Dec. 9.
1779. Jas. Harris, aft. ld. and E. of Malmesbury, Feb. 24.
M.-gen. Hector Monro, Mar. 23.
Randal Wm., 6th E., aft. 1st M. of Antrim, May 5.
1780, Nov. 13. Lt.-gen. Rd. Peirson.
Thos. Wroughton.
1780. Adm. sir Geo. Bridges Rodney, bt., aft. ld. Rodney, Nov. 14.
1781. Lt.-gen. Edwd., 2nd visc. Ligonier, Dec. 17.
1782. Capt. John Jervis, aft. E. of St. Vincent, May 29.
1783, Jan. 8. Gen. Geo. Augs. Elliot, aft. ld. Heathfield.
Gen. Chas. Grey, aft. ld. and E. Grey.
1785. Lt.-gen. Robt. Boyd, Jan. 28.
Lt.-gen. Fred. Haldimand, Sept. 30.
M.-gen. Archd. Campbell, Sept. 30.
1786, Dec 20. Lt.-gen. Wm. Fawcett.
Robt. Monckton, 4th visc. Galway.
1788, May 7. Sir Geo. Yonge, bt.
V.-adm. Alexr. Hood, aft. ld. and visc. Bridport.
1788. Lt.-gen. Robt. Sloper, June 6.
1791. Morton Eden, aft. ld. Henley, Dec. 16.
1792, Aug. 15. Lt.-gen. Wm. Augs. Pitt.
Lt.-gen. Hon. John Vaughan.
M.-gen. Wm. Medows.
M.-gen. Robt. Abercromby.
1793. Chas. Whitworth, aft. ld. Whitworth, Sept. 27.
1794, May 30. R.-adm. Hon. Geo. Keith Elphinstone, aft. ld. and visc. Keith.
Capt. sir John Borlase Warren, bt.
1794. M.-gen. Adam Williamson, Nov. 18.
1795. Sir Jos. Banks, bt., July 1.
M.-gen. Ralph Abercromby, July 22.

1796. R.-adm. Hugh Cloberry Christian, Feb. 17.
1797, M.-gen. Alured Clarke.
Jan. 14. M.-gen. Jas. Hy. Craig.
1797. R.-adm. Horatio Nelson, aft. ld. and visc. Nelson, May 27.
1798. V.-adm. John Colpoys, Feb. 14.
1799. Lt.-gen. Hon. Chas. Stuart.
1800, V.-adm. Hy. Harvey.
Jan. 8. V.-adm. sir Andr. Mitchell.
1801. R.-adm. Thos. Graves, May 14.
M.-gen. Hon. John Hely-Hutchinson, aft. ld. Hutchinson, and 2nd E. of Donoughmore, May 28.
1801, Lt.-gen. Thos. Trigge.
June 6. R.-adm. John Thos. Duckworth.
1801. R.-adm sir Jas. Saumarez, bt., Sept. 5.
1802. M.-gen. Eyre Coote, May 19.
1803. M.-gen. John Fras. Craddock, Feb. 16.
Lt.-gen. sir David Dundas, Apr. 28.
1804. Hon. Arth. Paget, May 21.
M.-gen. hon. Arth. Wellesley, aft. D. of Wellington, Aug. 28.
1804, M.-Gen. hon. Geo. Jas. Ludlow.
Sept. 26.
M.-gen. John Moore.
Commod. Saml. Hood.
1806, R.-adm. Wm., 7th E. of Northesk.
Jan. 29.
R.-adm. sir Richd. John Strachan, bt.
1806. R.-adm. hon. Alexr. Forrester Inglis Cochrane, Mar. 29.
M.-gen. sir John Stuart, Sept. 13.
Philip Francis, Oct. 29.
Sir Geo. Hilario Barlow, bt., Oct. 29.
1808. Percy Clinton Sydney, 6th visc. Strangford, Mar.
R.-adm. Richd. Goodwin Keats, Oct 15.
1809, Lt.-gen. sir David Baird, bt.
Apr. 21. Lt.-gen. Geo. Beckwith.
Lt.-gen. hon. John Hope, aft. ld. Niddry.
M.-gen. Brent Spencer.
1809, Capt. Thos. Cochrane, c.c. ld
Apr. 21. Cochrane, aft. 10th E. of Dundonald; exp. July 15, 1814 but re-adm. as G.C.B., Sept 22, 1847.
1809. M.-gen. John Cope Sherbrooke Sept. 16.
1810. Lt.-gen. Wm. Carr Beresford aft. ld. Beresford, Oct. 16.
1812, Lt. gen. Thos. Graham, aft. ld
Feb. 22. Lynedoch.
Lt.-gen. Rowland Hill, aft. ld and visc. Hill.
M.-gen. sir Saml. Auchmuty.
1812. Hy. Wellesley, aft. ld. Cowley Mar. 10.
Lt.-gen. Hon. Edwd. Paget, Jun 12.
Lt.-gen sir Stapleton Cotton, bt aft. ld. and visc. Combermere Aug. 21.
Chas. Stuart, aft. ld. Stuart of Rothsay, Sept. 26.
M.-gen. Isaac Brock, Oct. 10.
1813, Adm. hon. Geo. Cranfield Berkley.
Feb. 1.
Lt.-gen. sir Geo. Nugent, bt.
Lt.-gen. Wm. Keppel.
Lt.-gen. sir John Doyle, bt.
Lt.-gen. Wm. Cavendish Bentinck, c.c. ld. W. C. B.
M..gen. Jas. Leith.
M.-gen. Thos. Picton.
M.-gen. hon. Galbraith Lowry Cole.
M.-gen. hon. Chas. Wm. Stewart aft. ld. Stewart and 3rd M. Londonderry.
1813, Lt.-gen. hon. Alexr. Hope.
June 29. M.-gen. Hy. Clinton.
1813, Lt.-gen Geo., 9th E. of Dalhousie.
Sept. 11.
Lt.-gen. hon. Wm. Stuart.
M.-gen. Geo. Murray.
M.-gen. hon. Edwd. Michl. Pakenham.
1814. Adm. Wm. Young, July 12.
Col. Wm. Fredk. Hy. of Nassau hered. pr. of Orange, aft. Wm. I., K. of the Netherlands, Au 16.

Order Remodelled, Jan. 2, 1815.

See Introduction, *ante*, p. 753.

KNIGHTS GRAND CROSS—MILITARY DIVISION.

(G.C.B.)

George III.

Former Knights of the Bath declared to be Knights Grand Cross under the new division of the Order.

1815, Fredk., D. of York.
Jan. 2. Adm. John, E. of St. Vincent.
Gen. sir Robt. Abercromby.
1815, Adm. Geo., visc. Keith.
Jan. 2. Adm. sir John Borlase Warren bt.

1815, Jan. 2. Gen. sir Alured Clarke.
Adm. sir John Colpoys.
Gen. ld. Hutchinson.
Adm. sir John Thos. Duckworth.
Adm. sir Jas. Saumarez.
Gen. sir Eyre Coote.
Gen. sir John Fras. Cradock.
Gen. sir David Dundas.
F.M. Arth., D. of Wellington.
Gen. Geo. Jas., E. of Ludlow.
V.-adm. sir Saml. Hood.
Adm. Wm., 7th E. of Northesk.
V.-adm. sir Richd. John Strachan.
V.-adm. hon. sir Alex. Cochrane.
Lt.-gen. sir John Stuart.
V.-adm. sir Richd. Goodwin Keats.
Gen. sir David Baird.
Gen. sir Geo. Beckwith.
Lt.-gen. John, ld. Niddry.
Lt.-gen. sir Brent Spencer.
Lt.-gen. sir John Cope Sherbrooke.
Lt.-gen. Wm. Carr., ld. Beresford.
Lt.-gen. Thos., ld. Lynedoch.
Lt.-gen. Rowland, ld., aft. visc. Hill.
Lt.-gen. sir Saml. Auchmuty.

1815, Jan. 2. Lt.-gen. sir Edwd. Paget.
Lt.-gen. Stapleton, ld., aft. visc. Combermere.
Adm. hon. sir Geo. Cranfield Berkeley.
Gen. sir Geo. Nugent, bt.
Gen. sir Wm. Keppel.
Lt.-gen. sir John Doyle, bt.
Lt.-gen. Wm. Cavendish Bentinck, c.c. ld. W. C. B.
Lt.-gen. sir Jas. Leith.
Lt.-gen. sir Thos. Picton.
Lt.-gen. hon. sir Galbraith Lowry Cole.
Lt.-gen. Chas. Wm., ld. Stewart aft. 3rd M. of Londonderry.
Lt.-gen. hon. sir Alexr. Hope.
Lt.-gen. sir Hy. Clinton.
Lt.-gen. Geo., 9th E. of Dalhousie.
Lt.-gen. hon. Wm. Stewart.
M.-gen. sir Geo. Murray.
M.-gen. hon. sir Edwd. Michl. Pakenham.
Gen. Wm. Fredk. Hy. of Nassau, hered. Pr. of Orange, aft. Wm. I., K. of the Netherlands.

Subsequent appointments.

1815, Jan. 2. Adm. Wm. Hy., D. of Clarence, aft. Wm. IV.; actg. Great Master, 1827.
F.M. Edwd., D. of Kent.
F.M. Ernest Augs., D. of Cumberland.
F.M. Adolphus Fredk., D. of Cambridge.
F.M. Wm. Fredk., D. of Gloucester.
Adm. sir Wm. Young.
Adm. Saml., visc. Hood.
Adm. sir Richd. Onslow, bt.
Adm. hon. Wm. Cornwallis.
Adm. Wm., ld. Radstock.
Adm. sir Roger Curtis, bt.
Adm. Geo. Montagu.
Lt.-gen. Hy. Wm., E. of Uxbridge, aft. M. of Anglesey.
Lt.-gen. Robt. Brownrigg.
Lt.-gen. sir Harry Calvert, bt.
Lt.-gen. hon. Thos. Maitland.
Lt.-gen. Wm. Hy. Clinton.

1815. Richd., 2nd E. of Clancarty, Apr. 1.
Lt.-gen. hon. sir John Abercromby, Apr. 7.
M.-gen. hon. sir Chas. Colville, Apr. 7.
Adm. Jas., 1st ld. Gambier, June 7.

1815, Aug. 18. F.M. Pr. Schwartzenburg.
F.M. Alb. Louis Leopold, Pr. Blucher.

1815, Aug. 18. F.M. count Barclay de Tolly.
F.M. sir Chas. Philip, Pr. Wrede.
Gen. Wm. Fredk. Chas., Pr. and aft. K. Wm. I. of Wurtemburg.

1815. M.-gen. sir Jas. Kempt, June 22.

1816. Adm. Edwd., 1st ld. Exmouth, Mar. 16.
Gen. Leop. Geo. Fredk., D. of Saxe, &c.; aft. Leop. I., K. of the Belgians, May 23.
M.-gen. sir David Ochterlony, bt. Dec. 10.

1817. Lt.-gen. sir Gordon Drummond, Jan. 7.
M.-gen. sir Geo. Townshend Walker, bt., Mar. 11.

1818, Feb. 20. Adm. sir Chas. Morice Pole, bt.
R.-adm. sir Thos. Fras. Fremantle.
R.-Adm. sir Geo. Cockburn, aft. bt.

1818, Oct 14. Gen. Fras. Rawdon, 1st M. of Hastings.
Lt.-gen. sir Thos. Hislop.

1819, Apr. 17. Gen. Pr. Volkonsky.
Gen. count Woronzow.
Gen. count Zieten.
Gen. baron Frimont.

1819. M.-gen. sir Jno. Malcolm, Nov. 20.

GEORGE IV.

1820. Lt.-gen. Kenneth Alexr., 11th ld. Howard of Effingham, Mar. 17.
1820, May 16. Adm. sir Wm. Domett.
V.-Adm. sir Thos. Foley.
1820, May 20. Gen. Wm., 2nd E. Harcourt.
Adm. sir Benjn. Caldwell.
Adm. sir Richd. Rodney Bligh.
Gen. sir Hy. Johnson, bt.
Gen. Hy., 1st E. of Mulgrave.
Adm. sir Chas. Hy. Knowles, bt.
Adm. hon. sir Thos. Pakenham.
Gen. Geo., 1st ld. Harris.
Gen. sir Banastre Tarleton, bt.
Gen. sir Geo. Hewett, bt.
Gen. sir Geo. Don.
Gen. Jas. St. Clair, 2nd E. of Rosslyn.
Gen. Geo., ld. Gordon, c.c. M. of Huntly; aft. 5th D. of Gordon.
Lt.-gen. sir Chas. Cregan Craufurd.
Lt.-gen. sir Hildebrand Oakes, bt.
1820. Adm. sir Geo. Campbell, Jun 8.
Gen. Chas., count Alten, Au 12.
1821. V.-adm. sir Geo. Martin, Fe 23.
1822, Sept. 14. V.-adm. sir Thos. Boulde Thompson, bt.
V.-adm. sir Harry Neale, bt.
1824. Lt.-gen. sir John Oswald, Fe 25.
1825, Jan. 11. Adm. sir Edwd. Thornbrough.
Adm. sir Eliab Harvey.
1825. V.-adm. sir Wm. Johnstone Hop Oct. 4.
1826. Lt.-gen. sir Hy. Vane, Jan. 24.
M.-gen. sir Archd. Campbell, bt Dec. 26.
1827. V.-adm. sir Edwd. Codringto Nov. 13.
1830. V.-adm. sir Thos. Byam Marti Mar. 3.

WILLIAM IV.

1830. Bernard, D. of Saxe-Weimar, Aug. .
1830, Nov. 17. Adm. sir Jas. Hawkins Whitshed, bt.
Adm. sir Philip Chas. Henderson-Durham, aft. Calderwood-Henderson-Durham.
1831. Ernest Fredk. Herbert, Ct. Münster, Feb. 16.
1831, Feb. 24. Lt.-gen. sir Wm. Houstoun, bt.
Lt.-gen. sir Edwd. Barnes.
Lt.-gen. sir John Byng.
1831. Adm. sir Hy. Trollope, May 19.
1831, June 6. Adm. hon. sir Robt. Stopford.
Adm. sir Benjn. Hallowell Carew.
1831, Sept. 13. Gen. hon. sir Hy. Geo. Grey.
Gen. sir Ronald Craufurd Ferguson.
Gen. sir Hy. Warde.
Adm. sir Thos. Williams.
Adm. sir Wm. Hargood.
Lt.-gen. hon. sir Wm. Lumley.
Lt.-gen. sir Jas. Willoughby Gordon, bt.
R.-adm. sir Thos. Masterman Hardy, bt.
1833. Adm. sir Davidge Gould, Jan. 24.
Adm. sir Chas. Tyler, Jan. 29.
V.-adm. sir Pulteney Malcolm, Apr. 24.
1833, July 29. Lt.-gen. sir Geo. Anson.
Lt.-gen. sir John Ormsby Vandeleur.
1833. Lt.-gen. sir Thos. Dallas, Aug. 1.
1834. Lt.-gen. sir Herbert Taylor, Ap 16.
F.M. Chas., Archd. of Austri May 23.
Lt.-gen. ct. Walmoden, Aug. 19
Adm. sir John Wells, Oct. 6.
Lt.-gen. sir Robt. Edwd. H Somerset, c.c. ld. R. E. Somerset, Oct. 17.
Lt.-gen. sir Wm. Hy. Pringl Dec. 19.
1835. Lt.-gen. hon. sir Edwd. Stopfor Mar. 28.
Adm. sir Amelius Beauclerk, c. ld. A. Beauclerk, Aug. 3.
1835, Aug. 29. Lt.-gen. Ernest, &c., Pr. Hesse.
Lt.-gen. Ernest, Pr. of Hess Philippsthal-Barchfield.
1836. V.-adm. sir Graham Moore, Ma 11.
Gen. Louis Wm. Fredk., Landg of Hesse-Homburg, June 11.
Lt.-gen. Matth. Whitworth, 4 ld. Aylmer, Sept. 10.
1837. Lt.-gen. sir Thos. Makdoug Brisbane, bt., Feb. 6.
Adm. sir Lawrence Wm. Halste Feb. 24.
1837, Mar. 10. Lt.-gen. sir John Doveton.
M.-gen. sir John Whittingt Adams, nom.; but *d.* Mar. 1837, in India.
1837. Lt.-gen. sir Richd. Husse Vivian, bt., May 30.

VICTORIA.

1837. Pr. Paul Anthy. Esterhazy, July 12.
1838. Lt.-gen. sir John Colborne, aft. ld. Seaton, Jan. 29.
Lt.-gen. sir Thos. Bradford, Feb. 15.
M.-gen. sir Hy. Worsley, Feb. 16.
Lt.-gen. sir Fredk. Philipse Robinson, Apr. 20.
1838, July 19. Adm. sir Wm. Sidney Smith.
Lt.-gen. sir John Lambert.
Lt.-gen. hon. sir Robt. Wm. O'Callaghan.
1838, July 20. M.-gen. sir Alexr. Caldwell.
M.-gen. sir Jas. Law Lushington.
1838. M.-gen. sir Alexr. I. Dickson, July 23.
1839. Lt.-gen. Fredk. Geo. Augs., D. of Saxe Coburg and G., June 12.
Lt.-gen. sir John Keane, aft. ld. Keane, Aug. 12.
Adm. sir Hy. Wm. Bayntun, Oct. 25.
1840. M.-gen. sir Willoughby Cotton, Jan. 21.
F.M. Fras. Albert Augs. Chas. Emanuel, Consort of Q. Vict., Mar. 6.
1840, June 20. Lt.-gen. sir Fredk. Adam.
Lt.-gen. Benjn. D'Urban.
Lt.-gen. Andr. Fras. Barnard.
1840, July 4. Adm. Sir Wm. Hotham.
Adm. sir Josias Rowley, bt.
V.-adm. sir Chas. Rowley, bt.
V.-Adm. sir David Milne.
1840. Gen. Baldomero Espartero, Ct. of Luchana, &c., July 20.
1841. M.-gen. sir Jos. O'Halloran, Feb. 12.
M.-gen. Hugh, ld. Gough, aft. visc. Gough; Oct. 14.
1842, Feb. 23. Adm. hon. sir John Talbot.
Adm. sir Robt. Barlow.
Adm. sir Hy. Digby.
1842. Lt.-gen. Ct. Mensdorf, May 30.
Col. sir Robt. Hy. Sale, June 16.
Archduke Fredk. Chas. of Austria, Nov. 5.
1842, Dec. 2. V.adm. sir Wm. Parker.
M.-gen. Geo. Pollock.
M.-gen. Wm. Nott.
1843. M-.gen. Chas. Jas. Napier, July 4.
Pr. Fredk. Wm. Chas. of Prussia, Aug. 18.
1845, May. 8. Adm. sir Robt. Waller Otway, bt.
V.-adm. sir Edwd. Wm. Campbell Richd. Owen.
1846. Col. sir Hy. Geo. Wakelyn Smith, Apr. 7.
1847, May 22. V.-adm. Thos., 10th E. of Dundonald; (*see* "Cochrane" under K.B., Apr. 21, 1809, *ante*, p. 766.)
1847, Sept. 17. Lt.-gen. Fitzroy Jas. Hy. Somerset, c.c. ld. Fitzroy Somerset, aft. ld. Raglan.
Lt.-gen. sir John Macdonald.
1847. Gen. sir Colin Halket, Dec. 30.
1848. M.-gen. sir John Hunter Littler, Jan. 31.
Sir Jas. Lillyman Caldwell, Aug. 25.
1849. Lt.-gen. sir Edwd. Blakeney, May 7.
1849, June 5. M.-gen. sir Jos. Thackwell.
M.-gen. sir Walter Raleigh Gilbert.
1852, Apr. 6. Adm. sir Chas. Ekins.
Gen. sir Peregrine Maitland.
Adm. sir Thos. Bladen Capel.
Lt.-gen. sir Alexr. Woodford.
Lt.-gen. sir Hy. Fredk. Bouverie.
V.-adm. sir Chas. Bullen.
Lt.-gen. sir Jno. Fox Burgoyne.
1855, July 5. Lt.-gen. sir Geo. Brown.
V.-adm. Jas. Whitley Deans Dundas.
Geo. Wm. Fredk. Chas., D. of Cambridge.
Lt.-gen. sir De Lacy Evans.
Lt.-gen. sir Richd. England.
Lt.-gen. sir Colin Campbell, aft. ld. Clyde.
R.-adm. sir Edmd. Lyons, bt.
Adm. sir Graham Eden Hamond.
Adm. sir Jas. Alexr. Gordon.
Gen. sir Jas. McDonell.
Gen. sir Hew Dalrymple Ross.
1855. Le Comte Vaillant, Marshal of France, Oct. 16.
Gen. Jas. Simpson, Oct. 16.
Gen. Marmora, Oct. 25.
Marshal Pelissier, Nov. 12.
1856, Jan. 3. Gen. Bosquet.
Gen. de Salles.
Gen. MacMahon.
Gen. Regnault de St. John d'Angély.
Gen. Morris.
1857. Pr. Fredk. Wm. Louis of Prussia. aft. K. Wm. I. of Prussia and Emp. Wm. I. of Germany, Jan. 1.
Adm. Ferd. Alphonse Hamelin, May 7.
Lt.-gen. sir Jas. Outram, July 30
1858, July 6. M.-gen. sir Hugh Hy. Rose, aft. ld. Strathnairn.
H.H. Maharajah Bahadoor Koonwar Ranajee.
1859. R.-adm. sir Michl. Seymour, May 20.
Jas. Howard, 3rd E. of Malmesbury, Jan. 15.

1859. Sir John Pakington, bt., June 15.
1859, Gen. sir Thos. McMahon, bt.
June 21. Gen. Chas. Murray, 3rd E. Cathcart.
Gen. sir Wm. Maynard Gomm.
Gen. sir Robt. Wm. Gardiner.
1860, Adm. sir John West.
May 18. Adm. sir Wm. Hall Gage.
Adm. sir Fras. Wm. Austen.
Gen. sir Jas. Douglas.
Gen. sir Geo. Scovell.
Gen. Ulysses, ld. Downes.
Adm. sir Thos. John Cochrane.
Adm. sir Geo. Fras. Seymour.
Gen sir Fredk. Stovin.
Gen. sir Jas. Fergusson.
Lt.-gen. sir John Bell.
1860. Lt.-gen. sir Chas. Yorke, June 29.
Lt.-gen. Jas. Hope Grant, Nov. 9.
1861. M.-gen. sir Patrick Grant, Mar. 1.
1861, Gen. sir Arthur Benjn. Clifton.
June 28. Adm. sir Phipps Hornby.
Gen. sir Jas. Archd. Hope.
Gen. sir Thos. Wm. Brotherton.
Gen. sir Saml. Benjn. Auchmuty.
Adm. sir Barrington Reynolds.
Gen. sir Thos. Will, bt.
V.-adm. sir Maurice Fredk. Fitzhardinge Berkeley.
Lt.-gen. sir Harry David Jones.
1862, Gen. sir John Wright Guise, bt.
Nov. 10. Gen. sir John Forster FitzGerald.
Adm. Anthy., 10th E. of Lauderdale.
Adm. sir Edwd. Tucker.
1865. Albert Edwd., Pr. of Wales, Feb. 10.
1865, Adm. sir Edwd. Harvey.
Mar. 28. Adm. sir Fairfax Moresby.
Gen. sir Wm. Rowan.
Adm. sir Houston Stewart.
Gen. sir Wm. John Codrington.
Gen. sir Geo. Augs. Wetherall.
Adm. sir Hy. Ducie Chads.
Gen. sir Jas. Fredk. Love.
Gen. sir Jas. Jackson.
Lt.-gen. sir John Cheape.
Lt.-gen. Hy., 3rd visc. Melville.
V.-adm. hon. sir Fredk. Wm. Grey.
V.-adm. sir Jas. Hope.
1865. Adm. sir Geo. Robt. Lambert, June 7.
1867, Adm. sir Stephen Lushington.
May 13. Lt.-gen. sir John Lysaght Pennefather.
Lt.-gen. sir Richd. Airey.
Adm. sir Chas. Howe Fremantle.
M.-gen. sir Archdale Wilson, bt.
Lt.-gen. sir Edwd. Lugard.

1867, Gen. sir John Aitchison.
May 13. Gen. hon. sir Chas. Gore.
Gen. Geo., 8th M. of Tweeddale.
1868. Lt.-gen. sir Robt. Cornelis Napier, aft. ld. Napier of Magdala, Apr. 27.
1869, Adm. sir Hy. Prescott.
June 2. Gen. Geo. Chas., 3rd E. of Lucan.
Gen. sir Richd. Jas. Dacres.
Lt.-gen. hon. sir Jas. Yorke Scarlett.
Lt.-gen. sir Geo. Buller.
V.-adm. sir Augs. Leopold Kuper.
1870. Lt.-gen. sir Wm. Rose Mansfield, aft. ld. Sandhurst, May 14.
1871, Adm. hon. sir Hy. Keppel.
May 20. Gen. sir Wm. Fenwick Williams bt.
Adm. sir Alexr. Milne.
Adm. sir Sydney Colpoys Dacres
Gen. sir Robt. John Hussey Vivian.
Lt.-gen. sir John Michel.
Lt.-gen. Wm. Paulet, c.c. ld Wm. Paulet.
1873, Gen. sir Hy. Geo. Andrew
May 24. Taylor.
Gen. sir Geo. Bowles.
Adm. sir Provo Wm. Parry Wallis.
Adm. sir Wm. Fanshawe Martin.
Gen. sir Abraham Roberts.
Gen. sir Jas. Chas. Chatterton bt.
Thos., 11th E. of Lauderdale.
Adm. sir Lewis Tobias Jones.
Gen. sir Wm. Hy. Elliott.
Lt.-gen. sir Sydney John Cotton.
Lt.-gen. sir John Bloomfield.
Lt.-gen. sir Duncan Alexr Cameron.
1875, Gen. sir Thos. Reed.
May 29. Gen. Hy. ld. Rokeby.
Gen. sir John Bloomfield Gough.
Gen. sir Chas. Thos. Van Straubenzee.
Lt.-gen. hon. sir Augs. Almeric Spencer.
V.-adm. sir Hastings Regd. Yelverton.
Lt.-gen. sir Chas. Shepherd Stuart.
Lt.-gen. sir John Garvock.
Lt.-gen. sir Neville Bowles Chamberlain.
M.-gen. sir Alfd. Hastings Horsford.
1877. Gen. Jioji Rao Sindia Maharaja of Gwalior, Jan. 1.
1877, Adm. sir Geo. Rodney Mundy.
June 2. Gen. sir Wm. Wyllie.
Lt.-gen. sir Fredk. Edwd. Chapman.

1877, Lt.-gen. sir Fredk. Paul Haines.
June 2. Lt.-gen. sir David Edwd. Wood.
M.-gen. sir John Douglas.
1878. Gen. sir Arth. Augs. Thurlow Cunynghame, June 13.
Gen. Pr. Fredc. Chas. Nichs. of Prussia, July 3.
Gen. sir John Lintorn Arabin Simmons, July 29.
1879. M.-gen. Fredc. Augs., 2nd ld. Chelmsford, Aug. 19.
1880, Adm. sir Geo. Rose Sartorius.
Apr. 23. Adm. sir Thos. Mathew Chas. Symonds.
Adm. hon. sir Jas. Robt. Drummond.
Lt.-gen. sir Garnet Josh. Wolseley, aft. visc. Wolseley, June 19.
Lt.-gen. Donald Martin Stewart, Sept. 21.
M.-gen. Fredk. Sleigh Roberts, Sept. 21
1881, Gen. Wm. Lygon, 4th E. of Longford.
May 24. V.-adm. sir Fredk. Beauchamp Paget Seymour.
1882. Gen. sir Chas. Hy. Ellice, Apr. 15.
Lt.-gen. sir John Miller Adye, Nov. 17.
Adm. sir Anthy. Cooper Key, Nov. 24.
Adm. sir Wm. Robt. Mends, Nov. 24.
1883. F.M. Fredk. Wm. Nichs. Chas., Cr. Pr. of Prussia, aft. Emp. Fredk. III. of Germany and K. of Prussia, Jan. 25.
1884, Gen. sir Chas. Wm. Dunbar
May 24. Staveley.
Gen. sir Collingwood Dickson.
Gen sir Arthr. Borton.
1884, Gen. sir Hy. Chas. Barnston
May 24. Daubeney.
Gen. sir Jas. Brind.
1885. M.-gen. sir Peter Stark Lumsden, July 3.
Gen. Pr. Alexr. Louis Geo. Fredk. Emile of Hesse, July 22.
Adm. sir Geoffrey Thos. Phipps Hornby, Dec. 19.
1886. Gen. sir Fredk. Chas. Arthr. Stephenson, Jan. 30.
1886, Adm. Clarence Edwd. Paget, c.c.
May 29. ld. Clarence Paget.
Gen. Geo. Fredk., visct. Templetown.
Gen. sir Wm. Jones.
Gen. sir Chas. Reid.
Gen. sir Geo. Malcolm.
Gen. sir Danl. Lysons.
Lt.-gen. sir Fredk. Fras. Maude.
1886. Adm. John Hay, c.c. ld. John Hay, July 30.
Pr. Alexr. of Bulgaria, Dec. 10.
1887, Adm. sir Geo. Greville Welles-
June 21. ley.
Adm. sir Edwd. Gennys Fanshawe.
Gen. sir Edwd. Cooper Hodge.
Gen. sir Thos. Montagu Steele.
Gen. sir Edwin Beaumont Johnson.
Gen. sir Hy. Wylie Norman.
Adm. sir Wm. Houston Stewart.
Adm. sir John Edmd. Commerell.
Lt.-gen. sir Chas. Lawrence D'Aguilar.
Lt.-gen. sir Archd. Alison, bt.
Lt.-gen. sir Chas. Hy. Brownlow.
Gen. Pr. Wm. Augustus Edwd. of Saxe Weimar.
1887. Adm. Ernest Leopold, &c., Pr. of Leiningen, July 1 and Sept. 27.

KNIGHTS GRAND CROSS—CIVIL DIVISION.

(G.C.B.)

George III.

1815, Sir Robt. Gunning.
Jan. 2. Jas., E. of Malmesbury.
Morton, ld. Henley.
Chas., ld. Whitworth.
Sir Jos. Banks, bt.
Sir Arth. Paget.
Sir Philip Francis.
Sir Geo. H. Barlow.
Percy Clinton Sydney, visc.
1815, Strangford in Ir.; aft. ld Pens-
Jan. 2. hurst in Gr. Brit.
Hon. sir Hy. Wellesley, aft. 1st ld. Cowley.
Hon. sir Chas. Stewart.
1816. Sir Robt. Linton, Oct. 21.
1819. Sir Wm. A'Court, bt., aft. ld. Heytesbury, Oct. 20.

GEORGE IV.

1820, Sir Chas. Long.
May 20. Sir Chas. Bagot.
1822. Sir Edwd. Thornton, Mar. 8.
M.-gen. sir Benjn. Bloomfield, aft. 1st ld. B., Apr. 1.
1825. Granville, 1st visc. and E. Granville, May.
1827. Fredc. Jas. Lamb, aft. ld. Beauvale and visc. Melbourne, Dec 13.
1829, Sir Stratford Canning, aft. visc.
Dec. 7. Stratford de Redcliffe.
Sir Robt. Gordon.

WILLIAM IV.

1831. Sir Robt. Adair, Aug. 3.
1832. Hy. John, 3rd visc. Palmerston, June 6.
1833. Chas. Manners Sutton, aft. visc. Canterbury, Aug. 31.
1834. John, 2nd ld., and aft. 1st visc. Ponsonby, Mar. 3.
1834. Gilbert, 2nd E. of Minto, Sept 16.
1835. Geo., 2nd ld., aft. 1st E. of Auckland, Aug. 29.
Sir Chas. Theoph. Metcalfe, bt., Sept. 12.

VICTORIA.

1837. John Geo., 1st E. of Durham, June 27.
Geo. Wm. Fredk. Villiers, aft. 4th E. of Clarendon, Oct. 19.
Augs. Fredk., D. of Sussex; app. first G.C.B., Dec. 15, and actg. Gr. Mast., Dec. 16.
1838, Achd., 2nd E. of Gosford.
July 19. Col. Geo. Wm. Russell, c.c. ld. G. W. Russell.
Chas. Augs., 6th ld. Howard de Walden.
1838. Richd. Jenkins, July 20.
1839. John McNeill, Apr. 15.
1841. Lt.-gen. sir Howard Douglas, bt., Aug. 27.
Chas. Wm., 1st ld. Sydenham, Aug. 19.
Lt.-gen. sir Lionel Smith, bt., Aug. 27.
1842. M.-gen. sir Hy. Pottinger, bt., Dec. 2.
1843. Arth. Aston, Nov. 10.
1844. Lt.-gen. sir Hy. Hardinge, aft. visc. H., June 1.
Capt. sir Edmd. Lyons, bt., R.N., July 10.
Edwd., 1st E. of Ellenborough, Oct. 30.
1845. Chas. Cecil Cope, 3rd E. of Liverpool, Dec. 11.
1846. Lt.-gen. John, 11th E. of Westmorland, June 24.
1847. Sir Geo. Hy. Seymour, Jan. 21.
Constantine Hy., M. of Normanby, Dec. 10.
1849. Sir Geo. Grey, bt., Mar. 31.
1851. Sir Hy. Lytton Earle Bulwer; aft. ld. Dalling and Bulwer, Mar. 1.
1852. John Cam, ld. Broughton, Feb. 23.
1853. Hy. Richd. Chas., 2nd ld. and 1st E. Cowley, Feb. 21.
1854. Sir Jas. Robt. Geo Graham, bt., Apr. 15.
1855. Fox, 2nd ld. Panmure; aft. 11th E. of Dalhousie, Oct. 29.
1856. Sir Chas. Wood, bt., aft. visc Halifax.
1857. Edwd. Granville, 3rd E. of St. Germans, Jan. 24.
Sir John Laird Mair Lawrence, aft. ld. Lawrence, Nov. 11.
1858. M.-gen. John Hobart, ld. Howden, Mar. 5.
John Arth., 2nd ld. Bloomfield Sept. 3.
Jas., 8th E. of Elgin, and 12th E. of Kincardine, Sept. 28.
1859. Chas. John, visc. Canning, Mar. 31.
John, ld. Elphinstone.
1862. Richd. Bickerton Pemell, 2nd ld. and aft. 1st visc. Lyons, Jan. 24.
1863. John Robt., 3rd visc. and aft. 1st E. Sydney, Mar. 10.
Sir Jas. Hudson, Aug. 11.
1864. M.-gen. Sir Hy. Knight Storks, July 1.
1865. Hon. Sir Fredk. Wm. Adolphus Bruce, Mar. 17.
The Bey of Tunis, June 1.
1866. Sir Robt. Peel, bt., Jan. 5.
Capt. Ernest Leopold, &c., Pr. of Leiningen, R.N., Jan. 29.
Fras. Paul Chas. Louis Alexr., Pr. of Teck, June 12.
1866, Sir Andr. Buchanan.
July 6. Hon. Augs. Wm. Fredk. Spencer Loftus, c.c. ld. Augs. Loftus.
Sir Arth. Chas. Magenis.

1866. Ismail Pacha, Viceroy of Egypt, Dec. 18.
1867. Pr. Hohenlohe-Langenburg, May 8.
1868. Sir John Young, bt., Nov. 13.
1869. Hy. Geo. Elliott, Nov. 22.
1872. Robt. Vernon, 1st ld. Lyveden, July 13.
Hy. Fras. Howard, July 13.
1873. Sir Alexr. Jas. Edmd. Cockburn, bt., ld. ch. just., K.B.
Hon. Odo Wm. Leopold Russell, c.c. ld. Odo Russell; aft. ld. Ampthill.
1876. Sir Hy. Bartle Edwd. Frere, aft. bt., May 17.
The Hered. Gr. D. of Mecklenburg-Strelitz, Apr. 17.
Edwd. Robt. Lytton, 2nd ld. and aft. 1st E. of Lytton, Jan. 1.
Austen Hy. Layard, June 11.
1879. Gen. Fras. Hugh Geo., M. of Hertford, Jan. 24.
Pr. Alexr. Jos. of Battenberg, Pr. Elect of Bulgaria, June 6.
1880, Stephen Cave.
Apr. 20. Richd. Assheton Cross, aft. visc. Cross.
Sir Stafford Hy. Northcote, bt., aft. E. of Iddesleigh.
Hon. John Jas. Robt. Manners, c.c. ld. John Manners; aft. 7th D. of Rutland.
1881. Pr. Hy. of Prussia, Aug. 13.
Hy. Bouverie Wm. Brand, aft. visc. Hampden, Sept. 20.
1883. Fredk. Temple, E. of Dufferin, aft. M. of Dufferin and Ava, June 15.
1883, Sir Edwd. Thornton.
Aug. 21. Sir Augs. Berkeley Paget.
1884. Sir John Alexr. Macdonald, Nov. 1.
1885. Hy. Austin, ld. Aberdare, Jan. 7.
Geo. Augs. Constantine, M. of Normanby, Jan. 9.
Sir John Savile Lumley, June 15.
Chas., visc. Eversley, June 30.
Robt., visc. Sherbrooke, June 30.
1886. Fredk. Arth. Stanley, aft. ld. Stanley of Preston, Feb. 2.
Sir Edwd. Baldwin Malet, Feb. 2.
1887, Gr. D. Serge Alexandrovitch of
June 21. Russia.
Ern. Louis Chas. Albert Wm., Hered. Gr. D. of Hesse.
Bernard Fredk. Wm. Albt. Geo., Hered. Pr. of Saxe-Meiningen.
Mehemed Tewfik, Viceroy or Khedive of Egypt.
Gen. Hon. sir Hy. Fredk. Ponsonby.
V.-Adm. Victor Ferd., &c., Pr. of Hohenlohe-Langenburg.
Pr. Louis Alexr. of Battenberg.
1887. Sir Robt. Burnett David Morier, Sept. 30.
1888. Pr. Christian Fredc. Wm. Chas., Cr. Pr. of Denmark, Mar. 10.
Sir Wm. Arth. White, June. 21.

KNIGHTS COMMANDERS—MILITARY DIVISION.

(K.C.B.)

GEORGE III.

1815, Adm. Jas., ld. Gambier.
Jan. 2. Adm. sir Chas. Maurice Pole, bt.
Adm. Jas. Hawkins Whitshed.
Adm. sir Robt. Calder, bt.
Adm. sir Richd. Bickerton, bt.
Adm. John Knight.
Adm. Edwd. Thornbrough.
Adm. Geo. Campbell.
Adm. sir Albemarle Bertie, bt.
Adm. Edwd., 1st ld. Exmouth.
V.-adm. Wm. Domett.
V.-adm. Geo. Murray.
V.-adm. John Sutton.
V.-adm. Wm. Essington.
V.-adm. Eliab Hervey.
V.-adm. sir Edm. Nagle.
V.-adm. Richd. Grindall.
V.-adm. sir Geo. Martin.
V.-adm. sir Wm. Sydney Smith.
1815, Lt.-gen. Gordon Drummond.
Jan. 2. V.-adm. Herbert Sawyer.
Lt.-gen. hon. John Abercromby.
V.-adm. hon. Robt. Stopford.
V.-adm. Thos. Foley.
Lt.-gen. Ronald Craufurd Ferguson.
Lt.-gen. Hy. Warde.
V.-adm. Chas. Tyler.
V.-adm. Alan Hyde, ld. Gardner.
V.-adm. Wm. Mitchell.
V.-adm. sir Thos. Williams.
V.-adm. sir Thos. Boulden Thompson, bt.
Lt.-gen. Wm. Houston.
Lt.-gen. Wm. Lumley.
Lt.-gen. Wroth Palmer Acland.
Lt.-gen. Miles Nightingale.
Lt.-gen. Hy. Fredk. Campbell.
V.-adm. Wm. Hargood.

1815, Jan. 2. V.-adm. Robt. Moorsom.
V.-adm. Lawrence Wm. Halsted.
V.-adm. sir Harry Neale, bt.
V.-adm. sir Jos. Sidney Yorke.
V.-adm. hon. Arth. Kaye Legge.
M.-gen. Alan Cameron.
M.-gen. hon. Chas. Colville.
M.-gen. Hy. Fane.
M.-gen. Geo. Anson.
M.-gen. Kenneth Alexr. Howard, aft. 11th ld. Howard of Effingham.
R.-adm. Thos. Fras. Fremantle.
R.-adm. sir Fras. Laforey, bt.
R.-adm. Philip Chas. Durham.
R.-adm. Israel Pellew.
M.-gen. Hy. Bell.
M.-gen. John Oswald.
M.-gen. sir Wm. Anson, bt.
M.-gen. Edwd. Howorth.
M.-gen. Chas. Wale.
M.-gen. John Ormsby Vandeleur.
M.-gen. hon. Edwd. Stopford.
M.-gen. Geo. Townshend Walker.
R.-adm. Benjn. Hallowell.
R.-adm. Geo. Hope.
R.-adm. Amelius Beauclerk, c.c. ld. A. Beauclerk.
R.-adm. Jas. Nicoll Morris.
R.-adm. Thos. Byam Martin.
M.-gen. Jas. Kempt.
M.-gen. Robt. Rollo Gillespie, nom., but *d.* in India, Oct. 31, 1814.
M.-gen. Wm. Hy. Pringle.
R.-adm. Wm. Johnstone Hope.
R.-adm. Hy. Paulet, c.c. ld. Hy. Paulet.
R.-adm. Geo. Cockburn.
R.-adm. Graham Moore.
R.-adm. Hy. Wm. Bayntun.
R.-adm. sir Richd. King, bt.
R.-adm. Richd. Lee.
M.-gen. Fredk. Philipse Robinson.
M.-gen. Edwd. Barnes.
M.-gen. hon. Wm. Ponsonby.
M.-gen. John Byng.
M.-gen. Thos. Brisbane, aft. Makdougall-Brisbane.
M.-gen. Denis Pack.
M.-gen. Robt. Edwd. Hy. Somerset, c.c. ld. R. E. H. Somerset.
M.-gen. Thos. Bradford.
M.-gen. John Lambert.
M.-gen. Jas. Willoughby Gordon.
M.-gen. Manley Power.
M.-gen. Saml. Gibbs.
M.-gen. Matth., 5th ld. Aylmer.
R.-adm. Wm. Hotham.
R.-adm. Pulteney Malcolm.
R.-adm sir John Gore.
R.-adm. hon. Hy. Hotham.
R.-adm. Geo. Burlton.
R.-adm. Horne Popham.

1815, Jan. 2. R.-adm. sir Josias Rowley, bt.
R.-adm. Edwd. Codrington.
R.-adm. sir Chas. Rowley, bt.
M.-gen. Colquhoun Grant.
M.-gen. sir Thos. Sidney Beckwith.
M.-gen. hon. Robt. Wm. O'Callaghan.
M.-gen. Jno. Keane.
M.-gen. Colin Halkett.
M.-gen. sir Hy. Edwd. Bunbury, bt.
M.-gen. Richd. Hussey Vivian.
M.-gen. Hy. Torrens.
Capt. sir Geo. Eyre.
Capt. sir Chas. Brisbane.
Capt. John Talbot.
Capt. sir Edwd. Berry, bt.
Capt. sir Edwd. Hamilton.
Caps. Edwd. Wm. Campbell Richd. Owen.
Capt. sir Thos. Masterman Hardy, bt.
Capt. sir Jahleel Brenton, bt.
Capt. Sir Michael Seymour.
Capt. sir Thos. Laire.
Capt. sir Philip Bowes Vere Broke, bt.
Capt. sir Wm. Hoste, bt.
Capt. sir Christopher Cole.
Capt. sir Geo. Ralph Collier, bt.
Capt. sir Jas. Lind.
Capt. Jas. Alexr. Gordon.
Capt. sir Thos. Staines.
Capt. sir Edwd. Tucker.
Capt. sir Jas. Lucas Yeo.
Col. Jno. Elley.
Col. Chas. Philip Belson.
Col. Wm. Howe Delancey
Col. Benjn. Durban.
Col. Geo. Ridout Bingham.
Col. hon. Chas. Jas. Greville.
Col. Haylett Framingham.
Col. Andr. Fras. Barnard.
Col. Wm. Robe.
Col. Hy. Walton Ellis.
Col. John Cameron.
Col. hon. Robt. Le Poer Trench.
Col. Chas. Pratt.
Col. Edwd. Blakeney.
Col. John M'Lean.
Col. Richd. Downes Jackson.
Col. Wm. Douglas.
Col. Colin Campbell.
Col. John Colborne.
Col. Archd. Campbell.
Col. Thos. Arbuthnot.
Col. Hy. Fredk. Bouverie.
Lt.-col. Wm. Williams.
Lt.-col. Hy. Hollis Bradford.
Lt.-col. Alexr. Leith.
Lt.-col. hon. Robt. Lawrence Dundas.
Lt.-col. Robt. Arbuthnot.
Lt.-col. sir Chas. Sutton.
Lt.-col. Jas. Douglas.

1815, Lt.-col. Hy. Hardinge, aft. visc. H.
Jan. 2. Lt.-col. Geo. Hy. Fredk. Berkeley.
Lt.-col. Jeremiah Dickson.
Lt.-col. sir John Milley Doyle.
Lt.-col. sir Thos. Noel Hill.
Lt.-col. Robt. Macara.
Lt.-col. hon. Alexr. Gordon.
Lt.-col. Hy. Wm. Carr.
Lt.-col. Chas. Broke Vere.
Lt.-col. Fitzroy Jas. Hy. Somerset, c.c. ld. Fitzroy Somerset; aft. ld. Raglan.
Lt.-col. Jas. Wilson.
Lt.-col. Alexr. I. Dickson.
Lt.-col. John May.
Lt.-col. Geo. Scovell.
Lt.-col. Wm. Maynard Gomm.
Lt.-col. Ulysses Burgh.
Lt.-col. Fras. D'Oyley.
Lt.-col. Richd. Williams.
Lt.-col. Jas. Malcolm.
Lt.-col. Jas. Archd. Hope.
Lt.-col. Augs. Frazer.
Lt.-col. Hew Dalrymple Ross.
Lt.-col. Edm. Keynton Williams.
Lt.-col. Maxwell Grant.
Lt.-col. Fredk. Stovin.
Lt.-col. Jos. Hugh Carncross.
Lt.-col. Robt. Gardiner.
Lt.-col. John Dyer.
Lt.-gen. Chas., baron Linsingen.
Lt.-gen. count Walmoden.
Lt.-gen. count Nugent.
M.-gen. Sigismund, baron Low.
M.-gen. Chas., baron Alten.
M.-gen. Hy. de Hinuber.
M.-gen. Wilhelm de Dornberg.
Col. Fredk., baron de Arentschildt.
Lt.-col. Fredk. Augs. de Hertzberg.
Lt.-col. Julius Hartmann.
1815, Lt.-gen. Moore Disney.
Apr. 7. M.-gen. Wm. Inglis.
M.-gen. Jas. Lyon.
Lt.-gen. John Macdonald.
M.-gen. Robt. Blair.
M.-gen. Geo. Wood.
1815, M.-gen. Hector McLean.
Apr. 7. M.-gen. Thos. Dallas.
M.-gen. John M. Chalmers.
M.-gen. John Horsford.
M.-gen. Hy. White.
M.-gen. Gabriel Martindell.
M.-gen. Geo. Sackville Browne.
M.-gen. Geo. Holmes.
M.-gen. David Ochterlony.
Col. John Malcolm.
Col. Augs. Floyer.
Col. Robt. Barclay.
1815. V.-adm. sir Davidge Gould, June 7.
M.-gen. Geo. Cooke, June 20.
M.-gen. Peregrine Maitland, June 22.
M.-gen. Fredk. Adam, June 22.
Lt.-gen. Miguel Alava, Oct. 10.
Lt.-gen. Bar. de Muffling, Oct. 20.
1816. R.-Adm. Chas. Vinicombe Penrose, Jan. 3.
M.-gen. sir Hudson Lowe, Jan. 23.
R.-adm. sir David Milne, Sept. 19.
V.adm. Bar. Van de Capellen, Oct. 4.
1817. Lt.-gen. sir Alexr. Campbell, bt., Jan. 7.
Lt.-gen. Richd. Jones, Feb. 3.
Lt.-gen. Robt. Macfarlane, Mar. 11.
1818. Lt.-gen. Thos. Hislop, Sept. 5.
M.-gen. Dyson Marshall, Oct. 14.
M.-gen. Rufane Shaw Donkin, Oct. 14.
1819, Gen. Nichs. Chas., baron Vincent.
Apr. 17. Gen. count Pozzo de Borgo.
Gen. De Reede.
Lt.-gen. — Lamotte.
1819, V.-adm. Manley Dixon.
Aug. 12. R.-adm. hon. sir Hy. Blackwood, bt.
R.-adm. sir John Poo Beresford, bt.
1819, M.-gen. sir Thos. Munro, bt.
Nov. 26. M.-gen. Wm. Toone.
M.-gen. John Doveton.

George IV.

1820. Lt.-gen. sir Hy. Tucker Montresor, Mar. 17.
1820, Adm. sir Hy. Trollope.
May 20. Adm. Hy. D'Esterre Darby.
V.-adm. John Wells.
V.-adm. Hy. Nicholls.
Capt. sir Robt. Barlow.
Capt. hon. sir Geo. Grey, bt.
1822, M.-gen. sir Wm. Kerr Grant.
Dec. 3. M.-gen. Jas. Campbell.
M.-gen. Lionel Smith, aft. bt.
M.-gen. Theoph Pritzler.
1823. M.-gen. Thos. Brown, July 23.
1825. R.-adm. Wm. Chas. Fahie, Jan 13.
1826. R.-adm. Robt. Waller Otway, June 8.
1826, M.-gen. Thos. Reynell.
Dec. 26. M.-gen. Jasper Nicholls.
M.-gen. sir Saml. Ford Whittingham.
1827, M.-gen. sir Thos. McMahon, bt.
Jan. 18. Lt.-gen. Thos. Bowser
M.-gen. John Arnold.
1827. Lt.-gen. Baron de Hugel, Oct. 2.
1828, Adm. Louis, Count de Heiden.
Mar. 14. R.-adm. H. Re Rigny.

WILLIAM IV.

1830, Nov. 17. V.-adm. sir Willoughby Thos. Lake.
R.-adm. sir Fredk. Lewis Maitland.
1831. V.-adm. Hy. Digby. Mar. 14.
1831, May 19. V.-adm. Edwd. Griffith Colpoys.
V.-adm. Edwd. Jas. Foote.
1831, June 8. V.-adm. Chas. Ekins.
R.-adm. Thos. Baker.
1831, Sept. 13. Lt.-gen. Saml. Venables Hinde.
M.-gen. John. Wright Guise.
M.-gen. Jas. Bathurst.
M.-gen. Jas. Stevenson Banks.
R.-adm. Sir Robt. Laurie, bt.
M.-gen. John Macdonald.
M.-gen. Alexr. Woodford.
M.-gen. hon. Fredk. Cavendish Ponsonby.
R.-adm. Geo. Scott.
R.-adm. Thos. Dundas.
R.-adm. sir Graham Eden Hamond, bt.
M.-gen. John Buchan.
M.-gen. Hugh Gough, aft. ld. and visc. Gough.
M.-gen. Chas. Ashworth.
M.-gen. Chas. Bruce.
M.-gen. John Foster Fitzgerald.
M.-gen. John Ross.
M.-gen. Dugald Little Gilmour.
M.-gen. Wm. Macbean.
M.-gen. Geo. Elder.
1831, Sept. 26. M.-gen. Alexr. Knox.
M.-gen. sir John Whittington Adams.
M.-gen. Hy. Worsley.
M.-gen. Hopton Stratford Scott.
M.-gen. Robt. Scot.
M.-gen. Andr. Macdonald.
1832, Feb. 20. John Tremayne Rodd.
R.-adm. hon. Thos. Bladen Capel.
1832. M.-gen. John Waters, Mar. 1.
M.-gen. Hugh Fraser, Apr. 7.
1833. Adm. sir Chas. Hamilton, bt., Jan. 29.
1833, Apr. 24. R.-adm. Thos. Harvey.
R.-adm. Richd. Hussey Hussey.
1833, June 1. V.-adm. John Harvey.
V.-adm. Geo. Parker.
1833, Sept. 16. M.-gen. Arth. Brooke.
M.-gen. sir John Alex. Wallace, bt.
1834. Sir Wm. Parker, July 14.
R.-adm. Edwd. Bruce, Oct. 6.
M.-gen. John Taylor, Oct. 17.
1835. M.-gen. Richd. Bourke, Jan. 26.
M.-gen. hon. Hy. King, Mar. 28.
R.-adm. Chas. Adam, Aug. 10.
1836. R.-adm. Patrick Campbell, Apr. 11.
M.-gen. Wm. Thornton, Sept. 16.
M.-gen. Hy. Sheehy Keating, Dec. 21.
1837. M.-gen. sir John Wilson, Feb. 6.
1837, Feb. 28. V.-adm. Ross Donnelly.
R.-adm. Fras. Wm. Austen.
R.-adm. Geo. Mundy.
1837, Mar. 10. M.-gen. Jas. Lillyman Caldwell.
M.-gen. Alexr. Caldwell.
M.-gen. David Leighton.
M.-gen. Chas. Deacon.
M.-gen. Jos. Russell.
M.-gen. Sir Jos. O'Halloran.
M.-gen. Robt. Houstoun.
M.-gen. Robt. Stevenson.
M.-gen. Wm. Casement.
M.-gen. Jas. Law Lushington.

VICTORIA.

1837. M.-gen. Wm. Johnston, June 2.
1838. Col. De Lacy Evans, Feb. 13.
M.-gen. John Fane, c.c. ld. Burghersh, Feb. 15.
M.-gen. Donald Macleod, Feb. 16.
1838, Apr. 20. M.-gen. Chas. Somerset Manners, c.c. ld. C. Manners.
M.-gen. sir Jas. Macdonnell.
1838, July 19. Adm. John Lawford.
M.-gen. Andr. Pilkington.
M.-gen. John Gardiner.
M.-gen. Sir Arth. Benjn. Clifton.
M.-gen. Chas. Murray Cathcart, c.c. ld. Greenock.
M.-gen. Willoughby Cotton.
M.-gen. Sir John Geo. Woodford.
M.-gen. Patr. Lindesay.
1838, July 19. M.-gen. Chas. Jas. Napier.
M.-gen. Sir Evan John Murray Macgregor, bt.
M.-gen. Edwd. Gibbs.
M.-gen. Geo. Thos. Napier.
M.-gen. Hon. Hercules Robinson Pakenham.
M.-gen. Sir John Thos. Jones, bt.
M.-gen. John Hervey.
M.-gen. Leonard Greenwell.
M.-gen. Robt. Hy. Dick.
M.-gen. Neil Douglas.
R.-adm. John Acworth Ommaney.
M.-gen. Alexr. Cameron.
M.-gen. John Fox Burgoyne.
1838, July 20. M.-gen. John Rose.
M.-gen. Thos. Corsellis.

1838, M.-gen. Wm. Richards.
July 20. M.-gen. Thos. Whitehead.
M.-gen. John Doveton.
M.-gen. David Foulis.
M.-gen. Thos. Anburey.
1839, R.-adm. sir Chas. Bullen.
Apr. 18. R.-adm. sir Saml. Warren.
1839. Lt.-gen. Jas Watson, July 5.
1839, R.-adm. Saml. Pym.
Oct. 25. M.-gen. sir John Boscawen Savage.
1839, Col. Thos. Willshire.
Dec. 20. Col. Jos. Thackwell.
Col. Robt, Hy. Sale.
1840, V.-adm. John West.
July 4. R.-adm. sir Chas. Dashwood.
R.-adm. sir John Wentworth Loring.
R.-adm. sir Robt. Barrie.
R.-adm. sir Jas. Hillyar.
R.-adm. Wm. Fitzroy, c.c. ld. Wm. Fitzroy.
1840, Lt.-gen. sir Edwd. Kerrison, bt.
July 18. Lt.-gen. sir Howard Douglas, bt.
1840. Commod. Chas. Napier, Dec. 4.
1841, R.-adm. Fras. Baron de Bandiera.
Jan. 12. Capt. Baldwin Wake Walker.
1841, V.-adm. John Chambers White.
June 29. R.-adm. Chas. Richardson.
R.-adm. Sir Arth. Farquhar.
Commod. sir Jas. John Gordon Bremer.
1841. R.-adm. Fras. Mason, Aug. 24.
Capt. Thos. Herbert, R.N., Oct. 14.
1842, M.-Gen. Alexr. Geo., 16th ld.
Dec. 24. Saltoun.
Col. Robt. Bartley (? Bartlay).
Col. Jas. Holmes Schœdde.
Capt. Thos. Bourchier.
Col. John McCaskill.
1843, Lt-gen. Jas. Baron de Washing-
July 12. ton.
Lt.-gen. Maxn. Schreibershofer.
1843, M.-gen. sir Chas. Felix Smith.
Sept. 23. Col. Richd. England.
1844, M.-gen. John Grey.
May 2. M.-gen. Hy. Geo. Wakelyn Smith.
M.-gen. Jas. Rutherford Lumley.
M.-gen. John Hunter Littler.
1844, Col. Jas. Dennis.
Oct. 30. Col. Thos. Valiant.
1845. R.-adm. sir Edwd. Chetham, aft. Chetham-Strode, May 8.
1846. Capt. Chas. Hotham, Mar. 9.
M.-gen. Walter Raleigh Gilbert, Apr. 3.
M.-gen. Chas. Wm. Pasley, Dec. 21.
1847. R.-adm. sir Hugh Pigot, July 8.
R.-adm. sir Thos. John Cochrane, Oct. 29.
1848, M.-gen. sir Dudley St. Ledger
Mar 2. Hill.
M.-gen. John Rolt.
1848. M.-gen. Wm. Fras. Patr. Napier, Apr. 27.
M.-gen. Archd. Galloway, Aug. 25.
1849, Col. hon. Hy. Dundas.
June 5. Col. Colin Campbell, aft. ld. Clyde.
M.-gen. Wm. Samson Whish.
Col. John Cheape.
1850, Sir John Bisset.
Aug. 16. Sir Jas. McGregor, bt.
Sir Wm. Burnett.
Jas. Thomson.
Col. Hugh Massey Wheeler.
1851. M.-gen. Geo. Bowles, July 22.
1852. M.-gen. John Owen, Feb. 23.
1852, Lt.-gen. sir Thos. Downman.
Apr. 6. V.-adm. sir Geo. Fras. Seymour.
V.-adm. hon. sir Anthy. Maitland.
Lt.-gen. sir Archd. Maclaine.
Lt.-gen. Geo. Chas. D'Aguilar.
Lt.-gen. sir Richd. Armstrong.
Lt.-gen. Hy. Goldfinch.
Lt.-gen. John Bell.
Lt.-gen. Geo. Brown.
R.-adm. Phipps Hornby.
R.-adm. Wm. Fairbrother Carroll.
Col. Jas. Tennant.
1852. Lt.-gen. Chas. McLeod, June 29.
1853, Hon. Geo. Cathcart.
May 30. M.-gen. Hy. Somerset.
1853, M.-gen. Hy. Godwin.
Dec. 9. Brig.-gen. Scudamore Winde Steel.
Commander Geo. Robt. Lambert.
1854, Lt.-gen. hon. Geo. Cathcart.
May 30. M.-gen. Hy. Somerset.
1855, Lt.-gen. Geo. Chas., 3rd E. of
July 5. Lucan.
Lt.-gen. Hy. J. W. Bentinck.
Lt.-gen. John Lysaght Pennefather.
R.-adm. Houston Stuart.
R.-adm. Jos. Hanway Plumridge.
M.-gen. Geo. Wm. Fredk. Bruce, c.c. E. of Cardigan; aft. 2nd M. of Ailesbury.
M.-gen. Wm. John Codrington.
M.-gen. Richd. Airey.
M.-gen. hon. Jas. Yorke Scarlett.
M.-gen. Harry David Jones.
M.-gen. Arthur Wellesley Torrens.
M.-gen. Geo. Buller.
M.-gen. Wm. Eyre.
M.-gen. Richd. J. Dacres.
R.-adm. Hon. Montagu Stopford.
R.-adm. Hy. Ducie Chads.
R.-adm. Michael Seymour.
R.-adm. Hy. Byam Martin.
Capt. Stephen Lushington.
Adm. Fredk. Wm. Aylmer.

1855, Gen. Edwd. Nicolls.
July 5. Lt.-gen. Jas. Fergusson.
Lt.-gen. Thos. Wm. Brotherton.
V.-adm. Hy. Hope.
V.-adm. John Hy. Coode.
R.-adm. Maurice Fredk. Fitzhardinge Berkeley.
R.-adm. Fairfax Moresby.
1855. M.-gen. Hugh Hy. Rose, aft. ld. Strathnairn; Oct. 16.
1856, Gen. de Martimprey.
Jan. 3. Gen. F. A. Thiry.
Gen. Niel.
Gen. Camon.
Gen. Paté.
Gen. d'Antemarre d'Ervillé.
Gen. d'Allonville.
Gen. Levaillant.
Gen. Dulac.
Gen. Dalesme.
Gen. Herbillon.
Gen. Bouat.
Adm. Rigault de Genouilly.
Gen. d'Aurelles de Paladines.
Gen. Mellinet.
Adm. Penaud.
1856, Gen. Jas. W. Sleigh.
Feb. 5. Lt.-gen. Richd. Goddard Hare Clarges.
V.-adm. Hy. Prescott.
Lt.-gen. John McDonald.
Lt.-gen. Wm. Rowan.
V.-adm. Barrington Reynolds.
Lt.-gen. Wm. Geo. Moore.
M.-gen. Jas. Fred. Love.
M.-gen. Jas. Jackson.
M.-gen. Chas. Yorke.
R.-adm. hon. Richd. Saunders Dundas.
M.-gen. Lovell Benj. Lovell.
M.-gen. Wm. Fenwick Williams, aft. bt.
M.-gen. Geo. Augs. Wetherall.
Sir Geo. Maclean.
John Hall.
1856, M.-gen. Hy. Wm. Barnard.
May 3. Hy., ld. Rokeby.
1857, Lt.-gen. Sam. Benj. Auchmuty.
Jan. 2. Lt.-gen. Nathl. Thorn.
R.-adm. Chas. Howe Fremantle.
R.-adm. hon. Fredk. Wm. Grey.
Col. Robt. Garrett.
Col. Hy. Storks.
Lt.-gen. Geo. Petre Wymer.
Lt.-gen. Patrick Grant.
Jas. Macauley Higginson.
V.-adm. Leonard Victor Jos. Charner.
Adm. Marie Jos. Alphonse Odet-Pellion.
Adm. Jean Lugeol.
Adm. Louis Edouard Bouet Willaumez.
Adm. Octave Pierre Antoine De Chabannes Curton.
1857, Adm. Jean Pierre Edmond Julien
Jan. 2. de la Graviere.
Lt.-gen. Chevalier Giovanni Durando.
Lt.-gen. Chevalier Ardingo Trotti.
1857. M.-gen. Robt. John Hussey Vivian, Jan. 22.
M.-gen. John Bennett Hearsey, July 4.
R.-adm hon. Hy. Keppel, Sept. 12.
M.-gen. Hy. Havelock, Nov. 11.
Col. Archdale Wilson, Nov. 14.
1858, M.-gen. John Eardley Wilmot
Jan. 21. Inglis.
Capt. Wm. Peel, R.N.
Col. Edwd. Lugard.
1858, Col. Jas. Hope Grant.
Mar. 24. Col. Sidney John Cotton.
Col. Wm. Rose Mansfield, aft. ld. Sandhurst.
Col. Thos. Seaton.
1858. M.-gen. Chas. Thos. Van Straubenzee, June 18.
M.-gen. Thos. Harte Franks, July 27.
Col. Robt. Cornelius Napier, aft. ld. Napier of Magdala, July 27.
Capt. Adolphus Slade, R.N., Aug. 18.
R.-adm. sir Hy. John Leeke, Oct. 1.
Col. John Jones, Nov. 16.
1859. Sir John Young, bt., Feb. 4.
Sir Thos. Hastings, Mar. 9.
M.-gen. John Michel, Mar. 22.
Col. Chas. Shepherd Stuart, Mar. 22.
1859, Col. Robt. Walpole.
May 16. Col. Geo. Robt. Barker.
Col. John Douglas.
M.-gen. Hy. Gee Roberts.
M.-gen. Geo. Cornish Whitlock.
1859. John Macandrew, June 10.
Gen. Hy. Wyndham, June 21.
Lt.-gen. John Aitchison, June 21.
Col. David Edwd. Wood, Aug. 17.
1860. Col. Alfd. Hastings Horsford, May 9.
1860, Gen. hon. Hy. Murray.
May 18. Lt.-gen. Philip Bainbrigge.
Lt.-gen. Thos. Erskine Napier.
Lt.-gen. hon. Chas. Gore.
Lt.-gen. Edwd. Chas. Whinyates.
Lt.-gen. Saml. Burdon Ellis.
V.-adm. Arthur Fanshawe.
V.-adm. Provo Wm. Parry Wallis.
Lt.-gen. Geo. Judd Harding.
R.-adm. Robt. Lambert Baynes.
1860. Col. Anthy. Coningham Sterling, July 21.
Col. Richd. Denis Kelly, July 30.

1860. V.-adm. Jas. Hope, Nov. 9.
1861. M. Guillaume Marie Appoline Antonine Cousin-Montauban, Mar. 1.
1861, June 28. Adm. Edwd. Harvey.
Lt.-gen. Wm. Hy. Sewell.
Lt.-gen. Geo. Wm. Paty.
Lt.-gen. Jas. Shaw Kennedy.
Lt.-gen. Geo. Leigh Goldie.
Lt.-gen. John Michell.
V.-adm. Hy. Wm. Bruce.
V.-adm. Wm. Fanshawe Martin.
M.-gen. Wm. Brereton.
R.-adm. Lewis Tobias Jones.
Col. Wm. Lygon, E. of Longford.
1861. M.-gen. Thos. Simson Pratt, July 16.
1862. M.-gen. Stuart Corbett, Jan. 28.
1862, Nov. 10. Adm. hon. Geo. Elliott.
Gen. hon. Hugh Arbuthnot.
Gen. sir John Hanbury.
Gen. Geo., 8th M. of Tweeddale.
Adm. sir Lucius Curtis, bt.
Gen. Wm. Greenshields Power.
Gen. Hy. Geo. Andrew Taylor.
Adm. Wm. Bowles.
Gen. Alexr. Lindsay.
Gen. sir Jas. Hy. Reynett.
Gen. Richd. Llewellyn.
Gen. Chas. Grere Ellicombe.
Lt.-gen. Geo. Turner.
V.-adm. Wm. Jas. Hope Johnstone.
Lt.-gen. Jas. Freeth.
Lt.-gen. John Low.
Lt.-gen. sir Jas. Chas. Chatterton, bt.
Lt.-gen. Alexr. Kennedy Clark Kennedy.
Lt.-gen. Michl. White.
Lt.-gen. David Capon.
V.-adm. Jas. Scott.
M.-gen. sir Abr. Josias Cloete.
R.-adm. Chas. Talbot.
M.-gen. Wm. Hy. Elliott.
R.-adm. John McDougall.
R.-adm. Geo. Rodney Mundy.
Lt.-gen. Saml. Robt. Wesley.
1863. Col. Neville Bowles Chamberlain, Apr. 11.
Commissy.-gen. John Wm. Smith, Dec. 31.
1864. Sir John Liddell, Feb. 9.
M.-gen. Duncan Alexr. Cameron, Feb. 20.
R.-adm. sir Alexr. Milne, Feb. 25.
R.-adm. Augs. Leopold Kuper, Feb. 25.
M.-gen. John Garvock, Aug. 25.
1865. V.-adm. Jean Louis Chas. Jaures, Feb. 23.
1865, Mar. 28. Gen. Wm. Wood.
Gen. Thos. Kenah.
Adm. sir Geo. Rose Sartorius.
Gen. Abr. Roberts.
Lt.-gen. Thos. Monteath Douglas.
Lt.-gen. Wm. Cator.
Lt.-gen. Patr. Montgomerie.
Lt.-gen. Thos. Reid.
Lt.-gen. John Scott.
Lt.-gen. Wm. Wyllie.
Lt.-gen. Chas. Ash Windham.
V.-adm. Thos., 11th E. of Lauderdale.
V.-adm. Robt. Smart.
V.-adm. John Kingcome.
V.-adm. Horatio Thos. Austin.
Lt.-gen. John Edwd. Dupuis.
Lt.-gen. Fortescue Graham.
R.-adm. Sidney Colpoys Dacres.
M.-gen. ld. Wm. Paulet.
M.-gen. hon. Augs. Almeric Spencer.
M.-gen. Robt. Wm. Honner.
Col. John Wm. Gordon.
Col. Edwd. Harris Greathed.
Col. Chas. Wm. Dunbar Staveley.
Jas. Brown Gibson.
Wm. Linton.
Wm. Jas. Tyrone Power.
1865. Gen. Chas. Menzies, Apr. 19.
M.-gen. Chas. Warren, Apr. 19.
Robt. Gilmore Colquhoun, May 3.
Adm. Edwd. Collier, June 7.
V.-adm. Peter Richards, June 7.
Alexr. Bryson, June 7.
1867, Mar. 13. V.-adm. Hy John Codrington.
V.-adm. Josh. Nias.
V.-adm. sir Edwd. Belcher.
Lt.-gen. Edmd. Finucane Morris.
Lt.-gen. Peter Edmondstone Cragie.
Lt.-gen. John Bloomfield Gough.
Lt.-gen. Geo. Hy. Lockwood.
M.-gen. Maurice Stack.
M.-gen. Edwd. Green.
Lt.-gen. Geo. Brooke.
M.-gen. Jas. Rowland Smyth.
Adm. Fredk. Thos. Michell.
V-adm. Thos. Matthew Chas. Symonds.
R.-adm. Wm. Hutcheon Hall.
M.-gen. Geo. Bell.
Col. Fredk. Edwd. Chapman.
David Deas.
Lt.-gen. Thos. Holloway.
Capt. sir Wm. Saltonstall Wiseman.
Lt.-gen. Wm. Bell.
Lt.-gen. John Bloomfield.
Lt.-gen. Anthy. Blaxland Stransham.
M.-gen. Wm. Bates Ingilby.
M.-gen. Trevor Chute.
1868. M.-gen. Hy. Tombs, Mar. 14.
M.-gen. Geo. Malcolm, Aug. 14.
Capt. Leopold Geo. Heath, Aug. 14.

1869, V.-adm. Wm. Ramsay.
June 2. Lt.-gen. Geo. Fredk. visc. Templetown.
V.-adm. Clarence Edwd. Paget, c.c. ld. Clarence Paget.
Lt.-gen. Edwd. Huthwaite.
V-adm. Hy. Kellett.
M.-gen. Fredk. Horn.
M.-gen. Arthur Augs. Thurlow Cunynghame.
M.-gen. ld. Geo. Augs. Fredk. Paget.
M.-gen. Arthur Johnstone Lawrence.
M.-gen. Horatio Shirley.
R.-adm. Hastings Regd. Yelverton.
M.-gen. Wm. Jones.
R.-adm. Barth. Jas. Sulivan.
M.-gen. John St. George.
M.-gen. Edwd. Chas. Warde.
M.-gen. Jas. Brind.
M.-gen. Percy Egerton Herbert.
M.-gen. John Lintorn Arabin Simmons.
M.-gen. Archd. Little.
Col. Alfd. Thos. Wilde.
Thos. Galbraith Logan.
1871, Lt.-gen. Jas. Alexander.
May 20. Lt.-gen. Edwd. Walter Forestier Walker.
Lt.-gen. John Fowler Bradford.
M.-gen. David Russell.
M.-gen. Hy. Wm. Stisted.
M.-gen. Chas. Richd. Earl de la Warr.
M.-gen. Fredk. Paul Haines.
M.-gen. Thos. Montagu Steele.
M.-gen. Collingwood Dickson.
M.-gen. Chas. Reid.
M.-gen. Jas. Wm. Fitzmayer.
M.-gen. Hy. Chas. Barnston Daubeney.
R.-adm. Wm. Robt. Mends.
R.-adm. Wm. King Hall.
David Dumbreck.
Wm. Hy. Drake.
1871. Alexr. Armstrong, June 17.
1872, M.-gen. Geo. Bourchier.
Sept. 10. Col. Chas. Hy. Brownlow.
1873, Adm. Hy. Smith.
May 24. Adm. sir Thos. Sabine Pasley, bt.
Adm. Chas. Eden.
Lt.-gen. Fras. Warde.
V.-adm. Geo. St. Vincent King.
Lt.-gen. Fredk. Wm. Hamilton.
V.-adm. hon. Jas. Robt. Drummond.
Lt.-gen. Arth. Mitford Beecher.
Lt.-gen. Chas. Trollope.
Lt.-gen. Edwd. Cooper Hodge.
Lt.-gen. hon. Alexr. Hamilton Gordon.
Lt.-gen. John Fordyce.

1873, Lt.-gen. Philip Melmoth Nelson
May 24. Guy.
M.-gen. Hy. Hugh Manvers Percy, c.c. ld. Hy. Percy.
M.-gen. Chas. Hy. Ellice.
M.-gen. Richd. Wilbraham.
R.-adm. Astley Cooper Key.
M.-gen. Jas. Duncan Macpherson.
M.-gen. Edmd. Haythorne.
M.-gen. Hy. Drury Harness.
R.-adm. John Walter Tarleton.
R.-adm. Chas. Fredk. Alexr Shadwell.
M.-gen. Hy. Wylie Norman.
Col. John Miller Adye.
Surg.-gen. Wm. Mure Muir.
1874, M.-gen. sir Garnet Josh. Wolse-
Mar. 31. ley; aft. visc. Wolseley.
Capt. John Edmd. Commerell.
Capt. Wm. Nathan Wrighte Hewett.
Col. sir Archd. Alison.
Col. John Chetham McLeod.
Dep.-surg.-gen. Anthy. Dickson Home.
1875, Lt..gen. Burke Cuppage.
May 29. V.-adm. Richd. Collinson.
V.-adm. Claude Hy. Mason Buckle.
V.-adm. Geo. Giffard.
Lt.-gen. hon. Geo. Cadogan.
V.-adm. Wm. Loring.
Lt.-gen. sir Fras. Seymour, bt.
Lt.-gen. Wm. O'Grady Haly.
V.-adm. Edward Southwell Sotheby.
Lt.-gen. Edwd. Alan Holdich.
M.-gen. Edwin Beaumont Johnson.
M.-gen. Hy. Dominick Daly.
Surg.-gen. John Campbell Brown.
1876. M.-gen. hon. Fras. Colborne, Mar. 23.
1877, Adm. Geo. Elliot.
June 2. Lt.-gen. Arth. Borton.
Lt.-gen. Richd. Waddy.
V.-adm. Fredk. Beauchamp Paget Seymour.
Lt.-gen. Hy. Dalrymple White.
M.-gen. Wm. Sherbrooke Ramsay Norcott.
M.-gen. Daniel Lysons.
M.-gen. Chas. Lawrence D'Aguilar.
M.-gen. Jas. Talbot Airey.
M.-gen. Alexr. Taylor.
M.-gen. Michl. Galwey.
M.-gen. Geo. Wade Guy Green.
R.-adm. Wm. Houston Stewart.
M.-gen. Thos. Hurdle.
Wm. Richd. Edwin Smart.
1878. Lt.-gen. Sir Arnold Burrowes Kemball, July 29.
V.-adm. Geoffrey Thos. Phipps Hornby, Aug. 12.

1878. M.-gen. Fredk. Augs. ld Chelmsford, Nov. 11.
1879. Col. Hy. Evelyn Wood, June 23.
Commiss.-gen. Edwd. Strickland, June 23.
Gen. Hy. Bates, June 28.
1879, July 25. Lt.-gen. Donald Martin Stewart.
Lt.-gen. Sir Saml. Jas. Browne.
Lt.-gen. Fredk. Fras. Maude.
M.-gen. Michl. Anthy. Shrapnel Biddulph.
M.-gen. Fredk. Sleigh Roberts.
Col. Peter Stark Lumsden.
1879. R.-adm. Fras. Wm. Sullivan, Nov. 27.
1880. Col. Chas. Patton Keyes, Mar. 6.
Col. Campbell Clay Grant Ross, Mar. 6.
Adm. Geo. Greville Wellesley, Apr. 23.
M.-gen. Fredk. Alexr. Campbell, Apr. 23.
1881, Feb. 22. Lt. - gen. Robt. Onesiphorus Bright.
M -gen. Jno. Ross.
M.-gen. Jas. Hills.
M.-gen. Robt. Phayre.
Col. Herbert Taylor Macpherson.
Col. Chas. Hy. Palliser.
Col. Chas. Jno. Stanley Gough.
Col. Thos. Durand Baker.
Col. Chas. Metcalfe Macgregor.
Col. Hugh Hy. Gough.
1881, May 24. Adm. Hon. Chas. Gilbert Jno. Brydone Elliot.
Adm. Edwd Gennys Fanshawe.
Gen. Geo. Colt Langley.
Gen. Wm. Montagu Scott M'Murdo.
Gen. Mark Kerr, c.c. ld. Mark Kerr.
Gen. Pr. Wm. Augs. Edwd. of Saxe Weimar.
Gen. Jno. Thornton Grant.
Lt.-gen. Geo. Vaughan Maxwell.
Lt.-gen. Alexr. Macdonell.
Lt.-gen. Chas. Pyndar Beauchamp Walker.
Lt.-gen. Jno. Forbes.
V.-adm. Jno. Hay, c.c. ld. Jno. Hay.
M.-gen. Hon. Jno. Coke.
Capt. Fredk. Wm. Richards, R.N.
Col. Chas. Geo. Arbuthnot.
Col. Chas. Cooper Johnson.
1882. Capt. Walter Jas. Hunt-Grubbe, Aug. 14.
1882, Nov. 17. V.-adm. Wm. Montagu Dowell.
Lt.-gen. Geo. Harry Smith Willis.
Lt.-gen. Sir Edwd. Bruce Hamley.
R.-adm. Anthy. Hiley Hoskins.
Commiss -gen. Edwd. Morris.
M.-gen. Gerald Graham.
M.-gen. Drury Curzon Drury-Lowe.
1882, Nov. 17. Col. Chas. Butler Peter Nugent Hodges Nugent.
Col. Oriel Vivash Tanner.
Col. Sir Baker Creed Russell.
Dep. Surg.-gen. Jas. Arthur Hanbury.
1882, Nov. 24. Col. Cromer Ashburnham.
Lt.-gen. Rd. Chambre Hayes Taylor.
Lt.-gen. Arthur Jas. Herbert.
Lt.-gen. Edmd. Augs. Whitmore.
M.-gen. Chas. Wm. Adair.
Jno. Watt Reid.
M -gen. Sir Jno. Carstairs McNeill.
1884, May 21. Lt.-gen. Fredk. Chas. Arthur Stephenson.
Col. Herbert Stewart.
Adm. Alfd. Phillips Ryder.
V.-adm. Geo. Ommanney Willes.
1885. Adm. Sir Jno. Chas. Dalrymple Hay, Aug. 11.
1885, Aug. 25. M.-gen. Sir Geo. Richards Greaves.
M.-gen. Sir Redvers Hy. Buller.
Col. Jno. Hudson.
Col. Hy. Peter Ewart.
Col. Sir Chas Wm. Wilson.
1885. Capt. Robt. Hy. More Molyneaux, Nov. 7.
M.-gen. Harry North Dalrymple Prendergast, Dec. 8.
V.-adm. Arthur William Acland Hood, Dec. 19.
1886. Gen. hon. Arth. Edwd. Hardinge, Jan. 9.
Lt.-gen. hon. sir Leicester Smyth, Jan. 16.
Alfd. Ern. Alb., D. of Edinburgh, Feb. 18.
M.-gen. Edwd. Gascoigne Bulwer, Apr. 1.
1886, May 29. Gen. Frank Turner.
Adm. Arth. Farquhar.
Gen. Hy. Jas. Warre.
Lt.-gen. hon. Sir Geo. Gerald Foley.
Lt.-gen. Hy. Errington Longden.
Gen. Wm. Olpherts.
Adm. Jno. Corbett.
V.-adm. Sir Geo. Hy. Richards.
Lt.-gen. Julius Richd. Glyn.
Lt.-gen. Wm. Pollexfen Radcliffe.
Lt.-gen. Wm. Payn.
M.-gen. Jno. Watson.
1886, Nov. 25. Col. Fras. Booth Norman.
Col. Fras. Wallace Grenfell.
Col. Wm. Fras. Butler.
Col. Geo. Stewart White.
1887, June 21. Adm. Hy. Chads.
Gen. Jas Macleod Bannatyne Fraser-Tytler.
Adm. Chas. Farrell Hillyar.
Gen. Penrose Chas. Penrose.
Adm. Sir Edwd. Augustus Inglefield.

1887, Adm. Arth. Cumming.
June 21. Gen. Wm. Parke.
Adm. Sir Regd. John Macdonald.
Gen. John Alexr. Ewart.
Adm. Edwd. Bridges Rice.
Adm. Augs. Phillimore.
Adm. Richd. Jas., E. of Clanwilliam.
Gen. Chas. London Barnard.
Lt.-gen. John Luther Vaughan.
Lt.-gen. Lothian Nicholson.
M.-gen. Sir Hy. Marshman Havelock-Allan, bt.
Lt.-gen. Robt. Hume.
Lt.-gen. Hy. D'Oyley Torrens.
V.-adm Richd. Vesey Hamilton.
V.-adm. Thos. Brandreth.

1887, Surg.-gen. John Harrie K
June 21. Innes.
V.-adm. Wm. Graham.
V.-adm. Nowell Salmon.
M.-gen. Geo. Hutt.
Insp.-gen. of Hospitals Wr Mackenzie.
Insp.-gen. of Hospitals and Flee Jas. Jenkins.
M.-gen. Martin Dillon.
M.-gen. Geo. Byng Harman.
R.-adm. Geo. Tryon.
1887, Col. Robt. Cunliffe Lowe.
July 1. Wm. Stephen Alexr. Lockhart.
1888. M.-gen. Regd. Gipps, C.B., Ja 16.

KNIGHTS COMMANDERS—CIVIL DIVISION.

(K.C.B.)

Under Statute of Apr. 1, 1847

See Introduction, *ante*, p. 753.

VICTORIA.

* * Count Alexr. Mensdorf.
1848. Hy. Lytton Earle Bulwer, aft. ld.
Apr. 27. Dalling and Bulwer.
Hy. Ellis.
Richd. Pakenham.
Jas. Brooke.
Geo. Russell Clerke.
Hy. Light.
Geo. Grey.
Chas. Edw. Trevelyan.
Sir Randolph Isham Routh.
V.-adm. Beaufort.
Jas. Stephen.
M.-gen. Wm. Morison.
Lt.-col. Hy. Montgomery Lawrence.
1848, Lt.-gen. Duncan McGregor.
Dec. 26. Lt.-col. Chas. Rowan.
1849. Hy. Miers Elliot, June 5.
Thos. Nichs. Redington, Aug. 28.
1850. Saml. Geo. Bonham, Nov. 22.
Sir Geo. Wm. Anderson, Nov. 22.
1851, Jno. Arth., 2nd ld. Bloomfield.
Mar. 1. Hy. Rd. Chas., 2nd ld., aft. 1st E. Cowley.
Geo. Nicholls.
Sir Hy. Watkin Wm. Wynn, bt.
Hon. Wm. Temple.
Hon. Ralph Abercromby.
1851, Lt.-col. Wm. Reid.
Oct. 25. Richd. Mayne.
1852. Jno. Hobart, 2nd ld. Howden, Feb. 23.
Wm. Gore Ouseley, June 29.
Bedford Hinton Wilson, Dec. 23.
1853. Hy. Barkly, July 18.
Jas. Cosmo Melvill, Sept. 5.

1854. Sir Chas. Augs. Fitz Roy, June 1
Sir Jno. Fras. Davis, June 12.
Proby Thos. Cautley, July 29.
1855. Lt.-col. Justin Sheil, Jan. 23.
Jas. Hudson, Mar. 2.
1856, Maj. Hy. Creswick Rawlinson.
Feb. 5. Jno. Laird Mair Lawrence, af ld. Lawrence.
M.-gen. Wm. Hy. Sleeman.
M.-gen. Jas. Outram.
Benj. Hawes.
1856. Lt.-gen. Mark Cubbon, May 26.
Lt.-col. sir Wm. Thos. Deniso July 19.
R.-adm. Chas. Elliot, July 19.
Hon. Jno. Duncan Bligh, Sept. 3
Arthur Chas. Magenis, Sept. 30
Jno. Fiennes Crampton, Sept. 3
1857. Jno. Geo. Shaw-Lefevre, Jan. 2
Hon. Thos. Wyse, Mar. 27.
Col. Alexr. Murray Tulloch, Ap 17.
1858. Col. Hon. Chas. Beaumont Phipp Jan. 21.
Andr. Smith, July 9.
Richd. Madox Bromley, Sept. 6.
Thos. Tassell Grant, Sept. 6.
R.-adm. Alexr. Milne, Dec. 20.
1859. Col. Joshua Jebb, Mar. 25.
Hy. Bartle Edwd. Frere, May 2
Robt. Montgomery, May 20.
1860. Rowland Hill, Feb. 10.
1860, Fredk. Jas. Halliday.
May 18. Sir Robt. North Collie Hamilton, b
M.-gen. Richd. Jas. Hollwe Birch.
Col. Peter Melvill Melvill.
Lt.-Col. Herbert Benjn. Edwarde

1860. Chas. Lennox Wyke, May 22.
Andr. Buchanan, May 25.
M.-gen. Thos. Aiskew Larcom, June 19.
Geo. Lloyd Hodges, Aug. 6.
Richd. Bickerton, ld., aft. visc. Lyons, Dec. 11.
Sir Edmd. Walker Head, bt., Dec. 11.
1861. Fredk. Temple, ld. Dufferin & Claneboye, aft. E. of Dufferin and M. of Dufferin and Ava, June 18.
M.-Gen. Geo. Hall McGregor, June 25.
1862. Jno. Peter Grant, Feb. 14.
Jno. Hay Drummond Hay, May 20.
Harry Smith Parkes, June 20.
Rutherford Alcock, June 20.
1862, Wm. Stevenson.
July 23. Philip Edmd. Wodehouse.
Chas. Hy. Darling.
M.-gen. Edwd Macarthur.
1862. Augs. Wm. Fredk. Spencer Loftus, c.c. ld. Augs. Loftus, Dec. 12.
Hon. Fredk. Wm. Adolphus Bruce, Dec. 12.
1863. Sir Roderick Impey Murchison, Feb. 3.
Henry Fras. Howard, Mar. 3.
Col. Thos. Myddelton Biddulph, Mar. 10.
Augs. Berkeley Paget, Mar. 17.
1863. Capt. Pr. Ern. Leop., &c., of Leiningen, Aug. 7.
Jas. Douglas, Aug. 11.
Geo. Fredk. Edmonstone, Dec. 11.
1864. M.-gen. Wm. Marcus Coghlan, June 7.
1865. Lt.-gen. Sir Jno. Gaspard Le Marchant, Aug. 9.
Maj. Jno. Clayton Cowell, Aug. 23.
Wm. Hutt, Nov. 27.
1866. Pr. Victor Ferd., &c., of Hohenlohe-Langenburg, Jan. 29.
1866, Sir Alexr. Malet, bt.
June 23. Hon. Chas. Augs. Murray.
Hon. Jno. Hy. Thos. Manners-Sutton.
1866, Sir Jas. Clark, bt.
July 6. Thos. Erskine May, aft. ld. Farnborough.
Chas. Pressly.
1867. Gen. Wm. Thos. Knollys, Apr. 3.
Jno. Alexr. Macdonald, June 29.
Wm. Rose, Oct. 14.
1868, R.-adm. Jas. Craufurd Caffin.
Dec. 7. V.-adm. Robt. Spencer Robinson.
1869, Antony Panizzi.
July 27. Lt.-gen. Edwd. Sabine.
1870. M.-gen. Wm. Erskine Baker, Feb. 1.
M.-gen. Geo. Balfour, June 24.
Edwd. Thornton, Aug. 9.
Wm. Geo. Anderson, Dec. 6.
Col. Jno. Stewart Wood, Dec. 19.
1871. M.-gen. Thos. Townsend Pears, June 13.
Lt.-col. Howard Craufurd Elphinstone, July 3.
Wm. Hy. Stephenson, Nov. 7.
1872. Sir Wm. Jenner, bt., Jan. 20.
Geo. Biddell Airy, June 17.
V.-adm. Hon. Edwd. Alfred Jno. Harris, July 13.
Arth. Helps, July 18.
1873, Hy. Thring, aft. ld. Thring.
Mar. 27. Alfd. Power.
1874. Lt.-col. Jas. Macnaghten Hogg, aft. McGarel-Hogg and ld. Magheramorne, May 16.
1875. Hy. Cole, Mar. 25.
Col. Hy. Atwell Lake, Mar. 25.
Thos. Fras. Wade, Nov. 25.
1876. Chas., 5th ld. Suffield, May 17.
Capt. Geo. Strong Nares, Nov. 29.
1877. Col. Jno. Stokes, July 23.
1877, Lt.-col. Edmd. Fredk. Du Cane.
Aug. 6. Col. sir Lewis Pelly.
Commiss.-gen. Hy. Wm. Gordon.
1878. Edmd. Yeamans Walcot Henderson, Mar. 15.
Chas. Stuart Aubrey, 3rd ld. Tenterden, July 29.
Jno. Savile Lumley, Oct. 10.
Sir Rd. Wallace, bt., Nov. 14.
1879. Lt.-gen. Hy. Fredk. Ponsonby, Mar. 12.
1879, Sir Fras. Rd. Sandford.
May 31. Ralph Robt. Wheler Lingen, aft. ld. Lingen.
Jno. Lambert.
1879. Maj. Pierre Louis Napoleon Cavagnari, July 19.
Sir Hy. Drummond Wolff, Sept. 24.
1880. Theodore Martin, May 20.
Hon. Adolph. Fredc. Octavius Liddell, Apr. 20.
Jno. Tilley, Apr. 20.
Luitbert Alexr. Geo. Lionel Alphonse Freiher Von Pawel-Rammingen, May 24.
Edwd. Jas. Reed, Aug. 14.
Hy. Brougham Loch, Sept. 18.
Chas. Jno. Herries, Oct. 27.
1881, Lt.-col. Wm. Fitzwilliam Lenox
May 24. Conyngham.
Lt.-col. Hambleton Fras. Custance.
Lt.-col. Thos. Heron, visc. Ranelagh.
Lt.-col. Robt. Loyd Lindsay.
Thos. Brassey, aft. ld. Brassey.
Capt. Fredk. Jno. Owen Evans.
Alfd. Comyns Lyall.
1881. Edwin Baldwin Malet, Oct. 8.

1882. Jas. Caird, June 2.
Ralph Wood Thompson, June 2.
Geo. Kettilby Rickards, June 24.
Robt. Burnett David Morier, Oct. 16.
Robt. Geo. Wyndham Herbert. Dec. 26.
1882. Regd. Earle Welby, Dec. 26.
1883. Lyon Playfair, Apr. 9.
Col. Jno. Graham McKerlie, Sept. 15.
1884. Prof. Richd. Owen, Jan. 5.
Robt. Geo. Crookshank Hamilton, Jan. 12.
Robt. Hawthorn Collins, Apr. 15.
Prince Louis Alexr. of Battenburg, Apr. 29.
Hon. Spencer Cecil Brabazon Ponsonby-Fane, May 24.
Hy. Wentworth Acland, M.D., May 24.
1885. Nathl. Barnaby, June 15.
Augs. Keppel Stephenson, June 30.
Gen. Alexr. Nelson, visc. Bridport, July 22.
Ralph Allen Gosset, Aug. 11.
Arthur Lawrence Halliburton, Aug. 25.
Thos. Crawford, Aug. 25.
Philip Hy. Wodehouse Currie, Dec. 1.
1885. Geo. Edwd. Paget, Dec. 26.
1886, Feb. 2. Col. Jas. Fraser.
Wm. Stuart Walker.
1886. Fras. Brockman Morley, Feb. 2.
Col. Fredk. Winn Knight, Feb. 5
Hy. Robinson, May 29.
Sir Fras. Philip Cunliffe Owen, June 28.
Algernon Edwd. West, July 30.
Col. Donald Matheson.
1887. June 21. Lt.-gen. sir Dighton Macnaghten Probyn.
Maj. sir Evelyn Baring.
Stevenson Arthur Blackwood.
Chas. Thos. Newton.
John Simon.
Hugh Owen.
Wm. Fraser.
Chas. Lister Ryan.
Sir Edwd. Walter.
Capt. Douglas Galton.
Maj. Fleetwood Isham Edwards.
Arthur Mitchell.
Col. Geo. Ashley Maude.
Col. Walter Rice Olivey.
Lt.-col. Donald Matheson.
1888, Jan. 7. Sir Robt. Rawlinson.
Sir Chas. Warren.
1888, June 2. Edwd. Geo. Jenkinson.
Sir Julian Pauncefote.
1888. Edw. Blount, June 15.

OFFICERS OF THE BATH.

Deans.

1725, May 23. Saml. Bradford, dean of Westminster, and his successors.

See "Deans of Westminster," *ante*, p. 471.

Genealogists.

John Anstis (No. 2), May 1725.
Sackville Fox, Feb. 28, 1755.
John Suffield Brown, June 30, 1757.
Geo. Nayler, aft. sir G., June 15, 1792.
Walter Aston Blount, Nov. 22, 1831; re 1859; no succ. app.

See "" Blanc Couriers Heralds," *ante*, p. 339.

Registrars.

1725. Hon. Edwd. Young, aft. K. Arms, May 23.
1745. Col. Thos. Kokayne.
1750. Chas. Newton.

See "Registrars and Secretaries," *infra*.

Secretaries.

1725. Edwd. Montagu.
1749. Sir Jno. Jenour, bt.

See "Registrars and Secretaries," *infra*.

Registrars and Secretaries.

1755. Wm. Whitehead (Poet Laur.).
1785. Wm. Fauquier, Sept. 24.
1805. Maj. hon. Chas. Banks Stahope.

1809. Jno Chas. Herries, Jan.
1822. Lt.-col. Wm. Lewis Herries, aft. Sir W., Aug. 31.
1827. Capt. Michl. Seymour, aft. r.-adm. sir M.; Apr. 4.
1859. Alb. Wm. Woods, aft. sir A.

KINGS OF ARMS.

See "Bath and Gloucester Kings of Arms," *ante*, p. 330.

Grey Longueville, May 1725.
Hon. Edwd. Young, form. regr., Dec. 5, 1745.
Wm. Woodley, 1756-7.
Saml. Horsey, Jan. 12, 1757.
Thos. Gery Cullum, aft. bt., Dec. 14, 1771.
Fras. Townsend. deputy, 1788-1812.
John Palmer Cullum, Apr. 3, 1801.
Maj. Algn. Greville, Aug. 20, 1829.
V.-adm. hon. Geo. Grey, 1865.

THE ORDER OF THE GUELPHS—HANOVER.

THIS Order was instituted on Aug. 12, 1815, to commemorate the raising of Hanover into a kingdom. The kings of England being also kings of Hanover, the Order was often conferred upon British subjects; but when, on the accession of Queen Victoria in 1837, the two kingdoms became separated, the Order thenceforth became entirely a foreign one.

The Order consisted of the King of Hanover as Sovereign and Grand Master, and of three classes of knights not limited in number—Knights Grand Cross, Knights Commanders, and Knights, each class being also sub-divided into civil and military divisions.

The officers of the Order were—

CHANCELLOR.
VICE-CHANCELLOR.
SECRETARY.
KING OF ARMS.

The Order was styled—

"THE ORDER OF THE GUELPHS."

The following lists are confined to British subjects, and stop on the separation of Hanover from England in 1837. Those entered as appointed by King Ernest of Hanover were nominated by William IV., who died before their appointments were completed.

MEMBERS OF THE ORDER OF THE GUELPHS.

*Those marked "**C**" belong to the Civil Divisions.*

KNIGHTS GRAND CROSS OF THE ORDER OF THE GUELPHS.

(G.C.H.)

1815, Aug. 12. Fredk., D. of York and Albany.
Wm. Hy., D. of Clarence, aft. Wm. IV.
Edwd., D. of Kent.
1815, Aug. 12. Ernest Augs., D. of Cumberland.
Aug. Fredk., D. of Sussex, nom., but did not accede until 1830.
Adolph. Fredk., D. of Cambridge.

1815, Wm. Fredk., D. of Gloucester.
Aug. 12. Geo. Fredk. P., D. of Cumberland, aft. K. of Hanover.
1815. Geo. Fredk Wm. Chas., aft. D. of Cambridge.
1816. Pr. Leopold of Saxe-Coburg, aft. K. of the Belgians, Mar. 22.
F.M. Arth., D. of Wellington.
Gen. Hy., M. of Anglesea.
Gen. Chas. Wm., ld. Stewart, aft. M. of Londonderry.
Thos. Trevor, visc. Hampden, **C.**
Robt., ld. Castlereagh, aft. M. of Londonderry, **C.**
Lt.-gen. Sir Hy. Clinton.
Gen. hon. Sir Chas. Colville.
Lt.-gen. sir Jas. Kempt.
Gen. Rowland, ld. Hill.
Gen. sir Geo. Don.
Lt.-gen sir Geo. Murray.
Gen. Chas., 3rd E. of Harrington.
Geo. Jas. M. of Cholmondeley, **C.**
1817. Gen. sir Thos, Maitland.
V.-adm. sir Edmd. Nagle.
Gen. sir Harry Calvert, bt.
Gen. ld. Wm. Cavendish-Bentinck.
Gen. sir Jas. Campbell, bt.
Lt.-gen. sir Jas. Lyon.
Lt.-gen. Jno., ld. Burghersh.
Gen. sir Alexr. Mackenzie, bt.
Gen. sir Edwd. Howorth.
Gen. Stapleton, visc. Combermere.
Lt.-gen. sir Hy. Tucker Montresor.
Gen sir Jno. Murray, bt.
1818. Gen. sir Hy. Fredk. Campbell.
Gen. Wm. Carr, visc. Beresford.
V.-adm. sir Thos. Fras. Fremantle.
Gen. Fras., 1st M. of Hastings.
1819. Fras. Chas., E. of Yarmouth, aft. M. of Hertford, **C.**
Jno., E. of Mayo, **C.**
Adm. sir Jno. Borlase Warren, bt.
Gen. sir Chas. Hastings, bt.
Sir Geo. Rose, **C.**
Alleyne, ld. St. Helens, **C.**
F.M. sir Saml. Hulse.
Lt.-gen. Benj., ld. Bloomfield.
1820. Lt.-gen. sir Colin Halkett.
Gen. sir Jno. Macleod.
Lt.-gen. sir Jno. Hope.
1821. Lt.-gen. sir Chas. Asgill, bt.
Richd., E. of Clancarty, **C.**
Gen. Hy., M. Conyngham.
1822. Sir Brook Taylor, **C.**
1823. Jas., E. of Fife, **C.**
Fras. Nathl., E. of Mount Charles, aft. M. Conyngham, **C.**
Sir Wm. Knighton, bt., **C.**
1824. Sir Fras. Nathl. Burton, **C.**
Gen. sir Rufane Shaw Donkin.
Percy Sidney Clinton, visc. Strangford, **C.**
1824. Lt.-gen. sir Jas. Willoughb Gordon, bt.
Lt.-gen. sir Herbert Taylor.
1826. Richd., 3rd E. of Clanwilliam, **C**
Lt.-gen. sir Jno. Byng, aft. ld Strafford.
1827. Gen. sir Fras. Thos. Hammond.
Gen. sir Tomkyns Hilgrove Tuner.
Lt.-gen. sir Jos. Fuller.
Gen. sir Wm. Houston, bt.
Sir Wm. Fremantle.
Lt.-gen., ld. Geo. Thos. Beresfor
Gen., 3rd E. of Ashburnham.
1829. Sir Robt. Gordon, **C.**
1830. Wm. Geo., 16th E. of Erroll, **C.**
Rd. Wm., E. Howe, **C.**
Sir Hy. Halford, bt., **C.**
Sir Jonn. Wathen Waller, bt., **C**
Jno. Delaval, E. of Tyrconnell,
Wm., ld. Maryborough.
Gen. sir Jas. Stewart, bt.
Geo., 4th E. of Glasgow, **C.**
1831. Gen. Hon. sir Hy. Geo. Grey.
Lt.-gen. sir Richd. Hussey Vivia bt.
Adm. sir Wm. Hargood.
Adm. ld. Amelius Beauclerk.
Lt.-gen. sir Edwd. Kerrison, bt
Lt.-gen. sir Thos. Macdougall.
Lt.-gen. sir Jno. Keane, aft. l Keane.
Lt.-gen. sir Thos. Bradford.
Lt.-gen. sir Colquhoun Grant.
Geo. Hamilton, E. of Belfast, a 3rd M. of Donegal, **C.**
Lucius Bentinck, 10th visc. Falkland, **C.**
V.-adm. ld. Jas. O'Bryen.
Sir Robt. Wilmot Horton, bt.,
Lt.-gen. sir Jno. Smith.
Gen. Geo. Cockburn, aft. bt.
Sir Gore Ouseley, bt., **C.**
Sir Philip Chas. Sidney, aft. De L'Isle and Dudley, **C.**
Ld. Fred. FitzClarence, **C.**
Sir Hy. Watkin Williams Wy bt., **C.**
Sir Edwd. Cromwell Disbrov **C.**
1832. Gen. sir Josiah Champange.
Gen. sir Martin Hunter.
Gen. sir Jno. Fraser.
Capt. ld. Adolphus FitzClarence
V.-adm. hon. sir Chas. Paget.
Constantine Hy., E. of Mulgra aft. M. of Normanby, **C.**
Adm. sir Isaac Coffin, bt.
V.-adm. sir Peter Halkett, bt.
V.-adm. sir Edwd. W. C. R. Ow
* * V.-adm. hon. sir Hy. Blackwo *d.* 1832.
1833. Gen. sir Fredk. Augs. Wether
Wm. Basil Percy, E. of Denbigh
Gen. hon. sir Alexr. Duff.

1833. Sir Chas. Richd. Vaughan, **C.**
Geo. Wm., D. of Argyll, **C.**
Wm. Chas., E. of Albemarle, **C.**
Lt.-gen. sir Andr. F. Barnard.
1834. Sir Thos. Cartwright, **C.**
Lt.-gen sir Hy. Bayly.
Adm. sir Chas. Edmd. Nugent.
M.-gen. sir Hy. Wheatley.
Lt.-gen. sir Robt. Bolton.
V.-adm. sir Wm. Hall Gage.
Jno., 1st E. Brownlow, **C.**
Sir Robt. Grant, **C.**
Capt. sir Geo. Fras. Seymour.
M.-gen. sir Benjn. Chas. Stephenson.
Wm. Pitt, 1st E. Amherst, **C.**
Geo., 5th E. of Jersey, **C.**
1835. Thos., 2nd E. of Wilton, **C.**
Richd., M. of Chandos, aft. D. of Buckingham and Chandos, **C.**
Gen. sir Jno. Slade, bt.
V.-adm. sir Jno. Gore.
Lt.-gen. sir Wm. Keir Grant.
1835. Jno., E. of Clare.
M.-gen. sir Jas. Cockburn, bt.
Lt.-gen. sir Ralph Darling.
V.-adm. sir Chas. Rowley, bt.
1836. V.-adm. Richd. Dacres.
Sir Geo. Hamilton Seymour, **C.**
Gen. sir Saml. Hawker.
Adm. sir Jno. Poo Beresford, bt.
Jno. 13th ld. Elphinstone, **C.**
Sir Astley Paston Cooper, **C.**
Lt.-gen. sir Edwd. Blakeney.
Capt. ld. Jno. Fredk. Gordon, R.N., **C.**
Lt.-gen. sir Lionel Smith, bt.
Lt.-gen. sir Jno. Colborne, aft. ld. Seaton.
1837. Lt.-col. sir Richd. Church.
M.-gen. Alexr. Geo., 16th ld. Saltoun.
Gen. sir Jno. Gustavus Crosbie.
Sir Chas. Edwd. Grey.
Lt.-gen. sir Chas. Wm. Doyle.

APPOINTED BY KING ERNEST OF HANOVER.

See Introduction, *ante*, p. 785.

1837. Jos. Planta, **C.**
1837. M.-gen. sir Chas. Wade Thornton.

KNIGHTS COMMANDERS OF THE ORDER OF THE GUELPHS.

(K.C.H.)

1816. M.-gen. sir Jas. Lyon.
M.-gen. sir Benjn. Bloomfield.
Lt.-gen. sir Robt. Bolton.
M.-gen. sir Colquhoun Grant.
M.-gen. sir Colin Halkett.
Col. Philip Roche.
M.-gen. sir Rd. Hussey Vivian, bt.
M.-gen. sir Geo. Adam Wood.
1817. M.-gen. sir Alexr. Dickson.
Sir Wm. Congreve, bt.
1818. Lt.-gen. sir Benjn. D'Urban.
R.-adm. sir Home Riggs Popham.
1819. Lt.-gen. sir Jno. Elley.
M.-gen. sir Andrew F. Barnard.
Lt.-gen. sir Fras. Thos. Hammond.
Before M.-gen. Herbert Taylor.
1820. Lt.-gen. sir Tomkyns Hilgrove Turner.
R.-adm. hon. Chas. Paget.
M.-gen. sir Haylett Framingham.
Col. sir Wm. Rose.
1820. Col. sir Robt. Wm. Gardiner.
M.-gen. Jas., ld. Glenlyon.
Lt.-gen. Sir Geo. Airey.
1821. Lt.-gen. sir Chas. Wm. Doyle.
Lt.-gen. sir Saml. Ford Whittingham.
Lt.-gen. sir Geo. Augs. Quentin.
Col. Thos. Hy. Browne.
M.-gen. sir Wm. Keir Grant.
Col. sir Hy. Fredk. Cooke.
Gen. Geo. Cockburn, aft. bt.
M.-gen. sir Edwd. Kerrison, bt.
1822. Lt.-Col. sir Richd. Church.
M.-gen. Louis Wm., visc. Chabot.
M.-gen. sir Jno. May.
1824. Col. sir Jas. Hy. Reynett.
M.-gen. sir Jno. Harvey.
1826. Col. sir Wm. Lewis Herries.
1827. Sir Fredk. Beilby Watson, **C.**
Sir Jno. Conroy, bt.
Col. sir Jno. Macra, **C.**
Before Sir Hy. Halford, M.D., **C.**
1828. Sir Jonn. Wathen Waller, bt.
1828. Capt. hon. Robt. Cavendish Spencer.
1829. M.-gen. sir Jas. Carmichael Smyth, bt.
Ld. Albert Conyngham, **C.**
1830. Col. Augs. Fredk. D'Este, **C.**
Hon. John Kennedy Erskine.
M.-gen. sir Willoughby Cotton.
Sir Philip Chas. Sidney, **C.**
M.-gen. sir Alexr. Bryce.
1831 M.-gen. hon. sir Fredk. Cavendish Ponsonby.
Lt.-gen. sir Jas. Chas. Dalbiac.
M.-gen. sir Chas. Wade Thornton.
M.-gen. sir John Brown.
M.-gen. sir Jas. Campbell.
Sir John Hall, **C.**
Sir Geo. Harrison, **C.**
Col. sir Wm. Gosset.
Capt. sir Geo. Fras. Seymour.
Capt. sir Thos. Ussher.
Sir Matth. Tierney, bt., **C.**

1831. Col. sir Hy. Wheatley.
M.-gen. sir Benjn. Chas. Stephenson.
Col. sir Jos. Whatley.
M.-gen. sir Steph. Remnant Chapman.
Sir Wm. Burnett, M.D., **C.**
Lt.-col. hon. Edwd. Cust.
Sir Geo. Baillie Hamilton, **C.**
Lt.-gen. sir Phineas Riall.
Lt.-gen. sir Wm. Hutchinson
Lt.-gen. sir Lewis Grant.
Lt.-gen. sir Geo. Pownall Adams.
M.-gen. sir Amos Godsill Robt. Norcott.
M.-gen. sir Jas. Cockburn, bt.
Col. sir Michael McCreagh.
M.-gen. sir Evan John Murray MacGregor, bt.
M.-gen. sir Thos. Downman.
M.-gen. sir Neil Douglas.
Col. sir Archd. Christie.
Capt. sir Wm. Howe Mulcaster.
M.-gen. Wm. Tuyll.
Sir John Bedingfield, **C.**
Lt.-gen. sir Saml. Hawker.
M.-gen. sir Geo. Bulteel Fisher.
Sir Wm. Pym, M.D., **C.**

1832. M.-gen. sir Jas. Hay.
Gen. sir Warren Marmaduke Peacocke.
Lt.-gen. sir Chas. Bulkeley Egerton.
Lt.-gen. Wm. Sheridan.
M.-gen. sir John Fredk. Sigismond Smith.
Lt.-gen. sir Wm. Paterson.
Lt.-gen. sir Wm. Nicolay.
M.-gen. sir Arth. Benjn. Clifton.
M.-gen. sir Geo. Whitmore.
M.-gen. sir Leonard Greenwell.
M.-gen. sir Robt. Hy. Dick.
M.-gen. sir Fredk. Wm. Trench.
Capt. sir Wm. Augs. Montague.
Sir Wm. Franklin, **C.**
Sir Hy. Seaton, **C.**
Lt.-gen. sir John Macleod.
Lt.-gen. sir Fredk. Wm. Mulcaster.
M.-gen. Fras., count Rivarola.
M.-gen. sir Wm. Parker Carrol.
M.-gen. sir John Hanbury.
M.-gen. sir David Ximenes.
Capt. sir John Marshall.
Sir John Webb, M.D., **C.**
Lt.-gen. sir Jos. Straton.
M.-gen. sir John Geo. Woodford.
Sir Geo. Hamilton Seymour, **C.**
M.-gen. sir Wm. Douglas.
Lt.-gen. sir Thos. Browne.
M.-gen. sir Wm. Cornwallis Eustace.
Capt. sir Nisbet Josiah Willoughby.
Capt. sir Andr. Pellet Green.

1832. R.-adm. sir Arth. Farquhar
Commiss.-gen. sir John Bisset, **C.**
Sir John Deas Thompson, **C.**
Capt. sir Chas. Marsh Schomberg.
Sir Geo. Jackson, **C.**
Capt. sir Humphrey Fleming Senhouse.
V.-adm. hon. Courtenay Boyle.

1833. Lt.-gen. sir David Latimer Tinling Widdrington.
Lt.-gen. Wm. Geo., ld. Harris.
R.-adm. sir Edwd. Durnford King.
Capt. sir Fras. Augs. Collier.
Capt. sir Richd. Spencer.
M.-gen. sir John Boscawen Savage.
Capt. sir John Saml. Brooke Pechell, bt.
Lt.-gen. sir Hy. John Cumming.

1834. Lt.-gen. sir Evan Lloyd.
Lt.-gen. sir Thos. Gage Montresor.
Lt.-gen. sir Saml. Trevor Dickens.
M.-gen. sir Jas. Kearney.
M.-gen. sir Lorenzo Moore.
M.-gen. sir Jas. Viney.
M.-gen. sir Hy. Willoughby Rooke.
M.-gen. sir Patr. Ross.
M.-gen. sir Hy. King.
R.-adm. sir John Ferris Devonshire.
R.-adm. sir Jas. Hillyar.
R.-adm. sir Salusbury Davenport.
Commiss.-gen. sir Wm. Hy Robinson, **C.**
Commiss.-gen. sir Robt. Hugh Kennedy, **C.**
Sir John Woolmore, **C.**
Lt.-gen. sir Jos. Maclean.
R.-adm. sir Hugh Pigot.
R.-adm. sir Robt. Barrie.
Col. sir Saml. Gordon Higgins.
Lt.-col. sir Edmd. Currey.
M.-gen. sir Patr. Lindesay.

In 1834. Capt. hon. sir Hy. Duncan.

1835. R.-adm. sir Chas. Bullen.
Capt. sir Wm. Hy. Dillon.
Capt. sir Wm. Elliott.
Capt. sir Edmd. Lyons, bt.
M.-gen. sir Thos. Bligh St George.
Col. Patr. Doherty.
M.-gen. sir Thos. Pearson.
M.-gen. sir Maurice Chas O'Connell.
M.-gen. sir Octavius Cary.
Capt. ld. Jas. Townshend.
Col. hon. Horatio Geo. Powys Townshend.
R.-adm. sir Saml. Warren.
V.-adm. sir Robt. Lewis Fitzgerald.

1835. Maj. sir. Fras. Bond Head, bt., **C.**
1836. Lt.-gen. sir Wiltshire Wilson.
M.-gen. sir Chas. Wm. Maxwell.
M.-gen. sir Wm. Gabriel Davy.
Capt. hon. Fleetwood Broughton Reynolds Pellew.
Capt. hon. Jas. Ashley Maude.
Capt. sir John Strutt Peyton.
Capt. Richd. O'Conor.
Capt. sir Hy. Hart.
Capt. sir Jas. John Gordon Bremer.
Sir Robt. Ker Porter, **C.**
Capt. sir John Franklin, **C.**
Sir John Nicol Robt. Campbell, **C.**
1837. Lt.-gen. sir Alexr. Halkett.
1837. Lt.-gen. sir Robt. Barton.
Lt.-gen. sir Augs. De Butts.
Lt.-gen. sir Thos. Hawker.
V.-adm. sir Adam Drummond.
Capt. sir David Dunn.
Capt. sir Edwd. Chetham.
Capt. sir Thos. Mansell.
Sir Woodbine Parish, **C.**
M.-gen. sir Edwd. Bowater.
M.-gen. sir Jas. Macdonell.
M.-gen. sir Robt. McCleverty.
R.-adm. sir John Wentworth Loring.
Col. sir Geo. Arthur.
Sir David Davies, M.D., **C.**
Wm. Fredk. Chambers, M.D., **C.**
Capt. Thos. Barker Devon.

APPOINTED BY KING ERNEST OF HANOVER.

See Introduction, *ante*, p. 785.

1837. M.-gen. sir Fredk. Walker.
Capt. sir John Duff Markland.
Col. sir Wm. Verner.
Sir Chas. Ferd. Forbes, M.D., **C.**
1837. Capt. sir Watkin Owen Pell.
Col. sir Wm. Chalmers.
Sir Robt. Alexr. Chermside, M.D., **C.**

KNIGHTS OF THE ORDER OF THE GUELPHS.

(K.H.)

1816. Sir Geo. Nayler, York Her., aft. Garter; K.A. of the Order.
Col. Peter Augs. Lautour.
Maj. Wm. Havelock.
Sir Jas. Robt. Grant, M.D., **C.**
Capt. Thos. Carey.
Capt. Arthur Farquhar.
Lt.-col. Sir Wm. Osborne.
Lt.-col. John Mervin Cutliffe.
1817. Col. Stephen Remnant Chapman.
Col. Archd. Christie.
Col. Richd. D. Hanagan.
1818. Capt. Andr. Pellet Green.
Col. Chas. Ashe A'Court.
Col. Chas. Philip de Bossett.
Col. Gideon Gorrequer.
Col. Sir Felton Elwill Bathurst Hervey.
Lt.-col Jas. Reynett.
Lt.-col. Nathl. Eckersley.
Lt.-col. Thos. Hy. Brown.
1819. Col. Sir Alexr. Bryce.
Lt.-col. Wm. Thornhill.
Lt.-col. Archd. McDonald.
Lt.-col. Chas. Wade Thornton.
Capt. Jas. MacGlashan.
1820. Capt. Thos. Barker Devon.
Sir Andr. Halliday, **C.**
Benjn. Chas. Stevenson, **C.**
1821. Capt. Vicomte Thos. De Grenier Fonblanque.
Col. Sir Evan John Murray McGregor.
1822. Maj. Robt. Hutchinson Orde.
Capt. D'Arcy Todd.
1823. Sir Danl. Bayley.
1823. Lt.-col. Edwd. Chas. Whinyates.
Sir David Scott, bt., **C.**
John Hall, **C.**
1824. M.-gen. Geo. Jas. Reeves.
Lt.-col. Sir Wm. Davison.
1825. Maj. Roche Meade.
Sir John Meade, M.D., **C.**
Maj. Richd. Hardinge.
Sir Jonn. Wathen Waller, bt., **C.**
1827. Lt.-col. Edwd. Anthy. Angelo.
1828. Capt. hon. Chas. Southwell.
Timothy Brent, **C.**
1830. Lt.-col. Sir John Mark Fredk. Smith.
Col. Sir Jas. Maxwell Wallace.
Lt.-col. John Hobart, ld. Howden.
Capt. Wm. Augs. Montague.
Col. Thos. Noel Harris.
Col. Saml. Gordon Higgins.
1831. Col. Jas. Robertson Arnold.
Lt.-col. Jas. Jones.
Capt. Edwd. Sparshott.
Capt. Andr. Atkins Vincent.
Col. Geo. Cowper.
Lt.-col. Mathias Everard.
Lt.-col. Chas. Wright.
Col. John Mordlyon Wilson.
Lt.-col. John Hastings Mair.
Col. Jas. Fredk. Love.
Lt.-col. Robt. Simson.
Col. Geo. Brown.
Sir Robt. Alexr. Chermside, M.D., **C.**
Wm. Taylor Money, **C.**
Maj. Thos. Hy. Shadwell Clerke.

1831. Lt.-col. Alexr. Kennedy Clark Kennedy.
Lt.-col. Chas. Menzies.
Chas. König.
Sir John. Fredk. Wm. Herschel, bt., **C.**
Sir. Chas. Bell, **C.**
Jas. Ivory, **C.**
Sir David Brewster, **C.**
Sir John Leslie, **C.**
Lt.-col. Chas. Diggle.
Lt.-col. Alexr. Campbell.
Sir Nichs. Harris Nicolas, **C.**
In 1831. Lt.-col. Gustavus du Plat.
1832. Col. Wm. Riddall.
Col. Hy. Rainey.
Lt.-col. St. John Augs. Clerke.
Lt.-col. Jas. Considine.
Lt.-col. Wm. Thorn.
Lt.-col. John Cox.
Lt.-col. Digby Mackworth.
Maj Wm. Beckwith.
Sir Saml. Rush Meyrick, **C.**
Sir John Whiteford, **C.**
Richd. Mellish, **C.**
Capt. Robt. Smart.
Col. Robt. Ross.
Col. Hy. Daubeney.
Col. Walter Tremenheere.
Col. Geo. Wm. Paty.
Col. Robt. Nickle.
Lt.-col. Hy. Madox.
Lt.-col. Geo. Graydon.
Lt.-col. John Reed,
Lt.-col. Thos. Eccles.
Lt.-col. Chas. Barker Turney.
Lt.-col. Sir Michl. Creagh.
Maj. Archd. Stewart.
Maj. Jas. Waller Samo Waller.
Col. Nathl. Thorn.
Col. Wm. Chalmers.
Col. Edwd. Walker,
Col. Hy. Jas. Riddell.
Lt.-col. Wm. Beresford.
Lt.-col. Jas. Chas. Chatterton.
Lt.-col. Robt. Christr. Mansell.
Lt.-col. John Peddie.
Lt.-col. Leslie Walker.
Stepney Cowell, **C.**
Lt.-col. Steph. Holmes.
Maj. Wm. Onslow.
Lt.-col. Geo. E. Jones.
Lt.-col. John Marshall.
Sir Fredk. Madden, **C.**
Nichs. Carlisle, **C.**
Sir Fras. Palgrave, **C.**
Sir Hy. Ellis, **C.**
Edmd. Lodge (Clarencieux K.A.) **C.**
1833. M.-gen. Sir Geo. Teesdale.
Lt.-col. Saml. Dales.
Lt.-col. Robt. Bull.
Col. Thos. Staunton St. Clair.
Lt.-col. Chas. Archd. Macalister.
Col. Geo. Augs. Wetherall.
1833. Lt.-col. Edwd. Thos. Fitzgeral
Col. Alexr. Fisher Macintosh.
Lt.-col. Hy. Hanmer.
Lt.-col. Jas. Freeth.
Lt.-col. Chas. King.
Lt.-col. Chas. Holland Hastin
Lt.-col. Sir Robt. Moubray.
Commdr. Chas. Haultain.
Lt.-col. John Wright.
Col. John Owen.
Lt.-col. John Garland.
Maj. Wm. Fredk. Forster.
Maj. John Arnaud.
Lt.-col. John Chas. Hope.
Maj. John Fitzmaurice.
Maj. Jeremiah Ratcliffe.
Lt.-col. Ronald Regd. Macdona
Col. Fras. Maule.
John Clarke, M.D., **C.**
Maj. Geo. Doherty.
Capt. Sir Geo. Tyler.
Sir Chas. Wilkins, **C.**
Sir Graves Chamney Haughton,
Robt. Wm. St. John, **C.**
1834. Col. Wm. Greenshield Power.
Lt.-col. Wm. Gardner Freer.
Col. John Hare.
Col. Sir Andr. Leith Hay.
Lt.-col. Warner Westenra Higgi
Lt.-col. Alexr. Hope Pattison.
Lt.-col. Jas. McMair.
Col. Robt. Burd Gabriel.
Lt.-col. Chas McGrigor.
Col. Hy. Somerset.
Lt.-col. John Cross.
Maj. Barth. Vigors Derinzy.
Col. Sir Joseph Thackwell.
Lt.-col. Wm. Gordon Cameron
Lt.-col. Rice Jones.
Lt.-col. Nathan Wilson.
Maj. Wm. Mackie.
Lt.-col. Robt. Winchester.
Maj. Geo. Antoine Ramsay.
Maj. Sir Fras. Bond Head.
Commdr. Joseph Chappell W nough.
Col. Thos. Abernethie.
Capt. Edwd. Lloyd.
Sir Geo. Magrath, M.D., **C.**
Col. Fras. Sherlock.
Lt.-col. Wm. McAdam.
Lt.-col. Wm. Granville Eliot.
Lt.-col. John Elliot Cairnes.
Lt.-col. Sir Thos. Stephen Sor
Col. Harry Bulteel Harris.
Capt. Robt. Fair.
Capt. John Toup Nicolas.
Lt.-col. Jos. Vallack.
Capt. Sir Eaton Travers.
Lt. Col. Chas. Hamilton Smith
Sir Wm. Woods (Garter K. A.),
Sir Alexr. Ferrier.
Lt. Col. Sir Wm. Macbean G Colebrooke.
1835. Col. Saml. Rice.

1835. Col. Wm. Wood.
Capt. Wm. Willmott Henderson.
Lt.-col. John Jordan.
Col. Richd. Roberts.
Lt.-col. Chichester W. Crookshanks.
Lt.-col. Edwd. Jackson.
Col. Thos. Bunbury.
Lt.-col. John Spink.
Lt.-col. Wm. Pearce.
Lt.-col. Wm. Bush.
Lt.-col. ld. Robt. Kerr.
Lt.-col. Lovell Benjn. Lovell.
Lt.-col. Chas. Stisted
Col. Wm. Jervois.
Col. Robt. Barclay Macpherson.
Lt.-col. Jas. Harvey.
Lt.-col. Sir John Rowland Eustace.
Lt.-col. John Tyler.
Lt.-col. Geo. Disbrowe.
Lt.-col. Thos. Hy. Morice.
Lt.-col. Thos. Wm. Nicholson.
Lt.-col- Sir Hy. Bayly.
Lt.-col. Fredk. MacBean.
Lt.-col. Wm. Cox.
Maj. Jos. Anderson.
Maj. Arthur Hill Trevor.
Maj. Donald John McQueen.
Maj. Thos. Ryan.
Maj. Saml. Thorpe.
Lt-col. Pringle Taylor.
Lt.-col. Wm. Freke Williams.
Maj. Jas. Forlong.
Maj. Robt. Mullen.
Maj. Robt. Bidwell Edwards.
Commdr. Sir Wm. Brown.
Commdr. Walter Kirby.
Lt.-col. Hy. Booth.
Lt.-col. John Campbell.

1836. M.-gen. Love Parry Jones Parry.
Col. Nathl. Burslem.
Col. Sir Chas. Webb Dance.
Col. John Potter Hamilton.
Col. Miller Clifford.
Col. Steph. Arth. Goodman.
Lt.-col. Harris Corke Hailes.
Col. Thos. Thornbury Wooldrige.
Col. Geo. Dean Pitt.
Lt.-col. Saumarez Brock.
Col. Thos. Valiant.
Col. Nichs. Hamilton.
Lt.-col. Gervase Turbervill.
Lt.-col. Geo. Gore.
Col. Geo. Augs. Henderson.
Lt.-col. Chas. Leslie.
Lt.-col. Robt. Anderson.
Col. John McCaskill.
Lt.-col. Alexr. Findlay.
Lt.-col. Paul Phipps.
Col. Jas. Campbell.
Col. Richd. England.
Lt.-col. John Geddes.
Col. hon. Chas Gore.
Lt.-col. John Christr. Harrison.
Col. Alexr. Munro.

1836. Lt.-col. John Oldfield.
Lt.-col. Edwd. Wildman.
Lt.-col. Thos. Weare.
Lt.-col. Cudbert French.
Col. Sir Hy. Geo. Macleod.
Lt.-col. Archd. Montgomery Maxwell.
Lt.-col. Alexr. Clerke.
Col. Hy. Balneavis.
Lt.-col. Edwd. Thos. Fitzgerald.
Lt.-col. Norcliffe Norcliffe.
Maj. John. Wilson.
Maj. Jas. Henderson.
Maj. John Robyns.
Lt.-col. Wm. Hy. Newton.
Lt.-col. Edwd. Charleton.
Lt.-col. Hy. Herbert Manners.
Maj. John Paul Hopkins.
Maj. Nichs. Wilson.
Maj. Robt. Edwd. Burrowes.
Maj. Wm. Edwd. Page.
Maj. Geo. Pipon.
Maj. Thos. Molyneux Williams.
Maj. Plomer Young.
Lt.-col. Alexr. Barton.
Lt.-col. Arth. Du Bourdieu.
Maj. Chas. Cornwallis Michell.
Maj. Robt. Garrett.
Maj. John Salisbury Jones.
Capt. Wilson Braddyll Bigland.
Capt. Stanhope Lovell.
Capt. Buckland Stirling Bluett.
Capt. John Carpenter.
Capt. Sir Hy. John Leeke.
Capt. Saml. Radford.
Capt. Wm. Hotham.
Capt. Alexr. Barkclay Branch.
Commdr. Jos. Sherer.
Maj. Jas. Butler.
Lt.-col. Abrm. Josias Cloete.
Geo. Fredk. Beltz (Lancaster Her.), **C.**
Sir Wm. Jackson Hooker, **C.**
Capt. John Hindmarsh.
Commdr. Sir Jas. Pearl.
Commdr. Alexr. Maconochie.
Sir Jos. de Courcy Laffan., bt., **C.**
John M. Brackenbury, **C.**
Maj. Fredk. Chidley Irwin.
Sir John Robison, **C.**

1837. Capt. Jas. Ryder Burton.
Capt. Jas. Wm. Gabriel.
Capt. Chas. Warde.
Commdr. Benjn. Morton Festing.
Capt. Wm. John Cole.
Commdr. John Powney.
Commdr. Christr. Knight.
Capt. Wm. Slaughter.
Lt.-col. Geo. Paris Bradshaw.
Lt.-col. Turtcliff Boger.
Lt.-col. Chas. Cadell.
Col. John Carter.
Lt.-col. Alexr. Cairncross
Lt.-col. John Crowder.
Lt.-col. Wm. Elliott.

1837. Col. Chesborough Grant Falconar.
Lt.-col. Jas. Forrest Fulton.
Lt.-col. Geo. Gawler.
Lt.-col. John Hodge.
Col. Thos. Phipps Howard.
Lt.-col. Jas. Jackson.
Lt.-col. John Leslie.
Lt.-col. Thos. Marten.
Lt.-col. Donald Macpherson.
Lt.-col. John Moore.
Lt.-col. Jas. Poole Oates.
Lt.-col. Thos. Powell.
Lt.-col. Wm. Sall.
Lt.-col. Robt. Walton.
Lt.-col. Geo. Wilkins.
Maj. J. Jocelyn Anderson.
Lt.-col. John Austen.
Maj. Hy. Andrews.
Lt.-col. Hy. Baynes.
Maj. Wm. Bruce.
Maj. Jas. Briggs.
Maj. John Bogue.
Maj. Wm. Burney.
Lt.-col. Wm. Brereton.
Maj. Peter Bishop.
Lt.-col. Andr. Clarke.
Maj. Robt. Noble Crosse.
Maj. Eyre John Crabbe.
Maj. John Clark.
Lt.-col. John Crowe.
Maj. Chas. Deane.
Maj. Wm. Hy. Elliott.
Maj. Robt. Fraser.
Lt.-col. Wm. Green.
Maj. —— Grove.
Maj. Alexr. Grant.

1837. Maj. John. Wm. Henderson.
Maj. Jos. Mark Harty.
Maj. Jas. Price Hely.
Lt.-col. Bissell Harvey.
Maj. Norman Lamont.
Maj. Hy. Fredk. Lockyer.
Maj. Robt. Law.
Maj. Piearce Lowen.
Lt.-col. Chas. Levinge.
Maj. Monson Molesworth Madde
Lt.-col. Geo. Marshall.
Lt.-col. Wm. Miller.
Lt.-col. John Pennycuick.
Maj. Edwd. Jonn. Priestley.
Lt.-col. Jas. Hy. Philps.
Maj. Jas. Kerr Ross.
Maj. John Singleton.
Maj. Geo. Fitzgerald Stack.
Maj. Jos. Clavell Sladdon Sl field.
Maj. Peregrine Fras. Thorne.
Maj. Jas. Travers.
Maj. Jas. Badham Thornhill.
Maj. Abrm. Beresford Taylor.
Maj. Robt. Hy. Willcocks.
Lt.-col. Wm. Leighton Wood.
Jas. Arthur, M.D., **C.**
Wm. Durie, **C.**
Robt. Purkis Hillyar, **C.**
Chas. F. Forbes, M.D., **C.**
Capt. Sir Spencer Lambe Hunter Vassall.
Lt.-col. John Falconar Briggs.
Sheffield Grace, **C.**
Jas. Burns, M.D., **C.**
Sir Chas. Augs. Fitzroy, **C.**

Appointed by King Ernest of Hanover.

See Introduction, *ante*, p. 785.

1837. Commdr. Thos Gordon.
Capt. H. S. Stephens.
Capt. Geo. Gosling.
Lt.-col. Benjn. Orlando Jones.
Lt.-col Thos. Cox Kirby.
Capt. Jas. Morgan.

1837. Maj. R. Wilkinson.
Maj. Geo. John Belson.
Col. John Rolt.
Lt.-col. Anthy. Singleton King.
Maj. Arth. Gore.
Maj. North Ludlow Beamish.

OFFICERS OF THE ORDER OF THE GUELPHS.

Chancellors.

1815. Earnest Fredk. Hy., Count Munster, Aug. 12; res. 1831.

1831. Louis Conrad Geo., Bar Ompteda; res. 1837.

Vice-Chancellors.

1815. G. H. Nieper; res. 1824.

1824. Geo. Ernest Fredk. Hoppenstec

Secretaries.

1815. John Geo. Lewis Moeller, Aug.; res. 1833.

1833. Geo. Christr. Lichenburg; re 1837.

KINGS OF ARMS.

1815, Aug.	Geo. Nayler, aft. Sir G.; York and Blanc Coursier Her., and aft. Clarencieux and Garter K.A.; *d.* Oct. 28, 1831.	* *	Augs. Neubourg.

THE ORDER OF ST. MICHAEL AND ST. GEORGE.

THIS ORDER has probably undergone more changes than any other. It was originally instituted by Statutes of Apr. 27, 1818, and was then confined to "natives of the United States, of the Ionian islands, and of the island of Malta and its dependencies, and to such other subjects of his Majesty as may hold high and confidential situation in the Mediterranean."

The Order at first consisted of the King of the United Kingdom as Sovereign, the Grand Master, 8 Knights Grand Cross (including the Grand Master), 12 Knights Commanders, and 24 Knights. It was enlarged by Statutes of Aug. 16, 1832, and then consisted of the Sovereign, who was also Grand Master, 15 Knights Grand Cross, 20 Knights Commanders, and 25 Companions. Under Letters Patent of Dec. 31, 1850, and Statutes of Jan. 31, 1851, the constitution of the Order was modified, but it still remained confined to the Ionian Islands and Malta.

The Ionian islands were ceded to Greece in 1863, and shortly afterwards the Order was completely reconstituted.

By Statutes of Dec. 4, 1868 (gazetted July 1, 1869), as modified by Statutes of Apr. 3, 1869 (gazetted July 1, 1869), the persons admissible into the Order were to be natural-born or naturalized British subjects who had held office in or rendered services in relation to the Colonies. By the same Statutes the Order was declared to consist of the Sovereign, the Grand Master, 25 Knights Grand Cross, 60 Knights Commanders, and 100 Companions, with power to the Sovereign to appoint extra members of the first and second classes, and to increase the numbers of each class.

By Statutes of May 30, 1877, (gazetted same day), the numbers were increased to 35 Knights Grand Cross, 120 Knights Commanders, and 200 Companions, with power to appoint extra and honorary members.

By Statutes of May 24, 1879, the Order was extended to reward services rendered to the Crown in relation to foreign affairs, and the numbers were again increased to 50 Knights Grand Cross, 150 Knights Commanders, and 260 Companions, power to appoint extra members and to increase the numbers being still reserved to the Sovereign. By Statute of June 28, 1886, 8 Knights Commanders and 9 Companions were added as additional members, and by a later Statute of Mar. 21, 1887, these were made ordinary members, the numbers of the Order being increased to this extent.

The officers of the Order now are—

PRELATE.	SECRETARY.	REGISTRAR.
CHANCELLOR.	KING OF ARMS.	OFFICER OF ARMS.

The Order is styled—

THE MOST DISTINGUISHED ORDER OF ST. MICHAEL AND ST. GEORGE.

MEMBERS OF THE ORDER OF ST. MICHAEL AND ST. GEORGE.

GRAND MASTERS AND PRINCIPAL KNIGHTS GRAND CROSS OF THE ORDER OF ST. MICHAEL AND ST. GEORGE.

1818. Lt.-gen. Sir Thos. Maitland, gr. mast., Apr. 27 ; *d.* 1824.
1825. F.M. Adolphus Fredk., D. of Cambridge, gr. mast., June 20; decl. 1st. or ppal. G.C.M.G., Aug. 16, 1832 ; *d.* July 8, 1850.
1851. Geo. Wm. Fredk. Chas., D. o Cambridge, app. 1st or ppal G.C.M.G. ; re-app. as gr. mast and 1st or ppal. G.C.M.G., May 23, 1869, **G.**, and May 30, 1877 **G.**

KNIGHTS GRAND CROSS OF THE ORDER OF ST. MICHAEL AND ST. GEORGE.

(G.C.M.G.)

1818. Lt.-gen. sir Thos. Maitland, Apr. 27 (Gr. M.).
1818, Nov. 18. Emanuel Baron Theotoky.
Stamo Calichispulo.
Antonio, Ct. Comuto.
1818. Dec. 16. V.-adm. sir Chas. Vinicombe Penrose.
Giuseppe Borg Olivier.
Raffaele Crispino Xerri.
1819. V.-adm. sir Thos. Fras. Fremantle, Oct. 26.
Fredk, 6th E. of Guildford, Oct. 26.
1820. Adm. sir Graham Moore, Sept. 28; res. 1823 ; re-inv. Aug. 24, 1832.
1821. Lt.-gen. sir Fredk. Adam, Dec. 27.
1823. Ct. Nicolo Anino, Mar. 1.
1824. Adm. sir Harry Burrard Neale, bt., Jan. 16 ; res. 1826 ; re-inv. Aug. 24, 1832.
1825. F.M. Pr. Adolphus Fredk. D. of Cambridge (Gr.M., &c.), June 20.
Marino Veja, July 30.
1827. Adm. sir Edwd. Codrington, Apr. 23 ; res. 1828 ; re-inv. Aug. 24, 1832.
1828. M.-gen. hon. sir Fredk. Cavendish Ponsonby, Nov. 5.
1829. Adm. sir Pulteney Malcolm, Jan. 21 ; res. 1831 ; re-app. Aug. 16, 1832.
1831. V.-adm. hon. sir Hy. Hotham, July 4.
1832. Giuseppe Calcedonio Debono, May 28.
Giovanni Cappadoca, June 6.
Angiolo Condari, June 6.
Sir Jas. Macdonald, bt., June 22.
Lt.-gen. sir Alexr. Woodford. June 30.
Geo., &c., ld. Nugent (son of Geo., 2nd E. Temple and 1st M. of Buckingham), Aug. 12.
1833. Col. Fredk. Hankey, May 4.
R.-adm. Thos. Briggs, June 26.
Spiridion Vittor, Ct. Bulgari, July 7.
1834. Adm. sir Josias Rowley, bt Feb. 22.
1835. Lt.-gen. sir Howard Douglas, bt Mar. 18.
1836. Paolo, Ct. Parisio, Apr. 2.
Lt. gen. sir Hy. Fredk. Bouverie, Sept. 28.
1837, May 10. Gen. Hy. Pigot.
Gen. Thos., ld. Lynedoch.
Adm. hon. Robt. Stopford.
Adm. sir Geo. Martin.
Gen. sir Martin Hunter.
Gen. Wm. Wilkinson.
Lt.-gen. sir Chas. Bulkeley Egerton.
Gen. sir John Oswald.
Lt.-gen. sir Hudson Lowe.
V.-adm. sir Richd. Hussey Hussey.
M.-gen. sir Patr. Ross.
1838. Pietro Petrezzopulo, Apr. 26.
V.-adm. sir Geo. Eyre, May 2.
1839. Sir Vittor Caridi, Aug. 31.
1840. Sir Francisco Muzzan, July 7.
Sir Pietro Coidan, July 7.
Sir Nichs. Harris Nicolas, Oct.
1842. Pr. Fras. Albt. Augs. Chas. Emanuel, Pr. of Saxe-Coburg and Gotha, Consort of Q. Victoria, Jan. 15.
Demetrio, Ct. Della Decima, J. 21.
Sir Agostino Randon, Mar. 18.
1843. Lt.-gen. John, ld. Seaton, July
Lt.-gen. hon. Patr. Stuart, J. 3.
1844. Antonio, Ct. Theotoky, Dec. 1

1845. Pr. Geo. Fredk. Wm. Chas., aft. D. of Cambridge, June 26; aft. Gr. M.
1850. Spiridione Facco Stefano.
Hy. Geo. Ward.
Demetrio, Ct. Salomon, Sept. 7.
1853. Candiano, Ct. Roma.
Demetrio, Ct. Carrusa.
1854. Vincenzo Casolani.
1855. Alessandro Damaschini.
Sir John Young, bt.
1856. Sir Ignatius Gavin Bonavita.
Giuseppe Maria, Baron de Piro.
1857. Sir Demetrio Valsamachi.
Dionisio, Ct. Flamburiari.
1860. Col. Hy. Knight Storks.
M.-gen. John Gaspard Le Marchant.
Geo. Fergusson Bowen, Apr. 16.
Sir Paolo Dingli.
1864. Sir Pietro Armeni Braila, May 21.
1867. Sir Georgio Marcoran.
1868. Sir Adriano Dingli, Apr. 24.
Sir Edwd. Victor Houlton, Apr. 24.
Lt.-gen. sir Patr. Grant, Sept.
1869. Chas. Stanley, 4th visc. Monck, June 23.
1869, June 30. Edwd. Geoffr., 14th E. of Derby.
Hy. Geo., 3rd E. Grey.
John, 1st E. Russell.
Alf. Ern. Alb., D. of Edinburgh, July 2.
1870. Edwd. Geo. Earle Lytton, 1st ld. Lytton, Jan. 15.
Pr. Arth. Wm. Patr. Alb., aft. D. of Connaught, &c., Apr. 16.
1873. John Hy. Thos., 3rd visc. Canterbury, June 25.
1874. Sir Hy. Barclay, Mar. 9.
Sir John Peter Grant, Mar. 9.
M.-gen. sir Garnet Jos. Wolseley, aft. visc. Wolseley, Mar. 31.
John Hawley Glover, May 8.
1875. Sir Hercules Geo. Robt. Robinson, Jan. 28.
1876. Sir Datu Tummongong Abubakr Sri, Mahar. of Johore, May 1.
Fredk. Temple, E. of Dufferin, &c., aft. M. of Dufferin and Ava, May. 26.
1877, May 30. Alb. Edwd., Pr. of Wales.
Geo. Aug. Constantine, 2nd M. of Normanby.
1878. Lt.-gen. sir Arthur Purves Phayre, Jan. 24.
Hon. sir Arth. Hamilton Gordon, Feb. 6.
M.-gen. sir Wm. Fras. Drummond Jervois, May 25.
Sir Alexr. Tilloch Galt, May 25.
Sir Hy. Drummond Wolff, Aug. 15.
The King of Siam, Sept. 7.
Sir John Douglas Sutherland Campbell, c.c. M. of Lorne, Sept. 23.
Sir John Rose, bt., Oct. 29.
1879, May 24. Richd. Bickerton, ld. Lyons.
Odo Wm. Leopold Russell, c.c. ld. Odo Russell; aft. ld. Ampthill.
Sir Antonio Micallef.
1879, Aug. 29. Sir Chas. Lennox Wyke.
Sir Richd. Wood.
1879. Nuba Pasha, Oct. 9.
Somditch Pra Paramindr Maha. Chulalonkorn, K. of Siam, Nov. 22.
1880, May 28. Pr. Leopold Geo. Duncan Albt., aft. D. of Albany.
Gen. sir Arth. Borton.
1881, May 24. Sir Arth. Edwd. Kennedy.
Gen. sir Harry St. George Ord.
1881. Kalakana, K. of the Hawaiian Islands, July 23.
Sir Harry Smith Parkes, Nov. 26.
1882. M.-gen. sir Hy. Evelyn Wood, Feb. 17.
John Hy. Brand, Pres. Orange Fr. St., Mar. 23.
1883, May 24. Fred., ld. Blachford.
Sir Hy. Ernest Bulwer.
Sir Jas. Robt. Longden.
1883. Seyyid Barghash-bin-Said, Sultan of Zanzibar, Oct. 29.
1884. Hy. Chas. Keith, 5th M. of Lansdowne, Jan. 28.
Sir Robt. Richd. Torrens, May 24.
Sir Alfred Stephen, May 24.
Sir John Hay Drummond Hay, Dec. 4.
1885, June 6. Chas. Robt., 3rd ld. Carrington.
M.-gen. sir Andr. Clarke.
Sir Anthy. Musgrave.
Sir Fredk. Aloysius Weld.
1885. Sir Edwd. Baldwin Malet, June 26.
Lt.-gen. sir Gerald Graham, Aug. 25.
M.-Gen. sir Chas. Warren, Oct. 4.
Sir Julian Pauncefote, Dec. 1.
1886. Sir Wm. Arthur White, Jan. 28.
Sir Hy. Thurstan Holland, bt., aft. ld. Knutsford, Jan. 28.
Sir Chas. Tupper, Feb. 1.
Sir John Kirk, Feb. 2.
Sir Robt. Burnett David Morier, Feb. 13.
1886, May 29. Lt.-gen. sir Robt. Biddulph.
Sir Fras. Clare Ford, May 29.
1887. M.-gen. sir Geo. Cumine Strahan, Jan. 29.
1887, May 24. Gen. sir John Lintorn Arabin Simmons.
Gen. sir Hy. Wylie Norman.
Sir Hy. Brougham Loch.
Sir Wm. Cleaver Fras. Robinson.
1887, June 21 Sir Edwd. Wm. Stafford.
Sir Thos. Elder.

1888. Sir Ronald Ferguson Thomson, Jan. 10.
Sir Hy. Parkes, Jan. 28.
Sir Hy. Turner Irving, May 24.
Sir Danl. Cooper, bt., May 24.
1888. Sir Evelyn Baring, June 2.
Sir Chas. Johnson Brooke, June 2
The Sultan of Zanzibar.
Mortimer, ld. Sackville, Sept. 10
1889. Sir Hugh Lowe, Jan.

KNIGHTS COMMANDERS OF THE ORDER OF ST. MICHAEL AND ST. GEORGE.

(K.C.M.G.)

1818, Nov. 18. Vittor Caridi.
Antonio, Ct. Theotoky.
Dionizio Bulzo.
Col. Fredk. Hankey.
1818. Giuseppe Nicolo Zammit, Dec. 16.
Rd. Plasket, Dec. 16.
1819. M.-gen. sir Patr. Ross, Nov. 9.
1820, Feb. 26. Capt. hon. Anthy Maitland.
Nicolo, Ct. Anino.
Giovanni Cappadoca.
Marino Veja.
Col. sir Fredk. Stovin.
Alexr. Wood.
1820. Basilio Zavo, July 19.
1821. Demetrio, Ct. Foscardi, Mar. 14.
Giacomo Calichiopulo Manzaro, Mar. 14.
1822. Paolo, Ct. Parisio, Jan. 31.
1823. M.-gen. Robt. Travers, Feb. 20.
Francesco Muzzan, Mar. 1.
1825. Pietro Coidan, June 30.
Angiolo Condari, June 30.
1832. Jos. Russell, June 22.
Sir Nichs. Harris Nicolas (with rank of senior K.C.M.G.), Aug. 16.
1833, Feb. 9. Vincenzo Casolani.
Giuseppe Marq. Testaferrata.
Spiridion Vittor, Ct. Bulgari.
Pietro Petrizzopulo
1833. Edwd. Stuart Baynes, June 26.
Vincenzo, Ct. Manduca, July 17.
1835. Claudio Vincenzo Bonnici, June 11.
1836. Ignatius Gavin Bonavita, Apr. 2.
1839. Hector Greig, Jan. 26.
Stamo Gangadi, Aug. 30.
Agostino Randon, Aug. 30.
M.-gen. Fras., Ct. Rivarola, Nov. 30.
1840. Demetrio, Ct. Della Decima, July 7.
Altavilla Calichiopulo, Sept. 14.
1842. Angiolo Calichiopulo, Jan. 21.
Giuseppe Maria, Baron de Piro, Mar. 18.
1844, May 27. Demetrius Valsamachi.
Plato Petrides.
Dionisio, Ct. Flamburiari.
1844. Georgio Cazzaiti, Dec. 16.
1849. Antonio, Ct. Dusmani, Dec.
1850. Anastasio Tipaldo Xidian.
Alessandro Damaschini.
Agostino Portelli.
1854. Georgio Marcoran.
1854. Jno. Fraser.
1855. Spiridione Valsamachi.
1856. Pietro Armeni Braila.
Wm. H. Thornton.
Geo. Fergusson Bowen.
Paolo Dingli.
1857. Demetrio, Ct. Curcumelli, July 9
Andrea Mustoxidi.
1859. Jas. Philip Lacaita, Mar. 30.
Sir Chas. Eurwicke Douglas, bt. Apr. 4.
1860. Antonio Micallef.
Adriano Dingli.
Victor Houlton.
Peter Smith.
1862. Spiridione Valaoriti, July 14.
Hy. Drummond Wolff.
1864. Chas. Sebright, May 27.
Major Wilfred Brett, Oct. 13.
1868. Ct. Nichs. Scebarras Bologna.
1869, June 23. Col. Thos. Gore Browne.
Fras. Hincks.
Jas. Walker.
M.-gen. Chas. Hastings Doyle.
1869, June 30. Paul Edmd. de Strzlecki.
Geo. Wm., Baron Lyttelton.
Fredk. Peel.
Chas Bowyer Adderley, aft. ld Norton.
Sir Fredc. Rogers, bt.
Sir Hercules Geo. Robt. Robinson
Alexr. Tilloch Galt.
Hy. Taylor.
Thos. Fredk. Elliot.
1870. Jno. Rose, Jan. 15.
Thos. Wm. Clinton Murdoch Jan. 15.
Hon. Wm. Coutts Keppel, c.c visc. Bury; aft. ld. Ashford Aug. 24.
Lt.-gen. hon. Jas. Lindsay, Dec. 22
Col. Garnet Jos. Wolseley, aft visc. Wolseley, Dec. 22.
1871. Hon. Arth. Hamilton Gordon Feb. 23.
Sir Rd. Graves MacDonnell, Feb 23.
Sir Arth. Edwd. Kennedy, Sept. 29
Sir Benjn. Chilley Campbell Pine Sept. 29.
1872. Chas. Cowper, Feb. 23.
Geo. Fredc. Verdon, Feb. 23.
Somerset, Rd., E. of Belmore Mar. 27.

1872. Robt. Rd. Torrens, Aug. 31.
Hy. Ayers, Nov. 30.
1873. Col. Andr. Clarke, Mar. 27.
1874, Mar. 9. Geo. Augs. Constantine, M. of Normanby.
Sir Alfr. Stephen.
Sir Jas. McCulloch.
Jno. O'Shanassy.
Jno. Scott.
1874. Col. Fras. Worgan Festing, May 8.
1874, May 28. Col. Stephen Jno. Hill.
Col. Wm. Fras. Drummond Jervois.
Penrose Goodchild Julyan.
Hy. Ernest Bulwer, July 23.
Donald Maclean, July 23.
1874, Sept. 28. Sir Jas. Fergusson, bt.
Edwd. Deas Thomson.
Jno. Sealy.
1875, Mar. 5. Chas. Du Cane.
Geo. Macleay.
1875, May 28. Fras. Fortescue Turville.
Hon. Geo. Wm. Hamilton, c.c. visc. Kirkwall; aft. E. of Orkney.
Chas. Sladen.
Julius Vogel.
1875, Aug. 30. Anthy. Musgrave.
Rawson Wm. Rawson.
1876. Wm. Hy. Gregory, Feb. 19.
Jas. Robt. Longden, Mar. 13.
Chas. Peter Layard, Mar. 13.
Theophilus Shepstone, Aug. 14.
1877, May 1. Sir Hy. Thurstan Holland, bt., aft. ld. Knutsford.
Wm. Wellington Cairns.
Lt.-col. Hy. Fitzharding Berkeley Maxse.
Wm. Fitzherbert.
1877, May 30. M.-gen. sir Harry St. Geo. Ord.
Sir Redmond Barry.
Sir Hy. Watson Parker.
Jno. Bayley Darvall.
Steph. Walcott.
Wm. Cleaver Fras. Robinson.
Maj. Robt. Miller Mundy.
M.-gen. Patr. Leonard M'Dougall.
M.-gen. Jno. Hy. Lefroy.
M.-gen. Edwd. Selby Smyth.
Brig.-gen. Robt. Michael Laffan.
Jno. Robertson.
Hy. Parkes.
Arthur Blyth.
1877, Dec. 10. Sir Chas. Gavan Duffy.
Gen. Jno. Jarvis Bisset.
Rd. Wood.
1878, May 25. Albert Smith.
Hy. Turner Irving.
Sanford Freeling.
Sir Jas. Milne Wilson.
Jno. Hay.
Archd. Michie.
Fredk. B. T. Carter.
1878. Fras. Philip Cunliffe Owen, Oct. 29.

1879. Somditch Chas. Phya Sura-wongse, formerly regent of Siam, Jan. 29.
The Raja Ahmed Taj Udin bin Sultan Zain Alrashid Kedah, Apr. 30.
1879, May 24. Rachad Pacha.
Sir Narcisse Fortunat Belleau.
Wm. Taylour Thomson.
Wm. Pearce Howland.
Chas. Tupper.
Saml. Leonard Tilley.
Geo. Buckley Mathew.
Geo. Welsh Kellner.
M.-gen. Edwd. Wolstenholme Ward.
Dr. Ferdinand Von Mueller.
Geo. Brown.
Alexr. Campbell.
Rd. Jno. Cartwright.
Edwd. Wm. Stafford.
Wm. Fox.
1879. Riaz Pasha, July 31.
Sir Danl. Brooke Robertson, Aug. 29.
Jno. Luke Geo., E. of Donoughmore, Oct. 9.
M.-gen. hon. Hy. Hugh Clifford, Dec. 19.
Col. Chas. Knight Pearson, Dec. 19.
1880. Sir Julian Pauncefote.
M.-gen. Edwd. Bruce Hamley, Jan. 12.
Chas. Rivers Wilson, Jan. 12.
Col. Wm. Owen Lanyon, Apr. 6.
Col. Baker Creed Russell, Apr. 6.
Thos. Geo. Knox, Apr. 12.
M.-gen. Robt. Biddulph, Apr 12.
Jno. Pope Hennessy, Apr. 21.
Surg.-Maj. Saml. Rowe, Apr. 21.
Maj. Geo. Cumine Strahan, May 28.
Frdk. Aloysius Weld, May 28.
Wm. Vallance Whiteway, May 28.
Chao Phya Bhanuwongse Maha Kosa Tibodi Phraklang, July 10.
Col. Jno. Carstairs McNeill, Aug. 17.
Sir Danl. Cooper, bt., Oct. 25.
Patrick Jennings, Oct. 25.
Virgile Naz, Nov. 3.
1881. Spenser St. John, Mar. 28.
1881, May 24. Sir Fras. Dillon Bell.
Geo. Berkeley.
Hector Louis Langevin.
M.-gen. Geo. Richd. Greaves.
Arthur Hunter Palmer.
Lt.-gen. Jno. Summerfield Hawkins.
Lt.-col. Chas Wm. Wilson.
1881. Donald Currie, July 25.
Patr. Jos. Keenan, July 25.
Jno. Kirk, Sept. 5.
Joshua Peter Bell, Nov. 24.
Auckland Colvin, Nov. 26.

1882. Gen. Edwd. Stanton, Feb. 1.
Sir Jno. Hy. De Villiers, Feb. 17.
V.-adm. Richd. Jas., E. of Clanwilliam, Mar. 3.
Fras. Savage Reilly, Apr. 17.
Robt. Hart, Apr. 17.
1882, May 24. Cornelius Hendericksen Kortright.
Wm. Brampton Gordon.
Col. Wm. Bellairs.
Geo. Stoddart Whitmore.
Saul Samuels.
Count Giorgio Sérafino Ciantar (Palislogo) Barone di San Giovanni.
Jno. Hall.
1882. Edwd. Mortimer Archibald, Aug. 12.
1882, Aug. 18. Jno. Chas. Molteno.
Wm. Chas. Sargeaunt.
M.-gen. Archd. Edwd. Harbord Anson.
Mohamed Sultan Pasha, Oct. 28.
Wm. McArthur, Nov. 17.
Thos. McIlwraith, Nov. 17.
Col. Redvers Hy. Buller, Nov. 24.
1883, May 24. Wm. Robinson.
Geo. Wm. Des Vœux.
Col. Robt. Wm. Harley
Chas. Cameron Lees.
Fredk. Palgrave Barlee.
Jno. Douglas.
Chas. Hutton Gregory.
Lt.-col. Chas. Bullen Hugh Mitchell.
Hugh Low.
Wm. Morgan.
Ambrose Shea.
Col. Chas. Warren.
1883. Constantine Geo. Zerondacchi, July 9.
1884, Feb. 1. Lt.-gen. hon. Leicester Smyth.
Sir Geo. Wigram Allen.
Fredk. Whitaker.
Lt.-col. Fras. Walter de Winton.
1884. Sir Chas. Augs. Hartley, Feb. 19.
Surg.-gen. Wm. Guyer Hunter.
1884, May 24. Thos. Chas. Scanlen.
Col. Wm. Crossman.
Fredk. Napier Broome.
Arthur Elibank Havelock.
1884. David Lewis Macpherson, July 28.
Ronald Ferguson Thomson, Aug. 14.
Moustapha Bey Jawer, Mudir of Dongola, Dec. 3.
1885. Wm. Arthur White, Mar. 16.
Hy. Percy Anderson, Mar. 16.
Gerald FitzGerald, May 15.
1885, June 6. Adams Geo. Archibald.
Chas. Mills.
M.-gen. Peter Hy. Scratchley.
Alexr. Stuart.
1885, June 26. Hon. Lionel Sackville Sackville West.
1885. Fras. Clare Ford.
June 26. Thos. Villiers Lister.
1885. Halliday Macartney, Aug. 10.
1885, Aug. 25. Josh. Phillippe René Adolphe Caron.
M.-gen. Fredk. Dobson Middleton.
Edwd. Zohrab Pasha.
1885. Jno. Fowler, Sept. 1.
Col. Jno. Underwood Bateman-Champain, Dec. 31.
1886. Frank Cavendish Lascelles, Jan. 28.
Hon. Fras. Rd. Plunkett, Feb. 13.
Capt. Rd. Fras. Burton, Feb. 13.
1886, May 29. Abdul Samat Samat, Sultan of Selangore.
Sir Jno. Coode.
Lt.-col. Marshall Jas. Clarke.
Cecil Clementi Smith.
Donald Alexr. Smith.
Robt. Stout.
Hon. Wm. Stuart.
Chas. Crespigny, ld. Vivian.
Hon. Edmd. Jno. Monson.
Lt.-col. Robt. Lambert Playfair.
1886, June 28. Sir Saml. Devonport.
Fras. Knollys.
Arth. Nonus Birch.
Arth. Hodgson.
Jno. Fras. Julius Von Haast.
Augs. Jno. Adderley.
Jas. Fras. Garrick.
Graham Berry.
1886. Saml. Walker Griffith, July 23.
Sir Horace Rumbold, Aug. 6.
Francis Ottiwell Adams, Aug. 6.
Francis Beilby Alston, Aug. 6.
Sir Wm. Foster Stawell, Oct. 25.
Jno. Gordon Sprigg, Oct. 25.
Jno. Staples (ld. may. London), Nov. 9.
Walter Lawry Buller, Nov. 9.
1887, Apr. 18. Robt. Thorburn.
Jno. W. Downer.
Thos. Upington.
Jas. Lorimer.
Robt. Wisdom.
1887, May 24. Wm. Hillier, E. of Onslow.
Jenico Wm. Jos., visc. Gormanstown.
Jas. Hector.
Wm. Brandford Griffith.
Lt.-col. Jno. Terence Nicolls O'Brien.
Col. Fredk. Carrington.
Jno. Bates Thurston.
1887, June 21. Edwd. Newton.
Malcolm Fraser.
Wm. Hy. Marsh.
Sidney Godolphin Alexr. Shippard.
Jno. Wm. Akerman.
Jas. Alexr. Grant.
1887, June 21. M.-gen. Christr. Chas. Teesdale.
Col. Colin Campbell Scott Moncrieff.

1887, Wm. Kirby Green.
June 21. Col. Chas. Edwd. Mansfield.
Clement Lloyd Hill.
Jno. Hy. Fawcett.
Geo. Dashwood Taubman Goldie.
Mustapha Fehmy Pasha.
Jno. Antoinadis.
1887. Edgar Vincent, Aug. 1.
Sir Thos. Hy. Sanderson, Aug. 18.
1888. Col. Robt. Murdoch Smith, R.E., Jan. 2.
John Pender, Jan. 2.
1888, Geo. Smyth Baden-Powell.
Jan. 28. Harry Albert Atkinson.
Edwin Thos. Smith.
Fredk. Young.
1888, Michael Hy. Gallwey.
May 24. Hon. Walter Francis Hely-Hutchinson.
1888, John Fredk. Dickson.
May 24. Edwd. Noel Walker.
Capt. John Chas. Ready Colomb.
1888, Chas. Alfred Cookson.
June 2. Jas. Wm. Redhouse.
Alfred Dent.
Fredk. Wm. Smythe.
Zulfikar Pasha.
Osman Pasha Orphi.
John Sparrow David Thompson.
Jas. Spearman Winter
John. Hy. Gibbs Bergne.
1888. Hy. Arth. Blake, Nov. 7.
1889, Sir Herbert Bruce Sandford.
Jan. Roger Tuckfield Goldsworthy.
Jos. Wm. Trutch.
Lt.-gen. Thos. Lionel John Gallwey.

OFFICERS OF THE ORDER OF ST. MICHAEL AND ST. GEORGE.

Prelates.

1818. Viscoro Macario, Prelate in Ionian Islands, Nov. 17; *d.* Sept. 14. 1827.
1818. Giuseppe Bartolomeo Xerri, prelate in Malta, Dec. 15; *d.* Nov. 28, 1841.
1840. Crissanthos Masullo, abp. of Corfu, May 21, and the abps. of Corfu for the time being until
1877. Geo. Augs. Selwyn, bp. of Lichfield, May 30, **G.**
1878. Chas. Perry, bp. of New Zealand, May 25, **G.**

Chancellors.

1832. Sir Nichs. Harris Nicolas, Aug. 16; *d.* 1848.
Duties performed by ch. clk. in Colonial Office until
1877. Chas. Cox, aft. Sir C., May 30, **G.**

Secretaries.

1818. Col. Fredk. Hankey, Nov. 17, res. June 20, 1833.
Duties performed by ch. clk. in Colonial Office until
1877. Robt. Geo. Wyndham Herbert, aft. Sir R., May 30., **G.**

Kings of Arms.

1818. Sir Geo. Nayler (Garter K. A.), Nov. 17; *d.* Oct. 28, 1831.
1832. Sir Nichs. Harris Nicolas, May 20; made Chanc. Aug. 16, 1832.
Chas. Eurwicke Douglas, aft. Sir C., Oct. 12.
1859. Hy. Drummond Wolff, aft. Sir H., Apr. 5.
1869. Albert Wm. Woods, aft. sir A.; on reconstitution of order, *ut. supra.*

Registrars.

1818. Capt. Wm. Richd. Pepper Arden, Nov. 17; res. 1822.
1822. Lieut. Hy. Dundas Maclean, Feb. 20; res. 1824.
1826. Lt.-col. Jos. Rudsdell, aft. Sir J., Apr. 10; res. 1832.
1832. Geo. Hildeyard Tennyson Deyncourt, Nov. 12; res. Apr. 1839.
Duties performed by ch. clk. in Colonial Office until
1877. Hon. Robt. Hy. Meade, May 30 **G.**

THE ORDER OF THE STAR OF INDIA.

This Order was instituted by Letters Patent dated Feb. 23, 1861 (gazetted June 25, 1861), and is, as its name implies, essentially an Order connected with the British Empire in India. As originally constituted the Order consisted of the Sovereign, a Grand Master, and 25 Knights, together with such extra and honorary knights as the Sovereign should appoint, with power to confer the Order on native princes and chiefs of India. The Viceroy of India for the time being was made *ex-officio* Grandmaster of the Order.

By Letters Patent dated March 28, 1866 (gazetted May 25, 1866), the Order was reconstituted so as to consist of the Sovereign, the Grand Master, 25 Knights Grand Commanders, 50 Knights Commanders, and 100 Companions, with power to appoint extra and honorary members.

The constitution of the Order was again extended in 1875 and 1876, and now consists of the Sovereign, the Grand Master, 30 Knights Grand Commanders, 72 Knights Commanders, and 144 Companions, with power to appoint extra and honorary members as before.

The Statutes enable the Sovereign to confer the dignity of Knight Grand Commander upon princes and chiefs of India who have entitled themselves to the Royal favour, and upon such British subjects as have by important and loyal services rendered by them to the Indian Empire, merited the Royal favour; and to confer the dignity of Knight Commander and Companion upon persons who by their conduct or services in the Indian Empire have merited the Royal favour.

The officers of the Order are—

Registrar. Secretary.

The Order is styled—

The Most Exalted Order of the Star of India.

MEMBERS OF THE ORDER OF THE STAR OF INDIA.

GRAND MASTERS OF THE ORDER OF THE STAR OF INDIA.

1861. June 25. Chas. Jno., visc. Canning, Viceroy of India, and his successors in that office.

See "Viceroys of India," *ante*, p. 649.

KNIGHTS GRAND COMMANDERS OF THE ORDER OF THE STAR OF INDIA.

(G.C.S.I.)

Promotion of Knights Commanders on the Enlargement of the Order in 1866, *ut supra*.

1866, May 24. Albert Edwd., Pr. of Wales.
Nizam-ool-Moolk Nuwab Tuzinat Ali Khan, Nizam of Hyderabad.
Gen. Hugh Visc. Gough.
Jyajee Rao Sindhia, Mahar. of Gwalior.

1866, May 24. Geo. Fras. Robt., 3rd ld. Harris.
Mahar. Dhuleep Sing.
Runbeer Singh, Mahar. of Cashmere.
Sir Geo. Russell Clerk.
Tookoojee Rao Holkar, Mahar. of Indore.

1866, May 24. Mahar. Khunde Rao, Guicowar of Baroda.
Sir John Laird Mair Lawrence, bt., aft. ld. Lawrence.
Nuwab Sekunder, Begum of Bhopal.
Gen. Sir Hugh Hy. Rose, aft. ld. Strathnairn.
Yoosuf Ali Khan, Nuwab of Rampore.
Gen. Sir Geo. Pollock, bt.
Seramudi Rajahye Hindostan Raj.
Rajender Sree Mahar. Dheeraj

1866, May 24. Sewall Ram Sing, Bahadoor of Jyepore.
Furgund Dilbund Rasekhul Itgad Dowlut-i-Englishia, &c., Bahadoor of Kuppoorthulla.
Mahar. Rughoo Raj Sing, Bahadoor of Reevar.
Sir Hy. Bartle Edwd. Frere.
The Mahar. of Joudpore.
Sir Robt. Montgomery.
The Mahar. of Travancore.
Gen. Sir Wm. Rose Mansfield, aft. ld. Sandhurst.
The Mahar. of Kerowlee.

SUBSEQUENT APPOINTMENTS.

1867. Krishnar Raj. Wadyah, Mahar. of Mysore, May 24.
Lt.-gen. Sir Robt. Napier, aft ld. Napier of Magdala, Sept. 16.
1868. Ismail Pasha of Egypt, Aug 27.
Sir Wm. Robt. Seymour Vesey FitzGerald, Dec. 8.
1869. The Rana of Dholepore, June 2.
1870. Alfred Ernest Albert, D. of Edinburgh, Feb. 7.
Mohender Sing Mahar. of Puttiala, May 28.
The Nawab Salar Jung Bahadoor, May 28.
Ferd. de Lesseps, Aug. 19.
1871. Dheraj Sumbho Sing, Mahar. of Oodeypore, May 20.
The Rao Pragmuljee of Cutch, May 20.
1872. Thos. Geo., E. of Northbrook, May 3.
The Newab Shah Jehan, Begum of Bhopal, May 31.
1873, May 24. Mahar. Jung Bahadoor Kunwar Ranajee.
Gen. sir Jno. Low.
Lt. gen. sir Neville Bowles Chamberlain.
1873. Hajee Murza Hussein Khan, July 4.
1875. Pr. Tewfik Pasha, aft. Khedive of Egypt, May 3.
1875, Dec. 31. Raj. Rajessur Mahar. Dhiraj. Jeswunt Sing, Bahadoor of Jodhpur.
Furzund Dilpizir Nawab Mahummad Kulb Ali Khan, Bahadoor of Rampore.
Furzund Dilbund Rasekhul Itgad Dowlut-i-Englishia Raj. Rugbir Sing, Bahadoor of Jheend.
1876. Edwd. Robt. Lytton, E. of Lytton, Apr. 12.
·1876, June 28. Rd. Plant., &c., D. of Buckingham and Chandos.
Sir Philip Edmd. Wodehouse.
1877, Jan. 1. Arth. Wm. Patr. Albert, D. of Connaught.

1877, Jan. 1. Ram Sing, Mahar. of Bundi.
Jaswant Sing, Mahar. of Bhurtpore.
Shri Prasad Sing Narain, Mahar. of Benares.
Azim Jah Bahadoor Zapir-ud-dowla, Pr. of Arcott.
1877. Pr. Leopold Geo. Duncan Albert, aft. D. of Albany, Jan. 25.
Geo. Wm. Fredk. Chas., D. of Cambridge, June 2.
1878, Jan. 1. Cherif Pasha.
Sir Rd. Temple, bt.
1878. Sir Jno. Strachy, Apr. 30.
Safvet Pasha, Aug. 27.
1879, July 29. Mir Khodadad, Khan of Khelat.
Gen. sir Fredk. Paul Haines.
The Raj. of Nabha.
1880. Gathorne, visc. Cranbrook, Apr. 20.
The Nawab of Bahawulpur, Nov. 9.
1881. Sujjun Sing, Mahar. of Udaipur, May 24.
1882, May 23. The Mahar. of Travancore.
Nawab Ikbal-ud-dowlah of Oudh (Bagdad).
1884. Chama Rajendra Wadeir, Mahar. of Mysore, May 23.
Asaf Jah, Nizam of Hyderabad, Nov. 17.
1885. Sir Jas. Fergusson, bt., Feb. 25.
Abdul Rahman Khan, Amir of Afghanistan, Apr. 11.
Gen. sir Donald Martin Stewart, bt., Dec. 7.
1886, Jan. 1. Syud Toorkee, Sultan of Muscat.
Mahar. Mangal Sing of Ulwar
Takht Sinhji Thaken, Sahib of Bhaunagar
1887, July 28. Sir Mountstuart Elphinstone Grant-Duff.
1887, Feb. 15. Mahar. Sayaji Rao, Bahadoor, Gaekwar of Baroda.
The Maharana Futteh Sing Bahadoor of Meywar, Oodeypore.
Raja Shamsher Prakash, Bahadoor of Sirmur (Nahun).

1887. The Mahar. Holkar of Indore, June 30.
Massond Mirza Yemin-ed-dowleh, Zil-es, Sultan of Persia, Nov. 1.

1888. The Mahar. Sawai Madhu Sin of Jeypore, Jan. 1.
The Mahar. Rama Varma o Travancore, May 24.

KNIGHTS COMMANDERS OF THE ORDER OF THE STAR OF INDIA.

Original Knights.

1861, June 25. Fras. Albert, &c., Pr. Consort of Q. Victoria.
Albert Edwd., Pr. of Wales.
Nizam Ool Moolk Nuwab Tuyinat Ali Khan, Nizam of Hydrabad.
Gen. Hugh, visc. Gough.
Jyajee Rao Sindhia, Mahar. of Gwalior.
Geo. Fras. Robt., 3rd ld. Harris.
Mahar. Duleep Sing.
Gen. Colin, ld. Clyde.
Runbeer Sing, Mahar. of Cashmere.
Sir Geo. Russell Clerk.

1861, June 25. Tookoojee Rao, Holkar, Mahar. Indore.
Mahar. Khunde Rao, Guicowar o Baroda.
Sir Jno. Laird Mair Lawrence bt., aft. ld. Lawrence.
Nurendur Sing, Mahar. of Putiala
Lt.-gen. sir Jas. Outram.
— Nerwab Segumder, Begum Bhopal.
Gen. sir Hugh Hy. Rose, aft. l Strathnairn.
Yoosuf Ali Khan, Nuwab of Ran pore.

Subsequent Appointments.

1861, Aug. 19. F. M. Stapleton, visc. Combermere.
Gen. sir Geo. Pollock, aft. bt.

1863, Nov. 11. Seramudi Rajahye Hindostan Raj. Rajender Sree Mahar. Dheeraj Sewall Ram Sing, Bahadoor of Jyepore.
Furzund Dilbund Rasekool Ilahgad Dowlut-i-Englishia Raj. Suroop Sing Bahadoor of Jheend.

1864, Dec. 10. Fuzzund Dilbund Rasekhul Itgad Dowlut-i-Englishia, Bahadoor of Kuppoorthulla.
Mahar. Rughoo Raj. Sing, Bahadoor of Reevar.

1866, Feb. 12. Sir Hy. Bartle Edwd. Frere.
The Mahar. of Joudpore.
Sir Robt. Montgomery.
The Mahar. of Travancore.
Gen. sir Wm. Rose Mansfield, aft. ld. Sandhurst.
The Mahar. of Kerowlee.

1866, May 24. The Rajah Shreemun Mahar. Chuttroputtee Shahabe Dam Altaphoo.
Cecil Beadon.
The Nawab Jung Salar, Bahadoor of Hyderabad.
Donald Friell McLeod.
The Mahar. Jeypercash Sing, Bahadoor of Deo in Behar.
Hy. Ricketts.
The Mahar. Mirza Gajapoti Raz Maune, Sultan Zemindar of Vizianagram Bahadoor.
Hy. Byng Harrington.
The Mahar. Dig Bijye Sing.

1866, May 24. Walter Elliot.
Sharf-ul-Omrah Bahadoor.
Thos. Pycroft.
Rajah Jymungal Sing.
John Macpherson McLeod.
The Raj. Dinkur Rao.
M.-gen. Isaac Campbell Coffin.
The Raj. Redhakauth Deb.
M.-gen. Geo. St. Patrick Law rence.
The Raj. of Drangadra.
M.-gen. Geo. Moyle Sherer Shere
Rajah Deo Narain Sing.
M.-gen. sir Arth. Thos. Cotton.
Meer Shere Mahomed.
M.-gen. sir Neville Bowles Chamberlain.
The Raj. Sahib Dyal Missar.
Geo. Udny Yule.
Tanjore Madava Rao Dewan.
Chas. John Wingfield.
The Thakoor Rawul Jeswu Singjee.
Col. sir Herbert Benj. Edwarde
Hakeem Saadut Ali Khan.
Col. Arnold Burrowes Kemball
Sirdar Nihal Sing Chachi.
Lt.-col. Thos. Wilkinson.
Lt.-col. Robt. Wallace.
Lt.-col. Wm. Hy. Rhodes Green
Maj. Geo. Wingate.

1866. Datu Tummongong Abubakr S Mahar. of Johore, Sept. 17.

1867, Feb. 8. Col. Hy. Marion Durand.
Wm. Muir.

1867, May 24. The Mahar. Sree Jowan Singjee
Danl. Eliott.
Geo. Fredk. Harvey.

1867, M.-gen. Wm. Hill.
May 24. M.-gen. Vincent Eyre.
The Raj. Jodhbir Chund, of Nadown.
Hy. Lacon Anderson.
Richd. Temple, aft. bt.
1867, Col. Arthur Purves Phayre.
Sept. 16. The Mahar. Maun of Oude Sing.
Col. Edwd. Robt. Wetherall.
Col. Wm. West Turner.
1867. Wm. Robt. Seymour Vesey Fitz-Gerald, Oct. 22.
1868, M.-gen. Edwd. Lechmere Rus-
Aug. 24. sell.
Col. Wm. Lockyer Merewether.
1869, The Raj. of Cochin.
June 2. Lt.-gen. John Campbell.
M.-gen. Geo. Le Grand Jacob.
1870, Wm. Grey.
May 28. Pr. Gholam Mahomed.
1871, The Newab Mohsin-ood Dowlah,
May 20. Bahadoor of Oude.
Mohubut Khan Newab of Joonag-hur.
M.-gen. Geo. Inglis Jameson.
John Wm. Kaye.
Hy. Sumner Maine.
1871. Col. Fredk. John Goldsmid, Nov. 1.
1872, John Strachey.
May 31. John Cracroft Wilson.
1873. Lt.-col. Fredk. Richd. Pollock, Feb. 6.
1873, Nawab Khan Bahadoor Khwajah
May 24. Muhammed Khan Kuttuk.
Geo. Campbell.
Alexr. John Arbuthnot.
M.-gen. Harry Burnett Lumsden.
1873, Robt. Hy. Davies.
May 30. Col. Richd. John Meade.
Col. Lewis Pelly.
1874. Thos. Douglas Forsyth, July 27.
1875. Barrow Helbert Ellis, Oct. 5.
1875, Wm. Rose Robinson.
Dec. 31. Rudur Pertab Sing Mahundur Bahadoor, Mahar. of Punnah.
Shamshir Prakash Bahadoor, Rajah of Nahun.
Rao Kasee Rao Holkar Dad, Saheb of Indore.
Gen. Rumodeep Sing Rana Bahadoor.
Rao Raj. Ganput Rao Kirkee Shamshir Bahadoor Dewan of Gwalior.
Messutaz-ud-Dowlah Nawab Ma-hummad Faiz Ali Khan Baha-door, Prime Min. of Kotah.
Col. hon. Hy. Ramsay.
1876, M.-gen. Saml. Jas. Browne.
May 7. M.-gen. Dighton Macnaghten Probyn.
Surg.-gen. Jos. Fayrer.
1877, Shivaji Chatrapati, Raj. of Kol-
Jan. 1. hapore.
1877, Jas. Fitzjames Stephen.
Jan. 1. Raja Anand Puar, Rao of Dhar.
Arthur Hobhouse.
Man Singjee Sahib, Raj. of Drangdra.
Edwd. Clive Bayley.
The Vibhajee Jam Shri of Nauna-gar.
Sir Geo. Ebenezer Wilson Couper, bt.
R.-adm. Regd. Jno. Macdonald.
1877, Josh. Dalton Hooker, M.D.
June 2. Thos. Lawrence Seccombe.
1878. M.-gen. Mich. Kavanagh Kennedy, Jan. 1.
1878, Hon. Ashley Eden.
May 25. Stuart Colvin Bayley.
1879, Robt. Eyles Egerton.
July 29. Lt.-col. Owen Tudor Burne.
Col. Geo. Pomeroy Colley.
Maj. Robt. Groves Sandeman.
The Nawab Gholam Hussun Khan Alazai Khan Bahadoor.
1880. Mahar. Kirtee Sing of Munee-pore, Feb. 18.
Sirdar Dewa Sing, Dec. 9.
1881, Gen. Orfeur Cavenagh.
May 24. Chas. Umpherston Aitchison.
Tukht Singh Thakur, Saheb of Bhaunagar.
Jas. Davidson Gordon.
Jno. Forsyth.
Lepel Hy. Griffin.
1881. Moneshur Bux Sing, Mahar of Domraon, Oct. 29.
1882, The Mahar. Jotendro Mohun
May 23. Tagore.
Lt.-col. Oliver Beauchamp Coventry St. John.
1882, R.-adm. sir Wm. Nathan Wrighte
Nov. 17. Hewett.
M.-gen. sir Herbert Taylor Mac-pherson.
1883. Jno. Hy. Morris, May 24.
Maj. Evelyn Baring, Aug. 4.
1885, Augs. Rivers Thompson.
Jan. 1. Chas. Grant.
1885. Col. Edwd. Ridley Colbourne Bradford, June 6.
Col. Josh. West Ridgeway, July 20.
1886. Mahar. Pertab Sing. Jan 1.
Juland Danvers, Feb 8.
1886, Theodore Cracroft Hope
May 29. Chas. Edwd. Bernard.
Nawab Khwaja Abdul Ghani Meeah of Dacca.
Wm. Chicheley Plowden.
1887, Chas. Alfd. Elliott.
Feb. 15. Wm. Wilson Hunter.
Mahar. Sri Keshri Sing of Idar.
Wm. Geo. Davies.
Jas. Johnstone.
1888. Jas. Braithwaite Peile, Jan. 1.

1888, Moulvi Saiyid Ahmad Bahadoor.
Jan. 1. Jas. Browne.
1888, Jas. Broadwood Lyall.
May 24. Chas. Hankes Tod Crosthwaite.
1889, David Miller Barbour.
Jan. 1. Nawab Muhammad Akram Khan of Amb.

OFFICERS OF THE ORDER OF THE STAR OF INDIA.

Registrar.

1861. Alb. Wm. Woods, aft. sir A.

Secretaries.

1861. Col. Hy. Marion Durand, aft. sir H.
1865. Wm. Muir, aft. sir W.
1868. Sir Rd. Temple, bt.
1869. Chas. Umpherston Aitchison, aft. sir C.
1876. Thos. Hy. Thornton (?).
1877. C. U. Aitchison, *again* (?).
1878. Alf. Comyns Lyall, aft. sir A.
1881. Chas. Grant.
1885. Hy. Mortimer Durand, aft. sir H.

THE ORDER OF THE INDIAN EMPIRE.

This Order was instituted on Jan. 1, 1878, by Royal warrant dated Dec. 31, 1877. It is intended to reward services rendered to the Queen's Indian Empire, and to commemorate Her Majesty's adoption of the title of Empress.

As originally constituted the Order consisted of the Sovereign, the Grand Master, and Companions only. The Viceroy of India for the time being was *ex-officio* Grand Master, and Members of the Council of India were *ex-officio* and for life Companions of the Order.

By Letters Patent dated August 2, 1886, (gazetted Feb. 15, 1887), the constitution of the Order was altered so as to consist of the Sovereign, the Grand Master, 50 Knights Commanders, and Companions not limited in number. Power was given to appoint descendants of Geo. I. as extra Knights Commanders.

By Letters Patent dated June 1, 1887, (gazetted June 21, 1887), the constitution of the Order was further altered, and it now consists of the Sovereign, the Grand Master, 25 Knights Grand Commanders, 50 Knights Commanders, and Companions not limited in number, with power to the Sovereign to appoint any prince of the blood royal being descendants of Geo. I. as extra Knights Grand Commanders.

The officers of the Order are—

Registrar. Secretary.

The Order is styled—

The Most Eminent Order of the Indian Empire.

MEMBERS OF THE ORDER OF THE INDIAN EMPIRE.

GRAND MASTERS OF THE ORDER OF THE INDIAN EMPIRE.

1878, Jan. 1. Edwd. Robt. Lytton, ld., aft. E. of Lytton, Viceroy of India, and his successors.

See "Viceroys of India," *ante*, p. 649.

KNIGHTS GRAND COMMANDERS OF THE ORDER OF THE INDIAN EMPIRE.

(G.C.I.E.)

ORIGINAL KNIGHTS ON THE ENLARGEMENT OF THE ORDER, JUNE 21, 1887, *ut supra.*

1887, June 21. Albert Edwd., Pr. of Wales.
Alfred Ernest Albert, D. of Edinburgh.
Arth. Wm. Patr. Albert, D. of Connaught.

1887, June 21. Geo. Wm. Fredk. Chas., D. of Cambridge.
Donald Jas., ld. Reay.
Robt., ld. Connemara.
Gen. sir Fredk. Sleigh Roberts, bt.

SUBSEQUENT APPOINTMENTS.

1887. The Rao of Kutch, June 30.
1888. Mahar. Nripendra Narayan Bhup, Bahadoor of Kuch Behar, Feb. 23.

KNIGHTS COMMANDERS OF THE ORDER OF THE INDIAN EMPIRE.

(K.C.I.E.)

ORIGINAL KNIGHTS ON THE ENLARGEMENT OF THE ORDER, FEB. 15, 1887, *ut supra.*

1887, Feb. 15. Gen. sir Fredk. Sleigh Roberts, bt.
Hon. Edmd. Drummond.
Sir Alfred Comyns Lyall.
Robt. Anstruther Dalyell.
Maxwell Melvill.
M.-gen. Alexr. Cunningham.
Thakur Saheb Bhakwut Sing of Gondal.
Rana Shankar Baksh Sing Bahadoor.
Dietrich Brandis.
Sir Monier Williams.
Mahar. Pasupati Ananda Gajapati, Raj of Vizianagram.
Alexr. Meadows Rendel.

1887, Feb. 15. Donald Campbell Macnabb.
Nawab Munir-ud-Daula Salar Jung Bahadoor.
Sir Geo. Christr. Molesworth Birdwood.
Raja Ranjit Sing of Rutlam.
Surj.-gen. Benjn. Simpson.
Albert Jas. Leppoc Cappel.
Nawab Ali Kadir Sayid Husan Ali Bahadoor, of Moorshedabad.
Mahar. Lachmessur Sing Bahadoor, of Darbhanga.
Bapu Sahib Avar.
Donald Mackenzie Wallace.
Alfred Woodley Croft.
Bradford Leslie.

SUBSEQUENT APPOINTMENTS.

1887, June 30. The Thakore Sahib of Morvi.
The Thakore Sahib of Limri.
1887. Gerald Seymour Vesey Fitzgerald, Aug. 17.
1888, Jan. 1. Chas. Arthur Turner.
Nawab Bushir-ud-Dowla Amir-i-Akbar Asman Jah Bahadoor.
Nawab Shams-ul-Amara Amir-i-Kabir Khushed Jah Bahadoor.
Sir Edwin Arnold.
Mahar. Radha Prosad Sing of Dumraon.
Viankerala Varma Elarga, Raja of Cochin.
1888. Arthur Nicolson, Mar. 20.
1888, May 24. Raymond West.
Nawab Nawazish Ali Khan.
Guilford Lindsay Molesworth.

1888, May 24. Fredk. Russell Hogg.
Sirdar Naoroz Khan, of Kharan.
Surg.-gen. Wm. Jas. Moore.
Nawab Imam Baksh Khan.
Sirdar Atar Sing, of Bhadour.
Raja Velugoti Sri Krishna Yachendra, of Ventagiri.
1888, June 28. Mahar. Harendra Kisher Sing Bahadoor, of Bettia.
Sir Gregory Chas. Paul.
Mahar. Narendra Krishna Deb Bahadoor.
1889, Jan. 1. Hy. Mortimer Durand.
Mahar. Krishna Partab Sahi, Bahadoor of Hatwa.
Arth. Geo. Macpherson.
Wm. Markby.
Hy. Stuart Cunningham.

COMPANIONS OF THE ORDER OF THE INDIAN EMPIRE.

(C.I.E.)

EX-OFFICIO COMPANIONS.

See "Members of the Council of India," *ante*, pp. 646–7.

Ordinary Companions.

Original Companions, Jan. 1, 1878.

1878, Jan. 1. Mir Mahmud, Khan of Khelat.
Louis Steuart Jackson.
Col. Sir Rd. John Meade.
Rao Bahadoor Bukht Sing, Rao of Bedea.
John Muir.
Dietrich Brandis.
Sri Rajamani Raja Deo, Zemindar of Mandasa, Madras.
Sir Chas. Arth. Turner.
Mir Ali Khan of Lus Beyla, Khelat.
Gregory Chas. Paul.
Sirdar Asad Khan, Chief of the Sarawan Brahuis, Khelat.
Col. Sir Owen Tudor Burne.
Sirdar Gohur Khan, chief of the Jalawan Brahuis, Khelat.
Richd. Kaye Puckle.
Dep.-surg. Wm. Jameson.
Syud Wilayut Ali Khan of Panta.
Col. Wm. Geo. Mainwaring.
Rai Bahadoor Rajendra Lala Mitra.
Surg.-gen. John Fullarton Beatson.
Surg.-gen. Jas. Tyrell Carter Ross.
Norman Robt. Pogson.
Wm. Wilson Hunter.
Col. Chas. S. Hearn.

1878, Jan. 1. Col. Edwd. Chas. Sparshott Williams.
Rai Bahadoor Kristodas Pal.
M.-gen. Alexr. Cunningham.
R.-Adm. John Bythesea.
Morarji Gokuldas.
Col. Bendyshe Walton.
Col. Hy. Moore.
Tiruvarur Muthiswami Aiyar.
Col. Wm. Gordon.
Khan Bahadoor Saleh Hindi of Joonaghur.
Donald Graham.
Surg.-Maj. Thos. Gillham Hewlett.
Cettepaliem Ranga Charloo.
Col. Chas. Metcalfe Macgregor.
Robt. Berkeley Shaw.
Johann Geo. Buhler.
Bapu Diva Shastri.
Patr. Carnegy.
Thos. Maltby.
Thos. Mitchell Gibbon.
Ebenezer Roper Lethbridge.
Babu Bhuder Mukerji.
Geo. Smith.
John Hy. Rivett-Carnac.
Capt. Hon. Geo. Campbell Napier.
Roscoe Bocquet.
Jas. Blackburn Knight.
Pundit Nain Sing.

Subsequent Appointments.

1879. Jan. 1. Geo. Wm. Allen.
Bahmanji Tamasji Dastur.
Wm. Digby,
Fredk. Salmon Growse.
Lt.-col. Shaikh Hidayat Ali.
Lt.-col. Eugene Clutterbuck Impey.
Baba Khem Sing.
Maj. Edwd. Saml. Ludlow.
Raja Mangal Sing Bahadoor.
Guilford Lindsay Molesworth.
Moung Oon.
Surg. Danl. Robt. Thompson.
Col. Jas. Fras. Tennant.
Andr. Wingate.

1879, Pierre Francois Henri Nanquette.
June 30. Sir Fras. Philip Cunliffe Owen.

1880, Jan. 1. Sirdar Atar Sing.
Arth. Coke Burnell.
Surg.-Maj. Wm. Robt. Cornish.
Lt..gen. Sir Hy. Dominick Daly.
Pandit Ishwara Chandra, Vidya Ságárá.
Rev. Eugene Lafont.
Steph. Paget Walter Vyvyan Luke.

1880, Jan. 1. Chas. Jas. Lyall.
Chas. Gordon Welland Macpherson.
Mir Humayun Jah Bahadoor.
Thos. Ormeston.
Chas. Edwd. Pitman.
M.-gen. Sir Fredk. Sleigh Roberts.
Pandit Surup Narain.
Kazi Shahab-ud-din.
Geo. Sibley.
Babu Sourindio Mohun Tagore.

1880, Apr. 19. Ronald Ferguson Thomson.
Monier Williams.
Capt. Wm. John Williamson.

1880. Johann Eliza de Vry, July 14.

1880, Nov. 9. Sirdar Jugjat Sing, of Jhind.
The Dewan Bishen Sing, of Nabha.
Sirdar Nabhi Bakhsh, of Kuppurtalla.

1881, Feb. 5. David Ross.
Maurice Le Breton.
Richd. Isaac Bruce.
Alexr. Fredk. Douglas Cunningham.
Jas. Thos. Christie.

1881. Husein Ali Khan, Feb. 5.
1881, Jas. Ferguson.
May 24. Sir Steuart Colvin Bayley.
Dep.-insp.-gen. Chas. Morehead.
Pandit Mohesh Chandra Nyaratna.
Dep.-surg.-gen. Norman Chevers.
Capt. Wm. Hutt Curzon Wyllie.
Mirza Ghulam Ahmad.
Surg.-M. Edwd. John Waring.
Maj. Trevor John Chichele Plowden.
Brig.-surg. Oliver Barnett.
Shahzadah Sultan Jan Suddozaie.
Surg.-Maj. John Anderson.
Shorabji Shapurji Bengali.
Surg. Chas. Wm. Owen.
1882, Hy. Lucius Dampier.
Jan. 1, M.-gen. Jno. Aug. Fuller.
Jno. Lambert.
Rao Bahadoor Mahadeo Vasudeo Barvé.
Geo. Felton Mathew.
Harry Marten.
Wm. Patr. Andrew.
Mirza Abbas Khan.
Rao Bahadoor Tantia Gorey.
Rao Bahadoor Hittu Ram.
Abdul Hak.
Khan Bahadoor Saivad Aulad Husain.
Khan Bahadoor Pestonji Jahangir.
Capt. hon. Jno. Robertson.
1882, Wm. Mackinnon.
May 23. Syud Lutf Ali Khan.
Moung Shway Kyee.
Rana Shankar Bakhsh Sing Bahadoor.
Dep.-surg.-gen. Wm. Jas. Moore.
Edwd. Ronald Douglas.
1882, Ressaldar Major Tahour Khan
Nov. 18. Sirdar Bahadoor.
Subadar Major Mowladad Sirdar Bahadoor.
1883, Ali Kuli Khan, the Mukhbar-ud-
Jan. 1. Dowla of Persia.
Anund Rao Puar, Mahar. of Dhar.
Hy. Christr. Mance.
Hy. Geo. Keene.
Surg.-maj. Jas. Edwd. Tierney Aitchison.
Mohendro Lall Sircar.
Nawab Abdul Lateef.
Raghunath Narayen Khote.
Syed Bakir Ali Khan.
Maj. Oliver Probyn.
Capt. Claude Clerk.
Caspar Purdon Clarke.
Surg.-maj. Geo. Bidie.
1883, Lt.-col. Dav. Wilkinson Campbell.
May 24. Lt.-col. Fredk. Peterson.
Lt.-col. Thos. Ross Church.
Lt.-col. Saml. Jackson.
Fredk. Chas. Berry.
Alexr. Grant.
1883, Fras. Langford O'Callaghan.
May 24. Thakur Bichu Sing of Dholpur.
Fredk. Augs. Hugh Elliot.
1884, Baden Hy. Baden Powell.
Jan. 1. Nawab Imam Baksh Khan.
Sirdar Ajit Sing.
Geo. Alfd. Barnett.
Navroji Fardunji.
The Zemindar of Punganur.
Babu Chota Lall Sijwar.
Diwan Het Ram.
Jno. Faithful Fleet.
Col. Robt. Home.
1884, Alfd. Woodley Croft.
May 23. Rev. Wm. Miller.
Kashinath Trimbak Talang.
Benjn. Lewis Rice.
Geo. O'Brien Theodore Carew.
Sheikh Shuruf-ud-din Raees of Sheikhuppur.
Rai Bahadoor Kanai Lal Dé.
Col. Chas. Edwd. Stewart.
Durga Charan Laha.
Edwd. Thomas.
1885, François Alfd. Puton.
Jan. 1. Lucien Boppé.
Maj. Lewis Conway-Gordon.
Rev. Kistna Mohun Banarji.
Jas. Macnabb Campbell.
Rao Saheb Mahipatram Rupram Lilkanth.
Ralph Thos. Hotchkin Griffith.
Kanwar Harnam Sing.
Peter Mitchell.
Nawab Nawazish Ali Khan.
Resseldar Major Isri Pershad Sardar Bahadoor.
Demetrius Panioty.
1885, Maj. Robt. Parry Nisbet.
June 6. Fras. Day.
Jas. Baboneau Nickterlien Hennessey.
Dulputram Dayabhoy.
Capt. Adelbert Cecil Talbot.
Jas. Burgess.
Geo. Hamnett.
Ramaswami Mudalier.
1886, Mortimer Sloper Howell.
Jan. 1. Mohammed Hassan Khan.
Baboo Sarat Chandra Das.
Colin Arrott Robertson Browning.
Dharain Narain Pandit.
Raja Jung Bahadoor Khan.
Lt.-col. Andrew Higgins.
M.-gen. Wm. Leslie de la Poer Beresford.
Sirdar Bahadoor Man Sing Ressaldar.
Sir Frank Hy. Souter.
Artb. Naylor Wollaston,
1886. Sir Arthur Edwd. Hardinge, Jan. 22.
Maj. HughRd., visc. Downe, Mar. 10.
1886, Surg.-gen. Michael Cudmore Fur-
May 29 nell.

1886, Leichman Das Seth, of Muttra.
May 29. Edwd. Spence Symes.
Rao Bahadoor Ranchoulal Chotolal of Ahmedabad.
Dep.-surg.-gen. Alexr. Morrison Dallas.
Fredk. Chas. Kennedy.
1886, Jas. Watt.
June 28. Jno. Wm. Tyler.
Col. Augs. Le Messurier.
Maj. Rd. Nevill.
Mancherjee Nerwanjee Bhownaggree.
Jos. Ralph Edwd. Jno. Royle.
1887, Colman Patr. Louis Macaulay.
Jan. 1. Sirdar Jewan Sing Buria.
Jno. Lockwood Kipling.
Franz Kielhorn.
Rai Mahta Punno Lall.
Brig.-surg. Hy. Elmsley Busteed.
Pestonji Hormusji Cama.
1887, Carl Ludolph Griesbach.
Feb. 15. Capt. Fredk. Duncan Raikes.
Rao Bahadoor Mahadeo Govind Ranadè.
Wm. Wordsworth.
Capt. Albt. Fredk. de Laessöe.
Sirdar Shere Ahmed Khan.
Sirdar Muhammad Aslam Khan.
Hy. Montagu Matthews.
Palle Chentsal Rao Puntulu.
Col. John Stewart, R.A.
Syud Ameer Ali.
Hy. Seymour King.
Geo. Jamieson Swann.
Thos. Beatson Christie, M.D.
Wm. Jas. Maitland.
Moung U Pe Zi Linkedaw Myo Wun.
1887. Kumar Sri Kalooba, June 30.
1887, Capt. Chas. Wemyss Muir.
July 25. Ressaldar Major Nizamuddin Khan, Sirdar Bahadoor.
Ressaldar Shir Sing.
Ressaldar Jafar Ali Khan.
1887, Col. Geo. Ritso Goodfellow.
Aug. 8. Col. Chas. Wodehouse.
1887. M.-gen. Thos. Dennehy, Sept. 17.
1888, Frank Forbes Adam.
Jan. 1. Munshi Newab Kishore.
Rao Bahadoor Krishnaji Lakshaman Nulkar.
Col. Hy. Constantine Evelyn Ward.
Fredk. Thos. Granville Walton.
Ney Elias.
Shahzada Nadir.
Kazi Syud Ahmed Khan Bahadoor.
Syed Ameer Hosseni.
Reinhold Rost.
1888. Col. Chas. Smith Maclean, Mar. 20.
1888, Edmd. Forster Webster.
May 24. Alexr. John Lawrence.
Col. Jas. Cavan Berkeley.
Edwd. Chas. Kayll Ollivant.
Heera Sahib Lall Ramanuj Pershad Sing.
Maj. Wm. Sinclair Smith Bisset.
Meirjibai Kuvarji, Dewan of Kholapur.
Chas. Hy. Tawney.
Col. Thos. Weldon.
Hy. Irwin.
Capt. Buchanan Scott.
Arth. Hedding Hildebrand.
Jas. Walker.
Ressaldar Major Muzaffar Khan, Sirdar Bahadoor.
1888. Jas. McFerran, Nov. 19.
1889, Lt.-col. Edwin Hy. Hayter Collen.
Jan. 1. S. Subramaniya Aiyer, Rai Bahadur.
Edwin Felix Thos. Atkinson.
Capt. John Hext.
Ramkrishna Gopal Bhandarkar.
Wm. Brereton Hudson.
Surg.-maj. John Findlay.
Saiyid Mihrban Ali.
Hy. Josiah Whymper.
Raja Sudhal Deo of Bamva.
Fredk. Wm. Stevens.
Babu Protab Chunder Rai.
Alfred Wallis Paul.

OFFICERS OF THE ORDER OF THE INDIAN EMPIRE.

Registrar.

1878, Jan. 1. Sir Alb. Wm. Woods, Garter King of Arms.

Secretaries.

1878. Alfd. Comyns Lyall, aft. sir A.
1881. Chas. Grant.
1885. Hy. Mortimer Durand.

THE ORDER OF THE CROWN OF INDIA.

This Order was instituted on Jan. 1, 1878 by Royal Warrant dated Dec. 31, 1877, and gazetted Jan. 4, 1878. It is exclusively for ladies, and is intended to commemorate the assumption by the Queen of the title of Empress of India. It consists of the Sovereign and of the following ladies as the Sovereign may think fit:—(1) Princesses of the Royal House, (2) the wives and other female relatives of Princes of the Indian Empire, (3) other Indian ladies, and (4) the wives and other female relatives of any persons who have held or may hold the office of Viceroy and Governor-General of India, Governor of Madras or Bombay, or Principal Secretary of State for India.

The 1st of January in every year is to be deemed the anniversary of the institution of the Order.

The only officer of the Order is the Registrar.

The Order is styled—

The Imperial Order of the Crown of India.

MEMBERS OF THE ORDER OF THE CROWN OF INDIA. (Cr.I.)

Original Appointments. Jan. 1, 1878.

1878, Jan. 1. The Prss. of Wales.
The Cr. Prss. of Germany, aft. Empress Fredk.; Prss. Roy. of Gt. Britain and Ireland.
The Grd. Dss. of Hesse, Prss. Alice of Gt. Britain and Ireland; *d.* Dec. 1878.
Prss. Christian of Schleswig-Holstein, Prss. Helena of Gt. Britain and Ireland.
Prss. Louise, Mss. of Lorne.
Prss. Beatrice, aft. Prss. Hy. of Battenberg.
Marie Alexandrovna, Dss. of Edinburgh, Gr. Dss. of Russia.
Augusta Wilhelmnia Louisa, Dss. of Cambridge; *d.* 1889.
Augusta, &c., Gr. Dss. of Mecklenburg Strelitz; Prss. Augusta of Cambridge.
Mary, &c., Dss. of Teck; Prss. Mary of Cambridge.
The Maharanee Dhuleep Sing.
Nawab Shahjihan, Begum of Bhopal.
Maharanee Seta Velass Dewajee Ammanee Anaro of Mysore.
Maharanee Jumna Bai Saheb Gaekwar of Baroda.

1878, Jan. 1. Dilawar un-Nissar, Begum Saheb of Hyderabad.
Nawab Kudsia, Begum of Bhopal.
Vijaya Mohenu Mukta Boyi Ammanee, Rajah Saheb of Tanjore.
Maharanee Hai Nornoyee of Cossimbazar.
Eliz. Georgiana, Dss. of Argyll; *d.* May 1878.
Georgina Caroline, Mss. of Salisbury.
Henrietta Anne Theodosia, Mss. of Ripon.
Lady Mary Temple-Nugent-Brydges-Chandos-Grenville.
Mary Louisa, Countess Dowager of Elgin and Kincardine.
Blanche Julia, Countess of Mayo.
Lady Susan Georgina Bourke, aft. Lady Connemara.
Mary, viscss. Halifax.
Mary Catherinie, Lady Hobart.
Lady Jane Emma Baring.
Anne Jane Charlotte, Baroness Napier, aft. Napier and Ettrick.
Edith, Baroness, aft. Countess of Lytton.
Harriette Katherine, Baroness Lawrence.

1878, Jan. 1. Cecilia Frances, Lady Northcote, aft. Countess of Iddesleigh.
Catherine, Lady Frere.

1878, Jan. 1. Mary Augusta, Lady Temple.
Caroline Lucy, Lady Denison.
Katherine Jane, Lady Strachey.

Subsequent Appointments.

1878. Jane, viscss. Cranbrook, Apr. 20.
Prss. Frederica of Hanover, June 27.
Prss. Mary of Hanover, June 27.

1879. Thyra, Dss. of Cumberland, Feb. 25.
Louise Margt., &c., Dss. of Connaught, Mar. 13.

1879, May 31. Mary Cecilia, Baroness Napier of Magdala.
Fras. Eliz., Lady Cunynghame, c.c. the hon. Lady Cunynghame.
Susanna Maria, Dowager Lady Pottinger; *d.*

1881. Lakshmi Bhayie, Senior Rani of Travancore, Mar. 2.

1881, Oct. 8. Olive, Lady Fergusson; *d.*
Emily Eliza Adam, aft. Lady Adam.

1882. Helene Frederica Augusta, Dss. of Albany, Apr. 26.

1883, May 2. Florence, Countess of Kimberley.
Anna Julia Grant Duff, aft. Lady Grant Duff.
Sidh-Sri-Maharaj Kumari Patela Wali Maharani Sateba Kunwar Devi of Dholpur.

1884. Edith Helen Fergusson, Sept. 4.
Harriet Georgina, Countess of Dufferin, aft. Mss. of Dufferin and Ava, Dec. 15.

1885, Aug. 18. Jennie Churchill, c.c. Lady Randolph Churchill.
Fanny Georgina Jane, Baroness Reay.

1886. Georgina, viscss. Cross, Aug. 24.

1887. Maharanee Sunity Devee of Kuch Behar, Mar. 18.

1887, Aug. 6. Prss. Louisa Victoria Alexandra Dagmar of Wales.
Prss. Alexandra Olga Mary of Wales.

1889. Maud Evelyn, Mss. of Lansdowne.

OFFICER OF THE ORDER OF THE CROWN OF INDIA.

Registrar.

1878, Jan. 1. Sir Alb. Wm. Woods, Garter King of Arms.

PART XIV. NAVAL.

LORD HIGH ADMIRALS AND LORDS COMMISSIONERS OF THE ADMIRALTY.

See Part III., *ante*, p. 169.

SECRETARIES TO THE ADMIRALTY.

See Part III., *ante*, p. 186.

TREASURERS OF THE NAVY.

See Part III., *ante*, p. 256.

CONTROLLERS AND SURVEYORS OF THE NAVY.

See Part III., *ante*, p. 257.

JUDGES OF THE HIGH COURT OF ADMIRALTY, ENGLAND.

See Part III., *ante*, p. 422.

ADMIRALTY ADVOCATES.

See Part III., *ante*, p. 423.

JUDGES OF THE HIGH COURT OF ADMIRALTY, SCOTLAND.

See Part IX., *ante*, p. 524.

JUDGES OF THE HIGH COURT OF ADMIRALTY, IRELAND.

See Part X., *ante*, p. 587.

ADMIRALS.

The Admirals are arranged according to the following Lists :—

LIST A.

Admirals from the Restoration to 1836, with the dates of their first promotion as Rear Admirals.

LIST B.

Admirals of the Fleet from 1837.

LIST C.

Admirals of the United Kingdom from 1837.

LIST D.

Admirals of the Red, White, and Blue from 1837 to the discontinuance of the division into three Squadrons in 1864.

LIST E.

Admirals on the Active List from 1864.

LIST F.

Promotion of Admirals transferred from the Active to the Retired List.

LIST G.

Admirals on the Reserve Half-Pay List from 1851 to the closing of the List.

LIST H.

Captains promoted to the List of Retired Admirals.

LIST A.

ADMIRALS.

From the Restoration to the end of the year 1836.

The dates refer to the time when the officers were appointed Rear-Admirals.

* * Geo. Monk. aft. D. of Albemarle; *d.* 1670.
* * Pr. Rupert, D. of Cumberland, &c.; *d.* 1682.
* * Sir Jno. Lawson, *d.* 1665.
* * Edwd., E. of Sandwich, *d.* 1672.
* * Sir Richd. Stayner.
1661. Sir Robt. Holmes.
Sir Thos. Allen.
Sir Wm. Penn.
1665. Robt. Sampson.
Sir Thos. Tyddiman.
Sir Geo. Ayscue.
Sir Wm. Berkeley, *d.* 1666.
Sir Jos. Jordan.
Sir Christr. Mings, *d.* 1666.
Sir Jno. Herman.
Sir Jeremiah Smith.
1666. Sir Edwd. Spraggs, *d.* 1673.
Sir Wm. Jennings.
Robt. Utber (Uthurt ?), *d.* 1699.
Sir Jno. Kempthorne.
1670. Thos., E. of Ossory, son of the D. of Ormond.
Sir Fretcheville Holles, *d.* 1672.
Sir Jno. Chicheley, ld. admy., 1682.
1675. Sir Jno. Narborough.
1683. Geo., ld. Dartmouth.
Wm. Davies.
Sir Jno. Berry.
Sir Roger Strickland.
1688. Arthur Herbert, aft. E. of Torrington.
Sir Richd. Haddock, comptr. navy; *d.* 1714.
Jno., ld. Berkeley of Stratton; *d.* 1697.
Hy. Killigrew, ld. admy., 1693.
1690. Edwd. Russell, aft. E. of Orford, &c., first ld. admy.
Sir Cloudesley Shovel, *d.* 1707.
Sir Ralph Delaval, ld. admy., 1693.
Sir John Ashby.
Sir Geo. Rooke, ld. admy., 1702; *d.* 1709.
1691. Richd. Carter, *d.* 1692.
Matth. Aylmer, aft. ld. Aylmer; ld. admy., and r.-adm. Gr. Br.; *d.* 1720.
Sir David Mitchell, *d.* 1710.
1692. Sir Fras. Wheeler, *d.* 1694.
Hon. Edwd. Nevill, bro. to ld. Abergavenny.
1693. Sir Thos. Hopson, *d.* 1717.
1694. John Benbow, *d.* 1702.
Peregrine, M. of Carmarthen, aft. D. of Leeds; *d.* 1729.
Geo. Meeze.
1698. Sir John Munden.
1701. Geo. Churchill, bro. to John, D. of Marlborough; ld. admy.
Sir Stafford Fairborne.
1702. John Graydon, dism.
Sir Wm. Whetstone, dism. 1706.
1703. Sir John Leake, r.-adm. Gr. Br., and commr. admy.; *d.* 1720.
Sir Geo. Byng, aft. visc. Torrington, r.-adm. Gr. Br., and first ld. admy.
Sir Thos. Dilkes, *d.* 1707.
Basil Beaumont, *d.* 1704.
Sir Jas. Wishart, dism. 1715.
1705. Sir John Jennings, r.-adm. Gr. Br., 1732; *d.* 1745.
Chas., E. of Peterborough and Monmouth.
Sir Edwd. Whitaker, dism. 1715.
1706. Sir John Norris, ld. admy., and adm. fl.; *d.* 1749.
1707. Jas., visc. Dursley, aft. E. of Berkeley, v.-adm. Gr. Br., and first ld. admy.; *d.* 1736.
1708. John Baker, *d.* 1716.
Jas. Littleton, *d.* 1722.
Sir Chas. Wager, treasr. navy, and first ld. admy.; *d.* 1743.
1710. Sir Hovenden Walker, dism. 1715; *d.* 1725.
Sir Thos. Hardy, *d.* 1732.
1718. Chas. Cornewall, *d.* same year.
Geo. Delaval, *d.* 1723.
Jas. Mighells, res. to be a commr navy.
1722. Fras. Hosier, *d.* 1727.
1723. Sir Geo. Walton, res.
Chas. Strickland, *d.* 1724.
1727. Salmon Maurice, res. 1734; *d.* 1741.
Robt. Hughes, *d.* 1728.
Edwd. Hopson, *d.* 1728.
Philip Cavendish, ld. admy.; *d.* 1743.
Sir John Balchan, *d.* 1744.
Edwd. St. Looe, *d.* 1729.
Hon. Chas. Stewart, son of visc. Mountjoy; *d.* 1740.
Thos. Matthews, dism. Feb. 1744; *d.* 1748.
Sir Geo. Saunders, commr. navy; *d.* 1734

1734. Nichs. Haddock, *d.* 1746.
Sir Tancred Robinson, bt., res. 1741; *d.* 1754.
Geo., ld. Forbes, aft. E. of Granard, govr. Leeward isl.; *d.* 1765.
John Hagar, res. 1748.

1739. Edwd. Vernon, dism. 1746; *d.* 1757.

1740. Sir Chaloner Ogle, adm. fleet; *d.* 1751.

1743. Jas. Stewart, adm. fleet, 1751; *d.* 1757.
Richd. Lestock.
Sir Chas. Hardy, ld. admy.; *d.* 1744.
Thos. Davers, *d.* 1747.
Hon. Geo. Clinton, son of the E. of Lincoln; govr. New York, 1742; *d.* 1761.
Sir Wm. Rowley, K.B., ld. admy., 1751; adm. fleet, 1762; *d.* 1768.

1744. Wm. Martin, *d.* 1756.
Isaac Townshend, govr. Greenwich hosp.; *d.* 1765.
Hy. Medley, *d.* 1846.
Lord Vere Beauclerk, aft. ld. Vere, ld. admy.; quitted the service; *d.* 1781.
Geo. Anson, aft. ld. Anson, first ld. admy., 1751; adm. fleet, 1761; *d.* 1762.
Perry Mayne, *d.* 1761.

1745. Sir Peter Warren, K.B., *d.* 1752.
Hon. John Byng, shot by sentence of ct.-martl. on board the *Monarch*, at Portsmouth, Mar. 14, 1757.
Hy. Osborne, v.-adm. Gr. Br., 1763; *d.* 1771.
Hon. Fitzroy Hy. Lee, son of the E. of Lichfield; *d.* 1752.
Thos. Smith, *d.* 1762.
Thos. Griffin, *d.* 1771.

1747. Sir Edwd. Hawke, K.B., aft. ld. Hawke, first ld. admy. 1766; res. 1771; *d.* 1781.
Wm. Chambers, *d.* 1753.
Sir Chas. Knowles, bt., r.-adm. Eng., 1765; *d.* 1777.
Hon. John Forbes, ld. admy.; gen. of marines, 1762; adm. fleet, 1781.
Hon. Edwd. Boscawen, son of visc. Falmouth; gen. of marines, 1760; ld. admy. from 1751 to his death, 1761.
Robt. Mitchell, *d.* before 1758.
Chas. Watson, *d.* 1757.

1755. Temple West, ld. admy.; *d.* 1757.
Sir Geo. Pocock, K.B., res. 1766; *d.* 1792.
Hon. Geo. Townshend, *d.* 1769.

1755. Savage Mostyn. comptr. navy, 1749; *d.* 1757.
Fras. Holburne, ld. admy.; govr. Greenwich hosp.; *d.* 1771.

1756. Hy. Harrison, *d.* 1759.
Thos. Cotes, *d.* 1767.
Sir Thos. Frankland, bt., *d.* 1784.
Lord Harry Poulett, aft. D. of Bolton.
Hy. Norris.
Thos. Broderick, *d.* 1769.
Sir Chas. Hardy, govr. New York, 1756; *d.* 1780.
Geo., E. of Northesk, *d.* 1792.
Sir Chas. Saunders, K.B., lt.-gen. of marines, 1760; ld. admy., 1765; first ld. admy., 1766; *d.* Dec. 1775.

1758. Sir Thos. Pye, lt.-gen. of marines, 1781; *d.* 1785.
Chas. Stevens, *d.* 1761.
Philip Durell, *d.* 1766.
Chas. Holmes, *d.* 1761.
Sir Saml. Cornish, bt., *d.* 1770.
Sir Fras. Geary, bt., *d.* 1796.

1759. Smith Callis, *d.* 1761.
Sir Geo. Brydges Rodney, aft. ld. Rodney; v.-adm. Gr. Br.; *d.* 1792.

1761. Pr. Edwd. Augs., D. of York; bro. of Geo. III.; r.-adm. blue, 1761; v.-adm. blue, 1762; *d.* 1767.

1762. Sir Wm. Burnaby, kt. and bt., *d.* 1776.
Jas. Young, *d.* 1789.
Sir Piercy Brett, ld. admy.; *d.* 1781.
Sir John Moore, K.B. and bt., *d.* 1779.
Richd. Tyrrell, *d.* 1765.
Alexr., ld. Colville, *d.* 1770.
Sir Jas. Douglas, kt., aft. bt., *d.* 1787.
Sir John Bentley, *d.* 1770.
Wm. Gordon, *d.* 1768.
Geo., ld. Edgcumbe, aft. visc. Mount Edgcumbe and Valletort, *d.* 1795.
Robt. Swanton, *d.* Aug. 1765.
Saml. Graves, *d.* 1787.
Wm. Parry, *d.* 1779.
Hon. Augs. Keppel, aft. visc. Keppel, made first ld. admy., 1782; *d.* 1786.

1764. John Amherst, *d.* 1778.
Hy., D. of Cumberland and Strathearn, *d.* 1790.

1770. Sir Peter Dennis, bt., *d.* 1778.
Robt. Hughes, *d.* 1774.
Matth. Buckle, *d.* 1784.
Robt. Mann, ld. admy.; *d.* 1783.
Clerk Gayton, *d.* 1785.
John Barker, *d.* 1777.
Sir Richd. Spry, *d.* 1775.

1770. Lucius O'Brien, *d.* 1771.
John Montagu, *d.* Sept. 1795.
Hon. Thos. Craven, bro. to ld. Craven; *d.* 1772.
Sir Robt. Harland, bt., ld. admy.; *d.* 1784.
Jas. Sayer, *d.* 1777.
Richd. Howe, visc. and E. Howe, first ld. admy., 1783; *d.* 1799.

1775. Washington, E. Ferrers, *d.* 1778.
Hugh Pigot, ld. admy.; *d.* 1793.
Molineux Shuldham, aft. ld. Shuldham, *d.* 1798.
Sir Jos. Knight, *d.* 1775.
John Vaughan, *d.* 1789.
John Lloyd, *d.* 1778.
Robt. Duff, d. 1787.
John Reynolds. *d.* 1788.
Sir Hugh Palliser, bt., lt.-gen. marines, ld. admy., govr. Greenwich hosp.; *d.* 1796.
Hon. John Byron, *d.* 1786.
Augs. John, E. of Bristol, *d.* 1779.

1777. Geo. Mackenzie, *d.* 1780.
Matth. Barton, *d.* 1795.
Sir Peter Parker, kt. and bt., adm. fleet, Sept. 16, 1799; *d.* 1811.

1778. Hon. Saml. Barrington, lt.-gen. marines, 1786; *d.* 1800.
Marriot Arbuthnot, *d.* 1793.
Robt. Rodham, adm. red; *d.* 1808.
Geo. Darby, r.-adm. Gr. Br.; ld. admy., 1781; *d.* Feb. 1790.
John Campbell, govr. Newfoundland, 1782 to 1784; *d.* 1791.
Christr. Hill, *d.* 1778.
Jas. Gambier, *d.* 1788.
Wm. Lloyd, *d.* 1796.
Fras. Wm. Drake, *d.* 1788.
Sir Edwd. Hughes, K.B., *d.* 1795.
Sir Hyde Parker, bt. (No. 1), disapp. 1782.

1779. John Evans, *d.* 1796.
Mark Milbanke, *d.* 1804.
Nichs. Vincent, *d.* adm. red., 1809.
John Storr, *d.* 1783.
Sir Edwd. Vernon, *d.* 1794.
Joshua Rowley, cr. bt., 1786; *d.* 1790.
Richd. Edwards, *d.* 1794.
Thos. Graves, aft. ld. Graves, *d.* Feb. 1802.
Hon. Robt. Digby; *d.* adm. red, 1814.
Sir John Lockhart Ross, bt., *d.* 1790.

1780. Chas. Webber, *d.* 1783.
Wm. Langdon, *d.* 1785.
Benjn. Marlow, *d.* 1794.
Alexr. Hood, aft. ld. and visc. Bridport, v.-adm. Gr. Br. and gen. marines; *d.* 1814.

1780. Sir Chaloner Ogle, kt., aft. bt.; *d.* senior adm. of Br. navy, 1816.
Sir Saml. Hood, bt., aft. ld. and visc. Hood; *d.* adm. red, 1816.
Matth. Moore, *d.* 1787.
Sir Richd. Hughes, bt.; *d.* adm. red, 1812.
Richd. Kempenfelt, *d.* 1782.

1784. Sir Edmd. Affleck, bt., *d.* 1789.

1787, Sept. 14. John Elliot, *d.* adm. red, 1809.
Wm. Hotham, aft. ld. Hotham; *d.* adm. red, 1813.
Sir John Lindsay, K.B., *d.* June 1788.
Jos. Peyton, *d.* 1804.
John Carter Allen, *d.* 1800.
Sir Chas. Middleton, bt., aft. ld. Barham, ld. admy., 1794; *d.* adm. red, 1813.
Sir John Laforey, bt., *d.* 1796.
John Dalrymple, *d.* 1798.
Herbert Sawyer, *d.* 1798.
Sir Richd. King, bt., *d.* 1806.
Jonthn. Faulknor, *d.* 1795.
Philip Affleck, *d.* 1799.
Sir Richd. Bickerton, kt., aft. bt., *d.* 1792.
Hon. John Leveson Gower, *d.* 1792.
Sir John Jervis, aft. ld. and E. St. Vincent, G.C.B., first ld. admy., 1801; adm. fleet, 1821; *d.* 1823.
Adam Duncan, aft. visc. Duncan, *d.* 1804.
Sir Chas. Douglas, bt., *d.* 1789.
Sir Geo. Bowyer, bt., *d.* Dec. 1800.

1790, Sept. 21. Richd. Braithwaite, *d.* 1805.
Phillips Cosby, *d.* adm. red, 1808.
Saml. Pitchford Cornish, *d.* adm. red, 1816.
Thos. Fitzherbert, *d.* 1794.
John Brisbane, *d.* 1807.
John Houlton, *d.* 1791.
Chas. Wolseley, *d.* adm. red, 1808.
Chas. Inglis, *d.* Oct. 1791.
Saml. Cranston Goodall, *d.* 1801.
Hon. Keith Stewart, *d.* 1794.

1790, Dec. 3. Wm. Hy., D. of Clarence, aft. Wm. IV.; adm. fleet, Dec. 24, 1811; ld. h. adm., May 2, 1827; res. latter rank, Aug. 12, 1828; *d.* June 20, 1837.

1793, Feb. 1. Sir Richd Onslow, bt., G.C.B., *d.* adm. red. 1817.
Sir Robt. Kingsmill, bt., *d.* 1805.
Sir Geo. Collier, *d.* Apr. 1795.
Sir Hyde Parker (No. 2), *d.* 1807.
Rowland Cotton, *d.* 1794.
Benjn. Caldwell, *d.* adm. red, 1820.
Hon. sir Wm. Cornwallis, G C.B., *d.* r.-adm. U. K., 1819.

1793, Feb. 1. Wm. Allen, *d.* 1805.
John M'Bride, *d.* 1800.
Geo. Vandeput, *d.* 1800.
Chas. Bucknor, *d.* adm. red, 1811.
Wm. Dickson, *d.* 1803.
John Gell, *d.* 1806.
Sir Alan Gardner, aft. ld. Gardner, ld. admy., 1790; *d.* Dec. 1808

1794, Apr. 11. John Lewis Gidoin, *d.* 1796.
Geo. Gayton, *d.* 1797.
Geo. Murray, senr., *d.* 1797.
Robt. Linzee, *d.* 1804.
Sir Jas. Wallace, *d.* 1803.
Wm. Peere Williams Freeman, adm. fleet, 1830; *d.* 1832.
Thos. Pasley, aft. bt., *d.* 1808.
John Symons, *d.* 1799.
Sir Thos. Rich, bt., *d.* 1803.
Chas. Thompson, aft. bt., *d.* 1803.
Jas. Cumming, *d.* 1808.
John Ford, *d.* 1796.
Sir John Colpoys, G.C.B., ld. admy., 1804; *d.* adm. red, 1821.
Skeffington Lutwidge, *d.* adm. red, 1814.
Archd. Dickson, aft. bt., *d.* 1803.
Sir Geo. Montagu, G.C.B., *d.* adm. red, 1829.
Thos. Dumaresque, *d.* 1801.
Hon. sir Geo. Keith Elphinstone, aft. visc. Keith; G.C.B., *d.* adm. red, 1823.

1794, July 4. Jas. Pigot, *d.* adm. red, 1822.
Wm. Waldegrave, aft. ld. Radstock, *d.* adm. red, 1825.
Thos. Pringle, *d.* 1803.
Thos. Mackenzie, *d.* 1813.
Hon. Wm. Clement Finch, *d.* 1794.
Roger Curtis, aft. kt. and bt.; *d.* adm. red, 1816.
Sir Hy. Harvey, K.B., *d.* 1811.
Robt. Mann, junr., *d.* adm. red, 1813.
Wm. Parker, aft. bt., *d.* 1804.
Chas. Holmes Everett Calmady, *d.* 1807.
John Bourmaster, *d.* Dec. 1807.
Sir Geo. Young, *d.* 1810. His son was created a bt. in 1813.
John Henry, *d.* adm. red, 1829.
Sir Richd. Rodney Bligh, G.C.B. *d.* adm. red, 1821.

1795, June 1. Alexr. Græme, *d.* adm. red, 1818.
Geo. Keppel, *d.* 1805.
Saml. Reeve, *d.* 1803.
Robt. Biggs, *d.* 1803.
Fras. Parry, *d.* 1803.
Isaac Prescott, *d.* adm. red, 1830.
John Bazeley, *d.* 1809.
Christr. Mason, *d.* 1802.

1795, June 1. Thos. David Spry, *d.* adm. red, 1828.
Sir John Orde, bt., *d.* adm. red, 1824.
Sir Wm. Young, G.C.B., ld. admy. 1795; *d.* adm. red, 1821.
Jas. Gambier, aft. ld. Gambier G.C.B. Three times ld. admy; adm. fl. 1830; *d.* April 1833.
Sir Andr. Mitchell, K.B., *d.* 1806.
Chas. Chamberlaine, *d.* 1810.
Peter Rainier, *d.* 1808.
Sir Hugh Cloberry Christian, K.B. *d.* 1799.
Wm. Truscott, *d.* 1798.
Lord Hugh Seymour, *d.* 1801.
John Stanhope, *d.* 1800.
Christr. Parker, *d.* 1804.
Philip Patton, *d.* adm. red, Dec. 1815.
Sir Charles Morice Pole, G.C.B.; ld. admy, 1806; *d.* adm. red, 1830.
John Browne, *d.* 1808.
John Leigh Douglas, *d.* 1810.

1797, Feb. 20. Wm. Swiney, *d.* adm. red, 1829.
Sir Chas. Edmd. Nugent, G.C.H.; adm. fl. 1833 (see List B., *post*); *d.* 1844.
Wm. Fooks, *d.* 1798.
Chas Powell Hamilton, *d.* adm. red, 1825.
Edmd. Dod, *d.* 1815.
Sir Horatio Nelson, aft. ld. and visc. Nelson, and D. of Brontë, *d.* 1805.
Thos. Lenox Frederick, *d.* 1799.
Sir Geo. Home, bt. *d.* 1803.
Sir Chas. Cotton, bt., *d.* 1812.
Matth. Squire, *d.* 1800.
Roddam Home, *d.* 1800.

1799, Feb. 14. John Thomas, *d.* 1810.
Jas. Brine, *d.* 1814.
Sir Erasmus Gower, *d.* 1814.
John Holloway, d. adm. red, 1826.
John Blankett, *d.* 1801.
Geo. Wilson, *d.* adm. red, 1826.
Sir Chas. Hy. Knowles, bt., G.C.B., *d.* adm. red, 1831.
Hon. sir Thos. Pakenham, G.C.B., *d.* adm. red, 1836.
Robt. Deans, *d.* Jan. 1815.
Cuthbert Collingwood, aft. ld. Collingwood, *d.* 1810.
Sir Jas. Hawkins Whitshed, bt., G.C.B.; adm. fl. 1844 (see List B., *post*); *d.* 1849.
Arth. Kempe, *d.* adm. red, 1823.
Smith Child, *d.* 1813.
Chas., ld. Lecale, second son of Jas., D. of Leinster; *d.* 1810.
Thos. Taylor, *d.* 1812.
Sir John Thos. Duckworth, *d.* 1817.

1799, John Knowles, *d.* 1800.
Feb. 14. John Willett Payne, *d.* 1803.
Sir Robert Calder, bt., K.C.B., *d.* 1818.
Jas. Richd. Dacres, senr., *d.* 1810.
Hon. sir Geo. Cranfield Berkeley, G.C.B., *d.* Feb. 1818.
Thos. West, *d.* Feb. 1821.
Jas. Douglas, *d.* adm. red, 1839.
Peter Aplin, *d.* 1817.
Hy. Savage, *d.* adm. red, 1823.
Barth. Saml. Rowley, *d.* Oct. 1811.
Sir Richd. Hussey Bickerton, bt., K.C.B., *d.* adm. red, 1832.
Geo. Bowen, *d.* adm. red, 1823.
Robt. Montagu, *d.* adm. red, 1830.
John Fergusson, *d.* 1818.
John Howorth, *d.* 1799.
Edwd. Edwards, *d.* 1815.
Sir John Borlase Warren, G.C.B., *d.* 1822.
1801, Edwd. Tyrrell Smith, *d.* 1824.
Jan. 1. Sir Thos. Graves, K.B., *d.* 1814.
Thos. Macnamara Russell, *d.* 1834.
Sylverius Moriarty, *d.* 1809.
Sir Hy. Trollope, G.C.B., *d.* adm. red, 1839.
Hy. Edwyn Stanhope, aft. bt., *d.* 1814.
Robt. M'Dowell, *d.* 1816.
Billy Douglas, *d.* 1817.
John Wickey, *d.* adm. red, 1833.
John Inglis, *d.* 1807.
John Fish, *d.* adm. red, 1834.
Jahleel Brenton, senr., *d.* 1802.
Sir John Knight, K.C.B., *d.* adm. red, 1831.
Sir Edwd. Thornbrough, G.C.B., *d.* adm. red, 1834.
Jas. Kempthorne, *d.* 1808.
Sampson Edwards, *d.* adm. red, 1840.
Sir Geo. Campbell, G.C.B., *d.* adm. red, Jan. 1821.
Thos. Hicks, *d.* 1801.
Hy. Cromwell, *d.* 1814.
Arth. Philip, *d.* Aug. 1814.
Sir Wm. Geo. Fairfax, *d.* 1813.
Thos. Totty, *d.* 1802.
Sir Jas. Saumarez, bt., aft, ld. de Saumarez, G.C.B., v.-adm. Eng., 1831; *d.* 1836.
1804, Thos. Drury, *d.* adm. red, Sept.
April 23. 1832.
Sir Albemarle Bertie, bt., G.C.B., *d.* Feb. 1824.
Wm., E. of Northesk, G.C.B., *d.* r.-adm. Gr. Br., 1831.
Jas. Vashon, *d.* 1827.
Sir Wm. Hy. Douglas, bt., *d.* 1809.
Thos. Wells, *d.* 1812.
1804, Sir Edwd Pellew, bt., aft. visc.
Apr. 23. Exmouth, G.C.B.; v.-adm. Eng., 1832, *d.* 1833.
Sir Isaac Coffin, bt., G.C.H., *d.* adm. red, 1839.
John Aylmer, *d.* adm. red, 1841.
Saml. Osborne, *d.* 1816.
Richd. Boger, *d.* 1822.
Jonn. Faulknor, jun., *d.* 1809.
John Child Purvis, *d.* 1825.
Theoph. Jones, *d.* Nov. 1835.
Sir Wm. Domett, G.C.B., *d.* 1828.
Wm. Wolseley, *d.* adm. red, 1842.
John Manley, *d.* 1816.
Sir Geo. Murray, K.C.B., *d.* 1819.
Sir John Sutton, K.C.B., *d.* 1825.
Robt. Murray, *d.* 1834.
Hon. sir Alexr. Inglis Forrester Cochrane, G.C.B., *d.* 1832.
Sir Thos. Troubridge, bt.; ld. admy., 1801; *d.* 1810.
John Markham, ld. admy., 1801 *et seq.*; *d.* 1827.
Chas. Stirling, *d.* 1833.
Sir Hy. D'Esterre Darby, K.C.B., *d.* 1823.
Edwd. Bowater, *d.* 1829.
Geo. Palmer, *d.* 1834.
Wm. O'Bryen Drury, *d.* 1811.
Sir Wm. Essington, K.B., *d.* 1816.
Sir Thos. Louis, *d.* 1807.
1805, John M'Dougal, *d.* adm. red,
Nov. 9. 1814.
Jas. Alms, *d.* June 1816.
Sir Eliab Harvey, G.C.B., *d.* Feb. 1830.
John Peyton. *d.* July 1809.
Sir Edmd. Nagle, G.C.B., *d.* 1830.
Sir John Wells, G.C.B., *d.* adm. red, 1841.
Sir Richd. Grindall, K.C.B., *d.* 1820.
Sir Geo. Martin, G.C.B.; aft. adm. fl. and v.-adm. U.K. (see Lists B. and C., *post*); *d.* 1847.
Sir Alexr. John Ball, bt., *d.* 1809.
Sir Richd. John Strachan, bt., G.C.B., *d.* 1828.
Sir Wm. Sidney Smith, G.C.B., *d.* 1840.
Thos. Sotheby, *d.* 1831.
Edwd. O'Brien, *d.* 1809.
Nathan Brunton, *d.* 1814.
Wm. Hancock Kelly, *d.* 1811.
John Schanck, *d.* 1823.
Hon. Michl. de Courcey, *d.* 1824.
Wm. Bentinck, *d.* 1813.
Paul Minchin, *d.* 1810.
Philip D'Auvergne, Pr. of Bouillon, *d.* 1816.
1807, John Hunter, *d.* 1821.
Oct 2. Fras. Pender, *d.* 1820.
Wm. Albany Otway, *d.* 1814.
Geo. Lumsdaine, *d.* 1812.

1807, Oct. 2. Sir Saml. Hood, bt., K.B., *d.* 1814.
Sir Hy. Nicolls, K.C.B., *d.* 1830.
Sir Herbert Sawyer, K.C.B. *d.* 1833.
Sir Davidge Gould, G.C.B., aft. v.-adm. U. K. (see List C., *post*); *d.* 1847.
Sir Richd. Godwin Keats, G.C.B., govr. Newfoundland, 1813; *d.* 1834.

1808, April 28. Robt. Devereux Fancourt, *d.* 1826.
Sir Edwd. Buller, bt., *d.* 1824.
Hon. sir Robt. Stopford, G.C.B., aft. r.-adm. U. K. (see List C., *post*); *d.* 1847.
Mark Robinson, *d.* 1834.
Thos. Revell Shivers, *d.* 1827.
Chas. Cobbe, *d.* 1809.
Fras. Pickmore, *d.* 1818.
John Stevens Hall, *d.* 1814.
John Dilkes, *d.* 1827.
Wm. Lechmere, *d.* 1816.
Sir Thos. Foley, G.C.B., *d.* 1833.
Sir Charles Tyler, G.C.B., *d.* 1835.
Robt. Carthew Reynolds, *d.* 1811.
Robt. Watson, *d.* 1819.
Alan Hyde Gardner, aft. visc. Gardner, *d.* 1815.
Sir Manley Dixon, bt., K.C.B., *d.* Feb. 1837.
Geo. Losack, *d.* 1829.
Sir Wm. Mitchell, K.C.B., *d.* 1816.
Geo. Hart, *d.* 1812.
Thos. Bertie, aft. sir T., *d.* 1825.

1809, Oct. 25. Rowley Bulteel *d.* 1820.
Wm. Luke, *d.* 1819.
Isaac Geo. Manley, *d.* adm. red, 1837.
John Osborne, *d.* Jan. 1820.
Edmd. Crawley, *d.* 1834.
Chas. Boyles, *d.* 1816.
Sir Thos. Williams, G.C.B.; *d.* 1841.
Thos. Hamilton, *d.* 1815.
Sir Thos. Boulden Thompson, bt., G.C.B., *d.* 1828.
Geo. Countess, *d.* 1811.

1810, July 31. John Laugharne, *d.* 1819.
Sir Wm. Hargood, G.C.B., G.C.H., *d.* 1839.
Geo. Gregory, *d.* 1814.
John Ferrier, *d.* 1836.
Richd. Incledon Bury, *d.* 1825.
Sir Robt. Moorsom, K.C.B., *d.* 1835.
Sir Chas. Hamilton, bt., *d.* sen. adm. red, 1849.
Hon. Hy. Curzon, *d.* adm. red, 1846.
Wm. Bligh, *d.* 1817.
Sir Lawrence Wm Halsted, G.C.B., *d.* 1841.
Sir Edwd. Oliver Osborne, *d.* 1820.

1810, July 31. Sir Harry Burrard Neale, bt., G.C.B., ld. admy., 1804 *et seq.*; *d.* 1840.
Sir Joseph Sidney Yorke, bt., K.C.B., ld. admy., 1810 *et seq.*; *d.* 1831.
Hon. sir Arth. Kaye Legge, K.C.B., *d.* 1835.
Fras. Fayerman, *d.* 1820.
Geo., E. of Galloway, K.T., *d.* 1834.
Sir Thos. Fras. Fremantle, G.C.B., ld. admy., 1806; *d.* 1819.
Sir Fras. Laforey, bt., K.C.B., *d.* June 1835.
Sir Robt. Barlow, G.C.B., *d.* adm. red, 1843.
Sir Philip Chas. Calderwood Henderson Durham, G.C.B., *d.* adm. red, 1845.
Sir Israel Pellew, K.C.B., *d.* 1832.

1811, Aug. 1. Alexr. Frazer, *d.* 1829.
Sir Benjn. Hallowell Carew, G.C.B., *d.* 1834.
Sir Geo. Johnstone Hope, K.C.B., ld. admy., 1812 *et seq.*; *d.* 1817.
Lord Amelius Beauclerk, G.C.B., G.C.H., *d.* adm. red, 1846.
Wm. Taylor, *d.* adm. red, 1842.
Sir James Nicol Morris, K.C.B. *d.* 1830.
Geo. Burdon, *d.* 1815.
Wm. Browne, *d.* 1814.
Sir Thos. Byam Martin, G.C.B. aft. adm. fl. and v.-adm. U. K (see Lists B. and C., *post*).
Sir John Lawford, K.C.B., *d.* adm. red, 1842.
Frank Sotheron, *d.* 1839.
Thos. Wolley, *d.* 1826.

1812, Aug. 12. Sir Wm. Johnstone Hope, G.C.B. ld. admy., 1807 *et seq.*; *d* 1831.
Lord Hy. Paulet, K.C.B.; ld admy., 1813, *et seq.*; *d.* Jan 1832.
Chas. Wm. Paterson, *d.* adm. red 1841.
Sir Geo. Cockburn, G.C.B.; ld admy., 1818 *et seq.*; aft. adm fl. and r.-rdm. U. K. (see List B. and C., *post*).
Thos. Surridge, *d.* 1820.
Saml. Hood Linzee, *d.* 1820.
Jas. Carpenter, *d.* 1845.
Robt. Barton, *d.* 1831.
Sir Graham Moore, G.C.B.; ld admy., 1816 *et seq.*; *d.* 1843.
Matth. Hy. Scott, *d.* 1836.
Jos. Hanwell, *d.* 1839.
Sir Hy. Wm. Bayntun, G.C.B., *d.* 1840.
Hon. Fras. Farrington Gardner *d.* July 1821.

1812, Aug. 12. Sir Richd. King, bt., K.C.B., *d.* 1834.
Sir Edwd. Griffith Colpoys, K.C.B., *d.* 1832.
Sir Edwd. Jas. Foote, K.C.B., *d.* 1833.
Sir Richd. Lee, K.C.B., *d.* 1837.
Wm. Pierrepont, *d.* 1813.
Sir Peter Halkett, bt., G.C.H., *d.* 1839.
Wm. Bedford, *d.* 1827.

1813, Dec. 4. Philip Wilkinson Stephens, *d.* 1846.
Wm. Shield, *d.* 1842.
Hon. Chas. Elphinstone Fleeming, *d.* 1840.
Sir Chas. Vinicombe Penrose, K.C.B., *d.* 1830.
Sir Wm. Hotham, G.C.B., *d.* adm. red, 1848.
Geo. Hopewell Stephens, *d.* 1820.
Sir Pulteney Malcolm, G.C.B., *d.* 1838.
Wm. Nowell, *d.* 1828.
John Bazeley, *d.* 1828.
Jas. Bissett, *d.* 1824.
John Clements, *d.* 1825.
Sir John Gore, K.C.B., G.C.H., *d.* 1836.
Sir John Harvey, K.C.B., *d.* 1837.

1814, June 4. Hon. sir Hy. Hotham, K.C.B., *d.* 1833.
Sir Geo. Burlton, K.C.B.
Chas. Dudley Pater, *d.* 1818.
Sir Home Riggs Popham, K.C.B., *d.* 1820.
Sir Josias Rowley, bt., G.C.B., *d.* 1842.
Sir Edwd. Codrington, G.C.B., *d.* adm. red, 1851.
Sir Geo. Parker, K.C.B., *d.* adm. red, 1847.
Fredk. Watkins, ret.
Robt. Pamplin, *d.* 1834.
Edwd. Leveson Gower, res. 1821.
Hon. sir Hy. Blackwood, bt., K.C.B., *d.* 1832.
John Erskine Douglas, *d.* adm. red, 1847.
Geo., visc. Torrington, *d.* 1831.
Sir Ross Donnelly, K.C.B., *d.* 1840.
Sir John Poo Beresford, bt., K.C.B., G.C.H., *d.* 1844.
Hy. Lidgbird Ball, *d.* 1818.
Thos. Eyles, *d.* 1835.
Thos. Le Marchant Gosselin, *d.* adm. red.
Sir Chas. Rowley, bt., G.C.B., G.C.H., *d.* 1845.
Thos. Rogers.
Saml. Jas. Ballard, *d.* 1829.
Robt. Rolles, *d.* 1839.
Walter Locke, *d.* 1835.
Sir David Milne, G.C.B., *d.* 1845.
Geo. Dundas.

1814, June 4. Jas. Young, *d.* 1833.
Jas. Macnamara, *d.* 1826.
Donald Campbell, *d.* 1819.
Sir Robt. Waller Otway, bt., G.C.B., *d.* 1846.
Richd. Dacres, G.C.H., *d.* 1837.
Thos. Western.
John Wm. Spranger, *d.* 1822.
Wm. Lukin Windham, *d.* 1833.
Shuldham Peard, *d.* 1832.
Edwd. Fellowes, *d.* 1841.

1819, Aug. 12. Sir Willoughby Thos. Lake, K.C.B., *d.* 1847.
Sir Chas. Ogle, bt., aft. adm. fl. (see List B., *post*).
Hy. Raper, *d.* 1845.
Sir Wm. Chas. Fahie, K.C.B., *d.* 1833.
Sir Geo. Eyre, K.C.B., *d.* 1839.
Robt. Lambert, *d.* 1836.
Jos. Bingham, *d.* 1825.
Robt. Dudley Oliver, *d.* adm. red, 1850.
D'Arcy Preston, *d.* 1847.
Man Dobson, *d.* 1847.
Thos. Boys, *d.* 1832.
John Clarke Searle, *d.* 1824.
Sir Chas. Brisbane, K.C.B., *d.* govr. St. Vincent, 1829.
Hon. sir John Talbot, G.C.B., *d.* adm. red.
John Richd. Delap Tollemache, *d.* July 1837.
John Giffard, *d.* adm. red.
Sir John West, K.C.B., aft. adm. fl. (see List B., *post*).
Joseph Bullen, *d.* adm. red.
Stephen Poyntz, *d.* 1847.
John, ld. Colville, *d.* sen. adm. white, 1849.
John Cochet, *d.* adm. red.
Sir Archd. Collingwood Dickson, bt., *d.* 1827.
Robt. Winthrop, *d.* 1832.
Sir Hy. Digby, G.C.B., *d.* 1842.
Sir Chas. Ekins, K.C.B.
John Sprat Rainier, *d.* 1822.
Benjn. Wm. Page, *d.* 1845.
Hon. Philip Wodehouse, *d.* 1838.
Thos. Alexander, *d.* 1843.

1821, July 19. Andr. Smith, *d.* 1831.
Sir Edwd. Berry, bt., K.C.B., *d.* 1831.
Sir Wm. Prowse, G.C.B., *d.* 1826.
Lord Mark Robt. Kerr, *d.* 1840.
Sir Jas. Athol Wood, *d.* 1829.
Sir Thos. Harvey, K.C.B., *d.* 1842.
Richd. Hussey Moubray Hussey, *d.* 1842.
Hy. Richd. Glynn, *d.* adm. red.
John Bligh, C.B., *d.* 1831.
Peter Puget, *d.* 1822.
Sir Edwd. Hamilton, bt., K.C.B., *d.* 1851.
Sir Thos. Baker, K.C.B.

1821, Saml. Sutton, *d.* 1832.
July 19. Hy. Evans, *d.* 1842.
Hon. sir Courtenay Boyle, K.C.H., *d.* 1844.
Sir Robt. Laurie, bt., K.C.B., *d.* 1848.
Sir Wm. Hall Gage, G.C.H., ld. admy., Sept. 1841 to July 1846; aft. adm. fl. and adm. U. K. (see Lists B. and C., *post*).
John Maitland, *d.* 1836.
Stair Douglas, *d.* 1826.
Wm. Cuming, C.B., *d.* 1824.
Jas, Walker, C.B., *d.* 1831.
1823, The hon. sir Chas. Paget, G.C.H.,
Apr. 9. *d.* 1839.
Robt. Williams, *d.* 1827.
Richd. Worsley, *d.* 1838.
1825, Aiskew Paffard Hollis, *d.* 1844.
May. 27. Sir Hy. Heathcote.
Andr. Fitzherbert Evans, *d.* 1826.
Sir Edwd. Wm. Campbell Rich Owen, G.C.B., G.C.H., *d.* 1849.
Geo. Fredk. Ryves, *d.* 1826.
Geo. Jas. Shirley, *d.* Aug. 1845.
Sir Geo. Scott, K.C.B., *d.* 1841.
Sir Thos. Dundas, K.C.B., *d.* Mar. 1841.
Geo. Fowke, *d.* 1832.
Richd. Harrison Pearson, *d.* 1838.
Geo. Astle, *d.* 1830.
Sir John Tremayne Rodd, K.C.B., *d.* 1838.
Sir Thos. Masterman Hardy, bt., G.C.B., *d.* 1839.
Wm. Cumberland, *d.* 1832.
Jas. Keith Shepard, *d.* 1843.
Sir Graham Eden Hamond, bt., K.C.B., aft. adm. fl. and adm. U. K. (see Lists B. and C., *post*).
Robt. Honyman, *d.* 1848.
Sir Robt. Lewis Fitzgerald, K.C.H., *d.* 1844.
Volant Vashon Ballard, *d.* 1832.
Hugh Downman.
Hon. sir Thos. Bladen Capel, K.C.B.
Wm. Hanwell, *d.* 1830.
Thos. Manby, *d.* 1834.
Lord Jas. O'Bryen, G.C.H., aft. M. of Thomond.
Richd. Matson, *d.* 1848.
Richd. Raggett, *d.* 1829.
John Mackellar.
Geo. Barker.
Sir Chas. Adam, K.C.B., ld. admy. Nov. 1834 to Sept. 1841.
1830, John Styles, *d.* 1830.
July 22. Wm. Granger, *d.* 1848.
Sir John Chambers White, K.C.B., *d.* 1845.
1830, Hy. Garrett, *d.* 1846.
July 12. Sir Adam Drummond, K.C.H., *d.* 1849.
Robt. Hall, *d.* 1842.
John Chesshyre, *d.* 1843.
Robt. Lloyd, *d.* 1846.
Sir Thos. Livingstone, bt.
Sir Lucius Ferdinand Hardyman, *d.* 1834.
Joshua Sydney Horton, *d.* 1835.
Sir Edwd. Brace, K.C.B., *d.* 1843.
Sir Jahleel Brenton, jun., bt., K.C.B., *d.* 1844.
Sir Fras. Wm. Austen, K.C.B., aft. adm. fl. and adm. U. K. (see Lists B. and C., *post*).
Sir Bendall Robt. Littlehales, *d.* 1847.
Sir Patrick Campbell, K.C.B., *d.* 1841.
Narborne Thompson, *d.* 1844.
Sir Michl. Seymour, bt., K.C.B., *d.* 1834.
Edwd. Stirling Dickson, *d.* 1844.
Thos. Jas. Maling, *d.* 1848.
Sir John Acworth Ommanney, K.C.B.
Hy. Stuart, *d.* 1840.
Zacchary Mudge.
Hy. Hill, *d.* 1849.
Chas. Wollaston, *d.* 1845.
Alexr. Wilmot Schomberg, *d.* 1850.
Sir Edwd. Durnford King, K.C.H.
Hy. Vansittart, *d.* 1843.
Sir Geo. Mundy, K.C.B.
Geo. Sayer, *d.* 1831.
Sir Philip Bowes Vere Broke, bt., K.C.B., *d.* 1841.
Chas. Tinling, *d.* 1840.
Sir Fredk. Lewis Maitland, K.C.B., *d.* 1839.
Fredk. Warren, *d.* 1848.
Richd. Peacocke, *d.* 1846.
Jas. Carthew.
Sir Thos. Briggs, G.C.M.G.
John Broughton, *d.* Oct. 1837.
Hon. Geo. Heneage Lawrence Dundas, *d.* 1834.
Thos., E. of Dundonald, G.C.B. (late ld. Cochrane), aft. r.-adm. U. K. (see List C., *post*); *d.* 1860.
Nichs. Tomlinson, *d.* 1847.
Sir Wm. Parker, bt., G.C.B., ld. admy., Nov. 1834 *et seq.*; aft. adm. fl. and r.-adm. U. K. (see Lists B. and C., *post*).
Sir Robt. Tristram Rickets, bt., *d.* 1842.
Geo. M'Kinley.
Jas. Katon, *d.* 1845.
Sir Chas. Dashwood, K.C.B., *d.* 1847.

LIST B.

ADMIRALS OF THE FLEET.

From 1837 to the present time.

Name.	Promoted from List.	Adml. Fl.
Sir Chas. Edmd. Nugent, G.C.H.	A.	24 Apr. 33.
Sir Jas. Hawkins Whitshed, G.C.B.	A.	8 Jan. 44.
Sir Geo. Martin, G.C.B.	C.	9 Nov. 46.
Sir Thos. Byam Martin, G.C.B.	C.	13 Oct. 49.
Sir Geo. Cockburn, G.C.B.	C.	1 Jul. 51.
Sir Chas. Ogle, bt.	A.	8 Dec. 57
Sir Jno. West, K.C.B.	A.	25 Jun. 58.
Sir Wm. Hall Gage, G.C.B., G.C.H.	C.	20 May 62.
Sir Graham Eden Hamond, bt., G.C.B.	C.	10 Nov. 62.
Sir Fras. Wm. Austen, G.C.B.	C.	27 Apr. 63.
Sir Wm. Parker, bt., G.C.B.	C.	,,
Sir Lucius Curtis, bt., K.C.B.	D.	11 Jan. 64.
Sir Thos. Jno. Cochrane, G.C.B.	C.	23 Sep. 65.
Sir Geo. Fras. Seymour, G.C.B., G.C.H.	C.	20 Nov. 66.
Sir Jas. Alexr. Gordon, G.C.B. (*Reserved List*)	D.	3 Feb. 68.
Sir Wm. Bowles, K.C.B.	C.	15 Jan. 69.
Sir Geo. Rose Sartorius, K.C.B.	C.	2 Jul. 69.
Sir Fairfax Moresby, G.C.B.	C.	21 Jan. 70.
Sir Houston Stewart, G.C.B.	D.	20 Oct. 72.
Sir Provo Wm. Parry Wallis, G.C.B.	C.	11 Dec. 75.
Sir Hy. Jno. Codrington, K.C.B.	E.	22 Jan. 77.
Hon. sir Hy. Keppel, G.C.B.	E.	5 Aug. 77.
Thos., E. of Lauderdale, G.C.B.	E.	27 Dec. 77.
Sir Geo. Rodney Mundy, G.C.B.	E.	,,
Sir Thos. Matt. Chas. Symonds, K.C.B.	E.	15 Jun. 79.
Sir Jas. Hope, G.C.B.	E.	,,
Sir Alexr. Milne, bt., G.C.B.	E.	10 Jun. 81.
Hon. sir Chas. Gilbert Jno. Brydone Elliot, K.C.B.	E.	1 Dec. 81.
Sir Alf. Phillipps Ryder, K.C.B.	E.	29 Apr. 85.
Alb. Edw. Pr. of Wales (*Honorary*)	—	18 Jul. 87.
Sir Geoffr. Thos. Phipps Hornby, G.C.B.	E.	1 May 88.
Lord Jno. Hay, G.C.B.	E.	15 Dec. 88.

LIST C.

ADMIRALS OF THE UNITED KINGDOM.

From 1837 to the present time.

R.A.U.K.—Rear-Admiral of the United Kingdom.
V.A.U.K.—Vice-Admiral of the United Kingdom.

Name.	Promoted from List	R.A.U.K.	V.A.U.K.	Promoted to List
Sir Geo. Martin, G.C.B.	A.	......	28 Jan. 33.	B.
Hon. sir Robt. Stopford, G.C.B.	A.	Bef. 1837.	......	...
Sir Davidge Gould, G.C.B.	A.	......	1846.	...
Sir Thos. Byam Martin, G.C.B.	A.	......	1847.	B.
Sir Geo. Cockburn...	A.	1847.	......	B.
Sir Wm. Hall Gage...	A.	24 Oct. 53.	6 Nov. 54.	B.
Thos., 10th E. Dundonald, G.C.B. ...	A.	6 Nov. 54.	......	...
Sir Graham Eden Hamond, bt., G.C.B.	A.	22 Nov. 60.	5 Jun. 62.	B.
Sir Fras. Wm. Austen, G.C.B.	A.	5 Jun. 62.	11 Dec. 62.	B.
Sir Wm. Parker, bt., G.C.B.	A.	11 Dec. 62.	......	B.
Sir Thos. Jno. Cochrane, G.C.B.	D.	......	16 May 63.	B.
Sir Geo. Fras. Seymour, G.C.B.	D.	16 May 63.	23 Sep. 65.	B.
Sir Wm. Bowles, K.C.B.	D.	23 Sep. 65.	26 Nov. 66.	B.
Sir Wm. Phipps Hornby, G.C.B.	D.	26 Nov. 66.	......	..
Sir Geo. Rose Sartorius, K.C.B.	D.	......	1 Mar. 69.	B.
Sir Fairfax Moresby, G.C.B.	D.	20 Apr. 67.	17 Jul. 69.	B.
Sir Provo Wm. Parry Wallis, K.C.B.	D.	17 Jul. 69.	12 Feb. 70.	B.
Sir Wm. Jas. Hope Johnstone, K.C.B.	D.	12 Feb. 70.	......	...
Sir Michl. Seymour, G.C.B.	D.	......	15 Jan. 76.	...
Sir Wm. Fanshawe Martin, bt., G.C.B.	D.	19 Sep. 78.	......	...

LIST D.

ADMIRALS OF THE RED, WHITE, AND BLUE.

From 1837 to the discontinuance of the three Squadrons in 1864.

R.A.B.—Rear-Admiral of the Blue.
R.A.W.— ,, ,, ,, White.
R.A.R.— ,, ,, ,, Red.

V.A.B.—Vice-Admiral of the Blue.
V.A.W.— ,, ,, ,, White.
V.A.R.— ,, , ,, Red.

A.B.—Admiral of the Blue.
A.W.— ,, ,, White.
A.R.— ,, ,, Red.

* Those marked thus were on the Retired List when raised to flag rank.

Name.	R.A.B.	R.A.W.	R.A.R.	V.A.B.	V.A.W.	V.A.R.	A.B.	A.W.	A.R.	Promoted in List
*Jno. Winne	10 Jan. 37.	......	......	......	......	......	......	......	......	......
Richd. Curry	......	10 Jan. 37.	......	......	9 Nov. 46.	......	......	......	......	G.
Wm. Skipsey	......	,,	......	......	......	......	......	......	......	......
Hon. Fredk. Paul Irby	......	,,	......	......	......	......	......	......	......	......
Sir John Wentworth Loring K.C.B., K.C.H.	......	,,	......	9 Nov. 46.	......	......	8 Jul. 51.	......	......	......
Sir Robt. Howe Bromley, bt. ...	......	,,	......	,,	......	......	21 Aug. 51.	21 Jan. 54.	......	......
Hon. Duncombe Pleydell Bouverie	......	,,	......	,,	......	......	......	......	......	......
*Richd. Poulden	10 Jan. 37.	......	......	......	......	......	......	......	......	......
John Dick...	......	10 Jan. 37.	......	9 Nov. 46.	......	......	19 Jan. 52.	......	......	......
*Peter Ribouleau	10 Jan. 37.	......	......	,,	......	......	......	......	......	......
*Matth. Buckle (No. 2)	,,	......	......	,,	......	......	......	......	......	G.
*John Allen	,,	......	......	,,	......	......	......	......	......	G.
*Jas. Noble	,,	......	......	,,	......	......	......	......	......	......
Sir Saml. Warren, K.C.B., K.C.H.	......	10 Jan. 37.	......	,,	......	......	......	......	......	......
Anselm John Griffiths	......	,,	......	......	......	......	......	......	......	......
*Fras. Holmes Coffin	10 Jan. 37.	......	......	......	......	......	......	......	......	......
*Jeffery, ld. Raigersfeld ...	,,	......	......	......	......	......	......	......	......	......
*Christr. John Williams Nesham	,,	......	......	9 Nov. 46.	......	......	......	......	......	G.
Sir Chas. Bullen, K.C.B., K.C.H.	......	10 Jan. 37.	......	,,	......	......	30 Jul. 52.	......	......	......
Richd. Byron	10 Jan. 37.	......	......	......	......	......	......	......	......	......
Geo. Tobin	......	10 Jan. 37.	......	......	......	......	......	......	......	......
Wm. Hy. Webley-Parry	......	,,	......	......	......	......	......	......	......	......
*John Wight	10 Jan. 37.	......	......	9 Nov. 46.	......	14 Jan. 50.	......	......	......	G.
*Hy. Folkes Edgell	,,	......	......	......	......	......	......	......	......	......

Name.	R.A.B.	R.A.W.	R.A.R.	V.A.B.	V.A.W.	V.A.R.	A.B.	A.W.	A.R.	Promoted in List
*Cornelius Quinton	10 Jan. 37.	......	......	......	......	......	......	......	......	......
*Wm. Butterfield	,,	......	......	......	......	......	......	......	......	......
*Wm. Young	,,	......	......	9 Nov. 46.	......	......	......	......	......	......
*Wm. Hy Darnell	,,	......	......	......	......	......	......	......	......	......
*Jacob Walton	,,	......	......	......	......	......	......	......	......	......
Augs. Brine	,,	......	......	......	......	......	......	......	......	......
Edwd. Galwey	......	10 Jan. 37.	......	......	......	......	......	......	......	......
John Hayes	......	,,	......	......	......	......	......	......	......	......
Saml. Campbell Rowley	10 Jan. 37.	......	......	......	......	......	......	......	......	......
*Bulkeley Mackworth Praed	,,	......	......	9 Nov. 46.	......	2 Sep. 50.	......	......	......	......
*Saml. Mottley	,,	......	......	......	......	......	......	......	......	......
*Edwd. Walpole Browne	,,	......	......	......	......	......	......	......	......	......
*John Ronett Smollett	,,	......	......	......	......	......	......	......	......	......
*Hon. Wm. Le Poer Trench	,,	......	......	......	......	......	......	......	......	......
*Edwd. Sneyd Clay	,,	......	......	......	......	......	......	......	......	......
*Chas. Carter	,,	......	......	9 Nov. 46.	......	......	......	......	......	......
Thos Browne	,,	......	......	11 Dec. 46.	......	6 Nov. 50.	......	......	......	......
*Fras Godolphin Bond	,,	......	......	......	......	......	......	......	......	......
*Wm. Hy. Browne Tremlett	,,	......	......	22 Jan. 47.	......	21 Mar. 51.	......	......	......	G.
Sir Saml. Pym, K.C.B.	,,	......	......	13 Feb. 47.	......	8 Apr. 51.	17 Dec. 52.	3 Jul. 55.	......	......
*Saml. Butcher	,,	......	......	19 Feb. 47.	......	......	......	......	......	......
Robt. Jackson	,,	......	......	8 Mar. 47.	......	29 Apr. 51.	......	......	......	......
Sir Robt. Barrie, K.C.B., K.C.H.	,,	......	......	......	......	......	......	......	......	......
Chas. Payne Hodgson Ross, C.B.	,,	......	......	24 Apr. 47.	......	......	......	......	......	......
*Robt. O'Brien	,,	......	......	......	......	......	......	......	......	......
Sir Chas. Malcolm	,,	......	......	28 Apr. 47.	......	......	......	......	......	......
Fras. Wm. Fane	,,	......	......	......	......	......	......	......	......	......
Hon. Geo. Elliot	,,	......	......	13 May 47.	......	8 Jun. 51.	5 Mar. 53.	4 Jul. 55.	......	......
Wm. D'Urban	,,	......	......	......	......	......	......	......	......	......
Sir Jas. Hillyar, K.C.B., K.C.H.	,,	......	......	......	......	......	......	......	......	......
Ld. Wm. Fitzroy, K.C.B.	,,	......	......	26 Jun. 47.	......	......	2 Apr. 53.	9 Jul. 55.	......	......
Ld. Geo. Stuart	,,	......	......	......	......	......	......	......	......	......
*Matthew Godwin	,,	......	......	26 Jul. 47.	......	......	......	......	......	......

Name.	R.A.B.	R.A.W.	R.A.R.	V.A.B.	V.A.W.	V.A.R.	A.B.	A.W.	A.R.	Promoted in List
*Jas. Master	10 Jan. 37.	......	......	......	......	......	......	......	......	......
Sir Hugh Pigot, K.C.B., K.C.H. ...	,,	......	......	6 Aug. 47.	......	......	4 Jul. 53.	27 Sep. 55.	......	......
John Tower	,,	......	......	......	......	......	......	......	......	......
*Sir Salusbury Pryce Humphrys Davenport, K.C.H.	,,	......	......	......	......	......	......	......	......	......
Edwd. Hawker	,,	......	......	22 Sep. 47.	......	8 Jul. 51.	17 Sep. 53.	3 Oct. 55.	......	......
Sir Chas. Richardson, K.C.B. ...	,,	......	......	17 Dec. 47.	......	......	......	......	......	......
*Fras. Temple	,,	......	......	21 Dec. 47.	......	......	......	......	......	G.
Sir Arth. Farquhar	,,	......	......	......	......	......	......	......	......	......
Hy. Gordon	,,	......	......	27 Dec. 47.	......	......	......	......	......	G.
Sir Jas. Alexr. Gordon, K.C.B....	,,	......	......	......	......	8 Jan. 48.	21 Jan. 54.	......	......	......
Hon. Frdk. Wm. Aylmer, aft. ld. Aylmer	,,	......	......	3 Jan. 48.	......	......	......	......	......	G.
Richd. Thomas	,,	......	......	8 Jan. 48.	14 Jan. 50.	21 Aug. 51.	11 Sep. 54.	14 May 57.	... .	......
Jas. Richd. Dacres	28 Jun. 38.	......	......	20 Mar. 48.	2 Sep. 50.	19 Jan. 52.	......	......	......	......
*John Surman Carden	,,	......	......	23 Mar. 48.	6 Nov. 50.	......	......	......	......	G.
John Sykes	,,	......	......	1 Jun. 48.	11 Nov. 50.	4 Jun. 52.	3 Jul. 55.	9 Jul. 57.	......	......
*John Wentworth Holland ...	,,	......	......	......	......	......	......	......	......	......
*John Impey	,,	......	......	1 Aug. 48.	21 Mar. 51.	......	......	......	......	G.
*Hy. Manaton Ommanney ...	,,	......	......	24 Jan. 49.	8 Apr. 51.	......	......	......	......	G.
*Archd. Duff	,,	......	......	3 Mar. 49.	29 Apr. 51.	......	......	......	......	G.
John Hancock	,,	......	......	......	......	......	......	......	......	......
Hon. Donald Hugh Mackay ...	,,	......	......	......	......	......	......	......	......	......
Sir Fras. Mason, K.C.B.	,,	......	......	9 May 49.	11 Jun. 51.	30 Jul. 52.	......	......	......	......
*Hon. Major Jacob Henniker ...	,,	......	......	......	......	......	......	......	......	......
Thos. Brown	,,	......	......	8 Jun. 49.	16 Jun. 51.	17 Dec. 52.	4 Jul. 55.	......	......	......
Alexr. Shippard	,,	......	......	......	......	......	......	......	......	......
Robt. Henderson	,,	......	......	......	......	......	......	......	......	......
Sir Lucius Curtis, bt.	,,	......	......	15 Sep. 49.	......	5 Mar. 53.	9 Jul. 55.	30 Jul. 57.	1 Nov. 60.	B.
Sir John Louis, bt.	,,	......	......	9 Oct. 49.	......	2 Apr. 53.	27 Sep. 55.	22 Aug. 57.	......	......
Brian Hodgson	,,	......	......	18 Oct. 49.	......	......	......	......	......	G.
Hood Hanway Christian... ...	,,	......	......	......	......	......	......	......	......	......
Sir Josiah Coghill Coghill, bt. ...	23 Nov. 41.	......	......	30 Oct. 49.	......	......	......	......	......	......

Name.	R.A.B.	R.A.W.	R.A.R.	V.A.B.	V.A.W.	V.A.R.	A.B.	A.W.	A.R.	Promoted in List
Nathl. Day Cochrane	23 Nov. 41.	......	......	......	......	......	......	......	......	......
John Ayscough	,,	......	......	24 Dec. 49.	8 Jul. 51.	28 May 53.	3 Oct. 55.	28 Nov. 57.	18 Feb. 61.	......
Sir Thos. John Cochrane ...	,,	......	......	14 Jan. 50.	21 Aug. 51.	4 Jul. 53.	31 Jan. 56.	8 Dec. 57.	15 Jan. 62.	C.
Wm. Furlong Wise	,,	......	......	......	......	......	......	......	......	......
Edmd. Boger	,,	......	......	......	......	......	......	......	......	......
Wm. Jones Lye	,,	......	......	......	......	......	......	......	......	......
Sir Geo. Fras. Seymour, G.C.H.	,,	......	......	27 Mar. 50.	19 Jan. 52.	17 Sep. 53.	14 May 57.	13 Feb. 58.	20 May 62.	C.
Hon. Geo. Poulett, aft. Sir G. ...	,,	......	......	21 Jun. 50.	4 Jun. 52.	21 Jan. 54.	......	......	......	......
Jas. Haldane Tait	,,	......	......	......	......	......	......	......	......	......
Sir Wm. Beauchamp Proctor, bt.	,,	......	......	2 Sep. 50.	......	......	......	......	......	G.
Chas. Jas. Johnstone	,,	......	......	6 Nov. 50.	30 Jul. 52.	16 Feb. 54.	......	......	......	......
Edwd Ratsey	,,	......	......	11 Nov. 50.	......	......	......	......	......	G.
Richd. Turner Hancock... ...	,,	......	......	......	......	......	......	......	......	......
Chas. Philip Butler-Bateman ...	,,	......	......	21 Mar. 51.	......	......	......	......	......	G.
Mauritius Adolphus Newton de Starck	,,	......	......	......	... ..	......	......	......	......	......
Arth. Lysaght	,,	......	......	8 Apr. 51.	......	......	......	......	......	G.
Hon. Josceline Percy	,,	......	......	29 Apr. 51.	17 Dec. 52.	15 Apr. 54.	......	......	......	......
Hon. sir Anthy. Maitland, K.C.M.G., aft. E. of Lauderdale	,,	......	......	11 Jun. 51.	5 Mar. 53.	11 Sep. 54.	18 Jun. 57.	6 Mar. 58.	10 Nov. 62.	......
Hon. Granville Leveson Proby, aft. E. of Carysfort	,,	......	......	16 Jun. 51.	......	......	......	......	......	G.
Granville Geo., ld. Radstock ...	,,	......	......	......	2 Apr. 53.	3 Jul. 55.	......	......	......	......
Geo., E. Cadogan	,,	......	......	......	22 Apr. 53.	4 Jul. 55.	9 Jul. 57.	25 Jun. 58.	23 Mar. 63.	......
Sir Edwd. Tucker, K.C.B. ...	,,	......	......	8 Jul. 51.	28 May 53.	9 Jul. 55.	30 Jul. 57.	......	......	......
Wm. Maude	,,	......	......	......	......	......	......	......	......	......
Saml. Hood Inglefield	,,	......	......	......	......	......	......	......	......	......
Sir Wm. Augs. Montague, K.C.H.	,,	......	......	21 Aug. 51.	......	......	......	......	......	......
Valentine Collard	,,	......	......	......	......	......	......	......	......	......
Sir Edwd. Chetham Strode ...	,,	......	......	19 Jan. 52.	4 Jul. 53.	27 Sep. 55.	22 Aug. 57.	2 May 60.	......	......
Reuben Callaud Mangin... ...	,,	.. ....	......	......	......	......	......	......	......	......
Wm. Croft	,,	......	......	......	......	......	......	......	......	G.
Fras. Beauman	,,	......	......	......	......	......	......	......	......	......

Name	R.A.B.	R.A.W.	R.A.R.	V.A.B.	V.A.W.	V.A.R.	A.B.	A.W.	A.R.	Promoted in List
Jas. Robt. Philips	23 Nov. 41.	......	......	......	......	......	......	......	......	......
Pringle Stoddart	,,	......	......	......	......	......	......	......	......	......
Wm. Bowles, aft. sir W. ...	,,	......	......	8 Mar. 52.	17 Sep. 53.	3 Oct. 55.	28 Nov. 57.	1 Nov. 60.	27 Apr.'63.	C.
Hyde Parker (No. 3)	,,	......	......	4 Jun. 52.	21 Jan. 54.	......	......	......	......	......
Chas. Sibthorpe John Hawtayne	,,	......	......	30 Jul. 52.	11 Feb. 54.	31 Jan. 56.	......	......	......	......
Jas. Whitley Dean Dundas, aft. sir J.	,,	......	......	17 Dec. 52.	15 Apr. 54.	21 Oct. 56.	8 Dec. 57.	11 Feb. 61.	......	......
Saml. Jackson	,,	......	......	......	......	......	......	......	......	......
Sir Edwd. Thos. Troubridge, bt.	,,	......	......	......	......	......	......	......	......	......
Chas. Gordon	,,	......	......	......	......	......	......	......	......	G.
Jas. Murray Gordon	9 Nov. 46.	......	14 Jan. 50.	......	......	......	......	......	......	......
Sir Wm. Hy. Dillon, K.C.H. ...	,,	......	27 Mar. 50.	5 Mar. 53.	26 May 54.	12 May 57.	......	......	......	......
Thos. Searle	,,	......	......	......	......	......	......	......	......	......
Hy. Hope, aft. sir H.	,,	......	21 Jun. 50.	2 Apr. 53.	11 Sep. 54.	14 May 57.	20 Jan. 58.	15 Jan. 62.	27 Apr. 63.	......
Sir Thos. Usher, K.C.H.... ...	,,	......	......	......	......	......	......	......	......	......
Wm. Ward	,,	......	2 Sep. 50.	......	......	......	......	......	......	G.
Sir Saml. John Brooke Pechell, bt.	,,	......	......	......	......	......	......	......	......	......
Robt. Elliott	,,	......	6 Nov. 50.	......	......	......	......	......	......	G.
Cuthbt. Featherstone Daley ...	,,	......	11 Nov. 50.	......	......	......	......	......	......	......
Hon. sir Fleetwood Broughton Reynolds Pellew	,,	......	30 Dec. 50.	22 Apr. 53.	3 Jul. 55.	18 Jun. 57.	13 Feb. 58.	......	......	......
Sir Fras. Augs. Collier, K.C.H. ...	,,	......	......	......	......	......	......	......	......	......
Hon. Jas. Wm. King	,,	......	......	......	......	......	......	......	......	......
Sir Chas. Napier, K.C.B. ...	,,	......	21 Mar. 51.	28 May 53.	4 Jul. 55.	9 Jul. 57.	6 Mar. 58.	......	......	......
John Brett Purvis	,,	......	8 Apr. 51.	4 Jul. 53.	9 Jul. 55.	30 Jul. 57.	......	......	......	......
Wm. Hy. Shirreff	,,	......	......	......	......	......	......	......	......	......
Richd. Arthur	,,	......	29 Apr. 51.	17 Sep. 53.	......	......	......	......	......	......
Wm. Phipps Hornby, aft. sir W.	,,	......	11 Jun. 51.	21 Jan. 54.	27 Sep. 55.	22 Aug. 57.	25 Jun. 58.	12 Apr. 62.	24 Nov. 63.	C.
Hon. Wm. Gordon	,,	......	16 Jun. 51.	11 Feb. 54.	3 Oct. 55.	10 Sep. 57.	......	......	......	......
Chas. John Austen	,,	......	8 Jul. 51.	......	......	......	......	......	......	......
Philip Browne	,,	......	......	......	......	......	......	......	......	G.
Hy. Prescott, aft. sir H. ...	24 Apr 47.	......	21 Aug. 51.	15 Apr.'54.	31 Jan. 56.	10 Sep. 57.	2 May 60.	......	......	......
Sir Nesbit Josiah Willoughby, K.C.H.	28 Apr. 47.	......	......	......	......	......	......	......	......	......

Name.	R.A.B.	R.A.W.	R.A.R.	V.A.B.	V.A.W.	V.A.R.	A.B.	A.W.	A.R.	Promoted in List
Edwd. Wallis Hoare	13 May 47.	......	......	......	......	......	......	......	......	G.
John Coode	26 Jun. 47.	......	19 Jan. 52.	26 May 54.	......	......	......	......	......	......
Sir Thos. Fellowes	26 Jul. 47.	......	......	......	......	......	......	......	......	G.
Edwd. Hy. A'Court Repington...	6 Aug. 47.	......	......	......	......	......	......	......	......	G.
John Pasco	22 Sep. 47.	......	8 Mar. 52.	......	......	......	......	......	......	......
Wm. Fisher	2 Dec. 47.	......	4 Jun. 52.	......	......	......	......	......	......	......
Edwd. Harvey, aft. sir E. ...	17 Dec. 47.	......	30 Jul. 52.	11 Sep. 54.	21 Oct. 56.	2 Oct. 57.	9 Jun. 60.	20 May 62.	3 Dec. 63.	......
Wm. Fitzwilliam Owen	21 Dec. 47.	......	1 Oct. 52.	27 Oct. 54.	......	......	......	......	......	......
Manley Hall Dixon	27 Dec. 47.	......	8 Oct. 52.	7 Feb. 55.	......	......	......	......	......	G.
Hon. Alexr. Jones	3 Jan. 48.	......	......	......	......	......	......	......	......	G.
Peter John Douglas	7 Jan. 48.	14 Jan. 50.	26 Oct. 52.	3 Jul. 55.	......	......	......	......	......	......
Barrington Reynolds, aft. sir B.	8 Jan. 48.	27 Mar. 50	17 Dec. 52.	4 Jul. 55.	12 May 57.	28 Nov. 57.	1 Nov. 60.	......	......	......
Hon. Geo Alfd. Crofton... ...	30 Jan. 48.	21 Jun. 50.	5 Mar. 53.	9 Jul. 55.	......	......	......	......	......	......
Villiers Fras. Hatton	14 Feb. 48.	2 Sep. 50.	......	......	......	......	......	......	......	G.
Chas. Sotheby	20 Mar. 48.	6 Nov. 50.	2 Apr. 53.	......	......	......	......	......	......	......
Sir Aug. Wm. Jas. Clifford, bt....	23 Mar. 48.	11 Nov. 50.	22 Apr. 53.	27 Sep. 55.	14 May 57.	8 Dec. 57.	7 Nov. 60	4 Oct. 62.	11 Jan. 64.	......
Sir Joshua Rickets Rowley, bt...	3 Apr. 48.	30 Dec. 50.	28 May 53.	3 Oct. 55.	......	......	......	......	......	......
Alex. Renton Sharpe	1 Jun. 48.	21 Mar. 51.	4 Jul. 53.	30 Nov. 55.	18 Jun. 57.	......	......	......	......	......
Gordon Thos. Falcon	1 Aug. 48.	8 Apr. 51.	17 Sep. 53.	......	......	......	......	......	......	......
Sir Watkin Owen Pell	5 Sep. 48.	29 Apr. 51.	17 Nov. 53.	28 Dec. 55.	......	......	......	......	......	G.
Wm. Fairbrother Carroll, aft. sir W.	24 Jun. 49.	11 Jun. 51.	5 Dec. 53.	......	......	......	......	......	......	......
Sir Andr. Pellat Green, K.C.H...	3 Mar. 49.	16 Jun. 51.	......	......	......	......	......	......	......	G.
Wm. Bowen Mends	19 Mar. 49.	21 Aug. 51.	12 Jan. 54.	31 Jan. 56.	......	......	......	......	......	G.
Geo. Ferguson	4 May 49.	......	......	......	......	......	......	......	......	G.
Sir Geo. Rose Sartorius	9 May 49.	19 Jan. 52.	21 Jan. 54.	31 Jan. 56.	9 Jul. 57.	20 Jan. 58.	11 Feb. 61.	10 Nov. 62.	.. ...	C.
Robt. Wauchope	21 May 49.	8 Mar. 52.	27 Jan. 54.	21 Jul. 56.	30 Jul. 57.	11 Feb. 58.	29 Jul. 61.	......	......	......
Sir John Gordon Sinclair, aft. bt.	8 Jun. 49.	4 Jun. 52.	11 Feb. 54.	17 Oct. 56.	22 Aug. 57.	13 Feb. 58.	5 Aug. 61,	23 Mar. 63.	......	......
Geo. Edwd. Watts	1 Sep. 49	......	......	......	......	......	......	......	......	G.
Sir Jas. John Gordon Bremer, K.C.B.	15 Sep. 49.	......	......	......	......	......	......	......	......	......
Ralph Randolph Wormeley ...	9 Oct. 49.	......	......	......	......	......	......	......	......	......
Hayes O'Grady	18 Oct. 49	......	......	......	......	......	......	......	......	G.

Name.	R.A.B.	R.A.W.	R.A.R.	V.A.B.	V.A.W.	V.A.R.	A.B.	A.W.	A.R.	Promoted in List
Maurice Fred. Fitzhardinge Berkeley, aft. sir M. and ld. Fitzhardinge	30 Oct. 49.	30 Jul. 52.	15 Apr. 54.	21 Oct. 56.	10 Sep. 57.	6 Mar. 58.	15 Jan. 62.	27 Apr. 63.	......	......
Sir David Dunn, K.C.H.	5 Nov. 49.	4 Oct. 52.	......	......	......	......	......	......	......	G.
Fairfax Moresby, C.B., aft. sir F.	24 Dec. 49.	8 Oct. 52.	26 May 54.	12 Nov. 56.	10 Sep. 57.	25 Jun. 58.	12 Apr. 62.	27 Apr. 63.	......	C.
Geo Anson, ld. Byron	24 Dec. 49.	... ..	......	......	......	......	......	......	......	G.
Sir Edmd. Lyons, bt., G.C.B., K.C.H., aft. ld. Lyons	14 Jan. 50.	26 Oct. 52.	11 Sep. 54.	19 Mar. 57.	2 Oct. 57.	......	......	......	......	......
Sir Chas. Sullivan, bt.	15 Feb. 50.	,,	27 Oct. 54	12 May 57.	28 Nov. 57.	2 May 60.	20 May 62.	......	......	......
Sir John Marshall, C.B., K.C.H. ...	27 Mar. 50.	.....	......	......	......	......	......	......	......	......
Jas. Erskine Wemyss	21 Jun. 50.	......	......	......	......	......	......	......	... ..	......
Fras. Erskine Loch	2 Sep. 50.	17 Dec. 52.	7 Feb. 55.	14 May 75.	8 Dec. 57.	9 Jun. 60.	16 Jun. 62.	......	......	......
Edwd. Collier	1 Oct. 50.	5 Mar. 53.	3 Jul. 55.	18 Jun. 57.	......	......	......	......	......	G.
David Price	6 Nov. 50.	2 Apr. 53.	......	......	......	......	......	......	......	......
Algn., D. of Northumberland ...	11 Nov. 50.	......	......	......	......	......	......	......	......	G.
John Toup Nicolas, C.B., K.H. ...	30 Dec. 50.	......	......	......	......	......	......	......	......	......
Wm. Willmott Henderson, C.B., K.H.	21 Mar. 51.	22 Apr. 53.	......	......	......	......	......	......	......	......
Sir John Hill	2 Apr. 51.	28 May 53.	......	......	......	......	......	......	......	......
John Carter	8 Apr. 51.	......	......	......	......	......	......	......	......	G.
Hy. Meynell	29 Apr. 51.	......	.. ...	......	......	......	......	......	......	G.
Arth. Fanshawe, C.B., aft. sir A.	11 Jun. 51.	4 Jul. 53.	4 Jul. 55.	9 Jul. 57.	5 Jan. 58.	1 Nov. 60.	4 Oct. 62.	24 Nov. 63.	......	......
Houston Stewart, C.B., aft. sir H.	16 Jun. 51.	17 Sep. 53.	9 Jul. 55.	30 Jul. 57.	20 Jan. 58.	7 Nov. 60.	10 Nov. 62.	14 Nov. 63.	......	B.
Sir Jas. Stirling	8 Jul. 51.	17 Nov. 53.	27 Sep. 65.	22 Aug. 57.	11 Feb. 58.	11 Feb. 61.	22 Nov. 62.	3 Dec. 63.	......	......
Ld John Hay	21 Aug. 51	......	......	......	......	......	......	......	......	......
Provo Wm. Parry Wallis, aft. sir P.	27 Aug. 51.	5 Dec. 53.	3 Oct. 55.	10 Sep. 57.	13 Feb. 58.	29 Jul. 61.	21 Mar. 63.	11 Jan. '64.	......	C.
Wm. Walpole	19 Jan. 52.	12 Jan. 54.	30 Nov. 55.	,,	......	......	......	......	......	G.
Armar Lowry Corry	8 Mar. 52.	21 Jan. 54.	......	......	......	......	......	......	......	......
Sir Wm. Edwd. Parry	4 Jun. 52.	27 Jan. 54.	......	......	......	......	......	......	......	......
Hy. Wm. Bruce, aft. sir H. ...	30 Jul. 52.	11 Feb. 54.	28 Dec. 55.	2 Oct. 57.	6 Mar. 58.	5 Aug. 61.	27 Apr. 63.	......	......	......
Wm. Jas. Mingaye	1 Oct. 52.	15 Apr. 54.	31 Jan. 56.	4 Nov. 57.	25 Jun. 58.	......	......	......	......	G.
Jas. Hanway Plumridge, aft sir J.	8 Oct. 52.	26 May 54.	,,	28 Nov. 57.	24 Nov. 58.	15 Jan. 62.	27 Apr. 63.	......	......	......
Sir John Franklin, K.C.H. ...	26 Oct. 52.	......	......	......	......	......	......	......	......	......
Sir Thos. Herbert, K.C.B. ...	......	13 Jul. 54.	31 Jan. 56.	8 Dec. 57.	16 May 59.	......	......	......	......	......

Name.	R.A.B.	R.A.W.	R.A.R.	V.A.B.	V.A.W.	V.A.R.	A.B.	A.W.	A.R.	Promoted in List
Hon. Hy. John Rous	17 Dec. 52.	11 Sep. 54.	21 Jul. 56.	5 Jan. 58.	2 May 60.	12 Apr. 62.	25 Jun. 63.	15 Jun. 64.	......	......
Edwd. Boxer, C.B.	5 Mar. 53.	27 Oct. 54.	......	......	......	......	......	......	......	......
Geo. Fredk. Rich...	2 Apr. 53.	24 Nov. 54.	17 Oct. 56.	20 Jan. 58.	......	......	......	......	......	G.
Wm. Jas. Hope Johnstone, aft. sir W.	22 Apr. 53.	22 Jan. 55.	21 Oct. 56.	11 Feb. 58.	9 Jun. 60.	20 May 62.	24 Nov. 63.	......	......	C.
Wm. Fanshawe Martin, aft. sir W.	28 May 53.	7 Feb. 55.	12 Nov. 56.	13 Feb. 58.	1 Nov. 60.	16 Jun. 62	14 Nov. 63.	......	......	C.
Hon. Richd. Saunders Dundas, C.B., aft. sir R.	4 Jul. 53.	2 May 55.	19 May 57.	1 Mar. 58.	7 Nov. 60.	......	......	......	......	......
Ld. Adolph. FitzClarence, G.C.H.	17 Sep. 53.	6 Jun. 55.	......	......	......	......	......	......	......	......
Hy. Dundas	17 Nov. 53	3 Jul. 55.	12 May 57.	6 Mar. 58.	11 Feb. 61.	4 Oct. 62.	......	......	......	......
Hon. Montagu Stopford, aft. sir M.	5 Dec. 53.	4 Jul. 55.	14 May 57.	25 Jun. 58.	4 Jun. 61.	10 Nov. 62.	30 Nov. 63.	......	......	......
Hy. Ducie Chads, C.B., aft. sir H.	12 Jan. 54.	9 Jul. 55.	18 Jun. 57.	24 Nov. 58.	29 Jul. 61.	22 Nov. 62.	3 Dec. 63.	......	......	......
Sir Geo. Robt. Lambert, K.C.B...	21 Jan. 54.	,,	9 Jul. 57.	16 May 59.	5 Aug. 61.	23 Mar. 63.	15 Dec. 63.	......	......	......
Alexr. Thos. Emeric Vidal ...	27 Jan. 54.	27 Sep. 55.	30 Jul. 57.	27 Jun. 59.	,,	......	......	......	......	......
John Leith	11 Feb. 54.	......	......	......	......	......	......	......	......	......
Chas. Hope	1 Apr. 54.	......	......	27 Feb. 60.	......	......	......	......	......	......
Hy. John Leeke aft. sir H. ...	15 Apr. 54.	......	......	2 May 60.	15 Jan. 62.	27 Apr. 63.	11 Jan. 64.	......	......	......
Chas. Howe Fremantle, aft. sir C.	15 Apr. 54.	......	22 Aug. 57,	9 Jun. 60.	12 Apr. 62.	23 Mar. 63.	9 Feb. 64.	......	......	......
Michl. Seymour, aft. sir M. ...	26 May 54.	30 Nov. 55.	10 Sep. 57.	1 Nov. 60.	20 May 62.	25 Jun. 63.	5 Mar. 64.	......	......	C.
Hy. Byam Martin, C.B., aft. sir H.	13 Jul. 54.	28 Dec. 55.	,,	7 Nov. 60.	16 Jun. 62.	12 Sep. 63.	15 Jun. 64.	......	......	......
Hy. Eden	7 Aug. 54.	31 Jan. 56.	2 Oct. 57.	11 Feb. 61.	4 Oct. 62.	24 Nov. 63.	......	......	......	E.
Fredk. Wm. Beechey	11 Sep. 54.	,,	......	......	......	......	......	......	......	......
Jas. Scott, C.B., aft. sir J. ...	26 Oct. 54.	,,	4 Nov. 57.	4 Jun. 61.	10 Nov. 62.	14 Nov. 63.	......	......	......	E.
Wm. Sandom	27 Oct. 54.	19 May 56.	28 Nov. 57.	......	......	......	......	......	......	......
Geo. Wm. Conway Courtenay ...	24 Nov. 54.	21 Jul. 56.	8 Dec. 57.	29 Jul. 61.	22 Nov. 62.	......	......	......	......	......
Hon. Fredc. Wm. Grey, C.B., aft. sir F.	22 Jan. 55.	17 Oct. 56.	5 Jan. 58.	5 Aug. 61.	6 Feb. 63.	30 Nov. 63.	......	......	......	E.
Robt. Lambert Baynes, C.B., aft. sir R.	7 Feb. 55.	21 Oct. 56.	20 Jan 58.	,,	23 Mar. 63.	3 Dec. 63.	......	......	......	E.
Thos. Bennett	2 May 55.	12 Nov. 56.	11 Feb. 58.	15 Jan. 62.	1 Apr. 63.	......	......	......	......	G.
Peter Richards, C.B.	6 Jun. 55.	1 Dec. 56.	......	......	......	......	......	......	......	G.
Hy. Smith, C.B.	3 Jul. 55.	14 Feb. 57.	13 Feb. 58.	12 Apr. 62.	27 Apr. 63.	15 Dec. 63.	......	......	......	E.
Steph. Lushington, aft. sir S. [illegible]	[illegible]	19 Mar. 57.	1 Mar. 58.	......	......	......	......	......	......	G.

Name.	R.A.B.	R.A.W.	R.A.R.	V.A.B.	V.A.W.	V.A.R.	A.B.	A.W.	A.R.	Promoted in List
Jno. Alexr. Duntze	9 Jul. 55.	12 May 57.	6 Mar. 58.	20 May 62.	27 Apr. 63.	11 Jan. 64.	......	......	......	E.
Fred. Thos. Michell, C.B. ...	,,	14 May 57.	25 Jun. 58.	16 Jun. 62.	25 Jun. 63.	9 Feb. 64.	......	......	......	E.
Sir Thos. Hastings, C.B.... ...	27 Sep. 55.	18 Jun. 57.	24 Nov. 58.	4 Oct. 62.	12 Sep. 63.	5 Mar. 64.	......	......	......	......
Charles Ramsay Drinkwater Bethune, C.B.	3 Oct. 55.	9 Jul. 57.	16 May 59.	10 Nov. 62.	24 Nov. 63.	15 Jun. 64.	......	......	......	E.
Chas. Graham, C.B.	30 Nov. 55.	30 Jul. 57.	......	......	......	......	......	......	......	......
Chas. Talbot, aft. sir C.... ...	28 Dec. 55.	22 Aug. 57.	27 Jun. 59.	22 Nov. 62.	3 Nov. 63.	......	......	......	......	E.
Thos. Wren Carter, C.B. ...	31 Jan. 56.	10 Sep. 57.	2 May 60.	6 Feb. 63.	14 Nov. 63.	......	......	......	......	F.
Sir Thos. Sabine Pasley, bt. ...	,,	,,	9 Jun. 60.	23 Mar. 63.	30 Nov. 63.	......	......	......	......	E.
Christr. Wyvill	,,	2 Oct. 57.	1 Nov. 60.	......	......	......	......	......	......	......
Hy. Fras. Greville, C.B.	19 May 56.	4 Nov. 57.	7 Nov. 60.	1 Apr. 63.	......	......	......	......	......	......
Lord Geo. Paulet	21 Jul. 56.	19 Nov. 57.	11 Feb. 61.	3 Apr. 63.	3 Dec. 63.	......	......	......	......	F.
Lord Edwd. Russell, C.B. ...	17 Oct. 56.	28 Nov. 57.	4 Jun. 61.	27 Apr. 63.	15 Dec. 63.	......	......	......	......	E.
Hy. Wolsey Bayfield	21 Oct. 56.	8 Dec. 57.	29 Jul. 61.	,,	11 Jan. 64.	......	......	......	......	F.
Hon. Geo. Grey	12 Nov. 56.	5 Jan. 58.	5 Aug. 61.	25 Jun. 63.	9 Feb. 64.	......	......	......	......	F.
Sir Jas. Clarke Ross	1 Dec. 56.	20 Jan. 58.	,,	......	......	......	......	......	......	......
Jos. Nias, C.B., aft. sir J. ...	14 Feb. 57.	11 Feb. 58.	15 Jan. 62.	12 Sep. 63.	5 Mar. 64.	......	......	......	......	F.
Hy. Jno. Codrington, C.B., aft. sir H.	19 Mar. 57	13 Feb. 58.	4 Apr. 62.	14 Nov. 63.	15 Jun. 64.	......	......	......	......	E.
Jno. M'Dougall, aft. sir J. ...	12 May 57.	1 Mar. 58.	12 Apr. 62.	3 Nov. 63.	......	......	......	......	......	......
Michl. Quin	14 May 57.	6 Mar. 58.	19 May 62.	14 Nov. 63.	......	......	......	......	......	G.
Sir Thos. Maitland, C.B., aft. E. of Lauderdale	18 Jun. 57.	21 Jun. 58.	20 May 62.	30 Nov. 63.	......	......	......	......	......	E.
Robt. Smart, K.H., aft. sir R. ...	9 Jul. 57.	24 Nov. 58.	16 Jun. 62.	3 Dec. 63.	......	......	......	......	......	E.
Geo. Rodney Mundy	30 Jul. 57.	16 May 59.	4 Oct. 62.	15 Dec. 63.	......	......	......	......	......	E.
Hon. Hy. Keppel, C.B., aft. sir H.	22 Aug. 57.	27 Jun. 59.	10 Nov. 62.	11 Jan. 64.	......	......	......	......	......	E.
Jno. Jervis Tucker	10 Sep. 57.	2 May 60.	22 Nov. 62.	9 Feb. 64.	......	......	......	......	......	G.
Jno. Kingcome, aft. sir J. ...	,,	9 Jun. 60.	30 Jan. 63.	5 Mar. 64.	......	......	......	......	......	F.
Fredk. Bullock	12 Oct. 57.	1 Nov. 60.	6 Feb. 63.	28 Mar. 64.	......	......	......	......	......	......
Jno. Elphinstone Erskine ...	4 Nov. 57.	7 Nov. 60.	23 Mar. 63.	15 Jun. 64.	......	......	......	......	......	E.
Jas. Hope, C.B., aft. sir J. ...	19 Nov. 57.	11 Feb. 61.	1 Apr. 63.		......	......	......	......	......	E.
Horatio Thos. Austin, C.B. ...	28 Nov. 57.	4 Jun. 61.	3 Apr 63.	......	......	......	......	......	......	E.
Wm. Ramsey, C.B., aft. sir W. ...	8 Dec. 57.	29 Jul. 61.	27 Apr. 63.	......	......	......	......	......	......	E.

Name.	R.A.B.	R.A.W.	R.A.R.	V.A.B.	V.A.W.	V.A.R.	A.B.	A.W.	A.R.	Promoted in List
Sir Baldwin Wake Walker. bt., K.C.B.	5 Jan. 58.	5 Aug. 61.	27 Apr. 63.	......	......	......	......	......	......	E.
Alexr. Milne, aft. sir A.... ...	20 Jan. 58.	,,	25 Jun. 63.	......	......	......	......	......	......	E.
Lord Clarence Edwd. Paget, C.B.	11 Feb. 58.	15 Jan. 62.	12 Sep. 63.	......	......	......	......	......	......	E.
Richd. Laird Warren	13 Feb. 58.	4 Apr. 62.	24 Nov. 63.	......	......	......	......	......	......	E.
Geo. Elliot	1 Mar. 58.	12 Apr. 62.	3 Nov. 63	......	......	......	......	......	......	E.
Hon. Fred. Thos. Pelham, C.B.	6 Mar. 58.	......	......	......	......	......	......	......	......	......
Sidney Colpoys Dacres, C.B., aft. sir S.	25 Jun. 58.	19 May 62.	14 Nov. 63.	......	......	......	......	......	......	E.
John Shepherd	24 Nov. 58.	20 May 62.	......	......	......	......	......	......	......	......
Thos. Henderson...	16 May 59.	16 Jun. 62.	30 Nov. 63.	......	......	......	......	......	......	......
Lewis Tobias Jones, C.B., aft. sir L.	27 Jun. 59.	4 Oct. 62.	3 Dec. 63.	......	......	......	......	......	......	E.
Robt. Fanshawe Stopford ...	2 May 60.	10 Nov. 62.	15 Dec. 63.	......	......	......	......	......	......	E.
Robt. Spencer Robinson, aft. sir R.	9 Jun. 60.	22 Nov. 62.	11 Jan. 64.	......	......	......	......	......	......	E.
Thos. Matth. Chas. Symonds, C.B., aft. sir T.	1 Nov. 60.	30 Jan. 63.	9 Feb. 64.	......	......	......	......	......	......	E.
Thos. Leeke Massey	7 Nov. 60.	6 Feb. 63.	5 Mar. 64.	......	......	......	......	......	......	F.
Sir Edwd. Belcher, C.B.... ...	11 Feb. 61.	23 Mar. 63.	28 Mar. 64.	......	......	......	......	......	......	F.
Jas. John Stopford	4 Jun. 61.	1 Apr. 63.	15 Jun. 64.	......	......	......	......	......	......	E.
Woodford, John Williams ...	22 Jun. 61.	3 Apr. 63.	......	......	......	......	......	......	......	E.
Augs. Leopold Kuper, C.B., aft. sir A.	29 Jul. 61.	,,	......	......	......	......	......	......	......	E.
Chas. Eden, C.B.	5 Aug. 61.	27 Apr. 63.	......	......	......	......	......	......	......	E.
Hon. Chas. Gilbert John Brydone Elliott, C.B.	,,	,,	......	......	......	......	......	......	......	E.
Hon. Jos. Denman	15 Jan. 62.	25 Jun. 63.	......	......	......	......	......	......	......	E.
Geo. St. Vincent King, C.B., aft. sir G.	4 Apr. 62.	12 Sep. 63.	......	......	......	......	......	......	......	E.
Edwd. Pellew Halsted	12 Apr. 62.	24 Nov. 63.	......	......	......	......	......	......	......	E.
Geo. Goldsmith	19 May 62.	3 Nov. 63.	......	......	......	......	......	......	......	F.

Name.	R.A.B.	R.A.W.	R.A.R.	V.A.B.	V.A.W.	V.A.R.	A.B.	A.W.	A.R.	Promoted in List
Hy. Kellett, C.B.	16 Jun. 62.	30 Nov. 63.	......	......	......	......	......	......	......	F.
Wm. Hy. Anderson Morshead, C.B.	4 Oct. 62.	3 Dec. 63.	......	......	......	......	......	......	......	E.
Richd. Collinson, C.B., aft. sir R.	10 Nov. 62.	15 Dec. 63.	......	......	......	......	......	......	......	E.
Geo. Ramsay, C.B., aft. E. of Dalhousie	22 Nov. 62.	11 Jan. 64.	......	......	......	......	......	......	......	E.
Hastings Regd. Yelverton ...	30 Jan. 63.	9 Feb. 64.	......	......	......	......	......	......	......	E.
John Adams	6 Feb. 63.	5 Mar. 64	......	......	......	......	......	......	......	......
Geo. Hy. Seymour	23 Mar. 63.	28 Mar. 64.	......	......	......	......	......	......	......	E.
Fredk. Hutton	1 Apr. 63.	15 Jun. 64.	......	......	......	......	......	......	......	......
Wm. Hutcheon Hall, C.B., aft. sir W.	3 Apr. 63.	......	......	......	......	......	......	......	......	F.
Geo. Greville Wellesley, C.B. ...	,,	......	......	......	......	......	......	......	......	E.
Hon Geo. Fowler Hastings, C.B.	27 Apr. 63.	......	......	......	......	......	......	......	......	E.
Hon. Swynfen Thos. Carnegie ...	,,	......	......	......	......	......	......	......	......	E.
Hy. Lyster	25 Jun. 63.	......	......	......	......	......	......	......	......	......
Fredk. Warden, C.B.	12 Sep. 63.	......	......	......	......	......	......	......	......	......
Edwd. Gennys Fanshawe ...	3 Nov. 63.	......	......	......	......	......	......	......	......	E.
Claude Hy. Mason Buckle, C.B...	14 Nov. 63.	......	......	......	......	......	......	......	......	F.
Arth. Lowe	24 Nov. 63	......	......	......	......	......	......	......	......	F.
Hon Thos. Baillie	30 Nov. 63.	......	......	......	......	......	......	......	......	E.
Geo. Giffard, C.B.	3 Dec. 63.	......	......	......	......	......	......	......	......	F.
Sir Fredk. Wm. Erskine Nicholson, bt., C.B.	15 Dec. 63.	......	......	......	......	......	......	......	......	E.
Hon. Jas. Robt. Drummond, C.B., aft. sir J.	11 Jan. 64.	......	......	......	......	......	......	......	......	E.
John Lort Stokes...	9 Feb. 64.	......	......	......	......	......	......	......	......	F.
Hy. Mangles Denham, aft. sir H.	5 Mar. 64.	......	......	......	......	......	......	......	......	F.
Arth. Forbes	28 Mar. 64.	......	......	......	......	......	......	......	......	F.
Hy. Edmd. Edgell	15 Jun. 64.	......	......	......	......	......	......	......	......	F.

By Order in Council dated July 9, and gaz. Oct. 18, 1864, the division of the fleet into Red, White, and Blue Squadrons was discontinued, and a uniform flag adopted.

LIST E.

ADMIRALS ON THE ACTIVE LIST.

From the discontinuance of the division of the Fleet into Red, White, and Blue Squadrons in 1864 to the present time.

See note at foot of List D, *ante*, p. 833.

Name.	Continued from List	V.-Adm.	Adm.	Continued in List
Hy. Eden	D.	......	16 Sep. 64.	...
Sir Jas. Scott	D.	......	10 Feb. 65.	...
Hon. sir Fredc. Wm. Grey, C.B.	D.	......	24 Apr. 65.	...
Sir Robt. Lambert Baynes	D.	......	5 May 65.	...
Hy. Smith, C.B.	D.	......	12 Sep. 65.	...
John Alexr. Duntze	D.	......	2 Dec. 65.	...
Chas. Ramsay Drinkwater Bethune ...	D.	......	2 Apr. 66.	...
Sir Chas. Talbot, K.C.B.	D.	......	,,	...
Sir Thos. Sabine Pasley, bt...	D.	......	20 Nov. 66.	...
Lord Edwd. Russell	D.	......	20 Mar. 67.	...
Sir Hy. John Codrington, K.C.B.	D.	......	18 Oct. 67.	B.
Thos., E. of Lauderdale	D.	......	8 Apr. 68.	B.
Sir Robt. Smart, K.H.	D.	......	15 Jan. 69.	...
Geo. Rodney Mundy	D.	......	26 May 69.	B.
Hon. sir Hy. Keppel, K.C.B....	D.	......	2 Jul. 69.	B.
John Elphinstone Erskine	D.	......	10 Sep. 69.	...
Sir Jas. Hope, K.C.B.	D.	16 Sep. 64.	21 Jan. 70.	B.
Horatio Thos. Austin, C.B.	D.	20 Oct. 64.	......	...
Wm. Ramsey, C.B.	D.	12 Nov. 64.	......	F.
Sir Baldwin Wake Walker, bt., K.C.B. ...	D.	10 Feb. 65.	27 Feb. 70.	...
Sir Alexr. Milne	D.	13 Apr. 65.	1 Apr. 70.	B.
Lord Clarence Edwd. Paget	D.	24 Apr. 65.	,,	...
Richd. Laird Warren...	D.	5 May 65.	,,	...
Geo. Elliot	D.	12 Sep. 65.	,,	...
Sir Sidney Colpoys Dacres	D.	17 Nov. 65.	,,	...
Sir Lewis Tobias Jones	D.	2 Dec. 65.	......	F.
Robt. Fanshawe Stopford	D.	2 Apr. 66.	......	F.
Robt. Spencer Robinson, aft. sir R... ...	D.	,,	......	F.
Thos. Matth. Chas. Symonds, C.B., aft. sir T.	D.	,,	14 Jul. 71.	B.
Jas. John Stopford	D.	,,	......	...
Woodford John Williams	D.	,,	......	F.
Sir Augs. Leop. Kuper	D.	6 Apr. 66.	20 Oct. 72.	...
Chas. Eden, C.B.	D.	,,	......	F.
Hon. Chas. Gilbert John Brydone Elliott, C.B.	D.	,,	8 Feb. 73.	B.
Hon. Jos. Denman	D.	20 Nov. 66.	......	...
Sir Geo. St. Vincent King	D.	20 Mar. 67.	20 Apr. 75.	...
Edwd. Pellew Halsted	D.	24 May 67.	......	...
Chas. Frederick	D.	18 Oct. 67.	......	F.
Hy. Kellett, C.B.	D.	8 Apr. 68.	......	...
Wm. Hy. Anderson Morshead, C.B.... ...	D.	15 Jan. 69.	......	F.
Richd. Collinson, C.B.	D	17 Mar. 69.	......	F.
Geo. Ramsay, C.B., aft. 12th E. of Dalhousie	D.	,,	......	F.
Hastings Regd. Yelverton	D.	26 May 69.	30 Jul. 75.	...
Geo. Hy. Seymour	D.	2 Jul. 69.	......	...
Geo. Greville Wellesley, C.B.	D.	26 Jul. 69.	11 Dec. 75.	...
Hon. Geo. Fowler Hastings, C.B.	D	10 Sep. 69.	......	...
Hon. Swynfen Thos. Carnegie	D.	21 Jan. 70.	......	F.
Edwd. Gennys Fanshawe	D.	1 Apr. 70.	18 Jan. 76.	..
Arth. Lowe	D.	27 Feb. 70.	......	F.
Hon. Thos. Baillie	D.	1 Apr. 70.	......	F
Sir Fredk. Wm. Erskine Nicolson, bt., C.B.	D.	,,	......	F
Hon. sir Jas. Robt. Drummond, K.C.B. ...	D.	2 Jun. 70.	22 Jan. 77.	...

Name.	R.-Adm.	V.-Adm.	Adm.	Continued in List
Fred. Hy. Hastings Glasse, C.B.	16 Sep. 64.	......	.. ...	F.
Chas. Gepp Robinson...	20 Oct. 64.	......	......	F.
Geo. Thos. Gordon	28 Oct. 64.	......	......	F.
Erasmus Ommaney	12 Nov. 64.	14 Jul. 71.	......	F.
Douglas Curry	10 Feb. 65.	......	......	...
Geo. Wm. Douglas O'Callaghan	11 Apr. 65.	......	......	F.
Chas. Wise	13 Apr. 65.	......	......	F.
Thos. Pickering Thompson	24 Apr. 65.	......	......	F.
Wallace Houstoun	5 May 65.	......	......	F.
Wm. John Cavendish Clifford, C.B., aft. bt.	12 Sep. 65.	1 Oct. 71.	......	F.
Thos. Fisher	17 Nov. 65.	......	......	F.
Thos. Harvey	2 Dec. 65.	......	......	...
Wm. Loring, C.B., aft. sir W.	7 Mar. 66.	2 Nov. 71.	1 Aug. 77.	...
Sir Wm. Hoste, bt.	2 Apr. 66.	......	......	...
John Fulford	,,	......	......	F.
Alf. Phillipps Ryder	,,	7 May 72.	5 Aug. 77.	B.
Hy. Chads, aft. sir H.	,,	20 Oct. 72.	16 Sep. 77.	...
Fras. Scott	,,	8 Feb. 73.	......	...
Sir Adolphus Slade, K.C.B.	,,	......	......	F.
Arth. Farquhar	,,	6 Apr. 73.	9 Mar. 78.	...
Edwin Clayton Tennyson D'Eyncourt ...	,,	......	......	F.
Thos. Hy. Mason	,,	......	......	F.
Sidney Grenfell	6 Apr. 66.	......	......	F.
Richd. Strode Hewlett, C.B.	,,	......	......	F.
Sir John Chas. Dalrymple Hay, bt... ...	,,	......	......	F.
Jas. Horsford Cockburn	,,	......	......	...
Jas. Willcox, C.B.	,,	......	......	F.
Hugh Dunlop, C.B.	,,	......	......	F.
Astley Cooper Key, aft. sir A.	20 Nov. 66.	30 Apr. 73.	21 Mar. 78.	...
Fredk. Byng Montresor	20 Mar. 67.	......	......	F.
Chas. Farrel Hillyar	24 May 67.	29 May 73.	26 Sep. 78.	...
Edwd. Codd	,,	......	......	F.
Thos. Hope	31 May 67.	......	......	...
Edwd. Southwell Sotheby, C.B.	1 Sep. 67.	......	......	F.
Michl. De Courcy	18 Oct. 67.	......	......	F
John Walter Tarleton, C.B., aft. sir J. ...	8 Apr. 68.	25 Aug. 73.	......	F.
Lord Fredc. Herbert Kerr	9 Apr. 68.	......	......	F.
Edmd. Heathcote	1 Jan. 69.	1 Jan. 74.	......	F.
Geoffr. Thos. Phipps Hornby, aft. sir G ...	,,	1 Jan. 75.	15 Jun. 79.	B.
Chas. Fred. Alexr. Shadwell, C.B., aft. sir C.	15 Jan. 69.	20 Apr. 75.	2 Aug. 79.	...
Wm. King Hall, C.B., aft. sir W.	17 Mar. 69.	30 Jul. 75.	2 Aug. 79.	...
Thos. Wilson, C.B	,,	......	......	F.
Edwd. Augs. Inglefield, aft. sir E.... ...	26 May 69.	11 Dec. 75.	27 Nov. 79.	...
Wm. Edmonstone, C.B., aft. bt.	2 Jul. 69.	......	......	F.
Jas. Fras. Ballard Wainwright	26 Jul. 69.	......	......	
Jas. Newburgh Strange	10 Sep. 69.	......	......	F.
Jas. Chas. Prevost	16 Sep. 69.	......	......	F.
Sir Wm. Saltonstall Wiseman, bt., K.C.B. ...	12 Nov. 69.	......	......	...
Jas. Aylmer Paynter	21 Jan. 70.	......	......	F.
Arth. Cumming, C.B.	27 Feb. 70.	22 Mar. 76.	9 Jan. 80.	...
Arth. Parry Eardley Wilmot, C.B.	1 Apr. 70.	......	......	F.
Robt. Coote	,,	18 Jun. 76.	3 Jan. 81.	...
John Bourmaster Dickson	,,	......	......	...
Wm. Houston Stewart, C.B., aft. sir W. ...	,,	12 Nov. 76.	23 Nov. 81.	...
Hon. Arth. Auckland Leop. Pedro Cochrane, C.B.	,,	12 Nov. 76.	1 Dec. 81.	...
Fredk. Archd. Campbell	,,	......	......	...

Name.	R.-Adm.	V.-Adm.	Adm.	Continued in List
Fred. Beauchamp Paget Seymour, C.B., aft. sir F. and ld. Alcester	1 Apr. 70.	31 Dec. 76.	6 May 82	...
Hon. John Welbore Sunderland Spencer	,,	......	......	F.
Regd. John Jas. Geo. Macdonald, aft. Macdonald-Blomfield and sir R.	1 Apr. 70.	22 Jan. 77.	9 Jun. 82.	...
Geo. Hy. Richards, aft. sir G.	2 Jun. 70.	......	......	F.
Sir Fras. Leopold McClintock	1 Oct. 71.	5 Aug. 77.	7 Jul. 84.	...
Sir Leopold Geo. Heath, K.C.B.	20 Dec. 71.	......	......	F.
Hy. Schank Hillyar, C.B.	11 Feb. 72.	16 Sep. 77.	......	F.
Geo. Granville Randolph, C.B.	24 Apr. 72.	,,	......	F.
Lord John Hay, C.B.	7 May 72.	31 Dec. 77.	8 Jul. 84.	B.
Geo. Hancock	20 Oct. 72.	......	......	...
Hon. Fras. Egerton	8 Feb. 73.	......	......	F.
Edw. Bridges Rice	12 Feb. 73.	9 Mar. 78.	27 Oct. 84.	...
Thos. Miller	6 Apr. 73.	21 Mar. 78.	......	F.
Hon. Geo. Disney Keane, C.B.	30 Apr. 73.	......	......	F.
Sherard Osborn, C.B.	29 May 73.	......	......	...
Rowley Lambert, C.B.	25 Aug. 73.	21 Mar. 78.	......	...
Augs. Phillimore, aft. sir A.	1 Jan. 74.	30 Jan. 79.	30 Oct. 84.	...
Wm. Chas. Chamberlain	19 Jan. 74.	.. ...	......	...
Geo. Ommanney Willes, C.B., aft. sir G.	11 Jun. 74.	1 Feb. 79.	27 Mar. 85.	...
Wm. Garnham Luard, C.B.	1 Jan. 75.	15 Jun. 79.	31 Mar. 85.	...
John Corbett, C.B.	20 Apr. 75.	2 Aug. 79.	7 Apr. 85.	...
Edwd. Winterton Turnour, C.B.	25 Apr. 75.	9 Sep. 79.	......	F.
Algn. Fred. Rous De Horsey	7 May 75.	27 Nov. 79.	29 Apr. 85.	...
Hy. Boys	30 Jul. 75.	9 Jan. 80.	1 Jun. 85.	...
Robt. Jenkins, C.B.	4 Nov. 75.	......	......	F.
Wm. Montague Dowell, C.B., aft. sir W.	11 Dec. 75.	20 Jan. 80.	1 Jul. 85.	...
Arth. Wm. Acland Hood, C.B., aft. sir A.	22 Mar. 76.	23 Jul. 80.	18 Jan. 86.	...
Chas. Fellowes, C.B.	18 Jun. 76.	31 Dec. 80.	......	...
Chas. Wake	21 Sep. 76.	3 Jan. 81.	......	F.
Sir John Edmd. Commerell, K.C.B., V.C.	12 Nov. 76.	19 Jan. 81.	12 Apr. 86.	...
Richd. Jas., ld. Gilford, aft. E. of Clanwilliam	31 Dec. 76.	26 Jul. 81.	22 Jun. 86.	...
Hon. Fitzgerald Algn. Chas. Foley	,,	23 Nov. 81.	......	F.
Ernest, &c., pr. of Leiningen, G.C.B.	,,	1 Dec. 81.	7 Jul. 87.	...
Fred. Hy. Stirling	22 Jan. 77.	31 Dec. 81.	......	...
Chas. Webley Hope	1 Aug. 77.	......	......	...
Wm. Gore Jones, C.B.	5 Aug. 77.	6 May 82.	15 Jul. 87.	...
Hon. Hy. Carr Glyn, C.B., C.S.I.	16 Sep. 77.	9 Jun. 82.	......	...
Richd. Vesey Hamilton, aft. sir R.	27 Sep. 77.	17 Feb. 84	18 Oct. 87.	...
Chas. Ludovic Darley Waddilove	31 Dec. 77.	1 Apr. 84.	1 May 88.	...
John Dobree McCrea	,,	.....	......	...
Leveson Eliot Hy. Somerset	28 Feb. 78.	7 Jul. 84.	19 Jun. 88.	...
John Eglinton Montgomorie	9 Mar. 78.	......	......	F.
Sir Wm. Nathan Wrighte Hewett, K.C.B., V.C.	21 Mar. 78.	8 Jul. 84.	......	...
Algn. McLellan Lyons	26 Sep. 78.	27 Oct. 84.	15 Dec. 88	...
Alf. Ern. Alb., D. of Edinburgh	30 Dec. 78.	30 Nov. 82.	18 Oct. 87.	...
Thos. Brandreth	31 Dec. 78.	30 Oct. 84.	......	...
Thos. Bridgeman Lethbridge	,,	27 Mar. 85.	......	...
Fras. Wm. Sullivan, C.B., C.M.G., aft. sir F.	,,	31 Mar. 85.	......	...
Edwd. Hardinge, C.B.	30 Jan. 79.	7 Apr. 85.	......	...
Wm. Graham, C.B.	1 Feb. 79.	29 Apr. 85.	......	...
Anthy. Hiley Hoskins, C.B., aft. sir A.	15 Jun. 79.	1 Jun. 85.	......	...
Nowell Salmon, V.C., C.B.	2 Aug. 79.	1 Jul. 85.	......	...
John Clark Soady	9 Sep. 79.	24 Nov. 85.	......	...
Edw. Henry Howard	27 Nov. 79.	26 Nov. 85.	......	...

Name.	R.-Adm.	V.-Adm.	Adm.	Continued in List
John Kennedy Erskine Baird	31 Dec. 79.	18 Jan. 86	......	...
Chas. Thos. Curme	1 Jan. 80.	9 Mar. 86.	......	...
Geo. Willes Watson	9 Jan. 80.	12 Apr. 86.	......	...
Hy. Dennis Hickley	20 Jan. 80.	22 Jun. 86.	......	...
Fred. Anstruther Herbert	14 Feb. 80.	......	......	...
Hy. Bourchier Phillimore	8 Apr. 80.	24 May 87.	......	...
Hon. Wm. John Ward	23 Jul. 80.	7 Jul. 87.	......	...
Hy Rushworth Wratislaw	31 Dec. 80.	15 Jul. 87.	......	...
Wm. Hy. Whyte	3 Jan. 81.	18 Oct. 87.	......	...
Hy. Duncan Grant, C.B.	19 Jan. 81.	6 Jan. 88.	......	...
John Moresby	26 Jul. 81.	1 May 88.	......	...
John Crawford Wilson	23 Nov. 81.	......	......	...
Sholto Douglas, C.B.	1 Dec. 81.	......	......	...
Wm. Hy. Edye	31 Dec. 81.	14 May 88.	......	...
Arth. Thos. Thrupp	,,	......	......	...
Sir Michl. Culme Seymour, bt.	6 May 82.	19 Jun. 88.	......	...
Sir Fredk. Wm. Richards, K.C.B.	,,	25 Oct. 88.	......	...
Ralph Peter Cator	31 Dec. 82.	......	......	...
Hon. Walter Cecil Carpenter	,,	8 Nov. 88.	......	...
Theod. Morton Jones...	,,	......	......	...
Robt. Gordon Douglas	8 Jan. 83.	15 Dec. 88.	......	...
Chas. Trelawney Jago	20 Mar. 83.	......	......	...
Wm. Saml. Brown, aft. W. S. Grieve ...	17 Feb. 84.	......	......	...
Geo. Tryon, C.B., aft. sir G.	1 Apr. 84.	......	......	...
Algern. Chas. Fieschi Heneage	7 Jul. 84.	......	......	...
Sir Walter Jas. Hunt-Grubbe, K.C.B. ...	8 Jul. 84.	......	......	...
Chas. John Rowley	27 Oct. 84.	......	......	...
Richd. Wells	30 Oct. 84.	......	......	...
Thos. Le Hunte Ward, C.B.	27 Mar. 85.	......	......	...
Wm. Arthur, C.B.	31 Mar. 85.	......	......	...
Hon. Edm. Robt. Fremantle, C.B., C.M.G. ...	7 Apr. 85.	......	......	...
John Ommaney Hopkins	29 Apr. 85.	......	......	...
Geo. Caulfield D'Arcy Irvine, C.B.	1 Jun. 85.	......	......	...
Hy. Fairfax, C.B.	1 Jul. 85.	......	......	...
Wm. Elrington Gordon	5 Jul. 85.	......	......	...
Alf. John Chatfield	1 Jan. 86.	......	......	...
Thos. Barnardiston	,,	......	......	...
Lindesay Brine	,,	......	......	...
Jas. Elphinstone Erskine	18 Jan. 86.	......	......	...
Geo. Lydiard Sulivan	9 Mar. 86.	......	......	...
Wm. Codrington, C.B.	12 Apr. 86.	......	......	...
Hy. Fredk. Nicholson, C.B.	22 Jun. 86.	......	......	...
Alexr. Buller, C.B.	1 Jan. 87.	......	......	...
Loftus Fras. Jones	,,	......	......	...
Geo. Stanley Bosanquet	,,	......	......	...
Wm. Hy. Cuming	6 Apr. 87.	......	......	...
Fras. Mowbray Prattent	24 May 87.	......	......	...
Edwd. Kelly	10 Jun. 87.	......	......	...
Fredk. Chas. Bryan Robinson	7 Jul. 87.	......	......	...
Edwd. Stanley Adeane, C.M.G.	1 Jan. 88.	......	......	...
Richd. Edwd. Tracey	,,	......	......	...
Chas. Fredk. Hotham, C.B.	6 Jan. 88.	......	......	...
Lord Chas. Thos. Montague Douglas Scott, C.B.	3 Apr. 88.	......	......	...
Sir Robt. Hy. More Molyneux, K.C.B. ...	1 May 88.	......	......	...
Robt. O'Brien Fitzroy, C.B.	14 May 88.	......	......	...
Nathl. Bowden-Smith	19 Jun. 88.	......	......	...

LIST F.

PROMOTIONS OF ADMIRALS TRANSFERRED FROM THE ACTIVE TO THE RETIRED LIST.

Under Order of 24th March 1866.

R.V.A., Retired Vice-Admiral. Retd. A., Retired Admiral.

Name.	Promoted from List	R.V.A.	Retd. A.
Thos. Wren Carter, C.B.	D.	......	20 Nov. 66.
Lord Geo. Paulet, C.B.	D.	......	20 Mar. 67.
Hy. Wolsey Bayfield	D.	......	18 Oct. 67.
Hon. Geo. Grey	D.	......	,,
Sir Jos. Nias. K.C.B.	D.	......	,,
Sir John Kingcombe, K.C.B.	D.	......	10 Sep. 69.
Sir Wm. Ramsay	E.	......	27 Feb. 70.
Sir Lewis Tobias Jones	E.	......	14 Jul. 71.
Robt. Fanshawe Stopford	E.	......	,,
Sir Robt. Spencer Robinson, K.C.B.	E.	......	,,
Thos. Leeke Massey	D.	......	20 Oct. 72.
Sir Edwd. Belcher	D.	......	,,
Woodford Jas. Williams	D.	......	,,
Chas. Eden, C.B.	E.	......	8 Feb. 73.
Geo. Goldsmith, C.B.	D.	18 Oct. 67.	30 Jul. 75.
Chas. Frederick	E.	......	,,
Wm. Hy. Anderson Morshead, C.B.	E.	......	,,
Sir Richd. Collinson, K.C.B.	E.	......	,,
Geo., 12th E. of Dalhousie	E.	......	,,
Sir Wm. Hutcheon Hall, K.C.B.	D.	26 Jul. 69.	11 Dec. 75.
Hon. Swynfen Thos. Carnegie, C.B.	E.	......	18 Jun. 76.
Arth. Lowe	E.	......	,,
Hon. Thos. Baillie	E.	......	22 Jan. 77.
Claude Hy. Mason Buckle, C.B., aft. sir C. ...	D.	1 Apr. 70.	,,
Geo. Giffard, C.B., aft. sir G.	D.	,,	,,
Sir Fredk. Wm. Erskine Nicolson, bt., C.B. ...	E.	......	,,
John Lort Stokes	D.	14 Jul. 71.	1 Aug. 77
Sir Hy. Mangles Denham	D.	,,	,,
Arth. Forbes	D.	,,	,,
Harry Edmd. Edgell	D.	,,	......
Fredk. Hy. Hastings Glasse, C.B.	E.	,,	1 Aug. 77.
Chas. Gepp Robinson	E.	,,	......
Geo. Thos. Gordon	E.	,,	1 Aug. 77
Erasmus Ommaney	E.	.....	,,
Geo. Wm. Douglas O'Callaghan, C.B.... ...	E.	1 Oct. 71.	,,
Chas. Wise	E.	,,	,,
Thos. Pickering Thompson	E.	,,	,,
Wallace Houstoun	E.	,,	,,
Sir Wm. John Cavendish Clifford, bt. C.B. ...	E.	......	,,
Thos. Fisher	E.	2 Nov. 71.	,,
John Fulford	E.	7 May 72.	5 Aug. 77.
Sir Adolph. Slade, bt., K.C.B.	E.	6 Apr. 73.	......
Edwin Clayton Tennyson D'Eyncourt ...	E.	30 Apr. 73.	21 Mar. 78.
Thos. Hy. Mason	E.	,,	,,
Sidney Grenfell, C.B.	E.	,,	,,
Richd. Strode Hewlett, C.B.	E.	,,	......
Sir John Chas. Dalrymple Hay, bt., C.B. ...	E.	,,	21 Mar. 78.
Jas. Willcox, C.B.	E.	,,	......
Hugh Dunlop, C.B.	E.	30 Apr. 73.	21 Mar. 78.

Name.	Promoted from List	R.V.A.	Retd. A.
Fredk. Byng Montresor	E.	29 May 73.	26 Sep 78.
Edwd. Codd	E.	25 Aug. 73.	,,
Edwd. Southwell Sotheby, C.B., aft. sir E. ...	E.	,,	15 Jun. 79.
Michl. De Courcy, C.B.	E.	,,	,,
Sir John Walter Tarleton, K.C.B.	E.	......	,,
Lord Fredk. Herbt. Kerr	E.	1 Jan. 74.	,,
Sir Wm. Robt. Mends (ret. r.-adm. 1 Jan. '69.*)	...	,,	,,
Edmd. Heathcote	E.	......	,,
Thos. Wilson, C.B.	E.	11 Dec. 75.	27 Nov. 79.
Sir Wm. Edmonstone, bt., C.B.	E.	22 Mar. 76.	9 Jan. 80.
Jas. Newburgh Strange	E.	,,	,,
Jas. Chas. Prevost	E.	,,	......
Jas. Aylmer Paynter	E.	,,	......
Arth. Parry Eardley-Wilmot, C.B.	E.	18 Jun. 76.	......
Hon. John Welbore Sunderland Spencer ...	E.	22 Jan. 77.	......
Sir Geo. Hy. Richards, C.B.	E.	5 Aug 77.	......
Sir Leopold Geo. Heath, K.C.B.	E.	16 Sep. 77.	8 Jul. 84.
Hy. Schank Hillyar, C.B.	E.	......	......
Geo. Granville Randolph, C.B.	E.	......	......
Hon. Fras. Egerton	E.	9 Mar. 78.	......
Thos. Miller	E.	21 Mar. 78.	30 Oct. 84.
Hon. Geo. Disney Keane	E.	,,	,,
Edwd. Winterton Turnour, C.B.	E.	......	29 Apr. 85.
Robt. Jenkins, C.B.	E.	20 Jan. 80.	1 Jul. 85.
Chas. Wake	E.	......	12 Oct. 86.
Hon. Fitzgerald Algernon Foley	E.	......	24 May 87.
John Eglinton Montgomerie, C.B.	E.	8 Jul. 84.	15 Dec. 88

* Special appointment. *See* Gazette.

LIST G.

ADMIRALS ON THE RESERVE HALF-PAY LIST.

Under Order of June 25, 1851; gaz. June 27, and July 1, 1851.

THIS LIST IS NOW CLOSED.

R A., R.H.P.L., Rear-Admiral Reserve Half-Pay List. V.A., R.H.P.L., Vice-Admiral Reserve Half-Pay List. A., R.H.P.L., Admiral Reserve Half-Pay List.

Name.	Promoted from List	V.A., R.H.P.L.	A., R.H.P.L.
Fredk. Watkins	A.	......	1 Jul. 51.
Jno. Giffard	A.	......	,,
Hy. Rd. Glynn...	A.	......	,,
Sir Hy. Heathcote	A.	......	,,
Hugh Downman	A.	......	,,
Jno. Mackellar	A.	......	,,
Matth. Buckle (No. 2)	D.	......	30 Jul. 52.
Jno. Allen	D.	......	,,
Christopher Jno. Wms. Neshan	D.	......	,,
Rd. Curry	D.	......	1 Jul. 51.
Jno. Wight	D	......	17 Dec. 52.
Wm. Hy. Browne Tremlett	D.	......	,,
Fras. Temple	D.	......	21 Jan. 54.
Hy. Gordon	D.	......	,,
Fredk. Wm., ld. Aylmer	D.	1 Jul. 51.	11 Sep. 54.
Jno. Surman Carden	D.	......	3 Jul. 55.
Jno. Impey	D.	......	4 Jul. 55.
Hy. Manaton Ommaney	D.	......	,,
Archd. Duff	D.	......	,,
Brian Hodgson...	D.	22 Apr. 53.	......
Sir Wm. Beauchamp Proctor, bt.	D.	......	18 Jun. 57.
Edwd. Ratsey	D.	......	,,
Chas. Philip Butler Bateman	D.	......	,,
Arth. Lysaght	D.	......	,,
Granville Leveson, E. of Carysfort...	D.	......	9 Jul. 57.
Wm. Croft	D.	8 Mar. 52.	28 Nov. 57.
Chas. Gordon, C.B.	D.	5 Mar. 53.	20 Jan. 58.
Wm. Ward	D.	22 Apr. 53.	......
Robt. Elliott	D.	22 Apr. 53.	......
Philip Browne	D.	15 Apr. 54.	......
Edwd. Wallis Hoard	D.	26 May 54.	9 Jun. 60.
Edwd. Hy. A'Court Repington	D.	11 Sep. 54.	......
Manley Hall Dixon	D.	......	1 Nov. 60.
Hon. Alexr. Jones	D.	3 Jul. 55.	,,
Villiers Fras. Hatton	D.	27 Sep. 55.	......
Sir Watkin Owen Pell	D.	......	11 Feb. 61.
Sir Andr. Pellat Green, K.C.H.	D.	27 Sep. 55.	......
Wm. Bowen Mends	D.	......	11 Feb. 61.
Geo. Ferguson	D.	31 Jan. 56.	,,
Geo. Edwd. Watts, C.B.	D.	21 Oct. 56.	......
Hayes O'Grady...	D.	,,	15 Jan. 62.
Sir David Dunn, K.C.H.	D.	12 Nov. 56.	......
Geo. Anson, ld. Byron	D.	19 Mar. 57.	20 May 62.
Edwd. Collier, C.B.	D.	......	4 Oct. 62.
Algn., D. of Northumberland, K.G....	D.	9 Jul. 57.	,,
Jno. Carter	D.	,,	,,
Hy. Meynell	D.	,,	,,
Wm. Walpole	D.	......	27 Apr. 63.
Wm. Jas. Mingaye	D.	......	,,
Geo. Fredk. Rich.	D.	......	24 Nov. 63.

Name.	Promoted from List	V.A., R.H.P.L.	A., R.H.P.L.
Thos. Bennett	D.	......	12 Sep. 65.
Peter Richards, aft. sir P.	D.	12 Apr. 62.	,,
Sir Steph. Lushington, K.C.B.	D.	1 Oct. 65.	2 Dec. 65.
Michl. Quin	D.	......	8 Apr. 68.
Jno. Jervis Tucker	D.	......	10 Sep. 69.

	R.A., R.H.P.L.	V.A., R.H.P.L.	A., R.H.P.L.
Sir Jno. Ross, C.B.	8 Jul. 51.	......	......
Constantine Richd. Moorsom	27 Aug. 51.	10 Sep. 57.	......
Geo. Jas., 6th E. of Egmont...	,,	,,	23 Mar. 63.
Sir Geo. Augs. Westphal	,,	,,	,,
Donat Henchy O'Brien	8 Mar. 52.	2 Oct. 57.	......
Edwd. Lloyd, K.H.	,,	......	......
Benedictus Marwood Kelly	,,	2 Oct. 57.	27 Apr. 63.
Norwich Duff	8 Oct. 52.	28 Nov. 57.	......
Sir Chas. Christr. Parker, bt.	,,	,,	27 Apr. 63.
Jno. Edwd. Walcot	,,	,,	,,
Fredk., Earl Spencer, K.G., C.B.	,,	,,	......
Sir Geo. Tyler, K.H.	26 Oct. 52.	8 Dec. 57.	......
Sir Geo. Richd. Brooke Pechell, bt. ...	17 Dec. 52.	5 Jan. 58.	......
Herbert Brace Powell...	,,	......	......
Jas. Ryder Burton, K.H.	28 May 53.	13 Feb. 58.	14 Nov. 63.
Percy Grace	17 Nov. 53.	6 Mar. 58.	......
Chas. Philip, E. of Hardwicke	12 Jan. 54.	24 Nov. 58.	3 Dec. 63.
Chas., ld. Colchester	1 Apr. 54.	2 May 60.	11 Jan. 64.
Sir Hy. Jno. Leeke, K.H.	15 Apr. 54.	......	......
Thos. Martin	,,	9 Jun. 60.	9 Feb. 64.
Hy. Edwards	,,	,,	,,
Wm. Keats	,,	2 May 60.	11 Jan. 64.
Richd. Augs. Yates	13 Jul. 54.	7 Nov. 60.	15 Jun. 64.
Edwd. Le Cras Thornbrough	,,	......	......
Chas. Grenville Randolph	,,	7 Nov. 60.	15 Jun. 64.
Edwd. Richd. Williams	,,	,,	,,
Saml. Thornton	11 Sep. 54.	......	......
Octavius Vernon Harcourt	26 Oct. 54.	4 Jun. 61.	......
Hy. Jno. Chetwynd, E. Talbot, C.B., aft. E. of Shrewsbury and Talbot	,,	,,	10 Feb. 65.
Sir Wm. Symonds, C.B.	,,	......	......
Sir Richd. Grant	7 Feb. 55.	......	......
Hon. Geo. Fredk. Hotham	,,	......	......
Sir Jno. Burnet Dundas	,,	5 Aug. 61.	5 May 65.
Follett Walrond Pennell	2 May 55.	15 Jan. 62.	12 Sep. 65.
Wm. Alexr. Baillie Hamilton	,,	,,	,,
Edwd. Purcell	2 May 55.	,,	,,
Chas. Elliot, aft. sir C.	,,	,,	,,
Hy. Gossett	3 Jul. 55.	12 Apr. 62.	,,
Jno. Furneaux	,,	,,	......
Jodrell Leigh	,,	,,	......
Josh. O'Brien	,,	,,	12 Sep. 65.
Hy. Algn. Eliot	27 Sep. 55.	......	......
Jas. Wigston	,,	4 Oct. 62.	2 Apr. 66.
Geo. Fredk. Ryves, C.B.	,,	......	......
Hon. Thos. Best	3 Oct. 55.	10 Nov. 62.	......
Hon. Geo. Jno. Cavendish	28 Dec. 55.	22 Nov. 62.	......
Sir Jno. Hindmarsh, K.H.	,,	......	......
Chas. Hamlyn Williams	19 May 55.	......	......
Jno. Milligan Laws	21 Jul. 55.	......	......

Name.	R.A., R.H.P.L.	V.A., R.H.P.L.	A., R.H.P.L.
Sir Burton Macnamara	21 Jul. 55.	3 Apr. 63.	20 Mar. 67.
Jno., Marq. Townshend	1 Dec. 55.	......	......
Hon. Arth. Duncombe	,,	12 Sep. 63.	18 Oct. 67.
Robt. FitzRoy	14 Feb. 57.	,,	......
Hon. Jno. Fredk. FitzGerald de Ros	,,	......	......
Chas. Hy. Swinburne	,,	12 Sep. 63.	18 Oct. 67.
Hy. Dundas Trotter	19 Mar. 57.	......	......
Sir Geo. Back	,,	24 Nov. 63.	18 Oct. 67.
Wm. Hillyar	,,	,,	......
Lord Jno. Fredk. Gordon Hallyburton, G.C.H. ...	12 May 57.	4 Nov. 63.	8 Apr. 68.
Wm. Fredk. Lapidge	14 May 57.	......	......
Jas. Brazier or Brasier	,,	14 Nov. 63.	......
Rchd. Contart McCrea	,,	,,	8 Apr. 68.
Jno. Balfour Maxwell	18 Jun. 57.	30 Nov. 63.	,,
Jno. Rivett-Carnac	,,	,,	,,
Wm. Hargood	9 Jul. 57.	3 Dec. 63.	15 Jan. 69.
Sir Thos Raikes Trigg Thompson, bt.	,,	,,	......
Sir Wm. Dickson, bt.	22 Aug. 57.	11 Jan. 64.	......
Wm. Sydney Smith	,,	,,	2 Jul. 69.
Edwd. Hinton Scott	10 Sep. 57.	......	......
Geo. Augs. Elliott	,,	9 Feb. 64.	10 Sep. 69.
Wm. Holt	,,	......	......
Brunswick Popham	2 Oct. 57.	28 Mar. 64.	10 Sep. 69.
Thos. Ogle	,,	,,	,,
Geo. Evans	,,	,,	,,
Jno. Hackett	,,	,,	......
Julius Jas. Farmer Newell	,,	......	......
Russell Elliott	4 Nov. 57.	15 Jun. 64.	10 Sep. 69.
Edwd. Stanley	5 Jan. 58.	10 Feb. 65.	27 Feb. 70.
Hon. Edwd. Howard	20 Jan. 58.	13 Apr. 65.	1 Apr. 70.
Richd. Crozier	11 Feb. 58.	24 Apr. 65.	,,
Richd. Hy. King	13 Feb. 58.	......	......
Hon. Plantagenet Pierrepoint Cary	1 Mar 58.	12 Sep. 65.	1 Apr. 70.
Robt. Cragie	,,	,,	,,
Jno. Bunch Bonne Maison McHardy	,,	,,	,,
Nichs. Cory	24 Nov. 58.	......	......
Fras. Decimus Hastings	27 Jun. 59.	2 Dec. 65.	......
Geo. Hathorn	,,	,,	14 Jul. 71.
Sackett Hope	2 May 60.	2 Apr. 66.	......
Patr. Jno. Blake	4 Jun. 61.	,,	20 Oct. 72
Wm. Warren, C.B.	,,	,,	......
Jno. Venour Fletcher	29 Jul. 61.	6 Apr 66.	20 Oct. 72
Talavera Vernon Anson	,,	,,	,,
Josh. Gape	12 Apr. 62.	24 May 67.	30 Jul. 75
Mark Jno. Currie	,,	,,	......
Wm. Burdett Dobson	,,	,,	......
Wm. Turner	,,	,,	......
Fredk. Moore Boultbee	,,	24 May 67.	30 Jul. 75
Josh. Sherer, K.H.	,,	,,	,,
Edmd. Yonge	,,	,,	......
Hon. Edwd. Thornton Wodehouse	,,	,,	......
Wm. Langford Castle	,,	,,	......
Jas. Beckford Lewis Hay	,,	,,	30 Jul. 75.
Hon. Edwd. Alfr. Jno. Harris, aft. sir E.	,,	,,	,,
Wm. Ward Percival Johnson	,,	,,	,,
Digby Marsh	,,	......	......
Jno. Washington	,,	......	......
Hon. Keith Stewart	19 May 62.	18 Oct. 67.	30 Jul. 75.
Geo. Wm. Chas. Lydiard	,,	,,	......
Wm. Griffin	20 May 62.	18 Oct. 67.	......

Name.	R.A., R.H.P.L.	V.A., R.H.P.L.	A., R.H.P.L.
Hon. Hy. Anthy. Murray	20 May 62.	......	......
Jno. Hallowes	,,	18 Oct. 67.	30 Jul. 75.
Sir Robt. Hagan	22 Nov. 62.	......	......
Andr. Drew	30 Jan. 63.	26 May 69.	30 Jul. 75.
Jas. Vashon Baker	,,	,,	,,
Edwd. Josh. Bird	6 Feb. 63.	2 Jul. 69.	11 Dec. 75.
Wm. Smyth	23 Mar. 63.	,,	,,
Geo. Dobson	,,	,,	,,
Richd. Hy. Stopford	27 Apr. 63.	21 Jan. 70.	18 Jun. 76
Jas. Paterson Bower	12 Sep. 63.	27 Feb. 70.	,,
Jno. Russell	30 Nov. 63.	......	......
Barth. Jas. Sulivan, C.B.. aft sir B.	3 Dec. 63.	1 Apr. 70.	22 Jan. 77
Hy. Bagot	,,	,,	,,
Hon. Walter Bourchier Devereux	,,	......	......
Sir Geo. Nathl. Brooke Middleton, bt., C.B.... ...	,,	1 Apr. 70.	22 Jan. 77
Sir Geo. Graham Otway, bt.	11 Jan. 64.	2 Jun. 70.	,,
Sir Andrew Snape Hamond, bt.	,,	,,	......
Edwd. Barnett	9 Feb. 64.	14 Jul. 71.	1 Aug. 77.
Chas. Geo. Edwd. Patey	,,	,,	,,
Hy. Broadhead	,,	,,	,,
Alexr. Leslie Montgomery	,,	,,	,,
Thos. Sparke Thompson	15 Jun. 64.	,,	......
Horation Beauman Young	16 Sep. 64.	,,	1 Aug. 77.
Edwd., ld. Dunsany	12 Nov. 64.	,,	,,
Cospatrick Baillie Hamilton, C.B.	17 Nov. 65.	2 Nov. 71.	,,
Jas. Crawford Caffin, C.B., aft. Sir J.	2 Dec. 65.	,,	,,
Robt. Tryon	,,	,,	,,
Thos. Fras. Birch	20 Mar. 67.	......	......

LIST H.

CAPTAINS PROMOTED TO LIST OF RETIRED ADMIRALS.

Under Orders of Sept. 1, 1846, Oct. 31, 1846, Apr. 24, 1847, June 25, 1851, May 7, 1858, Aug. 1, 1860, July 9, 1864, March 24. 1866, and Feb. 22, 1870.

R.R.A., Retired Rear-Admiral. R.V.A., Retired Vice-Admiral. Ret.A., Retired Admiral.

Those marked * were appointed R.V.A. May 17, 1858, with seniority from the dates given in the List.

Name.	R.R.A.	R.V.A.	Ret.A.
Jas. Wilkes Maurice	1 Oct. 46.	......	......
Jas. Prevost	,,	......	......
Sir Fras. Beaufort, K.C.B.	,,	......	......
Spelman Swayne	,,	......	......
Thos. White	,,	......	......
Jas. Lillicrap	,,	......	......
Walter Grosset	,,	......	......
*Jno. Thompson	,,	27 May 54.	9 Jun. 60.
Thos. Folliott Baugh	,,	......	......
Saml. Martin Colquitt	,,	......	......
Gust. Stupart	,,	......	......
*Thos. Fras. Chas. Mainwaring	,,	11 Sep. 54.	......
Wm., Earl Waldegrave	,,	,,	......
*Jno. Hollinworth	,,	,,	9 Jun. 60.
Clement Sneyd...	,,	......	......
Jno. Duff Markland	,,	......	......
*Abel Ferris	,,	11 Sep. 54.	......
*Robt. Merrick Fowler	,,	27 Oct. 54.	......
Donald Campbell	,,	......	......
Sir Hy. Hart, K.C.H.	,,	......	......
*Geo. Henderson	,,	3 Jul. 55.	1 Nov. 60.
Thos. Tudor Tucker, C.B.	,,	......	......
Hy. Bourchier	,,	......	......
*Robt. Worgan Geo. Festing, C.B	,,	4 Jul. 55.	1 Nov. 60.
Geo. Morris	,,	......	......
Jno. Tancock	,,	......	......
*Jas. Pattison Stewart, C.B....	,,	27 Sep. 55.	7 Nov. 60.
Christr. Bell, C.B.	,,	......	......
Jas. Stevenson...	,,	......	......
*Hon. Edm. Sexton Pery Knox	,,	27 Sep. 55.	7 Nov. 60.
*David, E. of Leven & Melville	,,	,,	......
Colin Campbell	,,	......	......
Jos. Symes	,,	......	......
Hon. Wm. Hy. Percy	,,	......	......
*Jas. Pringle	,,	27 Sep. 55.	......
Saml. Leslie	,,	......	......
Edw. Ellicott	,,	......	......
Peter Rye	,,	......	......
Jas. Gifford	,,	......	......
*Geo. Le Geyt, C.B.	,,	3 Oct. 55.	11 Feb. 61.
Hy. Gage Morris	,,	......	......
Edw. Aug. Down	,,	......	......
Thos. Whinyates	,,	......	......
Jno. Wm. Andrew, C.B.	,,	......	......
*Robt. Mitford...	,,	28 Dec. 55.	11 Feb. 61.

Name.	R.R.A.	R.V.A.	Ret.A.
*Henderson Bain	1 Oct. 46.	28 Dec. 55.	11 Feb 61.
Clement Milward	,,	......	......
*Jos. Needham Tayler, C.B.	,,	28 Dec. 55.	11 Feb. 61.
Jno. Fordyce Maples, C.B.	,,	......	......
Robt. Bloye, C.B.	,,	......	......
*Thos. Edwd. Symonds	,,	28 Dec. 55.	11 Feb. 61.
*Lewis Hole	,,	31 Jan. 56.	,,
Jas. M'Kerlie	,,	......	......
Fred. Jennings Thomas	,,	......	......
*Hy. Thos. Davies	3 Mar. 49.	31 Jan. 56.	11 Feb. 61.
*Hon. Hy. Dilkes Byng	,,	,,	......
*Geo. Gustavus Lennock	4 May 49.	,,	11 Feb. 61.
*Robt. Gambier	1 Sep. 49.	21Oct. 56.	15 Jan. 62.
Chas. Fred. Payne	,,	......	......
Colin Macdonald	,,	......	......
Abrm. Lowe	15 Sep. 49.	......	......
Chas. Bertram	9 Oct. 49.	......	......
Geo. Hills	,,	......	......
Hy. Fanshawe	,,	......	......
*Isaac Hawkins Morrison	,,	21 Oct. 56.	......
Geo. Barne Trollope, C.B.	,,	......	......
Sir Thos. Mansell, K.C.H.	,	......	......
Thos. Groube	,	......	......
Hercules Robinson	,,	21 Oct. 56.	15 Jan. 62.
Wm. Black	,,	......	......
Jno. Harper	18 Oct. 49.	......	......
*Thos. Dick	30 Oct. 49.	21 Oct. 56.	15 Jan. 62.
Wm. Isaac Scott	,,	,,	......
*Bertie Cornelius Cator	5 Nov. 49.	12 Nov. 56.	12 Apr. 62.
*Fred. Edw. Vernon Harcourt	24 Dec. 49.	19 Mar. 57.	20 May 62.
Kenelm, ld. Somerville	14 Jan. 50.	,,	,,
Hy. Jenkinson	27 Mar. 50.	14 May 57.	16 Jun. 62.
Edwd. Saurin	21 Jun. 50.	,,	,,
John Hardy Godby	,,	......	......
Christr. Strachey	,,	......	......
Arden Adderley	2 Sep. 50.	14 May 57.	16 Jun. 62.
Sir Richd. O'Connor	,,	......	......
Thos. Ball Sulivan, C.B.	1 Oct. 50.	......	......
David Scott	,,	......	......
Nichs. Lechmere Pateshull	6 Nov. 50.	......	......
Rowland Money	,,	9 Jul. 57.	......
John Sheridan	,,	,,	......
Sir Hy. Loraine Baker, bt.	,,	,,	......
Geo. Wm. Hughes D'Aeth	,,	,,	4 Oct. 62.
Robt. Ramsay	,,	......	......
John Chas. Gawen Roberts, aft. Roberts-Gawen	,,	9 Jul. 57.	4 Oct. 62.
Archd. Tisdall	11 Nov. 50.	......	......
Jos. Gulston Garland	,,	......	......
Wm. Stanhope Lovell, K.H.	30 Dec. 50.	9 Jul. 57.	......
Jos. Digby	21 Mar. 51.	,,	......
Chas. Warde, K.H.	,,	,,	4 Oct. 62.
Wm. Ffarington	,,	,,	,,
Jas. Rattray	,,	,,	,,
John Allen	,,	......	......
Arth. Philip Hamilton	11 Jun. 51.	9 Jul. 57.	4 Oct. 62.
Danl. Lawrence	,,	......	......
Robt. Henley Rogers	,,	......	......
Geo. Bentham	,,	9 Jul. 57.	......
Jas. Arth. Murray	16 Jun. 51.	30 Jul. 57.	......
Hy. Higman	,,	,,	......
Geo. Hewson	,,	,,	......

Name.	R.R.A.	R.V.A.	Retd. A.
John Macpherson Ferguson	16 Jun. 51.	......	......
John Gourly	,,	......	......
*Augs. Baldwin	,,	30 Jul. 57.	10 Nov. 62.
*Hy. Colins Deacon	,,	,,	,,
*Edwd. Barnard	8 Jul. 51.	22 Aug. 57.	22 Nov. 62.
*Wm. Bateman Dashwood	,,	,,	,,
*Martin White	,,	,,	,,
John Cookesley	,,	......	......
*Chas. Geo. Rodney Phillott	,,	22 Aug. 57.	22 Nov. 62.
*Wm. Wolrige	,,	,,	,,
*Geo. Brine	21 Aug. 51.	10 Sep. 57.	23 Mar. 63.
*Hon. John Gordon	27 Aug. 51.	,,	,,
*Wm. Popham	,,	,,	,,
Jas. Hay	,,	......	......
Sir Chas. Thos. Jones	,,	......	......
*Robt. Riddell Carre	,,	10 Sep. 57.	......
*Hugh Patton	19 Jan. 52.	,,	27 Apr. 63.
*Hon. Chas. Orlando Bridgman	,,	,,	......
Sir Hy Shiffner, bt.	,,	......	......
Hy. Forbes	,,	......	......
*Alexr. Montgomerie	8 Mar. 52.	2 Oct. 57.	7 Apr. 63.
*John Wm. Montagu	,,	,,	,,
Hon. Geo. Pryse Campbell	,,	......	......
*Wilson Braddyll Bigland, K.H.	,,	2 Oct. 57.	......
*Geo. Cornish Gambier	,,	,,	27 Apr. 63.
John Gore	,,	......	......
John Gedge	,,	......	......
*Sir Chas. Burrard	1 Oct. 52.	4 Nov. 57.	27 Apr. 63.
*Thos. Ladd Peake	8 Oct. 52.	28 Nov. 57.	,,
Wm. Hendry	,,	......	......
*Hy. Theodosius Browne Collier	17 Dec. 52.	5 Jan. 58	25 Jun. 63.
*John Brenton	,,	,,	......
Wm. Ramsden	,,	......	......
*Hy Stanhope	,,	5 Jan. 58.	25 Jun. 63.
*John Townshend Coffin	,,	,,	,,
*Edwd. Curzon, C.B.	,,	,,	......
Septimus Arabin	,,	......	......
*Thos. Ball Clowes	5 Mar. 53.	5 Jan. 58.	24 Nov. 63.
*Wm. Hy. Smyth	28 May 53.	13 Feb. 58.	14 Nov. 63.
*Richd. Saumarez	,,	,,	,,
*Jas. Montague	4 Jul. 53.	24 Feb. 58.	30 Nov. 63.
Thos. Prickett	17 Sep. 53.	......	......
*Alexr. Dundas Young Arbuthnot, aft. sir A.	,,	6 Mar. 58.	30 Nov. 63.
Wm. Hotham, K.H.	5 Dec. 53.	25 Jun. 58.	,,
John Shekel	12 Jan. 54.	......	......
Geo. Ourry Lempriere	,,	24 Nov. 58.	3 Dec. 63.
John Gore	21 Jan. 54.	16 May 59.	15 Dec. 63.
Chas. Bowen	,,	......	......
John Geo. Graham	27 Jan. 54.	......	......
John Geo. Aplin	15 Apr. 54.	14 May 60.	......
John Pakenham	13 Jul. 54.	7 Nov. 60.	15 Jun. 64
Fredk. Augs. Wetherall	,,	......	......
Hy. Litchfield	,,	,,	,,
Wm. Webb	,,	,,	,,
Chas. Simeon	,,	......	......
Robt. Patton	7 Aug. 54.	11 Feb. 61.	16 Sep. 64.
Robt. Aitchison	,,	,,	......
John FitzGerald Studdert	27 Oct. 54.	29 Jul. 61.	25 Apr. 65.
Chas. B. Gordon	22 Jan. 55.	5 Aug. 61.	,,
Theobald Jones	2 May 55.	15 Jan. 62.	12 Sep. 65.
Geo. Lloyd	,,	......	......

Name.	R.R.A.	R.V.A.	Retd. A.
bt. White Parsons	3 Jul. 55.	......	......
orm. Crawford	,,	12 Apr. 62.	12 Sep. 65.
ussell Hy. Manners	,,	,,	,,
s. Thorne	,,	,,	,,
Eaton Travers, K.H.	9 Jul. 55.	......	......
m. Morier	,,	16 Jan. 62.	......
o. Scott	,,	,,	2 Apr. 66.
m. Bohun Bowyer	,,	......	......
ilip Parker King	27 Sep. 55.	......	......
urtenay Wm. Edmd. Boyle	,,	......	......
owland Mainwaring	,,	......	......
hn Wyatt Watling	,,	4 Oct. 62.	2 Apr. 66.
chd. Pridham	,,	,,	......
o. Lyons	,,	,,	2 Apr. 66.
ilip Westphal	,,	,,	,,
lwd. Sparshott, K.H.	,,	,,	,,
m. Blight	,,	......	......
o. Woollcombe	,,	4 Oct. 62.	......
hn Wilson	30 Nov. 55.	22 Nov. 62.	2 Apr. 66.
drew Atkins Vincent, K.H.	19 May 56.	......	......
ml. Radford, K.H.	,,	......	......
s. Harrison	21 Jul. 56.	......	......
. Shovell Jones Marsham	21 Oct. 56.	27 Apr. 63.	18 Oct. 67.
as. Crowdy	,,	,,	,,
os. Mansell	,,	,,	,,
m. Townsend Dance	12 Nov. 56.	,,	,,
n. Hamley	1 Dec. 56.	12 Sep. 63.	......
rm. Mills Hawkins	14 Feb. 57.	......	......
hn Drake	,,	12 Sep. 63.	......
wd. Augs. Frankland	,,	......	......
s. Burney	19 Mar. 57.	24 Nov. 63.	18 Oct. 67.
s. Morgan	,,	......	......
n. Slaughter, K.H.	14 May 67.	14 Nov. 63.	8 Apr. 68.
os. Gill	,,	,,	,,
n. Allan Herringham	,,	,,	......
bt. Gordon	,,	,,	8 Apr. 68.
chd. Owen	18 Jun. 57.	......	......
n. Robertson	9 Jul. 57.	......	......
. Ommaney Love	22 Aug. 57.	11 Jan. 64.	2 Jul. 69.
hn Fredk. Appleby	10 Sep. 57.	9 Feb. 64.	10 Sep. 69.
chd. Devonshire	,,	......	......
as. Rich	,,	9 Feb. 64.	......
bt. Deans	,,	,,	......
n. Richardson	,,	,,	......
o. Chas. Blake	,,	,,	10 Sep. 69
n. Pearce Stanley	,,	......	......
n. Hy. Pierson	,,	......	......
n Parker	2 Oct. 57.	28 Mar. 64.	......
r. Luckraft	4 Nov. 57.	15 Jun. 64.	10 Sep. 69.
wd. Chappell	20 Jan. 58.	......	......
n Monday	,,	13 Apr. 65.	......
os. Bushby	6 Mar. 58.	......	......
n. Shepheard	16 May 59.	2 Dec. 65.	......
n. Luckraft	,,	......	......
nl. Perkins Pritchard	29 Jul. 61.	6 Apr. 66.	......
. Stroud	12 Apr. 62.	24 May 67.	30 Jul. 75.
n. Hext	,,	......	......
n. Haydon	,,	......	......
n. Benj. Suckling	,,	......	......
n. Gordon	,,	24 May 67.	......
os. Sanders	,,	......	......

Name.	R.R.A.	R.V.A.	Ret. A.
Douglas Cox	12 Apr. 62.	......	......
Edwin Ludlow Rich	,,	24 May 67.	......
Evan Nepean	,,	......	......
Geo. Vernon Jackson	,,	24 May 67.	30 Jul. 75
Chas. Colville Frankland	,,	,,	,,
Wm. Geo. Hyndman Whish	,,	,,	,,
Edwd. Reeves Philip Mainwaring	,,	......	......
Thos. Fraser	,,	24 May 67.	......
Fras. Deane Hutcheson	,,	,,	30 Jul. 75
Chas. Basden	,,	......	......
Hy. Edwd. Coffin	,,	24 May 67.	30 Jul. 75
Fras. Vere Cotton	,,	,,	,,
Chas. Smith	,,	,,	,,
Fras. Harding	,,	,,	......
John Williams Aldridge	,,	,,	......
Wm. Allen	,,	......	......
John Baker Porter Hay	,,	24 May 67.	30 Jul. 7
Edwd. Iggulden Parry	30 Jan. 63.	......	......
Chas. Keele	,,	......	......
Edwd. Burnaby Tinling	23 Mar. 63.	......	......
Wm. Kelly	,,	2 Jul. 69.	......
Jas. Pulling	27 Apr. 63.	......	......
Wm. Nevill	15 Dec. 63.	1 Apr. 70.	......
Joseph Pearse	,,	,,	.....
Regd. Yorke	9 Feb. 64.	......	......
Geo. Guy Burton	15 Jun. 64.	......	......
Hy. Layton	,,	14 Jul. 71.	1 Aug. 7
Wm. Hewgill Kitchen	,,	......	......
Robt. Fitzgerald Gambier	,,	14 Jul. 71.	1 Aug. 7
Sir Cornwallis Ricketts, bt.	,,	,,	,,
Wm. Hy. Jervis	,,	,,	......
Jas. Hamilton Ward	16 Sep. 64.	,,	......
Edwd. St. Leger Cannon	,,	,,	1 Aug. 7
Ralph Barton	,,	,,	,,
Richd. Burridge	,,	......	......
Wm. Louis	28 Oct. 64.	14 Jul. 71.	1 Aug. 7
Chas. John Bosanquet	,,	,,	......
Courtney Osborne Hayes	,,	,,	1 Aug. 7
Wm. Knighton Stephens	10 Apr. 65.	1 Oct. 71.	,,
Geo. Hy. Parlby White	,,	,,	,,
Wm. Windham Hornby	,,	,,	,,
David Peat	13 Apr. 65.	,,	,,
Thos. Vernon Watkins	24 Apr. 65.	......	......
Wm. Clark	2 Dec. 65.	......	......
Thos. Lewis Gooch	,,	2 Nov. 71.	.....
Geo. Anthy. Halsted	,,	,,	......
Robt. Sharpe	,,	......	......
Wm. Louis Sherringham	17 Dec. 65.	2 Nov. 71.	......
Geo. Knyvett Wilson	2 Apr. 66.	......	......
John Thos. Talbot	,,	6 Apr. 73.	......
Alexr. Murray	,,	......	......
John Hay	,,	6 Apr. 73.	9 Mar. 7
Wm. Radcliffe	,,	......	......
Chas. Edmunds	,,	......	......
Robt. Kerr	6 Apr. 66.	30 Apr. 73.	21 Mar. 7
Jas. Anderson	,,	,,	,,
John McDougall	,,	......	......
Sir Robt. J. Le M. McClure, C.B.	20 Mar. 67.	29 May 73.	......
Herbert Schomberg	,,	......	......
Thos. Saumarez Brock	,,	......	......
Geo. Davies	,,	29 May 73.	......

Name.	R.R.A.	R.V.A.	Ret. A.
Edwd. Codd	24 May 67.	29 May 73.	26 Sep. 78.
Chas. Fredk. Schomberg	,,	,,	......
Fredk. Patten	,,	,,	......
Arth. Wm. Jerningham	,,	,,	26 Sep. 78.
Archd. McMurdo	,,	,,	......
Hy. Jno. Douglas	,,	......	......
Wm. Brown Oliver	,,	29 May 73.	......
Thos. Edwd. Law Moore	,,	......	......
Richd. Robt. Quin	31 May 67.	......	......
Jas. Gabriel Gordon	1 Jul. 67.	......	......
Jno. Reeve	,,	......	......
Geo. Flower Herbert	,,	......	......
Thos. Geo. Forbes	1 Sep. 67.	......	......
Wm. Newton Fowell	,,	......	......
Geo. Sumner Hand, C.B.	18 Oct. 67.	25 Aug. 73.	15 Jun. 79
Hy. Harvey	9 Apr. 68.	1 Jan. 74.	,,
Louis Symonds Tindal	,,	,	......
Colson Festing	17 Mar. 69.	......	......
Edmd. Gardiner Fishbourne, C.B.	,,	30 Jul. 75.	2 Aug. 79.
Thos. Chaloner	,,	,,	,,
Wm. Cornwallis Aldham, C.B.	,,	,,	......
Colin Yorke Campbell	,,	11 Dec. 75.	27 Nov. 79.
Nichs. Lefebore	2 Jul. 69.	22 Mar. 76.	9 Jan. 80.
Lord Wm. Compton, aft. M. of Northampton	26 Jul. 69.	,,	,,
Hy Richd. Foote	,,	,,	,,
Thos. Baldock	10 Sep. 69.	......	......
Geo. Augs. Bedford	,,	22 Mar. 76.	......
Jas. Stoddart	16 Sep. 69.	,,	9 Jan. 80.
Edwd. Tatham	1 Apr. 70.	12 Nov. 76.	......
Hy. Chas. Otter, C.B.	,,	......	......
Geo. Wodehouse	,,	31 Dec. 76.	......
Edwd. Hollinworth Delafosse	,,	......	......
Thos. Furber	,,	29 May 73.	......
Jno. Cornwall	,,	......	......
Spencer Smyth	,,	29 May 73.	26 Sep. 78.
Chas. Calmady Dent	,,	......	......
Robt. Loney	,,	25 Aug. 73.	15 Jun. 79.
Chas. Wilson Riley	,,	30 Jul. 75.	......
Godfrey Lamplugh Wolley	,,	......	......
Cheesman Hy. Binstead	,,	30 Jul. 75.	......
Wm. Cheselden Browne	,,	22 Mar. 76.	9 Jan. 80.
Hy. Duncan Twysden	,,	......	......
Geo. Parker	20 Oct. 72.	9 Mar 78.	27 Oct. 84.
Richd. Aldworth Oliver	,,	,,	,,
Edwd. Philips Charlewood	,,	,,	,,
Geo. Williams	,,	,,	......
Thos. Abel Bremage Spratt, C.B.	,,	,,	......
Arth. Mellersh	,,	,,	27 Oct. 84.
Chas. Jos. Fredk. Ewart, C.B.	8 Feb. 73.	......	......
Fredk. Chevallier Syer	12 Feb. 73.	......	......
Richd. Ashmore Powell, C.B.	6 Apr. 73.	21 Mar. 78.	......
Jno. Borlase, C.B.	,,	,,	......
Vincent Amcotts Massingberd	,,	,,	30 Oct. 84.
Jas. Rawstone	,,	,,	......
Robt. Hall, C.B.	30 Apr. 73.	21 Mar. 78.	
Jno. Montagu Hayes, C.B.	,,	,,	......
Chas. Luxmoore Hockin	25 Aug. 73.	,,	30 Oct. 84.
Hy. Alexr. Story	,,	,,	......
Edwd. Pelham Brenton Von Donop	,,	,,	......
Oliver Jno. Jones	,,	......	......
Octavius Cumberland, C.B.	,,	......	......

Name.	R.R.A.	R.V.A.	Ret.A.
Geo. Wm. Preedy, C.B.	1 Jan. 74.	30 Jan. 79.	......
Thos. Etheridge	,,	,,	30 Oct. 84.
Fredk. Lamport Barnard	,,	,,	......
Jas. Edwd. Katon	19 Jan. 74.	1 Feb. 79.	27 Mar. 85
Edwd. Westby Vansittart, C.B.	,,	,,	......
Wm. Abdy Fellowes...	,,	......	......
Jno. Jas. Kennedy, C.B.	,,	1 Feb. 79.	......
Jno. Barling Marsh	,,	,,	......
Matthew Stainton Nolloth	,,	,,	......
Hy. Gage Morris	,,	,,	27 Mar. 85
Richd. Dunning White	,,	,,	......
Alexr. Bridport Beecher	,,	......	......
Jno. Ormsby Johnson...	11 Jun. 74.	1 Feb. 79.	......
Alan Hy. Gardner, C.B.	,,	......	......
Wm. Jas. Saml. Pullen	,,	1 Feb. 79.	......
Hon. Geo. Hy. Douglas	,,	,,	27 Mar. 85
Geo. Le Geyt Bowyear, C.B.	,,	,,	......
Jas Dirom	,,	......	......
Hy. Croft	,,	1 Feb. 79.	27 Mar. 85
Fredk. Augs. Buchanan Craufurd	,,	......	......
Augs. Hy. Ingram	1 Jan. 75.	15 Jun. 79.	31 Mar. 85
Hy. Dumaresq...	,,	......	......
Wm. Ellis	,,	15 Jun. 79.	31 Mar. 85
Jas. Geo. Mackenzie	,,	......	......
Chas. Starmer...	,,	15 Jun. 79.	......
Geo. Stewart Reynolds	,,	,,	......
Jno Bettinson Cragg	,,	......	......
Augs. Sinclair Booth	,,	15 Jun. 79.	31 Mar. 85
Wm. Hoseason	,,	......	......
Wm. Heriot Maitland Dougall	,,	15 Jun. 79.	31 Mar. 85
Edwd. Peirse	,,	,,	......
Steph. Smith Lowther Crofton	,,	,,	......
Gilbert Brydone Rutherford...	,,	,,	31 Mar. 85
Albert Heseltine	,,	,,	,,
Chas. Richardson Johnson	,,	,,	......
Gerard Jno. Napier	,,	,,	......
Lewis Maitland	,,	......	......
Richd. Brydges Beechey	,,	15 Jun. 79.	31 Mar. 85
Wm. Hugh Dobbie	,,	,,	,,
Hy. Need	,,	......	......
Richd. Purvis...	,,	......	......
Thos. Cochran...	20 Apr. 75.	2 Aug. 79.	......
Edwd. King Barnard	,,	,,	......
Jas. Hosken	,,	,,	......
Jas. Saml. Akid Dennis	,,	,,	......
Jos. Martin Mottley	,,	,,	......
Edwd. Franklin	,,	......	......
Philip Somerville	,,	2 Aug. 79.	......
Arthur Trevor Macgregor	,,	,,	7 Apr. 85
Alexr. Boyle	,,	,,	......
Byron Drury	,,	,,	7 Apr. 85
Wm. Morris	,,	......	......
Wm. Rae Rolland	25 Apr. 75.	9 Sep. 79.	......
Richd. Moorman	7 May 75.	27 Nov. 79.	29 Apr. 85
Fredk. Augs. Maxse	4 Nov. 75.	20 Jan. 80.	1 Jul. 85
David Robertson, aft. Robertson-Macdonald ...	11 Dec. 75.	,,	,,
Saml. Mercer	,,	,,	......
Wm. Norton Taylor	,,	20 Jan. 80.	1 Jul. 85
Geo. Clarke Mends	,,	,,	......
Jonas Archer Abbott	,,	,,	1 Jul. 85
John Luke Richd. Stoll	,,	......	......

Name.	R.R.A.	R.V.A.	Ret.A.
Philip Augs. Helpman	11 Dec. 75.	......	......
John Ross Ward	,,	20 Jan. 80.	1 Jul. 85.
Edwd. Banbury Nott	,,	......	......
Wm. Boys	,,	......	......
Geo. Johnson	,,	20 Jan. 80.	1 Jul. 85.
Matth. Connolly	,,	,,	......
Jas. Archd. Macdonald	,,	......	......
Geo. Mason	,,	......	......
Alexr. Crombie Gordon	,,	20 Jan. 80.	......
Robt. Robertson	,,	,,	1 Jul. 85.
Jasper Hy. Selwyn	,,	,,	,,
Fras. Hy. Shortt	,,	,,	......
Robt. Jocelyn Otway	,,	,,	......
Victor Grant Hickley...	21 Sept.76.	3 Jan. 81.	12 Apr. 86.
Julian Foulston Slight, C.B.	,,	,,	,,
Wm. Hy. Haswell	,,	,,	......
Thos. Saumarez, C.B.	,,	,,	12 Apr. 86.
Saml. Hoskins Derriman, C.B.	,,	,,	,,
Peter Fredk. Shortland	,,	,,	......
Fredk. Leopold Augs. Selwyn	,,	,,	......
Chas. Hy. May	,,	,,	......
Richd. Wm. Courtenay	12 Nov. 76.	19 Jan. 81.	......
Donald McLeod Mackenzie	31 Dec. 76.	23 Nov. 81.	......
John Seccomb	,,	,,	......
Pr. Victor Ferd., &c., of Hohenlohe, c.c. Count Gleichen	,,	,,	24 May 87.
Jos. Grant Bickford	,,	......	......
Wm. Everard Alphonso Gordon, C.B.	,,	23 Nov 81	24 May 87.
Robt. Dawes Aldrich	,,	,,	......
Hy. Trollope	,,	......	......
Jack Hy. Murray	1 Aug. 77.	......	......
Jno. Orlebar	,,	6 May 82.	15 Jul. 87.
Fras. Marten	,,	......	......
Wm. Andrew Jas Heath, C.B.	,,	......	......
Jno. Wm. Dorville	,,	6 May 82	15 Jul. 87.
Elphinston D'Oyly D'Auvergne Aplin	,,	,,	......
Wm. Cornish Bowden	,,	,,	15 Jul. 87.
Geo. Hy. Gardner	,,	......	......
Jno. Clarke Byng	,,	......	......
Jno. Bythesea, V.C., C.B.	5 Aug. 77.	......	......
Hy. Saml. Hawker	,,	6 May 82.	15 Jul. 87.
Fras. Arden Close	,,	,,	,,
Arth. Wilmshurst, C.B.	,,	,,	......
Wm. Wood	,,	,,	15 Jul. 87.
Hy. Jno. Blomfield	27 Sep. 77.	17 Feb. 84.	18 Oct. 87.
Jno. Fras. Campbell Mackenzie	,,	,,	,,
Jas Beautine Willoughby	,,	,,	......
David Spain	,,	,,	......
Jno. Rashleigh Rodd	31 Dec. 77.	1 Apr. 84.	1 May 88.
Geo. Otway Popplewell	,,	,,	,,
Fredk. Thos. Chetham Strode	,,	,,	,,
Jno. Wallace Douglas M'Donald	,,	,,	,,
Jas. Minchin Bruce	,,	,, (?)	......
Wm. Horton, C.B.	,,	......	......
Richd. Bulkeley Pearse	,,	7 Jul. 84.	19 Jun. 88.
Herbert Philip de Kantzow	,,	,,	,,
Geo. Augs. Cooke Brooker, C.B.	,,	......	......
Norman Bernard Bedingfeld	9 Mar. 78.	8 Jul. 84.	......
Hy. Wm. Hire, C.B.	,,	......	......
Wm. Alfd. Rumbledon Pearse	,,	......	......
Jos. Hy. Marryat, C.B.	,,	......	......

Name.	R.R.A.	R.V.A.	Ret.A.
Trevenen Penrose Coode	9 Mar. 78.	8 Jul. 84.	......
Chas. Murray Aynsley, C.B.	,,	,,	......
Montague Fredk. O'Reilly	,,	......	......
Edwd. Lacy	,,	8 Jul. 84.	......
Montagu Buccleuch Dunn	,,	......	......
Sir Malcolm McGregor, bt.	,,	......	......
Jas. Richd. Veitch	,,	8 Jul. 84.	15 Dec. 88
Hy. Fredk. McKillop	,,	......	......
Hy. Jas. Raby, V.C., C.B.	21 Mar. 78	......	......
Jno. Fras. Ross	,,	......	......
Fredk. Wm. Pleydell-Bouverie	31 Dec. 78.	30 Oct. 84.	......
Edwd. Jas. Bedford	,,	,,	......
Hy. Christian	,,	,,	......
Chas. Wright Bonham	,,	,,	......
Jno. Halliday Cave, C.B.	,,	,,	......
Saml. Hood Henderson	,,	......	......
Jno. Edwd. Parish	,,	30 Oct. 84.	......
Richd. Dawkins	,,	......	......
Wm. Chas. Fabie Wilson, C.B.	,,	30 Oct. 84.	......
Hon. Thos. Alexr. Pakenham	,,	......	......
Herbert Fredk. Winnington Ingram...	,,	......	......
Francisco Sangro Tremlett	,,	......	......
David Miller	,,	......	......
Hubert Campion, C.B....	,,	......	......
Lewis Jas. Moore	30 Jan. 79.	......	......
Benj. Spencer Pickard	2 Aug. 79.	1 Jul. 85.	......
Fredk. Wm. Gough, C.B.	27 Nov. 79.	26 Nov. 85.	......
Richd. Chas. Mayne, C.B.	,,	......	......
John Wm. Whyte	,,	......	......
Mark Robt. Pechell	,,	26 Nov. 85.	......
Hy. Hamilton Beamish, C.B.	9 Jan. 80.	......	......
Fredk. Harrison Smith	23 Jul. 80.	7 Jul. 87.	......
Arthur Lukis Mansell	23 Nov. 81.	14 May 88.	......
Hugh Maxn. Elliott	,,	......	......
John Laisné Perry	31 Dec. 81.	......	......
Thos. Hutchinson Mangles Martin	9 Jun. 82.	25 Oct. 88.	......
Wm. Fitzherbert Ruxton	,,	,,	......
Chas. Bayley Calmady Dent	,,	,,	......
Geo. Teal Sebor Winthrop	,,	,,	......
Wm. Hy. Fenwick	31 Dec. 82.	8 Nov. 88.	......
Hon. Maurice Horatio Nelson	,,	......	......
Geo. John Malcolm	,,	......	......
Wm. Cox Chapman	,,	15 Dec. 88.	......
Hon. Armar Lowry Corry	,,	,,	......
Chas. Fenton Fletcher Boughey	8 Jan. 83.	,,	......
Geo. Hy. Parkin	,,	,,	......
Jas Andrew Robt. Dunlop	,,	,,	......
D'Arcy Spence Preston	,,	......	......
Hy. Bedford Woollcombe	,,	15 Dec. 88.	......
Philip Saumarez	20 Mar. 83.	......	......
Stapleton Jas. Greville	,,	......	......
Chas. Matth. Buckle	,,	......	......
Cortland Herbert Simpson	,,	......	......
Fras. Regd. Purvis	17 Feb. 84.	......	......
Chas. Richd. Fox Boxer	,,	......	......
Alexr. Phillips...	7 Jul. 84.	......	......
Robt. Anthy. Edwd. Scott	27 Mar. 85.	......	......
Fredk. Wm. Sidney	,,	......	......
Jos. Saml. Hudson	,,	......	......
Wm. Burley Grant	29 Apr. 85.	......	......
Thos. Baker Martin Sulivan...	,,	......	......

Name.	R.R.A.	R.V.A.	Ret. A.
Iountford Steph. Lovick Peile	29 Apr. 85.	......	......
Iacleod Baynes Cockcraft	1 Jun. 85.	......	......
'has. David Lucas, V.C.	,,	......	......
Ioratio Lawrence Arth. Lennox Maitland... ...	,,	......	......
ohn Wm. Pike	1 Jul. 85.	......	......
dwin John Pollard	,,	......	......
aml. Philip Townsend	,,	......	......
ichd. Bradshaw, C.B.	,,	......	......
'hos. Edwd. Smith	,,	......	......
edford Clapperton Tryvellion Pim	5 Jul. 85.	......	......
'hos. Hounsom Butler Fellows, C.B.	1 Jan. 86.	......	......
Iarcus Lowther	,,	......	......
ouis Hutton Vesturme	,,	......	......
alph Abercrombie Otho Brown	9 Mar. 86.	......	......
obt. Owen Leach	,,	......	......
rth. Woodall Gillett...	,,	......	......
Iy. Wandesford Comber	,,	......	......
dwd. Field	,,	......	......
ichd. Carter	,,	......	......
Iorgan Singer	12 Apr. 86.	......	......
Iy. McClintock Alexander	,,	......	......
ir Geo. Strong Nares, K.C.B.	1 Jan. 87.	......	......
'alentine Otway Inglefield	,,	......	......
eo. Doherty Broad	,,	......	......
lb. Hy. Wm. Battiscombe	,,	......	......
has. Jas. Bullock	,,	......	......
Iy. Anthy. Trollope	,,	......	......
Iy Matth. Miller	6 Apr. 87.	......	......
'hilip Howard Colomb	,,	......	......
Iamilton Edwd. Geo. Earlie	24 May 87.	......	......
'hilip Ruffle Sharpe	10 Jun. 87	......	......
libank Harley Murray	,,	......	......
as. Augs. Poland	1 Jan. 88.	......	......
no. Parry Jones Parry	,,	......	......
as. Wylie East	,,	......	......
Iy. Lowe Holder	,,	......	......
has. Fras. Walker	,,	......	......
redk. Wm. Hallowes	3 Apr. 88.	......	......
no. Child Purvis	,,	......	......
eo. Northland	19 Jun. 88.	......	......

GOVERNORS OF GREENWICH HOSPITAL.

1708. Sir Wm. Gifford.
1714. Adm. Matth. Aylmer.
1720. Adm. sir John Jennings.
1744. Adm. sir John Balchan.
1746. Ld. Archd. Hamilton.
1754. Adm. Isaac Townsend.
1765. Adm. sir Geo. Bridges Rodney, bt.
1771. Adm. Fras. Holburne.
Adm. sir Chas. Hardy.
1780. Adm. sir Hugh Palliser.
1796. Adm. Saml. visc. Hood, Mar. 20.
1816. Adm. sir John Colpoys, Feb. 9.
1821. Adm. sir Richd. Godwin Keats, G.C.B., Apr. 5.
1834. R.-adm. sir Thos. Masterman Hardy, bt., G.C.B., Apr. 9.
1837. Adm. hon. Chas. Elphinstone Fleming, Oct. 12.
1841. Adm. hon. sir Robt. Stopford, G.C.B., Apr. 7.
1847. V.-adm. sir Chas. Adam, K.C.B., July 3.
1853. V.-adm. sir Jas. Alexr. Gordon, K.C.B., Oct. 28.
1869. Adm. sir Houston Stewart, G.C.B., Feb. 15.
1872. Adm. sir Sydney Colpoys Dacres, G.C.B., Dec. 2.
1884. Adm. sir Lewis Tobias Jones, G.C.B., Mar. 25.

LIEUTENANT-GOVERNORS OF GREENWICH HOSPITAL.

1704. Capt. John Clements.
1705. Capt. Robt. Robinson.
1718. Capt. Thos. Cleasby.
Capt. Jos. Soanes.
1737. Capt. Teudor Trevor.
1740. Capt. Chas. Smith.
1750. Capt. Fras. Dansays.
1754. Capt. Jas. Lloyd.
1761. Capt. Wm. Boys.
1774. Capt. Thos. Baillie.
1778. Capt. Jarvis Maplesden.
1781. Capt. Broderick Hartwell.
1784. Capt. Jas. Ferguson.
1793. Capt. Wm. Locker.
1800. Capt. sir Richd. Pearson.
1805. Capt. Jno. Bourchier.
1809. Capt. Wm. Browell.
1831. R.-adm. sir Jahleel Brenton, K.C.B. aft. bt., Aug. 8.
1840. R.-adm. sir Jas. Alexr. Gordon, K.C.B., July 6.
1853. R.-adm. sir Wm. Edwd. Parry, Dec 6.
1855. R.-adm. sir Wm. Fairbrother Carroll K.C.B., Aug. 13.
1862. R.-adm. sir Stephen Lushington K.C.B., May 17.

Office abolished Sept. 1865, by 28 & 29 Vict. cap. 89.

PART XV. MILITARY.

COMMANDERS-IN-CHIEF.

1674. Jas., D. of Monmouth (nat. son of Chas. II.), Mar. 30; beheaded 1685.
1690. John, E., aft. D. of Marlborough, June 3; *d.* 1722.
1691. Meinhardt, D. of Leinster, Apr. 30.
1695. Meinhardt, D. of Leinster, now D. of Schomberg, K.G., May 9; *d.* 1719.
1711. Jas., D. of Ormond, Jan. 1; attainted 1715; *d.* 1746.
1744. John, E. of Stair, K.T., Jan. 1; *d.* May 1747.
1745. Geo. Wade, Mar.; *d.* 1748.
1757. John, visc., aft. E. Ligonier, Oct. 24 to 1759; *d.* 1770.
The office vacant.
1766. John, M. of Granby, son of John, 3rd D. of Rutland, Aug. 13; *res.* 1769; *d.* 1770.
The office vacant.
1778. Jeffrey, ld. Amherst, gen. on the staff, Mar. 19.
1782. Hon. Hy. Seymour Conway, Mar. 29; *d.* 1795.
1793. Jeffrey, ld. Amherst, *again*, gen. on the staff, Jan. 21; *d.* 1797.
1795. Fredk., D. of York, F.M. on the staff, Feb. 11; comm. ch., Apr. 3, 1798.
1809. Sir David Dundas, bt., Mar. 25, *d.* 1820.
1811. Fredk., D. of York, *again*, May 29, to Jan. 5, 1827, when he *d.*
Vacant to Jan. 21, 1827.
1827. Arthur, D. of Wellington, K.G., G.C.B., Jan. 22, to May 5, same year.
Vacant from May 6 to Aug. 26, 1827.
1827. Arthur, D. of Wellington, *again*, Aug. 27, to Feb. 14, 1828.
Vacant to Feb. 24, 1828.
1828. Rowland, visc. Hill, G.C.B., G.C.H., gen. on the staff, Feb. 25, to Aug. 14, 1842; *d.* Dec. 1842.
1842. Arth., D. of Wellington, *again*, Aug. 15, by L.P.
1852. Hy., 1st visc. Hardinge, G.C.B., gen. on the staff, Dec. 28; *res.* and *d.* 1856.
1856. Geo. Wm. Fred. Chas., D. of Cambridge, K.G., &c., gen. on the staff, July 15; comm. ch., Nov. 26, 1887.

CAPTAINS-GENERAL.

1660. Geo., D. of Albemarle, Aug. 3.
1678. Jas., D. of Monmouth, Apr. 27, to Sept. 11, 1679; *d.* 1685.
1702, Jno., E., aft. D. of Marlborough, Apr. 24, to Feb. 19, 1711.
1711. Jas., D. of Ormond, Feb. 20, to Sept. 22, 1714.
1714. Jno., D. of Marlborough, *again*, Sept. 23, to 1717; *d.* 1722
1744. Wm. Aug., D. of Cumberland, Mar. 8, to 1757; *d.* 1765.
1799. Fredk., D. of York, Sept. 4 to Mar. 24, 1809.

This title is now become obsolete.

FIELD-MARSHALS.

1736, Jan. 14. Geo., E. of Orkney, govr. of Edinburgh Castle; *d.* 1737.
Jno., D. of Argyll and Greenwich; *d.* 1743.
1739, •uly 2. Richd., visc. Shannon.
Fras., M. de Montandre.
1742, Mar. 28. Jno., E. of Stair.
Richd., visc. Cobham; *d.* 1749.
1743. Geo. Wade, Dec. 14; *d.* 1748.
1757. Nov. 28. Sir Robt. Rich, bt.; *d.* 1768.
Richd., visc. Molesworth; *d.* 1758.
Jno., ld., aft. visc. and E. Ligonier; *d.* 1770.
1763. Jas., ld. Tyrawley, June 10; *d.* 1773.
1793, Oct. 12. Hon. Hy. Seymour Conway; *d.* 1795.
Wm. Hy., D. of Gloucester, K.G.; *d.* 1805.
Sir Geo. Howard, K.B.; *d.* 1796.
1795. Fredk., D. of York and Albany, K.G., Feb. 10.
1796, July 30. Jno., D. of Argyll; *d.* 1806.
Jeffrey, ld. Amherst, K.B.; *d.*1797.
Jno. Griffin, ld. Howard de Walden; *d.* 1797.
Studholme Hodgson, *d.* 1798.
Geo., Marq. Townshend; *d.* 1807.
Ld. Fredk. Cavendish, *d.* 1803.
Chas., D. of Richmond, K.G.; *d.* 1806.
1805, Sept. 5. Edwd., D. of Kent and Strathern, K.G.; *d.* 1820.
1813. Arth., D. of Wellington, K.G., June 21.
1813, Nov. 26. Ernest Aug., D. of Cumberland, K.G. (K. of Hanover in 1837).
Adolphus Fredk., D. of Cambridge, K.G.; *d.* 1850.
1816, May 24. Wm. Fredk., D. of Gloucester, K.G.; *d.* 1834.
Leopold Geo. Fredk., D. of Saxe and Pr. of Coburg Saalfeld, K.G.; aft. K. of the Belgians.
1821, July 19. Chas., M. of Drogheda, K.P.; *d.* 1822.
Wm., E. Harcourt, K.C.B.; *d.* 1830.
1830, July 22. Sir Alured Clarke, G.C.B; *d.* 1832.
Sir Saml. Hulse, G.C.H, G.C.M.G.; *d.* 1837.
1840. Fras. Albert Aug. Charles Emanuel (Consort of Her Majesty Queen Victoria), D. of Saxony, Pr. of Saxe-Coburg and Gotha, K.G., K.T., K.P., &c.; *d.* 1861.
1845, July 28. Wm. II., K. of the Netherlands, K.G.; *d.* 1849.
1846, Nov. 9. Sir Geo. Nugent, bt., K.C.B.; *d.* 1849.
Thos. Grosvenor; *d.* 1850.
Hy. Wm., M. of Anglesey, K.G., G.C.B.; G.C.H.
1854, Nov. 5. Fitzroy, Jas. Hy., ld. Raglan, G.C.B.; *d.* 1855.
1855, Oct. 2. Stapleton, visc. Combermere, G.C.B.; *d.* 1865.
Jno., E. of Strafford, G.C.B.; *d.* 1860.
Hy., visc. Hardinge, G.C.B.; *d.* 1856.
1860, Apr. 1. Jno., ld. Seaton, G.C.B., G.C.M.G.; *d.* 1863.
1862, Nov. 9. Sir Edw. Blakeney, G.C.B., G.C.H.; *d.* 1868.
Hugh, visc. Gough, K.P., G.C.B., K.S.I.; *d.* 1869.
Geo. Wm. Fred. Chas., D. of Cambridge, K.G., K.P., G.C.B., &c.
Colin, ld. Clyde, G.C.B., K.S.I.; *d.* 1863.
1868, Jan. 7. Sir Alexr. Woodford, G.C.B., G.C.M.G.; *d.* 1870.
Sir Wm. Maynard Gomm, G.C.B. *d.* 1875.
Sir Hew Dalrymple Ross, G.C.B. *d.* 1868.
Sir Jno. Fox Burgoyne, bt. G.C.B.; *d.* 1871.
1870, May 24. Sir Geo. Pollock, bt., G.C.B. G.C.S.I.; *d.* 1872.
1875, May 29. Sir Jno. Forster FitzGerald, G.C.B. *d.* 1877.
Geo., M. of Tweeddale, K.T. G.C.B.; *d.* 1876.
Alb. Edw., Pr. of Wales.
1877, June 2. Sir Wm. Rowan, G.C.B.; *d.* 1879.
Sir Chas. Yorke, G.C.B.; *d* 1880.
Hugh Hy., ld. Strathnairn, G.C.B. G.C S.I.; *d.* 1885.
1883, Jan. 1. Robt. Cornelis, ld. Napier of Magdala, G.C.B., G.C.S.I.
1883. Sir Patr. Grant, G.C.B., G.C.M.G. June 24.
1886, Mar. 27. Sir Rd. Jas. Dacres, G.C.B.; *d* 1887.
Sir Jno. Michel, G.C.B.; *d.* 1886.
1886. Wm. Paulet, c.c. ld. Wm. Paulet July 10.
1887. Geo. Chas., E. of Lucan, G.C.B. June 21; *d.* 1888.

GENERALS.

The Generals are arranged according to the following lists:—

LIST A.

Officers who attained the rank of General, down to June 1854.

LIST B.

Officers who attained the rank of Lieutenant-General, down to November 1846.

LIST C.

Officers who attained the rank of Major-General, down to January 1837.

LIST D.

Major-Generals from 1837, with their subsequent promotions to Lieutenant-Generals and Generals.

LIST A. GENERALS.

Officers who attained the rank of General, down to June 1854.

1690. Fredk., D. of Schomberg, Apr. 19; *d.* 1690.
Chas., D. of Schomberg, his son, May 29; *d.* 1693.
1703. Meinhardt, D. of Schomberg, bro. of the last-named, Aug. 16; *d.* 1719.
1704. Hy. de Massue, E. of Galway, July 3; *d.* 1720.
1705. Chas., E. of Peterborough; *d.* 1735.
1707. Chas. Churchill, bro. of John, D. of Marlborough, Jan. 1.
1708. Richd., E. Rivers, Apr. 22; *d.* 1712
1709. Danl. Hervey, Jan. 1.
1711, Wm. Stewart.
Jan. 30. Thos. Erle.
David, E. of Portmore, govr. of Gibraltar; *d.* 1730.
Hon. Hy. Lumley.
1712. Chas. Ross, Apr. 1.
John Richmond Webb, June 16.
1714. Chas., ld. Tyrawley, Nov. 13.
1717. Wm., ld., aft. E. Cadogan, July 12.
1727. Geo., E. of Cholmondeley, Mar. 1; *d.* 1733.
1730, Sir Chas. Wills, K.B.; *d.* 1746
July 2. Thomas Wetham.
Jos. Sabine.
Wm. Evans.
1743, Sir Philip Honywood, K.B.; *d.*
Feb. 1. 1752.
Lord Mark Ker.
1745. Sir Robt. Rich, bt., Mar. 29.
John, E. of Dunmore, May 30; *d.* 1752.
1746. Richd., visc. Molesworth, Dec. 28; *d.* 1758.
Sir John Ligonier, aft. ld., visc., and E. Ligonier, Dec. 30.
1747. Robt. Dalzell, Mar. 24.
Gervase Parker, Mar. 24.
Alg., D. of Somerset, Mar. 26; *d.* 1750.
John, D. of Montagu, Mar. 28; *d.* 1749.
Wm., E. of Harrington, Mar. 30; *d.* 1756.
1758, Chas., D. of Marlborough; *d.*
July 10. 1758.
David Montolieu, baron de St. Hippolite.

1761, John, E. of Westmorland, *d.* 1774.
Mar. Roger Handasyde, *d.* 1763.
Jas., ld. Tyrawley.
Chas. Otway, *d.* 1764.
Chas., ld. Cadogan, *d.* 1776.
Hon. Jas. St. Clair.
John Guise.
1765, John, E. of Rothes, *d.* 1773.
Feb. 22. Harry Pulteney, *d.* 1767.
Hon. sir Chas. Howard, K.B.; *d.* 1765.
John, D. of Argyll, K.T.; *d.* 1770.
Jas. Edwd. Oglethorpe, *d.* 1785.
John, E. De la Warr, K.B.; *d.* 1776.
1770, Sir John Mordaunt, K.B.
Apr. 13. Hon. Jas. Cholmondeley, *d.* 1775.
Peregrine Lascelles, *d.* 1772.
Ld. John Murray.
John, E. of Loudoun, *d.* 1782.
Wm., E. of Panmure, *d.* 1781.
Wm. Hy., M. of Lothian, K.T.; *d.* 1775.
Wm., E. of Harrington, *d.* 1779.
Hugh Warburton.
1772, Cuthbert Ellison.
May 26. Peregrine Bertie, D. of Ancaster and Kesteven, *d.* 1778.
Evelyn, D. of Kingston, K.G.; *d.* 1773.
Hugh, visc. Falmouth, *d.* 1782.
Simon, Earl Harcourt, *d.* 1777.
Hy. Arth. Herbert, E. of Powis, *d.* 1772.
Michl. O'Brien Dilkes, *d.* 1775.
John, E. of Sandwich, *d.* 1792.
Hon. Hy. Seymour Conway, *d.* 1795.
Jas. Abercrombie, *d.* 1781.
Geo., E. of Albemarle, K.G.; *d.* 1772.
Fras. Leighton, *d.* 1773.
Ld. Robt. Manners, *d.* 1782.
John Mostyn.
John, E. Waldegrave, *d.* 1784.
Wm. Hy., D. of Gloucester, K.G.; *d.* 1805.
1777, Sir. Geo. Howard, K.B.
Sept. 6. Hon. sir Jos. Yorke, aft. ld. Dover, K.B.; *d.* 1792.
Wm. Belford, *d.* 1780.
Ld. Robt. Bertie, *d.* 1782.
Philip Honywood, *d.* 1785.
1778, John, D. of Argyll, *d.* 1806.
Mar. 19. Hon. John Fitzwilliam, *d.* 1789.
Wm. A'Court Ashe.
Jeffrey, ld. Amherst, K.B.; *d.* 1797.
1778, John Griffin, ld. Howard de
Apr. 2. Walden, *d.* 1797.
Studholme Hodgson.
Geo. Augs. Elliot, K.B., aft. ld. Heathfield; *d.* 1790.
1782, John Lambton, *d.* 1794.
Nov. 20. John Parslow, *d.* 1786.
1782, Hon. Thos Gage, *d.* 1787.
Nov. 20. Geo., Marq. Townshend, *d.* 1807.
Ld. Fredk. Cavendish.
Chas., D. of Richmond, Lenox, and Aubigny, K.G.; *d.* 1806.
Hy., E. of Pembroke, *d.* 1794.
John Severn, *d.* 1787.
Sir John Sebright, bt., *d.* 1794.
Hon. Geo. Cary.
1783, Hon. Jas. Murray, *d.* 1794.
Feb. 19. Cyrus Trapaud, *d.* 1801.
Sir Wm. Boothby, bt., *d.* 1787.
Benjn. Carpenter, *d.* 1788.
Bygoe Armstrong.
Wm., E. of Shelburne, *d.* 1805.
Wm. Haviland, *d.* 1784.
Sir John Irwin, K.B.; *d.* 1788.
Chas. Vernon, *d.* 1810.
David Græme, *d.* 1792.
1793. Fredk., D. of York, K.G.; Apr. 12.
1793, Robt. Melville, *d.* 1809.
Oct. 25. Moriscoe Frederick, *d.* 1801.
Robt. Dalrymple Horn Elphinstone, *d.* 1794.
Jas. Johnstone.
Jas. Johnston.
Chas., M. of Drogheda, *d.* 1821.
Sir Wm. Augs. Pitt, K.B.; *d.* 1809.
Lord Adam Gordon, *d.* 1801.
Hon. sir Alexr. Maitland, bt., *d* 1820.
Archd., E. of Eglintoun, *d.* 1796
Hunt Walsh.
Guy, ld. Dorchester, K.B., govr of Canada; *d.* 1808.
Sir Chas. Thompson, bt.
Robt. Clerk.
Robt. Cunninghame, aft. ld. Rossmore; *d.* 1801.
Hon. sir Wm. Howe, K.B., aft visc. Howe; *d.* 1814.
Ld. Geo. Hy. Lenox, *d.* 1805.
Hy. Fletcher, *d.* 1803.
1793, Jno. Hale, *d.* 1806.
Oct. 25. Sir Robt. Boyd, K.B., govr. o Gibraltar; *d.* 1794.
Sir Hy. Clinton, K.B.; *d.* 1795.
Chas., ld. Southampton; *d.* 1797
Bernard Hale, *d.* 1798.
Fras. Craig, *d.* 1811.
Hugh, D. of Northumberland K.G.; *d.* 1817.
Wm. Taylor.
Chas., Marq. Cornwallis, K.G.; *d* 1805.
1796, Sir David Lindsay, bt.; *d.* 1797.
May 3. Edwd. Maxwell Brown, *d.* 1803.
Jas. Robinson.
Eyre, ld. Clarina; *d.* 1804.
Geo. Warde, *d.* 1803.
Flower Mocher, *d.* 1801.
Sir Robt. Sloper, K.B.; *d.* 1802.
Staates Long Morris, *d.* 1800.
Ralph, E. of Ross; *d.* 1802.

1796, May 3. Sir Jno. Dalling, bt., K.B.; *d.* 1798.
Russel Manners, *d.* 1800.
Thos. Hall, *d.* 1809.
James Grant, *d.* 1806.
Sir Wm. Faucett, K.B.; *d.* 1804.
Wm. Jno., M. of Lothian; *d.* 1815.
Sir Chas. Grey, K.B., aft. E. Grey; *d.* 1807.
Sir Thos. Spencer Wilson, bt.; *d.* 1798.
Geo. Morrison, *d.* 1799.
Thos. Clarke, *d.* 1799.
Chas. Rainsford, *d.* 1809.

1797, Jan. 26. Edwd. Matthew, *d.* 1805.
Jas Pattison, *d.* 1805.
Hon. Hy. St. John, *d.* 1818.
Jno. Campbell, *d.* 1807.
Sir Geo. Osborne, bt.; *d.* 1818.

1798, Jan. 1. Sir Thos. Shirley, bt.; *d.* 1800.
Patr. Tonyn, *d.* 1804.
Gabriel Christie, *d.* 1799.
Jno. Reid, *d.* 1807.
Sir Wm. Green, bt.; *d.* 1811.
Geo. Scott, *d.* 1811.
Chas. O'Hara, lt.-govr. and aft. govr. of Gibraltar; *d.* 1802.
Loftus Anthy. Tottenham, *d.* 1810.
Wm. Rowley, *d.* 1807.
Peter Bathurst.
Hon. Wm. Gordon, *d.* 1815.
Robt. Prescott, *d.* 1815.
Hon. Wm. Harcourt, *d.* 1830.
Hy. Lawes, E. of Carhampton; *d.* 1821.
Wm. Dalrymple, *d.* 1807.
Wm. Picton, *d.* 1811.
Sir Hector Munro, K.B.; *d.* 1806.
Hon. Wm. Hervey, *d.* 1815.
Jno. Fletcher Campbell, *d.* 1808.
Fras. Lascelles, *d.* 1799.
Sir Wm. Medows, K.B.; *d.* 1813.

1799. Edwd. D. of Kent, K.G., May 10; *d.* 1820.

1801, Jan. 1. Edwd. Smith, *d.* 1808.
Thos. Bland, *d.* 1816.
Felix. Buckley, *d.* 1823.
Geo. Ainslie, *d.* 1804.
Benj. Gordon, *d.* 1803.
Jas. Adeane, *d.* 1802.
Hy. Watson Powell.
Sir Thos. Stirling, bt.; *d.* 1808.
Geo. Garth, *d.* 1819.
Richd. Grenville, *d.* 1823.

1802, Apr. 29. Jno. Leland, *d.* 1808.
Jas. Hamilton, *d.* 1803.
Jno. Stratton, *d.* 1803.
Jas. Rooke, *d.* 1805.
Chas. Crosbie, *d.* 1807.
Jno., E. of Suffolk; *d.* 1820.
Hon, Chapple Norton, *d.* 1818.
Geo. Hotham, *d.* 1806.

1802, Apr. 29. Sir David Dundas, K.B.; *d.* 1820.
Sir Robt. Abercromby, G.C.B.; *d.* 1827.
Gerard Lake, aft. ld. and visc. Lake; *d.* 1808.
Sir Thos. Musgrave, *d.* 1812.
Jas. Coates, *d.* 1822.
Ralph Dundas, *d.* 1814.
Richd. Whyte, *d.* 1807.
Sir Alured Clarke, K.B.; *d.* 1832.

1803, Sept. 25. Wm. Shirreff, *d.* 1804.
Saml. Hulse, G.C.H.
Hon. Albemarle Bertie, aft. E. of Lindsey: *d.* 1818.
Chas. Valancey, *d.* 1802.
Jno. Thos., E. of Clanricarde; *d.* 1808.
Sir Jas. Steuart (Denham), bt., G.C.H.; *d.* 1839.
Thos. Carleton, *d.* 1817.
Jas. Marsh, *d.* 1804.
Wm. Grinfield.
Cavendish Lister, *d.* 1823.
Chas. Leigh, *d.* 1815.
Jas. Ogilvie.
Sir Robt. Laurie, bt.; *d.* 1804.
Wm. Edmeston, *d.* 1804.
David Home, *d.* 1810.
Hugh Debbeig, *d.* 1808.
Montgomery Agnew, *d.* 1813.
Alexr., E. of Balcarres; *d.* 1825.
Cornelius Cuyler, aft. bt.; *d.* 1819.
Chas., E. of Harrington, G.C.B., G.C.H.; *d.* 1829.
Hon. Richd. Fitzpatrick, *d.* 1813.
Nisbet Balfour, *d.* 1823.
Edmd. Stevens, *d.* 1825.
Sir Thos. Trigg, K.B., lt.-govr., and aft. govr. of Gibraltar; *d.* 1814.
Fras., E. of Moira, aft. M. of Hastings, govr.-gen. of India, and subsequently govr. of Malta; *d.* 1826.
Peter Craig, *d.* 1810.
Ernest Aug., D. of Cumberland, K.G., K.P., G.C.B., aft. K. of Hanover.
Adolphus Fredk., D. of Cambridge, K.G., G.C.B., G.C.H.

1808, Apr. 25. Edmd. Fanning, *d.* 1818.
Hy. Johnson, aft. bt., G.C.B.; *d.* 1835.
Hon. Hy. Edwd. Fox, lt.-govr. of Gibraltar; *d.* 1811.
Jno. Watson Tad. Watson, *d.* 1826.
Lowther Pennington, aft. ld. Muncaster; *d.* 1818.
Fras. Edwd. Gwin, *d.* 1822
Robt. Morse, *d.* 1818.

1808, Apr. 25. Fras., ld. Heathfield; *d.* 1813.
Thos. Sloughter Stanwix, *d.* 1815.
Sir Jas. Pulteney, bt.; *d.* 1811.
Wm. Fredk, D. of Gloucester, K.G.

1809, Oct 25. Robt. Donkin, *d.* 1821.
Jas. Balfour, *d.* 1823.
Sir Jas. Duff, knt.; *d.* 1839.
Hy., ld. Mulgrave, aft. E. of Mulgrave, G.C.B.; *d.* 1831.
Grice Blakeney.

1811, July 31. Arth., visc., aft. E., M., and D. of Wellington, K.G., G.C.B., G.C.H.

1812, Jan. 1. Sir Paulus Æmilius Irving, bt.; *d.* 1828.
Geo. Harris, G.C.B., aft. ld. Harris; *d.* 1829.
Richd. Vyse, *d.* 1825.
Wm., visc., aft. E. Cathcart, K.T.; *d.* 1843.
Sir Banastre Tarleton, bt., G.C.B.; *d.* 1833.
Sir Hew Dalrymple, bt.; *d.* 1830.
Gordon Forbes, *d.* 1828.
Sir John Floyd, bt.; *d.* 1818.
Oliver de Lancey, *d.* 1822.
Sir Jas. Hy. Craig, K.B.; *d.* 1812.
Anthony Farrington, aft. bt.; *d.* 1823.
Jas. Stuart.
John White.
Andr. John Drummond.
John Wm., E. of Bridgewater; *d.* 1823.
Ellis Walker.
Sir Wm. Maxwell, *d.* 1837.
Geo., E. of Pembroke, K.G.; *d.* 1827.
John, E. of Chatham, K.G., govr. of Gibraltar; *d.* 1835.
Alex. Campbell, *d.* 1832.
Wm. Morshed, *d.* 1822.
Fras. Dundas, *d.* 1824.
Alex. Ross, govr. of Fort George; *d.* 1827.
Hon. Fras. Needham, aft. visc. and E. Kilmorey; *d.* 1832.
Sir Hy. Pigot, G.C.M.G.; *d.* 1840.

1813, June 4. Geo. Bernard, *d.* 1820.
Sir Geo. Nugent, bt., K.B.
John Barclay, *d.* 1823.
Wm. Macarmick, *d.* 1815.
Sir Robt. Stuart, bt.
Sir Wm. Keppel, G.C.B., govr. of Guernsey; *d.* 1834.
John, ld. Hutchinson, G.C.B., aft. E. of Donoughmore; *d.* 1832.
John Hamilton, *d.* 1835.
Alexr. Leith Hay, *d.* 1838.
Jas. Stewart, *d.* 1815.
Sir Chas. Hastings, bt., G.C.H.; *d.* 1823.
Robt. Manners, *d.* 1823.
Wm. Loftus, *d.* 1831.

1813, June 4. Oliver Nicolls, *d.* 1829
Alexr. Mercer, *d.* 1816.
Sir Geo. Hewett, bt., G.C.B.; *d.* 1840.

1814, June 4. Philip Martin; *d.* 1821.
Sir Eyre Coote, K.C.B., K.H.
Chas., D. of Richmond, K.G., ld. lt. of Ir., govr.-gen. of the Canadas; *d.* 1819.
John Adolphus Harris, *d.* 1827.
Wm. John Arabin, *d.* 1828.
Sir Geo. Don, G.C.B., G.C.H., lt.-govr. of Gibraltar; *d.* 1832.
Sir John Fras. Cradock, or Caradoc, G.C.B., K.H., aft. ld. Howden; *d.* 1839.
Lord Chas. Fitz-Roy, *d.* 1829.
Napier Christie Burton, *d.* 1835.
Richd. Rich Wilford, *d.* 1822.
Edwd. Morrison, *d.* 1843.
Sir Chas. Asgill, bt., G.C.H; *d.* 1823.
Thos. Garth, *d.* 1829.
Vaughan Lloyd.
Jas., E. of Rosslyn, G.C.B.; *d.* 1837.
Andr. Cowell, *d.* 1821.
Jos. Dusseaux, *d.* 1823.
Colin Mackenzie, *d.* 1815.
John Dickson, *d.* 1816.
John Money.
Sir Geo. Beckwith, G.C.B., govr of Barbadoes in 1808; *d.* 182[illegible]
Thos. Murray, *d.* 1816.
Thos. Roberts.
Geo. Jas., Earl Ludlow, G.C.B. *d.* 1842.
Richd., E. of Cavan, K.B.; [illegible] 1837.
Sir David Baird, bt., G.C.B.; [illegible] 1829.
Hon. Fredk. St. John, *d.* 1844
Ld. Chas. Hy. Somerset; gov[illegible] of Cape of Good Hope; *d.* 183[illegible]
John Despard, *d.* 1829.
Wm. Wemyss, *d.* 1839.

1814, July 25. Wm. Fredk. Hy., hered. Pr. [illegible] Orange, G.C.B.; aft. K. of t[illegible] Netherlands.

1816, May 2. Leopold Geo. Fredk., D. of Sa[illegible] and Pr. of Coburg Saalfel[illegible] K.G.; aft. K. of the Belgians.

1819, Aug. 12. Hon. Robt. Taylor, *d.* 1839.
Geo. Milner, *d.* 1836.
Geo., M. of Huntly, G.C.B., a[illegible] D. of Gordon; *d.* 1836.
Hon. Edwd. Finch, *d.* 1843.
Isaac Gascoyne, *d.* 1841.
David Douglas Wemyss, *d.* 183[illegible]
Hon. John Leslie Cuming, 1824
Hy. Wynyard, *d.* 1838.
Duncan Campbell, *d.* 1837.
Thos. Grosvenor.
John Calcraft, *d.* 1829.

1819, Aug. 12. John, E. of Hopetoun, G.C.B.; *d.* 1823.
Jas., ld. Forbes; *d.* 1843.
Hy. Wm., M. of Anglesey, K.G., G.C.B., G.C.H.
Sir John Doyle, bt., G.C.B.; *d.* 1834.
Sir Robt. Brownrigg, bt., G.C.B.; *d.* 1833.
Wm. Knollys, *d.* 1834.
Hon. Edmd. Phipps, *d.* 1837.
Wm. Cartwright, *d.* 1827.
Ferd., Ct. Homspesch; *d.* 1831.
Sir Baldwin Leighton, bt.; *d.* 1828.
John Coffin, *d.* 1838.
John Murray, *d.* 1824.
Sir Chas. Green, bt.; *d.* 1831.
Thos. Hartcup, *d.* 1820.

1821, July 19. Sir Thos. Blomefield, bt.; *d.* 1822.
Gother Mann, *d.* 1830.
John Pratt.
Sir Josiah Champagné, G.C.H.; *d.* 1840.
Sir Harry Calvert, bt., G.C.B., G.C.H.; *d.* 1826.
Sir Geo. Cockburn, G.C.H.; *d.* 1847.
Edwd. Dunne, *d.* 1844.
Jas. Drummond, *d.* 1831.
Wm. Dowdeswell, *d.* 1828.
Sir Alexr. Mackenzie, bt., G.C.H.
Geo. Moncrieff, govr. of Carrickfergus; *d.* 1830.
Thos. Meyrick, *d.* 1830.
Thos. Graham, ld. Lynedoch, G.C.B.; *d.* 1843.
Geo. Hy. Vansittart, *d.* 1824.
Hon. Chas. Fitz-Roy, *d.* 1831.
Fras. Hugonin, *d.* 1836.

1825, May 27. Wm. Scott, *d.* 1836.
Fras. Fuller *d.* 1841.
Sir Jas. Affleck, bt.; *d.* 1833.
Geo. Vaughan Hart, *d.* 1832.
Geo. Warde, *d.* 1830.
Mervyn Archdall, *d.* 1839.
Sir John Cope Sherbrooke, G.C.B. govr. of Canada; *d.* 1830.
Sir Gordon Drummond, G.C.B.; govr. of Canada.
Jas. Wharton, *d.* 1841.
Sir Wm. Payne, bt., *d.* 1831.
Hon. Edwd. Bligh, *d.* 1840.
Ld. Wm. Cav. Bentinck, G.C.B., G.C.H.; *d.* 1839.
Edmd, E. of Cork, K.P.
Hon. sir Hy. Geo. Grey, G.C.B., G.C.H.; *d.* 1845.
Hon. sir Edwd. Paget, G.C.B., govr. of Ceylon; *d.* 1849.
Sir Brent Spencer, G.C.B.; *d.* 1828.
Stapleton, ld., aft. visc. Combermere, G.C.B., G.C.H.
Saml. Dalrymple, *d.* 1832.
Hon. Wm. Stapleton, *d.* 1826.

1825, May 27. Denzil Onslow, *d.* 1838.
Sir John Murray, bt., G.C.H.; *d.* 1827.
Wm. Twiss, *d.* 1827.
Hon. Chas. Hope, *d.* 1828.
Sir Geo. Pigot, bt.; *d.* 1841.
Rowland, visc. Hill, G.C.B., G.C.H. *d.* 1842.
Fredk. Maitland, *d.* 1848.
Sir Martin Hunter, G.C.H.; *d.* 1846.
Wm. Carr, visc. Beresford, G.C.B., G.C.H.; govr. of Jersey.

1830, July 22. Geo. E. of Dalhousie, G.C.H.; *d.* 1838.
Thos. Baker, *d.* 1849.
Hy. Williams, *d.* 1845.
Hy., M. of Conyngham, K.P., G.C.H.; *d.* 1833.
Hon. sir Alexr. Hope, G.C.B.; *d.* 1837.
Sir John Fraser, G.C.H.; *d.* 1843.
Peter Heron, *d.* 1848.
John Ramsay, *d.* 1845.
Sir John Delves Broughton, bt.; *d.* 1847.
Wm. Dyott, *d.* 1847.
Sir Ronald Craufurd Ferguson, G.C.B.; *d.* 1841.
Sir Robt. Macfarlane, K.C.B., G.C.H.; *d.* 1843.
Sir John Gustavus Crosbie, G.C.H.; *d.* 1843.
Edwd. Stack, *d.* 1833.
Hon. John Brodrick, *d.* 1842.
Sir Hy. Warde, G.C.B., govr. of Barbadoes; *d.* 1834.
Jas. Durham, *d.* 1840.
Hon. David Leslie, *d.* 1838.
John Manners Ker, *d.* 1843.
Thos. Scott, *d.* 1842.
Sir Hillgrove Turner, G.C.H.; *d.* 1843.
Christr. Chowne, *d.* 1834.
Hon. Wm. Mordaunt Maitland, *d.* 1841.
John, ld. Crewe, *d.* 1835.
Hon. sir Galbraith Lowry Cole, G.C.B.; *d.* 1842.
Quin Jno. Freeman, *d.* 1834.
Geo., E. of Granard, *d.* 1837.
Fras. Moore.
Robt. Edwd., visc. Lorton.
Sir Wm. Hy. Clinton, G.C.B.; *d.* 1846.

1837, Jan. 10. Sir Fras. Thos. Hammond, G.C.B.; *d.* 1850.
Robt. Dudley Blake, *d.* 1850.
Hon. Robt. Meade, *d.* 1849.
Sir Wm. Houston, or Houstoun, bt., G.C.B. and G.C.H.; lt.-govr. of Gibraltar; *d.* 1842.
Geo. Michel, *d.* 1846.
Sir Thos. Hislop, bt., G.C.B.; *d.* 1843.

1837, Jan. 10. Thos., E. of Elgin: *d.* 1841.
David Hunter, *d.* 1846.
Sir Jno. Slade, bt., G.C.H.
Sir Fredk. Augs. Wetherell, G.C.H.; *d.* 1842.
Jno. Daniell Arabin, *d.* 1838.
Hon. sir Wm. Lumley, G.C.B.; *d.* 1850.
Sir Moore Disney, K.C.B.; *d.* 1846.
Jno. M'Kenzie.
Alexr. Graham Stirling, *d.* 1849.
Jno. Michel, *d.* 1844.
Sir Wm. Wilkinson, G.C.M.G.; *d.* 1840.
Sir Hy. Tucker Montresor, K.C.B., K.C.H.; *d.* 1837.
Jno. Hodgson, *d.* 1846.
Richd. Thos. Nelson, *d.* 1842.
Sir Jas. Hay, K.C.H.; *d.* 1837.
Jas. Robertson, *d.* 1845.
Edwd. Wm. Leyburn Popham, *d.* 1843.
Sir Fitzroy Jeffries Grafton Maclean, bt., *d.* 1847.
Sir Hy. Fredk. Campbell, K.C.B., G.C.H.
Wm. Burnett, *d.* 1839.
Chas. Wm., M. of Londonderry, G.C.B., G.C.H.
Sir Jno. Smith, G.C.H.; *d.* 1837.
Lewis Bayly Wallace, *d.* 1848.
Jno. Sulivan Wood, lt. Tow. of Lond.
Hon. sir Chas. Colville, G.C.B., G.C.H.; *d.* 1843.
Fredk. Chas. White.
Gore Browne, *d.* 1843.
Sir Hy. Fane, G.C.B.; *d.* 1840.
Sir Geo. Anson, G.C.B.; *d.* 1849.
Kenneth Alexander, E. of Effingham, G.C.B.; *d.* 1845.
Thos. R. Charleton, *d.* 1849.
Wm. Thos. Dilkes, *d.* 1841.
Sir Jno. Oswald, G.C.B., G.C.M.G.; *d.* 1840.
Pinson Bonham.
Sir Wm. Anson, bt., K.C.B.; *d.* 1847.
Chas. Terrot, *d.* 1839.

1838, June 28. Sir Thos. Saumarez, *d.* 1845.
Campbell Callendar, *d.* 1845.
Jas. Meredyth, *d.* 1841.
Robt. Hill Farmar, *d.* 1839.
Jno. Stratford Saunders, *d.* 1846.
Geo. Wilson, *d.* 1841.
Sir Warren Marmaduke Peacocke, K.C.B.; *d.* 1849.
Jno. Pare, *d.* 1839.
Sir Chas. Wale, K.C.B.; *d.* 1845.
Sir Jno. Ormsby Vandeleur, G.C.B.; *d.* 1849.
Chas. Pye Douglas, *d.* 1844.
Robt. Browne Clayton, *d.* 1845.

1838, June 28. Alexr. Jno. Goldie, *d.* 1848.
Sir Roger Hale Sheaffe, bt.
Hon. sir Alexr. Duff, G.C.H.; *d.* 1851.
Sir Rufane Shawe Donkin, K.C.B., G.C.H.; *d.* 1841.
Wm. Eden.
Sir Geo. Townshend Walker, bt., G.C.B.; *d.* 1842.
Sir Jno. Hamilton Dalrymple, aft. E. of Stair.

1841, Nov. 23. Sir Geo. Murray, G.C.B., G.C.H.; *d.* 1846.
Sir Jas. Kempt, G.C.B., G.C.H.; lt.-govr. of Fort William.
Sir Evan Lloyd, K.C.H.; *d.* 1846.
Matthew Sharpe, *d.* 1845.
Richd. Blunt.
Sir Hy. Bayly, G.C.H.; *d.* 1846.
Fras. Slater Rebow, *d.* 1845.
Gerrard Gosselyn.
Sir Fredk. Philips Robinson, G.C.B.
Sir Arth. Richd. Dillon, bt.; *d.* 1845.
Duncan Darroch; *d.* 1847.
Sir Phineas Riall, K.C.H.; *d.* 1850.
Wm. Brooke, *d.* 1843.
John Vincent, *d.* 1848.
Jos. Walker, *d.* 1848.
Sir Wm. Hutchinson, K.C.H.; *d.* 1845.
John, ld., aft. E. of Strafford, G.C.B., G.C.H.
Sir Thos. Macdougall Brisbane, bt., G.C.B., G.C.H.
Sir Alexr. Halkett, K.C.H.
Sir Wm. Keir Grant, K.C.B., G.C.H.
Ld. Robt. Edwd. Hy. Somerset, G.C.B.; *d.* 1842.
Hon. Arth. Annesley, *d.* 1849.
Boyle Travers.
Sir Thos. Bradford, G.C.B., G.C.H.
Jno. Granby Clay, *d.* 1846.
Gage John Hall.
Hon. Wm. De Blaquiere, aft. ld. De Blaquiere.
Sir Thos. Browne, K.C.H.; *d.* 1843.
Sir John Lambert, G.C.B.; *d.* 1847.
Sir Jas. Willoughby Gordon, bt., G.C.B., G.C.H.; *d.* 1851.
Sir Thos. Gage Montresor, K.C.H.
Sir Ralph Darling, G.C.H.
Sir Robt. Thos. Wilson, govr. of Gibraltar; *d.* 1849.
Matthew, ld. Aylmer, G.C.B., govr. of Canada, &c.; *d.* 1850.

1846, Nov. 9. Sir Chas. Imhoff.
Gabriel Gordon.
Chas. Craven, *d.* 1850.

1846, Jas. Orde, *d.* 1850.
Nov. 9. Sir Chas. Bulkeley Egerton, G.C.M.G., G.C.H.
Sir Hy. John Cumming, K.C.H.
Thos. Birch Reynardson, *d.* 1847.
John, E. of Carysfort.
Sir Peregrine Maitland, K.C.B., govr. at the Cape, &c.
Hon. Thos. Edwd. Capel.
Godfrey Basil Mundy, *d.* 1848.
Sir Colin Halkett, G.C.B., G.C.H.
Sir Fredk. Adam, G.C.B., G.C.H., G.C.M.G.

1851, Sir Lewis Grant.
Nov. 11. Peter Carey.
Sir John Alexr. Wallace, bt., K.C.B.
Hastings Fraser, C.B.
Sir Geo. Pownall Adams.
Sir Loftus Wm. Otway, C.B.
Sir Edwd. Kerrison, bt., K.C.B., G.C.H.
Sir Robt. Barton.
Sir John Wright Guise, bt. K.C.B.
Paul Anderson, C.B.
Sir Andr. Jno. Fras. Barnard, G.C.B.
Richd. Pigot.
Sir Jas. Watson, K.C.B.
Sir Aug. De Butts.
Sir Richd. Bourke, K.C.B.
Hon. sir Patrick Stuart, G.C.M.G.
Hy. Otway, ld. Dacre, C.B.
Sir Howard Douglas, G.C.B. G.C.M.G.
Hon Arth. Percy Upton, C.B.
Samuel Huskisson.
Hy. Monckton.
John Maister.
Samuel Browne.
Dennis Herbert.
John Bruce Richd., visc. O'Neill.
Sir Edwd. Blakeney, G.C.B., G.C.S.I.
Sir Thos. Hawker, K.C.S.I.
Sir John Wilson, K.C.B.
John, ld. Seaton, G.C.B., G.C.M.G., G.C.S.I.
Sir Thos. McMahon, bt., K.C.B.
Sir Alexr. Woodford, G.C.B., G.C.M.G.
John, E. of Westmorland, G.C.B., G.C.S.I.

1854, Fitzroy Jas. Hy., ld. Raglan, G.C.B.
June 20. Ld. Chas. Somerset Manners, K.C.B.
Robt. Ellice.
Cosmo Gordon.
Hugh, visc. Gough, G.C.B.
Sir Jas. Macdonell, K.C.B., K.C.S.I.
Jas. Wallace Sleigh, C.B.
Sir Wm. Gabriel Davy, C.B., K.C.S.I.
Jonathan Yates.
Sir John Forster Fitzgerald, K.C.B.
Sir Arthur Benj. Clifton, K.C.B., K.C.S.I.
Wm. Cornwallis Eustace, C.B., K.C.S.I.
Chas. Murray, E. Cathcart, K.C.B.
Sir Alexr. Leith, K.C.B.
Sir Jno. Brown, K.C.S.I.
Hon. Hugh Arbuthnott, C.B.
Sir Jas. Douglas, K.C.B.
Sir Wm. Macbean, K.C.B.
Hy. visc. Hardinge, G.C.B.
Sir Willoughby Cotton, G.C.B., K.C.S.I.
Sir Jno. Hanbury, K.C.S.I.
Hy. Beauchamp, E. Beauchamp.
Hon. Edwd. Pyndar Lygon, C.B.
Sir Geo. Whitmore.
Hy. Shadforth.
Jno. Millet Hamerton, C.B.
Sir Wm. Tuyll, K.C.H.
Sir Geo. Hy. Fredk. Berkeley, K.C.B.
Sackville Hamilton Berkeley.
Helier Touzel.
Sir Hy. King, C.B., K.C.H.
Sir Geo. Thos. Napier, K.C.B.
Sir Geo. Scovell, K.C.B.
Ulysses, ld. Downes.
Geo., M. of Tweeddale, K.T., C.B.
Sir Fredk. Wm. Trench, K.C.H.
Hy. Wyndham.
Fredk. Rennell Thackeray, C.B.
Jno. Fras. Birch.
Gustavus Nicolls.
Hy. Evelegh.
Hon. Wm. Hy. Gardner.
Geo. Wright.
Fredk. Walker.
Sir Edwd. Bowater.
Jos. Webbe Tobin.
Sir Wm. Maynard Gomm.

LIST B. LIEUTENANT-GENERALS.

Officers who attained the rank of Lieutenant-General, down to November 1846.

* * Geo., E. of Linlithgow.
1678, Wm., E. of Craven.
May 1. Geo., E. of Dunbarton.
1688, Sir Jno. Lanier, *d.* 1692.
Nov. 6. Jas. Douglas, *d.* 1692.
1689. Arth., E. of Granard. Jan. 10.
1690. Wm. Hy., E. of Rochford, Sept. 12.
1690, Piercy Kirke.
Dec. 22. Robt. Mackay
1693, Jas. FitzJames, D. of Berwick;
Apr. 3. *d.* 1734.
1693, Jas., E. of Arran and D. of
Apr. 16. Hamilton; *d.* 1712.
Aubrey, E. of Oxford.
1694. Thos. Talmash, Jan. 8; *d.* 1694.
1694, Sir Hy. Bellasyse.
Oct. 24. Richd., E. of Scarborough.
Hy., E. of Romney.
Hon. sir Fras. Compton.
1696, Wm., visc. Montgomery, M. of
June 2. Powis.
1704, Jno., ld. Cutts.
Jan. 1. Thos. visc. Tiviot.
Geo. Ramsay.
Richd. Ingoldsby.
M. of Miremont.
Fras. Langston.
1706. David, E. of Leven, Apr. 6.
1707, Hy. Withers.
Jan. 1. Cornelius Wood.
Thos., E. of Strafford.
Chas., E. of Arran.
Algn., E. of Essex.
Edmd. Mayne.
Wm. Seymour.
Hatton Compton.
Robt. Echlyn.
Wm., M. of Lothian.
Jno. Tidcomb.
Hugh Windham.
1709, Jas. Maitland.
Jan. 1. Thos., visc. Windsor.
Thos. Meredyth.
Fras. Palmer.
Jas., E. Stanhope.
Geo. Macartney.
Jno., visc. Mordaunt.
Hon. Harry Mordaunt.
Thos. Farrington.
Wm., visc. Mountjoy.
1710, Richd. Gorges.
Jan. 10. Nichs. Sankey.
Jno., E. of Crawford.
Hy. Holt.
1710, Geo., D. of Northumberland, K.G.
Jan. 10. Geo., ld. Carpenter.
Chas., ld. Mohun; *d.* 1712.
1711, Jas., E. of Barrymore.
Mar. 12. Wm., ld. North and Grey.
Geo., E. Marischal.
Sir Wm. Douglas.
1712. Geo. Kellum, Apr. 5.
1715. Jno., E. of Sutherland, Nov. 16.
1727, Owen Wynne.
Mar. 1. Wm. Tatton.
Hayman Rooke.
Thos. Pearce.
1735, Richd. Sutton.
Oct. 17. Andr. Bisset.
Humphrey Gore.
Hy. Gore.
1735, Robt. Napier.
Nov. 2. Jas. Dormer.
Thos. Panton.
1739, Geo. Preston.
July 2. Albt. Borgard.
Fras. Columbine.
Richd. Franks.
Chas. Churchill.
Wm. Barrel.
Jasper Clayton.
Piercy Kirke.
Jas. Tyrrell.
Edmd. Fielding.
Jno. Peter Desbordes.
Wm. Ker.
Richd., E. of Scarborough.
1742, Hy., E. of Pembroke.
Feb. 18. Sir Daniel O'Carrol, bt.
Hon. sir Jas. Campbell, K.B.; *d.* 1745.
1743, Clement Nevill.
Feb. 1. Sir Jno. Arnot, bt.
Wm. Hargrave.
Hy. Cornwall.
Hy. Harrison.
Thos. Howard.
Sir Jno. Cope, K.B.
1743, Peter Campbell.
Mar. 26. Jas. Scott.
Jno. Jones.
Richd. Philips.
Hy. Hawley.
1745, Joshua Guest.
May 27. Phineas Bowles.
Philip Anstruther.
1745, Jno. Foliot.
June. Adam Williamson.
Thos. Wentworth.

1745, June. Chas., D. of Richmond, Lenox, and Aubigny, K.G.
Wm. Anne, E. of Albemarle.
1745. Chas., D. of Bolton, Dec. 24.
1747, Aug. Geo. Read.
Archd. Hamilton.
Richd. Onslow.
Philip Bragg.
Jno. Huske.
1747, Sept. Chas. Frampton.
Alexr. Irwine.
Richd. St. George.
Wm., ld. Blakeney, K.B.
Humphrey Bland.
Jno., E. of Crawford
Geo. Churchill.
Hy. Skelton.
Jno. Johnson.
Edwd. Wolfe.
Jno. Wynyard.
1754. Thos. Bligh, Mar. 23.
Thos. Fowke, Apr. 30, *d.* 1765.
Hy. de Grangues, May 3.
1758, Jan. Jas. Cochrane.
Jno. Brown.
Sir Jno. Bruce Hope, bt.
Jno. Foliot.
Hon. Thos. Murray.
Hon. Jas. Stuart, *d.* 1768.
Maurice Bocland.
Ld. Geo. Beauclerk, *d.* 1768.
Ld. Geo. Sackville, *d.* 1785.
1759, Jan. 30. Wm. Shirley.
Sir Wm. Pepperell, bt.
1759, Feb. 4. Jno., D. of Guilford, K.G.; *d.* 1771.
Jno., M. of Granby; *d.* 1771.
Geo., E. of Cholmondeley, K.B.
Geo., E. of Halifax, K.G.; *d.* 1771.
Wm., E. of Home, govr of Gibraltar; *d.* 1766.
1759, Mar. 28. Jas. Kennedy.
Lewis Dejean.
1759, Apr. 17. Hy. Holmes.
Sir Andr. Agnew, bt.; *d.* 1771.
Robt. Napier.
Sir Richd. Lyttelton, K.B.; *d.* 1770.
Edwd. Pole.
1760, Feb. 22. Hon. Edwd. Cornwallis, govr. of Gibraltar; *d.* 1776.
Edwd. Carr.
Hon. Geo. Boscawen, *d.* 1775.
Thos., E. of Effingham, *d.* 1763.
Sir Robt. Rich, bt.; *d.* 1785.
Sir Jno. Whiteford, bt.
Wm. Kingsley.
Chas., ld. Cathcart, K.T.; *d.* 1776.
Wm. Whitmore.
Alexr. Duroure.
Hon. Bennet Noel, *d.* 1766.
Jno. Adlercron, *d.* 1766.
Thos. Dunbar.

1760, Dec. Jas. Durand.
Jno., M. of Lorne.
1765, Jan. 19. Danl. Webb, *d.* 1773.
Jas. Paterson.
Robt. Anstruther.
Sir Chas. Montagu, K.B.; *d.* 1777.
Geo., E. of Granard.
Jno. Stanwix, *d.* 1796.
Chas. Jeffreys.
Wm. Strode, *d.* 1776.
Jos. Hudson, *d.* 1773.
Sir Hy. Erskine, bt.; *d.* 1765.
Robt. Armiger, *d.* 1770.
Sir David Cunningham, bt.
Hon. Thos. Brudenell, *d.* 1767.
1770, Apr. 30. Wm. Skinner.
Hon. Robt. Monckton, govr. New York; *d.* 1782.
Jno. Hy. Bastide.
Edwd. Sandford.
Theodore Dury.
Jno. Parker.
Hon. Chas. Colville, *d.* 1775.
Wm. Browne.
Jno., E. De la Warr; *d.* 1777.
Hy. Whitley.
Sir Jno. Clavering, K.B.; *d.* 1778.
Sir Geo. Grey, bt.; *d.* 1773.
Jas. Adolphus Oughton, aft. sir J.
Jas., D. of Leinster; *d.* 1773.
1772, May 26. Jas. Prescott Mackay.
Jno. Gore, *d.* 1773.
Geo. Williamson, *d.* 1781.
Hon. Wm. Keppel, *d.* 1782.
Sir Richd. Pierson, K.B.; *d.* 1781.
Jno. Owen, *d.* 1775.
Edwd. Harvey.
Wm. Rufane, *d.* 1773.
Hamilton Lambert.
Cadwallader, ld. Blaney; *d.* 1775.
Wm. Gansell, *d.* 1774.
Edwd. Urmston.
1777, Aug. 29. Robt. Melville.
Wm. Evelyn, *d.* 1783.
Jas. Gisborne.
Fras. Grant.
Wm. Alexr. Sorrell.
Richd., E. of Cavan; *d.* 1778.
Hon. Simon Fraser, *d.* 1782.
Thos. Desaguliers, *d.* 1780.
Geo. Preston, *d.* 1784.
Jno. Thomas.
Hon. Philip Sherrard, *d.* 1790.
Hon. Geo. Lane Parker, *d.* 1791.
Sir Fredk. Haldimand, K.B.
Hon. Alexr. Mackay.
Jno. Pomeroy, *d.* 1790.
Sir Wm. Draper, K.B., govr. of Minorca; *d.* 1787.
Sir Robt. Hamilton, bt.
Edwd., E. Ligonier, *d.* 1782.
Sir Eyre Coote, K.B.; *d.* 1783.

1779, Wm. Amherst, *d.* 1782.
Feb. 27. Jordan Wren.
Launcelot Baugh, *d.* 1792.
Hy. Smith, *d.* 1794.
Jno. Bell, *d.* 1798.
Robt. Watson, *d.* 1791.
Danl. Jones.
Jno. Mackenzie, *d.* 1791.
Sir Jno. Burgoyne, bt.; *d.* 1785.
1782, Hezekiah Fleming, *d.* 1784.
Nov. 20. Wm. Stile.
Hy. Lister.
Robt. Skene.
Thos. Calcraft.
Sir Chas. Thompson, bt.
Robt. Robinson.
Wm. Taylor, *d.* 1794.
Edwd. Maxwell.
Wm. Tryon, *d.* 1788.
Jas. Cuninghame.
Jos. Gabbett.
Hon. Jno. Vaughan.
Sir Robt. Pigot, bt.; *d.* 1796.
Sir Robt. Murray Keith, K.B.; *d.* 1795.
Richd. Prescott.
1787, Spencer Cowper.
Sep. 26. Wm. Wynyard, *d.* 1789.
Rd. Burton Phillipson, *d.* 1792.
Fras. Smith, *d.* 1791.
Jno. Douglas, *d.* 1795.
Hon. Alex. Leslie, *d.* 1794.
Saml. Cleveland.
Sir Wm. Erskine, bt.; *d.* 1795.
1793, Thos. Osbert Mordaunt, *d.* 1808.
Oct. 12. Jos. Broome, *d.* 1796.
Chas. Ross.
Jno. Mansell, *d.* 1794.
1796, Anthy. Geo. Martin, *d.* 1800.
May 3. Hon. Thos. Bruce.
Chas. Wilson Lyon, *d.* 1799.
1797, Wynter Blathwayte, *d.* 1801.
Jan. 16. Sir Ralph Abercromby, K.B.; *d.* 1801.
1799, Wm. Gardiner, *d.* 1806.
June 16. Jas. Lumsdaine, *d.* 1807.
Wm. Spry, *d.* 1802.
1801, Horatio Spry, *d.* 1811.
Jan. 1. Wm. Souter Johnston.
Harry Innes, *d.* 1806.
Alexr. Campbell, *d.* 1808.
Jas. Fras. Perkins, *d.* 1803.
Fras. D'Oyly, *d.* 1803.
Maurice Wemyss.
Andrew Gordon, *d.* 1806.
Jno. Graves Simcoe, *d.* 1806.
Chas. Horneck, *d.* 1804.
Hy. Bowyer, *d.* 1808.
Jos. Walton, *d.* 1808.
Abraham d'Aubant, *d.* 1805.
1802, Duncan Drummond, *d.* 1805.
June 29. Count C. D. de Meuron, *d.* 1806.
Philip Goldsworthy.
1803, Baron Chas. Homspech, *d.* 1812.
Sep. 25. Jno. Bowater.
1803, Thos. Avarne, *d.* 1805.
Sep. 23. Jas. Hethersett, *d.* 1812.
Jas. Campbell, *d.* 1808.
Chas. Tarrant.
Jno. Freke.
Richd. England, *d.* 1812.
Thos. Goldie, *d.* 1804.
Robt. Douglas.
Simon Fraser, *d.* 1813.
Thos. Davies, *d.* 1812.
Sir Wm. Myers, bt.; *d.* 1805.
1805, Wm. Borthwick, *d.* 1808.
Jan. 1. Harry Burrard, aft. sir H.; *d.* 1813.
Arth. Ormsby, *d.* 1808.
Hy. Read, *d.* 1821,
Jeffrey Amherst, *d.* 1815.
Count Pierre Fredk. de Meuron, *d.* 1812.
1805. Lucius Barber, June 8; *d.* 1808.
1805, Jas. Ferrier, *d.* 1809.
Oct. 30. Archd. Robertson.
Miles Staveley.
Edwd. Jas. Urquhart, *d.* 1810.
Geo. Churchill, *d.* 1808.
Hon. Eyre Power Trench, *d.* 1808.
Sir Jno. Moore, K.B.; *d.* 1809.
Hon. Hy. Astley Bennet; *d.* 1815.
Sir Chas. Ross, bt.; *d.* 1814.
Jno. Whitelocke.
Hay Macdowall, *d.* 1810.
Wm. Anne Villettes, *d.* 1808.
1808, Garret Fisher, *d.* 1810.
April 25. Geo. Benson.
Geo., ld. Southampton; *d.* 1810.
Fras., ld. Seaforth.
Hon. sir Brydges Trecothick Heniker, *d.* 1816.
Wm. Thornton, *d.* 1841.
Sir Jno. Stuart, K.B., and Count of Maida (Sicilian title); *d.* 1815.
Hon. Vere Poulett, *d.* 1812.
Chas. Barton, *d.* 1819.
Alex. Makenzie Fraser, *d.* 1809.
Sir Wm. Congreve, bt., K.C.H.; *d.* 1814.
1809, Fredk. Wm., D. of Brunswick;
July 1. *d.* 1815.
1809, Geo. Elliott, *d.* 1820.
Oct. 25. Richd. Chapman, *d.* 1812.
Richd. Armstrong.
Wm. St. Leger, *d.* 1818.
Richd. Northey Hopkins, *d.* 1845.
1810, Patr. Sinclair, *d.* 1820.
July 25. Wm. Orch. Huddlestone, *d.* 1814.
Geo. Fead, *d.* 1815.
Jas. Sowerby, *d.* 1811.
Donald M'Donald, 1812.
Forbes Champagne, *d.* 1816.
Sir Chas. G. Craufurd.
1811, Fredc., bar. Dreschsel, German
June 4. Legion; *d.* 1826.
Chas., bar. Linsengen, K.C.B., G.C.H.; *d.* 1830.
Geo. Rochfort, *d.* 1821.

1811, June 4. Fras. Grose.
Hy. Richmond Gale.
Jno. Spens, *d.* 1821.
Robt. Tipping, *d.* 1823.
Archd. Campbell.
Alex. Trotter.
Jno. Robinson, *d.* 1819.
Hon. Thos. Maitland, G.C.B., govr. of Malta and the Ionian Islands; *d.* 1824.
Richd. Bright, *d.* 1831.
Wm. Ramsay, *d.* 1827.
Jas. Campbell.
Jno. Skerrett.
Sir Hildebrand Oakes, bt., G.C.B.; *d.* 1822.
Sir Colin Campbell.
Sir Geo. Prevost, bt.; *d.* 1816.
Wm. Waller, *d.* 1819.
Wm., E. of Craven; *d.* 1825.
Lord Wm. Bentinck.
Arthur Whetham, *d.* 1813.

1812, Jan. 1. Wm. Johnstone.
Jno. Leveson Gower; *d.* 1816.
Richd., E. of Donoughmore; *d.* 1825.
Hon. Jno. Abercromby, G.C.B.; *d.* 1817.

1813. Count Walmoden, Jan. 21; *d.* 1818.

1813, June 4. Jno. Evelegh, *d.* 1815.
Geo. Porter, aft. bar. de Hochefried; *d.* 1828.
Sir Jas. Erskine, *d.* 1825.
Robt. Lawson, *d.* 1816.
Thos. Peter, *d.* 1828.
Hon. Montague Matthew, *d.* 1819.
Andrew Gammell, *d.* 1815.
Sir Saml. Auchmuty, K.B.; *d.* 1822.
Sir Jas. Leith, K.B.; *d.* 1816.
Wm. Robertson, *d.* 1821.
Matth. Baillie, *d.* 1825.
Wm. Simson.
Wm. Munro, *d.* 1821.
Sir Jas. Campbell, bt.; *d.* 1819.
Sir Thos. Picton, K.B., K.C.H.; *d.* 1815.
Jno. Gordon Cuming Skene, *d.* 1828.
Sir Gonville Bromhead, bt.; *d.* 1822.
Stafford Lightburne, *d.* 1827.
Jno. Hy. Loft.
Edwd. Stephens, *d.* 1815.
Hon. sir Wm. Stewart, K.B.; *d.* 1827.

1814, June 4. Sir Jno. Hamilton, bt., *d.* 1835.
Robt. Douglas, *d.* 1827.
Jno. Prince, *d.* 1824.
Jno. Macleod, *d.* 1833.
Walter Cliffe, *d.* 1816.
Wm. Wynyard, *d.* 1819.
Alexr. Wood, *d.* 1817.
Alexr. Dirom, *d.* 1830.
Anthy. Lewis Layard, *d.* 1823.

1814, June 4. Jno., E., aft. M. of Breadalbane; *d.* 1834.
Wm. Spencer, *d.* 1829.
Saml. Graham, *d.* 1831.
Jas. Montgomerie, *d.* 1829.
Wm. Wright, *d.* 1818.
Wm. Buchanan, *d.* 1830.
Wm. Murray, *d.* 1818
Robt. Brereton, *d.* 1818.
Jno. Timms Hervey Elwes, *d.* 1824.
Wm. Thomas, *d.* 1848.
Fredc., count von der Decken, G.C.H.; *d.* 1840.
Christr. Darby, *d.* 1832.
Sir Albt. Gledstanes, *d.* 1818.
Chas. Stevenson, *d.* 1828.
Sir Wrothe Palmer Acland, or Ackland, K.C.B.; *d.* 1816.
Nichs. Nepean, *d.* 1824.
Jas. Taylor, *d.* 1825.
Sir Miles Nightingall, K.C.B.; *d.* 1829.
Wm. Cockell, *d.* 1831.
Leonard Shafto Orde, *d.* 1820.
Richd. Bingham, *d.* 1829.
Jno. Lee, *d.* 1821.
Sir Hy. Clinton, G.C.B., G.C.H.; *d.* 1829.
Jno. Sontag, *d.* 1816.
Jas. Dunlop, *d.* 1832.
Walter Kerr, *d.* 1833.
Sir Alexr. Campbell, bt., K.C.B.; *d.* 1824.

1819, Aug. 12. Wm. Cuppage, *d.* 1832.
Thos. Seward, *d.* 1831.
Fras. Laye, *d.* 1828.
Bayly Willington, *d.* 1823.
Jno. Croker, *d.* 1833.
Sir Jno. Hope, G.C.H.; *d.* 1836.
Geo. Meyrick.
Sir Alan Cameron, K.C.B.; *d.* 1828.
Thos. Andrew, ld. Blaney; *d.* 1834.
Hon. Stephen Mahon, *d.* 1828.
Danl. O'Meara, *d.* 1821.
Fras., bar. Rottenburg, *d.* 1832.
Lewis Lindenthal, *d.* 1837.
Roger Cochlan, *d.* 1834.
Sir Robt. Bolton, G.C.H.; *d.* 1836.
Robt. Cheney, *d.* 1820.
Sir Harry de Hinüber, K.C.B., K.C.H.; *d.* 1833.
Sir Hy. Bell, K.C.B.; *d.* 1835.
Thos. Strickland, *d.* 1828.
Thos., ld. Hartland, *d.* 1835.
Sir J. Shaw Maxwell, bt., *d.* 1830.
Hy. Rudyerd, *d.* 1828.
Wm. Doyle, *d.* 1823.
Jno. Hatton, *d.* 1821.
Sir Edwd. Howorth, K.C.B.; *a.* 1827.

1819, Jno. Dorrien, *d.* 1825.
Aug. 12. Thos. Desbrisay, *d.* 1823.
Wm. Fyers, *d.* 1829.
Geo. Glasgow, *d.* 1820.
Robt. Winter, *a.* 1822.
1821, Wm. Bentham, *d.* 1826.
July 19. Edwd. Stehelin, *d.* 1827.
Jno. Augustus Schalch, *d.* 1828.
Hy. Hutton.
Jno. Simon Farley, *d.* 1824.
Jno. Jenkinson, *d.* 1830.
Theoph. Lewis, *d.* 1833.
Fras. Delaval, *d.* 1828.
Richd. Williams.
Lawrence Desborough, *d.* 1825.
Jno. Mackelcan, *d.* 1838.
Jno. Thos. Layard, *d.* 1828.
Jno. Skinner.
Watkin Tench, *d.* 1833.
Lachlan Maclean, *d.* 1829.
Saml. Rimington, *d.* 1826.
David Ballingall, *d.* 1833.
David Shank, *d.* 1830.
Jno. Jas. Barlow.
Christr. Jeaffreson, *d.* 1824.
Wm. Minet, *d.* 1829.
Sir Wm. Cockburn, bt., *d.* 1835.
W. Waldegrave Pelham Clay, *d.* 1822.
Jno. Le Couteur, *d.* 1835.
Robt. Burne, *d.* 1825.
Sir Wm. Ayllett, knt., *d.* 1834.
Jno. Rigby Fletcher, *d.* 1830.
Hugh Mackay Gordon, *d.* 1823.
Robt. Ballard Long, *d.* 1825.
Jno. Hughes, *d.* 1832.
Sir Geo. Airey, knt., K.C.H. ; *d.* 1833.
Hon. sir Edwd. Stopford, G.C.B. ; *d.* 1837.
Sir Geo. Cooke, K.C.B. ; *d.* 1837.
Thos. Jos. Backhouse, *d.* 1828.
Fras. Gerard, visc. Lake, *d.* 1836.
Richd. Stovin, *d.* 1825.
Sir Kenneth Mackenzie Douglas, *d.* 1833.
Sir Fras. Jno. Wilder, *d.* 1823.
Geo., ld. Walsingham ; *d.* 1831.
Sir Saml. Hawker, G.C.H., *d.* 1838.
1825, Wm. Raymond, *d.* 1830.
May 27. Terence O'Loghlin, *d.* 1843.
Chas. N. Cookson, *d.* 1830.
Wm. Johnston, *d.* 1827.
Jno. Burton, *d.* 1830.
Sir D. Latimer Tinling Widdrington, K.C.B., *d.* 1839.
Wm. Guard, *d.* 1830.
Sir Thos. Richd. Dyer, bt. ; *d.* 1838.
Hy. Conran, *d.* 1829.
Sir Wm. Hy. Pringle, G.C.B. ; *d.* 1840.
Philip Kearney Skinner, *d.* 1826.

1825, Jno. Grey, *d.* 1837.
May 27. Jno. Murray, *d.* 1841.
Arth. Aylmer, *d.* 1831.
Jno. Mackenzie, *d.* 1833.
Sir Edwd Barnes, G.C.B., govr. of Ceylon; *d.* 1838.
Edm. Reiley Cope, *d.* 1835.
Sir Thos. Molyneux, bt. ; *d.* 1841.
Geo. Andr. Armstrong, *d.* 1834.
Sir Augustine Fitzgerald, bt. ; *d.* 1834.
Benjn. Forbes Gordon, *d.* 1840.
Wm. Peachy, *d.* 1838.
Jas. Butler, *d.* 1836.
Sir Wm. Inglis, K.C.B. ; *d.* 1835.
Geo. Lewis, *d.* 1828.
Robt. Lethbridge, *d.* 1831.
Danl. Seddon, *d.* 1839.
Geo. Robt. Ainslie, *d.* 1839.
Richd. O'Donovan, *d.* 1829.
Chas. Neville, *d.* 1837.
Hon. Thos. Wm. Fermor, aft. E. of Pomfret ; *d.* 1833.
Hugh Swayne, *d.* 1836.
Hon. Wm. Fitzroy, *d.* 1837.
Chas. Griffiths, *d.* 1829.
Fredk. Wm. Buller.
Alexr. Cosby Jackson, *d.* 1827.
Michl. Head, *d.* 1829.
Sir Jos. Fuller, G.C.H. ; *d.* 1841.
Sir Manley Power, K.C.B. ; *d.* 1826.
Geo. Horsford, *d.* 1840.
Sir Herbert Taylor, G.C.B., G.C.H. ; *d.* 1839.
1830, Jno. Humfrey, *d.* 1832.
July 22. Alexr. Adams, *d.* 1834.
Godfrey, ld. Macdonald ; *d.* 1832.
Saml. Nead, *d.* 1839.
Edwd. Webber, *d.* 1845.
Thos. L'Estrange, *d.* 1845.
Jos. Foveaux, *d.* 1846.
Geo. Kinnaird Dana, *d.* 1837.
Jas. Moore, *d.* 1848.
Sir Hy. Maghall Mervyn Vavasour, bt. ; *d.* 1838.
Hy. Raleigh Knight, *d.* 1836.
Sir Saml. Venables Hinde, K.C.B. ; *d.* 1837.
Thos. Norton Wyndham, *d.* 1839.
Berkenhead Glegg, *d.* 1842.
Hon. Jas. Ramsay, *d.* 1837.
Lewis Mosheim, *d.* 1830.
Sir Colquhoun Grant, K.C.B., G.C.H. ; *d.* 1835.
Sir Jas. Lyon, K.C.B., G.C.H. ; *d.* 1842.
Sir Thos. Sydney Beckwith, K.C.B. ; *d.* 1831.
Sir Chas. Phillips, knt. ; *d.* 1846.
Hy. Bruce, *d.* 1837.
Sir Wm. Sheridan, bt. ; *d.* 1836.
Hon. sir Robt. Wm. O'Callaghan, G.C.B., K.C.H. ; *d.* 1840.

1830, July 22. Sir Jno. Keane, G.C.B., G.C.H., aft. ld. Keane; *d.* 1844.
Ld. Geo. Thos. Beresford, G.C.H.; *d.* 1839.
Robt. Campbell. *d.* 1837.
Robt. Balfour, *d.* 1837.
Robt. Alexr. Dalzell, E. of Carnwath; *d.* 1839.
Jas. Cuming, *d.* 1839.
Hy. Eustace, *d.* 1844.
Sir Hy. Edwd. Bunbury, bt., K.C.B.
Sir Hudson Lowe, K.C.B., G.C.M.G., govr. of St. Helena; *d.* 1844.
Sir Hussey Vivian, G.C.B., G.C.H.; *d.* 1842.
Benj., ld. Bloomfield, G.C.B., G.C.H.; *d.* 1846.
Geo. Cookson, *d.* 1835.

1837, Jan. 10. Sir Jno. Elley, K.C.B., K.C.H.; *d.* 1839.
Sir Hy. Sheehy Keating, K.C.B.; *d.* 1847.
Sir Arth. Brooke, K.C.B.; *d.* 1843.
Hy. Shrapnel, *d.* 1842.
Jno. M'Nair, C.B.; *d.* 1840.
Sebright Mawby, *d.* 1850.
Jno. Montague Mainwaring; *d.* 1842.
Hon. Jno. Meade; *d.* 1849.
Sir John M'Leod, K.C.H.
Hy. Elliott, *d.* 1841.
Overington Blunden, *d.* 1837.
Sir Benj. D'Urban, G.C.B., G.C.H.; *d.* 1849.
Jno. Locke, *d.* 1837.
Geo. Wulff, *d.* 1846.
Sir Jno. Taylor, K.C.B.; *d.* 1843.
Sir Saml. Trevor Dickens, K.C.H.; *d.* 1847.
Sir Willshire Wilson, K.C.H.; *d.* 1842.
Sir Thos. Reynell, bt., K.C.B.; *d.* 1848.
Sir Wm. Nicolay, C.B., K.C.H.; *d.* 1842.
Sir Lionel Smith, bt., K.C.B., K.C.H.; *d.* 1842.
Sir Wm. Paterson, K.C.H.; *d.* 1849.
Sir Chas. Wm. Doyle, G.C.H.; *d.* 1842.
Sir Jas. Bathurst, K.C.B.; *d.* 1850.
Jas., ld. Glenlyon, K.C.H.; *d.* 1837.
Spencer Claudius Parry, *d.* 1845.
Geo. Wm. Phipps, *d.* 1841.
Wm. Millar, *d.* 1838.
Sir Jas. Stevenson Barns, K.C.B., K.C.; *d.* 1850.
Wm. Geo., ld. Harris, K.C.H.; *d.* 1845.
Sir Theophilus Pritzler, K.C.B.; *d.* 1839.

1837, Jan. 10. Montagu Burrows, *d.* 1848.
Sir Jno. Cameron, K.C.B.; *d.* 1844.
Geo. Salmon, *d.* 1848.
Hon. Geo. Murray, *d.* 1848.
Sir Hy. Askew, bt.; *d.* 1847.
Hon. Wm. Stuart, *d.* 1837.
Sir Jasper Nicolls, K.C.B.; *d.* 1849.

1838, June 28. Jno. Ross, *d.* 1843.
Hon. sir Hy. King, K.C.B.; *d.* 1839.
Sir Wm. Thornton, K.C.B.; *d.* 1840.
Sir Jos. Maclean, K.C.H.; *d.* 1839.
Richd. Dickinson, *d.* 1846.
Sir Jno. Macdonald, G.C.B.; *d.* 1850.
Anthy. Salvin, *d.* 1844.
Anthy. Walsh, *d.* 1839.
Sir Wm. Johnston, K.C.B.; *d.* 1844.
Fras. Newbery, *d.* 1847.
Alexr. Armstrong.
Danl. Fras. Blommart, *d.* 1844.
Sir Jos. Straton, K.B., K.C.H.; *d.* 1840.
Sir Jas. Chas. Dalbiac, K.C.H.; *d.* 1847.
Sir Jno. Maclean, K.C.B.; *d.* 1848.
Jas. Home, *d.* 1849.
Sir Richd. Downes Jackson, *d.* 1845.
Sir Geo. Augs. Quentin, K.C.H.
Sir Colin Campbell, K.C.B.; *d.* 1847.
Sir Saml. Ford Whittingham, K.C.B., K.C.H.; *d.* 1841.
Sir Archd. Campbell, bt., G.C.B.; *d.* 1843.
Sir Thos. Arbuthnot, K.C.B.; *d.* 1849.
Sir H. F. Bouverie, K.C.B., G.C.M.G.
Hy. Evatt.
Sir Fredk. Wm. Mulcaster, K.C.H., R.A.; *d.* 1846.

1841, Nov. 23. Sir Jno. Buchan, K.C.B.; *d.* 1850.
Edwd. Pritchard,; *d.* 1845.
Sir Maurice Chas. O'Connell, *d.* 1848.
Sir Andrew Pilkington, K.C.B.
Alexr. Bethune, *d.* 1848.
Sir Jno. Gardiner, K.C.B.
Geo. Middlemore, *d.* 1850.
Jas. Lomax, *d.* 1848.
Alexr. Nesbitt, *d.* 1849.
Sir Chas. Wm. Maxwell, K.C.H.; *d.* 1848.
Robt. Beevor, R.A.; *d.* 1843.
Mark Napier, *d.* 1843.
Jno. Wardlaw, *d.* 1848.
Wm. Augs. Johnson, ret. 1842.
Sir Jas. Kearney, K.C.H.; *d.* 1846.
Thos. Foster, *d.* 1843.

1841, Nov. 23. Jno. Le Mesurier, *d.* 1843.
Hon. Jno. Ramsay, *d.* 1842.
Robt. Owen, *d.* 1846.
Jas. Shortall, *d.* 1846.
Robt. Crawford, *d.* 1850.
Effingham Lindsay, *d.* in France, 1848.
Philip Philpot, *d.* 1843.
Count sir Fras. Rivarola, K.C.H.
Hon. sir Robt. Laurence Dundas, K.C.B. ; *d.* 1844.
Sir Robt. Arbuthnot, K.C.B.
Geo. Guy Carleton L'Estrange, *d.* 1848.
Sir Thos. Pearson, K.C.H. ; *d.* 1847.
Sir Dugald Little Gilmour, K.C.B. ; *d.* 1847.
Sir Gregory Holman Bromley Way ; *d.* 1844.
Sir Jno. Waters, K.C.B. ; *d.* 1842.
Sir Wm. Parker Carroll, K.C.H. ; *d.* 1842.
Jno. Clitherow.

1846, Nov. 9. Elias Walker Durnford, *d.* 1850
Arth. Lloyd.
Parry Jones Parry, K.C.H.
Sir David Ximenes, K.C.H. ; *d* 1848.
Daniel Colquhoun, *d.* 1848.
Chas. Nicol, *d.* 1850.
Sir Chas. Jas. Napier, G.C.B
Sir Jeremiah Dickson, K.C.B. ; *d* 1848.
Sir Chas. Wade Thornton, K.C.H
Sir Edwd. Gibbs, K.C.B. ; *d.* 1847
Hon. sir Hercules Robt. Pakenham, K.C.B. ; *d.* 1850.
Sir Jno. Harvey, K.C.B., K.C.H.
Sir Thos. Downman, K.C.H.
Sir Neil Douglas, K.C.B., K.C.H.
Alexr. Geo., ld. Saltoun and Abernethy, K.C.B., K.C.H.
Sir Steph. Remnant Chapman K.C.H. ; *d.* 1851.
Sir Jos. Hugh Carncross, K.C.B. *d.* 1847.
Alexr. Watson, *d.* 1849.
Edwd. Vaughan Worsley, *d.* 1850

LIST C. MAJOR-GENERALS.

Officers who attained the rank of Major-General, down to January 1837.

1690. Chas. Trelawney, Dec. 2.
1696, Mar. 30. Arnold Joost, E. of Albemarle; *d.* 1718.
Michl. Richards.
1696, June 1. Richd. Leveson.
Wm. Lloyd.
Wm., Count de Marton.
1697. Geo., Pr. of Hesse-Darmstadt, June 27; *d.* 1705.
1702. Wm. Selwyn, June 10.
1704, Jan. 1. Gusts., visc. Boyne; *d.* 1723.
Jno. Shrimpton.
Hy. Cunningham, *d.* 1706.
Arth. E. of Donegal; *d.* 1706.
Sir Bevil Granville, govr. of Barbadoes.
Jas., E. of Derby.
Fredk. Hamilton.
1705, Jan. 1. Robt. Killigrew, *d.* 1707.
Jas. Ferguson.
1707, Jan. 1. Emanl. Howe.
Thos. Brudenell.
Wm., visc. Charlemont; *d.* 1728.
Chas., ld. Baltimore.
1709. Samson de Lalo, Jan. 1; *d.* 1709.
1710, Jan. 1. Thos. Handasyde.
Jno. Bayne.
Barth. Ogilvy.
Sherrington Davenport.
Jno. Livesay.
Edwd. Braddock.
Gilbert Primrose.
Edwd. Pearce.
Roger Elliot.
Jno. Pepper.
Jos. Wightman.
Jno. Newton.
Thos. Crowther.
Chas. Sybourgh.
Richd. Holmes.
Chas., E. of Orrery.
Thos. Pulteney.
1712. Christr. ld. Slane, Jan. 1.
Jno. Hill, July 27; *d.* 1732.
1727, Mar. Hy., E. of Deloraine.
Richd. Russel.
Robt. Wroth.
Nichs. Price.
Ld. Jno. Ker, *d.* 1728
Thos. Stanwix.
Jas. Crofts.
Danl. Creighton.
Andr. Wheeler.
Robt. Hunter.
1735. Sir Jas. Wood, bt., Oct. 27.
1735, Nov. 4. Paul de Gually.
Jas. Moyle.
1739, July 2. Jno. Cavalier.
Balthazar Rivas de Foisac.
Jas. Douglas.
Jno. Orfeur.
Jno. Armstrong.
Chas., ld. Cathcart; *d.* 1740.
1743. Hon. Steph. Cornwallis, *d.* 1743.
Fras., E. of Effingham, *d.* 1763.
Fras. Fuller.
Hon. Hy. Ponsonby, *d.* 1745.
1745, May. Wm. Merrick.
Anthy. Lowther.
1747, Sep. Sir Wm. Gooch, bt.
Sir Chas. Armand Poulett, K.B.; *d.* 1765.
Geo., ld. Torrington; *d.* 1750.
Jas. Fleming.
Jno. Price.
1754, Mar. Richd. O'Farrel.
Edwd. Richbell.
Edwd. Braddock, *d.* 1755.
1755. Hon. Wm. Herbert, Feb. 21.
Richd, ld. Edgcumbe, Mar. 10
1757. Alexr. Drury, Feb. 2; *d.* 1758.
1757, Feb. 9. Hedworth Lambton.
Peregrine Thos. Hopson, *d.* 1759.
Ld. Chas. Hay, *d.* 1760.
1758. Paul Mascareen.
Granville Elliott, *d.* 1759.
1759. Jas. Wolfe, *d.* 1759.
1759, May 14. Jno. Parsons.
Julius Cæsar, *d.* 1762.
Geo. Walsh.
1759, June 25. Andr. Robinson.
Ld. Chas. Manners.
David Watson.
Hon. Jno. Barrington.
Sir Jas. Lockhart Ross, bt.
Borgard Michelson.
Jno. Grey.
1760. Stringer Lawrence, Dec. 9; *d.* 1775.
1761, Feb. Edwd. Whitmore.
Alexr., ld. Lindores.
1761, Mar. Hon. Sharrington Talbot, *d.* 1766.
Wm. Petitot.
Hon. Jno. Boscawen, *d.* 1767.
Jno. Lafusille, *d.* 1763.
Jno. Toovey.
1762, June 10. Jno. Furbar.
Ralph Burton.
Marcus Smith.

1764. Robt., ld. Clive, May 11; *d.* 1774.
1770, Apr. 30. Wm., E. of Glencairn; *d.* 1775.
Wm. Deane, *d.* 1775.
Jno. Salter, *d.* 1787.
Thos. Erle, *d.* 1777.
Richd. Worge, *d.* 1774.
Nevill Tatton.
Richd. Bendysh.
Jno. Scott, *d.* 1775.
1772, May 26. Wm. Napier.
Thos. Townshend.
Jno. Bradstreet, *d.* 1774.
1777, Aug. 29. Jno. Barlow.
Val. Jones.
Wm. Phillips.
David Erskine
1779, Feb. 27. Wm. Thornton.
Aug. Prevost, *d.* 1786.
Geo. Ogilvie.
1781, Oct. 19. Jas., E. of Loudoun.
Jas. Bramham, *d.* 1786.
Arth. Preston.
Robt. Sandford.
Jno. Roberts.
Anthy. St Leger.
Jas. Stuart, *d.* 1793.
Archd. McNab.
Wm. Roy, *d.* 1790.
Chas. Ross.
Harry Trelawney.
1782, Nov. 20. Jas. Paterson.
Hy. Gladwin.
Sir Jno. Burgoyne, bt.; *d.* 1785.
Thos., ld. Say and Sele; *d.* 1788.
Humphrey Stevens, *d.* 1791.
Jno. Mackenzie, ld. Macleod; *d.* 1789.
Sir Hy. Calder, bt., govr. of Gibraltar; *d.* 1792.
Hy. Pringle, *d.* 1800.
Sir Jno. Wrottesley, bt.; *d.* 1787.
Jas. D'Auvergne.
Arth. Tucker Collins, *d.* 1793.
Hon. Jas. Murray, *d.* 1794.
Saml. Townsend.
Arth. Geo. Martin.
West Hyde.
Hon. Thos. Bruce.
Walter Carruthers.
Philip Skene.
Thos. Marriott.
Thos. Cox.
Sir Archd. Campbell, K.B.; *d.* 1791.
Hon. Edwd. Stopford.
1787, Sept. 28. Thos., E. of Lincoln, aft. D. of Newcastle; *d.* 1795.
Jno. Campbell, *d.* 1794.
Alan Campbell, *d.* 1794.
Saml. Birch.
Jno. Martin.
Alexr. Rigby.
Jno. Gunning.
1790, Apr. 28. Gust. Guy Dickens.
Jno. Mansel.
Geo. Morgan.
Alexr. Stewart, *d.* 1794.
Jas. Hugonin, *d.* 1817.
1793, Oct. 12. Hon. Mark Napier, *d.* 1809.
Thos. Jones, *d.* 1801.
Jno. Phipps, *d.* 1798.
Patr. Bellew, *d.* 1799.
Benjn. Stehelin, *d.* 1796.
1794, Oct. 3. Fras. Richmond Humphreys, *d.* 1812.
Jno. Hughes, *d.* 1796.
Wm. Fawcett, *d.* 1826.
Wm. Crosbie, *d.* 1798.
Jno. Small, *d.* 1796.
Robt. Mason Lewis, *d.* 1800.
1795, Feb. 26. Welbore Ellis Doyle.
Alexr. Ross, *d.* 1801.
Chas. Graham, *d.* 1800.
Jno. St. Leger, *d.* 1800.
Richd. Bettesworth, *d.* 1801.
Wm. Johnstone.
Geo. Campbell.
Wm. Robt., visc. Fielding; *d.* 1799.
1796, May 3. Thos. Duval, *d.* 1807.
Wm. Maddox Richardson, *d.* 1822.
Wm. Lewis, *d.* 1798.
Thos. Davis.
Jas. Hartley, *d.* 1800.
Colebrooke Nesbit, ret. 1798.
Hon. Chas. Monson, *d.* 1800.
Wm. Brady, *d.* 1800.
1798, Jan. 1. Mackay Hugh Baillie, *d.* 1804.
Chas. Jackman.
Jno. Joinour Ellis, *d.* 1804.
Wm. Wemyss, *d.* 1799.
Robt. Douglas, ret. 1799.
1798, June 18. Archd. Robertson.
Bryan Blundell.
Hon. Jno. Knox, *d.* 1800.
Jas. Campbell.
Wm. Gooday Strutt, *d.* 1848.
1801, Jan. 1. Jno. Stewart, *d.* 1807.
Hy. Magan, *d.* 1806.
Chas. Barnett, *d.* 1804.
W. D. Maclean Clephane, *d.* 1803.
1802, Nov. 2. Steph. Poyntz, *d.* 1837.
Ilay Ferrier, *d.* 1824.
Geo. Cunninghame, *d.* 1803.
Fredk. Halkett, *d.* 1803.
Wm. Caulfield Archer, *d.* 1807.
Wm. Knollys, called E. of Banbury.
1803, Sept. 25. Duncan Campbell, *d.* 1809.
Patr. Wauchope, *d.* 1807.
Patr. Sinclair, *d.* 1808.
Jno. Smith, *d.* 1807.
1795, Feb. 26. Alexr. Mackay, *d.* 1809.
Edwin Hewgill, *d.* 1810.
Thos. Pakenham Vandeleur, *d.* 1804.

1804. Otto, bar. Schutte, Aug. 18.; ret. 1810.
1805, Hy., visc. Gage, *d.* 1808.
Jan. 1. Chas. Wm. Este, *d.* 1812.
Roger Aytoun, *d.* 1811.
Jas. Webber, *d.* 1808.
Geo., E. of Craufurd, *d.* 1808.
Stair Park Dalrymple, *d.* 1808.
Sir Wm. Clarke, bt.; *d.* 1808.
Jas. Hall.
Coote Manningham, *d.* 1809.
1805, Richd. Mark Dickens, *d.* 1808.
Oct. 30. Sir Geo. Chas. B. Boughton, bt., *d.* 1810.
1808, Chas. Baillie, *d.* 1810.
Apr. 25. Edwd. Fage, *d.* 1809.
Jas. Thewles, *d.* 1811.
Hugh Lyle Carmichael.
Jno. Randoll M'Kenzie, *d.* 1809.
Sir Wm. Erskine, bt.; *d.* 1813.
Nathl. Wm., ld. Clarina; *d.* 1810.
1809, Fredk. de Watteville.
Oct. 25. Jno. Barnes, *d.* 1810.
Archd., ld. Montgomerie; *d.* 1814.
David Hunter.
1810, Wm. Balfour, *d.* 1812.
July 27. Lawrence Bradshaw, ret.
Geo. Wm. Rich Harcourt.
Andr. Burn.
Augs., bar. Veltheim; *d.* 1829.
Geo., bar. Bock.
Thos. Trotter, *d.* 1825.
Peter du Plat, *d.* 1824.
Augs., bar. Honstedt.
Victor, bar. Alten; *d.* 1820.
Sigismund, bar. Low, K.C.B., K.C.H.; *d.* 1846.
Adolphus, bar. Barsse; *d.* 1834.
Chas., bar. Alten; *d.* 1840.
Wm. Grant, *d.* 1812.
Sir Montague Burgoyne, bt.; *d.* 1817.
Danl. Hoghton, *d.* 1811.
Barnard Foord Bowes, *d.* 1812.
1811. Benj. Fisher, *d.* 1814.
June 4. Thos. Nepean, *d.* Nov. 1816.
Sir Chas. Shipley, *d.* 1815.
J. Gaspard Le Marchant, *d.* 1812.
Jas. M. Hadden, *d.* 1817.
John Bouchier.
Sir Isaac Brock, K.B., *d.* 1812.
Geo. Wm. Ramsay, *d.* 1819.
Robt. Craufurd, *d.* 1812.
Thos. Barrow, *d.* 1820.
Jno. Wood, dism. 1817.
Horace Churchill, *d.* 1817.
Thos. Dunbar, *d.* 1815.
Alexr. Keith, *d.* 1812.
Æneas Shaw, *d.* 1815.
Geo. Dyer, *d.* 1817.
Andr. Hay, *d.* 1814.
Sir Jno. Douglas, *d.* 1814.
Trevor Hull, *d.* 1816.
Jas. Kemmis, *d.* 1820.

1811, Jno. Wilson.
June 4. Jno. Agmond Vesey, *d.* 1812.
1812, Flower M. Sproule.
Apr. 1. Wm. Borthwick, *d.* 1820.
Harry Chester, *d.* 1821.
Jno. Lindesay, *d.* 1820.
Richd. Hulse, *d.* 1813.
Geo. Stracey Smith.
Hon. Sir Edwd. M. Pakenham, G.C.B.; *d.* 1815.
Hy. M'Kinnom, *d.* 1812.
Sir Robt. Rollo Gillespie, K.C.B; *d.* 1814.
Jos. Baird, *d.* 1816.
Wm. Wheatley, *d.* 1812.
Jas. Hare, *d.* 1820.
Oliver Thos. Jones, *d.* 1815.
Andr. Ross, *d.* 1813.
1813, Wm. Kersteman, *d.* 1820.
June 4. Wm. Alexander, *d.* 1825.
Chas. Campbell, *d.* 1822.
Fras. Stewart.
Hy. Davis.
Hon. sir Wm. Ponsonby, K.C.B.; *d.* 1815.
Benj. Gordon Forbes.
Haviland Smith, *d.* 1817.
Wm. Fredk. Spry.
Hy. Procter, *d.* 1822.
Jno. Browne, *d.* 1816.
Jno. Hall, *d.* 1823.
Jno. Byrne Skerrett, *d.* 1814.
Sir Denis Pack, K.C.B.; *d.* 1823.
Sir Granville Thos. Calcraft, *d.* 1820.
Jno. Picton, *d.* 1815.
Edwd. Scott, *d.* 1844.
Wm. M'Caskill, *d.* 1815.
Jno. Crowgy, *d.* 1815.
Thos. Gerard Elrington.
Wm. Lockhart, *d.* 1817.
Robt. Ross, *d.* 1814.
Hy. Green Barry, *d.* 1838.
Lewis de Watteville, *d.* 1836.
Adam Gordon.
Matth. Chit. Darby Griffith, *d.* 1823.
Jno. Fras. Kelly, *d.* 1814.
Randolph Marriott, *d.* 1821.
Lachlan Maquarie, *d.* 1824.
Sir Saml. Gibbs, K.C.B.; *d.* 1815.
Sir Robt. Thos. Wilson, rem. 1821; subseq. rest. See "Generals," 1841.
Digby Hamilton, *d.* 1820.
1814, Sir Chas. Holloway, ret. 1824; *d.*
Jun. 4. 1827.
Archd. Stewart, *d.* 1823.
Thos. Norton Poulett, *d.* 1824.
Sir Edwd. Ger. Butler, *d.* 1825.
Michl. Edwd. Jacob, *d.* 1815.
Sir Thos. Brooke Pechell, bt., *d.* 1826.
Wm. Latham, *d.* 1823.
David Dewar.

1814, Edwd. Baynes, ret. 1828; *d.* 1829.
June 4. Jas. Stirling, *d.* 1834.
Robt. Young, *d.* 1815.
Edwd. Vicars, *d.* 1820.
J. Millar, ret.
Wm. Geo. Dacres, *d.* 1824.
Robt. Douglas, *d.* 1828.
Fras. Streicher, *d.* 1828.
Chas. Auriol, 1821.
Wm. Gifford, *d.* 1829.
I., baron de Sonnenberg, ret.
Chas. Irvine, *d.* 1820.
Sir Wm. Nicholson, bt., *d.* 1820.
Thos. Carey, *d.* 1824.
Wm. Grant, *d.* 1826.
Geo. Johnstone, *d.* 1826.
Wm. John, visc. Molesworth, *d.* 1815.
Wm. Hy. Beckwith, *d.* 1844.
Dugald Campbell, *d.* 1824.
Richd. Augs. Seymour.
Sir Hy. Torrens, K.C.B.; *d.* 1828.
1819, Ld. Fredk. Bentinck, *d.* 1828.
Aug. 12. Isaac Pattison Tinling, *d.* 1822.
Sir Wm. Douglas, K.C.H.; *d.* 1834.
Thos. Wm. Kerr, *d.* 1825.
Fredk. Hardyman, *d.* 1821.
John Fredk. Sigism. Smith, K.C.H., *d.* 1834.
Wm. Mutge.
Saml. Warren, *d.* 1833.
Patr. Mackenzie, *d.* 1820.
Wm. Needham, *d.* 1844.
Robt. Walter, ld. Blantyre, K.C.B.; *d.* 1830.
Sir Jas. Campbell, K.C.B., K.C.H.; *d.* 1835.
Edwd. Codd, *d.* 1829.
Robt. Sewell, *d.* 1835.
Chas. Amadée Harcourt, *d.* 1831.
Geo. Hill, *d.* 1830.
Saml. Swinton, *d.* 1832.
Sir C. Philip Belson, K.C.B., *d.* 1830.
Wm. Augs. Prevost.
Sir J. Pringle Dalrymple, bt.; *d.* 1829.
Robt. Kelso, *d.* 1823.
Jno. Nugent Smyth, *d.* 1838.
Jno. Lamont, ret. 1824; *d.* 1829.
Wm. Armstrong, *d.* 1837.
Robt. D'Arcy, ret. 1824; *d.* 1827.
Geo. Brydges.
Geo. Wm. Dixon, *d.* 1836.
Sir G. Ridout Bingham, K.C.B.; *d.* 1833.
Sir Thos. Bligh St. George, C.B., K.C.H.; *d.* 1836.
Jno. Murray, *d.* 1832.
Hon. sir Chas. Jas. Greville, K.C.B.; *d.* 1836
Alexr. Mark Ker Hamilton, *d.* 1842.
Sir Geo. Leith, bt., *d.* 1842.

1819, Sir Geo. Allan Madden, *d.* 1828.
Aug. 12. Jno. Miller, *d.* 1825.
Jno. Dalrymple, *d.* 1835.
Brooke Young, *d.* 1835.
Sir Haylett Framingham, K.C.B. *d.* 1820.
1821, Allen Hampden Pye, *d.* 1833.
Jul. 19. John Shaw, *d.* 1835.
Geo. Ramsay, *d.* 1834.
Jno. Lemoine.
Jno. Rowley, *d.* 1824.
Martin Campbell Cole, *d.* 1835.
Robt. Evans, *d.* 1833.
Richd. Harry Foley, *d.* 1825.
Jno. Thos., ld. Muskerry, ret 1823; *d.* 1824.
Hon. Hy. Brand.
Jas. Graves, ret. 1826.
Jos. Gubbins, ret. 1829; *d.* 1832
Geo. Duncan Robertson, ret. 1828 *d.* 1842.
John Nugent, *d.* 1830.
Louis Wm., visc. de Chabot, ret
Wm. Binks, *d.* 1833.
Sir Patr. Ross, G.C.M.G.; *d.* 185[illegible]
David Walker, ret. 1827; *d.* 184[illegible]
Chas. Turner, *d.* 1826.
Fras. Hepburn, C.B.; *d.* 1835.
Hy. Darling, *d.* 1835.
Wm. Hy. Rainsford, *d.* 1822.
Wm. Stewart, ret. 1831; *d.* 183[illegible]
1825, Hy. Chas. Darling, ret. 1829; [illegible]
May 27. 1845.
John Harris, *d.* 1833.
Sir Geo. Adam Wood, K.C.H.; [illegible] 1831.
Hy. Tolley, C.B., *d.* 1837.
Sir Chas. Pratt, K.C.B.; *d.* 183[illegible]
Nathl. Blackwell, *d.* 1833.
David Stewart, *d.* 1829.
Alexr. Murray Macgregor, re[illegible] and *d.* 1827.
Hon. Granville Anson Chetwy[illegible] Stapylton, ret. 1825; *d.* 1834
Richd. Buckby, *d.* 1830.
Robt. Stewart, *d.* 1837.
Lewis Davies, *d.* 1828.
Sampson Freeth, *d.* 1835.
Sir Alexr. Bryce, K.C.B.; *d.* 183[illegible]
Fras. Burke, *d.* 1827.
John Pyne Coffin, *d.* 1829.
Sir Geo. Bulteel Fisher, K.C.H *d.* 1834.
Sir Neil Campbell, *d.* 1827.
Sir Thos. Hawker, K.C.B.
Sir Jas. Campbell, K.C.H.
Geo. Mackie, *d.* 1831.
Sir Robt. Travers, C.B.; 1834.
Hon. sir Fredk. Cavendish Po[illegible] sonby, K.C.B., K.C.H.; *d.* 183[illegible]
Chas. Palmer, ret.
Hon. Hy. Augs. Berkeley Crav[illegible] *d.* 1836.
Geo., visc. Forbes, *d.* 1836.

1825, May 27. Sir Jas. Carmichael Smyth, bt., C.B., K.C.H.; *d.* 1838.
Robt. Pilkington, *d.* 1834.
Wm. Hy. Ford, *d.* 1829.
1830, July 22. Norman M'Leod, *d.* 1831.
Jas. Patr. Murray, ret. 1831; *d.* 1834.
Sir Jas. Viney, C.B., K.C.H. *d.* 1841.
Geo. Elliot Vinicombe, *d.* 1841.
Sir Lorenzo Moore, C.B., K.C.H.; *d.* 1837.
Thos. Marlay, *d.* 1831.
Sir Wm. Williams, K.C.B.; *d.* 1832.
Sir Chas. Ashworth, K.C.B.; *d.* 1832.
Archd. Campbell, C.B.; *d.* 1838.
Edwd. Jas. O'Brien, ret.
Jas. Alexr. Farquharson, *d.* 1834.
Sir Amos Godsill Robt. Norcott, C.B., K.C.H.; *d.* 1838.
Sir Chas. Bruce, K.C.B.; *d.* 1832.
Richd. Legge, *d.* 1834.
Wm. Stewart, ret. 1841.
Sir John Ross, K.C.B.; *d.* 1835.
Lord Robt. Wm. Manners, C.B.; *d.* 1835.
Sir. Geo. Elder, K.C.B.; *d.* 1836.
Sir Hy. Willoughby Rooke, K.C.H.; ret. 1832.
1837, Jan. 10. Sir Geo. Woodford, K.C.B., K.C.H.; ret. 1841.
Sir Howard Elphinstone, bt., *d.* 1846.
John Pringle, ret.
1837, Jan. 10. Sir Jas. Kyrle Money, bt., *d.* 1843.
Jno. Stafford, *d.* 1846.
Sir Patr. Lindesay, K.C.B., K.C.H.; *d.* 1839.
Sir Octavius Carey, K.C.H.; *d.* 1844.
Hy. Fredk. Cooke, C.B., K.C.H.; *d.* 1837.
Sir Evan Jno. Murray MacGregor, bt., K.C.B., K.C.H.; *d* 1841.
Sir Chas. Broke Vere, K.C.B.; *d.* 1843.
Sir Alexr. Dickson, G.C.B. K.C.H.; *d.* 1840.
Sir Jno. Thos. Jones, bt., *d.* 1843.
Sir Leonard Greenwell, K.C.B., K.C.H.; *d.* 1844.
Sir Robt. Hy. Dick, K.C.B., K.C.H.; *d.* 1846.
Wm. Keith Elphinstone, C.B.; *d.* 1842.
Sir Jno. Boscawen Savage, K.C.H.; *d.* 1843.
Cornelius Mann, *d.* 1840.
Steph. Galway Adye, C.B.; *d.* 1838.
Hy. Phillot, C.B.; *d.* 1839.
Peter Fyers, *d.* 1846.
Jno. Hassard, C.M.G.; *d.* 1838.
Alexr. Macdonald, C.B.; *d.* 1840.
Sir Robt. M'Cleverty, C.B., K.C.H.; *d.* 1838.
Clement Hill, *d.* 1845.
Percy Drummond, *d.* 1843.

LIST D.

MAJOR-GENERALS.

From 1837, with their subsequent promotions to LIEUTENANT-GENERALS AND GENERALS.

Note.—The Indian General Officers are included in this list.

Name.	M.-Gen.	L.-Gen.	Gen.
Hugh Stacey Osborne	10 Jan. 37.	9 Nov. 46.	20 Jun. 54.
Sir Jas. Lillyman Caldwell, K.C.B.	,,	,,	,,
Geo. Carpenter	,,	,,	......
Sir Alexr. Caldwell, K.C.B.	,,	......	......
Wm. Roome	,,	......	......
Jno. Luther Richardson	,,	9 Nov. 46.	......
Sir David Leighton, K.C.B.	,,	,,	20 Jun. 54
Wm. Blackburn	,,	......	.... .
Sir Chas. Deacon, K.C.B.	,,	......	......
Jas. Welsh	,,	9 Nov. 46.	20 Jun. 54.
Wm. Brooks	,,	......	......
Thos. Corsellis...	,,	......	......
Jno. Nichs. Smith	,,	......	......
Chas. Farran	,,	......	......
Sir Jas. Russell, K.C.B.	,,	9 Nov. 46.	20 Jun. 54
Donald Macleod	,,	......	......
Sir Jos. O'Hallaran, K.C.B.	,,	......	......
Martin White	,,	9 Nov. 46.	20 Jun. 54.
Edwd. Boardman	,,	......	......
Geo. Wahab	,,	......	......
David Courtenay Kenny	,,	9 Nov. 46.	......
Josiah Marshall	,,	......	......
Richd. Podmore	,,	9 Nov. 46.	20 Jun. 54.
Sir Robt. Houston, K.C.B.	,,	,,	,,
Arth. Molesworth	,,	......	......
Jno. Greenstreet	,,	9 Nov. 46.	20 Jun. 54.
Sir Robt. Stevenson, K.C.B.	,,	......	......
Christr. Fagan...	,,	......	......
Sir Wm. Casement, K.C.B.	,,	......	......
Wm. Croxton	,,	......	......
Jas. Rutherford Lumley	,,	......	......
Wm. Comyn	,,	......	......
Sir Geo. M. Cox, bt.	,,	......	......
Manasseh Lopez Pereira	,,	9 Nov. 46.	......
Thos. Pollock	,,	,,	......
Jno. Rose	,,	,,	......
Wm. Munro	,,	......	......
Geo. Rees Kemp	,,	9 Nov. 46.	20 Jun. 54
Hy. Roome	,,	......	......
Jno. Munro	,,	9 Nov. 46.	20 Jun. 54
Jno. Cunningham	,,	......	......
Chas. Thos. Geo. Bishop	,,	9 Nov 46.	......
Jno. Alexr. Paul Macgregor...	,,	,,	20 Jun. 54
Alexr. Limond	,,	......	......
Jas. David Greenhill	,,	......	......
Jeffrey Prendergast, aft. sir J.	,,	9 Nov. 46.	20 Jun. 54
Wm. Richards	,,	,,	,,
Alexr. Duncan	,,	,,	,,

Name.	M.-Gen.	L.-Gen.	Gen.
Thos. Whitehead	10 Jan. 37.	9 Nov. 46.	......
Robt. Jas. Latter	,,	,,	20 Jun. 54.
Thos. Stewart	,,	,,	......
Jerry Fras. Dyson	,,	,,	20 Jun. 54.
Wm. Douglas Cleiland	,,	,,	......
Wm. Hill Perkins	,,	,,	......
Jno. Doveton	,,	,,	20 Jun. 54.
Alexr. Fair	,,	,,	,,
David Foulis	,,	......	......
Duncan M'Pherson	,,	9 Nov. 46.	......
Clements Brown	,,	......	......
Wm. Farquhar	,,	......	......
Wm. Hopper	,,	......	......
Sir Thos. Anburey	,,	......	......
Sir Jas. Law Lushington, K.C.B.	,,	9 Nov. 46.	20 Jun. 54.
Benj. Wm. Dowden Sealy	,,	,,	......
Wm. Chas. Fraser	,,	,,	20 Jun. 54.
Wm. Gilbert	,,	,,	,,
Hy. D'Oyly	28 Jun. 38.	11 Nov. 51.	30 Jan. 55.
Foster Coulson	,,	......	......
Richd. Uniacke	,,	11 Nov. 51.	16 Dec. 56.
Geo. Irving	,,	,,	,,
Sir Francis Hastings Doyle, bt.	,,	......	......
Wm. Gray	,,		......
Edwd. Darley	,,	11 Nov. 51.	......
Wm. Vincent Hompesch	,,	......	
Christr. Hamilton, C.B.	,,	......	......
Sir Geo. Teesdale, K.H.	,,	......	......
Geo. Jas. Reeves, K.H.	,,		......
Hon. Hy. Murray	,,	11 Nov. 51.	16 Feb. 55.
Hon. Lincoln Stanhope	,,	......	......
Sir Jno. Grey, K.C.B.	,,	11 Nov. 51.	20 Feb. 55
Sir Alexr. Cameron, K.C.B.	,,	......	......
Matth. Mahon	,,	......	......
Sir Jas. Wilson, K.C.B.	,,	......	......
Sir Jno. May, K.C.B., K.C.H.	,,	......	......
Sir John Fox Burgoyne, K.C.B.	,,	11 Nov. 51.	5 Sep. 55.
Thomas Dalmer	,,	,,	......
Sir Hy. Watson	,,	......	......
Edwd. Walker, K.H.	,,	......	......
Thos. Evans	,,	11 Nov. 51.	18 May 55.
Brackley Kennett	,,	,,	28 Nov. 55.
Wm. Innes	,,	......	......
Jno. P. Dunbar	,,	......	......
Andrew Aitcheson	,,	......	......
Wm. Turner	,,	......	......
Adam Hogg	,,	......	......
Christr. Hodgson	,,	......	......
Richd. Whish	,,	11 Nov. 51.	......
Aug. Andrews	,,	,,	16 Mar. 55.
Gabriel Richd. Penny	,,	......	......
Jas. Ahmuty	,,	11 Nov. 51.	15 Sep. 55.
Jas. Cock	,,	......	......
Wm. Hull	,,	......	......
Sir Jas. Limond	,,	......	......
Chas. M'Leod	,,	11 Nov. 51.	......
Thos. Garner	,,	......	......
Robt. Pitman	,,	......	......
Christr. Sullivan Fagan	,,	......	......
Edmund W. Shuldham	,,	11 Nov. 51.	......
Wm. Saml. Heathcote	,,	......	......

Name.	M.-Gen.	L.-Gen.	Gen.
Richd. H. Yates	28 Jun. 38.	......	......
Jno. Mayne	,,	......	......
Anthy. Monin	,,	......	......
Wm. Sandwith...	,,	11 Nov. 51.	......
Mossem Boyd	,,	,,	9 Apr. 56.
Jno. M'Innes	,,	,,	4 Jul. 56.
Jas. Fallowfield Salter	,,	,,	18 Jul. 56.
Sir Ephraim G. Stannus	,,	......	......
Patr. Byers	,,	11 Nov. 51.	......
Wm. Burgh	,,	......	......
Edmund Cartwright	,,	11 Nov. 51.	......
Hy. Geo. Andr. Taylor	,,	,,	23 Sep. 57.
Alfr. Richards	,,	,,	......
Sir Jas. Sutherland	,,	......	......
Herbert Bowen	,,	......	......
Archd. Watson	,,	11 Nov. 51.	......
Wm. Dickson	,,	......	......
Jno. Wells Fast	,,	......	......
Wm. Phillips Price	,,	......	......
Jas. Durant	,,	......	......
Robt. Hampton	,,	......	......
Jno. Staples Harriott	,,	......	......
Brook Bridges Parlby	,,	11 Nov. 51.	13 Oct. 57.
Hy. Hodgson	,,	,,	......
Fetcheville Dykes Ballantine	,,	......	......
Fras. Jas. Thos. Johnstone	,,	......	......
Wm. G. Pearse...	,,	......	......
Sir Robt. Hy. Cunliffe, bt.	,,	11 Nov. 51.	13 Oct. 57.
Wm. Clapham	,,	......	......
Jno. Truscott	,,	11 Nov. 51.	27 Jan. 58.
Jno. Woulfe	,,	,,	......
Edwd. Edwards	,,	......	......
Thos. Webster	,,	......	......
Gilbert Waugh...	,,	......	......
Thos. Hatcher Smith...	,,	......	......
Edwd. Millian Gullifer Showers	,,	11 Nov. 51.	4 Mar. 58.
Wm. Woodhouse	,,	......	......
Hy. Faithfull	,,	......	......
Fras. Wm. Wilson	,,	11 Nov. 51.	......
Jno. Tombs	,,	......	......
Jno. Hickie Collett	,,	11 Nov. 51.	.....
Geo. L. Wahab	,,	......	......
Patr. Cameron	,,	11 Nov. 51.	24 Oct. 58.
Jno. Carfrae	,,	,,	5 Mar. 59.
Richd. West	,,	,,	......
Geo. Jackson	,,	,,	13 Mar. 59.
Saml. Goodfellow	,,	,,	30 May 59.
Chas. A. Walker	,,	......	......
Richd A. Willis	,,	......	......
Fredk. Bowes	,,	......	......
Jas. Stewart Fraser	,,	11 Nov. 51.	2 Jun. 60.
Isaac Kinnersley	,,	......	......
Peter de la Motte	,,	11 Nov. 51.	16 Jun. 60.
Hy. Huthwaite	,,	,,	......
Thos. Wilson	,,	,,	......
Felix Vincent Raper	,,	......	......
Geo. Swiney	,,	11 Nov. 51.	15 May 59.
Geo. Pollock, aft. sir G.	,,	,,	17 May 59.
Alexr. Lindsay	,,	,,	11 Sep. 59.
Jas. Alexander	,,	......	......
Vans Kennedy	,,	......	......

Name.	M.-Gen.	L.-Gen.	Gen.
Walter Raleigh Gilbert, aft. sir W. bt. ...	28 Jun. 38.	11 Nov. 51.	......
Thos. Paterson Smith	,,	,,	......
Edwd. Frederick	,,	,,	26 Jun. 60.
Geo. Benj. Brocks	,,	,,	30 Aug. 60.
Archd. Robertson	,,	......	......
Wm. Clinton Baddeley	,,	......	......
Hy. Bowdler...	,,	......	......
Peter Lodevick	,,	11 Nov. 51.	25 Jan. 61
Jas. Fullerton Dundas	,,	......	......
Jas. Morse	,,	11 Nov. 51.	......
Edwd. H. Simpson	,,	......	......
Jas. Hackett	,,	......	......
Thos. Newton	,,	......	......
Jno. Andr. Biggs	,,	......	......
Edwd. H. Bellasis	,,	......	......
Wm. Nott	,,	......	......
Geo. Cooper	,,	......	......
Suetonius Hy. Todd	,,	11 Nov. 51.	30 Jan. 61.
Jno. Briggs	,,	,,	6 Feb. 61.
Harry Thompson	,,	,,	21 Feb. 61.
Sir Archd. Maclain	23 Nov. 41.	,,	5 Jun. 55.
Jas. Hay	,,	,,	......
Wm. Wood, K.H.	,,	,,	31 Aug. 55.
Sir Wm. Warre	,,	,,	......
Chas. Ashe A'Court Repington, K.H.	,,	,,	20 Feb. 56.
Geo. Chas. D'Aguilar	,,	,,	......
Sir Chas. Wm. Pasley, K.C.B.	,,	,,	20 Sep. 60.
Jacob Glen Cuyler	,,	,,	......
Geo. O'Malley	,,	......	......
Edwd. Rowland Jos. Cotton	,,	......	......
Charles Turner	,,	11 Nov. 51.	......
Wm. Fras. Bentinck Loftus...	,,	,,	......
Geo. Burrell	,,	,,	......
James Ogilvie	,,	......	......
James Farrer	,,	......	......
Thos. Brabazon Aylmer	,,	11 Nov. 51.	25 Sep. 56.
Hy. Jas. Riddell, K.H.	,,	,,	26 Sep. 57.
Richd. Goodall Elrington	,,	......	......
Hy. Chas. Edwd. Vernon	,,	11 Nov. 51.	2 Apr. 59.
John Ready	,,	......	......
Sir Jas. Archd. Hope, K.C.B.	,,	11 Nov. 51.	12 Jun. 59.
Sir Robt. Jno. Harvey	,,	,,	17 Jul. 59.
Sir Hew Dalrymple Ross, K.C.B.	,,	,,	28 Nov. 54.
Sir Dudley St. Ledger Hill, K.C.B.... ...	,,	......	......
Sir Edmd. K. Williams, K.C.B.	,,	......	......
Sir Burges Camac	,,	......	......
Robt. M'Douall	,,	......	......
Sir Richd. Armstrong	,,	11 Nov. 51.	......
Sir Fredk. Stovin, K.C.B.	,,	,,	14 Aug. 59.
Sir Guy Campbell, bt.	,,	......	......
Richd. Goddard Hare Clarges	,,	11 Nov. 51.	......
Sir Chas. Felix Smith, K.C.B.	,,	,,	......
Alexr. Thompson	,,	,,	......
Chas. Grene Elicombe	,,	,,	20 Apr. 61.
Hy. Goldfinch	,,	,,	.. ...
Jas. Webber Smith	,,	,,	......
Fredk. Geo. Heriot	,,	,,	......
Wm. Crosse	,,	......	......
Sir Wm. Fras. Patrick Napier, K.C.B. ...	,,	11 Nov. 51.	17 Oct. 59.
John Duffy	,,	,,	......
Hy. Daubeney, K.H.	,,	,,	......

Name.	M.-Gen.	L.-Gen.	Gen.
Douglas Mercer	23 Nov. 41.	11 Nov. 51.	......
Fras. Miles Milman	”	”	......
John Reeve	”	”	7 Dec. 59.
Jacob Tonson	”	......	......
Wm. Alexr. Gordon	”	11 Nov. 51.	......
Steph. Arth. Goodman, K.H.	”	......	......
Thos. Kenah	”	11 Nov. 51.	26 Dec. 59.
Sir Robt. Wm. Gardiner, K.C.B.	”	”	28 Nov. 54.
Saml. Lambert	”	......	......
Jno. Wm. Fremantle...	”	......	......
Ld. Geo. Wm. Russell, G.C.B.	”	......	......
Edwd. Buckley Wynyard	”	11 Nov. 51.	28 Jan. 60.
Jas. Fergusson, aft. sir J.	”	”	13 Feb. 60.
Thos. Wm. Brotherton, aft. sir T.	”	”	1 Apr. 60.
Sir Adolphus Jno. Dalrymple, bt.	”	”	11 Apr. 60.
Sir Jas. Hy. Reynett, K.C.H.	”	”	5 May 60.
Wm. Smelt	”	”	......
Jas. Robertson Arnold, K.H.	”	”	......
Wm. Wemyss	”	”	......
Geo., E. of Munster	”	......	......
Robt. Pym	”	......	......
Walter R. Tremenheere, K.H.	”	11 Nov. 51.	28 Nov. 54.
Hy. Percival Lewis	”	......	......
John Bell, aft. sir J.	”	11 Nov. 51.	15 Jun. 60.
Saml. Benj. Auchmuty	”	”	19 Jun. 60.
Thos. Lightfoot	”	”	......
Alured Dodsworth Faunce	”	......	......
George Brown, K.H., aft. sir G.	”	11 Nov. 51.	7 Sep. 56.
Ld. Fredk. Fitz-Clarence, K.C.H.	”	”	......
Geo. Prescott Wingrove	”	......	......
Richd. Secker Brough	”	11 Nov. 51.	16 Dec. 56.
Andr. Bredin	”	......	......
Jas. Power	”	......	......
Chas. Younghusband	”	......	......
Geo. Crawford	”	......	......
Jno. Aitchison, aft. sir J.	”	11 Nov. 51.	30 Jul. 60.
Jas. Kennedy	”	”	......
Benj. Roope	”	”	......
Philip Le Fevre	”	......	......
Sir Jeremiah Bryant	”	......	......
Chas. Wm. Hamilton	”	11 Nov. 51.	2 Sep. 61.
Thos. Murray	”	......	......
Edmd. Fredk. Waters	”	11 Nov. 51.	17 Sep. 61.
Jos. Nesbitt	”	......	......
Wm. Martin Burton	”	11 Nov. 51.	......
Jas. Wahab	”	......	......
Wm. Samson Whish	”	11 Nov. 51.	......
Wm. Battine	”	......	......
Geo. Hunter	”	11 Nov. 51.	......
Richd. Collyer Andrée	”	”	2 Nov. 61.
Archd. Galloway	”	......	......
Edgar Wyatt	”	......	......
Geo. Mackenzie Steuart	”	11 Nov. 51.	......
Mark Cubbon	”	”	......
Saml. Roger Strover	”	”	......
Horatio Thos. Tapp	”	......	......
Thos. Shubrick	”	11 Nov. 51.	6 Apr. 62.
Wm. Hy. Kemm	”	”	......
Thos. King	”	”	......
Wm. Monteith...	”	......	......
Michl. Riddell	”	......	......

Name.	M.-Gen.	L.-Gen.	Gen.
Jno. Turner Trewman	23 Nov. 41.	......	......
Peter Fearon	,,	......	......
Richd. Lacy Evans	,,	......	......
Wm. Morison	,,	......	......
Thos. Morgan	,,	11 Nov. 51.	......
Lechmere Coore Russell	,,	......	......
Duncan Macleod	,,	11 Nov. 51.	......
Jno. Dun	,,	......	......
Wm. Cullen	,,	......	......
Wm. Dunlop	,,	......	......
Johnstone Napier	,,	......	......
David Barr	,,	11 Nov. 51.	......
Jno. Ogilvie	,,	......	......
Robt. Hume	,,	......	......
Jno. Hunter Littler, aft. sir J.	,,	11 Nov. 51.	......
Wm. Vincent	,,	,,	......
Thos. Manett	,,	,,	......
Jno. Anthy. Hodgson...	,,	......	......
Saml. Smith	,,	11 Nov. 51.	......
Thos. Hy. Paul	,,	,,	22 Nov. 62.
Ezekiel Barton...	,,	,,	......
Hy. Tuffrel Roberts	,,	,,	......
Jno. Thos. Gibson	,,	......	......
Fras. Farquharson	,,	11 Nov. 51.	6 Jan. 63.
Fredk. Rome	,,	......	......
Foster Walker...	,,	......	......
Sir Hy. Pottinger, bt....	,,	11 Nov. 51.	......
Jas. Caulfield	,,	,,	......
Richd. Tickell...	,,	,,	......
Pr. Geo. Wm. Fredk. Chas. of Cambridge, aft. D. of Cambridge	7 May 45.	19 Jun. 54.	15 Jul. 56.
Sir Hy. Geo. Wakelyn Smith, bt., G.C.B. ...	7 Apr. 46.	10 Sep. 47.	......
Chas Edwd. Conyers	9 Nov. 46.	20 Jun. 54.	......
Geo. Augs. Henderson, K.H., ...	,,	,,	......
Geo. Parke	,,	......	......
Robt. Barclay Macpherson, K.H.	,,	20 Jun. 54.	......
Philip Jas. Hay	,,	......	......
Jno. Slessor	,,	......	......
Jas. Irving	,,	20 Jun. 54.	4 Feb. 57.
Jas. Allen	,,	......	......
Archd. Money	,,	20 Jun. 54.	......
David Forbes	,,	......	......
Jno. Fredk. Ewart	,,	20 Jun. 54.	......
Hy. Adolphus Proctor	,,	,,	......
Wm. Jervoise, K.H.	,,	,,	3 Aug. 60.
Wm. Riddall, K.H.	,,	......	......
Thos. Fenn Addison	,,	......	......
Sir Fras. Cockburn	,,	20 Jun. 54.	12 Nov. 60.
Thos. Steele	,,	......	......
Carlo Jos. Doyle	,,	......	......
Thos. Charretie	,,	......	......
Hon. sir Geo. Robt. Arthur, bt., K.C.H. ...	,,	20 Jun. 54.	......
Patr. Campbell	,,	......	......
Edwd. Parkinson	,,	20 Jun. 54.	......
Thos. Hunter Blair	,,	......	......
Richd. Lleuellyn	,,	20 Jun. 54.	18 Jan. 61.
Peter Augs. Latour, K.H.	,,	,,	9 Mar. 61.
Jno. Hare	,,	......	......
Richd. Egerton	,,	20 Jun. 54.	......
Sir Wm. Chalmers, K.C.H.	,,	,,	......
Jno. Boteler Parker	,,	......	......

Name.	M.-Gen.	L.-Gen.	Gen.
Chas. Beckwith	9 Nov. 46.	......	......
Wm. Campbell	,,	......	......
Jas. Claude Bourchier	,,	20 Jun. 54.	......
Jas. Grant	,,	......	......
Thos. Wm. Taylor	,,	......	......
Lawrence Arguimbau	,,	20 Jun. 54.	......
Felix Calvert	,,	,,	......
Wm. Staveley	,,	......	......
Sir De Lacy Evans, K.C.B.	,,	20 Jun. 54.	10 Mar. 61.
Wm. Hy. Scott	,,	,,	23 Mar. 61.
Hugh Percy Davison	,,	......	......
Sir Thos. Willshire, bt., K.C.B.	,,	20 Jun. 54.	20 Apr. 61.
Hon. Hy. Edwd. Butler	,,	,,	......
Edwd. Fleming	,,	,,	......
Sir Wm. Gossett, K.C.B., K.C.H.	,,	......	......
Sir Jno. Rolt, K.C.B.	,,	20 Jun. 54.	......
Geo. Cardew	,,	......	......
Philip Bainbrigge, aft. sir P.	,,	20 Jun. 54.	24 Aug. 61.
Wm. Greenshields Power, K.H.	,,	,,	4 Feb. 57.
Thos. Erskine Napier, aft. sir T.	,,	,,	20 Sep. 61.
Nathl. Thorn, K.H.	,,	,,	......
Wm. Hy. Sewell, aft. sir W.	,,	,,	10 Nov. 61.
Wm. Lindsay Darling	,,	,,	15 Dec. 61.
Sir Jos. Thackwell, G.C.B., K.H.	,,	,,	.....
Alexr. Macdonald	,,	......	......
Sir Wm. Lewis Herries, K.C.H.	,,	20 Jun. 54.	......
Jno. M'Donald, aft. sir J.	,,	,,	7 Mar. 62.
Thos. Staunton St. Clair, K.H.	,,	......	......
Geo. Wm. Paty, K.H., aft. sir G.	,,	20 Jun. 54.	14 Mar. 62.
Lord Jas. Hay...	,,	,,	1 Jun. 62.
Thos. Jas. Wemyss	,,	,,	......
Robt. Burd Gabriel, K.H.	,,	......	......
Hy. Thomas	,,	20 Jun. 54.	......
Wm. Rowan, aft. sir W.	,,	,,	13 Aug. 62.
Jas. Shaw Kennedy, aft. sir J.	,,	,,	19 Aug. 62.
Arth. Wm., ld. Sandys	,,	,,	......
Sir Thos. Hy. Browne, K.C.H.	,,	,,	......
Richd. W. H. Howard Vyse	,,	......	......
Thos. Phipps Howard, K.H.	,,	......	......
Archd. Maclachlan	,,	20 Jun. 54.	......
Robt. Wm. Mills	,,	......	......
Edwd. Nicolls	,,	20 Jun. 54.	28 Nov. 54.
Fredk. Ashworth, aft. sir F.	,,	,,	......
Robt. Bryce Fearon	,,	......	......
Hy. Balneavis, C.M.G., K.H.	,,	20 Jun. 54.	......
Vincent Edwd. Eyre	,	......	......
Jno. Whetham	,,	......	......
Thos. Thornbury Wooldridge, K.H. ...	,,	......	......
Geo. Lee Goldie, C.B., aft. sir G.	,,	20 Jun. 54.	6 Nov. 62
Geo. Powell Higginson	,,	,,	9 Nov. 62
Geo. Bowles, aft. sir G.	,,	,,	,,
Thos. Bunbury	,,	,,	......
Hon. Hy. Fredk. Compton Cavendish ...	,,	,,	9 Nov. 62
Philip Ray	,,	......	......
Jno. Wm. Aldred	,,	20 Jun. 54.	......
Hy. Godwin	,,	......	......
Thos. Wm. Robbins	,,	20 Jun. 54.	9 Nov. 62
Roderick M'Neil, or Macneil	,,	,,	21 Dec. 63
Geo. Dean Pitt	,,	......	......
Wm. Sutherland	,,	20 Jun. 54.	......
Hy. Rainey, K.H.	,,	,,	......

Name.	M.-Gen.	L.-Gen.	Gen.
Hon. Chas. Gore, K.H.	9 Nov. 46.	20 Jun. 54.	12 Feb. 63.
Robt. Dalyell	,,	......	......
Wm. Lovelace Walton	,,	20 Jun. 54.	13 Feb. 63.
Thos. Fyers	,,	......	......
Edwd. Fanshawe	,,	......	......
Thos. Cunningham	,,	......	......
Thos. Jno. Forbes	,,	......	3 Jan. 59.
Alexr. Munro	,,	......	......
Jas. Pattison Cockburn	,,	......	......
Thos. Colby	,,	......	......
Robt. Hy. Birch	,,	......	......
Chas. Richd. Fox	,,	20 Jun. 54.	6 Mar. 63.
Jas. Armstrong	,,	......	......
Thos. Paterson	,,	......	......
Nathl. Wm. Oliver	,,	......	......
Richd. Jno. Jas. Lacy	,,	......	......
Geo. Lewis	,,	......	......
Elias Lawrence	,,	20 Jun. 54.	20 Jun. 55.
Geo. Jones	,,	,,	,,
Thos. Benjn. Adair	,,	......	......
Wm. Hallett Connolly	,,	20 Jun. 54.	20 Jun. 55.
Chas. Augs. Shawe	,,	,,	6 Mar. 63.
Peter Brown	,,	......	......
Geo. Beatty	27 Dec. 46.	20 Jun. 54.	20 Jun. 55.
Albert Edwd., Pr. of Wales...	......	......	9 Nov. 62.
Hy. Somerset	16 May 51.	26 Jan. 55.	......
Thos. Adams Parke, C.B.	11 Nov. 51.	20 Jun. 55.	6 Feb. 57.
Fredk. Campbell	,,	28 Nov. 54.	25 Sep. 59.
Chas. Menzies	,,	20 Jun. 55.	1 Jul. 57.
Mildmay Fane...	,,	30 Jan. 55.	27 Mar. 63.
Jno. Martin	,,	......	......
Sir Jas. Maxwell Wallace	,,	6 Feb. 55.	8 Jun. 63.
Hon. Jno. Finch, C.B.	,,	20 Feb. 55.	......
Jas. Lindsay	,,	18 May 55.	......
Wm. Geo. Moore	,,	5 Jun. 55.	......
Sir Hy. Floyd, bt.	,,	......	......
Jas. Campbell	,,	......	......
Wm. Geo. Cochrane	,,	5 Dec. 56.	......
Hy. Somerset, C.B., aft. sir H.	,,	29 Jan. 57.	......
Nichs. Wodehouse	,,	5 Sep. 57.	......
Hy., D. of Cleveland, C.B.	,,	8 Sep. 57.	23 Oct. 63.
Geo. Aug. Wetherall, C.B., aft. sir G. ...	,,	,,	,,
Wm. Douglas	,,	23 Nov. 58.	3 Apr. 62.
Jas. Simpson, aft. sir J.	,,	29 Jun. 55.	8 Sep. 55.
Jas. Fredk. Love, C.B., aft. sir J.	,,	26 Sep. 57.	10 Aug. 64.
Hon. Geo. Anson	,,	......	......
Sir Duncan McGregor, K.C.B.	,,	12 Dec. 57.	28 Oct. 64.
Nichs. Hamilton	,,	11 Jan. 58.	......
Sir Jas. Dennis, K.C.B.	,,	......	......
Chas. Anthy. Ferd. Bentinck	,,	15 Jan. 58.	......
Jno. Gregory Baumgardt, C.B.	,,	......	......
Sir Robt. Nickle	,,	......	......
Griffith Geo. Lewis, C.B.	,,	......	......
Geo. Judd Harding, C.B.	,,	......	......
Chas. Geo. James Arbuthnot	,,	13 Mar. 58.	25 Nov. 64.
Christr. Grant Falconar	,,	20 Jul. 58.	......
Sir Richd. England, K.C.B.	,,	4 Jun. 56.	6 Jul. 63.
Chas. Middleton	,,	......	......
Alexr. Fisher Mackintosh	,,	2 Aug. 58.	27 Dec. 64.
Beaumont, ld. Hotham	,,	26 Aug. 58.	12 Jan. 65.
Jos. Paterson	,,	,,	......

Name.	M.-Gen.	L.-Gen.	Gen.
Geo. Turner, C.B., aft. sir G.	11 Nov. 51.	28 Nov. 54.	24 Jan. 63.
Sir Jno. Owen, K.C.B., K.H.	,,	......	......
Jno. Wright, K.H.	,,	......	......
Geo. Alexr. Reid	,,	......	......
Jno. Home	,,	22 Sep. 58.	......
Mathias Everard, C.B.	,,	......	......
Cecil Bishopp, C.B.	,,	......	......
Sir Wm. Robt. Clayton, bt.	,,	26 Oct. 58.	12 Jan. 65.
Hon. Geo. Cathcart	,,	......	......
Jno. Spink	,,	26 Oct. 58.	12 Jan. 65.
Jas. Jackson, aft. sir J.	,,	,,	6 Feb. 65.
Robt. Christr. Mansell	,,	......	......
Geo. Paris Bradshawe	,,	......	......
Jno. Drummond	,,	26 Oct. 58.	10 Feb. 65.
Jas. Freeth, aft. sir J.	,,	,,	9 Mar. 65.
Sir Chas. Routledge O'Donnell	,,	,,	2 Apr. 65.
Jno. Leslie	,,	,,	......
Robt. Bartlett Coles	,,	,,	31 May 65.
Edwd. Pery Buckley	,,	,,	17 Aug. 65.
Sir Richd. Doherty	,,	,,	......
Edwd. Byam	,,	16 Nov. 58.	......
Wm. Rogers	,,	......	......
Chas. O'Neil Prendergast	,,	......	......
Geo. Chas., E. of Lucan	,,	14 Dec. 58.	28 Aug. 65.
Chas. Yorke, aft. sir C.	,,	13 Feb. 59.	5 Sep. 65.
Jno. Hy. Richardson	,,	2 Apr. 59.	12 Jan. 66.
Sir Jno. Rowland Eustace	,,	,,	......
Berkeley Drummond	,,	9 Apr. 59.	......
Hon. sir Edwd. Cust	,,	,,	12 Jan. 66.
Dennis Daly	,,	12 Jun. 59.	......
Wm. Chamberlayne	,,	17 Jul. 59.	14 Jan. 66.
Hy. Dwyer	20 Jun. 54.	......	......
Jeremiah Taylor	,,	17 Jul. 59.	......
Fras. Jno. Davies	,,	14 Aug. 59.	......
Jno. Fraser	,,	17 Oct. 59.	......
Jonathan Peel	,,	7 Dec. 59.	......
Marcus Beresford	,,	7 Dec. 59.	4 Mar. 66.
Jas. Chas. Chatterton, aft. sir J.	,,	13 Dec. 59.	31 Mar. 66.
Jno. Hobart, ld. Howden, K.C.B., K.H. ...	,,	26 Dec. 59.	......
Robt. Douglas	,,	28 Nov. 54.	25 Sep. 59.
Jas. Alexr., E. of Rosslyn	,,	26 Dec. 59.	20 Apr. 66.
Wm. Thos. Knollys	,,	11 Jan. 60.	17 Jun. 66.
Edwd. Studd	,,	......	......
Chas. Stuart Campbell, C.B.	,,	......	......
Sir Hy. Robt. Ferguson Davy, bt.	,,	28 Jan. 60.	25 Jun. 66.
Ernest Fred. Gascoigne	,,	13 Feb. 60.	20 Jan. 67.
Lovell Benj. Lovell, aft. sir L.	,,	1 Apr. 60.	......
St. John Aug. Clarke, K.H.	,,	11 Apr. 60.	8 Mar. 67.
Sir Jas. Holmes Schædde, K.C.B.	,,	23 Apr. 60.	......
Hy. Jno. Wm. Bentinck, aft. sir H. ...	,,	24 Apr. 60.	8 Dec. 67.
Alexr. Kennedy Clark Kennedy, C.B. ...	,,	3 May 60.	......
Thos. Reed, C.B., aft. sir T.	,,	4 May 60.	1 Jan. 68.
Hy., visc. Melville, K.C.B.	,,	5 May 60.	,,
Horatio Geo. Broke or Brooks	,,	15 May 60.	......
Edwd. Chas. Whinyates, C.B., K.H., aft. sir E.	,,	1 Jun. 56.	10 Dec. 64.
Thos. Hutchessen	,,	......	......
Jno. Oldfield, K.H.	,,	10 May 59.	3 Apr. 62.
Thos. Dynely, C.B.	,,	......	......
Sir Colin Campbell, K.C.B. aft. ld. Clyde ...	,,	4 Jun. 56.	14 May 58.
Geo. Petre Wymer, aft. sir G.	,,	8 Jun. 56.	9 Sep. 63.
Wm. Pattle	,,	18 Jul. 56.	9 Oct. 63.

Name.	M.-Gen.	L.-Gen.	Gen.
:dm. Finucane Morris, C.B....	20 Jun. 54.	17 Jun. 56.	13 Mar. 68.
'eter Edmonstone Craigie, C.B., aft. sir P.	,,	19 Jun. 56.	21 Jan. 68.
Iy. Colvile	,,	20 Jun. 56.	27 Mar. 68.
ieo. Cobbe	,,	4 Feb. 57.	15 Dec. 64.
lexr. Cavalie Mercer	,,	29 Aug. 57.	9 Feb. 65.
brm. Roberts	,,	13 Oct. 57.	3 Oct. 64.
:verard Wm. Bouverie	,,	30 Jul. 60.	9 Apr. 68.
Ion. Thos. Ashburnham, C.B.	,,	3 Aug. 60.	19 Apr. 68
Iichl. White, C.B.	,,	31 Aug. 60.	......
no. Scott, C.B., aft. sir J.	,,	13 Oct. 60.	1 May 68.
no. Lysaght Pennefather, C.B., aft. sir J....	,,	12 Nov. 60.	9 May 68.
'hos. Perronet Thompson	,,	27 Dec. 60.	12 Jul. 68.
Vm. Bush, K.H.	,,	......	......
'red. Thos. Buller	,,	......	......
Iy. Despard, C.B.	,,	......	......
ir Jno. Mark Fredk. Smith...	,,	25 Oct. 59.	3 Aug. 63.
dw. Wells Bell	,,	27 Dec. 60.	12 Jul. 68.
no. Reid	,,	......	......
as. Jones, K.H.	,,	......	......
dw. Carlyon	,,	......	......
ir Wm. Macbean Geo. Colebrook, C.B., K.H.	,,	16 Jan. 59.	26 Dec. 65.
hos. Burke	,,	18 Jan. 61.	......
hos. Saml. Trafford...	,,	......	......
y. Bristow	,,	......	......
Vm. Cator, aft. sir W.	,,	25 Sep. 59.	5 Apr. 66.
eo. Saunders Thwaites	,,	13 Feb. 61.	......
os. Jerrard	,,	......	......
rth. Morris	,,	......	......
as. Thos., E. of Cardigan	,,	13 Feb. 61.	......
Vm. Cowper Coles	,,	9 Mar. 61.	......
ir Michl. Creagh, K.H.	,,	......	......
ohn Eden, C.B.	,,	9 Mar. 61.	25 Aug. 68.
umphrey Robt. Hartley	,,	......	......
y. Wm. Barnard	,,	......	......
as. Campbell, K.H.	,,	......	......
on. Chas. Grey	,,	10 Mar. 61.	29 Aug. 68.
'm. Lennox Lascelles, aft. ld. De Ros ...	,,	12 Mar. 61.	10 Nov. 68.
no. Geddes, K.H.	,,	23 Mar. 61.	......
'm. Hy. Cornwall	,,	......	......
hilip Spencer Stanhope	,,	20 Apr. 61.	22 Nov. 68.
lexr. Maclachlan	,,	22 Jun. 60.	......
has. Murray Hay	,,	24 Aug. 60.	......
y., ld. Rokeby	,,	20 Sep. 61.	8 Mar. 69.
has. Gilmour...	,,	......	......
y. Edw. Porter	,,	10 Nov. 61.	5 Sep. 69.
no. Dawson Rawdon...	,,	15 Nov. 61.	......
'm. Beckwith, K.H.	,,	26 Nov. 61.	28 Oct. 69
y. Edw. Robinson	,,	......	......
y. Wm. Breton	,,	15 Dec. 61.	18 Dec. 69.
llan T. McLean	,,	20 Dec. 61.	......
eph. Kirby	,,	......	......
rth. Rd., D. of Wellington	,,	2 Feb. 62.	......
no. Julius Wm. Angerstein...	,,	,,	......
no. Wilson Kettlewell	,,	......	......
hos. Martin, K.H.	,,	16 Feb. 62.	......
atth. Chas. Dixon	,,	......	......
atr. Doull Calder	,,	......	......
hos. Gerrard Ball	,,	7 Mar. 62.	10 Jan. 70.
aton Monins	,,	......	......
ny Carlton Coffin	,,	......	......
m. Cox, K.H.	,,	......	......

Name.	M.-Gen.	L.-Gen.	Gen.
Jas. Stokes Bastard	20 Jun. 54.	24 Jan. 57.	......
Geo. Morton Eden	,,	14 Mar. 62.	......
Geo. Dixon	,,	30 May 62.	1 Apr. 70
Fred. Maunsell	,,	1 Jun. 62.	9 Aug. 70
Wm. Jno. Codrington..	,,	6 Jun. 56.	27 Jul. 63
Duncan Grant	,,	......	......
Hy. Alexr. Scott	,,	24 Jan. 63.	12 May 66
Wm. Wylde	,,	22 Feb. 63.	24 Aug. 66
Wm. Turnor	,,	......	......
Wm. Fludyer	,,	3 Jun. 62.	......
Jno. Wharton Frith	,,	13 Aug. 62.	......
Thos. Falls	,,	......	......
Hy. Chas. Russell	,,	......	......
Wm. Ferguson...	,,	......	......
Jno. Hall	,,	19 Aug. 62.	10 Oct. 70
Peter Margetson Wallace	,,	28 Nov. 54.	22 Feb. 63
Richd. Jones, (? sir)	,,	,,	......
Jno. Mitchel, or Mitchell, C.B. aft. sir J. ...	,,	,,	27 Jun. 64
Jno. Henry	,,	3 Aug. 55.	......
Chas. Ramsay Skardon	,,	22 Aug. 55.	......
Saml. Swinhoe...	,,	15 Sep. 55.	29 Jun. 63
Jno. Anderson (No. 1)	,,	5 Dec. 55.	13 Jan. 64
Fredk. Young	,,	18 Feb. 56.	28 Mar. 65
Thos. Monteath Douglas	,,	18 Mar. 56.	9 Apr. 65
Wm. R. C. Costley	,,	2 Apr. 56.	13 Jun. 65
Chas. Herbert	,,	9 Apr. 56.	26 Apr. 6[illegible]
Geo. Petre Wymer	,,	8 Jun. 56.	......
Alexr. Dick	,,	4 Jul. 56.	3 May 6[illegible]
Wm. Pattle	,,	18 Jul. 56.	......
Thos. Fiddes	,,	15 Sep. 56.	......
Jas. Perry	,,	6 Dec. 56.	......
Hugh Ross	,,	29 May 57.	......
Jno. Anderson (No. 2)	,,	23 Sep. 57.	......
Jas. Kitchen	,,	13 Oct. 57.	......
Abrm. Roberts, C.B.	,,	,,	......
Jno. Morgan, C.B.	,,	27 Jan. 58.	27 May 6[illegible]
Chas. Arth. Grenado Wallington	,,	4 Mar. 58.	12 Jun. 6[illegible]
Thos. Oliver	,,	4 May 58.	19 Jun. 6[illegible]
Michl. Edwd. Bagnold	,,	......	......
Duncan Gordon Scott...	,,	23 Jul. 58.	......
Hy. Hall, C.B.	,,	24 Oct. 58.	23 Jul. 6[illegible]
Julius Geo. Griffith	,,	4 Feb. 59.	17 Sep. 6[illegible]
Saml. Shaw	,,	5 Feb. 59.	......
Fredk. Larkins Doveton	,,	......	......
Jas. Henderson Dunsterville...	,,	......	......
Chas. Butler James	,,	15 May 59.	6 Dec. 6[illegible]
Matthew Coombs Paul	,,	17 May 59.	......
Chas. Payne	,,	......	......
Jno. Polgase James	,,	......	......
Sir Jno. Cheape, K.C.B.	,,	26 May 59.	......
Jno. Low, C.B., aft. sir J.	,,	30 May 59.	18 Jan. 6[illegible]
Jos. Harris	,,	29 Aug. 59.	......
Jno. Tulloch, C.B.	,,	11 Sep. 59.	6 Mar. 6[illegible]
Richd. Powney	,,	21 Sep. 59.	.. ...
Sir Hugh Massey Wheeler, K.C.B.	,,	......	......
Geo. Edwd. Gowan, C.B.	,,	27 Sep. 59.	......
Patr. Montgomerie, C.B.	,,	21 Dec. 59.	......
Jas. Stuart, C.B.	,,	......	......
Chas. Orans .., ...	,,	......	......
Wm. Hy. Hewitt	,,	30 Dec. 59.	......
Jno. Home	,,	......	......

Name.	M.-Gen.	L.-Gen.	Gen.
Goo. Wm. Aylmer Lloyd, C.B.	20 Jun. 54.	2 Jun. 60.	......
Alexr. Tulloch, C.B.	,,	16 Jun. 60.	......
Archd. Brown Dyce	,,	26 Jun. 60.	......
Jno. Wheeler Cleveland	,,	30 Aug. 60.	6 Mar. 68.
Robt. Blackall...	,,	18 Dec. 60.	......
David Capon, C.B.	,,	25 Jan. 61.	......
Wm. Donald Robertson	,,	30 Jan. 61.	......
Duncan Sim	,,	6 Feb. 61.	......
Geo. Sandys	,,	21 Jan. 61.	......
Sir Patr. Grant, G.C.B.	28 Nov. 54.	24 Oct. 62.	19 Nov. 70.
Sir Robt. Vivian, K.C.B.	,,	,,	22 Nov. 70.
Wm. Wylie, C.B.	,,	,,	24 Feb. 70.
Geo. Conran	,,	24 Jan. 65.	......
Edwd. Garstin...	,,	21 Dec. 65.	1 Mar. 67.
Sir Geo. Brooke, K.C.B.	,,	19 Jun. 66.	24 May 70.
Fred. Frankland Whinyates	,,	14 Jul. 67.	21 Jan. 72.
Adam Fife Crawford	,,	......	......
Chas. Montauban Carmichael, C.B.... ...	,,	14 Apr. 62.	18 Jan. 70.
Wm. Bolden Dundas, C.B.	,,	......	......
Hy. Wm. Gordon, C.B.	,,	19 May 63.	......
Fredk. Markham, C.B.	,,	......	......
Geo. Hy. Lockwood, aft. Sir G.	,,	3 Sep. 62.	22 Oct. 70.
Jos. Darby	,,	27 Jun. 64.	1 Jan. 68.
Jas. Eckford, C.B.	,,	24 Apr. 64.	......
Mathew Soppitt	,,	29 Apr. 64.	6 Mar. 68.
Andr. Hervey, C.B.	,,	23 Jul. 64.	......
Sir Scudamore Windo Steel, K.C.B.	,,	2 Sep. 64.	......
Jos. Leggett	,,	......	......
Fredk. Schuler	,,	17 Sep. 64.	......
Geo. Moore	,,	2 Nov. 61.	......
Foster Stalker, C.B.	,,	......	......
Maurice Tweedie	,,	6 Apr. 62.	......
Hy. Lechmere Worrall	,,	10 Jun. 62.	30 Mar. 69.
Jno. Bennet Hearsey, C.B.	,,	......	......
Geo. Richd. Pemberton	,,	6 Sep. 62.	......
Donald Macleod	,,	2 Oct. 62.	......
Steph. Davis Riley	,,	5 Oct. 62.	......
Christr. Godby, C.B.	,,	22 Nov. 62.	......
Nichs. Penny, C.B.	,,	......	......
David Cunninghame	,,	......	......
Chas. Dennis Dun	,,	6 Jan. 63.	......
Jas. Parsons, C.B.	,,	18 Mar. 63.	......
Geo. Warren	,,	6 Apr. 63.	23 Aug. 69.
Hy. Fisher Salter, C.B.	,,	14 Apr. 63.	......
Richd. Benson, C.B.	,,	......	......
Thos. Mathew Taylor	,,	17 Apr. 63.	8 Feb. 70.
Howard Dowker	,,	21 Apr. 63.	......
Hy. Sargent	,,	29 Jun. 63.	......
Geo. Jas. Wilson	,,	13 Jan. 64.	......
Lewis Wentworth Watson	,,	......	......
Jos. Garnault	,,	25 Jun. 64.	22 Feb. 70.
Robt. Hawkes...	,,	17 Aug. 64.	25 Jun. 70.
Archd. Fullerton Richmond, C.B.	,,	21 Oct. 64.	......
Jos. Bell	,,	8 Jan. 65.	25 Jun. 70.
Geo. Conran	,,	......	......
Patr. Grant, C.B.	,,	......	......
Christr. Dixon Wilkinson, C.B.	,,	12 Mar. 65.	25 Jun. 70.
Wm. Taylor	,,	28 Mar. 65.	......
Westrop Watkins	,,	......	......
Jno. Laurie	,,	......	......
Fredk. Parkinson Lester	,,	......	......

Name.	M.-Gen.	L.-Gen.	Gen.
Jas. Edwin Williams	28 Nov. 54.	5 Jun. 65.	25 Jun. 70.
Fras. Turnley Farrell	,,	13 Jun. 65.	......
Wm. Hy. Marshall	,,	23 Jul. 65.	......
Robt. Alexander	,,	22 Aug. 65.	25 Jun. 70.
Jno. Day Stokes	,,	......	......
Roger Williamson Wilson, C.B. ...	,,	......	......
Fras. Spencer Hawkins, C.B.	,,	......	......
Wm. Jno. Butterworth, C.B.	,,	......	......
Jno. Kynaston Luard, C.B.	,,	20 Nov. 65.	25 Jun. 70.
Jno. Graham	,,	......	......
Edwd. Garstin	,,	......	......
Adolphus Derville	,,	22 Dec. 65.	25 Jun. 70.
Richd. Home	,,	......	......
Robt. Jno. Hussey Vivian	,,	......	......
Thos. Littleton Green	,,	26 Apr. 66.	25 Jun. 70.
Alexr. Carnegy, C.B.	,,	......	......
Geo. Tomkyns...	,,	29 Apr. 66.	25 Jun. 70.
Hy. Geo. Roberts	,,	......	......
Wm. Cavaye	,,	3 May 66.	25 Jun. 70.
David Forbes	,,	......	......
Jno. Jas. Farrington	,,	......	......
Fras. Straton	,,	27 May 66.	25 Jun. 70.
Chas. Richd. Wm. Lane, C.B.	,,	12 Jun. 66.	,,
Wm. Jno. Gairdner, C.B.	,,	......	......
Geo. Brooke, C.B.	,,	......	......
Jno. Yaldwyn	,,	23 Jul. 66.	25 Jun. 70.
Benj. Robertson Hitchins	,,	26 Aug. 66.	......
Steph. Moody	,,	......	......
Watkin Lewis Griffies Williams, aft. bt. ...	,,	17 Sep. 66.	25 Jul. 70.
Eyre Evans Bruce	,,	6 Nov. 66.	3 Sep. 71.
Hy. Coningham	,,	6 Dec. 66.	......
Wm. Justice	,,	,,	......
Jno. Clough	,,	......	......
Thos. Dickinson	,,	......	......
Hy. Chambers Murray Cox	,,	18 Jan. 67.	9 Dec. 71.
Jno. Hoggan, C.B.	,,	......	......
Geo. Huyshe, C.B.	,,	12 Feb. 67.	19 Feb. 72.
Fredk. Blundell, C.B.	,,	......	......
Jno. Campbell. C.B., aft. sir J.	,,	1 Mar. 67.	21 Mar. 72.
Thos. Bowes Foster	,,	3 Jul. 67.	......
Fras. Frankland Whinyates	,,	14 Jul. 67.	......
Jas. Adam Howden	,,	9 Dec. 67.	......
Augs. Clarke	,,	15 Dec. 67.	23 Apr. 72.
Chas. Hamilton, C.B.	,,	30 Jan. 68.	16 May 72.
Edwd. Armstrong	,,	6 Mar. 68.	9 Dec. 72.
Chas. Waddington, C.B.	,,	......	......
Wm. Hy. Sleeman	,,	......	......
Alexr. Thomson Reid, C.B.	,,	......	......
Maurice Stack, C.B., aft. sir M.	,,	6 Mar. 68.	8 Mar. 73.
Jas. Outram, C.B.	,,	......	......
Wm. Wyllie, C.B.	,,	......	......
Walter John Browne, C.B.	,,	6 Mar. 68.	29 Aug. 73.
Sir Chas. Hopkinson, C.B.	,,	......	......
Hanbury Raynsford	,,	......	......
Brice Wakeford Lee	,,	......	......
Hy. Smith	,,	......	......
Geo. Augs. Litchford...	,,	......	......
Wm. Miles	,,	......	.....
Andr. Campbell	,,	......	......
Thos. Dickinson	,,	......	......
Stanley Bullock	,,	......	......

Name.	M.-Gen.	L.-Gen.	Gen.
Richd. Airey, aft. sir R.	12 Dec. 54.	24 Oct. 62.	9 Apr. 71.
Jas. Bucknall Bucknall Estcourt	,,	......	......
Hugh Hy. Rose, C.B., aft. sir H. and ld. Strathnairn	,,	28 Feb. 60.	4 Feb. 67.
Hy. Wm. Adams, C.B....	,,	......	......
Hon. Jas. Yorke Scarlett, aft. sir J. ...	,,	9 Nov. 62.	25 Oct. 71.
Sir Jno. Campbell, bt.	,,	......	......
Harry David Jones, aft. sir H.	,,	6 Jul. 60.	......
Arth. Wellesley Torrens	,,	......	......
Geo. Buller, C.B., aft. sir G....	,,	9 Nov. 62.	25 Oct. 71.
Wm. Eyre, C.B.	,,	......	......
Wm. Jas. Jones	13 Dec. 54.	......	......
Wm. Hy. Slade	,,	......	......
Richd. Thos. King	,,	27 Jun. 64.	......
Chas. Dixon	,,	20 Sep. 60.	......
Thos. Grantham	,,	......	......
Thos. Blanshard, C.B.	16 Dec. 54.	......	......
Wm. Brereton. C.B., K.H., aft. sir W. ...	,,	27 Jun. 64.	......
Sherburne Williams	,,	20 Sep. 60.	1 Jan. 68.
Jas. C. Victor	,,	......	......
Hy. Robt. Milner	29 Dec. 54.	......	......
Fras. Rawdon Chesney	6 Jan. 55.	28 Jul. 64.	1 Jan. 68.
Irwin Whitty	,,	......	......
Chas. Dalton	,,	......	......
Richd. Burne Rawnsley	,,	......	......
Jno. Heneage Grubbe	9 Jan. 55.	......	......
Philip Barry	13 Jan. 55.	......	......
Fred W. Whinyates	,,	......	......
Edwd. Vicars	,,	......	......
Jno. Hawkshaw	,,	......	......
Jno. Bloomfield Gough, C.B.	30 Jan. 55.	......	......
Wm. Furneaux...	7 Feb. 55.	......	......
R. G. B. Wilson	,,	......	......
Hon. Arth. Upton	20 Feb. 55.	......	......
Philip Fras. Story, C.B.	13 Apr. 55.	6 Mar. 68.	17 Nov. 73.
Alexr. Woodburn, C.B.	1 May 55.	......	......
Jno. D. Syers	7 May 55.	......	......
Jas. Archd. Chalmer	15 May 55.	......	......
Ambrose Lane...	18 May 55.	......	......
Anthy. Emmett	21 May 55.	......	......
Marcus Antonius Waters	,,	......	......
Walt. Powell	20 Jun. 55.	.. ...	......
Abrm. Hy. Gordon	,,	......	......
Jno. Montresor Pilcher	,,	......	......
Thos. Stevens...	,,	......	......
David Anderson Gibsone	,,	......	......
Jno. Rawlings Coryton	,,	6 Feb. 57	8 Sep. 58.
Robt. Mercer	,,	......	......
Saml. Burdon Ellis, C.B.	,,	......	......
Jno. Robyns, K.H.	,,	......	......
Jos. Walker	,,	......	......
Jas. Whylock	,,	......	......
Thos. Waring	,,	......	......
Geo. Butt Bury	,,	......	......
Jas. Irwin Willes	,,	......	......
David McAdam	,,	......	......
Chas. Compton Pratt	,,	......	......
Donald Campbell	,,	......	......
Hy. Jas. Gillespie	,,	......	......
Saml. Garmston	,,	......	......
Jno. Harvey Stevens	,,	......	.....

Name.	M.-Gen.	L.-Gen.	Gen.
Thos. Scott Reignolds	22 Jun. 55.	......	
Sir Richd. Jas. Dacres, K.C.B.	29 Jun. 55.	10 Dec. 65.	2 Feb. 68.
Jno. Jos. Hollis	6 Jul. 55.	......	......
Hugh Evans	10 Jul. 55.	......	......
Hy. Ivatt Delacombe	14 Jul. 55.	22 Dec. 60.	28 May 66.
Geo. Grantham	3 Aug. 55.	6 Mar. 68.	......
Hy. Cracklow	22 Aug. 55.	,,	28 Mar. 74.
Jas McHaffie	31 Aug. 55.	12 Nov. 62.	......
Robt. Blake Lynch	,,	......	......
Fras. Campbell	,,	......	......
Cassius Matth. Johnson	,,	......	......
Chas. Diggle, K.H.	,,	......	......
Jno. Murray Belshes	,,	12 Nov. 62.	......
Benjn. Orlando Jones...	,,	,,	......
Thos. Peacocke	,,	......	......
Danl. Baby	,,	......	.. ..
Geo. Nicholls	,,	......	......
Wm. Crokat	,,	21 Dec. 62.	25 Oct. 71.
Robt. Bateman	,,	......	......
Peter Dudgeon...	,,	......	......
Jno. Mitchell	,,	......	......
Norcliffe Norcliffe, K.H.	,,	......	......
Robt. Martin Leake	,,	21 Dec. 62.	25 Oct. 71.
Sir Abrm. Josias Cloëtte, C.B., K.H. ...	,,	,,	,,
Geo. Macdonald	7 Sep. 55.	29 Jan. 63.	,,
Barth. Vigors Derinzy, K.H....	,,	......	......
Chas. Ash Windham, C.B.	8 Sep. 55.	5 Feb. 63.	......
Wm. Prescott	15 Sep. 55.	25 Jun. 70.	10 Apr. 74.
Patr. Yule	9 Oct. 55.	......	......
Fras. Haultain	18 Oct. 55.	......	......
Jas. Gordon	27 Oct. 55.	......	.. ..
Jno. Ashmore	29 Oct. 55.	......	......
Chas. Otway	2 Nov. 55.	15 Dec. 64.	......
Sir Wm. Fenwick Williams, K.C.B., aft. bt.	,,	,,	2 Aug. 68.
Jno. Edwd. Dupuis, C.B., aft. sir J. ...	,,	9 Feb. 65.	......
Hy. Lawrence	5 Dec. 55.	25 Jun. 70.	23 May 74.
Jno. Cox	18 Dec. 55.	......	......
Richd. Budd	10 Feb. 56.	25 Jun. 70.	8 Jul. 74.
Geo. Hicks, C.B.	18 Feb. 56.	......	......
Hy. Fras. Caley	18 Mar. 56.	......	......
Hope Dick	2 Apr. 56.	25 Jun. 70.	28 Apr. 75.
Jos. Nash, C.B.	9 Apr. 56.	23 Mar. 69.	......
Wm. Hy. Law	16 May 56.	......	......
Jas. Alexander, C.B., aft. sir J.	18 May 56.	6 Mar. 68.	1 Aug. 72.
Sir Wm. Reid, K.C.B.	30 May 56.	......	......
Anthy. Marshall	,,	20 Apr. 61.	......
Robt. Sloper Piper	,,	,,	......
Robt. Andrews	7 Jun. 56.	......	......
Jno. Theoph. Lane	8 Jun. 56.	6 Mar. 68.	6 Oct. 72.
Fredk. Hy. Baddeley	10 Jun. 56.	......	......
Peter Faddy	14 Jun. 56.	20 Sep. 65.	7 Feb. 70.
Hassel Richd. Moore	,,	......	......
Edw. Sabine	,,	20 Sep. 65.	......
Fras. Ringler Thomson	14 Jun. 56.	......	......
Jas. Robertson Crawfurd	19 Jun. 56.	12 Feb. 63.	25 Oct. 71.
Geo. Hutton	4 Jul. 56.	......	......
Robt. Clarke	7 Jul. 56.	......	......
C. Brownlow Cumberland	8 Jul. 56.	......	......
Robt. Geo. Hughes	11 Jul. 56.	......	......
Andr. Spens	18 Jul. 56.	......	......
Thos. Budgeon	1 Aug. 56.	......	......

Name.	M.-Gen.	L.-Gen.	Gen.
'ennel Cole	11 Aug. 56.	......	......
Vm. Stewart Balfour...	22 Aug. 56.	13 Feb. 63.	......
Vm. Yorke Moore	5 Sep. 56.	......	......
Edw. Matson	10 Sep. 56.	......	......
Robt. Stewart	15 Sep. 56.	......	......
Vm. Booth	23 Sep. 56.	......	......
Edw. Pettingal	4 Nov. 56	......	......
Richd. Greaves	9 Nov. 56.	......	......
Iy. Hancock	28 Nov. 56.	25 Jun. 70.	......
'no. Alves	5 Dec. 56.	......	......
Iy. Jno. Wood, C.B.	6 Dec. 56.	......	......
Alexr. Fraser	8 Dec. 56.	27 Jul. 63.	......
d. Chas. Wellesley	,,	......	......
'hos. Gordon Higgins	24 Jan. 57.	26 Dec. 65.	......
Vm. Hy. Elliott, K.H., aft. sir W.	29 Jan. 57.	27 Jul. 63.	25 Oct. 71.
Saml. Hawkins	2 Feb. 57.	......	......
'no. Alexr. Philips	6 Feb. 57.	29 May 63.	......
'ortescue Graham	20 Feb. 57.	11 Mar. 65.	10 Nov. 66.
as. Clarke	,,	......	......
no. Tothill	,,	......	......
'no. Eyre	23 Feb. 57.	......	......
Edw. Huthwaite, C.B.	14 Mar. 57.	6 Mar. 68.	......
'os. Childs	31 Mar. 57.	......	......
'eter Edwards	14 Apr. 57.	9 Oct. 63.	19 Nov. 71.
Vm. Freke Williams, K.H.	,,	......	......
Vm. Cartwright	16 May 57.	9 Oct. 63.	19 Nov. 71.
rth. Gore	,,	,,	......
David Goodsman	,,	,,	......
oftus Owen	,,	......	......
'ringle Taylor...	,,	9 Oct. 63.	19 Nov. 71.
'hos. Orlando Cator	26 May 57.	......	......
saac Campbell Coffin, aft. sir I.	29 May 57.	25 Jun. 70.	......
'hos. Robt. Swinburne	4 Jun. 57.	31 Jan. 64.	......
Geo. Whichcote	,,	,,	5 Dec. 71.
as. Arth. Butter	,,	,,	,,
'hos. Hy. Johnston	,,	31 Jan. 64.	5 Dec. 71.
Geo. Cornish Whitlock, aft. sir G.	27 Jun. 57.	9 Apr. 64.	......
no. McArthur	1 Jul. 57.	......	......
aml. Robt. Wesley	,,	11 Apr. 62.	......
Iy. Aitchison Hankey	6 Jul. 57.	29 Apr. 64.	......
no. Campbell...	9 Jul. 57.	4 Jul. 64.	......
'lomer Young, K.H.	17 Jul. 57.	......	......
Iy. Havelock, C.B., aft. bt.	30 Jul. 57.	......	......
'redk. Geo. Lister	22 Aug. 57.	......	......
Vm. Dunn	29 Aug. 57.	......	......
Vm. Bell	,,	27 Feb. 66.	31 Jan. 72.
as. Fogo	,,	,,	......
Ion. Wm. Arbuthnot...	,,	,,	29 Mar. 73.
Iy. Blachley	,,	,,	......
Geo. Jno. Belson	,,	,,	......
Robt. Franck Romer	,,	,,	29 Mar. 73.
Richd. C. Molesworth	,,	......	......
'has. Ogle Streatfeild	2 Sep. 57.	......	......
Iy. Dive Townshend	5 Sep. 57.	8 Aug. 64.	31 Dec. 71.
'hos. Wright, C.B.	8 Sep. 57.	10 Aug. 64.	......
ir Archdale Wilson, bt., K.C.B.	14 Sep. 57	6 Mar. 68.	......
David Downing	15 Sep. 57.	25 Jun. 70.	23 Aug. 75.
'hos. Macknight Cameron	3 Oct. 57.	......	......
Vm. Nugent Thos. Smee	13 Oct. 57.	2 Jan. 70.	26 Nov. 75.
'hos. Chase Parr	,,	25 Jun. 70.	15 Feb. 76.
'redk. Hervey Sandys	15 Oct. 57.	25 Jun. 70.	......

Name.	M.-Gen.	L.-Gen.	Gen.
Jos. Ellison Portlock	25 Nov. 57.	......	......
Sir Jno. Eardley Wilmot Inglis, K.C.B. ...	26 Nov. 57.	......	......
Hy. Prior	2 Dec. 57.	......	......
Michl. Johnson	3 Dec. 57.	......	......
Fredk. Chas. Griffiths	12 Dec. 57.	......	......
Jno. Hungerford Griffin	22 Dec. 57.	......	......
Thos. Wood	11 Jan. 58.	9 Sep. 64.	1 Jan. 72.
Wm. Hassall Eden	15 Jan. 58.	10 Sep. 64.	4 Mar. 72.
Jno. Moule	27 Jan. 58.	......	......
Edwd. A. Parker	24 Feb. 58.	11 Sep. 64.	......
Sir Jas. Hope Grant, K.C.B.	26 Feb. 58.	3 Oct. 64.	23 Apr. 72.
Louis Saunders Bird	4 Mar. 58.	25 Jun. 70.	......
Jos. Clarke	16 Mar. 58.	28 Oct. 64.	......
Sir Jno. Gaspard Le Marchant	22 Mar. 58.	29 Oct. 64.	6 May 72.
Hale Young Wortham	1 Apr. 58.	......	......
Chas. Gascoyne	3 Apr. 58.	25 Nov. 64.	10 May 72.
David Birrell	25 Apr. 58.	25 Jun. 70.	23 Jul. 76.
Thos. Polwhele	1 May 58.	,,	13 Dec. 76.
Richd. Jas. Holwell Birch, C.B.	4 May 58.	......	......
Sir Wm. Rose Mansfield, aft. ld. Sandhurst	18 May 58.	27 Dec. 64.	23 May 72.
Wm. Fraser	5 Jun. 58.	......	......
Geo. Moncrieff...	14 Jun. 58.	22 Jun. 64.	......
Jas. Casimir Harold	1 Jul. 58.	......	......
Geo. Campbell, C.B.	4 Jul. 58.	11 Dec. 68.	21 Jul. 74
Peter Innes	13 Jul. 58.	25 Jun. 70.	......
Thos. Hartz Franks, aft. sir T., C.B. ...	20 Jul. 58.	......	......
Sir Edwd. Lugard, K.C.B.	,,	12 Jan. 65.	24 Oct. 72.
Alexr. Wm. Lawrence	,,	......	......
Sir Fredk. Abbott, C.B.	23 Jul. 58.	......	......
Jno. Fowler Bradford, C.B., aft. sir J. ...	,,	25 Jun. 70.	19 Dec. 76
Thos. Jas. Valiant	6 Aug. 58.	......	......
Poole Vallancey England	9 Aug. 58.	5 Apr. 66.	29 Mar. 73
Jno. Gordon	,,	......	......
Wm. Cuthbert Ward	12 Aug. 58.	20 Sep. 60.	......
Geo. Elliott	24 Aug 58.	......	......
Wm. Bookey Langford	,,	......	......
Marcus Jno. Slade	26 Aug. 58.	6 Feb. 65.	......
Harry Meggs Graves	27 Aug. 58.	......	......
Jno. Tatton Brown	8 Sep. 58.	28 Nov. 65.	13 Feb. 67
Geo. Hy. MacKinnon, C.B.	22 Sep. 58.	10 Feb. 65.	19 Jan. 73
Benj. Fras. Dalton Wilson	10 Oct. 58.	......	......
Chas. Grant, C.B.	14 Oct. 58.	14 Dec. 68.	1 Oct. 77
Archd. Spiers Logan	24 Oct. 58.	25 Jun. 70.	......
Saml. Brandam Boileau	26 Oct. 58.	......	......
Hon. Geo. Fredk. Upton, C.B., aft. visc. Templetown	,,	9 Mar. 65.	......
Hon. Arth. Alexr. Dalzell, aft. E. of Carnwarth	,,	2 Apr. 65.	14 Apr. 73
Thos. Simson Pratt, C.B.	,,	31 May 65.	26 May 73
Orlando Felix	,,	......	......
Wm. Nelson Hutchinson	,,	17 Aug. 65.	29 May 73
Hy. F. Lockyer, C.B....	,,	......	......
Simcoe Baynes...	,,	28 Aug. 65.	......
Montague Cholmondley Johnstone	,,	5 Sep. 65.	29 Dec. 73
Fredk. Meade	,,	......	......
Wm. Fredk. Forster	,,	24 Oct. 65.	6 Jan. 74
Fredk. Johnstone	,,	12 Jan. 66.	7 Jan. 74
Albert Goldsmid	,,	......	......
Edwd. Macarthur, C.B., aft. sir E.	,,	14 Jan. 66.	......
Day Hort Macdowall	,,	4 Mar. 66.	......
J. Price Hely	,,	......	......

Name.	M.-Gen.	L.-Gen.	Gen.
Chas. Robt. Bowers	26 Oct. 58.	10 Mar. 66.	......
J. Arnauld	,,	......	......
Fredk. Towers..	,,	......	......
Sir Robt. Garrett, K.C.B.	,,	10 Mar. 66.	......
Richd. Connop...	,,	31 Mar. 66.	......
Thos. Molyneux Williams	,,	,,	......
W. Nepean	,,	......	......
Arth. Hill Trevor	,,	......	......
Richd. Rich Wilford Brett	,,	......	......
W. Holmes Dutton	,,	......	......
Geo. Thos., E. of Albemarle	,,	31 Mar. 66.	7 Feb. 74
Geo. Thos. Colomb	,,	,,	,,
Fras. Nathl., M. of Conyngham, K.P. ...	,,	20 Apr. 66.	21 Mar. 74.
Sir Sydney Jno. Cotton, K.C.B.	,,	,,	......
Maurice Barlow	,,	24 Apr. 66.	21 Mar. 74
Jno. Napper Jackson...	,,	......	......
Botet Trydell	,,	......	......
Jno. Clark, K.H.	,,	......	......
Redmond W. Brough...	,,	......	......
Edwd. Hungerford Delaval Elers Napier ...	,,	6 May 66.	......
Edwd. Harvey...	,,	......	......
Jas. Robt. Young	,,	17 Jun. 66.	......
Geo. Brooke, aft. sir G.	,,	19 Jun. 66.	......
Jno. Michell, C.B., aft. sir J.	,,	25 Jun. 66.	28 Mar. 74.
Robt. Percy Douglas, aft. bt.	,,	6 Jan. 67.	14 Apr. 74.
Chas. Craufurd Hay	,,	20 Jan. 67.	......
Wm. Longworth Dames	,,	4 Feb. 67.	......
Chas. Warren, C.B.	,,	......	......
Geo. Alexr. Malcolm, C.B.	,,	8 Mar. 67.	16 May 74.
Robt. Hy. Wynyard, C.B.	,,	......	......
Geo. Durnford	,,	24 Aug. 66.	......
Richd. Hardinge, K.H.	,,	......	......
Jos. Hanwell	,,	24 Aug. 66.	......
Philip Sandilands	,,	,,	......
Browne Willis	,,	1 Mar. 64.	......
Benj. Hutchison Vaughan Arbuckle ...	,,	24 Aug. 66.	......
Jno. Harbridge Freer...	,,	,,	......
Archd. White Hope	,,	,,	......
Jno. Louis Smith	,,	,,	......
W. Cochrane Anderson	,,	(?)	......
Wm. Redman Ord	1 Nov. 58.	20 Apr. 61.	......
Chas. Æneas Shirreff	14 Nov. 58.	......	......
Hy. Eyre	16 Nov. 58.	3 Sep. 67.	23 Sep. 74.
Hy. Jno. Savage	23 Nov. 58.	3 Apr. 62.	......
Edwd. Messiter	,,	25 Jun. 70.	8 Feb. 77.
Ld. Wm. Paulet, C.B., aft. K.C.B.	13 Dec. 58.	8 Dec. 67.	7 Oct. 74.
Philip M'Pherson, C.B.	24 Dec. 58.	......	......
Nath. Massey Stack	,,	......	......
Richd. Say Armstrong	16 Jan. 59.	......	......
Stuart Corbett, C.B.	4 Feb. 59.	......	......
Chas. Wm. Ridley, C.B.	13 Feb. 59.	......	......
Jno. Patton	20 Feb. 59.	1 Jan. 68.	10 Oct. 74.
Hugh Manley Tuite	2 Mar. 59.	......	......
Hy. Macan	5 Mar. 59.	25 Jun. 70.	24 May 77.
Wm. Sage	13 Mar. 59.	......	......
Duncan Alexr. Cameron, C.B., aft. Sir D. ...	25 Mar. 59.	1 Jan. 68.	5 Dec. 74
Thos. Matheson	2 Apr. 59.	21 Jan. 68.	......
Geo. Bell, C.B., aft. Sir G.	9 Apr. 59.	28 Jan. 68.	8 Mar. 75.
Sir Justin Sheil	26 Apr. 59.	25 Jun. 70.	......
Horatio Nelson Vigors	1 May 59.	......	......
Chas. Wahab	6 May 59.	25 Jun. 70.	......

Name.	M.-Gen.	L.-Gen.	Gen.
Crighton Grierson	10 May 59.	3 Aug. 63.	......
Lewis Alexr. Hall	,,	,,	......
Robt. Richardson Robertson, C.B.	14 May 59.	31 Jan. 68.	13 Apr. 75.
Jas. Manson	15 May 59.	......	......
Geo. Twemlow	17 May 59.	......	......
Thos. Assheton Duke	26 May 59.	25 Jun. 70.	1 Oct. 77
Nathl. Jones	30 May 59.	......	......
Saml. Braybrooke	12 Jun. 59.	21 Feb. 68.	16 Apr. 75.
Danl. Bolton	20 Jun. 59.	......	......
Augs. Flemyng	8 Jul. 59.	......	......
Robt. Law	17 Jul. 59.	13 Mar. 68.	......
Edwd. L'Estrange	19 Jul. 59.	......	......
Jas. Clarke Charnock Gray	20 Jul. 59.	25 Jun. 70.	1 Oct. 77.
Usher Williamson	5 Aug. 59.	......	......
Sir Chas. Thos. Van Straubenzee, K.C.B. ...	14 Aug. 59.	27 Mar. 68.	29 Apr. 75.
Hy. Wm. Parke	23 Aug. 59.	......	......
Thos. David Carpenter	29 Aug. 59.	......	......
Sir Alexr. Murray Tulloch, K.C.B.	9 Sep. 59.	......	......
Thos. Alexr. Augs. Munsey...	11 Sep. 59.	......	......
Edwd. Hely Hutchinson	16 Sep. 59.	......	......
Jno. Bloomfield, aft. sir J.	25 Sep. 59.	12 May 66.	26 Nov. 75.
Robt. Thorpe	27 Sep. 59.	......	......
Alexr. Jardine	7 Oct. 59.	......	......
Wm. Geo. Gold	17 Oct. 59.	29 Mar. 68.	......
Thos. Foster	25 Oct. 59.	8 Feb. 66.	8 Jun. 71.
Jas. Scott	,,	......	......
Charlton Holl	28 Nov. 59.	25 Jun. 70.	......
Thos. Hurdle, C.B.	2 Dec. 59.	......	......
Thos. Peard Dwyer	,,	......	......
Jno. Hamilton Stewart	,,	......	......
Hon. Robt. Bruce	7 Dec. 59.	......	......
Arth. Cunliffe Van Notten Pole	13 Dec. 59.	9 Apr. 68.	......
Chas. Hewetson	21 Dec. 59.	25 Jun. 70.	......
Edwd. Walter Forrestier Walker, C.B. ...	26 Dec. 59.	19 Apr. 68.	13 May 75.
Morden Carthew	30 Dec. 59.	,,	1 Oct. 77.
Augs. Abbott, C.B.	,,	......	......
Jno. Forbes	1 Jan. 60.	......	......
Thos. Armstrong Drought	11 Jan. 60.	21 Apr. 68.	29 May 75.
Robt. Hy. Lowth, C.B.	24 Jan. 60.	......	......
Chas. Stuart	28 Jan. 60.	1 May 68.	29 May 75.
Hy. Powell Wulff	31 Jan. 60.	......	......
Hon. Augs. Almeric Spencer, aft. sir A. ...	13 Feb. 60.	9 May 68.	14 Sep. 75.
Philip Austin Smyly	14 Feb. 60.	......	......
Jno. Singleton...	21 Feb. 60.	......	......
Chas. Ashmore	1 Mar. 60.	12 Jul. 68.	19 Oct. 75.
Anthy. Robinson Harrison	8 Mar. 60.	......	......
Hy. Richd. Wright	,,	......	......
Fras. Warde, aft. sir F.	,,	24 Aug. 66.	15 Apr. 77.
Augs. Geo. Blachford	9 Mar. 60.	......	......
Hy. Keane Bloomfield	1 Apr. 60.	13 Aug. 68.	......
Jno. Lawrenson	6 Apr. 60.	25 Aug. 68.	2 Nov. 75.
Studholme Jno. Hodgson	11 Apr. 60.	29 Aug. 68.	2 Feb. 76.
Augs. Abbott	13 Apr. 60.	......	......
Jno. Douglas Johnstone, C.B.	17 Apr. 60.	......	......
Chas. Franklyn, C.B.	23 Apr. 60.	......	......
Godfrey Chas. Mundy	24 Apr. 60.	......	......
Jno. Glasfurd	27 Apr. 60.	......	......
Robt. Farquhar, C.B.	,,	......	......
Jas. Edwd. Gordon Morris	30 Apr. 60.	......	......
Fras. Hugh Geo. Seymour, aft. M. of Hertford	4 May 60.	10 Nov. 68.	10 Feb. 76.
Wm. Anson M'Cleverty	,,	22 Nov. 68.	17 Mar. 76.

Name.	M.-Gen.	L.-Gen.	Gen.
Lewis Duncan Williams	5 May 60.	23 Nov. 68.	......
Chas. Wright	17 May 60.	......	......
Jas. Edw. Gordon Morris	2 Jun. 60.	......	......
Robt. Blucher Wood, C.B.	3 Jun. 60.	10 Dec. 68.	......
Claud Douglas...	4 Jun. 60.	25 Jun. 70.	1 Oct. 77.
Chas. Emilius Gold	15 Jun. 60.	27 Dec. 68.	......
Josh. Hale	16 Jun. 60.	23 Feb. 69.	......
Chas. Algn. Lewis	19 Jun. 60.	......	5 Apr. 76.
Wm. Bates Ingilby, aft. sir W.	22 Jun. 60.	1 Jan. 68.	1 Oct. 77.
Hy. Goodwyn	26 Jun. 60.	1 Mar. 67.	14 Jul. 71.
Wm. Fanshaw Bedford	3 Jul. 60.	......	......
Geo. Conolly Ponsonby	,,	......	......
Michl. Francklyn Willoughby, C.B. ...	,,	......	......
Fras. Chas. Wells	,,	......	......
Chas. Jas. Green	,,	......	......
Jno. Grant	,,	......	......
Geo. Fk., &c., D. of Cumberland, K. of Hanover	......	......	27 May 76.
Chas. Campbell	3 Jul. 60.	......	......
Edwin Hy. Atkinson	,,	......	......
Sir Joshua Jebb, K.C.B.	6 Jul. 60.	......	......
Hy. Sandham	,,	3 Aug. 66.	......
Wm. Geo. White	,,	25 Jun. 70.	1 Oct. 77.
Richd. French...	11 Jul. 60.	......	......
Chas. Gostling...	13 Jul. 60.	......	......
Wm. Parlby	17 Jul. 60.	21 Mar. 69.	22 May 76.
Geo. Congreve...	20 Jul. 60.	......	......
Wm. Hy. Pickering	21 Jul. 60.	......	......
Jno. Thos. Hill	30 Jul. 60.	14 Jun. 69.	24 Jun. 76.
Geo. Evans Hunt	31 Jul. 60.	......	......
Thos. Coryndon Luxmore	2 Aug. 60.	7 Sep. 67.	8 Jul. 71.
Wm. Faris	,,	,,	,,
Montgomery Williams	,,	,,	12 Apr. 72.
Jno. Longfield, C.B.	3 Aug. 60.	5 Sep. 69.	19 Jul. 76.
Jas. Fitzgerald	30 Aug. 60.	25 Jun. 70.	......
Chas. Wm. Morley Balders, C.B.	31 Aug. 60.	28 Oct. 69.	......
Fred. Wm. Hamilton, C.B., aft. sir F. ...	,,	18 Dec. 69.	21 Nov. 76.
Coghill Glendower Ottley	11 Sep. 60.	......	......
Chas. Hastings Doyle, aft. sir C.	15 Sep. 60.	10 Jan. 70.	15 Mar. 77.
Thos. Hore	20 Sep. 60.	1 Jan. 68.	......
Richd. Jno. Stotherd...	,,	1 Jan. 68.	19 Jun. 72.
Chas. Edw. Michel	21 Sep. 60.	......	......
Clement Clemons	29 Sep. 60.	......	......
Chas. Haldane...	7 Oct. 60.	......	......
Fred. Horn, aft. sir F.	13 Oct. 60.	18 Jan. 70.	2 Jun. 77.
Alexr. Hy. Edmonstone Boileau	18 Oct. 60.	......	......
Jno. Skardon Ramsay	6 Nov. 60.	......	......
Jno. Fras. Glencairn Campbell, C.B. ...	12 Nov. 60.	3 Feb. 70.	......
Fred. Brooke Corfield	18 Nov. 60.	25 Jun. 70.	1 Oct. 77.
Ld. Fredk. Paulet	13 Dec. 60.	12 Feb. 70.	......
Edw. Green, C.B., aft. sir E....	18 Dec. 60.	25 Jun. 70.	2 Jun. 77.
Wm. Clendon	22 Dec. 60.	......	......
Anthy. Blaxland Stransham, aft. sir A. ...	,,	23 Aug. 66.	1 Apr. 70.
Jno. Rowland Smyth, C.B.	,,	1 Apr. 70.	......
Wm. Jas. D'Urban	27 Dec. 60.	20 Jun. 70.	......
Benj. Crispin	15 Jan. 61.	......	......
Hy. Jno. French	18 Jan. 61.	9 Aug. 70.	......
Geo. Farquharson	25 Jan. 61.	25 Jun. 70.	......
Wm. Robt. Corfield	30 Jan. 61.	25 Jun. 70.	1 Oct. 77.
Robt. St. John...	4 Feb. 61.	......	......
Richd. Horsford	6 Feb. 61.	......	......
Terence O'Brien	13 Feb. 61.	......	......

Name.	M.-Gen.	L.-Gen.	Gen.
Sir Robt. Cornelis Napier, K.C.B., aft. ld. Napier of Magdala	15 Feb. 61.	1 Mar. 67.	1 Apr. 74.
Chas. Wm. Wingfield	21 Feb. 61.	......	......
Jno. Ffolliott Crofton...	9 Mar. 61.	21 Aug. 70.	23 Aug. 77.
Jno. Grattan	10 Mar. 61.	15 Sep. 70.	......
Hon. Jas. Lindsay	12 Mar. 61.	10 Oct. 70.	......
Wm. Sullivan, C.B.	23 Mar. 61.	......	......
Josh. Webb Goldsworthy	29 Mar. 61.	......	......
Herbert Jacob	,,	......	......
Richd. Rodney Ricketts	,,	......	......
Edw. Hume Hart	,,	......	......
Edw. Trevor	1 Apr. 61.	......	......
Alex. Gordon	20 Apr. 61.	......	......
Jno. Hankey Bainbrigge	,,	22 Oct. 70.	1 Oct. 77.
Arth. Aug. Thurlow Cunynghame, C.B., aft. sir A.	,,	,,	,,
Arth. Mitford Becher, C.B., aft. sir A. ...	27 Apr. 61.	25 Jun. 70.	2 Jun. 77.
Jno. Fordyce	29 Apr. 61.	21 Jan. 72.	......
Wm. Jas. King	1 May 61.	......	......
Wm. Abraham Le Mesurier	,,	19 Nov. 70.	......
Jno. Swinburn...	,,	......	......
Thos. Kelly	,,	......	......
Jas. Kerr Ross	,,	19 Nov. 70.	......
Eardley Wilmot	,,	,,	......
Edw. Basil Brooke	,,	......	......
Jno. FitzMaurice	7 May 61.	......	......
Fredk. Hope	,,	......	......
Stanhope Wm. Jephson	24 May 61.	......	......
Hy. Poole	5 Jun. 61.	......	......
Lewis Alexr. During	17 Jun. 61.	19 Nov. 70.	1 Oct. 77.
Joshua Simmons Smith	,,	,,	,,
Thos. Ferguson Flemyng	11 Jul. 61.	25 Jun. 70.	......
Fras. Wheler, aft. Sir F.	21 Jul. 61.	,,	1 Oct. 77.
Jno. Studholme Hodgson	23 Jul. 61.	......	......
Thos. Townsend Pears, C.B....	6 Aug. 61.	......	......
Sir Andr. Scott Waugh	,,	......	......
Hy. Arth. O'Neill	,,	22 Nov. 70.	......
Horatio Shirley, C.B.	8 Aug. 61.	......	......
Arth. Johnstone Lawrence, C.B.	14 Aug. 61.	......	......
Richd. Parker...	24 Aug. 61.	2 Jan. 71.	1 Oct. 77.
Jno. Kennedy McCausland	29 Aug. 61.	......	......
Jno. Hobson	2 Sep. 61.	25 Jun. 70.	11 Jul. 77.
Walter Scott	5 Sep. 61.	1 Mar. 67.	31 Mar. 75.
Robt. Wm. Honnor, C.B.	17 Sep. 61.	......	......
Chas. Trollope, C.B.	20 Sep. 61.	24 Feb. 71.	1 Oct. 77.
Geo. St. Patrick Lawrence, C.B.	25 Sep. 61.	......	......
Wm. Halpin	8 Oct. 61.	......	......
Jas. Somers Down	2 Nov. 61.	25 Jun. 70.	......
Andrew T. Hemphill...	10 Nov. 61.	......	......
Ld. Geo. Aug. Fredk. Paget, C.B.	11 Nov. 61.	28 Feb. 71.	1 Oct. 77.
Peter Hamond...	15 Nov. 61.	......	......
Wm. Hy. Miller, C.B....	,,	......	......
Brook Jno. Taylor	,,	9 Apr. 71.	1 Oct. 77.
Burton Daveney	13 Dec. 61.	......	......
Jas. Stuart	,,	......	......
Geo. Thos. Conolly Napier, C.B.	15 Dec. 61.	30 Apr. 71.	......
Edwd. Sterling Farmar	31 Dec. 61.	......	......
Willoughby Trevelyan	1 Jan. 62.	25 Jun. 70.	......
Fras. Rowcroft, C.B.	,,	,,	......
Jno. Macoustie Shortt	,,	......	......
Jas. Matthie	,,	......	......

Name.	M.-Gen.	L.-Gen.	Gen.
Edwd. Rowley Hill	2 Feb. 62.	27 May 71.	1 Oct. 77.
Geo. Wm. Key	6 Feb. 62.	30 Jul. 71.	,,
Edw. Pole	16 Feb. 62.	25 Oct. 71.	,,
Arth. Shirley	7 Mar. 62.	......	......
Fred. Holl Robe	14 Mar. 62.	......	......
Edwd. Rea	25 Mar. 62.	......	......
Sandy Stawell Walsh, C.B.	,,	......	......
Wm. Biddlecombe Marlow	26 Mar. 62.	......	......
Alexr. Anderson	,,	10 Nov. 66.	1 Apr. 70.
Benj. Spicer Stehelin...	3 Apr. 62.	17 Mar. 68.	......
Chas. Alfr. Browne	6 Apr. 62.	......	......
Robt. Jno. McKillop	11 Apr. 62.	......	......
Sir Arth. Thos. Cotton	14 Apr. 62.	1 Mar. 67.	20 Mar. 76.
Geo. Macan	20 Apr. 62.	......	......
Sir Robt. Walpole, K.C.B.	30 May 62.	25 Oct. 71.	......
Noel Thos. Lake, C.B.	,,	......	......
Arth. Johnstone Lawrence, C.B., aft. sir A.	1 Jun. 62.	25 Oct. 71.	1 Oct. 77.
Hon. Geo. Cadogan, C.B.	3 Jun. 62.	,,	,,
Thos. Chas. Cotton Moore	10 Jun. 62.	......	......
Hugh Troup	,,	25 Jul. 70.	1 Oct. 77.
Geo. Inglis Jameson	15 Jun. 62.	18 Apr. 71.	......
Fred Darby Cleaveland	20 Jun. 62.	......	......
Simon Fraser	24 Jun. 62.	......	......
Jno. Chas. Hope Gibsone	28 Jun. 62.	25 Oct. 71.	1 Oct. 77.
Alexr. Cunningham	30 Jun. 62.	......	......
Wm. Maule Ramsay	1 Jul. 62.	11 May 71.	......
Chas. P. Ainslie	7 Jul. 62.	25 Oct. 71.	1 Oct. 77.
Piercy Benn	16 Jul. 62.	......	......
Humphrey Lyons	,,	20 May 71.	......
Jno. Fraser	18 Jul. 62.	.....	......
Sir Archd. Bogle	2 Aug. 62.	20 May 71.	......
Freeman Murray	13 Aug. 62.	25 Oct. 71.	1 Oct 77.
Hon. Alexr. Nelson Hood, aft. visc. Bridport	19 Aug. 62.	,,	,,
David Russell, C.B., aft. sir D.	3 Sep. 62.	,	,,
Richd. Albt. Bayley	6 Sep. 62.	4 Jul. 71.	1 Oct. 77.
Arnold Edwd. Burmester, C.B.	23 Sep. 62.	......	......
David Simpson	2 Oct. 62.	3 Sep. 71.	......
Horatio Shirley, C.B., aft. sir H.	24 Oct. 62.	25 Oct. 71.	1 Oct. 77.
Wm. Saml. Newton, aft. sir W.	6 Nov. 62.	,,	,,
Geo. Dixon, C.B.	7 Nov. 62.	......	......
Hamilton Vetch	,,	......	......
Arth. Sanders	,,	......	......
Egerton Chas. Wm. Miles Milman	9 Nov. 62.	......	......
Spencer Perceval	,,	25 Oct. 71.	......
Hy. Cooper	,,	,,	1 Oct. 77.
Randal Rumley	,,	,,	,,
Sir Hy. Knight Storks, K.C.B., G.C.M.G. ...	12 Nov. 62.	,,	......
Edwd. Altham Cumberlege	22 Nov. 62.	17 Sep. 71.	......
Fredk. Gaitskell, C.B.	23 Nov. 62.	......	......
Jno. Macdonald	12 Dec. 62.	25 Oct. 71.	1 Oct. 77.
Thos. Charlton Smith	21 Dec. 62.	25 Oct. 71.	1 Oct. 77.
Wm. Sutton, C.B.	,,	......	......
Stephen Pott	31 Dec. 62.	......	......
Chas. Jno. Cooke	6 Jan. 63.	......	......
Andr. Rowland	,,	1 Aug. 72.	1 Oct. 77.
Jno. Hill	13 Jan. 63.	......	......
Hy. Jos. Morris	20 Jan. 63.	......	......
Hy. Pester	24 Jan. 63.	11 Sep. 64.	......
Hon. Geo. Cecil Weld Forester, c.c. ld. G. F.	29 Jan. 63.	25 Oct. 71.	1 Oct. 77.
Edwd. Cooper Hodge, C.B., aft. sir E. ...	30 Jan. 63.	,,	,,
Thos. Crombie	5 Feb. 63.	,,	,,

Name.	M.-Gen.	L.-Gen.	Gen.
Philip Jno. Bainbrigge	6 Feb. 63.	......	......
Hy. Edwd. Doherty, C.B.	8 Feb. 63.	25 Oct. 71.	1 Oct. 77.
Aug. Halifax Ferryman, C.B.	12 Feb. 63.	19 Nov. 71.	,,
Jno. Wray Mitchell	,,	......	......
Wm. Jno. Ridley	13 Feb. 63.	......	......
Fras. Burton Boileau	20 Feb. 63.	......	......
Geo. James	22 Feb. 63.	2 Feb. 68.	......
Hy. Palliser	,,	......	......
Wm. Raikes Faber	9 Mar. 63.	5 Dec. 71.	1 Oct. 77.
Fras. Claude Burnett	10 Mar. 63.	......	......
Sir Chas. Shepard Stuart, K.C.B.	12 Mar. 63.	25 Oct. 71.	......
Jno. Walpole	17 Mar. 63.	......	......
Thos. Hy. Shuldham	18 Mar. 63.	15 Nov. 71.	......
Thos. Jas. Galloway	27 Mar. 63.	7 Dec. 71.	1 Oct. 77.
Jno. Garvock, aft. sir J.	1 Apr. 63.	29 Dec. 71.	......
Jno. Butler	3 Apr. 63.	9 Dec. 71.	......
Wm. Jones, C.B., aft. sir W.	,,	31 Dec. 71.	1 Oct. 77.
Wm. Barclay Goodfellow	6 Apr. 63.	14 Jul. 71.	,,
Chas. Edwd. Faber	7 Apr. 63.	......	......
Sir Wm. Marcus Coghlan, K.C.B.	14 Apr. 63.	6 Oct. 72.	1 Oct. 77.
Geo. Burney	17 Apr. 63.	......	......
Thos. Anderson	21 Apr. 63.	......	......
Geo. Munro	1 May 63.	......	......
Sir Wm. Fenwick Williams, K.C.B.	19 May 63.	......	......
Thos. Holloway, C.B.	29 May 63.	10 Nov. 66.	1 Apr. 70.
Hon. Alexr. Hamilton Gordon, C.B., aft. Sir A.	8 Jun. 63.	1 Jan. 72.	1 Oct. 77.
Geo. Maxwell	12 Jun. 63.	......	......
Haughton James	19 Jun. 63.	14 Dec. 71.	......
Wm. Lang	29 Jun. 63.	......	......
Fredk. Spence, C.B.	30 Jun. 63.	......	......
Corbet Cotton	6 Jul. 63.	5 Jan. 72.	1 Oct. 77.
Jas. Bowen Woosnam	13 Jul. 63.	......	......
Hy. Servanté	3 Aug. 63.	7 Nov. 68.	27 Aug. 72.
Vincent Eyre, C.B.	1 Sep. 63.	......	......
Jno. Maxwell Glasse	,,	......	......
Robt. Croft Wormald...	,,	......	......
Jno. Pottinger, C.B.	,,	......	......
Edwd. Wm. Smyth Scott	,,	......	......
Wm. Barr	,,	......	......
Bladen West Black	,,	......	......
Edwd. Lacon Ommanney	,,	......	......
Hy. Joshua Margary	,,	......	......
Gore Boland Munbee	,,	......	......
Wm. Ilbert Birdwood	,,	......	......
Chas. Becher Young	,,	......	......
Saml. Edgar Owen Ludlow	,,	......	......
Matth. Smith	9 Sep. 63.	4 Mar. 72.	......
Chas. Bertie Symons	20 Sep. 63.	......	......
Hy. Bates	9 Oct. 63.	8 Mar. 72.	1 Oct. 77.
Hy. Owen Crawley	11 Oct. 63.	......	......
Alf. Geo. Goodwyn	13 Oct. 63.	......	......
Jno. Mac Duff, C.B.	23 Oct. 63.	......	......
Edmd. Neal Wilford	2 Nov. 63.	......	......
Thos. Charlton Smith	21 Dec. 63.	......	......
Wm. Sutton, C.B.	,,	......	......
Jno. Twiss	5 Jan. 64.	......	......
Edwd. Frome	,,	20 Apr. 70.	21 Nov. 74.
Thos. Maitland Wilson	7 Jan. 64.	23 Apr. 72.	1 Oct. 77.
Geo. Staunton	12 Jan. 64.	,,	,,
St. Geo. Danl. Showers, C.B.	13 Jan. 64.	......	......
Chas. Cornwallis Johnstone	15 Jan. 64.	......	......

Name.	M.-Gen.	L.-Gen.	Gen.
Wm. Couperus Macleod	18 Jan. 64.	19 Feb. 72.	1 Oct. 77.
Geo. King	19 Jan. 64.	......	......
Chas. Crutchley	31 Jan. 64.	23 Apr. 72.	1 Oct. 77.
Walter Hamilton, C.B.	3 Feb. 64.	......	......
Richd. Jno. Nelson	5 Feb. 64.	......	......
Fras. Dick	12 Feb. 64.	......	......
Edwd. Thos. Lloyd	15 Feb. 64.	......	......
Chas. Rochfort Scott	21 Feb. 64.	......	......
Jas. Hy. Burke	27 Feb. 64.	......	......
Archd. Macbean	1 Mar. 64.	2 Feb. 68.	......
Robt. Longmore Garstin	,,	,,	......
Burke Cuppage	,,	,,	......
Mark Kerr Atherley	12 Mar. 64.	6 May 72.	1 Oct. 77.
Trevor Chute, aft. sir T.	9 Apr. 64.	10 May 72.	,,
Fredk. English, C.B.	19 Apr. 64.	......	......
Wm. Gust. Brown	29 Apr. 64.	23 May 72.	1 Oct. 77.
Hy. Jervis	17 May 64.	24 Oct. 72.	,,
Hy. Aylmer	20 May 64.	......	......
Colin Troup, C.B.	26 May 64.	21 Mar. 72.	......
Geo. Alexr. Baillie	28 May 64.	23 Apr. 72.	1 Oct. 77.
Jno. Welchman	25 Jun. 64.	......	......
Robt. Burn	27 Jun. 64.	2 Aug. 68.	1 Oct. 77.
Michl. Wm. Smith, C.B.	4 Jul. 64.	19 Jan. 73.	,,
Richd. Beaumont Burnaby	21 Jul. 64.	10 Nov. 68.	......
Wm. How Hennis	,,	,,	......
Danl. Thorndike	,,	,,	......
Harry Stow	28 Jul. 64.	7 Feb. 70.	......
Chas. Hy. Mee...	,,	......	......
Wm. Wallace D'Arley	,,	7 Feb. 70.	......
Jno. Tylden	,,	......	......
Geo. Hoolton Hyde	,,	7 Feb. 70.	1 Oct. 77.
Thos. Petres Flude	,,	,,	,,
Sir Neville Bowles Chamberlain, K.C.B. ...	5 Aug. 64.	1 May 72.	,,
Jno. Noble Arbuthnot Freese	,,	......	......
Jno. Maxwell Perceval, C.B.	8 Aug. 64.	14 Feb. 73.	1 Oct. 77.
Hy. Wm. Stisted, C.B., aft. sir H.	10 Aug. 64.	15 Feb. 73.	......
David Babington	17 Aug. 64.	16 May 72.	......
Philip Nelson Melmoth Guy, C.B., aft. sir P.	9 Sep. 64.	6 Apr. 73.	1 Oct. 77.
Fras. Seymour, C.B., ft. sir F.	10 Sep. 64.	14 Apr. 73.	,,
Jno. Mitchell	20 Sep. 64.	......	......
Chas. Steuart, C.B.	3 Oct. 64.	6 May 73.	......
Wm. Robt. Andr. Freeman	21 Oct. 64.	2 Oct. 72.	......
Chas. Fredk. North	24 Oct. 64.	......	......
Jno. Leslie Dennis	28 Oct. 64.	15 Oct. 72.	1 Oct. 77.
Chas. Richd. Sackville, ld. West, C.B., aft. E. de la Warr	29 Oct. 64.	......	......
Wm. Friend Hopkins, C.B.	4 Nov. 64.	......	......
Jno. Geo. Aug. Ayles...	,,	......	......
Fredk. Paul Haines, aft. sir F.	25 Nov. 64.	23 May 73.	1 Oct. 77.
Wm. Radcliff	9 Dec. 64.	......	......
Alexr. Tulloh	10 Dec. 64.	5 Jul. 67.	......
Hy. Geo. Teesdale	15 Dec. 64.	21 Jun. 71.	......
Thos. Akers Shone	18 Dec. 64.	13 Sep. 71.	1 Oct. 77.
Ashton Ashton Shuttleworth	,,	,,	......
Jno. Arth. Lambert, aft. Sir J.	27 Dec. 64.	26 May 73.	1 Oct. 77.
Wm. Fergusson Beatson	8 Jan. 65.	......	......
Wm. O'Grady Haly, aft. sir W.	12 Jan. 65.	26 May 73.	1 Oct. 77.
Saunders Alexius Abbott	24 Jan. 65.	......	......
Chas. Saml. Reid	,,	5 Apr. 73.	......
Hy. Phipps Raymond...	6 Feb. 65.	26 May 73.	1 Oct. 77.
Chas. Herrick Burnaby	9 Feb. 65.	31 Jan. 72.	,,

Name.	M.-Gen.	L.-Gen.	Gen.
Jno. Geddes Walker	9 Feb. 65.	31 Jan. 72.	......
Jno. McCoy	,,	......	......
Ld. Hy. Hugh Manvers Percy, c.c. visc. Percy	10 Feb. 65.	29 May 73.	1 Oct. 77.
Wm. C. E. Napier	9 Mar. 65.	22 Aug. 73.	,,
Thos. Lemon, C.B.	11 Mar. 65.	......	......
Jno. Edmonstoune Landers	12 Mar. 65.	9 Dec. 72.	1 Oct. 77.
Chas. Hy. Ellice, C.B., aft. sir C.	23 Mar. 65.	28 Sep. 73.	,,
Edwd. Rowland Mainwaring...	28 Mar. 65.	......	......
Richd. Cornwallis Moore, C.B.	29 Mar. 65.	10 May 74.	1 Oct. 77.
Hy. Richmond Jones, C.B.	2 Apr. 65.	5 Dec. 74.	,,
Ferd. Whittingham, C.B.	7 Apr. 65.	......	......
Auchmuty Tucker, C.B.	9 Apr. 65.	14 Dec. 73.	1 Oct. 77.
Harry Rivers	14 Apr. 65.	......	......
Hy. Austin Turner	19 Apr. 65.	......	......
Sir Thos. Myddelton Biddulph, K.C.B. ...	31 Apr. 65.	29 Dec. 73.	1 Oct. 77.
Geo. Balfour, C.B., aft. sir G.	5 Jun. 65.	21 Jul. 74.	,,
Geo. Aug. Fred. De Rinzy	,,	......	......
Gallway Byng Payne	12 Jun. 65.	......	......
Philip Harris	13 Jun. 65.	......	......
Wm. Wynne Lodder	18 Jul. 65.	......	......
Jas. Travers	23 Jul. 65.	5 Feb. 73.	1 Oct. 77.
Chas. Hagart, C.B.	28 Jul. 65.	6 Jan. 74.	,,
Wm. Erskine Baker, aft. sir W.	2 Aug. 65.	1 Apr. 74.	,,
Thos. Montague Steele, C.B., aft. sir T. ...	17 Aug. 65.	7 Jan. 74.	,,
Jno. Liptrap	22 Aug. 65.	8 Mar. 73.	,,
Wm. Chambré...	28 Aug. 65.	26 Mar. 73.	......
Hon. Arth. Chas. Legge	,,	,,	1 Oct. 77.
Melville Dalyell	,,	,,	,,
Jno. Birtwhistle	,,	......	......
Jas. Creagh	,,	26 Jan. 74.	......
Robt. Fitzgerald Crawford, aft. Copland-Crawford	31 Aug. 65.	31 Jan. 72.	1 Oct. 77.
Hy. Sykes Stephens	5 Sep. 65.	7 Feb. 74.	,,
Jas. McQueen	,,	,,	,,
Chas. Smith	,,	......	......
Fras. Westenra	,,	......	......
Edgar Gibson	,,	......	......
Edwd. Last	,,	......	......
Jno. St. George, C.B., aft. sir J.	20 Sep. 65.	29 Mar. 73.	1 Oct. 77.
Fras. Plunket Dunne	26 Sep. 65.	7 Feb. 74.	,,
Rawdon Jno. Popham Vassall	,,	,,	1 Oct. 77
Jas. Pattoun Sparke, C.B.	,,	,,	,,
Jno. Wm. Grey	10 Oct. 65.	......	......
Hubert Marshall	,,	11 May 73.	1 Oct. 77.
Jno. Liddell	12 Oct. 65.	......	......
Richd. Chetwode	24 Oct. 65.	......	......
Jno. Parson Westropp	,,	20 Feb. 74.	1 Oct. 77.
Geo. Marm. Reeves, C.B.	,,	......	......
Wm. Henderson	1 Nov. 65.	......	......
Thos. Tapp	4 Nov. 65.	......	......
Wm. Hy. March	20 Nov. 65.	......	......
Edw. Darvall	,,	20 Feb. 74.	1 Oct. 77
Hy. Carr Tate...	28 Nov. 65.	1 Apr. 70.	22 Jul. 75.
Aug. Dover Lyddon Farrant	12 Dec. 65.	......	......
Hy. Blois Turner	21 Dec. 65.	1 Apr. 74.	21 Dec. 77.
Geo. Hy. Swinly	22 Dec. 65.	......	......
Wm. Robt. Nedham	26 Dec. 65.	......	......
Edwd. Chas. Fletcher	12 Jan. 66.	......	......
Edwd. Bagot	,,	......	......
Jas. Scargill	,,	21 Mar. 74.	......
Robt. Lewis	,,	......	......

Name.	M.-Gen.	L.-Gen.	Gen.
Saml. Tryon	14 Jan. 66.	......	......
Thos. Williams, C.B.	,,	......	......
Richd. Clement Moody	25 Jan. 66.	......	......
Richd. Wilbraham, C.B., aft. sir R.... ...	26 Jan. 66.	21 Mar. 74.	1 Oct. 77.
Fredk. Aug. Yorke	2 Feb. 66.	......	......
Hy. Palmer	7 Feb. 66.	28 Mar. 74.	1 Oct. 77.
Chas. Edmd. Wilkinson	8 Feb. 66.	......	......
David Pott	15 Feb. 66.	14 Apr. 74.	1 Oct. 77.
Edwd. Chas. Warde, C.B., aft. sir E. ...	27 Feb. 66.	17 Nov. 75.	,,
Wm. Irwin	3 Mar. 66.	14 Apr. 74.	,,
Frank Adams, C.B.	4 Mar. 66.	......	......
Jas. Robt. Brunker	10 Mar. 66.	......	......
Hy. Darby Griffith, C.B.	31 Mar. 66.	14 Apr. 74.	1 Oct. 77.
Jno. Wm. Ormsby	5 Apr. 66.	......	......
Wm. Turnbull Renwick	10 Apr. 66.	8 Jun. 71.	27 Feb. 76.
Geo. Freeman Murray	17 Apr. 66.	......	......
Jas. Webber Smith, C.B.	20 Apr. 66.	15 May 74.	1 Oct. 77.
Luke Smyth O'Connor, C.B.	24 Apr. 66.	......	......
Chas. Lncas	26 Apr. 66.	......	......
Hy. Chas. Gosling	3 May 66.	......	......
Fredk. Darley George, C.B.	6 May 66.	17 May 74.	1 Oct. 77.
Arth. Jos. Taylor	12 May 66.	24 Oct. 70.	......
Peter. Thos. Cherry	27 May 66.	17 Nov. 73.	1 Oct. 77
John Wm. Croggan	12 Jun. 66.	10 Apr. 76.	......
John Hind, C.B.	15 Jun. 66.	......	......
John Yorke, C.B.	17 Jun. 66.	1 Aug. 74.	1 Oct. 77.
Jas. Abbott	19 Jun. 66.	27 Feb. 77.	,,
Hy. Dunn O'Halloran...	25 Jun. 66.	......	......
Pr. Fredk. Christian Chas. Aug. of Schleswig Holstein	3 Jul. 66.	14 Aug. 74.	1 Oct. 77.
Wm. Thos. Blewett Mountstephen	20 Jul. 66.	......	......
Fras. Gregor Urquhart	,,	......	......
Philip Kearney McGregor Skinner, C.B. ...	23 Jul. 66.	14 Aug. 74.	1 Oct. 77.
Chas Beamish	27 Jul. 66.	......	......
Sir John Wm. Gordon, K.C.B.	3 Aug. 66.	......	......
Chas. Jas. Buchanan Riddell, C.B.	8 Aug. 66.	......	......
John Hawkins Gascoigne	23 Aug. 66.	1 Apr. 70.	22 Dec. 75.
Collingwood Dickson, C.B., aft. sir C. ...	24 Aug. 66.	8 Jun. 76.	1 Oct. 77.
Wm. Edwd. Mulcaster	26 Aug. 66.	31 Aug. 74.	,,
John Hamilton Elphinstone Dalrymple ...	28 Aug. 66.	23 Sep. 74.	,,
Orfeur Cavanagh	17 Sep. 66.	7 Sep. 74.	,,
John Stafford Paton	29 Oct. 66.	7 Oct. 74.	,,
Hy. Jos. Pelly...	6 Nov. 66.	10 Oct. 74.	,,
Geo. Colt Langley	10 Nov. 66.	23 Feb 75.	7 May 77.
Jos. Oates Travers, C.B.	,,	......	......
Wm. Robt. Maxwell	,,	......	......
Jas. Macleod Bannatyne Fraser Tytler ...	13 Nov. 66.	10 Oct. 74.	1 Oct. 77.
John Coussmaker Heath	,,	......	......
Robt. Romer Younghusband	6 Dec. 66.	,,	,,
Arth. Geo. Burrows	,,	......	......
Danl. Rainier	6 Jan. 67.	......	......
Frank Turner, C.B.	18 Jan. 67.	4 May 77.	1 Oct. 77.
Hy. Hope Graham, C.B.	20 Jan. 67.	20 Nov. 74.	,,
Jas. Duncan Macpherson	24 Jan. 67.	......	......
Hy. Renney	2 Feb. 67.	5 Dec. 74.	1 Oct. 77.
Geo. Campbell, C.B.	4 Feb. 67.	8 Mar. 75.	
Hayes Marriott	13 Feb. 67.	7 Mar. 77.	1 Oct. 77.
Robt. Nichs. Faunce	26 Feb. 67.	......	......
Sir Hy. Marion Durand, C.B., K.C.S.I. ...	1 Mar. 67.	......	......
Edwd. Lawford	,,	......	......
Chas. Wm. Tremenhere, C.B.	,,	......	......

Name.	M.-Gen.	L.-Gen.	Gen.
Jno. Jarvis Bisset, C.B.	8 Mar. 67.	13 Apr. 75.	1 Oct. 77
Sir Hy. Tombs, K.C.B.	11 Mar. 67.	......	......
Jas. Walker Bayley	13 Mar. 67.	......	......
Hy. Willoughby Trevelyan, C.B.	25 Mar. 67.	......	......
Sir Chas. Reid	5 Apr. 67.	16 Apr. 75.	1 Oct. 77
Geo. Gardiner Alexander, C.B.	9 Apr. 67.	......	......
Geo. Briggs	6 May 67.	......	......
Jas. Brind, C.B., aft. sir J.	1 Jun. 67.	1 Oct. 77.	1 Oct. 77
Jno. Armstrong, C.B.	6 Jul. 67.	......	......
Sir David Edwd. Wood, K.C.B.	,,	26 Nov. 76.	1 Oct. 77
Chas. Vansittart Cockburn	,,	......	......
Alexr. Irving, C.B.	,,	......	......
Thos. Rawlings Mould	,,	......	......
Edmd. Twiss Ford	,,	......	......
Wm. Hamilton Elliot	,,	......	......
Pierrepont Hy. Mundy	,,	......	......
David Wm. Paynter, C.B	,,	......	......
Wm. Bethel Gardner	,,	......	......
Andrew Beatty	,,	......	......
Hy. Paget Christie	,,	......	......
Jas. Benj. Dennis	,,	......	......
Jas. Wm. Gosset	,,	......	......
Græme Alexr. Lockhart, C.B.	13 Jul. 67.	......	......
Robt. Raikes Kinleside	14 Jul. 67.	......	......
Thos. Josephus Deverell	31 Jul. 67.	......	......
Geo. Graydon	19 Aug. 67.	......	......
Chas. Harris Blunt	,,	......	......
Edwd. Alan Holdich, aft. sir E.	3 Sep. 67.	28 Apr. 75.	1 Oct. 7
Sir Fred. Edwd. Chapman, K.C.B.	7 Sep. 67.	12 Apr. 72.	,,
Sir Chas. Wm. Dunbar Stavely, K.C.B.	25 Sep. 67.	29 Apr. 75.	,,
Alf. Huyshe	31 Oct. 67.	1 Oct. 77.	,,
Richd. Geo. Conolly	29 Nov. 67.	......	......
Robt. Newton Philips	8 Dec. 67.	13 May 75.	1 Oct. 7
Geo. Palmer Whish	9 Dec. 67.	29 May 75.	,,
Geo. Malcolm, aft. sir G.	15 Dec. 67.	,,	,,
Jas. Wm. Fitzmayer, aft. sir J.	29 Dec. 67	15 Apr. 77.	,,
Sir Alfr. Hastings Horsford, K.C.B.	1 Jan. 68.	2 Aug. 75.	,,
Walt. D. Phillips Patton, aft. Patton-Bethune	,,	14 Sep. 75.	,,
Wm. Harrison Askwith	,,	20 Apr. 77.	27 Jun. 7
Wm. Edwd. Delves Broughton	,,	19 Jun. 72.	1 Oct. 7
Wm. Elliot Morton	,,	......	......
Albert Geo. Austen	10 Jan. 68.	......	......
Geo. Jackson Carey, C.B.	21 Jan. 68.	......	......
Hon. Percy Egerton Herbert, C.B.. aft. sir P.	28 Jan. 68.	22 Sep. 75.	......
Edwd. Lechmere Russell, aft. sir E.	30 Jan. 68.	23 Aug. 75.	1 Oct. 7
Arthur Borton, C.B., aft. sir A.	31 Jan. 68.	19 Oct. 75.	4 Dec. 7
Franklin Dunlop, C.B.	2 Feb. 68.	23 Apr. 68.	......
David Elliot Mackirdy	21 Feb. 68.	2 Nov. 75.	19 Mar. 7
Hy. Fredk. Dunsford, C.B.	22 Feb. 68.	11 Dec. 75.	1 Oct. 7
Chas. Fras. Skyring	4 Mar. 68.	......	......
Conolly McCausland	,,	......	......
Thos. Kensington Whistler	5 Mar. 68.	1 Oct. 77.	1 Oct. 7
Jno. Studholme Brownrigg	6 Mar. 68.	2 Feb. 76.	20 Mar. 7
Jno. Lintorn Arabin Simmons, aft. sir J.	,,	27 Aug. 72.	1 Oct. 7
Wm. Montague McMurdo	,,	10 Feb. 76.	20 May 7
Wm. Munro, C.B.	,,	,,	25 Jun. 7
Arnold Chas. Errington	,,	,,	10 Aug. 7
Clement Alexr. Edwards, C.B.	,,	17 Mar. 76.	,,
Saml. Tolfrey Christie, C.B.	,,	5 Apr. 76.	......
Chas. Jas. Dalton	,,	1 Oct. 77.	......
Wm. Mark Wood	,,	22 May 76.	16 Sep. 7

Name.	M.-Gen.	L.-Gen.	Gen.
Hy. Smyth, C.B.	6 Mar. 68.	24 Jun. 76.	29 Sep. 78.
Lord Mark Kerr, C.B.	,,	13 Jul. 76.	11 Nov. 78.
Fred. Marow Eardley Wilmot	,,	1 Oct. 77.	......
Hy. Wase Whitfield	,,	19 Jul. 76.	......
Jno. Wilkie	,,	6 Oct. 76	21 Dec. 78.
Hy. Percival de Bathe	,,	8 Oct. 76.	1 Jan. 79.
Richd. Waddy, C.B.	,,	21 Nov. 76	5 Feb. 79.
Jno. Hy. Francklyn, C.B.	,,	1 Oct. 77.	13 Nov. 80.
Thos. Holmes Tidy	,,	......	......
Edmd. Haythorne	,,	23 Dec. 76.	15 Mar. 79.
Thos. A. Brooke	,,	15 Mar. 77.	27 Apr. 79.
Hy. Dalrymple White, C.B.	,,	31 Mar. 77.	27 May 79.
Wm. Sherbrooke Ramsay Norcott, C.B. ...	,,	2 Jun. 77.	11 Jul. 79.
Geo. Wm. Young Simpson	,,	1 Oct. 77.	1 Oct. 77.
Jno. Maitland	,,	,,	......
Danl. Lysons, aft. sir D.	,,	2 Jun. 77.	14 Jul. 79.
Wm. Lygon, E. of Longford, K.C.B. ...	,,	,,	31 Jul. 79.
Pr. Wm. Aug. Edwd. of Saxe Weimar ...	,,	6 Jul. 77.	14 Nov. 79.
Gloucester Gambier, C.B.	,,	......	......
Archd. Little, C.B., aft. sir A.	,,	11 Jul. 77.	21 Jun. 80.
Saml. Netterville Lowder, C.B.	,,	1 Oct. 77.	2 Dec. 77.
Jno. Douglas, C.B., aft. sir J.	,,	23 Aug. 77.	30 Jan. 80.
Hy. Chas. Barnson Daubeney, C.B., aft. sir H.	,,	1 Oct. 77.	4 Mar. 80.
Hon. Richd. Wm. Penn Curzon, C.B., aft. E. Howe...	,,	,,	16 Mar. 80.
Thos. Tapp, C.B.	,,	2 Oct. 74.	......
Hy. Forster, C.B.	,,	......	......
Sir Thos. Westropp McMahon, C.B. ...	,,	1 Oct. 77.	12 Apr. 80.
Alexr. Maxwell, C.B.	,,	,,	19 Apr. 80.
Richd. Thos. Farren, C.B.	,,	,,	29 Apr. 80.
Hy. Sebastian Rowan, C.B.	,,	,,	......
Robt. Wardlaw, C.B.	,,	,,	8 May 80.
Jno. Thornton Grant, C.B.	,,	,,	21 May 80.
Alexr. Low, C.B.	,,	,,	22 May 80.
Percy Hill, C.B.	,,	,,	......
Sir Edwd. Harris Greathed, K.C.B.... ...	,,	,,	1 Jul. 80.
Sir Jno. Jones, K.C.B.	,,	,,	......
Gilbert Jno. Lane Buchanan	,,	......	
Edwd. Wm. Durnford	,,	1 Apr. 74.	1 Oct. 77.
Wm. Neville Custance, C.B.	,,	1 Oct. 77.	7 Sep. 80.
Arth. Cavendish Bentinck	,,	,,	......
Sir Richd. Denis Kelly, K.C.B.	,,	,,	5 Nov. 80.
Jno. Ramsay Stuart, C.B.	,,	,,	3 Dec. 80.
Hon. Robt. Rollo	,,	,,	19 Dec. 80.
Geo. Lambrick	,,	,,	25 Dec. 77.
Geo. Augs. Schomberg, C.B....	,,	......	......
Sir Hy. James...	,,	21 Nov. 74.	......
Geo. Wynne	,,	27 Feb. 76.	1 Oct. 77.
Arth. Broome, C.S.I.	,,	......	......
Evelyn Hy. Fredk. Pocklington ...	,,	1 Oct. 77.	......
Hy. Jas. Warre, C.B.	,,	,,	26 Dec. 80.
Julius Edmd. Goodwyn, C.B.	,,	,,	10 Jan. 81.
Rodolph De Salis, C.B.	,,	,,	......
Alfr. Thos. Hayland	,,	,,	12 Apr. 81.
Geo. Vaughan Maxwell, C.B.	,,	,,	18 Jun. 81.
Edwd. Selby Smyth, aft. sir E.	,,	,,	9 Mar. 81.
Thos. Becket Fielding Marriott	,,	,,	......
Edmd. Richd. Jeffreys, C.B.	,,	,,	1 Jul. 81.
Hon. Fras. Colborne, C.B., aft. sir F. ...	,,	,,	1 Apr. 81.
Hy. Drury Harness, C.B., aft. sir H. ...	,,	7 May 77.	1 Oct. 77.
Hon. St. Geo. Gerald Foley, C.B.	,,	1 Oct. 77.	1 Jul. 81.

Name.	M.-Gen.	L.-Gen.	Gen.
Hy. Rigby	6 Mar. 68.	31 Mar. 75.	15 Aug. 78.
Calledon Richd. Egerton	,,	......	......
Chas. Elmhirst	,,	1 Oct. 77.	25 Oct. 82.
Richd. Strachey	,,	23 Feb. 75.	......
Richd. Chambre Hays Taylor, C.B., aft. sir R.	,,	1 Oct. 77.	1 Apr. 83.
Hon. Arth. Edwd. Hardinge, C.B.	,,	,,	,,
Robt. Newport Tinley	,,	......	......
Edwd. Arth. Somerset	,,	1 Oct. 77.	1 Aug. 83.
Arth. Cyril Goodenough	,,	,,	......
Patr. Leonard McDougall, aft. sir P. ...	,,	,,	1 Oct. 83.
Chas. Erskine Ford	,,	,,	1 Oct. 77.
Thos. Elwyn	,,	......	......
Chas. Alexr. Orr	,,	20 Mar. 76.	......
Chas. Jas. Wright	,,	1 Oct. 77.	13 Feb. 81.
Alexr. Macdonell, aft. sir A....	,,	,,	1 Apr. 82.
Regd. Edwd. Knatchbull	,,	1 Aug. 72.	......
Anthy. Benn	,,	......	......
Julius Aug. Robt. Raines	,,	1 Oct. 77.	1 Jul. 81.
Jno. Alfr. Street, C.B.	,,	,,	23 Oct. 83.
Chas. Herbert, C.B.	,,	,,	......
Jno. Wm. Sidney Smith, C.B.	,,	,,	1 Jul. 81.
Fras. Pym Harding, C.B.	,,	......	......
Edwd. Stopford Claremont; C.B.	,,	1 Oct. 77.	1 Jul. 81.
Geo. Ramsey	,,	,,	1 Oct. 77.
Hy. Prichard	,,	,,	20 Aug. 78.
Crawford Trotter Chamberlain	,,	,,	1 Jan. 80.
Harry Burnett Lumsden, aft. sir H. ...	,,	1 Dec. 73.	,,
Chas. Cameron Shute, C.B.	,,	1 Oct. 77.	1 Jul. 81.
Jas. Wells Armstrong, C.B.	,,	,,	......
Thos. Sydenham Conway, C.B.	,,	,,	1 Jul. 81.
Lord Alfred Paget	,,	,,	,,
Chas. Hind	,,	,,	......
Aug. Fras. Ansell	,,	,,	1 Jul. 81.
Wm. Jas. Smythe	,,	,,	,,
Edwd. Kaye, C.B.	,,	1 Aug. 72.	......
Geo. Sandham...	,,	1 Oct. 77.	13 Nov. 80.
Thos. Hooke Pearson, C.B.	,,	,,	1 Jul. 81.
Lawrence Fyler, C.B.	,,	......	......
Sir Jas. Edwd. Alexander	,,	1 Oct. 77.	1 Jul. 81.
Percival Brown	,,	......	......
Richd. Hy. Jno. Beaumont	,,	......	......
Alexr. Hy. Louis Wyatt	,,	......	......
Chas. Lawrence D'Aguilar, C.B., aft. sir C.	,,	1 Oct. 77.	1 Apr. 84.
Robt. Gorges Hamilton	,,	,,	1 Jul. 81.
Jaspar Byng Creagh	,,	,,	......
Edwd. Angier Godfrey Muller	,,	......	......
Archd. Inglis Lockhart, C.B....	,,	1 Oct. 77.	......
Thos. Edgar Lacy	,,	,,	......
Geo. Wynell Mayow, C.B.	,,	......	......
Edwd. Blagden Hale, C.B.	,,	1 Oct. 77.	......
Jno. Alexr. Ewart, C.B.	,,	,,	13 Jan. 84.
Wm. Chas. Hadden	,,	,,	1 Jul. 81.
Wm. Parke, C.B.	,,	,,	1 Apr. 82.
Chas. L. Barnard, C.B., aft. sir C.	,,	......	5 Oct. 86.
Chas. Fredk. Parkinson	,,	......	......
Edwin Beaumont Johnson, aft. sir E. ...	,,	1 Oct. 77.	1 Oct. 77.
Geo. Bent, C.B.	,,	23 May 73.	......
Eustace Fane Bourchier	,,	1 Jun. 73.	... ..
Hy. Errington Longden, C.B., C.S.I.... ...	,,	1 Oct. 77.	1 Jul. 81.
Hy. Alexr. Carleton, C.B.	,,	,,	10 Jul. 79.
Mountford S. H. Lloyd	,,	......	......

Name.	M.-Gen.	L.-Gen.	Gen.
John Roche	6 Mar. 68.	1 Oct. 77.	1 Jul. 81.
Hy. Roxby Benson, C.B.	,,	,,	,,
Wm. M'Pherson	,,	......	......
Wm. Robt. Haliday	,,	1 Oct. 77.	......
Jas. Talbot Airey, C.B., aft. sir J. ...	,,	,,	1 Jul. 81.
Wilmot Hy. Bradford	,,	,,	,,
Chas. Lennox Brownlow Maitland	,,	,,	1 Dec. 84.
Wm. Twisleton Layard	,,	,,	1 Jul. 81.
Jos. Hy. Laye	,,	,,	,,
Wm. Chas. Forrest	,,	,,	,,
Arth. Thos. Phillpotts	,,	,,	23 May 81.
Hy. Jas. Stannus, C.B.	,,	,,	25 Jun. 79.
Geo. Prince Sealy	,,	,,	8 Dec. 79.
Hon. Jas. Wm. Bosville Macdonald, C.B. ...	,,	,,	1 Jul. 81.
Robt. Julian Baumgartner, C.B.	,,	,,	,,
Geo. Calvert Clarke, C.B.	,,	,,	,,
Chas. F. Fordyce, C.B.	,,	,,	,,
Fredk. Amelius Whimper, C.B.	,,	,,	......
Robt. Wm. Disney Leith, C.B.	,,	,,	1 Jul. 81.
Wm. Richd. Preston	,,	,,	,,
Edwd. Stanton, C.B	,,	,,	,,
Thos. Conyngham Kelly, C.B.	,,	,,	,,
Hy. Fredk. Ponsonby	,,	,,	,,
Edmd. Ogle	,,	,,	,,
Oliver Paget Bourke	,,	,,	......
Geo. Erskine	,,	,,	1 Jul. 81.
Edwd. Geo. Wynyard	,,	,,	,,
Thos. Pattle, C.B.	,,	,,	......
Wm. Lenox Ingall, C.B.	,,	,,	1 Jul. 81.
Chas. Pyndar Beauchamp Walker, C.B. ...	,,	,,	7 Oct. 84.
Wm. Clarke	,,	,,	1 Jul. 81.
Arth. Jas. Herbert, C.B., aft. sir A. ...	,,	,,	19 Mar. 85.
Jas., ld. Seaton	,,	,,	1 Jul. 81.
Nathan Smith Gardiner	,,	......	......
Saml. Wells, C.B.	,,	4 Dec. 77.	1 Jul. 81.
Hy. Geo. Hart	,,	,,	......
Robt. Pratt, C.B.	,,	12 Dec. 77.	......
Hon. Leicester Smyth, C.B., aft. sir L. ...	,,	13 Feb. 78.	18 Jul. 85.
Jno. Williams Reynolds	,,	......	......
Fredk. Chas. Arth. Stephenson, aft. sir. F.	,,	23 Feb. 78.	12 Jan. 86.
Edmd. Aug. Whitmore, C.B., aft. sir E. ...	,,	18 Mar. 78.	19 Mar. 86.
Ld. Alexr. Geo. Russell	,,	20 Mar. 78.	7 Apr. 86.
Jno. Cameron, C.B.	,,	1 Oct. 77.	......
Jno. Summerfield Hawkins	,,	,,	1 Jul. 81.
Jno. Reid Becher, C.B.	,,	7 Oct. 76.	29 Nov. 78.
Harry Wainwright Bax Bell...	,,	30 Mar. 76.	......
Alexr. Taylor, C.B., aft. sir A.	,,	1 Oct. 77.	31 Dec. 78.
Sir Garnet Jos. Wolseley, K.C.M.G., C.B.; aft. visc. Wolseley	,,	25 Mar. 78.	18 Nov. 82.
Robt. Maclagan	,,	1 Oct. 77.	31 Dec. 78.
Chas. Jas. Conway Mills	,,	25 Jun. 78.	1 Jul. 81.
Jno. Josiah Hort, C.B., aft. bt.	,,	10 Aug. 78.	,,
Sir Arnold Burrowes Kemball, K.C.S.I., C.B.	,,	1 Oct. 77.	26 Feb. 80.
Jno. Simpson, C.B.	,,	29 Aug. 78.	......
Hy. Garner Rainey	,,	9 Sep. 78.	1 Jul. 81.
Jno. Amber Cole	,,	16 Sep. 78.	,,
Richd. Waltr. Lacy	,,	29 Sep. 78.	,,
Fredk. Fras. Maude, C.B., V.C., aft. sir F.	,,	1 Oct. 78.	5 Nov. 85.
Edwd. Herbert Maxwell, C.B.	,,	11 Nov. 78.	1 Jul. 81
Jno. McNeill Walter	,,	21 Dec. 78.	,,
Jos. Edwin Thackwell, C.B.	,,	22 Dec. 78.	,,

Name.	M.-Gen.	L.-Gen.	Gen.
David Reid	6 Mar. 68	......	......
Jno. Douglas Campbell, C.B.	,,	1 Jul. 77	
Jos. Edwd. Addison	,,	1 Jan. 79	1 Jul. 81.
Edmd. Roche	,,	5 Feb. 79.	,,
Wm. Inglis	,,	15 Mar. 79.	,,
Lawrence Shadwell	,,	27 Apr. 79.	,,
Chas. Jno. Foster	,,	27 May 79.	13 Mar. 85.
Geo. Fredk. Stephenson Call, C.B.	,,	14 Jul. 79.	1 Jul. 81.
Jas. Croft Brooke, C.B.	,,	......	......
Robt. Bruce	,,	31 Jul. 79.	1 Jul. 81.
Regd. Younge Shipley, C.B.	,,	11 Aug. 79.	30 Sep. 82.
Horace Wm. Montagu, C.B.	,,	1 Oct. 77.	1 Jul. 81.
Jno. Elias. Collings, C.B.	,,	18 Sep. 79.	,,
Ralph Budd	,,	14 Nov. 79.	,,
Hy. Bingham	,,	......	......
Hy. Hamilton, C.B.	,,	30 Nov. 79.	1 Oct. 81.
Thos. Addison, C.B.	,,	30 Jan. 80.	1 Jul. 81.
Wm. Stratton Aslett	,,	......	......
Michl. Kavanagh Kennedy, aft. sir M.	,,	21 Dec. 77.	10 May 81.
Colin Campbell McIntyre, C.B.	,,	4 Mar. 80.	1 Oct. 81.
Jas. Maurice Primrose, C.S.I.	,,	,,	1 Apr. 82.
Fredk. Robt. Elrington, C.B.	,,	14 Mar. 80.	1 Jul. 81.
Geo. Warren Walker	,,	15 Aug. 78.	28 Nov. 85.
Chas. Lavallin Nugent	,,	16 Mar. 80.	1 Jul. 81.
Jno. Hy. Lefroy, C.B., aft. sir J.	,,	1 Oct. 77.	10 May 82.
Percy Archer Butler, C.B.	,,	12 Apr. 80.	1 Jul. 81.
Robt. Onesiphorus Bright, C.B., aft. sir R.	,,	13 Apr. 80.	1 Oct. 87.
Edwd. Wm. Derrington Bell, C.B., V.C.	,,	......	......
Wm. Sankey	,,	19 Apr. 80.	1 Jul. 81.
Edmd. Wodehouse	,,	25 Apr. 80.	,,
Fowler Burton, C.B.	,,	,,	,,
Christr. Birdwood	,,	18 Feb. 76.	1 Oct. 77.
Hy. Wm. Matthews	,,	19 Dec. 76.	22 Dec. 77.
Jno. Drummond Stewart	,,	......	......
Chas. Prior	,,	8 Feb. 77.	20 Aug. 78.
Geo. De Saumarez	6 Apr. 68.	23 Mar. 77.	20 Aug. 78.
Fred. Wm. Burroughs	20 Apr. 68.	24 May 77.	18 Jul. 79.
Wm. Knox Babington	22 Apr. 68.	1 Jan. 77.	......
Alfred de Lisle	12 May 68.	......	......
Wm. Gordon, C.B.	28 Jun. 68.	29 Apr. 80.	1 Jul. 81
Stephen Chas. Briggs	,,	......	......
Geo. Harry Smith Willis, C.B., aft. sir G.	,,	8 May 80.	11 May 87
Jno. Hope Wingfield	,,	19 May 80.	1 Jul. 81
Ld. Augs. Chas. Lennox Fitzroy, C.B.	,,	21 May 80.	,,
Jas. Daubeney, C.B.	,,	22 May 80.	,,
Robt. Warden, C.B.	,,	7 Jun. 80.	,,
Chas. Hy. Morris, C.B.	,,	1 Jul. 80.	,,
Chas. Wm. Thompson	,,	5 Oct. 80.	,,
Michl. Bruce	,,	31 Oct. 80.	,,
Julius Richd. Glyn, C.B., aft. sir J.	,,	5 Nov. 80.	1 Oct. 86
Wm. Olpherts, C.B., V.C.	,,	1 Oct. 77.	31 Mar. 83
Arth. Scudamore, C.B.	,,	......	......
Sir Jno. Miller Adye, K.C.B.	,,	27 Jun. 79.	20 Nov. 84
Steph. Chas. Briggs	,,	1 Oct. 77.	15 Dec. 80
Edwd. Price, C.B.	,,	27 May 80.	1 Jul. 81
Robt. Walter Macleod Fraser	,,	3 Dec. 80.	,,
Jas. Conolly, C.B.	,,	26 Dec. 80.	19 Feb. 85
Geo. Wm. Powlett Bingham, C.B.	,,	19 Dec. 80.	1 Jul. 81
Wm. Hope, C.B.	,,	10 Jan. 81.	,,
Chas. Fanshawe	,,	1 Jul. 78.	,,
Jno. Archd. Ballard, C.B.	,,	......	......

Name.	M.-Gen.	L.-Gen.	Gen.
Hy. Hamilton Maxwell, C.B....	16 Aug. 68.	1 Oct. 77.	31 Mar. 83.
Wm. Fredk. Curtis	,,	8 May 81.	......
Jno. Archd. Ballard	,,	29 Nov. 78.	31 Dec. 78.
Wm. Arden Crommelin, C.B....	,,	31 Dec. 78.	......
Lionel Stephen Hough	,,	......	......
Peter Maclean	22 Aug. 68.	......	......
Allan Hamilton Graham	,,	......	......
Richd. Hy. Crofton	,,	......	......
Thos. Knox	,,	......	......
Hon. Geo. Talbot Devereux	30 Sep. 68.	......	......
Hugh Archd. Beauchamp Campbell, C.B. ...	,,	......	......
Robt. Talbot	,,	......	......
Hy. Wm. Blake	19 Oct. 68.	1 Oct. 77.	18 Jul. 79.
Thos. Edmd. Knox	28 Oct. 68.	8 May 81.	1 Jul. 81.
Wm. Jas. Loftus, C.B.	,,	18 May 81.	,,
Jas. Wm. Domville	,,	......	......
Edwd. Westby Donovan	,,	18 Jun. 81.	1 Apr. 87.
Hy. Poole Hepburn, C.B.	,,	1 Jul. 81.	1 Jul. 81.
Richd. Mordesley Best	,,	,,	......
Richd. Knox	,,	..	......
Richd. King Clavell	,,	......	......
Wm. David Aitken	,,	1 Oct. 77.	31 Mar. 83.
Wm. Jno. Chamberlayne	,,	13 Jul. 81.	15 Jan. 82.
Jas. Edmd. Tannatt Nicolls	,,	31 Dec. 78.	......
David Anderson	,,	15 Jan. 82.	17 Jul. 88.
Fredk. Green Wilkinson	,,	9 Dec. 81.	......
Wm. Pollexfen Radcliffe, C.B.	,,	9 Mar. 82.	1 Apr. 87.
Reynell Geo. Taylor	,,	1 Oct. 77.	15 Dec. 80.
Thos. Hy. Pakenham...	,,	1 Apr. 82.	......
Fred. Alexr. Campbell, aft. sir F.	,,	8 Nov. 80.	5 Jul. 86.
Wm. Payn, C.B., aft. sir W.	,,	1 Apr. 82.	12 Aug. 88.
Thos. Ross	,,	14 Nov. 81.	......
Sir Wm. Thos. Dennison, K.C.B.	7 Nov. 68.	23 Nov. 70.	......
Fitzwilliam Walker	,,	......	......
Hy. Edwin Weare, C.B.	9 Nov. 68.	12 Aug. 81	......
Hy. Meade Hamilton, C.B.	,,	1 Jul. 81.	......
Chas. Bondler Fuller...	,,	,,	31 Mar. 83.
Hy. Philip Goodenough	,,	......	......
John Turner, C.B.	,,	13 Nov. 80.	......
Geo. Sandham	10 Nov. 68.	1 Oct. 77.	......
Chas. Duesbury Robertson	,,	......	......
Hon. Fredk. Aug. Thesiger, C.B., aft. ld. Chelmsford	,,	1 Apr. 82.	16 Feb. 88.
Michl. Galway, C.B., aft. sir M.	,,	1 Oct. 77.	......
Hon. Chas. Dawson Plunkett	18 Nov. 68.	......	......
Broadley Harrison	,,	23 Mar. 82.	......
Edw. Wm. De Lancey Lowe, C.B.	,,	......	......
Albert Fytche, C.S.I.	,,	1 Oct. 77.	......
Walter Birch	28 Nov. 68.	......	......
Geo. Malcolm	15 Dec. 68.	......	......
Hon. Aug. Geo. Chas. Chichester	24 Dec. 68.	2 Jun. 82.	......
Wm. Albert Stratton...	,,	14 Apr. 82.	......
Wm. Hy. Seymour, C.B.	,,	30 Sep. 82.	1 Jan. 84.
Sir Wm. Russell, bt., C.B.	,,	......	......
Spencer Westmacott	,,	1 Jul. 81.	13 Aug. 81.
Penrose Chas. Penrose, C.B....	,,	2 Sep. 78.	4 Jun. 79.
Danl. Geo. Robinson	,,	......	......
Donald Martin Stewart, C.B....	,,	1 Oct. 77.	......
John Harley Maxwell	31 Dec. 68.	......	......
Wm. Fras. Foote	27 Feb. 69.	......	......
Sir Edwd. Robt. Wetherall, C.B., K.C.S.I. ...	8 Mar. 69.	......	......

Name.	M.-Gen.	L.-Gen.	Gen.
Jyrmyn Chas. Symonds	17 Mar. 69.	......	......
Matth. Chas. Dixon	19 Mar. 69.	......	......
Sir Fredk. Wellington Jno. FitzWygram, bt.	23 Mar. 69.	1 Apr. 83.	......
Jno. Christr. Guise, C.B., V.C.	,,	1 Jul. 81.	......
Jno. Wm. Cox, C.B.	,,	21 Sep. 82.	......
Fras. Hornblow Rundall	,,	31 Dec. 78.	28 Nov. 85.
Hy. Wylie Norman, aft. Sir H.	,,	1 Oct. 77.	......
Hy. Lynedoch Gardiner	30 Mar. 69.	26 Nov. 80.	1 Oct. 82.
Michl. Anthy. Shrapnel Biddulph, C.B., aft. sir M.	,,	13 Feb. 81.	1 Nov. 86.
Alfr. Augs. Chapman	,,	1 Jul. 81.	......
Geo. Wade Guy Green, aft. sir G.	,,	1 Oct. 77.	11 Jun. 79.
Chas. Hy. Gordon, C.B.	1 Apr. 69.	......	......
Sir Harry St. George Ord, C.B.	16 Apr. 69.	......	......
Robt. Fredk. Mountain	5 May 69.	......	......
Richd. Hamilton, C.B.	8 May 69.	1 Oct. 77.	......
Hy. White Hitchins	12 May 69.	......	......
Geo. Wm. Alexr. Higginson, C.B.	17 May 69.	1 Apr. 83.	......
Thos. Geo. Alexr. Oakes, C.B.	,,	......	......
Robt. Hume, C.B.	,,	1 Aug. 83.	......
Chas. Wm. Green	,,	1 Jul. 81.	......
Andr. Browne, C.B.	,,	,,	......
Jno. Gwilt, C.B.	,,	......	......
Fras. Peyton	,,	1 Oct. 83.	30 Sep. 85.
Barth. O'Brien, C.B.	,,	1 Jul. 81.	......
Robt. Parker Radcliffe	,,	1 Sep. 83.	......
Chas. Wright Younghusband	,,	......	......
Edwd. Bruce Hamley, C.B., aft. sir E. ...	,,	10 May 82.	......
Saml. Enderby Gordon, C.B....	,,	25 May 82.	1 Nov. 82.
Hon. Edwd. Thos. Gage, C.B.	,,	1 Nov. 82.	......
Chas. Stuart Henry, C.B.	,,	1 Oct. 82.	......
Cadwallader Adams, C.B.	,,	23 Oct. 83.	......
Geo. Whitworth Talbot Rich, C.B.... ...	,,	1 Jul. 81.	......
Alexr. Robt. Manson...	,,	1 Oct. 79.	23 Aug. 84.
Jas. Mitchell MacDonald	6 Jun. 69.	......	......
Jno. Fraser	23 Jun. 69.	......	......
Jno. Wellesley Thomas, C.B.	18 Jul. 69.	1 Jul. 81.	......
Wm. Thos. Dickson	,,	,,	......
Wm. Wilby, C.B.	,,	1 Apr. 82.	......
Alfr. Thos. Wilde, aft. sir A.	,,	1 Oct. 77.	......
Hy. Harpur Greer, C.B.	22 Jul. 69.	1 Jul. 81.	......
Hy. Bird	,,	,,	......
Robt. Carey, C.B....	,,	......	......
Robt. Wm. Lowry, C.B.	,,	1 Oct. 82.	......
Hy. Jas. Barr	,,	1 Oct. 77.	......
Thos. Lightfoot, C.B.	1 Aug. 69.	27 Dec. 82.	......
Hon. Hy. Hugh Clifford, C.B.	,,	......	......
Hy. D'Oyley Torrens, C.B.	,,	13 Jan. 84.	......
Wm. Forbes Macbean	,,	1 Oct. 82.	......
Wm. Templer Hughes	3 Aug. 69.	1 Oct. 77.	......
Chas. Wilson Moore	15 Aug. 69.	......	......
Doveton Hodson, C.B....	19 Aug. 69.	......	......
Wm. Augs. Tyers, C.B.	23 Aug. 69.	1 Jul. 81.	......
Jno. Forbes, C.B., aft. sir J.	,,	1 Oct. 77.	3 Feb. 86.
Roger Stewart Beatson	20 Oct. 69.	......	......
Agmondisham Jno. A. Vesey Kirkland ...	24 Nov. 69.	......	......
Edwd. Mourrice Boxer	20 Dec. 69.	......	......
Chas. Scudamore Longden	,,	......	......
Edwd. Jno. Lake, C.S.I.	1 Jan. 70.	......	......
Wm. Drysdale, C.B.	2 Jan. 70.	1 Jul. 81.	......
Jas. Chas. Innes	,,	1 Oct. 77.	....

Name.	M.-Gen.	L.-Gen.	Gen.
Hy. Hope Crealock, C.B.	2 Jan. 70	4 Sep. 84.	......
Hy. Dominick Daly aft. sir H.	4 Jan. 70.	1 Oct. 77.	1 Dec. 88.
Chas. Sawyer	11 Jan. 70.	1 Jul. 81.	......
Jno. Neptune Sargent, C.B.	,,	7 Oct. 84.	......
Richd. Geo. Amherst Luard	,,	1 Dec. 84.	......
Hy. Milne	,,	1 Oct. 77.	......
Edwd. Seager, C.B.	15 Jan. 70.	1 Jul. 81.	......
Dudley Chas., ld. de Ros	,,	,,	......
Hy. Ralph Browne	,,	1 Jan. 85.	8 Jul. 85.
Jno. Luther Vaughan, aft. sir J.	,,	1 Oct. 77.	1 Dec. 88.
Chas. Hy. Hutchinson...	5 Feb. 70.	......	......
Thos. Robt. Crawley	6 Feb. 70.	......	......
Arnold Thompson	,,	......	......
Wm. Humphreys Kirby	,,	1 Jul. 81.	......
Geo. Jno. Peacocke	,,	1 Oct. 82.	......
Jas. Robt. Steadman Sayer, C.B.	,,	13 Mar. 85.	......
Wm. Collier Menzies	,,	1 Jul. 81.	19 Oct. 81.
Saml. Jas. Browne, aft. sir S.	,,	1 Oct. 77.	1 Dec. 88.
Sir Robt. Michael Laffan, K.C.M.G.... ...	8 Feb. 70.	1 Jul. 81.	......
Alexr. Cunningham Robertson, C.B.... ...	,,	,,	......
Geo. Saml. Montgomery, C.S.I.	,,	1 Oct. 77.	3 Feb. 86
Jas. Frankfort Manners Browne, C.B. ..	22 Feb. 70.	13 Aug. 81.	12 Feb. 88
Alaster McIan McDonald	,,	19 Mar. 85.	......
Chas. Cureton	,,	1 Oct. 77.	1 Dec. 88.
Robt. White, C.B.	1 Mar. 70.	8 Jul. 85.	......
Jno. Blick Spurgin, C.B., C.S.I.	,,	......	......
Augs. Wm. Murray, C.B.	,,	18 Jan. 82.	......
Dominick Jacotin Gamble, C.B.	,,	18 Jul. 85.	......
Geo. Bryan Milman, C.B.	,,	30 Dec. 84.	......
Edwd. Hy. Fisher	,,	......	......
Eyre Challoner Hy., ld. Clarina	,,	5 Nov. 85.	......
Jno. Ross, C.B., aft. sir J.	,,	12 Jan. 86.	......
Wm. Freeland Brett	,,	1 Jul. 81.	......
Robt. Beaufoy Hawley	,,	18 Apr. 83.	......
Fredk. Arth. Willis, C.B.	,,	19 Mar. 86.	......
Wm. Philip Hampton...	,,	1 Oct. 77.	......
Fras. Carey	,,	1 Jul. 81.	......
Chas. Edwd. Parke Gordon, C.B.	,,	,,	......
Jas. Robt. Gibbon, C.B.	18 Mar. 70.	......	......
Wm. Fredk. Marriott	,,	1 Oct. 77.	......
Robt. Stuart Baynes	26 Mar. 70.	1 Jul. 81.	......
Chas. Douglas...	,,	1 Oct. 77.	1 Jul. 81.
Hy. Edwd. Landor Thuillier, C.S.I., aft. sir H.	,,	10 Jul. 79.	,,
Hy. Radford Norman, C.B.	,,	1 Jul. 81.	......
Granville Geo. Chetwynd Stapylton ...	,,	,,	......
Geo. Courtenay Vialls, C.B.	,,	......	......
Lousada Barrow	,,	1 Oct. 77.	......
Jno. Hy. Lefroy	1 Apr. 70.	......	......
Wm. Kinnaird Worcester	30 Apr. 70.	......	......
Jas. Hy. Craig Robertson	16 May 70.	1 Jul. 81.	......
Chas. Arth. Barwell	,,	1 Oct. 77.	......
Hon. Percy Robt. Basil Feilding, C.B. ...	26 May 70.	7 Apr. 86.	......
Wm. Thos. Laird Patterson	,,	1 Jul. 81.	......
Herbert Edw. Stacy Abbott...	13 Jun. 70.	1 Oct. 77.	......
Sir Chas. Wm. Dunbar Staveley, K.C.B. ...	20 Jun. 70.	......	......
Hy. Blankley Harrington Rogers	1 Jul. 70.	......	......
Jno. Harvey Elwyn	4 Jul. 70.	......	......
Dighton Macnaghten Probyn, C.B., V.C., aft. sir D....	25 Jul. 70.	1 Oct. 77.	1 Dec. 88.
Robt. Jno. Eagar, C.B.	,,	1 Jul. 81.	......
Jno. Guize Rogers Aplin	,,	,,	......

Name.	M.-Gen.	L.-Gen.	Gen.
Chas. Hood	25 Jul. 70.	1 Jul. 81.	......
Chas. Crauford Fraser, V.C., C.B.	,,	1 Oct. 86.	......
Hon. Somerset Jno. [Gough] Calthorpe ...	,,	1 Jul. 81.	......
Jas. Pickard	1 Aug. 70.	......	......
Robt. Hughes	12 Aug. 70.	......	......
Chas. Edwd. Dawton Hill	15 Oct. 70.	......	......
Chas. Scott	17 Oct. 70.	......	......
Jno. Arthur Gildea	24 Dec. 70.	......	......
Jas. Geo. Balmain	31 Dec. 70.	......	......
Robt. Patton	1 Jan. 71.	......	......
Jno. Richd. Anderson, C.B.	15 Mar. 71.	......	......
Brooke Boyd	18 Apr. 71.	1 Oct. 77.	1 Dec. 88.
Fras. Elliot Voyle	11 May 71.	......	......
Jno. Liptrott	20 May 71.	1 Oct. 77.	1 Dec. 88.
Andr. Hunter	10 Jun. 71.	......	......
Edwd. Jno. Rickards...	,,	......	......
Thos. Elwyn	21 Jun. 71.	20 Jul. 81.	......
Colin Mackenzie, C.B....	4 Jul. 71.	1 Oct. 77.	......
Paul Bernard Whittingham	12 Jul. 71.	......	......
Wm. Hamilton Cox	20 Jul. 71.	......	......
Sir Arthur Purves Phayre, K.C.S.I., C.B. ...	9 Aug. 71	1 Oct. 77.	......
Fredk. Octavius Salusbury	19 Aug. 71.	......	......
Hy. Young Darracott Scott, C.B.	,,	......	......
Wm. Rice Dickinson	1 Sep. 71.	......	......
Fredk. Maitland	3 Sep. 71.	......	......
Hy. Arth. White	13 Sep. 71.	......	......
Hy. Nott	17 Sep. 71.	1 Oct. 77.	......
Fras. Hutchinson Synge	20 Sep. 71.	......	......
Edwd. Arth. Green	,,	......	......
Jno. Talbot Shakespear	26 Sep. 71.	20 Oct. 77.	......
Mortimer R. S. Whitmore	1 Oct. 71.	......	......
Edw. Adams	16 Oct. 71.	......	......
Wm. Hy. Delamain	31 Sep. 71.	......	......
Lewis Grant	18 Nov. 71.	......	......
Jas. Holt Freeth	14 Dec. 71.	......	......
Jno. Barrett	,,	2 May 78.	......
Wm. Manley Hall Dixon, C.B.	23 Dec. 71.	......	......
Evan Maberly, C.B.	17 Jan. 72.	......	......
Wm. Geo. Hamley	27 Jan. 72.	......	......
Hy. Craigie Brewster	3 Feb. 72.	......	......
Wm. Hindley Crighton, C.B....	17 Feb. 72.	......	......
Edwd. Patr. Lynch	19 Feb. 72.	20 Aug. 78.	......
Hy. Clerk	24 Apr. 72.	......	......
Richd. Lloyd Thompson	,,	......	......
Jno. Jas. Jenkins	,,	......	......
Jas. Campbell	1 May 72.	......	......
Robt. Jno. Hawthorne	,,	18 Jul. 79	1 Dec. 88.
Edwd. Moubray	15 May 72.	......	......
Wm. Stewart Furneaux	8 Jun. 72.	......	... ...
Hy. Philip Tyacke	19 Jun. 72.	......	......
Sampson Freeth	26 Jun. 72.	......	......
Chas. Vyvyan Cox, C.B.	1 Aug. 72.	......	......
John Hall Smyth, C.B.	,,	......	......
Sir Geo. Bourchier, K.C.B.	,,	......	......
Jos. Lyon Barrow, C.B.	,,	......	......
Hy. Hammond...	,,	......	......
Ernle Kyrle Money	,,	......	......
Gerard Potter Eton	,,	......	......
Wm. Maxwell	,,	......	......
Thos. Brougham	,,	......	......

Name.	M.-Gen.	L.-Gen.	Gen.
Thos. Hay Campbell	1 Aug. 72.	......	......
John Eliot	,,	......	......
Hy. Lewis	,,	......	......
Geo Eliot Voyle	,,	......	......
Alfr. Wintle	,,	......	......
Fredk. Geo. Nuthall	,,	......	......
Anthy. Maxtone Murray	,,	......	......
Chas. Saml. Woodcock	,,	......	......
Wm. Bainbrigge Marshall	,,	......	......
Hickman Thos. Molesworth	,,	......	......
Walker King Fooks	,,	......	......
Robt. Geo. Hunter Grant	,,	......	......
Chas. Vincent Bowie	,,	......	......
Hy. Regd. Courtenay	,,	......	......
Fredk. Conybeare	,,	......	......
Donald McNeill	,,	......	......
Hy. Erskine Hicks	,,	......	......
Edwd. Atlay, C.B.	,,	......	......
Robt. Alexr. Morse	,,	......	......
David Greenhill Anderson	,,	......	......
Jos. Skekleton...	,,	......	......
Chas. Jas. Barton	,,	......	......
Colin Cookworthy	,,	......	......
Geo. Maister	,,	......	......
Geo. Brown Melhuish	,,	......	......
John Ramsay Sladen	,,	......	......
Hy. Friend Kennedy	21 Aug. 72.	......	......
Fras. Percy Nott	1 Oct. 72.	......	......
David Watson	5 Oct. 72.	......	......
John Cowell Bartley	,,	......	......
Steph. Fras. Macmullen	31 Dec. 72.	18 Jul. 79.	1 Dec. 88.
Sir Thos. Peyton, bt....	15 Jan. 73.	......	......
Gibbes Rigaud...	1 Feb. 73.	......	......
Burdett Richd. Powell	5 Feb. 73.	13 Aug. 79.	......
Thos. Hy. Clifton	12 Feb. 73.	......	......
Millington Hy. Synge	8 Mar. 73.	......	......
Hy. Reynolds Werge	26 Mar. 73.	......	......
Geo. Sturrock	13 Apr. 73.	......	......
Evelyn Bradford	23 Apr. 73.	......	......
John Wedderburn	,,	......	......
Wm. Murray	,,	......	......
Miller Clifford	21 Jun. 73.	......	......
John Hamilton Cox, C.B.	5 Jul. 73.	......	......
Thos. Bernard Collinson	2 Aug. 73.	......	......
Chas. Triganee Franklin, C.B.	9 Aug. 73.	......	......
Fras. Gilbert Hamley...	,,	......	......
Chas. Louis	18 Sep. 73.	......	......
Wm. Driscoll Gosset	24 Sep. 73.	......	......
Andr. Pellett Scrimshire Green	8 Oct. 73.	......	......
Jas. Robt. Mann	18 Oct. 73.	......	......
Fredk. Macgowan	12 Nov. 73.	......	......
Thos. de Courcy Hamilton, V.C.	21 Jan. 74.	......	......
Robt. Barlow M'Crea	4 Feb. 74.	......	......
Augs. Fredk. Fras. Lennox	11 Mar. 74.	......	......
Fredk. Llewellyn Alexander ...	8 Apr. 74.	......	......
Jas. Edwd. Westropp...	,,	......	......
Albt. Hy. Andr. Hervey	10 Apr. 74.	......	......
Paget Bayly	13 May 74.	......	......
Arth. Comyn Pigou	17 Jun. 74.	......	......
Gother Fredk. Mann, C.B.	13 Aug. 74.	......	......
Stapylton Robinson	31 Oct. 74.	......	......

Name.	M.-Gen.	L.-Gen.	Gen.
Hy. Chas. Adlam	25 Nov. 74.	......	......
Wm. Russell Eliott	,,	......	......
Jno. Wm. Bristow	,,	......	......
Robt. Unwin	,,	......	......
Chas. Fredc. Smith	,,	......	......
Jno. Elphinstone Fraser	,,	......	......
Henley Thos. Bartlett	,,	......	......
Wm. Skene Row	,,	......	......
Hy. Boileau Adolph. Poulton	,,	......	......
Chas. Stephen Fowle	,,	......	......
Alexr. Mackay Mackenzie	,,	......	......
Geo. Delane	,,	......	......
Hy. Jno. Templar	,,	......	......
Chas. Wm. Miles	,,	......	......
Hy. Duncan Twysden	,,	......	......
Arth. Loftus Steele	,,	......	......
Chas. Jno. Bradley	,,	......	......
Fras. Mitchell Haultain	,,	......	......
Wm. Dacres Stanley	,,	......	......
Lumley Hodgson Huskisson Holland ...	,,	......	......
Jas. Orr	,,	......	......
Chas. Thos. Harkness	,,	......	......
Wm. Sidney Smith Mulcaster	,,	......	......
Arth. Sage	,,	......	......
Jno. Hy. Lyte Kerr	,,	......	......
Horatio Edwd. Walpole	,,	......	......
Chas. Osbaldiston Lukin	,,	......	......
Geo. Paxton	,,	......	......
Chas. Pulley	,,	......	......
Alexr. Cannan	,,	......	......
Saml. Thacker	,,	......	......
Ross Balfour Moore	,,	......	......
Hy. Burdon Hodgson	,,	......	......
Jno. Hy. Reynolds	,,	......	......
Jas. Black	,,	......	......
Wm. Abercrombie Dick	,,	......	......
Walter Montrion	,,	......	......
Jas. Fras. Eaton Travers	13 Jan. 75.	......	......
Edwin Alexr. Rowlatt	23 Jan. 75.	......	......
Hy. Mein Wilson	,,	......	......
Chas. Basil Gibbons Bacon	,,	......	......
Davd. Briggs	,,	......	......
Jno. Anstruther Angus	,,	......	......
Sir Chas. Walters D'Oyly, bt.	,,	......	......
Wm. Hy. Stubbs	,,	......	......
Wm. Elwyn	,,	......	......
Chas. Andrews	,,	......	......
Chas. Fredk. Browne	,,	......	......
Hy. Provost Babbage	,,	......	......
Chas. Holroyd	,,	......	......
Geo. Edwd. Holmes	,,	......	......
Jas. Dawson MacDonald	,,	......	......
Roderick Donald Macpherson	,,	......	......
Holled Wallace Hy. Coxe	,,	......	......
Jno. Seymour Dunbar	,,	......	......
Jno. Innes Gibbs	,,	......	......
Jas. Young Gowan	,,	......	......
Chas. Irvine	,,	......	......
Chas. Murray	,,	......	......
Neil Edmonstone Boileau	,,	......	......
Hugh Lowman Pester	,,	......	......

Name.	M.-Gen.	L.-Gen.	Gen.
Fredk. Nepean Smith...	23 Jan. 75.	......	......
Jno. Geo. Palmer	,,	......	......
Wm. Powell Stuart Smyth	,,	......	......
Wm. Herbert Cuming	,,	......	......
Wm. Graves	,,	......	......
Thos. Clerk	,,	......	......
Dillon Gustavus Pollard	,,	......	......
Alexr. Robt. Fraser	,,	......	......
Jno. Daniel	,,	......	......
Hy. Hoseason	,,	......	......
Sir Fredk. Jno. Goldsmid, C.B., K.C.S.I. ...	,,	......	......
Chas. Wm. Taylor	,,	......	......
Edwd. Augs. Saunders	,,	......	......
Hy. Rhodes Morgan	,,	......	......
Wm. Napper Pace	,,	......	......
Chas. Richd. Baugh	,,	......	......
Wm. Saml. Jones	,,	......	......
Jno. Daniel Williams	,,	......	......
Wm. Ashburner	,,	......	......
Wm. Edmonstone Macleod	,,	......	......
Jas. Jno. Combe	,,	......	......
Wm. Pirie	,,	......	......
Sir Wm. Hy. Rodes Green, C.B., K.C.S.I. ...	,,	......	......
Geo. McBain Barnes Farquharson	,,	......	......
Jno. Guillam Scott	,,	......	......
Edwd. Hope Smith Bowdich...	,,	......	......
Fras. Edwd. Francis	,,	......	......
Jno. Wm. Playfair	3 Feb. 75.	......	......
Edwd. Andrée Wyld	8 Feb. 75.	......	......
Webber D. Harris	25 Feb. 75.	......	......
Geo. Bucknall Shakspear	10 Mar. 75.	......	......
Guy Rotton	,,	......	......
Valentine Thos. Mairis	1 Apr. 75.	......	......
Chas. Jas. Hodgson	3 May 75.	......	......
Geo. Remington Cookson	5 Jun. 75.	......	......
Chas. Need	,,	......	......
Wm. Robt. Cunningham	,,	......	......
Regd. Ouseley	,,	......	......
Richd. Wellesley Chambers	,,	......	......
Geo. Fullerton Carnegie	,,	......	......
Wm. Briggs	,,	......	......
Jermy Chas. West	,,	......	......
Hy. Imlach Bett	,,	......	......
Robt. Maxwell Johnstone	,,	......	......
Hugh Geo. Robison	,,	......	......
Wm. Gray	,,	......	......
Wm. Croughton Stileman	,,	......	......
Albert Balcombe Beatson	23 Jun. 75.	......	......
Geo. Faithfull	,,	......	......
Alexr. Steuart Allen	,,	......	......
Barnett Ford	,,	......	......
Geo. Davison	,,	......	......
Jno. Robt. Mackenzie...	7 Jul. 75.	......	......
Geo. Hy. Vesey	24 Jul. 75.	......	......
Jno. Geo. Boothby	,,	......	......
Jno. Singleton	,,	......	......
Geo. Ward	1 Sep. 75.	......	......
Wm. Forbes	,,	......	......
Jno. Nisbett	,,	......	......
Wm. Fullerton	,,	......	......
Hy. Larkins Robertson	,,	......	......

Name.	M.-Gen.	L.-Gen.	
Hy. Le Poer Trench	1 Sep. 75.	......	......
Linnæus Tripe	,,	......	......
Chas. Wm. Cox	,,	......	......
Wm. Selwood Hewett	,,	......	......
Gustavus Hamilton Lockwood Milman	8 Sep. 75.	......	......
Fras. Montagu Maxwell Ommaney	,,	......	......
Jno. Baillie	6 Oct. 75.	......	......
Edwd. Hy. Blomfield	,,	......	......
Geo. Harper Saxton	,,	......	......
Octavius Hamilton	23 Oct. 75.	......	......
Edmd. Hy. Cullen Wintle	,,	......	......
Wm. Jno. Tweedie	,,	......	......
Edwin Luddington Scott	,,	......	......
Willoughby Lake Briggs, C.B.	,,	......	......
Evan Murray McGregor	,,	......	......
Wm. Hy. Shadwell Earle	13 Nov. 75.	......	......
Edwd. Smalley	,,	......	......
Jno. Fras. Stafford	,,	......	......
Richd. King Freeth	17 Nov. 75.	......	......
Wm. Vine	26 Nov. 75.	13 Jan. 81.	1 Dec. 88.
Bannastre Pryce Lloyd	1 Dec. 75.	......	......
Richd. Godfrey Jones	,,	......	......
St. Jno. O'Neill Muter	,,	......	......
Thos. Milles	18 Dec. 75.	......	......
Alexr. Kennedy Clark-Kennedy	5 Jan. 76.	......	......
Jas. Price Clarkson	,,	......	......
Jno. Wellwood Rutherford	,,	......	......
Edmd. David Russell Ross	,,	......	......
Hugh Lindsay Christie	,,	......	......
Edwd. Bannerman Ramsay	,,	......	......
Mathew Bligh Ford	15 Jan. 76.	......	......
Wm. Jno. Doveton	26 Feb. 76.	......	......
Hy. Manning Eliott	,,	......	......
Arth. Chauncy Phillips	,,	......	......
Fras. Rawdon Chesney	1 Apr. 76.	......	......
Chas. Parker Catty	31 May 76.	......	......
Alexr. Wm. Gordon	,,	......	......
Augs. Kay Moffat	14 Jun. 76.	......	......
Herbert Raban	,,	......	......
Geo. McAndrew	,,	......	......
Fredk. Hy. Smith	,,	......	......
Fras. Geo. Stainforth	,,	......	......
Wm. Ruxton Eneas Alexander	,,	......	......
Jno. Peter Wm. Campbell	,,	......	......
Jno. Richardson Auldjo	,,	......	......
Geo. Hutchinson, C.B., C.S.I.	,,	......	......
Fras. Applegath	,,	......	......
Fredk. Phillips	,,	......	......
Hamilton Robt. Hathway	,,	......	......
Patr. Maxwell	,,	......	......
Alexr. Thos. Armstrong	,,	......	......
Chas. Jas. Stewart Wallace	15 Jul. 76.	......	......
Wm. Geo. Owen	4 Aug. 76.	1 Jul. 81.	1 Dec. 88.
Hy. Mills	12 Aug. 76.	......	......
Thos. Wollams Holland	,,	......	......
Thos. Pierce	,,	......	......
Hugh Norris Hodgson	,,	......	......
Augs. Prichard	,,	......	......
Roberts Michael Westropp	,,	......	......
Geo. Elliot Ashburner	,,	......	......
Wm. Boyd Irwin	26 Aug. 76.	......	......

Name.	M.-Gen.	L.-Gen.	Gen.
Wm. Jno. Ward	26 Aug. 76.	......	......
Chas. Maxton Shakespear	,,	......	......
Thos. Hy. Stoddard	,,	......	......
Edmond Tudor Boddam	,,	......	......
Arthur Jacob Macan Rainey	,,	......	......
Jno. Shaw Kemball	,,	......	......
Evelyn Waddington	,,	......	......
Angelo Edwd. Osborne	28 Oct. 76.	......	......
Jno. Robertson Pughe	,,	......	......
Edwd. Norman Perkins	,,	......	......
Fredk. Jno. Ellis	,,	......	......
Wm. Agnew	,,	......	......
Geo. Gill Moxon	,,	......	......
Gordon Cavenagh	,,	......	......
Wm. Paske	,,	......	......
Jas. Roper Boswall	,,	......	......
Jno. Duncan Campbell Wallace	,,	......	......
Jas. Geo. Roche Forlong	,,	......	......
Chas. Wm. Dun	,,	......	......
Edmund Antoine Hy. Bacon	,,	......	......
Wm. Thos. Bowen	,,	......	......
Hy. Ebenezer Jacob	,,	......	......
Jno. Ruggles	11 Nov. 76.	......	......
Josh. Fletcher Richardson, C.B.	,,	......	......
Chas. Chester Dandridge	,,	......	......
Edwd Chas. Marston	,,	......	......
Chamberlen Wm. Walker	,,	......	......
Wm. Vine	26 Nov. 76.	......	......
Chas. Scrope Hutchinson	30 Dec. 76.	......	......
Jioji Rao Sindia	......	......	1 Jan. 77.
Rambir Singh	......	......	,,
Hy. Clyde Fletcher	17 Jan. 77.	......	......
Geo. Markham Carter	,,	......	......
Robt. Jno. Baker	,,	......	......
Jas. Edmund Mayne	31 Jan. 77.	......	......
Chas. Crauford Mason	,,	......	......
Walter Weldon	,,	......	......
Hy. Jno. Thos. Neild	,,	......	......
Saml. Brougham Faddy	8 Feb. 77.	1 Jul. 81.	1 Dec. 88.
Richd. Andr. Doria	,,	,,	,,
Arthur Butcher	10 Mar. 77.	......	......
Jas. Creighton Wood	4 Apr. 77.	......	......
Sir Arthur Hy. Freeling, bt.	7 Apr. 77.	......	......
Chas. Hodgkinson Smith, C.B.	18 Apr. 77.	......	......
Thos. Augs. Carey	24 Apr. 77.	8 Feb. 78.	3 Nov. 78.
Stephen Jas. Keate Whitehill	2 May 77.	2 May 78.	......
Geo. Drury	3 May 77.	......	......
Hamilton Chas. Smith	5 May 77.	......	......
Jas. Anthy. Steel	,,	......	......
Wm. Nembhard	,,	......	......
Jno. Beresford Smyly	,,	......	......
Jno. Jerome	23 May 77.	......	......
Jno. Fendall	,,	......	......
Alexr. Geo. Davidson	,,	......	......
Jas. Davidson	,,	......	......
Jno. Desborough, C.B.	30 May 77.	......	......
Jno. Everett Thring	,,	......	......
Robt. Corcyra Romer...	11 Jun. 77.	......	......
Jas. Cockburn...	28 Jun. 77.	......	......
Hy. Wm. Holland, C.B.	30 Jun. 77.	......	......
Sydney Jos. Hire	,,	......	......

Name.	M.-Gen.	L.-Gen.	Gen.
Wm. Walker	30 Jun. 77.	......	......
Alexr. Irvine	,,	......	......
Josh. Miles	,,	......	......
Geo. Shaw, C.B.	1 Jul. 77.	......	......
Ralph Young	4 Jul. 77.	......	......
Chas. Vanbrugh Jenkins	11 Jul. 77.	......	......
Fras. Robt. Glanville...	14 Jul. 77.	......	......
Robt. Boyle, C.B.	20 Jul. 77.	......	......
Edwd. Wolstenholme Ward, C.M.G.	11 Aug. 77.	......	......
Wm. Bolton Girdlestone	16 Aug. 77.	......	......
Richd. Armstrong Roberts	22 Aug. 77.	......	......
Antonio Mattei, C.M.G.	5 Sep. 77.	......	......
Saverio Gatt	,,	......	......
Hy. Ferrers Waddington	,,	......	......
Jno. Alfred Brereton	,,	......	......
Jas. Puckle	,,	......	......
Jno. Elphinstone	,,	......	......
Alexr. Jas. Bruce	,,	......	......
Arthur Francis	,,	......	......
Jno. Fredk. Berthon	,,	......	......
Jas. Hyde Champion	,,	......	......
Jno. Pitcairn Sandwith	,,	......	......
Wm. Browne Salmon	1 Oct. 77.	2 May 78.	......
Jas. Knox Spence	,,	20 Aug. 78.	......
Geo. Mytton Hill	,,	3 Nov. 78.	......
Thos. Stock	,,	11 Jun. 79.	......
Geo. Jackson	,,	17 Nov. 79.	......
Wm. Geo. Woods, C.S.I.	,,	,,	......
Robt. Napier Raikes	,,	18 Dec. 79.	......
Edwd. Every Miller	,,	......	......
Geo. Selby	,,	8 Dec. 79.	1 Jul. 81.
Geo. Verner	,,	1 Jan. 80.	......
Edwd. Wray, C.B.	,,	31 Dec. 78.	......
Hon. sir Hy. Ramsay, K.C.S.I., C.B. ...	,,	1 Jan. 80.	......
Alexr. Boyd	,,	16 Jan. 80.	......
Richd. Chas. Lawrence, C.B.	,,	25 Jan. 80.	......
Hy. Nicoll	,,	25 May 80.	......
Jno. Worgan	,,	31 Dec. 78.	......
Wm. Sparkes Hatch	,,	26 Feb. 80.	12 May 82.
Andrew Wm. Macintire, C.B.	,,	1 Sep. 81.	31 Mar. 83.
Jno. Gordon Petrie, C.B.	,,	31 Dec. 78.	......
Goodricke Armstrong Fisher	,,	14 Jul. 80.	......
Crawford Cooke	,,	21 Jul. 80.	......
Jno. Wilson	,,	15 Dec. 80.	......
Septimus Harding Becher	,,	18 Dec. 80.	......
Fredk. Dayot Atkinson	,,	21 Dec. 80.	......
Annesley Knox Gore	,,	......	......
Chas. Harris	,,	18 May 81.	......
Fras. Hy. Scott	,,	......	......
Jno. Saml. Drury Tullock	,,	......	......
Geo. Wm. Russell	,,	......	......
Molyneux Capel Spottiswood	,,	......	......
Hy. Man	,,	......	......
Chas. Lionel Showers...	,,	......	......
Augs. Turner	,,	......	......
Hy. Grice de Tessier	,,	1 Sep. 81.	31 Mar. 83.
Craven Hildesley Dickens, C.S.I.	,,	31 Dec. 78.	......
Donald Campbell Vanrenen	,,	,,	......
Fredk. Wm. Swinhoe...	,,	,,	......
Wm. Chas. Robertson Macdonald, C.B. ...	,,	......	......
Chas. Fitzroy Miller Mundy	,,	......	......

Name.	M.-Gen.	L.-Gen.	Gen.
Anthy. Robt. Thornhill	1 Oct. 77.	......	......
Jno. Patk. Redmond, C.B.	,,	1 Jul. 81.	......
Edwd. Gascoigne Bulwer, C.B., aft. sir E. ...	,,	21 Jan. 87.	......
Jno. Chiop Brooke	,,	......	......
Robt. Woolley...	,,	......	......
Edwd. Tuite Dalton, C.S.I.	,,	......	......
Hy. Le Geyt Bruce, C.B.	,,	31 Dec. 78.	......
Lothian Nicholson, C.B.	,,	19 Oct. 81.	......
Hon. Hussey Fane Keane, C.B.	,,	......	......
Geo. Hy., M. of Conynghame	,,	1 Jul. 81.	......
Wm. Hardy, C.B.	,,	1 Oct. 82.	......
Jno. Walpole D'Oyly	,,	1 Jul. 81.	......
Alexr. Tod Cadell	,,	31 Dec. 78.	......
Edwd. Fellowes	,,	......	......
Robt. Richards	,,	......	......
Coote Synge Hutchinson	,,	1 Jul. 81.	......
Pearson Scott Thompson, C.B.	,,	......	......
Jno. Hy. Ford Elkington	,,	1 Apr. 87.	......
Augs. Fredk. Steele	,,	1 Jul. 81.	......
Augs. Hy. Lane Fox-Pitt-Rivers	,,	1 Oct. 82.	......
Hy. Grierson	,,	1 Jul. 81.	......
Stephen Fras. Chas. Annesley	,,	,,	......
Hon. Jno. Jocelyn Bourke	,,	1 Oct. 82.	......
Sir Archd. Alison, K.C.B.	,,	18 Nov. 82.	......
Lindsay Farrington	,,	1 Oct. 82.	......
Jno. Bayly, C.B.	,,	23 Mar. 82.	26 Apr. 82.
Sir Wm. Fraser Drummond Jervois, C.B., K.C.M.G.	,,	......	......
Thos. Brydges Rodney, C.B....	,,	......	......
Peregrine Hy. Fellowes	,,	4 Jun. 79.	1 Feb. 86.
Jno. Wm. Collman Williams, aft. sir J. ...	,,	5 Oct. 86.	21 May 88.
Augs. Barnard Hankey	,,	1 Oct. 82.	......
Thos. Raikes	,,	......	......
Edwd. Newdigate Newdegate, C.B.	,,	11 May 87.	......
Wm. Fredk., ld. Abinger, C.B.	,,	1 Oct. 82.	......
Chas. Wm. Adair. C.B., aft. sir C.	,,	7 Nov. 85.	18 Jul. 86.
Chas. Vaughan Wilkinson	,,	......	......
Wm. Wilberforce Harris Greathed, C.B. ...	,,	......	......
Gordon Caulfield	,,	1 Jul. 81.	1 Dec. 88.
Fras. Faithful Warden	,,	,,	......
David Scott Dodgson, C.B.	,,	,,	1 Dec. 88.
Chas. Edwd. Beale	,,	......	......
Wm. Hy. Freese	,,	1 Jul. 81.	......
Alexr. Crombie Silver	,,	,,	1 Dec. 88.
Jno. Penrose Coode	,,	,,	,,
Edwd. Dayot Watson...	,,	,,	,,
Jno. Wm. Schneider, C.B.	,,	,,	,,
Douglas Hamilton	,,	20 Mar. 82.	1 Dec. 88.
Jno. Sherbrooke Gell...	,,	......	......
David Brown	,,	20 Mar. 82.	1 Dec. 88.
Wm. Jno. Dorehill	,,	......	......
Jas. Cockburn...	,,	......	......
Geo. Staple Dobbie	2 Oct. 77.	1 Apr. 82.	......
Chas. Robt. West Hervey	,,	......	......
Edwd. Harrison	4 Oct. 77.	......	......
Arth. Newbolt Rich	11 Oct. 77.	1 Apr. 82.	1 Dec. 88.
Jas. Eardley Gastrell	,,	......	......
Olaus Jno. Macleod Farrington	13 Oct. 77.	......	......
Robt. Thos. Leigh	,,	......	......
Geo. Swiney	,,	......	......
Chas. Geo. Hy. Coote...	,,	......	......

Name.	M.-Gen.	L.-Gen.	Gen.
Jno. Fredk. Lester	13 Oct. 77.	......	......
Thos. Smith Warden...	,,	......	......
Jno. Crawford Millar...	,,	......	......
Geo. Edwd. Thomas	,,	......	......
Gustavus Nigle Kingscote Anker Yonge ...	19 Oct. 77.	1 Jul. 81.	......
Augs. Wm. Hy. Meyrick	,,	,,	......
Fredk. Marshall, C.M.G.	20 Oct. 77.	5 Sep. 84.	......
Jno. Roe	31 Oct. 77.	......	......
Sussex Chas. Milford	,,	......	......
Wm. Lacy	1 Nov. 77.	......	......
Jas. Baillie	,,	......	......
Hy. Cole Faulkner	,,	......	......
Danl. Hy. Loudoun Mackinnon	,,	......	......
Jas. Cockburn	,,	......	......
Edwd. Harrison	24 Nov. 77.	......	......
Wm. Lewis Devenish Meares	,,	......	......
Edwd. Abbott Anderson	26 Nov. 77.	......	......
Jno. Hy. Stewart	2 Dec. 77.	......	......
Fredk. Mould	5 Dec. 77.	......	......
Rodk. Bannatyne MacLeod	8 Dec. 77.	......	......
Archd. Hugh Hope	,,	......	......
Jno. Fredk. Stoddard	,,	......	......
Josh. Hume Spry Pierce	,,	......	......
Robt. Renton	,,	......	......
Alfred Bassano, C.B.	12 Dec. 77.	......	......
Jno. Alexr. Dalzell	19 Dec. 77.	......	......
Chas. Spalding S. Evans Gordon	,,	......	......
Hy. St. Clair Wilkins...	21 Dec. 77.	31 Dec. 78.	18 Jan. 82.
Geo. Wm. Forbes	25 Dec. 77.	......	......
Hy. Augs. Adams	1 Jan. 78.	1 Apr. 82.	1 Dec. 88.
Robt. Hamilton Currie	23 Jan. 78.	......	......
Benj. Geo. Vander Gucht	,,	......	......
Edwd. Jno. Wild	,,	......	......
Blair Thos. Reid	2 Feb. 78.	......	......
Hy. Dimsdale Manning	,,	......	......
Fredk. Duffin	,,	......	......
Geo. Money Battye	,,	......	......
Wm. Hy. Paget	,,	......	......
Jno. Dwyer	,,	......	......
Thos. Thompson	8 Feb. 78.	......	......
Wm. Hy. Beaumont De Horsey	13 Feb. 78.	13 Feb. 83.	......
Wm. McBean, V.C.	16 Feb. 78.	......	......
Hy. Hyde	17 Feb. 78.	......	......
Lennox Jas. Farquharson	2 Mar. 78.	......	......
Robt. Patr. Anderson	,,	......	......
Wm. Cornwallis Phillips	,,	......	......
Percy Lee Holmes	,,	......	......
Fras. Geo. Hodgson	,,	......	......
Wm. Hy. Hessey	,,	......	......
Archd. Wm. Graham	,,	......	......
Wm. Carmichael Russell	13 Mar. 78.	......	......
Jno. Bean	18 Mar. 78.	......	......
Sir Hy. Marshman Havelock, bt., V.C., C.B.; aft. Havelock-Allan	,,	9 Dec. 81.	......
Edwd. Jno. Dickson	20 Mar. 78.	......	......
Richd. Buckley Prettejohn, C.B.	,,	1 Jul. 81.	......
Conyers Tower, C.B.	,,	......	......
Alexr. Mackenzie, C.B.	27 Mar. 78.	......	......
Valentine Fredk. Story	1 Apr. 78.	......	......
Geo. Butler Stoney	,,	......	......
Geo. Mein	3 Apr. 78.	......	......

Name.	M.-Gen.	L.-Gen.	Gen.
no. Goddard	17 Apr. 78.	......	......
no. Lawrence Bolton	,,	......	......
no. Wm. Alexr. Kennedy	20 Apr. 78.	......	......
has. Hopkins Byers	,,	......	......
eo. Alexr. St. Peter Fooks...	,,	......	......
no. Wm. Younghusband, C.S.I.	,,	......	......
'm. Josh. Fitzmaurice Stafford, C.B. ...	1 May 78.	......	......
obt. Alexr. Napper	,,	......	......
hos. Hardy Chamberlain	,,	......	......
oodson Adye	,,	......	......
y. Shewell	,,	......	......
eo. Fredk. Moore	,,	......	......
has. Powlett Lane	,,	......	......
artin Dillon, C.S.I.; aft. sir M.	,,	22 Nov. 87.	......
has. Edwd. Astell	4 May 78.	......	......
y. Drummond	1 Jun. 78.	......	......
rth. Stevens	12 Jun. 78.	......	......
m. Gordon Cameron, C.B.	25 Jun. 78.	17 Jul. 88.	......
hos. Lionel Jno. Gallwey	1 Jul. 78.	26 Apr. 82.	......
redk. Wm. Graham	7 Aug. 78.	......	......
s. Geo. Fife	15 Aug. 78.	31 Dec. 78.	......
eo. Alexr. Leckie	20 Aug. 78.	......	......
has. Baring	23 Aug. 78.	1 Jul. 81.	......
nkin Jones	24 Aug. 78.	31 Dec. 78.	......
'm. Hill	29 Aug. 78.	1 Jul. 81.	......
y. Campbell Johnstone	31 Aug. 78.	......	......
y. Arth. Dwyer	,,	......	......
obt. Farquhar Webster	,,	......	......
eonard Raisbeck Christopher	,,	......	......
ras. Lane Magniac	,,	......	......
leetwood Jno. Richards	2 Sep. 78.	1 Feb. 85.	......
m. Cosmo Trevor, C.B.	16 Sep. 78.	25 Jul. 84.	......
ras. Jno. Richards	,,	......	......
has. Herbert	25 Sep. 78.	......	......
aml. Crozier Law	,,	......	......
dmd. Lewin Taverner	,,	......	......
aml. Josh. Thorp	,,	......	......
dwd. Burgoyne Cureton	29 Sep. 78.	1 Jul. 81.	......
r Jno. Chetham McLeod, K.C.B.	2 Oct. 78.	12 Aug. 88.	......
m. Tod Brown, C.B.	16 Oct. 78.	......	......
y. Buckley Jenner Wynyard	1 Nov. 78.	......	......
y. Dyett Abbott, C.B.	3 Nov. 78.	......	......
m. Warden Anderson	,,	1 Apr. 82.	1 Dec. 88.
ark Walker, V.C., C.B.	11 Nov. 78.	16 Dec. 88.	......
y. Wellington Palmer	13 Nov. 78.	......	......
enj. Parrott	,,	......	......
m. Chas. Rich	,,	......	......
y. Ambrose Hare	,,	......	......
hos. Gordon Moore Lane	,,	......	......
lfr. Becher	,,	......	......
ugs. Phillip Chesshyre	,,	......	......
hos. Darling Ker	,,	......	......
y. Lowther Chermside, C.B.	16 Nov. 78.	......	......
arry Vince Timbrell...	,,	......	......
ras. Wm. Stubbs	,,	......	......
has. Waterloo Hutchinson	29 Nov. 78.	31 Dec. 78.	28 Nov. 85.
m. Conrad Hamilton	30 Nov. 78.	......	......
drian Hugh Paterson	,,	......	......
incent Jno. Shortland	,,	......	......
m. Calcott Clarke	,,	......	......
dmund L'Estrange	,,	......	......

Name.	M.-Gen.	L.-Gen.	Gen.
Jno. Fraser Raper	9 Dec. 78.	......	......
Alfr. Hales Heath	,,	......	......
Alfr. Digby Denniss	14 Dec. 78.	......	......
Hy. Andrew Sorel, C.B.	22 Dec. 78.	1 Nov. 85.	......
Sir Wm. Russell	24 Dec. 78.	1 Jul. 81.	......
Edwd. Archd. Foord	30 Dec. 78.	31 Dec. 78.	......
Saml. Stallard...	31 Dec. 78.	......	......
Hy. Francis	,,	......	......
Alfr. Light	,,	......	......
Chas. Stirling Dundas	,,	......	......
Chas. Metcalf Young	,,	......	......
David Jno. Falconer Newall	,,	......	......
Jno. Stewart Tulloch	,,	......	......
Geo. Rodney Brown	,,	......	......
Geo. Alexr. Renny, V.C.	,,	......	......
Chas. Hy. Cookes	,,	......	......
Hy. Parlett Bishop	,,	......	......
Chas. Mcwhirter Mercer	,,	......	......
Wallis Dowell	,,	......	......
Andrew Vance Falls	,,	......	......
Fredk. Wm. Bond	,,	......	......
Chas. Macleod Jno. Thornton	,,	......	......
Edwd. Wm. Dance	,,	......	......
Lancelot Fras. Chas. Thomas	,,	......	......
Douglas Gaye	,,	......	......
Hill Wallace, C.B.	,,	......	......
Geo. Gleig Brown	,,	......	......
Jno. Clements Hailes	,,	......	......
Jas. Hy. Reid	,,	......	......
Thos. Jas. Maclachlan	,,	......	......
Thos. Carlisle Crowe	,,	......	......
Robt. Cadell	,,	27 Feb. 82.	31 Mar. 8
Jas. Thos. Walker	,,	10 May 81.	12 Jan. 8
Alexr. Fraser, C.B.	,,	18 Jan. 82.	16 Sep. 8
Wm. Fras. Clarke Gosling	,,	12 May 82.	31 Dec. 8
Jno. Augs. Fuller	,,	1 Feb. 82.	......
Jas. Crofton	,,	17 May 82.	......
Jno. Anthy. Angelo	,,	......	......
Alexr. Cadell	,,	28 Jan. 82.	......
Arth. Bunny, C.B.	,,	......	......
Wm. Jno. Gray	,,	......	......
Hy. Wm. Gulliver	,,	16 Sep. 82.	......
Napier Geo. Campbell	,,	31 Mar. 83.	......
Fredk. Richd. Maunsell, C.B.	,,	12 Jan. 84.	21 Feb. 8
Chas. Pollard	,,	......	......
Fredk. Sleigh Roberts, aft. bt.	,,	26 Jul. 83.	......
Jno. Mackenzie Macintyre	,,	11 Sep. 82.	......
Peter Pierce Lyons-O'Connell	,,	......	......
Fras. Jno. Moberly	,,	......	......
Jno. Salusbury Trevor	,,	......	......
Wm. Stirling Oliphant	,,	......	......
Felix Thackeray Haig	,,	......	......
Arthur Scott Moberly	,,	......	......
Alexr. Davidson	,,	......	......
Alexr. Urquhart Hamilton Finch	,,	......	......
David Thomson	,,	......	......
Randal Josh. Feilden, C.M.G.	1 Jan. 79.	5 Jan. 83.	......
Regd. Onslow Farmer	,,	......	......
Chas. Brenton Basden	,,	......	......
Wm. Ramsay	,,	......	......
Chas. Jno. Fullerton	,,	......	......

Name.	M.-Gen.	L.-Gen.	Gen.
·edk. Jas. Stephenson	29 Jan. 79.	......	......
m. Byrie Alexander	,,	......	......
ɔuglas Scott	,,	......	......
ıo. Bedingfield Knocker	18 Feb. 79.	......	......
ıo. Lindridge Elgee	19 Feb. 79.	......	......
y. Stuart Bivar	,,	......	......
m. Hy. Binny	,,	......	......
.s. Sebastian Rawlins	,,	......	......
ɘo. Bligh Bowen	,,	......	......
lwd. Macalister Gilbert Cooper	,,	......	......
·nj. Jno. Chouvel Prior	,,	......	......
ɘo. Owen Bowdler	15 Mar. 79.	......	......
y. Cadogan Craigie	,,	......	......
r Roger Wm. Hy. Palmer, bt.	,,	1 Jul. 81.	......
ıas. M'Arthur	13 Apr. 79.	9 May 86.	15 Apr. 87.
r Seymour Jno. Blane, bt., C.B.	27 Apr. 79.	1 Jul. 81.	......
ıul Winsloe Phillips-Treby	17 May 79.	......	......
ıvid Blair Lockhart	,,	......	......
lwd. Laws Pym	4 Jun. 79.	18 Jul. 86.	22 Jun. 87.
o. Field, C.B.	11 Jun. 79.	1 Apr. 82.	1 Dec. 88.
lwd. Wm. Boudier	,,	......	......
ed. Geo. Pym, C.B.	7 Jul. 79.	......	......
.s. Hills, C.B., V.C., aft. sir Jas. Hills-Johnes, K.C.B.	10 Jul. 79.	31 Dec. 83.	......
·chd. Richd. Harenc	11 Jul. 79.	25 Oct. 82.	......
.s. Gubbins	14 Jul. 79.	1 Jul. 81.	......
ıo. Gusts. Halliday	18 Jul. 79.	1 Apr. 82.	1 Dec. 88.
ɘrald Littlehales Goodlake, V.C.	11 Aug. 79.	1 Jul. 81.	......
ıo. Gordon	13 Aug. 79.	7 May 82.	1 Dec. 88.
r Jno. Clayton Cowell, K.C.B.	1 Sep. 79.	......	......
chd. Burnaby	13 Sep. 79.	......	......
ɔn. Richd. Monck	18 Sep. 79.	......	......
o. Crosbie Graves	17 Oct. 79.	......	......
m. Thos. Williams	18 Oct. 79.	1 Jul. 82.	1 Dec. 88.
s. Clerk Rattray, C.B.	14 Nov. 79.	1 Jul. 81.	......
lomon Richards	17 Nov. 79.	......	......
sley Jno. Batten	20 Nov. 79.	16 Dec. 79.	......
ıas. Wilson Randolph	30 Nov. 79.	1 Jul. 81.	......
o. Richd. Hume	6 Dec. 79.	......	......
lwd. Walker Ellis Walker	8 Dec. 79.	......	......
ɔntagu Jas. Turnbull	18 Dec. 79.	1 Jul. 81.	......
ıncelot Fras. Chas. Thomas	31 Dec. 79.	......	......
ɔbt. Phayre, C.B.	1 Jan. 80.	......	......
o. Hy. Melville Babington...	16 Jan. 80.	......	......
ıas. Campbell McCullum	25 Jan. 80.	......	......
y. Geo. Woods	30 Jan. 80.	30 Jan. 85.	......
y. Woodbine Parish, C.B.	25 Feb. 80.	......	......
ɘo. Godfrey Pearse	26 Feb. 80.	7 Sep. 85.	......
·as. Locker Whitmore	4 Mar. 80.	1 Jul. 81.	......
ɔn. Wm. Hy. Adalbert Feilding	,,	......	......
chd. D'Oyly Compton Bracken	11 Mar. 80.	......	......
·ed. Wm. Burroughs, C.B.	16 Mar. 80.	1 Jul. 81.	......
s. Emerson	24 Mar. 80.	......	......
o. Fulton	25 Mar. 80.	5 Nov. 83.	......
ıas. Fredk. Torrens Daniell	12 Apr. 80.	......	......
m. Kelty McLeod	19 Apr. 80.	3 Apr. 85.	......
lwd. Howard Vyse	25 Apr. 80.	25 Apr. 85.	......
ıo. Jeffreys Fulton	,,	......	......
lexr. Abercromby Nelson, C.B.	29 Apr. 80.	10 Oct. 83.	......
lwyn Sherard Burnaby	,,	......	......
m. Wigram Barry, C.B.	1 May 80.	1 Apr. 84.	......

Name.	M.-Gen.	L.-Gen.	Gen.
Hon. David Macdowall Fraser, C.B.... ...	1 May 80.	1 Apr. 84.	1 Jul. 85
Hy. Peel Yates, C.B.	,,	24 Nov. 84.	1 May 85
Jno. Edwd. Michell, C.B.	,,	......	......
Nathl. Octavius S. Turner, C.B.	,,	......	......
Edwd. Arth. Williams, C.B.	,,	1 May 85.	......
Percy Scudamore Cunningham	,,	......	......
Fras. Walker Drummond	3 May 80.	1 Jul. 82.	1 Dec. 88
Wm. Roberts	4 May 80.	21 Aug. 83.	......
Jonathan Keer...	8 May 80.	......	......
Wm. Rickman...	19 May 80.	1 Apr. 85.	......
Fredk. Geo. Thos. Deshon	21 May 80.	1 Jul. 81.	......
Thos. Greenaway	25 May 80.	......	......
Geo. Vanderheyden Johnson...	27 May 80.	10 Dec. 83.	......
Arth. Wm. Patr. Alb., D. of Connaught and Strathern	29 May 80.	......	......
Hy. Peter Sykes	,,	......	......
Geo. Dean-Pitt...	7 Jun. 80.	30 Aug. 82.	......
Hy. Hilhouse Firth	11 Jun. 80.	......	......
Walter Rathbone Lambert	,,	......	......
Geo. Neeld Boldero	1 Jul. 80.	1 Jul. 85.	......
Hamond Weston Gwyn	4 Jul. 80.	15 Apr. 87.	......
Chas. McClintock Cotton	8 Jul. 80.	......	......
John Peel	11 Jul. 80.	11 Jul. 85.	......
Chas. Malcolm Barrow, C.B.	14 Jul. 80.	1 Apr. 82.	......
Danl. Boyd	21 Jul. 80.	,,	......
St. Geo. Mervyn Nugent	,,	......	......
Chas. Fredk. Parkinson	,,	......	......
Jno. Ingle Preston	4 Aug. 80.	......	......
Fras. Chas. Trevor	1 Sep. 80.	......	......
Hercules Atkin Welman	1 Oct. 80.	......	......
Jno. Theoph. Ussher...	,,	......	......
Lewis Edwd. Knight	5 Oct. 80.	......	......
Wm. Earle, C.S.I.	31 Oct. 80.	......	......
Patr. Robertson-Ross, C.B.	5 Nov. 80.	......	......
Jas. Farrell Pennycuick, C.B.	8 Nov. 80.	1 Jul. 85.	4 Jan. 86
Philip Gosset Pipon, C.B.	13 Nov. 80.	4 Jan. 86.	1 Apr. 86
Geo. Thos. Field	26 Nov. 80.	16 Dec. 85.	......
Fras. Young	15 Dec. 80.	......	......
Jno. Colpoys Haughton, C.S.I.	18 Dec. 80.	......	......
Richd. Herbert Gall, C.B.	19 Dec. 80.	......	......
Geo Saml. Young	,,	18 Nov. 86.	......
Thos. Fourness Wilson, C.B., C.I.E. ...	21 Dec. 80.	......	......
Shurlock Henning, C.B.	26 Dec. 80.	26 Dec. 86.	......
Alfr. Wm. Lucas, C.B.	31 Dec. 80.	......	......
Hy. Hastings Affleck Wood, C.B.	13 Jan. 81.	......	......
Horace Parker Newton	13 Feb. 81.	......	......
Jno. Dennis Swinburne, ch. Paymr.; to rank as M.-Gen.	1 Apr. 81.	......	......
Cecil Robt. St. Jno. Ives	6 Apr. 81.	......	......
Arthur Wombwell	8 May 81.	1 Jul. 81.	......
Chas. Thornton Stewart	10 May 81.	26 May 83.	......
Fras. Adams Ellis Loch, C.B.	18 May 81.	......	......
Chas. Tyrwhitt, C.B.	,,	1 Jul. 81.	......
Horatio Harbord Morant	,,	1 Apr. 85.	......
Wm. Lambert, C.B.	8 Jun. 81.	......	......
Geo. Wolfe	29 Jun. 81.	......	......
Alexr. Robinson	1 Jul. 81.	......	......
Fras. G. Kempster	,,	......	......
C. P. Moloney	,,	......	......
H. Hopkinson, C.S.I.	,,	......	......
R. R. Mainwaring	,,	......	......

Name.	M.-Gen.	L.-Gen.	Gen.
M. T. Ffrench	1 Jul. 81.	......	......
Alfr. Fox Place	,,	......	......
H. K. Burne, C.B.	,,	......	......
W. S. Simpson	,,	......	......
C. T. Aitchison, C.B.	,,	......	......
Sir R. J. Meade, K.C.S.I., C.I.E.	,,	......	......
J. M. McGregor	,,	......	......
Geo. Holroyd	,,	......	......
J. R. McMullen	,,	......	......
F. J. B. Priestley	,,	......	......
F. P. Layard	,,	......	......
Alfr. Cooper	,,	......	......
Arth. Howlett, C.B.	,,	......	......
Geo. S. Alexr. Anderson	,,	......	......
Sir Chas. Hy. Brownlow	,,	......	......
Sir Chas. Patton Keyes, K.C.B.	,,	20 Dec. 86.	......
Wm. Domett Morgan	,,	,,	......
Thos. Wright, C.B.	,,	,,	......
Geo. Cliffe Hatch, C.S.I.	,,	8 Jan. 87.	......
Sweedland Mainwaring	,,	......	......
Augs. Hy. Ternan	,,	8 Jan. 87.	......
Sir Campbell Claye Grant Ross, K.C.B. ...	,,	,,	......
Sir Peter Stark Lumsden, K.C.B., C.S.I. ...	,,	,,	......
Jno. Watson, C.B., aft. sir J.	,,	14 Jan. 87.	......
Edwd. Jas. Lawder	,,	,,	......
Andr. MacQueen	,,	......	......
Geo. Robt. Phillips	,,	14 Jan. 87.	......
Robt. Nixon Tronson	,,	......	......
Wm. Coussmaker Anderson, C.S.I.	,,	14 Jan. 87.	......
Edmd. Fras. Burton	,,	,,	......
Geo. Uvedale Price	,,	,,	......
Robson Benson	,,	,,	......
John Matth. Cripps	,,	,,	......
Julius Bentall Dennys...	,,	,,	......
John Cockburn Hood...	,,	,,	......
Fras Mardall	,,	......	......
Geo. Baldock	,,	14 Jan. 87.	......
Wm Legh Cahusac	,,	,,	......
Chas. Curtis Drury	,,	,,	......
Edwd. Thos. Fasken...	,,	,,	......
John Allen Wright	,,	......	......
Richd. Drapes Ardagh	,,	14 Jan. 87.	......
Fredk. Saml. Blythe, C.B.	,,	1 Jul. 86.	......
Jno. Hart Dunne	,,	......	......
Thos. Casey Lyons, C.B.	,,	......	......
Regd. Gipps, C.B.	,,	......	......
Alexr. J. H. Elliot, C.B.	,,	......	......
Hugh Rowlands, V.C., C.B.	,,	......	......
Robt. Abrm. Logan, C.B.	,,	6 May 82.	......
Wm. Wilkinson Taylor	,,	19 Mar. 83.	1 Dec. 88.
Geo. Strangways	,,	19 Mar. 83.	,,
Fredk. Chas. Maisey...	,,	,,	,,
Hy. Borlase Stevens	,,	16 Jul. 83.	,,
Jas. Buchanan...	,,	,,	,,
Wm. Hy. Watts	,,	,,	,,
Geo. Travis Radcliffe...	,,	1 Aug. 83.	,,
Chas. Raper Stainforth	,,	......	......
Chas. Jackson...	,,	......	......
Wredenhall Queiros Pogson	,,	23 Aug. 84.	......
Ffolliott Walker Baugh	,,	,,	......
Thos. Rochfort Snow...	,,	3 Feb. 86.	......

Name.	M.-Gen.	L.-Gen.	Gen.
Chas. Dumbleton	1 Jul. 81.	3 Feb. 86.	......
Chas. Gibson Anderson	,,	,,	......
Geo. Reynolds Scott Burrows	,,	,,	......
Edwd. Wm. Blackett...	,,	......	......
Saml. Peters Jarvis, C.M.G.	,,	......	......
Hy. Butler	,,	......	......
John Nason	10 Jul. 81.	1 Apr. 85.	......
Sir Chas. Geo. Arbuthnot, K.C.B.	16 Jul. 81.	1 Apr. 86.	......
Raymond Herb. White	27 Jul. 81.	......	......
Sir H. Evelyn Wood, V.C., K.C.B.	12 Aug. 81.	......	......
Wilbraham Oates Lennox, V.C., C.B. ...	13 Aug. 81.	12 Feb. 88.	......
Geo. Skene Hallowes	14 Aug. 81.	......	......
Robt. Thos. P. Cuthbert	15 Aug. 81.	......	......
Hy. Prim. Hutton	24 Aug. 81.	......	......
Jas. Nowell Young	,,	14 Jan. 87.	......
Edwd. Douglas Harvest	,,	......	......
Abingdon Augs. Bayley	1 Sep. 81.	7 Sep. 85.	......
Thos. Maunsell, C.B.	10 Sep. 81.	......	......
Fras. Edwd. Drew	14 Sep. 81.	......	......
Josh. Reay	1 Oct. 81.	......	......
Wm. Winson	,,	......	......
Hy. Fras. Williams	11 Oct. 81.	25 Sep. 85.	......
Gerald Graham, C.B., aft. sir G.	19 Oct. 81.	21 May 84.	......
Wm. Chas. Gott	1 Nov. 81.	18 May 86.	......
John Loudon	,,	14 Jan. 87.	......
Græme Auchmuty Fulton	8 Nov. 81.	......	......
Geo. Byng Harman, C.B.	14 Nov. 81.	......	......
Frank Chaplin	19 Nov. 81.	......	......
Benjn. Bousfield Herrick	3 Dec. 81.	......	......
Philip Harris	,,	......	......
Drury Curzon Drury-Lowe, C.B., aft. sir D.	,,	......	......
Herbert Dawson Slade	,,	......	......
Hy. Fras. Williams	10 Dec. 81.	......	......
Hy. Alexander	17 Dec. 81.	......	......
Hugh Heefke O'Connell	10 Jan. 82.	14 Jan. 87.	......
Chas. Jas. Merriman, C.S.I.	18 Jan. 82.	21 Jun. 84.	22 Feb. 87.
Wm. Taylor Corrie	,,	......	......
Wm. Hy. Hore West	24 Jan. 82.	......	......
Edw. Wm. Bray, C.B.	28 Jan. 82.	......	......
Richd. Temple Godman	31 Jan. 82.	......	......
Edmd. Jno. Scovell	8 Feb. 82.	......	......
Thos. Scovell Bigge	22 Feb. 82.	......	......
Wm. Alexr. Riach	1 Mar. 82.	14 Jan. 87.	......
Augs. Ritherdon	,,	,,	......
Jonn. Augs. Spry Faulknor	,,	1 Jul. 86.	......
Jno. Irvine Murray, C.B.	2 Mar. 82.	14 Jan. 87.	......
Percy Fortescue Gardiner	,,	,,	......
Wm. Hy. Crompton-Stansfield	7 Mar. 82.	......	......
Duncan Jas. Baillie	9 Mar. 82.	9 Mar. 87.	......
Wm. Barwell Browne Barwell	11 Mar. 82.	......	......
Valentine Ryan	18 Mar. 82.	......	......
Chas. Geo. Gordon, C.B.	23 Mar. 82.	......	......
Jno. Hackett	1 Apr. 82.	......	......
Chas. A. Boswell Gordon	,,	......	......
Jas. Sinclair Thomson	,,	2 Dec. 82.	......
Chas. Osborne Creagh-Osborne, C.B. ...	,,	20 Dec. 85.	......
Arth. Jas. Lyon-Freemantle	,,	......	......
Thos. Gillian	,,	22 Jan. 87.	......
Lewis Pelly, aft. sir L.	,,	,,	......
Chas. Joc. Cecil Sillery	,,	......	......
Anthy. Chas. Cooke, C.B	7 Apr. 82.	......	......

Name.	M.-Gen.	L.-Gen.	Gen.
eo. Bayles Heastey	13 Apr. 82.	......	......
y. Adair	,,	......	......
y. Wray, C.M.G.	26 Apr. 82.	......	......
redk. Thos. Whinyates	,,	......	......
lexr. Hugh Cobbe, C.B.	6 May 82.	......	......
y. Pye Phillips	,,	......	......
has. Richd. Ogden Evans	10 May 82.	28 Mar. 83.	......
as. Edw. Cordner	12 May 82.	31 Dec. 88.	......
dw. Josh. Ridgway Conolly	4 Jun. 82.	......	......
y. Rawlings Drew	29 Jun. 82.	22 Jan. 87.	......
has. Hayes Abdy	,,	,,	......
no. Thos. Francis	1 Jul. 82.	,,	......
ugs. Fraser Baird	,,	,,	......
as. Marquis	,,	,,	......
lfr. Butler Little	,,	,,	......
no. Louis Nation, C.B.	,,	4 Mar. 87.	......
llen Bayard Johnson, C.B.	,,	,,	......
r Herb. Taylor Macpherson, K.C.B., K.C.S.I.	,,	......	......
o. Ponsonby Watts, C.I.E.	,,	1 Jul. 87.	......
m. Gordon, C.S.I.	,,	,,	......
s. Gathorne Cookson	,,	20 Dec. 86.	......
tr. Geo. Scot	,,	,,	......
wen Lewis Cope Williams	21 Jul. 82.	21 Dec. 86.	......
o. Harrington Hawes	,,	......	......
as. Clarke	,,	1 Oct. 82.	......
bt. Russell Woodhouse	1 Sep. 82.	......	......
o. Wimburn Laurie	13 Sep. 82.	31 Dec. 87.	......
arry North Dalrymple Prendergast, V.C., C.B.	16 Sep. 82.	28 Nov. 85.	21 Feb. 87.
chd. Thos. Glyn, C.B., C.M.G.	30 Sep. 82.	30 Sep. 87.	......
as. Wm. Hastings	1 Oct. 82.	5 Jul. 86.	1 Oct. 87.
o. Hyde Page	,,	1 Apr. 85.	......
o. Edw. Baynes	,,	10 Dec. 85.	......
m. Cooper	,,	......	......
Jno. Carstairs McNeill, K.C.M.G., V.C., C.B.	,,	......	......
as. Lyons-Montgomery	,,	1 Jul. 87.	......
exr. Dawson	,,	19 Jan. 83.	......
iot Minto Playfair	,,	31 Dec. 88.	......
. Thornhill	,,	......	......
th. Thornton Gratwicke Pearse	,,	......	......
os. Priaulx Carey	,,	......	......
exr. Hadden Hutchinson	,,	......	......
. Edw. Ruck-Keene	,,	......	......
. Alexr. Cockburn	,,	20 Dec. 86.	......
Geo. Richards Greaves, K.C.M.G., C.B.	25 Oct. 82.	......	......
. Murray Miller, C.B.	31 Oct. 82.	......	......
. Augs. Smyth	1 Nov. 82.	......	......
. Jas. Charlemagne Dormer, C.B.	18 Nov. 82.	......	......
. Martin Cafe	28 Nov. 82.	25 Dec. 86.	......
nnes Middleton Colville, C.B.	2 Dec. 82.	12 Oct. 87.	......
e Hunt Bowles	5 Jan. 83.	14 May 87.	......
lter Doyly Kerrick	19 Jan. 83.	31 Dec. 88.	......
t. Straker Turton	2 Feb. 83.	......	......
wd. Chippindall, C.B.	13 Feb. 83.	22 Dec. 86.	......
id Jas. Welsh	24 Feb. 83.	......	......
. Bagot	23 Mar. 83.	......	......
Robt. Biddulph, K.C.M.G., C.B.	28 Mar. 83.	1 Oct. 87.	......
hd. Robertson Gloag	31 Mar. 83.	21 May 84.	......
Chas. Knight Pearson, K.C.M.G., C.B.	1 Apr. 83.	......	......
. Chas. Bancroft	3 Apr. 83.	31 Dec. 87.	......

Name.	M.-Gen.	L.-Gen.	Gen.
Alexr. Chas. Hector Stewart	10 Apr. 83.	......	......
Somerville Geo. Cam. Hogge	14 Apr. 83.	......	......
Jno. Ignatius Macdonell	18 Apr. 83.	27 Mar. 86.	......
Philip Edw. Victor Gilbert	1 May 83.	......	......
Robt. Jno. Hughes, C.B.	5 May 83.	......	......
Wm. Andr. Armstrong	13 May 83.	......	......
Jas Fras. Tennant, C.I.E.	26 May 83.	10 Jan. 84.	......
Richd. Hieram Sankey, C.B.	4 Jun. 83.	11 Jan. 84.	......
Geo. Fredk. de Berry	13 Jun. 83.	......	......
Jno. Thos. Dalyell	27 Jun. 83.	2 Oct. 86.	......
Chas. Van Notten Pole	1 Jul. 83.	......	......
Hy. Way Mawbey	3 Jul. 83.	......	......
Wm. Hy. Worthy Bennett	4 Jul. 83.	......	......
Jno. Julius Johnstone	21 Jul. 83.	......	......
Thos. Ignatius Maria Hog	26 Jul. 83.	11 Feb. 85.	......
Jno. Davis	1 Aug. 83.	......	......
Wm. Hy. Knight	7 Aug. 83.	......	......
Fras. Edwd. Edwards Wilson	8 Aug. 83.	......	......
Claud Alexander	21 Aug. 83.	......	......
Geo. Leslie	1 Sep. 83.	22 Apr. 87.	......
Edmd. Hy. Cox	3 Sep. 83.	5 Oct. 86.	21 May 8
Chas. Bulkeley Nurse	8 Sep. 83.	......	......
Edwd. Langford Dillon	14 Sep. 83.	......	......
Geo. Fredk. Campbell Bray	26 Sep. 83.	......	......
Hy. Fras. Bythesea	1 Oct. 83.	27 Mar. 86.	......
Hy. Kent	23 Oct. 83.	28 Aug. 86.	......
Sidney Chalmers	24 Oct. 83.	4 Mar. 87.	......
Chas. Fitzgerald	30 Oct. 83.	......	......
David MacFarlan	5 Nov. 83.	31 Dec. 88.	......
Hy. Cardew	16 Nov. 83.	......	......
Needham Thompson Parsons	17 Nov. 83.	......	......
Edwd. Horatio Hy. Foster	28 Nov. 83.	......	......
Edmond Fredk. Waterman	10 Dec. 83.	1 Jul. 87.	......
Chas. Phayre Hildebrand	,,	6 Mar. 87.	......
Jno. March Earle	16 Dec. 83.	1 Jul. 87.	......
Edwd. Saml. Jackson	,,	,,	......
Chas. Shaw de Neufville Lucas	31 Dec. 83.	......	......
Geo. Smart	1 Jan. 84.	2 Aug. 87.	......
Jas. Cadogan Parkinson Baillie	,,	2 Sep. 87.	......
Robt. Blair	,,	,,	......
Fredk. Schneider	,,	1 Jul. 87.	......
Fredk. Alexander	,,	,,	......
Geo. Byres Mainwaring	,,	,,	......
Chas. Hight	,,	,,	......
Geo. Pringle	,,	,,	......
Richd. Harte Keatinge	,,	,,	......
Jno. Dovan	,,	,,	......
Harry Smith Obbard	,,	,,	......
Chas. Thos. Palin	,,	,,	......
Hugh Rose	,,	,,	......
Robt. Mackenzie Macdonald	,,	,,	......
Jno. Gray Touch	,,	,,	......
Chas. Thompson	,,	,,	......
Chas. Fredk. Hicks	,,	,,	......
Alexr. Carnegie	,,	,,	......
Cuthbert Ward Burton	9 Jan. 84.	......	......
Jno. Fredk. Fischer	11 Jan. 84.	16 Sep. 86.	27 Jan. 8
Wm. West Goodfellow	12 Jan. 84.	22 Jan. 87.	......
Jos. Alexr. Smith	29 Jan. 84.	......	......
Hy. Jno. Maclean	1 Feb. 84.	......	......
Richd. Bateson	7 Feb. 84.	8 Jun. 87.	......

Name.	M.-Gen.	L.-Gen.	Gen.
Knox Rowan Niven	5 Mar. 84.	......	......
Wm. Alexr. Patr. Wyllie	12 Mar. 84.	......	......
Wm. Roberts Farmar	14 Mar. 84.	......	......
Robt. Crosse Stewart, C.B.	15 Mar. 84.	......	......
Gaspard Le Marchant Tupper	1 Apr. 84.	25 Oct. 87.	......
Hy. Jas. Bell	23 Apr. 84.	......	......
Sydney Darling	24 Apr. 84.	......	......
Jno. Edwd. Swindley	29 Apr. 84.	......	......
Sir Andr. Clarke	21 May 84.	27 Jul. 86.	......
Duncan Jno. McGregor	,,	,,	......
Sir Redvers Hy. Buller	,,	,,	......
Jno. Jas. Silverston O'Neill	9 Jun. 84.	......	......
Horace Alb. Browne	10 Jun. 84.	20 Sep. 87.	......
Fredk. Ernest Appleyard, C.B.	11 Jun. 84.	......	......
Hy. Fras. Hancock	21 Jun. 84.	......	......
Alfr. Wm. Adcock	2 Jul. 84.	......	......
Geo. Farquhar Kaye	16 Jul. 84.	......	......
Jno. Mullins	20 Jul. 84.	8 Sep. 86.	......
Julius Geo. Medley	,,	......	......
Hy. Miller	29 Jul. 84.	......	......
Thos. Netherton Harward	1 Aug. 84.	20 Mar. 85.	......
Wm. Robt. Houghton...	23 Aug. 84.	31 Mar. 88.	......
Wm. Butler Butler Shawe	,,	20 Sep. 87.	......
Geo. Chas. Girardot	27 Aug. 84.	......	......
Sir Wm. Bellairs, K.C.M.G.	4 Sep. 84.	7 Dec. 87.	......
Chas. Renny Blair	7 Sep. 84.	19 Oct. 87.	......
Lewis Wm. Buck, C.B.	,,	31 Mar. 88.	......
Chas. Jas. Hope Johnstone	10 Sep. 84.	......	......
Jas. Murray Straton	,,	......	......
Hon. Chas. Wemyss Thesiger	7 Oct. 84.	......	......
Edwd. Wm. Lloyd Wynne	11 Oct. 84.	......	......
Arth. Becher Marsack	25 Nov. 84.	31 Mar. 88.	......
Chas. Scott Elliot	,,	,,	......
Harry Cortlandt Anderson	,,	,,	......
Wm. Watts Corban	26 Nov. 84.	......	......
Alexr. Geo. Montgomery Moore	30 Dec. 84.	......	......
Sir Herbert Stewart, K.C.B.	19 Jan. 85.	......	......
Chas. Brisbane Ewart, C.B.	27 Jan. 85.	20 Jul. 88.	......
Fitzwilliam Fredk. Hunter	30 Jan. 85.	......	......
Thos. Elliott Hughes	11 Feb. 85.	......	......
Andr. Nugent	19 Feb. 85.	13 Nov. 86.	......
Stephen Hy. Edwd. Chamier	26 Feb. 85.	27 Oct. 86.	......
Thos. Andr. Lumsden Murray	1 Mar. 85.	......	......
Chas. Jas. Horne	4 Mar. 85.	......	......
Herbert Henderson James	14 Mar. 85.	31 Mar. 88.	......
Wm. Fraser Stephens	,,	,,	......
Fras. Fisher Hamilton, C.B.	19 Mar. 85.	......	......
Edwd. Marcus Beresford	20 Mar. 85.	......	......
Sir Wm. Hamilton, bt.	,,	......	......
Geo. Tito Brice	1 Apr. 85.	......	......
Fredk. Hardy	,,	......	......
Hon. Wm. Hy. Herbert	3 Apr. 85.	......	......
Horatio C. N. Blanckley	,,	......	......
Hon. Bernard Mathew Ward	25 Apr. 85.	2 Oct. 86.	......
Wm. Edmd. Moyses Reilly	1 May 85.	......	......
Sir Jno. Stokes	6 May 85.	25 Jan. 87.	......
Jno. Jago Trelawney	13 May 85.	......	......
Wm. Hy. Edgcom	24 May 85.	......	......
Thos. Nuttall	31 May 85.	1 Dec. 88.	......
Robt. W. Bland Hunt	4 Jun. 85.	......	......
Hy. Brackenbury, C.B.	15 Jun. 85.	1 Apr. 88	......

Name.	M.-Gen.	L.-Gen.	Gen.
Jas. Archd. Ruddell	21 Jun. 85.	......	......
Jno. Fredk. Sanders	,,	......	......
Chas. Patr. Stokes	23 Jun. 85.	......	......
Jos. Jordan, C.B.	24 Jun. 85.	......	......
Chas. Elgee	27 Jun. 85.	......	......
Walter Tuckfield Goldsworthy	1 Jul. 85.	......	......
Geo. Hy. Jno. Alexr. Fraser	,,	1 Apr. 88.	......
Fredk. Dobson Middleton, C.B.; aft. sir F.	,,	4 Nov. 87.	......
Jno. Prevost Battersby	2 Jul. 85.	......	......
Andrew C. K. Lock	,,	......	......
Richd. Preston, C.B.	,,	......	......
Geo. Fuller Walker	,,	......	......
Jas. Blair	,,	......	......
Mowbray Thomson	,,	......	......
Sir Chas. Jno. Stanley Gough, K.C.B.	,,	......	......
Chas. Hereford	8 Jul. 85.	......	......
Geo. Vincent Watson	,,	31 Dec. 87.	......
Brymer Fras. Schreiber, C.B.	11 Jul. 85.	......	......
Hon. Savage Mostyn, C.B.	,,	......	......
Jno. Sprot	18 Jul. 85.	19 Oct. 87.	......
Chas. Edmund Webber, C.B.	22 Jul. 85.	......	......
Wm. Starke	15 Aug. 85.	......	......
O'Bryen Bellingham Woolsey	26 Aug. 85.	......	......
Richd. Lewis Dashwood	6 Sep. 85.	......	......
Thos. Nicholl	7 Sep. 85.	......	......
Hy. Edwd. Jerome, V.C.	9 Sep. 85.	......	......
Cecil Mangles, C.B.	,,	......	......
Chas. Elphinstone Rennie	16 Sep. 85.	......	......
Cornwallis Oswald Maude	19 Sep. 85.	......	......
Jno. Alexr. Matth. Macdonald	,,	......	......
Arth. Drury	,,	......	......
Geo. Scougall Macbean	,,	......	......
Jno. Irwin Willes	,,	......	......
Wm. Geo. Mainwaring	,,	......	......
Wm. Anthy. Gib, C.B.	,,	......	......
Somerset Molyneux Wiseman Clarke	25 Sep. 85.	......	......
Jas. Sturgeon Hamilton Algar	9 Oct. 85.	......	......
Denzill Hammill	10 Oct. 85.	......	......
Robt. Nevill Gream	28 Oct. 85.	......	......
Michael Tweedie	1 Nov. 85.	......	......
Hon. Jas. Charlemagne Dormer	,,	......	......
Sylvester W. F. Moor Wilson	5 Nov. 85.	......	......
Edwd. M. Manningham-Buller	,,	......	......
Stanley De Burgh, C.B.	6 Nov. 85.	......	......
Jno. Michl. De Courcy Meade	7 Nov. 85.	22 Jun. 87.	......
Dawson Stockley Warren, C.B.	16 Nov. 85.	......	......
Fras. Eteson	17 Nov. 85.	......	......
Robt. Comyn Lavie	20 Nov. 85.	......	......
Jas. Jno. McLeod Innes, V.C.	28 Nov. 85.	16 Mar. 86.	......
Wm. Nassau Lees	,,	......	......
Wm. Paterson	6 Dec. 85.	......	......
Noel Hamlyn Harris	9 Dec. 85	......	......
Thos. John	,,	......	......
Fredk. Richd. Solly Flood, C.B.	10 Dec. 85.	......	......
Chas. Vernon Jenkins	11 Dec. 85.	......	......
Walter Coningham	,,	......	......
Robt. Jno. Hay	16 Dec. 85.	......	......
Arth. Tulloch	18 Dec. 85	......	......
Robt. Hale	20 Dec. 85.	......	......
Rowley Sale Hill	,,	......	......
Edwd. Hy. Clive	26 Dec. 85.	......	......

Name.	M.-Gen.	L.-Gen.	Gen.
Wm. Jno. Williams. C.B.	4 Jan. 86.	......	......
Geo. F. Blake	5 Jan. 86.	......	......
Hy. Blakeney Hayward	13 Jan. 86.	......	......
Nathl. Stevenson	14 Jan. 86.	......	......
Geo. Wm. Fraser	,,	......	......
Hungerford Meyer Boddam	,,	......	......
Alexr. Bond	,,	......	......
Wm. Chase Parr	,,	......	......
Geo. Herbert Murray Aynsley	,,	......	......
Sir Chas. Cooper Johnson	,,	......	......
Geo. Crommelin Hawkin	,,	......	......
Edwd. Winterton Dun	,,	......	......
Abrm. Chas. Bunbury	,,	......	......
Fras. Dawson	,,	......	......
Geo. Forbes Hogg	,,	......	......
Clifford Parsons	17 Jan. 86.	......	......
Edwd. Thos. S. Lawrence McGwire... ...	21 Jan. 86.	......	......
Jno. Granvill Harkness	29 Jan. 86.	......	......
Geo. Briggs	31 Jan. 86.	......	......
Fras. Wm. Thomas	1 Feb. 86.	......	......
Chas. Wm. Campbell	,,	......	......
Harry Chippindale Plunkett Rice	,,	......	......
Chas. Pulteney Forbes	3 Feb. 86.	......	......
Fredk. Roome	4 Feb. 86.	......	......
Brooking Soady	6 Feb. 86.	......	......
Thos. Gilbert Kennedy	,,	......	......
Geo. Hearn	10 Feb. 86.	......	......
Howard Codrington Dowker...	,,	......	......
Hy. Evelyn Coningham	12 Feb. 86.	......	......
Fras. Towry Adeane Law	13 Feb. 86.	......	......
Mangles Jas. Brander	16 Feb. 86.	......	......
Jas. Michael, C.S.I.	,,	......	......
Saml. Black	,,	......	......
Lewis Blyth Hole	24 Feb. 86.	......	......
Robt. Andrew Cole	28 Feb. 86.	......	......
Cyril Hugh Pennycuick Ducat	3 Mar. 86.	......	......
Robt. Holt Truell	,,	......	......
Sir Geo. Tomkyns Chesney, C.S.I.	16 Mar. 86.	10 Mar. 87.	......
Andr. Robt. Clephane	17 Mar. 86.	......	......
Robt. Stephenson Mosely	,,	......	......
Ern. Augs. Wm., &c. D. of Cumberland, K.G.	19 Mar. 86.	......	......
Hy. Jas. Buchanan	,,	......	......
Robt. Cotton Money	20 Mar. 86.	......	......
Fitzmaurice Beauchamp	27 Mar. 86.	......	......
Hon. Chas. Jno. Addington	,,	......	......
Hales Wilkie	,,	......	......
Wm. Howley Goodenough	1 Apr. 86.	......	......
Jno. Chas. Hay	,,	......	......
Woulfe Hay	4 Apr. 86.	......	......
Geo. Hy. Waller	7 Apr. 86.	......	......
Geo. Lodwick Warder	8 Apr. 86.	......	......
Brownlow Hugh Mathew	9 Apr. 86.	......	......
Jno. Gordon Graham	10 Apr. 86.	......	......
Geo. Fergus Graham	,,	......	......
Philip Bedingfield	20 Apr. 86.	......	......
Edwd. Harnett	23 Apr. 86.	......	......
Alexr. Hy. Edwd. Campbell	1 May 86.	......	......
Geoffrey Mairis	9 May 86.	......	......
David Wilson Laughton	10 May 86.	......	......
Chas. Hy. Hall	18 May 86.	......	......
Edwd. Owen Leggatt.	,,	......	......

Name.	M.-Gen.	L.-Gen.	Gen.
Richd. Alexr. Moore	18 May 86.	......	......
Chas. Edwd. Bates	,,	......	......
Jno. Miles	,,	......	......
Wm. Chas. Robt. Mylne	,,	......	......
Chas. Nedham...	,,	......	......
Jno. Wood Rideout	,,	......	......
Walter Theodore Chitty	,,	......	......
Thos. Mowbray Baumgartner	,,	......	......
Robt. Murray, C.S.I.	,,	......	......
Jas. Kempt Couper	,,	......	......
Wm. Jas. Pratt Barlow	,,	......	......
Regd. Quinton Mainwaring	,,	......	......
Chas. Batchelor	,,	......	......
Hy. Geo. White	19 May 86.	......	......
Thos. Parkyns Smith...	25 May 86.	......	......
Jas. Richd. Knox Tredennick	26 May 86.	......	......
Chas. Edwd. Oldershaw	29 May 86.	......	......
Wm. Hy. Graham	,,	......	......
Wm. Hall Noble	31 May 86.	......	......
Harry de Brett	,,	......	......
Jno. Jas. Heywood	,,	......	......
Jas. Black Reid	1 Jun. 86.	......	......
Edwd. Lindsay Hawkins	,,	......	......
Hardress Edmond Waller	3 Jun. 86.	......	......
Augs. Kirkwood Comber	12 Jun. 86.	......	......
Wm. Robt. Gordon	,,	......	......
Jas. Burn	,,	......	......
Alfr. Fitzhugh...	14 Jun. 86.	......	......
Fredk. Peere Williams Freeman	15 Jun. 86.	......	......
Ernest Archd. Berger	18 Jun. 86.	......	......
Augs. Fredk. De Butts Dixon	23 Jun. 86.	......	......
Jas. Lawson	29 Jun. 86.	......	......
Chas. Annesley Benson	1 Jul. 86.	......	......
Fredk. Cortland Anderson	,,	......	......
Montgomery Hunter	,,	......	......
Philip Smith	,,	......	......
Edwd. Dandridge	,,	......	......
Chas. Jas. Jennings	,,	......	......
Jas. Nichs. Brutton Hewett	,,	......	......
Patr. Jno. Campbell	5 Jul. 86.	......	......
Hy. McDonell De Went Douglas	10 Jul. 86.	......	......
Regd. Colvil Wm. Mitford	,,	......	......
Howard Sutton Jones	18 Jul. 86.	......	......
Fredk. Robt. Cameron Crofton	21 Jul. 86.	......	......
Gordon Douglas Pritchard	27 Jul. 86.	......	......
Edwd. Jno. Oldfield	28 Jul. 86.	......	......
Alured Clarke Johnson	29 Jul. 86.	......	......
Clennell Collingwood	11 Aug. 86.	......	......
Wm. Godfrey Dunham Massy	28 Aug. 86.	......	......
Dawson Kelly Evans	,,	......	......
Sir Thos. Durand Baker, K.C.B.	1 Sep. 86.	......	......
Geo. Brydges	3 Sep. 86.	......	......
Jno. Wm. Cleland-Henderson	4 Sep. 86.	......	......
Edwd. Morris Cherry	6 Sep 86.	......	......
Hy. Alexr. Brownlow	8 Sep. 86.	25 Nov. 86.	......
Hy. Wortham	,,	......	......
Sir Cromer Ashburnham	13 Sep. 86.	......	......
Edwd. Tanner	15 Sep. 86.	......	......
Edwd. Chas. Sparshott Williams	16 Sep. 86.	......	......
Wm. Stafford Bailey	19 Sep. 86.	......	......

Name.	M.-Gen.	L.-Gen.	Gen.
Chas. Jas. Hughes	26 Sep. 86.	......	......
Geo. Buchanan Bevan	27 Sep. 86.	......	......
Jno. Newbold Wilson...	28 Sep. 86	......	......
Thos. Obbard	30 Sep. 86.	......	......
Geo. Robt. Fitzroy	1 Oct. 86.	......	......
Edwd. McLaughlin	,,	......	......
Wm. Hanbury Hawley	2 Oct. 86.	......	......
Arth. Lyttelton Lyttelton Annesley ...	,,	......	......
Chas. Lorrain Woodruffe	19 Oct. 86.	......	......
Jno. Thos. Twigge	,,	......	......
Regd. Gother Thorold	,,	......	......
Geo. Stanley Hooper	20 Oct. 86.	......	......
Thos. Edwd. Gordon, C.B., C.S.I.	21 Oct. 86.	......	......
Benjn. Lumsden Gordon, C.B.	27 Oct. 86.	......	......
Fredk. Close	1 Nov. 86.	......	......
Jas. Miller	4 Nov. 86.	......	......
Robt. Stanwix Robertson	5 Nov. 86.	......	......
Hy. Barlow Maule	6 Nov. 86.	......	......
Townsend Aremberg de Moleyns	,,	......	......
Wm. Hy. Wardell	,,	......	......
Thos. Trophinus Hodges	,,	......	......
Geo. Fredk. Gildea	10 Nov. 86.	......	......
Emeric Streatfield Berkeley...	11 Nov. 86.	......	......
Jno. Keith Fraser	13 Nov. 86.	......	......
Fras. Gellie	,,	......	......
Hy. Fanshawe Davies	18 Nov. 86.	......	......
Fras. Edwd. Halliday	22 Nov. 86.	21 May 88.	......
Jos. Bonus	25 Nov. 86.	......	......
Robt. Hoskins Phelips	1 Dec. 86.	......	......
Sir Jno. Wm. Campbell	8 Dec. 86.	......	......
Arth. Stewart Hunter	,,	......	......
Richmond Houghton	9 Dec. 86.	......	......
Alexr. McGoun	12 Dec. 86.	......	......
Wm. Bannerman	20 Dec. 86.	......	......
Thos. Spence Hawkes	,,	......	......
Isaac Forsyth MacAndrew	,,	......	......
Jno. Jas. Hood Gordon	,,	......	......
Hy. Melvill	,,	......	......
Edwd. Staveley	21 Dec. 86.	......	......
Hy. Edmeades...	,,	......	......
Hy. Richd. Legge Newdigate	22 Dec. 86.	......	......
Wm. Munnings Lees	25 Dec. 86.	......	......
Edwd. Melville Lawford	,,	......	......
Lord Jno. Hy. Taylour	29 Dec. 86.	......	......
Richd. Barter	8 Jan. 87.	......	......
Geo. Julius Melliss	,,	......	......
Wm. Smith	11 Jan. 87.	......	......
Douglas Gordon Seafield St. Jno. Grant ..	14 Jan. 87.	......	......
Mostyn de la Poer Beresford	16 Jan. 87.	14 Dec. 87.	......
Richd. Crundel Brook	17 Jan. 87.	......	......
Godfrey Clerk...	21 Jan. 87.	......	......
Sir Chas. Metcalfe MacGregor	22 Jan. 87.	......	......
Fras. Wm. Hamilton	23 Jan. 87.	......	......
Chas. Grant	28 Jan. 87.	......	......
Sir Howard Craufurd Elphinstone, K.C.B., C.M.G.	29 Jan. 87.	......	......
Thos. Mansell Warren	,,	......	.....
Wm. Edwd. Marsden...	31 Jan. 87.	......	......
Hon. Raymond H. de Montmorency ...	1 Feb. 87.	......	......
Jas. Kiero Watson	2 Feb. 87.	......	.....

Name.	M.-Gen.	L.-Gen.	Gen.
Geo. Andr. Walker	6 Feb. 87.	......	......
Geo. Arnold Laughton	,,	......	......
Robt. Mallaby...	,,	......	......
Brudyshe Walton	,,	......	......
Sir Hugh Hy. Gough...	,,	......	......
Jno. Edwd. Allen	12 Feb. 87.	......	......
Richd. Longford Leir	,,	......	......
Fredk. Karslake	,,	......	......
Walter Newman	15 Feb. 87.	......	......
Chas. Jos. McMahon	17 Feb. 87.	......	......
Geo. Ayton Crastor	21 Feb. 87.	......	......
Jno.Le Mesurier	22 Feb. 87.	24 Mar. 87.	......
Archd. Geo. Douglas Logan...	,,	......	......
Wm. Hy. Abbott	2 Mar. 87.	......	......
Alan Murray	4 Mar. 87.	......	......
Jno. Pringle Sherriff	,,	......	......
Jas. Gunter	7 Mar. 87.	......	......
Luke O'Connor	9 Mar. 87.	......	......
Hy. Clement Wilkinson	,,	......	......
Æneas Perkins	,,	......	......
Lewis Percival...	11 Mar. 87.	......	......
Chas. Picot	16 Mar. 87.	......	......
Jas. Briggs	18 Mar. 87.	......	......
Jno. Hubbard White	24 Mar. 87.	......	......
Thos. Edmd. Byrne	31 Mar. 87.	......	......
Julian Hamilton Hall...	1 Apr. 87.	......	......
Wm. Wiltshire Lynch...	,,	......	......
Lionel Smith Warren...	,,	......	......
Geo. Nesbitt Stephens	,,	......	......
Wm. Harris Burland	,,	......	......
Arth. Donald Butter	,,	......	......
Jno. Ormsby Vandeleur	5 Apr. 87.	......	......
Wm. Dobree Carey	8 Apr. 87.	......	......
Hon. Edwd. Archd. Brab. Acheson... ...	13 Apr. 87.	......	......
Jas. Morris Toppin	,,	......	......
Fredk. Gasper Le Grand	15 Apr. 87.	......	......
Sir Christr. Chas. Teesdale	22 Apr. 87.	......	......
Chas. Augs. Fitzgerald Creagh	23 Apr. 87.	......	......
Robt. Jno. Jocelyn Stewart	30 Apr. 87.	......	......
Archd. Lewis Playfair	1 May 87.	......	......
Wm. Knox Leet	,,	......	......
Robt. Bennett	5 May 87.	......	......
Jno. Blaksley	7 May 87.	......	......
Herbert Le Cocq	12 May 87.	......	......
Geo. Digby Barker	14 May 87.	......	......
Wm. Booth	,,	......	......
Fredk. Wm. Best Parry	,,	......	......
Hugh Shaw	22 May 87.	......	......
Edmd. Davidson Smith	30 May 87.	......	......
Wm. Jno. Chads	8 Jun. 87.	......	......
Chas. Lewis Raikes	,,	......	......
Saml. Jas. Graham	22 Jun. 87.	......	......
Algn. Augs. Stewart	24 Jun. 87.	......	......
Nathl. Cricklow Ramsay	27 Jun. 87.	......	......
Horatio Gordon Robley	,,	......	......
Thos. Talbot	29 Jun. 87.	......	......
Wm. Stewart Richardson	30 Jun. 87.	......	......
Harry Hammon Lyster	1 Jul. 87.	......	......
Sir Geo. Stewart White	,,	......	......
Jno. Pennock Campbell	,,	......	......
Jno. Wm. Green	,,	......	......

Name.	M.-Gen.	L.-Gen.	Gen.
Basil Clifton Westby	1 Jul. 87.	......	......
Jno. Charley	,,	......	......
Arth. Hales	,,	......	......
Astley Fellowes Terry	,,	......	......
Arth. Hy. Taylor	,,	......	......
Wm. Moore Dickinson	4 Jul. 87.	......	......
Wm. Richd. White	6 Jul. 87.	......	......
Hugh Mackenzie	7 Jul. 87.	......	......
Geo. Shepherd Stevens	12 Jul. 87.	......	......
Wm. Cooke O'Shaughnessy	,,	......	......
Wm. Octavius Foord	16 Jul. 87.	......	......
Thos. Lynden Bell	21 Jul. 87.	......	......
Thos. Wm. Sneyd	,,	......	......
Jas. Landon Watt	30 Jul 87.	......	......
Thos. Lowndes...	1 Aug. 87.	......	......
Geo. Farquhar Irving Graham	,,	......	......
Stephen Wm. Barrow Sherman	,,	......	......
Sir Jno. Hudson, K.C.B.	2 Aug. 87.	......	......
Fredk. Edwd. Sotheby	9 Aug. 87.	......	......
Hy. Geo. Delafosse	10 Aug. 87.	......	......
Josias Dunn	12 Aug. 87.	......	......
Edwd. Birch	19 Aug. 87.	......	......
Robt. Fras. Firth	20 Aug. 87.	......	......
Wm. Edwd. Montague	24 Aug. 87.	......	......
Thos. Prittie Cosby	27 Aug. 87	......	......
St. John Bally...	31 Aug. 87.	......	......
Chas. Edwd. Blowers...	1 Sep. 87.	......	......
Hy. Moore, C.B., C.I.E.	2 Sep. 87.	......	......
Norman Macdonald	,,	......	......
Fredk. Fras. Daniell	5 Sep. 87.	......	......
Chas. Edmd. Layard	6 Sep. 87.	......	......
Jno. Crossland Hay	17 Sep. 87.	......	......
Hy. Thos. Arbuthnot	21 Sep. 87.	......	......
Hugh Parker Montgomery	22 Sep. 87.	......	......
Fredk. Wheeler	24 Sep. 87.	......	......
Arth. Fredk. Warren	30 Sep. 87.	......	......
Wm. Stirling	1 Oct. 87.	......	......
Chas. Jas. Tyler	,,	......	......
Jas. Peattie Morgan	,,	......	......
Richd. Sadlier	,,	......	......
Chas. David Chalmers	,,	......	......
Thos. Clarke	,,	......	......
Edmd. Ghuznee Morrogh	,,	......	......
Hy. Spencer Palmer	,,	......	......
Robt. Barton	,,	......	......
Robt. Owen Jones	,,	......	......
Talbot Bradford Middleton Glascock ...	5 Oct. 87.	......	......
Wm. de Wilton Roche Thackwell	,,	......	......
Jas Harwood Rocke	12 Oct. 87.	......	......
Fredk. Horace Arth. Seymour	,,	......	......
Thos. Alphonso Cary	,,	......	......
Colin Mackenzie	16 Oct. 87.	......	......
Hy. Holden Steward	17 Oct. 87.	......	......
Wm. Drummond Scrase Dickins	19 Oct. 87.	......	......
Hy. Ellenborough Dyneley	,,	......	......
Geo. Hy. Wm. Fagan	,,	......	......
Grant Blunt	21 Oct. 87.	......	......
Chas. Edwd. Luard	,,	......	......
Chas. O'Loughlin Prendergast	24 Oct. 87.	......	......
Richd. Oldfield	25 Oct. 87.	......	......
Arth. Hill	26 Oct. 87.	......	......

Name.	M.-Gen.	L.-Gen.	Gen.
Jas. Gibbons Smyth	26 Oct. 87.	......	......
Wm. Lambert Yonge	29 Oct. 87.	......	......
Geo. Stewart	31 Oct. 87.	......	......
Geo. Carden	,,	......	......
Clement Jas. Griffiths	1 Nov. 87.	......	......
Oliver Richardson Newmarch	,,	......	......
Markham Le Fer Taylor	,,	......	......
Edwd. Keate	,,	......	......
Donald Roderick Cameron	,,	......	......
Hy. Bond	,,	......	......
Jno. Thompson	4 Nov. 87.	......	......
Jas. Bevan Edwards	5 Nov. 87.	......	......
Alex. Lyon Emerson	9 Nov. 87.	......	......
Jas. Murray Thos. Simpson	,,	......	......
Jno. Charlton Kinchant	19 Nov. 87.	......	......
Edw. Dorrien Newbolt	,,	......	......
Fredk. Wm. Lambton	22 Nov. 87.	......	......
Edwd. Wm. Saunders	23 Nov. 87.	......	......
Wm. Morritt Barn. Bond	24 Nov. 87.	......	......
Alfred Templeman	30 Nov. 87.	......	......
Sir Hy. Peter Ewart	7 Dec. 87	......	......
Wm. Jno. Gillespie	,,	......	......
Wm. Hy. Deedes	,,	......	......
Robt. Children Whitehead, C.B.	14 Dec. 87.	......	......
Jno. Haughton...	,,	......	......
Eust. Beaum. Burnaby	,,	......	......
Hy. Chamberlayne Farrell	,,	......	......
Geo. Alf. Wilson	,,	......	......
Jno. Macvicar Burn	,,	......	......
Fitzroy Somerset Talbot	,,	......	......
Richd. Carruthers Budd	15 Dec. 87.	......	......
Wm. Keith	17 Dec. 87.	......	......
Hy. Darley Crozier	,,	......	......
Wm. Hy. Brooke Peters	,,	......	......
Jno. Byron	21 Dec. 87.	......	......
Fredk. Chenevix Trench	,,	......	......
Jno. Tilly	,,	......	......
Jno. Ryder Oliver	,,	......	......
Fredk. Milkington Kenyon Stow	,,	......	......
Wm. Fredk. Sandwith	23 Dec. 87.	......	......
Edwd. Jno. McNair	24 Dec. 87.	......	......
Nadolig Ximenes Gwynne	25 Dec. 87.	......	......
Geo. Hay Moncrieff	31 Dec. 87.	......	......
Fredk. Wm. Edwd. Forestier Walker ...	,,	......	......
Robt. Rollo Gillespie	,,	......	......
Geo. Balfour Traill	,,	......	......
Maunsell Mark Prendergast	,,	......	......
Robt. Wheeler	,,	......	......
Wm. Bally	,,	......	......
Ponsonby Sheppard	,,	......	......
Robt. Sandham	,,	......	......
Percy Guillemard Llewellyn Smith	,,	......	......
Edwd. Hy. Courtney	,,	......	......
Edwd. Micklem	,,	......	......
Jno. Fretcheville Dykes Donnelly	,,	......	......
Wm. Chas. F. Molyneux	,,	......	......
Richd. Wm. Erskine Dawson	,,	......	......
Arth. Phelps	13 Jan. 88.	......	......
Jno. Woulfe Keogh	18 Jan. 88.	......	......
Clement Metcalfe Browne	31 Jan. 88.	......	......

Name.	M.-Gen.	L.-Gen.	Gen.
Wm. Jas. Stuart	12 Feb. 88.	......	......
Arth. Edwd. Augs. Ellis	23 Feb. 88.	......	......
Alexr. Gordon Duff	17 Mar. 88.	......	......
Philip Story	23 Mar. 88.	......	......
Lionel D'Arcy Dunsterville	31 Mar. 88.	......	......
Chas. Doxat Clementson	,,	......	......
Thos. Wm. West Pierce, C.B.	,,	......	......
Thos. Lamb	,,	......	......
Hastings Fraser	,,	......	......
Wm. Munro	,,	......	......
Chas. Alexr. McMahon	,,	......	......
Jervis Harpur	31 Mar. 88.	......	......
Thos. Edwd. Webster	,,	......	......
Griffith Turner Jones...	,,	......	......
Wm. Hy. Apostoly Buttler	,,	......	......
Alb. Hy. Wilmot Williams	1 Apr. 88.	......	......
Harry McLeod	7 Apr. 88.	......	......
Hy. Brasnell Tuson, C.B.	21 May 88.	......	......
Wm. Cooper	11 Jul. 88.	......	......
Simpson Hackett	17 Jul. 88.	......	......
Geo. Alexr. Arbuthnot	19 Jul. 88.	......	......
Rd. Harrison	20 Jul. 88.	......	......
Hy. Cook	5 Aug. 88.	......	......
Chas. Mansfield Clarke	12 Aug. 88.	......	......
Ardley Hy. Falwasser Barny	29 Aug. 88.	......	......
Herbert Mark Garrett Purvis	12 Sep. 88.	......	......
Geo. Battye Fisher	8 Oct. 88.	.....	.. ..
Richd. Jas. Combe Marter	24 Nov. 88.	......	......
Chas. Thos. Haig	30 Nov. 88.	.....	......
Jno. Brenton Cox	1 Dec. 88.	......	......
Rowland Robt. Wallace	,,	......	.....
Ernest Aug. Green	,,	......	......
Octavius Ludlow Smith	,,	......	......
Jno. Durham Hall	,,	......	......
Wm. Turton Fagan	,,	.. ...	... ..
Thos. Wolrich Stansfeld	,,	......	......
Adam Hugh Montgomery Dickey	,,	......	......
Clements Robt. Shaw...	,,	......	......
Clement Jno. Smith	,,	......	......
Edwd. Lewis Hankin	3 Dec. 88.	......	......
Thos. Fras. Lloyd	16 Dec. 88.	......	......
Brabazon Hy. Pottinger	31 Dec. 88.	......	......

GOVERNORS OF CHELSEA HOSPITAL.

1691. Sir Thos. Ogle, Mar. 3.
1702. Col. Jno. Hales, Nov. 10.
1714. Brig.-gen. Thos. Stanwix, Jan. 13.
1720. Col. Chas. Churchill, June 6.
1727. Lt.-gen. Wm. Evans, June 20.
1740. Sir Robt. Rich, bt., May 6.
1768. Lt.-gen. sir Geo. Howard, Feb. 13.
1795. Gen. Geo., Marq. Townshend, July 6.
1796. Gen. sir Wm. Fawcett, K.B., July 12.
1804. Gen. sir David Dundas, K.B., Apr. 3.
1820. Gen. sir Saml. Hulse, Feb. 19.
1837. Gen. hon. sir Edwd. Paget, G.C.B., Jan. 10.
1849. Gen. sir Geo. Anson, G.C.B., May 18.
1849. Gen. sir Colin Halkett, K.C.B., Nov. 26.
1856. Gen. sir Edwd. Blakeney, G.C.B., Sept. 25.
1868. F. M. sir Alexr. Woodford, G.C.B., G.C.M.G., Aug. 3.
1870. Gen. sir Jno. Lysaght Pennefather, G.C.B., Aug. 27.
1872. Lt.-gen. sir Sydney Jno. Cotton, K.C.B., May 10.
1874. Gen. sir Patr. Grant, G.C.B., G.C.M.G., Feb. 24.

LIEUTENANT-GOVERNORS OF CHELSEA HOSPITAL.

1695. David Craufurd, Jan. 1.
1715. Col. Thos. Chudleigh, Jan. 14.
1726. Col. Wm. Wyndham, Apr. 15.
1730. Col. Thos. Norton, Apr. 22.
1748. John Cossley, July 3.
1765. Nathl. Smith, Nov. 6.
1773. John Campbell, Feb. 11.
1777. Bernard Hale, May 1.
1798. Gen. Wm. Dalrymple, Mar. 28.
1846. Gen Sir Geo. Anson, G.C.B., Feb. 23.
1849. Lt.-gen. Sir Andrew Fras. Barnard, G.C.B., G.C.H., Nov. 26.
1855. Gen. Sir Edwd. Blakeney, G.C.B., G.C.H. Feb. 6.
1856. Gen. Sir Alexr. Woodford, G.C.B., G.C.M.G., Sept. 25.
1807. Gen. Saml. Hulse, Mar.
1820. Lt.-gen. Sir Harry Calvert, bt. G.C.B., Feb. 19.
1826. Lt.-gen. Hon. Sir Alexr. Hope, G.C.B., Sept. 6.
1837. Lt.-gen. Sir Geo. Townshend Walker, bt., G.C.B., May 24.
1842. Gen. Sir Wm. Hy Clinton, G.C.B., Nov. 17.
1868. Col. Chas. Lennox Brownlow Maitland, May 9.
1874. Col. Richd. Herbert Gall, C.B., Mar. 1.
1881. Col. Richd. Wadeson, Mar. 26.
1855. Col. Edwd. Andr. Stuart, Mar. 13.

JUDGE-ADVOCATES GENERAL.

THE Judge-Advocate General and Judge Martial of all the Forces is an officer of considerable responsibility. He is the legal adviser of the sovereign and of the commander-in-chief in military cases, and by his authority all general courts-martial are held. In his office are deposited the originals of all such proceedings, and on his receipt of them they are examined, and either deposited as correct, or communicated upon, or submitted by the Judge Advocate General to Her Majesty for royal approval, or for pardon, or revision, as, in the opinion of this officer, the case may require.

The office has for many years been a political one, the holder resigning on a change of ministry.

Judge-Advocates General.

Down to 1847 the dates are those of the actual entrance upon office, not of the appointment, which is usually a few days earlier; or of the patent, commonly some days later than those adopted in this list. From 1847 the dates are those of the *Gazette* notices of the appointment.

1666. Dr. Saml. Barrowe, Jan.
1684. Geo. Clarke.
1705. Thos. Byde.
1715. Edwd. Hughes.
1734. Sir Hy. Hoghton, bt.
1741. Thos. Morgan.
1768. Chas. Gould, aft. sir Chas. Gould-Morgan, bt.; knt. 1779; cr. a bar. 1792, when he assumed the name of Morgan.
1806. Nathl. Bond, Mar 8.
1807. Richd. Ryder, Dec. 4.
1809. Chas. Manners-Sutton, Nov. 8.
1817. John Beckett, aft. bt., June 25.
1827. Jas. Abercromby, May 12; aft. ld. Dunfermline.
1828. Sir John Beckett, bt., *again*, Feb. 2.
1830. Robt. Grant, aft. sir R., Dec. 2.
1834. Robt. Cutlar Fergusson, July 7.
1834. Sir Jno. Beckett, bt., *again*, Dec. 22.
1835. Robt. Cutlar Fergusson, *again*, Apr. 25.
1838. Wm. St. Julien Arabin, Nov. 6.
1839. Sir Geo. Grey, bt., Feb. 21.
1841. Richd. Lalor Shiel, June 26.
Jno. Nicholl, Sep. 14.
1846. Jas. Stuart Wortley, Jan. 31.
Chas. Buller, July 14.
1847. Wm. Goodenough Hayter, aft. sir W., Dec. 30.

1849. Sir David Dundas, May 26, **G.**
1852. Geo. Bankes, Feb. 28, **G.**
Hon. Chas. Pelham Villiers, Dec. 30, **G.**
1858. Jno. Robt. Mowbray, Mar. 13, **G.**
1859. Thos. Emerson Headlam, June 24, **G.**
1866. Jno. Robt. Mowbray, *again*, July 12, **G.**
1868. Sir Colman Michael O'Loghlen, Dec. 16, **G.**
1870. Jno. Robt. Davison, Dec. 28, **G.**
1871. Sir Robt. Jos. Phillimore, D.C.L., Judge of the Admy. Court, May 17, **G.** Held the office pending a re-arrangement of its duties.
1873. Acton Smee Ayrton, Aug. 21, **G.**
1874. Stephen Cave, Mar. 7, **G.**
1875. Geo. Augs. Fredk. Cavendish-Bentinck, Nov. 24, **G.**
1880. Geo. Osborne Morgan, May 7, **G.**
1885. Wm. Thackeray Marriott, aft. sir W., July 13, **G.**
1886. Jno. Wm. Mellor, Feb. 22, **G.**
1886. Wm. Thackeray Marriott, aft. sir W., *again*, Aug. 9, **G.**

PART XVI. MISCELLANEOUS.

UNDER this heading are included a few lists which cannot be classified under any of the preceding titles, and which, indeed, can hardly be considered as strictly of an official character.

PRESIDENTS OF THE ROYAL COLLEGE OF PHYSICIANS OF ENGLAND.

PHYSICIANS were first incorporated in 1518 under letters patent, followed by acts of parliament, 32 Hen. VIII., cap. 40 (1540), and 1 Mary, sess. 2, cap. 9 (1553). The title of "ROYAL" was first adopted in 1858.

PRESIDENTS OF THE ROYAL COLLEGE OF PHYSICIANS OF ENGLAND FROM 1800.

1796. Thos. Gisborne.
1804. Sir Lucas Pepys.
1811. Sir Fras. Milman, bt.
1813. John Latham.
1820. Sir Hy. Halford, bt.
1844. John Ayrton Paris.
1857. Thos. Mayo.
1862. Thos. Watson, aft. bt.
1867. Jas. Alderson, aft. sir J.
1871. Geo. Burrows, aft. bt.
1876. Jas. Risdon Bennett, aft. sir J.
1881. Sir Wm. Jenner, bt.
1888. Sir Andr. Clark, bt.

MASTERS AND PRESIDENTS OF THE ROYAL COLLEGE OF SURGEONS OF ENGLAND.

BARBERS AND SURGEONS were first incorporated in 1540 under 32 Hen. VIII., cap 42. In 1745 the SURGEONS were formed into a separate corporation under 18 Geo. II., cap. 15. The title of "ROYAL" was first adopted under a charter obtained in 1843.

MASTERS OF THE ROYAL COLLEGE OF SURGEONS FROM 1800.

1800. Chas. Hawkins.
Wm. Long.
1801. Geo. Chandler.
1802. Thos. Keate.
1803. Sir Chas. Blicke.
1804. David Dundas, aft. bt.
1805. Thompson Forster.
1806. Chas. Hawkins, *again.*
1807. Sir Jas. Earle.
1808. Geo. Chandler, *again.*
1809. Thos. Keate, *again.*
1810. Sir Chas. Blicke, *again.*
1811. David Dundas, *again*
1812. Thompson Forster, *again.*
1813. Sir Everard Home, bt.
1814. Sir Wm. Blizard.
1815. Hy. Cline.
1816. Wm. Norris.
1817. Sir Jas. Earle, *again.*
Geo. Chandler, *again.*
1818. Thos. Keate, *again.*
1819. Sir David Dundas, bt., *again.*
1820. Thompson Forster, *again.*

PRESIDENTS OF THE ROYAL COLLEGE OF SURGEONS.

1821 Sir Everard Home, bt., *again.*
1822. Sir Wm. Blizard, *again.*
1823. Hy. Cline, *again.*
1824. Wm. Norris, *again.*
1825. Wm. Lynn.
1826. John Abernethy.
1827. Sir Astley Paston Cooper, bt.
1828. Sir Anthony Carlisle.
1829. Honoratus Leigh Thomas.
1830. Richd. Clement Headington.
Robt. Keate.
1831. Ditto.
1832. John Painter Vincent.
1833. Geo. Jas. Guthrie.
1834. Anthony White.
1835. John Goldwyer Andrews.
1836. Sir Astley Paston Cooper, bt., *again.*
1837. Sir Anthony Carlisle, *again.*
1838. Honoratus Leigh Thomas, *again.*
1839. Robt. Keate, *again.*
1840. John Painter Vincent, *again.*
1841. Geo. Jas. Guthrie, *again.*
1842. Anthony White, *again.*
1843. John Goldwyer Andrews, *again.*
1844. Sir Benj. Collins Brodie, bt.
1845. Saml. Cooper.
1846. Wm. Lawrence.
1847. Benj. Travers.
1848. Edwd. Stanley.
1849. Jos. Hy. Green.
1850. Jas. Moncrieff Arnott.
1851. John Flint South.
1852. Cæsar Hy. Hawkins.
1853. Jas. Luke.
1854. Geo. Jas. Guthrie, *again.*
1855. Wm. Lawrence, *again.*
1856. Benjn. Travers, *again.*
1857. Edwd. Stanley, *again.*
1858. Jos. Hy. Green, *again.*
1859. Jas. Moncrieff Arnott, *again.*
1860. John Flint South, *again.*
1861. Cæsar Hy. Hawkins, *again.*
1862. Jas. Luke, *again.*
1863. Fredc. Carpenter Skey.
1864. Jos. Hodgson.
1865. Thos. Wormald.
1866. Richd. Partridge.
1867. John Hilton.
1868. Richd. Quain.
1869. Edwd. Cock.
1870. Sir Wm. Fergusson, bt
1871. Geo. Busk.
1872. Hy. Hancock.
1873. Thos. Blizard Curling.
1874. Fredk. Le Gros Clark.
1875. Sir Jas. Paget, bt.
1876. Prescott Gardner Hewett, aft. bt
1877. John Birkett.
1878. John Simon, C.B.
1879. Luther Holden.
1880. John Eric Ericsen.
1881. Sir Wm. Jas. Erasmus Wilson
1882. Thos. Spencer Wells, aft. bt.
1883. John Marshall.
1884. John Cooper Forster.
1885. Wm. Scovell Savory.
1886. Ditto.
1887. Ditto.
1888. Ditto.

PRESIDENTS OF THE ROYAL SOCIETY.

The Royal Society was established about 1660, and incorporated by Chas. II. by Charters dated July 15, 1662, April 22, 1663, and April 8, 1669, under the title of "The President, Council, and "Fellowship of the Royal Society of London for improving Natural "Knowledge."

Presidents of the Royal Society.

(From *Haydn's Dictionary of Dates.*)

1660. Sir Robt. Moray, up to incorporation.
1663. Wm., visc. Brouncker, 1st Pres. aft. incorporation.
1677. Sir Jos. Williamson.
1680. Sir Christr. Wren.
1682. Sir Jno. Hoskins.
1683. Sir Cyril Wyche.
1684. Saml. Pepys.
1686. John, E. of Carberry.
1689. Thomas, E. of Pembroke
1690. Sir Robt. Southwell.
1695. Chas. Montague, aft. E. of Halifax.
1698. John, ld. Somers.
1703. Sir Isaac Newton.
1727. Sir Hans Sloane.
1741. Martin Folkes.
1752. Geo., E. of Macclesfield.
1764. Jas., E. of Morton.
1768. Jas. Burrow.
1768. Jas. West.
1772. Jas. Burrow, *again*.
1772. Sir Jno. Pringle.
1778. Sir Jos. Banks.
1820. Wm. Hyde Wollaston.
Sir Humphry Davy
1827. Davis Gilbert.
1830. Aug. Fredk., D. of Sussex.
1838. Spencer Josh. Alwyne, M. of Northampton.
1848. Wm., E. of Rosse.
1854. Jno., ld. Wrottesley.
1858. Sir Benj. Collins Brodie, bt.
1861. M.-Gen. sir Edw. Sabine.
1871. Geo. Biddell Airy, aft. sir G.
1873. Jos. Dalton Hooker, aft. sir J.
1878. Wm. Spottiswoode.
1883. Thos. Hy. Huxley.
1886. Geo. Gabriel Stokes, aft. bt.

PRESIDENTS OF THE ROYAL INSTITUTION

The Royal Institution was established in March 1799 and incorporated by Geo. III., Jan. 13, 1800, under the title of "The Royal Institution "of Great Britain for the diffusing knowledge and facilitating the "general introduction of useful mechanical inventions and improvements, "and for teaching by courses of philosophical lectures and experiments "the application of science to the common purposes of life." Its constitution was enlarged in 1810 under 50 Geo. III., cap. 51 (*Loc. and Pers.*)

Presidents of the Royal Institution.

1799. Sir Jos. Banks.
1800. Geo., E. of Winchilsea and Nottingham.
1813. Geo. Jno., E. Spencer.
1815. Thos., E. of Chichester.
1817. Edwd. Adolphus, D. of Somerset.
1842. Algn., ld. Prudhoe, aft. D. of Northumberland.
1865. Sir Hy. Holland, bt.
1873. Algn. Geo., D. of Northumberland.

PRESIDENTS OF THE ROYAL ACADEMY OF ARTS.

The Royal Academy was incorporated Dec. 10, 1768. Previous to this there had been a Society of Artists which met in St. Peter's Court, St. Martin's Lane about 1739, and was afterwards established as the Society of Incorporated Artists, which held its first exhibition in 1760.

Presidents of the Royal Academy.

(From *Haydn's Dictionary of Dates.*)

1768. Joshua Reynolds, aft. sir J.
1792. Benjn. West, res. 1805.
1805. Jas. Wyatt.
1806. Benjn. West, *again*.
1820. Sir Thos. Lawrence.
1830. Martin Archer Shee, aft. sir M.
1850. Chas. Lock Eastlake, aft. sir C.
1866. Sir Edwin Landseer, elect. but decl.
Fras. Grant, aft. sir F.
1878. Fredk. Leighton, aft. sir F.

ASTRONOMERS ROYAL.

(From *Haydn's Dictionary of Dates.*)

1675. John Flamsteed.
1719. Edmd. Halley.
1742. Jas. Bradley.
1762. Nathl. Bliss.
1765. Nevil Maskelyne.
1811. John Pond.
1835. Geo. Biddell Airy, aft. sir G,
1881. Wm. Hy. Mahoney Christie.

ADDENDUM.

AMBASSADORS TO ECUADOR.

(Accidentally omitted from p. 135.)

1854. Walter Cope, ch d'a. and C.G., Oct. 11.
1861. Geo. Fagan, ch. d'a. and C.G., Apr. 7.
1865. Lt.-col. Edwd. St John Neale, ch. d'a. and C.G., Aug. 14.
1867. Fredc. Hamilton, ch. d'a. and C.G. Feb. 9; min. res. and C.G., Dec. 12, 1872.
1883. Christian Wm. Lawrence, min. res. and C.G., Apr. 28.

INDEX OF NAMES.

The names appear in this Index, as in the body of the work, according to the actual style or title of the official at the date of his appointment to each particular office. Cross references are given to each of his prior or subsequent titles, *provided his name appears in the body as holding office whilst enjoying that title* :—*ex. gr.*

Pole, Hon. Wm. Well., aft. ld. Maryborough and 3rd E. of Mornington, *q.v.*, P.C. 208; C. Treas. Ir. 561; Ch. Ex. Ir. 561; Ch. Sec. Ir. 563.
Maryborough, Wm., ld., form. Hon. W. W. Pole, *q.v.*, aft. 3rd E. of Mornington, *q.v.*; L.T. 160; M.B.H. 303; Postm. G. 238.
Mornington, Wm., 3rd E. of, form. Hon. W. W. Pole and ld. Maryborough, *q.v.*, G.C.H. 786.

Therefore, to obtain a complete list of all the offices held by each person, reference must be made to each title.

It is believed that, except in the case of cross references, each entry refers to a separate and distinct person. Cases of doubtful identity are noted thus :—

* **Michael,** bp. Clr. 596.
* ——— bp. Gall. 538.
* Prob. same pers.

* **Methven,** Jno., Ld. Chanc. Ir. 576.
* ——— Jno., M. Chy. 396.
* ? same pers.

Some observations will be found in the Preface as to the variations in spelling, particularly amongst the earlier names. As far as possible the risk of a fruitless search for a name actually in the Index has been avoided, either by grouping the names under the most usual mode of spelling with cross references to the others, *ex. gr.*

MacGregor and **MacGrigor**
* * *
MacGrigor, *see* MacGregor

or by cross references only, *ex. gr.*

Marston, *see also* Merston

The former mode is adopted where it was found that the name of the same *person* had been variously spelt in different parts of the book ; the latter where it was found that although the *name* itself was spelt differently, the name of each person bearing it was spelt alike throughout.

The variations in spelling are, however, so numerous that the reader must, to some extent, rely on himself, and, if he cannot find a name under the expected heading, try under some other letter frequently substituted for it ; *ex. gr.*—I. and J., I. and Y., U. and V., Æ. and E., are frequently used indifferently both at the beginning and in the middle of a name. The names of the earlier ecclesiastical and legal dignitaries are sometimes used in their English and sometimes in their Latin form. Emperors, Kings, &c., and also Royal Princes are entered under their Christian names; but where English Princes have been created Dukes or Earls, they are entered under their later titles also.

Where a name applies both to surnames and to titles of nobility, the latter are grouped together at the end of the former;—*ex. gr.*

Gordon, Adam, 1st ld.,

follows

Gordon, Wm.

Considerations of space have necessitated the use of the shortest possible abbreviation of each dignity. Wherever practicable, a form has been adopted the meaning of which is obvious, but, to provide for any case of difficulty or uncertainty, a complete list of the abbreviations is here given.

LIST OF ABBREVIATIONS USED IN INDEX OF NAMES.

Abbreviation.	Dignity.
A.D. Aus.	Archduke of Austria.
A.G.	Attorney General.
A.G. Ir.	—— Ireland.
Abp.	archbishop, *see* bp. (bishop).
Acct. G.	Accountant General.
Adm. (A.)	Admiral, List A.
—— (B.)	„ „ B.
—— (C.)	„ „ C.
—— (D.)	„ „ D.
—— (E.)	„ „ E.
—— (F.)	„ „ F.
—— (G.)	„ „ G.
—— (H.)	„ „ H.
Adm. Adv.	Admiralty Advocate.
Adm. Ind.	Administrator of India.
Amb.	Ambassador, &c. to—
—— Abyss.	—— Abyssinia.
—— Arg.	—— Argentine Confederation or Republic.
—— Aus.	—— Austria.
—— B. St.	—— Barbary States.
—— Bdn.	—— Baden.
—— Bga.	—— Bulgaria.
—— Bgm.	—— Belgium.
—— Bno.	—— Borneo.
—— Bol.	—— Bolivia.
—— Bva.	—— Bavaria.
—— Bzl.	—— Brazil.
—— C. Am.	—— Central America.
—— C. R.	—— Costa Rica.
—— Ch.	—— China.
—— Ch. and Cor.	—— China and Corea.
—— Chi.	—— Chili.
—— D. pr.	—— Danubian principalities.
—— Dk.	—— Denmark.
—— Dom Rep.	—— Dominican Republic.
—— Ecr.	—— Ecuador.
—— Eg.	—— Egypt.
—— Fr.	—— France.
—— G. St.	—— German States.
—— Gr.	—— Greece.
—— Gmy.	—— Germany.
—— Guat.	—— Guatemala.
—— H. Dt.	—— Hesse Darmstadt.
—— H. Tns.	—— Hanse Towns.
—— Hnr.	—— Hanover.
—— Hti.	—— Hayti.
—— It.	—— Italy.
—— Jap.	—— Japan.
—— Lca.	—— Lucca.
Amb.	Ambassador, &c. to—
—— Mco.	—— Morocco.
—— Mda.	—— Modena.
—— Mex.	—— Mexico.
—— Mgo.	—— Montenegro.
—— Msct.	—— Muscat.
—— N.G.	—— New Grenada.
—— Nds.	—— Netherlands.
—— Pers.	—— Persia.
—— Pgl.	—— Portugal.
—— Pgy.	—— Paraguay.
—— Pld.	—— Poland.
—— Pma.	—— Parma.
—— Pr.	—— Prussia.
—— Pu.	—— Peru.
—— R. Pl.	—— Rio de la Plata.
—— Rep. Col.	—— Republic of Colombia.
—— Rma.	—— Roumania.
—— Russ.	—— Russia.
—— Scy.	—— Two Sicilies.
—— Sd. Is.	—— Hawaiian or Sandwich Islands.
—— Sda.	—— Sardinia.
—— Si.	—— Siam.
—— Sp.	—— Spain.
—— Sva.	—— Servia.
—— Sw.	—— Sweden.
—— Sw. and N.	—— Sweden and Norway.
—— Swz.	—— Switzerland.
—— Sxy.	—— Saxony.
—— Tky.	—— Turkey.
—— Tun.	—— Tunis.
—— Tusc.	—— Tuscany.
—— Txs.	—— Texas.
—— U.S.A.	—— United States of America.
—— U.S.C.	—— —— Columbia.
—— Ugy.	—— Uruguay.
—— Vce.	—— Venice.
—— Vza.	—— Venezuela.
—— Wbg.	—— Wurtemburg.
—— Zr.	—— Zanzibar.
Ant. P.A.	Antelope Pursuivant.
Arund. H.	Arundel Herald.
Ass. C. and A.	Assistant Comptroller and Auditor.
Astr. Roy.	Astronomer Royal.
Ath. P.A.	Athlone Pursuivant.
Aud. Ex.	Auditor of the Exchequer.
B.C.	Member of the Board of Control.
B. Ex.	Baron of Exchequer.

Abbreviation.	Dignity.
B. Ex. Ir.	Baron of Exchequer, Ireland.
—— Sc.	—— Scotland.
B. and G. K.A.	Bath and Gloucester King of Arms.
B.T.	Member of the Board of Trade.
B. Tun.	Bey of Tunis.
Barnes P.A.	Barnes Pursuivant.
Bath K.A.	Bath King of Arms.
Berw. P.A.	Berwick Pursuivant.
Bl. C. H.	Blanc-Coursier Herald.
Bl. L. P.A.	Blanch-Lion Pursuivant.
Bl. M. P.A.	Bluemantle Pursuivant.
Bl. Sang. P.A.	Blanch Sanglier Pursuivant.
Blf. Gsey.	Bailiff of Guernsey.
—— Jsey.	—— Jersey.
bp. bp. suff.	} *vide infra.*
abp. bp. bp. suffr. dn.	archbishop bishop bishop suffragan dean } The names of the various sees are abbreviated as below.
—— Abdn.	—— Aberdeen.
—— Abdn. and Ork.	—— Aberdeen and Orkney.
—— Ach.	—— Achonry.
—— Adel.	—— Adelaide.
—— Alg.	—— Algona.
—— Antig.	—— Antigua.
—— Ard.	—— Ardagh.
—— Ardf. and Agh.	—— Ardfert and Aghadoe.
—— Arg.	—— Argyll.
—— Arg. and Isl.	—— Argyll and the Isles.
—— Arm.	—— Armagh.
—— Arm. and Clr.	—— Armagh and Clogher.
—— Athab.	—— Athabasca.
—— Auckl. N.Z.	—— Auckland, N.Z.
—— Austr.	—— Australia.
—— B. and W.	—— Bath and Wells.
—— Ball.	—— Ballarat.
—— Bbay.	—— Bombay.
—— Bdoes.	—— Barbadoes.
—— Bedf.	—— Bedford.
—— Berw.	—— Berwick.
—— Bgr.	—— Bangor.
—— Bhurst.	—— Bathurst.
—— Blfn.	—— Bloemfontein.
—— B. Kaffr.	—— Kaffraria.
—— Brisb.	—— Brisbane.
—— Brl.	—— Bristol.
—— Brn.	—— Brechin.
—— C. Afr.	—— Central Africa.
—— C. Tn.	—— Cape Town.
—— Calc.	—— Calcutta.
—— Caled.	—— Caledonia.
—— Cant.	—— Canterbury.
—— Carl.	—— Carlisle.
—— Cash.	—— Cashel.
—— Cash. and Eml.	—— Cashel and Emly.
—— Cash., E., W. and L.	—— Cashel, Emly, Waterford and Lismore.
—— Cbia.	—— Columbia.
—— Chest.	—— Chester.
—— Chich.	—— Chichester.
—— Chr. Ch. Dbln.	—— Christ Church, Dublin.
—— Chr. Ch. N.Z.	—— Christ Church, N.Z.
—— Chr. Ch. Oxf.	—— Christ Church, Oxford.
—— Cld.	—— Clonard.
—— Clonf.	—— Clonfert.
—— Clonf. and K.	—— Clonfert and Kilmacduagh.
—— Clonm.	—— Clonmacnois.

Abbreviation.	Dignity.
abp. bp. or dn.	archbishop, bishop, or dean
—— Cloy.	—— Cloyne.
—— Clr.	—— Clogher.
—— Cmbo.	—— Colombo.
—— Cness.	—— Caithness.
—— Cnr.	—— Connor.
—— Cnwall.	—— Cornwall.
—— Colch.	—— Colchester.
—— Crk.	—— Cork.
—— Crk. and Cl.	—— Cork and Cloyne.
—— Crk., Cl. and R.	—— Cork, Cloyne and Ross.
—— Crk. and R.	—— Cork and Ross.
—— Dbln.	—— Dublin.
—— Dbln. and Gl.	—— Dublin and Glendalough.
—— Dbln., G. and K.	—— Dublin, Glendalough and Kildare.
—— Dev.	—— Devonshire.
—— Dham.	—— Durham.
—— Dkld.	—— Dunkeld.
—— Dkld. and Dnbl.	—— Dunkeld and Dunblane.
—— Dnbl.	—— Dunblane.
—— Dorch.	—— Dorchester.
—— Dorch. and Sir.	—— Dorchester and Sidnacester.
—— Dov.	—— Dover.
—— Down.	—— Down.
—— Down and Cnr.	—— Down and Connor.
—— Down, C. and D.	—— Down, Connor and Dromore.
—— Drom	—— Dromore.
—— Dry.	—— Derry.
—— Dry. and Rph.	—— Derry and Raphoe.
—— Dun.	—— Dunedin.
—— Dunw.	—— Dunwich.
—— E. Ang.	—— East Angles.
—— E. Eq. Afr.	—— Eastern Equatorial Africa.
—— Edinb.	—— Edinburgh.
—— Elm.	—— Elmham.
—— Elm. and Dunw.	—— Elmham and Dunwich.
—— Elph.	—— Elphin.
—— Ely	—— Ely.
—— Emly	—— Emly.
—— Enachd.	—— Enachdune.
—— Ex.	—— Exeter.
—— Falk. Isl.	—— Falkland Islands.
—— Fcton.	—— Fredericton.
—— Ferns	—— Ferns.
—— Ferns and L.	—— Ferns and Leighlin.
—— Fife.	—— Fife.
—— Fife, D. and D.	—— Fife, Dunkeld and Dunblane.
—— Gall.	—— Galloway.
—— Gibr.	—— Gibraltar.
—— Glasg.	—— Glasgow
—— Glasg. and Gall.	—— Glasgow and Galloway
—— Glend.	—— Glendalough.
—— Glr.	—— Gloucester.
—— Glr. and Br.	—— Gloucester and Bristo
—— Goulb.	—— Goulburn.
—— Grtn.	—— Grahamstown.
—— Graft. and Arm.	—— Grafton and Armidale.
—— Guiana	—— Guiana.
—— Guildf.	—— Guildford.
—— Her.	—— Hereford.
—— Hex.	—— Hexham.
—— Honol.	—— Honolulu.
—— Hull	—— Hull.

Abbreviation.	Dignity.
abp. bp. or dn.	archbishop, bishop, or dean
— Huron	— Huron.
— Ipsw.	— Ipswich.
— Isl.	— Of the Isles.
— Jam.	— Jamaica.
— Jpn.	— Japan.
— Jslm.	— Jerusalem.
— Kild.	— Kildare.
— Kilf.	— Kilfenora.
— Killa.	— Killala.
— Killa. and Ach.	— Killala and Achonry.
— Killoe.	— Killaloe.
— Killoe. and Kilf.	— Killaloe and Kilfenora.
— Killoe., K., Cl. and K.	— Killaloe, Kilfenora, Clonfert and Kilmacduagh.
— Kilm.	— Kilmore.
— Kilm. and Ard.	— Kilmore and Ardagh.
— Kilm., E. and A.	— Kilmore, Elphin and Ardagh
— Kilmacd.	— Kilmacduagh.
— Labn.	— Labuan.
— Leic.	— Leicester.
— Lhore.	— Lahore.
— Lich.	— Lichfield.
— Lich. and Cov.	— Lichfield and Coventry.
— Lim.	— Limerick.
— Lim., A. and A.	— Limerick, Ardfert and Aghadoe.
— Linc.	— Lincoln.
— Lindisf.	— Lindisfarne.
— Lism.	— Lismore.
— Llff.	— Llandaff.
— Llin.	— Leighlin.
— Lond.	— London.
— Lpl.	— Liverpool.
— M.-Ch.	— Mid-China.
— M. Riv.	— Mackenzie River.
— Mad.	— Madagascar.
— Manch.	— Manchester.
— Marlb.	— Marlborough.
— Mayo	— Mayo.
— Mburg.	— Maritzburg.
— Mdras.	— Madras.
— Melan.	— Melanesia.
— Melb.	— Melbourne.
— Mont.	— Montreal.
— Moos.	— Moosonee.
— Mor.	— Moray.
— Mor. and Ross	— Moray and Ross.
— Mor., R. and C.	— Moray, Ross and Caithness.
— Mortl.	— Mortlach.
— Mth.	— Meath.
— Mtius.	— Mauritius.
— N. Ch.	— North China.
— N. Q. Land	— New Queensland.
— N. Sc.	— Nova Scotia.
— N. Westr.	— New Westminster.
— N.Z.	— New Zealand.
— Nass.	— Nassau.
— Nat.	— Natal.
— Nels.	— Nelson.
— Newc., N.S.W.	— Newcastle, New South Wales.
— Newc. T.	— Newcastle-on-Tyne.
— Newfd.	— Newfoundland.
— Niag.	— Niagara.
— Nig. Dist.	— Niger District.
— Norw.	— Norwich.
— Nottm.	— Nottingham.
— Ont.	— Ontario.
— Ork.	— Orkney.
— Oss.	— Ossory.
— Oss., F. and L.	— Ossory, Ferns and Leighlin.
abp. bp. or dn.	archbishop, bishop, or dean
— Oxf.	— Oxford.
— Pboro.	— Peterborough.
— Penr.	— Penrith.
— Perth, W.A.	— Perth, Western Australia.
— Pret.	— Pretoria.
— Qu'app.	— Qu'appelle.
— Queb.	— Quebec.
— Rang.	— Rangoon.
— Rip.	— Ripon.
— Riv.	— Riverina.
— Roch.	— Rochester.
— Ross	— Ross.
— Ross and C.	— Ross and Caithness.
— Rph.	— Raphoe.
— Rup. Ld.	— Rupert's Land.
— S. and M.	— Sodor and Man.
— Saig.	— Saiger.
— Sal.	— Salisbury.
— Sask.	— Saskatchewan.
— Sels.	— Selsey.
— Shaft.	— Shaftesbury.
— Shbn.	— Sherborne.
— Shrewsb.	— Shrewsbury.
— Si. Le.	— Sierra Leone.
— Sidr.	— Sidnacester.
— Sing., L. and S.	— Singapore, Labuan and Sarawak.
— Southwell	— Southwell.
— St. Alb.	— St. Alban's.
— St. Andr.	— St. Andrew's.
— St. Andr., Dkld. and Dnbl.	— St. Andrew, Dunkeld and Dunblane.
— St. As.	— St. Asaph.
— St. Dav.	— St. David's.
— St. Hel.	— St. Helena.
— St. P.	— St. Paul's.
— St. Patr.	— St. Patrick's.
— Syd.	— Sydney.
— Tasm.	— Tasmania.
— Taun.	— Taunton.
— Thetf.	— Thetford.
— Tm.	— Tuam.
— Tm., K. and A.	— Tuam, Killaloe and Achonry.
— Tor.	— Toronto.
— Tr.	— Travancore.
— Tr. and Coch.	— Travancore and Cochin.
— Trin.	— Trinidad.
— Tru.	— Truro.
— Vict. (H. Kong)	— Victoria (Hong Kong).
— Welln.	— Wellington.
— Wells	— Wells.
— Westr.	— Westminster.
— Wfield.	— Wakefield.
— Wford.	— Waterford.
— Wford. and L.	— Waterford and Lismore.
— Winch.	— Winchester.
— Winds.	— Windsor.
— Wltn.	— Wilton.
— Worc.	— Worcester.
— Wpu.	— Waiapu.
— Yk.	— York.
— Zld.	— Zululand.
C. and A.G.	Comptroller and Auditor-General.
C. Acc. Ir.	Commissioner of Accounts, Ireland.
C. Alçn.	Count of Alençon.
C. Anht.	— Anhalt.
C. Anj.	— Anjou.
C.B. Ex.	Chief Baron, Exchequer.
— Ir.	— Ireland.
— Sc.	— Scotland.

Abbreviation.	Dignity.
C.C. Bbay.	Commander-in-Chief, Bombay.
—— Bgal.	—— Bengal.
—— Ind.	—— India.
—— Mdras.	—— Madras.
C.C.J.	County Court Judge.
C.C.P.	Chief Commissioner of Police.
C. Ch.	Commander-in-Chief.
C. Cus.	Commissioner of Customs.
—— Ir.	—— Ireland.
—— Sc.	—— Scotland.
C.D.L.	Chancellor of the Duchy of Lancaster.
C. Exc.	Commissioner of Excise.
—— Ir.	—— Ireland.
—— Sc.	—— Scotland.
C. Fld.	Count of Freisland.
C. Flrs.	—— Flanders.
C.G.A.	Captain of Gentlemen-at-Arms.
C.G. Ex.	Comptroller-General of Exchequer.
C.G.P.	Captain, Gentlemen Pensioners.
C.G.S.	Commissioner of Great Seal.
—— Ir.	—— Ireland.
—— Sc.	—— Scotland.
C. Hld.	Count of Holland.
C. Hlt.	—— Hainault.
C.I.E.	Companion, order Indian Empire.
C.I.R.	Commissioner of Inland Revenue.
C.J. Bank.	Chief Judge, Bankruptcy.
—— Bbay.	Chief Justice of Bombay.
—— Bgal.	—— Bengal.
—— C.P.	—— Common Pleas.
—— —— Ir.	—— —— Ireland.
—— Chest.	—— County Palatinate Chester.
—— K.B.	—— King's Bench.
—— —— Ir.	—— —— Ireland.
—— Mdras.	—— Madras.
—— N.W. Pr.	—— North-West Provinces.
—— Q.B.	—— Queen's Bench.
—— —— Ir.	—— —— Ireland.
C. Lux.	Count of Luxemburg.
C.P.R.	Count Palatine of the Rhine.
C. Ro.	Consul of Rome.
C. Sec.	Colonial Secretary.
C. St.	Commissioner of Stamps.
—— Ir.	—— Ireland.
C. St. and Tx.	Commissioner of Stamps and Taxes.
C. Svy.	Count of Savoy.
C. Treas. Ir.	Commissioner of Treasury, Ireland.
—— Sc.	—— Scotland.
C. Tx.	Commissioner of Taxes.
C.W.F. &c.	Commissioner of Woods, Forests and Land Revenue.
C.W.P.B.	Commissioner of Works and Public Buildings.
C.Y.G.	Captain of the Yeomen of the Guard.
Cal. P.A.	Calais Pursuivant.
Capt. Gen.	Captain-General.
Carl. H.	Carlisle Herald.
Ch. Com. Ass.	Chief Commissioner of Assam.
—— Bma.	—— Burma.
—— Cent. Pr.	—— Central Provinces.
—— Oudh.	—— Oudh.
—— Pjab.	—— Punjab.
Ch. Ex.	Chancellor of the Exchequer.
—— Ir.	—— Ireland
Ch. Jr.	Chief Justiciary.
Ch. Lond.	Chancellor, Diocese of London.
Ch. Sec. Ir.	Chief Secretary for Ireland.
Chambn. Ex.	Chamberlain of the Exchequer.
—— Lond.	—— London.
Chanc. Gart.	Chancellor, Order of the Garter.
—— Guelph.	—— Order of the Guelphs.
—— M.G.	—— Order of St. Michael and St. George.
Chest. H.	Chester Herald.
Chn. E.I. Co.	Chairman of the East India Company.
Clar. K.A.	Clarencieux King-of-Arms.
Clk. O.	Clerk of the Ordnance.
—— Pells.	Clerk of the Pells.
Coff. H.	Cofferer of the Household.
Com. Io. Isl.	Commissioner to the Ionian Islands.
Comf. P.A.	Comfort Pursuivant.
Comm. F. Ir.	Commander of the Forces in Ireland.
Commr. Ir.	Commissioner, Lord Lieutenancy of Ireland.
Comm. Serjt. Lond.	Common Serjeant of London.
Comm. Tr. Ir.	Commissioner of the Treasury, Ireland.
—— —— Sc.	—— —— Scotland.
Compt. H.	Comptroller of the Household.
—— N.	—— Navy.
—— Sc.	—— Scotland.
Const. T.L.	Constable of the Tower of London.
—— W. Cast.	—— Windsor Castle.
Cph. Aba.	Caliph of Arabia.
Cr. I.	Member Ord. Crown of India.
Csl. Fr.	Consul of France.
Curs. B. Ex.	Cursitor Baron of Exchequer.
D. Alçn.	Duke of Alençon.
D. Ant.	—— Anhalt.
D. Arch.	Dean of Arches.
D. Aus.	Duke of Austria.
D. Bbt.	—— Brabant.
D. Bdy.	—— Burgundy.
D. Bma.	—— Bohemia.
D. Bck.	—— Brunswick.
D. Bry.	—— Bretagne or Brittany.
D. Bva.	—— Bavaria.
D. Chanc. Ir.	Deputy Chancellor, Ireland.
D. Fac. Sc.	Dean of Faculty of Advocates, Scotland.
D. Fca.	Duke of Franconia.
D. Hnr.	—— Hanover.
D.L.K. Ir.	Deputy Lord Keeper, Ireland.
D. Lca.	Duke of Lucca.
D. Lne.	—— Lorraine.
D. Mda.	—— Modena.
D. Nass.	—— Nassau.
D. Ndy.	—— Normandy.
D. Obg.	—— Oldenburg.
D. Pld.	—— Poland.
D. Pma.	—— Parma.
D. Pr.	—— Prussia.
D. S. Alt.	—— Saxe-Altenberg.
D. S.C.G.	—— Saxe-Coburg and Gotha.
D. S.G.A.	—— Saxe-Gotha-Altenberg.
D. S. Mgn.	—— Saxe-Meiningen.
D. S. Wr.	—— Saxe-Weimar.
D. Su.	—— Suabia.
D. Svy.	—— Savoy.
D. Sxy.	—— Saxony.
D. Tny.	—— Tuscany.
D. Wbg.	—— Wurtemberg.
Dec. Ro.	Decemvir of Rome.
Dep. E.M.	Deputy Earl Marshal.
Dep. L.G.C.	—— Great Chamberlain.
Dep. Tr. Sc.	—— Treasurer, Scotland.
Dn.	Dean; *see* bp. (bishop).

Abbreviation.	Dignity.
Dn. Thist.	Dean, Order of Thistle.
Dt. Mex.	Dictator of Mexico.
—— Pgy.	—— Paraguay.
—— Pu.	—— Peru.
—— Ro.	—— Rome.
E.M.	Earl Marshal.
E.S.P.	Examiner of Stage Plays.
El. Bva.	Elector of Bavaria.
—— Hnr.	—— Hanover.
—— H. Csl.	—— Hesse-Cassel.
—— Sxy.	—— Saxony.
Emp. Aus.	Emperor of Austria.
—— Bzl.	—— Brazil.
—— Ch.	—— China.
—— E.E.	—— Eastern Empire.
—— Fr.	—— France.
—— Gmy.	—— Germany.
—— Hti.	—— Hayti.
—— Mex.	—— Mexico.
—— Ro.	—— Rome.
—— Russ.	—— Russia.
—— Tzde.	—— Trebizonde.
—— W.E.	—— Western Empire.
F.M.	Field-Marshal.
F. Sec.	Foreign Secretary.
Fitzal. P.A.	Fitzalan Pursuivant.
G. Antig.	Governor Antigua.
G. Antig. &c.	—— Antigua, &c.
G. Auck. Isl.	—— Auckland Islands.
G. Bah. Isl.	—— Bahama Islands.
G. Basut.	—— Basutoland.
G. Bbay.	—— Bombay.
G. Bdoes.	—— Barbadoes.
G. Bdoes, &c.	—— Barbadoes, &c.
G. Berb.	—— Berbice.
G. Bmda.	—— Bermuda.
G. Br. Bland.	—— British Bechuanaland.
G. Br. Cbia.	—— —— Columbia.
G. Br. Gu.	—— —— Guiana.
G. Br. Hond.	—— —— Honduras.
G. Br. Kaffr.	—— —— Kaffraria.
G. Br. N. Bno.	—— —— North Borneo.
G. Br.N.Guin.	—— —— New Guinea.
G.C.B.	Knight Grand Cross of the Bath.
G.C.G.H.	Governor of the Cape of Good Hope.
—— &c.	—— Cape of Good Hope and High Commissioner for South Africa.
G.C.H.	Knight Grand Cross Order of the Guelphs.
G.C.I.E.	Knight Grand Commander, Order Indian Empire.
G.C.M.G.	Knight Grand Cross St. Michael and St. George.
G.C.S.I.	Knight Grand Commander Star of India.
G. Can.	Governor of Canada.
G. Ceyl.	—— Ceylon.
G. Ch. Hosp.	—— Chelsea Hospital.
G. Ch. Isl.	—— Channel Islands.
G. Cypr.	—— Cyprus.
G. D. Bdn.	Grand Duke of Baden.
—— H. Dt.	—— Hesse Darmstadt.
—— M. Sch.	—— Mecklenburg-Schwerin.
—— M. Str.	—— Mecklenburg-Strelitz.
—— Obg.	—— Oldenburg.
—— S. Wr.	—— Saxe Weimar.
—— Tny.	—— Tuscany.
G. Dem. and Ess.	Governor of Demerara and Essequibo.
G. Dnca.	—— Dominica.
G. Falk. Isl.	—— Falkland Islands.
G. Fiji	—— Fiji.
G.G. Can.	Govr. Genl. of Canada.
G.G. Ind.	—— —— India.
G.G. N. Am. Prov.	—— —— North American Provinces.
G. Gamb.	Governor of Gambia.

Abbreviation.	Dignity.
G. Gibr.	Governor of Gibraltar.
G. Gld. Cst.	—— Gold Coast.
G. Gld.Cst.Col.	—— —— Colony.
G. Gr. Hosp.	—— Greenwich Hospital.
G. Gr.ld. W.	—— Griqualand West.
G. Gren.	—— Grenada.
G. Gsey.	—— Guernsey.
G. H. Kong.	—— Hong Kong.
G. Hgld.	—— Heligoland.
G. I. Man.	—— Isle of Man.
G. Jam.	—— Jamaica.
G. Jsey.	—— Jersey.
G. Labn.	—— Labuan.
G. Lag.	—— Lagos.
G. Leew. Isl.	—— Leeward Islands.
G. Mart.	—— Martinique.
G. Mdras.	—— Madras.
G. Mlta.	—— Malta.
G. Monts.	—— Montserrat.
G. Mtius.	—— Mauritius.
G. Mtoba.	—— Manitoba.
G. N. Brk.	—— New Brunswick.
G. N.S.W.	—— New South Wales.
G. N.Sc.	—— Nova Scotia.
G. N.W. Terr.	—— North-West Territory.
G. N.Z.	—— New Zealand.
G. Nat.	—— Natal.
G. Nev.	—— Nevis.
G. Newfd.	—— Newfoundland.
G. Ont.	—— Ontario.
G. Pr. Ed. Isl.	—— Prince Edward Island.
G. Q. Land.	—— Queensland.
G. Queb.	—— Quebec.
G. Seych. Isl.	—— Seychelles Islands.
G. S. Austr.	—— South Australia.
G. Si. Le.	—— Sierra Leone.
G. St. Hel.	—— St. Helena.
G. St. Luc.	—— St. Lucia.
G. St. Vin.	—— St. Vincent.
G. St. Xtr.	—— St. Christopher.
G. St. Xtr., &c.	—— St. Christopher, &c.
G. St. Xtr. and Nev.	—— St. Christopher and Nevis.
G. Str. Sett.	—— Straits Settlements.
G. T.and C. Isl.	—— Turks and Caicos Islands.
G. Tasm.	—— Tasmania.
G. Tob.	—— Tobago.
G. Trin.	—— Trinidad.
G. Upp. Can.	—— Upper Canada.
G. V. D. ld.	—— Van Diemen's Land.
G. Vanc. Isl.	—— Vancouver Island.
G. Vict.	—— Victoria.
G. Virg. Isl.	—— Virgin Islands.
G. W. Afr. Sett.	—— West Africa Settlement.
G. W. Austr.	—— Western Australia.
G. W. Pacif.	—— Western Pacific.
G. Wwd. Isl.	—— Windward Islands.
Gart. K.A.	Garter King of Arms.
Gen. (A.)	General, List A.
—— (B.)	" " B.
—— (C.)	" " C.
—— (D.)	" " D.
Geneal. Bath.	Genealogist, order of the Bath.
—— St. Patr.	—— order of St. Patrick.
Gr. M. Bath	Great Master, order of the Bath.
Gr. M. M.G.	—— —— St. Michael and St. George.
Gr. St.	Groom of the Stole.
Guelph K.A.	Guelph King of Arms.
Guis. P.A.	Guisnes Pursuivant.
H.C.P. Sc.	Lord High Commissioner to Parliaments of Scotland.
H. Mva.	Hospodar of Moldavia.
H. Rma.	—— Roumania.
H. Sec.	Home Secretary.
H. Wca.	Hospodar of Wallachia.
Han. H.	Hanover Herald.

Abbreviation.	Dignity.
Hps. P.A.	Hampnes Pursuivant.
Ir. K.A.	Ireland King of Arms.
J.A.G.	Judge-Advocate General.
J. Adm. Court	Judge Admiralty Court.
—— Ir.	—— Ireland.
—— Sc.	—— Scotland.
J. Bank.	Judge in Bankruptcy.
J. Bank Ir.	—— Ireland.
J.C.P.	Justice, Common Pleas.
J.C.P. Ir.	—— Ireland.
J.C.P.D.	Justice, Common Pleas Division, High Court of Justice.
J.C.P.D. Ir.	—— —— Ireland.
J. Ch. D.	Justice, Chancery Division, High Court of Justice.
J. Ch. D. Ir.	—— —— Ireland.
J. Chest.	Justice, County Palatine of Chester.
J. Div.	Judge, Divorce Court.
J. Ex. D.	Justice, Exchequer Division, High Court of Justice.
J. Ex. D. Ir.	—— Ireland.
J. It.	Justice Itinerant.
J.K.B.	Justice, King's Bench.
J.K.B. Ir.	—— —— Ireland.
J.P.D.A.	Judge of Probate, Divorce and Admiralty Division, High Court of Justice.
J. P. and M. Ir.	Judge of Probate and Matrimonial Causes Ireland.
J. Pr. Ct.	Judge of the Prerogative Court of Canterbury.
J. Prob.	Judge Probate Court.
J.Q.B.	Justice, Queen's Bench.
J.Q.B. Ir.	—— Ireland.
J.Q.B.D.	Justice, Queen's Bench Division, High Court Justice.
J.Q.B.D. Ir.	—— —— Ireland.
Jud. Com. P.C.	Judicial Committee of Privy Council.
Jy.	Justiciary.
Jy. Sc.	Judge of Justiciary, Scotland.
K. Adv.	King's Advocate.
K. Arr.	King of Arragon.
K.B.	Knight Companion of the Bath.
K. Bdy.	King of Burgundy.
K. Bgm.	—— the Belgians.
K. Bma.	—— Bohemia.
K. Bva.	—— Bavaria.
K.C.	King's Counsel.
K.C.B.	Knight Commander of the Bath.
K.C.E.	King Consort of England.
K.C.H.	Knight Commander, order of the Guelphs.
K.C.I.E.	—— order Indian Empire.
K.C.M.G.	—— St. Michael and St. George.
K.C.S.I.	—— Star of India.
K. Cle.	King of Castile.
K. Dk.	—— Denmark.
K.E.	—— England.
K. Fr.	—— France.
K.G.	Knight of the Garter.
K. Gr.	King of Greece.
K.H.	Knight, order of the Guelphs.
K. He.	King of the Hellenes.
K. Hgy.	—— Hungary.
K. Hnr.	—— Hanover.
K. Ir.	—— Ireland.
K. It.	—— Italy.
K. Jsm.	—— Jerusalem.
K. Lmd.	—— the Lombards.
K. Mad.	—— Madagascar.
K. Man.	—— Isle of Man.
K. Nav.	—— Navarre.
K. Nds.	—— the Netherlands.
K. Nls.	—— Naples.
K.P.	Knight of St. Patrick.
K. Pers.	King of Persia.
K. Pgl.	—— Portugal.
K. Pld.	—— Poland.
K. Pr.	—— Prussia.
K. Rma.	—— Roumania.
K. Ro.	—— Rome.
K. S. and N.	—— Sweden and Norway.
K. Sc.	—— Scotland.
K. Scy.	—— Sicily.
K. Sd. Is.	—— the Sandwich Islands.
K. Sda.	—— Sardinia.
K. Si.	—— Siam.
K. Sp.	—— Spain.
K. Sva.	—— Servia.
K. Sw.	—— Sweden.
K. Sxy.	—— Saxony.
K.T.	Knight of the Thistle.
K. 2 Scy.	King of the Two Sicilies.
K. Wbg.	—— Wurtemberg.
K. Wls.	—— Wales.
Kt. Mar. Sc.	Knight Marischal of Scotland.
L. Admy.	Lord or Commissioner of the Admiralty.
L. App.	Lord of Appeal.
L.C.H.	Lord Chamberlain of the Household.
L.D. Ir.	Lord Deputy of Ireland.
L.G. Bgal.	Lieut.-Governor of Bengal.
L.G.C.	Lord Great Chamberlain.
—— Sc.	—— of Scotland.
L.G. Ch. Hosp.	Lieut.-Governor of Chelsea Hospital.
—— Gr. Hosp.	—— Greenwich Hospital.
—— N.W. Pr.	—— North-West Provinces.
—— —— and Oudh	—— —— and Oudh.
L.G.O.	Lieutenant - General of the Ordnance.
L.G. Pjab.	Lieut.-Governor of the Punjab.
L.H.A.	Lord High Admiral.
—— Sc.	—— of Scotland.
L.H.C.K. Sc.	Lord High Commissioner to Kirk of Scotland.
L.H. Const.	Lord High Constable.
—— Sc.	—— Scotland.
L.H.S.	Lord High Steward.
—— Sc.	—— Scotland.
L.H.T.	Lord High Treasurer or Lord Treasurer.
—— Sc.	—— Scotland.
L.J. App.	Lord Justice of Appeal.
—— App. Ir.	—— Ireland.
—— Clk.	Lord Justice Clerk.
—— Gen.	—— General.
—— Ir.	—— Ireland.
L.K.	Lord Keeper.
—— Ir.	—— Ireland.
—— Sc.	—— Scotland.
L.L.—	Lord Lieutenant of—
—— Abdn.	—— Aberdeenshire.
—— Ang.	—— Anglesey.
—— Arg.	—— Argyleshire.
—— Arm.	—— Armagh.
—— Ant.	—— Antrim.
—— Ayrsh.	—— Ayrshire.
—— Beds.	—— Bedfordshire.
—— Berks.	—— Berkshire.
—— Berw.	—— Berwickshire.
—— Bffsh.	—— Banffshire.
—— Brec.	—— Breconshire.
—— Bucks.	—— Buckinghamshire.
—— Butesh.	—— Buteshire.
—— Cambs.	—— Cambridgeshire.
—— Card.	—— Cardiganshire.
—— Carlow	—— Carlow.
—— Carm.	—— Carmarthenshire.
—— Carn.	—— Carnarvonshire.
—— Cav.	—— Cavan.

Abbreviation.	Dignity.
L.L.—	Lord Lieutenant of—
—— Chesh.	—— Cheshire.
—— Clare.	—— Clare.
—— Clkmn.	—— Clackmannanshire.
—— Cnwall.	—— Cornwall.
—— Cness.	—— Caithness-shire,
—— Crk.	—— Cork.
—— Crom.	—— Cromarty.
—— Cumb.	—— Cumberland.
—— Dbln.	—— Dublin.
—— Dby.	—— Derbyshire.
—— Denb.	—— Denbighshire.
—— Devon.	—— Devonshire.
—— Dgal.	—— Donegal.
—— Dham.	—— Durham.
—— Dors.	—— Dorsetshire.
—— Downsh.	—— Downshire.
—— Dumb.	—— Dumbartonshire.
—— Dumfr.	—— Dumfries-shire.
—— Edinb.	—— Edinburgh.
—— Elgn.	—— Elginshire.
—— Esx.	—— Essex.
—— Ferm.	—— Fermanagh.
—— Fifesh.	—— Fifeshire.
—— Flints.	—— Flintshire.
—— Forf.	—— Forfarshire.
—— Galw.	—— Galway.
—— Glam.	—— Glamorganshire.
—— Glouc.	—— Gloucestershire.
—— Hadd.	—— Haddingtonshire.
—— Hants.	—— Hampshire.
—— Hav.	—— Haverfordwest.
—— Heref.	—— Herefordshire.
—— Herts.	—— Hertfordshire.
—— Hunts.	—— Huntingdonshire.
—— Inv.	—— Inverness-shire.
—— Ir.	—— Ireland.
—— K. Co.	—— King's County.
—— Kent	—— Kent.
—— Kerry	—— Kerry.
—— Kild.	—— Kildare.
—— Kilk.	—— Kilkenny.
—— Kinc.	—— Kincardineshire.
—— Kinr.	—— Kinross-shire.
—— Kirkc.	—— Kirkcudbright.
—— Lanc.	—— Lancashire.
—— Leic.	—— Leicestershire.
—— Leitr.	—— Leitrim.
—— Lim.	—— Limerick.
—— Linc.	—— Lincolnshire.
—— Linlithg.	—— Linlithgowshire.
—— Lnrk.	—— Lanarkshire.
—— Londy.	—— Londonderry.
—— Longf.	—— Longford.
—— Louth	—— Louth.
—— Mayo	—— Mayo.
—— Meath	—— Meath.
—— Mdx.	—— Middlesex.
—— Mer.	—— Merionethshire.
—— Mid-L.	—— Mid-Lothian.
—— Monaghan	—— Monaghan.
—— Monm.	—— Monmouthshire.
—— Montg.	—— Montgomeryshire.
—— Nbland.	—— Northumberland.
—— Norf.	—— Norfolk.
—— Notts.	—— Nottinghamshire.
—— Nrnsh.	—— Nairnshire.
—— Nton.	—— Northamptonshire.
—— N. Wales	—— North Wales.
—— Ork.and Z.	—— Orkney and Zetland.
—— Oxon.	—— Oxfordshire.
—— Pbls.	—— Peebleshire.
—— Pemb.	—— Pembrokeshire.
—— Prth.	—— Perthshire.
—— Q. Co.	—— Queen's County.
—— Radn.	—— Radnorshire.
—— Rnfw.	—— Renfrewshire.
—— Rosc.	—— Roscommon.
—— Ross	—— Ross-shire.
—— Roxb.	—— Roxburghshire.
L.L.—	Lord Lieutenant of—
—— Rutl.	—— Rutlandshire.
—— Salop	—— Shropshire.
—— Selk.	—— Selkirkshire.
—— Sligo	—— Sligo.
—— Soms.	—— Somersetshire.
—— Staffs.	—— Staffordshire.
—— Stirl.	—— Stirlingshire.
—— Suff.	—— Suffolk.
—— Surr.	—— Surrey.
—— Suss.	—— Sussex.
—— Suth.	—— Sutherlandshire.
—— S. Wales	—— South Wales.
—— Tipp.	—— Tipperary.
—— Tyr.	—— Tyrone.
—— Warw.	—— Warwickshire.
—— Wexf.	—— Wexford.
—— Wford.	—— Waterford.
—— Wickl.	—— Wicklow.
—— Wigt.	—— Wigtonshire.
—— Wilts	—— Wiltshire.
—— W. Meath	—— Westmeath.
—— Wmland.	—— Westmoreland.
—— Worc.	—— Worcestershire.
—— Yorks, E.R.	—— Yorkshire, East Riding.
—— Yorks, N. R.	—— —— North Riding.
—— Yorks, W. R.	—— —— West Riding.
L.M.	Lord Marshal.
L.M. Dbln.	Lord Mayor of Dublin.
L.M. Lond.	—— London.
L.P.C.	Lord President of the Council.
L.P. Ct. Sess.	—— Court of Session.
L.P.S.	Lord Privy Seal.
L.P.S. Sc.	—— of Scotland
L. Prov. Edinb.	Lord Provost of Edinburgh.
L.S.H.	Lord Steward of the Household.
L.T.	Lord of the Treasury, or Commissioner of the Treasury.
L. Treas. Ir.	Lord Treasurer of Ireland.
L.W.S.	Lord Warden of the Stannaries.
Lanc. H.	Lancaster Herald.
Land Comm.Ir.	Land Commissioner, Ireland.
Land J. Ir.	Land Judge, or Judge of Landed Estates Court, Ireland.
Ld. Adv.	Lord Advocate.
Ld. Chanc.	Lord Chancellor.
—— Ir.	—— Ireland.
—— Sc.	—— Scotland.
Ld. Clk. Reg.	Lord Clerk Register.
Ld. Man.	Lord of Isle of Man.
Ld. Sess.	Lord of Session.
Leic. H.	Leicester Herald.
Lg. H. Csl.	Landgrave of Hesse-Cassel.
—— H. Dt.	—— Hesse-Darmstadt.
—— H. Hbg.	—— Hesse-Homburg.
—— Hse.	—— Hesse.
Lt. Edinb.	Lieutenant of Edinburgh.
—— T.L.	—— Tower of London.
Ly. Dep.	Lyon Depute.
—— K.A.	—— King of Arms.
M. Aus.	Margrave of Austria.
M.B.H.	Master of the Buckhounds.
M. Bdn.	Margrave of Baden.
—— Brg.	—— Brandenberg.
M.C.I.	Member of the Council of India.
M. Chy.	Master in Chancery.
M. Fa.	Marquis of Ferrara.
M.G. K.A.	King of Arms, Order St. Michael and St. George.
M.G.O.	Master General of the Ordnance.
M.G.W.	Master of the Great Wardrobe.

.bbreviation.	Dignity.
.H.	Master of the Horse.
. Jap.	Mikado of Japan.
.M.	Master of the Mint.
.R.	—— Rolls.
— Ir.	—— —— Ireland.
. Robes	Mistress of the Robes.
ait. H.	Malta Herald.
ast. Coll. Surg.	Master, Royal College of Surgeons.
ch. K.A.	Marche King of Arms.
od. K. Sc.	Moderator of General Assembly of Kirk of Scotland.
owb. H.	Mowbray Herald.
t. Org. P.A.	Mont-Orgueil Pursuivant.
orf. H.	Norfolk Herald.
orr. K.A.	Norroy King of Arms.
ottm. P.A.	Nottingham Pursuivant.
ff. Nap.	Officer of Napoleon Buonaparte.
C.	Privy Councillor.
L.C.	Poor Law Commissioner.
Laur.	Poet Laureate.
P.	Holder of Patent of Precedence.
Ro.	Pope of Rome.
ym. G.	Paymaster-General.
rtr. Lond.	Portreeve of London.
rtsm. P.A.	Portsmouth Pursuivant.
stm. G.	Postmaster-General.
— Ir.	—— Ireland.
— Sc.	—— Scotland.
r. Bga.	Prince of Bulgaria.
— Bp. Sc.	—— "Primus" Bishop of Scotland.
— E.	Prince or Princess of England.
— Fr.	—— France.
— L. Dtd.	—— Lippe-Detmold.
— L. Sch.	—— Lippe-Schaumberg.
— Ltn.	—— Liechtenstein.
— M. Sch.	—— Mecklenburg-Schwerin.
— M. Str.	—— Mecklenburg-Strelitz.
— Mgo.	—— Montenegro.
— Mkg.	—— Mecklenburg.
— Mno.	—— Monaco.
— Nass.	—— Nassau.
— Or.	—— Orange.
— R. Gr.	—— Reuss-Greiz.
— R. Sch.	—— Reuss-Schleiz.
— Rma.	—— Roumania.
— S. Rdt.	—— Schwarzburg-Rudolstadt.
— S. Son.	—— Schwarzburg-Sonderhausen.
— Sva.	—— Servia.
— Tva.	—— Transylvania.
— W.E.	—— Wales (son of Sovereign of England).
— W. Pyr.	—— Waldeck Pyrmont.
— Wls.	—— Wales (native).
rel. M.G.	Prelate, ord. St. Michael and St. George.
rem.	Premier or Prime Minister.
res. Arg.	President of Argentine Republic.
— B. Ay.	—— Buenos Ayres.
— B.C.	—— Board of Control.
— B.H.	—— —— Health.
— B.T.	—— —— Trade.
— Bol.	—— Bolivia.
— C.P.D.	—— Common Pleas Division, High Court of Justice.
— C.P.D. Ir.	—— —— Ireland.
— C.R.	—— Costa Rica.
— Chi.	—— Chili.
— Coll. Ph.	—— Royal College of Physicians.
— Coll. Surg.	—— Royal College of Surgeons.
— Dn. Rep.	—— Dominican Republic.
— Ecr.	—— Ecuador.

Abbreviation.	Dignity.
Pres. Ex. D.	President, Exchequer Division, High Court of Justice.
—— Ex. D. Ir.	—— —— Ireland.
—— Fr.	—— French Republic.
—— Gua.	—— Guatemala.
—— Hdas.	—— Honduras.
—— Hti.	—— Hayti.
—— L.G.B.	—— Local Government Board.
—— Lib.	—— Liberia.
—— Mex.	—— Mexico.
—— N.G.	—— New Grenada.
—— Nic.	—— Nicaragua.
—— O.F.S.	—— Orange Free State.
—— P.C. Sc.	—— Privy Council, Scotland.
—— P.L.B.	—— Poor Law Board.
—— Pan.	—— Panama.
—— Pgy.	—— Paraguay.
—— Pjab.	—— Punjab.
—— Pu.	—— Peru.
—— Q.B.D.	—— Queen's Bench Division, High Court of Justice.
—— Q.B.D. Ir.	—— —— Ireland.
—— R.A.	—— Royal Academy of Arts.
—— R. Inst.	—— Royal Institution.
—— R. Soc.	—— Royal Society.
—— S. Dom.	—— St. Domingo.
—— S. Salv.	—— San Salvador.
—— Sp.	—— Spanish Republic.
—— Sw. C.	—— Swiss Confederation.
—— Trl.	—— Transvaal.
—— U.S.A.	—— United States of America.
—— U.S.C.	—— —— Columbia.
—— Ugy.	—— Uruguay.
—— V. Cr.	—— Vera Cruz.
—— Vzla.	—— Venezuela.
Prot. E.	Protector of England.
Ptc. P.A.	Portcullis Pursuivant.
Q. Adv.	Queen's Advocate.
Q. Arr.	Queen of Arragon.
Q.C.	Queen's Counsel.
Q.C.E.	Queen Consort of England.
Q. Cle.	Queen of Castile.
Q. Dk.	—— Denmark.
Q.E.	—— England.
Q. Jsm.	—— Jerusalem.
Q. Mad.	—— Madagascar.
Q. Nav.	—— Navarre.
Q. Pgal.	—— Portugal.
Q. Pld.	—— Poland.
Q. Sc.	—— Scotland.
Q. Sd. Is.	—— Sandwich Islands.
Q. Sp.	—— Spain.
Q. Sw.	—— Sweden.
R. Bl. P.A.	Rose Blanche Pursuivant.
R. Cr. P.A.	Rouge-croix Pursuivant.
R. Dr. P.A.	Rouge-Dragon Pursuivant.
R. Nds.	Ruler of the Netherlands, *i.e.* either Governor or Stadtholder.
R. Rge. P.A.	Rose Rouge Pursuivant.
R. Russ.	Ruler of Russia prior to the title of Emperor assumed in 1721 by Peter I.
Rbk. P.A.	Risebank Pursuivant.
Rec. Dbln.	Recorder of Dublin.
—— Lond.	—— London.
Regr. Bath	Registrar, order Bath.
—— Cr. I.	—— —— Crown of India.
—— Gart.	—— —— Garter.
—— I.E.	—— —— Indian Empire.
—— M.G.	—— —— St. Michael and St. George.
—— S.I.	—— —— Star of India.
—— and Sec. Bath.	—— and Secretary, order of Bath.
Rel. Nap.	Relative of Napoleon Bonaparte.
Richm. H.	Richmond Herald.
Rose P.A.	Rose Pursuivant.

Abbreviation.	Dignity.
S.G.	Solicitor-General.
—— Ir.	—— Ireland.
—— Sc.	—— Scotland.
S.G.O.	Surveyor-General of the Ordnance.
S.L.	Serjeant-at-Law.
—— Ir.	—— Ireland.
S.L.R.	Surveyor of Land Revenues.
S. Mco.	Sultan of Morocco.
S. St.	Secretary of State.
S. Tky.	Sultan of Turkey.
S.W.F.	Surveyor of Woods and Forests.
S. Zr.	Sultan of Zanzibar.
Sc. bp.	Scotch Bishop without see.
Sec. Adm.	Secretary to the Admiralty.
—— at W.	—— at War.
—— B.C.	—— Board of Control.
—— B.T.	—— —— Trade.
—— Bath	—— order of the Bath.
—— Guelph	—— —— the Guelphs.
—— I.E.	—— —— Indian Empire.
—— Ind.	—— of State for India.
—— L.G.B.	—— Local Government Board.
—— M.G.	—— order St. Michael and St. George.
—— P.L.B.	—— Poor Law Board.
—— P.O.	—— Post Office.
—— S.I.	—— order Star of India.
—— Sc.	—— for Scotland.
—— St. Ir.	—— of State, Ireland.
—— St. Patr.	—— order St. Patrick.
—— St. Sc.	—— of State, Scotland.
—— Thist.	—— order Thistle.
—— Tr.	—— Treasury.
—— Tr. Ir.	—— —— Ireland.
Sh. Pers.	Shah of Persia.
Som. H.	Somerset Herald.
Sp. H.C.	Speaker of the House of Commons.
Sr. N.	Surveyor of the Navy.

Abbreviation.	Dignity.
St. O.	Storekeeper of the Ordna
Suff. H.	Suffolk Herald.
Surr. H.	Surrey Herald.
Tell. Ex.	Teller of the Exchequer.
Tr. Ch.	Treasurer of the Chambe
Tr. H.	—— Household.
Tr. N.	—— the Navy.
Tr. Rome	Triumvir of Rome.
Trib. Rome	Tribune of Rome.
U.S. C.	Under Secretary, Colonies
U.S. F.	—— Foreign.
U.S. Home	—— Home.
U.S. Ind.	—— India.
U.S. Ir.	—— for Ireland.
U.S. S.	—— of State.
U.S. War	—— War.
U.S. W. and C.	—— War and Colonies.
Ulst. K.A.	Ulster King of Arms.
V.A. Sc.	Vice-Admiral of Scotland.
V.C.H.	Vice-Chamberlain of Household.
V. Chanc.	Vice-Chancellor.
—— Guelph	—— order of the Guelphs.
—— Ir.	—— Ireland.
V. Eg.	Viceroy of Egypt.
V.P.B.T.	Vice-President, Board Trade.
V. P. Ed.	—— Education Committe the Privy Council.
V.P. Ed. Sc.	—— —— Scotland.
V. Treas. Ir.	Vice-Treasurer Ireland.
Vic. Gen.	Vicar-General to archbis of Canterbury.
W.C.P.	Warden of the Cinque Por
W. and C. Sec.	War and Colonial Secreta
W. Sec.	Secretary of State for Wa
Wdn. Chr. Ch. Manch.	Warden of Christ Chu Manchester.
Wdn. M.	Warden of the Mint.
Winds. H.	Windsor Herald.
Yk. H.	York Herald.

INDEX.

A.

A—— bp. Cness. 531
Aba, K. Hgy. 59
Abbadie, Jas., dn. Killoe. 637
Abbas, V. Eg. 98
— I. to III., Sh. Pers. 99
Abbasides, Cph. Aba. 98
Abbingworth, Gilb. de, J It. 366
Abbot, *see also* Abbott.
— Chas., aft. 1st ld. Colchstr., *q.v.*, C. Treas. Ir. 561; Ch. Sec. Ir. 563; P.C. 207; Sec. St. Ir. 562; Sp. H.C. 250
— Geo., abp. Cant. 431; bp. Lich. & Cov. 444; bp. Lond. 452; dn. Winch. 471.
— Robt., bp. Sal. 467
— Thos., L.M. Dbln. 642
Abbott, *see also* Abbot.
— Aug., gen. (**D**) 894
— Ch. and Sir C., aft. 1st ld. Tenterden, *q.v.* C.J.K.B. 370; J.C.P. 380; J.K.B. 373; P.C. 210; S.L. 413
— sir Fk., gen. (**D**) 892
— Geo., L.T. 154
— Hy. Dy., gen. (**D**) 919
— Herb. Ed. S., gen. (**D**) 909
— Jas., gen. (**D**) 901
— Jonas A., adm. (**H**) 850
— sir Maur., L.M. Lond. 491
— Saund. Alex., gen. (**D**) 899
— Wm. Hy., gen. (**D**) 932
Abd-er Rhaman, S. Mco. 101
Abdul-Ahmed, I. and II., S. Tky. 98
— -**Aziz,** S. Tky. 98; K.G. 745
— -**Medjid,** S. Tky. 98; K.G. 744
Abdy, Anthy. T., K.C. 415
— Ch. Hayes, gen. (**D**) 925
— Jno. Th., C.C.J. 405
A'Becket, Th., abp. Cant. 430; Ld. Chanc. 353
Abel, bp. St. Andr. 529
— K. Dk. 93
— Jno., B. Ex. 383
Abendon (or Abyndon), Rd. de, B. Ex. 383
Abercorn, E. M. and D. of
— Jas., 7th E. of, P.C. 198
— Jno. Jas., 9th E. aft. 1st M. of, K.G. 743

Abercorn, E., M., and D. of—*cont.*
—— Jas., 2nd M. aft. 1st D. of, L.L. Dgal. 569; L.L. Ir. 558; K.G. 744; P.C. 214
—— Jas., 2nd D. of, L.L. Dgal. 569
Abercrombie and **Abercromby**
—— Alex., Ld. Sess. 520
—— sir Geo., C. Ex. Sc. 505
—— Geo., *see* ld. A., *infra*.
—— hon. Geo. Ralph. *see* ld. A. *infra*.
—— Jas., gen. (**A**) 858
—— Jas., C.B., Ex. Sc. 523
—— Jas., aft. 1st ld. Dunfermline, *q.v.*, J.A.G. 937; M.M. 247; P.C. 211; Sp. H.C. 250
—— hon. Jno. and sir J., C.C. Bbay. 660; C.C. Mdras. 657; G. Mdras. 658; gen. (**B**) 867; G.C.B. 767; K.C.B. 773
—— Ralph and sir R., Comm. F. Ir. 564; G. Trin. 722; Gen. (**B**) 866; K.B. 765
—— hon. Ralph and sir R., aft. 2nd ld. Dunfermline, *q.v.*, Amb. G. St. 122; Amb. Nds. &c. 123; Amb. Sda. 114; Amb. Tusc., &c., 115; K.C.B. 782
—— Rt. and sir R., C.C. Bbay. 659; C.C. Bgal. 652; C.C. Ind. 650; G. Bbay. 659; gen. (**A**) 859; K.B. 765; G.C.B. 766
Abercromby, lds.
—— Geo., 2nd ld., L.L. Stirl. 512
—— hon. Geo. Ralph, aft. 3rd ld. A., L.L. Clkmn. 509
Aberdare, Hy. Aust., ld., form. H. A. Bruce, *q.v.*, G.C.B. 773
Aberdeen, E. of
—— Geo., 1st E. of, form. sir G. Gordon, *q.v.*, Ld. Chanc. Sc. 515
—— Geo., 4th E. of, Amb. Aus. 117; C.D.L. 243; F. Sec. 228; K.G. 744; K.T. 748; L.L. Abdn. 508; L.T. 161; P.C. 209; Prem. 148; W. & C. Sec. 231
—— Jno. Campbell, 7th E. of, L.H.C.K. Sc. 546; L.L. Abdn. 508; L.L. Ir. 558; P.C. 220
Abergavenny, lds., E. and M. of
Beauchamp Family.
—— Wm., 1st ld., form. W. Beauchamp, *q.v.*, K.G. 734
Neville Family.
—— Geo., 3rd ld., K.G. 737; W.C.P. 319
—— Hy., 4th ld., K.B. 760
—— Geo., 15th ld. aft. 1st E. of, L.L. Suss. 312
—— Hy., 2nd E. of, K.T. 748

Abergavenny—*cont.*
—— Wm., 5th E. aft. 1st M. of, K.G. 745
Abernethie, Th., K.H. 790
Abernethy, Jno., bp. Cness. 532
—— Jno., Pres. Coll. Surg. 939
—— ld., *see* Saltoun and A.
Abetot, Hugh, K.B. 755
Abin, G. D'., Pres. Dom. Rep. 105
Abingdon, *see also* Abyngdone
Abingdon, E. of
—— Montg., 2nd E. of, Const. T.L. 321; P.C. 195
—— Montg., 5th E. of, L.L. Berks, 306
—— Montg., 6th E. of, L.L. Berks, 306
Abinger, Jas., 1st. ld., form. sir J. Scarlett, *q.v.*
—— Wm. Fk., 3rd ld., gen. (**D**) 917
Abling, Johan Cornelis d', G.C.G.H. 678
Abney, Th. and sir T., B. Ex. 385; J.C.P. 379; K.C. 415; S.L. 412.
—— sir Th., L.M. Lond. 491
Abool-Fatteh-Khan, Sh. Pers. 99
Aboyne, Geo., 5th E. of, also M. of Huntley, *q.v.*; aft. D. of Gordon, *q.v.*, K.T. 748
***Abraham,** bp. St. As. 462
*—— bp. Dnbl. 532
*—— bp. St. Dav. 464
* Prob. some same pers. Comp. dates.
—— Ch. Jno., bp. Welln. 710
Abree (or Leycester), Fras., dn. Pboro. 458
Abrincis, Wm. de, J. It. 365
Abubeker, Cph. Aba. 98
Abyndon, *see* Abendon
Abyngdone, *see also* Abingdon
—— Steph. de, L.M. Lond. 489
Acca, *see also* Ecca
—— bp. Dunw. 454
—— (Saint) bp. Hex. 480
Accursii, F., S. St. 222
Achaicus, L. M., C.Ro. 44
Achaius, K.Sc. 18
Acha, J. M. d', Pres. Bol. 109
Achard, Wm., J. It. 366
Acheson, *see also* Atcheson and Aicheson
—— sir Archd., Ld. Sess. 517, 519; Sec. St. Sc. 502
—— Hon. Ed. Archd. Brab., Gen. (**D**) 932
Achmet, *see* Ahmed
Acilius, M., C. Ro. 47
Ackland, *see* Acland

For List of Abbreviations, see pp. 944-952.

Ackworth, Jacob and sir J., Sr. N. 257
Acland, Ch. T. Dyke, Sec. B.T. 269
—— Hy. Wentw., K.C.B. 784
—— sir Th. Dyke, P.C. 220
—— (or Ackland,) Wroth. Palm. and sir W., gen. (**B**) 867; K.C.B. 773
Acle, Regd. de, J. It. 368
Acosta, S., Pres. U.S.C. 107
A'Court, Ch. Ashe, K.H. 789
—— Wm. and sir W., aft. 1st ld. Heytesbury *q.v.*, Amb. B. St. 131; Amb. Pgl. 125; Amb. Scy. 115; Amb. Sp. 124; G.C.B. 771; P.C. 209
Acton, sir Wm., L.M. Lond. 491
Adair, Archd., dn. Rph. 602; bp. Killa. and Ach. 613; bp. Wford. and L. 627
—— Ch. Wm. and sir C., gen. (**D**) 917; K.C.B. 781
—— Hy., gen. (**D**) 925
—— Jas., C.J. Chest. 386; Rec. Lond. 494; S.L. 412
—— Rt. and sir R., Amb. Aus. 117; Amb. Bgm. 123; Amb. Pr. 168; Amb. Tky. 129; G.C.B. 772: P.C. 211
—— Thos. B., gen. (**D**) 883
Adalbert, I. to III., D. Tny. 57
***Adam,** bp. Brn. 531; Ld. Chanc. Sc. 515
*—— bp. Cness. 531
*—— bp. Cnr. 603
*—— bp. Gall. 538
*—— bp. St. As. 462
*—— bp. Winch. 470
*—— J.C.P. 376
* Prob. some same pers. Comp. dates.
—— Ch. and sir C., adm. (**A**) 820; G. Gr. Hosp. 854; K.C.B. 776: L. Admy. 182-3; L.L. Kinr. 510
—— Emily Eliz., aft. lady A., Cr. Ind. 810
—— Frank F., C.I.E. 808
—— Fk. and sir F., Com. Io. Isl. 129; G.C.B. 769; G.C.M.G. 794; G. Mdras. 657; gen. (**A**) 863; K.C.B. 775; P.C. 212
—— Jas., Jy. Sc. 523; Ld. Sess. 521
—— hon. Jno., G.G. Ind. 648
—— Wm., Bar. Ex. Sc. 524; P.C. 209
—— Wm., K.C. 415
—— Wm., L.L. Kinr. 510
—— Wm. Geo., Acct. G. and M. Chy. 397; K.C. 416
—— Wm. Patr., C.W.P.B. 272; G. Mdras. 657; L.T. 161-2; P.C. 218; Paym. G. 245
Adams, Alex., gen. (**B**) 868
—— Arth. R., Q.C., 418
—— Bern., bp. Kilf. 635; bp. Lim. 638
—— Cadw., gen. (**D**) 908
—— Ed., gen. (**D**) 910
—— Fras. Ott. and sir F., Amb. Fr. 113; Amb. Swz. 114; K.C.M.G. 798
—— Frank, gen. (**D**) 901
—— Geo. E., Lanc. H. 333; R. Dr. P.A. 338
—— sir Geo. Powis, gen. (**A**) 863; K.C.H. 788
—— Hy. Augs., gen. (**D**) 918
—— Hy. Wm., gen. (**D**) 889
—— Jesse, Q.C. 418
—— Jas., L. Admy. 180
Adams—*cont.*
—— Jno., Adm. (**D**) 833
—— Jno., Pres. U.S.A. 102
—— Jno., P.P. 416; S.L. 413
—— Jno. Q., Pres. U.S.A. 102
—— sir Jno. Whitt., G.C.B. 768; K.C.B. 776
—— sir Rd., B. Ex. 385; Rec. Lond. 494; S.L. 412
—— Saml., dn. Cash. 627
—— sir Th., L.M. Lond. 491
—— Wm. D., C.W.F. &c. 271-2
—— Wm. Pitt, Amb. Bol. 135; Amb. Pu. 135
Adamson, Jno., L.M. Dbln. 641
—— Patr., abp. St. Andr. 529
Adawaldus, K. Lmd. 49
Adcock, Alf. Wm., gen. (**D**) 927
Adda, K.E. 2
Addenbrook, Jno., dn. Lich. 445
Adderley, Arden, Adm. (**H**) 845
—— Aug. Jno., K.C.M.G. 798
—— Chas., M.H. 302
—— Chas. B., aft. sir C. and 1st ld. Norton, *q.v.*, P.C. 216; K.C.M.G. 796; P.C. 216; Pres. B.H. 255; Pres. B.T. 269; U.S.C. 235; V.P. Ed. 255
Addington, hon. Ch. Jno., gen. (**D**) 929
—— Hav. Jno., C. St. 284
—— Hy., aft. hon. H., Cl. Pells 168
—— Hy., aft. 1st visc. Sidmouth *q.v.*, Ch. Ex. 165; L.T. 158; P.C. 205; Prem. 144; Sp. H.C. 250
—— Hy. Unw., Amb. G. St. 122; Amb. Spn. 124; P.C. 216; U.S.F. 230
—— Jno. Hiley, B.C. 252; L.T. 158; P.C. 207; Paym. G. 245; Sec. Tr. 163; U.S. Home, 227
Addison, Jno., C.C.J. 403
—— Jno. Edm. Wentw., Q.C. 419
—— Jos., B.T. 264; P.C. 197
—— Jos., S. St. 224; U.S.S. 225
—— Jos. Ed., gen. (**D**) 906
—— Lanc., dn. Lich. 445
—— Th., gen. (**D**) 906
—— Th. F., gen. (**D**) 881
Adeane, Ed. Stanley, adm. (**E**) 837
—— Jas., gen. (**A**) 859
Adela (dau. Wm. I.), Pr. E. 9
Adelaide, Q.C.E. 8
Adelbert, abp. Yk. 485
Adelicia, Q.C.E. 7
Adelmare, Hy., dn. Ely, 435
Adelmus and **Ardhelm,** *see also* Athelm
—— (or Ascelimus), dn. Linc. 447
Adelwalch, K.E. 1
Adeodatus, P. Ro. 33
—— (St.) abp. Cant. 429
Aderton, Rd., G. I. Man, 666
Adhelm (or Aldhelm) (St.) bp. Shbn. 466
Adil, Sh. Pers. 99
Adlam, Hy. Ch., gen. (**D**) 912
Adlercron, Jno., gen. (**B**) 865
Adolphus, C.P.R. 68
—— D. Nass. 76
—— E. Gmy. 62
—— (of Cleves) K. Nds. 82
—— I. to IV., Pr. Nass. 75
—— -Fredk., K. Sw. 92
Adolphus—*cont.*
—— -Fredk., Pr. E. (son Geo III.), aft. D. Cambridge, *q.v.* 15
—— -Fredk., Pr. Mkg. 74
—— -Fredk., II. to IV., Pr. M. Str. 75
—— -Fredk. III. (Pr. M. Str.) K.G. 742
—— -Geo., Pr. L. Sch. 73
—— Jno. Leyc., C.C.J. 404
Adored, bp. Worc. 472
Adrian, abp. Cant. 430
—— bp. St. Andr. 528
—— Emp. Ro. 47
—— I. to VI., P. Ro. 33-4-5
Adryan, Jno., L.M. Lond. 48
***Adulfe,** abp. Yk. 485; bp. Worc. 472
***Adulfus** (or Aldulfus), bp. Roch. 459
***Adulphus,** abp. Lich. 443
*—— abp. Yk. 485; bp. Worc 472
***Adulse,** abp. Yk. 485
*Prob. some same pers. Comp. dates.
Ady, Jno., J.C.P. Ir. 581
Adye, A. C., G. Gren. 724
—— Goods., gen. (**D**) 919
—— Jno. Mili., and sir J., G.C.B. 771; G. Gibr. 670; gen. (**D**) 906; K.C.B. 780; S.G.O. 260
—— Steph. Galw., gen. (**C**) 875
Æ, *see also* under **E**
Ædan, Pr. Wls. 16
Ædgene, bp. Kild. 616
Ædulphus (2), bp. Dev. 436
Ælfgar, bp. Lich. 443
Ælfstan, *see* Œlfstan
Ælphunus, bp. Dunw. 454
Æmilianus, Emp. Ro. 48
—— Q. F. M., C. Ro. 44
Æneanus, K. Sc. 18
Æsc, K.E. 1
Æthelnotus, *see* Ethelnoth
Affleck, sir Edm., adm. (**A**) 81
—— sir Jas., gen. (**A**) 861
—— Ph., adm. (**A**) 815; L. Admy. 180
Afghanistan, Amir of, G.C.S.I. 801
Africanus, L., C. Ro., 46
—— P. C. S. (2), C. Ro. 43-4
Aga - Mahommed - Khan Sh. Pers. 99
Agapetus I. and II., P. Ro 33-4
Agar, Chas., aft. visc. Somerton and E. of Normanton *q.v.*, bp. Cash. and Eml. 626 bp. Cloy. 631; dn. Kilm. 609
—— Jas., aft. 1st ld. and visc Clifden, *q.v.*, C. Cus. Ir. 565 C. Exc. Ir. 566
—— Jno., S.L. 412.
—— Laur., S. L. 411
—— Th., S.W.H. 271
—— Welb. Ell., C. Cus. 276
—— Wm., K.C. 415
Agar-Ellis, *see* Ellis
Agatha (dau. Wm. I.), Pr E. 9
Agatho, P. Ro. 33
Agelred, *see* Ethelricus
Aghton, Wm., M. Chy. 394
Agila, K. Sp. 85
Agilbertus, bp. Dorch. 446
—— bp. Winch. 470
Agilulphus, K. Lmd. 49
Aglionby, Geo., dn. Cant. 43
—— Wm., K.C. 415
—— Wm., U.S.S. 225

For List of Abbreviations, see pp. 944-952.

Agna, Eust. de, dn. Lim. 639
Agnes, D. Bva. 67
Agnew, sir Andr., gen. (**B**) 865
— Montg., gen. (**A**) 859
— Wm., gen. (**D**) 915
Agrippa, M. (3), C. Ro. 46-7
Aguero, J. de la R., Pres. Pu. 109
Aguila (or Aquila), Nichs. de, bp. Chich. 432; dn. Chich. 433
Aguilar, *see* Daguilar
Aguillon, Rd. de, L.H.A. 170
Aguirre, A. C., Pres. Ugy. 111
Ahala, C. S. S., C. Ro. 38-9
— Q. S. (2), C. Ro. 40; Dt. Ro. 40
Ahenorbarbus, C. D., C. Ro. 43-4-5-7
— L. D., C. Ro. 45-6
Ahmed I. to III., S. Tky. 97
Ahmedabad, Rao of, C.I.E. 808
Ahmuty, *see* also Auchmuty
— Jas., gen. (**D**) 877
Ai—, *see also* Ay—
Aicheson and **Aichison,** *see* Aitcheson and Acheson
Aichiley, Rd., L.M. Lond. 490
*__Aid__ (St.), bp. Kild. 616
*__Aidan,__ bp. Glend. 615
*— (St.), bp. Clr. 596; bp. Lindisf. 478
*— bp. Mayo, 611
* Prob. some same pers. Comp. dates.
Aidanus, K. Sc. 18
Aikins, Jas. Cox, G. Mtoba. 696
Ailbe, St., bp. Emly, 625
Ailchu, bp. Cld. 598.
Aildergoidh, K. Ir. 20
Ailesbury, E. and M. of
—Robt., 1st E. of, L.C.H. 295; P.C. 191-2
— Th., 2nd E. of, L.C.H. 295
— Th., 4th E. of, form. ld. Bruce, *q.v.*, K.T. 748; L.L. Wilts. 313
— Chas., 5th E. aft. 1st M. of, K.T. 748
— Geo. Wm. Fk., 2nd M. of, form. E. of Cardigan, *q.v.*, K.G. 744; L.L. Wilts. 313; M.H. 302; P.C. 216
— Ern. A.C., 3rd M. of, form. ld. E. Bruce, *q.v.*, L.L. Bucks. 306
Ailil, bp. Clr. 596
Ailild (2), bp. Arm. 595
Ailnothus, bp. Dorch. and Sidr. 446
Ailred, K.E. 2
Ailsa, M. of
— Archd., 1st M. of, form. E. of Cassilis, *q.v.*
— Archd., 2nd M. of, K.T. 748; L.L. Ayrsh. 508
Ailstone, Rt. le, L.H.T. 153
Aimon, C. Svy. 54
Ainmereach, K. Ir. 21
Ainmire, bp. Arm. 595
Ains—, *see also* **Ayns—**
Ainsley, Jno., L.M. Lond. 402
Ainslie, Chas. P., gen. (**D**) 897
— Geo. gen. (**A**) 859
— Geo. Rt., gen. (**B**) 868
— R., G. Gren. 725
— sir Rt., Amb. Tky. 129
Airey, *see also* Airy
— sir Geo., gen. (**B**) 868 K.C.H. 787
— Jas. Talb., and sir J., gen. (**D**) 905; K.C.B. 780
— Rd. and sir R., G., Gibr. 670; gen. (**D**) 889; G.C.B. 770; K.C.B. 777
Airlie, E. of
— Dav., 8th E. of, L.L. Forff. 510
— Dav. Gr. Dr., 9th E. of, K.T. 749; L.H.C.K. Sc. 546
Airmeadach, bp. Clr., 596
Airy, *see also* Airey
— Geo. Bidd., Astr. Roy. 941; K.C.B. 783; Pres. R. Soc. 940
Aiscough, *see* Ayscough
Aislabie, Jno., L.T. 156; Ch. Ex. 165; L. Admy. 177; L.T. 156; P.C. 196; Tr. N. 256
Aitcheson, *see* Aitchison and Acheson
Aitchison, Andr., gen. (**D**) 877
— C. T., gen. (**D**) 923
— Ch. Umph. and sir C., Ch. Com. Bma. 655; K.C.S.I. 803; L.G. Pjab. 654; Sec. S. I. 804
— Jas. Ed. T., C.I.E. 807.
— Jno. and sir J., gen. (**D**) 880; G.C.B. 770; K.C.B. 778.
— Rt., Adm. (**H**) 846
Aitken, Wm. Dav., gen. (**D**) 907
Aitkin, Jas., bp. Gall. 539; bp. Mor. 534
Akerman, Jno. Wm., K.C.M.G. 798
Akers-Douglas, *see* Douglas
Aket, sir Cuthb., L.M. Lond. 491
Alain, III. to V., D. Bry. 27-8
— -Fergent, D. Bry. 28
Alan, bp. Arg. 537
— dn. Kild. 619
— (abb. of Tewkesbury), J. It. 366
Aland, Jno. Fort. and sir., J., aft. ld. Fortescue, *q.v.*, B. Ex. 364; J.C.P. 379; J.K.B. 373; S.G. 401; S.L. 411
Alard, Gerv., L.H.A. 170
— Steph., L.H.A. 171
Alaric, I. and II., K. Sp. 84-5
Alava, Mig., K.C.B. 775
Albanus, bp. Bgr. 425
Albany, D. of, *see also* York
— Rt., D. of, L.G.C. Sc. (1383) 509
— Alexr., D. of, L.H.A. Sc. (1482), 499
— Leop., &c., D. of, *see* Leopold, Pr.
— Hel. Fred. Aug., Dss. of, Cr. Ind. 810
Albemar, Ph. de, G. Ch. Isl. 667
Albemarle, Wm. de, K.B. 754
Albemarle, E. and D. of
— Wm., E. of (1189), form. Wm. Mandeville, *q.v.*, aft. E. of Essex, *q.v.*
Plantagenet Family.
— Edwd., D. of, form. E. of Rutland, *q.v.*, aft. D. of York, *q.v.*; Const. T. L. 320
— Th., 9th E. of, also D. of Clarence, *q.v.*, K.G. 734
Monck Family.
— Geo., 1st D. of, form. sir G. Monk, *q.v.*; L.T. 155; B.T. 263; M.H. 302; L.L. Esx. 308;
Albemarle, E. and D. of—*cont.* L.L. Ir. 555; K.G. 748; capt. gen. 855
—Chris., 2nd D. of, P.C. 191; L.L. Esx. 308; G. Jam. 712; K.G. 740
Keppel Family.
— Arn. J., 1st E. of, gen. (**D**) 871; K.G. 741
— Wm. A., 2nd E. of, gen. (**B**) 865; Gr. St. 304; K.B. 764; K.G. 742; P.C. 199
— Geo., 3rd E. of, gen. (**A**) 858; K.G. 742; P.C. 200
— Wm. Ch., 4th E. of, G.C.H. 787; M.B.H. 303; M.H. 302; P.C. 211
— Geo. Th., 6th E. of, gen. (**D**) 893
Albert, Pr. (consort of Q. Victoria); Const. W. Cast. 322; F.M. 856; G.C.B. 769; G.C.M.G. 794; K.C.E. 7; K.C.S.I. 802; K.G. 744; K.P. 751; K.T. 748; L.W.S. 323; P.C. 214
*— (of Cologne), abp. Arm. 595
*— abp. Yk. 485
*— (Alberthus), bp. Dunw. 454
*— (Albertus), bp. Her. 441
* Prob. some same pers. Comp. dates.
— C. Hld. 82
— (C. P. R.) K.G. 734
— (d'Alsace) D. Lne. 29
— K. Bma. 59
— K. Hgy. 60
— (of Mkg.) K. Sw. 92
— K. Sxy. 78; K.G. 745
— Pr. Nass. 75
— Pr. S. Rdt. 79
— (of Austria) R. Nds. 82
— (of Saxony) (2) R. Nds. 82-3
— I. and II., Emp. Gmy. 62
— I. and II., D. Brk. 69
— I. and II., M. Aus. 58
— I. to III., D. Bva. 68
— I. to III., El. Sxy. 77
— I. to III., M. Brg. 65
— I. to IV., Pr. Mkg. 74
— I. to V., D. Aus. 58
— II. (D. Aus., aft. E. Gmy.); K.G. 735
— VI., A.D. Aus. 58
— -Edward (son of Q. Vict.); Pr. E. 15; Pr. W. E. 9. *See also* Pr. of Wales
— -Jno. Ch. F. Alfr. Geo. (g. son Q. Victoria), Pr. E. 16
— -Victor Chr. Ed. (g. son Q. Victoria), Pr. E. 15. *See* Pr. of Wales
— -Wm. Hy. (g. son Q. Victoria), Pr. E. 15
Alberthus, *see* Albert
Alberto, M. Fa. 53
Albertus and **Alberus,** *see* Albert
Albin (or Alwyn), bp. Brn. 530
Albini, *see also* Earls of Arundel
— Sir Ph. de, L.H.A. 170
— Wm. de, 2nd E. of Arundel, Const. W. Cast. 322; J. It. 366
Albinus, A. P., C. Ro. 42-4-5
— L. P. (3), C. Ro. 43-4
— S. P., C. Ro. 40-1-4-5
Alboinus, K. It. 49
Albright, Jno., dn. Rph. 602
Albrincis, Wm. de, W.C.P. 317

For List of Abbreviations, see pp. 944-952.

Albus, *see* White
Alcantara, F. L., Pres. Vzla. 108
Alcester, Fk.B., 1st ld., form. Sir F. B. Seymour, *q.v.*, L. Admy. 186
Alcfrid, K.E. 2
Alcock, Alex., dn. Lism. 629
—— Geo., L.M. Dbln. 641
—— Hugh, dn. Bgr. 426
—— Jno., dn. Ferns. 623
—— Jno., bp. Ely, 435; bp. Roch. 460; bp. Worc. 473; Ld. Chanc. 355; M.R. 387
—— Ruth. and Sir R., Amb. Ch. 131; Amb. Jap. 131; K.C.B. 783
Aldan, K. Sc. 18
Alday, Wdn. Chr. Ch. Manch. 481
Aldberry, Jno., bp. Linc. 446
Aldbertus, *see* Albert
Aldeburgh, Rd. de, A.G. 398; J.C.P. 377; K.B. 755; S.L. 406
Alderbury, Walt. de, dn. St. P. 453
Alderman, Jac., L.M. Lond. 488
Alderson, Edw. H. and Sir E. B. Ex. 385; J.C.P. 380; S.L. 413
—— Jas. and Sir J., Pres. Coll. Ph. 938
Aldham, Wm. Cornw., adm. (**H**) 849
Aldithley, *see* Audley
Aldovrandino, I. and II., M. Fa. 53
Aldreby, Jno. d', bp. Linc. 446
Aldred and **Aldredus**
* —— abp. Yk. 485; bp. Worc. 472
*—— (2) bp. Cnwall. 436
*—— bp. Dorch. 446
*—— bp. Lindisf. 478
* Poss. some same pers. Comp. dates.
—— Jno. Wm., gen. (**D**) 882
Aldrich, Hy., dn. Chr. Ch. Oxf. 457
—— Rt., bp. Carl. 475
—— Rt. Dawes, adm. (**H**) 851
—— Wm., L.M. Dbln. 641
Aldridge, Jno., Clk. O. 260; St. O. 260
—— Jno. Wms., adm. (**H**) 848
—— Rt. Cl., Regr. Gart. 746
Aldulf and **Aldulfus,** *see also* Adulfus
—— K.E. 2
Aldune, *see* Aldwin
Aldwin, Aldwinus, or **Aldune,** bp. Dham. 478; bp. Lindisf. 478; bp. Lond. 451
Aldworth, Rd. N., U.S.S. 226
Aldwulf, K.E. 2
Aldwyn, bp. Lich. 443
Alen, Jno., Ch. Ex. Ir. 561
Alencon, Jno. de, Ld. Chanc. 353
—— Herb. d', J. It. 367
***Alexander,** bp. Gall. 538
*—— bp. Linc. 446
*—— (2) bp. Ross, 535
*—— dn. Wells, 428
* Prob. some same pers. Comp. dates.
—— (Farnese), D. Pma. 53
—— (de Medici) D. Tny. 57
—— Emp. E.E. 50
—— K. Pld. 91
—— L.J. gen. 522

Alexander—*cont.*
—— (Carageorgevics), Pr. Sva. 95
—— (of Parma), R. Nds. 82
—— (Nevski), R. Russ. 89
—— (g. son Q. Vict.), Pr. E. 15
—— I., H. Rma. 95
—— I., Pr. Bga. 95; G.C.B. 771
—— I. to III. (Emp. Russ.), 90
—— I. (Emp. Russ.), K.G. 743
—— II. (Emp. Russ.), K.G. 745
—— III. (Emp. Russ.), K.G. 745
—— I. to III., K. Sc. 19
—— III., K. Sc., K.B. 754; K. Man, 665
—— I. to VIII., P. Ro. 32-4-5-6
—— -Albert (g. son Q. Vict.), Pr. E. 16
—— -Chas., D. Anht. 66
—— Claud, gen. (**D**) 926
—— Fk., gen. (**D**) 926
—— Fk. Llew., gen. (**D**) 911
—— Geo. Gard., gen. (**D**) 902
—— Hy., gen. (**D**) 924
—— Hy. McCl., adm. (**H**) 853
—— Jas., gen. (**D**.) 878
—— Jas. and sir J., gen. (**D**) 890; K.C.B. 780
—— Sir Jas. Ed., gen. (**D**) 904
—— Sir Jerome, J.C.P. Ir. 581
—— Jno., bp. Dkld. 542
—— M. S., bp. Jslm. 677
—— Nathl., bp. Clonf. and K. 636; bp. Down and Cnr. 604; bp. Killoe. and Kilf. 635
—— Rt., gen. (**D**) 888
—— Rt., K.C. 416
—— Th., adm. (**A**) 819
—— Wm., bp. Dry. and Rph. 602; dn. Emly, 628
—— Wm., gen. (**C**) 873
—— Wm., L.M. Dbln. 641
—— Wm., *see* ld. A. *infra*
—— Wm. and sir W., C.B. Ex. 382; Jud. Com. P.C. 360; K.C. 415; M. Chy. 397; P.C. 210; S.L. 413
—— Sir Wm., Sec. St. Sc. (1626) 502
—— Wm. Byr., gen. (**D**) 921
—— Wm. Jno., Q.C. 417
—— Wm. Rux. E., gen. (**D**) 914
Alexander, ld.
—— Wm., ld., aft E. of Stirling, *q.v.*, Ld. Sess. (1635) 517
Alexandra-Louise-Olg.-Vict. (g. dau. Q. Vict.), Pr. E. 16
Alexis, D. Anht. 66
—— R. Russ. 90
—— I. to III., Emp. E.E. 51
—— I. to IV., Emp. Tzde. 98
Aleyne, *see* Alleyne
Alf—, *see also* Alph—
Alfgar, *see* Wulfgar
Alfhelmus, bp. Dorch. and Sidr. 446
Alfine, bp. Lindisf. 478
Alfonso and **Alphonso,** C. Anj. 27
—— (son of Count of Denia), K.B. 755
—— (son of Edw. I.), Pr. E. 10
—— K. Nav. 85
—— K. Scy. 86; *also* K. Nls.
—— I. and II., K. Nls. 56
—— II. (K. Nls.), K.G. 737
—— I. to IV., D. Mda. 53
—— I. to V., K. Arr. 86
—— V. (K. Arr.), K.G. 735
—— I. to VI., K. Pgl. 88
—— V. (K. Pgl.), K.G. 735
—— I. to XIII., K. Sp. 85-6-7
—— XII. (K. Sp.), K.G. 745

Alford, Ch. Rd., bp. Vict. (H.K.) 674
—— Hy., dn. Cant. 432
—— Laur., Bl. M. P.A. 336; R. Bl. P.A. 344
***Alfred,** bp. Dev. 436
*—— bp. Sels. 432
*—— bp. Shbn. 466
* Prob. some same pers. Comp. dates.
—— K.E. 3; L.H.A. 170
—— (son Geo. III.) Pr. E. 15
—— -Ern.-Alb. (son Q. Vict.) Pr. E. 16; K.G. 744; K.T. 749; *see also* D. of Edinburgh
—— -Alex.-Wm.-Ern.-Alb., Pr. E. 16
Alfredus, *see* Alfred
***Alfric** (or Elfric, or Aluricius), abp. Cant. 430; bp. Wltn. 466; abp. Yk. 485
*—— bp. Elm. and Dunw. 454
*—— bp. Her. 441
*—— bp. Shbn. 466
***Alfrid,** bp. Elm. and Dunw. 454 * Prob. some same pers. Comp. dates.
Alfstan, *see* Ealstan
*—— bp. Wltn. 466
***Alfstanus,** bp. Roch. 459
* Poss. same pers.
Alfsius, bp. Winch. 470
Alfwine, bp. Winch. 470
Alfwold (2) bp. Dev. 436
—— (or Elfwold), bp. Shbn. 466
—— K.E. 2
Alfwoldus, *see* Alfwold
Alfwolfus, bp. Dev. 436
Alfwy, bp. Lond. 451
Algar, bp. Dev. 436
—— bp. Elm. and Dunw. 454
—— Jas. Sturg. Ham., gen. (**D**) 928
Algarus, *see* Algar
Algericus, bp. Sels. 432
Algnied, bp. Cld. 598
Alherdus, bp. Elm. 454
Alhmund, bp. Winch. 470
—— bp. Her. 480
Alhnael, abp. St. Dav. 463
Ali, Cph. Aba. 98
Alice (dau. Wm. I.), Pr. E. 9
—— (dau. Edw. I.), Pr. E. 10
—— -Mary-Vict.-Aug.-Paul. (g dau. Q. Vict.), Pr. E. 16
—— -Maud-Mary (dau. Q. Vict. Gr. Dss. of Hesse), Pr. E. 15; Cr. Ind. 809
Alifregus, bp. Elm. and Dunw. 454
Ali-Moorad-Khan, Sh. Pers 99
Alison, sir Archd., M.C.I. 647 gen. (**D**) 917; G.C.B. 771 K.C.B. 780
—— Ch., Amb. Pers. 130
Allan, *see also* Alan, Allen and Allin
*—— bp. C'ness. 531; Ld. Chanc Sc. 515
*—— bp. Isl. 539; bp. S. and M 483
* ? Same pers.
—— L.J. gen. 522
—— sir Hy. Marshn. Havelock K.C.B. 782. *See also* Havelock
—— Th., C. Cus. 276; C. Cus Ir. 565
—— Wm., L. Prov. Edinb. 548
Allanson, sir Geo. Wy., B Ex. Sc. 524
Allunton, Rt., Ld. Chanc. I 575

llen, *see also* Allan and Allin
— bp. Isl. 539; bp. S. and M. 483
— K. Man. 664
— Alex. St., gen. (**D**) 913
— Anthy, M. Chy. 396
— sir Geo. Wigr., K.C.M.G. 798
— Geo. Wm., C.I.E. 806
— Hy. Geo., Q.C. 419
— Hugh, bp. Down and Cnr. 604; bp. Ferns, 621
— Jas., dn. St. Dav. 465
— Jas., gen. (**D**) 881
— Jno., adm. (**D**) 823; (**G**) 840
— Jno., adm. (**H**) 845
— Jno., M.R. Ir. 585
— Jno., aft. sir J., abp. Dbln. and Gl. 616; L.K. and Ld. Chanc. Ir. 576
— sir Jno., L.M. Lond. 490
— Jno. Cart., adm. (**A**) 815
— Jno. Edw., gen. (**D**) 932
— Jno. Hast., dn. Killoe. 637
— Jos., bp. Brl. 439; bp. Ely, 435
— sir Josh., L.M. Dbln. 640
— Nichs., bp. Meath, 599; L. Treas. Ir. 558
— Rt., P.P. 417; S.L. 413
— Th., dn. Chest. 477
— sir Th., adm. (**A**) 813
— sir Tim., L.M. Dbln. 641
— Wm., adm. (**A**) 816
— Wm., adm. (**H**) 848
— sir Wm., L.M. Lond. 490
— Wm. Fern, L.M. Lond. 492
lerthorpe, Lawr., B. Ex. 83
ley, Jno., L.M. Dbln. 641
— Wm., bp. Exr. 437
leyne and **Aleyne,** *see also* llen
— sir Jas., C.J.C.P. Ir. 580
— Jno., B. Ex. 383
— Jno., dn. St. Pat. 618
— Jno. Fost., G. Bdoes. 720
— Py., L.M. Lond. 488
— sir Th., L.M. Lond. 491
libone, Rd. and sir R., K.B. 372; K.C. 415; S.L. 411
in, *see also* Allan and Allen
— Jos and sir J., Sr. N. 257
ington, Giles, K.B. 759
— Wm., L. Treas. Ir. 558
— Wm., Sp. H.C. 248-9
— Wm. ld., Const. T.L. 321
ix, Pet., dn. Ely, 435; dn. r. 440
ot, Jno., L.M. Lond. 491
— Rd., dn. Rph. 603
onville, gen. d', K.C.B. 778
naly or **Almary,** Walt., . Winds. 474
naric, K. Sp. 85
nary, *see* Almaly
as, Jas., adm. (**A**) 817
eto, Jno. de, bp. Rph. 601
ewick and **Alnwick,** m., bp. Linc. 446; bp. rw. 455; S. St. 222
s, Jos., Pr. Ltn., 73
h—, *see also* Alf—
hage, *see* Elphege
hege, *see* Elphege
hegus, *see* Elphegus
honso, *see* Alfonso
nwuld, K.E. 2
n, bp. Dnbl., 532
ne, K. Sc. 19
d, K.E. 2
c, K.E. 1.
na, V., pres. Arg. 110; s. B. Ay. 110

Alsius, bp. Lindisf. 478
Alsop, Rd., L.M. Lond. 492
Alston, Fras. Beilb., K.C.M.G. 798
Altamont, Jno. Denis, 3rd E. of, aft. 1st M. of Sligo, *q.v.*, K.P. 750
Altaphoo, Raj. Shreemun, &c., K.C.S.I. 802
Alten, Chas., bar. or count, gen. (**D**) 873; G.C.B. 768; K.C.B. 775
— Vict., bar., gen. (**C**) 873
Altham, Jas. and sir J., B.Ex. 384; K.B. 764; S.L. 409
— Rd., ld., form. hon. R. Annesley, *q.v.*
Althorpe, visc.
— Geo. Jno., visc., aft. 2nd E. Spencer, *q.v.*, L.T. 158
— Jno. Ch., visc., aft. 3rd E. Spencer, *q.v.*, Ch. Ex. 165; L.T., 158, 160; P.C. 211
Alubertus or **Alubrithus,** bp. Sels. 432
Alured, bp. Worc. 472
— K.E. 2.
Aluricius, *see* Alfric
Alvanley, Rd. P., ld., form. sir R. P. Arden, *q.v.*
Alverez, J., Pres. Mex. 103
Alves, John, gen. (**D**) 890
Alwi, *see* also Alwy
Alwigh, bp. Sidr. 446
***Alwinus** (or Ealfwyn), bp. Wells 427
*— bp. St. Andr. 528
*— bp. Worc. 472
Alword, *see* Elfward
Alwyn, *see also* Albin
*— bp. Elm and Dunw. 454
*Prob. some same pers. Comp. dates
— Nich., L.M. Lond. 490
Amadeus, K. Sp. 87
— I. to VII., C. Svy. 54
— VIII. and IX., D. Svy. 54
Amalgaid, bp. Arm. 595
Amaurus, I. and II., K. Jsm. 97
Amb, Nawab of, K.C.S.I., 804
Amberkeletus, K. Sc. 18.
Ambler, Ch., K.C. 415
Ambly, Wm. de, J. It. 367
Ambrose, Wm., Q.C. 419
Ambustus, C. F., C. Ro. 40
— M. F., C. Ro. (3), 40; Dt. Ro. 40
— Q. F. V., C. Ro. 39; Dt. Ro. 41
Amcotes, sir Hy., L.M. Lond. 490
Amelia (dau. Geo. III.) Pr. E. 15
— -Eliz., Lg. H. Csl. 72
— -Soph., (dau. Geo. II.) Pr. E. 14
Amertes, Rd., K.B. 761
Amherst, Jeffr., gen. (**B**) 866
— Jeffr., *see* ld. A. *infra*
— Jno., adm. (**A**) 814
— Rd., S. L. 409
— Wm., gen. (**B**) 866
Amherst, lds. and E.
— Jeffr. and sir J., aft. 1st ld. A., C. Ch. 855; F.M. 856; G. Gsey. 669; gen. (**A**) 858; K.B. 765; L.G.O. 259; P.C. 202.
— Wm. Pitt, 2nd ld. and 1st E.; Amb. Ch. 131; Amb. Scy. 114; G.C.H. 787; G.G. Ind. 649; P.C. 209
Amlave, abp. Arm. 595

Amos, Andr., C.C.J. 403
Ampadan, bp. Glend. 615
Amphibalus, bp. Isl. 539
Amphlett, Rd. P. and sir R., P.C. 219; B. Ex. 385; J. Ex. D. 385; Jud. Com. P.C. 361; L.J. App. 389; Q.C. 418; S.L. 414
Ampthill, Odo. Wm. L., ld., form. ld. Odo. Russell, *q.v.*
Amucaid, bp. Kild. 616
Amund (Colbrenner), K. Sw. 92
— (Slemme), K. Sw. 92
Amurath, I. to V., S. Tky. 97-8
Amyand, Cl., C. Cus. 276; U.S.S. 226
Amye, sir Jno., M. Chy. 395
Anacletus, P. Ro. 32
Anarawd, Pr. Wls. 16
Anastatius, I. and II., Emp. E.E. 50
— I. to IV., P. Ro. 33-4
Anburey, Th. and sir T., gen. (**D**) 877; K.C.B. 777
Ancaster [and Kesteven], D. of
— Peregr., 2nd D. of, L.G.C. 285; P.C. 197
— Peregr., 3rd D. of, gen. (**A**) 858; L.G.C. 288; L.L. Linc. 310; M.H. 302; P.C. 198
— Robt., 4th D. of, form. E. and M. of Lindsey, *q.v.*, L.G.C. 288; L.L. Linc. 310; P.C. 203
— Brownl., 5th D. of, L.L. Linc. 310
Ancelin or **Ancelinus,** dn. Her. 442
Ancram or **Ancrum,** E. of
— Rt., 1st E. of, form. Rt. Kerr, *q.v.*
— Wm., E. of, aft. 6th M. of Lothian, *q.v.*
Ancus-Martius, K. Ro. 36
Anderdon, Th. Ol., Q.C. 417
Anderson, Ad., D. Fac. Sc. 527; Jy. Sc. 523; Ld. Adv. 526; Ld. Sess. 521; S. G. Sc. 527
— Alexr., gen. (**D**) 897
— Ch. Gibs., gen. (**D**) 924
— Ch. Hy., Q.C. 420
— Dav., bp. Rup. Ld. 697
— Dav., gen. (**D**) 907
— Dav. Gr., gen. (**D**) 911
— Edm. and sir E., C.J.C.P. 375; S.L. 408
— Edw. Abb. gen. (**D**) 918
— Fk. Cortl., gen (**D**) 930
— Geo. S. Alex., gen. (**D**) 923
— Geo. Wm. and sir G., G. Bbay 659; G. Ceyl. 672; G. Mtius. 684; K.C.B. 782
— Harry Cortl. gen. (**D**) 927
— Hy. Lac., K.C.S.I. 803
— Hy. Perc., K.C.M.G. 798
— Jas., adm. (**H**) 848
— Jas., Q.C. 417
— Jno., gen. (**D**) 886
— Jno., Surg., C.I.E. 807
— Jno. Rd., gen. (**D**) 910
— sir Jno. Wm., L.M. Lond. 492
— J. Josc., K.H. 792
— Jos., K.H. 791
— Paul, gen. (**A**) 863
— Rt., K.H. 791
— Rt. Patr., gen. (**D**) 918
— Th. gen. (**D**) 898
— W. Cochr. gen. (**D**) 893
— Wm. Couss., gen. (**D**) 923
— Wm. Geo. and sir W., Ass. C. and A. 169; K.C.B. 783
— Wm. Ward, gen. (**D**) 919

For List of Abbreviations, see pp. 944-952.

Andover, visc.
— Th., visc., aft. 1st E. of Berkshire, *q.v.*, K.G. 739
— Cl., visc., form. Ch. Howard, *q.v.*, aft. 3rd E. of Berkshire, *q.v.*
Andreas, bp. Dnbl. 532
Andrée, Rd. Coll., gen. (**D**) 880
Andreossi, Off. Nap. 26
***Andrew,** bp. Arg. 537
*— (2) bp. Cness, 531
*— bp. Drom. 604
*— bp. Gall. 538
*— bp. Ork. 535
*— bp. St. Dav. 464
*— dn. Kilm. 609
*— (abb. of Melrose), L.H.T Sc. 496
* Prob. some same pers. Comp. dates.
— I. and II., R. Russ. 89
— I. to III., K. Hgy. 59-60
— (or Andrews), Geo., bp. Ferns and L. 622; dn. Lim. 639
— Jas., L.M. Lond. 489
— Jno., Ch. Lond. 422
— Jno. Wm., adm. (**H**) 844
— Wm., bp. Ach. 612; bp. Mth. 599
— Wm. Patr., C.I.E. 807
Andrews, Aug. gen. (**D**) 877
— Biggs, K.C. 416
— Ch., gen. (**D**) 912
— Ed. Bull., G. Gld. Cst. 686
— (or Andrew) Geo. *See* Andrew
— Ger., dn. Cant. 431
— Hy., K.H. 792
— Jno. Goldw., Pres. Coll. Surg. 939
— Lanc., bp. Chich. 433; bp. Ely, 435; bp. Winch. 471; dn. Westr. 469
— Rd., dn. Yk. 487
— Rt., gen. 890
— Th., L.M. Dbln. 641
— Th., L.M. Lond. 491
— Th., P.P. 416; S.L. 413
— Wm. Dr., J. Ex. D. Ir. 584
Andronicus, I. to III. Emp. E.E. 51
— I. to III. Emp. Tzde. 98
Andros, Sir Edm., G. Gsey. 668
Angarville (or Bury), Rd. de, bp. Dham. 478; dn. Wells 428; L.H.T. 153; Ld. Chanc. 354
Angelbeck, Joh. Ger. Van, G. Ceyl. 672
Angelo, Ed. Anthy. K.H. 789
— Jno. Anthy. gen. (**D**) 920
Angers, Aug. Réal, G. Queb. 694
Angerstein, Jno. Julius Wm., gen. (**D**) 885
Angharad (2), Pr. Wls. 16-7
Angle, Guich. D'., aft. E. of Huntingdon, *q.v.*, K.G. (1372) 733
Anglesey, E. and M. of
Annesley Family.
— Arth., 1st. E. of, form. ld. Annesley, and 1st visc. Valentia, *q.v.*, L. Admy. 175; L.P.S. 240; P.C. 191; Tr. N. 256
— Jno., 4th E. of, P.C. 195; V. Treas. Ir. 559
— Arth., 5th E. of, P.C. 196; V. Treas. Ir. 559
Anglesey, E. and M. of—*cont.*
Paget Family.
— Hy. Wm., 1st M. of, form. E. of Uxbridge, *q.v.*, F.M. 856; G.C.H. 786; gen. (**A**) 861; K.G. 743; L.H.S. 287; L.L. Ang, 314; L.L. Ir. 557; L.L. Staffs. 312; M.G.O. 259; P.C. 210
— Hy., 2nd M. of, form. E. of Uxbridge, *q.v.*
Anglicus, Jno., dn. Yk. 486
Anguish, Th., M. Chy. 396; Acct. G. 397
Angus, Jno. Anst., gen. (**D**) 912
Angus, lds. and E. of
— Archd., 5th E. of, L.H.A. Sc. 499; Ld. Chanc. Sc. 515
— Archd., 6th E. of, Ld. Chanc. Sc. 514
— Archd., ld. (son of Wm., 11th E., aft. E. of Ormond), Ld. Sess. 517
Angusianus, K. Sc. 18
Angusius (2), bp. Isl. 539
Anian and **Anianus,** *see also* Enion.
*— abp. St. Dav. 463
*— bp. Bgr. 425
*— (2) dn. St. As. 462
* Prob. some same pers. Comp. dates.
Anicetus, P. Ro. 32
Anino, Ct. Nic., G.C.M.G. 794; K.C.M.G. 796
Anluain, bp. Saig. 620
Anna, Emp. Tzde, 98
— K.E. 2
Annaly, lds.
Gore Family.
— Jno., ld., form. Jno. Gore, *q.v.*
White Family.
— Hy., 1st ld., form. H. White, *q.v.*
— Luke, 2nd ld., form. L. White, *q.v.*, K.P. 752
Annas, K.E. 2
Annandale, Wm., E., aft. 1st M. of, Commr. Tr. Sc. 497-8; K.T. 747; L.H.C.K. Sc. 546; L.K. Sc. 503; L.P.S. Sc. 501; Ld. Sess. 517; P.C. 196; Pres. P.C. Sc. 500; Sec. St. Sc. 502
Anne, D. Bry. 28
— E. Russ. 90
— (iss. Edw. III.) (2) Pr. E. 10-11
— (dau. Edw. IV.), Pr. E. 12
— (dau. Chas. I.), Pr. E. 13
— (dau. Jas. II.), Pr. E. 13; Q.E. 6
— (dau. Geo. II.), Pr. E. 14
— (of Bohemia), Q.C.E. 7
— (Boleyn), Q.C.E. 8
— (of Cleves), Q.C.E. 8
— (of Denmark), Q.C.E. 8
— (Hyde), Q.C.E. 8
— (of Warwick), Q.C.E. 8
— -Sophia (dau. of Q. Anne), Pr. E. 14
— Alexr, Rec. Lond. 493
Annesley, Arth., *see* ld. A., *infra*
— hon. Arth., gen. (**A**) 862
— Arth. Lytt. L., gen. (**D**) 931
— Sir Fras., aft. ld. Mountnorris, *q.v.*, Sec. St. Ir. 562; V. Treas. Ir. 559
— Hon. Rd., aft. ld. Altham, *q.v.*, dn. Exr. 437
— Hon. Rd., *see* E. of A., *infra*
Annesley—*cont.*
— Steph. Fras. Ch., gen. 917
— Hon. Wm., dn. Down,
Annesley, lds. and E. of
— Arth., aft. ld. A. and 1s of Anglesey, *q.v.*, Comm. 554; P.C. 190
— Rd., aft. 2nd E. of, C. Ir. 565; C. Exc. Ir. 566
Ansell, Aug. Fras., gen. 904
Anselm (Saint), abp. C 430
Anson, hon. Adelb. Jno. bp. Qu'App. 698
— Archd. Edw. Harb., G. Edw. Isl. 699; G. Str. 675; K.C.M.G. 798
— Fk., dn. Chest. 477
— Geo., *see* ld. A. *infra*
— Geo. and sir G., gen. 862; G. Ch. Hosp. 936; G 768; K.C.B. 774; L.G. Hosp. 936
— Hon. Geo., C.C. Ma 657; C.C. Ind. 651; Cl 260; gen. (**D**) 883; St. O.
— Talav. Vern., adm. 842
— Sir Wm., gen. (**A**) K.C.B. 774
Anson, lds. and visc.
— Hon. Geo., aft. 1st ld adm. (**A**) 814; Clk. O. 26 Admy. 178; P.C. 199
— Thos. Wm., 2nd visc. 1st. E. of Lichfield, M.B.H. 303; P.C. 212
Anstie, Jas., Q.C. 419
Anstis, Jno. (No. 1), K.A. 327; Norf. H. 341
— Jno. (No. 2), Bl. C.H. Gart. K.A. 327; Geneal. 784
Anstruther, sir A., P.C.
— Jno. and sir J., C.J. 652; K.C. 415
— Ph., gen. (**B**) 864
— Rt., gen. (**B**) 865
— Sir Rt., L.L. Fifesh.
— Wm., K.B. 761; Ld. 520
Anterus, P. Ro. 32
Anthelm (Saint), bp. W 470
Anthemius, Emp. W.E
Anthony, *see also* Anto
— bp. Rph. 601
— K. Pgl. 88
— Pr. Mno. 31
— -Clement T., K. Sxy.
— -Ulric, D. Brk. 70
— -Ulric, D. S. Mgn. 79
Anthun, K.E. 1
Antoinadis, Jno., K.C 799
Anton I. (or Anton Gu D. Obg. 76.
Antoninus-Pius, Em 47
Antonius, dn. Cash. 627
— Tr. Ro. 46
— C., C. Ro. 46
— M. (2) C. Ro. 45-6
Antony, *see also* Antho
— C. Lux. 84
— D. Bbt. 29
— D. Lne. 30
— D. Pma. 53
Antrim, Rand. Wm., and 1st M. of, K.B. 765 750

For List of Abbreviations, see pp. 944-952.

A.odh (3) K. Ir. 21
—— -Ruadh, K. Ir. 20
—— -Uaireodhnach, K. Ir. 21
Aongus-Olmuchac K. Ir. 20
—— Tiurimheach, K. Ir. 21
Aplin, Elph. D'Oyl. D'Auv., adm. (**H**) 851
—— Jno. Geo., adm. (**H**) 846
—— Jno. G. Rog., gen. (**D**) 909
—— Pet., adm. (**A**) 817
Appleby, Jno. de, dn. St. P. 453
—— Jno. Fk., adm. (**H**) 847
—— Th. de, bp. Carl. 475
Applegath, Fras., gen. (**D**) 914
Appleyard, Fk. Ern., gen. (**D**) 927
Appuleius, S., C. Ro. 47
April, Jno., G. Gsey. 668
Apsley, sir All., Lt. T. L. 321
—— sir Pet., Coff. H. 293
Apsley, lds.
—— Hy., ld. aft. 2nd E. Bathurst, *q.v.*, L.T. 158; Ld. Chanc. 357; P.C. 202
—— Hy., ld. aft. 3rd E. Bathurst, *q.v.*, B.C. 252; L. Admy. 180; P.C. 205; Tell. Ex. 168
—— Hy. Geo., ld., aft. 4th E. Bathurst, *q.v.*, B.C. 253
Apulia, Sim. de, bp. Exr. 436; dn. Yk. 486
Aquablanca, Jno. de, dn. Her. 442
Aquila (or Aguila), Nichs. de, bp. Chich. 432; dn. Chich. 433
Aquilinus, L. H., C. Ro. 38
—— T. H., C. Ro. 37
Aquilius, M., C. Ro. 45
Arabin, Jno. Danl., gen. (**A**) 862
—— Jno. L., L.M. Dbln. 642
—— Septimus, adm. (**H**) 846
—— Wm. Jno., gen. (**A**) 860
—— Wm. St. Jul., J.A.G. 937; P.P. 416; S.L. 413
Aram, Th., C. Exc. 279
Araric, K. It. 49
Arbuckle, Benj. Hutch. V., gen. (**D**) 893
Arbuthnot, Alex., C. Cus. Sc. 504
—— Alexr., bp. Killoe. and Kilf. 635; dn. Cloy. 633
—— Alexr. Dundas Young and sir A., adm. (**H**) 846
—— Alexr. Jno. and sir A., K.C.S.I. 803; M.C.I. 647
—— Ch., Amb. Sw. 126; Amb. Tky. 129; B.T. 268; C.D.L. 243; Sec. Tr. 163; P.C. 207; U.S.F. 229
—— Ch. Geo. and sir C., C.C. Bbay. 660; C.C. Mdras. 658; gen. (**D**) 924; K.C.B. 781
—— Ch. Geo. Jas., gen. (**D**) 883
—— Geo. Alexr., gen. (**D**) 935
—— Hy. Th., gen. (**D**) 933
—— hon. Hugh, gen. (**A**) 863; K.C.B. 779
—— Jno., *see* visc. A., *infra*
—— Marr., adm. (**A**) 815; G. N. Sc. 695
—— Rt. and sir Rt., gen. (**B**) 870; K.C.B. 774
—— Th. and sir T., gen. (**B**) 869; K.C.B. 774
—— Wm. and sir W., L. Prov. Edinb. 548
—— hon. Wm., gen. (**D**) 891
—— Wm. Urq., M.C.I. 646
Arbuthnot, visc.
—— Jno., 8th visc. L.L. Kinc. 510
Arcadius, Emp. E.E. 50
Archbold, *see* Archebold
Archdall, Merv., gen. (**A**) 861
Archebold, Wm., B. Ex. Ir. 583
Archer, Ch. Palm., L.M. Dbln. 642
—— E. C., G. Trin. 722
—— Jno. and sir J., J.C.P. 379; S.L. 410
—— Jno. le, L.D. Ir. 551; Ld. Chanc. Ir. 574
—— Th., dn. Oss. 622
—— Wm. Caulf., gen. (**C**) 872
—— Wm. Hy., L.M. Dbln. 641
Archibald, bp. Cness. 531
—— bp. Mor. 534
—— Adams Geo. and sir A., G. Mtoba. 696; G. N. Sc. 695; K.C.M.G. 798
—— Ed. Mort., K.C.M.G., 798
—— Th. D., aft. sir T., J.C.P. 380; J.C.P.D. 380; J.Q.B. 374; S.L. 414
Arcott, Azim, &c., Pr. of, G.C.S.I. 801
Arcy, *see* Darcy
Ardagh, Huny of, bp. Dry. 601
—— Rd. Dr., gen. (**D**) 923
Arden, Jno., K.B. 756
—— Ralph de, J. It. 366
—— Rd. de, J. It. 366
—— Rd. Pepp. and sir R., aft. ld. Alvanley, *q.v.*, A.G. 400; B.T. 268; C.J.C.P. 376; C.J. Chest. 386; K.C. 415; M.R. 388; P.C. 204; S.G. 402; S.L. 412
—— Wm. Rd. Pepp., Regr. M.G. 799
Arden, lds.
—— Ch. Geo., 1st ld., form. Hon. C. G. Perceval, *q.v.*, B.C. 252; L. Admy. 180; L.L. Surr. 312; M.M. 247
Arderne, Jas., B. Ex. 383; dn. Chest. 477
—— Pet., C.B. Ex. 381; J.C.P. 378; S.L. 407
Ardulf, K.E. 2
Areskine, *see* Erskine
Arentschildt, Fk., bar. de, K.C.B. 775
Aressey, Norm. de, J. It. 367
Arfastus (or Herefast), bp. Elm. and Dunw. 454; Ld. Chanc. 352
Argadus, L.J. Gen. 522
Argentine, Giles de, J. It. 368
—— Regd. de, J. It. 366; Jy. 364
Arguimbau, Lawrence, gen. (**D**) 882
***Argusteil,** bp. St. Dav. 464.
***Argwistil,** bp. Llff. 448
* ? Same pers.
Argyll, sir Jno. of, L.H.A. (1311) 170
Argyll, E., M., and D. of. *See also* M. of Lorne
—— Col., 1st E. of, Ld. Chanc. Sc. 515
—— Col., 3rd E. of, L.J. Gen. 522
—— Archd., 4th E. of, L.J. Gen. 522
—— Archd., 5th E. of, Ld. Chanc. Sc. 515
—— Gilespick, E. of, L.J. Gen. (1567) 522
—— Col., 6th E. of, L.J. Gen. 522; Ld. Chanc. Sc. 515
—— Archd., 7th E. of, L.J. Gen. 522
Argyll, E., M., and D. of—*cont.*
—— Archd., 8th E. and 1st M. of, Comm. Tr. Sc. 497; Ld. Sess. 517
—— Archd., 9th E. of, Ld. Sess. 517
—— Archd., 10th E. aft. 1st D. of, C.G.S. Sc. 515; Comm. Tr. Sc. 497; Ld. Sess. 517
—— [and Greenwich] Jno., 2nd D. of, F.M. 856; H.C.P. Sc. 508; K.G. 741; K.T. 747; L.S.H. 290; Ld. Sess. 517; M.G.O. 259; P.C. 195
—— Archd. 3rd D. of, form. E. of Islay, *q.v.*
—— Jno., 4th D. of, gen. (**A**) 858; K.T. 747; P.C. 201
—— Jno., 5th D. of, F.M. 856; gen. (**A**) 858; L.L. Arg. 508
—— Geo. Wm., 6th D. of, G.C.H. 787; L.S.H. 290; L.K. Sc. 503; L.L. Arg. 508; P.C. 212
—— Jno. D. E. N., 7th D. of, L.K. Sc. 503
—— Geo. Dougl., 8th D. of, K.G. 745; K.T. 748; L.L. Arg. 508; L.P.S. 241; P.C. 216; Postm. G. 239; Sec. Ind. 236
—— Eliz. Georg., Dss. of, Cr. Ind. 809; M. Robes, 304
Arias, C., Pres. Hdas. 106
Aribert, I. and II., K. Lmd. 49
Arista, M., Pres. Mex. 103
Ariwaldus, K. Lmd. 49
Arlington, Hy., 1st ld. and E. of, form. sir Hy. Bennet, *q.v.*, K.G. 740; L. Admy. 175; L.C.H. 295; P.C. 191
Armiger, Robt., gen. (**B**) 865
Armstrong, Alex. and sir A., gen. (**B**) 869; K.C.B. 780
—— Alex. Th., gen. (**D**) 914
—— Bygoe, gen. (**A**) 858
—— Edw., gen. (**D**) 888
—— Geo. Andr., gen. (**B**) 868
—— Jas., gen. (**D**) 883
—— Jas. Wells, gen. (**D**) 904
—— Jno., bp. Gr. Tn. 680
—— Jno., dn. Kilf. 637
—— Jno., gen. (**D**) 902
—— Jno., gen. (**C**) 871; S.G.O. 259
—— Rd., gen. (**B**) 866
—— Rd., S.L. Ir. 593
—— sir Rd., C.C. Mdras. 657; gen. (**D**) 879; K.C.B. 777
—— Rd. Say., gen. (**D**) 893
—— Rt. B., Q.C. 417
—— Wm., gen. (**C**) 874
—— Wm. Andr., gen. (**D**) 926
Arnauld, J., gen. (**D**) 893
Arnaud, Jno., K.H. 790
Arnold, sir Edwin, K.C.I.E. 805
—— Jas. Hy., Adm. Adv. 423; Vic. gen. 422
—— Jas. Robn., gen. (**D**) 880; K.H. 789
—— Jno., K.C.B., 775
—— Sir Nichs., L.J. Ir. 554
Arnot, Dav., bp. Gall. 538
—— Hy., L.H.T. Sc. 496
—— Sir Jno., gen. (**B**) 864
—— Rt., Compt. Sc. 498
Arnott, Jas. Monc., Pres. Coll. Surg. 939
Arnulf and **Arnulph.** *See also* Ernostus and Ranulph
—— C. Fld. 82
—— C. Hlt. 81
—— D. Bva. 67

Arnulf and Arnulph—*cont.*
—— E. Gmy. 61
—— I. to III., C. Fers. 81
Arosemena, J., Pres. Pan. 107
Arouse, Jno., L.P.S. Sc. 500; Ld. Clk. Reg. 525; Sec. St. Sc. 501
Arran, Earls of
Stewart Family.
—— Jas., 1st E. of, L.H.A. Sc. 499; Ld. Chanc. Sc. 515; Ld. Sess. 517
Butler Family.
1st Creation.
—— Rd., 1st E. of, L.D. Ir. 555
2nd Creation.
—— Chas., 1st E. of, gen. (**B**) 864
—— Jas., E. of, aft. 4th D. of Hamilton, *q.v.*, gen. (**B**) 864; K.T. 747; M.G.W. 296
Gore Family.
—— Arth. Saund., 2nd E. of, K.P. 750
—— Ph. Y., 4th E. of, K.P. 751
—— Arth. S. W. C., 5th E. of, form. visc. Sudley, *q.v.*, L.L. Mayo, 570
Arrighi, Off. Nap. 26
Arses, K. Pers. 99
Artabanus, K. Pers. 99
Art-Aonfhir K. Ir. 21
Artaxerxes, I. and II., K. Pers. 99
Arthur (son Hy. II.), Pr. E. 9
—— (son Hy. VII.), Pr. E. 12; Pr. W.E. 8. *See also* Pr. of Wales
—— I. to III., D. Bry. 28
—— -Fk.-Patr.-Alb. (g. son Q. Vict.), Pr. E. 16
—— Wm.-Patr.-Alb. (son Q. Vict.), aft. D. of Connaught and Strathearn, *q.v.*, Pr. E. 16; K.G. 745; K.P. 751; K.T. 749; P.C. 218
—— C. A., Pres. U.S.A. 103
—— Dav., dn. Lim. 639
—— Geo. and sir G., G. Bbay. 659; G. Br. Hond. 714; G. N.S.W. 703; G. Upp. Can. 692; G. V.D. Ld. 708; K.C.H. 789; P.C. 215
—— Hon. sir Geo. Rt., gen. (**D**) 881
—— Jas., K.H. 792
—— Rd., adm. (**D**) 827
—— Th., bp. Lim. 638
—— Wm., adm. (**E**) 837
Arthvael, abp. St. Dav. 463
Artrigius, bp. Arm. 595
Arundel, Arundell, and **Arundelle**
—— Jno., bp. Chich. 433
—— Jno., bp. Exr. 436; bp. Lich. and Cov. 444; dn. Exr. 437
—— Jno., dn. Winds. 474
—— Jno. (3), K.B. 756-7-8
—— Jno. de, K.B. 756
—— Sir Jno., K.G. 735
—— Jno. (of Trerico), K.B. 759
—— Hon. Rd., L.T. 157; M.M. 247; Tr. Ch. 294
—— Rog., J. It. 366
—— Th., K.B. 758
—— Th., K.B. 760
—— Th. de, abp. Cant. 430; abp. Yk. 485; bp. Ely, 435; Ld. Chanc. 354-5
—— (or Fitzalan), sir Wm., K.G. (1396) 734
Arundel, Earls of. *Search also* under Fitzalan, Maltravers, Norfolk, and Surrey
—— Wm., 2nd E. of, Const. W. Cast. 322
—— Wm., 3rd E. of, Jy. 364
Fitzalan Family.
—— Rd., 8th E. of (also E. of Surrey, *q.v.*), L.H.A. 172
—— Rd., 9th E. of, K.G. 734; L.H.A. 173; L.H.T. 153; Ld. K. 354
—— Th., 10th E. of, K.B. 755; K.G. 734; L.H.T. 153; W.C.P. 318
—— Jno., 12th E. of (also ld. Maltravers, *q.v.*), K.G. 735
—— Wm., 14th E. of, K.G. 736; W.C.P. 318
—— Th., 15th E. of, form. ld. Maltravers and ld. Fitzalan, *q.v.*, K.B. 756
—— Wm., 16th E. of, K.G. 737; L.C.H. 294 (?)
—— Hy., 17th E. of, K.G. 738; L.C.H. 294 (?); L.H. Const. 289; L.L. Suss. 312; L.S.H. 290.
—— Th., 19th E. of, C.G.S. 356; E.M. 326; K.G. 739; L.L. Surr. 312; L.L. Suss. 312; L.S.H. 290
—— Hy. Fk., 20th E. of, E.M. 326
—— Hy., E. of, aft. 7th D. of Norfolk, *q.v.*, Const. W. Cast. 322; L.L. Surr. (1682) 312
Arundel of Wardour, lds.
—— Hy., 3rd ld. L.P.S. 240; P.C. 193
Arvina, A. C. C. (2), C. Ro. 40; Dt. Ro. 41
—— P. C. (2), C. Ro. 41
Asaph (St.), bp. St. As. 462
Ascelimus (or Adelmus), dn. Linc. 447
Ascelyn, bp. Roch. 459
Ascham, *see* Askam
Ascue, *see also* Aiscue, Ayscue, and Askew
—— Wm., K.B. 759
Ascwardby, Ad. de., J. It. 367
Ascwinus, bp. Dorch. and Sidr. 446
Asgill, sir Ch., G.C.H. 786; gen. (**D**) 860
—— Sir Ch., L.M. Lond. 492
Ash, *see also* Ashe
—— St. Geo., bp. Clr. 596; bp. Cloy. 631; bp. Dry. 601
Ashbourne, Ed., ld., form. Ed. Gibson, *q.v.*, P.C. 220
Ashburner, Geo. Ell., gen. (**D**) 914
—— Wm., gen. (**D**) 913
Ashburnham, Bertr. de, W.C.P. 317
—— Cromer and sir C., gen. (**D**) 930; K.C.B. 781
—— sir Denny, C. Exc. 278
—— Elias de, C.J.K.B. Ir. 577
—— Hon. Th., gen. (**D**) 885
—— Wm. and sir W., bp. Chich. 433; dn. Chich. 434
—— Sir Wm., Chambn. Ex. 166; Coff. H. 293
Ashburnham, lds. and E. of
—— Jno., 3rd ld., aft. 1st E. of C.Y.G. 298
—— Jno. 2nd E. of, Gr. St. 304; M.G.W. 296; L.L. Suss. 312; P.C. 201; Gr. St. (1775) 304
Ashburnham, lds. & E. of—*cont.*
—— Geo. 3rd E. of, G.C.H. 786; K.G. 743
Ashburton, lds.
Dunning Family.
—— Jno., ld., form. Jno. Dunning, *q.v.*, C.D.L. 243
Baring Family.
—— Alex., 1st ld., form. A. Baring, *q.v.*, Amb. U.S.A. 132
—— Wm. B., 2nd ld., form. hon. W. B. Baring, *q.v.*
Ashby, sir Jno., adm. (**A**) 81[illegible]
—— Nichs., bp. Llff. 449
—— Wm., Ch. Ex. 153
Ashe, *see also* Ash
—— Alanus, B. Ex. 383
*—— Ed., B.T. 264
*—— Ed., Clk. O. 260
*—— Ed., G. Bdoes. 720
* Prob. same pers.
—— Wm. A'Court, gen. (**A**) 85[illegible]
Asher, Alex., S.G. Sc. 527
Ashford, Wm. C., ld., form[illegible] visc. Bury, *q.v.*
Ashley, hon. Anth. E. M., Sec[illegible] B.T. 269; U.S.C. 235
—— hon. Anthy. Jno., Q.C. 41[illegible]
—— Fras., S.L. 409
Ashley, lds.
—— Anthy. A., 1st ld., form. si[illegible] A. A. Cooper, *q.v.*, aft. 1s[illegible] E. of Shaftesbury, *q.v.*; Ch[illegible] Ex. 164; L.L. Dors. 30[illegible] L.T. 155
—— Anthy., ld., aft. 7th E. [illegible] Shaftesbury, *q.v.*, B.C. 253; [illegible] Admy. 182
Ashley-Cooper, *see* Coope[illegible]
Ashman, Rt., L.H.A. 171
Ashmole, Elias, Winds. H. 1[illegible]
Ashmore, Ch., gen. (**D**) 894
—— Jno., gen. (**D**) 890
Ashraff, Sh. Pers. 99
Ashton and **Assheton,** *s[illegible] also* Aston
—— Jno., K.B. 755
—— Rd., G. I. Man, 666
—— Rd., wdn. Chr. Ch. Manc[illegible] 481
—— Rd. or Rt. and sir [illegible] L.H.A. 172; L.H.T. 153; L[illegible] Ir. 551; Ld. Chanc. Ir. 5[illegible] W.C.P. 318. These referenc[illegible] apparently all relate to t[illegible] same person, although t[illegible] names differ. Comp. date[illegible]
Ashurst, Sir Hy., C. Exc. 2[illegible] 279
—— Sir Wm., C. Exc. 279
—— Sir Wm. Hy. C.G.S. 3[illegible] J.K.B. 373; S.L. 412
Ashway (or Aswy), Ra[illegible] L.M. Lond. 488
Ashwell, Jno., Clar. K.A. [illegible]
—— Jno. de, A.G. 398
Ashworth, Ch. and sir [illegible] gen. (**C**) 875; K.C.B. 776
—— Fk. and sir F. gen. [illegible] 882
Asiaticus, L. C. S., C. Ro. 45
Asicus (St.) bp. Elph. 608
Asina, C. C. S. (2), C. Ro. 4[illegible]
—— P. C. S., C. Ro. 43
Ask (or Aske), Rd., J.K.B. [illegible] S.L. 409
Askam and **Askham**
—— Walt., S.L. 407
—— Wm., L.M. Lond. 489
Aske, *see* Ask
Askeby, Robt. de, Ld. Ch[illegible] Ir. 574; M. Chy. 393

Askew, *see also* Ascue, Ayscue, &c.
—— Sir Chr., L.M. Lond. 490
—— Sir Hy., gen. (**B**) 869
Askham, *see* Askam
Askwith, Wm. Harr., gen. (**D**) 902
Aslett, Wm. Str., gen. (**D**) 906
Aspinall, Jno., S.L. 412
—— Jno. Br., Q.C. 418
Aspland, Linds. M., Q.C. 420
Assenburg, Louis Van, G.C.G.H. 678
***Asser,** abp. St. Dav. 463
*—— bp. Shbn. 466
* Poss. same pers.
Asserius, Reg. de, bp. Winch.
Assheton, *see* Ashton
Asshebournham, *see* Ashburnham
Assiat, bp. Arm. 595
Astell, Ch. Ed., gen. (**D**) 919
—— Wm., Chn. E.I. Co. 645
Astle, Geo. Adm. (**A**) 820
Astley, Herb., dn. Norw. 456
—— sir Jacob, B.T. 264
—— sir Jno., K.G. 736
Astolphus, K. Lmd. 49
Aston, *see also* Ashton
—— Arth. and sir A., Amb. Fr. 113; Amb. Spn. 124; G.C.B. 772
—— Jas. Jones, Q.C. 419
—— Jno., K.B. 759
—— Rd. and sir R., C.G.S. 357; C.J.C.P. Ir. 581; J.K.B. 373; K.C. 415; S.L. 412
—— Rog., Const. T.L. 320; Lt. T.L. 321
—— Theod., Q.C. 419
—— Walt., K.B. 761
—— sir Wm., J.K.B. Ir. 579
Astry, Jas., M. Chy. 396
—— (or Ostrich), Rauf., L.M. Lond. 490
Astwolfus, bp. Dunw. 454
Asty, Hy., C.B. Ex. 381; J.C.P. 378
Aswy, *see* Ashway
Atanagildo, K. Sp. 85
Atar Sing, &c., C.I.E. 806; K.C.I.E. 805
Ataulfo, K. Sp. 84
Atcherley-Jones, *see* Jones
Atcheson, *see also* Acheson and Aicheson
Athalaric, K. It. 49
Athelard (or Ethelard), abp. Cant. 430; bp. Winch. 470
Athelm (or Adelmus), abp. Cant. 430; bp. Wells 427
Athelred (or Ethelred), abp. Cant. 430; bp. Winch. 470
Athelric, bp. Shbn. 466
***Athelstan** (2), bp. Cnwll. 436
*—— bp. Elm. and Dunw. 454
*—— bp. Her. 441
* Poss. some same pers. Comp. dates.
—— K.E. 3; L.H.A. 170
Athelwald, abp. Yk. 485
Athelward (or Athelwolf), bp. Carl. 475
Athelwolfus, bp. Elm, 454
Athequa (or Attien), Geo., bp. Llff. 449
Atherley, *see also* Hatherley
—— (or Hatherley), Jno., L.M. Lond. 490
—— Mark. Kerr, gen. (**D**) 899
Atherton, Jno., bp. Wford. and L. 627
Atherton—*cont.*
—— Wm. and sir W., A.G. 400; Q.C. 417; S.G. 402
Athey, John de and sir J., L.H.A. 170, 171
Athill, Ch. H., Bl. M. P.A. 337
Athirco, K. Sc. 18
Athlumney, Wm. Mered., 1st ld., form. sir Wm. Somerville, *q.v.*, aft. ld. Meredyth, *q.v.*
Athol, Athole, or **Atholl,** E., M., and D. of
—— Jno. Stewart, E. of, Ld. Chanc. Sc. (1578) 515
—— Jno., 5th E., aft. 1st M. of, Comm. Tr. Sc. 497; K.T. 747; L.P.S. Sc. 501; L.J. gen. 522; Ld. Sess. 517
—— Jno., 2nd M., aft. 1st D. of, form. 6th E. of Tullibardine, *q.v.*; K.T. 747; L.H.C.K. Sc. 546; L.P.S. Sc. 501; Ld. Sess. 517
—— Jas., 2nd D. of, K.T. 747; L.K. Sc. 503; L.P.S. Sc. 501; Ld. Man. 665; P.C. 198
—— Jno., 3rd D. of, K.T. 747; Ld. Man. 665
—— Jno., 4th D. of, G. I. Man. 666; K.T. 748; L.L. Prth. 511; P.C. 206
—— Geo. Aug. Fred. Jno., 6th D. of, K.T. 748
—— Jno. Jas. Hugh Hy., 7th D. of, K.T. 749; L.L. Prth. 511
—— Anne, Dss. of, M. Robes, 304
Athowe, Th., S.L. 409
Athulf, bp. Elm. and Dunw. 454; bp. Her. 441
Atkins and **Atkyns**
—— Ed. and sir E. (No. 1), B. Ex. 384; C. Exc. 277; J.C.P. 379; S.L. 409
—— Ed. and sir E. (No. 2); B. Ex. 384; C.B. Ex. 381; S.L. 410
—— Jno., L.M. Lond. 492
—— Jno. Tr., Curs. B. Ex. 386
—— G. Gsey. 668
—— Sir Jonn., G. Bdoes. 719; G. Gsey. 668
—— Rt. and sir R., C.B. Ex. 381; J.C.P. 379; K.B. 764; S.L. 410
—— Sir Th., L.M. Lond. 491
—— Wm., dn. Ferns, 623
Atkinson and **Atkynson**
—— Ed., Bl. M. P.A. 336; Hps. P.A. 343; Som. H. 332
—— Ed. Hy., gen. (**D**) 895
—— Ed. Tindal, Q.C. 420
—— Edwin Fel. Th., C.I.E. 808
—— Fk. Day, gen. (**D**) 916
—— Geo., S.L. 413
—— Harry Alb., K.C.M.G. 799
—— Hy. Tindal, C.C.J. 405; S.L. 414
—— Jno., R. Cr. P.A. 335; Som. H. 332
—— Rd., L.M. Dbln. 642
Atkyns, *see* Atkins
Atkynson, *see* Atkinson
Atlay, Ed., gen. (**D**) 911
—— Jas., bp. Her. 442
Atratinus, A. S. (2), C. Ro. 37
—— C. S., C. Ro. 39
—— L. S. (2), C. Ro. 38, 46
Atterbury, Fras., bp. Roch. 460; dn. Carl. 476; dn. Chr. Ch. Oxf. 457; dn. Westr. 469
Atticus, A. M. T. (2), C. Ro. 42
Attien, *see* Athequa
Atwater, Wm., bp. Linc. 447; dn. Sal. 468; Regr. Gart. 746
Aubant, Abrm. d', gen. (**B**) 866
Auberville, Wm. de, Jy. 363
Aubigny, *see* Richmond, Lenox, and A.
Aubrey, *see also* Awbrey
—— Geo., L.L. Glam. 315
—— Jno. and sir J., L. Admy. 180; L.T. 158
—— Wm., M. Chy. 395; Vic.Gen. 421
Aucher, Hy. Fitz., Const. T.L. 320
Auchinleck, sir Geo., Ld. Sess. 519
Auchmuty, *see also* Ahmuty
—— Jas., dn. Arm. 597; dn. Emly, 628
—— Saml. and sir S., C.C. Bgal. 652; C.C. Ind. 650; C.C. Mdras. 657; Comm. F. Ir. 564; G.C.B 767; gen. (**B**) 867; K.B. 766
—— Saml. Benj. and sir S., gen. (**D**) 880; G.C.B. 770; K.C.B. 778
Auckland, lds. and E. of
—— Wm., 1st. ld., form. Wm. Eden, *q.v.*, Amb. Nds. &c. 122; Postm. G. 238; Pres. B.T. 268
—— Geo., 2nd ld., aft. 1st E. of, Aud. Ex. 167; G.C.B. 772; G.G. Ind. 649; Ld. Admy. 182-3; M. M. 247; P.C. 211; Pres. B.T. 268
—— Rt. Jno., 3rd ld., form. hon. R. J. Eden, *q.v.*, bp. B. and W. 428
Audeley and **Audley**
—— Edmd., bp. Her. 441; bp. Roch. 460; bp. Sal. 467
—— (or Aldithley), Jas. de, and sir J., J. It. 368; L.J. Ir. 550
—— sir Jas., K.G. 733
—— Maur. de, Jy. 364
—— Th. and sir T., aft. ld. A. of Walden, K.G. 738; Ld. K. and Ld. Chanc. 355; S.L. 408; Sp. H.C. 249
Audomare, Hy. de P., Jy. 364
Augereau, Off. Nap. 26
Augurinus, L. M. E., C. Ro. 38; Dec. Ro. 38
—— M. G., C. Ro. 38
—— M. M., C. Ro. 37
—— P. M., C. Ro. 37
—— Q. M. E., C. Ro. 38
—— T. G., C. Ro. 38; Dec. Ro. 38
—— T. M., C. Ro. 41
Augusta (g. dau. Geo. II.), Pr. E. 14
—— -Car.-Charl.-Eliz. (g. dau. Geo. III.), Pr. E. 15; Cr. Ind. 809
—— -Soph. (dau. Geo. III.), Pr. E. 15
Augustin and **Augustine**
—— abp. Cant. 429
—— bp. Wford. 626
—— Emp. Mex. 103
Augustulus, R., Emp. W. E. 49
Augustus, *see also* Octavianus
—— (2) D. Brk. 70
—— dn. Drom. 606
—— El. Sxy. 78
—— Emp. Ro. 36
—— (2) G. D. Obg. 76
—— Fredk., D. S. Mgn. 79
—— (son Geo. III.), aft. D. Sussex, *q.v.* Pr. E. 15; K.G. 742

Augustus—*cont.*
—— -Wm., D. Brk. 70
—— -Wm.-Geo., M. Bdn. 67
Auldjo, Jno. R., gen. (**D**) 914
Aumari, Rt. de, Jy. 364
Aungerville or **Aungervyle,** *see* Angarville
Aungier, sir Fras., aft. ld. A., L.K. Ir. 576; M.R. Ir. 585
Auntreseye, Rog. de, J. It. 367
Aure, Jno. de, J. It. 368
Aurelian, Emp. Ro. 48
Aurelio, K. Sp. 85
Aurelius, K. Sp. 85
—— -Caracalla A., Emp. Ro. 47
—— M., Emp. Ro. 47
Auriol, Ch., gen. (**C**) 874
Auruncus, P. C. (2), C. Ro. 37
Aust, Geo., U.S.F. 230
Austen, Alb. Geo., gen. (**D**) 902
—— Ch. Jno., adm. (**D**) 827
—— Fras. Wm. and sir F., adm. (**A**) 820; (**B**) 821; (**C**) 822; G.C.B. 776; K.C.B. 776
—— Jno., K.H. 792
—— Rd., L. Admy. 176
Austin, Ch., P.P. 417
—— Hor. Th., adm. (**D**) 831; (**E**) 834; K.C.B. 779
—— sir Jno., C. Cus. 274
—— Jno. Gard., G. Br. Hond. 714; G. H. Kong, 673
—— Wm. P., bp. Guiana, 715
Austria, Ch., Archd. of, G.C.B. 768
—— Fk. Ch., Archd. of, G.C.B. 769
Auverquerque, Hy. de N. d', M.H. 302
Autharis, K. Lmd. 49
Avalon, Jno., visc., L.L. Surr. 312
Avarne, Th., gen. (**B**) 866
Aveland, lds.
—— Gilb. J., 1st ld., L.L. Linc. 310
—— Gilb. Hy., 2nd ld., Dep. L.G.C. 288; P.C. 219
—— Clema. Eliz., lady, aft. lady Will. de Eresby, *q.v.*, L.G.C. 288
Avellaneda, N., Pres. Arg. 110
Avenbury, Giles de, dn. Her. 442
Avenon, Alexr., L.M. Lond. 490
Aventinensis, C.G. C. Ro. 40
—— L. G., C. Ro. 40-1
Averell (or Averill), Jno., bp. Lim. A. and A. 639; dn. Emly, 628; dn. Lim. 640
Averenches, Wm. de, W.C.P. 317
Averill, *see* Averell
Aviles, J. M., Pres. Ecr. 108
Avisa, Q.C.E. 7
Avitus, M. M., Emp. W. E. 49
Avonmore, Barry, ld. and visc., form. B. Yelverton, *q.v.*
Awbrey, *see also* Aubrey
—— Andr., L.M. Lond. 489
—— Wm., M. Chy. 395; Vic. Gen. 421
Awdry, sir J. W., C.J. Bbay, 660
Awkeburne, Lawr. de, bp. Sal. 467
Ay—, *see also* Ai—
Aydanus, bp. Llff. 448
Ayers, Hy., K.C.M.G. 797
Ayles, Jno. Geo. Aug., gen. (**D**) 899
Aylesbury, *see* Ailesbury
Aylesford, E. of
—— Heneage, 1st E. of, form. Hen. Finch and 1st ld. Guernsey, *q.v.*, C.D.L. 242
—— Heneage, 4th E. of, B.T. 267; L.S.H. 290; C.G.P. 300; C.Y.G. 298; L.S.H. 290; P.C. 204
Ayleston, Rt. de, B. Ex. 383
Aylett, Rt., M. Chy. 395
—— sir Wm., gen. (**B**) 868
Aylmer, Arth., gen. (**B**) 868
—— hon. Fk. Wm., *see* ld. A. *infra.*
—— Gerald and sir G., C. B. Ex. 583; C.J.K.B. Ir. 577; J.C.P. Ir. 581; L.J. Ir. 553
—— Hy., gen. (**D**) 899
—— Jno., adm. (**A**) 817
—— Jno., bp. Lond. 451
—— Matth., *see* ld. A., *infra*
Aylmer, lds.
—— Matth., aft. 1st ld. A., 177; adm. (**A**) 813; G. Gr. Hosp. 854; L. Admy. 177
—— Matth., 5th ld., G. Can. 691; gen.(**A**) 862; G.C.B. 768; K.C.B. 774
—— hon. Fk. Wm., aft. 6th ld. A., adm. (**D**) 825; (**G**) 840; K.C.B. 777
—— Thos. Br., gen. (**D**) 879
Ayloff, or **Ayloffe,** Wm., J.Q.B. 372; S.L. 408
—— Wm., S.L. 409
Ayns—, *see also* Ains—
Aynsley, Ch. Murray, adm. (**H**) 852
—— Geo. Herb. Murr., gen. (**D**) 929
Ayremin, Ayremyn, and **Ayremynne**
—— Rd. de, M.R. 387
—— Wm., bp. Carl. (?) 475; bp. Norw. 454; L.H.T. 153; Ld. K. 354; M.R. 387
Ayrton, Acton Sm., C.W.P.B. 272; J.A.G. 937; P.C. 218; Sec. Tr. 164
Ayscoghe, Wm., J.C.P. 378
Ayscough, Fras., dn. Brl. 440
—— Jno., adm. (**D**) 826
—— Jno., G. Jam. 712
—— Wm., bp. Sal. 467
Ayscue, sir Geo., adm. (**A**) 813; G. Bdoes. 719
Ayshton, Rd. or Nichs., J.C.P. 378; S.L. 407
Ayton, Andr., Ld. Sess. 519
Aytoun, Rog., gen. (**C**) 873
Azzo, VI. to VIII., M. Fa. 52-3

B.

Baalun, Jno. de, J. It. 367
—— Rog. de, J. It. 367
Babbage, Hy. Prev., gen. (**D**) 912
Baber, Ed., S.L. 408
Babington, Brut., bp. Dry. 601
—— Dav., gen. (**D**) 899
—— Gerv., bp. Exr. 437; bp. Llff. 449; bp. Worc. 473
—— Jno. Hy. Melv., gen. (**D**) 921
—— Wm., A. G. 398; C.B. Ex. 381; C.J.C.P. 375; J.C.P. 378; K.B. 756; S.L. 407
—— Wm. Kn., gen. (**D**) 906
Babthorpe, Wm., A.G. 398
Baby, Danl., gen. (**D**) 895
Babynghe, Jno., abp. Tm. 611
Baccus, *see* Backhouse
Bache, Alexr., bp. St. As. 462
—— Anthy., M.M. 246
Back, sir Geo., adm. (**G**) 842
Backhouse, Jno., C. Exc. 282
—— (or Baccus) Jno., K.B. 763
—— Jno., U.S.F. 230
—— Th. Jos., gen. (**B**) 868
Bacon, Ch., B.G., gen. (**D**) 912
—— Edm. Ant. Hen., gen. (**D**) 915
—— Edw., B.T. 265
—— Fras. and sir F., aft. ld. Verulam, and visc. St. Albans, *q.v.*, A.G. 399; J.K.B. 372; K.C. 414; Ld. Chanc. and L.K. 356; Q.C. 414; S.G. 401; S.L. 409
—— Fras. Hy., C.C.J. 405
—— Jas. and sir J., C.J. Bank. 392; Jud. Com. P.C. 362; P.C. 221; Q.C. 417; V. Chanc. 390
—— Jno., J.C.P. 377
—— Nath., J. Adm. Ct. 423
—— Nath., K.B. 763
—— Nichs., K.B. 764
—— sir Nichs., L.P.S. 240; L.K. 356
—— Th., J.C.P. 377; J.K.B. 371; K.B. 755
Baddeley, Fk. Hy., gen. (**D**) 890
—— Wm. Cl., gen. (**D**) 879
Baden, Giles, dn. Ardf. 640
Baden-Powell, *see* Powell
Badlesmere, Barth. de, aft. ld. Burghersh, *q.v.*, W.C.P. 318
Baduilla, K. It. 49
Baez, B., Pres. Dom. Rep. 105
Baggallay, Rd. and sir R., A.G. 400; Jud. Com. P.C. 361; L.J. App. 389; P.C. 219; Q.C. 418; S.G. 402-3
Bagley, Ch. Jno., G. Bah. Isl. 716
Bagnold, Michl. Ed., gen. (**D**) 886
Bagod, *see* Bagot
Bagot, hon. Chas. and sir C., Amb. Aus. 117; Amb. Fr. 113; Amb. Nds.&c. 123; Amb. Russ. 125; Amb. U.S.A. 132; G.C.B. 772; G. Can. 692; P.C. 209; U.S.F. 229
—— Danl., dn. Drom. 606
—— Ed., gen. (**D**) 900
—— Geo., gen. (**D**) 925
—— Hy., adm. (**G**) 843
—— Lewis, bp. Brl. 439; bp. Norw. 455; bp. St. As. 462; dn. Chr. Ch. Oxf. 457
—— Rd., C. Exc. 280
—— hon. Rd., bp., B.andW. 428; bp. Oxf. 457: dn. Cant. 432
Bagot, Bagod, Bigod, *or* Bigot, Rt., J.C.P.Ir. 581; J.K.B. Ir. 578
Bagshawe, Hy. Red., C.C.J 404; Q.C. 417

Bagshawe—*cont.*
—— Wm. H. G., C.C.J. 405; Q.C. 419
Bagwell, Jno., L.T. 161
—— Rd., dn. Clr. 598; dn. Kilmacd. 638
Bahawulpur, Nawab of, G.C.S.I. 801
Bahmanji, T. Dastur, C.I.E. 806
Bailey, *see also* Baily, Bayley, and Bayly
—— Fk., Q.C. 419
—— sir Jos. Russ., L.L. Brec. 315
—— Wm., C. St. 283-4
—— sir Wm., L.M. Lond. 490
—— Wm. Staff., gen. (**D**) 930
Baillie, Ch., gen. (**C**) 873; Jy. Sc. 523; Ld. Adv. 526; Ld. Sess. 521; S.G. Sc. 527
—— Cuthb., L.H.T., Sc. 497
—— Dunc. Jas., gen. (**D**) 924
—— Geo., B.T. 264; Dep. Tr. Sc. 498; L. Admy. 177; L.T. 156
—— Geo. Alex., gen. (**D**) 899
—— Hamilton W.A., Sec. Adm. 187
—— Hans., L.M. Dbln. 641
—— Hy. Jas., P.C. 217; Sec. B.C. 254; U.S. Ind. 236
—— Hugh Dunc., L.L. Ross. 512
—— Jas., gen. (**D**) 918
—— Jas. Cad. Parkn., gen. (**D**) 926
—— Jno., gen. (**D**) 914
—— Mack. Hugh, gen. (**C**) 872
—— Matth., gen. (**B**) 867
—— Hon. Thos., adm. (**D**) 833; (**E**) 834; (**F**) 838; L.G. Gr. Hosp. 854
—— Wm. (Provand), L.P. Ct. Sess. 516; Ld. Sess. 518
—— (Polkemmit), Ld. Sess. 520
Baillie-Hamilton, *see* Hamilton
Bailol, Josc. de, bp. Sal. 466
Baily, *see also* Bailey, Bayley and Bayly
—— Jno., Q.C. 417
—— Wm., bp. Clonf. and K. 636
Bain, Edwin Sand, S.L. 413
—— Hend., adm. (**H**) 845
Bainbridge and **Bainbrigge**
—— Chr., abp. Yk., 486; bp. Dham. 478; dn. Winds. 474; dn. Yk. 487; M.R. 387
—— Jno. Hank., gen. (**D**) 896
—— Ph. and sir P., gen. (**D**) 882; K.C.B. 778
—— Ph. Jno., gen. (**D**) 898
Baines, *see also* Banes and Baynes
—— Matth. Talbot, C.D.L. 243; P.C. 215; Pres. P.L.B. 262; Q.C. 417
—— Ralph., bp. Lich. and Cov. 444
—— Wm., C.C.J. 403
Baird, Augs. Fraser, gen. (**D**) 925
—— Sir Dav., Comm. F. Ir. 564; G.C.G.H. 679; gen. (**A**) 860; G.C.B. 767; K.B. 766
—— Sir Jno., Ld. Sess. 519-20
—— Jno. Kennedy Erskine, adm. (**E**) 837
—— Jos., gen. (**C**) 873
Baitan, bp. Clonm. 599
Bajazet, I. and II., S. Tky. 97
Bajocis, Rd. de, K.B. 755
Baker, —, S.L. 408
—— Geo., bp. Wford. and L. 627
—— sir Hy. Lorraine, adm. (**H**) 845
—— Jas. Vashon, adm. (**G**) 843
—— Jno., adm. (**A**) 813
—— Jno. and sir Jno., A.G. 398; Rec. Lond. 493; Sp. H.C. 249
—— Matth., G. Jsey. 667
—— Rt. Jno., gen. (**D**) 915
—— Th., gen. (**A**) 861
—— Th. and sir Th., adm. (**A**) 819; K.C.B. 776
—— Th. Dur. and sir Th., gen. (**D**) 930; K.C.B. 781
—— Wm., bp. Bgr. 426; bp. Norw. 455
—— Wm. Ersk. and sir W., gen. (**D**) 900; K.C.B. 783; M.C.I. 646
Balam, Rd. de, dn. Lich. 445
Balbinus, Emp. Ro. 47
Balbus, L. C., C. Ro. 46
—— L. N., C. Ro. 45
—— M.A., C. Ro. 44-5
Balcanquall, Walt., dn. Dham. 479; dn. Roch. 461
Balcarras or **Balcarres,** E. of
—— Alexr., 1st E. of, Sec. St. Sc. 502
—— Colin, 3rd E. of, Comm. Tr. Sc. 497
—— Alexr., 6th E. of, G. Jam. 712; gen. (**A**) 859
Balchan, sir Jno., adm. (**A**) 813; G. Gr. Hosp. 854
Balders, Ch. Wm. Morl., gen. (**D**) 895
Baldewyn, *see* Baldwin
Baldoc and **Baldock**
—— Geo., gen. (**D**) 923
—— (or Baudake), Ralph de, bp. Lond. 451; dn. St. P. 452; Ld. Chanc. 353-4
—— Rt. de, bp. Norw. 454; Ld. Chanc. 354
—— Rt. and sir R., J.K.B. 372; S.L. 410
—— Th., adm. (**H**) 849
Baldred, K.E. 1
Baldric (or Galdric), Ld. Chanc. 353
—— (or Baldry) sir Th., L.M. Lond. 490
Baldwin, Baldwyn, and **Baldewyn**
—— abb. Cant. 430; bp. Worc. 472
—— (son of Stephen), Pr. E. 9
—— I. and II., Emp. E.E. 51
—— I. to V., K. Jsm. 97
—— I. to VI., C. Hlt. 81
—— I. to IX., C. Flrs. 81
—— Augs., adm. (**H**) 846
—— Jno. and sir J., C.J.C.P. 375; S.L. 408
—— Maur. S., bp. Huron, 693
—— Saml., S.L. 410
—— Tim., M. Chy. 396
—— (Baldewyne), Wm., J.C.P. Ir. 581
Bale, Jno., bp. Oss. 620
Balfour, Arth. Jas., Ch. Sec. Ir. 563; L.K. Sc. 503; P.C. 220; Pres. L.G.B. 256; Sec. Sc. 502; V.P. Ed. Sc. 500
—— Blayn. Townl., G. Bah. Isl. 716
—— Sir Dav., Ld. Sess. 519
Balfour—*cont.*
—— Geo. and sir G., gen. (**D**) 900; K.C.B. 783
—— Jas., gen. (**A**) 860
—— Jas., Ld. Sess. 517-8
—— Sir Jas., L.P. Ct. Sess. 516; Ld. Clk. Reg. 525
—— Sir Jas., Ly. K.A. 513
—— Sir Jas., Sec. St. Sc. 502
—— Jno., bp. Brn. 531
—— Jno. Bl., P.C. 220; D. Fac. Sc. 527; Ld. Adv. 526; P.C. 220; S.G. Sc. 527
—— Lowry V. Townl., Sec. St. Patr. 752
—— Michl., Sec. St. Sc. 502
—— Nisb., gen. (**A**) 859
—— Rt. (c.c. ld. Burleigh), Comm. Tr. Sc. 497
—— Rt., gen. (**B**) 869
—— Wm., G. N. Brk. 695; gen. (**C**) 873
—— sir Wm., Lt. T.L. 321
—— Wm. St., gen. (**D**) 891
Balfourn, —, G. Tob. 723
Balguy, Jno., K.C. 416
Baliconingham, Jno. de, bp. Cork, 630
Baliol, *see also* Bailol
*—— Alexr., Ld. Chanc. Sc. 514
*—— sir Alexr., L.G.C. Sc. 506
* ? Same pers.
—— Ed., K. Sc. 19
—— Hy. de, L.G.C. Sc. 506
—— Jno., K. Sc. 19
Balizon, Greg., G. Ch. Isl. 667
Ball, Alexr. Jno. and sir A., adm. (**A**) 817; G. Mlta. 671
—— Hy., R. Cr. P.A. 335; Winds. H. 331
—— Hy. Lidgb., adm. (**A**) 819
—— Jno., S.L. Ir., 592
—— Jno., U.S.C. 235
—— Jno. Thos., A.G. Ir. 588; Ld. Chanc. Ir. 577; S.G. Ir. 590
—— Nichs., A.G. Ir. 588; J.C.P. Ir. 582; S.L. Ir. 593
—— Th., dn. Chich. 434
—— Thos. Gerrard, gen. (**D**) 885
Ballantine, Fletchv. Dykes, gen. (**D**) 878
—— Wm., P.P. 418; S.L. 413
Ballard, Jno. Archd., gen. (**D**) 907
—— Ph., dn. Worc. 473
—— Saml. Jas., adm. (**A**) 819
—— Vol. Vash., adm. (**A**) 820
—— Wm., Mch. K.A. 339
Ballaricus, Q. C. M., C. Ro. 45
Balleine, Geo. Or., dn. Jsey. 668
Ballenden and **Bellenden**
—— Adam, bp. Abdn. 530; bp. Dnbl. 532
—— sir Jno., L.J. Clk. 516; Ld. Sess. 518
—— sir Lew., L.J. Clk. 516; Ld. Sess. 518
—— Th., L.J. Clk. 516
—— Th. (2), Ld. Sess. 518
Ballingall, Dav., gen. (**B**) 868
Ballivian, A., Pres. Bol. 109
—— J., Pres. Bol. 109
Bally, St. Jno., gen. (**D**) 933
—— Wm., gen. (**D**) 934
Ballyganrin, Jno. de, dn. Oss. 622

For List of Abbreviations, see pp. 944-952.

Balmaceda, J. M., Pres. Chi. 111
Balmain, Jas., C. Exc. Sc. 505
—— Jas. Geo., gen. (**D**) 910
Balmerino, lds.
—— Jas., 1st ld., form. Jas. Elphinstone and sir J., *q.v.*, L.P. Ct. Sess. 516
—— Jno. Jas., 2nd ld. H.C.P. Sc. 507; Ld. Sess. 517
—— Jno., 5th ld., form. hon. Jas. Elphinstone, *q.v.*
Balmyle, Nichs. de, bp. Dnbl. 532; Ld. Chanc. Sc. 515
Balnavis, Balneaves, and **Balneavis**
—— Hy., gen. (**D**) 882; K.H. 791
—— Hy. (No. 1) L.J. Clk. 516; Ld. Adv. 526; Ld. Sess. 518
—— Hy. (No. 2) Ld. Sess. 518
Balreput, Wm. de, dn. Oss. 622
Balsch, T. R., H. Mva. 94
Balscot, Alexr., bp. Mth. 599; bp. Oss. 620; L.J. Ir. 551; L. Treas. Ir. 558; Ld. Chanc. Ir. 574
Balsham, Hugh de, bp. Ely, 434
Balta, J., Pres. Pu. 109
Balthazar, Pr. Mkg. 74
—— Pr. Nass. 75
Baltimore, lds.
—— Geo., 1st ld., form. sir G. Calvert, *q.v.*
—— Chas., 4th ld., gen. (**C**) 871
—— Ch., 6th ld., L. Admy. 178
Baltroddi, Walt. de, bp. Cness. 531
Bamme, Ad., L.M. Lond. 489
Bampfield, Th., Sp. H.C. 249
Banarji, Kistna Moh. C.I.E. 807
Banastre and **Banaustre,** *see also* Banister
—— Alard., J. It. 365
—— Th., K.G. 734
—— Th., B. Ex. 383
Banaustre, *see* Banastre and Banister
Banbury, E. of
—— Wm., 1st E. of, form. ld. Knollys and 1st visc. Wallingford, *q.v.*
—— Wm. Knollys, called E. of, gen. (**C**) 872
Bancroft, Jno., bp. Oxf. 456
—— Rd., abp. Cant. 431; bp. Lond. 452
—— Wm. Ch., gen. (**D**) 925
Bandinthel, Dow., dn. Jsey. 668
Bandiora, Fras., bar. de, K.C.B. 777
Bandon, E. of
—— Jas., 2nd E. of, L.L. Cork, 569
—— Fras., 3rd E. of, L.L. Cork, 569
—— Jas. Fr., 4th E. of, L.L. Cork, 569
Banent, Hugh, Ch. Sec. Ir. 561; L. Treas. Ir. 558
Banes, *see also* Baines and Baynes
—— Jos. Fk. Wall. Des., G. Pr. Ed. Is. 699
Banington, Hy., K.B. 758
Banister and **Bannister,** *see also* Banastre and Banaustre
—— Wm. and sir W., B. Ex. 384; S. L. 411
Banke, Rd., B. Ex. 383
—— Th., B. Ex. 383
Bankes and **Banks**
—— Geo., B.C. 253; Curs. B. Ex. 386; J.A.G. 937; L.T. 159-60; P.C. 215; Sec. B.C. 254
*—— Hy., C. Cus. 276
*—— Hy., K.C. 415
* ? same pers.
—— Jas. Stev., K.C.B. 776
—— Jno. and sir J., A.G. 399; C.J.C.P. 375; L.L. Dors. 307; L.J. 154; S.L. 409
—— sir Jos., B. Tr. 268; G.C.B. 771; K.B. 765; P.C. 206; Pres. R. Inst. 940; Pres. R. Soc. 940
—— Th., dn. St. As. 463
Bankhead, Ch., Amb. Mex. 133; Amb. Tky. 129
Banks, *see* Bankes
Bankwell (or Baukwell), Jno. de, J. It. 368
—— Rog. de, J.K.B. 371
Bannatyne, Jas., Ld. Sess 519
—— Th., Ld. Sess. 518
—— Wm. McL., Ld. Sess. 520
Bannerhassett, sir Jno., B. Ex. Ir. 584
Bannerman, Alexr. and sir A., G. Bah. Isl. 716; G. Newfd. 700; G. Pr. Ed. Isl. 669
—— Hy. Campbell-, Ch. Sec. Ir. 563; P.C. 220; Sec. Adm. 187; U.S. War, 233; W. Sec. 232
—— Wm., gen. (**D**) 931
Bannister, *see* Banister
Banquel, Jno. de, B. Ex. 383
Baodan, K. Ir. 21
Bapthorpe, Wm., K.B. 760
Baptist, Jno., bp. Drom. 604
Bapu Diva Shastri, C.I.E. 806
—— Sahib Avar, K.C.I.E. 805
Bar, Alexr., bp. Mor. 534
Barantin, Hugh de, Const. W. Cast. 322
Barbar, Jno., J. Pr. Ct. 421
Barbatus, M. H., C. Ro. 38
—— P. C. S., C. Ro. 41; Dt. Ro. 41
—— T. Q. C. (6), C. Ro. 38-9
Barber, C. Chapman, C.C.J. 405
—— Ch. Hy., K.C. 416
—— Jno., L.M. Lond. 491
—— Luc., gen. (**B**) 866
—— Wm., Q.C. 419
Barbour, Dav. Mill, K.C.S.I. 804
Barbula, L. Æ., C. Ro. 42
—— M. Æ., C. Ro. 43
—— Q. Æ., C. Ro. 41
Barbutt, Jno. D., Sec. P.O. 239
Barclay and **Berclay,** *see also* Barkly and Berkeley
—— sir Hy., G.C.M.G. 795
—— Jno., gen. (**A**) 860
—— Jos., bp. Jslm. 677
—— Rt., dn. Clr. 597
—— Rt., K.C.B. 775
—— Walt. de, L.G.C. Sc. 506
Bard, Pet., L.H.A. 170-1
Barde, Gauteur de, M.M. 246
Bardelby, Rt. de, L.K. 354; M. Chy. 393
—— Wm. de, M.R. Ir. 585
Bardolf, Hugh, J. It. 366; Jy. 363
—— Th., K.B. 754
—— sir Wm., L.H.A. 174
Bardolph, Wm., ld., form. sir Wm. Philips, *q.v.*
Bardsey, Arth. de, dn. Bg 426
Bardsley, Jno. W., bp. S. a M. 484
Bareiro, C., Pres. Pgy. 110
Barentyne, Dr., L.M. Lon 489
Barford, *see* Bereford
Bargash, B. S., S. Zr. 102
Bargrave, Is., dn. Cant. 431
Barham, Nichs., S.L. 408
—— Ch., 1st ld. form. sir Middleton, *q.v.*, Compt. 257; L. Admy. 180; P.C. 20
Barillas, M. L., Pres. Gua. 1
Baring, Alexr., aft. 1st Ashburton, *q.v.*, M.M. 24 P.C. 213; Pres. B.T. 268
—— Ch., bp. Dham. 479; Gl. and Br. 439
—— Ch., gen. (**D**) 919
—— Evel. and sir E., Amb. 130; G.C.M.G. 796; K.C. 784; K.C.S.I. 803
—— Fras., Chn. E.I. Co. 644
—— Fr. Th. and sir F., aft. ld. Northbrook, *q.v.*, Ch. 165; L. Admy. 183; L.T. 1 P.C. 214; Sec. Tr. 163
—— Hy. B., L.T. 160-1
—— Jane Emma, lady, Cr. I 809
—— Walt., Amb. Mgo. 128
—— Wm. B., aft. 2nd ld. A burton, *q.v.*, P.C. 214; Pay G. 244; Sec. B.C. 254
—— hon. Thos. Geo., aft. 2 ld. and 1st E. Northbro *q.v.*, L. Admy. 183-4; S Adm. 187; U.S. Home, 2 U.S. Ind. 236
Bark—, *see also* Berk—
Barkeley, *see* Barkley a Berkeley
Barker, Chr., Cal. P.A. 3 Gart. K.A. 327; K.B. 7 Norr. K.A. 329; R. Dr. P 337; Richm. H. 333
—— Ed., Curs. B. Ex. 386
—— Fk., bp. Syd. 703
—— Geo., adm. (**A**) 820
—— Geo. Digb., gen. (**D**) 932
—— Geo. Rt., K.C.B. 778
—— Jno., adm. (**A**) 814
—— Just., R. Cr. P.A. 335; R P.A. 344
—— Rt., K.B. 761; S.L. 409
—— Wm., dn. Rph. 603
Barkey, Anthy., L.M. Db 641
Barkham, sir Ed., L.M. Lo 491
—— Geo., Lanc. H., 333
Barking, Rd. de, B. Ex. 3 L.H.T. 152
Barkley, *see also* Barclay a Berkeley
—— Mor., K.B. 759
—— sir Rd., Lt.T.L. 321
—— Wm., K.B. 758
—— Arth. Cec. St., G. Falk. 731; G. Hlgld. 670; G. Sey Isl. 684
—— Hy. and sir H., G. Br. 715; G. C.G.H. 674; G. J 713; G. Mtius. 684; G. V 704; K.C.B. 782
Barlee, Fk. Palgr. and sir G. Br.Hond. 714; G. T 723; K.C.M.G. 798
Barlow, sir Geo. Hil., G Ind. 648; G. Mdras. G.C.B. 771; K.B. 766

Barlow—*cont.*
— sir Jas., L.M. Dbln. 641
— Jno., dn. Worc. 473
— Jno., gen. (**C**) 872
— Jno. Jas., gen. (**B**) 868
— Maur., G. Trin. 722; gen. (**D**) 893
— Ralph, dn. Llin. 623; dn. Wells 429
— Rand., abp. Tm. 611; dn. Chr. Ch. Dbln. 618
— sir Rt., adm. (**A**) 818; G.C.B. 769; K.C.B. 775
— Th., bp. Linc. 447
— Wm. (No. 1), bp. B. & W. 428; bp. Chich. 433; bp. St. As. 462; bp. St. Dav. 464
— Wm. (No. 2), bp. Linc. 447; bp. Roch. 460; dn. Chest. 477
— Wm. Jas. Pr., gen. (**D**) 930
Barnaby, Nath., K.C.B. 784
Barnard, *see also* Bernard
— Andr. [Jno.] Fras. and sir A., gen. (**A**) 863; G.C.B. 769; G.C.H. 787; K.C.B. 774; K.C.H. 787; L.G. Ch. Hosp. 936
— Ch. L. and sir C., gen. (**D**) 904; K.C.B. 782
— Ed. King, adm. (**H**) 850
— Fk. Lamp., adm. (**H**) 850
— Hy. Wm., gen. (**D**) 885; K.C.B. 778
— sir Jno., L.M. Lond. 491
— Thos., *see* Bernard
— (or Bernard), Wm., bp. Dry. 601; bp. Rph. 602; dn. Roch. 461
Barnardiston, Arth., M. Chy. 395
— Th., adm. (**E**) 837; S.L. 412
Barne, Barne, C. Tx. 285
— sir Geo., L.M. Lond. 490
— Snowd., C. Cus. 276; L.T. 159
Barnes and **Barns**
— Ed. and sir E., C.C. Ind. 651; G. Ceyl. 672; gen. (**B**) 868; G.C.B. 768; K.C.B. 774
— sir Geo., L.M. Lond. 490
— sir Jas. St., gen. (**B**) 869
— Jno., gen. (**C**) 873
— (or Bernes) Jno., L.M. Lond. 489
— Jno. Gor., Q.C. 420
— Rd., bp. Carl. 475; bp. Dham. 479; bp. Suff. Nottm. 447
— (or Barons), Wm., bp. Lond. 451; L.K. 355; M.R. 387
Barnes, lds.
— Jno., ld., *see* Berners
Barnet, Jno., bp. B. & W. 428; bp. Ely 435; bp. Roch. 460; bp. Worc. 472; L.H.T. 153
Barnett, Ch., gen. (**C**) 872
— Ed., adm. (**G**) 843
— Geo. Alfr., C.I.E. 807
— Ol., C.I.E. 807
Barnewall, *see also* Bernevall
— Barnaby, J.C.P. Ir. 581
— Ch., S.L. Ir. 591
— Chr., L. Treas. Ir. 558
— Ed., Ch. Ex. Ir. 561
— Jas., A.G. Ir. 588
— sir Jno., B. Ex. Ir. 584; Rec. Dbln. 642; S.L. Ir. 591
— sir Jno., aft. ld. Trimleston, *q.v.*
— Patr., M.R. Ir. 585; S.G. Ir. 589; S.L. Ir. 591
— Nichs., C.J.C.P. Ir. 580
— Th., B. Ex. 383
Barney, Geo., G. N. Aust. 705
Barns, *see* Barnes
Barny, Ardl. Hy. Falw., gen. (**D**) 935
Baroda, Gaekwar of (No. 1), G.C.S.I. 801
— Gaekwar of (No. 2), G.C.S.I. 801
— Gaekwar of (No. 3), K.C.S.I. 802
— Maharanee of, Cr. Ind. 809
Baron, Jno., dn. Norw. 456
— Jno. le, dn. Oss. 622
— Milo, bp. Oss. 620
— Rt., bp. Ork. 535
— Rol., abp. Cash. 625
Barons, *see* Barnes
Barowe, *see also* Barrow
— Th., L.K. 355; M. Chy. 394; M.R. 387
Barquerel, Rt., Portr. Lond. 488
Barr, Dav., gen. (**D**) 881
— Hy. Jas., gen. (**D**) 908
— Jas., Modr. K. Sc. 547
— (or Finbarr), St., bp. Cork 630
— Wm., gen. (**D**) 898
Barré, Isaac, Cl. Pells, 168; P.C. 202; Paym. G. 245; Tr. N. 256; V. Treas. Ir. 560
— Rd., Jy. 363
Barrel, Wm., gen. (**B**) 864
Barrell (or Barwell). Fras., S.L. 410
Barret, Andr., bp. Llff. 449
— Patr., bp. Ferns, 621; Ld. Chanc. Ir. 575
— sir Paul, S.L. 410
— Th., bp. Elph. 608
— Wm., bp. Kild. 617
Barret, of Newburgh, ld., *see* Newburgh
Barrett, Jno., gen. (**D**) 910
— MacWm., dn. Killa. 614
— Rd., bp. Killa. 612
Barrie, sir Rt., adm. (**D**) 824; K.C.B. 777; K.C.H. 788
Barrington, Benj., dn. Arm. 597
— hon. Daines, J. Chest. 387; K.C. 415
— hon. Geo., L. Admy. 182
— Jno. and sir J., L.M. Dbln. 642
— hon. Jno., gen. (**C**) 871
— sir Jonah, J. Admy. Ct. Ir. 587
— hon. Saml., adm. (**A**) 815
— hon. Shute, bp. Dham. 479; bp. Llff. 449; bp. Sal. 467
Barrington, visc.
— (or Shute) Jno. aft. 1st visc. B., M.R. Ir. 585
— Wm. W. 2nd visc., Ch. Ex. 165; L.H.A. 178; L.T. 157; M.G.W. 296; P.C. 200; Postm. G. 238; Sec. at W. 233; Tr. N. 256
— Geo. Wm. 7th visc., C.G.A. 300; C.Y.G. 298; P.C. 219; V.C.H. 292
Barrios, G., Pres. S. Salv. 106
— J. F., Pres. Gua. 106
Barrow and **Barrowe,** *see also* Barowe
— Ch. Malc. gen. (**D**) 922
— Fras., C.C.J. 405
— Is., bp. S. and M. 484; bp. St. As. 462; G. I. Man, 666
— Jno. and sir J., Sec. Admy. 187
— Jos. Ly., gen. (**D**) 910
Barrow and Barrowe—*cont.*
— Lous., Ch. Com. Oudh, 654; gen. (**D**) 909
— Rt. Kn., G. Lag. 687
— Saml., J.A.G. 937
— Th., G. Br. Hond. 714; gen. (**C**) 873
— Wm., bp. Bgr. 426; bp. Carl. 475
Barry, Alfr., bp. Syd. 703
— Ch. Rt., A.G. Ir. 589; J.Q.B. Ir. 579; J.Q.B.D. Ir. 579; L.J. App. Ir. 586; S.G. Ir. 590; S.L. Ir. 593
— sir Dav. de, L.J. Ir. 550
— Ger. de, bp. Cork, 630; dn. Cork, 632
— Hy. Gr., gen. (**C**) 873
— Jas. aft. sir J. and ld. Santry, *q.v.*, B. Ex. Ir. 584; C.J.K.B. Ir. 578; S.L. Ir. 591
— Jno., A.G. Ir. 588
— Jno., dn. Elph. 609
— Jno. Mac, L.T. 159; C. Treas. Ir. 561; L.T. 159
— Ph., gen. (**D**) 889
— Redm., C. Acc. Ir. 567
— sir Redm., G. Vict. 705; K.C.M.G. 797
— Rd., dn. Cash. 627
— Th., bp. Oss. 620; L. Treas. Ir. 558
— Wm. Wigr., gen. (**D**) 921
Barrymore, Jas. 4th E. of, gen. (**B**) 864
Barsse, Adolp., bar., gen. (**C**) 873
Bartane. Jno., Ld. Sess. 518
Barter, Rd., gen. (**D**) 931
Barthon, *see* Barton
Bartlay (or Bartley), Rt., K.C.B. 777
Bartlett, Ell. Ashm., L.Admy. 186
— Henl. Th., gen. (**D**) 912
Bartley, *see also* Bartlay
— Jno. Cow., gen. (**D**) 911
Barton, Alexr., K.H. 791
— Benj., L.M. Dbln. 641
— Ch., gen. (**B**) 866
— Ch. Jas., gen. (**D**) 911
— Cutts, dn. Brl. 440
— Ezek., gen. (**D**) 881
— Hy., L.M. Lond. 489-90
— Jno., dn. Ard. 609
— Jno. de, J. It. 368
— Jno. (No. 1), Rec. Lond. 493; S.L. 407
— Jno. (No. 2), S.L. 410
— Matth., adm. (**A**) 815
— Pet. de, M. Chy. 393
— Ralph, adm. (**H**) 848
— Rt., adm. (**A**) 818
— Rt., gen. (**D**) 933
— Rt. de, dn. St. P. 452
— Rt. and sir R., Compt. Sc. 498; L.H.T. Sc. 497
— Sir Rt., gen. (**A**) 863; K.C.H. 789
Barty, Jas. S., Modr. K. Sc. 547
Barvé, Rao B. M., C.I.E. 807
Barwell, Ch. Arth., gen. (**D**) 909
— (or Barrell), Fras., S.L. 410
— Wm. B. Br., gen. (**D**) 924
Barwick, Jno., dn. Dham. 479; dn. St. P. 453
— Saml., G. Bdoes. 720
Basden, Ch., adm. (**H**) 848
— Ch. Br., gen. (**D**) 920
Bash, sir E., Chambn. Ex. 166
— Ralph, K.B. 764

Basil, Emp. Tzde. 98
— I. to V., R. Russ. 89
— Wm., A.G. Ir. 588; C.J.K.B. Ir. 578
Basilius, I. and II., Emp. E.E. 50
Basing, de, *see* Kingsmill
— Ad., L.M. Lond. 488
— Saml., L.M. Lond. 488
Baskevyle, Walt., K.B. 759
Bassano, Alfr., gen. (**D**) 918
Bassenet, Ed., dn. St. Pat. 618
Basset and **Bassett**
— Alan, Jy. 364
— Fulke, bp. Lond. 451; dn. Yk. 486
— Jno., K.B. 759
— Jno. Jarv., K.C.M.G. 797
— Ph., Ch. Jr. 363; Const. T.L. 320
— Ralph, Ch. Jr. 362; Jy. 363
— Ralph, W.C.P. 318
— Ralph, *see* ld. B. *infra*
— Rd., Ch. Jr. 362; Jy. 363
— sir Rd., G. Br. Hond. 714
— Rt., L.M. Lond. 490
— Sim., J. It. 366
— Th.(No.1), J. It. 366; Jy. 363
— Th. (No. 2), J.K.B. 371; Jy. 365
— Th. (No. 3), W.C.P. 317
— Wm. (No. 1), J. It. 365; Jy. 363
— Wm. (No. 2), J. It. 367
— Wm. (No. 3) J.C.P. 377; J.K.B. 371
Bassett of Drayton, Ralph, 4th ld., K.G. 733; W.C.P. 318
Bassingborne, Humphr. de, J. It. 366
Bastard, Jas. S., gen. (**D**) 886
— Wm., J. It. 365
Bastide, Jno. Hy., gen. (**B**) 865
Bat (or Bate), Ger., L.M. Lond. 488
Bataile, Pet. de, M.M. 246
Batche, *see* Bathe
Batchelor, Ch., gen. (**D**) 930
Bate—, *see also* Bat—
— Jno., M. Chy. 394
Bateley, Wm., Sr. N. 257
Bateman, Ch. Ph., adm. (**D**) 826, (**G**) 840
— sir Anthy., L.M. Lond. 491
— sir Jas., L.M. Lond. 491
— Rt., gen. (**D**) 890
— Wm. (Wm. de Norwich), bp. Norw. 455; dn. Linc. 448
Bateman, lds. and visc.
— Wm., 1st visc., K.B. 764
— Jno., 2nd visc., L. Admy. 178; L.L. Heref. 308; M.B.W. 303; P.C. 200; Tr. H. 291
— Wm. B., 1st ld., L.L. Heref. 308
— Wm. B., 2nd ld., L.L. Heref. 308
Bateman-Champani, *see* Champain
Baterley, Jno., abp. Tm. 611
Bates, Ch. Edw., gen. (**D**) 930
— Hy. and sir H., gen. (**D**) 898; K.C.B. 781
— Joah, C. Cus. 276
Batesford, Jno. de, J. It. 368
Bateson, Rd., gen. (**D**) 926
— Th., L.T. 161
Bath, Nath. de, K.B. 755
— Wm., V. Treas. Ir. 559
Bath, E. and M. of—
— Ed., 5th E. of, form. E. Fitzwarine, *q.v.*
Bath, E. and M. of—*cont.*
— Jno., 7th E. of, form. sir J. Grenville, *q.v.*, also visc. Landsdowne, *q.v.*, Gr. St. 303; L.L. Cnwall. 307; P.C. 190, 192
— Wm., 10th E. of, form. Wm. Pulteney, *q.v.*, Coff. H. 293; L.L. Salop, 311; L.T. 142; Prem. 142
— Th., 1st M. of, form. 3rd visc. Weymouth, *q.v.*, 742
— Th., 2nd M. of, K.G. 743; L.L. Soms. 311
— Jno. A., 4th M. of, Amb. Pgl. 125
Bathe, Hy. Perc. de, gen. (**D**) 903
— Jas., C.B. Ex. Ir. 583
— Jno. and sir J., A.G. Ir. 588; C.J.C.P. Ir. 580; Ch. Ex. Ir. 561; S.G. Ir. 589; S.L. Ir. 591
— Laur., *see* Booth
— Th. (No. 1), C.B. Ex. Ir. 582
— (or Batche), Th. (No. 2), C.B. Ex. Ir. 582; L. Treas. Ir. 558
— Wm., J.C.P. Ir. 581
Bathonia, Hy. de, Ch. Jr. 363; J.C.P. 376; J.K.B. 371; Jy. 364
Bathurst, *see also* Bragge
— Benj., Amb. Aus. 117
— sir Benj., Coff. H. 293
— Ch., C.D.L. 243; M.M. 247; Pres. B.C. 253
— Hy., bp. Norw. 455
— Hy., *see* Earl B., *infra.*
— Jas. and sir J., G. Virg. Isl. 731; gen. (**B**) 869; K.C.B. 776
— Peter, gen. (**A**) 859
— Ralph, dn. Wlls. 429
Bathurst, lds. and E.
— Allen, 1st ld., aft. 1st E. C.G.P. 299; P.C. 198
— hon. Hy., aft. 1st ld. Apsley, *q.v.*, and 2nd earl B., C.G.S. 357; J.C.P. 379; K.C. 415; L.H.S. 287; L.P.C. 188; Ld. Chanc. 357; S.L. 412
— Hy., 3rd. E., form. ld. Apsley, *q.v.*, F. Sec. 228; Jud. Com. P.C. 360; K.G. 743; L.P.C. 188; M.M. 247; Pres. B.T. 268; W. and C. Sec. 231
Batline, Wm., Adm. Adv. 423
Battail, Jno. de, Ld. Chanc. and L.K. Ir. 574
Battayle, Rt., L.H.A. 171
Batte, Nich., L.M. Lond. 489
Batten, Sisley Jno., gen. (**D**) 921
Battenberg, Pr. Alexr. Jos. of, G.C.B. 773
— Pr. Hy. Maur. of, K.G. 745
— Pr. Louis Alex. of, G.C.B. 773; K.C.B. 784
Battersby, Jno. Prev., gen. (**D**) 928
Battine, Wm., gen. (**D**) 880
Battiscombe, Alb. Hy. Wm., adm. (**H**) 853
Battle, L., Pres. Ugy. 111
Battye, Geo. Mon., gen. (**D**) 918
Baudake, *see* Baldoc
Baugh, Ch. Rd., gen. (**D**) 913
— Ffoll. Walk., gen. (**D**) 923
— Launc., gen. (**B**) 866
— Thos. Foll., adm. (**H**) 844
Baukwell, *see* Bankwell
Baumburgh, Th. de, L.K. 354; M. Chy. 393
Baumgardt, Jno. Gregory, gen. (**D**) 883
Baumgartner, Rt. Jul., gen. (**D**) 905
— Th. Mowbr., gen. (**D**) 930
Bavant, Ralph, Lt. T.L. 321
Bavier, S., Pres. Sw. C. 31
Bawde, Th., K.B. 759
Bawtry, L., S.L. 409
Bax, Joh., G. C.G.H. 678
Baxter, Mart., dn. Cnr. 605
— Wm. E., Sec. Adm. 187; Sec. Tr. 164; P.C. 218
Bayeux, Jno. de, J. It. 366
Bayfield, Hy. Wolsey, adm. (**D**) 831; (**F**) 838
Bayford, Rt. Aug., Q.C. 420
Bayham, Jno. Jeff., visc., form. hon. J. J. Pratt, *q.v.*, aft. 2nd E. and 1st M. Camden, *q.v.*, B.T. 268; L. Admy. 180; L.T. 158; P.C. 205
Baylie, *see* Baillie and Bayly
Baylis, Rt. and sir R., C. Cus. 274-5; L.M. Lond. 491
— Th. Hy., Q.C. 419
Bayley, Baylie and **Bayly,** *see also* Bailey and Baily
— Abingd. Augs., gen. (**D**) 924
— sir Danl., K. H. 789
— Ed., dn. Ardf. 640
— Ed. Cl., K.C.S.I. 803
— Fras., C.C.J. 404
— sir Hy., gen. (**A**) 862; G.C.H. 787; K.H. 791
— Jno., dn. Killoe. 637; dn. Lism. 629
— Jno., gen. (**D**) 917
— Jno. and sir J., B. Ex. 385; J.K.B. 373; Jud. Com. P.C. 360; P.C. 212; S.L. 412
— Jas. Walt., gen. (**D**) 902
— Lewis, bp. Bgr. 426
— sir Nichs., L.L. Ang. 314
— Paget, gen. (**D**) 911
— Rd., dn. Sal. 468
— Rd. Alb., gen. (**D**) 897
— Stu. Colv. and sir S., C.I.E. 807; Ch. Com. Ass. 656; L.G. Bgal. 652; K.C.S.I. 803
— Th., bp. Killa. and Ach. 613; dn. Down, 605
— Wm. Butt, Chn. E.I. Co. 645; G.G. Ind. 649
Baynard, Fulco., J. It. 367
— Rd., Sp. H.C. 248
— Rt., J.K.B. 371
Baynbrigge, *see* Bainbrigge
Bayne, Jno., gen. (**C**) 871
— Ralph, bp. Lich. and Cov. 444
Baynes, *see also* Baines and Banes
— Ed., gen. (**C**) 874
— Ed. Stu. and sir E., Amb. Tun. 132; K.C.M.G. 796
— Geo. Ed., gen. (**D**) 925
— Hy., K.H. 792
— Jno., S.L. 411
— Rt. Lamb. and sir R., adm. (**D**) 830; (**E**) 834; K.C.B. 778
— Robt. St., gen (**D**) 909
— Simc., gen. (**D**) 892
Bayning, Ch., ld., form. Ch. Townshend, *q.v.*
Baynton, Ed., K.B. 763
Bayntun, Hy. Wm. and sir H., adm. (**A**) 818; G.C.B. 769; K.C.B. 774
Bazalgette, Evel., Q.C. 418
Bazeley, Jno., adm. (**A**) 816
— Jno., adm. (**A**) 819

For List of Abbreviations, see pp. 944-952.

Beach, sir Michl. Ed. Hicks-, Ch. Ex. 166; Ch. Sec. Ir. 563; L. T. 162; P.C. 219; Pres. B.T. 269; U.S. Home, 228
Beachcroft, sir Rt., L.M. Lond. 491
Beaconsfield, Benjn., E. of, form. B. Disraeli, *q.v.*, Amb. Gmy. and Pr. 116; K.G. 745; L.T. 162
Beadon, Cecil, aft. sir C., K.C.S.I. 802; L.G. Bgal. 652
—— Rd., bp. B. and W. 428; bp. Glr. 438
Beale, Ch. Ed., gen. (**D**) 917
—— Wm., dn. Ely, 435
—— Wm. Ph., Q.C. 420
Beales, Edmd., C.C.J. 405
Bealknap (or Belknap), Rt., C.J.C.P. 375; J. It. 369; S.L. 407
Beames, Jno., K.C. 416
Beamish, Ch., gen. (**D**) 901
—— Hy. Ham., adm. (**H**) 852
—— North Lindl., K.H. 792
Bean, Jno., gen. (**D**) 918
Beanus (St.), bp. Mortl. 530
Bearcroft, Edw., C.J. Chest. 386; K.C. 415
Beard, Hy., G. Berb. 715
Beare, Geo., S.L. 410
Bearngall, K. Ir. 20
Beasley, Wm. Cole, Q.C. 419
Beaton, *see also* Bethune
—— Dav. and sir D., L.H.T. Sc. 496; L.P.S. Sc. 501
Beatrice, D. Tny. 57
—— (dau. Hy. III.), Pr. E. 10
—— (dau. Edw. I.), Pr. E. 10
—— -Leop. Vict. (G. dau. Q. Vict.), Pr. E. 16
—— -Mary Vict. Feod. (dau. Q. Vict.), Pr. E. 16; Cr. Ind. 809
Beatson, Albert B., gen. (**D**) 913
—— Jno. Full., C.I.E. 806
—— Rog. Stew., gen. (**D**) 908
—— Wm. Ferg., gen. (**D**) 899
Beatty, Andr., gen. (**D**) 902
—— Geo., gen. (**D**) 883
Beauchamp, Fitzm., gen. (**D**) 929
—— Jno., K.B. 757
—— Jno., Ptc. P.A. 337
*—— Jno. de, Const. T.L. (1360) 320
*—— sir Jno., K.G. (1360) 733
*—— sir Jno., L.H.A. (1349) 172
*—— sir Jno., W.C.P. (1361) 318
* Prob. some same pers.
—— Rd., bp. Her. 441; bp. Sal. 467; Chanc. Gart. 745; dn. Winds. 474
—— Rd. de, aft. E. of Warwick, *q.v.*, K.B. 755; K.G. (1400) 734
—— (or Bello Campo), Rt. de, J.C.P. 376; Jy. 364
—— Th., K.B. 755
—— Walt. de, J. It. 367
—— sir Walt., Sp. H.C. 248
—— (or Bello Campo), Wm. de, B. Ex. 382
—— sir Wm., K.B. 765
—— Wm., aft. 1st ld. Abergavenny, *q.v.*, K.G. (1378) 734
Beauchamp of Hache, lds. and visc.
—— Ed., 1st visc., form. sir Ed. Seymour, *q.v.*, G. Jsey. 667
—— Ed. Seym., ld. aft. E. of Hertford, *q.v.*, K.B. (1616) 762

Beauchamp, Fras., visc., aft. E. of Yarmouth, *q.v.*, and 2nd M. of Hertford, *q.v.*, Ch. Sec. Ir. 562; Coff. H. 294; L.T. 157-8; P.C. 203

Beauchamp of Powyck, lds. and E.
—— Jno., 1st ld., K.G. 735; L.H.T. 153
—— Hy., 4th E., gen. (**A**) 863
—— Fk., 6th E., L.L. Worc. 313; L.S.H. 290; P.C. 218; Paym. G. 245
Beauclerk, ld. Amel., adm. (**A**) 818; G.C.B. 768; G.C.H. 786; K.C.B. 774
—— ld. Geo., G. Gibr. 669; gen. (**B**) 865
—— ld. Jas., bp. Her. 442
—— ld. Sidn., P.C. 198; V.C.H. 297
—— ld. V., aft. ld. Vere, *q.v.*, adm. (**A**) 814; L. Admy. 178
Beaudake, *see* **Baldoc**
Beaudyn, sir Rt., L.H.A. 171
Beaufort, Fras. and sir F., adm. (**H**) 844; K.C.B. 782
—— Hy. de, bp. Linc. 446; bp. Winch. 470; dn. Wells, 429; Ld. Chanc. 355
—— sir Jno., aft. E. of Somerset and M. of Dorset, *q.v.*, K.G. (1397) 734
—— sir Th., aft. E. of Dorset and D. of Exeter, K.G. (1402) 734; L.H.A. 173; Ld. Chanc. 355
Beaufort, D. of
—— Hy., 1st D. of, form. 7th E. and 3rd M. of Worcester, *q.v.*
—— Hy., 2nd D. of, C.G.P. 299; K.G. 741
—— Hy., 5th D. of, K.G. 742; L.L. Brec. 315; L.L. Leic. 305; L.L. Monm. 310
—— Hy. Ch., 6th D. of, K.G. 743; L.L. Brec. 315; L.L. Glouc. 308; L.L. Monm. 310
—— Hy., 7th D. of, K.G. 744
—— Hy. Ch. F., 8th D. of, M.H. 302; K.G. 745; L.L. Monm. 310; P.C. 216
Beaufoy, Hy., Sec. B.C. 254
Beaulieu, Ed., ld. and E., form. E. H. Montagu, *q.v.*
Beauharnais, Eug. de, Rel. Nap. 26
Beauman, Fras., adm. (**D**) 826
Beaumond, *see* Beaumont
Beaumont, Bas., adm. (**A**) 813
—— (or Beaumond) Fras., J.C.P. 378; S.L. 408
—— Geo., dn. Dry. 602
—— sir Geo., L. Admy. 177; L.P.S. 240
—— Hy., dn. Pboro. 458; dn. Winds. 474
—— sir Hy., Sp. H.C. 248
—— J. de, M.R. 388
—— Lew. de, bp. Dham. 478
—— Rd. Hy. Jno., gen. (**D**) 904
Beaumont, lds. and visc.
—— Jno., 4th ld., K.G. 734; L.H.A. 173; W.C.P. 318
—— Hy., 5th ld., K.B. 755
—— Jno., 6th ld. and 1st visc., K.G. 735
Beaupel, sir Rt., L.H.A. 172
Beauvale, Fk. Jas. ld., form. hon. F. J. Lamb, *q.v.*, aft. visc. Melbourne, *q.v.*

Beauvoir, Pet., G. Gsey. 668
Beaw, Wm., bp. Llff. 449
Bebb, Jno., Chn. E.I.Co. 645
Bec, *see* Beck and Bek
Becan, bp. Cld. 598
Beccles, Jno. All., G. Bdoes. 720
Beche, Nichs. de la, Const. T.L. 320
Becher, *see also* Beecher
—— Alfr., gen. (**D**) 919
—— Ath. M. and sir A., gen. (**D**) 896; K.C.B. 780
—— Jno. Reid, gen. (**D**) 905
—— Sept. Hard., gen. (**D**) 916
Beck, *see also* Bek
—— Anthy. de (No. 1), bp. Dham. 478; K. Man. 665
—— Anthy. (No. 2), bp. Norw. 455; dn. Linc. 448
—— Th., bp. St. Dav. 464; L.H.T. 152
Becke, Hy., dn. Brl. 440
Becker, Henrich, Adm. Ind. 647; G. Ceyl. 672
Becket and **Beckett,** *see also* A'Becket
—— Jno. and sir J., J.A.G. 937; L.T. 160; P.C. 209; U.S. Home 228
—— Th., J. It. 365
—— Wm., S.L. Ir. 591
Beckford, Pet., G. Jam. 712
—— Wm., L.M. Lond. 492
Beckingham, Elias de, J.C.P. 377; J. It. 368; S.L. 406
Beckington, Th., bp. B. & W. 428; S. St. 222
Beckles, Ed. H., bp. Si. Leo. 686
Beckwith, Ch., gen. (**D**) 882
—— Geo. and sir G., Comm. F. Ir. 564; G. Bdoes. 720; G. Bmda. 701; G. St. Vin. 725; gen. (**A**) 860; G.C.B. 767; K.C.B. 774
—— sir Th. Sidn., C.C. Bmbay. 660; gen. (**B**) 868; K.C.B. 774
—— Wm., gen. (**D**) 885; K.H. 790
—— Wm. Hy., gen. (**C**) 874
Beckyngton, *see* Beckington
Bective, Th., 2nd E. of, aft. 1st M. of Headfort, *q.v.*, K.P. 750
Bedea, Rao of, C.I.E. 806
Bedell, Wm., bp. Ard. 608; bp. Kilm. & Ard. 607
Bedenfield, *see* Bedingfield
Bedenoth, bp. Roch. 459
Bedford, Geo. Aug., adm. (**H**) 849
—— Ed. Jas., adm. (**H**) 852
—— Rt. de, dn. Glend. 619
—— Wm., adm. (**A**) 819
—— Fansh., gen. (**D**) 895
Bedford, E. and D. of
—— Ingelr. de Courcy, E. of, K.G. (1366) 733
—— Jno. Plantagenet, D. of (son of Hen. IV., *see* Pr. Jno.), also E. of Kendal, *q.v.*, G. Ch. Isl. 667; K.B. 755; K.G. 734; L.H.A. 174
—— Jasp. Tudor, D. of, form. E. of Pembroke, *q.v.*, L.L. Ir. 553

Russell Family.
—— Jno., 1st E. of, form. sir Jno. and ld. Russell, *q.v.*, L.W.S. 323
—— Fras., 2nd E. of, K.G. 738; L.L. Dors. 307; L.W.S. 323

Bedford, E. and D. of—*cont.*
— Wm., 5th E. of, form. W. Russell, *q.v.*, aft. M. of Tavistock, *q.v.*, and 1st D. of B., K.G. 740; P.C. 193
— Wrioth., 2nd D. of, K.G. 741; L.H. Const. 289
— Jno., 4th D. of, Amb. Fr. 112; gen. (**B**) 865; K.G. 742; L. Admy. 178; L.H. Const. 289; L.L. Beds. 306; L.L. Dev. 307; L.L. Ir. 557; L.P.C. 188; L.P.S. 241; P.C. 199; S. St. 224
— Jno., 6th D. of, K.G. 743; L.L. Ir. 557; P.C. 208
— Fras., 7th D. of, K.G. 744; L.L. Beds. 306; P.C. 215
— Fras. Ch. H., 9th D. of, K.G. 745; L.L. Hunts. 309
— Eliz., Dss. of, M. Robes, 304
Bedingfield, Edm., K.B. 758
— Hy. and sir H., C.J.C.P. 375; J.C.P. 379; S.L. 410
— sir Hy. Lt. T.L. 321
— sir Jno., K.C.H. 788
— Norm. Bern., adm. (**H**) 851
— Ph., gen. (**D**) 929
— sir Rt., L.M. Lond. 491
— Th., J.C.P. 379; S.L. 409-10
— Th., K.B. 759
Bedmar, M., R. Nds. 83
Bedoya, J. D. de, Dt. Pgy. 110
Bedwell, Fras. A., C.C.J. 405
Bedwinus, bp. Elm. 454
Beecher, *see also* Becher
— Alexr. Br., adm. (**H**) 850
— sir Ed., L.M. Lond. 491
Beechey, Fk. Wm., adm. (**D**) 830
— Rd. Brydg., adm. (**H**) 850
Beere, sir Jno., S.L. Ir. 591
Beeston, sir Wm., G. Jam. 712
Beete, captn., G. W. Austr. 707
Beevor, Rt., gen. (**B**) 869
Beg or **Begg,** Jno. J.K.B. Ir. 578
Beglatneu, bp. Cld. 598
Behar, Maharanee of, Cr. Ind. 810
Beide, Walt. de, Ld. Chanc. Sc. 514
Bek, *see also* Beck
— Anthy., Const. T.L. 320
— (or Beke) Th., bp. Linc. 446
— Th., M. Chy. 393
Bela, I to IV., K. Hgy. 59, 60
Belaguier, —, U.S.S. 226
Belasyse, *see also* Bellasyse
— Rowl., aft. E. Fauconberg, *q.v.*
Belasyse, lds.
— Jno., 1st ld., C.G.P. 299; L.T. 155; P.C. 193
— Hy., aft. 2nd ld. B., K.B., 763
Belcher, sir Ed., adm. (**D**) 832; (**F**) 838; K.C.B. 779
— J., G.N. Sc. 695
Beleanquall, Walt., *see* Balcanquall
Beler, Rog., B. Ex. 383
Belers, Matth., W.C.P. 317
Belet, Michl., B. Ex. 382
— Michl., J. It. 366; Jy. 363
Belfast, Geo., E. of, aft. 1st ld. Ennishowen and 3rd M. of Donegal, *q.v.*, G.C.H. 786; L.L. Ant. 578; P.C. 211; V.C.H. 292
Belfield (or Benfield), Jno., S.L. 411
Belford, Wm., gen. (**A**) 858
Belgrave, Rt., visc., aft. 2nd E. Grosvenor and 1st M. of Westminster, *q.v.*, B.C. 252; L. Admy. 180; L.L. Flints. 314
Belhaven, lds.
— Jno., 2nd ld., L.H.T. Sc. 498; Ld. Clk. Reg. 525
— Jno., 3rd ld., G. Bdoes. 720
— Robt. Montg., 8th ld., K.T. 749; L.H.C.K. Sc. 546; L.L. Lnrk. 511
Beli, Jago Ab., dn. Bgr. 426
Belknap, *see* Bealknap
Bell, Andr., Modr. K. Sc. 547
— sir Ch., K.H. 790
— Chr., adm. (**H**) 844
— Ed. Wells, G. Jam. 713; gen. (**D**) 885
— Ed. Wm. Derr., gen. (**D**) 906
— sir Fras. Dill., K.C.M.G. 797
— Geo. and sir G., gen. (**D**) 893; K.C.B. 779
— Harry W. Bax, gen. (**D**) 905
— Hy., gen. (**B**) 867; K.C.B. 774
— Hy. Jas., gen. (**D**) 927
— Jno., bp. Mayo, 612
— Jno., bp. Worc. 473
— Jno., dn. Ely, 435
— Jno., gen. (**B**) 866
— Jno., K.C. 415
— Jno. and sir J., G. Gsey. 669; gen. (**D**) 880; G.C.B. 770; K.C.B. 777
— Jos., gen. (**D**) 887
— Josh. Pet., G. Qland. 706; K.C.M.G. 797
— Ph., G. Bdoes. 719; G. Bmda. 701
— Rd., bp. Carl. 475
— Rt. and sir R., C.B. Ex. 381; S.L. 408; Sp. H.C. 249; U.S.S. 226
— Th., L.M. Dbln. 641
— Th. Lynd., gen. (**D**) 933
— Wm., bp. St. Andr. 529
— Wm., gen. (**D**) 891; K.C.B. 779
Bellaforgo, Rog. de, J. It. 369
Bellairs, Wm. and sir W., gen. (**D**) 927; K.C.M.G. 798
Bellamont, Ch., 5th ld. Coote, *q.v.*, and 1st E. of, Postm. G. Ir. 564
Bellamy, sir Ed., L.M. Lond. 491
Bellasis, Anthy., M. Chy. 395
— Ed., Bl. M. P.A. 337; Lanc. H. 333
— Ed., S.L. 413
— Ed. H., gen. (**D**) 879
Bellasyse, *see also* Belasyse
— sir Hy., gen. (**B**) 864
Belleau, sir Narc. Fort., G. Queb. 694
Belleganach, Ferq., bp. Cness, 531
Bellenden, *see* Ballenden
Bellew, Patr., gen. (**C**) 872
— sir Patr., L.L. Louth, 570
— Rd. M., L.T. 161
Belley, Jno., M. Chy. 395
Belling, *see* Bellyng
Bellingham, Danl. and sir D., L.M. Dbln. 640; M.M. 247
— sir Ed., L.J. Ir. 553
Bellini, Fr. G., Pres. Dom. Rep. 105
Bellishall, Rd. de, S.L. 406
Bello-Campo, *see* Beauchamp
Bellot, Hugh, bp. Bgr. 426; bp Chest. 476
Bellyng, Rd., S.G. Ir. 589
Belmis, Rd. de Beaum., bp Lond. 451
Belmont, Ch., E. of, form. Ch Cook, *q.v.*
Belmore, E. of
— Som., 2nd E. of, G. Jam 713
— Som. Rd., 4th E. of, G N.S.W. 703; K.C.M.G. 796 U.S. Home, 228
Beloigne, Rd. de, Const. T.L 320
Belper, Ed., 1st ld., form. Ed Strutt, *q.v.*, L.L. Notts, 311
Belsches, sir Alexr., Ld. Sess 519
Belshes, Jno. Murr., gen. (**D** 890
Belson, Ch. Ph. and sir C gen. (**C**) 874; K.C.B. 774
— Geo. Jno., gen. (**D**) 891 K.H. 792
Beltz, Geo. Fk., K.H. 791 Lanc. H. 333; Ptc. P.A. 337
Belwood, Rog., S.L. 411
Belzu, M. I., Pres. Bol. 109
Benares, Mahar. of, G.C.S.I 801
Benbow, Jno., adm. (**A**) 813
Bende, Jno., C. Exc. 278
Bendysh, Rd., gen. (**C**) 872
Bendings, Wm. de, J. It. 366 Jy. 363
Bendlowes, Wm., S.L. 408
Benedict, bp. Ach. 612
— bp. Ross, 631
— I. to XIV., P. Ro. 33-6
Benefacta, Rd. de, Ch. Jr. 36
Benet, *see* Benedict, Benne and Bennett
Benfield (or Belfield), Jno S.L. 411
Benham, Dav., bp. St. Andr 529; L.G.C. Sc. 506
— Hugh de, bp. Abdn. 530
Benjamin, Jud. Ph., P.P. 41
Benley, Wm., dn. Winds. 474
Benen (St.), bp. Arm., 595
Benn, Anthy., gen. (**D**) 904
— Anthy. and sir A., Re Lond. 494
— Piercy, gen. (**D**) 897
— Wm., L.M. Lond. 491
Bennet, Bennett and **Bene**
— Ld. Chanc. 353
— captn. —, G. Bmda. 701
— sir Hy., aft. 1st ld. and I of Arlington, *q.v.*, P.C. 190 S. St. 223
— hon. Hy. Aste., gen. (**B**) 86
— Jas., bp. St. Andr. 529 L.G.C. Sc. 506
— Jas. Risd. and sir J., Pre Coll. Ph. 938
— Jno., bp. Cork and Cl. 631
— Jno., J.K.B. Ir. 579
— Jno., K.B. 764
— Jno., M. Chy. 396; S.L. 4
— sir Jno., J. Pr. Ct. 421; I Chy. 395
— Rt., bp. Her. 441; dn. Wind 474
— Rt., gen. (**D**) 932
— Th., adm. (**D**) 830; (**G**) 84
— Th., M. Chy. 395-96
— sir Th., L.M. Lond. 491
— Wm., bp. Cloy. 631; b Cork and R. 632
— sir Wm., C. Exc. Sc. 504

Bennet, Bennett, and Benet—*cont.*
— Wm. Hy. Worthy, gen. (**D**) 926
Benolte, Th., Clar. K.A. 328; Norr. K.A. 329; R. Cr. P.A. 335; Winds. H. 331
Bense, L. Admy. 175
Benson, Ch. Ann., gen. (**D**) 930
— Et. A., Pres. Lib. 100
— Ed. W., abp. Cant. 431; bp. Tru. 469; Jud. Com. P.C. 362; P.C. 220
— Geo., dn. Her. 442
— Geo., gen. (**B**) 866
— Hy. Roxb., gen. (**D**) 905
— Mart., bp. Glr. 438
— Rd., gen. (**D**) 887
— Robs., gen. (**D**) 923
— Rt., aft. 1st ld. Bingley, *q.v.*, Ch. Ex. 165; L.T. 156; P.C. 196
— Wm., dn. Westr. 469
Benstede, Jno. de, J.C.P. 377; L.K. 353; S. St. 222
Bent, Geo., gen. (**D**) 904
Bentham, Geo., adm. (**H**) 845
— Th., bp. Lich. and Cov. 444
— Wm., gen. (**B**) 868
Bentinck, Arth. Cav., gen. (**D**) 903
— Ch. Anty. Ferd., gen. (**D**) 883
— ld. Fk., gen. (**C**) 874
— Geo. Aug. Fk. Cav., J.A.G. 937; P.C. 219; Sec. B.T. 269
— Hy., G. Dem. and Ess. 715
— Hy. Jno. Wm., gen. (**D**) 884; K.C.B. 777
— Hy. Wm., G. St. Vin. 725
*— Wm., adm. (**A**) 817
*—Wm., G. St. Vin. 725
* Prob. same. pers.
— Wm., aft. 1st visc. Woodstock and 1st E. of Portland, *q.v.*, P.C. 193
— ld. Wm. Hy. Cavendish- (*d.* 1839), Amb. Scy. 114; C.C. Ind. 651; G.C.B. 767; G.C.H. 786; G.G. Ind. 649; G. Mdras. 656; gen. (**A**) 861; (**B**) 867; K.B. 766; P.C. 211
— ld. Wm. Ch. Cav., P.C. 209; Tr. H. 291
Bentley, sir Jno., adm. (**A**) 814
Benyon, Saml. Y., K.C. 415
Beonna, bp. Her. 441
Beorhtric, K.E. 2
Beorn, K.E. 2
Beornegus, bp. Sels. 432
Beornmod (or Boernredus), bp. Roch. 459
Beornred, K.E. 3
Beornredus, *see* Beornmod
Beornulf, K.E. 3
Berangera, *see* Berengara
Berclay, *see* Barclay
Bere, Mont., C.C.J. 405; Q.C. 418
Bereford, *see also* Beresford
— (or Berford), Edmd. de, S.L. Ir. 590
— Ralph, J. It. 369
— Rd. de, J. It. 369; L. Treas. Ir. 558; Ld. Chanc. Ir. 574
— Wm. de, C.J.C.P. 375; J.C.P. 377; J. It. 368
Berengara (or Berangera), (dau. Edw. I.), Pr. E. 10
Berengaria, Q.C.E. 7
Berenger (de Rennes), D. Bry. 28
— I. and II., K. Lmd. 49
Beresford, *see also* Bereford
— ld. Ch. W. de la P., L. Admy. 186
— Ed. Marc., gen. (**D**) 927
— Geo. de la P., bp. Clonf. and K. 636; bp. Kilm. and Ard. 607; dn. Kilm. 609
— ld. Geo. Th., Compt. H. 293; G.C.H. 786; gen. (**B**) 869; P.C. 209
— hon. Jno., B.T. 268; C. Cus. Ir. 565; C. Exc. Ir. 566; C. Treas. Ir. 560; P.C. 204
— Jno. Cl., L.M. Dbln. 641
— ld. Jno. Geo. de la P., abp. Arm. 596; abp. Arm. and Clr. 597; abp. Dbln. and Gl. 616; bp. Clr. 596; bp. Cork and R. 632; bp. Rph. 602; dn. Clr. 598
— Jno. M. Massey-, dn. Kilm. 609
— sir Jno. Pov., adm. (**A**) 819; G.C.H. 787; K.C.B. 775; L. Admy. 182
— Marc., gen. (**D**) 884
— Marc. Gerv., abp. Arm. and bp. Clr. 597; bp. Kilm. E. and A. 608
— Most. de la P., gen. (**D**) 931
— Wm., C.C.J. 405
— Wm., K.H. 790
— Wm., P.C. 215; Sec. at W. 234
— hon. Wm., abp. Tm. 611; bp. Drom. 605; bp. Oss. 620
— Wm. Gesl. de la P., C.I.E. 807
Beresford, ld. and visc.
— Wm. Carr, ld. aft. visc., gen. (**A**) 861; G.C.B. 767; G.C.H. 786; K.B. 766; L.G.O. 259; M.G.O. 259; P.C. 210
Beresford-Hope, *see* Hope
Berew, Jno., dn. Her. 442
Berewyk, Jno. de, J. It. 368
Berested (or Berstede), Walt. de, J.C.P. 377; J. It. 368; Jy. 365; W.C.P. 317
Berford, *see* Burford and Bereford
Bergavenny, *see* Abergavenny
Berger, Ern. Archd., gen. (**D**) 930
Berghsted, Th. de, dn. Chich. 434
Bergne, Jno. Hy. G., K.C.M.G. 799
Berk—, *see also* Bark—
Berkeley, *see also* Barkley and Barclay
— Arn. de, B. Ex. 382
— Ch., *see* E. of B., *infra*
— sir Ch., aft. visc. Fitzhardinge and E. of Falmouth, *q.v.*, Compt. H. 292; P.C. 190
— Ch. L. G., Sec. P.L.B. 262
— Ed., K.B. 758
— Emer. Str., gen. (**D**) 931
— Geo., bp. Cloy. 631; dn. Drom. 606; dn. Dry. 602
— Geo. and sir G., G. Leew. Isl. 728; G. St. Vin. 725; G. W. Afr. Sett. 688; K.C.M.G. 797
— hon. Geo. Cr. and sir G., adm. (**A**) 817; G.C.B. 767; K.B. 766; S.G.O. 260
— Geo. Hy. Fk. and sir G., C.C. Mdras. 657; gen. (**A**) 863; K.C.B. 775; S.G.O. 260
Berkeley—*cont.*
— Gilb., bp. B. and W. 428
— Granv. C. L., C. Cus. 277
— hon. Hy., M.H. 302
— Hugh de, L.J. Gen. 522
— Jas. de, bp. Exr. 436
— Jas. Cav., C.I.E. 808
— Jno., K.B. 761
— Jno. de, K.B. 754
— Josh., dn. Tm. 613
— Maur. de, Const. T.L. 320
— Maur. de, J. It. 366
— hon. Maur. Fk. Fitzh., aft. sir M. and ld. Fitzhardinge, *q.v.*, adm. (**D**) 828; G.C.B. 770; K.C.B. 778; L. Admy. 182-3; P.C. 216
— Norb., aft. ld. Bottetourt, *q.v.*, L.L. Glouc. 308
— Rt. de, J. It. 366
— sir Rt., J.K.B. 372; S.L. 409
— Sackv. Ham., gen. (**A**) 863
— Wm., *see* ld. B. of Stratton, *infra*
— Wm., K.B. 757
— Wm., K.B. 758
— sir Wm., adm. (**A**) 813
Berkeley, lds. and E.
— Th., 5th ld., L.H.A. 173
— Jas., 6th ld., K.B. 756
— Hy., 12th ld., K.B. 760
— Th., ld. (son of Hy., 12th ld.), K.B. 761
— Geo., 13th ld., aft. 1st E., B.C. 263; P.C. 191-2
— Ch., 2nd E. of, form. Ch. Berkeley and visc. Dursley, *q.v.*, K.B. 763; L.J. Ir. 555; L.L. Surr. 312
— Jas., 3rd E. of, form. visc. Dursley, *q.v.*, K.G. 741; L. Admy. 177; P.C. 197
— Aug., 4th E. of, K.T. 747
— Fk. A., 5th E. of, L.L. Glouc. 308
Berkeley of Stratton, lds.
— Jno., 1st ld., L.L. Ir. 555; M.G.O. 258; P.C. 190
— Jno., 3rd ld., adm. (**A**) 813
— Wm., 4th ld., form. Wm. B., C.D.L. 242; M.R. Ir. 585; Pres. B.T. 264
— Jno., 5th ld., C.G.P. 299; C.Y.G. 298; Const. T.L. 321; P.C. 199; Tr. H. 291
Berkshire, E. of
Norreys Family.
— Fras. Norreys, E. of, form. ld. Norris or Norreys (1603), *q.v.*
Howard Family.
— Th., 1st E. of, form. Th. Howard and ld. H. and visc. Andover, *q.v.*, P.C. 190
— Hy. B., 4th E. of, Dep. E.M. 327
Berkstead, Jno., Lt. T.L. 322
Berkstede, Sim. de, bp. Chich. 432
Bermingham and **Bermyngham**, *see also* Birm—
— Jno. de, D. Chanc. Ir. 575; J.K.B. Ir. 578; S.L. Ir. 591
— Jos. Ald., dn. Kilmacd. 638
— Patr., C.J.K.B. Ir. 577
— Ph., C.J.C.P. Ir. 580
— Rd. de, J. It. 369
— sir Walt., L.J. Ir. 551
— Wm. de, abp. Tm. 611
— Wm. de, C.J.K.B. 577
— Wm. de, dn. Her. 442

Bernadotte, K. S. and N. 92; Off. Nap. 26
Bernard and **Bernhard**, *see also* Barnard
*—— bp. Ach. 612
*—— bp. Carl. 475
*—— bp. S. and M. 483
*—— (Bernardus), bp. St. Dav. 464
* Poss. some same pers. Comp. dates.
—— C. Anht. 66
—— D. Brk. 69
—— D. S. Mgn. 79
—— (bp. Bayonne), L.H.A. 170
—— Ld. Chanc. Sc. 515
—— I. and II., D. Sxy. 77
—— III., El. Sxy. 77
—— I. to IV., M. Bdn. 67
For non-reigning Dukes of this name, *see* under the title of their Dukedoms.
—— Andr., P. Laur. 300
—— hon. Ch. Brod., bp. Tm. K. and A. 613
—— Ch. Ed. and sir C., Ch. Com. Bma. 655; K.C.S.I. 803
—— Ch. Ed., K.C.S.I. 803
—— Ed., adm. (**H**) 846
—— -Erich, D. S. Mgn. 79; K.G. 743
—— Fras. and sir F., C. Cus. Ir. 565; C. Exc. Ir. 566; J.C.P. Ir. 581; S.G. Ir. 589; S.L. Ir. 592
—— Geo., gen. (**A**) 860
—— J., G. Bmda. 701
—— Jno., C. St. 283
—— Mont., Jud. Com. P.C. 361; P.C. 218
—— Nichs., dn. Ard. 609; dn. Kilm. 609
—— hon. Rd. Boyle, dn. Llin. 624
—— Rt. and sir R., S.L. 409-10
—— Scr., U.S.H. 228
—— (or Barnard) Th., bp. Killoe. and Kilf. 35; bp. Lim. A. and A. 639; dn. Dry. 602
—— Th., L.L. K. Co. 570
—— Wm., *see* Barnard
Bernardus, *see* Bernard
Berners, Ralph de, Const. T.L. 320
Berners, lds.
—— Jno., 1st ld., Const. W. Cast. 322; K.G. 736
—— (or Barnes), Jno., ld., K.B. 757
Bernes, *see* Barnes
Bernevall (or Barnewall) Chr., C.J.K.B. Ir. 577; J.K.B. Ir. 578
Bernhard, *see* Bernard
Bernred, K.E. 3
Bersald, C. Svy. 54
Berridge, J. S., G. St. Xtr. 729
Berro, B. P., Pres. Ugy. 111
Berry, sir Ed., adm. (**A**) 819; K.C.B. 774
—— Fk. Ch., C.I.E. 807
—— Geo., R. Cr. P.A. 335
—— Geo. Fk. de, gen. (**D**) 926
—— Grah., K.C.M.G. 798
—— sir Jno., adm. (**A**) 813
Bersted (or Berstede), *see* Berested
Berthgwyn, bp. Llff. 448
Berthier, Off. Nap. 26
Berthold, D. Bva. 67
Berthon, Jno. Fk., gen. (**D**) 916
Berthulf, K.E. 3
Berthun, K.E. 1
—— bp. Lich. 443
Bertie, hon. Albem., aft. 9th E. of Lindsey, gen. (**A**) 859
—— sir Albem., adm. (**A**) 817; K.C.B. 773
—— Mont., aft. 2nd E. of Lindesey, *q.v.*, K.B. 762
—— Peregr., K.B. 762
—— hon. Peregr., P.C. 194; Tell. Ex. 167; V.C.H. 296-7
—— ld. Rt., gen. (**A**) 858
—— Rog., K.B. 763
—— Th. and sir T., adm. (**A**) 818
—— Vere, B. Ex. 384; J.C.P. 379; S.L. 410
Bertram, dn. Lich. 445
—— Ch., adm. (**H**) 845
—— Geo. Clem., Blf. Jsey. 668
—— Rog., J. It. 367
—— Wm., G. Ch. Isl. 667
—— Wm., Sec. Thist. 749
Bertric, K.E. 2
Bertulf, bp. Winch. 470
—— K.E. 3
Berwick, sir Rt., L.P. Ch. Sess. 516
—— Saml., G. Bdoes. 719
—— Walt., J. Bank. Ir. 587; S.L. Ir. 593
Berwick, ld. and D. of
—— Jas., D. of, gen. (**B**) 864; K.G. (?) 740; Pr. E. 14
—— —, ld., form. — Hill, *q.v.*
Besborough, *see* Bessborough
Besley, Rt., L.M. Lond. 492
Besliz, Matth., W.C.P. 317
Bessborough, E. of
—— Brab., 1st E. of, L.J. Ir., 557
—— Wm., 2nd E. of, form. Visc. Duncannon, *q.v.*; P.C. 201; Postm. G. 238
—— Jno. Wm., 4th E. of, form. ld. and visc. Duncannon, *q.v.*; L.L. Ir. 557
—— Jno. Geo. Br., 5th E. of, L.L. Carl. 568; L.S.H. 290; M.B.H. 303; P.C. 215
Besset, Jas., Modr. K. Sc. 547
Bessieres, Off. Nap. 26
Best, sir Elias, L.M. Dbln. 640
—— Jno., bp. Carl. 475
—— Jno., C.Y.G. 298
—— J. R., G. Bdoes. 720
—— Rd. Mord., gen. (**D**) 907
—— hon. Th., adm. (**G**) 841
—— Wm. Dr., aft. sir W. and ld. Wynford, *q.v.*, C.J.C.P. 376; C.J. Chest. 386; J. Chest. 387; J.K.B. 373; P.C. 210; S.L. 412
Bestia, L.C., C. Ro. 45
Bethell, Chr., bp. Bgr. 426; bp. Exr. 437; bp. Glr. 439; dn. Chich. 434
—— Rd. and sir R., aft. ld. Westbury, *q.v.*; A.G. 400; 1st Ld. Chanc. 358; Q.C. 417; S.G. 402
—— Slingsby, L.M. Lond. 492
Betham, W. and sir W., Ulst. K.A. 572
Bethune, *see also* Beaton
—— Alex., gen. (**B**) 869
—— A. N., bp. Tor. 693
—— Ch. Rams. Dr., adm. (**D**) 831; (**E**) 834
—— Dav., abp. St. Andr. 529; Ld. Chanc. Sc. 515
—— (or Beaton), Jas. (No. 1), abp. Glasg. 537; abp. St. Andr. 529; bp. Gall. 538; Ld. Chanc. Sc. 515
Bethune—*cont.*
—— Jas. (No. 2), abp. Glasg. 537
—— Patton-, form. Patton, *q.v.*
—— Robt. de, bp. Her. 441
Betour, Wm. de, L.H.A. 170
Bett, Hy. Iml., gen. (**D**) 913
Bettesworth, Jno., Adm. Adv. 423; Ch. Lond. 422; D. Arch. 420; J. Pr. Ct. 421; Vic. Gen. 421
—— Rd., gen. (**C**) 872
—— Rd., S.L. Ir. 592
Bettia, Mahar. of, K.C.I.E. 805
Betts, Rd., bp. Kilf. 635
Betun, *see* Bethune and Beaton
Bevan, Ch. D., C.C.J. 404
—— Geo. Buch., gen. (**D**) 931
—— Hy., L.M. Dbln. 641
Bever, Th., Adm. Adv., 423
Beveridge, W., bp. St. As. 462
Beverley, St Jno. of, abp. Yk. 485; bp. Hex. 480
Beverley, E. of
—— Geo., 2nd E. of, form. ld. Lavaine, *q.v.*, C.Y.G. 298; P.C. 214
Beversham, Wm., M. Chy. 396
Bevill, Rt., K.B. (1603) 761
—— Rt., K.B. (1625) 763
Bevir, Ed. Jas., Q.C., 419
Bewcham, Gilb., K.B. 756
Bewes, Thos., Arund. H. 339
Bexhall, Jno., dn. Chich. 434
Bexley, Nichs., ld., form. N. Vansittart, *q.v.*
Bexstede, Pet. de, K.B.. 754
Beynvill, Rd. de, J. It. 367
Beyts, H. N. D., G. Mtius. 684
Bhaunagar, Sah. of, G.C.S.I. 801; K.C.S.I. 803
Bhopal (Kudsia), Beg. of, Cr. Ind. 809
—— (Shahsihan), Beg. of, Cr. Ind. 809
—— (Segumde), Beg. of, G.C.S.I. 801; K.C.S.I. 802
—— (Shah Jehan), Beg. of, G.C.S.I. 801
Bhownaggree, Manch. Nerw. C.I.E. 808
Bhurtpore, Mahar. of, G.C.S.I. 801
Biarn, bp. Ork. 535
Bibesco, Geo., H. Wca. 94
Bibulus, M. C., C. Ro. 46
Bickersteth, Ed., dn. Lich. 445
—— Ed. Hy., bp. Exr. 437; dn. Glr. 440
—— Ed. Wm., bp. Jpn. 677
—— Hy., aft. ld. Langdale, *q.v.*; Jud. Com. P.C. 360; K.C. 416; M.R. 388; P.C. 213
—— Rt., bp. Rip. 482
Bickerton, sir Rd., adm. (**A**) 815; K.C.B. 773; Ld. Admy. 181
—— Sir Rd. Huss., adm. (**A**) 817
Bickford, Josh. Gr., adm. (**H**) 851
Bickley, Th., bp. Chich. 433
Bicknell, Rt., M. Chy. 397
Bicknor, Byknore, or Bython, Alexr. de, abp. Dbln. and Gl.

Bicknor, Byknore, or Bython —*cont.* 615; dn. St. Patr. 617; L.D. Ir. 551; L. Treas. Ir. 558; Ld. Chanc. Ir. 574
Bidder, Geo. Park., Q.C. 419
Biddulph, Michl. Anthy. Shr. and sir M., gen. (**D**) 908; K.C.B. 781
— Midd., L.L. Denb. 314
— Rt. and sir R., G. Cypr. 671; gen. (**D**) 925; G.C.M.G. 795; K.C.M.G. 797
— Rt. Midd., L.L. Denb. 314
— Th. Mydd. and sir T., gen. (**G**) 900; K.C.B. 783; P.C. 219
Bidie, Geo., C.I.E. 807
Bidun, Rd., or Walt. de, bp. Dkld. 533; Ld. Chanc. Sc. 514
Bifus, bp. E. Ang. 454
Biggar, Walt., L.G.C. Sc. 506
Bigge. Th. Sc., gen. (**D**) 924
Biggs, Jno. Andr., gen. (**D**) 879
— Rt., adm. (**A**) 816
Bigham, Jno. Ch., Q.C. 420
Bigland, Ed., S.L. 410
— Ralph (No. 1), Bl. M. P.A. 336; Clar. K.A. 328; Gart. K.A. 328; Norr. K.A. 329; Som. H. 332
— Ralph (No. 2), Gart. K.A. 328; Norr. K.A. 330; R. Dr. P.A. 338; Richm. H. 334
— Wils. Bradd., adm. (**H**) 846; K.H. 791
Bigod, *see* Bagod and Bigot
Bigot and **Bigod**
— Hugh, or Rog. de, Ch. Jr. 363; Const. T.L. 320; W.C.P. 317
— Roger (2), aft. E. Norfolk, *q.v.*
Bill, Wm., dn. Westr. 469
Billers, sir Wm., L.M. Lond. 491
Billesdon, Nichs., dn. Sal. 468
— Rt., L.M. Lond. 490
Billing, Rt. Cl., bp. Suff. Beds. 452
— (or Billyng), Th. and sir T., C.J.K.B. 370; J.K.B. 371; Rec. Lond. 493; S.L. 407
Billingsly, sir Hy., L.M. Lond. 491
Billington, sir Wm., L.M. Dbln. 640
Billyng, *see* Billing
Bilson, Th., bp. Winch. 471; bp. Worc. 473
Bimon, sir Geo., C. Exc. 277-8
Binckes, *see also* Binks
— Wm., dn. Lich. 445
Bindley, Jas., C. St. 283-4
— Jno., C. Exc. 280
Bindon, Thos., dn. Lim. 640
Bindon, visc. and E. of
— Hy., 1st E. of, form. Hy. Howard and ld. Walden, *q.v.*, aft. E. of Suffolk, *q.v.*, Dep. E.M. 327; P.C. 195
— visc., *see* Howard of Bindon
Binge, Th., M. Chy. 395
Bingham, Geo. Rid. and sir G., gen. (**C**) 874; K.C.B. 774
— Geo. Wm. P., gen. (**D**) 906
— Hy., gen. (**D**) 906
— Jno., G. Gsey. 668
— Jos., adm. (**A**) 819
— Rd., gen. (**B**) 867
— Rd., J.K.B. 371; K.B. 757; S.L. 407
Bingham—*cont.*
— hon. Rd. C., Amb. Vza. 134
— Rt. de, bp. Sal. 466
Bingley, Rt. 1st ld., form. R. Benson, *q.v.*, P.C. 198; Tr. H. 291
Binks, *see also* Binckes
— Wm., gen. (**C**) 874
Binney, Hibb., bp. N. Sc. 695
Binning, Dav. M., C. Cus. 277
Binning, lds.
— Th. H., 1st ld., form. sir T. H. Hamilton, *q.v.*, aft. 1st E. of Melrose, *q.v.*, L.P. Ch. Sess. 516
— Th., ld., aft. 9th E. of Haddington, *q.v.*, B.C. 252-3; P.C. 209
Binny, Wm. Hy., gen. (**D**) 921
Binstead, Cheesman Hy., adm. (**H**) 849
Birch, —, G. Bah. Is. 716
— Arth. Non. and sir A., G. Ceyl. 673; K.C.M.G. 798
— Ed., gen. (**D**) 933
— Ed., S.L. 410
— Jno., B. Ex. 384; S.L. 408
— Jno., Curs. B. Ex. 386; S.L. 411
— Jno., C. Exc. 278
— Jno. Fras., gen. (**A**) 863
— Rd. Jas. Holw., K.C.B. 782; gen. (**D**) 892
— Rt. Hy., gen. (**D**) 883
— Saml., gen. (**C**) 872
— Saml., L.M. Lond. 492
— Th. and sir T., J.C.P. 379; S.L. 411
— Th. Fras., adm. (**G**) 843
— Th. J., C.C.J. 403
— Walt., gen. (**D**) 907
— Wm., Wdn. Chr. Ch. Manch. 481
Birchall, Jno., G. I. Man, 666
Bird, Birde and **Byrde**
— Ed. Josh., adm. (**G**) 843
— Hy., gen. (**D**) 908
— Jno., bp. Bgr. 426; bp. Chest. 476; bp. Suff. Penr. 482
— (or Brid), Jno., bp. Cloy. 630
— Jno., C. St. 283
— Louis Sand., gen. (**D**) 892
— Th., M. Chy. 396
— (or Byrd), sir Wm., D. Arch. 420; J. Pr. Ct. 421; M. Chy. 395
— Wm. Wilb., G.G. Ind. 649
Birdwood, Chr., gen. (**D**) 906
— sir Geo., Chr. M., K.C.I.E. 805
— Wm. Ilb., gen. (**D**) 898
Birger II., K. Sw. 92
Birine (or Birinus), Saint, bp. Dorch. 446; bp. Winch. 470
Birkbeck, Wm. Ll., Q.C. 420
Birkett, Jno., Pres. Coll. Surg. 939
Birkhead. Edm., bp. St. As. 462
Birlaco, Wm. de, M. Chy. 393
Birmingham, *sec* Bermingham
Birnie, sir Andr., Ld. Sess. 519
Biron, *see also* Byron
— Nichs., K.B. 759
— Rt. Jno., Q.C. 419
Birrell. Dav., gen. (**D**) 892
Birtwhistle, Jno., gen. (**D**) 900
Bishop, Ch. Th. Geo., gen. (**D**) 876
Bishop—*cont.*
— Hy. Parl., gen. (**D**) 920
— Jno., C.C.J. 405
— Pet., K.H. 792
— Wm., G. Bdoes. 720
Bishopp, Cecil, gen. (**D**) 884
— sir Geo., dn. Lism. 629
Bisse, Ph., bp. Her. 442; bp. St. Dav. 465
Bisset and **Bissett**
— Andr., gen. (**B**) 864
— Jas., adm. (**A**) 819
— sir Jno., K.C.B. 777; K.C.H. 788
— Jno. Jarv., gen. (**D**) 902
— Wm., bp. Rph. 602
— Wm. Sinc. Sm., C.I.E. 808
Bisshopp, *see* Bishopp
Bisus, bp. E. Ang. 454
Bitton (or Button), Wm. (2), bp. B and W. 427
Bivar, Hy. St., gen. (**D**) 921
Blacadder, *see* Blackadder
Blach, *see* Black
Blachford, Aug. Geo., gen. (**D**) 894
— B. P., L. Admy. 181
— Jno., L.M. Lond. 492
Blachford, lds.
— Fk., 1st ld., form. sir F. Rogers, *q.v.*, G.C.M.G. 795
Blachley, Hy., gen. (**D**) 891
Black, Adam, L. Prov. Edinb. 548
— Bladen West, gen. (**D**) 898
— Jas., gen. (**D**) 912
— (or Blach), Patr., dn. Enachd. 613
— Saml., gen. (**D**) 929
— Wm., adm. (**H**) 845
Black—, *see also* Blak—
Blackadder, Rt., bp. Abd. 530; abp. Glasg. 537
Blackall, *see also* Blackhall
— Rt., gen. (**D**) 887
— Saml. Wensl., G. Dnca. 730; G. Qland. 705; G.W. Afr. Sett. 688
Blackburn and **Blackburne**
— Colin, *see* ld. B., *infra*
— Fras., A.G. Ir. 588; C.J.Q.B. Ir. 578; L.J. App. Ir. 585; Ld. Chanc. Ir. 577; M.R. Ir. 585; S.L. Ir. 593
— Jno., K.C. 416
— Lanc., abp. Yk. 486; bp. Exr. 437; dn. Exr. 437; P.C. 197
— Nichs., L.H.A. 173
— Pet., bp. Abdn. 530
— Pet., L.T. 161
— Th., Wdn. Chr. Ch. Manch. 481
— Wm., gen. (**D**) 876
Blackburn, lds.
— Colin and sir C., aft. 1st. ld., J.Q.B. 373; J.Q.B.D. 374; Jud. Com. P.C. 361; L. App. 358; P.C. 219; S.L. 414
Blacker, Stew., dn. Llin. 624
Blackett, Ed. Wm., gen. (**D**) 924
Blackhall, *see also* Blackall
— Geo., L.M. Dbln. 640
— Offs., bp. Exr. 437
— sir Th., L.M. Dbln. 641
Blackleach, Huan, bp. S. and M. 483
Blackston, Jno., L. Treas. Ir. 558
Blackstone, Wm. and sir W., J.C.P. 379; J.K.B. 373; K.C. 415; S.L. 412

For List of Abbreviations, see pp. 944-952.

Blackwall, Rt., M. Chy. 394
Blackwell, Jno., L.T. 154
—— Nathl., G. Tob. 723; gen. (**C**) 874
Blackwood, hon. Hans, C. Acc. Ir. 567
—— hon. sir Hy., adm. (**A**) 819; G.C.H. 786; K.C.B. 775
—— S. A. and sir S., K.C.B. 784; Sec. P.O. 239
Bladen, Mart., B.T. 264
—— Th., dn. Ardf. 640
Bladus (St.), bp. Isl. 539; bp. S. and M. 483
Blæsus, C. S., C. Ro. 42
Blagge, Rt., B. Ex. 383
Blague, Th., dn. Roch. 461
Blaine, Del. Rt., C.C.J. 405
Blair, Ch. Renny, gen. (**D**) 927
—— Jas., gen. (**D**) 928
—— Jas. Hunter, L. Prov. Edin. 548
—— Jas. K., C.C.J. 404
—— Rt., gen. (**D**) 926; K.C.B. 775
—— Rt., D. Fac. Sc. 527; L.P. Ct. Sess. 516; S.G. Sc. 526
—— Th. H., gen. (**D**) 881
—— Wm., C. St. 283; C. Tx. 284; L.P.S. 241
Blakburn, *see* Blackburn
Blake, Geo. Ch., adm. (**H**) 847
—— Geo. F., gen. (**D**) 929
—— Hy. Arth. and sir H., G. Bah. Isl. 716; G. Jam. 713; G. Newfd. 700; G. Qland. 706; K.C.M.G. 799
—— Hy. Wm., gen. (**D**) 907
—— Patr. Jno., adm. (**G**) 842
—— Rt., Ld. Admy. 175; W.C.P. 319
—— Rt. Dudl., gen. (**A**) 861
—— Walt., bp. Clonm. 600
Blakedon, Jas., bp. Ach. 612; bp. Bgr. 426
Blakeley, Theoph., dn. Ach. 614; dn. Cnr. 605; dn. Down 605
Blakeney and **Blakeny**
—— Ed. and sir E., Comm. F. Ir. 564; F.M. 856; G.C.B. 769; G.C.H. 787; G. Ch. Hosp. 936; gen. (**A**) 863; K.C.B. 774; L.G. Ch. Hosp. 936
—— Grice, gen. (**A**) 860
—— Jas., Ch. Ex. Ir. 561
—— Jno., C.J.C.P. Ir. 580
Blakeney, ld.
—— Wm., aft. ld. B., gen. (**B**) 865; K.B. 765
Blakesley, Jos. Wms., dn. Linc. 448
Blaksley, Jno., gen. (**D**) 932
Blakiston, sir Matth., L.M. Lond. 492
Blanch and **Blanche**
—— (dau. Edw. I.), Pr. E. 10
—— (de la Tour—dau. Edw. III.), Pr. E. 10
—— (dau. Hy. IV.), Pr. E. 11
—— Q. Nav., 87
Blanchard, Rd., G. Vanc. Isl. 699
—— Th., G. Mtius. 684
Blanche, *see* Blanch
Blancke, sir Th., L.M. Lond. 490
Blanckley, Hor. C. N., gen. (**D**) 927
Blanco, A. G., Pres. Vzla. 108
Bland, Hy., dn. Dham. 479
—— Jas., dn. Ardf. 640
—— Humph., G. Gibr. 669; gen. (**B**) 865
—— Th., gen. (**A**) 859
Blandford, Walt., bp. Oxf. 456; bp. Worc. 473
Blandford, M. of, *see also* D. of Marlborough
—— Geo., M. of, aft. 4th D. of Marlborough, *q.v.*, L.T. 158
Blane, sir Seym. Jno., gen. (**D**) 921
Blaney, *see* Blayney
Blankett, Jno., adm. (**A**) 816
Blanshard, Th., gen. (**D**) 889
—— Wm., C.C. J. 404
Blantyre, lds.
—— Walt., 1st ld., form. W. Stewart, *q.v.*, L.H.T. Sc. 497; Ld. Sess. 517
—— Wm., 2nd ld., form. Wm. Stewart, *q.v.*
—— Rt. Walt., 11th ld., gen. (**C**) 874; L.L. Rnfw. 511
Blaquiere, sir Jno., aft. 1st ld. de Bl., Ch. Sec. Ir. 562; K.B. 765
—— Hon. Wm., aft. 3rd ld. de Bl., gen. (**A**) 862
Blasio, C. C. (2), C. Ro. 42
Blaston, Th. de, B. Ex. 383
Blathmac, K. Ir. 21
Blathwayte, Wm., B.T. 263; Sec. at W. 233
—— Wynt., gen. (**B**) 866
Blaundeston (or Brandeston), Hy. de, bp. Sal. 467; dn. Sal. 468
Blayne, Maur., dn. St. As. 463
Blayney and **Blaney**
—— Ch. Talb., dn. Killoe. 637
Blayney, lds.
—— Cadw., 9th ld., gen. (**B**) 865
—— Andr. Th., 11th ld., gen. (**B**) 867
Blebury, Jno. de, M. Chy. 393
Bleddyn, Pr. Wls. 16
—— (ab Cynvyn), Pr. Wls. 17
Bledri, bp. Llff. 449
Bleithud, bp. St. Dav. 464
Blencowe, Jno. and sir J., B. Ex. 384; J.C.P. 378; S.L. 411
Blennerhassett, Arth., J.K.B. Ir. 579; S.L. Ir. 592
—— sir Jno., C.B. Ex. Ir. 583
—— Rt., S.L. Ir. 591
Blesinton, Murr., visc., L.J. Ir. 555
Blethyn, Wm., bp. Llff. 449
Blicke. sir Ch., Mast. Coll. Surg. 939
Bligh, Hon. Ed., gen. (**A**) 861
—— Jno., adm. (**A**) 819
—— Hon. Jno. Dunc. and sir J., Amb. G. St. 122; Amb. Hnr. 120; Amb. Nds. &c. 123; Amb. Russ. 126; Amb. Sw. & N. 127; K.C.B. 782
—— sir Rd. Rodney, adm. (**A**) 816; G.C.B. 768
—— Rt., dn. Elph. 609
—— Th., gen. (**B**) 865
—— Wm., adm. (**A**) 818; G. N.S.W. 702
Blight, Wm., adm. (**H**) 847
Bliss, Hy., Q.C. 417
—— J. M., G. N. Brk. 695
—— Nath., Astr. Roy. 941
Blizzard, sir Wm., Mast. & Pres. Coll. Surg. 939
Blockley, Jno. de, B. Ex. 383
Blodwell, Dav., dn. St. As. 463
—— Jno., dn. St. As. 463
Bloet (or Bluet), Rt., bp. Linc. 446; Ch. Jr. 362; Ld. Chanc. 353
—— Sim., dn. Linc. 447
Blois, Hy. de, bp. Winch. 470
—— Wm. de, bp. Linc. 446; bp. Worc. 472
Blomefield, *see also* Blomfield and Bloomfield
—— sir Th., gen. (**A**) 861
Blomfield, *see also* Blomefield and Bloomfield
—— Ch. Jas., bp. Chest. 477; bp. Lond. 452; Jud. Com. P.C. 360; P.C. 211
—— Ed. Hy., gen. (**D**) 914
—— Hy. Jno., adm. (**H**) 851
—— **-Macdonald,** form. Macdonald, *q.v.*
Blommart, Danl. Fras., gen. (**B**) 869
Bloncat, Nichs., K.B. 756
Blonde, Jno. le, bp. Cork, 630; dn. Cloy. 632
Blondy, Rd., bp. Ex. 436
Blood, Nept. (2), dn. Kilf. 637
Bloomfield, *see also* Blomfield and Blomefield
—— Alf., bp. Suff. Colch. 461
—— sir Benjn., *see* ld. Bl., *infra*
—— Hy. Kean., G. N.S.W. 703; gen. (**D**) 894
—— Jno. and sir J., gen. (**D**) 894; G.C.B. 770; K.C.B. 779
—— Jno. A. D., *see* ld. B., *infra*
Bloomfield, lds.
—— sir Benj., aft. 1st ld. B., Amb. Sw. & N. 127; gen. (**B**) 869; P.C. 209; G.C.B. 772; G.C.H. 786; K.C.H. 787; P.C. 209
—— Hon. Jno. Arth. D., aft. 2nd ld., Amb. Aus. 117; Amb. Pr. 118; Amb. Russ. 126; G.C.B. 772; K.C.B. 782; P.C. 217
Blosse, Hy. Lynch, dn. Llff. 450
Blossett, sir Rt. H., C.J. Bgal. 652
Blount, Ed., K.C.B. 784
—— Ed. le, K.B. 755
—— Geo., C. Tx. 284-5
—— Jno., L.M. Lond. 489
—— sir Jno., K.G. 735
—— sir Michl., St. T.L. 321
—— sir Rd., Lt. T.L. 321
—— (or Blunt), St. Jno., K.B. 763
—— sir Walt., aft. ld. Mountjoy, *q.v.*, K.B. 757; L.H.T. 153
—— Walt. A., Bl. C. H. 339; Chest. H. 331; Clar. K.A. 328; geneal. Bath, 784; Norr. K.A. 330
Blowers, Ch. Ed., gen. (**D**) 933
Bloxham, Mark, L.M. Dbln. 641
Bloye, Rt., adm. (**H**) 845
Bloyon, Ralph de, K.B. 755
Blucher, Alb. Louis P. Pr., G.C.B. 767
Bludworth, sir Th., L.M. Lond. 491
Bluet, *see* Bloet
Bluett, Buckl. St., K.H. 791
Blund, Peter de, Const. T.L. 320
Blundell, sir Archd., V. Treas. Ir. 559
—— Br., gen. (**C**) 872
—— Dix, dn. Kild. 619
—— Fred., gen. (**D**) 888
Blunden, Over., gen. (**B**) 869
Blundeville (or Blunvill), Th. de, bp. Norw. 454; Const. T.L. 320
Blundy, Rd., abp. Cant. (desig.) 430

Blunt, Ch. Harris, gen. (**D**) 902
— Fras. Theoph., G. Seych. Isl. 684
— Grant, G. St. Hel. 682; gen. (**D**) 933
— Jno. Elij., M. Chy. 397
— Rd., gen. (**A**) 862
— (or Blount), St. Jno., K.B. 763
Blunvill, *see* Blundeville
Blyth and **Blythe**
— Arth., K.C.M.G. 797
— Fk. Saml., gen. (**D**) 923
— Geoff., bp. Lich. & Cov. 444; dn. Yk. 487
— Geo. Fras. P., bp. Jslm. 677
— Jno., bp. Sal. 467; Chanc. Gart. 745; M.R. 387
— Rt. bp. Down. &. Cnr. 604
Boardman, Ed., gen. (**D**) 876
Boate, Godf., J.K.B. Ir. 579; S.L. Ir. 592
Bobi, Hugh de, J. It. 366; Jy. 364
Bock, Geo., Bar., gen. (**C**) 873
Bocland, Geoffr. de, Jy. 363-4
— Hugh de, Ch. Jr. 362; Jy. 363
— Hugh de, J. It. 365
— Maur., gen. (**B**) 865
Bocquet, Rosc., C.I.E. 806
Boddam, Edmond Tud., gen. (**D**) 915
— Hung. Mey., gen. (**D**) 929
— Rawson H., G. Bbay. 659
Bodeco, *see* Dudoco
Bodekin, Chr., abp. Tm. 611; bp. Kilmacd. 636
Boden, Geo., Q.C. 418
Bodenham, Rog., K.B. 761
Bodmin, Jno., visc., form. ld. Robartes, *q.v.*, aft. E. of Radnor, *q.v.*
Bodryngham, Hy., K.B. 757
Boeff, Wm., S.L. 407
Boerley, Wm., Sp. H.C. 248
Boger, Edmd., adm. (**D**) 826
— Rd., adm. (**A**) 817
— Turtcl., K.H. 791
Bogle, sir Archd., gen. (**D**) 897
Bogran, L., Pres. Hdas. 106
Bogue, Jno., K.H. 792
Bohun, Jno. de, K.B. 754
— sir Wm. de, aft. E. of Northampton, *q.v.*, L.H.A. 172
Boileau, Alex. Hy. Edm., gen. (**D**) 895
— Fras. Bart., gen. (**D**) 898
— Neil Edm., gen. (**D**) 912
— Saml. Brand., gen. (**D**) 892
Boircech (Tigernach), bp. Cld. 599
Boiroimhe, K. Ir. 22
Boisel, bp. Worc. 472
Bokerell, Andr., L.M. Lond. 488
Bokingham, Jno. de, dn. Lich. 445; bp. Linc. 446
Bolayne, *see* Boleyn
Bolcomp, Jno., bp. Wford. and L. 627
Boldero, Geo. Neeld, gen. (**D**) 922
— Hy. Geo., Clk. O. 260
Bole, Jno., abp. Arm. 595
Bolebec, Hugh de, J. It. 367
Boleslas, I. to III., D. Bma. 59
— I. to IV., K. Pld. 90-1
Boleyn (or Boleine), Geoffr., L.M. Lond. 490
— (or Bo len), Geo., dn. Lich. 445
— Th., K.B. 759
— (or Bullen), sir Thos., aft. visc. Rochford and E. of Wiltshire and Ormond, *q.v.*, K.B. 758; K.G. 737; Tr. H. 291
Bolingbroke, Nichs. de, J. It. 369
Bolingbroke, visc. and E. of
— Ol., 1st E. of, form. O. St. John, *q.v.*, C.G.S. 356
— Hy., 1st visc., form. H. St. John, *q.v.*
Bolivar, Dt. Pu. 109
Bolland, Wm., aft. sir W., B. Ex. 385; S.L. 413
Bollen, *see* Boleyn
Bolles, Geo., L.M. Lond. 491
Bolling, Wm., B. Ex. 383
Bologna, Ct. Nichs. Sceb., K.C.M.G. 796
Bolter, Rog., dn. Exr. 437
Bolton, Danl., gen. (**D**) 894
— sir Ed., C.B. Ex. Ir. 583; S.G. Ir. 589
— Hugh, dn. Wford. 628
— Jas. Cl., S.L. 412
— Jno., dn. Dry. 602
— Jno. Lawr., gen. (**D**) 919
— Rd. and sir R., C.B. Ex. Ir. 583; Ld. Chanc. Ir. 576; Rec. Dbln. 642; S.G. Ir. 589
— Rt., dn. Carl. 476
— sir Rt., gen. (**B**) 867; G.C.H. 787; K.C.H. 787
— Theoph., abp. Cash. and Eml. 626; bp. Clonf. and K. 636; bp. Elph. 608
— Th., L.M. Dbln. 641
— Wm., dn. Ross. 633
— Wm., M. Chy. 394
— sir Wm., L.M. Lond. 491
Bolton, lds. and D. of
— Chas., 2nd D. of, form. M. of Winchester, *q.v.*; K.G. 741; L.C.H. 275; L.J. Ir. 555; L.L. Dors. 307; L.L. Ir. 556; P.C. 194
— Ch., 3rd D. of, C.G.P. 299; Const. T.L. 321; K.G. 746; gen. (**B**) 865; L.L. Dors. 307; L.L. Glam. 315; P.C. 197
— Harry, 4th D. of, form. ld. H. Poulett, *q.v.*, P.C. 199
— Ch., 5th D. of, form. C. Poulett and M. of Winchester, *q.v.*, L.L. Hants. 311
— Harry, 6th D. of, form. ld. H. Poulett, *q.v.*, L.L. Hants. 311; P.C. 202

— Th., 1st ld., form. Th. Orde, *q.v.*, L.L. Hants. 311
Bompas, Ch. Carp., P.P. 416; S.L. 413
— Hy. Mason, Q.C. 419
— Wm. Carp., bp. Athab. 697; bp. M. Riv. 697
Bonaparte, *see* Buonaparte
Bonar, Alf. G. G., Amb. Swz. 114
Bonaventure, bp. Ross. 631
Bonavita, Ign. Gav. and sir I., G.C.M.G. 795; K.C.M.G. 796
Boncour, *see* Bonquer
Bond, Alexr., gen. (**D**) 929
— Fras., G. Bdoes. 719
— Fras. God., adm. (**D**) 824
— Fk. Wm., gen. (**D**) 920
Bond—*cont.*
— Geo., S.L. 412
— sir Geo., L.M. Lond. 490
— Hy., gen. (**D**) 934
— Jas. Forw., dn. Ross. 633
— Jno., M. Chy. 395
— Nathl., B.T. 268; J.A.G. 937; K.C. 415; L.T. 158; P.C. 207; V.P.B.T. 269
— Nathl., S.L. 411
— Wens., dn. Ross. 633
— Wm. de, Ld. Chanc. Sc. 514
— Wm. Benn., bp. Montr. 694
— Wm. Morr. Barn., gen. (**D**) 934
Bondelez, Nig., dn. Bgr. 426
Bondington, Wm. de, bp. Glasg., 536; Ld. Chanc. Sc. 514
Boneville, Wm. de, A.G. 398
Bonfoy, Capt., G. Newfd. 700
Bongay, Raym. or Reg., L.M. Lond. 488
Bonham, Ch. Wr., adm. (**H**) 852
— Fras. Rt., St. O. 261
— Pins., gen. (**A**) 862
— Saml. Geo. and sir S., Amb. Ch. 131; G. H. Kong 673; K.C.B. 782
Bonham-Carter, *see* Carter
Bonhault, Greg., M. Chy. 395
Boniface (of Savoy), abp. Cant. 430
— bp. E. Ang. 454
— C. Svy. 54
— I. and II., D. Tny. 57
— I. to IX., P. Ro. 33-4-5
Bonner, Edmd., bp. Her. 441; bp. Lond. 451
— Pet., M. Chy. 396
— Rd. B.M., dn. St. As. 463
Bonnici, Cl. Vinc., K.C.M.G. 796
Bonnor, *see* Bonner
Bonquer (or Boncour), Wm., J.C.P. 377; Jy. 365
Bonus, Jos., gen. (**D**) 931
Bonvill, Wm., 1st. ld., K.G. 736
Bonython, Ch., S.L. 411
Booker, Fras., L.M. Dbln. 641
Boone, Gilb., S.L. 409
— Th., C. Cus. 276
Booth, Aug. Sincl., adm. (**H**) 850
— Ch., bp. Her. 441
— Geo., C. Cus. 274
— Geo. Scl., P.C. 219; Pres. L.G.B. 256; Sec. P.L.B., 262; Sec. Tr. 164
— Hy., K.H. 791
— Jas. Sec. B.T. 270
*— Jno., bp. Exr. 436
*— Jno., Wdn. Chr. Ch. Manch. 481
* Prob. same pers.
— Lawr., abp. Yk. 486; bp. Dham. 478; dn. St. P. 453; Ld. Chanc. 355
— Pen., dn. Winds. 474
— hon. Rt., dn. Brl. 440
— sir Robt., C.J.C.P. Ir. 580; C.J.K.B. Ir. 578; J.C.P. Ir. 581
— Wm., abp. York 486; bp. Lich. and Cov. 444
— Wm., gen., (**D**) 891
— Wm., gen. (**D**) 932
Boothby, Jno. Geo., gen (**D**) 913
— Wm. and sir W., C. Cus. 276-7; C. Cus. Ir. 566
— sir Wm., gen. (**A**) 858

For List of Abbreviations, see pp. 944-952.

Bootle, Ed., S.L. 412
— sir Rt., L.L. Sligo, 571
— Th., K.C. 415
Boppé, Lucien, C.I.E. 807
Bordeaux, Oliver de, Const. W. Cast. 322
Boreham (or Borham), Herv. de, B. Ex. 382; J.C.P. 377; Jy. 365
Borgard, Alb., gen. (**B**) 864
Borghorst, Jac., G. C.G.H. 678
Borgo, Ct. Pozzo de, K.C.B. 775
Borham, *see* Boreham
Boris-Gordonof, R. Russ. 90
Borlase, Jno., adm. (**H**) 849
— sir Jno., L.J. Ir. 554
— Wm. C., Sec. L.G.B. 256
Borough (or Boroughs), Jas., Mowb. H. 340
— Thos., ld., *see* Burgh
Borrero, A., Pres. Ecr. 108
Borrett, Jno., M. Chy. 396
Borso, D. Mda. 53
Borthwick, Dav., Ld. Sess. 518
— Wm., gen. (**B**) 866
— Wm., gen. (**C**) 873
Borton, Arth., and sir A., G. Mlta. 671; gen. (**D**) 902; G.C.B. 771; G.C.M.G. 795; K.C.B. 780
Borzivoi, I. and II., D. Bma. 59
Bosa, *see also* Osa
— (Saint), Abp. Yk. 485
Bosanquet, Ch. Jno., adm. (**H**) 848
— Fk. Alb., Q.C. 420
— Geo. Stanley., adm. (**E**) 837
— Jac., Chn. E.I.Co. 644
— Jno. B. and sir J., C.G.S. 358; J.C.P. 380; Jud. Com. P.C. 360; P.C. 212; S.L. 413
Bosbury, Th. de, dn. Her. 442
Boscawen, hon. Edw., adm. (**A**) 814; Ld. Admy. 178; P.C. 200
— hon. Geo., gen· (**B**) 865
— Hugh, *see* ld. B., *infra*
— hon. Jno., gen. (**C**) 871
Boscawen, ld.
— Hugh, aft. ld B. and 1st visc. Falmouth, *q.v.*, Compt. H. 292; L.W.S. 323; P.C. 193; V. Treas. Ir. 559
Boscehall, Wm. de, J. It. 368
Bosch, Wm. de, Ld. Clk. Reg. 524
Bosco, *see also* Wood
— Jno. de, A.G. 398; J. It. 368
— Wm. de, *see* Wood
Bosel (or Boselus), bp. Worc. 472
Boson, D. Tny. 57
Bosquet, gen.; G.C.B. 769
Bossett, Ch. Ph. de, K.H. 789
Bostock, Majr., G. Trin. 722
Boswall, Jas. Rop., gen. (**D**) 915
Boswell, Alexr., Jy. Sc. 522; Ld. Sess. 520
— Cl. Irv., Ld. Sess. 520
— Rt., Ly. Dep. 513
Bosworth, sir Wm., Chambn. Lond. 493
Boteler, *see also* Butler and Botiller
— Alexr. le, J. It. 365
— Jno., J.C.P. 378; K.B. 756; S.L. 407

Boteler—*cont.*
— Nichs. le, J. It. 367
— Ralph, aft. ld. Sudeley, *q.v.*, K.G. 735
— Wm. F., K.C. 416
Botetourt, Jno. de, and sir J. J. It. 369; L.H.A. 170
— Odo, K.B. 755
— Wm. de, K.B. 754
Botetourt, ld.
— Norb., 3rd ld., form. N. Berkeley, *q.v.*
Botevillin, Rt., dn. Yk. 486
Both, *see* Booth
Bothe, Ph., K.B. 759
— Rt., dn. Yk. 487
Botheby, Jno. de, Ld. Chanc. Ir. 574
Bothwell, Adam, bp. Ork. 535; Ld. Sess. 517-8
— Fras., Ld. Sess. 518
— Jno., Ld. Sess. 518
— Rd., Ld. Sess. 518
Bothwell, Earls of
Hepburn Family.
— Patr., 1st E. of, L.H.A. Sc. 499
— Adam, 2nd E. of, L.H.A. Sc. 499
— Patr., 3rd E. of, L.H.A. Sc. 499
— Jas., 4th E. of and D. of Orkney, *q.v.*; L.H.A. Sc. 499
Stewart Family.
— Fras., 1st E. of, L.H.A. Sc. 499
Botiller, *see also* Boteler and Butler
— Jas., K.B. 754
Bottlesham, Jno. de, bp. Roch. 460
— Wm., bp. Llff. 449; bp. Roch. 460
Bouat, Genl., K.C.B. 778
Boucher, Desf., G. Mtius. 683
Bouchier, *see also* Bourchier
— Jno., gen. (**C**) 873
— maj. L., G. Trin. 722
Boudier, Ed. Wm., gen. (**D**) 921
Boudon, Wm. de, B. Ex. 383
Boughey, Ch. Fent. Fl., adm. (**H**) 852
Boughton, sir Geo. C. B., gen. (**C**) 873
Bouillon, Phil. D'Auvergne, Pr. of, adm. (**A**) 817
Boukton, Jno. de, L. Treas. Ir. 558
Bouland, Jno. de, M. Chy. 393
Boulger, Barn., dn. Oss. 623
Boulogne, Eust., E. of., L.H.A. 170; W.C.P. 317
Boultbee, Fk. Moore, adm. (**G**) 842
Boulter, Hugh or Hugo, abp. Arm. 596; bp. Brl. 439; dn. Chr. Ch. Oxf. 457; L.J. Ir. 556
Boulton, Hy. Cr., Chn. E.I. Co. 644
Bound, Jno., R. Cr. P.A. 335
Bourchier, *see also* Bouchier
— Eust. Fane, gen. (**D**) 904
— Geo. and sir G., gen. (**D**) 910; K.C.B. 780
— Hy., adm. (**H**) 844
— Hy., aft. 2nd E. of Essex, K.B. 757
— Jas. C., gen. (**D**) 882
— Jno., L.G. Gr. Hosp. 854
— (or Bousser) Jno. de, J.C.P. 377

Bourchier—*cont.*
— (or Burgchier), sir Rt., Ld. Chanc. 354
— Th., K.C.B. 777
— Th., abp. Cant. 431; bp. Ely 435; bp. Worc. 473; L.H.T. 153; L.K. and Ld. Chanc. 355
— Th. (or Jno.), K.B. 757
— sir Th., Const. W. Cast. (1474) 322
— sir Wm., Const. T.L. 320
Bourchier, lds. and visc.
— Jno., 2nd ld., K.G. 734
— Hugh, 4th ld., K.G. 735
— Lewis, 5th ld., form. sir L. Robsart, *q.v.*
— Hy., 1st visc., aft. E. of Essex, K.G. 735; L.H.T. 153
Bourde, *see* Bourne
Bourdieu, Arth. Du, K.H. 791
Bourdon, Jno., G. Jam. 712
Bourmaster, Jno., adm. (**A**) 816
Bourke, *see also* Burke
— Jno., aft. 1st ld. Naas and 1st E. Mayo, *q.v.*, C. Cus. Ir. 565; C. Exc. Ir. 566
— hon. Jno. Joc., gen. (**D**) 917
— hon. Jos., dn. Oss. 623
— hon. Jos. Deane, aft. 3rd E. of Mayo, *q.v.*, abp. Tm. 611; bp. Ferns. and L. 622; Dn. Drom. 606; dn. Killoe 637
— Oliver Pag., gen. (**D**) 905
— hon. Rt., aft. ld. Connemara, *q.v.*, G. Mdras. 657; P.C. 219; U.S.F. 230
— Rd. and sir R., G. C.G.H. 679; G. N.S.W. 703; gen. (**A**) 863; K.C.H. 776
— hon. Rd., dn. Ard. 609; bp. Wford. and L. 627
— lady Susan Georg., aft. lady Connemara, Cr. Ind. 809
— Sir Th., L.D. Ir. 551
Bourn (or Bourde), Gilb., bp. B. and W. 428
Bourne, sir Jno., S. St. 223
— Rd., dn. Tm. 613
— Roger de, K.B. 754
— Wm. Sturges, B.C. 253 C.W.F. &c. 271; H. Sec. 227, L.T. 158; P.C. 209; Sec. Tr 163
Bousser, *see* Bourchier
Bousfield, Hy. Br., bp. Pret 682
Bouverie, hon. Dunc. Pl. adm. (**D**) 823
— hon. Ed. Pl., P.C. 216 Paym. G. 245; Pres. P.L.B 262; U.S. Home 228; V.P.B.T 269
— Everard Wm., gen. (**D**) 88[illegible]
— Fk. Wm., adm. (**H**) 852
— Hy., C. St. 284
— Hy. Fk. and sir H., G. Mlta 671; gen. (**B**) 869; G.C.B. 769 G.C.M.G. 794; K.C.B. 774
— Hy. Jas., C. Cus. 277
Bouvet, *see* Lozier-Bouvet
Bovill, St. Sew. de, abp. Yk 485; dn. Yk. 486
— Wm. and sir W., P.C. 217 C.J.C.P. 376; Jud. Com. P.C 361; P.C. 217; Q.C. 417; S.G 402; S.L. 414
— Wm. Jno., Q.C. 419
Boville, Jno. de, Const. T.I 320
Bovington, Walt. de, J. I[illegible] 366

Bowater, Ed., adm. (**A**) 817
— sir Ed., gen.(**A**) 863; K.C.H. 789
— Jno., gen. (**B**) 866
Bowden, Jno. Wm., C. St. 284; C. St. and Tx. 285; C. Tx. 285
— Wm. Cornish-, adm. (**H**) 851
Bowden-Smith, *see* Smith
Bowditch, Edw. Hope Sm., gen. (**D**) 913
Bowdler, Geo. Ow., gen. (**D**) 921
— Hy., gen. (**D**) 879
Bowen, Ch., adm. (**H**) 846
— Ch. S. C. and sir C., J.Q.B.D. 374; Jud. Com. P.C. 362; L.J. App. 389; P.C. 220
— Ed., dn. Rph. 603
— Geo., adm. (**A**) 817
— Geo. Bl., gen. (**D**) 921
— Geo. Ferg. and sir G., G. H. Kong. 673; G. Mtius. 684; G. Qland. 705; G. Vict. 705; G. N.Z. 709; G.C.M.G. 795; K.C.M.G. 796; P.C. 221
— Herb., gen. (**D**) 878
— Jas. Wm., Q.C. 419
— Jno., bp. Si. Le. 686
— Wm. Th., gen. (**D**) 915
Bower, Fost., K.C. 415
— Jas. Paterson, adm. (**G**) 843
Bowerman, Jno., dn. Ard. 609
Bowers, Ch. R., gen. (**D**) 893
— Geo. Hall, dn. Manch. 481
— Th., bp. Chich. 433
Bowes, Barn. Foord, gen. (**C**) 873
— Fk., gen. (**D**) 878
— sir. Geo., L.L. Dham. 308
— Jno., Sp. H. C. 248
— Jno., *see* Wm., *infra*
— Jno., *see* ld. B., *infra*
— Mart. and sir S., L.M. Lond. 490; M.M. 246
— sir Rt., M.R. 388
— Wm. or Jno., Rec. Lond. 493
Bowes, ld.
— Jno., aft. ld. B., A.G. Ir. 588; C. Acc. Ir. 567; C.B. Ex. Ir. 583; L.J. Ir. 557; Ld. Chanc. Ir. 576; S.G. Ir. 589; S.L. Ir. 592
Bowet and **Bowett**
*— Hy., abp. Yk. 485; bp. B. and W. 428; L.H.T. 153
*— Hy., dn. St. Patr. 617
* ? same person.
Bowie, Ch. Vinc., gen. (**D**) 911
Bowlby, Th., C. Ex. 280
Bowle, *see* Bowles
Bowles, Geo. and sir G., gen. (**D**) 882; G.C.B. 770; K.C.B. 777; Lt. T.L. 322
— (or Bowle), Jno., bp. Roch. 460; dn. Sal. 468
— Phin., gen. (**B**) 864
— Phin., Sec. Adm. 186
— Vere Hunt, gen. (**D**) 925
— Wm. and sir W., adm. (**B**) 821; (**C**) 822; (**D**) 827; K.C.B. 779
Bowley, Rt., M.M. 246
Bowring and **Bowryng**
— Jno. and sir J., Amb. Ch. 131; Amb. Si. 131; G. H. Kong. 673
— Th., C.J.C.P. Ir. 580
Bowser, Th., C.C. Mdras. 657; K.C.B. 775
Bowstead, Jas., bp. Lich. 444; bp. S. and M. 484
Bowyear, Geo. Lely, adm. (**H**) 850
Bowyer, sir Geo., adm. (**A**) 815
— Hy., gen. (**B**) 866
— Jno. Wyndh., C. Exc. 280-1
— sir Wm., L.M. Lond. 490
— Wm. Bohun, adm. (**H**) 847
Boxall and **Boxhall**
— Jno., dn. Norw. 455; dn. Pboro. 458; dn. Winds. 474; S. St. 223
Boxer, Ch. Rd. Fox, adm. (**H**) 852
— Ed., adm. (**D**) 830
— Ed. Mourr., gen. (**D**) 908
Boxhall, *see* Boxall and Buxhull
Boyce, Jos., L.M. Dbln. 642
Boyd, Alexr., gen. (**D**) 916
— Andr., bp. Arg. 538
— Arch., dn. Exr. 438
— Brooke, gen. (**D**) 910
— Ch., C. Cus. Ir. 566
— Danl., gen. (**D**) 922
— Jas., abp. Glasg. 537
— Moss, gen. (**D**) 878
— Rt., J.K.B. Ir. 579
— Rt. and sir R., G. Gibr. 670; gen. (**A**) 858; K.B. 765
— Th. J. and sir T., L. Prov. Edinb. 548
— Walt., J. Bank. Ir. 587
Boyd, lds.
— Robt., 1st ld., L.G.C. Sc. 506; Ld. Chanc. Sc. 515
— Rt., 4th ld., Ld. Sess. 517
Boydell, Jno., L.M. Lond. 492
Boyer, Jno. Pet., Pres. Hti. 105; Pres. S. Dom. 105
Boyland, Rd. de, J. It. 368
Boyle, Alexr. R., adm. (**H**) 850
— Bellingham, C. Cus. Ir. 565; C. Ex. Ir. 566
— hon. Court. and sir C., adm. (**A**) 820; K.C.H. 788
— Court. Wm. Edmund, adm. (**H**) 847
— Dav., Jy. Sc. 523; L.J. Clk. 516; L.P. Ct. Sess. 516; Ld. Sess. 520; P.C. 210; S.G. Sc. 526
— Dav., *see* ld. B., *infra*
— Geo. Dav., dn. Sal. 468
— Hy., *see* visc. B., *infra*
— hon. Hy., aft. ld. Carleton, *q.v.*, Ch. Ex. 165; L.T. 155; L. Treas. Ir. 559
— Hy., P.C. 194; S. St. 224
— Jas., C. Exc. Sc. 504
— Jas., bp. Cork, Cl. and R. 631
— Michl., abp. Arm. 596; abp. Dbln. and Gl. 616; bp. Cork, Cl. and R. 631; bp. Wford. and L. 627; dn. Cloy. 633; dn. Lism. 629; L.J. Ir. 555; Ld. Chanc. Ir. 576
— hon. Patr., Ld. Sess. 520
— Rd., abp. Tm. 611; bp. Cork, Cl. and R. 631; bp. Ferns and L. 622; dn. Lim. 639; dn. Wford. 628
— Rt., gen. (**D**) 916
— hon. Rt. Ed., Sec. St. Patr. 752
— Roger, bp. Clr. 596; bp. Down and Cnr. 604; dn. Cork, 632
— Wm., C. Cus. Sc. 503
Boyle, lds. and visc.
— Dav., ld., Dep. Tr. Sc. 498
Boyle, lds. and visc.—*cont.*
— Dav., ld., aft. E. of Glasgow, *q.v.*
— Hy., aft. 1st visc. B. and E. of Shannon, *q.v.*, Ch. Ex. Ir. 562; L.J. Ir. 556
Boyles, Ch., adm. (**A**) 818
Boyne, Gusts., visc., gen. (**C**) 871
Boynton, sir Jno., S.L. 410
Boys, Hy., adm. (**E**) 836
— Jno., C. Exc. 279
— Jno., dn. Cant. 431
— Th., adm. (**A**) 819
— Wm., adm. (**H**) 851; L.G. Gr. Hosp. 854
Brabazon, Rog. de or le, C.J.K.B. 369; J. It. 368; J.K.B. 371
— Wm. and sir W., L.J. Ir. 553; V. Treas. Ir. 559
Brabœuf, Wm. de, J. It. 368
Brabourne, E. H., ld., form. E. H. Knatchbull-Hugessen, *q.v.*
Brace, sir Ed., adm. (**A**) 820
Brackell (or Bracknell), Walt., bp. Oss. 620
Bracken, Rd. D'Oyl., Compt. gen. (**D**) 921
Brackenbury, Hy., gen. (**D**) 927
— Jno. M., K.H. 791
— Rt., M.M. 246
— sir Th., Const. T.L. 320
Bracklesham, Wm. de, dn. Chich. 434
Brackley, ld. and visc.
— Jno., ld., aft. 3rd E. of Bridgewater, *q.v.*, K.B. 763
— Th., visc., form. sir T. Egerton, *q.v.*, and ld. Ellesmere
Bracknell, *see* Brackell
Bracton, *see also* Breton and Britton
— Hy. de, Ch. Jr. 363; J. It. 368; Jy. 364
Bradbridge, Wm., bp. Exr. 437; dn. Sal. 468
Braddock, Ed., gen. (**C**) 871
Bradstreet, sir Saml., Rec. Dbln. 642
Bradbury, Geo., Curs. B. Ex. 386
— Th., L.M. Lond. 490
Bradeston, Th. de, K.B. 755
Bradfield, Jno. de, bp. Roch. 459
Bradford, Ed. Ridl. Colb., K.C.S.I. 803
— Evel., gen. (**D**) 911
— Hy. Holl., K.C.B. 774
— Jno. Fowl. and sir J., gen. (**D**) 892; K.C.B. 780
— Saml., bp. Carl. 476; bp. Roch. 460; dn. Westr. 469
— Th. and sir T., C.C. Bbay. 660; gen. (**A**) 862; G.C.B. 769; G.C.H. 786; K.C.B. 774
— Wilm. Hy., gen. (**D**) 905
Bradford, E. of
Newport Family.
— Fras., 1st E. of, form. ld. and visc. Newport, *q.v.*, Compt. H. 292; Tr. H. 291
— Rd., 2nd E. of, P.C. 195
Bridgeman Family.
— Orl. G. C., 3rd E. of, form. visc. Newport, *q.v.*, L.C.H. 295; L.L. Salop, 311; M.H. 302

For List of Abbreviations, see pp. 944-952.

Bradley, Ch. Jno., gen. (**D**) 912
—— Geo. Gr., dn. Westr. 469
—— Hy., G. I. Man. 666
—— Jas., Astr. Roy. 941
—— Jno., bp. suff. Shaft. 467
Bradshaw, Geo. Paris, gen. (**D**) 884; K.H. 791
—— Hy., A.G. 398; C.B. Ex. 381; S.G. 401
—— Jno., C.D.L. 242; C.G.S. 356; C.J. Chest. 386; S.L. 409
—— Jno., R. Cr. P.A. 335; R. Rge. P.A. 344; Winds. H. 331
—— Lawr., gen. (**C**) 873
—— Rd., adm. (**H**) 853
—— Th., C. Tx. 284; L. Admy. 179; Sec. Tr. 163
—— Th. Jos. C., C.C.J. 405
—— Wm., bp. Brl. 439; dn. Chr. Ch. Oxf. 457
—— Wm. Rigby, C. Tx. 285
Bradstreet, Jno., gen. (**C**) 872
—— sir Saml., C.G.S. Ir. 576; J.K.B. Ir. 579
Bradwardine, Th., abp. Cant. 430
Brady, Hugh, bp. Meath, 599
—— Jno. or Rd., bp. Kilm. 607
—— Maz., A.G. Ir. 588; C.B. Ex. Ir. 583; Ld. Chanc. Ir. 577; S.G. Ir. 590
—— Nichs., bp. Kilm. 607
—— sir Nichs. Wm., L.M. Dbln. 642
—— Rd. or Jno., bp. Kilm. 607
—— Rod., bp. Kilm. 607
—— Th., bp. Kilm. 607
—— Wm., dn. Ard. 609
—— Wm.. gen. (**C**) 872
Bragg, Ph., gen. (**B**) 865
Bragge, Ch., aft. Bragge-Bathurst, B.T. 268; P.C. 207; Pres. B.C., 253; Sec. at W. 234; Tr. N. 256
Braila, Pietr. Arm. and sir P., G.C.M.G. 795; K.C.M.G. 796
Braiosa, Wm. de, J. It. 365-6
Brailsford, Matth., dn. Wells, 429
Braithwaite, Rd., adm. (**A**) 815
Bramhall, Jno., abp. Arm. 596; bp. Dry. 601
Bramham, Jas., gen. (**C**) 872
Brampston, *see* Bramston
Brampton, Ed., G. Gsey. 668
Bramston, Bramstone, and **Brampstone**
—— Fras. and sir F., B. Ex. 384; S.L. 410
—— Jno., dn. Winch. 471
—— Jno., K.B. 764
—— Jno., U.S.C., 236
—— Jno. and sir J., C.J.K.B. 370
Bramwell, Geo. W. W. and sir G., aft. ld. B., B. Ex. 385; J. Ex. D. 385; Jud. Com. P.C. 361; L.J. App. 389; Q.C. 417; S.L. 413
Branch, Alexr. Barcl., K.H. 791
—— Ch. Jas., bp. Antig. 728
Branche, sir Jno., L.M. Lond. 490
Brand, hon. Hy., gen. (**C**) 874
—— hon. Hy. B. W. and sir H., aft. visc. Hampden, *q.v.*; G.C.B. 773; L.T. 161; P.C. 217; Sec. Tr. 163; Sp. H.C. 251
—— hon. Hy. Rt., S.G.O. 260
—— Jno. Hy. and sir J., Pres. O.F.S. 101; G.C.M.G. 795
Brandan (St.), bp. Isl. 539
Brander, Mangles Jas., gen. (**D**) 929
Brandesford, Wolst. de, bp. Worc. 472
Brandeston (or Blaundeston), Hy. de, bp. Sal. 467; dn. Sal. 468
Brandis, Dietr., C.I.E. 806; K.C.I.E. 805
Brandon, Ch., K.B. 760
—— sir Ch., aft. D. of Suffolk, *q.v.*, K.G. 737
—— sir Th., K.G. 737
Brandon, D. of, *see* Hamilton and Br.
Brandreth, Jn., dn. Arm. 597; dn. Emly, 628
—— Th. and sir T., adm. (**E**) 836; Compt. N. 258; L. Admy. 185-6; K.C.B. 782
Brandt, Rt., C.C.J. 403
Branketre, Jno. de, M. Chy. 393
Brann, Geo., bp. Drom. 604; bp. Elph. 608
Branthwaite, Rd., S.L. 408
Branthwayt, Wm., S.L. 411
Braos, Ph. de, S.L. Ir. 550
Braose, *see* Bruse
Brasier (or Brazier), Jas., adm. (**G**) 842
Brasnell, G. Tob. 723
Brassey, Th., aft. sir T. and ld. B., K.C.B. 783; L. Admy. 185-6; Sec. Adm. 187
Braun, Col., Amb. Swz. 113
Braundon, Reg. de, M. Chy. 393
Bravo, Dt. Mex. 103
Bray, sir Edmd., Const. T.L. 321
—— Ed. Wm., gen. (**D**) 924
—— Geo. Fk. Campb., gen. (**D**) 926
—— Jno., M. Chy. 393
—— Jno., *see* ld. B. *infra*
—— sir Reg., K.B. 758; K.G. 737; C.D.L. 242; L.H.T. 154; Sp. H.C. 249
—— Steph., C.B. Ex. Ir. 582; C.J.C.P. Ir. 580; C.J.K.B. Ir. 577
—— Th., dn. Rph. 603
Bray, ld.
—— Jno., ld., C.G.P. 299
Bray - broc, - broke, & - brooke
*—— Hy. de, J. It. 367; Jy. 364; W.C.P. 317
* (?) all same pers.
—— Rt., bp. Lond. 451; dn. Sal. 468; J. It. 366; Ld. Chanc. 354; Ld. Chanc. Ir. 575; S. St. 222
—— Saml., gen. (**D**) 894
Braybrooke, ld.
—— Rd., 3rd ld., L.L. Ess. 308
Braylegh, Rd. de, dn. Exr. 437
Brayton, Th. de, L.K. 354
—— (or Drayton), Th. de, M. Chy. 393
Brazier, *see* Brasier
Breadalbane, E. and M. of
—— Jno., 2nd E. of, L.H.T. Sc. 497
—— Jno. 3rd E. of, form. visc. Glenorchy, *q.v.*, L.P.S. Sc. 501; P.C. 202; V.A. Sc. 499
—— Jno., 4th E. aft. 1st M. of, gen. (**B**) 867
Breadalbane, E. and M. of—*cont.*
—— Jno., 2nd M. of, Amb. Pr. 118; K.T. 748; L.C.H. 295; L.L. Arg. 508; P.C. 215
—— Gavin, 7th E. of, P.C. 219; Tr. H. 292
Breaute, Faukes de, J. It. 367
Brechin, Thos., E. of, form. T. Erskine, *q.v.*
Brecknock, Geo. Ch., E. of, aft. 2nd. M. Camden, *q.v.*, T. Admy. 182
Bredin, Andr., gen. (**D**) 880
Bree, Herb., bp. Bdoes. 721
Breen, H. Heg., G. St. Luc. 725
Bregwin, abp. Cant. 430
Breitenbach, Coenr. Van, G. C.G.H. 678
Brekdene, Jno., B. Ex. Ir. 583
Brembyr, Nichs., L.M. Lond. 489
Bremer, sir Jas. Jno. Gord., adm. (**D**) 828; K.C.B. 777; K.C.H. 789
Brenchesley, Wm., J.C.P. 378; K.B. 755; S.L. 407
Brendinus, bp. S. and M. 483
Brendoc, Dav., bp. Clonm. 600
Brendan, bp. Ardf. and Agh. 639; dn. Ardf. 640
Brens, Rt. de, K.B. 755
Brent, Humphr., C. Cus. 275; C. Cus. Sc. 503
—— sir Nathl., Vic. Gen. 421
—— Tim., K.H. 789
Brente, Rt., K.B. 755
Brentford, Patr., E. of, P.C. 189
Brentingham, Th., bp. Exr. 436; L.H.T. 153
Brenton, Jahl. (No. 1), adm. (**A**) 817
—— Jahl. (No 2) and sir J., adm. (**A**) 820; K.C.B. 774; L.G. Gr. Hosp. 854
—— Jno., adm. (**H**) 846
Brereton, sir Jno., S.L. Ir. 891
—— Jno. Alf., gen. (**D**) 916
—— Rt., gen. (**B**) 867
—— Wm. and sir W., gen. (**D**) 889; K.C.B. 779; K.H. 792
—— sir Wm., L.J. Ir. 553
Brerewood, Rt. and sir R., J.K.B. 372; S.L. 409
Bret, *see* Brett
Bretayne, Rd., L.M. Lond. 489
Breteville, Rd. de, A.G. 398
Brethemain, *see* MacBreohan
Bretislas, I. to III., D. Bma. 59
Breton, *see* Bretton
Brett and **Bret**
—— Ch., L. Admy. 179-80
—— Gerard de la, K.B. 755
—— Harry de, gen. (**D**) 930
—— sir Piercy, adm. (**A**) 814 L. Admy. 179
—— Rd., C. Exc. 278
—— Rd. Rich Wilf., gen. (**D**) 893
—— Wilf., K.C.M.G. 796
—— Wm. B. and sir W., aft. 1st ld. Esher, *q.v.*, J.C.P. 380; J.C.P.D. 380; Jud. Com. P.C. 361; L. J. App. 389; M.R. 388; P.C. 219; Q.C. 418; S.G. 402; S.L. 414
—— Wm. Fr., gen. (**D**) 909

Brettan, Jno., B. Ex. Ir. 583
Bretton and **Breton,** *see also* Bracton
— M. Chy. 395
— Fras. le, dn. Jsey. 668
— (or Bracton), Hy. de, Jy. 364
— Hy. Wm., gen. (**D**) 885
— Jno. and sir J., L.M. Lond. 489
— (or Bretun, or Bracton), Jno. de or le, bp. Her. 441; J.C.P. 377; J.K.B. 371; Jy. 365
— Jno. le, J. It. 369
— Maur. le, C.I.E. 806
— Peter, K.B. 755
— Rd., C. Cus. 274
— Thos. le, dn. Jsy. 668
— sir Th. le (2), Blf. Jsy. 668
— (or Brito), Wm. le, J. It. 368; Jy. 364
— Wm. Corb. le, dn. Jsy. 668
Breugel, Alb. Van, G.C.G.H. 678
Breuse, Hugh de, dn. Her. 442
Brevint, Danl., dn. Linc. 448
Brewce, *see* Bruce
Brewer, Wm., bp. Exr. 436
Brewster, Abraham, A.G. Ir. 588; L.J. App. Ir. 585; Ld. Chanc. Ir. 577; S.G. Ir. 590
— sir Dav., K.H. 790
— sir Fras., L.M. Dbln. 640
— Hy. Cr., gen. (**D**) 910
Brian, *see* Bryan
Brice, dn. Arm. 597
— (or Bricius), bp. Mor. 534
— Geo. Tito, gen. (**D**) 927
— Hugh, M.M. 246
— Jno., Bl. M. P.A. 336
— Sew. Wm., Q.C. 420
Bricius, *see* Brice
Brictius, bp. Lim. 638
Brid, *see* Bird
Brideoake, Ralph, bp. Chich. 433; dn. Sal. 468
Bridgeman, hon. Ch. Orl., adm. (**H**) 846
— Hy., bp. S. and M. 484; dn. Chest. 477
— Jno., bp. Chest. 477
— sir Jno., C.J. Chest. 386; S.L. 409
— sir Orl., B.T. 264; C.B. Ex. 381; C.J.C.P. 375; L.K. 357; P.C. 190; S.L. 410
— Wm., Sec. Adm. 186; U.S.S. 225
Bridgen, Wm., L.M. Lond. 492
Bridges, *see also* Brydges
For members of the Chandos Peerage, *see* Brydges
— — G. Bah. Isl. 716
— Jno., bp. Oxf. 456; dn. Sal. 468
— Jno., C. Cus. 274
— Th., K.B. 764
— sir Th., Lt. T.L. 321
— Wm., C. Exc. 278
Bridget (dau. Ed. IV.), Pr. E. 12
Bridgewater, Earls of
— Hy. Daubeney, E. of, form. ld. Daubeny, *q.v.*
Egerton Family.
— Jno., 1st E. of, form. J. Egerton, *q.v.*
— Jno., 2nd E. of, B.T. 263; L.L. Chesh. 306; L.L. Herts, 309; P.C. 190-1
Bridgewater, Earls of—*cont.*
— Jno., 3rd E. of, form ld. Brackley, *q.v.*; B.T. 263; L. Admy. 176; P.C. 194
— Jno. Wm., 7th E. of, gen. (**A**) 860
Bridgman, *see* Bridgeman
Bridport, Giles de, bp. Sal. 466; dn. Wells, 428
Bridport, lds. and visc.
— Alex., 2nd ld. and 1st visc. (1st Cr.); form. Alex. Hood, *q.v.*
— Alex. N., 3rd ld. and 1st visc. (2nd Cr.); form. A. N. Hood, *q.v.*, K.C.B. 784
Briesley, Sim. de, dn. Lich. 445; dn. Linc. 448
Briggs, Dav., gen. (**D**) 912
— Geo., gen. (**D**) 902
— Geo., gen. (**D**) 929
— Jas., gen. (**D**) 932; K.H. 792
— Jno., gen. (**D**) 879
— Jno. Falc., K.H. 792
— Steph. Ch., gen. (**D**) 906
— Th., S.L. 407
— Th. and sir T., adm. (**A**) 820; G.C.M.G. 794
— Will. Lake, gen. (**D**) 914
— Wm., gen. (**D**) 913
Bright, Geo., dn. St. As. 463
— Jno., C.D.L. 243; P.C. 218; Pres. B.T. 269
— Rd., gen. (**B**) 867
— Rt. On. and sir R., gen. (**D**) 906; K.C.B. 781
— Th., bp. Down, 603
Brigid or **Brigidian,** Moel (No. 1), bp. Kild. 616
— Moel (No. 2), bp. Kild. 616
See also Moelbrigidian
Brigilsus, bp. E. Ang. 454
Brihtwald, abp. Cant. 430
Brillanne, Chev. de Guir de la, G. Mtius. 683
Brind, Jas. and sir J., gen. (**D**) 902; G.C.B. 771; K.C.B. 788
Brine, Aug., adm. (**D**) 824
— Geo., adm. (**H**) 846
— Jas., adm. (**A**) 816
— Lindesay, adm. (**E**) 837
Brinkley, Jno., bp. Cloy. 631
Brinstan (St.), bp. Winch. 470
Brinton, Th. de, bp. Roch. 460
Brisbane, sir Ch., adm. (**A**) 819; G. St. Vin. 725; K.C.B. 774
— Jno., adm. (**A**) 815
— Th. and sir T., aft. Makdougall-Brisbane, G. N.S.W. 703; gen. (**A**) 862; G.C.B. 768; K.C.B. 774
Bristol, E. and M. of
Digby Family.
— Jno., 1st E. of, form. sir J. Digby, *q.v.*
— Geo., 2nd E. of, K.G. 740; P.C. 189
— Jno., 3rd E. of, L.L. Dors. 307
Hervey Family.
— Geo. Wm., 2nd E. of, Amb. Spn. 123; Gr. St. 304; L.L. Ir. 557; L.P.S. 241; P.C. 202
— Aug. Jno., 3rd E. of, form. hon. A. J. Hervey, *q.v.* adm. (**A**) 815
— Fk. Augs., 4th E. of, form. hon. F. A. Hervey, *q.v.*
Bristol, E. and M. of—*cont.*
— Fk. Wm., 5th E. of, aft. 1st E. Jermyn (*q.v.*) and 1st M. of Br.; form. ld. Hervey, *q.v.*
— Fk. Wm. Jno., 3rd M. of, L.L. Suff. 312
Bristow and **Bristowe**
— Hy., gen. (**D**) 885
— Hy. Fox, Q.C. 418
— Jno. Wm., gen. (**D**) 912
— Saml. B., C.C.J. 405; Q.C. 419
Brithelm and **Brithelmus**
— bp. Winch. 470
— bp. Lond. 451
*— bp. Wells, 427
*— bp. Winch. 470
* Poss. same pers.
Brithman, D., Ld. Sess. 518
Brithmar, bp. Lich. 443
Brithwaldus, *see* Burwoldus
Brithwold (St.), bp. Winch. 470; bp. Wlton. 466
Brithwyn (2), bp. Shbn. 466; bp. Wells, 427
Britland, Reg., S.L. 411
Brito, Rd., J. It. 366
— (or Breton), Wm. le, J. It. 368; Jy. 364
Briton and **Britton**
— Jas., dn. Oss. 623
— Ralph, J. It. 366
Brittany, Jno., D. of, *see* E. of Richmond
Britteagus, bp. Worcs. 472
Britton, *see* Briton
Britwynus, bp. Cnwall. 436
Briwer, Wm., B. Ex. 382; J. It. 366; Jy. 363
Briwes, Jno. de, Jy. 364
— Rt. de, J.C.P. 377
Broad, Geo. Doh., adm. (**H**) 853
Broadhead, Hy., adm. (**G**) 843
Broadhurst, Hy., U.S. Home 228
Brocas, Jno., dn. Killa. 614
— sir Rd., L.M. Lond. 491
— Theoph., dn. Killa. 614
Brock, *see also* Brok
— Danl. de L., Blf. Gsey. 669
— Isaac, gen. (**D**) 873; K.B. 766
— Saum., K.H. 791
— Th. Saum., adm. (**H**) 848
Broclesby, Wm. de, B. Ex. 383
Broder, Ph., dn. Cash. 627
Broderick, *see* Brodrick
Brodie, Alexr., Ld. Sess. 519
— Alexr., Ly. K.A. 513
— sir Benj. Coll., Pres. Coll. Surg. 939; Pres. R. Soc. 940
— Hugh Fife Ashley, L.L. Nrnsh. 511
— Jas., L.L. Nrnsh. 511
— Jas. Campb. Jno., L.L. Nrnsh. 511
— Th., Ly. Dep. 513
— Wm., L.L. Nrnsh. 511
Brodrick, Alan, aft. 1st ld. and visc. Midleton, *q.v.*, A.G. Ir. 588; C.J.Q.B. Ir. 578; L.J. Ir. 556; Ld. Chanc. Ir. 576; S.G. Ir. 589; S.L. Ir. 591
— Allan, C. Cus. 275
— hon. Ch., abp. Cash. and Eml. 626; bp. Clonf. and K. 636; bp. Kilm. 607
— Jno. or St. Jno., S.L. 411
— hon. Jno., G. Mart. 719; gen. (**A**) 861

Brodrick—*cont.*
—— Th., adm. (**A**) 814
—— hon. Th., U.S. Home
—— Wm., S.L. Ir. 592
—— hon. Wm., Sec. B.C. 254; L.T. 158-9
—— hon. Wm. Jno., aft. 7th visc. Midleton, *q.v.*, dn. Exr. 438
—— Wm. St. J. F., U.S. War, 233
Brogan, Steph. de, dn. St. Pat. 617
Brogden, Jas., L.T. 159
Broghill, Roger Ld., Comm. Ir. 555
Brok, *see also* Brock
—— Lawr. del, Jy. 365
Broke, *see also* Brooke
—— hon. Geo., gen. (**D**) 884
—— sir Ph. Bowes Vere, adm. (**A**) 820; K.C.B. 774
—— Willoughby de, *see* W.
Bromby, Ch. Hy., bp. Tasm. 708
Brome, *see also* Broome
—— Ad. de, J. It. 369; M. Chy. 393
Bromfeld and **Bromfield**
—— Edmd., bp. Llff. 449
—— sir Ed., L.M. Lond. 491
—— Leol. de, bp. St. As. 462
—— Wm., M.M. 247
Bromhead, sir Gonv., gen. (**B**) 867
Bromley, Ed. and sir E., B. Ex. 384; S.L. 409
—— Nichs., dn. St. Patr. 617
—— Rd. Madd., K.C.B. 782
—— sir Rt. Howe, adm. (**D**) 823
—— Rog., Bl. M. P.A. 336; Chest. H. 330
—— Th. and sir T. (No. 1), C.J.Q.B. 370; J.K.B. 372; S.L. 408
—— Th. (No. 2), Ld. Chanc. 356; Rec. Lond. 493; S.G. 401
—— Wm., K.B. 764
—— Wm., P.C. 196; S. St. 224; Sp. H.C. 250
—— Wm. de, Ch. Ex. Ir. 561; dn. St. Patr. 617; L.K. Ir. 574; L. Treas. Ir. 558
Bromwich, Jno. de, L.J. Ir. 551
Bron, *see* Brown
Bronscombe, Walt., bp. Exr. 439
Bronte, *see* Nelson and B.
Brokley, Jno., L.M. Lond. 490
Brook and **Brooke,** *see also* Broke
——, —— (2), S.L. 408
—— Arth. and sir A., gen. (**B**) 869; K.C.B. 776
—— sir Ch. Johnson, G.C.M.G. 796
—— Dav. and sir D., C.B. Ex. 381; S.L. 408
—— Ed. Bas., gen. (**D**) 896
—— Geo. and sir G., gen. (**D**) 887; K.C.B. 779
—— Hy. Rd., *see* Earl Br., *infra*
—— Jas. and sir J., Amb. Bno. 131; G. Labn. 675; K.C.B. 782
—— Jas. Cr., gen. (**D**) 906
—— Jno. Ch., R. Cr. P. A. 335; Som. H. 332
—— Jno. Chiop., gen. (**D**) 917
—— Ralph, R. Cr. P.A. 335; Yk. H. 334
—— (or Broke), Rd. C.B. Ex. 381; J.C.P. 378; Rec. Lond. 493; S.L. 408

Brook and Brooke—*cont.*
—— Rd. Cr., gen. (**D**) 931
—— (or Broke), Rt. and sir R., C.J.C.P. 375; Comm. Serjt. Lond. 495; J.K.B. (?) 372; Rec. Lond. 493; S.L. 408; Sp. H.C. 249
—— Th., dn. Chest. 477
—— Th. A., gen. (**D**) 903
—— Wm., C.G.S. Ir. 577
—— Wm., gen. (**A**) 862
—— Wm., K.B. 763
Brooke, lds. and E., *see also* Warwick
—— Fulke, 1st ld., form. F. Greville, *q.v.*
—— (and Warwick), Fras., 1st E. of, K.T. 747
—— Hy. Rd. aft. 3rd E. of, K.T. 748
—— *see also* Willoughby de Broke
Brooker, Geo. Aug. Cooke, adm. (**H**) 851
Brookes and **Brooks**
—— B., G. Trin. 722
—— Geo., gen. (**D**) 888
—— Geo. Benj., gen. (**D**) 879
—— (or Broke), Hor. Geo., gen. (**D**) 884
—— Jas., bp. Glr. 438
—— Maur., L.M. Dbln. 642
—— Wm., gen. (**D**) 876
Brooksbank, Stamp, C. Exc. 281
—— Josh., dn. Clonf. 637
Broome, Arth., gen. (**D**) 903
—— Fk. Nap., G. Mtius. 684; G. W. Austr. 707; K.C.M.G. 798
—— Jos., gen. (**B**) 866
—— (or Brome) Th., S.L. 410
Brotherton, Th. Wm. and sir T., gen. (**D**) 880; G.C.B. 770; K.C.B. 778
Brothwick, Dav., Ld. Adv. 526
Brough, Redm. W., gen. (**D**) 893
—— Rd. Seck., gen. (**D**) 880
—— Wm., dn. Glr. 440
Brougham, Hy., dn. Lism. 629
—— Hy., *see* ld. B. *infra.*
—— Jno., C. Exc. 279
—— Th., gen. (**D**) 910
—— Wm., M. Chy. 397
Brougham, ld.
—— Hy., aft. ld. B. and Vaux, Jud. Com. P.C. 360; K.C. 416; Ld. Chanc. 358; P.C. 211; P.P. 416
Broughton, Jno., adm. (**A**) 820
—— sir Jno. Delves, gen. (**A**) 861
—— Rt., K.B. 758
—— Th., C. Exc. Sc. 504
—— Wm. Ed. D., gen. (**D**) 902
—— Wm. Gr., bp. Austrl. 703; bp. Syd. 703
Broughton, ld.
—— Jno. Cam., ld., form. J. C. Hobhouse, *q.v.*, G.C.B. 772
Broun, *see* Brown
Brouncker, Ed., dn. Lism. 629
Brouncker, visc.
—— Wm., visc., L. Admy. 175; Pres. R. Soc. 940
Browell, Wm., L.G. Gr. Hosp. 854
Brown and **Browne**
—— Maj.-Gen. —, G. Bdoes. (1884) 721

Brown and Browne—*cont.*
—— —, G. Tob. (1764) 723
—— Lt.-Col. —, G. Trin. (1846) 722
—— Andr., gen. (**D**) 908
—— Andr., Modr. K. Sc. 547
—— Anthy., Chambn. Lond. 493
—— Anthy., K.B. (1547) 760
—— Anthy., K.B. (1603) 761
—— Anthy., L.M. Lond. 492
—— Anthy. and sir A., C.J.C.P. 375; J.C.P. 378; S.L. 408
—— sir Anthy., C.G.P. 299; K.G. 738; M.H. 301
—— Arth., C. Acc. Ir. 567; S.L. Ir. 592
—— Clem., gen. (**D**) 877
—— Clem. Metc., gen. (**D**) 934
—— Ch. Alf., gen. (**D**) 897
—— Ch. Fk., gen. (**D**) 912
—— Dav., gen. (**D**) 917
—— Denis, dn. Emly. 628
—— Dom., aft. ld. Oranmore and Br., *q.v.*, L.L. Mayo, 570
—— Dougl., Q.C. 418
—— Ed., dn. Tm. 613
—— Ed. Har., bp. Ely, 435; bp. Winch. 471
—— Ed. Mavor, gen. (**A**) 858
—— Ed. Walp., adm. (**D**) 824
—— Fras., dn. Elph. 609
—— Geo., abp. Dbln. and Gl. 616
—— Geo., Bl. M. P.A. 336
—— Geo., bp. Dkld. 533
—— Geo., C. Exc. Sc. 505
—— Geo., G. Bbay. 659
—— Geo., K.B. 763
—— Geo., K.C.M.G. 797
—— Geo., Ld. Sess. 520; Jy. Sc. 523
—— Geo., Q.C. 419
—— Geo., S.L. 408
—— Geo. and sir G., Comm. F. Ir. 564; gen. (**D**) 880; G.C.B. 769; K.C.B. 777; K.H. 789
—— Geo. Gl., gen. (**D**) 920
—— Geo. Rodn., gen. (**D**) 920
—— Geo. Sackv., K.C.B. 775
—— Gore, gen. (**A**) 862
—— Hy., Amb. Ch. 130
—— Hy., C. Cus. 274
—— Hy. Mont., dn. Lism. 629
—— Hy. Ralph, gen. (**D**) 909
—— Horace Alb., gen. (**D**) 927
—— Hugh, S.L. Ir. 590
—— Humphr. and sir H., J.C.P. 378; S.L. 408
—— Jas., S.L. Ir. 592
—— sir Jas., K.C.S.I. 804
—— Jas. Fr. Manners, gen. (**D**) 909
—— Jemm., abp. Tm. 611; bp. Cork and R. 632; bp. Drom. 605; bp. Elph. 608; bp. Killoe. 634; dn. Ross 633
—— Jno., adm. (**A**) 816
—— Jno., gen. (**B**) 865
—— Jno., gen. (**C**) 873
—— Jno., K.B. 758
—— Jno., L.M. Lond. 490
—— Jno., M. Chy. 394
—— Jno., S.L. 408
—— sir Jno., gen. (**A**) 863; K.C.H. 787
—— Jno. Campb., K.C.B. 780
—— Jno. Hutt. Balf., Q.C. 420
—— Jno. Suff., Bl. C.H. 339; Geneal. Bath, 784
—— Jno. Tatt., gen. (**D**) 892
—— Jonn., dn. Her. 442
—— Jos., Q.C. 418

Brown and Browne—*cont.*
— Malc. J., G. Lag. 687
— Matth., K.B. 758
— Mountf., G. Bah. Isl. 716
— Perc., gen. (**D**) 904
— Pet., bp. Cork and R. 632
— Pet., dn. Ferns, 623
— Pet., gen. (**D**) 883
— Ph., adm. (**D**) 827; (**G**) 840
— Ralph Abercr., adm. (**H**) 853
— (or Broun), Rd., J.C.P. Ir. 581
— sir Rd., C. Exc. 277; L.M. Lond. 491
— Rt., B. Ex. 384
— (or Bron), Rt., dn. Wford. 628
— Rt., Bl. M. P.A. 336; Guis. P.A. 343; R. Cr. P.A. 335; Richm. H. 333
— Saml., gen. (**A**) 863
— Saml. and sir S., C.G.S. 356; J.C.P. 379; J.K.B. 372; P.P. 414; S.L. 409-10
— Saml. Jas. and sir S., gen. (**D**) 909; K.C.B. 781; K.C.S.I. 803
— Steph., bp. Ross, 631
— Steph., L.M. Lond. 490
— Th., adm. (**D**) 824
— Th., adm. (**D**) 825
— Th., Bl. M. P.A. 336
— Th., bp. Norw. 455; bp. Roch. 460; dn. Sal. 468
— Th., Clar. K.A. 328; Gart. K.A. 328; Lanc. H. 333
— Th., Norr. K.A. 329
— Th. and sir T., gen. (**A**) 862; K.C.B. 775; K.CH. 788
— Th. Gore and sir T., G. Bmda. 701; G. N.Z. 709; G. St. Hel. 682; G. Tasm. 708; K.C.M.G. 796
— Th. Hy., gen. (**D**) 882; K.C.H. 787; K.H. 789
— Walt., L. Prov. Edinb. 548
— Walt. Jno., gen. (**D**) 888
— Wm., adm. (**A**) 818
— Wm., G. Bmda. 701
— Wm., G. Gsey. 669
— Wm., gen. (**B**) 865
— Wm., and sir W., L.M. Lond. 490
— sir Wm., K.H. 791
— Wm. Cheselden, adm. (**H**) 849
— Wm. Gust., gen. (**D**) 899
— Wm. Laur., dn. Thist. 749
— Wm. Saml., aft. W. S. Grieve, adm. (**E**) 837
— Wm. Todd, gen. (**D**) 919
Browning, Col. Air. R., C.I.E. 807
— Jno., M. Chy. 396
— Saml., M. Chy. 396
Brownlow, Ch. Hy. and sir C., gen. (**D**) 923; G.C.B. 771; K.C.B. 780
— Hy. Alex., gen. (**D**) 930
— Jno., dn. Clonm. 600
Brownlow, lds. and E.
— Jno., 2nd ld., aft. 1st E., G.C.H. 787; L.L. Linc. 310
— Adelb. W. B., 3rd E., L.L. Linc. 310; P.C. 221; Paym. G. 245; Sec. L.G.B. 256
Brownrigg, Jno. Stud., gen. (**D**) 902
— Ralph, bp. Exr. 437
— Rt. and sir R., G. Ceyl. 672; G.C.B. 767; gen. (**A**) 861
Bruce, *see also* Bruse
— Alexr. Jas., gen. (**D**) 916

Bruce—*cont.*
— Andr., bp. Dkld. 533; bp. Ork. 535
— Ch., G. Br. Gu. 715; G. Mtius. 684
— Ch. and sir C., gen. (**C**) 875; K.C.B. 776
— Ch. L. C., Sec. B.C. 254
— ld. Ch. W. B., P.C. 219; V.C.H. 297
— Dav., K. Sc. 19
— Ed., K.B. 762
— Ed., K.C.B. 776
— Ed., aft. ld. Kinloss, *q.v.*, Ld. Sess. 519; M.R. 388
— ld. Ern. Augs. Ch., aft. 3rd M. of Ailesbury, *q.v.*, P.C. 214; V.C.H. 297
— Eyre E., gen. (**D**) 888
— hon. Fk. W. A. and sir F., Amb. Bol. 135; Amb. Ch. 131; Amb. U.S.A. 132; Amb. Ugy. 137; G. Newfd. 700; G.C.B. 772; K.C.B. 783
— Gainsf., Q.C. 420
— Geo. Wyndh. H. Knight-, bp. Blfn. 681
— Hy., gen. (**B**) 868
— Hy. Aust., aft. 1st ld. Aberdare, *q.v.*, H. Sec. 227; Jud. Com. P.C. 361; L.P.C. 188; P.C. 217; U.S. Home, 228; V.P. Ed. 255
— sir Hy. Herv., L.L. Londy. 570
— Hy. Le G., gen. (**D**) 917
— Hy. Wm. and sir H., adm. (**D**) 829; K.C.B. 779
— Jas., bp. Dkld. 533; bp. Glasg. 536; Ld. Chanc. Sc. 515
— Jas. Lewis Knight- and sir J., Jud. Com. P.C. 360; K.C. 416; L.J. App. 388; P.C. 214; V. Chanc. 390
— Jas. Minchin, adm. (**H**) 851
— Jno., G. W. Austr. 707
— Jno., Sec. B.C. 254
— Jonn, dn. Kilf. 637; dn. Tm. 613
— Michl., gen. (**D**) 906
— Rd. Is., C.I.E. 806
— Rt., gen. (**D**) 906
— Rt., K. Sc. 19
— Rt., Ld. Sess. 519
— Rt., J. Sc. 523; Ld. Sess. 520
— hon. Rt., gen. (**D**) 894
— sir Stew., Geneal. St. Patr. 752
— Th., C. Cus. Sc. 504
— Th., K.B. 757
— hon. Th., gen. (**B**) 866
— hon. Th., gen. (**C**) 872
— Wm., K.H. 792
Bruce, lds.
— Th., ld., aft. E. of Ailesbury, *q.v.* (cr. 1776), P.C. 203
Bruchilla, *see* Burghill
Brudenell and **Brudnell**
— Edmd., A.G. 398
— hon. Jas., B.T. 264
— Rt., C.J.C.P. 375; J.C.P. 378; J.K.B. 372; S.L. 408
— Th., gen. (**C**) 871
— hon. Th., gen. (**B**) 865
Bruera, Gilb. de, dn. St. P. 453
Bruere, Geo. Jas., G. Bmda. 701
Bruge, sir Jno., L.M. Lond. 490

Bruges, *see* Bridges
Brugge, Walt. de, B. Ex. Ir. 583
— (or Brugges), sir Wm., Gart. K.A 327
Brun, From. le, Ld. Chanc. Ir. 574
Brune, Dav., Compt. Sc. 498
Brundish, Rt., J.K.B. 371
Brunker, Jas. Rt., gen. (**D**) 901
Bruno, D. Lne. 29
— J. de, G. Trin. 721
Brunton, Alexr., Modr. K. Sc. 547
— Nathl., adm. (**A**) 817
Brus, Pet. de (2), J.It. 367-8
— Rt. de, C.J.K.B. 369; Jy. 364
Bruse, *see also* Bruce
— (or Braose), Giles de, bp. Her. 441
— Wm. de, bp. Llff., 449
Brusele, Hy. de, M.M. 245-6
Brutus, C. J. B. (3), C. Ro. 41; Dt. Ro. 41
— D. J., C. Ro. 44-5
— L. J., C. Ro. 37
— M. J., C. Ro. 44
Bruyn, sir Hy., L. Treas. Ir. 558
Bruynink, Wilh. M., G. Ceyl. 672
Bryan and **Brian**
— Boromy, K. Ir. 22
— sir Fras., L.J. Ir. 553
— Guy, *see* ld. G., *infra*
— Regd., bp. St. Dav. 464; bp. Worc. 472
— Th., C.J.C.P. 375; K.B. 757; S.L. 407
Bryan, lds.
— Guy and sir G., aft. ld. B., K.G. (1370) 733; L.H.A. 172
Bryant, sir Jerem., gen. (**D**) 880
Bryce, sir Alex., gen. (**C**) 874; K.C.H. 787; K.H. 789
— Hugh, L.M. Lond. 490
— Jas., U.S.F. 230
Brydges, *see also* Bridges
— Geo., gen. (**C**) 874
— Geo., gen. (**D**) 930
— Geo., L.M. Lond. 492
— sir H. Jones-, form. Jones, amb. Pers. 130; P.C. 213
— hon. Jas., aft. E. of Carnarvon and D. of Chandos, *q.v.*, L. Admy. 177; Paym. G. 244
— sir Jno., aft. ld. Chandos, *q.v.*, Lt. T.L. 321
— Wm., S.G.O. 259
— Wm., S.L. 411
Brykenell, Th., K.B. 760
Bryson, Alexr., K.C.B. 779
Bubbewith, Bubbewyth, or **Bubwith**, Nichs., bp. B. and W. 428; bp. Lond. 451; bp. Sal. 467; L.H.T. 153; M. Chy. 394; M.R. 387
Bubulcus, C. J. B. (2), C. Ro. 41-2
Buccleuch, D. of, *see also* Monmouth and Queensberry
— Fras., 2nd D. of, form. E. of Dalkeith, *q.v.*
— Hy., 3rd D. of, K.G. 742; K.T. 747; L.L. Mid.-L. 509; L.L. Roxb. 512
— Chas. Wm. Hy., 4th D. of, form. E. of Dalkeith, *q.v.*; K.T. 748; L.L. Mid-L. 509

Buccleuch, D. of—*cont.*
—— Walt. Fr., 5th D. of, Jud. Com. P.C. 360; K.G. 743; K.T. 748; L.L. Mid-L. 509; L.L. Roxb. 512; L.P.C. 188; L.P.S. 241; P.C. 214
—— Wm. Hy. W., 6th D. of, form. E. of Dalkeith, *q.v.*
—— Louisa J., Dss. of, M. Robes (1885) 304
—— Charlotte, Dss. of, M. Robes (1841) 304
Buchan, Jno. and sir J., gen. (**B**) 869; K.C.B. 776
Buchan, Earls of
Comyn or Cummin Family.
—— Wm., 1st E. of, L.J. Gen. 522
—— Alexr., 2nd E. of, L.J. Gen. 522
—— Jno., 3rd E. of, Sec. St. Sc. 501
Stewart Family.
—— Jno., 2nd E. of, L.G.C. Sc. (*d.* 1424) 506
Stewart and Erskine Families.
—— Jas., 1st E. of, L.G.C. 506
—— Jas., 7th E. of, form. J. Erskine, *q.v.*
—— Dav., 4th ld. Cardross and 9th E. of, L.H.C.K. Sc. 546
Buchanan, Andr. and sir, A., Amb. Aus. 117; Amb. Dk. 127; Amb. Nds. &c. 123; Amb. Pr. 118; Amb. Russ. 126; Amb. Spn. 124; Amb. Swz. 113; G.C.B. 772; K.C.B. 783; P.C. 217
—— Geo., L.P.S. Sc. 501
—— Gilb. Jno. L., gen. (**D**) 903
—— Hy. Jas., gen. (**D**) 929
—— Jas., C. Cus. Sc. 504
—— Jas., gen. (**D**) 923
—— Jas., Pres. U.S.A. 102
—— Wm., dn. Ach. 614; dn. Killa. 614; dn. Tm. 613
—— Wm., gen. (**B**) 867
Buchanan-Riddell, *see* Riddell
Buche, capt. Piers or Jno. de, K.G. 733
Buchevet, Andr., Portr. Lond. 488
Buck, Lew. Wm., gen. (**D**) 927
Buckby, Rd., gen. (**C**) 874
—— (Bugby or Buckleby), W., S.L. 410
Buckeridge, Jno., bp. Ely, 435; bp. Roch. 460
Buckhurst, lds.
—— Th., 1st ld., aft. 1st E. of Dorset, *q.v.*, C.G.S. 356; E.M. 326; K.G. 739; L.H.T. 154; Ld. Chanc. 356
—— Rd., ld., aft. 3rd E. Dorset, *q.v.*, L.L. Suss. 312
—— Ch., ld., aft. 6th E. of Dorset, *q.v.*, L.L. Suss. 312
Buckingham, Jno. de, B. Ex. 383
—— sir Owen, L.M. Lond. 491
Buckingham, E., M., and D. of
Plantagenet Family.
—— Th., E. of, aft. D. of Gloucester (son of Ed. III.), K.G. 734
Stafford Family.
—— Humphr., 1st D. of, form. (1429) E. Stafford, *q.v.*, W.C.P. 318
—— Hy., 2nd D. of, K.B. 757; K.G. 736; W.C.P. 319
—— Ed., 3rd D. of, form. E. Stafford, *q.v.*, K.G. 737
Buckingham, E., M., and D. of —*cont.*
Villiers Family.
—— Geo., 1st E., M., and D. of, form. Geo. Villiers, sir G. and visc. V., *q.v.*, Const. W. Cast. 322; E.M. 326; L.H.A. 174; L.H. Const. 289; M.H. 302; W.C.P. 319
—— Geo., 2nd D. of, K.G. 740; L. Admy. 175; M.H. 302; P.C. 189-90
—— Rd. C., D. of, form. (1806) E. Temple, *q.v.*
Nugent-Temple-Grenville Family.
—— Geo., 1st M. of, form. Geo. Grenville, Geo. Nugent, and 2nd E. Temple, *q.v.*, K.G. 742; L.L. Ir. 557
—— Rd., 2nd M. of, aft. 1st D. of, form. E. Temple, *q.v.*, K.G. 743; L.L. Bucks. 306; L.S.H. 290
—— Rd., 2nd D. of, form. M. of Chandos, *q.v.*, K.G. 740; L.P.S. 241; P.C. 214
—— Rd., 3rd D. of, form. M. of Chandos, *q.v.*, C. Sec. 235; G.C.S.I. 801; G. Mdras. 657; Jud. Com. P.C. 361; L.L. Bucks. 306; L.P.C. 188; P.C. 217
Buckinghamshire, E. and D. of. *See also* Normanby
Sheffield Family.
—— Jno., 1st D., form. E. Mulgrave and M. of Normanby, *q.v.*, L.P.C. 188; L.S.H. 290
Hobart Family
—— Jno., 1st E. of, form. sir Jno. and ld. Hobart, *q.v.*
—— Jno., 2nd E. of, form. ld. Hobart, *q.v.*, Amb. Russ. 125; L.L. Ir. 557
—— Rt., 3rd E. of, form. hon. R. and ld. Hobart, *q.v.*, C.D.L. 243; Postm. G. 238; Pres. B.C. 253
Buckland, Wm., dn. Westr. 469
Buckle, Ch. Hy. Mason and sir C., adm. (**D**) 833; (**F**) 838; K.C.B. 780
—— Ch. Matth., adm. (**H**) 852
—— sir Cuthb., L.M. Lond. 491
—— Matth. (No. 1), adm. (**A**) 814
—— Matth. (No. 2), adm. (**D**) 823; (**G**) 840
Buckleby, *see* Buckby
Buckler, Ch. Alb., Surr. H. 334
Buckley, Ed. Pery, gen. (**D**) 884
—— Felix, gen. (**A**) 859
—— Hy. Burt., Q.C. 420
Buckner, Jno., bp. Chich. 433
Bucknill, Th. Towns., Q.C. 420
Bucknor, Ch., adm. (**A**) 816
Buckworth, sir Jno., C. Cus. 273-4
—— Theoph., bp. Drom. 604
Budd, Ralph, gen. (**D**) 906
—— Rd., gen. (**D**) 890
—— Rd. Carr., gen. (**D**) 934
Budgeon, Th., gen. (**D**) 890
Buerlaco, Wm. de, Ld. Chanc. Ir. 574
Bugby, *see* Buckby
Bugwell, Reg. de, dn. Exr. 437
Buhler, Joh. Geo., C.I.E. 806
Buiric, bp. Roch. 459
Buist, Geo., Modr. K. Sc. 547
Bulbus, C. A. (2), C. Ro. 42
—— Bulfin P., L.M. Dbln. 642
Bulgari, count Sp. Vitt., G.C.M.G. 794; K.C.M.G. 796
Bulkeley, Arth., bp. Bgr. 426
—— Lanc., abp. Dbln and Gl. 616
—— R., G. N. Sc. 695
—— sir Rd. B.W., L.L. Carn. 314
Bulkeley, visc.
—— Th. Jas., 7th visc., L.L. Carn. 314
Bull, Danl., C. Tx. 284
—— Fk., L.M. Lond. 492
—— Geo., bp. St. Dav. 465
—— Geo., dn. Cnr. 605
—— Rt., K.H. 790
—— Wm. bp. Ardf. and Agh. 639; dn. Cork, 632
Bullen, *see also* Boleyn
—— Ch. and sir C., adm. (**D**) 823; G.C.B. 769; K.C.B. 777; K.C.H. 788
—— Jos., adm. (**A**) 819
—— **-Smith,** *see* Smith
Buller, Alex., adm. (**E**) 837
—— Chas., J.A.G. 937; Pres. P.L.B. 262; Q.C. 417; Sec. B.C. 254
—— sir Ed., adm. (**A**) 818
—— Ed. M. Mann., gen. (**D**) 92[illegible]
—— Fras. and sir F., J.C.P. 379; J. Chest. 387; J.K.B. 373; K.C. 415; S.L. 412
—— Fk. Th., gen. (**D**) 885
—— Fk. Wm., gen. (**B**) 868
—— Geo. and sir G., gen. (**D**) 889; G.C.B. 770; K.C.B. 777
—— Jas., L. Admy. 181
—— Jno., C. Cus. 276; C. Exc. 281; L. Admy. 179; L.T. 158
—— Redv. Hy. and sir R., gen. (**D**) 927; K.C.B. 781; K.C.M.G. 798; U.S. Ir. 563
—— Walt. Lawr., K.C.M.G. 798
—— Wm., bp. Exr. 437; dn. Cant. 431; dn. Exr. 438
Bullingham, Jno., bp. Brl. 439; bp. Glr. 438
—— Nichs., bp. Linc. 447; bp. Worc. 473
Bullock, Ch. Jas., adm. (**H**) 853
—— Ed., Comm. Serjt. Lond. 495
—— Fk., adm. (**D**) 831
—— Stanley, gen. (**D**) 888
—— Th., dn. Norw. 456
—— sir Wm. L.G.C. Sc. 506
Bulnès, M., Pres. Chi. 111
Bulstrode, Th., M. Chy. 396
Bulteel, Rowl., adm. (**A**) 818
Bulwer, Ed. Gasc. and sir E., gen. (**D**) 917; K.C.B. 781
—— Hy. Ernest Gasc. and sir H., G. Cypr. 671; G. Dnc. 730; G. Labn. 675; G. Na[illegible] 680; G.C.M.G. 795; K.C.M.[illegible] 797
—— Hy. Lytt. and sir H., aft. ld. Dalling and B., *q.v.*; Amb. Fr. 113; Amb. Bgm. 123; Amb. Spn. 124; Amb. Tky. 12[illegible]; Amb. Tusc. 115; Amb. U.S. 132; G.C.B. 772; K.C.B. 78[illegible]; P.C. 214
—— Jas. Redf., Q.C. 418
Bulwer-Lytton, *see* Lytton

Bulzo, Dion., K.C.M.G. 796
Bunbury, Abrm. Ch., gen. (**D**) 929
—— Hy. Ed. and sir H., gen. (**B**) 869; K.C.B. 774; U.S.W. and C. 231
—— Th., dn. Lim. 640
—— Th., gen. (**D**) 882; K.H. 791
Bunch, Rt., Amb. C. Am. 134; Amb. U.S.C. 134; Amb. Vza. 135
Bundi, Mahar. of, G.C.S.I. 801
Bunny, Anth., gen. (**D**) 920
Buonaparte, Annon. Car., Rel. Nap. 26
—— Eliz., Rel. Nap. 26
—— Jer., Rel. Nap. 25
—— Joseph, Rel. Nap. 25; K. Nls. 56; K. Sp. 86
—— Louis, Pr. Or. 83
—— Louis N., Emp. Fr. 24-5
—— Lucien, Rel. Nap. 25
—— Maria-Paul. 26
—— Nap., Emp. Fr. &c. 24-5; *see also* Napoleon
Burchardt, I. and II., D. Su. 80
Burchett, Josh., Sec. Adm. 186
Burchull, *see* Buxhill
Burdett, Geo., dn. Llin. 623
—— Jno., dn. Clonf. 637
Burdon, Geo., adm. (**A**) 818
—— Jno. Sh., bp. Vict. (H.K.) 674
Burdred, K.E. 3
Burford, Ch., E. of, aft. 2nd D. of St. Albans, *q.v.*, K.B. 764
—— Ed., bar. of, *see* Ed. Cornwall
Burge, Wm., K.C. 416
Burgers, T. F., Pres. Trl. 101
Burges, Jno. Sm., Chn. E.I. Co. 644
Burgess, Geo., C. Exc. Sc. 505
—— Jas., C.I.E. 807
—— Jas. B., L.P.S. 241; U.S.F. 229
—— Rt. de, W.C.P. 318
—— Saml., dn. Llin. 623
—— Th., bp. Sal. 467; bp. St. Dav. 465
Burgh, *see also* Burke
—— Geoffr. de, bp. Ely, 434
—— Herb. de, bp. Lim. 638
—— Hubert de and sir H., aft. E. of Kent, *q.v.*, L.H.A. 170; W.C.P. 317
—— Hugh, L. Treas. Ir. 558
*—— Hugh de, B. Ex. Ir. 583; C.B. Ex. Ir. 582
*—— Hugh de, M. Chy. 393
* Prob. same pers.
—— Jno. de, Const. T.L. 320
—— Lucas de, S.L. 406
—— Raym. de, bp. Emly, 625
—— Rd. de, L.D. Ir. 550
—— Stanl. de, gen. (**D**) 928
—— Th., bp. Emly, 625
—— Th., C. Acc. Ir. 567; C. Cus. Ir. 565-6; Sec. Tr. Ir. 561
—— sir Th. de, L.D. Ir. 551; L. Treas. Ir. 558
—— Th., *see* ld. B., *infra*
—— Th. Jno., dn. Cloy. 633
—— Ulyss., bp. Ard. 608; dn. Emly, 628
—— Ulysses and sir U., aft. ld. Downes, *q.v.;* K.C.B. 775; S.G.O. 260

Burgh—*cont.*
—— Walt. Huss., C.B. Ex. Ir. 583; S.L. Ir. 592
—— Wm., gen. (**D**) 878
—— Wm., J.C.P. 378; K.B. 755
—— Wm. de, bp. Llff. 449
Burgh, lds.
—— sir T., aft. 1st ld. B., K.G. 736
—— Th., 5th ld., K.G. 739; L.D. Ir. 554
Burghersh, Barth., *see* ld. B., *infra*
—— Hy. de, bp. Linc. 446; L.H.T., 153; Ld. Chanc. 354
—— Rt. de (? 1 or 2), W.C.P. 318
—— sir Wm., L.H.A. 171
Burghersh, lds.
Burghersh Family.
—— Barth., 1st ld., form. B. Burghersh, or Badlesmere, W.C.P. 318
—— Barth., 2nd ld., Const. T.L. 320; K.G. 733
Fane Family.
—— Mildm. F., ld., aft. 2nd E. of Westmoreland, *q.v.*; K.B. 762
—— Jno., ld., aft. 11th E. of Westmoreland, *q.v.*; Amb. Pr. 118; Amb. Scy. 115; Amb. Tusc. &c. 115; G.C.H. 786; K.C.B. 776; P.C. 210
Burghill, Fras., Mowb. H. 340; Som. H. 332
—— (or Bruchilla) Jno., bp. Lich. and Cov. 444; bp. Llff. 449
Burghley, *see* Burleigh
Burgo, Dav. de, bp. Clonf. 636
—— Hub. de, L.H.T. 152
—— Jno. de, abp. Tm. 611
—— Milo. de, dn. Lim. 639
—— Rol. de, bp. Clonf. 636; bp. Elph. 608; dn. Clonf. 637
—— Th. de, bp. Clonf. 635
Burgon, Jno. Wm., dn. Chich. 434
Burgoyne, Jno. and sir J., Comm. F. Ir. 564; gen. (**B**) 866; (**C**) 872
—— Jno. Fox and sir J., Const. T.L. 321; F.M. 856; gen. (**D**) 877; G.C.B. 769; K.C.B. 776
—— Mont., Chambn. Ex. 166
—— sir Mont., gen. (**C**) 873
—— Wm., C.D.L. 242
Burgundy, Ch., D. of, K.G. 736
—— Ph. le Bon., D. of, K.G. 735
Burhred, K.E. 3
Burke, *see also* Bourke and Burgh
—— Edm., P.C. 203; Paym. G. 245
—— Fras., gen. (**C**) 874
—— Hy. F., R. Cr. P.A. 336; Som. H. 332
—— Jas. Hy., gen. (**D**) 899
—— Jas. St. Geo., Q.C. 418
—— Jno. Bern. and sir J., Ulst. K.A. 572
—— Pet., S.L. 414
—— Rd., Sec. Tr. 163
—— (or Bourke) Th., dn. Elph. 609
—— Th., gen. (**D**) 885
—— Th. Hy., U.S. Ir. 563
—— Wm., U.S.S. 226
—— (or Burgh) sir Wm., L.L. Ir. 550

Burland, Jno. and sir J., B. Ex. 385; S.L. 412
—— Wm. Harr., gen. (**D**) 932
Burleigh and **Burghley,** *see also* Burley
—— Wm., dn. Emly, 628
—— Wm. A. C., *see* ld. B., *infra*
Burleigh, lds.
Cecil Family.
—— Wm., 1st ld., form. sir Wm. Cecil, *q.v.*, C.G.S. 356; E.M. 326; K.G. 738; L.H.T. 154; L.K. 356
—— Th., 2nd ld., aft. 1st E. of Exeter, *q.v.*, K.G. 739
—— Brownl., ld., aft. 9th E. of Exeter, *q.v.*, L.L. Rutl. 311
—— Wm. Allen Cecil, c.c. ld., P.C. 217; Tr. H. 292
Balfour Family.
—— Robt., ld., Comm. Tr. Sc. (1649) 497
Burley, *see also* Burleigh
—— sir Jno., K.G. 734
—— sir Rd., K.G. 734
—— sir Sim. de, Const. W. Cast. 322; K.G. 734; W.C.P. 318
—— Th., Ld. Chanc. Ir. 574
—— Wm., dn. Clonm. 600
Burlington, E. of
Boyle Family.
(*See also* E. of Cork.)
—— Rd., 1st E. of, *also* E. of Cork, *q.v.*
—— Ch., 2nd E. of, P.C. 194
—— Rd., 3rd E. of, C.G.P. 299; K.G. 741; P.C. 197
Cavendish Family.
—— Wm., 2nd E. of, L.L. Lanc. 309
Burlton, Geo. and sir G., adm. (**A**) 819; K.C.B. 774
Burmester, Arn. Edw., gen. (**D**) 897
Burn, *see also* Burne
—— Andr., gen. (**C**) 873
—— Jas., gen. (**D**) 930
—— Jno. Macv., gen. (**D**) 934
—— Rt., gen. (**D**) 899
Burnaby, Ch. Herr., gen. (**D**) 899
—— Ed. Sh., gen. (**D**) 921
—— Eust. Beaum., gen. (**D**) 934
—— Jno. D., C.C.J. 403
—— Rd., gen. (**D**) 921
—— Rd. Beaum., gen. (**D**) 899
—— Sherr. B., Vic. Gen. 422
—— sir Wm., adm. (**A**) 814
Burne, *see also* Burn
—— H. K., gen. (**D**) 923
—— Owen Tud. and sir O., C.I.E. 806; K.C.S.I. 803; M.C.I. 647
—— Rt., gen. (**B**) 868
—— Wm. de, J.C.P. 377
Burnell, Arth. Coke, C.I.E. 806
—— Hy., J.K.B. Ir. 579; Rec. Dbln. 642
—— Hugh, *see* ld. B., *infra*
—— Jno., L.M. Lond. 492
—— Rd., B. Ex. Ir. 583
—— Rt., abp. Cant. 430; bp. B. and W. 427; L.H.T. 152; Ld. Chanc. 353
—— Wm., dn. Wells, 428
Burnell, lds.
—— Hugh, 2nd ld., K.G. 734
Burnet, Alexr., abp. Glasg. 537; abp. St. Andr. 529; bp. Abdn. 530; Ld. Sess. 517
—— Gilb., bp. Sal. 467
—— Gilb., C. Exc. Sc. 504

Burnet—*cont.*
—— Rt., Ld. Sess. 519
—— Th. and sir T., J.C.P. 379; S.L. 412
Burnett, Fras. Cl., gen. (**D**) 898
—— Geo., Ly. Dep. 513; Ly. K.A. 513
—— Jas., Ld. Sess. 520
—— sir Jas. Horn, L.L. Kinc 510
—— Jno., J. Adm. Sc. 524
—— sir Th., L.L. Kinc. 510
—— Wm. and sir W., gen. (**A**) 862; K.C.B. 777; K.C.H. 788
Burney, Geo., gen. (**D**) 898
—— Jas., adm. (**H**) 847
—— Wm., K.H. 792
Burnham, Al. de, dn. St. P. 452
—— Jno. de, L. Treas. Ir. 578
—— Th. de, J. It. 369
Burnley, Jos. H., Amb. Sxy. 121
Burns, Jas., K.H. 792
Burnton, Wm. de, J. It. 368
Burnwulf, K.E. 3
Burrard, sir Ch., adm. (**H**) 846
—— Harry and sir H., gen. (**B**) 866
Burrell, Geo., gen. (**D**) 879
—— Pet., S.L.R. 271
—— sir Pet. aft. ld. Gwydyr, *q.v.*, Dep. L.G.C. 288
—— Wm., C. Exc. 280-1
Burrhieus (or Burrie), bp. Roch. 459
Burridge, Rd., adm. (**H**) 848
Burrie, *see* Burrhieus
Burrough, Jas. and sir J., J.C.P. 380; K.C. 415; S.L. 413
Burroughs, Fk. Wm., gen. (**D**) 906
—— Fk. Wm., gen. (**D**) 921
—— Jno. and sir J., Gart. K.A., 327; Norr. K.A. 329
—— Saml., M. Chy. 396
Burrow, Jas., Pres. R. Soc. 940
Burrowes, Hy., L.M. Dbln. 641
—— Rt., dn. Cork, 632
—— Rt. Ed., K.H. 791
Burrows, Arth. Geo., gen.(**D**) 901
—— Geo. and sir G., Pres. Col. Ph. 938
—— Geo. Reyn. Sc., gen. (**D**) 924
—— Mont., gen. (**B**) 869
Burscough, Wm., dn. Lism. 629; bp. Lim. A. and A. 639
Burslem, Nathl., K.H. 791
Burstall, Wm., M.R., 387
Burston, Danl., dn. Wford. 628
Burt, Wm. H., G. Leew. Isl. 727
Burton, S.L. 406
—— Benj., C. Cus. Ir. 565; C. Exc. Ir. 566
—— Benj., L.M. Dbln. 641
—— Ch., J.K.B. Ir. 579; S.L. Ir. 593
—— sir Ch., L.M. Dbln. 641
—— Cuthb. Ward, gen. (**D**) 926
—— Edm., dn. Killa. 614
—— Edm. Fras., gen. (**D**) 923
—— Fowl., gen. (**D**) 906
—— Fras., J. Chest. 387; K.C. 415
—— sir Fras. N., G.C.H. 786
Burton—*cont.*
—— Geo. Guy, adm. (**H**) 848
—— Hy., K.B. 761
—— Jas. Ryder, adm. (**G**) 841; K.H. 791
—— Jno., gen. (**B**) 868
—— Jno. de, M.R. 387
—— Nap. Chr., gen. (**A**) 860
—— Ralph, gen. (**C**) 871
—— Rd. Fras., K.C.M.G. 798
—— Th., bp. S. and M. 483
—— Wm., C. Exc. 280
—— Wm., C. Treas. Ir. 561
—— Wm. Mart., gen. (**D**) 880
—— sir Wm. W., G. N.S.W. 703
Burton, lds.
—— Hy., ld., form. H. Paget, *q.v.*, aft. E. of Uxbridge, *q.v.*
Burwaldus or **Burwold,** bp. Wells, 427
Burwoldus (or Brithwaldus), bp. Cnwall. 436
Bury, Ad. de, L.M. Lond. 489
—— Geo. Butt, gen. (**D**) 889
—— Rd. de, *see* Angarville
—— Rd. Inc., adm. (**A**) 818
—— Th. and sir T., B. Ex. 384; C.B. Ex. 382; S.L. 411
—— Wm., Commr. Ir. 555
Bury, visc.
—— Wm. Coutts, visc., aft. ld. Ashford, K.C.M.G. 796; P.C, 216; Tr. H. 291; U.S. War. 232
Busby, Wm. Beaum., dn. Roch. 461
Bush, Bushe, and **Busshe**
—— Ch. Kend., C.J.K.B. Ir. 578; S.G. Ir. 589; S.L. Ir. 592
—— Fras. Whitt., Q.C. 420
—— Gerv. Park., C. Acc. Ir. 567; C. Cus. Ir. 565; C. Exc. Ir. 566
—— Jno., M. Chy. 393
—— J. Scott, G. Trin. 722-3
—— Paul, bp. Brl. 439
—— Wm., gen. (**D**) 885; K.H. 791
Bushby, Th., adm. (**H**) 847
Bushe, *see* Bush
Bushell, Th., M.M. 246
Bushey, sir Jno., Sp. H.C. 248
Bushir - ud - Dowlah, &c., K.C.I.E. 805
Busk, Geo., Pres. Coll. Surg. 939
Busshe, *see* Bush
Bussy, Myles, K.B. 759
***Bustamente,** Pres. Mex. 103
*—— M. B., Pres. Ugy. 111
* ? same pers.
Bustamento, Jno. de, bp. Ach. 612
Busteed, Hy. Elmo., C.I.E. 808
Buszard, Marst. Cl., Q.C. 419
Butcher, Arth., gen. (**D**) 915
—— Saml., adm. (**D**) 824
—— Saml., bp. Meath, 599
Bute, E and M. of
—— John, 3rd E. of, Gr. St. 304; K.G. 742; K.T. 747; L.T. 157; P.C. 200; Prem. 143; S. St. 224
—— Jno., 4th E. and 1st M. of, form. visc. Mountstuart, *q.v.*; Amb. Spn. 124; L. L. Butesh. 508; L. L. Glam. 315
—— Jno., 2nd M. of, K.T. 748; L.H.C.K. Sc. 546; L.L. Butesh. 508; L.L. Glam. 315
—— Jno. Patr., 3rd M. of, K.T. 749
Buteo, M. F., C. Ro. 42; Dt Ro. 43
—— N. F., C. Ro. 42
Buthtir, G. Tob. 723
Butiler, *see* Butler
Butler, *see also* Boteler
—— Barth., Hps. P.A. 343; R. Cr. P.A. 335; Ulst. K.A. 572; Yk. H. 334
—— Ch., K.C. 416
—— Edmd., abp. Cash. 625
—— Edmd., A.G. Ir. 588; J.K.B. Ir. 578
—— (or Boteler), sir Edmd., L.L. Ir. 550
—— sir Ed. Ger., gen. (**C**) 873
—— Geo., dn. Pboro. 459
—— Hy., gen. (**D**) 924
—— hon. Hy. Ed., gen. (**D**) 882
—— Hy. Mont., dn. Glr. 440
—— Jas., gen. (**B**) 868
—— Jas., K.C. 414
—— Jas., K.H., 791
—— Jas., aft. visc. Thurles, and 9th E. of Ormond, *q.v.*; L. Treas. Ir. 559
—— Jas. Arth., gen. (**D**) 891
—— Jno., bp. Her. 442; bp. Oxf. 456
—— Jno., gen. (**D**) 898
—— Jno., K.B. 763
—— Jos., bp. Brl. 439; bp. Dham. 479; dn. St. P. 453
—— Lill., dn. Ard. 609
—— Capt. N., G. Bmda. 701
—— Sir Nichs., C. Cus. 273-4; P.C. 193
—— Percy Archd., gen. (**D**) 906
—— Ph., Ath. P.A. 341
—— Ph., K.B. 763
—— Regd., bp. Her. 441; bp Lich. and Cov. 444
—— Rd., dn. Clonm. 600
—— Saml., bp. Lich. and Cov. and Lich. 444
—— Theob. and sir T., L.J. Ir. 550; S.G. Ir. 589; S.L. Ir. 591
—— Th., dn. Tm. 613
—— Th., dn. Winds. 474
—— Th., K.B. 758
—— Wm., K.B. 755
—— Sir Wm., L.M. Lond. 490
—— (or Boteler), Wm. Fitz-Thos. le, L.D. Ir. 552
—— Wm. Fras., K.C.B. 781
—— Wm. Hy. Ap., gen. (**D**) 935
—— Wm. Jno., dn. Linc. 448
Butler-Bateman, *see* Bateman
Butson, Chr., bp. Clonf. and K. 636; bp. Killoe. K. Cl. and K. 636; dn. Wford. 628
—— Chr. Hy. G., dn. Kilmacd. 638
Butt, Chas. P., and sir C. J.P.D.A. 391; Q.C. 418
—— Geo. Medd, Q.C. 417
Butter, Arth. Don., gen. (**D**) 932
Butterfield, Wm., adm. (**D**) 824
Butterworth, Wm. J., gen. (**D**) 888
Buttler, *see* Butler
Buttolph, Th., dn. Rph. 602
Button, *see also* Bitton
—— Th. de, bp. Exr. 436; dn. Wells 428
Butts, sir Augs. de, gen. (**A**) 863; K.C.H. 789
—— Eyt., dn. Cloy. 633
—— Rt., bp. Ely, 435; bp. Norw. 455; dn. Norw. 456

Buxhill, Buxhull, or **Burchull,** Alan, Const. T.L. 320; K.G. 734
Byam, Ed., gen. (**D**) 884
— Sir Wm., G. Antig. 728
Byde, Th., J.A.G. 937
Byerly, Rt., L.P.S. 240
Byers, Ch. Hopk., gen. (**D**) 919
— Patr., gen. (**D**) 878
Byknore, *see* Bicknor
Byles, Jno. Barn. and sir J., J.C.P. 380; Jud. Com. P.C. 361; P.C. 218; P.P. 417; S.L. 413
Byng, Sir Geo., *see* ld. B., *infra*
— Capt. Geo. Stev., aft. visc. Enfield, *q.v.*, and ld. and 2nd E. Strafford, *q.v.*; Compt. H. 293; L.T. 160; P.C. 213; Sec. B.C. 254; Tr. H. 291
— Sir Jno., aft. 1st ld. and E. Strafford. *q.v.*; G.C.H. 786
— hon. Hy. Dilke, adm. (**H**) 845
— Jno. and sir J., Comm. F. Ir. 564; G.C.B. 768; K.C.B. 774
— hon. Jno., aft. 5th visc. Torrington. *q.v.*; C. St. 284
— hon. Jno., adm. (**A**) 814; G. Newf. 700
— Jno. Clarke, adm. (**H**) 851
— hon. Pattee, aft. 2nd visc. Torrington, *q.v.*; P.C. 198; Tr. N. 256
— Hon. Rt., G. Bdoes. 720
— Th., D. Arch. 420
Byng, lds.
— sir Geo., aft. ld. B. and 1st visc. Torrington, *q.v.*, adm. (**A**) 813; L. Admy. 177; P.C. 197; Tr. N.
Byngham, *see* Bingham
Bynteworth, *see* Wentworth
Byrd, *see* Bird
Byrne, Edm. Widd., Q.C. 420
— Jas., dn. Clonf. 637
— Th. Edm., gen. (**D**) 932
Byron, *see also* Biron
— Hy., G. I. Man. 665
— Jno., gen. (**D**) 934
— hon. Jno., adm. (**A**) 815; G. Newfd. 700
— Jno. and sir J., K.B. 763; Lt. T.L. 321
— Nichs., K.B. 757
— Rd., adm. (**D**) 823
Byron, lds.
— Geo. Ans., 7th ld., adm. (**D**) 829; (**G**) 840
Byshe, — Winds. H. 331
— Ed. and sir E., Clar. K.A. 328; Gart. K.A. 327; Lanc. H. 333
Bysley, Th., Bl. M. P.A. 336; Rbk. P.A. 344; Yk. H. 334
Bysse, Jno., C.B. Ex. Ir. 583; Rec. Dbln. 642
Bythesea, Hy. Fras., gen. (**D**) 926
— Jno., adm. (**H**) 851; C.I.E. 806
Bython, *see* Bicknor

C.

Cabanas, T., Pres. Hdas. 106
Cabellero, B., Pres. Pgy. 110
Cabhthaick, K. Ir. 21
Cabral, J. M., Pres. Dn. Rep. 105
Caceres, A. A., Dt. Pu. 109
Cadamo, Jno. de, M. Chy. 393
Cadar, abp. Lond. 450
Caddel, Jno., Rec. Dbln. 642
Cadell (2), Pr. Wls. 17
— Alexr., gen. (**D**) 920
— Alexr. Tod., gen. (**D**) 917
— Ch., K.H. 791
— Rt., gen. (**D**) 920
Cadeth (2), Pr. Wls. 17
Cadmano, J. M. P., Pres. Ecr. 108
Cadogan, hon. Cl. Sl., *see* ld. C., *infra*
— hon. Geo., gen. (**D**) 897; K.C.B. 781
Cadogan, lds. and E.
1st Creation.
— Wm., aft. 1st ld. and E. Cad., Clk. O. 260; gen. (**A**) 857; K.T. 747; Lt. T.L. 322; M.G.O. 258; P.C. 197
— Ch., 2nd ld., gen. (**A**) 858
2nd Creation
— hon. Ch. Sl., aft. 3rd ld. and 1st E. Cad., M.M.C. 247
— Geo., 3rd E., adm. (**D**) 826
— Hy. Ch., 4th E., C.Y.G. 298; P.C. 217
— Geo. Hy., 5th E., L.P.S. 241; P.C. 220; U.S.C. 235; U.S. War, 232
Caducan (2), bp. Bgr. 425
Cadwallon ab Jevaf, Pr. Wls. 16
Cadwgan ab Bleddyn (2), Pr. Wls. 17
Cæ—, *see also* **Cea**
Cæcus, A. C. (2), C. Ro. 41
Cædicius, Q., C. Ro. 42
Cæna, abp. Yk. 485
Cænfelad, bp. Emly, 625
Cæpio, *see also* Scipio
— C. S., C. Ro. 42-3
— Q. S., C. Ro. 44-5
Caer (Cahir or Carr), Jas. dn. Tm. 613
Caermerin, bp. St. Dav. 464
Cæsar, *see also* Octavianus and Augustus
— Ch., Tr. N. 256
— sir Ch., M. Chy. 395; M.R. 388
— C. J. (5), C. Ro. 46; (4) Dt. Ro. 46; Tr. Ro. 46
— (d'Este), D. Mda. 53
— Hy., dn. Ely, 435
— Jul., gen. (**C**) 871
— Jul. and sir J., J. Adm. Ct. 422
— Jul. and sir Jul., C.G.S. 356; M. Chy. 395; M.R. 388
— L. J., C. Ro. 45-6
— S. J., C. Ro. 44-5
— Th., Curs. B. Ex. 386
Cæsominus, L.C.P., C. Ro. 44-5-6
Cafe, Wm. Mart., gen. (**D**) 925
Caffin, Jas. Crawf. and sir J., adm. (**G**) 843; K.C.B. 783
Cahir, *see* Caer
Cahusac, Wm. Legh., gen. (**D**) 923
Cailan (St.), bp. Down, 603
Caillard, Camille F. D., C.C.J. 404
Caine, lt.-col., G. H. Kong, 673
— Wm. S., L. Admy. 186
Cairbre-Cinncait, K. Ir. 21
— -Liffeachair, K. Ir. 21
Caird, Jas., K.C.B. 784
Cairioll, K. Ir. 21
Cairlan, bp. Am. 595
Cairncross, *see also* Carncross
— Alexr., abp. Glasg. 537; bp. Brn. 531; bp. Rph. 601
— Alexr., K.H. 791
— Rt., bp. Ross. 535; L.H.T. Sc. 497
Cairnes, Jno. Ell., K.H. 790
Cairns, Hugh, *see* ld. C. *infra.*
— Wm. Welln. and sir W., G. Br. Hond. 714; G. Nev. 730; G. Qland. 706; G. S. Austr. 706; G. St. Xtr. 729; G. Trin. 722; K.C.M.G. 797
Cairns, lds. and E.
— Hugh McC., aft. sir H. and 1st ld. and E. Cairns, A.G. 400; Jud. Com. P.C. 361; Ld. Chanc. 358; L.J. App. 389; P.C. 217; Q.C. 417; S.G. 402
Cairny, Rt. de, bp. Dkld. 533
Caithness, E. of, *see also* E. of Orkney
— Geo., E. of, L.H.A. Sc. 499
— Wm., E. of, L.H.A. Sc. 499
— Jas., 12th E. of, L.L. Cness. 509; Postm. G. Sc. 503
— Alexr., 13th E. of, L.L. Cness. 509
— Jas., 14th E. of, L.L. Cness. 509
— Geo. Ph. Alexr., 15th E. of, L.L. Cness. 509
Caius, Pr. Ro. 33
Calatinus, A. A. (2), C. Ro. 42; Dt. Ro. 42
Calcraft, sir Granv. Th., gen. (**C**) 873
— Hy. Geo., Sec. B.T. 270
— Jno., Clk. O. 260; P.C. 211; Paym. G. 244
— Jno., gen. (**A**) 860
— Th., gen. (**B**) 866
Calder, sir Hy., G. Gibr. 670; gen. (**C**) 872
— sir Jas., C. St. 283
— Patr. D., gen. (**D**) 885
— sir Rt., adm. (**A**) 817; K.C.B. 773
— Wm., L. Prov. Edinb. 548
Calderon, F. G. Pres. Pu. 109
Calderwood, sir W., Ld. Sess. 520
Calderwood - Henderson - Durham, *see* Durham
Caldus, C. C., C. Ro. 45
Caldwall, Wm., Ld. Chanc. Sc. 515
Caldwell, Alexr. and sir A., gen. (**D**) 876; G.C.B. 769; K.C.B. 776
— Benj., adm. (**A**) 815; G.C.B. 768

Caldwell—*cont.*
— Jas. Lill. and sir J., gen. (**D**) 876; G.C.B. 769; K.C.B. 776
— Matth., G. I. Man. 666
Caledon, Dupré, 2nd E. of, G.C.G.H. 679; K.P. 751; L.L. Tyr. 571
Calenus, Q. F., C. Ro. 46
Caleto, Jno. de, Jy. 365
Caley, Hy. Fras., gen. (**D**) 890
Calfe, Rd. (2), bp. Down, 603
Calfhill, Jno., bp. Worc. 473
Calichiopulo, Alt., K.C.M.G. 796
— Ang., K.C.M.G. 796
— Stamo, G.C.M.G. 794
Caligula, Emp. Ro. 47
Calixtus, I. to III., P. Ro. 32, 34-5
Call, Geo. Fk. H., gen. (**D**) 906
Callaghan, Jerem. Th. Fitz-G., G. Labn. 675
— Th. Fitz-G., G. Bah. Isl. 716; G. Falk. Isl. 731; G. Gamb. 686
Callan, Geo. Field, visc., K.B. (1625) 762
Callaway, Hy., bp. Br. Kaffr. 681
Callendar, Campb., gen. (**A**) 862
Callice, Rt., S.L. 409
Callis, Smith, adm. (**A**) 814
Callow, Wm., J.C.P. 378
Callwey, Wm., K.B. 759
Calmady, Ch. Holmes Ev., adm. (**A**) 816
Calowe (or Collow), Wm., S.L. 407
Calpurnianus, M. P. P., C. Ro. 46
Calthorp and **Calthorpe**
— Ch. and sir C., A.G. Ir. 588; J.C.P. Ir. 581
— Chr., K.B. 763
— Hy., K.B. 764
— Le S., S.L. 410
— (or Colthrop) Mart., L.M. Lond. 491
— hon. Som. Jno. (Gough), gen. (**D**) 910
— Walt., bp. Norw. 454
— Wm., K.B. 757
Calthrop, Hy., Rec. Lond. 494
Calverley, sir Hugh, L.H.A. 173
Calvert, Felix, C. Exc. 278; gen. (**D**) 882
— Fk., Q.C. 417
— sir G., aft. ld. Baltimore, *q.v.*, S. St. 223
— sir Harry, G.C.B. 767; G.C.H. 786; gen. (**A**) 861; L.G. Ch. Hosp. 936
— Pet., D. Arch. 421; J. Pr. Ct. 421; Vic. Gen. 422
— Th. J., Wdn. Chr. Ch. Manch. 481
— sir Wm., L.M. Lond. 492
Calvilegh, Hugh, G. Ch. Isl. 667
Calvinus, C. D. (4), C. Ro. 40, 46
— C. S., C. Ro. 45
— T. V. (2), C. Ro. 40-1
Calvo, B., Pres. Pan. 107
Calvus, C. C. S., C. Ro. 43
— L. C. M., C. Ro. 44
Calwylegh, Dav. de, dn. St. As. 463
Camac, sir Burg., gen. (**D**) 879
Camargo, S., Pres. C.R. 106
Cambacérès, Csl. Fr. 24; Off. Nap. 26
Cambell, *see also* Campbell
— sir Jas., L.M. Lond. 491
— sir Th., L.M. Lond. 491
Cambhou, Walt. de, J. It. 368
Cambrege, Wm., L.M. Lond. 489
Cambrensis, Gir., bp. St. Dav. 464
Cambridge, Jno. de, K.B. 755
Cambridge, E. and D. of
Plantagenet Family.
— Edmd., 1st E. of, aft. D. York, *q.v.*, K.G. 733; W.C.P. 318
Hamilton Family.
— Jas., 1st E. of, also 2nd M. of Hamilton, *q.v.*
— Wm., 3rd E. of, also 2nd D. Hamilton, *q.v.*, K.G. 740
Stuart Family.
— Jas., 1st D. of, K.G. 740
Issue of Geo. III.
— Pr. Adolph Fk., 1st D. of (*see also* Adolphus), F.M. 856; G.C.B. 767; G.C.H. 785; G.C.M.G. 794; gen. (**A**) 859; Gr. Mast. M.G. 794; K.G. 742; P.C. 207
— Pr. Geo. Wm. Fk. Ch., 2nd D. of (*see also* George), C. Ch. 855; F.M. 856; G.C.B. 769; G.C.H. 786; G.C.I.E. 805; G.C.M.G. 795; G.C.S.I. 801; gen. (**D**) 881; Gr. Mast. M.G. 794; K.G. 743; K.P. 751; K.T. 749; P.C. 216
— Augusta W. L., Dss. of, Cr. Ind. 809
Cambuslang, Walt., bp. Dnbl. 532
Cambyses, K. Pers. 99
Camden, Wm., Clar. K.A. 328; Richm. H. 333
Camden, lds., E., and M.
— Ch., 1st ld. and 1st E., form. sir Ch. Pratt, *q.v.*, L.P.C. 188; Ld. Chanc. 357
— Jno. Jeffr., 2nd E. and 1st M., form. J. J. Pratt and visc. Bayham, *q.v.*, Jud. Com. P.C. 360; K.G. 743; L.L. Ir. 557; L.L. Kent, 309; L.P.C. 188; W. and C. Sec. 230
— Geo. Ch., 2nd M., form. E. of Brecknock, *q.v.*, K.G. 744; L.L. Brec. 315
Camelford, Th., ld., form. Th. Pitt, *q.v.*
Camell, *see also* Cammell
— Wm. de, dn. Wells 428
Camera, Wm. de, LJ. Clk. 516
Camerinus, S. S., C. Ro. 39
Cameron, Alan and sir A., gen. (**B**) 867; K.C.B. 774
— Alexr. and sir A., gen. (**D**) 877; K.C.B. 776
— Ch., G. Bah. Isl. 716; G. Mlta. 671
— Don., L.L. Ind. 510
— Don. Rod., gen. (**D**) 934
— Duncan Alexr. and sir D., gen. (**D**) 893; G.C.B. 770; K.C.B. 779
— Ed. Jas., G. Virg. Isl. 731
— Jno. bp. Glasg. 536; Ld. Chanc. Sc. 515; L.P.S. Sc. 500; Sec. St. Sc. 501
— Jno., gen. (**D**) 905
Cameron—*cont.*
— Jno. and sir J., gen. (**B**) 869; K.C.B. 774
— Patr., gen. (**D**) 878
— Th. Mackn., gen. (**D**) 891
— Wm. Gord., gen (**D**) 919; K.H. 790
Camidge, Ch. Ed., bp. Bhurst. 704
Camillus, L. F. (2), C. Ro. 40-1; Dt. Ro. (2) 40
— M. F. (5), Dt. Ro. 39-40
Cammell, *see also* Camell
— Jno., M. Chy. 394
Camois and **Camoys**
— Ralph de, W.C.P. 318
— Rd., K.B. 755
— Th. de, or ld. C., K.G. (1415) 735
Camon, gen., K.C.B. 778
Campbell, *see also* Cambell, Cammell, and Camell
— — G. Tob. (1810) 723
— Alan., gen. (**C**) 872
— Alexr., bp. Brn. 531
— Alexr., C. Exc. 281-2
— Alexr., gen. (**A**) 860
— Alexr., gen. (**B**) 866
— Alexr., K.H. 790
— Alexr. and sir A., C.C. Mdras. 657; gen. (**B**) 867; K.C.B. 775; G. Ont. 692; K.C.M.G. 797
— sir Alexr. (Cesnock), aft. 2nd E. of Marchmont, *q.v.*, Ld. Sess. 520
— Alexr. Hy. Ed., gen. (**D**) 929
— hon. Alexr. Hume, K.C. 415; Ld. Clk. Reg. 525
— Andr., gen. (**D**) 888
— Archd. and sir A., C.C. Mdras. 657; G. Jam. 712; G. Mdras. 656; gen. (**C**) 872; K.B. 765
— sir Archd., G.C.B. 768; G. N. Brk. 695; gen. (**B**) 869; K.C.B. 774
— Archd., gen. (**B**) 867
— Archd., gen. (**C**) 875
— Archd., L.L. Renfw. 511
— Archd., Ld. Sess. 520
— hon. Archd., bp. Abdn. 540; Sc. bp. 545
— ld. Archd., Comm. Tr. Sc. 498
— Ch., gen. (**C**) 873
— Ch., gen. (**D**) 895
— Ch. Stuart., gen. (**D**) 884
— Ch. Wm., gen. (**D**) 929
— Colin, adm. (**H**) 844
— Colin, C. Cus. 275; C. Cus. Sc. 504
— Colin and sir C., aft. ld. Clyde, *q.v.*, C.C. Ind. 651; G.C.B. 769; gen. (**D**) 884; K.C.B. 777
— Colin and sir C., G. Ceyl. 672; G. N. Sc. 695; G. Tob. 723; gen. (**B**) 869; K.C.B. 774
— sir Colin, G. Gibr. 670; gen. (**B**) 867
— sir Colin, Ld. Sess. 520
— Colin Yorke, adm. (**H**) 849
— Dav. Wilk., C.I.E. 807
— Den., dn. Lim. 639; bp. Dry. 601
— Donald, adm. (**A**) 819
— Donald, adm. (**H**) 844
— Donald, bp. Brn. 531; Ld. Sess. 518
— Donald, gen. (**D**) 889

Campbell—*cont.*
— sir Donald, G. Pr. Ed. Isl. 699
— Dug., gen. (**C**) 874
— Dunc., gen. (**A**) 860
— Dunc., gen. (**C**) 872
— Fras., gen. (**D**) 890
— Fk., gen. (**D**) 883
— ld. Fk., B.C. 252; B.P. 267; Ch. Sec. Ir. 562; L.P.S. Sc. 501; Ld. Clk. Reg. 525; P.C. 201; V. Treas. Ir. 560
— Fk. Archd., adm. (**E**) 835
— Fk. Alexr. and sir F., gen. (**D**) 907; K.C.B. 781
— Geo., gen. (**C**) 872
— Geo., gen. (**D**) 892
— Geo., gen. (**D**) 901
— Geo. and sir G., adm. (**A**) 817; G.C.B. 768; K.C.B. 773
— Geo., Ch. Com. Cent. Pr. 655; K.C.S.I. 803; L.G. Bgal. 652; M.C.I. 647
— hon. Geo. Pryse, adm. (**H**) 846
— sir Guy, gen. (**D**) 879
— sir Hy., C. Tx. 285
— Hy. Dund., G. Si. Le. 685
— Hy. Fk. and sir H., gen. (**A**) 862; G.C.H. 786; K.C.B. 773
— sir Hew, Ld. Sess. 519
— Hugh Archd. B., gen. (**D**) 907
— Ilay, Ld. Adv. 526; L.P. Ch. Sess. 516; S.G. Sc. 526
— J., L.M. Dbln. 642
— Jas., gen. (**B**) 866
— Jas., gen. (**B**) 867
— Jas., gen. (**C**) 872
— Jas., gen. (**D**) 883
— Jas., gen. (**D**) 885; K.H. 791
— Jas., gen. (**D**) 910
— Jas. and sir J., G. Ceyl. 672; G. Gren. 724; gen. (**C**) 874; K.C.B. 775; K.C.H. 787
— hon. Jas. aft. sir Jas., gen. (**B**) 864; K.B. 764
— sir Jas., C. Cus. 275; C. Cus. Sc. 503
— sir Jas., Compt. Sc. 498
— sir Jas., G.C.H. 786; gen. (**B**) 867
— sir Jas., gen. (**C**) 874
— sir Jas., Ly. K.A. 513
— Jas. C., bp. Bgr. 426
— Jas. Macn., C.I.E. 807
— Jno., *see* ld. C. *infra*
— Jno., Acct G. 397; M. Chy. 397
— Jno., adm. (**A**) 815; G. Newfd. 700
— Jno., bp. Arg. 538
— Jno., bp. Isl. 539
— Jno., C. Cus. 275; C. Cus. Sc. 503
— Jno., gen. (**A**) 859
— Jno., gen. (**C**) 872
— Jno., gen. (**D**) 891
— Jno., Jy. Sc. 523; Ld. Sess. 520
— Jno., K.H. 791
*— Jno., L. Admy. 178
*— Jno., L.T. 157
* Poss. same. pers.
— Jno., L.G. Ch. Hosp. 936
— Jno., L.M. Dbln. 642
— Jno., Modr. K. Sc. 547
— Jno. and sir J. (of Lundy), L.H.T. Sc. 497; Ld. Sess. 518
— Jno. and sir J., gen. (**D**) 888; K.C.S.I. 803

Campbell—*cont.*
*— sir Jno., G. St. Vin. 725
*— sir Jno., gen. (**D**) 889
* Prob. same pers.
— Jno. Dougl., gen. (**D**) 906
— Jno. Fl., gen. (**A**) 859
— Jno. Fras. Gl., gen. (**D**) 895
— Jno. Hooke, Ly. K.A. 513
— sir Jno. Nichs. Rt., K.C.H. 789
— Jno. Penn., gen. (**D**) 932
— Jno. Pet. Wm., gen. (**D**) 914
— sir Jno. Wm., gen. (**D**) 931
— Melf., G. Nev. 730
— Napier Geo., gen. (**D**) 92
— Neil, bp. Arg. 538
— Neil, bp. Isl. 540
— sir Neil, G. Si. Le. 685; gen. (**C**) 874
— Patr., gen. (**D**) 881
— Patr., Ld. Sess. 520
— Patr. and sir P., adm (**A**) 820; K.C.B. 776
— Patr. Jno., gen. (**D**) 930
— Pet., gen. (**B**) 864
— Pryse, L.T. 157
— Rt., gen. (**B**) 869
— Rt. and sir R., Chn. E.I. Co. 645
— Theoph., dn. Drom. 606
— Th. Hay, gen. (**D**) 911
— Wm., C. St. Ir 568
— Wm., G. Bmda. 701
— Wm., gen. (**D**) 882
Campbell, lds.
— Jno., aft. sir J. and 1st ld. C., A.G. 400; C.D.L. 243; C.J.Q.B. 370; Jud. Com. P.C. 360; K.C. 416; Ld. Chanc. 358; Ld. Chanc. Ir. 577; P.C. 214; Q.C. 417; S.G. 402; S.L. 413
Campbell-Bannerman, *see* Bannerman
Campejus, Lawr., bp. Sal. 467
Camperdown, Rt. Dund., 1st E. of, K.T. 748
— Rt. A. P. H., 3rd E. of, L. Admy. 185
Campero, N., Pres. Bol. 109
Campion and **Campyon**
— Abrm., dn. Linc. 448
— Hub., adm. (**H**) 852
— (or Champion), Wm., dn. Ferns, 623
— W. B., S.L. Ir. 593
Campo, R., Pres. S. Salv. 106
Campyon, *see* Campion
Camvill, Ger. de, J. It. 366
— Rd. de, L.H.A. 170
— Th. de, Jy. 364
Canal, B., Pres. Hti. 105
Canalizo, Pres. Mex. 103
Candy, Geo., Q.C. 420
Cane, Maur., C. Acc. Ir. 567
Canina, C. C. (2), C. Ro. 41
Caning or **Canings,** Th., L.M. Lond. 490
Canmore, Ev., Ld. Chanc. Sc. 514
Cannan, Alexr., gen. (**D**) 912
Canning, Geo., Amb. Pgl. 124; B.C. 252; Ch. Ex. 165; F. Sec. 228; G.G. Ind. 648; L.T. 159; P.C. 206; Paym. G. 244; Prem. 146; Pres. B.C. 253; Tr. N. 256; U.S.F. 229
— Geo., aft. 1st ld. Garvagh, *q.v.*
— Hy., Amb. G. St. 122; Amb. H. Tns. 120

Canning—*cont.*
— Stratford and sir S., aft. ld. Str. de Redcliffe, *q.v.* Amb. Bgm. 123; Amb. G. St. 122; Amb. Gr. &c. 128; Amb. Russ. 125; Amb. Spn. 124; Amb. Swz. 113; Amb. Tky. 129; Amb. U.S.A. 132; G.C.B. 772; P.C. 210
Canning, visc. and E.
— Ch. J., 2nd visc., aft. 1st E., C.W.F. &c. 272; G.C.B. 772; G.G. Ind. 649; K.G. 744; P.C. 215; Postm. G. 239; U.S.F. 230
Cannon, Ed. St. Leger., adm. (**H**) 848
— Rt., dn. Linc. 448
Canseco, P. D., Pres. Pu. 109
Cant, Andr. or Dav., bp. Glas. 543; Sc. Bp. 545
Cantelon, Nichs. de, K.B. 754
Cantebrig, Jno. de, J.C.P. 377; S.L. 406
— Th. de, B. Ex. 383; C.B. Ex. 381
Cantelewe, Wm., K.B. 757
Canterbury, Ch., 1st visc., form. C. Manners-Sutton, *q.v.*
— Jno. Hy. Th., 3rd visc., form. hon. J. H. Manners Sutton, *q.v.*; G.C.M.G. 795
Cantilupe, Arn. F. de, dn. St. P. 453
— (or Normannus), Sim. de, L.K. 353
— Th. de, bp. Her. 44 Chanc. 353
— Walt. de, bp. Worc. 472; J. It. 367
— Wm. de, J. It. 367; Jy. 364
Cantock, Th., bp. Emly, 625; Ld. Chanc. Ir. 574
Cantok, Jno., dn. Cloy. 632
Canton, Gerald, bp. Cloy. 630
Cantrell, Jos. T., C.C.J. 403
Cantwell, Jno., abp. Cash. 625
— Ol., bp. Oss. 620
Canute, K.E. 4
— K. Sw. 92
— II. to VI., K. Dk. 93
Caolbhach, K. Ir. 21
Capadose, Maj., G. Trin. 722
Capel and **Capell,** *see also* Cappel
— Ed., E.S.P. 301
— Hy., *see* ld. C. *infra*
— hon. Th. Bl. and sir T., adm. (**A**) 820; G.C.B. 749; K.C.B. 776
— hon. Th. Ed., gen. (**A**) 863
— sir Wm., L.M. Lond. 490
Capel, lds.
— Hy. and sir H., aft. ld. C. of Tewkesbury, K.B. 763; L. Admy. 175; L.J. Ir. 555; L.T. 155; P.C. 192-3
Capella, *see* Cappela and Rupella
Capellanus, Petr., dn. Kild. 619
— Wm., Ld. Clk. Reg. 524
Capellen, bar. Van de, K.C.B. 775
Capenhurst, Th. de, M. Chy. 393
Capito, C. F., C. Ro. 47
Capitolinus, M. M., C. Ro. 39
— P. M., Dt. Ro. 40
— S. T. M., C. Ro. 38
— T. Q. C., Dt. Ro. 39
Capon, Dav., gen. (**D**) 887; K.C.B. 779

For List of Abbreviations, see pp. 944-952.

Cappadoca, Giov., G.C.M.G. 794; K.C.M.G. 796
Cappel, *see also* Capel
— Alb. Jas. Lepp., K.C.I.E. 805
Cappela, Rd. de, bp. Her. 441
Caprarius, C. C. M., C. Ro. 45
Caractacus, K. Sc. 18
Caradoc, *see also* Cradock
— Jno. Fras. and sir J., aft. 1st ld. Howden, *q.v.*, C.C. Mdras. 657; G. C.G.H. 679; gen. (**A**) 860; G.C.B. 767; K.B. 766
— hon. Jno. Hob., aft. 2nd ld. Howden, *q.v.*, Amb. Bgm. 123; Amb. Tky. 129
Carberry or **Carbery**
— Rd., ld. Vaughan, and 2nd E. of, P.C. 190
— Jno., 3rd E. of, L. Adm'y. 176; Pres. R. Soc. 940
Carbo, C. P. (3), C. Ro. 45
Carbonel, Rd., K.B. 756
Carden, Geo., gen. (**D**) 934
— Jno. Surm., adm. (**D**) 825; (**G**) 840
— sir Rt. Walt., L.M. Lond. 492
— sir Th., Lt. T.L. 321
Cardenas, A., Pres. Nic. 106
Cardew, Geo., gen. (**D**) 882
— Hy., gen. (**D**) 926
Cardiff, E. of
— Hy., ld., aft. E. of Pembroke, *q.v.* K.B. 760
Cardigan, E. of
— Geo., 4th E. of, aft. 1st D. of Montagu, *q.v.*, Const. W. Cast. 322; K.G. 742
— Jas., 5th E. of, Const. W. Cast. 322
— Jas. Th., 7th E. of, gen. (**D**) 885
— Geo. Wm. Fk., 8th E. of, also 2nd M. of Ailesbury, *q.v.*, K.C.B. 777
Cardonnell, Jas., C. Cus. Sc. 504
— Mansf., C. Cus. Sc. 504
Cardross, lds., *see* E. of Buchan
Cardwell, Edw., aft. 1st visc., C.D.L. 243; C. Sec. 235; Ch. Sec. Ir. 563; P.C. 216; Pres. B.T. 269; Sec. Tr. 163; W. Sec. 232
Carent, Nichs., dn. Wells, 429
Carew and **Carewe**
— sir Benj. Hall., adm. (**A**) 818; G.C.B. 768
— Fras. (2), K.B. 763
— Geo., dn. Brl. 440; dn. Chr. Ch. Oxf. 457; dn. Exr. 437; dn. Winds. 474
— Geo., M. Chy. 395
— sir Geo., aft. E. of Totnes, *q.v.*, L.G.V. 259
— ld Geo., *see* ld. Clapton
— Geo. O'Br. Theod., C.I.E. 807
— Hy., Tell. Ex. 167
— sir Jno. de, L.J. Ir. 551
— sir Matth., M. Chy. 395
— Nichs., C. St. 283
— sir Nichs., Chambn. Ex. 166
— sir Nichs., K.G. 737; M.H. 301
— Reg. P., B.T. 268; P.C. 207; U.S. Home, 227
— Rd. de, bp. St. Dav. 464
— sir Th., L.H.A. 173
— Wym., K.B. 760
Carew, lds.
— Rt. Sh., 2nd ld., K.P. 751; L.L. Wexf. 571
Carey and **Cary**
— Fras., gen. (**D**) 909
— Geo., dn. Exr. 437
— sir Geo., L.J. Ir. 554
— hon. Geo., gen. (**A**) 858
— Geo. Jackson, G. Vict. 704; gen. (**D**) 902
— Hy. and sir Hy., aft. 1st visc. Falkland, *q.v.*, Compt. H. 292; K.B. 762
— Hy., aft. 1st visc. Rochford, and 1st E. of Dover, *q.v.*, K.B. 762
— Jas., bp. Exr. 436; bp. Lich. and Cov. 444
— Jno., B. Ex. 383; C.B. Ex. 381; S.L. 407
— Jno., aft. visc. Rochford, and 2nd E. of Dover, *q.v.*, K.B. 763
— Mordecai, bp. Clonf. and K. 636; bp. Killa. and Ach. 613
— sir Oct., gen. (**C**) 875; K.C.H. 788
— Pet. Stafford, aft. sir P., Blf. Gsey. 669; gen. (**A**) 863
— hon. Plant. P., adm. (**G**) 842
— Rt., gen. (**D**) 908
— Th., B. Ex. Ir. 584
— Th., K.H. 789
— Th., gen. (**C**) 874
— Th. Alph., gen. (**D**) 933
— Th. Aug., gen. (**D**) 915
— Th. Pr., gen. (**D**) 925
— Val., bp. Exr. 437; dn. St. P. 453
— Walt., B.T. 264
— Wm., bp. Exr. 437; bp. St. As. 462
— Wm. Dob., gen. (**D**) 932
Carfrae, Jno., gen. (**D**) 878
Carhampton, E. of
— Hy. L., 2nd E. of, Comm. F. Ir. 564; gen. (**A**) 859
— Jno., 3rd E. of, form. hon. J. Luttrell and Luttrell-Olmius, *q.v.*, C. Cus. 282
Caridi, sir Vitt., G.C.M.G. 794; K.C.M.G. 796
Carilefo (or Carilepho), Wm. de, bp. Dham. 478; Ch. Jr. 362
Carinus, Emp. Ro. 48
Carhill, Chr., Carl. H. 339; Norr. K.A. 329
Carlaverock, sir Eum. M., ld., L.G.C. Sc. (1258) 506
Carleton and **Carlton,** *see also* Karleton
— Dudley, *see* ld. C. *infra*
— Geo., bp. Chich. 433; bp. Llff. 449
— Ger., dn. Pboro. 458
— Guy, bp. Brl. 439; bp. Chich. 433; dn. Carl. 476
— Guy and sir Guy, aft. 1st ld. Dorchester, *q.v.*, G. Can. 691; G. N. Brk. 695; G. N. Sc. 695; K.B. 765
— Hy. Alexr., gen. (**D**) 904
— Hugh, C.G.S. Ir. 576; C.J.C.P. Ir. 581; S.G. Ir. 589; S.L. Ir. 592
— Jno., L.M. Dbln. 641
— Jno. de, B. Ex. Ir. 583
— Jno. de, dn. Wells, 428
— Pet., dn. Killoe. 637
— Rt., dn. Cork, 632
Carleton and Carlton—*cont.*
— (or Charleton), Rt. de, C.J.C.P. 375; K.B. 755
— Th., gen. (**A**) 859
— (or Karleton), Wm. de, B. Ex. 382; C.B. Ex. (?) 381
Carlton, lds.
Carleton Family.
— Dudley and sir D., aft. ld. C. and visc. Dorchester, *q.v.*, S. St. 223; V.C.H. 296
Boyle Family.
— Hy., 1st ld., form. hon. Hy. Boyle, *q.v.*, L.P.C. 188; L. Treas. Ir. 559; P.C. 196
Carlingford, Chich. S., ld., form. Chichester S. Fortescue, *q.v.*, aft. 2nd ld. Clermont, *q.v.*, Jud. Com. P.C. 362; L.P. 752; L.P.C. 188; L.P.S. 241
Carlisle, sir Anthy., Pres. Coll. Surg. 939
— Nichs., K.H. 790
Carlisle, Earls of
Hay Family.
— Jas., 1st E. of, form. ld. Hay, *q.v.*; K.G. 739
Howard Family.
— Ch., 1st E. of, G. Jam. 712
— Ch., 3rd E. of, Const. T.L. 321; Const. W. Cast. 322; Dep. E.M. 327; L.T. 155-6; P.C. 194
— Hy., 4th E. of, K.G. 742
— Fk., 5th E. of, K.G. 742; K.T. 747; L.L. Ir. 557; L.L. Yorks. E.R. 313; L.P.S. 241; L.S.H. 290; P.C. 203; Pres. B.T. 266; Tr. H. 291
— Geo., 6th E. of, form. visc. Morpeth, *q.v.*; C.W.F. &c. 271; K.G. 743; L.P.S. 241
— Geo. W. F., 7th E. of, form. ld. Morpeth, *q.v.*; C.D.L. 243; K.G. 744; L.L. Ir. 557-8
Carloman (2), K. Fr. 23
Carlos, D. Pma. 53
Carlton, *see* Carleton
Carlyon, Ed., gen. (**D**) 885
Carmarthen, M. of
— Th., 1st M. of, form. Th. and ld. Osborne, visc. Latimer, and E. of Danby, *q.v.*, aft. 1st D. of Leeds, *q.v.*; L.H.S. 286
— Pereg., M. of, aft. 2nd D. of Leeds, *q.v.*, adm. (**A**) 813
— Fk. G., M. of, aft. 5th D. of Leeds, *q.v.*, H. Sec. 226; Amb. Fr. 112; L.L. Yorks. E.R. 313; P.C. 203
Carmichael, Ch. M., gen. (**D**) 887
— sir Danl., Comm. Tr. Sc. 497
— Geo., bp. Glasg. 536
— Hugh Lyle, gen. (**C**) 873
— sir Jas., Comm. Tr. Sc. 497; L.J. Clk. 516; Ld. Sess. 519
— hon. Wm., abp. Dbln. and Gl. 616; bp. Clonf. and K. 636; bp. Ferns and L. 622; bp. Meath, 599
Carmichael, lds.
— Jno., ld., aft. E. Hyndford, *q.v.*, L.H.C.K. Sc. 546; L.P.S. Sc. 501
Carnac, Jas. Rivett- and sir J., Chn. E.I. Co. 645; G. Bbay. 659
— Jno. Rivett-, adm. (**G**) 842
— Jno. Hy. Rivett-, C.I.E. 806

For List of Abbreviations, see pp. 944-952.

Carnarvon, E. and M. of
Brydges Family.
—— Hy., M. of, aft. 2nd D. of Chandos. *q.v.*, K.B. 764
Herbert Family.
—— Hy., 1st E. of, M.H. 302; P.C. 208
—— Jas., M. of, aft. 1st D. of Chandos, *q.v.*, L.L. Hants, 311
—— Hy. H. M., 4th E. of, C. Sec. 235; L.L. Hants, 311; L.L. Ir. 558; P.C. 217; U.S.C. 235
Carncross, *see also* Cairncross
—— Jos. Hugh and sir J., gen. (**B**) 870; K.C.B. 775
—— Ed. and sir E., M. Chy. 394
Carnegie and **Carnegy**
—— Alexr., gen. (**D**) 888
—— Alexr., gen. (**D**) 926
—— Dav., Ld. Sess., aft. ld. C. and 1st E. of Southesk, 517
—— Geo. Full., gen. (**D**) 913
—— sir Jas., aft. E. of Southesk, *q.v.*, (1855), L.L. Kinc. 510
—— Patr., C.I.E. 806
—— sir Rt., Ld. Sess. 518
—— hon. Swynf. Th., adm. (**D**) 833; (**E**) 834; (**F**) 838; L. Admy. 184; L.T. 161
Carney (or Kerney), sir Rd., Ulst. K.A. 572
Carnot, M. F. Sadi-, Pres. Fr. 25
Carnoth, Jno. de, bp. Brn. 531
Carnwarth, Rt. Alex., 7th E. of, gen. (**B**) 869
—— Arth. Alex., 10th E. of, form. hon. A. A. Dalzell, *q.v.*
Carnsto, Th. de, Ld. Chanc. Sc. 515
Caro, J. J., Pres. Mex. 103
Caroline (2), Q.C.E. 8
—— -Augusta-Maria (iss. Geo. II.), Pr. E. 14
—— -Matilda (g. dau. Geo. II.), Pr. E. 14
Caron, Josh. Ph., K.C.M.G. 798
—— R. E., G. Queb. 694
Carpenter, Benj., gen. (**A**) 858
—— Geo., gen. (**D**) 876
—— Jas., adm. (**A**) 818
—— Jno., bp. Worc. 473
—— Jno., K.H. 791
—— Th. Dav., gen. (**D**) 894
—— hon Walt. Cec., adm. (**E**) 837
—— Wm. Boyd, bp. Rip. 482
Carpenter, lds.
—— Geo., ld., gen. (**B**) 864
Carr and **Carre**, *see also* Caer and Kerr
—— Ch., bp. Killoe. 634
—— Ed., gen. (**B**) 865
—— Geo., Ld. Sess. 520
—— Hy. Wm., K.C.B. 775
—— (or Kerr), Jno., dn. Ard. 609
—— Rd., aft. E. of Somerset, *q.v.*, K.B. (1603) 761
—— sir Rt., C.D.L. 242; P.C. 191-2
—— Rt. Riddell, adm. (**H**) 846
—— Rt. Jas., bp. Chich. 433; bp. Worc. 473; dn. Her. 442
—— Th., bp. Bbay. 661
—— Wm., C. Exc. 279
—— Wm., Curs. B. Ex. 386
Carrell, Jno., S.L. 408
Carrera, R., Pres. Gua. 105
Carrerg, Alexr. de, Ld. Clk. Reg. 524
Carrick, sir Jno., Ld. Chanc. Sc. 515
Carrinas, C., C. Ro. 46
Carrington, Fk., K.C.M.G. 798
—— Jno. Worr., G. Tob. 724
Carrington, lds.
—— Rt. Jno., 2nd ld., L.L. Bucks, 306
—— Ch. Rt., 3rd ld., C.G.A. 300; G.C.M.G. 795; G. N.S.W. 703; L.G.C. 288; P.C. 220
—— Charl. A. A., lady, L.G.C. 288
Carrion, G., Pres. Ecr. 108
Carroll, sir Geo., L.M. Lond. 492
—— Redm., L.M. Dbln. 642
—— Wm. and sir W., L.M. Dbln. 642
—— Wm. Fairbr. and sir W., adm. (**D**) 828; K.C.B. 777; L.G. Gr. Hosp. 854
—— sir Wm. Park, gen. (**B**) 870; K.C.H. 788
Carrow, Jno. M., C.C.J. 403
Carrusa, Ch. Demet., G.C.M.G. 795
Carruthers, Walt., gen. (**C**) 872
Carson, Th., dn. Kilm. 609; bp. Kilm. E. and A. 609
Carswell, Jno., bp. Isl. 539
Cartaret, *see* Carteret
Carter, Ch., adm. (**D**) 824
—— Fk. Bowk. Tedd. and sir F., G. Newfd. 700; K.C.M.G. 797
—— Geo. Markh., gen. (**D**) 915
—— Gilb. T., G. Gamb. 686
—— Jno., adm. (**D**) 829; (**G**) 840
—— Jno., K.H. 791
—— Jno., L.M. Lond. 492
—— Jno. Bonham-, L.T. 161
—— Lawr. and sir L., B. Ex. 384; S.L. 411
—— Rd., adm. (**A**) 813
—— Rd., adm. (**H**) 853
—— Th., dn. Tm. 613
—— Th., M.R. Ir. 585; Sec. St. Ir. 562
—— Th. Wren, adm. (**D**) 831; (**F**) 838
Carteret and **Cartaret**, Ed. Postm. G. 238
—— sir Geo., B.T. 263; G. Jsey. 667; L. Admy. 175; P.C. 190; Tr. N. 256; V.C.H. 296; V. Treas. Ir. 559
—— Ph. de, G. Ch. Isl. 667
Cartaret, lds.
Carteret Family.
—— Jno., ld., aft. 2nd visc. C. and E. Granville, *q.v.*, L.L. Ir. 556
Thynne Family.
—— Hy. Fk., aft. 1st ld. C., form. hon. H. F. Thynne, *q.v.*, Blf. Jsey. 668; Postm. G. 238
—— Jno., ld., form. ld. Jno. Thynne, *q.v.*
Carthage (St.), bp. Lism. 626
Carthagh (St.), bp. Oss. 620
Carthew, Jas., adm. (**A**) 820
—— Mord., gen. (**D**) 894
—— Th., S.L. 411
Carthilinthus, K. Sc. 18
Cartier, Jno., adm. Ind. 648
Cartwright, Edm., gen. (**D**) 878
—— Rd. Jno., K.C.M.G. 797
—— Th., bp. Chest. 477; dn. Rip. 482
—— Th. and sir T., Amb. G. St. 122; Amb. Nds. &c. 123; Amb. Sw. and N. 127; G.C.H. 787
—— Wm., gen. (**A**) 861
—— Wm., gen. (**D**) 891
Carus, M. A., Emp. Ro. 48
—— Th., J.Q.B. 372; S.L. 408
Carwen, *see* Curwen and Curwyn
Cary, *see* Carey
Caryl, Jno., S.L. 408
Carysfort, lds. and E. of
—— Jno., 1st ld., K.B. 765; L. Admy. 178-9
—— Jno. Josh., 2nd ld. and 1st E. of, Amb. Pr. 118; B.C. 252; B.T. 268; K.P. 750; M.R. Ir. 585; P.C. 208; Postm. G. 238
—— Jno., 2nd E. of, gen. (**A**) 863
—— Granv. Lev., 3rd E. of, form. hon. G. L. Proby, *q.v.*
—— Granv. Lev., 4th E. of, K.P. 751
—— Wm., 5th E. of, K.P. 751
Cas—, *see also* **Cass—**
Casamajor, Lewis, Amb. Russ. 125
Casberd, Rd. M., J. Chest. 387; K.C. 416; P.P. 416
Casement, Wm. and sir W., gen. (**D**), 876; K.C.B. 776
Casey, Jno., dn. Lich. 445
—— Wm., bp. Lim. 638
Cash, Jno., L.M. Dbln. 641
Cashel, Carm. O. M., bp. Killoe. 634
Cashel, Th., visc., form. Th. Somerset (1605) *q.v.*
Cashmere, Mahar. of, G.C.S.I. 800; K.C.S.I. 802
Casimir, I. to V., K. Pld. 90-1
—— IV. (K. Pld.), K.G. 735
—— Jno., K.G. 738
Casolani, Vinc., G.C.M.G. 795; K.C.M.G. 796
Cassels, Andr., M.C.I. 647
Cassey, *see* Cassy
Casilis, E. of
—— Gilb., 3rd E. of, L.H.T. Sc. 497
—— Jno., 6th E. of, Comm. Tr. Sc. 497; L.J. Gen. 522; Ld. Sess. 517
—— Jno., 7th E. of, Comm. Tr. Sc. 497
—— Archd., 12th E. of, aft. 1st M. of Ailsa, *q.v.*, K.T. 748
Cassineto, Wm. R. de, dn. Tal. 468
Cassy (or Cassey), Jno., C.B. Ex. 381
Castanaga, M. of, R. Nds. 83
Castel-Rodrigo, M. of (2), R. Nds. 83
Castelar, E., Pres. Sp. 87
Castellanos, V., Pres. Hdas. 106; Pres. Hti. 105
Castello, Adrian de, bp. B. & W. 428; bp. Her. 441
Castilion, Jno., dn. Roch. 461
Castilla, M. S. del, Pres. S. Salv. 106
—— R., Pres. Pu. 109

For List of Abbreviations, see pp. 944-952.

Castle, Edm., dn. Her. 442
—— Ed. Jas., Q.C. 420
—— Wm. Langf., adm. (**G**) 842
Castlecomer, Chr W., visc., Sec. at W. 233
Castlecoote, C. H., 1st ld., form. C. H. Coote, *q.v.*, C. Cus. Ir. 565-6
Castlemaine, lds. and E. of
—— Rog., E. of, P.C. (1686) 193
—— Rd., 4th ld., L.L. Wmeath, 571
Castlereagh, visc.
—— Rt., visc., aft. 2nd M. of Londonderry, *q.v.*, Amb. Aus. 117; Amb. Pr. 118; Amb. Russ. 125; C. Treas. Ir. 560 and 561; Ch. Sec. Ir. 563; F. Sec. 228; G.C.H. 786; K.G. 743; P.C. 206; Pres. B.C. 252; Sec. St. Ir. 562; W. and C. Sec. 231
—— Fk. Wm. Rt., visc., aft. 4th M. of Londonderry, *q.v.*, L. Admy. 182; L.L. Downsh. 569; P.C. 213; V.C.H. 297
Castlerosse, Val. Aug., visc., aft. 4th E. of Kenmare, *q.v.*, Compt. St. 293; L.L. Kerry, 569; P.C. 216; V.C.H. 297
Castleton, sir Jno., L.M. Dbln. 640
—— Wm., dn. Norw. 455
Castletown, Jno. W., 1st ld., form. J. W. Fitzpatrick, *q.v.*
Castreton, Ad. de, Jy. 365
Castro, Gerv. de, bp. Bgr. 426
—— J., Pres. Vzla. 108
—— J. M., Pres. C. R. 106
Caswell, Tim., C. Exc. 281
Catalan, P. Mno. 31
Catasach (2), bp. Arm. 595
Catellus, *see* Catullus
Catelyn, Catlin and **Catlyn**
—— Nathl. and sir N., Rec. Dbln. 642; S.L. Ir. 591
—— Rd., S.L. 408
—— Rt. and sir R., C.J.Q.B. 370; J.C.P. 378; S.L. 408
Catesby, Jno. and sir J., J.C.P. 378; S.L. 407
—— Wm., K.B. 756
—— Wm., Sp. H.C. 249
Catguaert, bp. Llff. 448
Cathal, bp. Cork, 630
Catharine and **Catherine,** *see also* Katharine
—— (dau. Hy. III.), Pr. E. 10
—— (g. dau. Edw. III.), Pr. E. 11
—— (dau. Jas. II.), Pr. E. 13
—— (of Braganza), Q.C.E. 8
—— Q. Nav. 85
—— Q. Nav. 88
—— I. and II., E. Russ. 90
—— -Laura (dau. Jas. II.), Pr. E. 13
Cathart, Dav., Ld. Sess. 520
Cathcart, hon. Fred., Amb. 121; G. St. 122; Amb. Russ. 125
—— hon. Geo. and sir G., G. C.G.H. 679; gen. (**D**) 884; K.C.B. 777
Cathcart, lds., visc. and E. *See also* lds. Shaw
—— Ch., 8th ld., gen. (**C**) 871
—— Ch. S., 9th ld., Amb. Russ. 125; gen. (**B**) 865; K.T. 747; L.H.C. K. Sc. 546; P.C. 202
—— Wm. S., 10th ld., aft. 1st visc. and E., Amb. Aus. 117; Amb. Russ. 125; Comm. F.

Cathcart, lds., visc. and E.—*cont.*
Ir. 564; gen. (**A**) 860; K.T. 748; L.L. Clkmn. 509; P.C. 206
—— Ch. Murr., 2nd E., G.C.B. 770; G. Can. 692; gen. (**A**) 863
Catherine, *see* Catharine
Catherlough, Rt., 1st E. of, K.B. (1767) 765
Cathmogan, bp. Cork, 630
Cathoire, Mor., K. Ir. 21
Cathrow, Jas., aft. Cathrow-Disney, R. Dr. P.A. 338; Som. H. 332
Catlin and **Catlyn,** *see* Catelyn
Cato, C. P., C. Ro. 45
—— L. P., C. Ro. 45
—— M. P., C. Ro. 43, 45
Cator, Bertie Corn., adm. (**H**) 845
—— Ralph Pet., adm. (**E**) 837
—— Th. Orl., gen. (**D**) 891
—— Wm. and sir W., gen. (**D**) 885; K.C.B. 779
Catryk, Jno., *see* Ketterick
Catty, Ch. Park., gen. (**D**) 914
Catullus, abp. St. Dav. 46
Catulus, C. L., C. Ro. 42-3
—— Q. L., C. Ro. 45
—— Roger Malus, Ld. Chanc. 353
Caturco, Jno. de, M.M. 245
Catus, S. Æ. P., C. Ro. 43
Cauchon, J. E., G. Mtoba. 696
Caudex, A. C., C. Ro. 42
Caudinus, L.C.L., C. Ro. 42
—— P.C.L., C. Ro. 42
Caulaincourt, Off. Nap. 26
Caulfeild, Ch., bp. Nass. 717
—— Jas. M., L.L. Arm. 568
Caulfield, Gord., gen. (**D**) 917
—— Jas., gen. (**D**) 881
—— St. Geo., A.G. Ir. 588; C.J.K.B., Ir. 578; S.G. Ir. 589
—— Wm., J.K.B. Ir. 579; S.L. Ir. 591
Caundish, *see also* Cavendish
—— Rt., S.L. 407
—— Steph., L.M. Lond. 489
Caunton, sir Jno. de, L.H.A. 170
Caurden, Rd., dn. Chich. 434
Causton, Rt. de, L.H.A. 172
Cautley, Prob. Th., and sir P., K.C.B. 782; M.C.I. 646
Cavagnari, Pierre L. Nap. and sir P., K.C.B. 783
Cavalier, Jno., gen. (**C**) 871
Cavan, E. of
—— Rd., 6th E. of, gen. (**B**) 865
—— Rd., 7th E. of, form. visc. Kilcoursie, *q.v.*, gen. (**A**) 860
Cavanagh and **Cavenagh** *see also* Kavanagh
—— Danl., bp. Llin. 622
—— (or Kavenagh), Derm., dn. Llin. 623
—— Gord., gen. (**D**) 915
—— Orf., gen. (**D**) 901; K.C.S.I. 803
Cavaye, Wm., gen. (**D**) 888
Cavaza, E., Pres. Nic. 106
Cave, sir. Amb., C.D.L. 242
—— Hugh de, J. It. 368
—— Jno. de, J.K.B. 371
—— Jno, de, Jy. 365
—— Jno. Halliday, adm. (**H**) 852

Cave—*cont.*
—— Lewis Wm. and sir L., J. Bank. 392; J.Q.B.D. 374; Q.C. 419
—— Steph. and sir S., Amb. Eg. 130; G.C.B. 773; J.A.G. 937; P.C. 217; Paym. G. 245; V.P.B.T. 269
Cavenagh, *see* Cavanagh
Cavendish, *see also* Caundish
—— ld. Fk., F.M., 856; gen. (**A**) 858
—— ld. Fk. Ch., Ch. Sec. Ir. 563; L.T. 162; Sec. Tr. 164
—— hon. Geo., Sec. Tr. Ir. 561
—— hon. Geo. Jno., adm. (**G**) 841
—— ld. Geo., Compt. H. 292; L.L. Dby. 307; P.C. 201
—— sir Hy., C. Treas. Ir. 560
—— hon. Hy. Fk. Compt., gen. (**D**) 882
—— Jno., K.B. (1616) 762
—— Jno. de, C.J.K.B. 370; J.C.P. 378; J. It. 369; S.L. 407
—— ld. Jno., Ch. Ex. 165; L.T. 157; L.T. 158; P.C. 203
—— Ph., adm. (**A**) 813; L. Admy. 178
—— Rd., C. Cus. 275-6
—— hon. Sp. Compt., c.c. ld. Hartington, *q.v.*
—— Wm., K.B. (1625) 763
—— Wm., aft. visc. Mansfield, and E. of Newcastle, *q.v.*, K.B. (1610) 762
Cavendish, lds.
—— Wm., ld., P.C. (1679) 192
—— Wm., ld. form. c.c. M. of Hartington, *q.v.*, aft. 4th D. of Devonshire, *q.v.*
Cavendish-Bentinck, Bentinck
Cawdor, E. of
—— Jno. Fk., 1st E., L.L. Carm. 315
—— Jno. Fk. V., 2nd E., L.L. Carm. 315
Caxton, Jer. de, Jy. 364
Cay, R. H., J. Adm. Sc. 524
Cayley, Jno., C. Cus. Sc. 503
—— Wm., C. Exc. 280
Cazzaiti, Georgio, K.C.M.G. 796
Cea—, *see also* **Cæ—**
Ceadda, St. (or St. Chad), bp. Lond. 450
Ceadwal, K.E. 2
Cearmna, K. Ir. 20
Ceawlin, K.E. 2-3
Ceballos, M.J., Pres. Mex. 103
Cecil, Ch., bp. Bgr. 426; bp. Brl. 439
—— Ed., *see* ld. C., *infra*
—— ld. Eust. B. H. C., S.G.O 260
—— Rt., B.T. 263
—— Rt., aft. sir Rt. and 1st E. of Salisbury, *q.v.*, C.D.L. 242; S. St. 223
—— Wm., aft. 2nd E. of Salisbury, *q.v.*, K.B. 761
—— sir Wm., aft. 1st ld. Burleigh or Burghley, *q.v.*, Chanc Gart. 745; S. St. 223
Cecil, lds.
—— sir Ed., aft. 1st ld. C. and 1st visc. Wimbledon, *q.v.*
Cedde, bp. Her. 441
Ceili, bp. Ard. 607
Cele, Pet., bp. Arm. 595
Celer, Q. C. M., C. Ro. 46
Celestine, I. to V., P. Ro 33-4-5

Cellach, bp. Emly, 625
—— bp. Lich. 443
Celman, M. J., Pres. Arg. 110
Celmund, bp. Her. 441
Celred, K.E. 3
Celsus, bp. Arm. 595
Celwold, K.E. 2
Cely, Jno., bp. Down 603
Cemeliauc, *see* Cimeliau
Cenauc, abp. St. Dav. 463
Cendred, *see* Cenred
Cenelm, K.E. 3
Ceneu, abp. St. Dav. 463
Cenfada, bp. Emly. 625
Cenfail (St.), bp. Clr. 596
Cenred (or Cendred), K.E. 2-3
Censorinus, L. M., C. Ro. 44, 46
Centho, C. C., C. Ro. 42; dt. Ro. 43
Centumalus, C. F. M., C. Ro. 41, 43; dt. Ro. 42
Centwine, K.E. 2
Cenulf, K.E. 3
Cenwal, K.E. 2
Cenwald, K.E. 2
Cenwalh, K.E. 2
Ceolulfus (or Kenulphus), bp. Dorch. 446; bp. Dorch. and Sidr. 446
Ceolbertus, bp. Lond. 451
Ceolnoth, abp. Cant. 430
Ceolred, K.E. 3
Ceolredus, bp. Dorch. 446
Ceolric, K.E. 2
Ceolwulf (3), K.E. 2-3
Ceorl, K.E. 3
Cerco, Q. L., C. Ro. 42
Cerdicus, K.E. 2-3
Cerenhire, bp. Llff. 448
Ceresole, P., Pres. Sw. C. 31
Cerna, V., Pres. Gua. 106
Cerretanus, Q. A. (2), C. Ro. 41
Cerpain, bp. Ardf. and Agh. 639
Cestria, *see also* Chester
—— Jno. de, A.G. 398
Cethegus, C. C., C. Ro. 43
—— M. C., C. Ro. 43-4
—— P, C., C. Ro. 44
Ceynemundus, *see* Cunemund
Cettepaliem, Charloo, C.I.E. 806
Chabot, Louis Wm., visc. de, gen. (**C**) 874; K.C.H. 787
Chachi, Sird. N. S., K.C.S.I. 802
Chaçon, José Mar. de, G. Trin. 721
Chad (St.), abp. Yk. 485; bp. Lich. 443
—— Geo. Wm., Amb. G. St. 122; Amb. Nds. &c. 123; Amb. Pr. 118; Amb. Rep. Col. 134; Amb. Sxy. 120
Chaddesworth, *see* Chadsworth
Chaderton, Ed., M. Chy. 394
—— Wm., bp. Chest. 476; bp. Linc. 447; Wdn. Chr. Ch. Manch. 481
Chads, Hy. and sir H., adm. (**E**) 835· K.C.B. 781
—— Hy. Ducie and sir H., adm. (**D**) 830; G.C.B. 770; K.C.B. 777
—— Wm. Jno., gen. (**D**) 932
Chadsworth (or Chaddesworth) Th. de, abp. Dbln. and Gl. 615; dn. St. Patr. 617
Chadwick, Geo. Alexr., dn. Arm. 597
—— Jas., C. Cus. 274
Chadworth, Jno., bp. Linc. 447
Chaffe, Rt., dn. Ardf. 640
Chaine, Jno., dn. Cnr. 605
Chalenor, *see* Chaloner
Challis, Th., L.M. Lond. 492
Challoner, *see* Chaloner
Chalmer, Jas. A., gen. (**D**) 889
Chalmers, Ch. Dav., gen. (**D**) 933
—— Dav. (2), Ld. Sess. 518
—— Jno. M., K.C.B. 775
—— M. D., C.C.J. 405
—— Sidn., gen. (**D**) 926
—— Th., Mod. K. Sc. 547
—— Wm. and sir W., gen. (**D**) 881; K.C.H. 789; K.H. 790
Chaloner, Challoner and **Chalenor**
—— Jas., G. I. Man, 666
—— Jno., Sec. St. Ir. 562
—— Rt., Bl. M. P.A. 336; Lanc. H. 333
—— Th., adm. (**H**) 849
Chalons, Rt., K.B. 756
Chalton, Th., L.M. Lond. 490
Chalyner, Jno., Rec. Lond. 493
Chamberlain-e and **Chamberlayn-e**
—— Ch., adm. (**A**) 816
—— Crawf. Trott, gen. (**D**) 904
—— Ed., Sec. Tr. 163
—— Fras., G. Gsey. 668
—— Jno., M. Chy. 394
—— Jos., P.C. 219; Pres. B.T. 269; Pres. L.G.B. 256
—— Sir Leon., G. Gsey. 668
—— Nev. B. and sir N., C.C. Mdras. 658; G.C.B. 770; G.C.S.I. 801; gen. (**D**) 899; K.C.B. 779; K.C.S.I. 802
—— Rt., K.B. 761
—— Tank., J.C.P. Ir. 582; J.K.B. Ir. 579
—— Th., dn. Brl. 440
—— Th. and sir T., C.J. Chest. 386; J.C.P. 379; J.K.B. 372; S.L. 409
—— Th. Hardy, gen. (**D**) 919
—— Wm., gen. (**D**) 884
—— sir Wm., K.G. 736
—— Wm. Ch., adm. (**E**) 836
—— Wm. Jno., gen. (**D**) 907
Chambers, Jno., bp. Pboro. 458
—— Mont., Q.C. 417
—— Rd. Well., gen. (**D**) 913
—— sir Rt., C.J. Bgal. 652
—— Th. and sir T., Comm. Serjt. Lond. 495; Q.C. 418; Rec. Lond. 494
—— Walt., bp. Labn. 675; bp. Sing. L. and S. 676
—— Wm., adm. (**A**) 814
—— Wm., L. Prov. Edin. 548
—— Wm., L. Treas. Ir. 558
—— Wm. Fk., K.C.H. 789
Chambre, Alan and sir A., B. Ex. 385; J.C.P. 380; S.L. 412
—— Jno. de la, dn. Winds. 474
—— Wm., dn. St. Patr. 617
—— Wm., gen. (**D**) 900
Chamier, sir Anthy., U.S.S. 226
—— Steph. Hy. Ed., gen. (**D**) 927
Chamorro, F., Pres. Nic. 106
—— P. J., Pres. Nic. 106
Champagne, ——, Off. Nap. 26
—— Arth., dn. Clonm. 600
—— Forbes, gen. (**B**) 866
—— sir Josiah, G.C.H. 786; gen. (**A**) 861
Champain, Jno. Und. Bateman, K.C.M.G. 798
Champion, *see also* Campion
—— Jas. Hyde, gen. (**D**) 916
—— sir Rd., L.M. Lond. 490
Champflower, Walt., L.K. Ir. 575
Champneis, sir Jno., L.M. Lond. 490
Champneys, Wm. Weld., dn. Lich. 445
Chandeler and **Chandler**
—— E. B., G.N. Brk. 696
—— Ed., bp. Dham. 479; bp. Lich. and Cov. 444
—— Geo., dn. Chich. 434
—— Geo., Mast. Coll. Surg. 939
—— Jno., bp. Sal. 467; dn. Sal. 468
—— Rd., C. Cus. 275
—— Th., dn. Her. 442
Chandless, Th., Q.C. 417
Chandos, sir Jno., K.G. 733
Chandos of **Sudeley,** lds
—— Jno., 1st ld., form. sir J. Bridges, *q.v.*; Lt. T.L. 321
—— Edm. (2nd), ld.. K.G. 738
—— Grey, 5th ld., K.B. 761
Chandos, M. and D. of; *see also* Buckingham
—— Rd., M. of, aft. 1st D. of Buckm. and C., *q.v.*, G.C.H. 787
—— R. P. C. T. N., M. of, aft. 2nd D. of Buckm. and C., *q.v.*; L.T. 161
—— Jas., 1st D. of, form. hon. Jas. Bridges, *q.v.*; L.L. Heref. 308
—— Hy., 2nd D. of, form. M. of Carnarvon, *q.v.*
—— Jas., 3rd D. of, form. M. of Carnarvon, *q.v.*; L.S.H. 290; P.C. 203
Chandra Das, C.I.E. 807
Channell, Arth. M., Q.C. 420
—— Wm. F. and sir W., B. Ex. 385; P.P. 417; S.L. 413
Chantrell, Wm., S.L. 407
Chanvill, Wm., Jy. 364
Chaplin, sir Fras., L.M. Lond. 491
—— Frank, gen. (**D**) 921
—— Hy., C.D.L. 243; P.C. 220
Chapman, Alfr. Augs., gen. (**D**) 908
—— sir Benj. Jas., L.L. W. Meath
—— Fredk. Edw. and sir F., G. Bmda. 701; G.C.B. 770; K.C.B. 779; gen. (**D**) 902
—— Jas., bp. Cmbo. 673
—— sir Jno., L.M. Lond. 491
—— Rd., gen. (**B**) 866
—— Steph. Remn. and sir S., G. Bmda. 701; gen. (**B**) 870; K.C.H. 788; K.H. 789
—— Th., S.L. 409
—— Wm. Cox, adm. (**H**) 852
Chappel, Chappell, and **Chapple**
—— Ed., adm. (**H**) 847
—— Jno., dn. Ross, 633
—— Wm., bp. Cork and R. 631; dn. Cash. 627
—— Wm. and sir Wm., J.K.B. 373; S.L. 411

Chardelaw, *see* Shardelow
Charden, Jno., bp. Down and Cnr. 604
Charebert, K. Fr. 22
Charlemagne, E. Gmy. 61; K. Fr. 23
Charlemont, visc. and E. of
— Wm., 2nd visc., gen. (**C**) 871
— Jas., 1st E. of, K.P. 750
— Fras. Wm., 2nd E. of, K.P. 751; L.L. Tyr. 571
— Jas. Mol., 3rd E. of, K.P. 751; L.L. Tyr. 571
***Charles,** bp. Kilf. 635; dn. Kilf. 637
*— dn. Ard. 609
*— dn. Killoe. 637
* Poss. some same pers. Comp. dates.
— C. Ang. 27
— C. Flrs. 81
— C. Lux. 84
— (the Bold), D. Bdy. 29; K.G. 736
— D. Brk. 70
— (de Blois), D. Bry. 28
— (of France), D. Lne. 29
— (archd. of Austria), G.C.B. 768
— K. Bma. 59
— (Martel), K. Fr. 23
— K. Hgry. 60
— (of Austria), K. Nls. 56
— (of Spain), K. Nls. 56
— (of Anjou), K. Scy. 55
— K. Wbg. 81
— Lg. H. Csl. 72
— (son Jas. I.), aft. D. of York and Chas. I., *q.v.*, Pr. E. 13
— (son Chas. I.), aft. Chas. II., *q.v.*, Pr. E. 13
— (son Jas. II.), Pr. E. 13
— Pr. Mkg. 74
— Pr. and K. Rma. 95
— (Gunther), Pr. S. Son. 79
— R. Nds. 83
— (Pr. of Lorraine), R. Nds. 83
— I. and II., K.E. 6
— II. (K.E.), L.H.A. 176
— I. and II., M. Bdn. 67
— I. to III., D. Svy. 54
— I. to III., K. Nav. 85, 87
— I. to III., K. Nls. 56
— I. to III., Pr. Mno. 31
— I. to IV., C. Alçn. 26
— I. to IV., D. Lne. 29, 30
— I. to IV., K. Sp. 86
— I. to VII., Emp. Gmy. 61–2
— V. (Emp. Gmy.), K.G. 737
— I. to X., K. Fr. 23–4–5
— IX. (K. Fr.), K.G. 738
— X. (K. Fr.), K.G. 743
— II., C.P.R. 68; K.G. 740
— II. and III., D. Pma. 54
— VII. to XIV., K. Sw. 92
— XIII. to XV., K. S. and N. 92
— XI. (K.Sw.), K.G. 740
— -Albert, El. Bva. 68
— -Albert, K. Sda. 55
— -Alexr., D. Wbg. 81
— Arth. and sir A., J.Q.B.D. 374; Q.C. 419
— -Alex-Aug., G.D. S. Wr. 79
— -Aug., D. S. Wr. 79
— -Aug., G.D. S. Wr. 79
— -Aug., Pr. Nass. 76
— -Christian, Pr. Nass. 76
— -Edward (g. son Jas. II.), Pr. E. 14

Charles—*cont.*
— -Emmanuel, I. and II., D. Svy. 55
— -Emmanuel, I. and II., K. Sda. 55
— -Eugene, D. Wbg. 81
— -Felix, K. Sda. 55
— -Frederick, D. S. Mgn. 79
— -Frederick, G.D. Bdn. 67
— -Frederick, G.D. S. Wr. 79
— -Frederick, M. Bdn. 67
— -Frederick (M. of Brandenburg Anspach), K.G. 742
— Fk. W. A., D. Brk. 71
— -Leopold, Pr. M. Sch. 74
— -Leopold Fred., G. D. Bdn. 67
— Lewis (g. son Jas. I.), Pr. E. 13
— -Louis, C.P.R. 68; K.G. 739
— -Louis, D. Lca. 52
— -Louis, G.D. Tny. 57
— -Louis-Fred., G.D. Bdn. 67
— -Louis-Fred., G.D.M. Str. 75
— -Louis-Fred., I. and II., Pr. M. Str. 75
— (or Carles), Nichs. Bl. L. P.A. 341; Lanc. H. 333
— -Philip, C.P.R. 68
— -Philip (iss. Jas. I.), Pr. E. 13
— -Theodore, C.P.R. 68; El. Bva. 68
— -Wm., M. Bdn. 67
— -Wm.-Ferd., D. Brk. 70; K.G. 742
— -Wm.-Fk. (Pr. of Leiningen), K.G. 744
Charleton, *see* Charlton
Charlewood, Ed. Ph., adm. (**H**) 849
Charley, Jno., gen. (**D**) 933
— Wm. T. and sir W., Comm. Serjt. Lond. 495; Q.C. 419
Charlotte, Q.C.E. 8
— (g. dau. Jas. I.), Pr. E. 13
— -Augusta Matilda (dau. Geo. III.), Pr. E. 14
— -Augusta-Louisa (dau. Wm. IV.), Pr. E. 15
— -Caroline-Augusta (dau. Geo. IV.), Pr. E. 15
— -Maria (dau. Jas. II.), Pr. E. 13
Charlton and **Charleton,** *see also* Carleton
— Andr., L.P.S. 240
— Ed., K.H. 791
— Job and sir J., C.J. Chest. 386; J.C.P. 379; S.L. 410; Sp. H.C. 249.
— sir Jno., L.J. Ir. 551
— Lewis de, bp. Her. 441
— Rd., K.B. 757
— Rt. de, C.J.C.P. 375; K.B. 755
— Th., bp. Her. 441; L.D., Ir. 551; Ld. Chanc. Ir. 574; L.H.T. 153
— sir Th., Sp. H.C. 248
— Th. R., gen. (**A**) 862
Charnels, Wm., bp. Ferns, 621
Charner, Leon. Vict. Jos., K.C.B. 778
Charobert, K. Hgy. 60
Charretie, Th., gen. (**D**) 881
Chase, Th., L.K. Ir. 575
Charteris, hon. Fras. W., L.T. 161
Charterpool, Hy., ld., also 6th E. of Suffolk, *q.v.*

Chastillon, Hy. de, Jy. 364
Chatfield, Alf. Jno., adm. (**E**) 837
— Fk., Amb. Guat. and C.R. 133
Chatham, E. of
— Wm., 1st E. of, form. W. Pitt (No. 1), *q.v.*; L.P.S. 241; Prem. 143
— Jno., 2nd E. of, G. Gibr. 670; G. Jsey. 667; gen. (**A**) 860; Jud. Com. P.C. 360; K.G. 742; L. Admy. 180; L.P.C. 188; L.P.S. 241; M.G.O. 259; P.C. 204
Chatterton, Hedges Eyre, A.G. Ir. 588; J. Ch. D. Ir. 586; S.G. Ir. 590; V. Chanc. Ir. 586
— Jas., S.L. Ir. 592
— Jas. Ch. and sir J., gen. (**D**) 884; G.C.B. 770; K.C.B. 779; K.H. 790
Chatworth, Th., L.M. Lond. 490
Chaucer, Geoffr., P. Laur. 300
— Th., Sp. H.C. 248
Chaucomb, Hugh de, J. It. 366
Chauncey, Hy., S.L. 411
Chause, Rt., bp. Carl. 475
Chavo, Maur. Pasq. de, G.C.G.H. 678
Chaworth, sir Rd., Ch. Lond. 422
Chawry, Rd., L.M. Lond. 490
Cheale, Jno., Arund. H. 339; Norr. K.A. 329
Cheap, Th., Chn. E.I. Co. 644
Cheape, Jno. and sir J., gen. (**D**) 886; G.C.B. 770; K.C.B. 777
Chediok, Th., K.B. 756
Cheek, Th., Lt. T.L. 322
Cheetham, *see also* Chetham
— Hy., bp. Si. Le. 686
Cheevers (or Chevyrs), Wm., D. Chanc. Ir. 575; J.K.B. Ir. 578; L. Treas. Ir. 558
Cheeke, sir J., S. St. 223
Chelmsford, lds.
— Fk., 1st ld., form. sir F. Thesiger, *q.v.*, Jud. Com. P.C. 361; Ld. Chanc. 358
— Fk. Aug., 2nd ld., form. F. A. Thesiger, *q.v.*, G.C.B. 771; K.C.B. 781; Lt. T.L. 322
Chelred, K.E. 3
Chelreye, Edm., J. It. 369
Chene, Cheyne, Cheney, and **Cheyney,** *see also* Chesney
— Ch., C. Cus. 273
— sir Edm. de, G. Ch. Isl. 667
— Edw., dn. Sal. 468
— Fras., K.B. 759
— Jno. (of Canterbury), K.B. 757
— sir Jno., K.G. 736; Sp. H.C. 248
— Ralph, L.D. Ir. 551; L.K. Ir. 575
— Rd., bp. Brl. 439; bp. Glr. 438
— Rt., gen. (**B**) 867
— Rt. de, bp. Linc. 446
— Th., Const. W. Cast. 322
— Th., dn. Linc. 448; dn. Winch. 471
— Th., K.B. 758
— sir Th., K.G. (1539, *d.* 1558) 738; Tr. H. 291; W.C.P. 319
— Wm., K.B. 755
— Wm., L.P.S. 240; Rec. Lond. 493

For List of Abbreviations, see pp. 944-952.

Chene, Cheyne, Cheney, and Cheyney—*cont.*
—— Wm. and sir W., C.J.K.B. 370; J.C.P. 378; J.K.B. 371; K.B. 756; S.L. 407
Chenevix, Rd., bp. Killoe. 634; bp. Wford. & L. 627
Cheney, *see* Chene
Cheoke, *see* Chooke
Cheolmund, bp. Roch. 459
Cheorl, K.E. 3
Cherif Pasha, G.C.S.I. 801
Cherleton of Powis, Ed. ld., K.G. (1407) 735
Chermside, Hy. Lowth, gen. (**D**) 919
—— sir Rt. Alex., K.C.H. 789; K.H. 789
Chernstone, Jno. de, K.B. 755
Cherry, Ed. Morris, gen. (**D**) 930; Pet. Th., gen. (**D**) 901
Chertsey, abb. of, J. It. 365
Cheryton, Th., bp. Bgr. 426
Cheshire, Jno., S.L. 411
Chesney, *see also* Chene
—— Fras. Rawd., gen. (**D**) 889
—— Fras. Rawd., gen. (**D**) 914
—— sir Geo. Tomk., gen. (**D**) 929
Chesshyre, Augs. Ph., gen. (**D**) 919
—— Jno., adm. (**A**) 820
Chester, *see also* Cestria
—— Harry, gen. (**C**) 873
—— Hy., K.B. 764
—— Jno. de, A.G. 398
—— Pet. de, B. Ex. 382; J. It. 368
—— Th., bp. Elph. 608
—— sir Wm., L.M. Lond. 490
—— Wm. Benn., bp. Killoe. K. Ch. & K. 636
Chester, E. of
—— Ran. Blundevil, E. of, Jy. (1193-4) 363
Chesterfield, E. of
—— Phil., 2nd E. of, P.C. 192
—— Phil., 3rd E. of, P.C. 197
—— Phil. D., 4th E. of, form. ld. Stanhope, *q.v.*, C.Y.G. 298; K.G. 741; L.L. Ir. 556; L.S.H. 290; S. St. 224
—— Phil., 5th E. of, Amb. Spn. 123; Postm. G. 238; L.L. Bucks, 306; K.G. 743; M.H. 302; M.M. 247; P.C. 204
—— Geo., 6th E. of, M.B.H. 303; P.C. 213
Chestrefeld, Jno. de, M. Chy. 393
Chetham, *see also* Cheetham
—— sir Edw. aft. Chetham-Strode, *q.v.*, K.C.B. 777; K.C.H. 789
—— Hy., S.L. 411
—— **-Strode,** *see* Strode
Chetwode, Rd., gen. (**D**) 900
Chetwood, Kn., dn. Glr. 440
Chetwynd, U.S.S. 226
—— Ed., dn. Brl. 440
—— Jno., B.T. 264
—— Wm., E.S.P. 301
Chetwynd, lds. and visc.
—— hon. Wm. Rd., aft. 3rd visc. C., L. Admy. 177; M.M. 247
—— —, ld., Sec. B.T. 270
Cheverel, Rt. de, bp. Carl. 475
Chevars, Jno., dn. Llin. 623
Chevers, Nichs., bp. Llin. 621
—— Norm., C.I.E. 807
Chevreuse, Claude de Loraine, D. de, K.G. 739
Chevyrs, *see* Cheevers
Chewton, Geo., visc., aft. 5th E. of Waldegrave, *q.v.*, P.C. 203; V.C.H. 297
Cheyam, Jno. de, bp. Glasg. 536
Cheyn, Cheyne, and **Cheyney,** *see* Chene
Chi—, *see also* **Chy—**
Chibon, Jno., S.L. 409
Chichelee, Rd., L.M. Lond. 489
Chicheley, *see also* Chycheley
—— Hy., abp. Cant. 431; bp. St. Dav. 464
—— sir Jno., adm. (**A**) 813; L. Admy. 175-6; M.G.O. 258
—— Rt., L.M. Lond. 489
—— sir Th., C.D.L. 242; L. Admy. 175; M.G.O. 258; P.C. 191-2
Chichester and **Chychester**
—— sir Arth. (*see* ld. C., *infra*)
—— hon. Aug. Geo. Ch., gen. (**D**) 907
—— sir Ch., G. Trin. 722
—— ld. Ed., dn. Rph. 603
—— Jno., L.M. Lond. 489; M.M. 246
—— Rt., bp. Exr. 436; dn. Sal. 468
—— Rt., K.B. 761
Chichester, lds. and E. of
—— sir Arth., aft. ld. C., L.D. Ir. 554; L. Treas. Ir. 559
Leigh Family.
—— Fras., 1st E. of, form. ld. Dunsmore, *q.v.*
—— Hy. Th., 3rd E. of, L.L. Suss. 312
Pelham Family.
—— Th., 1st E. of, form. hon. T. Pelham, *q.v.*
—— Th., 2nd E. of, form. hon. T. and ld. Pelham, *q.v.*, Postm. G. 238; Pres. R. Inst. 940
Chidley, Rt., S.L. 408
Child, sir Fras., L.M. Lond. 491
—— sir Lacon. Wm., M. Chy. 396
—— Lawr., bp. St. As. 462
—— Sm., adm. (**A**) 816
—— Wm., M. Chy. 395-6
Childebert, I. to III., K. Fr. 22-3
Childeric, I. to III., K. Fr. 22-3
Childers, Hugh C. E., C.D.L. 243; Ch. Ex. 166; H. Sec. 227; L. Admy. 184-5; L.T. 162; P.C. 218; Paym. G. 245; Sec. Tr. 163; W. Sec. 232
Childs, Jos., gen. (**D**) 891
Chillenden, Wm., abp. Cant. 430
Chillery, Edmd., S.L. 407
Chillingworth —, G. Bah. Isl. 716
Chilperic, K Bdy. 28
—— I. and II., K. Fr. 22-3
Chilton, Geo., C.C.J. 404; K.C. 416
Chineferth, bp. Roch. 459
Chinnery, Geo., bp. Cloy. 631; bp. Killoe. and Kilf. 635; dn. Cork, 632
—— **-Haldane,** *see* Haldane
Chipman, Ward, G. N. Brk. 695
Chippindall, Edw., gen. (**D**) 925
Chisholm, *see also* Chisolme
—— Jas., bp. Dnbl. 532
—— Wm. (2), bp. Dnbl. 532
Chishull, Gilb. de, M. Chy. 393
—— Jno. de, bp. Lond. 451; dn. St. P. 452; L.H.T. 152; L.K. 353
Chisolme, *see also* Chisholm
—— Wm., Ld. Sess. 518
Chitterne, Jno. de, M. Chy. 394
Chitting, Hy., Chest. H. 331
Chitty, Jos. W. and sir J., J. Ch. D. 391; Q.C. 419
—— sir Th., L.M. Lond. 492
—— Walt. Theod., gen. (**D**) 930
Chiverton, Rd., L.M. Lond. 491
Chlorus, C., Emp. Ro. 48
Choke, Rd. and sir R., C.J.C.P. (?) 375; J.C.P. 378; K.B. 757; S.L. 407
Cholmeley, Ran., Rec. Lond. 493; S.L. 408
—— sir Rog., C.B. Ex. 381; C.J.K.B. 370; Rec. Lond. 493; S.L. 408
Cholmondeley, Geo. Jas., C. St. 283; C. Exc. 281
—— Hugh, dn. Chest. 477
—— hon. Jas., gen. (**A**) 858
—— sir Rd., Lt. T.L. 321
Cholmondeley, lds., visc., E. and M. of
—— Hugh, ld. and 2nd visc., aft. 1st E. of, Compt. H. 292; L.L. Chesh. 306; L.L. N. and S. Wales, &c. 314; P.C. 195; Tr. H. 291
—— Geo., 2nd E. of, G. Gsey. 668; gen. (**A**) 857; L.L. Chesh. 306; L.L. N. and S. Wales, &c. 314
—— Geo., 3rd E. of, form. visc. Malpas, *q.v.*, C.D.L. 242; gen. (**B**) 865; L.L. N. and S. Wales, &c. 314; L.P.S. 241; P.C. 198; V. Treas. Ir. 560
—— Geo. Jas., 4th E., aft. 1st M. of, Amb. Pr. 118; C.Y.G. 298; G.C.H. 786; K.G. 743; L.L. Chesh. 306; L.S.H. 290; P.C. 204
—— Geo. Jas. Horatio, 2nd M. of, L.G.C. 288; P.C. 211
—— Wm. Hy. Hugh, 3rd M. of, L.G.C. 288
—— Georgina, Ctss., aft. Mss. of, L.G.C. 288
Chomeley, H., S.L.R. 271
Chooke (or Cheoke), Jno., K.B. 759
Chorleton, sir Job, *see* Charlton
Chouiski, V., R. Russ. 90
Chowne, Chr., gen. (**A**) 861
Chri—, *see also* **Chry—**
***Christian,** bp. Ardf. and Agh. 639
*—— bp. Emly, 625
*—— bp. Gall. 538
*—— bp. Isl. 539
*—— bp. Kilf. 635
* Poss. some same pers. Comp. dates.
—— D. Brk. 70; K.G. 739
—— (of Schleswig-H.), Pr., K.G 745
—— K. Sw. 92
—— (iss. Jas. I.), Pr. E. 13
—— I. and II., El. Sxy. 78
—— I. to IX., K. Dk. 93-4

Christian—*cont.*
—— IV. (K. Dk.), K.G. 739
—— V (K. Dk.), K G. 740
—— IX. (K. Dk.), K.G. 744
—— VIII., D. Obg. 76
—— Ed., G. I. Man, 666
—— -Ernest, D. S.C. and G. 78
—— Evan, G. I. Man, 666
—— F. W. C., Pr., *see* Denmark
—— Hy., adm. (**H**) 852
—— Hood Hanw., adm. (**D**) 825
—— Hugh Clobb. and sir H., adm. (**A**) 816; K.B. 766
—— Jonn., J.C.P. Ir. 582; L.J. App. Ir. 585; S.G. Ir. 590; S.L. Ir. 593
—— -Louis, D. Brk. 70
—— -Louis, Pr. Mkg. 74
—— -Louis, II., Pr. M. Sch. 75
—— Vict. Alb. Ludw. Ern. Anton. (g. son Q. Vict.), Pr. E. 16
—— Wm., G. I. Man, 666
Christianus, *see* Christian
Christie, Archd. and sir A., K.C.H. 788; K.H. 789
—— Gabr., gen. (**A**) 859
—— Hy., Sc. bp. 545
—— Pag., gen. (**D**) 902
—— Hugh Linds., gen. (**D**) 914
—— Jas. Th., C.I.E. 806
—— Saml. Tolfr., gen. (**D**) 902
—— Th. Beats., C.I.E. 808
—— Wm. D., Amb. Arg. 136; Amb. Bzl. 135; Amb. Pgy. 136
—— Wm. Hy. Mahoney, Astr. Roy. 941
Christina, Q. Sw. 92
Christophe, H., Pres. and Emp. Hti. 104
Christopher, bp. Drom. 604
—— D. Wbg. 80
—— Emp. E. E. 50
—— P. Ro. 34
—— I., M. Bdn. 67
—— I. to III., K. Dk. 93
—— III., K. Sw. 92
—— -Bathori, pr. Tva. 60
—— Griff., bp. Lism. 626
—— Leon. Raisb., gen. (**D**) 919
—— Rt. A., C.D.L. 243; P.C. 215
Christopherson, Jno., bp. Chich. 433; dn. Norw. 455
Christy, *see* Christie
Chry—, *see also* **Chri—**
Chrystal, Jas., Modr. K. Sc. 547
Chudleigh, Th., C. Cus. 273-4
—— Th., L.G. Ch. Hosp. 936
Chudworth, Jno., ld., L.L. Glouc. 308
Church, sir Rd., G.C.H. 787; K.C.H. 787
—— Rd. Wm., dn. St. P. 453
—— Th. Ross, C.I.E. 807
Churchill, Ch., G. Ch. Hosp. 936; gen. (**B**) 864
—— Ch., G. Gsey. 668; gen. (**A**) 857; Lt. T.L. 322
—— Geo., adm. (**A**) 813; L. Admy. 176-7
—— Geo. (2), gen. (**B**) 865-6
—— Horace, gen. (**C**) 873
—— Jno. and sir J., K.C. 414; M.R. 388
—— Jno. Sp., G. Dnca. 731; G. Monts. 729; G. Nev. 730; G. Virg. Isl. 731
—— ld. Rand. H. S., Ch. Ex. 166; L.T. 162; P.C. 220; Sec. Ind. 236
—— lady Rand., Cr. Ind. 810
Churchill, lds.
—— Jno., ld., aft. 1st E. and 1st D. of Marlborough, *q.v.*, P.C. 193
Churton, Ed. Towns., bp. Nass. 717
Chute, Chaloner, Sp. H.C. 249
—— Trev. and sir T., G. N.S.W. 703; gen. (**D**) 899; K.C.B. 779
—— Wm., L.L. Hants 311
Chwang-lei, Emp. Ch. 100
Chy—, *see also* **Chi—**
Chycheley, *see* Chicheley
Chychester, *see* Chichester
Chyckwell, Ham., L.M. Lond. 489
Chyne, sir Reyn., L.G.C. Sc. 506
Chyrinton, Wm. de, M. Chy. 393
Cibber, Colley, P. Laur. 301
Cicely (dau. Wm. I.), Pr. E. 9
—— (dau. Ed. IV.), Pr. E. 12
Cicero, M. T., C. Ro. 46-7
Ciceter, Pet. de, dn. Wells 428
Cicurinus, C. V. G., C. Ro. 38
—— P. V. G., C. Ro. 37
—— S. V. C., Dec. Ro. 38
—— T. V. G., C. Ro. 37-8
Cillenius, bp. Ferns, 621
Cimeliau (or Cemeliauc), bp. Llff. 448
Cincinnatus, C. M., C. Ro. 38
—— L. Q., C. Ro. 38 Dt. Ro. 38-9
—— T. Q., Dt. Ro. 39
—— T. Q. P. (2), C. Ro. 39
Cindasuinto, K. Sp. 85
Cineferth, bp. Lich. 443
Cinna, L. C. (4), C. Ro. 45
Cionaoth, K. Ir. 21
Cionfaola, K. Ir. 21
Cissa, K.E. 1
Claggett, Nichs., bp. Exr. 437; bp. St. Dav. 465; dn. Roch. 461
Clanbrassil, E. of
—— Jas., E. of, K.P. (1783) 750
Clancy, Boet., dn. Killoe. 637
—— Jno. de, L.H.T. 152
—— Jos. de, L.H.T. 152
Clancarty, E. of
—— Rd., 2nd E. of, form. visc. Dunlo, *q.v.*, Amb. Aus. 117; Amb. Nds. &c. 122-3; B.T. 268; G.C.B. 767; G.C.H. 786; M.M. 247; P.C. 208; Postm. Gen. 238; Postm. G. Ir. 564; Pres. B.T. 268
Claneboye, *see* Dufferin and C.
Clanricarde, E. and M. of
—— Ulick, 5th E. aft. M. of, L.D. Ir. 554
—— Wm., 7th E. of, L.J. Ir. 555
—— Hy., 12th E. aft. M. of, K.P. 750
—— Jno. Th., 13th E. of, gen. (**A**) 859
—— Ulick J., 14th E. aft. M. of, Amb. Russ. 126; C.Y.G. 298; K.P. 751; L.L. Galw. 569; L.P.S. 241; P.C. 212; Postm. G. 238; U.S.F. 230
Clanwilliam, E. of
—— Rd., 3rd E. of, Amb. Pr. 118; G.C.H. 786; U.S.F. 229
—— Rd. Jas., 4th E. of, form. ld. Gilford, *q.v.*, K.C.B. 782; K.C.M.G. 798
Clapham, Wm., gen. (**D**) 878
Clappa, K.E. 2
Clapton, ld. Geo. Carew, bar. de, G. Gsey. 668
Clare, Ralph, K.B. 763
—— Rd. (or Matth.) de, W.C.P. 317
Clare, visc. and E. of; *see also* D. of Newcastle
Nugent Family.
—— Rt., 1st visc., form. R. Nugent, *q.v.*, aft. E. Nugent, *q.v.*, V. Treas. Ir. 560
Clare Family.
—— Rog., 5th E. of, J. It. 365
Holles Family.
—— Jno., 4th E. of, aft. D. of Newcastle, *q.v.*
Fitzgibbon Family.
—— Jno., 1st E. of, form. Jno., ld. and visc. Fitzgibbon, *q.v.*
—— Jno., 2nd E. of, G. Bbay. 659; G.C.H. 787; K.P. 751; P.C. 211
—— Rd. Hob., 3rd E. of, form. R. H. Fitzgibbon, *q.v.*
Clare, de, *see* Earls of Pembroke
Claremont, Ed. H., gen. (**D**) 904
Clarence, E. and D. of
—— Th., E. of, *see* Th. Lancaster
—— Lion., D. of (son of Ed. III.), K.G. 733; L.L. Ir. 551
—— Th., D. of (son of Hen. IV.), form. Pr. Th., *q.v.*; also E. of Albemarle, *q.v.*, K.G. 734
—— Geo., D. of (bro. of Ed. IV.), form. Pr. Geo., *q.v.*, K.B. 756; K.G. 736; L.L. Ir. 552
—— Wm. Hy., D. of, aft. Wm. IV., *q.v.*, adm. (**A**) 815; G.C.B. 767; G.C.H. 785; Gr. M. Bath, 754; L.H.A. 182; P.C. 205
Clarendon, Earls of; *see also* Rochester
Hyde Family.
—— Ed., 1st E. of, form. sir E. Hyde, *q.v.*, also visc. Cornbury; L.H.S. 286
—— Hy., 2nd E. of, form. ld. Hyde, *q.v.*, L.L. Ir. 555; L.P.S. 240; P.C. 191; P.C. 192
—— Ed., 3rd E. of, P.C. 196
—— Hy., 4th E. of, form. ld. Hyde, *q.v.*
Villiers Family.
—— Th., 1st E. of., form. ld. Hyde, *q.v.*, B.T. 267; C.D.L 243; Postm. G. 238
—— Geo. Wm. F., 4th E. of. form. G. W. F. Villiers, *q.v.*, Amb. Fr. 113; Amb. Pr. 118; C.D.L. 243; F. Sec. 229; K.G. 744; L.L. Ir. 557; L.P.S. 241; P.C. 214; Pres. B.T. 269
Clarges, Rd. Godd. Hare, gen. (**D**) 879; K.C.B. 778
Clarina, lds.
—— Eyre, 1st ld., gen. (**A**) 858
—— Nath. Wm., 2nd ld., gen (**C**) 873
—— Eyre Cl. Hy., 4th ld., gen (**D**) 909
Clark and **Clarke,** *see also* Clerc, Clerk, and Clerke
—— G. Bah. Isl. 716
—— Alured and sir Al., C.C. Bgal. 652; C.C. Ind. 650; C.C. Mdras. 657; F.M. 856; G.C.B. 767; G.G. Ind. 648; gen. (**A**) 859; K.B. 766
—— Alured, dn. Exr. 438

Clark and Clarke—*cont.*
— Andr. and sir A., G.C.M.G. 795; G. Str. Sett. 675; G. W. Austr. 707; gen. (**D**) 927; K.C.M.G. 797; K.H. 792
— sir Andr., Pres. Coll. Ph. 938
— Andr. Ruth., D. Fac. Sc. 527; Ld. Sess. 521; S.G. Sc. 527
— Aug., gen. (**D**) 888
— Casp. Purd., C.I.E. 807
— Ch., B. Ex. 385; S.L. 412
— Ch., gen. (**D**) 925
— Ch., Q.C. 419
— Ch. Mansf., gen. (**D**) 935
— Ed., C. Exc. 279
— Ed., M. Chy. 395
— sir Ed., L.M. Lond. 491
— Ed. Geo. and sir E., Q.C. 419; S.G. 403
— Fk. Le Gros, Pres. Coll. Surg. 939
— Geo., J.A.G. 937; L. Admy. 177; Sec. Adm. 187; Sec. at W. 233
— Geo. Calv., gen. (**D**) 905
— Hy., S.L. 409
— Jas., gen. (**D**) 891
— sir Jas., K.C.B. 783
— Jno., *see* Clerk
— Jno., dn. Sal. 468
— Jno., G. Gsey. 668
— Jno., gen. (**D**) 893; K.H. 792
— Jno., K.H. 790
— Jos., gen. (**D**) 892
— Marsh. Jas. and sir M., C. Basut. 681; K.C.M.G. 798
— Nathl. G., K.C. 415
— Nathl. R., C.C.J. 403; S.L. 413
— Rd., Chambn. Lond. 493; L.M. Lond. 492
— Rt., dn. Tm. 613
— Rt., gen. (**D**) 890
— Rt. and sir R., B. Ex. 384; S.L. 408
— St. Jno. Augs., gen. (**D**) 884; K.H. 790
— Saml., C. Cus. 273-4
— Saml., dn. Clonm. 600
— Saml., M. Chy. 396
— Som. Molyn. W., gen. (**D**) 928
— Th., gen. (**A**) 859
— Th., gen. (**D**) 933
— Th. and sir T., L. Prov. Edinb. 548
— sir Th., M.R. 388; P.C. 199
— Th. Jas., Q.C. 418
— Wm., adm. (**H**) 848
— Wm., dn. Winch. 471
— Wm., gen. (**D**) 905
*— Wm., J. Adm. Ct. 423; J. Pr. Ct. 421
*— Wm. and sir W., Sec. at W. 233
* ? same person.
— sir Wm., gen. (**C**) 873
— Wm. Calc., gen. (**D**) 919
— Wm. Stanl., Chn. E.I. Co. 645
Clark-Kennedy, *see* Kennedy
Clarkson, Eug. Com., Q.C. 419
— Jas. Pr., gen. (**D**) 914
Claude, D. Bry. 28
Claudia, Pr. Mno. 31
Claudius, I. and II., Emp. Ro. 47-8
Claudus, C. Q., C. Ro. 42
Claughton, Piers. Calv., bp. Cmbo. 673; bp. St. Hel. 680
— Th. Lee, bp. Roch. 460; bp. St. Alb. 461
Clavell, Rd. King, gen. (**D**) 907
Claver, Jno., J. It. 369
Clavering, Jno. and sir J., C.C. Ind. 650; gen. (**B**) 865; K.B. 765
— Rt., bp. Llff. 449; bp. Pboro. 458; dn. Her. 442
Clay, Edmd. del, C.J.C.P. Ir. 580; S.L. 407
— Ed. Sneyd, adm. (**D**) 824
— Jno. Gr., gen. (**A**) 862
— Steph. de, J. It. 366
— Wm. and sir W., Sec. B.C. 254
— W. Wald. Pelh., gen. (**B**) 868
Claydon, Rt., M. Chy. 394
Clayton and **Cleyton**
— Jasp., G. Gibr. 669; gen. (**B**) 864
— Jno., dn. Kild. 619
— Ralph, S.L. 412
— Rd., C.J.C.P. Ir. 581; K.C. 415
— Rd., dn. Pboro. 458
— Rt., bp. Clr. 596; bp. Cork and R. 632; bp. Killa. and Ach. 613
*— sir Rt., C. Cus. 274
*— sir Rt., L.M. Lond. 491
* Prob. same pers.
— Rt. Br., gen. (**A**) 862
— Wm., aft. ld. Sundon, *q.v.*, L.T. 156
— sir Wm. Rt., gen. (**D**) 884
Cleasby, Anthy. and sir A., B. Ex. 385; J. Ex. D. 385; Q.C. 418; S.L. 414
— Th., L.G. Gr. Hosp. 854
Cleaveland, *see also* Cleveland
— Fk. Darby, gen. (**D**) 897
Cleaver, Euseby, abp. Dbln. and Gl. 616; bp. Cork and R. 632; bp. Ferns and L. 622
— Wm., bp. Bgr. 426; bp. Chest. 477; bp. St. As. 462
Cleborne, Wm., dn. Kild. 619
Cledauc or **Cledauke,** abp. St. Dav. 463
Clederon, Nichs. or Jno., bp. Bgr. 426
Cleere, Dav., dn. Oss. 623
— Jas., dn. Oss. 622
Cleeve, Dav., dn. Wford. 628
Cleghorn, R. B., G. Nev. 729
Cleiland, Wm. Dougl., gen. (**D**) 877
Cleland, Wm., C. Cus. Sc. 503
Cleland - Henderson, *see* Henderson
Clement, bp. Dnbl. 532
— I. to XII., P. Ro. 32, 34, 35, 36
Clements, Hy. Jno., C. Treas. Ir. 561
— Jno., adm. (**A**) 819; L.G. Gr. Hosp. 854
— Rt., aft. 1st ld., visc., and E. of Leitrim, *q.v.*, C. Cus. Ir. 565
Clementson, Ch. Dox., gen. (**D**) 935
Clemons, Clem., gen. (**D**) 895
Clen, Hy. le, bp. Abdn. 530
Clench, Jno., B. Ex. 384; J.Q.B. 372; S.L. 408
Clendon, Wm., gen. (**D**) 895
Cleophis, K. It. 49
Clephane, Andr. Rt., gen. (**D**) 929
— Dav., C. Exc. Sc. 505
Clephane—*cont.*
— Wm. Dougl. McL., G. Gren. 724; gen. (**C**) 872
Clepsina, C. G. (2), C. Ro. 42
— L. G., C. Ro. 42
Clerach, Muredach, bp. Killa. 612
Cleragh (or Clerk), Th., bp. Killa. 612
Clerc, *see* Clerk
Clere, Rt., K.B. 759
Clerk, Clerke and **Clerc,** *see also* Clarke
— Alexr., K.H. 791
— Barth., D. Arch. 420
— Claude, C.I.E. 807
— Ed., dn. Cloy, 633
— Ed., K.C. 415
— sir Geo., Clk. O. 260; L Admy. 181-2; M.M. 247; P.C. 214; Sec. Tr. 163; U.S. Home, 227; V.P.B.T. 269
— Geo. Russ. and sir G., G. Bbay. 659; G.C.S.I. 800; K.C.B. 782; K.C.S.I. 802; M.C.I. 646; Sec. B.C. 254; U.S. Ind. 236
— Godfr., gen. (**D**) 931
— Hy., gen. (**D**) 910
— Jas., B. Ex. Sc. 524
— Jno., B. Ex. 383
— Jno., bp. B. and W. 428; dn. Winds. 474
— Jno., L.T. 154
— Jno., M.R. 387
— Jno., Q.C. 418
— Jno., S.G. Sc. 526; Ld. Sess. 520
— Jno., S.L. 409
— Jno. le, J. It. 365
— Nichs. le, L. Treas. Ir. 558
— Rt., gen. (**A**) 858
— St. Jno. Aug. (*see* Clark)
— (or Cleragh) Th., bp. Killa. 612
— Th., dn. Chest. 477
— Th., gen. (**D**) 913
— Th., K.C. 415
— Th. Hy. Shadw., K.H. 789
Clermont, lds. and E. of
— Chich. S., 2nd ld., form. Chich. S. Fortescue, *q.v.*, and ld. Carlingford, *q.v.*
— Wm. Hy., 1st E. of, K.P. (1795) 750; Postm. G. Ir. 564
Cletheroe, *see* Clitheroe
Cleveland, *see also* Cleaveland
— Gr., Pres. U.S.A. 103
— Jno., Sec. Adm. 186-7
— Jno. W., gen. (**D**) 887
— Saml., gen. (**B**) 866
Cleveland, E. and D. of
Wentworth Family.
— Th., E. of, form. ld. Wentworth, *q.v.*, C.G.P. 299
Fitzroy Family.
— Ch., 2nd D. of, form. E. of Southampton, *q.v.*
Vane Family.
— Wm. Hy., 1st D. of, form. 3rd E. of Darlington, *q.v.*, K.G. 744
— Hy., 2nd D. of, gen. (**D**) 883; K.G. 744
— Harry Geo., 4th D. of, K.G. 744
Cleyton, *see* Clayton
Cli—, *see also* **Cly—**
Cliderhou (or Clyderhou), Rd., L.H.A. 173
— Rt. de, J. It. 369

For List of Abbreviations, see pp. 944-952.

Clifden, *see also* Clifton
—— Rt., K.B. 757
—— Jas., 1st ld., aft. 1st visc., form. Jas. Agar, *q.v.*, C. Cus. Ir. 565; C. Exc. Ir. 566; Postm. G. Ir. 564
Cliff—e and **Clyff—e**
—— Hy. de, L.K. 354; M.R. 387
—— Jno., S.L. Ir. 592
—— Rt., Wdn. Chr. Ch. Manch. 481
—— Walt., gen. (**B**) 867
—— Wm. de, M. Chy. 393
—— (or Clifford), Wm. de, B. Ex. 382
Cliffer, Walt., L.J. Gen. 522
Clifford and **Clyfford**
—— sir Aug. Wm. Jas., adm. (**D**) 828
—— Hy., K.B. 759
—— hon. Hy. Hugh and sir H., G. C.G.H. &c. 679; gen. (**D**) 908; K.C.M.G. 797
—— Jno., K.B. 757
—— sir Lew., K.G. 734
—— Mill., gen. (**D**) 911; K.H. 791
—— Rd., bp. B. and W. 428; bp. Lond. 451; bp. Worc. 472; dn. Yk. 486
—— Rt. de, L.M. 325
—— Rog. de (2), J. It. 368
—— S., Tell. Ex. 167
—— sir Th , *see* ld. Clifford of Chudleigh, *infra*
—— Wm. de. bp. Emly, 625
—— (or Cliff) Wm. de, B. Ex. 382
—— Wm. Jno. Cav., adm. (**E**) 835; (**F**) 838
Clifford, lds.
—— Jno., 11th ld., K.G. 735
—— Hy., 14th ld., K.B. 758
—— Hy., 15th ld., K.B. 760
—— Fras. ld., aft. 4th E. of Cumberland, *q.v.*. K.B. 761
—— Hy. ld., aft. 5th E. of Cumberland, *q.v.* K.B. 762
Clifford of Chudleigh, sir Th. C., aft. ld., Compt. H. 292; L.H.T. 140; L.T. 155; Tr. H. 291; P.C. 190; Prem. 140
Clifton, *see also* Clifden
—— sir Arth. Benj., gen. (**A**) 863; G.C.B. 770; K.C.B. 776; K.C.H. 788
—— Gam., dn. Her. 442
—— Gerv. (2), K.B. 758
—— Rt., K.B. 757
—— Rt. and sir R., K.B. 764
—— Th., L.L. Cambs. 306
—— Th. Hy., gen. (**D**) 911
—— (of Notts.) Wm. or Gerv., K.B. 761
Cline, *see also* Clyne
—— Hy., Mast. and Pres. Coll. Surg. 939
Clinton and **Clynton**
—— Geoffr. de, Ch. Jr. 362; Jy. 363; L.H.T. 152
—— hon. Geo., adm. (**A**) 814
—— Hy., K.B. 760
—— Hy. and sir H., gen. (**B**) 867; G.C.B. 767; G.C.H. 786; K.B. 766
—— sir Hy., G. Gibr. 670; gen. (**A**) 858; K.B. 765
—— (or Clynton), Pet., B. Ex. Ir. 583
—— Rog. de, bp. Lich. and Cov. 443
—— Wm. de and sir W., aft. E. of Huntingdon, *q.v.*, L.H.A. 171-2; W.C.P. (1331) 318
Clinton and Clynton—*cont.*
—— Wm. Hy. and sir W., G.C.B. 767; gen. (**A**) 861; L.G. Ch. Hosp. 936; L.G.O. 259
Clinton, lds. and E.
—— Jno., ld., K.B. (1501) 759
—— Ed., ld., aft. 1st E. of Lincoln, Const. T.L. 320; K.G. 738; L.H.A. 174
—— Theoph., c.c. ld. C., aft. 4th E. of Lincoln, K.B. 762
—— Ed., c.c. ld. C., aft. 5th E. of Lincoln, K.B. 763
—— Hugh, ld., aft. 1st E. of, K.B. (1725) 764
—— Ch. Rod., ld., form. hon. C. R. Trefusis, *q.v.*
—— C. H. R., ld., L.L. Dev. 307; U.S. Ind. 236
Clipping, Jno., bp. Chich. 432; dn. Chich. 433
Clitheroe and **Cletheroe**
—— sir Chr., L.M. Lond. 491
Clitherow, Jno., gen. (**B**) 870
Clive and **Clyve**
—— Ed. and sir E., B. Ex. 385; J.C.P. 379; S.L. 412
—— Ed. Hy., gen. (**D**) 928
—— Geoffr. de, bp. Her. 441
—— Geo., C.C.J. 403
—— Geo., Curs. B. Ex. 386
—— Geo., U.S. Home, 228
—— sir Geo., Ch. Ex. Ir. 561
—— Hy., U.S. Home, 227
—— Rt., *see* ld. C., *infra*
—— Wm., dn. Chest. 477
Clive, lds.
—— Rt., aft. 1st ld. C., Adm. Ind. 647-8; gen. (**C**) 872; K.B. 765; L.L. Montg. 315; L.L. Salop, 311
—— Ed., 2nd ld., aft. E. of Powis, *q.v.*, G. Mdras. 656; L.L. Salop, 311
Cloal, Nichs., dn. Llin. 623
Clodianus, C. C. L., C. Ro. 46
Clodion, K. Fr. 22
Clodius, K. Fr. 22
—— Emp. Ro. 47
Clodomir, K. Fr. 22
Clœte, Abrm. Jos. and sir A., gen. (**D**) 890; K.C.B. 779; K.H. 791
Clogh, Don. or Rt., dn. Clr. 597
Clonbrock, Rt., ld., L.L.Galw. 569
Clone (or Clove), Jno. de, A.G. 398
Clonin, Nehemh., bp. Clr. 596
Clonmel, Jno., V. and E. of, form. Jno. Scott, and ld. Earlsfort, *q.v.*
Cloos, Jno., dn. Chich. 434
Clopton and **Cloptone**
—— Hugh or Hy., Bl. L. P.A. 341; R. Dr. P.A. 338
—— Hugh, L.M. Lond. 490
—— Rt., L.M. Lond. 490
—— Walt. de and sir W., C.J.K.B. 370; K.B. 755; S L. 407
Close, Fras., dn. Carl. 476
—— Fras. Arden, adm. (**H**) 851
—— Fk., gen. (**D**) 931
—— Nichs., bp. Carl. 475; bp. Lich. and Cov. 444
Clotaire, I. to IV., K. Fr. 22-3
Clough, Ch. Butl., dn. St. As. 463
—— Jno., gen. (**D**) 888
Clove, *see* Clone
Clovis, I. to III., K. Fr. 22-3
Clowes, Th. Ball, adm. (**H**) 846
Clutterbuck, hon. Th., L. Admy. 178; L.T. 156; P.C. 198; Tr. N. 256
Cluvius, C., C. Ro. 47
Clux, sir Hy. Van, K.G. 735
Cly—, *see also* **Cli—**
Clyde, Colin, ld., form. Sir C. Campbell, *q.v.*; F.M. 856; K.C.S.I. 802
Clyderhou, *see* Cliderhou
Clyff, *see* Cliff
Clyfford, *see* Clifford
Clyne, *see also* Cline
—— Dav., Ly. Dep. 513
Clynton, *see* Clinton
Clyve, *see* Clive
Coates, *see also* Cootes
—— Jas., gen. (**A**) 859
Cobbe, Alex. Hugh, gen. (**D**) 925
—— Ch., abp. Dbln. and Gl. 616; bp. Drom. 605; bp. Kild. 617; bp. Killa. and Ach. 613; dn. Ard. 609; dn. Chr. Ch. Dbln. 618
—— Ch., adm. (**A**) 818
—— Geo., gen. (**D**) 885
Cobbeham, *see* Cobham
Cobethorn, Jno., dn. Exr. 437
Cobham and **Cobbeham**
—— Hy. de, J. It. (1218-9) 367
—— Hy. de, G. Ch. Isl. 667; W.C.P. 318
—— Hy. de, W.C.P. (2) 318
—— Jno. de. B. Ex. 352; J.C.P. 376; J.K.B. 371; Jy. 365; S.L. 406
—— Jno. de, Jy. 364
—— sir Jno., L.H.A. 171
—— Regd., K.B. 756
—— Regd., *see* ld. C., *infra*
—— Regd. de, J. It. 368; W.C.P. 317
—— Th., abp. Cant. 430; bp. Worc. 472
—— Wm. de, J. It. 368
Cobham, lds. and visc.
Cobham Family.
—— Regd. and sir R., aft. 1st ld. C., K.G. 733; L.H.A. 172; W.C.P. 318
Brooke Family.
—— Geo., 4th ld., K.G. 738
—— Wm., 5th ld., C.G.S. 356; K.G. 738; L.L. Kent, 309; L.K. 356; W.C.P. 319
—— Hy., 6th ld., K.G. 739; L.L. Kent, 309; W.C.P. 319
Temple and Grenville Families.
—— Rd., 1st ld. and visc., form. sir R. Temple, *q.v.*; Const. W. Cast. 322; F.M. 856; P.C. 196
Cobledyk or **Cobledyl**, Alexr. de, K.B. 755
Cobthach, bp. Saig, 620
Cocherne, *see* Cochrane
Cochet, Jno., adm. (**A**) 819
Cochin, Raj. of, K.C.I.E. 805; K.C.S.I. 803
Cochlan, Rog., gen. (**B**) 867
Cochrane (or Cocherne), Ly. K.A. 513
—— hon. Alex. Ingl. Forr. and sir A., adm. (**A**) 817; G.C.B. 767; K.B. 766
—— hon. Arth. Auckl. D. Leop., adm. (**E**) 835
—— Bas., C. Cus. Sc. 504; C. Exc. Sc. 505; G. I. Man, 666
—— Jas., gen. (**B**) 865
—— Jno. Hy., C. Cus. Sc. 504

Cochrane (or Cocherne)—*cont.*
—— Nathl. Day, adm. (**D**) 826
—— Th., adm. (**H**) 850
—— Th., *vide* ld C., *infra*
—— sir Th. Jno., adm. (**B**) 821; (**C**) 822; (**D**) 826; G.C.B. 770; G. Newfd. 700; K.C.B. 777
—— Wm. Geo., gen. (**D**) 883
Cochrane, lds.
—— Jno., ld., aft. 2nd E. of Dundonald, *q.v.*, Comm. Tr. Sc. 497
—— Th., ld., aft. 6th E. of Dundonald, *q.v.*, C. Ex. Sc. 505
—— Th., ld., aft. 10th E. of Dundonald, *q.v.*, K.B. 766
Cock—, *see also* **Cok—**
Cock and **Cocke**
—— Alf., Q.C. 420
—— Ch. Geo., J. Adm. Ct. 423; J. Pr. Ct. 421
—— Ed., Pres. Coll. Surg. 939
—— Jas., gen. (**D**) 877
—— Jno., Lanc. H. 333; Ptc. P.A. 337
Cockain, Cockayne, and **Cokayne**
—— Fras., L.M. Lond. 492
—— Geo. E., Lanc. H. 333; Norr. K.A. 330
—— Jno., C.B. Ex. 381; J.C.P. 378
—— Th., Rec. Lond. 493
—— sir Wm., L.M. Lond. 491
Cockburn—e & **Cokburn—e**
—— Ad., L.J. Clk. 516; Dep. Tr. Sc. 498; Ld. Sess. 520
—— Alex., Amb. G. St. 121; Amb. H. Tns. 120; Amb. Rep. Col. 134
—— Alex. and sir A., J. Adm. Sc. 524; Ld. Chanc. Sc. 515
—— Alex. Jas. E. and sir A., A.G. 400; C.J.C.P. 376; C.J.Q.B. 370; G.C.B. 773; Jud. Com. P.C. 361; P.C. 216; Pres. Q.B.D. 371; Q.C. 417; S.G. 402; S.L. 413
—— Archd., Bar. Ex. Sc. 524
—— Ch., C. Ex. Sc. 504
—— Ch. Vansitt., gen. (**D**) 902
—— Fras. and sir F., G. Bah. Isl. 716; G. Br. Hond. 714; gen. (**D**) 881
—— Geo., Compt. N. 257
—— Geo. and sir G. (No. 1), adm. (**A**) 818; (**B**) 821; (**C**) 822; G.C.B. 767; K.C.B. 774; L. Admy. 181-2-3; P.C. 210
—— Geo. and sir G., bt. (No. 2), G.C.H. 786; gen. (**A**) 861; K.C.H. 787
—— Hy., J. Sc. 523; Ld. Sess. 520; S.G. Sc. 527
—— Hy. Alex., gen. (**D**) 925
—— Jas., Compt. Sc. 498
—— Jas., gen. (**D**) 917
—— Jas. and sir J., G. Bmda 701; G.C.H. 787; K.C.H. 788; U.S.W. & C. 231
—— Jas. Horsf., adm. (**E**) 835
—— Jas. P., gen. (**D**) 883
—— Jno., B.T. (1715) 264
—— Jno., L. Admy. (1730) 177-8
—— Jno., Ld. Sess. 517-8
—— Jno. and sir Jno., L.J. Clk. 516
—— Rd. and sir Rd., L.P.S. Sc. 501; Ld. Sess. 518; Sec. St. Sc. 502
—— Rt., bp. Ross. 535
—— Wm., dn. Yk. 487
—— sir Wm., gen. (**B**) 868
Cockcraft, Macleod R. Baynes, adm. (**H**) 853
Cocke, *see* Cock
Cockell, Wm., gen. (**B**) 867
—— Wm., S.L. 412
Cockerell, sir Ch., B.C. 253
Cocks, sir Ch., aft. ld. Somers, *q.v.*, Clk. O. 260
—— sir Hy., Coff. H. 293
—— Rd., C. Exc. 279
Cockys, Jno., D. Arch. 420; Vic. Gen. 421
Cocq, Herb. Le, gen. (**D**) 932
Codd, Ed., adm. (**E**) 835; (**F**) 839
—— Ed., adm. (**H**) 849
—— Ed., G. Br. Hond. 714; gen. (**C**) 874
Codrington, Chr., G. Bdoes. 719; G. Leew. Isl. 727
—— Ed. and sir E., adm. (**A**) 819; G.C.B. 768; G.C.M.G. 794; K.C.B. 774
—— Hy. de, M. Chy. 393
—— Hy. Jno. and sir H., adm. (**B**) 821; (**D**) 831; (**E**) 834; K.C.B. 779
—— Jno. de, M. Chy. 393
—— Lath., dn. Kilf. 637
—— Wm., adm. (**E**) 837; L. Admy. 186
—— Wm. Jno. and sir W., G.C.B. 770; G. Gibr. 670; K.C.B. 777; gen. (**D**) 886
Cœ—, *see also* **Cæ—**
Cœliomontanus, C & Dt. Ro., *see* Tricostus
Coell, Jno., M. Chy. 396
Cœmgene, *see* Kevin
Cœna, abp. Yk. 485
Cœnredus, bp. Sels. 432
Coffin, sir Isaac, adm. (**A**) 817; G.C.H. 786
—— Isaac Camp., and sir I., gen. (**D**) 891; K.C.S.I. 802
—— Fras. Holmes, adm. (**D**) 823
—— Guy C., gen. (**D**) 885
—— Hy. Ed., adm. (**H**) 848
—— Jno., gen. (**A**) 861
—— Jno. Pyne, gen. (**C**) 874
—— Jno. Townshend, adm. (**H**) 846
Cogan, Jno., L.J. Ir. 550
Coghill, sir Josh. Cogh., adm. (**D**) 825
—— Marm., Ch. Ex. Ir. 562
Coghlan, Wm. Marc. and sir W., gen. (**D**) 898; K.C.B. 783
Cogley, Patr. M.R. Ir. 585
Cohen, Arth., Q.C. 419
Coidan, Pietr. and sir P., G.C.M.G. 794; K.C.M.G. 796
Coigley, Qu., bp. Drom. 604
Coimbaoth, K. Ir. 20
Coimbra, Pet., D. of, K.G. 735
Cok—, *see also* **Cock—**
Cokam (or Cokeyn), Jno., Rec. Lond. 493
Cokburn—e, *see* Cockburn—e
Cokayne, *see* Cockaine
Coke, *see also* Cook and Cooke
—— Edw., aft. sir E., A.G. 399; C.J.C.P. 375; C.J.K.B. 370; Rec. Lond. 494; S.G. 401; S.L. 409; Sp. H.C. 249
—— sir Jno., L. Admy. 175; L.T. 154; S. St. 223
—— hon. Jno., gen. (**D**) K.C.B. 781
—— Th., aft. ld. Lovell, visc. Coke and E. of Leicester, *q.v.*, K.B. 764; P.C. 195; Postm. G. 238; Tell. Ex. 167; V.C.H. 297
Coke—*cont.*
—— (or Cooke) Wm., J.C.P. 378; M. Chy. 395; S.L. 408
Cokefield (or Cokefeud), Jno. de, J.C.P. 377; J.K.B. 371; Jy. 365
—— Rt. de, J. It. 367
Cokesay, Th., K.B. 758
Cokeyn, *see* Cokam
Colborne, hon. Fras. and sir F., gen. (**D**) 903; K.C.B. 780
—— Jno. and sir J., aft. ld. Seaton, *q.v.*, G.C.B. 769; G.C.H. 787; G.G. N. Am. Prov. 692; G. Upp. Can. 692; K.C.B. 774
—— Wm., R. Dr. P A. 338; Yk. H. 334
Colby, Th., gen. (**D**) 883
—— Wm. de, dn. Yk. 486
Colchester, lds. and visc.
Savage Family.
—— Th., 1st visc., aft. 1st E. Rivers, *q.v.*, L.L. Esx. 308
—— Rd., visc., aft. 4th E. Rivers, *q.v.*, L.L. Chesh. 306
Abbot Family.
—— Ch., 1st ld., form. C. Abbot, *q.v.*
—— Ch., 2nd ld., adm. (**G**) 841; P.C. 215; Paym. G. 245; Postm. G. 239; V.P.B.T. 269
Coldwell, Jno., bp. Sal. 467; dn. Roch. 461
Cole, Ch., Chambn. Ex. 166
—— sir Chr., K.C.B. 774
—— hon. Galbr. Lowry and sir G., G.C.B. 767; G.C.G.H. 679; G. Mtius. 683; gen. (**A**) 861; K.B. 766
—— Hy., D. Arch. 420; Vic. Gen. 421; J. Pr. Ct. 421; dn. St. P. 453
—— Hy., K.C.B. 783
—— Hy. Th., Q.C. 418
—— Hy. Warn., C.C.J. 405; Q.C. 418
—— Jno. Amb., gen. (**D**) 905
—— Mart. Campb., gen. (**C**) 874
—— Pennel, gen. (**D**) 891
—— Rt. Andr., gen. (**D**) 929
—— Th., dn. Norw. 456
—— Wm., dn. Linc. 448
—— Wm. Jno., K.H. 791
—— hon. Wm. Montg., dn. Wford. 628
Colebrooke, Rt., Amb. H. Tns. 120; Amb. Tky. 129
—— sir Th. Ed., L.L. Lnrk. 511
—— Wm. Macbean Geo. and sir W., G. Antig. &c. 727; G. Bah. Isl. 716; G. Bdoes. &c. 719-20-21; G. Br. Gu. 715; G. N. Brk. 696; gen. (**D**) 885; K.H. 790
Colenso, Jno. Wm., bp. Nat. 680
Colepeper and **Colepepper,** *see also* Culpeper
—— Jno. (No. 1), J.C.P. 378; S.L. 407
—— Jno. (No. 2), *see* ld. C., *infra*
—— Mart., dn. Chich. 434
Colepeper, lds.
—— sir Jno. (No. 2), aft. 1st ld. C., Ch. Ex. 154; M.R. 388; P.C. 189
—— Th., 2nd ld., B.T. 263; L.T. 155
Coleridge, Jno. D., *see* ld. C., *infra*

Coleridge—*cont.*
—— Jno. T. and sir J., J.K.B. 373; Jud. Com. P.C. 361; P.C. 216; P.P. 416; S.L. 413
—— W. H., bp. Bdoes. 721
Coleridge, lds.
—— Jno. D. and sir J., aft. ld. C., A.G. 400; C.J.C.P. 376; Jud. Com. P.C. 361; P.C. 218; Pres. C.P.D. 376; Pres. Q.B.D. 371; Q.C. 418; S.G. 402; S.L. 414
Coles, Rt. Bartlett, gen. (**D**) 884
—— Wm. Cowp., gen. (**D**) 885
Colet, Hy., L.M. Lond. 490
—— Jno., dn. St. P. 453
Coleton, Rog. de, dn. Exr. 437
Coleville, *see* Colville
Colla-Uais, K. Ir. 21
Collard, Val., adm. (**D**) 826
Collatinus, L. T., C. Ro. 37
Collen, Edwin Hy. Hayt., C.I.E. 808
—— Geo. W., Ptc. P.A. 337
Coller, Bl. M. P.A. 336
Colleton, sir Pet., G. Bdoes. 719
Collett, Jno. Hick., gen. (**D**) 878
Colley, *see also* Cowley
—— Geo. Pom. and sir G., G Nat. 680; K.C.S.I. 803
Collier, *see also* Collyer
—— Ed., adm. (**D**) 829; (**G**) 840; K.C.B. 779
—— sir Fras. Aug., adm. (**D**) 827; K.C.H. 788
—— Geo., Wdn. Chr. Ch. Manch. 481
—— sir Geo., adm. (**A**) 815
—— sir Geo. Ralph, K.C.B. 774
—— Hy. Theod. Br., adm. (**H**) 846
—— Jno. Fr., C.C.J. 405
—— Rt. Porr. and sir R., aft. ld. Monkhouse, *q.v.*, A.G. 400; J.C.P. 380; Jud. Com. P.C. 361; P.C. 218; P.P. 417; S.G. 402; S.L. 414
Collings, Jesse, Sec. L.G.B. 256
—— Jno. El., gen. (**D**) 906
Collingham, Hugh, dn. St. As. 463
—— Jno., bp. Emly. 625
Collingwood, Clennell, gen. (**D**) 930
—— Cuthb., *see* ld. C., *infra*
—— Ralph, dn. Lich. 445
Collingwood, lds.
—— Cuthb., aft. ld. C., adm. (**A**) 816
Collins, Arth. Jno. Hamm. and sir A., C.J. Mdras. 658; Q.C. 419
—— Arth. Tuck., gen. (**C**) 872
—— Dav., G. V.D.Ld. 708
—— Jas., dn. Killa. 614
—— Rd. Henn., Q.C. 420
—— Rt. Hawth., K.C.B. 784
—— Wm. Anthy., Q.C. 418
Collinson, Rd. and sir R., adm. (**D**) 833; (**E**) 834; (**F**) 838; K.C.B. 780
—— Th. Bern., gen. (**D**) 911
Collow (or Colowe), Wm., S.L. 407
Collyer, *see also* Collier
—— Jno., C.C.J. 403
—— Th., Clar. K.A. 328; Ir. K.A. 338
Collyne, Jno., dn. Wford. 628
*__Colman__ bp. Cld. 598
*—— bp. Clonm. 599
*—— bp. Lindisf. 478
*—— (or Mocholmoc), bp. Lism. 626
*—— (St.), bp. Clonf. 635
*—— (St.), bp. Cloy. 630
*—— (St.), bp. Drom. 604
*—— (St.), bp. Kilmacd. 636
* Prob. some same pers. Comp. dates.
—— Geo., E.S.P. 301
Colneye, Wm. de, J. It. 369
Colocair, bp. Clonm. 599
Coloman, K. Hgy. 59
Colomb, Geo. Th., gen. (**D**) 893
—— Jno. Ch. Ready, K.C.M.G. 799
—— Phil. How., adm. (**H**) 853
Colonsay, Duncan, ld., form. D. McNeill, *q.v.*
Colowe, *see* Collow
Colpoys, Ed. Gr. and sir E., adm. (**A**) 819; K.C.B. 776
—— Jno. and sir J., adm. (**A**) 816; G.C.B. 767; G. Gr. Hosp. 854; K.B. 766; L. Admy. 180
Colquhoun, Archd., Ld. Adv. 526
—— Dan., gen. (**B**) 870
—— sir Jas., L.L. Dumb. 509
—— Jno. and sir J., Compt. Sc. 498; L.G.C. Sc. 506
—— sir Patr. MacC., Q.C. 418
—— Rt., bp. Arg. 537
—— Rt. Gilm. and sir R., Amb. D. Pr. 128; Amb. Eg. 130; K.C.B. 779
Colquitt, Saml. Mart., adm. (**H**) 844
Colthrop, *see* Calthrop
Coltman, Th. and sir T., J.C.P. 380; K.C. 416; S.L. 413
Colton, Jno., abp. Arm. 595; dn. St. Pat. 617; L.J. Ir. 551; L. Treas. Ir. 558; Ld. Chanc. Ir. 574
Columbariis and **Columbiers,** Gilb. de, J. It. 366
—— Matth. de, J. It. 368
Columbine, Fras., G. Gibr. 669; gen. (**B**) 864
Colvile, Colvill—e, and **Coleville**
—— Alexr. (2), Ld. Sess. 518
—— hon. Ch., gen. (**B**) 865
—— hon. Ch. and sir Ch., C.C. Bbay. 660; G.C.B. 767; G.C.H. 786; G. Mtius. 683; gen. (**A**) 862
—— Fiennes M., gen. (**D**) 925
—— Gilb. de, Jy. 363
—— Hy., gen. (**D**) 885
—— Hy. de, J. It. 368
—— sir Jas., Compt. Sc. 498
—— sir Jas., Ld. Sess. 518
—— sir Jas. Wm., C.J. Bgal. 652; Jud. Com. P.C. 361; P.C. 216
—— Jno., Ld. Sess. 518
—— Rt., L.P.S. Sc. 501
Colville of Culross, lds
—— Alexr., 5th ld., adm. (**A**) 814
—— Jno., 7th ld., adm. (**A**) 819
—— Ch. Jno., 8th ld., K.T. 749; M.B.H. 303; P.C. 217
Colvin, Auckl. and sir A., K.C.M.G. 797; L.G. N.W.Pr. and Oudh, 654
—— Jno. Russ., L.G. N.W.Pr. 653
Coman, bp. Ferns, 621
Combe, Jas. Jno., gen. (**D**) 913
Comber, Augs. Kirkw., gen. (**D**) 930
—— Hy. Wandesford, adm. (**H**) 853
—— Th., dn. Dham. 479
Combermere, Stapleton, 1st ld. and visc., form. sir S. Cotton, *q.v.*, C.C. Ind. 650; Comm. F. Ir. 654; Const. T.L. 321; F.M. 856; G. Bdoes. 720; G.C.B. 767; G.C.H. 786; gen. (**A**) 861; K.C.S.I. 802; P.C. 213
Comegern, *see* Comergius
Comerford, Edm., bp. Ferns, 621; dn. Oss. 622
—— Ger., B. Ex. Ir. 584
—— Wm., dn. Oss. 622
Comergius (or Comegern), bp. Llff. 448
Comin—s, *see* Comyn—s
Commerell, Jno. Edm. and sir J., adm. (**E**) 836; G.C.B. 771; K.C.B. 780; L. Admy. 185
Commodus, Emp. Ro. 47
Comonfort, Ig., Pres. Mex. 103
Comuto, Ant. Ct., G.C.M.G. 794
Compton, ld. Alwyne, bp. Ely, 435; dn. Worc. 474
—— hon. sir Fras., gen. (**B**) 864
—— hon. Geo., aft 6th E. of Northampton, *q.v.*, L.T. 157
—— Hatt. and sir H., gen. (**B**) 864; Lt. T.L. 322
—— Hy., bp. Lond. 452; bp. Oxf. 456; P.C. 191-2-3
—— Hy., K.B. 761
—— sir R. H. A.D., C.J. Bbay. 660
—— Sp., K.B. 762
—— hon. Sp., aft. ld. and E. of Wilmington, *q.v.*, K.B. 764; P.C. 196; Paym. G. 244; Sp. H.C. 250
—— ld. Wm., aft. 1st. E. of Northampton, *q.v.*, K.B. 761
—— ld. Wm., aft. 4th M. of Northampton, *q.v.*, adm. (**H**) 849
—— sir Wm., Ld. Chanc. Ir. 575
—— sir Wm., M.G.O. 258; P.C. 190
Comyn and **Comyns**
—— Jno., abp. Dbln. 615
—— sir Jno., B. Ex. 384; C.B. Ex. 382; J.C.P. 379; S.L. 411
—— Nichs., bp. Ferns, 621; bp. Wford. and L. 627
—— Rd., S.L. 411
—— sir Rt. Buckl., C.J. Mdras. 658
—— Wm., gen. (**D**) 876
Conaire, K. Ir. 21
—— -Mor, K. Ir. 21
Conall-Claon, K. Ir. 21
—— Jno. de, dn. Kild. 619
Conan and **Conanus**
—— abp. Lond. 450
*—— bp. Cnwall. 436
*—— bp. S. and M. 483
* Prob. same pers.
—— (St.) bp. Isl. 539
—— K. Wls. 16
—— I. to IV., D. Bry. 28
Conant, *see* Pigott-Conant
Conarus, K. Sc. 18
Conchabhar, K. Ir. 21

*Conchovar, bp. Saig. 620
*Concovar, Fiachry, bp. Cld. 599
* Poss. same pers.
Condari, Ang., G.C.M.G. 794; K.C.M.G. 796
Conduit, Jno., M.M. 247
Conduyte, Reyn., L.M. Lond. 489
Coney, Rd., G. Bmda. 701
Congal - Cionmaghair, K. Ir. 21
Congall, K. Ir. 22
Congallus, I. to III., K. Sc. 18
Congleton, sir Hy. B. and ld. C., form. sir H. B. Parnell, *q.v.*
Congreve, Geo., gen. (**D**) 895
— Ralph, G. Gibr. 669
— sir Wm., gen. (**B**) 866; K.C.H. 787
Congusa, bp. Arm. 595
Coniers, *see* Conyers
Conindicus or **Conindrius**, bp. Isl. 539; bp. S. and M., 483
Coningham, *see also* Conyngham
— Hy., gen. (**D**) 888
— Hy. Ev., gen. (**D**) 929
— Walt., gen. (**D**) 928
Coningsby and **Conyngsby**
— Humph., J.K.B. 372; S.L. 407
— Th., *see* ld. C. *infra*
— Wm., J.K.B. 372; S.L. 408
Coningsby, lds. and E.
— Th., aft. ld. and Earl C., L.J. Ir. 555; L.L. Heref. 308; P.C. 194; V. Treas. Ir. 559
Conlaeth (St.), bp. Kild. 616
*Conmach, bp. Arm. 595
*— bp. Saig. 620
* Poss. same pers.
Conmaol, K. Ir. 20
Connaught [and Strathearn], Arth. W. P. A., D. of (son Q. Vict.), *see also* Pr. Arthur, C.C. Bbay. 660; G.C.I.E. 805; G.C.M.G. 795; G.C.S.I. 801; gen. (**D**) 922; K.T. 749; P.C. 218
— Louise Margt., Dss. of, Cr. Ind. 810
Conn-Ceadchadhach, K. Ir. 21
Connell, Jno. and sir J., J. Adm. Sc. 524
Connemara, Rt. ld., form. R. Bourke, *q.v.*; G.C.I.E. 805
— Susan, lady, form. lady Susan Bourke, *q.v.*
Connesburgh, Edmd., abp. Arm. 595
Connolly, *see* **Conolly**,
Connop, Rd., gen. (**D**) 893
Connor, K. Ir. 21
— Geo. Hy., dn. Winds. 474
— K. of Chenow and de Erpe., K.B. (1394) 755
Conober, D. Bry. 27
Conolly and **Connolly**
— Edw. Josh. R., gen. (**D**) 925
— Jas., gen. (**D**) 906
— Matth., adm. (**H**) 851
— Rd. Geo., gen. (**D**) 902
— Wm., L. J. Ir. 556
— Wm. H., gen. (**D**) 883
Conon, P. Ro. 33
Conrad, C.P.R. 68
— (2), D. Lne. 29
— D. Tny. 57
Conrad—*cont.*
— K. Bdy. 28
— K. Jsm. 97
— I. and II., C. Lux. 841
— I. and II., D. Bma. 59
— I. and II., D. Bva. 67
— I. and II., K. Scy. 55
— I. to IV., D. Su. 80
— I. to IV., E. Gmy. 61
— I. to VII., D. Fca. 71
Conradin, D. Su. 80
Conran, Geo., gen. (**D**) 887
— Hy., gen. (**B**) 868
Conroy, sir Jno., K.C.H. 787
Considine, Jas., K.H. 790
Constable, Jno., dn. Linc. 448
— Rt., S.L. 407
— Th., K.B. 756
Constance, D. Bry. 28
— (dau. Wm. I.), Pr. E. 9
— (g. dau. Edw. III.), Pr. E. 11
— Jno. de, bp. Worc. 472
Constans, Emp. Ro. 48
— II., Emp. E.E. 50
Constantine, P. Ro. 33
— R. Russ. 89
— I. and II., Emp. Ro. 48
— I to IV., K. Sc. 18-9
— III. to XIII., Emp. E.E. 50-1
— Earl. Ld. Chanc. Sc. (1094) 514
Constantiis, Walt. de, bp. Linc. 446; Ch. Jr. 362; Jy. 363; Ld. Chanc. 353
Constantius, I. and II., Emp. Ro. 48
Contentus (St.), bp. Isl. 539; bp. S. and M. 483
Continisanus, L. H. A., C. Ro. 38
Conuil, *see* O'Cnail
Conveal, K. Ir. 20
Conway, Comte de, G. Mtius. 683
— Ed., *see* ld. C., *infra*
— hon. Hy. Seym., C. Ch. 855; F.M. 856; gen. (**A**) 858; P.C. 201; S.G.O. 259; S. St. 224
— Ed., M. Chy. 396
— Hugh and sir H., K.B. 758; L. Treas. Ir. 559
— Th. Syd., gen. (**D**) 904
Conway, lds., visc. and E. of
— sir Ed., aft. 1st ld. and visc., S. St. 223
— Ed., 3rd visc. and 1st E. of, P.C. 192; S .St. 223
Conway-Gordon, *see* Gordon
— Seymour-, *see* Hertford
Conybeare, Fredk., gen. (**D**) 911
— Jno., bp. Brl. 439; dn. Chr. Ch. Oxf. 457
— W. D., dn. Llff. 450
Conyers and **Coniers**
— Ch. Edw., gen. (**D**) 881
— sir Ger., L.M. Lond. 491
— Jno., K.C. 415
— sir Jno., K.G. 736
— sir Jno., Lt. T.L. 321
— Trist., S.L. 410
— Wm., S.L. 409
Conyngsby, *see* Coningsby
Conyll, Nichs., dn. Kild. 619
Conyngham, *see also* Coningham and Cunyngham
— ld. Alb., K.C.H. 787
— ld. Fras., *see* Marq. C. *infra*
Conyngham—*cont.*
— Wm. Burt, C. Treas. Ir. 560
— Wm. Fitz Len., K.C.B. 783
Conyngham, M.
— Hy., 1st M., Const. W. Cast. 322; G.C.H. 786; gen. (**A**) 861; K.P. 750; L.S.H. 290; P.C. 210
— Fras. N., 2nd M., form. ld. Fras. C. and E. of Mountcharles, *q.v.*; gen. (**D**) 893; K.P. 751; L.C.H. 295; L.L. Meath, 570; P.C. 213; Postm. G. 238; U.S.F. 229
— Geo. Hy., 3rd M. of, gen. (**D**) (1877) 917
Coode, Jno. or Jno. Hy., adm. (**D**) 828; K.C.B. 778
— sir Jno., K.C.M.G. 798
— Jno. Penr., gen. (**D**) 917
— Trev. Penr., adm. (**H**) 852
Cook and **Cooke**, *see also* Coke
— Anthy., K.B. 760
— Anthy. Ch., gen. (**D**) 924
— Ch. and sir C., B.T. 264
— Ch., aft. E. of Belmont, *q.v.*, K.B. 765
— Ch. Jno., gen. (**D**) 897
— Crawf., gen. (**D**) 916
— Danl., L.M. Dbln. 641
— Ed., C.C.J. 404
— Ed., U.S.F. 229; U.S. Ir. 563; U.S.W. and C. 231
— (or Coke), Geo., bp. Brl. 439; bp. Her. 442
— Geo., dn. Thist. 749
— Geo., Modr. K. Sc. 547
— Geo., Paym. G. 245
— Geo. and sir G., gen. (**B**) 868; K.C.B. 775
— Hy., gen. (**D**) 935
— Hy. Fk. and sir H., gen. (**C**) 875; K.C.H. 787
*— Jno., J.K.B. Ir. 579
*— Jno., S.G. 401
* Prob. same pers.
— Jno., L.M. Dbln. 641
— Jno., Modr. K. Sc. 547
— Jno. and sir J., D. Arch. 420; K. Adv. 422; Vic. Gen. 421
— Miles, M. Chy. 396
— sir Rd., Ch. Ex. Ir. 562; Sec. St. Ir. 562
— Rt., Chest. H. 331; Clar. K.A. 328; R. Bl. P.A. 344
— sir Saml., L.M. Dbln. 641
— Th., K.B. 757
— Th., L.M. Lond. 490
— Wm., D. Arch. 420; J. Adm. Ct. 422; J. Pr. Ct. 421
— Wm., dn. Ely 435
— Wm., K.C. 415
— Wm. (*see* Coke)
— W. G., G. St. Xtr. 729
— Wm. Hy., C.C.J. 405; Q.C. 418
Cookes, Ch. Hy., gen. (**D**) 920
Cookesley, Jno., adm. (**H**) 846
Cookson, Ch. Alf., K.C.M.G. 799
— Ch. N., gen. (**B**) 868
— Geo., gen. (**B**) 869
— Geo. Rem., gen. (**D**) 913
— Jas. Gast., gen. (**D**) 925
— Mont. H., aft. Cookson-Crackanthorpe, Q.C. 419
Cookworthy, Colin, gen. (**D**) 911
Coombe, Harv. Chr., L.M. Lond. 492

Coombe—*cont.*
— Jno., C.J. Chest. 386; J. Chest. 387
Coomber, Th., dn. Call. 476
Cooper, Alfr., gen. (**D**) 923
— sir A. A., aft. ld Ashley and E. of Shaftesbury, *q.v.*, P.C. 189
— sir Ast. Past., G.C.H. 787; Pres. Coll. Surg. 939
— Ch. Purt., K.C. 416
— hon. Cropl. Ashl., Clk. O. 260
— sir Danl., G.C.M.G. 796; K.C.M.G. 797
— E. H., L.L. Sligo 571
— Edw. Mac. Gilb., gen. (**D**) 921
— Geo., gen. (**D**) 879
— Grey and sir G., L.T. 158; P.C. 206; Sec. Tr. 163
— Hy., gen. (**D**) 897
— Jno., S.L. 408
— Jno. S., C. St. Ir. 568
— Saml., Pres. Coll. Surg. 939
— Th., K.C. 415
— Wm., gen. (**D**) 925
— Wm., gen. (D) 935
Coorteyse, Rd., dn. Chich. 434
Coote, Ch., dn. Kilf. 637
— sir Ch., aft. E. of Mountrath, *q.v.*, Comm. Ir. 555
— Chas. Geo. Hy., gen. (**D**) 917
—Ch. Hy., aft. ld. Castlecoote, *q.v.*, C. Acc. Ir. 567; C. Cus. Ir. 565; C. Exc. Ir. 566; Geneal. St. Patr. 752
— Eyre and sir E. (No. 1), C.C. Ind. 650; G. Jam. 713; gen. (**B**) 865; K.B. 765
— Eyre and sir E. (No. 2), G.C.B. 767; gen. (**A**) 860; K.B. 766
— Rt., adm. (**E**) 835
— Th., C.G.S. Ir. 576; J.K.B. Ir. 579; Rec. Dbln. 642
— Th., R. Rge. P.A. 344
— Wm., dn. Down. 605
Coote, lds.
— Ch., 5th ld. *see* E. of Bellamont
Cootes (or Coates), L.M. Lond. 490
Cope, Anthy., dn. Arm. 597
— Anthy., dn. Elph. 609
— Edm. Ril., gen. (**B**) 868
— Jno. and sir J., K.B. 764; gen. (**B**) 864
— Walt.. Amb. Ecr. 942
— Walt., bp. Clonf. and K. 636; bp. Ferns and L. 622; dn. Drom. 606
Copeland, Wm. P., L.M. Lond. 492
Copinger, *see* Coppinger
Copland, Crawford-, form. Crawford, *q.v.*
Copleston, Ed., bp. Llff 449; dn. Chest. 477; dn. St. P. 453
— Reg. Steph., bp. Cmbo. 673
Copley, Jno. Rt., dn. Kilf. 637
— Jno. S. and sir J., aft. ld. Lyndhurst, *q.v.*, A.G. 400; C.J. Chest. 386; Ld. Chanc. 357; M.R. 388; P.C. 210; S.G. 402; S.L. 413
Copping, Jno., dn. Clr. 597
Coppinger and **Copinger,**
— Maur., S.L. Ir. 592
— sir Wm., L.M. Lond. 490
Corach, Fintan, bp. Clonf. 635
Corban, Wm. Watts, gen. (**D**) 927
Corbet and **Corbett**
— Ed., K.B. 761
— Ed., S.L. 411
— Edwin, Amb. Bzl. 135; Amb. C. Am. 134; Amb. Gr. 129; Amb. Sw. and N. 127; Amb. Swz. 114
— Fras., dn. St. Patr. 618
— Jno., adm. (**E**) 836; K.C.B. 781
— Jno., S.L. 410
— Miles, C.B. Ex. Ir. 583; C.G.S. Ir. 576; Comm. Ir. 554-5
— Regd., J.Q.B. 372; S.L. 408
— Rd., bp. Norw. 455; bp. Oxf. 456; dn. Chr. Ch. Oxf. 457
— Rt., K.B. 759
— sir Rt., C. Cus. 275
— (of Murtone), Roger, K.B. 757
— Stuart, gen. (**D**) 893; K.C.B. 779
— Th., Sec. Adm. 186-7
— Uvedale, C.C.J. 403
Corbiere, —, U.S.S. 225
Corbois (or Corbyl), Wm., abp., Cant. 430
Corbred, I. and II., K. Sc. 18
Corbridge or **Corbrigge,** Th., abp. 485
Corbyl, *see* Corbois
Cordell, Wm. and sir W., M.R. 388; S.G. 401; Sp. H.C. 249
Cordner, Jas. Ed., gen. (**D**) 925
Cordova, G., Pres. Bol. 109
Corfield, Fk. Br., gen. (**D**) 895
— Wm. Rt., gen. (**D**) 895
Cork, E. *See also* Burlington and Orrery
— Rd, 1st E. of, L.J. Ir. 554; L. Treas. Ir. 559
— Rd, 2nd E. of, L. Treas. Ir. 559
— Ch., 3rd E. of, L. Treas. Ir. 559
— Rd., 4th E. of, L. Treas. Ir., 559-60
— Edm., 8th E. of, gen. (**A**) 861; K.P. 751
— Rd. Edm. St. L., 9th E. of, K.P. 751; L.L. Soms. 311; M.B.H. 303; M.H. 302; P.C. 217
***Cormac** and **Cormacus**
*— bp. Ach. 612
*— bp. Ard. 607
*— bp. Arm. 595
*— (2), bp. Cld. 598
*— bp. Dbln. 615
*— bp. Dkld. 533
*— bp. Mortl. 530
*— bp. Saig. 620
* Prob. some same pers. Comp. dates.
Cormac-Ulfhada, K. Ir. 21
Cormailles, Jno. de, K.B. 754
Cornbury, visc., *see* E. of Clarendon
***Cornelius,** abp. Arm. 595
*— abp. Tm. 611
*— bp. Ach. 612
*— bp. Cnr. 604
*— bp. Drom. 604
*— bp. Elph. 608
Cornelius—*cont.*
*— bp. Kilmacd. 636
*— dn. Cash. 627
*— dn. Llin. 623
* Prob. some same pers. Comp. dates
— P. Ro. 32
— L., C. Ro. 47
Corner, Rd. de la, bp. Mth. 559
— Wm. de, bp. Sal. 467
Cornet, sir Pet., G. Ch. Isl. 667
Cornewall, *see* Cornwall
Cornewallis, *see* Cornwallis
Cornhill, Gerv. de, J.It 365; Jy. 363
— Hyde, dn. St. P. 452
— Regd. de, Jy. 364
— (or Cornhull), Wm. de, bp. Lich. and Cov. 443; J. It. 366
Cornhull, *see* Cornhill
Cornicen, P. Æ. E., C. Ro. 39
— S. O., Dec. Ro. 38
Cornificius, L., C. Ro. 46
Cornish, Hy., C. St. 283
— Rt. K. Kestell- (*see also* Kestell), bp. Madr. 689
— sir Saml., adm. (**A**) 814
— Saml. Pitchf., adm. (**A**) 815
— Wm. Rt., C.I.E. 806
Cornutus, Q.S.C., C. Ro. 37
— S. S. C., C. Ro. 37-8; Dec. Ro. 38
Cornvale, Jno., K.B. 756
Cornwall and **Cornewall**
— Ch., adm. (**A**) 813
— Ch. W., L.T. 157-8; P.C. 203; Sp. H.C. 250
— Clem. Fras., G. Br. Cbia. 698
— Edmd. de, K.B. 755
— Edmd. (bar. of Burford), K.B. 758
— F. H. W., bp. Brl. 439; bp. Her. 442; bp. Worc. 473; dn. Cant. 431
— Hy., gen. (**B**) 864
— Jas., C. Exc. 282
— Jno., adm. (**H**) 849
— sir Jno., aft. ld. Fanhope, *q.v.*, K.G. 735
— Wm. Hy., gen. (**D**) 885
Cornwall, D. of, *see* Pr. of Wales
Cornwall, E. of
— Piers Gaveston, E. of (*see also* Gaveston), L.L. Ir. 550
Cornwallis and **Cornewallis**
— hon. Ed., G. Gibr. 670; G. N. Sc. 694; gen. (**B**) 865
— Fk., *see* ld. C., *infra*
— hon. Fk., abp. Cant. 431; bp. Lich. and Cov. 444; dn. St. P. 453; P.C. 202
— (or Cornewalsche), Jas., L.H.A. 173
— (or Cornewalsh), Jas., C.B. Ex. Ir. 582
— hon. Jas., *see* E. of C., *infra*
— hon. Steph., gen. (**C**) 871
— sir Th., Compt. H. 292
— hon. Wm. and sir W., adm. (**A**) 815; G.C.B. 767
Cornwallis, lds., E. and M.
— sir Fk., aft. 1st ld. C., P.C. 190; Tr. H. 291
— Ch., aft. 2nd ld. C.. K.B. 763

Cornwallis, lds., E. and M.—*cont.*
— Ch., 3rd ld., L. Admy. 176; P.C. 194
— Ch., 4th ld., Paym. G. 244; Postm. G. 238
— Ch., 5th ld., aft. 1st E., Const. T.L. 321; P.C. 198
— Ch., 2nd E., aft. 1st M., Amb. Fr. 112; C.C. Ind. 650; Comm. F. Ir. 564; Const. T.L. 321; G.G. Ind. 648; gen. (**A**) 858; K.G. 742; L.L. Ir. 557. M.G.O. 259; P.C. 202; V. Treas. Ir. 560
— Ch., 3rd E. and 2nd M., M.B.H. 303
— hon. Jas., aft. 4th Earl C., bp. Lich. and Cov. 444; dn. Cant. 431; dn. Dham. 479; dn. Winds. 474
Cornwalsche, *see* Carnwallis
Cornwalshe, *see* Cornwallis
Corr, Rd., bp. Lism. 626
Corre, Dav., bp. Clonf. 635
Corrie, Danl., bp. Mdras. 658
— Wm. Tayl., gen. (**D**) 924
Corrin, Dav., dn. Llin. 623
Corry, *see also* Cory
— hon. Arm. Lowr., adm. (**D**) 829; adm. (**H**) 852
— hon. Hy. Th. Lowr., Compt. H. 293; L. Admy. 183-4; P.C. 213; Sec. Adm. 186-7; V.P. Ed. 255
— Isaac, B.T. 268; C. Cus. Ir. 565; C. Treas. Ir. 560-1; Ch. Ex. Ir. 562; P.C. 206
Corsellis, Th., gen. (**D**) 876; K.C.B. 776
Coruncanius, T., C. Ro. 42; Dt. Ro. 42
Corvinus, M., K. Hgy. 60
— M. V. M., C. Ro. 41, 47
Corvus, L. F., C. Ro. 41
— M. V. (6), C. Ro. 40-1; Dt. Ro. 40-1
Cory, *see also* Corry
— Milo, bp. Clonm. 600
— Nichs., adm. (**G**) 842
Corye, Arthr., S.L. Ir. 591
Coryngham, Jno., L. Treas. Ir. 558
Coryton, Jno. R., gen. (**D**) 889
Cosby, D. A. S., aft. ld. Sydney, *q.v.*, Amb. Dk. 127
— Phillips, adm. (**A**) 815
— Th. Pri., gen. (**D**) 933
Coshalett, Wm. de, B. Ex 383
Cosin and **Cosyn**
— Jno., bp. Dham. 479; dn. Pboro. 458
— Rd., D. Arch. 420; M. Chy. 395; Vic. Gen. 421
— Wm., dn. Wells, 429
Cosmo, I. to III., G.D. Tny. 57
Cossigny, Dav. Ch. de, G. Mtius. 683
Cossimbazar, Maharanee of, Cr. Ind. 809
Cossley, Jno., L.G. Ch. Hosp. 936
Cossus, A. C., C. Ro. 39; Dt. Ro. 39
— C. C., C. Ro. 39
— P. C. M., C. Ro. 39
— P. C. R., Dt. Ro. 39
Coster, Wm. Jac., G. Ceyl. 672
Costley, Wm. R. C., gen. (**D**) 886
Cosyn, *see* Cosin
Cot—, *see also* **Cott—**
Coterell, *see* Cotterell
Cotes, Ch. C., L.T. 162
— Geo., bp. Chest. 476
— Jno. de, dn. Lim. 639
— Th., adm. (**A**) 814
— Wash., dn. Lism. 629
Cotesmore, *see* Cottesmore
Cotgrave, Hugh, R.Cr. P.A. 335; Richm. H. 333
Cotismore, *see* Cottesmore
Cott—, *see also* Cot—
Cotta, C. A., C. Ro. 42, 43, 46
— L. A., C. Ro. 44-5-6
— M. A., C. Ro. 46
Cottenham, Ch. Chr., 1st ld. and E. of, form. sir C. C. Pepys, *q.v.*, Ld. Chanc. 358
Cotterel, Cotteril and **Coterell**
— sir Ch., L.P.S. 240
— Patr., L.H.A. 173
— Rt., J.K.B. Ir. 578
— Steph. and sir St., L.P.S. 241; Sec. B. T. 270
— Walt., S.L. Ir. 591
— Wm., bp. Ferns and L. 622; dn. Rph. 602
Cotterill, Hy., bp. Edinb. 543; bp. Gr. Tn. 680
Cottesloe, T. F., ld., form. sir T. F. Fremantle, *q.v.*
Cottesmore (or Cotismore), Jno., C.J.C.P. 375; J.C.P. 378; S L. 407
Cottingham and **Cotyngham**
— Hy., dn. Clonm. 600
— Th. de, L.K. 354; M. Chy. 393
Cottington, Fras., ld., Ch. Ex. 154; Const. T.L. 321; L. Admy. 175; L.H.T. and L.T. 140; L.L. Dors. 307; P.C. 189; S. St. 223
Cotton, sir All., L.M. Lond. 491
— sir Arth. Th., gen. (**D**) 897; K.C.S.I. 802
— sir Ch., adm. (**A**) 816
— Ch. McCl., gen. (**D**) 922
— Corb., gen. (**D**) 898
— Edw. Rowl. Jos., gen. (**D**) 879
— Fras. Vere, adm. (**H**) 848
— Geo., dn. Chest. 477
— Geo. Ed. L., bp. Calc. 653
— Hy., bp. Sal. 467
— Hy., dn. Lism. 629
— Hy. and sir H., Jud. Com. P.C. 361; L.J. App. 389; P.C. 219; Q.C. 418
— Jno., Chn. E.I. Co. 645
— Jno. Hy., dn. Bgr. 427
— sir Jno. Hinde, B.T. 264; Tr. Ch. 294
— sir Rt., Postm. G. 237
— Rowl., adm. (**A**) 815
— Stanh., G. Gibr. 669
— sir Stapleton, aft. ld. and visc. Combermere, *q.v.*, K.B. 766
— Syd. Jno. and sir S., G.C.B. 770; G. Ch. Hosp. 936; gen. (**D**) 893; K.C.B. 778
— Wm., bp. Exr. 437
— Wm. Jas. R., L.M. Lond. 492
— Willoughby and sir W., C.C. Bbay. 660; G.C.B. 769; gen. (**A**) 863; K.C.B. 776; K.C.H. 787
Cottrell, *see* Cotterell
Cotyngham, *see* Cottingham
Couch, Rd. and sir R., C.J. Bbay. 660; C.J. Bgl. 653; Jud. Com. P.C. 362; P.C. 219
Coulson, Foster, gen. (**D**) 877
— Walt., Q.C. 417
Coulter, Wm., L. Prov. Edinb. 548
Countess, Geo., adm. (**A**) 818
Coupar, Wm., bp. Gall. 538
Coupar, ld.
— Jno., ld., Ld. Sess. 517
Couper, *see also* Cooper and Cowper
— Geo. Eb. W. and sir G., C.C. Oudh. 654; Ch. Com. Oudh, 654; K.C.S.I. 803; L.G. N.W. Pr. 653; L.G. N.W. Pr. and Oudh, 654
— Jas. Kempt., gen. (**D**) 930
Couplith, Jas., bp. Cnr. 604
Couraud, Jno., U.S.S. 225
Courcey and **Courcy**
— Edmd., bp. Clr. 596 bp. Ross, 631
— hon. Michl. de, adm. (**A**) 817; (**E**) 835; (**F**) 839
Courtenay and **Courteney,** *see also* Courtney
— Geo. Wm. Conway, adm. (**D**) 830
— Hy. Reg., bp. Brl. 439; bp. Exr. 437
— Hy. Reg., gen. (**D**) 911
— Hugh, *see* ld. C., *infra*
— Jno., L.T. 158
— Jno., S.G.O. 260
— Pet, bp. Exr. 436; bp. Winch. 470; dn. Exr. 437; dn. Winds. 474
— Pet. de, Const. W. Cast. 322; K.G. 734
— Ph., K.C. 416
— Ph. de and sir P., L.H.A. 172-3; L.L. Ir. 551
— Regd., bp. Jam. 713
— Rd., dn. St. As. 463; dn. Wells, 429; bp. Norw. 455
— Rd. Wm., adm. (**H**) 851
— Th. P., B.C. 253; P.C. 211; Sec. B.C. 254; V.P.B.T. 269
— Wm., abp. Cant. 430; bp. Her. 441; bp. Lond. 451; Ld. Chanc. 354; M. Chy. 397
Courtenay, lds.
— Hugh de, aft. 5th ld. C. and 1st E. of Devon (1st Cr.), *q.v.*, K.B. 755
— sir Hugh (son of 2nd E. of Devon), K.G. 733
— Hugh, aft. 4th E. of Devon, *q.v.*, K.B. 755
— Wm., ld., aft. 2nd E. of Devon (2nd Cr.), *q.v.*, K.B. 758
— Wm. Reg., visc., aft. 3rd E. of Devon (3rd Cr.), *q.v.*, Sec. P.L.B. 262
Courteney, *see* Courtenay
Courthorpe, Wm., R. Cr. P.A. 336; Som. H. 332
Courtney, *see also* Courtenay
— Ed. Hy., gen. (**D**) 934
— F., bp. N. Sc. 695
— Leon. H., Sec. Tr. 164; U.S.C. 235; U.S. Home, 228
Courtown, E. of
— Jas., 2nd E. of, K.P. 750; P.C. 204; Tr. H. 291
— Jas. Geo., 3rd E. of, form. visc. Stopford, *q.v.*, C.G.P. 300; C.Y.G. 298; K.P. 751
Cousin-Montauban, *see* Montauban

Couteur, Jno. Le, gen. (**B**) 868
Couza, Pr. A. J., H. Rma. 95
Coveley, Th., A.G. 398
Coventre, *see* Coventry
Coventry, Hy. and sir H., B.T. 263; L. Admy. 175; P.C. 191-2; S. St. 223
— Jno., K.B. 763
— Jno., L.M., 490
— Millis, C.C.J. 406
— Th. and sir Th., J.C.P. 378; S.L. 409
— Th., *see also* ld. C., *infra*
— sir Wm., L.T. 155
Coventry, lds and E. of *Villiers Family.*
— Geo., 1st E. of, form. M. and aft. D. of Buckingham, *q.v.*
— sir Th., aft. 1st ld. C., A.G. 399; L.K. 356; Rec. Lond. 494; S.G. 401
— Wm., 5th E. of, P.C. 197
— Geo. W., 6th E. of, L.L. Worc. 313
— Geo. Wm., 7th E. of, form. visc. Deerhurst, *q.v.*
— Geo. W., 9th E. of, C.G.A. 300; M.B.H. 303; P.C. 219
Coverdale, Miles, bp. Exr. 436
Covingham, Jno., Regr. Gart. 746
Covinis, Rog. de, dn. Lich. 445
Cowan, sir Ed. Port., L.L. Ant. 568
— Jas., L. Prov. Edinb. 548
— Jno., Jy. Sc. 523; Ld. Sess. 521; S.G. Sc. 527
— sir Jno., L.M. Lond. 492
Coward, Wm., S.L. 411
Cowell, Andr., gen. (**A**) 860
— Jno., Vic. Gen. 421
— Jno. Cl. and sir J., gen. (**D**) 921; K.C.B. 783; P.C. 221
— Stepn., K.H. 790
Cowen, *see* Cowan
Cowie, Benj. M., dn. Exr. 438; dn. Manch. 481
— Hugh, Q.C. 419
— Th. H., Q.C. 419
— Wm. Gard., bp. Auckl. (N.Z.) 709
Cowland, Rd., dn. Bgr. 426
Cowley, *see also* Colley
— Rt., M.R. Ir. 585
— Walt., S.G. Ir. 589
Cowley, lds and E.
— Hy., 1st. ld., form. hon. H. and sir H. Wellesley, *q.v.*, Amb. Fr. 113
— Hy. Rd. Ch., 2nd ld. and 1st E., form. hon. H. R. C. Wellesley, *q.v.*, Amb. Aus. 117; Amb. Fr. 113; Amb. G. St. 122; Amb. Swz. 113; K.C.B. 782; K.G. 745; G.C.B. 772; P.C. 215
Cowper, *see also* Couper
— Ch., G. N.S.W. 703; K.C.M.G. 796
— Geo., C. St. 283
— Geo., K.H. 789
— Sp., C.J. Chest. 386; J.C.P. 379; S.L. 411
— Sp., gen. (**B**) 866
— hon. Sp., dn. Dham. 479
— Th., dn. Chr. Ch. Oxf. 457; dn. Glr. 440; bp. Linc. 447; bp. Winch. 471
Cowper—*cont.*
— hon. Wm. F., aft. ld. Mount-Temple, *q.v.*, C.W.P.B. 272; L. Admy. 183; L.T. 160; P.C. 216; Paym. G. 245; Pres. B.H. 255; V.P.B.T. 269; V.P. Ed. 255
Cowper, lds. and E.
— Wm., aft. sir W., visc. Fordwick, *q.v.*, and 1st ld. and 1st Earl C., K.C. 415; Ld. Chanc. 357; L.H.S. 286; L.K. 357; L.L. Herts. 309; P.C. 195
— Geo. Aug., 6th E., L.L. Kent, 309
— Fras. Th. de Gr., 7th E., C.G.A. 300; K.G. 744; L.L. Beds. 306; L.L. Ir. 558; P.C. 218
Cox and **Coxe,** *see also* Cocks
— Ch. and sir C., Chanc. M.G. 799
— Ch. Vyv., gen. (**D**) 910
— Ch. Wm., gen. (**D**) 914
— col. —, G. Gsey. 668
— Dougl., adm. (**H**) 848
— Edm. Hy., gen. (**D**) 926
— Ed. Wm., S.L. 414
— sir Geo. M., gen. (**D**) 876
— Hy. Ch. M., gen. (**D**) 888
— Holl. Wall. Hy., gen. (**D**) 912
— Homersham, C.C.J. 405
*— Jno., gen. (**D**) 890
*— Jno., K.H. 790
* ? same pers.
— Jno. Br., gen. (**D**) 935
— Jno. Ham., gen. (**D**) 911
— Jno. Wm., gen. (**D**) 908
— Michl., abp. Cash. and Eml. 626; bp. Oss. 620
— Rd., bp. Ely, 435; bp. Norw. 455; dn. Chr. Ch. Oxf. 457; dn. Westr. 469
— sir Rd., C. Cus. Ir. 565; C. Exc. Ir. 566
— sir Rd., C.J.C.P. Ir. 580; C.J.Q.B. Ir. 578; J.C.P. Ir. 581; L.J. Ir. 555; Ld. Chanc. Ir. 576
— Saml., G. Bdoes. 720
— Saml. Compt., M. Chy. 397
— Th., dn. Ferns, 623
— Th., gen. (**C**) 872
— Wm., gen. (**D**) 885; K.H. 791
— Wm. Ham., gen. (**D**) 910
Coxe, *see* Cox
Coyn (or Quin), Jno., bp. Lim. 638
Cozens, Alex., R. Cr. P.A. 335
— -Hardy, *see* Hardy
Crabbe, Eyre Jno., K.H. 792
Crackanthorpe, see Cookson-Crackanthorpe
Crackhall, Jno., L.H.T. 152
Cracklow, Hy., gen. (**D**) 890
Craddock and **Cradock,** *see also* Caradoc
— Jno., abp. Dbln. and Gl. 616; bp. Kilm. 607
— Rog., bp. Llff. 449; bp. Wford. 626
— capt. T., G. Bmda. 701
— Wm., dn. St. Patr. 618
Cradock, *see* Craddock
Cragg, Jno. Bettinson, adm. (**H**) 850
Craggs, Jas., P.C. 197; Postm. G. 238; S. St. 224; Sec. at W. 233; Sec. P.O. 239
Craig, Fras., gen. (**A**) 858
— Jas. Hy., G. C.G.H. 678; G. Can. 691; G. Gsey. 669; gen. (**A**) 860; K.B. 766
— sir Lew., Ld. Sess. 519
— Peter, gen. (**A**) 859
— Rd., Ld. Clk. Reg. 525
— Rd. Davis, Q.C. 417
— Wm., J. Sc. 523; Ld. Sess. 520
— Wm. Gibs. and sir W., L.T. 161; Ld. Clk. Reg. 525; P.C. 217
Craigie, Geo. Clerk, Ly. Dep. 513
— Hy. Cad., gen. (**D**) 921
— Peter Edmonstone, gen. (**D**) 885; K.C.B. 779
— Rt., adm. (**G**) 842
— Rt., L.P. Ct. Sess. 516; Ld. Adv. 526; Ld. Sess. 520
Craik and **Craike**
— Alexr., bp. Kild. 617; dn. St. Patr. 618
— Jas., Modr. K. Sc. 547
Craike, *see* Craik
Crail, Adam, bp. Abdn. 530
Cramahé, Hect. C., G. Cam. 691
Crambeth, Matthw. de, bp. Dkld. 533
Cramer, Jno. A., dn. Carl. 476
Crampton, Jno. F. T. and sir J., Amb. Hnr. 120; Amb. Russ. 126; Amb. Spn. 124; Amb. U.S.A. 132; K.C.B. 782
— Ph., L.M. Dbln. 641
— Ph. Cecil, J.K.B. Ir. 579; S.G. Ir. 590
Cranborne, visc.
— Ch., visc. (son of 2nd E. of Salisbury), K.B. 762
— Jas., visc., aft. 6th E. of Salisbury, *q.v.*, L.L. Herts, 309
— Jas., visc., aft. 7th E. and 1st M. of Salisbury, *q.v.*, Tr. H. 291
— Jas. Br. Wm., visc., aft 2nd M. of Salisbury, *q.v.*, B.C. 253
— Rt. A. T., visc., aft. 3rd M. of Salisbury, *q.v.*, P.C. 217; Sec. Ind. 236
Cranbrook, Gathorne, 1st visc., form. G. Hardy, *q.v.*, C.D.L. 243; G.C.S.I. 801; Jud. Com. P.C. 362; L.P.C. 188; Pres. P.L.B. 262; W. Sec. 232
— Jane, Viscss., Cr. Ind. 810
Crancumb, Geoff. de, Const. T. L. 320
Crane, sir Fras., Chanc. Gart. 746
Cranfield, Randal, M.M. 246
Cranfield, ld.
— Lionel, 1st ld., aft. E. of Middx., *q.v.*, L.H.T. 139, 154
Cranley, Th., abp. Dbln. and Gl. 616; L. J. Ir. 552; Ld. Chanc. Ir. 575
Cranley, lds. and visc.
— Geo., 1st ld. and Visc., form. Geo. Onslow, *q.v.*, aft. 4th ld. and 1st Visc. Onslow, *q.v.*
Cranmer, Th., abp. Cant. 431
Cranston, hon. Capt., G. I. Man. 666
Cranstoun, Geo., Fac. Sc. 527; Ld. Sess. 520

Cranworth, Rt. Mons., ld., form. sir R. M. Rolfe, *q.v.*; L.J. App. 388; Ld. Chanc. 358
Crassus, —, Tr., Ro. 46
— C. L., C. Ro. 44
— C.P., C. Ro. 39
— L. L., C. Ro. 45
— L. P. (3), C. Ro. 39, 40, 41; Dt. Ro. 40
— M. L. (3), C. Ro. 46-7
— M. O., C Ro. 42
— M. P., C. Ro. 39; Dt. Ro. 40
— P. C., C. Ro. 46
— P. L., C. Ro. 44-5
—Rd., bp. Lich. and Cov. 444; L.K. 353
— T. O. (2), C. Ro. 42
Crastor, Geo. Ayt., gen. (**D**) 932
Crathilinthus, K. Sc. 18
Craucombe, Jno. de, M. Chy. 393
Crauford, and **Craufurd;** *see also* Crawford
— Arch., Ld. Sess. 518
— sir Ch. Cregan, G.C.B. 768; gen. (**B**) 866
— Fk. Augs. Buch., adm. (**H**) 850
— Jas., Jy. Sc. 523
— Jas., Ld. Sess. 521; S.G. Sc. 527
— sir Jas., amb. Dk. 127; amb. G. St. 121; amb. H. Tns. 120
— Rt., gen. (**C**) 873
Crauford, lds. and E. of
— Dav., ld., L.G.C. Sc. (1256) 506
— Dav., 5th E. of, aft. D. of Montrose, *q.v.*, L.H.A. Sc. 499; L.J. Gen. 522
— Jno., 17th E. of, Comm. Tr. Sc. 497; Ld. Sess. 517
— Wm., 18th E. of. Comm. Tr. Sc. 497; Pres. P.C. Sc. 500
— Jno., 19th E. of, gen. (**B**) 864
— Jno. 20th E. of, gen. (**B**) 865
— Geo., 22nd E. of, gen. (**C**) 873; L.L. Fifesh. 510
Craufurd, *see* Crauford
Craven, Ch., gen. (**A**) 862
— hon. Hy. Aug. Berk., gen. (**C**) 874
— hon. Th., adm. (**A**) 815
— sir Wm., L.M. Lond. 491
Craven, lds. and E. of
1st Creation.
— Wm., 1st ld. and 1st E. of, B.T. 263; gen. (**B**) 864; L. Admy. 175; P.C. 190, 192
— Wm., 6th ld., L.L. Berks. 306
2nd Creation.
— Wm., 7th ld. and 1st E. of, gen. (**B**) 867; L.L. Berks. 306
— Wm., 2nd E. of, L.L. Warw. 312
— Geo. Gr., 3rd E. of, L.L. Berks. 306
Crawford and **Crawfurd,** *see also* Crauford
— Abraham, adm. (**H**) 847
— Adam Fife, gen. (**D**) 887
— Archd., L.H.T. Sc. 496
— Dav., L.G. Ch. Hosp. 936
— Geo., gen. (**D**) 880
Crawford and Crawfurd—*cont.*
— Gibbs, Clk. O. 260
— Jas., G. Bmda. 701
— Jas. R., gen. (**D**) 890
— Jno. W., G. Ont. 692
— Nichs., L.J. Clk. 516; Ld. Sess. 518
— Rt., gen. (**B**) 870
— Rt. F., aft. Copland-Crawford, *q.v.* (**D**) 900
— Th., K.C.B. 784
— Th., Modr. K. Sc. 547
Crawford, lds. and E. of, *see* Crauford
Crawley, Edm., adm. (**A**) 818
— Fras., Curs. B. Ex. 386
— Fras. and sir F., J.C.P. 379; S.L. 409
— Hy. Ow., gen. (**D**) 898
— Th. Rt., gen. (**D**) 909
Crayford, Jno., dn. Emly. 628
Creagh, Andr., dn. Lim. 639
— Ch. Augs. Fitzg., gen. (**D**) 932
— Ch. Vand., G. Br. N. Bno. 676
— Dav., Abp. Cash. 625
— Jas., gen. (**D**) 900
— Jaspar Byng, gen. (**D**) 904
— sir Michl., gen. (**D**) 885; K.H. 790
— sir Michl., L.M. Dbln. 640
— Wm., bp. Lim. 638
Creagh-Osborne, *see* Osborne
Crealock, Hy. Hope, gen. (**D**) 909
Creech, Wm., L. Prov. Edinb. 548
Creevy, Th., Sec. B.C. 254
Creighton, Abm., Ld. Sess. 518
— Danl., gen. (**C**) 871
— Jno., dn. Ferns. 623
— Rt., bp. B. & W. 428; dn. Wells, 429
— (or Crichton), Rt., Ld. Adv. 526; Ld Sess. 518
Crepping, Rd. de, J. It. 368
— Walt. de, J. It. 366; Jy. 364
Cresheld, Rd., J.C.P. 379; S.L. 409
Crespo, J., Pres. Vzla., 108
Cresset (or Cressett), Ed., bp. Llff. 449; dn. Clr. 597; dn. Her. 442
Cressi, *see* Cressy
Cressingham, Hugo de, J. It. 368
Cressy and **Cressi**
— Hugh, dn. Llin. 623
— Hugh, J.K.B. Ir. 579
— Hugh de, J. It. 366; Jy. 363
— Wm. de (2), J. It. 367, 369
Cresswell and **Creswell**
— Cressw. and sir C., J.C P. 380; J. Div. 391; J. Prob. 391; Jud. Com. P.C. 361; K.C. 416; P.C. 216; S.L. 413
— Jno., J.C.P. 379
— (or Treswell), Rt., Som. H. 332
Creswick, Saml., dn. Brl. 440; dn. Wells, 429
Creticus, Q. C. M., C. Ro. 46
Crevequer, Ham. de, W.C.P. 317
Crew and **Crewe**
— Nthl., *see* ld. C. *infra*
— Ran. and sir R., C.J.K.B. 370; S.L. 409; Sp. H.C. 249
— Th. and sir T., S.L. 409; Sp. H.C. 249
Crewe of Stene, lds.
— Nathl., aft. 3rd ld. C., bp. Dham. 479; bp. Oxf. 456; dn. Chich. 434; L.L. Dham. 308; P.C. 191, 193
Crewe of Crewe, lds.
— Jno., 2nd. ld., gen. (**A**) 861
Creye, Wm. de, L.H.A. 170
Crichton, *see also* Crighton and Creighton
— Geo., bp. Dkld. 533; L.P.S. Sc. 501
— sir Jas., L.G.C. Sc. 506
— Rt., bp. Dkld. 533
— (or Creighton), Rt., Ld. Adv. 526; Ld. Sess. 518
Crichton, lds.
— sir Wm., aft. ld. C., Ld. Chanc. Sc. 515
Crida, K.E. 3
Cridda, K.E. 3
Crigan, Cl., bp. S. & M. 484
Crighton, *see also* Crichton and Creighton
— Jno., aft. E. of Erne, *q.v.*, L.L. Ferm. 569
— Wm. Hindl., gen. (**D**) 910
— Jno. Hy., visc., L.T. 162
Criol (or Crioyle), Bert. de, Const. T.L. 320; W.C.P. 317
— Nichs. de, B. Ex. 382; W.C.P. 317
Criomthan, K. Ir. 21
Crioyle, *see* Criol
Cripps, Hy. Wm., Q.C. 418
— Jno. Matth., gen. (**D**) 923
— Wm., L.T. 160-1
Crispe, Hy., Comm. Serjt. Lond. 495
— sir Nichs., C. Cus. 273
Crispin and **Cryspyn**
— Benj., gen. (**D**) 895
— Wm., dn. Llin. 623
Crispinus, T. Q. P. C., C. Ro. (2) 40, 43; Dt. Ro. 40
Crispyn, *see* Crispin
Croft and **Crofte,** *see also* Crofts
— Alf. Woodl., C.I.E. 807; K.C.I.E. 805
— sir Archer, B.T. 264
— Hy., adm. (**H**) 850
— Herb., bp. Her. 442; dn. Her. 442
— Hugh de, K.B. 754
— sir Jas., L.D. Ir. 553
— sir Rd., Tr. H. 291
— Th., M. Chy. 396
— Wm., adm. (**D**) 826; (**G**) 840
Crofton, Fk. Rt. C., gen. (**D**) 930
— hon. Geo. Alf., adm. (**D**) 828
— Jas., gen. (**D**) 920
— Jno. Foll., gen. (**D**) 896
— Rd. Hy., gen. (**D**) 907
— Steph. Sm. Lowth., adm. (**H**) 850
— Th., dn. Elph. 609
Crofts, *see also* Croft
— Jas., gen. (**C**) 871
— sir Jas., Compt. H. 292
— Jno., dn. Norw. 456
Croggan, Jno. Wm., gen. (**D**) 901
Crokat, Wm., gen. (**D**) 890
Croke and **Crooke**
— Geo. and sir G., J.C.P. 379; J.K.B. 372; S.L. 409
— Jno., Ch. Lond. 422
— Jno. and sir J., J.K.B. 372; Rec. Lond. 494; S.L. 409; Sp. H.C. 249

For List of Abbreviations, see pp. 944-952.

Croke and Crooke—*cont.*
—— Jno., M. Chy. 395
—— Rd., Nottm. P.A. 343; R. Dr. P.A. 338
—— Rd., S.L. 410
—— Unton, S.L. 409
—— Wm., S.L. 408
Crokedayk, Ad. de, J It. 368
Crokefield, Rt. de, J. It. 367
Croker, Jno., gen. (**B**) 867
—— Jno. Wils., P.C. 211; Sec. Adm. 186
Crokesley, Jno. de, J. It. 368
—— Rd. de, B. Ex. 382
Cromarty, Geo., 1st E. of, form. G. Mackenzie and visc. Tarbat, *q.v.*, L.J. Gen. 522
Crombie, Jno., Modr. K. Sc. 547
—— Th., gen. (**D**) 897
Cromer, Geo., abp. Arm. 595; Ld. Chanc. Ir. 576
Crommelin, Wm. Ard., gen. (**D**) 907
Cromp, Lawr., Ptc. P.A. 337; Yk. H. 334
Crompton, Ch. and sir C., J.Q.B. 373; Q.C. 419; S.L. 413
—— Th. and sir T., Ch. Lond. 422; J. Adm. Ct. 422; M. Chy. 395; Vic. Gen. 421
—— **-Stansfield,** *see* Stansfield
Cromwell, *see also* Crumwell
—— Hy., adm. (**A**) 817
—— Hy., Comm. Ir. 554; L.L. Ir. 555
—— sir Jno. de, L.H.A. 171
—— Ol. (of Huntingdonshire), K.B. 761
—— Ol., L.L. Ir. 554; Prot. E. 6
—— Rd., Prot. E. 6
—— Th., *see* ld. C. *infra*
Cromwell of Tatshall, lds.
—— Ralph, 3rd ld., L.H.T. 153
Cromwell of Wimbledon, lds.
1st Creation.
—— Th., aft. 1st ld. C. and E. of Essex, *q.v.*, dn. Wells, 429; K.G. 738; L.H.T. and Ch. Ex. 154; L.P.S. 240; M.R. 388; S. St. 223
2nd Creation.
—— Greg., 1st ld., K.B. 760
Cronan (St.), bp. Lism. 626
Cronyn, Benj., bp. Huron, 693
Crooke, *see* Croke
Crookshank, Alexr., J.C.P. Ir. 582
—— Chich. W., K.H. 791
Cropery, bp. Clonm. 599
Crosbie and **Crosby**
—— Brass., L.M. Lond. 492
—— Ch., gen. (**A**) 859
—— Jno., bp. Ardf. and Agh. 639
—— (or Crosseby), Jno. de, M. Chy. 393
—— sir Jno. Gust., G.C.H. 787; gen. (**A**) 861
—— hon. Maur., dn. Lim. 640
—— Wm., gen. (**C**) 872
—— Wm. Arth., C. St. Ir. 568
Cross and **Crosse**
—— Fras., M. Chy. 397
—— Jno., K.H. 790
—— Jno. and sir J., J. Bank. 392; S.L. 413
—— Jno. Kyn., U.S. Ind. 236
—— Rd. A., *see* visc. C., *infra*
—— Rt. Noble, K.H. 792
Cross and Crosse—*cont.*
—— Wm., dn. Ferns, 623; dn. Lism. 629; dn. Llin. 623
—— Wm., gen. (**D**) 879
Cross, visc.
—— Rd. Assh., aft. visc. C., G.C.B. 773; H. Sec. 227; P.C. 218; Sec. Ind. 236
—— Georg., viscss., Cr. Ind. 810
Crosseby, *see* Crosbie
Crossley, Jno. Th., Q.C. 419
Crossman, Saml., dn. Brl. 440
—— Wm., K.C.M.G. 798
Crosthwaite, Ch. H. T., Ch. Com. Bma. 655; Ch. Com. Cent. Pr. 655; K.C.S.I. 804
Crow and **Crowe**
—— Ch., bp. Cloy. 631
—— Jno., K.H. 792
—— Metf., G. Bdoes. 720
—— Th. Carl., gen. (**D**) 920
—— Wm., dn. Clonf. 637
Crowder, Jno., K.H. 791
—— Jno., L.M. Lond. 492
—— Rd. B. and sir R., J.C.P. 380; K.C. 416; S.L. 413
Crowdy, Ch., adm. (**H**) 847
Crowe, *see* Crow
Crowgy, Jno., gen. (**C**) 873
Crowmer, Wm., K.B. 760
—— Wm., L.M. Lond. 489-90
Crowne, Wm., R. Dr. P.A. 338
Crowther, Saml. Adj., bp. Nig. Dist. 689
—— Th., gen. (**C**) 871
Croxton, Wm., gen. (**D**) 876
Crozier, Hy. Darl., gen. (**D**) 934
—— Rd., adm. (**G**) 842
Crudare, Hendr., G. C.G.H. 678
Crum-Ewing, *see* Ewing
Crump, Fk. Oct., Q.C. 420
Crumwell, *see also* Cromwell
—— Jno. de, Const. T.L. 320
Crunmoel, bp. Kild. 616
Crus, L. C. L., C. Ro. 46
Crutchley, Ch., gen. (**D**) 899
Cryspyn, *see* Crispin
Cuadra, V., Pres. Nic. 106
Cuan, bp. Emly, 625
Cubbon, Mark, gen. (**D**) 880; K.C.B. 782
Cubitt, Geo., P.C. 219
—— Wm., L.M. Lond. 492
Cucathach, bp. Saig. 620
Cuddon, Th., M. Chy. 397
—— sir Th., Chambn. Lond. 493
Cudiniscus, bp. Arm. 595
Cuff (or Cuyt), Jno., K.B. 760
Culenus, K. Sc. 19
Culeworth, *see also* Culwurth
—— Wm. de, J.C.P. 376; Jy. 364
Culfwolf, bp. Her. 441
Cullen, K. Sc. 19
—— Arch., K.C. 416
—— Ch., dn. Oss. 623
—— Rt., Jy. Sc. 523; Ld. Sess. 520
—— Wm., gen. (**D**) 881
Culliford, Wm., C. Cus. 274; C. Cus. Sc. 503
Cullin, Patr., bp. Clr. 596
Cullum, Jno. Palm., B. and Gl. K.A. 330; Bath K.A. 785
—— Th. G., B. and Gl. K.A. 330; Bath K.A. 785
Cully, Geo., C.W.F. &c. 273
Culme, Benjn., dn. St. Patr. 618
Culpeper and **Culpepper,** *see also* Colepeper
—— Nichs., K.B. 757
Culross, Abbot of, Ld. Sess. 518
Culross, lds.
—— *see* Colville of C.
Culto, Abrm., C. Exc. Ir. 567
Culwurth, *see also* Culeworth
—— Rd. de, Const. T.L. 320
Cumasach, bp. Arm. 595
Cumba, Jno. de, bp. Cloy. 630
Cumberlege, Ed. Alth., gen. (**D**) 897
Cumberland, C. Br., gen. (**D**) 890
—— Den., bp. Clonf. and K. 636; bp. Kilm. 607
—— Octavius, adm. (**H**) 849
—— Rd., bp. Pboro. 458
—— Wm., adm. (**A**) 820
Cumberland, E. and D. of
Search also under their Christian names
—— Hy., 1st E. of, K.G. 737
—— Geo., 3rd E. of, K.G. 739
—— Fras., 4th E. of, form. Fr. Clifford, *q.v.*
—— Hy., 5th E. of, form. ld. Clifford, *q.v.*
—— Rupert, D. of, *see* Pr. Rupert
—— Geo., D. of (cons. of Q. Anne), *see* Pr. George of Denmark
—— Wm. Aug., D. of (*d.* 1765), capt. gen. 855; K.B. 764; K.G. 741; P.C. 198
—— Hy. Fk., D. of (*d.* 1790), adm. (**A**) 814; K.G. 742; P.C. 202
(*Descendants of K. Geo. III.*)
—— Ern. Aug., 1st D. of, aft. K. of Hanover, *q.v.*, F.M. 854; G.C.B. 767; G.C.H. 785; gen. (**A**) 859; K.P. 751; P.C. 206
—— Pr. Geo. Fk., &c. of, aft. 2nd D. of C. and K. of Hanover, *q.v.*, G.C.H. 786; K.G. 743
—— Pr. Ern. Aug. Wm., &c. of, aft. 3rd D. of C. and Pr. of Hanover, gen. (**D**) 929; K.G 745
—— Thyra, Dss. of, Cr. Ind. 810
Cumbert (Saint), bp. Lich. 443
Cumin, *see* Cummin
Cumine, —, G. Tob. 723
Cuming, *see* Cumming
Cummin and **Cumin**
—— Jno., J. It. 365; Jy. 363
—— Th., Ld. Adv. 526
—— Wm., L J. Gen. 522
Cumming, Cuming and **Cumyng**
—— Arth., adm. (**E**) 835; K.C.B. 782
—— sir Hy. Jno., gen. (**A**) 863; K.C.H. 788
—— Jas., adm. (**A**) 816
—— Jas., gen. (**B**) 869
—— hon. Jno. Lesl., gen. (**A**) 860
—— Wm., adm. (**A**) 820
—— Wm., Ld. Chanc. Sc. 514
—— sir Wm., Ly. K.A. 513
—— Wm. Hy., adm. (**E**) 837
—— Wm. Herb., gen. (**D**) 913

For List of Abbreviations, see pp. 944-952.

Cunemund (orCeynemundus), bp. Her. 441
Cunibert, K. Lmd. 49
Cunliffe, sir Rt. Hy., gen. (**D**) 878
Cunningham—e, *see also* Cunyngham
—— A., dn. Rph. 602
—— Ad., Ld. Sess. 519
—— Alex., C.I.E· 806; gen. (**D**) 897; K.C.I.E. 805
—— Alex. Fk. D., C.I.E. 806
—— C. J., G. Antig. 728
—— Ch., G. St. Xtr. 729
—— Dav., bp. Abdn. 530
—— Dav., gen. (**D**) 887
—— sir Dav., gen. (**B**) 865
—— Geo., gen. (**C**) 872
—— Hy., G. Jam. 712
—— Hy., gen. (**C**) 871
—— Hy. Sta., K.C.I.E. 805
—— Jas., G. Bdoes. 720
—— Jas., gen. (**B**) 866
—— Jno., gen. (**D**) 876
—— Jno., Ld. Sess. 520; S.G. Sc. 527
—— Jno., Modr. K. Sc. 547
—— Percy Sc., gen. (**D**) 922
—— Rt., aft. ld. Rossmore, *q.v.*, Comm. F. Ir. 564; gen. (**A**) 858
—— Th;, gen. (**D**) 883
—— Wm., bp. Arg. 538
—— Wm. Rt., gen. (**D**) 913
Cunyngham—e, *see also* Cunningham—e
—— Arth. Aug. Thurl. and sir A., G.C.B. 771; G. C.G.H. 679; gen. (**D**) 896; K.C.B. 780
—— hon. Fras. Eliz., Cr. Ind. 810
Cuppage, Burke, G. Jsey. 668; gen. (**D**) 899; K.C.B. 780
—— Geo., dn. Cnr. 605
—— Wm., gen. (**B**) 867
Curcumelli, Dem., Ct., K.C.M.G. 796
Cureton, Ch., gen. (**D**) 909
—— Edw., Burg., gen. (**D**) 919
Curio, L. S., C. Ro. 45
Curk, *see* Cusack
Curle (or Curll), Walt., bp. B. and W. 428; bp. Roch. 460; bp. Winch. 471; dn. Lich. 445
Curling, Th. Bl., Pres. Coll. Surg. 939
Curll, *see* Curle
Curme, Ch. Th., adm. (**E**) 837
Curragh, Pet., bp. Lim. 638; L. Treas. Ir. 558
Curran, Dav., dn. Llin. 623
—— Jno. Philp., M.R. Ir. 585
Currey, sir Edm., K.C.H. 788
Currie, Bert. Wodeh., M.C.I. 647
—— Don., K.C.M.G. 797
—— sir Fk., Chn. E. I. Co. 646; M.C.I. 646
—— Mark Jno., adm. (**G**) 842
—— Phil. H. W. and sir P,. K.C.B. 784; U.S.F. 230
—— Rt. Ham., gen. (**D**) 918
Curry, Doug., adm. (**E**) 835
—— Rd., adm. (**D**) 823; (**G**) 840
—— Wm., S.L. Ir. 593
Cursor, L. P.(5), C. Ro. 40-1-2; Dt. Ro. 41
Curteis, sir Th., L.M. Lond. 490
Curteys, Rd., bp. Chich. 433; dn. Chich. 434
Curthopp, Jas., dn. Pboro. 458
Curtis, sir Luc., adm. (**B**) 821; (**D**) 825; K.C.B. 779
—— Rog. and sir R., adm. (**A**) 816; G.C.B. 767
—— Th., L.M. Dbln. 641
—— Wm., and sir W., L.M. Lond. 492
—— Wm. Fk., gen. (**D**) 907
Curton, Oct. P. A. de Ch., K.C.B. 778
Curvus, *see* Corvus
Curwen, Curwin, and **Curwyn**
—— Dav., dn. Llin. 623
—— Hugh, abp. Dblin. & Gl. 616; bp. Oxf. 456; dn. Her. 442; L.J. Ir. 553; Ld. Chanc. Ir. 576
—— Th., K.B. 759
Curzon, Ed., adm. (**H**) 846
—— hon. Hy., adm. (**A**) 818
—— hon. Rd. Wm. P., aft. Earl Howe, *q.v.*, gen. (**D**) 903
—— Rt., B. Ex. 384
Cusack and **Cusake**
—— Ad., J.C.P. Ir. 581
—— (or Curk), Jno., dn. Oss. 622
—— sir Jno., M.R. Ir. 585
—— Nichs., bp. Kild. 616
—— Rt., B. Ex. Ir. 583
—— Th. and sir T., Ch. Ex. Ir. 561; J.C.P. Ir. 581; L.J. Ir. 553; L.K. Ir. 576
Cusake, *see* Cusack
Cusans, Wm. de, L.H.T. 153
Cuserugge, Baldw. de, J. It. 366
Cust, Arth. P. Purey-, dn. Yk. 487
—— hon. Ed. and sir E., gen. (**D**) 884; K.C.H. 788
—— Fras. C., K.C. 415
—— sir Jno., P.C. 201; Sp. H.C. 250
—— Rd., dn. Linc. 448; dn. Roch. 461
—— hon. Wm., C. Cus. 277
Custance, Hamb. Fras.,K.C.B. 783
—— Wm. Nev., gen. (**D**) 903
Cutch, Rao of, G.C.S.I. 801
Cuthard (or Cutheard), bp. Lindisf. 478
Cuthbert, abp. Cant. 430; bp. Her. 441
—— (St.), bp. Lindisf. 478
—— Dav., C. Ex. Sc. 505
—— Jno., S.L. 411
—— Rt. Th. P., gen. (**D**) 924
Cutheard, *see* Cuthard
Cutherwolf, bp. Roch. 459
Cuthfrid, bp. Lich. 443
Cuthred, K.E. 1, 2
Cuthwynus, bp. Dunw. 454
Cutler, Ed., Q.C. 420
—— Jno., S.L. 408
—— Wm., S.L. 408
Cutliffe, Jno. Merv., K.H. 789
Cutto, Abrm., C. Exc. 282
Cutts, Jno., ld., gen. (**B**) 864; L.J. Ir. 555
Cuyler, Corn. and sir C., gen. (**A**) 859
—— Jacob Gl., gen. (**D**) 879
Cuyt, *see* Cuff
Cwichelm, K.E. 2
Cygony, Eug. de, Const. W Cast. 322
Cynan, K. Wls. 16
Cynegils, K.E. 2
Cynewolf, bp. Lindisf. 478
Cynewulf, K.E. 2
Cynric, K.E. 2, 3
Cyrus, K. Pers. 99

D.

D', *see* De
D***, dn. Emly, 628
Daborne, Rt., dn. Lism. 629
Dabrichcourt, *see* Daubrichcourt
Dacca, Meeah of, K.C.S.I. 803
Daccombe, Jno. and sir J., C.D.L. 242
Dachuan (or Mochuan Luachra), bp. Ferns, 621
Dacre, Ran. de, Const. T.L. 320
Dacre, Lords
Fienes Family.
—— Rd., 1st ld., Const. T.L. 320
—— Th., 2nd ld., K.B. 758
—— Hy. Otw., 15th ld., gen. (**A**) 863
—— Th. Cr. Wm., 16th ld., L.L. Esx. 308
Dacre Family.
—— (of the North) Th., 2nd ld., K.B. (1503) 759
—— (of Gillesland) Th., 2nd ld., KG. (1518) 737
Dacres, Jas. Rd., adm. (**A**) 817; (**D**) 825
—— Rd., adm. (**A**) 819; G.C.H. 787
—— Rd. Jas. and sir R., Const. T.L. 321; F.M. 856; G.C.B. 770; gen. (**D**) 890; K.C.B. 777
—— Sydn. Colp., and sir S., adm. (**D**) 832; (**E**) 834; G.C.B. 770; G. Gr. Hosp. 854; K.C.B. 779; L. Admy. 184-5
—— Wm., Geo., gen. (**C**) 874
Daeth, Geo. Wm. Hughes, adm. (**H**) 845
Dagnall, Allen, Guis. P.A. 343; Ptc. P.A. 337; Yk. H. 334
Dagobert, I. to III., K. Fr. 23
Daguilar, Ch. Law. and Sir C., G.C.B. 771; gen. (**D**) 904; K.C.B. 780
—— Geo. Ch., gen. (**D**) 879; K.C.B. 777.
Daivill, Jno. de, J. It. 367
Dakin, Th. and sir T., L.M. Lond. 492
Dalam, Rd de, dn. Lich. 445
Dalbiac, sir Jas. Ch., gen. (**B**) 809; K.C.H. 787
Dale, Rt., Bl. L. P.A. 341; Rich. H. 334
—— Th., dn. Roch. 461

For List of Abbreviations, see pp. 944-952.

Dale—*cont.*
— Val., dn. Wells, 429; J. Adm. Ct. 422
Dales, Saml., K.H. 790
Dalesme, Genl., K.C.B. 778
Daley, *see* Daly
Dalhousie, E. & M. of
— Geo., 8th E. of, L.H.C. K. Sc. 546
— Geo., 9th E. of, C.C. Ind. 651; G.C.B. 767; G. Can. 691; G. N. Sc. 695; gen. (**A**) 861; K.B. 766
— Jas. Andr., 10th E. and 1st M. of, G.G. Ind. 649; K.T. 748; Ld. Clk. Reg. 525; P.C. 214; Pres. B.T. 269; V.P.B.T. 269; W.C.P. 319
— Fox, 11th E., form. Fox Maule and ld. Panmure, *q.v.*
— Geo., 12th E. of, form. Geo. Ramsay, *q.v.*, adm. (**F**) 838
— Jno. Wm., 13th E. of, K.T. 749; L.K. Sc. 503; P.C. 221; Sec. Sc. 502; V.P.Ed Sc. 500
Dalison, Ch., S.L. 410
— Wm., J.Q.B. 372; S.L. 408
Dalkeith, Earls of
— Jas., E. of, son of 1st D. of Buccleugh, K.T. 747
— Fras., E. of, aft. 2nd D. Buccleugh, *q.v.*, K.T. 747
— Ch. W. Hy., E. of, aft. 4th D. Buccleugh, *q.v.*, L.L. Dumfr. 509; L.L. Selk. 512
— Wm. Hy. W., E. of, aft. 6th D. of Buccleugh, *q.v.*, K.T. 249; L.L. Dumfr., 509
Dallas, Alexr. Morr., C.I.E. 808
— Geo., K.C. 415
— Rt. and sir R., C.J.C.P. 376; C.J. Chest. 386; J.C.P. 380; P.C. 210; S.G. 402; S.L. 413
— Th. and sir T., G.C.B. 768; K.C.B. 775
Dalling, Jno. and sir J., C.C. Mdras. 657 G. Jam. 712; gen. (**A**) 859
Dalling and **Bulwer,** Hy. &c., ld., form. sir H. L. Bulwer, *q.v.*
Dalmaticus, L. C. M., C. Ro. 45
Dalmeny, A., ld., L. Adm. 182-3
Dalmer, Th., gen. (**D**) 877
Dalrymple, sir Adolph. Jno., gen. (**D**) 880
— Ch., L.T. 162
— col. —, G. Mtius. (1818) 683
— Dav. (Westhall), Ld. Sess. 520
— sir Dav. (Hailes), Jy. Sc. 523; Ld. Sess. 520
— sir Dav., Ld. Adv. 526
— Hy., Jy. Sc. 522
— Hew. Ld. Sess. 520
— sir Hew, G. Gsey. 669; gen. (**A**) 860
— sir Hew, L.P. Ct. Sess. 516
— Jno., adm. (**A**) 815
— Jno., gen. (**C**) 874
— Jno., L. Prov. Edinb. 548
— sir Jno., Bar. Ex. Sc. 524
— Jno. Ham. Elph., gen. (**D**) 901
— sir J. Pr., gen. (**C**) 874
— Jas. and sir J., aft. 1st visc. Stair, *q.v.*, L.P. Ch. Sess. 516; Ld. Sess. 519
— hon. Jno., and sir J., aft. 2nd visc. and 1st E. of Stair, *q.v.*, L. J. Clk. 516; Ld. Adv. 524; Ld. Sess. 520; Sec. St. Sc. 502
Dalrymple—*cont.*
— Jno., visc., aft. 6th E. of, Stair, *q.v.*, Amb. Pld. 126; Amb. Pr. 118
— sir Jno. Ham., aft. 8th E. of Stair, *q.v.*, gen. (**A**) (1838) 862
— Jno. Ham., aft. visc. D. and 10th E. of Stair, *q.v.*, L.L. Wigt. 512
— Saml., gen. (**A**) 861
— Stair Park, gen. (**C**) 873
— Wm., gen. (**A**) 859; L.G. Ch. Hosp. 936
Dalrymple, visc., *vide supra*
Dalton, Ch., gen. (**D**) 889
— Ch. Jas., gen. (**D**) 902
— Ed. Tuite, gen. (**D**) 917
— Jno., dn. Wford. 628
— Laur., Cal. P.A. 342; R. Cr. P.A. 335; Norr. K.A. 329; Richm. H. 333
— Rt. de, Const. T.L. 320
— Th., C.B. Ex. Ir. 583
Daly and **Daley**
— Cuthb. Feath., adm. (**D**) 827
— Dennis, gen. (**D**) 884
— Denis, J.C.P. Ir. 581
— Dom. and sir D., G. Pr. Ed. Isl. 699; G. S. Austr. 706
— Fk., G. Tob. 723
— Hy. Dom. and sir H., C.I.E. 806; gen. (**D**) 909; K.C.B. 780
— Rt., bp. Cash. E. W. and L. 627; dn. St. Patr. 618
— Rt., bp. Kild. 617
— St. Geo., B. Ex. Ir. 584; J.K.B. Ir. 579; S.L. Ir. 592
Dalyell, Jno. Th., gen. (**D**) 926
— Melv., gen. (**D**) 900
— Rt., gen. (**D**) 883
— Rt. Anstr., K.C.I.E. 805; M.C.I. 647
Dalzell, hon. Arth. Alexr., aft. E. of Carnwarth, *q.v.*; gen. (**D**) 892
— Jno. Alexr., gen. (**D**) 918
— Rt., gen. (**A**) 857
Damaschini (or Damoschini), Aless., G.C.M.G. 795; K.C.M.G. 796
Damasus, I. and II., P. Ro. 33-4
Damer, hon. Geo. L. Dawson-, Compt. H. 293; P.C. 214
— Jno., C. Acc. Ir. 567
Dames, Wm. Longw., gen. (**D**) 893
Damianus, bp. Roch. 459
Dammartin, Mans. de, J. It. 365
Damoschini, *see* Damaschini
Dampier, Hy. and sir H., J.K.B. 373; S.L. 412
— Hy. Luc., C.I.E. 807
— Th., bp. Ely, 435; bp. Roch. 460; dn. Dham. 479; dn. Roch. 461
Dana, Geo. Kinn., gen. (**B**) 868
Danby, Rt. and sir R., C.J.C.P. 375; J.C.P. 378; K.B. 757; S.L. 407
Danby, lds. and Earls of
Danvers family.
— Hy., 1st E. of, form. ld. Danvers, *q.v.*, G. Gsey. 668; K.G. 739
Osborne family.
— Th., 1st E. of, form. visc. Latimer, *q.v.*, aft. M. of Carmarthen, and D. of Leeds, *q.v.*, L. Admy. 175; L.P.C. 187; K.G. 740
Dancaster, Jno., B. Ex. 384
Dance, sir Ch. Webb, K.H. 791
— Edw. Wm., gen. (**D**) 920
— Wm. Towns., adm. (**H**) 847
Dandridge, Ch. Chest., gen. (**D**) 915
— Ed., gen. (**D**) 930
Danesport, Th., G. I. Man. 665
Danett, Th., dn. Winds. 474; Regr. Gart. 746
Dangely, Regn. de St. John, G.C.B. 769
Daniel and **Daniell**
*— (or St. Daniel), bp. Bgr. 425
*— bp. Cloy. 630
*— bp. Kilf. 635
*— bp. Llin. 621
*— bp. Ross, 631
*— bp. Sels. 432
*— bp. Winch. 470
*— dn. Kild. 619
* Prob. some same pers. Comp. dates
— (3) K. Ir. 21-2
— I., P. Mgo. 95
— -Alexandrowitz, R. Russ. 89
— capt., G. W. Austr. 707
— Edw., dn. Her. 442
— Ch. Fk. Torr., gen. (**D**) 921
— Fk. Fras., gen. (**D**) 933
— Jno., gen. (**D**) 913
*— Rd., dn. Arm. 597
*— Rd., dn. Down, 605
* Prob. same pers.
— Saml., P. Laur. 301
— Ter., dn. Arm. 597
— Wm., abp. Tm. 611
— Wm. and sir W., J.C.P. 378; S.L. 408
— Wm. Th. Sh., C.C.J. 404; Q.C. 417
Dansays, Fras., L.G. Gr. Hosp. 854
Dantsey, bp. Meath, 599; L.D. Ir. 552; L. Treas. Ir. 558
Danvers, Hy., *see* ld, D., *infra*
— Jno., C. Exc. 279
— Juland, K.C.S.I. 803
— Rt., Comm. Sergt. Lond. 495; J.C.P. 378; K.B. 757; Rec. Lond. 493; S.L. 407
— Wm., J.C.P. 378; S.L. 407
Danvers, lds.
— Hy., ld., aft. 1st E. of Danby, *q.v.*
Dany, Jno., S.L. 409
Darbhanga, Mahar of, K.C.I.E. 805
Darby, Chr., gen. (**B**) 867
— Geo., adm. (**A**) 815; L. Admy. 179
— Hy. D'Est. and sir H., adm. (**A**) 817; K.C.B. 775
— Jno. Lion, dn. Chest. 477
— Jos., gen. (**D**) 887
Darcey, Darcie and **Darcy**
— sir Arth., G. Jsey. 667; Lt. T.L. 321
— hon. Conyers and sir C., Compt. H. 292; K.B. 764; M.H. 302; P.C. 198

For List of Abbreviations, see pp. 944-952.

Darcie, Darcy, and Darcey—*cont.*
—— Geo. Abb. K., G. Falk. Isl. 731; G. Gamb. 686
—— Hy., L.M. Lond. 489
—— (or Ducie), Hugh, K.B. 764
—— Jno. (2), Const. T.L. 320
—— Jno., L.M. Dbln. 642
—— sir Jno., L.D. Ir. 551; L.J. Ir. 551
—— sir Ph., L.H.A. 173
—— Rt., gen. (**C**) 874
—— Rt., K.B. 757
—— Rog. and sir R., L.J. Ir. 551; L.K. Ir. 574
—— Th., dn. St. Patr. 618; M.R. Ir. 585
—— Th., *see* ld. D., *infra*
Darcy of Chiche, lds.
—— Th. and sir T., aft. 1st ld., C.Y.G. 298; K.G. 738; L.C.H. 294; V.C.H. 296
—— Jno., 2nd ld., K.B. 761
Darcy of Darcy, lds.
—— Th., aft. 1st ld., K.B. 758 (?); K.G. 737
—— Jno., 3rd ld., K.B. 761
Dardanus, K. Sc. 18
Dardys, Barth., J.C.P. Ir. 581
Darell, Nathl., G. Gsey. 668
Darelle, Geo., K.B. 757
Darius, I. to III., K. Pers. 99
Darley, Ed., gen. (**D**) 877
—— Fk., L.M. Dbln. 641
—— Jno. R., bp. Kilm., E. and A. 609
—— Wm. Wall, gen. (**D**) 899
Darling, Chas. Hy. and sir C., G. C.G.H. 679; G. Jam. 713; G. Newfd. 700; G. St. Luc. 725; G. Vict. 704; K.C.B. 783
—— Ch. Jno., Q.C. 420
—— Hy., gen. (**C**) 874
—— Hy. Ch., G. Bdoes. 720; G. Tob. 723; gen. (**C**) 874
—— Jno., dn. Emly, 628
—— Moir Tod. St., S.G. Sc. 527
—— Ralph and sir R., G.C.H. 787; G. Mtius. 683; G. N.S.W. 703; G. V.D.Ld. 708; gen. (**A**) 862
—— Syd., gen. (**D**) 927
—— Wm. L., gen. (**D**) 882
Darlington, E. of
—— Hy., 1st E. of, form. hon. Hy. Vane, *q.v.*; L.L. Dham. 308; L.T. 157, Paym. G. 244
—— Hy., 2nd E. of, L.L. Dham. 308
—— Wm. Hy., 3rd E. of, aft. D. of Cleveland, *q.v.*, L.L. Dham., 308
Darnall (or Darnell), Jno., B. Ex. 384; S.L. 411
Darnell, Wm. Hy., adm. (**D**) 824
Darnley, Ed., 5th E. of, L.L. Meath, 570
Daron, Jno. D., dn. Bgr. 426
Darragh, Jno., L.M. Dbln. 641
Darrell, sir Marm., Coff. H. 293
Darroch, Dunc., G. N.Sc. 695; gen. (**A**) 862
Dartas, Samps., Ch. Ex. Ir. 561
Dartasso, Jas., L.H.A. 173
Dartmouth, lds. and E. of
—— Geo., 1st ld., form. Geo. Legge, *q.v.*, adm. (**A**) 813; Const. T.L. 321; L.G.O. 259
Dartmouth, lds. and E. of—*cont.*
—— Wm., 2nd ld., aft. visc. Lewisham and 1st E. of D., B.T. 263; L.P.S. 240; P.C. 195; Pres. B.T. 265; S. St. 224
—— Wm., 2nd E. of, C. Sec. 234; L.P.S. 241; L.S.H. 290; P.C. 201
—— Geo., 3rd E. of, form. visc. Lewisham, *q.v.*, K.G. 743; L.C.H. 295; L.S.H. 290; Pres. B.C. 252
—— Wm. Wals., 5th E. of, L.L. Staffs. 312
Dartrey, Rd., 3rd ld. aft. 1st E., K.P. 751; L.L. Monaghan, 570
Darvall, Ed., gen. (**D**) 900
—— Jno. Bayl., K.C.M.G. 797
Dasent, Jno. B., C.C.J. 404
Dashwood, sir Ch., adm. (**A**) 820; K.C.B. 777
—— sir Fras., aft. ld. le Despencer, *q.v.*, Ch. Ex. 165; L.T. and C.E. 157; P.C. 200; Tr. Ch. 294
—— sir Hy. Wm., L.L. Oxon. 311
—— Rd. Lew., gen. (**D**) 928
—— sir Sl., C. Exc. 279
—— sir Wm., L.M. Lond. 491
—— Wm. Bateman, adm. (**H**) 846
Date, sir Thos., L.D. Ir. 551
Dathy, K. Ir. 21
Daubeny, Giles, K.B. 755
—— Giles, *see* ld. D., *infra*
—— Hy., gen. (**D**) 879; K.H. 790
—— Hy. Ch. B. and sir H., G.C.B. 771; gen. (**D**) 903; K.C.B. 780
—— Jas., gen (**D**) 906
—— Ralph, K.B. 755
—— Wm., K.B. 755
Daubeny, lds.
—— Giles, aft. 1st ld. D., K.B. 757; K.G. 736; M.M. 246
—— Hy., 2nd ld., aft. E. of Bridgwater, *q.v.*, Const. W. Cast. 322; K.B. 759
Dauber, Rd., C. Exc. Sc. 505
Daubrichcourt and **Dabrichcourt**
—— sir Jno., Const. T.L. 320; K.G. 735
—— sir Sanchet, K.G. 733
Dauncey, Ph., P.P. 415
Daunt, Achill., dn. Cork, 632
Dauvergne, J., G. Hlgld. 670
—— Jas., gen. (**C**) 872
Davall, Pet., M. Chy. and Acct. G. 396
Davenant, Ch., C. Exc. 278
—— Jno., bp. Sal. 467
—— sir Wm., P. Laur. 301
Davencester, Ph. de, Jy. 363
Daveney, Burt., gen. (**D**) 896
Davenport, Humph. and sir H., C.B. Ex. 381; J.C.P. 379; S.L. 409
—— sir Salusb. Price Humph., adm. (**D**) 825; K.C.H. 788
—— Sherr., gen. (**C**) 871
—— Th., K.C. or P.P. 415; S.L. 412
Davers, Th., adm. (**A**) 814
Davey, *see also* Davy and Davie
—— Horace and sir H., Q.C. 419; S.G. 403
—— Th., G. V.D. Ld. 708
***David** (St.), abp. St. Dav. 463
*—— (2), bp. Ach. 612
David—*cont.*
*—— bp. Arg. 537
*—— bp. Arm. 595
*—— bp. Bgr. 425
*—— bp. Cness. 531
*—— bp. Dkld. 533
*—— (of Chirbury), bp. Drom. 604
*—— bp. Kild. 617
*—— (of Emly), bp. Killoe. 634
*—— bp. Mor. 534
*—— (4), bp. St. As. 462
*—— bp. Wford. 626
*—— dn. Cash. 627
*—— dn. Kilmacd. 637
*—— dn. St. As. 462
*—— dn. Wford. 628
* Prob. some same pers. Comp. dates.
—— Emp. Tzde. 98
—— (abb. of Aberbrothock), L.P.S. Sc. 501
—— ab Llewelyn, Pr. Wls. 17
—— ab Owain Gwynedd, Pr. Wls. 16
—— I. and II., K. Sc. 19
—— Mont., G. Mtius. 683
Davidson, *see also* Davison
—— Alexr., G. Mdras. 656
—— Alexr., gen. (**D**) 920
—— Alexr. Geo., gen. (**D**) 915
—— Dunc., L.L. Ross. 512
—— Jas., gen. (**D**) 915
—— Rand. T., dn. Winds. 474
Davie, *see also* Davy and Davey
—— sir Hy. Robt. Ferguson, gen. (**D**) 884
Davies, Davis and **Davys**
—— Danl. Gaten., bp. Antig. 728
—— sir Dav., K.C.H. 789
—— Fras., bp. Llff., 449
—— Fras. Jno., gen. (**D**) 884
—— Geo., bp. Pboro. 458; dn. Chest. 477
—— Geo., adm. (**H**) 848
—— Hart, C. Exc. 282
—— Hy., gen. (**C**) 873
—— Hy. Fansh., gen. (**D**) 931
—— Hy. Th., adm. (**H**) 845
—— Jno., gen. (**D**) 926
—— Jno., S.L. 409
—— sir Jno., A.G. Ir. 588; S.G. Ir. 589; Sec. St. Ir. 562
—— sir Jno., C. Exc. 278
—— Jno. Fras. and sir J., Amb. Ch. 131; G. H. Kong 673; K.C.B. 782
—— Lewis, gen. (**C**) 874
—— sir Paul, Sec. St. Ir. 562
—— Rd., bp. St. As. 462; bp. St. Dav. 464
—— Rd., L.L. Ang. 314
—— Rt. Hy. and sir R., Ch. Com. Oudh, 654; K.C.S.I. 803; L.G. Pjab. 654; M.C.I. 647
—— Rowl., dn. Cork, 632; dn. Ross. 633
—— Th., bp. St. As. 462
—— Th., gen. (**B**) 866
—— Th., gen. (**C**) 872
—— sir Th., L.M. Lond. 491
—— Wm., adm. (**A**) 813
—— sir Wm., C.J.K.B. Ir. 578 Rec. Dbln. 642; S.L. Ir. 591
—— sir Wm. Geo., K.C.S.I. 803
Davis, *see* Davies
Davison and **Davyson,** *see also* Davidson
—— Archd., dn. Thist. 749
—— Geo., gen. (**D**) 913

Davison and Davyson—*cont.*
—— sir Hy., C.J. Bbay. 660; C.J. Mdras. 658
—— Hugh P., gen. (**D**) 882
—— Jno., dn. Sal. 468; dn. Winds. 474
—— Jno., M. Chy. 394
—— Jno. Rt., J.A.G. 937; P.C. 218; Q.C. 418
—— Wm., S. St. 223
—— sir Wm., K.H. 789
Davoust, Off. Nap. 26
Davranches, Alv. de Alm., Count, K.G. 735
Davy, *see also* Davie and Davey
—— sir Humph., Pres. R. Soc. 940
—— Wm., S.L. 412
—— sir Wm. Gabr., gen. (**A**) 863; K.C.H. 789
Davys, *see* Davies
Davyson, *see* Davison
Dawes, Th., R. Cr. P.A. 335
—— sir Wm., abp. Yk. 486; bp. Chest. 477; P.C. 196
Dawkins, Ed. Jas., Amb. Gr. 128
—— Hy., C.W.F. &c. 271-2
—— Rd., C. Exc. 281-2
—— Rd., adm. (**H**) 852
Dawnay, hon. Guy C., S.G.O. 260
Daws, Rd., dn. Her. 442
Dawson, Alexr., Adm. Ind. 647
—— Alexr., gen. (**D**) 925
—— Arth., B. Ex. Ir. 584; C. Acc. Ir. 567
—— Ch., L.M. Dbln. 642
—— Fras., gen. (**D**) 929
*—— Geo. Rt., C. Cus. 277
*—— Geo. Rt., P.C. 212; Sec. Adm. 186; Sec. Tr. 163; U.S. Home, 227
* ? same pers.
—— Hy. Rd., dn. St. Pat. 618
—— Rd., G. I. Man, 666
—— R. Peel, L.L. Londy. 570
—— Rd. Wm. Ersk., gen. (**D**) 934
—— Rt., bp. Clonf. and K. 636; dn. Down 605; dn. Drom. 606
—— Th. Vesey, dn. Clonm. 600; dn. Killa. 614
Day, Fras., C.I.E. 807
—— Geo., bp. Chich. 433
—— Jno. Ch. and sir J., J.Q.B.D. 374; Q.C. 419
—— Jno. Godfr., dn. Ardf. 640
—— Maur. Fitzg., bp. Cash. E. W. and L. 627; dn. Lim. 640
—— Rt., J.K.B. Ir. 579
—— Saml., G. Bmda. 701
—— Wm., bp. Winch. 471; dn. Winds. 474
Dayabhoy, Dulp., C.I.E. 807
Daza, H., Pres. Bol. 109
De and **D'**
Names with these prefixes will be found under the subsequent surname—*e.g.* for Jno. De Courcy, *see* Courcy, Jno. de
Deacon, Ch. and sir C., gen. (**D**) 876; K.C.B. 776
—— Hy. Colins, adm. (**H**) 846
Dealtry, Th., bp. Mdras. 658
Dean and **Deane,** *see also* Dene
—— —, L. Admy. 175
—— Ch., K.H. 792
—— (or Dene), Hy. (No. 1), abp. Cant. 431; bp. Sal. 467; L.K. 355

Dean and Deane—*cont.*
—— Hy. (No. 2), bp. Bgr. 426; Ld. Chanc. Ir. 575; L.J. Ir. 553
—— Jas. Park. and sir J., Adm. Adv. 423; Q.C. 418; Vic. Gen. 422
—— Jos., C.B. Ex. Ir. 583
—— Rd., bp. Oss. 620; dn. Oss. 623
—— sir Rd., L.M. Lond. 491
—— Rd. B., C. Cus. 276-7
—— Th., dn. Cloy. 633
—— Wm., G. Bdoes. 719
—— Wm., gen. (**C**) 872
—— **-Pitt,** *see* Pitt
Deane, *see* Dean
Deans, Rt., adm. (**A**) 816
—— Rt., adm. (**H**) 847
Deas, Dav., K.C.B. 779
—— Geo., Ld. Sess. 521; S.G. Sc. 527
—— Jno., Jy. Sc. 523
Deasy, Rickard, A.G. Ir. 588; B. Ex. Ir. 584; L.J. App. Ir. 586; S.G. Ir. 590; S.L. Ir. 593
Debbeig, Hugh, gen. (**A**) 859
Debono, Guiss. Calc., G.C.M.G. 794
Decaen, Ch., G. Mtius. 683
Decan, Ad., dn. Bgr. 426
Decianus, C. P. (2), C. Ro. 41
Decima, Ct. Della, G.C.M.G. 794; K.C.M.G. 796
Decius, M., Emp. Ro. 47
Decken, Fredc. Count von der, gen. (**B**) 867
Decula, M. T., C. Ro. 45
Dedder, Louis, dn. Oss. 622
Dedwin (or Theodwin), abp. Lond. 450
Dee, Dunc., Comm. Serjt. Lond. 495
—— Fras., bp. Pboro. 458; dn. Chich. 434
—— Jno., Wdn. Chr. Ch. Manch. 481
Deedes, Wm. Hy., gen. (**D**) 934
Deerhurst, Geo. W., visc., aft. 7th E. of Coventry, *q.v.*, L.L. Worc. 313
De Eresby, *see* Willoughby de Eresby
Deering, *see* Dering
Deey, Rt., L.M. Dbln. 640
Deicola, bp. Emly, 625
Dejean, Lew., gen. (**B**) 865
Delabere, Jno., bp. St. Dav. 464
—— Rd., K.B. 758
Delacombe, Hy. W., gen. (**D**) 890
Delafield, —, dn. Oss. 622
Delafosse, Ed. Hollinw., adm. (**H**) 849
—— Hy. Geo., gen. (**D**) 933
Delahyde, Rd., C.J.C.P. Ir. 580; Ch. Ex. Ir. 561
—— Chr., J.K.B. Ir. 578
Delamain, Wm. Hy., gen. (**D**) 910
Delamere, Hy., 2nd ld., aft. 1st E. of Warrington, *q.v.*, Ch. Ex. 164; L.L. Chesh. 306; L.T. and Ch. Ex. 155; P.C. 193
Delancey, Wm. Howe, K.C.B. 774
Delane, Geo., gen. (**D**) 912
Delaney, —, G. Tob. 723
Delany, Patr., dn. Down, 605

Delaval, Fras., gen. (**B**) 868
—— Fras. Bl., K.B. 765
—— Geo., adm. (**A**) 813
—— sir Ralph, adm. (**A**) 813; L. Admy. 176
Delawarr, lds. and E.
1st Creation.
—— Th., 8th ld., K.B. 757; K.G. 737
—— Th., 9th ld., K.G. 738
2nd Creation.
—— Jno., 6th ld., P.C. 198; Tell. Ex. 167; Tr. Ch. 294
—— Jno., 7th ld. and 1st E., G. Gsey. 668; gen. (**A**) 858; K.B. 764; Tr. H. 291
—— Jno., 2nd E., gen. (**B**) 865
—— Geo. J., 5th E., L.C.H. 295; P.C. 214
—— Ch. Rd., 6th E., form. ld. West, *q.v.*, K.C.B. 780
Delisle and **Dudley,** Ph. Ch., 2nd ld., form. sir P. C. Sidney, *q.v.*
Delme, sir Pet., L.M. Lond. 491
Deloraine, Hy., 1st E. of, gen. (**C**) 871; K.B. 764
Delves, Jno., J.C.P. 377
Delvin, lds. and visc.
—— Rd. Nug., 1st ld., L.D. Ir. 553
—— Geo. Fred. Nug., visc., aft. 7th E. of Westmeath, *q.v.*, Sec. St. Patr. 752
Demetrius, I. to III., R. Russ. 89, 90
Dempster, Geo., Sec. Thist. 749
Den, Th., bp. Ferns, 621
—— (or Dene), Wm., L.J. Ir. 550
Denbigh, E. of
—— Wm., 1st E. of, form. ld. and visc. Fielding, *q.v.*
—— Bas., 4th E. of, Tell. Ex. 168
—— Bas., 6th E. of, P.C. 200
—— Wm. Bas. P., 7th E. of, G.C.H. 786; P.C. 212
Dendy, Ed. S., Chest. H. 331; R. Dr. P.A. 338; Surr. H. 334
Dene, *see also* Dean and Den
—— Pet. de, M. Chy. 393
—— Ralph de, J. It. 365
Denebert, bp. Worc. 472
Denefrith, bp. Shbn. 466
Denewulf, bp. Winch. 470
Denham, Hy. Mangles and sir H., adm. (**D**) 833, (**F**) 838
—— Jno., K.B. 764
—— Jno. and sir J., B. Ex. 384; C.B. Ex. Ir. 583; C.J.K.B. Ir. 578; L.J. Ir. 554; S.L. 409
Denier, Ph. J., M.M. 246
Denis, *see also* Dennis
—— bp. Clonf. 636
*—— (or Dionysius), dn. Arm. 597
*—— dn. Tm. 613
* Poss. same pers.
—— K. Pgl. 88
—— (O'Brian), K. Ir. 22
—— Walt., K.B. 758
Denison and **Dennison**
—— Car. Lucy, lady, Cr. Ind. 810
—— Edm. Beck., aft. ld. Grimthorpe, *q.v.*, Q.C. 417
—— Ed., bp. Sal. 467
—— Jno. Evel., aft. visc. Ossington, *q.v.*, L. Admy. 182; P.C. 216; Sp. H.C. 250

Denison and Dennison—*cont.*
—— Th. and sir T., J.K.B. 373; S.L. 412
—— Wm. Th. and sir W., G. Mdras. 657; G. N.S.W. 703; G. V. D. ld. 708; gen. (**D**) 907; K.C.B. 782
Denman, hon. Geo., J.C.P. 380; J.C.P.D. 380; J.Q.B.D. 374; Q.C. 418; S.L. 414
—— hon. Josh., adm. (**D** & **E**) 832, 834
—— Th., *see* ld. D., *infra*
Denman, lds.
—— Th., aft. sir T. and 1st ld. D., A.G. 400; C.J.K.B. 370; Ch. Ex. 165; Comm. Serjt. Lond. 495; Jud. Com. P.C. 360; L.H.S. 287; P.C. 212; P.P. 416; S.L. 413
Denmark, Christian Fk. Wm. Ch., Cr. Pr. of, G.C.B. 773
—— Geo., Pr. of, also styled D. of Cumberland, *q.v.*, Const. W. Cast., 322; L.H.A. 176-7; P.C. 192; W.C.P. 319
Denn, Vinc., S.L., 411
Dennehy, Th., C.I.E. 808
Dennis, *see also* Denis and Dennys
—— bp. Ross, 631
—— Alf. Digb., gen. (**D**) 920
—— Jas. and sir J., gen. (**D**) 883; K.C.B. 777
—— Jas., aft. ld. Tracton, *q.v.*, C.B. Ex. Ir. 583; S.L. Ir. 592
—— Jas. Benj., gen. (**D**) 902
—— Jas. Saml. Akid, adm. (**H**) 850
—— Jno. Lesl., gen. (**D**) 899
—— sir Pet., adm. (**A**) 814
Dennison, *see* Denison
Denny, Ed., B. Ex. 383
Dennys, *see also* Dennis
—— Jul. Bent., gen. (**D**) 923
Densell, Jno., S.L. 408
Dent, Alfr., K.C.M.G. 799
—— Ch. Bayl. Calm., adm. (**H**) 852
—— Ch. Calm., adm. (**H**) 849
—— Digby, Compt. N. 257
—— Th. de, C.J.C.P. Ir. 580
Denta, L. C. M., C. Ro. 42
Dentatus, M. C. (3), C. Ro. 41-2
Denter, M. L., C. Ro. 41
Denton, Alexr., J.C.P. 379; S.L. 411
—— Jas., dn. Lich. 445
Denum, Jno. de, S.L. 406
—— Wm. de, B. Ex. 383; K.B. 755; S.L. 406
Deodatus, *see also* Adeodatus and Deus-dedit
—— bp. Mth. 599
Deo-in-Behar, Bah. of, K.C.S.I. 802
Deo Narain, Raj., K.C.S.I. 802
Deora, *see* Diora
Deorlaf, bp. Her. 441
Depeden, Jno., Regr. Gart. 746
Depham, Rog. de, Rec. Lond. 493
Deping, Jno., bp. Wford. and L. 626
Derby, Jno., M. Chy. 394
*—— Jno. de, dn. Lich. 445
*—— Jno. de, M. Chy. 393
* Prob. same pers.
—— Wm., B. Ex. 383
Derby, Earls of
—— Hy., E. of, aft. K. Hy. IV., *q.v.*, K.G. 734
Stanley Family.
Search also under lds. Strange.
—— Thos., 1st E. of, form. ld. Stanley, *q.v.*, K. Man. 665
—— Thos., 2nd E. of, form. Th. Stanley, *q.v.*, K. Man. 665
—— Ed., 3rd E. of, K.B. 760; K.G. 738; L.L. Chesh. 306; L.P.S. 240; Ld. Man. 665
—— Hy., 4th E. of, K.G. 738; L.L. Chesh. 306; Ld. Man. 665
—— Ferd., 5th E. of, Ld. Man. 665
—— Wm., 6th E. of, K.G. 739; L.L. Chesh. 306; Ld. Man. 665
—— Jas., 7th E. of, form. ld. Strange, *q.v.*, K.G. 740; L.L. Chesh. 306; Ld. Man. 665
—— Ch., 8th E. of, L.L. Chesh. 306; Ld. Man. 665
—— Wm. R. G., 9th E. of, L.L. Chesh. 306; L.L. N. and S. Wales, &c. 314; Ld. Man. 665
—— Jas., 10th E. of, C.D.L. 242; C.Y.G. 298; gen. (**C**) 871; Ld. Man. 665; P.C. 195-6
—— Ed., 12th E. of, C.D.L. 243; P.C. 204, 212
—— Ed. Sm., 13th E. of, K.G. 744; L.L. Lanc. 309
—— Ed. G., 14th E. of, form. ld. Stanley, *q.v.*; G.C.M.G. 795; K.G. 744; L.T. 161; Prem. 148
—— Ed. Hy., 15th E. of, form. ld. Stanley, *q.v.*; C. Sec. 235; F. Sec. 229; K.G. 745; U.S.F. 230
Dereham, Th., A.G. 398
Derham, ld., *see* Dynham
Dering and **Deering**
—— Ch., C. Tx. 284-5
—— sir Ed., C. Cus. 273; L.P.S. 240; L.T. 155
—— Heneage, dn. Rip. 482
Derinzy, Barth. Vigors, gen. (**D**) 890; K.H. 790
Derlington, Jno. de, abp. Dbln. and Gl. 615
Dermod, bp. Kilm. 607
—— (St.), bp. Arm. 595
Dernot, dn. Dry. 602
Derqui, S., Pres. Arg. 110
Derrick, sir Gilb., Gart. K.A. 327
Derriman, Saml. Hoskins, adm. (**H**) 851
Derville, Adolph., gen. (**D**) 888
Desaguliers, Th., gen. (**B**) 865
Desart, Jno. Olway, 2nd E. of, L.T. 159
Desbordes, Jno. Pet., gen. (**B**) 864
Desborough, Jno., gen. (**D**) 915
—— Jno., W.C.P. 319
—— Lawr., gen. (**B**) 868
Desbrisay, Th., gen. (**B**) 868
Deshon, Fk. Geo. Th., gen. (**D**) 922
Desiderius, K. Lmd. 49
Deskford, lds.
—— Jas., ld., aft. 1st visc. and 4th E. of Seafield, *q.v.*, Sec. St. Sc. 502
Deskford, lds.—*cont.*
—— Jas., ld., aft. 6th E. of Findlater, and 3rd E. of Seafield, *q.v.*, C. Cus. Sc. 504
Desmond, E. of—
—— Jas., 15th E. of, L. Treas. Ir. 559
—— Rd., E. of, form. R. Preston. *q.v.* (K.B. 1603)
Desmyniers, Jno., L.M. Dbln. 640
—— Lewis, L.M. Dbln. 640
Despard, Ed. Marc., G. Br. Hond. 714
—— Hy., gen. (**D**) 885
—— Jno., gen. (**A**) 860
Despencer, search also under Spencer
—— Hugh le, Ch. Jr. 363; Const. T.L. 320; J. It. 368
—— sir Hugh le, aft. E. of Gloucester, *q.v.*, L.H.A. 171
Despencer, lords le
Despencer Family.
—— Ed., 5th ld. le, K.G. 733
—— Th., 6th ld. le, aft. E. of Gloucester, *q.v.*, K.G. 734
—— Rd., 7th ld., K.B. 756
Dashwood Family.
—— Fras., ld., form. sir Fras. Dashwood, *q.v.*; L.L. Bucks, 306; M.G.W. 296; Postm. G. 238
Dessalinis, J. J., Emp. Hti. 104
Deste, Aug. Fk., K.C.H. 787
Dethick, Gilb., Hps. P.A. 343; Norr. K.A. 329; R. Cr. P.A. 335; Richm. H. 333
—— Hy., R. Cr. P.A. 335; Richm. H. 333
—— Jno., L.M. Lond. 491
—— Nich., Bl. M. P.A. 336; Winds. H. 331
—— Wm., Gart. K. A. 327; R. Cr. P.A. 335; Som. H. 332; Yk. H. 334
Deucher, A., Pres. Sw. C. 31
Deus-dedit, P. Ro. 33. *See also* Adeodatus and Deodatus
Devaynes, Wm., Chn. E.I. Co. 644
Devenesche, Jno., bp. Winch. 470
Devenish, Rt., Norr. K.A. 329; Yk. H. 334
Devereil, Th. Jos., gen. (**D**) 902
Devereux, Alex., bp. Ferns. 621
—— hon. Geo. Talb., gen. (**D**) 907
—— Jno., bp. Ferns, 621; dn. Ferns 623
—— Jno., K.B. 757
—— sir Jno. or ld., W.C.P. 318; K.G. 734
—— Rd., K.B. 760
—— hon. Walt. Bourch., adm. (**G**) 843
Devon, Thos. Bark., K.C.H. 789; K.H. 789
Devon and **Devonshire,** E. of—
Courtenay Family.
—— Ed., E. of, L.H.A. (succ. 1387) 173
—— Hugh, E. of, form. H. Courtenay, *q.v.* (succ. 1419), K.B. 755
—— Ed., E. of (succ. 1485), K.G. 737
—— Hy., E. of, aft. M. of Exeter, *q.v.* (succ. 1511), K.G. 737

Devon and Devonshire, E. of—*cont.*
—— Ed., E. of, aft. M. of Exeter, *q.v.* (succ. 1553), K.B. 760
—— Ch., E. of, form. ld. Mountjoy, *q.v.* (succ. 1603); M.G.O. 258; E.M. 326
—— Wm. Reg., E. of, form. visc. Courtenay (succ. 1859), *q.v.*, C.D.L. 243; P.C. 917; Pres. P.L.B. 262; Sec. P.L.B. 262
Cavendish Family.
See Devonshire.
Devonport,, sir Saml., K.C.M.G. 798
Devonshire, sir Jno. Ferr., K.C.H. 778
—— Rd., adm. (**H**) 847
Devonshire, E. and D. of—
Courtenay Family.
See Devon.
Cavendish Family
—— Wm., 3rd E. of, B.T. 263
—— Wm., 4th E. of, aft. M. of Hartington, *q.v.*, and 1st D. of D., K.G. 741; L.H.S. 286; L.S.H. 290; P.C. 193
—— Wm., 2nd D. of, form. M. of Hartington, *q.v.*; K.G. 741; L.P.C. 188; L.S.H. 290; P.C. 195
—— Wm., 3rd D. of, form. M. of Hartington, *q.v.*; C.G.P. 299; K.G. 741; L.L. Ir. 556; L.P.S. 240; L.S.H. 290; P.C. 198
—— Wm., 4th D. of, form. M. of Hartington, *q.v.*; K.G. 742; L.C.H. 295; L.L. Dby. 307; L.T. 157; L. Treas. Ir. 560; Prem. 142
—— Wm., 5th D. of, K.G. 742; L.L. Dby. 307; L. Treas. Ir. 560
—— Wm. S., 6th D. of, Amb. Russ. 126; K.G. 743; L.C.H. 295; L.L. Dby. 307; P.C. 210
—— Wm., 7th D. of, K.G. 744; L.L. Dby. 307; P.C. 219
Dewan, Tanj. Mad. Rao., K.C.S.I. 802
Dewar, Dav., gen. (**C**) 873
—— sir J., C.J. Bbay. 660
Dewdney, Edg., G. N.W. Terr. 697
Deyn, Wm. de, bp. Abdn. 530
D'Eyncourt, Edmd., J. It. 369
—— Edwin Clayton Tenn., adm. (**E**) 835; (**F**) 838
—— Geo. Hild. Tenn., Regr. M.G. 799
—— Roger, K.B. 754
—— Ralph, 3rd ld., K.B. 755
—— form. Tennyson D'Eyncourt, *see* Tennyson.
Dhar, Mahar. of, C.I.E. 807
—— Rao of, K.C.S.I. 803
Dheeraj, Mahar., G.C.S.I. 801
Dhiraj, Mahar., G.C.S.I. 801
Dholepore, Rana of, G.C.S.I. 801
Dholpur, Maharanee, Cr. Ind. 810
—— Thakur, &c. of, C.I.E. 807
Dhuleep Sing, Mahar., G.C.S.I. 800
—— —— Maharanee of, Cr. Ind. 809
Diadematus, P. C. M., C. Ro. 45
Diarmuid (2), K. Ir. 21
Diaz, M. M., Pres. Pan. 107
—— P., Pres. Mex. 104
Diceto, Ralph de, dn. St. P. 452
Dick, Alexr., gen. (**D**) 886
—— Fras., gen. (**D**) 899
—— Geo., G. Bbay. 659
—— Hope, gen. (**D**) 890
—— Jno., adm. (**D**) 823
—— sir Rt. H., gen. (**C**) 875; K.C.B. 776; K.C.H. 788
—— Th., adm. (**H**) 845
—— Wm. Aberc., gen. (**D**) 912
Dickens and **Dickins**
—— Crav. Hild., gen. (**D**) 916
—— Gust. Guy, gen. (**C**) 872
—— Rd. Mark, gen. (**C**) 873
—— sir Saml. Trev., gen. (**B**) 869; K.C.H. 788
—— Wm. Drumm. S., gen. (**D**) 933
Dickenson and **Dickinson**
—— Ch., bp. Mth. 599
—— Jas., Q.C. 418
—— Marshl., L.M. Lond. 492
—— Rd., gen. (**B**) 869
—— Th., gen. (**D**) 888
—— Th., gen. (**D**) 889
—— Th. P., C. Cus. 277
—— Wm., C. Cus. 273-4
—— Wm., L. Admy. 180-1
—— Wm. Moore, gen. (**D**) 933
—— Wm. Rice, gen. (**D**) 910
Dickey, Ad. Hugh M., gen. (**D**) 935
Dickins, *see* Dickens
Dickinson, *see* Dickenson
Dickson, *see also* Dixon
—— Alex. I. and sir A., G.C.B. 769; gen. (**C**) 875; K.C.B. 775; K.C.H. 787
—— Archd , adm. (**A**) 816
—— sir Archd. Coll., adm. (**A**) 819
—— Coll. and sir C., gen. (**D**) 901; G.C.B. 771; K.C.B. 780
—— Ed. Jno., gen. (**D**) 918
—— Ed. St., adm. (**A**) 820
—— Jas., dn. Elph. 609; dn. Down, 605
—— Jerem. and sir J., gen. (**B**) 870; K.C.B. 775
—— Jno., gen. (**A**) 860
—— Jno., Ld. Sess. 519
—— Jno. Bourne, adm. (**E**) 835
—— Jno. Fk., K.C.M.G. 799
—— sir Rt., C. Cus. Sc. 503
—— Wm., adm. (**A**) 816
—— Wm., bp. Down and Cnr. 604
—— Wm., gen. (**D**) 878
—— Wm., L.M. Dbln. 641
—— sir Wm., adm. (**G**) 842
—— Wm. J., Amb. U.S.C. 134
—— Wm. Th., gen. (**D**) 908
Didier, K. Lmd. 49
Didius, T., C. Ro. 45
Difthefield, sir —, G. Gsey. 668
Dig-Bijye, Mahar., K.C.S.I. 802
Digby, Essex, bp. Drom. 605; dn. Cash. 627
—— Hy. and sir H., adm. (**A**) 819; G.C.B. 769; K.C.B. 776
—— sir Jno., *see* ld. D., *infra*
—— Jos., adm. (**H**) 845
—— hon. Rt., adm. (**A**) 815
—— Simon, bp. Elph. 608; bp. Lim., A. and A. 639; dn. Kild. 619
—— Wm., C.I.E. 806
—— hon. Wm., dn. Clonf. 637; dn. Dham. 479; dn. Worc. 474
Digby of Sherborne, lds.
—— sir Jno., aft. 1st ld. D. of S. and 1st E. of Bristol, *q.v.*, Lt. T.L. 321; V.C.H. 296
—— Geo., ld., aft. 2nd E. of Bristol, *q.v.*; S. St., 223
Digby of Geashill, lds. and E.
—— Hy., 7th ld., aft. 1st E., L. Admy. 179; L.L. Dors. 307
—— Ed., 8th ld. and 2nd E., L.L. Dors. 307
Digges and **Diggs,** sir Dudl., M. Chy. 395; M.R. 388
—— Rd., S.L. 409
Diggle, Ch., gen. (**D**) 890; K.H. 790
Diggs, *see* Digges
Dighton, Wm. de, L.K. 354
Dilke, sir Chas. Wentw., P.C. 220; Pres. L.G.B. 256; U.S.F. 230
Dilkes, Jno., adm. (**A**) 818
—— Michl. O'Br., gen. (**A**) 858
—— sir Th., adm. (**A**) 813
—— Wm. Th., gen. (**A**) 862
Dillon, —, G. Tob. 723
—— sir Arth. Rd., gen. (**A**) 862
—— Barthw. and sir B., C.B. Ex. Ir. 582; C.J.K.B. Ir. 577; J.K.B. Ir. 578; V. Treas. Ir. 559
—— Ed., dn. Kild. 619
—— Ed. Longf., gen. (**D**) 926
—— Ger., J.K.B. Ir. 579; Rec. Dbln. 642; S.L. Ir. 591
—— Lucas, A.G. Ir. 588; C.B. Ex. Ir. 583
—— Martin and sir M., gen. (**D**) 919; K.C.B. 782
—— Rd., J.K.B. Ir. 578
*—— Rt., B. Ex. Ir. 584
*—— Rt., Ch. Ex. Ir. 561
* Prob. same pers.
—— Rt. and sir R., A.G. Ir. 588; C.J.C.P. Ir. 580; J.C.P. Ir. 581; J.K.B. 578
—— Th., bp. Kild. 617
—— Th., J.C.P. Ir. 581
—— sir Wm. Hy., K.C.H. 788; adm. (**D**) 827
Dillon, lds. and visc.
—— Rt., ld., L.J. Ir. 554; L.K. Ir. 576
—— Chas., 12th visct., K.P. 750
Diman, bp. Kild. 616
Dimmock, *see* Dymock
Dimsdale, F. T., C.C.J. 403
Dinan, *see* Dynham
Dinely, Rt., G. I. Man. 666
Dingli, Andr. and sir A., G.C.M.G. 795; K.C.M.G. 796
—— Paolo and sir P., G.C.M.G. 795; K.C.M.G. 796
Dingwall, Jno., Ld. Sess. 518
Dinkin, Rao Raj., K.C.S.I. 802
Diocletian, Emp. Ro. 48
Dionysius (or Denis), dn. Arm. 597; dn. Crk. 632; dn. Ferns, 623
—— K. Pgl. 88
—— P. Ro. 32
Diora (or Deora), bp. Roch. 459
Diothorba, K. Ir. 20
Diratus, bp. Ferns, 621
Dirle (or Dule), Wm., dn. Ferns, 623
Dirom, Alex., gen. (**B**) 867
—— Jas., adm. (**H**) 850

For List of Abbreviations, see pp. 944-952.

Disbrowe, Edw. Cr. and sir E., Amb. Nds., &c. 123; Amb. Russ. 126; Amb. Sw. and N.. 127; Amb. Swz. 113; G.C.H. 786
—— Geo., K.H. 791
—— Jno., L.T. 154
Disibode, bp. Dbln. 615
Disney, Brab. Wm., dn. Arm. 597; dn. Emly, 628
—— Moore and sir M., gen. (**A**) 862; K.C.B. 775
—— *see* Cathrow-Disney
Disraeli, Benj., aft. E. of Beaconsfield, *q.v.*, Ch. Ex. 166; L.P.S. 241; L.T. 161-2; P.C. 215; Prem. 150
—— Jas., C.I.R. 286
Diuma, bp. Lich. 443
Dives, L.C., C. Ro. 46
—— P. L. C., C. Ro. 43
Dix, Macn., G. St. Luc. 725
Dixie, sir Wolst., L.M. Lond. 490
Dixon, *see also* Dickson
—— Augs. Fredk. De B., gen. (**D**) 930
—— Ch., gen. (**D**) 889
—— Geo., gen. (**D**) 885
—— Geo., gen. (**D**) 897
—— Geo. Wm., gen. (**C**) 874
—— Manley and sir M., adm. (**A**) 818; K.C.B. 775
—— Manl. Hall, adm. (**D**) 828; (**G**) 840
—— Matt. Ch., gen. (**D**) 886
—— Matt. Ch., gen. (**D**) 908
—— Nichs., B. Ex. 383
—— Rd., bp. Cork and Cl. 631
—— Rt., J.C.P. Ir. 581; S.L. Ir. 592
—— Wm. Manl. H., gen. (**D**) 910
Dobbes, *see* Dobbs
Dobbie, Geo. St., gen. (**D**) 917
—— Wm. Hugh R., adm. (**H**) 850
Dobbs and **Dobbes**
—— Rd., dn. Cnr. 605
—— sir Rd., L.M. Lond. 490
—— Wm. Carey, Land J. Ir. 587
Dobson, Geo., adm. (**G**) 843
—— Man., adm. (**A**) 819
—— Wm. Burdett, adm. (**G**) 842
Dod, *see also* Dodd
—— Edmd., adm. (**A**) 816
—— Rog., bp. Mth. 599
—— Th., dn. Rip. 482
Dodd, *see also* Dod
—— sir Saml., C.B. Ex. 382; S.L. 411
Dodds, Greg., dn. Exr. 437
Doderidge, Jno. and sir J., J.K.B. 372; S.G. 401; S.L. 409
Dodgson, *see also* Dodson
—— Ch., bp. Elph. 608; bp. Oss. 620
—— Dav. Sc., gen. (**D**) 917
Dodington, Geo., L. Admy. 177
—— Geo. Bubb, aft. ld. Melcombe, *q.v.*, L.T. 156; P.C. 199; Tr. N. 256
Dodinsele, *see* Odinsele
Dodmer, Ralph, L.M. Lond. 490
Dodson, *see also* Dodgson
—— Jno. and sir J., adm. Adr. 423; D. Arch. 421; J. Pr. Ct. 421; Jud. Com. P.C. 360; K. Adv. 422; P.C. 215; Vic. Gen. 422
Dodson—*cont.*
—— Jno. Geo., aft. ld. Monk-Bretton, *q.v.*, C.D.L. 243; P.C. 218; Pres. L.G.B. 256; Sec. Tr. 164
Dodswell, Rd., C. Exc. Sc. 505
Dodwell, Hy., dn. Killa. 614
Doffelde, Sim., L.M. Lond. 489
Dogworth, Jno. de, K.B. 754
Doherty, Geo., K.H. 790
—— Hy. Ed., gen. (**D**) 898
—— Jno., C.J.C.P. Ir. 581; S.G. Ir. 589
—— Patr., K.C.H. 788
—— Rd. and sir R., G. Si. Le. 685; G. St. Vin. 725; G. Trin. 722; gen. (**D**) 884
Dolabella, C. C., C. Ro. 44-5
—— P. C., C. Ro. 46
Dolben, Dav., bp. Bgr. 426
—— sir Gilb., J.C.P. Ir. 581
—— Jno., abp. Yk. 486; bp. Roch. 460; dn. Westr. 469
—— Wm. and sir W., J.K.B. 372; Rec. Lond. 494; S.L. 410
Dolgfinnus, bp. Ork. 535
Dollon, Lew., G. Gsey. 668
Domangard, K. Sc. 18
Domett, Wm. and sir W., adm. (**A**) 817; G.C.B. 768; K.C.B. 773; L. Admy. 181
Domingue, M., Pres. Hti. 105
Dominique, Paul, B.T. 264
Dominus, Marc. Ant. de, dn. Winds. 474
Domitian, Emp. Ro. 47
Domraon, Mahar. of, K.C.S.I. 803
Domville, Jas. Wm., gen. (**D**) 907
—— Wm. and sir W., L.M. Lond. 492
—— sir Wm., A.G. Ir. 588
Don, *see also* Donne
—— Geo. and sir G., G.C.B. 768; G.C.H. 786; G. Gibr. 670; gen. (**A**) 860
—— The O. Conn., L.T. 161
Donagh and **Donnagh**
—— K. Ir. 21
—— K. Ir. 22
Donald, bp. Arm. 595
—— bp. Dry. 601
—— dn. Rph. 602
—— I. to VII., K. Sc. 18-9
Donat, bp. Dbln. 615
—— bp. Kilm. 607
—— bp. Llin. 621
Donative, Jno., M.M. 246
Doncaster, Jno. de, J.C.P. 377
Doncaster, visc. and E. Search under D. of Buccleuch, E. of Dalkeith, ld. Hay, and D. of Monmouth
Donchad, K. Ir. 21
Donegal, E. and M. of—
—— Arth., 3rd E. of, gen. (**C**) 871
—— Geo. Aug., 2nd M. of, K.P. 751; L.L. Dgal. 569
—— Geo. H., 3rd M. of, form. E. of Belfast and ld. Ennishowen, *q.v.*, C.Y.G, 298; K.P. 751; L.L. Ant. 568
Donell, dn. Louth, 598
Donellan, Jas. and sir J., C.J.C.P. Ir. 580; J.C.P. Ir. 581
—— Nehem., abp. Tm. 611
—— Nehem., B. Ex. Ir. 584; C.B. Ex. Ir. 583; C.G.S. Ir. 576; Rec. Dbln. 642; S.L. Ir. 591
Dongal, K. Sc. 18
Dongan, Jno., bp. Dry. 601; bp. Down, 603
—— Th., B. Ex. Ir. 584; J.K.B. Ir. 579
—— Wm., Rec. Dbln. 642
Dongardus, K. Sc. 18
Dongola, Mudir of, K.C.M.G. 798
Donkan, Jno., bp. S. and W. 483
Donkin, Rt., gen. (**A**) 860
—— Ruf. Sh. and sir R., G. C.G.H. 679; gen. (**A**) 862; K.C.B. 775; G.C.H. 786; S.G.O. 260
Donnagh, *see* Donagh
Donne, *see also* Don
—— Jno., dn. St. P. 453
—— Wm. B., E.S.P. 301
Donnelly, Jno. Fr. D., gen. (**D**) 934
—— Ross and sir R., adm. (**A**) 819; K.C.B. 776
Donop, Ed. Pelh. br. Von, adm. (**H**) 849
Donortius, bp. Mortl. 530
Donough (2), K. Ir. 22
Donoughmore, lds., visc. and E. of
—— Rd. Hely, 2nd ld. and 1st visc. and E. of, form. Rd. Hely Hutchinson, *q.v.*, B.T. 268; C. Cus. Ir. 565; C. Exc. Ir. 566; gen. (**B**) 867; P.C. 208 Postm. G. Ir. 564
—— Jno., 2nd E. of, form. Jno. and ld. Hutchinson, *q.v.*, K.B. 766
—— Jno., 3rd E. of, K.P. 751; L.L. Tipp. 571
—— Rd. Jno., 4th E. of, P.C. 216; Paym. G. 245; Pres. B.T. 269; V.P.B.T. 269
—— Jno. Luke Geo., 5th E. of, K.C.M.G. 797
Donovan, Ed. Westb., gen. (**D**) 907
Donus, I. and II., P. Ro. 33-4
Dopping, Anthy., bp. Kild, 617; bp. Meath 599; bp. Oss. 620; dn. Clonm. 600
Doran, Maur., bp. Llin. 622
Dorchester, lds. and visc.
Carlton Family.
—— Dudley, visc., form. sir D. and ld. Carleton, *q.v.*
—— Guy, 1st ld., form. G. Carleton, *q.v.*, gen. (**A**) 858
Pierrepoint Family.
1st Creation.
—— Hy., 1st M. of, E.M. 326; P.C. 190
2nd Creation.
—— Evelyn, 1st M. of, aft. D. of Kingston, *q.v.*, P.C. 195
Damer Family.
—— Geo. 2nd E. of, form. visc. Milton, *q.v.*, L.L. Dors. 307
Dore, Peter, Bl. M. P.A. 336; Norr. K.A., 329; Richm. H. 334
Dorehill, Wm. Jno., gen. (**D**) 917
Doresme, Arn. de, S.L. 406
Doreword, Jno., Sp. H.C. 248
Doria, Rd. Andr., gen. (**D**) 915
Dorislaus, Is., J. Adm. Ct. 423
Dormer, Fleetw., M. Chy 396
—— Jas., gen. (**B**) 864

Dormer—*cont.*
— hon. Jas. Ch., gen. (**D**) 925
— sir Michl., L.M. Lond. 490
— Rt. and sir R., J.C.P. 379; S.L. 411
— Wm., K.B. 760
Dornadilla, K. Sc. 17
Dornberg, Wilh. de, K.C.B. 775
Dornburgh, Did. Van., G. Ceyl. 672
Dorrien, Jno., gen. (**B**) 868
Dorrill, Capt., G. Newfd. 700
Dorsell, Rt., dn. Chest. 477
Dorset, E., M. and D. of
— St. Osm., E. of, bp. Sal. (1078, *d.* 1099) 466, *see also* Osmund
Beaufort Family.
1st Creation.
— Jno., 1st E. and M. of, form. sir J. Beaufort, *q.v.*; L.H.A. 173; W.C.P. 318
— Th. 2nd E. of, form. sir T. Beaufort, *q.v.*, aft. D. of Exeter, *q.v.*; L.H.A. 173
2nd Creation.
— Ed. B., 1st E. and M. of, form. E. of Morton, *q.v.*, aft. D. of Somerset, *q.v.*; Const. W. Cast. 322
Grey Family.
— Th., 1st M. of, form. E. of Huntingdon, *q.v.*; Const. T.L. 320; K.B. 757; K.G. 736
— Th., 2nd M. of, K.G. 737
— Hy., 3rd M. of, aft. 1st D. of Suffolk, *q.v.*, K.B. 760; K.G. 738 L.H. Const. 289
Sackville Family.
— Th., 1st E. of, form. ld. Buckhurst, *q.v.*; E.M. 326
— Ed., 4th E. of, form. ld. Sackville, *q.v.*; K.G. 739; L. Admy. 175; L.C.H. 295; L.L. Suss. 312
— Rd., 5th E. of, L.L. Suss. 312
— [and Middlesex], Ch., 6th E. of, K.G. 741; L.C.H. 295; L.L. Suss. 312; P.C. 193
— Lionel Cr., 7th E. and 1st D. of, Gr. St. 303; K.G. 741; L.H.S. 287; L.P.C. 188; L.L. Ir. 556-7; L.L. Kent 309; L.S.H. 290; M.H. 302; P.C. 196; W.C.P. 319
— Ch., 2nd D. of, form. E. of Middlesex, *q.v.*; L.L. Kent 309; P.C. 202
— Jno. Fk., 3rd D. of, amb. Fr. 112; C.Y.G. 298; K.G. 742; L.L. Kent 309; L.S.H. 290; P.C. 203
— Ch., 5th D. of, K.G. 743; M.H. 302; P.C. 210
Dorso, M. F., C. Ro. 40
Dorville, Jno. Wm., adm (**H**) 851
Dotin, Jas. (or Jno.), G. Bdoes. 720
Doubleday, Edw., M.M. 246
Doubridge, Wm., B. Ex. 383
Douet, bp., Jam. 713
Dougal, bp. Dnbl. 532
— K. Sc. 18
Dougall, Wm. Heriot Maitl., adm. (**H**) 850
Doughes, Th. de, B. Ex. Ir. 583
Doughtie, Ed., dn. Her. 442
Douglas, Alex., bp. Mor. 534
— Andr., Amb. Nds., &c. 123
— Archd., Ld. Sess. 518
— Archd., Postm. G. Sc. 502
— Archd. and sir A., L.H.T. Sc. 497; L.J. Gen. 522; L.P.S. Sc. 501
— Aretas Akers-, Sec. Tr. 164
— hon. Arth. Gasc., bp. Abd. and Ork. 541
— Billy, adm. (**A**) 817
— Ch., gen. (**D**) 909
— sir Ch., adm. (**A**) 815
— Ch. Eurw. and sir C., K.C.M.G. 796; M.G.K.A. 799
— Chas., aft. 5th M. of Queensberry, *q.v.*
— Ch. Pye., gen. (**A**) 862
— Claud, gen. (**D**) 895
— Dav. Ld. Sess. 520
— Ed. Archd., dn. Ardf. 640
— Ed. Ron., C.I.E. 807
— Fras. Br., L. Prov. Edinb. 548
— Gavin, bp. Dkld. 533
— Geo., bp. Mor. 534
— hon. Geo. Hy., adm. (**H**) 850
— Hy. Alex., bp. Bbay. 661
— Hy. Jno., adm. (**H**) 849
— Hy. McDonell de W., gen. (D) 930
— sir Howard, Com. Io. Isl. 129; G.C.B. 772; G.C.M.G. 794; G. N. Brk. 695; gen. (**A**) 863; K.C.B. 777
— Jas., adm. (**A**) 817
— Jas., C. Ex. Sc. 505
— Jas., gen. (**B**) 864
— Jas., gen. (**C**) 871
— Jas., G. Br. Cbia. 698; G. Vanc. Isl. 699; K.C.B. 783
— Jas. and sir J., G.C.B. 770; G. Gsey. 669; gen. (**A**) 863; K.C.B. 774
— sir Jas., adm. (**A**) 814
— Jno., abp. St. Andr. 529
— Jno., bp. Carl. 476; bp. Sal. 467; dn. Winds. 474
— Jno., gen. (**B**) 866
— Jno. and sir J., gen. (**D**) 903; G.C.B. 771; K.C.B. 778
— Jno. and sir J., G. Ceyl. 673; K.C.M.G. 798
— sir Jno., gen. (**C**) 873
— Jno. Ersk., adm. (**A**) 819
— Jno. Leigh, adm. (**A**) 816
— sir Kenn. Mack., gen. (**B**) 868
— Neil and sir N., gen. (**B**) 870; K.C.B. 776; K.C.H. 788
— Pet. Jno., adm. (**D**) 828
— Rt., bp. Brn., 531; bp. Dnbl. 532
— Rt., gen. (**B**) 866
— Rt., gen. (**B**) 867
— Rt., gen. (**C**) 872
— Rt., gen. (**C**) 874
— Rt., gen. (**D**) 884
— Rt. Gord., adm. (**E**) 837
— Rt. Percy and sir R., G. C.G.H. 679; G. Jsey. 668; gen. (**D**) 893
— Sholto, adm. (**E**) 837
— Stair, adm. (**A**) 820
— Sylv., aft. ld. Glenbervie, *q.v.*, B.C. 252; B.T. 268; Ch. Sec. Ir. 563; K.C. 415; L.T. 158; P.C. 205
— Th. Mont., gen. (**D**) 886; K.C.B. 779
— Walt., G. Leew. Isl. 727
Douglas—*cont.*
— Wm., gen. (**D**) 883
— Wm., K.C.B. 774
— Wm., Ld. Sess. 518
— sir Wm., C. Ex. Sc. 504
— sir Wm., gen. (**B**) 864
— sir Wm., gen. (**C**) 874; K.C.H. 788
— sir Wm. Hy., adm. (**A**) 817
— Wm. Rt. K., L. Admy. 181-2
Douglas, lds., E. and M. of
— Jas., E. of, K.G. 736
— Archd., ld., aft. 9th D. of Hamilton, *q.v.*, LL. Forf. 510
— Alexr., M. of, aft. 10th D. of Hamilton, *q.v.*, Amb. Russ. 125; L.L. Lnrk. 511; P.C. 208
— Wm. Alexr., &c., M. of, aft. 11th D. of Hamilton, *q.v.*, Kt. Mar. Sc. 507
Doune, Jas., ld., Ld. Sess. 517
Dounton, Wm. de, K.B. 754
Douvedale, Jno., K.B. 754
Dovan, Jno., gen. (**D**) 926
Dove, Th., bp. Pboro. 458; dn. Norw. 455
Dovedall, Th., *see* Dowdall
Dover, Jno. le, J. It. 365
Dover, Earls of, *see also* Queensberry
Carey Family.
— Hy., 1st. E. of, form Hy. Carey, and visc. Rochford, *q.v.*
— Jno., 2nd E. of, form. visc. Rochford, *q.v.*
Jermyn Family.
— Hy., 1st ld., aft. ld. Jermyn, *q.v.*, C. Treas. Ir. 559; L.T. 155; P.C. 193
Yorke Family.
— Jos., 1st ld., form. hon. sir J. Yorke, *q.v.*
Doveton, Fred. L., gen. (**D**) 886
— Jno., gen. (**D**) 877; K.C.B. 777
— Jno. and sir J., G.C.B. 768; K.C.B. 775
— Wm. Jno., gen. (**D**) 914
Dovey (or O'Dove), Maur., dn. Arm. 597
Dowdall, Geo., abp. Arm. 595
— Jas., C.J.K.B. Ir. 578; J.C.P. Ir. 581; J.K.B. Ir. 578; S.G. Ir. 589
— Rt., C.J.C.P. Ir. 580; S.L. Ir. 591
— (or Dovedall), Th., M.R. Ir. 585
Dowden, Jno., bp. Edinb. 543
Dowdeswell, Geo. M., Q.C. 418
— Jno. E., M. Chy. 397
— Wm., Ch. Ex. 165; L.T. 157; P.C. 201
— Wm., G. Bah. Isl. 716
— Wm., gen. (**A**) 861
Dowell, Wallis, gen. (**D**) 920
— Wm. Mont. and sir W., adm. (**E**) 836; K.C.B. 781
Dowker, Howard, gen. (**D**) 887
— Howard Codr., gen. (**D**) 929
Dowling, Alf. S., C.C.J. 404; S.L. 413
Down, Ed. Aug., adm. (**H**) 844
— Jas. Somers, gen. (**D**) 896
Downe, visc.
Ducie Family.
— Wm., 1st visc., form. sir W. Ducie, *q.v.*

Downe, visc.—*cont.*
Dawnay Family.
— Hugh Rd., 8th visc., C.I.E. 807
Downer, Jno. W, K.C.M.G. 798
Downes, Lewis, dn. Kilm. 609
— Rt., bp. Down and Cnr. 604; bp. Ferns and L. 622; bp. Rph. 602; dn. Dry. 602
Downes, lds.
— Wm., aft. ld. D., C.J.K.B. Ir. 578; J.K.B. Ir. 579
— Ulysses, ld., form. U. de Burgh or Borough, *q.v.*, G.C.B. 770; gen. (**A**) 863; S.G.O., 260
Downham, Geo., bp. Dry. 601
— Jas., dn. Arm. 597
Downing, Dav., gen. (**D**) 891
— Geo. and sir G. (No. 1), C. Cus. 273; Tell. Ex. 167
— Geo. and sir G. (No. 2) Tell. Ex. 167
— sir Geo. (No. 3) K.B. 764
Downman, Hugh, adm. (**A**) 820; (**G**) 840
— sir Th., gen. (**B**) 870; K.C.B. 777; K.C.H. 788
— Wm., bp. Chest. 476
Downs, Dive, bp. Crk. and R. 632
— Dudl., R. Dr. P.A. 338
— Hy., bp. Dry. 601; bp. Elph. 608; bp. Killa. and Ach. 613; bp. Mth. 599
Downshire, M. of
— Wills., 1st M. of, form. E. of Hillsborough, *q.v.*
— Arthr., Bl. S. T., 3rd M. of, K.P. 751; L.D. Downsh. 569
Dowse, Jno. Rt., dn. Ferns, 623
— Rd., A.G. Ir. 589; B. Ex. Ir. 584; J. Ex. D. Ir. 584; S.G. Ir. 590; S.L. Ir. 593
Dowtford, Rt. de, dn. St. P. 452
Doyle, Ch. Hast. and sir C., G. N. Brk. 696; G. N.Sc. 695 gen. (**D**) 895; K.C.M.G. 796
— Ch. Jos., G. Gren. 724; gen. (**D**) 881
— sir Ch. Wm., G.C.H. 787; gen. (**B**) 869; K.C.H. 787
— sir Fras. Hast., gen. (**D**) 877
— sir Fras. H. Ch., C. Cus. 277; C. Exc. 281-2
— sir Jno., G.C.B. 767; G. Gsey. 669; gen. (**A**) 861; K.B. 766
— sir Jno. Mill., K.C.B. 775
— P. W., Amb. Mex. 133
— Welb. Ell., gen. (**C**) 872
— Wm., gen. (**B**) 867
Doyley and **Doyly**
— sir Ch. Walt., gen. (**D**) 912
— Chr., U.S.C. 255
— Fras., gen. (**B**) 866; K.C.B. 775
— Geo., G. Jam. 712
— Hy., gen. (**D**) 877
— Jno. Walt., gen. (D) 917
— Th., P.P. 416; S.L. 413
— sir Wm., C. Exc. 277; Tell. Ex. 167
Doyne, Ch., dn. Llin. 623
— Robert, C.B. Ex. Ir. 583; C.J.C.P. Ir. 580
Doythwal, abp. St. Dav. 463
Drangdra, Raj. of, K.C.S.I. 802
— Raj. of, K.C.S.I. 803
Draiton, *see* Drayton
Drake, capt. —, G. Newfd. 700
— Fras., Amb. G. St. 121; Amb. Vce. 116
— sir Fras. S., L. Admy. 180
— Fras. Wm., adm. (**A**) 815
— Jno., adm. (**H**) 847
— Rog., Adm. Ind. 647
— sir Wm., L. Admy. 177
— Wm. Hy., K.C.B. 780
Draper, sir Chr., L.M. Lond. 490
— Rd., S.L. 412
— Rt., bp. Ard. 608; bp. Kilm. and Ard. 607
— Wm. and sir W., gen. (**B**) 865; K.B. 765
Draycote (or Draycott), Hy., B. Ex. Ir. 583; Ch. Ex. Ir. 561; M.R. Ir. 585
Drayton and **Draiton**
— Nichs. de, B. Ex. 383
— (or Brayton), Th. de, M. Chy. 393
— sir Th., L.H.A. 171
— Wm., D. Chanc. Ir. 574
Drelincourt, Pet., dn. Arm. 597
Dreschel, Fredc. Bar., gen. (**B**) 866
Drew, Andr., adm. (**G**) 843
— Ed., Rec. Lond. 494; S.L. 408
— Fras. Ed., gen. (**D**) 924
— Hy. Rawl., gen. (**D**) 925
Droes, Hugh de, J. It. 367
Drogheda, E. and M. of
— Hy., 3rd E. of, L.J. Ir. 555
— Ch., 6th E., aft. 1st M. of, Ch. Sec. Ir. 562; F.M. 856; gen. (**A**) 858; K.P. 750; L.J. Ir. 557; Postm. G. Ir. 564
— Hy. Fr., 3rd M. of, K.P. 751; L.L. Kild. 569
Drogo, D. Bry. 28
— K. Scy. 55
— L.K. 353
Drokenesford, Jno. de, A.G. 398; bp. B. and W. 427; L.H.T. 152
Drope, Rt., L.M. Lond. 490
Drought, Th. Armstr., gen. (**D**) 894
Drouss, Rt., L.H.A. 172
Droz, N., Pres. Sw. C. 31
Dru, Laur., A.G. 398
Druce, Geo., Q.C. 418
Druck, H., Pres. Sw. C. 31
Drumlanrig, E. and visc.
— Jas., E. of, aft. 2nd D. of Queensberry, *q.v.*, L.H.T. Sc. 497
— Archd. Wm., visc., aft. 7th M. Queensberry, *q.v.*, Compt. H. 293; L.L. Dumf. 509; P.C. 216
Drummond, sir Ad., adm. (**A**) 820; K.C.H. 789
— Alexr., Ly. K.A. 513
— sir Alexr., Ld. Sess. 517
— Andr. Jno., gen. (**A**) 860
— Berkeley, gen. (**D**) 884
— Dunc., gen. (**B**) 866
— hon. Edm. K.C.I.E. 805; L.G. N.W. Pr. 653; M.C.I. 647
— Fras. Walk., gen. (**D**) 922
— Geo., C. Cus. 275; C. Exc. Sc. 504
Drummond—*cont.*
— Geo., C. Exc. Sc. 505
— Geo., L. Prov. Edinb. 548
— Geo., Sec. Thist. 749
— Gord. and sir G., G.C.B. 767; G. Can. 691; gen. (**A**) 861; K.C.B. 773
— Hy., gen. (**D**) 919
— Jas., bp. Brn. 531
— Jas., gen. (**A**) 861
— hon. Jas. Rt., and sir J., adm. (**D**) 833; (**E**) 834; G.C.B. 771; K.C.B. 780; L. Admy. 184
— Jno., gen. (**D**) 884
— Jno., aft. visc. Melfort, &c. *q.v.*, P.C. 192
— Percy, gen. (**C**) 875
— hon. Rt., abp. Yk. 486; bp. Sal. 467; bp. St. As. 462; P.C. 200
— Th., U.S. Ir. 563
— Vict. A. W., Amb. Bva. 119
— Walt., Ld. Clk. Reg. 525
— Wm., Amb. Scy. 114; Amb. Tky. 129; P.C. 207
— hon. Wm., aft. visc. Strathallan, *q.v.*, Comm. Tr. Sc. 497
— Wm. Abern., bp. Brn. 541; bp. Edinb. 542
Drummond, lds.
— Jno. Ld., L.J. Gen. 522
Drummond-Hay, *see* Hay
Drury, Alexr., gen. (**C**) 871
— Arth., gen. (**D**) 928
— Byron, adm. (**H**) 850
— Ch. Cort., gen. (**D**) 923
— sir Dr., Lt. T.L. 321
— Geo., gen. (**D**) 915
— Rt., Sp. H.C. 249
— Th., adm. (**A**) 817
— Wm., J. Pr. Ct. 421
— sir Wm., L.J. Ir. 554
— Wm. O'Br., adm. (**A**) 817
Drury-Lowe, *see* Lowe
Drusus, C. L., C. Ro. 44
— M. L., C. Ro. 45
Drusy, Th., K.B. 756
Dryby, Simon de, L.H.A. 171
Dryden, Jno., P. Laur. 301
Drysdale, Jas. Vic., G. Tob. 723
— Wm., gen. (**D**) 908
Duach-Fionn, K. Ir. 20
Dubdalethy, I. to III., bp. Arm. 595
Dubritius (St.), bp. Llff. 448
Dubs, J., Pres. Sw. C. 31
Dubtach, I. and II., bp. Arm. 595
Duc, Rog. le, L.M. Lond. 488
Ducane, Ch. and sir C., C. Cus. 277; G. Tasm. 708; K.C.M.G. 797; L. Admy. 184
— Edm. Fk., K.C.B. 783
Ducasse, Pasch (or Paul), dn. Clr. 597; dn. Ferns, 623
Ducat, Cyril Hugh Penn, gen. (**D**) 929
Ducie and **Ducy**
— (or Darcy), Hugh, K.B. 764
— sir Rt., L.M. Lond. 491
— sir Wm., aft. visc. Downe, *q.v.*, K.B. (1661) 763
Ducie, ld. and E. of
— Matth., 2nd ld., form. M. Morton, *q.v.*, L.L. Glouc. 308
— Hy. Jno., 3rd E. of, C.Y.G. 298; L.L. Glouc. 308; P.C. 216

*__Duck,__ Arth., M. Chy. 395
*__Ducke,__ Arth., Ch. Lond. 422
* ? Same pers.
__Ducket,__ sir Lionel, L.M. Lond. 490
__Duckett,__ Geo., C. Exc. 279-80
__Duckworth,__ Jno. Th. and sir J., adm. (__A__) 816; G.C.B. 767; G. Newfd. 700; K.B. 766
— Saml., M. Chy. 397
__Ducy,__ *see* Ducie
__Dudda,__ bp. Winch. 470
__Dudgeon,__ Peter, gen. (__D__) 890
__Dudley,__ sir Andr., K.G. 738
— Edm., Sp. H.C. 249
— sir Matth., C. Cus. 274
— sir or ld. Rt., aft. E. of Leicester, *q.v.*, Const. W. Cast. 322; K.G. 738; M.H. 302
— Wm., bp. Dham. 478; dn. Winds. 474
— sir Wm., Ld. Chanc. Ir. 575
__Dudley,__ lds.
Sutton family.
— Jno., 4th ld., Const. T.L. 320; K.G. 736; L.L. Ir. 552
— Ed., 5th ld., K.B. 758; K.G. 737
__Dudley__ and __Ward,__ Jno. Wm., 4th visc., aft. Earl D., P.C. 210; F. Sec. 228
__Dudoco__ or Bodeca, bp. Wlls. 427
__Duẽnas,__ F., Pres. S. Salv. 106
__Duff,__ K. Sc. 19
— hon. sir Alex., gen. (__A__) 862; G.C.H. 786; L.L. Elgn. 509
— Alex. Gord., gen. (__D__) 935
— Anna Jul. Grant, aft. Lady Grant D., Cr. Ind. 810
— Archd., adm. (__D__) 825; (__G__) 840
— Geo. Skene, L.L. Elgn. 509
— sir Jas., gen. (__A__) 860
__Duff,__ Jas., aft. 5th E. of Fife, *q.v.*, L.L. Bffsh. 508
— Mountst. Elph. Grant- and sir M., G. Mdras. 657; G.C.S.I. 801; P.C. 219; U.S.C. 235; U.S. Ind. 236
— Norwich, adm. (__G__) 841
— Rt., adm. (__A__) 815; G. Newfd. 700
— Rt. Wm., L. Admy. 186; L.T. 162
__Dufferin,__ Fk. T., 5th ld., aft. 1st E. and 1st M. of D. and Ava, form. Fk. and ld. Temple, *q.v.*, Amb. Eg. 130; Amb. Russ. 126; Amb. Tky. 130; C.D.L. 243; G.C.B. 773; G.C.M.G. 795; G.G. Can. 692; G.G. Ind. 650; K.C.B. 783; K.P. 751; L.L. Downsh. 569; P.C. 218; Paym. G. 245; U.S. Ind. 236
— Harr. Georg., Ctss. of, aft. Mss. of D. and Ava, 810
__Duffield,__ *see* Doffelte
__Duffin,__ Fk., gen. (__D__) 918
__Duffus,__ K. Sc. 19
__Duffe,__ Comp. with O'Dubhai and O'Duffy.
— sir Ch. Gord., K.C.M.G. 797
— Jno., gen. (__D__) 879
__Dugdale,__ Jno. and sir J., Mowb. H. 340; Norr. K.A. 329; Winds. H. 331
Dugdale—*cont.*
— Jno. Str., Q.C. 420
— Wm., Chest. H. 331; Gart. K.A. 327; Norr. K.A. 329; R. Cr. P.A. 335
__Dugmore,__ Wm., Q.C. 418
__Duilius,__ C., C. Ro. 42; Dt. Ro. 43
— K., C. Ro. 40
__Duina__ (or Dunnus), bp. Roch. 459
__Duke,__ sir Jas., L.M. Lond. 492
— Th. Assh., gen. (__D__) 894
__Duket,__ Rd., J. It. 367
__Dulac,__ Genl., K.C.B. 778
__Dule,__ *see* Dirle
__Duma,__ bp. Lich. 443
__Dumaresq,__ Hy., adm. (__H__) 850
— Jno. D. A., G. Lag. 687
__Dumaresque,__ Th., adm. (__A__) 816
__Dumas,__ Mons., G. Mtius. 683
__Dumbarton,__ Gec., 1st. E. of, gen. (__B__) 864; K.T. 747
__Dumbert,__ *see* Dunbert
__Dumblane,__ Th., visc., form. sir T. Osborne, *q.v.*, aft. E. of Danby, &c., *q.v.*
__Dumbleton,__ Ch., gen. (__D__) 924
__Dumbreck,__ Dav., K.C.B. 780
__Dumfries,__ E. of, *see* E. of Stair
__Dummer,__ Edmd., Sr. N. 257
__Dumraon,__ Mahar of, K.C.I.E. 805
__Dun,__ Chas. D., gen. (__D__) 887
— Ch. Wm., gen. (__D__) 915
— sir Dan., D. Arch. 420; J. Adm. Ct. 423
— Ed. Wint., gen. (__D__) 929
— Jno., gen. (__D__) 881
__Dunbar,__ Archd., Ld. Sess. 518
— Columba, bp. Mor. 534
— Gavin, abp. Glasg. 537; bp. Abdn. 530; Ld. Chanc. 515; Ld. Clk. Reg. 525 (not Dav. as in body)
— Jno. P., gen. (__D__) 877
— Jno. Seym., gen. (__D__) 912
— Rt. de, Ld. Clk. Reg. 524
— Th., gen. (__B__) 865
— Th., gen. (__C__) 873
— Wm., bp. Abdn, 540; bp. Mor. 544
— sir Wm., C. and A.G. 169; C.G. Ex. 169; L.T. 161
__Dunbar,__ E. of
— Geo., 1st E. of, form. ld. Hume of B., *q.v.*, K.G. 739; L.H.T. Sc. 497
__Dunbarton,__ *see* Dumbarton
__Dunbert__ (or Dumbert), bp. Winch. 470
__Duncan,__ bp. Dkld. 533
— I. and II., K. Sc. 19
— Adam, *see* visc. D., *infra*
— Alexr., bp. Glasg. 543; gen. (__D__) 876
— Andr., Mod. K. Sc. 547
— Hy., Mod. K. Sc. 547
— hon. Hy. and sir H., Lt. O. 261; K.C.H. 788
— Jno., bp. Isl. 539
— Jonn., G. Bbay. 659
__Duncan,__ visc.
— Adam, aft. 1st. visc. D., Adm. (__A__) 815
— Adam, c.c. visc. D., L.T. 161
__Duncannon,__ visc.
— Wm., visc., aft. 2nd E. of Bessborough, *q.v.*, L. Admy. 168-9-80; L.T. 157
Duncannon, visc.—*cont.*
— Jno. Wm., visc., aft. 4th E. of Bessborough, *q.v.*, C.W.F., &c. 272; H. Sec. 227; L.L. Carlow, 568; L.L. Kilk. 570; L.P.S. 241; P.C. 212
__Duncombe,__ hon. Arth., adm. (__G__) 842; L. Admy. 183
— hon. Aug., dn. Yk. 487
— sir Ch., L.M. Lond. 491
— sir Jno., Ch. Ex. 164; L.T. 155; M.G.O. 258; P.C. 190
— Wm., L.J. Ir. 555
__Dundas,__ Chas. St., gen. (__D__) 920
— Dav. and sir D., C. Ch. 855; G. Ch. Hosp. 936; G. Gsey. 669; G.C.B. 767; gen. (__A__) 859; K.B. 766
— sir Dav., J.A.G. 937; P.C. 215; Q.C. 417; S.G. 402
— sir Dav., Mast. Coll. Surg. 939
— Dunc., Ly. K.A. 513
— Fras. and sir F., G. C.G.H. 678; gen. (__A__) 860
— Fk., L.L. Ork. and Z. 511
— Geo., adm. (__A__) 819
— Geo., G. Bdoes. 721; G. St. Vin. 725
— Geo., G. Pr. Ed. Isl. 699
— Geo., Ld. Sess. 521
— hon. Geo. Heneage Lawr. adm. (__A__) 820; Compt. N. 257 L. Admy. 182
— Hy., adm. (__D__) 830
— Hy., aft. 1st visc. Melville, *q.v.*, B.C. 252; B.T. 267; H. Sec. 226; L.P.S. Sc. 501; Ld. Adv. 526; Pres. B.C. 252; P.C. 203; Tr. N. 256; P.C. 203; W. and C. Sec. 230
— Hy., aft. 3rd visc. Melville, *q.v.*, K.C.B. 777
— Jas., bp. Down and Cnr. 604
— Jas., Ld. Sess. 520
— sir Jas., Ld. Sess. 519
— Jas. Full., gen. (__D__) 879
— Jas. Wh. Deans, and sir J., adm. (__D__) 827; Clk. O. 260; G.C.B. 769; L. Admy. 183
— Jno., Ly. Dep. 513
— sir Jno. Burnet, adm. (__G__) 841
— Jno. Chas., L.L. Ork. and Z. 511
— hon. Jno. Ch., L.L. Ork. and Z. 511
— sir Laur., *see* ld. D., *infra*
— Ralph, gen. (__A__) 859
— Ralph Pet., C. Exc. Ir. 566
— hon. Rd. Saunders and sir R., adm. (__D__) 830; K.C.B. 778; L. Admy. 183-4
— Rt. (No. 1), L.P. Ct. Sess. 516; Ld. Adv. 526; Ld. Sess. 520
— Rt. (No. 2), L.P. Ct. Sess. 516; Ld. Adv. 526
— Rt. (No. 3), Ld. Adv. 526
— hon. Rt. Laur. and sir R., gen. (__B__) 870; K.C.B. 774
— Rt. Sand, aft. 2nd visc. Melville, *q.v.*, C.B. Ex. Sc. 523; Ch. Sec. Ir. 563; P.C. 208; Pres. B.C. 252-3
— Th., Ly. Dep. 513
— sir Th., adm. (__A__) 820; K.C.B. 776
— Th., *see* ld. D., *infra*

Dundas—*cont.*
*—— Wm., B.C. 252; Ld. Clk. Reg. 525; P.C. 206; Sec. at W. 234
*—— Wm., L. Admy. 181
* ? same pers.
—— Wm. Bolden, gen. (**D**) 887
Dundas, lds.
—— sir Th., aft. 1st ld. D., L.L. Ork. and Z. 511
—— Lawr., 2nd ld., aft 1st E. of Zetland, *q.v.*, L.L. Ork. and Z. 511; P.C. 202
—— Th. Jno., ld., aft. 2nd E. of Zetland, L.L. Yorks. N.R. 313
Dundemore, Steph. de, bp. Glasg. 536
—— (or Dundumore), Th. de, bp. Ross. 535
Dundonald, E. of
—— Jno., 2nd E. of, Comm. Tr. Sc. 497
—— Thos., 8th E. of, form. Th. Cochrane, *q.v.*
—— Th., 10th E. of, form. ld. Cochrane, *q.v.*; adm. (**A**) 820; (**C**) 822; G.C.B. 769
Dundumore, *see* Dundemore
Dune, Rog. de la, Const. T.L. 320
Dunetus, L.J. Gen. 522
Dunfermline, lds. and E. of
—— Geo., E. of, form. (1533) ld. Fyvie, *q.v.*
—— Alexr., 1st E. of, form. sir Alexr. Seton and ld. Urquhart, *q.v.*; Ld. Chanc. Sc. 515
—— Ch., 2nd E. of, L.H.C. K. Sc. 546; L.P.S. Sc. 501
—— Jno. 3rd E. of, Ld. Sess. 517
Abercromby Family.
—— Jas., 1st ld., form. Jas. Abercromby, *q.v.*
—— Ralph, 2nd ld., form. sir R. Abercromby, *q.v.*
Dunflower, Walt. de, M.M. 245
Dungannon, Arth., 1st visc., form. hon. A. Trevor, *q.v.*, C. Cus. Ir. 565
Dunglass, lds.
—— Cosp. A., ld., aft. 11th E. of Home, *q.v.*, U.S.F. 230
—— Ch. Alexr., ld., aft. 12th E. of Home, *q.v.*, L.L. Berw. 508
Dungarvan, Ch., visc. (son of 5th E. of Cork), L. Treas. Ir. 559
Dunker, sir Walt., G. Ch. Isl. 667
Dunkit, Robt. de, dn. Oss. 622
Dúnlo, Rd., visc., aft. 2nd E. of Clancarty, *q.v.*, B.C. 252
Dunlop, Frankl., gen. (**D**) 902
—— Hugh, adm. (**E**) 835; (**F**) 839
—— Jas., gen. (**B**) 867
—— Jas. Andr. Rt., adm. (**H**) 852
—— Wm., gen. (**D**) 881
Dunmore, E. of
—— Jno., 4th E. of, G. Bah. Isl. 716; gen. (**A**) 857
—— Ch. Adolph., 7th E. of, L.L. Stirl. 512
Dunn, sir Dav., adm. (**D**) 829; (**G**) 840; K.C.H. 789
—— Josias, gen. (**D**) 933
—— Mont. Buccl., adm. (**H**) 852
—— Wm., gen. (**D**) 891
—— Wm., L.M. Dbln. 641
Dunne, Ed., gen. (**A**) 861
—— Fras. P., Clk. O. 260; gen. (**D**) 900
—— Jeremh., L.M. Dbln. 642
—— Jno. Hart., gen. (**D**) 923
Dunning, Jno., aft. 1st ld. Ashburton, *q.v.*, P.C. 203; S.G. 402
Dunnus, *see* Duina
Dunow, Jno., bp. Limk. 638
Dunraven, E. of
—— Edw. Rd., 3rd E. of, K.P. 751; L.L. Lim. 570
—— Windh. Th., 4th E. of, K.P. 751; U.S.C. 235
Dunsany, lds.
—— Ed. W., 14th ld., L.L. Meath, 570
—— Ed., 16th ld., adm. (**G**) 843
Dunsford, Hy. Fk., gen. (**D**) 902
Dunsmore, Fras., 1st ld., aft. 1st E. of Chichester, *q.v.*, C.G.P. 299
Dunstan, *see also* Kitchin
—— (St.), abp. Cant. 430; bp. Lond. 451; bp. Worc. 472
Dunstavil, *see* Dunsterville
Dunsterville, Jas. H., gen. (**D**) 886
—— Lion. D'Arcy, gen. (**D**) 935
—— (or Dunstavil) sir Rt., K.G. (?) 734
Duntze, Jno Alexr. adm. (**D**) 831; (**E**) 834
Duport, Jas. dn. Pboro. 458
Duppa, Br., bp. Chich. 433; bp. Sal. 467; bp. Winch. 471; dn. Chr. Ch. Oxf. 457
Dupré, Ed., dn. Jsey. 668
Dupplin, visc.
—— Geo., 1st visc., form. sir Geo., and 1st ld. Hay., *q.v.*, aft. 1st E. of Kinnoull, *q.v.*
—— Geo., Hy., visc., aft. 7th E. of Kinnoull, *q.v.*, Tell. Ex. (1711) 167
—— Th., visc., aft. 8th E. of Kinnoull, *q.v.*, B.T. 264-5; C.D.L. 243; L.T. 157; P.C. 200; Paym. O. 244
Dupuis, Jno. Ed. and sir J., gen. (**D**) 890; K.C.B. 779
Duquerry, Hy., S.L. Ir. 592
Durand, Hy. Mar. and sir H., gen. (**D**) 901; K.C.S.I. 802; L.G. Pjab. 654; M.C.I. 646; Sec. S.I. 804
—— Hy. Mort. and sir H., K.C.I.E. 805; Sec. I.E. 808; Sec. S.I. 804
—— Jas., gen. (**B**) 865
Durando, Giov., K.C.B. 778
Durant, Jas., gen. (**D**) 878
—— Raym., K.B. 754
—— Th., M. Chy. 393
***Duras,** ld., K.B. (1464) 757
*—— Gaillard de Durefort, ld. of, K.G. 736
* Poss. same pers.
D'Urban, Benj., and sir B., G. Antig., &c. 727; G. Br. Gu. 715; G. C.G.H. 679; G. Dem. and Ess. 715; G.C.B. 769; gen. (**B**) 869; K.C.B. 774; K.C.H. 787
—— Wm., adm. (**D**) 824
—— Wm. Jas., gen. (**D**) 895
Durdent, Walt., bp. Lich. and Cov. 443
Durdin, Rt. G., L.M. Dbln. 642
Duredent, Walt., J. It. 367
Durell, Jno., dn. Winds. 474
—— Ph., adm. (**A**) 814
Durem, Jno., B. Ex. 383
Durham, sir Alexr., Ly. K.A. 513
—— Jas., gen. (**A**) 861
—— sir Ph. Ch. Calderwood-Henderson-, adm. (**A**) 818; G.C.B. 768; K.C.B. 774
Durham, lds. and E. of
—— Jno. Geo., 1st ld., aft. 1st E. of, form. J. G. and visc. Lambton, *q.v.*, Amb. Aus. 117; Amb. Pr. 118; Amb. Russ. 126; G.C.B. 772; G.G. N. Am. Prov. 692; L.P.S. 241; P.C. 211
—— Geo. F. D'A., 2nd E. of, L.L. Dham. 308
—— Jno. Geo., 3rd E. of, L.L. Dham. 308
Durie, Andr., bp. Gall. 538; Ld. Sess. 518
—— Geo., Ld. Sess. 518
—— Wm., K.H. 792
During, Lewis Alexr., gen. (**D**) 896
Durnford, Ed. Wm., gen. (**D**) 903
—— Elias Walk., gen. (**B**) 870
—— Geo., gen. (**D**) 893
—— Rd., bp. Chich. 433
Durninge, Jno., B. Ex. Ir. 583
Duroc, Off. Nap. 26
Duroure, Alex., gen. (**B**) 865
Dursley, visc.
—— Ch., visc., aft. 2nd E. Berkeley, *q.v.*, P.C. 194
—— Jas., visc., aft. 3rd E. of Berkeley, *q.v.*, adm. (**A**) (1707) 813
Durstus, K. Sc. 17
Dury, Theod., gen. (**B**) 865
Durward, Jno., K.B. 757
Dusmani, Ant., Count, K.C.M.G. 796
Dusseaux, Jos., gen. (**A**) 860
Duthac (St.), bp. Ross, 535
Dutton, Pet., G. I. Man, 665
—— sir Rd., G. Bdoes. 719
—— W. Holmes, gen. (**D**) 893
—— Alex., c.c. ld. D., also c.c. M. of Douglas and Cl., *q.v.*, aft. 10th D. of Hamilton, *q.v.*
Duval, Th., gen. (**C**) 872
Dwyer, Hy., gen. (**D**) 884
—— Hy. Arth., gen. (**D**) 919
—— Jno., gen. (**D**) 918
—— Th. Peard., gen. (**D**) 894
Dwyna, bp. Lich. 443
Dyacon, Michl., bp. St. As. 462
Dyal-Missar, Rajah, K.C.S.I. 802
Dyce and **Dyche,** *see* Dyke
Dyer, Archd. B., gen. (**D**) 887
—— sir Ed., Chanc. Gart. 746
—— Geo., gen. (**C**) 873
—— Jas. and sir J., C.J.C.P. 375; J.C.P. 378; J.Q.B. 372; S.L. 408; Sp. H.C. 249
—— Jno., K.C.B. 775
—— sir Th. Rd., gen. (**B**) 868
Dyes, Fras., Bl. M. P.A. 336; Winds. H. 331
Dyett, J. P. L., G. Nev. 730
—— R. H., G. Virg. Isl. 731
Dyke, Dyce and **Dyche**
—— Rt., L.K. Ir. 575; M.R. Ir. 585

Dyke, Dyce, and Dyche—*cont.*
— sir Wm. Hart-, Ch. Sec. Ir. 563; P.C. 219; Sec. Tr. 164; V.P. Ed. 255
Dymock (or Dimmock), Andr., B. Ex. 383; S.G. 401
— Th., K.B. 756
Dyneley, Hy. Ell., gen. (**D**) 933
Dynely, Th., gen. (**D**) 884
Dynevil, Barth., K.B. 754
Dynevor, Geo., 4th ld., L.L. Carm. 315
Dynham (or Derham), Jno., aft. ld. D., (*d.* 1509), K.G. 736; L.H.T. 154; Chanc. Ir. 575
Dyott, Rd., C. St. 283
— Wm., gen. (**A**) 861
Dysart, E. of
— Lion., 3rd E. of, K.T. 747
— Wm. J. M., 8th E. of, L.L. Rutl. 311
Dyson, Jer., B.T. 265-6; Coff. H. 294; L.T. 157; P.C. 203; Sec. Tr. 163
— Jerry Fras., gen. (**D**) 877
Dyvnwal, K. Wls. 16

E.

E—, *see also* Æ—
Ead—, *see also* Ed—
Eadbald and **Eadbaldus,** K.E. 1
— bp. Lond. 451
Eadbert and **Eadbertus**
— (St.), bp. Lindisf. 478
— bp. Sels. 432
— bp. Worc. 472
— K.E. 1-2
Eadbrightus, bp. Lond. 451
Eadfarthus, bp. Dunw. 454
Eadfrid (St.), bp. Lindisf. 478
Eadhedus, bp. Sidr. 446
Eadhelmus, bp. Sels. 432
Eadhericus, bp. Dorch. & Sidr. 446
Eadilfridus, bp. Elm. 454
Eadmerus, bp. St. Andr. 528
Eadmund, *see* Edmund
Eadna-Airgtheach, K. Ir. 20
Eadnothus, bp. Dev. 436
— (2) bp. Dorch. & Sidr. 446
Eadred, bp. Dham. 478
Eadsige (or Eadsinus), abp. Cant. 430
Eadsinus, bp. Winch. 470
Eadstanus, bp. Lond. 451
Eadulphus, I. and II., bp. Sidr. 446
Eagar, Rt. Jno., gen. (**D**) 909
Eagle, Fras. K., C.C.J. 403
Ealdferth, K.E. 2
Ealfwyn, *see* Alwinus
Ealstan (or Alfstan), bp. Shbn. 466
Eamer, sir Jno., L.M. Lond. 492
Eames, Jno., C. Tx. 284-5
— Jno., M. Chy. 397
Eanbald (2), abp. Yk. 485
Eanbert, bp. Hex. 480
— bp. Lindisf. 478
Eanfrid, K.E. 2
Eardley-Wilmot, *see* Wilmot
Earduff, bp. Roch. 459
Eardulph, bp. Lindisf. 478
Earl, Ed., C. Cus. 277; C. Cus. Ir. 504
— Th., L.J. Ir. 555
Earle, *see also* Erle
— Alfr., bp. suff. Marlb. 452
— Aug., C. Exc. 280
— (or Erle), Erasm., S.L. 409-10
— Giles, L.T. 156
— sir Jas., Mast. Coll. Surg. 939
— Jno., bp. Sal. 467; bp. Worc. 473; dn. Westr. 469
— Jno. March, gen. (**D**) 926
— Ralph A., Sec. P.L.B. 262
— Wm., L. Admy. 175
— Wm., gen. (**D**) 922
— Wm., S.L. 411
— Wm. Hy. Sh., gen. (**D**) 914
— Wm. R., Clk. O. 260
Earlie, Hamilton Ed. Geo., adm. (**H**) 853
Earlsfort, Jno., 1st ld., form. Jno. Scott, *q.v.*, aft. 1st V. & E. of Clonmel, *q.v.*
Earn, sir Hy., K.G. 733
Earnulph (St.), bp. Roch. 459
East, sir Ed. Hyde, C.J. Bgal. 652; Jud. Com. P.C. 360; P.C. 212
— Jas. Wyl., adm. (**H**) 853
Eastlake, Ch. L. and sir C., Pres. R.A. 941
Easton, Ad., dn. Yk. 486
Eastwick, Wm. Jos., M.C.I. 646
Eastwood, Jno., L.M. Dblin. 640
Eata (or Estata), St., bp. Hex. 480; bp. Lindisf. 478
Eatheadus, bp. Lich. 443
Eathored, bp. Worc. 472
Eberhard, D. Bva. 67
— I. to III., D. Fca. 71; D. Wbg. 80-1
— Louis, D. Wbg. 81
Ebrington, Hugh, visc., aft. 2nd E. Fortescue, *q.v.*, L.L. Dev. 307; L.L. Ir. 557; L.T. 161; P.C. 213; Sec. P.L.B. 262
Ebroicis, Steph. de, J. It. 367
Eburnus, Q. F. M., C. Ro. 45
Ebury, Rt., 1st ld., form. hon. R. Grosvenor, *q.v.*
Ecbert, *see also* Egbert
— K.E. 1
Ecca (or Acca), bp. Her. 441
Eccles, sir Jno., L.M. Dbln. 641
— Th., K.H. 790
Ecclesia, Wm. de St. Maria, bp. Lond. 451; Jy. 363
Ecfrid, K.E. 2
Echénique, J. R., Pres. Pu. 109
Echlin, sir Hy., B. Ex. Ir. 584; J.K.B. Ir. 579; S.L. Ir. 591.
— Rt., bp. Down. & Cnr. 604; dn. Tm. 613
Echlyn, Rt., gen. (**B**) 864
Eck, Lubb. Jan. baron Van, G. Ceyl. 672
Eckersley, Nathl., K.H. 789
Eckford, Jas., gen. (**D**) 887
Ed—, *see also* Ead—
Edan, St., bp. Ferns. 621
Edbert and **Edbertus**
— bp. Dorch. 446
— K.E. 1
Eddeville, St. de, Const. T.L. 320
Eddis, Arth. Sh., C.C.J. 405; Q.C. 418
Eddisbury, E. J., ld., form. E. J. Stanley, *q.v.*, aft. ld. St. of Alderley, *q.v.*
Eden, hon. Ash. and sir A., Ch. Com. Bma. 655; K.C.S.I. 803; L.G. Bgal. 652; M.C.I. 647
— Ch., adm. (**D**) 832; (**E**) 834; (**F**) 838; K.C.B. 780; L. Admy. 184
— Geo. Mort., gen. (**D**) 886
— Hy., adm. (**D**) 830; (**E**) 834; L. Admy. 183-4
— Jno., gen. (**D**) 885
— Morton and sir M., aft. 1st ld. Henley, *q.v.*, Amb. Dk. 127; Amb. G. St. 121; Amb. Gmy. 117; Amb. Pr. 118; Amb. Spn. 124; Amb. Sxy. 120; K.B. 765; P.C. 206
— Rt., bp. Mor. Ross and Cness. 544; Pr. bp. Sc. 540
— Rt. Henley, aft. 2nd ld. Henley, *q.v.*, M. Chy. 397
— hon. Rt. Jno., aft. 3rd ld. Auckl., *q.v.*, bp. S. and M. 484
— Th., L. Admy. 175
— Th., M. Chy. 395
— Wm., gen. (**A**) 862
— Wm., M. Chy. 396
— Wm., aft. 1st ld. Auckland, *q.v.*, Amb. Fr. 112; Amb. Spn. 123; B.T. 266-7; Ch. Sec. Ir. 562; P.C. 204; U.S.S. 226; V. Treas. Ir. 560
— hon. Wm. Fk., Tell. Ex. 168
— Wm. Hass., gen. (**D**) 892
Edendon, *see* Edington
Edenham, Geoff., J.K.B. 371
Edenstowe, Hy. de, M. Chy. 393
Ederus, K. Sc. 18
Edgar and **Edgarus**
*— bp. Her. 441
*— bp. Lond. 451
*— bp. Sidr. 446
* Prob. some same pers. Comp. dates.
— K.E. 3; L.H.A. 170
— K. Sc. 19
— (son Jas. II.), Pr. E. 13
— Hy., bp. Fife, 543
— Jas., C. Cus. Sc. 504
Edgcom, Wm. Hy., gen. (**D**) 927
Edgcombe and **Edgecumbe,** *see also* Mount-Edgcumbe
— G., *see* ld. E., *infra*
— Piers., K.B. 759
— Rd., K.B. 763
— Rd., *see* ld. E., *infra*
— sir Rd., Compt. H. 292
Edgcumbe, lds.
— hon. Rd., aft. 1st ld. E., C.D.L. 243; L.L. Cnwall. 307; L.T. 156; P.C. 199; V. Treas. Ir. 559-60
— hon. Rd., aft. 2nd ld. E., B.T. 265; Compt. H. 292; gen. (**C**) 871; L. Admy. 178; P.C. 200

Edgcumbe, lds.—*cont.*
—— Geo., 3rd. ld., aft. 1st visc. Mount Edgcumbe and Valletort, adm. (**A**) 814; C.G.P. 299; L.L. Cnwall. 307; P.C. 201; Tr. H. 291; V. Treas. Ir. 560
Edge, Jas. Br., C.C.J. 406
—— Jno. and sir J., C.J. N.W. Pr. 654; Q.C. 420
Edgell, Harry Edmd., adm. (**D**) 833; (**F**) 838
—— Hy. Folker., adm. (**D**) 823
Edgeworth, Ed., bp. Down and Cnr. 604
Edgore, Geo., S.L. 408
Edigein or **Edigen,** Th., dn. Elph. 609
Edilbinus, bp. Llff. 448
Edilwach, K.E. 1
Edilwald, K.E. 1-2
Edinburgh, Pr. Ern. Alb., aft. D. of, *q.v.*; *see also* Pr. Alfred; adm. (**E**) 836; G.C.I.E. 805; G.C.M.G. 795; G.C.S.I. 801; K.C.B. 781; K.P. 751; K.T. 749; P.C. 217
—— Marie Alex., Dss. of, Cr. Ind. 809
Edington (or Evendon), Wm., abp. Cant. 430; bp. Winch. 470; L.H.T. 153; Ld. Chanc. 354
Edisbury, Jno. or Jas., M. Chy. 396
Edlin, Pet. H., aft. sir P., Q.C. 418
Edline, Ed., Bar. Ex. Sc. 524
Edmeades, Hy., gen. (**D**) 931
Edmeston, Wm. gen. (**A**) 859
Edmondes, sir Th., Compt. H. 292; Tr. H. 291
Edmonds, Hy., K.B. 763
Edmondson, Jos., Mowb. H. 340
Edmonstone, Geo. Fk., K.C.B. 783; L.G. N.W. Pr. 653
—— Wm., adm. (**E**) 835; (**F**) 839
Edmund and **Eadmund**
*—— bp. Dham. 478
*—— bp. Lim. 638
*——(or St. Hamund), bp. Shbn. 466
*—— bp. Winch. 470
* Prob. some same pers. Comp. dates.
—— (son Hy. III.), Pr. E. 9
—— (son Ed. I.), Pr. E. 10
—— (son Ed. III.), Pr. E. 10
—— (iss. Ed. III.), Pr. E. 10, 11
—— (son Hy. VII.), Pr. E. 12
—— (Mortimer) (iss. Ed. III.), Pr. E. 10
—— (Tudor) (son Owen Tudor), Pr. E. 11
—— I. and II., K.E. 3, 4
Edmundi, *see* Fitzedmund
Edmunds, Ch., adm. (**H**) 848
Ednam, Th., bp. Bgr. 426
Ednevet, Howell Ap., bp. St. As. 462
Edred, K. E. 3
Edric, K.E. 1
—— (Duke), L.H.A. 170
Edulph, bp. Her. 441
Edwal ab Meyric, Pr. Wls. 16
—— Voel, Pr. Wls. 16
Edward, bp. Abdn. 530
*—— bp. Brn. 531
Edward—*cont.*
*—— L.G.C. Sc. 506
*—— L.H. Const. Sc. 507
*—— Ld. Chanc. Sc. 514
* Prob. some same pers. Comp. dates.
—— C. Svy. 54
—— D. Pma. 53
—— K. Pgl. 88; K.G. 735
—— K. Sc. 19
—— M. Bdn. 67
—— (the Confessor), K.E. 4
—— (the Elder), K.E. 3
—— (the Martyr), K.E. 3
—— I. to VI., K.E. 4, 5; *see also* under Princes of Wales and Princes of England, *infra*
—— III. (K.E.), K.G. 733; K.B. 755; L.H.A. 172
—— (son of Hy. III.), aft. Ed. 1st, *q.v.*, G. Ch. Isl. 667; L.J. Ir. 550; Pr. E. 9
—— (son Ed. I), aft. Ed. II., *q.v.*, K.B. 754; Pr. E. 10; Pr. W.E. 8
—— (son Ed. II.), aft. Ed. III., *q.v.*, Pr. E. 10
—— (Blk. Pr., son Ed. III.), Pr. E. 10; Pr. W.E. 8
—— (g. son Ed. III.), aft. D. of York, *q.v.*; Pr. E. 11
—— (iss. Ed. III.) (2), Pr. E. 11
—— (son of Blk. Pr.), Pr. E. 10
—— (son Hy. VI.), Pr. E. 12; Pr. W.E. 8
—— (son Ed. IV.), aft. Ed. V., *q.v.*, Pr. E. 12; Pr. W.E. 8
—— (son Rd. III.), Pr. E. 12; Pr. W.E. 8
—— (son Hy. VIII.), aft. Ed. VI., *q.v.*, Pr. E. 12; Pr. W.E. 8
—— (g. son Jas. I.), Pr. E. 13
—— -Augustus (g. son Geo. II.), aft. D. of York, *q.v.*, Pr. E. 14; K.G. 742
—— (son Geo. III.), aft. D. of Kent, *q.v.*, Pr. E. 14; K.G. 742; K.P. 750
—— Pr. (Ct. Pal. Rh.), KG. 740
—— -Charles, L.H.A. 170
Edwarde, Rd., B. Ex. Ir. 583
—— Wm., L.M. Lond. 490
Edwardes and **Edwards**
—— Arth. Wm., dn. Cork, 632
—— capt., G. Newfd. 700
—— Clem. Alex., gen. (**D**) 902
—— Ed., adm. (**A**) 817
—— Ed., gen. (**D**) 878
—— Fl. Ish., K.C.B. 784
—— hon. Geo. Warr., G. Labn. 675
—— Hy., adm. (**G**) 841
—— Hy., M. Chy. and Acct. G. 396
—— Hy. Th., dn. Bgr. 427
—— Herb. Benj. and sir H., K.C.B. 782; K.C.S.I. 802
—— sir Jas., L.M. Lond. 491
—— Jas. Bev., gen. (**D**) 934
—— Jno., Q.C. 419
—— Pet., gen. (**D**) 891
—— Rd., adm. (**A**) 815; G. Newfd. 700
—— Rd., M. Chy. 396
—— hon. Rd., Amb. Arg. 136; Amb. G. St. 122; Amb. Vza. 134
—— Rt. Bidw., K.H. 791
—— Samps., adm. (**A**) 817
—— Th., Ch. Lond. 422
—— Wm., S.L. 411
Edwin, K.E. 2, 3
—— (St.), bp. Worc. 472
—— sir Humphrey, C. Exc. 279; L.M. Lond. 491
Edwy, K.E. 3
Edye, Wm. Hy., adm. (**E**) 837
Eedes, Rd., dn. Worc. 473
Eeles, Jno., dn. Wford. 628
Effingham, Nichs. de, bp. Cloy. 630
Effingham, lds. Howard of, *see* Howard of Eff.
Effingham, Earls of
1st Creation.
—— Fras., 1st E. of, form. 7th ld. Howard of E., *q.v.*, Dep E.M. 327; gen. (**C**) 871
—— Th., 2nd E. of, Dep. E.M. 327; gen. (**B**) 865
—— Th., 3rd E. of, B.T. 267; Dep. E.M. 327; G. Jam. 712; M.M. 247; P.C. 203; Tr. H. 291
2nd Creation.
—— Kenn. Alexr., 1st E. of, form. 11th ld. Howard of E. *q.v.*, gen. (**A**) 862
Egbald, bp. Winch. 470
Egbert, *see also* Ecbert
—— (St.), abp. Yk. 485
—— (2), bp. Lindisf. 478
—— K.E. 1, 2, 3
Egeblaunch (or Egueblank), Pet. de, bp. Her. 441
Egelmar, bp. Elm. and Dunw. 454
Egelric, bp. Dham. 478
Egelwine, bp. Dham. 478
Egerton, hon. Algn. F., Sec. Adm. 187
—— Call. Rd., gen. (**D**) 904
—— sir Ch. Bulk., G.C.M.G. 794; gen. (**A**) 863; K.C.H. 788
—— Ed. C., U.S.F. 230
—— Edwin Hy., Amb. Fr. 113
—— hon. Fras., adm. (**E**) 836; (**F**) 839
—— ld. Fras., form. ld. F. L. Gower, *q.v.*, aft. 1st E. of Ellesmere, *q.v.*, Sec. at W. 234
—— hon. Hy., bp. Her. 442
—— hon. Jno., bp. Bgr. 426; bp. Dham. 479; bp. Lich. and Cov. 444; dn. Her. 442
—— Jno., aft. 2nd visc. Brackley, and 1st E. of Bridgewater, *q.v.*, K.B. 761
—— Rd., gen. (**D**) 881
—— Rt. Eyles and sir R., K.C.S.I. 803; L.G. Pjab. 654
—— Th., M.M. 246
—— sir Th., aft. 1st ld. and E. of Ellesmere, and visc. Brackley, *q.v.*, A.G. 399; L.K. 356; M.R. 388; S.G. 401
—— Wm., K.B. 763
Egerton of Tatton, Wm. T., 1st ld., L.L. Chesh. 307
Egferth, K.E. 3
Egfrid, bp. Lindisf. 478
—— K.E. 2-3
Egica or **Egiza,** K. Sp. 85
Eglasius, bp. Dunw. 454
Eglescliffe, Jno. de, bp. Cnr. 604; bp. Llff. 449
Eglinton and **Eglintoun,** E. of
—— Alexr., 6th E. of, Commr. Tr. Sc. 497
—— Alexr., 9th E. of, L.H.T. Sc. 498
—— Archd., 11th E. of, gen. (**A**) 858; L.L. Ayrsh. 508

Eglinton and Eglintoun—*cont.*
—— Hugh, 12th E. of, K.T. 748; L.L. Ayrsh. 508
—— Archd. Wm., 13th E. of, K.T. 748; L.L. Ayrsh. 508; L.L. Ir. 557-8; P.C. 215
Egmont, E. of
—— Jno., 2nd E. of, L. Admy. 179; P.C. 199; Postm. G. 238
—— Jno. Jas., 3rd E. of, L.L. Soms. 311
—— Geo. Jas., 6th E. of, adm. (**G**) 841
Egremont, *see* Hertford
Egremont, E. of
—— Ch., 2nd E. of, L.L. Suss. 312; P.C. 200; S. St. 224
—— Geo. O'Br., 3rd E. of, L.L. Suss. 312
Egric, K.E. 2
Egueblank, *see* Egeblaunch
Egwolfus, bp. Lond. 450
Egwyn (St.), bp. Worc. 472
Egypt, M. T., Khedive of, G.C.B. 773
Eithrial, K. Ir. 20
Ekins, Chas. and sir C., adm. (**A**) 819; G.C.B. 769; K.C.B. 776
—— Jeffr., dn. Carl. 476
—— Jno., dn. Sal. 468
Elanc, abp. St. Dav. 463
Elappea, K.E. 2
Elcho, lds.
—— Dav., ld., aft. 3rd E. of Wemys, *q.v.*, Comm. Tr. Sc. 498
—— Fras., ld., aft. 9th E. of Wemyss, *q.v.*, L.T. 161
Elde, Fras., M. Chy. 396
Elder, Geo. and sir G., gen. (**C**) 875; K.C.B. 776
—— Th., L. Prov. Edin. 548
—— Th., Postm. G. 502
—— Th. and sir T., G.C.M.G. 795
Eldon, Jno., 1st ld. and E. of, form sir Jno. Scott, *q.v.*; Jud. Com. P.C. 360; Ld. Chanc. 357
Eldridge, Ch. Monr., G. Antig. 728; G. Dnca. 731; G. Leew. Isl. 728; G. St. Xtr. and Nev. 729
Eldunen, abp. St. Dav. 463
Eleanor, Q. Nav. 85, 87
—— (of Aquitaine), Q.C.E. 7
—— (of Castile), Q.C.E. 7
—— (of Provence), Q.C.E. 7
—— (dau. K. John), Pr. E. 9
—— (dau. Hen. II.), Pr. E. 9
—— (g. dau. Hen. II.), Pr. E. 9
—— (dau. Edw. I.) (2), Pr. E. 10
—— (dau. Edw. II.), Pr. E. 10
—— (iss. Edw. III.), Pr. E. 10
—— (g. dau. Hy. VII.), Pr. E. 12
Elerius, B. Ex. 382
Eleutherius, bp. Cld. 599
—— (St.), bp. Winch. 470
Eleutherus, P. Ro. 32
Elffine, bp. Winch. 470
Elfric, *see* Alfric
Elfsig, bp. Lindisf. 478
Elfsinus (St.), bp. Winch. 470
Elfward (or Alword), bp. Lond. 451
Elfwinus, dn. St. P. 452
Elfwold, *see* Alfwold
Elgee, Ch., gen. (**D**) 928
—— Jno. Lindr., gen. (**D**) 921
Elgin, *see also* Ailesbury and Kincardine
Elgin, E. of
—— Th., 7th E. of, Amb. G. St. 121; Amb. Gmy. 117; Amb. Pr. 118; Amb. Tky. 129; gen. (**A**) 862; L.L. Fifesh. 510; P.C. 206
—— Jas., 8th E. of, Amb. Ch. 131; Amb. Jap. 131; Amb. U.S.A. 132; G.C.B. 772; G. Can. 692; G.G. Ind. 649; G. Jam. 713; K.T. 748; L.L. Fifesh. 510; P.C. 216; Postm. G. 239
—— Vict. Alexr., 9th E. of, C.W.P.B. 273; L.L. Fifesh. 510; P.C. 220; Tr. H. 292
—— Mary L., Css. dow. of, Cr. Ind. 809
Elgistil, bp. Llff. 448
Elguen or **Elgune,** bp. St. Dav. 464
Elias, bp. Clonm. 600
—— Ney, C.I.E. 808
Elibank, Alexr., 7th ld., L.L. Pbls. 511
Elicombe, *see* Ellicombe
Elim, K. Ir. 21
Elingham, Th. de, M. Chy. 393
Elion, Hubert, M.M. 245
Eliot and **Eliott,** *see* Elliot
Elisæus, bp. Gall. 538
Eliud, *see* Thelian
Elizabeth, C. Lux. 84
—— E. Russ. 90
—— Q.E. 5
—— (Woodville), Q.C.E. 7
—— (of York), Q.C.E. 8
—— (dau. Edw. I.), Pr. E. 10
—— (g. dau. Edw. III.), Pr. E. 11
—— (iss. Edw. III.), Pr. E. 10
—— (iss. Edw. III.), Pr. E. 11
—— (dau. Edw. IV.), Pr. E. 12
—— (dau. Hy. VII.), Pr. E. 12
—— (dau. Hy. VIII., aft. Q. E.), *q.v.*, Pr. E. 12
—— (dau. Chas. I.), Pr. E. 13
—— (dau. Jas. I.), Pr. E. 13
—— (g. dau. Jas. I.), Pr. E. 13
—— (g. dau. Q. Vict.), Pr. E. 15
—— (dau. Geo. III.), Pr. E. 15
—— -Caroline (dau. Geo. II.), Pr. E. 14
—— -Caroline (g. dau. Geo. II.), Pr. E. 14
—— Georg. Adel. (dau. Wm. IV.), Pr. E. 15
Elkington, Jno. Hy. Ford, G. Gsey. 669; gen. (**D**) 917
Ella, bp. Lich. 443
—— K. E. 1, 2, 3
Ellan, Den., dn. Kild. 619
Ellarker, Jno., S.L. 407
Ellauri, J., Pres. Ugy. 111
Ellenborough, lds. and E. of
—— Ed., 1st ld., form. Ed. Law., *q.v.*, Ch. Ex. 165; P.C. 207
—— Edw., 2nd ld., aft. 1st E. of, G.C.B. 772; G.G. Ind. 649; L. Admy. 183; L.P.S. 241; L.T. 160; P.C. 211; Pres. B.C. 253-4
Ellerker, sir Jno. de, L. Treas. Ir. 558
Ellesmere, Rog., bp. Cork, 630
Ellesmere, lds. and E. of
—— Th., 1st ld., form. sir T. Egerton, *q.v.*, aft. visc. Brackley, *q.v.*, L.T. 154
—— Fras., 1st E. of, form. ld. F. L. Gower, and ld. F. Egerton, *q.v.*, K.G. 744; L.L. Lanc. 309; Sec. at W. 234; U.S.W. & C. 231
Ellesworth, Sim. de, J. It. 368
Elletson, Rog. Hope, G. Jam. 712
Elley, Jno. and sir J., gen. (**B**) 869; K.C.B. 774; K.C.H. 787
Ellice, *see also* Ellis and Ellys
—— Ch. Hy. and aft. sir C., gen. (**D**) 900; G.C.B. 771; K.C.B. 780
—— Ed., P.C. 212; Sec. at W. 234; Sec. Tr. 163
—— Rt., gen. (**A**) 863
—— Russ., Chn. E.I.Co. 646
Ellicombe, Ch. Gr., gen. (**D**) 879; K.C.B. 779
Ellicott, *see also* Elliott
—— Ch. Jas., bp. Gl. and Br. 439; dn. Exr. 438
—— Ed., adm. (**H**) 844
Elliot, Elliott, Eliot, and **Eliott**
—— Alexr. J. H., gen. (**D**) 923
—— Ch. and sir C., adm. (**G**) 841; Amb. Txs. 132; G. Bmda. 701; G. St. Hel. 682; G. Trin. 722; K.C.B. 782
—— Ch. Alfr. and sir C., Ch. Com. Ass. 656; K.C.S.I. 803
—— Ch. Sc., gen. (**D**) 927
—— hon. Ch. Gilb. Jno. Bryd. and sir C., adm. (**B**) 821; (**D**) 832; (**E**) 834; K.C.B. 781
—— Danl., K.C.S.I. 802
—— Ed., B.T. 265-6
—— hon. Ed. Jas., B.C. 252; L.T. 158
—— Ed. King, Ch. Com. Cent. Pr. 655
—— Fk. Augs. H., C.I.E. 807
—— Geo., adm. (**D**) 832; (**E**) 834; K.C.B. 780
—— Geo., gen. (**B**) 866
—— Geo., gen. (**D**) 892
—— hon. Geo., adm. (**D**) 824; K.C.B. 779; Sec. Adm. 186
—— Geo., aft. sir G., and 1st ld. Heathfield, *q.v.*, Comm. F. Ir. 564; G. Gibr. 670; gen. (**A**) 858; K.B. 765
—— Geo. Augs., adm. (**G**) 842
—— Gilb., dn. Brl. 440
—— sir Gilb. (No. 1), Jy. Sc. 522; Ld. Sess. 520
—— sir Gilb. (No. 2), Ld. Sess. 520; L.J. Clk. 516
—— Gilb. and sir G. (No. 3), L. Admy. 178; L.T. 157; P.C. 201; Tr. Ch. 294; Tr. N. 256
—— sir Gilb. (No. 4), aft. 1st ld. and E. of Minto, *q.v.*, P.C. 205
—— Granv., gen. (**C**) 871
—— Hy., gen. (**B**) 869
—— Hy. Algn., adm. (**G**) 841
—— hon. Hy. Geo. and sir H., Amb. Aus. 117; Amb. Dk. 127; Amb. Gr. 129; Amb. It. 114; Amb. Scy. 115; Amb. Tky. 130; G.C.B. 773; P.C. 217
—— Hy. Maur., gen. (**D**) 914
—— Hy. Miers, K.C.B. 782
—— Hugh (No. 1), Amb. Dk. 127; Amb. G. St. 121; Amb. Pr. 118; Amb. Scy. 114; Amb. Sxy. 120
—— Hugh (No. 2), G. Bdoes. 720; G. Mdras. 656; G. Leew. Isl. 727; P.C. 209
—— Hugh Maxn., adm. (**H**) 852
—— Jno., adm. (**A**) 815; G. Newfd. 700
—— Jno., gen. (**D**) 911
—— sir Jno., B. Ex. Ir. 584

Elliot, Elliott, Eliot, and Eliott —*cont.*
—— hon. Jno. E., Sec. B.C. 254
—— Rd., C. Exc. 279-80
—— Rd., J.C.P. 378; S.L. 408
—— Rt., adm. (**D**) 827; (**G**) 840
—— (or Elyot), Rt., bp. Wford. 626
—— Rog., G. Gibr. 669; gen. (**C**) 871
—— Russ., adm. (**G**) 842
—— Th. Fk. and sir T., K.C.M.G. 796; U.S. C. 236
—— Walt., K.C.S.I. 802
—— Wm., C. Treas. Ir. 561; Ch. Sec. Ir. 563; P.C. 208
—— Wm., M.R. 387
—— Wm. and sir W., K.C.H. 788; K.H. 791
—— Wm., *see* ld. E., *infra*
—— Wm. Granv., K.H. 790
—— Wm. Ham., gen. (**D**) 902
—— Wm. Hy. and sir W., G.C.B. 770; gen. (**D**) 891; K.C.B. 779; K.H. 792
—— Wm. Russ., gen. (**D**) 912
Eliot, lds.
—— Wm., ld., form. hon. Wm. Eliot, *q.v.*, aft. 2nd E. of St. Germans, *q.v.*, Amb. G. St. 121; Amb. Nds., &c. 122; L. Admy. 180; L.T. 158-9; U.S. F. 229
—— Ed. Gr., ld., aft. 3rd E. of St. Germans, *q.v.*, Amb. Spn. 124; Ch. Sec. Ir. 563; L.T. 159-60; P.C. 214
Ellis and **Ellys,** *see also* Ellice
—— Anthy., bp. St. Dav. 465
—— Arth. Ed. Augs., gen. (**D**) 935
—— Barr. Helb. and sir B., K.C.S.I. 803; M.C.I. 647
—— Bern., G. Gsey. 668
—— Fras., aft. Ellis-McTaggart, C.C.J. 404
—— Fk. Jno., gen. (**D**) 915
—— Geo. J. W., C.W.F. &c. 272; P.C. 211
—— Hy., G. N.Sc. 695
—— Hy. and sir H., Amb. Bzl. 135; Amb. Ch. 131; Amb. Pers. 130; B.C. 253; Clk. Pells, 168; K.C.B. 782; K.H. 790; P.C. 212
—— Hy. Walt., K.C.B. 774
—— Jno., dn. Her. 442; U.S.S. 225
—— Jno. Join., gen. (**C**) 872
—— Jno. W. and sir J., L.M. Lond. 492
—— Saml. Burd., gen. (**D**) 889; K.C.B. 778
—— Th., dn. Kild. 619
—— Welbore, bp. Kild. 617; bp. Mth. 599; dn. Chr. Ch. Dbln. 618
—— Welbore, aft. 1st ld. Mendip, *q.v.*, C. Sec. 234; L. Admy. 178; P.C. 200; Sec. at W. 233; Tr. N. 256; V. Treas. Ir. 560
—— Wm., A.G. 398
—— Wm., adm. (**H**) 850
—— Wm. B., Ex. 383
—— (or Ellys) Wm. and sir W., J.C.P. 379; S.G. 401; S.G. Ir. 589; S.L. 410
Ellison, Cuthb., gen. (**A**) 858
—— Th., C.C.J. 404
Ellys, *see* Ellis and Ellice
Elmarus, bp. Sels. 432
Elmer, bp. Shbn. 466
Elmham, sir Wm. de, L.H.A. 173
Elmhirst, Ch., gen. (**D**) 904
Elmsley, Wm., C.C.J. 404; Q.C. 417
Elnaeth, abp. St. Dav. 463
Elphege and **Elphegus,** *see also* Alphege and Alphage
*—— (St.), abp. Cant. 430; bp. Winch. 470
*—— bp. Lich. 443; bp. Wells, 427
* Poss. same pers. Comp. dates.
Elphinstone, Alexr., *see* ld E., *infra*
—— sir Geo., L.J. Clk. 516
—— hon sir Geo. Keith, aft. 1st ld. and visc. Keith, *q.v.*, adm. (**A**) 816; K.B. 765
—— sir How., gen. (**C**) 875
—— How. Crawf. and sir H., gen. (**D**) 931; K.C.B. 783
—— Jas., aft. 1st ld. Balmerino, *q.v.*, Ld. Sess. 518; Sec. St. Sc. 502
—— sir Jas. Dalrymple How., L.T. 162
—— Jno., gen. (**D**) 916
—— hon. Jno., aft. 5th ld. Balmerino, *q.v.*, Ld. Sess. 520
—— hon. Mountst., G. Bbay. 659
—— Robt. Dalr. Horn., gen. (**A**) 858
—— Wm., bp. Abdn. 530; bp. Ross. 535; L.P.S. Sc. 500; Ld. Chanc. Sc. 515
—— sir Wm., L.J. Gen., 522; Ld. Sess. 519
—— hon. Wm. Fullerton, Chn. E.I. Co. 645; L.L. Dumb. 509
—— Wm. Keith, gen. (**C**) 875
Elphinstone, lds.
—— Alexr., Master of, and aft. 4th ld. E., L.H.T. Sc. 497; Ld. Sess. 517
—— Jno., 11th ld., L.L. Dumb. 509
—— Jno., 12th ld., L.L. Dumb. 509
—— Jno., 13th ld., G. Bbay. 659; G.C.B. 772; G.C.H. 787; G. Mdras. 657; P.C. 213
Elrington, Fredk. Rt., gen. (**D**) 906
—— Jno., K.B. 757
—— Rd. Good., gen. (**D**) 879
—— Th., bp. Ferns and L. 622; bp. Lim. A. and A. 639
—— Th. Ger., gen. (**C**) 873
Elsley, Ch. H., C.C.J. 403
Elstan, *see* Leovingus
Elstanus, bp. Lond. 451
Elton, Ch. Is., Q.C. 420
Eltonhead or **Eltonhed,** Ed. M. Chy. 395
—— Jno., S.L. 409
Eludgeth, abp. St. Dav. 463
Eluid, abp. St. Dav. 463
Elva, L. Æ., C. Ro. 38
—— T. Æ., C. Ro. 37
Elvanus, abp. Lond. 450
Elvaoth, abp. St. Dav. 463
Elves, sir Jno., C. Exc. 278
Elvoed, abp. St. Dav. 463
Elvogus, bp. Llff. 448
Elwaed, abp. St. Dav. 463
Elwald, K.E. 2
Elwes, Jno. Timms H., gen. (**B**) 867
Elwyn, Jno. Harv., gen. (**D**) 909
—— Th., gen. (**D**) 904
—— Th., gen. (**D**) 910
—— Wm., gen. (**D**) 912
Ely, Nichs. de, bp. Winch. 470; bp. Worc. 472; L.H.T. 152; Ld. Chanc. 353; L.K. 353
—— Philip de, L.H.T. 152
—— Ralph de, B. Ex. 382
—— Rd. de, L.H.T. 152
—— Wm. de, Jy. 364; L.H.T. 152
—— Adam, visc. Loftus of, *see* Loftus
Ely, E. and M. of
1st Creation.
—— Hy. 1st E. of, form 4th visc. Loftus, *q.v.*, K.P. 750
2nd Creation.
—— Ch., 1st E. aft. 1st M. of, form. ld. and visc. Loftus, *q.v.*, Postm. G. Ir. 564
—— Jno., 2nd M. of, K.P. 750
Elyot (or Eliot), Rt., bp. Wford. 626
Emanuel and **Emmanuel**
—— K. Pgl. 88; K.G. 737
—— Philibert, D. Svy. 54; K.G. 738; R. Nds. 82
Embercus, bp. Sidr. 446
Emeldon, Rt. de, Ch. Ex. Ir. 561
Emelden, Wm. de, M. Chy. 393
Emeric, K. Hgy. 59
Emerson, Alexr. Lyon, gen. (**D**) 934
—— Jas., gen. (**D**) 921
—— Th., L.M. Dbln. 641
Emilius-Augustus, D. S.G.A. 78
Emly, Ed., dn. Dry. 602
Emly, lds.
—— Wm., ld., form W. Monsell, *q.v.*
Emma (g. dau. Hen. I.), Pr. E. 9
Emmanuel, *see* Emanuel
Emmett, Anth., gen. (**D**) 889
Empson, Rd. and sir R., Sp. K.C. 249; C.D.L. 242
—— Wm., L.M. Dbln. 641
Enderby, Ch., G. Auck. Isl. 710
—— Wm., K.B. 758
Eneuris, bp. St. Dav. 464
Enfant, Walter L', C.J.K.B. Ir. 577
Enfield, visc.
—— Geo. Stev., visc., form. hon. G. S. Byng, *q.v.*, ld. and aft. 2nd E. of Strafford, *q.v.*
—— Geo. Hy. Ch., visc., aft. ld. and 3rd E. of Strafford, *q.v.*, L.L. Mdx. 310; Sec. P.L.B. 262; U.S.F. 230; U.S. Ind. 236
Engaine, Warn., J. It. 368
Engilbert, R. Nds. 82
England, Poole Vall., gen. (**D**) 892
—— Rd., gen. (**B**) 866; K.H. 791
—— Rd. and sir Rd., gen. (**D**) 883; G.C.B. 769; K.C.B. 777
Englefeld and **Englefield**
—— Alan de, J. It. 367
—— Matth. de, bp. Bgr. 425
—— Th., J.C.P. 378; S.L. 408
—— Th. and sir T., Sp. H.C. 249
—— Wm. de, J. It. 368; Jy. 365

For List of Abbreviations, see pp. 944-952.

English, Fk., gen. (**D**) 899
Enion (or Anian, *q.v.*) (2), bp. St. As. 462
Ennishowen, Geo. Ham., ld., form. E. of Belfast, *q.v.*, aft. 3rd M. of Donegal, *q.v.*
Enniskillen, Jno. Will., 2nd E. of, K.P. 751; L.L. Ferm. 569
Entrecasteaux, Chev. de Br. d', G. Mtius. 683
Eochaidh, K. Ir. 21
—— -Eadgothac, K. Ir. 20
—— -Gunait, K. Ir. 21
—— -Moidhmeodhain, K. Ir. 21
—— -Mumho, K. Ir. 20
Eolla, bp. Sels. 432
Eorpwald, K.E. 2
Er, K. Ir. 20
Erard (St.), bp. Ard. 607
Ercenbert, K.E. 1
Erchenwin, K.E. 2
Erchwine, K.E. 2
Ercole, *see also* Hercules
—— I. to III., D. Mda. 53
Ercombert, K.E. 1
Erdington, Giles de, J.C.P. 377; Jy. 364
Erdulf, K.E. 2
Eresby, *see* Willoughby de Eresby
Ergham or Erghum, Ralph, bp. B. and W. 428; bp. Sal. 467; C.D.L. 242
Eric and **Erich,** D. Brk. 69
—— Pr. Mkg. 74
—— I to IX., K. Dk. 93
—— X. to XIV., K. Sw. 92
—— X. (K. Dk.), K.G. 734
Ericsen, Jno. Eric, Pres. Coll. Surg. 939
Erispoe, D. Bry. 27
Erkenwald (St.), bp. Lond. 450
Erle, *see also* Earle
—— Erasm., S.L. 409
—— Pet. P.C. 218; Q.C. 417
—— Th., gen. (**A**) 857; L.G.O. 259; P.C. 195
—— Th., gen. (**C**) 872
—— Wm. and sir W., C.J.C.P. 376; J.C.P. 380; J.Q.B. 373; Jud. Com. P.C. 361; K.C. 416; P.C. 216; S.L. 413
Ermenric, K.E. 1
Ermensind, C. Lux. 84
Ermyn, Wm., B. Ex. 383
Ernald, bp. St. Andr. 528
Erne, E. of
—— Jno., 3rd E. of, form. J. Crichton or Crighton, *q.v.*, K.P. 751
—— Jno. Hy., 4th E. of, K.P. 752
Ernest, D. Bva. 68
—— D. S. Alt. 78
—— El. Sxy. 77
—— M. Aus. 58
—— M. Bdn. 67
—— R. Nds. 82
—— I., D. S.G.A. 78
—— II., D.S.C. and G. 78; K.G. 744
—— I. and II., D. Brk. 69-70
—— I. and II., D. Su. 80
—— -Anthony, D. S.C. and G. 78; K.G. 744
—— -Aug., D.S.W. 79
—— -Aug., D. Hnr. 70; El. Hnr. 70
—— -Aug. (bro. of Geo. I., bp. of Osnaburg and D. of York), K.G. 741; Pr. E. 13

Ernest—*cont.*
—— -Aug., Pr., aft. D. of Cumberland, *q.v.*, and K. Hnr.; K.G. 742; K. Hnr. 71; P.C. 206; Pr. E. 15
—— -Aug. Const., D. S. Wr. 79
—— -A. W., &c., D. Brk. 71
—— -Casimir, Pr. Nass. 76
—— -Fredk., D.S.C. and G. 78
—— -Fredk., M. Bdn. 67
—— -Fredk., I. and II., D. S. Alt. 78
—— -Fredk. Chas., D. S. Alt. 78
—— -Fredk., P.G., D. S. Alt. 78
—— -Louis, Lg. H. Dt. 72
—— Louis I. and II., D.S. Mgn. 79
—— -Louis Ch. Alb. Wm. (g. son Q. Vict.), Pr. E. 15
—— -Louis Fk., D.S.G.A. 78; K.G. 742

For non-reigning Dukes and Princes, see under their territorial names.

Ernle and **Ernley**
—— Jno., A.G. 398; C.J.C.P. 375; S.G. 401
—— sir Jno., B.T. 263; Ch. Ex. 164; L. Admy. 175; L.T. 155; P.C. 191-2
Ernostus (or Arnulph), bp. Roch. 459
Erpingham, sir Th., K.G. 734; W.C.P. 318
Erpwald, K.E. 2
Errazuriz, F., Pres. Chi. 111
Errington, Arnold Ch., gen. (**D**) 902
Erroll, family of
—— L.H. Const. Sc. 507
Erroll, E. of
—— Gilb., E. of (1321), form. sir G. Hay, *q.v.*
—— Wm., 15th E. of, Kt. Mar. Sc. 507; L.H.C. K.Sc. 546
—— Wm. Geo., 16th E. of, G.C.H. 786; K.T. 748; Kt. Mar. Sc. 507; L.L. Abdn. 508; L.S.H. 290; M.B.H. 303; P.C. 212
Erskine or **Areskine**
—— sir Alexr., Ly. K.A. 513
—— Ch., Jy. Sc. 522; L.J. Clk. 516; Ld. Adv. 526; Ld. Sess. 520
—— sir Ch., Ly. K.A. 513
—— Dav., gen. (**C**) 872
—— Dav., Ld. Sess. 520
—— hon. Ed. M., Amb. Gr. 129; Amb. Sw. and N. 127
—— Geo., gen. (**D**) 905
—— sir Geo., Ld. Sess. 519
—— hon. Hy., Ld. Adv. 526
—— hon. Jas., Kt. Mar. Sc. 507
—— sir Jas., gen. (**B**) 867
—— Jas. Elphinstone, adm. (**E**) 837; L. Admy. 186
—— Jno., dn. Cork, 632
—— Jno. Elphinstone, adm. (**D**) 831; (**E**) 834
—— Jno. Kenn., K.C.H. 787
—— sir Hy., gen. (**B**) 865; Sec. Thist. 749
—— hon. Hy. Dav., dn. Rip. 482
—— Jas., Bar. Ex. Sc. 524
—— Jas., L.J. Clk. 516
—— Jas., Ld. Sess., 520
—— hon. Jas., Ld. Sess. 520
*—— Rt. (ld. of Erskine), L.G.C. Sc. 506
*—— Rt. de, L.J. Gen. 522
* Prob. same pers.

Erskine or Areskine—*cont.*
—— Th. and sir T., aft. E. of Brechin, Ld. Sess. 518; Sec. St. Sc. 502
—— hon. Th., C.J. Bank. 392 J.C.P. 380; Jud. Com. P.C 360; K.C. 416; P.C. (1831), *see errata* for p. 212; S.L. 413
—— hon. Th., *see* ld. E., *infra*
—— sir Th., aft. 1st visc. Fenton and E. of Kellie, *q.v.*, C.Y.G. 298
—— Wm., abp. Glasg. 537
—— Wm., Ld. Sess. 520
—— sir Wm., gen. (**B**) 866
—— sir Wm., gen. (**C**) 873
Erskine, lds., *see also* E. of Mar

Scotch Title.
—— Jno., ld., Ld. Sess. 517
—— Jno., ld., K.B. 762; Ld. Sess. 517
—— Th. ld., aft. E. of Buchan, K.B. 761
—— Jas., ld., aft. 7th E. of Buchan, K.B., *q.v.*, 762

English Title.
—— hon. Th., aft. 1st ld. E., K.C. 415; K.T. 748; L.H.S. 287; Ld. Chanc. 357; P.C. 208
—— Dav. Montagu, 2nd ld., Amb. Bva. 119; Amb. U.S.A. 132
Ert, bp. Ardf. and Agh. 639
Erville, gen. de Ant. d', K.C.B. 778
Ervigio, K. Sp. 85
Ervigius, K. Sp. 85
Ervin, bp. St. Dav. 464
Esca (or Escus), K.E. 1
Eschaid, bp. Arm. 595
Escobar, Pres. Pgy. 110
Escuris, Matth. de, J. It. 365
Escus, *see* **Esca**
Escwine, K.E. 2
Esdaile, sir Jas., L.M. Lond. 492
Esher, Wm. B., ld., form. sir W. B. Brett, *q.v.*
Esmond, Jno., bp. Emly, 625; bp. Ferns, 621
Esmonde, Jno., L.T. 161
Esna, bp. Her. 441
Espartero, Bald., Ct. of Luchana, &c., G.C.B. 769
Espernon, Bern. de N. de F. D. D', K.G. 740
Espinasse, Jas., C.C.J. 403
Espinosa, X., Pres. Ecr. 108
Esquilinus, *see also* Tricostas
—— L. S., Dec. Ro. 38
Esquivel, A., Pres. C.R. 106
Esseby, Rt. de, Jy. 364
Esseburne, Rt. de, J.C.P. 376
Esseby, Jord. de, J. It. 367
Essendon, sir Wm. de, L. Treas. Ir. 558
Essex, lds. and E. of
—— Hy de, or E. of, J. It. (1155-6) 365; W.C.P. 317

Mandeville Family.
—— Wm., 1st E. of, L.H.A. 170

Fitz-Peter or Fitz-Piers Family.
—— Geoff., 1st E. of, form. G. Fitz-Peter, *q.v.*, J. It. 365
—— Geoff., 2nd E. of, form. G. Fitz-Piers, *q.v*

De Bohun Family.
—— Humphr., 1st E. of, *see* Hereford and Essex

Essex, lds. and E. of—*cont.*
Bourchier Family.
— Hy., 1st E. of, form. 1st visct. Bourchier, *q.v.*; L.H.T. 153; L.K. 355
— Hy., 2nd E. of, C.G.P. 299; K.G. 737
Cromwell Family.
— Th., E. of, form. Thos. and ld. Cromwell, *q.v.*
Parr Family.
— Wm., 1st E. of, form. ld. Parr, of Kendal, *q.v.*, aft. M. of Northampton, *q.v.*
Devereux Family.
— Walt., 1st E. of, form. 2nd visc. Hereford, *q.v.*
— Rt., 2nd E. of, E.M. 326; K.G. 739; L.L. Ir. 554; M.G.O. 258; M.H. 302
— Rt., 3rd E. of, L.C.H. 295
Capel Family.
— Arth., 1st E. of, L. Admy. 175; L.L. Ir. 555; L.L. Herts, 309; L.T. 155; P.C. 191-2; Prem. 140
— Alg., 2nd E. of, Const. T.L. 321; gen. (**B**) 864; L.L. Dors. 307; L.L. Herts, 309; P.C. 195
— Wm., 3rd E. of, C.Y.G. 298; K.G. 741; K.T. 747; P.C. 198
— Wm. Anne. H., 4th E. of, L.L. Herts, 309
— Geo., 5th E. of, L.L. Heref. 308
Essington, Wm. and sir W., adm. (**A**) 817; K.C.B. 773
Estata, *see* Eata
Estcourt, Jas. Bucknall Bucknall, gen. (**D**) 889
— Th., M. Chy. 395-6
— Th. H. S. Sotheron-, H. Sec. 227; P.C. 216; Pres. P.L.B. 262
Este, Ch., bp. Oss. 620; bp. Wford. and L. 627
— Ch. Wm., gen. (**C**) 873
Esterhazy, Pr. Paul Anthy., G.C.B. 769
Estfeld or **Estfield,** Wm., L.M. Lond. 490
Esturmy, Th., K.B. 754
— sir Wm., Sp. H.C. 248
Eteson, Fras., gen. (**D**) 928
Etfinus, K. Sc. 18
Eth, *see* Ath and Aeth
— K. Sc. 19
Ethelan, bp. Worc. 472
Ethelard (or Athelard), abp. Cant. 430; bp. Winch. 470
— K.E. 2
Ethelbald, abp. Yk. 485
— (2) bp. Shbn. 466
— K.E. 3
Ethelbert and **Ethelbertus**
— bp. Gall. 538
— bp. Hex. 480
— K.E., 1, 2, 3
— Pryn, K.E. 1
Ethelbyrht, K.E. 2
Etheleage, bp. Shbn. 466
Ethelfrith, K.E. 2
Ethelgarus, abp. Cant. 430; bp. Sels. 432
— bp. Dev. 436
Ethelheard, K.E. 2
Ethelhere, K.E. 2
Ethelhune, bp. Worc. 472
Ethelmar, bp. Elm. and Dunw. 454
Ethelmen, abp. St. Dav. 463
Ethelnoth and **Ethelnothus**
— (or Æthelnotus), abp. Cant. 430
— bp. Lond. 451
Ethelred, abp. Cant. 430
— (several) K.E. 2, 3
Ethelric (2), K.E. 2
Ethelricus (or Agelred), bp. Sels. 432
Ethelsius, bp. Shbn. 466
Ethelstan, bp. Wltn. 466
Ethelulphus, bp. Sels. 432
Ethelwald and **Ethelwold**
*— bp. Lich. 443
*— (St.) bp. Lindisf. 478
*— (2) bp. Shbn. 466
*— (St.) bp. Winch. 470
* Prob. some same pers. Comp. dates.
— K.E. 2
Ethelwardus, bp. Lond. 451
Ethelwold, *see* Ethelwald
Ethelwolf, K.E. 3
Ethelwin and **Ethelwinus**
*— bp. Sidr. 446
*— bp Wltn. 466
*— bp. Wells, 427
* Prob some same pers. Comp dates.
Etheridge, Th., adm. (**H**) 850
Ethodius I. and II., K. Sc. 18
Ethus, K. Sc. 19
Eton, Gerard Pott., gen. (**D**) 910
Ettrick, *see* Napier and E.
Etwal, abp. St. Dav. 463
Euan-Smith, Ch. B., amb. Zr. 132
Eudes, K. Fr. 23
— I. to IV., D. Bdy. 28
Eudocia, Emp. E.E. 51
Eugene, *see also* Eugenius
*— abp. Arm. 595
*— bp. Ach. 612
*— bp. Arm. 595
*— bp. Cld. and Meath, 599
*— bp. Cnr. 604
*— dn. Cloyne, 632
* Prob. some same pers. Comp. dates.
— (Pr. of Savoy), R. Nds. 83
Eugenius, *see also* Eugene
— dn. Cloy. 632
— Emp. W.E. 49
— I. to IV., P. Ro. 33-4-5
— I. to VIII., K. Sc. 18
Eunan, St., bp. Rph. 601
Eure, Th. de, dn. St. P. 453
Euric, K. Sp. 85
Eusden, Laur., P. Laur. 301
Eusebius, P. Ro. 33
Eustace and **Eustachius**
— bp. Cnr. 603; L. Treas. Ir. 558
— bp. Ely 434; dn. Sal. 468; Jy. 364; Ld. Chanc. 353
— (son Stephen), Pr. E. 9
— Hy., gen. (**B**) 869
— sir Jno. Rowl., gen. (**D**) 884; K.H. 791
— sir Maur., L.J. Ir. 555; Ld. Chanc. Ir. 576; M.R. Ir. 585; S.L. Ir. 591
— Wm. Cornw. and sir W., gen. (**A**) 863; K.C.H. 788
Euston, Geo. Hy., E. of, aft. 4th D. of Grafton, *q.v.*, L.L. Suff. 312
Eutychianus, P. Ro. 33
Evaldus, bp. Arg. 537
Evance, Steph., C. Exc. 279
Evandale, And., 1st ld., Ld. Chanc. Sc. 515
Evans, Andr. Fitzh., adm. (**A**) 820
— Ch. Rd. Ogd., gen. (**D**), 925
— Dav., dn. St. As. 463
— Daws. Kelly, gen. (**D**) 930
— De Lacy and sir D., G.C.B. 769; gen. (**D**) 882; K.C.B. 776
— Fk., G. Lag. 687
— Fk. Jno. Owen, K.C.B. 783
— Geo., adm. (**G**) 842
— Hy., adm. (**A**) 820
— Herb. Davies, L.L. Card. 315
— Hugh, dn. St. As. 463
— Hugh, gen. (**D**) 890
— Jno., adm. (**A**) 815
— Jno., bp. Bgr. 426; bp. Mth. 599
— Jno., K.C. 416
— Rd. L., gen. (**D**) 881
— Rt., gen. (**C**) 874
— Rt., dn. Bgr. 426
— Th., gen. (**D**) 877
— Wm., G. Ch. Hosp. 936; gen. (**A**) 857
Evarico, K. Sp. 85
Evaristus, P. Ro. 32
Evatt, Hy., gen. (**B**) 869
— Jno., dn. Elph. 609
Evelegh, *see also* Everleigh
— Hy., gen. (**A**) 863
— Jno., gen. (**B**) 867
Evelyn, Jno., L.P.S. 240
— sir Jno., C. Cus. 274-5; Postm. G. 238
— Wm., dn. Emly, 628
— Wm., gen. (**B**) 865
Evenus I. to III., K. Sc. 17-18
Everard, bp. Norw. 454
— Jno., J.K.B. Ir. 579
— Matth., gen. (**D**) 884; K.H. 789
— Th., C. Ex. 279
Everdon, Jno. de, B. Ex. 383; dn. St. P. 453
— Silv. de, bp. Carl. 475; J. It. 368; L.K. 353
— Th. de, dn. St. Patr. 617; M.R. Ir. 585; V. Chanc. Ir. 575
— Wm. de, B. Ex. 383
Everleigh, *see also* Evelegh
— Jno., dn. Ross, 633
Everett, Ed., C.C.J. 403
Evereux, Wm. de, K.B. 755
Everitt, Fras. W. E., Q.C. 419
Eversden, *see* Everdon
Eversley, Ch., 1st visc., form. C. Shaw-Lefevre, *q.v.*, G.C.B. 773
Everus, bp. St. Dav. 464
Every, Th. de, dn. St. P. 453
Evesham, Jno. de, bp. Worc. 472
— Simon de, bp. Ferns, 621
— Siv. de, bp. Worc. 472
— Th. de, M.R. 387
Evesk, Hy. de, J. It. 367
Evre, *see* Eyre
Evres, W., 2nd ld., K.B. 761
Evynden, Rd., bp. Bgr. 426
Ewart, Ch. Brisb., G. Jsey. 668; gen. (**D**) 927
— Ch. Jos. Fk., adm. (**H**) 849
— Hy. Pet. and sir H., gen. (**D**) 934; K.C.B. 781
— Jno. Alexr., gen. (**D**) 904; K.C.B. 782

For List of Abbreviations, see pp. 944-952.

Ewart—*cont.*
— Jno. Fk., gen. (**D**) 881
— Jos., Amb. Pr. 118
Ewe, Rd., E. of, W.C.P. 317
Ewens, Matth., B. Ex. 384; S.L. 408
Ewer, Jno., bp. Bgr. 426; bp. Llff. 449
Ewing, Alexr., bp. Arg. and Isl. 541
— Humphrey Ewing Crum-, L.L. Dumb. 509
— Rt., dn. Emly, 628
Exeter, Rd. d', L.J. Ir. 550
Exeter, lds, E., M., and D. of
Holland Family (1).
— Jno., 1st D. of, form. Jno. Holand, *q.v.*, and E. of Huntingdon, *q.v.*
Beaufort Family.
— Th., D. of, form. Th. Beaufort, sir T., and E. of Dorset, *q.v.*
Holland Family (2).
— Jno., 1st D. of, form. E. of Huntingdon, *q.v.*, Const. T.L. 320; L.H.A. 174
— Hy., 2nd D. of, L.H.A. 174
Courtenay Family.
— Hy., 1st M. of, form. 8th E. of Devonshire, *q.v.*
Cecil Family.
— Th., 1st E. of, form. Th. Cecil, *q.v.*, and ld. Burghley, *q.v.*
— Wm., 2nd E. of, K.G., 739
— Brownl., 9th E. of, form. ld. Burleigh, *q.v.*
— Brownl., 2nd M. of, K.G. 743; L.C.H. 295; L.L. Nton. 310; L.L. Rutl. 311; L.S.H. 290; P.C. 214
— Wm. A., 3rd M. of, C.G.A. 300
Exmewe, sir Th., L.M. Lond. 490
Exmouth, Edw., 1st ld. and visc., form. sir E. Pellew, *q.v.*, G.C.B. 767; K.C.B. 773
Exon (or Oxon) Jno., bp. Winch. 470
— Rd. de, C.J. C.P. Ir. 580
Exshaw, Jno., L.M. Dbln. 641
Exton, Ev., R. Cr. P.A. 335; Richm. H. 333
— Jno., J. Adm. Ct. 423
— Nich., L.M. Lond. 489
— sir Th., Ch. Lond. 422; D. Arch. 420; J. Adm. Ct. 423
Eyer, Sim., L.M. Lond. 490
Eyles, Irwin, Amb. Ch. 130
— sir Jno., L.M. Lond. 491; Postm. G. 238
— Th., adm. (**A**) 819
Eynefeld, Hy. de, J. It. 368
Eyre, Ed. Jno., G. Antig. 728; G. Jam. 713; G. N.Z. 709; G. St. Vin. 725
— sir Geo., adm. (**A**) 819; G.C.M.G. 794; K.C.B. 774
— Giles, dn. Chich. 434
— Giles and sir G., J.K.B. 373; S.L. (1689) 411
— Giles or Eyles, S.L. (1724) 411
— Hy., gen. (**D**) 893
— sir Jas., bp. Ex. 385; C.B. Ex. 382; C.G.S. 357; C.J.C.P. 376; P.C. 205; Rec. Lond. 494; S.L. 412
— Jno., gen. (**D**) 891
— Jul. or Giles, dn. Killoe, 637

Eyre—*cont.*
— Rt., C. Exc. 280
— Rt. and sir Rt., C.B. Ex. 382; C.J.C.P. 376; J.Q.B. 373; P.C. 197; Q.C. 415
— Samps., S.L. 409

F.

Faber, Ch. Ed., gen. (**D**) 898
— Wm. Raikes, gen. (**D**) 898
Fabian, P. Ro. 32
Fachman (St.), bp. Ross, 63
Factna, bp. Arm. 595
Faddy, Peter, gen. (**D**) 890
— Saml. Br., gen. (**D**) 915
Fagan, Chr., gen. (**D**) 876
— Chr. Sull., gen. (**D**) 877
— Geo., Amb. C. Am. 133 Amb. Ecr. 942; Amb. Vza. 135
— Geo. Wm. Hy., gen. (**D**) 933
— Wm. Turt., gen. (**D**) 935
Fage, Ed., gen. (**C**) 873
Fahie, Wm. Ch. and sir W., adm. (**A**) 819; K.C.B. 775
Fair, Alex., gen. (**D**) 877
— Rt., K.H. 790
Fairborne, Staff. and sir S., adm. (**A**) 813; L. Admy. 177
Fairfax, Brian, C. Cus. 275
— Ch., dn. Down, 605
— Guy or Guido, J.K.B. 372; K.B. 757; S.L. 407
— Hy., adm. (**E**) 837
— Hy., dn. Norw. 456
— Rt., L. Admy. 177
— Th., K.B. 759
— Th., S.L. 408
— Th., *see* ld. Fairfax, *infra.*
— Wm., J.C.P. 378; S.L. 408
— sir Wm. Geo., adm. (**A**) 817
Fairfax, lds.
— Th. and sir T., aft. 3rd ld., Const. T.L. 321; Ld. Man, 665
Fairfowl, Andr., abp. Glasg. 537
Fairlewe (or Fellow), Nichs., Cal. P.A. 342
Fairley, Jas., bp. Arg. 538
Faithfull, Geo., gen. (**D**) 913
— Hy., gen. (**D**) 878
Faithman, bp. Cld. 598
Falcon, Gord. Th., adm. (**D**) 828
— J. C., Pres. Vza. 108
Falconar and **Falconer** — *see also* Falkiner, Faulkner, Faulknor and Fawconer
— sir Alexr., Ld. Sess. 519
— hon. Ch. J. Keith-, C.I.R. 286
— Chesb. Gr., K.H. 792
— Christr. Grant, gen. (**D**) 883

Falconar and Falconer—*cont.*
— Colin, bp. Arg. 538; bp. Mor. 534
— sir Dav., L.P. Ct. Sess. 516; Ld. Sess. 519
— Jas., Ld. Sess. 520
— Jno., Sc. bp. 545
— Th., C.C.J. 404
— Wm., bp. Cness. 541; bp. Edinb. 542; bp. Mor. 544; bp. Ork. 545; pr. bp. Sc. 540
Falconbridge, *see* Fauconbridge
Falconburgh, *see* Fauconberg
Falconer, *see* Falconar
Faleise, Wm. de, Jy. 364
Falk, Iman Wilh., G. Ceyl. 672
Falkiner, *see also* Falconer, &c.
— Danl., L.M. Dbln. 641
— sir Fk. Jno., Sec. St. Patr. 752
— Fk. Rd., Rec. Dbln. 642
Falkingham, Ed., Compt. N. 257
Falkland, visc.
— Hy., 1st visc., form. Hy. Carey, *q.v.*, L.D. Ir. 554
— Luc., 2nd visc., S.St. 223
— Anthy., 5th visc., L. Admy. 176; P.C. 194; Tr. N. 256
— Luc., 10th visc., C.Y.G. 298; G. Bbay. 659; G.C.H. 786; G. N.Sc. 695; P.C. 213
Fallan, Wm. B.Ex. 383
Falls, Andr. V., gen. (**D**) 920
— Th., gen. (**D**) 886
Falmouth, visc. and E. of
Berkeley Family.
See also Berkeley.
— Chas., E. of, form. visc. Fitzharding, *q.v.*
Boscawen Family.
— Hugh, 1st visc., form. Hugh and ld. Boscawen, *q.v.*, V. Treas. Ir. 559; C.Y.G. 298; Gen. (**A**) 858; P.C. 200
— Geo. Ev., 3rd visc., C.G.P. 300; P.C. 205
Falquez, Man., G. Trin. 721
Falshaw, Jas. and sir J., L. Prov. Edinb. 548
Falstaff (or Fastolf), sir Jno., K.G. 735
Falstoffe, Th., bp. St. Dav. 464
Falto, P. V., C. Ro. 42
— Q. V., C. Ro. 42
Fancourt, Chas. St. J., G. Br. Hond. 714
— Rt. Dev., adm. (**A**) 818
Fane, Fras., B.T. 264-5
— Fras., K.B. 763
— Fras., aft. 1st E. of Westmorland, *q.v.*, K.B. 761
— Fras. Wm., adm. (**D**) 824
— Hy., aft. sir H., C.C. Ind. 651; gen. (**A**) 862; K.C.B. 774; S.G.O. 260
— sir Hy., C. Exc. 278
— Jno., C. Tx. 284
— hon. Jul. Hy. Ch., Amb. Fr. 113
— Mildm., gen. (**D**) 883
— Ponsonby-, hon. Sp. Cec. Br., K.C.B. 784
Fanhope, Jno. ld., form. sir J. Cornwall, *q.v.*
Fanning, Edmd., gen. (**A**) 859; G. Pr. Ed. Isl. 699
— P., G. N.Sc. 695

For List of Abbreviations, see pp. 944-952.

Fanshawe, Arth., adm. (**D**) 829; K.C.B. 778
—— Ch., gen. (**D**) 906
—— Ed., gen. (**D**) 883
—— Ed. Genn. and sir E., adm. (**D**) 833; (**E**) 834; G.C.B. 771; K.C.B. 781; L. Admy. 184
—— Hy., adm. (**H**) 845
—— sir Rd., Chanc. Gart. 746; P.C. 190
—— Th., K.B. 763
—— Th., K.B. 764
Faranan, bp. Arm. 595
Farncomb, Th., L.M. Lond. 492
Fardunji, Navr., C.I.E. 807
Farebrother, Ch., L.M. Lond. 492
Farewell, Jno., Lt. T.L. 322
Farges, Bertr. de, dn. Sal. 468
Farias, Pres. Mex. 103
Faringdon, *see* Faryngdone
Faris, Wm., gen. (**D**) 895
Farish, Jas., G. Bbay. 659
Farington, *see* Farrington
Farley, Jno. Sim, gen. (**B**) 868
Farmar, Ed. Sterl., gen. (**D**) 896
—— Rt. Hill, gen. (**A**) 862
—— Wm. Roberts, gen. (**D**) 927
—— (? Turner) Jno., G. Bdoes. 720
Farmer, Regd. Onsl., gen. (**D**) 920
Farnborough, lds.
Long Family.
—— Ch., 1st ld., form. Ch. Long and sir C., *q.v.*, Paym. G. 244
May Family.
—— Th. E., 1st ld., form. T. E. May, *q.v.*
Farnese (3), D. Pma. 53
Farnham, Nichs. de, bp. Dham. 478
Farnham, lds.
—— Hy., 7th ld., K.P. 751
Farquhar, Arth. and sir A., adm. (**D**) 825; K.C.B. 777; K.C.H. 788; K.H. 789
—— Arth., adm. (**E**) 835; K.C.B. 781
—— Rt., gen. (**D**) 894
—— Rt. Towns., G. Mtius. 683
—— Wm., gen. (**D**) 877
***Farquharson,** col., G. Trin. 722
*—— Fras., gen. (**D**) 881
* ? same pers.
—— Geo., gen. (**D**) 895
—— Geo. McB. Barnes, gen. (**D**) 913
—— Jas. Alexr., G. St. Luc. 725; gen. (**C**) 875
—— Lenn. Jas., gen. (**D**) 918
Farran, Ch., gen. (**D**) 876
Farrant, Aug. Dov. Lydd., gen. (**D**) 900
Farrar, *see also* Farrer
—— Wm., K.C. 415
Farrell, Ferg., L.M. Dbln. 642
—— Fras. T., gen. (**D**) 888
—— Hy. Chamberl., gen. (**D**) 934
Farren, Rd. Th., gen. (**D**) 903
Farrer, *see also* Farrar and Ferrar
—— Jas., gen. (**D**) 879
—— Jas. Wm., M. Chy. 397
—— Th. H. and sir T., Sec. B. T. 270
Farrington, Ffarrington and **Faryngton**
—— Anthy., S.L. 410
—— Anthy. and sir A., gen. (**A**) 860
—— Hugh de, B. Ex. Ir. 583
—— Jno. J., gen. (**D**) 888
—— Linds., gen. (**D**) 917
—— Olaus. Jno. M., gen. (**D**) 917
—— Rt. de, L. Treas. Ir. 558; M. Chy. 394
—— Th., C. St., 283; C. Exc. 280
—— Th., gen. (**B**) 864
—— Wm., adm. (**H**) 845
Faryngdone, Nichs., L.M. Lond. 489
Faryngton, *see* Farrington
Fasken, Ed. Th., gen. (**D**) 923
Fast, Jno. Wells, gen. (**D**) 878
Fastidius, abp. Lond. 450
Fastolf, *see also* Falstaff
—— Nichs., J. It. 369; J.K.B. Ir. 378
Faucett, *see* Fawcett
Fauconberg and **Fauconbridge,** Eust. de, bp. Lond. 451; Jy. 364; L.H.T. 152
—— Walt. de, K.B. 754
Fauconberg, lds., visc. and E. of
Neville family.
—— Wm., ld., form. W. Neville, *q.v.*, aft. E. of Kent, *q.v.*; K.G. 735
Belasyse family.
See also Belasyse.
1st Creation.
—— Th., 2nd visc., aft. 1st E. L.L. Dham. 308; C.G.P. 299; P.C. 191–2–3
2nd Creation.
—— Hy., 2nd E., L.L. Yorks, N.R. 313
Faukes, Jno., M. Chy. 394
Faulkner and **Faulknor,** *see also* Falc—
—— (or Falconer), Jno., M.M. 246-7
—— Jonn., adm. (**A**) 815
—— Jonn., adm. (**A**) 817
—— Jonn. Augs. Spr., gen. (**D**) 924
—— Hy. Cole, gen. (**D**) 918
Faunce, Alured Dods, gen. (**D**) 880
—— Rt. Nichs., gen. (**D**) 901
Faunt, Wm., J.K.B. 371
Fauquier, F. D., bp. Alg. 693
—— Wm., Regr. and Sec. Bath, 784
Faustin, Emp. Hti. 105
Faux, Jno., dn. Winds. 474
Favila, K. Sp. 85
Fawcett and **Faucett**
—— Hy., P.C. 219; Postm. G. 239
—— Jno. Hy., K.C.M.G. 799
—— Wm. and sir Wm., gen. (**C**) 872; G. Ch. Hosp. 936; gen. (**A**) 859; K.B.765; P.C. 206
Fawconer, Jno. le, A.G. 398
—— Th., L.M. Lond. 489
Fawkner, *see also* Falc— and Falk—
—— Everard and sir E., Postm. G. 238; C. St. 284
*—— Wm., Amb. Pgl. 124; Amb. Russ. 125; Amb. Tusc. 115
*—— Wm., Sec. B.T. 270
* ? same pers.
Faye, Chas. de la, U.S.S. 225
Fayerman, Fras., adm. (**A**) 818
Fayery, Rt., Ptc. P.A. 337
Fayrer, Jos., K.C.S.I. 803
Fazakerley, Jno., G. I. Man. 665
—— sir Wm., Chambn. Lond. 493
Fead, Geo., gen. (**B**) 866
Fearaidhach, Fionfachtna, K. Ir. 21
Feargal, K. Ir. 21
Feargna, K. Ir. 20
Feargus (2), K. Ir. 21
—— -Forthamhuil, K. Ir. 21
Fearne, Ch., Sec. Adm. 187
Fearon, K. Ir. 20
—— Peter, gen. (**D**) 881
—— Rt. Br., gen. (**D**) 882
Featherston, *see* Fetherston
Feckenham, Jno., dn. St. P. 453
Feidhlimhidh, K. Ir. 21
Feidlimid, bp. Cl. 596
Feil—, *see* Fiel—
Feilden, Rand. Josh., gen. (**D**) 920
Felbrigge, Sir Sim., K.G. 734
Felde, Th., dn. Her. 442
Feldyng, Geoffr., L.M. Lond. 490
***Felix,** bp. Lism. 626
*—— bp. Mor. 534
*—— (St.), bp. E. Ang. 454
*—— (St.) bp. Oss. 620
* Prob. some same pers. Comp. dates.
—— I. to V., P. Ro., 32, 33, 35
—— L. C. S., C. Ro. 45; *see also* Sulla
—— Orl., gen. (**D**) 892
Fell, Jno., bp. Oxf. 456; dn. Chr. Ch. Oxf. 457
—— Saml., dn. Chr. Ch. Oxf. 457; dn. Lich. 445
—— Th., C.D.L. 242; J. Chest. 386
Fellow, *see also* Fairlewe
—— Hy., Guis. P.A. 343
Fellowes and **Fellows**
—— Ch., adm. (**E**) 836
—— Edw., adm. (**A**) 819
—— Edw., gen. (**D**) 917
—— Peregr. Hy., gen. (**D**) 917
—— sir Th., adm. (**D**) 828
—— Th. Hounson Butler, adm. (**H**) 853
—— Wm., Guis. P.A. 343; Lanc. H. 332; Norr. K.A. 329; Ptc. P.A. 337
—— Wm., M. Chy. 396
—— Wm. Abdy, adm. (**H**) 850
Felter, Wm., dn. Yk. 487
Felton, Anthy., K.B. 761
*—— Jno. de, K.B. 754
*—— sir Jno., L.H.A. 171
* Prob. same pers.
—— Nichs., bp. Brl. 439; bp. Ely, 435
—— Th., K.G. 734
—— sir Th., Compt. H. 292
Fencotes, Jno. de, J. It. 369; S.L. 407
—— Th. de, J.C.P. 377; K.B. 755; S.L. 406
Fendall, Jno., gen. (**D**) 915
Fenn, sir Rd., L.M. Lond. 491
Fenner, Ed. and sir E., J.Q.B. 372; S.L. 408
Fenrother, Rt., M.M. 246
Fenton, sir Geoffr., Sec. St. Ir. 562

Fenton, visc.
—— Thos., visc., form. sir Th. Erskine, *q.v.*, aft. E. of Kellie, *q.v.*, K.G. 739
Fenwick, Hy., L. Admy. 184
—— Wm. Hy., adm. (**H**) 852
Fenys, *see* Finnis
Feodor, *see* Theodore
Ferchard, I. and II., K. Sc. 18
Ferdachry, bp. Arm. 595
Ferdinand, C. Flrs. 81
—— D. Pma. 53
—— Emp. Aus. 58
—— (2), K. Arr. 86
—— (2), K. Scy. 56
—— (Pr. Brk.), K.G. 742
—— Pr. Bga. 95
—— R. Nds. 82-3
—— I., K. Bma. 59
—— I., K. Pgl. 88
—— I. to III., E. Gmy. 62
—— I. (E Gmy.), K.G. 737
—— I. to IV., G. D. Tny. 57
—— I. to IV., K. Nls. 56
—— II. (K. Nls.), K.G. 736
—— I. to V., K. Cle. 56, 85-86
—— I. to V., K. Hgy. 60
—— I. to VII., K. Sp. 85-6
—— V. (K. Sp.), K.G. 736
—— VII. (K. Sp.), K.G. 743
—— II., K. 2 Scy. 56
—— V., K. Nav. 88
—— -Albrecht, D. Brk. 70
—— -Hy. Fk., Lg. H. Hbg. 73
—— -Mary, El. Bva. 68
Ferdomnac, bp. Kild. 616
—— bp. Tm. 611
Feredach, bp. Saig. 620
Fergie, *see* Forgie
Fergus (St.), bp. Down, 603
—— I. to III., K. Sc. 178
Ferguson and **Fergusson**
—— —, G. Tob. 723
—— sir Ad., B.T. 266
—— Edith Hel., Cr. Ind. 810
—— Geo., adm. (**D**) 828; (**G**) 840
—— Geo., Ld. Sess. 520
—— Jas., C.I.E. 807
—— Jas., gen. (**C**) 871
—— Jas., L.G. Gr. Hosp. 854
—— Jas., Ld. Sess. 520
—— Jas. and sir J., G.C.B. 770; G. Gibr. 670; gen. (**D**) 880; K.C.B. 778
—— sir Jas., G. Bbay. 659; G.C.S.I. 801; G. N.Z. 709; G. S. Austr. 706; K.C.M.G. 797; P.C. 218; U.S.F. 230; U.S. Home, 228; U.S. Ind. 236
—— sir Jas., Jy. Sc. 522; Ld. Sess. 520
—— Jno., adm. (**A**) 817
—— Jno. Macpherson, adm. (**H**) 846
—— Olive, lady, Cr. Ind. 810
—— Rt., L.L. Fifesh. 510
—— sir Rt. A., L.L. Londy. 570
—— Rt. Cutl., J.A.G. 937; P.C. 213
—— Ron. Crauf. and sir R., gen. (**A**) 861; G.C.B. 768; K.C.B. 773
—— Wm., G. Si. Le. 685
—— Wm., gen. (**D**) 886
—— sir Wm., Pres. Coll. Surg. 939
Feria, D. of, R. Nds. 83
Feringes, Geoff. De, dn. St. P. 452
Ferings, Rd. de, abp. Dbln. and Gl. 615
Fermanagh, Ralph, visc. aft. ld. Verney, *q.v.*
Fermbaud, Nichs., J. It. 369
Fermor, hon. Th. Wm., aft. E. of Pomfret, *q.v.*, gen. (**B**) 868
Fermoy, Edm. B., 1st ld., L.L. Crk. 569
Fernandez, P., Pres. C.R. 106
Ferne, Hy., bp. Chest. 477; dn. Ely, 435
Ferquhard, bp. Isl. 539
Ferral, Lisach, bp. Ard. 608
—— (or O'Ferrall), Rd., bp. Ard. 607; dn. Ard. 609
Ferrall, *see* O'Ferrall
Ferrar (or Farrer), Rt., bp. S. and M. 483; bp. St. Dav. 464
Ferrara, Herc. d'Esté, D. of, K.G. 736
Ferrard, visc., *see* Massareene and F.
Ferrariis, Th. de, G. Ch. Isl. 667
Ferrant, Jno., Mch. K.A. 339
Ferrars
—— sir Ralph, L.H.A. 172
Ferrers of Chartley, lds. and E.
—— Walt., 7th ld., K.G. 736
—— Walt., 8th ld., aft. visc. Hereford, *q.v.*, K.G. 737
—— Robt., 13th ld., aft. visc. Tamworth, *q.v.*, and E. Ferrers, P.C. 194
—— Geo., 16th ld., aft. E. of Leicester and M. of Townshend, *q.v.*, C.G.P. 229; P.C. 203
—— Wasl., 5th E., adm. (**A**) 815
Ferri, I. to IV., D. Lne. 29
Ferriby, Th., B. Ex. 383
Ferrier, sir Alex., K.H. 790
—— Ilay, gen. (**C**) 872
—— Jas., gen. (**B**) 866
—— Jno., adm. (**A**) 818
—— L. H., C. Cus. Sc. 504
Ferris, Abel, adm. (**H**) 844
Ferte, Ralph de la, J. It. 367
Ferrure, Hy. de, G. Ch. Isl. 667
Ferryman, Aug. Hal., gen. (**D**) 898
Fesch (Cardinal), Rel. Nap., 26
Feschamp, St. Rem. de, bp. Dorch., Sidr. and Linc. 446
Festing, Benj. Mort., K.H. 791
—— Colson, adm. (**H**) 849
—— Fras. Worg., K.C.M.G. 797
—— Rt. Worg. Geo., adm. (**H**) 844
Feth-Ali, Sh. Pers. 99
Fethelmachus, K. Sc. 18
Fetherston, Fras., L.M. Dbln. 641
—— Jno., dn. Llin. 623
Fettes, Wm., L. Prov. Edinb. 548
Feversham, Louis, 2nd E. of, K.G. 740
Fevre, Ph. Le, gen. (**D**) 880
Ff—, *see* F—
Fi—, *see also* Fy—
Fiachade-Labhriun, K. Ir. 20
Fiachadh (2), K. Ir. 20
—— -Fion, K. Ir. 21
—— -Fionohudh, K. Ir. 21
—— -Fionsgothach, K. Ir. 20
Fiachre, bp. Cld. 598
Fidatra, Donato, abp. Arm. 595; bp. Clr. 596
Fiddes, Th., gen. (**D**) 886
Fidenas, L. S. (2), C. Ro. 39
—— Q. S. P. S. (2), Dt. Ro. 39
Fiedlimid, bp. Arm. 595
Field, Ed., adm. (**H**) 853
—— Ed., bp. Newfd. 700
—— Geo. Th., gen. (**D**) 922
—— Jno., gen. (**D**) 921
—— Rd., dn. Glr. 440
—— Theoph., bp. Her. 441; bp. Llff. 449; bp. St. Dav. 464
—— Th., bp. Llin. 622
—— Wm. Ventr. and sir W., J.Q.B. 374; J.Q.B.D. 374; Q.C. 418; S.L. 414
Fielding and **Feilding**; *see also* Fyldyng
—— Edmd., gen. (**B**) 864
—— hon. Percy Rt. Bas., gen. (**D**) 909
—— hon. Wm. Hy. Ad., gen. (**D**) 921
—— Bas., ld., aft. 2nd E. of Denbigh, K.B. 762
—— Wm., visc., aft. 3rd E. of Denbigh, M.G.W. 296
—— Wm. Rt., visc., son of 6th E. of Denbigh, gen. (**C**) 872
Fienes and **Fiennes**
—— Alan de, W.C.P. 317
—— Ingelr. de, W.C.P. 317
—— Jas. de (2), W.C.P. 317
—— Jas. de., aft. 1st ld. Say and Sele, *q.v.*
—— Jno. de, W.C.P. 317
—— Nathl., called ld. F., C.G.S. 356
—— Th., K.B. 758
Fife, Jas. Geo., gen. (**D**) 919
Fife, E. of
—— Const., E. of, L. J. Gen. (11—) 522; Ld. Chanc. Sc. 514
—— Jas., 2nd E. of, L.L. Bffsh. 508
—— Jas., 4th E. of, G.C.H. 786; K.T. 748; L.L. Bffsh. 508
—— Jas., 5th E. of, form. Jas. Duff, *q.v.*; K.T. 748
—— Alexr. Wm. Geo., 6th E., aft. 1st D. of, form. visc. Macduff, *q.v.*; C.G.A. 300; K.T. 749; P.C. 219
—— Louise, dss. of, *see* Prss. Louise of Wales
Fifyne, Th. de, bp. Ross. 535
Figueras, Pres. Sp. 87
Figulus, C. M., C. Ro. 46
Fillmore, M., Pres. U.S.A. 102
Fimbria, C. F., C. Ro. 45
Finan (St.), bp. Lindisf. 478
Finanus, K. Sc. 17
Finbarr, *see* Barr
Finch, —, S.L. 410
—— Alexr. Urq. Ham., gen (**D**) 920
—— Danl., *see* ld. F., *infra*
—— hon. Ed., gen. (**A**) 860
—— Fras., C. Exc. 278
—— Heneage, and sir H., Rec. Lond. 494; S.L. 409; Sp. H. Co 249
—— hon. Heneage, S.G. 401
—— Heneage, aft. ld. Guernsey and E. of Aylesford, *q.v.*
—— Heneage, *see* ld. F., *infra*
—— Hy., dn. Yk. 487
—— Hy., S.L. 409
—— hon. Jno., gen. (**D**) 883
—— Jno., *see* ld. F. *infra*
—— Nath., S.L. 409
—— Wm., bp. suff. Taunton, 428
—— hon. Wm., P.C. 198; V.C.H 297

Finch—*cont.*
— hon. Wm. Cl., adm. (**A**) 816
Finch of Fordwich, lds.
— Jno., aft. sir J. and ld. F., C.J.C.P. 375; J.C.P. 379; K.C. 414; L.K. 356; S.L. 409; Sp. H.C. 249
Finch of Daventry, lds.
— Heneage, aft. sir H. and 1st ld. F., and 1st E. of Nottingham, *q.v.*; A.G. 399; L. Admy. 175; L.H.S. 286; Ld. Chanc. 357; L.K. 357; P.C. 191; S.G. 401
— hon. Danl., aft. 2nd E. of Nottingham, and E. of Winchelsea, *q.v.*, L. Admy. 175; P.C. 192
— Danl., ld., aft. 3rd E. of W. and N., *q.v.*, Compt. H. 292; L.T. 156; P.C. 197
Finch-Hatton, *see* Hatton
Finchad (St.), bp. Ross, 631
Fincham, *see* Fyncham
Fincormachus, K. Sc. 18
Findlater and **Finlater,** E. of, *see also* Deskford and Seafield
— Jas., 3rd E. of, K.T. 747
— Jas., 4th E. of, form visc. and E. of Seafield, *q.v.*; L.K. Sc. 503; P.C. 197
— Jas., 5th E. of, V.A. Sc. 499
Findlay and **Finlay**
— bp. Arg. 537; bp. Dnbl. 532
— Alexr., K.H. 791
— Jno., C.I.E. 808
— Rt. Bann., Q.C. 419
Findochus, K. Sc. 18
Fineux (or Fineaux), Jno. and sir J., C.J.K.B. 370; J.C.P. 378; S.L. 407
Fingal, K. Man, 664
Fingal, E. of
— Arth. Jas., 8th E. of, K.P. 751
— Arth. Jas., 9th E. of, K.P. 751; L.L. Meath, 570
Fingask, Thos. de, bp. Cness. 531
Finglas, *see also* Fynglass
— Rd., S.G. Ir. 589; S.L. Ir. 591
Finian (St.), bp. Cld. 598
Finlater, *see* Findlater
Finlay, *see* Findlay
Finlayson, Jas., Mod. K. Sc. 547
Finnachta, bp. Ferns, 621
Finnis, Th. Q., L.M. Lond. 492
— (or Fenys), Wm., K.B. 759
Finniss, Boyle Trav., G.S. Austr. 706
Finny (or Phinny), Geo., G. Bah. Isl. 716
Finucane, Matts., J.C.P. Ir. 582
Fion-Fin, K. Ir. 20
Fionachta, K. Ir. 20
— -Fleadha, K. Ir. 21
Firth, Hy. Hilh., gen. (**D**) 922
— Rt. Fras., gen. (**D**) 933
— Wm., S.L. 413
Fischer, *see* Fisher
Fish, Jno. adm. (**A**) 817
Fishbourne, Edmd. Gard., adm. (**H**) 849
Fishburn, Th., J. It. 368
Fisher and **Fischer**
— Benj., gen. (**C**) 873
— Chr., bp. Elph. 608
*— Ed., C. Exc. 281
*— Ed., U.S.F. 229
* Poss. same pers.
— Ed. Hy., gen. (**D**) 909
— Garret, gen. (**B**) 866
— Geo. Batt., gen. (**D**) 935
— sir Geo. Bult., gen. (**C**) 874; K.C.H. 788
— Goodr. Armst., gen. (**D**) 916
— Jno., bp. Exr. 437; bp. Sal. 467
— Jno., bp. Roch. 460
— Jno., J.C.P. 378; S.L. 407
— Jno. Fk., gen. (**D**) 926
— Rt. A., C.C.J. 405
— Th., adm. (**E**) 835; (**F**) 838
— Th. Halh., Q.C. 419
— Wm., adm. (**D**) 828
— Wm., C. St. 283
Fishide, Wm. de, S.L. 407
Fitch, *see also* Fytche
— Col., Lt. T.L. 322
Fitton, sir Alexr., Lord Chanc. Ir. 576; L.J. Ir. 555
— sir Edw., V. Treas. Ir. 559
Fitz —
Search also under the name without this prefix.
Fitz-Adam, Jno., C.J.C.P. Ir. 580
Fitz-Ailwyn, *see* FitzAlwyn
Fitz-Alan, *see also* under Arundel, E. of
— Brian, J. It. 367
— sir Rd., L.H.A. 172
— (or Arundel), Th., abp. Cant. 430
— Wm., J. It. 366
— (or Arundel), sir Wm., K.G. 734
Fitz-Alan, lds.
— Thos., ld., aft. E. of Arundel, K.B. (1461) 756
Fitz-Aldelm (or Andelm), Wm., Jy. 363; L.L. Ir. 550
Fitz-Alexander, Nig., Jy. 363
Fitz-Alwyn, Hy., Jy. 364; L.M. Lond. 488
— Rog., L.M. Lond. 488
Fitz-Bernard, Rt., J. It. 366
— Th., J. It. 366; Jy. 363
Fitz-Clarence, ld. Adolph., adm. (**D**) 830; G.C.H. 786
— ld. Fk., C.C.Bbay. 660; G.C.H. 786; gen. (**D**) 880; Lt. T.L. 322
— Geo., aft. E. of Munster, *q.v.*
Fitz-Edmund, Jno., bp. Cork and Cl. 631
— Jno., dn. Cloy. 632
Fitz-Ernise, Ph., J. It. 365
Fitz-Eustace, sir Ed., L.D. Ir. 552; Ld. Chanc. Ir. 575
— Rt. L., L. Treas. Ir. 558
— Roland and sir R., aft. ld. Portlester, *q.v.*, L.D. Ir. 552; L. Treas. Ir. 558
— sir Rd. (2), Ld. Chanc. Ir. 575
Fitzgerald and **Fitzgerold**
— sir Aug., gen. (**B**) 868
— Ch., G. Gamb. 686; G. W. Austr. 707
— Ch., gen. (**D**) 926
— ld. Ch., C. Cus. Ir. 565
— Dav., bp. St. Dav. 464
— Dav. Fitzjas., dn. Cloy. 632
Fitzgerald and Fitzgerold—*cont.*
— Ed., C. St. Ir. 568
— Ed. Th., K.H. 790
— Fras. Alex., B. Ex. Ir. 584; J. Ex. D. Ir. 584
— Ger., K.C.M.G. 798
— Ger., L. Treas. Ir. 559
— Ger. Fitzjas., dn. Lism. 629
— Ger. Seym. Ves., K.C.I.E. 805
— Hy., J. It. 365; Jy. 363
— ld. Hy., Postm. G. Ir. 564
— Hy. Ves., *see* ld. F., *infra*
— Jas., gen. (**D**) 895
— Jas., S.L. Ir. 592
— sir Jas., L.D. Ir. 553
— Jno., bp. Ardf. and Agh. 639
— Jno., dn. Cork, 632
— Jno. Dav., *see* ld. F. *infra*
— sir Jno. Forster, F.M. 856; G.C.B. 770; gen. (**A**) 863; K.C.B. 776
— Maur., abp. Cash. 625
— Maur., C. Cus. Ir. 565; C. Treas. Ir. 561; L. Adm. 182; L.T. 159
— Maur., L.J. Ir. 550
— Maur. and sir M., L.D. Ir. 553
— ld. Maur. L.L. Wexf. 571
— Maur. Fitzm. L.J. Ir. 550
— ld Otho., Compt. H. 293; P.C. 217; Tr. H. 292
— Pat., J.C.P. Ir. 581; Rec. Dbln. 642
— Rt., S.L. Ir. 592
— sir Rt. Lew., adm. (**A**) 820; K.C.H. 788
— ld. Rt. S., Amb. Dk. 127; Amb. Pgl. 124; Amb. Swz. 113
— Th., D. Chanc. Ir. 575; Ld. Chanc. Ir. 575
— Th. Burt., C. St. Ir. 568
— Th. Maur., L.J. Ir. 550
— Wm., bp Clonf. and K. 636; bp. Cork, Cl. and R. 632; bp. Killoe, K,. Cl. and K. 636; dn. Cloy. 633
— Wm. Rt. Seym. Ves., G. Bbay. 659; G.C.S.I. 801; K.C.S.I. 803; P.C. 217; U.S.F. 230
— Wm. Ves., *see* ld. F., *infra*
Fitzgerald, lds.
— Jno. D., aft. ld F., A.G. Ir. 588; J.Q.B. Ir. 579; J.Q.B.D. Ir. 579; Jud. Com. P. C. 362; L. App. 358; P.C. 220; S.G. Ir. 590
Fitzgerald and Vesci, lds.
— Wm. Vesey, aft. 1st ld. F. and V.; amb. Sw. and N. 127; C. Treas. Ir. 561; Ch. Ex. Ir. 562; L.L. Clare, 569; L.T. 159; P.C. 209; Paym. G. 244; Pres. B.C. 254; Pres. B.T. 268; Tr. N. 257
— Hy. Vesey, aft. 2nd ld. F. and V., dn. Emly. 628; dn. Kilm. 609
Fitzgerold, *see* Fitzgerald
Fitzgibbon, Ger., L.J. App. Ir. 586; S.G. Ir. 590; S.L. Ir. 593
Fitzgibbon, lds. and visc.
— Jno., aft. ld. and visc. F., and 1st E. of Clare, *q.v.*, A.G. Ir. 588; L.J. Ir. 557; Ld. Chanc. Ir. 577; P.C. 205
— hon. Rd. Hob., aft. 3rd. E. of Clare, *q.v.*, L.L. Lim. 570

Fitz-Gilbert, Rd., Ch. Jr. 362
— Wm., Ld. Chanc. 353
Fitz-Guido, (or FitzGuy) Wm., dn. St. Pat. 617
Fitzharding, visc. and E.
— Ch., visc., form. sir C. Berkeley, *q.v.*, aft. E. of Falmouth, *q.v.*, Tr. Ch. 294; Tr. H. 291
— Jno., visc., Tell. Ex. 168
— Wm. F. E., form. ld. Segrave, *q.v.*
— Maur. F. F., 1st ld., form. sir Maur. Berkeley, *q.v.*
Fitzharris, Jas. Ed., visc., aft. 2nd E. of Malmesbury, *q.v.*, L.T. 158; U.S.F. 229
Fitz-Helton, Wm., J. It. 365
Fitz-Henry, Meiler, L.J. Ir. 550
— Ran., J. It. 367
Fitzherbert, Alleyne, aft. ld. St. Helens, *q.v.*, Amb. St. G. 121; Amb. Nds. &c. 122; Amb. Russ. 125; Ch. Sec. Ir. 563; P.C. 204
— Anthy., J.C.P. 378; S.L. 408
— Matth., J. It. 367
— Matth., K.B. 754
— Th., adm. (**A**) 815
— Wm., B.T. 265-6
— Wm., K.C.M.G. 797
Fitz-Hervey, Hy., J. It. 366
— Osb., J. It. 366; Jy. 363
Fitzhugh, Alf., gen. (**D**) 930
— Geo., dn. Linc. 448
— Jno., Jy. 364
— Rt., bp. Lond. 451
Fitzhugh, lds.
— Hy., 3rd ld., K.G. 735; L.H.T. 153
— Geo., 7th ld., K.B. 759
Fitz-James, Jno. and sir J., A.G. 398; C.B. Ex. 381; C.J.K.B. 370; J.K.B. 372; S.L. 408
— Rd., bp. Chich. 433; bp. Lond. 451; bp. Roch. 460
Fitz-Joceline, Reg., abp. Cant. 430; bp. B. and W. 427
— War., J. It. 367; Jy. 364
Fitz-John, Milo, bp. Cork, 630; dn. Cork, 632
— Nichs., dn. Oss. 622
— Rd., dn. Cash. 627
— Th., J. It. 368
— Wm., abp. Cash. 624; bp. Oss. 620; L.L. Ir. 551; Ld. Chanc. Ir. 574
— Wm., J. It. 365
Fitz-Martin, Wm., J. It. 365; Jy. 363
Fitzmaurice, ld. Edmd. G. P., U.S.F. 230
— Jas., bp. Ardf. and Agh. 639
— Jno., gen. (**D**) 896; K.H. 790
— Ulyss., G. Gren. 724
Fitzmayer, Jas. Wm. and sir J., gen. (**D**) 902; K.C.B. 780
Fitz-Moore, Edm., Q.C. 418
Fitz-Neale or **Fitz-Nigel,** Rd., bp. Lond. 451; dn. Linc. 447; J. It. 365; Jy. 363
— Wm., J. It. 365
Fitz-Oger, Oger, Jy. 364
Fitz-Osborne, Wm., E. of Hereford, Ch. Jr. (Wm. 1.) 362
Fitz-Other, Walt., Const. W. Cast. 322
Fitz-Otho, Hugh, Const. T.L. 320
Fitzpatrick, Denn., Ch. Com. Ass. 656
— Jno. Wils., aft. ld. Castletown, *q.v.*, L.L. Q. Co. 571
— Patr. P., C. Exc. 282
— hon. Rd., Ch. Sec. Ir. 562; gen. (**A**) 859; L.G.O. 259; P.C. 204; Sec. at W. 234
Fitz-Peter, Geoff., aft. E. of Essex, *q.v.*, Ch. Jr. (1198) 362; J. It. 366; Jy. 363; W.C.P. 317
— Sim., Jy. 363
Fitz-Pier, *see* Fitz-Peter
Fitz-Ralph, Ger., J. It. 365
— Rd., abp. Arm. 595; dn. Lich. 445
— Rt., bp. Worc. 472
— Simon, K.B. 755
— Wm., J. It. 365; Jy. 363
Fitz-Ranulph, Ralph, J. It. 368
Fitz-Reginald, Ralph, J. It. 367
Fitz-Renfred, or Fitz-Reinfred, or Fitz-Reinfrey, Rog., Const. T.L. 320; J. It. 366; Jy. 363
Fitz-Richard, Gerald, bp. Crk. and Cl. 631
— Sim., C.J.C.P. Ir. 580; J.C.P. Ir. 581; K.B. 755; S.L. Ir. 590
— Wm., J. It. 365-6
— Wm., L.M. Lond. 489
Fitz-Robert, Jno., B. Ex. 382; J. It. 367
— Ph., J. It. 366
— Rand., J. It. 367
— Walt., J. It. 366; Jy. 363
— Walt., J. It. 367
Fitz-Roger, Rt., J. It. 366; Jy. 364
— Rog., L.M. Lond. 488
— Wm., J. It. 367
Fitz-Rosceline, Wm., J. It. 367
Fitzroy, ld. Augs. Ch. Lenn., gen. (**D**) 906
— hon. Ch., gen. (**A**) 861
— ld. Ch., gen. (**A**) 860
— ld. Ch., P.C. 213; V.C.H. 297
— Ch. Augs. and sir C., G. Antig. &c. 727; G. N. Austr. 705; G. N.S.W. 703; G. Pr. Ed. Isl. 699; K.C B. 782; K.H. 792
— Geo. Rt., gen. (**D**) 931
— Hy., aft. E. of Nottingham, and D. of Richmond and Somerset, *q.v.*, K.G. (1525) 737
— hon. Hy., C.W.P.B. 272; L. Admy. 183; P.C. 216; U.S. Home, 228
— Rt., adm. (**G**) 842; G.N.Z. 709
— Rt. O'Brien, adm. (**E**) 837
— hon, Wm., gen. (**B**) 868
— ld. Wm., adm. (**D**) 824; K.C.B. 777
Fitzsimon, Fitzsimons, and **Fitzsymon**
— Ed., A.G. Ir. 588; M.R. Ir. 585; S.L. Ir. 591
— Osb., Jy. 364
— Rd., J. It. 367
— sir Rd., K.G. 733
— Turst., J. It. 365; Jy. 363
— Walt., abp. Dbln. and Gl. 616; L.D. Ir. 553; Ld. Chanc. Ir. 575
Fitz-Stephen, Ralph, J. It. 365; Jy. 363
— Wm., J. It. 366; Jy. 363
Fitzsymon, *see* Fitzsimon
Fitz-Thomas, Jno., dn. Ardf. 640
— Maur., K.B. 755
— Th., L.M. Lond. 489
— Wm., Ld. Chanc. Ir. 575
Fitz-Torold, Nichs., J. It. 366
Fitz-Walter, sir Walt., L.H.A. 173
— Wm., Const. W. Cast. 322
Fitz-Walter, lds. and E.
— Benj., 1st Earl, L.L. Esx. 308; P.C. 198; Pres. B.T. 264; Tr. H. 291
— Jno., 12th ld., K.B. (1485) 758
— Rt., 13th ld., aft. 1st visc. F. and E. of Sussex, *q.v.* K.B. 759; K.G. 737
— Hy., ld., aft. 2nd E. of Sussex, *q.v.*, K.B. 760
— Th., visc., aft. 3rd E. of Sussex, *q.v.*, L.D. Ir. 553
— Hy. Ratcliff, ld., K.B. (1610) 762
Fitz-Warine, Falco., Jy. 365
— Wm., J. It. 367
— sir Wm., K.G. 733
Fitz-Warine, lds.
— Jno., 11th ld., K.B. 758
— Ed., ld., aft. 4th E. of Bath, *q.v.*, K.B. 762
Fitzwarren, *see* Fitzwarine
Fitzwigram, *see* Fitzwygram
Fitzwilliam and **Fitzwilliams**
— Adam, J. It. 367; Jy. 364
— Geo., K.B. 760
— Hugh de, J. It. 368
— hon. Jno., gen. (**A**) 858
— Osb., Jy. 364
— Otho., Jy, 363
— Ralph, J. It. 369
— Rd., G. Bah. Isl. 716
— Rt., J. It. 367
— Th. and sir T., Rec. Lond. 493; Sp. H.C. 249
— sir Th., V. Treas. Ir. 559
— Wm., Ch. Ex. Ir. 561
— Wm., dn. Wells, 429
— sir Wm., L.D. Ir. and L.J. Ir. 554; L.K. Ir. 576
— sir Wm., aft. 1st E. of Southampton, *q.v.*, C.D.L. 242; K.G. 737; Tr. H. 291
Fitzwilliam, E.
— Wm., 4th E., L.L. Tr. 557; L.L. Yorks, W.R. 313; L.P.C. 188; P.C. 205
— Chas. Wm., 5th E., K.G. 744
— Wm. Th. Sp., 6th E., form. visc. Milton, *q.v.*; K.G, 744
Fitzwilliam of Meryon, visc.
— Rd., 6th visc., C. Treas. Ir. 559; K.B. 764
FitzWygram, sir Fk. Well. Jno., gen. (**D**) 908
Flaccinator, M. F., C. Ro. 41
Flaccus, C. F., C. Ro. 44
— C. N., C. Ro., 46
— C. V., C. Ro. 45
— C. V. P., C. Ro. 40
— L. V., C. Ro., 42-3-4-5
— M. F., C. Ro. 42, 45
— P. V., C. Ro. 43
— Q. F. (4) C. Ro. 42-3-4; Dt. Ro. 43
— S. F., C. Ro. 44

Flaithbheartagh, K. Ir. 21
Flambard, Ralph or Ran., bp. Dham. 478; Ch. Jr. 362; L.H.T. 152
Flamburiari, Ct. Dion., G.C.M.G. 795; K.C.M.G. 796
Flaminius, C., C. Ro. 43-4
Flamininus, L. Q., C. Ro. 43
— T. Q., C. Ro. 43-4-5
Flamsteed, Jno., Astr. Roy. 941
Flan-Febla, bp. Arm. 595
Flannagan, Steph. W., Land. J. Ir. 586-7; P.C. 220
— Wm., dn. Ach. 614; dn. Killa. 614
Flandrensis, Rd., Jy. 364
Flann-Sionna, K. Ir. 22
Flannan (St.), bp. Killoe. 634
Flathguss, bp. Ferns, 621
Flathlem, bp. Saig. 620
Flavius, L., C. Ro. 47
Flavus, L. L., C. Ro. 39
— S. L., C. Ro. 37
— T. L., C. Ro. 37; Dt. Ro. 37
Fleeming, *see* Fleming
Fleet, sir Jno., L.M. Lond. 491
— Jno. Faithf., C.I.E. 807
Fleetwood, Ch., Comm. Ir. 554; W.C.P. 319
— Jas., bp. Worc. 473
— Wm., bp. Ely 435; bp. St. As. 462
— Wm., Rec. Lond. 494; S.L. 408
Fleming and **Flemyng**
— Aug., gen. (**D**) 894
— (or Fleeming), hon. Ch. Elph., adm. (**A**) 819; G. Gr. Hosp. 854
— Chr., A.G. Ir. 588
— Ed., gen. (**D**) 882
— Fras., G. Mtius. 684
— Geo. and sir G., bp. Carl. 476; dn. Carl. 476
— Hy., Sec. L.G.B. 256; Sec. P.L.B. 262
— Hez., gen. (**B**) 866
— Hor. Towns., dn. Cloy. 633
— Jas., gen. (**C**) 871
— Jas., Q.C. 418
— Jno., G. I. Man. 666
— Jno. Smyth, L.M. Dbln. 641
— Michl. le, dn. Lism. 628
— Nichs., abp. Arm. 595
— Rd., abp. Yk. 485
— Rd., bp. Linc. 446
— Rd., bp. Llin. 621
— Rt., dn. Linc. 448
— Th., bp. Llin. 622
— Th., L.M. Dbln. 641
— (or Flemyng), Th. and sir T., C.B. Ex. 381; C.J.K.B. 370; Rec. Lon. 494; S.G. 401; S.L. 408
— Th. Ferg., gen. (**D**) 896
— sir Val., G. Tasm. 708
— Walt. le, dn. Lism. 628
— Wm., C. Ex. 279
— Wm. le, bp. Lism. 626
Fleming, lds.
— Jno., 2nd ld., L.G.C. Sc. 506
— Malc., 3rd ld., L.G.C. Sc. 506
— Jas., 4th ld., L.G.C. Sc. 506
— Jno., 5th ld., L.G.C. Sc. 506
Flemyng, *see* Fleming
Fleshmonger, Wm., dn. Chich. 434
Fletcher, Andr., L.J. Clk. 516; Ld. Sess. 520
— sir Andr., Ld. Sess. 519
— Dav., bp. Arg. 538
— Ed., G. I. Man, 666
— Ed. Ch., gen. (**D**) 900
— Geo., Yk. H. 334
— Hy., gen. (**A**) 858
— Hy. and sir H., Chn. E.I.Co. 644
— Hy. Ch., gen. (**D**) 915
— sir Jno., Ld. Adv. 526
— Jno. Rigg, gen. (**B**) 868
— Jno. Venour, adm. (**G**) 842
— Ph., dn. Kild. 619
— Rd., bp. Brl. 439; bp. Lond. 451; bp. Worc. 473; dn. Pboro. 458
— Th., bp. Drom. 605; bp. Kild. 617; dn. Down, 605; dn. Chr. Ch. Dbln. 618
— Th., S.L. 409
— Wm., dn. Kild. 619
— Wm., J.C.P. Ir. 582
Fleur, Chev. de, G. Mtius. 683
Flint, Th., S.L. 410
Flood, sir Fk., C. Acc. Ir. 567
— Fk. Rd. Solly, gen. (**D**) 928
— Hy., P.C. 203; V. Treas. Ir. 560
— Ward., A.G. Ir. 588; C.J. K.B. Ir. 578; J. Admy. Ct. Ir. 587; S.G. Ir. 589
***Florence,** bp. Cloy. 630
*— bp. Emly, 625
*— bp. Glasg. 536; Ld. Chanc. Sc. 514
*— bp. Ross. 631
*— dn. Rph. 602
* Prob. some same pers. Comp. dates.
— I., C. Fld. 82
— I. to V., C. Hld. 82
Florentius, *see* Florence
Flores, J. J., Pres. Ecr. 108
— Juan de, G. Trin. 721
— V., Pres. Ugy. 111
Florestan, I., Pr. Mno. 31
Florez, *see* Flores
Florian, Emp. Ro. 48
Florus, C. A., C. Ro. 42
Flower, Ch. and sir C., L.M. Lond. 492
— Cyril, L.T. 162
— Ph., dn. Kilf. 637
— Rt., Som. H. 332
— Rog., Sp. H.C. 248
— Wm., Chest. H. 331; Guis. P.A. 343; Norr. K.A. 329; R. Cr. P.A. 335
Flowerdew, Ed., B. Ex. 384; S.L. 408
Floyd, sir Hy., gen. (**D**) 883
— sir Jno., gen. (**A**) 860
Floyde, Maj., G. I. Man, 666
Floyer, Aug., K.C.B. 775
Flude, Th. Pet., gen. (**D**) 899
Fludyer, sir Saml., L.M. Lond. 492
— Wm., gen. (**D**) 886
Flyn, Wm., dn. Clonm. 600
Foche, Jno., C. Exc. 279
Foda, Cumin, bp. Clonf. 635
Fœldobar, bp. Clr. 596
Fœndelach, bp. Arm. 595
Fogamair, O'Mœl, bp. Killa. 612
Fogartach, K. Ir. 21
— (2) bp. Saig. 620
Fogg, Laur., dn. Chest. 477
Fogo, Jas., gen. (**D**) 891
Foisac, Balt. R. de, gen. (**C**) 871
Foix, Jno. de, aft. E. of Kendal, *q.v.*, K.G. (1435) 735
— Pet. de la, K.B. 754
Folan, Jno., bp. Lim. 638
Folco, M. Fa. 53
Foley, hon. Fitz. Algn. Ch., adm. (**E**) 836; (**F**) 839
— Paul, Sp. H.C. 250
— Rd. Harry, gen. (**C**) 874
— Rt., dn. Worc. 474
— hon. St. Geo. Ger., G. Gsey. 669; gen. (**D**) 903; K.C.B. 781
— Saml., bp. Down and Cnr. 604; dn. Ach. 614
— Th. and sir Th., adm. (**A**) 818; G.C.B. 768; K.C.B. 773
Foley, lds.
Foley Family.
2nd Creation.
— Th., 3rd ld., C.G.P. 300; L.L. Worc. 313; P.C. 212; Postm. G. 238
— Th. Hy., 4th ld., C.G.A. 300; C.G.P. 300; L.L. Worc. 313
Foliot, Gilb. or Rt., bp. Her. 441; bp. Lond. 451
— Hugh, Jy. 364
— Jno., gen. (**B**) 864
— Jno., gen. (**B**) 865
— Rt. or Gilb., bp. Her. 441; bp. Lond. 451
— Walt., J. It. 367
Foljambe, Jeffr., J.K.B. Ir. 578
Folkes, Mart., Pres. R. Soc. 940
Folkestone, Wm., visc., son of 4th E. of Radnor, P.C. 220; Tr. H. 292
Folkyngham, Jno. de, M. Chy. 394
Follett, Brent. Sp., Q.C. 417
— Wm. W. and sir W., A.G. 400; K.C. 416; S.G. 402
Formosus, P. Ro. 33
Fonblanque, Jas., P.P. 415-16
— visc. Th. de Gr., K.H. 789
Fontaine, Jan. de la, G. C.G.H. 678
Fontibus, Jus. de, bp. Ely, 434; L.H.T. 152
Fontinalis, A. A. V., C. Ro. 38
Fooks, Geo. Alex. St. P., gen. (**D**) 919
— Walk. King, gen. (**D**) 911
— Wm., adm. (**A**) 816
— Wm. Crac., Q.C. 418
Foord, *see also* Ford
— Ed. Archd., gen. (**D**) 920
— Wm. Oct., gen. (**D**) 933
Foote, Ed. Jas. and sir E., adm. (**A**) 819; K.C.B. 776
— Hy. Rd., adm. (**H**) 849
— Th., L.M. Lond. 491
— Walt., L.P.S. Sc. 500
— Wm. Fras., gen. (**D**) 907
Forannan, St., bp. Kild. 616
Forbes, Alexr., bp. Abdn. 530; bp. Cness. 532
— Alexr., C. Exc. Sc. 504
— Alexr. Penr., bp. Brn. 541
— Arth., adm. (**D**) 833; (**F**) 838
— sir Arth., L.J. Ir. 555
— Benj. Gord., gen. (**C**) 873
— Ch. Ferd. and sir C., K.C.H. 789; K.H. 792
— Ch. Pult., gen. (**D**) 929
— Dav., gen. (**D**) 881
— Dav., gen. (**D**) 888
— Dunc., L.P. Ct. Sess. 516; Ld. Adv. 524

Forbes—*cont.*
—— sir Fras., L.M. Lond. 491
—— hon. Fras. Reg., Amb. Aus. 117; Amb. Bzl. 135; Amb. G. St. 122; Amb. Sxy. 120-21
—— Geo., L.M. Dbln. 641
—— Geo. Wm., gen. (**D**) 918
—— Gord., gen. (**A**) 860
—— Hy., adm. (**H**) 846
—— Jno., G. Bah. Isl. 716
—— Jno., gen. (**D**) 894
—— Jno., L.M. Dbln. 641
—— Jno., Q.C. 419
—— Jno. and sir J., gen. (**D**) 908; K.C.B. 781
—— hon. Jno., adm. (**A**) 814; L. Admy. 178-9
—— Jno. Hay, Jy. Sc. 523; Ld. Sess. 520
—— Lewis W., Modr. K. Sc. 547
—— Patr., bp. Cness. 532 and 541
—— Patr., Modr. K. Sc. 547
—— Rt., bp. Ork. 545; bp. Ross and Cness. 545
—— Th. Geo., adm. (**H**) 849
—— Th. Jno., gen. (**D**) 883
—— Wm., bp. Edinb. 533
—— Wm., gen. (**D**) 913
—— Wm., L.M. Dbln. 641
Forbes, lds. and visc.
—— Jas. Och., 17th ld., gen. (**A**) 861; L.H.C. K. Sc. 546

—— Geo., ld., aft. 3rd E. of Granard, *q.v.*, adm. (**A**) 814
—— Geo. Jno., visc., son of 6th E. of Granard, gen. (**C**) 874; L.L. Longf. 570; Sec. St. Patr. 752
Forbes-Mackenzie, *see* Mackenzie
Ford, *see also* Foord
—— Barn., gen. (**D**) 913
—— Ch. Ersk., gen. (**D**) 904
—— Edm. Tw., gen. (**D**) 982
—— Fras. Cl. and sir F., Amb. Arg. 136; Amb. Bzl. 135; Amb. Gr. 129; Amb. Spn. 124; Amb. Ugy. 137; G.C.M.G. 795; K.C.M.G. 798
—— Jno., adm. (**A**) 816
—— Matth. Bl., gen. (**D**) 914
—— sir Rd., L.M. Lond. 491
—— Wm., B. Ex. 383
—— Wm. Hy., gen. (**C**) 875
Fordham (or Frodsham), Jno., bp. Dham. 478; bp. Ely, 435; dn. Wlls. 428
Fordhere, bp. Shbn. 466
Fordwich, Geo. Augs. F., visc., aft. 6th E. Cowper, *q.v.*, U.S.F. 230
Fordyce, Ch. F., gen. (**D**) 905
—— Jno., gen. (**D**) 896; K.C.B. 780
—— Jno., S.L.R. 271
Foreman, *see also* Forman
—— Andr., abp. St. Andr. 529; bp. Mor. 534; Ld. Chanc. Sc. 514
Forest, *see* Forrest
Forester, *see* Forrester
Forfar, Archd., 2nd E. of, L.H.T. Sc. 498; L.P.S. Sc. 501
Forgie (? Fergie), Rt., dn. Killa. 614
Forlong, Jas., K.H. 791
—— Jas. Geo. R., gen. (**D**) 915
Forman, *see also* Foreman
—— sir Rt., Ly. K.A. 513
—— Wm., L.M. Lond. 490
Formay, Walt., bp. Ross, 631
Fornerod, Pres. Sw. C. 31
Forrest and **Forest**
—— Ch., L.M. Dbln. 641
—— Jas. and sir J., L. Prov. Edinb. 548
—— Jno., dn. Wells, 429
—— Jno., L.M. Dbln. 640
—— Wm. Ch., gen. (**D**) 905
Forrester and **Forester**
—— Ad., L.J. Clk. 516
—— sir Andr., Sec. Thist. 749
—— Dunc., Compt. Sc. 498
—— G. C. W., *see* ld. F., *infra*
—— sir Jno., Ld. Chanc. Sc. 515; L.G.C. Sc. 506
—— Walt., bp. Brn. 531
Forrester, lds.
—— Jno. Geo., 2nd ld., C.G.A. 300; P.C. 214
—— hon. Geo. Cecil Weld., aft. 3rd ld. F., Compt. H. 293; gen. (**D**) 897; P.C. 215
Forster, *see also* Foster
—— Hy., gen. (**D**) 903
—— captn. J., G. Bmda. 701
—— Jas., S.L. 412
—— Jno., A.G. Ir. 588; C.J.C.P. Ir. 580; Rec. Dbln. 642; S.G. Ir. 589
—— Jno. Coop., Pres. Coll. Surg. 939
—— Nichs., bp. Killoe. 634; bp. Rph. 602
—— Steph., L.M. Lond. 490
—— Thomps., Mast. Coll. Surg. 939
—— Wm., bp. S. and M. 483
—— Wm., dn. Kilmacd. 638
—— Wm., K.B. 761
—— Wm. Edw., Ch. Sec. Ir. 563; P.C. 218; U.S.C. 235; V.P. Ed. 255
—— Wm. Fk., gen. (**D**) 892; K.H. 790
Forsyth, Jno., K.C.S.I. 803
—— Th. Dougl., K.C.S.I. 803
—— Wm., Q.C. 417
Fort, Th., bp. Ach. 612
Fortescue, Chich., aft. sir C., Ulst. K.A. 572
—— Chich. Saml., aft. 1st ld. Carlingford and 2nd ld. Clermont, *q.v.*, Ch. Sec. Ir. 563; L.L. Esx. 308; L.T. 161; P.C. 217; Pres. B.T. 269; U.S.C. 235
—— Fras., K.B. 761
—— Ger., Ulst. K.A. 572
—— Hy., C.J.K.B. Ir. 577
—— hon. Hugh, *see* ld. F., *infra*
—— Jno. and sir J., C.J.K.B. 370; S.L. 407
—— sir Jno., C.D.L. 242; Ch. Ex. 154
—— Lew., B. Ex. 384
—— Matt., C.C.J. 404
—— Wm. and sir W., B. Ex. 385; J.C.P. 379; K.C. 415; M.R. 388; P.C. 198; S.L. 412
Fortescue, lds. and E.
—— Jno. F., 1st ld., form. sir J. F. Aland, *q.v.*
—— Hugh, 3rd ld. and 1st E., form. visc. Ebrington, *q.v.*; L.L. Dev. 307
—— Hugh, 2nd E., form. visc. Ebrington, *q.v.*; K.G. 744; L.S.H. 290; Sec. P.L.B. 262
—— Hugh, 3rd E., form. visc. Ebrington, *q.v.*
Forth, M. Chy. 395
—— Jno. D., Ptc. P.A. 337
Forth—*cont.*
—— Wm., C. Exc. 278
Fortze, Wm. de, L.H.A. 170
Forward, Rt., dn. Drom. 606
Forwood, Arth. B., Sec. Adm. 187
Foscardi, Demetr. Ct., K.C.M.G. 796
Foster, *see also* Forster
—— Anthy., C. Acc. Ir. 567; C.B. Ex. Ir. 583
—— Aug. Jno. and sir A., Amb. Dk. 127; Amb. Sda. 114; Amb. U.S.A. 132; P.C. 210
—— Ch. Jno., gen. (**D**) 906; M.C.I. 647
—— Edw. Hor. Hy., gen. (**D**) 926
—— Jno., K.B. 759
—— Jno., L.J. Ir. 557
—— Jno., aft. ld. Oriel, *q.v.*, B.T. 268; C. Treas. Ir. 561; Ch. Ex. Ir. 562; L.T. 158-9; P.C. 204
—— Jno. Fitzg., G. Vict., 704
—— Jno. Lesl., B. Ex. Ir. 584
—— Michl. and sir M., J.K.B. 373; S.L. 412
—— (or Fostin), bp. Elph. 608
—— Rt. and sir R., C.J.K.B. 370; J.C.P. 379; S.L. 409
—— Th., gen. (**B**) 869
—— Th. B., gen. (**D**) 888
—— Th., gen. (**D**) 894
—— Th. and sir T., J.C.P. 378; S.L. 409
—— Th. Campb., Q.C. 419
—— hon. Th. Hy., C. Cus. Ir. 565; C. Treas. Ir. 561
—— Wm., bp. Clr. 596; bp. Cork and R. 632; bp. Kilm. 607
Fostin, *see* Foster
Fothadus, bp. St. Andr. 528
Fotherby, Ch., dn. Cant. 431
—— Martin, bp. Sal. 467
Fotheringham, Fk., C. Exc. Sc. 505
Fouché, Off. Nap. 26
Foulis and **Fowlis**
—— Dav., gen. (**D**) 877; K.C.B. 777
—— Jas. or Jno. (Collington), Ld. Adv. 526; Ld. Clk. Reg. 525; Ld. Sess. 518
—— sir Jas. (Collington), L.J. Clk. 516; Ld. Sess. 519
—— sir Jas. (Reidfurd), Ld. Sess. 519
—— Jno. or Jas., *see* Jas. *supra*
—— Wm., L.P.S. Sc. 500; Sec. St. Sc. 501
Foulkes (or Ffoulkes), Wm. W., C.C.J. 405
Foung-Chih, Emp. Ch. 100
Fountain, Jno., C.G.S. 356; S. L. 410
Fountayne, Jno., dn. Yk. 487
Foveaux, Jos., G. N.S.W. 702; gen. (**B**) 868
Fowell. Wm. Newton, adm. (**H**) 849
Fowke, Geo., adm. (**A**) 820
—— Th., G. Gibr. 669; gen. (**B**) 865
Fowkes, Jno., L.M. Lond. 491
Fowle, Ch. St., gen. (**D**) 912
—— Jno., C. Exc. 279-80
Fowler, Ed., bp. Glr. 438
—— Hy., G. Br. Hond. 714; G. Lag. 687
—— Hy. H., P.C. 221; Sec. Tr. 164; U.S. Home, 228

Fowler—*cont.*
— Jno., K.C.M.G. 798
— Moses, dn. Rip. 482
— Rd., K.B. 759
— Rd. and sir R., C.D.L. 242; S.G. 401
— Rt., abp. Dbln. and Gl. 616; bp. Killoe and Kilf. 635; C.G.S. Ir. 576
— Rt., bp. Oss. F. and L. 622
— Rt., dn. St. Pat. 618
— Rt. Merr., adm. (**H**) 844
— Rt. Nichs. and sir R., L.M. Lond. 492
Fowlis, *see* Foulis
Fownes, sir Wm., L.M. Dbln. 641
Fox, Ch., Paym. G. 244
— hon. Ch. Jas., F. Sec. 228; L. Admy. 179; L.T. 157; P.C. 203, 208; Prem. (?) 144
— Ch. Rd., gen. (**D**) 883; S.G.O. 260
— Ed., bp. Her. 441
— Ed., M.M. 247
— Hy., aft. 1st ld. Holland, *q.v.*, L.T. 157; P.C. 199; Paym. G. 244; S. St. 224; Sec. at W. 233
— hon. Hy. Ed. (son of 1st ld. Holland), Amb. Scy. 114; Comm. F. Ir. 564; G. Gibr. 670; gen. (**A**) 859
— hon. Hy. Ed., aft. 4th ld. Holland, *q.v.*, Amb. Aus. 117; Amb. G. St. 122; Amb. Tusc. &c. 115
— Hy. Steph., Amb. Bzl. 135; Amb. R. Pl. 136; Amb. U.S.A. 132
— Luke, J.C.P. Ir. 582
— Rd., bp. B. and W. 428; bp. Exr. 436; bp. Dham. 478; bp. Winch. 471; L.P.S. 240; S. St. 223
— Sackv., Bl. C.H. 339; Geneal. Bath, 784
— sir Steph., L.T. 155; Paym. G. 244
— Wm., K.C.M.G. 797
Fox-Pitt-Rivers, *see* Rivers
Fox - Strangways, *see* Strangways
Foxall, Jno., abp. Arm. 595
Foxfoord, Rd., Ch. Lond. 422
Foxle, Jno. de, B. Ex. 383
— Th. de, Const. W. Cast. 322
Foy, Nathl., bp. Wford. and L. 627
Framingham, Hayl. and sir H., gen. (**C**) 874; K.C.B. 774; K.C.H. 787
Frampton, Ch., gen. (**B**) 865
— Rt., B. Ex. 383
— Rt., bp. Glr. 438; dn. Glr. 440
Franc, sir Stand. de, K.G. (?) 734
Frances (gr. dau. Hy. VII.), Pr. E. 12
Franch (or Franke), Hy., Yk. H. 334
Ffranche, or Franke, Th., Bl. M. P.A. 336; Guis. P.A. 343
Francia, J. G. R., Dt. Pgy. 110
Francillon, Jas., C.C.J., 403
Francis, *see also* Fraunceys
— Pr. Mno. 30
— I. (of France), D. Bry. 28
— I., D. Pma. 53
Francis—*cont.*
— I. (form. Fras. II. of Germany), Emp. Aus. 58; K.G. 743
— I., K. Hgy. 60
— I. and II., D. Bry. 28
— I. and II., D. Lne. 30
— I. and II., Emp. Gmy. 62
— I. and II., K. Fr. 24
— I. (K. Fr.), K.G. 737
— I. and II., K. 2 Scy. 56
— I. to V., D. Mda. 53
— -Augs. Ch. Em., Pr. Cons. of Engl., *see* Albert
— Arth. gen. (**D**) 916
— Fras. Ed., gen. (**D**) 913
— -Fk., D.S.C.G. 78
— Hy., gen. (**D**) 920
— -Hyacinth, D. Svy. 55
— Jno., dn. Llin. 623
— Jno., dn. Lism. 629
— Jno. Th., gen. (**D**) 925
— -Joseph, D.S.C. and G. 78
— -Joseph, Emp. Aus. 58; K.G. 745*
— -Joseph, K. Hungary, 60
— -Mary, I. and II., G. D. Tny. 57
— Ph. and sir P., G.C.B. 771; K.B. 766
— -Phœbus, K. Nav. 85, 88
— Rd., K.B. 756
— Rd., bp. Wford. 626
— -Sforza (D. Milan), K.G. 736
— -Steph., D. Lne. 30
Francisca - Josepha, &c. (g. dau. Q. Vict.), Pr. E. 16
Francisco-Mello, R. Nds. 83
Franck—, *see* Franc—
Franco, G., Pres. Ecr. 108
Frank, Jno., M. Chy. 394
Franke, *see* Franche
Frankfort, Lodge, ld., form. L. Morris, *q.v.*, C. Treas. Ir. 561
Frankland, Ch. Colv., adm. (**H**) 848
— Ed. Aug., adm. (**H**) 847
— Fk., C. Exc. 280
— Jno., dn. Ely 435; dn. Glr. 440
— Rd., C. Tx. 284
— Th. and sir T., B.T. 264; C. Cus. 274; C. Exc. 279; L. Admy. 177-8; Postm. G. 237-8
— sir Th., adm. (**A**) 814
— W., L. Admy. 181
Franklin and **Franklyn**
— Ch., gen., (**D**) 894
— Ch. Tr., gen. (**D**) 911
— Ed., adm. (**H**) 850
— Jno., M. Chy. 396
— sir Jno., adm. (**D**) 829; G. V.D.Ld. 708; K.C.H. 789
— Jno. H., gen. (**D**) 903
— M., G. N.Sc. 695
— Wm., dn. Winds. 474
— sir Wm., K.C.H. 788
Franks, Rd., gen. (**B**) 864
— Thos. Hartz. and sir T., gen. (**D**) 892; K.C.B. 778
Fraser and **Frazer**
— Alexr., adm. (**A**) 818
— Alexr., gen. (**D**) 891
— Alexr., gen. (**D**) 920
— Alexr. and sir A., Jy. Sc. 522; Ld. Sess. 520
— sir Alexr., L.G.C. Sc. 506
— Alexr. Mack, gen. (**B**) 866
— Alexr. Rt., gen. (**D**) 913
— Aug., K.C.B. 775
— Ch. Cr., gen. (**D**) 910
Fraser and Frazer—*cont.*
— Ch. Hy., Amb. G. St. 121; Amb. H. Tns. 120; Amb. Spn. 123
— hon. Dav. Macd., gen. (**D**) 922
— Geo. Hy. Jno. Alex., gen. (**D**) 928
— Geo. Wm., gen. (**D**) 929
— Hast., gen. (**A**) 863; K.C.B. 776
— Hast., gen. (**D**) 935
— Hugh, Amb. Chi. 137; Amb. Jap. 131
— Jas., bp. Manch. 480
— Jas., K.C.B. 784
— Jas. St., gen. (**D**) 878
— Jno., bp. Ross. 535
— Jno., gen., (**D**) 884
— Jno., gen. (**D**) 897
— Jno., gen. (**D**) 908
— Jno., K.C.M.G. 796
— Jno., Ld. Clk. Reg. 525
— sir Jno., gen. (**A**) 861; G.C.H. 786
— Jno. Elph., gen. (**D**) 912
— Jno. F., C.C.J. 403
— Jno. Keith, gen. (**D**) 931
— Malc., K.C.M.G. 798
— Patr., D. Fac. Sc. 527; Ld. Sess. 521
— Rt., K.H. 792
— Rt. Walt. Macl., gen. (**D**) 906
— Simon, gen. (**B**) 866
— Simon, gen. (**D**) 897
— hon. Simon., gen. (**B**) 865
— hon. Simon, aft. ld. Lovat, *q.v.*, L.L. Inv. (1873) 510
— Th., adm. (**H**) 848
— Wm., bp. St. And. 529; Ld. Chanc. Sc. 514
— Wm., gen. (**D**) 892
— Wm., K.C.B. 784
— Wm., L.P.S. 241; U.S.F. 229; U.S.S. 226
— Wm. Ch., gen. (**D**) 877
Fraser-Tytler, *see* Tytler
Fraunceis, *see* Fraunceys
Fraunces, Jno., L.M. Lond. 489
Fraunceys, *see also* Francis
— Ad., L.M. Lond., 489
— (or Fraunces), Jno., L.K. 354
— Jno. le, M. Chy. 393; B. Ex. 382; Jy. 365
— Sim., L.M. Lond. 489
Fraunke, Jno., M.R. 387
Fray, Jno., B. Ex. 383; C.B. Ex. 381; Rec. Lond. 493
Frazer, *see* Fraser
Freake, *see* Freke
Frecknam, Jno., abb. or dn. Westr. 469
Frederic and **Frederick**
— A.D. Aus. 58
— (Ct. Pal. Rh., aft. K. of Bohem.) K.G. (1612) 739
— C. Lux. 84
— D. Anht. 66
— D. Bma. 59
— D. Brk. 69, 70
— D. Fca. 71
— (of Luxemburg), D. Lne. 29
— D. Pr. 65
— D. S. Alt. 78
— D. Tny. 57
— K. Jsm. 97
— (son Geo. III.), bp. Osnaburgh, aft. D. of Yk. and Alb., *q.v.*, Pr. E. 14; K.B. 765; K.G. 742; P.C. 204

For List of Abbreviations, see pp. 944-952.

Frederic and Frederick—*cont.*
—— Pr. Nass. 76
—— Pr. M. Sch. 75
—— I., K. Sw. 92
—— I., K. Wbg. 81
—— I., M. Fa. 52
—— I. and II., D. Lne. 29
—— I. and II., D. Wbg. 81
—— I. (D. Wbg.), K.G. 739
—— I. and II., K. Pr. 65
—— I. (K. Pr.), K.G. 741
—— I. and II., Lg. H. Csl. 72
—— I. (Lg. H. Csl.), K.G. 741
—— I. and II., M. Brg. 65
—— I. to III., D. Aus. 58
—— I. to III., El. Sxy. 77
—— I. to III., K. Scy. 55-6
—— I. to IV., D. S.G.A. 78
—— III. (D. S.G.A.), K.G. 742
—— I. to IV., E. Gmy. 61-2
—— IV. (E. Gmy.), K.G. 736
—— I. to V., C.P.R. 68
—— I. to VI., D. Su. 80
—— I. to VII., K. Dk. 93-4
—— II. (K. Dk.), K.G. 738
—— VI. (K. Dk.), K.G. 743
—— II. to VII., M. Bdn. 66-7
—— III., K. Nls. 56
—— -Aug., D. Obg. 76
—— -Aug. (iss. Jas. I.), Pr. E. 13
—— -Aug., I. and II., K. Pld. 91
—— -Aug., I. and II., K. Sxy. 78
—— -Aug., II. (K. Sxy.), K.G. 744
—— -Aug., I. to III., El. Sxy. 78
—— Ch. and sir C., adm. (**D**) 832; (**E**) 834; (**F**) 838; L. Admy. 184; K.B. 765; S.G.O. 260
—— -Ch. (Pr. Pruss.), G.C.B. 771
—— -Ch. (Archd. Austr.), G.C.B. 769
—— -Ch. Augs. (Pr. of Schl. Holst.), gen. (**D**) 901
—— -Chr., El. Sxy. 78
—— Ed., gen. (**D**) 879
—— -Eug., D. Wbg. 81
—— -Fras., Pr. M. Sch. 75
—— -Fras., I. to III. G.D.M. Sch. 75
—— -Geo. (D. Saxe-C. and G.), G.C.B. 769
—— -Gunther, Pr. S. Rdt. 79
—— -Hy. (g. son Jas. I.), Pr. E. 13
—— -Hy., Pr. Or. 83; R. Nds. 83; K.G. 739
—— Jno., C. Cus. 276
—— sir Jno., L.M. Lond. 491
—— -Jos., Lg. H. Hbg. 73
—— -Lewis (son Geo. II.), aft. D. of Glouc. and Pr. of Wales, *q.v.*, Pr. E. 14; Pr. W.E. 9; P.C. 197; K.G. 741
—— -Louis V., Lg. H. Hbg. 73
—— Morisc., gen. (**A**) 858
—— Th. Len., adm. (**A**) 816
—— -Ulrick, D. Brk. 70
—— -Wm., D. Nass. 76
—— -Wm., D. Brk. 70; gen. (**B**) (1809) 866
—— -Wm., D. Pr. 65
—— -Wm., El. H. Csl. 72
—— -Wm. (g. son Geo. II.), Pr. E. 14
—— -Wm. (g. son Q.Vic.), Pr. E. 15
—— -Wm., Pr. M. Sch. 74
—— -Wm., Pr. Mkg. 74
—— -Wm., Pr. Nass. 76
—— -Wm., I. to IV. K. Pr. 65
—— -Wm., III. (K. Pr.) K.G. 743
—— -Wm., IV. (K. Pr.) K.G. 744

Frederic and Frederick—*cont.*
—— -Wm.-Nich.-Ch., Pr. of Pruss., aft. Fk. III., Emp. of Ger., and K. of Pruss. G.C.B. 771; K.G. 744
—— -Wm.-Ch. &c., G.D. M. Str. 75; K.G. 744
—— -Wm.-Leop., Pr. L. Dtd. 73
—— -Wm. (Marg. and El. of Brandenburg), K.G. 740
—— -Wm.-Louis (Pr. of Pruss., aft. K. Pr. and Emp. Gmy.), G.C.B. 769
—— -Wm.-Vict.-Alb. (g. son Q. Vict., aft. Emp. Wm. II. of Gmy.) Pr. E. 15; K.G. 745
Frederica (Prss. of Han.), Cr. Ind. 810
Frederika - Wilh. - Am. - Vict. (g. dau. Q. Vict.) Pr. E. 15
Freebairn, Dav., bp. Edinb. 542; bp. Gall. 543; Pr. Bp. Sc. 540
Freeling, sir Arth. Hy., gen. (**D**) 915
—— Fras., Sec. P.O. 239
—— sir Geo. Hy., C. Cus. 277
—— Sanf. and sir S., G. Bdoes. 721; G. Dnca. 730; G. Gld. Cst. Col. 686; G. Gren. 724; G. Trin. 723; K.C.M.G. 797
Freeman, Fk. P. Wms., gen. (**D**) 930
—— Geo., K.B. 764
—— Hy. Stanh., G. Lag. 687
—— Quin, Jno., gen. (**A**) 861
—— Ralph. and sir R., L.M. Lond. 491; M.M. 246
—— Rd., C.B. Ex. Ir. 583; L.J. Ir. 555; Ld. Chanc. Ir. 576
—— Saml., dn. Pboro. 458
—— Wm. P. Wms., adm. (**A**) 816
—— Wm. Rt. Andr., gen. (**D**) 899
Freemantle, *see* Fremantle
Freer, *see also* Frere
—— Jno. Harbr., gen. (**D**) 893
—— Wm. Gard., K.H. 790
Freese, Jno. Nob. Arb., gen. (**D**) 899
—— Wm. Hy., gen. (**D**) 917
Freeth, Jas., aft. sir J., gen. (**D**) 884; K.C.B. 779; K.H. 790
—— Jas. Holt., gen. (**D**) 910
—— Rd. King, gen. (**D**) 914
—— Samps., gen. (**C**) 874
—— Samps., gen. (**D**) 910
Freind, *see* Friend
Freire, Dt. Chi. 111
Freke and **Freake**
—— Edmd., bp. Norw. 455; bp. Roch. 460; bp. Worc. 473; dn. Roch. 461; dn. Sal. 468
—— Jno., gen. (**B**) 866
Fremantle and **Freemantle**
—— Arth. Jas. Lyon-, gen. (**D**) 924
—— Ch. Howe and sir C., adm. (**D**) 830; G.C.B. 770; K.C.B. 778
—— hon. Edmd. Rt., adm. (**E**) 837
—— Hy., Sec. Tr. 163
—— Jno. Wm., gen. (**D**) 880
—— Thos. Fras., aft. sir T. (No. 1), adm. (**A**) 818; G.C.B. 767; G.C.H. 786; G.C.M.G. 794; K.C.B. 774; L. Admy. 181
—— sir Th. Fras. (No. 2), aft. ld. Cottesloe, *q.v.*; C. Cus. 277; Ch. Sec. Ir. 563; P.C. 214; Sec. Tr. 163; Sec. at W. 234

Fremantle and Freemantle—*cont.*
—— Wm. Hy. and sir W., B.C. 253; G.C.H. 786; P.C. 210; Tr. H. 291
—— Wm. Rt., dn. Rip. 482
French and **Ffrench**
—— Cudb., K.H. 791
—— Danl. O'C., Q.C. 420
—— Fk. Wm., St. O., 261
—— Hy. Jno., gen. (**D**) 895
—— Humphr., L.M. Dbln. 641
—— Jno., C. St. Ir. 568
—— Jno., L.M. Lond. 489
—— Jno., dn. Elph. 609
—— Jno., dn. Rph. 602
—— M.T., gen. (**D**) 923
—— Rd., gen. (**D**) 895
—— Rd., L.M. Dbln. 641
—— Rt., J.C.P. Ir. 582
—— Th. V., bp. Lhore. 655
—— Val., dn. Ross. 633
—— Wm., dn. Ard. 609
Frenchvill, Wm. de, J. It. 367
Frenyngham, Ralph de, J.C.P. 377
Freodwulf, K.E. 2
Frere, *see also* Freer
—— Barth., Amb. Spn. 124 Amb. Tky. 129
—— Cath., Lady, Cr. Ind. 810
—— (or Frier), Guy, Const. T.L. 320
—— Hy., G. Bdoes. 720
—— Hy. B.E. and sir H., Amb. Msct. 130; Amb. Zr. 132; G. Bbay. 659; G.C.B. 773; G. C.G.H., &c. 679; G.C.S.I. 801; K.C.B. 782; K.C.S.I. 802; M.C.I. 646; P.C. 218
—— Jno., G. Bdoes. 720
—— Jno. H., Amb. Pgl. 124; Amb. Pr. 118; Amb. Spn. 124; P.C. 207; U.S.F. 229
—— Wm., S.L. 412
Fresne, Chev. de, G. Mtius. 683
Frethewaldus, bp. Gall. 538
Frethome, *see* Fretton
Freton and **Fretton**
—— (or Frethome), Jno. de, M. Chy. 393
—— Rog. de, dn. Chich. 434
Frevyle, Geo., B. Ex. 384
Frewen, Acc., abp. Yk. 486; bp. Lich. and Cov. 444; dn. Glr. 440
Frewin, Rd., C. Cus. 276
Frey, Jas., dn. Arm. 597
Freyne, Arth., 1st ld. de, L.L. Rosc. 571
Frias, T., Pres. Bol. 109
Friend and **Freind**
—— Jno., C. Exc. 278
—— Wm., dn. Cant. 431
Frier, *see* Frere
Frilington, sir Jno., Const. W. Cast. 322
Frimont, Baron, G.C.B. 767
Frisby, Wm., S.L. 407
Friskeney, Walt. de, B. Ex. 383; J.C.P. 377; J.K.B. 371
Frith, *see also* Fryth
—— Jno. Wharton, gen. (**D**) 886
Fritharis, K. Sc. 17
Frithebert, bp. Hex. 480
Frithstan (St.), bp. Winch. 470
Frodsham, *see* Fordham
Froila, I. and II., K. Sp. 85
Frome, Ed., gen. (**D**) 898; G. Gsey. 669

Fromiata, M. of, R. Nds. 83
Frowcester, Edm., dn. Her. 442
Frow, *see* Froweck
Frowde, Philip, Postm. G. 237
Froweck, Frowick, and **Frowyck**
— Hy., K.B. 759
— (or Frow), Hy., L.M. Lond. 490
— Jno. de, Ld. Chanc. Ir. 574
— Th., C.J.C.P. 375; S.L. 407
— Th., K.B. 758
Frugi, L. C. P., C. Ro. 44
Fry, Ed. and sir E., Jud. Com. P.C. 362; Just. Ch. D. 391; L.J. App. 389; P.C. 220; Q.C. 418
Fryer, sir Jno., L.M. Lond. 491
Fryseby, Rd. de, A.G. 398
Fryston, Rd., M. Chy. 394
Fryth, *see also* Frith
— Rowl., Mowb. H. 340; Lanc. H. 333
Fulburn, Steph. de, bp. Wford. 626; L.D. Ir. 550; L. Treas. Ir. 558
— Walt. de, bp. Wford. 626; dn. Wford. 628; Ld. Chanc. Ir. 574
— Wm. de, B. Ex. 383
Fulford, Fras., bp. Montr. 694
— Humphr., K.B. 759
— Jno., adm. (**E**) 835; (**F**) 838
— Jno. de, bp. Llff. 449
Fullarton, *see* Fullerton
Fuller, Ch. Bondl., gen. (**D**) 907
— Maj. F., G. Trin. 722
— Fras., gen. (**A**) 861
— Fras., gen. (**C**) 871
— Fras., S.L. 411
— Jno. Aug., C.I.E. 807; gen. (**D**) 920
— sir Jos., G.C.H. 786; gen. (**B**) 868
— Rd., Adm. Adv. 423
— Saml., dn. Linc. 448
— Th. B., bp. Niag. 693
— Wm., bp. Ardf. and Agh. 639; bp. Lim. A. and A. 639; bp. Linc. 447; dn. Dham. 479; dn. Ely, 435; dn. St. Pat. 618
Fullerton and **Fullarton**
— Ch. Jno., gen. (**D**) 920
*— Jno., bp. Edinb. 542; Pr. Bp. Sc. 540
*— Jno., Sc. Bp. 545
* Prob. same pers.
— Jno., Ld. Sess. 520
— Th., C. Cus. Sc. 503
— Wm., G. Trin. 722
— Wm., gen. (**D**) 913
Fullerton-Elphinstone, *see* Elphinstone
Fulton, Græme Auchm., gen. (**D**) 924
— Jas. Forr., K.H. 792
— Jno., gen. (**D**) 921
— Jno. Jeffr., gen. (**D**) 921
Fulc, *see* Fulke
Fulco, J.C.P. 377
— I. to IV., C. Anj. 27
Fulcon, Rt., Jy. 365
Fulertach, bp. Cld. 598
Fulke, K. Jsm. 97
— (or Fulc), Rt., J.C.P. 377
Fulke-Greville, *see* Greville
Fullo, L. A., C. Ro. 43
Fulthorp and **Fulthorpe**
— Rt., or Rog. de, J.C.P. 378; J. It. 369; S.L. 407
— Th., J.C.P. 378
— Th., S.L. 407
Fulvianus, M. A., C. Ro. 44
Fulwar, Th., abp. Cash. and Eml. 626; bp. Ardf. and Agh. 639
Fundulus, C. F., C. Ro. 42
Furbar, Jno., gen. (**C**) 871
Furber, Th., adm. (**H**) 849
Furneaux, Jno., adm. (**G**) 841
— Wm., gen. (**D**) 889
— Wm. St., gen. (**D**) 910
Furneis, Adam de, dn. St. Patr. 617
Furnell, Michl. Cudm., C.I.E. 807
Furnellis, Alan de, J. It. 366; Jy. 363
— Hy. de, Jy. 364
— Sim. de, J. It. 368
— Wm. de, Jy. 364
Furner, Wm., C.C.J. 403
Furnese, Hy., L.T. 157
Furnius, C., C. Ro. 47
Furnival, Th., ld., L.H.T. 153
Furrer, J., Pres. Sw. C. 31
Furzer, Dan., Sr. N. 257
Fust, *see* Jenner
Fusus, A. F. M., C. Ro. 38
— C. F. P., C. Ro. 39
— L F. M., C. Ro. 38
— P. F. M., C. Ro., 38
— Sex. F. M., C. Ro. 37
— Sp. F. M., C. Ro. 37-8
Fy—, *see also* Fi—
Fyche, Geo., dn. St. Patr. 618
Fyers, Pet., gen. (**C**) 875
— Th., gen. (**D**) 883
— Wm., gen. (**B**) 868
Fyldynge, *see also* Fielding
— Geo. or Ger., K.B. 759
Fyler, Lawr., gen. (**D**) 904
Fyllioll, Wm., K.B. 759
Fyncham, Ad. de, A.G. 398
Fyncheden (or Fynchedon), Wm. de, C.J.C.P. 375; J.C.P. 378; S.L. 407
Fyngale, Geoff. de, A.G. 398
Fynglass, *see also* Finglas
— Patr., C.B. Ex. Ir. 583; C.J.K.B. Ir. 577
Fytche, Alb., Ch. Com. Bma. 655; gen. (**D**) 907
— Wm., Adm. Ind. 647
Fyvie, Geo., ld., aft. E. of Dunfermline, *q.v.*, L.P.S. Sc. 501

G.

G*** (son of Peter), B. Ex. 382
G***, bp. Brn. 531
G***, dn. Crk. 632
Gabbett, Jos., gen. (**B**) 866
Gabinios, A., C. Ro. 46
Gabriel, I. and II., Pr. Tva. 60
— Jas. Wm., K.H. 791
— Rt. B., gen. (**D**) 882; K.H. 790
— Th. and sir T., L.M. Lond. 492
Gadderar, Jas., bp. Abdn. 540
Gaerst, Hugh de, J. It. 366; Jy. 363
Gafney, Chr., bp. Oss. 620
Gage hon. Ed. Th., gen. (**D**) 908
— hon. Th., gen. (**A**) 858
— sir Jno., C.D.L. 242; Compt. H. 292; Const. T.L. 320-21; K.G. 738; V.C.H. 296
— sir Wm., K.B. 764
— sir Wm. Hall, adm. (**A**) 820; (**B**) 821; (**C**) 822; G.C.B. 770; G.C.H. 787; L. Admy. 183
Gage, visc.—
— Hy., 3rd visc., gen. (**C**) 873
Gage-Hall, *see* Hall
Gainsborough, Wm. de, bp. Worc. 472
Gainsborough, E. of
— Ch. Geo., 2nd E. of, L.L Rutl. 311
Gairdner, *see also* Gardiner and Gardner
— Wm. J., gen. (**D**) 888
Gaisford, Th., dn. Chr. Ch. Oxf. 457
Gaitskell, Fk., gen. (**D**) 897
Galba, S. S., C. Ro. 44-5; Emp. Ro. 47
Galbraith, Rt., Ld. Sess. 518
Galdric, *see* Baldric
Gale, Ch. Jas., C.C.J. 403
— Geo., M.M. 246
— Hy. Richm., gen. (**B**) 867
— Rog., C. Exc. 279-80; C. St. 283
— Th., dn. Yk. 487
Galeatius, bp. Drom. 604
Galerius, M., Emp. Ro. 48
Galfragus, Wm., bp. Elm. & Dunw. 454
Galfrid and **Galfridus**, *see also* Geoffrey
*— bp. Abdn. 530
*— bp. Llff. 449
*— bp. St. As. 462
*— Ld. Clk. Reg. 524
*Prob. some same pers. Comp. dates.
Galinole, Th., M.M. 246
Gall, Rd. Herb., gen. (**D**) 922; L.G. Ch. Hosp. 936
Gallakan, Redm., bp. Killa. 612
Gallienus, Emp. Ro. 48
Galloway, All. de, L.H. Const. Sc. 507
— Archd. and Sir A., Chn. E.I. Co. 645; gen. (**D**) 880; K.C.B. 777
— Th. Jas., gen. (**D**) 898
Galloway, E. of
— Jas., 5th E. of, L.H.T. Sc. 498
— Jno., 7th E. of, form. ld. or visc. Garlies, *q.v.*, K.T. 748; L.L. Wight, 512
— Geo., 8th E. of, form. ld. or visc. Garlies, *q.v.*, adm. (**A**) 818; K.T. 748; L.L. Kirkc. 510; L.L. Wigt. 512
— Rand., 9th E. of, form. visc. Garlies, *q.v.*
— Al. Plant., 10th E. of, K.T. 749; L.H.C. K. Sc. 546

Gallus, C. S., C. Ro. 42, 44
— Hostilius, Emp. Ro. 47
— L. A., C. Ro. 44
— L. C., C. Ro. 46
— P. V. A., C. Ro. 38
— Q. O., C. Ro. 42; Dt. Ro. 42
Gallwey, *see also* Galwey
— Th. Lion. Jno., G. Bmda. 701; gen. (**D**) 919; K.C.M.G. 799
— Michl. Hy., K.C.M.G. 799
Galsagus, Wm., bp. Elm. & Dunw. 454
Galt, Alex. Till. and sir A., G.C.M.G. 795; K.C.M.G. 796
Galton, Dougl., K.C.B. 784
Galway and **Galwey,** *see also* Gallwey
— Ed., adm. (**D**) 824
— Michl. and sir M., gen. (**D**) 907; K.C.B. 780
Galway, visc. and E. of
— Hy. de Mass., 1st E. of, gen. (**A**) 857; L.J. Ir. 555-6; P.C. (1715) 196
— Jno., 1st visc., S.L.R. 271
— Rt. M. A., 4th visc., Amb. G. St. 121; Compt. H. 293; K.B. 765; P.C. 204
Gamaliel, bp. Isl. 539; bp. S. & M. 483
Gamarra, A., Pres. Pu. 109
Gambier, sir Ed. J., C.J. Mdras. 658
— Geo. Cornish, adm. (**H**) 846
— Glouc., gen. (**D**) 903
— Jas., adm. (**A**) 815
— Jas., *see* ld. G., *infra.*
— Rt., adm. (**H**) 845
— Rt. FitzG., adm. (**H**) 848
Gambier, lds.
— Jas., aft. 1st ld. G., adm. (**A**) 816; G. Newfd. 700; G.C.B. 767; K.C.B. 773; L. Admy. 180-1
Gamble, Dom. J., G. Bdoes. 721; G. Jam. 713; gen. (**D**) 909
Gameline, bp. St. Andr. 529; Ld. Chanc. Sc. 514
Gammell, Andr., gen. (**B**) 867
Gane, Jno. Lawr., Q.C. 420
Gangadi, Stamo, K.C.M.G. 796
Gansell, Wm., gen. (**B**) 865
Gant, Maur. de, J. It. 367
— Rt. de, dn. Yrk. 486; Ld. Chanc. 353
Gape, Josh., adm. (**G**) 842
Gapper, Abrm., S.L. 412
Garbh, St. Senach, bp. Clonf. 635
Garcia, M., Pres. Gua. 106
Garcias, I. to IV., K. Nav. 85 and 87
— -Ramirez, K. Nav. 85
— -Ximenes, K. Nav. 87
Garden, Alex., Compt. Sc. 498
— Fras., Jy. Sc. 523; Ld. Sess. 520
Gardener and **Gardiner,** *see also* Gardner
— sir Brocas C. St. 283
— Geo., dn. Norw. 455
— Hy. Lyn., gen. (**D**) 908
— Jno. and sir J., gen. (**B**) 869; K.C.B. 776
— Matth., Mod. K. Sc. 547
— Nathan Sm., gen. (**D**) 905
— Percy Fort., gen. (**D**) 924
— Rd., L.M. Lond. 490
— Rd., dn. St. Patr. 617
— Rt. and sir R., C.J.K.B. Ir. 578; L.J. Ir. 554
Gardener and Gardiner—*cont.*
— Rt. Wm. and sir R., G.C.B. 770; G. Gibr. 670; gen. (**D**) 880; K.C.B. 775; K.C.H. 787
— Steph., bp. Winch. 471; Ld. Chanc. 355; S. St. 223
— Th. and sir T., A.G. 399; Rec. Lond. 494; S.G. 401
— Wm., Amb. Pld. 126
— Wm., gen. (**B**) 866
— sir Wm., K.B. 763
Gardner, *see also* Gardener
— Alan, *see* ld. G., *infra*
— Alan Hy., adm. (**H**) 850
— Anthy. W., Pres. Lib. 100
— hon. Fras. Far., adm. (**A**) 818
— Geo. Hy., adm. (**H**) 851
— Jno., bp. Linc. 447
— Rt., S.L. 408
— Wm. Beth., gen. (**D**) 902
— Hon. Wm. Hy., gen. (**A**) 863
Gardner, lds. and visc.
— Alan, aft. sir A. and 1st ld. G., adm. (**A**) 816; L. Admy. 180
— Al. Hyde, aft. 2nd ld. and (?) 1st visc. G., adm. (**A**) 818; K.C.B. 773
Garfield, J. A., Pres. U.S.A. 103
Gargrave, sir Th., Sp. H.C. 249
Garland, Hy. de, dn. Chich. 434
— Jno., K.H. 790
— Jno. de, J. It. 366
— Jos. Gulston, adm. (**H**) 845
Garlies, lds. and visc.
— Jno., ld. or visc., aft. 7th E. of Galloway, *q.v.*, B.T. 266
— Geo., ld. or visc., aft. 8th E. of Galloway, *q.v.*, L. Admy. 181; L.L. Kirkc. 510
— Rand., visc., aft. 9th E. of Galloway, *q.v.*, L.L. Kirkc. 510; L.L. Wigt. 512
Garlike, Benj., Amb. Dk. 127; Amb. Pr. 118; Amb. Russ. 125
Garmston, Saml.. gen. (**D**) 889
Garnault, Jos., gen. (**D**) 887
Garner, C. Hlt. 81
— Rd., M.M. 246
— Th., gen. (**D**) 877
Garnet, Jno., bp. Clr. 596; bp. Ferns and L. 622
Garnett, Jno., dn. Exr. 438
Garnier, Th., dn. Linc. 448; dn. Rip. 482; dn. Winch. 471
Garrard, sir Saml., L.M. Lond. 491
— Th., Comm. Serjt. Lond. 495
Garratt, Jno., L.M. Lond. 492
Garrett, Hy., adm. (**A**) 820
— Rt. and sir R., gen. (**D**) 893; K.C.B. 7781; K.H. 791
Garrick, Jas. Fras., K.C.M.G. 798
Garrow, Wm. and sir W., A.G. 400; B. Ex. 385; C.J. Chest. 386; Jud. Com. P.C. 360; K.C. 415; P.C. 212; S.G. 402; S.L. 413
Garstin, Ed., gen. (**D**) 888
— Rt. Longm., gen. (**D**) 899
Garth, Ch., C. Exc. 281
— Geo., gen. (**A**) 859
— Rd. and sir R., C.J. Bgal. 653; P.C. 221; Q.C. 418
— Th., gen. (**A**) 860
Garthshore, W., L. Admy. 180
Garton, Th. de, B. Ex. 383
Garvagh, Geo., 1st ld., form. G. Canning, L.L. Londy. 570
Garvey or **Garvie**
— Jno., abp. Arm. 595; bp. Kilm. 607; dn. Chr. Ch. Dbln. 618; dn. Ferns, 623
Garvock, Jno. and sir J., G.C.B. 770; gen. (**D**) 898; K.C.B. 779
Garway, sir Hy., L.M. Lond. 491
— Wm., C. Cus. 273
Gascoigne and **Gascoyne**
— Bamber, B.T. 265-6; L. Admy. 179
— Ch., gen. (**D**) 892
— sir Crispe, L.M. Lond. 492
— Edmd. de, W.C.P. 317
— Ern. Fk., gen. (**D**) 884
— Is., gen. (**A**) 860
— Jno. or Wm., K.B. 758
— Jno. Hawk, gen. (**D**) 901
— Rt. de, W.C.P. 317
— Wm. or Jno., K.B. 758
— Wm. and sir W., C.J.K.B. 370; S.L. 407
Gaselee, Steph., (No. 1), S.L. 413
— Steph. (No. 2), and sir S., J.C.P.; 380 K.C. 416; S.L. 413
Gasey, Jno., dn. Lich. 445
Gaskell, Jas. M., L.T. 160
Gaskin, J. S., G. Bdoes. 720-1
Gasper, bp. Ach. 612
Gastrell, Fras., bp. Chest. 477
— Jas. Eardl., gen. (**D**) 917
— J. P. Harris-, Amb. U.S.C. 134
Gate, *see* Gates
Gatel, Ralph de, Const. T.L. 320
Gates (or Gate), sir Jno., C.D.L. 242; V.C.H. 296
— Ph. C., C.C.J. 405; Q.C. 419
— Th., B. Ex. 384; S.L. 409
Gatesden, Jno. de, J.C.P. 376; Jy. 364
Gatt, Sav., gen. (**D**) 916
Gatta, Laur. de la, R. Cr. P.A. 335
Gatty, Alf. S., R. Dr. P.A. 338; Yk. H. 334
Gaudeby, Hugh de, M. Chy. 394
Gauden, Jno., bp. Exr. 437; bp. Worc. 473
Gaunt, Jno. de, A.G. 398
Gauntstede, Sim., L.K. 355; M. Chy. 394; M.R. 387
Gaudy and **Gawdy**
— Fras. and sir F., C.J.C.P. 375; J.Q.B. 372; S.L. 408
— Hy., K.B. 761
— Th., J.Q.B. 372; S.L. 408
— Th. (senr.), S.L. 408
Gaveston, Piers, *see* E. of Cornwall
Gawdy, *see* Gaudy
Gawen, Roberts-, form. Roberts, *q.v.*
Gawler, Geo., G. S. Aus. 706; K.H. 792
Gaye, Dougl., gen. (**D**) 920
Gayer (or Gayre), Rt., K.B. 764
Gaynesburg, Wm., bp. Worc. 472
Gayre, *see also* Gayer
— sir Jno,, L.M. Lond. 491

Gayton, Clerk, adm. (**A**) 814
—— Geo., adm. (**A**, 816
Geale, Benj., L.M. Dbln. 641
Geary, sir Fras., adm. (**A**) 814
Gebethorpe, Wm., K.B. 756
Geddes, Jno., gen. (**D**) 885; K.H. 791
Gedding, Ralph de, Jy. 363
Gedge, Jno., adm. (**H**) 846
Gedney, Jno, L.M. Lond. 490
Gee, Ed., dn. Linc. 448
—— Wm., dn. Pboro. 458
Geeres, Th., S.L. 411
Geffrey, *see* Geoffrey
Geffrard, N. F., Pres. Hti. 105
Geide-Olgothach K. Ir. 20
Geils, Lt.-Col., G. V.D. Ld. 708
Geisa, I. and II., K. Hgy. 59
Gelasius, abp. and bp. Arm. 595
—— bp. Down, 603
—— I. and II., P. Ro. 33-4
Gell, Fk., bp. Mdras. 658
—— Jno., adm. (**A**) 816
—— Jno. Sh., gen. (**D**) 917
Gellian, Th., dn. Oss. 622
Gellie, Fras., gen. (**D**) 931
Gemeticensis, Rt., abp. Cant. 430
Geminus, C. S., C. Ro. 43
—— M. S. P., C. Ro. 43
—— P. S. (2), C. Ro. 42
Geneville, sir Geoffr. de, L.J. Ir. 550
Genouilly, Rigault de, K.C.B. 778
Gent, Th., B. Ex. 384; S.L. 408
Geoffrey, *see also* Galfrid and Jeffrey
*—— bp. Lim. 638
*—— (of Monmouth), bp. St. As. 462
*—— (of Turvill), bp. Oss. 620
*—— bp. St. Dav. 464
*—— (bp. Coutance), Ch. Jr. 362
*—— dn. Chich. 433
*—— (archdn. Berks.), J. It. 366
*—— (archdn. Norw.), L.H.T. 152
*—— L.K. 353
* Prob. some same pers. Comp. dates.
—— (g. son Hy. I.), Pr. E. 9
—— (son Hy. II.), Pr. E. 9
—— (2), dn. Her. 442
—— I. to III., D. Bry. 28
—— I. to VI., C. Anj. 27
George, bp. Kild. 616
—— Emp. Tzde. 98
—— (son of ld. Hastings), K.B. (1501) 759
—— cons. of Q. Anne, also Pr. of Denmark, D. of Cumberland, *q.v.*, K.C.E. 7; K.G. 740; P.C. 192
—— (abb. of Holyrood House) L.P.S. Sc. 501
—— (iss. Ed. III.), Pr. E. 11
—— (son Ed. IV.), Pr. E. 12
—— (son Q. Anne), Pr. E. 14
—— I., K. He. 96; K.G. 745
—— I. and II., Sg. H. Dt. 72
—— I. and II., Pr. Tva. 60
—— I. to III., R. Russ. 89
—— I. to IV., K.E. 6, *see also under* George, Pr. W. E., P. E., El. Hnr. and K. Hnr.
—— II. (K.E.), K.G. 741
—— II., D.S. Mgn. 79
George—*cont.*
—— -Albert, Pr. S. Rdt. 79
—— -Aug. (aft. Geo. II., K.E.), El. Hnr. 71; K.G. 741; P.C. 196; Pr. E. 14; Pr. W. E. 9
—— -Aug. Fred. (s., aft. Geo. IV., K.E.) Pr. E. 14; Pr. W. E. 9; K. Hnr. 71
—— -Ch. Fk., D.S. Alt. 78
—— Den., B. Ex. Ir. 584; Rec. Dbln. 642
—— -Fk., D.S. Mgn. 79
—— -Fk., M. Bdn. 67
—— -Fk. Ch. Jos., G.D. M. Str. 75
—— -Fk. Darl., gen. (**D**) 901
—— -Fk. Ern. Alb. (g. son Q. Victoria), Pr. E. 15
—— -Fk. &c., form. D. of Cumb. *q.v.*, K. Hnr. 71; gen. (**D**) 895
—— -Fk. Hy., Pr. W. Pyr. 80
—— -Fk. Wm. Ch. (g. son Geo. III.), Pr. E. 15
—— Jno., J.Q.B. Ir. 579; S.G. Ir. 590
—— -Lewis (aft. Geo. I., K.E.), El. Hnr. 70; K.G. 741; Pr. E. 13
—— -Podiebrad, K. Bma. 59
—— -Victor, Pr. W. Pyr. 80
—— -Wm. (c.c. D. of Zell), D. Brk. 70; K.G. 741
—— -Wm., D. Pr. 65
—— -Wm. (son Geo. II.), Pr. E. 14
—— -Wm., Pr. L. Sch. 73
—— Wm., dn. Linc. 448
—— -Wm. Fk. Pr., (aft Geo. III.), El. Hnr. 71; K.G. 742; K. Hnr. 71; Pr. E. 14; Pr. W. E. 9
***Gerald,** bp. Cork, 630
*—— bp. Cork and Cl. 631
*—— (St.), bp. Mayo, 611
*—— dn. Ard. 609
* Prob. same pers. Comp. dates.
Geran, bp. Saig. 620
Gerard and **Gerrard**
—— abp. Yk. 485; bp. Her. 441
—— bp. Drom. 604
—— (d. Alsace), D. Lne. 29
—— (abp. Aix), L.H.A. 170
—— And., bp. Abdn. 540
—— sir Ch., G I. Man, 666
—— Cuthb., G. I. Man, 666
—— Gilb., K.B. 762
—— Gilb., Mod. K. Sc. 547
—— sir Gilb., A.G. 398; Ld. Chanc. 356; M.R. 388
—— sir Gilb., C.D.L. 242
—— sir Jno., L.M. Lond. 491
—— Radd. G. I. Man, 666
—— Th., G. I. Man, 665-6
—— Wm., dn. St. Pat. 618; Ld. Chanc. Ir. 576
—— sir Wm., L.M. Lond. 490
Gerawan, Flor., bp. Clonm. 600
Gerlach, Pr. Nass. 75
Germaine, *see* ld. Geo. Sackville; *see also* Jermyn and St. Albans
Germanus, bp. Isl. 539; bp. S. and M. 483
Gernemue, Ad. de, J. It. 365
Gernoun, Jno., C.J.C.P. Ir. 580
Gernum, Ralph, J. It. 367
Gerrard, *see* Gerard
Gervais, Isaac, dn. Tm. 613
Gervase, bp. Drom. 604
—— bp. St. Dav. 464
Gery, Th., M. Chy. 396
Gesalric, K. Sp. 85
Gese, Jno., bp. Wford. and L. 627
Gestling, Jno. de, Jy., 364
Geta, C. L., C. Ro. 45
—— S., Emp. Ro. 47
Gethin, Abs., dn. Oss. 623
Gettour, Wm., L.H.A. 171
Gex, Jno. Pet. de, aft. sir J. Q.C. 418
Geyt, Geo. le, adm. (**H**) 844
Gheast, Edm., bp. Roch. 460; bp. Sal. 467
Ghika, A., H. Wca. 94
—— Pr. A. D., H. Wca. 94
—— G. A., H. Mva. 94
Ghinucci, Jer. de, bp. Worc. 473
Gholam Hussun, &c., Nawab, K.C.S.I. 803
Ghulam, Mirza, C.I.E., 807
Gib, Wm. Anthy., gen. (**D**) 928
—— Gavin, Modr. K. Sc. 547
Gibbervin, Geoff., Jy. 364
Gibbon, Gybon, and **Gybbon**
—— Ed., B.T. 266
—— Ed. H., Mowb. H. 340; Norr. K.A. 330; Yk. H. 334
—— Jas. Rt., gen. (**D**) 909
—— Jno., Bl. M. P.A. 336
—— Jno., L.H.A. 172
—— Matth. C. H., Richmd. H. 334
—— Ph., S.L.R. 271
—— Th., dn. Carl. 476
—— Th., S.L. 411
—— Th. Mitch., C.I.E. 806
Gibbons, Ed., C. Cus. 274
—— sir Jno., K.B. 765
—— Phil., L.T. 157
—— Sills, J. and sir S., L.M. Lond. 492
—— Wm., L.M. Dbln. 641
Gibbs, Ed. and sir E., G. Jsey. 668; gen. (**B**) 870; K.C.B. 776
—— Fk. Waym., Q.C. 419
—— Jno. Innes, gen. (**D**) 912
—— Michl., L.M. Lond. 492
—— Saml. and sir S., gen. (**C**) 873; K.C.B. 774
—— Vic. and sir V., A.G. 400; C.B. Ex. 382; C.J.C.P. 376; C.J. Chest. 386; J.C.P. 380; K.C. 415; P.C. 209; S.G. 402; S.L. 412
Gibson, sir Alex., Ld. Clk. Reg. 525; Ld. Sess. 519
—— Edg., gen. (**D**) 900
—— Edm., bp. Linc. 447; bp. Lond. 452; P.C. 197
—— Ed., aft. ld. Ashbourne, *q.v.*, A.G. Ir. 589; Ld. Chanc. Ir. 577
—— Jas. Brown, K.C.B. 779
—— Jno. dn. Down. 605
—— sir Jno., J. Pr. Ct. 421
—— Jno. Geo., A.G. Ir. 589; J.Q.B.D. Ir. 580; S.G. Ir. 590; S.L. Ir. 593
—— Jno. Th., gen. (**D**) 881
—— Th. Milner, P.C. 215; Pres. B.T. 269; V.P.B.T. 269
—— Wm., Ld. Sess. 518
Gibsone, Dav. A., gen. (**D**) 889
—— Jno. Ch. Hope, gen. (**D**) 897
Gidney, Jno., L.M. Lond. 490
Gidoin, Jno. Lew., adm. (**A**) 816
Giffard, *see also* Gifford
—— Geo., adm. (**D**) 833; (**F**) 838; K.C.B. 780
—— Geo. M. and sir G., Jud. Com. P.C. 361; L.J. App. 389; P.C. 218; Q.C. 418; V. Chanc. 390

For List of Abbreviations, see pp. 944-952.

Giffard—*cont.*
—— Godfr., bp. Worc. 472; J. It. 368; Ld. Chanc. 353
—— Hard. St., aft. sir S. and ld. Halsbury, *q.v.*, Jud. Com. P.C. 362; Ld. Chanc. 358; P.C. 220; Q.C. 418; S.G. 403
—— Hy. Alexr., Q.C. 419
—— Hugh, Const. T.L. 320; J.C.P. 376; Jy. 364
—— Jno., adm. (**A**) 819
—— Jno., adm. (**G**) 840
—— Jno., K.B. 754
—— Jno. W. de L., C.C.J. 405
—— Nichs., K.B. 755
—— Rd., J. It. 366
—— Walt., abp. Yk. 485; bp. B. & W. 427; Const. T.L. 320; L.H.T. 152; Ld. Chanc. 353
—— Wm., bp. Winch. 470; Ld. Chanc. 352-3
Gifford, *see also* Giffard
—— Ad., Ld. Sess. 521
—— Godfr., *see* Giffard
—— Jas., adm. (**H**) 844
—— (or Gyfford), Jno., K.B. 759
—— Rt., *see* ld. G., *infra*
—— Th., bp. Kild. 616
—— Wm., gen. (**C**) 874
—— sir Wm., C. Exc. 279; G. Gr. Hosp. 854
—— Gifford, lds.
—— Rt., aft. sir R. and ld. G., A.G. 400; C.J.C.P. 376; M.R. 388; P.C. 210; S.G. 402; S.L. 413
Gigles, Jno., bp. Worc. 473
—— Silv., bp. Worc. 473
Gilbert, Gillebert, and **Giselbert**
*—— abp. Arm. 595; bp. Rph. 601
*—— bp. Ardf. & Agh. 639; dn. Ardf. 640
*—— bp. Brn. 530
*—— bp. Clonm. 600
*—— bp. Cork, 630
*—— bp. Dkld. 533
*—— bp. Gall. 538
*—— bp. Isl. 539
*—— (Gille or Gillebert), bp. Lim. 638
*—— (Universalis), bp. Lond. 451
*—— bp. St. As. 462
*—— (of Galloway), bp. S. and M. 483
*—— dn. Clonm, 600
*—— dn. Cloy. 632
* Prob. some same pers. Comp. dates.
—— C. Lux. 84
—— D. Bdy. 28
—— D. Lne. 29
—— Ash. T., bp. Chich. 433
—— Davis, Pres. R. Soc. 940
—— Geoffr. or Jeff. and sir G., B. Ex. 384; C.B. Ex. 382; C.B. Ex. Ir. 583; J.K.B. Ir. 579; L.K. and C.G.S. 357; S.L. 411
—— Jno., abp. Yk. 486; bp. Llff. 449; bp. Sal. 467; dn. Exr. 438; P.C. 200
—— Jno., bp. Bgr. 426; bp. Her. 441; bp. St. Dav. 464; L.H.T. 153
—— Ph. Ed. V., gen. (**D**) 926
—— Rt., bp. Lond. 451; dn. Yk. 487
—— Walt. Ral. and sir W., gen. (**D**) 879; G.C.B. 769; K.C.B. 777
—— Wm., gen. (**D**) 877
Gilbertus, *see* Gilbert
Gildea, Geo. Fk., gen. (**D**) 931
—— Jno. Arth., gen. (**D**) 910
Giles (or Gyles), Edm., M. Chy. 395
Gilford. Rd. Jas., ld., aft. 4th E. of Clanwilliam, *q.v.*, adm. (**E**) 836; L. Admy. 185
Gill, J. B., Pres. Pgy. 110
—— Th., adm. (**H**) 847
—— Wm., L.M. Lond. 492
Gillan, Jno., bp. Dnbl. 542; Sc. bp. 545
—— Rt., Modr. K. Sc. 547
Gille and **Gillebert,** *see* Gilbert
Gillespie, Hy. Jas., gen. (**D**) 889
—— Rt. Rollo and sir R., gen. (**C**) 873; (**D**) 934; K.C.B. 774
—— Wm. Jn., gen. (**D**) 934
Gillett, Arth. W., adm. (**H**) 853
Gillot (or Gyllot), Jno., K.B. 759
Gillian, Th., gen. (**D**) 924
Gillies, Ad., Ld. Sess. 520
Gillus, K. Sc. 17
Gilmore, sir Ch., B.T. 264
Gilmour, Ch., gen. (**D**) 885
—— Dug. Little. and sir D., gen. (**B**) 870; K.C.B. 776
—— sir Jno., L.P. Ct. Sess. 516
Gilpin, Ch., Sec. P.L.B. 262
Gipps, sir Geo., G. N.S.W. 703
—— Regd., gen. (**D**) 923; K.C.B. 782
Girardot, Geo. Ch., gen. (**D**) 927
Girdler, Jos., S.L. 411
Girdlestone, Saml., Q.C. 417
—— Wm. Bolt., gen. (**D**) 916
Giró, J. F.., Pres. Ugy. 111
Gisborne, Jas., gen. (**B**) 865
—— Th., Pres. Coll. Ph. 938
Giselbert, *see* Gilbert
Giselham, Wm. de, A.G. 398; J.C.P. 377; S.L. 406
Giselherus, bp. Sels. 432
Giso, bp. Wlls. 427
Gisors, or Gysors
—— Jno. de, Const. T.L. 320
—— Jno. de, L.M. Lond. 488-9
Glabrio, M. A., C. Ro. 43-4-6
Gladstanes, Gladstaines and **Gladstone,** *see also* Gledstanes
—— Geo., abp. St. Andr. 529; bp. Cness. 531
—— Herb. Jno., L.T. 162; U.S. War, 233
—— Jno., Ld. Sess. 518
—— sir Th., L.L. Kinc. 510
—— Wm. Ewart, Ch. Ex. 166; Com. Io. Isl. 129; L.P.S. 241; L.T. 160-1-2; M.M. 247; P.C. 214; Prem. 150-1; Pres. B.T. 269; U.S.W. and C. 231; V.P. B.T. 269; W. and C. Sec. 231
—— Wm. Hy., L.T. 162
Gladwin, Hy., gen. (**C**) 872
Glahaul, Hugh de, J. It. 367
Glamis, lds.
—— Jno., 1st ld., L.G.C. Sc. 506; Ld. Chanc. Sc. 515
—— Jno., 3rd ld., L.J. Gen. 522
—— Jno., 8th ld., Ld. Chanc. Sc. 515; Ld. Sess. 517
Gland, Jno., B. Ex. Ir. 583
Glandie, Jno., dn. Cash. 627
Glandore, Jno., 2nd E. of, M.R. Ir. 585
Glanville, Barth. de, J. It. 367
—— Fras. Rt., gen. (**D**) 916
—— Gilb. de, bp. Roch. 459 J. It. 366; Jy. 363
—— Jno. J.C.P. 378; S.L. 408
—— Jno. and sir J., Sp. H.C. 249; S.L. 409
—— Osb. de, Jy. 363
—— Ran. de, Ch. Jr. 362; J. It. 366; Jy. 363
—— Wm. de, Jy. 364
Glappa, K.E. 2
Glascock and **Glasscock**
—— Ed., C. St. Ir. 568
—— Talb. Br. M., gen. (**D**) 933
—— Wm., M. Chy. 395-6
Glasfurd, Jno., gen. (**D**) 894
Glasgow, Geo., gen. (**B**) 868
Glasgow, E. of
—— Dav., 1st. E. of, form. Dav. and ld. Boyle, *q.v.*, L.H.C.K. Sc. 546; Ld. Clk. Reg. 525; Tr. Dep. Sc. 498
—— Jno., 3rd E. of, L.H.C.K. Sc. 546
—— Geo., 4th E. of, G.C.H. 786; L.L. Ayrsh. 508; L.L. Rnfw. 511
—— Jas., 5th E. of, L.L. Rnfw. 511
—— Geo. Fk., 6th E. of, Ld. Clk. Reg. 525
Glasscock, *see* Glascock
Glasse, Fk. Hy. Hastings, adm. (**E**) 835; (**F**) 838
—— Jno. Maxw., gen. (**D**) 898
—— Wm. B., Q.C. 417
Glastonbury, Jas., ld., form. Jas. Grenville, *q.v.*
Gledstanes, *see also* Gladstanes
—— sir Alb., gen. (**B**) 867
Glegg, Berk., gen. (**B**) 868
Gleichen, ct., *see* Hohenlohe, Pr. Vict. Ferd. of
Gleig, Geo., bp. Brn. 541; Pr. Bp. Sc. 540
Glenbervie, Sylv., ld., form. S. Douglas, *q.v.*, B.C. 252; C.W.F. &c. 271; G.C.G.H. 678; L.T. 158; Paym. G. 245; S.W.F. 271; V.P.B.T. 269
Glencairn, E. of
—— Wm., 9th E. of, Comm. Tr. Sc. 497; L.J. Gen. 522; Ld. Chanc. Sc. 515; P.C. 190
—— Wm., 12th E. of, gen. (**C**) 872
Glendoning, Matth., bp. Glasg. 536
Glenelg, Ch., 1st ld, form. Ch. Grant, *q.v.*
Glenham, Hy., bp. St. As. 462; dn. Brl. 440
Glenlyon, Jas., 1st. ld., form. Jas. Murray, *q.v.*, gen. (**B**) 869; K.C.H. 787
Glenorchy, Jno., visc., aft. 3rd E. of Breadalbane, *q.v.*, K.B. 764; L. Admy. 178
Glentworth, lds.
—— Wm. Cecil, 1st ld., form. W. C. Pery, *q.v.*
—— Edmd. Hy., ld., aft. 1st visc. and E. of Limerick, *q.v.*, Sec. St. Ir. 562
Glicia, M. C., Dt. Ro. 42
Gloag, Archd. R., gen. (**D**) 925
Gloucester, Milo, *see* E. of Hereford
—— Walt. de, B. Ex. 383; J. It 369; dn. Chich. 434

Gloucester, E. and D. of
— Hugh de Audley, E. of (1327), form. sir H. le Despencer, *q.v.*
— Th. Plantagenet, D. of, (6th son of Edw. III.), form. E. of Buckingham and 6th ld. le Despencer, *q.v.*, L.L. Ir. 551
— Humphr. Plantagenet, D. of (son of Hen. IV.), form. E. of Pembroke, *q.v.*, K.G. 734; G. Ch. Isl. 667; K.B. 755; Ld. K. 355; W.C.P. 318; *see also* Pr. Humphrey
— Rd. Plantagenet, D. of (aft. Rd. III., *q.v.*), K.B. 756; K.G. 736; L.H.A. 174; W.C.P. 318
— Hy., D. of (son of Ch. I), K.G. 740; P.C. 189
— Wm., D. of (son of Q. Anne), K.G. 741
— Wm. Hy., D. of (g. son of Geo. II.), F.M. 856; gen. (**A**) 858; K.G. 742; P.C. 201
— Wm. Fk., D. of, son of last D., F.M. 856; G.C.B. 767; G.C.H. 786; gen. (**A**) 860; K.G. 742; P.C. 207
Glover, Jno. Hawl. and sir J., G.C.M.G. 795; G. Lag. 687; G. Leew. Isl. 728; G. Newfd. 700
— Rt., Ptc. C.A. 337; Som. H. 332
— Wm., S.L. 413
Glycerius, Emp. W.E. 49
Glyn, Glynn, and **Glynne**
— hon. Geo., aft. 2nd ld. Wolverton, *q.v.*, Sec. Tr. 164
— hon. Hy. Carr, adm. (**E**) 836
— Hy. Rd., adm. (**A**) 819
— Jno., dn. Bgr. 426
— Jno., S.L. 412
— Jno. and sir J., C.J.K.B. 370; Rec. Lond. 494; S.L. 409-10
— Julius Rd. and sir J., gen. (**D**) 906; K.C.B. 781
— sir Rd., L.M. Lond. 492
— sir Rd. Carr, L.M. Lond. 492
— Rd. Th., gen. (**D**) 925
— sir St. Rd., L.L. Flints, 314
— Wm., bp. Bgr. 426
Goare, sir Jno., L.M. Lond. 491
Gobat, Saml., bp. Jslm. 677
Godbolt, Jno., J.C.P. 379; S.L. 409
Godby, Chr., gen. (**D**) 887
— Jno. Hardy, adm. (**H**) 845
Goddard, Captn., G. Bmda. 701
— Guib., S.L. 410
— Jno., gen. (**D**) 919
— Th., M.M. 247
Godefridus, *see* Godfrey
***Godeleigh,** Jno., bp. Exr. (nom.) 436
*— Jno. de, dn. Wells, 428
* Prob. same pers.
Goderede, Wm., J.K.B. 371; S.L. 407
Goderick, *see* Goodricke
Goderich, *see also* Goodrich
— Fk. Jno., visc., form. F. J. Robinson, *q.v.*, aft. E. of Ripon, *q.v.*; L.T. 159; W. and C. Sec. 231
Godericus, bp. St. Andr. 528
Godfrey, Godfridus, and **Godefridus**
— bp. B. and W. 427
— (or Wm.) bp. Chich. 432
— bp. St. As. 462
— C. Hlt. 81
— D. Tny. 57
— (de Bouillon), K. Jsm. 97
— I. to IX., D. Lne. 29
— Rd., M. Chy. 396
Godley, Jno. Arth., C.I.R. 286; U.S. Ind. 236
Godman, Jos., Sec. P.O. 239
— Rd. Temp., gen. (**D**) 924
Godmundus, bp. Roch. 459
Godolphin, Ch., C. Cus. 274
— Hy., dn. St. P. 453
— Fras., K.B. 763
— Fras., *see* E. of G., *infra*
— Jno., J. Adm. Ct. 423; J. Pr. Ct. 421
Godolphin, lds. and E. of
— Sydney, aft. 1st ld. and E. of G., and visc. Rialton, *q.v.*, Ch. Ex. 164; K.G. 741; L.H.T. 140; L.T. 141, 155; L.L. Cnwall. 307; P.C. 192, 4; Prem. 140-1; S. St. 224
— hon. Fras., visc. Rialton, *q.v.*, aft. 2nd E. of G., Coff.H. 293; Gr. St. 303-4; L.P.S. 240; P.C. 197; Tell. Ex. 167
Godred (Crovan) I., K. Man. 665
— (Crovan) II., K. Man. 665
Godschal, sir Rt., L.M. Lond. 491
Godson, Rd., Q.C. 417
Godwin, Godwinus, and **Godwyn**
*— bp. Lich. 443
*— dn. St. P. 452
*— (3) bp. Norw. 459
*— (3) bp. Roch. 459
*— Fras., bp. Her. 441; bp. Llff. 449
* Prob. some same pers. Comp. dates.
— Hy., gen. (**D**) 882; K.C.B. 777
— Matt., adm. (**D**) 824
— Th., abp. B. and W. 428; dn. Cant. 431; dn. Chr. Ch. Oxf. 457
— Tim., bp. Cash. and Eml. 626; bp. Kilm. and Ard. 607
Goe, Field Pl., bp. Melb. 705
Goens, Ryck. Van (No. 1), G. Ceyl. 672
— Ryck. Van (No. 2), G. Ceyl. 672
Gogan, *see* Gorgan
Gogh, Jno., M. Chy. 393
Gogwan (or Gucanor or Gucanus), bp. Llff. 449
Gohur, &c., C.I.E. 806
Golafre, Jno., G. Ch. Isl. 667
Golborne, Chr., dn. Kild. 619
Golbourn, Wm., bp. Kild. 617
Gold, Ch. Emil., gen. (**D**) 895
— Wm. Geo., gen. (**D**) 894
Goldbeter, Barth., M.M. 246
Goldesburgh, *see* Goldsborough
Goldfinch, Hy., gen. (**D**) 879; K.C.B. 777
Goldie, Alexr. Jno., gen. (**A**) 862
— Geo. Dashw. T., K.C.M.G., 799
— Geo. L., gen. (**D**) 882; K.C.B. 779
— Th., gen. (**B**) 866
Golding, Ed., B.C. 252; L.T. 158
— Walt., B. Ex. Ir. 583
Goldington, Wm. de, J. It. 369
Goldsborough and **Goldesburgh**
— Ed., B. Ex. 383
— Godfr., bp. Glr. 438
— sir Jno., Sp. H.C. 248
— Th., B. Ex. 383
Goldsmid, Alb., gen. (**D**) 892
— Fras. Hy., Q.C. 418
— Fk. Jno. and sir F., gen. (**D**) 913; K.C.S.I. 803
Goldsmith, Ed., dn. Elph. 609
— Geo., adm. (**D**) 832; (**F**) 838
— Is., dn. Cloy. 633
— Leofst., Portr. Lond. 488
Goldsworthy, Burrington, C. St. 283
— Josh. Webb., gen. (**D**) 896
— Ph., gen. (**B**) 866
— Rog. Tuckf. and sir R., G. Br. Hond. 714; G. Gren. 724; G. Nev. 730; G. St. Luc. 725; K.C.M.G. 799
— Walt. Tuckf., gen. (**D**) 928
Goldwell, Jas., bp. Norw. 455; dn. Sal. 468; Regr. Gart. 746
— Th., bp. Oxf. 456; bp. St. As. 462
Gollenesse, Jul. Val. St. Van, G. Ceyl. 672
Gomensoro, T., Pres. Ugy. 111
Gomm, Wm. Mayn. and sir W., C.C. Ind. 651; Const. T.L. 321; F.M. 856; G.C.B. 770; G. Mtius. 683; gen. (**A**) 863; K.C.B. 775
Gondemar, K. Bdy. 28
Gondibert, K. Lmd. 49
Gondulph, K. Sc. 19
Gonshull, Th. de, K.B. 754
Gontran, K. Fr. 22
Gonzales, Ig., Pres. Dom. Rep. 105
— M., Pres. Mex. 104
— St. J., Pres. S. Salv. 106
Gooch, Th., bp. Brl. 439; bp. Ely, 435; bp. Norw. 455
— Th. Lewis, adm. (**H**) 848
— sir Wm., gen. (**C**) 871
Goodacre, Hugh, abp. Arm. 595
Goodall, Sam. Cranst., adm. (**A**) 815
Goode, Wm., dn. Rip. 482
Goodenough, Arth. Cyr., gen. (**D**) 904
— Edm., dn. Wlls. 429
— Geo. Tr., C. Tx. 285
— Hy. Ph., gen. (**D**) 907
— Saml., bp. Carl. 476; dn. Roch. 461
— Wm. Howl., gen. (**D**) 929
Goodfellow, Chr., S.L. 410
— Geo. Ritso, C.I.E. 808
— Saml., gen. (**D**) 878
— Wm. Barke, gen. (**D**) 898
— Wm. West, gen. (**D**) 926
Goodier, sir —, C.Y.G. 298
Goodinge, Th., S.L. 411
Goodlake, Ger. Litt., gen. (**D**) 921
Goodman, Gabr., dn. Westr. 469
— Godfr., bp. Glr. 438; bp. Her. 441; dn. Roch. 461
— Jno., dn. Wlls. 429
— Steph. Arth., gen. (**D**) 880; K.H. 791

For List of Abbreviations, see pp. 944-952.

Goodrich and **Goodricke,** *see also* Goderich
— Fras., K.C. 414
— sir Hy., L.G.O. 259; P.C. 194
— sir Jno., Amb. Sw. 126; B.T. 267; P.C. 203
— Rd., M. Chy. 395
— Th., bp. Ely, 435; Ld. K. and Ld. Chanc. 355
Goodsman, Dav., gen. (**D**) 891
Goodwin and **Goodwyn**
— Alfr. Geo., gen. (**D**) 898
— Harv., bp. Carl. 476; dn. Ely, 435
— Hy., gen. (**D**) 895
— Julius Edm., gen. (**D**) 903
— Rt., Comm. Ir. 554
— Wm., dn. Chr. Ch. Oxf. 457
Goold, Th., S.L. Ir. 593
Goranus, K. Sc. 18
Gordianus, I. to III., Emp. Ro. 47
Gordon, Abrm. Hy., gen. (**D**) 890
— Ad., gen. (**C**) 873
— ld. Adam, gen. (**A**) 858
— Alexr., bp. Abdn. 530; L.P.S. Sc. 500
— Alexr., bp. Gall. 538; bp. Isl. 539; Ld. Sess. 517
— Alexr., gen. (**D**) 896
— hon. Alexr., K.C.B. 775
— hon. Alexr., Ld. Sess. 520
— Alexr. Crombie, adm. (**H**) 851
— sir Alexr. Duff, C.I.R. 285
— hon., Alexr. Ham. and sir A., gen. (**D**) 898; K.C.B. 780
— Alexr. Wm., gen. (**D**) 914
— Andr., gen. (**B**) 866
— hon. Arth. Ham. and sir A., G.C.M.G. 795; G. Ceyl. 673; G. Fiji, 711; G. Mtius. 684; G. N. Brk. 696; G. N.Z. 709; G. Trin. 722; G. W. Pacif. 711; K.C.M.G. 796
— Benj., gen. (**A**) 859
— Benj. Forbes, gen. (**B**) 868
— Benj. Lumsd., gen. (**D**) 931
— Ch., adm. (**D**) 827; (**G**) 840
— Ch. A. Bosw., gen. (**D**) 924
— Ch. B., adm. (**H**) 846
— Ch. Ed. P., gen. (**D**) 909
— Ch. Geo., gen. (**D**) 924
— Ch. Hy., gen. (**D**) 908
— Ch. Sp. S. E., gen. (**D**) 918
— Cosm., B. Ex. Sc. 524
— Cosm., gen. (**A**) 863
— Edw. Str., *see* ld. G. *infra*
— Gabr., G. Br. Hond. 714; gen. (**A**) 862
— Geo., dn. Exr. 438; dn. Linc. 448
— sir Geo., aft. 1st ld. Haddo and E. of Aberdeen, *q.v.*, L.P. Ct. Sess. 516; Ld. Sess. 519; Pres. P.C. Sc. 500
— Geo. Jno. Robt., Amb. Hnr. 120; Amb. Sw. and N. 127; Amb. Swz. 114; Amb. Ugy. 137
— Geo. Th., adm. (**E**) 835; (**F**) 838
— Hy., adm. (**D**) 825; (**G**) 840
— Hy. Wm., gen. (**D**) 887; K.C.B. 783
— Hugh Mack., gen. (**B**) 868
— Jas., gen. (**D**) 890
— Jas. Alexr. and sir J., adm. (**B**) 821; (**D**) 825; G.C.B. 769; G. Gr. Hosp. 854; K.C.B. 774; L.G. Gr. Hosp. 854

Gordon—*cont.*
— Jas. Dav., K.C.S.I. 803
— Jas. Gabr., adm. (**H**) 849
— Jas. Murr., adm. (**D**) 827
— Jas. Will. and sir J., G.C.B. 768; G.C.H. 786; gen. (**A**) 862; K.C.B. 774
— Jno., bp. Gall. 538
— Jno., bp. Gall. 539
— Jno., dn. Sal. 468
— Jno., gen. (**D**) 892
— Jno., gen. (**D**) 921
— hon. Jno., adm. (**H**) 846
— ld. Jno. Fk., G.C.H. 787
— Jno. Jas. Hood, gen. (**D**) 931
— Jno. Wm. and sir J., gen. (**D**) 901; K.C.B. 779
— Lewis, Ld. Sess. 520
— Lewis, Modr. K. Sc. 547
— Lewis Conway, C.I.E. 807
— Rt., adm. (**H**) 847
— Rt., B.C. 253; Sec. B.C. 254; Sec. Tr. 163
— Rt., G. Berb. 715
— Rt., Mod. K. Sc. 547
— hon. Rt. and sir R., Amb. Aust. 117; Amb. Bzl. 135; Amb. Tky. 129; G.C.B. 772; G.C.H. 786; P.C. 210
— Saml. Edw., gen. (**D**) 908
— Th., K.H. 792
— Th. Ed., gen. (**D**) 931
— Wm., adm. (**A**) 814
— Wm., adm. (**H**) 847
*— Wm., K.B. 765
*— Wm. and sir W., Amb. G. St. 121; Amb. Dk. 127
* ? Same pers.
— Wm., bp. Abdn. 530
— Wm., C.C.J. 403
— Wm., C.I.E. 806; gen. (**D**) 925
— Wm., gen. (**D**) 906
— hon. Wm., adm. (**D**) 827; L. Admy. 183
— hon. Wm., gen. (**A**) 859
— ld. Wm., V.A. Sc. 499
— Wm. Alexr., gen. (**D**) 880
— Wm. Br., K.C.M.G. 798
— Wm. Elr., adm. (**E**) 837
— Wm. Evr. Alph. adm. (**H**) 851
— Wm. Rt., gen. (**D**) 930
Gordon, lds. and D. of. *See also* Richmond and Gordon
— Ed. Str., aft. ld. G., D. Fac. Sc. 527; Jud. Com. P.C. 361; L. App. 358; Ld. Adv. 526; P.C. 219; S.G. Sc. 527
— Geo., ld., aft. 2nd M. of Huntley, *q.v.*, K.B. 762
— Geo., 1st D. of, K.T. 747
— Cosmo Geo., 3rd. D. of, K.T. 747
— Alexr., 4th D. of, K.T. 748; L.K. Sc. 503; L.L. Abdn. 508
— Geo., 5th D. of, form. E. of Aboyne and M. of Huntley, *q.v.*, L.K. Sc. 503; P.C. 211; L.L. Abdn. 508
Gordon-Lennox, *see* Lennox
Gore, Ann. Kn., gen. (**D**) 916
— Arth., gen. (**D**) 891; K.H. 792
— Arth. Kn., L.L. Sligo, 571
— Augs. Fk., G. St. Vin. 725; G. Tob. 724
— hon. Ch. and sir C., G.C.B. 770; gen. (**D**) 883; K.C.B. 778; K.H. 791
— hon. Ch. Alexr., C.W.F. &c. 272-3

Gore—*cont.*
— Fras., G. Bmda. 701; G. Upp. Can. 692
— Geo., A.G. Ir. 588; J.C.P. Ir. 581
— Geo., K.H. 791
— hon. Geo., dn. Killa. 614
— Hy., gen. (**B**) 864
— Hugh, bp. Wford. and L. 627; dn. Lism. 629
— Humph., gen. (**B**) 864
— sir Jno., adm. (**A**) 819; G.C.H. 787; K.C.B. 774
— (2) Jno., adm. (**H**) 846
— Jno., gen. (**B**) 865
— Jno., aft. ld. Annaly, *q.v.*, C.J.K.B. Ir. 578; S.G. Ir. 589
— Ralph, L.M. Dbln. 641
— sir Ralph, Ch. Ex. Ir. 562; L.J. Ir. 556
— Rd., C. Cus. Ir. 565
— hon. Rt., Amb. Arg. 136; Amb. Ugy. 136
— Wm., bp. Clonf. and K. 636; bp. Elph. 608; bp. Lim., A. and A. 639; dn. Cash. 627
— Wm., C. St. Ir. 568
— Wm., dn. Clr. 597; dn. Down, 605
— sir Wm., L.M. Lond. 491
Gorgan (or Gogan), abp. St. Dav. 463
Gorges, Edm., K.B. 758
— Ralph de, L.D. Ir. 551
— Rd., gen. (**B**) 864
— Rt., dn. Kilmacd. 638
— Saml., J.C.P. Ir. 581
Goring, Geo., 1st ld., aft. E. of Norwich, *q.v.*, V.C.H. (1640), 296
Gormanstown, visc.
— Rt., 1st visc., L.D. Ir. 553
— Wm., 2nd visc., L.J. Ir. 553
— Jen., 7th visc., C. Treas. Ir. 559
— Jen. Wm. Jos., 14th visc. G. Br. Gu. 715; G. Leew. Isl. 728; K.C.M.G. 798
Gormo, K. Dk. 93
Gorrequer, Gid., K.H. 789
Gorst, Jno. Eld. and sir J. Q.C. 419; S.G. 403; U.S. Ind. 236
Gorwysc or **Gorwyst,** abp. St. Dav. 463
Goschen, Geo. J., Amb. Tky. 130; C.D.L. 243; Ch. Ex. 166; L. Admy. 185; L.T. 162; P.C. 217; Paym. G. 245; Pres. L.G.B. 256; Pres. P.L.B. 262; V.P.B.T. 269
Gosselin, Th. Le M., adm. (**A**) 819
Gosselyn, Ger., gen. (**A**) 862
Gosset and **Gossett**
— Hy., adm. (**G**) 841
— Jas. Wm., gen. (**D**) 902
— Raph. All. and sir R., K.C.B. 784
— sir Wm., gen. (**D**) 882; K.C.H. 787; U.S. Ir. 563
— Wm. Dr., gen. (**D**) 911
Gosford, E. of.
— Archd., 2nd E. of, C.Y.G. 298; G.C.B. 772; G. Can. 691; L.L. Arm. 568; P.C. 213
— Archd., Br. Sp. 4th E. of, K.P. 751; L.L. Arm. 568
Goske, Ysbr., G. C.G.H. 678
Gosling, Geo., K.H. 792
— Hy. Ch., gen. (**D**) 901
— Wm. Fras. Cl., gen. (**D**) 920

Gosnel or **Gosnold,** Jno., M. Chy. 395; S.G. 401
Gostling, Ch., gen. (**D**) 895
Gote, Reg. de, dn. Yk. 486
Goth, Raym. de la, dn. Linc. 448; dn. Sal. 468; dn. St. P. 452
Gothelon, I. and II., D. Lne. 29
Gott, Jno., dn. Worc. 474
—— Wm. Ch., gen. (**D**) 924
Goubert, P. J.. Pres. Trl. 101
Gough, Ch. Jno. and sir C., gen. (**D**) 928; K.C.B. 781
—— Fras., bp. Lim. 638
—— Fk. Wm., adm. (**H**) 852
—— Hugh, *see* visc. G. *infra*
—— sir Hugh Hy., gen. (**D**) 932; K.C.B. 781
—— Jno. Bloomf. and sir J., G.C.B. 770; gen. (**D**) 889; K.C.B. 779
—— Th. Bunb., dn. Dry. 602
Gough, lds. and visc.
—— Hugh, aft. sir H. and ld. and visc. G., C.C. Ind. 651; C.C. Mdras. 657; F.M. 856; gen. (**A**) 863; G.C.B. 769; G.C.S.I. 800; K.C.B. 776; K.C.S.I. 802; P.C. 216
Goulburn, Ed., P.P. 416; S.L. 413
—— Ed. Meyr., dn. Norw. 456
—— Fk., C. Cus. 277
—— Hy., Ch. Ex. 165; Ch. Sec. Ir. 563; H. Sec. 227; L.T. 159, 60, 61; P.C. 210; U.S. Home, 227; U.S. W. and C. 231
Gould, Ch. and sir C. Gould-Morgan, J.A.G. 937; *see also* Morgan
—— sir Davidge, adm. (**A**) 818; (**C**) 822; G.C.B. 768; K.C.B. 775
—— G. F., Amb. Sva. 128
—— Hy., S.L. 411
—— Hy. and sir H., B. Ex. 385; J.C.P. 379; K.C. 415; S.L. 412; J.K.B. 373
Gouldsbury, Val., G. Gamb. 686
Goulston, Jos., dn. Chich. 434
Gourly, Jno., adm. (**H**) 846
Gournay, sir Matth. de, K.G. 734
Gowan, Geo. E., gen. (**D**) 886
—— Jas. Young, gen. (**D**) 912
Gowen, Th., dn. Clr. 597
Gower, hon. Bapt. Leveson, B.T. 264
—— Ed. Lev., adm. (**A**) 819
—— sir Erasm., adm. (**A**) 816; G. Newfd. 700
—— ld. Fras. Leveson, c. c. ld. Fras. Egerton, *q.v.*, aft. 1st E. of Ellesmere, *q.v.*, Ch. Sec. Ir. 563; L.T. 159; P.C. 211; Sec. at W. 234; U.S.W. and C. 321
—— Geo. Gr. Lev., L.T. 162
—— ld. Gr. Lev., aft. 1st visc. and E. Granville, *q.v.*, Amb. Pr. 118; Amb. Russ. 125; L.T. 158; P.C. 207; Sec. at W. 234
—— Hy., bp. St. Dav. 464
—— Jno. Lev., gen. (**B**) 867
—— hon. Jno. Lev., adm. (**A**) 815; L. Admy. 180
—— hon. Jno. Lev., *see* ld. G., *infra*
—— hon. Rd. Lev., U.S.S. 226
Gower, lds. and E.
—— sir Jno. Lev., aft. 1st ld. G., C.D.L. 242; P.C. 195
—— Jno. Lev., 2nd ld., aft. 1st E., L.P.S. 241; P.C. 198
—— Gr. Lev., 2nd Earl, c.c. ld. or visc. Trentham, *q.v.*, aft. 1st M. of Stafford, *q.v.*; K.G. 742; L.C.H. 295; L.L. Staffs. 312; L.L. Suth. 512; L.P.C. 188; L.P.S. 241; M.G.W. 296; M.H. 302; P.C. 200
—— Geo. Gr., c.c. ld. or Earl G., aft. 2nd M. of Stafford, and 1st D. of Sutherland, *q.v.*; Amb. Fr. 112; L.L. Staffs. 312; L.L. Suth. 512; P.C. 205; Postm. G. 238
—— Geo. Gr., c.c. Earl G., aft. M. of Stafford, and 2nd D. of Sutherland, *q.v.*, L.L. Suth. 512
Gowrie, Wm. Ruthven, aft. 1st E. of, L.H.T. Sc. 497
Graaff, Corn. Jac. van de, G. C.G.H. 678
—— Wilh. Jac. van de, G. Ceyl. 672
Gracchus, T. S. (3), C. Ro., 42, 3, 4
Grace, Percy, adm. (**G**) 841
—— Sheff., K.H. 792
Græme, Alex., adm. (**A**) 816
—— Dav., gen. (**A**) 858
—— Hy. Sull., G. Mdras. 656
—— maj. Laur., G. Nev. 729; G. Tob. 723
Grafton, D. of.
—— Hy., 1st D. of, K.G. 740; L.H. Const. 289
—— Chas., 2nd D. of, K.G. 741; L.C.H. 295; L.H.S. 286; L.J. and L.L. Ir. 556; P.C. 196
—— Aug. Hy., 3rd D. of, K.G. 742; L.L. Suff. 312; L.P.S. 241; L.T. 157; P.C. 201; Prem. 143; S. St. 224
—— Geo. Hy., 4th D. of, form. E. of Euston, *q.v.*; K.G. 743
—— Augs. Chas. Lenn., 7th D. of, K.G. 745
Graham, Allan Ham., gen. (**D**) 907
—— Andr., bp. Dnbl. 532
—— Archd., bp. Isl. 540
—— Archd. Wm., gen. (**D**) 918
—— Ch., adm. (**D**) 831
—— Ch., gen. (**C**) 872
—— Cyr. Ch., G. Gren. 724
—— Don., C.I.E. 806
—— Fort., gen. (**D**) 891; K.C.B. 779
—— Fk. Wm., gen. (**D**) 919
—— Geo., bp. Dnbl. 532; bp. Ork. 535
—— Geo., L.L. Kinr. 510
—— ld. Geo.. G. Newf. 708
—— Geo. Farq. Irv., gen. (**D**) 933
—— Geo. Ferg. gen. (**D**) 929
—— Ger. and sir G., G.C.M.G. 795; gen. (**D**) 924; K.C.B. 781
—— Hy. Hope, gen. (**D**) 901
—— Jas., Ld. Sess. 520
—— sir Jas. Rt. Geo., G.C.B. 772; H. Sec. 227; L. Admy. 182-3; P.C. 212
—— Jno., bp. Chest. 477
—— Jno., gen. (**D**) 888
—— Jno., Ld. Sess. 518
—— Jno., Modr. K. Sc. 547
—— hon. Jno., G. Gsey. 668
—— Jno. Geo., adm. (**H**) 846
Graham—*cont.*
—— Jno. Gord., gen. (**D**) 929
—— Jos., Q.C. 419
—— Patr., bp. Brn. 531; abp. St. Andr. 529
—— Rd., C. Exc. 278
—— Rd., R. Cr. P.A. 335
—— Rt., C. Exc. Sc. 505
—— Rt., L.T. 160
—— Rt. and sir R., B. Ex. 385; Jud. Com. P.C. 360; K.C. 415; P.C. 212; S.L. 412
—— Saml., gen. (**B**) 867
—— Saml. Jas., gen. (**D**) 932
—— Th., M.M. 247
—— Th., aft. ld. Lynedoch, *q.v.*, K.B. 766
—— Wm. and sir W., adm. (**E**) 836; Compt. N. 258; K.C.B. 782; L. Admy. 186
—— Wm., dn. Carl. 476; dn. Wlls. 429
—— Wm. Hy., gen. (**D**) 930
Graham, E. of, *see* Montrose
Graham, M. of.
—— Jas., M. of, aft. 3rd D. of Montrose, *q.v.*, L.L. Hunts, 309; L.T. 158; P.C. 205; Paym. G. 244; Pres. B.T. 268; V.P. B.T. 269
—— Jas., M. of, aft. 4th. D. of Montrose, *q.v.*, B.C. 253; P.C. 210; V.C.H. 297
Gramston, *see* Granston
Granard, visc. and E. of.
—— Arth., 1st visc., aft. 1st E. of, L.J. Ir. 555; gen. (**B**) 864
—— Geo., 3rd E. of, form. ld Forbes, *q.v.*
—— Geo., 4th E. of, gen. (**B**) 865
—— Geo., 6th E. of, gen. (**A**) 862
—— Geo. Arth. Hast., 7th E. of, K.P. 751; L.L. Leitr. 570
Granby, M. of.
—— Jno, M. of (son of 3rd D. of Rutland, *d.v.p.*), M.G.O. 259
—— Jno., M. of (son of 4th D. of Rutland, *d.v.p.*), C. Ch. 855; gen. (**B**) 865; L G.O. 259; L.L. Dby. 307; M.G.O. 259; P.C. 200
—— Ch. C. J., M. of, aft. 6th D. of Rutland, *q.v.*, L.L. Linc 310
Grancurt, Wm. de, B. Ex. 382
Granden, Warr. de, J. It. 367
Grandison, Jno., bp. Exr. 436
—— sir, or Bar. Otho or Otto de, G. Ch. Isl. 667; L.H.A. 171
—— W.C.P. 318
Grandison, visc.
—— Oliver, 1st visc., form sir Oliv. St. John *q.v.*, L. Treas. Ir. 559
—— Geo., 4th visc., C.Y.G. 298
Graney, Leonard, ld. Grey and visc., L.D. Ir. 553
Granger, Th. C., Q.C. 417
—— Wm., adm. (**A**) 820
Grangues, Hy. de, gen. (**B**) 865
Granston (or Gramston), Th., K.G. 733
Grant, Alexr., K.H. 792
—— Alexr., C.I.E. 807
—— sir Alexr. C., B.C. 253
—— Andr., Modr. K. Sc. 547
—— Ch., Chn. E.I. Co. 645
—— Ch., gen. (**D**) 892

For List of Abbreviations, see pp. 944-952.

Grant—*cont.*
—— Ch., gen. (**D**) 931
—— Ch., K.C.S.I. 803; Sec. I.E. 808; Sec. S.I. 804
—— Ch., aft. ld. Glenelg, *q.v.*, Ch. Sec. Ir. 563; L.T. 159; Pres. B.C. 253; Pres. B.T. 268; P.C. 210; Tr. N. 257; V.P.B.T. 269; W. and C. Sec. 231
—— Colq. and sir C., G.C.H. 786; gen. (**B**) 868; K.C.B. 774; K.C.H. 787
—— Dougl. Gord. S. St. J., gen. (**D**) 931
—— Dunc., gen. (**D**) 886
—— Fras., gen. (**B**) 865
—— Fras., aft. sir F., Pres. R.A. 941
—— sir Fras., ld. Sess. 520
—— hon. Fras. Wm., aft. 6th E. of Seafield, *q.v.*, L.L. Inv. 510
—— Hy. Dunc. adm. (**E**) 837
—— J. M., G. St. Luc. 725
—— Jas., gen. (**A**) 859
—— Jas., gen. (**D**) 882
—— Jas., Modr. K. Sc. 547
—— Jas. Alexr., K.C.M.G. 798
—— Jas. Hope and sir J., C.C. Mdras. 658; G.C.B. 770; gen. (**D**) 892; K.C.B. 778
—— sir Jas. Jno., L.L. Inv. 510
—— sir Jas. Rt., K.H. 789
—— Jno., Bar. Ex. Sc. 524
—— Jno., gen. (**D**) 895
—— Jno. Pet. and sir J., G.C.M.G. 795; G. Jam. 713; K.C.B. 783; L.G. Bgl. 652
—— Jno. Thornt., gen. (**D**) 903; K.C.B. 781
—— Lewis, gen. (**D**) 910
—— Lewis and sir L., G. Bah. Isl. 716; G. Trin. 722; gen. (**A**) 863; K.C.H. 788
—— Maxw., K.C.B. 775
—— Patr. and sir P., C.C. Mdras. 658; F.M. 856; G.C.B. 770; G. Ch. Hosp. 936; G.C.M.G. 795; G. Mlta. 671; gen. (**D**) 887; K.C.B. 778
—— Patr., Jy. Sc. 522
—— Patr., Ld. Sess. 520
—— (or Weathershed), Rd., abp. Cant. 430
—— sir Rd., adm. (**G**) 841
—— Rt. and sir R., B.C. 253; G. Bbay. 659; G.C.H. 787; J.A.G. 937; P.C. 212
—— Rt. Geo. H., gen. (**D**) 911
—— Th. Tass., K.C.B. 782
—— Ulyss. S., Pres. U.S.A. 103
—— Wm. and sir W., C.J. Chest. 386; K.C. 415; M.R. 388; P.C. 207; S.G. 402
—— Wm., gen. (**C**) 873
—— Wm., gen. (**C**) 874
—— Wm., Jy. Sc. 523; Ld. Adv. 526; Ld. Sess. 520
—— Wm. Burl., adm. (**H**) 852
—— sir Wm. K., G.C.H. 787; gen. (**A**) 862; K.C.B. 775; K.C.H. 787
Grant-Duff, *see* Duff
Grantham, Geo., gen. (**D**) 890
—— (or Grauntham), Jno. L.M. Lond. 489
—— Th., gen. (**D**) 889
—— Wm. and sir W., J.Q.B.D. 374; Q.C. 419
Grantham, lds. and E. of
—— Hy. of Nassau, E. of, P.C. 197
Grantham, lds. and E. of—*cont.*
—— Th., 1st ld., form. sir T. Robinson, *q.v.*, M.G.W. 296; Postm. G. 238
—— Th., 2nd ld., form. hon. Th. Robinson, *q.v.*, Amb. Spn. 123; B.T. 267; H. Sec. 226; Pres. B.T. 266
—— Th. Ph., 3rd ld., aft. E. de Grey, *q.v.*, L.L. Beds. 306
Grantley, Fl., 1st ld., form. sir F. Norton, *q.v.*, B.T. 267
Granville, sir Bev., G. Bdoes. 720; gen. (**C**) 871
—— Den., dn. Dham. 479
—— Geo., aft. ld. Lansdowne, *q.v.*. Sec. at W., 233
Granville, lds. and E.
Granville Family.
—— sir Jno., ld. Gr., aft. 1st E. of Bath, *q.v.*, L.W.S. 323
—— hon. Jno., aft. ld. Gr. of Potheridge, L.G.O. 259; L.L. Cnwall. 307; L.W.S. 323; P.C. 195
Carteret Family.
—— Jno., 2nd E., form. ld. Carteret, *q.v.*, K.G. 742; L.P.C. 188; S. St. 224
Leveson-Gower Family.
—— Granv., 1st visc. and E. Gr., form. ld. Gr. Leveson-Gower, *q.v.*, Amb. Fr. 113; Amb. Nds. &c. 123; G.C.B. 772; Sec. at W. 234
—— Gr. Geo., 2nd E., form. ld. Leveson, *q.v.*, Amb. Russ. 126; C.D.L. 243; C. Sec. 235; F. Sec. 228-9; Jud. Com. P.C. 361; K.G. 744; L.P.C. 188; M.B.H. 303; P.C. 215; Paym. G. 244; U.S.F. 230; V.P.B.T. 269; W.C.P. 319
Gras, Jno. de, K.B. 754
—— Nichs. le, J. It. 368
Gratian, Emp. W.E. 49
Grattan, Jas., Rec. Dbln. 642
—— Jno., gen. (**D**) 896
—— sir Rd., L.M. Dbln. 641
Grauntham, *see* Grantham
Grave, Rt., bp. Ferns and L., 622; bp. Llin. 622; dn. Cork, 632
Graves, Ch., bp. Lim. A. and A. 639; dn. Clonf. 637
—— Harry Meggs, gen. (**D**) 892
—— Jas., gen. (**C**) 874
—— Jno. Cr., gen. (**D**) 921
—— Nichs., dn. Drom. 606
—— Rd., dn. Ard. 609
—— Saml., adm. (**A**) 814
—— Th., dn. Cnr. 605
—— Th. and sir Th., adm. (**A**) 817; K.B. 766
—— Th., *see* ld. G., *infra*
—— Wm., gen. (**D**) 913
—— Wm., M. Chy. 397
Graves, lds.
—— Th., aft. 1st ld. G., adm. (**A**) 815
—— Thos. N., 2nd ld., C. Exc. 282
Gravesend, Ben. or Rd. de, bp. Linc. 446; bp. Lond. 451; dn. Linc 448
—— Steph. de, bp. Lond. 451
Graviere, Jean P. E. J. de la, K.C.B. 778
Graville, Jno. G. F. de M. Count de, K.G. 740
Gray, *see also* Grey
—— Edmd. Dwyer, L.M. Dbln. 642
Gray—*cont.*
—— Fras., *see* ld. Gr., *infra*
—— sir Jas., Amb. Scy. 114; Amb. Spn. 123; K.B. 765; P.C. 202
—— Jas. Cl. Charm., gen. (**D**) 894
—— Jno., Ld. Clk. Reg. 524
—— Jno., Q.C. 418
—— Rt., bp. Brl. 439
—— Ralph, K.B. 756
—— Ralph, K.B. 759
—— Rd., K.B. 756
—— Rt., bp. C. Tn. 679
—— Rog., L.J. Ir. 552
—— Th., dn. Ardf. 640; dn. Wford. 628
—— Wm., gen. (**D**) 877
—— Wm., gen. (**D**) 913
—— Wm. Jno., gen. (**D**) 920
Gray, lds.
—— Andr. Ld., L.J. Gen. (1504) 522
—— Patr. Ld., Ld. Sess. (1584) 517
—— hon. Fras., aft. ld. G., Postm. G. Sc. (1807) 503
Graydon, Geo., gen. (**D**) 902; K.H. 790
—— Jno., adm. (**A**) 813
Gream, Rt. Nev., gen. (**D**) 928
Greathed, Ed. Harr. and sir E., gen. (**D**) 903; K.C.B. 779
—— Wm. Wilb. H., gen. (**D**) 917
Greaves, Ch. Spr., Q.C. 417
—— Geo. Richards and sir G., gen. (**D**) 925; K.C.B. 781; K.C.M.G. 797
—— Jno. Ern., L.L. Carn. 314
—— Rd., gen. (**D**) 891
—— Th., dn. Ardf. 640
Grecielus, bp. Llff. 448
Greeke, Th., B. Ex. 384
Green, Greene, and **Grene**
—— Andr. Pell. and sir A., adm. (**D**) 828; (**G**) 840; gen. (**D**) 911; K.C.H. 788; K.H. 789
—— Ch., Lanc. H. 333
—— Ch. and sir C., G. Gren. 724; gen. (**A**) 861
—— Ch. Jas., gen. (**D**) 895
—— Ch. Wm., gen. (**D**) 908
—— Ed. and sir E., gen. (**D**) 895; K.C.B. 779
—— Ed. Arth., gen. (**D**) 910
—— Ern. Aug., gen. (**D**) 935
—— Geo. Wade Guy and sir G., gen. (**D**) 908; K.C.B. 780
—— G., L. Admy. 175
—— Hy., Leic. H. and K.A. 340
—— Hy. and sir H., C.J.K.B. 369; J.C.P. 377; S.L. 406
—— Hy. Dav., Q.C. 420
—— Jas., Bl. M. P.A. 336
—— Jno., bp. Linc. 447; dn. Linc. 448
—— Jno., bp. S. and M. 483
—— Jno., bp. Worc. 472
*—— Jno., Rec. Lond. 494
*—— Jno., S.L. 409
* Prob. same pers.
—— Jno., S.L. 411
—— Jno., Sp. H.C. 248
—— Jno. and sir J., Amb. D. Pr. 128; Amb. Rma. 128
—— Jno. S. T., C.C.J. 403
—— Jno. Wm., gen. (**D**) 932
—— sir Jonas, Rec. Dbln. 642
—— Jos. Hy., Pres. Coll. Surg. 939

Green, Greene, and Grene—*cont.*
— Rd. Wilson, A.G. Ir. 588; B. Ex. Ir. 584; S.G. Ir. 590; S.L. Ir. 593
— Th., bp. Ely, 435; bp. Norw. 455
— Th., dn. Sal. 468
— Th., L.M. Dbln. 641
— Th. L., gen. (**D**) 888
— Th. W., Q.C. 418
— Wm., dn. Ach. 614
— Wm., K.H. 792
— sir Wm., gen. (**A**) 859
— Wm. Con., dn. Chr. Ch. Dbln. 619
— Wm. Hy. R. and sir W., gen. (**D**) 913; K.C.S.I. 802
— Wm. Kirby, Amb. Mco. 132; Amb. Mgo. 128; K.C.M.G. 799
Greenaway, Th., gen. (**D**) 922
Greene, *see* Green
Greenfeld and **Greenfield,** *see also* Grinfield
— Jno., S.L. 407
— (or Grenville) Th., K.B. 759
— Wm. de, abp. Yk. 485; dn. Chich. 434; Ld. Chanc. 353; M. Chy. 393
Greenford, Jno. de, bp. Chich. 432; dn. Chich. 433
Greenhalgh, Jno., G. I. Man, 666
Greenhill, Jas. Dav., gen. (**D**) 876
Greenhow, Wm. T., C.C.J. 405
Greenlaw, Gilb., bp. Abdn. 530; bp. St. Andr. 529; Ld. Chanc. Sc. 515
Greenock, ld. Ch. Murr. Cathc., K.C.B. 776
Greenstreet, Jno., gen. (**D**) 876
Greenwell, Leon., and sir L., gen. (**C**) 875; K.C.B. 776; K.C.H. 788
Greenwich, D. of, *see* Argyll and Gr.
Greenwood, Jno., Q.C. 417
Greer, Hy. Harp., gen. (**D**) 908
Greg, Wm. R., C. Cus. 277
Gregg, Jno.' bp. Cork, Cl. and R. 632
— Rt. Saml., bp. Cork, Cl. and R. 632; bp. Oss. F. and L. 622
Gregorius and **Gregory**
*— abp. Tm. 611; bp. Elph. 608
*— bp. Brn. 530
*— bp. Cork, 630
*— bp. and abp. Dbln. 615
*— (No. 1), bp. Dkld 533; Ld. Chanc. Sc. 514
*— (No. 2), bp. Dkld. 533
*— bp. Mor. 534
*— bp. Ross. 535
*— bp. St. Andr. 528
*— Ld. Clk. Reg. 524
* Prob. same pers. Comp. dates.
— K. Sc. 19
— I. to XVI., P. Ro. 33-4-5-6
— Ch. Hutt., K.C.M.G. 798
— Dav., dn. Chr. Ch. Oxf. 457
— Geo., adm. (**A**) 818
— Geo., St. O. 260
— Jas., dn. Kild. 619
— Jno., G. Bah. Isl. 716
Gregorius and Gregory—*cont.*
— Jno., G. Jam. 712
— Rt., Chn. E.I. Co. 644
— Wm., C. Exc. Ir. 566; U.S. Ir. 563
— Wm., L.M. Lond. 490
— Wm. and sir W., B. Ex. 384; J.C.P. 379; J.K.B. 373; S.L. 410; Sp. H.C. 249
— Wm. Hy., G. Ceyl. 673
— Wm. Hy., K.C.M.G. 797
Gregson, Wm., U.S. Home 227
Greig, Hect., K.C.M.G. 796
Greinville, *see* Grenville
Greisley, Jno., K.B. 755
Grene, *see* Green
Grenefeld and **Grenefield,** *see* Greenfeld
Greneford, *see* Greenford
Grenehurst, Ralph, M. Chy. 394
Grenfell, Fras. Wall., K.C.B. 781
— Sidn., adm., (**E**) 835; (**F**) 838
Grenville and **Greinville,** *see also* Granville and Temple
— Ad. de, J.C.P. 377; J. It. 368; Jy. 365
— Eust. de, Const. T.L. 32
— hon. Geo., aft. Nugent-Temple, 2nd E. Temple and 1st M. of Buckingham, *q.v.*, Tell. Ex. 167; Ch. Ex. 165; L. Admy. 178; L.T. 157; P.C. 199; Prem. 143; S. St. 224; Tr. N. 259
— hon. Geo. Nev., dn. Winds. 474
— hon. Hy., Amb. Tky. 129; C. Cus. 276; G. Bdoes. 720
— Jas., aft. ld. Glastonbury, B.T. 267; L.T. 158; P.C. 204
— hon. Jas., B.T. 264-5; Coff. H. 294; L.T. 157; P.C. 200; V. Treas. Ir. 560
— lady Mary J. N. B. C., Cr. Ind. 809
— Rd., gen. (**A**) 859
— (or Grenefield), Th., K.B. 759
— Thos., Ld. Admy. 181; P.C. 206; Pres. B.C. 252
— Wm. Wyndh., aft. ld. G., Aud. Ex. 167; B.C. and Pres. B.C. 252; B.T. 267; C. Treas. Ir. 561; Ch. Sec. Ir. 562; F. Sec. 228; H. Sec. 226; L.T. 158; Pres. B.C. 252; P.C. 204; Paym. G. 245; Prem. 144; Sp. H.C. 250; V.P.B.T. 269
Gresham, sir Jno., L.M. Lond. 490
— sir Rd., L.M. Lond. 490
Gretton, Geo., dn. Her. 442
Greville and **Grevyl**
— Algn., Bath K.A. 785; B. and Gl. K.A. 330
— Algn. W. F., *see* ld. Gr., *infra*
— hon. Chas., P.C. (1783) 204; Tr. H. 291; B.T. 266; U.S. Home 227
— Ch. Fulke, V.C.H. 297
— hon. Ch. Fras., L. Admy. 179
— hon. Ch. Jas. and sir C., gen. (**C**) 874; K.C.B. 774
— Fulke, Amb. G. St. 121
— sir Fulke, aft. 1st ld. Brooke, Ch. Ex. 154; K.B. 761
Greville and Grevyl—*cont.*
— ld. Geo., aft. 2nd E. of Warwick, *q.v.*, B.T. 266
— Hy. Fras., adm. (**D**) 83
— Stapl. Jas., adm. (**H**) 852
— Wm. J.C.P. 378; S.L. 408
Greville of Clonyn, lds.
— Fulke, S., 1st ld., L.L. W. Meath, 571
— hon. Algn. W. Fulke, aft. 2nd ld. G., L.T. 162
Grévy, F. P. J., Pres. Fr. 25
Grevyl, *see* Greville
Grey, *see also* Gray
— hon. Ch., gen. (**D**) 885
— hon. Ch., *see* ld. G., *infra*
— sir Ch., G.J. Bgal. 652
— sir Ch. Ed., G. Bdoes., &c. 719-20; G.C.H. 787; G. Jam. 713; G. Trin. 722; P.C. 213
— hon. Edw., bp. Her. 442; dn. Her. 442
— hon. Fc. Wm. and sir F., adm. (**D**) 830; (**E**) 834; K.C.B. 778; G.C.B. 770; L. Admy. 184
— Geo., K.B. 757
— hon. Geo., adm. (**D**) 831; (**F**) 838; B. and Gl. K.A. 330; Bath K.A. 785
— hon. Geo. and sir G., G. C.G.H. 679; G. N.Z. 709; G. S. Austr. 706; K.C.B. 782
— sir Geo., C.D.L. 243; C. Sec. 234; G.C.B. 772; H. Sec. 227; J.A.G. 937; P.C. 213; U.S.W. and C. 231
— sir Geo., gen. (**B**) 865
— hon. sir Geo., K.C.B. 775
— Hy. Geo. and sir H., G.C.B. 768; G. C.G.H. 679; G.C.H. 786; gen. (**A**) 861
— Jno. de, abp. Cant. (nom.) 430; bp. Norw. 454; J. It. 368; Jy. 364; L.J. Ir. 550
— Jno., dn. Lism. 629
— Jno., gen. (**B**) 868
— Jno., gen. (**C**) 871
— Jno., K.B. 758
— Jno. and sir J., C.C. Bbay. 660; gen. (**D**) 877; K.C.B. 777
— sir Jno. de, K.G. 735; L.L. Ir. 552
— Jno. Wm., gen. (**D**) 900
— Ralph, *see* ld. Gr., *infra*
— Ralph W., Sec. P.L.B. 262; C. Cus. 277
— Rd., G. Ch. Isl. 667
— Rd., K.B. 754
— Rd., K.B. 757
— Rd. de, W.C.P. 317
— Sim. de, W.C.P. 318
— Th. de. B.T. 266; U.S.C. 235
— sir Th., E.M. 326
— Walt. de, abp. Yk. 485; bp. Lich. and Cov. 443; bp. Worc. 472; Const. T.L. 320; Jy. 364; L.H.T. 152; Ld. Chanc. 353
— Wm., bp. Ely, 435; bp. Linc. 446; bp. Lond. 451; dn. Yk. 487
— Wm. and sir W., G. Jam. 713; K.C.S.I. 803; L.G. Bgal. 652
— Wm. de, aft. sir Wm. and ld. Walsingham, *q.v.*, A.G. 399; C.J.C.P. 376; K.C. 415; P.C. 202; S.G. 402; S.L. 412
— hon. Wm. G., Amb. Fr. 113
Grey, lds., *see* North and Grey

Grey of Codnor, lds.
— Jno., 3rd ld., K.G. 733
— Rd., 4th ld., K.G. 734; L.H.A. 173
Grey of Howick, lds. and E.
— Ch., aft. 1st ld. and 1st E. Gr., G. Gsey. 669; gen. (**A**) 859; K.B. 765; P.C. 206
— hon. Ch. (visc. Howick, *q.v.*) aft. 2nd Earl Grey; K.G. 743; L. Admy. 181; L. T. 160; P.C. 208; Prem. 146.
— Hy. Geo., 3rd E., form. visc. Howick, *q.v.*, G.C.M.G. 795; K.G. 744; L.L. Nbland. 310; W. & C. Sec. 231
Grey of Ruthyn, lds.
— Edm., 4th ld., aft. E. of Kent, *q.v.*, L.H.T. 153
— Rd., 6th ld., aft. E. of Kent, *q.v.*, K.B. 758
Grey of Wake or Werke, lds.
— Wm., 1st ld., C.D.L. 242; C.G.S. 356
— hon. Ralph, aft. 4th ld. Grey of W., G. of Bdoes. 720
Grey of Wilton, lds.
— Wm., 13th ld., K.G. 738
— Arth., 14th ld., K.G. 738; L.D. Ir. 554
Grey and **Ripon**
— Th. Ph., 2nd E. de, form. 3rd ld. Grantham, *q.v.*, K.G. 744; L. Admy. 182; L.L. Ir. 557; P.C. 213
— Geo. Fk. Saml., 3rd E. de, and 2nd E. of Ripon, aft. M. of Ripon, *q.v.*, form. G. F. S. Robinson, *q.v.* and ld. Grantham, Jud. Com. P.C. 361; K.G. 745; L.P.C. 188; P.C. 217; Sec. Ind. 236; U.S. War. 232; W. Sec. 232
Grey-Wilson, *see* Wilson
Greyley, Th. de, K.B. 754
Greystanes, Rt., bp. Dham. 478
Greystoke, Hy. de, A.G. 398; B. Ex. 383
Grierson, Crighton, gen. (**D**) 894
— Hy., gen. (**D**) 917
Griesbach, Carl Lud., C.I.E. 808
Griesley, Sim. de, *see* Briesley
Grieve, Jno., L. Prov. Edinb. 548
— R—, C. Exc. Sc. 505
— W. S., form. W. S. Browne, *q.v.*
Griffri, bp. St. Dav. 464
Griffin, —, S.L. (1504) 408
— Ed., A.G. 398; S.G. 401
— Ed., K.B. 761
— sir Ed., Tr. Ch. 294
— Hy., bp. Lim. A. & A. 639
— Jno., bp. Llin. 621; bp. Oss. 620
— Jno. Gr., aft. 4th ld. Howard de Walden, *q.v.*, K.B. 765
— Jno. Hung., gen. (**D**) 892
— Lep. Hy., K.C.S.I. 803
— Maur., bp. Roch. 460
— Michl. C.B. Ex. Ir. 582
— Nichs., K.B. 759
— Ralph, dn. Linc. 448
— Th., adm. (**A**) 814
— Wm., adm. (**G**) 842
Griffith, Griffiths, Gryffith, Gryffiths, and **Grufydd**
— ap Conan (or Cynan), Pr. Wls. 16
Griffith, Griffiths, Gryffith, Gryffiths, and Grufydd—*cont.*
— ab Llewelyn (2), Pr. Wls. 16
— ab Meredydd, Pr. Wls. 17
— ab Rhys, Pr. Wls. 17
— ap Ryce, K.B. 754
— (or Griffin), ap Yerward, bp. Bgr. 425
— (ld. Rhys), Pr. Wls. 17
— Anselm Jno., adm. (**D**) 823
— Ch., gen. (**B**) 868
— Ch. Marsh, Q.C. 419
— Clem. Jas., gen. (**D**) 934
— Edm., bp. Bgr. 426; dn. Bgr. 426
— Fk. Ch., gen. (**D**) 892
— Geo., bp. St. As. 462
— G. H., G. Seych. Isl. 684
— Hy. Darb., gen. (**D**) 901
— Jno., dn. St. As. 463
— Jno., G. Bbay. 659
— Jul. Geo., gen. (**D**) 886
— Lewis, dn. Glr. 440
— Matt. Ch. D., gen. (**C**) 873
— Ph., Amb. N.G. 134
— Ralph Th. Ho., C.I.E. 807
— Rd., dn. Ross. 633
— Rt., S.L. Ir. 591
— Saml. Walk., K.C.M.G. 798
— Sylv., dn. Her. 442
— Th. Ris., G. Seych. Isl. 684
— Walt., K.B. 758
— Wm., K.B. 758
— Wm., M. Chy. 395
— Wm., G. Gld. Cst. Col. 687; G. Lag. 687; K.C.M.G. 798
— Wm. Downes, C.C.J. 405
Griffits, Jas. O., Q.C. 419
Grimaldo, I. to IV., Pr. Mno. 30
Grimbald, Pet. de, B. Ex. 382
— Rt., J. It. 368
Grimesby (or Grymesby)
— Edm. de, M. Chy. 393
— Elias de, M. Chy. 393
Grimoald, K. Lmd. 49
Grimsby, *see* Grimesby
Grimstead, —, M. Chy. 395
Grimstone (or Grymstone)
— Ed., M. Chy. 395
— sir Harb., M.R. 388; Sp. H.C. 249
Grimthorpe, Edm. Beck., ld., form. E. B. Denison, *q.v.*
Grimus, K. Sc. 19
Grindal or **Grindall,** Edmd., abp. Cant. 431; abp. Yk. 486; bp. Lond. 451
— Rd. and sir R., adm. (**A**) 817; K.C.B. 773
Grinfield, *see also* Greenfield
— Wm., gen. (**A**) 859
Grinkettel or **Grinketellus,** bp. Elm. and Dunw. 454; bp. Sels. 432
Grinwode, Rd., R. Cr. P.A. 335
Gronow, Hyw. Ab., dn. Bgr. 426
Gros, Anc. le, bp. St. Dav. 464
— Raym. le, L.L. Ir. 550
Grose, capt. F., G. N.S.W. 702
— Fras., gen. (**B**) 867
— Fras., Richm. H. 334
— Nash and sir N., J.K.B. 373; S.L. 412
Grosseld, Geoff., bp. Ferns, 621
Grosset, Walt., adm. (**H**) 844
Grosthead, Rt., bp. Linc. 446
Grosvenor, ld. Rd., P.C. 218; Sec. Tr. 164; V.C.H. 297
— ld. Rt., aft. ld. Ebury, *q.v.*, Compt. H. 293; P.C. 212; Tr. H 291
— ld. Rt., *see* E. Gr., *infra*
— Th. F.M. 856; gen. (**A**) 860
Grosvenor, E.
— Rt., 2nd E., form. visc. Belgrave, *q.v.*, aft. 1st M. of Westminster, *q.v.*
Groube, Th., adm. (**H**) 845
Grouchy, Off. Nap. 26
Grouthed, Rt., bp. Linc. 446
Grove, —, K.H. 792
— Jas. or Jno., S.L. 411
— Rt., bp. Chich. 433
— Wm. Rt. and sir W., J.C.P. 380; J.C.P.D. 380; J.Q.B.D. 374; Jud. Com. P.C. 362; P.C. 221; Q.C. 417; S.L. 414
Groves, capt. Th., G. Newfd. 700
Growse, Fk. Salm., C.I.E. 806
Grubbe, Jno. Hen., gen. (**D**) 889
— Walt. Jas. Hunt- and sir W., adm. (**E**) 837; K.C.B. 781
Grufydd, *see* Griffith
Gry—, *see* Gri—
Gryffith, *see* Griffith
Grymesty, *see* Grimesty
Grymstone, *see* Grimstone
Gual, P., Pres. Vzla. 108
Gualafer, bp. Dbln. 615
Gually, Paul de, gen. (**C**) 871
Gualterius, *see* Walter
Guard, Wm., gen. (**B**) 868
Guarden, W. W. H., C. Treas. Ir. 561
Guardia, Sant. de la, Pres. Pan. 107
— Tom., Pres. C.R. 106
Guardiola, S., Pres. Hdas. 106
Guarinus, *see* Warine
Gubbins, Jas., gen. (**D**) 921
— Jos., gen. (**C**) 874
Gucanor or **Gucanus,** *see* Gogwan
Gucht, Benj. Geo. van der, gen. (**D**) 918
Guelderland, W., D. of, K.G. 734
Guelph, D. Tny. 57
— I. and II., D. Bva. 67
Guerdain, Aar., M.M. 246
Guernsey, Hen., ld., form. Hen. Finch, *q v.*, aft. E. of Aylesford, *q.v.*, P.C. 195
Gueroc, de Nantes, D. Bry. 28
Guerrero, Dt. Mex. 103; Pres. Mex. 103
Guest, Josh., gen. (**B**) 864
Guidelium (or Guiteline), abp. Lond. 450
Guido, *see also* Guy
— I. and II., Pr. Mno. 30
Guildford and **Guilford**
— sir Ed., W.C.P. 319
— sir Hy., C.Y.G. 298; K.G. 737
— sir Rd., K.G. 737
Guilford, lds. and E. of
— Fras., 1st ld., form. F. North, *q.v.*
— Fras., 2nd ld., P.C. 196; Pres. B.T. 264
— Fk., 2nd E. of, form. ld. North, *q.v.*

For List of Abbreviations, see pp. 944-952.

Guilford, lds. and E. of—*cont.*
— Fk., 5th E. of, form. hon. Fk. North, *q.v.*, Chambn. Ex. 166; G.C.M.G. 794
Guilermus, dn. St. P. 452
Guilford, *see* Guildford
Guille, Jno., Blf. Gsey. 669
Guillermo, C., Pres. Dom. Rep. 105
Guinness, Benjn. Lee and sir B., L.M. Dbln. 642
Guise, Jno., gen. (**A**) 858
— Jno. Chr., gen. (**D**) 908
— Jno. Wr. and sir J., G.C.B. 770; gen. (**A**) 863; K.C.B. 776
Guiteline, *see* Guidelium
Guldeford, Hy. de, J.C.P. 377; J. It. 368
Gulfridus, bp. Llff. 448
Gulielmus, *see* William
Gulliver, Hy. Wm., gen. (**D**) 920
Gully, Wm. Court., Q.C. 419
Gulston, Wm., bp. Brl. 439
Gundebaud, K. Bdy. 28
Gundemar, K. Sp. 85
Gunderic, K. Bdy. 28
Gundevil, Hugh de, J. It. 365
Gundicar, K. Bdy. 28
Gundred (dau. Wm. I.), Pr. E. 9
Gundry, Nathl. and sir N., J.C.P. 379; K.C. 415; S.L. 412
Gundulph, bp. Roch. 459
Gunter, Jas., gen. (**D**) 932
Gunther II., Pr. S. Son. 79
Gunthorpe, Jno., dn. Wells, 429; M. Chy. 394
— Wm., B. Ex. 383
Gunning, Jno., gen. (**C**) 872
— Pet., bp. Chich. 433; bp. Ely, 435
— Rt. and sir R., Amb. Dk. 127; Amb. Pr. 117; Amb. Russ. 125; G.C.B. 771; K.B. 765
Guodloiu, bp. Llff. 448
Gurdon, Adam, J. It. 368
Gurges, Q. F. M. (3), C. Ro. 41-2
Gurmallion, D. Bry. 28
Gurney, Jno. and sir J., B. Ex. 385; K.C. 416; S.L. 413
— sir Rd., L.M. Lond. 491
— Russ., P.C. 217; Q.C. 417; Rec. Lond. 494
Gurnven, abp. St. Dav. 463
Gurvan, bp. Llff. 448
— (de Rennes), D. Bry. 27
Gustavus (g. son Jas. I.), Pr. E. 13
— I. to IV., K. Sw. 92
— II. (K. Sw.), K.G. 739
— -Adolphus Fredk., Lg. H. Hbg. 73
— (Vasa), K. Sw. 92
Guthard, bp. Sels. 432
Guthred, K.E. 1
Guthrie, Dav. and sir D., Compt. Sc. 498; L.H.T. Sc. 496; Ld. Clk. Reg. 525
— Geo. Jas., Pres. Coll. Surg. 939
— Hy., bp. Dkld. 533
— Jno., bp. Mor. 534
Gutierraz, S., Pres. U.S.C. 107
Guttred, K. Man. 664
Guy (or Guido), bp. Bgr. 425
— D. Tny., 57
— (dn. of Waltham), Jy. 363
— de Dampierre, C. Flrs. 81
Guy (or Guido)—*cont.*
— de Lusignan, K. Jsm. 97
— de Tours, D. Bry. 28
*— Hy., C. Cus. 274
*— Hy., M.H. 302
* Prob. same pers.
— Ph. Melm. Nels., and sir P., G. Jsey 668; gen. (**D**) 899; K.C.B. 780
Guyse, Jno., K.B. 758
Guzman, F., Pres. Nic. 106
Gwalior, Mahar of, G.C.B. 770; G.C.S.I. 800; K.C.S.I. 802
— Raj. of, K.C.S.I. 803
Gwent, Rd., D. Arch. 420
Gwenwinwin or **Gwenwynwyn**, Pr. Wls. 17
Gwillim, Jno., Portsm. P.A. 344; R. Cr. P.A. 335
Gwilt, Jno., gen. (**D**) 908
Gwin, *see* Gwyn and Gwynne
Gwrgant, Nichs. ap, bp. Llff. 449
Gwydyr, lds.
— Pet., 1st ld., form. sir P. Burrell, *q.v.*, Dep. L.G.C. 288
— Pet. Rt., 2nd ld., aft. ld. Willoughby De Eresby, P.C. 210
Gwyn and **Gwin**, *see also* Gwynne
— Jno., dn. Dry. 602; dn. Rph. 603
— sir Rowl., Tr. Ch. 294
— Fras., B.T. 264; Sec. at War, 233
— Fras. Ed., gen. (**A**) 859
— Ham. West., gen. (**D**) 922
— Rice, S.L. 409
Gwynne, *see also* Gwyn
— Marm., C. St. 283
— Mad. Xim., gen. (**D**) 934
Gybbon and **Gybon**, *see* Gibbon
Gyfford, *see* Giffard and Gifford
Gyles, *see* Giles
Gyllot, *see* Gillot
Gyndell or **Gyndwelle**, Jno., bp. Linc. 446
Gysors, *see* Gisors

H.

Haast, Jno. Fras. Jul. Von, K.C.M.G. 798
Hac Huargusa, Maneus, bp. Emly. 625
Hachet, Geoff., J. It. 366
Hacket, Andr., M. Chy. 396
— Dav., bp. Oss. 620
— Jno., bp. Lich. and Cov. 444
— Nichs., dn. Oss. 622
— Pet., abp. Cash. 625
— Rd., dn. Killoe. 637
— Th., bp. Down and Cnr. 604
— sir Th., L.M. Dbln. 640
Hackett, Jas., gen. (**D**) 879
— Jno., adm. (**G**) 842
— Jno., gen. (**D**) 924
— Simps., gen. (**D**) 935
Hackins, Pieter, G. C.G.H. 678
Hackrell, Th., dn. Cork, 632
Hadden, Jas. M., gen. (**C**) 873; S.G.O. 260
— Wm. Ch., gen. (**D**) 904
Haddington, E. of
— Th., 1st E. of, form. sir T. Hamilton, *q.v.*, L.P.S. Sc. 501; Sec. St. Sc. 502
— Th., 6th E. of, K.T. 747
— Ch., 8th E. of, L.L. Hadd. 510
— Th., 9th E. of, form. ld. Binning and ld. Melros, *q.v.*, B.C. 253; C.D.L. 243; K.T. 748; L. Adm. 183; L.L. Ir. 557; L.P.S. 241
— Geo., 10th E. of, L.H.C.K. Sc. 546
— Geo., 11th E. of, L.L. Hadd. 510
Haddo, Geo., 1st ld., form. sir Geo. Gordon, *q.v.*, aft. E. of Aberdeen, *q.v.*
Haddock, Nichs., adm. (**A**) 814
— Rd. (No. 1), Compt. N. 257
— sir Rd. (No. 2), adm. (**A**) 813; Compt. N. 257
Haddon, Jas., dn. Exr. 437
— sir Rd., L.M. Lond. 490
— Walt., J. Pr. Ct. 421
Hadenham, Alexr. de, A.G. 398
Hadfield, Oct., bp. Welln. 710
— Walt. de, J. It. 365
Hadley, Jno., L.M. Lond. 489
Hadlow, *see* Handlo, Nichs.
Hadrian, *see* Adrian
Haernunen, abp. St. Dav. 463
Hagan, sir Rt., adm. (**G**) 843
Hagar, Jno., adm. (**A**) 814
Hagart, Ch., gen. (**D**) 900
Haghman, *see* Hawman
Haig, Ch. Th., gen. (**D**) 935
— Felix Thack., gen. (**D**) 920
Hailes, *see also* Hales
— Danl., Amb. Dk. 127; Amb. Fr. 112; Amb. Pld. 126; Amb. Sw. 126
— Harris C., K.H. 791
— (or Halles), Jas., K.B. 760
— Jno. Cl., gen. (**D**) 920
Haines, *see also* Heynes
— Fk. Paul and sir F., C.C. Ind. 651; C.C. Mdras. 658; G.C.B. 771; G.C.S.I. 801; gen. (**D**) 899; K.C.B. 781
Hak, Abd., C.I.E. 807
Hakeem, Saadut, &c., K.C.S.I. 802
Hakenshawe, Rog., J.K.B. Ir. 578
Hakewell, Wm., M. Chy. 395
Halcombe, Jno., S.L. 413
Haldane, Ch., gen. (**D**) 895
— Jas. Rt. A. Chinnery-, bp. Arg. and Isl. 541
— Jno., C. Cus. Sc. 503
— Jno., L.J. Gen. 522
— Patr., C. Exc. 279
— Rt., Mod. K. Sc. 547
Halden, Wm. de, Rec. Lond. 493
Haldimand, Fk. and sir Fk., G. Can. 691; gen. (**B**) 865; K.B. 765

Hale, Bern., gen. (**A**) 858; L.G. Ch. Hosp. 936
— Bern. and sir B., B. Ex. 384; C.B. Ex. Ir. 583; S.L. 411
— Ed. Bl., gen. (**D**) 904
— Frank Van, K.G. 733
— Hy., C. Cus. 275
— Jno., gen. (**A**) 858
— Josh., gen. (**D**) 895
— Matth. and sir M., C.B. Ex. 381; C. Exc. 277; C.J.K.B. 370; J.C.P. 379; S.L. 409-10
— Matth. Bl., bp. Brisb. 786; bp. Perth W.A. 707
— Rt., gen. (**D**) 928
— Sim. de, J. It. 367
— Warr. St., L.M. Lond. 492
Hales, *see also* Hailes
— Arth., gen. (**D**) 933
— (or Halys), Chr., A.G. 398; M.R. 388; S.G. 401
— Ed. and sir E., L. Admy. 175-6; Lt. T.L. 322
— Humphr., Bl. M.P.A. 336; Yk. H. 334
— Jas. and sir J., J.C.P. 378; S.L. 408
— (or Halys), Jno., B. Ex. 383
— (or Hals), Jno., bp. Lich. and Cov. 444; dn. Exr. 437
— Jno., G. Ch. Hosp. 936
— sir Rt., L.H.A. 172
— Steph., K.B. 764
Hales, lds.
— Patr. Ld., L.J. Gen. 522
Halford, sir Hy., G.C.H. 786; K.C.H. 787; Pres. Coll. Ph. 938
Halghton, *see* Halton
Haliburton, *see* Halliburton
Haliday, *see* Halliday
Halifax, Saml., bp. Gbr. 438; bp. St. As. 462
— sir Th., L.M. Lond. 492
Halifax, lds., visc., E. and M.
Saville Family.
— Geo., 1st visc., E., and M. of. B.T. 263; L.P.C. 187; L.P.S. 240; Pl. 191; P.C. 192; P.C. 193
Montague and Dunk Families.
— Ch., 1st ld. and 1st E. of (1st Cr.), form. Ch. Montague, *q.v.*, K.G. 741; L.L. Surr. 312; L.T. 156; Prem. 141
— Geo., 2nd ld. and 1st E. of (2nd Cr.), form. Geo. Montague, *q.v.*, K.B. 764; P.C. 197
— Geo., 2nd E. of, form. Geo. Montague, *q.v.*, gen. (**B**) 865; K.G. 742; L. Admy. 179; L.L. Ir. 557; L.L. Nton. 310; L.P.S. 241; P.C. 199; Pres. B.T. 265; S. St. 224-5
Wood Family.
— Ch., 1st visc., form. sir C. Wood, *q.v.*, L.P.S. 241
— Mary, viscss. of, Cr. Ind. 809
Halket and **Halkett**
— sir Alex., gen. (**A**) 862; K.C.H. 789
— Col. and sir C., C.C. Bbay. 660; G.C.B. 769; G.C.H. 786; G. Ch. Hosp. 936; gen. (**A**) 863; K.C.B. 774; K.C.H. 787
— Fk., gen. (**C**) 872
— Jno., G. Bah. Isl. 716; G. Tob. 723
— sir Peter, adm. (**A**) 819; G.C.H. 786
— Wm., L.J. Clk. 16
Hall, sir Benjn., aft. ld. Llanover, *q.v.*, C.W.P.B. 272; P.C. 216; Pres. B.H. 255
— Ch., Q.C. 419
— Ch. and sir C., V. Chanc. 390
— Ch. Hy., dn. Chr. Ch. Oxf. 457; dn. Dham. 479
— Ch. Hy., gen. (**D**) 929
— Geo., bp. Chest. 477
— Geo., bp. Drom. 605
*— Hy., bp. Killa and Ach. 613
*— Hy., dn. Cork, 632
* Prob. same pers.
— Hy., gen. (**D**) 886
— Jas., gen. (**C**) 873
— Jno., bp. Brl. 439
— Jno., gen. (**C**) 873
— Jno., gen. (**D**) 886
— Jno., K.C.B. 778
— Jno., K.C.M.G. 798
— Jno. and sir J., K.C.H. 787; K.H. 789
— Jno. Durh., gen. (**D**) 935
— Jno. Gage, G. Mtius. 683; gen. (**A**) 862
— Jno. Stev., adm. (**A**) 818
— Jos., bp. Ex. 437; bp. Norw. 455; dn. Worc. 473
— Jul. Ham., gen. (**D**) 932
— Lewis A., gen. (**D**) 894
— Rt., adm. (**A**) 820
— Rt. adm. (**H**) 849; Compt. N. 258; L. Admy. 185; Sec. Admy. 187
— Saml., Q.C. 420
— Th., C. Cus. 274; C. Exc. 279
— Th., gen. (**A**) 859
— Tim., bp. Oxf. 456
— Wm., S.L. 407
— Wm., S.L. 411
— Wm. Hutch., adm. (**D**) 833; (**F**) 838; K.C.B. 779
— Wm. King and sir W., adm. (**E**) 835; K.C.B. 788
Hallam, Hy., C. St. 284
— Jno., dn. Brl. 440
— (or Hallum), Rt., abp. Yk. (nom.) 485; bp. Sal. 467
Halles, *see* Hailes
Halley, Edmd., Astr. Roy. 941
Halliburton, **Haliburton**, and **Hallyburton**
— Arth. Lawr., K.C.B. 784
— Geo., bp. Abdn. 530; bp. Brn. 531
— Geo., bp. Dkld. 533
— Geo. and sir G., Ld. Sess. 519
— ld. Jno. Fk. Gord., adm. (**G**) 842
— sir Walt. de, L.H.T. Sc. 496
Halliday and **Haliday**
— maj., G. Trin. 722
— sir And., K.H. 789
— Fras. Ed., gen. (**D**) 931
— Fk. Jas. and sir F., K.C.B. 782; L.G. Bgal. 652; M.C.I. 646
— Jno. Gust., gen. (**D**) 921
— Wm. Rt., gen. (**D**) 905
Hallowell, Benj., K.C.B. 774
Hallowes, Fk. Wm., adm. (**H**) 853
— Geo. Sk., gen. (**D**) 924
— Jno., adm. (**G**) 843
Halloway, *see* Holloway
Halls (or Hals), Jno., J.C.P. 378; J.K.B. 371; S.L. 407
Hallum, *see* Hallam
Halpin, Wm., gen. (**D**) 896
Hals, *see* Halls and Halse
Halsay, Th., bp. Llin. 622
Halsbury, Hard. St., 1st ld., form. sir H. S. Giffard, *q.v.*, Ld. Chanc. 358; P.C. 220
Halse (or Hals), Jno., bp. Lich. and Cov. 444; dn. Exr. 437
Halsey, Jno., M. Chy. 396
Halstan, K. Sw. 92
Halsted, Ed. Pell., adm. (**D**) 832; (**E**) 834
— Geo. Anth., adm. (**H**) 848
— Lawr. Wm. and sir L., adm. (**A**) 818; G.C.B. 768; K.C.B. 774
Haltoft, Gilb., B. Ex. 383
Halton (or Halghton), Jno. de, bp. Carl. 475
— Rt., S.L. 408
Haly, Wm. O'Gr. and sir W., gen. (**D**) 899; K.C.B. 780
Halys, *see* Hales
Hambury, Hy. de, C.J.C.P. Ir. 580
Hamelin, Ferd. Alph., G.C.B. 769
— Th., Bl. L.P.A. 341
Hamelinus, dn. Linc. 447
Hameltone, *see* Hamilton
Hamerton, Jno. Mill., gen. (**A**) 863
Hamilton, Alexr. Mark K., gen. (**C**) 874; G. Br. Hond. 714
— sir Andr., Ld. Sess. 519
— Archd., abp. Cash. and Eml. 626; bp. Killa. and Ach. 613
— Archd., gen. (**B**) (1747) 865
— ld. Archd., G. Gr. Hosp. 854; G. Jam. 712; L. Admy. 177-8
— Arth. Ph., adm. (**H**) 845
— Ch., bp. Niag. 693
— Ch., gen. (**D**) 888
— sir Ch., adm. (**A**) 818; G. Newfd. 700; K.C.B. 776
— Ch. Jas. H., Amb. Fr. 113
— Ch. Pow., adm. (**A**) 816
— Ch. Wm., gen. (**D**) 880
— Chr., gen. (**D**) 877
— ld. Claude J., L.T. 161; P.C. 215; Tr. H. 291; V.C.H. 297
— Cosp. Baill., adm. (**G**) 843
— Dav., bp. Arg. 538
— Digby, gen. (**C**) 873
— Dougl., gen. (**D**) 917
— sir Ed., adm. (**A**) 819; K.C.B. 774
— Fras. Fisher, gen. (**D**) 927
— Fras. Wm., gen. (**D**) 931
— Fc., Amb. Ecr. 942
— Fc., G. Leew. Isl. 727; gen. (**C**) 871
— Fk. Wm. and sir F., gen. (**D**) 895; K.C.B. 780
— Gav., bp. Gall. 538
— Gav., Ld. Sess. 517
— Geo., B. Ex. Ir. 584; S.L. Ir. 592
— Geo., Mod. K. Sc. 547
— Geo. A., P.C. 218; Sec. Tr. 163-4
— sir Geo. Baill., Amb. Tusc. 115; K.C.H. 788
— ld. Geo. F., L. Admy. 186; P.C. 219; U.S. Ind. 236; V.P. Ed. 255
— Ham. Ch. J., Amb. Bzl. 135; Amb. R. Pl. 136

Hamilton—*cont.*
— Hy., C. Cus. Ir. 566
— Hy., G. Bmda. 701; G. Dnca. 730
— Hy., gen. (**D**) 906
— Hy. Meade, gen. (**D**) 907
— Hy. P., dn. Sal. 468
— Hugh, bp. Clonf. and K. 636; bp. Oss. 621; dn. Arm. 597
— Jas., bp. Arg. 538
— Jas., bp. Gall. 538
— Jas., gen. (**A**) 859
— Jas., L.M. Dbln. 641
— Jas., Ld. Sess. 520
— Jas. Archd., dn. Cloy. 633
— Jno., abp. St. Andr. 529; bp. Dkld. 533; L.H.T. Sc. 497; L.P.S. Sc. 501; Ld. Chanc. Sc. 515; Ld. Sess. 518
— Jno., dn. Drom. 606
— Jno., gen. (**A**) 860
— sir Jno., gen. (**B**) 867
— sir Jno. (Orbieston), L.J. Clk. 516; Ld. Sess. 519
— sir Jno. (Magdalens), Ld. Clk. Reg. 525; Ld. Sess. 517; Ld. Sess. 519
— sir Jno. (abb. of Paisley) Ld. Sess. 518
— sir Jno. (Halcraig), Ld. Sess. 520
— Jno. Pott., K.H. 791
— Ker Baill., G. Antig., &c. 727; G. Bdoes. 721; G. Gren. 724; G. Newfd. 700
— lt.-col. —, G. Hlgld. (1814) 670
— Malc., abp. Cash. and Eml. 626
— Nichs., gen. (**D**) 883; K.H. 791
— Oct., gen. (**D**) 914
— Patr., Compt. Sc. 498
— sir Patr., L.M. Dbln. 641
— Rd., gen. (**D**) 908
— Rd. Ves. and sir R., adm. (**E**) 836; K.C.B. 782
— Rt., dn. Thist. 749
— Rt., Ld. Sess. 520
— sir Rt. gen. (**B**) 865
— Rt. Geo. Cr. and sir R., G. Tasm. 708; K.C.B. 784; U.S. Ir. 563
— Rt. Gorg, gen. (**D**) 904
— sir Rt. North Coll., K.C.B. 782
— Sackv., U.S. Ir. 563
— Th., adm. (**A**) 818
— Th., Ld. Sess. 519
— Th., S. St. 223
— sir Thos., aft. ld. Binning and Byres, 1st E. of Melros and of Haddington, *q.v.*, Ld. Adv. 526; Ld. Clk. Reg. 525; Ld. Sess. 518
— Th. de C., gen. (**D**) 911
— Walk. K., bp. Sal. 467
— Walt., gen. (**D**) 899
— Walt., L. Prov. Edinb. 548
— Wm. de, dn. Yk. 486; J. It. 368; L.K. and Ld. Chanc. 353; M. Chy. 393
— Wm. and sir W., Amb. Scy. 114; K.B. 765; P.C. 205
— sir Wm., gen. (**D**) 927
— sir Wm. (Whitelaw), L.J. Clk. 516; Ld. Sess. 520
— sir Wm. (Sanquhar) Ld. Sess. 518
— Wm. Alexr. Baillie, adm. (**G**) 841
— Wm. Conr., gen. (**D**) 919

Hamilton—*cont.*
— Wm. Gerard, B.T. 265; C. Acc. Ir. 567; Ch. Ex. Ir. 562; Ch. Sec. Ir. 562
— Wm. Rd., Amb. Scy. 115; U.S.F. 230
Hamilton, M. and D. of
— Jas., 2nd M. of, and 1st E. of Cambridge, *q.v.*, H.C.P. Sc. 507; K.G. 739; L.S.H. 290
— Jas., 3rd M. and 1st D., also 2nd E. of Cambridge, *q.v.*, (*d.* 1649), H.C.P. Sc. 507; K.G. 739; L.H.C.K. Sc. 546; M.H. 302
— Wm., 2nd D. of and 3rd E. of Cambridge, *q.v.*, form. E. of Lanark, *q.v.*, K.G. 740; P.C. 189
— Wm., 3rd D. of, form. E. of Selkirk, *q.v.*, C.G.S. Sc. 515; Comm. Tr. Sc. 497; H.C.P. Sc. 507; L.H.A. Sc. 499; Ld. Sess. 519; P.C. 193
— Jas., 4th D. of, and 1st D. of Brandon, *q.v.*, form. 3rd E. of Arran, *q.v.*, K.G. 741; M.G.O. 258
— Jas., 5th D. of and 2nd D. of Brandon, K.T. 747
— Jas., 6th D. of and 3rd D. of Brandon, K.T. 747
— Dougl., 8th D. of and 5th D. of Brandon, K.T. 748; L.L. Lnrk. 511
— Archd., 9th D. of and 6th D. of Brandon, L.L. Lnrk. 511
— Alexr., 10th D. of and 7th D. of Brandon, form. M. of Douglas and Cl., and ld. Dutton, *q.v.*, K.G. 743; L.H.S. 287
— Wm. Alexr. &c., 11th D. of and 8th D. of Brandon, form. M. of Douglas and Cl., *q.v.*, L.L. Lnrk. 511
— Alexr. L. S., 12th D. of and 9th D. of Brandon, K.T. 749
Hamilton,Baillie-, *see* Baillie-Hamilton
Hamley, Ed. Br. and sir E., G. S. Austr. 706; gen. (**D**) 908; K.C.B. 781; K.C.M.G. 797
— Fras. Gilb., gen. (**D**) 911
— Wm., adm. (**H**) 847
— Wm. Geo., gen. (**D**) 910
Hammer, B., Pres. Sw. C. 31
— Th., K.C. 414
Hammersley, sir Hugh, L.M. Lond., 491
Hammill, Denz., gen. (**D**) 928
Hammond and **Hamond**
— sir Andr. Sn., adm. (**G**) 843; Compt. N. 257; G. N. Sc. 695
— Edmd., *see* ld. H., *infra*
— sir Fras. Th., G.C.H. 786; gen. (**A**) 861; K.C.H. 787
— Geo., Amb. U.S.A. 132; U.S.F. 230
— sir Grah. Eden, adm. (**A**) 820; (**B**) 821; (**C**) 822; G.C.B. 769; K.C.B. 776
— Hy., gen. (**D**) 910
— Jno., Blf. Jsey. 668
— Jno., Ch. Lond. 422
— Jno., L.M. Lond. 489
— Pet., gen. (**D**) 896
— Th., S.L. 408
Hammond, lds.
— Edm., aft. ld. H., P.C. 217; U.S.F. 230
Hamnett, Geo., C.I.E. 807

***Hamo,** dn. Linc. 447
*— dn. Yk. 486
* ? Same pers.
Hamond, *see* Hammond
Hampden, Renn. D., bp. Her. 442
*— Rd., Ch. Ex. 164; L.T. 155
*— Rd., P.C. 197; Tell. Ex. 168; Tr. N. 256
* ? same pers.
— hon. Rt., Postm. G. 238
Hampden, visc.
Trevor Family.
— Th., 2nd visc., G.C.H. 786
Brand Family.
— Hy. B. W., 1st visc., form. sir H. B. W. Brand, *q.v.*, L.L. Suss. 312
Hampson, Rd., S.L. 410
Hampton, Chr., abp. Arm. 596
— Jno. Steph., G. W. Austr. 707
— Rt., gen. (**D**) 878
— Th., G. Ch. Isl. 667
— Wm., L.M. Lond. 490
— Wm. Ph., gen. (**D**) 909
Hampton, lds.
— Jno. S., 1st ld., form. sir J. S. Pakington, *q.v.*
Hamund, *see* Eadmund
Hanagan, Rd. D., K.H. 789
Hanbury, Hy. de, J.K.B. 371
— Jas. Arth., K.C.B. 781
— sir Jno., gen. (**A**) 863; K.C.B. 779; K.C.H. 788
— Th., S.L. 411
Hanbury-Tracy, *see* Tracy
Hancock and **Handcock**
— Geo., adm. (**E**) 836
— Hy., gen. (**D**) 891
— Hy., Pres. Coll. Surg. 939
— Hy. Fras., gen. (**D**) 927
— Jno., adm. (**D**) 825
— Rd., dn. Ach. 614
— Rd. S., adm. (**D**) 826
— Steph., dn. Clonm. 600; dn. Kilmacd. 638
— sir Wm., Rec. Dbln. 642
Hand, Geo. Sumn., adm. (**H**) 849
Handasyde and **Handyside**
— Rt., Jy. Sc. 523; Ld. Sess. 521; S.G. Sc. 527
— Rog., gen. (**A**) 858
— Th., G. Jam. 712; gen. (**C**) 871
Handcock, *see* Hancock
Handlo (or Hadlow) Nichs. de, J.C.P. 377; J.K.B. 371; Jy. 365
Handyside, *see* Handasyde
Hanemere, Dav., J.K.B. 371
Hankey, Augs. Barn., gen. (**D**) 917
— Fredk., G.C.M.G. 794; K.C.M.G. 796; Sec. M.G. 799
Hankford, Wm. and sir W., C.J.K.B. 370; J.C.P. 378; K.B. 755; S.L. 407
Hankin, Ed. Lew., gen. (**D**) 935
Hanlain, Ph., dn. Tm. 613
Hanmer, Hy., K.H. 790
— Jno., bp. St. As. 462
— Jno., G. I. Man, 666
— sir Th., Sp. H.C. 250
Hannemere, Dav., S.L. 407
Hannen, Jas. and sir J., J.P. and D. 391; J.P.D.A. 391; J.Q.B. 373; Jud. Com. P.C. 361; P.C. 218; S.L. 414

Hannibal, Hanybal, and **Hennibal**
—— Matth., K.B. 754
—— Th., bp. Worc. 472
—— Th., M.R. 387
Hannington, Jas., bp. E. Eq. Afr. 688
Hanson, sir R. D., G. S. Austr. 706
—— sir Reg., L.M. Lond. 492
—— sir Rt., L.M. Lond. 491
Hanwell, Jos., adm. (**A**) 818
—— Jos., gen. (**D**) 893
—— Wm., adm. (**A**) 820
Hanybal, *see* Hannibal
Harald, *see also* Harold
—— bp. Arg. 537
—— I. to III., K. Dk. 93
Harbert, sir Jno., J. Adm. Ct. 422
Harbord, sir C., S.L.R. 271
*—— Wm., P.C. 193; V. Treas. Ir. 559
*—— Wm., S.L.R. 271
* Prob. same pers.
—— Wm. A., aft. 2nd ld. Suffield, *q.v.*, L.L. Norfolk, 310
—— sir Wm. Mord., K.B. 764
Harby, sir Job, C. Cus. 273
Harcourt, Harecourt, and **Hardecourt**
—— Ch. Am., gen. (**C**) 874
—— hon. Ed. Ven. Vernon-, abp. Yk. 486; bp. Carl. 476; Jud. Com. P.C. 360; P.C. 208
—— Fk. Ed. Vernon-, adm. (**H**) 845
—— Geo. Wm. R., gen. (**C**) 873
—— Oct. Vernon, adm. (**G**) 841
—— Ph. de, dn. Linc. 447
—— Rd., K.B. 757
—— (or Hardecourt), Rt., K.B. 759
—— sir Rt., K.G. 736
—— Sim., *see* ld. H., *infra*
—— hon. Wm., gen. (**A**) 859
—— Wm. G. G. Ven. Vernon and sir W., Ch. Ex. 166; H. Sec. 227; L.T. 162; P.C. 219; Q.C. 418; S.G. 402
Harcourt, lds. and E.
—— sir Sim., aft. 1st ld. H., A.G. 399; Ld. Chanc. 357; Ld. K. 357; P.C. 195; S.G. 401
—— Sim., 2nd ld. and 1st E., Amb. Fr. 112; gen. (**A**) 858; L.L. Ir. 557; P.C. 199
—— Wm., 3rd E., F.M. 856; G.C.B. 768
Hardecourt, *see* Harcourt
Hardell, Rd., L.M. Lond. 489
—— Wm., L.M. Lond. 488
Harden, Jno. W., C.C.J. 403
Hardicanute, K.E. 4
Hardie, *see also* Hardy
—— Rt., M.C.I. 647
Harding, Fras., adm. (**H**) 848
—— Fras. Pym, G. N. Brk. 696; gen. (**D**) 904
—— Geo., K.C. 415
—— Geo. Judd, G. Gsey. 669; gen. (**D**) 883; K.C.B. 778
—— Jno., bp. Bbay. 661
—— Jno. Dorn. and sir J., Q. Adv. 422; Q.C. 418
Hardinge, hon. Arth. Ed. and sir A., C.C. Bbay. 660; C.I.E. 807; G. Gibr. 670; gen. (**D**) 904; K.C.B. 781
—— Ed., adm. (**E**) 836
—— Hy., *see* visc. H., *infra*
—— Rd., gen. (**D**) 893; K.H. 789
Hardinge, visc.
—— Hy., aft. sir H. and 1st visc. H., C. Ch. 855; Ch. Sec. Ir. 563; Clk. O. 260; F.M. 856; G.C.B. 772; G.G. Ind. 649; gen. (**A**) 863; K.C.B. 775; M.G.O. 259; P.C. 211; Sec. at W. 234
—— Ch. St., 2nd visc., U.S. War, 232
Hardres, Rt. de, J. It. 366
—— (or Hardy) Th., S.L. 410
Hardulfus, bp. Dunw. 454
Hardwick, lds. and E.
—— Phil., 1st ld. and E., form. Ph. Yorke and sir P., *q.v.*, L.H.S. 287; Ld. Chanc. 357
—— Ph., 2nd E. of, form. hon. Ph. Yorke, and visc. Royston, *q.v.*
—— Ph., 3rd E. of, K.G. 743; L.L. Cambs. 306; L.L. Ir. 557; P.C. 206
—— Ch. Ph., 4th Earl of, adm. (**G**) 841; L.L. Cambs. 306; L.P.S. 241; P.C. 215; Postm. G. 239
—— Ch. Ph., 5th E. of, M.B.H. 303
Hardy, *see also* Hardie
—— Benj., Q.C. 418
—— sir Ch., adm. (**A**) 814; G. Gr. Hosp. 854; G. Newfd. 700; L. Admy. 178
—— Fk., gen. (**D**) 927
—— Gath., aft. visc. Cranbrook, *q.v.*, H. Sec. 227; P.C. 217; Pres. P.L.B. 262; Sec. Ind. 236; U.S. Home, 228; W. Sec. 232
—— Herb. H. Cozens-, Q.C. 419
—— Nathl., dn. Roch. 461
—— (or Hardres), Th., S.L. 410
—— sir Th., adm. (**A**) 813
—— sir Th. Mast., adm. (**A**) 820; G.C.B. 768; G. Gr. Hosp. 854; K.C.B. 774; L. Admy. 182
—— Wm., gen. (**D**) 917
Hardyman, Fk., gen. (**C**) 874
—— sir Luc. Herd., adm. (**A**) 820
Hare, Fras., bp. Chich. 433; bp. St. As. 462; dn. St. P. 453; dn. Worc. 473
—— Hy. Ambr., gen. (**D**) 919
—— Jas., Amb. Pld. 126
—— Jas., gen. (**C**) 873
—— Jno., G. C.G.H. 679; gen. (**D**) 881; K.H. 790
—— Jno., R. Dr. P.A. 338; Richm. H. 334
—— sir Nichs., M.R. 388; Sp. H.C. 249
—— Ralph, K.B. 761
—— Th., dn. Oss. 623
Harecourt, *see* Harcourt
Harenc, Archd. Rd., gen. (**D**) 921
Hareng, Ralph, Jy. 364
Harewell, *see also* Harwell
—— Jno., bp. B. and W. 428
Harewood, E. of
—— Hy., 2nd E. of, form. visc. Lascelles, *q.v.*
—— Hy., 3rd E., L.L. of Yorks. W.R. 313
Hargood, Wm., adm. (**G**) 842
—— Wm. and sir W., adm. (**A**) 818; G.C.B. 768; G.C.H. 786; K.C.B. 773
Hargrave, Fras., K.C. 415
—— Wm., G. Gibr. 669; gen. (**B**) 864
Hargraves, Jas., dn. Chich. 434
Hargreave, Ch. Jas., Land. J. Ir. 587; Q.C. 417
Harington, *see* Harrington
Harkness, Ch. Th., gen. (**D**) 912
—— Jno. Granv., gen. (**D**) 929
Harland, sir Rt., adm. (**A**) 815; Ld. Admy. 179
Harlardus, bp. Dorch. 446
Harlech, Wm. Rd., 2nd ld., L.L. Leitr. 570
Harlewin (or Herlewin), bp. Llin. 621
Harley, Ed., K.B. 763
—— Jno., bp. Her. 441
—— hon. Jno., bp. Her. 442; dn. Winds. 474
*—— Rt., K.B. (1603) 761
*—— sir Rt., M.M. (1625) 246
* ? same pers.
—— Robt., aft. 1st E. of Oxford and Mortimer, *q.v.*, Ch. Ex. 165; L.T. 156; P.C. 195; S. St. 224; Sp. H.C. 250
—— Rt. Wm. and sir R., G. Bdoes. 721; G. Br. Hond. 714; G. Gld. Cst. 686; G. Gren. 724; G. Tob. 724; K.C.M.G. 798
—— hon. Th., L.M. Lond. 492; P.C. 202; B.T. 267; L.L. Radn. 316
Harlowe, sir Rt., Lt. T.L. 321
Harman, Cutts, dn. Wford. 628
—— Ed. Rt. King-, L.L. Rosc. 571; U.S. Ir. 564
—— Geo. Byng, gen. (**D**) 924; K.C.B. 782
—— J., *see* Veysey
Harness, Hy. Dr., and sir H., gen. (**D**) 903; K.C.B. 780
Harnett, Ed., gen. (**D**) 929
Harnhall, Hy. de, K.B. 754
Harold, *see also* Harald
—— bp. Lim. 638
—— K. Man, 665
—— (g. son Q. Vict.), Pr. E. 16
—— I. and II., K.E. 41
—— II. (K.E.), L.H.A. 170; W.C.P. 317
—— Jas. Cas., gen. (**D**) 892
—— Jno., dn. Her. 442
Haroun-Al-Raschid, Cph. Aba. 98
Harper and **Harpur**
—— Jerv., gen. (**D**) 935
—— Jno., adm. (**H**) 845
—— H. Jno. Chitty Chr., bp. Ch. N.Z. 709
—— Rd., J.C.P. 378; S.L. 408
—— sir Wm., L.M. Lond. 490
Harpisfield, *see* Harpsfield
Harpole and **Harpoll**
—— (or Hartpoole), Walt., dn. Llin. 623
Harpsfield and **Harpisfield**
—— Jno., dn. Norw. 455
—— Nichs., D. Arch. 420
Harpur, *see* Harper
Harrac-Rohrau, C. of, R. Nds. 83
Harrington and **Harington**
—— Hy. Byng, K.C.S.I. 802
—— Jas., dn. Yk. 487
—— Jno., K.B. 761
—— Rd. and sir R., C.C.J. 405
—— Wm., M. Chy. 395
—— sir Wm., K.G. 735

Harrington, lds. and E. of
—— Wm., 1st ld. and E. of, form. Wm. Stanhope, *q.v.*, gen. (**A**) 857; L.L. Ir. 556; L.P.C. 188; S. St. 224
—— Wm., 2nd E. of, gen. (**A**) 858
—— Ch., 3rd E. of, Amb. Aus. 117; Amb. Pr. 118; Comm. F. Ir. 564; Const. W. Cast. 322; G.C.H. 786; gen. (**A**) 859; P.C. 206
Harriott, *see also* Haryot
—— Jno. St., gen. (**D**) 878
Harris, —, M. Chy., 395
—— Ch., gen. (**D**) 916
—— hon. Ch. Am., bp. Gibr. 670
—— sir Ed., J.K.B. Ir. 579
—— hon. Ed. Alfr. Jno., and sir E., Amb. Chi. 137; adm. (**G**) 841; Amb. Nds., &c. 123; Amb. Pu. 135; Amb. Swz. 114; K.C.B. 783
—— Geo., Adm. Adv. 423
—— Geo. *see* ld. H., *infra*
—— Hy., C. St. 283
—— Harry Boot., K.H. 790
—— Jas. L. Admy. 179; L.T. 157
—— Jas. and sir J., aft. 1st ld. and E. of Malmesbury, *q.v.*, Amb. Nds. &c. 122; Amb. Pr. 118; Amb. Russ. 125; Amb. Spn. 123; K.B. 765; P.C. 204
—— Jno., bp. Llff. 449; dn. Wells 429
—— Jno., gen. (**C**) 874
—— Jno., S.L. 408
—— Jno. Adolph., gen. (**A**) 860
—— Jos., gen. (**D**) 886
—— Noel Haml., gen. (**D**) 928
—— Ph., gen. (**D**) 900
—— Ph., gen. (**D**) 924
—— Rd., Q.C. 420
—— Th., M. Chy. 396
—— Th., S.L. 408-9
—— Th. Noel, K.H. 789
—— Webber D., gen. (**D**) 913
Harris, lds.
—— Geo., 1st ld. G.C.B. 768; G. Mdras. 656; gen. (**A**) 860
—— Wm. Geo., 2nd ld., gen. (**B**) 869; K.C.H. 788
—— Geo. Fras. R., 3rd ld., G.C.S.I. 800; G. Mdras. 657; G. Trin. 722; K.C.S.I. 802
—— G. R. C. 4th ld. U.S. Ind. 236; U.S. War. 232
Harris - Gastrell, *see* Gastrell
Harrison, Anth. Robn. gen. (**D**) 894
—— Broadl., gen. (**D**) 907
—— Ed., gen. (**D**) 917
—— Ed., gen. (**D**) 918
—— Ed., Post. G. 238
—— Geo., Bl. M. P.A. 336; Clar. K.A. 328; Norr. K.A. 330; Winds. H. 331
—— Geo. and sir G. K.C.H. 787; Sec. Tr. 164
—— Geo. and sir G., L. Prov. Edinb. 548
—— Geo. H. Rogers-, Bl. M. P.A. 337; Winds. H. 332
—— Hy., adm. (**A**) 814
—— Hy., gen. (**B**) 864
—— Jno., Chn. E.I. Co. 644
—— sir Jno., C. Cus. 273
—— Jno. Chr., K.H. 791
—— Josh., adm. (**H**) 847
Harrison—*cont.*
—— Michl., J. Bank. Ir. 587; J.C.P.D. Ir. 582; J.Q.B.D. Ir. 580; S.G. Ir. 590
—— Rd., gen. (**D**) 935
—— Theoph., dn. Clonm. 600
—— Th., C. Exc. 282; C.I.R. 285; C. St. and Tx. 285
—— sir Th., Chambn. Lond. 493
—— Wm., K.C. 415
—— Wm. Geo., Q.C. 419
—— Wm. Hy., Pres. U.S.A. 102
—— Wm. T., bp. Glasg. and Gall. 544
Harrowby, lds. and E.
—— Dudley, 2nd ld. and 1st E., also 1st visc. Sandon, *q.v.*, form. hon. D. Ryder, *q.v.*, C.D.L. 243; Amb. Pr. 118; Amb. Russ. 125; F. Sec. 228; Jud. Com. P.C. 360; L.P.C. 188; Pres. B.C. 252
—— Dudley, 2nd E. of, form. Dudley Ryder, and visc. Sandon, *q.v.*, C.D.L. 243; K.G. 744; L.P.S. 241; P.C. 216
—— Dudl. Fr. St., 3rd E. of, form. visc. Sandon, *q.v.*, L.P.S. 241
Harsnet, Saml., abp. Yk. 486; bp. Norw. 455; bp. Chich. 433
Hart, Anthy. and sir A., K C. 415; Ld. Chanc. Ir. 577; P.C. 210; V. Chanc. 390
—— Ed. Hume, gen. (**D**) 896
—— Geo., adm. (**A**) 818
—— Geo. Vaugh., gen. (**A**) 861
—— Hy., K.B. 763
—— Hy., L.M. Dbln. 641
—— sir Hy., adm. (**H**) 844; K.C.H. 789
—— Hy. Geo., gen. (**D**) 905
—— Jno., Chest. H. 331
—— Jno., G. Leew. Isl. 727
—— sir Jno., L.M. Lond. 491
—— sir Rt., Amb. Ch. and Cor. 131; K.C.M.G. 798
—— Walt., bp. Norw. 455
—— Wm., Ld. Adv. 526
Hart-Dyke, *see* Dyke
Hartcup, Th., gen. (**A**) 861
Hartington, M. of, *see also* Cavendish and Devonshire
—— Wm., M. of, aft. 2nd D. of Dev., *q.v.*, C.Y.G. 298
—— Wm., M. of, aft. 3rd D. of Dev., *q.v.*, C.G.P. 299
—— Wm., M. of, aft. 4th D. of Dev., *q.v.*, L.L. Ir. 557; L. Treas. Ir. 560; M.H. 302; P.C. 199
—— Spenc. Compt. Cav., c.c. M. of, son of 7th D. of Dev., Ch. Sec. Ir. 563; L. Admy. 184; P.C. 217; Postm. G. 239; Sec. Ind. 236; U.S. War. 232; W. Sec. 232
Hartland, Th., ld., gen. (**B**) 867
Hartley, sir Ch. Aug., K.C.M.G. 798
—— Humphr. Rt., gen. (**D**) 885
—— Jas., gen. (**C**) 872
Hartman, Jul., K.C.B. 775
Hartpoole, *see* Harpoll
Hartstonge, Jno., bp. Dry. 601; bp. Oss. 620
—— sir Stand., B. Ex. Ir. 584
Hartwell, Brod., L.G. Gr. Hosp. 854
—— Wm., K.B. 759
Harty, Jos. Mark, K.H. 792
—— sir Rt. Way, L.M Dbln. 642
Harvest, Ed. Dougl., G. W. Austr. 707; gen. (**D**) 924
Harvey, Harvie, and **Hervey**
—— (or Hervœus), bp. Bgr. 425; bp. Ely, 434
—— (or Hausir) bp. Ork. 535
—— Albt. Hy. Andr., gen. (**D**) 911
—— ld. Alf., L.T. 161
—— Andr., gen. (**D**) 887
—— ld. Arth. Ch., bp. B. and W. 428
—— hon. Aug. Jno., aft. 3rd E. of Bristol, *q.v.*, L. Admy. 179; Ch. Sec. Ir. 562
—— Biss., K.H. 792
—— Ch. Rt. W., gen. (**D**) 917
—— Danl., G. Gsey. 668; gen. (**A**) 857
—— Ed. and sir E., adm. (**D**) 828; G.C.B. 770; K.C.B. 779
—— Ed., gen. (**B**) 865
—— Ed., gen. (**D**) 893
—— Eliab, K.C. 415
—— Ellab and sir E., adm. (**A**) 817; G.C.B. 768; K.C.B. 773
—— sir Felt. Elw. B., K.H. 789
—— Fras. and sir F., J.C.P. 379; S.L. 409
—— hon. Fk. Augs., aft. 4th E of Bristol, *q.v.*, bp. Cloy. 631; bp. Dry. 601
—— Fk., *see* ld. H., *infra*
—— sir Geo., Lt. T.L. 321
—— Geo. Fk., K.C.S.I. 802
—— Hy., adm. (**H**) 849
—— Hy., M. Chy. 395
—— Hy. and sir H., adm. (**A**) 816; K.B. 766
—— sir Hy., D. Arch. 420
—— Jas., K.H. 791
—— sir Jas., L.M. Lond. 490
—— Jno., dn. Her. 442
—— Jno. and sir J., adm. (**A**) 819; K.C.B. 776
—— Jno. and sir J., G. N. Brk. 695; G. N. Sc. 695; G. Newfd. 700; G. Pr. Ed. Isl. 699; gen. (**B**) 870; K.C.B. 776; K.C.H. 787
—— Jno. A., *see* ld. H., *infra*
—— Jno. Spr., M. Chy. and Acct. G. 397
—— Lionel, Amb. Spn. 124
—— sir Rt. Jno., gen. (**D**) 879
—— sir Seb., L.M. Lond. 491
—— Steph., K.B. 763
—— Th., adm. (**E**) 835
—— Th. and sir T., adm. (**A**) 819; K.C.B. 776
—— sir Walt., L.M. Lond. 489
—— Wm., Bl. M.P.A. 336; Clar. K.A. 328; Hps. P.A. 343; Norr. K.A. 329; Som. H. 332
—— hon. Wm., gen. (**A**) 859
—— ld. Wm., Amb. Fr. 113
Hervey, lds., *see also* Jermyn
—— Jno., ld., son of 1st E. of Bristol, L.P.S. 240; P.C. 198 V.C.H. 297
—— Jno. Augs., ld., son of 4th E. of Bristol, Amb. Tusc. 115
—— Fk. Wm., ld., aft. 5th E. and 1st M. of Bristol, *q.v.*, U.S.F. 229
Harvie, *see* Harvey

Harward, Ch., dn. Chich. 434; dn. Exr. 438
—— Th. Neth., gen. (**D**) 927
Harwedon, Rt. de, J. It. 369
Harwell, *see also* Harewell
—— Ed., K.B. 761
Harwood, *see also* Harewood
—— Ch., C.C.J. 403
Harynton, *see also* Harrington
—— Th. Grey, ld., K.B. (1491) 758
Haryot, *see also* Harriott
—— Wm., L.M. Lond. 490
Hascard, Greg., dn. Winds. 474
Haseley, Jno., dn. Chich. 434
Haselshaw, Walt. de, bp. B. and W. 427; dn. Wells, 428
Haskett, Elias, G. Bah. Isl. 716
Hassal, Jno., dn. Norw. 456
Hassan, Cph. Aba. 98
—— (Muley), S. Mco. 101
—— (Mohammed) C.I.E. 807
Hassard, Jno., gen. (**C**) 875
Hastings, sir Ch., G.C.H. 786; gen. (**A**) 860
—— Ch. Holl., K.H. 790
—— Ed., K.B. (1400) 756
—— Ed. (son of Wm. 1st ld. H.), K.B. (1475) 757
—— Ed., *see also* ld. H., *infra*
—— Fras. Dec., adm. (**G**) 842
—— Fras. Wm., gen. (**D**) 925
—— Geo., K.B. 759
—— hon. Geo. Fowl., adm. (**D**) 833; (**E**) 834
—— Grah., Q.C. 419
—— Hy., Som. H. 332; R. Cr. P.A. 335
—— Jas., dn. Ach. 614
—— Jno., K.B. 758
—— sir Th., adm. (**D**) 831; K.C.B. 778; St. O. 261
—— Warren, Adm. and G.G. Ind. 648; P.C. 209
—— Wm., Nottm. P.A. 343; Ptc. P.A. 337; Som. H. 332
Hastings, lds., *see also* Hoo and H.
—— Wm., 1st ld., K.G. 736; M.M. 246
—— Fras., ld., aft. 2nd E. of Huntingdon, *q.v.*, K.B. 760
—— Hy., ld., aft. 3rd E. of Huntingdon, *q.v.*, K.B. 760
—— Fras., 1st M. of, form. E. of Moira, *q.v.*, Const. T.L. 321; G. Mlta. 671; G.C.B. 767; G.C.H. 786; M.G.O. 259
Hastings of Loughborough, sir Edw., aft. ld., K.G. 738; L.W.S. 323
Haswell, Wm. Hy., adm. (**H**) 851
Hatch, Geo. Cl., gen. (**D**) 923
—— Wm. Sp., gen. (**D**) 916
Hatchard, Th. Goodw., bp. Mtius. 684
Hatchell, Jno., A.G. Ir. 588; S.G. Ir. 590
Hatcliffe, W., S. St. 222
Hatfield, Th. de, bp. Dham. 478
—— Walt., dn. Llin. 623
Hatherley, *see also* Atherley
—— Wm. P., ld., form. sir W. P. Wood, *q.v.*
Hatherton, Ed. Jno., ld., form. E. J. Littleton, *q.v.*, L.L. Staffs, 312
Hathorn, *see also* Hawthorn
—— Geo., adm. (**G**) 842
Hathway, Ham. R., gen. (**D**) 914
Hatsell, Hy. and sir H., B. Ex. 384; S.L. 411
Hatton, hon. Ch., G. Gsey. 668
—— Chr., K.B. (1603) 761
—— sir Chr., C.Y.G. 298; K.G. 739; Ld. Chanc. 356; V.C.H. 296
—— Chr., *see also* ld. H., *infra*
—— Ed. Finch-, C. St. 284; U.S. Home, 227
—— Geo., C. St. Ir. 568
—— Jno., gen. (**B**) 867
—— Rd., M. Chy. 394
—— (or Hutton), Rt., S.L. 409
—— Villiers Fras., adm. (**D**) 828; (**G**) 840
Hatton, lds.
—— Chr., aft. sir C. and ld., Compt. H. 292; G. Gsey. 668; K.B. 763; P.C. 190
Hatwa, Mahar. of, K.C.I.E. 805
Haugh, Jno., J.C.P. 378
Haughton, sir Graves C., K.H. 790
—— Jno., gen. (**D**) 934
—— Jno. Colp., gen. (**D**) 922
Hault, Nichs., G. Ch. Isl. 667
Haultain, Ch., K.H. 790
—— Fras., gen. (**D**), 890
—— Fras. Mitch., gen. (**D**) 912
Haunsar, Wm. de, J. It. 367
Hausir, *see* Harvey
Hauteyn, Ham., J. It. 368
Havelock, Arth. Elib. and sir A., G. Nat. 680; G. Nev. 730; G. Trin. 723; G. W. Afr. Sett. 688; K.C.M.G. 798
—— Hy. and sir H., gen. (**D**) 891
—— sir Hy. M., aft. Havelock-Allan, gen. (**D**) 918; K.C.B. 778
—— Wm., K.H. 789
Havelock-Allan, *see* Allan
Haverhull, Wm., L.H.T. 152
Havers, Jno., Bl. M. P.A. 337
Haversham, Jno., 1st ld., L. Admy. 176
Haviland and **Havilland**
—— Jno. V. S. de, R. Cr. P.A. 336; Yk. H. 334
—— Pet. de and sir P., Blf. Gsey. 669
—— T. H., G. Pr. Ed. Isl. 699
—— Wm., gen. (**A**) 858
Hawarden, Corn., 4th visc., aft. 1st E. de Montalt, *q.v.*, L.L. Tipp. 571
Hawes, Benj. and sir B., Dep. Sec. at W. 234; K.C.B. 782; U.S. W. and C. 231; U.S. War, 233
—— Geo. Har., gen. (**D**) 925
—— Jas., L.M. Lond. 490
Hawford, Ph., dn. Worc. 473
Hawick, Andr. de, Sec St. Sc. 501
Hawise, Q.C.E. 7
Hawke, sir Ed., aft. 1st. ld. H., adm. (**A**) 814; K.B. 765; L. Admy. 179; P.C. 202
Hawker, Ed., adm. (**D**) 825
—— Hy. Saml., adm. (**H**) 851
—— Jos., Clar. K.A. 328; Norr. K.A. 330; R. Cr. P.A. 335; Richm. H. 334
—— sir Saml., gen. (**B**) 868; G.C.H. 787; K.C.H. 788
Hawker—*cont.*
—— sir Th., gen. (**A**) 863; (**C**) 874; K.C.H. 789
Hawkes, Rt., gen. (**D**) 887
—— Th. Sp., gen. (**D**) 931
Hawkesbury, lds.
—— Ch., 1st ld., form. C. Jenkinson, *q.v.*, aft. 1st E. of Liverpool, *q.v.*, C.D.L. 243; Pres. BT. 268; Sec. at W. 234
—— Rt. B., ld. (R. B. Jenkinson), aft. 2nd E. of Liverpool, *q.v.*, B.C. 252; B.T. 268; F. Sec. 228; H. Sec. 227; M.M. 247; P.C. 206; W.C.P. 319
Hawkeslow, Wm., Clar. K.A. 328
Hawkey, Hy. Aitch., gen. (**D**) 891
Hawkin, Geo. Cr., gen. (**D**) 929
Hawkins, Abrm. Mills, adm. (**H**) 847
—— Cæs. Hy., Pres. Coll. Surg. 939
—— Ch., Mast. Coll. Surg. 939
—— Ed. Linds., gen. (**D**) 930
—— Fras., dn. Chich. 434
—— Fras. S., gen. (**D**) 888
—— Hy. and sir H., J. Ex. D. 386; J.Q.B.D. 374; Q.C. 418
—— Jas., bp. Drom. 605; bp. Rph. 602; dn. Emly, 628
—— Jno., Ulst. K.A. 572
—— Jno. Summ., gen. (D) 905; K.C.M.G. 797
—— Saml., gen. (**D**) 891
—— Th., dn. Clonf. 637
—— Wm., S.L. 411
—— Wm. (No. 1), Ulst. K.A. 572
—— Wm. and sir W. (No. 2), Ulst. K.A. 572
Hawkshaw, Jno., gen. (**D**) 889
Hawles, Jno. and sir J., K.C. 415; S.G. 401
Hawley, Hy., G. Bdoes. 719
—— Hy., gen. (**B**) 864
—— Rt. Beauf., gen. (**D**) 909
—— Th., Carl. H. 339; Clar. K.A. 328; R. Bl. P.A. 344; R. Cr. P.A. 335
—— Wm., G. Bdoes. 719
—— Wm. Hamb., G. Mtius. 684; gen. (**D**) 931
Hawman (or Haghman), Nichs., B. Ex. 383
Haws, Jno., S.L. 407
Hawtayne, Ch. Jno. Sibth., adm. (**D**) 827
Hawte, Th., K.B. 759
—— Wm., K.B. 757
Hawthorne, Ch. St., C. Exc. Ir. 567
—— Rt. Jno., gen. (**D**) 910
Haxey, Th., M. Chy. 394
Hay —, *see also* Hey—
Hay, *see also* Haye
—— Alexr. and sir A. (Easter Kennet), Ld. Clk. Reg. 525; Ld. Sess. 518
—— Alexr. (Fosterseat), Ld. Sess. 519
—— Alexr. and sir A. (Newton), Ld. Sess. 519; Sec. St. Sc. 502
—— sir Alexr. (Whitburgh), Ld. Clk. Reg. 525
—— sir Alexr. (Landor), Ld. Clk. Reg. 525
—— sir Alexr., S. St. (1609) 223
—— Alexr. Leith, gen. (**A**) 860

Hay—*cont.*
— Andr., gen. (**C**) 873
— Andr. L. and sir A., Clk. O. 260; G. Bmda. 701; K.H. 790
— Ch., Ld. Sess. 520
— ld. Ch., gen. (**C**) 871
— Ch. Cr., gen. (**D**) 893
— Ch. Murr., G. Mtius. 684; gen. (**D**) 885
— hon. Ed., Amb. Pgl. 124; G. Bdoes. 720
— Ed. Hay Drummond- and sir E., G. St. Xtr. 729; G. St. Hel. (1854) 682
— Ed. Wm. Aur. Drummond-, Amb. Mxco. 132
— Fras., c.c. ld. H., K.B. (1610) 762
— Geo., L. Admy. 178-9
— Geo., Ld. Sess. 518
— Geo. and sir G., Ch. Lond. 422; D. Arch. 421; J. Adm. Ct. 423; J. Pr. Ct. 421; K. Adv. 422; Vic. Gen. 422
— sir Geo., aft. 1st visc. Dupplin, and 1st E. of Kinnoull, *q.v.*, Ld. Chanc. Sc. 515; Ld. Clk. Reg. 525
— sir Gilb., aft. c.c. E. of Erroll, *q.v.*, L.H. Const. Sc. (1321) 507
— Jas., adm. (**H**) 846
— Jas., bp. Ross, 535
— Jas., gen. (**D**) 879
— sir Jas., Compt. Sc. 498
— sir Jas., gen. (**A**) 862; K.C.H. 788
— ld. Jas.. gen. (**D**) 882
— Jas., c.c. ld. H., aft. 1st. visc. Doncaster and E. of Carlisle, *q.v.*, M.G.W. 296; K.B. (1625) 762
— Jas. Beckford Lew., adm. (**G**) 842
— Jas. Shaw, G. Gamb. 686; G. Si. Le. 685
— Jno., adm. (**H**) 848
— Jno., K.C.M.G. 797
— sir Jno., Ld. Sess. 517 and 519
— ld. Jno., adm. (**B**) 821; (**D**) 829; (**E**) 836; G.C.B. 771; K.C.B. 781; L. Admy. 183-4-5-6
— Jno. Bak. Port., adm. (**H**) 848
— Jno. Ch., gen. (**D**) 929
— Jno. Ch. Dalr. and sir C., adm. (**E**) 835; (**F**) 838; K.C.B. 781; L. Admy. 184-5; P.C. 219
— Jno. Cr., gen. (**D**) 933
— Jno. H. Drummond- and sir J., Amb. Mco. 132; G.C.M.G. 795; K.C.B. 783; P.C. 221
— Lor. Geddes, G. Tob. 724
— Ph. Jas., gen. (**D**) 881
— Rt. Jno., gen. (**D**) 928
— Rt. Wm., U.S.C. 235; U.S.W. and C. 232
— Th., dn. Ferns, 623
— Th., Ld. Sess. 518
— Th., Sec. St. Sc. 502
* Prob. all same pers.
— Th., Ld. Sess. 520
— Wm., bp. Cnr. 604
— Wm., bp. Mor. 534
— Wm., C.C.P. 261
— Wm., C. Cus. 276
— Woulfe, gen. (**D**) 929
Hay of Yester, lds., *see* Yester
Haya, Rt. de, J. It. 368
Haydell, Jno. de, A.G. 398
Haydock, Gilb., M. Chy. 394
— sir Hy. de, C.D.L. 242
Haydon, *see also* Heydon
Haydon—*cont.*
— sir Jno., G. Bmda. 701
— Wm., adm. (**H**) 847
— sir Wm., L.G.O. 259
Haye, *see also* Hay
— Jno. de la, K.B. 754
— Wm. de la, L.D. Ir. 550
Hayes, Courtn. Osb., adm. (**H**) 848
— Edmd., S.G. Ir. 590; J.Q.B. Ir. 579
— Geo. and sir G., J.Q.B. 373; P.P. 418; S.L. 413
— Horace, C. Tx. 285
— Jas. Th., bp. Trin. 723
— Jno., adm. (**D**) 824
— sir Jno., L.M. Lond. 491
— Jno. Mont., adm. (**H**) 849
— Ruth. B., Pres. U.S.A. 103
— Saml., C. St. Ir. 568
Hayland, Alfr. Th., gen. (**D**) 903
Hayley, Th., dn. Chich. 434
— Wm., dn. Chich. 434
Hayme, *see* Heym
Haynes, *see* Haines and Heynes
Hayter, sir Arth. D., L.T. 162; U.S. War, 233
— Thos., bp. Lond. 452; bp. Norw. 455; P.C. 200
— Wm. Good. and sir W., J.A.G. 937; P.C. 215; P.P. 417; Sec. Tr. 163
Haythorne, Edm., gen. (**D**) 903; K.C.B. 780
Hayton, W., S. St. 222
Hayward, *see also* Heyward
— Abm., Q.C. 417
— Hy. Blak., gen. (**D**) 929
— Jno., M. Chy. 395
— Wm., S.L. 412
Haywood, *see* Heywood
Head, sir Edm. Walk., G. Can. 692; G. N. Brk. 696; K.C.B. 783; P.C. 216; P.L.C. 262
— sir Fras. Bond, G. Upp. Can. 692; K.C.H. 789; K.H. 790; P.C. 217
— Jno., dn. Killoe. 637
— Michl., gen. (**B**) 868
Headfort, E. and M. of
— Th., 1st M. of, form. 2nd E. of Bective, *q.v.*, K.P. 750
— Th., 2nd M. of, K.P. 751; L.L. Cav. 569
— Th., 3rd M. of, K.P. 752; L.L. Meath, 570
Headington, Rd. Cl., Pres. Coll. Surg. 939
Headlam, Th. Em., J.A.G. 937; P.C. 216; Q.C. 417
Headley, Th., S.L. 409
***Headda,** bp. Lich. 443
*— (St.), bp. Winch. 470
* Prob. same pers.
Headulacus, bp. Elm. 454
Heald, Geo., K.C. 416
Heale, Jno., S.L. 408
Heard, Isaac and sir I., Bl. M. P.A. 336; Clar. K.A. 328; Gart. K.A. 328; Lanc. H. 333; Norr. K.A. 329
Heardred, bp. Dunw. 454
— bp. Hex. 480
Hearn, Ch. S., C.I.E. 806
— Geo., gen. (**D**) 929
Hearsey, Jno. B., gen. (**D**) 887; K.C.B. 778
Heastey, Geo. Bayles, gen. (**D**) 925
Heath, Alf. Hales, gen. (**D**) 920
— Dougl. D., C.C.J. 403
Heath—*cont.*
— Ed. K.B. 764
— Geo. Th., P.P. 416; S.L. 413
— Jno. and sir J., J.C.P. 379; S.L. 412
— Jno. Coulson, gen. (**D**) 901
— sir Leop. Geo., adm. (**E**) 836; (**F**) 839; K.C.B. 779
— Nichs., abp. Yk. 486; bp. Roch. 460; bp. Worc. 473; Ld. Chanc. 355
— Rd. and sir R., B. Ex. 384; S.L. 410
— Rt. and sir R., A.G. 399; C.J.C.P. 375; C.J.K.B. 370; J.K.B. 372; Rec. Lond. 494; S.G. 401; S.L. 409
— Th., M. Chy. 395
— Wm. Andr. Jas., adm. (**H**) 851
Heathcote, Edm., adm. (**E**) 835; (**F**) 839
— Geo., C. Tx. 284
— Geo., L.M. Lond. 491
— sir Gilb., L.M. Lond. 491
— sir Hy., adm. (**A**) 820; (**G**) 840
— Ralph, Amb. G. St. 121
— sir Wm., L.L. Hants, 311
— sir Wm., P.C. 218
— Wm. Saml., gen. (**D**) 877
Heathfield, lds.
— Geo. Augs., 1st ld., form. hon. Ceo. Elliot, *q.v.*
— Fras. Augs., 2nd ld., gen. (**A**) 860
Heathobertus, *see* Hecbertus
Heathored or **Heathured,** bp. Lindisf. 478
Heaton, *see also* Heton
— Rd., dn. Clonf. 637
Heber, K. Ir. 20
— Reg., bp. Calc. 653
Heca, bp. Sels. 432
Hecbertus (or Heathobertus), bp. Lond. 451
Hector, Jas., K.C.M.G. 798
Hedda, bp. Sels. 432
Hedges, Ch. and sir C., J. Adm. Ct. 423; J. Pr. Ct. 421; P.C. 194; S. St. 224
Hedian, *see* Hodian
Hedwige, Q. Pld. 91
Heende (or Hyende or Hind), Jno., L.M. Lond. 489
Heer, Gerr. de, G. Ceyl. 672
— J., Pres. Sw. C. 31
Heera, Sahib, &c. C.I.E. 808
Hegham, Rog. de, A.G. 398; B. Ex. 383
Hegwood, Rt., G. I. Man, 666
Heiden, Louis Count de, K.C.B. 775
Heigham, Nichs., dn. Linc. 448
Helena-Aug.-Vict. (dau. Q. Vict.), Pr. E. 16; Cr. Ind. 809
Heliogabalus, Emp. Ro. 47
Hellen, Rt., J.C.P. Ir. 582; S.G. Ir. 589
Hellmuth, Isaac, bp. Huron, 693
Helmstan, bp. Winch. 470
Helot, Wilh., G. C.G.H. 678
Helpman, Ph. Augs., adm. (**H**) 851
Helps, Arth., K.C.B. 783
Helwais, sir Gerv., Lt. T.L. 321
Hely, Jas. Pr., gen. (**D**) 892; K.H. 792
— sir Jno., C.B. Ex. Ir. 583
— sir Jno., C.J.C.P. Ir. 580

Hely-Hutchinson, *see* Hutchinson
Helynn or **Helyun,** Walt. de, J.C.P. 377; J. It. 368; J.K.B. 371; Jy. 365
Hemel, bp. Lich. 443
Hemenhale, Th. de, bp. Norw. 454
Hemery, Jas., dn. Jsey. 668
Hemming, Geo. Wirgm., Q.C. 419
Hemphill, Andr. T., gen. (**D**) 896
—— C. H., S.L. Ir. 593
Hempsham, Walt. de, abp. Cant. 430
Hemynborgh, Rt., A.G. Ir. 588
Henchman, Humphr., bp. Lond. 452; bp. Sal. 467; P.C. 190
—— Humphr., Ch. Lond. 422; J. Adm. Ct. 423
Henden, Ed. and sir E., B. Ex. 384; S.L. 409
Henderson, Alexr., L. Prov. Edinb. 548
—— C. A., Amb. Pgy. 136
—— Edm. Y. W. and sir E., C.C.P. 261; K.C.B. 783
—— Geo., adm. (**H**) 844
—— Geo. Aug., gen. (**D**) 881; K.H. 791
—— Jas., K.H. 791
—— Jas., L.J. Clk. 516; Ld. Adv. 525
—— Jno. Wm., K.H. 792
—— Jno. Wm. Cleland, gen. (**D**) 930
—— Rt., adm. (**D**) 825
—— Saml. Hood, adm. (**H**) 852
—— Th., adm. (**D**) 832
—— Th., Ld. Sess. 519
—— Wm., gen. (**D**) 900
—— Wm. Geo., dn. Carl. 476
—— Wm. Willmott, adm. (**D**) 829; K.H. 791
Henderson - Durham, *see* Durham
Hendry, Wm., adm. (**H**) 846
Hene, Hy., B. Ex. Ir. 584; C.B. Ex. Ir. 583; S.L. Ir. 591
Heneage, Algn. Ch. F., adm. (**E**) 837
—— Edw., C.D.L. 243; P.C. 220
—— Geo., dn. Linc. 448
—— sir T., C.D.L. 242; V.C.H. 296
Hengham, Ralph de, C.J.C.P. 375; C.J.K.B. 369; J.C.P. 377; J.K.B. 371; Jy. 365
—— Wm. de, J. It. 367
Henghell, Danl. van den, G. C.G.H. 678
Hengist, K. E. 1, 3
Heniker, *see* Henniker
Henley, Jos. Warn., P.C. 215; Pres. B.T. 269
—— Rt., C. Cus. 274
—— Rt., *see* ld. H. *infra*
Henley, lds.
Henley Family.
—— Rt. and sir R., aft. 1st ld. H. and E. of Northington, *q.v.*, A.G. 399; K.C. 415; L.H.S. 287; Ld. Chanc. 357; L.K. 357; P.C. 200
—— hon. Rt., aft. 2nd E. of Northington, *q.v.*, Tell. Ex. 168
Eden Family.
—— Morton, 1st ld., form. sir M. Eden, *q.v.*, G.C.B. 771
Henley, lds.—*cont.*
—— Fk. Mort., 2nd ld., B.T. 268
Henlyn, Wm., L.M. Lond. 490
Henn, Wm., J.K.B. Ir. 579
Hennessey, Jas. Bab. Nicks., C.I.E. 807
—— Jno. Pope and sir J., G. Bah. Isl. 716; G. Bdoes. 719; G. Bdoes. &c. 721; G. H. Kong, 673; G.Labn. 675; G. Mtius. 684; G. W. Afr. 688; K.C.M.G. 797
Hennibal, *see* Hannibal
Henniker and **Heniker**
—— Albor., Q.C. 419
—— hon. sir Br. Tr., gen. (**B**) 866
—— hon. major Jacob, adm. (**D**) 825
Henning, Shurl. gen. (**D**) 922
Henningberg, Rt. de, Ld. Chanc. Ir. 574
Hennington, Rd. de, J. It. 368; Jy. 365
Hennis, Wm. How., gen. (**D**) 899
Henrietta (g. dau. Jas. I.), Pr. E. 13
—— (dau. Jas. II.), Pr. E. 13
—— -Maria (dau. Chas. I.), Pr. E. 13
—— -Maria, Q.C.E. 8
***Henry** (of London), abp. Dbln. 615; Jy. 364
*—— bp. Clonm. 600
*—— bp. Emly, 625
*—— (2), bp. Gall. 538
*—— (of Wessenberch), bp. Kild. 616
*—— (or Maurice), bp. Kilf. 635
*—— bp. Llff. 449
*—— (2), bp. Ork. 535
*—— bp. Ross. 535
*—— bp. Wford. 626
*—— dn. Her. 442
*—— dn. Sal. 468
* Prob. some same pers. Comp. dates.
*—— (of Saxe), C.P.R. 68
*—— (2), D. Brk. 69
—— (2), D. Tny. 57
—— (Pr. Pruss.), G.C.B. 773
—— K. Bma. 59
—— K. Jsm. 97
—— (2), K. Pgl. 88
—— K. Pld. 91
—— K. Scy. 55
—— Ld. Sess. 517
—— (son Wm. I.), Pr. E. 9
—— (g. son Hen. I., aft. Hen. II.), Pr. E. 9
—— (son Hen. II.), Pr. E. 9
—— (son K. John, aft. Hen. III.), Pr. E. 9
—— (son Hen. III.), Pr. E. 9
—— (son of Edw. I.), Pr. E. 10
—— (g. son. Edw. III.), Pr. E. 11
—— (iss. Edw. III.), Pr. E. 11
—— (son. Hen. IV., aft. Hen. V.), Pr. E. 11; Pr. W.E. 8
—— (son Hen. V.), Pr. E. 11
—— (iss. of Hen. V., aft. Hen. VII.), Pr. E. 12
—— (son Hen., VII., aft. Hen. VIII.), Pr. E. 12; Pr. W.E. 8
—— (g. son Hen. VII.), Pr. E. 12
—— (son Hen. VIII.), Pr. E. 12
—— (son Chas. I.), Pr. E. 13
—— I., Emp. E.E. 51
—— I., Emp. Hti. 105
Henry—*cont.*
—— I., M. Brg. 65
—— I., C. Anht. 66
—— I. and II., D. Bdy. 28
—— I. and II., D. Lne. 29, 30
—— I. and II., D. Su. 80
—— I. to III., D. Sxy. 77
—— I. to III., K. Nav. 88
—— I to IV., D. Brk. 69
—— I. to IV., K. Cle. 85-6
—— III. (K. Cle.), K.G. 734
—— I. to V., C. Lux. 84
—— . to V., K. Fr. 23-4-5
—— II. (K. Fr.), K.G. 738
—— III. (K. Fr.), K.G. 738
—— IV. (K. Fr.), K.G. 739
—— I. to VI., Pr. Mkg. 74
—— I. to VII., E. Gmy. 61-2
—— I. to VIII., K.E. 4, 5
(*See also under* Pr. Wales, [illegible] York and Pr. E, *supra*)
—— I. and II. (K.E.), L.H.A. 1[illegible]
—— II. (K.E.), K. Ir. 22
—— VI. (K.E.), K.B. 756
—— I. to X., D. Bva. 67
—— II., D. Aus. 58
—— II., M. Aus. 58
—— II. to IV., D. Bbt. 29
—— XI. to XIV., Pr. R. Sch. 7[illegible]
—— XX. to XXII., Pr. R. G[illegible] 76
—— -Benedict (g. son Jas. II[illegible] Pr. E. 14
—— -Borwin, I. and II., [illegible] Mkg. 74
—— -Crassus, K. Nav. 85
—— -Fredk. (son Jas. I.), Pr. [illegible] 12; Pr. W.E. 8
—— -Fredk. (g. son Geo. II., a[illegible] D. of Cumb., *q.v.*), Pr. E. 14
—— -Julius, D. Brk. 70
—— Chas. St., gen. (**D**) 908
—— Jno., adm. (**A**) 816
—— Jno., gen. (**D**) 886
—— Wm., dn. Killoe. 637
Henryson, Ed., Ld. Sess. 5[illegible]
Henslow, Jno., Sr. N. 25
Henshawe, Jos., bp. Pbo[illegible] 458; dn. Chich. 434
Henyngham, Jno., K.B. 75[illegible]
Heodwulf, K.E. 2
Hepburn, sir Ad., Ld. Se[illegible] 519
—— Fras., gen. (**C**) 874
—— Geo., bp. Isl. 539; L.H. Sc. 497
—— Geo. Buch., Bar. Ex. [illegible] 524; J. Adm. Sc. 524
—— Hy. Poole, gen. (**D**) 907
—— Jas., bp. Mor. 534; L.H. Sc. 497
—— Jno., bp. Brn. 531
—— Jno., bp. Dnbl. 532
—— Patr., bp. Mor. 534; Sec. [illegible] Sc. 502
—— Rd., C. Cus. Sc. 504
—— Wm., Ld. Clk. Reg. 525
Heppescotes, Th. de, J.C[illegible] 377
Hepton, *see* Hopton
Heraclius, I. and II., E[illegible] E.E. 50
Herbert, bp. Glasg. 53[illegible] L.G.C. Sc. 506; Ld. Cha[illegible] Sc. 514
—— Arth., *see* ld. H. of Torb[illegible] *infra*
—— Arth. Jas. and sir A., g[illegible] (**D**) 905; K.C.B. 781
—— Ch., gen. (**D**) 886
—— Ch., gen. (**D**) 904
—— Ch., gen. (**D**) 919
—— Denn., gen. (**A**) 863

Herbert—*cont.*
— Ed. and sir E., A.G. 399; S.G. 401
— sir Ed., C.J.C.P. 375
— sir Ed., C.J. Chest. 386; C.J.K.B. 370; K.C. 415; P.C. 192; S.L. 411
— Ed., *see* ld. H. of Chirbury, *infra*
— Fk. Anstr., adm. (**E**) 837
— hon. Geo., dn. Her. 442
— Geo. Flower, adm. (**H**) 849
— Hy., *see* ld. H. of Chirbury, *infra*
— Hy. Arth., Ch. Sec. Ir. 563; L.L. Kerry, 569; P.C. 216
— Jno., A.G., 398
— Jno., dn. Wells, 429
— sir Jno., Chanc. Gart. 746; S. St. 223
— Jno. M., C.C.J. 403
— hon. Percy Eg. and sir P., gen. (**D**) 902; K.C.B. 780; P.C. 217; Tr. H. 292
— Ph., K.B. 763
— *see also* ld. H. of Cardiff, *infra*
— Rd. (?), K.B. 757
— Rd. Townsh., C. Acc. Ir. 567; C. St. Ir. 568
— Rt., S.L.R. 271
— hon. Rt., B.T. 264-5
* Prob. same pers.
— Rt. Geo. Wyndh. and sir R., K.C.B. 784; Sec. M.G. 799; U.S.C. 235-6
— hon. Sidn., *see* ld. H. of Lea, *infra*
— Th. and sir T., adm. (**D**) 829; K.C.B. 777; L. Admy. 183
— Wm., K.B. 756
— Wm., aft. ld. Powys, *q.v.*, K.B. (1603) 761
— hon. Wm., dn. Manch. 481; Wdn. Chr. Ch. Manch. 481
— hon. Wm., G. Gibr. 669; gen. (**C**) 871
— hon. Wm. Hy., gen. (**D**) 927

Herbert of Chepstow, lds.
Herbert Family.
— Wm., 1st ld., aft. E. of Pembroke, *q.v.*, K.G. 736
Somerset Family.
— Ch., ld., form. sir Ch. Somerset, *q.v.*, aft. 1st E. of Worcester, *q.v.*, L.C.H. 294
— Wm. and sir W., aft. ld. W., and 3rd E. of Worcester, *q.v.*, K.B. (1547) 760; M.H. 301

Herbert of Chirbury, lds.
1st Creation.
— Ed., aft. 1st ld. H. of C., K.B. 761
2nd Creation.
— Hy., 1st ld., B.T. 263-4; Coff. H. 293

Herbert of Cardiff, lds.
— sir Wm., aft. 1st ld. H. of C., and 1st E. of Pembroke, *q.v.*, K.G. 738
— Ph., aft. 4th E. of Pembr. and 1st E. of Montg., *q.v.*, K.B. 761
— Ch., c.c. ld. H. of C. (son of Ph., 4th E. of Pembr. and 1st E. of Montg.), K.B. 762
— Geo. Aug., ld., aft. 11th E. of Pembr., &c., *q.v.*, P.C. 204; V.C.H. 297

Herbert of Lea, lds.
— Sidney, ld., form. hon. S. Herbert, C. Sec. 234; H. Sec. 227; L.T. 162; P.C. 214; Sec. Adm. 186; Sec. at W. 234; Sec. B.C. 254; W. Sec. 232

Herbert, of Torbay, lds.
— Arth. and hon. A., aft. ld. H. of T. and E. of Torrington, *q.v.*, adm. (**A**) 813; L. Admy. 176; P.C. 193

Herbillon, Genl., K.C.B. 778

Hercules, *see also* Ercole
— D. Mda. 5
— I. and II., Pr. Mno. 31

Herefast, *see* Arfastus

Hereford, Ch., gen. (**D**) 928
— Geoff., bp. Kild. 617

Hereford, Earls of
— Wm. FitzOsborne, E. of, Ch. Jr. (Wm. I.) 362
De Bohun Family.
— Humphr. de B., 1st E. of, W.C.P. 317
— Humphr. de B., 2nd E. of, J. It. 368
— Humphr. de B., 7th E. of, K.G. 733
Devereux Family.
— Walt., 1st visc., form. ld. Ferrers of Chartly, *q.v.*
— Walt., 2nd visc., aft. E. of Essex, *q.v.*, K.G. 738
— Hy., 14th visc., C.G.A. 300; C.G.P. 300; P.C. 211

Herefrid, bp. Winch. 470

Heremon, K. Ir. 20

Herennius, M., C. Ro. 45

Herewald, bp. Llff. 449
— bp. Shbn. 466

Herewin, bp. Lich. 443

Herford, Rt. de, Ch. Ex. Ir. 561

Herierd (or Heriet), Rd. de, Jy. 363

Heriot, Fk. Geo., gen. (**D**) 879

Herlaston, Wm. de, J. It. 369; L.K. 354; M. Chy. 393

Herle, sir Rt., L.H.A. 172; W.C.P. 318
— Th., Wdn. Chr. Ch. Manch. 481
— Wm. de, C.J.C.P. 375; J.C.P. 377; S.L. 406

Herlewin, *see* Harlewin

Herman, bp. Sal. 466; bp. Wltn. 466
— C. Hlt. 81
— I. to IV., D. Su. 80
— I. to IX., M. Bdn. 66-7
— Billing, D. Sxy. 77
— sir Jno., adm. (**A**) 813

Hermenric, K.E. 1

Hermington, Ad. de, L. Treas. Ir. 558

Hernun, bp. St. Dav. 464

Heron, D. C., S.L. Ir. 593
— Ed., and sir E., B. Ex. 384; K.B. 761; S.L. 408
— Hy., K.B. 763
— Pet., gen. (**A**) 861
— sir Rd., Ch. Sec. Ir. 562

Herosee, F. F., Pres. Sw.C. 31

Herrera, J. J., Pres. Mex. 103
— V., Pres. C.R. 106

Herrick, Benj. B. gen. (**D**) 921

Herries, Ch. Jno., C. Exc. 282; C.I.R. 285; C. St. and Tx. 285; K.C.B. 783

Herries—*cont.*
*— Jno. Ch., Ch. Ex. 165; L.T. 159; M.M. 247; P.C. 211; Pres. B.C. 254; Pres. B.T. 268; Sec. Tr. 163; Sec. at W. 234
*— Jno. Ch., Reg. and Sec. Bath 785
(?) same pers.
— Wm. Lew. and sir W., gen. (**D**) 882; K.C.H. 787; Regr. and Sec. Bath 785

Herries, lds.
— Marm., ld., L.L. Kirkc. 510; L.L. Yorks. E.R. 313

Herring, Thos., abp. Cant. 431; abp. Yk. 486; bp. Bgr. 426; dn. Roch. 461; P.C. 199
— Wm., dn. St. As. 463

Herringham, Wm. Allan, adm. (**H**) 847

Herschel and **Herschell**
— Farr., *see* ld. H., *infra*
— sir Jno. Fk. Wm., K.H. 790; M.M. 247

Herschell, lds.
— Farr. and sir F., aft. 1st ld. H., Jud. Com. P.C. 362; Ld. Chanc. 358; P.C. 220; Q.C. 419; S.G. 403

Hertelpole (or Hertpoll), Geoffr. de, J. It. 369; Rec. Lond. 493
— Jno., M. Chy. 394

Hertenburg, Jno., G. Ceyl. 672

Hertesburg, Giles de, M.M. 245

Hertford, *see also* Herford
— Rt. de, dn. Sal. 468
— Rt. de, J.C.P. 377

Hertford, E. and M. of
Seymour Family.
1st Creation.
— Ed., 1st E. of, form. visc. Beauchamp, *q.v.*, *also* D. of Somerset, *q.v.*, K.B. 760; K.G. 738; L.H.T. 139, 154
2nd Creation.
— Wm., 2nd E. of, form. Wm. Seymour, *q.v.*, aft. 1st M. and D. of Somerset, *q.v.*, K.G. 740; P.C. 190
— Algn., 7th E. of, form. ld. A. Percy, *q.v.*, aft. E. of Northd., Egremont, &c., *q.v.*
Seymour-Conway Family.
— Fras., 1st E. of., form. 2nd ld. Conway, aft. 1st E. of Yarmouth, and M. of Hertford, *q.v.*, K.G. 742; L.C.H. 295; L.L. Ir. 557; L.L. Montg. 315; L.L. Warw. 312; M.H. 302; P.C. 201
— Fras. 2nd M. of, L.C.H. 295; L.L. Warw. 312; L.W.S. 323; K.G. 743; M.H. 302
— Fras. Ch., 3rd M. of, form. E. of Yarmouth, *q.v.*, K.G. 743
— Rd., 4th M. of, form. E. of Yarmouth, *q.v.* K.G 744
— Fras. H. G., 5th M. of, form. F. H. G. Seymour, *q.v.*, G.C.B. 773; L.C.H. 295; P.C. 218

Hertley, Jno. de, bp. Roch. 460

Hertpoll, *see* Hertelpole

Hertzburg, Fk. Aug. K.C.B. 775

Hervey, *see* Harvey

Herwynton, Ad. de, M. Chy. 393

Heseltine, Alb., adm. (**H**) 850
Hesill, Wm., B. Ex. 383
Hesketh, Jno., Lanc. (**H**) 333; Ptc. P.A. 337
Hesse, Alexr., Pr. of, G.C.B. 771
—— Ern., gr. D. of, G.C.B. 773
—— Ern., Pr. of, G.C.B. 768
—— Fk. Wm. Louis, Pr., aft. gr. D. of, K.G. 744
Hesse-Barchfield, Ph. Ern., Pr. of, G.C.B. 768
Hesse-Darmstadt, Geo. Pr. of, G. Gibr. 669; gen. (**C**) 871
Hessein, Sh. Pers. 99
Hessey, Wm. Hy., gen. (**D**) 918
Hethersett, Jas., gen. (**B**) 866
Heton, *see also* Heaton
—— Mart., dn. Winch. 471; bp. Ely 435
Hett, Jno., M. Chy. 397
Heureaux, U., Pres. Dom. Rep. 105
Hewetson, Chas., gen. (**D**) 894
Hewett and **Hewitt**
—— Geo. and sir G., C.C. Ind. 650; C.C. Mdras. 657; Comm. F. Ir. 564; G.C.B. 768; gen. (**A**) 860
—— Jas., aft. ld. and visc. Lifford, *q.v.*, J.K.B. 373; Ld. Chanc. Ir. 576; S.L. 412
—— hon. Jas., C. Acc. Ir. 567; C. Exc. 282; C. Exc. Ir. 566-7
—— hon. Jas., dn. Arm. 597
—— Jas. Nichs. Br., gen. (**D**) 930
—— hon. Jno., dn. Cloy. 633
—— hon. Jos., J.K.B. Ir. 579; S.L. Ir. 592
—— Presc. Gardn. and sir P., Pres. Coll. Surg. 939
—— Th., S.W.F. 271
—— Wm., C. St. 283
—— sir Wm., Amb. Abyss. 131
—— Wm. Hy., gen. (**D**) 886
—— Wm. Nath. Wri. and sir W., adm. (**E**) 836; K.C.B. 780; K.C.S.I. 803; L. Admy. 186
—— Wm. Selw., gen. (**D**) 914
Hewgill, Edwin, gen. (**C**) 872
Hewlett, Rd. Strode, adm. (**E**) 835; (**F**) 838
—— Th. Gill., C.I.E. 806
Hewson, Geo., adm. (**H**) 845
Hewys, Th. de, L.H.A. 170
Hext, Jno., C.I.E. 808
—— Wm., adm. (**H**) 847
Hey—, *see also* Hay—
Heydon, *see also* Haydon
—— Benj., dn. Wells, 429
—— Hy., K.B. 758
—— Jno., K.B. 760
—— Th. de, Jy. 364
Heyforde, Humphr., L.M. Lond. 490
Heygarth (or Heygate), Jno., dn. Llin. 623
Heygate, Wm. and sir W., L.M. Lond. 492; Chambn. Lond. 493
Heym and **Hayme**
—— Pet., J. It. 368
—— Steph., J.C.P. 377; Jy. 365
Heyn, Jno., bp. Clonf. 635
Heynes, *see also* Haines
—— Sim., dn. Exr. 437
Heyrick, Rd., Wdn. Chr. Ch. Manch. 481
Heyrun, Jord., J. It. 367
Heytesbury, Wm., 1st ld., form. sir W. A'Court, *q.v.*, Amb. Russ. 126; G.G. Ind. 649; L.L. Ir. 557
Heyward, *see also* Hayward
—— sir Rowl., L.M. Lond. 490
Heywood and **Haywood**
—— Jno. Jas., gen. (**D**) 930
—— J. M., L. Admy. 180
—— Pet., G. Jam. 712
—— Saml., S.L. 412
—— Th., dn. Lich. 445
Heyworth, Wm., bp. Lich. and Cov. 444
Hibbert, Jno. T., P.C. 220; Sec. Adm. 187; Sec. L.G.B. 256; Sec. Tr. 164; U.S. Home, 228
Hibbotts, Th., Ch. Ex. Ir. 562
Hiccocks, Jno., M. Chy. 396
—— Wm., C. Exc. 278
Hicham, Rt., S.L. 409
Hickes, *see* Hicks
Hickley, Hy. Denn., adm. (**E**) 837
—— Vict. Gr., adm. (**H**) 851
Hickman, Ch., bp. Dry. 601
—— Hy., M. Chy. 395
—— Thos. Windsor-, aft. visc. Windsor, *q.v.*
—— sir Wm., M.G.O. 258
Hicks and **Hickes**
—— Ch. Fk., gen. (**D**) 926
—— Geo., dn. Worc. 473
—— Geo., gen. (**D**) 890
—— Hy. Ersk., gen. (**D**) 911
—— Th., adm. (**A**) 817
Hickson, R. M., G. Virg. Isl. 731
Hicks-Beach, *see* Beach
Hidayat, Shaik Ali, C.I.E. 806
Hiddesley, Mark, bp. S. and M. 484
Hien-fung, Emp. Ch. 100
Hierologus, bp. Lism. 626
Higate, Jas., bp. Kilf. 635
Higbald, bp. Lindisf. 478
Higbert (2), bp. Lich. 443
Higden and **Hygden**
—— Br., dn. Yk. 487
—— Jno., dn. Chr. Ch. Oxf. 457
Higgin, Wm., bp. Dry. and Rph. 602; bp. Lim. A. and A. 639
—— Wm. Housm., Q.C. 418
Higgins, Andr., C.I.E. 807
—— Anthy., dn. Rip. 482
—— Clem., Q.C. 420
—— Dem. O', Pres. Chi. 111
—— Jos. Nap., Q.C. 419
—— Saml. Gord. and sir S., K.C.H. 788; K.H. 789
—— Th., gen. (**D**) 891
—— Warn. West., K.H. 790
—— Wm., dn. Lim. 640
Higginson, Geo. P., gen. (**D**) 882
—— Geo. Wm. Alexr., gen. (**D**) 908
—— Jas. Mac., G. Antig., &c. 727; G. Mtius. 684; K.C.B. 778
Higgs, Griff., dn. Lich. 445
Higham, Clem. and sir C., C.B. Ex. 381; Sp. H.C. 249
—— Rd., S.L. 407
—— sir Rog., L.H.A. 171
Hight, Ch., gen. (**D**) 926
Higman, Hy., adm. (**H**) 845
Hilary and **Hillary**
—— abp. Lond. 450
—— abp. Yk. 485; bp. Chic 432
—— P. Ro. 33
—— Rog. C.J.C.P. 375; J.C. 377
Hildebrand, K. Lmd. 49
—— Arth. Hedd., C.I.E. 808
—— Ch. Phayre, gen. (**D**) 926
Hildersley, Jno. de, B. E 383
Hildeyerd, Hy., Chambn. E 166
—— P., Chambn. Ex. 166
Hildyard, Jno., C.C.J. 403
—— Rt. Ch., Q.C. 417
Hill, Abr., B.T. 263
—— Alex., Mod. K. Sc. 547
—— Alex. St., Q.C. 418
—— Arth., Ch. Ex. Ir. 562
—— Arth., gen. (**D**) 933
—— ld. Arth. M. C., Compt. H 293; P.C. 214; Tr. H. 291
—— ld. Arth. Wm., Compt. H 293; P.C. 220
—— Ch. Ed. Dawt., gen. (**D** 910
—— Chr., adm. (**A**) 815
—— Clem., gen. (**C**) 875
—— Clem. Ll., K.C.M.G. 799
—— sir Dudl. St. Leg., G. S Luc. 725; gen. (**D**) 879; K.C. 777
—— Ed. Rowl., gen. (**D**) 897
—— Geo., dn. Thist. 749
—— Geo., gen. (**C**) 874
—— Geo., S.L. 412
—— sir Geo. Fitz-Ger., Treas. Ir. 561; G. St. Vi 725; G. Trin. 722; P.C. 209
—— Geo. Mytt., gen. (**D**) 916
—— Hy, adm. (**A**) 820
—— Hy., R. Dr. P.A. 338; Wind H. 331
—— Hy. Worsl., G. Gld. Cs 686
—— Hugh, aft. sir H., J.Q. 373; Q.C. 417; S.L. 413
—— Jno., C. Cus. 275
—— Jno., dn. Kilm. 609
—— Jno., gen. (**C**) 871; L.G. 259; P.C. 196
—— Jno., gen. (**D**) 897
—— (or Hull), Jno., J.C.P. 37 J.K.B. 371; S.L. 407
—— sir Jno., adm. (**D**) 829
—— Jno. Th., gen. (**D**) 895
—— Matth. Dav., P.P. 416
—— Nichs., dn. St. Pat. 617
—— Percy, gen. (**D**) 903
—— Rd., bp. Lond. 451
—— Rd., L. Admy. 177; L. 155
—— (or Hull), Rt., J.C.P. 37 S.L. 407
—— Rog., B. Ex. 384; J.K. 372; S.L. 410
—— Rowld. and sir R., K.C. 782; Sec. P.O. 239; L.M. Lon 490
—— sir Rowld., *see* ld. H. *infr*
—— Rowley, bp. S. and M. 484
—— Rowley Sale, gen. (**D**) 928
—— Steph. Jno. and sir S., Antig. &c. 727; G. Gld Cs 686; G. Newfd. 700; G. Si. L 685; K.C.M.G. 797
—— Th., dn. Oss. 623
—— sir Th. Noel, K.C.B. 775
—— Wm., gen. (**D**) 919; K.C.S. 803
—— Wm., M. Chy. 394

For List of Abbreviations, see pp. 944-952.

Hill—*cont.*
— Wm., Sec. Tr. 164
— hon. Wm., aft. 3rd ld. Berwick, Amb. G. St. 121; Amb. Scy. 115; Amb. Sda. 114; P.C. 210
Hill, lds. and visc.
— Rowl., aft. 1st ld. and visc. H., C. Ch. 855; G.C.B. 767; G.C.H. 786; gen. (**A**) 861; K.B 766; P.C. 211
— Rowl, 2nd visc., L.L. Salop, 311
Hillam, —, S.L. 407
Hillary, *see* Hilary
Hills, Geo., adm. (**H**) 845
— Geo., bp. Cbia. 698
— Jas., aft. sir Jas. Hills-Johnes, gen. (**D**) 921; K.C.B. 781
Hillsborough, Wills, 1st E. of, aft. M. of Downshire, *q.v.*, C. Sec. 234; Compt. H. 292; P.C. 199; Postm. G. 238; Pres. B.T. 265-6; S. St. 225; Tr. Ch. 294
Hillyar, Ch. Farr., adm. (**E**) 835; K.C.B. 781
— Hy. Sch., adm. (**E**) 836; (**F**) 839
— sir Jas., adm. (**D**) 824; K.C.B. 777; K.C.H. 788
— Rt. Purk., K.H. 792
— Wm., adm. (**G**) 842
Hilsey, Jno., bp. Roch. 460
Hilton, Adam de, J. It. 368
— Jno., Pres. Coll. Surg. 939
— Wm., B. Ex. Ir. 584; J.C.P. Ir. 581
***Hinchcliffe,** Jno., bp. Pboro. 458
*— Jno., dn. Dham. 479
* ? same pers.
Hinchinbroke, Jno. visc., aft. 5th E. of Sandwich, *q.v.*, M.B.H. 303; P.C. 202; V.C.H. 297
Hincks, Fras. and sir F., K.C.M.G. 796; G. Bdoes. &c. 719, 721; G. Br. Gu. 715
Hind and **Hinde,** *see also* Heende
— Ch., gen. (**D**) 904
— Jno., gen. (**D**) 901
— Jno., J.C.P. 378; S.L. 408
— Saml. Ven. and sir S., gen. (**B**) 868; K.C.B. 776
Hindmarch, Wm. M., Q.C. 418
Hindmarsh, Jno. and sir J., adm. (**G**) 841; G. Hlgld. 670; G. S. Austr. 706; K.H. 791
Hinds, Saml., bp. Norw. 455; dn. Carl. 476
— Saml., G. Bdoes. 720
Hinton, Jno., dn. Tm. 613
Hinton, visc.
— Jno., 1st visc., form. 4th ld. and aft. 1st E. Poulett, *q.v.*
Hinüber, Harry de and sir H., gen. (**B**) 867; K.C.B. 775
Hire, Hy. Wm., adm. (**H**) 851
— Sydn. Jos., gen. (**D**) 915
Hirtius, A., C. Ro. 46
Hisketh, Huan., bp. S. and M. 483
Hislop, Th. and sir T., C.C. Bbay. 660; C.C. Mdras. 657; G.C.B. 767; G. Gren. 724; G. Trin. 722; gen. (**A**) 861; K.C.B. 775
Hispallus, C. C. S., C. Ro. 44
Hispania, *see* Ispania
Hitch, Rt., dn. Yk. 487
Hitchins, Benj. R., gen. (**D**) 888
— Hy. Wh., gen. (**D**) 908
Hittu, Ram Rao Bah., C.I.E. 807
Hoadley, Benj., bp. Bgr. 426; bp. Her. 442; bp. Sal. 467; bp. Winch. 471
— Jno., abp. Arm. 596; abp. Dbln. and Gl. 616; bp. Ferns and L. 622; L.J. Ir. 556
Hoard (or Hoare), Ed. W., adm. (**D**) 828; (**G**) 840
Hoare, *see also* Hore and Hoard
— Ed. New., dn. Ach. 614; dn. Wford. 628
— sir Rd., L.M. Lond. 491
Hobart, hon. Geo. Vere, G. Gren. 724
— Hy. and sir H., A.G. 399; C.J.C.P. 375; S.L. 409
— sir Hy., C. Cus. 274
— hon. Hy. Lew., dn. Winds. 474
— Jno., *see* ld. H., *infra*
— Miles, K.B. 763
— Nathl., M. Chy. 395-6
— Rt., *see* ld. H., *infra*
Hobart, lds.
— sir Jno., aft. 1st ld. H. and 1st E. of Bucks, *q.v.*, B.T. 264; G.C.P. 299; K.B. 764; P.C. 199; Tr. Ch. 294
— Jno., ld., aft. 2nd E. of Bucks, *q.v.*, Compt. H. 292; P.C. 200
— Rt., aft. ld. H. and 4th E. of Bucks, *q.v.*, C. Treas. Ir. 560; Ch. Sec. Ir. 563; G. Mdras. 656; P.C. 205; W. and C. Sec. 230
— Vere Hy., ld., son of 6th E. of Bucks, G. Mdras. 657
— Mary Cath., lady, Cr. Ind. 809
Hobbes or **Hobbys,** Th., dn. Exr. 437; dn. Winds. 474
Hobhouse, Arth., *see* ld. H., *infra*
— Benj. and sir B., Sec. B.C. 254
— Ed., bp. Nels. 710
— Hy., P.C. 211; U.S. Home, 228
— sir Jno. Cam, aft. ld. Broughton, *q.v.*, C.W.F. &c. 272; Ch. Sec. Ir. 563; P.C. 212; Pres. B.C. 253-4; Sec. at W. 234
Hobhouse, lds.
— Arth., aft. sir A. and ld. H., Jud. Com. P.C. 362; K.C.S.I. 803; P.C. 220; Q.C. 418
Hobrugg, Gerv. D., dn. St. P. 452
***Hobson,** Jno., gen. (**D**) 896
*— Jno., or Wm., G. N.Z. 709
* ? same pers.
Hoby, sir Ph., dn. Ardf. 640
Hochefried, Geo. Bar. de, form. Geo. Porter, *q.v.*
Hockin, Ch. Luxm., adm. (**H**) 849
Hodge, Ed. Coop. and sir E., G.C.B. 771; gen. (**D**) 897; K.C.B. 780
— Jno., K.H. 792
Hodges, Geo. Ll., K.C.B. 783
— Hugh, S.L. 411
Hodges—*cont.*
— col. L., Amb. H. Tns. 120
— Th., dn. Her. 442
— Th. Troph., gen. (**D**) 931
— Wm., L.M. Dbln. 642
Hodges-Nugent, *see* Nugent
Hodgkins, Jno., bp. suffr. Bedf. 452
Hodgson, *see also* Hodson
— Arth., K.C.M.G. 798
— Brian, adm. (**D**) 825; (**G**) 840
— Ch. Jas., gen. (**D**) 913
— Chr., gen. (**D**) 877
— Fras. Geo., gen. (**D**) 918
— Hy., C. Tx. 285
— Hy., gen. (**D**) 878
— Hy. Burd., gen. (**D**) 912
— Hugh Norr., gen. (**D**) 914
*— Jno., G. Bmda. 701
*— Jno., gen. (**A**) 862
* ? same pers.
— Jno., Q.C. 417
— Jno. Anthy., gen. (**D**) 881
— Jno. Studh., gen. (**D**) 896
— Jos., Pres. Coll. Surg. 939
— Rt., dn. Carl. 476; dn. Chest. 477
— sir Rt., G. Pr. Ed. Isl. 699
— Studh., F.M. 856; gen. (**A**) 858
— Studh. J., gen. (**D**) 894
Hodian (or Hedian), Jno., dn. Cash. 627
Hodson, *see also* Hodgson
— Doveton, gen. (**D**) 908
Hody, sir Jno., C.J.K.B. 370
— Wm., A.G. 398; C.B. Ex. 381; S.L. 407
Hoel, V. and VI., D. Bry. 28
Hoese, Simon or Harry, W.C.P. 317
Hoffman, J. T., Pres. O.F.S. 101
Hog, *see* Hogg
Hogan, Donat, dn. Emly, 628
— Hugh, dn. Emly, 628
— (or Hogar), Rd., bp. Clonm. 600; bp. Killoe. 634
Hogar, *see* Hogan
Hogg, Hog, and **Hogge**
— Ad., gen. (**D**) 877
— Fk. Russ., K.C.I.E. 805
— Geo. Forbes, gen. (**D**) 920
— Jas. Macn., aft. McGarel-Hogg and ld. Magheramorne, K.C.B. 783
— Jas. Weir and sir J., Chn. E.I. Co. 645-6; M.C.I. 646; P.C. 218
— sir Rog., Ld. Sess. 519
— Som. Geo. Cam., gen. (**D**) 926
— Th. Ign. M., gen. (**D**) 926
Hoggan, Jno., gen. (**D**) 888
Hogge, *see* Hogg
Hoggins, Chr. A., Q.C. 417
Hoghton, *see* Houghton
Hohenlohe, (Ct. Gleichen), *see* Victor
Holand, *see* Holland
Holbeach, Holbeche, and **Holbeck**
— Hy., bp. Linc. 447; bp. Roch. 460; bp. suffr. Brl. 43?; dn. Worc. 473
— Hugh, dn. St. As. 463
Holburne, Fras., adm. (**A**) 814; G. Gr. Hosp. 854; L. Admy. 179
Holcrofte, Hy., Ch. Ex. Ir. 562
— Jno., K.B. 760

For List of Abbreviations, see pp. 944-952.

Holden, Luther, Pres. Coll. Surg. 939
Holder, Hy. Lowe, adm. (**H**) 853
Holdernesse, Alexr. de, J. It. 367
— Rog. de, dn. Yk. 486
Holdernesse, E. of
— Rt., 3rd E. of, P.C. 197; Pres. B.T. 264
— Rt., 4th E. of, L.L. Yorks. N.R. 313; P.C. 199; S. St. 224; W.C.P. 319
Holdich, Ed. Alan and sir E., gen. (**D**) 902; K.C.B. 780
Holdsworth, R., dn. Worc. 473
Hole, Lewis, adm. (**H**) 845
— Lewis Bl., gen. (**D**) 929
— Saml. Reyn., dn. Roch. 461
Holford, Geo. P., Sec. B.C. 254
— Pet., M. Chy. 396
— Rd., M. Chy. 396
— Th. (No. 1), Ptc. P.A. 337; Winds. H. 331
— Th. (No. 2), Bl. L. P.A. 341; Ptc. P.A. 337
Holgate, Rt., abp. Yk., 486; bp. Llff. 449
Holgin, Greg., dn. Kild. 619
Holgrave, Jno., B. Ex. 383
Holiday, *see* Hollyday
Holkar (Mahar. of Indore), K.C.S.I. 802; G.C.S.I. 802
Holker, Jno. and sir J., A.G. 400; Jud. Com. P.C. 362; L.J. App. 389; P.C. 220; Q.C. 418; S.G. 403
Holl, Charlt., gen. (**D**) 894
— Wm. H., C.C.J. 405; Q.C. 419
Holland and **Holand**, *see also* Hollond
— C., L.T. 154
— Geo., dn. Dry. 602
— sir Hy., Pres. R. Inst. 940
— Hy. Ed., Amb. Tusc. &c. 115
— Hy. Thurston, aft. sir H. and ld. Knutsford, *q.v.*, C. Sec. 235; G.C.M.G. 795; K.C.M.G. 797; P.C. 220; Sec. Tr. 164; U.S.C. 236; V.P. Ed. 255
— Hy. Wm., gen. (**D**) 915
— sir Jno., Compt. H. 292; P.C. 195
— Jno., aft. E. of Huntington, and 1st D. of Exeter, *q.v.*,
— Jno. or Ph., Ptc. P.A. 337; R. Rge. P.A. 344
— Jno. Wentw., adm. (**D**) 825
— Luml. H. H., gen. (**D**) 912
— sir Otho., K.G. 733
— Ph. or Jno., *see* Jno., *supra*
— Rd., K.B. 756
— sir Rt., L.H.A. 171
— Seth, dn. Worc. 473
— Th., G. Ch. Isl. 667
— sir Th., aft. E. of Kent (*d.* 1360), K.G. 733
— Th. Woll., gen. (**D**) 914
Holland, lds. and E. of
Rich Family.
— Hy., 1st E. of, form. Hy. Rich, and ld. Kensington, *q.v.*, C.Y.G. 298; K.G. 739; Const. W. Cast. 322
Fox Family.
— Hy., 1st ld., form. Hy. Fox, *q.v.*
— Hy. Rd., 3rd ld., C.D.L. 243; P.C. 208; L.P.S. 241
Holland, lds. and E. of—*cont.*
— Hy. E., 4th ld., form. hon. H. E. Fox, *q.v.*
Holles, *see also* Hollis
— Denz., *see* ld. H., *infra*
— sir Fretch., adm. (**A**) 813
— sir Wm., L.M. Lond. 490
Holles, lds.
— Denzil, aft. 1st ld. H., P.C. 190, 192; L.L. Dors. 307
Holliday, *see* Hollyday
Holligan, J. R., G. St. Xtr. 729
Hollingworth, Jno., Bl. M. P.A. 336; Rbk. P.A. 344
— Rand. or Rod., dn. Ach. 614
— Th., Yk. H. 334
Hollinworth, Jno., adm. (**H**) 844
Hollis, *see also* Holles
— Aysc. Paff., adm. (**A**) 820
— D., L. Admy. 175
— Jno. Jos., gen. (**D**) 890
Hollist, Rd., K.C. 415
Hollond, *see also* Holland
— E. J., G. Mdras. 656
— Jno., G. Mdras. 656
Holloway and **Halloway**
— Ch., S.L. 410
— sir Ch., gen. (**C**) 873
— Jno., adm. (**A**) 816; G. Newfd. 700
— Rd. and sir R., J.K.B. 372; S.L. 410
— Th., gen. (**D**) 898; K.C.B. 779
Hollyday, sir Hy., L.M. Lond. 491
Holme, Jno., B. Ex. 383
— Th. and sir T., Clar. K.A. 328; Winds. H. 331
Holmes and **Holms**
— Ch., adm. (**A**) 814
— Geo., K.C.B. 775
— Geo. Ed., gen. (**D**) 912
— Gilb., dn. Ardf. 640
— Hy., gen. (**B**) 865
— Hugh, A.G. Ir. 589; J.C.P.D. Ir. 582; J.Q.B.D. Ir. 580; S.G. Ir. 590
— Jno., L.T. 162; Sec. B.T. 269
— Percy L., gen. (**D**) 918
— Pet., C. Acc. Ir. 567; C. St. Ir. 568
— Rd., gen. (**C**) 871
— Rt., dn. Winch. 471
— sir Rt., adm. (**A**) 813
— Steph., K.H. 790
— Wm., dn. Exr. 438
Holmewood, Ed., G. I. Man, 666
Holroyd, Ch., gen. (**D**) 912
— Geo., gen. (**D**) 923
— Geo. S. and sir G., J.K.B. 373; S.L. 413
— Hy., C.C.J. 405
Holstein, Aug., D. of, K.G. 738
Holt, Fras. Ludl., K.C. 416
— Hy., gen. (**B**) 864
— Jno., J.C.P. 378; K.B. 755; S.L. 407
— Jno. and sir J., C.G.S. 357; C.J.K.B. 370; P.C. 194; Rec. Lond. 494; S.L. 411
— Rd., G. I. Man, 665
— Th., S.L. 410
— Wm., adm. (**G**) 842
Holwell, Jno. Zeph., Adm. Ind. 647
Holworthy, Maj. —, G. Trin. 722
Holyman, Jno., bp. Brl. 439
Holywode, Rt. de, B. Ex. Ir 583; C.B. Ex. Ir. 582
Home, Anthy. Dicks, K.C.B 780
— Dav., gen. (**A**) 859
— Dav., Ld. Sess. 520
— sir Ev., Mast. and Pres Coll. Surg. 939
— sir Geo., adm. (**A**) 816
— Hy., Jy. Sc. 522; Ld. Sess 520
— Jas., gen. (**B**) 869
— Jas., Ly. Dep. 513
— Jno., gen. (**D**) 886
— Jno. Home, gen. (**D**) 884
— Nin., G. Gren. 724
— Rd., gen. (**D**) 888
— Rt., C.I.E. 807
— Rodd., adm (**A**) 816
Home, E. of
— Wm., 8th E. of, G. Gib 669; gen. (**B**) 865
— Alexr., 10th E. of, L.I Berw. 508
— Cosp. Alexr., 11th E. o form. ld. Dunglass, *q.v.*, L.I Sc. 503
— Ch. Alexr., 12th E. o form. ld. Dunglass, *q.v.*
Homewood, *see* Holmewoo
Homspesch, Wm. Vinc., ge (**D**) 877
— Bar. Ch., gen. (**B**) 866
— Count Ferd., gen. (**A**) 861
Hone, Jno., M. Chy. 395
— Nathl., L.M. Dbln. 641
Honey—, *see* Hony—
Honner or **Honnor**, R Wm., gen. (**D**) 896; K.C.B. 7
Honore, Hy., dn. Bgr. 426
Honorius (St.), abp. Cant. 4
— Emp. W.E. 49
— I. to IV., P. Ro. 33-4-5
— I. to V., Pr. Mno. 31
Honstedt, Augs., bar., ge (**C**) 873
Honyman, Andr., bp. Or 535
— sir Geo. Ess., J.C.P. 38 Q.C. 418; S.L. 414
— Rt., adm. (**A**) 820
— sir Wm., Jy. Sc. 523; L Sess. 520
Honywood, Mich., dn. Lir 448
— Ph., gen. (**A**) 858
— Ph. and sir P., gen. (857; K.B. 764
Hoo, Jno., S.L. 411
— Th., aft. ld. Hoo and Ha ings, K.G. 735
Hood, Alexr., aft. 1st ld. a 1st visc. Bridport, *q.v.*, ad (**A**) 815; K.B. 765
— hon. Alexr. Nelson, aft. 3 ld. and 1st visc. Bridp (2nd Cr.), *q.v.*, gen. (**D**) 897
— Arth. Wm. Acl. and sir adm. (**E**) 836; K.C.B. 781; Admy. 185-6
— Ch., gen. (**D**) 910
— Jno. Cockb., gen. (**D**) 92
— Rd., dn. Kilmacd. 638
— Saml. and sir S., adm. 818; G.C.B. 767; G. Trin. 7 K.B. 766
— sir Saml., *see* ld. H., *inf*
Hood, lds. and visc.
— sir Saml., aft. ld. and v H., adm. (**A**) 815; G. Hosp. 854; G.C.B. 767; Admy. 180

For List of Abbreviations, see pp. 944-952.

Hook, Jas., dn. Worc. 474
—— Jno., S.L. 411
—— Walt. F., dn. Chich. 434
Hooke-Campbell, *see* Campbell
Hooker, Josh. Dalt. and sir J., K.C.S.I. 803; Pres. R. Soc. 946
—— Rog., dn. Llin. 623
—— sir Wm., L.M. Lond. 491
—— sir Wm. Jacks., K.H. 791
Hooper, Ed., C. Cus. 275-6
—— Geo., bp. B. and W. 428; bp. St. As. 462; dn. Cant. 431
—— Geo. Stanl., gen. (**D**) 931
—— Jas. J., C.C.J. 405
—— Jno., bp. Glr. 438; bp. Worc. 473
—— Jno. Kinn., L.M. Lond. 492
—— Nichs. (or Rd.), S.L. 411
Hope, hon. Alex. and sir A., Amb. Dk. 127; G.C.B. 767; gen. (**A**) 861; K.B. 766; L.G. Ch. Hosp. 936
—— Alexr. Jas. B. Beresford-P.C. 219
—— Archd., Ld. Sess. 520
—— Archd. Hugh, gen. (**D**) 918
—— Archd. Wh., gen. (**D**) 893
—— Ch., adm. (**D**) 830
—— Ch., L.J. Clk. 516; L.P. Ct. Sess. 516; Ld. Adv. 526; P.C. 210
—— hon. Ch., G. I. Man, 666
—— hon. Ch., gen. (**A**) 861
—— Ch. Webl., adm. (**E**) 836
—— Fk., gen. (**D**) 896
—— Geo., K.C.B. 774
—— Geo. Johnst. and sir G., adm. (**A**) 818; L. Admy. 181
—— Geo. W., U.S.W. and C. 231
—— Hy. and sir H. adm. (**D**) 827; K.C.B. 778
—— Jas. and sir J., adm. (**B**) 821; (**D**) 831; (**E**) 834; K.C.B. 779; G.C.B. 770
—— sir Jas., Ld. Sess. 519
—— Jas. Archd. and sir J., gen. (**D**) 879; G.C.B. 770; K.C.B. 775
—— Jas. Rt., P.P. 417
—— Jno., D. Fac. Sc. 527; L.J. Clk. 516; P.C. 214; S.G. Sc. 527
—— sir Jno., G. I. Man, 666
—— hon. Jno. and sir J., aft. ld. Niddry, and 4th E. of Hopetoun, *q.v.*, Comm. F. Ir. 564; G.C.H. 786; gen. (**B**) 867; K.B. 766
—— Jno. or Th., *see* Th.
—— Jno. Bruce and sir J., G. Bmda. 701; gen. (**B**) 865
—— Jno. Ch., K.H. 790
—— Sackett, adm. (**G**) 842
—— Theod. Cr., K.C.S.I. 803
—— Th., adm. (**E**) 835
—— Th., or Jno.
*—— L.H.C., K. Sc. 546
*—— L.J. Gen. 522
*—— Ld. Adv. 526
*—— Ld. Sess. 510
*—— Ld. Sess. 519
* *Note.*—There is some confusion in these names. Compare dates.
—— Wm., gen. (**D**) 906
—— Wm. Johnst. and sir W., adm. (**A**) 818; G.C.B. 768; K.C.B. 774; L. Admy. 181, 182; P.C. 212
Hope-Johnstone, *see* Johnstone
Hopetoun, E. of
—— Ch., 1st E. of, K.T. 747; L.H.C., K. Sc. 546
—— Jno., 2nd E. of, L.H.C., K. Sc. 546
—— Jas., 3rd E. of, L.L. Linlithg. 511
—— Jno., 4th E. of, form. sir Jno. Hope, and ld. Niddry, *q.v.*, gen. (**A**) 861; L.L. Linlithg. 511
—— Jno., 5th E. of, L.L. Linlithg. 511
—— Jno. Al., 6th E. of, L.L. Linlithg. 511
—— Jno. Ad. L., 7th E. of, L.H.C. K. Sc. 546
Hopkins, Benjn., Chambn. Lond. 493
—— Ezek., bp. Dry. 601; bp. Rph. 601
—— Jno., L.M. Lond. 492
—— Jno. Omm., adm. (**E**) 837; Compt. N. 258
—— Jno. Paul, K.H. 791
—— Rd., L. Admy., 179, 180; L.T. 158
—— sir Rd., S.L. 410
—— Rd. North., gen. (**B**) 866
—— Th., U.S.S. 225
—— Wm. Fr., gen. (**D**) 899
Hopkinson, sir Ch., gen. (**D**) 888
—— H., gen. (**D**) 922
Hoppenstedt, Geo. Ern. Fk., V. Chanc. Guelph, 792
Hopper, Wm., gen. (**D**) 877
Hopson, Ed., adm. (**A**) 813
—— Peregr. Th., G.N. Sc. 694; gen. (**C**) 871
—— sir Th., adm. (**A**) 813
Hopton, Arth., K.B. 761
—— Jno., bp., Norw. 455
—— sir Owen, Lt. T.L. 321
—— Ralph, *see* ld. H., *infra*
—— Walt. de., B. Ex. 382; J. It. 368; J.K.B. 371
—— (or Hepton), Wm. de, A.G. 398; S.L. 406
Hopton, lds.
—— Ralph, aft. 1st ld. H., K.B. 763; P.C. 189
Hopwood, Ch. Hy., Q.C. 419
Horan, Jas., L.M. Dbln. 641
Horden, Jno., bp. Moos. 697
Hore, *see also* Hoare
—— Rt., A.G. Ir. 588
—— Th., gen. (**D**) 895
Horley (or Horsey), Geo., dn. Ross, 633
Hormisdas, P. Ro. 33
Horn, *see* Horne
Hornby and **Horneby**
—— Geoffr. Th. Phipps, and sir G., adm. (**B**) 821; (**E**) 835; G.C.B. 771; K.C.B. 780; L. Admy. 185
—— Nathl., C. Exc. 278, 279
—— Phipps and sir P., G.C.B. 770; K.C.B. 777; L. Admy. 183
*—— Wm. de, A.G. 398
*—— Wm., S.L. 407
* Poss. same pers.
—— Wm. Ph. and sir W., adm. (**C**) 822; (**D**) 827
—— Wm. Windh., adm. (**H**) 848
Horncastle, Jus. de, bp. Carl. 475
Horne and **Horn**
—— Alexr., G. I. Man, 666
—— Ch. Jas., gen. (**D**) 927
—— Fk., and sir F., gen. (**D**) 895; K.C.B. 780
—— Geo., bp. Norw. 455; dn. Cant. 431
—— Jno. de, K.B. 754
—— Rt., bp. Winch. 471; dn. Dham. 479
—— Rt., D. Fac. Sc. 527
—— Wm., L.M. Lond. 490
—— Wm. and sir W., A.G. 400; K.C. 416; M. Chy. 397; S.G. 402
Hornebrock, R., Bl. M. P.A. 336
Horneby, *see* Hornby
Horneck, Ch., gen. (**B**) 866
Horse, Pet. de la, K.B. 754
Horsey, Algn. Fk. R. de, adm. (**E**) 836
—— (or Horley), Geo., dn. Ross. 633
—— Saml., B. and Gl. K.A. 330; Bath K.A. 785; Han. H. 340
—— Wm. Hy. B. de, gen. (**D**) 918
Horsfall, Jno., bp. Oss. 620
Horsford, Alf. Hast., G.C.B. 770; gen. (**D**) 902; K.C.B. 778
—— Geo., gen. (**B**) 868
—— Jno., K.C.B. 775
—— Rd., gen. (**D**) 895
Horsley, Saml., bp. Roch. 460; bp. St. As. 462; bp. St. Dav. 465; dn. Westr. 469
—— Wm., Clar. K.A. 328
Horsman, Ed., Ch. Sec. Ir. 563; L.T. 160; P.C. 216
Hort, Jno. Jos., gen. (**D**) 905
—— Josiah, abp. Tm. 611; bp. Ferns and L. 622; bp. Kilm. and Ard. 607; dn. Ard. 609; dn. Cloy. 633
Hortensius, L., C. Ro. 45
—— Q., C. Ro. 46; Dt. Ro. 41
Horton, Jas., G. I. Man, 666
—— Josh. Sydn., adm. (**A**) 820
—— Rt. Jno. Wilm. and sir R., G.C.H. 786; G. Ceyl. 672; U.S.W. and C. 231
—— Rog., J.C.P. 378; J.K.B. 371
—— Th., G. I. Man, 666
—— Wm., adm. (**H**) 851
Hose, Geoff., J. It. 366
—— Geo. Fk., bp. Sing. L. and S. 676
Hoseason, Hy., gen. (**D**) 913
—— Wm., adm. (**H**) 850
Hosier, Fras., adm. (**A**) 813
Hosken, Jas., adm. (**H**) 850
Hoskins, Anthy. Hiley and sir A., adm. (**E**) 836; K.C.B. 781; L. Admy. 185-6
—— Edm. or Edw., S.L. 410
—— Jno., M. Chy. 396
—— Jno., S.L. 409
—— sir Jno., Pres. R. Soc. 940
Hospitali, Ralph de, J. It. 365
Hoste, sir Wm., adm. (**E**) 835; K.C.B. 774
Hotham, Beaum., aft. sir B. (7th Bart.), C. Cus. 275-6
—— Beaum., *see* ld. H. *infra*
—— Ch. and sir C., Amb. Arg. 136; Amb. Bol. 135; Amb. Pgy. 136; Amb. Ugy. 137; G. Vict. 704; K.C.B. 777
—— sir Ch., K.B. 765
—— Ch. Fk., adm. (**E**) 837; L. Admy. 186

For List of Abbreviations, see pp. 944-952.

Hotham—*cont.*
—— Geo., gen. (**A**) 859
—— hon. Geo. Fredc., adm. (**G**) 841
—— hon. Hy. and sir H., L. Admy. 181-2; adm. (**A**) 819; G.C.M.G. 794; K.C.B. 774
—— Jno. (No. 1), bp. Clr. 596; bp. Oss. 620
—— Jno. (No. 2), bp. Ely, 434; L.H.T. 152; L. Treas. Ir. 558; Ld. Chanc. 354
—— Jno. de, K.B. 755
—— Wm. de, abp. Dbln. and Gl. 615
—— Wm., adm. (**H**) 846; K.H. 791
—— Wm. and sir W., adm. (**A**) 819; G.C.B. 769; K.C.B. 774
—— Wm., *see* ld. H. *infra*
Hotham, lds.
—— Wm., aft. 1st ld. H., adm. (**A**) 815
—— sir Beaum., aft. 2nd ld. H., B. Ex. 385; C.G.S. 357; S.L. 412
—— Beaum., 3rd ld., gen. (**D**) 883
Hothfield, Hy. Jas., 1st ld., form. sir H. J. Tufton, *q.v.*
Houblon, sir Jno., L. Admy. 176; L.M. Lond. 491
Houbrug, Wm. de, J. It. 367
Hough, Jno., bp. Lich. and Cov. 444; bp. Oxf. 456; bp. Worc. 473
—— Lionel St., gen. (**D**) 907
Houghton and **Hoghton**
—— Ad., bp. St. Dav. 464; Ld. Chanc. 354
—— Danl., gen. (**C**) 873
—— sir Hy., J.A.G. 937
—— Richm., gen. (**D**) 931
—— Rt. and sir R., J.K.B. 372; S.L. 409
—— Wm. Rt., gen. (**D**) 927
Houghton, lds.
—— R. M., 1st ld., form. R. Monckton-Milnes, *q.v.*
Houlditch, Rd., C. St. 283
Houlton, Ed. Vict. and sir E., G.C.M.G. 795; K.C.M.G. 796
—— Jno., adm. (**A**) 815
Houston and **Houstoun**
—— Alex., G. Gren. 724
—— Andr., G. Gren. 724
—— Rt. and sir R., gen. (**D**) 876; K.C.B. 776
—— Wallace, adm. (**E**) 835; (**F**) 838
—— Wm. and sir W., G.C.B. 768; G.C.H. 786; G. Gibr. 670; gen. (**A**) 861; K.C.B. 773
Houton, Jno. de, B. Ex. 383; J. It. 367
How, *see also* Howe
—— Th., L.M. Dbln. 641
—— Wm. W., bp. Wfield. 484; bp. Suff. Bedf. 452
Howard, Ch., P.C. 190
—— hon. Ch. and sir C., gen. (**A**) 858; K.B. 765
—— Ch., *see* ld. H., *infra*
—— hon. Ch. Kenn., C.W.F. &c. 273
—— Ed., K.B. (1616) 762
—— sir Ed., or ld. Ed., K.G. 737; L.H.A. 174
—— hon. Ed., adm. (**G**) 842
—— Ed. Hy., adm. (**E**) 836
—— ld. Ed. G. F., *see* ld. H. Glossop, *infra*
—— Ed. Staff., U.S. Ind. 236

Howard—*cont.*
—— Fk. Chris., C. Exc. 278
—— sir Geo., F.M. 856; G. Ch. Hosp. 936; gen. (**A**) 858; K.B. 765; P.C. 206
—— Hy., aft. ld. Maltravers, *q.v.*, K.B. (1616) 762
—— hon. Hy. Ed. Jno., dn. Lich. 445
—— Hy. Fras. and sir H., Amb. Bva. 119; Amb. Bzl. 135; Amb. Hnr. 120; Amb. Pgl. 125; Amb. Pr. 118; G.C.B. 773; K.C.B. 783
—— hon. Hy. Geo., Amb. Tusc. 115
—— Hy. Thos. Mol., Dep. E.M. 327
—— hon. Hugh, C. St. Ir. 568
—— Jas., *see* ld. H., *infra*
*—— sir Jno., L.H.A. 171
*—— sir Jno., L.H.A. 172
* Poss. same pers.
—— Jno., *see* ld. H., *infra*
—— Jno. Morgan, C.C.J. 406; Q.C. 419
—— Jos. Jacks., Malt. H. 335
—— sir P., bp. Jam. 712
—— Rt., bp. Elph. 608; bp. Killa. and Ach. 613; dn. Ard. 609
—— Rt., K.B. (1616) 762
—— sir Rt., Aud. Ex. 166; P.C. 193
—— Th., gen. (**B**) 864
—— Th., aft. D. of Norfolk, *q.v.*, K.B. 757 (*d.* 1524)
—— Th., aft. D. of Norfolk, *q.v.*, K.B. 760 (*d.* 1572)
—— Th., Tell. Ex. 167
—— Th. Ph., gen. (**D**) 882; K.H. 792
—— Wm., J.C.P. 377; J. It. 368
—— Wm., K.B. (1616) 762
—— Wm., K.B. (1625) 763
Howard, lds. and visc.
—— Jno., ld., aft. D. of Norfolk, K.G. 736 (*d.* 1475)
—— Jno. ld., aft. D. of Norfolk, *q.v.*, Const. T.L. 320; E.M. 326 (*d.* 1485)
Howard of Bindon, visc.
—— Th., 3rd visc., L.L. Dors. 307; K.G. 739
Howard of Castlerising, lds.
—— Hy., ld., aft. D. of Norfolk, *q.v.*, E.M. 326 (1692)
Howard of Charleton, lds.
—— Th., 1st ld., aft. 1st E. of Berkshire, *q.v.*, K.B. (1605) 761
—— Ch., aft. visc. Andover and 2nd E. of Berkshire, K.B. 763
Howard of Effingham, lds.
—— Wm., 1st ld., L.H.A. 174; K.G. 738; L.C.H. 294; L.P.S. 240
—— Ch., 2nd ld., aft. E. of Nottingham, *q.v.*, E.M. 326; K.G. 738
—— Ch., ld., aft. 2nd E. of Nottingham, *q.v.*, L.H.A. 174; L.L. Surr. 312
—— Kenn. Alex., 11th ld., K.C.B. 774; G.C.B. 768
Howard of Glossop, lds.
—— ld. Ed. G. Fitz-A., aft. ld. H. of Gl., Dep. E.M. 327; P.C. 215; V.C.H. 297
Howard de Walden, lds.
—— Th., 1st ld., aft. E. of Suffolk, *q.v.*, Const. T.L. 321; K.G. 739; L.H.T. 154

Howard de Walden, lds.—*cont.*
—— Theop., 2nd ld., aft. E. of Suffolk, *q.v.*, C.G.P. 299
—— Jas. (son of ld. H. de W.), aft. 3rd ld. H. de W., K.B. 763
—— Jno. Gr., 4th ld., form. J. G. Griffin, *q.v.*, F.M. 856; gen. (**A**) 858; L.L. Esx. 308
—— Ch. Aug., 6th ld. and ld. Seaford, *q.v.*, Amb. Bgm. 123; Amb. Pgl. 125; Amb. Sw. and N. 127; G.C.B. 772; U.S.F. 229
Howard-Elphinstone, *see* Elphinstone
Howarth, *see also* Howorth
—— Hy., K.C. 415
Howden, Jas. A., gen. (**D**) 888
Howden, lds.
—— Jno. Fras., 1st ld., form. sir J. F. Cradock or Caradoc, *q.v.*
—— Jno. Hob., 2nd ld., form. hon. J. H. Caradoc, *q.v.*, Amb. Arg. 136; Amb. Bzl. 135; Amb. Spn. 124; Amb. Ugy. 136; G.C.B. 772; gen. (**D**) 884; K.C.B. 782; K.H. 789
Howe, *see also* How
—— Emanl., gen. (**C**) 871
—— Jno., P.C. 195; Paym. G. 244
—— Jos., G. N. Sc. 695
—— Rd., *see* visc. H., *infra*
—— Wm., *see* visc. H., *infra*
Howe, visc. and E.
—— Eman. Scr., 2nd visc., G. Bdoes. 720
—— Rd., 4th visc. and 1st Earl H. (1st Cr.), adm. (**A**) 815; B.T. 267; K.G. 743; L. Admy. 179-80; P.C. 200; Tr. N. 256
—— hon. sir Wm., aft. 5th visc. H., gen. (**A**) 858; L.G.O. 259; K.B. 765; P.C. 203
—— Rd. Wm., aft. 1st E. (2nd Cr.), G.C.H. 786; P.C. 212
—— Rd. W. P., 3rd E. (2nd Cr.) form. R. W. P. Curzon, *q.v.*, L.L. Leic. 309
Howel and **Howell**
—— (2), bp. Bgr. 425-6
—— ap. Jevaf, Pr. Wls. 16
—— Dha (3), Pr. Wls. 16, 17
—— Fulk ap, Guis. P.A. 343; Lanc. H. 333; R. Dr. P.A. 337
—— Jno. and sir J., Rec. Lond. 494; S.L. 410
—— Mort. Sl., C.I.E. 807
—— Th., bp. Brl. 439
—— Wm., M. Chy. 396
Howie, Jas., dn. Cloy. 633
Howick, visc.
—— Ch., visc., form. hon. C. and aft. 2nd E. Grey, *q.v.*, F. Sec. 228; P.C. 213; Sec. a. W. 234
—— Hy., visc., aft. 3rd E. Grey, *q.v.*, U.S. Home, 227; U.S. W. and C. 231
Howison, Hy., L.M. Dbln. 641
Howland, Rd., bp. Pboro. 458
—— Wm. Pearce and sir W., G. Ont. 692; K.C.M.G. 797
Howlett, Arth., gen. (**D**) 923
—— Rd., dn. Cash. 627
Howley, Jno., S.L Ir. 593
—— Wm., abp. Cant. 431; B.T. 268; bp. Lond. 452; Jud. Com. P.C. 360; P.C. 209

For List of Abbreviations, see pp. 944-952.

Howorth, *see also* Howarth
— Ed. and sir E., G.C.H. 786; gen. (**B**) 867; K.C.B. 774
— Jno., adm. (**A**) 817
Howson, Jno., bp. Dham. 479; bp. Oxf. 456
— Jno. S., dn. Chest. 477
Howth, lds. and E. of
— Nichs., ld., form. N. St. Lawrence, *q.v.*, Ld. Chanc. Ir. 575
— Thos., 3rd E. of, K.P. 751; L.L. Dbln. 569
— Wm. Ul. Tr., 4th E. of, K.P. 752
Hoyte, Geo., L.M. Dbln. 642
Huarach, bp. Emly, 625
Hubarthorne, sir Hy., L.M. Lond. 490
Hubbard, Jac., A.G. 398
— Jno. Gell., P.C. 219
Hubert, bp. St. Dav. 464
— bp. Worc. 472
— D. Tny. 57
— Pr. Mno. 30
— Jas., K.B. 759
— Jas.. M. Chy. 394
— Walter, abp. Cant. 430; Ch. Jr. 362
Huddersfield, Jno., S.L. 407
— Wm., A.G. 398
Huddleston and **Hudleston**
— Jno., K.B. 760
— Jno. W. and sir J., B. Ex. 385; J.C.P. 380; J. Ex. D. 385; J.Q.B.D. 374; Q.C. 417; S.L. 414
— Wm. Orch., gen. (**B**) 866
Hudson, Ed. Gust., dn. Arm. 597
— Jas. and sir J., Amb. Bzl. 135; Amb. It. 114; Amb. Sda. 114; Amb. Tusc. 115; G.C.B. 772; K.C.B. 782
— Jno., bp. Elph. 608; dn. Clr. 597
— Jno. and sir J., gen. (**D**) 933; K.C.B. 781
— Jos., gen. (**B**) 865
— Josh. Saml., adm. (**H**) 852
— Wm. Br., C.I.E. 808
Hudsor, Wm., bp. Meath, 599
Hue, Corbet, dn. Jsey. 668
Huet, sir Wm., L.M. Lond. 490
Hugel, Bar. de, K.C.B. 775
Hugessen, sir Ed. H. Knatchbull-, form. sir E. H. Knatchbull, *q.v.*, aft. ld. Brabourne; *q.v.*, L.T. 161; P.C. 218; U.S. Home, 228; U.S.C. 235
Hugh and **Hugo**
*— bp. Linc. 446
*— (3) bp. Oss. 620
*— bp. St. Andr. 528
*— bp. St. As. 462
*— (or Odo), dn. Oss. 622
*— dn. Yk. 486
* Prob. some same pers. Comp. dates
— (the black), D. Bdy. 28
— (the Great), D. Bdy. 28
— D. Su. 80
— D. Tny. 57
— K. Fr. 23
— K. Ir. 21
— K. Lmd. 49
— I. to V., D. Bdy. 28
— -Alain, K. Ir. 21
— -Capet, K. Fr. 23
— -Fionnliath, K. Ir. 22
Hugh and Hugo—*cont.*
— Jno. Fitz-, Const. W. Cast. 322
— (-Slaine), K. Ir. 21
Hughes, Ch. Jas., gen. (**D**) 931
— Ed., J.A.G. 937
— Ed., K.B. 765
— sir Ed., adm. (**A**) 815
— Hy. Geo., B. Ex. Ir. 584; S.G. Ir. 590
— Hugh, dn. Bgr. 427
— Hugh Rt., L.L. Flints. 314
— Jno., gen. (**B**) 868
— Jno., gen. (**C**) 872
— Josh., bp. St. As. 462
— R., G. N. Sc. 695
— sir Rd., adm. (**A**) 815
— Rt., adm. (**A**) 813
— Rt., adm. (**A**) 814
— Rt., gen. (**D**) 910
— Rt. Geo., gen. (**D**) 890
— Rt. Jno., gen. (**D**) 926
— Th., C.C.J. 405; Q.C. 418
— Th. Ell., gen. (**D**) 927
— Wm., bp. St. As. 462
— Wm. Temp., gen. (**D**) 908
Hugo, *see* Hugh
Hugonin, Fras., gen. (**A**) 861
— Jas., gen. (**C**) 872
Huick (or Huyck), Th., Ch. Lond. 422; M. Chy. 395
Huitta, bp. Lich. 443
Hulin, Off. Nap. 26
Hull, sir Ed., K.G. 736
— (or Hill), Jno., J.C.P. 378; J.K.B. 371; S. L. 407
— (or Hill), Rt., J.C.P. 378; S. L. 407
— Rt. Trev.. gen. (**C**) 873
— Wm., gen. (**D**), 877
Hullock, Jno. and sir J., B. Ex. 385; S.L. 413
Hulot, Rd., bp. Kild. 616
Hulse, Hugh, J.K.B. 371
— Jno., J.C.P. 378
— Rd., gen. (**C**) 873
— Saml. and sir S., F.M. 856; G.C.H. 786; G. Ch. Hosp. 936; gen. (**A**) 859; L.G. Ch. Hosp. 936; V.C.H. 297
Humbert, (St.), bp. Elm. 454
— (2) bp. Lich. 443
— I., K. It. 51; K.G. 745
— I. to III., C. Svy. 54
Humbryct, bp. Elm. 454
Hume, hon. Alexr., Dep. Tr. Sc. 497
— sir Andr., Ld. Sess. 520
— Dav., U.S.S. 226
— sir Geo., Compt. Sc. 498
— Jas., C. Cus. 276
— Jno., bp. Brl. 439; bp. Oxf. 456; bp. Sal. 467; dn. St. P. 453
— Jno., dn. Dry. 602
— Jno., Ld. Sess. 519
— sir Jno.. Comm. Tr. Sc. 498
— Jno. Rd., gen. (**D**) 921
— Jos. D., Sec. B.T. 270
— Patr., Compt. Sc. 498
— sir Patr., aft. ld. Polworth, *q.v.*
— Rt., gen. (**D**) 881
— Rt. gen. (**D**) 908; K.C.B. 782
Hume, lds.
— Alex., ld., L.G.C. Sc. (1488) 506
— (of Berwick), Geo., ld., aft. E. of Dunbar, *q.v.*, Ch. Ex. 154; M.G.W. 296
Humfrey, Humphrey, and **Humphry**
— (or Humfridus), bp. Winch. 470
— K. Scy. 55
— Ld. Chanc. Sc. 514
— Pr. (son of Hen. IV., aft. E. of Pembr. and D. of Glouc., *q.v.*, Pr. E. 11; K.B. 755; K.G. 734
— Jno., gen. (**B**) 868
— Jno., L.M. Lond. 492
— Laur., dn. Glr. 440; dn. Winch. 471
— Lebbens Ch., Q.C. 417
— Jos., M. Chy. 397; Q.C. 417
Humphreys, Fras. Richm., gen. (**C**) 872
— Humph., bp. Bgr. 426; bp. Her. 442; dn. Bgr. 426
— Rt., dn. Kilf. 637; dn. Killoe. 637
— sir Wm., L.M. Lond. 491
Hulton, Wm. A., C.C.J. 403
Humston, Rt., bp. Down. & Cnr. 604
Hunden, Jno., bp. Llff. 449
Hunferthus, bp. Elm. 454
Hungerford, Ed., K.B. 763
— Rt., K.B. 756
— Th., K.B. 758
— sir Th., Sp. H.C. 248
— Walt., *see* ld. H., *infra*
Hungerford, lds.
— Walt., aft. sir W. and ld. H., Const. W. Cast. 322; K.B. 756; K.G. 735; L.H.A. 174; L.H.T. 153; Sp. H.C. 248
Hunks, sir Hy., G. Bdoes. 719
Hunsdon, lds.
— Hy., 1st ld., C.G.P. 299; E. M. 326; K.G. 738; L.C.H. 294; L.K. and C.G.S. 356
— Geo., 2nd ld., C.G.P. 299; K.G. 739; L.C.H. 294
Hunt and **Hunte**
— Ed., Sr. N. 257
— Geo. Ev., gen. (**D**) 895
— Geo., Ruthv. le, G. Dnca. 731
— Geo. Ward, Ch. Ex. 166; L. Admy. 185; L.T. 161; P.C. 217; Sec. Tr. 164
— Jno., C.J.K.B. Ir. 577
— Jno., or Wm., *see* Wm., *infra*
— Percival, L.M. Dbln. 641
— Rd., A.G. 398
— Rd., dn. Dham. 479
— Rt. W. Bl., gen. (**D**) 927
— Rog., B. Ex. 383; Sp. H.C. 248
— Wm. le, S.L. 411
— Wm. or Jno., M.Ch[illegible] 5
Hunt-Grubbe, *see* Grubbe
Hunter, Andr , gen. (**D**) 910
— Arth. Stew.(gen. (**D**) 931
— Cl. Steph. and sir C., L.M. Lond. 492
— Dav., gen. (**A**) 862
— Dav., gen. (**C**) 873
— Fitzw. Fk., gen. (**D**) 927
— Geo., gen. (**D**) 880
*— Jno., adm. (**A**) 817
*— Capt. —, G. N.S.W. (1795) 702
* ? same pers.
— Jno., Chn. E.I. Co. 644
— Mart. and sir M., G.C.H. 786; G.C.M.G. 794; G. N. Brk. 695; gen. (**A**) 861
— Montg., gen. (**D**) 930
— Pet., G. Br. Hond. 714

For List of Abbreviations, see pp. 944-952

Hunter—*cont.*
— Rt., G. Jam. 712; gen. (**C**) 871
— Th. O., L. Admy. 178-9; L.T. 157
— Wm., L.M. Lond. 492
— Wm. Guyer, K.C.M.G. 798
— Wm. Wils. and sir W., C.I.E. 806; K.C.S.I. 803
Huntercombe, Th. de, Const. W. Cast. 322
Huntingdon, Jno., Wdn. Chr. Ch. Manch. 481
— Rt., bp Rph. 601
— Rt., C. Exc. 278
— Wm. de, Ld. Chanc. Sc. 514
Huntingdon, E. of
— Dav., 5th E. of, bro. of Wm., K. of Scotland, L.J. Gen. 522 (*d.* 1219)
— Wm., E. of, form. Wm. Clinton and sir W., *q.v.*, L.H.A. 172
— Guich. E. of, form. G. D'Angle, *q.v.*
Holland Family.
— Jno., 1st E. of, form. Jno. Holand, *q.v.*, aft. 1st D. Exeter, *q.v.*, L.H.A. 173
— Jno., 2nd E. of, aft. D. of Exeter, *q.v.*, K.B. 756; K.G. 735; L.H.A. 174
Grey Family.
— Th., E. of, aft. M. of Dorset, *q.v.*, K.B. (1475) 757
Hastings Family.
— Fras., 2nd E. of, form. Fras. Hastings, *q.v.*, K.G. 738
— Hy., 3rd E. of, form. Hy. Hastings, *q.v.*, K.G. 738
— Theoph., 7th E. of, C.G.P. 299; P.C. 192
— Fras., 10th E. of, Gr. St. 304; M.H. 302; L.L. Yorks. W.R. 313; P.C. 200
— Hans Fras., 11th E. of, G. Dnca. 730
Huntingfield, Rog. de, J. It. 366
— Wm. de, J. It. 366; W.C.P. 317
Huntingford, Geo. Is., bp. Glr. 439; bp. Her. 442
Huntley and **Huntly**
— Hy. Vere and sir H., G. Pr. Ed. Isl. 699
Huntly, E. and M. of
— Geo., 2nd E. of, L.J. Gen. 522; Ld. Chanc. Sc. 515
— Geo., 4th E. of, Ld. Chanc. Sc. 515
— Geo., 5th E. of, Ld. Chanc. Sc. 515
— Geo., 2nd M. of, form. ld. G. Gordon, and visc. Aboyne, *q.v.*
— Geo., M. of, and E. of Aboyne, aft. 5th D. of Gordon, *q.v.*, G.C.B. 768; gen. (**A**) 860; K.T. 748
— Ch., 10th M. of, L.L. Abdn. 508
— Ch., 11th M. of, C.G.A. 300; P.C. 219
Hurd, Rd., bp. Lich. and Cov. 444; bp. Worc. 473
Hurdle, Th., gen. (**D**) 894; K.C.B. 780
Hurley, Th., bp. Emly, 625
Husain, Husein, and **Hussein**
— Ali Khan, C.I.E. 807
— Kh. Bah. Sair., C.I.E. 807
— Kh. Haj. Murz., G.C.S.I. 801
Husato, Hub. de, W.C.P. 317
Huscarl, Rt. or Rog., Jy. 364
Huse, *see* Husse and Hussey
Husee, *see also* Hussey
— Anthy., J. Adm. Ct. 422
Husein, *see* Husain
Huske, Jno., gen. (**B**) 865
Huskisson, sir Jno. Ralph, form. Milbanke, *q.v.*
— Saml., gen. (**A**) 863
— Wm., B.T. 268; C.W.F. &c. 271; P.C. 209; Pres. B.T. 268; Sec. Tr. 163; Tr. N. 256; U.S.W. 231; W. and C. Sec. 231
Husse and **Hussey**
— —, M. Chy. 395
— Hy., dn. Wlls. 428
— Dudl., Rec. Dbln. 642
— Jas., B. Ex. 383
— Lawr., M. Chy. 395
— Rd., K.C. 415
— sir Rd. Huss., aft. Hussey-Vivian, *see* Vivian
— Rd. Huss. Moubr., adm. (**A**) 819; G.C.M.G. 794; K.C.B. 776
— Th., S.L. 412
— Walt., B. Ex. Ir. 583
— (or Huse, or Husse), Wm. and sir W., A.G. 398; C.J.K.B. 370; S.L. 407
Husseburn, Th. de, J. It. 366; Jy. 363
Hussein, *see* Husain
Hussey, *see* Husse
Hussey-Vivian, *see* Vivian
Hustaart, Jac., G. Ceyl. 672
Hutchens, *see* Hutchins
Hutchenson, *see* Hutchinson
Hutchessen, Th., gen. (**D**) 884
Hutchins, Geo. and sir G., C.G.S. 357; S.L. 411
Hutchinson and **Hutchenson**
— hon. Abr. Hely-, C. Cus. 277; C. Cus. Ir. 565-6
— Alexr. Hadd., gen. (**D**) 925
— Arch., B.T. 264
— Ch. Hy., gen. (**D**) 909
— Ch. Scr., gen. (**D**) 915
— Ch. Wat., gen. (**D**) 919
— Coote Sy., gen. (**D**) 917
— Ed. Hely-, gen. (**D**) 894
— Fras., Arund. H. 339; Chest. H. 331
— Fras., bp. Down and Cnr. 604
— Geo., gen. (**D**) 914
— Jno. Hely-, P.C. 204; S.L. Ir. 592; Sec. St. Ir. 562
— Jno. Hely-, *see* ld. H., *infra*
— Rd. Hely-, aft. 2nd ld., 1st visc., and 1st E. of Donoughmore *q.v.*, C. Acc. Ir. 567; C. Cus. Ir. 565
— Saml., bp. Killa. and Ach. 613; dn, Drom. 606
— hon. Walt. Fras. Hely-, K.C.M.G. 799
— sir Wm., gen. (**A**) 862; K.C.H. 788
— Wm. Nels., gen. (**D**) 892
Hutchinson, lds.
— Jno. Hely-, aft. ld. H. and 2nd E. of Donoughmore, *q.v.*, Amb. Pr. 118; G.C.B. 767; gen. (**A**) 860; K.B. 766
Hutchison, Fras. Deane, adm. (**H**) 848
— Geo., Modr. K. Sc. 547
Huthwaite, Ed., gen. (**D**) 891; K.C.B. 780
— Hy., gen. (**D**) 878
Hutt, Geo., K.C.B. 782
— Jno., G. W. Austr., 707
— Wm., K.C.B. 783; P.C. 217; Paym. G. 245; V.P.B.T. 269
Hutton, Cr., C.C.J. 405
— Fk., adm. (**D**) 833
— Geo., gen. (**D**) 890
— Hy., gen. (**B**) 868
— Hy., L.M. Dbln. 641
— Hy. Pr., gen. (**D**) 924
— Jno., Bl. M. P.A. 336; Guis. P.A. 343
— Matth. (No. 1), abp. Yk. 486; bp. Dham. 479; dn. Yk. 487
— Matth. (No. 2), abp. Cant. 431; abp. Yk. 486; bp. Bgr. 426; P.C. 199
— Rd. and sir R., J.C.P. 378; S.L. 409
— Rt., S.L. 409
— Th., M. Chy. 394
Huxley, Th. Hy., Pres. R. Soc. 940
Huxtable, Hy. Const., bp. Mtius. 684
Huycke, *see* Huick
Huyshe, Alfr., gen. (**D**) 902
— Geo., gen. (**D**) 888
Hy—, *see* Hi—
Hyde, —, S.L. 410
— Alexr., bp. Sal. 467; dn. Winch. 471
— Ed., dn. Winds. 474
— Ed., *see* ld. H., *infra*
— Fk., S.L. 410
— Geo., K.B. 761
— Geo. Hoolt., gen. (**D**) 899
— Hy., gen. (**D**) 918
— Hy., aft. 2nd E. of Clarendon, *q.v.*. K.B. 763
— Laur., *see* visc. H., *infra*
— Nichs. and sir N., C.J.K.B. 370; S.L. 409
— Rt. and sir R., C.J.K.B. 370; J.C.P. 379; S.L. 409
— Th., J. Adm. Ct. 423
— Th. de la, J. It. 369
— West, gen. (**C**) 872
Hyde, lds. and visc.
Hyde Family.
— Ed., aft. 1st ld. H., visc. Cornbury, and E. of Clarendon, *q.v.*, B.T. 263; Ch. Ex. 154; L.T. 155; L.K. 356; P.C. 189
— Hy., aft. 2nd E. of Clarendon, *q.v.*, K.B. 763
— Hy., ld., aft. 4th E. of Clarendon, and 2nd E. of Rochester, *q.v.*, P.C. 195; Prem. 140; V. Treas. Ir. 559
— hon. Laur., aft. 1st visc. H. and E. of Rochester (New Cr.), *q.v.*, Ch. Ex. 164; L.T. 155; P.C. 192
Hyde of Hindon, lds.
Villiers Family.
— Th., ld., aft. 1st E. of Clarendon, *q.v.*, C.D.L. 243; P.C. 201; Postm. G. 238
Hyderabad, Salar Jung, Bah. of, K.C.I.E. 805
— Begum of, Cr. Ind. 809
— Niz. of, G.C.S.I. 800
— Niz. of, G.C.S.I. 801
— Niz. of, K.C.S.I. 802
— Salar Jung, Bah. of K.C.S.I. 802
Hyende, *see* Heende

Hygden, *see* Higden
Hyginus, P. Ro. 52
Hygons, Ed., M. Chy. 394
Hylle, Th., L.M. Lond. 490
Hylton, Wm. Geo., ld., form. Wm. Geo. Hylton-Jolliffe, *q.v.*
Hyndestone, Wm., S.L. 407
Hyndford, E. of
— Jno., 1st E. of, form. 2nd ld. Carmichael, *q.v.*, Sec. St. Sc. 502
— Jno., 3rd E. of, K.T. 747; L.H.C.K. Sc. 546; P.C. 199; V.A. Sc. 499
Hyngham, —, K.B. 757
Hypsœus, C. P. V. (2), C. Ro. 40
— M. P., C. Ro. 45
Hythe, Haymo de, bp. Roch. 460
Hywel, *see also* Howel
—Pr. Wls. 17
— ab Jevav, Pr. Wls. 16
— Dha (3), Pr. Wls. 16, 17

I.

Iago, *see* Jago
Ibbestock or **Ibbestoke,** Laur. de, dn. Lich. 445
Ibbetson, sir H. J. Selw., P.C. 220; Sec. Tr. 164; U.S. Home, 228
Ibbotson, Jno., Sec. Adm. 187
Ibrahim, S. Tky. 97
— V. Eg. 98
Icomaid, Jno., bp. Kilmacd. 636
Ida, K.E. 2
Idar, Mahar of, K.C.S.I. 803
Iddesleigh, E. of
— Staff. Hy., 1st E. of, form. sir S. H. Northcote, *q.v.*, F. Sec. 229; L.L. Dev. 307; L.T. 162
— Walt. Staff., 2nd E. of, form. W. S. Northcote, and visc. St. Cyres, *q.v.*
— Countess of, form. Lady Northcote, *q.v.*
Iddesworth, Hy. de, M. Chy. 393
Idle, —, C.B. Ex. Sc. 523
Idunan, bp. Cld. 599
Idwallo, K. Wls. 16
Ifeld, Jno. de, J. It. 369
Iglesias, M., Dt. Pu. 109
Igor, R. Russ. 89
Ilay, E. of, *see* Isla
Ileyan, Greg., bp. Kilmacd. 636
— Maur., bp. Kilmacd. 636
— Nichs., bp. Kilmacd. 636
Ilchester, Ad. de, dn. Sal. 468
Ilchester, E. of
— Steph., 1st E. of, form. St. Fox-Strangways, *q.v.*, P.C. 201
Ilchester, E. of—*cont.*
— Hy. Steph., 3rd E. of, C.Y.G. 298; L.L. Soms. 311; P.C. 213
— Wm. Th. H., 4th E. of, form. W. T. H. Fox-Strangways, *q.v.*
— Hy. E., 5th E. of, C.G.A. 300; L.L. Dors. 307; P.C. 218
Illingworth, sir Rd., C.B. Ex. 381; K.B. 757
— Temp., dn. Emly, 628
Iltute, abp. Lond. 450
Imam Baksh, &c., C.I.E. 807; K.C.I.E. 805
Imhoff, sir Ch., gen. (**A**) 862
— Gust. W. Van, G. Ceyl. 672
Imperiosus, C. M. C. (2), C. Ro. 40
— L. M. C., Dt. Ro. 40
Impey, sir Elij., C.J. Bgal. 652
— Eugene, Cl., C.I.E. 806
— Jno., adm. (**D**) 825, (**G**) 840
Imurily (or Smurily), Jno., bp. Ross. 631
Ina, K.E. 2
Inas, K.E. 2
Ince, Hy. Br., Q.C. 419
— Jno., G. Bdoes. 720
Incent, Jno., dn. St. P. 453
Inchiquin, lds. and E. of
— Murr., 5th ld. and 1st E. of, form. M. O'Brien, *q.v.*, P.C. 189
— Wm., 2nd E. of, G. Jam. 712
— Wm., 4th E. of, K.B. 764
— Murr., 5th E. of, aft. 1st M. of Thomond, *q.v.*, K.P. 750
— Luc., 13th ld., form. L. O'Brien, *q.v.*
— Ed. D., 14th ld., L.L. Clare, 569
Inderwick, Fk. Andr., Q.C. 419
Indore, Mahar of, G.C.S.I. 800
— Mahar of, *see* Holkar
— Saheb of, K.C.S.I. 803
Indrect, bp. Kilmacd. 636
Indulfus, K. Sc. 19
Ingaldesthorpe, *see* Inglethorpe
Ingall, Wm. Len., gen. (**D**) 905
Inge, Hugh, abp. Dbln. and Gl. 616; bp. Mth. 599; Ld. Chanc. Ir. 576
— Jno., J.C.P. 377
— Wm., A.G. 398; C.J.K.B. 369; J.C.P. 377; J. It. 368; S.L. 406
Ingelby, *see* Ingleby
Ingeld, K. Sw. 92
Ingelram or **Ingelramus,** bp. Glasg. 536; Ld. Chanc. Sc. 514
Ingham, Ern. Gr., bp. Si. Le. 686
— Rt., Q.C. 417
— Theoph. H., C.C.J. 403
Ingilfield, *see* Inglefield
Ingilby, *see* Ingleby
Ingleby, Ingelby, and **Ingilby**
— Ch. and sir C., B. Ex. 384; B. Ex. Ir. 584; S.L. 411
— Jno., bp. Llff. 449
— Th. de, J.C.P. 378; J.K.B. 371
— Wm. Bates and sir W., gen. (**D**) 895; K.C.B. 779
Inglefield and **Ingilfield**
— Ed. Augs. and sir E., adm. (**E**) 835; K.C.B. 781
— Saml. Hood, adm. (**D**) 826
— Th., K.B. 759
— Val. Otw., adm. (**H**) 853
Inglesham, Rt. de, Jy. 363
Inglethorpe (or Ingaldesthorpe), Th. de, bp. Roch. 459; dn. St. P. 452
Inglis, Alexr., bp. Dkld. 533; Compt. Sc. 498; Ld. Clk. Reg. 525; Sec. St. Sc. 502
— Ch., adm. (**A**) 815
— Ch., bp. N. Sc. 695
— Hugh and sir H., Chn. E.I. Co. 644-5
— J., bp. N. Sc. 695
— Jno., adm. (**A**) 817
— Jno., Chn. E.I. Co. 645
— Jno., D. Fac. Sc. 527; L.J. Clk. 516; L.P. Ct. Sess. 516; Ld. Adv. 526; P.C. 216; S.G. Sc. 527
— Jno., Mod. K. Sc. 547
— Jno. Eardl. Wilm. and sir J., gen. (**D**) 892; K.C.B. 778
— Jno. Forbes Dav., Ch. Com. Oudh. 654
— sir Rt. H., P.C. 216
— Wm., gen. (**D**) 906
— Wm. and sir W., gen. (**B**) 868; K.C.B. 775
Ingo, I. and II., K. Sw. 92
Ingoldesby, Jno., B. Ex. 383
— Rd., gen. (**B**) 864; L.J. Ir. 555-6
— Rd., K.B. 764
Ingram, sir Arth., Coff. H. 293
— Aug. Hy., adm. (**H**) 850
— Herb. Fk. Winn., adm. (**H**) 852
— sir Th., C.D.L. 242; P.C. 190
Ingualdus, bp. Lond. 450
Innerkeithing and **Inverkeithing**
— Rd. de, bp. Dkld. 533; Ld. Chanc. Sc. 514
Innermeath, Jas., ld., Ld. Sess. 517
Innes, Geo., bp. Brn. 541
— Harry, gen. (**B**) 866
— Jas. Ch., gen. (**D**) 908
— Jas. Jno. McL., gen. (**D**) 928
— Jno., bp. Cness. 531
— Jno., bp. Mor. 534
— Jno. Harr. K., K.C.B. 782
— Pet., gen. (**D**) 892
— Rt., Ly. Dep. 513
— Wm., gen. (**D**) 877
Innocent I. to XIII., P. Ro. 33-4-5-6
Insula, Brian de, J. It. 367
— Godfr. de, Jy. 364
— Jno. de, B. Ex. 383; J. It. 368
— Pet. de, M. Chy. 393
— Rog. de, dn. Yk. 486
— Rt. de, bp. Dham. 478
— Sim. de, Jy. 364
— Wm. de, J. It. 367; Jy. 364
Inverkeithing, *see* Innerkeithing
Inwardby, Geo., K.B. 759
Ippegrave, Th. de, Const. T.L. 320
Irby, hon. Fk. Paul, adm. (**D**) 823

Ireland, Jno., dn. Westr. 469
—— Jno., G. I. Man, 666
—— sir Jno., G. I. Man, 665
Irene, Emp. E.E. 50
—— Emp. Tzde. 98
—— -Marie-Louisa-Anna(g.dau. Q. Vict.), Pr. E. 15
Ireton, Hy., L.D. Ir. 554
—— sir Jno., L.M. Lond. 491
—— Rod. de, bp. Carl. 475
Irgalach, bp. Saig. 620
Ironside, Ed., L.M. Lond. 492
—— Gilb., bp. Brl. 439; bp. Her. 442
Irvine, *see also* Irving
—— Ch., gen. (**C**) 874
—— Alex., gen. (**D**) 916
—— Ch., gen. (**D**) 912
—— Geo. Caulf. D'A., Adm. (**E**) 837
—— sir J., Comm. F. Ir. 564
—— Wm., Sc. Bp. 545
Irving, *see also* Irvine
—— Alex., gen. (**D**) 902
—— Alex., Ld. Sess. 520
—— capt. —, G. W. Austr. 707
—— Geo., gen. (**D**) 877
—— Hy. Turn. and sir H., G. Br. Gu. 715; G.C.M.G. 796; G. Leew. Isl. 727; G. Trin. 722; K.C.M.G. 797
—— lt.-col. —, G. Gsey. 669
—— Paul Æ., G. Can. 491; gen. (**A**) 860
Irwin, Alex., dn. Ardf. 640
—— Fk. Chidl., K.H. 791
—— Hy., C.I.E. 808
—— Jno. and sir J., G. Gibr. 670; gen. (**A**) 858; K.B. 765
—— lt.-col. —, G. W. Austr. 707
—— Wm., gen. (**D**) 901
—— Wm. Boyd, gen. (**D**) 914
Irwin, visc.
—— Rd., visc., G. Bdoes. (1720-1) 720
Irwine, Alex., gen. (**B**) 865
Isaac (of Newcastle-upon-Tyne), bp. Cnr. 603
—— I. and II., Emp. E.E. 51
***Isaacson,** Jas., C. Cus. Sc. 503
*—— Jas., C. St. 283
* Prob. same pers.
Isabel (dau. K. John), Pr. E. 9
—— (dau. Edw. III.), Pr. E. 10
—— (iss. Edw. III.), Pr. E. 11
Isabella (dau. Jas. II.), Pr.E.13
—— (of Angoulême), Q.C.E. 7
—— (of France), Q.C.E. 7
—— (of Valois), Q.C.E. 7
—— Q. Jsm. 97
—— R. Nds. 83
—— I. and II., Q. Sp. 86
Isauricus, P. S. V. (2), C. Ro. 46
Iscanus, Barth., bp. Exr. 436
Isenei, Garn. de, Const. T.L. 320
Isham, Jno., U.S.S. 225
—— Edm., Adm. Adv. 423
Ishwara Chandra, &c., C.I.E. 806
Isjialaw, I. and II., R. Russ. 89
Isla or **Islay,** Archd., E. of, aft 3rd D. of Argyll, *q.v.*, L.J. Gen. 522; L.K. Sc. 503; L.P.S. Sc. 501; Ld. Clk. Reg. 525; Ld. Sess. 517; P.C. 196
Islip, Sim., abp. Cant. 430
Ismail, Sh. Pers. 99
—— Meerza, Sh. Pers. 99
—— Pacha, V. Eg. 98; G.C.B. 773; G.C.S.I. 801
Ispania, Jas. de, dn. St. Pat. 617
Istlep or **Isteley,** Walt. de, L. Tr. Ir. 558
Ithamar, Saint, bp. Roch. 459
Iturvide, A., Emp. Mex. 103
Ivan I. to V., R. Russ. 89, 90
—— VI., E. Russ. 90
Ives, Cec. Rt. St. Jno., gen. (**D**) 922
—— Jno., Suff. H. 341
Ivo, dn. Wells, 428
Ivory, Jas., Jy. Sc. 523; K.H. 790; Ld. Sess. 520; S.G. Sc. 527
Ivyn, *see* Juyn

J.

J * * *, dn. Lim. 639
Jackman, Ch., gen. (**C**) 872
Jackson, Alexr. Cosb., gen. (**B**) 868
—— Andr., Pres. U.S.A. 102
—— Ch., dn. Chr. Ch. Dbln. 618
—— Ch., gen. (**D**) 923
—— Ch., bp. Ferns and L. 622; bp. Kild. 617
—— Cyr., dn. Chr. Ch. Oxf. 457
—— Ed., K.H. 791
—— Ed. Saml., gen. (**D**) 926
—— Fras. J., Amb. Dk. 127; Amb. Fr. 112; Amb. Pr. 118; Amb. Tky. 129; Amb. U.S.A. 132
—— Geo., gen. (**D**) 916
—— Geo. and sir G., gen. (**D**) 878; K.C.H. 788
—— sir Geo., Sec. Adm. 187
—— Geo. Vern., adm. (**H**) 848
—— Hy. M., and sir H., J.Q.B.D. 374; Q.C. 419
—— Hy. Moore, G. T. and C. Isl. 713
—— J., C. Exc. Sc. 505
—— Jas. and sir J., gen. (**D**) 884; G.C.B. 770; K.C.B. 778; K.H. 792
—— Jas. Ed., dn. Arm. 597
—— Jno., bp. Linc. 447; bp. Lond. 452; Jud. Com. P.C. 361; P.C. 218
—— Jno., G. C.G.H. 679
—— Jno. Napp, gen. (**D**) 893
—— Jos. Dev., J.C.P. Ir. 582; S.G. Ir. 590; S.L. Ir. 593
—— Louis Sten., C.I.E. 806
—— Rand., Chest. H. 330; Mt. Org. P.A. 343
—— Rd., K.C. 415
—— Rd., L.T. 158
—— Rd. Downes and sir R., gen. (**B**) 869; K.C.B. 774
—— Rt., adm. (**D**) 824
—— Saml., adm. (**D**) 827
—— Saml., C.I.E. 807
—— Th., Amb. Sda. 114
Jackson—*cont.*
—— Th., dn. Pboro. 458
—— Wm., Amb. Ch. 130
—— Wm., bp. Oxf. 457
—— Wm., C. Exc. 281
—— Wm., dn. Killa. 614
—— Wm. L., Sec. Tr. 164
—— Wm. Walr., bp. Antig. 728
Jacob, *see also* Jacobe
—— Ed., K.C. 416
—— Geo. Legr., K.C.S.I. 803
—— Hy. Eb., gen. (**D**) 915
—— Herb., gen. (**D**) 896
—— sir Jno., C. Cus. 273
—— Matth. Penn., C. St. Ir. 568
—— Michl. Ed., gen. (**C**) 873
Jacobe, *see also* Jacob
—— sir Rt., S.G. Ir. 589
Jacobson, Wm., bp. Chest. 477
Jacobus, *see* James
Jacopin, Laur. Pet., bp. Ach. 612
Jacquelina, C. Hld. 82
Jaenbert, *see* Lambert
Jaffir Khan, Sh. Pers. 99
Jago and **Iago**
—— Pr. Wls. 16
—— ab Edwal, Pr. Wls. 16
—— Ch. Trel., adm. (**E**) 837
Jahangir, Kh. Bah. Pest., C.I.E. 807
James and **Jacobus**
*—— (abb. of Dunfermline) Compt. Sc. 498
*—— dn. Clonf. 637
*—— dn. Tm. 613
*—— dn. Oss. 622
* Prob. some same pers. Comp. dates
—— (g. son Hy. VII.), Pr. E. 12
—— (son Chas. I.), Pr. E. 13
—— D. of Monmouth, *q.v.*, (son Chas. II.) Pr. E. 13
—— (son Jas. II.), Pr. E. 13
—— [Fras. Ed.] (son Jas. II.), Pr. E. 13
—— I., Emp. Hti. 104
—— I., K. Scy. 55
—— I., M. Bdn. 67
—— I. and II., K. Arr. 86
—— I. and II., K.E. 5, 6
—— II. (K. E.), form. D. of Yk., *q.v.*, L.H.A. 176
—— I. to VI., K. Sc. 19-20
—— I. (K. Sc.), K.B. 756
—— V. (K. Sc.), K.G. 737
—— VI. (K. Sc.), K.G. 739 (*see* Jas. I., K.E.)
—— Bart., L.M. Lond. 490
—— Ch. B., gen. (**D**) 886
—— Edwd., Q.C. 417
—— Edwin Jno., Q.C. 417
—— Fras., M. Chy. 395
—— Geo., gen. (**D**) 898
—— Haught., gen. (**D**) 898
—— Hy. and sir H., A.G. 400; P.C. 220; Q.C. 418; S.G. 402
—— sir Hy., gen. (**D**) 903
—— Herb. Arm., dn. St. As. 463
—— Herb. Hend., gen. (**D**) 927
—— Jno., Amb. Nds. &c. 122
—— sir Jno., C. Exc. 278
—— sir Jno. K., L.M. Dbln. 641-2
—— Jno. Th., bp. Calc. 653
—— Jno. Polg., gen. (**D**) 886
—— sir Walt. J., Wdn. M. 245
—— Wm., bp. Dham. 479; dn. Chr. Ch. Oxf. 457; dn. Dham. 479

James and Jacobus—*cont.*
— Wm., L.M. Dbln. 641
— Wm. and sir W., Chn. E.I. Co. 644
— Wm. M. and sir W., Jud. Com. P.C. 361; L.J. App. 389; P.C. 218; Q.C. 417; V. Chanc. 390
Jameson, Geo. Ingl., gen. (**D**) 897; K.C.S.I. 803
— Wm., C.I.E. 806
Jamieson, Rt., Modr. K. Sc. 547
Jamys, Jno., M. Chy. 394
Jane, C. Flrs. 81
— C. Hlt. 82
— D. Bbt. 29
— (Seymour), Q.C.E. 8
— Th., bp. Norw. 455
— Wm., dn. Glr. 440
Janisch, Huds. Ralph, G. St. Hel. 682
Jansens, Jan. W., G. C.G.H. 678
Janssen, sir Steph. Theoph., Chambn. Lond. 493; L.M. Lond. 492
Jaraslaw I. to III., R. Russ. 89
Jardine, Alexr., gen. (**D**) 894
— Jno., dn. Thist. 749
Jarlath (St.), bp. Arm. 595; bp. Tm. 611
Jaromir, D. Bma. 59
Jaropalk I. and II., R. Russ. 89
Jaruman, bp. Lich. 443
Jarvis, B. E., G. Antig. 728
— Saml. Pet., gen. (**D**) 924
Jasper Tudor (son of Owen Tudor), Pr. E. 12
Jaures, Jean Louis Ch., K.C.B. 779
Jay, Rd., S.L. 407
Jayne, Fras. Jno., bp. Chest. 477
Jeaff—, *see* Jeff—
Jebb, Jno, bp. Lim., A. and A. 639
— Jno., dn. Cash. 627
— Jos. and sir J., gen. (**D**) 895; K.C.B. 782
— Rd., J.K.B. Ir. 579; S.L. Ir. 593
Jefferay, *see* Jeffrey
Jefferies, *see* Jeffreys
Jefferson, Jeffreson, and **Jeffreyson**
— Chr., gen. (**B**) 868
— Jno. and sir J., C.G.S. Ir. 576; J.C.P. Ir. 581; S.L. 410
— T., Pres. U.S.A. 102
Jeffery, *see* Jeffrey
Jeffrey, Jeffery, and **Jefferay**
— Fras., D. Fac. Sc. 527; Ld. Adv. 526; Ld. Sess. 520
— Jno. and sir J., C.B. Ex. 381; J.Q.B. 372; S.L. 408
— sir Rt., L.M. Lond. 491
Jeffreson, *see* Jefferson
Jeffreys, Jeffries, and **Jefferies**
— Ch., gen. (**B**) 865
— Ed., J. Chest. 387; Q.C. 415
— Edmd. Rd., gen. (**D**) 903
— Geo., *see* d. J., *infra*
— Jas., C. Cus. 276
— Jno., Wdn. M. 245
— St. Jno., C. Acc. Ir. 567
Jeffreys, lds.
— Geo., aft. sir G. and ld. J., C.J. Chest. 386; C.J.K.B. 370; Comm. Sergt. Lond. 495; K.C. 414; L.H.S. 286; Ld. Chanc. 357; P.C. 192; Rec. Lond. 494; S.L. 410
Jeffreyson, *see* Jefferson
Jeffries, *see* Jeffreys
Jeggon or **Jegon,** Jno., bp. Norw. 455; dn. Norw. 455
Jekyll, Jos., M. Chy. 397
— Jos. and sir J., C.G.S. 357; C.J. Chest. 386; K.C. 415; M.R. 388; P.C. 197; S.L. 411
Jelf, Arth. Rd., Q.C. 419
Jellett, H. P., S.L. Ir. 593
Jenkin, Mered., L.M. Dbln. 641
Jenkins and **Jenkyns,** Ch. Vanbr., gen. (**D**) 916
— Ch. Vern., gen. (**D**) 928
— Jas., K.C.B. 782
— Jno. Jas., gen. (**D**) 910
— sir Leol., J. Adm. Ct. 423; J. Pr. Ct. 421; P.C. 192; S. St. 223
— Lewis, C. St. 284
— Rd., Chn. E.I. Co. 645; G.C.B. 772
— Rd., dn. Wells, 429
— Rt., adm. (**E**) 836; (**F**) 839
Jenkinson, Ch., aft. 1st ld. Hawkesbury, and 1st E. of Liverpool, *q.v.*, B.T. 267; L. Admy. 179; L.T. 157; P.C. 202; Sec. at W. 234; Sec. Tr. 163; U.S.S. 226; V. Treas. Ir. 560
— hon. Ch. C. C., aft. 3rd E. of Liverpool, *q.v.*, U.S. Home, 227; U.S.W. and C. 231
— Ed. Geo., K.C.B. 784
— Hy., adm. (**H**) 845
— Jno., gen. (**B**) 868
— Jno. B., bp. St. Dav. 465; dn. Dham. 479; dn. Worc. 474
— hon. Rt. B., aft. ld. Hawkesbury, and 2nd E. of Liverpool, *q.v.*, B.C. 252
Jenkyns, *see* Jenkins
Jenner, Hy. Lasc., bp. Dun. 710
— Herb., aft. sir H., aft. Jenner-Fust, D. Arch. 421; J. Pr. Ct. 421; Jud. Com. P.C. 360; K. Adv. 422; P.C. 213; Vic. Gen. 422
— sir Th., B. Ex. 384; J.C.P. 379; Rec. Lond. 494; S.L. 410
— sir Wm., K.C.B. 783; Pres. Coll. Ph. 938
Jenney and **Jenny**
— Chr. and sir C., J.C.P. 378; S.L. 408
— Wm., J.K.B. 372; S.L. 407
Jennings, Ch. Jas., gen. (**D**) 930
— Jno., K.B. 763
— sir Jno., adm. (**A**) 813; G. Gr. Hosp. 854; L. Admy. 177
— Patr., K.C.M.G. 797
— Wm., dn. Glr. 440
— Wm. (No. 1), Berw. P.A. 341; R. Cr. P.A. 335
— Wm. (No. 2), Lanc. H. 332; Guis. P.A. 343
— Wm., Q.C. 415
— sir Wm., adm. (**A**) 813
Jenny, *see* Jenney
Jenour, sir Jno., Sec. Bath 784
Jenyns, Soame, B.T. 265-6
— Steph., K.B. 760; L.M. Lond. 490
Jephson, Michl., dn. St. Pat. 618
— Stanh. Wm., gen. (**D**) 896
— Wm., dn. Lism. 629
— Wm., S.L. 412
Jeremie, Jas. A., dn. Linc. 448
— Jno., G. Si. Le. 685; *see also* Jermey
Jermey, *see also* Jeremie
— Hy., K.B. 760
Jermin and **Jermyn**
— Hugh Will., bp. Brn. 541; bp. Cmbo. 673; Pr. Bp. Sc. 540
— Ph., J.K.B. 372; S.L. 409
— Thos. and sir T., Compt. H. 292; G. Jsey. 667; K.B. 761; V.C.H. 296
Jermyn, lds. and E.
Jermyn Family.
— Hy., aft. 1st ld. J. and 1st E. of St. Albans, *q.v.*, G. Jsey. 667; P.C. 189
— Th., 2nd ld., G. Jsey. 667
— Hy., 3rd ld., form. ld. Dover, *q.v.*
Hervey Family.
— Fredk. Wm., E., form. ld. Hervey, *q.v.*, aft. 1st M. of Bristol, *q.v.*, P.C. 214; Tr. H. 291
Jerningham, Arth. Wm., adm. (**H**) 849
— hon. Geo. S. S., Amb. Nds. &c. 123; Amb. Spn. 124; Amb. Sw. and N. 127
— Hy. and sir H., C.Y.G. 298; K.B. 760; M.H. 301
— hon. W. G. S., Amb. Pu. 135
Jerome, Hy. Ed., gen. (**D**) 928
— Jno., gen. (**D**) 915
Jerraw, Jos., gen. (**D**) 885
Jersey, E. of
— Ed., 1st E. of, form. ld. and visc. Villiers, *q.v.*, L.C.H. 295; L.J. Ir. 555; P.C. 194; S. St. 224
— Wm., 3rd E. of, P.C. 199
— Geo. B., 4th E. of, form. visc. Villiers, *q.v.*, C.G.P. 299; M.B.H. 303
— Geo., 5th E. of, G.C.H. 787; L.C.H. 295; M.H. 302; P.C. 211
— Vict. Alb. Geo., 7th E. of, L.L. Oxon, 311
Jervis, Hy., gen. (**D**) 899
— sir Humphr., L.M. Dbln. 640
— sir Jno., aft. ld. and E. St. Vincent, *q.v.*, adm. (**A**) 815; K.B. 765
— Jno., and sir J., A.G. 400; C.J.C.P. 376; Jud. Com. P.C. 215; P.P. 416; S.G. 402; S.L. 413
— Th., J. Chest. 387; P.P. 415; K.C. 416
— Wm. Hy., adm. (**H**) 848
Jervoise, Wm., G. H. Kong, 673; gen. (**D**) 881; K.H. 791
— Wm. Fras. Dr. and sir W., G.C.M.G. 795; G. N.Z. 709; G. S. Austr. 707; G. Str. Sett. 675; gen. (**D**) 917; K.C.M.G. 797

Jessel, Geo. and sir G., Jud. Com. P.C. 361; M.R. 388; P.C. 218; Q.C. 418; S.G. 402
Jessop, Wm., J. Chest. 387
Jeswunt, Thakoor R., K.C.S.I. 802
Jeune, Fras., bp. Pboro. 458; dn. Jsey. 668; dn. Linc. 448
—— Fras. Hy., Q.C. 420
Jevaf (or Jevav), Pr. Wls. 16
Jevan, bp. St. Dav. 464
Jevav, *see* Jevaf
Jewan, Sing Buria, C.I.E. 808
Jewell, Jno., bp. Sal. 467
Jeypore, Mahar of, G.C.S.I. 802
Jheend, Bah. of, G.C.S.I. 801; K.C.S.I. 802
Jioji, Sindia Rao, gen. (**D**) 915
Joachim I. and II., M. Brg. 65
—— -Ernest, C. Anht. 66
—— -Fredk., M. Brg. 65
Joan, Q. Cle. 86
—— (dau. Hy. II.), Pr. E. 9
—— (dau. K. John), Pr. E. 9
—— (dau. Edw. I.), Pr. E. 10
—— (dau. Edw. II.), Pr. E. 10
—— (dau. Edw. III.), Pr. E. 10
—— (g. dau. Edw. III.), Pr. E. 11
Joanna (of Navarre), Q.C.E. 7
—— I. and II., Q. Nls. 56
—— I. to III., Q. Nav. 87-8
Jobson, sir Fras., Lt. T.L. 321
Joceline and **Joseline,** *see also* Jocelyn, Josselynt, and Josselynn
—— bp. Glasg. 536; bp. B. and W. 427; Jy. 363
Jocelyn, *see also* Jocelinè, Josceline, Josselyn, and Josselyne
—— hon. Geo., C. Acc. Ir. 567
—— hon. Jno., C. Cus. Ir. 565-6
—— hon. Percy, bp. Clr. 596; bp. Ferns and L. 622
—— Rt., *see* visc. J., *infra*
Jocelyn, visc.
—— Rt., aft. ld. Newport, *q.v.*, and 1st visc. J., A.G. Ir. 588; L.J. Ir. 556; L.J. Ir. 557; Ld. Chanc. Ir. 576; S.G. Ir. 589; S.L. Ir. 592
—— Rt., visc., aft. 3rd E. of Roden, *q.v.*, P.C. 209; Tr. H. 291; V.C.H. 297
—— Rt., visc. (son of 3rd E. of Roden), Sec. B.C. 254
Joddrell, Paul, K.C. 415
Jodhpur, Bah. of, G.C.S.I. 801
Jofreir, bp. Ork. 535
***John,** abp. Cant. (desig.) 430
*—— (St.) of Beverley, abp. Yk. 485
*—— bp. Abdn. 530
*—— (2), bp. Ardf. and Agh. 639
*—— bp. Arg. 537
*—— bp. Clonf. 635
*—— bp. Clonm. 600
*—— bp. Cness. 531
*—— (2), bp. Cnr. 604
*—— bp. Dry. 601
*—— bp. Down and Cnr. 604
*—— bp. Drom. 604
*—— bp. Dkld. 533
*—— bp. Elph. 608
*—— bp. Exr. 436
*—— bp. Gall. 538

John—*cont.*
*—— bp. Glas. 536; Ld. Chanc. Sc. 514
*—— (5), bp. Isl. 539
*—— (of Taunton), bp. Kild. 616
*—— bp. Kilmacd. 636; dn. Kilmacd. 637
*—— bp. Kilmacd. 636
*—— bp. Kilm. 607
*—— bp. Llin. 621
*—— (of Tatenale), bp. Oss. 620
*—— bp. Rph. 601
*—— (2), bp. Roch. 459
*—— (2), bp. Ross. 535
*—— (2), bp. St. As. 462
*—— (2), bp. S. and M. 483
*—— bp. Wford. and L. 627
*—— dn. Ard. 609
*—— dn. Cloy. 632
*—— dn. Kild. 619
*—— dn. Oss. 622
* Prob. some same pers. Comp. dates.
—— C. Anj. 27
—— (D'Avennes), C. Hlt. 82
—— C. Lux. 84
—— D. S. Wr. 79
—— D. Hnr. 70
—— D. Bdy. 29
—— (the Constant), El. Sxy. 77
—— K. Bma. 59
—— K. Dk. 93; K.G. 737
—— (form. E. of Mortain, *q.v.*), K.E. 4; Ld. Tr. 550; L.H.A. 170
—— (De Brienne), K. Jsm. 97
—— K. Scy. 56
—— K. Sxy. 78
—— (abb. of Peterborough), L.H.T. 152
—— (prior of St. Andrews), L.P.S. Sc. 500
—— (son of Hy. II.), aft. K. John, *q.v.*, Pr. E. 9
—— (son of Hy. III.), Pr. E. 9
—— (son of Edw. I.), Pr. E. 10
—— (son of Edw. II.), Pr. E. 10
—— (g. son of Edw. III.), Pr. E. 11
—— (of Gaunt) (son of Edw. III.), Pr. E. 10
—— (Mortimer) (iss. Edw. III.), Pr. E. 10
—— (iss. Edw. III.), Pr. E. 11
—— (son of Hy. IV.), aft. E. of Kendal and D. of Bedford, *q.v.*, Pr. E. 11; K.B. 755; K.G. 734
—— Pr. Nass. 75
—— of Austrla (2), R. Nds. 82-3
—— I. and II., C. Hld. 82
—— I. and II., D. Alçn. 26
—— I. and II., D. Bva. 68
—— I. and II., D. Lne. 29
—— I. and II., K. Arr. 86
—— I. and II., K. Cle. 86
—— I. (K. Cle.), K.G. 733
—— I. and II., K. Fr. 24
—— I. and II., K. Nav. 85, 87
—— I. and II., Pr. Mkg. 74
—— I. and II., Pr. Mno. 31
—— I. to III., K. Pld. 91
—— I. to III., K. Sw. 92
—— I. to III., M. Brg. 65
—— I. to IV., D. Bbt. 29
—— I. to IV., Emp. Tzde. 9
—— I. to V., R. Russ. 89, 90
—— I. to VI., D. Bry. 28
—— I. to VI., Emp. E.E. 50-1
—— . to VI., K. Pgl. 88-9
—— I. (K. Pgl.), K.G. 735

John—*cont.*
—— II. (K. Pgl.), K.G. 736
—— VI. (K. Pgl.), K.G. 743
—— I. to XXIII., P. Ro. 33-4-5
—— II., Pr. Ltn. 73
—— -Adolph (D. of Saxe Weissenfels), K.G. 742
—— -Albert I., Pr. Mkg. 74
—— d'Albret, K. Nav. 85
—— (Baliol), K. Sc. 19
—— -Ernest, D. S.C. and G. 78
—— -Ernest, Pr. Nass. 76
—— -Ernest, I. and II., D. S. Wr. 79
—— -Fredk., D. Wbg. 11
—— -Fredk., El. Sxy. 78
—— -Gastone, G. D. Tny. 57
—— -George, M. Brg. 65
—— -George, I. to IV.. El. Sxy. 78
—— -George II. (El. Sxy.), K.G. 740
—— -George IV. (El. Sxy.), K.G. 741
—— -Kemin, Pr. Tva. 60
—— -Louis, Pr. Nass. 75
—— -Sigism., M. Brg. 65
—— -Sigism., Pr. Tva. 60
—— -Sigism., D. Pr. 65
—— Th., gen. (**D**) 928
—— -Wm., D. S. Wr. 79
—— -Wm., C.P.R. 68
—— Zapoly, Pr. Tva. 60
Johnes, *see also* Jones
—— Arth. J., C.C.J. 403
—— Hills-, form. Hills, *q.v.*
—— Jno., C.C.J. 403
—— Th , L.L. Card. 315
—— Th., L.L. Carm. 315
Johnson, *see also* Jonson
—— Allen Bay., gen. (**D**) 925
—— Alured Clarke, gen. (**D**) 930
—— Andr., Pres. U.S.A. 103
—— Cass. Matt., gen. (**D**) 890
—— Ch. Coop. and sir C., gen. (**D**) 929; K.C.B. 781
—— Ch. Rich., adm. (**H**) 850
—— Ed. Ralph., bp. Calc. 653
—— Edwin Beaum. and sir E., gen. (**D**) 904; G.C.B. 771; K.C.B. 780; M.C.I. 647
—— Geo., adm. (**H**) 851
—— Geo., J. Chest. 387; M.R. 388; S.L. 410
—— Hy. S., dn. Wells 429
—— Geo. Vand., gen. (**D**) 922
—— Hy. and sir H., G.C.B. 768; gen. (**A**) 859
—— H. R. W., Pres. Lib. 100
—— Jas., bp. Glr. 438; bp. Worc. 473
—— Jno., gen. (**B**) 865
—— Jno., L.M. Lond. 492
—— Jno. Jas., Q.C. 418
—— Jno. Ormsby, adm. (**H**) 850
—— Michl., gen. (**D**) 892
—— Nathl., G. Leew. Isl. 727
—— Nichs., Paym. G. 244
—— Rt., B. Ex. Ir. 584
—— Rt., bp. Cloy. 631; dn. Tm. 613
—— Rt., J.C.P. Ir. 581
—— Rt., J.C.P. Ir. 582
—— Th., L.M. Lond. 492
—— Wentw., G. Bah. Isl. 716
—— Wm., dn. Oss. 623
—— Wm., J.C.P. Ir. 582; S.L Ir. 593
—— Wm. Aug., gen. (**B**) 869
—— Wm. Moore, A.G. Ir. 589; J.Q.B.D. Ir. 580; S.G. Ir. 590
—— Wm. Ward Percival, adm. (**G**) 842

Johnston and **Johnstone**
*—— —, G. Tob. 723
*—— hon. Andr. Cochr., G. Dnca. 730
* ? same pers.
—— sir Alexr., Jud. Com. P.C. 360; P.C. 212
—— sir Archd., Ld. Adv. 526; Ld. Clk. Reg. 525; Ld. Sess. 519
—— Ch. Cornw., gen. (**D**) 898
—— Ch. Jas., adm. (**D**) 826
—— Ch. Jas. Hope, gen. (**D**) 927
—— Ed. Jno., C. St. 284
—— Fras. Jas. Th., gen. (**D**) 878
—— Fk., gen. (**D**) 892
—— Geo., B.C. 252
—— Geo., G. N.S.W. 702; gen. (**C**) 874
—— Hy. Campb., gen. (**D**) 919
—— Jas., G. Can. 691; G. N. Brk. 495; gen. (**A**) 858
—— Jas., gen. (**A**) 858
*—— Jas., Ld. Clk. Reg. 525
*—— Jas., Sec. St. Sc. 502
* Poss. same pers.
—— Jas., K.C.S.I. 803
—— Jno. Dougl., gen. (**D**) 894
—— Jno. Jul., gen. (**D**) 926
—— Mont. Cholm., G. Mtius. 684; gen. (**D**) 892
—— Rt. Maxw., gen. (**D**) 913
—— Th. Hy., gen. (**D**) 891
—— Wm., gen. (**B**) 867
—— Wm., gen. (**B**) 868
—— Wm., gen. (**C**) 872
—— Wm. and sir W., gen. (**B**) 869; K.C.B. 776
—— Wm. and sir W., L. Prov. Edinb. 548
—— Wm. Jas. Hope- and sir W., adm. (**C**) 822; adm. (**D**) 830; K.C.B. 779
—— Wm. Sout., gen. (**B**) 866
Johore, Mahar. of, G.C.M.G. 795; K.C.S.I. 802
Jolantha, D. Lne. 30
Jolles, sir Jno., L.M. Lond. 491
Jolliffe, Hy., dn. Brl. 440
—— Wm., B.T. 266; L. Admy. 180
—— sir Wm. Geo. Hylton, aft. ld. Hylton, *q.v.*, P.C. 216; Sec. Tr. 163; U.S. Home, 228
Jolly, Alexr., bp. Mor. 544
Jonathan, bp. Dnbl. 532
Jones, *see also* Johnes
—— hon. Alexr., adm. (**D**) 828; (**G**) 840
—— Ambr., bp. Kild. 617
—— Barzillai, dn. Lism. 629
—— Benj. Orl., gen. (**D**) 890; K.H. 792
—— Cadw., G. Bah. Isl. 716
—— Ch. Chad., S.L. 413
—— sir Ch. Th., adm. (**H**) 846
—— Danl., gen. (**B**) 866
—— Dav. Br., C.C.J. 405
—— Dav. Fras. Atcherly-, P.P. 416; S.L. 413
—— Drury, L.M. Dbln. 641
—— Ed., bp. Cloy. 630; bp. St. As. 462; dn. Lism. 629
—— sir Fras., L.M. Lond. 491
—— Geo., gen. (**D**) 883
—— Geo. E., K.H. 790
—— Geo. Lewis, bp. Kild. 617; bp. Kilm. 607; dn. Chr. Ch. Dbln. 619
—— Griff. Turn., gen. (**D**) 935

Jones—*cont.*
—— Harry Dav. and sir H., gen. (**D**) 889; G.C.B. 770; K.C.B. 777
—— Hy., bp. Clr., 596; bp. Mth. 599; dn. Ard. 609; dn. Kilm. 609
—— sir Hy., aft. Jones-Brydges, Amb. Pers. 130; P.C. 213
—— Hy. Richm., gen. (**D**) 900
—— Herb. Geo., C.C.J. 404; S.L. 413
—— How. Sutt., gen. (**D**) 930
—— Hugh, bp. Llff. 449
—— Hugh Val., C. Cus. Ir. 565; U.S.S. 226
—— J—, dn. Bgr. 426
—— Jas., gen. (**D**) 885; K.H. 789
—— Jenk., gen. (**D**) 919
—— Jno., Comm. Ir. 554-5
—— Jno., gen. (**B**) 864
—— Jno. and sir J., gen. (**D**) 903; K.C.B. 778
—— Jno. Salisb., K.H. 791
—— sir Jno. Th., gen. (**C**) 875; K.C.B. 776
*—— Lewis, bp. Killoe. 634
*—— Lewis, dn. Ard. 609
*—— Lewis, dn. Cash. 627
* Prob. same pers.
—— Lewis Tobias, aft. sir L., adm. (**D**) 832; (**E**) 834; (**F**) 838; G.C.B. 770; G. Gr. Hosp. 854; K.C.B. 779
—— Llew., bp. Newf. and Bmda. 700
—— Loftus Fras., adm. (**E**) 837
—— Michl., Comm. Ir. 554
—— Nathl., gen. (**D**) 894
—— Oliver, J.C.P. Ir. 581; J.K.B. Ir. 579
—— Oliver Jno., adm. (**H**) 849
—— Oliver Th., gen. (**C**) 873
—— Ph., Yk. H. 334
—— Rice, K.H. 790
—— Rd., aft. visc. and E. of Ranelagh, *q.v.*, Ch. Ex. Ir. 562
—— Rd., dn. Elph. 609; dn. Wford. 628
—— Rd., gen. (**D**) 886
—— Rd., K.C.B. 775
—— Rd. Godfr., gen. (**D**) 914
—— Rd. Ow., gen. (**D**) 933
—— Theob., adm. (**H**) 846
—— Theod. Mort., adm. (**E**) 837
—— Theoph., adm. (**A**) 817
—— Th., abp. Dbln. and Gl. 616; bp. Mth. 599; dn. St. Pat. 618; L.J. Ir. 554; Ld. Chanc. Ir. 576
—— Th., gen. (**C**) 872
—— Th., Q.C. 418
—— Th. and sir T., C.J.C.P. 375; J.K.B. 372; K.C. 414-5; S.L. 410
—— Val., gen. (**C**) 872
—— Wm. and sir W., A.G. 399; K.C. 414; S.G. 401; C.J.K.B. Ir. 578; J.C.P. 378; J.K.B. 372; L.K. Ir. 576; S.L. 409
—— Wm. and sir W., gen. (**D**) 898; G.C.B. 771; K.C.B. 780
—— Wm. Basil, bp. St. Dav. 465
—— Wm. Br., Ch. Com. Cent. Pr. 655
—— Wm. Gore, adm. (**E**) 836

Jones—*cont.*
—— Wm. Jas., gen. (**D**) 889
—— Wm. Saml., gen. (**D**) 913
—— Wm. West, bp. C. Tn. 679
Jong, Jac. de, G. Ceyl. 672
Jonson, *see also* Johnson
—— Ben, P. Laur. 301
Joonaghur, Newab of, K.C.S.I. 803
—— Saleh Hindi of, C.I.E. 806
Jordan, bp. Cloy. 630; bp. Cork and Cl. 631
—— dn. Sal. 468
—— Jno., K.H. 791
—— Jos., gen. (**D**) 928
—— sir Jos., adm. (**A**) 813
—— Th. H., C.C.J. 405
Jorse, Roland, abp. Arm. 595
—— Walt. de, abp. Arm. 595
Josceline and **Joscelyn,** *see* Jocelyn and Josselyn
***Joseph,** bp. Arm. 595
*—— bp. St. Dav. 464
*—— bp. Clonm. 599
*—— bp. Llff. 449
*—— dn. Arm. 597
* Prob. some same pers. Comp. dates.
—— K. Pgl. 88
—— (Buonaparte) K. Sp. 86
—— I. and II., E. Gmy. 62-3
—— I. and II., K. Hgy. 60
—— Geo. Fk., D.S. Alt. 78
Josephine, Emp. Fr. 25
Josina, K. Sc. 17
Josselyn and **Josselyne,** *see also* Joceline and Jocelyn
—— Ralph or Rauf, K.B. 757; L.M. Lond. 490
—— Th., K.B. 760
Jossus, C. Lux. 84
—— E. Gmy. 62
—— (the Beardless), M. Brg. 65
Joubert, P. J., Pres. Trl. 101
Joudpore, Mahar. of, G.C.S.I. 801; K.C.S.I. 802
Jourdan, Off. Nap. 26
Jovellanos, S., Pres. Pgy. 110
Jovian, Emp. Ro. 48
Jowan, Mahar., K.C.S.I. 802
Joy, *see also* Shioy
—— Hy., A.G. Ir. 588; C.B. Ex. Ir. 583; S.G. Ir. 589; S.L. Ir. 593
—— Hy. Hall, K.C. 416
Joyce, Saml., Q.C. 419
Joyner, Jno., Comf. P.A. 342; R. Cr. P.A. 335; Norr. K.A. 329; Richm. H. 333
Joynour, Wm., L.M. Lond. 488
Joynt, Wm. Lane, L.M. Dbln. 642
Juan, Juan San, G. Trin. 721
Juanna (2), Q. Nav. 85
Juarez, Ben., Dt. Mex. 104; Pres. Mex. 104; Pres. V. Cr. 104
Jude, sir Andr., L.M. Lond. 490
Judicael, de Rennes, D. Bry. 27
Jugjat Sing, C.I.E. 806
Jukel, Jno., J. It. 365
Julian, *see also* Julyan
—— Emp. Ro. 48
Julianus, D., Emp. Ro. 47
Julius, D. Brk. 70
—— I. to III., P. Ro. 33, 35
Julus, C. J. (4), C. Ro. 37-8-9; Dec. Ro. 38; Dt. Ro. 40
—— L. J., C. Ro. 39
—— V. J., C. Ro. 38

Julyan, *see also* Julian
— Penr. Goodch., K.C.M.G. 797
Jung, Nawab Salar, G.C.S.I. 801
— &c., C.I.E. 807
Junot, Off. Nap. 26
Justice, Wm., gen. (**D**) 888
Justin I. and II., Emp. E.E. 50
Justinian I. and II., Emp. E.E. 50
Justus (St.), abp. Cant. 429; bp. Roch. 459
Juxon, Wm., abp. Cant. 431; bp. Her. 441; bp. Lond. 452; dn. Worc. 473; L.H.T. 154; P.C. 190
Juyn or **Ivyn**
— Jno. and sir J., C.B. Ex. 381; C.J.C.P. 375; C.J.K.B. 370; K.B. 756; J.C.P. 378; S.L. 407
Jyepore, Bah. of, G.C.S.I. 801; K.C.S.I. 802
Jymungal, Raj., K.C.S.I. 802

K.

K—, *see also* C—
Kalakaua, K. Sd. Is. 111; G.C.M.G. 795
Kamehameha I. to V., K. Sd. Is. 111
Kanai, Lal Dé, C.I.E. 807
Kane, Jos., L.M. Dbln. 641
— Nathl., L.M. Dbln. 641
— Rd., G. Gibr. 669
Kang-he, Emp. Ch. 100
Kantzow, Herb. Ph., adm. (**H**) 851
Kanwar-Harnam, C.I.E. 807
Kardeston, Wm. de, J. It. 369
Karleol, Wm. de, C.B. Ex. 381
Karleton, *see* Carleton
Karlett, Wm. de, B. Ex. Ir. 583
Karnicke, Th., dn. Wells, 429
Karslake, Ed. K., Q.C. 418
— Fk., gen. (**D**) 932
— Jno. B. and sir J., A.G. 400; P.C. 219; Q.C. 418; S.G. 402
— Wm. Wall., Q.C. 419
Katharine and **Katherine,** *see also* Catharine
— (of Arragon), Q.C.E. 8
— (of Braganza), Q.C.E. 8
— (Howard), Q.C.E. 8
— (Parr), Q.C.E. 8
— (of Valois), Q.C.E. 7
— (dau. Ed. IV.), Pr. E. 12
Katon, Jas., adm. (**A**) 820
— Jas. Ed., adm. (**H**) 850
Kaune, Regd. D., J. It. 367
Kavanagh, *see also* Cavanagh
— Arth. McM., L.L. Carl. 568
Kay, Ed. Eben. and sir E., Just. Ch. D., 391; Q.C. 418
— (or Key), Jno., P. Laur. 300
— Jos., Q.C. 418
Kay - Shuttleworth, *see* Shuttleworth
Kaye, Ed., gen. (**D**) 904
— Geo. Farq., gen. (**D**) 927
— Jno., bp. Brl. 439; bp. Linc. 447
— Jno. Wm., K.C.S.I. 803
— sir Rd., dn. Linc. 448
Kazi Syud, &c. C.I.E. 808
Kean and **Keane,** *see also* Keen
— Dav. D., Q.C. 418
— Geo. Disn., adm. (**E**) 836; (**F**) 839
— hon. Hussey Fane, gen. (**D**) 917
— Jno., *see* ld. K., *infra*
Keane, lds.
— sir Jno., aft. ld. K., C.C. Bbay. 660; G.C.B. 769; G.C.H. 786; G. St. Luc. 725; gen. (**B**) 869; K.C.B. 774
Kearney, *see also* Kerney
— sir Jas., gen. (**B**) 869; K.C.H. 788
— Jno., bp. Oss. 621
Keate, Ed., gen. (**D**) 934
— Rt., Pres. Coll. Surg. 939
— Rt. Wm., G. Gren. 724; G. Nat. 680; G. Trin. 722; G. W. Afr. Sett. 688
— Th., Mast. Coll. Surg. 939
Keating and **Keatinge**
— Cad., dn. Clr. 598
— Hy. Sh. and sir H., gen. (**B**) 869; K.C.B. 776
— Hy. Sing. and sir H., J.C.P. 380; Jud. Com. P.C. 361; P.C. 219; Q.C. 417; S.G. 402; S.L. 414
— Jno., C.J.C.P. Ir. 580
— Jno. Wm., dn. Tm. 613; dn. St. Pat. 618
— Michl. Jno., dn. Kilf. 637
— Rd., J. P. and M. Ir. 587
— Rd., S.L. Ir. 593
— Rd. Hart., Ch. Com. Ass. 656; gen. (**D**) 926
Keats, Rd. Godw. and sir R., adm. (**A**) 818; G.C.B. 767; G. Gr. Hosp. 854; G. Newfd. 700; K.B. 766
— Wm., adm. (**G**) 841
Keble and **Keeble**
— Hy., L.M. Lond. 490
— Rd., C.G.S. 356; S.L. 409
— Th., S.L. 407
— Walt., S.L. 407
Keck, Anthy. and sir A., C.G.S. 357; S.L. 412
— Saml., M. Chy. 396
Kedah, Raja Ahmed, &c., K.C.M.G. 797
Keeble, *see* Keble
Keele, Ch., adm. (**H**) 848
Keeling, *see* Kelyng
Keen and **Keene,** *see also* Kean
— Benj., B.T. 264; K.B. 765
— Ch., Amb. Sw. 126
— Edmd., bp. Chest. 477; bp. Ely, 435
— Hy. Geo., C.I.E. 807
— Jno., S.L. 411
— Jno. Ed. Ruck-, gen. (**D**) 925
— Wh., B.T. 266; L. Admy. 180
Keenan, Nichs., bp. Ardf. and Agh. 639
— Patr. Jos., K.C.M.G. 797
Keene, *see* Keen
Keen-lung, Emp. Ch. 100
Keer, Jno., gen. (**D**) 922
Kegworth, Sim. de, A.G. 398
Keightley, Th., C.G.S.Ir. 576; L.J. Ir. 555
Kei-King, Emp. Ch. 100
Keilwey, *see also* Keylway
— Rt., S.L. 408
Keith (family of), E.M. Sc. 507
— Alexr., gen. (**C**) 873
— Alexr., Kt. Mar. Sc. 507
— Alexr. and sir A., Kt. Mar. Sc. 507
— sir Bas., G. Jam. 712
— Geo., H.C.P. Sc. 507
— Rt., bp. Cness. 541; bp. Fife, 543; bp. Ork. 545; Pr. Bp. Sc. 540
— Rt. Murr. and sir R., Amb. Dk. 127; Amb. Gmy. 116; Amb. Russ. 125; Amb. Sxy. 120; gen. (**B**) 866; K.B. 765; P.C. 205
— Wm., gen. (**D**) 934
— Wm. (E. Marischal), Ld. Sess. (1541) 517
— Wm. (E. Marischal), Ld. Sess. (1561) 517
— Wm. (E. Marischal), L.P.S Sc. (1660) 501
Keith, lds. and visc.
— Geo., ld. and visc., form hon. Geo. K. Elphinstone, *q.v.*, G.C.B. 766
Keith-Falconer, *see* Falconer
Kekewich, Arth. and sir A., Just. Ch. D. 391; Q.C. 419
— Geo. G., C.C.J. 403
Kelet, Wm., M. Chy. 394
Kellach, bp. Killa. 612
— bp. St. Andr. 528
Kellawe, Rd. de, bp. Dham. 478
Kellerman, Off. Nap. 26
Kellesay, Rd. de, J. It. 367
Kelleshull, Rd. de, J.C.P. 377
Kellett, Hy., adm. (**D**) 833; (**E**) 834; K.C.B. 780
Kellie, *see also* Kelly
Kellie, E. of
— Thos. E. of, form. visc. Fenton, *q.v.* (1615), and sir T. Erskine, *q.v.* (1603)
— Th., E. of, L.L. Fifesh. (1824) 510
Kellner, Geo. Welsh, K.C.M.G. 797
Kellum, Geo., gen. (**B**) 864
Kelly, *see also* Kellie
— Bened. Marw., adm. (**G**) 841
— Ed., adm. (**E**) 837
— Fitzr. and sir F., A.G. 400; C.B. Ex. 382; Jud. Com. P.C. 361; K.C. 416; P.C. 217; Pres. Ex. D. 382; S.G. 402; S.L. 414
— Jas. Butl., bp. Mor., Ross. and Cness. 544; bp. Newfd. 700
— Jno. Fras., gen. (**C**) 873
— Ralph, abp. Cash. 625
— Rd. Den and sir R., gen. (**D**) 903; K.C.B. 778
— Th., gen. (**D**) 896
— Th., J.C.P. Ir. 582; Ir. 592

Kelly—*cont.*
— Th., L.M. Lond. 492
— Th. Cunn., gen. (**D**) 905
— Th. F., J. Admy. Ct. Ir. 587
— Wm., adm. (**H**) 848
— Wm. Hanc., adm. (**A**) 817
Kelsall, Hy., C. Tx. 284
Kelso, Rt., gen. (**C**) 874
Kelyng and **Kelynge**
— Jno. and sir J. (No. 1), C.J.K.B. 370; J.K.B. 372; S.L. 410
— Jno. and sir J. (No. 2), K.C. 414; S.L. 410
Kemball, Arn. Burr. and sir A., gen. (**D**) 905; K.C.B. 780; K.C.S.I. 802
— Jno. Sh., gen. (**D**) 915
Kemble, Ch., E.S.P. 301
— Jno. Mitch., E.S.P. 301
Kemm, Wm. Hy., gen. (**D**) 880
Kemmis, Jas., gen. (**C**) 873
Kemp, Geo. Rees, gen. (**D**) 876
— Jno., abp. Cant. 431
— Th., K.B. 759
— Th. R., Q.C. 419
Kempe, Arth., adm. (**A**) 816
— Jno., abp. Yk. 486; bp. Chich. 433; bp. Lond. 451; bp. Roch. 460; Ld. Chanc. 355
— Th., bp. Lond. 451
— Wm., S.L. 412
Kempenfelt, Rd., adm. (**A**) 815
Kemplay, Jas., Q.C. 419
Kempster, Fras. G., gen. (**D**) 922
Kempt, Jas. and sir J., G.C.B. 767; G.C.H. 786; G. Can. 691; G. N. Sc. 695; gen. (**A**) 862; K.C.B. 774; M.G.O, 259; P.C. 212
— Jno., G. N.S.W. 703
Kempthorne, Jas., adm. **A** 817
— sir Jno., adm. (**A**) 813
Ken, Th., bp. B. and W. 428
Kenah, Th., gen. (**D**) 880; K.C.B. 779
Kendal, H. de, M. Chy. 393
— Jas., L. Admy. 176
— Jas., S. St. 223
Kendal, E. of
— Jno., E. of, also D. of Bedford, *q.v.* (son of Hen. IV.), K.G. 734
— Jno., E. of, form. Jno. de Foix, *q.v.*
— Jno. (Beaufort), E. of, E. and aft. D. of Somerset, *q.v.*; (*d.* 1444)
Kendall, Jas,, G. Bdoes. 719
— Rt. de, W.C.P. 318
Kendred, K.E. 3
Kendrek, Jno., L.M. Lond. 491
Kenealey, Ed. Vaugh., Q.C. 418
Kenelm, K.E. 3
Kenewold, *see* Kenwold
Kenferth, bp. Lich. 443
Kenmare, E. of
— Val., 2nd E. of, L.L. Kerry, 569
— Val. Aug., 4th E. of, form. visc. Castlerosse, *q.v.*; K.P. 751; L.C.H. 295
Kennedy, Alexr. Kenn. Clarke- (No. 1), gen. (**D**) 884; K.C.B. 779; K.H. 790
Kennedy—*cont.*
— Alexr. Kenn. Clarke- (No. 2), gen. (**D**) 914
— Arth. Ed. and sir E., G.C.M.G. 795; G. Gamb. 686; G. H. Kong, 673; G. Qland. 706; G. Si. Le. 685; G. Vanc. Isl. 699; G. W. Afr. Sett. 688; G. W. Austr. 707; K.C.M.G. 796
— Ed. Mitch., dn. Clonf. 637
— Fk. Ch., C.I.E. 808
— Hy. Fras., gen. (**D**) 911
— Jas., bp. Dkld. 533; bp. St. Andr. 529; Ld. Chanc. Sc. 515
— Jas., gen. (**B**) 865
— Jas., gen. (**D**) 880
— Jas. Sh. and sir J., gen. (**D**) 882; K.C.B. 779
— Jno. Jas., adm. (**H**) 850
— Jno. Wm. Alex., gen. (**D**) 919
— Michl. Kav. and sir M., gen. (**D**) 906; K.C.S.I. 803
— sir Rd., B. Ex. Ir. 584
— sir Rt. Hugh, K.C.H. 788
— Th. Fras., C.W.F. &c. 272-3; Clk. O. 260; L.T. 160
— Th. Gilb., gen. (**D**) 929
— Th. Le B., dn. Clghr. 598
— Vans, gen. (**D**) 878
— Wm. Rann, Q.C. 420
Kennedy, lds.
— Jno., 2nd ld., L.J. Gen. 522
Kennet and **Kennett**
— Brackley, gen. (**D**) 877
— Brackley, L.M. Lond. 492
— White, bp. Pboro. 458; dn. Pboro. 458
Kenneth I. to III. K. Sc. 18, 19
Kennett, *see* Kennet
Kenney, *see* Kenny
Kennion, *see also* Kenyon
— Geo. Wyndh., bp. Adel. 707
Kenny and **Kenney**
— Arth. Hy., dn. Ach. 614
— Dav. Courtn., gen. (**D**) 876
— sir Ed., G. N. Sc. 695
Kenric, K.E. 2, 3
Kenrick, Ad. E., dn. Bgr. 426
— Jno., C. St. 283
— Matth., C. St. 283
Kensington, lds.
Rich Family.
— Hy., 1st ld., aft. 1st E. of Holland, *q.v.*
Edwardes Family.
— Wm., 2nd ld., L. Admy. 181
— Wm., 3rd ld., L.L. Pemb. 316
— Wm., 4th ld., Compt. H. 293; L.L. Pemb. 316; P.C. 219
Kent, Hy., gen. (**D**) 926
— Jno., C. Cus. Sc. 503
— Th., M. Chy. 394
Kent, E., M., and D. of
— Odo, E. of, Ch. Jr. 362; L.H.T. 152; W.C.P. 317
— Godw., E. of, W.C.P. 317
— Hub., E. of, form. H. de Burgh, *q.v.* (*d.* 1243), Ch. Jr. 362; L.J. Ir. 550; Const. T.L. 320
— Edmd. (of Woodstock), E. of (*d.* 1332), W.C.P. 318
— Th., E. of, form. sir T. Holland, *q.v.* (*d.* 1360)
— Th., E. of (*d.* 1397), K.G. 734
Kent, E., M., and D. of—*cont.*
— Th., E. of, and D. of Surrey, *q.v.* (*d.* 1400), E.M. 326; K.G. 734; L.L. Ir. 552
— Edm., E. of (*d.* 1407), K.G. 734; L.H.A. 173
— Wm., E. of, form. ld. Fauconberg (*d.* 1463), L.H.A. 174
— Edm., E. of, form. ld. Grey of Ruthyn, *q.v.* (*d.* 1488)
— Rd., E. of (*d.* 1523), K.G. 737
— Hy., E. of (*d.* 1651), C.G.S. 356
— Hy., E., aft. M. and D. of (*d.* 1740), Const. W. Cast. 322; K.G. 741; L.C.H. 295; L.L. Heref. 308; L.P.S. 240; L.S.H. 290; P.C. 195
— Ed., D. of (son of Geo. III.), form. Pr. Ed., *q.v.* (*d.* 1820), F.M. 856; G.C.B. 767; G.C.H. 785; G. Gibr. 670; gen. (**A**) 859; P.C. 206
Kentigern, bp. St. As. 462
Kentwode, Reg., dn. St. P. 453
***Kenulf** and **Kenulfus**
*— bp. Lindisf. 478
*— bp. Winch. 470
*— (or Ceolulfus), bp. Dorch. 446
* Poss. same pers. Comp. dates.
— K.E. 3
Kenwálchus, bp. Lond. 451
Kenwold, bp. Worc. 472
Kenwulf, K.E. 2
Kenyon, *see also* Kennion
— Jno. Rt., Q.C. 418
— Ll., *see* ld. K., *infra*
— Rog., G. I. Man, 666
Kenyon, lds.
— Ll., aft. sir L. and 1st ld. K., A.G. 399; B.T. 267; C.J. Chest. 386; C.J.K.B. 370; K.C. 415; L.L. Flints. 314; M.R. 388; P.C. 204; S.L. 412
Keogh, Jno. Woulfe, gen. (**D**) 934
— Wm., A.G. Ir. 588; J.C.P. Ir. 582; J.C.P.D. Ir. 582; S.G. Ir. 590
Keppel, Aug., *see* visc. K., *infra*
— hon. Fk., bp. Exr. 437; dn. Winds. 474
— Geo., adm. (**A**) 816
— hon. Hy. and sir H., adm. (**B**) 821; (**D**) 831; (**E**) 834; G.C.B. 770; K.C.B. 778
— hon. Wm., gen. (**B**) 865
— Wm. and sir W., G.C.B. 767; G. Gsey. 669; gen. (**A**) 860; K.B. 766; P.C. 211
Keppel, visc.
— hon. Aug., aft. visc. K, adm. (**A**) 814; L. Admy. 179-80; P.C. 203
Keppock or **Keppok,** Jno., C.J.K.B. Ir. 577; J.K.B. Ir. 578; D. Chanc. Ir. 574
Ker and **Kerr,** *see also* Carr
— Andr., Ld. Sess. 519
— sir Andr., Ld. Sess. 517
— ld. Fc. Herb., adm. (**E**) 835; (**F**) 839
— Geo., Ld. Sess. 518
— (or Carr), Jno., dn. Ard. 609
— ld. Jno., gen. (**C**) 871
— Jno. Hy. Lyte, gen. (**D**) 912

Ker and Kerr—*cont.*
— Jno. M., gen. (**A**) 861
— Mark, Ld. Sess. 517
— Mark, aft. 1st E. of Lothian, *q.v.*, Ld. Sess. 517
— ld. Mark, gen. (**A**) 857
— ld. Mark, gen. (**D**) 903; K.C.B. 781
— ld. Mark Rt., adm. (**A**) 819
— Rt., adm. (**H**) 848
— Rt., aft. E. of Ancrum, *q.v.*, K.B. (1603) 761
— ld. Rt., K.H. 791; Sec. Thist. 749
— Th., G. Falk. Isl. 731; G. Gren. 724
— Th. Darl., gen. (**D**) 919
— Th. Wm., gen. (**C**) 874
— Walt., gen. (**B**) 867
— Wm., gen. (**B**) 864
Keran (or Kyran), dn. Cash. 627
Kerdiffe, Ed., S.L. Ir. 591
— Jno., dn. Clonm. 600
— Walt., J.C.P. Ir. 581
Kerney, *see also* Kearney
— Jas., bp. Cnr. 604
— (or Carney), sir Rd., Ulst. K.A. 572
Kerovan, Steph., bp. Clonf. 636; bp. Kilmacd. 636
Kerowler, Mahar. of, G.C.S.I. 801; K.C.S.I. 802
Kerr, *see* Ker and Carr
***Kerrich,** Walt. Cheese D'Oyl., gen. (**D**) 925
*— Walt. Cheese D'Oyl., gen. (**D**) 935
* ? same pers.
Kerrison, sir Ed., gen. (**A**) 863; G.C.H. 786; K.C.B. 777; K.C.H. 787
Kersteman, Wm., gen. (**C**) 873
Kervel, Adr. von, G. C.G.H. 678
Keshan, Jno., L.M. Dbln. 642
Kestell-Cornish, *see* Cornish
Kesteven, D. of, *see* Ancaster and K.
Ket, —, *see also* Kett—
Ketene, Jno. de, bp. Ely, 434
Keterich, *see* Ketterich
Kettel, Th., bp. Down, 603
Ketterich (or Catryk), Jno., bp. Exr. 436; bp. Lich. and Cov. 444; bp. St. Dav. 464
Kettle, Jno., Winds. H. 331
— Rup. A. and sir R., C.C.J. 404
Kettleby, Rt. J., S.L. 412
Kettleseye, R. de, M. Chy. 393
Kettlewell, Jno. W., gen. (**D**) 885
Kevenagh, *see* Kavanagh and Cavanagh
Kevin (or Coemgene), St., bp. Glend. 615
Key, Astl. Coop. and sir A., adm. (**E**) 835; G.C.B. 771; K.C.B. 780; L. Admy. 185-6; P.C. 220
— Bransb. Lanc., bp. Br. Kaffr. 681
— Geo. Wm., gen. (**D**) 897
— (or Kay), Jno., P. Laur. 300
— sir Jno., Chambn. Lond. 493; L.M. Lond. 492
Keyes, Ch. Patt. and sir C., gen. (**D**) 923; K.C.B. 781
Keylway, *see also* Keilwey
— Rt., M. Chy. 395
Keys, Hy., M. Chy. 394
Keyser, Pol. de and sir P., L.M. Lond. 492
Khalif, S. Zr. 102
Kharan, Sirdar of, K.C.I.E. 805
Khelat, Khan of, G.C.S.I. 801
— Khan of (Mir Ali), C.I.E. 806
— Khan of (Mir Mahmud), C.I.E. 806
Khem Singh, C.I.E. 806
Kholapur, Dewan of, C.I.E. 808
Khote, Ragh. Nar., C.I.E. 807
Kiaran (St.), bp. Clonm. 599; bp. Saig. 620
Kidder, Rd., bp. B. and W. 428; dn. Pboro. 458
Kidwelly (or Kydwell), Morg., A.G. 398; K.B. 759
Kielhorn, Franz, C.I.E. 808
Kilconcath, Wm. de, bp. Brn. 530
Kilcoursie, F. E. G., visc., aft. 9th E. of Cavan, *q.v.*, P.C. 220; V.C.H. 297
Kildare, E. and M. of
— Th., 2nd E. of, L.D. Ir. 551
— Maur., 4th E. of, L.D. Ir. 551
— Ger., 5th E. of, L.L. Ir. 552
— Th., 7th E. of, L.D. Ir. 552; Ld. Chanc. Ir. 575
— Ger., 8th E. of, K.G. 737; L.D. Ir. 553
— Ger., 9th E. of, L.J. and L.D. Ir. 553
— Rt., 19th E. of, C.G.S. Ir. 576; L.J. Ir. 556
— Jas., 20th E. of, aft. 1st M. of K. and 1st D. of Leinster, *q.v.*
Kildelicht, Rt., Ld. Chanc. Sc. 514
Kildesby (or Kyldesbury), Wm. de, L.K. 354; M. Chy. 393
Kilgour, Rt., bp. Abdn. 541; Pr. Bp. Sc. 540
Kilkenny, Andr. de, dn. Exr. 437
— Wm. de, bp. Ely, 434; L.K. 353; M. Chy. 393
Killach, Mel., bp. Emly. 625
Killene (St.), bp. Ferns, 621; bp. Oss. 620
Killigrew, Hy., adm. (**A**) 813; L. Admy. 176
— Rt., gen. (**C**) 871
Killingbury, Rd., L.M. Lond. 489
Killingworth, Wm., S.L. 411
Kilmain, Jas., ld., also 2nd ld. Tyrawley, *q.v.*
Kilmallock, Dom., ld., form. sir D. Sarsfield, *q.v.*
Kilmorey, Fras., 12th visc. and 1st E. of, form. hon. F. Needham, *q.v.*
Kilmyngton, Rd. de, dn. St. P. 453
Kilwardby, Rt., abp. Cant. 430
Kilwarden, Arth., visc., form. Arth. Wolfe, *q.v.*
Kimberley, Jonn., dn. Lich. 445
Kimberley, E. of
— Jno., E. of, form. Jno. and ld. Wodehouse, *q.v.*; C.D.L. 243; C. Sec. 235; K.G. 745; L.P.S. 241; Sec. Ind. 236; U.S.F. 230
Kimberley, E. of—*cont.*
— Florence, Css. of, Cr. Ind. 810
Kinahan, Rt. Hy., L.M. Dbln. 642
Kincaird, Alexr., L. Prov. Edinb. 548
Kincardine, E. of, *see also* Elgin and K.
— Alexr., 2nd E. of, Comm. Tr. Sc. 497; Ld. Sess. 517; P.C. 191; V.A. Sc. 499
Kindale, Rt. de, W.C.P. 318
Kindersley, Rd. Tor. and sir R., Jud. Com. P.C. 361; K.C. 416; M. Chy. 397; P.C. 217; V. Chanc. 390
Kinchant, Jno. Charl., gen. (**D**) 934
Kinebert, or Kineberth, or Kinebertus, bp. Lich. 443
— bp. Winch, 470
— bp. Sidr. 446
Kinehard, bp. Winch. 470
Kinewaldus (or Kinewardus), bp. Wells, 427
Kineward, bp. Winch. 470
Kinewardus, *see* Kinewaldus
Kinfauns, Chart. de, Ld. Chanc. Sc. 515
King and **Kyng**
— Abrm. Bradley and sir A., L.M. Dbln. 641
— sir Anthy. L.M. Dbln. 641
— Anthy. Sing., K.H. 792
— Ch., K.H. 790
— Col. —, Lt. T.L. 322
— Ed., bp. Elph. 608; dn. Elph. 609
— Ed., bp. Linc. 447
— sir Ed. Durnf., adm. (**A**) 820; K.C.H. 788
— Geo., gen. (**D**) 899
— Geo. St. Vincent and sir G., adm. (**D**) 832; (**E**) 834; K.C.B. 780
— Gilb., L.M. Dbln. 641
— Greg., Lanc. H. 333; R. Dr. P.A. 338
— Hy., bp. Chich. 433; dn. Roch. 461
— hon. Hy. and sir H., G. Hlgld. 670; gen. (**B**) 869; K.C.B. 776
— sir Hy., gen. (**A**) 863; K.C.H. 788
— Hy. Seym., C.I.E. 808
— Hult. Smith, C. Acc. Ir. 567; C. Cus. 277; C. Cus. Ir. 566
— J. H., G. St. Xtr. 729
— Jas., dn. Rph. 603
— hon. Jas. Wm., adm. (**D**) 827
— Jno., bp. Lond. 452; dn. Chr. Ch. 457
— Jno., dn. Tm. 613
— Jno., K.C. 414
— Jno., Sec. Tr. 163
— Jno., U.S. Home, 228
— Oliver, bp. B. and W. 428; bp. Exr. 436; dn. Her. 442; Regr. Gart. 746; S. St. 223
— Captn. P. G., G. N.S.W. 702
— Peter, *see* ld. K., *infra*
— Ph. Park., adm. (**H**) 847
— sir Rd. (No. 1), adm. (**A**) 815; G. Newfd. 700
— sir Rd. (No. 2), adm. (**A**) 819; K.C.B. 774

For List of Abbreviations, see pp. 944-952.

King and Kyng—*cont.*
— Rd. Hy., adm. (**G**) 842
— Rd. Th., gen. (**D**) 889
— Rt., bp. Oxf. 456
— sir Rt., Comm. Ir. 554
— Th., gen. (**D**) 880
— Th., M.M. 246
— Th. W., R. Dr. P.A. 338; Yk. H. 334
— Walt., bp. Roch. 460
— Wm., abp. Dbln. and Gl. 616; bp. Dry. 601; C.G.S. Ir. 576; dn. St. Pat. 618; L.J. Ir. 556
— Wm. Jas., gen. (**D**) 896
— Wm. Sm., dn. Llin. 624
King, lds.
— Peter, aft. sir P. and ld. K., C.J.C.P. 376; L.H.S. 286; Ld. Chanc. 357; P.C. 196; Rec. Lond. 494; S.L. 411
King-Harman, *see* Harman
Kingcome, Jno., adm. (**D**) 831; (**F**) 838; K.C.B. 779
Kingdom, Rd., C. Exc. 278
Kingdon, Holl. Tull., bp. Fcton. 696
— Th. K., Q.C. 418
Kingestone, *see* Kingston
Kinglake, Jno. Alexr., P.P. 417; S.L. 413
Kingscote, Col. R. N. F., C.W.F. &c. 273
Kingscotes, Jno., bp. Carl. 475
Kingsdown, Th. Pemb., ld., form. T. P. Leigh, *q.v.*
Kingsley, Wm., gen. (**B**) 865
Kingsmill, Geo. and sir G., J.C.P. 378; S.L. 408
— Jno., J.C.P. 378; S.L. 407
— sir Rt., adm. (**A**) 815
— (or De Basing), Wm., dn. Winch. 471
Kingston and **Kingstone**
— Ad. de, dn. St. Patr. 617
— Hy. de, J. It. 366
— Jno., C. St. 284
— Th., dn. Winds. 474
— sir Wm., Const. T.L. 320; K.G. 738; C.Y.G. 298
Kingston, E. and D. of
King-Tenison Family.
— Hy. Ern. N., 8th E. of, L.L. Rosc. 571
Pierrepoint Family.
— Ev., 1st D. of, form. M. of Dorchester, *q.v.*, K.G. 741; L.P.C. 188; L.P.S. 240
— Ev., 2nd D. of, gen. (**A**) 858; K.G. 742; L.L. Notts, 311
Kinleside, Rt. Raikes, gen. (**D**) 902
Kinloss, Ed., ld., form. sir E. Brace, *q.v.*
Kinnaird, Geo. Wm. F., 9th ld., M.B.H. 303; P.C. 214; K.T. 748; L.L. Prth. 511
Kinnatellus, K. Sc. 18
Kinnear, Alexr. Sm., D. Fac. Sc. 527; Ld. Sess. 521
Kinnersley, Is., gen. (**D**) 878
Kinninmund, or Kynninmund
— Alexr. (2), bp. Abdn. 530
— Jno. de, bp. Brn. 531
— Matth. de, bp. Abdn. 530
Kinnoull, E. of
— Geo., 1st E. of, form. sir G. Hay, and 1st visc. Dupplin, *q.v.*
— Geo., 2nd E. of, C.Y.G. 298

Kinnoull, E. of—*cont.*
— Th., 8th E. of, form. visc. Dupplin, *q.v.*
— Rt. Aur., 9th E. of, Ly. K.A. 513; P.C. 206
— Th. Rt., 10th E. of, L.L. Prth. 511; Ly. K.A. 513
Kinsey, or **Kinsius**
— bp. Lich. 443
— abp. Yk. 485
Kinton, Godfr. de, *see* Ludham
Kintore, E. of
— Jno., 1st E. of, Dep. Tr. Sc. 497; L.P.S. Sc. 501
— Anthy., 5th E. of, L.L. Kinc. 510
— Fras. Alexr., 8th E. of, L.L. Abdn. 508; L.L. Kinc. 510
— Algn. H. T., 9th E. of, C.Y.G. 298; G. S. Austr. 707; P.C. 221
Kipling, Jno. Lockw., C.I.E. 808
— Th., dn. Pboro. 458
Kirby, *see also* Kirkeby
— Cranl. Th., S.L. 412
— Jno., Ir. K.A. 338
— Steph., gen. (**D**) 885
— Th. Cox, K.H. 792
— Walt., K.H. 791
— Wm. Humphr., gen. (**D**) 909
Kirk, *see also* Kirke
— Jno. and sir J., Amb. Zr. 132; G.C.M.G. 795; K.C.M.G. 797
Kirkaldie, sir Jas., L.H.T. Sc. 497
Kirke, *see also* Kirk
— Piercy, gen. (**B**) 864
Kirkeby, *see also* Kirby
— Gilb. de, J. It. 368
— Jno. de, bp. Carl. (*d.* 1353), 475
*— Jno. de, bp. Ely, 434; bp. Roch. 459; J.C.P. 376; J. It. 367; Jy. 364; L.H.T. 152; Ld. Chanc. 353; M. Chy. 393
* It is doubtful whether these all refer to the same pers. Compare dates, and see *Foss's Judges*
— Jno., M.R. Ir. 585
— Th. de, M.R. 387
Kirketon, Jno. de, K.B. 754
— Rog. de. J.C.P. 378; S.L. 407
Kirkham, Rt., L.K. 355; M. Chy. 394; M.R. 387
— Walt. de, bp. Dham. 478; dn. Yk. 486
Kirkland, Agmond Jno. A. V., gen. (**D**) 908
Kirkwall, Geo. Wm. H., visc., aft. 6th E. of Orkney, *q.v.*, K.C.M.G. 797
Kirmington, Josc. de, dn. Linc. 448
Kirtling, Geoff., dn. Linc. 447
Kirwan, Anth. La T., dn. Kilmacd. 638; dn. Lim. 640
— Walt. Bl., dn. Killa. 614
Kitchen and **Kitchin**
— (or Dunstan), Anth., bp. Llff. 449
— Geo. Wm., dn. Winch. 471
— Jas., gen. (**D**) 886
— Wm. Hewg., adm. (**H**) 848

Kite, Jno., abp. Arm. 595; bp. Carl. 475
— sir Rt., L.M. Lond. 492
Ki-tsiang, Emp. Ch. 100
Kittenstein, Jac. Van, G. Ceyl. 672
Knapp, Fras., dn. Klla. 614
Knatchbull, sir Ed., P.C. 213; Paym. G. 244
— sir Ed. Hug., aft. Knatchbull-Hugessen and ld. Brabourne, *see* Hugessen
— sir Jno., L.P.S. 240
— Reg. Ed., gen. (**D**) 904
Knatchbull-Hugessen, *see* Hugessen
Knesworth, Th., L.M. Lond, 490
Knevet, *see* Knyvet
Knight, Chr., K.H. 791
— Edmd., Chest. H. 331; Norr. K.A. 329; R. Dr. P.A. 338
— Fk. Wm., Sec. P.L.B. 262
— col. Fk. Winn, K.C.B. 784
— Hy. Edm., aft. sir H., L.M. Lond. 492
— Hy. Ral., gen. (**B**) 868
— J. A. Gil., G. Trin. 721
— Jas. Blackb., C.I.E. 806
— Jas. Lew., aft. Knight-Bruce, *see* Bruce
— Jno. and sir J., adm. (**A**) 817; K.C.B. 773
— sir Jos., adm. (**A**) 815
— Lewis Ed., gen. (**D**) 922
— Th., Chest. H. 331; R. Cr. P.A. 335
— Th., M.M. 246
— Wm., bp. B. and W. 428
— Wm., S. St. 223
— Wm. Br., dn. Llff. 450
— Wm. Hy., gen. (**D**) 926
Knight-Bruce, *see* Bruce
Knightby, Rd., K.B. 759
— Val., K.B. 760
Knightley, Edm., S.L. 408
— Rd., K.B. 763
— Th., V. Treas. Ir. 559
Knighton, sir Wm., G.C.H. 786
Knivet, *see* Knyvet
Knocker, Jno. Bed., gen. (**D**) 921
Knoll, Ed. de la, dn. Wells, 428
Knolles, Th., L.M. Lond. 489
Knollys, *see also* Knowles and Knowlys
— Clem. C., G. St. Luc. 725
— Fras. and sir F., K.C.M.G. 798; C.Y.G. 298; Compt. H. 292; K.G. 739; Tr. H. 291
— sir Rt., K.G. (?) 734
— Wm., gen. (**A**) 861
— Wm., called E. of Banbury, gen. (**C**) 872
— sir Wm., *see* ld. K., *infra*
— Wm. Th. and sir W., G. Gsey. 669; gen. (**D**) 884; K.C.B. 783; P.C. 218
Knollys, lds.
— sir Wm., aft. 1st ld. Kn., 1st. visc. Wallingford, *q.v.*, and 1st E. of Banbury, *q.v.*, Compt. H. 292; K.G. 739; Tr. H. 291
Knovill, Gilb. de, J. It. 369
Knowles, *see also* Knollys and Knowlys
— Ch. and sir C., adm. (**A**) 814; G. Jam. 712
— sir Ch. Hy., adm. (**A**) 816; G.C.B. 768

Knowles—*cont.*
— Jno., adm. (**A**) 817
— Rt., K.B. 761
Knowley, Ch. Jas., Q.C. 417
Knowlys, *see also* Knowles and Knollys
— Newn., Comm. Sergt. Lond. 495; Rec. Lond. 494
— sir Wm., L.H.T. Sc. 496
Knox, Alex., K.C.B. 776
— Andr., bp. Isl. 540; bp. Rph. 601
— hon. Edm., bp. Killoe. and Kilf. 635; bp. Lim. A. and A. 639; dn. Down, 605
— hon. Edm. Sext. Pery, adm. (**H**) 844
— hon. Geo., C. Cus. Ir. 565; C. Treas. Ir. 561
— hon. Jno., gen. (**C**) 872
— sir Jno., L.M. Dbln. 640
— Rd., gen. (**D**) 907
— Rt. Bent., abp. Arm. 597; bp. Down, C. and D. 605
— Th., bp. Isl. 540
— Th., gen. (**D**) 907
— Th. Edm., gen. (**D**) 907
— Th. Geo., Amb. Si. 131; K.C.M.G. 797
— Wm., U.S.C. 235
— Hon. Wm., bp. Killoe. and Kilf. 635; bp. Dry. 601
Knyvet, Knyvett, Knevit, and **Knivet**
— sir Anthy., Lt. T.L. 321
— Jno., K.B. 763
— Jno. and sir J., C.J.K.B. 370; J.C.P. 377; Ld. Chanc. 354; S.L. 407
— Th. and sir T., K.B. 759; M.H. 301
— Wm., K.B. 757
Knyvet, lds.
— Th., ld., M.M. 246
Knüsel, M., Pres. Sw. C. 31
Knutsford, Hy. T., ld., form. sir H. T. Holland, *q.v.*
Koe, Jno. H., C.C.J. 403; Q.C. 417
Koenigseck, C. of, R. Nds. 83
Kokayne, *see also* Cokayne
— Th., Regr. Bath. 785
Kolhapore, Raj. of, K.C.S.I. 803
Komei Tonno, M. Jap. 100
König, Ch., K.H. 790
Koonwar, Ranajee, G.C.B. 769; G.C.S.I. 801
Kortright, Corn. Hend. and sir C., G. Br. Gu. 715; G. Gamb. 686; G. Gren. 724; G. Tob. 724; G. Trin. 722; G. Virg. Isl. 731; G. W. Afr. Sett. 688; K.C.M.G. 798
Krishnaji, &c., C.I.E. 808
Kristodas Pal, C.I.E. 806
Kroma, Ph., &c., K. Si. 100
Krüger, S. J. P., Pres. Trl. 101
Kuangsu, Emp. Ch. 100
Kuch, Behar Bah. of, G.C.I.E. 805
Kuclinus (or Ruclinus), bp. St. Dav. 464
Kumar, Sri Kalooba, C.I.E. 808
Kunill, Wm. de, Jy. 364
Kunwar, *see* Koonwar
Kuper, Aug. Leop. and sir A., adm. (**D**) 832; (**E**) 834; G.C.B. 770; K.C.B. 779
Kuppoorthulla, Bah. of, G.C.S.I. 801; K.C.S.I. 802
— Sird. of, C.I.E. 806
Kureem, Khan, Sh. Pers. 99
Kutch, Rao of, G.C.I.E. 805
Kuttuck, Nawab, K.C.S.I. 803
Ky—, *see also* Ki—
Kyee, Moung Sher., C.I.E. 807
Kydwell, *see* Kidwelly
Kyffen, How. ab M., dn. St. As. 463
Kyffin, Rd., dn. Bgr. 426
Kyldesbury, *see* Kildesby
Kyle, Saml., bp. Cork, Cl. and R., 632
Kyme, Sim. de, J. It. 366
Kymer, Gilb., dn. Sal. 468
Kynaston, Wm., Curs. B. Ex. 386; M. Chy. 396
Kyndelw, dn. Bgr. 426
Kyng, *see* King
Kyngton, Jno., M. Chy. 394
Kyran, *see* Keran
Kyriel, sir Nich., L.H.A. 171
Kyriell, sir T., K.G. (1460). *See Errata for p.* 736
Kyrketon, *see* Kirketon
Kyrkham, *see* Kirkham
Kyrkin, Geo., M.M. 245

L.

La. For names with this prefix search under the name next following; *ex. gr.*, La Brise under Brise
Labeo, Q. F., C. Ro. 44
Laborde, Ed., G. Gren. 724; G. Tob. 724; G. St. Luc. 725; G. St. Vin. 725
Labouchere, Hy., aft. ld. Taunton, *q.v.*, C. Sec. 235; Ch. Sec. Ir. 563; L. Admy. 182; M.M. 247; P.C. 213; Pres. B.T. 268-9; V.P.B.T. 269; U.S.W. and C. 231
Labourdonnais, Mahé de, G. Mtius. 683
Lacaita, Jas. Ph., K.C.M.G. 796
Lacere, Rd., L.M. Lond. 489
Lacey, *see* Lacy
Lack, Th., Sec. B.T. 270
Lacu, Pet. de Mals. J. It. 369
Lacy and **Lacey**
— Edm., bp. Exr. 436; bp. Her. 441
— Ed., adm. (**H**) 852
— Hugh de, aft. E. of Ulster, *q.v.*, L.J. Ir. 550
— (or Lees) Hugh, bp. Lim. 638
— Jno. de, aft. 1st E. of Lincoln, *q.v.*, J. It. 367
— Jno. de, L.J. Ir. 550
— Jno. de, M. Chy. 393
— Rd. Jno. Jas., gen. (**D**) 883
— Rd. Walt., gen. (**D**) 905
— Rog. de, J. It. 366
— Th. Edg., gen. (**D**) 904
— Wm., gen. (**D**) 918
Ladbroke, sir Rt., L.M. Lond. 491
Ladislas and **Ladislaus**
— A.D. Aus. 58
— D. Aus. 58
— K. Nls. 56
— I. to VI., K. Hgy. 59, 60
— I. to VII., K. Pld. 90-1
— II. to IV., D. Bma. 59
— V. and VI., K. Bma. 59
Lælius, C., C. Ro. 43
Lænas, C. P. (2), C. Ro. 44
— M. P. (4), C. Ro. 40, 41, 44
— P. P., C. Ro. 45
Laessöe, Alb. Fk. de, C.I.E. 808
Lævinus, C. V., C. Ro. 44
— M. V., C. Ro. 43
— P. V., C. Ro. 42
Laffan, sir Jos. de C., K.H. 791
— Rt. Mich. and sir R., G. Bmda. 701; gen. (**D**) 909; K.C.M.G. 797
Lafont, Eug., C.I.E. 806
Laforey, sir Fras., adm. (**A**) 818; K.C.B. 774
— sir Jno., adm. (**A**) 815
Lafusille, Jno., gen. (**C**) 871
Lagman, K. Man. 665
Lago, Ralph, Bl. M. P.A. 336
Lagysse, Ralph, Cal. P.A. 342; Ptc. P.A. 337; Yk. H. 334
Laha, Durg. Ch., C.I.E. 807
Laidgnen, bp. Ferns. 621
Laighne, K. Ir. 20
Laing, *see also* Lang and Leng
— Jno., bp. Glasg. 536; L.H.T. Sc. 496; Ld. Chanc. Sc. 515; Ld. Clk. Reg. 525
— Saml., Sec. Tr. 163
Laird, Dav., G. N.W. Terr. 697
Laire, sir Th., K.C.B. 774
Lake, Arth., bp. B. and W. 428; dn. Worc. 473
— Ed. Jno., gen. (**D**) 908
— Ger., *see* ld. L. *infra*
— Hy. Atw., K.C.B. 783
— Jno., bp. Brl. 439; bp. Chich. 433; bp. S. and M. 484
— Noel Th., gen. (**D**) 897
— sir Th., S. St. 223
— Walt., S.L. 408
— Warw., C. St. 284
— Wm. Ch., dn. Dham. 479
— sir Will. Th., adm. (**A**) 819; K.C.B. 776
Lake, lds. and visc.
— Ger., aft. 1st ld. and 1st visc. L., C.C. Bgal. 652; C.C. Ind. 650; gen. (**A**) 859
— Fk. Ger., 2nd visc., gen. (**B**) 868
Laken or **Lakene,** Wm., J.K.B. 371; S.L. 407
Lakyn, Rd., K.B. 758
Lalo, Sams. de, gen. (**C**) 871
Laly, *see* Mullaly and O'Mullaly
Laman, Pres. Pu. 109
Lamb, And., bp. Brn. 531; bp. Gall. 538
— hon. Fk. Jas., aft. 1st ld. Beauvale and 3rd visc. Melbourne, *q.v.*, Amb. Aus. 117; Amb. Bva. 119; Amb. G. St. 121; Amb. Pgl. 125; Amb. Scy. 114; Amb. Spn. 124; G.C.B. 772; P.C. 210
— hon. Geo., U.S. Home, 227

Lamb—*cont.*
— Jno., dn. Brl. 440
— Jno., dn. Ely, 435
— sir Jno., D. Arch. 420
— Matt., K.C. 415
— Rt., bp. Pboro. 458; dn. Pboro. 458
— Th., gen. (**D**) 935
— Th. D., C. Tx. 285
— Wm., Ld. Sess. 518
— hon. Wm., aft. 2nd visc. Melbourne, *q.v.*, Ch. Sec. Ir. 563; P.C. 210
Lambard, sir Nich., L.M. Lond. 490
— Wm., M. Chy. 395
Lambarde, Wm., Rbk. P.A. 344
Lambart, Gust. Wm., Sec. St. Pat. 752
— Gust. Fras. Wm., Sec. St. Pat. 752
Lambert (or Jaenbert), abp. Cant. 430
— D. Tny. 57
— L.D. Ir. 554
— Danl., L.M. Lond. 491
— Geo. Rt., and sir G., adm. (**D**) 830; G.C.B. 770; K.C.B. 777
— Ham., gen. (**B**) 865
— Jas., L.M. Dbln. 642
— Jno., C.I.E. 807; W.C.P. 319
— Jno. and sir J., G.C.B. 769; gen. (**A**) 862; K.C.B. 774; K.C.B. 783; P.C. 220; Sec. L.G.B. 256
— Jno. Arth. and sir J., gen. (**D**) 899
— Ralph, bp. Drom. 605; bp. Mth. 599; dn. Down. 605
— Rt., adm. (**A**) 819
— Rowley, adm. (**E**) 836
— Saml., gen. (**D**) 880
— Walt. Rathb., gen. (**D**) 922
— Wm., gen. (**D**) 922
Lamberton, Wm., bp. St. Andr. 529
Lambley, Rand. de, bp. Abdn. 530
Lambrick, Geo., gen. (**D**) 903
Lambton, Fk. Wm., gen. (**D**) 934
— Hedw., gen. (**C**) 871
— Jno., gen. (**A**) 858
Lambton, visc.
— J. G., aft. visc. L. and ld. and E. of Durham, *q.v.*
Lamont, Dav., Modr. K. Sc. 547
— Jno., gen. (**C**) 874
— Norm., K.H. 792
Lamotte, Lt. Gen. K.C.B. 775
Lamplugh, Th., abp. Yk. 486 bp. Exr. 437; dn. Roch. 461
Lamport, Hugh, bp. Ferns, 621
Lamvallei, Wm. de, J. It. 366
Lanark, Wm., E. of, aft. D. of Hamilton, *q.v.*, Sec. St. Sc. (1641) 502
Lanatus, A.M., C. Ro. 37, 39
— L. M., C. Ro. 39
— T. M., C. Ro. 38
Lancaster, Jno., bp. Wford. and L. 627
— Jno. de, W.C.P. 318
— Rt. de, bp. St. As. 462
Lancaster—*cont.*
— Th., abp. Arm. 595; bp. Kild. 617; dn. Oss. 623
— Th. de, and sir Th., aft. D. of Clarence, *q.v.*, L.H.A. (1405) 173; L.L. Ir. 552
— Wm. de, J. It., 367
Lancaster, D. of
— Hy., 2nd. D. of (*d.* 1362) K.G. 733
— Jno. of Gaunt, D. of, also E. of Richmond, *q.v.*, K.G. 733
Lancey, Oliver de, gen. (**A**) 860
Lancy, Benjn., *see* Lant
Landaff, *see* Llandaff
Landell, Wm., bp. St. Andr. 529
Landers, Jno. Edm., gen. (**D**) 900
Lando (or Landonius), P. Ro. 34
Landon, Wh., dn. Exr. 438
Landseer, sir Ed., Pres. R.A. (?) 941
Lane, Ambr., gen. (**D**) 890
— Ch. Powl., gen. (**D**) 919
— Ch. R. W., gen. (**D**) 888
— Edmd., bp. Kild. 617
— sir Geo. (? Jas.), aft. 1st visc. Lanesborough, *q.v.*, Sec. St. Ir. 562
— Hy. M., Bl. M.P.A. 337; Chest. H. 331
— Jno. Theoph., gen. (**D**) 890
— Rd. and sir R., C.B. Ex. 381; L.K. 356; P.C. 189; S.L. 409
— Th., M. Chy. 396
— Th. and sir T., L.M. Lond. 491
— Th. Gord. M., gen. (**D**) 919
Lanesborough, visc. and E. of
Lane Family.
— Geo. (? Jas.), 1st visc., form. sir Geo. Lane, *q.v.*
Butler-Danvers Family.
— Br., 2nd E. of, form. ld. Newtown, *q.v.*
— Jno. V. D., 6th E. of, L.L. Cav. 569
Laney, Benj., *see* Lant
Lanferthus, bp. Elm. 454
Lanfranc (St.), abp. Cant. 430; Ch. Jr. 362
Lang, *see also* Laing
— Rd., bp. Kild. 617
— Wm., gen. (**D**) 898
Langdale, Hy., ld., form. H. Bickersteth, *q.v.*, C.G.S. 358
Langdon, Jno., bp. Roch. 460
— Wm., adm. (**A**) 815
Langevin, Hect. Louis, K.C.M.G. 797
Langford, Ch., dn. Her. 442
— Ralph de, dn. St. P. 452
— Walt. de, dn. St. P. 452
Langham, Simon, abp. Cant. 430; bp. Ely, 434; L.H.T. 153; Ld. Chanc. 354
Langland, *see* Longland
Langley, *see also* Longley
— Geo. Colt., gen. (**D**) 901; K.C.B. 781
— sir Jno., L.M. Lond. 490
— Ralph, Wdn. Chr. Ch. Manch. 481
— Wm. de, A.G. 398
— Th., *see* Longley
L'Anglois, Benj., B.T. 266; St. O. 260; U.S.S. 226
Langman, Ralph, Ptc. P.A. 337; Yk. H. 334
Langport, Rd., M. Chy. 394
Langrishe, Herc. and sir H., C. Cus. Ir. 565; C. Exc. Ir. 566
— Jas., dn. Ach. 614
— Rt. and sir R., C. Exc. Ir. 566-7
Langston, Fras., gen. (**B**) 864
Langton, Jno. de, bp. Chich. 432; Ld. Chanc. 353-4; M.R. 387
— Jno., bp. St. Dav., 464
— Sim. de, abp. Yk. 485
— Steph., abp. Cant. 430; Const. T.L. 320
— Th., abp. Cant. 431; bp. Sal. 467; bp. St. Dav. 464; bp. Winch. 470; Chanc. Gart. 745
— Th., K.B. 761
— Walt. de, bp. Lich. and Cov. 444; L.H.T. 152
— Wm., dn. Clr. 598
— (or Langueton), Wm. de, abp. Yk. (?) 485; dn. Yk. 486
Langueton, *see* Langton
Lanier, sir Jno., G. Jsey. 667; gen. (**B**) 864
Lannes, Off. Nap. 26
Lansdowne, ld., visc., and E. of, *see also* Granville
— Ch. Granville, visc., aft. 2nd E. of Bath, *q.v.*, L.L. Cnwall. 307
— (of Bideford), Geo., ld., form. Geo. Granville, *q.v.*, Compt. H. 292; P.C. 196; Tr. H. 291
— Wm., 1st M. of, form. 2nd E. of Shelburne, *q.v.*
— Hy., 3rd M. of, form. ld. H. Petty, *q.v.*, H. Sec. 227; Jud. Com. P.C. 360; K.G. 743; L.L. Wilts, 313; L.P.C. 188
— Hy., 4th M. of, form. E. of Shelburne, *q.v.*, K.G. 744; U.S.F. 230
— Hy. Ch. K., 5th M. of, G.C.M.G. 795; G.G. Can. 692; G.G. Ind. 650; L.T. 161-2; U.S. War, 232
— Maud. Ev., Mss. of, Cr. Ind. 810
Lant, Lancy, or **Laney,** Benj., bp. Ely, 435; bp. Linc. 447; bp. Pboro. 458; dn. Roch. 461
— Th., Ptc. P.A. 337; Winds. H. 331
Lanyon, Wm. Owen and sir W., Gr. Ld. W. 681; K.C.M.G. 797
Laoghaire, K. Ir. 21
— Lorck, K. Ir. 21
Lapidge, Wm. Fk., adm. (**G**) 842
Lapuerta, L., Pres. Pu. 109
Larcom, Th. Aisk and sir T., K.C.B. 783; U.S. Ir. 563
Large, Rt., L.M. Lond. 490
Largisius, bp. Kild. 616
Larke, Th., dn. Chich. 434
Larken, Arth S., Ptc. P.A. 337; Richm. H. 334
Laronius, L., C. Ro. 47
Larpent, Fras. S., C. Cus. 277
— Jno., E.S.P. 301
Lascelles, Fras., gen. (**A**) 859
— F. C. and sir F., Amb. Bga. 128; Amb. Rma. 128; K.C.M.G. 798

Lascelles—*cont.*
— Peregrine, gen. (**A**) 858
— Th., S.G.O. 259
— Wm. Lenn., aft. ld. De Ros, *q.v.*, gen. (**D**) 885
— hon. Wm. Sebr., Compt. H. 293; P.C. 215
Lascelles, visc.
— Hy., visc., aft. 2nd E. of Harewood, *q.v.*, L.L. Yorks W.R. 313
Laserian (St.), bp. Clr. 596; bp. Llin. 621
Lasingby, Wm., C.B. Ex. 381
Last, Ed., gen. (**D**) 900
Lateef, Naw. Abd., C.I.E. 807
Lateranus, L. S. S., C. Ro. 40
Latham, Jno., Pres. Coll. Ph. 938
— Wm., gen. (**C**) 873
— Wm., Q.C. 420
Lathelle, Nichs., B. Ex. 383
Lathom, Ed., 1st E. of, form. 2nd ld. Skelmersdale, *q.v.*, C.Y.G. 298; L.C.H. 295
Latimer and **Latymer**
— Hugh, bp. Worc. 473
— Th. de. K.B. 754
— Wm., dn. Pboro., 458
Latimer, lds.
Latimer and Nevill Families.
— Wm., 4th ld., K.G. 733; W.C.P. 318
— Jno., ld. (? Jno. ld. Nevill), K.B. (1400) 755
— Jno., 5th ld., K.B. (1426) 756
Nevill Family.
— Rd., 2nd ld., K.B. 757
Osborne Family.
— Th., visc., form. Th. Osborne, and sir T. and ld. O., *q.v.*, aft. E. of Danby, M. of Carmarthen, and D. of Leeds, *q.v.*, L. Admy. 175; L.H.T. 158; Prem. 140
Latorre, L., Pres. Ugy. 111
Latour (or Lautour), Pet. Aug., gen. (**D**) 881; K.H. 789
Latrobe, Ch. Jos., G. V.D. Ld. 708; G. Vict. 704
Latter, Rt. Jas., gen. (**D**) 877
Latymer, *see* Latimer
Laud, Wm., abp. Cant. 431; bp. B. & W. 428; bp. Lond. 452; bp. St. Dav. 464; dn. Glr. 440; L.T. 140, 154
Lauder, *see also* Lawder
— Geo., bp. Arg. 537
— Hy., Ld. Sess. 518
— sir Jno., Ld. Sess. 520
— Rt., bp. Dnbl. 532
— Rt. de, L.J. Gen. 522
— Wm., bp. Glasg. 536; Ld. Chanc. Sc. 515
— Wm. Bern., dn. Llin. 624
Lauderdale, lds., visc. E. and D. of
— Hugo de Morville, ld. of, Ld. Chanc. Sc. 514
— Jno., 2nd ld., aft. 1st visc. and E. of, Ld. Sess. 517, 519
— Jno., 2nd E., aft. 1st D. of, Comm. Tr. Sc. 497; H.C.P. Sc. 507; K.G. 740; L. Admy. 175; Ld. Sess. 517; P.C. 190, 192; Pres. P.C. Sc. 500; Sec. St. Sc. 502
— Jno., 5th E. of, form. sir J. Maitland, *q.v.*
— Jas., 8th E. of, Amb. Fr. 112; K.T. 748; L.K. Sc. 503; P.C. 208
Lauderdale, lds., visc., E. and D. of—*cont.*
— Jas., 9th E. of, L.L. Berw. 508
— Anthy., 10th E. of, form. hon. sir A. Maitland, *q.v.*, G.C.B. 770
— Th., 11th E. of, form. sir T. Maitland, *q.v.*, adm. (**B**) 821; (**E**) 834; G.C.B. 770; K.C.B. 779
Laugharne, Jno., adm. (**A**) 818
Laughton, Dav. Wilson, gen. (**D**) 929
— Geo. Arn., gen. (**D**) 932
Launfare, Jno. de, B. Ex. 382
Laurence and **Laurentius,** *see also* Lawrence
*— (St.), abp. Cant. 429
*— bp. Arg. 537
*— bp. Cork, 630
*— bp. Dnbl. 532
*— bp. Isl. 539
*— bp. Ross. 631
*— bp. S. and M. 483
* Prob. some same pers. Comp. dates.
— P. Ro. 33
Laurentio, Barth. de S., dn. Exr. 437
Laurentius, *see* Laurence
Laurie, Gilb., C. Ex. Sc. 505; L. Prov. Edinb. 548
— Jno., gen. (**D**) 887
— Jno., Woodb., gen. (**D**) 925
— sir Pet., L.M. Lond. 492
— Rt., bp. Brn. 531
— Rt., Clar. K.A. 328; Norr. K.A. 330; R. Cr. P.A. 335; Winds. H. 332
— sir Rt., Kt. Mar. Sc. 507
— sir Rt., adm. (**A**) 820; K.C.B. 776
— sir Rt., gen. (**A**) 859
Lautour, *see* Latour
Laval, Danl. de, Amb. Dk. 127
Lavie, Rt. Com., gen. (**D**) 928
Lavington, Geo., bp. Exr. 437
Lavington, lds.
— Ralph, ld., form. R. Payne and sir R., *q.v.*, G. Leew. Isl. 727; K.B. 765; P.C. 206
Law, hon. Ch. Ew., Comm. Serjt. Lond. 495; K.C. 416; Rec. Lond. 494
— Edm., bp. Carl. 476
— sir Ed., aft. 1st ld. Ellenborough, *q.v.*, A.G. 400; C.J.K.B. 370; K.C. 415; S.L. 412
— Fras. Towry Ad., gen. (**D**) 929
— Geo. Hy., bp. B. & W. 428; bp. Chest. 477
— Hy., dn. Glr. 440
— Hugh, Ld. Chanc. Ir. 577; S.G. Ir. 590
— Jas., abp. Glasg. 537; bp. Ork. 535
— Jas., Sec. St. Sc. 502
— Jno., bp. Clonf. & K. 636; bp. Elph. 608; bp. Killa. & Ach. 613
— Rt., gen. (**D**) 894: K.H. 792
— Saml. Cr., gen. (**D**) 919
— Wm., L. Prov. Edinb. 548
— Wm. Hy., gen. (**D**) 890
Lawder, *see also* Lauder
— Alexr., bp. Dkld. 533
— Ed. Jas., gen. (**D**) 923
— Th., bp. Dkld. 533
Lawes, Ed. Hobs. Vitr., S.L. 413
— sir Nichs. G. Jam. 712
— Vitruv., P.P. 416; S.L. 413
Lawford, Ed., gen. (**D**) 901
— Ed. Melv., gen. (**D**) 931
— Jno. and sir J., adm. (**A**) 818; K.C.B. 776
Lawless, Steph., bp. Lim. 638
— Wm., dn. St. Pat. 617
Lawley, sir Fas., C. Cus. 273
Lawrance, Jno. Compt., Q.C. 419
Lawrence, *see also* Laurence
— Alexr. Jno., C.I.E. 808
— Alexr. Wm., gen. (**D**) 892
— Arth. Johnst. and sir A., gen. (**D**) 896; K.C.B. 780
— Chas., G. N. Sc. 694
— Chr. Wm., Amb. Ecr. 942
— Danl., adm. (**H**) 845
— Elias, gen. (**D**) 883
— Geo. St. Patr., gen. (**D**) 896; K.C.S.I. 802
— Hy., gen. (**D**) 890
— Hy. Montg., K.C.B. 782; Pres. Pjab. 654
— Jas. Cl. and sir J., L.M. Lond. 492
— Jno., L.M. Lond. 491
— Jno. L.M., *see* ld. L., *infra*
— Rd., abp. Cash. and Eml. 626; abp. Cash., E. W. and L. 627
— Rd. Ch., gen. (**D**) 916
— Sould. and sir S., J.C.P. 379; J.K.B. 373; S.L. 412
— Str., gen. (**C**) 871
— Th., K.B. 759
— sir Th., Pres. R.A. 941
— Wm., Ld. Sess. 519
— Wm., Pres. Coll. Surg. 939
— Wm. and sir W., L.M. Lond. 492
Lawrence, lds.
— Jno. L. M., aft. sir J. and ld. L., Ch. Com. Pjab. 654; G.C.B. 772; G.C.S.I. 801; G.G. Ind. 649; K.B. 782; K.C.S.I. 802; M.C.I. 646; P.C. 216
— Harriet Kath., Baroness, Cr. Ind. 809
Lawrenson, Jno., gen. (**D**) 894
Laws, Jno. Milligan, adm. (**G**) 841
Lawson, Ch., L. Prov. Edinb. 548
— Jas.. gen. (**D**) 930
— Jas., Ld. Sess. 518
— Jas. Anthy., A.G. Ir. 588; J.C.P. Ir. 582; J.C.P.D. Ir. 582; J.Q.B.D. Ir. 580; P.C. 218; S.G. Ir. 590; S.L. Ir. 593
— sir Jno., adm. (**A**) 813
— Just., C.G.S. Ir. 577
— Rd., L.J. Clk. 516; Ld Adv. 525
— Rt., gen. (**B**) 867
Laxton, sir Wm., L.M. Lond. 490
Layard, Anthy. Lew., gen. (**B**) 867
— Austen Hy. and sir A., Amb. Spn. 124; Amb. Tky. 130; C.W.P.B. 272; G.C.B. 773; P.C. 218; U.S.F. 230
— Ch. Edm., gen. (**D**) 933
— Ch. Pet., dn. Brl. 440 K.C.M.G. 797
— F. P., gen. (**D**) 923
— Jno. Th., gen. (**B**) 868
— Wm. Tw., gen. (**D**) 905

Laye, Rog. de la, *see* Leye
— Fras., gen. (**B**) 867
— Jos. Hy., gen. (**D**) 905
Layton, Hy., adm. (**H**) 848
— Rd., dn. Yk. 487; M. Chy. 394
Lazo, R. Z. Y., Pres. S. Salv. 106
Le— For names with this prefix search under the name next following; *ex. gr.*, Le Neve under Neve
Leach, *see also* Leech
— Jno. and sir J., C.J. Chest. 386; Jud. Com. P.C. 360; K.C. 415; M.R. 388; P.C. 209; V. Chanc. 390
— Rt. Owen, adm. (**H**) 853
Leahy, Dav., C.C.J. 403
Leake, *see also* Leeke
— Geo. M., Chest. H. 331
— sir Jno., L. Admy. 177; adm. (**A**) 813
— Jno. M., Chest. H. 331
— Rt. Mart., gen. (**D**) 890
— Steph. M. (No. 1), Clar. K.A. 328; Gart. K.A. 328; Lanc. H. 333; Norr. K.A. 329
— Steph. M. (No. 2), Norf. H. 341
— (or Leeke), Wm., B. Ex. 384; S.L. 410
Lear, Fras., dn. Sal. 468
Learmonth, sir Jas., Ld. Sess. 519
— Jno., L. Prov. Edinb. 548
L'Eau, de, *see* Waters
Leblanc, Sim. and sir S., J.K.B. 373; S.L. 412
Le Breton, *see* Breton
Lebrun, Csl. Fr. 24; Off. Nap. 26
Lecale, Chas. ld., adm. (**A**) 816
Lech. sir Ph., L.H.T. 153
Lechlade, Ralph de, dn. Wells, 428
— Th. de, dn. Exr. 437
Lechmere (or Letchmere), Nichs. (No 1), B. Ex. 384; S.L. 411
— Nichs. (No. 2), *see* ld. L., *infra*
— Wm., adm. (**A**) 818
Lechmere, lds.
— Nichs. and sir N. (No. 2), aft. ld. L., A.G. 399; C.D.L. 242; P.C. 197; S.G. 401
Leck, Jno., abp. Dbln. and Gl. 615; L. Treas. Ir. 558
Leckie, Geo. Alexr., gen. (**D**) 919
Leconteur, Clem., dn. Jsey. 668
— Ph., dn. Jsey. 668
Ledbury, Steph. de, dn. Her. 442
Ledenham, Eust. de, J. It. 366
Le Despencer, *see* Despencer
Ledgard, Fredk. T. D., Q.C. 420
Ledisham, Th., dn. Oss. 623; dn. Wford, 628
Ledred, Rd., bp. Oss. 620
Ledrede, Rt., L.H.A. 172
Ledwick, Edw., dn. Kild. 619
Lee, *see also* Leye and Leigh
— —, E.S.P. 301
— Brice W., gen. (**D**) 888
— Edw., abp. Yk. 486
— hon. Fitzr. Hy., adm. (**A**) 814

Lee—*cont.*
— G., L. Admy. 178
— (or Ley), Geo., dn. Cork, 632
— sir Geo., D. Arch. 420; J. Pr. Ct. 421; P.C. 199
— sir Hy., K.G. 739
— Jas. Pr., bp. Manch. 480
— Jno., A.G. 399; K.C. 415; S.G. 402
— Jno., gen. (**B**) 867
— Jno., Q.C. 418
— Jno. (of Wiltshire), K.B. 759
— Jno., Modr. K. Sc. 547
— Rd., Clar. K.A. 328; Ptc. P.A. 337; Richm. H. 333
— Rd., L.M. Lond. 490
— Rd. and sir R., adm. (**A**) 819; K.C.B. 774
— Rt., L.M. Lond. 491
— Rt., Ld. Sess. 521
— Rowl., bp. Lich. and Cov. 444; M. Chy. 394
— Th., Chest. H. 331
— sir Th., L. Admy. 175-6
— Ussh., dn. Kilmacd. 638; dn. Wford. 628
— Wm., Sr. N. 257
— Wm. and sir W., J.K.B. 373; C.J.K.B. 370; Ch. Ex. 165; P.C. 198; S.L. 411
— Wm., Q.C. 417
Leech, *see also* Leach
— Arth. Hy., dn. Cash. 627
— Ed., M. Chy. 395
— Sim., K.B. 764
***Leeds,** Ed., M. Chy. 397
*— Ed., S.L. 412
* Poss. same pers.
— Th., K.B. 761
Leeds, D. of
— Th., 1st D. of, form. Th. Osborn, sir T. and ld. O., visc. Latimer, E. of Danby, and M. of Carmarthen, *q.v.*
— Per., 2nd D. of, form. M. of Carmarthen, *q.v.*
— Th., 4th D. of, Coff. H. 293-4; K.G. 742; P.C. 200
— Fras. God., 5th D. of, form. M. of Carmarthen, *q.v.*, K.G. 742
— Geo. Wm. Fk., 6th D. of, K.G. 743; L.L. Yorks, N.R. 313; M.H. 302
Leeke, *see also* Leake
— Hy. Jno. and sir H., adm. (**D**) 830; (**G**) 841; K.C.B. 778; K.H. 791; L. Admy. 184
— Th., Curs. B. Ex. 386
— Wm., *see* Leake
Lees, Ch. Cam. and sir C., G. Bah. Isl. 716; G. Bdoes. 721; G. Gld. Cst. Col. 686; G. Labn. 675; G. Lag. 687; G. Leew. Isl. 728; K.C.M.G. 798
— Hugh (*see* Lacy)
— Jas. Cam., dn. Thist. 749
— Wm. Munn., gen. (**D**) 931
— Wm. Nass., gen. (**D**) 928
Leeson, Wm., M. Chy. 395
— sir Wm. Ed., Geneal. St. Patr. 752
Leet, Wm. Kn., gen. (**D**) 932
Lefanu, Th. Ph., dn. Emly, 628
Lefebore, Nichs., adm. (**H**) 849
Lefebre, Off. Nap. 26
Lefevre, Ch. Shaw-, aft. visc. Eversley, *q.v.*, P.C. 213; Sp. H.C. 250

Lefevre—*cont.*
— Geo. J. Shaw-, C.W.P.B. 272; L. Admy. 184; P.C. 219; Postm. G. 239; Sec. Adm. 187; Sec. B.T. 269
— Jno. Geo. Shaw-, K.C.B. 782; P.L.C. 262; Sec. B.T. 270; U.S.W. &c. 231
Lefroy, G., dn. Drom. 606
— Jeffr., dn. Drom. 606
— Jno. Hy. and sir J., G. Bmda. 701; G. Tasm. 708; gen. (**D**) 906; K.C.M.G. 797
— Th., B. Ex. Ir. 584; C.J.Q.B. Ir. 578; S.L. Ir. 593
— Th. E. P., C.C.J. 405
Legard, Rt., M. Chy. 396
Leggatt, *see also* Leggett
— Ed. Owen, gen. (**D**) 929
Legge, hon. Arth. Ch., gen. (**D**) 900
— hon. Arth. K. and sir A., adm. (**A**) 818; K.C.B. 774
— Colin, L.G.O. 259
— hon. Ed., bp. Oxf. 457; dn. Winds. 474
— Fras., G. N.Sc. 695
— Geo., aft. 1st ld. Dartmouth, *q.v.*, L.G.O. 259; M.G.O. 258; P.C. 192
— Heneage, C. Exc. 281
— hon. Heneage, B. Ex. 385; K.C. 415; S.L. 412
— hon. Heneage, C. Cus. 277
— Hy., S.W.F. 271
— hon. Hy. Bils., Ch. Ex. 165; L. Admy. 178; L.T. 157; P.C. 199; Tr. N. 256
— Rd., gen. (**C**) 875
— Th., L.M. Lond. 489
— Th., M. Chy. 395
— Wm., M.G.W. 296
Leggett, *see also* Leggatt
— Jos., gen. (**D**) 887
Legh, *see also* Leigh
— Th. and sir T., M. Chy. 394
Leghe (of Stokewell), Jno., K.B. 759
Legrand, Alexr., C. Cus. Sc. 504
— Fk. Gasp., gen. (**D**) 932
Leheup, Isaac, C. Cus. 275
Leia, Pet. de, bp. St. Dav. 464
Leicester, *see also* Lester and Leycester
— Jno. of, bp. Dkld. 533
— Petr. de, B. Ex. 382; L.H.T. 152
— Rog. de, J.C.P. 377; B. Ex. 382
— (or Lester, or Lyster), Wm., dn. Clonm. 600
Leicester, E. of
Beaumont or Bellamont Family.
— Rt. de Beaumont, 2nd E. of, Ch. Jr. (1154) 362; J. It. 365
Dudley Family.
— Rt., E. of, form. sir R. or ld. R. Dudley, *q.v.*, L.S.H. 290; L.K. 356
Sydney Family.
— Rt., 1st E. of, form. ld. Sydney, and visc. Lisle, *q.v.*
— Rt., 2nd E. of, L.L. Ir. 554; P.C. 190
— Jno., 6th E. of, C.Y.G. 298; Const. T.L. 321; K.B. 764; P.C. 198; L.L. Kent, 309; W.C.P. 319

For List of Abbreviations, see pp. 944-952.

Leicester, E. of—*cont.*
Coke Family.
1st Creation.
—— Th., E. of, form. Th. Coke, and ld. Lovel, *q.v.*, Postm. G. 238
Townshend Family.
—— Geo., 1st E. of, form. ld. de Ferrers, *q.v.*, aft. M. Townshend, *q.v.*, B.T. 267; L.S.H. 290; M.M. 247; Postm. G. 238
Coke Family.
2nd Creation.
—— Th. Wm., 2nd E. of, K.G. 745; L.L. Norf. 310
Leige, sir Ferd., G. I. Man, 666
Leigh, *see also* Legh
—— Capel Hanb., L.L. Monm. 310
—— Ch., G. Leew. Isl. 727; gen. (**A**) 859
—— hon. Ed. Chand., Q.C. 419
—— Fras., K.B. 761
—— Joddrell, adm. (**G**) 841
—— Rd., S.L. 412
—— Rt. Th., gen. (**D**) 917
—— (or Lee) sir Th., L.M. Lond. 490
—— Th. Pemb., aft. ld. Kingsdown, *q.v.*, Jud. Com. P.C. 360; P.C. 214. *See also* Pemberton
—— Wm., dn. Her. 442
Leigh, lds.
—— Wm. H., 2nd ld. (2nd Cr.), L.L. Warw. 312
Leighton, sir Baldw., gen. (**A**) 861
—— Dav. and sir D., gen. (**D**) 876; K.C.B. 776
—— Fras., gen. (**A**) 858
—— Fk. and sir F., Pres. R.A. 941
—— Hy. de, bp. Abdn. 530; bp. Mor. 534
—— Rt., abp. Glasg. 537; bp. Dnbl. 532
—— sir Th., G. Gsey. 668
—— sir Wm., L.M. Lond. 492
Leiningen, Ern. Leop. &c., Pr. of, adm. (**E**) 836; G.C.B. 771-2; K.C.B. 783
Leinster, D. of
Schomberg Family.
—— Meinh., 1st D. of, aft. 3rd D. of Schomberg, *q.v.*, C. Ch. 855
Fitzgerald Family.
—— Jas., 1st D. of, form. 20th E. of Kildare, *q.v.*, gen. (**B**) 865
—— Wm. Rt., 2nd D. of, K.P. 750; M.R. Ir. 585
—— Augs. Fk., 3rd D. of, L.L. Kild. 569; P.C. 212
Leir, Rd. Longf., gen. (**D**) 932
Leishman, Matth., Mod. K. Sc. 547
Leith, Alexr. and sir A., gen. (**A**) 863; K.C.B. 774
—— sir Geo., gen. (**C**) 874
—— Jas. and sir J., G. Bdoes. 720; G.C.B. 767; G. Leew. Isl. 727; gen. (**B**) 867; K.B. 766
—— Jno., adm. (**D**) 830
—— Jno. Farl., Q.C. 419
—— Patr., Ld. Clk. Reg. 525
—— Rt. Wm. Disn., gen. (**D**) 905
Leitrim, lds. and E. of
—— Rt., 1st ld. and E. of, form. R. Clements, *q.v.*
Leitrim, lds. and E. of—*cont.*
—— Nathl., 2nd E. of, K.P. 751; L.L. Leitr. 570
Leiva, P., Pres. Hdas. 106
Leland, Jno., gen. (**A**) 859
Leman, sir Jno., L.M. Lond. 491
Le Marchant, *see* Marchant
Le Mesurier, *see* Mesurier
Lemoine, Jno., gen. (**C**) 874
Lemon, J., L. Admy. 180
—— Th., gen. (**D**) 900
Lempedlar, Gilb. de, L.G.C. Sc. 506
Lempriere, Geo. Ourry, adm. (**H**) 846
Lendivord, abp. St. Dav. 463
Le Neve, *see* Neve
L'Enfant, *see* Enfant
Leng, Jno. (? Laing), bp. Norw. 455
Lennard, *see also* Leonard
—— Samps., Bl. M. P.A. 336; R. Rge. P.A. 344
Lenne, *see* Lynn
Lennock, Geo. Gust., adm. (**H**) 845
Lennox and **Lenox**
—— ld. Arth., Clk. O. 260; L.T. 160
—— Augs. Fk. Fras., gen. (**D**) 911
—— ld. Geo. Hy., Const. T.L. 321; gen. (**A**) 858; P.C. 202
—— ld. Hy. Ch. Geo. Gord., C.W.P.B. 272; L.T. 161; P.C. 219; Sec. Adm. 187
—— Wilbr. O., gen. (**D**) 924
Lennox, D. of, *see also* Richmond
Stuart Family.
—— Esmy., 1st D. of, L.G.C. Sc. 506
—— Ludovick, 2nd D. of, aft. E. of Newcastle-on-Tyne, and D. of Richmond, *q.v.*
—— Esmé, 3rd D. of, form. E. of March, *q.v.*, K.G. 739; *see* D. of Richmond
—— Jas., 4th D. of, and 2nd E. of March; *see* D. of Richmond
—— Esmey, 5th D. of; *see* D. of Richmond
—— Ch., 6th D. of; *see* D. of Richmond
Lennox Family.
—— Ch., 1st D. of, and 1st D. of Richmond, *q.v.*
Lens, Jno., S.L. 412
Lenthall, Wm., C.D.L. 242; C.G.S. 356; M.R. 388; Sp. H.C. 249
Lentulus, *see also* Clodianus Sura
—— C. C., C. Ro. 43-4-5
—— C. C. P., C. Ro. 45
—— L. C., C. Ro. 41-2-3; Dt. Ro. 41
—— P. C., C. Ro. 44
—— S. C., C. Ro. 41
Leo I. to VI., Emp. E. E. 50
—— I. to XIII., P. Ro. 33-4-5-6
Leofardo, Jno. de S., dn. Chich. 434
Leoffius, bp. Worc. 472
Leofgar, *see also* Leovegard
—— bp. Lich. 443
Leofric, bp. Dev., Cnwall. and Exr. 436
Leofwin, bp. Lich. 443
Leofwynus, bp. Dorch. and Sidr. 446
Leolinus Magnus, Pr. Wls. 16
Leonard, *see also* Lennard
—— J. It. 365
—— Patr. M., C.C.J. 405
Leonius, dn. Wells, 428
Leontius, Emp. E. E. 50
Leopardo, St. Gilb. de S., bp. Chich. 432
Leopold, D. Lne. 30
—— Pr. L. Dtd. 73
—— R. Nds. 83
—— I. and II., D. Bva. 67
—— I. and II., E. Gmy. 62-3
—— I. and II., G. D. Tny. 57
—— I. and II., K. Bgm. 83
—— I. (K. Bgm.), form. Pr. Leop. of S. Coburg, F.M. 856; G.C.B. 767; G.C.H. 786; gen. (**A**) 860; K.G. 743; P.C. 209
—— II. (K. Bgm.), K.G. 745
—— I. and II., K. Hgy. 60
—— I. to VIII., M. Aus. and D. Aus. 58
—— -Ch.-Ed.-Geo. Alb. (g. son Q. Victoria), Pr. E. 16
—— -Geo.-Dunc.-Alb., Pr., aft. D. of Albany, *q.v.*, G.C.M.G. 795; G.C.S.I. 801; K.G. 745; K.T. 749; P.C. 219; Pr. E. 16
—— Fk., D. Anth. 66
—— Fk. Fras., D. Anht. 66
Leosgar, bp. Lich. 443
***Leovegard** (or Leofgar) (St.), bp. Her. 441
***Leovegarus,** dn. St. P. 452
* Poss. same pers.
Leovingus, *see also* Livingus
—— abp. Cant. 430; bp. Wells, 427
Lepidus, Tr. Ro. 46
—— M. Æ., C. Ro. 41-3-4-5-6
—— P. Æ., C. Ro. 46
Lere, Banco de, K.B. 755
Lesko, IV., D. Pld. 90
—— V. and VI., K. Pld. 91
Lesley and **Leslie**
—— Alexr., Compt. Sc. 498
—— hon. Alexr., gen. (**B**) 866
—— Bradf., K.C.I.E. 805
—— Ch., K.H. 791
—— Ch. Pow., L.L. Monaghan, 570
—— hon. Dav., gen. (**A**) 861
—— Geo., gen. (**D**) 926
—— Hy., bp. Down and Cnr. 604; bp. Mth. 599; dn. Down, 605
—— Hy., dn. Cnr. 605
—— Hy., dn. Drom. 606
—— Jas., bp. Lim. A. and A. 639
—— Jno., bp. Clr. 596; bp. Isl. 540; bp. Rph. 601; dn. Rph. 602
—— Jno., bp. Drom. 605; bp. Elph. and Kilm. E. and A. 608; dn. Cork, 632
—— Jno., bp. Ross, 535; Sec. St. Sc. 502
—— Jno., dn. Drom. 606
—— Jno., dn. Dry. 602
—— Jno., gen. (**D**) 884; K.H. 792
—— Jno., Ld. Sess. 518
—— sir Jno., K.H. 790
—— sir Jno., Ld. Sess. 519
—— sir Leon, L.H. Const. Sc. 507
—— Rt., bp. Clr. 596; bp. Drom. 604; bp. Rph. 601
—— Saml., adm. (**H**) 844
Lestock, Rd., adm. (**A**) 814
Lesseps, Count Ferd. de, G.C.S.I. 801

Lester, *see also* Leicester
— Fk. P., gen. (**D**) 887
— Jno. Fk., gen. (**D**) 918
— Rd., *see* Lyster
Lestrange, *see also* Strange
— Edmd., gen. (**D**) 919
— Ed., gen. (**D**) 894
— Geo. Guy Carl, gen. (**B**) 870
— Th., gen. (**B**) 868
Letham, Jno., Ld. Sess. 518
Lethbridge, Eben. Rop., C.I.E. 806
— Rt., gen. (**B**) 868
— Th. Br., adm. (**E**) 836
Letherland, Jno., G. I. Man, 665
Lettsom, W. G., Amb. Bol. 135; Amb. Mex. 133; Amb. Ugy. 137
Leuchars, Pat. de, bp. Brn. 531; Ld. Chanc. Sc. 515
Leuknore, *see also* Lewkenor
— Geoffr. de, J.C.P. 377; J. It. 368; Jy. 365
Leutbert, K. Lmd. 49
Leuvigildo, K. Sp. 85
Levaillant, genl., K.C.B. 778
Levelyn, J., L. Admy. 175
Leven, E. of, *see also* Melville
— Dav., 2nd E. of, gen. (**B**) 864
— Alexr., 5th E. of, L.H.C.K. Sc. 546; Ld. Sess. 520
— Dav., 6th E. of, L.H.C.K. Sc. 546
— Dav., 8th E. of, adm. (**H**) 844
Leverous, *see* Liverous
Levesham, Wm., B. Ex. 383
Leveson, Rd., gen. (**C**) 871
Leveson, visc.
— Gr. Geo., visc., aft. 2nd E. Granville, *q.v.*, U.S.F. 230
Leveson-Gower, *see* Gower and Granville
Levin, *see* Levinz
Leving, Tim., S.L. 409
Levinge, Cr., *see* Levinz
— Bapt., bp. S. and M. 484
— Ch., K.H. 792
— sir Rd., A.G. Ir. 588; C.J.C.P. Ir. 580; S.G. Ir. 589
Levins, *see* Levinz
Levington, (or Levinton), Rd. de, J. It. 367
Levingston, Th., K.C. 414
Levinz, Levins, or **Levin**
— Cress. and sir C., A.G. 399; J.C.P. 379; K.C. 414; S.L. 410
— Wm., C. Cus. 275-6
Levett, sir Rd., L.M. Lond. 491
— Wm., dn. Brl. 440
Levua, K. Sp. 85
Lewen, Just. and sir J., M. Chy. 395-6
— Wm., J. Pr. Ct. 421; M.Chy. 395
— sir Wm., L.M. Lond. 491
Lewes, *see* Lewis
Lewin, sir Geo. A., Q.C. 417
Lewis and **Lewes,** *see also* Louis
— (2), bp. Bgr. 425-6
— (g. son Jas. I.), Pr. E. 13
— Ch. Algn., gen. (**D**) 895
— (or Lewes), Dav., J. Adm. Ct. 422; M. Chy. 395
— Erasm., U.S.S. 225
— Evan, dn. Bgr. 427
Lewis and Lewes—*cont.*
— Geo., gen. (**B**) 868
— Geo., gen. (**D**) 883
— Geo. Corn. and sir G., Ch. Ex. 166; H. Sec. 227; L.T. 161; P.C. 216; P.L.C. 262; Sec. B.C. 254; Sec. Tr. 163; U.S. Home, 228; W. Sec. 232
— Geo. Pitt-, Q.C. 420
— Griffith Geo., gen. (**D**) 883
— Hy., gen. (**D**) 911
— Hy. Perc., gen. (**D**) 880
— Jno., dn. Oss. 623
— Jno. Trav., bp. Ont. 693
— Matth., Dep. Sec. at War. 234
— Pet., dn. Lism. 629
— Rd., bp. Llff. 447
— Rt., gen. (**D**) 900
— Rt. Mas., gen. (**C**) 872
— Theoph., gen. (**B**) 868
— Th. Fr., and sir T., P.C. 211; P.L.C. 262; Sec. Tr. 163; Tr. N. 257; V.P.B.T. 269
— sir Watk., L.M. Lond. 492
— Wm., gen. (**C**) 872
— Wm. Dav., Q.C. 418
Lewisham, visc.
— Wm., 1st visc., form. 2nd. ld., and aft. 1st E. of Dartmouth, *q.v.*
— Geo., visc., ld., and aft. 4th E. of Dartmouth, *q.v.*, L.W.S. 323; P.B.C. 252; P.C. 207
— Wm. Heneage, visc. (son of 5th E. of Dartmouth), P.C. 220; V.C.H. 297
Lewkenor and **Lewknor,** *see also* Leuknore
— Jno., K.B. 763
— Rd. and sir R., C.J. Chest. 386; S.L. 408
— Roger, K.B. 756
— Roger, K.B. 758
— Th., K.B. 758
Lewkyn (or Loufkin), Jno., L.M. Lond. 489
Lewson, Rd., K.B. 763
Lexington and **Lexinton**
— Hy. de, bp. Linc. 446; dn. Linc. 448
— Jno. de, Jy. 364; L.K. 353
— Rt. de, C.J.C.P. 375; Ch. Jr. 363; Jy. 364
— Wm. de, dn. Linc. 448
Lexinton, lds.
— Rt., 2nd ld., B.T. 263; P.C. 194
Ley and **Leye,** *see also* Lee
— Jas. and sir J., aft. ld. and E. of Marlborough, *q.v.*; C.G.S. 356; C.J.K.B. 370; C.J.K.B. Ir. 578; L.H.T. 154; L.K. Ir. 576; S.L. 409
— Rog. de la, B. Ex. 382; dn. St. P. 452
Leyat, Rd., dn. Sal. 468
Leyborne, Leybourn, Leybourne, and **Leyburn**
— sir Rt., L.H.A. 171
— Rog., bp. Carl. 475
— Rog. de, Const. T.L. 320; W.C.P. 317
— sir Wm. de, L.H.A. 170
— Wm. Leyb., G. Gren. 724; G. St. Vin. 725; G. Tob. 723
Leycester and **Leycestre,** *see also* Leicester
— Fras., *see* Abree
— Hugh, K.C. 415
Leycester and Leycestre—*cont.*
— Jno. de, A.G. Ir. 588
— Wm. de, M. Chy. 393
Leye, *see* Ley
Leynagh, Jno., bp. Lism. 626
Leys, Pet., G. Labn. 675
Leyson, Griff., D. Arch. 420; J. Adm. Ct. 422
Li—, *see also* Ly—
Libba, *see* Molibba
Liberius, P. Ro. 33
Libiau, bp. Llff. 448
Libo, L. J., C. Ro. 42
— L. S., C. Ro. 46
— M. P., C. Ro. 41
Lichenburg, Geo. Chr., Sec. Guelph, 792
Lichfield, *see also* Litchfield
— Th. de, dn. Chich. 433
Lichfield, E. of
Stuart Family.
— Chas., E. of, aft. 3rd D. of Richmond, *q.v.*
Lee Family.
— Geo. H., 3rd E. of, C.G.P. 299; P.C. 201
Anson Family.
— Th. Wm., 1st E. of, form. 2nd visc. Anson, *q.v.*, Postm. G. 238
— Geo. Th., 2nd E. of, L.L. Staffs. 312
Licinus, C. F. D., C. Ro. 42
— L. P., C. Ro. 44
— M. F., C. Ro. 42
Licinius, C., Trib. Ro. 39
— F. V., Emp. Ro. 48
Liddell and **Lidell**
— hon. Adolph. Fk. Oct., and sir A., K.C.B. 783; Q.C. 418; U.S. Home, 228
— Hy. Geo., dn. Chr. Ch. Oxf. 457
— Jno., gen. (**D**) 900
— sir Jno., K.C.B. 779
— Th., bp. Down, 603
Lidiard, *see* Lydiard
Lifford, Jas., 1st ld. and visc., form. Jas. Hewitt, *q.v.*, C. Acc. Ir. 567; L.J. Ir. 557
Light, Alfr., gen. (**D**) 920
— Hy., G. Br. Gu. 715
— Hy., G. Antig. 728
— Hy., K.C.B. 782
Lightbourn, Jas., M. Chy. 396
Lightburne, Staff., gen. (**B**) 867
— Wm., dn. Dry. 602
— Wm., L.M. Dbln. 641
Lightfoot, Ellis, G. Bah. Isl. 716
— Jos. Barb., bp. Dham. 479
— Th., gen. (**D**) 880
— Th., gen. (**D**) 908
Ligonier, lds. visc. and E.
— Jno. and sir J., aft. 1st ld. visc. and E. of L., C. Ch. 855; F.M. 856; G. Gsey. 668; gen. (**A**) 857; K.B. 764; L.G.O. 259; M.G.O. 259; P.C. 199
— Ed., 2nd visc. and 1st E. of (2nd Cr.), gen. (**B**) 865; K.B. 765
Ligus, P. Æ., C. Ro. 44
Lilburne, G. Bah. Isl. 716
Lilkanth, R. S. M. R., C.I.E. 807
Lill, Godfr., J.C.P. Ir. 582; S.G. Ir. 589; S.L. Ir. 592
Lillicrap, Jas., adm. (**H**) 844
Lillington, Geo., G. Bdoes. 720

Lilly, Hy., R. Cr. P.A. 335; R. Rge. P.A. 344
Limberg, Ad. de, Ld. Chanc. Ir. 574
Limerick, Edmd. Hy., 1st visc. and E. of, form. ld. Glentworth, *q.v.*
Limesey, Rt. de, bp. Lich. 443
Limond, Alexr., gen. (**D**) 876
—— sir Jas., gen. (**D**) 877
Limri, Thakore Sahib of, K.C.I.E. 805
Linares, J. M., Pres. Bol. 109
Linch, *see* Lynch
Lincoln, Abr., Pres. U.S.A. 102-3
—— Alured de (2), J. It. 365, 367
—— Jno. de, A.G. 398
—— Th. de, S.L. 406
Lincoln, Earls of
Lacy Family.
—— Jno., 1st E. of, form. Jno. de Lacy, *q.v.*
De la Pole Family.
—— Jno., E. of, K.B. (1475) 757; L.L. Ir. 553
Clinton Family.
—— Ed., 1st E. of, form. ld. Clinton, *q.v.*, L.H.A. 174
—— Ed., 5th E. of, form ld. Clinton, *q.v.*
—— Hy., 7th E. of, Coff. H. 293; Const. T.L. 321; K.G. 741; P.C. 196; Paym. G. 244
—— Hy., 9th E. of, aft. 2nd D. of Newcastle, *q.v.*, Aud. Ex. 167; Coff. H. 293; K.G. 742
—— Th., E. of, aft. 4th D. of Newcastle, *q.v.*, gen. (**C**) 872
—— Hy., E. of, aft. 5th D. of Newcastle, *q.v.*, C.W.F. &c. 272; Ch. Sec. Ir. 563; L.T. 160; P.C. 214
Lind or **Lynde**
—— Geo., L. Prov. Edinb. 548
—— sir Jas., K.C.B. 774
—— Jno. de la, Const. T.L. 320
Lindenthal, Lew., gen. (**B**) 867
Lindesay and **Lindesey**, *see* Lindsay and Lindsey
Lindley, Nathl. and sir N., J.C.P. 380; J.C.P.D. 380; J.Q.B.D. 374; Jud. Com. P.C. 362; L.J. App. 389; P.C. 220; Q.C. 419; S.L. 414
Lindores, Abb. of, Ld. Sess. 518
Lindores, lds.
—— Alexr., ld., gen. (**C**) 871
Lindsay, Lindsey, Lindesay, and Lindesey
—— — G. Tob. 723
—— Alexr., bp. Dkld. 533
—— Alexr., gen. (**D**) 878; K.C.B. 779
—— Col. —, G. N.S.W. 703
—— hon. Ch. Dalr., bp. Kild. 617; bp. Killoe. and Kilf. 635; dn. Chr. Ch. Dbln. 619
*—— Dav., bp. Brn. 531; bp. Edin. 533
*—— Dav., bp. Ross. 535
* Prob. same pers.
—— Dav. de, L.J. Gen. 522
—— sir Dav., gen. (**A**) 858
—— sir Dav., Ld. Sess. 519
—— sir Dav. (3), Ly. K.A. 513
—— Eff., gen. (**B**) 870
—— hon. Hugh, Chn. E.I. Co. 645

Lindsay, Lindsey, Lindesay, and Lindesey—*cont.*
—— Ingeram, bp. Abdn. 530
—— Jas., bp. Dkld. 533
—— Jas., gen. (**D**) 883
—— Jas., L.P.S. Sc. 500
—— hon. Jas., gen. (**D**) 896; K.C.M.G. 796
—— sir Jerome, Ly. K.A. 513
—— Jno., bp. Glasg. 536; L.G.C. Sc. 506
—— Jno., gen. (**C**) 873
—— Jno., aft. ld. Wolmerstown, *q.v.*, K.B. 761
—— Jno., Ld. Sess. 518
—— sir Jno., adm. (**A**) 815; K.B. 765; L. Admy. 180
—— sir Jno., Sec. St. Sc. 502
—— Patr., abp. Glasg. 537; bp. Ross. 535; Ld. Sess. 517
—— Patr., G. I. Man, 666
—— Patr. and sir P., gen. (**C**) 875; K.C.B. 776; K.C.H. 788
—— Rt., J.C.P. Ir. 581
—— Rt. Jas. Loyd-, aft. ld. Wantage, *q.v.*, K.C.B. 783; U.S. War, 233
—— Th., abp. Arm. 596; bp. Killoe. 634; bp. Rph. 602; dn. St. Pat. 618; L.J. Ir. 556
—— Walt. (Ld. St. John), Ld. Sess. 518
—— Wm., Amb. Vce. 116
—— Wm. de, Ld. Chanc. Sc. 514
—— sir Wm., L.G.C. Sc. 506
—— Wm. Alexr., Ptc. P.A. 337
Lindsay of the Byres, lds. and E. of
—— Jno., 1st ld., L.J. Gen. 522
—— Jno., 5th ld., Ld. Sess. 517
—— Jno., 10th ld. aft. E. of, L.H.T. and Comm. Tr. Sc. 497; Ld. Sess. 517
Lindsey, E. and M. of
Bertie Family.
—— Rt. B., E. of, form. ld. Will. de Eresby, *q.v.*, K.G. 739; L. Admy. 175; P.C. 190
—— Mont., 2nd E. of, form. M. Bertie, *q.v.*, E.M. 326; K.G. 740; L.G.C. 287; P.C. 190
—— Rt., 3rd. E. of, L.G.C. 288; P.C. 192-3
—— Rt., 4th E. of, aft. 1st. M. of Lindsey and D. of Ancaster and K., *q.v.*, P.C. 194; L.G.C. 288
—— Albem., 5th E. of, form. A. Bertie, *q.v.*
Lindsell, Aug., bp. Her. 441; bp. Pboro. 458; dn. Lich. 445
Lindsey, *see* Lindsay
Lingard, Rd., dn. Lism. 629
—— Jno., Comm. Serjt. Lond. 495
Lingen, Ralph Rt. Wh., aft. sir R. and ld. L., K.C.B. 783; Sec. Tr. 164
Linlithgow, E. of
—— Geo., 3rd E. of, gen. (**B**) 864; L.H.A. Sc. 499
—— Geo., 4th E. of, L.H.T. Sc. 497
Linsengen, or **Linsingden**, Ch. Bar., gen. (**B**) 866; K.C.B. 775
Linton, Bern. de, bp. Isl. 539
—— sir Rt., G.C.B. 771
—— Syd., bp. Riv. 704
—— Wm., K.C.B. 779
Linus, P. Ro. 32

Linzee, Rt., adm. (**A**) 816
—— Sam. Hood, adm. (**A**) 818
Lion, *see* Lyon
Lionel (son of Edw. III.), Pr. E. 10
Lionello, M. Fa. 53
Lipscomb, Chr., bp. Jam. 713
Liptrap, Jno., gen. (**D**) 900
Liptrott, Jno., gen. (**D**) 910
Lisburne, Wilm., 4th visc. and 1st E. of, form. hon. W. Vaughan, *q.v.*, B.T. 266; L. Admy. 179
Lisgar, Jno., 1st ld., form. Jno. Young, *q.v.*, L.L. Cav. 569
Lisieux, Th., dn. St. P. 453
Lisle, *see also* Lyle
—— Alfr. de, gen. (**D**) 906
—— Gerard de, K.B. 755
—— Jno., called ld. L., C.G.S. 356
—— Jno., K.B. 755
—— Jno. de, Const. W. Cast. 322
—— Jno., L. Admy. 175; L.T. 154
—— Jno., *see* ld. L., *infra*
—— Saml., bp. Norw. 455; bp. St. As. 462
—— Th., bp. Ely, 434
—— Wm., M. Chy. 396
Lisle of Rugemont, lds.
—— sir Jno., aft. 2nd ld., K.G. (1327) 733
Lisle, lds. and visc.
Talbot Family.
—— Th., visc., K.B. (1464) 757
Grey Family.
—— Jno., visc., K.B. (1503) 759
Plantagenet Family.
—— Arth., visc., K.G. (1524) 737; W.C.P. 319
Dudley Family.
—— Jno., ld. and visc., aft. E. of Warwick, and D. of Northumberland, *q.v.*, K.B. (1547) 760; K.G. 738; L.H.A. 174
Sydney Family.
—— Rt., visc., aft. 1st E. of Leicester, *q.v.*, K.G. 739
—— Phil., ld., aft. 3rd E. of Leicester, *q.v.*, L.L. Ir. 554
Lisley, Nichs., K.B. 758
Lismore, Geo. Pons., 2nd visc., L.L. Tipp. 571
Lister, *see also* Lyster
—— Cav., gen. (**A**) 859
—— Fk. Geo., gen. (**D**) 891
—— Hy., gen. (**B**) 866
—— Th. Vill. and sir T., K.C.M.G. 798; U.S.F. 230
Liston, Rt. and sir R., Amb. Dk. 127; Amb. Nds. &c. 122; Amb. Spn. 123; Amb. Sw. 126; Amb. Tky. 129; Amb. U.S.A. 132; P.C. 209
Listowel, E. of
—— Wm., 2nd E. of, K.P. 751
—— Wm., 3rd E. of, K.P. 751
Litchford, Geo. A., gen. (**D**) 888
Litchfield, *see also* Lichfield
—— Hy., adm. (**H**) 846
Lithington, Wm., dn. Chich. 434
Litten, *see* Lytton
Little, Alfr. Butler, gen. (**D**) 925
—— Archd. and sir A., gen. (**D**) 903; K.C.B. 780
—— Geo., Q.C. 418

Littlebiri, Mart. de, J.C.P. 377; J. It. 368; J.K.B. 371; Jy. 365
Littlebury, sir Humph., L.H.A. 171
Littledale, Jos., aft. sir J., J.K.B. 373; Jud. Com. P.C. 360; P.C. 214; S.L. 413
Littlehales, sir Bend. Rt., adm. (**A**) 820
Littler, Jno. Hunt. and sir J., gen. (**D**) 881; G.C.B. 769; K.C.B. 777
— Ralph D. M., Q.C. 419
Littleton, *see* Lyttleton
Litton, *see also* Lytton
— Ed. Falc., Land Comm. Ir. 588
Liuva I. and II., K. Sp. 85
Liverance, Galfr., bp. Dkld. 533
Liverous (or Leverous), Th., bp. Kild. 617; dn. St. Pat. 618
Liverpool, E. of
— Ch., 1st E. of, form. C. Jenkinson, and ld. Hawkesbury, *q.v.*
— R. B., 2nd E. of, form. ld. Hawkesbury, *q.v.*; C. Treas. Ir. 561; K.G. 743; L.T. 159; Prem. 145-6; W.C.P. 319; W. and C. Sec. 231
— Ch. Cec. Cope, 3rd E. of, form. hon. C. C. C. Jenkinson, *q.v.*; G.C.B. 772; L.S.H. 290; P.C. 214; U.S. Home, 227
Livesay, Jno., gen. (**C**) 871
Livianus, M. Æ. L., C. Ro. 45
Livingston and **Livingstoun**
— Adam, Ld. Sess. 517
— Dav., L.P.S. Sc. 500
— Jas., bp. Dkld. 533; Ld. Chanc. Sc. 515
*— Rt. de, Compt. Sc. 498
*— Rt., L.H.T. Sc. 496
* ? same pers.
— sir Th., adm. (**A**) 820
— sir Wm., Ld. Sess. 519
Livingston, lds. and mast. of
— Jas., 1st ld., L.G.C. Sc. 506
— Alexr., 5th ld., Ld. Sess. 517
— Alexr., mast. of, Ld. Sess. 517
Livingus, *see also* Leovingus
— (or Livyngus), bp. Dev. and Cnwall. 436; bp. Worc. 472
Livinius, bp. Dbln. 615
Llandaff, Fras. Jas., 2nd E. of, K.P. 751
Llanover, Benj., ld., form. sir B. Hall, *q.v.*, L.L. Monm. 310
Llewelyn ap Griffith, Pr. Wls. 17
— ab Sitsyllt (2), Pr. Wls. 16-17
— Ll., dn. St. Dav. 465
— Rd., gen. (**D**) 881; K.C.B. 779
— Rt. Baxt., G. St. Vin. 725; G. T. and C. Isl. 713; G. Tob. 724
Lloyd and **Loyd**
— Arth., gen. (**B**) 870
— Bann. Pr., gen. (**D**) 914
— Ch., bp. Oxf. 457
— Chr., dn. Elph. 609
— Cliff., G. Mtius. 684
— Dav., dn. St. As. 463
— Ed., adm. (**G**) 841; K.H. 790
Lloyd and Loyd—*cont.*
— Ed., C. St. 283
— Ed. Jno., C.C.J. 404; Q.C. 417
— hon. Ed. Most., aft. ld. Mostyn, *q.v.*, L.L. Mer. 314
— Ed. Th., gen. (**D**) 899
— Eug. or Owen, dn. Cnr. 605
— sir Ev., gen. (**A**) 862; K.C.H. 788
— Geo., adm. (**H**) 846
— Geo., bp. Chest. 477; bp. S. and M. 483
— Geo. Aug., Amb. Bol. 135
— Geo. Wm. A., gen. (**D**) 887
— Hy., S.L. 411
— Hor., C.C.J. 405; Q.C. 418
— Hugh, bp. Llff. 449
— Humph., bp. Bgr. 426; dn. St. As. 463
— Jas., L.G. Gr. Hosp. 854
— Jno., adm. (**A**) 815
— Jno., bp. St. Dav. 464
— Jno., dn. St. As. 463
— Jno., K.C. 415
— Jno., S.L. 409
— Jno., S.L. Ir. 593
— Marm., J. Chest. 386
— Morg., Q.C. 419
— Mountf. S. H., gen. (**D**) 904
— Nathl. and sir N., Adm. Adv. 423; K. Adv. 422
— Owen, *see* Eug., *supra*
— Ph., dn. Norw. 456
— Rd. and sir R. (No. 1), Adm. Adv. 423; D. Arch. 420; J. Adm. Ct. 423
— Rd. and sir R. (No. 2), B. Ex. 385; K.C. 415; S.G. 402; S.L. 412
— Rt., adm. (**A**) 820
— sir Rt., G. Gibr. 670
— Th., dn. Bgr. 427
— Th., L.L. Card. 315
— Th. Fras., gen. (**D**) 935
— Vaughan, gen. (**A**) 860
— Wm., adm. (**A**) 815
— Wm. (No. 1), bp. Killa. and Ach. 613; dn. Ach. 614
— Wm. (No. 2), bp. Lich. and Cov. 444; bp. St. As. 462; bp. Worc. 473; dn. Bgr. 426
— Wm. (No. 3), bp. Llff. 449; bp. Norw. 455; bp. Pboro. 458
Loch, Fras. Ad. Ell., gen. (**D**) 922
— Fras. Ersk., adm. (**D**) 829
— Geo., Q.C. 418
— Hy. B. and sir H., C.W.F. &c. 273; G.C.M.G. 795; G. I. Man, 666; G. Vict. 705; K.C.B. 783
— Jno., Chn. E.I. Co. 645
Lochin, bp. Kild. 616
Lock, Andr. C. K., gen. (**D**) 928
Locke, Jno., B.T. 263
— Jno., gen. (**B**) 869
— Jno., Q.C. 417
— Matth., Sec. at W. 233
— Th., Clar. K.A. 328; Lanc. H. 333; Norr. K.A. 330; R. Dr. P.A. 338
— Walt., adm. (**A**) 819
Locker, Wm., L.G. Gr. Hosp. 854
Lockhart, Alan Eliot, L.L. Selk. 512
— Alexr., Ld. Sess. 520
— Archd. Ingl., gen. (**D**) 904
Lockhart—*cont.*
— Dav. Bl., gen. (**D**) 921
— sir Geo., L.P. Ct. Sess. 516; Ld. Sess. 520
— Græme Alexr., gen. (**D**) 902
— sir Jas., Ld. Sess. 519
— sir Jno., Ld. Sess. 519
— sir Steph., Ld. Clk. Reg. 525
— Th., C. Exc. Sc. 505
— Wm., gen. (**C**) 873
— sir Wm., Ld. Sess. 519
— Wm. Steph. Alexr., K.C.B. 782
Lockwood, Frank, Q.C. 420
— Geo. Hy., gen. (**D**) 887; K.C.B. 779
— Th., dn. Chr. Ch. Dbln. 618
Lockyer, Fras., dn. Pboro. 458
— Hy. Fk., gen. (**D**) 892; K.H. 792
Loco, Hugh de B., bp. Carl. 475
Locock, Sidn., Amb. Bzl. 135; Amb. C. Am. 134; Amb. Sva. 128
Locton, *see* Lokton
Lodder, Wm. Wynne, gen. (**D**) 900
Lodelow, Th. de, C. B. Ex. 381; Rec. Lond. 493
Loder, Hugh, K.B. 759
Lodevick, Pet., gen. (**D**) 879
Lodge, Edm., Bl. M. P.A. 337; Clar. K.A. 328; K.H. 790; Lanc. H. 333; Norr. K.A. 330
— sir Th., L.M. Lond. 490
Lodington, Wm. de, A.G. 398; J.C.P. 378; S.L. 407
Lodowic, *see also* Ludowick
— Jno., M.M. 246
Lodowis, Th., bp. Killa. 612
Loft, Jno. Hy., gen. (**B**) 867
Loftus, Adam (No. 1), abp. Arm. 595; abp. Dbln. and Gl. 616; dn. St. Patr. 618; L.J. Ir. 554; L.K. and Ld. Chanc. Ir. 576
— Adam (No. 2), aft. visc. L. of Ely, L.J. Ir., 554; Ld. Chanc. Ir. 576; V. Treas. Ir. 559
— sir Adam (No. 3), L.K. Ir. 576
— ld. Augs. Wm. Fk. Sp., Amb. Aus. 117; Amb. Bva. 119; Amb. G. St. 122; Amb. Pr. 118; Amb. Russ. 126; G.C.B. 772; G. N.S.W. 703; K.C.B. 783
— Ed., Rec. Dbln. 642; S.L. Ir. 591
— Hy., C. Acc. Ir. 567
— Wm., gen. (**A**) 860; Lt. T.L. 322
— Wm. Fras. B., gen. (**D** 879
— Wm. Jas., gen. (**D**) 907
— ld. W. F. S., P.C. 217
Loftus, of Ely, visc.
— Adam, visc., *see* Adam Loftus (No. 2), *supra*
Loftus, lds. and visc.
— Ch., 1st ld., form. C. Tottenham, *q.v.*, aft. 1st E. and M. of Ely, *q.v.*, K.P. 750; Postm. G. Ir. 564
— Jno., ld., aft. visc. L. and 2nd M. of Ely, *q.v.*, C. Treas. Ir. 561

Logan, Archd. Sp., gen. (**D**) 892
— Archd. Geo. Dougl., gen. (**D**) 932
— Jno., bp. Down, 603
— Rt. Abr., gen. (**D**) 923
— Th. Galbr., K.C.B. 780
Logie, Andr., Ld. Adv. 526
Logore, Th. de, M. Chy. 393
Loingseach, K. Ir. 21
Loizaga, C., Dt. Pgy. 110
Lokton (or Locton), Jno. de, J.K.B. 371; S.L. 407
Lomax, Jas., gen. (**B**) 869
Lombard, *see also* Lumbard
— Rt., dn. Wford. 628
Lombardini, Pres. Mex. 103
Lomtuil, bp. Kild. 616
London and **Londres**
— Edmd. de, M. Chy. 393
— Hy. de, abp. Dbln. & abp. Dbln. & Gl. 615; L.J. Ir. 550
— Jno., M. Chy. 394
— Lucas de, dn. Wford. 628
— Walt. de, dn. St. P. 452; dn. Wells, 428
— Wm. de, J. It. 367; Jy. 364
Londonderry, lds. and M. of
Pitt Family.
— Th., ld., form. Th. Pitt, *q.v.*, G. Leew. Isl. 727
Stewart and Vane Tempest Family.
— Rt., 2nd M. of, form. visc. Castlereagh, *q.v.*
— Ch. Wm., 3rd M. of, form. hon. C. W. and ld. Stewart, *q.v.*, gen. (**A**) 862; K.G. 744; L.L. Dham. 308
— Fk. Wm. Rt., 4th M. of, form. visc. Castlereagh, *q.v.*, K.P. 751
— Geo. Hy. Rt. Ch. Wm., 5th M. of, K.P., 751; L.L. Dham. 308
— Ch. Stu., 6th M. of, K.G. 745; L.L. Ir. 558; P.C. 221
Londres, *see* London
Lone, sir Rd., G. Gsey. 668
Lonergan, *see* Longain
Loney, Rt., adm. (**E**) 849
Long, Ch., aft. 1st ld. Farnborough, *q.v.*, C.Treas. Ir. 561; B.T. 268; Ch. Sec. Ir. 563; G.C.B. 772; L.T. 158; P.C. 207; Paym. G. 245; Sec. Tr. 163
— Jno., abp. Arm. 595
— Lisleb. and sir L., Rec. Lond. 494; Sp. H.C. 249
*— Rt., P.C. 189
*— sir Rt., Aud. Ex. 166; L.T. 155; Ch. Ex. 164; P.C. 191
* ? same pers.
— Rt. Ball, gen. (**B**) 868
— Th., dn. Cork, 632
— Th., K.B. 759
— Walt. H., Sec. L.G.B. 256
— Wm., Mast. Coll. Surg. 939
Longchamp, Hy., K.B. 754
— Wm. de, bp. Ely, 434; Ch. Jr. 362; Const. T.L. 320; Const. W. Cast. 322; Jy. 363; Ld. Chanc. 353; W.C.P. 317
Longden, Ch. Sc., gen. (**D**) 908
— Hy. Err., gen. (**D**) 904; K.C.B. 781
— Jas. Rt. and sir J., G. Br. Gu. 715; G. Br. Hond. 714; G. Ceyl. 673; G. Dnca. 730; G. Trin. 722; G.C.M.G. 795; K.C.M.G, 797
Longespee, Nichs., bp. Sal. 467
— Rog. de (or de Molend), bp. Lich. and Cov. 444; L.H.T. 152
— Steph. de, L.J. Ir. 550
— Wm. (E. of Salisbury), L.H.A. 170
Longfield, Jno., gen. (**D**) 895
— Mountefort, C. Cus. Ir. 565
— Mountefort, Land. J. Ir. 587
— Rd., C. Cus. Ir. 565; C. Ex. Ir. 566-7
Longford, Ralph, K.B. 756
— Wm. Book., gen. (**D**) 892
Longford, visc. and E. of
— Chr., 1st visc., form. 22nd ld. Slane, *q.v.*
— Th., 2nd E. of, K.P. 751
— Wm. Lygon, 4th E. of, gen. (**D**) 903; G.C.B. 771; K.C.B. 779; L.L. Longf. 570; U.S. War. 232
Longinus, K. It. 49
— C. C., C. Ro. 44-5
— L. C., C. Ro. 45
— Q. C., C. Ro. 44
Longland (or Langland), Jno., bp. Linc. 447; dn. Sal. 468
Longley, *see also* Langley
— Ch. T., abp. Cant. 431; abp. Yk. 486; bp. Dham. 479; bp. Rip. 482; Jud. Com. P.C. 361; P.C. 217
— Jno., G. Dnca. 730
— (or Langley), Th., abp. Yk. 485; bp. Dham. 478; dn. Yk. 486; L.K. & Ld. Chanc. 355
Longstrother, Jno., L.H.T. 153
Longtoft, Jno. de, M. Chy. 393
Longueville, Grey, B. & Gl. K.A. 330; Bath K.A. 785; Han. H. 340
Longueville, E. of
— Gast. de Foix, E. of, K.G. 735
Longus, C. S., C. Ro. 40-1; Dt. Ro. 41
— K. D., Dec. Ro. 38
— L. M. V., C. Ro. 42
— M. T., C. Ro. 37
— T. S., C. Ro. 43
Longworth, Fras Tr. D., L.L. K. Co. 570
— Jno. A., Amb. Sva. 128
— Rd., dn. Chest. 477
Lonison, Jno., M.M. 246
Lonsdale, Jas. Jno., C.C.J. 404
— Jno., bp. Lich. 444
Lonsdale, lds., visc., and E. of
— Jno., 1st ld. and visc., form. sir J. Lowther, *q.v.*, L.P.S. 240
— Hy., 3rd visc., Const. T.L. 321; L.P.S. 240; P.C. 197
— Jas., E. of, form. sir J. Lowther, *q.v.* (*d.* 1802)
— Wm., E. of, form. visc. Lowther, *q.v.* (*d.* 1844), K.G. 743
— Wm., 2nd E. of, form. visc. Lowther, *q.v.* (*d.* 1872), Jud. Com. P.C. 360; L.P.C. 188; L.L. Cumb. 307; L.L. Wmland. 313
— Hy., 3rd E. of, form. Hy. Lowther, *q.v.* (*d.* 1876)
Looft-Ali-Khan, Sh. Pers. 99
Lopes, Hy. C. and sir H., J.C.P.D. 380; J.Q.B.D. 374; Jud. Com. P.C. 362; L.J. App. 389; P.C. 220; Q.C. 418
— sir Mass., L. Admy. 185; P.C. 220
Lopez, C. A., Dt. Pgy. 110
— F. S., Dt. Pgy. 110
— V., Pres. Arg. 110
Lopham, Th., S.L. 407
Loraine, Walch. de, E. of Northumberland, bp. Dham. 478
Lord, Ed., G. V.D. Ld. 708
— Jas., B. Ex. 384
Lorimer, Jas., K.C.M.G. 798
Lorin or **Loring,** sir Nele, K.G. 733
— sir Jno. Wentw., adm. (**D**) 823; K.C.B. 777; K.C.H. 789
— Wm. and sir W., adm. (**E**) 835; K.C.B. 780
Lorne, lds. and M. of, *see also* Argyll
— Archd., ld., aft. 8th E. of Argyll, *q.v.*, Ld. Sess. 517
— Jno., M. of, aft. 5th D. of Argyll, *q.v.*, gen. (**B**) 865
— Jno., G. E. H. D. S., M. of, son of 8th D. of Argyll, G.C.M.G. 795; G.G. Can. 692; K.T. 749; P.C. 219
— Prss. Louise, Mss. of, Cr. Ind. 809; *see* Princess Louise
Lorton, Rt. Ed., 1st visc., gen. (**A**) 861; L.L. Rosc. 571
Losack, Geo., adm. (**A**) 818
Lose, Terric de, M.M. 245
Losh, Jas., C.C.J. 404
Losing, Rt., bp. Her. 441
Losinga, Herb., bp. Elm. Dunw. and Norw. 454
Loten, Joan Gid., G. Ceyl. 672
Lothair and **Lothaire**
— D. Sxy. 77
— K.E. 1
— K. Fr. 23
— K. Lmd. 49
— I. and II., E. Gmy. 61
Lother, K.E. 1
Lothebury, Rd. de, M.M. 245
Lothian, E. and M. of
— Mark, 1st E. of, form. Mark Ker, *q.v.*
— Wm., 3rd E. of, Sec. St. Sc. 502
— Robt., 4th E., aft. 1st M. of, H.C.P. Sc. 508; L.H.C. K. Sc. 546; L.J. Gen. 522
— Wm., 2nd M. of, gen. (**B**) 864; K.T. 747
— Wm., 3rd M. of, K.T. 747; L.H.C. K. Sc. 546; Ld. Clk. Reg. 525
— Wm. Hy., 4th M. of, gen. (**A**) 858; K.T. 748
— Wm. Jno., 5th M. of, gen. (**A**) 859; K.T. 748
— Wm., 6th M. of, form. E. of Ancrum, *q.v.*, K.T. 748; L.L. Mid-L. 509; L.L. Roxb. 512
— Jno. Wm. Rt., 7th M. of, C.Y.G. 298; L.L. Roxb. 512; P.C. 214
— Sch. Hy., 9th M. of, K.T. 749; L.K. Sc. 503; L.P.S. Sc. 501; P.C. 220; Sec. Sc. 502; V.P. Ed. Sc. 500
Loudham, Wm., J. It. 367

Loudon and **Loudoun**
— Jno. de, Const. W. Cast. 322
— Jno., gen. (**D**) 924
Loudoun, E. of
— Jno., 1st E. of, Comm. Tr. Sc. 497; Ld. Chanc. Sc. 515; Pres. P.C. Sc. 500
— Hugh, 3rd E. of, K.T. 747; L.H.C. K. Sc. 546; L.H.T. Sc. 498; L.K. Sc. 503; Ld. Sess. 517; P.C. 195; Sec. St. Sc. 502
— Jno., 4th. E. of, gen. (**A**) 858
— Jas., 5th E. of, gen. (**C**) 872
Loufkin, *see* Lewkyn
Loughborough, Alexr., ld., form. A. Wedderburn, *q.v.*, aft. 1st E. of Rosslyn, *q.v.*, C.G.S. 357; L.H.S. 287
Lougher, Rt., M. Chy. 395
Loughlin, Arilan., dn. Clonf. 637
Louis, D. Svy. 54
— D. Wbg. 81
— G.D. Tny. 57
— (the Great), K. Hgy. 60
— K. Lmd. 49
— (Hutin), K. Nav. 85
— K. Nav. 87
— K. Pld. 91
— K. Sp. 86
— (de Requisens), R. Nds. 82
— I., K. Bma. 59
— I., K. Hgy. 60
— I., K. Pgl. 89; K.G. 744
— I., K. Scy. 56
— I., Pr. Mno. 31
— I. and II., C. Flrs. 81
— I. and II., K. Bva. 68
— I. and II., M. Brg. 65
— I. and II., Pr. Nass. 75
— I. to III., D. Bva. 67
— I. to IV., E. Gmy. 61-2
— I. to IV., G.D. H. Dt. 72
— III. (G.D. H. Dt.), K.G. 744
— I. to XVIII., K. Fr. 23-4
— XVIII. (K. Fr.), K.G. 743
— II., G.D. Bdn. 67
— II. to VI., C.P.R. 68
— V. to X., Lg. H. Dt. 72
— -Buonaparte, Pr. Or. 83
— Ch., gen. (**D**) 911
— -Eugene, D. Wbg. 81
— -Fredk., Pr. S. Rdt. 79
— -George, M. Bdn. 67
— -Hippolyta, Pr. Mno. 31
— sir Jno., adm. (**D**) 825
— -Napoleon, aft. Nap. III., *q.v.*, Pres. Fr. 25
— -Phillippe, K. Fr. 24-5; K.G. 744
— sir Th., adm. (**A**) 817
— Wm., adm. (**H**) 848
— -Wm., M. Bdn. 67
— -Wm.-Augs., G.D. Bdn. 67
— -Wm.-Fk., Lg. H. Hbg. 73; G.C.B. 768
Louisa (dau. Geo. II.), Pr. E. 14
— -Anne, (g. dau. Geo. II.), Pr. E. 14
— -Caroline-Alb., (dau. Q. Victoria), Pr. E. 16; Cr. Ind. 809; aft. Mss. of Lorne, *q.v.*
— -Hollandia (g. dau. Jas. I.), Pr. E. 13
— -Maria-Th. (dau. Jas. II.), Pr. E. 14
— -Vict.-Alex.-Dagm. (g. dau. Q. Vict.), Pr. E. 15
Louth, *see* Lowth
Louther, *see* Lowther
L'Ouverture, Touss., Pres. Hti. 104
Lovaine, lds.
— Geo. ld., aft. 2nd E. of Beverley, and 5th-6th D. of Northumberland, *q.v.*, B.C. 252-3; L.T. 158
— A. G., ld., aft. 6th-7th D. of Northumberland, *q.v.*, L. Admy. 184; Paym. G. 245; P.C. 216; V.P.B.T. 269
Lovat, lds.
— Th. Alexr., ld., K.T. (1864) 749; L.L. Inv. 510
— Simon, ld., form. hon. S. Fraser, *q.v.* (succ. 1875)
Love, Hyg., dn. Kilf. 637
— Hy. Omm., adm. (**H**) 847
— Jas. Fk. and sir J., G.C.B. 778; G. Jsey. 668; gen. (**D**) 883; K.C.B. 778; K.H. 789
— Rd., dn. Ely, 435
Loveday, Rog., J.C.P. 377; J. It. 368
Lovel, *see* Lovell
Lovelace, Wm., S.L. 408
Lovelace, lds. and E.
Lovelace Family.
— Jno., 3rd ld., G.C.P. 299
King Family.
— Wm., 1st E. of, L.L. Surr. 312
Lovel and **Lovell**
— Fulke, bp. Lond. 451
— Hy. de, dn. Ch. 434
— Jno., J. It. 368; J.K.B. 371
— Benj., and sir L., gen. (**D**) 884; K.C.B. 778; K.H. 791
— Ph., L.H.T. 152
— Sal. and sir S., B. Ex. 384; J. Chest. 387; Rec. Lond. 494; S.L. 411
*— sir Th., Const. T.L. 320; K.G. 737; Tr. H. 291
*— Th., Sp. H.C. 249
* ? same pers.
— Wm. Stanh., adm. (**H**) 845; K.H. 791
Lovel, lds.
Lovel Family.
— Jno., 8th ld., K.G. 734
— Fras., 9th ld. and 1st visc., K.G. 736
Coke Family.
— Th., ld., form. T. Coke, *q.v.*, aft. E. of Leicester, *q.v.*, Postm. G. 238
Lovet, Chr., L.M. Dbln. 640
Lovetot, Jno. de, J.C.P. 377
Lovibond, Hy., M. Chy. 396
Loving, J., Tell. Ex. 167
Low, *see* Lowe
Lowder, Saml. Nett., gen. (**D**) 903
Lowe and **Low**
— Abrm., adm. (**H**) 845
— Alexr., gen. (**D**) 903
— Arth., adm. (**D**) 833; (**E**) 838; (**F**) 834
— Dav., bp. Mor. and Ross. 544; bp. Ross. 545
— Drury, Curz. Drury-, aft. sir Dr., gen. (**D**) 924; K.C.B. 781
— Ed., aft. sir E., M. Chy. 396
— Edw. Wm. De L., gen. (**D**) 907
— sir Huds., G. Antig. 728; G. St. Hel. 682; G.C.M.G. 794; gen. (**B**) 869; K.C.B. 775
Lowe and Low—*cont.*
— Hugh and sir H., G.C.M.G. 796; G. Labn. 675; K.C.M.G. 798
— Jno., bp. Roch. 460; bp. St. As. 462
— Jno. and sir J., G.C.S.I. 801; gen. (**D**) 886; K.C.B. 779
— (or Lupus), Jno. de, dn. Oss. 622
— Rt., aft. visc. Sherbrooke, *q.v.*, Ch. Ex. 166; H. Sec. 227; L.T. 161; P.C. 216; Paym. G. 245; Sec. B.C. 254; V.P. B.T. 269; V.P. Ed. 255
— Rt. Cunl., K.C.B. 782
— Sigism. Bar., gen. (**C**) 873; K.C.B. 775
— sir Th., L.M. Lond. 491
— Th. Hill., dn. Exr. 438
Lowen, Piearce, K.H. 792
Lowndes, Ch., Sec. Tr. 163
— Th., gen. (**D**) 933
— Wm., C. Exc. 280-1; C. Tx. 284-5
— Wm., C.C.J. 403
— Wm. L., Q.C. 417
Lowry, Rt. Wm., gen. (**D**) 908
Lowth and **Louth**
— Rt., B.T. 267; bp. Lond. 452; bp. Oxf. 456; bp. St. Dav. 465; P.C. 203
— Rt. Hy., gen. (**D**) 894
Louth, E. of
— sir Jno. Bermingham, E. of, L.J. Ir. (1321) 551
Lowther and **Louther**
— Anthy., gen. (**C**) 871
— Ger. and sir G., B. Ex. Ir. 584; C.G.S. Ir. 576; C.J.C.P. Ir. 580; J.C.P. Ir. 581
— Hy., *see* ld. L., *infra*
— Hugh de, A.G. 398; J. It. 369
— Jas., Ch. Sec. Ir. 563; P.C. 219; U.S.C. 235
— Jas., St. O. 260
— Jno., *see* ld. L., *infra*
— sir Lanc., B. Ex. Ir. 584
— Luke, L.M. Dbln. 640
— Marc., adm. (**H**) 853
— Rt., G. Bdoes. 720
— Th. de, J.K.B. 371
— Wm., Amb. Arg. 136
— sir Wm., C. Cus, 273
Lowther, lds. and visc.
— sir Jno., aft. 1st ld. L. and visc. Lonsdale, *q.v.* (*d.* 1700), L. Admy. 176; L.T. 155; P.C. 193; V.C.H. 296
— sir Jas., aft. ld. and visc. L. and E. of Lonsdale, *q.v.* (*d.* 1802), L.L. Cumb. 307; L.L. Wmland. 313
— Wm., visc., aft. E. of Lonsdale, *q.v.* (*d.* 1844), L.L. Cumb. 307; L.L. Wmland. 313
— Wm., visc., aft. 2nd E. of Lonsdale, *q.v.* (*d.* 1872), B.C. 253; C.W.F. &c. 271; L Admy. 181; L.T. 159; P.C 211; Postm. G. 238; Tr. N. 257; V.P.B.T. 269
— Hy., aft. 3rd E. Lonsdale (*d.* 1876) L.L. Cumb. 307; L.L. Wmland. 313
Lowys, Jno., M.M. 246
Loyd, *see* Lloyd
Loyd-Lindsay, *see* Lindsay
Lozier-Bouvet, Mons. de, G. Mtius. 683

Luard, Ch. Ed., gen. (**D**) 933
—— Jno., Kyn., gen. (**D**) 888
—— Rd. Geo. Amb., gen. (**D**) 909
—— Wm. Garnh., adm. (**E**) 836
Lucan, Geo. Ch., 3rd E. of, F.M. 856; gen. (**D**) 884; G.C.B. 770; K.C.B. 777; L.L. Mayo, 570
Lucas, Alfr. Wm., gen. (**D**) 922
—— Anthy., C. Exc. 280-1
—— Ch., gen. (**D**) 901
—— Ch. Dav., adm. (**H**) 853
—— Ch. Sh. de N. gen. (**D**) 926
—— Ed., U.S. Ir. 563
—— Matth. P., L.M. Lond. 492
—— Th., S.G. 401
—— sir Th., called ld. L., Const. T.L. (1688) 321
Luci, *see* Lucy
Lucian, Pr. Mno. 31
Lucius I. to III., P. Ro., 32, 34
Luckraft, Alf., adm. (**H**) 847
—— Wm., adm. (**H**) 847
Luctacus, K. Sc. 18
Lucullus, L. L., C. Ro. 44; C. Ro. 46
—— M. T. V., C. Ro. 46
Lucy and **Luci**
—— sir Anth., L.L. Ir. 551
—— Geoffr. de, dn. St. P. 452
—— sir Geoffr. de, L.H.A. 170
—— Godfr. de, bp. Winch. 470; J. It. 366; Jy. 363
—— Regd. de, J. It. 365
—— Rd. de, Ch. Jr. 362; Const. T.L. 320; Const. W. Cast. 322; J. It. 365; Jy. 363
—— Rt. de, J. It. 365
—— Steph. de, J. It. 367
—— Wm., bp. St. Dav. 464
—— Wm., K.B. 758
Luda, Wm. de, bp. Ely, 434
Ludecan, K.E. 3
Ludeham (or Ludham, or Kinton), Godfr. de, abp. Yk. 485; dn. Yk. 486
Ludlam, sir Geo., Chambn. Lond. 493
Ludlow, Eben., P.P. 416; S.L. 413
—— Edm., Comm. Ir. 554-5
—— Ed. Saml., C.I.E. 806
—— Geo. Jas. } *See* E. of L.,
—— Peter, } *infra*
—— Rd., K.B. 757
—— Saml. Edg. Ow., gen. (**D**) 898
—— Walt. de, dn. Wford. 628
Ludlow, lds. and E. of
—— Peter, 1st ld. and E. of, Compt. H. 293; P.C. 203
—— Geo. Jas., 3rd E. of, G.C.B. 767; gen. (**A**) 860; K.B. 766
Ludolph, D. Su. 80
Ludowick, *see also* **Lodowick**
—— Rodolph. D. Brk. 70
Luedwith, abp. St. Dav. 463
Lugard, sir Ed., G.C.B. 770; gen. (**D**) 892; K.C.B. 778; P.C. 218; U.S. War. 233
Lugeol, Jean, K.C.B. 778
Lughaidh (2), K. Ir. 21
—— Riebdearg, K. Ir. 21
Lugthacus, K. Sc. 18
Luic, Alex. N. de, M.M. 245
Luighne, K. Ir. 20
Luiredus, dn. St. P. 452
Luitpert, K. Lmd. 49
Luitprandus, K. Lmd. 49
***Luke,** abp. Dbln. & Glr. 615
*—— bp. Kilmacd. 636
*—— dn. Killoe. 637
*—— dn. Lim. 639
* Prob. some same pers. Comp. dates.
—— Jas., Pres. Coll. Surg. 939
—— Nichs., B. Ex. 384
—— Steph. Pag. Walt. Viv. C.I.E. 806
—— Wm. (or Walt.), J.K.B. 372
—— Wm., adm. (**A**) 818
Lukin, Ch. Osb., gen. (**D**) 912
—— Geo. Wm., dn. Wells, 429
—— Wm., G. Dnca. 730
Lullimore, *see* Lynn
Lumbard, *see also* Lombard
—— Jno., J.K.B. Ir. 578
Lumley, hon. Jas., M.H. 302
—— Jas. Ruth., gen. (**D**) 876; K.C.B. 777
—— Jno., *see* ld. L., *infra*
—— Jno. Savile-, and sir J., Amb. Bgm. 123; Amb. It. 114; Amb. Swz. 114; Amb. Sxy. 121; G.C.B. 773; K.C.B. 783; P.C. 220
—— Marm., bp. Carl. 475; bp. Linc. 447; L.H.T. 153
—— sir Mart., L.M. Lond. 491
*—— Hy., G. Jsey. 667
*—— hon. Hy., gen. (**A**) 857
* Poss. same pers.
—— Rd., *see* ld. L., *infra*
—— Wm., and sir W., G. Bmda. 701; gen. (**A**) 862; G.C.B. 768; K.C.B. 773
—— Wm. Gold., Q.C. 418
Lumley, lds. and visc
—— Jno., ld., K.B. (1553) 760
—— Rd., 2nd visc., aft. E. of Scarborough, *q.v.*, L.L. Dham. 308; P.C. 193
Lumsdaine, Geo., adm. (**A**) 817
—— Jas., gen. (**B**) 866
Lumsden, Andr., bp. Edinb. 542; Pr. Bp. Sc. 540
—— Harry Burn. and sir H., gen. (**D**) 904; K.C.S.I. 803
—— Pet. St. and sir P., gen. (**D**) 923; G.C.B. 771; K.C.B. 781; M.C.I. 647
Lunalilo I., Q. Sd. Isl. 111
Lunapeius, bp. Llff. 448
Lundin, sir Rt., L.H.T. Sc. 496
Lundyne, Wm. de, Ld. Chanc. Sc. 514
Lunsford, Col. —, Lt. T.L. 321
Lunverd, bp. St. Dav. 464
Lupton, Rog., M. Chy. 394
Lupus, L. C. L., C. Ro. 44
—— (or de Low), Jno., dn. Oss. 622
—— P. R., C. Ro. 45
Lurgan, Ch., 2nd. ld., K.P. 751; L.L. Arm. 568
Luscinus, C. F. (3), C. Ro. 42
Luscus, T. A., C. Ro. 44
Lush, Rt. and sir R., J.Q.B. 373; J.Q.B.D. 374; Jud. Com. P.C. 361; L.J. App. 389; P.C. 219; Q.C. 417; S.L. 414
Lushborough (or Luxemburgh), Louis de, bp. Ely, 435
Lushington, Godfr., U.S. Home, 228
—— Jas. Lawr. and sir J., Chn. E.I. Co. 645; G.C.B. 769; gen. (**D**) 877; K.C.B. 776
Lushington—*cont.*
—— Steph. and sir S. (No. 1), Chn. E.I. Co. 644-5
—— Steph. (No. 2), Ch. Lond. 422; D. Arch. 421; J. Adm. Ct. 423; Jud. Com. P.C. 360; P.C. 213
—— Steph. and sir S. (No. 3), adm. (**D**) 830; (**G**) 841; G.C.B. 770; K.C.B. 777; L.G. Gr. Hosp. 854
—— Steph. Geo., C. Cus. 277
—— Steph. Rumb., G. Mdras. 657; P.C. 211; Sec. Tr. 163
—— Vern., C.C.J. 405; Q.C. 418; Sec. Adm. 187
Lusk, Andr. and sir A., L.M. Lond. 492
Luttrell, Fras. F., C. Cus. 276 C. Tx. 284
—— Hugh, K.B. 758
—— hon. Jas., S.G.O. 260
—— Jno., K.B. 755
—— Rt., V. Chanc. Ir. 574
—— Th. and sir T., C.J.C.P. Ir. 580; S.G. Ir. 589; S.L. Ir. 591
Luttrell-Olmius, *see* Olmius and Carhampton
Lutwidge, Skeff., adm. (**A**) 816
Lutwyche, Ed. and sir E., C.J. Chest. 386; J.C.P. 379; S.L. 410
—— Th., Q.C. 415
Luxemburgh, *see* Lushborough
Luxmoore and **Luxmore**
—— C. Sc., dn. St. As. 463
—— Jno., bp. Brl. 439; bp. Her. 442; bp. St. As. 462; dn. Glr. 440
—— Th. Corynd., gen. (**D**) 895
Lyall, *see also* Lyell
—— Alfr. Com. and sir A., K.C.B. 783; K.C.I.E. 805; L.G. N.W.Pr. and Oudh. 654; M.C.I. 647; Sec. I.E. 808; Sec. S.I. 804
—— Ch. Jas., C.I.E. 806
—— Geo., Chn. E.I. Co. 645
—— Jas. Broadw. and sir J., K.C.S.I. 804; L.G. Pjab. 654
—— Wm. R., dn. Cant. 432
Lydiard, Geo. Wm. Ch., adm. (**E**) 842
—— Ralph de, J. It. 367
Lydington, Jno. de, B. Ex. Ir. 583
Lye, Wm. Jones, adm. (**D**) 826
Lyell, *see also* Lyall
—— Rd., J. Adm. Ct. 422; M. Chy. 395
Lygh, Rog., Clar. K.A. 328
Lygon, hon. Ed. Pind., gen. (**A**) 863
—— hon. Fk., L. Admy. 184
Lyhert, Walt., bp. Norw. 455
Lyle, *see also* Lisle
—— Acheson, L.L. Londy. 570
—— Rt. ld., L.J. Gen. (1488) 522
Lymbergh, Ad. de, B. Ex. 383
Lymington, Jno., visc., form. Jno. Wallop, *q.v.*, aft. E. of Portsmouth, *q.v.*
Lynch and **Linch**
—— Andr. H., M. Chy. 397
—— Dav., J. Bank. Ir. 587; Land. J. Ir. 587
—— Ed. Patr., gen. (**D**) 910

Lynch and Linch—*cont.*
—— Germ., M.M. 246
—— sir Hy., B. Ex. Ir. 584
—— Jno., bp. Elph. 608
—— Jno., dn. Cant. 431
—— Marc., dn. Clonm. 600
—— Rt. Bl., gen. (**D**) 890
—— Rol., bp. Clonf. 636; bp Clonf. and K. 636; bp. Kilmacd. 636
—— Stan. J., Land Comm. Ir. 588
—— sir Th., G. Jam. 712
—— Wm. and sir W., Amb. Sda. 114; K.B. 765; P.C. 203
—— Wm. Wiltsh., gen. (**D**) 932
Lynde, *see* Lind
Lyndhurst, J. S., ld., form. J. S. Copley, *q.v.*; C.B. Ex. 382; Jud. Com. P.C. 360; Ld. Chanc. 358
Lyndon, Jno., J.K.B. Ir. 579; S.L. Ir. 591
Lynedoch, Th., ld., form. Th. Graham and sir T., *q.v.*, G.C.B. 767; G.C.M.G. 794; gen. (**A**) 861
Lynn, Wm., Pres. Coll. Surg. 939
—— Wm., S.L. 410
—— (or Lenne or Lullimore), Wm. de, bp. Chich., 432; bp. Worc. 472; dn. Chich. 434
Lynom, Th., S.G. 401
Lyns (? Lyus), Adam, bp. Ard. 607
Lynwood, Wm., bp. St. Dav. 464
Lyon and **Lion**
—— Ch. Wils., gen. (**B**) 866
—— sir Jas., G. Bdoes. 720; G.C.H. 786; gen. (**B**) 868; K.C.B. 775; K.C.H. 787
—— sir Jno., L.M. Lond. 490
—— sir Patr., Ld. Sess. 520
—— Th. and sir T., Ld. Sess. 517
—— sir Th., L.H.T. Sc. 497; Ld. Sess. 518
—— Wm., bp. Cork, Cl. and R., 631; bp. Ross. 631
Lyon-Fremantle, *see* Fremantle
Lyons, Algn. McLell., adm. (**E**) 836
—— Edm., *see* ld. L. *infra*
—— Humph., gen. (**D**) 897
—— Jno., adm. (**H**) 847
—— Rd. B. P., *see* ld. L. *infra*
—— Th. Cas., gen. (**D**) 923
Lyons, lds. and visc.
—— sir Edm., aft. 1st ld. L., adm. (**D**) 829; Amb. Gr. 128; Amb. Sw. and N. 127; Amb. Swz. 113; G.C.B. 769; G.C.B. 772; K.C.H. 788
—— Rd. Bick. P., 2nd ld., aft. 1st visc., Amb. Fr. 113; Amb. Tky. 130; Amb. Tusc. 115; Amb. U.S.A. 132; G.C.B. 772; G.C.M.G. 795; K.C.B. 783; P.C. 217
Lyons - Montgomery, *see* Montgomery
Lysaght, Arth., adm. 826; (**D** and **G**) 840
Lysons, Danl. and sir D., G.C.B. 771; gen. (**D**) 903; K.C.B. 780
Lyster, *see also* Leicester and Lister
—— Harry Hamm., gen. (**D**) 932

Lyster—*cont.*
—— H. Y., adm. (**D**) 833
—— Jas., dn. Llin. 624
—— (or Lester), Rd., A.G. 398; C.B. Ex. 381; C.J.K.B. 370; S.G. 401
Lythegrenes, Jno. de, J. It. 368
Lyttelton, Littleton, and **Lyttleton**
—— Ch., bp. Carl. 476; dn. Exr. 438
—— sir Ch., G. Jam. 712
—— Ed., *see* ld. L. *infra*
—— Ed. Jno., aft. ld. Hatherton, *q.v.*, Ch. Sec. Ir. 563; P.C. 212
—— Fish., Adm. Adv. 423
—— Geo. } *see* ld. L. *infra*
—— Geo. Wm. } *see* ld. L. *infra*
—— Jas., adm. (**A**) 813
—— Jas., M. Chy. 395
—— hon. Rd. and sir R., G. Gsey. 668; gen. (**B**) 865; K.B. 765
—— Th., J.C.P. 378; K.B. 757; S.L. 407
—— sir Th. (No. 1), L. Admy. 175; L.T. 155; Sp. H.C. 250; Tr. N. 256
—— sir Th. (No. 2), L. Admy. 177-8
—— Tim. and sir T., B. Ex. 384; S.L. 410
—— Wm., S.L. 409
—— Wm., *see* ld. L. *infra*
—— Wyb. de, dn. Wells, 428
Lyttelton, lds.
1st Creation.
—— Ed. and sir E., aft. ld. L., C.J.C.P. 375; L.T. 154; L.K. 356; Rec. Lond. 494; S.G. 401; S.L. 409
2nd Creation.
—— sir Geo., aft. 1st ld. L., Ch. Ex. 165; Coff. H. 293; L.T. 157; P.C. 199
—— Th., 2nd ld., P.C. 203
3rd Creation.
—— Wm. Hy., aft. ld. Westcote and 1st ld. L., Amb. Pgl. 124; G. Jam. 712
—— Wm. Hy., 3rd ld., L.L. Worc. 313
—— Geo. Wm., 4th ld., K.C.M.G. 796; L.L. Worc. 313; P.C. 218; U.S. W. and C. 231
Lytton, *see also* Litton
—— Rt., K.B. 759
—— Rt., K.B. 760
—— sir Rd., L.L. Herts. 308
—— Bulwer-, *see* Bulwer
Lytton, lds. and E.
—— Ed. Geo. E. L., 1st ld., form. sir E. Bulwer, *q.v.*, C. Sec. 235; G.C.M.G. 795; P.C. 216
—— Ed. Rt. L., 2nd ld., aft. 1st E., Amb. Fr. 113; Amb. Pgl. 125; G.C.B. 773; G.C.S.I. 801; G.G. Ind. 649; P.C. 221
—— Edith Bss., aft. Ctss. of, Cr. Ind. 809
Lyus, *see* Lyns
Lyveden, Rt., ld., form. R. Vernon-Smith, *q.v.*, G.C.B. 773
Lywarch, bp. St. Dav. 464

M.

M*** bp. Dnbl. 532
—— dn. Llin. 623
Maberly, Ev., gen. (**D**) 910
—— Wm. L., C. Cus. 277; Clk. O. 260; S.G.O. 260; Sec. P.O. 239
M'—Mc—and **Mac**—
McAdam, Dav., gen. (**D**) 889
—— Wm., K.H. 790
MacÆda, Malachy, abp. Tm. 611; bp. Elph. 608
MacÆdain, Cormac, bp. Clonf. 635
MacAiblen, Gilla, bp. Clonf. 635
MacAilild, Colman, bp. Cld. 598
MacAirthir, bp. Lism. 626
MacAlister, Ch. Archd., K. H. 790
Macallycan, Thos., Ld. Sess. 518
Macan, Geo., gen. (**D**) 897
—— Hy., gen. (**D**) 893
—— Jno., J. Bank. Ir. 587
Mac-an-Crossain, Hy., bp. Rph. 601
McAndrew, Geo., gen. (**D**) 914
—— Is. Fors., gen. (**D**) 931
—— Jno., K.C.B. 778
Macara, Rt., K.C.B. 775
Macario, Vic., Prel. M.G. 799
Macarmick, Wm., gen. (**A**) 860
Macarroll, Jno., L.M. Dbln. 641
M'Arthur, Ch., gen. (**D**) 921
MacArthur, Ed. and sir E., G. Vict. 704; gen. (**D**) 892; K.C.B. 783
—— Jno., gen. (**D**) 891
—— Wm., K.C.M.G. 798; L.M. Lond. 492
Macartin (St.), bp. Clr. 596
Macartney, Geo., *see* ld. M. *infra*
Maçartney, lds., E., and M.
—— Geo. and sir G. and ld., visc., and Earl M., gen. (**B**) 864; Amb. Ch. 130; Amb. Russ. 125; Ch. Sec. Ir. 562; G. C.G.H. 678; G.G. Ind. 648; G. Gren. 724; G. Mdras. 656; K.B. 765; P.C. 205
—— Hall, K.C.M.G. 798
—— Jas., J.C.P. Ir. 581; J K.B. 579
Macaulay, Colm. Patr. L., C.I.E. 808
—— Kenn., Q.C. 417
—— Th. B., *see* ld. B. *infra*
Macaulay, lds.
—— Th. B., aft. ld. M., B.C. 253; P.C. 214; Paym. G. 244; Sec. at W. 234; Sec. B.C. 254
MacAward, Mœlisa, bp. Clonf. 635
MacBaithen, Dungal, bp. Glend. 615

For List of Abbreviations, see pp. 944-952.

M'—Mc— and Mac—
Macbean, Archd., gen. (**D**) 899
—— Fk., K.H. 791
—— Geo., gen. (**D**) 928
—— Wm., gen. (**D**) 918
—— Wm. and sir W., gen. (**A**) 863; K.C.B. 776
—— Wm. Forbes, gen. (**D**) 908
Macbeth, bp. Ross, 535
—— K. Sc. 19
MacBrady, Andr., bp. Kilm. 607
—— Gilb., bp. Ard. 607
MacBreohan (or Brethemain), Eug., bp. Mayo, 612
M'Bride, Jno., adm. (**A**) 816
MacBrien, *see also* MacBruyn
—— Ch., bp. Emly, 625
—— Malachy, bp. Elph. 608
McBruyn (or McBrien), Arth., dn. Dry. 602
MacCaghwell, *see also* MacCamaill
—— Jas., abp. Cash. 625; abp. Cash. and bp. Emly, 626
MacCamaill and **MacCamæil**
—— Arth., bp. Clr. 596
—— Bern., bp. Clr. 596
—— (or McKamyll), Edmd., dn. Arm. 597
—— Eug., bp. Clr. 596; dn. Clr. 597
—— (or McKathmoyll), Jno., dn. Clr. 597
—— (or MacCaghwell), Wm., dn. Clr. 597
—— Wm., dn. Dry. 602
MacCarmacan, Menel., bp. Rph. 601; dn. Rph. 602
MacCarmic, Corn., bp. Rph. 601
—— Jno., bp. Rph. 601
McCarthy, Ch., G. Si. Le. 685
—— Ch. Just. and sir C., G. Ceyl. 672-3
—— Jno. Geo., Land. Comm. Ir. 588
—— Thady, bp. Cork and Cl. 631
—— Conamail, bp. Emly, 625
MacCarvill and **MacCarwill,** *see also* O'Carrol
—— Dav., abp. Cash. 624; dn. Cash. 627
—— (or O'Carrol), Jno., abp. Cash. 625; bp. Cork, 630; bp. Meath, 599; dn. Cork, 632
—— Maur., abp. Cash. 624
MacCasac, Wm., bp. Ard. 607
McCaskill, Jno., K.C.B. 777; K.H. 791
—— Wm., gen. (**C**) 873
MacCatasaid, Matth. (2), bp. Clr. 596
—— Nichs., bp. Clr. 596
MacCathan, Conan, bp. Ferns, 621
MacCathasach, Rumold, bp. Cld. 598
McCausland, Con., gen. (**D**) 902
—— Jno. Kenn., gen. (**D**) 896
MacCellaid, Feolan, bp. Emly, 625
MacCenfeolad, Owen, bp. Emly, 625
MacCiarucain, Colum, bp. Cork, 630
Macclerig, Eugene, bp. Tm. 611
Macclesfield, Nichs., L.H.A. 173

M'—Mc— and Mac—
Macclesfield, lds. and E. of
Gerard Family.
—— Ch., form. ld. Gerard, and visc. Brandon, *q.v.*, L.L. N. and S. Wales, &c. 314; P.C. 193
Parker Family.
—— Th., 1st E. of, form. sir T., ld. and visc. Parker, *q.v.*
—— Geo., 2nd E. of, Pres. R. Soc. 940
—— Geo., 4th E. of, form. Geo. and visc. Parker, *q.v.*, C.G.P. 300; C.Y.G. 298; L.L. Oxon. 311
McClintock, sir Fras. Leop., adm. (**E**) 836
—— Jno., aft. ld. Rathdonnell, *q.v.*, L.L. Louth, 570
McClure, sir Rt. J. Le M., adm. (**H**) 848
MacCoghlan, Corm., dn. Clonm. 600
MacColgan, bp. Ferns, 621
MacConail, Flan., bp. Emly, 625
MacConoma, Corn., bp. Kilm. 607
MacCormac, Cathald, bp. Clonf. 635
MacCoughlan, Corm., bp. Clonm. 600
McCoy, Jno., gen. (**D**) 900
MacCragh, Donat, bp. Killoe. 634
—— Matth., bp. Killoe. 634; dn. Killoe. 637
—— Thady, bp. Killoe. 634
McCrea, Jno. Dobree, adm. (**E**) 836
—— Rd. Contart, adm. (**G**) 842
—— Rt. Barl., gen. (**D**) 911
McCreagh, sir Michl., K.C.H. 788
MacCrossain, Rd., bp. Rph 601
MacCuanach, Arect., bp. Ferns, 621
MacCulenan, Cormac, bp. Lism. 626
—— Cormac, bp. Cash. 624
MacCulloch, Edg., Blf. Gsey. 669
—— Jas., Ulst. K.A. 572
—— sir Jas., K.C.M.G. 797
McCullum, Ch. Campb., gen. (**D**) 921
MacDermot, The, S.G. Ir. 590
—— Ter., L.M. Dbln. 640
—— Th. MacFerall, bp. Elph. 608
MacDomnuil, Dermod, bp. Ross. 631
M'Donagh, McMulr., dn. Ach. 614
McDonald and **Macdonald,** *see also* Macdonell
—— —, G. Tob. 723
—— Off. Nap. 26
—— A. A., G. Pr. Ed. Isl. 699
—— Alaster McIan, gen. (**D**) 909
*—— Alexr., G. Br. Hond. 714
*—— Alexr., gen. (**C**) 875
* ? same pers.
—— Alexr., gen. (**D**) 882
—— Andr., K.C.B. 776
—— Archd., K.H. 789
—— Archd. and sir A., A.G. 400; C.B. Ex. 382; K.C. 415; P.C. 205; S.G. 402; S.L. 412

M'—Mc— and Mac—
McDonald and Macdonald—*cont.*
—— Ch., C. Acc. Ir. 567
—— Colin, adm. (**H**) 845
—— Coll. Amb. Pers. 130
—— D. A., G. Ont. 692
—— Don., gen. (**B**) 866
*—— Geo., G. Dnca. 730
*—— Geo., gen. (**D**) 890
* ? same pers.
—— sir Jas., B.C. 253; Com. Io. Isl. 129; G.C.M.G. 794
—— gen. sir Jas., *see* Macdonell
—— Jas. Archd., adm. (**H**) 851
—— Jas. Daws., gen. (D) 912
—— Jas. Mitch., gen. (**D**) 908
—— hon. Jas. Win. Bosv., gen. (**D**) 905
—— Jno., gen. (**D**) 197
—— Jno., K.C.B. 775
—— Jno. and sir J. (No. 1), G.C.B. 769; gen. (**B**) 869; K.C.B. 776
—— Jno. and sir J. (No. 2), gen. (**D**) 882; K.C.B. 778
—— Jno. Alexr. and sir J., G.C.B. 773; K.C.B. 783; P.C. 219
—— Jno Alexr. Matth., gen. (**D**) 928
—— Jno. Hay A. and sir J., D. Fac. Sc. 527; L.J. Clk. 516; Ld. Adv. 526; P.C. 220; S.G. Sc. 527
—— Jno. Wall. Dougl., adm. (**H**) 851
—— Norm., gen. (**D**) 933
—— Norm. H., U.S. Ir. 563
—— Norm. Wm., Si. Le. 685
—— Regd. Jno. and sir R., K.C.B. 782; K.C.S.I. 803
—— Regd. Jno. Jas. Geo., aft. Macdonald-Blomfield, adm. (**E**) 836
—— Rt. Mack., gen. (**D**) 926
—— Ron. Reg., K.H. 790
—— Wm. Ch. R., gen. (**D**) 916
Macdonald, lds.
—— Godfr., 3rd ld., gen. (**B**) 868
Macdonald-Robertson, *see* Robertson
MacDonegan, Florence, bp. Drom. 604
—— Nelan, bp. Ferns, 621
Macdonell and **Macdonnell,** *see also* McDonald
—— Alexr. and sir A., gen. (**D**) 904; K.C.B. 781
—— sir Ed., L.M. Dbln. 642
—— Hugh Guion, Amb. Bva. 119; Amb. Bzl. 135; Amb. Dk. 127
—— (or McDonald), sir Jas., G.C.B. 769; gen. (**A**) 863; K.C.B. 776; K.C.H. 789
—— Jno. Cott., dn. Cash. 627
—— Jno. Ign., gen. (**D**) 926
—— Rd. Graves and sir R., G. Gamb. 686; G. H. Kong, 673; G. N. Sc. 695; G. S. Austr. 706; G. St. Vin. 725; K.C.M.G. 796
MacDonennach, Laigdene, bp. Saig. 620
MacDongail, bp. Kild. 616
Macdonnell, *see* Macdonell
Macdonogh, Rt., bp. Cork, 630
M'Douall, Rt., gen. (**D**) 879
McDougall, Fras. Th., bp. Labn. 675; bp. Sing. L. and S. 676

M'—Mc— and Mac—
McDougall—*cont.*
— Jno., adm. (**A**) 817
— Jno., adm. (**H**) 848
— Jno. and sir J., adm. (**D**) 831; K.C.B. 779
— Patr. Leon and sir P., gen. (**D**) 904 ; K.C.M.G. 797
— sir Th., G.C.H. 786
Macdowal, Andr., Ld.Sess.520
Macdowall, Day Hort., gen. (**D**) 892
— Ferg., Ld. Clk. Reg. 525
— H., C.C. Mdras. 657
— Hay, gen. (**B**) 866
— Wm., L.L. Rnfw. 511
M'Dowell, Rt., adm. (**A**) 817
Macduff, Jno., gen. (**D**) 898
Macduff, visc.
— Alexr. Wm. Geo., visc., aft. 6th E. and 1st D. of Fife, *q.v.*, L.L. Elgn. 509
MacDuibne, Fursey, bp. Kilm. 607
— Matth., bp. Kilm. 607
MacDunchad, Tola, bp. Cld. 598
MacDunecan, Condla, bp. Llin. 621
Macedonicus, Q. C. M., C. Ro. 44
MacElchade, Corn., bp. Ross. 631
MacEneol, Cong., bp. Kilm. 607
Macerinus, M. G. (3), C. Ro. 38-9
— P. G., C. Ro. 39
— T. G., C. Ro. 37
Mcfarlan and **Macfarlane**
— Andr., bp. Mor. 544; bp. Ork. and Ross. 545
— Dav., gen. (**D**) 926
— Dunc. (2), Mod. K. Sc. 547
— Jas., Mod. K. Sc. 547
— Patr., Mod. K. Sc. 547
— Rt., Ld. Sess. 521
— Rt. and sir R., gen. (**A**) 861 ; G.C.H. 786 ; K.C.B. 775
MacFergus, Dubenr., bp. Ferns. 621
McFerran, Jas., C.I.E. 808
MacFingail, Rudgall, bp. Emly, 625
MacFintan, Tuenoch, bp. Ferns, 621
MacFlamchellaic, Flan., bp. Emly, 625
MacFlanagan, Ferdomnach, bp. Cld. 598
MacFlan, Murechad, bp. Kild. 616
MacFlin, Florence, abp. Tm. 611
MacFitzbran, Cormac, bp. Glend. 615
MacFœlan, Mured, bp. Kild. 616
McGanysa, Conn., dn. Down, 605
M'Garel-Hogg, *see* Hogg
MacGee, *see* Magee
MacGelany, Cornelius, bp. Kild. 616
McGenis, *see also* Magennis
— (or McGinnis), Conn., dn. Down, 605
MacGilbride, Jno., bp. Rph. 601
Macgill, Dav. (Cranston Riddel), Ld. Adv. 526; Ld. Sess. 519
— Dav. (Nisbet) Ld. Sess. 518

M'—Mc— and Mac—
Macgill—*cont.*
— Jas. (Rankeilor Nether), Ld. Clk. Reg. 525; Ld. Sess. 518
— sir Jas. (Cranston Riddel), Ld. Sess. 519
— Rt., Ld. Sess. 519
— Stev., Mod. K. Sc. 547
McGillewride, Corn., dn. Rph. 602
MacGinnis, *see* MacGennis
MacGirthid, Fienmale, bp. Cld. 598
MacGlashan, Jas., K.H. 789
MacGorman, Matth., bp. Emly, 625
McGoun, Alexr., gen. (**D**) 931
Macgowan, Fk., gen. (**D**) 911
MacGragh, *see* Magragh
M'Graidin, Pierce, dn. Ard. 609
MacGraith and **MacGrath,** *see* Magrath
MacGregor and **MacGrigor**
— Alexr. Murr., gen. (**C**) 874
— Arth. Trev., adm. (**H**) 850
— Ch., K.H. 790
— Ch. Metc. and sir C., C.I.E. 806; gen. (**D**) 931; K.C.B. 781
— Dunc. and sir D., gen. (**D**) 883; K.C.B. 782
— Dunc. Jno., gen. (**D**) 927
— Evan, Sec. Adm. 187
— sir Ev. Jno. Murray, G. Antig., &c. 727; G. Bdoes., &c. 719-20; G. Dnca. 730; G. Trin. 722; gen. (**C**) 875; K.C.B. 776; K.C,H. 788; K.H. 789
— Ev. Murr., gen. (**D**) 914
— Geo. Hall, K.C.B. 783
— J. M., gen. (**D**) 923
— sir Jas., K.C.B. 777
— Jno., Sec. B.T. 270
— Jno. Alexr. Paul, gen. (**D**) 876
— sir Malc., adm. (**H**) 852
— Wm., G. Br. N. Guin. 711
MacGuffan, Fin., bp. Kild. 616
MacGuire, *see* Maguire
McGwire, Ed. Th. St. Lawr., gen. (**D**) 929
Machabæus, *see* Matthæus
Machadh-Mongruadh, Q. Ir. 20
Machado, Rog., Clar. K.A. 328; Norr. K.A. 329; Richm. H. 333
McHaffie, Jas., gen. (**D**) 890
M'Hardy, Jno. Bunch Bonne Maison, adm. (**G**) 842
Machatus (St.), bp. Isl. 539
Machilla, bp. S. and M. 483
Machonochie, *see* Maconochie
Mackray, Rt., bp. Rup. Ld. 697
Machutus, bp. S. and M. 483
McIlwraith, Th., K.C.M.G. 798
MacInclodnai, Mœlmorda, bp. Emly, 625
MacInlianaig, Ch., bp. Elph. 608
— Gelasius, bp. Elph. 608
M'Innes, Jno., gen. (**D**) 878
MacIntire, *see* MacIntyre
Macintosh, *see* Mackintosh
MacIntire and **MacIntyre**
— Æn. Jno., Q.C. 419
— Andr. Wm., gen. (**D**) 916
— Colin Camp., gen. (**D**) 906
— Jno. Mack., gen. (**D**) 920

M'—Mc— and Mac—
Mackarness, Geo. Rd., bp. Arg. and Isl. 541
— Jno. F., bp. Oxf. 457
McKathmoyll, *see* McCamaill
McKamyll, *see* McCamaill
Mackay, Alexr., gen. (**C**) 872
— hon. Alexr., gen. (**B**) 865
— D. J., aft. 1st ld. Reay, *q.v.*
— hon. Don. Hugh, adm. (**D**) 825
— Jas. Pr., gen. (**B**) 865
— Rt., gen. (**B**) 864
Mackelcan, Jno., gen. (**B**) 868
MacKellach, Culean, bp. Kild. 616
Mackellan, Ang., Mod. K. Sc. 547
— Jno., adm. (**A**) 820; (**G**) 840
MacKelly, Dav., abp. Cash. 624; bp. Cloy. 630; dn. Cash. 627
McKenny, Th., L.M. Dbln. 641
Mackenzie, Alexr., Ch. Com. Cent. Pr. 655
— Alexr., gen. (**D**) 918
— sir Alexr., G.C.H. 786; gen. (**A**) 861
— Alexr. Mack., gen. (**D**) 912
— C. F., bp. C. Afr. 688
*— Col., —, C.C. Bgal. 652; C.C. Ind. 650
*— Colin, gen. (**A**) 860
* ? same pers.
— Colin, gen. (**D**) 910
— Colin, gen. (**D**) 933
— Colin Jas., L.L. Pbls. 511
— Don., Ld. Sess. 521
— Don. McLeod, adm. (**H**) 851
— Dougl., bp. Z. Ld. 681
— Fras. Humb., aft. ld. Seaforth, *q.v.*, L.L. Ross. 512
— Geo., adm. (**A**) 815
— sir Geo., aft. visc. Tarbat and E. of Cromarty, *q.v.*, L.J. Gen. 522; Ld. Adv. 526; Ld. Clk. Reg. 525; Ld. Sess. 519
— sir Hed., L.L. Ross, 512
— Hy., bp. suffr. Nottm. 447
— Holt., B.C. 253; P.C. 212
— Hugh, gen. (**D**) 933
— sir Jas., Ld. Sess. 520
— Jas. Alexr. St., B.C. 253; Com. Io. Isl. 129; G. Ceyl. 672; P.C. 213; Sec. B.C. 254
— Jas. Geo., adm. (**H**) 850; G. Falk. Isl. 731; G. Nev. 730; G. St. Xtr. 729
— hon. Jas. St., Amb. Sda. 114; L.P.S. Sc. 501; P.C. 200
— sir Jas. Wemyss, L.L. Ross. 512
— Jno., gen. (**A**) 862
— Jno., gen. (**B**) 866
— Jno., gen. (**B**) 868
— Jno. Fras. Campb., adm. (**H**) 851
— Jno. Rand., gen. (**C**) 873
— Jno. Rt., gen. (**D**) 913
— Jno. Stuart, L.P.S. Sc. 501
— Josh. Hy., Jy. Sc. 523; Ld. Sess. 520
— Kenn. Aug. M., Q.C. 420
— sir Kenn. Sm., L.L. Ross. 512
— Kinc., L. Prov. Edinb. 548

For List of Abbreviations, see pp. 944-952.

M'—Mc— and Mac—
Mackenzie—*cont.*
—— Murd., bp. Mor. 534; bp. Ork. 535
—— Patr., gen. (**C**) 874
—— Pet., Modr. K. Sc. 547
—— Rod., L.J. Clk. 516; Ld. Sess. 520
—— Th., adm. (**A**) 816
—— Th., Ld. Sess. 521; S.G. Sc. 527
—— Wm., K.C.B. 782
—— Wm. Forbes-, L.T. 160; Sec. Tr. 163
McKeogh, Sim., dn. Clonf. 637
M'Kerlie, Jas., adm. (**H**) 845
—— Jno. Gr., K.C.B. 784
Mackeson, Wm. W., Q.C. 418
Mackeston (or Makeson), Geo., dn. Arm. 597
Mackey, Jas. W. and sir J., L.M. Dbln. 642
Mackie, Geo., G. St. Luc. 725; gen. (**C**) 874
—— Wm., K.H. 790
McKillop, Hy. Fk., adm. (**H**) 852
—— Rt. Jno., gen. (**D**) 897
MacKinede, Olchobar, bp. Emly, 625
MacKinfalaid, Malduin, bp. Rph. 601
M'Kinley, Geo., adm. (**A**) 820
M'Kinnom, Hy., gen. (**C**) 873
Mackinnon, Danl. Hy. L., gen. (**D**) 918
—— Geo. Hy., gen. (**D**) 892
—— Wm., C.I.E. 807
Mackintosh and **Macintosh**
—— Alexr. Fisher, gen. (**D**) 883; K.H. 790
—— sir Jas., B.C. 235; P.C. 211
—— Rt. Jas., G. Antig., &c. 727; G. St. Xtr. 729
—— Wm., D. Fac. Sc. 527
Mackirdy, Dav. Ell., gen. (**D**) 902
Macknight, Th., Modr. K. Sc. 547
Mackworth and **Macworth**
—— Digb., K.H. 790
—— Humphr., J. Chest. 386
—— Jno., dn. Linc. 448
Maclachlan, Alexr., gen. (**D**) 885
—— Archd., gen. (**D**) 882
—— Th. Jas., gen. (**D**) 920
MacLactnan, Bechan, bp. Cld. 598
—— Finnacht, bp. Ferns, 621
Mac Cladach, Corm., bp. Saig. 620
Maclagan, Rt., gen. (**D**) 905
—— Wm. D., bp. Lich. 444
MacLagenan, Columb, bp. Emly, 625
MacLaghlin, Michl., bp. Dry. 601
Maclain-(e), Archd. and sir A., gen. (**D**) 879; K.C.B. 777
MacLaisir, bp. Arm. 595
McLaren, Dunc., L. Prov. Edinb. 548
—— Jno., Jy. Sc. 523; Ld. Adv. 526; Ld. Sess. 521
McLaughlin, Ed., gen. (**D**) 931
Maclaurin, Jno., Ld. Sess. 520
McLean, Allan T., gen. (**D**) 885
—— Ch. Sm., C.I.E. 808

M'—Mc— and Mac—
McLean—*cont.*
—— Don., K.C.M.G. 797
—— Fras. Wm., Q.C. 420
—— sir Fitzroy Jeff. Gr., gen. (**A**) 862
—— sir Geo., K.C.B. 778
—— Hect., bp. Arg. 538
—— Hect., K.C.B. 775
—— Hy. Dund., Regr. M.G. 799
—— Hy. Jno., gen. (**D**) 926
—— Jno., bp. Sask. 697
—— Jno., G. Br. Kaffr. 630; G. Nat. 680
—— Jno. and sir J., gen. (**B**) 869; K.C.B. 774
—— sir Jos., gen. (**B**) 869; K.C.H. 788
—— Lachl., gen. (**B**) 868
—— Pet., gen. (**D**) 907
—— Rod., bp. Isl. 539
Macleay, Geo., K.C.M.G. 797
McLelan, A. W., G. N. Sc. 695
McClelland, Jas., B. Ex. Ir. 584; S.G. Ir. 589
M'Leod, Ch., gen. (**D**) 877; K.C.B. 777
—— Don., gen. (**D**) 876; K.C.B. 776
—— Don., gen. (**D**) 887
—— Don. Friell., K.C.S.I 802; L.G. Pjab. 654
—— Dunc., gen. (**D**) 881
—— Harry, gen. (**D**) 935
—— Hy. Geo. and sir H., G. St. Xtr. 729; G. Trin. 722; K.H. 791
—— Jno., Dn. Thist. 749
—— Jno., gen. (**B**) 867
—— Jno., Modr. K. Sc. 547
—— sir Jno., G.C.H. 786; gen. (**B**) 869; K.C.H. 788
—— Jno. Cheth. and sir J., gen. (**D**) 919; K.C.B. 780
—— Jno. Macph. and sir J., K.C.S.I. 802; P.C. 218
—— J. M., *see* ld. M., *infra*
—— Jos. Add., Q.C. 419
—— Nor., Dn. Thist. 749
—— Nor. (2), Modr. K. Sc. 547
—— Nor., gen. (**C**) 875
—— Rt. Br. Æn., L.L. Crom. 509
—— Rod., L.L. Crom. 509
—— Rod. Bann., gen. (**D**) 918
—— Wm. Coup., gen. (**D**) 899
—— Wm. Edm., gen. (**D**) 913
—— Wm. Kelly, gen. (**D**) 921
Macleod, lds.
—— Jno. Mark, aft. ld. M., gen. (**C**) (1782) 872
Maclerk, *see* Mauclerk
M'Clery, Miler, dn. Clonm. 600
M'Cleverty, sir Rt., gen. (**C**) 875; K.C.H. 789
—— Wm. Ans., C.C. Mdras. 658; gen. (**D**) 894
MacLoingle, bp. Arm. 595
MacLongsee, Murchertach, bp. Cld. 599
MacLubney, Killene St., bp. Saig. 620
MacMaelfin, Tibraid, bp. Emly, 625
McMahon, Ch. Alexr., gen. (**D**) 935
—— Ch. Jos., gen. (**D**) 932
—— Dav., bp. Killoe. 634; dn. Killoe. 637
*—— Jno. and sir J., P.C. 209
*—— Jno., St. O. 261
* ? same pers.

M'—Mc— and Mac—
McMahon—*cont.*
—— Mar. Patr. Maur., G.C.B. 769; Pres. Fr. 25
—— Patr., bp. Ard. 608
—— sir Th., C.C. Bbay. 660; G.C.B. 770; gen. (**A**) 863; K.C.B. 775
—— sir Th. Westr., gen. (**D**) 903
—— Wm. and sir W., M.R. Ir. 585; S.L. Ir. 593
McMair, Jas., K.H. 790
MacManus, G. I. Man, 665
MacMasson, Th., bp. Dry. 601
Mac Mel Brenan, Derm., bp. Ardf. and Agh. 639
Mac Mic Oeducan, *see* Oeducan
MacMoëlmorra, Fergall, bp. Saig. 620
MacMogtigern, Lanfran, bp. Kild. 616
MacMolissa, Nichs., abp. Ann. 595
McMorine, Wm., Modr. K. Sc. 547
McMullen, J. R., gen. (**D**) 923
—— Steph. Fras., gen. (**D**) 911
McMurdo, Arch., adm. (**H**) 849
—— Wm. Mont. Sc., gen. (**D**) 902; K.C.B. 781
MacMurrough, Arth., K. of Leinster, K.B. (1394) 755
McNab, Archd., gen. (**C**) 872
Macnabb, Don. Campb., K.C.I.E. 805
MacNaghten, Don., bp. Dkld. 533
—— Edm. Alexr., C. Treas. Ir. 561; L.T. 159
—— Ed., *see* ld. M., *infra*
—— Ell., Chn. E.I. Co. 646; M.C.I. 646
—— sir Wm. Hay, G. Bbay. 659
Macnaghten, lds.
—— Ed., aft. ld. M., Jud. Com. P.C. 362; L. App. 358; P.C. 221; Q.C. 419
McNair, Ed. Jno., gen. (**D**) 934
—— Jno., gen. (**B**) 869
Macnamara, sir Burt., adm. (**G**) 842
—— Hy. T. J., C.C.J. 405
—— Jas., adm. (**A**) 819
MacNaserda, Robertæ, bp. Kild. 616
Macnaughton, *see* Macnaghten
Macneale, Macneil, Macneile, and **McNeill**
—— Don., gen. (**D**) 911
—— Dunc., aft. ld. Colonsay, *q.v.*, D. Fac. Sc. 527; Jy. Sc. 523; L.P. Ct. Sess. 516; Ld. Adv. 526; Ld. Sess. 521; P.C. 216; S.G. Sc. 527
—— Hugh, dn. Rip. 482
—— Jno., Amb. Pers. 130
—— Jno., dn. Down, 605
—— Jno. and sir J., G.C.B. 772; P.C. 216
—— Jno. Carst. and sir J., gen. (**D**) 925; K.C.B. 781; K.C.M.G 797
—— Rod., gen. (**D**) 882
Macnisius, Ængus (St.), bp. Cnr. 603
Macoge, bp. Lism. 626

For List of Abbreviations, see pp. 944-952.

M'—Mc— and Mac—
Macon, K. Man, 664
Maconochie and **Machonochie**
— Alexr., C. Cus. Sc. 504
— Alex., Jy. Sc. 523; Ld. Adv. 526; Ld. Sess. 520; S.G. Sc. 527
— Alexr., K.H. 791
— All., Jy. Sc. 523; Ld. Sess. 520
— Jas., C.C.J. 406
Mac O'Reghty, Hy., bp. Ach. 612
Macphail, Jno., G. Antig. 728; G. Dnca. 730
Macpherson, Arth. Geo., K.C.I.E. 805
— Ch. Gord. W., C.I.E. 806
— Dav. Lew., K.C.M.G. 798
— Don., K.H. 792
— Dunc., gen. (**D**) 877
— Herb. Tayl. and sir H. C.C. Mdras. 658; gen. (**D**) 925; K.C.B. 781; K.C.S.I. 803
— Jas. Dunc., gen. (**D**) 901; K.C.B. 780
— Jno. and sir J., G.G. Ind. 648
— Ph., gen. (**D**) 893
— Rod. Don., gen. (**D**) 912
— Rt. Barcl., gen. (**D**) 881; K.H. 791
— Wm., gen. (**D**) 905
Macquarrie, Lachl., G. N.S.W. 703; gen. (**C**) 873
Macquay, Geo., C. Exc. Ir. 566
MacQueen, Andr., gen. (**D**) 923
— Don. Jno., K.H. 791
— Jas., gen. (**D**) 900
— Jno. Fras., Q.C. 418
— Rt., Jy. Sc. 523; L.J. Clk. 516; Ld. Sess. 520
Macra, sir Jno., K.C.H. 787
MacRaik, Matth., bp. Clonf. 636
Macrinus, M. O., Emp. Ro. 47
Macrobius, *see* Malchus
MacRonan, bp. Ardf. and Agh. 639
Macrorie, Wm. Kenn., bp. Mburg. 680
MacScanlain, Edchada, bp. Emly, 625
MacScelagai, Gelasius, bp. Kilmacd. 636
MacSmarhadhan, bp. Ard. 607
McSwiney, Pet. Paul, L.M. Dbln. 642
MacSwiny, Kenfœlad de, bp. Saig. 620
McTaggart, Wm., dn. Dry. 602
— Ellis-, *see* Ellis
Macvicar, Neil, L. Prov. Edinb. 548
Macworth, *see* Mackworth
Madan, Spenc., bp. Brl. 439; bp. Pboro. 458
Madden, Dodgs. Ham., S.G. Ir. 590; S.L. Ir. 593
— sir Fk., K.H. 790
— sir Geo. All., gen. (**C**) 874
— Jno., S.W.F. 271
— Jno., dn. Kilm. 609
— Mons. Mol., K.H. 792
— Saml. Owen, dn. Cork, 632
Maddingley, Rt. de, J. It. 369
Maddison, *see also* Madison
— Geo., U.S.F. 229
Maddocks, Jno., K.C. 415
Maddox and **Madox**
— Hy., K.H. 790
— Is., bp. St. As. 462; bp. Worc. 473; dn. Wells, 429
Madenew, abp. St. Dav. 463
Madison, *see also* Maddison
— J., Pres. U.S.A. 102
Madoc ab Meredydd, Pr. Wls. 17
— Leol. ap, bp. St. As. 462; dn. St. As. 462
Madock, Jno., bp. Kild. 616
Madox, *see* Maddox
Mæ—, *see also* Mœ—
Mælfinan, bp. Emly, 625
— bp. Kild. 616
Mælschwythe, abp. St. Dav. 463
Mænius, C., C. Ro. 40; Dt. Ro. (2) 41
Magan, Hy., gen. (**C**) 872
Magee (or Mageoir), Jno., bp. Ard. 607
— Wm., abp. Dbln. and Gl. 616; bp. Rph. 602; dn. Crk. 632
— Wm. Conn., bp. Pboro. 458; dn. Crk. 632
Magellus, L.P. (3), C. Ro. 41
Magenis and **Magennis**
— Arth., bp. Drom. 604
— Arth. Ch. and sir A., Amb. Aus. 117; Amb. Pgl. 125; Amb. Scy. 115; Amb. Sw. and N. 127; Amb. Swz. 113; G.C.B. 772; K.C.B. 782
— Conn., dn. Down, 605
— Eug., bp. Down and Cnr. 604; bp. Dry. 601
— Rd. (2), C. Acc. Ir. 567
— Wm., dn. Kilm. 609
Mageoir, *see* Magee
Magheramorne, Jas., ld., form. Jas. McGarel-Hogg, *q.v.*
Maglathin, Jeffr., bp. Dry. 601
Magminot, Wak. de, W.C.P. 317
Magnay, Chr., L.M. Lond. 492
— Wm. and sir W., L.M. Lond. 492
Magniac, Fras. Lane, gen. (**D**) 919
Magnus, D. Sxy. 77
— K. Dk. 93; K. Man. 665
— K. Man. 665
— I. and II., D. Brk. 69
— I. and II., K. Sw. 92
— I. and II., Pr. Mkg. 74
— C. P. (2), C. Ro. 46
— S. P. A., C. Ro. 44
Magodaig, Brendan, bp. Ard. 607
— Jos., bp. Ard. 607
Magon, Mons., G. Mtius. 683
Magonail, Donat, bp. Rph. 601
— Patr., bp. Rph. 601
Magragh and **Macgragh**
— abp. Cash. and Eml. 626; bp. Ach. and Kill. and Ach. 612; bp. Clr. 596; bp. Wford. and L. 627
Magrath, sir Geo., K.H. 790
*— Sim., bp. Ard. 607
*— Sim., dn. Elph. 609
* ? same pers.
Maguire, *see also* MacGwire
— Ch., dn. Clr. 597
— Ed., dn. Down, 605
— Nichs. bp. Llin. 622
Maguire—*cont.*
— Pet., bp. Clr. 596
— Rog., bp. Clr. 596
Mahadeo, &c., C.I.E. 808
Mahmoud, Sh. Pers. 99
Mahmud (2), S. Tky. 97-8
Mahomed (2), Sh. Pers. 99
— I. to V., S. Tky. 97
— Aslam, &c., C.I.E. 808
— Es Sadok, B. Tun. 101
— Ghol., K.C.S.I. 803
— Meer Sh., K.C.S.I. 802
— Sidy, B. Tun. 101
— Sult. Pash., K.C.M.G. 798
Mahon, D'Arcy, C. St. Ir. 568
— Jas., dn. Drom. 606; dn. Tm. 613
— Jno., C. Acc. Ir. 567
— Matth., gen. (**D**) 877
— Pet., dn. Elph. 609
— hon. Steph., gen. (**B**) 867
Mahon, visc.
— Ph. Hy., visc., aft. 5th E. Stanhope, *q.v.*, U.S.F. 230
— Arth. Ph. Hy., visc., aft. 6th E. Stanhope, *q.v.*, L.T. 162
Mahta, Punno Lall, C.I.E. 808
Maida, Jno., Ct. of, *see* Jno. and sir J. Stuart
Maidstone, Jno. de, dn. Linc. 448
— (or Maydenstune), Ralph de, bp. Her. 441; dn. Her. 442
— (or Maydenstune), Walt., bp. Worc. 472
Maihewe, *see also* Mayhew
— Rd., M. Chy. 394
Mail, K. Ir. 21
Maillart, Wm., *see* Mullart
Maine, *see also* Mayne
— Hy. Jas. Sumn. and sir H., K.C.S.I. 803; M.C.I. 646 U.S. Home (?) 228
Mainus, K. Sc. 17
Mainwaring, Mainweringe, Manwaring, and **Maynwaring**
— Arth., C. Cus. 274
— Ed. Reeves Ph., adm. (**H**) 848
— Ed. Rowl., gen. (**D**) 900
— Geo., Richm. H. 333
— Geo. Byres, gen. (**D**) 926
— Jno. Mont., G. St. Luc. 725; gen. (**B**) 869
— Ph. and sir P., L.K. Ir. 576; Sec. St. Ir. 562
— Regd. Quinton, gen. (**D**) 930
— R. R., gen. (**D**) 922
— Rog., B. Ex. Ir. 583
— Rog., bp. St. Dav. 464; dn. Worc. 473
— Rowl., adm. (**H**) 847
— Sweedl., gen. (**D**) 923
— sir Th., M. Chy. 395
— Th. Fras. Ch., adm. (**H**) 844
— Wm. Geo., gen. (**D**) 928; C.I.E. 806
Mair, Jno. Hast., G. Dnca. 730; G. Gren. 724; K.H. 789
Mairis, Geoffr., gen. (**D**) 929
— Val. Th., gen. (**D**) 913
Maisey, Fk. Ch., gen. (**D**) 923
Maister, Geo., gen. (**D**) 911
— Jno., gen. (**A**) 863
Maitland, Hon. sir Alexr., gen. (**A**) 858

Maitland—*cont.*
— hon. sir Anthy., aft. 10th E. of Lauderdale, *q.v.*, adm. (**D**) 826; K.C.B. 777; K.C.M.G. 796
— Chas., Ld. Sess. 519
— hon. Ch., Dep. Tr. Sc. 497
— Chas. Lenn. Br., gen. (**D**) 905; L.G. Ch. Hosp. 936; Lt. T.L. 322
— Ed. F., Ld. Sess. 521; S.G. Sc. 527
— Fk., G. Gren. 724; gen. (**A**) 861; L.G. Dnca. 730
— Fk., gen. (**D**) 910
— sir Fk. Lew., adm. (**A**) 820; K.C.B. 776
— Horatio Lawr. Arth. Lenn., adm. (**H**) 853
— Jas., Modr. K. Sc. 547
— Jas., gen. (**B**) 864
— Jno., adm. (**A**) 820
— Jno., gen. (**D**) 903
— Jno., L.P.S. Sc. 501; Ld. Sess. 518
— Jno. and sir J., Ld. Chanc. Sc. 515; Ld. Sess. 518; Sec. St. Sc. 502
— Sir Jno. aft. 5th E. of Lauderdale, *q.v.*, Ld. Sess. 520.
— Lew., adm. (**H**) 850
— Peregr. and sir P., C.C. Mdras. 657; G.C.B. 769; G. C.G.H. 679; G. N. Sc. 695; G. Upp. Can. 692; gen. (**A**) 863; K.C.B. 775
— Rd., aft. 4th E. of Lauderdale, Dep. Tr. Sc. 497
— sir Rd. (Lethington), L.P.S. Sc. 501; Ld. Sess. 517-8
— sir Rd. (Pittrichie) Ld. Sess. 519
— Rt., Ld. Sess. 518
— Th., Ld. Sess. 521; S.G. Sc. 527
— hon. Th. and sir T., B.C. 252; Com. Io. Isl. 129; G.C.B. 767; G.C.H. 786; G.C.M.G. 794; G. Ceyl. 672; G. Mlta. 671; gen. (**B**) 867; Gr. M. M.G. 794; P.C. 207
— sir Th., aft. 11th E. of Lauderdale, *q.v.*, adm. (**D**) 831; (**E**) 834
— Wm. and sir W., Ld. Sess. 517-8; Sec. St. Sc. 502
— Wm. Jas., C.I.E. 808
— hon. Wm. Mord., gen. (**A**) 861
Majendie, Hy. Wm., bp. Bgr. 426; bp. Chest. 477
Majorianus, J. V., Emp. W.E. 49
Majoribanks, *see* Marjoribanks
Makdougall, *see* Macdougall
Makdougall-Brisbane, *see* Brisbane
Makellan, *see* Mackellan
Makenade, Wm., Rec. Lond. 493
Makeson, *see* Mackeston
Mal, K. Ir. 21
Malachy (O'Morgair), bp. Arm. 595; bp. Cnr. 603; bp. Down, 603
— (3), bp. Down, 603
— I. and II., K. Ir. 22
Malakine, Nichs. M.M., 246
Malalo, Th., A.G. Ir. 588
Malartic, Comte de, G. Mtius. 683
Malberthorp, Rt. de, C.J.K.B. 369; J.C.P. 377; J.K.B. 371
Malcallan, bp. Clonf. 635
****Malchus** (or Macrobius), bp. Glend. 615
*— (St.), bp. Isl. 539
*— bp. Lism. 626
*— (St.), bp. S. & M. 483
*— bp. Wford. 626
* Prob. some same pers. Comp. dates.
Malclerk, *see* Mauclerk
Malcolm, bp. Cness. 531
— I. to IV., K. Sc. 19
— Alexr., Ld. Sess. 520
— sir Ch., adm. (**D**) 824
— Geo. and sir G. (No. 1), G.C.B. 771; gen. (**D**) 902; K.C.B. 779
— Geo. and sir G. (No. 2), gen. (**D**) 907
— Geo. Alexr., gen. (**D**) 893
— Geo. Jno., adm. (**H**) 852
— Jas., K.C.B. 775
— Jno. and sir J., G. Bbay. 659; G.C.B. 767; K.C.B. 775
— Pult. and sir P., adm. (**A**) 819; G.C.B. 768; G.C.M.G. 794; K.C.B. 774
— W. R., U.S.C. 236
Malduinus, bp. St. Andr. 528
— K. Sc. 18
Malduit, *see* Mauduit
Malebysse, Rd., J. It. 366
Malepilys, B. de, M.M. 246
Malet and **Mallet**
— sir Alexr., Amb. G. St. 122; K.C.B. 783
— Baldw., S.G. 401; S.L. 408
— Ed. B. and sir E., Amb. Bgm. 123; Amb. Eg. 130; Amb. Gmy. and Pr. 116; Amb. Tky. 130; G.C.B. 773; G.C.M.G. 795; K.C.B. 783; P.C. 220
— Fras., bp. Sal. 467; dn. Linc. 448
— Jno., Clar. K.A. 328
— Jno., K.B. 761
— sir Louis, M.C.I. 647; P.C. 220; U.S. Ind. 236
— Rt., J.K.B. 371
— Th. and sir T., J.K.B. 372; S.L. 409
Malfechin, bp. Cld. 598
Maling, Chr. T., C. Exc. 281
— Irw. Ch., G. Gren. 724
— Th. Jas., adm. (**A**) 820
Malins, Rd. and sir R., Jud. Com. P.C. 362; P.C. 220; Q.C. 417; V. Chanc. 390
Malisius (2), bp. St. Andr. 528
Mallaby, Rt., gen. (**D**) 932
Mallarino, M. M., Pres. N.G. 107
Malleolus, M. P., C. Ro. 43
Mallet, *see* Malet
Mallory, Th., dn. Chest. 477
Malmesbury, lds., visc., and E.
Wharton Family.
— Th., visc., form. Th. Wharton and ld. E. and M. of W., *q.v.* (*d.* 1715)
Harris Family.
— Jas., 1st ld. and E. of, form. sir J. Harris, *q.v.*; Amb. Fr. 112; Amb. Pr. 118; G.C.B. 771; L.L. Hants, 311
— Jas. Ed., 2nd E. of, form. visc. Fitz-Harris, *q.v.*
Malmesbury, lds., visc., and E. —*cont.*
— Jas. How., 3rd E. of, F. Sec. 228-9; G.C.B. 769; L.P.S. 241; P.C. 215
Malmore, bp. St. Andr. 528
Malo, *see* Mauley
****Malone**, Anthy., Ch. Ex. Ir. 562
*— Anthy., S.L. Ir. 592
* Prob. same pers.
— Edmd., J.C.P. Ir. 582; S.L. Ir. 592
— Rd., S.L. Ir. 592
— (or O'Molan), Odo, dn. Clonm. 600
Malore (or Malorre), Pet., J.C.P. 377; J.K.B. Ir. 578
Malorie, sir Rd., L.M. Lond. 490
Malorre, *see* Malore
Malpas, Hy., M. Chy. 394
Malpas, lds. and visc.
— Geo., visc. (aft. 3rd E. of Cholmondeley, *q.v.*, K.B. 764; L.H.A. 177; L.L. Chesh. 306
— Geo., visc. (son of 3rd E. of Cholmondeley), L.T. 156
Malscoed, abp. St. Dav. 463
Maltby, Ed., bp. Chich. 433 bp. Dham. 479
— Th., C.I.E. 806
Malton, Rt., B. Ex. 383
Malton, E. of
— Th. Wats., 1st E. of, form. T. W. Wentworth, *q.v.*, aft. M. of Rockingham, *q.v.*
Maltravers, lds. *Refer also to* E. of Arundel and D. of Norfolk
— Jno. FitzAlan, ld., L.M. (1377 and 1383) 325
— —, ld., K.B. (1426) 756
— Jno., ld., K.B. (1464) 757
— Th., ld. (aft. E. of Arundel), K.B. (1489) 758; K.G. (1474) 736
— Hy., ld., aft. E. of Arundel, K.B. (1547) 760
— Jas., ld., K.B. (1616) 762
— Hy., ld., form. H. Howard, *q.v.* (1616)
— Hy. C., ld., form. E. of Surrey, *q.v.*, aft. D. of Norfolk, *q.v.* (succ. 1842)
Maluginensis, L. C., C. Ro. 38
— M. C., Dec. Ro. 38
Malvane (or O'Malone) Malach, dn. Kild. 619
Malvoisine, Wm., bp. Glasg. 536; bp. St. Andr. 529; Ld. Chanc. Sc. 514
Malyverer, *see* Mauleverer
Mamercinus, L. Æ. (2), C. Ro. 40
— L.P., C. Ro. 38; M. Æ., C. Ro. 39; Dt. Ro. (3), 39
— P. P., C. Ro. 37
— T. Æ., C. Ro. 40
Mamercus, L. Æ. (3), C. Ro. 37-8
— T. Æ., C. Ro. 38
Man, *see* also Mann
— Alexr., bp. Cness. 531
— Hy., gen. (**D**) 916
— Jno., dn. Glr. 440
Manby, Pet., dn. Dry. 602
— Th., adm. (**A**) 820
Mance, Hy. Chr., C.I.E. 807
Manchester, Wm. de, dn. Lich. 445

Manchester, E. and D. of
— Hy., 1st E. of, form. H. Montagu, and 1st visc. Mandeville, *q.v.*, L.P.S. 240; L.T. 154
— Ed., 2nd E. of, C.G.S. 356; E.M. 326; K.G. 740; L.C.H. 295; P.C. 190
— Chas., 3rd E., aft. 1st D. of, C.Y.G. 298; P.C. 194; S. St. 224
— Wm., 2nd D. of, C.Y.G. 298; K.B. 764
— Rt., 3rd D. of, L.L. Hunts. 309
— Geo., 4th D. of, Amb. Fr. 112; L.C.H. 295; L.L. Hunts. 309; P.C. 203
— Wm., 5th D. of, G. Jam. 713; L.L. Hunts. 309; Postm. G. 238
— Wm. Dr., 7th D. of, K.P. 751
— Louise F. A., Dss. of, M. Robes, 304
Manchin, bp. Llin. 621
Mancinus, A. H., C. Ro. 44
— C. H., C. Ro. 44
— L. H., C. Ro. 44
Manclares, F., G. Trin. 721
Mandasa, Zem. of, C.I.E. 806
Manders, Rd., L.M. Dbln. 641
Manderstone, Jno. L. Prov. Edinb. 548
Mandevil and **Mandeville**
— Geoffr. de (1, 2, 3), Const. T.L. 320
— Geoffr. de (No. 2), E. of Essex, J. It. 365
— Jno., dn. Pboro. 458
— J. H., Amb. R. Pl. 136; Amb. Tky. 129
— Wm. de, Const. T.L. (Hen. I.) 320
— Wm. de, E. of Albemarle and E. of Essex, *q.v.*, Ch. Jr. 362
Mandeville, visc.
— Hy., 1st visc., form. ld. Montagu, *q.v.*, aft. 1st E. of Manchester, *q.v.*, C.G.S. 356
Manduca, Vinc. Ct., K.C.M.G. 796
Manett, Th., gen. (**D**) 881
Manfeld, Rt., M.M. 246
Manfield, Rt., M. Chy. 394
Manfred, K. Scy. 55
Mangal, Sing, C.I.E. 806
Mangin, Reuben Call., adm. (**D**) 826
Mangles, Cec., gen. (**D**) 928
— Ross Don., Chn. E.I. Co. 646; M.C.I. 646
Manilius, M., C. Ro. 44
— P., C. Ro. 45
Manisty, Hy. and sir H., J. Q.B.D. 374; Q.C. 417
Manley, sir Fras., S.L. 410
— Isaac Geo., adm. (**A**) 818
— J., S.L.R. 271
— Jno., adm. (**A**) 817
— Pet. de, J. It. 369
— Wm., S.L. 412
— Wm., C. Exc. 281-2
Mann, *see also* Man
— Corn., gen. (**C**) 875
— Goth., gen. (**A**) 861
— Gother Fk., gen. (**D**) 911
— Hy., bp. S. and M. 483; dn. Chest. 477
— sir Horace, Amb. Tusc. 115; K.B. 765

Mann—*cont.*
— Isaac, bp. Cork and R. 632
— Jas. Rt., gen. (**D**) 911
— Rt. (No. 1), adm. (**A**) 814; L. Admy. 179
— Rt. (No. 2), adm. (**A**) 816; L. Admy. 180
Manners, ld. Ch., gen. (**C**) 871
— ld. Ch. Hy. Som., gen. (**A**) 863; K.C.B. 776
— Fras., aft. 6th E. of Rutland, *q.v.*, K.B. 761
— Hy. Herb., K.H. 791
— ld. Jno. J. R., aft. 7th D. of Rutland, C.D.L. 243; C.W.P.B. 272; G.C.B. 773; P.C. 215; Postm. G. 239
— Rt., gen. (**A**) 860
— ld. Rt. Wm., gen. (**A**) 858
— ld. Rt. Wm., gen. (**C**) 875
— Russ., gen. (**A**) 859
— Russ. Hy., adm. (**H**) 847
Manners, lds.
— Th., 1st ld., form. Th. Manners-Sutton, *q.v.*, P.C. 208, 210
Manners-Sutton, *see* Sutton
Mannesin, Pet., bp. Oss. 620
Manning, Hy. Dimsd., gen. (**D**) 918
— Jas., C.C.J. 403; P.P. 417; S.L. 413
— Th., bp. Suff. Ipsw. 455
— Th., dn. Winds. 474
*— Th., M. Chy. 394
*— Th., S. St. 222
* Prob. same pers.
Manningham, —, adm. Ind. 647
— Ch. Wm., Tell. Ex. 168
— Coote, gen. (**C**) 873
— Th., bp. Chich. 433; dn. Winds. 474
Manningham-Buller, *see* Buller
Manny, Walt. de, aft. ld. M., K.B. 755; K.G. 733; L.H.A. 171-2
Mansel and **Mansell**
— Arth. Lukis, adm. (**H**) 852
— Hy. Longv., dn. St. P. 453
*— Jno., Const. T.L. 320; L.K. 353
*— Jno., W.C.P. 317
* Poss. same pers.
— Jno., gen. (**B**) 866
— Jno., gen. (**C**) 872
— Rt. Chr., gen. (**D**) 884; K.H. 790
— Th. (No. 1), adm. (**H**) 847
— Th. (No. 2) and Sir T., adm. (**H**) 845; K.C.H. 789
— Th., *see* ld. M., *infra*
— Wm. L., bp. Brl. 439
Mansell, lds.
— Th. and sir T., aft. ld. M., Compt. H. 292; L.T. 156; P.C. 195; Tell. Ex. 167
Mansfield, Ch. Ed. and sir C., Amb. Pu. 135; Amb. Rma. 128; Amb. U.S.C. 134; Amb. Vza. 135; K.C.M.G. 799
— Hy. de, dn. Linc. 448
— Jas. and sir J., C.J.C.P. 376; C.J. Chest. 386; K.C. 415; P.C. 207; S.G. 402; S.L. 412
— Wm. Rose and sir R., aft. ld. Sandhurst, *q.v.*, C.C. Bbay. 660; C.C. Ind. 651; Comm. F. Ir. 564; G.C.B. 770; G.C.S.I. 801; gen. (**D**) 892; K.C.B. 778; K.C.S.I. 802

Mansfield, lds., visc. and E.
Cavendish Family.
— Wm., visc., aft. E. of Newcastle, form. W. Cavendish (1610), *q.v.*
Murray Family.
— Wm., 1st ld., form. Wm. Murray, *q.v.*, aft. 1st E. of Mansfield; Ch. Ex. 165; P.C. 200
— Dav., 2nd E. of, form. visc. Stormont, *q.v.*, L.P.C. 188
— Dav. Wm., 3rd E. of, K.T. 748; L.L. Clkmn. 509
— Wm. Dav., 4th E. of, K.T. 748; L.H.C.K. Sc. 546; L.L. Clkmn. 509
Man Sing Ressaldar, C.I.E. 807
Manson, Alexr. Rt., gen. (**D**) 908
— Jas., gen. (**D**) 894
— (or Monson), Jno., K.B. 763
Mant, Rd., bp. Down and Cnr. 604; bp. Down, C. and D. 605; bp. Killoe and Kilf. 635
Mantaners, Jno., G. Ch. Isl. 667
Mantel, Rt., J. It. 365; Jy. 363
Manuel, I. and II., Emp. E.E. 51
— I. to III., Emp. Tzde. 98
Manwaring, *see* Mainwaring
Manwood, Pet., K.B. 761
— Rog., C.B. Ex. 381; J.C.P. 378; S.L. 408
Manzaro, Giac. Cal., K.C.M.G. 796
Maol-Ceachlin, I. and II., K. Ir. 21
Maolcobha, K. Ir. 21
Map, Walt., J. It. 365
Mapenore, Hugh de, bp. Her. 441; dn. Her. 442
Mapilton, Hugh de, bp. Oss. 620; dn. St. Pat. 617; Ld. Treas. Ir. 558
— Jno., M. Chy. 394
Maples, Jno. Ford., adm. (**H**) 845
Maplesden, Jarv., L.G. Gr. Hosp. 854
Mapletoft, Rt., dn. Ely, 435
Maq—, *see* Macq—
Mar, Rt., bp. Brn. 530
Mar, E. of
— Wm., E. of, L.G.C. Sc. (1266) 506
— Th., E. of, L.G.C. Sc. (1358) 506
— Jno. E. of (*d.* 1632), L.H.T. 497; K.G. 739
— Jno., E. of (*d.* 1732), K.T. 747; P.C. 195; Sec. St. Sc. 502
Mara, *see* Mare
Marbury, *see* Merbury
Marcellinus, P. Ro. 33
— C. C. L., C. Ro. 46
Marcellus I. and II., P. Ro. 33, 35
— C. C. (2), C. Ro. 46
— M. C., C. Ro. 40, 41, 43, 44, 46; Dt. Ro. 41
— Q. C., C. Ro. 43
Marceur, Jno., M.M. 246
March, Wm. Hy., gen. (**D**) 900
March, E. of, *see also* E. of Wemyss and E. of Ulster
Mortimer Family (*see also under* Mortimer).
— Rog., 1st E. of, form. R. Mortimer, *q.v.*

For List of Abbreviations, see pp. 944-952.

March, E. of—*cont.*
— Rog., 2nd E. of, K.G. 733; L.L. Ir. 551-2; W.C.P. 318
— Edmd., 3rd E. of, L.L. Ir. 551
— Rog., 4th E. of, K.B. 755
— Edm., 5th E. of, K.B. 756; L.H.A. 174; L.L. Ir. 552
Stuart Family.
— Esmé, 1st E. of, aft. D. of Lenox (1624), *q.v.*
— Jas., 2nd E. of, aft. D. of Lenox (1633), *q.v.*; also D. of Richmond, *q.v.*
Douglas Family.
— Wm., 3rd E. of, aft. 4th D. of Queensberry, *q.v.*, K.T. 747; V.A. Sc. 499
Gordon-Lennox Family.
— Ch. Hy., E. of, aft. 6th D. of Richmond and G., *q.v.*
Marchant, E. of, *see* Campbell
Marchant, Le,
— Den. and sir D., Sec. B.T. 270; Sec. Tr. 163; U.S. Home, 228
— Jno. Gasp. and sir G. (No. 1), G. Mlta. 671; G.N. Sc. 695; G. Newfd. 700; gen. (**C**) 873
— sir Jno. Gasp. (No. 2), C.C. Mdras. 658; G.C.M.G. 795; gen. (**D**) 892; K.C.B. 783
— Rt. Porr., Blf. Gsey. 669
Marchia, Wm. de, bp. B. and W. 427; L.H.T. 152
Marcianus, Emp. E.E. 50
Marchmont, E. of
— Patr., 1st E. of, form. P. Polwarth and 8th ld. P., *q.v.*; Comm. Tr. Sc. 497; L.H.C.K. Sc. 546
— Alexr., 2nd E. of, K.T. 747; P.C. 197
— Hugh, 3rd E. of, L.K. Sc. 503; P.C. 201
Marcluith, bp. Llff. 448
Marcoran, Georgio and sir G., G.C.M.G. 795; K.C.M.G. 796
Marcus and **Mark**
— (or Maurice), bp. Isl. 539; bp. S. and M. 483; Ld. Ch. Sc. 515
— P. Ro. 33
Mardall, Fras., gen. (**D**) 923
Mare and **Mara**
— Hy. de la, C.J.C.P. 375; J.C.P. 376; Jy. 364
— sir Peter de la, Sp. H.C. 248
— Regd. de la, K.B. 755
Marescall and **Mareschall,** *see also* Marischal and Marshall
— Ger. le, bp. Lim. 638
— (or Marescallus), Jno., J. It. 367
— Th. de, S.L. 406
— Wm. de, B. Ex. 382
— Wm., Jy. 363
— Wm., E. of Pembroke, W.C.P. (1138-9) 317
Maret, Off. Nap. 26
Marett, Rt. Pip., Blf. Jsey. 668
Mareyn (or Marnia), Angel, K.B. 760
Margall, Pres. Sp. 87
Margaret, C. Hld. 82
— C. Hlt. 82
— (of Anjou), Q.C.E. 7
Margaret—*cont.*
— (of France), Q.C.E. 7
— Q. Dk. 93
— Q. Sc. 19
— Q. Sw. 92
— (of Austria) (2), R. Nds 82
— (dau. Hy. III.), Pr. E. 9
— (dau. Edw. I.), Pr. E. 10
— (dau. Edw. III.), Pr. E. 10
— (iss. Edw. III.), Pr. E. 11
— (iss. Edw. III.), Pr. E. 11
— (dau. Edw. IV.), Pr. E. 12
— (dau. Hy. VII.), Pr. E. 12
— (g. dau. Hy. VII.), Pr. E. 12
— (dau. Jas. I.), Pr. E. 13
— I. and II., C. Flrs. 81
— -Beatr.-Feod. (g. dau. Q. Victoria), Pr. E. 15
— Vict.-Aug.-Charl.-Nora-Maud (g. dau. Q. Victoria), Pr. E. 16
Margary, Hy. Josh., gen. (**D**) 898
Margetson, Jas., abp. Arm. 596; abp. Dbln. and Gl. 616; dn. Chr. Ch. Dbln. 618; dn. Dry. 602; dn. Wford. 628
Maria, *see also* Mary
— I. and II., Q. Pgl. 88-9
— -Beatrix, D. Mda. 53
— -Louisa, D. Luc. 52
— -Louisa, D. Pma. 54
— -Louisa, Emp. Fr. 25
— -Theresa, E. Gmy. 62
— -Theresa, Q. Hgy. 60
Marie-Alexandra-Victoria (g. dau. Q. Victoria), Pr. E. 16
Marines, Hugh de, dn. St. P. 452
Marinus, *see also* Martin
— P. Ro. 33
Maris, Wm. de, dn. St. P. 452
Mareschall, *see* Marescall
Marischal, Earls, *see also* Marescall
— Wm., E., L.P.S. Sc. (1660) 501
— Geo., E., gen. (**B**) (1711) 864
Marisco, Geoffy. de, L.L. Ir. 550
— sir Jno. Fitz-Geoffr. de, L.J. Ir. 550
— Rd. de, B. Ex. 382; bp. Dham. 478; Jy. 364; Ld. Chanc. 353
— Wm de S., bp. Llff. 449
Mariscis, Rt. de, dn. Linc 448
Marius, C. (7), C. Ro. 45
Marjoribanks and **Majoribanks**
— Campb., Chn. E.I. Co. 645
— hon. Ed., Compt. H. 293; P.C. 220
— Jno., L. Prov. Edinb. 548
— Th. and sir T., Ld. Clk. Reg. 525; Ld. Sess. 518
Mark, *see* Marcus
Markby, Wm., K.C.I.E. 805
Markham, Fk., gen. (**D**) 887
— Geo., dn. Yk. 487
— Jno., adm. (**A**) 817; L. Admy. 180-1
— Jno., J.C.P. 378; S.L. 407
— Jno. and sir J., C.J.K.B. 370; J.K.B. 371; K.B. 756; S.L. 407
— sir Jno., Lt. T.L. 321
— Rt., K.B. 757
Markham—*cont.*
— Wm., abp. Yk. 486; bp. Chest. 477; dn. Chr. Ch. Oxf. 457; dn. Roch. 461; P.C. 203
Markland, Jno. D. and sir J., adm. (**H**) 844; K.C.H. 789
Marlay and **Marley**
— Geo., bp. Drom. 605
— Rd., bp. Wford. and L. 627; bp. Clonf. and K. 636; dn. Ferns, 623
— Th., A.G. Ir. 588; C.B. Ex. Ir. 583; C.J.K.B. Ir. 578; S.G. Ir. 589
— Th., gen. (**C**) 875
Marlebergh, Th. de, K.B. (1324) 754
Marlborough, E. and D. of
Ley Family.
— Jas., 3rd E. of, form. sir Jas. and ld. Ley, *q.v.*, B.T. 263
Churchill Family.
— Jno., 1st E. and D. of, form. ld. Churchill, *q.v.*, C. Ch. 855; Capt. Gen. 855; K.G. 741; M.G.O. 258; P.C. 193-4
— Ch., 3rd D. of and 5th E. of Sunderland, gen. (**A**) 857; K.G. 741; L.S.H. 290; L.P.S. 241; M.G.O. 259; P.C. 199
— Geo., 4th D. of, K.G. 742; L.C.H. 295; L.L. Oxon. 311; L.P.S. 241; P.C. 201
— Geo., 6th D. of, L.L. Oxon. 311
— Jno. Winst., 7th D. of, Jud. Com. P.C. 361; K.G. 745; L.L. Ir. 558; L.L. Oxon. 311; L.P.C. 188; L.S.H. 290; P.C. 217
— Sarah, Dss. of, Gr. St. and M. Robes. 303
Marley, *see* Marlay
Marlow, Benj., adm. (**A**) 815
— Wm. Bidd., gen. (**D**) 897
Marlowe, Rd., L.M. Lond. 489
Marmion, Rt., J. It. 366; Jy. 363
Marmont, Off. Nap. 26
Marmora, Genl., G.C.B. 769
Marney, sir Hy., aft. 1st ld. M., C.D.L. 242; C.Y.G. 298; K.B. 759; K.G. 737; L.P.S. 240
Marnia, *see* Mareyn
Marny, Hugh de, dn. St. P. 452
Maroffe, Mart., Cal. P.A. 342; R. Dr. P.A. 338; Yk. H. 334
Marowe, Wm., L.M. Lond. 490
Marquis, Jas., gen. (**D**) 925
Marr, E. of, *see* Mar
Marriott, Hayes, gen. (**D**) 901
— Jas. and sir J., J. Adm. Ct. 423; K. Adv. 422
— Rand., gen. (**C**) 873
— Th., gen. (**C**) 872
— Th. Beck. F., gen. (**D**) 903
— Wm. Fk., gen. (**D**) 909
— Wm. Thad. and sir W., J.A.G. 937; P.C. 220; Q.C. 419
Marryat, Jos. Hy., adm. (**H**) 851
— Saml., K.C. 416
Marrow, Th., S.L. 408
Marsack, Arth. Bech., gen (**D**) 927

For List of Abbreviations, see pp. 944-952.

Marsden, Alexr., C. Exc. Ir 566; U.S. Ir. 563
— Saml. Ed., bp. Bhurst., N.S.W. 704
— Wm,. Sec. Adm. 186-7
— Wm. Ed., gen. (**D**) 931
Marsh, Digby, adm. (**G**) 842
— Fras., abp. Dbln. and Gl. 616; bp. Ard. 608; bp. Kilm. and Ard. 607; dn. Arm. 597; dn. Cnr. 605
— Herb., bp. Llff. 449; bp. Pboro. 458
— Jas., gen. (**A**) 859
— Jerem., dn. Kilm. 609
— Jno. Barling, adm. (**H**) 850
— Narc., abp. Arm. 596; abp. Dbln. and Gl. 616; abp. Cash. and Eml. 626; bp. Ferns and L. 622; L.J. Ir. 555
— Ralph de, J. It. 368
— Rd., dn. Yk. 487
— Wm. Hy. and sir W., G. H. Kong, 673; K.C.M.G. 798
Marshal and **Marshall,** *see also* Marescall
— Anthy., gen. (**D**) 890
— sir Chapm., L.M. Lond. 492
— Dyson, K.C.B. 775
— Fk., gen. (**D**) 918
— Geo., K.H. 792
— Geo. W., R. Cr. P.A. 336
— sir Hy., L.M. Lond. 491
— Hy., bp. Exr. 436; dn. Yk. 486
— Hub., gen. (**D**) 900
— Jno., bp. Llff. 449
— Jno., K.H. 790
— Jno.. L.M. 325
— Jno., Ld. Sess. 521
— Jno., Pres. Coll. Surg. 939
— sir Jno., adm. (**D**) 829; K.C.H. 788
— Josiah, gen. (**D**) 876
— Rd., dn. Chr. Ch. Oxf. 457
— Rt., J.C.P. Ir. 582; S.L. Ir. 592
— Saml., J. Chest. 387; S.L. 412
— Th., dn. Glr. 440
— Th. H., C.C.J. 403
— Wm., aft. 2nd E. of Pembroke, *q.v.*, L.M. (1199) 325
— Wm. Bainbr., gen. (**D**) 911
— Wm. Hy., gen. (**D**) 888
Marsham, Hy. Shov. Jones, adm. (**H**) 847
Marston, *see also* Merston
— Ed. Cl., gen. (**D**) 915
Martel, Ph., M. Chy. 393
Marten, *see also* Martin
— Alfr. Geo., Q.C. 419
— Fras., adm. (**H**) 851
— Harry, C.I.E. 807
— Hy., *see* Martin
Marter, Rd. Jas. Combe, gen. (**D**) 935
Martimprey, Genl. de, K.C.B. 778
Martin, *see also* Marten and Martyn
— bp. Arg. 537
— bp. Killa. 612
— K. Arr. 86
— I. and II., K. Scy. 56
— I. to V., P. Ro. 33-4-5
— Anthy., bp. Mth. 599; dn. Wford. 628
— Anthy. Geo., gen. (**B**) 866
— Arth. Geo., gen. (**C**) 872
— Edm., dn. Worc. 473
— Ed., dn. Ely, 435
Martin—*cont.*
— Fras., Bl. M. P.A. 337; Clar. K.A. 328; Norr. K.A 330; Winds. H. 332
— sir Geo., adm. (**A**) 817; (**B**) 821; (**C**) 822; G.C.B. 768; G.C.M.G. 794; K.C.B. 773
— Hy., K.C. 415
— Hy., M. Chy. 397
— (or Marten), Hy. and sir H., Ch. Lond. 422; D. Arch. 420; J. Adm. Ct. 423; J. Pr. Ct. 421
— sir Hy., Compt. N. 257
— Hy. Byam and sir H., adm. (**D**) 830; K.C.B. 777
— Jno., gen. (**C**) 872
— Jno., gen. (**D**) 883
— Jno., J.C.P. 378; S.L. 407
— Lom., S.L. 412
— Moel, bp. Kild. 616
— Nathl., C. Exc. 278
— Pet., J.C.P. Ir. 581
— Ph., gen. (**A**) 860
— Rd., bp. St. Dav. 464
— Rd., bp. Wford and L. 627
— Rd., C. Acc. Ir. 567
— Rd., Rec. Lond. 494
— sir Rd., L.M. Lond. 491; M.M. 246
— Rd. Junr., M.M. 246
— sir Rog., L.M. Lond. 490
— Saml., Sec. Tr. 163
— Saml. and sir S., B. Ex. 385; Jud. Com. P.C. 361; P.C. 218; Q.C. 417; S.L. 413
— Theod., K.C.B. 783
— Th., gen. (**D**) 885; K.H. 792
— Th., adm. (**G**) 841
— Th. Byam and sir T., adm. (**A**) 818; (**B**) 821; (**C**) 822; Compt. N. 257; G.C.B. 768; K.C.B. 774
— Hutch. Mang., adm. (**H**) 852
— Wm., adm. (**A**) 814
— Wm. Fansh. and sir W., adm. (**C**) 822; (**D**) 830; G.C.B. 770; K.C.B. 779; L. Admy. 184
Martindell, Gabr., K.C.B. 775
Martineau, Alf., C.C.J. 405
Martinez, T., Pres. Nic. 106
Martinier, Th., G. I. Man, 666
Martival, Rog. de, dn. Linc. 448; bp. Sal. 467
Martley, Hy., Land. J. Ir. 587
Marton, Jno. de, M. Chy. 393
— Wm. de, count, gen. (**C**) 871
Martyn, *see also* Martin
— Dav., bp. St. Dav. 464
— Edm., M. Chy. 394
— J., dn. Bgr. 426
— Rd., C. St. 283
— Rd., M. Chy. 394
— Wm., J. It. 369
*— Wm., K.B. 759
*— Wm., L.M. Lond. 490
* Poss. same pers.
Martyns, *see* Mertins
Mary (of Hanover), Prss., Cr. Ind. 810
— (dau. Stephen), Pr. E. 9
— (dau. Edw. I.), Pr. E. 10
— (dau. Edw. III.), Pr. E. 10
— (dau. Edw. IV.), Pr. E. 12
— (dau. Hy. VII.), Pr. E. 12
— (dau. Hen. VIII.), Pr. E. 12; aft. Q.E. *vide infra*
Mary—*cont.*
— (dau. Jas. I.), Pr. E. 13
— (dau. of Ch. I.), Pr. E. 13
— (dau. Q. Anne) (2) Pr. E. 14
— (dau. Jas. II.), Pr. E. 13
— (dau. Geo. II.), Pr. E. 14
— (dau. Geo. III.), Pr. E. 15
— (de Bohun), Q.C.E. 7
— (of Modena), Q.C.E. 8
— (2) Q.E. 5-6
— Q. Hgy. 60
— Q. Sc. 19
— Q. Scy. 56
— (of Aus.), R. Nds. 82
— -Adel.-Wilh.-Eliz. (g. dau. Geo. III.), aft. Dss. Teck, Pr. E. 15; Cr. Ind. 809
— -Anne (of Aus.), R. Nds. 83
— -Christina, R. Nds. 83
— -Eliz., R. Nds. 83
— -Vict. (g. dau. Q. Victoria), Pr. E. 16
Maryborough, Wm., ld., form. Hon. W. Wellesley-Pole, *q.v.*, aft. E. of Mornington, *q.v.*, G.C.H. 786; L.T. 160; M.B.H. 303; Postm. G. 238
Masca, Pand., bp. Norw. 454; Const. T.L. 320
Mascareen, Paul., gen. (**C**) 871
Maschal, Rt., bp. Her. 441
Mascoed, abp. St. Dav. 463
Maseres, Fras., Curs. B. Ex. 386
Masham, Fras. C., M. Chy. and Acct. G. 396
— Saml., *see* ld. M., *infra*,
Masham, lds.
— Saml., aft. ld. M. Coff. H., 293
Maskelyne, Nev., Astr. Roy. 941
Maso, C. P., C. Ro. 43
Mason, Ch. Cr., gen. (**D**) 915
— Chr., adm. (**A**) 816
— Edm., dn. Sal. 468
— Fras. and sir F., adm. (**D**) 825; K.C.B. 777
— Geo., adm. (**H**) 851
— Geo., bp. S. and M., 484
— sir Jno., dn. Winch. 471
— Jno. Monk, C. Cus. Ir. 565; C. Exc. Ir. 566; C. Treas. Ir. 560
— Rt., Rec. Lond. 494
— Th. Hy., adm. (**E**) 835; (**F**) 838
Massena, Off. Nap. 26
Massereene and **Ferrard,** visc.
— Jno. Skeff., visc. (succ. 1831), K.P. 751
— Clotw. Jno. E., visc. (succ. 1863), L.L. Louth, 570
Massey and **Massy**
— Ch., dn. Lim. 640
— Jno., dn. Chr. Ch. Oxf. 457
— Wm. Godf. Dunh., gen. (**D**) 930
— Wm. N., P.C. 217; U.S. Home, 228
Massey - Beresford, *see* Beresford
Massie, Th. Leeke, adm. (**D**) 832; (**F**) 838
Massingberd, Vinc. Amc., adm. (**H**) 849
Masson, Louis Fras. Rod., G. Queb. 694
Massy, *see* Massey
Master, Jas., adm. (**D**) 825

For List of Abbreviations, see pp. 944-952.

Masters, —, G. Tob. 723
Masullo, Criss., Prel. M.G. 799
Mathair, Concen, bp. Emly, 625
Matham, Wm., L.T. 154
Mathew, *see* Matthew
Matheson, Don., K.C.B. 784
— sir Jas., L.L. Ross. 512
— Th., gen. (**D**) 893
Matho, M. P. (2), C. Ro. 43
Matilda, *see also* Maud
— D. Tny. 37
— (of Boulogne), Q.C.E. 7
— (of Flanders), Q.C.E. 7
— (of Scotland), Q.C.E. 7
Matson, Ed., gen. (**D**) 891
— Rd., adm. (**A**) 820
Matsoyker, Jno., G. Ceyl. 672
Mattei, Ant., gen. (**D**) 916
Matthæus (or Machabæus), bp. Ross. 535
Matthew and **Mathew**
*— bp. Cloy. 630
*— bp. Kilmacd. 636
*— bp. Ross, 631
*— bp. W'ford. 626
*— (2) dn. Chich. 433
* Prob. some same pers. Comp. dates.
— I. and II., D. Lne. 29
— Brownl. Hugh, gen. (**D**) 929
— Ed., G. Gren. 724; gen. (**A**) 859
— Geo. B. and sir G., Amb. Arg. 136; Amb. Bzl. 135; Amb. C. Am. 134; Amb. Pgy. 136; Amb. U.S.C. 134; K.C.M.G. 797
— Geo. Benv., G. Bah. Isl. 716
— Geo. Felt, C.I.E. 807
— Hy. Jas., bp. Lhore, 655
— Jas. Ch. and sir J., J. Q.B.D. 374
— Jno., L.M. Lond. 490
— hon. Mont., gen. (**B**) 867
— Tob., abp. Yk. 486; bp. Dham. 479; dn. Chr. Ch. Oxf. 457; dn. Dham. 479
— sir Wm. (No. 1), G. Leew. Isl. 727
— Wm. (No. 2), G. Leew. Isl. 727
Matthews, Hy., H. Sec. 227; P.C. 221; Q.C. 418
— Hy. Mont., C.I.E. 808
— Hy. Wm., gen. (**D**) 906
— Rt., S.L. 413
— Th., adm. (**A**) 813
— Wilk., Q.C. 417
Matthias, E. Gmy. 62
— I. and II., K. Hgy. 60
— Emm., Amb. H. Tns. 120
Matthie, Jas., gen. (**D**) 896
Maturin, Gabr. Jas., dn. Kild. 619; dn. St. Patr. 618
— Pet., dn. Killa. 614
Malclerk or **Mauclerk,** Walt., bp. Carl. 475; J. It. 367; L.H.T. 152
Malduit, *see* Mauduit
Maud, *see also* Matilda (dau. Hy. I.), Pr. E. 9
— (dau. Stephen), Pr. E. 9
— (dau. Hy. II.), Pr. E. 9
— -Charl.-Mary-Vict. (g. dau. Q. Victoria), Pr. E. 15
— Cornw. Osw., gen. (**D**) 928
— Fk. Fras. and sir F., G.C.B. 771; gen. (**D**) 905; K.C.B. 81
Maud—*cont.*
— Geo. Ashl., K.C.B. 784
— Jas. Ashl., K.C.H. 789
— hon. Rt. Wm. Hy. dn. Clr. 598
— Wm., adm. (**D**) 826
Maudesley, Rt., G.I. Man. 666
Mauduit and **Malduit,**
— Jno., J. It. 366; Jy. 363
— Peers, R. Dr. P.A. 338; Winds. H. 331
— Rt., Jy. 364
— Wm., Jy. 363
Maugere, bp. Worc. 472
Maughold, bp. S. and M. 483
Mauhan, Ger., M.M. 245
Maule, Fras. K.H. 790
— hon. Fox, aft. 2nd ld. Panmure, and 11th E. of Dalhousie, *q.v.*, L.L. Forf. 510; P.C. 214; Pres. B.C. 254; Sec. at W. 234; U.S. Home, 227; V.P.B.T. 269
— Hy., bp. Cloy. 631; bp. Drom. 605; bp. Meath, 599; dn. Cloy. 633
— Hy. Barl., gen. (**D**) 931
— Jno., Bar. Ex. Sc. 524
— Jno. Bl., Q.C. 418
— hon. L., S.G.O. 260
— Wm. Hy. and sir W., B. Ex. 385; J.C.P. 380; Jud. Com. P.C. 361; K.C. 416; P.C. 216; S.L. 413
Mauleverer or Malyverer, A., K.B. 759
Mauley or Malo Lacu, Pet. de, J. It. 369
Mauley, lds.
— Pet., 7th ld., K.B. (1400) 755
Maunsell, Fk., gen. (**D**) 886
— Fk. Rd., gen. (**D**) 920
— Geo., dn. Llin. 624
— J., S. St. 222
— Th., gen. (**D**) 924
Mauntelle, Walt., K.B. 757
Maupin, Mons. de, G. Mtius. 683
Mauregato, K. Sp. 85
***Maurice,** abp. Cash. 624
*— bp. Ardf. and Agh. 639
*— bp. Arm. 595
*— (or Hy.), bp. Kilf. 635
*— bp. Kilm. 607
*— (of Blanchville), bp. Llin. 621
*— bp. Lond. 451; Ld. Chanc. 352
*— (2) bp. Ross. 631
*— (or Marcus), Ld. Chanc. Sc. 515
* Prob. some same pers. Comp. dates.
— El. Sxy. 78
— Emp. E.E. 50
— Lg. H. Csl. 72
— (g. son. Jas. I.), Pr. E. 13
— Pr. Or. 83
— (Pr. of Nassau), R. Nds. 83 K.G. 739
— Pr. (Ct. Pal. Rhine), K.G. 740
— Andr., dn. St. As. 463
— Ed., bp. Oss. 620
— Jas. Wilkes, adm. (**H**) 844
— Pet., dn. Bgr. 427
— Salm., adm. (**A**) 813
Mauritius (or Meuricus), bp. Bgr. 425
— bp. Dnbl. 532
— (or Maurus), dn. Arm. 597
Maurus, *see* Mauritius
Mawbey, Hy. Way., gen. (**D** 926
— Sebr., gen. (**B**) 869
Mawe, Leon., bp. B. and W 428
Mawley, *see* Mauley
Mawson, Ch., Chest. H. 331; R. Cr. P.A. 335
— Matth., bp. Chich. 433; bp. Ely, 435; bp. Llff. 449
— Rd., Ptc. P.A. 337; Winds. H. 331
Maxentius, Emp. Ro. 48
Maxey, Anthy., dn. Winds. 474
Maximianus, H., Emp. Ro. 48
Maximilian, A.D. Aus. 58
— El. Bva. 68
— Emp. Mex. 104
— K. Hgy. 60
— Wm. (iss. Jas. I.), Pr. E. 13
— I. and II., E. Gmy. 62
— I. (E. Gmy.), K.G. 737
— II. (E. Gmy.), K.G. 738
— -Emanuel, El. Bva. 68
— -Joseph I. and II., El. Bva. 68; K. Bva. 68
Maximinus, C. J. V., Emp. Ro. 47
Maximus, C. D. C., C. Ro. 42; Dt. Ro. 42
— C. M., C. Ro. 45
— M. V., C. Ro. 41-2
— M. V. L., C. Ro. 38
— M. V. V., Dt. Ro. 37
— P., Emp. W. E. 49
— P. C. D., C. Ro. 42
— P. S. G., C. Ro. 43; Dt. Ro. 43
— Q. F., C. Ro. 43, 45; C. Ro. 46
— S. C., C. Ro. 41, 42, 43
Maxse, Fk. Aug., adm. (**H**) 850
— Hy. Fitz-Berk., and sir H., G. Hlgld. 670; G. Newfd. 700; K.C.M.G. 797
Maxwell, Alexr., gen. (**D**) 903
— Arch. Montg., K.H. 791
*— Ch., G. Si. Le. (1811) 685
*— Ch., G. St. Xtr., &c. (1819) 727
* ? same pers.
*— Ch. Wm., G. Dnca. 730
*— Ch. Wm., gen. (**B**) 869; K.C.H. 789
* Prob. same pers.
— Ed., gen. (**B**) 866
— Ed. Herb., gen. (**D**) 905
— Geo., gen. (**D**) 898
— Geo. Cl., C. Cus. Sc. 504
— Geo. Vaughan, gen. (**D**) 903; K.C.B. 781
— hon. Hy., bp. Drom. 605; bp. Mth. 599; dn. Kilm. 609
— sir Herb. Eust., L.T. 162
— Hy. Ham., gen. (**D**) 907
— Jas., Sec. St. Sc. 502
— Jno., abp. Tm. 611; bp. Killa. and Ach. 613; bp. Ross. 536; Ld. Sess. 517
— Jno., G. Bah. Isl. 710
— sir Jno., Comm. Tr. Sc. 497-8; Ld. Sess. 520
— sir Jno., L.G.C. Sc. 506
— Jno. Balfour, adm. (**G**) 842
— Jno. Harl, gen. (**D**) 907
— sir Jno. Shaw, gen. (**B**) 867

Maxwell—*cont.*
— Rt., bp. Ard. 608; bp. Kilm. and Ard. 607; dn. Arm. 597
— Rt., bp. Ork. 535
— Rt., *see* ld. M., *infra*
— sir Murr., G. Pr. Ed. Isl. 699
— Patr., gen. (**D**) 914
— Wm., gen. (**D**) 910
— sir Wm., gen. (**A**) 860
— Wm. Rt., gen. (**D**) 901
— sir Wm. Stirling-, K.T. 749
Maxwell, lds.
— Rt., ld., L.H.A. Sc. (bet. 1502 and 1511) 499
— Rt., ld., Ld. Sess. (1541) 517
May, Ch. Hy., adm. (**H**) 851
— Geo. Aug. Ch., A.G. Ir. 589; C.J.Q.B. Ir. 578; Pres. Q.B.D. Ir. 578
— sir Hy., V.C.H. 296
— sir Humphry, C.D.L. 242; M.R. 388
— Jno. and sir J., K.C.B. 775; K.C.H. 787
— Rd. and sir R., Curs. B. Ex. 386; B. Ex. 384
— Th., Chest. H. 331; R. Dr. P.A. 338
— Th. Ersk., aft. ld. Farnborough, *q.v.*, K.C.B. 783; P.C. 220
— Wm., abp. Yk. 486; dn. St. P. 453
Mayart, Saml., J.C.P. Ir. 581
Maydenhithe, Jno. de, dn. Chich. 434
Maydenstune, *see* Maidstone
Mayes, Jenk., dn. Oss. 623
Mayhew, *see also* Maihewe
— (or Mayo), Rd.. bp. Her. 441
Maynard, Hy., Tell. Ex. 167
— Jno., K.B. 763
— Jno. and sir J., C.G.S. 357; S.L. 409-10
— Th., C. Cus. 274-5
— W., G. Nev. 730
Maynard, lds. and visc.
— Wm., 2nd ld., Compt. H. 292; P.C. 191
— Ch., 6th ld., aft. 1st visc., L.L. Suff. 312
— Hy., 3rd visc., L.L. Esx. 308
Mayne, *see also* Maine
— Edmd., gen. (**B**) 864
— Ed., J.C.P. Ir. 582; J.K.B. Ir. 579
— Jas. Edmd., gen. (**D**) 915
— Jno., gen. (**D**) 878
— Perry, adm. (**A**) 814
— Rd. and sir R., C.C.P. 261; K.C.B. 782
— Rd. Ch., adm. (**H**) 852
Maynewaring, *see* Mainwaring
Mayo, *see also* Mayhew
— Th., Pres. Coll. Ph. 938
Mayo, visc. and E. of
— Jno., 1st visc. and E. of, form. Jno. Bourke and ld. Naas, *q.v.*
— Jos. Deane, 3rd E. of, form. hon. J. D. Bourke, *q.v.*
— Jno., 4th E. of, form. ld. Naas, *q.v.*, L.C.H. 786
— Rd. Southw., 6th E. of, form. ld. Naas, *q.v.*, G.G. Ind. 649; K.P. 751
— Bl. Jul., Css. of, Cr. Ind. 809
Mayow, Geo. Wyn., gen. (**D**) 904
Mead and **Meade**
— Fk., gen. (**D**) 892
— Jas., G. Monts. 729
— hon. Jno., gen. (**B**) 869
— sir Jno., K.H. 789
— Jno. Michl. de C., gen. (**D**) 928
— Nathl., S.L. 411
— Rd. Jno. and sir R., C.I.E. 806; gen. (**D**) 923; K.C.S.I. 803
— hon. Rt., G. C.G.H. 679; gen. (**A**) 861
— Rt. Hy., Regr. M.G. 799; U.S.C. 236
— Rochr., K.H. 789
— Saml., C. Cus. 275-6
— Th., J.C.P. 378; S.L. 408
— Th., L.M. Dbln. 641
— Wm., dn. Cork, 632
Meadows, *see also* Medows
— Ed., C. Tx. 285
— sir Ph., B.T. 263; C. Exc. 279
Meagh and **Miagh**
— Wm., bp. Kild. 617; dn. Kild. 619
Meagher, Wm., L.M. Dbln. 642
Meales, *see* Meyler
Meares, Wm. Lew. Dev., gen. (**D**) 918
Mearns, D., Modr. K. Sc. 547
Meath, E. of
— Jno. Chambre, 10th E. of, K.P. 751; L.L. Dbln. 569
— Wm., 11th E. of, L.L. Wickl. 571
Meautis, sir Pet., G. Gsey. 668
Meaux, Nichs. de, bp. S. and M. 483
Mecklenburg-Strelitz, Hered. Gr. D. of, G.C.B. 773
For reigning Dukes see under their Christian names.
Medici, *see page* 57
Medicis, Jul. de, bp. Worc. 473
Medina, J. M., Pres. Hdas. 106
Medjid, S. Zr. 102
Medley, Hy., adm. (**A**) 814
— Jno., bp. Fcton. 696
— Jul. Geo., gen. (**D**) 927
Medlicott and **Medlycott**
— Jas., M. Chy. 396
Medows, *see also* Meadows
— Wm. and sir W., C.C. Bbay. 659; C.C. Mdras. 657; Comm. F. Ir. 564; G. Bbay. 659; G.G. Ind. 648; G. Mdras. 656; gen. (**A**) 859; K.B. 765
Medullinus, L. F. (2), C. Ro. 39
Mee, Ch. Hy., gen. (**D**) 899
Meeres, sir J., L. Admy. 175-6
Meeze, Geo., adm. (**A**) 813
Meggott, Rd., dn. Winch. 471
Mehemet Ali, V. Eg. 98
Meiklejohn, Hugh, Modr. K. Sc. 547
Mein, Geo., G. Trin. 722; gen. (**D**) 918
Melbourne, visc.
— Wm., 2nd visc., form. hon. Wm. Lamb, *q.v.*, H. Sec. 227; L.T. 160; Prem. 146-7
Melbourne, visc.—*cont.*
— F. J., 3rd visc., form. hon. F. J. Lamb, *q.v.*, and ld. Beauvale *q.v.*
Melchiades, P. Ro. 33
Melchuo, St., bp. Ard. 607
Melcombe, Geo., ld., form. G. Dodington, *q.v.*
Meldrum, Jas., Ld. Sess. 518
— Walt., bp. Brn. 531
Meleborne, Jord. de, dn. Chich. 433
Melfort, Jno., 1st visc. and E. of, form. Jno. Drummond, *q.v.*, K.T. 747; Sec. St. Sc. 502
Melgarejo, M., Pres. Bol. 109
Melhuish, *see also* Mellish
— Geo. Br., gen. (**D**) 911
Mell (St.), bp. Ard. 607
Meller, *see* Mellor
Mellersh, Arth., adm. (**H**) 849
Mellinet, Genl., K.C.B. 778
Mellish, *see also* Melhuish
— Ch., C. St. 284
— Ed., dn. Her. 442
— Geo. and sir G., Jud. Com. P.C. 361; L.J. App. 389; P.C. 218; Q.C. 418
— Rd., K.H. 790
*— Wm., C. Exc. 280
*— Wm., Sec. Tr. 163
* Prob. same pers.
Melliss, Geo. Jul., gen. (**D**) 931
Mellitus (or Miletus), (St.), abp. Cant. 429; bp. Lond. 45
Mellor and **Meller**
— Jno., M. Chy. 396
— Jno. and sir J., J.Q.B. 373; J.Q.B.D. 374; Jud. Com. P.C. 361; P.C. 919; Q.C. 417; S.L. 414
— Jno. Wm., J.A.G. 937; P.C. 221; Q.C. 419
Melross, *see* Hamilton
Melton, Wm. de, abp. Yk. 485; L.H.T. 153; L.K. 354; S. St. 222
Meluginensis, M. C., C. Ro. 39
— S. C. C., C. Ro. 37
Melun, Rt. de, bp. Her. 441
Melvill and **Melville**
— hon. Alexr., Comm. Tr. Sc. 497
— Hy., gen. (**D**) 931
— Jas. Cosm., K.C.B. 782
— Jno. and sir J., L. Prov. Edinb. 548
— Maxw., K.C.I.E. 805
— Pet. Melr., K.C.B. 782
— Rt., G. Gren. 724; G. St. Vin. 725; G. Tob. 723; gen. (**A**) 858; (**B**) 865
— sir Rt., Ld. Sess. 517
— Wm., Ld. Sess. 518
Melville, lds., visc. and E. of, *see also* Leven and Melville
Melville Family.
— Geo., 4th ld., aft. 1st E. of, H.C.P. Sc. 508; L.P.S. 501; Pres. P.C. Sc. 500; Sec. St. Sc 502
Dundas Family.
— Hy., 1st visc. form. H. Dundas, *q.v.*, L. Admy. 180 P.C. 203, 208; Pres. B.C. 252
— Rt. S., 2nd visc., K.T. 748; L. Admy. 181-2; L.P.S. Sc. 501; Pres. B.C. 253
— Hy., 3rd visc., G.C.B. 770; gen. (**D**) 884

Melwer, Conrad, M.M. 246
Memmius, C., C. Ro. 46
Mendip, Welbore, 1st ld., form. Welbore Ellis, *q.v.*
Mends, Geo. Clarke, adm. (**H**) 850
— Wm. Bower, adm. (**D**) 828; (**G**) 840
— Wm. Rt. and sir W., adm. (**F**) 839; G.C.B. 771; K.C.B. 780
Menendez, F., Pres. S. Salv. 106
— M., Pres. Pu. 109
Mensdorf, Ch., G.C.B. 769
— Ct. Alexr., K.C.B. 782
Menteith, E. of, *see also* Monteith
— Wm., E. of, L.J. Gen. (1628) 522; Ld. Sess. 517
Mento, C. J., C. Ro. 39
Menzies, Archd., C. Cus. Sc. 404
— Ch., gen. (**D** 883; K.C B. 779; K.H. 790
— Th., Compt. Sc. 498
— Wm. Coll., gen. (**D**) 909
Meones, Nichs., J.K.B. Ir. 578
Mepeham, Sim., abp. Cant. 430
Mepham, Rd., dn. Linc. 448
Merbury (or Marbury), Laur., D. Chanc. Ir. 575; L. Treas. Ir. 558
Mercer, Alexr., gen. (**A**) 860
— Alexr. C., gen. (**D**) 885
— Ch. McW., gen. (**D**) 920
— Dougl., gen. (**D**) 880
— Rt., gen. (**D**) 889
— Saml., adm. (**H**) 850
— Wm. T., G. H. Kong, 673
Mercier, Wm., bp. Cnr. 604
Merdyth, *see* Meredith
Mere, *see* Delamere
Meredith, Meredyth, and **Meridyth;** *see also* Meredydd
— (ab Owain), Pr. Wls. 17
— (ap Owen), Pr. Wls. 16
— (ap Owen), Pr. Wls. 17
— Ch., dn. Ardf. 640
— sir Ch., Ch. Ex. Ir. 562
— sir Hy., Ch. Ex. Ir. 562
— sir Hy., J. Admy. Ct. Ir. 587
— Jas., gen. (**A**) 862
— Rd., bp. Llin. 622; dn. St. Patr. 618
— Rd., dn. Wlls. 429
— sir Rt., Comm. Ir. 554
— Rog., M. Chy. 396
— Th., gen. (**B**) 864
— sir Wm., L. Admy. 179
— sir Wm., P.C. 203; Compt. H. 292
Meredith, lds.
— Wm., ld., form. ld. Somerville, *q.v.*
Meredydd, *see also* Meredith
— Pr. Wls. 17
— (ab Bleddyn), Pr. Wls. 17
— (ab Owain) (2), Pr. Wls. 16, 17
— (ap. Owain), Pr. Wls. 16
Merefield, Jno., S.L. 410
Merelay, Rog. de, J. It. 367
Merenda, T. A., Dec. Ro. 38
— S. C., C. Ro. 42
Meres, Rog. de, J.C.P. 378; J. It. 369; S.L. 407
Mereschall, *see* Marescall
Merewell, Hy. de, bp. Winch.
Merewether, Ch. Geo., Q.C. 419
— Hy. Alw., Q.C. 417; S.L. 413
— Jno., dn. Her. 442
— Wm. Lock. and sir W., K.C.S.I. 803; M.C.I. 647
Merewith, bp. Wells, 427
Merfyn, *see* Mervyn
Merick, *see* Merrick
Merington, Wm. de, A.G. 398
Merino, F. A. de, Pres. Dom. Rep. 105
Meriton, Geo., dn. Pboro. 458; dn. York, 487
Merivale, Ch., dn. Ely, 435
— Herm., U.S.C. 235; U.S. Ind. 236; U.S. W. and C. 232
Merkes, Th., bp. Carl. 475
Merlin, Ed., Ptc. P.A. 337
Merovæus, K. Fr. 22
Merrick and **Merick,** *see also* Meyrick
— Jno., bp. S. and M. 483
— Rowl., bp. Bgr. 426
— Wm., gen. (**C**) 871
— sir Wm., J. Pr. Ct. 421
Merriman, Ch. Jas., gen. (**D**) 924
— Jno., bp. Down and Cnr. 604
— N. J., bp. Gr. Tn. 680
Merry, Anth., Amb. Dk. 127; Amb. Fr. 112; Amb. Sw. 126; Amb. U.S.A. 132
— Wm., Dep. Sec. at W. 234
Mershton, *see* Merston
Merston, *see also* Marston
— Hy., B. Ex. 383
— (or Mershton), Wm. de, A.G. 398
Mertins (or Martyns), sir Geo., L.M. Lond. 491
Merton, Jno. de, M. Chy. 393
— (or Myrton), Th. de, L.H.T. Sc. 496
— Walt. de, bp. Roch. 459; Jy. 365; Ld. Chanc. 353; L.K. 353
— Wm. de, dn. Wells, 428
Merula, L. C., C. Ro. 43, 45
Mervin, Mervyn, and **Merfyn**
— K. Wls. 16
— Pr. Wls. 17
— sir Audl., S.L. Ir. 591
— Edm. or Edw., J.K.B. 372; S.L. 408
Merwe, Walt., M.M. 246
Messala, M. V., C. Ro. 43-4
— P. V., C. Ro. 47
Messenden, Rog. de, J.C.P. 377; Jy. 365
Messing, Rd., bp. Drom. 604
Messiter, Ed., gen. (**D**) 893
Messutaz-ud-Dowlah, &c., Pr. Min. of Kotah, K.C.S.I. 803
Mesurier, Augs. Le, C.I.E. 808
— Jno. Le, gen. (**B**) 870
— Jno. Le, gen. (**D**) 932
— Paul Le, L.M. Lond. 492
— Wm. Abrm. Le, gen. (**D**) 896
Metallanus, K. Sc. 18
Metcalfe, C. T., *see* ld. M., *infra*
— Th., C.D.L. 242
— Wm. Jas., C.C.J. 405; Q.C. 419
Metcalfe, lds.
— sir Ch. Theoph, aft. ld. M., G.C.B. 772; G. Can. 692; G.G. Ind. 649; G. Jam. 713; P.C. 213
Metellus, C. C., C. Ro. 45
— L. C., C. Ro. 42, 44, 45, 46; Dt. Ro. 43
— M. C., C. Ro. 45
— P. C., C. Ro. 45
— Q. C., C. Ro. 44-5-6; Dt. Ro. 43
Metford, *see* Mitford
Metge, Pet., B. Ex. Ir. 584; S.L. Ir. 592
Metham, Th., K.B. 759
Methuen, Methven, and **Methwen**
*— Jno., B.T. 263
*— Jno., Ld. Chanc. Ir. 576
*— Jno., M. Chy. 396
* Poss. same pers.
*— Jno., Sec. St. Sc. 501
*— sir Jno. Ld. Clk. Reg. 525
* Prob. same pers.
— Paul and sir P., Compt. H. 292; K.B. 764; Ld. Admy. 177; L.T. 156; P.C. 196; S. St. 224; Tr. H. 291
Methwold, Wm. and sir W., C.B. Ex. Ir. 583; L.K. Ir. 576; S.L. 409
Metingham, Jno. de, C.J.C.P. 375; J.K.B. 371; S.L. 406
Meuricus, *see* Mauritius
Meuron, Count C. D. de, gen. (**B**) 866
— Count Pierre F. de, gen. (**B**) 866
Mew or **Mews,** Pet., bp. B. and W. 428; bp. Winch. 471; dn. Roch. 461
Mexborough, Jno., E. of, form. Jno. Savile and ld. Pollington, *q.v.*
Mey, Jno., abp. Arm. 595; L.D. Ir. 552
— Jno., bp. Carl. 475
Meyden, Adr. Van der, G. Ceyl. 672
Meyler (or Meales), Wm., dn. Clonm. 600
Meynell, Edg. J., C.C.J. 405
— Hy., adm. (**D**) 829; (**G**) 840
— Rt., S.L. 408
Meyners, Rt. de, L.G.C. Sc. 506,
Meyrick, *see also* Merrick
— Augs. Wm. Hy., gen. (**D**) 918
— Geo., gen. (**B**) 867
— sir Saml. R., K.H. 790
— Th., gen. (**A**) 861
Meywar, Bah. of, G.C.S.I. 801
Miagh, *see* Meagh
Micallef, Ant. and sir A., G.C.M.G. 795; K.C.M.G. 796
***Michael,** bp. Clr. 596
*— bp. Gall, 538
*— bp. Isl. 539
*— (of Exeter), bp. Oss. 620
*— bp. S. and M. 483
* Prob. some same pers. Comp. dates.
— Emp. Tzde. 98
— I. and II., Pr. Tva. 60
— I. to III., Pr. Sva. 95
— I. to III., R. Russ. 89
— I. to VIII., Emp. E.E. 50-1
— -Fedorowitz, R. Russ. 90
— -Koributh-Wiesnowiski, K. Pld. 91

Michael—*cont.*
— Jas., gen. (**D**) 929
— Wm. Hy., Q.C. 419
Michel and **Michell,** *see also* Mitchell
— Ch. Ed., gen. (**D**) 895
— Geo., gen. (**A**) 861
— Jno., gen. (**A**) 862
— Jno. and sir J., Comm. F. Ir. 564; F. M. 856; G.C.B. 770; gen. (**D**) 893; K.C.B. 778
— Ch. Cornw., K.H. 791
— Fc. Th., adm. (**D**) 831; K.C.B. 779
— Hy., A.G. Ir. 588; C.B. Ex. Ir. 582; C.J.C.P. Ir. 580
— Jno., K.C.B. 779
— Jno „L.M. Lond. 490
— Jno., M. Chy. 395
— Jno. Ed., gen. (**D**) 922
Michelson, Borgard, gen. (**C**) 871
Michie, Archd., K.C.M.G. 797
— Jno., Chn. E.I. Co. 644
Micklejohn, *see* Meiklejohn
Micklem, Ed., gen. (**D**) 934
Micklethwaite, Th., L.G.O. 259; L.T. 156
Middlemore, Geo., G. Gren. 724; G. St. Hel. 682; gen. (**B**) 869
Middlesex, E. of, *see also* Dorset and M.
— Lion., E. of, form. ld. Cranfield, *q.v.*
— Ch., E. of, aft. 2nd D. of Dorset, *q.v.*, L.T. 157
Middleton, Midleton, and **Myddleton**
— Ad. de, J. It. 369
— Ch., gen. (**D**) 883
— Ch. and sir C., aft. 1st ld. Barham, *q.v.*, adm. (**A**) 815; Compt. 257; L. Admy. 180
— Chr., J. Adm. Ct. 422
— Fk. Dobs. and sir F., gen. (**D**) 928; K.C.M.G. 798
— sir Geo. Nat. Br., adm. (**G**) 843
— Jno. de, dn. Her. 442
— Jno. de, S.L. 407
— Marm., bp. St. Dav. 464; bp. Wford. and L. 627
— Pet. de, J. It. 369
— Rd., L.L. Denb. 314
— Rd. de, J.C.P. 377; Jy. 365; L.K. and Ld. Chanc. 353
— R. T. C., Amb. Vza. 135
— Th. de, M. Chy. 394
— sir Th., L.M. Lond. 491
— Th. Fansh., bp. Calc. 653
— Wm. de, B. Ex. 382
— Wm. de, bp. Norw. 454
Middleton, E. of
Middleton Family.
— Jno., 1st E. of, H.C.P. Sc. 507; Ld. Sess. 517; P.C. 190
— Ch., 2nd E. of, Ld. Sess. 517; P.C. 192; S. St. 224; Sec. St. Sc. 502
Midleton, visc.
Brodrick Family.
— Alan, 1st visc., form. ld. Brodrick, *q.v.*, L.J. Ir. 556
— Geo., 4th visc., L.L. Surr. 312
— Wm. Jno., 7th visc., form. hon. W. J. Brodrick, *q.v.*
Middylton, *see* Middleton
Midleton, *see* Middleton
Miecislas, I., D. Pld. 90; K. Pld. 90-1
Mighells, Jas., adm. (**A**) 813; Compt. N. 257
Miguel, K. Pgl. 89
Milan IV., K. Sva. 95
— Fras. Sf., D. of, K.G. 736
Milbanke and **Millbanke**
— Jno., C. Cus. Ir. 565
— Jno. Ralph, aft. sir J. R. Milbanke-Huskisson, *q.v.*, Amb. Aus. 117; Amb. Bva. 119; Amb. G. St. 122; Amb. Nds., &c., 123; Amb. Russ. 126
— Mark, adm. (**A**) 815; G. Newfd. 700
Milborne, sir Jno., L.M. Lond. 490
Milbourne, Rd., bp. Carl. 475; bp. St. Dav. 464; dn. Roch. 461
Mildmay, Benj., C. Exc. 279
— sir Wm., Ch. Ex. 154
Miles, Ch. Wm., gen. (**D**) 912
— Jno., gen. (**D**) 930
— Josh., gen. (**D**) 916
— Wm., gen. (**D**) 888
Miletus, *see* Mellitus
Milford, Sussex Ch., gen. (**D**) 918
Milford, lds.
1st Creation.
— Rd., 1st ld., form. sir R. Phillipps, *q.v.*, L.L. Pemb. 316
2nd Creation.
— Rd. B., 1st ld., form. R. B. Phillipps, *q.v.*
Millar, *see also* Miller
— Arth., bp. Edinb. 542; Pr. Bp. Sc. 540
— Fk. Ch. Jas., Q.C. 419
— J., gen. (**C**) 874
— Jno., Jy. Sc. 523; Ld. Sess. 521; S.G. Sc. 527
— Jno. Cr., gen. (**D**) 918
— Wm., gen. (**B**) 869
Millars, Wm. de, Const. W. Cast. 322
Millbanke, *see* Milbanke
Miller, *see also* Millar
—, K.C. 414
— Alexr. Ed. and sir A., Q.C. 419
— Coombe, dn. Chich. 434
— Dav., adm. (**H**) 852
— Ed., S.L. 411
— Ed. Ev., gen. (**D**) 916
— Geo. Murr., gen. (**D**) 925
— Hy., gen. (**D**) 927
— Hy. Matth., adm. (**H**) 853
— Jas., gen. (**D**) 931
— Jno., gen. (**C**) 874
— Jno., K.C. 416
— sir Jno., Chambn. Ex. 166
— Rt., C.C.J. 404; S.L. 413
— Stearne B., J. Bank. Ir. 587
— Th., adm. (**E**) 836, (**F**) 839
— Th., R. Dr. P.A. 337
— Th. and sir T., L.J. Clk. 516; L.P. Ct. Sess. 516; Ld. Adv. 526; Ld. Sess. 529
— Wm., C.I.E. 807
— Wm., K.H. 792
— Wm., *see* Millar
— sir Wm., Ld. Sess. 520
— Wm. Hy., gen. (**D**) 896
Milles, *see also* Mills
— Jer., dn. Exr. 438
— Th., bp. Wford. and L. 627
— Th., gen. (**D**) 914
— Th., K.C. 415
Milligan, Wm., Modr. K. Sc. 547
Milling, Th., bp. Her. 441
Millington, Fras., C. Cus. 273
— Jno., S.L. 410
Mills, *see also* Milles
— Ch., Chn. E.I. Co. 645
— Ch., M.C.I. 646
— Ch., K.C.M.G. 798
— Ch. Jas. Conw., gen. (**D**) 905
— Hy., gen. (**D**) 914
— Hy., Q.C. 418
— Rt. Wm., gen. (**D**) 882
Milman, Egerton Ch. Wm. Miles, gen. (**D**) 897
— sir Fras., Pres. Coll. Ph. 938
— Fras. Miles, gen. (**D**) 880
— Geo. Br., gen. (**D**) 909
— Gustavus Ham. L., gen. (**D**) 914
— Hy. Hart, dn. St. P. 453
— Rt., bp. Calc. 653
Milne, *see also* Mylne
*— Alexr., C.W.F. &c. 272
*— Alexr. and sir A., adm. (**B**) 821; (**D**) 832; (**E**) 834; G.C.B. 770; L. Admy. 183-4; K.C.B. 779, 782
* ? same pers.
— Alexr., L.P. Ct. Sess. 516
— sir Dav., adm. (**A**) 819; G.C.B. 769; K.C.B. 775
— Hy., gen. (**D**) 909
— sir Jno., G. Gsey. 668
Milner, *see also* Mylner
— Geo., gen. (**A**) 860
— Hy. Rt., gen. (**D**) 889
— Is., dn. Carl. 476
Milnes, Jno., Sec. Adm. 187
— Rt. Monckton, aft. ld. Houghton, *q.v.*
Milo (of Dunstable), bp. Ard. 607
Milosch, I. and II.. Pr. Sva. 95
Milred, bp. Lindisf. 478
— bp. Worc. 472
Milton, Chr. and sir Chr., B. Ex. 384; J.C.P. 379; S.L. 411
— Wm., dn. Chich. 434
Milton, visc.
Damer Family.
— Geo., visc., aft. 2nd E. of Dorchester, *q.v.*, Ch. Sec. Ir. 563; P.C. 206
Fitzwilliam Family.
— Wm. Th. Sp., visc., aft. 6th E. Fitzwilliam, *q.v.*, L.L. Yorks, W.R. 313
Miltown, Jos., 4th E. of, K.P. 751
Milvani, Th., Q.C. 420
Milward, Clem., adm. (**H**) 845
— Clem., Q.C. 418
— Rt., J. Chest. 387
— Rt., L.P.S. 240
— Th. and sir T., J. Chest. 386; S.L. 409
Minant, Hugh, bp. Lich. and Cov. 443
Minchin, Humphr., Clk. O. 260
— Paul, adm. (**A**) 817
Minet, Wm., gen. (**B**) 868
Mingaye, Wm. Jas., adm. (**D**) 829; (**G**) 840
Mings, sir Chr., adm. (**A**) 813
Minot, Th., abp. Dbln. and Gl. 616; dn. St. Pat. 61

Minto, lds., visc., and E. of
— Gilb.. 1st ld., visc. and E. of, form. sir G. Elliott, *q.v.*, Amb. Gmy. 117; G.G. Ind. 648; Pres. B.C. 252
— Gilb., 2nd E. of, Amb. Pr. 118; Amb. Scy. 115; Amb. Sda. 114; Amb. Swz. 113; Amb. Tusc., &c. 115; G.C.B. 772; L. Admy. 182-3; L.P.S. 241; P.C, 212
— Wm. Hugh, 3rd E. of, K.T. 749
Mir, Humayun, &c., C.I.E. 806
Miramon, M., Pres. Mex. 104
Mirehouse, Jno., Comm. Serjt Lond. 495
Miremont, M. of, gen. (**B**) 864
Mirfield, Wm. de, M. Chy. 393
Mirfine, Th., L.M. Lond. 490
Miscelus, bp. Emly, 625
Missenden, Jas., S.L. 408
Mitcham, Sim. de, dn. Sal. 468
Mitchell, *see also* Michel and Michell
—, —, M. Chy. 395
— Alexr. F., Mod. K. Sc. 547
— Andr. and sir A., adm. (**A**) 816; K.B. 766
— Andr. and sir A., Amb. Pr. 117; K.B. 765
— Arth., K.C.B. 784
— capt. —, G. Br. Hond. 714
— Ch. Bull. H. and sir C., G. Fiji, 711; G. Leew. Isl. 728; G. W. Pacif. 711; K.C.M.G, 798
— Dav., bp. Abdn. 530
— sir Dav., adm. (**A**) 813; L. Admy. 176-7
— Jno., gen. (**D**) 886
— Jno., gen. (**D**) 890
— Jno., gen. (**D**) 899
— Jno. Wr., gen. (**D**) 898
— sir Michl., L.M. Dbln. 640
— Pet., C.I.E. 807
— Rt., adm. (**A**) 814
— Wm. and sir Wm., adm. (**A**) 818; K.C.B. 773
Mitchinson, J., bp. Bdoes. 721
Mitford, sir Jno., aft. 1st ld. Redesdale, *q.v.*, A.G. 400; K.C. 415; Ld. Chanc. Ir. 577; P.C. 206; S.G. 402; Sp. H.C. 250
— Regd. C. W., gen. (**D**) 930
*— Rd., bp. Chich. 433; bp. Sal. 467; L. Treas. Ir. 558
*— (or Metford), Rd., bp. St. Dav. 464
* ? same pers.
— Rt., adm. (**H**) 844
— Rt., C. Tx. 285
— Walt., dn. Wells, 429
Mitre, B., Pres. Arg. 110; Pres. B. Ay: 110
Miza, Abbas Khan, C.I.E. 807
Moberly, Arth. Sc., gen. (**D**) 920
— Fras. Jno., gen. (**D**) 920
— Geo., bp. Sal. 467
Mocher, Flower, gen. (**A**) 858
Mocholmoc, *see* Colman
Mochuan, *see* Dachuan
Mocoach, bp. Saig. 620
Moctean, bp. Cld. 598
Modesley, Th., dn. Chest. 477
Modiford, Th. and sir T., G. Bdoes. 719; G. Jam. 712
Mœdogair, bp. Ferns, 621
Mœl-Brigid (or Brigidian), bp. Arm. 595; bp. Emly, 625; bp. Rph. 601
Mœlcob, bp. Arm. 595
Mœldarius, bp. Clonm. 599
Mœldoborean, bp. Kild. 616
Mœles, Jno. de, K.B. 755
***Mœlisa,** abp. Arm. 595; bp. Clr. 596
*— I., bp. Arm. 595
*— bp. Clr. 596
*— (O'Dorigh), bp. Rph. 601
* Prob. some same pers. Comp. dates.
Mœller, Jno. Geo. L., Sec. Guelph, 792
Mœlmorda, bp. Emly, 625
Mœlmury, bp. Arm. 595
Mœlpatrick, bp. Arm. 595
Mœls, Nichs. de, W.C.P. 317
Mœna (St.), bp. Clonf. 635
Mœngal, bp. Kild. 616
Moeran, Edw. B., dn. Down. 605
Moffat, Augs. K., gen. (**D**) 914
— Nichs. de, bp. Glasg. 536
Mogaldus, K. Sc. 18
Mohamed, *see* Mahomed
Mohesh, Chandra Nyaratna, C.I.E. 807
Mohun and **Moyun**
— sir Jno., K.G. 733
— Regd. de, J.C.P. 376; Jy. 364
— Ch., 5th ld., gen. (**B**) 864
Moigne, *see* Moygne
Moir, Alexr. Wils., G. Virg. Isl. 731
— Dav., bp. Brn. 541
Moira, Fras., E. of, aft. 1st M. of Hastings, *q.v.*, C.C. Ind. 650; Const. T.L. 321; G.G. Ind. 648; gen. (**A**) 859; K.G. 743; M.G.O. 259; P.C. 207
Molend, Rog. de; *see* Longespee, Rog. de
Moleston, Adam de, K.B. 754
Molesworth, Arth., gen. (**D**) 876
— Guilf. Linds., C.I.E. 806; K.C.I.E. 805
— Hender, G. Jam. 712
— Hickm. Th., gen. (**D**) 911
— Jno., *see* visc. M., *infra*
— Rd., *see* visc. M., *infra*
— Rd. C., gen. (**D**) 891
— Rt., *see* visc. M., *infra*
— sir Wm., C. Sec. 234; C.W.P.B. 272; P.C. 216
— Wm. Jno., *see* visc. M., *infra*
Molesworth, visc.
— Rt., aft. 1st visc. M., B.T. 264
— Jno., aft. 2nd visc. M., C. St. 283
— Rd., 3rd visc., F.M. 856; gen. (**A**) 857
— Rt., aft. 5th visc. M., C. Cus. Ir. 566
— Wm. Jno., 6th visc., gen. (**C**) 874
Moleton, sir Th. de, L.H.A. 170
Moleyns, *see also* Molins
— Towns. Aremb. de, gen. (**D**) 931
Molibba (or Libba), bp. Glend. 615
Molin (St.), bp. Ferns, 621
Molineux, *see* Molyneux
Molins (or Moleyns), Ad., bp. Chich. 433; dn. Sal. 468
Mollo, K.E. 2
Moloney, C. P., gen. (**D**) 922
— Corn. Alf., G. Gamb. 686; G. Gld. Cst. Col. 687; G. Lag. 687
Molteno, Jno. Ch., K.C.M.G. 798
Molyneux, Molineux, and **Molyneaux**
— Danl., Ulst. K.A. 372
— Edm. and sir E., J.C.P. 378; K.B. 760; S.L. 408
— hon. Fras. Geo., Amb. G. St. 122
— Rt., G. I. Man, 666
— Rt. Hy. Moore and sir R., adm. (**E**) 837; K.C.B. 781
— S., L. Admy. 177
— Th., Ch. Ex. Ir. 561
— sir Th., gen. (**B**) 868
— Wm. Ch. F., gen. (**D**) 934
Mona, Guy de, bp. St. Dav. 464; L.H.T. 153
Monagas, J. T., Pres. Vzla. 107-8
Monahan, Jas. Hy., A.G. Ir. 588; C.J.C.P. Ir. 581; S.G. Ir. 590
Monarchus, Geoff., Jy. 363
Moncell, *see also* Monsell
— Nichs., dn. Ferns, 623
Moncey, Off. Nap. 26
Monck, *see also* Monk
— Geo., aft. 1st D. of Albemarle, *q.v.*, adm. (**A**) 813; L.T. 154-5; P.C. 189; Prem. 140
— hon. Rd., gen. (**D**) 921
Monck, lds. and visc.
— ld., *see* Albemarle
— Ch. Stanl., 4th visc., G.C.M.G. 795; G. Can. 692; G.G. Can. 692; L.L. Dbln. 569; L.T. 161; P.C. 218
Monckton, Hy., gen. (**A**) 863
— Rt., B.T. 263-4
— hon. Rt., gen. (**B**) 865
Moncreiffe and **Moncrieffe**
— Col. Campb. Sc., K.C.M.G. 798
— Dav. Stewart, Bar. Ex. Sc. 524
— Geo., gen. (**A**) 861
— Geo., gen, (**D**) 892
— Geo. Hay, gen. (**D**) 934
— Hy. J., Ld. Sess. 521
— Jas., *see* ld. M., *infra*
— sir Jas. W., D. Fac. Sc. 527; Jy. Sc. 523; Ld. Sess. 520
— Rd., L.M. Dbln. 641
Moncrieff, lds.
— Jas., aft. ld. M., D. Fac. Sc. 527; L.J. Clk. 516; Ld. Adv. 526; P.C. 218; S.G. Sc. 527
Monday, *see also* Munday
— Jno., adm. (**H**) 847
Moneda, Pedr. de la, G. Trin. 721
Money, archd., gen. (**D**) 881
— Ernle Ky., gen. (**D**) 910
— sir Jas. Kyrle, gen (**C**) 875
— Jno., gen. (**A**) 860
— Rt. Cott., gen. (**D**) 929
— Rowl., adm. (**H**) 845
— Wm. Tayl., K.H. 789
Monin, Anthy., gen. (**D**) 878
Monins, Eaton, gen. (**D**) 885
— Matth., K.B. 763
Monk, *see also* Monck
— Jas. Hy., bp. Glr. and Br. 439; dn. Pboro. 458

For List of Abbreviations, see pp. 944-952.

Monk—*cont.*
—— Jno., Q.C. 417
—— Nichs., bp. Her. 442
Monk-Bretton, Jno. Geo., ld., form. J. G. Dodson, *q.v.*
Monkhouse, R. P., ld., form. R. P. Collier, *q.v.*
Monmouth, Jno. de, bp. Llff. 449
—— Jno. de, J. It. 367
Monmouth, E. and D. of; *refer also to* Buccleugh *and to* Peterborough
—— Jas., D. of (*see also* James), K.G. 740; M.H. 302; P. 191; C. Ch. 855; Ld. Admy. 175; capt. gen. 855; L.G.C. Sc. 506; Pr. E. 13; P.C. 191
—— Ch., E. of, form. 2nd visc. Mordaunt, *q.v.*, also E. of Peterborough, *q.v.*
Monoux, Geo., L.M. Lond. 490
Monro and **Monroe,** *see also* Munro
—— Alexr., bp. Arg. 538
—— Hect., K.B. 765
—— Jas., Pres. U.S.A. 102
—— Jno., L.J. App. Ir. 586; S.G. Ir. 590
Monsell, *see also* Moncell
—— Wm., aft. ld. Emly, *q.v.*, Clk. O. 260; L.L. Lim. 570; P.C. 216; Paym. G. 245; Postm. G. 239; Pres. B.H. 255; U.S.C. 235; V.P.B.T. 269
Monson, hon. Ch., gen. (**C**) 872
—— hon. Edm. Jno., amb. Arg. 136; amb. Dk. 127; amb. Pgy. 136; amb. Ugy. 137; K.C.M.G. 798
—— Jno., K.B. 763
—— Jno., *see* ld. M., *infra*
—— Rt., J.C.P. 378; S.L. 408
Monson, lds.
—— Jno., aft. 1st ld., K.B. 764; P.C. 198; Pres. B.T. 264
—— Wm. Jno., 7th ld., C.Y.G. 298; P.C. 218; Tr. H. 292
Montacute, Sim. de, bp. Ely, 434; bp. Worc. 472
—— sir Sim. de, K. Man, 665; L.H.A. 170
—— Th. de, dn. Sal. 468
—— Wm. de, aft. 1st E. of Salisbury, *q.v.*, Const. T.L. 320; K.B. 754; L.H.A. 171
—— sir Wm., aft. 2nd E. of Salisbury, *q.v.*, K. Man (*d.* 1397)
Montagu, Montague, Montagou, and **Mountague**
—— Basil, K.C. 416
—— Ch., aft. 1st ld. and E. of Halifax, *q.v.*, Aud. Ex. 167; Ch. Ex. 165; L.T. 155; P.C. Prem. 141; Pres. R. Soc. 940
—— Sir Ch., gen. (**B**) 865; K.B. 765
—— Chr., Aud. Ex. 166; Ch. Ex. 279, 280; C. St. 283
—— Ed., K.B. 762
—— Ed., called ld. M., L.T. (1654) 154
—— Ed., M. Chy. 397
—— Ed., Sec. Bath, 784
—— Ed., and sir E., C.J.C.P. 375; C.J.K.B. 370; S.L. 408
—— sir Ed., Tr. H. 291
—— Ed., aft. 1st E. of Sandwich, *q.v.*, K.G. 740; L.T. 155; P.C. 190
—— Ed., *see* ld. M. *infra*
Montagu, Montague, Montagou, and Mountague—*cont.*
—— Ed. Hass., aft. ld. and E. Beaulieu, K.B. (1753) 765
—— Ed. Wortl., L.T. 156
—— Fk., L.T., 158; P.C. 204
—— ld. Fredk., Postm. G. 238
—— Geo. and Sir G., adm. (**A**) 816; G.C.B. 767
—— Geo., aft. 2nd E. of Halifax, *q.v.*, Aud. Ex. 167
—— Hy., M. Chy. 396
—— Hy. and sir H., aft. ld. Kimbolton, visc. Mandeville and E. of Manchester, *q.v.*, C.J.K.B. 370; K.C. 414; L.H.T. 154; Rec. Lond. 494; S.L. 409
—— Hy. Seym., C. St. 284; C. St. and Tx. 285; C. Tx. 285
—— Horace Wm., gen. (**D**) 906
—— Jas., adm. (**H**) 846
—— Jas., bp. B. and W. 428; bp. Winch. 471; dn. Lich. 445; dn. Worc. 473
—— Jas. and sir J., A.G. 399; B. Ex. 384; C.B. Ex. 382; C.G.S. 357; Q.C. 415; S.G. 401; S.L. 411
—— Jno., adm. (**A**) 815; G. Newfd. 700
—— hon. Jno., dn. Dham. 479
—— Jno. Wm., adm. (**H**) 846
—— Ol., K.C. 415
—— Rd., bp. Chich. 433; bp. Norw. 455; dn. Her. 442
—— Rt., adm. (**A**) 817
—— ld. Rt., P.C. 217; V.P. Ed. 255
—— Wm. and sir W., C.B. Ex. 381; S.L. 410
—— Wm. de, G. Ch. Isl. 667
—— Wm. Aug. and sir W., adm. (**D**) 826; C. St. 284; K.C.H. 788; K.H. 789
—— Wm. Ed., gen. (**D**) 933
Montague, lds., E. and D. of
Neville Family.
—— Jno., ld., aft. E. of Northumberland, *q.v.*, and M. of Montague (*d.* 1471), K.G. 736
Browne Family.
—— Anthy., 1st visc., K.G. 738
Montagu Family.
—— Ed., aft. ld. M., K.B. (1603) 761
—— Ralph, aft. 3rd ld. and 1st E. and D. of M., C.G.P. 299; M.G.W. 296; P.C. 191, 193
—— Jno., 2nd D. of, C.G.P. 299; gen. (**A**) 857; Gr. M. Bath, 753; K.B. 764; K.G. 741; L.H. Const. 289; M.G.O. 259; M.G.W. 296; P.C. 198
Brudenell Family.
—— Geo., 1st D. of, form. E. of Cardigan, *q.v.*, L.L. Hunts, 309; M.H. 302; P.C. 203
—— Hy. Jas., ld., L.L. Selk. (1823, *d.* 1845) 512
Montaigne, *see* Monteigne
Montalt, Corn. Earl de, form. visc. Hawarden, *q.v.*, L.L. Tipp. 571
Montandre, Fras. M. de, F.M. 856; G. Gsey. 668
Montauban, Guill. M. A. A. Cousin-, K.C.B. 779
Monteagle, lds.
Stanley and Parker Families.
—— Ed., 1st ld., K.G. 737
—— Wm., 3rd ld., form. W. Stanley, *q.v.*
—— Hy., 5th ld., form. Hy. Parker, *q.v.*
Monteagle, lds.—*cont.*
Rice Family
—— Thos. Spring, 1st ld., form. Th. Spr. Rice, C.G. Ex. 169
—— Th. Spr., 2nd ld., K.P. 752
Montealegra, J. M., Pres. C.R. 106
Montealto, Jno. de, J. It. 368
Monteforti, Hy. de, Jy. 365
Monteigne, Geo., abp. Yk. 486; bp. Dham. 479; bp. Linc. 447; bp. Lond. 452; dn. Westr. 469
Monteith, *see also* Menteith
—— Wm., gen. (**D**) 880
Monte, Odorisio Inig. D'Av., Count de, K.G. 736
Monter, Rt., M. Chy. 394
Monteras, F. de la, G. Trin. 721
Monterei, C. of, R. Nds. 83
Montez, J. F., Pres. Hdas. 106
Montfichet, Rd. de, B. Ex. 382; J. It. 367
Montford (or Mundfort), Wm. de, dn. St. P. 452
—— (or Monteforti), Hy. de, J.C.P. 377; W.C.P. 317
—— Pet. de, Sp. H.C. 248
—— Simon, W.C.P. 318
Montgomerie and **Montgomery**
—— Alexr., adm. (**H**) 846
—— Alexr., L.M. Dbln. 642
—— Alexr. Lesl., adm. (**G**) 843
—— Alf., C. Exc. 282; C.I.R. 285; C. St. and Tx. 285
—— Ch. Lyons, gen. (**D**) 925
—— hon. Fras., L.H.T. Sc. 498
—— Geo., bp. Clr. 596; bp. Dry. 601; bp. Mth. 599; bp. Rph. 601; dn. Norw. 456
—— Geo. Saml., gen. (**D**) 909
—— sir Graham Gr., L.L. Kinr. 510; L.T. 161
—— sir Hy. Con., M.C.I. 646; P.C. 219
—— H. H., bp. Tasm. 708
—— Hugh Park., gen. (**D**) 933
—— Jas., G. Dnca. 730; gen. (**B**) 867
—— Jas. and sir J. (No. 1), Ld. Adv. 526; C.B. Ex. Sc. 523
—— sir Jas. (No. 2), Ld. Adv. 526
—— Jno., C. Exc. Sc. 504
—— Jno., K.B. 756
—— sir Jno. de, L.H.A. 172
—— Jno. Egl., adm. (**E**) 836; (**F**) 839
—— Nichs., K.B. 758
—— Patr., gen. (**D**) 886; K.C.B. 779
—— Rt., abp. Glasg. 537
—— Rt., bp. Arg. 538
—— Rt., C. Cus. Sc. 504
—— Rt. and sir R., Ch. Com. Oudh. 654, G.C.S.I. 801; K.C.B. 782; K.C.S.I. 802; L.G. Pjab. 654; M.C.I. 646
—— sir Th., K.G. 736
—— Wm., C. Exc. Ir. 566
Montgomery, lds., visc. and E. of; *see also* Pembroke
—— Archd., ld. (son of 12th E. of Eglinton), gen. (**C**) 873
—— Ph., E. of, form. P. Herbert, *q.v.*, aft. 4th E. of Pembroke, *q.v.*; K.B. 761; K.G. 739; L.C.H. 295; L.L. Kent, 309
—— Wm., visc., also E. and M. of Powis, *q.v.*, gen. (**B**) 804

Montjoy, *see* Mountjoy
Montmain, Rt., bp. Mth. 599
Montmorency, hon. Harv. de, dn. Ach. 614
— hon. Raym. H. de, gen. (**D**) 931
Montmorency, D. of
— Anne, D. of, and Ct. de Beaumont, K.G. 737
— Fras., D. of, K.G. 738
Montpesson, sir Th., L.P.S. 240
Montresor, Fk. Byng, adm. (**E**) 835; (**F**) 839
— sir Hy. Tuck, G.C.H. 786; gen. (**A**) 862; K.C.B. 775
— sir Th. Gage, gen. (**A**) 862; K.C.H. 788
Montrion, Walt., gen. (**D**) 912
Montrose, E. and D. of
Lindsay Family.
— Dav., D. of, form. 5th E. of Crauford *q.v.*, L.G.C. Sc. 506
Graham Family.
— Jno., 3rd E. of, H.C.P. Sc. 507; L.H.T. Sc. 497; Ld. Chanc. Sc. 515; Ld. Sess. 517
— Jno., 4th E. of, Pres. P.C. Sc. 500
— Jas., 1st M. of, K.G. 740
— Jas., 2nd M. of, Ld. Sess. 517
— Jas., 3rd M. of, Pres. P.C. Sc. 500
— Jas., 4th M., aft. 1st D. of, Comm. Tr. Sc. 498; L.H.A. Sc. 499; L.K. Sc. 503; L.P.S. Sc. 501; Ld. Clk. Reg. 525; P.C. 195; Pres. P.C. Sc. 500; Sec. St. Sc. 502
— Jas., 3rd D. of, form. M. of Graham, *q.v.*, B.C. 252; K.G. 743; K.T. 748; L.C.H. 295; L.J. Gen. 522; L.L. Dumb. 509; L.L. Stirl. 512; M.H. 502; Pres. B.T. 268; Postm. G. 238
— Jas., 4th D. of, form. M. of Graham, *q.v.*, C.D.L. 243; K.T. 748; L.L. Stirl. 512; L.S.H. 290; Postm. G. 239
— Dougl. B. M. R., 5th D. of, K.T. 749; L.L. Stirl. 512
Montt, M., Pres. Chi. 111
Montz, Hito, M. Jap. 100
Monymusk, Michl., bp. Dkld. 533; L.G.C. Sc. 506
Monypenny, Dav., Ld. Sess. 520; S.G. Sc. 527
Mooodie and **Moody**
— Jas., C. Exc. Sc. 504
— Rd. Clem., G. Falk. Isl. 731; gen. (**D**) 901
— Steph., gen. (**D**) 888
— Wm., bp. Cness. 531
Moon, Fras. Gr. and sir F., L.M. Lond. 492
Moor, Th., dn. St. P. 453
Moore, *see also* More
— Alexr. Geo. Mont., gen. (**D**) 927
— Arth., B.T. 264
— Arth., dn. Ach. 614
— Arth., J.C.P. Ir. 582; S.L. Ir. 592
— Ch. Wils., gen. (**D**) 908
— Fras., gen. (**A**) 861
— Fras., S.L. 409
— Geo., gen. (**D**) 887
— Geo. Fk., gen. (**D**) 919

Moore—*cont.*
— Gr. and sir G., adm. (**A**) 818; G.C.B. 768; G.C.M.G. 794; K.C.B. 774; L. Admy. 181
— Hass. Rd., gen. (**D**) 890
— Hy., C.I.E. 806; gen. (**D**) 933
— Hy., G. Jam. 712
— Jas., gen. (**B**) 868
— Jno., abp. Cant. 431; bp. Bgr. 426; dn. Cant. 431; P.C. 204
— Jno., bp. Ely, 435; bp. Norw. 455
— Jno., Comm. Ir. 554
— Jno., K.H. 792
— Jno., Norr. K.A. 329; Winds. H. 331
— Jno. and sir J., gen. (**B**) 866; K.B. 766
— sir Jno., adm. (**A** 814; K.B. 765
— sir Jno., L.M. Lond. 491
— Lewis Jas., adm. (**H**) 852
— sir Lorenzo, gen. (**C**) 875; K.C.H. 788
— Matth., adm. (**A**) 815
— Ogle Wm., dn. Cash. 627; dn. Clr. 598
— Rd., A.G. Ir. 588; J.Q.B. Ir. 579; S.G. Ir. 590; S.L. Ir. 593
— Rd., bp. Winch. 470
— Rd., dn. Emly, 628
— Rd., G. Bmda. 701
— Rd. Alex., gen. (**D**) 930
— Rd. Cornw., gen. (**D**) 900
— Rog., S.L. 411
— Ross. Balf., gen. (**D**) 912
— Th., Paym. G. 244
— Th. Ch. Cott., gen. (**D**) 897
— Th. Ed. Laws, adm. (**H**) 849; G. Falk. Isl. 731
— Wm., dn. Drom. 606
— Wm. Geo., gen. (**D**) 883; K.C.B. 778
— Wm. Jas., C.I.E. 807; K.C.I.E. 805
— Wm. Yorke, gen. (**D**) 891
Moorhouse, Jas., bp. Manch. 480; bp. Melb. 705
Moorman, Rd., adm. (**H**) 850
Moorshedabad, Bah. of, K.C.I.E. 805
Moorsom, Const. Rd., adm. (**G**) 841
— Jas. M., Q.C. 420
— Rt. and sir Rt., adm. (**A**) 818; K.C.B. 774; L. Admy. 181; S.G.O. 260
Mora, Jno. de, D. Chanc. Ir. 574
— J. R., Pres. C.R. 106
Morales, A., Pres. Bol. 109
Morant, Horatio Harb. gen. (**D**) 922
Morarji, Gokuldas, C.I.E. 806
Moravia, Andr. de, bp. Mor. 534
Moray, Dav., bp. Mor. 534
— Gilb., bp. Cness. 531; L.G.C. Sc. 506
— sir Rt., Pres. R. Soc. 940
Moray, Earls of
— Alexr., 5th E. of, H.C.P. Sc. 507; K.T. 747; Ld. Sess. 517; P.C. 192; Sec. St. Sc. 502
— Ch., 6th E. of, K.T. 747
— Jas., 8th E. of, K.T. 747
— Fras., 9th E. of, L.L. Elgn. 509
— Fras., 10th E. of, K.T. 748; L.L. Elgn. 509

Mordachus, K. Sc. 18
Mordant and **Mordaunt**
— Col., G. Gsey. 668
— Hon. Harry, gen. (**B**) 864
— Jno., S.L. 407
*— sir Jno., C.D.L. 242; K.B. 759
*— sir Jno., Sp. H.C. 249
* Prob. same pers.
— sir Jno., gen. (**A**) 858; K.B. 765
— Jno., *see* ld. M. *infra*
— Th. Osb., gen. (**B**) 866
Mordaunt of Turvey, lds.
— Jno., aft. 2nd ld. M., K.B. 760
Mordaunt of Avalon, &c., visc.
— Jno., 1st visc., Const. W. Cast. 322
— Ch., 2nd visc., aft. E. of Monmouth, and E. of Peterborough, *q.v.*, L.T., 155; P.C. 193; Prem. 140
— Jno., visc. (son of 2nd visc.), *d.v.p.*, gen. (**B**) 864
Morden, sir Jno., C. Exc. 279
Morden, lds.
— Chas., ld., *see* Hon. Chas. Yorke
Mordon, Sim., L.M. Lond. 489
More, *see also* Moore
*— sir Geo., Chanc. Gart. 746
*— sir Geo., Lt. T.L., 321
* Prob. same pers.
— Jno., J.C.P. 378; J.K.B. 372; S.L. 408
— Jno., S.L. 409
— sir Reg., L.G.C. Sc. 506
— Rd., bp. Winch. 470
— Rd., M. Chy. 395
— sir Thos., C.D.L. 242; Ld. Chanc. 355; Sp. H.C. 249
— Wm., L.M. Lond. 489
— Wm., bp. suff. Colch. 461
Morehead, Ch., C.I.E. 807
Moreman, Jno., dn. Exr. 437
Moreno, G. G., Pres. Ecr. 108
Moresby, Fairf. and sir F., adm. (**B**) 821; (**C**) 822; (**D**) 829; G.C.B. 770; K.C.B. 778
— Jno., adm. (**E**) 837
Moreton, *see* Morton
Morevill, *see* Morvill
Morewic, Hugh de, J. It. 366; Jy. 363
Morgair, Malachy O', *see* Malachy
Morgan, All., dn. Killoe. 637
— Ch., C.C. Bgal. 652; C.C. Ind. 650
— Ch., L.L. Brec. 315
— sir Ch. Gould, P.C. 207
— Fras., J.Q.B. 372; S.L. 408
— Fras. (or Geo.), Rec. Dbln. 642
— Geo., gen. (**C**) 872
— Geo. Osb., J. A. G. 937; P.C. 219; Q.C. 418; U.S.C. 235
— Hamon., J. It. 366
— Hy., bp. St. Dav. 464
— sir Hy., G. Jam. 712
— Hy. Rose, gen. (**D**) 913
— Hugh, dn. Bgr. 426
*— Jas., adm. (**H**) 847
*— Jas., K.H. 792
* Prob. same pers.
— Jas. Peatt., gen. (**D**) 933
— (or Young), Jno., bp. St. Dav. 464; Chanc. Gart. 745; dn. Winds. 474

Morgan—*cont.*
—— Jno., dn. Wford. 628
—— Jno., gen. (**D**) 886
—— Jno., L.L. Brec. 315; L.L. Monm. 310
—— Jno., M. Chy. 394
—— Ph., bp. Ely, 435; bp. Worc. 472
—— Rd. and sir R., C.J.C.P. 375; S.L. 408
—— Rt., bp. Bgr. 426
—— Th., gen. (**D**) 881
—— Th., J.A.G. 937
—— Th., L.L., Brec. 315; L.L. Monm. 310
—— Th., S.W.F., 271
—— sir Th., G. Jsey. 667
—— Walt. and sir W., C.J. Mdras. 658; C.J. N.W.Pr. 654
—— Wm., bp. Clff. 449; bp. St. As. 462
—— Wm., K.C.M.G. 798
*—— Wm. (No. 1), L.L. Brec. 315; L.L. Monm. 310
*—— Wm., and sir W. (No. 2), K.B. 764; L.L. Brec. 315; L.L. Monm. 310
* Prob. same pers.
—— Wm. Dom., gen. (**D**) 923
Morgan-Gould, form. Gould, *q.v.*
Morgeneu, bp. St. Dav. 464
Morgenveth, bp. St. Dav. 464
Moriarty, Silv., adm. (**A**) 817
—— Thos., Dn. Ardf. 640
Morice and **Morys,** *see also* Maurice
—— Humph., L.W.S. 323
—— Jno. and sir J., L.D. Ir. 551; Ld Chanc. Ir. 574
—— Th. Hy., K.H. 791
Morier, Dav. R., Amb. Swz. 113
—— Jas., Amb. Pers. 130
—— Jno. P., Amb. Sxy. 120
—— Rt. B. D. and sir R., Amb. Bva. 119; Amb. Pgl. 125; Amb. Russ. 126; Amb. Spn. 124; G.C.B. 773; G.C.M.G. 795; K.C.B. 784; P.C. 220
—— Wm. adm. (**H**) 847
Moriertach, Nehemh., bp. Cloy. 630
Morin, M.P., U.S.S. 226
—— Ralph, J. It. 366
Moris, *see* Morris
Morison, *see* Morrison
Morland, sir Saml., C.Exc. 278
—— (or Murland), Wm., dn. Winds. 474; M. Chy. 394; M.R. 387
Morley, Arnold, Sec. Tr. 164
—— Fras. Br., K.C.B. 784
—— Geo., bp. Winch. 471; bp. Worc. 473; dn. Chr. Ch. Oxf. 457; P.C. 191
—— Herb., Lt. T.L. 322
—— Jno., Ch. Sec. Ir. 563; P.C. 220
*—— Rt. de, Const. T.L. 320
*—— sir Rt., L.H.A. 172
* Prob. same pers.
—— Th., bp. suff. Marlb. 452
—— Th., S.L., 411
—— Wm., K.B. 764
Morley, lds. and E. of
—— Th., 4th ld., K.G. 735; L.H.A. 174
—— Hy., 7th ld., K.B. 757
—— Alb. Edm., 3rd E. of, C.W.P.B. 273; P.C. 220; U.S. War, 232
Morlière, Mag. de la, G. Mtius. 683
Mornington, E. of
—— Rd., 2nd E. of, aft. ld. and M. Wellesley, *q.v.*, B.C. 252; G.G. Ind. 648; K.P. 750; L.T. 158; P.C. 205
—— Wm., 3rd E. of, form. hon. W. Wellesley Pole, and ld. Maryborough, *q.v.*
Morpeth, visc.
—— Geo. H., visc., aft. 6th E. of Carlisle, *q.v.*, Amb. Pr. 118; B.C. 252; L.L. Yorks. E.R. 313; P.C. 208
—— Geo. Wm. Fk., visc., aft. 7th E. of Carlisle, *q.v.*, C.W.F. &c. 272; Ch. Sec. Ir. 563; L.L. Yorks. E.R. 313; P.C. 213
Morrell, Th. Baker, bp. Edinb. 543
Morrice, Humphr., Compt. H. 292; P.C. 201
—— sir Wm., L.T. 155; P.C. 189; S. St. 223
Morris and **Moris**
——, —, S.L. 407
—— Alexr., G. Mtoba. 696
—— Arth., gen. (**D**) 885
—— Ch. Hy., gen. (**D**) 906
—— Corbyn, C. Cus. 276
—— Den., dn. Lism. 629
—— Edm. Finucane, gen. (**D**) 885; K.C.B. 779
—— Edw., K.C.B. 781
—— Edw., M. Chy. 397
—— Genl., G.C.B. 769
—— Geo., adm. (**H**) 844
—— Hy. Gage (No. 1), adm. (**H**) 844
—— Hy. Gage (No. 2), adm. (**H**) 850
—— Hy. Jos., gen. (**D**) 897
—— Jas. Ed. Gord., gen. (**D**) 894
—— Jas. Nic. and sir J., adm. (**A**) 818; K.C.B. 774
—— Jno. Hy., Ch. Com. Cent. Pr. 655; K.C.S.I. 803
—— Lodge, aft. ld. and visc. Frankfort, *q.v.*, C. Treas. Ir. 560; U.S. Ir. 563
—— Michl and sir M., A.G. Ir. 588; J.C.P. Ir. 581; Pres. Q.B.D. Ir. 578; J.C.P. Ir. 582; S.G. Ir. 590
—— Pet., dn. Dry. 602
—— Staates Long, gen. (**A**) 858
—— Val., G. St. Vin. 725
—— Wm., adm. (**H**) 850
Morrison and **Morison**
—— Alexr., Ld. Sess. 519
—— Arth., L.M. Dbln. 642
—— (or Moryson), Ch., K.B. 761
—— Ed., G. Jam. 713; gen. (**A**) 860
—— Geo., gen. (**A**) 859
—— Is. Hawk., adm. (**H**) 845
—— sir Rd., M.G.O. 258
—— Wm., gen. (**D**) 881; K.C.B. 782
Morrogh, Edm. Gh., gen. (**D**) 933
Morse, Jas., gen. (**D**) 879
—— Rt., gen. (**A**) 859
—— Rt. Alexr., gen. (**D**) 911
Morshead, sir Jno., L.W.S. 323
—— Wm. Hy. Anders., adm. (**D**) 833; (**E**) 834; (**F**) 838
Morshed, Wm., gen. (**A**) 860
Mortain, Jno., E. of, aft. K. John of Eng. *q.v.*, G. Ch. Isl. 667
Moreton, *see* Morton
Mortier, Off. Nap. 26
Mortimer, Edm. de, K.B. 754
—— Geoff. de, K.B. 755
—— Rog., K.B. 756
*—— Rog. de, K.B. 754
*—— sir Rog., aft. E. of March, *q.v.*, L.J. Ir. 551
* Prob. same pers.
—— sir Th. de, C.J.K.B. Ir. 577
—— Wm. de, J. It. 368
Mortimer, lds. and E. of
—— Rt., E. of, form. Rt. Harley, *q.v.*, also E. of Oxford, *q.v.*
—— Edm., ld. (*d.* 1331), L.M. 325
Mortlock, sir Jno. Cheet., C. Exc. 281-82; C. Exc. Ir. 567
Morton and **Moreton**
—— sir Alb., S. St. 223
—— Jno., abp. Cant. 431; bp. Ely, 435; L.K. 355; M.R. 387
—— Jno., C.J. Chest. 386; K.C. 415
—— Matth. Ducie, aft. ld. Ducie, *q.v.*, V. Treas. Ir. 559
—— Rt., bp. Worc. 473; M.R. 387
—— Th., bp. Chest. 477; bp. Dham. 479; bp. Lich. and Cov. 444; dn. Glr. 440; dn. Winch. 471
—— Wm., bp. Mth. 599; bp. Kild. 617; dn. Chr. Ch. Dbln. 618
—— sir Wm., J.K.B. 372; S.L. 410
—— sir Wm., Rec. Lond. 494
—— Wm. Ell., gen. (**D**) 902
Morton, E. of,
—— Rt., E. of, Ch. Jr. (1078) 362
—— Jno., E. of, L.L. Ir. (1177-9) 550
—— Edm. (Beaufort), E. of, aft. E. of Dorset, and D. of Somerset, *q.v.* (*d.* 1455), K.G. 735
Douglas Family.
—— Jas., 4th E. of, L.H.A. Sc. 499; Ld. Chanc. Sc. 515
—— Wm., 9th E. of, C.Y.G. 298; K.G. 739; L.H.T. Sc. 497
—— Geo., 15th E. of, V.A. Sc. 499
—— Jas., 16th E. of, K.T. 747; Ld. Clk. Reg. 525; Pres. R. Soc. 940
—— Geo., 18th E. of, K.T. 748; L.H.C.K. Sc. 546; L.L. Fifesh. 510; L.L. Mid. L. 509
Reynolds-Moreton Family.
(*See* E. of Ducie.)
Morvael, abp. St. Dav. 463
Morvi, Thakore, Sahib of, K.C.I.E. 805
***Morvill,** Hugh de, J. It. 365;
*—— Hugh de, L.H. Const. Sc. 507; Ld. Chanc. Sc. 514
* ? same pers.
—— Rd. de, L.H. Const. Sc. 507
—— Wm. de, L.H. Const. Sc. 507
Morys, *see* Morris and Maurice
Moryson, *see* Morrison
Moseley, Rt. Stephenson, gen. (**D**) 929
—— Ed., Ld. Sess. 519

Moses, Wm., S.L., 411
Mosheim, Lew., gen. (**B**) 868
Mosley, sir Nichs., L.M. Lond. 491
Mosquera, T. C. de, Pres. N.G. 107; Pres. U.S.C. 107
Moss, Ch., bp. B. and W. 428; bp. St. Dav. 465
— Ch., bp. Oxf. 457
— Rt., dn. Ely, 435
Mossom, Rt., dn. Chr. Ch. Dbln. 618; bp. Dry. 601
— Rt., dn. Oss. 623
Mostyn, Jno., gen. (**A**) 858
— sir Rog., L.L. Flints. 314
— sir Rog., Tell. Ex. 168
— Sav., adm. (**A**) 814; Compt. N. 257; L. Admy. 178
— hon. Sav., gen. (**D**) 928
Mostyn, lds.
— Ed. M., 2nd ld., form. hon. E. M. Lloyd, *q.v.*
Motelow, Hy. de, J.C.P. 377
Mothel, Jno., bp. Lim. 638
Motte, Pet. de la, gen. (**D**) 878
Motteram, Jas., C.C.J. 405; Q.C. 419
Motteux, Jno., Chn. E.I. Co. 644
Mottley, Jos. Mart., adm. (**H**) 850
— Saml., adm. (**D**) 824
Moubray, *see* Mowbray
Mould, Fk., gen. (**D**) 918
— Th. Rawl., gen. (**D**) 902
Moule, Geo. E. V., bp. M. Ch. 676
— Jno., gen. (**D**) 892
Moulson, sir Th., L.M. Lond. 491
Moulton, A., G. N. Sc. 694
— Jno. Fl., Q.C. 420
Moulvi, Saiyid, &c., K.C.S.I. 804
Moung, U. Pe, &c., C.I.E. 808
— U. Oun, C.I.E. 806
Mounsey, Aug. Hy., Amb. U.S.C. 134
Mountague, *see* Montague
Mountain, Geo. Jehos., bp. Queb. 694
— I., bp. Queb. 694
— Rt. Fk., gen. (**D**) 908
Mount, Alexr. Hugh, E. of, L.J. Ir. (1702) 555
Mount-Charles, Fras. N., E. of, aft. 2nd M. of Conyngham, *q.v.*, G.C.H. 786; L.T. 159; U.S.F. 229
Mount-Edgcumbe, *see* Edgcumbe
Mount-Edgcumbe, visc. and E. of
— Geo., 1st visc., form ld. Edgcumbe, *q.v.*, V. Treas. Ir. 560
— Rd., 2nd E. of, C.G.P. 300; L.L. Cnwall. 307; P.C. 208
— Wm. H., 4th E. of, L.C.H. 295; L.L. Cnwall. 307; L.S.H. 290; P.C. 219
Mounteney, Rd., C. Acc. Ir. 567
Mountgryson, Rd. ld., K.G. (?) 736
Mountjoy and **Montjoy,** lds.
— M. B., ld., aft. 1st E. of Newport, *q.v.*
Blount Family.
— Walt., 1st ld., K.G. 736
— Jno., 3rd ld., K.B. 757
— Wm., 4th ld., K.B. 759; K.G. 737; M.M. 246
Mountjoy and Montjoy, lds.—*cont.*
— Jas., 6th ld., K.B. 760
— Ch., 8th ld., form. sir Ch. Blount, *q.v.*, aft. E. of Devon, *q.v.*, K.G. 739; L.D. Ir. 554
Stewart Family.
— Wm., 2nd visc., gen. (**B**) 864
Mountney, Rd., B. Ex. Ir. 584
Mountmorres, Herv., 4th visc., dn. Cloy. 633
Mountnorris, Fras., 1st ld., form. sir Fras. Annesley, *q.v.*
Mountrath, E. of
— Ch., 1st E. of, form. sir C. Coote, *q.v.*, L.J. Ir. 555
— Ch., 2nd E. of, L.J. Ir. 555
Mountstephen, Wm. Th. Bl., gen. (**D**) 901
Mountstewart and **Mountstuart**
— Jno., visc., aft. 4th E. and 1st M. of Bute, *q.v.*, Amb. Sda. 114; Amb. Spn. 123; L.L. Glam. 315; P.C. 203
Mowbray and **Moubray**
— Ed., gen. (**D**) 910
— Jno., K.B. 756
— Jno. de, J.C.P. 377; K.B. 755; S.L. 406
— Jno. Rt., J.A.G. 937; P.C. 216
— sir Rt., K.H. 790
— Th. Jno., K.B. 756
Mowbray, lds.
— Jno., ld., aft. 2nd D. of Norfolk, *q.v.*, E.M. (1412) 326; K.G. 735
Mowse, Wm., D. Arch. 420; J. Pr. Ct. 421; M. Chy. 395; Vic. Gen. 421
Moxon, Geo. Gill., gen. (**D**) 915
Moyers, Geo., L.M. Dbln. 642
Moygne (or Moigne), Th., bp. Ard. 608; bp. Kilm. and Ard. 607; dn. St. Patr. 618
Moylan, Denis, L.M. Dbln. 642
— Denis C., C.C.J. 403
Moyle, Jas., gen. (**C**) 871
— Rt., *see* Walt.
— Th., Sp. H.C. 249
— Walt. or Rt., J.C.P. 378
— Walt., K.B. 757; S.L. 407
Moyne, Jno. le, Jy. 365
Moyse, Shadr., C. Cus. Sc. 504
Moyun, *see* Mohun
Mubire, Rt., bp. Rph. 601
Mucegros, Milo de, J. It. 366
— Rd. de, Jy. 364
Mucellus, bp. Her. 441
Mucianus, P. L. C., C. Ro. 45
Mudalier, Ram., C.I.E. 807
Mudge, Zach., adm. (**A**) 820
Mueller, Ferd. von, K.C.M.G. 797
Muffling, Bar. de, K.C.B. 775
Mugge, Wm., dn. Winds. 474
Mugillanus, L. P. (2), C. Ro. 38-9
— M. P., C. Ro. 39
Muhammad, *see* Mahomed
Muimnech, Clothna, bp. Emly, 625
Muinheamhoin, K. Ir. 20
Muinimone, K. Ir. 20
Muir, *see also* Mure
— Alexr. Wils., G. St. Xtr. 729
— Ch. Wem., C.I.E. 808
— Jno., C.I.E. 806
— Wm., dn. Thist. 749
Muir—*cont.*
— Wm., Mod. K. Sc. 547
— sir Wm., M.C.I. 647; K.C.S.I. 802; L.G. N.W. Pr. 653; Sec. S.I. 804
— Wm. Mure, K.C.B. 780
Muirhead, Andr., bp. Glasg. 536
— Rd., Ld. Clk. Reg. 525; Sec. St. Sc. 502
Muirmhne, K. Ir. 20
Muirreadach, K. Ir. 20
— -Tireach, K. Ir. 21
Mukerji, Babu Bhuder, C.I.E. 806
Mulcaster, sir Fk. Wm., gen. (**B**) 869; K.C.H. 788
— Wm. Ed., gen. (**D**) 901
— sir Wm. Howe, K.C.H. 788
— Wm. Sidn. Sm., gen. (**D**) 912
Muleton, Th. de, C.J.C.P. 375; Ch. Jr. 363; J. It. 367; Jy. 364
Muley, &c. (3), S. Mco. 101
Mulgan, Jno., bp. Llin. 622
Mulfield, Rt., bp. Killoe. 634
Mulgrave, lds. and E. of
Sheffield Family.
— Edmd., 1st E. of, form. 3rd ld. Sheffield, *q.v.*
— Jno., 3rd E. of, aft. M. of Normanby, and D. of Buckinghamshire, *q.v.*, K.G. 740; L.C.H. 295; P.C. 192
Phipps Family.
— Const. J., 2nd ld., B.C. 252; B.T. 267; L. Admy. 179; P.C. 204; Paym. G. 244
— Hy., 3rd ld., aft. visc. Normanby and 1st E. of Mulgrave, *q.v.*, C.D.L. 243; F. Sec. 228; G.C.B. 768; gen. (**A**) 860; L. Admy. 181; L.L. Yorks. E.R. 313; M.G.O. 259; P.C. 207
— Const. Hy., 2nd E. of, aft. 1st M. of Normanby, *q.v.*, G.C.H. 786; G. Jam. 713; L.L. Ir. 557; L.P.S. 241; P.C. 212
— Geo. Aug., E. of, aft. 2nd M. of Normanby, *q.v.*, Compt. H. 293; G.N. Sc. 695; P.C. 215; Tr. H. 291
Mullaly (or Laly) Wm., abp. Tm. 611; dn. Tm. 613
Mullart (or Maillart), Wm., dn. Cash. 627
Mullen, Rt., K.H. 791
Muller, Ed. Anger. Godf., gen. (**D**) 904
Mullins, Jno., gen. (**D**) 927
Multon, Sim. de, M. Chy. 393
Munbee, Gore Bol., gen. (**D**) 898
Muncaster, lds.
— Lowth., 2nd ld., form. L. Pennington, *q.v.*
— Joselyn, Fr., 5th ld., L.L. Cumb. 307
Munchin (St.), bp. Lim. 638
Munday, *see also* Mundy and and Monday
— sir Jno., L.M. Lond. 490
Mundell, Wm. A., Q.C. 418
Mundella, Anth. Jno., P.C. 219; Pres. B.T. 269; V.P. Ed. 255
Munden, Jno. de, S.L. 406
— sir Jno., adm. (**A**) 813
Mundfort (or Montford), Wm. de, dn. St. P. 452
Mundy, *see also* Monday and Munday
— Ch. Fitz Mill., gen. (**D**) 916

Mundy—*cont.*
—— Geo., dn. Emly, 628
—— Geo. and sir G., adm. (**A**) 820; adm. (**B**) 821; K.C.B. 776
—— Geo. Rodn. and sir G., adm. (**D**) 831; (**E**) 834; G.C.B. 770; K.C.B. 779
—— Godfr. Bas., gen. (**A**) 863
—— Godfr. Ch., G. Jsey. 668; gen. (**D**) 894; U.S. War. 233
—— Jas., S.L. 411
—— Pierrepont Hy., gen. (**D**) 902
—— Rt. Mill., G. Bdoes. 721; G. Br. Gu. 715; G. Br. Hond. 714; G, Gren. 724; K.C.M.G. 797
Muneepore, Mahar. of, K.C.S.I. 803
Munro, *see also* Monro
—— Alex., gen. (**D**) 883; K.H. 791
—— sir Alexr., C. Cus. 276
—— Col. —, G. Trin. 722
—— Geo., gen. (**D**) 898
—— sir Hect., gen. (**A**) 859
—— Jno., gen. (**D**) 876
—— sir Th., G. Mdras. 656 K.C.B. 775
—— Wm., gen. (**B**) 867
—— Wm., gen. (**D**) 876
—— Wm., gen. (**D**) 902
—— Wm., gen. (**D**) 935
Munsey, Th. Alex. Aug., gen. (**D**) 894
Munshi, Newab Kishore, C.I.E. 808
Münster, Ern. Fk. Herb. Ct., Chanc. Guelph. 792; G.C.B. 768
Munster, Geo., 1st E. of, form. Geo. Fitz-Clarence, *q.v.*, Const. W. Cast. 322; gen. (**D**) 880; Lt. T.L. 322; P.C. 212
Munzinger, J., Pres. Sw. C. 31
Murat, Joach., K. Nls. 56; Off. Nap. 26
Murchison, sir Rod. Imp., K.C.B. 783
Murdac, *see also* Muredach
—— Hy., abp. Yk. 485
—— Hugh, J. It. 366
—— Ralph, J. It. 366; Jy. 363
Murdoch, Th. Wm. Cl., K.C.M.G. 796
Mure, *see also* Muir
—— Dav., Jy. Sc. 523; Ld. Adv. 526; Ld. Sess. 521; S.G. Sc. 527
—— Wm., Bar. Ex. Sc. 524
Murechan, bp. Arm. 595
Muredach, *see also* Murdac
—— bp. Arm. 595
—— bp. Mayo, 611
—— (St.), bp. Killa. 612
Murena, L. L., C. Ro. 46
Muriertagh, K. Ir. 22
Murland, *see* Morland
Murphy, Fras. S., P.P. 417; S.L. 413
—— Jas., J.C.P.D. Ir. 582; J.Q.B.D. Ir. 580
—— Jno. Patr., Q.C. 419
Murray, Alan, gen. (**D**) 932
—— Alex., adm. (**H**) 848
—— Alex., dn. Killa. 614
—— Alex., Ld. Sess. 520; S.G. Sc. 526
—— Andr., L.M. Dbln. 641
—— Andr., bp. Ross. 535

Murray—*cont.*
—— Anth. Maxt., gen. (**D**) 911
—— Augs. Wm., gen. (**D**) 909
—— Capt. —, G. V.D. Ld. 708
—— Ch., gen. (**D**) 912
—— hon. Ch. Augs. and sir C., Amb. Dk. 127; Amb. Pers. 130; Amb. Pgl. 125; Amb. Swz. 113; Amb. Sxy. 121; K.C.B. 783; P.C. 219
—— sir Dav., Compt. Sc. 498
—— Elibank Harl., adm. (**H**) 853
—— Freem., G. Bmda. 701; gen. (**D**) 897
—— Dav., aft. visc. Stormont, *q.v.*
—— Geo., bp. Roch. 460; bp. S. and M. 484; dn. Worc. 474
—— Geo. adm. (**A**) 816
—— Geo. and sir G. adm. (**A**) 817; K.C.B. 773
—— Geo. and sir Geo., Comm. F. Ir., 564; G.C.B. 767; G.C.H. 786; gen. (**A**) 862; K.B. 766; L.G.O. 259; M.G.O. 259; P.C. 211; W. and C. Sec. 231
—— hon. Geo., gen. (**B**) 869
—— ld. Geo., bp. St. Dav. 465
—— Geo. Fr., gen. (**D**) 901
—— sir Gid., Compt. Sc. 498; Ld. Sess. 519
—— hon. Hy., gen. (**D**) 877; K.C.B. 778
—— hon. Hy. Anth., adm. (**G**) 843
—— Herb. H., C. Cus. 277
—— Jack Hy., adm. (**H**) 851
—— Jas., aft. 1st ld. Glenlyon, *q.v.*
—— Jas., U.S.F. 230
—— Jas. and sir J., Ld. Clk. Reg. 525; Ld. Sess. 520
*—— hon. Jas., G. Can. 691; gen. (**C**) 872
*—— hon. Jas., G. I. Man, 666
*—— hon. Jas., gen. (**A**) 858
* ? same person.
—— Jas. Arth., adm. (**H**) 845
—— Jas. Patr., gen. (**C**) 875
—— Jas. Wolfe, J. Adm. Sc. 524; Ld. Sess. 520
—— Jno., Amb. Tky. 129; Amb. Vce. 116
—— Jno., dn. Killoe. 637
—— Jno., gen. (**A**) 861
—— Jno., gen. (**B**) 868
—— Jno., gen. (**C**) 874
—— Jno. (Drumcairn), Ld. Sess. 519
—— Jno. (Bowhill), Ld. Sess. 520
—— sir Jno., gen. (**A**) 861; G.C.H. 786
—— ld. Jno., gen. (**A**) 858
—— Jno. Archd. and sir J., Ld. Adv. 526; Ld. Sess. 520
—— Jno. Irv., gen. (**D**) 924
—— Jno. Walton, dn. Cnr. 605
*—— sir Patr., Bar. Ex. Sc. 524
*—— sir Patr., Sec. B.C. 254
* ? same pers.
—— Patr., aft. E. of Tullibardine, *q.v.*, K.B. (1603) 761
—— Rd., dn. Ard. 609
—— Rd., Wdn. Chr. Ch. Manch. 481
—— Rt., adm. (**A**) 817
—— Rt., gen. (**D**) 930
—— sir Rt., Comm. Tr. Sc. 497; L. J. Clk. 516; Ld. Sess. 519
—— Th., gen. (**A**) 860

Murray—*cont.*
—— Th., gen. (**D**) 880
—— hon. Th., gen. (**B**) 865
—— sir Th., Ld. Sess. 519
—— Th. Andr. L., gen. (**D**) 927
—— Wm., bp. Kilf. 635; bp. Llff. 449
—— Wm., gen. (**B**) 867
—— Wm., gen. (**D**) 911
—— sir Wm., Compt. Sc. 498
—— Hon. Wm., aft. 1st ld. and E. of Mansfield, *q.v.*, A.G. 399; C.J.K.B. 370; S.G. 401; S.L. 412
Murray, lds.
—— Jno., ld., aft. E. of Tullibardine (?), Sec. St. Sc. (1696), 502
Murray-Macgregor, *see* Macgregor
Murrieux, sir Thos.. Const. T.L. 320
Murtough (2), K. Ir. 21-2
—— -MacNeil-MacLachlin, K. Ir. 22
Mus, P. D. (4), C. Ro. 40-1
Musa-Chelebi, S. Tky. 97
Musard, Ralph, J. It. 367
Muscat, Sultan of, G.C.S.I. 801
Muschampe, Chr., B. Ex. 384
—— Geoffr. de, bp. Lich. and Cov. 443
Musgrave, Anthy., and sir A., G. Br. Cbia., 698; G. Jam. 713; G. Nat. 680; G. Newfd. 700; G. Nev. 730; G. Qland. 706; G. S. Austr. 706; G. St. Vin. 725; G.C.M.G. 795; K.C.M.G. 797
*—— Ch., Clk. O. 260
*—— sir Ch., L.G.O. 259
* Prob. same pers.
—— sir Chr., C.Y.G. 298
—— sir Chr., L.P.S. 240
—— sir Chr., M.G.O. 258
—— sir Chr., Tell. Ex. 167
—— sir Ph., G. I. Man, 666
—— Rd., K.B. 761
—— sir Rd. C., L.L. Wmland. 313
—— Th., abp. Yk. 486; bp. Her. 442; dn. Brl. 440; Jud. Com. P.C. 360; P.C. 215
—— Th., dn. Carl. 476
—— sir Th., gen. (**A**) 859
—— sir Wm., C. Cus. 276
Musgrove, Jno. and sir J., L.M. Lond. 492
Muskerry, Jno. Th., 2nd ld., gen. (**C**) 874
Muskham, Rt. de, M. Chy., 394
Mustapha, B. Tun. 101
—— I. to IV,. S. Tky. 97-8
—— Fehmy Pasha, K.C.M.G. 799
Mustoxide, Andrea, K.C.M.G. 796
Muter, St. John O'N., gen. (**D**) 914
Mutford, Jno. de, A.G. 398; J.C.P. 377; J. It. 369
Mutge, Wm., gen. (**C**) 874
Mutton, sir Peter, M. Chy. 395
Muttra, L. D. Seth of, C.I.E. 808
Muzaffar Khan, &c., C.I.E. 808
Muzzan, Franc. and sir F., G.C.M.G. 794; K.C.M.G. 796

My—, *see also* Mi—
Myburgh, Ph. Alb., Q.C. 419
Myddelton and **Myddleton,** *see* Middleton
Myers, sir Wm., gen. (**B**) 866
Mylne, *see also* Milne
— Louis Geo., bp. Bbay. 661
— Wm. Ch. Rt., gen. (**D**) 930
Mylner, *see also* Milner
— Th.. Cal. P. A. 342; Lanc. H. 332; R. Dr. P.A. 337
Mynne, Jno., Yk. H. 334
Myrton, *see* Merton
Mysore, Mahar. of (2), G.C.S.I. 801
— Maharanee of, Cr. Ind. 809

N.

Naas, lds.
— Jno., ld., form. Jno. Bourke, *q.v.*, aft. 1st E. of Mayo, *q.v.*
— Rd. Southwell, ld., aft. 6th E. of Mayo, *q.v.*, Ch. Sec. Ir., 563; P.C. 215
Nabha, Dewan Bishen, Sing of, C.I.E., 806
— Raj. of, G.C.S.I. 801
Nadir, Sh. Pers. 99
Nadown, Raj. of, K.C.S.I. 803
Nagle, Sir Edm., adm. (**A**) 817; G.C.H. 786; K.C.B. 773
— sir Rd., A.G. Ir. 588
Nahun, Raj. of, K.C.S.I. 803
Nain Sing, C.I.E. 806
Nairn and **Nairne**
— Alex., Compt. Sc. 498
— Alex., Ly. K.A. 513
*— sir Dav., C. Cus. 274
*— sir Dav., Sec. Thist. 749
* Poss. same pers.
— sir Rt., Ld. Sess. 519
— Wm. and sir W., Jy. Sc. 523; Ld. Sess. 520
Naish, *see also* Nash
— Jno., A.G. Ir. 589; L.J. App. Ir. 586; Ld. Chanc Ir. 577; S.G. Ir. 590
Namis, abp. St. Dav. 463
Namur, Rt. de, K.G. 733
Nanfan, Jno., G. Ch. Isl. 667
Nangle, Rd., bp. Clonf. 636
Nanose, Pres. Nic. 106
Nanquette, Pierre Franc. H., C.I.E. 806
Naomh Gilda na (2), bp. Glend. 615
Napier, sir Alex., Ld. Sess. 519
— sir Arch., Ld. Sess. 517, 519
— Ch. and sir C., adm. (**D**) 827; K.C.B. 777
— Ch. Jas. and sir C., C.C. Ind. 651; G.C.B. 769; G. Virg. Isl. 731; gen. (**B**) 870; K.C.B. 776

Napier—*cont.*
— Ed. Hung del El.. gen. (**D**) 893
— Fras., *see.* ld. N. *infra.*
— Hon. Geo. Campb. C.I.E. 806
— Geo. Th. and sir G., G. C.G.H. 679; gen. (**A**) 863; K.C.B. 776
— Geo. Th. Conolly, gen. (**D**) 896
— Ger. Jno., adm. (**H**) 850
— Johnstone, gen. (**D**) 881
— Josh. and sir J., A.G. Ir. 588; C.G.S. Ir. 577; Jud. Com. P.C. 361; Ld. Chanc. Ir. 577; P.C. 218
— Mark, gen. (**B**) 869
— Hon. Mark, gen. (**C**) 872
— Rt., gen. (**B**) 864
— Rt., gen. (**B**) 865
— Rt. C., *see* ld. N., *infra*
— Th. E. and sir T., gen. (**D**) 882; K.C.B. 778
— Wm., gen. (**C**) 872
— Wm., G. Labn. 675
— Wm. C. E., gen. (**D**) 900
— Wm. Fras. Patr. and sir W., G. Gsey. 669; gen. (**D**) 879; K.C.B. 777
Napier, lds.
— Fras., 7th ld., L.H.C.K. Sc. 546; L.L. Selk. 512
— Fras. 9th ld., aft. ld. N. and Ettrick, Amb. Nds. &c. 123; Amb. Russ. 126; Amb. Pr. 118; Amb. U.S.A. 132; G. Mdras. 657; K.T. 749; P.C. 217
— Anne Jane Ch., bss., aft. N. and E., Cr. Ind. 809
Napier of Magdala, lds.
— Robt. Corn. and sir R., aft. ld. N. of M., C.C. Bbay. 660; C.C. Ind. 651; Const. T.L. 321; F.M. 856; G.C.B. 770; G.C.S.I. 801; G. Gibr. 670; gen. (**D**) 896; K.C.B. 778
— Mary Cecilia, Bss., Cr. Ind. 810
Napoleon. *See also* Bonaparte
— I., Csl. Fr. 24; Emp. Fr. 24
— II. and III., Emp. Fr. 25
— III. (Emp. Fr.), K.G. 744
— (Pr. Imp.), Pr. Fr. 26
Napper, sir Rt., C. B. Ex. Ir. 583
— Rt. Alexr., gen. (**D**) 919
Narbon and **Narboone**
— Jno., Bl. M. P.A. 336; Rbk. P.A. 344; Richm. H. 333
— Nichs, Bl. M. P.A. 336; Richm. H. 333; Ulst. K.A. 572
Narborough, sir Jno., adm. (**A**) 813
Narendra Krishna, &c., K.C.I.E. 805
Nares, Geo. and sir G., J.C.P., 379; S.L. 412
— Geo. Str. and sir G. adm. (**H**) 853; K.C.B. 783
Narses, K. It. 49
Nash, *see also* Naish
— Jno. Hunter del, J.K.B. Ir. 578
— Jos., gen. (**D**) 890
— Wm., L.M. Lond. 492
Nasica, L. C. S., C. Ro. 43
— P. C. S. (2), C. Ro. 44-5
Nasmith, Dav., Q.C. 420
Nason, Jno., gen. (**D**) 924
Nasr-ul-Din, Sh. Pers. 99; K.G. 745

Nathalocus, K. Sc. 18
Nathan, bp. St. Dav. 464
Nathy, St. (or Nathy Cruimthir), bp. Ach. 612
Nation, Jno. Louis, gen. (**D**) 925
Naunagar, Vibhajee of, K.C.S.I. 803
Naunton, sir R., S. St. 223
Nawazish Ali Kahn, C.I.E. 807; K.C.I.E. 805
Nayler, Geo. and sir G., Bl. C.H. 339; Bl. M. P.A. 337; Clar. K.A. 328; Gart. K.A. 328; Geneal. Bath. 784; Guelph K.A. 793; K.H. 789; M.G.K.A. 799; Yk. H. 334
Naylor, Ch., dn. Winch. 471
— Rt., dn. Lim. 639; dn. Lism. 629
Naz, Virg., K.C.M.G. 797
Nead, Saml., gen. (**B**) 868
Neal and **Neale,** *see also* Neele and Neile.
— Ed. St. Jno., Amb. Ecr. 942
— Rd., *see* Neile
— Th., M.M. 247
Nearne, Jno., dn. Llin. 623
Neave, Wm., S.L. Ir. 591
Neaves, Ch., Jy. Sc. 523; Ld. Sess. 521; S.G. Sc. 527
Nectanus, bp. Mortl. 530
Nedham, Ch., gen. (**D**) 930
— Wm. Rt., gen. (**D**) 900
Need, Ch., gen. (**D**) 913
— Hy., adm. (**H**) 850
Needham, hon. Fras., aft. visc. and E. Kilmorey, gen. (**A**) 860
— Jno., J.C.P. 378; J.K.B. 371; K.B. 757; S.L. 407
— Wm., gen. (**C**) 874
Neele, Rd. and sir R., J.C.P., 378; J.K.B. 371; S.L. 407
Negreti, Dt. Mex. 103
Negus, Fras., M.H., 302
Nehemiah, bp. Cnr. 603; bp. Kild. 616
— dn. Killoe. 637
Neild, Hy. Jno. Th., gen. (**D**) 915
Neile, *see also* Neal and Neyle
— Jno., dn. Rip. 482
— (or Neale, or Neyle) Rd., abp. Yk. 486; bp. Dham. 479; bp. Lich. and Cov. 444; bp. Linc. 447; bp. Roch. 460; bp. Winch. 471; dn. Westr. 469
— sir Harry Burr., adm. (**A**) 818; G.C.B. 768; G.C.M.G. 794; K.C.B. 774; L. Admy 180-1
Nelson, Alex. Aberc., G. Gsey 669; gen. (**D**) 921
— Geo., L.M. Lond. 492
— Hor., *see* ld. N. *infra*
— Hugh, G. Br. Cbia. 698
— Hon. Maur. Hor., adm. (**H**) 852
— Rd. Jno., gen. (**D**) 899
— Rd. Th., gen. (**A**) 862
Nelson, lds. and visc.
— sir Hor., aft. ld. and visc. Nelson and D. of Bronte, adm. (**A**) 816; K.B. 766
Nelthorpe, Wm., C. Cus. Sc. 504
Nembhard, Wm., gen. (**D**) 915
Nemours, Jul. de Medicis, D. of, K.G. 737
Nepean, Evan adm. (**H**) 848

For List of Abbreviations, see pp. 944-952.

Nepean—*cont.*
— Evan and sir E., C. Treas. Ir. 561; Ch. Sec. Ir. 563; G. Bbay. 659; L. Admy. 180-81; L.P.S. 241; P.C. 207; Sec. Adm. 186; U.S. Home, 228; U.S.W. 231
— Nichs., gen. (**B**) 867
— Th., gen. (**C**) 873
— W., gen. (**D**) 893
Nepos, J., Emp. W.E. 49
— Q. C. M., C. Ro. 45
Neresford, sir Rt. de, W.C.P. 317
Nergu, bp. St. Dav. 464
Nero, C. C., C. Ro. 43
— T. C., C. Ro. 43; Emp. Ro. 47
Nerva, Emp. Ro. 47
— M. C., C. Ro. 46
Nesbit and **Nesbitt,** *see* Nisbet
Nesham, Chr. Jno. W., adm. (**D**) 823; (**G**) 840
Nessan (St.), bp. Cork 630
Nessefield, Wm. de, A.G. 398
Nethercoat, Wm., dn. Kilmacd. 638
Nettervill, Luke, abp. Arm. 595; J.K.B. Ir. 578
Neubourg, Aug. Guelph, K.A. 793
Neve, Pet. Le, Norr. K.A. 329; R. Cr. P.A. 335; Richm. H. 333
— Ph., S.L. 411
— Wm. Le and Sir W., Clar. K.A. 328; Mowb. H. 340; Norr. K.A. 329; Yk. H. 334
Nevell, *see* Nevill
Nevil, Nevill, Neville, and **Nevyll**
— Alan de (No. 1), Jy. 363
— Alan de (No. 2), J. It. 365
— Alexr., abp. 485
— Ch., gen. (**B**) 868
— Chr., K.B. 763
— Clem., gen. (**B**) 864
— Sir Ed., B. Ex. 384; J.C.P. 379; S.L. 410
— hon Ed., adm. (**A**) 813
— Geoffr. de, J. It. 368
— Geo., abp. Yk. 486; bp. Exr. 436; Ld. Chanc. 355
— Geo., *see* Wm., *infra*
— Hugh de, K.B. 754
— Jno. de, K.B. 754
— Jno., K.B. 755
— Jno., K.B. 756
— Joll. de. J.C.P. 376; J. It. 368; Jy. 364
— Laur., bp. Ferns, 621
— Phil. de, K.B. 754
— Ralph de, abp. Cant. 430; bp. Chich. 432; dn. Lich. 445; J. It. 367; Ld. Chanc. Ir. 574; L.K. and Ld. Chanc. 353
— Ralph de, Const. T.L. 320
— Ralph, L.T. 161
— Ralph, Q.C. 420
— Ralph, *see* ld. N. *infra*
— Rd., C. Acc. Ir. 567
— Rd., C.I.E. 808
— Rd., aft. E. of Warwick and Salisbury, *q.v.*, K.G. 736 (*d.* 1471)
— Rt., bp. Dham. 478; bp. Sal. 467
— Rt. de (No. 1), Jy. 364
— Rt. (No. 2), J. It. 368
— Saml. Tarr., bp. Duned. 710

Nevil, Nevill, Neville, and Nevyll—*cont.*
— (or Nevell), Th., dn. Cant. 431; dn. Pboro. 458
— (or Nevylle), Th., dn. Ferns, 623
— Th., K.B. 756
— Th., K.B. 760
— Th., K.B. 762
— Sir Th., Sp. H.C. 249
— Wm., adm. (**H**) 848
— Wm. or Geo., K.B. 758
— Wm., aft. ld. Fauconberg, *q.v.*, K.B. 756
— Sir Wm. de, L.H.A. 172
Neville of Raby, lds.
— Jno., 3rd ld. K.G. 733; L.H.A. 172
— Ralph, ld., aft. 3rd E. of Westmorland, *q.v.*
Nevoy, Sir Dav., ld. Sess. 519
Newall, Dav. Jno. F., gen. (**D**) 920
Newark (or Newerke), Hy. de, abp. Yk. 485; dn. Yk. 486
Newbald, *see also* Nymbolthey.
— (or Newbold), Geoff. de, J.C.P. 377; J. It. 368
Newbery, Fras., gen. (**B**) 869
Newblanch, Ph. Chab., E of, K.G. 737
Newbold, *see* Newbald
Newbolt, Ed. Dorr., gen. (**D**) 934
— Sir Jno. H., C.J. Mdras. 658
Newborough and **Newburgh**
— Rog., K.B. 759
Newborough, lds.
Wynn Family.
— Th., 1st ld.; form. Th. Wynne, *q.v.*
Newburgh, lds.
Barret Family.
— Ed., ld. Barret of, C.D.L. 242; Ch. Ex. 154
Newcastle, E., M., and D. of
Cavendish Family.
(*See also* Cavendish.)
— Wm., 1st E., M., and D. of, form. W. Mansfield, visc. Mansfield, *q.v.*, K.G. 740; P.C. 189
— Hy., 2nd D. of, form. E. of Ogle, *q.v.*; K.G. 740; P.C. 192
Holles Family.
— Jno., D. of, form. E. of Clare, *q.v.*, P.C. 195; K.G. 741; L.P.S. 240
Holles, Pelham, and Clinton Families.
— Thos., 1st D. of, form T. Pelham, ld. P. and E. of Clare, *q.v.* (*d.* 1768), K.G. 741; L.C.H. 295; L.L. Mdx. 310; L.L. Notts. 311; L.P.S. 241; L.T. 157; P.C. 197; Prem. 142; S. St. 224
— Hy., 2nd D. of, from E. of Lincoln. *q.v.*; L.L. Notts, 311; P.C. 202
— Th., 3rd D. of, form. E. of Lincoln, *q.v.*; L.L. Notts, 311
— Hy., 4th D. of, K.G. 743; L.L. Notts, 311
— Hy., 5th D. of, form. 2nd E. of Lincoln, *q.v.*, C. Sec. 235; K.G. 744; L.L. Notts, 311; L.W.S. 323; W. Sec. 232; W. and C. Sec. 231

Newcombe, Benj., dn. Roch. 461
— Danl., dn. Glr. 440
— Jno., dn. Roch. 461
— Rd., bp. Llff. 449; bp. St. As. 462
— Wm., abp. Arm. 596; bp. Drom. 605; bp. Oss. 620; bp. Wford. and L. 627
Newdigate, C. N., P.C. 220
— Ed. Newd., G. Bmda. 701; gen. (**D**) 917
— Hy. Rd. Legge, gen. (**D**) 931
— Jno., S.L., 408
— Rd. and sir R., C.J.K.B. 370; J.K.B. 372; S.L. 409, 410
Newell, Jul. Jas. Farm., adm. (**G**) 842
Newerk, *see* Newark
Newhaven, Ch. Visc., C.Cus. 273
Newland, Hy., dn. Ferns, 623
Newman, Hor. Towns., dn. Cork, 632
— Th., M. Chy. 394
— Walter, gen. (**D**) 932
Newmarch, Oliv., gen. (**D**) 934
Newmarket, Ad. de, J. It. 367
Newnham, Geo. Lew., K.C. 415
— Nath., L.M. Lond. 492
— Th. de, M. Chy. 393
— Wm. de, M. Chy. 393
Newport, And., C. Cus. 273
— Jno., S. L. 408
— sir Jno., C.G.Ex. 169; C. Treas. Ir. 561; Ch. Ex. Ir. 562; P.C. 208
— Pat. de, dn. St. P. 452
— Rd. de, bp. Lond. 451; dn. St. P. 453
— Hon. Th., aft. ld. Torrington, *q.v.*, C. Cus. 274; L.T. 156
— Wm., K.B. 756
Newport, E. of
Blount Family.
— Montj., 1st E. of, form. ld. Montjoy, *q.v.*, M.G.O. 258
Newport Family.
— Fras., 2nd ld., aft. 1st visc. N. and E. of Bradford, *q.v.*, Compt. 292; P.C. 190; P.C. 193; Tr. H. 291
— O. G. C., visc., aft. 3rd E. of Bradford, *q.v.*, P.C. 215; V.C.H. 297
Jocelyn Family.
— Rt., 1st ld., form. Rt. Jocelyn, *q.v.*, aft. 1st visc. J., *q.v.*, L.J. Ir. 557
Newry, Jno., dn. Chich. 434
Newton, Ad., dn. Dham. 479
— Ch., Regr. Bath, 784
— Ch. Th., K.C.B. 784
— Ed., G. Jam, 713; G. Mtius. 684; K.C.M.G. 798
— Fras., dn. Winch. 471
— Hy. and sir H., Adm. Adv. 423; Ch. Lond. 422; J.Adm.Ct. 423; M. Chy. 396
— Horace Park, gen. (**D**) 922
— Isaac and sir I., M.M. 247; Pres. R. Soc. 940
— Jno., gen. (**C**) 871
— Michl. and sir M., K.B. 764
— Rd., C.J.C.P. 375; J.C.P. 378; S.L. 407
— Th., bp. Brl. 439; dn. St. P. 453
— Th., gen. (**D**) 879

For List of Abbreviations, see pp. 944-952.

Newton—*cont.*
—— Wm. Hy., K.H. 791
—— Wm. Saml. and sir W., gen. (**D**) 897
Newtown, Brinsley, ld., aft. 2nd E. of Lanesboro', C. Cus. Ir. 565; C. Exc. Ir. 566
Ney, Off. Nap. 26
Neylan or **Neyland,** Danl., bp. Kild. 617; dn. Elph. 609; dn. Oss. 623
Neyle, *see also* Neile
—— Gilb. Nev., C. St. 284
Niall, K. Ir. 21
—— -Caillie, K. Ir. 21
—— -Freasach, K. Ir. 21
—— -Glundubh, K. Ir. 22
Nias, Jos. and sir J., adm. (**D**) 831; (**F**.) 838; K.C.B. 779
Niccolo, *see* Nicholas
Nicephorus, I. to III., Emp. E.E. 50
Nichol, *see* Nicholl
Nicholas, Nicolas, and **Nicolaus**
*—— (3), bp. Ardf. and Agh. 639
*—— bp. Cness. 531
*—— bp. Down, 603
*—— bp. Elph. 608
*—— bp. Emly. 625
*—— bp. Isl. 539
*—— bp. Kilmacd. 636
* Prob. some same pers. Comp. dates.
—— Ld. Chanc. Sc. 514; Ld. Clk. Reg. 524; Sec. St. Sc. 501
—— D. Lne. 29
—— I., E. Russ. 90; K.G. 743
—— I., K. Dk. 93
—— I., Pr. Mgo. 95
—— (or Niccolo), I. to III., M. Fa. 53
—— I. to V., P. Ro. 33-4-5
—— Ambr., L.M. Lond. 490
—— Ed., L.P.S. 240; Paym. G. 244
—— sir Ed., L.T. 155; P.C. 189; S. St. 223
—— Fras., D. Lne. 30
—— Jno., K.B. 763
—— Jno. Toup, adm. (**D**) 829; K.H. 790
—— Matth., dn. Brl. 440; dn. St. P. 453
—— sir Nich. Harr., Chanc. M.G. 799; G.C.M.G. 794; K.C.M.G. 796; K.H. 790; M.G. K.A. 799
—— Rt., B. Ex. 384; J.K.B. 372; S.L. 409
—— Rt., C. Exc. 281
Nicholl, Nichol, Nicoll, and **Nicol**
—— G. Tob. 723
—— Ch., gen. (**B**) 870
—— Ch. Gunt, K.B. 764
—— Fras., Modr. K. Sc. 547
—— Hy., gen. (**D**) 916
—— Jno. and sir J. (No. 1), B.T. 268; D. Arch. 421; J. Adm. Ct. 423; J. Pr. Ct. 421; Jud. Com. P.C. 360; K. Adv. 422; P.C. 208; Vic. Gen. 422
—— Jno. and sir J. (No. 2), B.T. 268; J.A.G. 937; L.T. 160; P.C. 214
—— Th., gen. (**D**) 928
Nichols, Nicholls, Nicols and **Nicolls**
—— Aug. and sir A., J.C.P. 378; S.L. 409
Nichols, Nicholls, Nicols, and Nicolls—*cont.*
—— Bened., bp. Bgr. 426; bp. St. Dav. 464
—— Ed., gen. (**D**) 882; K.C.B. 778
—— Geo., gen. (**D**) 890
—— Geo., K.C.B., 782; P.L.C. 262; Sec. P.L.B. 262
—— Gust., gen. (**A**) 863
—— Hy. and sir H., Adm (**A**) 818; Compt. N. 257; K.C.B. 775
—— Jas. Edm. Tarr., gen. (**D**) 907
—— Jasp. and sir J., C.C. Ind. 651; C.C. Mdras. 657; gen. (**B**) 869; K.C.B. 775
—— Oliv. C.C. Bbay. 660; gen. (**A**) 860
—— Wm., C.C.J. 404
—— Wm., dn. Chest. 477
Nicholson and **Nicolson**
—— Arth., K.C.I.E. 805
—— sir Fk. Wm. Ersk., adm. (**D**) 833; (**E**) 834; (**F**) 838
—— sir Geo., Ld. Sess. 519
—— Hy. Fk., adm. (**E**) 837
—— Jas., bp. Dkld. 533
—— Loth., G. Jsey. 668; gen. (**D**) 917; K.C.B. 782
—— sir Th. Ld. Adv. 526
—— Th. Wm., K.H. 791
—— Wm., abp. Cash. and Eml. 626; abp. Carl. 476; bp. Dry. 601
—— Wm., bp. Glr. 438
—— sir Wm., gen (**C**) 874
Nicholyn, Lotto, M.M. 240
Nickle, Rt. and sir R., gen. (**D**) 883; K.H. 790
Nicol, *see* Nicholl
Nicolas, *see* Nicholas
Nicolaus, *see* Nicholas
Nicolay, Wm. and sir W., G. Dnca. 730; G. Mtius. 683; G. St. Xtr. &c. 727; gen. (**B**) 869; K.C.H. 788
Nicoll, *see* Nicholl
Nicolls, *see* Nichols
Nicols, *see* Nichols
Nicolson, *see* Nicholson
Niddry, Jno., 1st ld., form. hon. J. Hope, *q.v.*, G.C.B. 767
Nieper, G. H., V. Chanc. Guelph, 792
Niel, Genl., K.C.B. 778
Nigel or **Nigellus,** bp. Ely, 434; dn. Linc. 447; Jy. 363; L.H.T. 152
Niger, M. V. M., C. Ro. 46
—— P., Emp. Ro. 47
—— Rog., bp. Lond. 451
Nightingale or **Nightingall**
—— Miles and sir M., C.C. Bbay. 660; gen. (**B**) 867; K.C.B. 773
Nikke or **Nikks,** Rd., *see* Nix
Nilson, Laur., C.C. Bbay. 659
Ninian (St.) (2), bp. Gall. 538
Nisbet, Nesbit, and **Nesbitt**
—— Alexr., gen. (**B**) 869
—— Colebr., gen. (**C**) 872
—— Jno., gen. (**D**) 913
—— sir Jno., Ld. Adv. 526; Ld. Sess. 519
—— Jos., gen. (**D**) 880
—— Patr., Ld. Sess. 519
—— Rt. Parry, C.I.E. 807
Nison, Fras. and sir F., Dep. Sec. at W. 234
Niven, Knox Rowan gen. (**D**) 927
Nix (or Nikks)
—— Rd., bp. Norw. 455; L.K. 355; Regr. Gart. 746
Nixon, Fras. Russ., bp. Tasm. 708
—— J. Lyons, G. Nev. 729; G. St. Xtr. 729; G. Virg. Isl. 731
Nizamuddin, &c., C.I.E. 808
Nobilior, M. F., C. Ro. 43-4
—— Q. F., C. Ro. 44
—— S. F. P., C. Ro. 42
Nobis, bp. Llff. 448
Noble, Jas., adm. (**D**) 823
—— Jno., dn. Exr. 437
—— Wm. Hall, gen. (**D**) 930
Noboa, D., Pres. Ecr. 108
Noctua, Q. C., C. Ro. 41
Noel, hon. Bennet, gen. (**B**) 865
—— hon. Gerard J., C.W.P.B. 272; L.T. 161; P.C. 219
—— Rown., dn. Sal. 468
—— hon. Wm., C.J. Chest., 386; J.C.P. 379; K.C. 415; S.L. 412
Noell, *see also* Nowell
—— Ed., C. Exc. 279
Nolan, Michl., K.C. 416; J. Chest. 387
Nolloth, Matth. S., adm. (**H**) 850
Nomenoe, D. Bry. 27
Nonis, abp. St. Dav. 463
Nood, Piet. Gysb., G. C.G.H. 678
Norcliffe, Norc., gen. (**D**) 890; K.H. 791
Norcott, sir Amos Gods. Rt., gen. (**C**) 875; K.C.H. 788
—— Edm., G. Gamb. 686
—— Wm. Sh. R., G. Jsey. 668; gen. (**D**) 903; K.C.B. 780
Norfolk, E. and D. of. *Refer also to* Arundel, Howard, Maltravers and Mowbray
Bigod Family.
(*See also* Bigod)
—— Rog. Big., 2nd E. of, Jy. 363
—— Rog., 4th E. of, J. It. 367; L.M. 325
—— Rog., 5th E. of, L.M. 325
Plantagenet Family.
—— Th. (De Brotherton), 1st E. of, L.M. 325
—— Margt., Ctss., aft. Dss. of, L.M. 325
Mowbray Family
—— Th., D. of, form. E. of Nottm., *q.v.* (*d.* 1399)
—— Jno., D. of, form. Jno. Mowbray, and E. of Nottm., *q.v.* (*d.* 1432)
—— Jno., D. of, form. E. of Nottm., *q.v.* (*d.* 1461), E.M. 326; K.G. 735
—— Jno., D. of (*d.* 1472), K.G. 736
Plantagenet Family.
—— Rd., D. of, *also* D. of York, *q.v.* (*d.* 1483)
Howard Family.
—— Jno., 1st D. of, form. ld. Howard, *q.v.*, L.H.A. 174
—— Th., 2nd D. of, form. ld. Howard and E. of Surrey, *q.v.*, L.H.A. 174
—— Th., 3rd D. of, E.M. 326; L.K. 355
—— Th., 4th D. of, E.M. 326; K.G. 738

For List of Abbreviations, see pp. 944-952.

Norfolk, E. and D. of—*cont.*
— Th., 1st E. of, form. E. of Arundel, *q.v.* (*d.* 1646)
— Hy., 7th D. of, form. E. of Arundel, *q.v.*, E.M. 326; K.G. 740; P.C. 193
— Th., 8th D. of, E.M. 326
— Ed., 9th D. of, E.M. 326
— Ch., 10th D. of, E.M. 326
— Ch., 11th D. of, form. E. of Surrey, *q.v.*, E.M. 326; L.L. Suss. 312
— Bern. Ed., 12th D. of, E.M. 326; K.G. 743; P.C. 211
— Hy. Ch., 13th D. of, form. E. of Surrey and ld. Maltravers, *q.v.*, E.M. 326; K.G. 744; L.S.H. 290; M.H. 302
— Hy. Gr., 14th D. of, E.M. 326
— Hy., 15th D. of, E.M. 326; K.G. 745

Norgate, Ed., Bl. M.P.A. 336; Winds. H. 331

Norman, Fras. Booth, K.C.B. 781
— Hy. Radf., gen. (**D**) 909
— Hy. Wyl. and sir H., G.C.B. 771; G.C.M.G. 795; G. Jam. 713; G. Qland. 706; gen. (**D**) 908; K.C.B. 780; M.C.I. 647
— Jno., L.M. Lond. 488
— Jno., L.M. Lond. 490
— Lion., C. Cus. Sc. 503

Normanby, visc. M. and D. of
Sheffield Family.
— Jno., 1st M. of, form. 3rd E. of Mulgrave, *q.v.*, aft. 1st D. of N., and D. of Bucks, *q.v.*, L.P.S. 240; P.C. 194-5
Phipps Family.
— Hy., 1st visc., form. ld. and aft. E. of Mulgrave, *q.v.*
— Const. Hy., 2nd visc., aft. 1st M. of, form. E. of Mulgrave, &c., *q.v.*, Amb. Fr. 113; Amb. Tusc. 115; G.C.B. 772; H. Sec. 227; K.G. 744; W. and C. Sec. 231
— Geo. Augs. Const., 2nd M. of, form. E. of Mulgrave, *q.v.*, C.G.A. 300; G.C.B. 773; G.C.M.G. 795; G. N.Z. 709; G. Qland. 706; G. Vict. 705; K.C.M.G. 797

Normandy, Hy., D. of, Ch. Jr. (1153) 362

Normannus, *see* Normanus

Normanton, Wm., M. Chy. 394

Normanton, E. of
— Ch., 1st E. of, form. Chas. Agar, and ld. and visc. Somerton, *q.v.*

Normannus and **Normanus,** *see also* Cantilupe
— (or De Cantilupe), Simon, L.K. 353
— Ulf., bp. Dorch. and Sidr. 446

Normanville, Th. de, J. It. 368

Norreis, *see* Norreys

Norreys, *see also* Norris
— (or Norreis), Pet., dn. St. Pat. 618
— Rt., Ch. Ex. Ir. 561

Norrie, Rt., bp. Glasg. 543

Norris, *see also* Norreys
— Hy., adm. (**A**) 814
— sir Jno., adm. (**A** 813; L. Admy. 177; P.C. 198

Norris—*cont.*
— Jno. Fr., Q.C. 419
— sir Th., L.J. Ir. 554
— Wm., K.B. 761
— Wm., Mast. and Pres. Coll. Surg. 939

Norris, lds.
— Fras., 2nd ld., aft. 1st E. of Berkshire, *q.v.*, K.B. (1605) 761

North, Br., bp. Lich. and Cov. 444; bp. Winch. 471; bp. Worc. 473; dn. Cant. 431
— Ch. Fk., gen. (**D**) 899
— Dudley, *see* ld. N., *infra*
— sir Dudl., L.T. 155
— Ford and sir F., J.Q.B.D. 374; Just. Ch. D. 391; Q.C. 419
— Fras. and sir F., aft. 1st ld. Guildford, *q.v.*, A.G. 399; C.J.C.P. 375; K.C. 414; L.K. 357; P.C. 192; S.G. 401; S.L. 410
— hon. Fk., aft. 7th E. of Guildford, *q.v.*, G. Ceyl. 672
— hon. Fk., *see* ld. N., *infra*
— hon. G., U.S.Home, 227
— Jno., K.B. 762
— Jno. Hy., J. Admy. Ct. Ir. 587
— Jno. Sidney, P.C. 221
— Rog., K.C. 414-5
— Rog., *see* ld. N., *infra*

North, lds.
— Rog., 2nd ld., K.B. 761; Tr. H. 291
— Dudl., aft. 3rd ld. N., K.B. 762; L. Admy. 175
— Wm., 6th ld., gen. (**B**) 864; P.C. 196
— hon. Fk., c.c. ld. North, aft. 4th E. of Guildford, *q.v.*, Ch.Ex. 165; Chambn. Ex. 166; H. Sec. 226; K.G. 742; L.L. Soms. 311; L.T. 157-8; Paym. G. 245; P.C. 202; Prem. 143; W.C.P. 319

Northalis, Rd., abp. Dbln. and Gl. 616; bp. Oss. 620; Ld. Chanc. Ir. 575

Northall, Rt. de, bp. Worc. 472

Northampton, Adam de, bp. Ferns, 621
— Hyde, J. It. 366.
— Jno. de, L.M. Lond. 489
— Rd. de, bp. Ferns, 621

Northampton, E. and M. of.
De Bohun Family.
— Wm., 1st E of, form. Sir W. de Bohun, *q.v.*, K.G. 733; L.H.A. 172
Parr Family.
— Wm., M. of, form. ld. Parr of Kendal, and E. of Essex, *q.v.*; C.G.P. 299
Howard Family.
— Hy., E. of, E.M. 326; K.G. 739; L.P.S. 240; L.T. 154; W.C.P. 319
Compton Family.
— Wm., 1st E of, form. ld. Compton, *q.v.*, K.G. 739
— Spencer, 2nd E. of, M.G.W. 296
— Jas., 3rd E. of, Const. T.L. 321; P.C. 191
— Geo., 4th E. of, Const. T.L. 321; P.C. 195
— Geo., 4th or 6th E. of, form. hon. G. Compton, *q.v.*
— Ch., 7th E. of, amb. Vce. 116

Northampton, E. and M. of—*cont.*
— Sp., 8th E. of, L.L. Nton. 310
— Ch., 9th E. aft. 1st M. of, L.L. Nton. 310
— Spenc. Jos. Alw., 2nd M. of, Pres. R. Soc., 940
— Wm., 4th M. of, form. ld. Wm. Compton, *q.v.*, K.G. 745

Northatus, K. Sc. 17

Northbertus, bp. Elm. 454

Northbrook, lds. and E. of
— Fras. T., 1st ld., form. sir F. T. Baring, *q.v.*
— Th. Geo., 2nd ld. aft. 1st E. of, form. hon. T. G. Baring, *q.v.*; amb. Eg. 130; G.C.S.I. 801; G. G. Ind. 649; L. Admy. 185-6; P.C. 218; Sec. Adm. 187; U.S. War. 232

Northbrugh or **Northburgh,** Rog. de, bp. Lich. and Cov. 444; L.H.T. 153

Northburg, Michl. de, bp. Lond. 451

Northbury, sir Jno., L.H.T. 153
— Wm. de, J. It. 368

Northcote, hon. Hy. Staff., aft. Sir H., S.G.O. 260; U.S. War. 233
— sir Staff. Hy., aft. 1st E. of Iddesleigh, *q.v.*, Ch. Ex. 166; G.C.B. 773; L.T. 162; P.C. 217; Pres. B.T. 269; Sec. Ind. 236
— Walt. Staff., aft. visc. St. Cyres, and 2nd E. of Iddesleigh, *q.v.*, C.I.R. 286
— Cec. Fras., lady, aft. Css. of Iddesleigh, Cr. Ind. 810

Northcott, Chas., dn. Kilmacd. 638

Northcote, E. of
— Dav., 4th E. of, L.H.T. Sc. 498
— Geo., 6th E. of, adm. (**A** 814
— Wm., 7th E. of, adm. (**A**) 817; G.C.B. 761; K.B. 766

Northey, sir Ed., A.G. 399
— Wm. B.T. 266

Northington, E. of
— Rt., 1st E. of, form. sir Rt. and ld. Henley, *q.v.*, L.L. Hants, 311; L.H.S. 287; L.P.C. 188
— Rd., 2nd E. of, form. hon. R. Henley, *q.v.*, K.T. 748; L.L. Tr. 557; P.C. 204

Northland, Geo., adm. 853

Northumberland, E. and D. of
— Walch. de Lovaine, E. of, bp. Dham. (1072) 478
— Hy., E. of (*d.* 1152), Ld. Chanc. Sc. 514
— Hugh Pudsey or Pusar, E. of (*d.* 1195), (*see* Pudsey)
Percy Family.
— Hy., 1st E. of, form. Hy. Percy, *q.v.* (*d.* 1408); K. Man, 665; L.H.A. 173
Nevill Family.
— Jno., E. of, form. ld. aft. M. of Montague, *q.v.*
Percy Family restored.
— Hy., 4th E. of (*d.* 1489), K.G. 736
— Hy., 5th E. of, K.B. (1489), 758; K.G. 737

For List of Abbreviations, see pp. 944-952.

Northumberland, E. and D. of —*cont.*
— Hy., 6th E. of, K.G. (1537), 737
Dudley Family.
— Jno., D. of, form. visc. Lisle and E. of Warwick, *q.v.* (*d.* 1553); E.M. 326; L.S.H. 290
Percy Family restored.
— Th., 7th E. of (*d.* 1572), K.G. 738
— Hy., 9th E. of (*d.* 1632), K.G. 739; C.G.P. 299
— Algn., 10th E. of (*d.* 1668), E.M. 326; K.G. 739; L.H.A. 175; L.H. Const, 289; L.L. Dham. 308; P.C. 190
Fitzroy Family.
— Geo., D. of (*d.* 1716), Const. W. Cast. 322; gen. (**B**) 864; K.G. 740; L.L. Surr. 312; P.C. 196
Seymour Family.
— Algn., E. of, form. ld. Algn. Percy and E. of Hertford, *q.v.* (*d.* 1750)
Smithson and Percy Families.
Note.—These Dukes commence with 1st according to Burke, and 2nd according to Nicolas.
— Hugh, E., aft. 1st-2nd D. of (*d.* 1786), K.G. 742; L.L. Ir. 557; L.L. Mdx. 310; L.L. Nbland. 310; M.H. 302; P.C. 201
— Hugh, 2nd-3rd D. of (*d.* 1817); gen. (**A**) 858; K.G. 742; L.L. Nbland, 310
— Hugh, 3rd-4th D. of (*d.* 1847), amb. Fr. 113; K.G. 743; L.L. Ir. 557; L.L. Nbland. 310; P.C. 210
— Algn., 4th-5th D. of, form. ld. Prudhoe, *q.v.* (*d.* 1865); adm. (**D**) 829; (**G**) 840; K.G. 744; Ld. Admy. 183; P.C. 215
— Geo., 5th-6th D. of, form. ld. Lovaine, and 2nd E. of Beverley, *q.v.*
— Algn. Geo., 6th-7th D. of, form. ld. Lovaine, *q.v.*, K.G. 745; L.L. Nbland, 310; L.P.S. 241; Pres. R. Inst. 940
Northwell, Wm. de, B. Ex. 383
Northwold, Hugh, bp. Ely, 434
— (or Northwood) Rog. de, B. Ex. 382; W.C.P. 317; Jy. 364
Northwood, *see* Northwold
Norton, hon. Chapple, gen. (**A**) 859
— sir Dudley, Ch. Ex. Ir. 562; Sec. St. Ir. 562
— Fletcher and sir F., aft. 1st ld. Grantley, *q.v.*, A.G. 399; K.C. 415; P.C. 202; S.G. 402; Sp. H.C. 250
— hon. Fl., Bar. Ex. Sc. 524
— Geo., K.B. 760
— Greg. de, Rec Lond. 493
— Jeff. de, Rec. Lond. 493
— Jno. de, A.G. 398
— Jno., K.B. 759
— Rd., C.J.C.P. 375; S.L. 407
— Th., L.G. Ch. Hosp. 936
— Wm., Amb. Swz. 113
Norton, lds.
— Ch. B., 1st ld, form. sir C. B. Adderley, *q.v.*
Norwich, Geoff. de, dn. Yk. 486.
— sir Jno. de, L.H.A. 171
— Ralph de, Jy. 364
— Rt. de, C.J.C.P. 375; J.C.P. 378; S.L. 408
— (or Norwico) W. de, B. Ex. 383; C.B. Ex. 381; L.H.T. 152, 153
— Wm. de, (W. Bateman), bp. Norw. 455; dn. Linc. 448
Norwich, E. of
Goring Family.
— Geo., 1st E of, form. ld. Goring, *q.v.*, C.G.P. 299; P.C. 190
— Chas., 2nd E. of, B.T. 263; C.Y.G. 298
Norwico, *see* Norwich
Nothelmus, abp. Cant. 430
Nott and **Notte**
— Ed. Banb., adm (**H**) 851
— Fett., S.L. 411
— Fras. Percy, gen. (**D**) 911
— Hy., gen. (**D**) 910
— Jno., L.M. Lond. 489
— Wm., G.C.B. 769; gen. (**D**) 879
Nottage, Geo. Sw., L.M. Lond. 492
Notte, *see* Nott.
Nottingham, Jno. de, dn. Linc. 448
— Rt. de, B. Ex. 383
— Rt. de, J.C.P. 376; Jy. 364
— Wm. de, A.G. 398; C.B. Ex. 383
— Wm., J. It. 368
Nottingham, E. of
Mowbray Family.
— Th., E. of, aft. D. of Norfolk, *q.v.*, E.M. 326; K.G. 734; L.M. 325
Plantagenet Family.
— Rd., E. of (1476), also D. of York, *q.v.*
Berkeley Family.
— Wm., E. of (*d.* 1492), E.M. 326
Fitzroy Family.
— Hy., E. of, form. Hy. Fitzroy, *q.v.*, aft. D. of Richmond and Somerset, *q.v.*
Howard Family.
— Chas., 1st E. of, form. ld. How. of Eff., *q.v.*, Const. W. Cast. 322; E.M. 326; L.H.A. 174; L.L. Suss. 312; L.S.H. 290
Finch Family.
— Heneage, 1st E. of, form. sir H. and ld. Finch, *q.v.*
— Danl., 2nd E. of, form. hon. D. and ld. Finch, *q.v.*, aft. 7th E. of Winchilsea, *q.v.*; Ld. Admy, 176; L.L. Kent, 309; L.P.C. 188; P.C. 195; S. St. 224
Notton, Wm. de, J.K.B. 371; S.L. 406
Novant, Hugh, bp. Lich. and Cov. 443
Novis, abp. St. Dav. 463
Novitianus, P. Ro. 32
Nowell, *see also* Noell
— Alex., dn. St. P. 453
— Hy., G. I. Man, 666
— Lawr., dn. Lich. 445
— Rd., G. I. Man, 666
— Wm.. adm. (**A**) 819
Noy, Wm., A.G. 399
Nuad, bp. Arm. 595
Nuadha-Fioun-Fail, K. Ir. 20
Nuba Pasha, G.C.M.G. 795
Nucells, ld., *see* Scales and N.
Nudd, bp. Llff. 448
Nugent, Andr., gen. (**D**) 927
— sir Ch. Edmd., adm. (**A**) 816; (**B**) 821; G.C.H. 787
— Ch. B. P. N. Hodges-, K.C.B. 781
— Ch. Lav., gen. (**D**) 906
— Count, K.C.B. 775
— Edm., bp. Kilm. 607
— sir Edm., L.M. Dbln. 642
— Geo., *see* ld. N., *infra*
— Geo. and sir G., C.C. Bgal. 652; C.C. Ind. 650; F.M. 856; G.C.B. 767; G. Jam. 713; gen. (**A**) 860; K.B. 766
*— Jno., G. Antig. 728
*— Jno., gen. (**C**) 874
* Poss. same pers.
— Nichs., B.Ex. Ir. 583; C.J. C.P. Ir. 580; S. G. Ir. 589
— Rd., L.D. Ir. 552
— Rt., *see* ld. N., *infra*
— St. Geo. M., gen. (**D**) 922
— Th., C.J.K.B. Ir. 578; J.K.B. Ir. 579
— Th., Comm. Serjt. Lond. 495
Nugent, lds. and E.
— Rt., aft. 1st ld. and E. Nugent and visc. Clare, *q.v.*, L.T. 157; P.C. 200; Pres. B.T. 266; V. Treas. Ir. 560
— Geo., ld., aft. 2nd E. Temple and 1st M. of Buckm., *q.v.*, L.L. Bucks. 306
— Geo., ld., son of 1st M. of Buckm., Com. Io. Isl. 129; G.C.M.G. 794; L.T. 160
Numa Pompilius, K. Ro. 36
Numerianus, Emp. Ro. 48
Numidicus, Q. C. M., C. Ro. 45
Nunant, Hugh, bp. Lich. and Cov. 443
Nünez, R., Pres. U.S.C. 107
Nurse, Ch. Bulk, gen. (**D**) 926
Nuthall, Fred. Geo., gen. (**D**) 911
Nutley, Rd., J.Q.B. Ir. 579
Nuttall, Enos bp. Jam. 713
— Jno., dn. Chest. 477
— Jos., L.M. Dbln, 641
— Th., gen. (**D**) 927
Nymbolthe (or Newbald), Sim., R. Cr. P.A. 335
Nyon, Mons. de, G. Mtius. 683

O.

O'—
See also under the name without this prefix, which is sometimes omitted in the original lists from which this book is compiled.
Oak—, *see* Oke—

Oakeley, *see* Oakley
Oakes, sir Hild., G.C.B. 768; G. Mlta. 671; gen. (**B**) 867; L.G.O. 259
— Rd., Amb. G. St. 121; Amb. Pld. 126
— Th. Geo. Alexr., gen. (**D**) 908
Oakham, *see* Okeham
Oakley and **Oakeley**
— sir Ch., G. Mdras. 656
— Jno., dn. Carl. 476; dn. Manch. 481
Oates, Jas. Poole, K.H. 792
Oatlawe, *see* Outlaw
Oatley, Ad., M. Chy. 376
O'Bainan, Patr., bp. Cnr. 603
— Gelasius, bp. Clr. 596
Obaldia, J. de, Pres. Pan. 107
Obando, J. M. y, Pres. N.G. 107
O'Bardain, dn. Kilm. 609
Obbard, Harry Sm., gen. (**D**) 926
— Th., gen. (**D**) 931
O'Beirn, Malachy, bp. Kild. 616
O'Beirne, Th. Lewis, bp. Meath, 599; bp. Oss. 621
O'Beoda, Donat, bp. Killa. 612
Obinus, abp. Lond. 450
Obizzo, II. and III., M. Fa. 53
Obligado, Pres. B. Ay. 110
O'Braion, bp. Clonm. 599
O'Braoin, Steph. W., bp. Mayo, 611
O'Brian, O'Brien, and **O'Bryen**
— Barth., gen. (**D**) 908
— Const., bp. Killoe. 634
— Don., bp. Clonm. 600
*— Don., bp. Killoe. 634
*— Don., bp. Lim. 638
* Poss. same pers.
— Don. Hinchy, adm. (**G**) 841
— Ed., adm. (**A**) 817
— Ed. Jas., gen. (**C**) 875
— Jas., J.Q.B. Ir. 579; J.Q.B.D. Ir. 579; S.L. Ir. 593
— ld. Jas., aft. 3rd M. of Thomond, *q.v.*, adm. (**A**) 820; G.C.H. 786
— Jas. Th., bp. Oss., F. and L. 622; dn. Cork, 632
— Jno. Ter. Nic. and sir J., G. Ceyl. 673; G. Hlgld. 670; G. Newfd. 700; K.C.M.G. 798
— Jos., adm. (**G**) 841
— Kenn., dn. Emly, 628
— Luc., adm. (**A**) 815
— sir Luc., aft. 13th ld. Inchiquin, *q.v.*, L.L. Clare, 569
— Marian, abp. Cash. 624; bp. Cork, 630
— Maur., bp. Kilf. 635; dn. Kilf. 637; bp. Killoe. 634
— Michl. Wm., S.L. 414
— Percy W., L.T. 157
— Pet., A.G. Ir. 589; S.G. Ir. 590; S.L. Ir. 593
— Rt., adm. (**D**) 824
— Terence (3), bp. Killoe, 634
— Terence, gen. (**D**) 895
— Thad., dn. Cash. 627
— Tim. and sir T., L.M. Dbln. 642
— Wm., J.C.P.D. Ir. 582; J.Q.B.D. Ir. 580
O'Brogan, Bened., bp. Ach. 612
— Dav., bp. Clr. 596
— Nehem., bp. Clr. 596
— Steph., abp. Cash. 624
O'Brogy, Greg., bp. Clonf. 635; dn. Clonf. 637
O'Brolcan, Flathbert, bp. Dry. 600
O'Bryen, *see* O'Brien
O'Buacalla, Chas., bp. Emly, 625
O'Cahan (or O'Cane), Corn., bp. Rph. 601
— (or O'Cane), Dennis, bp. Kilf. 635
O'Cairil, Corn., bp. Tm. 611
O'Callaghan, Fras. Langf., C.I.E. 807
— Geo. Wm. Dougl., adm. (**E**) 835; (**F**) 838
— Hon. Rt. Wm. and sir R., C.C. Mdras. 657; G.C.B. 769; gen. (**B**) 868; K.C.B. 774
O'Cane, *see* O'Cahan
O'Caran, Gilb., abp. Arm. 595; bp. Rph. 601
O'Carellan, *see* O'Cherballen
O'Carmacain, Gilc., dn. Elph. 609
O'Carolan, *see* O'Cherballen
O'Carrol, sir Danl., gen. (**B**) 864
— Jno., *see* MacCarrill
— Th., abp. Cash. 625; abp. Tm. 611
O'Cashin, Jno., bp. Killa. 612
O'Cassy, *see* O'Cuffy
O'Catan, Sluagad, bp. Llin. 621
O'Cathald, Muredach, bp. Kild. 616
O'Cathlan, Brigd., bp. Ferns, 621
— Mœlisa, bp. Ferns, 621
O'Cathsuigh, Cormac, bp. Kild. 616
O'Cellaic, Dungall, bp. Llin. 621
O'Cervallan, Hugh, bp. Clr. 596
O'Cherballen (or O'Carellan) Florence (2), bp. Dry. 600
— (or O'Carolan), Don., dn. Dry. 602
— (or Carellan), German or Gervase, bp. Dry. 601
Ocherlony, Alex., Bl. L. P.A. 341
Ochiltree, Michl., bp. Dnbl. 532
Ochterlonie, Ochterlony, and **Ouchterlonie**
— sir Dav., G.C.B. 767; K.C.B. 775
— Jno., bp. Brn. 541
Ochus, K. Pers. 99
O'Clerchen, Cellach, bp. Cld. 599
O'Clery, Gelisa, bp. Ach. 612
O'Cloghena, Florence or Finin, bp. Ross. 631
O'Clowan or **O'Cluan,** Malachy, bp. Killa. 612
O'Clumain, Oengus, bp. Ach. 612
O'Cnuil (or Conuil), Cat., bp. Tm. 611
O'Coffy, Amlave, bp. Dry. 600
— (or O'Dubthaic), Maur., bp Dry. 600
O'Coinderi, *see* O'Connery
O'Colman (or Kellach), Gelas., bp. Ferns, 621
O'Colweny, Michl., dn. Ardf. 640
O'Con—, *see also* O'Conn—
O'Conactain, Mœlisa, bp Elph. 608
O'Conacty, Florence, bp. Kilm. 607
O'Conaing, Donat, bp. Cash. 624
O'Conarchy, Christ., bp. Lism. 626
— Don., bp. Ardf. and Agh. 639
O'Concubhair, *see* O'Connor
O'Conellan, Abrm., abp. Arm. 595; dn. Arm. 597
O'Congalan, Th., bp. Ard., 607
O'Coning, Derm., bp. Killoe. 634
O' Conn—, *see also* O'Con—
O'Connell, Connor (2), bp. Killoe. 612
— Danl., L.M. Dbln. 642
— Hugh Heefke, gen. (**D**) 924
— Maur. Ch. and Sir M., G. N.S.W. 703; G. Qland. 705-6; gen. (**B**) 869; K.C.H. 788
— Pet. Pierce Ly., gen. (**D**) 920
O'Conner, *see* O'Connor
O'Connery, (or O'Coinderi), Th., dn. Kilm. 609
O'Connor, O'Conor, and **O'Conner**
— Ardg., bp. Elph. 608
— Bern., bp. Ross, 631
— Donat, bp. Elph. 608
— (or O'Concubhair), Donat, bp. Killa. 612
— Jno., L.M. Dbln. 642
— Luke, gen. (**D**) 932
— Luke S. M., G. Gamb. 686; gen. (**D**) 901
— Maur., bp. Elph. 608
— Milo, bp. Elph. 608
— N. R., Amb. Bga. 128
— Owen, bp. Killa. 612; dn. Ach. 614
O'Conolly, Patr., bp. Clr. 596
— Rd. and sir R., adm. (**H**) 845; K.C.H. 789
— Th., abp. Arm. 595
— Tn., abp. Tm. 611; bp. Elph. 608; dn. Ach. 614
O'Conor, *see* O'Connor
O'Conuil, *see* O'Cnuil
O'Corboy, Flan., bp. Ferns, 621
O'Corcroin, bp. Clr., 596
O'Cormacain, Is., bp. Killoe, 634; dn. Killoe. 637
— Th., bp. Killoe. 634
— Wm., abp. Tm. 611; B. Cfert, 635
O'Cormagan, Dav., dn. Killoe, 637
O'Corrin, Jas., bp. Killoe. 634
O'Corry, Maur., dn. Arm. 597
O'Coscry, Bened., bp., Killoe. 634; dn. Killoe. 637
Octa, bp. Gall. 538
— K.E. 1
Octavianus, *see also* Augustus
— Emp. Ro. 47
— C. J. C. (7), C. Ro. 46-7; Tr. Ro. 46
Octavius (son Geo. III.), Pr. E. 15
— C., C. Ro., 44-5
— (Farnese), D. Pma. 53
— L., C. Ro. 46
Octtan, G. I. Man, 665
O'Cuffy (or O'Cassy), Dav., bp. Emly, 625

For List of Abbreviations, see pp. 944-952.

O'Culean, Den., dn. Arm. 597
O'Cunga, Ultan, bp. Cld. 598
O'Cunlis, Corn., bp. Clonf. 636; bp. Emly, 625
O'Curran, Corn., dn. Llin. 623
O'Currin, Sim., bp. Kilf. 635
O'Daithil, Conaing, bp. Emly, 625
O'Daly, Lewis, bp. Clonm. 600
O'Dea, Corn., bp. Killoe. 634; bp. Lim. 638
— Denn., bp. Oss. 620
Odell, Th., C. Exc. Ir. 566-7
— Th., E.S.P. 301
— Wm., C. Treas. Ir. 561; L.T. 159
Odet-Pellion, *see* Pellion
Odiham, *see* Odyham
Odinsele (or Dodinsele), Wm. de, L.J. Ir. 550
O'Diocholla, Eudocius, bp. Kild. 616
Odlamh-Fodhla, K. Ir. 20
Odlum, S. S., G. Monts. 729
***Odo,** bp. Kilmacd. 636
*— bp. Mayo, 612
*— bp. Ross, 631
*— dn. Clr. 597
*— (or Hugh) dn. Oss. 622
* Prob. some same persons. Comp. dates.
— (bp. Bayeux and E. of Kent), Ch. Jr. 362
— H. Severus, bp. Wltn. 466
Odoacer, Emp. W.E. 49
— K. It 49
O'Doghertie, Phel., dn. Rph. 602
O'Doherty, Gilb., bp. Emly, 625; dn. Emly, 628
O'Donchada, Ch., dn. Cloy. 632
O'Donellan, Andr., dn. Emly, 628
O'Donnel and **O'Donnell**
— Sir Ch. Routl., gen. (**D**) 884
— Rodk., bp. Dry. 601; dn. Rph. 602
— Thirl., dn. Arm. 597
— Th. Mac Cormac, bp. Rph. 601
O'Donovan, Rd., gen. (**B**) 868
O'Dorigh, Mœlisa, bp. Rph. 601
O'Dove, M., *see* Dovey
O'Dowd, Const., dn. Tm. 613
O'Dowda, Manus Fitz Fult., bp. Killa, 612
— Wm., bp. Killa. 612
O'Dreain, Gill., dn. Elph., 609
O'Dubery, bp. Cloy. 630
O'Dubhai and **O'Duffy**
— Catholicus, abp. Tm. 611
— Cele, bp. Mayo, 611
— Don., bp. Clonm. 599; bp. Elph. 608; bp. Tm. 611
— Flanachan, bp. Elph. 608
— Maur. or Mur., bp. Tm. 611
— Wm., bp. Clonm., 600
O'Dubhin, bp. Kild. 616
O'Dubthaigh, Muredach, bp. Rph. 601
O'Duffy, *see* O'Dubhai
O'Duibditrib, Dav., bp. Ardf. and Agh. 639
O'Dullany, St. Felix, bp. Oss. 620
O'Dunan, Miler or Melm., bp. Cash. 624
O'Dunluing, Tuethal, bp. Cld. 599
O'Dwyer, Dav., dn. Cash, 627
Odyham, Walt. de, M. Chy. 393
Œ— *see also Æ*—
Œducan, Mac-Mic, bp. Lism. 626
Œlfstan (or Æfstan), bp. Lond. 451
O'Ergain, Ect., bp. Clonm. 599
O'Erodain, *see* O'Ronan
Œswy, bp. Dorch. and Sidr. 446
O'Etegan, Wm., bp. Elph. 608
O'Fallon, Don., bp. Dry. 601
O'Farrel, Rd., gen. (**C**) 871
O'Felan, Eug., bp. Killoe. 634
O'Ferral and **O'Ferrall**
— Ch., bp. Ard. 607
— Corn., bp. Ard. 607
— Florence, bp. Rph. 601
— Owen, bp. Ard. 607
— Rd., bp. Ard. 607; dn. Ard. 609
— Rd. More, G. Mlta. 671; L.T. 160; P.C. 215; Sec. Adm. 186; Sec. Tr. 163
— Wm., bp. Ard. 607
Offa, K.E. 2-3
Offaley, Th. ld., L.D. Ir. 553
Offley, sir Th., L.M. Lond. 490
— Wm., dn. Chest. 477
Offord, Andr. de, M. Chy. 393
— Jno. de, *see* Ufford
O'Fianacta, Suibney, bp. Kild. 616
O'Fin, Cormac, bp. Emly, 625
— Matth., bp. Ross, 631
O'Findan, Wm., bp. Clonm. 600
O'Findsa, Jno., bp. Elph. 608
O'Flaherty, Donat, bp. Killa. 612
— Donat, dn. Enachd. 613
O'Flain, Condla, Bp. Llin. 621
O'Flanagan and **O'Flannagan**
— bp. Cloy, 630
*— dn. Elph. 609
*— Barth., bp. Dry. 601
* Poss. same pers.
— Don., bp. Elph. 608
— Malach., dn. Elph. 609
O'Flanchua, bp. Emly, 625
O'Flanua, Regd., bp. Emly, 625
O'Fœlan, Dubdan, bp. Cld. 598
O'Fogarty, Don., bp. Oss. 620
O'Foglada, Mœlisa, bp. Cash. 624
O'Follanmuin, Tuathal, bp. Cld. 599
O'Follomar, bp. Cld. 599
O'Forannan, Cath., bp. Kild. 616
O'Fraic, Jno., bp. Ard. 607
O'Galachor, —, bp. Clonm. 600
— Laur. (2), bp. Rph. 601; dn. Rph. 602
O'Gallagher, Edm., dn. Rph. 602
Oger, J. It. 365
O'Gernidider, bp. Killoe. 634
O'Ghonelan, Jas., bp. Killoe. 634
Ogilvie and **Ogilvy**
— sir Alexr., Ld. Sess. 520
— Barth., gen. (**C**) 871
— Geo., gen. (**C**) 872
— Jas., gen. (**A**) 859
— Jas., gen. (**D**) 879
Ogilvie and Ogilvy—*cont.*
— Jas., *see* ld. O., *infra*
— Jno., gen. (**D**) 881
— Patr. de, L.H.T. Sc. 496; L.J. Gen. 522
— sir Patr., Ld. Sess. 519
— sir Walt. (2), L.H.T. Sc. 496-7
Ogilvie, lds.
— Jas., ld., Ld. Sess. 517
Ogle, sir Chall. (No. 1), adm. (**A**) 814
— sir Chall. (No. 2), adm. (**A**) 815
— sir Ch., adm. (**A**) 819; (**B**) 821
— Edmd., gen. (**D**) 905
— Newt., dn. Winch. 471
— Th., adm. (**G**) 842
— sir Th., G. Ch. Hosp. 936
Ogle, E. of
— Hy., E. of, aft. D. of Newcastle. *q.v.*, P.C. (1670) 191
Oglethorpe, Jas. Ed., gen. (**A**) 858
— Owen., bp. Carl. 475; dn. Winds. 474; Regr. Gart. 746
— sir Rt., B. Ex. Ir. 584
— Theoph., M.H. 302
O'Gorman, Finan, bp. Kild. 616
O'Grada and **O'Grady**
— Hayes, adm. (**D**) 828; (**G**) 840
— Jno., abp. Cash. 625
— Jno., abp. Tm. 611
— Jno., abp. Elph. 608
— Standish, A.G. Ir. 588 C.B. Ex. Ir. 583
O'Griffa, Matth. or Mahoun, bp. Killoe. 634
O'Hagan, Christian, bp. Cld. 599
— Jno., Land Comm. Ir. 588; S.L. Ir. 593
O'Hagan, lds.
— Th., aft. ld. O'H., A.G. Ir. 588; J.C.P. Ir. 582; K.P. 752; Ld. Chanc. Ir. 577; S.G. Ir. 590; S.L. Ir. 593
O'Hailgenen, Maclothod, bp. Cork, 630
O'Haingly, Don., bp. Dbln. 615
— Saml., bp. Dbln. 615
O'Halloran, Hy. Dunn., gen. (**D**) 901
— sir Jos., gen. (**D**) 876; G.C.B. 769; K.C.B. 776
O'Hamire, Melisa, bp. Wford. 626
O'Haneki, bp. Killa. 612; dn. Killa. 614
O'Hanmada, Gilla Mac-Aiblen, bp. Ardf. and Agh. 639
O'Hara, Ch., C. Acc. Ir. 567; C. Treas. Ir. 561; G. Gibr. 670; gen. (**A**) 859
— Murchard, bp. Ach. 612
O'Harachtain, Mœlisa, bp. Emly, 625
O'Harretaigh, Al., bp. Clonm. 599
O'Hathern, Alan., bp. Ardf. and Agh. 639
O'Haurecan, Fogdath, bp. Ferns, 621
O'Heany (or O'Heawo, or Shennagh), Don., dn. Kilf. 637
O'Hectigern, Christn., bp. Clonm. 599
O'Heda, bp. Lism. 626

For List of Abbreviations, see pp. 944-952.

O'Hedian, Jno., bp. Oss. 620
— Rd., abp. Cash. 625
— Wm., bp. Emly, 625
O'Hedram, Nichs., bp. Ach. 612
O'Heffernan, *see also* O'Hiffernan
— Æn.. bp. Emly, 625
O'Heidigein, Th., dn. Elph. 609
O'Heir, Colman, bp. Cld. 598
O'Heirnan (or O'Hiffernan), Th., dn. Cork, 632
O'Hene, Don., bp. Cash. 624
O'Heney, Ch., bp. Killoe. 634
— Corn., bp. Killoe. 634
—Matth., abp. Cash. 624
O'Henisy, Nichs., bp. Wford. and L. 627
O'Heoghain, Don., dn. Clr., 597
— Pet., dn. Clr. 597
O'Heothy, Christn., bp. Ard. 607
— Matth., bp. Ard. 607
O'Heremon, Aid., bp. Kild. 616
O'Herlihy, Th., bp. Ross, 631
O'Hethe, Jos., bp. Ferns, 621
O'Hiffernan, *see* O'Heirnan
O'Higin, —, bp. Mayo, 612
O'Higgin, Bern., bp. Elph. 608
— Eriell, dn. Elph. 609
O'Higgins, Dem., Pres. Chi. 111
O'Hinalan, Jno., bp. Kilf. 635
O'Hiraghty, Dav., abp. Arm. 595
O'Hislenan, bp. Ard. 607
O'Hogain, Matth., bp. Killoe. 634; dn. Killoe. 637
— Maur., bp. Killoe. 634
— Th., bp. Killoe. 634
O'Hogan, Hugh, dn. Killoe. 637
O'Hoisin, Aid, abp. Tm. 611; bp. Tm. 611
— Edan., bp. and abp. Tm. 611
O'Horan, Don., dn. Killoe. 737
O'Houlachan and **O'Hullachan**
— Don., abp. Cash. 624
— Jno., dn. Ross, 633
— Laur., bp. Ross, 631
— Pet., bp. Ross, 631
Oilliol, K. Ir. 20
— -Molt, K. Ir. 21
Oke—, *see also* Oak—
O'Keefe, Thadd., dn. Cloy. 632
Okeham, Jno de, B. Ex. 383
O'Kellach, Fœlan, bp. Kild. 616
— Murtogh, bp. Kild. 616
O'Kellechuir, Dunch., bp. Saig. 620
O'Keily, Edan, bp. Clr. 596
— Eochaid, bp. Cld. 599
— Maur., abp. Tm. 611; bp. Clonf. 635
— Michl. or Nichs., dn. Clonf. 637
— Th. (3), bp. Clonf. 635; abp. Tm. 611
O'Kennedy, Don., bp. Killoe. 634
O'Kerney, Carbrick, bp. Ferns, 621
O'Kerny, Christn., bp. Cnr. 603
O'Kerry, Patr., dn. Arm. 597
Oketon, Jno. de, J. It. 368; Jy. 365
Okey, sir Wm., C.D.L. 242
O'Killeen, Cormac, bp. Clonm. 599
Olaf, Skotkonung. K. Sw. 92
O'Lagenan, Mœlisa, bp. Emly, 625
O'Laghnan, Laur., bp. Elph. 608; bp. Kilmacd. 636
— Marian, abp. Tm. 611; dn. Tm. 613
O'Laidig (or O'Loyn), bp. Killa. 612
O'Laigdnen, Carbre, bp. Ferns, 621
— Constans, bp. Ferns, 621
— Corn., bp. Ferns, 621
— March., bp. Ferns, 621
— Ugair., bp. Ferns, 621
Olain, K. Man, 664
O'Laitin, Jno., bp. Killa. 612
O'Lannube, Jno., bp. Drom, 604;
O'Lapain, Ængus or Æneas, bp. Rph. 601
Olaus IV. and V., K. Dk. 93
Olave, I. to III., K. Man. 664-5
Oldais, Jno., bp. Clonm. 600
Oldershaw, Ch. Ed., gen. (**D**) 930
Oldfield, Ed. Jno., gen. (**D**) 930
— Jno. gen. (**D**) 882; K.H. 791
— Rd., gen. (**D**) 933
Oldhall, sir Wm., Sp. H.C. 248
Oldham (or Oldman), Hugh, bp. Exr. 436
— Rd., bp. S. and M. 483
Oldiss, *see* Oldyss
Oldman, *see* Oldham
Oldys, Wm., Nor. K.A. 329
Oldyss (or Oldiss), Wm., Adm. Adv. 423
O'Lean, Jno., bp. Clonf. 635
O'Leary, D. F., Amb. N.G. 134
Olega, R. Russ. 89
O'Liathan, Colman, bp. Lism. 626
Oliford, Walt. de, Ld. Chanc. Sc. 514
O'Ligbai, bp. Emly, 625
Oliphant, *see also* Ollivant
— Jas., Chn. E.I. Co. 646
— Jas., *see* Wm., *infra*
— Rt., Postm. G. Sc. 502
— Walt., L.J. Gen. 522
— Wm. or Jas. and sir W., Ld. Adv. 526; Ld. Sess. 519
— Wm. St., gen. (**D**) 920
Oliver, Jno., dn. Chr. Ch. Oxf. 457; M. Chy. 395
— Jno., dn. Worc. 473
— Jno. Ryd., gen. (**D**) 934
— Jord., J. It., 367
— Nathl. Wm., gen. (**D**) 883
— Rd. Aldw., adm. (**H**) 849
— Rt. Dudl., adm. (**A**) 819
— Th., gen. (**D**) 886
— Wm. Br., adm. (**H**) 849
Olivey, Walt. R., K.C.B. 784
Olivier, Giuss. Borg., G.C.M.G. 794
Ollivant, *see also* Oliphant
— Alfd., bp. Llff. 449
— Ed. Ch. K., C.I.E. 808
Olmius, Hon. Jno. Luttrell-, aft. E. of Carhampton, *q.v.*, C. Exc. 281
Olney, Jno., L.M. Lond. 490
O'Loghlan, Cong., bp. Kilf. 635
O'Loghlen, sir Colm. Michl., J.A.G. 937; P.C. 218; S.L. Ir. 593
— Michl. and sir M., A.G. Ir. 588; B.Ex. Ir. 584; M.R. Ir. 585; S.G. Ir. 590; S.L. Ir. 593
O'Loghlin, Rd., bp. Kilf., 635
— Ter., gen. (**B**) 868
O'Lonergan, Alan, bp. Cloy. 630
— Donat (3), abp. Cash. 624
— Ired, bp. Killoe. 634
— Thady. bp. Killoe. 634
O'Longain (or Lonugan), Th., dn. Clonf. 637
O'Lorchan, Don., dn Clonf. 637
O'Loyn, *see* O'Laidig
Olpherts, Wm., gen. (**D**) 906; K.C.B. 781
O'Luchan (or O'Lucheran), Th., dn. Arm. 597
O'Lumlin, Corm. or Ch., bp. Clonf. 635
Olybrius, F. A., Emp. W.E. 49
O'Macturan, Christn., bp. Clr. 596
O'Mail, Corm., bp. Glend. 615
O'Mailduib, Neil, bp. Cork, 630
O'Maily, Edan, bp. Clonm. 599
O'Malfagamair, Jno., bp. Killa. 612
O'Malgebry, Carthag, bp. Ferns, 621
O'Malley, Geo., gen. (**D**) 879
— Pet. Fr., Q.C. 417
O'Malone, Hugh, bp. Clonm 600
— (or O'Malvain), bp. Cloy 630
Omar, Cph. Aba. 98
O'Meara, Danl., gen. (**B**) 867
O'Meiciti (or O'Meleic), bp Emly. 625
O'Melider, Mor., bp. Clonm. 599
O'Miachan, Denn., bp. Ach. 612
— Th., bp. Ach. 612
O'Micthian, Walt., bp. Ross, 631
Ommaney and **Ommany**
— Ed. Lac., gen. (**D**) 899
— Erasm., adm. (**E**) 835; (**F**) 338
— Fras. Mont. Maxw., gen. (**D**) 914
— Hy. Man., adm. (**D**) 825; (**G**) 840
— Jno. Ackw. and sir J., adm. (**A**) 820; K.C.B. 776
Ommiades, Cph. Aba. 98
O'Modein, Mœl., bp. Clonm. 599
O'Mœil, Ph., bp. Clonm. 600
O'Mœlomair, Erc., bp. Tm 611
O'Moghan, Greg., abp. Tm. 611
O'Molan (or Malone), Odo, dn. Clonm. 600
O'Moran, Macrait, bp. Ard. 607
O'Morda, Den., bp. Elph., 608

For List of Abbreviations, see pp. 944-952.

O'Mordai, Petro, bp. Clonf. 635
O'Morgair, Christn., bp. Clr. 596
— Malachy, *see* Malachy
Ompteda, Louis Conr. Geo., baron, Chanc. Guelph, 792
O'Muctigern, Lœtan, bp. Kild., 616
O'Mugin, Gilla Æda, bp. Cork, 630
O'Muinic, Cleirec, bp. Llin. 621
O'Mulkyran, Denis, bp. Elph. 608
O'Mullaly (or Laly), Th., abp. Tm. 611
— Wm., abp. Tm. 611; dn. Tm. 613
O'Mulledy, Corn., bp. Emly, 625; bp. Clonf. 636
O'Mulloy, Albin, bp. Ferns, 621
O'Mulrony, Florence Mack., bp. Elph. 608
O'Muredach, Cobthack (St.), bp. Kild., 616
O'Murrechan, Mur., bp. Clonm. 599
O'Murredai, Adam, bp. Ard., 607
O'Murry, Don., abp. Tm. 611
O'Mutan, Mugron, bp. Cork, 630
Onacus (or Onachus), bp. Isl. 539; bp. S. and M. 483
O'Nathain, Th., bp. Rph. 601
O'Neale, K. of Meath, K.B. (1394) 755
— Odo, bp. Clr. 596
— Odo, bp. Dry. 601
O'Neil, O'Neile, and **O'Neill**
— sir Bryan, J.K.B. Ir. 579
— Hy. Arth., gen. (**D**) 896
— Jno. Jas. Silvn. gen. (**D**) 927
— Jno. Th., dn. Kilmacd. 638
O'Neill, visc. and E.
— Chas. Hy., 2nd visc. and 1st E., K.P. 750; L.L. Ant. 568; Postm. G. Ir. 564
— Jno., Br. Rd., 3rd visc., gen. (**A**) 863
O'Niellan, Ch., dn. Arm. 597
O'Nioc, Murchad, bp. Tm. 611
— Murg., bp. Tm. 611
Only, Roger. K.B., 754
Onslow, Alexr. Camb., G. W. Austr. 707
— Arth., dn. Worc., 474
— Arth., P.C. 197; Sp. H. C. 250
— Arth., S.L. 412
— Arth., Tr. N. 256
— Denz., gen. (**A**) 861
— Foot, C. Exc. 279
— Geo., *see* ld. O., *infra*
— Rd., gen. (**B**) 865
— Rd., Rec. Lond. 493; S.G. 401; Sp. H.C. 249
— Rd., *see* ld. O., *infra*
— sir Rd., adm. (**A**) 815; G.C.B. 767
— Th., *see* ld. O., *infra*
— Wm., K.H. 790
— Wm. H., *see* E. of O., *infra*
Onslow, lds. and E. of
— sir Rd., aft. 1st ld. O., Ch. Ex. 165; L. Admy. 176; L.L. Surr. 312; L.T. and Ch. Ex. 156; P.C. 195; Sp. H.C. 250; Tell. Ex. 167
Onslow, lds. and E. of—*cont.*
— Th., 2nd ld., L.L. Surr. 312; Tell. Ex. 168
— Rd., 3rd ld., K.B. 765; L.L. Surr. 312
— Geo., aft. 4th ld. O., 1st ld. and visc. Cranley, *q.v.*, and 1st E. of O., Compt. H. 292; L.L. Surr. 312; L.T. 157-8; P.C. 202; Tr. H. 291
— Wm. Hill., 4th E. of, G. N.Z. 709; K.C.M.G. 798; Sec. B.T. 269; U.S.C. 235
Oodeypore, Mahar. of, G.C.S.I. 801
— Maharanee of, G.C.S.I. 801
Openshaw, Rt., dn. Clr. 597; dn. Cnr. 605
Opimius, L., C. Ro. 45
— Q., C. Ro. 44
O'Quin, Th., bp. Clonm. 600
Orange, Pr. of, *see* under their Christian names
O'Raithnin, Slog., bp. Saig. 620
Oranmore and Browne, Dom., 1st ld., form. D. Browne, *q.v.*
Orans, Ch., gen. (**D**) 886
Orantes, J. M., Pres. Gua. 106
Orbegoso, L. J., Pres. Pu. 109
Orbha, K. Ir. 20
Orcadensis, Chr., bp. S. and M. 483
— Sim., bp. S. and M. 483
Orchan, S. Tky. 97
Ord, *see also* Orde
— Fras., M. Chy. 397
— Harry St. Geo. and sir H., G. Bmda. 701; G.C.M.G. 795; G. Dnca. 730; G. Str. Sett. 675; G. W. Austr. 707; K.C.M.G. 797; gen. (**D**) 908
— Rt., C.B. Ex. Sc. 523
— Wm. Hy., L.T. 160
— Wm. Redm., gen. (**D**) 893
Ordbrightus, bp. Sels. 432
Orde, *see also* Ord
— Jas., gen. (**A**) 863
— sir Jno., adm. (**A**) 816; G. Dnca. 730
— Leon. Sbr., gen. (**B**) 867
— Rt. Hutch., K.H. 789
— Th., aft. 1st ld. Bolton, *q.v.*, B.T. 267; Ch. Sec. Ir. 563; P.C. 204; Sec. Tr. 163; U.S.H. 227
Ordogno or **Ordono,** I. to IV., K. Sp. 85
O'Rebacain, Gilla-Mocuda bp. Lism. 626
— Mal-Duin, bp. Lism. 626
O'Reilly, Mont. Fk., adm. (**H**) 852
O'Reley, Jno., bp. Kilm. 607
— Rd., bp. Kilm. 607
Orestes, C. A., C. Ro. 46
— L. A., C. Ro., 44-5
Orevalle, *see* Orwell
Orfeur, Jno., gen. (**C**) 871
Orford, Rt. de, bp. Ely, 434
Orford, E. of
Russell Family.
— Ed., 1st E. of, form. E. Russell, *q.v.*, L. Admy. 176-7; P.C. 195
Walpole Family.
1st Creation.
— Rt., 1st E. of, form. sir R. Walpole, *q.v.*
— Rt., 2nd E. of, form. ld. Walpole, *q.v.*
Orford, E. of—*cont.*
— Geo., 3rd E. of, L.L. Norf. 310
— Horatio, 4th E. of, form. ld. Walpole, *q.v.*
2nd Creation.
— Horatio, 1st E. of, form. ld. Walpole, *q.v.*
O'Riagan, Flanagan, bp. Kild. 616
Orial, Pet. de, L.H.T. 152
Oribe, M., Pres. Ugy. 111
Oriel, Jno., 1st ld., form. Jno. Foster, *q.v.*
Orivallis, *see* Rivallis
Orkney, E. of, *see also* Caithness
Sinclair Family.
— Hy., 1st E. of (*d.* about 1418), L.H.A. Sc. 499
— Wm., 3rd E. of, L.J. Gen. 522; Ld. Chanc. Sc. 515
Bothwell Family.
— Jas., D. of, and E. of Bothwell, *q.v.*, L.H.A. Sc. (1567) 499
Hamilton and Fitzmaurice Families.
— Geo., 1st E. of, F.M. 856; K.T. 747; P.C. 196
— Geo. Wm. H., 6th E. of, form. visc. Kirkwall, *q.v.*
Orlebar, Jno., adm. (**H**) 851
*— Jno., C. Exc. 280
*— Jno., M. Chy. 396
* Poss. same pers.
Orleton, Ad. de, bp. Her. 441; bp. Winch. 470; bp. Worc. 472; L.H.T. 153
Ormathwaite, lds.
— Jno., 1st ld., form. sir J. Walsh, *q.v.*
— Arth., 2nd ld., form. hon. A. Walsh, *q.v.*
Orme, Alexr., dn. Ard. 609
— Ed., dn. Kilm. 609
— Fk. D., Amb. Bol. 135; Amb. Vza. 134
Ormesby, *see* Ormsby
Ormeston, Th., C.I.E. 806
Ormiston, Rog., K.B. 759
Ormond, sir —, L.H.A. 170
— Jas., *see* D. of O., *infra*
— Th., K.B. 758
Ormond, E., M., and D. of, *see also* under Wiltshire
— Jas. Butler, 1st E. of, L.L. Ir. 551
— Jas., 2nd E. of, L.J. Ir. 551
— Jas., 3rd E. of, L.D. Ir. 551-2
— Jas., 4th E. of, L.D. Ir. 552; L.L. Ir. 552
— Jas., 5th E. of, also 1st E. of Wiltshire, *q.v.*, K.G. 736; L.L. Ir. 552
— Pierce, 8th E. of, also E. of Ossory, *q.v.*, L.D. Ir. 553
— Jas., 9th E. of, form. Jas. Butler and visc. Thurles, *q.v.*, L. Treas. Ir. 559
— Th., 10th E. of, K.B. 760; K.G. 739; L. Treas. Ir. 559; L.J. Ir. 554
— Jas., 12th E., aft. 1st M. and D. of, K.G. 740; L. Admy. 175; L.H.S. 286; L.L. Ir. 554; L.L. Ir. 555; L.S.H. 290; P.C. 189, 92
— Jas., 2nd D. of, C. Ch. 855; Capt. Gen. 855; K.G. 740; L.H. Const. 289; L.L. Ir. 555-6; P.C. 194; W.C.P. 319

Ormond, E , M., and D. of—*cont.*
— Walt., 16th E. of, K.P. 750
— Jas., 19th E. and 1st M. of, (new Cr.), K.P. 751; L.L. Kilk. 570
— Jno., 2nd M. of, K.P. 751
— Jas. Edm. Wm. Theob., 3rd M. of, K.P. 752; L.L. Kilk. 570
Ormesby and **Ormsby**
— Arth., gen. (**B**) 866
— Coote, dn. Dry. 602
— Hy., A.G. Ir. 589; L.J. App. Ir. 586; Land J. Ir. 587; S.G. Ir. 590
— Jno. Wm., gen. (**D**) 901
— Wm. de, J.C.P. 377; J. It. 368; J.K.B. 371
O'Robhartaigh, dn. Louth, 598
O'Ronan, Kinad, bp. Glend 615
— (or O'Erodain), Magr., bp. Ardf. and Agh. 639
— Mel. Brandan, bp. Ardf. and Agh. 639
Orr, Ch. Alex., gen. (**D**) 904
— Jas., gen. (**D**) 912
Orrery, E. of, *see also* under Cork
— Rog., 1st E. of, L.J. Ir. 555; P.C. 190
— Ch., 4th E. of, gen. (**C**) 871; K.T. 747; P.C. 196
Orry, K. I. Man, 664
Orseth, sir Wm., G. Ch. Isl. 667
Orsini, Reyn., dn. Sal. 468
Orthanach, bp. Kild. 616
O'Ruadan, Felix, abp. Tm. 611
— Gillasius, bp. Ach. 612
— Imar, bp. Killa. 612
— Melruan, bp. Ach. 612
— Rugnad, bp. Kilmacd. 636
— Th., bp. Ach. 612
O'Rudican, Dermod, bp. Ferns. 621
O'Ruirk, Simon, bp. Kilm. 607
Orwell (or Orevalle), Hugh de, bp. Lond. 451
— Th., bp. Killa. 612
Orwell, lds. and visc.
— Fras., 1st ld. and visc., form. Fras. Vernon, *q.v.*, aft. E. of Shipbrooke, B.T. 265
Osa (or Bosa), bp. Sels. 432
Osbaldeston, Geoffr., J.K.B. Ir. 579
— Rd., A.G. Ir. 588
— Rd., bp. Carl. 476; bp. Lond. 452; dn. Yk. 487; P.C. 201
* **Osbert,** bp. Exr. 436; Ld. Chanc. 352
*— dn. Sal. 468
* Poss. same pers.
— bp. Dnbl. 532
Osborn and **Osborne**
— —, K.C. 415
— Alexr., C. Cus. Sc. 504
— Ang. Ed., gen. (**D**) 915
— Capt. —, G. Newfd. 700
— Ch., C. Cus. 273
— Ch., J.K.B. Ir. 579
— Ch. Osb. Creagh-, gen. (**D**) 924
— Ed., L.M. Lond. 490
— sir Ed. Ol., adm. (**A**)
— sir Geo., gen. (**A**) 859
— Hy., adm. (**A**) 814
— Hugh St., gen. (**D**) 876
Osborn and Osborne—*cont.*
— Jno., Amb. Sxy. 120
— Jno., adm. (**A**) 818
— Jno., C.C.J. 405; Q.C. 418
— Jno. and sir Jno., S.L. Ir. 591
— Jno. and sir J., L. Admy. 181
— sir Pet., G. Gsey. 668
— R. Bernal, Sec. Adm. 187
— Rt., dn. Ferns, 623
— Rt., Sec. Adm. 187
— Saml., adm. (**A**) 817
— Sherard, adm. (**E**) 836
— Sidney F. G., C.I.R. 286
— Th., *see* ld. O., *infra*
— sir Wm., C. Cus. Ir. 565; C. Ex. Ir. 566
— sir Wm., K.H. 789
Osborne, lds.
— sir Th., aft. ld. O., visc. Dunblane, visc. Latimer, E. of Danby, M. of Carmarthen, and D. of Leeds, *q.v.*, L.T. 155; P.C. 191; Tr. N. 256
O'Scanlan, Patr., abp. Arm. 595; bp. Rph. 601
Oscar, K. Sw. 92
— I. and II., K. S. and N. 92
— II. (K. S. and N.), K.G. 745
O'Scoba, Carbrac, bp. Rph. 601
O'Sedaghan, Dav., bp. Kilmacd. 636
O'Selbaic (2), bp. Cork, 630
— Cellach, bp. Cork, 630
— Clerech, bp. Cork, 630
— Moriertach, bp. Lism. 626
— Patr., bp. Cork, 630
O'Semican, Th., dn. Lim. 639
Osgodby or **Osgodeby,** Adam de, L.K. 353-4; M.R. 387
O'Shanassy, Jno., K.C.M.G. 797
O'Shaughnessy, Wm. Cooke, gen. (**D**) 933
O'Siagal, Conat, bp. Elph. 608
O'Sinadaig, Clemens, bp. Ach. 612
Oskitell, abp. Yk. 485
Osman I. and II., S. Tky. 97-8
— Pasha, K.C.M.G. 799
Osmund (St.) (E. of Dorset), bp. Sal. 466; Ld. Chanc. 352
Osmundus (or Oswynus), bp. Lond. 451
O'Solehan, Maur., bp. Cloy. 630
Ospina, M., Pres. N. G. 107
Osred (2), K.E. 2
Osric (2) K.E. (2)
Ossenius, bp. Cld. 598
Ossington, Jno. Ev., 1st visc., form. J. E. Denison, *q.v.*
Ossory, E. of; *see also* Ormond and Upper Ossory
— Pierce, E. of, *also* 8th E. of Ormond, *q.v.*, L.D. Ir. 553
— Th., E. of (son of Jas. 1st, D. of Ormond), adm. (**A**) 813; K.G. 740; L. Admy. 175; L.D. Ir. 555; P.C. 190, 192
Ossulston, Ch. Augs., ld., aft. 5th E. of Tankerville, *q.v.*, P.C. 208; Tr. H. 291
Ostforus, bp. Worc. 472
Ostrich, *see* Astry
Osulf, K.E. 2
O'Sullivan, Alan, bp. Cloy. 630; bp. Lism. 626
— Laur., bp. Cloy. 630
Osulph, bp. Wltn. 466
Oswald, K.E. 2, 3
— Ld. Chanc. Sc. 514
— (St.), abp. Yk. 485; bp. Worc. 472
— Jas., B.T. 265; L.T. 157; P.C. 201; V. Treas. Ir. 560
— Jno., bp. Clonf. and K. 636; bp. Drom. 605; bp. Rph. 602
— Jno. and sir J., gen. (**A**) 862; G.C.B. 768; G.C.M.G. 794; K.C.B. 774
Osweo, K.E. 2
Oswulf, K.E. 2
Oswy, K.E. 2, 3
Oswynus, *see* Osmundus
Otalora, T. E., Pres. U.S.C. 107
O'Tarpa, Carus, bp. Ach. 612
O'Tarpaid (or O'Torpy), Cormac, bp. Killa. 612
O'Teig, Teig, bp. Killoe. 634
Other, Walt. Fitz., Const. W. Cast. 322
Othman, Cph. Aba. 98
— S. Tky. 97
Otho, (the Illustrious), C.P.R. 68
— D. Aus. 58
— D. Bdy. 28
— (2), D. Brk. 69
— D. Fca. 71
— Emp. Ro. 47
— K. Gr. 96
— I., D. Lne. 29
— I. and II., D. Bva. 67
— I. to III., D. Su. 80
— I. to III., D. Sxy. 77
— I. to IV., E. Gmy. 61
— I. to V., M. Brg. 65
— Hy., C.P.R. 68
— Hugh Fitz, Const. T.L. 320
— Wm. Leopold, K. Bva. 68
O'Tiernay, *see* Tierney
O'Tigernach, Corn., bp. Ardf. and Agh. 639
— Florence, bp. Kilf. 635
O'Tirlenan, bp. Ard. 607
Otley, *see* Ottley
O'Toole (St. Laurence), abp. Dbln. 615
O'Tormaig, Jocelin, bp. Ard. 607
O'Torpy, *see* O'Tarpaide
O'Traffy (or Rory), Rod., bp. Ferns, 621
Otrington, Jno., L.M. Dbln. 640
Otter, Hy. Ch., adm. (**H**) 849
— Wm., bp. Chich. 433
Otterburn, Ad., L.J. Clk. 516; Ld. Adv. 526; Ld. Sess. 518
— Nicol., Ld. Clk. Reg. 525
— Wm., Sec. St. Sc. 501
Ottley and **Otley**
— Ad., bp. St. Dav. 465
— Coghill Gl., gen. (**D**) 895
— Rt. or Rog., L.M. Lond. 490
Ottoman, S. Tky. 97
Ottway and **Otway**
— Arth. J. and sir A., P.C. 220; U.S.F. 230
— Ch., gen. (**A**) 858
— Ch., gen. (**D**) 890
— sir G. Gr., adm. (**G**) 843
— J., K.C. 414
— L. C., Amb. Mex. 133
— sir Loft. Wm., gen. (**A**) 863
— Rt. Jocel., adm. (**H**) 851
— Rt. Wall., and sir R., adm. (**A**) 819; G.C.B. 769; K.C.B. 775

Ottway and Otway—*cont.*
—— Th., bp. Killa. and Ach. 613; bp. Oss. 620
—— Wm. Alb., adm. (**A**) 817
Ouchterlonie, *see* Ochterlonie
Oude, Bah. of, K.C.S.I. 803
—— Sing, Mahar. of, K.C.S.I. 803
—— Nawab of, G.C.S.I. 801
Oudenarde, Giles de, Lt. T.L. 321
Oudinot, Off. Nap. 26
Oudoceus, bp. Llff. 448
Oudtschoom, Pieter, &c., G. C.G.H. 678
Oughton, Jas. Adolph., and sir J., gen. (**B**) 865; K.B. 765
Ouldhal, Edm., bp. Meath, 599
Ourgham, Th., K.B. 755
Ouseley, sir Gore, Amb. Pers. 130; G.C.H. 786; P.C. 210
—— Regd., gen. (**D**) 913
—— Wm. Gore and sir W., Amb. Arg. 136; Amb. Bzl. 135; Amb. C. Am. 133; Amb. Ugy. 136; K.C.B. 782
Outlawe (or Oatlawe), Rog., L.J. Ir. 551; Ld. Chanc. Ir. 574
Outram, Jas., and sir J. Ch. Comm. Oudh, 653; G.C.B. 769; gen. (**D**) 888; K.C.B. 782; K.C.S.I. 802
Ovedale, Th., K.B. 757
Ovens, Ed., C.C.J. 404
Overal, Jno., bp. Lich. and Cov. 444; bp. Norw. 455; dn. St. P. 453
Overay, Th., G. Jsey. 667
Overbeck, Danl., G. Ceyl. 672
Overend, Wm., Q.C. 417
Overton, Benj., C. Cus. 274
—— Th., B. Ex. 383
—— Wm., bp. Lich. and Cov. 444
Owain, *see* Owen
Owden, Th. Sc. and sir T., L.M. Lond. 492
Owen and **Owain**
—— bp. Ard. 607
—— K. Hgy. 59
—— Yk. H. 334
—— ab Grufydd (2), Pr. Wls. 17
—— Ad., dn. Lim. 639
—— ap Howel (or Hywel), Dha, Pr. Wls. 17
—— Ch. Wm., C.I.E. 807
—— Ed. Wm. Camp. Rich. and sir E., adm. (**A**) 820; Clk. O. 260; G.C.B. 769; G.C.H. 786; K.C.B. 774; L. Admy. 182; S.G.O. 260
—— Fras. Ph. Cunl. and sir F., C.I.E. 806; K.C.B. 784; K.C.M.G. 797
—— Geo., Norr. K.A. 329; R. Cr. P.A. 335; Yk. H. 334
—— Gwynedd, Pr. Wls. 16
—— Hugh, K.C.B. 784
—— Hugh, L.L. Pemb. 316
—— Jno., bp. St. As. 462
—— Jno. Chr., dn. Oxf. 457
—— Jno., dn. Clonm. 600
—— Jno., gen. (**B**) 865
—— Jno. and sir J., gen. (**D**) 884; K.C.B. 777; K.H. 790
—— sir Jno., L.L. Pemb. 316
—— Loft., gen. (**D**) 891
—— Morg., bp. Llff. 449
—— Rd., adm. (**H**) 847
—— Rd., K.C.B. 784
—— Rt., gen. (**B**) 870
—— Th., J.C.P. 378; S.L. 408

Owen and Owain—*cont.*
—— Wm., K.C. 416
—— sir Wm., L.L. Hav. 316; L.L. Pemb. 316
—— Wm. Fitzwm., adm. (**D**) 828
—— Wm. Geo., gen. (**D**) 914
—— Wm. S., C.C.J. 405
Owens, Geo. Bolster and sir G., L.M. Dbln. 642
Owlgrave, Th., L.M. Lond. 490
Owtred, Hy., K.B. 759
Oxenbridge and **Oxonbridge**
—— Ed. or God., K.B. 760
—— sir Rt., Lt. T.L. 321
—— Th., S.L. 407
Oxenden, A., bp. Montr. 694
—— Geo., D. Arch. 420; Vic. Gen. 421
—— sir Geo., L.T. 156; L. Admy. 177
Oxenford, *see also* Oxynforde
—— Const. de, J. It. 366
Oxford, Jno. of, bp. Norw. 454; Ch. Jr. 362; dn. Sal. 468; J. It. 366
Oxford, E. of
De Vere Family.
—— Rt., 3rd E. of, form. Rt. de Vere, *q.v.*; J. It. 367
—— Thos., 8th E. of, form. Th. de Vere, *q.v.*
—— Rt., 9th E. of, K.G. 734; L.L. Ir. 551
—— Rd., 11th E. of, K.G. 735
—— Jno., 12th E. of, K.B. 756
—— Jno., 13th E. of, C.Y.G. 298; Const. T.L. 320; K.B. 757; K.G. 736; L.H.A. 174
—— Jno., 15th E. of, K.G. 737
—— Jno., 16th E. of, K.B. 760
—— Hy., 18th E. of, K.B. 762
—— Aubrey, 20th E. of, gen. (**B**) 864; K.G. 740; P.C. 191-2-3
Harley Family, see also Mortimer.
—— Rt., 1st E. of, also E. Mortimer, *q.v.*, form. Rt. Harley, *q.v.*, K.G. 741; L.H.T. 156; Prem. 141
—— Ed., 4th E. of, L.L. Radn. 316
Oxmanton, Wm., ld., aft. 3rd E. of Rosse, *q.v.*, L.L. K. Co. 570
Oxon—, *see also* Exon—
Oxonbridge, *see* Oxenbridge
Oxynforde, *see also* Oxenford
—— Jno. de, L.M. Lond. 489

P.

*P * * *, dn. Emly, 628
*P * * *, dn. Lim. 639
* Poss. same pers.
Pace, Rd., dn. Exr. 437; dn. St. P. 453; S. St. 223
—— Wm. Napp, gen. (**D**) 913

Pacheco, G., Pres. Bol. 109
Pacilus, C. F. (2), C. Ro. 39, 42
Pack, Chr., L.M. Lond. 491
—— Den. and sir D., gen. (**C**) 873; K.C.B. 774
Packhurst, sir Rt., L.M. Lond. 491
Packington, *see also* Pakington
—— Wm. de, dn. Lich. 445
***Paddesley,** Jno., L.M. Lond. 490
*—— Jno., M.M. 246
* Prob. same pers.
Paddy, Nichs., Lanc. H. 333; R. Dr. P.A. 338
Pade, Raym., dn. Sal. 468
Pado, Jno. or Jonn. de, K.B. 755
Pætinus, M. F., C. Ro. 41
—— M. F. C., C. Ro. 41
Pætus, C. Æ., C. Ro. 41
—— P. A., C. Ro., 40, 46, 47
—— P. Æ., C. Ro. 43
—— Q. Æ., C. Ro. 44
Paez, J. A., Pres. Vzla. 107-8
Page, Benj. Wm., adm. (**A**) 819
—— Fras. and sir F., B. Ex. 384; J.C.P. 379; J.K.B. 373; S.L. 411
—— Geo. Hyde, gen. (**D**) 925
—— Jno., L.M. Dbln. 641
*—— Jno., M. Chy. 395
*—— Jno. or Wm., Curs. B. Ex. 386
* Prob. same pers.
—— Rd., S.G. 401
—— Wm., *see* Jno., *supra*
—— Wm. Ed., K.H. 791
Pagerie, Steph. de la, Rel. Nap. 26
Paget, Lord Alfr., gen. (**D**) 904
—— hon. Arth. and sir A., Amb. G. St. 121; Amb. Gmy. 117; Amb. Scy. 114; Amb. Tky. 129; G.C.B. 771; K.B. 766; P.C. 207
—— Aug. B. and sir A., Amb. Aus. 117; Amb. Dk. 127; Amb. It. 114; Amb. Pgl. 125; Amb. Sw. and N. 127; Amb. Sxy. 121; G.C.B. 773; K.C.B. 783; P.C. 219
—— hon. Berk., C. Exc. 282; L.T. 159
—— Ch. and sir C., adm. (**A**) 820; G.C.H. 786; K.C.H. 787
—— ld. Clar. Ed., adm. (**D**) 832; (**E**) 834; G.C.B. 771; K.C.B. 780; P.C. 217; Sec. Adm. 187
—— hon. Ed. and sir E., C.C. Ind. 650; G.C.B. 767; G. Ceyl. 672; G. Ch. Hosp. 936; gen. (**A**) 861; K.B. 766
—— ld. Geo. Aug. Fred, gen. (**D**) 896; K.C.B. 780
—— Geo. Ed., K.C.B. 784
—— Hy., K.B. 760
—— hon. Hy., *see* ld. P., *infra*
—— Jas., Curs. B. Ex. 386
—— sir Jas., Pres. Coll. Surg. 939
—— Wm., K.B. 763
—— Wm., *see* ld. P., *infra*
—— Wm. Hy., gen. (**D**) 918
Paget, lds.
—— sir Wm., aft. 1st ld. P., C.D.L. 242; Compt. H. 292; K.G. 738; L.P.S. 240; S. St. 223

Paget, lds.—*cont.*
— Hy., aft. 7th ld. P., form. ld. Burton, *q.v.*, aft. 1st E. of Uxbridge, *q.v.*; C.Y.G. 298; L. Admy. 177; L.T. 156; P.C. 196
Pagham, Jno., bp. Worc. 472
Pain and **Paine,** *see* Payn and Payne
Painter, *see* Paynter
Pakenham, Jno., adm. (**H**) 846
— hon. Ed. Michl. and sir E., G.C.B. 767; gen. (**C**) 873; K.B. 766
— hon. F. J., Amb. Arg. 136; Amb. Chi. 137; Amb. Pgy. 136
— hon. Hy., dn. Chr. Ch. Dbln. 619; dn. St. Pat. 618
— hon. Herc. Rt. and sir H., gen. (**B**) 870; K.C.B. 776
— Rd. and sir R., Amb. Mex. 133; Amb. Pgl. 125; Amb. U.S.A. 132; K.C.B. 782; P.C. 214
— sir Th., S.L. Ir. 591
— hon. sir Th., adm. (**A**) 816; G.C.B. 768
— hon. Th. Alexr., adm. (**H**) 852
— Th. Hy., gen. (**D**) 907
Pakington, *see also* Packington
— Jno., S.L. 408
— sir Jno. Som., aft. 1st ld. Hampton, *q.v.*, G.C.B. 770; L. Admy. 184; P.C. 215; W. and C. Sec. 231; W. Sec. 232
Paladines, D'Aurelles de, K.C.B. 778
Palatio, Octavian de, abp. Arm. 595
Palgrave, sir Fras., K.H. 790
— Wm. G., Amb. Bga. 128; Amb. Si. 131; Amb. Ugy. 137
Palin, Ch. Th., gen. (**D**) 926
Palle, Chentsal, &c., C.I.E. 808
Palles, Chr., A.G. Ir. 589; C.B. Ex. Ir. 583; Pres. Ex. D. Ir. 583; S.G. Ir. 590
Palliser, Ch. Hy., K.C.B. 781
— Hy., gen. (**D**) 898
— Hugh and sir H., adm. (**A**) 815; Compt. N. 257; G. Gr. Hosp. 854; G. Newfd. 700; L. Admy. 179
— Wm., abp. Cash. and Eml. 626; bp. Cloy. 630
Palmer, Anthy., K.B. 761
— Arth., C.C.J. 403; S.L. 412
— Arth. Hunt. and sir A., G. Qland. 706; K.C.M.G. 797
— Ch., gen. (**C**) 874
— Felix, G. Gren. 724
— Fras., gen. (**B**) 864
— Geoffr. and sir G., A.G. 399; C.J. Chest. 386; S.G. 401
— Geo., adm. (**A**) 817
— Guy, S.L. 408
— Hy., gen. (**D**) 901
— Hy. Sp., gen. (**D**) 933
— Hy. Well., gen. (**D**) 919
— sir Jas., Chanc. Gart. 746
— Jno., dn. Pboro. 458
— Jno. Geo., gen. (**D**) 913
— Jno. Hinde, Q.C. 418
— Jos., dn. Cash. 627
— Pet., J.C.P. Ir. 581
— sir Ralph, C.J. Mdras. 658
Palmer—*cont.*
— Rog., K.B. 763
— sir Rog. Wm. Hy., gen. (**D**) 921
— Round., aft. sir R. and 1st ld. and E. Selborne, *q.v.*, A.G. 400; Ld. Chanc. 358; P.C. 218; Q.C. 417; S.G. 402
— Th., C. St. 283
Palmerston, visc.
— Hy., 2nd visc., B.T. 265; L. Admy. 179; L.T. 158
— Hy. Jno., 3rd visc., F. Sec. 228; G.C.B. 772; H. Sec. 227; K.G. 744; L. Admy. 181; L.T. 161; P.C. 208; Prem. 148-9; Sec. at W. 234; W.C.P. 319
Palmes, G., Tell. Ex. 167
Palmys, Brian, jun., S.L. 408
Paludius, abp. Lond. 450
Paman, *see* Payman
Pamplin, Rt., adm. (**A**) 819
Pandit, Dh. Nar., C.I.E. 807
Panioty, Demetr., C.I.E. 807
Paniter (or Panter), Dav., bp. Ross. 535; Sec. St. Sc. 502
— Patr., Sec. St. Sc. 502
Panizzi, Ant., K.C.B. 783
Panmure, ld. and E. of
— Wm., E. of, G. Gibr. (1756) 669; gen. (**A**) (1770) 858
— Fox, 2nd ld., form. hon. Fox Maule, *q.v.*, aft. 11th E. of Dalhousie, *q.v.*, G.C.B. 772; K.T. 748; L.P.S. Sc. 501; W. Sec. 232
Pansa, C. V., C. Ro. 46
— Q. A., C. Ro. 41
Panta, Synd. &c., of, C.I.E 806
Panter, D., *see* Paniter
Panton, Jas., J.K.B. 371
— Th., gen. (**B**) 864
Pantulf, Hugh, J. It. 366
Papelew, Rt., bp. Chich. 432
Paperna, M., C. Ro. 45
Papillon, Dav. (? 1 or 2), C. Exc. 280-1
Papus, L. Æ., C. Ro. 43
— M. Æ., Dt. Ro. 41
— Q. Æ. (2), C. Ro. 42
Par, *see also* Parr
— Rd. de, Portr. Lond. 488
Paramindr, &c. (K. Siam), G.C.M.G. 795
Pardishowe, Th. de, M. Chy. 393
Pare, Jno., gen. (**A**) 862
Paredes, Pres. Mex. 103
Parfew, Rt., *see* Purfoy
Pargeter, Wm., M. Chy. 396
Pargitor, sir Th., L.M. Lond 490
Parham, Benj., C.C.J. 403
Paris, Jno. Ayrt., Pres. Coll. Ph. 938
Parish, Hy. Woodb., gen. (**D**) 921
— Jno. Ed., adm. (**H**) 852
— Woodb. and sir W., C. Exc. 282; C. Exc. Sc. 505; K.C.H. 789
Parisio, Ct. Paolo, G.C.M.G. 794; K.C.M.G. 796
Park, Jas. Al. and sir J., J.C.P. 380; K.C. 415; S.L. 413
Parke, Col. —, G. Leew. Isl. 727
— Geo., gen. (**D**) 881
— Hy. Wm., gen. (**D**) 894
— Jas. and sir J., aft. ld. Wensleydale, *q.v.*, B. Ex. 385; J.K.B. 373; Jud. Com. P.C. 360; P.C. 212; S.L. 413
Parke—*cont.*
— Th. Adams, gen. (**D**) 883
— Wm., gen. (**D**) 904; K.C.B. 782
Parker, sir Ch. Chr., adm. (**G**) 841
— Chr., adm. (**A**) 816
— Ed. A., gen. (**D**) 892
— Geo., adm. (**H**) 849
— Geo., *see* visc. P., *infra*
— sir Geo., adm. (**A**) 819; K.C.B. 776
— hon. Geo. Lane, gen. (**B**) 865
— Gerv., gen. (**A**) 857
— Hy. (2), K.B. 760
— Hy., aft. 5th ld. Monteagle, *q.v.*, K.B. 762
— Hy. Perr., bp. E. Eq. Afr. 688
— sir Hy. Wats., K.C.M.G. 797
— sir Hyde (No. 1), adm. (**A**) 815
— sir Hyde (No. 2), adm. (**A**) 815
— Hyde (No. 3), adm. (**D**) 827; L. Admy. 183
— Jas. and sir J., Q.C. 417; V. Chanc. 390
— Jno., abp. Dbln. and Gl. 616; abp. Tm. 611; bp. Elph. 608
— Jno., adm. (**H**) 847
— Jno., B. Ex. 384; S.L. 409, 410
— Jno., dn. Llin. 623
— Jno., gen. (**B**) 685
— Jno., L.T. 160; P.C. 216; Sec. Adm. 186; Sec. Tr. 163
— Jno., M.R. Ir. 585
— Jno. B., gen. (**D**) 881
— Kenyon Stev., Q.C. 417
— Matth., abp. Cant. 431; dn. Linc. 448
— sir Peter, adm. (**A**) 815
— Rd., gen. (**D**) 896
— Rog., dn. Linc. 448
— Saml., bp. Oxf. 456
— Th. and sir T., B. Ex. 385; C.B. Ex. 382; J.C.P. 379; P.C. 202; S.L. 412
— Th., *see* ld. P., *infra*
— Wm., adm. (**A**) 816
— sir Wm., adm. (**A**) 820; (**B**) 821; (**C**) 822; G.C.B. 769; K.C.B. 776; L. Admy. 182-3
— Wm. and sir W., J. Pr. Ct. 421
Parker, lds. and visc.
— Th., and sir T., aft. 1st ld. P., and 1st E. of Macclesfield, *q.v.*, C.J.Q.B. 370; Ld. Chanc. 357; P.C. 195; S.L. 411
— Geo., aft. visc. P. and 2nd E. of Macclesfield, *q.v.*
— Geo., visc., aft. 4th E. of Macclesfield, *q.v.*, Tell. Ex. 167; Compt. H. 293; P.C. 205
Parkes, Harry Sm. and sir H., Amb. Ch. and Cor. 131; Amb. Jap. 131; G.C.M.G. 795; K.C.B. 783
— Hy. and sir H., G.C.M.G. 796; K.C.M.G. 797
Parkhurst, Jno., bp. Norw. 455
— sir Wm., M.M. 246
Parkin, Geo. Hy., adm. (**H**) 852
Parkinson, Ch. Fk., gen. (**D**) 904
— Ch. Fk., gen. (**D**) 922
— Ed., gen. (**D**) 881

Parlby, Brook Br., gen. (**D**) 878
— Wm., gen. (**D**) 895
Parma, Pr. of, R. Nds. 83
Parnell, Hy. Br., and sir H. aft. 1st ld. Congleton, *q.v.*, C. Treas. Ir. 561; Paym. G. 244; Sec. at W. 234; Tr. N. 257
— Jno., J.K.B. Ir. 579
— Jno. and sir J., C. Cus. Ir. 565; C. Exc. Ir. 566; C. Treas. Ir. 560; Ch. Ex. Ir. 562; P.C. 204
Parneys, Jno. L.M. Lond. 490
Parning or **Parnyng** Rt. and sir R., C.J.K.B. 369; J.C.P. 377; Ld. Chanc. 354; S.L. 406
Parr, *see also* Par
— Jno., G.I. Man, 666
— Jno., G. N. Sc. 695
— Rd., bp. S. and M. 483
— Th., K.B. 759
— Th. Chase, gen. (**D**) 891
— Wm. Chase, gen. (**D**) 929
Parr of Kendal, sir Wm., K.G., 736
— Wm., ld., aft. E. of Essex, and M. of Northampton, *q.v.*, K.G. (1543) 738
Parra, A., Pres. U.S.C. 107
Parrott, Benj., gen. (**D**) 919
Parry, Benj., bp. Oss. 620; dn. Oss. 623; dn. St. Pat. 618
— Dav., G. Bdoes. 720
— Ed., bp. Killoe. 634; dn. Lism. 629; dn. Wford. 628
— Ed., bp. Suff. Dov. 431
— Ed., Chn. E.I. Co. 645
— Ed. Igg., adm. (**H**) 848
— Fras., adm. (**A**) 816
— Fras., C. Exc. 278-9
— Fk. Wm. Best, gen. (**D**) 932
— Hy., bp. Glr. 438; bp. Worc. 473; dn. Chest. 477
— Hy. Hutt, bp. Perth, W.A. 707
— (or Pavy), Hugh, bp. St. Dav. 464
— Jno., bp. Oss. 620; dn. Chr. Ch. Dbln. 618
— Jno. Bill, C.C.J. 403; Q.C. 417
— Jno. H., P.P. 418; S.L. 413
— Jno. Parry Jones, adm. (**H**) 853
— Love Parry Jones, gen. (**B**) 870; K.H. 791
— Rd., bp. St. As. 462; dn. Bgr. 426
— Rt., dn. Lism. 629
— Spencer Cl., gen. (**B**) 869
— Th., bp. Bdoes. 721
— sir Th., C.D.L. 242
— sir Th., Compt. H. 292; Tr. H. 291
— Wm., adm. (**A**) 814
— sir Wm. Ed., adm. (**D**) 829; L.G. Gr. Hosp. 854
— Wm. Hy. Webley-, adm. (**D**) 823
Parslow, Jno., G. Gibr. 670; gen. (**A**) 858
Parsons, Cliff., gen. (**D**) 929
— sir Humphr., L.M. Lond. 491
— Jas., gen. (**D**) 887
— Jno., bp. Pboro. 458; dn. Brl. 440
— Jno., gen. (**C**) 871
Parsons—*cont.*
— sir Jno., L.M. Lond. 491
— sir Lawr., B. Ex. Ir. 584; C. Treas. Ir. 561
— Needh. Th., gen. (**D**) 926
— Rt. White, adm. (**H**) 847
— sir Wm., L.J. Ir. 554
Partridge, Hy., K.C. 415
— Rd., Pres. Coll. Surg. 939
Pascal I. and II., P. Ro. 33-4
Paschal, Jno., bp. Llff. 449
Pasco, Jno, adm. (**D**) 828
Pashley, Rt., Q.C. 417
Paske, Wm., gen. (**D**) 915
Paslen, Jno., K.B. 756
Pasley, Ch. Wm. and sir C., gen. (**D**) 879; K.C.B. 777
— Th., and sir T., adm. (**A**) 816
— sir Th. Sab., adm. (**D**) 831; (**E**) 834; K.C.B. 780
Pasquito (de Vannes), D. Bry. 27
Passele, Edm. de, B. Ex. 383; S.L. 406
Passelewe, Rt., Ch. Ex. 152
— Sim., B. Ex. 382
Paston or **Pastone,** Wm., J.C.P. 378; S.L. 407
Patchett, Wm., Q.C. 419
Paté, Genl. —, K.C.B. 778
Pate, Rd., bp. Worc. 473
Pater, bp. Llff. 448
— Ch. Dudl., adm. (**A**) 819
Paterculus, C. S., C. Ro. 42
Paterson and **Patterson**
— Adr. Hugh, gen. (**D**) 919
— Ch. Wm., adm. (**A**) 818
— Geo., G. Gren. 724
— Jas., gen. (**B**) 865
— Jas., gen. (**C**) 872
— Jno., abp. Glasg. 537; bp. Edinb. 533; bp. Gall. 539; bp. Ross. 536
— Jos., gen. (**D**) 883
— Marc., C.J.C.P. Ir. 581; S.G. Ir. 589; S.L. Ir. 592
— Th., gen. (**D**) 883
— Walt., G. Pr. Ed. Isl. 699
— Wm., C.C.J. 406
— Wm., dn. Carl. 476; dn. Exr. 437
*— Wm., G. N.S.W. 702
*— sir Wm., K.C.H. 788
* ? same pers.
— Wm., gen. (**D**) 928
— sir Wm., gen. (**B**) 869
— Wm. Th. L., gen. (**D**) 909
Pateshull and **Patteshull**
— Hugh de, bp. Lich. and Cov. 444; L.H.T. 152
— Mart. de, Ch. Jr. 363; dn. St. P. 452; Jy. 364
— Nichs. Lechm., adm. (**H**) 845
— Sim. de, J. It. 366; Jy. 363
— Walt. de, J. It. 367
Patey, *see also* Paty
— Ch. Geo. Ed., adm. (**G**) 843; G. Gamb. 686; G. Lag. 687; G. St. Hel. 682
Paton, Jas., bp. Dkld. 533
— Jno. Staff., gen. (**D**) 901
Patricio, Pres. Nic. 106
Patrick (St.), bp. Arm. 595
*— bp. Cloy. 630
*— bp. Dbln. 615
*— bp. Kilf. 635
*— bp. Kilm. 607
*— bp. Lim. 638
*— dn. Drom. 606
* Prob. some same pers. Comp. dates.
Patrick—*cont.*
— (Master of Gray), Ld. Sess. 517
— Sim., bp. Chich. 433; bp. Ely, 435; dn. Pboro. 458
Patrington, Steph., bp. Chich. 433; bp. St. Dav. 464
Patroe (St.), bp. Cnwall. 436
Patten, Fk., adm. (**H**) 849
— (or Waynflete), Jno., dn. Chich. 434
— Jno. Wils., C.D.L. 243; Ch. Sec. Ir. 563; P.C. 217
— Merc., Bl. M. P.A. 336
Patterson, *see* Paterson
Patteshull, *see* Pateshull
Patteson, Jno. and sir J., J.K.B. 373; Jud. Com. P.C. 360; P.C. 215; S.L. 413
— J. C., bp. Melan, 711
Pattinson, Rd., G. Hlgld. 670
Pattison, Alexr. Hope, K.H. 790
— Jas., Chn. E.I. Co. 645
— Jas., gen. (**A**) 859
Pattle, Th., gen. (**D**) 905
— Wm., gen. (**D**) 886
Patton, Geo., L.J. Clk. 516; Ld. Adv. 526; P.C. 217; S.G. Sc. 527
— Hugh, adm. (**H**) 846
— Jno., gen. (**D**) 893
— Phil., adm. (**A**) 816; L. Admy. 180-1
— Rt., adm. (**H**) 846
— Rt., gen. (**D**) 910
— Walt. D. Phillips, aft. Patton-Bethune, gen. (**D**) 902
Pattyn, *see* Patten and Waynflete
Paty, *see also* Patey
— Geo. Wm., gen. (**D**) 882; K.C.B. 779; K.H. 790
Paul and **Pauli**
— bp. Cnr. 604
— Emp. Russ. 90
— I. to V., P. Ro., 33, 35-6
— -Alexr. Leop., Pr. L. Dtd. 73
— Alf. Wall., C.I.E. 808
— -Fredk., G.D. M. Sch. 75
— Geo., K. Adv. 422; Vic. Gen. 422
— Gregory Ch. and sir G., C.I.E. 806; K.C.I.E. 805
— Jas., Modr. K. Sc. 547
— Jno., Modr. K. Sc. 547
— Matt. C., gen. (**D**) 886
— Th., dn. Cash. 627
— Th. Hy., gen. (**D**) 881
— Wm., bp. Oxf., 456; dn. Lich. 445
— Wm. de, bp. Mth. 599
Paule, the Lord of, K.B. (1400) 755
Paulet and **Pawlet,** *see also* Poulett
*— sir Amyas, Chanc. Gart. 745
*— sir Amias, G. Jsey. 667
* ? same pers.
— sir Anthy., G. Jsey. 667
— Ch., aft. 5th D. of Bolton *q.v.*, K.B. 765
— ld. Fk., gen. (**D**) 895
— ld. Geo., adm. (**D**) 831; (**F**) 838
— ld. Harry, aft. 4th D. of Bolton, *q.v.*, adm. (**A**) 814; L. Admy. 178
— ld. Hy., K.B. (1625) 762
— ld. Hy., adm. (**A**) 818 K.C.B. 774; L. Admy. 181
— sir Hugh, G. Jsey. 667

Paulet—*cont.*
— Jno., K.B. 759
— ld. Nass., K.B. (1725) 764
— ld. Wm., Tell. Ex. (1715) 168
— ld. Wm., F.M. (1886) 856; G.C.B. 770; gen. (**D**) 893; K.C.B. 779
— sir Wm., aft. ld. St. John of Basing, 1st E. of Wiltshire, and 1st M. of Winchester, *q.v.*, Tr. H. 291
— Wm., aft. 3rd M. of Winchester, *q.v.*, K.B. 760
Paulinus (St.), abp. Yk. 485; bp. Roch. 459
Paull, *see* Paul
Paullulus, S. P. A., C. Ro. 44
Paullus, L. Æ. (2), C. Ro. 43, 44, 46
— M. Æ., C. Ro. 41-2
Pauncefote, sir Jul., G.C.M.G. 795; K.C.B. 784; K.C.M.G. 797; U.S.F. 230; U.S.C. 236
Paunton, Jas. de, Jy. 365
Pauper, *see* Poor
Pavely, sir Walt., K.G. 733
Pavy (or Parry), Hugh, bp. St. Dav. 464
Pawel-Rammingen, L. A. G. L. A. F. von, K.C.B. 783
Pawlet, *see* Paulet and Poulett
Paxton, Geo., gen. (**D**) 912
Pay (or Pye), Adam, bp. Cloy. 630
Paye, Steph. de, bp. St. Andr. 529
Payham, J., bp. Worc. 472
Payman (or Paman), Clem., dn. Elph. 609
Payn, Payne, Pain, and **Paine**
— Ch., gen. (**D**) 886
— Ch. Fk., adm. (**H**) 845
— Fras., dn. Jsy. 668
— Gallw. B., gen. (**D**) 900
— Jno., bp. Mth. 599; M.R. Ir. 585
— Jas. S., Pres. Lib. 100
— Jno. Home, Q.C. 420
— Jno. Will., adm. (**A**) 817; L.W.S. 323
— sir Ralph, aft. ld. Lavington, *q.v.*, G. Leew. Isl. 727; K.B. 765
— Steph., dn. Exr. 437
— Wm., S.L. 413
— Wm. and sir W., gen. (**D**) 907; K.C.B. 781
— sir Wm., gen. (**A**) 861
Paynem, Clem., dn. Elph. 609
Paynswick, Rt., dn. Chr. Ch. Dbln. 618
Paynter, G. Bmda. 701
— Dav. Wm., gen. (**D**) 902
— Jas. Aylm., adm. (**E**) 835; (**F**) 839
Payridon, Pres. Arg. 110
Peacock, Barnes and sir B., C.J. Bgal. 652-3; Jud. Com. P.C. 361; P.C. 218; Q.C. 417
— Geo., dn. Ely, 435
— Geo. Jno., gen. (**D**) 909
— Reg., bp. Chich. 433; bp. St. As. 462
Peache, sir Th., W.C.P. 318
Peachy, Wm., gen. (**B**) 868
Peacock, Peacocke, and **Pecocke**
— Rd., adm. (**A**) 820
— sir Steph., L.M. Lond. 490
— Th., gen. (**D**) 890
— sir Warr. Marm., gen. (**A**) 862; K.C.H. 788
Peada, K.E. 3
Peake, Sir Hy., Tr. N. 257
— sir Jno., L.M. Lond. 491
— Th., P.P. 416; S.L. 413
— Th. Ladd, adm. (**H**) 846
— sir Wm., L.M. Lond. 491
Pearce, *see also* Pearse and Peirse
— sir Edm., M. Chy. 396
— Ed., gen. (**C**) 871
— Th., gen. (**B**) 864
— Wm., dn. Ely, 435
— Wm., K.H. 791
— Zach., bp. Bgr. 426; bp. Roch. 460; dn. Westr. 469; dn. Winch. 471
Peard, Shuldh., adm. (**A**) 819
Pearl, sir Jas., K.H. 791
Pears, Th. Towns., gen. (**D**) 896; K.C.B. 783
Pearse, *see also* Pearce and Peirse
— Arth. Th. Gr., gen. (**D**) 925
— Geo. Godfr., gen. (**D**) 921
— Josh., adm. (**H**) 848
— Rd. Bulk., adm. (**H**) 851
— Wm. Alf. Rumb., adm. (**H**) 851
— Wm. G., gen. (**D**) 878
Pearson, *see also* Peirson
— Alexr., Ld. Sess. 519
— sir Ch. Kn., gen. (**D**) 925; K.C.M.G. 797
— Jno., bp. Chest. 477
— Jno., L.M. Dbln. 641
— Jno. and sir J., Just. Ch. D. 391; Q.C. 418
— Jos. Br., bp. Newc. N.S.W. 704
— Nathl., L.M. Dbln. 641
— Nichs., dn. Sal. 468
— sir Rd., L.G. Gr. Hosp. 854
— Rd. Harr., adm. (**A**) 820
— sir Th., gen. (**B**) 870; K.C.H. 788
— Th. Hooke, gen. (**D**) 904
— Wm., Q.C. 419
Peat, Dav., adm. (**H**) 848
Pec, Rd. de, J. It. 366
Pecham (or Peche), Rt., bp. Lich. 443
Peche, Jno., L.M. Lond. 489
— sir Jno., W.C.P. 318
— Rd., bp. Lich. and Cov. 443; L.J. Ir. 550
— Rt., *see* Pecham
Pechell, sir Geo. Rd. Brooke, adm. (**G**) 841
— Mark Rt., adm. (**H**) 852
— Saml., M. Chy. 397
— sir Saml. Jno. Br., adm. (**D**) 827; K.C.H. 788; L. Admy. 182-3
— sir Th. Br., gen. (**C**) 873
Peck, *see* Pecke
Peckard, Pet., dn. Pboro. 458
Pecke, Ed., S.L. 410
Peckham, sir Edm., M.M. 246
— sir Hy., S.L. 410
— Jno., abp. Cant. 430
— Rt., L.M. Lond. 492
Peckwell, Rt. Hy., S.L. 412
Pecoce, Dunc., Sec. St. Sc. 501
Pecocke, *see* Peacock
Pecthelmus, bp. Gall. 538
Peddie, Jno., K.H. 790
Pede, Rd., dn. Her. 442
Pedius, Q., C. Ro. 46
Pedley, sir Nichs., S.L. 410
Pedor, Jno., dn. Worc. 473
Pedraza, Pres. Mex. 103
Pedro, all indexed under Peter
Peebles, Jno., bp. Dkld. 533; Ld. Chanc. Sc. 515
— Rt., L.G.C. Sc. 506
Peel, *see also* Peile
— Arth. Well., P.C. 220; Sec. B.T. 269; Sec. P.L.B. 262; Sec. Tr. 164; Sp. H.C. 251
— Fk. and sir F., K.C.M.G. 796; P.C. 216; Sec. Tr. 163; U.S.C. 231, 235; U.S.W. and C. 231; U.S. War, 232
— Jno., dn. Worc. 474
— Jno., gen. (**D**) 922
— Jonn., gen. (**D**) 884; P.C. 216; S.G.O. 260; W. Sec. 232
— Laur. and sir L., B.C. 253; C.J. Bgal. 652; Jud. Com. P.C. 361; P.C. 216
— Rt. and sir R. (No. 1), C. Treas. Ir. 561; Ch. Ex. 165; Ch. Sec. Ir. 563; H. Sec. 227; L.T. 160-1; P.C. 209; Prem. 147; U.S.W. and C. 231
— sir Rt. (No. 2), Ch. Sec. Ir. 563; G.C.B. 772; L. Admy. 183; P.C. 217
— Wm., K.C.B. 778
— Wm. Yates, B.C. 253; L.T. 160; P.C. 213; U.S. Home, 227
Peers, sir Ch., C. Cus. 274-5; L.M. Lond. 491
— Rd., G. Bdoes. 719
Peile, *see also* Peel
— Jas. Br., K.C.S.I. 803; M.C.I. 647
— Mountf. Steph. Lov., adm. (**H**) 853
Peirs, *see* Piers
Peirse, *see also* Pearce and Pearse
— Ed., adm. (**H**) 850
Peirson, *see also* Pearson
— Rd., K.B. 765
Pelagius, K. Sp. 85
— I. and II., P. Ro. 33
Pelayo, K. Sp. 85
Pelham, Edmd. and sir E., C.B. Ex. Ir. 583; L.K. Ir. 576; S.L. 409
— hon. Fk. Th., adm. (**D**) 832; L. Admy. 184
— hon. Geo., bp. Brl. 439; bp. Exr. 437; bp. Linc. 447
— Hy., C. Cus. 276
— Hy., Cl. Pells. 168
— Hy., L. Admy. 175
— hon. Hy., Ch. Ex. 165; L.T. 156-7; P.C. 197; Prem. 142; Paym. G. 244; Sec. at W. 233; Tr. Ch. 294
— hon. Jno. Th., bp. Norw. 455
— Th., B.T. 264
— Th., K.B. 755
— Th., *see* ld. P., *infra*
— sir Wm., L.J. Ir. 554
Pelham, lds.
— Th., aft. 1st ld. P., C. Cus. 274; L.T. 155
— Th., aft. 2nd ld. P. and 1st E. of Clare and 1st D. of Newcastle, *q.v.*, B.T. 265; Compt. H. 292; L. Admy. 179; M.G.W. 296; P.C. 201
*— hon. Th., aft. ld. P., and 2nd E. of Chichester, *q.v.*, C.D.L. 243; C.Y.G. 298; C. Treas. Ir. 560; Ch. Sec. Ir. 563; H. Sec. 226; P.C. 206; S.G.O. 260; Sec. St. Ir. 562
*— Th., B.C. 252

* ? same pers.

Pelissier, Marsh., G.C.B. 769
Pell, Alb. and sir A., J. Bank. 392; S.L. 412
—— sir Watk. Owen, adm. (**D**) 828; (**G**) 840; K.C.H. 789
Pellew, sir Ed., aft. 1st ld. and visc. Exmouth, *q.v.*, adm. (**A**) 817
—— hon. Fleet. Br. R. and sir F., adm. (**D**) 827; K.C.H. 789
—— Geo., dn. Norw. 456
—— Isr. and sir I., adm. (**A**) 818; K.C.B. 774
Pellion, Marie Jos. Alph. Odet—, K.C.B. 778
Pelly, Hy. Jos., gen. (**D**) 901
—— Lewis and sir L., gen. (**D**) 924; K.C.B. 783; K.C.S.I. 803
Pember, Ed. Hy., Q.C. 419
Pemberton, sir Fras., C.J.C.P. 375; C.J.K.B. 370; J.K.B. 372; P.C. 192; S.L. 410
—— Geo. R., gen. (**D**) 887
—— sir Jas., L.M. Lond. 491
—— Jno., M. Chy. 394
—— Jos., L.M. Dbln. 641
—— Th., aft. ld. Kingsdown, *q.v.*, K.C. 416
Pembridge, Pembrigg, or **Pembrugg,** sir Rd. de, W.C.P. 318; K.G. 733
Pembroke, Hy., dn. Oss. 622
—— Jno., B. Ex. Ir. 583
Pembroke, E. of, *see also under* Montgomery
De Clare Family.
—— Gilb. De Clare, 1st E. of, L.M. 325
—— Rd, (Strongbow), 2nd E. of, L.J. Ir. 550; L.M. 325
Marshal Family.
—— Wm., 1st E. of, L.D. Ir. 550; L.L. Ir. 550; W.C.P. 317
—— Wm., 2nd E. of, form. W. Marshall, *q.v.*, L.J. Ir. 550; L.M. 325
—— Rd., 3rd E. of, L.M. 325
—— Gilb., 4th E. of, L.M. 325
—— Walt., 5th E. of, L.M. 325
—— Anselm, 6th E. of, L.M. 325
Hastings Family.
—— Jno., 2nd E. of, K.G. 733
Plantagenet Family.
—— Humph., 1st E. of (son of Hy. IV.), aft. D. of Gloucester, *q.v.*, K.G. 734
Tudor Family.
—— Jasper, 1st E. of, form. J. Tudor, *q.v.*, aft. D. of Bedford, *q.v.*, K.B. 756; K.G. 736; L.L. Ir. 553
Herbert Family.
1st Creation.
—— Wm., 1st E. of, form. ld. Herbert of Chepstow, *q.v.*
2nd Creation.
—— Wm., 1st E. of, form. sir Wm. Herbert, and aft. ld. H. of Cardiff, *q.v.*, L.S.H. 290
—— Hy., 2nd E. of, form. ld. Cardiff, *q.v.*, K.G. 738
—— Wm., 3rd E. of, E.M. 326; K.G. 739; L.C.H. 294-95; L.S.H. 290; L.W.S. 323
—— Ph., 4th E. of, also 1st E. of Montgomery and 1st ld. Herbert of Shurland, *q.v.*, Const. W. Cast. 322; L.W.S. 323
The following were also E. of Montgomery:—
—— Wm. 6th E. of, B.T. 263

Pembroke, E. of—*cont.*
—— Th., 8th E. of, K.G. 741; L. Admy. 176; L.H.A. 176-7; L.L. Ir. 555; L.L. S. Wales, 315; L.P.C. 188; L.P.S. 240; P.C. 194; Pres. R. Soc. 940
—— Hy., 9th E. of, gen. (**B**) 864; Gr. St. 304; P.C. 198
—— Hy., 10th E. of, gen. (**A**) 858; L.L. Wilts, 313
—— Geo. Augs., 11th E. of, form. ld. Herbert, *q.v.*, Amb. Aus. 117; G. Gsey. 669; gen. (**A**) 860; K.G. 743; L.L. Wilts, 313
—— Geo. Rt. Chas., 13th E. of, U.S. War. 232
Pemery, Thor. Rd., K.B. 758
Penaud, Adm., K.C.B. 778
Pencestre or **Penchester,** Steph. de and sir S., J.C.P. 377; W.C.P. 318
Penda, K.E. 3
Pendarves, Alexr., S.L.R., 271
Pender, Fras., adm. (**A**) 817
—— Jno., K.C.M.G. 799
Pendergast, *see* Prendergast
Penfold, *see* Pinfold
Pengelly, Th. and sir T., C.B. Ex. 382; S.L. 411
Penkeston, Jas., J.K.B. Ir. 578
—— Walt., J.K.B. Ir. 578
Penn, sir Wm., adm. (**A**) 813
Pennant, sir Saml., L.M. Lond. 492
Pennefather, Ed., C.J.Q.B. Ir. 578; S.G. Ir. 590; S.L. Ir. 593
—— Jno. Lys. and sir J., G.C.B. 770; G. Ch. Hosp. 936; gen. (**D**) 885; K.C.B. 777
—— Rd., B. Ex. Ir. 584; C. St. Ir. 568; U.S. Ir. 563
Pennell, Foll. Walr., adm. (**G**) 841
Penney, *see* Penny
Pennington, Alderman, Lt. T.L. 321
—— sir Isaac, L.M. Lond. 491
—— sir Jos., C. Cus. 276
—— Lowth., aft. 2nd ld. Muncaster, *q.v.*, gen. (**A**) 859
Pennus, M. J., C. Ro. 44
Penny and **Penney**
—— Gabr. Rd., gen. (**D**) 877
—— Jno., bp. Bgr. 426; bp. Carl. 475
—— Nichs., dn. Lich. 445
—— Nichs., gen. (**D**) 887
—— Wm., Ld. Sess. 521
Pennycuick, Jas. Farr., gen. (**D**) 922
—— Jno., K.H. 792
Penrhyn, Ed. Gord., 1st ld., L.L. Carn. 314
Penrice, Hy., Adm. Adv. 423; J. Adm. Ct. 423
Penros and **Penrose**
—— Ch., gen. (**D**) 907; K.C.B. 781
—— Ch. Vin. and sir C., adm. (**A**) 819; G.C.M.G. 794; K.C.B. 775
—— Jno., C.J.K.B. Ir. 577; J.C.P. 378
Penshurst, Percy Cl. S., 1st ld., form. V. Strangford, *q.v.*
Penson, Wm., Chest. H. 331; Lanc. H. 333
Penton, Hy., L. Admy. 179
Penzance, Jas. Pl., 1st ld., form. J. P. Wilde, *q.v.*; D. Arch. 421

Pepin, K. Fr. 23
Peploe, Saml. (No. 1), Wdn. Chr. Ch. Manch. 481; bp. Chest. 477
—— Saml. (No. 2), Wdn. Chr. Ch. Manch. 481
Pepper, Jno., gen. (**C**) 871
Pepperell, sir Wm., gen. (**B**) 865
Pepys, Ch. Chr. and sir C., aft. 1st ld. and E. Cottenham, *q.v.*; C.G.S. 358; Jud. Com. P.C. 360; K.C. 416; Ld. Chanc. 358; M.R. 388; P.C. 213; S.G. 402
—— Hy., bp. S. and M. 484; bp. Worc. 473
—— sir Lucas, Pres. Coll. Ph. 938
—— Rd., B. Ex. 384; C.G.S. Ir. 576; C.J.K.B. Ir. 578; S.L. 409
—— Saml., Pres. R. Soc. 940; Sec. Adm. 186
—— Wm. W., M. Chy. 397
Pera, M. J., C. Ro. 43; Dt. Ro. 43
—— D. J., C. Ro. 42
Perbroun or **Perburn,** Jno. de, L.H.A. 171
Percehay (or Perchehay), Hy. de, B. Ex. 383; J.C.P. 378; S.L. 407
Perceval and **Percival**
—— Alexr., L.T. 160
—— hon. Ch. Geo., aft. 1st ld. Arden, *q.v.*, L. Admy. 180
—— (or Persevall), Hugh, dn. Ross. 633
—— Jno., L.M. Lond. 490
—— Jno. Maxw., G. N.S.W. 703; gen. (**D**) 899
—— Lew., gen. (**D**) 932
—— Sp., gen. (**D**) 897
—— Sp. and sir S., Clk. O. 260; Tell. Ex. 167; U.S. Home, 227
—— hon. Sp., A.G. 400; C.D.L. 243; C. Treas. Ir. 561; Ch. Ex. 165; K.C. 415; L.T. 158-9; P.C. 208; Prem. 145; S.G. 402
—— Wm., dn. Emly, 628
Perchard, Pet., L.M. Lond. 492
Perchehay, *see* Percehay
Percival, *see* Perceval
Percy, hon. Algn., Amb. Fr. 113; Amb. Swz. 113
—— Algn., *see* ld. P., *infra*
—— Allan, K.B. 761
—— Hy., K.B. 754
—— Hy. (Hotspur), K.B. 756; K.G. 734
—— Hy., K.B. (1426), 756
—— Hy., *see* ld. P., *infra*
—— hon. Hugh, dn. Cant. 432; bp. Carl. 476; bp. Roch. 460
—— hon. Josc., adm. (**D**) 826
—— Pet. de, J. It. 368; Jy. 365
—— Rt. de, J. It. 366
—— Th., bp. Drom. 605; dn. Carl. 476
—— Th., bp. Norw. 455
—— Th., aft. E. of Worcester, *q.v.* (*d.* 1402), K.G. 734; L.H.A. 173
—— (or Persey), Walt., S.L. 407
—— Wm., bp. Carl. 475
—— Wm. de, J. It. 366
—— Wm. de, K.B. 755
—— hon. Wm. Hy., adm. (**H**) 844; C. Exc. 282

Percy, lds., visc. and E.
— Hy., aft. ld. P. and E. Northbd., *q.v.* (*d.* 1408), K.G. 733; L.M. 325
— Algn., aft. ld. P. and D. of Northbd., *q.v.* (*d.* 1668), K.B. 762
— ld. Algn., aft. E. of Hertford, and E. of Northumber- and 7th D. of Somerset, *q.v.* (*d.* 1750), G. Gsey. 668
— Hy. Hugh Maur., visc. (son of Geo., 5th D. of Northbd.), gen. (**D**) 900; K.C.B. 780
— Hy. Geo., Earl, son of 6th D. of Northbd., P.C. 218; Tr. H. 292
Pereira, Pres. Ugy. 111
— Manass. Lop., gen. (**D**) 876
Perez, J. J., Pres. Chi. 111
— S., Pres. U.S.C. 107
Periam (or Peryam), Wm. and sir W., C.B. Ex. 381; J.C.P. 378; S.L. 408
Perkins, Æn., gen. (**D**) 932
— Chr., dn. Carl. 476
— Ed. Norm., gen. (**D**) 915
— Jas. Fras., gen. (**B**) 866
— Wm. Hill., gen. (**D**) 877
Perne, Andr., dn. Ely, 435
Perowne, Jno. Jas. S., dn. Pboro. 459
Perperna, M., C. Ro. 45
Perriam, *see* Periam
Perrin, *see also* Perryn
— Arth., L.M. Dbln. 642
— Louis, A.G. Ir. 588; J.K.B. Ir. 579; S.L. Ir. 593
Perring, Jno., L.M. Lond. 492
Perrot or **Perrott,** sir Geo., B. Ex. 385; K.C. 415; S.L. 412
— sir Jno., L.D. Ir. 554
Perry, Ch., bp. Melb. 705; Prel. M.G. 799
— Jas., gen. (**D**) 886
— Jno. Laisne, adm. (**H**) 852
— Mich., L.M. Lond. 491
— sir Th. Ersk., C.J. Bbay. 660; M.C.I. 646
Perryam, *see* Periam
Perryn, *see also* Perrin
— Rd. and sir R., B. Ex. 385; K.C. 415; S.L. 412
Persevall, *see* Perceval
Persey, Walt., *see* Percy
Persia, Mukhbar ud Dowlah of, C.I.E. 807
— Sult. of, G.C.S.I. 802
Pertab, Mahar. of, K.C.S.I. 803
Pertharitus, K. Lmd. 49
Perth, Jas., 4th E. of, Comm. Tr. Sc. 497; K.T. 747; L.J. Gen. 522; Ld. Chanc. Sc. 515; Ld. Sess. 517; P.C. 192
Pertinax, Emp. Ro. 47
Pery, Wm. Cecil, aft 1st ld. Glentworth, *q.v.*, bp. Killa. and Ach. 613; bp. Lim. A. and A. 639; dn. Killoe. 637; dn. Dry. 602
Peryam, *see* Periam
Pester, Hy., gen. (**D**) 897
— Hugh Loam., gen. (**D**) 912
Pessulano, Rt. de M., bp. Lich. and Cov. 444
Pestonji, &c., C.I.E. 808
Peter and **Pedro**
*— bp. Clonm. 600
*— (of Dunath), bp. Cnr. 604
*— bp. Lich. 443
Peter and Pedro—*cont.*
*— bp. Ork. 535
*— dn. Dry. 602
* Prob. some same pers. Comp. dates.
— (2), C. Alçn. 26
— C. Svy. 54
— (de Courtenay), Emp. E.E. 51
— (abb. of Tewkesbury), J. It. 367
— K. Cle. 86
— K. Hgy. 59
— K. Nav. 85
— P. Ro. 32
— (de Fuentes), R. Nds. 82
— I., G.D. Obg. 76
— I., R. Russ. 90
— I. and II., D. Bry. 28
— I. and II., Emp. Bzl. 108
— II. (Emp. Bzl.), K.G. 745
— I. and II. K. Scy. 55
— I. to III., E. Russ. 90
— I. to IV., K. Arr. 86
— I. to V., K. Pgl. 88-9
— V. (K. Pgl.), K.G. 744
— -Ernest, K. Nds. 82
— -Fred., D. Obg. 76
— -Fred.-Louis, D. Obg. 76; G.D. Obg. 76
— -Leopold, G.D. Tny. 57
— -Louis-Farnese, D. Pma. 53
— Th., gen. (**B**) 867
— Wm. and sir W., M. Chy. 394
Peterborough, E. of, *see also* Monmouth
— Hy., 2nd E. of, Gr. St. 303; K.G. 740; P.C. 191-2
— Ch., 3rd E. of, also E. of Monmouth, *q.v.*, adm. (**A**) 813; G. Jam. 712; gen. (**A**) 857; K.G. 741; P.C. 195
Peters, Wm. Hy. Br., gen. (**D**) 934
Petersdorff, Ch. E., C.C.J. 404; S.L. 413
Peterson, Fk., C.I.E. 807
— Wm., dn. Exr. 437
Petheram, Wm. Com. and sir W., C.J. Bgal. 653; C.J. N.W. Pr. 654; Q.C. 419
Peticus, C. S. (2), C. Ro. 39, 40
— C. S. (5), Dt. Ro. 40
Petion, A., Pres. S. Dom. 105
Petit and **Petyt**
— Dunc., Ld. Chanc. Sc. 515
— Jno., B. Ex. 383
— Jno., K.B. 755
— Th., dn. Ferns, 623
— Wm. le, S.L. Ir. 590; L.J. Ir. 550
Petitot, Wm., gen. (**C**) 871
Petow, Pet., bp. Sal. 467
Petre, Ed., P.C. 193
— Geo. Gl., Amb. Arg. 136; Amb. Pgl. 125; Amb. Pgy. 136; Amb. Scy. 115
— sir Wm., S. St. 223
Petre, lds.
— Jno., 1st ld., L.L. Esx. 308
Petrezzopulo, Pietr., G.C.M.G. 794; K.C.M.G. 796
Petrides, Plato, K.C.M.G. 796
Petrie, Arth., bp. Edinb. 542; bp. Mor. 544
— Jno. Gord., gen. (**D**) 916
— Wm., G. Mdras. 656
Petronilla, Q. Arr. 86
Petrus, *see* Peter
Pettingal, Ed., gen. (**D**) 891
Petty, ld. Hy., aft. 3rd. M. Lansdowne, *q.v.*, Ch. Ex. 165 L.T. 158; P.C. 207
Petyt, *see* Petit
Peverel, Peverell, and **Peveril**
— Hugh, Jy. 363
— Th., bp. Llff. 449; bp. Oss. 620; bp. Worc. 472
— Wm., K.B. 754
— Wm., W.C.P. 317
Peyton, Fras., gen. (**D**) 908
— Jno., adm. (**A**) 817
— sir Jno., G. Jsey. 667; Lt. T.L. 321
— sir Jno. Str., K.C.H. 789
— Jos., adm. (**A**) 815
— Th., dn. Tm. 613
— sir Th., gen. (**D**) 911
Pezet, J. A., Pres. Pu. 109
Pharamond, K. Fr. 22
Phayre, Arth. Purv. and sir A., Ch. Com. Bma. 655; G.C.M.G. 795; G. Mtius. 684; gen. (**D**) 910; K.C.S.I. 803
— Rt., gen. (**D**) 921; K.C.B. 781
Pheasant or **Phesant**
— Jasp., dn. Killoe. 637
— Pet., J.C.P. 379; Rec. Lond. 494; S.L. 409
Phelip, *see* Philip
Phelips, *see* Philips
Phelps, Arth., gen. (**D**) 934
— Rd., U.S.S. 226
Phesant, *see* Pheasant
Philbrick, Fk. Adolph., Q.C. 419
Philibert (de Chalons), Pr Or. 83
— I. and II., D. Svy. 54
— I. and II. M. Bdn. 67
Philip and **Phelip**
*— bp. Ardf. and Agh. 639
*— bp. Brn. 531
*— bp. Clonm. 600
*— (of Slane), bp. Cork, 630
*— (of Poictiers), bp. Dham. 478; Jy. 364
*— bp. Emly, 625
*— bp. Wford. 626; dn. Wford. 628
*— dn. Clr. 597
*— dn. Cork, 632
*— dn. Emly, 628
*— dn. Lism. 628
*— Ld. Chanc. 353
* Prob. some same pers. Comp. dates.
— (D'Alsace), C. Flrs. 81
— (the Hardy), C. Flrs. 81
— (the Ingenuous), C.P.R. 68
— (le Bon), D. Bbt. 29
— D. Pma. 53
— D. Su. 80
— D. Tny. 57
— Emp. Ro. 47
— E. Gmy. 61
— (Ph. II. Spn.), K.C.E. 7
— K. Cle. 86; K.G. 737
— (2), K. Nav. 85
— K. Sw. 92
— L.G.C. Sc. 506
— (the Generous) Lg. Hse. 72
— M. Bdn. 67
— (son Hy. II.), Pr. E. 9
— (gson. Jas. I.), Pr. E. 13
— Pr. L. Sch. 73
— (le Beau), R. Nds. 82
— I., C. Svy. 54
— I. to III., D. Bdy. 29
— III. (D. Bdy.), K.G. 735

Philip and Phelip—*cont.*
— I. to III., Pr. Nass. 75
— I. to V., K. Sp. 86
— II. (K. Sp.), K.C.E. 7; K.G. 738
— I. to VI., K. Fr. 23-4
— V., K. Nav. 87
— Arth., adm. (**A**) 817
— -Augs. -Fredk. -Lg., H. Hbg. 73
— (or Phelip), Jno. K.B. 756
— Matth., K.B. 757; L.M. Lond. 490
— Wm., C.P.R. 68
— Wm., Pr. Or. 83
Philipot, *see also* Philpot
— Jno., Bl. L.P.A. 341; R. Dr. P.A. 338; Som. H. 332
Philippa (g. dau. Edw. III.), Pr. E. 10
— (g. dau. Edw. III.), Pr. E. 11
— (Iss. Edw. III.), Pr. E. 10
— (dau. Hy. IV.), Pr. E. 11
— Q.C.E. 7
Philipps, *see* Phillips
Philippas, L. M., C. Ro. 45-6
— Q.M., C. Ro. 42, 44
Philips, *see* Phillips
Philipson, *see* Phillipson
Phillimore, Augs. and sir A., adm. (**E**) 836; K.C.B. 782
— Hy. Bourch., adm. (**E**) 837
— Jno. Geo., Q.C. 417
— Jos. and sir J., Adm. Adv. 423; B.C. 253
— Rt. Jos. and sir R., Adm. Adv. 423; D. Arch. 421; J.A.G. 937; J. Adm. Ct. 423; J.P.D.A. 391; Jud. Com. P.C. 361; P.C. 217; Q. Adv. 422; Q.C. 418
— Walt. Geo. F. and sir W., P.P. 420
Phillip, Capt. A., G. N.S.W. 702
Phillipicus-Bardanes, Emp. E.E. 50
Phillips, Phillipps, Philips, Philipps, and **Philips,** *see also* Philps
Phillips, Alex. R., adm. (**H**) 852
— Amb., S.L. 411
— Arth. Chaunc., gen. (**D**) 914
— Benj. S. and sir B., L.M. Lond. 492
— sir Ch., gen. (**B**) 868
— Ch., Ed. Grigg, L.L. Hav. 316
— Dav., G. Jsey. 667
— Ed. and sir E., M.R. 388; S.L. 409; Sp. H.C. 249
— Fk., gen. (**D**) 914
— Geo. Rt., gen. (**D**) 923
— Hy. Pye, gen. (**D**) 925
— Jas. M., R. Dr. P.A. 338
— Jas. Rt., adm. (**D**) 827
— Jno., bp. S. and M., 483
*— sir Jno., B.T. 264
*— sir Jno., P.C. 201
* ? same pers.
— Jno. Alex., gen. (**D**) 891
— Jno. Hy., aft. sir J. Phillips-Scourfield, L.L. Hav. 316
*— Rd., G. N.Sc. 694
*— Rd., gen. (**B**) 864
* Prob. same pers.
— Rd., U.S.C. 235
— sir Rd., aft. ld. Milford (1st Cr.), *q.v.*, L.L. Hav. 316
— sir Rd. Bulk., aft. ld. Milford (2nd Cr.), *q.v.*, L.L. Hav. 316

Phillips—*cont.*
— Rd. Ell., C. Cus. Sc., 504
— Rt., L.P.S. 240
— Rt. Hosk., gen. (**D**) 931
— Rt. Newt. gen. (**D**) 902
— Saml. March., P.C. 215; U.S. Home, 228
— sir Th., Q.C. 418
— Walt., dn. Roch. 461
— Wm., gen. (**C**) 872
— sir Wm., aft. ld. Bardolph, K.G. 735
— Wm. Cornw., gen (**D**) 918
Phillips-Treby, *see* Treby
Phillipson and **Philipson**
— Jno., S.W.F. 271
— Rd. Burt., gen (**B**) 866
— T., L. Admy. 178
Phillott, Ch. Geo. Rodn., adm. (**H**) 846
— Hy., gen. (**C**) 875
Phillpot, *see* Philpot
Phillpott-s, *see* Philpott-s
Philo, C. C., C. Ro. 38
— L. V. (2), C. Ro. 43; Dt. Ro. 43
— Q. P. (4), C. Ro. 40-1; Dt. Ro. 40
Philpot, Philpott, Phillpot, and **Phylpot,** *see also* Philipot
— Hy., bp. Worc. 473
— Jno., J.C.P. Ir. 581
— Jno., K.B. 759
— Jno., L.M. Lond. 489
— Ph., gen. (**B**) 870
Philpotts and **Phillpotts**
— Arth. Th., gen. (**D**) 905
— Hy., bp. Exr. 437; dn. Chest. 477
Philps, Jas. Hy., K.H. 792
Philus, L. F., C. Ro. 44
— P. F., C. Ro. 43
Phin, Kenn. M., Modr. K. Sc. 547
— Th., P.P. 417
— Th., Sec. Adm. 187
Phinny, *see* Finny
Phipps, hon. Aug., C. Ex. 281-2
— Benj., dn. Down, 605; dn. Ferns, 623
— hon. Ch. Beaum., K.C.B. 782
— sir Const., L.J. Ir. 556; Ld. Chanc. Ir. 576
— hon. Edm., gen. (**A**) 861
— hon. Edw., Q.C. 417
— Geo. Wm., gen. (**B**) 869
— Jno., gen. (**C**) 872
— Paul, K.H. 791
Phipson, Th. W., Q.C. 418
Phocas, Emp. E.E. 50
Phra-Bat, &c., K. Si. 100
Phraklang - Chao, &c., K.C.M.G. 797
Phyl—, *see* Phil—
Piastus, D. Pld. 90
Picard, *see* Pickard
Picens, M. H., C. Ro. 46
Picheford, Geoffr. de, Const. W. Cast. 322; J. It. 368
Pickard, Picard, and **Pycard**
— Benj. Sp., adm. (**H**) 852
— Hy., L.M. Lond. 489
— Jas., gen. (**D**) 910
Pickering and **Pykering,** *see also* Puckering
— sir Jas., Sp. H.C. 248
— J. A., G. Virg. Isl. 731
— Perc. Andr., Q.C. 417
— Rt. de, dn. Yk. 486; M. Chy. 393

Pickering and Pykering—*cont.*
— Wm. de, dn. Yk. 486; M. Chy. 393
— Wm. Hy., gen. (**D**) 895
Pickett, Wm., L. M. Lond. 492
Pickmore, Fras., adm. (**A**) 818; G. Newfd. 700
Picot, *see* Pycot
Picton, Jno., gen. (**C**) 873
— Th. and sir T., G.C.B. 767; G. Tob. 723; G. Trin. 722; gen. (**B**) 867; K.B. 766
— Wm., gen. (**A**) 859
Pictor, C. F., C. Ro. 42
— N. F., C. Ro. 42
Pictuinus, bp. Gall. 538
Piel, *see* Pyell
Pielat, Jac. Chr., G. Ceyl. 672
Pierce, *see also* Pearce
— F., Pres. U.S.A. 102
— Josh. Hume Spr., gen. (**D**) 918
— Th., dn. Sal. 468
— Th., gen. (**D**) 914
— Th. Wm. West, gen. (**D**) 935
— Wm., *see* Piers
Pierola, N. de, Dt. Pu. 109
Pierrepont, hon. Hy. M., Amb. Sw. 126; P.C. 208
— Wm., adm. (**A**) 819
Pierrot, Pres. Hti. 105
Piers, Jno., abp. Yk. 486; bp. Roch. 460; bp. Sal. 467; dn. Chr. Ch. Oxf. 457; dn. Chest. 477; dn. Sal. 468
— (or Pierce), Wm., bp. B. and W. 428; bp. Pboro. 458; dn. Pboro. 458
Pierse, *see also* Piers, Pearce, Pearse, and Pierce
— Dudl., dn. Kilmacd. 637
Pierson, *see also* Pearson and Peirson
— sir Rd., gen. (**B**) 865
— Wm. Hy., adm. (**H**) 847
Pietas, L. A., C. Ro. 46
Piggot, Piggott, Pigot, and **Pigott**
— —, G. Tob. 723
— sir Arth., A.G. 400
— Dav. Rd., A.G. Ir. 588; C.B. Ex. Ir. 583; S.G. Ir. 590
— Ed. F. S., E.S.P. 301
— Fras., aft. Pigott-Conant, G. I. Man, 666
— sir Geo., gen. (**A**) 861
— Gill. and sir G., B. Ex. 385; P.P. 417; S.L. 413
— Hy. and sir H., G.C.M.G. 794; gen. (**A**) 860
— Hugh and sir H., adm. (**A**) 815; (**D**) 825; K.C.B. 777; K.C.H. 788; L. Admy. 179, 180
— Jas., adm. (**A**) 816
— Rd., gen. (**A**) 863
— Rd., S.L. 407
*— Rt., Wdn. M. 245
*— sir Rt., gen. (**B**) 866
* ? same pers.
— Th., bp. Bgr. 426
— Th., S.L. 408
Pigou, Arth. Com., gen. (**D**) 911
— Fras., dn. Chich. 434
Pike and **Pyke**
— Jno. Wm., adm. (**H**) 853
— Rd., K.B. 754
Pikenot, Rt., J. It. 366

Pilborough, Jno., B. Ex. 384
Pilcher, Jno. M., gen. (**D**) 889
Pilkington and **Pilkynton**
— Andr. and sir A., gen. (**B**) 869; K.C.B. 776
— Jas., bp. Dham. 479
— Jno., K.B. 757
— Rt., gen. (**C**) 875
— sir Th., L.M. Lond. 491
Pillar, Jas., S.L.R. 271
Pilmore, Jno., bp. Mor. 534; bp. Ross. 535
Pilsworth, Wm., bp. Kild. 617
Pim, *see also* Pym
— Bedf. Clapp. Tryv. adm. (**H**) 853
Pincerna, Nichs. de, J. It. 367
Pinckney, L., Tell. Ex. 167
— W., Tell. Ex. 167
Pine, *see also* Pyne
— Benjn. Chill. Campb. and sir B., G. Antig., &c. 727; G. Gld. Cst. 686; G. Leew. Isl. 727; G. Nat. 680; G. St. Xtr. 729; G. W. Austr. 707; K.C.M.G. 796
— Jno., Bl. M. P.A. 336
— Rd., G. Gld. Cst. 686
Pineda, L., Pres. Nic. 106
Pinfold, Ch., Adm. Adv. 423
— Ch., G. Bdoes. 720
— Th., Adm. Adv. 423
Pingo, Benj., R. Dr. P.A. 338; Yk. H. 334
Pinkeni, Gilb. de, J. It. 365
Pinkham, Wm. Cypr., bp. Sask. 697
Pinson, Ph., abp. Tm. 611
Pinto, Pres. Arg. 110
— A., Pres. Chi. 111
Pipard, Gilb., J. It. 366
— Pet., L.J. Ir. 550
Pipe, Rd., L.M. Lond. 490
— Rt. Sl., gen. (**D**) 890
Pipon, Geo., K.H. 791
— Ph. Goss., gen. (**D**) 922
Pirie, Jno. and sir J., L.M. Lond. 492
— Wm., gen. (**D**) 913
— Wm. R., Mod. K. Sc. 547
Piro, Giuss. Mar. Bar. de, G.C.M.G. 795; K.C.M.G. 796
— Wm., bp. Glend. 615
Pirri, Martyn, M.M. 246
Piso, C. C., C. Ro. 44, 46
— Q. C., C. Ro. 44
Pitcairne, Rt., Ld. Sess. 518; Sec. St. Sc. 502
Pitman, Ch. Ed., C.I.E. 806
— Rt., gen. (**D**) 877
Pitt, Geo., aft. 1st ld. Rivers, *q.v.*, Amb. Sda. 114; Amb. Spn. 123
— Geo. Dean-, gen. (**D**) 882; K.H. 791
— Geo. Dean-, gen. (**D**) 922
*— Jno., B.T. 264-5
*— Jno., G. Bmda. 701
*— Jno., L. Admy. 178
*— Jno., S.W.F. 271
* Prob. some same pers. Comp. dates.
— Th., G. Jam. 712
— Th., aft. 1st ld. Camelford, *q.v.*, L. Admy. 179; L.W.S. 323
— Th., M. Chy. 396
— Th., aft. ld. Londonderry, *q.v.*
— Wm. (No. 1), aft. 1st E. of Chatham, *q.v.*, P.C. 199; Paym. G. 244; Prem. 142; V. Treas. Ir. 560; S. St. 224
Pitt—*cont.*
— Wm. (No. 2), B.C. 252; Ch. Ex. 165; L.T. 158; P.C. 203; Prem. 144; W.C.P. 319
— Wm. Augs. and sir W., Comm. F. Ir. 564; gen. (**A**) 858; K.B. 765
Pitt-Lewis, *see* Lewis
Pitt-Rivers, *see* Rivers
Pittenweem, Abbot of, Ld. Sess. 518
Pitts, Saml., B.T. 264
Piuntellus, Wm., Const. T.L. 320
Pius I. to IX., P. Ro. 32, 35, 36
— Q. C. M., C. Ro. 45
Place, Alfr. Fox, gen. (**D**) 923
Planché, Jas. R., R. Cr. P.A. 336; Som. H. 332
Plancus, L. M. (2), C. Ro. 46
Planta, Jos., B.C. 253; G.C.H. 787; L.T. 160; P.C. 213; Sec. Tr. 143; U.S.F. 230
Plantaganet, Geoffr., abp. Yk. 485; bp. Linc. 446; Ld. Chanc. 353
Plasket, Rd., K.C.M.G. 796
Plat, Gust. du, K.H. 790
— Pet. du, gen. (**C**) 873
Platt, Th. Josh. and sir T., B. Ex. 385; K.C. 416; S.L. 413
Playfair, Archd. Lew., gen. (**D**) 932
— Ell. Minto, gen. (**D**) 925
— Jno. Wm., gen. (**D**) 913
— Lyon and sir L., K.C.B. 784; P.C. 218; Postm. G. 239; V.P. Ed. 255
— Rt. Lamb, K.C.M.G. 798
Playnford, Rowl., Bl. M. P.A. 336; Yk. H. 334
Plegmund, abp. Cant. 430
Plessetis, Jno. de, Const. T.L. 320
Plessis, Hugh de, K.B. 754
Pleste, Rt. de, B. Ex. 383
— Wm. de, A.G. 398
Plesyngton, Rt. de, C.B. Ex. 381
Plettenberg, Joach. Van, G. C.G.H. 678
Pleydell - Bouverie, *see* Bouverie
Plomer, *see also* Plumer
— Jno., K.B. 757
— sir Wm., L.M. Lond. 492
Plot, Rt., Mowb. H. 340
Plowden, Trevor Jno. Chich., C.I.E. 807
— Wm. Chich., K.C.S.I. 803
Plumbe, Saml., L.M. Lond. 492
Plume, Isaac, dn. Drom. 606
Plumer, *see also* Plomer
— Rd., B.T. 264-5
— Th. and sir T., A.G. 400; K.C. 415; M.R. 388; P.C. 209; S.G. 402; V. Chanc. 390
Plumptre, Ed. H., dn. Wells, 429
— Jno., C. St. 283
— Jno., dn. Glr. 440
Plumridge, Jas. Hanw. and sir J., adm. (**D**) 829; K.C.B. 777
Plumstok, Rd. de, M. Chy. 393
Plunket and **Plunkett**
— Alexr., Ld. Chanc. Ir. 575
— hon. Ch. Daws., gen. (**D**) 907
— sir Chr., L.D. Ir. 552
Plunket and Plunkett—*cont.*
— hon. Dav. Rt., C.W.P.B. 273; P.C. 219; S.G. Ir. 590
— hon. Fras. R. and sir F., Amb. Fr. 113; Amb. Jap. 131; Amb. Sw. and N. 127; K.C.M.G. 798
— Jno., C.J.K.B. Ir. 578
— Jno. Hubert, G. N.S.W. 703
— hon. Patr., J. Bank. Ir. 587
— sir Nichs., L. Treas. Ir. 558
— Rd., C.J.K.B. Ir. 577; S.L. Ir. 591
— hon. Rt., dn. Tm. 613
— Th., C.J.K B. Ir. 577
— hon. Th., dn. Down, 605; bp. Tm. K. and A., 613
— sir Th. Fitz- Chr., S.L. Ir. 591
— Walt., M.M. 247
— Wm., C. Exc. 282; C. Exc. Ir. 567
— Wm. Con., *see* ld. P., *infra*
Plunket, lds.
— Wm. Con., aft. 1st ld. P., A.G. Ir. 588; C.J.C.P. Ir. 581; Ld. Chanc. Ir. 577; P.C. 211-2; S.G. Ir. 589
— Wm. Con., 3rd ld., abp. Dbln. G. and K. 617; bp. Mth. 599; dn. Chr. Ch. Dbln. 619
Plymouth, E. of
— Th., 1st E. of, P.C. 192
— Other L., 4th E. of, L.L. Glam. 315
Pocock, Geo. and sir G., adm. (**A**) 814; K.B. 765
— Rd., bp. Mth. 599; bp. Oss. 620
Pocklington, Ev. Hy. Fk., gen. (**D**) 903
— Jno., B. Ex. Ir. 584; J. Chest. 387
Podda, bp. Her. 441
Podmore, Rd., gen. (**D**) 876
Poer, *see also* Poor
— Miler le, bp. Llin. 621
— Rt. le, B. Ex. Ir. 583; C.J.C.P. Ir. 580
— Rt. le, bp. Wford. and L. 627; dn. Lim. 639
— Rt. le, L. Treas. Ir. 558
— Walt. le, J. It. 367
Pogson, Norman Rt., C.I.E. 806
— Wred. Quir., gen. (**D**) 923
Poitiers, Ern. de, K.B. 755
— Ph. de, bp. Dham. 478
— Rd., Archd. of, J. It. 365
Poland, Jas. Aug., adm. (**H**) 853
Pole, *see also* Poole
— Arth. Cunl. Van Nott., gen. (**D**) 894
— Ch. Mor. and sir C., adm. (**A**) 816; G.C.B. 767; G. Newfd. 700; K.C.B. 773; L. Admy. 181
— Ch. Van Nott., gen. (**D**) 926
— (or Poole), Dav., bp. Pboro. 458; D. Arch. 420; Vic. Gen. 421
— Edmd. de la, aft. D. of Suffolk, *q.v.*, K.B. (1483) 758
— Edw., gen. (**B**) 865
— Edw., gen. (**D**) 897
— sir Michl. de la, L.H.A. 172; Ld. Chanc. 354
— Ralph, J.K.B. 371; S.L. 407
— Regd., abp. Cant. 431; dn. Exr. 437

For List of Abbreviations, see pp. 944-952.

Pole—*cont.*
— sir Rd., K.G. 737
— Wm., S.L. 407
— Wm. de la, L.H.A. 174
— Wm. de la, B. Ex. 383
— hon. W. W., aft. ld. Maryborough and E. of Mornington, *q.v.*, C. Treas. Ir. 561; Ch. Ex. Ir. 562; Ch. Sec. Ir. 563; Clk. O. 260; L.T. 159; M.M. 247; P.C. 208; Sec. Adm. 186
Polhill, Ch., C. Exc. 279-80
Polirac, Bertr. de, M.M. 245
Polk, J. K., Pres. U.S.A. 102
Pollard, Ch., gen. (**D**) 920
— Dill. Gust., gen. (**D**) 913
— sir Hugh, Compt. H. 292; G. Gsey. 668; P.C. 190
— Jno., S.L. 408; Sp. H.C. 249
— Lewis, J.C.P. 378; S.L. 408
— Wm., dn. Bgr. 426
Pollexfen, Hy. and sir H., A.G. 399; C.J.C.P. 375; S.L. 411
— Jno., B.T. 263
— Nichs., C. Exc. 279
Pollington, Jno., 1st ld., form. Jno. Savile, *q.v.*, aft. E. of Mexboro', *q.v.*
Pollio, C. A., C. Ro. 46
Pollock, Ch. Ed., and sir C., B. Ex. 385; J. Ex. D. 385; J.Q.B.D. 374; Q.C. 418; S.L. 414
— Dav. and sir D., C.J. Bbay. 660; K.C. 416
— Fk. and sir F., A.G. 400; C.B. Ex. 382; Jud. Com. P.C. 360; K.C. 416; P.C. 214; S.L. 413
— Fk. Rd., K.C.S.I. 803
— Geo. and sir Geo., Const. T.L. 321; F.M. 856; G.C.B. 769; G.C.S.I. 801; gen. (**D**) 878; K.C.S.I. 802
— Jos., C.C.J. 404
— Pet., Ld. Sess. 517
— Th., gen. (**D**) 876
Poltimore, Aug. F. G. W., 2nd ld., P.C. 218; Tr. H. 292
Polton (or Pulton), Th., bp. Chich. 433; bp. Her. 441; bp. Worc. 473; dn. Yk. 486
Polwarth, lds.
— Patr., ld., form. sir P. Hume, *q.v.*, aft. 1st E. of Marchmont, *q.v.*, Comm. Tr. Sc. 497; Ld. Chanc. Sc. 515; Ld. Sess. 517
— Alexr., ld., aft. 2nd E. of Marchmont, *q.v.*, Ld. Clk. Reg. 525
— Hy. Fras., ld. (*d.* 1867), L.L. Selk. 512
— Walt. Hugh, ld. (succ. 1867), L.L. Selk. 512
Polwhele, Th., gen. (**D**) 892
Pomeroy, Arth., dn. Cork, 632
— Jno., gen. (**B**) 865
— Wm. de, K.B. 755
Pomery, Ed., K.B. 759
Pomfret, Jno., R. Cr. P.A. 335
Pomfret, E. of
— Th., 1st E. of, K.B. 764
— Geo., 2nd E. of, P.C. 202
— Th. Wm., 4th E. of, form. hon. T. Fermor, *q.v.*
Pompeius, Tr. Ro. 46
— C., C. Ro. 47
— Q., C. Ro. 44
— S., C. Ro. 46
Pompilius, N., K. Ro. 36
Pond, Jno., Astr. Roy. 941
Ponde, Jno. (or Th.), R. Cr. P.A. 335; Som. H. 332
Ponsonby, hon. Fk. Car. and sir F., G.C.M.G. 794; G. Mlta. 671; gen. (**C**) 874; K.C.B. 776; K.C.H. 787
— Geo., Ld. Chanc. Ir. 577; P.C. 208
— hon. Geo., L.T. 160
— Geo. Conw., gen. (**D**) 895
— hon. Hy. gen. (**C**) 871
— Hy. Fk. and sir H., G.C.B. 773; gen. (**D**) 905; K.C.B. 783; P.C. 219
— hon. Jno., C. Cus. Ir. 565; C. Exc. Ir. 566; L.J. Ir. 557
— Jno., *see* ld. P., *infra*
— hon. Rd., bp. Dry. 601; bp. Dry. and Rph. 602; bp. Killoe. and Kilf. 635; dn. St. Pat. 618
— hon. Wm. and sir W., gen. (**C**) 873; K.C.B. 774
— Wm. Br., Postm. G. Ir. 564
Ponsonby, lds. and visc.
— Jno., 2nd ld., aft. 1st visc., Amb. Aus. 117; Amb. Bgm. 123; Amb. Bzl. 135; Amb. R. Pl. 136; Amb. Scy. 115; Amb. Tky. 129; G.C.B. 772
Ponsonby-Fane, *see* Fane
Pont, Rt., Ld. Sess. 518
Ponte, Rd. de, J. It. 366
Pontianus, P. Ro. 32
Pontois, Jno. de, bp. Winch. 470
Poole, *see also* Pole
— Arth. Rusc., Q.C. 420
— Arth. Wm., bp. Jpn. 677
— Dav., S.L. 412
— Dav., *see* Pole
— Hy., gen. (**D**) 896
— Hy. and sir H., C. Exc. 280
— Jacob, L.M. Dbln. 641
Pooley, Jno., bp. Cloy. 631; bp. Rph. 601; dn. Oss. 623
— Rt., C. St. 283
Poor, Poore, and **Pauper** *See also* Poer.
— Herb. or Rt., bp. Sal. 466; Jy. 363
— Rd., bp. Chich. 432; bp. Dham. 478; bp. Sal. 466; dn. Sal. 468; J. It. 367
— Rog., Ld. Chanc. 353
Pope, Saml., Q.C. 418
— Wm., K.B. 761
Popham, Brunsw., adm. (**G**) 842
— Ed. Wm. Leyb., gen. (**A**) 862
— Alexr., C. Tx. 284-5
— Alexr., M. Chy. 397
*— Fras., K.B. 763
*— Fras., L. Admy. 175
* ? the same pers.
— Home Riggs and sir H., adm. (**A**) 819; K.C.B. 774; K.C.H. 787
— Jno. and sir J., A.G. 399; Jno., C.J.Q.B. 370; S.G. 401; S.L. 408; Sp. H.C. 248-9
— Wm., adm. (**H**) 846
Poplicola, *see also* Potitus
— L. G., C. Ro. 46
— M. V. (2), C. Ro. 40
— P. V., C. Ro. 37, 38, 40; Dt. Ro. 40
Popple, Alured, G. Bmda. 701
— Wm., G. Bmda. 701
Popplewell, Geo. Otw., adm. (**H**) 857
Porche, Perciv. de, M.M. 245
— Rt. de, M.M. 246
Porcher, Jno., M.M. 245
Porcina, M. Æ. L., C. Ro. 44
Port, Ad. de, J. It. 366
— Jno., J.K.B. 372; S.G. 401; S.L. 408
Portarlington, Hy. Jno., 3rd E. of, K.P. 751
Porte, Jno., K.B. 760
Portelli, Agost., K.C.M.G. 796
Porten, Stain. and sir S., C. Cus. 276; U.S.S. 226
Porter, Andr. M., A.G. Ir. 589; M.R. Ir. 585; S.G. Ir. 590
— sir Ch., L.J. Ir. 555; Ld. Chanc. Ir. 576
— Geo., aft. bar. de Hochefried, gen. (**B**) 867
— Geo. R., Sec. B.T. 270
— Hy. Ed., gen. (**D**) 885
— Jas., V.C.H. 296
— Jas. and sir J., Amb. G. St. 121; Amb. Tky. 129
— Jno., bp. Clr. 596; bp. Killa. and Ach. 613
— Jno., L.M. Dbln. 641
— Neale, G. Antig. 728; G. Leew. Isl. 728; G. Monts. 729
— sir Rt. Ker, Amb. Vza. 134; K.C.H. 789
Porterfield, Jno., abp. Glasg. 537
Porteseye, Ad. de, J. It. 367
Porteus, Beilby, B.T. 268; bp. Chest. 477; bp. Lond. 452; P.C. 204
Portington, Jno., J.C.P. 378; S.L. 407
Portland, Rt., bp. Emly, 625
Portland, E. and D. of
Weston Family.
— Rd., 1st E. of, form. ld. Weston, *q.v.*
— Jerome, 2nd E. of, P.C. 190
— Ch., 3rd E. of, B.T. 263
[*Bentinck* and *Cavendish-B. Families.*
— Wm., 1st D. of, form. Wm. Bentinck and visc. Woodstock, *q.v.*, Gr. St. 303; K.G. 741
— Hy., 2nd E., aft. 1st D. of, G. Jam. 712
— Wm., 2nd D. of, K.G. 742
— Wm. Hy., 3rd D. of, form. M. of Titchfield, *q.v.*, H. Sec. 226; K.G. 742; L.C.H. 295; L.L. Ir. 557; L.L. Notts. 311; L.P.C. 188; L.T. 158; P.C. 201; Prem. 144-5
— Wm. Hy., 4th D. of, Jud. Com. P.C. 360; L.P.C. 188; L.P.S. 241; P.C. 210
— Wm. J. A. C. J., 7th D. of, M.H. 302; P.C. 221
Portlester, Rowl., 1st ld., form. sir R. Eustace, *q.v.*, L. Treas. Ir. 559; Ld. Chanc. Ir. 575
Portlock, Jos. Ell., gen. (**D**) 892
Portman, Wm. and sir W., C.J.Q.B. 370; J.K.B. 372; K.B. 763; S.L. 408
Portman, lds. and visc.
— Ed. B., 1st ld., aft. 1st visc., L.L. Soms. 311; L.W.S. 323

Portmore, E. of
— Dav., 1st E. of, G. Gibr. 669; gen. (**A**) 857; K.T. 747; P.C. 196
— Ch., 2nd E. of, K.T. 747
Portsmouth, Jno., 1st E. of, form. Jno. Wallop and visc. Lymington, *q.v.*
Portu, Maurice de, abp. Tm. 611
Postumius, L., C. Ro. 42
Poterna, Jas. de, Jy. 364
Potitus, *see also* Poplicola
— L. V., C. Ro. 37-8-9
— M. V. M., C. Ro. 41
Pott, Dav., gen. (**D**) 901
— Steph., gen. (**D**) 897
Potter, Barn., bp. Carl. 475
— Chr., dn. Dham. 479; dn. Worc. 473
— Jno., abp. Cant. 431; bp. Oxf. 456; P.C. 198
— Jno., dn. Cant. 431
— Jno., U.S.S. 226
— Th., dn. Wford. 628
— Th., V. Treas. Ir. 560
— Wm., Q.C. 419
Pottinger, Brab. Hy., gen.(**D**) 935
— sir Hy., Amb. Ch. 131; G.C.B. 772; G.C.G.H. 679; H. Kong, 673; G. Mdras. 657; gen. (**D**) 881; P.C. 214
— Jno., gen. (**D**) 898
— Rd., J. Chest. 387
— Rd., U.S.S. 226
— Sus. Maria, Dow. Lady, Cr. Ind. 810
Potton, Rd. de, bp. Abdn. 530
Poulden, Rd., adm. (**D**) 823
Poulett and **Powlett,** *see also* Paulet
— Ch. Arm. and sir C., gen. (**C**) 871; K.B. 765
— Geo., L.L. Hants, 311
— hon. Geo. and sir G., adm. (**D**) 826
— Th. (or Wm.), S.L. 411
— Th. Nort., gen. (**C**) 873
— hon. Vere, gen. (**B**) 866
— Wm., S.L. 407
— Wm., S.L. 411
Poulett, lds. and E.
— Jno., 3rd ld., L.L. Dors. 307
— Jno., 4th ld., aft. visc. Hinton, *q.v.*, and 1st Earl P., K.G. 741; L.L. Soms. 311; L.T. 156; L.S.H. 290; P.C. 195
— Jno., 2nd E., L.L. Soms. 311
— Vere, 3rd E., L.L. Dev. 307
— Jno., 4th E., K.T. 748; L.L. Soms. 311
Poulett - Thompson, *see* Thompson
Poulton, Hy., Boil. A., gen. (**D**) 912
Poulteney, J., S.L.R. 271
Pounteney (or Pultney), Jno., L.M. Lond. 489
Povey, sir Jno., B. Ex. Ir. 584; C.J.K.B. Ir. 578
Powell, Baden Hy. Baden-, C.I.E. 807
— Burd. Rd., gen. (**D**) 911
— Geo. Sm. Baden-, K.C.M.G. 799
— Hy. Wats., gen. (**A**) 859
— Herb. Br., adm. (**G**) 841
— Jno., G. Bdoes. 719
— Jno. and sir J. (No. 1), J.C.P. 379; J.K.B. 372; S.L. 411

Powell—*cont.*
— Jno. and sir J. (No. 2), B. Ex. 384; J.C.P. 379; J.K.B. 373; S.L. 411
— Jno. Jos., C.C.J. 405; Q.C. 418
— Mos., dn. Llin. 623
— Nathl., K.C. 415
— Rh., dn. Bgr. 426
— Rd. Ashm., adm. (**H**) 849
— Th., K.H. 792
— Th. and sir T., B. Ex. 384; J.K.B. 372; S.L. 410
— Walt., gen. (**D**) 889
— Wm., dn. St. As. 463
— Wm., S.L. 409
— Wm. Ed., L.L. Card. 315
Power, Alfr., K.C.B. 783
— Dav., Q.C. 418
— Ed., dn. Lism. 629
*— Col. J—, G. Mtius. 683
*— Jas., gen. (**D**) 880
* ? same pers.
— Manl. and sir M. K.C.B. 774; gen. (**B**) 868
— Maur., G. St. Luc. 725
— Rd., B. Ex. Ir. 584
— Walt., M. Chy. 393
— Wm. Gr., K.C.B. 779; K.H. 790; gen. (**D**) 882
— Wm. Jas. Ty., K.C.B. 779
Powerscourt, visc.
— Rd., visc., form. Rd. Wingfield, *q.v.*
— Merv., 7th visc., K.P. 751
Powis and **Powys**
— hon. Hor., bp. S. and M. 484
— Lytt. H. and sir L., B. Ex. 384; J. Chest. 387; J.K.B. 373; S.L. 411
— Th., dn. Cant. 431
— Th. and sir T., A.G. 399; J.Q.B. 373; S.G. 401; S.L. 410-11
Powis, lds., E., and M. of
— Jno., ld. K.B. (1478) 757
Herbert Family.
1st Creation.
— Wm., 1st ld., form. W. Herbert and sir W., *q.v.*
— Wm., 1st E., aft. 1st M. of, P.C. 193
— Wm., visc. Montgomery, *q.v.*, and 2nd M. of, gen. (**B**) 864
Herbert Family.
2nd Creation.
— Hy. Arth., 1st ld. Herbert of Chirbury, aft. 1st E. of, Compt. H. 292; gen. (**A**) 858; L.L. Salop, 311; P.C. 200; Tr. H. 291
— Geo. Ed. H. A., 2nd E. of, L.L. Montg. 315
Clive and Herbert Families.
3rd Creation.
— Ed., 1st E. of, form. 2nd ld. Clive, *q.v.*, L.L. Ir. 557; L.L. Montg. 315; P.C. 207
— Edw., 2nd E. of, K.G. 744; L.L. Montg. 315
— Ed. Jas., 3rd E. of, L.L. Montg. 315
Powle, Hy. and sir H., M.R. 388; P.C. 192-3; Sp. H.C. 250
— Rd., K.B. 764
Powlett, *see* Poulett, Paulet, and Orde
***Pownall,** Jno., C. Cus. 276; C. Exc. 281
*— Jno., U.S.C. 235
* Prob. same pers.

Powney, Jno., K.H. 791
— Rd., gen. (**D**) 886
Powtrell, Nichs., S.L. 408
Powys, *see* Powis
Poynes, Nichs., K.B. 761
Poynet, Jno., bp. Roch. 460; bp. Winch. 471
Poynings, sir Ed., Compt. H. 292; K.G. 737; L.D. Ir. 553; W.C.P. 319
— Th,, K.B. 760
Poynton, Alexr. de, J. It. 366
Poyntz, Hugh de, K.B. 754
— Rt., K.B. 763
— Steph., adm. (**A**) 819
— Steph., gen. (**C**) 872
— Steph., P.C. 198
Poywick, Wm. de, J. It. 368; Jy. 365
Pracle, Pr. Jull. du, G. Ch. Isl. 667
Prado, Mar., Pres. Pu. 109
— Mar. Ign., Pres. Pu. 109
Praed, Bulk. Mackw., adm. (**D**) 824
— Wm. Mackw., C.C.J. 403; S.L. 412
— Winthr. M., Sec. B.C. 254
Pratt, Benj., dn. Down, 605
— Ch. and sir C., gen. (**C**) 874; K.C.B. 774
— Ch. and sir C., aft 1st ld. and E. Camden, *q.v.*, A.G. 339; C.J.C.P. 376; K.C. 415; P.C. 201; S.L. 412
— Ch. C., gen. (**D**) 889
— Jno., gen. (**A**) 861
— Jno. and sir J., C.G.S. 357; C.J.K.B. 370; Ch. Ex. 165; J.K.B. 373; P.C. 197; S.L. 411
— hon. Jno. Jeffr., aft. visc. Bayham, and 2nd E. and 1st M. Camden, *q.v.*, L. Admy. 180; Tell. Ex. 167
— Rt., gen. (**D**) 905
— Rt., M. Chy. 397
— Saml., dn. Roch. 461
— Th. Sims., gen. (**D**) 892; K.C.B. 779
— Wm., dn. Cloy. 633
Prattent, Fras. Mowbr., adm. (**E**) 837
Pratty, Rd., bp. Chich. 433
Preedy, Geo. Wm., adm. (**H**) 850
Premislas, K. Pld. 91
— I. and II., K. Bma. 59
Prendergast and **Pendergast**
— Ch. O'L., gen. (**D**) 933
— Ch. O'N., gen. (**D**) 884
— Harris, Q.C. 418
— Harry N. Dalr., gen. (**D**) 925; K.C.B. 781
— Jeffr. and sir J., gen. (**D**) 876
— Jno., dn. Lism. 629
— Mauns. Mark, gen. (**D**) 934
— Michl., Q.C. 417
— sir T., Postm. G. Ir. 564
— Wm., bp. Mayo, 612
Prene, Jno., abp. Arm. 595; dn. St. Pat. 617
Prentice, Saml., C.C.J. 405; Q.C. 418
Prescott, Hy. and sir H., adm. (**D**) 827; G.C.B. 770; G. Newfd. 700; K.C.B. 778; L. Admy. 183
— Isaac, adm. (**A**) 816
— Rd., gen. (**B**) 866

For List of Abbreviations, see pp. 944-952.

Prescott—*cont.*
—— Rt., G. Can. 691; gen. (**A**) 859
—— Wm., gen. (**D**) 890
Pressly, Ch., C. Exc. 282; C.I.R. 285; C. St. and Tx. 285; K.C.B. 783
Preston, Arth., gen. (**C**) 872
—— Arth. Jno., dn. Kild. 619; dn. Lim. 640
—— sir Ch., C. Cus. Sc. 504
—— D'Arcy, adm. (**A**) 819
—— D'Arcy Spence, adm. (**H**) 852
—— Geo., gen. (**B**) 864
—— Geo., gen. (**B**) 865
—— Gilb. de, C.J.C.P. 375; J.C.P. 376; J. It. 368; J.K.B. 371; Jy. 364
—— Jno., J.C.P. 378; Rec. Lond. 493; S.L. 407
—— Jno., L.M. Lond. 489
—— Jno. and sir J., L.P. Ct. Sess. 516; Ld. Sess. 518; Sec. St. Sc. 502
—— Jno. Ing., gen. (**D**) 922
—— Rd., gen. (**D**) 928
—— Rd., K.C. 416
—— Rt. de and sir R., C.J.C.P. 375; C.J.C.P. Ir. 580; D. Chanc. Ir. 575; L.D. Ir. 551; Ld. Chanc. and L.K. Ir. 575; S.L. Ir. 590
—— sir Rt., Ld. Sess. 519
—— Rd., aft. 1st E. of Desmond, *q.v.*, K.B. 761
—— Rd., *see* visc. Pr., *infra*
—— Rog. de, J.C.P. Ir. 581; J.K.B. Ir. 578
—— Th., Ptc. P.A. 337; Ulst. K.A. 572
—— Wm., bp. Ferns and L. 622; bp. Killa. and Ach. 613
—— Wm., L.D. Ir. 553
—— Wm. Rd., gen. (**D**) 905
Preston, visc.
—— Rd., 1st visc., P.C. 192; S. St. 224
Prestwyk, Wm., M. Chy. 394
Pretorius, M. W., Pres. Trl. 101
Prettejohn, Rich. Buckl., gen. (**D**) 918
Pretyman, Geo., *see* Tomline
Prevost, Aug., gen. (**C**) 872
—— Geo. and sir G., G. Can. 691; G. Dnca. 730; G. N. Sc. 695; G. St. Luc. 725; gen. (**B**) 867
—— Jas., adm. (**H**) 844
—— Jas. Ch., adm. (**E**) 835; (**F**) 839
—— Wm. Aug., gen. (**C**) 874
Price, Pryce, and **Pryse**
—— Arth., abp. Cash. and Eml. 626; bp. Clonf. and K. 636; bp. Ferns and L. 622; bp. Mth. 599; dn. Ferns, 623; dn. Lism. 629
—— Ch., L.M. Lond. 492
—— Cromw., C. Acc. Ir. 567
—— Dnl., dn. Her. 442
—— Dnl., dn. St. As. 463
—— Dav., adm. (**D**) 829
—— Ed., gen. (**D**) 906
—— (or Pryse), Ed. Lewis, L.L. Card. 315
—— Edwin Pl., C.C.J. 405; Q.C. 418
—— Geo. Uved., gen. (**D**) 923
—— Griff., K.C. 415
—— Hy., dn. Cash. 627
—— Jno., C. Exc. 279
Price, Pryce, and Pryse—*cont.*
—— Jno., gen. (**C**) 871
—— Jno., L.L. Glam. 315
—— Jno., V. Treas. Ir. 559
—— Nichs., gen. (**C**) 871
—— Rd., dn. Clonm. 600
—— Rt., bp. Ferns and L. 622; dn. Cnr. 605
—— Rt. and sir Rt., B. Ex. 384; J.C.P. 379; S.L. 411-2
—— Rt. Davis, L.L. Mer. 314
—— Th., abp. Cash. and Eml. 626; bp. Kild. 617
—— Th., G. Dnca. 730; G. St. Xtr. 729
—— Wm. Ph., gen. (**D**) 878
Prichard, *see also* Pritchard
—— Augs., gen. (**D**) 914
—— Hy., gen. (**D**) 904
—— sir Wm., L.M. Lond. 491
Prickett, Geo., S.L. 411
—— Th., adm. (**H**) 846
Prideaux, Ch. Gr., Q.C. 418
—— Edm., A.G. 399; C.G.S. 356; K.C. 414; S.G. 401
—— Humphr., dn. Norw. 456
—— Jno., bp. Worc. 473
—— Jno., S.L. 408
Pridham, Rd., adm. (**H**) 847
Priestley, Ed. Jonn., K.H. 792
—— F. J. B., gen. (**D**) 923
Priestman, H., L. Admy. 176
Prieto, Pres. Chi. 111
Prime, Saml., S.L. 412
Primrose, sir Archd., L.J. Gen. 522; Ld. Adv. 526; Ld. Sess. 519; Ld. Clk. Reg. 525
—— Gilb., gen. (**C**) 871
—— Jas. Maur., gen. (**D**) 906
Prince, Jno., gen. (**B**) 867
Pringle, Alexr., L.T. 160
—— And., Jy. Sc. 523; Ld. Sess. 520
—— Geo., gen. (**D**) 926
—— Hy., gen. (**C**) 872
—— Jas., adm. (**H**) 844
—— Jno., gen. (**C**) 875
—— Jno., Ld. Sess. 520
—— sir Jno., Pres. R. Soc. 940
—— Rt., Sec. at W. 233; U.S.S. 225
—— Rt. Edgf., Ld. Sess. 520
—— Th., adm. (**A**) 816
—— sir Walt., Ld. Sess. 520
—— Wm. Hy. and sir W., G.C.B. 768; gen. (**B**) 868; K.C.B. 774
Prinsep, Hy. Thoty, M.C.I. 646
Prior, Benj. Jno. C., gen. (**D**) 921
—— Ch., gen. (**D**) 906
—— Hy., gen. (**D**) 892
—— Matth., B.T. 263; C. Cus. 274; U.S.S. 225
Priscus, T. N., C. Ro. 38
Prisot, Jno., S.L. 407
Pritchard, *see also* Prichard
—— Ed., gen. (**B**) 869
—— Gord. Dougl., gen. (**D**) 930
—— (or Pritchet), Jno., bp. Glr. 438
—— Saml. Perk., adm. (**H**) 847
Pritchet, *see* Pritchard
Pritzler, sir Theoph., gen. (**B**) 869; K.C.B. 775
Privernas, L. Æ. M. (2), C. Ro. 40-1; Dt. Ro. 40-1
Probus, M. A., Emp. Ro. 48
Proby, sir Pet., L.M. Lond. 491
Proby, lds.
—— hon. Granville L., ld., aft. 3rd E. of Carysfort, adm. (**D**) 826; (**G**) 840
—— Granville L., ld., aft. 4th E. of Carysfort, *q.v.*, Compt. H. 293; P.C. 216
Probyn, Dight. Macn. and sir D., gen. (**D**) 909; K.C.B. 784; K.C.S.I. 803
—— Edm. and sir E., C.B. Ex. 382; J.K.B. 373; S.L. 411
—— Jno., dn. Llff. 450
—— Ol., C.I.E. 807
—— Th., G. St. Xtr. &c. 727
Procter and **Proctor**
—— Anth., dn. Ferns, 623
—— Hy., gen. (**C**) 873
—— Hy. A., gen. (**D**) 881
—— Rd., M. Chy. 396
—— sir Wm. Beaud., adm. (**D**) 826; (**G**) 840
Proculus, C. P., C. Ro. 40
Profit, J., S. St. 222
Prophet, Jno., dn. Her. 442; dn. Yk. 486
Prosper, bp. Cness. 531
Protab, Chunder Rai., C.I.E. 808
Proude, Nichs., dn. Clonf. 637
Prowde, Lewis, J.K.B. Ir. 579
Prowse, sir Wm., adm. (**A**) 819
Prudhoe, lds., *see also* Northumberland
—— Algn., ld., aft. D. of Northumb., *q.v.*, Pres. R. Inst. (1842) 940
Pry—, *see also* Pri—
Pryce, *see* Price
Prynne, Wm., C. Exc. 277-8
Pryse, *see* Price
Prysot, Jno., C.J.C.P. 375
Prytherg, Rd., J. Chest. 386
Pucelle, Ger. la, bp. Lich. and Cov. 443
Puckering, *see also* Pickering
—— sir Jno., Ld. K. 356; S.L. 408; Sp. H.C. 249
Puckle, Jas., gen. (**D**) 916
Pudsey, sir Geo., S.L. 410
—— Rd. K., C.I.E. 806
—— (or Pusar), Hugh, E. of Northbd., bp. Dham. 478; Ch. Jr. 362; Const. W. Cast. 322; J. It. 366; Jy. 363
Puella, Ger., bp. Lich. and Cov. 443
Puerta, L., Pres. Pu. 109
Puget, Pet., adm. (**A**) 819
Pugeys, Imb., Const. T.L. 320
Pughe, Jno. Rt., gen. (**D**) 915
Pugolas, Hy., Bl. M. P.A. 336; Richm. H. 334
Pulcher, A.C., C. Ro. 43-4-5-6
—— C. C., C. Ro. 44-5
—— P. C. C. Ro. 42, 44
Pulleine, Jno. Jas., bp. suff. Penr. 482
Puleston, Jno., J.C.P. 379; S.L. 409
Pullein, Hy., G. Bmda. 701
—— Saml., *see* Pullen
Pullen (or Pullein), Saml., abp. Tm. 611; dn. Clonf. 637
—— Tobias, bp. Cloy. 630; bp. Drom. 605; dn. Ferns, 623
—— Wm. Jas. Saml., adm. (**H** 850

Puller, Chr. and sir C., C.J. Bgal. 652; K.C. 416
Pulley, Ch., gen. (**D**) 912
Pulling, Alexr., S.L. 414
—— Jas., adm. (**H**) 848
Pullison, sir Ed., L.M. Lond. 490
Pullus, L. J., C. Ro. 42
Pully, Rd., bp. S. and M. 483
Pulman, Jas., Clar. K.A. 328; Norr. K.A. 330; Ptc. P.A. 337; Richm. H. 334
Pulteney, Danl., B.T. 264; L. Admy. 177
—— Harry, gen. (**A**) 858
—— sir Jas., gen. (**A**) 860; P.C. 208; Sec. at W. 234
—— Jno., B.T. 263-4; C. Cus. 274
—— Th., gen. (**C**) 871
—— Th., K.B. 758
—— Wm., aft. E. of Bath, *q.v.*, P.C. 196, 198; Sec. at W. 233
—— sir Wm., L.P.S. 240
Pultney (or Pounteney), Jno., L.M. Lond. 489
Pulton, Th., *see* Polton
Pulvillus, C. H. (2), C. Ro. 38
—— M. H. (2), C. Ro. 37
Punchard, Wm., dn. Kild. 619
Punganur, Zem. of, C.I.E. 807
Punnah, Mahar. of, K.C.S.I. 803
Puntoyse, Jno. de, M.M. 245
Pupienus, Emp. Ro. 47
Purcell, *see also* Pursell
—— Ed., adm. (**G**) 841
—— Jno. (2), bp. Ferns, 621
Purchase, Wm., L.M. Lond. 490
Purdon, Ed., L.M. Dbln. 642
—— Hy., S.L. Ir. 592
Purefoy, Wm., J. Pr. Ct. 421
Purey-Cust, *see* Cust
Purfoy, Parfew, or **Warton,** bp. Her. 441; bp. St. As. 462
Purley, Fras., S.L. 411
Purpureo, L. F., C. Ro. 43
Pursell, *see also* Purcell
—— Th., bp. Wford. and L. 627
—— Th., dn. Ferns, 623
Pursglove, Rt., bp. Suff. Hull, 486
Purvis, Fras. Reg., adm. (**H**) 852
—— Herb. Mark Garr., gen. (**D**) 935
—— Jno. Brett, adm. (**D**) 827
—— Jno. Child, adm. (**A**) 817
—— Jno. Child, adm. (**H**) 853
—— Rd., adm. (**H**) 850
—— Th., Q.C. 417
Pusar, *see* Pudsey
Puskin, Rd., dn. St. As. 463
Putiala, Mahar., G.C.S.I. 801; K.C.S.I. 802
Putnam, Geo., K.B. 759
Puton, Franç., Alfr., C.I.E. 807
Putta, abp. Yk. 485
—— bp. Dev. 436
—— bp. Her. 441; bp. Roch. 459
Puttiala, *see* Putiala
Py—, *see also* Pi—
Pybus, Ch. S., L. Admy. 180; L.T. 158
Pycard, *see* Picard and Pickard
Pychard, Jno., dn. Chich. 434
Pycot, Jno., dn. Exr. 437
Pycroft, Th., K.C.S.I. 802
Pye, Adam, *see* Pay
—— All. Hampd., G. Br. Hond. 714; gen. (**C**) 874
—— Hy. Jas., P. Laur. 301
—— Laur., G. Ceyl. 672
—— Rd., C. St. 283
—— sir Rt., Aud. Ex. 166
—— sir Th., adm. (**A**) 814
—— Wm., dn. Chich. 434
Pyell (or Piel), Jno., L.M. Lond. 489
Pykering, *see* Pickering
Pyke, *see* Pike
Pym, *see also* Pim
—— Ed. Lawr., gen. (**D**) 921
—— Fk. Geo., gen. (**D**) 921
—— Rt., gen. (**D**) 880
—— Saml. and sir S., adm. (**D**) 824; K.C.B. 777
—— sir Wm., K.C.H. 788
—— W. Rowl., G. Monts. 729
Pymme, *see* Pym and Pyne
Pympell, Steph. de, dn. Wells, 428
Pynchebek, Th., C.B. Ex. 381
Pyne, *see also* Pine
—— Rd. and sir R., C.J.K.B. Ir. 578; C.J.C.P. Ir. 580; L.K. Ir. 576
—— (or Pymme), B. Ex. 384
—— W. R., G. Trin. 722

Q.

Quail, Wm., L.M. Dbln. 641
Quain, Jno. Rd. and sir J., J.Q.B. 374; J.Q.B.D. 374; Q.C. 418; S.L. 414
—— Rd., Pres. Coll. Surg. 939
Qualberg, Corn. Van, G. C.G.H. 678
Quaplode, Wm., bp. Dry. 601
Quarme, Geo., C. Exc. 280; C. Tx. 284
Queensberry, M. and D. of, *see also* Buccleugh and Dover
—— Wm., 3rd E., aft. 1st M. and D. of, Comm. Tr. Sc. 497; H.C.P. Sc. 507; L.J. Gen. 522; Ld. Sess. 517; P.C. 192; Pres. P.C. Sc. 500
—— Jas., 2nd D. of, also D. of Dover, H.C.P. Sc. 508; K.G. 741; L.H.T. Sc. 497-8; L.P.S. Sc. 501; Ld. Sess. 517; P.C. 195; Sec. St. Sc. 502
—— Ch., 3rd D. of, also D. of Dover, L.J. Gen. 522; L.K. Sc. 503; P.C. 197; V.A. Sc. 499
—— Wm., 4th D. of, form. 3rd E. of March, *q.v.*, L.L. Dumfr. 509
For subsequent Dukes, *see* Buccleugh and Q.
Queensberry, M. and D. of—*cont.*
—— Ch., 5th M. of, form. sir C. Douglas, *q.v.*, K.T. 748; L.L. Dumfr. 509
—— Jno., 6th M. of, L.L. Dumfr. 509
—— Archd. Wm., 7th M. of, form. visc. Drumlanrig, *q.v.*
Quentin and **Quintin**
—— bp. Clonm. 600
—— sir Geo. Aug., gen. (**B**) 869; K.C.H. 787
Querceto, Rt. de, bp. Linc. 446
Quichelmus (or Gulielmus), bp. Roch. 459
Quin (or Coyn), bp. Lim. 638
—— Mark, L.M. Dbln. 640
—— Michl., adm. (**D**) 831; (**G**) 841
—— Rd. Rt., adm. (**H**) 849
—— Th., L.M. Dbln. 640
Quincey or **Quincy,** de, *see* E. of Winchester
—— Sim. de, Ld. Clk. Reg. 524
Quintillus, Emp. Ro. 48
Quintin, *see* Quentin
Quinton, Corn. adm. (**D**) 824
Quirinus, C. S., C. Ro. 46
Quivil, Pet., bp. Exr. 436

R.

R*,** dn. St. As. 462
Raban, Herb., gen. (**D**) 914
Rabuleius, M., Dec. Ro. 38
Raby, Hy. Jas., adm. (**H**) 852
—— Jno., S.L. 411
Raby, lds.
—— Th., 3rd ld., aft. visc. Wentworth and E. of Strafford, *q.v.*, P.C. 196
Rachad, Pacha, K.C.M.G. 797
Radama I. and II., K. Mad. 101
Radcliffe and **Radclyffe,** *see also* Ratcliffe
—— Geo. Tr., gen. (**D**) 923
—— Hy., G. I. Man, 665
—— Rd. (or Ratcliffe), Barnes P.A. 341; Bl. M. P.A. 336; Som. H. 332
—— (or Radclyf), Ralph, K.B. 756
—— Rt. Park, gen. (**D**) 908
—— (or Radclyff), Rog., dn. St. P. 453
—— Th., bp. Drom. 604
—— Wm., adm. (**H**) 848
—— Wm., gen. (**D**) 899
—— Wm., R. Cr. P.A. 335
—— Wm. Poll., gen. (**D**) 907; K.C.B. 781
Radeclyve, Th. de, J. It. 369
Radenhale, Jno. de, J. It. 369
Radeswell, Rt. de, M. Chy. 393

For List of Abbreviations, see pp. 944-952.

Radford, Saml., adm. (**H**) 847; K.H. 791
Radington, sir Jno., L.H.A. 173
Radley, W., *see* Raleigh
Radlington, sir Jno., L.H.A. 173
Radnor, Elias de, bp. Llff. 449
Radnor, E. of
Robartes Family.
— Jno., 1st E. of, form. Jno. Robartes, *q.v.*, L.P.C. 187
— Ch. B., 2nd E. of, L.L. Cnwall. 307; L.W.S. 323; P.C. 194; Tr. Ch. 294
— Hy., 3rd E. of, L.L. Cnwall. 307
— Jno., 4th E. of, form. ld. Robartes and visc. Bodmin, *q.v.*
Bouverie and Pleydell-B. Families.
— Jacob, 2nd E. of, L.L. Berks, 306
— Jacob, 4th E. of, L.L. Wilts, 313
Radstock, lds.
— Wm., 1st ld., form. sir Wm. Waldegrave, *q.v.*, G.C.B. 767
— Granv. Geo., 2nd ld., adm. (**D**) 826
Radulph and **Radulphus,** *see* Ralph
Rae, *see also* Ray
— Dav. and sir D., Jy. Sc. 523; L.J. Clk. 516; Ld. Sess. 520
— Wm., bp. Glasg. 536
— sir Wm., Ld. Adv. 526; P.C. 211
Raff, W., Pres. Sw. C. 31
Raggad or **Ragged,** Patr., bp. Cork, 630; bp. Oss. 620
Raggett, Rd., adm. (**A**) 820
Ragimbertus, K. Lmd. 49
Raglan, Fitzroy Jas. Hy., 1st ld., form. ld. F. Somerset, *q.v.*, F.M. 856; gen. (**A**) 863; P.C. 216
Raigersfeld, Jeff., ld., adm. (**D**) 823
Raikes, Ch. Lew., gen. (**D**) 932
— Fk. Dunc., C.I.E. 808
— Hy. Cec., P.C. 219; Postm. G. 239
— Rt. Nap., gen. (**D**) 916
— Th., gen. (**D**) 917
Rainald, C. Hlt. 81
Rainbow, Ed., bp. Carl. 475; dn. Pboro. 458
Raine, Jno., K.C. 415
Rainelm, bp. Her. 441
Rainer I. to III., Pr. Mno. 30-1
— Danl., gen. (**D**) 901
Raines, Julius Aug. Rt., gen. (**D**) 904
— Rd. and sir R., J. Adm. Ct. 423; J. Pr. Ct. 421
Rainey, *see also* Reiny
— Arth. Jac. M., gen. (**D**) 915
— Hy., gen. (**D**) 882; K.H. 790
— Hy. Garn., gen. (**D**) 905
Rainier, Jno. Spr., adm. (**A**) 819
— Pet., adm. (**A**) 816
Rainsford, *see* Raynsford
Rait, Jas., bp. Brn. 541
— Jno., bp. Abdn. 530
Raith, Alexr., ld., Dep. Tr. Sc. (1692) 497
Rajundra, Lala Mitra, C.I.E. 806
Ralee, Jno. de, K.B. 755
Raleigh, Walt., dn. Wells, 429
— sir Walt., C.Y.G. 298; G. Jsey. 667; L.W.S. 323
— Wm. de, bp. Lich. and Cov. 444; bp. Norw. 454; bp. Winch. 470; Jy. 364
Ralph, Raldulph and **Radulphus,** *see also* Rodolf
— abp. Cant. 430; bp. Roch. 459
*— bp. Brn. 530
*— bp. Chich. 432
*— bp. Dnbl. 532
*— bp. Down, 603
*— (of Kilmessan), bp. Down, 603
*— bp. Gall. 538
*— (of Bristol), bp. Kild. 616; dn. St. Patr. 617
*— (le Petit), bp. Mth., 599
*— bp. Norw. 454; Ld. Chanc. Ir. 574
*— bp. Ork. 535
*— dn. Chich. 433
*— (2), dn. Her. 442
*— dn. Linc. 447
*— (archd. of Hereford), Jy. 363
*— (archd. of Colchester), Jy. 363
* Prob. some same pers. Comp. dates
Ralston, *see* Raulston
Ram, sir Abel, L.M. Dbln. 640
— Diwan Het., C.I.E. 807
— Th. (No. 1), bp. Ferns and L. 622; dn. Cork, 632; dn. Ferns, 623
— Th. (No. 2), dn. Ferns, 623
Rambir, Singh, gen. (**D**) 915
Rambridge, Jno., dn. Lich. 445
Ramhar, Kell., bp. Saig. 620
Ramiro, I. and II., K. Arr. 86
— I. to III., K. Sp. 85
Ramkrishnar, &c., C.I.E. 808
Ramos, M.-gen. —, G. Gibr. 669
Rampore, Bah. of, G.C.S.I. 801
— Nawab of, G.C.S.I. 801; K.C.S.I. 802
Rampret, D. Tny. 57
Rampston (or Rempston), sir Th. de, Const. T.L. 320; K.G. 734; L.H.A. 173
Ramsay and **Ramsey**
— Andr., G. Bbay. 659
— sir Andr., Ld. Sess. 519
— Ed. Bann., gen. (**D**) 914
— Geo., gen. (**B**) 864
— Geo., gen. (**C**) 874
— Geo., gen. (**D**) 904
— Geo., *see* ld. R., *infra*
— Geo. Ant., K.H. 790
— Geo. Wm., G. Antig., &c., 727; gen. (**C**) 873
— hon. sir Hy., gen. (**D**) 916; K.C.S.I. 803
— Jas., bp. Dnbl. 532; bp. Ross, 536
— hon. Jas., gen. (**B**) 868
— Jno., gen. (**A**) 861
— hon. Jno., gen. (**B**) 870
— sir Jno., L.H.T. Sc. 496
Ramsay and Ramsey—*cont.*
— Jno. Sc., gen. (**D**) 895
— Nathl., gen. (**D**) 932
— Pet. de, bp. Abdn. 530
— Rt., adm. (**H**) 845
— R. Murray, G. Lag. 687
— sir Th., L.M. Lond. 490
— Wm., gen. (**B**) 867
— Wm., gen. (**D**) 920
— Wm. and sir W., adm. (**D**) 831; (**E**) 834; (**F**) 838; K.C.B. 780
— Wm. Maule, gen. (**D**) 897
Ramsay, lds.
— Geo., aft. ld. R. and 12th E. of Dalhousie, *q.v.*, adm. (**D**) 833; (**E**) 834; (**F**) 838
Ramsden, sir J. W., U.S. War, 232
— Th., U.S.S. 225-6
— Wm., adm. (**H**) 846
Ramsey, *see* Ramsay
Ramshay, Wm., C.C.J. 404
Ranajee, Mahar. Kunwar, G.C.S.I. 801
Ranavolona, I. to III., Q. Mad. 101
Randolf, (abb. of Evesham), J. It. 367
— Jno., J. It. 368
— Ch. Grenv., adm. (**G**) 841
— Ch. Wils., gen. (**D**) 921
— Geo. Granv., adm. (**E**) 836; (**F**) 839
— Hy., L.H.A. 171
— Jno., B.T. 268; bp. Bgr. 426; bp. Lond. 452; bp. Oxf. 456; P.C. 208
— Jno., J. It. 369
— sir Th., L.G.C. Sc. 506
Randon, Agost. and sir A., G.C.M.G. 794; K.C.M.G. 796
Ranelagh, visc. and E. of
— Rd., 3rd visc. and 1st E. of, form. Rd. Jones, *q.v.*, P.C. 194; Paym. G. 244
— Th. Hor., 7th visc., K.C.B. 783
Ranger, *see* Reinger
Rankin and **Rankine**
— Alexr., Mod. K. Sc. 547
*— Dav., bp. Glasg. 543
*— Dav., Sc. Bp. 545
* Prob. same pers.
— Jno., Mod. K. Sc. 547
Ranulph, *see also* Arnulph
— bp. Down, 603
— J. It. 366
— (or Arnulph), Ld. Chanc. 353
Ranutio, I. and II., D. Pma. 53
Raoul, D. Lne. 29
Raper, Felix Vinc., gen. (**D**) 878
— Hy., adm. (**A**) 819
— Jno. Fr., gen. (**D**) 920
Rapp, Off. Nap. 26
Rasoherina, Q. Mad. 101
Rastall, Saml., dn. Killoe. 637
— Wm., J.Q.B. 372; S.L. 408
Ratbod or **Radboton,** D. Tny. 57
Ratchis, K. Lmd. 49
Ratcliffe, *see also* Radcliffe
— Alexr., K.B. 763
— Geo., K.C. 414
— Hy., K.B. 760
— Jer., K.H. 790
— sir Jno., K.G. 735
— Rd., *see* Radcliffe
— sir Rd., K.G. 736
— Th., K.B. 762

Rathdonnell, Jno., 1st ld., form. J. McClintock, *q.v.*
Ratsay, Ed., adm. (**D**) 826; (**G**) 840
Rattray, Jas., adm. (**H**) 845
— Jas. Cl., gen. (**D**) 921
— Th., bp. Dkld. 542; Pr. Bp. Sc. 540
Raulston, Jno., bp. Dkld. 533; Sec. St. Sc. 501
Raven, Jno., R. Dr. P.A. 338; Richm. H. 333
Ravendale, Mich. de, M. Chy. 393
Ravenser, Rd. de, M. Chy. 393
Ravenshaw, Jno. Golds., Chn. E.I. Co. 645
Ravilla, L. C. L., C. Ro. 45
Ravis or **Ravys,** Th., bp. Glr. 438; bp. Lond. 452; dn. Chr. Ch. Oxf. 457
Rawdon, Jno. Daws., gen. (**D**) 885
Rawle, Rd., bp. Trin. 723
Rawlins, Jas. Seb., gen. (**D**) 921
— Rd., bp. St. Dav. 464
— Th., S.L. 410
Rawlinson, Chr. and sir C., C.J. Mdras. 658
— Hy. Cresw. and sir H., Amb. Pers. 130; K.C.B. 782; M.C.I. 646
— sir Rt., K.C.B. 784
— Th., L.M. Lond. 492
— sir Th., L.M. Lond. 491
— Wm. and sir W., C.G.S. 357; S.L. 411
Rawnsley, Rd. B., gen. (**D**) 889
Rawson, Geo., C.J. Ir. 568
— Jno., L. Treas. Ir. 559
— Rawson Wm. and sir R., G. Bah. Isl. 716; G. Bdoes. &c. 719, 721; K.C.M.G. 797
Rawstone, Jas., adm. (**H**) 849
Ray, *see also* Rae
— Hy., Berw. P.A. 341
— Ph., gen. (**D**) 882
Raymond, K. Arr. 86
— K. Cle. 85
— Hy. Ph., gen. (**D**) 899
— Rt., *see* ld. R., *infra*
— Th. and sir Th., B. Ex. 384; J.C.P. 379; J.K.B. 372; S.L. 410
— Wm., gen. (**B**) 868
Raymond, lds.
— Rt. and sir R., aft. 1st ld. R., A.G. 399; C.G.S. 357; C.J.K.B. 370; J.K.B. 373; P.C. 197; S.G. 401; S.L. 411
— Rt., 2nd ld., P.C. 200
Raymundus, *see* Reymundus
Raynsford and **Rainsford**
— Ch., gen. (**A**) 859
— Hanb., gen. (**D**) 888
— Jno., W.C.P. 318
— sir Mark, L.M. Dbln. 640
— Rd. and sir R., B. Ex. 384; C.J.K.B. 370; J.K.B. 372; S.L. 410
— Wm. H., gen. (**C**) 874
Raynton, sir Nichs., L.M. Lond. 491
Rea, Ed., gen. (**D**) 897
Reachta-Righdhearg, K. Ir. 21
Read, *see also* Reade, Rede, Reed and Reid
— Clare Sew., Sec. L.G.B. 256
Read—*cont.*
— Geo., gen. (**B**) 865
— Hy., gen. (**B**) 866
— Jno., S.L. 407
— Rd. and sir R., L.K. and Ld. Chanc. Ir. 576; M. Chy. 395
— Rt. and sir R., C.J.C.P. 375; J.K.B. 372; S.L. 407
— Saml., L.M. Dbln. 641
Reade, *see also* Read, &c.
— Hy., C. Tx. 284
— Rt., bp. Carl. 475; bp. Chich. 433; bp. Wford. and L. 626
— sir Th., Amb. Tun. 132
— T. F., Amb. Tun. 132
— Wm., bp. Chich. 432
Reader and **Reder**
— Enoch, dn. Emly, 628; dn. Kilm. 609
— Enoch, L.M. Dbln. 640
— (or Reder), Jno., dn. Wford. 628
— Rd., dn. Emly, 628; dn. Kilm. 609
Ready, Jno., G. I. Man, 666 G. Pr. Ed. Isl. 699; gen. (**D**) 879
Reay, Josh., gen. (**D**) 924
Reay, lds.
— Don. Jas., 1st ld., form. sir D. J. Mackay, *q.v.*, G. Bbay. 659; G.C.I.E. 805
— Fanny Georg. Jane, lady, Cr. Ind. 810
Rebilus, C. C., C. Ro. 46
Rebow, Fras. Sl., gen. (**A**) 862
Recaredo I. and II., K. Sp. 85
Recesuinto, K. Sp. 85
Rechila (2), C. Hlt. 81
Rede, *see also* Read, &c.
— Barth., *see* Reed
— Edm., K.B. 757
— Rd., C.B. Ex. Ir. 582; D. Chanc. Ir. 575
— Roger de, M.M. 245
— Walt. le, abp. Cash. 625; bp. Crk. 630
— Wm., K.B. 759
Redeford, sir Hy., Sp. H.C. 248
Redenesse, Jno. de, C.J.K.B. Ir. 577; J.K.B. Ir. 578
Reder, *see* Reader
Redesdale, Jno., 1st ld., form. sir J. Mitford, *q.v.*, B.T. 268
Redeswell, Jno. de, B. Ex. 383
Redeward, *see* Redward
Redhakauth, Deb. Raj., K.C.S.I. 802
Redhouse, Jas. Wm., K.C.M.G. 799
Redington, Th. Nichs. and sir T., K.C.B. 782; Sec. B.C. 254; U.S. Ir. 563
Redman, Rd., Sp. H.C. 248
— Rd., bp. Ely, 435; bp. Exr. 436; bp. St. As. 462
— Wm., bp. Norw. 455
— Wm., K.B. 758
Redmond, Jno. Patr., gen. (**D**) 917
Redwald, K.E. 23
Redward (or Redeward), abp. Yk. 485
Reed, *see also* Read, &c.
*— Barth., L.M. Lond. 490
*— Barth., M.M. 246
* Prob. same pers.
— Ed. Jas. and sir E., K.C.B. 783; L.T. 162
Reed—*cont.*
— Gen. de, K.C.B. 775
— Jno., gen. (**D**) 885; K.H. 790
— Th. and sir T., G.C.B. 770; gen. (**D**) 884; K.C.B. 779
Rees, *see* Rice
Reevar, Bah. of, G.C.S.I. 801; K.C.S.I. 802
Reeve and **Reve**
— sir Edm., J.C.P. 379; S.L. 409
— Jno., adm. (**H**) 849
— Jno., gen. (**D**) 880
— Saml., adm. (**A**) 816
— Th. le, bp. Lism. 626; bp. Wford. and L. 626; Ld. Chanc. Ir. 574
— Th. and sir T., C.J.C.P. 376; J.C.P. 379; K.C. 415; P.C. 198; S.L. 411
— Walt. le, dn. Wford. 628
Reeves, Geo. Jas., gen. (**D**) 877; K.H. 789
— Geo. Marm., gen. (**D**) 900
— Isaac Morg., dn. Ross. 633
— Wm., bp. Down, C. and D. 605; dn. Arm. 597
Refham, *see* Roffham
Regillensis, A. C. C., *see* Sabinus
— A. C. C., C. Ro. 40; Dt. Ro. 40
— A. C. S., C. Ro. 37-8
— A. P. A., C. Ro. 37-8; Dt. Ro. 37
— C. C. C., Dt. Ro. 40
— C. C. S., C. Ro. 38
— S. P. A., C. Ro. 38; Dec. Ro. 38
***Reginald,** bp. Cloy. 630; bp. Down. 603
*— bp. Cnr. 603
*— bp. Crk. 630
*— (2), bp. Isl. 539; bp. S. and M. 483
* Prob. some same pers. Comp. dates.
— D. Mda. 53
— (2), K. Man. 664-5
— (or Reynold), Walt., abp. Cant. 430; bp. Worc. 472; L.H.T. 152; Ld. Chanc. 354
Regner I. to V., C. Hlt. 81
Regnier, Off. Nap. 26
Regulus, C. A., C. Ro. 423
— M. A., C. Ro. 40-1-2-3; Dt. Ro. 43
Reichel, Ch. Pars., bp. Mth. 599; dn. Clonm. 600
Reid, *see also* Read, &c.
— Alexr. T., gen. (**D**) 880
— Blair Th., gen. (**D**) 918
— Ch. and sir C., G.C.B. 771; gen. (**D**) 902; K.C.B. 780
— Ch. Saml., gen. (**D**) 899
— Dav., C. Cus. Sc. 504
— Dav., gen. (**D**) 906
— Geo. Alexr., gen. (**D**) 884
— Jas. Bl., gen. (**D**) 930
— Jas. Hy., gen. (**D**) 920
— Jno., gen. (**A**) 859
— Jno. Walt., K.C.B. 781
— Lest. Rt., G. Bbay. 659
— Rt., bp. Ork. 535; L.P. Ct. Sess. 516; Ld. Sess. 518
— Rt. Thr., Q.C. 420
— Th., Chn. E. I. Co. 645
— Wm. and sir W., G. Bdoes. &c. 719-20; G. Bmda. 701; G. Mlta. 671; gen. (**D**) 890; K.C.B. 782

Reignolds, *see also* Reynolds
—— Th. Sc., gen. (**D**) 890
Reilly, Fras. Sav., K.C.M.G. 798; Q.C. 419
—— Jno., C. Acc. Ir. 567
—— Wm. Edmd. M., gen. (**D**) 927
Reinaldus, bp. Ross. 535
Reiner, abp. Arm. 595
Reinerus (or Reyner), bp. St. As. 462
Reinger, Jno., B. Ex. 382
—— Rd., Jy. 364
Reiny, *see also* Rainey
—— Jno. de, J. It. 367
Remington, *see* Reymington
Rempston, *see* Rampston
Rendel, Alexr. Mead., K.C.I.E, 805
—— Geo. W., L. Admy. 186
René (de Nassau), Pr. Or. 83
—— I. and II., D. Lne. 29
Renger, Rd., L.M. Lond. 488
Renney, Hy., gen. (**D**) 901
Rennell, Th., dn. Winch. 471
Rennie, Ch. Elph., gen. (**D**) 928
—— Geo., G. Falk. Isl. 731
—— Wm. Hepb., G. St. Vin. 725; G. Trin. 722
Renny, Geo. Alexr., gen. (**D**) 920
Renshaw, Th. Ch., Q.C. 419
—— Walt. Ch., Q.C. 420
Renton, Rt., gen. (**D**) 918
Renulphus, bp. Lond. 451
Renwick, Wm. Turnb., gen. (**D**) 901
Reodaigh, bp. Ferns, 621
Repingdon, Ph. de, bp. Linc. 446
Repington, Ch. Ashe A'Court, gen. (**D**) 879
—— Ed. Hy. A'Court, adm. (**D**) 828; (**G**) 840
Repps, Wm., bp. Norw. 455
Ressaldar, &c., C.I.E. 807
—— Jafar Ali Khan, C.I.E. 808
—— Shir Singh, C.I.E. 808
Rest, Jno., L.M. Lond. 490
Restitutus, abp. Lond. 450
—— bp. Lond. 450
Retford, Rt. de, J. It. 368
—— Wm. de, B. Ex. 383
Rethunus, bp. Dorch. 446
Reutha or **Reutherus,** K. Sc. 17
Reve, *see* Reeve
Reveley, Hy., C. Exc. 281
Rewys, Nichs., dn. Bgr. 426
Rex, Q. M., C. Ro. 45-6
Reygate, Jno. de, J.K.B. 371; Jy. 365
Reymington, Jno., L.M. Lond. 490
Reymundus (or Wymundus), bp. S. and M. 483
—— dn. Lim. 639
Reynardson, sir Abrm., L.M. Lond. 491
—— Th. Birch, gen. (**A**) 863
Reynel and **Reynell,** *see also* Reynolds
—— Carew, bp. Down. and Cnr. 604; bp. Dry. 601
—— (or Reynolds), sir Rd., C.J.K.B. Ir. 578; J.C.P. Ir. 581; J.K.B. Ir. 579; S.L. Ir. 591
—— Th. and sir T., gen. (**B**) 869; K.C.B. 775
Reyner, *see* Reinerus
Reynett, Jas. Hy. and sir J., gen. (**D**) 880; K.C.B. 779; K.C.H. 787; K.H. 789
Reynolds, *see also* Reignolds and Reynel
—— Barr., and sir B., adm. (**D**) 828; G.C.B. 770; K.C.B. 778
—— Ed., bp. Norw. 455; dn. Chr. Ch. Oxf. 457
—— Geo., L.M. Dbln. 641
—— Geo. Stew., adm. (**H**) 850
—— Jas. and sir J. (No. 1), C.B. Ex. 382; J.K.B. 373; S.L. 411
—— Jas. and sir J. (No. 2), B. Ex. 385; C.J.C.P. Ir. 581; S.L. 412
—— Jno., adm. (**A**) 815
—— Jno., dn. Linc. 448
—— Jno., L.M. Dbln. 642
—— Jno. Hy., gen. (**D**) 912
—— Jno. Wm., gen. (**D**) 905
—— Josh. and sir J., Pres. R.A. 941
—— Rd., bp. Bgr. 426; bp. Linc. 447; dn. Pboro. 458
—— sir Rd., *see* Reynell
—— Rt., A.G. 399; S.G. 401
—— Rt. Carth., adm. (**A**) 818
—— Th., bp. Her. 441; dn. Exr. 437
—— Walt., *see* Reginald
Reyson, Jno., L.M. Dbln. 641
Rhee, Th. Van, G. Ceyl. 672
Rheinhold, Rost, C.I.E. 808
Rhenius, Jno. Is., G. C.G.H. 678
Rhodes, *see also* Rodes
—— Chr., C. Exc. Sc. 505
—— Godfr., dn. Dry. 602
Rhodri, K. Wls. 16
Rhydderch, Pr. Wls. 17
—— ab Caradoc, Pr. Wls. 17
—— ab Jestyn, Pr. Wls. 17
Rhys, *see also* Rice
—— Pr. Wls. 17
—— ab Grufydd (2), Pr. Wls. 17
—— ab Tewdwr Mawr, Pr. Wls. 17
—— ab Owen, Pr. Wls. 17
Ri—, *see* Ry—
Riach, Wm. Alexr., gen. (**D**) 924
Riall, Phin., G. Gren. 724; gen. (**A**) 862; K.C.H. 788
Rialton, visc.
—— Sidney, 1st visc., form. 1st ld. and aft. 1st E. Godolphin, *q.v.*
—— Fras., ld., aft. 2nd E. of Godolphin, *q.v.*, L.W.S. 323
Riaz, Pasha, K.C.M.G. 797
Ribouleau, Pet., adm. (**D**) 823
Ribton, sir Geo., L.M. Dbln. 641
Rice, *see also* Rees and Rhys
—— Benj. Lew., C.I.E. 807
—— hon. Ed., dn. Glr. 440
—— Ed. Br., adm. (**E**) 836; K.C.B. 782
—— Fras., M.M. 247
—— Geo., B.T. 265-6; P.C. 202; Tr. Ch. 294
—— Jno. ap, L. Treas. Ir. 558
—— Harry Chipp. Pl., gen. (**D**) 929
—— Saml., K.H. 790
—— sir Steph., B. Ex. Ir. 584; C.B. Ex. Ir. 583; C. Treas. Ir. 559
—— hon. Steph. E. Spring, C. Cus. 277
Rice—*cont.*
—— Th. Spring, aft. ld. Monteagle, *q.v.*, Ch. Ex. 165; L.T. 160; P.C. 212; Sec. Tr. 163; U.S. Home, 227; W. and C. Sec. 231
—— hon. Th. C. W. Spring, U.S.F. 230
Rich and **Riche**
—— Arth. Newb., gen. (**D**) 917
—— Ch., adm. (**H**) 847
—— Edmd., abp. Cant. 430
—— Edwd., M. Chy. 395
—— Edwin Ludl., adm. (**H**) 848
—— Geo. Fk., adm. (**D**) 830; (**G**) 840
—— Geo. Wh. Talb., gen. (**D**) 908
—— Hy., L.T. 161
—— Hy., aft. 1st E. of Holland, *q.v.*, K.B. 762
—— Hugh, K.B. 760
—— J. B., Pres. Hti. 105
—— sir Pet., Chambn. Lond. 493
—— Rd., } *see* ld. R., *infra*
—— Rt., }
—— Rt., M. Chy. 395
—— sir Rt., G. Ch. Hosp. 936; gen. (**A**) 857; F.M. 856
—— sir Rt., gen. (**B**) 865
—— sir Rt., L. Admy. 176
—— sir Th., adm. (**A**) 816
—— Wm. Ch., gen. (**D**) 919
Rich, lds.
—— Rd., aft. 1st ld. R., Ld. Chanc. 355; S.G. 401; Sp. H.C. 249
—— Rt., aft. 2nd ld. R. (?), K.B. (1559) 761
—— Rt., ld., aft. 2nd E. of Warwick, *q.v.*, K.B. 761
—— Rt., ld., aft. 3rd E. of Warwick, *q.v.*, K.B. 762
***Richard,** abp. Cant. 430
*—— bp. Ach. 612
*—— bp. Bgr. 425
*—— (St.), bp. Chich. 432
*—— bp. Clonm. 600
*—— bp. Cnr. 604
*—— (de Prœbenda), bp. Dkld. 533; Ld. Chanc. Sc. 514
*—— (2), bp. Isl. 539
*—— bp. Lim. 638
*—— bp. Mor. 534
*—— bp. S. and M. 483
*—— bp. St. Andr. 528
*—— bp. St. As. 462
*—— bp. Wford. and L. 627
*—— (2), dn. Chich. 433
*—— dn. Her. 442
*—— dn. Lich. 445
*—— (Archd. Wilts), J. It. 366
* Prob. some same pers. Comp. dates.
—— D. Bdy. 28
—— K.B. 754
—— (son Wm. I.), Pr. E. 9
—— (son Hy. II.), aft. Rd. I., *q.v.*, Pr. E. 9
—— (son K. John), Pr. E. 9
—— (son Hy. III.), Pr. E. 9
—— (son Blk. Pr.), aft. Rd. II., Pr. E. 10; Pr. W. E. 8
—— (g. son Ed. III.), Pr. E. 11
—— (iss. Ed. III.), Pr. E. 11
—— (iss. Ed. III.), Pr. E. 11
—— (son Ed. IV.), Pr. E. 12
—— Rose P.A. 344
—— I. to III., D. Ndy. 30
—— I. to III., K.E. 4, 5
—— I. (K.E.), L.H.A. 551

Richard—*cont.*
— II. (K.E.), Ld. Ir. 551
— Jno. ap, dn. Her. 442
Richards, Alb. Nort., G. Br. Cbia. 698
— Alf., gen. (**D**) 878
— Ed. L., C.C.J. 403
— Ed. Vaugh., Q.C. 418
— Fleetw. Jno., gen. (**D**) 919
— Fras. Jno., gen. (**D**) 919
— Fk. Wm. and sir F., adm. (**E**) 837; K.C.B. 781; L. Admy. 186
— Geo. Hy. and sir G., adm. (**E**) 836; (**F**) 839; K.C.B. 781
— Griff., Q.C. 417
— Jno., A.G. Ir. 588; B. Ex. Ir. 584; S.G. Ir. 590
— Jno., dn. Ardf. 640
— Jno., L.L. Glam. 315
— Michl., gen. (**C**) 871; S.G.O. 259
— Pet. and sir P., adm. (**D**) 830; (**G**) 841; K.C.B. 779; L. Admy. 183
— Rd. and sir R., M. Chy. and Acct. G. 397
— Rd. and sir R., B. Ex. 385; C.B. Ex. 382; C.J. Chest. 386; K.C. 415; P.C. 209; S.L. 413
— Rt., gen. (**D**) 917
— Rt. Vaughan, Q.C. 417
— Sol., gen. (**D**) 921
— Wm., gen. (**D**) 876; K.C.B. 777
Richardson, Ch. and sir C., adm. (**D**) 825; K.C.B. 777
— Jas. Th. Stew. and sir J., Sec. Thist. 749
*— Jno., bp. Ard. 608
*— Jno., dn. Her. 442
* Prob. same pers.
— Jno., dn. Kilmacd. 638
— Jno. and sir J., J.C.P. 380; S.L. 413
— Jno. Hy., gen. (**D**) 884
— Jno. Luther, gen. (**D**) 876
— sir Jno. Stew., Sec. Thist. 749
— Josh. Fl., gen. (**D**) 915
— Rd., S.L. 411
— Rt., dn. Ard. 609
— Rt., L.H.T. Sc. 497
— Th. and sir T., C.J.C.P. 375; C.J.K.B. 370; S.L. 409; Sp. H.C. 249
— Wm., adm. (**H**) 847
— Wm., S.L. 410
— Wm. Madd., gen. (**C**) 872
— Wm. Stew., gen. (**D**) 932
Richbell, Ed., gen. (**C**) 871
Riche, *see* Rich
Richer I., C. Hlt. 81
Richense, Q. Pld. 90
Richey, Matth. H. J., G. N. Sc. 695
Richier, Isaac, G. Bmda. 701
Richm—, S.L. 407
Richmond, Archd. F., gen. (**D**) 887
— Hy., C. Cus. 276-7
— Rd., bp. S and M. 484
Richmond, E. and D. of, *see also* March, Lenox, Gordon and Nottingham
De Dreux Family.
— Peter de Savoy, 1st E. of, W.C.P. (1241) 317
— Jno. de Montford, 7th E. of, also D. of Brittany, K.G. (1376) 734
Richmond, E. and D. of—*cont.*
Plantagenet Family.
— Jno., E. of, aft. D. of Lancaster, *q.v.*, and K. Castile (*d.* 1399), K.G. 733
— Jno., E. aft. D. of, L.H.A. (1421) 174
Tudor Family.
— Edm., 1st E. of, form. E. Tudor, *q.v.*
Fitzroy Family.
— Hy., D. of, form. Hy. Fitzroy, and then E. of Nottingham, *q.v.* (*d.* 1536), L.H.A. 174; W.C.P. 319
Stuart Family.
1st Creation.
— Lud., 1st E. and D. of, also D. of Lenox, *q.v.*, C.G.S. 356; E.M. 326; H.C.P. Sc. 507; K.G. 739; L.G.C. Sc. 506; L.S.H. 290
2nd Creation.
— Jas., 1st D. of, also E. of March and D. of Lenox, K.G. 739; L.G.C. Sc. 506; L.H.A. Sc. 499; L.S.H. 290; W.C.P. 319
— Esmé, 2nd D. of, also D. of Lenox, L.G.C. Sc. 506
— Ch., 3rd D. of, form. E. of Lichfield, *q.v.*, also D. of Lenox, L.G.C. Sc. 506
Lenox Family.
— Ch., 1st D. of, K.G. 740; L.G.C. Sc. 506; L.H.A. Sc. 499; L.L. Kent, 309; M.H. 302
— Ch., 2nd D. of, gen. (**B**) 865; K.B. 764; K.G. 741; L.H. Const. 289; M.H. 302; P.C. 198
— Ch., 3rd D. of, Amb. Fr. 112; F.M. 856; gen. (**A**) 858; K.G. 742; L.L. Suss. 312; M.G.O. 259; P.C. 201; S. St. 224
— Ch., 4th D. of, G. Can. 691; gen (**A**) 860; K.G. 743; L.L. Ir. 557; L.L. Suss. 312; P.C. 208
— Ch., 5th D. of, K.G. 743; L.L. Suss. 312; P.C. 211; Postm. G. 238
— Ch. Hy., 6th D. of and 1st D. of Gordon, Jud. Com. P.C. 361; K.G. 745; L.K. Sc. 503; L.P.C. 188; L.L. Bffsh. 508; Pres. B.T. 269; Sec. Sc. 502; V.P. Ed. Sc. 500
Rickards, Ed. Jno., gen. (**D**) 910
— Geo. Kett., K.C.B. 784
Rickets and **Ricketts**
— sir Cornw., adm. (**H**) 848
— Geo. Poy., G. Bdoes. 720; G. Tob. 723
— Hy., K.C.S.I. 802
— Rd. Rodn., gen. (**D**) 896
— sir Rt. Tr., adm. (**A**) 820
Rickhill, Wm., J.C.P. 378; S.L. 407
Rickinghale, Jno., bp. Chich. 433
Rickman, Wm., gen. (**D**) 922
Riddall, Wm., gen. (**D**) 881; K.H. 790
Riddel, Riddell, and **Ridel**
— Ch. Jas. Buch., gen. (**D**) 901
— Geoffr. (No. 1), Ch. Jr. 362; Jy. 363
Riddel, Riddell, and Ridel—*cont.*
— Geoffr. (No. 2), bp. Ely, 434; Ch. Jr. 362; Jy. 363; L.H.T. 152
— Hy. Jas., gen. (**D**) 879; K.H. 790
— Michl., gen. (**D**) 880
— Rd., bp. Ely, 434; J. It. 366
— Steph., Ld. Chanc. Ir. 574
— sir Walt. Buchanan, C.C.J. 404
— Wm., Ld. Chanc. Sc. 514
Ridding, Geo., bp. Southwell, 468
Riddoch, Jas. Compt. Sc. 498
Ridel, *see* Riddel
Rideout, Jno. Wood, gen. (**D**) 930
Rider, *see* Ryder
Rideware, Wm. de, J. It. 366
Ridgeway, Josh. West and sir J., K.C.S.I. 803; U.S. Ir. 563
Ridley, Ch. Wm., gen. (**D**) 893
— sir Matth. W., Sec. Tr. 164; U.S. Home, 228
— Nichs., bp. Lond. 451; bp. Roch. 460
— Nichs., M. Chy. 397
— Th. and sir T., M. Chy. 395; Vic. Gen. 421
— Wm., bp. Caled. 698
— Wm. Jno., gen. (**D**) 898
Riebeck, Joh. Anthy. Van, G. C.G.H. 678
Rier, Geo., L.L. Carm. 315
Rigaud, Gibbes, gen. (**D**) 911
— Steph. Jord., bp. Antig. 728
Rigby, Alexr., B. Ex. 384; S.L. 409
— Alexr., gen. (**C**) 872
— sir Alexr., C. Cus. Sc. 503
— Chr., C. Tx. 284
— Ed., S.L. 410
— Jno., Q.C. 419
— Rd., B.T. 265; Ch. Sec. Ir. 562; M.R. Ir. 585; Paym. G. 244; V. Treas. Ir. 560
Riggs, Ed., C. Cus. 275
Righy, Hy., gen. (**D**) 904
Rigny, H. de, K.C.B. 775
Riley, *see also* Ryley
— Ch. Wils., adm. (**H**) 849
*— Ph., C. Exc. 279
*— Ph, S.W.F. 271
* ? same pers.
— Steph. D., gen. (**D**) 887
Rimington, Saml., gen. (**B**) 868
***Rinaldo,** D. Tny. 57
*— M. Fa. 53
* ? same pers.
Ringstede, Th. de, bp. Bgr. 426
Rinzy, Geo. Aug. Fk. de, gen. (**D**) 900
Ripariis, Rt. de, J. It. 368
— Walt. de, J. It. 367
— Wm. de, Ld. Chanc. Sc. 514
Ripon, E. and M. of, *see also* Earl De Grey
— Fk. Jno., 1st E. of, form. F. J. Robinson and visc. Goderich, *q.v.*, L.P.S. 241; Paym. G. 244; Pres. B.C. 254; Pres. B.T. 268

Ripon, E. and M. of—*cont.*
—— Geo. Fk., 1st M. of, form. E. De Grey and R. (*see* Grey), G.G. Ind. 650; L. Admy. 186; L.L. Yorks N.R. 313
—— Henr. Anne Theod., Mss. of, Cr. Ind. 809
Rishberry, Jno., bp. Emly, 625
Ritchie, Ch. T., P.C. 221; Pres. L.G.B. 256; Sec. Adm. 187
—— Dav., Mod. K. Sc. 547
—— Geo., Mod. K. Sc. 547
—— Rt., Amb. Vce. 116
—— Wm., Mod. K. Sc. 547
Ritherdon, Augs., gen. (**D**) 924
Rivallis, Ryevalis, or Orivallis, Pet. de, B. Ex. 382; L.H.A. 170; L. Treas. Ir. 558; W.C.P. 317
Rivarola, C. A., Dt. and Pres. Pgy. 110
—— Fras., Ct., gen. (**B**) 870; K.C.H. 788; K.C.M.G. 796
Rivera, F., Pres. Ugy. 111
Rivers, Augs. Hy. Lane Fox-Pitt-, gen. (**D**) 917
—— Harry, gen. (**D**) 900
—— Hy., U.S.S. 226
—— Jas., U.S.S. 226
—— sir Jno., L.M. Lond. 490
Rivers, lds. and E.
Widvile Family.
—— Rd., 1st ld., aft. 1st E., K.G. 735; L.H.T. 153
—— Anthy., 2nd E., form. ld. Scales and Nucells, *q.v.*
Darcy and Savage Families.
—— Th., 1st E., form. visc. Colchester, *q.v.*
—— Rd., 4th E., Const. T.L. 321; gen. (**A**) 857; M.G.O. 258; P.C. 195
Pitt Family.
—— Geo., 1st ld., form. Geo. Pitt, *q.v.*, L.L. Dors. 307; L.L. Hants. 311
Riverston, Th., ld., C. Treas. Ir. (1689) 559
Rivett-Carnac, *see* Carnac
Rizzio, Dav., Sec. St. Sc. 502
Roan or **Roane,** Jno., bp. Killoe. 634; dn. Clr. 597
Robaire, Bart. de, K.B. 757
Robartes and **Robarts**
—— Fras., Tell. Ex. 167
—— Russ., Tell. Ex. 167
Robartes, lds.
—— Jno., 2nd ld., aft. 1st visc. Bodmin and E. of Radnor, *q.v.*, B.T. 263; E.M. 326; L.D. and L.L. Ir. 555; L.P.S. 240; L.T. 155; P.C. 190, 192
Robbins, *see also* Robins and Robyns
—— Th. Wm., gen. (**D**) 882
Robe, Fk. H., G. S. Austr. 706 gen. (**D**) 897
—— Wm., K.C.B. 774
*__Robert__ (the Norman), abp. Cant. 430; bp. Lond. 451
*—— bp. Ard. 607
*—— bp. B. and W. 427
*—— (2), bp. Brn 531
*—— (2), bp. Clonf. 635
*—— (of Flanders) bp. Cnr. 605
*—— bp. Dkld. 533
*—— (de Prœbenda), bp. Dnbl. 532
*—— (of England), bp. Emly, 625
Robert—*cont.*
*—— bp. Isl. 539
*—— (of Askeaton), bp. Kild. 616
*—— bp. Killa. 612
*—— (2), bp. Lim. 638
*—— (of Bedford), bp. Lism. 626
*—— (4), bp. Ross. 535
*—— bp. Ross. 631; M.M. 246
*—— bp. St. Andr. 528
*—— (2), bp. Wford. 626
*—— dn. Ferns, 623
*—— dn. Llin. 623
*—— (2), dn. Sal. 468
*—— (abbot of Holyrood House), L.H.T. Sc. 497
* Prob. some same pers. Comp. dates.
—— (de Courtenay), Emp. E.E. 51
—— (the wise), K. Nls. 56
—— (son Wm. I.), Pr. E. 9
—— (son James I.), Pr. E. 12
—— I., D. Pma. 54
—— I. and II., D. Bdy. 28
—— I. and II., D. Ndy. 30
—— I. and II., K. Fr. 23
—— I. to III., C. Flrs. 81
—— I. to III., K. Sc. 19
—— (Guiscard), K. Scy. 55
Roberts, Abrm. and sir A., G.C.B. 770; gen (**D**) 885; gen. (**D**) 886; K.C.B. 779
—— Ed., Cl. Pells. 168
—— Fras. Alexr. Cr., bp. Nass. 717
—— Fk. Sl. and sir F., C.C. Ind. 651; C.C. Mdras. 658; C.I.E. 806; G.C.B. 771; G.C.I.E. 805; G. Nat. 680; gen. (D) 920; K.C.B. 781; K.C.I.E. 805
—— Hy., C.I.R. 285
—— Hy. G., gen. (**D**) 888; K.C.B. 778
—— Hy. Tuff., gen. (**D**) 881
—— Jno., B.T. 265-6
*—— Jno., Chn. E.I. Co. 644
*—— Jno., Chn. E.I. Co. 645
* ? same pers.
—— Jno., gen. (**C**) 872
—— J. C., U.S.S. 226
—— Jno. Ch. Gawen, aft. Roberts-Gawen, adm. (**H**) 845
—— J. J., Pres. Lib. 100
—— Rd., K.H. 791
—— Rd. Armstr., gen. (**D**) 916
—— Th., gen. (**A**) 860
—— Wm., bp. Bgr. 426
—— Wm., gen. (**D**) 922
—— Ulst., K.A. 572
Robertson, Alexr. Cunn., gen. (**D**) 909
—— Archd., gen. (**B**) 866
—— Archd., gen. (**C**) 872
—— Archd., gen. (**D**) 879
—— Ch. Duisb., gen. (**D**) 907
—— sir Danl. Br., K.C.M.G. 797
—— Dav., aft. Robertson-Macdonald, adm. (**H**) 850
—— Dav., L.L. Berw. 508
—— Geo. Dunc., gen. (**C**) 874
—— Hy. Lark., gen. (**D**) 913
—— Herc. Jas., Ld. Sess. 521
—— Jas., gen. (**A**) 862
—— Jas., Ld. Sess. 519
—— Jas., Mod. K. Sc. 547
—— Jas. Hy. Cr., gen. (**D**) 909
—— Jno., K.C.M.G. 797
—— hon. Jno., C.I.E. 807
Robertson—*cont.*
—— Patr. B., Ld. Adv. 526, S.G. Sc. 527
—— Patr., D. Fac. Sc. 527; Ld. Sess. 521
—— Rt., adm. (**H**) 851
—— Rt. Rich., gen. (**D**) 894
—— Rt. Stanw., gen. (**D**) 931
—— Th., dn. Dham. 479
—— Wm., adm. (**H**) 847
—— Wm., gen. (**B**) 867
—— Wm., Ld. Sess. 520
—— Wm., Postm. G. Sc. 502
—— Wm. D., gen. (**D**) 887
Robertson-Ross, *see* Ross
Robins, *see also* Robbins and Robyns
—— Jos. F., dn. Killoe. 637
Robinson, *see also* Robison
—— Alexr., gen. (**D**) 922
—— Andr., gen. (**C**) 871
—— Benj. C., P.P. 419; S.L. 414
—— Ch., J.K.B. Ir. 579
—— Ch. Gepp., adm. (**E**) 835; (**F**) 838
—— sir Chr., Adm. Adv. 423; Ch. Lond. 422; J. Adm. Ct. 423; K. Adv. 422; P.C. 211
—— Danl. Geo., gen. (**D**) 907
—— Fk. Ch. Br., adm. (**E**) 837
—— hon. Fk. J., aft. 1st visc. Goderich, and E. of Ripon, *q.v.*, B.T. 268; Ch. Ex. 165; L. Admy. 181; L.T. 159; Paym. G. 245; Pres. B.T. 268; Tr. N. 256; U.S.W. & C. 231; V.P.B.T. 269
—— Fk. Lacey, C.I.R. 286
—— Fk. Ph. and sir F. G.C.B. 769; G. Tob. 723; gen. (**A**) 862; K.C.B. 774
—— Geo., J.C.P. Ir. 581
—— Geo. Aberc. and sir G., Chn. E.I. Co. 645
—— Hy., bp. Carl., 475
—— Hy., C. Exc. Sc. 504
—— Hy., K.C.B. 784
—— Hy. Ed., gen. (**D**) 885
—— Herc., adm. (**H**) 845
—— Herc. Geo. Rt. and sir H., G.C.M.G. 795; G. Antig. 728; G. C.G.H. 679; G. Ceyl. 673; G. H. Kong, 673; G. Monts. 729; G. Mtius. 684; G. N.S.W. 703; G. N.Z. 709; G. St. Xtr. 729; K.C.M.G. 796; P.C. 220
—— Jas., gen. (**A**) 858
—— Jas., S.L. Ir. 593
—— Jno., bp. Brl. 439; bp. Lond. 452; dn. Winds. 474; L.P.S. 240; P.C. 196
—— Jno., S.W.F. 271
—— Jno., gen. (**B**) 867
—— Jno., Sec. Tr. 163
*—— sir Jno., Const. T.L. 321; Lt. T.L. 322
*—— sir Jno., L.M. Lond. 491
* Prob. same pers.
—— Jno. Bev., G. Ont. 692
—— sir Leon., Chambn. Lond. 493
—— Mark, adm. (**A**) 818
—— Nichs., bp. Bgr. 426
—— sir R., G. Bmda. 701
—— Rd., aft. 1st ld. Rokeby, *q.v.*, abp. Arm. 596; bp. Ferns and L. 622; bp. Kild. 617; bp. Killa. and Ach. 613; dn. Chr. Ch. Dbln. 618

Robinson—*cont.*
— Rt., gen. (**B**) 866
— Rt., L.G. Gr. Hosp. 854
— Rt. Spencer and sir R., adm. (**D**) 832; (**E**) 834; (**F**) 838; Compt. N. 258; K.C.B. 783; L. Admy. 185
— Saml., Chambn. Lond. 493
— Stapylt., gen. (**D**) 911
— T., Sec. P.O. 239
— sir Tancr., adm. (**A**) 814
— Th., dn. Kilm. 609
— sir Th., aft. 1st ld. Grantham, *q.v.*, B.T. 265; C. Exc. 280; G. Bdoes. 720; K.B. 764; M.G.W. 296; P.C. 199; S. St. 224
— hon. Th., aft. 2nd ld. Grantham, *q.v.*, B.T. 266; P.C. 202; V.C.H. 297
— Wm. and sir W., G. Bah. Isl. 716; G. Bdoes. &c. 719, 721; G. Trin. 723; K.C.M.G. 798
— Wm.Cl. Fras. and sir W., G. Falk. Isl. 731; G. Pr. Ed. Is. 699; G. S. Austr. 707; G. Str. Sett. 675; G. W. Austr. 707; G.C.M.G. 795; K.C.M.G. 797
— Wm. Foth., Q.C. 419
— sir Wm. Hy., K.C.H. 788
— Wm. Rose, K.C.S.I. 803
Robison, *see also* Robinson
— Hugh Geo., gen. (**D**) 913
— sir Jno., K.H. 791
Robitaille, Theod., G. Queb. 694
Robles, F., Pres. Ecr. 108
Robley, —, G. Tob. 723
— Hor. Gord., gen. (**D**) 932
Robsart, sir Jno., K.G. 735
— Lewis, aft. ld. Bourchier, *q.v.* (*d.* 1433), K.B. 756; K.G. 735
Robson, Sim., dn. Brl. 440
Roby, Bapt., dn. Lich. 445
Robyns, *see also* Robins and Robbins
— Jno., gen. (**D**) 889; K.H. 791
Roca, J. A., Pres. Arg. 110
— V. R., Pres. Ecr. 108
Rocafuerte, V., Pres. Ecr. 108
Roceline, Ld. Chanc. 353
Roch, sir Wm., L.M. Lond. 490
Roche, *see also* Roches
— Edm., gen. (**D**) 906
— Geo., abp. Cash. 625
— Hy., dn. Ferns, 623
— (or Rupe), Jno., bp. Cork, 630; dn. Cork, 632
— Jno., bp. Lism. 626
— Jno., gen. (**D**) 905
— (or Roches), sir Jno., L.H.A. 173
— Milo., bp. Llin. 622
— Ph., K.C.H. 787
— Th., B. Ex. 383
— Wm., bp. Cork and Cl. 631
Rocheford, *see* Rochford
Roches, *see also* Roche
— Chev. Des, G. Mtius. 683
— Jno. de, G. Ch. Isl. 667
Rochester, Rt. and sir R., C.D.L. 242; Compt. H. 292; K.B. 760; K.G. 738
— Solomon de, J. It. 368
Rochester, visc. and E. of, *see also* Clarendon and Somerset
Carr Family.
— Rt., 1st visc., form. Robt. Carr, *q.v.*, aft. E. of Somerset, *q.v.*, K.G. 739
Rochester, visc. and E of—*cont.*
Hyde Family.
— Laur., 1st E. of, form. hon. L., ld. and visc. Hyde, *q.v.*, L.L. Cnwall. 307; K.G. 740; L.H.T. and L.T. 155; L.L. Herts. 309; L.L. Ir. 555; L.P.C. 187-8; P.C. 194; Prem. 140
— Hy., 2nd E. of, form. ld. Hyde, *q.v.*, aft. E. of Clarendon, *q.v.*, L.L. Cnwall. 307; V. Treas. Ir. 559
Rochford and **Rocheford**
— Barth., K.B. 755
— Sayer de, K.B. 755
Rochford, lds., visc., and E. of
Boleyn Family.
— Th., 1st visc., form sir T. Boleyn, *q.v.*, aft. E. of Wiltshire and Ormond, *q.v.*
— Geo., ld. and visc. (son of Thos., 1st visc.), W.C.P. 319
Carey Family.
— Hy., 1st visc., form. Hy. Carey, *q.v.*, aft. 1st E. of Dover, *q.v*
— Jno., visc., form. Jno. Carey, *q.v.*, aft. 2nd E. of Dover, *q.v.*
Nassau (of Zulestein) Family, see also Zulestein.
— Wm. Hy., 1st E. of, form. W. H. Nassau de Zulestein, gen. (**B**) 864
— Wm. Hy. N., 4th E. of, Amb. Fr. 112; Amb. Spn. 123; Gr. St. 304; K.G. 742; L.L. Esx. 308; P.C. 200; S. St. 225
Rochfort, Geo., gen. (**B**) 866
— Maur., bp. Lim. 638; L.D. Ir. 551
— sir Maur., L.D. Ir. 550
— Rt., A.G. Ir. 588; C.B. Ex. Ir. 583; L.K. Ir. 576
— Rt., bp. Down and Cnr. 604
— Simon, bp. Mth. 599
— Th., dn. St. Pat. 618
Rock, Jas., R. Dr. P.A. 338
Rocke, Jas. Harw., gen. (**D**) 933
Rockele, Rt. de, J.C.P. 376; Jy. 364
Rockingham and **Rokyngham**
— Jno. de, M. Chy. 393
Rockingham, lds., E., and M. of
— Lewis, 3rd ld., aft. 1st E. of, L.L. Kent, 309
— Lewis, 2nd E. of, L.L. Kent, 309
— Th., 3rd E. of, L.L. Kent, 309
— Th., 1st M. of, form. T. W. Wentworth and 1st E. of Malton, *q.v.*
— Ch.. 2nd M. of, K.G. 742; L.L. Yorks, W.R. 313; L.T. 157-8; P.C. 201; Prem. 143-4
Rocomb, Rd., bp. Llin. 622
Rodborough, Milo de, J. It. 369
Rodd, Jno. Rashl., adm. (**H**) 851
— Jno. Trem. and sir J., adm. (**A**) 820; K.C.B. 776
Rodeburn, Th., bp. St. Dav. 464
Roden, E. of
— Rt., 2nd E. of, form. visc. Jocelyn, K.P. 750
— Rt., 3rd E. of, form. visc. Jocelyn, *q.v.*, K.P. 751
Roderham, Jno. de, M. Chy. 394
Rodes, *see also* Rhodes
— Fras., J.C.P. 378; S.L. 408
Roderic, Roderick, and **Rodheric**
— bp. St. Dav. 464
— (O'Connor), K. Ir. 22
— K. Sp. 85
— (2), K. Wls. 16
— Ch., dn. Ely, 435
Rodham, Rt., adm. (**A**) 815
Rodheric, *see* Roderic
Rodney, Geo. Br., *see* ld. R., *infra*
— Rd. de, K.B. 754
— Th. Br., gen. (**D**) 917
Rodney, lds.
— Geo. Br., aft. sir G. and 1st ld. R., adm. (**A**) 814; G. Gr. Hosp. 854; G. Newfd. 700; K.B. 765
— Geo., 3rd ld., L.L. Radn. 316
Rodoaldus, K. Lmd. 49
Rodolf, Rodolph, and **Rodolphus;** *see also* Ralph and Rudolph
— D. Aus. 58
— D. Bdy. 28
— D. Su. 80
— K. Bma. 59
— K. Fr. 23
— K. Hgy. 60
— K. Lmd. 49
— Pr. Tva. 60
— I. and II., C.P.R. 68
— I. and II., E. Gmy. 62
— II. (E. Gmy.), K.G. 738
— I. to III., El. Sxy. 77
— I. to III., K. Bdy. 28
— I. to X., M. Bdn. 67
— -Aug., D. Brk. 70
Rodrigo, K. Sp. 85
Rodwell, Benj. B. H., Q.C 418
— Edg., Q.C. 419
Roe, Geo., L.M. Dbln. 642
— Jno., gen. (**D**) 918
— Jno., S.L. 408
— sir Th., Chanc. Gart. 746
— Wm. Th., C. Cus. 276-7
Roebuck, Jno. Arth., P.C. 219; Q.C. 417
Roffham (or Refham), Rd., L.M. Lond. 489
***Roger,** abp. Yk. 485
*— bp. B. and W. 427
*— (of Appleby), bp. Oss. 620
*— (of Wexford), bp. Oss. 620; dn. Kild. 619
*— (2), bp. Ross. 535
*— bp. Sal. 466; Ch. Jr. 362; L.H.T. 152; Ld. Chanc. 353
*— bp. St. Andr. 528; Ld. Chanc. Sc. 514
*— bp. Wford. and L. 626
*— (son of Rt., E. of Glo'ster), bp. Worc. 472
*— dn. Sal. 468
* Prob. some same pers. Comp. dates.
— (O'Connor), K. Ir. 22
— I. and II., K. Scy. 55
— Lapine, M.M. 245
— (Mortimer) (iss. Ed. III.), Pr. E. 10

Rogers, Arund., C.C.J. 405
— sir Ed., Compt. H. 292; V.C.H. 296
— Fras. J. N., K.C. 416
— sir Fredc., aft. 1st ld. Blachford, *q.v.*, K.C.M.G. 796; P.C. 218; U.S.C. 235
— Hy., K.B. 759
— Hy. Bl. Harr., gen. (**D**) 909
— Rd., bp. suff. Dov. 431; dn. Cant. 431
— Rt. Henley, adm. (**H**) 845
— Th., adm. (**A**) 819
— Th., S.L. 407
— Wm., gen. (**D**) 884
— Wm., M. Chy. 396
— Woodes, G. Bah. Isl. 716
Rogers-Harrison, *see* Harrison
Rogerson, Jno., A.G. Ir. 588; C.J.K.B. Ir. 578; Rec. Dbln. 642; S.G. Ir. 589
— sir Jno., L.M. Dbln. 640
Roghened (or Roughead), Wm., bp. Emly, 625; dn. Emly, 628
Rokeby, Ralph, S.L. 408
— (or Rookby), Th. and sir T., J.C.P. 379; J.K.B. 373; S.L. 411
— sir Th., L.J. Ir. 551
— Wm., abp. Dbln. and Gl. 616; bp. Mth. 599; Ld. Chanc. Ir. 575-6
Rokeby, lds.
— Rd., 1st ld., form. R. Robinson, *q.v.*, L.J. Ir. 557
— Hy., 6th ld., gen. (**D**) 885; K.C.B. 778; G.C.B. 770
Rokel, S.L. 406
Rokesley or **Rokeslie,** Greg., L.M. Lond. 489; M.M. 245
Rokh, Sh. Pers. 99
Rokyngham, *see* Rockingham
Rolfe, Rt. M. and sir R., aft. ld. Cranworth, *q.v.*, B. Ex. 385; C.G.S. 358; Jud. Com. P.C. 360; K.C. 416; P.C. 215; S.G. 402; S.L. 413; V. Chanc. 390
— Th., S.L. 407
Roland, *see also* Rowland
— Jno., dn. Cash. 627; M. Chy. 394
Rolland, Wm. Rae, adm. (**H**) 850
Rolle, Hy., C.J.K.B. 370; J.K.B. 372; L.T. 154; S.L. 409
— J., L. Admy. 175
Rolles, Jno., K.B. 764
— Rt., adm. (**A**) 819
Rollo, D. Ndy. 30
— hon. Rt., gen. (**D**) 903
Rollock, Pet., bp. Dkld. 533; Compt. Sc. 498; Ld. Sess. 517
Rolt, Jno. and sir J., A.G. 400; Jud. Com. P.C. 361; L.J. App. 389; P.C. 217; Q.C. 417
— Jno. and sir J., gen. (**D**) 882; K.C.B. 777; K.H. 792
Rolveston, Rog. de, dn. Linc. 447
Roma, Ct. Cam., G.C.M.G. 795
Romachus, K. Sc. 18
Romaine, *see also* Romayne
— Wm. G., Sec. Adm. 187
Romanus, bp. Roch. 459
— K. Lmd. 49
— P. Ro. 34
— I. to III., Emp. E.E. 50
Romayne, *see also* Romaine
— Jno., abp. Yk. 485
— Th., L.M. Lond. 489
Rome, Fk., gen. (**D**) 881
— Jno., M. Chy. 394
Romer, Rt., Q.C. 419
— Rt. Corc., gen. (**D**) 915
— Rt. Fr., gen. (**D**) 891
Romesei, *see* Romsey
Romilly, Fk., C. Cus. 277
— Jno., *see* ld. R., *infra*
— Saml. and sir S., K.C. 415; S.G. 402
Romilly, lds.
— Jno. and sir J., aft. 1st ld. R., A.G. 400; Jud. Com. P.C. 360; M.R. 388; Q.C. 417; P.C. 215; S.G. 402
Romney, lds. and E. of
Sydney Family.
— Hy., E. of, form. Hy., ld. and visc. Sydney, *q.v.*, gen. (**B**) 864; Gr. St. 303
Marsham Family.
— Ch., 3rd ld., aft. 1st E., L.L. Kent, 309
Romsey (or Romesei), Nichs. de, J. It. 368
— Walt. de, J. It. 367
Romulus, bp. Isl. 539; bp. S. and M. 483
— K. Ro. 36
Ronan, bp. Lism. 626
Ronhale (or Rouhale), Rd., M. Chy. 394
Rookby, *see* Rokeby
Rooke, sir Geo., adm. (**A**) 813; L. Admy. 176-7; P.C. 195
— Giles and sir G., J.C.P. 379; S.L. 412
— Hayman, gen. (**B**) 864
— sir Hy. Will., gen. (**C**) 875; K.C.H. 788
— Jas., gen. (**A**) 859
Roolwer, bp. Isl. 539; bp. S. and M. 483
Roome, Fk., gen. (**D**) 929
— Hy., gen. (**D**) 876
— Wm., gen. (**D**) 876
Roope, Benj., gen. (**D**) 880
Roos, sir Jno., L.H.A. 171
Roos, lds.
— Wm., ld., 7th (12th), K.G. 734; L.H.T. 153
— Th., 9th (14th) ld., K.B. 756
— Th., 13th (18th) ld., aft. E. of Rutland, *q.v.*, K.G. 737
Roper, Hy., dn. Clonm. 600
— sir Hy., C.J. Bbay. 660
— Jno., A.G. 398
Rorey, Earl, Ld. Chanc. Sc. 514
Ros, sir Jno. de, L.H.A. 171
— hon. Jno. Fk. FitzGer. de, adm. (**G**) 842
— P. de, J. It. 366
— Rt. de, Jy. 364
Ros, lds. de
— Wm. Lenn., 20th ld. de, form. Wm. L. Lascelles. *q.v.*, C.Y.G. 298; P.C. 215
— Dudley Ch., 21st ld. de, gen. (**D**) 909
Rosas, J. M. de, Pres. Arg. 110
Roscommon, Wentworth, 4th E. of, C.G.P. 299
Rose, Alexr., bp. Edinb. 533; bp. Mor. 534; Pr. Bp. Sc. 540
— Ch., bp. Dkld. and Dnbl. 542; bp. Dnbl. 542
— Geo., B.T. 268; P.C. 207; Paym. G. 245; Sec. Tr. 163; Tr. N. 256; V.P.B.T. 269
Rose—*cont.*
— Geo. and sir G., J. Bank. 392; K.C. 416; M. Chy. 397
— Geo. Hy. and sir G., Amb. Bva. 119; Amb. Pr. 118; Amb. U.S.A. 132; G.C.H. 786; P.C. 210
— Jno., gen. (**D**) 876; K.C.B. 776
— Jno., L.M. Dbln. 641
— Jno. and sir J., G.C.M.G. 795; K.C.M.G. 796; P.C. 221
— Hy., J.K.B. Ir. 579
— Hugh, gen. (**D**) 926
— Hugh Hy. and sir H., aft. ld. Strathnairn, *q.v.*, C.C. Ind. 651; Comm. F. Ir. 564; G.C.B. 769; G.C.S.I. 801; gen. (**D**) 889; K.C.B. 778; K.C.S.I. 802
*— Jas., bp. Glasg. 543
*— Jas., Sc. bp. 545
* Prob. same pers.
— sir Jno. Wm., Rec. Lond. 494; S.L. 412
— Sl., C. Ex. 282; C. Ex. Sc. 505
— Wm., K.C.B. 783
— sir Wm., K.C.H. 787
— Wm. Anders. and sir W., L.M. Lond. 492
Rosebery, E. of
— Neil, 3rd E. of, K.T. 748
— Archd. Jno., 4th E. of, K.T. 748; L.L. Linlithg. 511; P.C. 212
— Archd. Ph., 5th E. of, C.W.P.B. 273; F. Sec. 229; L.L. Linlithg. 511; L.L. Mid. L. 509; L.P.S. 241; P.C. 220; U.S. Home, 228
Roslyn, *see* Rosslyn
Ross and **Rosse**
— Alexr., gen. (**A**) 860
— Alexr., gen. (**C**) 872; S.G.O. 260
— Andr., gen. (**C**) 873
— Arth., abp. Glasg. 537; abp. St. Andr. 529; bp. Arg. 538; bp. Gall. 539
— sir Campb. Cl. Gr., gen. (**D**) 923; K.C.B. 781
*— Ch., C. Exc. 282
*— Ch., L. Admy. 182; L.T. 160
* ? same pers.
— Ch., gen. (**A**) 857
— Ch., gen. (**B**) 866
— Ch., gen. (**C**) 872
— Ch. Payne Hodgs., adm. (**D**) 824
— Dav., C. Exc. Sc. 504
— Dav., C.I.E. 806
— Dav., Ld. Sess. 520
— Dav. Rt., G. Tob. 723
— Edm., G. Ch. Isl. 667
— Edm. Dav. Russ., gen. (**D**) 914
— Geo., *see* ld. R., *infra*
— Hew. Dalr. and sir H., F.M. 856; G.C.B. 769; gen. (**D**) 879; K.C.B. 775; L.G.O. 259
— Hugh, gen. (**D**) 886
— sir Jas. Clarke, adm. (**D**) 831
— Jas. Kerr, gen. (**D**) 896; K.H. 792
— sir Jas. Lockh., gen. (**C**) 871
— Jas. Tyr. Cart., C.I.E. 806

Ross and Rosse—*cont.*
—— Jno. de, bp. Carl. 475
—— Jno., bp. Down, 603
—— Jno., bp. Exr. 437
—— Jno., gen. (**B**) 869
—— Jno., Ld. Adv. 525
—— Jno. and sir J., gen. (**C**) 875; G. Gsey. 669; K.C.B. 776
—— Jno. and sir J., gen. (**D**) 909; K.C.B. 781
—— sir Jno., adm. (**G**) 841
—— Jno. Fras., adm. (**H**) 852
—— sir Jno. Lockh., adm. (**A**) 815
—— Matth., D. Fac. Sc. 527
—— sir Patr., G. Antig. 728; G.C.M.G. 794; G. St. Hel. 682; gen. (**C**) 874; K.C.H. 788; K.C.M.G. 796
—— Patr. Robertson, gen. (**D**) 922
—— Rt., C. Cus. Ir. 565; C. Exc. Ir. 566
—— Rt., gen. (**C**) 873
—— Rt., K.H. 790
—— Rt., L.M. Dbln. 641
—— Th., gen. (**D**) 907
Ross, lds., E., and D. of
—— Walt., E. of, L.J. Gen. (1239) 522
Stuart Family.
—— Jas., 1st D. of, abp. St. Andr. 529; Ld. Chanc. Sc. 515
—— Wm., 12th ld., L.H.C.K. Sc. 546; L.H.T. Sc. 498
—— Geo., aft. 13th ld. R., C. Cus. 275; C. Cus. Sc. 504; C. Exc. Sc. 504
Gore Family.
—— Ralph, 1st E. of, gen. (**A**) 858
—— Geo., 2nd E. of, C. Treas. Ir. 561
Rosse, E. of
—— Laur., 2nd E. of, Postm. G. Ir. 564
—— Wm.. 3rd E. of, form. ld. Oxmanton, *q.v.*; K.P. 751; Pres. R. Soc. 940
Rossell, Ch., L.M. Dbln. 641
Rosslyn, E. of
—— Alex., 1st E. of, form. A. Wedderburn and ld. Loughborough, *q.v.*
—— St. Cl. Jas., 2nd E. of, Amb. Pgl. 124; G.C.B. 768; gen. (**A**) 860; Jud. Com. P.C. 360; L.L. Fifesh. 510; L.P.C. 188; L.P.S. 241; L.T. 160; P.C. 211
—— Jas. A., 3rd E. of, gen. (**D**) 884; M.B.H. 303; P.C. 214
—— Rt. Fras., 4th E. of, G.C.A. 300; L.H.C.K. Sc. 546; P.C. 221
Rossmore, lds.
—— Rt., 1st ld., form. G. R. Cunningham, *q.v.*
—— Hy. Rt., 3rd ld., L.L. Monaghan, 570
Rostislaw, R. Russ. 89
Roswell, Wm. (error in body, Rd.), S.G. 401
Rotharis, K. Lmd. 49
Rotheachta (2), K. Ir. 20
Rothenhale, Jno., K.B. 756
Rotheram and **Rotherham**
—— Jno. and sir J., B. Ex. 384; S.L. 411
—— (or Scott), Th., abp. 486; bp. Linc. 447; bp. Roch. 460; Ld. Chanc. 355
Rotherfeld, Wm. de, bp. Carl. 475
Rotherham, *see* Rotheram
Rothes, E. and D. of
—— Wm. (? Geo.), 4th E. of, Ld. Sess. 517
—— Jno., 7th E., aft. 1st D. of, Comm. Tr. Sc. 497; H.C.P. Sc. 507; Ld. Chanc. Sc. 515; Ld. Sess. 517; P.C. 190; Pres. P.C. Sc. 500
—— Jno., 8th E. of, L.H.C.K. Sc. 546; V.A. Sc. 499
—— Jno., 9th E. of, Comm. F. Ir. 564; gen. (**A**) 858; K.T. 747
Rothesay, Stuart de, *see* Stuart
Rottenburg, Fras. Bar., gen. (**B**) 867
Rotton, Guy, gen. (**D**) 913
Roubury, Gilb. de, J.C.P. 377; J.K.B. 371
Roucliffe, Br., B. Ex. 383
Rouden, Wm., M. Chy. 394
Rouen, abp. of, Const. T.L. 320
Rough, Wm., S.L. 412
Roughhead, *see* Roghened
Rouhale, *see* Ronhale
Roupell, Geo. B., M. Chy. 397
—— Rt. Pr., Q.C. 417
Rous, Anthy., dn. Lich. 445
—— Fras., Sp. H.C. 249
—— hon. Hy. Jno., adm. (**D**) 830; L. Admy. 183
—— Jno. de, K.B. 755
—— Saml., G. Bdoes. 720
Rouse, C. W. B., Sec. B.C. 254
—— sir Edmd., L. and V. Treas. Ir. 559
—— F., L. Admy. 175
Routh, sir Rand. Ish., K.C.B. 782
Routhall, *see* Ruthal
Row, Wm. Sk., gen. (**D**) 912
Rowan, Ch., and sir C., C.C.P. 261; K.C.B. 782
—— Hy. Seb., gen. (**D**) 903
—— Wm. and sir W., F.M. 856; G.C.B. 770; gen. (**D**) 882; K.C.B. 778
Rowcliffe, Hy., Q.C. 419
Rowcroft, Fras., gen. (**D**) 896
Rowe, sir Hy., L.M. Lond. 491
—— Jno., G.I. Man. 666
—— Nichs., P. Laur. 301
—— Pet., C.J.K.B. Ir. 577
—— Saml. and sir S., G. Gamb. 686; G. Gld. Cst. Col. 687; G. W. Afr. Sett. 688; K.C.M.G. 797
—— sir Th., L.M. Lond. 490
—— sir Wm., L.M. Lond. 491
—— Wm. Carp., Q.C. 417
Rowland, *see also* Roland
—— Andr., gen. (**D**) 897
Rowlands, Hy., bp. Bgr. 426; dn. Bgr. 426
—— Hugh, gen. (**D**) 923
—— Wm. Bowen, Q.C. 419
Rowlatt, Edwin Alexr., gen. (**D**) 912
Rowlet, Ralph, M.M. 246
Rowley, Bart. Saml., adm. (**A**) 817
—— sir Chas., adm. (**A**) 819; G.C.B. 769; G.C.H. 787; K.C.B. 774; L. Admy. 182
—— Ch. Jno., adm. (**E**) 837
Rowley—*cont.*
—— Jno., gen. (**C**) 874
—— Josh., adm. (**A**) 815
—— sir Josh. Rick., adm. (**D**) 828
—— sir Josias, adm. (**A**) 819; G.C.B. 769; G.C.M.G. 794; K.C.B. 774
—— Saml. Campb., adm. (**D**) 824
—— Wm., C. Acc. Ir. 567; C. Cus. Ir. 565-6
—— Wm., gen. (**A**) 859
—— Wm. and sir W., adm. (**A**) 814; K.B. 765; L. Admy. 178
Rowthall, *see* Ruthal
Roxburgh, Fras. and sir F., C.C.J. 405; Q.C. 418
—— Hugo de, bp. Glasg. 536; Ld. Chanc. Sc. 514
Roxburgh, E. and D. of
—— Rt., 1st E. of, L.P.S. Sc. 501
—— Jno., 5th E., aft. 1st D. of, K.G. 741; L.P.S. Sc. 501; P.C. 195; Sec. St. Sc. 502
—— Jno., 3rd D. of, Gr. St. 304; K.G. 743; K.T. 748; L.L. Roxb. 512; P.C. 206
—— Jas. Hy. Rt., 6th D. of, K.T. 748; L.L. Berw. 508
—— Jas. Hy. Rt., 7th D. of, L.L. Roxb. 512
—— Anne, Dss. of, M. Robes, 304
Roy, Wm., gen. (**C**) 872
Royal, Jos., G. N.W. Terr. 697
Roye, Edw. J., Pres. Lib. 100
Royle, Jos. Ralph Ed. Jno., C.I.E. 808
Royse, Geo., dn. Brl. 440
Royston, Pet. Sor., bp. Mtius. 684
Royston, visc.
—— Ph., visc., form. hon. P. Yorke, *q.v.*, aft. 2nd E. of Hardwicke, *q.v.*, L.L. Cambs. 306; P.C. 200
—— Ch. Ph., visc., aft. 4th E. of Hardwicke, Compt. N. 293; P.C. 217
Ruby, Mons. de, Compt. Sc. 498; Ld. Chanc. Sc. 515
Ruchonnet, L., Pres. Sw. C. 31
Ruck-Keene, *see* Keene
Ruclinus, *see* Kuclinus
Rudd, Anthy., bp. St. Dav. 464; dn. Glr. 440
Ruddell, Jas. Archd., gen. (**D**) 928
Ruderfield, Wm. de, abp. Yk. 485
Rudhale, Wm., S.L. 408
Rudolf (Cr. Pr. Austr.), K.G. 745
Rudsdell, Jos. and sir J., Regr. M.G. 799
Rudstone, sir Jno., L.M Lond. 490
Rudyard, Wm., dn. St. Pat. 617
Rudyerd, Hy., gen. (**B**) 867
Rufane, Wm., gen. (**B**) 865
Rufinus, P. C. (2), C. Ro. 41-2; Dt. Ro. 40, 42
Rufus (2), bp. Lond. 451
—— C. Ro. and Dt. Ro.; *see also* Flavus and Mamercinus
—— A. C. C., C. Ro. 42
—— Cornelius, bp. Elph. 608
—— Geoffr., bp. Dham. 478; Ld. Chanc. 353

Rufus—*cont.*
— Guy, J. It. 365
— M. M., C. Ro. 43, 45
— P. R., C. Ro. 45
— Q. M., C. Ro. 43
— Q. P., C. Ro. 45
— Rd., J. It. 366
— S. L. F., C. Ro. 37
— S. S., C. Ro. 46
— S. S. C., C. Ro. 40
— T. A. L., C. Ro. 45
— Wm., J. It. 365; Jy. 363
Rugg, Hy., dn. Cloy. 633
— Wm., bp. Norw. 455
Ruggles, Jno., gen. (**D**) 915
Rugnett, sir Jas. Hy., G. Jsey. 668
Rule, Wm. de, bp. Lich. and Cov. 444
— sir Wm., Sr. N. 257
Rullianus, Q. F. M., C. Ro. (5) 41; Dt. Ro. (2) 41
Rumbold, sir Arth. C. H., G. Nev. 729; G. St. Xtr. 729; G. Virg. Isl. 731
— sir Geo. Berr., Amb. H. Tns. 120
— Hor. and sir H., Amb. Arg. 136; Amb. Chi. 137; Amb. Gr. 129; Amb. Sw. and N. 127; Amb. Swz. 114; K.C.M.G. 798
Rumley, Rand., gen. (**D**) 897
Rumodeep, Sing, K.C.S.I. 803
Rumold, St., bp. Dbln. 615
Rumpf, Isaac Aug., G. Ceyl. 672
Rundall, Fras. Hornbl., gen. (**D**) 908
Rundle, Th., bp. Dry. 601
Runnington, Ch., S.L. 412
Rupe, *see* Roche
Rupella (or Capella), sir Rd. de, L.J. Ir. 550
Rupert, E. Gmy. 62
— Pr. (g. son Jas. I), *see also* under D. of Cumberland; adm. (**A**) 813; C.P.R. 68; Const. W. Cast. 322; K.G. 740; L. Admy. 175; L.L. Surr. 312; P.C. 190-1; Pr. E. 13
— I. to III., C.P.R. 68
— III. (C.P.R., aft. Emp. Gmy.), K.G. 735
Rupibus, Pet. de, bp. Winch. 470; Ch. Jr. 362; Jy. 364; Ld. Chanc. 353
Rupilius, C. Ro. 45
Rurick, R. Russ. 89
Ruse or **Rushe,** Anthy., dn. Chich. 434
Rushedon, Th., S.L. 408
Rushooke, Th., bp. Chich. 433; bp. Llff. 449
Rushout, sir Jno., L.T. 157; P.C. 199; Tr. N. 256
Rushton, Rand., G. I. Man, 665
Rushworth, Ch. Powl., C. Exc. 282; C.I.R. 285; C. St. 284; C. St. and Tx. 285; C. Tx. 285
— Ed. Ever., G. Br. Gu. 715; G. Jam. 713; G. Trin. 722
Russe, Wm., M.M. 246
Russel and **Russell**
— ld. Alexr. Geo., gen. (**D**) 905
— A. J., Pres. Lib. 100
— Bak. Cr. and sir B., K.C.B. 781; K.C.M.G. 797
— Barth., J.K.B. Ir. 578
— Ch. Arth. and sir C., A.G. 400; Q.C. 419

Russel and Russell—*cont.*
— Dav. and sir D., gen. (**D**) 897; K.C.B. 780
— Ed. Lechm. and sir E., gen. (**D**) 902; K.C.S.I. 803
— Ed., aft. E. of Orford, *q.v.*, adm. (**A**) (1690) 813; L. Admy. 176; P.C. 193; Tr. Ch. 294; Tr. N. 256
— ld. Ed., adm. (**D**) 831; (**E**) 834
— El., L.M. Lond. 489
— Fras., K.B. 760
— hon. Fras., G. Bdoes. 719
— Geo. and sir G., C.C.J. 404
— Geo. Lake, C.C.J. 404
— Geo. Wm., gen. (**D**) 916
— Ld. Geo. Wm., Amb. Pr. 118; G.C.B. 772; gen. (**D**) 880
— Geo. W. E., Sec. L.G.B. 256
— sir Hy., C.J. Bgal. 652; P.C. 209
— Hy. Ch., gen. (**D**) 886
— Jas., Q.C. 417
— sir Jas., gen. (**D**) 876
— Jno., adm. (**G**) 843
— Jno., bp. Linc. 447; bp. Roch. 460; Ld. Chanc. 355
— Jno., Sp. H.C. 248
— Jno., *see* ld. and Earl R., *infra*
— Jno. Arch., C.C.J. 405; Q.C. 418
— Jos., K.C.B. 776; K.C.M.G. 796
— Lechm. C., gen. (**D**) 881
— Michl., bp. Glasg. 543
— ld. Odo Wm. Leop., aft. ld. Ampthill, *q.v.*, Amb. G. St. 122; Amb. Gmy. and Pr. 116; G.C.B. 773; G.C.M.G. 795; P.C. 218; U.S.F. 230
— Rd., gen. (**C**) 871
— Rt., G. Gsey. 668
— Rog., dn. Lism. 628
— Th. Macn., adm. (**A**) 817
— Wm., bp. Isl. 539; bp. S. and M. 483
— Wm., M. Chy. and Acct. G. 397
— Wm., *see* ld. R., *infra*
— sir Wm., gen. (**D**) 907
— sir Wm., gen. (**D**) 920
— sir Wm., L.D. Ir. 554
— ld. Wm., Amb. Pgl. 125; L. Admy. 181
— W. A., bp. N. Ch. 676
— Wm. Carm., gen. (**D**) 918
— Wm. Oldn. and sir W., C.J. Bgl. 652; S.L. 413
— ld. Wr., dn. Exr. 438
Russell, lds. and E.
— sir Jno., aft. ld. R. and 1st E. of Bedford, *q.v.*, Compt. H. 292; K.G. 738; L.H.A. 174; L.P.Y. 240
— Wm., ld., aft. 5th E. of Bedford, *q.v.*, K.B. 763
— ld. Wm., son of 5th E. of Bedford (beheaded 1683), P.C. 192
— ld. Jno., aft. 1st Earl R., Amb. Aus. 117; C. Sec. 234; F. Sec. 228-9; G.C.M.G. 795; H. Sec. 227; Jud. Com. P.C. 361; K.G. 744; L.P.C. 188; L.T. 161; P.C. 211; Paym. G. 244; Prem. 148-9; W. and C. Sec. 231
Russin, bp. Cork, 630
Rust, Geo., dn. Cnr. 605; bp. Drom. 605

Ruthal, Jno., L.H.T. 152
— or Routhall, or Rowthall, Th., bp. Dham. 478; dn. Sal. 468; L.P.S. 240; Regr. Gart. 746; S. St. 223
Rutherford and **Rutherfurd**
— Andr., aft. Rutherford-Clark, *q.v.*, Ld. Adv. 526; Ld. Sess. 521; P.C. 215; S.G. Sc. 527
— Gilb. Bryd. R., adm. (**H**) 850
— Jno. Wellw., gen. (**D**) 914
Ruthven, lds., *see also* E. of Gowrie
1st Creation.
— Wm., 2nd ld., L.P.S. Sc. 501; Ld. Sess. 517
— Wm., 4th ld., Ld. Sess. 517
2nd Creation.
— Dav., 2nd ld., Comm. Tr. Sc. 497
Ruthyn, ld. Grey of, *see* Grey
Rutilus, C. M., C. Ro. (4) 40-1; Dt. Ro. (2) 40
— C. N. (2), C. Ro. 38-9, 41
— S. N., C. Ro. 37, 41
— *see also* Tricostus, P. V.
Rutlam, Rajah of, K.C.I.E. 805
Rutland, E. and D. of
Plantagenet Family.
— Ed., 1st E. of (son of Edw. III.), aft. D. of, Albemarle and D. of York, *q.v.*, K.G. 734; L.H.A. 173; Const. T.L. 320
— Edmd., E. of (son of Rd., D. of York), G. Ch. Isl. (1397) 667
— Edmd., E. of, Ld. Chanc. Ir. (1460) 575
Manners Family.
— Th., 1st E. of, form. 13th (18th) ld. Roos, *q.v.*
— Hy., 2nd E. of, K.G. 738
— Ed., 3rd E. of, K.G. 738
— Fras., 6th E. of, form. F. Manners, *q.v.*, K.G. 739
— Jno., 2nd D. of, K.G. 741
— Jno., 3rd D. of, C.D.L. 242; K.G. 741; L.L. Leic. 309; L.S.H. 290; M.H. 302; P.C. 197
— Ch., 4th D. of, K.G. 742; L.L. Ir. 557; L.L. Leic. 309; L.P.S. 241; L.S.H. 290; P.C. 204
— Jno. Hy., 5th D. of, K.G. 743; L.L. Leic. 309
— Ch. C. J., 6th D. of, form. M. of Granby, *q.v.*, K.G. 745; L.L. Leic. 309
— Jno. Jas. Rt., 7th D. of, form. ld. Jno. Manners, *q.v.*
Rutmel, bp. Clonf. 635
Rutter, Saml., bp. S. and M. 484
Ruxton, Wm. Fitzh., adm. (**H**) 852
Ruydocus, bp. Cnwall. 436
Ry —, *see also* Ri —
Ryan, Ch. List. and sir C., Ass. C. and A. and C. and A.G. 169; K.C.B. 784
— Corn., dn. Killoe. 637
— Donagh, dn. Emly, 628
— sir Ed., B.T. 268; C.J. Bgl. 652; Jud. Com. P.C. 360; P.C. 214

Ryan—*cont.*
—— Th., K.H. 791
—— Val., gen. (**D**) 924
—— Vinc. Wm., bp. Mtius. 684
Rycarde, Jno., dn. St. Pat. 618
Ryder and **Rider**
—— Alfr. Ph. and sir A., adm. (**B**) 821; (**E**) 835; K.C.B. 781
—— sir Dudl., A.G. 399; C.J.K.B. 370; P.C. 199; S.G. 401; S.L. 412
—— hon. Dudley, aft. 2nd ld. and 1st E. of Harrowby *q.v.*, B.C. 252; B.T. 268; Compt. H. 293; P.C. 205; Paym. G. 244; Tr. N. 256; U.S. F. 229; V.P.B.T. 269
—— Hy., bp. Killoe. 634
—— hon. Hy., bp. Glr. 439; bp. Lich. and Cov. 444
—— hon. Hy., dn. Wells, 429
—— Jno. (No. 1), abp. Tm. 611; bp. Down and Cnr. 604; bp. Killoe. 634
—— Jno. (No. 2), bp. Killoe. 634; dn. St. Pat. 618
—— Jno., dn. Lism. 629
—— Ralph, K.B. 759
—— sir Wm., L.M. Lond. 491
—— hon. Rd., H. Sec. 227; J.A.G. 937; L.T. 158; P.C. 208
Rye, Pet., adm. (**H**) 844
Ryevalis, *see* Rivallis
Rygwallon, Pr. Wls. 16
Rykeman, Rog., M.M. 245
Ryle, Jno. Ch., bp. Lpool. 480; dn. Sal. 468
Ryley, *see also* Riley
—— —, Chest. H. 331
—— Wm., Bl. M. P.A. 336; Clar. K.A. 328; Lanc. H. 333; Norr. K.A. 329; R. Rge. P.A. 344
Rynwell, Wm., L.M. Lond. 490
Rytherch, Pr. Wls. 17
Rythmarch, bp. St. Dav. 464
Ryves, Br., dn. Chich. 434; dn. Winds. 474
—— Geo. Fk., adm. (**A**) 820; (**G**) 841
—— Jerome, dn. Killoe. 637; dn. St. Pat. 618
—— sir Rd., B. Ex. Ir. 584; L.K. Ir. 576; Rec. Dbln. 642; S.L. Ir. 591
—— sir Wm., A.G. Ir. 588; J.K.B. Ir. 579

S.

S*,** dn. Oss. 622
Sabert (St.), K.E. 2
Sabine, Ed. and sir E., gen. (**D**) 890; K.C.B. 783; Pres. R. Soc. 940
—— Fras., dn. Lich. 445
—— Jos., G. Gibr. 669; gen. (**A**) 857
Sabinianus, P. Ro. 33
Sabinus, *see also* Regillensis;
—— A. C. C. R. (2), C. Ro. 38; Dec. Ro. 38
—— C. C., C. Ro. 46
—— T. S., C. Ro. 37
Sabloil, Rt. de, L.H.A. 170
Sacheverell (or Sackveyle), Hy., K.B. 760
—— Wm., G. I. Man, 666; L. Admy. 176
Sackveyle, *see* Sacheverell
Sackville, *see also* Germaine
—— Ed., aft. 4th E. of Dorset, *q.v.*, K.B. 762
—— ld. Geo., gen. (**B**) 865
—— ld. Geo., *see* ld. S., *infra*
—— Jord. de, J. It. 367
—— Rd., sir R., Ch. Ex. 154; L.L. Suss. 312
—— Th., K.B. 763
Sackville, lds. and visc.
—— ld. Geo., aft. ld. Geo. Sackville-Germaine and 1st visc. Sackville, Pres. B.T. 266; C. Sec. 234; L.G.O. 259; L. Treas. Ir. 560; P.C. 200; P.C. 201
—— Mortim., ld., G.C.M.G. (1888) 796
Sackville-West, *see* West
Sadermen, abp. St. Dav. 463
Sadington, Rt. de, C.B. Ex. 381; Ld. Chanc. 354
—— (or Sodington), Th. de, J. It. 368
Sadleir, Jno., L.T. 161
—— Rd., gen. (**D**) 933
Sadler, Jno., M. Chy. 395
—— sir Ralph, C.D.L. 242; S. St. 223
Sadurnven, abp. St. Dav. 463
Sænius, L., C. Ro. 47
Safvet, Pasha, G.C.S.I. 801
Sage, Arth., gen. (**D**) 912
—— Jno., Sc. Bp. 545
—— Wm., gen. (**D**) 893
Saget, N., Pres. Hti. 105
Saham, Rd. de, B. Ex. Ir. 382; L. Treas. Ir. 558
—— Wm. de, J.K.B. 371
Saherus (*comes* Winton), B. Ex. 382
Sahuhie —, G. Tob. 723
Said, V. Eg. 98
Sainsbury, Th., L.M. Lond. 492
Saint, Ailm., K.B. 756
"Saint." For popes and bishops bearing this prefix, see under their Christian names. Where "St." forms part of the surname or title, the names are given below.
St. Albans, visc., E. and D. of
Bacon Family.
—— Fras., visc., form. Fras. Bacon and ld. Verulam, *q.v.*
Jermyn Family.
—— Hy., 1st E. of, form. Hy. Jermyn, *q.v.*, K.G. 740; L.C.H. 295; P.C. 190
Beauclerk Family.
—— Ch., 1st D. of, C.G.P. 299; K.G. 741
—— Ch., 2nd D. of, form. E. of Burford, *q.v.*, Const. W. Cast. 322; K.G. 741
—— Geo., 3rd D. of, L.L. Berks. 306
St. Albans, visc., E. and D. of—*cont.*
—— Wm., A. A. De V., 10th D. of, C.Y.G. 298; L.L. Notts. 311; P.C. 218
St. Amand, sir Alm., *see* ld. St. A., *infra*
—— Arn. de, G. Ch. Isl. 667
—— Rd., *see* ld. St. A., *infra*
St. Amand, lds.
—— sir Alm., aft. 2nd ld. St. A., L.J. Ir. 551
—— (or Scyntismond), Almaric, 3rd ld., K.B. 755
—— Rd., 4th ld., K.B. 757
St. Augustine (abb. of), J. It. 365
St. Barbara, Wm. de, bp. Dham. 478; dn. Yk. 486
St. Clair, *see also* Sinclair
—— hon. Jas., gen. (**A**) 858
—— Th. S., gen. (**D**) 882; K.H. 790
St. Clere, Guy, W.C.P. 318
St. Cyr, Off. Nap. 26
St. Cyres, Walt. S., visc., form. W. S. Northcote, *q.v.*, aft. 2nd E. of Iddesleigh, *q.v.*
St. Edmund, Rog. de, J. It. 366
—— Wm. de, Const. T.L. 320; Jy. 364
St. George, Arth., dn. Ross, 633
—— Hy. and sir H. (No. 1), Bl. M. P.A. 336; Gart. K.A. 327; Norr. K.A. 329; R. Rge. P.A. 344; Richm. H. 333
—— Hy. and sir H. (No. 2), Clar. K.A. 328; Gart. K.A. 327; Norr. K.A. 329; Richm. H. 333
—— Jno. and sir J., gen. (**D**) 900; K.C.B. 780
—— Rd., gen. (**B**) 865
—— Rd. and sir R., Berw. P.A. 341; Clar. K.A. 328; Norr. K.A. 329; Sec. St. Patr. 752; Ulst. K.A. 572; Winds. H. 331
—— sir Th., Gart. K.A. 327; Norr. K.A. 329; Som. H. 332
—— sir Th. Bl., gen. (**C**) 874; K.C.H. 788
St. German, Jno. de, bp. Worc. 472
St. Germans, E. of
—— Jno., 1st E. of, form. Jno. Eliot and 2nd ld. E., *q.v.*, U.S.F. 229
—— Wm., 2nd E. of, form. hon. Wm. Eliot, *q.v.*
—— Ed. Gr., 3rd E. of, form. ld Eliot, *q.v.*, G.C.B. 772; L.L. Ir. 557; L.S.H. 290; Postm. G. 238
St. Helena, Jno. de, J. It. 367
St. Helens, All., 1st ld., form. All. Fitzherbert, *q.v.*, Amb. Nds., &c. 122; Amb. Russ. 125; G.C.H. 786
St. Hippolite, Dav. M., baron de, gen. (**A**) 857
St. Jacobo, Steph. de, Jy. 363
St. John, hon Fk., gen. (**A**) 860
—— Fk. Rt., Amb. C. Am. 134; Amb. Sva. 128; Amb. U.S.C. 134; Amb. Vza. 135
—— Hy., *see* ld. St. J., *infra*
—— hon. Hy., gen. (**A**) 859
—— Jeffr., bp. Ferns, 621

St. John—*cont.*
— Jno. bp. Ferns, 621
— Jno. de, J. It. 367; L. Treas. Ir. 558
— Jno., K.B. 758
— Jno., S.L.R. 271
— Ol., A.G. 399; C.G.S. 356; C.J.C.P. 375; L.T. 154; S.G. 401; S.L. 409
— Ol., *see* ld. St. J., *infra*
— sir Ol., aft. 1st visc. Grandison, *q.v.*, L.D. Ir. 554
— Ol. Beauch. Cov., K.C.S.I. 803
— Pawlet, K.B. 763
— Rt., gen. (**D**) 895
— Rt. Wm., K.H. 790
— Rowl., K.B. 762
— hon. and rev. St. Andr., dn. Worc. 474
— St. Andr., U.S.F. 229
— St. Andr., *see* ld. St. J., *infra*
— Spens. and sir S., Amb. Bol. 135; Amb. Dom. Rep. 133; Amb. Hti. 133; Amb. Mex. 133; Amb. Pu. 135; K.C.M.G. 797
— Wm., dn. Ferns, 623
— Wm. de, G. Ch. Isl. 667
— Wm., *see* ld. St. J., *infra*
St. John, lds.
— Walt. Lindesay, ld., Ld. Sess. (1537) 518
St. John of Bletsho, lds.
— Ol., 4th ld., aft. 1st E. of Bolingbroke, *q.v.*, K.B. 762
— Ol., ld., aft. 2nd E. of Bolingbroke, *q.v.*, K.B. 762
— St. Andr., 13th ld., P.C. 208; C.G.P. 300
St. John of Lydiard Tregoze, lds.
— Hy., aft. 1st ld. and visc. St. John, and 1st visc. Bolingbroke, *q.v.*, P.C. 195; S. St. 224; Sec. at W. 233
St. John of Basing, lds.
Pawlet Family.
— Wm., ld., aft. E. of Wiltshire and M. of Winchester, *q.v.*, K.G. 738; L.C.H. 294; L.H.T. 139; L.S.H. 290; Ld. K. 355
St. Just, Luc. Let. de, G. Queb. 694
St. Lawrence, Lawr. de, Ld. Chanc. Ir. 575
— Nichs., aft. ld. Howth, *q.v.*
— Rt. de, Ch. Ex. Ir. 561; Ld. Chanc. Ir. 575
— (or Howth), Th., A.G. Ir. 588; J.K.B. Ir. 578
— hon. Th., bp. Cork and R., 632; dn. Cork, 632
St. Leger, —, Bl. Sang. P.A. 342
— Anthy., gen. (**C**) 872
— Anthy. and sir A., K.G. 738; L.D. Ir. 553; L.K. Ir. 576; M.R. Ir. 585
— Jeff., bp. Oss. 620
— Jno., gen (**C**) 872
— St. Jno., B. Ex. Ir. 584
— Th., bp. Mth., 599
— Th., K.B. 757
*— Wm., bp. Llin. 621
*— Wm., bp. Mth. 599
* ? same pers.
— Wm., gen. (**B**) 866
St. Leonards, Ed. B., 1st ld., form. sir E. B. Sugden, *q.v.*, Jud. Com. P.C. 360
St. Loe, sir Wm., C.Y.G. 298
St. Looe, Ed., adm. (**A**) 813
St. Martin, Lawr. de, bp. Roch. 459
— Ralph de, J. It. 366
— Rd. de, dn. St. Pat. 617
St. Omera, Wm. de, J. It. 368; J.K.B. 371; Jy. 365
St. Paul, Horace, Amb. Sw. 126
— Jno. de, abp. Dbln. and Gl. 615; Ld. Chanc. Ir. 574; Ld. K. 354; M.R. 387
St. Quintin and **St. Quinton**
— Walt. de, J. It. 366
*— sir Wm., C. Cus. 274
*— sir Wm., L.T. 156
*— sir Wm., V. Treas. Ir. 559
* Prob. all same pers.
St. Severino, (dn. of), M. Chy. 394
St. Valerico, Jno. de, B. Ex. 382
St. Vigore, Th. de, J. It. 368
St. Vincent, Jno., 1st ld. and E., form. sir J. Jervis, *q.v.*, Amb. Pgl. 124; G.C.B. 766; L. Admy. 180; P.C. 206
Sairt, Airtri, bp. Cork, 630
Sais, An, dn. Bgr. 426
Saisjed, Mihrban, C.I.E. 808
Salamon, *see also* Salomon
— D. Bry. 27
— K. Hgy. 59
Salar Jung, *see* Hyderabad, Bah. of, 802
Salavaria, Maria de, G. Trin. 721
Salaverry, F. S., Pres. Pu. 109
Salbiere, Comte de, G. Ch. Isl. 667
Salcedo, Juan José, G. Trin. 721
Salceto, Rt. de, J. It. 368
Salcott, Jno., bp. Bgr. 426; bp. Sal. 467
Sale, Rt. Hy., and sir R., G.C.B. 769; K.C.B. 777
Saleman, Jno., bp. Norw. 454
Salern, Walt. de, abp. Tm. 611; dn. St. P. 452
Salgar, E., Pres. U.S.C. 107
Salinator, C. L., C. Ro. 44
— M. L. (2), C. Ro. 43; Dt. Ro. 43
Salinguerra I. and II., M. Fa. 52
Salinis, Steph. de, K.B. 754
— Wm. de, dn. St. Patr. 617
Salis, Rod. de, gen. (**D**) 903
Salisbury, *see also* Salusbury
— Fulke., dn. St. As. 463
— Jno., bp. S. and M. 483; bp. suff. Thetf. 455; dn. Norw. 455
Salisbury, E. and M. of; *see also* Warwick
Longespée Family; *see also* Longespée.
— Wm., E. of (*d.* 1250), L.H. A. 170; W.C.P. 317
Montacute Family.
— Wm., 1st E. of, L.M. 325
— Wm., 2nd E. of, form. W. Montacute and sir W., *q.v.*, L.H.A. 172; K.G. 733; L.H.A. 172; L.M. 325
Salisbury, E. and M. of—*cont.*
— Jno., 3rd E. of, E.M. 326; K.G. 734
— Th., 4th E. of, K.G. 735
Nevill Family.
— Rd., 1st E. of, K.G. 735; Ld. Chanc. 355
Cecil Family.
— Rt., 1st E. of, form. ld. Cecil and visc. Cranborne, *q.v.*, K.G. 739; L.H.T. 154; L.L. Herts. 308
— Wm., 2nd E. of, form. Wm. Cecil, *q.v.*, C.G.P. 299; C.G.S. 356; K.G. 739; L.L. Dors. 307; L.L. Herts. 308
— Jas., 3rd E. of, K.G. 740; P.C. 191
— Jas., 5th E. of, L.L. Herts. 309
— Jas., 7th E., aft. 1st M. of, form. visc. Cranborne, *q.v.*, K.G. 742; L.C.H. 295; P.C. 203; Postm. G. 238
— Jas. Br. W., 2nd M. of, form. visc. Cranborne, *q.v.*, B.C. 253; Jud. Com. P.C. 361; K.G. 744; L.L. Mdx. 310; L.P.C. 188; L.P.S. 241; P.C. 210
— Rt. A. T., 3rd M. of, form. ld. R. Cecil and visc. Cranborne, *q.v.*, Amb. Gmy. and Pr. 116; Amb. Tky. 130; F. Sec. 229; K.G. 745; L.T. 162; Prem. 151; Sec. Ind. 236
— Geo. Car., Mss. of, Cr. Ind. 809
Salkeld, Lane, dn. Carl. 476
— Wm., S. L. 411
Sall, Wm., K.H. 792
Salles, Genl. de, G.C.B. 769
Salley (or Sawley), Miles, bp. Llff. 449
Salmeron, Pres. Sp. 87
Salmon, C. S., G. Nev. 730
— Geo., gen. (**B**) 869
— Jno., bp. Norw. 454; Ld. Chanc. 354
— Now., adm. (**E**) 836; K.C.B. 782
— Th., bp. Ferns and L. 622
— Wm. Br., gen. (**D**) 916
Salnave, S., Pres. Hti. 105
Salomon, *see also* Salamon
— Count Dem., G.C.M.G. 795
Salomons, Dav. and sir D., L.M. Lond. 492
Salt, Th., Sec. L.G.B. 256
Saltenstall, sir Rd., L.M. Lond. 491
Salter, Ed., M. Chy. 395
— Greg. de, dn. Kild. 619
— Hy. Fish., gen. (**D**) 887
— Jas. Fall., gen. (**D**) 878
— Jno., gen. (**C**) 872
— sir Jno., L.M. Lond. 491
— Wm. Talf., Q.C. 419
Saltoun, Alex. Geo., 16th ld., gen. (**B**) 870; G.C.H. 787; K.C.B. 777; K.T. 748
Saltu, Hugh de, bp. Ferns, 621
Salusbury, *see also* Salisbury
— Fk. Oct., gen. (**D**) 910
— Th., Adm. Adv. 423; J. Adm. Ct. 423
Salveine, Rog., K.B. 756
Salveyn, Ger., J. It. 369
Salvin, Anthy., gen. (**B**) 869
Salwey, Rd., L.T. 154
Sambach, sir Wm., S.G. Ir. 589

Samford, Th. de, Jy. 364
Sampson (St.), abp. St. Dav. 463
— bp. Brn. 530
— bp. Worc. 472
— Rd., bp. Chich. 433; bp. Lich. and Cov. 444; dn. Lich. 445; dn. St. P. 453; dn. Winds. 474; Regr. Gart. 746
— Rt., adm. (**A**) 813
— Th., dn. Chr. Ch. Oxf. 457
— Th., K.B. 759
Sams, Wm., J. Adm. Ct. 423
Samson, *see* Sampson
Samuels, Saul, K.C.M.G. 798
Sancho (Ramirez), K. Arr. 86
— I. and II., K. Pgl. 88
— I. to VII., K. Nav. 85-6-7
— II. to IV., K. Cle. 85-6
Sancroft, Wm., abp. Cant. 431; dn. St. P. 453; dn. Yk. 487; P.C. 191-2
Sancta, Fide Alan de, Ld. Chanc. Ir. 574
Sandale, Jno. de, bp. Winch. 470; Ch. Ex. 152; dn. St. P. 453; L.H.T. 152; Ld. Chanc. 354
Sandbach, sir Wm., S.L. Ir. 591
Sandeman, Rt. Gr., K.C.S.I. 803
Sanders, *see also* Saunders
— Arth., C. Cus. 277
— Arth., gen. (**D**) 897
— Jno. Fk., gen. (**D**) 928
— Matth., bp. Llin. 622
— Th., adm. (**H**) 847
Sanderson, *see also* Saunderson
— sir Jas., L.M. Lond. 492
— P., Amb. Rma. 128
— Rt., bp. Linc. 447
— sir Th. Hy., K.C.M.G. 799
Sandes, Geo., K.B. 763
— Steph. C., bp. Cash., E. W. and L. 627; bp. Killoe., K., Cl. and K. 636
Sandford, Ch. Wald., bp. Gibr. 670
— Danl., or Dav., bp. Edinb. 542
— Danl. Fox, bp. Tasm. 708
— Ed., gen. (**B**) 865
— Fras., Lanc. H. 333; R. Dr. P.A. 338
— sir Fras. Rd., K.C.B. 783; P.C. 220; U.S.C. 236
— Geo., dn. Ard. 609
— Hy. de, bp. Roch. 459
— sir Herb. Br., K.C.M.G. 799
— Nichs. de, dn. Ferns, 623
— Rt., gen. (**C**) 872
Sandham, Geo., gen. (**D**) 904
— Hy., gen. (**D**) 895
— Rt., gen. (**D**) 934
Sandhurst, lds.
— Wm. Rt., 1st ld., form. sir W. R. Mansfield, *q.v.*
— Wm., 2nd ld., U.S. War, 232
Sandilands, Phil., gen. (**D**) 893
Sandom, Wm., adm. (**D**) 830
Sandon, vist.
— Dudl., visc., aft. 2nd E. of Harrowby, *q.v.*, Sec. B.C. 254
— Dudl. Fras. St., visc., aft. 3rd E. of Harrowby, *q.v.*, P.C. 219; Pres. B.T. 269; V.P. Ed. 255
Sandwich, Hy. de, bp. Lond. 451; W.C.P. 317
— Ralph de, Const. T.L. 320; J.K.B. 371; L.M. Lond. 489; W.C.P. 318
— Sim. de, W.C.P. 317
— Sim. de and sir S., W.C.P. 318
Sandwich, E. of
— Ed., 1st E. of, form. Ed. and ld. Montagu, *q.v.*, adm. (**A**) 813; B.T. 263; M.G.W. 296
— Jno., 4th E. of, Amb. Spn. 123; gen. (**A**) 858; Ld. Admy. 178; P.C. 199; Postm. G. 238; S. St. 224-5; V. Treas. Ir. 560
— Jno., 5th E. of, form. visc. Hinchinbroke, *q.v.*, Postm. G. 238
— Jno. Wm., 7th E. of, C.G.A. 300; L.L. Hunts, 309; M.B.H. 303; P.C. 215
Sandwith, Jno. Pitc., gen. (**D**) 916
— Wm., gen. (**D**) 878
— Wm. Fk., gen. (**D**) 934
Sandys, Ed., *see* ld. S., *infra*
— Edwyn, abp. Yk. 486; bp. Lond. 451; bp. Worc. 473
— Fk. Herv., gen. (**D**) 891
— Geo., gen. (**D**) 887
— Saml., *see* ld. S., *infra*
— Wm., *see* ld. S., *infra*
Sandys of the Vine, lds.
— sir Wm., aft. 1st ld. S., K.G. 737; L.C.H. 294
Sandys of Ombersley, lds.
Sandys Family.
— Saml., aft. 1st ld. S., Ch. Ex. 165; Coff. H. 293; L.T. 157; P.C. 198; Pres. B.T. 265; Tr. Ch. 294
— hon. Edwin, aft. 2nd ld. S., L. Admy. 178
Hill Family.
— Arth. M. Wm., 2nd ld., gen. (**D**) 882
San Giovanni, Giorg., &c., Bar. de, K.C.M.G. 798
Sankey, Ed., L.M. Dbln. 641
— Hy. Gore, L.M. Dbln. 641
— Nichs. G.I. Man. 666; gen. (**B**) 864
— Rd. Hier., gen. (**D**) 926
— Wm., gen. (**D**) 906
San Martin, Pres. Pu. 109
— J. M., Pres. S. Salv. 106
Sanope, *see* Snape
San Ramon, Th., Pres. Pu. 109
Sansetun, Benet. de, bp. Roch. 459; Jy. 364
Santa Anna, A. L. de, Pres. and Dt. Mex. 103
***Santa Cruz,** Pres. Bol. 109
*— And., Pres. Pu. 109
* ? same pers.
Santa Maria, D., Pres. Chi. 111
Santana, P., Pres. Dom. Rep. 105
Santhey, Jno., B. Ex. Ir. 584; C.J.K.B. Ir. 578
Santos, M., Pres. Ugy. 111
Santry, Jas., 1st ld., form. sir J. Barry, *q.v*
Sapiens, L. L., C. Ro. 44
Saracenus, Jno., dn. Wells, 428
Sardar, Bahadoor, R. M. J. P., C.I.E. 807
Sardenne, Wm. de, M. Chy. 393
Sarel, Hy. Andr., G. Gsey. 669
Sargeaunt, Wm. Ch. and sir W., G. St. Vin. 725; K.C.M.G. 798
Sargent, sir Ch., C.J. Bbay. 660
— Hy., gen. (**D**) 887
*— Jno., Clk. O. 260
*— Jno., Sec. Tr. 163
* Prob. same pers.
— Jno. Nept., gen. (**D**) 909
Sargood, Aug., P.P. 419; S.L. 414
Sarmiento, D. F., Pres. Arg. 110; Pres. Ugy. 111
Sarnsfield, sir Nichs., K.G. 734
Sarsfield, sir Domnk., aft. 1st visc. Kilmallock, C.J.C.P. Ir. 580; J.K.B. Ir. 579
Sartorius, sir Geo. Rose, adm. (**B**) 821; adm. (**C**) 822; adm. (**D**) 828; G.C.B. 771; K.C.B. 779
Satow, Ern. M., Amb. Si. 131
Satrael or **Satrahel,** K. Sc. 18
Saumarez and **Sausmarez**
— Geo. de, gen. (**D**) 906
— Jas. de, *see* ld. S., *infra*
— Ph., adm. (**H**) 852
— Rd., adm. (**H**) 846
— Th., adm. (**H**) 851
— sir Th., gen. (**A**) 862
Saumarez, lds.
— sir Jas. de, aft. 1st ld. S., adm. (**A**) 817; G.C.B. 767; K.B. 766
Saunders, *see also* Sanders
— Aug. P., dn. Pboro. 459
— Ch., C.C.J. 404
— Ch. and sir C., adm. (**A**) 814; Compt. N. 257; K.B. 765; L. Admy. 179; P.C. 202
— Edm. and sir E., C.J.K.B. 370; S.L. 410
— sir Edw., C.B. Ex. 381; C.J.Q.B. 370; J.C.P. 378; S.L. 408
— Edw. Augs., gen. (**D**) 913
— Edw. Wm., gen. (**D**) 934
— sir Geo., adm. (**A**) 813
— Herb. Cliff., Q.C. 419
— Jno. Str., gen. (**A**) 862
— Morl., S.L. Ir. 591
— Rt., S.L. Ir. 591
Saunderson, *see also* Sanderson
— hon. Th., aft. 3rd E. of Scarborough, *q.v.*, K.B. 764
Saunford, Fulk. de, abp. Dbln. and Gl. 615
— Jno. de, abp. Dbln. and Gl. 615; dn. St. Pat. 617; J. It. 368; L.J. Ir. 550
Saurin, Ed., adm. (**H**) 845; C. Cus. 277; C. St. 284; C. St. and Tx. 285; C. Tx. 288
— Jas., bp. Drom. 605; dn. Cork, 632; dn. Dry. 602
— Lewis, dn. Ard. 609
— Wm., A.G. Ir. 588
Sausmarez, *see* Saumarez
Sausse, sir Matth. Rd., C.J. Bbay. 660
Sauvage, *see also* Savage
— Geoffr. le, Jy. 364
— Jas. le, J. It. 367
— Rog. le, Const. W. Cast. 322

Savage, *see also* Sauvage
— sir Arn., Sp. H.C. 248
— Hy., adm. (**A**) 817
— Hy. Jno., gen. (**D**) 893
— Jno. and sir J., K.B. 757; K.G. 737
— sir Jno. Bosc., gen. (**C**) 875; K.C.B. 777; K.C.H. 788
— Ph., Ch. Ex. Ir. 562
— Th., abp. Yk. 486; bp. Lond. 451; bp. Roch. 460
Savaricus, bp. B. and W. 427
Savary, Off. Nap. 26
Savell, Hy., K.B. 760
Savensby (or Stavensby), Alexr. de, bp. Lich. and Cov. 443
Saverrio, P. S., C. Ro. 41-2
Savile and **Saville**
*— Hy., L. Admy. 175-6
*— Hy., V.C.H. 296
* ? same pers.
— Jno., aft. 1st ld. Pollington and 1st E. of Mexboro', *q.v.*, K.B. 765
— Jno., *see* ld. S., *infra*
— Jno. and sir J., B. Ex. 384; S.L. 408
— sir Jno., form. Lumley, *q.v.*, P.C. 220
Savile, lds. and visc.
— sir Jno., aft. 1st ld. S. and E. of Sussex, *q.v.*, Compt. H. 292
— Th., 2nd ld., aft. 1st visc., Tr. H. 291
Savory, Wm. Scov., Pres. Coll. Surg. 939
Savoy, Bern. de, Const. W. Cast. 322
— Pet. of, bp. Worc. 472; dn. Sal. 468
Sawbridge, Jno., bp. Winch. 470
— Jno., L.M. Lond. 492
— Th., dn. Ferns, 623
Sawley, *see* Salley
Sawyer, Ch., gen. (**D**) 909
— Edm., M. Chy. 396
— sir Rt., A.G. 399; Sp. H.C. 249
— W. C., bp. Graft. and Arm. 704
— Herb., adm. (**A**) 815
— Herb. and sir H., adm. (**A**) 818; K.C.B. 773
Saxby (or Saxelby), Ed., B. Ex. 384
Saxe - Coburg, Pr. of, *see* Albert
Saxe-Meiningen, Bern. Fk. &c., Pr. of, G.C.B. 773
Saxe-Weimar, Bern., D. of, G.C.B. 768
— Pr. Wm. A. E. of, Comm. F. Ir. 564; G.C.B. 771; gen. (**D**) 903; K.C.B. 781
Saxelby, *see* Saxby
Saxey, Wm., J.K.B. Ir. 579
Saxred, K.E. 2
Saxton, sir Ch., U.S. Ir. 563
— Geo. Harp., gen. (**D**) 914
Saxulf (or Sexulf) (St.), bp. Lich. 443
Say and **Saye**
— Galfr. de, L.H.A. 171
— sir Geoff., L.H.A. 171
— Jno. and sir J., C.D.L. 242; K.B. 757
— Jno., Sp. H.C. 248-9
— Wm., dn. St. P. 453
— Wm., K.B. 758
— Wm. de, W.C.P. 317
Say and **Sele,** lds. and visc.
— Jas., 1st ld., form. Jas. de Fienes, Const. T.L. 320; L.H.T. 153; W.C.P. 318
— Wm., 1st visc., L. Admy. 175; L.P.S. 240; P.C. 190
— Th., 10th ld., gen. (**C**) 872
Sayer, Exton, Adm. Adv. 423; S.L.R. 271
— Geo., adm. (**A**) 820
— Jas., adm. (**A**) 815
— Jas. Rt. St., gen. (**D**) 909
— Jos., S.L. 412
Sayle, Capt. W., G. Bmda. 701
Scaccario, Matth. de, A.G. 398
Scæva, D. J. B., C. Ro. 41
— P. M., C. Ro. 44
Scævola, Q. M., C. Ro. 44-5
Scales, Th., ld., K.G. (1425) 735
Scales and **Nucells,** Anthy., ld., aft. 2nd E. Rivers, *q.v.*, K.G. (1466) 736
Scaly, Jno., K.C.M.G. 797
Scambler (or Scrambler), Edm., bp. Norw. 455; bp. Pboro. 458
Scammell, Walt., bp. Sal. 466; dn. Sal. 468
Scandalus (or Scannail), bp. Kild. 616
Scanlen, Th. Ch., K.C.M.G. 798
Scannail, *see* Scandalus
Scarborough, *see* Scardeburgh and Scorburgh
Scarborough, E. of
— Rd., 1st E. of, form. Rd., ld., and visc. Lumley, *q.v.*, C.D.L. 242; gen. (**B**) 864; L.L. Dham. 308; V. Treas. Ir. 559
— Rd., 2nd E. of, gen. (**B**) 864; K.G. 741; M.H. 302; P.C. 197; gen. (**B**) 864
— Rd., 4th E. of, Coff. H. 294; Dep. E.M. 327; P.C. 201; V. Treas. Ir. 560
— Jno., 8th E. of, L.L. Notts. 311
Scardeburgh, *see also* Scarborough
— Rt. de, dn. Yk. 486
— Rt. de, K.B. 755; J.C.P. 377; J.K.B. 371
— (or Scarborough), Rog. de, J. It. 367
Scardeville, Hy., dn. Cloy. 633
Scargill, Jas., gen. (**D**) 900
Scarle, Jno. de, Ld. Chanc. 354-5; M.R. 387
— sir Th., C.D.L. 242
Scarlett, Jas. and sir J., aft. 1st ld. Abinger, *q.v.*, A.G. 400; C.B. Ex. 312; Jud. Com. P.C. 360; K.C. 415; P.C. 213; S.L. 413
— sir Jas. Yorke, G.C.B. 770; gen. (**D**) 889; K.C.B. 777
— hon. Pet. C., Amb. Bzl. 135; Amb. Gr. 129; Amb. Mex. 133; Amb. Tusc. 115
Scarsdale, Robt., 3rd E. of, C.G.P. 299
Scaurus, M. A., C. Ro. 45
— M. Æ., C. Ro. 45
Scawen, Rt., C. Exc. 278
Sch—, *see also* Sh—
Schædde, *see* Schœdde
Schalch, Jno. Augs., gen. (**B**) 868
Schanck, Jno., adm. (**A**) 817
Schaw, *see* Shaw
Schenk, K., Pres. Sw. C. 31
Scherer, J. J., Pres. Sw. C. 31
Schives, Jno., Ld. Clk. Reg. 525
— Wm., abp. St. Andr. 529
Schneider, Fk., gen. (**D**) 926
— Jno. Wm., gen. (**D**) 917
Schœdde, sir Jas. Holmes, gen. (**D**) 884; K.C.B. 777
Scholey, Geo., L.M. Lond. 492
Schomberg, Alexr. Wilm., adm. (**A**) 820
— Ch. Fk., adm. (**H**) 849
— sir Ch. M, G. Dnca. 730; K.C.H. 788
— Geo. Augs., gen. (**D**) 903
— Herb., adm. (**H**) 848
— Jos. T., Q.C. 418
Schomberg, D. of
— Fk., 1st D. of, gen. (**A**) 857; K.G. 741; M.G.O. 258; P.C. 193
— Ch., 2nd D. of, gen. (**A**) 857
— Meinhardt, 3rd D. of, also D. of Leinster, *q.v.*, C. Ch. 855; gen. (**A**) 857; K.G. 741; P.C. 194
Schoolbred, Wm., Mod. K. Sc. 547
Schreiber, Brym. Fras., gen. (**D**) 928
Schreibershofer, Maxn., K.C.B. 777
Schrender, Jan, G. Ceyl. 672
Schuler, Fk., gen. (**D**) 887
Schultz, Jonn. Chrn., G. Mtoba. 696
Schute, *see* Shute
Schutte, Otto, bar., gen. (**C**) 873
Schutz, Jno., L.W.S. 323
Schwartzenburg, Pr., G.C.B. 767
Scipio, *see also* Africanus, Asiaticus, Barbatus, Cæpio, Calvus, and Nasica
— L. C., C. Ro. 40-1-2
— P. C., C. Ro. 43-4
— Q. C. M. P., C. Ro. 46
Scoble, Andr. Rd., Q.C. 419
Scorburgh or **Scoresburgh,** Rt. de, B. Ex. 383; J. It. (?); K.B. 755
Scory, Jno., bp. Chich. 433; bp. Her. 441; bp. Roch. 460
Scot, *see* Scott
Scothou, Wm. de, J. It. 369
Scotland, Colley Harm. and sir C., C.J. Mdras. 658
Scotre, Rog. de, B. Ex. 383; C.B. Ex. 381; S.L. 406
Scott and **Scot**
— Alexr., Ld. Clk. Reg. 525
— Benj., Chambn. Lond. 493
— Buch., C.I.E. 808
— Ch., gen. (**D**) 910
— Ch. Perry, bp. N. Ch. 676
— Ch. Rochf., G. Gsey. 669; gen. (**D**) 899
— ld. Ch. Th. Mont. Dougl., adm. (**E**) 837
— Cuthb., bp. Chest. 476
— Dav., adm. (**H**) 845
*— Dav., Chn. E.I. Co. 644-5
*— sir Dav., K.H. 789
* ? same pers.
— Dougl., gen. (**D**) 921
— Dunc. G. gen. (**D**) 886
— Ed., gen. (**C**) 873

For List of Abbreviations, see pp. 944-952.

Scott and Scot—*cont.*
—— Ed., K.B. 763
—— Ed. Hint., adm. (**G**) 842
—— Ed. Wm. Sm. gen. (**D**) 898
—— Edwin Ludd., gen. (**D**) 914
—— Fras., adm. (**E**) 835
—— Fras. H., gen. (**D**) 916
—— Geo., adm. (**H**) 847
—— Geo., gen. (**A**) 859
—— Geo. and sir G., adm. (**A**) 820; K.C.B. 776
—— Geo. Lewis, C. Exc. 280-1
—— Hy. Alexr., gen. (**D**) 886
—— Hy. Y. Darr., gen. (**D**) 910
—— Hopt. Stratf., K.C.B. 776
—— Jas., gen. (**B**) 864
—— Jas., gen. (**D**) 894
—— Jas., Ld. Sess. 518
—— Jas. and sir J., adm. (**D**) 830; (**E**) 834; K.C.B. 779
—— Jno., aft. ld. Earlsfort and visc. and E. of Clonmel, *q.v.*, A.G. Ir. 588; C.J.K.B. Ir. 578; S.G. Ir. 589; S.L. Ir. 592
—— Jno., B. Ex. 383; C.B. Ex. 381
—— Jno., bp. Dkld. 533
—— Jno., bp. St. Andr. 528
—— Jno., dn. Lism. 629
—— Jno., dn. Yk. 487
—— Jno., gen. (**C**) 872
—— Jno. and sir J., aft. 1st ld. and E. of Eldon, *q.v.*, A.G. 400; B.T. 268; C.J.C.P. 376; K.C. 415; P.C. 206; S.G. 402; S.L. 412
—— Jno. and sir J., G. Br. Gu. 715; G. Labn. 675; G. Nat. 680; K.C.M.G. 797
—— Jno. and sir J., gen. (**D**) 885; K.C.B. 779
—— sir Jno., Ld. Sess. 517, 519
—— sir Jno., W.C.P. 318
—— Jno. Guill., gen. (**D**) 913
—— Matth., bp. Abdn. 530; bp. Dkld. 533; Ld. Chanc. Sc. 514
—— Matth. Hy., adm. (**A**) 818
—— Patr. Geo., gen. (**D**) 925
—— Rt., dn. Roch. 461
—— Rt., K.C.B. 776
—— Rt. Anth. Ed. adm. (**H**) 852
—— Th., abp. York, &c.; *see* Rotheram
—— Th., gen. (**A**) 861
—— Th. (Pitgorn), L.J. Clk. 516
—— Th. (Abbotshall), Ld. Sess. 518
—— Th., L.M. Lond. 490
—— Walt., gen. (**D**) 896
—— Wm., B. Ex. Ir. 584; C. Acc. Ir. 567; J.K.B. Ir. 579; S.L. Ir. 592
—— Wm., gen. (**A**) 861
—— Wm. and sir W., aft. ld. Stowell, *q.v.*, Adm. Adv. 423; B.T. 268; Ch. Lond. 422; J. Adm. Ct. 423; P.C. 206; Vic. Gen. 422
—— Wm. and sir W., C.J.K.B. 369; J.C.P. 377; J.K.B. 371; S.L. 406
*—— Wm., K.B. 758
*—— sir Wm., W.C.P. 319
* Prob. same pers.
—— Wm. (Balwerie), Ld. Sess. 518
—— sir Wm. (Clerkintoun), Ld. Sess. 519
—— Wm. Carm., C.C.J. 404
—— Wm. Hy., gen. (**D**) 882
—— Wm. Is., adm. (**H**) 845
Scougal, Jas., Ld. Sess. 520
—— Jno., Ld. Sess. 519
—— Patr., bp. Abdn. 530
Scourfield, *see* Phillipps-Scourfield
Scovell, Edmd. Jno., gen. (**D**) 924
—— Geo. and sir G., G.C.B. 770; gen. (**A**) 863; K.C.B. 775
Scrambler, *see* Scambler
Scratchley, Pet. Hy., gen. (**D**) 1 Oct. 1882 (*see* Errata); K.C.M.G. 798
Scriven, Jno., P.P. 416; S.L. 413
Scrogie, Wm., bp. Arg. 538
Scroggs, Wm. and sir W., C.J.K.B. 370; J.C.P. 379; K.C. 414-5; S.L. 410
Scroop, Scroope, and **Scrope**
—— Adr., K.B. 763
—— Geoffr. le, A.G. 398; C.J.K.B. 369; J.C.P. 377; J.K.B. 371; S.L. 406
—— Hy. le, C.B. Ex. 381; C.J.K.B. 369; J.C.P. 377
—— Hy., *see* ld. S., *infra*
—— (of Castlecombe), Jno., K.B. 759
—— Jno., C.G.S. 357
*—— Rd., abp. Yk. 485; bp. Lich. and Cov. 444
*—— Rd. de, dn. Chich. 434
* Poss. same pers.
—— Rd., bp. Carl. 475
—— sir Steph. le, L.D. Ir. 552
—— Th., bp. Drom. 604
—— sir Th. le, L.D. Ir. 551
—— Wm., *see* ld. S., *infra*
Scrope of Bolton, lds.
—— Rd., 1st ld., L.H.T. 153; L.K. 354
—— Rd., 3rd ld., L.H.T. 153
—— Jno., 5th ld., K.G. 736
—— Hy., 7th ld., K.B. 759
—— Hy., aft. 9th ld. Scr., K.B. 760; K.G. 739
—— Th., 10th ld., K.G. 739
Scrope of Masham, lds.
—— Hy., 3rd ld., K.G. 735; L.H.T. 153
—— Jno., 4th ld., L.H.T. 153
—— sir Wm., aft. ld. Scr. and 1st E. of Wiltshire, *q.v.*, K.G. 734; K. Man. 665; L.H.T. 153
Scudamore, Arth., gen. (**D**) 906
—— F. I., Sec. P.O. 239
—— sir Jno., K.B. 763
Scurlock, Scurlog or **Scurloke,** Burnaby, A.G. Ir. 588
—— Th., D. Chanc. Ir. 574
Scyntismond, Alm., *see* St. Amand
Seachnasach, K. Ir. 21
Seadhna (2), K. Ir. 20
Seafield, visc. and E. of, *see also* E. of Findlater
—— Jas., 1st visc., aft. 1st E. of S., and 4th E. of Findlater, *q.v.*, form. ld. Deskford, *q.v.*, L.H.C.K. Sc. 546; L.H.T. Sc. 498; Ld. Chanc. Sc. 515; P.C. 195; Sec. St. Sc. 502; P.C. 195
—— Fras. Wm., 6th E. of, form. hon. F. W. Grant, *q.v.*
—— Jno. Ch., 7th E. of, K.T. 749
Seaford, Ch. Aug., 2nd ld., form. ld. Howard de Walden, *q.v.*, U.S.F. 229
Seaforth, lds. and E. of
Scotch Peerage.
—— Geo., 2nd E. of, Sec. St. Sc. 502
—— Kenn., 3rd E. of, K.T. 747
English Peerage.
—— Fr. Humb., 1st ld., form. F. H. Mackenzie, *q.v.*, G. Bdoes. 720; gen. (**B**) 866
Seager, Ed., gen. (**D**) 909
Seagram, Hy. Frowd, G. Gamb. 686
Seagrave, *see* Segrave
Sealy, Benj. Wm. Dowd., gen. (**D**) 877
—— Geo. Pr., gen. (**D**) 905
Seamer, sir Th., L.M. Lond. 490
Searle, *see also* Serle
—— Danl., G. Bdoes. 719
—— Jno. C., adm. (**A**) 819
—— Th., adm. (**D**) 827
Seaton, *see also* Seton
—— sir Hy., K.C.H. 788
—— Th., K.C.B. 778
Seaton, lds.
—— Jno., 1st ld., form. sir J. Colborne, *q.v.*, Comm. F. Ir. 564; Comm. Io. Isl. 129; F.M. 856; G.C.M.G. 794; gen. (**A**) 863
—— Jas., 2nd ld., gen. (**D**) 905
Sebastian, K. Pgl. 88
—— Off. Nap. 26
Sebba, K.E. 2
Sebbi, K.E. 2
Sebert (St.), K.E. 2
Sebright, Ch., K.C.M.G. 796
—— sir Jno., gen. (**A**) 858
Seccombe, Jno., adm. (**H**) 851
—— Th. Lawr., K.C.S.I. 803
Secker, Th., abp. Cant. 431 bp. Brl. 439; bp. Oxf. 456 dn. St. P. 453; P.C. 200
Sectabrat, bp. Emly, 625
Seculer, Alexr. le, B. Ex. 382
Seddon, Danl., gen. (**B**) 868
Sedgrave, *see* Segrave
Sedgwick, Ed., U.S.S. 226
*—— Jas., C. Exc. Sc. 505
*—— Jas., C. St. 284
* Prob. same pers.
Sedna (St.), bp. Saig, 620
Sedulius (St.), bp. Dbln. 615
—— (or Siedhul), bp. Kild. 616
Seel, Hy. How. Mol., Bl. M. P.A. 337; Richm. H. 334
Seele, Th., dn. St. Pat. 618
Seffride (or Seffridus) (2), bp. Chich. 432; dn. Chich. 433; J. It. 365
Sefton, E. of
—— Ch. Wm., 3rd E. of, L.L. Lanc. 309
—— Wm. Ph., 4th E. of, Amb. Pgl. 125; K.G. 745; L.L. Lanc. 309
Segar, Rt., C.C.J. 404
—— Th., Bl. M. P.A. 336
—— Wm. and sir W., Gart. K.A. 327; Norr. K.A. 329; Ptc. P.A. 337; Som. H. 332
Segda, Ph., dn. Cloy. 632
Segene, bp. Arm. 595
Segrave, Seagrave, Sedgrave, and **Sydgrave**
—— Gilb. de, bp. Lond. 451
—— Gilb. de, Jy. 364
—— Hugh de, L.K. 354
—— Nichs., *see* ld. S., *infra*
—— Patr., B. Ex. Ir. 584

For List of Abbreviations, see pp. 944-952.

Segrave, Seagrave, Sedgrave, and Sydgrave—*cont.*
*—— Rd., B. Ex. Ir. 583
*—— Rd., B. Ex. Ir. 584
*—— Rd., C.B. Ex. Ir. 582
*—— Rd., Ld. Chanc. Ir. 575
* Prob. some same pers. Comp. dates.
—— Steph.. abp. Arm. 595; dn. Lich. 445
—— Steph. de, Ch. Jr. 363; Const. T.L. 320; Jy. 364; W.C.P. 317
—— Walt. de, dn. Chich. 434
Segrave, lds.
Segrave Family.
—— Nichs., ld. (*d.* 1380), L.M. 325
Berkeley Family.
—— Wm. FitzH., ld., aft. 1st E. of FitzHardinge, *q.v.*, L.L. Glouc. 308
Seinges, Rd. de, J. It. 366; Jy. 364
Seintpoll, Geo., S.L. 408
Selangore, Sult. of, K.C.M.G. 798
Selbaic, *see* O'Selbaic
Selborne, Round., 1st ld. and 1st E., form. sir R. Palmer, *q.v.*, Jud. Com. P.C. 361; Ld. Chanc. 358
Selby, *see also* Seleby
—— Geo., gen. (**D**) 916
—— Hy., S.L. 410
—— Jas., Rec. Lond. (elect.) 494; S.L. 411
—— Ralph de, B. Ex. 383
Selden, J., L. Admy. 175
Seleby, *see also* Selby
—— Wm. de, A.G. 398
Selfe, Wm. Lyon, C.C.J. 405
Selim I. to III., S. Tky. 97-8
Selkirk, E. of
—— Wm., 1st E. of, aft. D. of Hamilton, *q.v.*
—— Ch., 2nd E. of, L.H.T. Sc. 498; Ld. Clk. Reg. 525; P.C. 198; Sec. St. Sc. 502
—— Th., 5th E. of, L.L. Kirkc. 510
—— Dunb. Jas., 6th E. of, L.K. Sc. 503; L.L. Kirkc. 510
Sellar, Jas., Modr. K. Sc. 547
Sellon, Baker Jno., S.L. 412
Selred, K.E. 2
Selwin and **Selwyn**
—— Ch. Jasp. and sir C., Jud. Com. P.C. 361; L.J. App. 389; P.C. 217; Q.C. 417; S.G. 402
—— Fk. Leop. Augs., adm. (**H**) 851
—— Geo. Augs., bp. Auckl. N.Z. 709; bp. Lich. 444; Prel. M.G. 799
—— G. Aug., S.L.R. 271
—— Jasp. Hy., adm. (**H**) 851
—— Jno. Rich., bp. Melan. 711
—— Wm., G. Jam. 712; gen. (**C**) 871
—— Wm., K.C. 415
—— Wm., K.C. 416
Selwin-Ibbetson, *see* Ibbetson
Sempringham, Ralph de, dn. Lich. 445
*__Senach,__ bp. Arm. 595
*—— bp. Cld. 598
* ? same pers.
Senchai, bp. Emly, 625
Sendall, Walt. Jos., G. Wwd. Isl. 719
Seneschallus, Walt., Ld. Chanc. Sc. 514
Senhouse, sir Humph. Fl. K.C.H. 788
—— Rd., bp. Carl. 475; dn. Glr. 440
Senior, Hy., G. Antig. 728
—— Nass. Wm., M. Chy. 397
Seppings, sir Rt., Sr.N. 257
Seramudi, &c., G.C.S.I. 801
Serapio, P. C. S. N., C. Ro. 44
Serbrethe, bp. Emly, 625
Serchfield, Rowl., bp. Brl. 439
Serge, Alexr., Gr. D. of Russ., G.C.B. 773
Sergius, I. to IV., P. Ro. 33-4
—— L. (2), C. Ro. 39
Serle, *see also* Searle
—— Rt., L.M. Lond. 488
Serlo, dn. Exr. 437
—— dn. Sal. 468
Serrano, Pres. Sp. 86
Serranus, A. A., C. Ro. 44
—— C. A., C. Ro. 45
—— S. A., C. Ro. 44
Serred, K.E. 2
Serrurier, Off. Nap. 26
Servante, Hy., gen. (**D**) 898
Servilianus, Q. F. M., C. Ro. 44
Servilius, C., C. Ro. 43; Dt. Ro. 43
Servius, Tullius, K. Ro. 36
Sesse, Rt., dn. Cloy. 633
Seton, *see also* Seaton
—— Alexr. (Kilcreuch), Ld. Sess. 519
—— Alexr. (Prior of Pluscardin), Ld. Sess. 517
—— sir Alexr. (Pitmedden), Ld. Sess. 519
—— sir Alexr., ld. Urquhart, aft. 1st E. of Dunfermline, *q.v.*, L.P. Ct. Sess. (1593) 516
—— Dav., Compt. Sc. 498
—— Jas., G. St. Vin. 725
—— Rog., *see* Seyton
—— sir Jno., Ld. Sess. 517
—— (or Setone), Th. de and sir T., C.J.K.B. 369; J.C.P. 377; J.K.B. 371; S.L. 406
Seton, lds.
—— Geo., ld., Ld. Sess. (1542) 517
Sevenoak, Wm., L.M. Lond. 489
Sever, Seveyer, or **Siveyer,** Wm., bp. Carl. 475; bp. Dham. 478
Severius, P. Ro. 33
Severn, Jno., gen. (**A**) 858
Severus, A., Emp. Ro. 47
—— F. V., Emp. Ro. 48
—— Lib., Emp. W.E. 49
—— Luc. Sept., Emp. Ro. 47
—— Od., abp. Cant. 430
Seveyer, *see* Sever
Seward, Th., gen. (**B**) 867
Sewell, Rt., gen. (**C**) 874
—— Th. and sir T., K.C. 415; M.R. 388; P.C. 201
—— Wm. Hy. and sir W., gen. (**D**) 882; K.C.B. 779
Sexburga, Q.E. 2
Sexhelm, bp. Lindisf. 478
Sexted, K.E. 2
Sextius, L., Trib. Ro. 39
Sexton, Th., L.M. Dbln. 642
Sexulf, *see* Saxulf
Sey and **Sele,** *see* Say and Sele
Seymour, Ch., dn. Dry. 602
—— Ch. Hy., dn. Tm. 613
—— Ed. and sir E., Compt. H. 292; L. Admy. 175; L.T. 155; P.C. 191, 192, 194; Sp. H.C. 249; Tr. N. 256
—— Edw. A., *see* ld. S., *infra*
—— Fras. and sir F., gen. (**D**) 899; K.C.B. 780
—— ld. Fras., dn. Wells, 429
—— Fras. Hugh Geo., aft. 5th M. of Hertford, *q.v.*, gen. (**D**) 894
—— Fk., G. Bmda. 701
—— Fk., G. Br. Cbia. 698; G. Br. Hond. 714
—— Fk., G. Nev. 729
—— Fk. Beauch. Pag. and sir F., aft. ld. Alcester, *q.v.*, adm. (**E**) 836; G.C.B. 771; K.C.B. 780; Ld. Admy. 185
—— Fk. Hor. Arth., gen. (**D**) 933
—— ld. Geo., C. Exc. 281-2
—— sir Geo. Fras., adm. (**B**) 821; (**C**) 822; (**D**) 826; G.C.B. 770; G.C.H. 787; K.C.B. 777; K.C.H. 787; L. Admy. 183
—— Geo. Ham. and sir G., Amb. Aus. 117; Amb. Bgm. 123; Amb. Pgl. 125; Amb. Russ. 126; Amb. Tusc. &c. 115; Amb. G. St. 121; G.C.H. 787; K.C.H. 788; P.C. 216
—— Geo. Hy., adm. (**D**) 833; (**E**) 834; G.C.B. 772; L. Admy. 184-5
—— Hy., K.B. 760
—— Hy. Danb., Sec. B.C. 254
—— Horace A. D., C. Cus. 277
—— ld. Hugh, adm. (**A**) 816; L. Admy. 180
—— sir Michl., adm. (**A**) 820; K.C.B. 774
—— Michl. (Culme-Seymour), and sir M., adm. (**C**) 822; (**D**) 830; (**E**) 837; G.C.B. 769; K.C.B. 777; Regr. and Sec. Bath, 785
—— Rd. Aug., G. St. Luc. 725; gen. (**C**) 874
—— Wm., gen. (**B**) 864
—— Wm., K.B. 759
—— Wm., aft. 2nd E. and 1st M. of Hertford, *q.v.*, K.B. 762
—— Wm. Digby, Q.C. 418
—— Wm. Hy., gen. (**D**) 907
—— Ed. Ad., c.c. ld. S., aft. 12th D. of Somerset, *q.v.*, C.W.F. &c. 272; C.W.P.B. 272; L.T. 160; P.C. 215; Sec. B.C. 254; U.S. Home, 227
Seymour of Sudley, lds.
—— Th., ld., K.G. 738; L.H.A. 174
Seymour of Trowbridge, lds.
—— Fras., 1st ld., C.D.L. 242; P.C. 190
Seymour-Conway, *see* Conway and Hertford
Seys, A. N., bp. Bgr. 425
—— Evan, S.L. 409; S.L. 410
Seyton or **Seytone,** Rog. de, C.J.C.P. 375; J.C.P. 377; Jy. 365
Seyyid, B.B.S., S. Zr. 102; G.C.M.G. 795
—— K., S. Zr. 102
—— M., S. Zr. 102
Shaa, Edm., L.M. Lond. 490
—— Jno. and sir J., L.M. Lond. 490; M.M. 246

Shadforth, Hy., gen. (**A**) 863
Shadwell, Ch. Fk. Alexr. and sir C., adm. (**E**) 835; K.C.B. 780
—— Lanc. and sir L., C.G.S. 358; Jud. Com. P.C. 360; K.C. 416; P.C. 211; V. Chanc. 390
—— Lawr., gen. (**D**) 906
—— Th., P. Laur. 301
Shadworth, Jno., L.M. Lond. 489
Shaftesbury, lds. and E. of
—— Anthy., 1st ld., form. sir A. A. Cooper, and ld. Ashley, *q.v.*, B.T. 263; L. Admy. 175; L.P.C. 187; Ld. Chanc. 357
—— Anthy., 2nd E. of, P.C. 191
—— Anthy., 4th E. of, L.L. Dors. 307; P.C. 200
—— Cropley, 6th E. of, P.C. 209
—— Anthy., 7th E. of, form. ld. Ashley, *q.v.*, K.G. 744; L.L. Dors. 307
Shaftoe, sir Rt., S.L. 410
Shahab-ud-din, Kazi, C.I.E. 806
Shahzada, Nadir, C.I.E. 808
Shakespear, Ch. Maxt., gen. (**D**) 915
—— Geo. Buckn., gen. (**D**) 913
—— Jno. Talb., gen. (**D**) 910
Shams - ul - Amara, &c. K.C.I.E. 805
Shand, Alexr. B., Ld. Sess. 521
Shank, Dav., gen. (**B**) 868
Shankar Bakhsh, &c., C.I.E. 807
—— &c., K.C.I.E. 805
Shannon, visc. and E. of
1st Creation.
—— Rd., 2nd visc., F.M. 856; L.J. Ir. 556
2nd Creation.
—— Hy., visc. Boyle, and 1st E. of Sh., form. Hy. Boyle, *q.v.*
—— Rd., 2nd E. of, C. Treas. Ir 560-61; K.P. 750; P.C. 203; V. Treas. Ir. 560
—— Hy., 3rd E. of, K.P. 750; L.L. Crk. 569
Shapcott, Rt., S.G. Ir. 589
Shapter, Jno., Q.C. 418
Shardelow (or Chardelawe), Jno. de, J.C.P. 377; J.K.B. 371; K.B. 755
—— Rt. de, Jy. 364
—— Th. de, A.G. 398
Shareshull, Wm. de and sir W., C.B. Ex. 381; C.J.K.B. 369; J.C.P. 377; J.K.B. 371; K.B. 755; S.L. 406
Sharf-ul-Omrah, K.C.S.I. 802
Sharp and **Sharpe**
—— Alex. Rent., adm. (**D**) 828
—— Hy., M. Chy. 394
—— Jas., abp. St. Andr. 529
—— Jno., abp. Yk. 486; dn. Cant. 431; dn. Norw. 456; P.C. 195
—— Jno., B.T. 264
—— Matth., gen. (**A**) 862
—— Phil. Ruff., adm. (**H**) 853
—— Rt., adm. (**H**) 848
—— Sutton, Q.C. 417
—— Wm., G. Bdoes. 720
Sharpeless, Jno., G. I. Man, 666
Sharrington, sir Wm., M.M. 246
Shaw and **Schaw**
—— Æn., gen. (**C**) 873
—— Alexr., G. I. Man, 666
—— Ch. Aug., gen. (**D**) 883
—— Cl. Rt., gen. (**D**) 935
—— sir Fk., Rec. Dbln. 642
—— Geo., gen. (**D**) 916
—— Geo., L.H.T. Sc. 496
—— Hugh., gen. (**D**) 932
—— Jas., Compt. Sc. 498
—— sir Jas., Chambn. Lond. 493; L.M. Lond. 492
—— Jno., gen. (**C**) 874
—— sir Jno., C. Cus. 273
—— sir Jno., S.L. 410
—— Meyr., C. St. 284
—— Rt., bp. Mor. 534
—— Rt., L.M. Dbln. 641
—— Rt. Bert., C.I.E. 806
—— Sam., gen. (**D**) 886
—— Wm., Q.C. 419
—— Wm. B., gen. (**D**) 927
Shaw, lds.
—— Ch., ld., aft. visc. and E. Cathcart, *q.v.*, V.A. Sc. 499
Shaw-Lefevre, *see* Lefevre
Shaxton, Nichs., bp. Sal. 467
Shea, *see also* Shee
—— Ambr. and sir A., G. Isl. 716; K.C.M.G. 798
Sheaffe, sir Rog. Hale, gen. (**A**) 862
Shecfield, —, M. Chy. 394
Shee, *see also* Shea
—— sir Geo., Amb. Pr. 118; Sec. Tr. Ir. 561; U.S.F. 230; U.S. Home, 227; U.S.W. and C. 231
—— Mart. Arch., Q.C. 418
—— Mart. Arch. and sir M., Pres. R.A. 941
—— Wm. and sir W., J.Q.B. 373; P.P. 417; S.L. 413
Sheffield, sir Rt., Rec. Lond. 493
—— sir Th., Sp. H.C. 249
—— Wm., dn. Yk. 487
Sheffield, lds. and E. of
Sheffield Family.
—— Jno., 2nd ld., K.B. 761
—— Edmd., ld., aft. 1st E. of Mulgrave, *q.v.*, K.G. 739
—— Edw., aft. 2nd E. of Mulgrave, *q.v.*, K.B. 762
Holroyd Family.
—— Jno., 1st ld., aft. 1st E. of, B.T. 268; P.C. 209
Sheikhuppur, Sheik of, C.I.E. 807
Sheil, *see* Shiel
Shekel, Jno., adm. (**H**) 846
Shekleton, Jos., gen. (**D**) 911
Shelburne, E. of
—— Wm., 2nd E. of, aft. 1st M. of Lansdowne, *q.v.*, gen. (**A**) 858; H. Sec. 226; K.G. 742; L.T. 158; P.C. 201; Prem. 144; Pres. B.T. 265; S. St. 224
—— Hy., E. of, aft. 4th M. of Lansdowne, *q.v.*, L.T, 161; U.S.F. 230
Sheldon, Gilb., abp. Cant. 431; bp. Lond. 452; P.C. 190
—— sir Jos., L.M. Lond. 491
—— Jno. or Ralph, K.B. 758
—— (or Shilton), Rd. and sir R., K.C. 414; S.G. 401
***Shelford,** Hy., dn. Her. 442
*—— Hy., M. Chy. 394
* Prob. same pers.
Shelley, Jno. and sir J., P.C. 202; Tr. H. 291
—— Rd., C. St. 283
—— Wm., J.C.P. 378; Rec. Lond. 493; S.L. 408
Shelton, Jno., K.B. 759
—— Rd., C. St. 283
Shelvocke, Geo., Sec. P.O. 239
Shennagh (or Heawo), Danl., dn. Kilf. 637
Shepard, *see* Sheppard
Shepey, *see* Sheppey
Shephard, Wm., S.L. 410
Shepheard Wm., adm. (**H**) 847
Shepherd, Arth., Bl. L.P.A 341; R. Dr. P.A. 338
—— Hy. J., K.C. 416
—— Jas., S.L. 411
—— Jas. Keith, adm. (**A**) 820
—— Jno.. adm. (**D**) 832
—— Jno., Chn. E. I. Co. 645-6; M.C.I. 646
—— Saml. and sir S., A.G. 400; C.B. Ex. Sc. 523; P.C. 210; S.G. 402; S.L. 412
Sheppard and **Shepard,** *see also* Shippard
—— Pons., gen. (**D**) 934
Sheppey, Jno. de, bp. Roch. 460; dn. Linc. 448; L.H.T. 153
Shepstone, Theoph., K.C.MG. 797
Sherborne (or Sherburn), Rt., bp. Chich. 433; bp. St. Dav. 464; dn. St. P. 453
Sherbrick, Th., gen. (**D**) 880
Sherbrooke, Jno. Cope and sir J., G.C.B. 767; G. Can. 691; G. N. Sc. 695; gen. (**A**) 861; K.B. 766
Sherbrooke, visc.
—— Rt., visc., form. Rt. Lowe, *q.v.*, G.C.B. 773
Sherburn, Rd. and sir R., G. I. Man, 666
—— Rt., *see* Sherborne
—— Th., G. I. Man, 666
Shere Ahmed Khan, C.I.E. 808
Sherer, Geo. Moyle Sh., K.C.S.I. 802
—— Josh., adm. (**G**) 842; K.H. 791
Sheridan, Jno., adm. (**H**) 845
—— Pat., bp. Cloy. 630; dn. Cnr. 605
—— Rd. Br., P.C. 208; Sec. Tr. 163; Tr. N. 256; U.S.F. 229
—— Wm., bp. Kilm. and Ard, 607; bp. Ard. 608; dn. Down, 605
—— Wm. and sir W., gen. (**B**) 868; K.C.H. 788
Sheriff and **Sherriff,** *see also* Shirreff
—— Jas. W., G. Nev. 730
—— Jno. Pr., gen. (**D**) 932
—— Th., R. Dr. P.A. 338
Sheriffs, Jas., Mod. K. Sc. 547
Sheringham, Wm. Louis., adm. (**H**) 848
Sherington, Walt., C.D.L. 242
—— Wm., K.B. 760
Sherlock, D., S.L. Ir. 593
—— Fras., K.H. 790
—— Nichs., dn. Kild. 619
—— Th., bp. Bgr. 426; bp. Lond. 452; bp. Sal. 467; dn. Chich. 434; dn. St. P. 453; P.C. 199

For List of Abbreviations, see pp. 944-952.

Sherman, Steph. Wm. B., gen. (**D**) 933
Sherrard, hon. Ph., gen. (**B**) 865
Sherriff, *see* Sheriff
Sherwood, Jno., bp. Dham. 478
—— Wm., bp. Mth. 599; L.D. Ir. 552; Ld. Chanc. Ir. 575
Shewell, Hy., gen. (**D**) 919
Sheyn, Matth., bp. Cork and Cl. 631
Shiel and **Sheil**
—— Jas., L.M. Dbln. 641
—— Justin and sir J., Amb. Pers. 130; gen. (**D**) 893; K.C.B. 782
—— Rd. Lal., Amb. Tusc. 115; J.A.G. 937; M.M. 247; P.C. 214; V.P.B.T. 269
Shield, Hugh, Q.C. 419
—— Wm., adm. (**A**) 819
Shioy (or Joy), Wm., abp. Tm. 611
Shiffner, sir Hy., adm. (**H**) 846
Shilton, Rd., *see* Sheldon
—— Rd., K.C. 414
Shipbrooke, Fras., 1st E. of, form. Fras. Vernon and visc. Orwell, *q.v.*
Shipley, sir Ch., G. Gren. 724; gen. (**C**) 873
—— Jno., bp. Llff. 449; bp. St. As. 462; dn. Winch. 471
—— Regd. Younge, gen. (**D**) 906
—— Wm. Dav., dn. St. As. 463
Shippard, *see also* Sheppard
—— Alexr., adm. (**D**) 825
—— Sidn. God. Alexr., G. Br. Bland. 680; K.C.M.G. 798
Shirland and **Shurland**
—— Alm. de, B. Ex. 383
—— sir Geoffr. de, W.C.P. 317
—— sir Rt. de, W.C.P. 318
Shirley and **Shurley**
—— Arth., gen. (**D**) 897
—— sir Geo. or sir Jno., C.J.K.B. Ir. 578
—— Geo. Jas., adm. (**A**) 820
—— Hor. and sir H., gen. (**D**) 897; K.C.B. 780
—— Jno., S.L. 409
—— Ralph., K.B. 756
—— Th. and sir T., G. Bah. Isl. 716; G. Dnca. 730; G. Leew. Isl. 727; gen. (**A**) 859
—— Walt. Aug., bp. S. and M. 484
—— Wm., G. Bah. Isl. 716; gen. (**B**) 865
Shirreff, *see also* Sheriff
—— Ch. Æn., gen. (**D**) 893
—— Wm., gen. (**A**) 859
—— Wm. Hy., adm. (**D**) 827
Shirton, *see* Sturton
Shivers, Th. Rev., adm. (**A**) 818
Shone, Saml., bp. Kilm. E. and A. 609
—— Th. Ak., gen. (**D**) 899
Shorabji, &c., C.I.E. 807
Shore, sir Jno., aft. 1st ld. Teignmouth, *q.v.*, G.G. Ind. 648
Shoredich, Jno. de, B. Ex. 383; K.B. 755
Shoreswood, Geo., bp. Brn. 531; Ld. Chanc. Sc. 515; Ld. Clk. Reg. 525; Sec. St. Sc. 501
Short, *see also* Shortt
—— Augs., bp. Adel. 707
—— Th. Vowl., bp. S. and M. 484; bp. St. As. 462
Shortall, Jas., gen. (**B**) 870
Shorthalls, Th., B. Ex. Ir. 583
Shorter, Jno., C. St. 283
—— sir Jno., L.M. Lond. 491
Shortland, Pet. Fk., adm. (**H**) 851
—— Vinc. Jno., gen. (**D**) 919
—— Will., G. N.Z. 709; G. Nev. 729; G. Tob. 723
Shortt, *see also* Short
—— Fras. Hy., adm. (**H**) 851
—— Jno. Mac., gen. (**D**) 896
Shotesbrooke, Jno., K.B. 756
Shottinden, Rt. de, Jy. 365
Shovel, sir Cloudesl., adm. (**A**) 813; L. Admy. 177
Shower, sir Barth., Rec. Lond. 494
Showers, Ch. Lion., gen. (**D**) 916
—— Ed. Mill. Gull., gen. (**D**) 878
—— St. Geo. Danl., gen. (**D**) 898
Shrapnel, Hy., gen. (**B**) 869
Shrewsbury, Ralph de, bp. B. and W. 428
—— Rt. de, bp. Bgr. 425
Shrewsbury, E. and D. of, *see also* Talbot
—— Jno., 1st E. of, form. sir Jno. and 12th ld. and Earl Talbot, *q.v.*
—— Jno., 2nd E. of, K.G. 736; L.H.T. 153; L.L. Ir. 552
—— Geo., 4th E. of, K.B. 757; K.G. 737; L.S.H. 289
—— Fras., 5th E. of, K.G. 738
—— Geo., 6th E. of, E.M. 326; K.G. 738
—— Gilb., 7th E. of, K.G. 739
—— Ch., 12th E., aft. 1st D. of, K.G. 741; L.C.H. 295; L.H.T. 156; L.L. Heref. 308; L.L. Herts, 309; L.L. Ir. 556; P.C. 193-4; Prem. 141; S. St. 224
—— Hy. Jno., (? 18th) E. of, also 3rd E. of Talbot, *q.v.*, C.G.A. 300
—— Chas. Jno., 19th (? 20th) E. of, C.G.A. 300; P.C. 219
Shriggely, Jno., B. Ex. Ir. 583; C.J.K.B. Ir. 577
Shrimpton, Jno., G. Gibr. 669; gen. (**C**) 871
Shuckburgh, Rd., dn. Cnr. 605
Shuldham, Edm. W., gen. (**D**) 877
—— Molyn., *see* ld. S., *infra*
—— Th. Hy., gen. (**D**) 898
Shuldham, lds.
—— Molyn., aft. 1st ld. S., adm. (**A**) 815; G. Newfd. 700
Shun-che, Emp. Ch. 100
Shurland, *see* Shirland
Shurley, *see* Shirley
Shute, Ch. Cam., gen. (**D**) 904
—— Jno., aft. Jno. Barrington-Shute and 1st visc. B., *q.v.*, C. Cus. 274; M.R. Ir. 585
—— (or Schute), Rt., B. Ex. 384; J.Q.B. 372; Rec. Lond. 494; S.L. 408
Shuttleworth, Asht. Asht., gen. (**D**) 899
—— Ph. N., bp. Chich. 433
—— Rd., S.L. 408
Shuttleworth—*cont.*
—— sir Ugh. J. Kay-, C.D.L. 243; P.C. 221; U.S. Ind. 236
Shutz, Jno., C. St. 283
Si—, *see also* Sy—
Siam, Surawongse Somd. C. P., Reg. of, K.C.M.G. 797
Sibley, Geo., C.I.E. 806
Sibthorpe, sir Chr., J.K.B. Ir. 579
—— Rt., bp. Kilf. 635; bp. Lim. 638
—— Th. de, M. Chy. 393
Siculus, Q. C. V., C. Ro. 37
Sidenham, *see* Sydenham
Sidi-Ali, B. Tun. 101
—— -Mohamed, S. Mco. 101
Sidmouth, Hy., 1st visc., form. H. Addington, *q.v.*, H. Sec. 227; Jud. Com. P.C. 360; L.P.C. 188; L.P.S. 241
Sidney, *see* Sydney
Siedhul, *see* Sedulius
Sigarus, bp. Wells, 427
Sigbert (2), bp. Lich. 443
Sigebert (4), K.E. 2
—— I. and II., K. Fr. 22-3
Sigebryt, K.E. 2
Sigefrid, C. Lux. 84
Sigehard, K.E. 2
Sigello, *see* Sigillo
Sigelmus (or Sigfridus), bp. Sels. 432
—— (or Swithelmus), I. and II., bp. Shbn. 466
Sigenard, K.E. 2
Sigered, K.E. 2
Sigeric (2), K.E. 2
Sigerico, K. Sp. 84
Sigfridus, *see* Sigelmus
Sigher, K.E. 2
Sigillo or Sigello
—— Hugh de, bp. Dkld. 533
—— Nichs. de, J. It. 365
—— Rt. de, bp. Lond. 451
Sigismund, E. Gmy. 62; K.G. 735
—— K. Bdy. 28
—— K. Bma. 59
—— K. Hgy. 60
—— K. Sw. 92
—— M. Brg. 65
—— (g. son Q. Vict.), Pr. E. 15
—— I. and II., D. Lne. 29
—— I. to III., K. Pld. 91
—— -Bathori, Pr. Tva. 60
—— -Ragotzski, Pr. Tva. 60
Sijwar, Babu, Ch. L., C.I.E. 807
Silanus, D. J., C. Ro. 46
—— M. J., C. Ro. 45
Silk, Wm., bp. Mth. 599
Sillery, Ch. Joc. Cec., gen. (**D**) 924
Sillitoe, Ad. W., bp. N. Westr. 698
Silo, K. Sp. 85
Silver, Alexr. Cr., gen. (**D**) 917
Silverius, P. Ro. 33
Silvester, *see* Sylvester
Sim, Dunc., gen. (**D**) 887
Simcocks, Th., dn. Cloy. 633
Simcoe, Jno. Gr., Amb. Pgl. 124; gen. (**B**) 866
Simeon and **Symeon**
—— -Breac, K. Ir. 20
—— Ch., adm. (**H**) 846
—— Geoff., dn. Chich. 434; dn. Linc. 448; M. Chy. 394
—— Jno., M. Chy. 397
Simmonds, *see also* Symonds
—— Wm., S.L. 408

Simmons, *see also* Symons
— Jno. Lint. Ar. and sir J., G.C.B. 771; G.C.M.G. 795; G. Mlta. 671; gen. (**D**) 902; K.C.B. 780
Simnevil, Jno. de, K.B. 754
***Simon,** bp. Dnbl. 532
*— bp. Dry. 601
*— bp. Gall. 538
*— bp. Isl. 539
*— (of Kilkenny), bp. Kild. 616
*— bp. Mor. 534
*— bp. Ross, 535
*— bp. Worc. 472
*— dn. Chich. 433
*— dn. Linc. 448
*— (abb. of Reading), J. It. 367
* Prob. some same pers. Comp. dates.
— (the Proud), R. Russ. 89
— Jno., K.C.B. 784; Pres. Coll. Surg. 939
— Jno., P.P. 418; S.L. 414
Simonds, *see* Symonds
Simons, *see* Symons
Simpkinson, Jno. Aug. F., K.C. 416
Simplicius, P. Ro. 33
Simpson and **Simson**
— Alexr. L., Mod. K. Sc. 547
— Benj., K.C.I.E. 805
— Cortl. Herb., adm. (**H**) 852
— Dav., gen. (**D**) 897
— Ed. and sir E., Ch. Lond. 422; D. Arch. 421; J. Pr. Ct. 421
— Ed. H., gen. (**D**) 879
— Frank, G. Lag. 687
— Geo. Wm. Y., gen. (**D**) 903
— Jas. and sir J., G.C.B. 769; gen. (**D**) 883
— Jas. Murr. Th., gen. (**D**) 934
— Jno., gen. (**D**) 905
— Jno., S.L. 410
— Rt., K.H. 789
— Th., Compt. Sc. 498
— Wm., Curs. B. Ex. 386
— Wm., gen. (**B**) 867
— Wm. Hy., G. Lag. 687
— W. S., gen. (**D**) 923
Sinclair, *see also* St. Clair
— Geo., Ld. Sess. 520
— Hy., bp. Ross, 535; L.P. Ct. Sess. 516; Ld. Sess. 518
— Jno., bp. Brn. 531; L.P. Ct. Sess. 516
— Jno., bp. Cness. 531
— Jno. (dean of Restalrig), Ld. Sess. 518
— sir Jno., P.C. 209
— hon. Jno. (Muckle), Ld. Sess. 520
— sir Jno. Gord., adm. (**D**) 828
— Patr., gen. (**B**) 866
— Patr., gen. (**C**) 872
— sir Rt., L.J. Clk. 516; Ld. Sess. 520
— Wm., bp. Dkld. 533
Sinell (St.), bp. Clr. 596
Singe, *see* Synge
Singer, Jos. Hend., bp. Mth. 599
— Morg., adm. (**H**) 853
— Wm., Mod. K. Sc. 547
Singh, Mahar. Dhul., K.C.S.I. 802
Singleton, Hy., C.J.C.P. Ir. 581; M.R. Ir. 585; S.L. Ir. 592
Singleton—*cont.*
— Jno., gen. (**D**) 894
— Jno., K.H. 792
— Jno., gen. (**D**) 913
— Mark, St. O., 260-1
Sinwell, Jno., bp. Linc. 446
Siorlamh, K. Ir. 20
Siorna-Saoghalach, K. Ir. 20
Sircar, Moh. Lall., C.I.E. 807
Sirdar-Ajit, C.I.E. 807
— Asad, &c., C.I.E. 806
— -Dewa, K.C.S.I. 803
Siricius, abp. Cant. 430; bp. Wltn. 466
— P. Ro. 33
Sirmur, Bah. of, G.C.S.I. 801
Sisebert, Sisibut, or Sisebuth, K. Sp. 85
Sisenando, K. Sp. 85
Sisinnius, P. Ro. 33
Siveyer, *see* Sever
Siward, bp. Roch. 459
Sixtus, I. to V., P. Ro. 32, 33, 35
Skardon, Ch. R., gen. (**D**) 886
Skeete, Jno. Br., G. Bdoes. 720
Skeffington, Th., bp. Bgr. 426
— sir Wm., L.D. Ir. 553
Skelmersdale, Ed., 2nd ld., aft. 1st E. of Lathom, *q.v.*, C.Y.G. 298; P.C. 219
Skelton, sir Bev., Lt. T.L. 322
— Hy., gen. (**B**) 865
— Jno., P. Laur. 300
Skene, Andr., S.G. Sc. 527
— Jas. and sir J., L.P. Ct. Sess. 516; Ld. Clk. Reg. 525; Ld. Sess. 519
— Jno. and sir J., Ld. Adv. 526; Ld. Clk. Reg. 525; Ld. Sess. 518
— Jno. Gord. C., gen. (**B**) 867
— Ph., gen. (**C**) 872
— Rt., gen. (**B**) 866
Skerk, Pet., K.B. 754
Skerrett, Jno., gen. (**B**) 867
— Jno. Burn., gen. (**C**) 873
Skerwing, Rog. de, bp. Norw. 454
Skey, Fc. Carp., Pres. Coll. Surg. 939
Skiddy, Rog., bp. Crk. and Cl. 631; dn. Lim. 639
Skilling, Michl., A.G. 398
Skinner and **Skynner**
— Allan M., C.C.J. 404; Q.C. 417
— Brindl., C. St. 283
— Jno., bp. Abdn. 541; Pr. Bp. Sc. 540
— Jno., gen. (**B**) 868
— Jno. and sir J., C.B. Ex. 382; J. Chest. 387; K.C. 415; P.C. 204; S.L. 412
— Matth., C.J. Chest. 386; S.L. 411
— Ph. K., gen. (**B**) 868
— Ph. K. McGr., gen. (**D**) 901
— Ralph, dn. Dham. 479
— Rt., bp. Brl. 439; bp. Oxf. 456; bp. Worc. 473
— Th., L.M. Lond. 491-2
— Wm., bp. Abdn. 541; Pr. Bp. Sc. 540
— Wm., gen. (**B**) 865
Skipp, *see* Skypp
Skipsey, Wm., adm. (**D**) 823
Skipton, Rd., M. Chy. 394
— Wm., dn. Killa. 614
Skipwith, sir Th., S.L. 410
— Wm. de, C.B. Ex. 381; C.J.K.B. Ir. 577; J.C.P. 377-8; K.B. 755; S.L. 406
Skirlaw or **Skirlow,** Walt., bp. B. and W. 428; bp. Dham. 478; bp. Lich. and Cov. 444; L.K. 354; M. Chy. 393
Skirrow, Walt., K.C. 416
Skrene, Wm., S.L. 407
Skynner, *see* Skinner
Skypp, Jno., bp. Her. 441
Skyring, Ch. Fras., gen. (**D**) 902
Slack, Ch. Maur., bp. Clr. 597
Slacke, Rd., Winds. H. 331
Slade, Adolph. and sir A., adm. (**E**) 835; (**F**) 838; K.C.B. 778
— Fk. Wm., Q.C. 417
— Herb. Daws., gen. (**D**) 924
— sir Jno., G.C.H. 787; gen. (**A**) 862
— Marc. Jno., G. Gsey. 669; gen. (**D**) 892
— Saml., dn. Chich. 434
— Th. and sir T., Sr. N. 257
— Wm. H., gen. (**D**) 889
Sladen, Ch., K.C.M.G. 797
— Jno. Rams., gen. (**D**) 911
Slake, Nichs., dn. Wells, 429
Slane, lds.
— Chr., 13th ld., L. Treas. Ir. 559
— Chr., 22nd ld., aft. 1st visc. Longford, *q.v.*, gen. (**C**) 871
Slaning, Nichs., K.B. 764
Slanoll, K. Ir. 20
Slany, sir Steph,, L.M. Lond. 491
Slaughter, Wm., adm. (**H**) 847; K.H. 791
Sledda, K.E. 2
Sleeman, Wm. H., gen. (**D**) 888; K.C.B. 782
Sleigh, Jas. Wall., gen. (**A**) 863; K.C.B. 778
— Wm. C., S.L. 414
Slessor, Jno., gen. (**D**) 881
Sley, Wm., dn. Arm. 597
Slight, Jul. Foulst., adm. (**H**) 851
Sligo, M. of
— Jno. Den., 1st M. of, form. E. of Altamont, *q.v.*
— Howe Pet., 2nd M. of, G. Jam. 713; K.P. 750; L.L. Mayo, 570; P.C. 212
Slingsby, Hy., M.M. 246-7
Sloane, Hans. and sir H., B.T. 266; Pres. R. Soc. 940
Sloper, Rt. and sir R., C.C. Ind. 650; C.C. Mdras. 657; gen. (**A**) 858; K.B. 765
— Wm., B.T. 265
Sluaig - O'Mail, bp. Lism. 626
Sluysken, Abr. Jos., G. C.G.H. 678
Slyfield, Jos. Cl. Sl., K.H. 792
Smalbroke, Rd., bp. Lich. and Cov. 444; bp. St. Dav. 465
Small, hon. Jno., G. Gsey. 669; gen. (**C**) 872
Smalley, Ed., gen. (**D**) 914
Smallridge or Smalridge
— Geo., bp. Brl. 439; dn. Carl. 476; dn. Chr. Ch. Oxf. 457
Smallwell, Ed., bp. Oxf. 456; bp. St. Dav. 465
— Matth., dn. Lich. 445

Smalridge, *see* Smallridge
Smart, Geo., gen. (**D**) 926
— Jas., gen. (**D**) 886
— Rt. and sir R., adm. (**D**) 831; (**E**) 834; K.C.B. 779; K.H. 790
— Wm. Rd. Ed., K.C.B. 780
Smedley, Jonn., dn. Clr. 597; dn. Killa. 614
Smee, Wm. Nug. Th., gen. (**D**) 891
Smelt, Corn., G. I. Man, 666
— Leon., Clk. O. 260
— Wm., gen. (**D**) 880
Smerdis, K. Pers. 99
Smert (or Swertz), Jno. Gart. K.A. 327
Smith, *see also* Smyth and Smythe
— Alb., K.C.M.G. 797
— Ad., C. Cus. Sc. 504
— Andr., adm. (**A**) 819
— Andr., K.C.B. 782
— Archd. Lev. and sir A., J.Q.B.D. 374
— Arthr., abp. Dbln. and Gl. 616; bp. Clonf. and K. 636; bp. Down and Cnr. 604; bp. Mth. 599; dn. Dry. 602; dn. Rph. 602
— Cecil Clem. and sir C., G. Ceyl. 673; G. Str. Sett. 675; K.C.M.G. 798
— Ch., adm. (**H**) 848
— Ch., gen. (**D**) 900
— Ch., L.G. Gr. Hosp. 854
— Ch. B. Euan-, Amb. Zr. 132
— Ch. Doug., G. Pr. Ed. Isl. 699
— Ch. Fk., gen. (**D**) 912
— sir Ch. F., G. Trin. 722; gen. (**D**) 879; K.C.B. 777
— Ch. Ham., K.H. 790
— Ch. Hodg., gen. (**D**) 915
— Chr., L.M. Lond. 492
— Clem. Jno., gen. (**D**) 935
— Colin, Mod. K. Sc. 547
— Culling Ch., C. Cus. 277; U.S.F. 229
— Don., L. Prov. Edinb. 548
— Don. Alex., K.C.M.G. 798
— D. T., G.T. and C.Isl. 713
— Edmd. Davidson, gen. (**D**) 932
— Ed., bp. Down and Cnr. 604; dn. St. Pat. 618
*— Ed., G. I. Man, 666
*— Ed., gen. (**A**) 859
* ? same pers.
— sir Ed., C.J.C.P. Ir. 580
— Ed. Fras., Q.C. 418
— Ed. Tyrr., adm. (**A**) 817
— Edwin Th., K.C.M.G. 799
— Fras., gen. (**B**) 866
— sir Fras., G. Tasm. 708
— Fk. Harris, adm. (**H**) 852
— Fk. Hy., gen. (**D**) 914
— Fk. Nep., gen. (**D**) 913
— Geo., B. Ex. Ir. 584; C. Acc. Ir. 567
— Geo., bp. Vict. (H.K.) 674
— Geo., C.I.E. 806
— Geo., Chn. E.I. Co. 645
— Geo. Str., G. N. Brk. 795; gen. (**C**) 873
— Ham. Ch., gen. (**D**) 915
— Hav., gen. (**C**) 873
— Hy., adm. (**D**) 830; (**E**) 834; K.C.B. 780
— Hy., gen. (**B**) 866
— Hy., gen. (**D**) 888

Smith—*cont.*
— Hy. Geo. W. and sir H., G.C.B. 769; G. C.G.H. 679; gen. (**D**) 881; K.C.B. 777
— Hugh, K.B. 764
— Jas., Modr. K. Sc. 547
— sir Jas., L.M. Lond. 491
— Jas. Carm., *see* Smyth
— Jas Rd. Bullen, M.C.I. 647
— Jas. Webb., gen. (**D**) 879
— Jas. Webb., gen. (**D**) 900
— sir Jer., adm. (**A**) 813
— Jno. (No. 1), B. Ex. 384
— Jno. (No. 2), B. Ex. 384; S.L. 411
— Jno., bp. Killa. and Ach. 613; dn. Lim. 639
— Jno., bp. Llff. 449
*— Jno., C. Exc. 279
*— Jno., Ch. Ex. 165; L.T. 155; P.C. 194; Sp. H.C. 250
* Poss. same pers.
— Jno., gen. (**C**) 872
— Jno., L.M. Dbln. 640
— Jno., P.C. 197; Tell. Ex. 167
— sir Jno., G.C.H. 786; gen. (**A**) 862
— Jno. Fk. Sig. and sir J., gen. (**C**) 874; K.C.H. 788
— Jno. Geo. S., C.C.J. 403
— Jno. Louis, gen. (**D**) 893
— sir Jno. Mark Fk., gen. (**D**) 885; K.H. 789
— Jno. Nichs., gen. (**D**) 876
— Jno. S., Amb. Tky. 129
— Jno. Wm., K.C.B. 779
— Jno. Wm. Sidn., gen. (**D** 904
— Jos. Alexr., gen. (**D**) 926
— Jos. Grace, C.C.J. 403
— Josh. Jonn., L.M. Lond. 492
— Josh. Simm., gen. (**D**) 896
— Josiah Wm., C.C.J. 404; Q.C. 418
— Lionel and sir L., G. Bah. Isl. 716; G. Bdoes. &c. 719-20; G. Br. Gu. 715; G. Mtius. 683; G. Jam. 713; G. St. Luc. 725; G. Trin. 722; G.C.B. 772; G.C.H. 787; gen. (**B**) 869; K.C.B. 775
— Luml., Q.C. 419
— Marc., gen. (**C**) 871
— Matth., gen. (**D**) 898
— Michl. and sir M., B. Ex. Ir. 584; M.R. Ir. 585
— Michl. Wm., gen. (**D**) 899
— Miles, bp. Glr. 438
— Mont. Ed. and sir M., J.C.P. 380; Jud. Com. P.C. 361; P.C. 218; Q.C. 417; S.L. 414
— Nathl., Chn. E.I. Co. 644
— Nathl., L.G. Ch. Hosp. 936
— Nathl. Bowden, adm. (**E**) 837
— Nichs., M. Chy. and Acct. G. 397
— Oct. Ludl., gen. (**D**) 935
— Perc. Guill. Ll., gen. (**D**) 934
— Pet., K.C.M.G. 796
— Ph., gen. (**D**) 930
— Rd. Hort., Q.C. 419
— Rt. Mard., K.C.M.G. 799
— Rt. Payne, dn. Cant. 432
— Rt. Vern., aft. ld. Lyveden, *q.v.*, L.T. 160; P.C. 214; Pres. B.C. 254; Sec. at W. 234; Sec. B.C. 254; U.S.W. and C. 231

Smith—*cont.*
— Saml., G. I. Man, 666
— Saml., gen. (**D**) 881
— Saml., dn. Chr. Ch. Oxf. 457
— Th., adm. (**A**) 814
— Th., bp. Carl. 476; dn Carl. 476
— Th., L.M. Lond. 492
— Th., aft. 1st visc. Strangford, *see* Smythe
— sir Th., Chanc. Gart. 745; S. St. 223
— sir Th., dn. Carl. 476
— Th. Assh., L.L. Carn. 314
— Th. Berry Cusack, A.G. Ir. 588; M.R. Ir. 585; S.G. Ir. 590
— Th. Charlton, gen. (**D**) 897
— Th. Ed., adm. (**H**) 853
— Th. Hatch., gen. (**D**) 878
— Th. Park., gen. (**D**) 930
— Th. Patr., gen. (**D**) 879
— Wm., bp. Killa. and Ach. 613; bp. Kilm. and Ard. 607; bp. Rph. 601; dn. Drom. 606
— Wm., bp. Lich. and Cov. 444; bp. Linc. 447
— Wm., dn. Chest. 477
— Wm., gen. (**D**) 931
— Wm., L.M. Dbln. 640
— Wm., R. Dr. P.A. 338
— Wm. Cusack and sir W., B. Ex. Ir. 584; S.G. Ir. 589
— Wm. Fk. Haynes, G. Br. Gu. 715; G. Leew. Isl. 728
— Wm. Hy., Ch. Sec. Ir. 563; L. Admy. 185; L.T. 162; P.C. 219; Sec. Tr. 164; W. Sec. 232
— Wm. Sydn., adm. (**G**) 842
— sir Wm. Sidn., adm. (**A**) 817; G.C.B. 769; K.C.B. 773
Smith-King, *see* King
Smith-Stanley, *see* Stanley and E. of Derby
Smollett, Jno. Rou., adm. (**D**) 824
Smurily, *see* Imurily
Smyly, Andr. Ferg., dn. Dry. 602
— Jno. Ber., gen. (**D**) 915
— Ph. Aust., gen. (**D**) 894
Smyth, *see also* Smythe and Smith
— Ed. Selb. and sir E., G. Mtius. 684; gen. (**D**) 903; K.C.M.G. 797
— (or Smith), Geo., B. Ex. Ir. 584; C. Acc. Ir. 56
— Geo., Ld. Sess. 519
— Hy., gen. (**D**) 903
— Hy. Augs., gen. (**D**) 925
— sir Jas. Carm., G. Bah. Isl. 716; G. Br. Gu. 715; gen. (**C**) 875; K.C.H. 787
— Jas. Gibb., gen. (**D**) 934
— Jas. Rowl., *see* Jno. Rowl.
— Jno., B.T. 268; L. Admy. 180; L.T. 158; M.M. 247; P.C. 207
— Jno., J.C.P. Ir. 581
— Jno. Hall, gen. (**D**) 910
— Jno. Hy., U.S. Home, 227
— Jno. Nug., G. Br. Hond. 714; G. N. Sc. 695; gen. (**C**) 874
— Jno. (or Jas.) Rowl., gen. (**D**) 895; K.C.B. 779
— hon. Leic. and sir L., G. C.G.H. &c. 679; gen. (**D**) 905; K.C.B. 781; K.C.M.G. 798
— Rd., L.M. Dbln. 641

Smyth—*cont.*
— Spenc., adm. (**H**) 849
— Th., bp. Lim., A. and A. 639; dn. Emly, 628
— Wm., adm. (**G**) 843
— Wm. Hy., adm. (**H**) 846
— Wm. Pow. St., gen. (**D**) 913
Smythe, *see also* Smyth and Smith
— Dav., Ld. Sess. 520
— Fk. Wm., K.C.M.G. 799
— hon. Geo. A. F. P. S., aft. visc. Strangford, *q.v.*, U.S.F. 230
— hon. Ph. Syd., dn. Dry. 602
— hon. Sidn. Staff. and sir S., B. Ex. 385; C.B. Ex. 382; C.G.S. 357; K.C. 415; P.C. 203; S.L. 412
— Th., aft. 1st visc. Strangford, *q.v.*, K.B. 763
— Th. (Bp.), *see* Smyth
— Wm., dn. Ardf. 640
— Wm, Jas., gen. (**D**) 904
Smythes, Jesse, S.G. Ir. 589
Smythies, Ch. Acan., bp. C. Afr. 688
Snagg and **Snagge**
— Th., A.G. Ir. 588; S.L. 408; Sp. H.C. 249
— Th. W., C.C.J. 405
Snape (or Sanope), Rd., K.B. 755
Sneath, Wm., K.B. 760
Snedbran, bp. Kild. 616
Snell, Th., bp. Oss. 620; bp. Wford. and L. 626
Sneterby, Reg., B. Ex. Ir. 583
Sneyd, Clem., adm. (**H**) 844
— Th. Wm., gen. (**D**) 933
Snigge, sir Geo., B. Ex. 384; S.L. 409
Snodgrass, K., G. N.S.W. 703; G. V.D. Ld. 708
Snow, Th. Rochf., gen. (**D**) 923
— Wm., dn. Brl. 440
Snowdon, Rt., bp. Carl. 475
Snyterton, Th. de, J. It. 369
Soady, Brooking, gen. (**D**) 929
— Jno. Clark, adm. (**E**) 836
Soame (or Some), sir Steph., L.M. Lond. 491
Soanes, Jos., L.G. Gr. Hosp. 854
Sobhair, K.E. 20
Sobiestas I. and II., D. Bma. 59
Socche, Godw., M.M. 245
Sodington, sir Rd., L.H.T. 153
— Th., *see* Sadington
Sogdianus, K. Pers. 99
Soilly, Hy. de, bp. Worc. 472
Solvathius, K. Sc. 18
Solyman, Sh. Pers. 99
— I. to III., S. Tky. 97
Some, *see* Soame
Somer, Hy., B. Ex. 383
Somers, Jno., *see* ld. S., *infra*
— Rd., C. Cus. 275; C. Cus. Sc. 504; C. Exc. Sc. 504
Somers, lds. and E.
Somers Family.
— Jno., aft. sir J. and ld. S., A.G. 399; L.H.S. 286; L.P.C. 188; Ld. Chanc. 357; L.K. 357; P.C. 194; Pres. R. Soc. 940; Rec. Lond. 494; S.G. 401
Somers, lds. and E.—*cont.*
Cocks and Somers-Cocks Families.
— Chas., 1st ld., form. sir C. Cocks
— Jno., 2nd ld., aft. 1st E. S., L.L. Heref. 308
— Jno., 2nd E., L.L. Heref. 308
Somerset, Ch. (3rd son of Edw., 4th E. of Worc.), K.B. 762
— sir Ch., 1st ld. Herb. and E. of Worcester, *q.v.*, C.Y.G. 298; K.G. 737; L.C.H. 294
— ld. Ch. Hy., G.C.G.H. 679; Compt. H. 293; gen. (**A**) 860; P.C. 206; Paym. G. 244
— Ed. (4th son of Edw., 4th E. of Worc.), K.B. 762
— Ed. Arth., gen. (**D**) 904
— ld. Fitzr. Jas. Hy., aft. ld. Raglan, *q.v.*, Amb. Fr. 113; G.C.B. 769; K.C.B. 775; M.G.O. 259
— ld. Gr. Ch. Hy., C.D.L. 243; C.W.F., &c. 272; L.T. 159-60; P.C. 213
— Gr. Rt. Hy., Q.C. 418
— Hy. de, dn. Exr. 437
— Hy. and sir H., C.C. Bbay. 660; gen. (**D**) 883; K.C.B. 777; K.H. 790
— ld. Hy. Rd. Ch., Compt. H. 293; P.C. 219
— Lev. El. Hy., adm. (**E**) 836
— ld. Rt. Ed. Hy., G.C.B. 768; gen. (**A**) 862; K.C.B. 774; L.G.O. 259; S.G.O. 260
— Th., aft. visc. Cashel, *q.v.*, K.B. 761
Somerset, E., M., and D. of; *see also* Nottingham and Richmond
Beaufort Family.
— Jno., 1st E. and M. of, form. sir J. Beaufort, *q.v.*, aft. M. of Dorset, *q.v.*
— Jno., 3rd E., aft. D. of, also E. of Kendal, *q.v.*, K.G. 735
— Ed., 4th E., aft. D. of, form. E. of Morton and E. of Dorset, *q.v.*; W.C.P. 318
Fitzroy Family.
— Hy. (nat. son of Hen. VIII.) D. of Richmond and G., also E. of Nottingham, *q.v.*
Carr Family.
— Rt., E. of, form. Rt. Carr and visc. Rochester, *q.v.*; L.C.H. 294; L.H.T. Sc. 497
Seymour Family.
— Ed., 1st D. of (cr. 1547), form. 1st E. of Hertford, *q.v.*; E.M. 326; K.B. 760; L.W.S. 323
— Wm. 2nd D. of, form. M. of Hertford, *q.v.*
— Ch., 6th D. of, K.G. 740; L.P.C. 188; M.H. 302; P.C. 194
— Alg., 7th D. of, form. ld. Percy, *q.v.*, also E. of Hertford and E. of Northbd., *q.v.*, gen. (**A**) 857; L.L. Suss. 312
— Ed., 9th D. of, P.C. 202
— Ed. Adolph., 11th D. of, K.G. 743; Pres. R. Inst. 940
— Ed. Adolph., 12th D. of, form. ld. Seymour, *q.v.*, K.G. 744; L. Admy. 184; L.L. Dev. 307
— Eliz., Dss. of, Gr. St. and M. Robes, 303
Somerton, Ed., S.L. Ir. 591
Somerton, visc.
— Ch., 1st visc., form. Ch. Agar, *q.v.*, aft. 1st E. of Normanton, *q.v.*, abp. Dbln. and Gl. 616
Somerville, Jas., L.M. Dbln. 641
— Ph., adm. (**H**) 850
— sir Wm. Mered., aft. 1st ld. Athlumny and ld. Meredyth, *q.v.*, Ch. Sec. Ir. 563; P.C. 215; U.S. Home, 228
Somerton, lds.
— Kenelm., 17th ld., adm. (**H**) 845
Sommers, *see* Somers
Sonnenberg, I., bar. de, gen. (**C**) 874
Sontag, Jno., gen. (**B**) 867
Soofe, Sh. Pers. 99
Sophia (dau. Jas. I.), Pr. E. 13
— (the Electress—g. dau. Jas. I.), Pr. E. 13
— (dau. Geo. III.), Pr. E. 15
— (D. of Zell.), Q.C.E. 8
— -Charlotte (iss. Jas. I.), Pr. E. 13
— -Dorothea (dau. Geo. I.), Pr. E. 14
— -Dor. Ulr. Alice (g. dau. Q. Vict.), Pr. E. 15
— -Matilda (iss. Geo. II.), Pr. E. 14
Sophus, P. S., C. Ro. 41-2
Soppitt, Matt., gen. (**D**) 887
Sorel and **Sorell**
— Hy. Andr., gen. (**D**) 920
— sir Th. St., K.H. 790
— Wm., G.V.D. Ld. 708
— Wm. Alexr., gen. (**B**) 865
Sorewell, Wm. de, J. It. 367
Sorrell, *see* Sorell
Sosius, C., C. Ro. 47
Sotehill, *see* Sotill
Soterus, P. Ro. 32
Sotheby, Ch., adm. (**D**) 828
— Ed. Southw., adm. (**E**) 835; (**F**) 839; K.C.B. 780
— Fk. Ed., gen. (**D**) 933
— Th., adm. (**A**) 817
Sothern, *see also* Southern
— Jno., J.K.B. Ir. 578
Sotheron, Frank, adm. (**A**) 818
Sotheron-Estcourt, *see* Estcourt
Sotherton, *see* Southerton
Sotill, Ger., K.B. 756
— (or Sotehill), Hy., A.G. 398
Soto, B., Pres. C.R. 106
— M. A., Pres. Hdas. 106
Soublette, C., Pres. Vzla. 107
Souillac, Vicomte de, G. Mtius. 683
Soulouque, F., Pres. and Emp. Hti. 105
Soult, Off. Nap. 26
Sourindio, &c., C.I.E. 806
Souter, *see also* Suter
— sir Frank Hy., C.I.E. 807
South, Jno. Fl., Pres. Coll. Surg. 939
Southampton, lds., E. and D. of
Fitzwilliam Family.
— Wm., 1st E of, form. sir Wm. Fitzwilliam, *q.v.*; L.H.A. 174; L.P.S. 240; K.H. 291

Southampton, lds., E. and D. of —*cont.*
Wriothesley Family.
— Thos., 1st E. of, form. ld. Wriothesley, *q.v.*
— Hy., 3rd E. of, K.G. 739
— Thos., 4th E. of, B.T. 263; E.M. 326; K.G. 740; L.H.T. and L.T. 155; P.C. 189
Fitzroy Family.
1st Creation.
— Ch. Fitzr., 1st E. of, aft. 1st D. of S. and of Cleveland, *q.v.*, K.G. 740
2nd Creation.
— Ch., 1st ld., gen. (**A**) 858
— Geo. F., 2nd ld., gen. (**B**) 866
— Ch., 3rd ld., L.L. Nton. 310
Southcote, Jno., J.Q.B. 372; S.L. 408
Southern, *see also* Sothern
— Hy., Amb. Arg. 136; Amb. Bzl. 135
— Jas., Sec. Admy. 186
Southerton and **Sotherton**
— Jno., B.E. 384; Curs. B. Ex. 386
— Now., Curs. B. Ex. 386
Southesk, Jas., E. of, form. sir Jas. Carnegie, *q.v.*, K.T. 749
Southey, Rd., G. Gr. Ld. W. 681
— Rt., P. Laur. 301
Southgate, Th., Q.C. 418
Southwell, Ch., K.H. 789
— Ed. (No. 1), L.P.S. 240; Sec. St. Ir. 562
— Ed. (No. 2), Sec. St. Ir. 562
— Rd., dn. Ardf. 640
— Rt. and sir R., B.T. 263; C. Cus. 274; C. Exc. 278; Pres. R. Soc. 940; Sec. St. Ir. 562
— sir Rt., M.R. 388
Southwell, visc.
— Th. Anthy., 3rd. visc., K.P. 751
— Th. Arth. Jos., 4th visc., K.P. 751; L.L. Leitr. 570
Souwche, *see* Zouch
Sowerby, Jas., gen. (**B**) 866
Sowler, Rt. Scarr., Q.C. 418
Spaigne, Nichs. de, M. Chy. 393
Spain, Dav., adm. (**H**) 851
Spakeston, Rd. de, dn. Wells, 428
Spaldewick, Wm. de, J. It. 368
Spalding, Jno. de, J. It. 368
Spankie, Rt., P.P. 416; S.L. 413
Sparke, Bowy. Ed., bp. Chest. 477; bp. Ely, 435; dn. Brl. 440
— Jas. Patt., gen. (**D**) 900
— Th., bp. suff. Berw. 479
— sir Wm., J.K.B. Ir. 579
Sparkford, Th., bp. Wford. and L. 626
Sparrow, Anthy., bp. Exr. 437; bp. Norw. 455
Sparshott, Ed., adm. (**H**) 847; K.H. 789
Spearman, Alex. Y. and sir A., P.C. 218; Sec. Tr. 164
Speed, Wm., Q.C. 420
Speeke, *see* Speke
Speechley, Jno. Mart., bp. Tr. and Coch. 676
Speke and **Speeke**
— Geo., K.B. 761
— Jno., K.B. 759
Spelman, Clem., Curs. B. Ex. 386
— Jno., J.K.B. 372; S.L. 408
Spence, Fk., gen. (**D**) 898
— Geo., K.C. 416
— Hy. D. M., dn. Glr. 440
— Jas. Kn., gen. (**D**) 916
— Jno., Compt. Sc. 498
— Jno., Ld. Adv. 526; Ld. Sess. 518
— Th., bp. Abdn. 530; bp. Gall. 538; L.P.S. Sc. 509
Spencer, *see also* Spenser
— Aubr. Geo., bp. Jam. 713; bp. Newfd. 700
— hon. Aug. Almer. and sir A., C.C. Bbay. 660; G.C.B. 770; gen. (**D**) 894; K.C.B. 779
— Brent. and sir B., G.C.B. 767; gen. (**A**) 861; K.B. 766
— ld. Ch., Compt. H. 292; L. Admy. 179; M.M. 247; P.C. 201; Postm. G. 238; Tr. Ch. 294; V. Treas. Ir. 560
— ld. Fras. A., B.C. 252
— Geo. Trev., bp. Mdras. 658
— Giles, G. Gsey. 668
— Hy. le, bp. Norw. 455
— ld. Hy. Jno., Amb. Nds. &c. 122; Amb. Pr. 118; Amb. Sw. 126
— sir Hugh de, aft. E. of Gloucester (?), *q.v.*, W.C.P. 318
— sir Jas., L.M. Lond. 490
— Jno., Adm. Ind. 648
— Jno., dn. Ely, 435
— sir Jno., L.M. Lond. 491
— hon. Jno. Welbore Sunderland, adm. (**E**) 836; (**F**) 839
— sir Rd., K.C.H. 788
— ld. Rt., B.T. 266; P.C. 203; S.W.F. 271; V. Treas. Ir. 560
— hon. Rt. Cav., K.C.H. 787
— Wm., gen. (**B**) 867
— Wm., *see* ld. Sp., *infra*
— Wm. Rt., C. St. 284
Spencer of Wormleighton, lds.
— Wm., aft. 1st ld. Sp., K.B. 762
Spencer of Althorpe, E.
— Geo. Jno., 2nd E., Amb. Gmy. 117; H. Sec. 227; K.G. 743; Ld. Admy. 180; L.P.S. 241; P.C. 206; Pres. R. Inst. 940
— Jno. Ch., 3rd E., form. visc. Althorpe, *q.v.*
— Fk., 4th E., adm. (**G**) 841; K.G. 744; L.C.H. 295; L.S.H. 290; P.C. 215
— Jno. Poyntz., 5th E., Jud. Com. P.C. 361; K.G. 744; L.L. Ir. 558; L.L. Nton. 310; L.P.C. 188; P.C. 216
Spens, Andr., gen. (**D**) 890
— Jno., gen. (**B**) 867
Spenser, *see also* Spencer
— Edm., P. Laur. 301
Sphothad, Ld. Chanc. Sc. 514
Spicer, Alexr., dn. Killoe. 637
— Wm., M. Chy. 396
Spiers, Alexr., L.L. Renfw. 511
Spigurnell, Hy., J.K.B. 371; S.L. 406
— sir Ralph, L.H.A. 172; W.C.P. 318
Spiller, Rd., C. Exc. 281
Spink, Jno.. gen. (**D**) 884; K.H. 791
Spinks, Fk. L., S.L. 414
— Th., Q.C. 418
Spinther, P. C. L., C. Ro. 46
Spitigneus I. and II., D.Bma. 59
Spittal, Jas. and sir J., L. Prov. Edinb. 548; Lt. Edinb. 509
Spofford or **Spofforth,** Th., bp. Her. 441; bp. Roch. 460
Spooner, Jno., G. Bdoes. 720
— Wm., C.C.J. 404
Spot, Nin., Compt. Sc. 498
Spottiswood, Jas., bp. Clr. 596
— Jno., abp. Glasg. 537; abp. St. Andr. 529; Ld. Chanc. Sc. 515; Ld. Sess. 517
— Molyn. Cap., gen. (**D**) 916
— sir Rt., L.P. Ct. Sess. 516; Ld. Sess. 517, 519; Sec. St. Sc. 502
— Wm., Pres. R. Soc. 940
Spraggs, sir Ed., adm. (**A**) 813
Spranger, Jno., M. Chy. 397
— Jno. Wm., adm. (**A**) 819
Sprat and **Spratt**
— Th., bp. Roch. 460; dn. Westr. 469
— Th. Ab. Br., adm. (**H**) 849
Spridelington (or Sprinlington), Wm. de, bp. St. As. 462; dn. St. As. 463
Sprigg, Jno. Gord., K.C.M.G. 798
Spring-Rice, *see* Rice
Springthorpe, Jno., M. Chy. 394
Sprinlington, *see* Spridelington
Sprint, Jno., dn. Brl. 440
Springthorpe, Jno., C.D.L. 242
Sprot, Jno., gen. (**D**) 928
Sprotton, Jno., bp. S. and M. 483
Sproule, Flower M., gen. (**C**) 873
Spry, Ch., *see* Wm.
— Hor., gen. (**B**) 866
— sir Rd., adm. (**A**) 814
— Th. Dav., adm. (**A**) 816
— Wm. (? Ch.), G. Bdoes. 720
— Wm., gen. (**B**) 866
— Wm. Fk., gen. (**C**) 873
Spurgin, Jno. Bl., gen. (**D**) 909
Spurinus, Q. P., C. Ro. 44
Spurling, Jno., S.L. 408
Spynie, Wm., bp. Mor. 534
Squibb, Arth., Clar. K.A. 328
— L., Tell. Ex. 168
Squire, Matth., adm. (**A**) 816
— Saml., bp. St. Dav. 465; dn. Brl. 440
Stack, Ed., gen. (**A**) 861
— Geo. FitzG., K.H. 792
— Jno., bp. Ardf. and Agh. 639
— Maur., gen. (**D**) 888; K.C.B 779
— Nath. Mass., gen. (**D**) 893
Stackpoole, Wm. Hy., dn. Kilf. 637
Stafford, —, K.B. 757
— Aug. O'Brien, Sec. Adm. 187
— Edm., bp. Exr. 436

Stafford—*cont.*
— Edm., Ld. Chanc. 354-5
— Edm., *see* E. of S., *infra*
— Ed., aft. D. of Buckingham, *q.v.*, K.B. (1485) 758
— Ed. Wm. and sir E., G.C.M.G. 795; K.C.M.G. 797
— Hugh (bro. to E. of St.), K.B. (1400) 755
— Jno., abp. Cant. 431; bp. B. and W. 428; dn. Wells, 429; L.H.T. 153; Ld. Chanc. 355
— Jno., dn. Oss. 622
— Jno., gen. (**C**) 875
— Jno., aft. E. of Wiltshire, *q.v.*, K.B. (1461) 756
— Jno. Fras., gen. (**D**) 914
— Nichs., bp. Ferns and L. 622
— Ralph, *see* ld. S., *infra*
— sir Th., M.G.O. 258
— Wm. Josh. Fitzm., gen. (**D**) 919
Stafford, lds., E., and M. of
Stafford Family.
— Ralph de, aft. 10th ld. and 1st E. of S., K.B. 755; K.G. 733
— Hugh, 2nd E. of, K.G. 734
— Th., 3rd E. of, K.B. 755
— Edm., 5th E. of, K.B. 755; K.G. 734
— Humph., 6th E. of, K.B. 756; K.G. 735
— Hy., ld. (son of 7th E.), aft. 1st E. of Wiltshire, *q.v.*, K.G. 737
Gower Family.
— Gr., 1st M. of, form. 2nd E. Gower, *q.v.*
— G. Gr. L., 2nd M. of, form. 3rd E. Gower, *q.v.*, aft. 1st D. of Sutherland, *q.v.*, K.G. 743
— Geo. Gr., M. of, form. E. Gower, *q.v.*, aft. 2nd D. of Sutherland, *q.v.*
— Geo. Gr. Wm., &c., M. of, aft. 3rd D. of Sutherland. *q.v.*, L.L. Crom. 509
Stag, Jno., B. Ex. 383
Stainer, *see* Stayner and Stanier
Staines, sir Th., K.C.B. 774
— sir Wm., L.M. Lond. 492
Stainforth, Ch. Rap., gen. (**D**) 923
— Fras. Geo., gen. (**D**) 914
Staingrave, Ad. de, J.C.P. 377; J.K.B. 371
Stair, visc.
— Jas., 1st visc., form. sir Jas. Dalrymple, *q.v.*
— Jno., 2nd visc. and 1st E. of, form. sir Jno. Dalrymple, *q.v.*
— Jno., 2nd E. of, form. visc. Dalrymple, *q.v.*, C. Ch. 855; F.M. 856; K.T. 747; P.C. 196; V.A. Sc. 499
— Wm., 4th E. of, also 4th E. of Dumfries, K.T. 747
— Jno. Ham., 8th E. of, form. sir J. H. Dalrymple, *q.v.*, K.T. 748; L.K. Sc. 503
— Jno. Ham., 10th E. of, form. visc. Dalrymple, *q.v.*, K.T. 749; L.H.C.K. Sc. 546; L.L. Ayrsh. 508
Staley, Th. Nett., bp. Honol. 712
Stalker, Foster, gen. (**D**) 887
Stallard, Saml. gen. (**D**) 920

Stamer, sir Lovel, bp. suff. Shrewsb. 444
— sir Wm., L.M. Dbln. 641
Stamford, Rog., Chest. H. 330
— Taur. de, dn. St. P. 452
Stamford, E. of
— Th., 2nd E. of, B.T. 263; C.D.L. 242; P.C. 194; Pres. B.C. 263
— [and Warrington], Geo. Harry, 5th E. of, L.L. Chesh. 306
— [and Warrington], Geo. Harry, 6th E. of, L.L. Chesh. 306-7
Stamp, sir Th., L.M. Lond. 491
Stämpfli, J., Pres. Sw. C. 31
Stanbery, Stanberry or **Stanbury,** Jno., bp. Bgr. 426; bp. Her. 441; bp. Norw. 455
Standish, M. Chy. 395
— Hy., bp. St. As. 462
— Jas., V. Treas. Ir. 559
Stanes, Rd. de, J.C.P. 377; J. It. 368; J.K.B. 371; Jy. 365
Stanhope, Arth., dn. Wford. 628
— Ch., *see* ld. S., *infra*
*— Ch., U.S.S. 225
*— hon. Ch., Tr. Ch. 294
* Prob. same pers.
— hon. Ch. Banks, Reg. and Sec. Bath, 784
*— sir Ed., Ch. Lond. 422; M. Chy. 395; Vic. Gen. 421
*— Ed., K.B. 761
* ? same pers.
— hon. Ed., C. Sec. 235; P.C. 220; Pres. B.T. 269; Sec. B.T. 269; U.S. Ind. 236; V.P. Ed. 255; W. Sec. 232
— Geo., dn. Cant. 431
— Hy., adm. (**H**) 846
— Hy. (son of Ph., ld. S.), K.B. 763
— Hy. Edwin, adm. (**A**) 817
— Jas., *see* Earl S., *infra*
— Jno., adm. (**A**) 816
— hon. Jno., L. Admy. 178
— Jno., *see* ld. S., *infra*
— hon. Linc., gen. (**D**) 877
— Lovel, U.S.S. 226
— Ph., Amb. G. St. 121; Amb. H. Tns. 120; Amb. Sxy. 120
— Ph. D., *see* ld. S., *infra*
— Ph. Spenc., gen. (**D**) 885
— Wm., K.B. 764
— Wm., aft. 1st ld. and E. of Harrington, *q.v.*, P.C. 197; V.C.H. 297
Stanhope of Harrington, lds.
— sir Jno., aft. 1st ld. S., V.C.H. 296
— Ch., aft. 2nd ld., K.B. 762
Stanhope of Elvaston and Mahon, lds., visc., and E.
— Jas., aft. 1st ld., visc., and Earl S., Ch. Ex. 165; gen. (**B**) 864; L.T. 156; P.C. 196; Prem. 141; S. St. 224
— Ph. Hy., 5th E. of, form. visc. Mahon, *q.v.*
Stanhope of Chesterfield, lds.
— Ph. D., ld., aft. 4th E. of Chesterfield, *q.v.*, C.Y.G. 298
Stanian, Temple, U.S.S. 225
Stanier (or Stainer), sir Saml., L.M. Lond. 491
Stanihurst, Jas., Rec. Dbln. 642

Stanislaus, D. Lne. 30
— I. and II., K. Pld. 91
Stanley, Arth. Penr., dn. West. 469
— C., G. I. Man, 666
— Ch. (g. son of 8th E. of Derby), K.B. 763
*— Edm., C. Acc. Ir. 567
*— Edm., S.L. Ir. 592
* Prob. same pers.
— sir Edm., C.J. Mdras. 658
— Ed., adm. (**G**) 842
— Ed., bp. Norw. 455
— Ed., K.B. 761
— Ed., Pres. Coll. Surg. 939
— Ed. G., *see* ld. St. of Bick., *infra*
— Ed. Hy., *see* ld. St. of Bick., *infra*
— Ed. Jno., *see* ld. St. of Ald., *infra*
— F. A., *see* d. St. of Prest. *infra*
— Geo., G. I. Man, 666
— Geo., K.B. 757
— Hans, Amb. Fr. 112; Amb. Russ. 125; Coff. H. 294; L. Admy. 179; P.C. 201
— Hy. (2), G. I. Man, 666
— Jas., bp. Ely, 435; Wdn. Chr. Ch. Manch. 481; bp. S. and M. 483
— Jas., M. Chy. 397
— Jno., G. Antig. 728
— Jno. and sir J., C. Cus. 274-5; C. St. 283
— sir Jno. (*d.* 1414), Const. W. Cast. 322; K.G. 734; K. Man, 665; L.L. Ir. 552
— sir Jno., K. Man (1414), 665
— sir Jno., Tell. Ex. (1700) 167
— Rand., G. I. Man, 666
— Rt., K.B. 763
— Th., bp. S. and M. 483
*— Th., dn. Wells, 429
*— Th., M.R. 387
* Prob. same pers.
— Th., G. I. Man (1663) 666
— sir Th., C.D.L. 242
— sir Th., G. I. Man (1537) 666
— sir Th., G. I. Man (1562) 666
— sir Th., L.L. Ir. (1431) 552
— sir Th., M.M. (1539) 246
— Th., *see* ld. St., *infra*
— Wm., dn. St. As. 463
— Wm., G. I. Man, 666
— Wm., K.B. 757
— sir Wm., L.D. Ir. 552
— Wm., aft. ld. Monteagle, *q.v.*, K.B. (1533) 760
— sir Wm., Ch. Ex. 154; K.G. 736; L.C.H. 294
— Wm., aft. 6th E. of Derby, *q.v.*, G. I. Man, 666
— Wm., *see* ld. St., *infra*
— Wm. Dac., gen. (**D**) 912
— hon. Wm. Owen, L.L.Ang. 314
— Wm. Pearce, adm. (**H**) 847
Stanley, lds., *see also* Strange and Derby
— Th., ld., aft. 1st ld. St. (*d.* 1459), K.G. 736; K. Man, 665
— Th., ld., aft. 1st E. of Derby, *q.v.*, 736
— Th., aft. ld. Strange and 2nd E. of Derby, *q.v.*, K.B. 758
— Ed., ld., aft. 12th E. of Derby, *q.v.*, L.L. Lanc. 309

Stanley of Bickerstaff, lds.
—— Ed., c.c. ld. St., aft. 1st ld. St. of B. and 13th E. of Derby, *q.v.*
—— hon. Ed. G., aft. ld. St. of B. and 14th E. of Derby, *q.v.*, Ch. Sec. Ir. 563; P.C. 212; U.S.W. and C. 231; W. and C. Sec. 231; C. Sec. 235
—— Ed. Hy., c.c. ld. St. and ld. St. of B., aft. 15th E. of Derby, *q.v.*, F. Sec. 229; P.C. 216; Pres. B.C. 254; Sec. Ind. 236; U.S.F. 230
Stanley of Alderley, lds.
—— Ed. Jno., 2nd ld., form. E. J. Stanley and ld. Eddisbury, *q.v.*, P.C. 214; Paym. G. 244-5; Postm. G. 239; Pres. B.T. 269; Sec. Tr. 163; U.S.F. 230; U.S. Home, 227; V.P.B.T. 269
Stanley of Preston, lds.
—— Fk. Arth., 1st ld., form. F. A. Stanley, C. Sec. 235; G.C.B. 773; G.G. Can. 692; L. Admy. 184-5; P.C. 219; Pres. B.T. 269; Sec. Tr. 164; U.S. War, 233; W. Sec. 232
Stannard, Eton (or Eaton), Rec. Dbln. 642; S.L. Ir. 592
Stannus, sir Ephr. G., gen. (**D**) 878
—— Hy. Jas., gen. (**D**) 905
—— Jas., dn. Ross. 633
Stanser, R., bp. N. Sc. 695
Stansfeld, Jas., C.C.J. 403; L.T. 161; P.C. 218; Pres. L.G.B. 256; Pres. P.L.B. 262; Sec. Tr. 164
—— Jas., junr., L. Admy. 184
—— Th. Wolr., gen. (**D**) 935
—— Wm. Hy. Crompton, gen. (**D**) 924
Stanton, Ed. and sir E., Amb. Bva. 119; Amb. Eg. 130; gen. (**D**) 905; K.C.M.G. 798
—— Geo. Hy., bp. N. Q. Land, 706
—— Herv. de, Ch. Ex. 152
Stanwey, Jno., dn. Her. 442
—— Wm. de, dn. Exr. 437
Stanwix, Jno., gen. (**B**) 865
*—— Th., G. Ch. Hosp. 936
*—— Th., gen. (**C**) 871
* Prob. same pers.
—— Th. Sl., gen. (**A**) 860
Stanyan, A., L. Admy. 177
Stanyford or **Stanyforth,** Th., S.L. 412
Stapelton and **Stapilton,** *see* Stapleton
Staple, Ad., L.M. Lond. 489
Staples, Ed., bp. Mth. 599
—— Jno., C. Cus. Ir. 565; C. Exc. Ir. 566
—— Jno. and sir J., K.C.M.G. 798; L.M. Lond. 492
Stapleton, Stapelton, and **Stapilton**
—— Aug. G., C. Cus. 277
—— Br., K.B. (1475) 757
—— Br., K.B. (1503) 759
—— sir Br., K.G. (1382) 734
—— sir Miles, C. Cus. 276
—— sir Miles, K.G. 733
—— Milo, } *see* ld. St., *infra*
—— Nichs., }
—— Ph., L. Admy. 175
—— Walt., bp. Exr. 436; Const. T.L. 320; L.H.T. 153
—— sir Wm., G. Leew. Isl. 727
—— hon. Wm., gen. (**A**) 861
Stapleton, lds.
—— Milo de, aft. 1st ld. St., J. It. 369
—— Nichs. de, aft. 2nd ld. St., J.K.B. 371
Stapleton-Cotton, *see* Cotton
Stapylton, hon. Granv. Ans. Chetw., gen. (**C**) 874
—— Granv. Geo. Chet., gen. (**D**) 909
—— Hy. D., C.C.J. 403
Starck, Maur. Adolph. N. de, adm. (**D**) 826
Starke, Wm., gen. (**D**) 928
Starkey, Humphr. and sir H., C.B. Ex. 381; J.C.P. 378; Rec. Lond. 493; S.L. 407
Starkie, Th., C.C.J. 403; K.C. 416
Starmer, Ch., adm. (**H**) 850
Statham or **Stathum,** Nichs., B. Ex. 383
Staunford, Wm., J.C.P. 378; S.L. 408
Staunton, Geo., gen. (**D**) 898
—— sir Geo. L., Amb. Ch. 130
—— Herv. or Hy. de, B. Ex. 383; C.B. Ex. 381; C.J.C.P. 375; C.J.K.B. 369; J.C.P. 377; J. It. 368
—— Jno., S.L. Ir. 592
—— Laur., dn. Linc. 448
—— Michl., L.M. Dbln. 642
—— Ph. de, bp. Llff. 449
—— Ph. de, K.B. 755
—— Wm. de, J. It. 368
Staurachius, Emp. E.E. 50
Staveley, Chas. Wm. Dunb. and sir C., C.C. Bbay. 660; G.C.B. 771; gen. (**D**) 902; gen. (**D**) 909; K.C.B. 779
—— Ed., gen. (**D**) 931
—— Wm., C.C. Mdras. 657; G. Mtius. 683; gen. (**D**) 882
—— Miles, gen. (**B**) 866
Stavensby, *see* Savensby
Staverton, Jno., B. Ex. 383
Stawell, *see also* Stowell
—— sir Wm. Foster, G. Vict. 705; K.C.M.G. 798
Stayner, *see also* Stainer
—— sir Rd., adm. (**A**) 813
Stebbing, Saml., R. Cr. P.A. 335; Som. H. 332
Stede, Edwin, G. Bdoes. 719
Steel and **Steele**
—— — S.L. 410
—— Arth. Loft, gen. (**D**) 912
—— Augs. Fk., gen. (**D**) 917
—— Ed., bp. C. Afr. 688
—— Jas. Anthy., gen. (**D**) 915
—— Rd., C. St. 283
—— Rt., M. Chy. 397
—— Scud. W. and sir S., gen. (**D**) 887; K.C.B. 777
—— Th., B.C. 252; P.C. 205; Paym. G. 245; Sec. Tr. 163
—— Th., gen. (**D**) 881
—— Th. Mont. and sir T., Comm. F. Ir. 564; G.C.B. 771; gen. (**D**) 900; K.C.B. 780
—— Wm., A.G. 399; C.B. Ex. 381; Comm. Ir. 555; Ld. Chanc. Ir. 576; Rec. Lond. 494; S.L. 409
Steere, Jno., bp. Ardf. and Agh. 639; bp. Kilf. 635
—— Wm., bp. Ardf. and Agh. 639; dn. Ardf. 640
Stefano, Sp. Facco, G.C.M.G. 795
Stehelin, Benjn., gen. (**C**) 872
—— Benj. Sp., gen. (**D**) 897
—— Ed., gen. (**B**) 868
Steinaüer, M., G. Mtius. 683
Stenkill, K. Sw. 92
***Stephen,** abp. Lond. 450
*—— bp. Brn. 531
*—— bp. Isl. 539
*—— (2), bp. Wford. 626; abp. Tm. 611
*—— dn. Kild. 619
*—— L. Treas. Ir. 558
* Prob. some same pers. Comp. dates.
—— D. Bva. 68
—— Emp. E.E. 50
—— K.E. 4
—— K. Pld. 91
—— (g. son of Wm. I.), Pr. E. 9
—— I. and II., Pr. Tva. 60
—— I. to IV., K. Hgy., 59, 60
—— I. to IX., P. Ro. 32-3-4
—— sir Alf., G. N.S.W. 703; G.C.M.G. 795; K.C.M.G. 797
—— Geo. Miln., G. S. Austr. 706
—— Hy. Jno., P.P. 416; S.L. 413
—— Jas., C.C.J. 405
—— Jas., M. Chy. 397
—— Jas. and sir J., B.T. 268; K.C.B. 782; P.C. 215; U.S.C. 235; U.S.W. and C. 232
—— Jas. Fitz. and sir J., J. Ex. D., 386; J.Q.B.D. 374; K.C.S.I. 803; Q.C. 418
—— Wm., J. Adm. Ct. 423
—— Wm., bp. Dnbl. 532
Stephens, *see also* Stevens
—— Archd. Jno., Q.C. 418 (*see ante* Stephen)
—— Ed., gen. (**B**) 867
—— Geo. Hopew., adm. (**A**) 819
—— Geo. Nesb., gen. (**D**) 932
—— Hy. Sykes, gen. (**D**) 900; K.H. 792
—— Pembr. Scott, Q.C. 419
—— Ph. and sir P., L. Admy. 180-1; Sec. Adm. 186-7
—— Phil. Wilk., adm. (**A**) 819
—— sir Rd., J.K.B. Ir. 579; S.L. Ir. 591
—— Wm. Fraser, gen. (**D**) 927
—— Wm. Kn., adm. (**H**) 848
Stephenson, *see also* Stevenson
—— Aug. Kepp, K.C.B. 784
—— Benj. Ch. and sir B., C.W. F. &c. 272; G.C.H. 787; K.C.H. 788; K.H. 789
—— sir Fk. Ch. Arth., G.C.B. 771; gen. (**D**) 905; K.C.B. 781
—— Fk. Jas., gen. (**D**) 921
—— Geo., dn. Kilf. 637
—— Hy. Fk., C. Exc. 282; C.I.R. 285; C. St. and Tx. 285
—— sir Wm., L.M. Lond. 492
—— Wm. Hy. and sir W., C.I.R. 286; K.C.B. 783
Stepney, Geo., B.T. 263
—— sir Jno., Amb. Pr. 118; Amb. Sxy. 120
Sterling, *see also* Stirling
—— Anthy. Con., K.C.B. 778
—— sir Saml., L.M. Lond 491

Sterne, Jno., bp. Clr. 596; bp. Drom. 605; dn. St. Pat. 618
—— Jno., bp. suff. Colch. 461
—— Rd., abp. Yk. 486; bp. Carl. 475
Steuart, *see also* Stewart and Stuart
—— Ch., gen. (**D**) 899
—— Dav., L. Prov. Edinb. 548
—— Geo. Mack., gen. (**D**) 880
—— sir Jas., *see* Stewart
—— Rt., L.T. 160
Stevens, *see also* Stephens
—— Arth., gen. (**D**) 919
—— Ch., adm. (**A**) 814
—— Edm., gen. (**A**) 859
—— Fk. Wm., C.I.E. 808
—— Geo. Shep., gen. (**D**) 933
—— Hy., S.L. 411
—— Hy. Borl., gen. (**D**) 923
—— Humph., gen. (**C**) 872
—— Jno. Harv., gen. (**D**) 889
—— Rt., dn. Roch. 461
—— Rt., S.L. 410
—— Th., gen. (**D**) 889
Stevenson, *see also* Stephenson
—— Ch., gen. (**B**) 867
—— Jas., adm. (**H**) 844
—— Jno., Ld. Sess. 518
—— Nathl., gen. (**D**) 929
—— Rd., G. I. Man, 666
—— Rt. and sir R., gen. (**D**) 876; K.C.B. 776
—— Rt. H., Mod. K. Sc. 547
—— Wm., G. Br. Hond. 714; G. Mtius. 684; K.C.B. 783
Steward, Gabr. T., C. Tx. 285
—— Hy. Hold., gen. (**D**) 933
—— (or Stewart), Sir Nichs., Chambn. Ex. 166
—— Rt., dn. Ely 435
Stewart, *see also* Steuart and Stuart
—— —, G. Tob. 723
—— Col. —, G. N.S.W. 703
—— Alexr., gen. (**C**) 872
—— Alexr. Ch. Hect., gen. (**D**) 926
—— Algn. Augs., gen. (**D**) 932
—— Andr. (No. 1), bp. Cness. 531; L.H.T. Sc. 497
—— Andr. (No. 2), bp. Cness. 531; bp. Dkld. 533; bp. Mor. 534; L.P.S. Sc. 500
—— Archd., gen. (**C**) 873
—— Archd., K.H. 790
—— Ch. (ld. Stuart de Rothesay), *see* Stuart
—— hon. Ch., adm. (**A**) 813
—— Ch. Ed., C.I.E. 807
—— C. J., bp. Queb. 694
—— Ch. Thornt., gen. (**D**) 922
—— Ch. Wm., *see* ld. St. and M. of Lond., *infra*
—— Dav., bp. Mor. 534
—— Dav., gen. (**C**) 874
—— Don. Mart. and sir D., C.C. Ind. 651; G.C.B. 771; G.C.S.I. 801; gen. (**D**) 907; K.C.B. 781; M.C.I. 647
—— Dug., Ld. Sess. 520
—— Ed., bp. Ork. 535
—— Ed., dn. Winch. 471
—— hon. Ed., C. Cus. 276
—— Fras., gen. (**C**) 873
—— Geo., gen. (**D**) 934
—— Gilb., Ly. K.A. 513
—— Hy., dn. Drom. 606
—— Herb. and sir H., gen. (**D**) 927; K.C.B. 781
Stewart—*cont.*
—— Houst. and sir H., adm. (**B**) 821; (**D**) 829; G.C.B. 770; G. Gr. Hosp. 854; K.C.B. 777; L. Admy. 183
—— Jas., adm. (**A**) 814
—— Jas., bp. Mor. 534; L.H.T. Sc. 496
—— Jas., gen. (**A**) 860
—— Jas., L. Prov. Edinb. 548
—— sir Jas., G.C.H. 786; gen. (**A**) 859
—— hon. Jas. Hy. Keith, C. Cus. 276-7; C. Cus. Ir. 566; C. St. 284; Sec. Tr. 164
—— Jas. Patt., adm. (**H**) 844
—— Jno., A.G. Ir. 588; S.G. Ir. 589
—— Jno., C.I.E. 808
—— Jno., gen. (**C**) 872
—— Jno., K.B. 756
—— Jno. Dr., gen. (**D**) 906
—— Jno. Ham., gen. (**D**) 894
—— Jno. Hy., gen. (**D**) 918
—— hon. Keith, adm. (**A**) 815
—— hon. Keith, adm. (**G**) 842
—— sir Michl. Shaw, L.L. Renfw. 511
—— sir Michl. Rt. Shaw, L.L. Renfw. 511
—— (or Steward), sir Nichs., Chambn. Ex. 166
—— Rd., dn. Llin. 623
—— Rt., Amb. N.G. 134
—— Rt., bp. Cness. 531
—— Rt., gen. (**C**) 874
—— Rt., gen. (**D**) 891
—— Rt., Ld. Sess. 520
—— Rt., M. Chy. 396
—— Rt. Cr., gen. (**D**) 927
—— Rt. Jno. Joc., gen. (**D**) 932
—— Th., gen. (**D**) 877
—— sir Th., Ld. Sess. 520
—— Walt., aft. 1st ld. Blantyre, *q.v.*, L.P.S. Sc. 501; Ld. Sess. 517
—— Wm., bp. Abdn. 530; L.H.T. Sc. 497
—— Wm., gen. (**A**) 857
—— Wm., gen. (**C**) 874
—— Wm., gen. (**C**) 875
—— Wm., aft. 2nd ld. Blantyre, *q.v.*, K.B. 762
—— sir Wm., L.M. Lond. 491
—— sir Wm., Ly. K.A. 513
—— hon. Wm., G.C.B. 767; gen. (**B**) 867; K.B. 766
—— Wm. Houston and sir W., adm. (**E**) 835; Compt. N. 258; G.C.B. 771; K.C.B. 780
—— sir Wm. Jas., Ld. Adv. 526
Stewart, lds.
—— hon. Ch. Wm., aft. ld St. and 3rd M. of Londonderry, *q.v.*, Amb. Aus. 117; G.C.B. 767; G.C.H. 786; K.B. 766; P.C. 209; U.S.W. and C. 231
Stewart - Moncreiffe, *see* Moncreiffe
Steyngrave, Ad. de, B. Ex. 383
Stibbert, Giles, C.C. Bgal. 652; C.C. Ind. 650
Stibbs, Ed., Chest. H. 331
Stidio, bp. Cnwall. 436
Stigand, abp. Cant. 430; bp. Elm. and Dunw. 454; bp. Winch. 470
—— bp. Sels. and Chich. 432
Stikesward, Rog. de, J. It. 366
Stile, sir Jno., V. Treas. Ir. 559
—— Wm., gen. (**B**) 866
Stileman, Wm. Cr., gen. (**D**) 913
Stiles, *see also* Styles
—— Wm., C. Cus. 276
Still, Jno., bp. B. and W. 428
—— Sim. Van der, G. C.G.H. 678
—— Wm. Adr. Van der, G. C.G.H. 678
Stillingfleet, Ed., bp. Worc. 473; dn. St. P. 453
—— Jas., dn. Worc. 473
Stillington, Rt., bp. B. and W. 428; Ld. Chanc. 355
Stirbey, D. B., H. Wca. 94
Stircheleye, Walt. de, J. It. 368
Stirling, *see also* Sterling
—— Alex. Gr., gen. (**A**) 862
—— sir Archd., Ld. Sess. 519
—— Ch., adm. (**A**) 817
—— Fk. Hy., adm. (**E**) 836
—— Jas., gen. (**C**) 874
—— Jas. and sir J., adm. (**D**) 829; G. W. Austr. 707
—— Jas. and sir J., Just. Ch. D. 391
—— Jas. and sir J., L. Prov. Edinb. 548
—— Jno., Mod. K. Sc. 547
—— sir Th., gen. (**A**) 859
—— Waite Hock., bp. Falk. Isl. 731
—— Wm., gen. (**D**) 933
Stirling, Wm., 1st visc., aft. 1st E. of, form. sir Wm. Alexander, *q.v.*, Ld. Sess. 517
Stirling-Maxwell, *see* Maxwell
Stisted, Ch., K.H. 791
—— Hy. Wm. and sir H., G. Ont. 692; gen. (**D**) 899; K.C.B. 780
Stitchell, Rt., bp. Dham. 478
Stivicle, Josc. de, Jy. 364
Stock, Jno. Sh. Ed., Q.C. 418
—— Jos., J. Admy. Ct. Ir. 587; S.L. Ir. 593
—— Jos., bp. Killa. and Ach. 613; bp. Wford. and L. 627
—— Th., gen. (**D**) 916
Stockenstrom, Andr. and sir A., G. C.G.H. 679
Stockesley, Jno., bp. Lond. 451
Stockton, Jno., L.M. Lond. 490
—— Th., J.K.B. Ir. 579
Stoddard, Jno. Fk., gen. (**D**) 918
—— Th. Hy., gen. (**D**) 915
Stoddart, Jas., adm. (**H**) 849
*—— Jas., C. Exc. Sc. 505
*—— Jas., L. Prov. Edinb. 548
* Prob. same pers.
—— Pringle, adm. (**D**) 827
Stody, Jno., L.M. Lond. 489
Stoke, Ralph de, Jy. 364
—— Rd. de, J. It. 367
Stokes, Al. de, dn. St. As. 463
—— Ch. Patr., gen. (**D**) 928
—— Geo. Gabr. and sir G., Pres. R. Soc. 940
—— Jno., M. Chy. 394
—— Jno. de, B. Ex. 383
—— Jno. and sir J., gen. (**D**) 927; K.C.B. 783
—— Jno. D., gen. (**D**) 888
—— Jno. Lort, adm. (**D**) 833; (**F**) 838
—— Rd., B. Ex. 383
Stoll, Jno. Luke Rd., adm. (**H**) 850

Stolo, C. L. C. (2), C. Ro. 40
Stondon, Wm., L.M. Lond. 489
Stone, Andr., B.T. 265; U.S.S. 225-6
—— Dav. Hy., L.M. Lond. 492
—— Geo., abp. Arm. 596; bp. Dry. 601; bp. Ferns and L. 622; bp. Kild. 617; dn. Chr. Ch. Dbln. 618; dn. Dry. 602; dn. Ferns, 623; L.J. Ir. 556-7
—— Jno., S.L. 409
—— Jno., S. St. 222
—— Wm. Hy., dn. Kilm. 609
Stonehewer, Rd., C. Exc. 280; U.S.S. 226
Stonehouse, sir Jno., Compt. H. 292; P.C. 196
***Stoner,** Wm., K.B. 757
*—— Lt. T.L. 321
* Prob. same pers.
Stoney, Geo. Butl., gen. (**D**) 918
Stonford, *see* Stouford
Stonor, Hy. Jas., C.C.J. 404
Stonore, Jno. de, C.B. Ex. 381; C.J.C.P. 375; J.C.P. 377; S.L. 406
Stopford, Ed., bp. Mth. 599
—— hon. Ed. and sir E., G.C.B. 768; gen. (**B**) 868; K.C.B. 774
—— hon. Ed., gen. (**C**) 872
—— Jas., bp. Cloy. 631; dn. Kilmacd. 638
—— Jas. Geo., *see* visc. St., *infra*
—— Jas. Jno., adm. (**D**) 832; (**E**) 834
—— hon. Mont., K.C.B. 777; adm. (**D**) 830
—— Rd. Hy., adm. (**G**) 843
—— hon. Rt. and sir R., adm. (**A**) 818; (**C**) 822; G.C.B. 768; G.C.M.G. 794; G. Gr. Hosp. 854; K.C.B. 773
—— Rt. Fansh., adm. (**D**) 832; (**E**) 834; (**F**) 838
—— hon. Th., bp. Cork and R. 632; dn. Ferns, 623; dn. Killoe. 637
Stopford, visc.
—— Jas. Geo., visc., aft. 3rd E. of Courtown, *q.v.*, Tr. H. 291
Stopynden, Jno., M.R. 387
Storer, Anthy., B.T. 266-7
Storey, *see* Story
Storke, Rd., Rbk. P.A. 344
Storks, Hy., C.C.J. 403; P.P. 416; S.L. 413
—— Hy. Kn. and sir H., Com. Io. Isl. 129; G.C.B. 772; G.C.M.G. 795; G. Jam. 713; G. Mlta. 671; gen. (**D**) 897; K.C.B. 778; P.C. 217; S.G.O. 260
Stormont, visc.
—— Dav., 7th visc., form. D. Murray, *q.v.*, aft. 2nd E. of Mansfield, *q.v.*; Amb. Fr. 112; Amb. Gmy. 116; Amb. Sxy. 120; K.T. 748; L. J. Gen. 522; L.P.C. 188; P.C. 201; S. St. 225
—— Wm. D., visc., aft. 4th E. of Mansfield, *q.v.*, L.T. 160
Storr, Jno., adm. (**A**) 815
Story and **Storey**
—— Ed., bp. Carl. 475; bp. Chich. 433
—— Geo. Walt., dn. Cnr. 605; dn. Lim. 639
—— Hy. Alexr., adm. (**H**) 849
—— Jos., bp. Killoe. 634; bp. Kilm. 607; dn. Ferns, 623

Story and Storey—*cont.*
—— Ph., gen. (**D**) 935
—— Ph. Fras., gen. (**D**) 889
—— Val. Fk., gen. (**D**) 918
Stote, sir Rd., S.L. 410
Stotherd, Rd. Jno., gen. (**D**) 895
Stouford, Stonford, or Stovard, Jno. de, C.B. Ex. 381; J.C.P. 377; S.L. 406
Stourdza, M., H. Mva. 94
Stourton, Wm., Sp. H.C. 248
—— Wm., *see* ld. S., *infra*
Stourton, lds.
—— Jno., aft. 3rd ld. St., K.B. 757
—— Wm., 4th ld., K.B. 758
—— Wm., aft. 10th ld. St., K.B. 762
Stout, Rt., K.C.M.G. 798
Stovard, *see* Stouford
Stovin, Fk. and sir F., gen. (**D**) 879; G.C.B. 770; K.C.B. 775; K.C.M.G. 796
—— Rd., gen. (**B**) 868
Stow, Fk. Milk., gen. (**D**) 934
—— Harry, gen. (**D**) 899
—— Th., dn. St. P. 453
—— Wm. de, B. Ex. 383
Stowell, Jno., K.B. 761
—— (or Stawell), Jno., K.B. 763
Stowell, lds.
—— Wm. ld., form. sir W. Scott, *q.v.*; Jud. Com. P.C. 360
***Stoyte,** sir Fras., L.M. Dbln. 641
*—— Fras., Rec. Dbln. 642
* ? same pers.
—— Jno., L.M. Dbln. 641
Strabo, C. F., C. Ro. 44-5
—— C. P., C. Ro. 45
Stracey, *see* Strachey
Strachan, *see also* Strahan
—— Dav., bp. Brn. 531
—— Dav., Ld. Sess. 518
—— Jas., Sec. St. Sc. 502
—— Jno., bp. Brn. 541
—— Jno., bp. Tor. 693
—— Jno. Mill., bp. Rangn. 655
—— sir Rd. Jno., adm. (**A**) 817; G.C.B. 761; K.B. 766
Strachey and **Stracey**
—— Chr., adm. (**H**) 845
—— Geo., Amb. Sxy. 121
—— Hy. and sir H., Sec. Tr. 163; St. O. 260; U.S. Home 227
—— Jno., Rec. Lond. 494
—— Jno. and sir J., Ch. Com. Oudh. 654; G.C.S.I. 801; K.C.S.I. 803; L.G. N.W. Pr. 653; M.C.I. 647
—— Kath. Jane, Lady, Cr. Ind. 810
—— Rd., gen. (**D**) 904; M.C.I. 647
Stradbroke. Jno. Ed. C., 2nd E. of, L.L. Suff. 312
Stradling, Ed., K.B. 755
—— Geo., dn. Chich. 434
Strafford, Edm. de, dn. Yk. 486
—— Nichs., *see* Stratford
Strafford, ld. and E. of
Wentworth Family.
1st Creation.
—— Thos., 1st E. of, form. ld. Raby and visc. Wentworth, *q.v.*, K.G. 740
—— Wm., 2nd E. of, K.G. 740; P.C. 191

Strafford, ld. and E. of—*cont.*
2nd Creation.
—— Th., 1st E. of, gen. (**B**) 864; K.G. 741; L. Admy. 177.
Byng Family.
—— Jno., 1st ld. and E., form. sir J. Byng, *q.v.*, F.M. 856; gen. (**A**) 862
—— Geo. S., 2nd E. of, form. hon. G. S. Byng, ld. Str. and visc. Enfield. *q.v.*
—— G. H. C., ld. and aft. 3rd E. of, form. visc. Enfield (in 1884) *q.v.*
Strahan, *see also* Strachan
—— hon. Ch., G. Gsey. 668
—— Geo. Cum. and sir G., G. Bdoes., &c. 719, 721; G.C.G.H. &c. 679; G. Gld. Cst. Col. 686; G. Tasm. 708; G.C.M.G. 795; K.C.M.G. 797
—— Wm., Adm. Adv. 423
Strall or **Stralley,** Wm., K.B. 756
Strang, *see* Strange
Strange, Eubulo le, K.B. 754
—— Guy le, J. It. 366
—— Jas. Newb., adm. (**E**) 835; (**F**) 839
—— (or Strang), Jno., dn. Oss. 622
—— Jno., Amb. Vce. 116
—— Jno. le, K.B. 754
—— Jno. and sir J., K.C. 415; M.R. 388; P.C. 199; Rec. Lond 494; S.G. 401
—— Rt., K.B. 759
—— Rog. le, J. It. 368
—— Rog. le, K.B. 755
—— (or Straunge), Th. and sir T., D. Chanc. and Ld. Chanc. Ir. 575; L.D. Ir. 552; L. Treas. Ir. 558
—— sir Th. A., C.J. Mdras. 658
Strange, lds.
Stanley and Murray Families.
(*See also* Stanley.)
—— Th., ld., form. Th. Stanley, *q.v.*, aft. 2nd E. of Derby, *q.v.*
—— Ed. Stanley, c.c. ld. Str. (gr. son of 3rd E. of Derby), K.B. 760
—— Jas., 1st ld., aft. 7th E. of Derby, *q.v.*, K.B. 762
—— Jas., ld. (? son of 2nd D. of Athole), C.D.L. (1762) 243; P.C. 201
—— Jno. Sm., c.c. ld. Str. (son of 11th E. of Derby), L.L. Lanc. 309
Strange of Knockyn, lds.
—— Jno., 12th ld., K.B. 756
—— Geo., 13th ld., K.G. 736
Strangeways, *see* Strangways
Strangford, visc.
—— Th., 1st visc., form. Th. Smith (1625), *q.v.*
—— Percy C., 6th visc., aft. ld. Penshurst, *q.v.*, Amb. Pgl. 124; K.B. 766; P.C. 208; G.C.B. 771; Amb. Sw. and N. 127; Amb. Tky, 129; G.C.H. 786; Amb. Russ. 126; Amb. Bzl. 135
—— Geo. A. F. P. S., 7th visc. form. hon. G. A. F. P. S Smythe, *q.v.*
Strangways and **Strangeways**
—— Geo., gen. (**D**) 923
—— Giles, P.C. 191

Strangways and Strangeways —*cont.*
— Jas., J.C.P. 378; S.L. 407
— sir Jas., Sp. H.C. 249
— hon. Wm. Th. H. Fox-, aft. 4th E. of Ilchester, *q.v.*, Amb. Aus. 117; Amb. G. St. 122; U.S.F. 230
Stranshom, Anthy. Bl. and sir A., gen. (**D**) 895; K.C.B. 779
Stratford, Fras. P., M. Chy. 397
— Hy. de, M. Chy, 393
— Jno. de, abp. Cant. 430; bp. Winch. 470; L.H.T. 153; Ld. Chanc. 354
*— Nichs., dn. St. As. 463
*— Nichs., Wdn. Chr. Ch. Manch. 481
* ? same pers.
— Ralph de, bp. Lond. 451
— Rt. de, bp. Chich. 432; Ld. Chanc. 354
Stratford de Redcliffe Stratf., visc., form. sir S. Canning, *q.v.*, K.G. 745
Strathallan, Wm., 4th ld. and 1st visc., form. hon. Wm. Drummond, *q.v.*
Strathbrock, Rt., bp. Cness. 531
Strathearn, *see* Connaught and Str., Cumberland and Str., and Kent and Str.
Strathmore, E. of
— Patr., 3rd E. of, Ld. Sess. 517
— Claude, 13th E. of, L.L. Forf. 510
Strathnairn, Hugh H., 1st ld., form. sir H. H. Rose, *q.v.*, F.M. 886
Straton and **Stratton**
— Ad. de, B. Ex. 382
— Alex., Amb. Sw. 126
— Fras., gen. (**D**) 888
— Jas. Murr., (gen. (**D**) 927
— Jno., gen. (**A**) 859
— sir Jos., gen. (**B**) 869; K.C.H. 788
— Rd. de, K.B. 754
— Wm. Alb., gen. (**D**) 907
Straubenzee, Ch. Th. Van and sir C., G.C.B. 770; G. Mlta. 671; gen. (**D**) 894; K.C.B. 778
Straunge, *see* Strange
Streatfeild, Ch. Ogle, gen. (**D**) 891
Street, Jno. Alfr., gen. (**D**) 904
— Th. and sir Th., B. Ex. 384; J.C.P. 379; S.L. 410
Streicher, Fras., gen. (**C**) 874
Stretely, Jno. de, dn. Linc. 448
Stretton, Rt., bp. Lich. and Cov. 444
— Th. de, dn. Lich. 445
Strickland, Ch., adm. (**A**) 813
— Ed., K.C.B. 781
— sir Rog., adm. (**A**) 813
— Th., gen. (**B**) 867
— Th., K.B. 761
— sir Th., L.P.S. 240
— (or Strykeland), Walt., K.B. 759
— Wm., bp. Carl. 475
— sir Wm., L.T. 156; P.C. 198; Sec. at W. 233
Striker, Th., dn. Cloy. 632
Stringer, sir Th., J.K.B. 372; S.L. 410
Stritche, Andr., dn. Lim. 639
Strode, Ch., S.W.F. 271
— sir Ed. Chetham-, form. Chetham, *q.v.*, adm. (**D**) 826
— Fk. Th. Chetham-, adm. (**H**) 851
— Geo., S.L. 410
— Jno. de la, J. It. 368
— Th., S.L. 410
— Wm., gen. (**B**) 865
Strong, Wm., C. Exc. 279
Stroud, Hy., adm. (**H**) 847
Strover, Saml. R., gen. (**D**) 880
Structus, *see also* Ahala
— P. S. P., C. Ro. 37-8
— Q. S. P. (2), C. Ro. 38; Dt. Ro. 39
— S. S. P., C. Ro. 38
Strutt, Ed., aft. 1st ld. Belper, *q.v.*, C.D.L. 243; P.C. 215
— Wm. Gooday, gen. (**C**) 872
Strykeland, *see* Strickland
Stryvelin, Gilb. de, bp. Abdn. 530
— Th. de, Ld. Chanc. Sc. 514
Strzlecki, Paul Edm. de, K.C.M.G. 796
Stuart, *see also* Steuart and Stewart
— family of, L.H.St. Sc. 505
— Alexr., abp. St. Andr. 529; Ld. Chanc. Sc. 515
— Alexr., bp. Mor. 534
— Alexr., K.C.M.G. 798
— Andr., B.T. 266
— Andr. (bps., &c.) *see* Stewart
— Ch., gen. (**D**) 894
— hon. Ch. and sir C., *see* ld. St. de Rothesay, *infra*
— Ch Sh. and sir C., gen. (**D**) 898; G.C.B. 770; K.C.B. 778
— hon. Ch., K.B. 766
— sir Don. M., *see* Stewart
— Ed. Andr., L.G. Ch. Hosp. 936
— Ed. Cr., bp. Wpu. 710
— Fras., K.B. 762
— ld. Geo., adm. (**D**) 824
— Hy., adm. (**A**) 820
— H. V., *see* ld. St. de Decies, *infra*
— Houst., *see* Stewart
— Jas., C.C. Bbay. 659; C.C. Mdras. 657; gen. (**A**) 860
— Jas., gen. (**C**) 872
— Jas., gen. (**D**) 896
— Jas., D. of Ross, *q.v.*
— Jas. (L.H.T. Sc.), *see* Stewart
— hon. Jas., gen. (**B**) 865
— Jas. Fk. D. C., L.L. Butesh. 508
— Jno. and sir J., Jud. Com. P.C. 361; P.C. 218; Q.C. 417; V. Chanc. 390
— Jno. and sir J. (Count of Maida), K.B. 766; G.C.B. 767; G. Gren. 724; gen. (**B**) 866
— sir Jno., C. Exc. Sc. 505
— Jno. Rams., gen. (**D**) 903
— hon. Patr. and sir P., G.C.M.G. 794; G. Mlta. 671; gen. (**A**) 863
— ld. Patr. Jas. Herb. Cr., L.L. Butesh. 508
— sir Nichs., *see* Stewart
— Rd., dn. Chich. 434
Stuart—*cont.*
— Rt., Amb. Dom. Rep. 133; Amb. Hti. 133
— Rt., C.J. N.W. Pr. 654
— Rt., Q.C. 418
— sir Rt., gen. (**A**) 860
— sir Simeon (2), Chambn. Ex. 166
— Th., bp. St. Andr. 529
— Walt., *see* Stewart
— hon. Wm., abp. Arm. 596; bp. St. Dav. 465; P.C. 206
— hon. Wm., Amb. Arg. 136; Amb. Gr. 129; Amb. Nds., &c. 123; Amb. Pgy. 136; Amb. Ugy. 137; K.C.M.G. 798
— hon. Wm., gen. (**B**) 869
— hon. Wm. and sir W., *see* Stewart
— Wm. Jas., gen. (**D**) 935
Stuart de Decies, lds.
— Hy. Vill., 1st ld., form. H. V. Stuart, L.L. Wford. 571
Stuart de Rothesay, lds.
— Ch., ld., form. Ch. Stuart and sir C., Amb. Fr. 112-13; Amb. Nds., &c. 122; Amb. Pgl. 124-25; Amb. Pr. 118; Amb. Russ. 126; G.C.B. 771; K.B. 766
Stuart-Wortley, *see* Wortley
Stuart-Mackenzie, *see* Mackenzie
Stubbs, Fras. Wm., gen. (**D**) 919
— Wm., bp. Chest. 477; bp. Oxf. 457
— Wm. Hy., gen. (**D**) 912
Stubin, Dav., dn. Kild. 619
Studd, Ed., gen. (**D**) 884
Studdert, Jno. Fitz Gu. adm. (**H**) 846
Stupart, Gust., adm. (**H**) 844
Sturges-Bourne, *see* Bourne
Sturmey or **Sturmy,** sir Jno., L.H.A. 170, 171
Sturrock, Geo., gen. (**D**) 911
Sturton (or Shirton), Rt., dn. Ross. 633
Stuteville, Rt. de, bp. Dkld. 533
— Rt. de, J. It. 365
— Wm. de, J. It. 366
Styles, *see also* Stiles
— Jno., adm. (**A**) 820
Suarez, J., Pres. Ugy. 111
Suatopluc, D. Bma. 59
Subadar, &c., C.I.E. 807
Subramaniya, &c., C.I.E. 808
Suchet, Off. Nap.
Suckling, Edm., dn. Norw. 456
— sir Jno., Coff. H. 293; Compt. H. 292
— Maur., Compt. N. 257
— Wm. Benj., adm. (**H**) 847
Sudbury, Jno., dn. Dham. 479
— Sim. de, abp. Cant. 430; bp. Lond. 451; Ld. Chanc. 354
— Th. de, dn. Wells, 428
Suddozaie, Shahzadah, &c., C.I.E. 807
Sudhal, Deo, &c., C.I.E. 808
Sudeley, lds.
Boteler Family.
— Ralph, 1st ld., form. R. Boteler, *q.v.*, L.H.T. 153
Hanbury-Tracey Family.
— Ch., 1st ld., form. Ch. Hanbury-Tracy, *q.v.*, L.L. Montg. 315

Sudeley, lds.—*cont.*
— Th. C., 2nd ld., form. hon. Th. Ch. Hanbury-Tracy, *q.v.*, L.L. Montg. 315
— Sud. Ch. Geo., 3rd ld., L.L. Montg. 315
— Ch. D. Rd., 4th ld., C.G.A. 300; P.C. 220
Sudley, Rt. de, J. It. 368
Sudley, visc.
— Ch. F., visc., aft. 5th. E. of Arran, *q.v.*, C. Cus. 277
Suebricht, K.E. 2
Suenfrid, K.E. 2
Suenon I. to III., K. Dk. 93
Suero, Pres. Bol. 109
Suffield, lds.
— Wm, A., 2nd ld., form. W. A. Harbord, *q.v.*
— Ch., 5th ld., K.C.B. 783; M.B.H. 303; P.C. 220
Suffolk, E., M., and D. of
Ufford Family.
— Rt., 1st E. of, form. sir Rt. Ufford, *q.v.*, K.G. 733; L.H.A. 172
— Wm., 2nd E. of, K.G. 734; L.H.A. 172
De la Pole Family.
— Michl., 1st E. of, K.G. (?) 734
— Wm., 4th E., aft. 1st M. and D. of, K.G. 735
— Jno., 2nd D. of, K.G. 736
— Edm., 6th E. of, form. E. de la Pole, *q.v.*, K.G. 737
Brandon Family.
— Ch., 1st D. of, form. sir C. Brandon. *q.v.*, E.M. 326; L.K. 355; L.S.H. 289
Grey Family.
— Hy., 1st D. of, form. M. of Dorset, *q.v.*
Howard Family.
— Th., 1st E. of, form. 1st ld. Howard de Walden, *q.v.*, C.G.P. 299; E.M. 326; L.C.H. 294
— Theoph., 2nd E. of, form. ld. Howard de Walden, *q.v.*, K.G. 739; L.L. Dors. 307; W.C.P. 319
— Jas., 3rd E. of, E.M. 326
— (and Bindon), Hy., 6th E. of, *also* ld. Chesterford, *q.v.*, Pres. B.T. 264; L.L. Esx. 308
— Ch. Wm., 7th E. of, L.L. Esx. 308
— (and Berkshire), Hy., 12th E. of, Dep. E.M. 327; K.G. 742; L.P.S. 241; P.C. 202; S. St. 225
— Jno., 15th E. of, gen. (**A**) 859
Sugden, Ed. B. and sir E., aft. 1st ld. St. Leonards, *q.v.*, K.C. 416; Ld. Chanc. 358; Ld. Chanc. Ir. 577; P.C. 213; S.G. 402
Suibhne-Mean, K. Ir. 21
Suibhney, bp. Arm. 595
Suintila, K. Sp. 85
Suithulfus, *see* Swithulfus
Sulby, *see* Sully
Sulgheim or **Sulgeheyn,** bp. St. Dav. 464
Sulhaithnay, abp. St. Dav. 463
Sulhidwr or **Sulhidyr,** bp. St. Dav. 464
Sulivan, *see also* Sullivan
— Barth. Jas. and sir B., adm. (**G**) 843; K.C.B. 780
Sulivan—*cont.*
— Geo. Lyd., adm. (**E**) 837
— Lawrence and sir L., P.C. 215; Dep. Sec. at W. 234
— Lawr., *see* Sullivan
— Steph. Hy., Amb. Chi. 137; Amb. Pu. 135
— Th. Baker Mart., adm. (**H**) 852
— Th. Ball, adm. (**H**) 845
Sulla, L. C. (2), C. Ro. 45; Dt. Ro. 45
— P. C., C. Ro. 46
Sulliard, *see* Sulyard
Sullivan, *see also* Sulivan
— sir Ch., adm. (**D**) 829
— Ed., bp. Alg. 693
— Ed. and sir E., A.G. Ir. 588; Ld. Chanc. Ir. 577; M.R. Ir. 585; S.G. Ir. 590; S.L. Ir. 593
— Fras. Wm. and sir F., adm. (**E**) 836; K.C.B. 781
— Jno., B.C. 252-3; B.T. 268; P.C. 207; U.S. W. and C. 231
— Laur., Chn. E.I. Co. 644
— Lawr., *see* Sulivan
— Tim. Danl., L.M. Dbln. 642
— Wm., gen. (**D**) 896
Sully (or Sulby), Jno., K.G. 733
Sulnay, abp. St. Dav. 463
Sulyard (or Sulliard), Jno., J.K.B. 372; S.L. 407
Sumeri, Rog. de, J. It. 368
Summerled, K. Man, 665
Sumner, Ch., C.C.J. 404
— Ch. Rd., bp. Llff. 449; bp. Winch. 471; dn. St. P. 453
— Geo. Hy. Guildf., bp. Suff. 471
— Jno. B., abp. Cant. 431 bp. Chest. 477; Jud. Com. P.C. 360; P.C. 215
Sumpter, Rt. de, dn. Exr. 437
Sunderland, E. of
— Rt., 2nd E. of, L.C.H. 295; K.G. 740; L.P.C. 187; P.C. 191; S. St. 223-4
— Ch., 3rd E. of, Gr. St. 303; K.G. 741; L.L. Ir. 556; L.P.C. 188; L.P.S. 240; L.T. 141, 156; P.C. 195; Prem. 141; S. St. 224; V. Treas. Ir. 559
— Ch., 5th E. of, also 3rd D. of Marlborough, *q.v.*
Sundon, Wm., 1st ld., form. Wm. Clayton, *q.v.*, L.T. 156
Sura, P. C. L., C. Ro. 46
Surien, sir Fras., K.G. 735
Surrey, lds., E., and D. of. *Search also under* Arundel, Maltravers, and Norfolk
Warenne Family.
(*See also* Warenne.)
— Rd., 8th E. of, form. E. of Arundel (1386), *q.v.*
— Th. de Holland, D. of, form. E. of Kent (1397), *q.v.*, E.M. 326; L.L. Ir. 552
— Th., E. of, aft. 2nd D. of Norfolk, *q.v.* (*d.* 1524), E.M. 326; K.G. 736; L.H.T. 154
— Th., ld. Howard and E. of, aft. 3rd D. of Norfolk, *q.v.* (*d.* 1554), K.G. 737; L.H.T. 154; L.L. Ir. 553
— Hy. Howard, c.c. E. of, K.G. (1541) 738
Surrey, lds., E., and D. of—*cont.*
— Ch., E. of, aft. 11th D. of Norfolk, *q.v.*, Dep. E.M. 327; L.L. Yorks, W.R. 313; L.T. 158
— Hy. Ch., E. of, aft. ld. Maltravers, *q.v.*, and 13th D. of Norfolk, *q.v.*, C.Y.G. 298; P.C. 213; Tr. H. 291
Surup, Narain, C.I.E. 806
Surridge, Th., adm. (**A**) 818
Sussex, E. and D. of
Ratcliffe Family.
— Rt., 1st E. of, form. visc. Fitzwalter, *q.v.*
— Hy., 2nd E. of, K.G. 738
— Th., 3rd E. of, form. visc. Fitzwalter, *q.v.*, C.G.P. 299; K.G. 738; L.C.H. 294; L.D. Ir. 553
— Hy., 4th E. of, K.G. 739
— Rt., 5th E. of, K.G. 739
Yelverton Family.
— Talb., 1st. E. of, Dep. E.M. 327; K.B. 764; P.C. 197

— Aug. Fk., D. of (son of Geo. III.), form. Pr. Aug. Fk., *q.v.*, Const. W. Cast. 322; G.C.B. 772; G.C.H. 785; Gr. M. Bath, 754; K.T. 748; P.C. 207; Pres. R. Soc. 940
Sutcliffe, Matth., dn. Exr. 437
Suter, Andr. Burn, bp. Nels. 710
Suther, Th. G., bp. Abdn. and Ork. 541
Sutherland, sir Jas., gen. (**D**) 878
— Wm., G. Mtius. 684; gen. (**D**) 882
Sutherland, E. and D. of
— Jno., 13th E. of, L.P.S. Sc. 501
— Geo., 14th E. of, C.G.S. Sc. 515
— Jno., 15th E. of, gen. (**B**) 864; K.T. 747; P.C. 197
— Geo. Gr., 1st. D. of, form. E. Gower and 2nd M. of Stafford, *q.v.*
— Geo. Gr., 2nd D. of, form. M. of Stafford, *q.v.*, K.G. 744; L.L. Salop, 311
— Geo. Gr. Wm., 3rd D. of, form. M. of Stafford, *q.v.*, K.G. 744; L.L. Suth. 512
— Harriett E. G., Dss. of, M. Robes, 304
— Anna, Dss. of, M. Robes, 304
Suthfield, Walt. de, bp. Norw. 454
Suthflete, *see* Wuldham
Suthill, Jno., J. It. 366
Suthworth, Matth. de, Rec. Lond. 493
Sutton and **Suttone**
— sir Ch., K.C.B. 774
— Ch. Manners-, abp. Cant. 431; bp. Norw. 455; dn. Pboro. 458; dn. Winds. 474; P.C. 207
— Ch. Manners- and sir C., aft. 1st visc. Canterbury, *q.v.*, G.C.B. 772; J.A.G. 937; P.C. 208; Sp. H.C. 250
— (Suttone), Elias de, J.K.B. 371
— Ferd., K.B. 762

For List of Abbreviations, see pp. 944-952.

Sutton and Suttone—*cont.*
*— Hy., dn. Dry. 602; dn. Wford. 628
*— Hy., dn. Lim. 639
* Poss. same pers.
— Jno., L.M. Dbln. 641
— Jno. de, K.B. 755
— Jno. and sir J., adm. (**A**) 817; K.C.B. 773
— hon. Jno. Hy. Th. Manners-, aft. 3rd visc. Canterbury, *q.v.*, G. N. Brk. 696; G. Trin. 722; G. Vict. 705; K.C.B. 783; U.S. Home, 228
— Ol., bp. Linc. 446; dn. Linc. 448
— Rd. G. Gsey. 668; gen. (**B**) 864
*— Rd., L.P.S. 241
*— sir Rd., L.T. 155
* Prob. same pers.
— Rt., D.L.K. Ir. 575; M.R. Ir. 585; V. Chanc. Ir. 575
— Rt., dn. St. Pat. 618
— Rt., U.S.S. 226
— Rt. and sir R., K.B. 764; P.C. 197
— Rog. de, M. Chy. 393
— Saml., adm. (**A**) 820
— sir Th. Manners-, aft. 1st ld. Manners, *q.v.*, B. Ex. 385; K.C. 415; Ld. Chanc. Ir. 577; S.G. 402; S.L. 412
— Wm., gen. (**D**) 897
— Wm., B. Ex. Ir. 583; M.R. Ir. 585
Swaffham, Jno. de, bp. Bgr. 426; bp. Cloy. 630
Swalchyne, Rt. de, Rec. Lond. 493
Swale, sir Rd., M. Chy. 395
Swan, Ed. Bell, C. Acc. Ir. 567
Swanland, Sim. L.M. Lond. 489
Swann, Geo. Jam., C.I.E. 808
Swanston, Clem. Tudw. (No. 1), K.C. 416
— Clem. Tudw. (No. 2), Q.C. 418
Swanton, Rt., adm. (**A**) 814
— Th., Compt. N. 257
Swayn, Jno., abp. Arm. 595
Swayne, Hugh, gen. (**B**) 868
— Spelm., adm. (**H**) 844
Sweatman, Arth., bp. Tor. 693
Sweeting, H. L., G. Mtius. 684
Sweetman, Milo, abp. Arm. 595
Sweit, sir Geiles, D. Arch. 420
Swellengrebel, Hendr., G. C.G.H. 678
Swereford, Alexr. de, B. Ex. 382
Swerendon, Wm., M. Chy. 394
Swerker I. and II., K. Sw. 92
Swertz, *see* Smert
Swetenham and **Swettenham**
— Edm. Q.C. 419
— Kilner, L.M. Dbln. 641
— Matth., L.H.A. 173
Sweyn I. and III., K. Dk. 93
Swi—, *see also* Swy—
Swiatopalk, R. Russ. 89
Swiatoslow, R. Russ. 89
Swift, Fras. Hy., dn. Clonm. 600
— Jonn., dn. St. Pat. 618
Swillington, Ralph, A. G. 398
Swinburn and **Swinburne**
— Ch. Hy., adm. (**G**) 842
— Jno., gen. (**D**) 896
— Jno. Denn., gen. (**D**) 922
— Th. Rt., gen. (**D**) 891
Swindley, Jno. Ed., gen, (**D**) 927
Swinefield, Rd., bp. Her. 441
Swiney, Geo., gen. (**D**) 878
— Geo., gen. (**D**) 917
— Wm., adm. (**A**) 816
Swinhoe, Fk.Wm., gen.(**D**) 916
— Saml., gen. (**D**) 886
Swinly, Geo. Hy., gen. (**D**) 900
Swinnerton and **Swynnerton**
— sir Jno., L.M. Lond. 491
— Rog. de, Const. T.L. 320
Swinton, Alexr., Ld. Sess. 520
— Jno., Ld. Sess. 519
— Jno., Ld. Sess. 520
— Saml., gen. (**C**) 874
Swithed, K.E. 2
Swithelm and **Swithelmus,** *see also* Sigelmus
— K.E. 2
Swithin (St.), bp. Winch. 470
Swithred, K.E. 2
*__Swithulf,__ bp. Roch. 459
*__Swithulfus,__ bp. Lond. 451
* ? same pers.
Swy—, *see also* Swi—
Swynford, Nichs., L.M. Lond. 489
Swynnerton, *see* Swinnerton
Sy—, *see also* Si—
Sybba, bp. Elm. 454
Sybourgh, Ch., gen. (**C**) 871
Sydall, El., bp. Glr. 438; bp. St. Dav. 465; dn. Cant. 431
Sydemanus, bp. Dev. 436
Sydenham and **Sidenham**
— Benj., C. Exc. 281
— Rd., J.C.P. 378
— Sim., bp. Chich. 433; dn. Sal. 468
— Th., Amb. Pgl. 124
— Wm., called ld. S., L.T. 154
Sydenham, lds.
— Ch., 1st ld., form. C. Poulett-Thompson, *q.v.*, G.C.B. 772; G. Can. 692
Sydeserf, Th., bp. Brn. 531; bp. Gall. 538; bp. Ork. 535
Sydgrave, *see* Segrave
Sydney and **Sidney**
— Fk. Wm., adm. (**H**) 852
— sir Hy., K.G. 738; L.J. Ir. 553; V. Treas. Ir. 559
— Hy., *see* ld. S., *infra*
— sir Ph. Ch., aft. ld. De L'Isle and Dudley *q.v.*, G.C.H. 786; K.C.H. 787
— Th., L.M. Lond. 492
— sir Wm., Lt. T.L. 321
Sydney of Penshurst, lds.
— Rt., ld., aft. E. of Leicester, K.B. 762
Sydney of Sheppey, lds. and visc.
— Hy., aft. ld. and visc. Syd., and 1st E. of Romney, *q.v.*, L.J. Ir. 555; L.L. Kent, 309; M.G.O. 258; P.C. 193; S. St. 224; W.C.P. 319
Sydney of Chislehurst, lds., visc., and E.
Townshend Family.
— Th., 1st ld. and visc., form. T. Townshend, *q.v.*, B.C. and Pres. B.C. 252; Pres. B.T. 267; Sec. at W. 234
Sydney of Chislehurst, lds., visc., and E.—*cont.*
— Jno. Rt., 3rd visc., aft. 1st E., Amb. Bgm. 123; C.Y.G. 298; G.C.B. 772; L.C.H. 295; L.L. Kent, 309; L.S.H. 290; P.C. 216
Sydney, lds.
Irish Peerage.
— Dudl. A. S., 1st ld., form. D. A. S. Cosby, *q.v.*
Sydnor, Rd., Regr. Gart. 746
Syed, Ameer Hoss., C.I.E. 808
— Bakir Ali Khan, C.I.E. 807
Syer, Fk. Chev., adm. (**H**) 849
Syers, Jno. D., gen. (**D**) 890
Sykes, Hy. Pet., gen. (**D**) 922
— Jno., adm. (**D**) 825
— Wm. Hy., Chn. E.I.Co. 646
Sylvester and **Silvester**
— I. and II., P. Ro. 33-4
— Jno., Comm. Serjt. Lond. 495; Rec. Lond. 494
— Rt., bp. Suff. Hull, 486
Symeon, *see* Simeon
Symes, Ed. Sp., C.I.E. 808
— Jos., adm. (**H**) 844
— Sutt., dn. Ach. 614
Symmachus, P. Ro. 33
Symonds and **Simonds**
— Jno., Rec. Lond. 493
— Jyrm. Ch., gen. (**D**) 908
— Th. Ed., adm. (**H**) 845
— Th. Matth. Ch. and sir T., adm. (**B**) 821; (**D**) 832; (**E**) 834; G.C.B. 771; K.C.B. 779
— sir Wm., adm. (**G**) 841; Sr. N. 257
Symons and **Simons**
— Ch. Bert., gen. (**D**) 898
— Corn. J., G. Ceyl. 672
— Jno., adm. (**A**) 816
Synge and **Singe**
— Ed. (No. 1). bp. Ardf. and Agh. 639; bp. Crk., Cl. and R. 631; bp. Lim. 638; dn. Elph. 609
— Ed. (No. 2), abp. Tm. 611; bp. Rph. 602; bp. Clonf. and K. 636; bp. Cloy. 631; bp. Elph. 608; bp. Ferns and L. 622
— Fras. Hutch., gen. (**D**) 910
— Geo., bp. Cloy. 630; dn. Drom. 606
— Mill. Hy., gen. (**D**) 911
— Saml., dn. Kild. 619
— Nichs., bp. Killoe. 634; Killoe. and Kilf. 635
Synterby, Nichs. de, B. Ex. Ir. 583; J.C.P. Ir. 581
Syred or **Syredus,** abp. Cant. (?) 430; dn. St. P. 452
Syud, Ameer Ali, C.I.E. 808
— Lutf. Ali Khan, C.I.E. 807

T.

T——, bp. Brn. 530
Taaf, Jno., abp. Arm. 595
Tablere, Danl. le, dn. Tm. 613
Tabley, Geo., 2nd ld. de, P.C. 218; Tr. H. 292
Tablir, Ralph, J. It. 367
Tachmon, Hugh de, bp. Mth. 599; L. Treas. Ir. 558
Tacina (dau. of Owen Tudor), Pr. E. 12
Tacitus, Emp. Ro. 48
Taddy, Wm., S.L. 413
Tadnoth, bp. Roch. 459
Tages, M. O., Pres. Ugy. 111
Tagore, Mahar. Jot. Moh., K.C.S.I. 803
Tailboys, *see* Talboys
Tailer, Wm., S.L.R. 271
Tailerand, dn. Yk. 486
Taillor, *see also* Taylor
—— Th., B. Ex. Ir. 580
Tait, *see also* Tate
—— Archd. C., abp. Cant. 431; bp. Lond. 452; dn. Carl. 476; Jud. Com. P.C. 361; P.C. 216
—— Geo., Ly. Dep. 513
—— Jas. Hold., adm. (**D**) 826
Talang, Kash. Tr., C.I.E. 807
Talbot, Adelb. Cec., C.I.E. 807
—— Bruno, C. Treas. Ir. 559; Ch. Ex. Ir. 562
—— Ch., dn. Exr. 438; dn. Sal. 468
—— hon Ch., *see* ld. T., *infra*
—— Ch. and sir C., adm. (**D**) 831; (**E**) 834; K.C.B. 779
—— Chr. Rice Mans., L.L. Glam. 315
—— Fitzr. Som., gen. (**D**) 934
—— Gilb. and sir G., J. It. 368; K.G. 737; L.H.A. 173; L.S.H. 289
—— Jas., Amb. Swz. 113
—— Jno., *see* ld. T., *infra*
—— hon. Jno., B.T. 265
—— hon. Jno., J. Chest. 387
—— hon. Jno. and sir J., adm. (**A**) 819; G.C.B. 769; K.C.B. 774
—— Jno. and sir J., *see* ld. T., *infra*
—— hon. Jno. C., Q.C. 417
—— Jno. C., *see* E. Talbot, *infra*
—— Jno. G., Sec. B.T. 269
—— Jno. Th., adm. (**H**) 848
—— Rd., bp. Lond. 451; dn. St. P. 452
*—— Rd., abp. Dbln. and Gl. 616; L.D. Ir. 552; Ld. Chanc. Ir. 575
*—— Rd., dn. Chich. 434
* Prob. same pers.
—— Rd., J.C.P. Ir. 581
—— Rd., aft. 1st E. and D. of Tyrconnel, *q.v.*
—— Rt., gen. (**D**) 907
—— hon. Sharr., gen. (**C**) 871
—— Th., D. Chanc. Ir. 575
—— Th., gen. (**D**) 932
—— Wm., bp. Dham. 479; bp. Oxf. 456; bp. Sal. 467; dn. Worc. 473; L.L. Dham. 308
Talbot—*cont.*
—— Wm., M.M. 247
—— Wm., Rec. Dbln. 642
—— sir Wm., M.R. Ir. 585
Talbot, lds. and E., *see also* Shrewsbury
—— Gilbert, 5th ld., K.G. (abt. 1413) 735
—— sir Jno., aft. 12th ld. T. and 1st E. of Shrewsbury, *q.v.*, K.G. 735; L.L. Ir. 552; Ld. Chanc. Ir. 575
—— Jno., aft. 2nd E. of Shr., *q.v.*, K.B. 756
—— Geo., ld., aft. 6th E. of Shr., *q.v.*, K.B. 760
Talbot of Hensoe, lds. and E.
—— hon. Ch., aft. 1st ld. T., Ld. Chanc. 357; P.C. 198; S.G. 401
—— Wm., 2nd ld., aft. Earl T. (1st Cr.), L.H.S. 287; L.S.H. 290; P.C. 200
—— Jno., 3rd ld. and 1st E. (2nd Cr.), B.T. 267
—— Chas., 2nd E. of, K.G. 744; K.P. 751; L.L. Ir. 557; L.L. Staffs. 312; P.C. 209
—— Hy. Jno., 3rd E., aft. E. of Shr. and T., *q.v.*, adm. (**G**) 841; C.G.A. 300; P.C. 216
Talboys (or Tailboys), Hy., K.B. 758
Talebot, *see* Talbot
Talfourd, Th. N. and sir T., J.C.P. 380; P.P. 416; S.L. 413
Talleyrand (de Perigord), Off. Nap. 26
Talmash, Th., gen. (**B**) 864
Tamasp or Thamas Sh. Pers. 99
Tametone, Wm. de, J. It. 367
Tamphilus, C. B., C. Ro. 44
—— M. B., C. Ro. 44
Tamworth, sir Nichs., L.H.A. 172
Tamworth, visc.
—— Rt., visc., form. ld., aft. E. Ferrers, *q.v.*
Tancock, Jno., adm. (**H**) 844
Tancred, K. Scy. 55
—— Hy. Wm., K.C. 416
Tanfield, Laur. and sir L., C.B. Ex. 381; J.K.B. 372; S.L. 409
Tanjore, Vijaya, &c., Rajah of, Cr. Ind. 809
Tankard, Jno., bp. Killa. 612
Tankerville, E. of
Grey Family.
1st Creation.
—— Jno., 1st E. of, K.G. (1419-20) 735; K.B. (1426) 756
2nd Creation.
—— Ford, 1st E. of, B.T. 263; L.P.S. 240; L.T. 155; P.C. 194
Bennet Family.
—— Ch., 1st E. of, K.T. 747; P.C. 196; Postm. G. 238
—— Ch., 2nd E. of, C.Y.G. 298; K.T. 747
—— Ch., 4th E. of, P.C. 204
—— Ch. Augs., 5th E. of, form. ld. Ossulston, *q.v.*
—— Ch., 6th E. of, C.G.A. 300; L.S.H. 290; P.C. 217
Tanks, Wm., C.B. Ex. 381
Tanner, Ed., gen. (**D**) 930
—— Jno., bp. Drom. 604; bp. Dry. 601
—— Oriel Viv., K.C.B. 781
—— Th., bp. St. As. 462
Tantia, Gorey Rav. Bah., C.I.E. 807
Tany, Wm., L.D. Ir. 551; Ld. Chanc. Ir. 574
Taong-Kwang, Emp. Ch. 100
Tapp, Hor. Th., gen. (**D**) 880
—— Th., gen. (**D**) 903
Tappulus, P. V., C. Ro. 43
Tapton, Jno., dn. St. As. 463
Tarbat, Geo., 1st visc., form. G. Mackenzie, *q.v.*, aft. 1st E. of Cromarty, *q.v.*, Comm. Tr. Sc. 497; Sec. St. Sc. 502
Tarbock, Ed., G. I. Man, 666
Tarente, Hy. Ch. de la Tremouille, Pr. of, K.G. 740
Tarkinus, bp. Isl. 539
Tarleton, sir Banastre, G.C.B. 768; gen. (**A**) 860
—— Jno. Walt., adm. (**E**) 835; (**F**) 839; K.C.B. 780; L.Admy. 185
Tarpey, Hugh, L.M. Dbln. 642
Tarquinius (Priscus), K. Ro. 36
—— (Superbus), K. Ro. 36
Tarrant or **Tarrent,** Ch., dn. Carl. 476; dn. Pboro. 458
—— Ch., gen. (**B**) 866
Tash, Th., C. Cus. 276
Tate, *see also* Tait
—— Hy. Carr, gen. (**D**) 900
—— Jno., L.M. Lond. 490
—— Jno., Rec. Lond. 494; S.L. 411
—— Nahum, P. Laur. 301
—— Rt., L.M. Lond. 490
Tatham, Ed., adm. (**H**) 849
Tatius, K. Ro. 36
Tatton, Nev., gen. (**C**) 872
—— Wm., gen. (**B**) 864
Tatwine, abp. Cant. 430
Taubman, Jno., G. I. Man, 666
Taunton, Jno. de, dn. St. Pat. 617
—— Rd., bp. suff. Dov. 431
—— Wm. E., aft. sir W., J.K.B. 373; K.C. 416; S.L. 413
Taunton, lds.
—— Hy., 1st ld., form. Hy. Labouchere, *q.v.*, C. Sec. 235; U.S. W. and C. 231
Taurello, M. Fa. 52
Taurus, T. S., C. Ro. 46
Taverner, Edm., L., gen. (**D**) 919
—— Jno., S. W. F. 271
Tavistock, Wm., 1st M. of, form. 5th E., aft. 1st D. of Bedford, *q.v.*
(*See also* D. of Bedford.)
Tawney, Ch. Hy., C.I.E. 808
Taxton, Jno., Ld. Chanc. Ir. 575
Taylor and **Taylour**
—— Abrm. Ber., K.H. 792
—— Alex. and sir A., gen. (**D**) 905; K.C.B. 780
—— Arth. Hy., gen. (**D**) 933
—— Arth. Jos., gen. (**D**) 901
—— Brooke and sir B., Amb. Bva. 119; Amb. Dk. 127; Amb. G. St. 121; Amb. Pr. 118; G.C.H. 786; P.C. 211
—— Brook Jno., gen. (**D**) 896
—— Ch. Wm., gen. (**D**) 913
—— Ed., C. Exc. Ir. 566
—— Geo., Rec. Dbln. 642
—— Hy., K.C.M.G. 796
—— Herb. and sir H., G.C.B. 768; G.C.H. 786; gen. (**B**) 868; K.C.H. 787; S.G.O. 260

For List of Abbreviations, see pp. 944-952.

Taylor and Taylour—*cont.*
— Hy. Geo. Andr. and sir H., G.C.B. 770; gen. (**D**) 878; K.C.B. 779
— Jas., gen. (**B**) 867
— sir Jas., L.M. Dbln. 641
— Jeremiah., gen. (**D**) 884
— Jeremy, bp. Down. and Cnr. 604; bp. Drom. 605
— Jno., bp. Linc. 447; dn. Linc. 448
— Jno., M.R. 387
— Jno. and sir J., gen. (**B**) 869; K.C.B. 776
— ld. Jno. Hy gen. (**D**) 931
— Jno. Pitt, C.C.J. 404
— Jos. Newh. adm. (**A**) 845
— Markh. Le F., gen. (**D**) 934
— Michl. Ang., P.C. 212
— Pringle, G., Jam. 713; gen. (**D**) 891; K.H. 791
— Reyn. Geo., gen. (**D**) 907
— Rd., S.L. 409
— Rd. Ch. H. and sir R., gen. (**D**) 904; K.C.B. 781
— Rt., dn. Clonf. 637
— hon. Rt., gen. (**A**) 860
— Saml., Q.C. 420
— Th. adm. (**A**) 816
— (or Taillor), Th., B. Ex. Ir. 583
— Th., L.M. Dbln. 641
— Th., Mod. K. Sc. 547
— Th. Ed., C.D.L. 243; L.T. 161; P.C. 217; Sec. Tr. 163
— Th. Matth., gen. (**D**) 887
— Th. Wm., gen. (**D**) 882
— Wm., adm. (**A**) 818
— Wm., gen. (**A**) 858
— Wm., gen. (**B**) 866
— Wm., gen. (**D**) 887
— Wm., L.M. Lond. 490
— Wm., Mod. K. Sc. 547
— Wm. Nort., adm. (**H**) 850
— Wm. Wilk., gen. (**D**) 923
— Z., Pres. U.S.A. 102
Teate, Jos., dn. Oss. 623
Teck, Fras., &c., D. of, G.C.B. 772
— Mary, Dss of, *see* Mary Adel. &c.
Tedfrid, bp. Dunw. 454
Tedder, Th., dn. Llin. 623
Teed, Jno., Godfr., C.C.J. 404; Q.C. 417
Teesdale, Chr. Ch. and sir C., gen. (**D**) 932; K.C.M.G. 798
— sir Geo., gen. (**D**) 877; K.H. 790
— Hy. Geo., gen. (**D**) 899
Teia, K. It. 49
Teignmouth, Jno., 1st ld., form. sir J. Shore, *q.v.*, B.C. 252-3; P.C. 208
Tejada, S. L. de, Pres. Mex. 104
Telesphorus, P. Ro. 32
Telius, *see* Thelian
Tempest, Th., A.G. Ir. 588
Templar, Hy. Jno., gen. (**D**) 912
Templarius, G., L.H.T. 152
Temple, Chr., C.C.J. 404; K.C. 416
— Fras., adm. (**D**) 825; (**G**) 840
— Fk., bp. Exr. 437; bp. Lond. 452; Jud. Com. P.C. 362; P.C. 220
— Fk., aft. ld. Dufferin, &c., *q.v.*, U.S. Ind. 236

Temple—*cont.*
*— sir Jno., A.G. Ir. 588
*— sir Jno., M.R. Ir. 585
*— sir Jno., S.G. Ir. 589
*— sir Jno., V. Treas. Ir. 559
* Prob. some same pers. Comp. dates.
— Leofr., Q.C. 419
— Oct., G. Si. Le. 685
— Rd. and sir R., Ch. Com. Cent. Pr. 655; G. Bbay. 659; G.C.S.I. 801; K.C.S.I. 803; L.G. Bgal. 652; Sec. S.I. 804
— sir Rd., C. Cus. 273-4; K.B. 763
— sir Rd., aft. ld. and visc. Cobham, *q.v.*, G. Jsey. 667
— Rt. Gr., C.C.J. 403
— Steph., Q.C. 417
— Wm. and sir W., M.R. Ir. 585
— sir Wm., P.C. 192
— hon. Wm. and sir W., Amb. Russ. 126; Amb. Scy. 115; K.C.B. 782
Temple, Earls
— Rd., 2nd E., K.G. 742; L. Admy. 178; L.L. Bucks. 306; L.P.S. 241; P.C. 200
— G. N., 3rd E., form. G. Grenville, *q v.*, aft. 1st M. of Buckm., *q.v.*, F. Sec. 228; L.L. Ir. 557; P.C. 203
— Rd., 4th E., aft. 2nd M. and 1st D. of Buckm., *q.v.*, B.C. 252; P.C. 207; Paym. G. 244; V.P.B.T. 269
— Mary Aug., lady, Cr. Ind. 810
Templeman, Alfr., gen. (**D**) 934
Templetown, Geo. Fk., 3rd visc., form. hon. G. F. Upton, *q.v.*, K.C.B. 780; G.C.B. 771
Tench, Watk., gen. (**B**) 868
Tenham, ld., *see* Teynham
Tenison, *see* Tennison and Tennyson
Tennant, Jas., K.C.B. 777
— Jas. Fras., C.I.E. 806; gen. (**D**) 926
Tennent, Jas. Emers. and sir J., G. Ceyl. 672; G. St. Hel. 682; Sec. B.C. 254; Sec. B.T. 270
Tennison and **Tenison,** *see also* Tennyson
— Ed., bp. Oss. 620
— Ed. K., L.L. Leitr. 570; L.L. Rosc. 571
— Rd., bp. Clr. 596; bp. Mth. 599; dn. Clr. 597; bp. Killa. and Ach. 613
— Th., abp. Cant. 431; bp. Linc. 447; P.C. 194
— Th., J.C.P. Ir. 582; S.L. Ir. 592
Tennyson, *see also* Tennison
— Alf., *see* ld. T., *infra*
— Ch., aft. Tennyson-D'Eyncourt, *q.v.*, Clk. O. 260; P.C. 212
Tennyson, lds.
— Alf., aft. 1st ld. T., P. Laur. 301
Tennyson-D'Eyncourt, *see* D'Eyncourt
Tenterden, lds.
— Ch., 1st ld., form. sir Ch. Abbot, *q.v.*
— Ch. S. A., 3rd ld., K.C.B. 783; U.S.F. 230

Teoldus, bp. Worc. 472
Tergusius, W.C.P. 317
Terlyng, Jno., M. Chy. 393
Ternan, Augs. Hy., gen. (**D**) 923
Ternay, Chev. d'Arz. de, G. Mtius. 683
Terrell, Th. H., C.C.J. 404
Terret, *see* Terrot
Terry, Astl. Fell., gen. (**D**) 933
Terrick, Rd., bp. Lond. 452; bp. Pboro. 458; P.C. 201
Terringham (or Tiringham), Wm., K.B. 763
Terrot, Ch., gen. (**A**) 862
— Ch. Hugh., bp. Edinb. 543; Pr. Bp. Sc. 540
Terryll, Th., C.G.S. 356
Testa, Vit. de, dn. St. P. 453
Testaferrata, Gius. Marq., K.C.M.G. 796
Tessier, Hy. Gr. de, gen. (**D**) 916
Teviot (or Tiviot), visc.
Spencer Family.
— Rt., visc., form. hon. Rt. Spencer, L.P.S. (1685) 240
Livingston Family.
— Th., visc., form. sir Th. Livingston, gen. (**B**) (1704) 864
Tew, Dav., L.M. Dbln. 641
— Jno., L.M. Dbln. 641
Tewfik, V. Eg. 98; G.C.S.I. 801
Teyes, Wal. de, W.C.P. 317
Teynham, lds.
— Jno., 1st ld., K.B. 762
— Chr., 5th ld., L.L. Kent, 309
Thacker, Saml., gen. (**D**) 912
Thackeray, Fk. Renn., gen. (**A**) 863
Thackwell, Jos. and sir J., G.C.B. 769; gen. (**D**) 882; K.C.B. 777; K.H. 790
— Jos. Edwin, gen. (**D**) 905
— Wm. de W. Roche, gen. (**D**) 933
***Thady,** bp. Ach. 612
*— bp. Down and Cnr. 604
*— bp. Drom. 604
*— bp. Killoe. 634
*— bp. Kilm. 607
*— bp. Ross, 631
* Prob. some same pers. Comp. dates.
Thakur, &c., K.C.I.E. 805
Thalna, M. J., C. Ro. 44
Thamas, *see* Tamasp
Thanet, E. of
— Th., 6th E. of, P.C. 195
— Hy., 11th E. of, L.L. Kent, 309
Thayer, Humphr., C. Exc. 280
Thean or **Theanus,** abp. Lond. 450
Thedred, abp. Lond. 450
Thefridus, bp. Dunw. 454
Thelian (or Telius, or Elad), bp. Llff. 448
Thelwall, Ewb., M. Chy. 395
— Th. de, C.D.L. 242; M. Chy. 393; M.R. Ir. 585
***Theobald,** abp. Cant. 430 Ld. Chanc. 353
*— bp. Worc. 472
* ? same pers.
— C. Lux. 84
— I. and II., D. Lne. 29
— I. and II., K. Nav. 85, 87

For List of Abbreviations, see pp. 944-952.

Theodat, K. Sp. 85
Theodatus, K. It. 49
Theodebald, K. Fr. 22
— K. It. 49
Theodebert I. and II., K. Fr. 22-3
Theodiscle, K. Sp. 85
Theodolinda, K. Lmd. 49
Theodora, Emp. E.E. 51
— Emp. Tzde. 98
Theodore, abp. Cant. 430
— P. Ro. 33
— I. and II., R. Russ. 90
— -Lascaris I. and II., Emp. E.E. 51
Theodoric, K. It. 49
— I. and II., K. Sp. 84
Theodorus I. and II., P. Ro. 33-4
*__Theodred,__ bp. Elm. and Dunw. 454
*__Theodredus,__ bp. Lond. 451
* ? same pers.
Theodric, K.E. 2
Theodosius I., Emp. W. E. 49
— I. to III., Emp. E.E. 50
Theodwin, *see* Dedwin
Theologild, abp. Cant. 430
Theonus, bp. Lond. 450
Theophilus, Emp. E.E. 50
Theotoky, Ct. Ant., G.C.M.G. 794; K.C.M.G. 796
— Bar. Em., G.C.M.G. 794
Thereus, K. Sc. 17
Thermus, Q. M., C. Ro. 43
Therry, Jno., C. Exc. Ir. 566-7
Thesiger, hon. Alfr. Hy., Jud. Com. P.C. 361; L.J. App. 389; P.C. 219; Q.C. 419
— hon. Ch. Wemyss, gen. (**D**) 927
— Fk. and sir F., aft. 1st ld. Chelmsford, *q.v.*, A.G. 400; K.C. 416; Ld. Chanc. 358; P.C. 216; S.G. 402
— hon. Fk. Aug., aft. 2nd ld. Chelmsford, *q.v.*, G. C.G.H. &c. 679; gen. (**D**) 907
Theudis, K. Sp. 85
Theudisela, K. Sp. 85
Theulph, bp. Worc. 472
Thewell, Wm. de, L.H.A. 171
Thewles, Jas., gen (**C**) 873
Thicknesse, Fras. Hy., bp. suff. Leic. 458
Thierry, C. Flrs. 81
— I. and II., D. Lne. 29
— I. to IV., K. Fr. 22-3
— I. to IV., C. Fld. 82
— V. to VII., C. Hld. 82
Thiers, L. A., Pres. Fr. 25
Thirkilby, *see* Thurkilby
Thirlby or **Thirleby,** bp. Ely, 435; bp. Norw. 455; bp. Westr. 469
Thirlwall, Conn., bp. St. Dav. 465
Thirij, F. A., K.C.B. 778
Thirninge •(or Thyrnynge), Wm., C.J.C.P. 375; J.C.P. 378
Thirwit, *see* Tirwit
Tholozaine, *see* Tolason
Thirkell, *see* Thyrkyll
*__Thomas__ (2), abp. Yk. 485
*— bp. Clonf. 635
*— (2) bp. Clonm. 600
*— bp. Down, 603
*— bp. Down and Cnr. 604
*— bp. Dnbl. 532
*— bp. E. Ang. 454
*— bp. Emly, 625

Thomas—*cont.*
*— (3), bp. Gall. 538
*— bp. Isl. 539
*— bp. Kild. 616
*— (2) bp. Killa. 612
*— bp. Kilm. 607
*— bp. Lism. 626
*— (2) bp. Llin. 621
*— bp. Ork. 535
*— bp. Ross. 535
*— (2), bp. S. and M. 483
*— (2), bp. St. As. 462
*— dn. Ardf. 640
*— dn. Cash. 627
*— dn. Clonm. 600
*— dn. Dry. 602
*— (of Woodford), dn. Lim. 639
*— dn. Tm. 613
*— (abb. of Winchecumbe), J. It. 367
* Prob. some same pers. Comp. dates.
— C. Svy. 54
— (son Edw. I.), Pr. E. 10
— (son Edw. III.), Pr. E. 10; K.G. 734
— (g. son Edw. III.), Pr. E. 11
— (iss. Edw. III.), Pr. E. 11
— (son Hy. IV.), aft. D. of Clarence, Pr. E. 11; K.B. 755
— sir Edm., B.T. 265; S.W.F. 271
— Ed., C.I.E. 807
— Fras. Wm., gen. (**D**) 929
— Fk. Jenn., adm. (**H**) 845
— sir Geo., G. Leew. Isl. 727
— Geo. Ed., gen. (**D**) 918
— Grant E., G. Bdoes. 721
— Griff. ap, K.B. 759
— Hy., gen. (**D**) 882
— Hor. L., Pres. Coll. Surg. 939
— Hugh, dn. Ely, 435
— Jas., Bl. M.P.A. 336; Chest. H. 331
— Jno., adm. (**A**) 816
— Jno. (No. 1), bp. Linc. 447; bp. Sal. 467; bp. St. As. 462; dn. Pboro. 458
— Jno. (No. 2), bp. Pboro. 458; bp. Sal. 467; bp. Winch. 471
— Jno. (No. 3), bp. Roch, 460 dn. Westr. 469
— Jno., gen. (**B**) 865
— Jno. Well., gen. (**D**) 908
— Lamb., dn. Chich. 434
— Lanc. Fras. Ch., gen. (**D**) 920
— Lewis, bp. suff. Shrewsb. 444
— Mes., bp. Goulb. 704
— Ralph, S.L. 413
— Rd., adm. (**D**) 825
— Rowl., dn. Bgr. 426
— sir Rys ap, K.G. 737
— Wm., bp. St. Dav. 464; bp. Worc. 473; dn. Worc. 473
— Wm., gen. (**B**) 867
— Wm. ap, K.B. 756
Thomian, bp. Arm., 595
Thomlinson, *see* Tomlinson
Thomond, Brian de, K. of Thomond, K.B. (1394) 755
Thomond, E. and M. of
— Hy., 8th E. of, L.L. Esx. 308
— Percy, 1st E. of, form. Percy Wyndham O'Brien, *q.v.*, 294; L.L. Soms. 311; P.C. 200; Tr. H. 291

Thomond, E. and M. of—*cont.*
— Murr., 1st M. of, form. 5th E. of Inchiquin, *q.v.*
— Wm., 2nd M. of, K.P. 750
— Jas., 3rd M. of, form. ld. Jas. O'Bryen, *q.v.*
Thompson, Thomson, and **Tomson**
— Maj. —, G. Trin. 722
— Alexr., and sir A., B. Ex. 385; C.B. Ex. 382; M. Chy. and Acct. G. 397; P.C. 209; S.L. 412
— Alexr., gen. (**D**) 879
— Anthy., dn. Rph. 603
— Arnold, gen. (**D**) 909
— Aug. Riv. and sir A., Ch. Com. Bma. 655; K.C.S.I. 803; L.G. Bgal. 652
— Benj., U.S.C. 235
— Ch., adm. (**A**) 816
— Ch., gen. (**D**) 926
— Ch., K.C. 415
— Ch., M. Chy., 397
— sir Ch., gen. (**A**) 858
— sir Ch., gen. (**B**) 866
— Ch. Hotham-, form. Hotham, *q.v.*
— Ch. Poulett-, aft. ld. Sydenham, *q.v.*, G.G. N. Am. Prov. 692; P.C. 212; Pres. B.T. 268; Tr. N. 257; V.P.B.T. 269
— Ch. Wm., gen. (**D**) 906
— Danl. Rt., C.I.E. 806
— Dav., gen. (**D**) 920
— Ed., L. Admy. 178
— Ed. Deas., K.C.M.G. 797
— Fras. Ringl., gen. (**D**) 890
— Giles, bp. Glr. 438; dn. Winds. 474
— Harry, gen. (**D**) 879
— Hy., Ly. K.A. 513
— Jas., K.C.B. 777
— Jas. Sinc., gen. (**D**) 924
— Jno., adm. (**H**) 844
— Jno., gen. (**D**) 934
— sir Jno., L.M. Lond. 491
— sir Jno. Deas, K.C.H. 788
— Jno. Sp. Dav., K.C.M.G. 799
— Jno. V., S.L. 413
— Mowbr., gen. (**D**) 928
— Narb., adm. (**A**) 820
— Pears. Sc., gen. (**D**) 917
— Ralph Wood and sir W., K.C.B. 784; U.S. War. 233
— Rd., dn. Brl. 440
— Rd. Ll., gen. (**D**) 910
— Rt., C. St. 283
— (or Tounson), Rt., bp. Sal. 467; dn. Westr. 469
— Ron. Ferg. and sir R., Amb. Pers. 130; C.I.E. 806; G.C.M.G. 796; K.C.M.G. 798
— Saml., Ptc. P.A. 337; Winds. H. 331
— Th., dn. Killa. 614
— Th., gen. (**D**) 918
— Th., Lanc. H. 333; R. Dr. P.A. 338
— sir Th. Bould. adm. (**A**) 818; Compt. N. 257; G.C.B. 768; K.C.B. 773
— Th. Perr., gen. (**D**) 885
— Th. Pick., adm. (**E**) 835; (**F**) 838
— Th. P. E., C.C.J. 405
— Th. Sp., adm. (**G**) 843
— sir Th. Raikes Tr., adm. (**G**) 842
— Wm., abp. Yk. 486; bp. Glr. and Br. 439; Jud. Com. P.C. 361; P.C. 217
— Wm., L.M. Lond. 492

Thompson, Thomson, and Tomson—*cont.*
— Wm., S.L. 411
— Wm. and sir W., B. Ex. 384; Curs. B. Ex. 386; Rec. Lond. 494; S.G. 401; S.L. 411
— sir Wm., C. Cus. 273
— W. A., Mod. K. Sc. 547
— Wm. T. and sir W., Amb. Chi. 137; Amb. Pers. 130; K.C.M.G. 797
Thoms, *see also* Toms
— Jno., dn. Ferns, 623
Thomson, *see* Thompson
Thonory, Jno., bp. Oss. 620
Thoralby, Jno., M. Chy. 394
Thorburn, Rt., K.C.M.G. 798
Thoresby, Jno. de, abp. Yk. 485; bp. St. Dav. 464; bp. Worc. 472; Ld. Chanc. 354; L.K. 354; M.R. 387
Thoresbye, Hy., M. Chy. 395
Thorimbergh (or Thurumberd), Aym., Const. T.L. 320
Thorismund, K. Sp. 84
Thoriz, Rog. de, dn. Exr. 437
Thorn and **Thorne**
— Jas., adm. (**H**) 847
— Nathl., gen. (**D**) 882; K.C.B. 778; K.H. 790
— Peregr. Fras., K.H. 792
— Steph. de, dn. Her. 442
— Wm., dn. Chich. 434
— Wm., K.H. 790
Thorndon, *see* Thornton
Thornborough, Thornbrough, Thornburg, and **Thornburgh**
— Ed. and sir E., adm. (**A**) 817; G.C.B. 768; K.C.B. 773
— Ed. Le Cras, adm. (**G**) 841
— Jno., bp. Brl. 439; bp. Lim. 638; bp. Worc. 473; dn. Yk. 487
— Th., Rec. Lond. 493
— Th., Winds. H. 331
— Walt. de, Ld. Chanc. Ir. 574
Thorndike, Danl., gen. (**D**) 899
Thorne, *see* Thorn
Thornhill, Anthy. Rt., gen. (**D**) 917
— Jas. Badh., K.H. 792
— Hy., gen. (**D**) 925
— Wm., K.H. 789
Thornton (or Thorndon), Ægedius, L. Treas. Ir. 558
— Ch. Macl. Jno., gen. (**D**) 920
— Ch. Wade and sir C., G.C.H. 787; gen. (**B**) 870; K.C.H. 787; K.H. 789
— Ed. and sir E. (No. 1), Amb. Dk. &c. 127; Amb. G. St. 121; Amb. H. Tns. 120; Amb. Pgl. 125; Amb. Pr. 118; Amb. Sw. 126; G.C.B. 772; P.C. 209
— Ed. and sir E. (No. 2), Amb. Arg. 136; Amb. Bzl. 135; Amb. N.G. 134; Amb. Pgl. 125; Amb. Pgy. 136; Amb. Russ. 126; Amb. Tky. 130; Amb. U.S.A. 132; Amb. Ugy. 137; G.C.B. 773; K.C.B. 783; P.C. 218
— Gilb. de, A.G. 398; C.J.K.B. 369; S.L. 406
— Jno., C.I.R. 285; C. St. 284; C. St. and Tx. 285; C. Tx. 285
— Peter de, K.B. 755
— Rt., Chn. E.I. Co. 645
Thornton—*cont.*
— Saml., adm. (**G**) 841
— Saml., bp. Ballt. 705
— Th. H., Sec. S.I. 804
— Wm., gen. (**B**) 866
— Wm., gen. (**C**) 872
— Wm. and sir W., gen. (**B**) 869; K.C.B. 776
— Wm. H., K.C.M.G. 796
Thorold, Anthy. Wils., bp. Roch. 460
— sir Geo., L.M. Lond. 491
— Regd. Goth., gen. (**D**) 931
Thorp and **Thorpe**
— Ch., L.M. Dbln. 641
— Fras., B. Ex. 384; S.L. 409
— Geo. de, K.B. 754
— Gerv., dn. Wford. 628
— Jno. de, J. It. 369
— Jno. Th., L.M. Lond. 492
— Rt., gen. (**D**) 894
— Rt. de (No. 1), J.C.P. 377
— Rt. de and sir R. (No. 2), C.J.C.P. 375; Ld. Chanc. 354; S.L. 406
— Rt. de (No. 3), J. It. 369
— Saml., K.H. 791
— Saml. Jos., gen. (**D**) 919
— (or Trop), Sim. de, J. It. 368
— Th., B. Ex. 383; Ch. Ex. 153; Sp. H.C. 248
— Wm. de and sir W., A.G. 398; B. Ex. 383; C.J.K.B. 369; J.C.P. 377; J.K.B. 371; S.L. 406
Thring, Jno. Ed., gen. (**D**) 915
— Hy., aft. 1st ld. T., K.C.B. 783
Throckmorton and **Throgmorton**
— sir Nichs., Chambn. Ex. 166
— Rt., K.B. 759
— Wm., M. Chy. 394
Thuillier, Hy. Ed. Land. and sir H., gen. (**D**) 909
Thurbone, Jno., S.L. 411
Thurkilby (or Thirkilby, Rog. de, Ch. Jr. 363; J.C.P. 376; J. It. 368; J.K.B. 371; Jy. 364
Thurland, sir Ed., B. Ex. 384; S.L. 410
Thurles, Jas., visc., form. J. Butler, *q.v.*, aft. 9th E. of Ormond, *q.v.*
Thurlow, Ed., Ch. Sec. Ir. 562
— Ed., *see* ld. T., *infra*
— hon. Th. Linc., bp. Dham. 479; bp. Linc. 447; dn. Roch. 461; dn. St. P. 453
Thurlow, lds.
— Ed., aft. 1st ld. E., A.G. 399; K.C. 415; L.H.S. 287; Ld. Chanc. 357; P.C. 203; S.G. 402; Tell. Ex. 168
— Thos. Jno., 5th ld., L.H.C. K. Sc. 546; P.C. 221; Paym. G. 245
Thursby, *see* Thoresby
Thurstan, abp. Yk. 485
Thurston, Jno. Bates and sir J., G. Fiji, 711; G. W. Pac. 711; K.C.M.G. 798
— Mark, M. Chy. and Acct. G. 396
Thrupp, Arth. Th., adm. (**E**) 837
Thurumburd, *see* Thorimbergh
Thuysz, Jan., G. Ceyl. 672
Thwaites, Geo. Saund., gen. (**D**) 885
— Th., C.D.L. 242
Thyn, *see* Thynne
Thynbegh, *see* Tynebegh
Thynne, Egr., S.L. 409
— Fras., Lanc. H. 333
— ld. Geo., aft. 2nd ld. Carteret, *q.v.*, B.T. 268; Compt. H. 293; L.T. 158; P.C. 207
— Hy., Tr. H. 292
— Hy. Fk. (No. 1), aft. 1st ld. Carteret, *q.v.*, C. Exc. 278; L.T. 155; P.C. 202
— ld. Hy. Fk. (No. 2), P.C. 219
— ld. Jno., aft. 3rd ld. Carteret, *q.v.*, B.T. 268; P.C. 207; V.C.H. 297
Thyrnynge, *see* Thirninge
Thyrkyll, Lanc., K.B. 759
Ti—, *see also* Ty—
Tibelot, Pain de, K.B. 754
Tiberius, bp. Down and Cnr. 604
— (3), Emp. Ro. 47
— II. and III., Emp. E.E. 50
Tichborne, *see also* Titchbourn
— sir Hy., L.G.O. 259; L.J. Ir. 554
— Rt., L.M. Lond. 491
Tickel, Rd., C. St. 283-4
Tickell, Rd., gen. (**D**) 881
— Th., U.S.S. 225
Tickhill, Th., A.G. 398
Tidcomb, Jno., gen. (**B**) 864
Tidhelm, bp. Her. 441
Tidy, Th. Holmes, gen. (**D**) 903
Tierney, Geo., M.M. 247; P.C. 207; Pres. B.C. 252; Tr. N. 256
— (or O'Tierney), Jno., dn. Kilmacd. 637
— sir Matth., K.C.H. 787
Tigermas, K. Ir. 20
***Tigernach** (Boircech), bp. Cld. 599
*— (O'Mœleoin), bp. Clonm. 599
*— (St.), bp. Clonm. 599
*— (St.), bp. Clr. 596
*— (2), bp. Drom. 604
* Prob. some same pers. Comp. dates.
Tighe, Ed., C. Acc. Ir. 567
— Hugh U., dn. Ard. 609; dn. Dry. 602; dn. Llin. 624
— W. Fk., L.L. Kilk. 570
Tilbury, Rd. de, Const. T.L. 320
Tildeslegh, *see also* Tyldsley
— Th., S.L. 407
Tilesworth, Wm., M.M. 246
Tilford, *see* Tydferth
Tilhere, bp. Hex. 480; bp. Worc. 472
Tilley and **Tilly**
— Hy., K.B. 754
— Jno., gen. (**D**) 934
— Jno., K.C.B. 783; Sec. P.O. 239
— Saml. Leon. and sir S., G. N. Brk. 696; K.C.M.G. 797
Tillotson, Jno., abp. Cant. 431; dn. Cant. 431; dn. St. P. 453; P.C. 194
Tilly, *see* Tilley
Tilred, bp. Lindisf. 478
Tilson, Geo., U.S.S. 225
— Hy., bp. Elph. 608; dn. Chr. Ch. Dbln. 618

For List of Abbreviations, see pp. 944-952.

Timbrell, Harry V., gen. (**D**) 919
Tindal, *see also* Tyndall
— Louis Sym., adm. (**H**) 849
— Nichs. C. and sir N., C.J.C.P. 376; Jud. Com. P.C. 360; P.C. 211; S.G. 402; S.L. 413
Tinker, Jno., G. Bah. Isl. 716
Tinley, Rt. Newt., gen. (**D**) 904
Tinling, Ch., adm. (**A**) 820
— Ed. Burn., adm. (**H**) 848
— Isaac Patt., gen. (**C**) 874
Tinningham, Ad. de, bp. Abdn. 530
Tinney, Wm. Hy., K.C. 416; M. Chy. 397
Tippetts, sir Jno., Sr. N. 257
Tipping, Rt., gen. (**B**) 867
Tiptoft, Jno. de and sir J., K.B. 755; L.H.T. 153; Sp. H.C. 248
— Jno., *see* ld. T., *infra*
— sir Rt., L.H.A. 170
Tiptoft, lds.
— Jno., ld., *see* E. of Worcester
Tirrtullus, bp. Her. 441
Tiringham, *see* Terringham
Tirloch, K. Ir. 22
Tirrey, Dom., bp. Crk. and Cl. 631
Tiruvarur, &c., C.I.E. 806
Tirwhit, *see* Tyrrwhitt
Tirwit (or Thirwit), Rt., J.C.P. 378; J.K.B. 371; S.L. 407
Tisdall, Archd., adm. (**H**) 845
— Ph., A.G. Ir. 588; S.G. Ir. 589; S.L. Ir. 592; Sec. St. Ir. 562
Tissyngton, Rd. de, M. Chy. 393
Titchbourn, *see also* Tichborne
— Col. —, Lt. T.L. 322
Titchfield, Wm. Hy., M. of, aft. 4th D. of Portland, *q.v.*, L.L. Mdx. 310; L.T. 158
Titcomb, Jonn. H., bp. Rangn. 655
Titilus, K.E. 2
Titius, M., C. Ro. 47
Titulus, K.E. 2
Titus (3), Emp. Ro. 47
Tiviot, *see* Teviot
Tobias, bp. Roch. 459
Tobin, Geo., adm. (**D**) 823
— Jos. Webbe, gen. (**A**) 863
Tocliffe, Rd., bp. Winch. 470; Ch. Jr. 362; J. It. 366; Jy. 363
Tod and **Todd**
— Anth., Sec. P.O. 239
— Darcy, K.H. 789
— Jno., bp. Down. and Cnr. 604; bp. Drom. 604; dn. Cash. 627; dn. Oss. 623
— Suet. Hy., gen. (**D**) 879
— Wm., dn. Drom. 606
Tola, bp. Kild. 616
Tolason (or Tholazaine), Jno., L.M. Lond. 489
Toler, Jno., A.G. Ir. 588; C.J.C.P. Ir. 581; S.G. Ir. 589; S.L. Ir. 592
Tollemache, Jno. Rd. Delap., adm. (**A**) 819
Toller, Saml. B., Q.C. 418
Tolly, Count Barcl. de, G.C.B. 767
*— lt.-col. —, G. Trin. 722
*— Hy., gen. (**C**) 874
* Prob. same pers.

Tombs, Hy. and sir H., gen. (**D**) 902; K.C.B. 779
— Jno., gen. (**D**) 878
Tomkyns, Geo., gen. (**D**) 888
Tomline, Geo. Pretyman, form. Pretyman, bp. Linc. 447; bp. Winch. 471; dn. St.P. 453
Tomlins, Rd., Curs. B. Ex. 386
Tomlinson and **Thomlinson**
— Geo., bp. Gibr. 670
— Matth., Comm. Ir. 554-5
— Nichs., adm. (**A**) 820
Toms *see also* Thoms
— Peter, Ptc. P.A. 337
Tomson, *see* Thompson
Tonei, Simeon de, bp. Mor. 534
Tong or **Tonge,** Th., Clar. K.A. 328; Norr. K.A. 329; Yk. H. 334
Tonson, Jacob, gen. (**D**) 880
— hon. Ludl., bp. Killoe., K., Cl. and K. 636
Tonstall, *see* Tunstall
Tony, Michl., L.M. Lond. 488
Tonyn, Patr., gen. (**A**) 859
Tooker, *see* Tucker
Toone, Wm., K.C.B. 775
Toovey, Jno., gen. (**C**) 871
Topcliffe, Jno., C.B. Ex. Ir. 582; C.J.K.B. Ir. 577
Topham, Anthy., dn. Linc. 448
Toppesfeld, Fras., B. Ex. Ir. 583
Toppin, Jas. Morr., gen. (**D**) 932
Topping, Jas., P.P. 415
Torbach, bp. Arm. 595
Torell, Wm., Jy. 363
Torgesius, bp. Lim. 638
Torkinus, bp. S. and M. 483
Tornoura, Ad. de, J. It. 366
Toro, M. M., Pres. U.S.C. 107
Torquatus, A. M., C. Ro. 44
— L. M., C. Ro. 46
— — T. M., C. Ro. 41-2-3-4; Dt. Ro. 43
— T. M. J. (3), C. Ro. 40; Dt. Ro. 40-1
Torr, Jno. B., Q.C. 419
Torre, M. G. de la, Pres. Ecr. 108
Torrens, Arth. Welles., gen. (**D**) 889; K.C.B. 777
— Hy. and sir H., gen. (**C**) 874; K.C.B. 774
— Hy. D'O. and sir H., G. C.G.H. &c. 679; G. Mlta. 671; gen. (**D**) 908; K.C.B. 782
— Rt., J.C.P. Ir. 582; S.L. Ir. 593
— Rt. Rd., and sir R., G.C.M.G. 795; K.C.M.G. 797
Torrington, Ph. de, abp. Cash. 625
Torrington, lds., visc., and E. of
Herbert Family.
— Arth., 1st E. of, form. Arth. Herbert, *q.v.*
Newport Family.
— Th., 1st ld., form. hon. T. and ld. Newport, *q.v.*, L.T. 156; P.C. 197; Tell. Ex. 167
Byng Family.
— Geo., 1st visc., form. sir G. and ld. Byng, *q.v.*, K.B. 764; L.H.A. 177-8

Torrington, lds., visc. and E. of—*cont.*
— Pattée, 2nd visc., form. hon. P. Byng, *q.v.*. C.Y.G. 298; V. Treas. Ir. 560
— Geo., 3rd visc., gen. (**C**) 871
— Geo., 4th visc., Amb. G. St. 121
— Geo., 6th visc., adm. (**A**) 819
— Geo., 7th visc., Amb. Bgm. 123; G. Ceyl. 672
Torrismund, K. Sp. 84
Torry, Patr., bp. Dkld. and Dnbl. 542; bp. Fife, Dkld., and Dnbl. 543
Tortherus, bp. Her. 441
Tostius, *see* Tuistius
Tota, *see* Totta
Tothill, Jno., gen. (**D**) 891
— Jno., M. Chy. 396
Totila, K. It. 49
Totington, Alexr., bp. Norw. 455
— Sams. de, J. It. 366
Totta and **Tota**
— bp. Dorch. 446
— bp. Sels. 432
Tottenham, Loft. Anthy., gen. (**A**) 859
— Ch., aft. ld. Loftus, *q.v.*, C. Cus. Ir. 565
— ld. Rt. Ponsonby, bp. Clr. 596; bp. Ferns and L. 622; bp. Killoe. and Kilf. 635
Totnes, Geo., 1st E. of, form. sir G. and ld. Carew, M.G.O. 258
Totty, sir Jno., L.M. Dbln. 640
— Th., adm. (**A**) 817
Touch, Jno. Gr., gen. (**D**) 926
Touchet, Ferd. or Merv., K.B. 762
— Jas., K.B. 757
Tounson, Rt., *see* Thompson
Tour, Sanch. de la, K.G. (?) 734
Tournay, Wm. de, dn. Linc. 447
Tourner, Tim., S.L. 410
Toutheby, Gilb. de, J. It. 369; S.L. 406
Touzel, Helier, gen. (**A**) 863
Tovar, M. F., Pres. Vzla. 108
Tovey, Wm., G. Gibr. 670
Tower and **Towre**
— Con., gen. (**D**) 918
— Jno., adm. (**D**) 825
— Rd. de la, R. Dr. P.A. 337
Towers, Fk., gen. (**D**) 893
— Jno., bp. Pboro. 458; dn. Pboro. 458
Towgood, Rd., dn. Brl. 440
Townley, Ch. and sir C., Bl. M. P.A. 336; Clar. K.A. 328; Gart. K.A. 328; Lanc. H. 333; Norr. K.A. 329; Yk. H. 334
— Ch. Watson, L.L. Cambs. 306
Townsend, *see* Townshend
Towre, *see* Tower
Towse, Wm., S.L. 409
Townshend and **Townsend**
*— Ch. (No. 1), L. Admy. 179; L.T. 167
*— Ch. (No. 2), Tr. N. 256
* Prob. same pers.
— Ch. (No. 3), aft. 1st ld. Bayning, *q.v.*, P.C. 203; V. Treas. Ir. 560

For List of Abbreviations, see pp. **944-952.**

Townshend and Townsend—*cont.*
— hon. Ch. (No. 4), B.T. 265; Ch. Ex. 165; L. Admy. 178; L.T. 157; P.C. 200; Paym. G. 244; Pres. B.T. 265; Sec. at W. 233; Tr. Ch. 294
— Ch., *see* visc. T., *infra*
— Ed., dn. Norw. 456
— Fras., Bath K.A. 785; R. Cr. P.A. 335; R. Dr. P.A. 338; Winds. H. 331
— Geo., C. Exc. 279; C. St. 283
— hon. Geo., adm. (**A**) 814
— Geo., *see* visc. and marq. T., *infra*
— H., J. Chest. 386
— Ham., dn. Ach. 614
— Hy. Dive, gen. (**D**) 891
— hon. Hor., C. Exc. 280
— hon. Hor. G. P., K.C.H. 788
— Isaac, adm. (**A**) 814; G. Gr. Hosp. 854
— Jas., L.M. Lond. 492
— ld. Jas., K.C.H. 788
— Jno., C. Cus. Ir. 565; C. Exc. Ir. 566
— hon. Jno., aft. ld. Jno. T., L. Admy. 179-80; P.C .208; Paym. G. 245
— Jno., *see* marq. T., *infra*
— Jno. Fitzhenry, J. Admy. Ct. Ir. 587
— hon. Jno. Th., aft. 2nd visc. Sydney, *q.v.*, L. Admy. 180; L.T. 158; U.S. Home, 227
— Rd., C. Cus. Ir. 565; C. Exc. Ir. 566
— Rt., S.L. 408
— Rog., J.C.P. 378; S.L. 407
— Saml., gen. (**C**) 872
— Saml. Ph., adm. (**H**) 853
— Steph., dn. Exr. 437
— Th., gen. (**C**) 872
— Th. (No. 1), Tell. Ex. 167; U.S.S. 225
— Th. (No. 2), aft. 1st ld. and 1st visc. Sydney, *q.v.*, F. Sec. 228; L.T. 157; P.C. 202; Paym. G. 245; Sec. at W. 234
— Th. Stew., bp. Mth. 599; dn. Wford. 628
— Wm. Chamb., dn. Tm. 613
— Wm. Ch., Q.C. 417
Townshend, visc. and M.
— Ch., 2nd visc., L.L. Ir. 556; L.P.C. 188; K.G. 741; P.C. 195; S. St. 224
— hon. Geo., aft. 4th visc. and 1st M., F.M. 856; G. Ch. Hosp. 936; gen. (**A**) 858; L.G.O. 259; L.L. Ir. 557; L.L. Norf. 310; M.G.O. 259; P.C. 200
— Geo., 2nd M., form. ld. de Ferrers and E. of Leicester, *q.v.*
— Jno., 4th M., adm. (**G**) 842
Tozer, Jno., S.L. 413
— Wm. Geo., bp. C. Afr. 688; bp. Jam. 713
Tracey, Ch. Hanbury, aft. 1st ld. Sudeley, *q.v.*
— Hy. de, B. Ex. 382; J. It. 367
— Rd. Ed., adm. (**E**) 837
— Rt. and sir R., B. Ex. 384; C.G.S. 357; J.C.P. 379; J.K.B. Ir. 579; S.L. 411
Tracton, Jas., 1st ld., form. J. Dennis, *q.v.*
Trafford and **Traford**
— Ed., K.B. 759
— Rd. L., C.C.J. 403
— Th. Saml., gen. (**D**) 885
Trahaern ab Caradoc, Pr. Wls. 16
Trail, Jas., bp. Down. and Cnr. 604
— Jas., E.S.P. 301
— Jas., U.S. Ir. 563
— Saml., Mod. K. Sc. 547
— Walt., bp. St. And. 529
Traill, Geo. Balf., gen. (**D**) 934
Trahern, *see* Traheyron
Traheron, Barth., dn. Chich. 434
Traheyron (or Trahern), Th., Nottm. P.A. 343; Ptc. P.A. 337; Som. H. 332
Trajan, Emp. Ro. 47
Tramerin, bp. St. Dav. 464
Trapaud, Cyrus, gen. (**A**) 858
Traquair, Jno., 1st E. of, H.C.P. Sc. 507; L.H.C. K. Sc. 546; L.H.T. Sc. 497; Ld. Sess. 517
Trau, Berm. Arn., &c., K.G. 734
Traunt, Patr., C. Exc. 278
Travancore, Mahar. of (2), G.C.S.I. 801; K.C.S.I. 802
— Rani of, Cr. Ind. 810
Travers, Benj., Pres. Coll. Surg. 939
— Boyle, gen. (**A**) 862
— Eaton and sir E., adm. (**H**) 847; K.H. 790
*— Jas., gen. (**D**) 900
*— Jas., K.H. 792
* ? same pers.
— Jas. Fras. Eaton, gen. (**D**) 912
— Jos. Oates, gen. (**D**) 901
— Pet., M.R. Ir. 585
— Rt. (No. 1), bp. Killoe. 634
— Rt. (No. 2), bp. Llin. 622
— sir Rt.. gen. (**C**) 874
— Saml., S.L.R. 271
Traverst, R., K.C.M.G. 796
Trayford, Edmd., K.B. 756
Trayner, Jno., Ld. Sess. 521
Treacher, Wm. Hood, G. Br. N. Bno. 676
Trebonius, C., C. Ro. 46
Treby, Geo., L.T. 156
— Geo. and sir G., A.G. 399; C.G.S. 357; C.J.C.P. 375; Rec. Lond. 494; S.G. 401; S.L. 411
— Geo. and sir G., Sec. at W. 233; Tell. Ex. 167
— Paul Winsl. Phillips, gen. (**D**) 921
Trecothick, Barl., L.M. Lond. 492
Tredegar, Ch. M. R., L.L. Brec. 315
Tredennick, Jas. Rd. Kn., gen. (**D**) 930
Treffnant (or Trevenant), Jno., bp. Her. 441
Trefusis, hon. Ch. Rod., aft. ld. Clinton, *q.v.*, C. Exc. 281, 282; C. Ex. Ir. 567
Tregonwell, Jno. and sir J., J. Adm. Ct. 422; M. Chy. 394
Tregrision, Ralph, dn. Exr. 437
Tregury, Michl., abp. Dbln. and Glr. 616; dn. St. Pat. 618
Trelawney, Ch., gen. (**C**) 871
*— Ed., C. Cus. 275
*— Ed., G. Jam. 712
* Poss. same pers.
— Ed., dn. Exr. 438
— Ham., G. St. Hel. 682
— Harry, gen. (**C**) 872
— Jno. Jago, gen. (**D**) 927
— sir Jonn., bp. Brl. 439; bp. Exr. 437; bp. Winch. 471
— sir Wm., G. Jam. 712
— sir Wm., L.L. Cnwall. 307
Trellick, *see* Trilleck
Tremayle, Th., J.K.B. 372; S.L. 407
Tremayne, Jno., Comm. Serjt. Lond. 495; Rec. Lond. 493; S.L. 411
Tremenhere and **Tremenheere**
— Ch. Wm., gen. (**D**) 901
— Walt. R., gen. (**D**) 880; K.H. 790
Tremlett, Franciso Sangro, adm. (**H**) 852
— Wm. Hy. Br., adm. (**D**) 824; (**G**) 840
Tremulus, Q.M. (2), C. Ro. 41
Trench, hon. Eyre Power, gen. (**B**) 866
— Fk. Chen., gen. (**D**) 934
— sir Fk. Wm., gen. (**A**) 863; K.C.H. 788
— Hy. Le Poer, gen. (**D**) 914
— hon. Power, abp. Tm. 611; abp. Tm. and bp. Kill. and Ach. 613; bp. Elph. 608; bp. Wford. and L. 627
— Rd. Chen., abp. Dbln. G. and K. 617; dn. Westr. 469
— hon. Rt. Le Poer, K.C.B. 774
— Th., dn. Kild. 619
— hon. Wm. Le Poer, adm. (**D**) 824
Trenchard, Jno., C. Tx. 284, 285
*— Jno., C.J. Chest. 386; S.L. 411
*— sir Jno., P.C. 194; S. St. 224
* Prob. same pers.
Trentham, Gr. L., visc., aft. 2nd E. Gower, *q.v.*, L.H.A. 178
Tresham, Wm. and sir W., C.D.L. 242; Sp. H.C. 248
Tresilian (or Tresylian), Rt. and sir R., C.J.K.B. 370 J.K.B. 371; S.L. 407
Treslove, Th. C., K.C. 416
Treswell, Andrew, S.W.F. 271
— (or Creswell), Rt., Bl. M. P.A. 336; Som. H. 332
— Rt., S.W.F. 271
Tresylian, *see* Tresilian
Trevaignon, Jno. de, J.C.P. 377; S.L. 406
Trevanyon, Jno., K.B. 759
Trevaur, Jno. (2), bp. St. As. 462
Trevelyan, Ch. Ed. and sir C., G. Mdras. 657; K.C.B. 782; Sec. Tr. 164
— Geo. Ott. and sir G., C.D.L. 243; Ch. Sec. Ir. 563; L. Admy. 185; L.K. Sc. 503; P.C. 220; Sec. Adm. 187; Sec. Sc. 502; V.P. Ed. Sc. 500
— Hy. Will., gen. (**D**) 902
— Jno., K.B. 759
— Will., gen. (**D**) 896
Trevenant, *see* Treffnant
Trevet, Th., J. It. 368; Jy. 365

Trevor, —, Sec. at W. 233
— hon. Arth., aft. 2nd V. Dungannon, *q.v.*, C. Cus. Ir. 565; C. Exc. Ir. 566
— Arth. Hill, gen. (**D**) 893; K.H. 791
— Ed., gen. (**D**) 896
— Fras. Ch., gen. (**D**) 922
— Hugh, L.M. Dbln. 641
— Jno., K.C. 415
— Jno. and sir J. (No. 1), C.G.S. 357; K.C. 414; M.R. 388; P.C. 194; Sp. H.C. 250
— sir Jno. (No. 2), P.C. 190; S. St. 223
— hon. Jno. (No. 3), L. Admy. 178
— hon. Jno. (No. 4), Amb. G. St. 121; Amb. Sda. 114; P.C. 206
— Jno. Sal., gen. (**D**) 920
— sir Rd., J. Adm. Ct. 423
— hon. Rd., bp. Dham. 479; bp. St. Dav. 465
— Teudor, L.G. Gr. Hosp. 852
— Th. and sir T., B. Ex. 384; S.L. 409
— Th., *see* ld. Tr., *infra*
— Wm. Cosm., G. Tasm. 708; gen. (**D**) 919
Trevor, lds.
— sir Th. and ld. T., A.G. 399; C.G.S. 357; C.J.C.P. 376; K.B. 763; L.P.C. 188; L.P.S. 240; P.C. 195, 197; S.G. 401; S.L. 411
Trewman, Jno. T., gen. (**D**) 881
Trewythosa, Sim. de, A.G. 398; S.L. 406
Trial-Faidh, K. Ir. 20
Tricipitinus, H. L., C. Ro. 39
— L. L., C. Ro. 38
— L. L. F., C. Ro. 39
— S. L., C. Ro. 37
— T. L. (2), C. Ro. 37
Tricostus, A. V., C. Ro. 37-8
— L. V., C. Ro. 39
— O. V., C. Ro. 37-8
— (Rutilus), P. V., C. Ro. 37
— S. V., C. Ro. 38
— T. V., C. Ro. 37-8
Tridianus, *see* Tyrcheanus
Trigeminus, P. C. F., C. Ro. 38; Dec. Ro. 38
Trigge, Th. and sir T., G. Gibr., 670; gen. (**A**) 859; K.B. 766; L.G.O. 259
Trikingham, Lamb. de, B. Ex. 383; J.C.P. 377; J. It. 368-9; J.K.B. 371
Trilleck or **Trillock,** Ad. de (2), dn. Oss. 622
— Jno., bp. Her. 441
— Th., bp. Roch. 460; dn. Her. 442; dn. St. P. 453
Trimingham, Jno., G. Bmda. 701
Trimleston, Jno., 3rd ld., form. sir Jno. Barnewall, *q.v.*, J.K.B. Ir. 578; L. Treas. Ir. 559; Ld. Chanc. Ir. 576
Trimmell, Wm., dn. Winch. 471
Trimnell, Ch., bp. Norw. 455; bp. Winch. 471
Trinder, Hy., S.L. 411
— Jno., M.M. 247
Tripe, Linn., gen. (**D**) 914
Tristram, Th. Hutch., Ch. Lond. 422; Q.C. 419
Trobe, *see* Latrobe
Trollope, Ch., gen. (**D**) 896; K.C.B. 780
— Ed., bp. suff. Nottm. 447
— Geo. Barne., adm. (**H**) 845
— Hy., adm. (**H**) 851
— sir Hy. adm. (**A**) 817; G.C.B. 768; K.C.B. 775
— Hy. Anthy., adm. (**H**) 853
— sir Jno., P.C. 215; Pres. P.L.B. 262
Tronson, Rt. Nix., gen. (**D**) 923
Trop, *see* Thorp
Trott, G. Bah. Isl. 716
Trotter, Alex., gen. (**B**) 867
— Hy. Dund., adm. (**G**) 842
— Rt., Postm. G. Sc. 502
— Th., gen. (**C**) 873
— Wm., L. Prov. Edinb. 548
Trotti, Ard., K.C.B. 778
Troubridge, sir Ed. Th., adm. (**D**) 827; L. Admy. 182, 183
— sir Th., adm. (**A**) 817; L. Admy. 180
Troup, Col., gen. (**D**) 899
— Hugh, gen. (**D**) 897
Troutbecke, Wm., C.D.L. 242
Trower, Jas., K.C. 415; M. Chy. 397
— Walt. Jno., bp. Gibr. 670; bp. Glasg. and Gall. 544
Truell, Rt. Holt., gen. (**D**) 929
Trujillo, J., Pres. U.S.C. 107
Trumbull, sir Wm., L.T. 155; P.C. 194; S. St. 224
Trumhere, bp. Lich. 443
Trumpington, Wm. de, J. It. 367
Truro, Thos., 1st ld., form. sir T. Wilde, *q.v.*
Truscott, sir Fras. W., L.M. Lond. 492
— Jno., gen. (**D**) 878
— Wm., adm. (**A**) 816
Trussell, Wm., J.C.P. 377; Jy. 365
*— Wm., Sp. H.C. 248
*— sir Wm., L.H.A. 172
* Prob. same pers.
Trutch, Jos. Wm., G. Br. Cbia. 698; K.C.M.G. 799
Trydell, Botet, gen. (**D**) 893
Tryon, Geo. and sir G., adm. (**E**) 837; K.C.B. 782; Sec. Adm. 187
— Rt., adm. (**G**) 843
— Saml., gen. (**D**) 901
— Wm., gen. (**B**) 866
Tsai-t'ien, Emp. Ch. 100
Tuadcar, bp. Kild. 616
Tuathal, bp. Clonm. 599
— -Maolgarbh, K. Ir. 21
— -Teachtmar, K. Ir. 21
Tubertus, A. P., Dt. Ro. 39
— P. P. (2), C. Ro. 37
Tubman, Nichs., Hps. P.A. 343; Lanc. H. 333; R. Cr. P.A. 335
Tucca, C. S., C. Ro. 42
Tucker, Auchm., gen. (**D**) 900
— Benj., Sec. Adm. 187
— Danl., G. Bmda. 701
— Ed., C. St. 283; C. Tx. 284
— Ed. and sir E., adm. (**D**) 826; G.C.B. 770; K.C.B. 774
— Hy. St. Geo., Chn. E.I.Co. 645
— Jno., U.S.S. 225
— Jno. Jerv., adm. (**D**) 831; (**G**) 841
— Jos., dn. Glr. 440
Tucker—*cont.*
— Jos., Tr. N. 257
— Steph. Is., R. Cr. P.A. 336; Som. H. 332
— Th. Tud., adm. (**H**) 844
— (or Tooker), Wm., dn. Lich. 445
Tuda, bp. Lindisf. 478
Tuditanus, C. S., C. Ro. 45
— M. S., C. Ro. 42, 44
— P. S., C. Ro. 43
Tudor, Edm., aft. E. of Richmond, *q.v.*, K.B. (1449) 756
— Jasp., aft. E. of Pembroke, *q.v.*, K.B. (1449) 756
— J. E., G. St. Xtr. 729
— Jos., C. Cus. Sc. 504
Tufnell and **Tuffnell**
— Ed. Wyndh., bp. Brisb. 706
— Hy., L.T. 160; P.C. 215; Sec. Tr. 163
Tufton, sir Hy. Jas., aft. 1st ld. Hothfield, *q.v.*, L.L. Wmland. 313
— sir Wm., G. Bdoes. 719
Tuistius (or Tostius), bp. Wford. 626
Tuite, Hugh Manl., gen. (**D**) 893
Tulbagh, Ryk., G. C.G.H. 678
Tulca, K. Sp. 85
Tulga, K. Sp. 85
Tullibardine, E. of
— Patr., 2nd E. of, form. P. Murray, *q.v.*
— Jno., 6th E. of, aft. 1st D. of Athole, *q.v.*, H.C.P. Sc. 508
Tullie, *see also* Tully
— Th., dn. Carl. 476
— Th., dn. Rip. 482
Tulloch, Alex., gen. (**D**) 887
— sir Alexr. Murr., gen. (**D**) 894; K.C.B. 782
— Arth., gen. (**D**) 928
— Jno., dn. Thist. 749
— Jno., gen. (**D**) 886
— Jno., Mod. K. Sc. 547
— Jno. St., gen. (**D**) 920
— Th. de, bp. Ork. 535
— Wm., bp. Mor. 534; bp. Ork. 535; L.P.S. Sc. 500
Tullock, Jno. Saml. Dr., gen. (**D**) 916
Tulloh, Alexr., gen. (**D**) 899
Tullus (Hostilius), K. Ro. 36
— L. V., C. Ro. 46-7
Tully, *see also* Tullie
— Rev. or Riv., dn. Clonf. 637
— Rt., bp. St. Dav. 464
Tulse, sir Hy., L.M. Lond. 491
Tumbert, bp. Hex. 480
Tumfriht, *see* Tunfrith
Tunbright, bp. Lich. 443
Tunfrith (or Tumfriht), bp Lich. 443
Tunis, The Bey of, G.C.B. 772
Tunstall, Cuthb., bp. Dham. 479; bp. Lond. 451; dn. Sal. 468; L.L. Dham. 308; L.P.S. 240; M.R. 387
*— sir Rd., K.G. 736
*— sir Rd., M.M. 246
* Prob. same pers.
Tuntgall, bp. Saig. 620
Tupper, Ch. and sir C., G.C.M.G. 795; K.C.M.G. 797
— Gasp. le M., gen. (**D**) 927
Turbervill, Gerv., K.H. 791
Turberville, Jas., bp. Exr. 437

Turbus, Wm., bp. Norw. 454
Turgesius, K. Ir. 21
Turgot, bp. St. Andr. 528
Turke, L.M. Lond. 489
Turlough I. and II., K. Ir. 22
— (O'Connor), K. Ir. 22
Turnbull, Hugh, dn. Chich. 434
— Mont. Jas., gen. (**D**) 921
— Wm., bp. Glasg. 536; bp. Dkld. 533; L.P.S. Sc. 500
Turnemire, Wm. de, M.M. 245
Turner, Turnor and **Turnour**
— Adolph, Amb. Ugy. 136
— Algn., Sec. P.O. 239
— Arth., J.C.P. Ir. 581
— Arth., S.L. 409
— Augs., gen. (**D**) 916
— Ch., G. Si. Le. 685; gen. (**C**) 874
— Ch., gen. (**D**) 879
— sir Ch., B.T. 264; L. Admy. 177; L.T. 156; Tell. Ex. 168
— Chas. Arth. and sir C., C.I.E. 806; C.J. Mdras. 658; K.C.I.E. 805; M.C.I. 647
— (or Turnor), Chr. and sir C., B. Ex. 384; C. Exc. 277; S.L. 410
— Edm. Rt., C.C.J. 405
— (or Turnour), sir Ed., C.B. Ex. 381; S.G. 401; S.L. 410; Sp. H.C. 249
— (or Turnour), Ed. Wint., adm. (**E**) 836; (**F**) 839
— Fras., bp. Ely, 435; bp. Roch. 460; dn. Winds. 474
— Frank, gen. (**D**) 901; K.C.B. 781
— Geo., gen. (**D**) 884; K.C.B. 779
— Geo. Jas. and sir G., Jud. Com. P.C. 360; L.J. App. 389; P.C. 215; Q.C. 417; V. Chanc. 390
— Hy., S.L. 411
— Hy. Aust., gen. (**D**) 900
— Hy. Bl., gen. (**D**) 900
— sir Hilgr., G. Bmda. 701; gen. (**A**) 861
— (or Turnor), J., G. Bmda. 701
— Jas. Fras., bp. Graft. and Arm. 704
— Jno., C. St. 283
— (? Farmer), Jno., G. Bdoes. 720
— Jno., gen. (**D**) 907
— Jno., S.L. 410
— sir Jno., L.T. 157
— Jno. M., bp. Calc. 653
— Jos., dn. Norw. 456
— Nathl. Oct. S., gen. (**D**) 922
— Saml., L.M. Lond. 492
— Steph., dn. Rip. 482
— Th., dn. Cant. 431; dn. Roch. 461
— Tim., C.J. Chest. 386
— sir Tomk. Hilgr., G.C.H. 786; K.C.H. 787
— Walt., dn. Ferns, 623
— Wm., adm. (**G**) 842
— Wm., Amb. N.G. 134; Amb. Rep. Col. 134; Amb. Tky. 129
— Wm., dn. Wells, 429
— Wm., gen. (**D**) 877
— (or Turnor), Wm., gen. (**D**) 886

Turner, Turnor, and Turnour —*cont.*
— Wm. and sir W., Adm. Adv. 423; J. Adm. Ct. 423; J. Pr. Ct. 421
— sir Wm., L.M. Lond. 491
— Wm. West, K.C.S.I. 803
Turney, Ch. Bark., K.H. 790
Turnham, sir Rt. de, L.H.A. 170
— Steph. de, Jy. 364; L.H.A. 170
Turnor, *see* Turner
Turnour, *see* Turner
Turpin, bp. Brn. 530
— Rd., Bl. M. P.A. 336; Hps. P.A. 343; Winds. H. 331
Turpington, Jno., K.B. 756
Turri, Jord. de, Jy. 364
— Nichs. de, Ch. Jr. 363; J.C.P., 377; Jy. 364
Turrinus, C. M., C. Ro. 42
Turton, Jno. and sir J., B. Ex. 384; J.K.B. 373; S.L. 411
— Rt. Str., gen. (**D**) 925
— Th., bp. Ely, 435; dn. Pboro. 459; dn. Westr. 469
Turvil and **Turville**
— Fras. Fortesc., K.C.M.G. 797
— Geoffr. de, L. Treas. Ir. 558; V. Chanc. Ir. 574
— Maur. de, J. It. 367
Tuscus, C. A., C. Ro. 37
Tuson, Hy. Brasn., gen. (**D**) 935
Tuthaldus, bp. St. Andr. 528
Tuttebury or **Tuttlebury** Th., B. Ex. 383; dn. Wells, 429
Tuyll, Wm. and sir W., gen. (**A**) 863; K.C.H. 788
Twedy, Hy., M.M. 246
Tweeddale, E. and M. of
— Jno., 2nd E., aft. 1st M. of, Comm. Tr. Sc. 497; H.C.P. Sc. 508; L.H.T. Sc. 497-8; Ld. Chanc. Sc. 515; Ld. Sess. 517; Pres. P.C. Sc. 500
— Jno., 2nd M. of, form. ld. Yester, *q.v.*, Ld. Chanc. Sc. 515; Ld. Clk. Reg. 525
— Jno., 4th M. of, L.J. Gen. 522; Ld. Sess. 517; P.C. 198; Sec. St. Sc. 502
— Geo., 7th M. of, L.L. Hadd. 510
— Geo., 8th M. of, C.C. Mdras. 657; F.M. 856; G.C.B. 770; G. Mdras. 657; gen. (**A**) 863; K.C.B. 779; K.T. 748; L.L. Hadd. 510
Tweedie, Maur., gen. (**D**) 887
— Michl., gen. (**D**) 928
— Wm. Jno., gen. (**D**) 914
Twells, Ed., bp. Blfn. 681
Twemlow, Geo., gen. (**D**) 894
Twigge, Jno. Th., gen. (**D**) 931
Twisden, *see also* Twysden
— Ph., bp. Rph. 602
— sir Th., J.K.B. 372; S.L. 409-10
Twistleton, Ed. T. B., P.L.C. 262
Twiss, Horace, K.C. 416; U.S.W. and C. 231
— Jno., gen. (**D**) 898
— Wm., gen. (**A**) 861
— Trav. and sir T., Adm. Adv. 423; Ch. Lond. 422; Q. Adv. 422; Q.C. 418; Vic. Gen. 422

Twylden, Jno., gen. (D) 899
Twynham, Walt., Ld. Chanc. Sc. 515
Twysden, *see also* Twisden
— Hy. Dunc., adm. (**H**) 849; gen. (**D**) 912
Ty—, *see also* Ti—
Tyacke, Hy. Ph., gen. (**D**) 910
Tyddiman, sir Th., adm. (**A**) 813
***Tydferth,** bp. Dunw. 454
*— (or Tilford), bp. Hex. 480
* ? same pers.
Tyers, Wm. Augs., gen. (**D**) 908
Tyery, Nichs., M.M. 246
Tyes, Theod. le, K.B. 754
Tyldsley, *see also* Tildeslegh
— Th., G. I. Man, 666
Tyler, Maj. —, G. Trin. 722
— Ch. and sir C., adm. (**A**) 818; G.C.B. 768; K.C.B. 773
— Ch. Jas., gen. (**D**) 933
— Geo. and sir G., adm. (**G**) 841; G. St. Vin. 725; K.H. 790
— Jno., bp. Llff. 449; dn. Her. 442
— Jno., K.H. 791
— Jno., Pres. U.S.A. 102
— Jno. Wm., C.I.E. 808
Tynbegh (or Thynbegh), Wm. de, A.G. Ir. 588; C.B. Ex. Ir. 582; C.J.C.P. Ir. 580; L. Treas. Ir. 558
Tyndall, *see also* Tindal
— Humphr., dn. Ely, 435
— J. M., M. Chy. 395
— Saml. Wm., L.M. Dbln. 642
*— Wm., Guis. P.A. 343; Lanc. H. 332; R. Dr. P.A. 337
*— Wm., K.B. 758
* ? same pers.
Tynebegh, *see* Tynbegh
Tyrawley, lds.
— Ch., 1st ld., gen. (**A**) 857
— Jas., 2nd ld., also ld. Kilmain, F.M. 856; G. Gibr. 669; gen. (**A**) 858; P.C. 201
Tyrcheanus, or **Tyrchan,** or **Tridianus,** bp. Llff. 448
Tyrconnel, E., visc. and D. of
Talbot Family.
— Rd., 1st E., aft. 1st D. of, L.L. Ir. 555; L. Treas. Ir. 559; P.C. 193
Brownlow Family.
— Jno., 1st visc., K.B. 764
Carpenter Family.
— Jno. Delaval, 4th E. of G.C.H. 786
Tyrell, *see* Tyrrell
Tyrone, Geo. de la Poer, 2nd E., aft. 1st M. of Waterford, *q.v.*, K.P. 750
Tyrrell and **Tyrell**
— Hy., K.B. 760
— Jas., gen. (**B**) 864
— Jas., L.P.S. 240
— Jno., C.C.J. 403
— Jno., S.L. Ir. 590
— Jno. and sir J., Sp. H.C. 248
— Ralph, Const. W. Cast. 322
— Rd., adm. (**A**) 814
— Th. and sir T., J.C.P. 379; S.L. 410
— Wm., bp. Newc. N.S.W 704

Tyrrwhitt, *see also* Tirwhit
— Ch., gen. (**D**) 922
— Th. and sir T., L.W.S. 323
Tytler, Alexr. Fr., Ld. Sess. 520
— Jas., Ly. Dep. 513
— Jas. Mc. L. Bann. Fraser, gen. (**D**) 901 ; K.C.B. 781

U.

Ubylwinus (or Unelbicus), bp. Llff. 448
Uchtred, *see also* Ughtred and Uhtred
— bp. Lindisf. 478
Udaipur, Mahar. of, G.C.S.I. 801
Udalric, D. Bma. 59
Udny, Alexr., C. Exc. Sc. 505
Uffa, K.E. 2
Ufflete, Gill. de, S.L. 407
Ufford (or Offord), Jno. de, abp. Cant. 430; dn. Linc. 448 ; Ld. Chanc. 354
— sir Ralph, L.J. Ir. 551
*— Rt. de, K.B. 754
*— sir Rt., L.H.A. 171
* ? same pers. and ? aft. 1st E. of Suffolk
— sir Rt. de, L. J. Ir. 550
— sir Th., K.G. 733
Ugaine-Mor, K. Ir. 21
Ughtred, *see also* Uchtred and Uhtred
— sir Anthy., G. Jsey. 667
*— sir Th., L.H.A. 171
*— Th., 1st ld., K.G. 733
* Prob. same pers.
Uhtred, *see also* Uchtred and Ughtred
— bp. Llff. 449
Ulderic, D. Tny. 57
Ulecot, Jno. de, J. It. 367
— Ph. de, J. It. 367
Ullock, Hy., dn. Roch. 461
Ulmannus, *see* Ulstanus
Ulric, D. Wbg. 80
Ulrick, D. of Holstein, K.G. 739
— Pr. Mkg. 74
Ulrica-Eleanora, Q. Sw. 92
Ulstan, or **Ulstanus** (or Ulmannus), dn. St. P. 453
Ulster, Earls of, *see also* March and Ulster
— Jno. de Courcy, E. of, L.D. Ir. (1185) 550
— Hugh, E. of, form. (1189) H. de Lacy, *q.v.*
— Lion., E. of, K.G. (1361) 733
Ulwar, Mahar. of, G.C.S.I. 801
Umfreville, sir Rt. de, K.G. 735
Umpton, Alexr., K.B. 760
— Ed., K.B. 761
Underdown, Emm. Mag., Q.C. 420
Underhill, Jno., bp. Oxf. 456
— Jos., Q.C. 419
Underwood, Rd., dn. Lism. 629
Unelbicus, *see* Ubylwinus
Uniacke, Rd., gen. (**D**) 877
Universalis, Gilb., bp. Lond. 451
Unwin, Rt., gen. (**D**) 912
Unwona, bp. Dorch. 446; bp. Sidr. 446
Upington, Th., K.C.M.G. 798
Upper-Ossory, Jno., 2nd E. of, L.L. Beds. 306
Upsale, Geoffr. de, J. It. 368
Upton, Anthy., J.C.P. Ir. 581
— hon. Arth., gen. (**D**) 889
— hon. Arth. Percy, gen. (**A**) 863
— hon. Geo. Fk., aft. 3rd visc. Templetown, *q.v.*, gen. (**D**) 892
— Jno., C. Cus. 273
Urban, bp. Bgr. 425; bp. Llff. 449
— I. to VIII., P. Ro. 32, 34-5-6
Urban, D', *see* Durban
Urbina, J. M., Pres. Ecr. 108
Urbino, Fk., D. of, K.G. 736
— Guido Ubaldo, D. of, K.G. 737
Urgeneu. bp. St. Dav. 464
Uriarte, H., Pres. Pgy. 110
Uriell, Jas., C.B. Ex. Ir. 582
Urlin, sir Sim., Rec. Lond. 494; S.L. 411
Urmston, Ed., gen. (**B**) 865
Urquhart, Ed. Jas., gen. (**B**) 866
— Fras. Gr., gen. (**D**) 901
— Th., bp. Ross, 535
Urquhart, lds.
— Alexr., ld., from. Alexr. Seton, *q.v.*, aft. 1st E. Dunfermline, *q.v.*, L.P. Ct. Sess. 516 ; Ld. Sess. 518
Urquiza, J. J., Pres. Arg. 110
Urraca, K. Cle. 85
Ursula (iss. Edw. III.), Pr. E. 11
Urswick or **Urswicke,** Chr., dn. Winds. 474 ; dn. Yk. 487 Regr. Gart. 746
Urswyke, Th., B. Ex. 383 ; C.B. Ex. 381 ; Comm. Serjt. Lond. 495 ; Rec. Lond. 493
Uscher, Usher and **Ussher**
— Ad., Ulst. K.A. 572
— Chr., Ulst. K.A. 572
— Hy., abp. Arm. 595
— Herb. Tayl., G. Gld. Cst. 686 ; G. Gld. Cst. Col. 687 ; G. Labn. 675 ; G. Tob. 724
— Jas., abp. Arm. 596 ; bp. Carl. 475 ; bp. Mth. 599
— Jno. Theoph., gen. (**D**) 922
— Rt., bp. Kild. 617
— sir Th., adm. (**D**) 827 ; K.C.H. 787
— Th. N., Amb. Hti. 133
Utber (or Uthert), Rt., adm. (**A**) 813
Utellus, bp. Her. 441
Utermark, Jno. de Hav., Blf. Gsey. 669
Uthert, *see* Utber
Uthwayte, Rd., C. St. 283
Utlagh, *see* Outlawe
Utlawe, *see* Outlawe
Utterton, Jno. Sutt., bp. suff. Guildf. 471
Uvedall, Wm., K.B. 758
Uxbridge, E. of
1st Creation.
— Hy., 1st E. of, form. hon. Hy. Paget and 7th ld. P., and 1st ld. Burton, *q.v.*, C.Y.G. 298 ; P.C. 196
— Hy., 2nd E. of, L.L. Ang. 314
2nd Creation.
— Hy., 1st E. of, L.L. Staffs, 312
— Hy. Wm., 2nd E. of, aft. 1st M. of Anglesey, *q.v.*, G.C.B. 767 ; L.L. Ang. 314
— Hy., E. of, aft. 2nd M. of Anglesey, *q.v.*, L.C.H. 295 ; P.C. 213

V.

Vache, sir Ph. de la, K.G. 734
— Rd. de la, Const. T.L. 320 ; Const. W. Cast. 322 ; K.G. 733
Vaillant, Count, G.C.B. 769
Valaoriti, Spir., K.C.M.G. 796
Valdez, J. de Dios, G. Trin. 721
Vale, Geoff. de la, K.B. 755
Valencey, Ch., gen. (**A**) 859
Valens, Emp. E.E. 49
Valentia, Geth., Aym., or Lud. de, bp. Winch. 470
Valentia, visc.
— Arth., 2nd visc., aft. 1st E. of Anglesey, *q.v.*, V. Treas. Ir. 559
Valentinian I. to III., Emp. W.E. 48-9
Valentinus, P. Ro. 33
Valerianus, Emp. Ro. 48
Valerius, N., C. Ro. 47
Valia, K. Sp. 84
Valiant, Th., K.C.B. 777 ; K.H. 791
— Th. Jas., gen. (**D**) 892
Vallack, Jos., K.H. 790
Valle, A., Pres. S. Salv. 106
— Jno. de, bp. Ardf. and Agh. 639
— Steph. de, bp. Lim. 638 ; bp. Mth. 599 ; dn. Lim. 639 ; L. Treas. Ir. 558
Valletort, *see* Mount-Edgcumbe and V.
Vallibus, Pet. de, Const. T.L 320
Valoignes, Waresius de, L.H.A. 171
Valoines, Theob. de, J. It. 367
Valois, Hamo de, L.J. Ir. 550
Valoniis, Ph. de, L.G.C. Sc. 506
— Wm. de, L.G.C. Sc. 506
Valsamachi, Demetr. and sir D., G.C.M.G. 795 ; K.C.M.G 796
— Spir., K.C.M.G. 796

Valverde, J. D., Pres. Dom. Rep. 105
Vamba, K. Sp. 85
Vampage, Jno., A.G. 398
Vanbrugh, Capt., G. Newfd. 700
— sir Jno., Clar. K.A. 328; Gart. K.A. 327
Vanburen, M., Pres. U.S.A. 102
Vance, Jas., L.M. Dbln. 641
— Patr., Ld. Sess. 518
Vandamme, Off. Nap. 26
Vandeleur, Jno. Ormsb. (No. 1), C. Cus. Ir. 565-6; C. Exc. Ir. 566
— Jno. Ormsb. and sir J. (No. 2), gen. (**A**) 862; G.C.B. 768; K.C.B. 774
— Jno. Ormsb. (No. 3), gen. (**D**) 932
— Th. B., J.K.B. Ir. 579; S.L. Ir. 593
— Th. Pak., gen. (**C**) 872
Vandepert, Geo., adm. (**A**) 816
Vanderesch, Jacob, C. St. 283
Vane, Fras., K.B. 763
— Hy. (g. son of E. of Westmoreland), K.B. (1661) 763
— sir Hy., G.C.B. 768
— sir Hy., Coff. H. 293; Compt. H. 292; L. Admy. 175; L.T. 154; Tr. H. 291; S. St. 223
— hon. Hy., aft. 2nd E. of Darlington, *q.v.*, L.T. 157; V. Treas. Ir. 560
— Vere, K.B. 763
Vangoens, Ryck, G. Ceyl. 672
Vanhomrigh, Barth., L.M. Dbln. 640
Vanmildert, Wm., bp. Dham. 479; bp. Llff. 449; dn. St. P. 453
Vannes, Pet., dn. Sal. 468
Vanrenen, Don. Campb., gen. (**D**) 916
Vansittart, Ed. Westby, adm. (**H**) 850
— Geo. Hy., gen. (**A**) 861
— Hy., adm. (**A**) 820
— Hy., G.G. Ind. 648
— Nich., aft. 1st ld. Bexley, C.D.L. 243; Ch. Ex. 165; Ch. Ex. Ir. 562; Ch. Sec. Ir. 563; C. Treas. Ir. 561; L.T. 159; P.C. 207; Sec. Tr. 163
Vantort, J., dn. Bgr. 426
Varela, P., Pres. Ugy. 111
Vargas, Pres. Vzla. 107
Varro, C. T., C. Ro. 43
Varus, C. C., C. Ro. 46
— C. L., C. Ro. 42
— C. Q., Dt. Ro. 40
— S. Q., C. Ro. 38
Vasali I. to V., R. Russ. 89
Vasconcelos, Pres. S. Salv. 106
Vashon, Jas., adm. (**A**) 817
Vassall, Rawd. Jno. P., gen. (**D**) 900
— sir Sp. L. H., K.H. 792
Vatia, P. S., C. Ro. 45
Vaticanus, P. S. C., C. Ro. 38; Dec. Ro. 38
— T. R. R., C. Ro. 38; Dec. Ro. 38
Vatinius, P., C. Ro. 46
Vaughan, —, M. Chy. 395
— Ch. Jno., dn. Llff. 450
Vaughan—*cont.*
— Ch. Rd. and sir C., Amb. Spn. 124; Amb. Swz. 113; Amb. Tky. 129; Amb. U.S.A. 132; G.C.H. 787; P.C. 210
— Ed., bp. St. Dav. 464
— Ed., L. Admy. 175
— Gwynn, C. Cus. 275-6
— Harl., S.L. 412
— sir Hugh, G. Jsey. 667
— Jas., dn. Ach. 614
— Jno., adm. (**A**) 815
— Jno., K.B. 763
— Jno., L.L. Carm. 315
— Jno. and sir J. (No. 1), C.J.C.P. 375; S.L. 410
— Jno. and sir J. (No. 2), B. Ex. 385; J.C.P. 380; Jud. Com. P.C. 360; P.C. 212; S.L. 412
— hon. Jno., gen. (**B**) 866; K.B. 765
— Jno. Luth. and sir J., gen. (**D**) 909; K.C.B. 782
— Pet., dn. Chest. 477
— Rd., bp. Bgr. 426; bp. Chest. 477; bp. Lond. 452
— Rd., K.B. 763
— Steph., M.M. 246
— Th., K.B. 757
— hon. Wm., aft. visc. and E. of Lisburne, *q.v.*, L.L. Card. 315; L.L. Mer. 314
Vaughan, lds.
— Rd., 1st ld. (also 2nd E. of Carbery, *q.v.*), P.C. 190
— Jno., ld., aft. 3rd E. of Carbery, *q.v.*, G. Jam. 712; L. Admy. 176
Vaus, Geo., bp. Gall. 538
— Th. de, Sec. St. Sc. 501
Vaux, Jno. de, J. It. 368
— Lawr., Wdn. Chr. Ch. Manch. 481
— Oliver de, J. It. 368
— Rt. de, J. It. 366
— T., G. Jsey. 667
Vaux of Harroden, lds.
— Th., 2nd ld., K.B. 760
Vavasour, Hy. le, K.B. 754
— sir Hy. Magh. M., gen. (**B**) 868
— Jno., J.C.P. 378; S.L. 407
— Wm., J. It. 366
— Wm. le, J. It. 369
Veele, Walt. de, bp. Kild. 616
Veintimilla, Ig. de, Pres. Ecr. 108
Veitch, Hy., C. Cus. Sc. 504
— Jas., Ld. Sess. 520
— Jas. Rd., adm. (**H**) 852
Veja, M., G.C.M.G. 794; K.C.M.G. 796
Velasco, Pres. Bol. 109
Veldon, Jno., Rec. Dbln. 642
Velson, Wm., Ld. Chanc. 352; *see* Welson
Veltheim, Aug. Var., gen. (**C**) 873
Venables, Add. Rt. P., bp. Nass. 717
— Geo. St., Q.C. 418
— Wm., L.M. Lond. 492
Venham, Gilb. de, Ld. Chanc. Ir. 575
Venno, L. P., C. Ro. 41
Venour, Wm., L.M. Lond. 489
Ventagiri, Raja of, K.C.I.E. 805
Ventidius, P., C. Ro. 46
Ventris, Peyt. and sir P., J.C.P. 379; S.L. 411
Vera, E. S. de L., G. Trin. 721
Verchild, Jas., G. Leew. Isl. 727
Verdan, *see* Verdun
Verdoen, sir Pet., L.M. Dbln. 641
Verdon, Geo. Fc., K.C.M.G. 796
Verdun, Bertr. de, J. It. 366; Jy. 363
— Jno. de, J. It. 368
— (or Verdan), sir Theob. de, L.L. Ir. 551
— Walt. de, Const. T.L. 320; J. It. 367
Vere, Alberic de, Ch. Jr. 362; Jy. 363
— Ch. Br. and sir C., gen. (**C**) 875; K.C.B. 775
— Rt. de (bro. to 12th E. of Oxford), K.B. 756
— Th. de, aft. 8th E. of Oxford, *q.v.*, K.B. 754
— Wm. de, bp. Her. 441; J. It. 366; Jy. 364
— Wm. de, Ld. Chanc. 353
Vere of Tilbury, lds.
— Horatio, 1st ld., M.G.O. 258
Vere of Hanworth, lds.
— Vere, 1st ld., form. ld. V. Beauclerk, *q.v.*, L.L. Berks. 306
Vereker, Ch., C. Treas. Ir. 561
— hon. Jno. Prend., L.M. Dbln. 642
Verelst, Hy., Adm. Ind. 648
Veremundo I. to III., K. Sp. 85
Vergu, bp. St. Dav. 464
Verner, Geo., gen. (**D**) 916
— sir Wm., K.C.H. 789
Verney, Geo., *see* ld. Willoughby de Broke
— Grev., K.B. 763
— sir H., P.C. 220
— Jno., dn. Lich. 445
— Jno., K.B. 758
— hon. Jno., C.J. Chest. 386; K.C. 415; M.R. 388; P.C. 198
— Ralph, *see* Earl V., *infra*
Verney, E.
— Rauf., L.M. Lond. 490
— Ralph, 1st E., form. visc. Fermanagh, *q.v.*, P.C. 201
Vernon, Ch., gen. (**A**) 858; Lt. T. L. 322
— Ed., adm. (**A**) 814
— Fras., aft. 1st E. of Shipbrooke, *q.v.*
— sir Ed., adm. (**A**) 815
— hon. Ed. Verron-, aft. Vernon Harcourt, *see* Harcourt
— Geo., K.B. 760
— Geo. and sir G., B. Ex. 384; J.C.P. 379; S.L. 409
— Hy., C. Exc. 280
— Hy., K.B. 758
— sir Hy., C. Exc. 277
— Hy. Ch. Ed., gen. (**D**) 879
— Jas., L.P.S. 240; P.C. 194; S. St. 224; Tell. Ex. 167 U.S.S. 225
— Jas. Jr., C. Exc. 279-80
— Rd., Sp. H.C. 248
— sir Rd., Coff. H. 293
— Th., B.T. 264
— Th., Tell. Ex. 168
— Wm. de, J. It. 367
Vernon-Harcourt, *see* Harcourt

Verrucosus, Q. F. M. (5), C. Ro. 43; Dt. Ro. 43
Verschoyle, Ham., bp. Kilm. E. and A. 609; dn. Ferns, 623
—— Jas., bp. Killa. and Ach. 613; dn. St. Pat. 618
Versluys, Steph., G. Ceyl. 672
Verulam, lds. and E. of
—— Fras., ld., form. Fras. Bacon, *q.v.*, aft. visc. St. Albans, *q.v.*
—— Jas. Walt., 1st E. of, L.L. Herts. 309
—— Jas. Walt., 2nd E. of, L.L. Herts. 309
Verus, L., Emp. Ro. 47
Vesci, Wm. de, L.J. Ir. 550
Vesci, visc. de
—— Jno., 2nd visc. de, L.L. Q. Co. 571
—— Jno. Rt. Wm., 4th visc. de, L.L. Q. Co. 571
Vesey, Geo. Hy., gen. (**D**) 913
—— Jno., abp. Tm. 611; bp. Limk., A. and A. 639; dn. Crk. 632; L.J. Ir. 556
—— Jno., *see* Voysey
—— Jno. Agm., gen. (**C**) 873
—— sir Th., bp. Killoe. 634; bp. Oss. 620
—— Wm. de, J. It. 368
Vesey-Fitzgerald, *see* Fitzgerald
Vespasian, Emp. Ro. 47
Vesturme, Louis Hutton, adm. (**H**) 853
Vetch, Ham., gen. (**D**) 897
—— Saml., G. N. Sc. 694
Veteriponte, Rt. de, J. It. 366-7
Vetus, C. A., C. Ro. 47
Veulle, Jno. de, Blf. Jsey. 668
Veym, Rd. de, J. It. 367
Veysey, *see* Voysey
Vialls, Geo. Court., gen. (**D**) 909
Vibal, Dt. Pgy. 110
Vibulanus, K. F. (3), C. Ro. 37-8
—— M. F. (2), C. Ro. 37-8; C. Ro. 39
—— N. F., C. Ro. 39
—— Q. F. (7), C. Ro. 37-8-9; Dec. Ro. 38
Vicars, Ed., gen. (**C**) 874
—— Ed., gen. (**D**) 889
Vicedominus, P. Ro. 35
Victor, Off. Nap. 26
—— I. to III., P. Ro. 32-4
—— -Amadeus, K. Scy. 56
—— -Amadeus I. and II., D. Svy. 55
—— -Amadeus I. and II., K. Sda. 55
—— -Emmanuel I. and II., K. Sda. 55
—— -Emmanuel II. (K. It.); K.G. 744
—— -Ferd., &c., Pr. of Hohenlohe - Langenbourg (Ct. Gleichen), adm. (**H**) 851; Const. W. Cast. 322; G.C.B. 773; K.C.B. 783
—— Jas. C., gen. (**D**) 889
Victoria, Q.E. 6; Pr. E. 15
—— -Adel.-Mary-Louisa (dau. Q. Vict.), Pr. E. 15; Cr. Ind. 809
—— -Alb.-Eliz.-Mat.-Mary (g. dau. Q. Vict.), Pr. E. 15
—— -Alex.-Olga-Mary (g. dau. Q. Vict.) Pr. E. 15
Victoria—*cont.*
—— -Alix-Helen-Louise-Beatr. (g. dau. Q. Vict.), Pr. E. 16
—— -Eliz.-Aug.-Charl. (g. dau. Q. Vict.), Pr. E. 15
—— -Eug.-Julia-Eva (g. dau. Q. Vict.), Pr. E. 16
—— -Louise-Sophia-Aug.-Am.-Hel. (g. dau. Q. Vict.), Pr. E. 16
—— -Mel. (g. dau. Q. Vict.), Pr. E. 16
—— -Patr.-Hel.-Eliz. (g. dau. Q. Vict.), Pr. E. 16
—— G., Pres. Mex. 103
Vidal, Alexr. Th. Em., adm. (**D**) 830
—— F. A., Pres. Ugy. 111
—— Owen Em., bp. Si. Le, 686
Vidone, Walt. de, Ld. Chanc. Sc. 514
Vie, sir Hy. de, Chanc. Gart. 746
Vigilius, P. Ro. 33
Vignoles, Ch., dn. Oss. 623
Vigors, Barth., bp. Ferns and L. 622; dn. Arm. 597; dn. Llin. 623
—— Hor. Nels., gen. (**D**) 893
Villahermosa, D. of, R. Nds. 83
Villemore, Barth., Compt. Sc. 498
Villettes, Arth., Amb. Swz. 113
—— Wm. Anne, G. Jam. 713; gen. (**B**) 866
Villiers, hon. Ch. Pelh., J.A.G. 937; P.C. 216; Pres. P.L.B. 262
—— sir Ed., M.M. 246
—— Fras., Tell. Ex. 168
—— sir Geo., *see* ld. V., *infra*
—— hon. Geo. W. F. and sir G., aft. 4th E. of Clarendon, *q.v.*, Amb. Spn. 124; C. Cus. 277; G.C.B. 772
—— hon. Hy. M., bp. Dham. 479; bp. Carl. 476
—— sir Hy., M.M. 246
—— hon. Jno. Chas., Amb. Pgl. 124; B.T. 268; Compt. H. 293; P.C. 204
—— sir Jno. Hy. de, K.C.M.G. 798
—— hon. Th., L. Admy. 178
—— Th. Hyde, Sec. B.C. 254
Villiers, lds. and visc.
—— sir Geo., aft. 1st visc. V. and E. M. and D. of Buckingham, *q.v.*, K.G. 739; M.H. 302
—— Ed., 1st ld. and visc., aft. 1st E. of Jersey, *q.v.*, L.J. Ir. 555
—— Geo. B., visc., aft. 4th E. of Jersey, *q.v.*, L.H.A. 179; P.C. 201; V.C.H. 297
Villula, Jno. de, bp. B. & W. 427
Vincent, *see also* St. Vincent
—— Andr. Atk., adm. (**H**) 847; K.H. 789
—— Aug., R. Cr. P.A. 335; R. Rge. P.A. 344; Winds. H. 331
—— Edg., K.C.M.G. 799
—— sir Fras., Amb. Vce. 116
—— sir Fras., U.S.F. 229
—— Jas. V., dn. Bgr. 427
—— Jno., gen. (**A**) 862
—— Jno. Paint., Pres. Coll. Surg. 939
—— Nichs., adm. (**A**) 815
Vincent—*cont.*
—— Nichs. Ch. Car., K.C.B. 775
—— Wm., dn. Westr. 469
—— Wm., gen. (**D**) 881
Vine, Wm., gen. (**D**) 914
Viney, sir Jas., gen. (**C**) 875; K.C.H. 788
Vinicombe, Geo. Ell., gen. (**C**) 875
Vinucius, L., C. Ro. 47
Violens, L. V. F. (2), C. Ro. 41
Vipont, Th., bp. Carl. 475
Viscellinus, S. C. (3), C. Ro. 37
Visen, Hy., D. of, K.G. 735
Visme, Louis de, Amb. G. St. 121; Amb. Sw. 126
Visolus, C. P. L., C. Ro. 40-1
—— Q. P. L., Dec. Ro. 38
Vitalianus, P. Ro. 33
Vitellius, Emp. Ro. 47
Vitericus, K. Sp. 85
Vitiges, K. It. 49
Vitiza, K. Sp. 85
Vitulus, L. M., C. Ro. 42
—— Q. M., C. Ro. 42
Vivian, Ch., C. St. 283
—— Ch. Cresp., *see* ld. V., *infra*
—— sir Hussey, *see* Hussey
—— Huss. Cresp., *see* ld. V., *infra*
—— hon. Jno. C. W., L.T. 161, 162; U.S. War. 233
—— Rd. Huss. and sir R., *see* ld. V., *infra*
—— sir Rt., gen. (**D**) 887
—— Rt. Jno. Huss. and sir R., gen. (**D**) 888; G.C.B. 770; K.C.B. 778; M.C.I. 646
Vivian, lds.
—— Rd. Huss., aft. 1st ld. V., Comm. F. Ir. 564; gen. (**B**) 869; G.C.B. 768; G.C.H. 786; K.C.B. 774; K.C.H. 787; M.G.O. 259; P.C. 213
—— Ch. Cr., 2nd ld., L.L. Cnwall. 307
—— hon. Huss. Cresp., aft. 3rd ld. V., Amb. Bgm. 123; Amb. Dk. 127; Amb. Eg. 130; Amb. Rma. 128; Amb. Swz. 114; K.C.M.G. 798
Vizianagram, Mahar. of, K.C.I.E. 805
—— Zem. of, K.C.S.I. 802
Vladimir I. and II., R. Russ. 89
Vodimus, abp. Lond. 450
Vœux, Geo. Wm. Des. and sir G., G. Bah. Isl. 716; G. Fiji, 711; G. H. Kong, 673; G. Newfd. 700; G. St. Luc. 725; G. Trin. 722; G. W. Pacif. 711; K.C.M.G. 798
Vogel, Jul., K.C.M.G. 797
Vogorides, N. S., H. Mva. 94
Volcan, Jno., bp. Drom. 604; bp. Oss. 620
Volkonsky, Pr., G.C.B. 767
Volusianus, Emp. Ro. 47
Volusus, C. V. P., C. Ro. 39
—— M. V., C. Ro. 37
Vosey, *see* Voysey
Voyle, Geo. El., gen. (**D**) 911
—— Fras. Ed., gen. (**D**) 910
Voysey, Vosey, or **Veysey,** Jno. (*alias* Harman), bp. Exr. 436-7; dn. Exr. 437; dn. Winds. 474; Regr. Gart. 746
Vreelandt, Ger. J., G. Ceyl. 672

Vry, Johann Eliza de, C.I.E. 806
Vulso, A. M., C. Ro. 38, 44; Dec. Ro. 38
— C. M., C. Ro. 43
— L. M. (2), C. Ro. 42
Vuyst, Petr., G. Ceyl. 672
Vyner, Th., dn. Glr. 440
— Rt. and sir R., M.M. 247; L.M. Lond. 491
— Th. and sir T., L.M. Lond. 491; M.M. 247
Vyse, Ed. How., gen. (**D**) 921
— Rd., gen. (**A**) 860
— Rd. W. H. Howard, gen. (**D**) 882

W.

W**, dn. Emly. 628
W**, dn. Lim. 639
* Prob. same pers.
Waad, sir Wm., Lt. T.L. 321
Wace, Wm., bp. Wford. 626; dn. Wford. 628
Waddell, Jno., Ld. Sess. 518
Waddilove, Ch. Lod., adm. (**E**) 836
— Rt. D., dn. Rip. 482
Waddington, Ch., gen. (**D**) 888
— Ed., bp. Chich. 433
— Evelyn, gen. (**D**) 915
— Geo., dn. Dham. 479
— Hy. Ferr., gen. (**D**) 916
— Hor., P. C., 217; U.S. Home, 228
Waddy, Rd., gen. (**D**) 903; K.C.B. 780
— Saml. D., Q.C. 419
Wade, Geo., C. Ch. 855; F.M. 856; L.G.O. 259; P.C. 198
— Th. Fras. and sir T., Amb. Ch., 131; G. C.G.H. 679; K.C.B. 783
Wadenhall, Ad. de, dn. St. Pat. 617
Wadeson, Rd., L.G. Ch. Hosp. 936
Wadham, Jno., J.C.P. 378; S.L. 407
Waferton (or Waverton), Th. de, dn. Oss. 622
Wafyr, Hy., K.B. 757
Wagenaar, Zach., G. C.G.H. 678
Wager, sir Ch., adm. (**A**) 813; Compt. N. 257; L. Admy. 177-8; P.C. 198; Tr. N. 256
Wagomai, Nichs., bp. Mayo, 612
Wahab, Ch., gen. (**D**) 893
— Geo., gen. (**D**) 876
— Geo. L., gen. (**D**) 878
— Jas., gen. (**D**) 880
Wainfleet, *see* Waynflete
Wainwright, Jno., B. Ex. Ir. 584
Wainwright—*cont.*
— Jas. Fras. Ball., adm. (**E**) 835
Waithman, Rt., L.M. Lond. 492
Wakbruge, —, S.L. 407
Wake, Ch., adm. (**E**) 836; (**F**) 839
— Th., Const. T.L. 320
— Wm., abp. Cant. 431; bp. Linc. 447; dn. Exr. 437; P.C. 196
Wakebrug, Wm. de, J. It. 369
Wakefield, Dl., K.C. 416
— Hy., bp. Worc. 472; L.H.T. 153
Wakeman, Jno., bp. Glr. 438
Wakering, Jno. de, bp. Norw. 455; C.D.L. 242; L.K. 355; M. Chy. 394; M.R. 387
Walcot, Walcott, and **Wallcott**
— Jno., L.M. Lond. 489
— Jno. Ed., adm. (**G**) 841
— Steph., K.C.M.G. 797
— Th. and sir T., J.K.B. 372; S.L. 410
Waldby, Rt., abp. Dbln. and Gl. 616; abp. Yk. 485; bp. Chich. 433; bp. S. and M. 483; Ld. Chanc. Ir. 575
Waldegrave, *see also* Walgrave
— sir Rd., Sp. H.C. 248
— hon. Saml., bp. Carl. 476
— hon. Wm., aft. 1st ld. Radstock, *q.v.*, adm. (**A**) 816; G. Newfd. 700
Waldegrave, lds. and E.
— Hy., 1st ld., Compt. H. 292
— Jas., 2nd ld. and 1st E., P.C. 198; K.G. 741
— Jas., 2nd E., K.G. 742; L.W.S. 323; P.C. 199; Tell. Ex. 168
— Jno., 3rd E., gen. (**A**) 858; L.L. Esx. 308
— Geo., 4th E., form. visc. Chewton, *q.v.*
— Wm., 8th E., adm. (**H**) 844
Waldemar, K. Sw. 92
— M. Brg. 65
— Gouth. Fk., P.L. Dtd. 73
— (g. son. Q. Victoria), Pr. E. 15
— I. to III., K. Dk. 93
Walden, Rog., abp. Cant. 430; bp. Lond. 451; dn. Yk. 486; L.H.T. 153
Walden, lds., *see* Howard de Walden
Waldern (or Waldren), Wm., L.M. Lond. 489-90
Waldherus, bp. Lond. 450
Waldhull, Sim. de, J. It. 366
Waldimir, *see* Vladimir
Waldric, Ld. Chanc. 353
Wale, Ch. and sir C., G. Mart. 719; gen. (**A**) 862; K.C.B. 774
— Jas., bp. Kild. 617
— sir Th., K.G. 733
Waledene, Humph. de, B. Ex. 383
Waleis, *see* Waleys
Waleran, Walerand, and **Walleran**
— C. Lux. 84
— D. Lne. 29
— bp. Roch. 459
— Jno., Const. T.L. 320
— Rt., Jy. 364; W.C.P. 317
Wales, Princes and Princesses of. *Search also* under their Christian names.
— Edw. Pr. of, aft. Edw. I., *q.v.*, W.C.P. 318
— Edw., Pr. of (Blk. Pr.), K.G. 733
— Rd., Pr. of, aft. Rd. II., *q.v.*, K.G. 734
— Hy., Pr. of, aft. Hy. V., *q.v.*, K.G. 734; W.C.P. 318
— Ed., Pr. of (son of Hy. VI.), *see* Pr. Ed.
— Ed., Pr. of, aft. Ed. V., *q.v.*, K.B. 757; K.G. 736; S.L. Ir. 553
— Arth., Pr. of, 1st son of Hy. VII., K.B. 758; K.G. 737
— Hy. Fk., Pr. of, son of Jas. I., K.G. 739
— Ch., Pr. of, aft. Ch. II., *q.v.*, K.G. 740
— Fk., Pr. of, son of Geo. II., *see also* Pr. Fredk., P.C. 197
— Geo. Augs., Pr. of, aft. Geo. IV., *q.v.*, K.G. 742; P.C. 204
— Alb. Ed., Pr. of (son of Q. Vict.), adm. (**B**) 821; F.M. 856; G.C.B. 770; G.C.I.E. 805; G.C.M.G. 795; G.C.S.I. 800; gen. (**D**) 883; K.C.S.I. 802; K.G. 744; K.P. 751; K.T. 749; P.C. 217
— Pr. Albert Vict. of, aft. D. of Clarence, K.G. 745; K.P. 752. *See also* Pr. Alb. Vict.
— Pr. Geo. Fk. Ern. Alb. of, K.G. 745
— Alexandra, Prss. of, Cr. Ind. 809
— Prss. Alex. Olga, &c. of, Cr. Ind. 810
— Prss. Louise, &c. of, aft. Dss. of Fife, Cr. Ind. 810
Waleys, Walleys, and **Waleis**
— Dav. le, dn. Wford. 628
— Hy., L.M. Lond. 489
— Rd. de, bp. Emly, 625
— Wm. de, J. It. 367
Walgrave, *see also* Waldegrave
— sir Ed., C.D.L. 242
— Wm., K.B. 759
Walkeline (or Walkin), bp. Winch. 470
Walker, Baldw. Wake and sir W., adm. (**D**) 832; (**E**) 834; Compt. N. 258; K.C.B. 777; Sr. N. 257
— Chamberl. Wm., gen. (**D**) 915
— Ch. A., gen. (**D**) 878
— Ch. Fras., adm. (**H**) 853
— Ch. Pynd. Beauch., gen. (**D**) 905; K.C.B. 781
— Dav., gen. (**C**) 874
— Ed., gen. (**D**) 877; K.H. 790
— Ed., Sec. at W., 233
— Ed. and sir E., Bl. L. P.A. 341; Chest. H. 331; Gart. K.A. 327; Norr. K.A. 329; R. Cr. P.A. 335
— Ed. Noel, K.C.M.G. 799
— Ed. Walk. Ell., gen. (**D**) 921
— Ed. Walt. Forr., gen. (**D**) 894; K.C.B. 780
— Ellis, gen. (**A**) 860
— Fitzwm., gen. (**D**) 907
— Foster, gen. (**D**) 881

Walker—*cont.*
— Fk., gen. (**A**) 863
— sir Fk., K.C.H. 789
— Fk. Wm. Ed. For., gen. (**D**) 934
— Geo. Andr., gen. (**D**) 932
— Geo. Full., gen. (**D**) 928
— Geo. Towns. and sir G., C.C. Mdras. 657; G.C.B. 767; G. Gren. 724; gen. (**A**) 862; K.C.B. 774; L.G. Ch. Hosp. 936
— Geo. Warr., gen. (**D**) 906
— sir Hov., adm. (**A**) 813
— Jas., adm. (**A**) 820
— Jas., bp. Edinb. 543; Pr. Bp. Sc. 540
— Jas., C.I.E. 808
— Jas. and sir J., G. Bah. Isl. 716; G. Bdoes. &c. 719, 721; G. Trin. 722; K.C.M.G. 796
— Jas. Th., gen. (**D**) 920
— Jno., L.M. Dbln. 641
— Jno., Q.C. 417
— Jno. Geddes, gen. (**D**) 900
— Jos., gen. (**A**) 862
— Jos., gen. (**D**) 889
— Lesl., K.H. 790
— Mark, gen. (**D**) 919
— Rog., dn. Chest. 477
— Saml., A.G. Ir. 589; S.G. Ir. 590
*— Th., C. Cus. 274-5
*— Th., S.L.R. 271
* Prob. same pers.
— Th., M. Chy. and Acct. G. 397; S.L. 412
— Walt., J. Adm. Ct. 423; J Pr. Ct. 421
— W., G. Br. Gu. 715
— Wm., C.C.J. 403
— Wm., gen. (**D**) 916
— Wm., L.M. Dbln. 641
— Wm., Rec. Dbln. 642
— Wm. Stu., K.C.B. 784
Walkin, *see* Walkeline
Walkingham, Al. de, A.G. 398; J. It. 368
Walkington, Ed., bp. Down and Cnr. 604
— Th., dn. Exr. 437
Wall, Geo., S.L. 408
— Jno., dn. Drom. 606
— Pet., bp. Clonm. 600
— Th. and sir T., Bl.M. P.A. 336; Berw. P.A. 341; Cal. P.A. 342; Gart. K.A. 327; Lanc. H. 332; Norr. K.A. 329; R. Cr. P.A. 335; Winds. H. 331
Wallace, Ad., Compt. Sc. 498
— Ch. Jas. St., gen. (**D**) 914
— Don. Mart., K.C.I.E. 805
— Hill, gen. (**D**) 920
— Jas., A.G. 399; K.C. 415; S.G. 402
— Jas., Mod. K. Sc. 547
— sir Jas., adm. (**A**) 816; G. Newfd. 700
— sir Jas. Maxw., gen. (**D**) 883; K.H. 789
— sir Jno. Alexr., gen. (**A**) 863; K.C.B. 776
— Jno. Dunc. Campb., gen. (**D**) 915
— Lewis Bail., gen. (**A**) 862
— M., G. N. Sc. 695
— Pet. M., gen. (**D**) 886
— sir Rd., K.C.B. 783
— Rt., bp. Isl. 540
— Rt., K.C.S.I. 802
— Rowl. Rt., gen. (**D**) 935

Wallace—*cont.*
— Th., *see* ld. W., *infra*
— sir Th., Ld. Sess. 519
Wallace, lds.
— Th., aft. 1st ld., B.C. 252-3; L. Admy. 180; M.M. 247; P.C. 207; V.P.B.T. 269
Wallcott, *see* Walcot
Wallensis, Th., bp. St. Dav. 464
Waller, Edm., Coff. H. 293
— Fk., Q.C. 419
— Geo., Hy., gen. (**D**) 929
— Hardress Edm., gen. (**D**) 930
— Jas. Wall. S., K.H. 790
— sir Jonn. Wathen, G.C.H. 786; K.C.H. 787; K.H. 789
— Rt., C. Cus. Ir. 565; C. Exc. Ir. 566
— sir Steph., G. Ch. Isl. 667
— Th., S.L. 410
— Th. W., Amb. Bgm. 123
— Wm., C. St., 283-4
— Wm., gen. (**B**) 867
Walleran, *see* Waleran
Walleys, *see* Waleys
Wallia, K. Sp. 84
Wallifly, Geffr., G. Gsey. 668
Wallinger, Arn., S.L. 413
Wallingford, Wm., 1st visc., form. ld. Knollys, *q.v.*, aft. E. of Banbury, *q.v.*
Wallington, Ch. Arth. G., gen. (**D**) 886
Wallis, Geo., Ulst. K.A. 572
— Hugo, bp. Linc. 446
— Jas., U.S.S. 226
— Prov. Wm. P. and sir P., adm. (**B**) 821; (**C**) 822; (**D**) 829; G.C.B. 770; K.C.B. 778
— Th., dn. Wford. 628
— Th., dn. Dry. 602
Wallop, sir Hy., L.J. Ir. 554; V. Treas. Ir. 559
— Jno., aft. 1st visc. Lymington and E. of Portsmouth, *q.v.*, L.T. 156
— sir Jno., K.G. 738
— Rd., Curs. B. Ex. 386
Wallore, *see* Wollore
Walmesley, Th. and sir T., J.C.P. 378; S.L. 408
Walmisley, Wm., dn. Lich. 445
Walmoden, Count, gen. (**B**) 867; G.C.B. 768; K.C.B. 775
Walmsley, *see* Walmesley
Walpole, Edw. and sir E., Cl. Pells. 168; K.B. 765
— Ed., K.B. 763
— Galfr., Postm. G. 238
— hon. Geo., U.S.F. 229
— Hor., *see* ld. W., *infra*
— Hor. Ed., gen. (**D**) 912
— Jno., gen. (**D**) 898
— Jno., S.L. 408
— hon. Jno., Amb. Chi. 137
— Ralph de, bp. Ely, 434; bp. Norw. 454
— Rt., *see* ld. W., *infra*
— Rt. and sir Rt., gen. (**D**) 897; K.C.B. 778
— hon. Rt., Amb. Pgl. 124
— Rt. and sir R., aft. 1st E. of Orford, *q.v.*, Ch. Ex. 165; K.B. 764; K.G. 741; L. Admy. 177; L.T. 156; P.C. 196; Paym. G. 244; Prem. 141-2; Sec. at W. 233; Tr. N. 256
— Spenc., G. I. Man, 666
— Spenc. Hor., H. Sec. 227; P.C. 215; Q.C. 417

Walpole—*cont.*
— hon. Th., Amb. G. St. 121
— Wm., adm. (**D**) 829; (**G**) 840
Walpole of Walpole, lds.
— Rt., 1st ld., aft. 2nd E. of Orford, *q.v.*, Aud. Ex. 167; Cl. Pells. 168; K.B. 764
Walpole of Wolterton, lds.
— Horatio, aft. 1st ld. W., Coff. H. 293; P.C. 198; Tell. Ex. 168; U.S.S. 225
— Horatio, ld., aft. 1st E. of Orford (2nd Creation), *q.v.*, Amb. Russ. 125; B.C. 253; L. Admy. 181
Walram, Pr. Nass. 75
Walrand, Rt., bp. Ferns, 621
Walrond, Wm. H., L.T. 162
Walsh and **Walshe**
— Abel, dn. Tm. 613
— Anthy., gen. (**B**) 869
— hon. Arth., aft. 2nd ld. Ormathwaite, *q.v.*, L.L. Radn. 316
— Dav., Mod. K. Sc. 547
— Fk. Wm., J. Bank. Ir. 587
— Geo., gen. (**C**) 871
— Hunt, gen. (**A**) 858
— Jno., dn. Crk. 632
— (or Welsh), Jno., J.C.P. 378; S.L. 408
— Jno., dn. Cnr. 605
— sir Jno., aft. 1st ld. Ormathwaite, *q.v.*, L.L. Radn. 316
— Jno. Ed., A.G. Ir. 588; M.R. Ir. 585
— Nichs., bp. Oss. 620
— sir Nichs., C.J.C.P. Ir. 580; J.K.B. Ir. 579
— Patr., bp. Wford. and L. 627; dn. Wford. 628
— Ralph, or Raphael, dn. Drom. 606
— Sandy St., gen. (**D**) 897
— Th., B. Ex. 383
— Walt., dn. Kild. 619
— Wm., bp. Mth. 599
— Wm., dn. Lism. 628
— Wm. Pak., bp. Oss., F. and L. 622; dn. Cash. 627
Walsham, sir Jno., Amb. Fr. 113; Amb. Ch. and Cor. 131
Walshe, *see* Walsh
Walshum, Rt. de, dn. St. As. 463
Walsingham, sir Ed., Lt. T.L. 321
— sir Fras., C.D.L. 242; Chanc. Gart. 745; L.K. 356; S. St. 223
— Rd. de, J. It. 369
Walsingham, lds.
— Wm., 1st ld., form. sir W. de Grey *q.v.*
— Th., 2nd ld., B.C. 252; B.T. 267; P.C. 204; Postm. G. 238; V. Treas. Ir. 560
— Geo., 3rd ld., gen. (**B**) 868
Walstodus (or Wastoldus), bp. Her. 441
Walter, *see also* Gualterius
*— bp. Dkld. 533
*— bp. Gall. 538
*— bp. Glasg. 536
*— bp. Her. 441
*— bp. Roch. 459
*— bp. St. Andr. 528
*— (3), bp. Wford. 626
*— (Prior of Blantyre), Compt. Sc. 498
*— (abp. Rouen), Const. W. Cast. 322

Walter—*cont.*
*— dn. Chich. 433
*— L.J. Gen. 522
*— Ld. Chanc. Sc. 514
* Prob. some same pers. Comp. dates.
— Dav., L.G.O. 259
— sir Ed., K.C.B. 784
— Hub., abp. Cant. 430; bp. Sal. 466; Ch. Jr. 362; dn. Yk. 486; Jy. 363; Ld. Chanc. 353
— Jno. and sir J., C.B. Ex. 381; S.L. 409
— Jno. McN., gen. (**D**) 905
— Theob., J. It. 366
Waltham, Jno., bp. Oss. 620
— Jno. de, bp. Sal. 467; L.H.T. 153; L.K. 354; M.R. 387
— Rog., B. Ex. 383
— Wm., M. Chy. 394
Walton, *see also* Wauton
— Bend., C.I.E. 806
— Br., bp. Chest. 477
— Brud., gen. (**D**) 932
— Fk. Th. Granv., C.I.E. 808
— sir Geo., adm. (**A**) 813
— Jac., adm. (**D**) 824
— Jno., G. I. Man, 665
— Jno., abp. Dbln. and Gl. 616
— Jos., gen. (**B**) 866
— Rt., K.H. 792
— Saml., L.M. Dbln. 641
— Sim. de, *see* Wauton
— Wm., K.C. 416
— Wm. L., gen. (**D**) 883
Walwaine, Wm., L.H.T. 153
Walworth, Wm. de and sir W., L.M. Lond. 489
Wamba, K. Sp. 885
Wandesford, Chr., L.J. Ir. 554; L.K. Ir. 576; M.R. Ir. 585
— Michl., dn. Dry. 602; dn. Lim. 639
Wangford, Wm., S.L. 407
Wangrave, Jno. de, Rec. Lond. 493
Wanley, Fras., dn. Rip. 482
Wantage, Rt. Jas., 1st ld., form. R. J. Lloyd-Lindsay, *q.v.*, L.L. Berks. 306
Waple, Jno., M. Chy. and Acct. G. 396
Warburton, Ch. Mong., bp. Cloy. 631; bp. Lim., A. and A. 639; dn. Ard. 609; dn. Clonm. 600
— Geo., dn. Glr. 440; dn. Wells, 429
— Hugh, gen. (**A**) 858
— Jno., Som. H. 332
— Pet. (No. 1), J.C.P. 378; S.L. 408
— Pet. (No. 2), J.C.P. 379; J. Chest. 386; J.K.B. 372; S.L. 409
— Wm., bp. Glr. 438; dn. Brl. 440
— Wm., dn. Elph. 609
Warcup, Leon., Berw. P.A. 341; Bl. M. P.A. 336; Carl. H. 339
Ward, *see also* Warde
— lt.-col. —, G. Trin. 722
— hon. Bern. Matth., gen. (**D**) 927
— sir Ed., A.G. 399; C.B. Ex. 382; C.G.S. 357; S.L. 411
— Ed. Michl., Amb. Sxy. 120; Amb. Pgl. 125; Amb. Russ. 125
Ward—*cont.*
— Ed. Wolst., gen. (**D**) 916; K.C.M.G. 797
— Geo., gen. (**D**) 913
— Hy. Const. Ev., C.I.E. 808
— Hy. Geo. and sir H., Com. Io. Isl. 129; G.C.M.G. 795; G. Ceyl. 673; G. Mdras. 657; Sec. Adm. 186
— Jas., dn. Cloy. 633
— Jas. Ham., adm. (**H**) 848
— Jno., Amb. H. Tns. 120
— Jno., Bl. M. P.A. 336
— Jno., J. Chest. 387; Q.C. 415
— Jno., L M. Dbln. 640
— sir Jno., L.M. Lond. 491
— Jno. Giff., dn. Linc. 448
— Jno. Ross, adm. (**H**) 851
— Knox, Clar. K.A. 328
— Michl., bp. Dry. 601; bp. Oss. 620; dn. Lism. 629
— Michl., J.K.B. Ir. 579
— sir Patience, C. Cus. 274; L.M. Lond. 491
— Rt., Clk. O. 260; L. Admy. 181; U.S.F. 229
— Rowl., S.L. 409
— Seth., bp. Exr. 437; Chanc. Gart. 746; bp. Sal. 467; dn. Exr. 437
— Th., dn. Cnr. 605
— Th. Le Hunt, adm. (**E**) 837
— Wm., adm. (**D**) 840; (**G**) 827
— Wm., bp. S. & M. 484
— Wm. Cuthb., gen. (**D**) 892
— Wm. Jno., gen. (**D**) 915
— hon. Wm. Jno., adm. (**E**) 837
Warde, *see also* Ward
— Ch., adm. (**H**) 845; K.H. 791
— Ed. Ch. and sir E., gen. (**D**) 901; K.C.B. 780
— Fras. and sir F., gen. (**D**) 894; K.C B. 780
— Geo., Comm. F. Ir. 564; gen. (**A**) 858
— Geo., gen. (**A**) 861
— Hy. and sir H., G. Bdoes. 720; G. Mtius. 683; gen. (**A**) 861; G.C.B. 768; K.C.B. 773
— Jno., L.M. Lond. 489
— Matth., dn. Kilmacd. 637
— Wm., B. Ex. 383
Wardell, Wm. Hy., gen. (**D**) 931
Warden, Fras. F., gen. (**D**) 917
— Fk., adm. (**D**) 833
— Rt., gen. (**D**) 906
— Th. Sm., gen. (**D**) 918
Warder, Geo. Lodw., gen. (**D**) 929
Wardlaw, Hy., bp. St. Andr. 529
— Jno., gen. (**B**) 869
— Rt., gen. (**D**) 903
— Walt., bp. Glasg. 536
Wardour, Wm., Cl. Pells. 168
Ware, Hy., bp. Chich. 433
— Jno. de la, bp. Llff. 449
— Jos., dn. Elph. 609
— Rd. de, J. It. 368
Warelwast and **Warlewast**
— Rt., bp. Exr. 436; dn. Sal. 468
— Wm., bp. Exr. 436
Waren, *see* Warren
Warenne, Jno., *see* Earl W., *infra*
— Regd. de, J. It. 365
— Wm. de, J. It. 366; Jy. 364
— Wm., *see* Earl W., *infra*
Warenne, Earls
— Wm. de, aft. Earl W. and Surrey, Ch. Jr. 362
— Jno. de, Earl W. and Surrey, J. It. 368
Warham, Ralph de, bp. Chich. 432
— Wm., abp. Cant. 431; bp. Lond. 451; Ld. K. and Ld. Chanc. 355; M.R. 387
Warine (or Guarinus), Ld. Chanc. or V. Chanc. 353
Waring, *see also* Warren
— Ed. Jno., C.I.E. 807
— Holt, dn. Drom. 606
— Th., gen. (**D**) 889
Warle, Warlee, or **Warlegh,** Ing. de, B. Ex. 383; L.K. 354
Warlewast, *see* Warelwast
Warmington, Corn. M., Q.C. 420
Warmistry, Th., dn. Worc. 473
Warner, D. B., Pres. Lib. 100; dn. Lich. 445
— sir Ed., Lt. T.L. 321
— Jno., bp. Roch. 460; dn. Lich. 445; dn. Winch. 471
— sir Jno., L.M. Lond. 491
— Ph., G. Leew. Isl. 727
— Th., C. St. 283
Warneville, Ralph de, Ld. Chanc. 353
Waroc, D. Bry. 27
Warr, De la, *see* De la Warr
Warr, Rd., K.B. 759
— Rd., U.S.S. 225
Warre, Hy. Jas., C.C. Bbay. 660; gen. (**D**) 903; K.C.B. 781
— sir Wm., gen. (**D**) 879
Warren and **Waren,** *see also* Warenne
— Arth. Fk., gen. (**D**) 933
— Ch., C.J. Chest. 386; K.C. 415
— Daws. St., gen. (**D**) 928
— Ch. and sir C. (No. 1), gen. (**D**) 893; K.C.B. 779
— Ch. and sir C. (No. 2), C.C.P. 261; G. B. Bland. 680; G.C.M.G. 795; K.C.B. 784; K.C.M.G. 798
— Ed., dn. Emly, 628; dn. Oss. 623
— Fk., adm. (**A**) 820
— Geo., gen. (**D**) 887
— Geo., K.B. 765
— Jno., bp. Bgr. 426; bp. St. Dav. 465; dn. Bgr. 427
— Jno., J. Chest. 387
— Jno. de, K.B. 754
— sir Jno. Borl., adm. (**A**) 817; Amb. Russ. 125; G.C.B. 766; G.C.H. 786; K.B. 765; P.C. 207
— Lion. Sm., gen. (**D**) 932
— Nathl., L.M. Dbln. 641
— Pet. and sir P., adm. (**A**) 814; K.B. 765
— sir Ralph, L.M. Lond. 490
— Rd. de, L.H.T. 152
— (Waryn or Waryng), Rd., dn. Lim. 639
— Rd. B., S.L. Ir. 593
— Rd. Laird., adm. (**D**) 832; (**E**) 834
— Rt. Rd., A.G. Ir. 588; J.P. and M. Ir. 587; S.G. Ir. 590
— sir Saml., adm. (**D**) 823; K.C.B. 777; K.C.H. 788
— Saml., gen. (**C**) 874
— Saml., L.M. Dbln. 642

Warren and Waren—*cont.*
—— Saml., Q.C. 417
—— Th. Mans., gen. (**D**) 931
—— Wm., adm. (**G**) 842
Warrender, sir Geo., B.C. 253; L. Admy. 181; P.C. 210
Warrington, Hy., 1st E. of, form. 2nd ld. Delamere, *q.v.*
Warry, Geo. D., Q.C. 420
Warsup, Rt., M. Chy. 396
Warton, *see also* Wauton
—— (or Parfew, or Purfoy), Rt., bp. Her. 441; bp. St. As. 462
—— Th., P. Laur. 301
Wartre, Nichs., bp. Drom. 604
Warwick, Nichs. de, A.G. 398; S.L. 406
Warwick, lds., E., and D. of
—— Jno. de Plessitis, E. of, J. It. (1250) 368
Beauchamp Family.
—— Th., E. of (*d.* 1369), K.G. 733; L.H.A. 172; L.K. 354; L.M. 325
—— Th., E. of (*d.* 1401), K.G. 734; L.H.A. 173; L.M. 325
—— Rd., E. of, form. R. Beauchamp, *q.v.* (*d.* 1439), K.B. 755
—— Hy. de Beauchamp, E. of, aft. D. of W. (*d.* 1445), G. Ch. Isl. 667
Nevill Family.
—— [and Salisbury], Rd., E. of, form. Rd. Nevill, *q.v.* (*d.* 1471). K.G. 736; L.H.A. 174; W.C.P. 318
Dudley Family.
—— Jno., E. of, form. visc. Lisle, *q.v.*, aft. D. of Northumberland, *q.v.* (*d.* 1553)
—— Ambr., E. of (*d.* 1589), K.G. 738; M.H. 301
Rich Family.
—— Rt., 1st E. of, form. R. Rich, *q.v.*
—— Rt., 2nd E. of, G. Gsey. 668; L. Admy. 175; L.H.A. 175; L.L. Esx. 308; W.C.P. 319
—— Rt., 3rd E. of, form. Rt. Rich, *q.v.*
Greville Family.
See also Brooke and Warwick.
—— [and Brooke], Geo., 2nd E. of, form. ld. Geo. Greville, *q.v.*, L.L. Warw. 312
—— Hy. R., 3rd E. of, L.L. Warw. 312
Waryn, *see* Warren
Wasand, *see* Watsand
Washington, Geo., Pres. U.S.A. 102
—— Jas., Bar. de, K.C.B. 777
—— Jno., adm. (**G**) 842
Wastoldus, *see* Walstodus
Water, Ph., dn. Lim. 639
Waterford, M. of
—— Geo. de la P., 1st M. of, form. 2nd E. of Tyrone, *q.v.*
—— Jno. Hy. de la P., 5th M. of, K.P. 751; L.L. Wford. 571; M.B.H. 303
—— Hy. de la P., 2nd M. of, K.P. 750
—— Hy. de la P., 3rd M. of, K.P. 751
—— Jno. Hy. de la P., 5th M. of, K.P. 751; L.L. Wford. 571; M.B.H. 303; P.C. 220
Waterhouse, Ch., G. Gsey. 668
—— sir Ed., Ch. Ex. Ir. 561
Waterlow, sir Syd. H., L.M. Lond. 492
Waterman, Edm. Fk., gen. (**D**) 926
—— sir Geo., L.M. Lond. 491
Waters, Ed. Fk., gen. (**D**) 880
—— (or de l'Eau), Eust., bp. Lim. 638; dn. Lim. 639
—— Jno., R. Bl. P.A. 344; R. Cr. P.A. 335; Yk. H. 334
—— Jno. and sir J., gen. (**B**) 870; K.C.B. 776
—— Marc. Ant., gen. (**D**) 890
—— Th., Carl. H. 339; R. Cr. P.A. 335
Waterton, Rt., K.B. 759
Waterville, Jno. de, K.B. 754
Watford, Rt. de, dn. St. P. 452
Wath, Michl. de, L.K. 354; M.R. 387
Watkins, Fk., adm. (**A**) 819; (**G**) 840
—— Jno., dn. Her. 442
—— Ll. Vaugh., L.L. Brec. 315
—— Th. Vern., adm. (**H**) 848
—— Westr., gen. (**D**) 887
Watling, Jno. Wyatt, adm. (**H**) 847
Wats, *see* Watts
Watsand (or Wasand), Al. de, J.C.P. 376; Jy. 364
Watson, Alexr., gen. (**B**) 870
—— Anthy., bp. Chich. 433; dn. Brl. 440
—— Archd., gen. (**D**) 878
—— Archd., Modr. K. Sc. 547
—— sir Arth. Townl., Q.C. 420
—— sir Br., L.M. Lond. 492
—— Ch., adm. (**A**) 814
—— Dav., gen. (**C**) 871
—— Dav., gen. (**D**) 911
—— Ed. Day., gen. (**D**) 917
—— sir Fras., G. Jam., 712
—— Fras. Metc., dn. Llin. 624
—— Fk. Beilb. and sir F., C. Cus. 277; K.C.H. 787
—— Geo., C. Exc. 281
—— Geo. Vinc., gen. (**D**) 928
—— Geo. Willes, adm. (**E**) 837
—— Hy., G. Br. Gu. 715
—— sir Hy., gen. (**D**) 877
—— Jas., S.L. 412
—— Jas. and sir J., gen. (**A**) 863; K.C.B. 777
—— Jas. K., gen. (**D**) 931
—— Jno., Bl. M.P.A. 336
—— Jno., bp. Winch. 471; dn. Winch. 471
—— Jno., dn. Ferns, 623
—— Jno. and sir J., gen. (**D**) 923; K.C.B. 781
—— Jno. Wats. Tad., gen. (**A**) 859
—— Jonn., bp. Dkld. and Dnbl. 542
—— Lewis W., gen. (**D**) 887
—— Rd., bp. Llff. 449
—— Rt., adm. (**A**) 818
—— Rt., gen. (**B**) 866
—— Th., bp. Linc. 447; dn. Dham. 479
—— Th., bp. St. Dav. 464
—— Th. and sir T., Pres. Coll. Ph. 938
—— Wm., *see* ld. W., *infra*
—— Wm. Hy. and sir W., B. Ex. 385; Q.C. 417; S.L. 413
Watson, lds.
—— Wm., aft. ld. W., D. Fac. Sc. 527; Jud. Com. P.C. 362; L. App. 358; Ld. Adv. 526; P.C. 219; S.G. Sc. 527
Watt, Jas., C.I.E. 808
—— Jas. Land., gen. (**D**) 433
Watteville, Fk. de, gen. (**C**) 873
—— Lewis de, gen. (**C**) 873
Watts and **Wats**
—— —, Adm. Ind. 647
—— Geo. Ed., adm. (**D**) 828; (**G**) 840
—— sir Jno., L.M. Lond. 491
—— Jno. Pons., gen. (**D**) 925
—— Rt., dn. Ferns, 623; dn. Oss. 623
—— Wm., L.M. Dbln. 640
—— Wm. Hy., gen. (**D**) 923
Wauchope, Jno., Ld. Sess. 519
—— Patr., gen. (**C**) 872
—— Rt., adm. (**D**) 828
Waude, Wm. de, dn. Sal. 468
Waugh, sir Andr. Sc., gen. (**D**) 896
—— Gilb., gen. (**D**) 878
—— Jno., bp. Carl. 476; dn. Glr. 440
—— Jno., dn. Worc. 473
Waughton, sir Th., Sp. H.C. 248
Wauton, *see also* Warton
—— Jno. de, J. It. 367
—— (or Walton), Sim. de, bp. Norw. 454; J.C.P. 376; J. It. 368; Jy. 364
Waveney, Rt. Al. St., 1st ld., L.L. Ant. 568
Waverton, *see* Waferton
Way, sir Greg. Holm. Br., gen. (**B**) 870
—— S. J., G. S. Austr. 706
Waykam, Wm., K.B. 754
Waynflete (or Patten), Jno., dn. Chich. 434
—— Wm. de, bp. Winch. 470; Ld. Chanc. 355
Weare, Hy. Edwin, gen. (**D**) 907
—— Th., K.H. 791
Wearg, sir Clem., S.G. 401
Weathershed (or Grant), Rd., abp. Cant. 430
Weaver, *see* Weever
Web, Webb and **Webbe**
—— All. Beech., bp. Blfn. 681; bp. Gr. Tn. 680
—— Ch. Locock, Q.C. 419
—— Danl., gen. (**B**) 865
—— Ezek., dn. Lim. 639
—— Geo., bp. Lim. 638
—— Jas., G. Newfd. 700
—— sir Jno., K.C.H. 788
—— Jno. Richm., gen. (**A**) 857; K.C. 415
—— Nichs., G. Bah. Isl. 716
—— Noah, dn. Llin. 623
—— Th., dn. Kilm. 609
—— Th., S.L. 411
—— Wm., adm. (**H**) 846
—— Wm., dn. Dry. 602
—— sir Wm., L.M. Lond. 491
Webber, Ch., adm. (**A**) 815
—— Ch. Edm., gen. (**D**) 928
—— Ed., gen. (**B**) 868
—— Fras., dn. Her. 442
—— Hy., dn. Exr. 437
—— Jas., dn. Rip. 482
—— Jas., gen. (**C**) 873
—— Wm. Thos. Th., bp. Brisb. 706
Webley-Parry, *se* Parry
Webster, Edm. Forst., C.I.E. 808
—— Rd. Ev. and sir R., A.G. 400; Q.C. 419

Webster—*cont.*
— Rt. Farq., gen. (**D**) 919
— Th., gen. (**D**) 878
— Th., Q.C. 418
— Th. Ed., gen. (**D**) 935
Wedderburn, Alex., aft. 1st ld. Loughborough and E. of Rosslyn, *q.v.*, A.G. 399; C.J.C.P. 376; K.C. 415; P.C. 203; S.G. 402; S.L. 412
— Alex., C. Exc. Sc. 504
— sir Dav., Postm. G. Sc. 503
— Jas., bp. Dnbl. 532
— Jas., S.G. Sc. 527
— Jno., gen. (**D**) 911
— Patr., Ld. Sess. 520
— sir Pet., Ld. Sess. 519
Weeks, Jno. Wills, bp. Si. Le. 686
— Ralph, G. Bdoes. 720
Weems, *see* Wemyss
Weever, Jno., Comm. Tr. 554
Welby, Reg. Earle and sir R., K.C.B. 784; Sec. Tr. 164
— Th. Earle, bp. St. Hel. 680
— Wm., K.B. 761
Welch, *see* Welsh
Welchman, Jno., gen. (**D**) 899
Weld, Fredk. Aloys. and sir F., G. Str. Sett. 675; G. Tasm. 708; G. W. Austr. 707; G.C.M.G. 795; K.C.M.G. 797
— sir Humphr., L.M. Lond. 491
— Jos., S.L. 411
Weldon, Th., C.I.E. 808
— Walt., gen. (**D**) 915
— Wm. Hy., R. Dr. P.A. 338; Winds. H. 332
Welford and **Welleford**
— Geoff. de, M. Chy. 393
— Ralph de, J. It. 366; Jy. 364
— Rd. G., C.C.J. 404
Welifed, Nichs., bp. Wford. 626; dn. Wford. 628
Welleford, *see* Welford
Welles, *see also* Wells
— (or Wellis), Jno., L.M. Lond. 490
— Rt., dn. Ely, 435
— Sim. de, bp. Chich. 432
— Wm., L.D. Ir. 552
— Wm. de, J. It. 367
Welles, lds. and visc.
— Leo (or Lionel), 6th ld., K.B. 756; K.G. 736; L.L. Ir. 552
— Jno., 1st visc., K.G. 736
Wellesley, Arth. and sir A., aft. 1st visc. E., M., and D. of Wellington, *q.v.*, C. Treas. Ir. 561; Ch. Sec. Ir. 563; K.B. 766; P.C. 208
— ld. Ch., gen. (**D**) 891
— Geo. Grev. and sir G., adm. (**D**) 833; (**E**) 834; G.C.B. 771; K.C.B. 781; L. Admy. 185
— hon. Ger., dn. Winds. 474
— hon. Hy. and sir Hy., aft. 1st ld. Cowley, *q.v.*, Amb. Aus. 117; Amb. Spn. 124; G.C.B. 771; K.B. 766; L.T. 158; Sec. Tr. 163; P.C. 209
— hon. H. R., aft. 2nd ld. and 1st E. Cowley, *q.v.*, Amb. Tky. 129
— Rd., *see* Marq. W., *infra*
— Walt., bp. Kild. 617
Wellesley, Marq.
— Rd., Marq., form. 2nd E. of Mornington, *q.v.*, Amb. Spn. 124; B.C. 252; C. St. 284; F. Sec. 228; K.G. 743; L.C.H. 295; L.L. Ir. 557; L.S.H. 290; L.T. 159
Wellington, visc., E., M., and D. of
— Arth., 1st visc., E., M., and D. of, form. sir A. Wellesley, *q.v.*, Amb Aus. 117; Amb. Fr. 113; Amb. Pr. 118; Amb. Russ. 125-6; C. Ch. 855; Const. T.L. 321; F.M. 856; F. Sec. 228; G.C.B. 767; G.C.H. 786; gen. (**A**) 860; K.G. 743; L.H. Const. 289; L.L. Hants. 311; L.T. 159-60; M.G.O. 259; Prem. 146; W.C.P. 319
— Arth. Rd., 2nd D. of, gen. (**D**) 885; K.G. 744; L.L. Mdx. 310; M.H. 302; P.C. 216
— Elizabeth, Dss. of, M. Robes, 304
Wellis, *see* Welles
Wells, *see also* Welles
— Fras. Ch., gen. (**D**) 895
— Hugh or Hugo de, bp. Linc. 446; J. It. 367; Jy. 364
— Jno., bp. Llff. 449
— Jno. and sir J., adm. (**A**) 817; G.C.B. 768; K.C.B. 775
— Josc. de, J. It. 367; Jy. 364
— Mord. L., S.L. 413
— Rd., adm. (**E**) 837
— Saml., gen. (**D**) 905
— Th., adm. (**A**) 817
— Th. Spencer and sir T., Pres. Coll. Surg. 939
— Wm. de, bp. Roch. 460
— sir Wm., D. Chanc. Ir. 575
Wellwood, Jno., dn. Rph. 602
Wellys, Rt., bp. Ach. 612
Welman, Herc. Atk., gen. (**D**) 922
Welsh, Dav. Jas., gen. (**D**) 925
— Jas., gen. (**D**) 876
— (or Walsh), Jno., J.C.P. 378
Welson, Wm , *see* Velson
Welti, E., Pres. Sw. C. 31
Welward, Wm., Ld. Chanc. Ir. 574
Wemyss, Andr., Ld. Sess. 518
— Dav. Dougl., gen. (**A**) 860
— (or Weems), Hy., bp. Gall. 538
— sir Jas., Ld. Sess. 519
— Jas. Ersk., adm. (**D**) 829; L.L. Fifesh. 510
— Jas. HayErsk., L.L. Fifesh. 510
— sir Jno., Ld. Sess. 519
— Maur., gen. (**B**) 866
— Th., Ld. Sess. 518
— Th. Jas., gen. (**D**) 882
— Wm., gen. (**A**) 860
— Wm., gen. (**C**) 872
— Wm., gen. (**D**) 880
Wemyss, E. of, *see also* E. of March
— Jno., 1st E. of, L.H.C.K. Sc. 546
— Dav., 3rd E. of, L. Admy., 177; L.H.A. Sc. 499; V.A. Sc. 499
— Fras., 7th E. of, aft. E. of W. and March, L.L. Pbls. 511
— (and March), Fras., 8th E. of, L.L. Pbls. 511
Wenceslas, D. Bbt. 29
— E. Gmy. 62
— M. Brg. 65
— I. and II., C. Lux. 84
— I. and II., D. Bma. 59
— III. to VI., K. Bma. 59
Wendy, *see* Windy
Wendover, Rd. de, bp. Roch. 459
Weneyve, Jno., C. St. 283
Wengham, *see* Wingham
Wenlock, sir Jno., K.G. (1460) *see* errata; L. Treas. Ir. 559; Sp. H.C. 248
— Walt., L.H.T. 152
Wenlock, lds.
— Paul B., 1st ld., L.L. Yorks. E.R. 313
— Beilby Rd., 2nd ld., L.L. Yorks. E.R. 313
Wensleydale, Jas., 1st ld., form. sir J. Parke, *q.v.*
Went, Jno., *see* West
Wentgrave, Jno., L.M. Lond. 489
Wentworth, Hy., K.B. 758
— Jno., G. N. Sc. 695
— Pet., dn. Arm. 597
— Pet., dn. Dry. 602
— Pet., K.B. 763
— sir Ph., K.G. 735
— Rd., K.B. 759
— (or Bynteworth), Rd. de, bp. Lond. 451; Ld. Chanc. 354
— Th., gen. (**B**) 864
— Th., K.B. 763
— Th., *see* ld. W., *infra*
— Th., aft. 1st E. of Malton, and 1st M. of Rockingham, *q.v.*, K.B. 764
Wentworth of Nettlested, lds.
— Th., 1st ld., L.C.H. 294
— Th., 4th ld., aft. 1st E. of Cleveland, *q.v.*, K.B. 762
Wentworth of Woodhouse, lds.
— Thos., visc., form. ld. Raby, *q.v.*, aft. E. of Strafford, *q.v.*, L.D. Ir. 554; P.C. 189
Werden, sir Jno., C. Cus. 273-4
Werefrid, bp. Worc. 472
Weremund, bp. Roch. 459; bp. Worc. 472
Weremundus, bp. Dunw. 454
Werge, Hy. Reyn., gen. (**D**) 911
Werinbertus, bp. Dorch. 464
Werstane or **Werstanus,** bp. Dev. 436; bp. Shbn. 466
Weseham, Rog. de, bp. Lich. and Cov. 444; dn. Linc. 447
Wesley, *see also* Westley
— Saml. Rt., gen. (**D**) 891; K.C.B. 779
West, Algn. E. and sir A., C.I.R. 286; K.C.B. 784
— Aug. Wm., dn. Ard. 609
— Benj., Pres. R.A. 941
— Ch. R. S., *see* ld. S., *infra*
— Edm., S.L. 410
— sir Ed., C.J. Bbay. 660
— Geo., Wdn. Chr. Ch. Manch. 481
— Hy. Wynd., Q.C. 418
— Jac., L.M. Dbln. 642
— Jas., Pres. R. Soc. 940
— Jas., Sec. Tr. 163
— Jermy. Ch., gen. (**D**) 913
— Jno., C. Cus. Sc. 504
— Jno., dn. Chr. Ch. Dbln. 619; dn. St. Pat. 618
— Jno. and sir J., adm. (**A**) 819; (**B**) 821; G.C.B. 770; K.C.B. 777

West—*cont.*
— (or Went, Jno., dn. Cloy. 632
— hon. Lionel. Sackv. Sackv. and sir L., Amb. Arg. 136; Amb. Fr. 113; Amb. Spn. 124; Amb. U.S.A. 132; K.C.M.G. 798
— Mart., G. Nat. 680
— Nichs., bp. Ely. 435; dn. Winds. 474; Regr. Gart. 746
— Raym., K.C.I.E. 805
— Regd., dn. Her. 442
— Rd., gen. (**D**) 878
— Rd., L.J. Ir. 556; Ld. Chanc. Ir. 576
— Temple, adm. (**A**) 814; L. Admy. 178
— Th., adm. (**A**) 817
— Th., K.B. 754
— Th., K.B. 756
— Th., K.B. 758
— Wm. Cornw., L.L. Denb. 314
— Wm. Hy. Hore, gen. (**D**) 924
West, lds.
— Ch. Rd. Sackv., ld., aft. 6th E. de la Warr, *q.v.*. gen. (**D**) 899
Westbury, Wm., J.C.P. 378; J.K.B. 371; S.L. 407
— Rd., 1st ld., form. sir R. Bethell, *q.v.*, Jud. Com. P.C. 361; P.C. 217
Westby, Barth., B.E. 383
— Bas. Cl., gen. (**D**) 933
— Ward. Geo., C. Cus. 275-6
Westcote, Jno. de, J. It. 369
Westcote, lds.
— Wm. Hy., 1st ld., (W. H. Lyttelton in 1761), L.T. 158
Westenra, Fras., gen. (**D**) 900
Western, Th., adm. (**A**) 819
— Th. Burch., L.L. Esx. 308
Westfield, Th., bp. Brl. 439
Westhorp, Th., M. Chy. 394
Westlake, Jno., Q.C. 419
Westley, *see also* Wesley
— sir Rt., L.M. Lond. 491
Westmacott, Sp., gen. (**D**) 907
Westmeath, E. of
— Th., 6th E. of, K.P. 750
— G. F., 7th E. of, form. visc. Delvin, *q.v.*
— Anthy. Fr., M. of, L.L. W. Meath, 571
Westminster, Ed. de, B. Ex. 382
Westminster, M. and D. of,
— Rt., 1st M. of, form. visc. Belgrave, and 2nd E. Grosvenor, *q.v.*, K.G. 744
— Rd., 2nd M. of, L.S.H. 290; K.G. 744; L.L. Chesh. 307; P.C. 215
— Hugh Lupus, 3rd M. and 1st D. of, K.G. 745; L.L. Chesh. 307; M.H. 302; P.C. 219
Westmoreland, E. of
Nevill Family.
(*See also* Nevill.)
— Ralph, 1st E. of, E.M. 326; K.G. 734
— Ralph, 2nd E. of, K.B. 756
— Ralph, 4th E. of, K.G. 737
— Hy. 5th E. of, K.G. 738; L.L. Dham. 308
Fane Family.
— Fras., 1st E. of, form. F. Fane, *q.v.*
Westmoreland, E. of—*cont.*
— Vere, 4th E. of, L.L. Kent, 309
— Th., 6th E. of, Pres. B.T. 264; P.C. 197
— Jno., 7th E. of, gen. (**A**) 858
— Jno., 10th E. of, form. ld. Burghersh, *q.v.*, K.G. 742; L.L. Ir. 557; L.L. Nton. 310; L.P.S. 241; M.H. 302; P.C. 205; Postm. G. 238
— Jno., 11th E. of, form. ld. Burghersh, *q.v.*, Amb. Aus. 117; Amb. Bgm. 123; Amb. G. St. 122; G.C.B. 772; gen. (**A**) 863
Weston, Ed., U.S.S. 225-6
— Fras., K.B. 760
— Hy., K.B. 761
— Hugh, dn. Westr. 469; dn. Winds. 474
— Jas. and sir J., B. Ex. 384; S.L. 409
— Jno. de, Const. T.L. 320
— Jno., S.L. 407
— Nichs., bp. Dry. 601
— Ph. de, dn. Yk. 486
— Rd. (No. 1), J.C.P. 378; S.G. 401; S.L. 408
— Rd. and sir R. (No. 2), B. Ex. 384; S.L. 409
— Rd. and sir R. (No. 3), B. Ex. 384; S.L. 410
— sir Rd., G. Gsey. 668
— sir Rd., *see* ld. W., *infra*
— Rt. and sir R., dn. Arch. 420; dn. St. Pat. 618; dn. Wells, 429; L.J. Ir. 554; Ld. Chanc. Ir. 576; M. Chy. 395
— Steph., bp. Exr. 437
— Th. de, K.B. 754
— Walt. de, G. Ch. Isl. 667
— sir Wm., C.J.C.P. Ir. 580
— sir Wm., G. Gsey. 668
Weston, lds.
— sir Rd., aft. 1st ld. W. and E. of Portland, *q.v.*, Ch. Ex. 154; K.G. 739; L. Admy. 175; L.H.T. 139; Ch. Ex. 154
Westphal, sir Geo. Aug., adm. (**G**) 841
— Ph., adm. (**H**) 847
Westphaling, Herb., bp. Her. 441
Westropp, Jas. Ed., gen. (**D**) 911
— Jno. Pars., gen. (**D**) 900
— sir Michl. R., C.J. Bbay. 660
— Roberts Michl., gen. (**D**) 914
Westwode, Rog., B. Ex. 383
Wetenhall, Ed., bp. Cork and R. 632; bp. Kilm. and Ard. 607
Wetham, *see also* Whetham
— Th., gen. (**A**) 857
Wetherall, *see also* Wetherell
— Ed. Rt. and sir R., gen. (**D**) 907; K.C.S.I. 803
— Fk. Augs., adm. (**H**) 846
— sir Fk. Aug., G.C.H. 786; gen. (**A**) 862
— sir G. R., U.S. Ir. 563
— Th., M. Chy. 394
Wetherby, Jno., dn. Cash. 627; dn. Emly, 628
Wetherell, *see also* Wetherall
— Ch. and sir C., A.G. 400; P.P. 415; K.C. 416; S.G. 402
— Fk. Aug. (2), *see* Wetherall
Wetherell—*cont.*
— Geo. Augs. and sir G., gen. (**D**) 883; G.C.B. 770; K.C.B. 778; K.H. 790
— Nath., dn. Her. 442
Wetherhead, Th., bp. Wford. and L. 627
Wetton, Rd., M. Chy. 394
Wexford, Rog. de, dn. Oss. 622
Weyland, Th. de, C.J.C.P. 375; J.C.P. 377; J. It. 368; S.L. 406
— Wm. de, J.C.P. 377; J. 368; Jy. 365
Weymouth, visc.
— Th., 1st visc. B. T. 63; P.C. 195
— Th., visc., aft. 3rd M. of Bath, *q.v.*, Gr. St. 304; K. 742; L.L. Ir. 557; P.C. 201 S. St. 224-5
Whalley, Captn. S., G. Bmda 701
Wharncliffe, lds.
— Jas. Arch., 1st ld., Jud. Com. P.C. 360; L.L. Yorks. W.R. 313; L.P.C. 188; L.P.S. 241; P.C. 213
— Jno., 2nd ld., form. hon. Jno. Stuart-Wortley, *q.v.*
Wharton, Geo., K.B. 761
— Goodw., L. Admy. 176
— Jas., gen. (**A**) 861
— sir M., L. Admy. 176
— Rd., Sec. Tr. 163
— Rt., C.C.J. 403
— Th., C. Exc. Sc. 505
— Th., K.B. 763
— Th., *see* ld. Wh., *infra*
Wharton, lds., E., and M. of
— hon. Th., aft. 5th ld. and 1st E. and M. of Wharton (also E. of Malmesbury, *q.v.*), Compt. H. 292; L.L. Ir. 555; L.P.S. 240; P.C. 193
Whateley and **Whately**
— Rd., abp. Dbln. G. and K. 617; abp. Dbln. and Gl. 616
— Th., B.T. 266; Sec. Tr. 163 U.S.S. 226
— Wm., Q.C. 417
Whatley, sir Jos., K.C.H. 788
Wheate, sir Th., St. O. 260
Wheatley, sir Hy., G.C.H. 787; K.C.H. 788
— Rt., G. Bdoes. 719
— Wm., gen. (**C**) 873
Wheeler, *see also* Wheler
— Andr., gen. (**C**) 871
— Ed., Chn. E.I. Co. 644
— sir Fras., adm. (**A**) 813
— Fk., gen. (**D**) 933
— Hugh Mass. and sir H., gen. (**D**) 886; K.C.B. 777
— Jonas (or Jas.), bp. Oss. 620; dn. Chr. Ch. Dbln. 618
— Rt., gen. (**D**) 934
— Th., C.C.J. 404; S.L. 414
— Th. Whitt., Q.C. 420
Wheelhouse, Wm. St. Jas. Q.C. 419
Whelan, sir Th., L.M. Dbln. 642
Wheler, *see also* Wheeler
— Fras. and sir F., gen. (**D**) 896
Whelpdale, Rog., bp. Carl. 475
Whetham, *see also* Wetham
— Arth., gen. (**B**) 867
— sir Ch., L.M. Lond. 492
— Jno., C. Exc. 279, 280; C. Exc. Sc. 504

Whetham—*cont.*
— Jno., dn. Lism. 629
— Jno., gen. (**D**) 882
Whetstone, sir Wm., adm. (**A**) 813
Whi—, *see also* Why—
Whichcote, Geo., gen. (**D**) 891
Whiddon (or Whyddon), Jno., J.Q.B. 372; S.L. 408
Whigham, Jas., C.C.J. 404
Whimper, *see also* Whymper
— Fk. Am., gen. (**D**) 905
Whinyates, Ch., Richm. H. 334
— Ed. C. and sir E., gen. (**D**) 884; K.C.B. 778; K.H. 789
— Fras. F., gen. (**D**) 888
— Fk. F., gen. (**D**) 887
— Fk. Th., gen. (**D**) 925
— Fk. W., gen. (**D**) 889
— Th., adm. (**H**) 844
Whish, Geo. Palm., gen. (**D**) 902
— Mart., C. Exc. 281; C. St. 283
— Rd., gen. (**D**) 877
— Wm. Geo. Hyndm., adm. (**H**) 848
— Wm. Sams., gen. (**D**) 880; K.C.B. 777
Whistler, Th. Kins., gen. (**D**) 902
Whitaker, sir Ed., adm. (**A**) 813
— Fk., K.C.M.G. 798
— Wm., S.L. 412
Whitby, *see* Whittey
Whitbread, Gord., C.C.J. 405
— Saml., L. Admy. 184
Whitchister (or Wircestre), Rog., J.C.P. 377; Jy. 365
Whitcock, *see* Whittock
Whitcombe, Jno., abp. Cash. and Eml. 626; bp. Clonf. and K. 636; bp. Down and Cnr. 604
White, *see also* Whyte and Albus
— Anthy., Pres. Coll. Surg. 939
— hon. Ch. W., L.L. Clare, 569
— Fras., bp. Carl. 475; bp. Ely, 435; dn. Carl. 476; bp. Norw. 455
— Fk. Ch., gen. (**A**) 862
— Fk. Meadows, Q.C. 419
— Geoffr., bp. Crk. 630
— Geo. Hy. Parlby, adm. (**H**) 848
— Geo. Stewart and sir G., gen. (**D**) 932; K.C.B. 781
— Hy., K.C.B. 775
— Hy., aft. 1st ld. Annaly, *q.v.*, L.L. Longf. 570
— Hy. Arth., gen. (**D**) 910
— Hy. Dalr., gen. (**D**) 903; K.C.B. 780
— Hy. Geo., gen. (**D**) 930
— Hy. Hopley, Q.C. 418
— (or Whyte), Jno., A.G. Ir. 588
— Jno., gen. (**A**) 860
— Jno., G. Jam. 712
— sir Jno., L.M. Lond. 490
— Jno. Chamb. and sir J., adm. (**A**) 820; K.C.B. 777
— Jno. Hubb., gen. (**D**) 932
— Luke, L.L. Longf. 570
— Luke, aft. 2nd ld. Annaly, *q.v.*, L.T. 161
— Mart., adm. (**H**) 846

White—*cont.*
— Mart., gen. (**D**) 876
— Michl., gen. (**D**) 885; K.C.B. 779
— Patr. and sir P., B. Ex. Ir. 583; J.K.B. Ir. 578
— Pet., dn. Wford. 628
— (or Albus), Ph., dn. Crk. 632
— Raym. Herb., gen. (**D**) 924
— Rd., L.D. Ir. 551; Ld. Chanc. Ir. 575
— Rd., L.M. Dbln. 641
— Rd. Dunn., adm. (**H**) 850
— Rt., bp. Dnbl. 542; bp. Fife, 543; pr. bp. Sc. 540
— Rt., gen. (**D**) 909
— Tayl., J. Chest. 387
— Th., adm. (**H**) 844
— Th., bp. Pboro. 458
— Th., Clk. O. 260
— Th., dn. Ard. 609
— sir Th. (2), L.M. Lond. 490, 492
— Wm., dn. Dry. 602
*— Wm., dn. Tm. 613
*— Wm., dn. Kilf. 637
* ? same pers.
— Wm., L.M. Lond. 490
— Wm. Arth. and sir W., Amb. Rma. 128; Amb. Sva. 128; Amb. Tky. 130; G.C.B. 773; G.C.M.G. 795; K.C.M.G. 798; P.C. 221
— Wm. Geo., gen. (**D**) 895
— Wm. Rd., gen. (**D**) 933
Whiteacre, Ch., S.L. 411
— Ed., S.L. 411
Whitefeld, *see also* Whitfield
— (or Witefeld), Rt. de, J. It. 366; Jy. 363
Whiteford, *see also* Whitford
— sir Geo., L.M. Dbln. 642
— sir Jno., gen. (**B**) 865
— sir Jno., K.H. 790
Whitehall, Launc., C. Cus. Sc. 503
Whitehead, Hugh, dn. Dham. 479
— Jas. and sir J., L.M. Lond. 492
— Rt. Ch., gen. (**D**) 934
— Th., gen. (**D**) 877; K.C.B. 777
— Wm., P. Laur. 301; Regr. and Sec. Bath, 784
Whiteheare (or Whytere), Jno., dn. Brl. 440
Whitehill, Steph. Jas. K., gen. (**D**) 915
Whitehorne, Jas. Ch., Q.C. 419
Whitehurst, Ch. H., Q.C. 417
Whitelock and **Whitelocke,** *see also* Whitlock
— Bulstr., called ld. W., C. Exc. 279; C.G.S. 356; Const. W. Cast. 322; L. Admy. 175; L.T. 154; S.L. 409
— Jas. and sir J., J.K.B. 372; S.L. 409
— Jno., gen. (**B**) 866
Whiteside, Jas., A.G. Ir. 588; C.J.Q.B. Ir. 578; S.G. Ir. 590
Whiteway, Wm. Vall., K.C.M.G. 797
Whitfield, *see also* Whitefield
*— maj.-gen. —, G. H. Kong, 673
*— Hy. Wasc., gen. (**D**) 903
* ? same pers.
— Ralph, S.L. 409

Whitford, *see also* Whiteford
— (or Whitworth), Walt., bp. Brn. 531
Whitgift, Jno., abp. Cant. 431; bp. Worc. 473; dn. Linc. 448
Whithers, *see also* Withers
— Ch., S.W.F. 271
Whiting, Th., Chest. H. 330
Whitlaw, Archd., Sec. St. Sc. 502
Whitley, Geoffr., dn. Ferns, 623
— Hy., gen. (**B**) 865
Whitlock, *see also* Whitelock
— Geo. Corn. and sir C., gen. (**D**) 891; K.C.B. 778
— Jas., C.J. Chest. 386
— Wm., K.C. 415
Whitmarsh, Jas. F., K.C. 416
Whitmore, Ch. S., C.C.J. 404; Q.C. 417
— Ed., gen. (**C**) 871
— Edm. Augs. and sir E., gen. (**D**) 905; K.C.B. 781
— Fras. Lock., gen. (**D**) 921
— Geo., C. St. 283
— sir Geo., gen. (**A**) 863; K.C.H. 788
— sir Geo., L.M. Lond. 491
— Geo. Stodd., K.C.M.G. 798
— Hy., L.T. 161
— Mort. R. S., gen. (**D**) 910
— Th., K.B. 764
— Wm., gen. (**B**) 865; Wdn. M. 245
Whitshed, Jas. Hawk. and sir J., adm. (**A**) 816; adm. (**B**) 821; G.C.B. 768; K.C.B. 773
— Wm., C.J.C.P. Ir. 581; C.J.K.B. Ir. 578; S.G. Ir. 589
Whittaker, *see* Whitaker
Whittey (or Whitby), Rt., bp. Ferns, 621
Whittingham, Ferd., gen. (**D**) 900
— Paul Bern., gen. (**D**) 910
— sir Saml. Ford., C.C. Mdras. 657; G. Dnca. 730; gen. (**B**) 869; K.C.B. 775; K.C.H. 787
— Wm., dn. Dham. 479
Whittington, Rd., L.M. Lond. 489
— Th., B. Ex. 383
Whittlesey (or Wittlesey), Wm. de, abp. Cant. 430; bp. Roch. 460; bp. Worc. 472
Whittock, Jno., bp. Cloy. 630; dn. Cloy. 632
Whitty, Irw., gen. (**D**) 889
Whitwell, sir Nathl., L.M. Dbln. 641
Whitwich, Jno., S.L. 409
— Th., Yk. H. 334
Whitworth, Ch., *see* ld. W., *infra*
— Fras., S.W.F. 271
— Walt., *see* Whitford
Whitworth, lds., visc., and E.
— Ch., aft. 1st ld., visc. and E., Amb. Dk. 127; Amb. Fr. 112; Amb. Pld. 126; Amb. Russ. 125; B.T. 268; G.C.B. 771; K.B. 765; L.L. Ir. 557; P.C. 206
Whorwode, Wm., A.G. 398; S.G. 401
Whorwood, Jas., Winds. H. 331
Why—, *see also* Whi—
Whyche, Hugh, K.B. 757

For List of Abbreviations, see pp. 944-952.

Whyddon, *see* Whiddon
Whyham, Wm. Hy., G. Nev. 730
Whylock, Jas., gen. (**D**) 889
Whymper, *see also* Whimper
— Hy. Jos., C.I.E. 808
Whyte, *see also* White and Albus
— Hy., Ld. Sess. 518
— (or White), Jno., A.G. Ir. 588
— Jno., bp. Linc. 447; bp. Winch. 471
— Jno. Wm., adm. (**H**) 852
— Nichs., M.R. Ir. 585
— Rd., gen. (**A**) 859
— Wm., dn. Kild. 619
— Wm., dn. Wford. 628
— Wm. Hy., adm. (**E**) 837
Whytere, *see* Whiteheare
Wi—, *see also* Wy—
Wiatschelıw, R. Russ. 89
Wibba, K.E. 3
Wich, *see also* Wyche
— Rd. de la, bp. Chich. 432
Wichinton, Hy. de, Jy. 364
— Wm. de, J. It. 367
Wickart, Jno., dn. Winch. 471
Wickens, Jno. and sir J., V. Chanc. 390
Wickey, Jno., adm. (**A**) 817
Wickford, *see* Wikeford
Wickham and **Wyckham,** *see also* Wykeham
— Lewis, C. St. and Tx. 285
— Tob., dn. Yk. 487
— Wm., Amb. Swz. 113; B.T. 268; C. Treas. Ir. 561; Ch. Sec. Ir. 563; L.T. 158; P.C. 207; U.S. Home, 227
— Wm., bp. Linc. 447; bp. Winch. 471; dn. Linc. 448
— Wm. de, *see* Wykeham
Wicklow, Wm. Forw., 4th E. of, K.P. 751; L.L. Wickl. 571
Wickwane, Wm., abp. Yk. 485
Widdrington, sir Dav. Lat. Tirl., gen. (**B**) 868; K.C.H. 788
— Th. and sir T., C.B. Ex. 381; C.G.S. 356; L.T. 154; S.L. 409; S.L. 410; Sp. H.C. 249
Widmore, Jno. Frost, K.C. 415
Wigard, abp. Cant. 429
Wigenholt, Jno., J. It. 367
Wighedus, bp. Lond. 450
Wight, Jno., adm. (**D**) 823; (**G**) 840
Wighthun, bp. Sels. 432
Wighteinus, bp. Winch. 470
Wightman, Jos., gen. (**C**) 871
— Wm., and sir W., J.Q.B. 373; S.L. 413
Wightred, K.E. 1
Wightwick, Th., Ptc. P.A. 337
Wiglaf, K.E. 3
Wigley, Fras. Sp., G. Nev. 730; G. St. Xtr. 729; G. St. Xtr. and Nev. 729
Wigmore, Th., G. Gsey. 668
Wigram, Jas. and sir J., Jud. Com. P.C. 360; K.C. 416; P.C. 214; V. Chanc. 390
— Jos. Cott., bp. Roch. 460
— Loft. Tott., Q.C. 417
— Wm., Chn. E.I.Co. 645
Wigston, Jas., adm. (**G**) 841
Wigthen, bp. Winch. 470
Wihtred, K.E. 1
Wikeford, *see* Wykford

Wilberforce, Ern. Rowl., bp. Newc. T. 481
— Saml., bp. Oxf. 457; bp. Winch. 471; dn. Westr. 469
Wilbert, bp. Shbn. 466
Wilbraham, Ed., Q.C. 417
— Rd., gen. (**D**) 901; K.C.B. 780
— Rog., S.G. Ir. 589
— Th., Rec. Lond. 494
Wilby, Wm., gen. (**D**) 908
Wilcocks, *see also* Willcocks
— Jos., bp. Glr. 438; bp. Roch. 460; dn. Westr. 469
Wilcox, *see also* Willcox
— Ed., S.W.F. 271
— Jno., C. Exc. 278, 279
Wild and **Wilde,** *see also* Wylde
— Alf. Th. and sir A., gen. (**D**) 908; K.C.B. 780; M.C.I. 647
— Ed. Jno., gen. (**D**) 918
— Geo., bp. Dry. 601
— Geo., S.L. 409
— Jas. P. and sir J., aft. ld. Penzance, *q.v.*, B. Ex. 385; J. Prob. and Div. 391; Jud. Com. P.C. 361; P.C. 217; Q.C. 417; S.L. 414
— Jno., C.B. Ex. 381; C.G.S. 356; K.C. 414; S.L. 409
— Th. and sir T., aft. ld. Truro, A.G. 400; C.J.C.P. 376; Jud. Com. P.C. 360; Ld. Chanc. 358; P.C. 215; S.G. 402; S.L. 413
— Wm. and sir W., J.C.P. 379; J.K.B. 372; Rec. Lond. 494; S.L. 410
Wildeman, *see* Wildman
Wilder, sir Fras. Jno., gen. (**B**) 868
Wildman, Ed., K.H. 791
— Jno., M.M. 246
— Rd., C.C.J. 403
Wilferus, abp. Yk. 485
Wilford, Edm. Neal, gen. (**D**) 898
— Fras., dn. Ely, 435
— Gerv. de, B. Ex. 383; C.B. Ex. 381
— Rd. Rich., gen. (**A**) 860
*__Wilfredus,__ bp. Dunw. 454
*__Wilfreth__ (2), bp. Worc. 472
*__Wilfride__ (2), abp. Yk. 485
*— bp. Sels. 432
*— bp. St. Dav. 464
*— bp. Worc. 472
* Prob. some same pers. Comp. dates.
Wiliby, } *see* Wilughby
Wilighby, }
Wilkes, Jno., Chambn. Lond. 493; L.M. Lond. 492
Wilkie, Hales, gen. (**D**) 929
— Jno., gen. (**D**) 903
Wilkins, Ch., P.P. 417; S.L. 413
— sir Ch., K.H. 790
— Geo., K.H. 792
— Hy. St. Cl., gen. (**D**) 918
— Jno., bp. Chest. 477; dn. Rip. 482
Wilkinson, —, G. Bmda. 701
— Andr., St. O. 260
— Ch. Edm., gen. (**D**) 901
— Ch. Vaughan, gen. (**D**) 917
— Chr. D., gen. (**D**) 887
— Fk. Gr., gen. (**D**) 907
— Geo. How., bp. Tru. 469
— Geo. Hutt., C.C.J. 403
— Hy. Cl., gen. (**D**) 932

Wilkinson—*cont.*
— R., K.H. 792
— Th., K.C.S.I 802
— Th., L.M. Dbln. 641
— Th. Ed., bp. Zld. 681
— Wm. and sir W., G.C.M.G. 794; gen. (**A**) 862
Will, Jno. Shiress, Q.C. 420
— sir Th., G.C.B. 770
Willaumez, Louis Ed. Bouet, K.C.B. 778
Willcock, Jno. W., Q.C. 417
Willcocks, *see also* Wilcocks
— Rt. Hy., K.H. 792
Willcox, *see also* Wilcox
— Jas., adm. (**E**) 835; (**F**) 838
Willeby, Pet., Ch. Ex. 152
Willes, *see also* Wills
— Ed., bp. B. and W. 428; bp. St. Dav. 465; dn. Linc. 448
— Ed., C. Acc. Ir. 567; C.B. Ex. Ir. 583
— Ed., J.K.B. 373; K.C. 415 S.G. 402; S.L. 412
— Geo. Omm. and sir G., adm. (**E**) 836; K.C.B. 781
— Jas. Irw., gen. (**D**) 889
— Jas. Sh. and J., J.C.P. 380; Jud. Com. P.C. 361; P.C. 218; S.L. 413
— Jno. and sir J., A.G. 399; C.G.S. 357; C.J.C.P. 376; C.J. Chest. 386; K.C. 415; J. Chest. 387; P.C. 198; S.L. 412
— Jno. Irw., gen. (**D**) 928
— Wm. Hy., C.C.J. 404
William, *see also* Gulielmus
*— abp. Yk. 485
*— bp. Arg. 537
*— bp. Brn. 531
*— bp. Bgr. 425
*— (or Godfrey), bp. Chich. 432
*— bp. Cness. 531
*— (of Port Royal), bp. Cnr. 604
*— (of Jerepont), bp. Cork, 630
*— (3), bp. Dnbl. 532
*— bp. Down, 603
*— bp. Drom. 604
*— bp. Emly, 625
*— bp. Isl. 539
*— bp. Kild. 616
*— (2) bp. Llff. 449
*— bp. Llin. 621
*— (the Norman), bp. Lond. 451
*— bp. Mor. 534
*— (6), bp. Ork. 535
*— (of Kilkenny), bp. Oss. 620
*— (Gulielmus or Quichelmus), bp. Roch. 459
*— bp. S. and M. 483
*— (abb. of Ross.), Compt. Sc. 498
*— (Commend. of Culross), Compt. Sc. 498
*— dn. Bgr. 426
*— dn. Chich. 433
*— (2), dn. Lich. 445
*— dn. St. P. 452
*— dn. Yk. 486
*— (archd. of Hereford), J. It. 366
*— (archd. of Totness), Jy. 363
*— (of York), Jy. 364
*— (prior of St. John's), Ld. Chanc. Ir. 574
*— Ld. Clk. Reg. 521
* Prob. some same pers. Comp. dates.

William—*cont.*
—— C. Anj. 27
—— (de Clito), C. Flrs. 81
—— C. Lux. 84
—— D. Aus. 58
—— (2) D. Brk. 69, 70
—— (Aug. L. &c.), D. Brk. 71; K.G. 743
—— (2), D. Ndy. 30
—— D.S. Wr. 79
—— E. Gmy. 62
—— (of Bavaria), K.G. 734
—— K. Sc. 19
—— (Earl Marischal), L.P.S. Sc. 501
—— M. Bdn. 67
—— (Rufus—son of Wm. I.), Pr. E. 9, aft. Wm. II., *q.v.*
—— (son of Hy. I.), Pr. E. 9
—— (g. son of Hy. I.), Pr. E. 9
—— (son of Stephen), Pr. E. 9
—— (son of Hy. II.), Pr. E. 9
—— (son of Hy. III.), Pr. E. 9
—— (son of Edw. III.), Pr. E. 10
—— (iss. of Edw. III.), Pr. E. 11
—— (g. son of Chas. I.), Pr. E. 13
—— (son of Q. Anne), Pr. E. 14
—— (de Croi), R. Nds. 82
—— (of Nassau), R. Nds. 83
—— I., E. Gmy. 63, 65; K. Pr. 65; K.G. 744
—— I., K. Wbg. 81; G.C.B. 767; K.G. 743
—— I. and II., D. Brk. 69
—— I. (D. Brk.), K.G. 735
—— I. and II., D. Bva. 68
—— I. and II., El. H. Csl. 72
—— I. to III., K. Scy. 55
—— I. to IV., K.E. 45-6
—— Pr. Or., aft. Wm. III. (K.E.), K.G. 740; and see Wm. III. (Pr. O.), *infra*
—— IV. (K.E.), form. D. of Clarence and Pr. Wm. Hy., *infra, q.v.*, K.G. 742; K. Hnr. 71; K.T. 748
—— I. to III., K. Nds. 83
—— II. (K. Nds.), F.M. 856; K.G. 745
—— III. (K. Nds.), *see* Wm. I. (Pr. O.), *infra*
—— I. to IV., R. Nds. 83
—— I. to VI., C. Hld. 82
—— I. to VI.,
Princes of Orange.
—— I., Pr. Or. 83; R. Nds. 83
—— II., Pr. Or. 83; K.G. 740; R. Nds. 83
—— III., Pr. Or. 83; K.E. 5; K.G. 740; R. Nds. 83
—— IV., Pr. Or. 83; K.G. 741; R. Nds. 83
—— V., Pr. Or. 83; K.G. 742
—— VI., Pr. Or. 83
—— -Fk. —, Pr. Or. 83; K. Nds. (Wm. I.), 83; gen. (**A**) 860; G.C.B. 767; K.B. 766; K.G. 743

—— IV. to IX., Lg. H. Csl. 72
—— IX. (Lg. H. Csl.), aft. Wm. I., El. H. Csl., *q.v.*, K.G. 742
—— -Aug. (son of Geo. II.), aft. D. of Cumb., *q.v.*, Pr. E. 14
—— -Ern., D.S. Wr. 79
—— -Fredk. (iss. of Geo. II.), Pr. E. 14
—— -Fredk., Pr. Or., *vide supra*
—— -Geo., D. Nass. 76
—— -Hy. (g. son of Geo. II.), Pr. E. 14

William—*cont.*
—— -Hy. (Wm. IV., K.E., *q.v.*), K. Hnr. 71; P.C. 205; Pr. E. 14
—— -Lewis, D. Wbg. 81
Williams, Albt. Hy. Wilm., gen. (**D**) 935
—— Benj. Fras., Q.C. 420
—— Benj. T., C.C.J. 405; Q.C. 419
—— Ch. Fk., K.C. 416
—— Ch. Haml., adm. (**G**) 841; K.B. 764; L.L. Heref. 308
—— Ch. J. Watk. and sir C., J.Q.B.D. 374; Q.C. 419
—— Dav. and sir D. (No. 1), J.K.B. 372; S.L. 408
—— Dav. (No. 2), M.R. 387
—— Edm. Keyn. and sir E., gen. (**D**) 879; K.C.B. 775
—— Ed. Arth., gen. (**D**) 922
—— Ed. Ch. Sp., C.I.E. 806; gen. (**D**) 930
—— Ed. Rd., adm. (**G**) 841
—— Ed. V. and sir E., J.C.P. 380; Jud. Com. P.C. 361; P.C. 217; S.L. 413
—— Geo., adm. (**H**) 849
*—— Griff., bp. Oss. 620
*—— Gr., dn. Bgr. 426
* Prob. same pers.
—— Gw., C.C.J. 405
—— Hy. or Rd., dn. Lich. 445
—— Hy., gen. (**A**) 861
—— Hy. Fras., gen. (**D**) 924
—— Jas. E., gen. (**D**) 888
—— Jas. Wm., bp. Queb. 694
—— Jno. (No. 1), abp. Yk. 486; bp. Linc. 447; dn. Sal. 468; dn. Westr. 469; L.K. 356
—— Jno. (No. 2), bp. Chich. 433
—— Jno., C. Cus. 276-7
—— Jno., dn. Bgr. 426
—— Jno., S.L. 412
—— Jno. and sir J., B. Ex. 385; J.K.B. 373; K.C. 416; S.L. 413
—— Jno. and sir J., Sr. N. 257
—— sir Jno., L.M. Lond. 491
—— Jno., aft. ld. W., L.C.H. 294
—— Jno. Danl., gen. (**D**) 913
—— Jno. Wm. Colm. and sir J., gen. (**D**) 917
—— Jos., dn. Clr. 597
—— Josh., Q.C. 418
—— Lew. Dunc., gen. (**D**) 895
—— Monier and sir M., C.I.E. 806; K.C.I.E. 805
—— Mont. Steph., Q.C. 420
—— Montg., gen. (**D**) 895
—— Owen Lew. Cope, gen. (**D**) 925
—— Penry, L.L. Brec. 315
—— Ph., K.C. 416
—— Rd. or Hy. dn. Lich. 445
—— Rd., gen. (**B**) 868; K.C.B. 775
—— Rt., adm. (**A**) 820
—— Rt. Griff., Q.C. 419
—— Rt. Vaugh., C.C.J. 404
—— Rowl., G. Leew. Isl. 727
—— Saml., G. Gren. 724
—— Sherb., gen. (**D**) 889
—— Th., dn. Llff. 450
—— Th., Sp. H.C. 249
—— Th., gen. (**D**) 901
—— sir Th., adm. (**A**) 818; G.C.B. 768; K.C.B. 773
—— Th. Molyn., gen. (**D**) 893; K.H. 791
*—— Watk., L.L. Denb. 314
*—— Watk., L.L. Mer. 314
* ? same pers.

Williams—*cont*
—— Watkin L. G. and sir W., gen. (**D**) 888
—— Wm., bp. Wpu. 710
*—— Wm., K.C. 415
*—— Wm., Sp. H.C. 249
*—— sir Wm., S G. 401
* ? same pers. Comp. dates.
—— Wm. and sir Wm., gen. (**C**) 875; K.C.B. 774
—— Wm. Fenw. (of Kars) and sir W., Const. T.L. 321; G.C.B. 770; G. Gibr. 670; G. N. Sc. 695; gen. (**D**) 890, 898; K.C.B. 778
—— Wm. Fr., gen. (**D**) 891; K.H. 791
—— Wm. Jno., gen. (**D**) 929
—— Wm. Th., gen. (**D**) 921
—— Woodf. Jno., adm. (**D**) 832; (**E**) 834; (**F**) 838
Williams-Wynn, *see* Wynn
Williamson, Ad., gen. (**B**) 864; K.B. 765
—— Cæs., dn. Cash. 627
—— Dav., Ld. Sess. 520
—— Geo., gen. (**B**) 865
—— sir Jos., L. Admy. 175; P.C. 191, 194; Pres. R. Soc. 940; S. St. 223
—— Rt., C. Cus. 274
—— Ush., gen. (**D**) 894
—— Wm. Jno., C.I.E. 806
Williby, *see* Willoughby
Willimot, *see* Wilmot
Willington, Bayly, gen. (**B**) 867
Willis, Alfr., bp. Honol. 712
—— Browne, gen. (**D**) 893
—— Ch., K.B. 764
—— Ed. Coop., Q.C. 419
—— Fras., dn. Worc. 473
—— Fras., U.S.S. 226
—— Fk. Arth., gen. (**D**) 909
—— Geo. Harry Sm. and sir G., gen. (**D**) 906; K.C.B. 781
—— Jas., C. Cus. 276
—— Rd., bp. Glr. 438; bp. Sal. 467; bp. Winch. 471; dn. Linc. 448
—— Rd. A., gen. (**D**) 878
—— Wm., Q.C. 419
Willmore, Grah., C.C.J. 404; Q.C. 417
Willmot, *see* Wilmot
Willock, sir Hy., Chn. E.I. Co. 645
Willoughby, Wilughby, and **Wyllughby**
—— —, K.B. 755
—— Chr., K.B. 758
—— Ed., dn. Exr. 437
—— Hy., G. Bdoes. 719
—— Jas. Beaut., adm. (**H**) 851
—— Jno. de, K.B. 755
—— Jno. Poll., M.C.I. 646
—— Michl. Fr., gen. (**D**) 895
—— sir Nesbit Josiah, adm. (**D**) 827; K.C.H. 788
—— (or Williby), Ph. de, dn. Linc. 448; B. Ex. 382
—— Rd. de, C.J.K.B. 369; J.C.P. 377; J.K.B. 371
—— Th., dn. Roch. 461
—— sir Th., J.C.P. 378; S.L. 408
—— Wm. de, K.B. 755
Willoughby de Broke, lds.
—— Rt., 1st ld., K.G. 737; L.S.H. 289
—— Rt., 2nd ld., K.B. 759
—— Geo., 4th ld., dn. Winds. 474

Willoughby de Eresby, lds.
— Wm., 5th ld., K.G. 734
— Rt., 6th ld., K.G. 735
— Rd. de Welles, ld. (husband of Joan, dau. of Rt., 6th ld. W. de E.), K.B. 759
— Rt. Bert., 10th (11th) ld., aft. E. of Lindesey, *q.v.*, K.B. 761; L.G.C. 287
— Mont., ld., aft. 2nd E. of Lindesey, *q.v.*, B.T. 263
— Rt., ld., aft. 3rd E. of Lindesey, *q.v.*, C.D.L. 242
— Prisc. Barb. Eliz., 17th (18th) lady, L.G.C. 288
— Pet. Rt., 18th (19th) ld., form. ld. Gwyder, *q.v.*, L.G.C. 288; L.L. Carn. 314
— Alberic, 19th (20th) ld., L.G.C. 288
— Clema. Eliz., 20th (21st) lady, form. lady Aveland, *q.v.*, L.G.C. 288
Willoughby of Parham, lds.
— Fras., 5th ld., G. Bdoes. 719
— Wm., 6th ld., G. Bdoes. 719; G. Leew. Isl. 727
Wills, *see also* Willes
— Alf. and sir A., J.Q.B.D. 374; Q.C. 419
— Ch. and sir C., gen. (**A**) 857; L.G.O. 259; P.C. 197
Willshire, *see also* Wiltshire
— Th. and sir T., gen. (**D**) 882; K.C.B. 777
Wilmington, Sp., 1st ld. and E. of, form. hon. Sp. Compton, *q.v.*, K.B. 764; K.G. 741; L.P.C. 188; L.P.S. 240; L.T. 157; Prem. 142
Wilmore, *see* Willmore
Wilmot and **Willmot**
— Arth. Parry Eardley, adm. (**E**) 835; (**F**) 839
— Eardl., gen. (**D**) 896
— Fk. Marr. Eardley, gen. (**D**) 903
— Jno., M. Chy. 397
— sir Jno. Eardley (No. 1), C.G.S. 357; C.J.C.P. 376; J.K.B. 373; P.C. 202; S.L. 412
— sir Jno. Eardley Eardley (No. 2), C.C.J. 404
— sir Jno. Eardley Eardley (No. 3), G. V. D. ld. 708
— Lemuel All., G. N. Brk. 696
— (or Willmot), Nich., S.L. 410
— Rt., G. N. Sc. 695
— (or Willimot), Rt., L.M. Lond. 491
— Rt. Dunc., G. N. Brk. 696
Wilmshurst, Arth., adm. (**H**) 851
Wilmund, abp. Yk. 485
Wilson, Archd. and sir A., gen. (**D**) 891; G.C.B. 770; K.C.B. 778
— Bedf. H. and sir B., Amb. Bol. 135; Amb. Vza. 134; K.C.B. 782
— Benj. Fras. Dalt., gen. (**D**) 892
— Ch. Riv., K.C.M.G. 797
— Ch. Wm. and sir W., K.C.B. 781; K.C.M.G. 797
— Chr. bp. Brl. 439
— Danl., bp. Calc. 653
— Fras. Ed. Edwards, gen. (**D**) 926
Wilson—*cont.*
— Fras. Wm., gen. (**D**) 878
— Geo., adm. (**A**) 816
— Geo., gen. (**A**) 862
— Geo., K.C. 415
— Geo., S.L. 412
— Geo. Alfr., gen. (**D**) 934
— Geo. Jas., gen. (**D**) 887
— Geo. Knyv., adm. (**H**) 848
— Giff. and sir G., J. Chest. 387; K.C. 416; M. Chy. 397
— Gl., C. Cus. 276-7
— Hy. Mein, gen. (**D**) 912
— Jas., bp. Crk., Cl. and R. 632
— Jas., dn. Tm. 613
— Jas., P.C. 216; Paym. G. 245; Sec. B.C. 254; Sec. Tr. 163; V.P.B.T. 269
— Jas. and sir J., gen. (**D**) 877; K.C.B. 775
— sir Jas. Milne, K.C.M.G. 797
— Jno., adm. (**H**) 847
— Jno., C.C.J. 403
— Jno., dn. Rip. 482
— Jno., gen. (**D**) 916
— Jno., G. Ceyl. 672; gen. (**C**) 873
— Jno. and sir J., C.G.S. 357; J.C.P. 379; S.L. 412
— Jno. and sir J., gen. (**A**) 863; K.C.B. 776; K.H. 791
— Jno. Cracr., K.C.S.I. 803
— Jno. Crawf., adm. (**E**) 837
— Jno. Mordl. K.H. 789
— Jno. Newb., gen. (**D**) 931
— Nathan, K.H. 790
— Nathl., bp. Limk., A. and A. 639; dn. Rph. 602
— Nichs., K. H. 791
— Rd., bp. Mth. 599
— Rt., dn. Ferns, 623
— R. G. B., gen. (**D**) 889
— sir Rt. Th., gen. (**A**) 862 (**C**) 873; G. Gibr. 670
— Rog. W., gen. (**D**) 888
— Saml., L.M. Lond. 492
— Sylv. W. F. M., gen. (**D**) 928
— Th., adm. (**E**) 835; (**F**) 839
*— Th., bp. S. and M. 484
*— Th., dn. Carl. 476
*— Th., dn. Dham. 479
*— Th., dn. Drom. 606
*— Th., dn. Lism. 629
*— Th., dn. Worc. 473
* Poss. some same pers. Comp. dates.
— Th., gen. (**D**) 878
— Th., S. St. 223
— Th. Fourn., gen. (**D**) 922
— Th. Maitl., gen. (**D**) 898
— sir Th. Sp., gen. (**A**) 859
— Wm. Ch. Fahie, adm. (**H**) 852
— Wm. Grey, G. St. Hel. 682
— sir Wm. Jas. Erasm., Pres. Coll. Surg. 939
— Wm. Sc., bp. Glasg. and Gall. 544
— sir Willshire, gen. (**B**) 869; K.C.H. 789
Wilton and **Wylton**
— (or Wyltone), Wm. de, C.J.C.P. 375; J.C.P. 376
— Gilb. de, bp. Carl. 475
— Laur. de, J. It. 367
— Rd. de, J. It. 365
— Wm. de, Ch. Jr. 363; Jy. 364
Wilton, E. of
— Th., 2nd. E. of, form. hon. Th. Grosvenor, *q.v.*, Amb. Sxy. 120; G.C.H. 787; L S.H. 290; P.C. 213
Wiltshire, E. of
Scroope or Le Scrope Family.
— Wm., 1st E. of, form. sir W. Scroope, or ld. Scrope, *q.v.*, L.H.T. 153
Butler Family.
— Jas., 1st E. of, also 5th E. of Ormond, *q.v.*, K.G. 736; L.H.T. 153
Stafford Family.
1st Creation.
— Jno., 1st E. of, form. Jno. Stafford, *q.v.*, K.G. 736
— Ed., 2nd E. of, K.B. 757
2nd Creation.
— Hy., 1st E. of, form. Hy. or ld. Stafford, *q.v.*
Boleyn Family.
— (and Ormond), Th., 1st E. of, form. sir Th. Boleyn and visc. Rochford, *q.v.*, L.P.S. 248; Tr. H. 291
Paulet Family.
See also Paulet.
— Wm., 1st E. of, form. 1st ld. St. John of Basing, *q.v.*, aft. 1st M. of Winchester, *q.v.*, L.H.T. 154
— Chas. Ing., E. of, aft. 13th M. of Winchester, *q.v.* L.L. Hants. 311
Wilughby, *see* Willoughby
Wimer, —, J. It. 365
Wimbledon, Ed., 1st visc., form. sir Ed. and ld. Cecil, *q.v.*, L.L. Surr. 312
Wimbush, *see* Wymbysh
Wina, bp. Lond. 450; bp. Winch. 470
Wincelaus, El. Sxy. 77
Winch and **Winche**
— Hy., Q.C. 420
— Humfr. and sir H., C.B. Ex. Ir. 583; C.J.K.B. Ir. 578; J.C.P. 378; S.L. 409
— sir Humph., L. Admy. 75-6
Winchecombe, Tideman de, bp. Llff. 449; bp. Worc. 472
Winchelsea and **Winchelsey,** *see* Winchilsea
Winchestede, Jno. de, J. It. 367
— Hy., L.M. Lond. 492
— Jno., bp. Mor. 534
— Rt., K.H. 790
Winchester, E. and M. of
De Quincey Family.
— Saher. de, E. of (1211-2) Jy. 364; L.H. Const. Sc. 507
— Rog., 2nd E. of, L.H. Const. Sc. 507
Paulet Family.
— Wm., 1st M. of, form. ld. St. Jno. of Basing, and E. of Wiltshire, *q.v.*, L.H.T. 154
— Wm., 3rd M. of, form. W. Paulet, *q.v.*, L.L. Dors. 307
— Ch., 6th M. of, aft. 1st D. of Bolton, *q.v.*, P.C. 191, 193
— Ch., M. of, aft. 2nd D. of Bolton, *q.v.*, L.J. Ir. 555; P.C. 194
— Ch. Paulet, M. of, aft. 5th D. of Bolton, *q.v.*, P.C. 200
— Ch. Ing., 13th M. of, Gr. St. 304; P.C. 209
— Jno., 14th M. of, L.L. Hants. 311

Winchilsea and **Winchilsey**
— Rt., abp. Cant. 430
Winchilsea, E. of, *see also* Nottingham and Paulet
— Heneage, 3rd E. of, L.L. Kent, 309
— Ch., 4th E. of, L.L. Kent, 309; P.C. 196; Pres. B.T. 264
— Danl., 7th E. of, form. ld. Finch, *q.v.*
— Danl. 8th E. of, K.G. 742; L.H.A. 178; L.P.C. 188
— Geo., 9th E. of, Gr. St. 304; K.G. 743; L.L. Rutl. 311; P.C. 207; Pres. R. Inst. 940
Winchingham, Wm. de, J.C.P. 378
Windebank, sir Fras., L. Admy. 175; L.T. 154; S. St. 223
— Jas., L.P.S. 240
Windell, Rt., bp. Emly, 625
Windham, *see* Wyndham
Windlesore, *see* Wyndlesore
Windsor, Andr., K.B. 759
— hon. Dixie, St. O. 260
— Th., Const. W. Cast. 322
— Th., K.B. 760
— Wm., K.B. 760
— sir Wm. de, L.L. Ir. 551
Windsor, lds. and visc.
— Th., 6th ld., K.B. 762
— Th., 7th ld., G. Jam. 712
— Th., visc. (son of Th., 7th ld. W. and 1st E. of Plymouth), form. Th. Windsor-Hickman, *q.v.*, gen. (**B**) 864
Windy (or Wendy), Th., K.B. 764
Wineffe, *see* Winniffe
Winfride, bp. Lich. 443
Wing, Jno. Wm., C.C.J. 403
Wingate, Andr., C.I.E. 806
— Ed., C. Exc. 278
— Geo., K.C.S.I. 802
Winger, *see* Wyngar
Wingfield, sir Anthy., C.Y.G. 298; Compt. H. 292; V.C.H. 296; K.G. 738
— Ch. Jno., Ch. Com. Oudh. 654; K.C.S.I. 802
— Ch. Wm., gen. (**D**) 896
— Ed., U.S.C. 236
— Fras., S.L. 410
— Jno., dn. Kilmacd. 637
— Jno., K.B. 757
— Jno., Yk. H. 334; Ptc. P.A. 337
— Jno. Hope, gen. (**D**) 906
— sir Rd., C.D.L. 242; K.G. 737
— sir Rd., aft. 1st visc. Powerscourt, *q.v.*, L.J. Ir. 554; L.L. Ir. 554
— (or Wyngfelde), Rt., K.B. 756
— Wm., K.C. 416; M. Chy. 397
Wingham (or Wengham), Hy. de, bp. Lond. 451; L.K. 353
Wingrove, Geo. Presc., gen. (**D**) 880
Winn, *see also* Wynn
— Rowl., L.T. 162
Winne, Jno., adm. (**D**) 823
Winniett, Wm. and sir W., G. Gld. Cst. 686
Winniffe (or Wineffe), Th., bp. Linc. 447; dn. Glr. 440; dn. St. P. 453
Winnington, sir Ed., St. O. 260
Winnington—*cont.*
— Fras. and sir F., K.C. 414; S.G. 401
— Th. and sir T., L. Admy. 177-8; L.T. 156; P.C. 198; Paym. G. 244; Sec. at War, 233
Winram, Geo., Ld. Sess. 519
Winsey (or Winsius), bp. Lich. 443
Winslow, E., G. N. Brk. 695
— Th. Ewing, Q.C. 419
Winson, Wm., gen. (**D**) 924
Winter, Jas. Sp., K.C.M.G. 799
— Rt., gen. (**B**) 868
— Sank., dn. Kild. 619
— Th., dn. Cloy. 633
— Th., dn. Wells, 429
Winterbotham, Hy. S. P., U.S. Home, 228
Winterbottom, Th., L.M. Lond. 492
Winterburne, *see* Wynterburne
Winthrop, Geo. Teale Teb., adm. (**H**) 852
— Rt., adm. (**A**) 819
Winthrope, Saml., G. Antig. 728
Wintle, Alfr., gen. (**D**) 911
— Edm. Hy. Cull., gen. (**D**) 914
Winton, Fras. Walt. de, K.C.M.G. 798
Winton, E. of, *see* E. of Winchester
Winwood, sir R., S. St. 223
Wircestre (or Whitchester), Rog. de, J.C.P. 377
Wire, Dav. Wms., L.M. Lond. 492
Wiro (or Wirus), St., bp. Dbln. 615
Wisdom, Rt., K.C.M.G. 798
Wise, *see also* Wyse
— Ch., adm. (**E**) 835; (**F**) 838
— Ed., K.B. 763
— Th., K.B. 761
— Wm. Furl., adm. (**D**) 826
Wisebex, Regd. de, J. It. 366
Wiseheart, and **Wisehart** *see* Wishart
Wiseman, Capel, bp. Drom. 605; dn. Rph. 602
*— sir Rt., C. Exc. 278
*— sir Rt., D. Arch. 420
*— sir Rt., J. Adm. Ct. 423
*— sir Rt., Vic. Gen. 421
* ? same pers.
— Wm., sir Saltonst., adm. (**E**) 835; K.C.B. 779
Wishart, Wisehart, and **Wiseheart**
— Geo., bp. Edinb. 533
— sir Jas., adm. (**A**) 813; L. Admy. 177
— Jas., L.J. Clk. 516; Ld. Adv. 525
— Jno., bp. Glasg. 536
— sir Jno., Compt. Sc. 498; Ld. Sess. 517
— Rt., bp. Glasg. 536
— Wm., bp. Glasg. 536; bp. St. Andr. 529; Ld. Chanc. Sc. 514
Witchester (or Wircestre), *see* Whitchester
Witefeld, *see* Whitefeld
Witham, sir Jno., G. Bdoes. 719
— Wm., dn. Wells. 429
Withenius, bp. Winch. 470
Witherington, Jno., S.L. Ir. 592
Withers, *see also* Whithers
— Hy., gen. (**B**) 864
— Rd., Guis. P.A. 343; Ptc. P.A. 337
— sir Wm., L.M. Lond. 491
Withlafe, R.E. 3
Withred, bp. Lindisf. 478
Witiza, K. Sp. 85
Witta, bp. Lich. 443
Witter, Danl., bp. Killoe. 634; dn. Ardf. 640; dn. Down, 605
Wittlesey, *see* Whittlesey
Witton, Jonn., G.I. Man, 666
Wivill, *see* Wyvill
Wo—, *see also* Woo—
Wode, Jno., Sp. H.C. 249
Wodeford, *see also* Woodford
— Th. de, dn. Lism. 628
Wodehouse, *see also* Woodhouse
— Ch., C.I.E. 808
— Edm., gen. (**D**) 906
— hon. Ed. Thornt., adm. (**G**) 842
— Geo., adm. (**H**) 849
— Jno. de, M. Chy. 393
— Jno., *see* ld. W., *infra*
— Jas. Hay, Amb. Sd. Is. 137
— Nichs., gen. (**D** 883
— hon. Ph., adm. (**A**) 819
— Ph. Edm. and sir P. Amb. Vza. 134; G. Bbay. 659; G. Br. Gu. 715; G. Br. Hond. 714; G. C.G.H. 679; G.C.S.I. 801; K.C.B. 783
— (or Woodhouse), Rt. de, B. Ex. 383; L.H.T. 153
Woodstock, lds.
— hon. Jno., aft. 2nd ld. W., L.L. Norf. 310
— Jno., 3rd ld., aft. 1st E. Kimberley, *q.v.*, Amb. Dk. 127; Amb. Russ. 126; L.L. Ir. 558; P.C. 217; U.S.F. 230
Wodestoke, *see also* Woodstock
— Jas de, J.C.P. 377
Wodewyk, Rd., K.B. 756
Wodhele, Rog., dn. Bgr. 426
Wodington, Ad., Ld. Chanc. Ir. 574
Wogan, Jno. and sir J., J. It. 368; L.J. Ir. 550
— Jno., K.B. 759
— Rd., Ld. Chanc. Ir. 575
Wogham, *see* Woogen
Wolesley, *see* Wolseley
Wolfe, *see also* Wolff and Woulfe
— Arth., aft. visc. Kilwarden, *q.v.*, A.G. Ir. 588; C.J.K.B. Ir. 578; S.G. Ir. 589
— Ed., gen. (**B**) 865
— Geo., gen. (**D**) 922
— Jas., gen. (**C**) 871
— Jno., C. Cus. Ir. 565
Wolfehelm, bp. Her. 441
Wolferstan, Ch., G. Bdoes. 719
Wolff, *see also* Wolfe and Woulfe
— Hy. Dr. and sir H., Amb. Eg. 130; Amb. Tky. 130; G.C.M.G. 795; K.C.B. 783; K.C.M.G. 796; M.G.K.A. 799; P.C. 220
Wolfi, bp. Cnwall. 436
Wolfius, bp. Lich. 443
Wolfstan, *see* Wolstan
Wollaston, Arth. Nayl., C.I.E. 807

Wollaston—*cont.*
— Ch., adm. (**A**) 820
— sir Jno., L.M. Lond. 491
— Wm. Hy. de, Pres. R. Soc. 940
Wollaveston, Hy. de, J. It. 368; Jy. 365
Wolley, *see also* Wooley
— Ed., bp. Clonf. and K. 636
— Godfr. Lampl., adm. (**H**) 849
— Th., adm. (**A**) 818
Wollore (or Wallore), Dav. de, L.K. 354; M.R. 357
Wolman, *see* Woolman
Wolmerstown, Jno., ld., form. Jno. Lindsay, *q.v.*, K.B. (1603) 761
Wolocus, bp. Cnwall. 436
Wolphelm or **Wolphelmus** (2), bp. Wells, 427
Wolrige, Wm., adm. (**H**) 846
Wolseley and **Wolesley**
— Ch., adm. (**A**) 815
— Garnet Jos., *see* ld. and visc. W., *infra*
— Jno., dn. Kild. 619
— Ralph, B. Ex. 383
— Wm., adm. (**A**) 817
— Wm., L.J. Ir. 555
Wolseley, lds. and visc.
— Garn. Jos., aft. sir G., and 1st ld. and visc. W., Amb. Gmy. and Pr. 116; G. Cypr. 671; G. Nat. 680; G.C.B. 771; G.C.M.G. 795; gen. (**D**) 905; K.C.B. 780; K.C.M.G. 796; K.P. 752; M.C.I. 647
Wolsey, *see also* Woolsey
— Rd., bp. Down and Cnr. 604
— Th., abp. Yk. 486; bp. B. and W. 428; bp. Dham. 478; bp. Linc. 447; bp. Winch. 471; dn. Her. 442; dn. Linc. 448; dn. Yk. 487; Ld. Chanc. 355; Regr. Gart. 746
Wolsius, abp. Yk. 485
Wolstan and **Wolstanus**
— (or Wolfstan) (2), abp. Yk. 485; bp. Worc. 472
— bp. Lond. 451
Wolstenholme, sir Jno., C. Cus. 273
Wolston, Guy de, K.B. 758
Wolton, *see* Woolton and Walton
Wolveden, Rt., dn. Lich. 445
Wolveridge, Jas. or Jno., M. Chy. 395
Wolverton, Geo. G., 2nd ld., form. hon. G. G. Glynn, *q.v.*, P.C. 218; Paym. G. 245; Postm. G. 239
Womach, Lawr., bp. St. Dav. 464
Wombwell, Arth., gen. (**D**) 922
— Geo. and sir G., Chn. E.I. Co. 644
Woo—, *see also* Wo—
Wood, Alex., D. Fac. Sc. 527; Jy. Sc. 523; Ld. Sess. 520
— Alex., gen. (**B**) 867
— Alex., K.C.M.G. 796
— Andr., bp. Cness. 532; bp. Isl. 540
— Andr., Compt. Sc. 498
— Andr., L.H.A. Sc. 499
— Ch. and sir C., aft. visc. Halifax, *q.v.*, Ch. Ex. 165; G.C.B. 772; L. Admy. 183-4; L.T. 161; P.C. 215; Pres. B.C. 254; Sec. Adm. 186; Sec. Ind. 236; Sec. Tr. 163

Wood—*cont.*
— Ch. Wm., Q.C. 419
— Corn., gen. (**B**) 864
— Dav., Compt. Sc. 498
— Dav. Ed. and sir D., gen. (**D**) 902; G.C.B. 771; K.C.B. 778
— Attiwell, S.L. Ir. 592
— Geo., K.C.B. 775
— Geo., S.L. 408
— Geo., and sir G., B. Ex. 385; S.L. 412
— Geo. and sir G., gen. (**C**) 874; K.C.H. 787
— Hy. Evel. and sir H., gen. (**D**) 924; G.C.M.G. 795; K.C.B. 781
— Hy. Hast. A., gen. (**D**) 922
— Hy. Jno., gen. (**D**) 891
— Jas., dn. Ely, 435
— sir Jas., gen. (**C**) 871
— sir Jas. Ath., adm. (**A**) 819
— Jas. Cr., gen. (**D**) 915
— Jno., C. Exc. 282; C.I.R. 285; C. St. 284; C. St. and Tx. 285; C. Tx. 285
— Jno., G. I. Man, 666
— Jno., gen. (**C**) 873
— Jno., Ld. Sess. 517
— Jno. Sul., gen. (**A**) 862; Lt. T L. 322
— Jno. Stew., K.C.B. 783
— Matth., L.M. Lond. 492
— Rd. and sir R., Amb. Tun. 132; G.C.M.G. 795; K.C.M.G. 797
— sir Rd., L.H.T. 153
— Rt., U.S.S. 226
— Rt. Bl., gen. (**D**) 895
— Rog., G. Bmda. 701
— Th., C.J.C.P. 375; J.C.P. 378; S.L. 407
— Th., gen. (**D**) 892
— Th., bp. Lich. and Cov. 444; dn. Lich. 445
— Wm., adm. (**H**) 851
— Wm., gen. (**D**) 879; K.H. 791
— Wm., K.C.B. 779
— (or Bosco), Wm. de, Ld. Chanc. Sc. 514
— Wm. Leight., K.H. 792
— Wm. Mark, gen. (**D**) 902
— Wm. Page and sir W., aft. 1st ld. Hatherley, *q.v.*, Jud. Com. P.C. 361; L.J. App. 389; Ld. Chanc. 358; P.C. 217; Q.C. 417; S.G. 402; V. Chanc. 390
Woodall, Wm., S.G.O. 260
Woodburn, Alex., gen. (**D**) 889
Woodcock, Ch. Saml., gen. (**D**) 911
— Jno., L.M. Lond. 489
Woodford, *see also* Wodeford
— Alexr. and sir A., F.M. 856; G.C.B. 769; G.C.M.G. 794; G. Ch. Hosp. 936; G. Gibr. 670; gen. (**A**) 863; K.C.B. 776; L.G. Ch. Hosp. 936
— sir Geo., gen. (**C**) 875
— Jas. R., bp. Ely, 435
— sir Jno. Geo., K.C.B. 776; K.C.H. 788
— Ralph, Amb. Dk. 127; Amb. H. Tns. 120
— sir Ralph J., G. Trin. 722
Woodforde, Woodf. F., C.C.J. 405
Woodhouse, *see also* Wodehouse
— capt—., G. Bmda. 701

Woodhouse—*cont.*
— Jno., C.D.L. 242
— Jno. C., dn. Lich. 445
— Rt., *see* Wodehouse
— Rt. Russ., gen. (**D**) 925
— Th., K.B. 759
— Wm., gen. (**D**) 878
Woodley, Wm., B. and Gl. K.A. 330; Bath K.A. 785; Han. H. 340; G. Antig. 728; G. Berb. 715
Woodloke, Hy., bp. Winch. 470
Woodrofe, sir Nichs., L.M. Lond. 490
Woodruffe, Ch. Lorr., gen. (**D**) 931
Woods, Alb. Wm. and sir A. (No. 1), Fitzal. P.A. 343; Gart. K.A. 328; Lanc. H. 333; M.G.K.A. 799; Ptc. P.A. 337; Regr. Cr. I. 810; Regr. I.E. 808; Regr. S.I. 804; Regr. and Sec. Bath, 785
— Alb. Wm. (No. 2), R. Dr. P.A. 338
— Eug., dn. Arm. 597
— Hy. Geo., gen. (**D**) 921
— Wm. and sir W., Bl. M. P.A. 337; Clar. K.A. 328; Gart. K.A. 328; K.H. 790; Norf. H. 341
— Wm. Geo., gen. (**D**) 916
Woodstock, *see also* Wodestoke
— Wm., 1st. visc., form. Wm. Bentinck, *q.v.*, aft. 1st D. of Portland, *q.v.*
Woodvile, Woodville, Wydvill, and **Wydville**
— Ed. and sir E., K.B. 757; K.G. 737
— Jno., K.B. 757
— Lion., bp. Sal. 467; Chanc. Gart. 745; dn. Exr. 437
— Rd., K.B. 757
Woodward, Rd., dn. Clr. 598; bp. Cloy. 631
— Rd., M. Chy. 394
— Rt., dn. Sal. 468
— Th., dn. Down. 605
Woogen (or Wogham), Wm., S.L. 411
Woolcombe and **Woollcombe**
— Geo., adm. (**H**) 847
— Hy. Bedf., adm. (**H**) 852
Wooley and **Woolley,** *see also* Wolley
— sir Jno., Chanc. Gart. 746; dn. Carl. 476
— Rt., gen. (**D**) 917
Woollcombe, *see* Woolcombe
Woolley, *see* Wooley
Woolman, Rd., dn. Wlls. 429; M. Chy. 394
Woolmore, sir Jno., K.C.H. 788
Woolnough, Jos. Ch., K.H. 790
Woolrich, Toby, M. Chy. 396
Woolridge, Th. Thornb. gen. (**D**) 882; K.H. 791
Woolrych, Humphry W., S.L. 413
Woolsey, *see also* Wolsey
— O'Bryen Bell., gen. (**D**) 928
***Woolton,** Jno., bp. Exr. 437
*— Jno., Wdn. Chr. Ch. Manch. 481
* ? same pers.
Woosnam, Jas. Bow., gen. (**D**) 898

Worcester, Wm. Kenn., gen. (**D**) 909
Worcester, E. and M. of
Percy Family.
— Th., 1st E. of, form. Th. Percy and sir T., *q.v.*, L.H.A. 173
Tiptoft Family.
— Jno., 1st E. of, form. ld. Tiptoft, *q.v.*, Const. T.L. 320; K.G. 736; L.H.T. 153; Ld. Chanc. Ir. 575; L.L. Ir. 552
Herbert Family.
— Ch., 1st E. of, form. sir C. Somerset and ld. Herbert, *q.v.*, Chanc. Gart. 745; L.C.H. 294
— Wm., 3rd E. of, form. ld. Herbert, *q.v.*, K.G. 738
— Ed., 4th E. of, E.M. 326; K.G. 739; L.H. Const. 289; L.P.S. 240; M.H. 302
— Hy., 3rd M. of, aft. 1st D. of Beaufort, *q.v.*, K.G. 740; L.L. N. and S. Wales, &c. 314; P.C. 191-2
— Hy., M. of, aft. 7th D. of Beaufort, *q.v.*, L. Admy. 181
Worcheley, Jno. de, Ld. Chanc. Ir. 574
Wordsworth, Ch., bp. St. Andr., Dkld., and Dnbl. 545
— Ch. F. F., Q.C. 417
— Chr., bp. Linc. 447
— Jno., bp. Sal. 467
— Wm., C.I.E. 808
— Wm., P. Laur. 301
Worgan, Jno., gen. (**D**) 916
Worge, Rd., gen. (**C**) 872
Wormald, Rt. Cr., gen. (**D**) 898
— Th., Pres. Coll. Surg. 939
Wormeley, Ralph Rand., adm. (**D**) 828
Worms, bar. Hy. de, Sec. B.T. 269; U.S.C. 235
Woronus, bp. Cnwall. 436
Woronzow, Count, G.C.B. 767
Worrall, Hy. L., gen. (**D**) 887
Worseley and **Worsley**
— Ed. Vaughan, gen. (**B**) 870
— Hy., G. Bdoes. 720
— Hy. and sir H., G.C.B. 769; K.C.B. 776
— Rd., adm. (**A**) 820
— sir Rd., Amb. Vce. 116; Compt. H. 292; P.C. 203
— Wm., dn. St. P. 453
Worth, Ed., bp. Killoe. 634; dn. Crk. 632
— Jno., dn. Kild. 619; dn. St. Patr. 618
— Jno., *see* Wrothe
— Wm., B. Ex. Ir. 584
Wortham, Hale Young, gen. (**D**) 892
— Hy., gen. (**D**) 930
Worthington, sir Wm., L.M. Dbln. 641
Wortledge, Jno., C.C.J. 404
Wortley, Ch. Balt. Stuart-, U.S. Home, 228
— hon. Jas. Archb. Stuart-, J.A.G. 937; P.C. 215; Q.C. 417; Rec. Lond. 494; S.G. 402
— hon. Jno. Stuart-, aft. 2nd ld. Wharncliffe, *q.v.*, Sec. B.C. 254
Wotton, Ed., *see* ld. W., *infra*
— Nichs., dn. Cant. 431; dn. Yk. 487; S. St. 223
— Nichs., L.M. Lond. 489-90
— Wm., B. Ex. 383
Wotton, lds.
— sir Ed., aft. 1st ld. W., Compt. H. 292; Tr. H. 291
Woulfe, *see also* Wolfe and Wolff
— Jno., gen. (**D**) 878
— Steph., A.G. Ir. 588; C.B. Ex. Ir. 583; S.G. Ir. 590; S.L. Ir. 593
Wrangham, Digby C., P.P. 417; S.L. 413
Wratislas I. and II., D. Bma. 59
Wratislau, Hy. Rushw., adm. (**E**) 837
Wray, Bourch., K.B. 763
— Chr., L. Admy. 175
— Chr. and sir C., C.J.Q.B. 370; J.C.P. 378; J.Q.B. 372; S.L. 408; Sp. H.C. 249
— Ed., gen. (**D**) 916
— Hy., G. Jsey. 668; gen. (**D**) 925
Wrede, Pr. Ch. Phil., G.C.B. 767
Wren, Chr., dn. Winds. 474
— sir Chr., Pres. R. Soc. 940
— Jord., gen. (**B**) 866
— Matth., bp. Ely, 435; bp. Her. 441; bp. Norw. 455; dn. Winds. 474
Wrench, Fk. S., Land Com. Ir. 588
Wrenfordsley, Hy. Th., G. W. Austr. 707
Wrexworth, Jno., Gart. K.A. 327
***Wright,** Ch., gen. (**D**) 895
*— Ch., K.H. 789
* ? same pers.
— Ch. Jas., gen. (**D**) 904
— Geo., gen. (**A**) 863
— Hy. Rd., gen. (**D**) 894
— Jas. and sir J., Amb. Vce. 116
— Jno., gen. (**D**) 884; K.H. 790
— Jno. All., gen. (**D**) 923
— Mart. and sir M., B. Ex. 385; J.K.B. 373; S.L. 411
— Nath. and sir N., L.K. 357; P.C. 194; S.L. 411
— Rt., bp. Brl. 439; bp. Lich. and Cov. 444
— Rt. and sir R., B. Ex. 384; C.J.C.P. 375; C.J.K.B. 370; J.K.B. 372; S.L. 410
— Th., gen. (**D**) 891
— Th., gen. (**D**) 923
— Th., L.M. Lond. 492
— Wm., gen. (**B**) 867
— Wm., M.M. 246
Wriothesley, *see also under* Wrythe
— Jas., c.c. ld. Wr., K.B. (1616) 762
— Jno., *see* Wrythe
— Th., *see* ld. Wr., *infra*
Wriothesley, lds.
— Jas., *see supra*
— Th., ld., aft. E. of Southampton, *q.v.*, K.G. 738; L.K. and Ld. Chanc. 355; S. St. 223
Writhe, *see* Wrythe
Writheseley, *see* Wrythe
Wroe, Rd., Wdn. Chr. Ch. Manch. 481
Wroth, –, S.L. 410
— (or Worth), Jno., L.M. Lond. 489
— Rt., gen. (**C**) 871
Wrotham, Wm. de, Jy. 364; W.C.P. 317
Wrottesley, sir Hugh, K.G. 733
— sir Jno., gen. (**C**) 872
— sir Rd., dn. Worc. 474
Wrottesley, lds.
— Jno., 2nd ld., Pres. R. Soc. 940
— Arth., 3rd ld., L.L. Staffs. 312
Wroughton, Th. and sir T., Amb. Pld. 126; Amb. Sw. 126; K.B. 765
Wrythe and **Writhe**
— Ch., Berw. P.A. 341; R. Cr. P.A. 335; Winds. H. 331
— (or Writhesley), Jno., Ant. P.A. 341; Gart. K.A. 327; R. Cr. P.A. 335
— (or Wriothesley), sir Th., Gart. K.A. 327
— (or Wriothesley), Wm., Yk. H. 334
Wrythens, Fras., K.C. 414
Wsewolod I. to III., R. Russ. 89
Wuffstan, bp. Lond. 451
Wuldham (or Suthflete), Th. de, bp. Roch. 459
Wulfehard, bp. Her. 441
Wulfelm, abp. Cant. 430
Wulff, Geo., gen. (**B**) 869
— Hy. Pow., gen. (**D**) 894
Wulfgar (or Alfgar), bp. Wltn. 466
Wulfhere, abp. Yk. 485
— K.E. 3
Wulfine and **Wulfinus**
— bp. Shbn. 466
— bp. Dorch. and Sidr. 446
Wulfius, abp. Yk. 485
— bp. Lond. 451
Wulfred, abp. Cant. 430
Wy—, *see also* Wi—
Wyatt, *see also* Wyott
— Alex. Hy. Lewis, gen. (**D**) 904
— Edg., gen. (**D**) 880
— Edwin, S.L. 410
— (or Wyotte), Hy., K.B. 759
— Jas., Pres. R.A. 941
Wyche, *see also* Wich
— sir Cyril, L.J. Ir. 555; Pres. R.C. 940
— Hugh, L.M. Lond. 490
— Jno., B. Ex. Ir. 583
— sir Pet., Compt. H. 292
Wychingham, Wm. de, S.L. 407
Wychyngham, Geoffr., L.M. Lond. 489
Wyckham, *see* Wickham
Wydvile and **Wydville,** *see* Woodville
Wye, Rd., bp. Cloy. 630
Wyfforde, Nichs., L.M. Lond. 490
Wyke, Ch. Lenn. and sir C., Amb. C. Am. 133; Amb. Dk. 127; Amb. Hnr. 120; Amb. Mex. 133; Amb. Pgl. 125; G.C.M.G. 795; K.C.B. 783; P.C. 220
Wykeham, *see also* Wickham
— Wm. de, bp. Winch. 470 Ld. Chanc. 354
Wykehampton, Rt. de, bp. Sal. 466; dn. Sal. 468
Wykford and **Wikeford**
— Rt. de, abp. Dbln. and Gl. 616; Ld. Chanc. Ir. 574; M. Chy. 393

Wyld and **Wylde,** *see also* Wild
— Ed. Andr., gen. (**D**) 913
— Th., C. Exc. 279-80
— Wm., gen. (**D**) 886
— Wm., *see* Wilde
Wyle, Walt. de la, bp. Sal. 466
Wylie, *see* Wyllie
Wylinton, Ralph de, K.B. 755
Wyllie, Wm. and sir W., gen. (**D**) 888; G.C.B. 770; K.C.B. 779
— Wm. Alexr. Patr., gen. (**D**) 927
— Wm. Hutt. Curz., C.I.E. 807
Wyllughby, *see* Willoughby
Wylton, *see* Wilton
Wymburne, Walt. de, J.K.B. 371
Wymbysh, Nichs., M. Chy. 394
— Geo. Petre and sir G., gen. (**D**) 884; K.C.B. 778
Wymond, abp. Yk. 485
Wymundham, Th. de, *see* Wyndham
Wymundus (or Reymundus), bp. Isl. 539; bp. S. and M. 483
Wynard, Wm., S.L. 407
Wyndham, Wymundham, and **Windham**
— Ch. Ash, gen. (**D**) 890; K.C.B. 779
— Fras., J.C.P. 378; S.L. 408
— hon. F. W., Amb. Tusc. 115
— Geo. H., Amb. Bzl. 135; Amb. Sva. 128
— Hy., gen. (**A**) 863; K.C.B. 778
— Hugh, gen. (**B**) 864
— Hugh and sir H., B. Ex. 384; J.C.P. 379; S.L. 409-10
— Jno., S.L. 410
— Th., C. Tx. 284
— Th., *see* ld. W., *infra*
— Th. de, B. Ex. 382; L.H.T. 152
— Th. Nort., gen. (**B**) 868
— Wadh. and sir W., J.K.B. 372; S.L. 410
— Wm., L.G. Ch. Hosp. 936
— Wm. (No. 1), Ch. Sec. Ir. 562; P.C. 206; Sec. at W. 234; W. and C. Sec. 231
— sir Wm. (No. 2), Ch. Ex. 165; P.C. 196; Sec. at W. 233
— Wm. Luk., adm. (**A**) 819
Wyndham, lds.
— Th., aft. 1st ld. W., C.J.C.P. Ir. 580; L.J. Ir. 556; Ld. Chanc. Ir. 576
Wyndlesore, Hugh de, Const. T.L. 320; W.C.P. 317
Wynford, W. D., 1st ld., form. sir W. D. Best, *q.v.*, Jud. Com. P.C. 360
Wyngar (or Winger), Jno., L.M. Lond. 490
Wyngfelde (or Wingfield), Rt., K.B. 756
Wynklegh, Rog. de, dn. Exr. 437
Wynn and **Wynne,** *see also* Winn
— Ed. Wm. Ll., gen. (**D**) 927
— Ch. Watk. Wms., C.D.L. 243; P.C. 210; Pres. B.C. 253; Sec. at W. 234; U.S. Home, 227
Wynn and Wynne—*cont.*
— Hy. Watk. and sir H., Amb. Dk. 127; Amb. Swz. 113; Amb. Sxy. 120; G.C.H. 786; K.C.B. 782; P.C. 210
— sir Watk. Wms. (4th bt.), L.L. Mer. 314
— sir Watk. Wms. (5th bt.), L.L. Denb. 314; L.L. Mer. 314
— sir Watk. Wms. (6th bt.), L.L. Mer. 314
— Geo., gen. (**D**) 903
— Jno., bp. B. and W. 428; bp. St. As. 462
— Jno., U.S. Ir. 563
— Owen, gen. (**B**) 864
— Owen, S.L. 410
— Rd., S.L. 411
— Rt., C. Cus. Ir. 565-6
— Th., aft. 1st ld. Newborough, *q.v.*, L.L. Carn. 314
— Wm. and sir Wm., B.T. 268; Ch. Lond. 422; D. Arch. 421; J. Pr. Ct. 421; K. Adv. 422; P.C. 205; S.L. 412; Vic. Gen. 422
— Wm. Hy., dn. Drom. 606
Wynterburne, Th., dn. St. P. 453
Wynyard, Ed. Buck., gen. (**D**) 880
— Ed. Geo., gen. (**D**) 905
— Hy., gen. (**A**) 860
— Hy. B. J., gen. (**D**) 919
— Jno., gen. (**B**) 865
— Rt. Hy., G.C.G.H. 679; G. N.Z. 709; gen. (**D**) 893
— Wm., gen. (**B**) 866
— Wm., gen. (**B**) 867
Wyott, *see also* Wyatt
— Ph., dn. Lism. 629
Wyredus, bp. Elm. and Dunw. 454
Wyrley, Wm., R. Cr. P.A. 335
Wyse, *see also* Wise
— Andr., V. Treas. Ir. 559
— Th. and sir T., Amb. Gr. 128; K.C.B. 782; L.T. 160; P.C. 215; Sec. B.C. 254
Wyseman, Rt., *see* Wiseman
Wythens, sir Fras., J.K.B. 372; S.L. 410
Wyther, Wm., J. It. 368
Wytter, Danl., *see* Witter
Wyvil, Wyvile, and **Wyville**
— Maj. —, M.M. 247
*— Chr., adm. (**D**) 831
*— Chr., C. Exc. Sc. 505
* ? same pers.
— Chr., dn. Rip. 482
— Jno. de, B. Ex. 382; J.C.P. 377; Jy. 365
— sir Marm., C. Exc. 279
— Rt., bp. Sal. 467

X.

Xerri, Gius. Bart., Prel. M.G. 799
— Raph. Cr., G.C.M.G. 794
Xerxes I. and II., K. Pers. 99
Xidian, Anast. Tip., K.C.M.G. 796
Ximenes, sir Dav., gen. (**B**) 870; K.C.H. 788
— J., Pres. C.R. 106

Y.

***Yale,** Th., D. Arch. 420; Vic. Gen. 421
*— Dav. or Th., M. Chy. 395
* Prob. same pers.
Yarborough, *see also* Yerborough
— Ch. A. W., 3rd E. of, L.L. Linc. 310
Yard, Rt., M. Chy. 396
— Rt., U.S.S. 225
Yardley, sir Wm., C.J. Bbay. 660
Yarford, sir Jas., L.M. Lond. 490
Yarmouth, E. of
Paston Family.
— Wm., 2nd E. of, Tr. H. 291
Seymour Conway Family.
— Fras., 1st E. of, aft. 1st M. of Hertford, *q.v.*, form. visc. Beauchamp, *q.v.*
— Fras. Ch., E. of, aft. 3rd M. of Hertford. *q.v.*, Amb. Fr. 112; G.C.H. 786; L.W.S. 323; P.C. 209; V.C.H. 297
— Hugh de Grey, E. of (son of 5th M. of Hertford), Compt. H. 293; P.C. 219
Yaldwyn, Jno., gen. (**D**) 888
Yates, Hy. Peel, gen. (**D**) 922
— Jno., K.B. 760
— Jonn., gen. (**A**) 863
— Jos. and sir J., J.C.P. 379; J.K.B. 373; S.L. 412
— Jos. St. J., C.C.J. 403
— Rd. Augs., adm. (**G**) 841
— Rd. H., gen. (**D**) 878
Yatington or **Yattenden,** Nichs. de, Const. W. Cast. 322; Jy. 365
Yaxley, Jno., S.L. 407
Yeamans, Jno., G. Antig. 728
Yeard, Jno., dn. Ach. 614
Yelverton, Barry, aft. 1st ld. and visc. Avonmore, A.G Ir. 588; C.B. Ex. Ir. 583
— Chr. and sir C., J.Q.B. 372; S.L. 408; Sp. H.C. 249
— Hast. Reg. and sir G., adm. (**D**) 833; (**E**) 834; G.C.B. 770; K.C.B. 780; L. Admy. 185
— Hy. and sir H., A.G. 399; J.C.P. 379; J.K.B. 372; S.G. 401; S.L. 409
— Wm., J.K.B. 371; K.B. 757; S.L. 407
Yeo, sir Jas. Lucas, K.C.B. 774

Yerborough, *see also* Yarborough
— sir Jno. De, C.D.L. 242
Yerward, Griff. ap, bp. Bgr. 425
Yester, lds.
— Jas. (? Jno.), Hay, ld., K.B. (1603) 761
— Jno., ld., aft 2nd M. of Tweeddale, *q.v.*, L.H.T. Sc. 497
Yonge, *see also* Young
— Edmd., adm. (**G**) 842
— sir Geo., G. C.G.H. 678; K.B. 765; L. Admy. 179; M.M. 247; P.C. 203; Sec. at W. 234; V. Treas. Ir. 560
— Gust. N. K. A., gen. (**D**) 918
*— Jno., dn. Chich. 434
*— Jno., dn. Yk. 487
*— Jno., M.R. 387
* ? same pers.
— Jno., L.M. Lond. 490
— Ph., bp. Brl. 439; bp. Norw. 455
— Th., *see* Young
— Wm. and sir W., Coff. H. 293; K.B. 764; L. Admy. 177; L.T. 156; P.C. 198; Sec. at W. 233; V. Treas. Ir. 560
— Wm. Lamb., gen. (**D**) 934
York and **Yorke**
— Ch. and sir C., Const. T.L. 321; F.M. 856; gen. (**D**) 884; G.C.B. 770; K.C.B. 778
— hon. Ch., aft. 1st ld. Morton, *q.v.*, A.G. 399; K.C. 415; Ld. Chanc. 357; P.C. 202; S.G. 402
— hon. Ch. Ph., H. Sec. 226; L. Admy. 181; P.C. 206; Sec. at W. 234; Tell. Ex. 168
— Fk. Augs., gen. (**D**) 901
— hon. Gr. M., dn. Worc. 474
— hon. Jas., bp. Ely, 435; bp. Glr. 438; bp. St. Dav. 465; dc. Linc. 448
— Jno., dn. Down, 605; dn. Kilmacd. 637
— Jno., gen. (**D**) 901
— Jno., M.M. 246
— hon. Jno., B.T. 265; L. Admy. 179
— hon. Jos. and sir J., aft. 1st ld. Dover, *q.v.*, Amb. Nds. &c. 122; B.T. 267; gen. (**A**) 858; K.B. 765; P.C. 202
— sir Jos. Sid., adm. (**A**) 818; K.C.B. 774; L. Admy. 181
— sir Ph., aft. 1st ld. and E. of Hardwicke, *q.v.*, A.G. 399; C.J.K.B. 370; P.C. 198; S.G. 401; S.L. 412
— hon. Ph., aft. visc. Royston and 2nd E. of Hardwicke, *q.v.*, Tell. Ex. 168
— Reg., adm. (**H**) 848
— Rog., S.L. 408
— Wm. de, bp. Sal. 466; Ch. Jr. 363; J. It. 367
— Wm. and sir W., C. Acc. Ir. 567; C.J.C.P. Ir. 581; Ch. Ex. Ir. 562; J.C.P. Ir. 582
York, D. of, *see also* Albany *Plantagenet Family.*
— Edm., 1st D. of, form. E. of Cambridge, *q.v.*
— Ed., 2nd D. of (g. son of Edw. III.), form. Pr. Edwd., E. of Rutland and D. of Albemarle, *q.v.*, Const. T.L. 320; G. Ch. Isl. 667; W.C.P. 318
York, D. of—*cont.*
— Rd., 3rd D. of, K.B. 756; K.G. 735

— Rd., D. of (2nd son of Edw. IV.), also E. of Nottingham, and D. of Norfolk, *q.v.*, E.M. 326; K.B. 757; K.G. 736; L.L. Ir. 552
— Hy., D. of, aft. Hen. VIII., *q.v.*, E.M. 326; K.B. 758; K.G. 737; L.L. Ir. 553; W.C.P. 312
— Ch., D. of, aft. Ch. I. *q.v.*, K.B. 761; K.G. 739
— Fk., D. of (son of Geo. III.), *see* Pr. Fredk.
— Jas., D. of, aft. Jas. II., *q.v.*, H.C.P. Sc. 507; K.G. 740; L.H.A. 175; L.H.A. Sc. 499; P.C. 189; W.C.P. 319
— Ed. Aug., D. of (bro. of Geo. III.), adm. (**A**) 814; P.C. 200
— Fk. D. of (son of Geo. III.), C. Ch. 855; Capt. Gen. 855; F.M. 856; G.C.B. 766; G.C.H. 785; gen. (**A**) 858; Gr. M. Bath, 754; K.B. 765; P.C. 204
Yotton, Jno., dn. Lich. 445
Young and **Younge,** *see also* Yonge
— Ad., C.I.R. 286
— Alexr., bp. Edinb. 533; bp. Ross. 536
— Aretas Wm., G. Pr. Ed. Isl. 699; G. Trin. 722
— Brooke, gen. (**C**) 874
— Ch. Becher, gen. (**D**) 898
— Ch. G. and sir C., Gart. K.A. 328; R. Dr. P.A. 338; Yk. H. 334
— Ch. Metc., gen. (**D**) 920
— Ed., bp. Drom. 605; bp. Ferns and L. 622; dn. Clr. 598
— Ed., C. Tx. 284
— Ed., dn. Exr. 437
— Ed., dn. Sal. 468
— Ed., S.W.F. 271
— hon. Ed., B. and Gl. K.A. 330 Bath K.A. 785; Han. H. 340; Regr. Bath, 784
— Fras., gen. (**D**) 922
— Fk., gen. (**D**) 886
— Fk., K.C.M.G. 799
— Geo. (? hon.), P.C. 218; Ld. Adv. 526; Ld. Sess. 521; S.G. Sc. 527; Jy. Sc. 523
— sir Geo., adm. (**A**) 816
— Geo. Saml., gen. (**D**) 922
— Hor. Beaum., adm. (**G**) 843
— Hy. Ed. Fox and sir H., G. C.G.H. 679; G. S. Austr. 706; G. Tasm. 708
— Jas., adm. (**A**) 814
— Jas., adm. (**A**) 819
— Jas. Now., gen. (**D**) 924
— Jas. Rt., gen. (**D**) 893
— Jno., bp. Arg. 538
— Jno., bp. Llin. 621
— Jno., bp. Roch. 460
— (or Morgan), Jno., bp. St. Dav. 464; Chanc. Gart. 745; dn. Winds. 474
— Jno., Bl. M. P.A. 336; Som. H. 332
— Jno., dn. Sal. 468
— Jno., dn. Winch. 471
— Jno., *see* Yonge
Young and Younge—*cont.*
— Jno., and sir J., aft. 1st ld. Lisgar, *q.v.*, Ch. Sec. Ir. 563; Com. Io. Isl. 129; G.C.B. 773; G.C.M.G. 795; G.G. Can. 692; G. N.S.W. 703; G. Pr. Ed. Isl. 699; K.C.B. 778; L.T. 160; P.C. 216; Sec. Tr. 163
— Matth., bp. Clonf. and K. 636
— Plomer, gen. (**D**) 891; K.H. 791
— Ralph, gen. (**D**) 916
— Rd., bp. Athab. 697
— Rd., bp. Bgr. 426; bp. Roch. 460
— Rt., gen. (**C**) 874
— Th., abp., 486; bp. St. Dav. 464
— (or Yonge), Th., J.C.P. 378; J.K.B. 371; S.L. 407
— sir Walt., C. Cus. 274-5
— Wm., adm. (**D**) 824
— Wm., G. Gren. 724; G. Tob. 723
— Wm. and sir W., adm. (**A**) 816; G.C.B. 767; K.B. 766; L. Admy. 180
— sir Wm. (bt.), G. Dnca. (*d.* 1788) 730
— sir Wm. (bt.), G. Tob. (*d.* 1811) 723
— Wm. Alexr. Geo., G. Br. Gu. 715; G. Gld. Cst. Col. 687; G. Jam. 713; G. Trin. 723
Younghusband, Ch., gen. (**D**) 880
— Ch, Wr., gen. (**D**) 908
— Jno. Wm., gen. (**D**) 919
— Rt. Rom., gen. (**D**) 901
Yugworth, Rd., bp. suff. Dov. 431
Yule, Geo. Udn., K.C.S.I. 802
— Hy., M.C.I. 647
— Patr., gen. (**D**) 890
Yung-ching, Emp. Ch. 100

Z.

Zacharius, P. Ro
Zaldua, F. J., Pres. U.S.C. 107
Zammit, Gius. Nic., K.C.M.G. 796
Zanzibar, Sult. of, G.C.M.G. 796
Zapolski, J., K. Hgy. 60
Zavala, J., Pres. Nic. 106
Zavo, Bas., K.C.M.G. 796
Zemb, J., Pres. Sw. C. 31
Zeno, Emp. E.E. 50
Zephirinus, P. Ro. 32
Zerrondacchi, Const. Geo K.C.M.G. 798

For List of Abbreviations, see pp. 944-952.

Zetland, Thos., 2nd E. of, form. ld. Dundas, *q.v.*, K.G. 745; K.T. 749
Ziemomislas, D. Pld. 90
Ziemovitus, D. Pld. 90
Zieten, Count, G.C.B. 767
Zohrab, Ed. Pasha, K.C.M.G. 798
Zosimus, P. Ro. 33
Zouche, Alan la, *see* ld. Z., *infra*
— Ed. la, *see* ld. Z. *infra*
— Jno. de la, bp. Llff. 449
— (or Souwche), Jno., K.B. (1559) 761
Zouche—*cont.*
— Rd., J. Adm. Ct., 423
— Wm., bro. of Jno., 8th ld. Z. of Haryngworth, K.B. (1483) 758
— Wm. la, or Wm. de la, abp. Yk. 485; dn. Yk. 486; L.H.T. 153
— Wm. la, *see* ld. Z., *infra*
Zouche of Ashby, lds.
— Alan la, aft. 4th ld. Z. of A., Const. T.L. 320; J.K.B. 371; Jy. 264; L.J. Ir. 550; L.M. Lond. 489
Zouche of Haryngworth, lds.
*— Wm. la, Const. T.L. 320
*— Wm. de, J. It. 369
* Most likely same pers., and also 2nd ld. Z. of H.
— Wm., 4th ld., K.G. 735
— Ed., 12th ld., G. Gsey. 668; W.C.P. 319
Zuinski, R. Russ. 90
Zulestein, Wm. Hy. Nassau de, aft. 1st E. of Rochford, *q.v.*
Zulfika, Pasha, K.C.M.G. 799
Zuloaga, F., Pres. Mex. 104

For List of Abbreviations, see pp. 944-952.